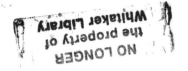
When it was published in 1976, *The World Encyclopedia of Comics* was the first comprehensive reference book about comic art. The work featured biographical entries on the most important authors and artists—detailing their lives and careers as well as their styles and contributions to the genre—plus entries on the landmark strips and characters of the form. The *Encyclopedia* quickly became recognized as the authoritative work on comic art.

This new, updated edition of *The World Encyclopedia of Comics* features new information on the most important cartoonists from all over the world, such as Art Spiegelman, Gary Larson, Lynn Johnston, and Frank Miller, as well as entries on important new strips or comic books like *Calvin and Hobbes*, *Dilbert*, *Spawn*, and *Mutts*. In addition, information has been added to many of the original *Encyclopedia* entries. Eighty pages of color comic art chart the development of the medium, from the *Katzenjammer Kids* of 100 years ago to the stylistic strips of today. As with the original volume, this edition of *The World Encyclopedia of Comics* includes an extensive glossary; a bibliography; essays on the history of the medium; listings of comic book publishers and comic strip syndicates; and indexes.

With over 1,400 entries and 1,000 illustrations, the new edition of *The World Encyclopedia of Comics* is not only comprehensive, it is definitive.

The World Encyclopedia of Comics

Edited by Maurice Horn

THE CONTRIBUTORS

Manuel Auad (M.A.), *The Philippines*
Bill Blackbeard (B.B.), *U.S.*
Gianni Bono (G.B.), *Italy*
Joe Brancatelli (J.B.), *U.S.*
MaryBeth Calhoun (M.B.C.), *U.S.*
Javier Coma (J.C.), *Spain*
Bill Crouch (B.C.), *U.S.*
Giulio Cesare Cuccolini (G.C.C.), *Italy*
Mark Evanier (M.E.), *U.S.*
Wolfgang Fuchs (W.F.), *Germany*
Luis Gasca (L.G.), *Spain*
Robert Gerson (R.G.), *U.S.*
Denis Gifford (D.G.), *Great Britain*
Paul Gravett (P.G.), *Great Britain*
Peter Harris (P.H.), *Canada*
Hongying Liu-Lengyel (H.Y.L.L.), *China*
Maurice Horn (M.H.), *France/U.S.*
Pierre L. Horn (P.L.H.), *U.S.*
Slobodan Ivkov (S.I.), *Yugoslavia (Serbia)*
Bill Janocha (B.J.), *U.S.*
Orvy Jundis (O.J.), *The Philippines*
Hisao Kato (H.K.), *Japan*
John A. Lent (J.A.L.), *Asia*
Richard Marschall (R.M.), *U.S.*
Alvaro de Moya (A.M.), *Brazil*
Kalmán Rubovszky (K.R.), *Hungary/Poland*
Ervin Rustemagić (E.R.), *Yugoslavia*
John Ryan (J.R.), *Australia*
Matthew A. Thorn (M.A.T.), *Japan*
Dennis Wepman (D.W.), *U.S.*

The World Encyclopedia of Comics

Edited by Maurice Horn

Chelsea House Publishers
Philadelphia

Acknowledgments

The editors of *The World Encyclopedia of Comics* wish to extend their sincere thanks to the following persons: Bill Anderson, Jerry Bails, Larry Brill, Mary Beth Calhoun, Frank Clark, Bill Crouch, Leonard Darvin, Tony Dispoto, Jacques Glénat-Guttin, Ron Goulart, George Henderson, Pierre Horn, Pierre Huet, S. M. "Jerry" Iger, Jessie Kahles Straut, Rolf Kauka, Heikki Kaukoranta, Roland Kohlsaat, Maria-M. Lamm, Mort Leav, Vane Lindesay, Ernie McGee, Jacques Marcovitch, Victor Margolin, Doug Murray, Pascal Nadon, Harry Neigher, Walter Neugebauer, Syd Nicholls, Tom Peoples, Rainer Schwarz, Silvano Scotto, Luciano Secchi, David Smith, Manfred Soder, Jim Steranko, Ernesto Traverso, Miguel Urrutía, Jim Vadeboncoeur, Jr., Wendell Washer, Peter Wiechmann, Mrs. John Wheeler and Joe Willicombe.

We would also like to thank the following collectors who donated reproductions of art from their collections: Wendy Gaines Bucci, Mike Burkey, Tony Christopher, Russ Cochran, Robert Gerson, Roger Hill, Bill Leach, Eric Sack, and Jim Steranko.

Special thanks also to Michel Mandry, Bernard Trout, José Maria Conget of Instituto Cervantes in New York, Four-Color Images Gallery, Frederik Schodt, David Astor, Alain Beyrand, Manuel Halffter, Dominique Petitfaux, Annie Baron-Carvais, Janice Silverman.

Our appreciation also to the following organizations: Associated Newspapers Ltd., Bastei Verlag, Bulls Pressedienst, Comics Magazine Association of America, Editions Dupuis, ERB Inc., Field Newspaper Syndicate, Globi Verlag, The Herald and Weekly Times Ltd., Kauka Comic Akademie, King Features Syndicate, Marvel Comics Group, San Francisco Academy of Comic Art, Strip Art Features, Walt Disney Archives and Walt Disney Productions.

Finally, we wish to thank Don Manza for his photographic work.

Chelsea House Publishers
1974 Sproul Road, Suite 400
P.O. Box 914
Broomall PA 19008-0914

Copyright 1999 Chelsea House Publishers. All rights reserved. Printed and bound in the United States of America.

Typeset by Alexander Graphics, Indianapolis IN

Library of Congress Cataloging-in-Publication Data

The world encyclopedia of comics / edited by Maurice Horn.
   p. cm.
   Includes bibliographical references and index.
   ISBN 0-7910-4854-3 (set). — ISBN 0-7910-4857-8 (v. 1). — ISBN
0-7910-4858-6 (v. 2). — ISBN 0-7910-4859-4 (v. 3). — ISBN
0-7910-4860-8 (v. 4). — ISBN 0-7910-4861-6 (v. 5). — ISBN
0-7910-4862-4 (v. 6). — ISBN 0-7910-4863-2 (v. 7)
   1. Comic books, strips, etc.—Dictionaries. I. Horn, Maurice.
PN6710.W6 1998
741.5'03—dc21   97-50448
                                                 CIP

Contents

Preface to the Second Edition

This is an updated, enlarged edition of what has become, since its publication more than 20 years ago, the standard reference work in the field of comics: *The World Encyclopedia of Comics*. Building upon that foundation, we have conserved all the entries as originally written, only updating those (some 600 of them) that needed updating. Additionally, over 200 entries on features, artists, and writers that have come to the forefront of the field in the past 20 years have been added to this edition, bringing the total number of entries to more than 1,400. Written by experts from around the world, some of them former contributors, some new to the *Encyclopedia*, these additional entries widen the panorama of world comic art as it has evolved over the last two decades. We are particularly proud to have made this edition even more encyclopedic and even more universal with the inclusion of entries on artists and comics from countries—mostly from Asia, Africa, and eastern Europe—that, for political or practical reasons, were absent from the first edition.

The front and back matter (history, chronology, bibliography, and essays) have also been updated to reflect the changes that have occurred since the first publication of the *Encyclopedia*. These updates will provide the reader with a global perspective and a current time line to a living art form that doesn't cease to reinvent itself. More than 120 new black-and-white illustrations and additions to the color section will further enhance the usefulness and pleasure provided by this *Encyclopedia*.

This edition of *The World Encyclopedia of Comics* is intended for use not only as a scholarly reference tool, being the most comprehensive survey of the medium ever realized, but also as an endless source of enjoyment for the reader. The information contained in this *Encyclopedia* covers the developments in the comic art field through December 1997. It is the intention of the publisher to further update and revise the work at periodic intervals.

Foreword to the First Edition

The World Encyclopedia of Comics is the first book to cover the entire field of comic art in all of its aspects—artistic, cultural, sociological, and commercial—on a global scale. To this purpose we have assembled an international team of 15 contributors from 11 different countries, each a recognized authority in his field. (Short biographies of these contributors may be found on pages 920-926 of this work.) The exhaustive data compiled for this book has, for the most part, been obtained firsthand by direct examination and reading of the sources, and through interviews with the artists, authors, editors and publishers involved. The text, therefore, is lively and fascinating reading, aside from its value as a straight reference work.

The more than 1200 cross-referenced entries constitute the main body of this encyclopedia. These entries have been organized alphabetically for easy reference, and fit in two classifications: biographical and bibliographical. The biographical entries deal with comic artists, writers and editors, and provide a succinct summary of the subjects, with emphasis on their work in the comics, their stylistic and thematic contributions, their influence on other artists or writers and their achievements in general. The bibliographical entries, which relate to the comic features themselves, contain a brief history, including the names of the artists and writers who created and worked on them, a summary of themes, plots and leading characters, a discussion of the place held by each particular feature in the history and art of the comics and their adaptations into other media. Many relevant anecdotes, parallels and asides are also included in the entries (which are valuative as well as informative).

To supplement the individual entries and give the reader a "bird's eye view" of the comic art form, the volume contains a number of informative articles, including a world history of the comics (providing a global overview of the more than 80 years of comic art), a chronology of important events in comics development, a history of newspaper syndication, an analytical summary dealing with the language, themes and structures of the comics and an extensive glossary of comic terms.

This book constitutes not only a definitive study of a very important and influential art form, it also illuminates many facets and peculiarities of 20th-century culture, and of Western civilization as a whole. It is, therefore, an invaluable tool for historians, sociologists, art instructors, folklorists and critics.

There are also a bibliography and a number of appendices included. Of particular usefulness are the indices which provide easy access to additional information on thousands of authors and titles apart from the individual entries in their names. Illustrated with over 700 black-and-white pictures and 100 color reproductions, the encyclopedia is the most extensive and representative anthology of comic works ever assembled.

The World Encyclopedia of Comics has been designed not only as a reference work on the subject, but also as a source of endless hours of enjoyment for scholars and laymen alike. The data contained herein covers the developments in the comic art field through December 1975. It is the intention of the publisher to update, revise and enlarge *The World Encyclopedia of Comics* accordingly, at a later date.

The Editors

Comics Around the World

A Short History
A World Chronology
An Analytical Summary

Comics of the World:
A Short History

The following essay represents the first attempt at a history of world comic art. The only other international history of the comics, *A History of the Comic Strip,* not only fails to deal with comic books, but is largely confined to the productions of the United States and Western Europe. This account presents a more balanced world picture, and while the American and European productions receive the largest share of attention, reflecting their preeminent position in the world of comics, they are placed in a wider context that includes the very important contributions made by Japanese comics, as well as those from countries of Asia, Latin America, and the Pacific, in a truly global overview of the 100 or more years of comic art.

In this historical narrative I have tried to chronicle the evolution of the world's comics, pinpoint their heights and valleys, describe their trends and cycles, and analyze their accomplishments and failings, in the context of 20th-century culture. I have also attempted to capture the spirit, feel, and flavor of comic history by concerning myself with the thrust of events and happenings, rather than with historical details. For more detailed information the reader should refer to the chronology and to the bio-bibliographical entries for the authors and features mentioned in the text.

William Hogarth, "Gin Lane."

Genesis

As cannot be sufficiently reiterated, the comic strip is emphatically *not* a medium of graphic narration. The narrative in the strip is not conveyed visually, but is expressed in both pictures and words. While emphasis may be given to one of the dual aspects of the strip over the other, the interest most often shifts back and forth, according to the demands of the action or the needs of characterization and atmosphere. It is therefore futile, as some uninformed critics still do, to relate the comics to early modes of visual narration: there is as much generic distance between the comics and the Trajan Column or Queen Mathilde's tapestry as exists between the cinema and shadow theater. They simply do not aim at the same effect. To pretend otherwise is to make a regrettable confusion of categories.

It is probably in Leonardo da Vinci's notebooks that one finds the first deliberate strivings toward a new language that would retain the cognitive and normative elements of the written word and flesh them out with visual expletives. Leonardo devised his scheme in answer not to an aesthetic problem, but to a philosophical dilemma. It was becoming apparent to the artists and thinkers of the Renaissance that the preeminence of the printed word was leading man to isolation from his fellow men. Leonardo thought that only the image, which bears an immediately recognizable relationship with external reality, could help liberate language from the alienating power (to use a modern phrase) of the printed word.

In spite of limited experiments, text and illustration followed different paths. It fell upon the genius of the English illustrator William Hogarth to reassemble the two heterogenous elements of text and image into a single whole. In his picture series, like *The Rake's Progress* or *Marriage à la Mode,* he reestablished the sequential nature of visual narrative, while at the same time depicting the action as if it were a stage play, thus giving it dramatic impact. His creations were so clearly different from the traditional illustrations of his time that a new name had to be coined for them, "cartoons." The dramatic setting of these cartoons clearly called for the systematic use of the balloon (a form that has been in use sporadically over a long period), and thus the definitive characteristics of the cartoon were established. Refined later by Thomas Rowlandson and introduced to the Continent by the fame of James Gillray, these techniques led in a roundabout way to the creation of the comic strip.

The 19th century witnessed a flourishing of illustrated narratives, spurred on by such technical innovations as zincography and, later, photoengraving. But these narratives ("Images d'Epinal" in France, "Bilderbogen" in Germany) still kept text and pictures separate from each other. Artistically these picture-stories

Wilhelm Busch, "Max und Moritz."

reached their highest point with the Swiss Rodolphe Töpffer, whose work, abundantly praised by Goethe, signaled not the beginning of a new art form, as some have contended, but the brilliant end of an already outdated artistic concept.

More important in the history of the comic strip was the German Wilhelm Busch, whose creation, *Max und Moritz*, contributed mightily (if accidentally) to the birth of the American comic strip. As H. Arthur Klein, Busch's talented translator, ably put it, "We may call Busch the stepfather, if not the father, of an important group of comics in the United States." Another early pioneer of the budding art of the comics, the Frenchman Georges Colomb (who used the pen name "Christophe"), introduced stylistic innovations such as actions depicted from odd angles and accelerated narratives, which foreshadow some of the techniques of the strip. His work was years ahead of such artistically disreputable frolics as W. F. Thomas's *Ally Sloper*.

At the end of the 19th century the stage was set for the grand entrance of a new mode of expression. It was to come from an altogether unexpected direction.

Birth of the comic form

From the vantage of hindsight, the birth and subsequent rise of the comic strip in the United States seem as inevitable as they are spectacular. At the end of the 19th century, however, nothing pointed to an American breakthrough in a field

Rudolph Dirks, "The Katzenjammer Kids."

that had been pioneered and explored almost exclusively by Europeans. American artists were lagging far behind their European counterparts in the art of pictorial storytelling. In fact, the original impetus came not from the artists themselves, but from the publishers, who, in the Sunday supplement, created the medium best suited for the expression of their artist's ideas.

Around 1880 a number of American daily newspapers started publishing on Sundays (despite a campaign for the continued observance of the Sabbath), but it was Joseph Pulitzer who first seized upon the Sunday supplement as a showcase for his newspaper, the *World*. To attract readers to his newspaper, Pulitzer made increasing use of color and illustrations, including cartoons. The conjunction of these innovations directly led to Richard Outcault's historic *Yellow Kid* on February 16, 1896 (actually, color had already been applied to Outcault's panel as early as July 1895, but the results had not been considered entirely satisfactory). *The Yellow Kid* was not yet a comic strip as we define it today, but its creation was pivotal, signaling as it did the birth of the comics as a distinct medium.

In the pages of the *World*, therefore, were gathered all the essential elements of the form—the sequential narrative, continuing characters, dialogue enclosed within the picture—but their synthesis was brought about not by Pulitzer, but by his redoubtable young competitor, William Randolph Hearst, who had just bought out the *Morning Journal* from Joseph's brother, Albert. Not only did Hearst share Pulitzer's conviction that the Sunday supplement had a remarkable future, but further, he saw that the cartoons constituted its main pillar of strength. As it turned out, he was right on both counts. Hearst's weapon against Pulitzer was to launch a new color supplement, *The American Humorist* (self-described as "eight pages of polychromatic effulgence that make the rainbow look like a lead pipe") in 1897. In these pages appeared the work of artists who, under the vigilant gaze of Hearst, unconsciously forged a new language that, together with the movies, brought a new way of looking at external reality. In these developments Hearst's role should not be slighted. Granted that his methods and ethics left something to be desired—at one point he bought out the entire staff of the *World*—his judgment and discrimination in selecting his artists were uncanny. He can rightly be regarded as the godfather of the new form (only much later to be called the "comics").

In the stable of artists assembled by Hearst for his *American Humorist* three stand out: Richard Outcault, James Swinnerton, and Rudolph Dirks, respectively the authors of *The Yellow Kid* (bought out along with its creator from the *World*), *The Journal Tigers*, and *The Katzenjammer Kids* (this last feature was probably the single most important creation in the entire history of the comic strip).

Every period of great innovation must be followed by a period of consolidation. The early cartoonists were developing new themes and creating new conventions at such a furious pace that they were in danger of outrunning themselves. Clearly, a new man was needed who would bring some order into the chaotic cartoon world, who would channel all the heady, bold, and often contradictory experiments going on at the same time into a distinct pattern and along a central direction. Such a man was Frederick Burr Opper. His Happy Hooligan prefigured Charlie Chaplin's tramp just as his Gloomy Gus already wore Buster Keaton's mask. His peculiar brand of dark humor and slapstick found further development in the comedies of Mack Sennett. Even his narrative techniques point in some of the directions that the movies later took.

Such were the four men most responsible for the art of the comic strip as we know it today. Their work might seem coarse and vulgar, but they were also vital and vibrant. They were pioneers, innovators. Delicacy of line, shade of meaning, subtlety of design were subordinated to the sheer joy of being able to express themselves in an entirely new idiom. Their creations were imbued with an overwhelming sense of discovery, a reckless abandon to the seemingly endless possibilities of the medium. They left to a new generation of cartoonists (and to their older selves) the task of refining and disciplining their artistic impulses. Improvisation and spontaneity, not skill and purpose, were their main concerns.

If their collective contributions can be summarized at all, it might be said that they stand in the history of comic art in the same position that the artists of the Quattrocento occupy in the history of Western art in general.

F. B. Opper, "Happy Hooligan, © King Features Syndicate.

The new order and the old

By the early years of the 20th century the rough outlines of the new medium were already apparent. The vital conventions and vocabulary of the comics—speech balloons, onomatopoeia, motion lines, frame-enclosed pictures—were already in use as the accepted norm and were finding their way into the public consciousness. Venturing forth, as they were, into unknown territory, the first practitioners of the medium sought to preserve a lifeline with the older and established form, the humor cartoon. This helps to explain the more than casual resemblance they bear to one another. In style, if not in intent and treatment, they remained close to their immediate sources—the linearity and simplicity of the cartoon. The next period (circa 1905) saw the first break between the comic strip and the cartoon, and the first conscious strivings for the creation of an altogether autonomous and original art form.

Winsor McCay was the artist who, above all others, proved to be the guiding genius of this aesthetic revolution. His single-minded and masterly research into new semantic structures and thematic variations, starting with *Little Sammy Sneeze* and deepening into *The Dreams of the Rarebit Fiend*, found its most accomplished and dazzling expression in *Little Nemo in Slumberland*.

In *Little Nemo* McCay achieved a unity between plot and theme that is rarely found among the comics (or in other art forms, for that matter).

The only artist of the period who could be compared to Winsor McCay was the German-American painter Lyonel Feininger. His two short-lived creations for the comic medium, *Wee Willie Winkie's World* and *The Kin-der-Kids,* endowed as they are with the artist's whimsical vision, seem in retrospect to have captured

Lyonel Feininger, "The Kin-der-Kids"

the *Zeitgeist* of the comic strip form, caught between its cartoony beginnings and its painterly aspirations. If in style Feininger owes little to the tradition of the American cartoon (and much to the school of German caricature), in spirit he is closer to Dirks (as the name "the Kin-der-Kids" indicates) than McCay was ever to be.

No man, however, has contributed to the basic "look" of the comic strip as much as George McManus, a young cartoonist who came into his own around the same time. McManus had begun unobtrusively in 1900, but as early as five years later he was already displaying his almost awesome mastery of line, his uncanny feel for situations, and his unerring ear for dialogue in such creations as *Panhandle Pete* and *The Newlyweds*, harbingers of things to come.

In a position somewhat apart from the others stands Charles William Kahles. At a time when all cartoonists were eager to stake out their own particular provinces, Kahles pursued his craft with self-indulgence. He seems to have been in love with the medium itself and was so intoxicated by its multivariegated possibilities that he could not tie himself to any one of the paths open to him.

Winsor McCay, "Little Nemo."

Louis Forton, "Les Pieds-Nickelés." © SPE.

Each of the four men discussed here brought his own unique contribution to the developing medium; each enlarged and greatly enriched the scope of the comic strip, refined its artistry, and invented many of the narrative and visual devices that are now part of the language of the comics. Their contributions may seem unequal, yet it was in the interaction of their diverging styles that they achieved a sense of unity. They bore more resemblance to one another than to any of the preceding generation of cartoonists. If their inspirations were disparate, their aims were similar, and together they lifted the comics to what was already recognizable as an exacting and original art form.

While all this was happening in the United States, Europe was lagging far behind. Even the more successful among European comic strips, such as *Weary Willie and Tired Tim* and *Airy Alf* in England, *Les Pieds-Nickelés* and *Bécassine* in France, and *Bilbolbul* in Italy, still did not make use of the balloon, but put captions of sometimes substantial size under the pictures, thereby divorcing the image from the text. It was some time before Europe (and the rest of the world) caught up with the United States in this field.

In Japan, on the other hand, Rakuten Kitazawa, founder of the famous *Tokyo Puck* (modeled on the American *Puck*) in 1905, wholeheartedly adopted the techniques and innovations brought about by the American cartoonists in his comic strip creations, such as *Doncia* and *Tonda Haneko*.

The advent of the daily strip

At about the same time that McCay and Feininger were bringing the comics to formal perfection, Bud Fisher firmly established the daily strip as one of the most important features in the newspaper. *Mutt and Jeff* (created in 1907 as *Mr. A. Mutt*) was not the first comic to appear across the page of a daily newspaper, but it was the first to do so with lasting success. After 1910, when it was evident that the daily strip was there to stay, many newspapers followed suit, timidly at first; then, as the new form met with growing readership, the practice of running daily comic strips inside the newspaper became general throughout the United States.

Bud Fisher, "Mutt and Jeff." © H. C. Fisher.

G. A. Van Raemdonck, "Bulletje en Bonestaak." Bulletje and Bonestaak "pay a visit" to Jopie Slim and Dickie Bigmans of the London Evening News. © Het Volk.

It was lucky for Fisher's reputation (as well as for his finances) that his "discovery" was so universally recognized, for his artistic standing was not on a par with that of his illustrious contemporaries. *Mutt and Jeff*'s style was clearly derivative of the conventions of the early cartoon. Even the characters (the mismatched duo) and the theme (the enjoyment of idleness) owed much to Opper. Fisher's contribution was more basic: by creating the black-and-white daily comic strip (by which name the whole medium soon became known), he opened up new aesthetic possibilities (not to mention almost endless commercial opportunities) that later cartoonists were able to explore and enlarge.

Still, the new format did not take hold immediately: the traditions of the Sunday color supplement and the comic page were strong. Only when a satisfactory way of tying daily and Sunday readership was found did the comic strip become the social phenomenon that it is today.

Parenthetically, it is interesting to note that *Mr. A. Mutt* and its most widely heralded predecessor, Clare Briggs's *A. Piker Clerk*, both started as horse-race tip sheets: they were conceived as part and parcel of the daily newspaper, and not as an extension of the weekly color comics to the black-and-white eight-column page.

At any rate, the progress of the newfangled feature was slow. The daily strip met with the opposition, if not downright hostility, of newspaper editors (a tradition still alive today). A few newspapers tried daily strips, but only Hearst (who had bought out Fisher and his strip in 1908) wholeheartedly embraced the new format (again showing both artistic judgment and business acumen). At first he used the black-and-white strips for experimental purposes (they were cheaper to produce than full-color Sundays). *Bringing Up Father* and *Krazy Kat*, for instance, originated in the daily newspaper pages, but, later, daily strips became established in their own right.

Captain Joseph Patterson, publisher of the Sunday-less *New York News* (at least until 1924), was instrumental in the growth of the daily strip. Not only did he help produce such standards as *The Gumps* and *Little Orphan Annie*, but, when the *News* finally added a Sunday section, he introduced the concept of the synchronized daily/Sunday comic feature. This was devised as a commercial ploy, but it definitively established the comics as an integral part of American newspapers.

The spread of the daily strip format to other parts of the world was slow and patternless. Outside the United States and Canada there existed no strong tradition of the Sunday supplement, and the daily strip provided the comics with their first foothold in the adult newspaper (they had been confined up to then mainly to children's publications). At first these were reprints of American imports (*Mutt and Jeff* appeared as early as 1910 in Argentina and Japan), but slowly a national production began to emerge in many countries. This progress is interesting to follow: England got its first original newspaper strip in 1915 (Charles Folkard's *Teddy Tail*, published in the *Daily Mail*), followed by Argentina (Arturo Lanteri's *El Negro Raul*, 1916) and Australia (*The Potts*, 1919).

With the general acceptance of the daily strip in American newspapers in the 1920s, the form grew rapidly abroad: in Sweden (*Adamson,* known as *Silent Sam* in the United States, 1920), the Netherlands (*Bulletje en Bonestaak*, 1921), Mexico (*Don Catarino*, 1921), and Japan (Yutaka Asō's *Nonkina Tousan*, 1924). A national newspaper strip production also began around that time in Canada, Denmark, and Finland.

There were important holdouts, however; the first French newspaper strip, *Le Professeur Nimbus*, appeared only in 1934, while the Italians had to wait until 1968 to see their first national strip (Bonvi's *Sturmtruppen*). As a form, however, the daily strip is now an accepted part of most newspapers throughout the world.

A time of consolidation

Every period of intense creation and daring innovation—such as characterized the first decade of the American comic strip—has to be followed by a breathing space, a time of recapitulation and consolidation. After 1910 the cartoonists, looking back on past achievements, went into a reflective or analytical pause, according to their particular temperament. Their mood was best exemplified by the work of the greatest artists of the period, George Herriman and George McManus, whose accomplishments, while seemingly divergent in purpose and outlook, were actually strikingly similar in form and substance. Both consciously sought to express themselves in the language of the comics and solely on its terms—and their inspiration (however literary it seemed at the outset) owed more to the art of the comic strip than to any exterior source.

So much ink has been spilled in praise of these two artists (especially Herriman, who in recent years has attained the status of a quasi-literary saint) that we forget how funny they were—and how their funniness directly derived from the bumptiousness of the early cartoons. In line, Herriman owed as much to Opper as McManus did to Swinnerton, while the brick tossed by Ignatz at Krazy Kat and the rolling pin thrown at Jiggs by Maggie were the logical extensions of the

George McManus, "Bringing Up Father." © King Features Syndicate.

George Herriman, "Krazy Kat." © King Features Syndicate.

One of Rube Goldberg's famed "inventions." © Reuben L. Goldberg.

traditions of slapstick and destruction ushered in by *The Katzenjammer Kids*. A fresh look at *Bringing Up Father* and *Krazy Kat* seems, therefore, in order.

In the world of comic art *Krazy Kat* and *Bringing Up Father* represent two aesthetic opposites. The questionings of the former are contrasted with the certainties of the latter. The same correspondence obtains in the dialogues, graphic styles, backgrounds, themes, situations, and attitudes. Herriman is lyrical and McManus is earthy, Herriman is complex and McManus is direct, Herriman is a dreamer and McManus is a pragmatist, and so on all the way down the line. They represent, almost ideally, the dual direction in which subsequent comic artists would travel. One may be called entertainment and the other may be called art, but they are indissolubly tied together by the very nature of the form. Intellectual snobbishness recognizes *Krazy Kat* as art, while popular success marks *Bringing Up Father* as entertainment, but the truth, as usual, lies somewhere in between. Herriman is as much an entertainer as he is an artist, and McManus teases the mind as much as he pleases the eye. Both reached a summit in comic strip expression, and their divergent styles were responses to the demands of the medium, as they perceived them.

This early chapter of the comics' turbulent history can best be summed up, however, by the feature that, in many ways, started it all—*The Katzenjammer Kids*. Due to some artistic cloning and legal acrobatics, the terrible twins had in the meantime duplicated themselves. One set (under the title *Hans and Fritz*, then *The Captain and the Kids*) remained under the direction of Rudolph Dirks; the other passed into the hands of Harold Hering Knerr, who also kept the original title—and the race was on! In trying to outdo each other, Knerr and Dirks, each in his own inimitable style, set the tone, pace, and flavor of the whole period, outrageously swiping characters, ideas, and entire situations from each other, exuberantly escalating the antics of their heroes, letting the action run wild, pulling out all stops—both of them encapsulating at once the vibrant spirit of the comics in the sublime effrontery of it all.

The comics bloomed in all directions in the second decade of the 20th century, testifying to the vigor of the form and the growing self-sufficiency of its practitioners. If Ray Ewer's *Slim Jim* prolonged the stylistic experiments of Feininger and McCay, the work of Milt Gross and Rube Goldberg amplified Opper's thematic concerns. The cartoonists' choice of themes—the escaped lunatic facing an even more insane outside world (*Count Screwloose of Tooloose*), the innocent set upon by a savage society (*Boob McNutt*), the little man trampled down by cruel fate (*Nize Baby*)—had a peculiarly disturbing, even neurotic, ring, showing that the comics, even at that time, were not as insulated from the intellec-

Two of Milt Gross's zany creations: "Looy Dot Dope" and "That's My Pop." © Milt Gross.

tual mainstream as their detractors pretended them to be. The underlying current of paranoia could be detected in even as innocuous a strip as *Abie the Agent*, which Arthur Brisbane once called (in a typical display of ignorance) "the first of the adult comics in America."

The end of the devil-may-care days of the medium occurred some time between 1920 and 1925. All of a sudden the comics grew into maturity. At the same time that they became an art form, they also became a business, big business, and the responsibility was to be taken from the artists, an unreliable and impractical lot, as everybody knows. Because of the enthusiastic efforts of the early cartoonists, the comics had evolved the most important elements of their vocabulary and their own syntax. To be sure, much *terra incognita* still remained to explore, but the shape and outline of the medium were now entirely known.

The family strip

By the 1920s the comics had become so vast a field that specialization was inevitable. The freewheeling days of the early decades, when each man could embark on wild flights of fancy taking him in all directions, were over. The powers-that-be decreed that each artist was to stick to his own theme (or, more often than not, to a given formula). If this resulted in an unhappy narrowing of focus for the strips concerned, it did not affect the medium as a whole. Strips like *The Katzenjammer Kids* or *Krazy Kat* remained as free and delightfully unpredictable as ever. What had changed was not the content but the spirit of the comics.

What brought about these changes was the generalization of the syndicate distribution system and the limitations that system entailed (a discussion of the syndicate system can be found in another part of this encyclopedia). The American newspaper had become a family institution, and to that institution the comics held the comforting illusion of a rose-colored looking glass. No one was more responsible for this trend than Captain Joseph Medill Patterson, publisher of the *New York Daily News*, who is said to have had an uncanny flair for identifying himself with the middle-class aspirations of the very audience he sought. Home from a (supposedly) bad day's work at factory or office, a father could chuckle at the doings and sayings of characters bearing enough resemblances to himself that they could elicit delighted glimmers of recognition; yet, they remained so unlike him in their stylized attire and stereotyped responses that he could laugh at them without laughing at himself. In turn, a mother could look appreciatively

Children of the Comics

From the outset, kids in the comics have been an unruly lot. They are lazy, conniving, sloppy, occasionally cruel, always rebellious. Fortunately, the advent of the family strip did not appreciably change the remarkably candid and realistic appraisal of children as cheerful barbarians. In a world beset with conformity and hypocrisy, there is a welcome absence of sham in the actions of the comics' children. In strips like Skippy, Reg'lar Fellers, *and the Sunday version of* Winnie Winkle, *the trend is glaringly exposed. Perry and his gang, Skippy, Puddin'head, and the others may not possess the diabolical imagination of the Katzies, but their revolt against the adult world is no less real for its being more concealed.*

The children of the comics retain enough innocence to believe in dreams, in the brotherhood of clubhouse pals, the vastness of nights under the stars, the magic of an afternoon at the circus; and they have acquired enough wisdom to know that the adult world is the enemy of dreams. Therefore they lie, cheat, and dissemble—the typical response of the bright and weak to the stupid and strong. But even in their deceit, delinquency, and self-aggrandizement, and in the hollowness of their victories, they are never made to look inane or ridiculous. We never laugh at the children as we do at their adult victims; we laugh with them.

This is not accidental, of course. The cartoonists are tipping the scales in favor of the kids. It is as if, in an act of like rebellion, they too are crying out against the stupidities and iniquities of middle-class life, which they are supposed to uphold and enshrine.

M.H.

at "funnies" which were not coarse or vulgar, but in which the wife, more often than not, was one up on her husband.

The archetype of this new wave of family strips was *The Gumps*, directly conceived and named by Captain Patterson. There is no doubt that the fearless captain intended the strip to be a shining example of his stewardship over the newly created Tribune-News Syndicate, as well as the prototype for the new comic strip age to come.

Sidney Smith, "The Gumps." © Chicago Tribune-New York News Syndicate.

It is well to remember that the family genre is not deplorable in itself and has produced a few masters who have managed to transcend both the limitations of the setting and the literalness of the situation by breathing into their creations the intents and characteristics of established and respected forms. Under the daily ludicrous happenings in *Blondie*, there is a lively comedy of manners that gives substance and meaning to the strip; the sense of the implacable flow of time overwhelms the gentle pieties of *Gasoline Alley*, while *Moon Mullins* turns the very facts of family life into the frightening structure of a black comedy.

Little Orphan Annie is the most extreme case of all. First designed as a story about an orphan (in the vein of the screen tearjerkers of the time), it was transformed by its creator into a dark parable of Good and Evil, a brooding metaphor of life, in which all characters took on the translucence of symbols, and all situations became permeated with a haunting sense of betrayal and doom—a far cry from the idyll of domestic romance!

The family-type comics were created to attract a female readership, and nowhere was this as apparent as in the so-called girl strips. Aimed particularly at the growing number of working girls, they presented a flattering self-picture of independence, attractiveness (even glamour), and poise, the image of self-reliance mixed with charm. Despite the implications of their titles *(Tillie the Toiler, Winnie Winkle, the Breadwinner)*, there was little depiction of their actual work in these strips, for they were more devoted to play and romance. A combination gossip column, fashion illustration, and advice for the lovelorn, most deserve only the sleep of oblivion.

A couple of girl strips have managed, however, to rise above the norm. Cliff Sterrett's *Polly and Her Pals* is notable for its very intricate design and composition and for its goofy and somewhat surreal atmosphere. The same pixieish charm can be found in *Winnie Winkle,* whose author, Martin Branner, was able to display a fine sense of comedy and irony.

The domestic strips met with growing (even astonishing) popularity in the United States, but failed to set the world of comics on fire. In the 1920s, when the family strip was at its zenith in North America, the rest of the world, by and large, failed to take notice. There were *The Potts* (originally *You and Me*) in Australia, *Don Pancho Talero* (*Bringing Up Father* with a Latin accent) in Argentina, *Dot and Carrie*, a misguided attempt to bring the American-type girl strip to the English masses, and that was about all. Even the genuine article, the American-grown domestic feature, often got short shrift abroad: in France, for instance, *The Gumps* was edged out after a few years by Alain Saint-Ogan's upstart *Zig et Puce*,

The "Gasoline Alley" cast of characters as seen by Dick Moores. © Chicago Tribune-New York News Syndicate.

Jim Russell, "The Potts." © The Herald and Weekly Times Ltd.

while only the Sunday page of *Winnie Winkle* (featuring the pranks of brother Perry and his pals) got published in France and the Netherlands.

One reason for this international failure was the fact that the comics, outside of the North American continent, were still aimed mainly at children, and the kids, with remarkable discernment, simply loathed the genre. Also, the figure of the *pater familias* was still very much respected in most parts of the world (especially in Japan). One can see how a Jiggs or an Andy Gump would have failed to fit the bill. (It took the American occupation of Japan to bring about the first Japanese family strip—*Sazae-san*—in 1946.) However, over the years a few non-American domestic strips made their appearances: *Vater und Sohn* (Germany), *La Familia Burrón* (Mexico), *Patatras* (as a replacement for *Gasoline Alley*, France), *La Familia Ulises* (Spain). But, as a genre, the family strip never really succeeded outside of the United States.

End of an era: 1929

By the end of the 1920s the comics had reached a high plateau of public adulation. They certainly rivaled the movies (which had just begun to talk—or stammer) in popularity, especially in the United States. Comic creation, while giving some signs of fatigue and repetition, continued at a fast pace. The years 1918-1928 were exceedingly fecund. Some of the comics produced in this period have been noted elsewhere; three American features deserve special mention at this point.

Billy DeBeck's *Barney Google* was an earthy example of the traditional comic strip. It exhibited a good-natured humor, as well as a graphic style that represented the epitome of the well-crafted cartoon strip. With *Little Orphan Annie* Harold Gray introduced a not entirely welcome innovation into the field of comic features: the advocacy of a political ideology (in this case, that of the Right) within the confines of his strip. Elzie Segar's *Thimble Theater* derived from the zaniness of Milt Gross and Rube Goldberg's comic creations and from the lyrical humor of *Krazy Kat*. Segar was a master of creating inimitable characters and bewildering situations.

The scene was not limited to the United States, however. The comic strip had by then assumed the proportions of a worldwide social and artistic phenomenon. In England, H. S. Foxwell with *Tiger Tim* (created by J. S. Baker), A. B. Payne with *Pip, Squeak and Wilfred*, and Mary Tourtel with *Rupert* brought the animal strip to new heights of popularity, while J. Millar Watt's *Pop* acquired international fame. At the other end of the globe, Japan produced many cartoonists of talent in this period, the most prolific being the aforementioned Yutako Asō.

In France, where children rather than animals were favorite subjects, Louis Forton (creator of the earlier *Les Pieds-Nickelés*) produced *Bibi Fricotin,* and Alain Saint-Ogan came out with *Zig et Puce,* the first French comic feature to make use of the balloon exclusively. Italian comics, on the other hand, remained faithful

Willy DeBeck, "Barney Google." © King Features Syndicate.

to the illustrated story with captions, in such creations as Sergio Tofano's *Signor Bonaventura*, Antonio Rubino's *Quadratino*, and Carlo Bisi's *Sor Pampurio*.

Comic strip production did not remain confined to its traditional bastions in the U.S.A., England, France, Italy, and Japan. National comic strips sprouted everywhere—in Spain (where K-Hito created the very funny *Macaco*), in Scandinavia *(Pekka Puupää* in Finland, *Adamson* in Sweden, and others), in Latin America (*Chupamirto* in Mexico, Arturo Lanteri's creations in Argentina), in Australia (*Ginger Meggs, Fatty Finn),* even in China, where an original comic strip production began as early as 1920 in Shanghai.

Thus, at the beginning of 1929 the world's comics presented an image of success and stability that was to be shattered that same year by the introduction of narrative techniques and stylistic devices of an altogether different type.

Mary Tourtel, "Rupert." © Beaverbrook Newspapers Ltd.

The adventure strip

Adventure and the unknown have always exercised a fascinating appeal upon the imagination and the human spirit. Ever responsive to popular aspirations, the comic strip was prompt to seize upon these dreams. If Charles Kahles was the first to mine this rich lode in his strips, he did not long remain the only prospector. The first decades of the century were a time of explorers and discoverers, and the travel accounts of these hardy spirits soon found their way into the comic pages. Poetically transposed or devastatingly parodied, they gave extra color to the erratic wanderings of Felix the Cat, the mock heroics of Boob McNutt, the round-the-world odyssey of the Gumps, and the cataclysmic cruise of the Katzenjammers.

The early strips, however, used adventure merely as an added fillip, a ploy aimed at setting off the familiar pyrotechnics of slapstick and buffoonery. Roy Crane was the first to break away from the confining conventions of caricature and broad humor by introducing to his strip *Wash Tubbs* the dashing figure of Captain Easy, soldier of fortune. A little later Harold Foster's *Tarzan* and Nowlan and Calkins's *Buck Rogers* completed this transformation. From that moment on, the adventure strip was going to play it straight (January 1929).

Some interesting aesthetic consequences arose from this deliberate choice of interpretation. Artistically, the new strip form abandoned the caricatural style and free-flowing line of the early cartoon and moved closer to magazine illustration (in its graphic design) and figurative art (in its composition), while aiming at duplicating the sequential flow of the cinema in its effect. This judicious blending of forms gave the new strips the illusion of movement, of reality, of life. At the same time the traditional forms of storytelling adopted by the older strips—the comic fable, the morality play, the familiar anecdote, the fairy tale— were discarded in favor of the narrative continuum of the novel and the heroic tone of the epic. Even as the movies were beginning to talk, the comics started to move. They had gone all the way from static entertainment to dynamic spectacle.

In one respect the continuity strip has a definite advantage over the movie. The uninterrupted flow of happenings unfolding day after day, week after week, gives the strip a quality of timelessness and a diversity of approaches within a single framework that the movie cannot possibly hope to equal. There is an excitement and expectation in the words "to be continued" that should not be dismissed. The adventures go on for all eternity, the end of each episode being but the starting point of the next one, and part of their fascination comes from watching this unceasing parade, this sea of characters, places, and incidents endlessly rolling on.

It has been said that the adventure strip confronts its readers with only a few basic situations. This is true, as it is true with all forms of narrative literature, but the variations exercised upon the primary themes were and are the measure of any artist. In this respect the cartoonists displayed an astonishing range and an unequaled evocative power. They took over and assimilated into their strips preexisting narrative forms; they drew upon the historical novel and the movie serial, the mythological legends and the pulp magazines, the wisdom of folklore and the sensationalism of dime novels, giving them unity and continuity within the unique structural framework of the comic strip.

Harold Foster, "Tarzan." © ERB, Inc.

Chester Gould, "Dick Tracy." © Chicago Tribune-New York News Syndicate.

While *Tarzan* and *Buck Rogers* both owed their inspiration to existing novels, in 1931 Chester Gould created the first successful, originally conceived adventure strip, *Dick Tracy*, a tale of mystery and detection. *Dick Tracy*'s importance lay in its plotting and its locale. It did not take place in some future century or some distant jungle, but in the here and now.

In quick succession, scores of adventure strips saw the light between 1929 and 1934. In addition to *Dick Tracy*, other strips of note were Frank Godwin's *Connie* (originally begun as a girl strip), Hal Forrest's *Tailspin Tommy* and Lyman Young's *Tim Tyler* (both started in 1928, but taking their definitive character only some time later), and *Brick Bradford*, a space strip drawn by Clarence Gray. The greatest artist of the time, however, proved to be Alex Raymond, who produced three strips of worldwide renown: *Secret Agent X-9*, *Jungle Jim*, and *Flash Gordon*, the latter being especially beloved.

Then came the flood. Lee Falk brought out two adventure strips of great originality: *Mandrake the Magician* (with Phil Davis) and *The Phantom* (with Ray Moore). Milton Caniff created the much-admired *Terry and the Pirates*; Foster went on to produce *Prince Valiant* while the talented Burne Hogarth took over *Tarzan*. This was also the time of *Radio Patrol*, *King of the Royal Mounted*, *Don Winslow*, *Charlie Chan*, *Red Ryder*, and Noel Sickles's *Scorchy Smith*, ably continued by Frank Robbins.

The spirit of adventure pervaded the whole comic field in the 1930s: even the humor strip turned to all-out derring-do. The classic example was provided by Segar, who developed the heroic (albeit comical) figure of Popeye the Sailor. Adventure was also present in the daily escapades of Mickey Mouse (who joined the comic pages in 1930) and of his predecessor from the cartoon film, Felix the Cat. Al Capp's *Li'l Abner* also started its satirical career on a fairly adventurous note and, of course, such features as *Alley Oop* and *Oaky Doaks* were conceived as strips of humorous adventure from the start.

The rapid development and extravagant popularity of the American adventure strip overwhelmed the fledgling competition from other comic-producing countries. By 1940 the American syndicates were inundating Europe and the rest of the world with their enormous output. The English strip was marking time, the South American production faltering, the Japanese set back; the French made a timid effort at renewing the outdated outlook of their comic features with René Pellos's imaginative science-fiction strip, *Futuropolis*, but this effort remained isolated. The Italians did better, following the ban of American comics by Musso-

Hergé (George Rémi), "Tintin." © Editions Casterman.

lini in 1938 with such excellent creations as *Kit Carson*, *Gino e Gianni*, *Virus*, and *Dottor Faust*. The best and most imaginative comic strip to come out of Europe in this period, however, was indisputably Hergé's *Tintin*, which was to become a worldwide success, rivaling even the best-known American features.

Spurred on by the success of American adventure comics, many publishers hastily decided to develop their own homegrown varieties, with mixed results. Thus, the decade witnessed the birth of action-oriented features all over the world: in England (*Buck Ryan*), Japan (*Hatanosuke Hinomaru*), Spain *(Cuto)*, Yugoslavia (*Stari Mačak*), Australia (*Larry Steele*), and Argentina (*Hernan el Corsario*). What checked the seemingly inexorable American expansion was not the desultory competition, but the outbreak of World War II. The American comic industry was cut off from its most lucrative markets in Europe and had its sales

Phil Nowlan and Dick Calkins, "Buck Rogers." © National Newspaper Syndicate.

影丸(かげまる)

眼力の百蔵(がんりきのひゃくぞう)
(眼づけの熊)

太郎(たろう)

しびれ　され

岩魚(いわな)

Cast of characters of "Ninja Bugeichō." © *Sanpei Shirato.*

further limited in those countries still open, because of paper rationing and embargoes on nonessential imports.

The rise of the comic book

Contrary to what many people believe, the comic book is not an American innovation of the 1930s. It may be argued that Rodolphe Töpffer's *Histoires en Estampes* was the first genuine attempt at collecting comic stories in book form. In Germany, in the second half of the 19th century, all of Wilhelm Busch's stories appeared within book covers, as did Christophe's creations a few years later.

In the United States comic strip reprinting started with *The Yellow Kid* as early as 1897. In the early 1900s F. A. Stokes published color reprints of *Buster Brown, The Katzenjammer Kids, Foxy Grandpa,* et al., in book form. Other books from different companies reproduced the *Mutt and Jeff* strips, Tad's comic creations, and others, all in black and white. These were succeeded by the Cupples and Leon books of the 1920s and 1930s, which reprinted such standards as *Bringing Up Father, Little Orphan Annie,* and *Dick Tracy.*

It was the Japanese, however, who published the first cheap, mass-produced, regularly scheduled comic books in the 1920s. Printed (sometimes in color) on pulp paper and distributed on a monthly basis, they actually predated the American comic book by a good 10 years. Eventually original material began to appear in these books, some of artistic merit—Suimei Imoto's *Nagagutsu no Sanjūshi* appeared there in 1930, for instance. The comic book format was soon so successful with Japanese children that it gave rise to lending libraries specializing exclusively in comic books, the "kashibonya manga." These special libraries then began to produce their own comic books for rent, and this practice was successful enough to last well into the 1960s. Many young cartoonists started their career in rental comic books: Gōseki Kojima, Sanpei Shirato, Hiroshi Hirata, Shinji Mizushima, among others. Several successful features also got their start in these limited-circulation comic books before graduating to regularly published, newstand-sold publications (*Hakaba no Kitarō* and *Ninja Bugeichō* being the two most notable).

The first modern American comic book, *Funnies on Parade,* appeared in 1933 as a promotional giveaway for Procter and Gamble. In May 1934 the Eastern Color Printing Company issued the first commercial comic book, *Famous Funnies,* a monthly collection of newspaper strip reprints. The next year saw the birth of the first comic book containing exclusively original material, all of it humorous, called *New Fun.* Adventure features were not far behind, and they ensured the success of the new format. In January 1937 *Detective Comics* was first with a comic book devoted to a single protagonist. By the end of the 1930s the comic book was clearly a medium in search of a hero; he finally appeared in the first issue (June 1938) of *Action Comics.* His name was Superman and he made comic history.

Superman was conceived as far back as 1933 by the writer/artist team of Jerry Siegel and Joe Shuster, who had unsuccessfully submitted it to every imaginable newspaper syndicate. When the lone survivor of the planet Krypton arrived in the pages of *Action Comics,* he became an immediate hit. Eventually *Superman* made countless millions for a number of people (but not for its creators, who had sold all their rights).

The phenomenal success of *Superman* spawned a host of imitations; by the time of America's entrance into World War II, the legion of superheroes had virtually taken over the comic book medium. Most of the creations were worthless, but a few managed to survive and even to flourish: Bob Kane's *Batman,* Carl Burgos's *The Human Torch,* Bill Everett's *Sub-Mariner,* and Jack Cole's *Plastic Man* have become classics of sorts. None of them, however, could compete in wit and imagination with C. C. Beck's 1940 creation, *Captain Marvel.*

The unholy proliferation of comic books was feverishly abetted by scores of entrepreneurs eager to cash in on the superhero craze. Two such men deserve special notice: Harry Donnenfeld, who single-handedly created the D.C. empire (now National Periodicals, part of Warner Communications), and S.M. "Jerry" Iger, an indefatigable discoverer of new comic book talent.

Among Iger's discoveries were Lou Fine, Jack Kirby, and Will Eisner, Iger's special protégé. In 1940 Eisner created *The Spirit,* not for sale on newsstands, but as

Jerry Siegel and Joe Shuster, "Superman." © *National Periodical Publications.*

part of a comic book supplement to be carried by Sunday newspapers. Both the feature and the format proved successful—so much so that comic book supplements were soon offered by King Features and the News-Tribune Syndicate (*Brenda Starr* first appeared there). This step was the newspaper syndicates' ultimate recognition that the comic book was there to stay.

World War II and the comics

Unlike World War I, which affected the American comic strip only superficially, World War II caused a profound and permanent upheaval in the comics. Most comic strip heroes rushed into the armed services and helped America's psychological war preparation. Joe Palooka, Jungle Jim, Captain Easy, and countless others found themselves enthusiastically battling against the Axis forces or fighting spies and saboteurs on the home front. Most typical was Caniff's *Terry and the Pirates*, whose episode dated October 17, 1943, was the first comic strip ever to be reprinted in the *Congressional Record*.

War comics, as distinct from the already existing adventure strips–turned–service features for the duration, became a staple of the times, the two most noteworthy being Roy Crane's *Buz Sawyer* and Frank Robbins's *Johnny Hazard*. In contrast, Crockett Johnson's poetic *Barnaby* was also born in this period.

The comic books, led by Joe Simon and Jack Kirby's *Captain America*, proved even more bellicose than the newspaper features. The titles of some of the books published in this period suffice to give a clue as to their character: *Spy Smasher, Commando Yank, Major Victory, Captain Flag, The Fighting Yank, The Unknown Soldier.* . . . But the war also gave rise to another phenomenon—comic strips especially created for servicemen. The most notable of these were George Baker's *The Sad Sack*, Milton Caniff's *Male Call*, and Dave Breger's *GI Joe*, whose title became a synonym for the average "buck private."

The American heroes of the comics were not alone in battling the Axis. The British comic characters had been at it since 1939, going to war in a spirit at first cheerful (one early war comic was called *Musso the Wop*) and, after the fall of France, with grim determination as well as humor. If *Derickson Dene* was a good example of the former, *Jane* (whose scantily clad heroine joined the British

Joe Simon and Jack Kirby, "Captain America." ® Marvel Comics Group.

equivalent of the WACs, to the enjoyment of soldiers of all ranks) provided much of the latter. Australia and Canada also helped with such contributions to the war effort as *Bluey and Curley* and *Rex Baxter*.

The Axis countries, however, were going tit for tat. Germany had no war comics, for Hitler loathed the form, but the Italians fielded *Romano il Legionario*, *Fulmine* (formerly *Dick Fulmine*), and *Il Mozzo del Sommergibile* ("The Submarine Cabin-Boy"), while the Japanese had *Norakuro* and a number of other war comics created for the occasion. The war also echoed in comic strips produced in neutral countries from Spain to Argentina, and Sweden to Switzerland.

Long after V-E and V-J days, the war continued to be fought in the comics, in some cases well into the 1950s, both in America and in liberated Europe. World War II thus proved the single most important real-life experience ever to be reflected in the comics.

A period of uncertainty: 1945-1950

Paradoxically, the end of World War II fostered among American cartoonists a feeling of malaise and a spirit of self-doubt that contrasted sharply with the self-assurance, even cockiness, of the war years. This disarray was perceptible everywhere, in comic books and in newspaper features, in gag strips as well as in adventure stories. As was noted in *A History of the Comic Strip*: "It is understandable that after a conflict that had cost 30 million human lives, humorists found it a bit difficult to be funny. The adventure strip authors, for their part, had a still more complex problem: compared with the silent heroism displayed by millions of combatants, famous or anonymous, the exploits of their characters suddenly seemed contemptible, futile, and almost unseemly."

The desire for change, for a new departure, was most sharply reflected among the adventure strip artists, who, unlike their colleagues working in the humorous vein, did not have a long tradition to fall back on. It is no surprise, therefore, that three of the most prestigious artists of the comics, Alex Raymond, Milton Caniff, and Burne Hogarth, decided at about the same time (1945-1947) to break with their own pasts and forge ahead with entirely new creations. In varying degrees, and for divergent reasons, all three features failed in their intent: Hogarth's *Drago* petered out after one year, Raymond's *Rip Kirby* was cut short by the untimely death of its creator (while ably continued by John Prentice, the feature lost most of its electricity and mystique), and Caniff's *Steve Canyon* sank into the morass of the Cold War. The American adventure strip proved unable to rejuvenate itself, and this portent (while it went unnoticed at the time) signaled the irremediable decline and ultimate death of the genre.

BUT BOOM-BOOM IS IMPATIENT AND FALLS FOR AN OLD TRICK... HIS SLUG DOES RIP'S HAT NO GOOD....

Alex Raymond, "Rip Kirby." © King Features Syndicate.

The funny strip and the comic book reacted differently to the changes wrought by the coming of peace. While only one worthwhile feature appeared in the humor field—Walt Kelly's *Pogo*, which more properly belonged to the next decade, the comic book publishers engaged in frenzied activity, dropping old titles, starting new categories, forever tampering with formats and concepts, but generally getting nowhere in the changed atmosphere of the postwar years.

The same confusion reigned in Europe, in Latin America, and in Japan. The desire to go back to things as they were before was strong; there was much repetitiveness, sterility, and imitation in the comics born in the immediate postwar era, but there were also the first stirrings of a youthful and exuberant creative spirit about to burst onto the claustrophobic scene. In France Raymond Poïvet and Roger Lécureux started the seemingly played-out science-fiction strip on a fresh path with *Les Pionniers de l'Espérance*; Hans Kresse started *Eric de Noorman* in Holland; in England Wally Fawkes (Trog) created the delightful *Rufus* (later retitled *Flook*), while Aurelio Galleppini in Italy perpetuated the Western myth with *Tex Willer*. But the newly found mood of creativity expressed itself strongest in tiny Belgium, where a whole new batch of exciting and enduring features saw the light of print between 1945 and 1950: Morris's classic of Western parodies, *Lucky Luke*, Jacques Martin's tale of the Roman empire, *Alix l'Intrépide*, Willy Vandersteen's endearing *Suske en Wiske*, and, best of all, E. P. Jacobs's scintillating science-fiction series, *Blake et Mortimer*.

After an initial period of prostration, the Japanese cartoonists also rebounded with their legendary resiliency. The American occupation had the beneficial effect of cutting the Japanese strip loose from some of its more desiccated storytelling traditions, and Japanese comics acquired a more occidental outlook, with forays into science fiction (*Fushigina Kuni no Putchā*), jungle adventure (*Shōnen Oja*), and even domestic humor (*Sazaesan*).

The late 1940s also witnessed a strong surge of interest in the cultural and social potentialities of the comic form (the first comprehensive survey of the medium, Coulton Waugh's *The Comics*, appeared in 1947). There was also widespread (if sometimes grudging) recognition of the contributions made by the comics to the folklore and mythology of our times; Superman, Krazy Kat, Popeye, Dagwood, and Li'l Abner were now perceived in a new light, not just as slapstick or cardboard characters, but as emblematic figures representative of deep nostalgia and longing. For the comics, the age of innocence was over.

Milton Caniff, "Steve Canyon." © Field Newspaper Syndicate.

E. P. Jacobs, "Blake at Mortimer." © Editions du Lombard.

The eventful decade of the 1950s

The 1950s were marked by the slow but irreversible decline of the American comic industry in terms of creativity, leadership, prestige, and viability. The causes for this erosion were many, but a few can be singled out.

The very popularity of the newspaper comics was, paradoxically, one cause of their decline. In order to capitalize on the comics' pull on their readers, many newspapers started cramming four, five, or even as many as eight features onto a standard page, resulting in an unseemly overcrowding of the comic page; like food piled up on a cafeteria tray, the mess eventually turned off all but the less discriminating customers. The daily strip fared no better, being further and further reduced in size to suit editors' whims. By the end of the 1950s the newspaper strips were a shambles. Older readers were slow to notice, but younger people gradually stopped reading them.

The action strip, which suffered most grievously from these strictures (the humor strip could adapt more easily to the reduction in format), was dealt a further blow by the retirement or death of some of its most outstanding practitioners (Burne Hogarth quit the field in 1950, Alex Raymond was killed in a car accident in 1956, Clarence Gray died in 1957, and Frank Godwin died in 1959). The American adventure strip never recovered from this quadruple loss.

The comic book, meanwhile, had its own problems. After the boom of the war years, readership fell off drastically. Many publishers went out of business, and those remaining had to fight fiercely to keep their share of the shrinking market. The novelty of the medium had by now worn thin, and its most popular feature, the superhero, was no longer able to pull in the customers—even Superman fared badly. In order to bolster sales, some publishers turned to unbridled violence, in the form of crime stories, or to horror. The most extreme case was that of William Gaines's E.C. Comics.

Some of the titles that E.C. put out in the early 1950s speak for themselves: *Crypt of Terror, The Vault of Horror, The Haunt of Fear.* Latter-day apologists of the E.C. horror comics speak in hushed tones of the high quality of art and writing that went into these books. There is some truth to their arguments, as far as they go. Most of the art and writing was only good in comparison to those in other comic books; furthermore, E.C. artists and editors, while arguably setting some

Comic Strip Mythology: Sadie Hawkins Day

Sadie Hawkins Day takes place annually in the Dogpatch of Al Capp's Li'l Abner strip every November, no particular date in November being "official." Essentially, it is a traditional mountain-culture ceremony, invented by Capp for his rural hill characters, in which all the eligible bachelors of the Dogpatch community are pursued, after being given a "fair" running start, by all the eligible females, age or physical condition notwithstanding. Males "drug" over the finish line in the heart of the town by midnight have to marry the girls who capture them; in the meantime, the men can hide anywhere, so long as they remain within the city limits of Dogpatch (which covers a good bit of open hill country). The girls may use any means they like to capture the man of their choice, from a club to tear gas—and almost every conceivable device has been used in the course of the Li'l Abner strip.

Introduced in a Li'l Abner narrative beginning on November 13, 1937, Sadie Hawkins Day was named for the daughter of "one of the earliest settlers of Dogpatch, Hekzebiah Hawkins," to quote Capp's text. Homely, Sadie had gone without suitors until she was 35, and her father was grimly furious. Taking a gun, he rounded up by cajolery and/or force all of the eligible young men in the town, laid down the rules (in Capp's initial version, the girl only had to catch the boy to be able to marry him; for drama's sake, Capp added the fin-

ish line a bit later), and fired his gun to start the boys running, then fired it again to set the girls on their trail a brief time later. The Dogpatch spinsters, Capp wrote, "reckoned it were such a good idea that Sadie Hawkins Day was made an annual affair." As presented in Li'l Abner, Abner was usually the fearful figure followed by the reader during the yearly event in the strip, until his actual marriage to Daisy Mae forced Capp to feature other characters in subsequent years' events.

For several decades, Capp reprinted the original two 1937 daily episodes, explaining the origin and rules of Sadie Hawkins Day every successive November. He deliberately left the date of the day in November unfixed, however, to permit himself continuity leeway from year to year. The dates announced in the narrative have varied from November 7 (1942) to November 25 (1967) and are obviously valid only for the year concerned. The Sadie Hawkins Day idea was seized upon almost from its inception by college, community, and office groups eager to dress up in hillbilly regalia and "switch" the roles of the sexes for a day. It has been estimated that 500 to 1,000 such parties or actual chases take place annually in the United States. Marriage, however, does not seem to be the pursuit of these get-togethers.

B.B.

A horror comic book. © E.C. Publications.

new trends in graphic storytelling, also displayed (in a succession of gruesome stories and gory covers) a callous disregard for civilized sensitivities. This trait, while acceptable, perhaps even desirable, in formats designed for mature readers (such as the later underground comics), was certainly objectionable in a popular medium overwhelmingly aimed at children. It seemed like a sure way to bring censure to the comic book.

The comics had always had their share of detractors (some were legitimately concerned educators, others were plain cranks), but these had proved no more than mere nuisances. Toward mid-century, however, the clouds above the comics grew increasingly more dark and threatening, and the horror comics bore the largest share of the blame. The controversy reached its crescendo in 1954 with the Estes Kefauver senatorial hearings and the publication of Dr. Frederic Wertham's *Seduction of the Innocent*. That same year, to fend off impending censorship, the publishers established the Comics Code Authority, a self-regulating body (the standards set forth by the code, as later revised, can be found in Appendix C). If it saved the industry from probable ruin (a fact conveniently overlooked by its more rabid critics), the establishment of the code also resulted in the total emasculation of the medium. As a creative force, the comic book simply ceased to exist for the remainder of the decade.

The newspaper strips fared somewhat better. There was a discernible loss of creativity, not only in the adventure field (the only noteworthy entry was *The Cisco Kid* and, symptomatically, it was drawn by a foreign artist, the Argentinian José-Luis Salinas), but in the traditional humor strip as well. *Beetle Bailey*, by Mort Walker, and *Dennis the Menace*, by Hank Ketcham, both appeared at the beginning of the decade and were the only strips whose popularity rivaled that of the established funny strips.

The 1950s also witnessed the rise of the soap-opera comics. Started as a genre in the 1930s (with *Mary Worth* as its standard-bearer), the soaps prospered and multiplied in this, America's most problem-ridden decade. There were *Judge Parker*, written by Dr. Nicholas Dallis (significantly, a psychiatrist and the author of the earlier *Rex Morgan, M.D.*), Stan Drake's *The Heart of Juliet Jones*, Leonard Starr's *On Stage*, and a host of others.

Comic Publishing in the Philippines in the 1970s: A Case Study

For several decades Ace Publications has been the dominant comic book company in the Philippines. It is controlled by Ramon Roces, the owner of Roces Publications and the most successful publisher in the field.

On June 14, 1947, the first issue of Pilipino Komiks *appeared in the Philippines, a country that has the most avid comic book readers in the world. Many of the comic publications were geared toward the masses; they catered to the tastes and demands of the adult population, as well as those of the younger generation.*

Pilipino Komiks *became such a tremendous hit that other comics were brought out in the 1950s.* Hiwaga, Espesyal Komiks, Tagalog Klasiks, Kenkoy Komiks, *and* Educational Klasiks *were added to the roster.*

The guiding force behind the success of Ace Publications was Tony Velasquez, the most popular cartoonist in the Islands. He wrote and illustrated Kenkoy, *the most famous cartoon character in the history of Philippine comics. Velasquez also had worked for* Halakhak, *the first comic book to be published in the country.*

Also working for Roces Publications were comic book pioneers Francisco Reyes (the illustrator of Kulafu, *the Filipino jungle hero), Carlos Francisco (the foremost muralist in the country), and Francisco V. Coching (the most imitated and admired writer-artist in the medium). Other early participants were Jesse Santos (of* DI 13 *fame), Larry Alcala (creator of* Kalabog en Bosyo, *the funniest duo to appear in komix), Noly Panaligan (one of the finest komik technicians), Fred Carillo, Teny Henson, Ruben Yandoc, and Elpidio Torres.*

The writers who joined the fold were Clodualdo del Mundo, Mars Ravelo, Gregorio Coching, Pablo Gomez, Virgilio Redondo, and Damy Velasquez. And some of the more well-known cartoonists were Deo Gonzales, Sabala Santos, Malang Santos, and Menny Martin. Among the list of top artists who became internationally known are Nestor Redondo, Alfredo Alcala, Tony Zuñiga, and Alex Niño.

Many of the classics of the Philippine graphic-novel appeared in the pages of the comics that carried the Ace insignia. Among them are Kabibe, Satur, Lapu-Lapu, El Indio, Barbaro, Dumagit, Maldita, Pulot-Gata, Waldas, Gigolo, Buhawi, Darna, Diwani, Ukala, Ifugao, Infanta Judith, Yamato, Warspite, Mikasa, Guerrero, Kurdapya, Monica, Pandora, Hokus-Pokus, Buntot-Page, Payaso, Brix Virgo, *and a host of others.*

Numerous other artists and writers have contributed their talents through the years to Ace. Among them are Federico Javinal, Alcantara, Jess Jodloman, P. Z. Marcelo, Rico Rival, Nestor Leonidez, Tuning Ocampo, Jim Fernandez, Tony Caravana, Rene Rosales, Manuel Carillo, Cirio H. Santiago, Rico Bello Omagap, and Jaime Vidal.

O.J.

Walt Kelly, "Pogo." © Walt Kelly.

Charles Schulz, "Peanuts." © United Feature
Syndicate.

Then the nation's fears, doubts, and hopes found their expression in a remarkable group of intellectual and sharply questioning new strips: *Peanuts, Feiffer, B.C.*
(to which should be added the earlier *Pogo*). Their authors, Charles Schulz, Jules
Feiffer, Johnny Hart, and Walt Kelly, often pioneered in their innovative use of
the medium, as well as in their sharp and unblinking commentary on contemporary social, political, and psychological ills. That they did indeed strike a
responsive chord is best exemplified by the extraordinary success of *Peanuts*.

The rest of the world was no longer taking its cue from the American comics,
however. National comic strip productions were again springing up everywhere.
This was hastened by the proliferation of comic weeklies, which turned more
and more to local talent to replace an American production grown increasingly
stale. Art, like nature, abhors a vacuum, and as the American production went
down, both quantitatively and qualitatively, non-American features correspondingly came to the fore.

This phenomenon was nowhere as apparent as with the action strips. While
American syndicates were dropping adventure titles right and left, the rest of the
world was busy turning out new ones. In the science-fiction field there were
Frank Hampson's *Dan Dare*, Sidney Jordan's *Jeff Hawke*, Osamu Tezuka's
Tetsuwan-Atom; the Western gave birth to Arturo Del Castillo's *Randall* and
Joseph Gillain's *Jerry Spring*; the police strip had *Ric Hochet* and *Gil Jourdan*. Other
types of adventure stories also found their representation in such strips as *Akadō*

Osamu Tezuka, "Tetsuwan-Atom." © Shōnen.

Arturo Del Castillo, "Randall." © Frontera.

Suzunosuke, *Air Hawk*, *El Capitan Trueno*, *Michel Tanguy*, and *Ninja Bugeicho*, to mention only the best or the most popular.

In the humor field the American strip also met with stiff competition from France (where *Astérix*, born in 1959, soon became a worldwide success), Belgium (*Gaston Lagaffe*, *Max*), Japan (*Kappa*), Germany (*Nick Knatterton*), Spain (*Mortadelo y Filemón*), Italy (*Cocco Bill*), and especially England, with Reg Smythe's *Andy Capp*, which has since conquered the American public.

Where America still held an advantage was in the realm of the sophisticated strip. No other country could boast of a feature as philosophical as *Pogo* or as penetrating as *Peanuts*. But, even there, the situation soon changed.

A shift in direction

After its brilliant, but essentially limited, renaissance in the 1950s, the American newspaper strip began to suffer from the worst artistic and economic slump in its history. In the 1960s and early 1970s few new strips achieved acclaim or notice, and only three reached the top of the lists: Johnny Hart and Brant Parker's *The Wizard of Id*, Garry Trudeau's *Doonesbury*, and Dik Browne's *Hägar the Horrible*. Economic disaster went hand in hand with artistic failure; the 1975 edition of *Editor & Publisher*'s syndicate directory listed less than 200 current strips being nationally syndicated, an all-time low. (Some syndicates also offered reprints of defunct comic features, such as Harold Gray's *Little Orphan Annie*, a most damning admission of creative failure.)

Granted that the economic factors that led to the syndicates' predicament (such as the declining readership of American newspapers) were not of their making (though it can be argued that, since the comic strip has historically been the most popular feature in newspapers, more people would have read the papers if they could find better comics in their pages), the unmitigated artistic disaster resulting was entirely the syndicates' own doing. Despite an undisputably large pool of new cartooning talent being turned out each year by the art schools (to mention only one source), the syndicate editors were unwilling or unable to tap these resources. Only a handful of nationally syndicated strip cartoonists were under 35 years of age, and only one, Garry Trudeau, was in his twenties (significantly, he was discovered by a small-time organization, which grew big, thanks to their judgment).

In point of fact a majority of cartoonists were in their sixties and seventies, and while old age is not necessarily synonymous with senility, it can hardly be looked upon as a fount of creative ideas. (Lest the reader gets the false impression that old-timers are paragons of productivity in their later years, one must hasten to add that most older cartoonists—and quite a few younger ones as well—resort to the infamous practice of "ghosting": they hire anonymous hacks to do their work while they play golf or watch their health.) It is no wonder, therefore, that the syndicate system literally crumbled under such appalling dead weight.

Garry Trudeau, "Doonesbury." © G.B. Trudeau.

Stan Lee and John Romita, "Spider-Man." © Marvel Comics Group.

In the 1960s the comic book broke with the pattern of repetitiveness and uni-formity that had become associated with the medium in the preceding decade. Editor/writer Stan Lee, particularly, started experimenting with new designs and concepts, with the help of a talented stable of artists that included Jack Kirby, Steve Ditko, and Jim Steranko. This was the famous age of Marvel's "super-heroes with problems," characters such as the Fantastic Four, Thor, and, espe-cially, Spider-Man, who became a symbol for a whole generation of college students. National also tried to revamp its comic book lineup to suit the new age of relevance, but with markedly less success.

In the 1970s the comic books came down from the high peak of their popu-larity. The publishers tried to diversify, with new titles coming out practically every month (some lasting only one or two issues), but only the adaptation in comic form of Robert Howard's *Conan the Barbarian* took hold with the readers. In 1975 the drawn-out legal battle between National and *Superman*'s creators was finally settled out of court, with National's parent company, Warner Com-munications, agreeing to pay Jerry Siegel and Joe Shuster a lifelong annuity—a welcome plus for an industry that has been plagued with much adverse pub-licity.

The foremost comic book innovations came, however, from the so-called underground comics (or "comix" as they are commonly called), which allied

"Hef's Pad." © Robert Crumb, Jay Lynch, Skip Williamson.

James Holdaway and Peter O'Donnell, "Modesty Blaise." © Beaverbrook Newspapers Ltd.

great freedom of subject matter (including pornography and scatology) with a return to the original sources. Begun in such publications as *The East Village Other* and *Zap Comix*, the undergrounds enjoyed a tremendous boom throughout the decade, despite harassment, censorship, and lawsuits. Eventually the underground cartoonists gained recognition, and some, like Robert Crumb (whose most popular creations are *Fritz the Cat* and *Mr. Natural*) and Gilbert Shelton (author of *The Fabulous Furry Freak Brothers*), became famous.

Some enthusiastic critics (this writer included) predicted a long and glorious future for the new breed. Unhappily, the undergrounders' staying power did not match their talent; most of them lacked the self-discipline indispensable to any artist, and soon many dropped out of the comix scene for the same reasons they had dropped out of straight society—out of adolescent self-indulgence. While the underground movement cannot be entirely written off, it is certainly no longer the model that it was in its heyday.

The 1960s and the first half of the 1970s witnessed the exuberant growth of the comic form in the rest of the world. The English cartoonists enjoyed a surge of creativity; British humor asserted itself in Frank Dickens's hilarious account of office life, *Bristow*, and reached new heights of outrageousness with such iconoclastic confections as Bill Tidy's *The Fosdyke Saga* and Nicholas Garland's *Barry McKenzie*. In a more serious vein were Peter O'Donnell and James Holdaway's fast-moving *Modesty Blaise*, Pat Tourret and Jenny Butterworth's lighthearted soap opera, *Tiffany Jones*, and the superlative creations of Frank Bellamy, England's most gifted draftsman (*Frazer of Africa* and *Heros the Spartan*).

Across the Channel the French comic strip flourished. Two excellent comic features, *Achille Talon* by Greg (Michel Régnier) and *Gai Luron* by Marcel Gotlib, saw the light of print in this period; adventure was well represented by such outstanding creations as *Lieutenant Blueberry*, Jean Giraud's brooding Western; *Philémon*, a delightful work of fantasy by Fred (Othon Aristides); and Jean-Claude Forest's sex-cum-science-fiction strip, *Barbarella*.

The other major French-speaking country, Belgium, contributed the adventure strip, *Bernard Prince*, and the Western, *Comanche*, both drawn by Hermann (Huppen) and written by Greg, as well as François Craenhals's period strip, *Chevalier Ardent*, and the whimsical *Les Schtroumpfs* by Peyo (Pierre Culliford).

Jean-Claude Forest, ''Barbarella.'' © J.C. Forest.

In Italy the 1960s saw the establishment of the ''black hero'' type of strip: *Diabolik* by Angela and Luciana Giussani opened the way, followed by *Kriminal* and others. The sick humor strip found its representation in Franco Bonvicini's *Sturmtruppen.* Two of the most remarkable artists of the comics came into their own in this period—Hugo Pratt, who injected new life into the adventure strip with *Una Ballata del Mare Salato* and *Corto Maltese,* and Guido Crepax, who revolutionized the content and style of the modern comic strip in such creations as *La Casa Matta, Bianca,* and, above all, the hauntingly beautiful *Valentina.*

Quality of design and draftsmanship was the hallmark of the Spanish cartoonists of this period: Carlos Giménez (*Delta 99, Dani Futuro*), Victor de la Fuente (*Haxtur*), and Esteban Maroto (*Cinco por Infinito, Wolff*) were the most outstanding. For his part, Enric Sío carried out interesting experiments with layout and color in his strips, *Nus* and *Sorang.*

European comic production was, in the 1970s, more vigorous and diversified than at any time in its history. Every European country seemed to be participat-

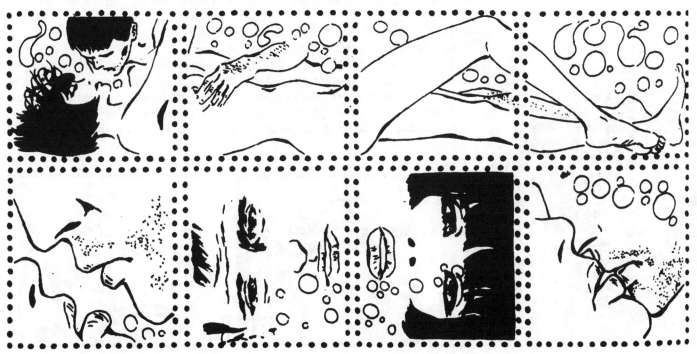

Guido Crepax, ''Valentina.'' © Crepax/Figure.

ing in the comic sweepstakes, from Denmark (*Rasmus Klump*) to Germany (*Roy Tiger*, Rolf Kauka's comic creations), from the Netherlands (*Dzjengis Khan*) to Yugoslavia (*Herlock Sholmes*). Even in the Soviet Union the comics enjoyed a modest boom. So excellent did the European features become that, while they did not reach the United States in any sizable number (the success of *Andy Capp* notwithstanding), they successfully competed with American comics in such traditional American markets as Canada and South America.

Japan was the only non-Western country with a major comics production. Japanese creations were both numerous and notable in the 1960s and the first half of the 1970s. Osamu Tezuka added to his string of successes with the allegorical *Hi no Tori*, but he received artistic and commercial competition from Sanpei Shirato (*Sasuke, Kamui Den*), Gōseki Kojima (*Kozure Okami*), Tetsuya Chiba (*Harisu no Kaze, Ashita no Joe*), and Takao Saitō (*Golgo 13*). Two remarkable draftsmen reached their stride in this period: Hiroshi Hirata, who excelled in the depiction of violent, pulsating action scenes, and Koo Kojima, a master of subtle eroticism. Modern brands of black comedy and nonsense found able exponents in Shunji Sonoyama (*Gyatoruzu*), Fujio Akatsuka (*Osomatsu-kun*), and Tatsuhiko Yamagami (*Gaki Deka*); while Shinji Nagashima created what may be the first autobiographical novel in comic form with his trilogy, *Kiiroi Namida*.

The comics are a world phenomenon. To cite every comic-producing country would be tantamount to a roll call at the United Nations. One must mention, however, the Philippines (*Voltar*), Mexico (*Alma Grande*), Argentina (*Mafalda*, a Latin version of *Peanuts*), and China, whose flourishing comic book productions are slowly finding their way into the West.

The comics today: a new perspective

One of the most significant developments in the recent history of comic art, and perhaps the one most likely to affect its course in the future, has come not from within the profession, but from without: the formation in the 1960s of groups devoted to the study and preservation of the comics. In the past there had been individuals who had written cogently on the subject, but their efforts remained isolated and they went largely unnoticed. Not so with those militant organizations whose voices became increasingly audible. Soon there were international comic conferences (the first one, held at Bordighera, Italy, in 1965, was followed by the yearly congresses in Lucca); major art exhibitions were organized (the 1967 "Bande Dessinée et Figuration Narrative" at the Louvre and the 1971 "75 Years of the Comics" at the New York Cultural Center were two milestones); comic art museums were established (the first one, the City Museum of Cartoon Art, opened in Omiya, Japan, in 1966); and specialized, professional magazines (succeeding the amateurish "fanzines") sprang up everywhere. Strong and articulate personalities emerged in the field and manifested themselves in scores of histories, essays, articles, and lectures.

This activity in turn brought about a heightened awareness among a substantial segment of the public (usually the young and the intellectuals), changing them into ardent readers and critics of the form (there are comicophiles as there are cinephiles). Put in simple terms, there has been created *a public*, whose enthusiasm and appreciation make up for their small (but growing) numbers.

A page from a Chinese comic book.

Shunji Sonoyama, "Gyatoruzu." © Sonoyama.

Like their counterparts in other disciplines, the comic critics fulfill two main functions. One is the rediscovery, reevaluation, and preservation of the past (the works and artistic reputations of Winsor McCay, Alex Raymond, and Burne Hogarth, among others, have all been saved from oblivion by this continuing process of reappraisal). Their second—and perhaps more important—function is to express an educated judgment on the current production. Here, too, the critics have been successful in pointing the way; certainly artists as diverse as J. C. Forest, Guido Crepax, Shinji Nagashima, and Robert Crumb owe a large part of the recognition they have received to perceptive critics and an enlightened public.

Twenty years of American comics

Starting in the late 1970s, however, there has been a strong resurgence of fresh, innovative humor strips. In 1977 the Pulitzer Prize-winning editorial cartoonist Jeff McNelly created *Shoe*, a hilarious newsroom satire in which the assorted characters are birds of a different plumage; and the following year Jim Davis's *Garfield*, the quintessential cat strip, made its appearance. The trend culminated with the publication of Berke Breathed's *Bloom County* (1980), starring, among other outlandish characters, a sententious penguin, a liquor- and drug-crazed cat, and a 10-year-old scientific genius and convicted hacker named Oliver Wendell Jones.

Other newspaper strips followed along the same path, including *Zippy the Pinhead*, an iconoclastic feature concocted by Bill Griffith for underground comic books in the 1970s and transplanted to the newspaper pages a decade later; Scott Adams's minimally drawn but brilliantly written office comedy *Dilbert*; and two by yet more Pulitzer Prize winners, Mike Peters's *Mother Goose and Grimm* and Doug Marlette's *Kudzu*. The most original, innovative, and delightful comic strip to come out in the last decade—perhaps in the last quarter-century—was *Calvin and Hobbes*, about a hyperactive six-year-old and his pet tiger, created by Bill Watterson in 1985 and ended much too soon 10 years later.

Doug Marlette, "Kudzu." © Jefferson Communications.

Women and minorities were finally given their due in the past 20 years. Following such pioneering strips of the 1960s and 1970s as Morrie Turner's *Wee Pals* and Ted Shearer's *Quincy*, the last decade witnessed an ample flowering of newspaper comics on black themes: mention should be made of Ray Billingsley's *Curtis*, Stephen Bentley's *Herb & Jamaal*, and Robb Armstrong's *Jump Start*. Similarly, two distinctive and award-winning features written and drawn by women, Cathy Guisewite's *Cathy* (1976) and Lynn Johnston's *For Better or For Worse* (1978) gained strong readership among both genders.

The story strips, however, have continued on a downward spiral. The last 20 years tolled the end for such long-lasting features as *Brick Bradford, Captain Easy, Secret Agent Corrigan,* and *Joe Palooka.* Bucking the trend, Tribune Media Services in 1995 revived *Terry and the Pirates* in a new, jazzed-up version. The year 1996 marked the 100th birthday of comics, with numerous celebrations taking place across the United States, including the issuance by the U.S. Postal Service of a 20-stamp set of "Newspaper Strip Classics," and this in turn may signal the resurgence of a form that some had already written off as dead a few short years ago.

With newsstand sales plummeting and many companies folding, the comic-book medium was only saved at the end of the 1970s by a revolutionary method of distribution: the so-called direct market, consisting of a network of specialized comic stores (totaling almost 5,000 by the mid-1990s) that bought comic-book titles on a nonreturnable basis. Thus bolstered by guaranteed sales of their product, comic-book publishers quickly rebounded.

Marvel preserved its dominant position in the comics industry with its incredibly successful line of *X-Men* comics; started as early as 1963, they only gained a large public following in the late 1970s. By the 1980s the series had spawned an entire line of spin-offs, most starting with the letter "X" (*X-Factor, X-Force,* etc.). Other Marvel titles of note have been *Alpha Flight, The New Mutants,* and the Frank Miller-scripted *Daredevil;* but overall the Marvel production suffered a sharp decline in both quality and popularity in the 1990s, a trend hastened by the flight of some of their top talents, who went on to form Image Comics. The spate of bad news culminated in December 1996, when Marvel filed for bankruptcy.

Meanwhile, DC Comics maintained a steady course, bolstered by their traditional titles, which were strongly helped by the box-office success of the *Superman* and *Batman* movies. This allowed them to experiment with new and interesting titles, such as *The New Teen Titans, Camelot 3000, Starman,* and especially *Watchmen* (1985) by the British team of Alan Moore and Dave Gibbons.

The direct market also allowed a host of small comic-book publishers, the so-called independents, to survive and occasionally flourish. Many of the most innovative creations emanated from the independents, including Howard Chaykin's *American Flagg!,* Harvey Pekar's *American Splendor,* and Dave Sim's *Cerebus,* not to mention the incredibly successful *Teenage Mutant Ninja Turtles.*

The period also saw the generalization of the graphic novel, an extended narrative told in comic-book style. The form allowed for some of the most powerful statements ever made on significant and/or controversial themes. *Maus,* done by Art Spiegelman over the span of 10 years, is an allegory of the Holocaust, in which the Jews are depicted as mice and the Nazis as cats. In 1995, Howard Cruse told a poignant coming-of-age (and coming-out-of-the-closet) tale with *Stuck Rubber Baby;* the following year Joe Kubert produced *Fax from Sarajevo,* a gripping story of the civil war in Bosnia; while Will Eisner has created several autobiographical novels (*A Contract with God, The Dreamer, Dropsie Avenue*). Comic books have finally grown up.

The last 17 years have witnessed what can only be called the "Hollywoodization of the comics," from the release of *Flash Gordon* in 1980 to the 1997 movie *Batman and Robin.* In the intervening years, these comic characters have made it onto the big screen: *Popeye, The Mask, Superman* and its sequels, *Dick Tracy, Barb Wire, The Phantom, Teenage Mutant Ninja Turtles, The Crow, Dennis the Menace,* even the British *Judge Dredd,* among others, with many more to come.

The globalization of the comics

The past two decades have been a period of great creativity in all parts of the planet, led, but no longer dominated by, the traditional comics-producing countries of western Europe, the United States, and Japan. In Britain the trend has been toward the creation of superpowered characters based on the American model, such as Judge Dredd and Marvelman. Across the Channel, French cartoonists continued to be active in all genres: social satire (*Les Bidochon,* about a lowbrow French family, is a good example), erotic humor (Georges Pichard's

Art Spiegelman, "Maus." © Art Spiegelman.

many creations), romantic adventure (François Boucq's *The Magician's Wife* and others), and science fiction (a genre in which Yugoslav-born Enki Bilal excels). Italy hasn't lagged far behind, with such creations as Vittorio Giardino's political thrillers (*Hungarian Rhapsody, Orient Gateway*), Stefano Tamburini and Tanino Liberatore's punk epic *Ranxerox*, the cartoon spoofs of Massimo Mattioli, and the many graphic novels of erotic fantasy by Milo Manara.

Following the death of the dictator General Francisco Franco, a remarkable flowering of the art took place in Spain. Mention should be made of Fernando Fernández, author of an impressive adaptation of *Dracula* (1984); of Daniel Torres, creator of the tongue-in-cheek futuristic adventures of Rocco Vargas; of the transplanted Argentinians Carlos Sampayo and José Muñoz, who uncannily re-created the mood of 1940s *film noir* in their thriller, *Alack Sinner*; and of Jordi Bernet, whose dynamic style has given distinction to the gangster tales of *Torpedo*. Other creations of note have come out of Germany (with the remarkable *Bell's Theorem* by Matthias Schultheiss), the Netherlands (where Jost Swarte holds sway with his surreal vignettes of daily life), Denmark (*Valhalla*, a tongue-in-cheek chronicle of the gods).

In the 1990s the western European production suffered a marked loss of creativity (and a consequent loss of readership), which was only partially offset by the emergence of new talent coming out of eastern Europe (Gzregorz Rosinski and Jerzy Wroblewski in Poland, Karel Saudek in the Czech Republic, and others). Even Russia, where comics had been frowned upon by the Soviet regime, enjoys a small but growing output of comic publications.

In the Americas, the Canadian Dave Sim is the author of the aforementioned *Cerebus the Aardvark*; Mauricio de Souza of Brazil spearheads a flourishing production of children's comics, of which *Monica* is the best known internationally; and Mexico continues to pour out an average but steady flow of comic *novelas*. While the Argentine output was temporarily put into artistic eclipse by the advent of the military regime in the late 1970s, the return of democracy has brought a renewal of the medium to the country. This is particularly true of Robin Wood, whose many creations have captured an international public, and of Alberto Breccia (1919-1993), who topped his long career with *Perramus*, a wrenching meditation on the meaning of life and memory.

Japan has now the distinction of being the largest producer of comic books in the world, in terms of number of copies sold. The Japanese comic books range from romance comics (Riyoko Ikeda's *The Rose of Versailles*) to thrillers (*Golgo 13* by Takao Sato) to whimsical comedy (Rumiko Takahashi's *Ranma 1/2*) to the very Japanese genre of "salary men" comics, depicting the tribulations of office workers. Of special note have been Shotaro Ishinimori's *Japan Inc.*, a fictional (or perhaps not so fictional) account of the workings of the Japanese economy, and *Gen of Hiroshima*, a very long narrative started in 1973 by Keiji Nakazawa and now totaling over 2,000 pages, about the horrors of nuclear war. Japanese comics (or *manga*) are sold in all parts of the world, including North America and western Europe.

For a long time Japan had inundated the rest of Asia with its production, but in recent years a vigorous comics industry has sprung up in every country of the region. It would be fastidious to name them all, but mention should be made of the Indonesian *Djon Domino* by Johnny Hidajat, of Rafiqun Nabi's *Tokai* in Bangladesh, of Lat's *Kampung Boy* in Malaysia. India has had a thriving comics industry, which is somewhat hampered by the number of regional dialects in the country. The cartoonist Pran has somehow surmounted this handicap with his many children's comics, which have earned him the title "Walt Disney of India." China's comics tradition goes back to the 1920s, but after the Communist takeover most of the comics industry was devoted to propaganda and nationalistic themes. A steady flow of comic strips (or rather "comic boxes," since Chinese comics usually come in a square rather than a horizontal format) has been produced since the 1950s, a production slowed (but not ended) by the Cultural Revolution. Of late, cartoonists such as Ye Quianyu and Zhang Leping have dealt with contemporary and even satirical themes in their comic strips.

Australia and New Zealand have maintained their long tradition of homespun newspaper strips. The former spawned Allan Salisbury's punning *Snake Tales*, while the latter harbors Murray Ball's barnyard-flavored *Footrot Flats*. The comics have now become a universally accepted form of expression, and examples can be found from South Africa (where the most popular newspaper strip, *Madam and Eve*, stars a white matron and her black maid) to Algeria, whose eminent cartoonist, Sid Ali Melouah, has won many awards in Europe for his comic strips. Most importantly, cartoonists and their creations are now transcending national borders, with European artists coming to the United States, American cartoonists working in Europe and Japan, and many national publications open to talent from the entire world. This trend can only continue well into the next century.

With festivals, exhibitions, and conventions (not to mention comic art museums) springing up all over the world, there now seems to be a universal acceptance of the comics as a legitimate form of popular culture, despite resistance in some academic circles, to validate the important contributions the comics have made to the consciousness and culture of people worldwide.

One of the more hopeful (as well as one of the more exciting) developments in recent years has been the introduction of comics on the Internet. There are now forums for discussion on the comics during which fans can voice their opinions and exchange views on the latest comics offerings, thereby providing word-of-mouth support to an art form too often neglected by mainstream media; just as importantly, comics old and new are being broadcast over the Net. Some of the syndicates offer daily installments of their most popular strips, and creators also use the Web to promote their strips, independently of their syndicates. As Lee Salem of Universal Press Syndicate recently noted, "Whatever cyberspace becomes may well afford cartoonists other creative outlets, and it's easy to envision thousands—even millions—of people subscribing to a cartoonist's work for a penny a day." The number of comic strips thus beamed out increases every day, and there has been a promising growth in the number of international, independent, and underground comics that have joined the ranks of more established features. It is possible that to a great extent the future of comics in the 21st century lies in that direction.

Maurice Horn

A World Chronology of Comic Art
From the 18th Century to the Present

1734:

William Hogarth's *A Harlot's Progress* published.

1735:

W. Hogarth's *A Rake's Progress* published.

1745:

W. Hogarth's *Marriage à la Mode* appears.

1790-1815:

James Gillray publishes his series of patriotic cartoons, extolling British virtues and excoriating the vices of Republican (and later Napoleonic) France.

1809:

Thomas Rowlandson produces his most famous cartoon series, *The Tour of Doctor Syntax*, with verses by William Combe.

1814:

First volume of *Hokusai Manga* ("The Hokusai Cartoons") published in Japan.

1815:

T. Rowlandson publishes his satirical cartoon series, *English Dance of Death*.

1841:

Punch magazine started in London.

1846-47:

Rodolphe Töpffer's picture-stories collected in book form as *Histoires en Estampes*.

1885:

Wilhelm Busch's *Max und Moritz* published in Germany.

First real newspaper syndicate, A. N. Kellogg News Company, established in the United States.

1867:

First adventure of *Ally Sloper* published in England by Charles Henry Ross.

1877:

English-language version of the comic weekly *Puck* published in the United States.

1881:

Judge magazine starts publication as *The Judge*.

1883:

Life magazine established.

James Gillray, "Tales of Wonder."

Richard Outcault, "The Yellow Kid."

1889:

Christophe's *La Famille Fenouillard à l'Exposition* published in France.

1890:

Comic Cuts and *Chips* started in England.

1893:

New York Recorder publishes its first color page, one week ahead of the *New York World*. James Swinnerton's *Little Bears* starts as a spot filler in the *San Francisco Examiner*.

1895:

R. F. Outcault's character, the Yellow Kid, makes his first appearance in the *World*.

1896:

The *Yellow Kid* definitively established as a weekly feature.

In England *Weary Willie and Tired Tim* created by Tom Browne.

1897:

Outcault leaves the *World* for the *Journal*. "The American Humorist," the *Journal*'s color Sunday supplement established (first issue features *The Yellow Kid* and Rudolph Dirks's *The Katzenjammer Kids*).

1900:

Carl "Bunny" Schultze creates *Foxy Grandpa* for the *New York Herald*. F. B. Opper's *Happy Hooligan* appears.

1902:

R. F. Outcault starts *Buster Brown* in the *New York Herald*.

J. S. Baker's *Casey Court* started in England.

First publication in France of *Le Jeudi de la Jeunesse* magazine.

First Swedish comic strip, *Mannen som gör vad som faller honom in* ("The Man who Does Whatever Comes to His Mind") by Oskar Andersson (O.A.), appears.

1903:

Gustave Verbeck's reversible strip, *The Upside Downs*, starts publication in the *Herald*. Clare Briggs's weekday strip, *A. Piker Clerk*, starts in the *Chicago American*.

1904:

George McManus creates *The Newlyweds*. *The Dream of the Rarebit Fiend* by Silas (Winsor McCay) starts in the *Evening Telegram*. James Swinnerton originates *Little Jimmy*.

J. S. Baker's *Tiger Tim* started in England.

Comic weekly *L'Illustre* (later changed to *Le Petit Illustrê*) established in Paris.

First French-Canadian newspaper strip, *Le Père Ladébauche*, started in *La Presse* by J. Charlebois.

C. W. Kahles, "Hairbreadth Harry."

1905:

Winsor McCay creates *Little Nemo in Slumberland* for the *Herald*. G. Verbeck starts *The Terrors of the Tiny Tads*.

Bécassine by Pinchon and Caumery published in France.

First publication of the comic magazine *O Tico Tico* in Brazil.

Tokyo Puck founded in Japan.

1908:

C. W. Kahles originates *Hairbreadth Harry*. From Germany, Lyonel Feininger creates *The Kin-der-Kids* and *Wee Willie Winkie's World* for the *Chicago Tribune*.

1907:

First successful daily strip, H. C. "Bud" Fisher's *Mr. A. Mutt* (later changed to *Mutt and Jeff*), appears in the *San Francisco Chronicle*.

1908:

The comic weekly *L'Epatant* established in Paris; in issue number 9 Louis Forton creates *La Bande des Pieds-Nickelés*.

In England *Billy Bunter* started by Frank Richards.

Il Corriere dei Piccoli established in Italy with Attilio Mussino's *Bilbolbul* featured in first issue.

1909:

L'Espiègle Lili created by Jo Valle and André Vallet (France).

1910:

Desperate Desmond created by Harry Hershfield. First appearance of George Herriman's *The Dingbat Family*.

Antonio Rubino's *Quadratino* published in Italy.

1911:

Sidney Smith creates *Old Doc Yak*.

1912:

International Feature Service founded by William Randolph Hearst. Rudolph Dirks leaves the *Journal*; Hearst starts lawsuit against Dirks to prevent him from drawing *The Katzenjammer Kids* for the *World*. Cliff Sterrett's *Polly and Her Pals* started as *Positive Polly*.

1913:

George McManus originates his most famous creation, *Bringing Up Father*. First appearance of George Herriman's *Krazy Kat* as a regular strip.

1914:

Hearst v. Dirks lawsuit settled in appeal; *The Katzenjammer Kids* remains in the *Journal* (illustrated by H. H. Knerr), while Dirks retains right to draw his characters for the *World*, under the title *Hans and Fritz* (changed to *The Captain and the Kids* during World War I). Harry Hershfield starts *Abie the Agent*.

1915:

Fontaine Fox definitively establishes *Toonerville Folks*. Rube Goldberg creates *Boob McNutt*. Merrill Blosser's *Freckles and His Friends* appears. King Features Syndicate founded by Moses Koenigsberg as a consolidation of International Feature Service and other Hearst newspaper interests.

First British daily strip, *Teddy Tail* by Charles Folkard, appears in the *Daily Mail*.

1916:

Arturo Lanteri's *El Negro Raul* started in Argentina.

1917:

Sidney Smith starts *The Gumps*.

In Italy *Il Signor Bonaventura* created by Sto (Sergio Tofano).

1918:

Frank King originates *Gasoline Alley*.

First professional association of cartoonists, the "Manga Kourakukai," founded by Rakuten Kitazawa in Japan.

1919:

Billy DeBeck creates *Barney Google*. *Thimble Theater* started by E. C. Segar. *Harold Teen* originated by Carl Ed.

Pip, Squeak and Wilfred created by Bertram Lamb and A. B. Payne in England.

The Potts (originally *You and Me*) started by Stanley Cross in Australia.

Sto (Sergio Tofano), "Il Signor Bonaventura." © Corriere dei Piccoli.

James Bancks, "Ginger Meggs." © Australian Consolidated Press Ltd.

1920:
Martin Branner creates *Winnie Winkle*.
Rupert created by Mary Tourtel in England.
Oscar Jacobsson's *Adamson* started in Sweden.

1921:
Ed Wheelan creates *Minute Movies*. Russ Westover originates *Tillie the Toiler*. *Out Our Way* started by J. R. Williams.
Birdseye Center started (as *Life's Little Comedies*) by James Frise in Canada.
John Millar Watt creates *Pop* in the *London Daily Sketch*.
First successful Dutch daily strip, *Bulletje en Bonestaak*, by G. A. Van Raemdonck, appears in *Het Volk* (preceded by a few months by the short-lived *Yoebje en Achmed*).
Ginger Meggs (originally *Us Fellers*) created by James Bancks in Australia.
Don Catarino daily strip started by Salvador Pruneda in Mexico.

1922:
Smitty created by Walter Berndt.
In Argentina Arturo Lanteri creates *Don Pancho Talero*.
Fatty Finn created by Syd Nicholls in Australia.

1923:
Pat Sullivan's *Felix the Cat* syndicated as a newspaper strip. *The Nebbs* started by Sol Hess, with drawings by W. A. Carlson. *Moon Mullins* created by Frank Willard. Ad Carter produces *Just Kids*.
Nonkina Tousan created by Yutaka Asō in Japan.

1924:
Harold Gray creates *Little Orphan Annie*. Roy Crane's *Wash Tubbs* started. *Boots and Her Buddies* created by Edgar Martin.
In France Louis Forton creates *Bibi Fricotin*.
Nonkina Tousan becomes Japan's first original daily strip.

1925:
Ella Cinders started by Charles Plumb and Bill Conselman. Alain Saint-Ogan creates *Zig et Puce* in France.
In Finland Ola Fogelberg starts *Pekka Puupää*.
Longest-running Australian strip, Mary Gibbs's *Bib and Bub*, appears.

1926:
In Mexico Jesús Acosta Cabrera creates *Chupamirto*.

1927:
Frank Godwin creates *Connie*.

1928:
Tim Tyler's Luck created by Lyman Young. Hal Forrest and Glen Chaffin introduce *Tailspin Tommy*. Ham Fisher starts *Joe Palooka*. Percy Crosby's *Skippy* syndicated by King Features.
Macaco created by K-Hito (Ricardo García López) in Spain.

1929:
The adventure strip definitively established in the comic pages with P. Nowlan and R. Calkins's *Buck Rogers* and Harold Foster's *Tarzan*. Popeye makes his appearance in Segar's *Thimble Theater*. Clifford McBride's *Napoleon* established.
In Belgium Hergé (Georges Rémi) creates *Tintin*.

Sor Pampurio created by Carlo Bisi in Italy.

Tony Velasquez's *Kenkoy* appears in the Philippines.

1930:

Walt Disney's *Mickey Mouse*, drawn by Ub Iwerks, starts syndication as a daily strip. Chic Young creates *Blondie*.

Speed Tarō created by Sako Shushido in *Japan*.

1931:

Chester Gould creates *Dick Tracy*.

Patoruzú started as an independent strip by Dante Quinterno in Argentina.

In Japan *Norakuro* created by Suihou Tagawa.

1932:

Martha Orr creates *Apple Mary* (later changed to *Mary Worth*). C. D. Russell's *Pete the Tramp* starts national syndication.

Norman Pett starts *Jane's Journal* (later *Jane*) for the *London Daily Mirror*.

Fiki-Miki created by Makusynski and Walentinowicz in Poland.

Globi, by J. K. Schiele and Robert Lips, appears in Switzerland.

In Sweden *91 Karlsson* started by Rudolf Petersson.

1933:

Funnies On Parade issued for Procter and Gamble. Zack Mosley starts *Smilin' Jack* (originally *On the Wing*). William Ritt and Clarence Gray create *Brick Bradford*. Milton Caniff starts *Dickie Dare*. *Alley Oop* created by V. T. Hamlin.

1934:

A bumper year for the American comic strip: *Flash Gordon* and *Jungle Jim* (both by Alex Raymond), *Secret Agent X-9* (by A. Raymond and Dashiell Hammett), *Mandrake the Magician* by Lee Falk and Phil Davis, *Li'l Abner* by Al Capp, *Terry and the Pirates* by Milton Caniff, *Red Barry* by Will Gould, *Don Winslow* by F. Martinek and L. Beroth. Noel Sickles takes over *Scorchy Smith* (created 1930). Otto Soglow's *Little King* starts syndication.

First French daily strip, *Le Professeur Nimbus*, created by A. Daix.

In Germany *Vater und Sohn* started by Erich Ohser (E. O. Plauen).

First Japanese superhero strip, *Tanku Tankurō*, created by Gajō.

1935:

Zane Grey's *King of the Royal Mounted* started by Allen Dean. Ralph Fuller creates *Oaky Doaks*. Publication of *New Fun* comic book. Bob Moore and Carl Pfeufer create *Don Dixon*. *Smokey Stover* started by Bill Holman.

In Spain Jesús Blasco originates *Cuto*.

Luis Palacio creates *Don Fulgencio* in Argentina.

1936:

Lee Falk and Ray Moore create *The Phantom*.

Martha Orr, "Apple Mary." © Publishers Syndicate.

K-Hito (Ricardo García López), "Macaco." © K-Hito.

Will Eisner, "The Spirit." © Will Eisner.

Ted McCall and C. R. Snelgrove originate *Robin Hood and Company* for the *Toronto Telegram*.

Riyūichi Yokoyama's *Edokko Ken-chan* (later changed to *Fuku-chan*) started in Japan.

1937:

Harold Foster creates *Prince Valiant*. Burne Hogarth takes over the *Tarzan* Sunday page. *Detective Comics* established.

Jack Monk starts *Buck Ryan* in England.

In France *Futuropolis* created by René Pellos.

In Italy Rino Albertarelli originates *Kit Carson*. Cesare Zavattini and Giovanni Scolari create *Saturno contro la Terra*.

Andrija Maurović's *Stari Mačak* published in Yugoslavia.

H. Dahl Mikkelsen's *Ferd'nand* appears in Denmark.

Creation of Gabriel Vargas's *La Familia Burron* in Mexico.

Larry Steele created by Reg Hicks in Australia.

1938:

Fred Harman creates *Red Ryder*. Fran Striker's *The Lone Ranger* adapted to the comics by Ed Kressy. Al Andriola begins *Charlie Chan*. *Superman*, by Jerry Siegel and Joe Shuster, appears in *Action Comics*. *The Shadow* started as a newspaper strip by Vernon Greene.

The comic weekly *Spirou* established in Belgium.

Mussolini enacts a law barring all American comics (except *Mickey Mouse*) from Italy. *Virus* created by Federico Pedrochhi and Walter Molino. *Dick Fulmine* originated by Carlo Cossio.

Just Jake started by Bernard Graddon in England.

Djordje Lobacev's *Princeza Ru* appears in Yugoslavia.

1939:

Batman, by Bob Kane and Bill Finger, created in *Detective Comics*. Carl Burgos creates *The Human Torch*. Bill Everett originates *Sub-Mariner* in *Marvel Mystery*.

Barlog creates *Die Fünf Schreickensteiner* for the *Berliner Illustrirte*.

1940:

Dale Messick creates *Brenda Starr*. Will Eisner produces *The Spirit*. Lou Fine's *The Black Condor* appears in *Crack Comics*. *Captain Marvel* created by Bill Parker and C. C. Beck. Gardner Fox and Harry Lampert start *The Flash*.

In Australia *Bluey and Curley* created by Alex Gurney. Stan Cross starts *Wally and the Major*.

1941:

Gus Arriola creates *Gordo*. *Vic Jordan* by Payne and Wexler starts. *Captain America* created by Joe Simon and Jack Kirby. *Wonder Woman*, by William Marston and H. G. Peter, appears in *All-Star Comics*. Jack Cole creates *Plastic Man* in *Police Comics*. Bob Montana starts *Archie*. *Green Arrow* created by Mort Weisinger and George Papp.

Fred Harman, "Red Ryder." © NEA Service.

In Spain Jesús Blasco creates *Anita Diminuta*.

1942:

George Baker creates *The Sad Sack*. Crockett Johnson starts *Barnaby*. Dave Breger introduces *G. I. Joe* (formerly *Private Breger*) in *Yank*. Charles Biro and Bob Wood start *Crimebuster*. Carl Barks begins his comic book association with *Donald Duck*.

1943:

Milton Caniff creates *Male Call* for Camp Newspapers. Roy Crane creates *Buz Sawyer*. *Captain Easy* taken over by Crane's assistant, Leslie Turner. Al Andriola starts *Kerry Drake*. Walt Kelly's *Pogo* appears in *Animal Comics*.

Garth started by Steve Dowling in England.

1944:

Frank Robbins creates *Johnny Hazard*.

Marijac's underground strip, *Les Trois Mousquetaires du Maquis*, appears in France.

1945:

Burne Hogarth creates *Drago*. Ray Bailey begins *Bruce Gentry*.

Les Pionniers de l'Espérance created by Raymond Poïvet and Roger Lécureux in France.

Willy Vandersteen starts *Rikki en Wiske* (later changed to *Suske en Wiske*) in Belgium.

1946:

Alex Raymond creates *Rip Kirby*. The National Cartoonists Society established, with Rube Goldberg as its first president.

In France Claude Arnal starts *Placide et Muzo* and Pierre Liquois originates *Guerre à la Terre*.

In Belgium Morris creates *Lucky Luke*. *Tintin* magazine started (in first issue E. P. Jacobs's *Blake et Mortimer* and Paul Cuvelier's *Corentin* appear).

El Coyote, by José Mallorqui and Francisco Batet, begins in Spain.

1947:

Milton Caniff creates *Steve Canyon*, leaving *Terry* to George Wunder. Coulton Waugh publishes the first book-length study of the American comic strip, *The Comics*.

In Belgium creation of *Buck Danny* by V. Hubinon and J. M. Charlier.

In Japan *Fushigira Kuni* started by Fukijiro Yokoi.

1948:

Walt Kelly's *Pogo* appears as a daily strip in the *New York Star*. *Rusty Riley* created by Frank Godwin. *Rex Morgan, M.D.* appears.

Jacques Martin creates *Alix l'Intrépide* (Belgium).

Shōnen Oja created by Soji Yamakawa in Japan.

Raymond Poïvet, "Les Pionniers de l'Espérance." © Editions Vaillant.

José-Luis Salinas and Rod Reed, "The Cisco Kid." © King Features Syndicate.

1949:

In England Trog (Wally Fawkes) creates *Rufus* (later retitled *Flook*).

1950:

Charles Schulz's *Peanuts* appears. Mort Walker creates *Beetle Bailey*. E. C. Comics launches its "new trend" of horror comics.

Eagle comic weekly started in England (*Dan Dare*, by Frank Hampson, appears in first issue).

1951:

Rod Reed and José-Luis Salinas start *The Cisco Kid*. In an interval of a few days, Hank Ketcham in the United States and David Law in England each create a different kid strip by the same name—*Dennis the Menace* (March 12 and 17).

In Japan *Tetsuwan-Atom* created by Osamu Tezuka.

1952:

Judge Parker started by N. Dallis and Dan Heilman. *Mad* magazine starts publication.

Eiichi Fukui creates *Igaguri-kun* in Japan.

1953:

In Belgium Raymond Macherot creates *Chlorophylle*.

Jimmy das Gummipferd started by Roland Kohlsaat in Germany.

1954:

Mort Walker and Dik Browne create *Hi and Lois*. Dr. Frederic Wertham publishes his anti-comic book essay, *Seduction of the Innocent*, in April; in October the Comics Code Authority is established as a reaction.

Jeff Hawke originated by Sydney Jordan in England.

In Japan *Akadō Suzunosuke* created by Eiichi Fukui.

1955:

Gus Edson and Irwin Hasen create *Dondi*.

Max l'Explorateur, by Bara, starts in the Paris daily *France-Soir*.

1957:

Leonard Starr creates *On Stage*. Mel Lazarus starts *Miss Peach*.

Reg Smythe creates *Andy Capp* in England.

Gaston Lagaffe created by André Franquin in England.

In Italy Benito Jacovitti originates *Cocco Bill*.

1958:

Johnny Hart creates *B.C.* John Dirks takes over *The Captain and the Kids* from his father, Rudolph Dirks. *Feiffer* begins national syndication. *Rick O'Shay* created by Stan Lynde. *Short Ribs* created by Frank O'Neal. Irving Phillips starts *The Strange World of Mr. Mum*.

China's longest-running strip, Shen Pei's *Little Tiger*, debuts.

1959:

Stephen Becker's *Comic Art in America* published by Simon and Schuster.

The French comic weekly *Pilote* started (in the first issue *Astérix*, by René Goscinny and Albert Uderzo, and *Michel Tanguy*, by J. M. Charlier and Uderzo, appear).

Ninja Bugeichō created by Sanpei Shirato in Japan.

John Dixon's *Air Hawk and the Flying Doctors* started in Australia.

Johnny Hart, "B.C." © Field Newspaper Syndicate.

1960:

Peyo's *Les Schtroumpfs* established in *Spirou*.

1961:

Stan Lee and Jack Kirby create *The Fantastic Four*. *Apartment 3-G* started by N. Dallis and Alex Kotzky.

Alma Grande produced by Pedro Zapiain and José Suárez Lozano in Mexico.

1962:

Harvey Kurtzman and Will Elder's *Little Annie Fanny* starts publication in *Playboy*. Stan Lee creates *Spider-Man*, with Steve Ditko, and *Thor*, with Jack Kirby.

Bristow started by Frank Dickens in England.

Creation of the Club des Bandes Dessinées in France. Marcel Gotlib starts *Gai Luron* (first called *Nanar et Jujube*). J. C. Forest creates *Barbarella*.

In Italy *Diabolik* created by Angela and Luciana Giussani.

1963:

In England creation of *Modesty Blaise* by Peter O'Donnell and James Holdaway. Alex Graham starts *Fred Basset*.

Achille Talon, by Greg, and *Fort Navajo* (later *Lieutenant Blueberry*), by Charlier and Gir (Jean Giraud), created in France.

Alfredo Alcala starts *Voltar* in the Philippines.

1964:

Johnny Hart and Brant Parker create *The Wizard of Id*.

Tiffany Jones started by Pat Tourret and Jean Butterworth in England.

SOCERLID established in France (among its founders were Pierre Couperie and Maurice Horn).

Maxmagnus and Bunker create *Kriminal* in Italy.

In Argentina Quino (Joaquin Lavado) creates *Mafalda*.

1965:

Wee Pals created by Morrie Turner. *Nick Fury, Agent of SHIELD* created by Jack Kirby in *Strange Tales*. First appearance in print of Robert Crumb's *Fritz the Cat*.

First International Comics Convention held in Bordighera, Italy. The comic monthly *Linus* starts publication in Milan. In its pages appears Guido Crepax's *Neutron* (later to become *Valentina*).

1966:

In Belgium creation of *Chevalier Ardent*, by François Craenhals, and *Bernard Prince*, by Greg and Hermann.

The City Museum of Cartoon Art opened in Omiya, Japan.

First version of China's most famous comic book, *The Red Detachment of Women*, published in Peking.

1967:

Redeye started by Gordon Bess. *Zap Comics* appears. Gilbert Shelton creates *The Fabulous Furry Freak Brothers*. Robert Crumb originates *Mr. Natural*. The Academy of Comic Art established by Bill Blackbeard in San Francisco.

The Musée des Arts Décoratifs (Palais du Louvre) shows a comprehensive exhibition of comic art, "Bande Dessinée et Figuration Narrative," organized by SOCERLID. Philippe Druillet's *Lone Sloane* appears in book form. *Philémon*, by Fred, established.

Comic monthly *Eureka* started in Italy.

In Japan *Hi no Tori* created by Osamu Tezuka.

1968:

The English version of *Bande Dessinée et Figuration Narrative, A History of the Comic Strip*, by Pierre Couperie and Maurice Horn, published. John Saunders and Al McWilliams start *Dateline: Danger! The Dropouts* created by Howard Post.

Bonvi's *Sturmtruppen*, Italy's first successful daily strip, appears.

Exhibition "La Historieta Mundial" organized in Buenos Aires, Argentina.

1969:

The Collected Works of Buck Rogers in the 25th Century published by Chelsea House Publishers, New York.

Golgo 13 created by Takao Saitō in Japan.

In Italy *Alan Ford* originated by Magnus and Bunker (Luciano Secchi and Roberto Raviola).

In India Pran creates his best-known strip, *Chacha Chaudary*.

Jack Kirby, "Thor." © Marvel Comics Group.

Takao Saitō, "Golgo 13." © Big Comic.

1970:

Broom Hilda created by Russell Myers. Garry Trudeau's *Doonesbury* starts national syndication. Jim Lawrence and Jorge Longaron produce *Friday Foster*. Marvel Comics starts comic book adaptation of *Conan*.

Corto Maltese created by Hugo Pratt for the French weekly *Pif*.

Djon Domino starts publication in Indonesia.

1971:

Maurice Horn organizes the exhibition "75 Years of the Comics" at the New York Cultural Center, the first comic exhibition ever held in a major American museum.

Stop Me! The British Newspaper Strip published by Denis Gifford in England.

1972:

Comics: Anatomy of a Mass Medium, by Reinhold Reitberger and Wolfgang Fuchs, appears in English translation.

Zack comic weekly starts publication in Germany.

1973:

Dik Browne creates *Hägar the Horrible*.

1974:

Joe Brancatelli starts *Inside Comics*, the first professional magazine on comic art in America. The Museum of Cartoon Arts opens in Greenwich, Connecticut.

Tatsuhiko Yamagami creates *Gaki Deka* in Japan.

1975:

The Cartoon Museum opens in Orlando, Florida.

First International Festival of Comics held at the University of Montreal, Canada.

Guido Crepax's *Histoire d'O* published simultaneously in Italy and France.

Mètal Hurlant magazine starts appearing on French newsstands: Jen Giraud, using the name "Moebius," will publish his most ground-breaking comics there.

Alack Sinner created by José Muñoz and Carlos Sampayo in Italy.

Dik Browne, "Hägar the Horrible." © King Features Syndicate.

1976:

Harvey Pekar begins his *American Splendor* comic-book series.
First edition of *The World Encyclopedia of Comics* published.

1977:

Jeff McNelly's *Shoe* starts syndication.
Dave Sim's *Cerebus* appears.
Publication of *The Smithsonian Collection of Newspaper Comics*.

1978:

First appearance of *Garfield*.
Wendy and Richard Pini begin publication of *Elfquest*.

1979:

For Better or For Worse first appears. *Little Orphan Annie* resurrected as *Annie*, following the success of the eponymous musical comedy.

1980:

Berke Breathed creates *Bloom County*.
The World Encyclopedia of Cartoons published.

1982:

Torpedo 1936 begins its long international run in Spain.
Martin Mystère produced in Italy.
In Japan creation of *Akira*.

1984:

Teenage Mutant Ninja Turtles launched.
In Argentina Alberto Breccia creates *Perramus*.
Duan Jifu's *Lao Ma* produced in China.
First issue of *Comic Art* magazine released in Rome.

1985:

Bill Watterson's spirit-renewing *Calvin and Hobbes* starts syndication.
Strip, Poreklo i Znacaj ("Comics, Their Origins and Importance") published in Yugoslavia.

Jim Davis, "Garfield." © United Feature Syndicate.

A Chinese "comic box": "Lao Ma's Adventures" by Duan Jifu. © Duan Jifu.

1986:

Alan Moore and Dave Gibbons produce *Watchmen*.

Monumental *Historia de los Comics* completed in Spain.

1989:

Scott Adams creates the extraordinarily successful *Dilbert*.

1991:

Jim Lee, Rob Liefeld, Todd McFarlane, and others found Image Comics (official announcement is made in January 1992).

First auction of comics and comic art held at Sotheby's Auction House in New York.

Javier Coma's *Diccionario de los Comics* published in Spain.

1994:

First three volumes of John A. Lent's four-volume *International Bibliography of Comic Art* released. (Fourth volume follows in 1996.)

1995:

Terry and the Pirates revived by Tribune Media Services.

In anticipation of the 100th anniversary of the comics, the U.S. Postal Service issues a 20-stamp set of "American Classic Comic Strips."

1996:

In this anniversary year of the birth of the comics the International Museum of Cartoon Art opens in Boca Raton, Florida; *100 Years of American Newspaper Comics* is published. The occasion is also marked by exhibitions in the United States and around the world, notably in Brussels, Barcelona, Buenos Aires, Tokyo, Belgrade, and Rome.

In December Marvel Comics files for reorganization under Chapter 11 of the U.S. bankruptcy laws.

1997:

For the first time in Spanish history, the National Library in Madrid organized a conference on the comics in January.

As of December 1997, the Marvel Comics legal proceedings were still not resolved.

The World of Comics:
An Analytical Summary

The following essay constitutes not a general theory of comic art (this will have to wait until such time as a new set of aesthetic principles specifically applying to 20th-century art forms, as well as to the traditional arts, has been formulated), but an inquiry into the nature and workings of the art form itself. My thoughts on the subject were first expressed in "What is Comic Art?", which I wrote as the introduction to the 1971 New York Cultural Center exhibition, "75 Years of the Comics." In turn, that introduction served as the basis of my lecture series, "Language and Structure of the Comics," which I have been giving at universities in North America and Europe since 1973.

The New York Cultural Center catalogue has been out of print for a number of years now (and the New York Cultural Center itself out of existence since 1975), but since then a number of writers have appropriated my positions (sometimes my very words) as their own, in publications from Montreal, Québec, to Buenos Aires, Argentina, and from Richmond, Virginia, to Rome, Italy. Imitation, as everyone knows, is the sincerest form of flattery, and I am flattered to see my ideas given such wide currency. However, I also feel that any personal body of ideas is best expressed in the words of its originator, so as to allow a reader to form an educated opinion and to evaluate the validity of such ideas in full knowledge of their exact formulation.

In the 20 years that have elapsed since the first publication of the *Encyclopedia*, there have been a few efforts to arrive at a definition of this medium, most of them by practicing cartoonists from the limited perspective of their craft. (Picasso once observed to fellow painter and budding art critic André Lhote that he could choose between being a good painter or becoming a good critic but couldn't be both. Lhote took the hint, abandoned painting, and turned himself into the leading modern art theoretician of the first half of the 20th century.) In this context I have decided to leave this essay in the form in which it originally appeared in the first edition of *The World Encyclopedia of Comics*.

The comics: a working definition

What is comic art? To this question it is already possible to give a tentative answer. It was Coulton Waugh who, in his pioneering book *The Comics* (1947),

Text and pictures reinforce each other: "Krazy Kat." © *King Features Syndicate.*

Panel: Paul Robinson, "Etta Kett." © King Features Syndicate.

first propounded an analytical definition that came to be widely accepted as the groundwork on which to build any serious study of the comics. Summarily put, the comics are a form necessarily including the following elements: a narrative told by way of a sequence of pictures, a continuing cast of characters from one sequence to the next, and the inclusion of dialogue and/or text within the picture.

Unfortunately, Waugh and his subsequent followers did not fully comprehend the significance of their discovery. Instead of realizing that they had just described the broad features of a new art form calling for an accordingly new set of standards, they kept trying to fit this newcomer into the alien mold of older and accepted forms. It is therefore not surprising that this conceptual aberration led its author into further and further aesthetic confusion. Thus Waugh, in the conclusion of his massive study, asked the question, "Is artistic and literary development [in the comics] possible?"—hardly an earthshaking pronouncement at the end of a 360-page volume.

Aside from the naiveness of believing content could somehow develop independently of form and structure (and elaborate structure at that), Waugh and his followers correlatively failed to recognize that the descriptive definition they themselves had given precluded any development outwards and that all subsequent improvements had to be organic to a preexistent and self-contained form. Within the external structure of the comics, there had to be an internal cohesiveness that could not be gained from surface observation.

Strip: Noel Sickles, "Scorchy Smith." © AP Newsfeatures.

The above definition, then, does not give us insight into the essence of the comics any more than the formula for *pi* gives us knowledge of the nature of the circle. It is as a methodological tool that it can be of invaluable use. By clearing away much of the semantic confusion surrounding the comics, it narrows the scope of research and puts the subject into a more accurate and more sharply defined focus.

The language of the comics

It would not occur to the serious scholar or critic to pronounce judgment on a novel on the evidence of a few paragraphs or to review a play on the basis of one or two scenes. Yet this practice is widely accepted in the criticism of the comics. Most art critics have not accepted the very simple and legitimate notion that a comic feature should be judged within its proper context, and on its own terms. In other words, a working knowledge of the language of the comics is necessary for any intelligent discussion of the subject, and because it is specialized knowledge, many a critic who sets out to expose the comics only succeeds in exposing his own ignorance.

Even when honestly trying to judge the comics, the unwitting critic is likely to evaluate the text and the pictures independently, whereas the most original feature of the comics is the blend of these two elements into one organic whole. Expression in the comics is the result of this interaction between word and picture, the product and not the sum of its component parts. The art and the writing reinforce (or pull down) each other in a variety of ways. When the writing (plot, situations, dialogue) is good, it can carry passable or even poor art along; conversely, good art can sometimes make up for any weakness in the writing. When both art and writing are exceptional, the result is a masterpiece (George Herriman's *Krazy Kat* is one good example); when art and writing are both terrible, the result validates all the criticism leveled at the comics (unfortunately, as in all arts, the bad is much more common than the good).

The basic element in the language of the comics is the panel, a simple drawing most often enclosed in a rectangular or square frame, that stands both in isolation from, and in intimate relation to, the others, like a word in a sentence. It is the simplest form of the comics, in the strict sense of gestalt, the contents of which are perceived as one unit. It is therefore futile to try to judge the artistry of a comic by the drawing of one panel (or a number of panels, each examined in isolation). To separate image content from narrative content is to do violence to the whole concept of the comics.

The panels themselves are grouped, again like words in a sentence, into strips (superficially a horizontal succession of panels) or pages whose format widely varies but whose chief characteristic, as opposed to a strip, is to present a vertical as well as a horizontal combination of frames. In turn these strips and pages articulate themselves, in a more or less complex manner, into sequences and episodes.

For their vocabulary the comics borrow both from common language and the language of (representational) art. Over the years they have developed a peculiar set of conventions, of which the balloon is the most widely known and used, and invented an array of new signs and symbols, mainly in the form of word-pictures and visual puns. Thus a lamp comes to represent a bright idea, a black cloud over the head of a character a feeling of grief or despair. The examples are endless.

Today the language of the comics, with its innovations, its symbols, its colorful onomatopoeia (pow, vroom, ka-boom!) is as familiar and commonly accepted as the language of the movies. Together they have forced upon Western man a new way of looking at external reality.

The comics as communication

Even before the advent of Marshall McLuhan, the comics were usually viewed in terms of communication, without much attention being paid to them as art, whether actual or potential. There is some validity in seeing the comics in this light exclusively, and this prejudice has been reinforced in no small measure by those organizations engaged in selling the comics as a product (the same atti-

Balloon: René Goscinny and Albert Uderzo, "Astérix." © Editions Dargaud.

Visual pun: H. H. Knerr, "The Katzenjammer Kids." © King Features Syndicate.

Comics used in advertising: Chester Gould, Autolite.

tude was also prevalent among the movie studios as regarded the motion pictures, and it contributed largely to the decline and fall of Hollywood).

The two main supports of the comics have historically been the book and the newspaper, and this resulted in the development of two different publics, with some overlap between them. As the heir to the picture book, the book of comics (and later the comic book narrowly defined) addressed itself mainly to younger readers, while the comic strip, being part and parcel of the daily newspaper, was generally conceived as a more adult form of expression. The gap, however, has been narrowing over the years, with the growth in the United States of comic books mainly destined for adults, and in Europe of illustrated weeklies encompassing a greater range of features. One of these papers styles itself, fittingly enough, "the newspaper of young people from 7 to 77."

There is no doubt that the public reads the comics primarily for their entertainment value, but even so one must make a distinction between routine readership (the reader who turns to the comics page from force of habit upon opening his newspaper) and active readership, which consists in looking at the comics for some form of specific satisfaction (it might be artistic, or nostalgic, or even campy). We find that those adults most interested in the comics are located at both ends of the educational spectrum. It would seem that the less educated enjoy the comics for their uncomplicated immediacy, and the sophisticates have increasingly adopted the medium (in Europe first, and now in the United States) for its anticultural qualities. If the medium is the message, then the message of the comics, with their flouting of the rules of traditional art and of civilized language, can only be subversion. (This point in one form or the other has always been the leading argument of the enemies of the comics. Now it is being utilized *a contario* by the exponents of the counterculture.)

A word must be said about the comics as specialized communication, however. The comics have been used in advertising ever since the Yellow Kid, and their utilization as propaganda has also been widespread, from the crude patriotizing of English and French comics in World War I to Steve Canyon and Buz Sawyer fighting the good fight in Vietnam, and American "imperialist" soldiers being lambasted in Chinese comics (at least before Nixon's visit to Peking).

Among its more sedate pursuits, the medium has been used in the dissemination of information ("Dennis-the-Menace and dirt" for the Soil Conservation Society of America and "Cliff Merritt sets the record straight" for the Brotherhood of Railroad Trainmen) and as a valuable teaching tool—two recent textbooks prepared by the University of Illinois for the teaching of the new math rely heavily on the comic form.

Compared to other forms of mass media, the comics are not a highly effective instrument of either suasion or enlightenment. They are not as overwhelming as the movies, as authoritative as the written word, or as pervasive as television. That they function best as a form of expression may be a commercial drawback, but that very fact also testifies to the integrity of their form.

The intellectual confusion about the comics

As has happened with the cinema, the popular success of the comics as a mass medium has obscured their preexistence as a form. Surveying the forest but ignoring the individual trees, the critics have seized upon the comics as a sociological object to be clinically studied, thereby denying *a priori* that aesthetic qualities could be attributed to them. This, of course, helped conceal the social critic's ignorance of the dynamics of creation in the comics.

Actually, the comics are a much more personal mode of expression than the movies, television, or even most modern manifestations of art and music. Whether there are several authors or only one, each feature is done in a craftsman's manner; this applies not only, as should be expected, to the writing and drawing, but to the lettering and tracing of the balloons also. Quite often this applies to the delineating of the frames surrounding each panel as well. While there exist some chemically pretreated materials, the cartoonist's instruments remain primarily ink, pen, brush, and paper. This, of course, does not give a comic strip a personal look unless the artist has some personal ideas to express, but it serves to prove that the comics are far from being the mechanized process that some pretend them to be. It is true that the comics are often a team effort,

Prince Valiant

IN THE DAYS OF
KING ARTHUR
BY
HAROLD R FOSTER

Synopsis: FOR MONTHS PRINCE VALIANT AND HIS COUNCIL HAVE SOUGHT A PLAN WHEREBY THEIR 7000 MEN MIGHT HOPE TO HALT THE 20,000 SAVAGE HUNS SENT TO CLEAR THE PASS AND OPEN THE WAY FOR FURTHER ONSLAUGHTS UPON EUROPE. A CHANCE REMARK OF SLITH'S GIVES VAL AN IDEA.

THE PLAN IS DARING, INSPIRED, DANGEROUS, BUT THEIR DESPERATE PLIGHT CALLS FOR A DESPERATE PLAN, AND VAL'S ENTHUSIASM FINALLY WINS CONSENT FROM THE COUNCIL.

DEFEAT WILL COST HIM HIS HEAD, SO KARNAK, CHIEFTAIN OF THE HUNS, HAS PROCEEDED CAREFULLY. HIS BASE IS FORTIFIED AND PILED HIGH WITH SUPPLIES.... HIS FIERCE WARRIORS ARE CLAMORING TO BE LOOSED UPON THEIR NIMBLE FOES.

AT DAWN THEY ISSUE FORTH, DRUMS THROBBING, SPEARS WAVING AND SWORDS CLASHING ON SHIELDS.

LIKE A GREAT OCTOPUS THE HUN ARMY MOVES SLOWLY UP THE WIDE VALLEY, ITS FAR-FLUNG ARMS SWEEPING EVERY FOLD AND HOLLOW OF THE ENCIRCLING HILLS.

"GENTLEMEN, THE HUN IS IN FRONT OF US, FAMINE LURKS BEHIND. TO-NIGHT WE BANQUET ROYALLY ON THE LAST OF OUR PROVISIONS..... AND TO-MORROW?.... DEATH OR PLENTY!"

FROM AMONG THE RANKS WILY SLITH CHOOSES ALL THOSE WHO MOST RESEMBLE HUNS, PUTS HUN COSTUMES OVER THEIR ARMOR, THEN, WITH A MYSTERIOUS PACK TRAIN DISAPPEARS SILENTLY INTO THE NIGHT.

BY NOON OF THIS, THE SECOND DAY, KARNAK IS WELL UP THE PASS AND STILL NO SIGN OF AN ENEMY, INDEED, THERE IS NO ENEMY, FOR.........

VAL HAD SAID TO HIS HUN-HUNTERS: "KARNAK'S WOLVES ARE AT THE MOUTH OF OUR CANYON. HULTA WILL LEAD US BY A SECRET WAY TO THE PLAINS BELOW, THERE TO PUT OUR PLAN TO THE TEST."

NEXT WEEK—
VAL INVITES KARNAK TO DINE!

Charles Schulz, "Peanuts." © United Feature Syndicate.

with assistants working on the backgrounds, the lettering, even the inking, and there is no denying that more often than not it is a case of too many cooks spoiling the broth. Predictably enough, the best authors are those who retain the strongest direction (Charles Schulz, for instance, does everything on *Peanuts*, including the lettering) and therefore give their features the most accomplished sense of unity.

Since artistic creation is present (or at least potential) in every feature of the comics, the temptation is great to apply to this new form the canons of traditional aesthetics, but again there is the danger of intellectual confusion. Because the comics present so many facets, each mirroring the rules of different art forms, they present some thorny epistemological problems that need to be cleared away if one desires to achieve any understanding of the form.

Guido Crepax, "La Casa Matta." © E.D.I.P.

The comics as graphic art

Since a comic, any comic, is first perceived visually, the tradition has always been to classify the comics as graphic art and to link them ("lump them" would probably be a more accurate choice of words) with illustration and caricature. And indeed, as one can see, there is a direct affiliation between the cartoon and the comic strip, just as there is a strong bond between the story strip and illustration. The differences, however, are obvious: the cartoon and the illustration highlight only one point, be it a punch line or the dramatic climax in a narrative, while the comics must keep the continuity of a whole sequence flowing.

This is not meant to play down the artistic skills required to draw a comic feature. Karl Fortess's assertions that "the comic strip artist is not concerned with art problems, problems of form, spatial relationships, and the expressive movement of line" and that "the comic strip has failed to produce a Daumier or a Hogarth" are utter nonsense. The best of the comic artists are very much concerned with artistic problems, although from a different vantage point than that of the traditional draftsman. On this score I simply let the illustrations in the color selections of this work speak for themselves. As for excellence of drawing, the comics can boast of a long line of outstanding artists from Winsor McCay to Burne Hogarth, from Frank Bellamy to Guido Crepax. All artistic currents have found expression in the comics, and a collection of the best works in this field presents an astonishing retrospective of the history of graphic art.

It would thus be perfectly possible to judge the comics entirely on their artistic merits, just as it would be feasible to judge a motion picture on its photography alone. Of course, that would mean that one is willing to place undue restrictions on other ways of appreciating the comics. But the image in the comics is not fixed in some point in time; rather, it inserts itself within the time flow of the narrative. It is a *diffuse* image whose projection in space, overlapping from one frame to another, mirrors a projection in time, forwards and backwards. Because of that fact the artistic concerns of the comic artist are not wholly coincidental with the concerns of the traditional artist, so it is only axiomatic to conclude that traditional aesthetics cannot be wholly coincidental with the aesthetics of the comics.

Mythology in comics: the legend of Theseus told in a Hungarian comic strip by Istvan Endrody.

The comics as narrative literature

Functionally, the comics would seem to belong to some literary discipline, as they are chiefly meant to be *read*, and the persistent public indifference to silent or pantomine strips bears this out. Some critics, therefore, have tried to link the comics with folk literature. There again similarities can be found; certainly the argument of many a comic sequence closely parallels such folk forms as the tale, the fable, or the parable. Harold Gray in *Little Orphan Annie*, Al Capp in *Li'l Abner*, and Walt Kelly in *Pogo* are especially fond of these forms. As one can see, however, the comics are the expression of individual artists and run counter to the collective processes that have contributed to the vast body of folk literature. What the comic artists have done is simply to weave these inchoate or unformed mythologies into their own scheme of things, in ways not dissimilar to those of artists and writers everywhere.

Winsor McCay, "Little Nemo."

Narration, however defined, remains the essence of the comics: their purpose is to tell a story. Because they aim at a large public, the comics have come to compete with, and eventually displace, older forms of popular literature like the dime novels, the pulps, and the magazine serials. Their superiority to these earlier forms comes not, as is widely assumed, from the fact that they can tell the story in graphic terms, but from the fact that, because of their graphic elucidation of detail and background, they can tell the story in more economical terms. As some wit put it, "They give you more bangs in less time."

Building on these premises, some authors have tried to fashion their comics into a monumental novel, with all that it implies in terms of a self-contained universe governed by its own laws, dynamics, and motivations. It would do them injustice to compare them exclusively with the picaresque novels. Some have deliberately aimed higher. Gray's *Little Orphan Annie* offers perhaps the closest example of a novel in comic form. Not only are there undertones of Dickens and Hugo, but the obsessing and rhythmic repetition of motif and echo is very close to the preoccupations of modern novelists. In *Gasoline Alley* Frank King sets out to describe the lives and times of a small midwestern community with a tenderness and serenity worthy of Goethe's *Wilhelm Meister*. Other examples could be cited with equal justification.

If I have insisted on the literary qualities present in the comics, it is because they are not so readily apparent as their graphic values. There again I must be careful not to beg the question and judge the comics in terms of literary standards alone. The comics is indeed a literary form, but one that should not be reduced to its literary elements lest its very raison d'être be subverted.

The comics as a dramatic form

A case can be made (and indeed has been made) for the comics being a latter-day outgrowth of the dramatic arts. It may be said without irony that the comics, more than any other 20th-century literary form, follow Aristotle's rule of a beginning, a middle, and an end. In the 80 years of their existence they have accomplished much the same progression as Western drama since the Middle Ages; starting with the farce or pantomime (*Yellow Kid, Katzenjammer Kids, Happy Hooligan*), they have assimilated the elements of the comedy of observation and manners (*Bringing Up Father, Moon Mullins*) before proceeding to the themes of the social comedy and the melodrama (*Mary Worth, Steve Canyon*) and the drama of ideas (*Little Orphan Annie*). The great dramatic currents of the 20th-century world have also found their spokesmen in the comics with the likes of George Herriman, Walt Kelly, Jules Feiffer, and Georges Wolinski.

The foregoing argument should not be slighted. Because of the ubiquitous use of the balloon, the dialogue constitutes the strongest and most prominent literary feature of the comics. While most cartoonists use dialogue chiefly as a means to convey essential information and to carry the plot forward, many others have become aware of its dramatic powers and played skillfully upon them. They have called upon dialogue to establish character and motivation (George McManus, Milton Caniff, Hergé), to create suspense and anticipation (Harold

Dream balloons: Mort Walker, "Beetle Bailey." © King Features Syndicate.

Theatrical strip: "Feiffer." © Jules Feiffer.

Gray, E. P. Jacobs, Milton Caniff), to reveal the central themes and ideas of their work (George Herriman, Walt Kelly, Charles Schulz), to establish tone and rhythm, and to give purpose to the action. The examples are endless, but dramatic conventions and stage devices are the special domain of two artists—George McManus and Walt Kelly, whose work has always been more dramatic than narrative.

In the context of action the balloon plays an ambivalent role: by function it is a dramatic device, by nature a graphic form, thus creating possibilities that great cartoonists have been prompt to explore. By using the graphic elements of the balloon (its shape, the lettering and the symbols within it) in a literal way, they are able to translate the nonverbal aspects of language: tone, pitch, rhythm, and accent. More importantly, the balloon can transcend speech, addressing itself to the naked thought (thought balloon), and even free itself of all the restraints of organized expression. Thus, one sees the balloon changing its form, slowly dissolving, or suddenly exploding. It is used as a ploy, a mask, a shield, an attack weapon. One also sees an analogy with the symbolic use of props in the modern theater.

Comics and cinema

For many reasons, some of which we have already mentioned, the comics come closer to the movies than to any other art form. Not only were they both born around the same time and from the same artistic and commercial preoccupations, but both tended to the same end: the creation of dialectical movement, either through optical illusion (cinema) or through kinetic suggestion (comics). It is well to point out at this juncture that many techniques which came to be called "cinematic" originated in the comics. Montage was the rule in the comics well before Eisenstein came along, and the techniques of cutting, framing, and panning were used by such early practitioners as Opper, McCay, and Feininger. As for the "audio," the comics had ample time to develop the voice-off, the

Cinematic Montage: Jim Steranko, "Nick Fury." © Marvel Comics.

Cinematic Montage: Jim Steranko, "Nick Fury." © Marvel Comics.

voice-over, and overlapping dialogue during the 30 years when the movies had at their disposal only the barbarous subtitle. Even the grammar of the comics and the movies was almost identical; the concepts of "shot" (as opposed to the static "scene") and "sequence," the variations of angle and perspective, and the possibility of tracking forward and backward are present in both forms.

The influence of the movies on the comics has been great; not only have they given the comics better techniques for the suggestion of movement in the transposition to paper of the equivalents of cinematic lighting, depth of field, silhouetted backgrounds, etc., but they also proved a major source of inspiration. The movie serials were as much the forerunners of the adventure strip as the dime novel or the pulps, and their distinctive syncopated rhythm became the hallmark of most of the action series of the 1930s.

Comic strips and animated cartoons

The constant cross-fertilization between the comics and the cinema soon produced its first legitimate offspring: the animated cartoon, a peculiarly modern union of art and technology. In their book *The Cinema as Art*, Ralph Stevenson and J. R. Debrix declare that "the accepted definition of an animated film is, not that it is drawn by hand, but that it is created frame-by-frame," which, of course, is how the comics are also created. This fact goes a long way toward proving that the animated cartoon owes more to the comics than to the cinema.

Another important point should also be made in this connection. Animation of still drawings predates the invention of the movie camera by quite a number of years. Using colored cartoons drawn on strips of paper (comic strips, literally!), such early inventors as the Belgian Plateau with his phenakistoscope, and the Englishman W. G. Horner with his zoetrope, were able to animate sequences of drawings as early as the 1830s.

The most important early pioneer in the field of animation was the Frenchman Emile Reynaud, who invented the praxinoscope and was the first to project animated cartoons onto a screen (his Théâtre Optique opened in 1892). In his study *Animation in the Cinema*, Ralph Stevenson unequivocally states, "He [Reynaud] not only invented a technique, he originated a genre and was the first to develop the animated film . . . into a spectacle." It was only years later, through the efforts of the American J. Stuart Blackton, that animation became irrevocably tied (for better and worse) to the cinema.

Many comic strip artists were also pioneers of the animated film; Winsor McCay is the most notable example, but Bud Fisher and George McManus also

Interdependent relationship between comics and animated cartoons: "Mutt and Jeff." © H. C. Fisher.

Interdependent relationship between comics and animated cartoons: "Popeye." © *King Features Syndicate.*

dabbled in animation, and Pat Sullivan worked on comic strips in Australia, England, and the United States before going into film cartooning.

The early cartoon films drew most of their inspiration and techniques from the comics, as well as many of their most popular characters: *Mutt and Jeff, The Katzenjammer Kids, Krazy Kat, Bringing Up Father, Happy Hooligan* (an early Blackton effort), *Les Pieds-Nickelés*, among others, were turned into successful cartoon series. In the 1920s, however, the animated cartoon started giving some of its own characters back to the comic strips with *Felix the Cat*. But even in the 1930s, when *Mickey Mouse, Donald Duck*, and other Disney creations massively invaded the comic pages, the comics were still contributing to screen animation in a notable way (with O. Soglow's *Little King* and especially E. C. Segar's *Popeye*).

In recent times animators have turned more and more toward experimentation and abstraction and away from the aesthetics of the traditional cartoon. Deprived of an important source of fresh ideas, commercial studios everywhere have again turned to the comics: in the United States (*Peanuts, Archie, Spider-Man*), France (*Astérix*), Belgium (*Tintin, Lucky Luke, Les Schtroumpfs*), Japan (*Tetsuwan-Atom*, alias "Astroboy"), and many other places. The romance between the comic strip and the animated cartoon is not over.

A search for new standards

By now it is apparent that the comics cannot be reduced to fit into any preconceived formula. By their very existence they seem to baffle any attempt at epistemological elucidation and offer an obdurate resistance to traditional aesthetics. One can very well sympathize with the resentment and frustration of the critic who finds all his neat little formulas of little or no use in any sane explication of the medium. The comics simply refuse to be pigeonholed. One solution (and it is the most frequent, if the least enlightening) is to put the comics beyond the pale, to write them off as non-art, non-literature, and non-significant. This approach is applied to the movie also, but to the astonishment of only the ignorant, both comics and movies have been able to survive the excommunication of the would-be defenders of Art, Truth, Beauty, and the preservation of the cultural status quo.

It is a peculiar form of intellectual perversity that consists in doggedly trying to berate the comics in the name of art or literature, in the face of overwhelming evidence that the comics do not answer to either. In the presence of an altogether new and original form, intrinsic values must be objectively assessed. This is no easy task, hardly easier than it has been with the movies. A thorough knowledge of the field must be obtained, with the same assiduity as is required of any other discipline; the *a priori* judgment that this is an inferior form only deserving of inferior scholarship is an especially galling piece of tortuous reasoning. It is only by serious study that one can arrive at an understanding of the underlying structures of the comics and formulate any critical conclusion.

Space and time in the comics

The problems of spatial representation have bedeviled the comic artist ever since the inception of the medium. Because the cartoonist deals not with one, but with an organic sequence of pictures, these problems cannot be solved by perspective alone. Simple perspective would give the same uniform depth value to all of the panels and thus tend to flatten them out, giving them the same

Chiaroscuro effect: Jim Steranko, "Nick Fury." © *Marvel Comics Group.*

appearance as the friezes on the walls of Egyptian mastabas. Some artists, notably Chester Gould, put this principle to good aesthetic use, but in the hands of less gifted craftsmen, this only produces a succession of still drawings.

In order to create depth, other artists have resorted to the effects of chiaroscuro, or to a manipulation of scale that subtly distorts traditional perspective and forces a perception of volume from the reader, much as a composed photograph does. In the Sunday pages (as well as in the comic books) foremost artists such as Winsor McCay, Burne Hogarth, and Hiroshi Hirata have created spatiality out of the multilinearity (horizontal, vertical, or diagonal) of the layout by means of expanding or projecting figures along carefully worked-out vectors. The drawings seem literally ready to burst out of their frames.

In the comics time is a function of space (this is their most important difference from the movies); the frames of a strip or page are divisions of time. Thus narrative flow, which is how the author conceives of the passing of time in a particular sequence, and time flow, which is how it is perceived by the reader, are seldom coincidental. Furthermore, they both must be weighed against actual (or reading) time, which may be very long (as in the case of many newspaper strips) or quite short (as with a comic book). The resulting confusion further adds to the sense of unreality that comics produce. Even a feature like *Gasoline Alley*, which purports to keep apace with real time and whose characters age along with the reader, does not escape the rule.

Time in the comics seems to have no organic function; all that happens happens not by necessity but by accident or chance. Time is limitless and open-ended; it can also be reversible: often the characters will go back 10, 20, or more years in time and start the cycle again in a different direction. The comics are ahistorical not because they refuse to deal with their times (they often do), but because real time is irrelevant to their purpose. There is an almost complete absence of teleology in the comics: the events that took place last year have not the slightest influence on the events taking place now, at least not in the strictly causative sense. The same can be argued of popular literature, but words have not the same suggestive power as pictures. By confronting us with a direct representation of reality, the image involves us much more closely in the process. As the Bogart cult demonstrates, only the movies might have been more effective than the comics in this respect, if actors were not made of mortal flesh. Thus the comics are uniquely qualified to take us into a paradoxical universe where time is neither consumed nor abolished: the universe of the eternal present tense.

Themes of the comics

Aesthetic preoccupations and commercial considerations have always conspired to limit the thematic range of the comics. Commercially, the comics are a mass medium, and their authors must give the public something immediately and easily recognizable. Yet at the same time the action must have a certain exemplarity if it is to rise above the level of the simple anecdote. The problem of creating a milieu at once ordinary and different is the lot of all mass media that also aspire to becoming art forms. To answer the challenge, the comics may resort to the wholesale creation of a mythical ontogeny, as in the case of Superman and most other superheroes, or of a dream kingdom (*Little Nemo* is the best example), but few are the comics that have not made some use of the device.

The protagonists of the comics, whether by design or by necessity, go back to the fount of our collective memories and aspirations. They represent some emblematic figure, some archetype linking us to the primeval drives and forces across the night of history. It is as if the comics had taken it upon themselves to embody all our collective longings and try to give them some channel for fulfillment. And yet at the same time it is asked that they toe the social line, and this dichotomy has often led to ambivalence and frustration.

However ridiculous the family may appear in *Bringing Up Father*, for instance, the notion of family itself is never under attack. As one press release once stated: "Jiggs never struck Maggie and will never divorce her." The same ambivalence can be noted in relation to society itself. The first comics were genuinely anarchistic and nihilistic (*The Katzenjammer Kids* is, of course, the classic example), but soon they learned to compromise and eventually to accept the rules of social

Mythical ontogeny: "Superman" and his cohorts.
© National Periodical Publications.

by EDGAR RICE BURROUGHS

WITH RIMALI AND HIS PARTY ON THE TRAIL AGAIN TOWARD THALIA, TARZAN TOOK TO THE TREES, RANGING FAR AHEAD OF HIS COMPANIONS. SUDDENLY HE PAUSED——————

——AND PEERED DOWN AT THE TRAIL BELOW. A GREAT BEAST MOVED SILENTLY ALONG THE TRAIL...... A LION...BEAUTIFULLY MANED AND BRILLIANTLY SPOTTED.

KEEPING PACE WITH THE LION, TARZAN SOON DISCOVERED THE PREY NUMA WAS STALKING.

CONTRARY TO THE HABIT OF MOST CARNIVORE ABOUT TO MAKE A KILL, THE SPOTTED LION SPRANG TOWARD ITS PREY IN UTTER SILENCE.

ALERTLY WATCHING THE DRAMA, TARZAN LEAPED IN THE PATH OF THE CHARGING FURY.

AS NUMA RENEWED THE ATTACK, TARZAN WHEELED, AND LEAPED FOR THE GREAT BEAST'S BACK.
2-6
HOGARTH

Well-balanced page: Burne Hogarth, "Tarzan." © ERB, Inc.

order, however ludicrous. The free spirit of the comics could not be kept down, however, and emerged among the so-called underground comics and in such creations as *Gaki Deka, Sturmtruppen,* or *Barry McKenzie.*

In one of the most revealing pages of *Pogo,* Walt Kelly says of the comics that they are "like a dream . . . a tissue of paper reveries . . . it glows and glimmers its way thru unreality, fancy an' fantasy." Even to an intellectual (by any standard) artist like Kelly, the intellectual limitations of the comics are apparent. But these limitations are also their strength. By their very inability to sustain for long any lofty and more relevant theme, they retain the virtue of timelessness, thus refusing to become another dreary exercise in ephemeral literature.

Stylistics

In order to shape the two heterogeneous elements of the comics into one artistic whole, each cartoonist has to evolve his own distinctive signature (at least those cartoonists who take some pride in their craft do). Two different approaches soon emerge: in the first one the picture takes precedence over the text and the story is told in purely narrative and graphic terms (this method was traditionally the trademark of the great draftsmen from McCay and Feininger to Foster and Hogarth; it can still be found in the work of cartoonists like Hirata and Maroto); the second solution to this stylistic problem gives primacy to the text, as happens in such features as *Little Orphan Annie, Li'l Abner,* and *Pogo.* On the other hand, a more fluid type of narrative emerged in the 1930s, with the use of dramatic dialogue and cinematic techniques combining to preserve a skillful if delicate balance between the literary and the graphic elements of the comics. Milton Caniff was its foremost exponent, and Hugo Pratt later became its most skilled practitioner.

To maintain the integrity of a sequential narrative within the framework of contiguous, but separate, pictures presents another set of problems. Of course the cartoonist can construct an exact visual correlative to the written narrative, but the redundancy and wastefulness of such a method are obvious. It would seem preferable by far to have text and picture carry the action alternately rather than simultaneously. Will Eisner and Milton Caniff are recognized masters of such techniques: in their features they use verbal understatement as a counterpoint to violent visual action or, conversely, they set off visual metaphors to relieve long stretches of dialogue or monologue.

The breaking down of the story into panels and sequences is also mainly a problem of style. The comic artist may prefer to carefully prepare and build up the action, as Harold Gray or Chester Gould do, or to collide head-on with the happenings, an aggressive approach more associated with the comic book and the underground comics. To endow his images with atmosphere, the cartoonist may choose the use of solid black masses or the ambiguous delineation of background; or, to the contrary, he may resort to visual objects violently etched into the foreground—the range is infinite. In this respect color can play an important role by calling attention to important points in the narrative; it can also help link dialectically different frames in a sequence by carrying the same tonal value from one picture to another.

The comics have also at their disposal the syntax of the other literary and artistic forms: iteration, distortion, amplification, stylization, etc. It is up to the artist to make a discreet use of these devices and to avoid the sins of overdramatization and redundancy. In the comics, as in all art, less is more.

A few words in conclusion

It is the fate of all new art forms to be greeted with derision. Attic tragedy was decried as sacrilegious, Italian opera put down as unseemly cacophony, and the cinema termed (not so long ago) "an art for drunken ilotes." Against the comics the laughter has been longest and loudest. For the major part of their 100-year existence the comics have everywhere been held up to public scorn, censure, and ridicule.

This is no longer so; scholarship and analysis have replaced prejudice and ignorance. Yet the comics' growing cultural acceptance has brought with it the added burden of responsibility. Now that they are no longer dismissed as grubby purveyors of mindless entertainment, the cartoonists and their employers must

Narrative redundancy: Harry Hall and Ted McCall, "Men of the Mounted." © Toronto Telegram.

expect to be called into account on aesthetic and ethical grounds (just as novelists, book publishers, playwrights, and filmmakers are). Some may resent this fact and yearn for the good old days when cartoonists could labor in reassuring obscurity and syndicates and publishers could peddle their wares in lucrative self-complacency; there is no turning back.

Maurice Horn

Alphabetical Entries

AASNES, HÅKON (1943-)

Håkon Aasnes, Norwegian comic artist, born February 13, 1943, in Oslo, grew up in the nearby village of Aurskog, and started drawing at the age of two—with a carpenter's pencil on wrapping paper. *The Phantom* fascinated him from his earliest years and made him want, at the age of five, to become a comic artist. He even drew his own *Phantom* stories, and at ten, he had created about 50 heroes of his own, abandoning them after two or three strips. At 17 he created a first version of *Tobram*. It was not until August 6, 1972, however, that an updated version, *Seidel og Tobram*, ("Seidel and Tobram") was first published in the Norwegian press. Before that came to pass, Aasnes tried his hand at a number of jobs, running the gamut from door-to-door salesman to industrial worker to foreign worker in Germany and South Africa. Here, he gained the experience on which to base his comic strip, in order to create an atmosphere of credibility and to flesh out the characters of his heroes.

Seidei og Tobram originally started out as two country bumpkins, but eventually developed into two members of the fictitious village of Ulvedal and are usually haunted by misfortune. *Seidel og Tobram* is a popular, robust comedy played out against the background of contemporary Norwegian provincial life. The strip is drawn in a simple, uncluttered style with speech balloons neatly integrated with the artwork. Håkon Aasnes's style is strongly influenced by Sy Barry's version of *The Phantom*. Aasnes had always been a fan of *The Phantom*, devouring the stories whenever he got to read them. When he discovered a Swedish *Phantom* comic book written and drawn by Swedish artists, he was irritated by the fact that they tried to emulate Barry's style but were never quite matching it. Thus, he sent in his own drawings, which in the end helped to land him his very own comic strip with Bull's Pressetjeneste (Bull's Press Service, the European affiliate of King Features Syndicate) for distribution to Norwegian newspapers. The strip, unfortunately, did not last into the 1980s, but the artist keeps trying. It is not easy to get wealthy drawing comic strips in Norway, however. Therefore Aasnes is holding down a regular job, besides doing what he dreamed of since he could hold a pencil.

W.F.

ABBIE AN' SLATS (U.S.)

Abbie an' Slats was the 1937 creation of young Al Capp, fresh from his success with *Li'l Abner*, and Raeburn van Buren, an accomplished magazine illustrator, who decided to enter comics partly on the strength of Capp's prophetic assertion that radio would kill the popular weeklies.

Capp wrote the continuities for the first nine years, followed by his brother Elliot Caplin in what the latter thought would be a temporary assignment; Caplin wrote *Abbie an' Slats* until the demise of the strip.

The strip took place in a small village and involved its local citizens, although adventures took them all over the world. Crabtree Corners, the locale, was never firmly placed in the minds of the readers or the creators; van Buren designed the surroundings as an amalgam of a New England fishing village and the small Ozark town that he visited every year of his professional life.

The characters included old spinster Aunt Abbie, who never emerged as a major character but who was always present, like her inspiration, an old schoolteacher of van Buren's—ugly, tough, and bighearted; Slats Scrapple, a ruggedly handsome country boy and well-meaning roughneck; his girlfriend Becky, an attractive dark-haired girl; her sister Sue, providing much of the glamour and romantic interest in later days; and the girls' father Bathless Groggins, one of the great comic creations.

Groggins had a walrus moustache and looked, acted, and presumably, smelled like a bum. His companions, including dumb Charlie, a fisherman, and the decidedly Scottish MacBagpipe, ranged from colorful eccentrics to outright swindlers. Like W. C. Fields, who surpassed Groggins only in malevolence, Groggins could only be loved by his fans. The Sunday page, devoted to humorous continuities separate from the dailies, became Groggins' own territory shortly after the strip's debut.

The story lines through the years were consistently good; the *Abbie an' Slats* world was a masterful mixture of suspense, action, and humor. Reader interest in the United Features' comic was always high, as evidenced by the "resurrection" of Bathless' pal Charlie, who was killed off but returned to the strip because of fan pressure.

"Abbie an' Slats," Raeburn van Buren. © United Feature Syndicate.

Van Buren's art was also a mixture of sophisticated illustration, slick beauty and broad humor. The attractiveness of his work on *Abbie* was due as much to his own senses of humor and adventure as it was to his illustration experience. And the merest excuse let an assortment of pretty girls pass through the panels of *Abbie an' Slats*. His world throbbed with action, beauty, and humor; Becker claimed his sense of fantasy was the best in the comics since Winsor McCay.

Abbie an' Slats began as a daily strip on July 7, 1937, and ended on January 30, 1971. The Sunday began on January 15, 1939, and expired several months before the daily version.

R.M.

ABIE THE AGENT (U.S.)   In the wake of his highly successful *Desperate Desmond*, Harry Hershfield ventured into a completely new area with *Abie the Agent*, launched as a daily strip in the *New York Journal* on Monday, February 2, 1914. Abe Mendel Kabibble, the portly, popeyed, moustached protagonist of *Abie* (earlier a minor character in *Desmond*), was the star of the first sympathetic ethnic comic strip. The Katzenjammers were bumbling Germans, Happy Hooligan and the Yellow Kid were caricatured shanty-town Irish, but Abie was at least as real and related to the actual Jewish world of his time as Abe Potash and Morris Perlmutter of the popular *Saturday Evening Post* series by Montague Glass. Like Glass' team, Abie Kabibble was fiercely enmeshed in the New York business world. A car salesman, or "agent" (he termed himself "President: Complex Auto Co."), Abie feverishly worked every angle to make his sales quota and percentage income. As a vital adjunct to this, Abie played politics in his businessman's lodge and, to a lesser degree, on a ward and city level. More than any other early strip, Hershfield's *Abie the Agent* reflects much of the quality of lower middle-class big-city life of the 1910s and '20s. Later in the strip, Abie makes it, and rises in the social strata. It is also often hilariously funny.

There is little doubt in retrospect that Hershfield found his real niche in *Abie*. The *Desmond/Durham* satire

was very inventive and often a graphic delight, but it was essentially pointless for so long sustained a work and wore thin at times, while the potential for humor and human involvement in *Abie* was as endless as that in everyday life. Hershfield himself was obviously happy with *Abie* and continued the strip, as a daily and later as a Sunday page, well into the 1930s. The public of the larger cities seemed to like *Abie* well enough to keep it in profitable print in many newspapers during most of its duration, but it had limited appeal in smaller towns, where *Abie* seemed as exotic as *Krazy Kat*.

Hershfield did not create any memorable characters in *Abie* other than Abie himself, but "that phooey Minsk," a business friend of Abie's; Benny Sparkman, agent for the competing Collapsible Car Co.; and Abie's girlfriend (later wife), Rosa Mine Gold Pearlman, are notable regulars in the strip. Abie's tangled syntax, an amusing element of the strip, was curiously dropped in an offshoot of the comic in the early 1930s called *Kabibble Kabaret*. This later feature, measuring about 1" × 2", was a daily comic page insert of text without art and consisted of make-believe readers' questions ("Dear Mr. Kabibble: Should I marry a blonde or a brunette?") and Abie's reply ("Positively NO!"). Some papers ran it with the strip, others separately.

Hershfield folded his Sunday *Abie* page, the last form of the strip, in 1940. It remained richly enjoyable right up to the last panel, and is one of the major comic strips that deserve to be reprinted complete in permanent form.

B.B.

ACHILLE TALON (France)   *Achille Talon* was created by Greg (Michel Regnier) on February 7, 1963, in the French magazine *Pilote*.

The middle-aged Achille Talon is the archetypal French *petit-bourgeois*: block-headed, pot-bellied, and bloated with self-importance, he talks in common phrases, acts in circles, and always appears as a boorish, superficially educated slob. His pompousness and empty intellectualism have no limits, and while he looks down his large nose upon people in a lower social position than his own, he stubbornly refuses to acknowledge any kind of superiority other than a crassly material one.

"Abie the Agent," Harry Hershfield. © King Features Syndicate.

"Achille Talon," Greg (Michel Régnier). © Editions Dargaud.

Achille's father, Alambic Dieudonné Corydon Talon, whose only goal in life is drinking as many mugs of beer as possible, listens with unbounded admiration and paternal pride to his son's fatuous pronouncements, and often aids and abets him in his wild-eyed schemes. But Talon's neighbor, Hilarion Lefuneste, remains unimpressed by the antics of his friend and often puts him in his place, a defeat that Talon accepts philosophically, in the knowledge that some day stupidity will rise again.

Achille Talon is one of the funniest European strips of the last several decades, as well as a brilliant satire on middle-class smugness and philistinism (and, in this respect, it has been compared to Flaubert's *Bouvard and Pécuchet*). So popular had the character become at one time that in 1975 he gave rise to his own weekly, *Achille Talon Magazine*, which lasted for about one year. Following this failure, his appearances have become scarcer, concentrating on longer stories rather than gags.

M.H.

ADAMS, NEAL (1941-   ) American comic book and comic strip writer and artist born June 6, 1941, on Governor's Island in New York. After studies at the School of Industrial Arts, Adams broke into both the comic book and syndicated strip fields in 1959, drawing features for various *Archie* titles and also working three months on the *Bat Masterson* strip. But his first major comic work came in 1962 when Newspaper Enterprise hired him to draw the *Ben Casey* medical strip. Based on the then-popular television series, Adams drew the strip from its November 26, 1962, start until its July 31, 1966, demise.

Adams then drew Lou Fine's *Peter Scratch* for a month before becoming the artist on National's *Deadman* feature in November 1967's *Strange Adventures*. Written by veteran Jack Miller, the strip dealt with circus performer Boston Brand, who could not achieve eternal rest until he avenged his own murder with a variety of spiritual powers. Although the premise was far-fetched, Miller's hard-hitting realistic dialogue kept the series plausible, and Adams' work made *Deadman* a superlative strip. His drawings were highly realistic and beautifully detailed, and he constantly experimented with page layout and composition.

When *Deadman* ended in February 1969, Adams began to branch out: he drew highly acclaimed stories for Marvel's *X-Men*, National's *Teen Titans* and *Superman*, and helped return *The Batman* to its original "creature of the night" bent. In April 1970, he and writer Denny O'Neil combined to produce the first in a new series for National, the highly publicized *Green Lantern/Green Arrow* feature. The strip broke away from standard comic book fare to tackle the serious issues of the day. Writer O'Neil's stories were hailed as the most advanced in comic books, and Adams' raw realism was rarely seen previously in comic book art. Unfortunately, Adams began missing deadlines, sales did not match the critics' raves, and it was finally cancelled in May 1972 after 13 stories.

Since the demise of *Green Lantern/Green Arrow*, Adams has become a powerful and respected force in the industry. His work has appeared in many National, Marvel, and Warren titles, and he has done considerable advertising work, designed the costumes for the science fiction play *Warp*, ghosted work for several syndicated strips, and been president of the Academy of Comic Book Arts.

J.B.

After working briefly on the *Big Ben Bolt* newspaper strip in the late 1970s, Adams founded Continuity Associates to promote his work in the fields of advertising, commercial art, and comic books. On the latter front he produced a number of titles, including *Crazyman* and *Mr. Mystic*, but clichéd writing and erratic scheduling disappointed many of Adams's fans, and the line was discontinued in the mid-1990s.

M.H.

ADAMSON (Sweden) *Adamson* is the best-known comic strip to come out of Sweden. It was created in 1920 for inclusion in *Söndags-Nisse* ("Sunday Troll"), a Swedish humor weekly. Swedish artist Oscar Jacobsson came up with Adamson, a stout little man who, except for three hairs, has a bald pate. He smokes a cigar continuously while trying to cope with whatever problem is at hand. With *Adamson*, Oscar Jacobsson continued and developed to perfection the tradition of the pantomime strip. This, in fact, earned the strip the title *Silent Sam* when, in 1922, it became the first Scandinavian comic strip to be published in the United States. Jacobsson also succeeded in selling his strip to China and Japan and to many European nations. Selections of his strip were published in Berlin (1925-1928), London (1928), and Paris (1929). In Sweden, where annuals first appeared in 1921, *Adamsons bästa under 25 år* ("The Best from 25 Years of Adamson") was issued in 1944. Earlier, a trip to Greece and Italy in 1925-1926 resulted in a book titled *Adamsons resa* ("Adamson's Journey").

Jacobsson's strip enjoyed an immense popularity thanks to his simple style and his bizarre, original, and witty ideas, which are as fresh today as when they were originally conceived. *Adamson*'s popularity helped the strip survive its creator, who died in 1945. *Adamson* was continued by Danish artist Viggo Ludvigsen, who preferred to work in anonymity. Since 1965 no new *Adamson* strips have been produced, but the old artwork is being revived.

Adamson's witty misadventures, because of their historic importance and international popularity, have resulted in the adoption of the Adamson character as a statuette—a Swedish analogy to the Shazam or Oscar awards—two of which are awarded annually to the best Swedish and foreign comic artists. This is a fitting tribute to the genius of Oscar Jacobsson and to the popularity of *Adamson*, the strip that also boasts the distinction of having been reprinted in one of the first of a line of pocket books in postwar Germany.

W.F.

"Adamson," Oscar Jacobsson. © Consolidated News Features.

ADAM STRANGE (U.S.) Space opera in comic art has always been a syndicated strip proposition. There was Raymond's *Flash Gordon*, Gray's *Brick Bradford*, and even Calkins' and Nowlan's *Buck Rogers*. On the other hand, comic book science fiction has never been done well: The Fiction House group's material was always more interested in scantily dressed ladies with obvious attributes; Orbit's science fiction was uninspired; and EC's work, generally regarded as comic books' best, was predominated by bug-eyed monsters. Even Basil Wolverton's promising *Spacehawk* was destroyed when *Target Comics'* publisher decided it was unpatriotic for Spacehawk to be in space during a world war.

So, it remained for artist Carmine Infantino and writer Gardner Fox to fill the gap when they created *Adam Strange* for National's *Mystery in Space* number 53 in August 1959. The strip's basic premise was simple: earth-bound scientist Adam Strange was struck by a "zeta" beam and instantaneously transported to the planet Rann in the Alpha Centauri galaxy. He instantly fell in love with Alanna, a raven-tressed Rann woman, became enthralled with the Rann civilization, and became a more-or-less permanent resident of the planet. He also adopted a red-and-white jumpsuit and a helmet and became Rann's greatest protector.

All the stories were written by Gardner Fox, who blended considerable scientific knowledge and research with soaring flights of fancy to create the *Adam Strange* adventures. Adam and Alanna, two beautiful people, spent issue after issue of *Mystery in Space* cavorting through the galaxy, solving crimes, protecting both Earth and Rann, and exchanging what appeared to be harmless kisses.

Artistically, Carmine Infantino handled the pencilling and Murphy Anderson handled most of the inking. (Bernard Sachs handled the inking on the first and several early stories.) Infantino utilized a series of impeccable Hal Foster-inspired layouts on the strips and a tight illustrating line to make the feature one of the best-drawn of the early 1960s. Most breathtaking on the feature were his magnificent futuristic cityscapes. Much like comic strip artist Leonard Starr used night city scenes, Infantino drew cityscapes for maxi-

mum drama. They were always in the background, lush and round and beautifully symmetrical.

Adam Strange lost Infantino and Anderson shortly before the end of its run—they were replaced by Lee Elias—and it last appeared in September 1965's 102nd issue of *Mystery in Space*. The feature has been sporadically revived by National (now DC) Comics from the 1970s through the 1990s, but it has never been as successful as it was in former years.

J.B.

ADDISON *see* Walker, Mort.

ADOLF (Japan) Osamu Tezuka's last major work and the one most widely circulated outside Japan, *Adolf* (in Japanese *Adolf ni Tsugu* or "Tell Adolf") was serialized in the prestigious *Shukan Bunshun* magazine between 1983 and 1985. In a torrential story that stretches over more than 1,000 pages, the author displayed the full panoply of narrative devices in a graphic style approximating illustration, though many caricatural distortions and cartoony shortcuts are evident.

The Adolf in question is Adolf Hitler, Fuehrer of Germany, evidence of whose Jewish ancestry has somehow been discovered by a Japanese exchange student in Berlin and sent by him to a correspondent in the Japanese port city of Kobe, thus providing the wellspring for the tortuous plot. In a circuitous way the Fuehrer's fate becomes intertwined with those of two young boys, friends growing up in Kobe and who also happen to be named Adolf: Adolf Kaufmann, the son of a German diplomat, and Adolf Kamil, son of a Jewish refugee couple from Germany. As the tentacles of the Gestapo reach into Kobe to suppress the proof of Hitler's non-Aryan origins and to silence all witnesses, the two young Adolfs are increasingly sucked into the vortex of Nazi insanity. Kaufmann will turn into a leader of the Hitler Youth and later of the S.S., while Kamil will become a dedicated Zionist.

"Adam Strange," Carmine Infantino. © DC Comics.

"Adolf," Osamu Tezuka. © Tezuka Productions.

Looming behind the almost nonstop action involving Hitler's missing birth documents is the awesome shadow of World War II. The plot, reflective of Greek tragedy, does not stop at war's end but continues to engulf the protagonists long after the general madness has ended. Kamil now lives in Israel and is an officer in the army, while Kaufmann fights on the side of the P.L.O. and Black September. At the conclusion, in a highly symbolic gesture, Kamil will kill his childhood friend.

An ardent pacifist, Tezuka posits a revisionist version of the conflict of World War II, blaming it all on Adolf Hitler (as the defendants at the Nuremberg trials also did, to little avail), and somewhat glosses over the willing role played by the great majority of the German (and Japanese) populace in the chronicle of aggression leading up to the outbreak of global war. The author seems to have felt that the Jewish identity (or "Jewish problem," as the Nazis and their sympathizers chose to term it) is at the heart of World War II, and indeed at the heart of most of this century's history. It is revealing to note in this context that of the three principals, the Jewish Adolf is the only one to survive at the end.

Adolf was made into a radio drama in 1993. In the United States it was produced in five volumes published by Cadence Books in 1995-96.

M.H.

ADVENTURES OF PATSY, THE   *see* Patsy.

AGACHADOS, LOS (Mexico) *Los Agachados* (which can be translated as "Those Who Stoop Down") was created in Mexico by Eduardo del Rio ("Rius") on September 14, 1968, in a twice-monthly comic book format. In the first two issues Rius carried over the characters he had earlier created in his series *Los Supermachos*, but afterwards each story treated a different theme.

"Los Agachados," Ríus (Eduardo del Rio). © Ríus.

The "agachados" are the Mexican people, the lower classes who take their siestas stooped down on the doorsteps of their churches and whom Rius wanted to politicize through his stories. There are no central characters since it is the people themselves who live and breathe through the pages. In this way each book deals with a relevant theme whose reality is graphically depicted by Rius. He narrates the history of his country, looks at the Spanish and later North American colonialism, and examines Mexico's customs, virtues, and faults. Christ, Lenin, the Olympic Games, the housing problem, Coca-Cola, and the Mexican comics are all themes that the author presents in his strip, in a popular and authentic dialect far removed from classical Castilian. The balloons are integrated within the panels, the layout of each page forms a whole entirely different from the conventional comic strip, and color delineates the different areas in a very personal rendering.

Rius has also written a book inspired by his series, *La Iglesia de los Agachados* ("The Church of the Agachados"). The political, social, and artistic significance of *Los Agachados* have made it the most important comic strip published in Mexico.

L.G.

AGHARDI (Spain) *Aghardi* was created in Spain by Enric Sio in 1969, and was being published simultaneously in the Italian monthly *Linus* and in the Spanish magazine *Mundo Joven*. The strip relates the expeditions of a group of scientists headed by anthropology professor Samantha Jordan and her assistant Martha, who are united by emotional ties with lesbian undertones. Steve, a photographer, and Jo, a humanities professor, are also in the team. All these characters weave their complex relationships in Mexico, Bolivia, and Peru, the situation reaching its climax in Tibet. Real history is continually intertwined with references to Mayan and Incan legends, especially the one relating to Matreya, the god of the subterranean kingdom of Aghardi.

In this experiment in black and white, Enric Sio relates a story of "realistic fantasy" based on traces possibly left by extraterrestrial beings who visited Earth. His narrative blends adventures and surreal circumstances at one level with well-defined sociopolitical opinions on another level. To this end he uses analytical montages, and the continual inclusion of legends illustrated in the style of old Mayan and Aztec codices.

The texts are written by Sio himself (the first time he has done his own scriptwriting). In this feature, where there can be found many aesthetic innovations, it is well to note that the two main protagonists were inspired by fashion model Veroushka and by singer Guillermina Motta. The difficulty of its language, the dialogues that differ from those ordinarily found in comics of the period, and the ground-breaking montages make *Aghardi* a work of exquisite complexity and beauty.

L.G.

AGUILA, DANI (1928-   ) According to his fellow artists, Dani Aguila is one of the busiest painter-cartoonists around. Born in the Philippines on September 24, 1928, he started to work on his first cartoon strip in 1949, when he was enrolled at the University of the Philippines. He graduated in 1952 with a Bach-

Dani Aguila, "Pinoy Moreno." © Filipino Reporter.

elor of Fine Arts degree. He then began his second strip, called *Student Life*, but he soon departed for the United States to continue his studies. In 1956 he attended graduate courses in mass communications at Syracuse University in New York. Returning to the Philippines, Aguila worked for the Philippine Rural Reconstruction Movement. There he did a cartoon strip called *Kamagong* (the name of a hard, black wood). He said that the name, though ironic, signified strength and uniqueness. The strip was about a rare, white water buffalo.

From 1960 to 1962 he did a series called *Barrio Breeze*, and from 1962 to 1965 he did a strip for *Asian Newsweekly Examiner* called *The Cock and Bull*. It was a political strip that gained an avid following.

After traveling back and forth between the Philippines and the United States, Aguila finally settled in Nashville, Tennessee, where he worked for a local television station as an art director and drew political cartoons for a Nashville periodical. Several of his panel cartoons have won editorial awards and have been included in anthologies. Recently he started a new comic strip for the *Filipino Reporter* (a Filipino-American weekly) called *Pinoy Moreno*. It is a humorous strip dealing with the lighter side of acculturation, integration, and assimilation. He is now back in the Philippines.

While in the Philippines, Dani Aguila was a leading force in the Society of Philippine Illustrators and Cartoonists. He edited a cartoon anthology that included the works of many of the most important names in the Philippine comic book and cartoon fields.

O.J.

AHERN, GENE (1895-1960) Gene Ahern called himself a southerner, as he pointed out that he had been born on the south side of Chicago, in 1895. As a boy, he wanted first to be a comedian, and then a "funny writer." He finally fell in love with comic strips and decided to work at his decidedly unmarked talent until he could make the funny pages. For three years he studied at the Chicago Art Institute, improving his basic technique to minimal competence—but that, as it proved, was unimportant. For Ahern, like Segar, Dorgan, and others, was a man who simply "drew funny": people laughed at his work on sight, regardless of his technical facility.

Gene Ahern, "Room and Board." © King Features Syndicate.

Newspaper and syndicate editors loved him and gave him sports page work in the early 1910s, with the NEA syndicate sending it to Scripps-Howard papers, among others throughout the country. He immediately began developing strip ideas and concepts, such as *Taking Her To The Ball Game* (a 1914 panel series poking fun at women reacting to the mysteries of baseball), *Fathead Fritz* (a dumb rookie on the diamond), and *Dream Dope* (comic panels on sports); the last two were unified under the running panel title of *Squirrel Food*, where Ahern's two longest-lasting characters, The Nut Brothers, Ches and Wal, eventually emerged.

The young cartoonist's big break came in 1923, when NEA began distributing his innovative daily panel, *Our Boarding House*. This often hilarious narrative strip was Ahern's big success with the public, and a Sunday page about the panel's star character, Major Hoople, soon followed. By 1936, Ahern was nationally famous and accepted a contract with King Features to do a variant on *Our Boarding House* for them. This new feature, called *Room and Board*, focused on a Hoople simulacrum named Judge Puffle. Like the Sunday *Boarding House* page's *Nut Brothers* topper, the new

Room and Board Sunday page carried a *Squirrel Cage* half-page about the same kind of characters, adding a new figure: the once-famed bearded hitchhiker with his "Nov Schmoz Ka Pop?" comment. Ahern died on November 17, 1960, and his King Features panel folded.

B.B.

AIRBOY (U.S.) Created by Charles Biro in November 1942, *Airboy* made its first appearance in Hillman's *Air-Fighters* number two. Featuring the exploits of Davy (Airboy) Nelson and his amazing airplane "Birdie," *Airboy* quickly became the premier boy's strip of all time, and, as an aviation strip, it was second only to Quality Comics' *Blackhawk*. Strangely enough, however, Airboy was never the main attraction in *Airboy*. That distinction fell to the plane, Birdie.

Created by a monk named Martier, Birdie was an amazing invention. It had gray, serrated wings that flapped like a bat, two massive 50-calibre machine guns, and unusual hovering abilities and remote-control devices. One of the many wartime patriotic comic features, *Airboy* dealt almost exclusively with Birdie's (and Airboy's) battles against hordes of Fascist-controlled planes. It was not unusual for Birdie to out-maneuver and destroy 50 or 60 Nazi or Japanese aircrafts in one dogfight. And, in fact, these herculean dogfights became the major selling point in *Airboy*. The air-war fantasy motif made the strip an escape from the real and horrible war. *AirFighters* comics eventually became *Airboy* comics in December 1945.

As originally scripted by Biro, personal conflict and interaction dominated *Airboy*. But under later writers, Birdie achieved such an exalted position that artists like Bernie Sachs, Carmine Infantino, and Tony DiPreta

"Airboy," Fred Kida. © Hillman Periodicals.

were hardly drawing people anymore. Fred Kida was the only artist who ever managed to develop the red, yellow, and blue-clad Airboy into a distinguishable character. He depicted Airboy as an older, more mature person and later portrayed him as a soldier-of-fortune rather than a child with a toy. Before these stories, which were always dark and moody, Airboy was a one-dimensional pilot, totally subservient to Birdie's remarkable machinery. Kida drew a majority of the stories between 1943 and 1946, and he is recognized as the strip's definitive artist.

There were very few recurrent villains in *Airboy*, as they were never allowed to develop. Airboy did have one outstanding adversary, Valkyrie, and she soon developed into the comic industry's answer to *Terry and the Pirates*' Dragon Lady. A beautiful and sexually agressive aviatrix, Valkyrie made her debut in November 1943. Bearing a remarkable resemblance to motion picture's Veronica Lake, she and her squadron of "Air Maidens" were originally exponents of the Nazi cause. She adopted a more pragmatic view of the war, however, and was constantly shifting from one side to the other. At times, she'd even change during a story, alternately trying to save and destroy Airboy and Birdie. Her coquettish flirtations were in sharp contrast to Airboy's often adolescent, flag-waving behavior.

The postwar years were troublesome for *Airboy*, however. Having outlived the war they were created to fight, Airboy and Birdie were floundering in a sea of common, everyday crimes. Birdie wasn't made to fight bank robbers, however, and the feature was discontinued in May 1953's *Airboy* number 111.

J.B.

In 1986 Eclipse Comics decided to bring back Airboy, pitting him against some of his old adversaries, such as Valkyrie and Skywolf. With sometimes excellent drawing by the likes of George Evans, Dan Spiegle, and Paul Gulacy, *Airboy* (and its collateral titles) managed to survive until the end of the decade.

M.H.

AIR HAWK AND THE FLYING DOCTORS (Australia) Created by former comic book artist John Dixon, the Sunday page was first published in the Sydney *Sun-Herald* on June 14, 1959. The popularity of the strip over the next four years led to the introduction of the daily strip in May 1963. Both versions are still running, making it the most successful adventure strip to be published in Australia. *Air Hawk* is the name of an air charter service operated by the tall blond ex-fighter ace, Jim Hawk. The charter service is based in Alice Springs, in the heart of the continent. In addition to operating this flight charter enterprise, Jim has been granted the franchise to supply a special Emergency Relief Unit to work in conjunction with the Royal Flying Doctor Service. The unit's function is to relieve any Flying Doctor Base in need of assistance and to be available for special emergencies. Dr. Hal Mathews, who has been seconded by the R.F.D.S. to work with the special unit, is a close friend of Hawk and has been with the strip since its inception. The romantic interest is provided by Sister Janet Grant, a former nurse with the Australian Inland Mission, who is now a full-time assistant to Dr. Mathews.

In Hawk, Dixon has successfully portrayed the tall, lean, suntanned, unflappable Australian of popular mythology and invested him with a better education and more technical skills than his legendary counter-

"Air Hawk," John Dixon. © The Herald and Weekly Times Ltd.

Sandy Highflier, "the airship man," was a young adventurer who roamed the world in his dirigible (made up of a motorboat suspended from a sausage balloon), in search of wrongs to redress and damsels to rescue. His adventures proved more humorous than suspenseful. His airship became tangled in telegraph wires and ran into church steeples, and, at one time, Sandy himself was plucked out of his ship by a mischievous giraffe. Sandy usually managed to outwit his

part. The scripts, written by Dixon, have always been solid with plenty of action, drama, suspense, and good characterization—but fairly conventional (i.e., conservative) in approach, avoiding any contentious areas. *Air Hawk* is played out against the background of cathedral-like ridges, barren landscapes, caverns, rivers, and waterholes of the Outback country. The locations allow for the introduction of native fauna, Aborigines, and their way of life. Dixon captures all these things with graphic authenticity. A great deal of the strip's popularity stems from the amount of time-consuming detail that Dixon depicts on his variety of airplanes—for the strip is, above all, an aviation strip. Apart from satisfying the reader's taste for realistically drawn adventure, *Air Hawk* offers the majority of readers (including the bulk of those in Australia) an opportunity to experience the far-off, exotic frontier of the rugged yet beautiful inland country. Dixon has taken great care to see that the hero has not strayed from his basic role of a flying adventurer.

Soon after the introduction of the daily strip, Mike Tabrett took over the Sunday page under Dixon's guidance. In March 1970, he was replaced by Hart Amos, a former comic book artist and illustrator, whose keen eye for depicting mechanical details almost equals Dixon's. As well as appearing in most Australian states, *Air Hawk* appears in New Zealand, Hong Kong, South Africa, Ireland, Italy, Spain, France, Germany, Sweden, and Argentina. To date, its U.S. appearances have been restricted to *The Menomonee Falls Gazette*, a weekly with limited circulation. Since the late 1970s every Australian artist worth his salt seems to have worked on the strip, including Paul Power, Keith Chatto, and Phil Belbin.

J.R.

AIRSHIP MAN, THE (U.S.) C. W. Kahles produced one of his first comic creations, *The Airship Man*, as a Sunday half-page for the *Philadelphia North American* from March 1902 to October 1903.

"The Airship Man," C. W. Kahles.

enemies, be they bloodthirsty pirates or spear-throwing cannibals, more by luck than by design. Some of his aerial stunts would later find their way into the author's celebrated *Hairbreadth Harry*.

The *Airship Man* stands out among early comic strips as one of the first (if not the very first) attempts at mixing derring-do with humor. As for Sandy Highflier, he deserves a niche of his own as the first air adventurer of the comics.

M.H.

AIRY ALF AND BOUNCING BILLY (G.B.) *The Adventures and Misadventures of Airy Alf and Bouncing Billy* began on the front page of *The Big Budget* number one, a jumbo-size three-in-one comic, 24 pages for one penny. The date was 19 June 1897, and so the edition was also a special one to celebrate Queen Victoria's Jubilee. Alf and Billy went on their bicycles and wound up in prison, a standard payoff for this pair. Tom Browne, then the top British comic artist, created them, and while physically they were fat and thin, resembling his established *Weary Willie and Tired Tim*, they were of a slightly higher class than those two tramps. They also reflected Browne's major hobby, bicycling, and for the year that he drew them, he cycled almost continuously. They even joined the Cycle Scouts section of the Volunteer Army Reserve. Their adventures reflected other aspects of Victorian society, and not only did they make dutiful appearances at the Oxford and Cambridge Boat Races, Henley Regatta, Lords Cricket Ground, etc., they also met such notables as Prime Minister Joseph Chamberlain and Dan Leno, and they ran the Cuban blockade.

Alf and Billy were taken over in 1898 by Ralph Hodgson, who signed himself "Yorick." At first he followed Browne's style closely, even going so far as to draw Alf and Billy meeting their rivals Willie and Tim! But having been made art editor of the *Big Budget*, Hodgson experimented in a number of styles, adding balloons in the American manner and dropping typeset captions. The strip ran until 1908. Many *Alf and Billy* episodes were reprinted in *Victorian Comics* (1975).

D.G.

"Airy Alf and Bouncing Billy," Ralph Hodgson.

AIZEN, ADOLFO (1907-1991) Brazilian editor, born in 1907 in Juazeiro, Bahia. At age 15, Adolfo Aizen moved to Rio de Janeiro, then the country's capital, and in 1933 he started his career as a journalist with *O Malho*. During a trip to the United States, he met the executives at King Features Syndicate and bought the Brazilian rights to King's properties. In March 1934 he started *Suplemento Juvenil* as a children's supplement to the newspaper *A Noite*, publishing such comics as *Jungle Jim, Flash Gordon, Tarzan, Mandrake*, and *Terry and the Pirates*; it became an instant hit. He later launched *O Mirim* along the same lines. This gave rise to a rival publication, *Gibi*, which became the synonym for comic book (even today children ask for a "gibi" from their newsstand vendor).

In the early 1940s Aizen brought American superheroes to Brazil, with the publication of *Superman* and *Batman*, and later of *Spider-Man* and *Thor*, among others. He also published the Brazilian edition of *Classics Illustrated*; after the title had folded in the United States, he hired Brazilian artists to illustrate the literary works of national authors such as Jorge Amado, José Lins do Rego and Machado de Assis. In the process he nurtured the talents of Andre Le Blanc (a former Will Eisner assistant), Manoel Victor Filho, Ziraldo, and others. In 1950 he published a co-edition of a Disney special with Argentina. This was the start of yet another publishing giant, Editora Abril, the authorized Disney publisher for Latin America, and today one of the largest publishers in South America. At his death in 1991, he was celebrated as the pioneer of comics publishing in Brazil.

A.M.

AKADŌ SUZUNOSUKE (Japan) *Akadō Suzunosuke* was created by Eiichi Fukui in the August 1954 issue of the Japanese comic monthly *Shōnen Gahō*. Eiichi Fukui died suddenly, before he could draw the second story, and was succeeded by Tsunayoshi Takeuchi, who was to draw the strip until its demise.

Akadō Suzunosuke was a young man living in the time of the samurais. He was trained in the Japanese art of fencing ("Kendō") at a small school in the country. Recognized as a promising swordsman by his mas-

"Akadō Suzunosuke," Eiichi Fukui.
© Shōnen Gahō.

ter Oshinosuke Yokomura, Suzunosuke became a pupil of the famous Chiba in Edo (the former name for Tokyo). Gentle and honest, Suzunosuke worked hard at his craft and earned the respect of his schoolmates, including that of his chief rival, Rainoshin Tatsumaki, whom he defeated in a sword contest and who later became his friend.

Suzunosuke (whose full name is Suzunosuke Kinno, but who received the nickname Akadō because of the red shield—"akadō"—which he uses) fought against brigands, plunderers and other villains (Namiemon Kuroshio, Kaiomaru, Madara-seij in, Naoto Maka, etc.), whom he invariably defeated by his intelligent tactics and his superior swordplay (which includes his favorite technique, the deadly "shinkūgiri" or "vacuum cut").

Akadō Suzunosuke has been made into a radio program, a television series and a number of animated films. In 1958 an Akadō festival was held in the Hibiya concert hall in Tokyo. Tsunayoshi drew his character to the accompaniment of a theme song that later became a hit recording. *Akadō Suzunosuke* was discontinued in the December 1960 issue of *Shōnen Gahō*.

H.K.

AKATSUKA, FUJIO (1935-   ) Japanese comic book artist, born September 1935 in China. After the Pacific War (World War II) his mother brought him back to Japan. Following graduation from high school, Fujio Akatsuka was employed by a chemical company; he hated it and in his spare time drew a number of comic strips, which he sent out to magazines. In 1955 he made his debut with a girl strip, *Arashio Koete*, which met with scant success. To support himself, he worked as an assistant to Mitsuteru Yokoyama from June 1955 to January 1958. Akatsuka describes these years as the most miserable of his life.

Finally Akatsuka was able to sell a gag strip to the monthly *Manga Ō*: it was *Namachan* (1958). In 1962 he followed with his first popular success, *Osomatsukun* (in which he brought to life some of his most famous characters: Iyami, Chibita, Dekapan, Hatabo, etc.). In 1962 he also created his most famous girl strip, *Himitsu no*

Akko chan. From this time on, Akatsuka produced one successful strip after another: *Otasukekun* (a humor strip, 1963), *Shibire no Skatan* (another humor strip, 1966), *Ijiwaru Ikka* ("The Spiteful Family," 1966), *Tensai Bakabon* (a humor strip again, and one of his best works, 1967), *Moretsu Ataro* (a 1967 humor strip in which he created some new characters such as Kemunpasu, Beshi, the Mad Policeman, Nyarome, and others), and *Waru Waru World* (1974).

Akatsuku's greatest merit was to uphold and renew the humor strip tradition at a time when the continuity strip was in its heyday. Next to Osamu Tezuka, he created the greatest number of popular comic characters, and he is, without a doubt, the greatest humor cartoonist working in Japan today. Many of his works (notably *Osomatsu-kun, Tensai Bakabon, Moretsu Ataro* and *Himitsu no Akkochan*) have been adapted into animated films. Akatsuka's graphic style is simple and basic, his characters are not superheroes, but antiheroes, and his stories are grounded in comedy, slapstick and nonsense. He has also promoted the work of other Japanese artists through his Fujio Productions; as Frederik Schodt wrote in *Manga! Manga!* (1983), "He is helping transform the humor of Japanese comics and, indirectly, of Japanese society."

H.K.

AKIM (Italy) In the period between 1950 and 1970, the *Tarzan* comic books and comic strips were only sparsely distributed in Italy. This situation offered a golden opportunity to unscrupulous imitators, and a swarm of spurious editions sprang up, all trying to take advantage of the success enjoyed by E. R. Burroughs' jungle hero in movie theaters all over Europe.

Among the many *Tarzan* imitations, only one became very popular and enjoyed wide circulation: *Akim*, conceived by Augusto Pedrazza and published for the first time in a 32-page comic book in the collection "Albo Gioello," by Edizioni Tomasina on February 10, 1950. In the first episode (which was palmed off as true fact to the readers), the origin of the character was given in lines identical to the story written by Burroughs. Here are some of the opening lines:

"Akim," Augusto Pedrazza. © Tomasina.

"... Son of the British Consul in Calcutta, Count Frederick Rank. During the journey back to England, the ship bearing Count Rank and his family sinks, due to the dereliction of a sailor: the only survivors are Mrs. Rank and her son Jim. Washed ashore on an unknown land, the mother builds a shelter for her son, but a panther tears her to pieces. But, as the panther is carrying the child into her den, a gorilla attacks the panther and the wounded beast is compelled to drop the child. The curious gorilla picks the child up."

Some 16 years later (so the story continues) a strapping young fellow is swinging from treetop to treetop: his name is Akim, the white ape. Of course he speaks the language of the animals and is respected and obeyed by all of them. Later Akim will befriend two other apes, Kar and Zug, and meet Rita, a white girl with whom he promptly falls in love; Akim also has a young ward whom he protects like his own son.

The only difference with the Tarzan saga is that Akim and Rita are not bound in wedlock (as are Tarzan and Jane). As for the rest, the plots totally follow the Tarzan stories, especially the movie scripts. There is the impact caused by civilization, whether in the jungle or in New York (to where Akim journeys), the love contest for Akim, and the stereotyped distinctions between good people and villains. Even the environment and the physical features of the characters are not very dissimilar, apart from the drawing style, which in the Italian version was always hurried and barely adequate (this was primarily due to Pedrazza's enormous output).

After more than 1,000 issues in comic books and one-shots, *Akim* disappeared from Italian newsstands, but continued being published abroad. In fact, Akim enjoyed his own comic book in France, which was drawn by the indefatigable if mediocre Pedrazza, although the texts were written for a while by Roberto Renzi. This version also eventually ended.

G.B.

ALACK SINNER (Argentina/Spain/Italy/France)
Alack Sinner is a prime example of the growing internationalization of comics, as well as one of the most innovative creations of the last 20 years. The brainchild of Argentinian-born José Muñoz and Carlos Sampayo working in Spain, it first appeared in the pages of the Italian magazine *Alter Alter* in 1975. Both authors had been raised on Dashiell Hammett and Raymond Chandler novels and on Humphrey Bogart movies, and they strove to re-create the dark atmosphere and bleak outlook of their early inspirations.

Scriptwriter Sampayo set his thriller in the New York of his imagination (only in 1981 did he visit the city for the first time). Alack Sinner, the nominal protagonist, was initially an ex-cop turned private investigator whose caseload included blackmail, kidnapping, and attempted murder. For a while he dropped out of the gumshoe business to become a taxi driver, but he later returned to his true calling. In the course of his business, he encountered other lost souls, including Sophie, a pathetic and engaging figure (and the protagonist of a later series of her own), whose lover he would become and whose daughter he would father. All the characters socialize, argue, deal, pair off, or collide at Joe's Bar, a sort of crossroads of the netherworld, a meeting place for society's outcasts. In that context even the anti-hero's name, so redolent of an Adamic fall from grace, seems to point to some cosmic disjunction.

"Alack Sinner," José Muñoz and Carlos Sampayo. © the authors.

Sampayo's narrative is uncannily matched by Muñoz's artwork—sulfurous, brutal, and unsparing. Employing only black and white with no halftones, Muñoz is able to conjure up images of bleak despair with a dispassionate minuteness that belies their white-hot intensity. As the critic Oscar Zarate noted, "Every visual element, even the smallest one, is a protagonist that fights to be listened to, becoming a threatening presence that haunts you."

Alack Sinner was greeted enthusiastically almost from the moment it came out. The series was snapped up by the French monthly *A Suivre* immediately after *Alter Alter* folded in 1980. In the United States, it has been published by Fantagraphics under the pared-down title *Sinner*, and it has been a great influence—even down to the title—on Frank Miller's critically acclaimed *Sin City*.

M.H.

ALAN FORD (Italy) Published for the first time in July 1969, *Alan Ford* is the most important phenomenon that the Italian comic industry has recorded in recent years.

From the inception, *Alan Ford* has enjoyed tremendous success and wide distribution, due to the imaginativeness of its authors, Max Bunker (Luciano Secchi) for the text, and Magnus (Roberto Raviola) for the drawing, who have created a comic book of high humor and picaresque adventure, as well as a satire on our dehumanizing society.

Alan Ford, the first existential nonhero in the history of Italian comics, was for years the only specimen

"Alan Ford," Luciano Secchi and Roberto Raviola. © Editoriale Corno.

of his kind. Built on solidly constructed texts, *Alan Ford* displays its rich fantasy in each of its 120-page comic books. Alan Ford, the handsome but shy and luckless protagonist, is a member of the shady secret organization known as TNT and is entrusted with the weirdest missions by his boss, the deathless Numero Uno. Numero Uno is an old man confined in a wheelchair who has lived through the ages and never lets anyone forget it. Bob Rock (modeled on Magnus) is the frustrated number-two man, resentful and petulant; the Cariatide (modeled after Bunker) is the symbol of the eternal bureaucrat; Il Conte (the Count) is the professional burglar, indispensable to any organization of the kind; Grunf is a nostalgic of the old times of free-booting adventure; Geremia is the perennial complainer; and the two animals Cirano and Squitty round out the zany outfit.

The TNT members are so hung up physically and psychologically that they always prove unable to successfully complete any assignment. Caught in awkward situations, tripped up by their own schemes, Alan Ford and his associates display the resignation of all losers. In the end we forgive them their shortcomings because they are no different from those of every inhabitant of this planet. *Alan Ford* remains a big seller in Italy, having reached issue number 300 in 1995.

G.B.

ALBERTARELLI, RINO (1908-1974) Italian cartoonist and illustrator, born in 1908 in Cesena. After many experiences in disparate fields—painter, ceramist, store clerk, actor, set designer—Rino Albertarelli went to Milan at the age of 20. There he met Antonio Rubino, who gave him the opportunity to work for the children's weekly *Il Balilla*. After military service, Albertarelli began working with several publishers, Paravia and Vallardi among them. His works also appeared in the magazines *Viaggi e Avventure* and *Cartoccino dei Piccoli,* and he assumed the editorship of the latter from 1933 to 1935. Starting in 1936, he published his first continuing comic stories: for Argentovivo he realized *I Pirati del Pacifico,* and for *L'Audace* he created *Capitan Fortuna* and *Big Bill.* In 1937 Albertarelli started working for Mondadori, bringing out his most famous cre-

ations: *Kit Carson, Gino e Gianni, Baghongi il Pagliaccio* ("Baghongi the Clown"), *Il Dottor Faust, Mefistofele, Un Gentiluomo di 16 Anni* ("A Gentleman of 16"), and *Gioietta Portafortuna,* all of which were published in the large-circulation weeklies *Topolino* and *Paperino,* along with his adaptations of Salgari's novels, the long saga of *Il Corsaro Nero* ("The Black Corsair") paramount among them.

In the meantime, Albertarelli had broadened his field to include satirical magazines such as *Il Bertoldo, Marc'Aurelio, Settebello, Il Galantuomo,* and *Fra Diavolo* and had become a member of the editorial staff of *Le Grande Firme.* In 1942 he was recalled to the army and, when the war ended, he tried his hand at a stage farce, *Il Simulatore,* written in collaboration with Pepino De Fillippo. In 1946 he resumed his Salgarian work, illustrating many of the master's stories for the periodical *Salgari.* These were practically his last comic stories for children and were drawn from 1946 to 1948.

Albertarelli experimented next with romance comics for the publisher Cino del Duca in 1948, and these works were published in the French magazine *Nous Deux.* After some collaboration with foreign publishers, Albertarelli devoted himself fully to illustration for didactic, religious, and western articles and stories. His work was published in *Successo, Historia, Tempo, Settimo Giorno, Visto,* and *Marie-Claire.* An important series of his wash drawings was published by Dardo in 1965. Only recently did Albertarelli come back to comic art, producing the series *I Protagonisti* for Daim Press, a collection of monographs of famous personages from Custer to Billy the Kid, all of them scrupulously documented. His sudden death on September 21, 1974, prevented Albertarelli from completing this work.

G.B.

ALCALA, ALFREDO P. (1925-   ) Filipino comic book illustrator and cartoonist, born August 23, 1925, in Talisay, Occidental Negros, Philippines. Alcala dropped out of school at an early age to pursue his first love, drawing. He started out painting signs. After a year he got a job working for a wrought-iron shop designing chandeliers, table lamps, hat racks, and garden furniture. At one time he designed a church pulpit. He copied and studied the works of Harold Foster's *Prince Valiant* and Alex Raymond's *Flash Gordon* until the early hours of the morning. However, it was Louis K. Fine (Lou Fine), the artist of *The Black Condor, Uncle Sam, The Dollman,* etc., who most influenced Alcala.

In October 1948, Alcala's first comic book illustration appeared in *Bituin Komiks* ("Star Comics"). By November of the same year he was illustrating for the largest publishing house in the Philippines: Ace Publications. They started out with two comic books titled *Filipino Komiks* and *Tagalog Klassiks,* and after a few years they expanded to two more titles: *Espesial Komiks* and *Hiwaga Komiks.* These books were published twice a month, and Alcala drew for all of these simultaneously. The stories that Alcala drew were serials that ran for several months. Their themes varied from superheroes to melodramatics, from comedy to fantasy. Because of his versatility, Alcala never had any problems adapting to these different stories. He is considered one of the fastest illustrators in the Philippines and has been known to work for 96 hours straight without sleep. Alcala always does his own pencilling, inking, and lettering. He very rarely uses an assistant.

As Alcala progressed, he studied American illustrators such as Howard Pyle, N.C. Wyeth, Dean Cornwell, Robert Fawcett, J.C. Leyendecker, and others. One of the strongest influences on Alcala was the great British muralist Frank Brangwyn.

In the early 1970s an American editor went to the Philippines to look over some of the work of the Filipino artists. Alcala was one of the first to be praised. Since then he has done work for two of the largest comic book publishers in the United States, D.C. National and Marvel Publications. He has also contributed to *Captain Marvel* and *House of Secrets*; in the late 1970s and early 1980s he also illustrated the *Rick O'Shay* and *Star Wars* newspaper strips.

M.A.

Mogenson draws another comic strip, *Poeten*, starring a writer and his family.

Alfredo, however, stars a black-haired, round-headed, moustachioed man who, although married to a domineering wife, has never given up flirting. Alfredo is shown in many different jobs, places, and epochs of history. He is the perennial Everyman living out everyone's fantasies. As such he has endeared himself to his readers and has become a perennial success.

W.F.

"Alix," Jacques Martin. © Editions du Lombard.

"Alfredo," Moco (Jørgen Morgenson and Cosper Cornelius). © PIB.

ALFREDO (Denmark) *Alfredo* is one of the European strips that enjoys worldwide fame because it is a pantomime strip with a universal appeal. The American title for the strip is *Moco* (Los Angeles Times Syndicate), a signature that combines the names of its artist/writers Jørgen Mogenson and Cosper Cornelius. The Danish comic strip *Alfredo* conquered a worldwide audience by following the example of H. Dahl Mikkelsen's *Ferd'nand* and Oscar Jacobsson's *Adamson*, which had long since proved the old adage that silence (especially that of pantomime) is golden.

Jørgen Mogenson had already embarked on a career as painter and sculptor and Cosper Cornelius had chosen the life of jazz musician when they got together in 1940 to devote their time to *Hudibras*, a satirical magazine founded by Cornelius as a forum for talented "crazy" artists. Mogenson's early work had one character that suited that idea fully: the Mad Artist. The Mad Artist's misadventures appeared in the form of a pantomime comic strip. Whatever the Mad Artist did became reality: When he is chased through the desert by a lion, a fat man he draws in the sand springs to life and serves as a decoy. The surrealistic strip had already won international renown when Mogenson decided to end it before he ran out of ideas. The pantomime style, however, was carried over into *Alfredo*, on which he and Cornelius have cooperated since the 1950s. Their collaboration is rather unusual. Mogenson and Cornelius each do three daily strips per week without comparing notes or sketches. Surprisingly enough, they never come up with the same gags. This method of collaboration leaves enough time for other pursuits.

ALIX L'INTRÉPIDE (Belgium) *Alix l'Intrépide* ("Alix the Fearless") was created by Jacques Martin in October 1948 for the Belgian weekly *Tintin*.

Alix is the son of a Gaul chieftain, Astorix but has been adopted by the Roman governor Honorus Galla, a friend and faithful lieutenant of Julius Caesar. This situation provides a built-in conflict of loyalties within Alix, which Martin knows how to put to good dramatic use. At the same time Alix's most persistent enemy is the Greek Arbaces, ambitious and cunning, and an ally of Caesar's enemy Pompey.

At first Alix was a lone wolf pursuing his own dreams and aspirations, but in 1949 he met the young Egyptian Enak and the two struck up a lasting friendship, in spite of misunderstandings and vicissitudes.

Alix has been pursuing his adventures almost uninterruptedly since 1948 from one end of the Roman Empire to the other; his exploits have carried him from Rome to Scythia, from Egypt to the German *limnes*. He has fought against the callous directives of the Roman Senate and the grand designs of Parthian and Egyptian usurpers, and he has even had to repress mutiny within the ranks of his own Gaul mercenaries.

Jacques Martin has been able to maintain the epic sweep of Alix's adventures for over a quarter of a century, without compromising historical authenticity or tampering with factual accuracy. *Alix* is an outstanding adventure strip depicted with an almost archaeological knowledge of the period. The adventures of Alix have been reprinted in book form by Editions du Lombard and Editions Casterman. The success of the series has continued unabated to this day and has given rise to a number of exegeses, notably *L'Odyssée d'Alix* (1987).

M.H.

ALLEN, DALE *see* Saunders, Allen.

ALLEY OOP (U.S.) Created by Vincent T. Hamlin and distributed by Newspaper Enterprise Association (NEA), *Alley Oop* premiered on August 7, 1933, as a daily strip, which was followed by a Sunday version on September 9, 1934.

Alley is a caveman, uncivilized and invincible in the tradition of Popeye (like Popeye he has gigantic forearms and tremendous strength). Mounted on his faithful pet dinosaur Dinny, he brings order to the Kingdom of Moo, which is going to pot under the inept leadership of King Guzzle (in turn, Guzzle is bedeviled by his scheming grand vizier, Foozy, and nagged by his wife, Queen Umpateedle). Oftentimes Alley must go and fight against Moo's many outside enemies, as well as against its unruly subjects. His martial feats and bullheaded sense of duty are only matched by his unswerving devotion to his sweetheart Oola, a piquant brunette whom he spends a good part of his time fighting over.

In 1939 Hamlin, tiring of all this prehistoric folderol, introduced two new protagonists: Professor Wonmug, inventor of a time machine, and his demented assistant Oscar Boom. In short order Alley and Oola found themselves transported to the 20th century (Alley's dinosaur was later to follow). In a series of screwball adventures, Hamlin made good use of the device: he had his hero meeting Cleopatra, fighting in the Crusades, crossing swords with 17th-century pirates, and rescuing settlers from attacking Indians. Alley Oop has also made a few reappearances in the Land of Moo, where his compatriots, cantankerous and rowdy as ever, seem unperturbed by all his comings and goings.

In 1971 Hamlin retired, and the strip was taken over by his former assistant Dave Graue, who did a credible job of continuation and preserved most of the feature's original flavor. Since 1993 *Alley Oop* has been drawn by Jack Bender, while Graue still continues to provide the scripting.

Alley Oop has been entertaining its readers for over 60 years now, and much of the credit must go to V. T. Hamlin's great vision. His strip has remained consistently imaginative both narratively and graphically (some of *Alley Oop*'s Sunday pages of 1936 through 1940 are models of innovative layout and skillful use of color) and must be ranked as one of the best comic creations to come out of the 1930s.

Alley Oop has been reproduced in comic books, and in 1960 it inspired a popular song of the same name.

M.H.

ALLY SLOPER (G.B.) The first British strip hero (or rather antihero), Alexander Sloper F.O.M. ("Friend of Man"), Ally for short—his name is a pun on the Victorian poor man's dodge of sloping off down the alley when the rent man is in sight—was born in the pages of *Judy*, a weekly cartoon and humor magazine clearly modeled on *Punch*. His first adventure, "Some of the Mysteries of Loan and Discount," a full-page strip, was published on August 14, 1867. It was drawn, somewhat crudely, by Charles Henry Ross, who was not known for his artistry. Ross was a popular literary hack who could reel off "penny dreadfuls" by the yard but who preferred wordplay of a humorous variety. Helping him with the inking, and taking over completely once the series was established, was Marie Duval, a French teenager whose real name was Emilie de Tessier, otherwise known as Mrs. Charles Henry Ross. Established from the start was Sloper's character, that of a seedy con man forever hatching new get-rich-quick schemes doomed to failure. So was his partner in crime Isaac Moses, otherwise known as Ikey Mo.

Sloper soon became a weekly fixture in *Judy*, and this resulted in the world's first comic book, a paperback reprint, *Ally Sloper: A Moral Lesson*, published in November 1873. The first original periodical to feature Sloper was the annual almanac *Ally Sloper's Comic Kalendar*, and 13 almanacs were published between December 1874 and 1887. Then came *Ally Sloper's Summer Number* (1880-1884); *Ally Sloper's Comic Crackers* (1883); and the ultimate triumph, the weekly comic paper *Ally Sloper's Half-Holiday*. This ran from May 3, 1884, to May 30, 1914, changed its title to *Ally Sloper* from June 6, 1914, to September 9, 1916, was revived as *Ally Sloper's Half-Holiday* again from November 5, 1922, to April 14, 1923, then turned up later as two one-shots in 1948 and 1949. There was also the annual extra edition, *Ally Sloper's Christmas Holidays* (1884-1913), and a short-lived weekly, *Ally Sloper's Ha'porth* (January 23 to March 21, 1899).

"Alley Oop," Vincent Hamlin. © NEA Service.

"Ally Sloper," Charles Ross and Marie Duval.

Ross benefited little from this exploitation, as he had sold all the copyrights to Gilbert Daziell, the former engraver turned publisher. However, it had made Ross the editor of *Judy* magazine along the way; and his son, Charles Jr., wrote pieces for the *Half-Holiday* under the guise of Tootsie Sloper. Tootsie was a member of the enlarged Sloper Family of Mildew Court, created for the *Half-Holiday* by W. G. Baxter. This inspired cartoonist died suddenly, at an early age, of alcoholism. Ally was taken over by W. F. Thomas, in similar style, and Thomas was to draw the strip into the 1920s.

Ally was also the first strip hero to be merchandised. There was the Sloper Keyless Watch, the Sloper Insurance Scheme, the F.O.S. ("Friend of Sloper") award with his colored certificate, the Sloper Pipe, the Sloper Club with bronze medallion, and the Sloper China Bust. He was also "toned down" for coloring books for children, had popular songs written about him, and was portrayed in early films.

D.G.

ALMA GRANDE (Mexico) *Alma Grande* ("Great Soul"), subtitled "El Yaqui Justiciero" ("The Justice-Fighting Yaqui"), was created in 1961 by the writer Pedro Zapiain, with illustrations by José Suárez Lozano, as a weekly comic book. As is usually the case with this type of Mexican comic book, the action goes on indefinitely without regard to chronological niceties, and without allowing the reader a moment of respite.

Alma Grande is the titular hero, a half-breed Yaqui and Caucasian, who has been brought up in the wild Yaqui Valley in Sonora, where he also experiences a great deal of his adventures, in the company of his friend "the Swede," the inseparable Culebra Prieta ("Black Serpent") and Marcelino. His sweetheart, the schoolteacher Alice, often provides Alma Grande with cause for alarm, being continually the target of the villains. These villains form a whole rogues' gallery, filled with psychopathic brutes. They are headed by Count Cieza, Alma Grande's mortal enemy, and by the beautiful and sadistic nyphomaniac Laura (who resembles movie actress María Felix), as cruel as her father, Colonel Venegas, ever was.

The epic flavor is constantly present in the scenarios written by Zapiain and Rafael Arenas, and in the drawings done by Suárez's successors, the illustrators Othon Luna, R. R. Zambrano, Angel José Mora, and Ricardo Reyna.

"Alma Grande," José Suárez Lozano. © Novedades.

Two movies were based on the strip: *Alma Grande, el Yaqui Justiciero* ("Alma Grande, the Justice-Fighting Yaqui," 1965), and *Alma Grande en el Desierto* ("Alma Grande in the Desert," 1966).

L.G.

"Alphonse and Gaston," F. B. Opper. © International Feature Service.

ALPHONSE AND GASTON (U.S.) A super-polite team of comic Frenchmen created by Fred Opper for the Hearst Sunday pages in the early 1900s, *Alphonse and Gaston* first appeared there early in 1902, initially as a weekly half-page gag strip with a descriptive subtitle, then with the addition of implicit or actual week-to-week continuity. The two leads (plus their Parisian friend, Leon, who entered the strip on July 13, 1902) traveled out West, then around the world through 1902 and 1903. Characterized by their flamboyant 19th-century French dandy clothing and their highly affected good manners ("You first, my dear Alphonse!" "No, no—*you* first, my dear Gaston!"), Alphonse and Gaston (and Leon, although he was rarely involved in the exchanges of *politesse*) were often trapped in brutal mishaps as the result of their undue attention to social proprieties in the face of an undeterred menace.

An original comic strip concept in the United States, *Alphonse and Gaston* became an immense hit with comic section readers and could have run for years as an individual strip had the Hearst Sunday space not been so limited. Opper's interest in trying new strip concepts, however, relegated Alphonse, Gaston, and Leon to occasional appearances in his other strips after 1904 (most notably, *Happy Hooligan* and *Maud*). Revived as feature characters in newspaper advertisements for a few months in the 1940s, the Frenchmen otherwise faded from the comic page with fewer appearances in Opper's work through the 1920s and early 1930s.

Surprisingly overlooked for film adaptation, the characters had one book of their own (*Alphonse and*

"American Splendor," Harvey Pekar. © Harvey Pekar.

Gaston, N.Y. American & Journal, 1905) as well as appearances in several Happy Hooligan and Maud titles of the same period. They are immortalized in the American idiom, however, as a universally understood symbol of excessive politeness.

B.B.

AMAZING MAN (U.S.) *Amazing Man*, alias *A-Man*, was created by Bill Everett and made its first appearance in Centaur's *Amazing Man* number five in September 1939. Although the character was slated to have a short run with a lackluster house, he has become one of the most fondly remembered heroes of the early days of comic books.

Amazing Man was really John Aman. According to his origin, the Tibetan " 'Council of Seven' selected an orphan of superb physical structure, and each did his part to develop in the child all the qualities of one who would dominate the world of men." Aman stayed with the council until he was 25, at which time he passed a grueling series of tests to earn his freedom and powers. He was also given the ability to turn into green mist. Dubbed the Amazing Man, Aman returned to America to battle crime. In one of the most interesting plot lines ever to appear in comics, Amazing Man was also forced to fight a psychological war with one member of the Council, The Great Question, who constantly bombarded Aman with telepathy. While most

comics were sticking to pedestrian villains, *Amazing Man* was the only strip using mental battles.

In several early adventures, Aman even abandoned the traditional superhero garb, opting instead for a simple, double-breasted blue suit. He eventually switched to trunks and crossed suspenders, and added a sidekick, Tommy, the Amazing Kid, in August 1941.

Creator Bill Everett handled the first two years of *Amazing Man*, and many consider his work on the strip superior to his *Sub-Mariner* material. He left the feature in 1940, however, and Paul Gustavson and Sam Glanzman produced the bulk of the remaining stories.

The *Amazing Man* feature ended after the 27th issue of *Amazing Man* in February 1942. The character also appeared in several issues of *Stars and Stripes* during 1941.

J.B.

AMERICAN SPLENDOR (U.S.) Harvey Pekar's work as an elevator operator, sales clerk, photocopier, and hospital file clerk provided the ideal background for his tales of grimly commonplace life in *American Splendor*. An occasional writer on jazz and other aspects of popular culture for such publications as *The Jazz Review*, *Downbeat*, and *Evergreen Review*, Pekar began composing realistic stories for underground comic books in 1975, with his contribution to *Bizarre Sex*, followed by *Flaming Baloney, Flamed-Out Funnies, Snarf*, and *Comix Book* in 1976. He has never been a fan of fantasy or superhero comics, he reports, but writes as he does in an effort "to push people into their lives rather than helping people escape from them."

Pekar's interest in the comic strip was first inspired by the work of pioneer underground cartoonist and fellow jazz fan Robert Crumb, whom he met in 1962 and about whose work he wrote articles for the *Journal of Popular Culture* in 1970 and *Jazzworld* in 1971. Self-described as "having no discernible skill as an illustrator" himself, Pekar called on Crumb and other comic book artists to draw the stories he wrote. He published his first independent collection of contemporary slices of life under the ironic title *American Splendor* in 1976, which included the artwork of Crumb and others, and he has produced collections annually ever since. The first 15 collections were published and distributed at his own expense, but as his initial audience has grown, his work has appeared in more prestigious trade imprints.

Doubleday issued two large volumes in paperback under their Dolphin imprint, *American Splendor: The Life and Times of Harvey Pekar* (1986) and *More American Splendor: From Off the Streets of Cleveland Comes . . .* (1987), and *New American Splendor Anthology* appeared in 1991. The strip has become a cult classic but has entered the American mainstream sufficiently to bring Pekar invitations to appear on national television talk shows.

After nearly two decades of recording the small irritations and frustrations of everyday life in his annual installments of *American Splendor*, Pekar and his wife Joyce Brabner collaborated on a poignant account of the writer's 1990 recovery from cancer. The 252-page novel, *Our Cancer Year* (1994), movingly drawn by Frank Stack, achieved great power through Pekar's characteristic focus on the small details of their ordeal. In his fragmentary one-page vignettes as well as his longer, more ambitious narratives, Pekar is unsparing in the light he throws on the littleness of life. An actor, and often the protagonist, in most of his modest dramas, he is merciless in his depiction of his own weakness. *American Splendor*'s unsparing candor and clarity of vision have contributed a new note to American comics and prompted critic R.C. Harvey to describe the series in *The Art of the Comic Book* (1996) as a "beacon for those who sought to make comics intimate and personal and therefore individually expressive in ways not hitherto attempted."

D.W.

AMOK (Italy) In the wake of the superhero comic books that the American troops brought with them to Italy, many Italian cartoonists were influenced by their American colleagues and produced characters that were similar in theme and artwork to those of the American comic scene. So, partly as imitations of the superheroes, partly as nostalgic remembrances of The Phantom, a whole slew of masked crime-fighters appeared in the months following the end of WWII; few of these are still remembered today.

Amok (subtitled "Il Gigante Mascherato"—the Masked Giant) is certainly one of the most celebrated. It appeared for the first time on the newsstands on October 17, 1947. It was written by Cesare Solini and drawn by Antonio Canale (who were respectively signing their work with the pen names "Phil Anderson" and "Tony Chan"), and it was published by the

Milanese firm of Agostino della Casa. The more than 50 books that told of the adventures of Amok, an Indian crime-fighter engaged in a war to the death against the evil "Scorpion" gang, met with immediate success. Amok and his inseparable companions, the newspaperman Bill Davidson, Amok's comic sidekick, and Kyo, Amok's faithful panther, soon became part of the comics' mythology.

The Scorpion band (which had stolen the treasure of the "Moon Pagoda" and kidnapped the beautiful Nikita) was pursued by Amok through ominous jungles and sinister cities as far as Sambaland Lake. After countless adventures, perils, fires, and gunfights, Amok, with the help of his friends and of his fiancée Edmea, finally put an end to the murderous Scorpion's depredations.

The last stories of the series were published by Dardo in December 1948 and written by Franco Baglioni. Two special issues, printed in full color and written by Giovanni Bonelli, the celebrated author of *Tex Willer*, were produced especially for the French publisher Sagédition, which had bought the rights to the strip. *Amok* was also published in Spain, Argentina, and Turkey.

G.B.

ANDERSON, CARL THOMAS (1865-1948) The renowned creator of the bald-headed, mute little boy who was the hero of *Henry*, Carl Thomas Anderson, was born on February 14, 1865, in the Norwegian district of Madison, Wisconsin, to immigrant parents. He took his first schooling in Janesville, Wisconsin, and continued it, after a family move, in Beatrice, Nebraska, where he became a carpenter's apprentice. Leaving school early, he traveled around the Middle West, working in planing mills. An expert cabinet-maker by age 25, Anderson invented a patented folding desk that is still being manufactured. After reading a correspondence school pamphlet promoting cartooning, he traveled to Philadelphia, where he enrolled in the Pennsylvania Museum and School of Industrial Art. To support himself, he took a job on the *Philadelphia Times* in 1894, drawing fashion pictures for $12.00 a week. In the late 1890s he was asked by Arthur Brisbane of the *New York World* to come to Manhattan to draw for the *World* Sunday pages. There he created a short-lived strip called *The Filipino and the Chick* before he was "raided" by Hearst's *Journal* and put to work on a strip called *Raffles and Bunny* for the *Journal*'s Sunday section. In 1903 he produced *Herr Spiegelberger, the Amateur Cracksman* for the McClure Syndicate.

Anderson's early work failed to catch the public fancy, however, and he turned to freelance work in the early 1900s, doing gag cartoons for *Judge, Life, Puck,* and *Collier's* over the next few decades. His income dwindled as his markets collapsed or changed, and, hit by the Depression like many others, Anderson finally left New York in 1932 to return to Madison, where his father was dying, determined to return to cabinetmaking. Teaching a night class in cartooning while he altered his sights, he made one final stab at a new market, sending the first rough sketches of a panel series about a scrawny-necked, egg-headed boy named Henry off to the *Saturday Evening Post*. The editors loved them, began to run them every week on the last page of text in the magazine, and demanded more. From 1932 through 1934, *Henry* appeared every week in the *Post*, where he was noticed by W. R. Hearst, who contacted Anderson in Madison and asked for a Sunday half-page and a daily strip based on the character. Anderson obliged and was signed by King Features. The public, already engaged by the *Post* series, was delighted by the new strip, and it was an enormous success over the next two decades. In 1942 Anderson was forced to retire because of ill-health and turned his feature over to his assistants, Don Trachte and John Liney. A lifelong bachelor, Anderson died in Madison on November 4, 1948. The strip was continued beyond his death by his assistants for some time.

B.B.

Lyman Anderson, magazine illustration.

ANDERSON, LYMAN (1907-1993) American illustrator and cartoonist, born May 4, 1907. Anderson studied at the Chicago Art Institute and graduated in 1928, when he moved to New York and enrolled at the Grand Central Art School to study under top illustrator Pruett Carter.

In 1929 Anderson began illustrating for pulp magazines—displaying his versatility in crime, science-fiction, love, and western titles—for various publishers, while pursuing his studies.

In the early 1930s Major Malcolm Wheeler-Nicholson, a publisher, conceived *New Fun*, a comic book. Anderson worked on the first two issues and left shortly before the magazine folded.

An associate on *New Fun* was Sheldon Stark, who, in 1934, contacted Anderson as a possible artist for a strip he was designing for King Features Syndicate, based on Edgar Wallace's detective stories. *Inspector Wade* was the result, and the collaboration appeared in daily newspapers later that year. Wade was the quintessential detective, a pipe-smoking case-solver, sophisticated and calm. Anderson's pulp style was well suited to the story line.

Anderson continued to study illustration with Harvey Dunn and Walter Biggs during his work on *Wade* (which he left in July 1938 to the pen of Neil O'Keefe). Top-flight illustration and advertising work followed, and later Anderson became a staff instructor with Famous Artists School in Westport, Connecticut. He retired, doing only occasional work; some of his illustrations appeared in the revived *Saturday Evening Post*. He died on May 30, 1993, at his home in Connecticut.

R.M.

ANDERSON, MURPHY (1926-) American comic book and comic strip artist, born 1926 in Asheville, North Carolina. Influenced by many of the slickest artists in the field—including Will Eisner, Lou Fine, and Alex Raymond—Murphy Anderson's only real training came at the Art Students League. He broke into comic books in 1944 at the Fiction House group, pencilling and inking strips like *Suicide Smith* (1944), *Sky Rangers* (1946), and *Star Pirate* (1944-1947). And it was here he received his only writing assignment, handling a minor Fiction House feature entitled *Life on Other Worlds*.

When Dick Calkins retired from the long-running *Buck Rogers* syndicated strip in 1947, Anderson assumed the artistic duties. Not quite the craftsman and innovator Calkins was, the young artist was a better draftsman and illustrator. His smooth, fine-line work on the 25th-century space adventure strip was among the best work the feature sported in its run. Anderson left *Buck Rogers* in 1949 but returned for another stint on the strip in 1958 and 1959.

After Anderson's first go-round on *Buck Rogers*, he returned to comic books in 1950 and drew for a number of houses, including Pines (1950-1953, science fiction), Marvel (1950, horror), St. John (1953, weird), Ziff-Davis (1950-1953, science fiction), and finally National. Joining the latter in 1950, he was with the company for years, primarily as their top-flight inker. He joined penciller—later publisher—Carmine Infantino on two strips of note, *Adam Strange* and *Batman*. Handling the former in the late 1950s and early 1960s, Anderson was the perfect choice for this science-fiction strip. He complemented Infantino's pencils, and together they produced the slickest, prettiest, and best-received science-fiction strip of the era. In 1964, when *Adam Strange* editor Julius Schwartz was handed the faltering giant *Batman*, he again called on penciller Infantino and inker Anderson. Together they broke away from the sometimes grotesque Kane-Robinson style and produced a slicker, more pristine Batman than had ever been seen before. This interpretation became so popular that an Infantino-Anderson drawing graced the cover of the *Batman* anthology published by Crown in 1971. After Infantino was promoted in 1966, Anderson went on to ink Gil Kane on *Green Lantern* and *Atom*, and eventually teamed with veteran penciller Curt Swan to revamp still another National giant, *Superman*. This Swan-Anderson rendition, clean, straightforward, and exciting, may well be the most popular style ever imposed on the "Man of Steel."

Anderson also had an illustrious career at National as a penciller. Between 1960 and 1964, he drew the *Atomic Knights* feature, a well-received "after-the-nuclear-holocaust" strip, and between 1963 and 1967, drew *Hawkman*. He and Joe Kubert, a more detailed and stylized artist, made the strip one of the finest illustrated of the 1960s. His work on one of the Spectre revivals in 1966 was also highly regarded. He retired from comics to devote more of his time to commercial art, to which end he founded Murphy Anderson Visual Concepts in the late 1980s.

J.B.

Oskar Andersson, "Mannen som gör vad som faller honom in."

ANDERSSON, OSKAR EMIL (1877-1906) Oskar Emil Andersson, Swedish cartoonist and comic artist, was born January 11, 1877, in Stockholm, Sweden. He grew up in Ekero near Stockholm. His father worked in the Royal Mint, and so did Andersson after he had finished school. He had plans to get an education in furniture designing, but his talent at drawing led him down another path. At the age of 20 Andersson tried selling his first cartoons to *Söndags-Nisse* (Sunday Troll), a Swedish humor weekly of the time. Realizing Andersson's talent, the editors of *Söndags-Nisse* employed him as a regular contributor. Oskar Andersson's initials, O.A., served as his pseudonym, which is still as well known as it was in his time.

O.A. read all the American comics he could lay his hands on: *Little Bears, The Yellow Kid, The Katzenjammer Kids*. In 1902, he created for *Söndags-Nisse* his now-legendary *Mannen som gör vad som faller honom in* (The man who does whatever comes to his mind), a comic strip some 20 episodes of which were published between 1902 and 1906. The man who does whatever comes to his mind is a kind of sour-faced libertarian living out his every whim in a protestation of man's free will against morals and mechanization. Thus, when it stops raining, he simply drops his opened umbrella to the ground; he pulls a folded car out of his coat pocket when he wants to go for a ride; he cuts off his fingers after shaking hands with a person he dislikes; or watches a dynamiting site at close proximity while others warn him from a safe distance. The latter incident is one of the few in which O.A. employed speech balloons.

Besides *Mannen som gör vad som faller honom in*, O.A. also drew *Urhunden* (the story of a prehistoric dog and his prehistoric owner in modern surroundings) and a large number of cartoons for *Söndags-Nisse*. He also made book illustrations. His pen-and-ink drawings show that he was a master of perspective and employed various styles. They also show a predilection for satire, irony, black humor, and morbid self-destruction. O.A.'s life ended in suicide on November 28, 1906. According to his own wishes, his headstone simply reads "Har vilar sig O.A." (Here rests O.A.).

W.F.

AND HER NAME WAS MAUD (U.S.) Fred Opper's classic kicking-mule strip, *And Her Name Was Maud* (a play on "and her name was mud"), technically began publication under that title as a Sunday page-topper with Opper's *Happy Hooligan* on May 23, 1926, consisting of two rows of about four panels each. Actually, however, Maud the mule was a feature character in many of Opper's Sunday page episodes going well back into the early 1900s, where her appearances about 12 times a year were interspersed between the occasional entries of Alphonse and Gaston and the more frequent appearances of Opper's chief character, Happy Hooligan (although all of these characters or a combination of them could be grouped together in a weekly episode from time to time).

Maud was a mule on the farm of a bespectacled, white-whiskered, patch-elbowed old tiller of the soil in a flat black hat named Si and his bun-haired wife, Mirandy, who first appeared on the comic page on Sunday, July 24, 1904 (although Si himself had appeared before as "Uncle Si" in Opper gag sequences before 1900). Si has just purchased Maud in the opening half-page episode for $10.00 and is showing his new barnyard acquisition off to Mirandy (who says nothing but a reiterated "Land Sakes Alive") when Maud first demonstrates her kicking proclivities by belting Si across a half acre of farmland, then emits the first of her many classic "Hee Haw's!"

The genius behind the concept of Maud lay in Opper's draftsmanship: the drawing of the grinning, demonic mule (whom Si cannot resell to anyone, try as he can) provokes a certain chuckle in the reader on every appearance, no matter how repetitive or flat the basic gag situation may be. Later, the mule does as much good for Si and Mirandy as she does harm, by kicking various undesirables off the farm, booting Si's car out of the way of a speeding freight train, etc., and becomes a fixture on the farm for some 30 years to come.

Dropped by Opper in the 1910s when the artist wanted to concentrate on continual weekly series about other characters, Maud was revived in May 1926, to run weekly until her final appearance in the Sunday pages in the early 1930s (most papers dropped the strip with the episode of August 14, 1932), when Opper went into semi-retirement. A classic figure in American graphic art, Maud deserves a sizable contemporary anthology to complement her now rare, early book appearances in such collections as *Maud*, *Maud the Mirthful Mule*, and *Maud the Matchless*, all before 1910.

B.B.

ANDRAX (Germany) *Andrax* is one of a number of German comic strips produced in Spain for Kauka comic books. Starting in No. 27/1973 of *primo*, just nine issues after the debut of *Kuma*, *Andrax* may well be the most interesting of the German adventure comics to come out of that year. Earlier reprints of adventure comics from the pages of the Spanish comics magazine *Trinca* helped establish contact with Spanish artists of the Bardon Art Studio. One of the ideas the editorial offices toyed around with was that of a science-fiction or fantasy series. It was proposed to Spanish artist Jorge Bernet, who, together with Miguel Cusso, came up with *Andrax*.

Andrax is a kind of modern Rip Van Winkle. In 1976, during the Montreal Olympics, he is still known as Michael Rush, decathlon winner supreme. The somewhat mad, wheelchair-bound professor Magor considers him to be the perfect specimen for his experiment and has him kidnapped. Rush is injected with a serum that is to keep him in suspended animation for two thousand years, so he can wake up as Andrax in a new, perfect civilization.

But Andrax does not wake to a super-civilization where peace reigns supreme. Instead he finds a desolate planet Earth that has returned to barbarism, presumably after a nuclear holocaust. His experience as a decathlon athlete comes in handy whenever he encounters giant rats or barbarian hordes. He wins in hand-to-hand combat with Holernes, who has dreams of world rule (which are soon tempered by Andrax's views about society and justice).

H. G. Wells, Isaac Asimov, Theodore Sturgeon, and Richard Matheson are some of the literary influences that helped create the *Andrax* myth, which holds up extremely well, both story and art wise, compared to similar fantasies of life in a post-holocaust future. The stories are fast-paced and offer splendid visuals with easy-flowing lines, perfect mastery of anatomy, vast

landscapes, perfect staging and lighting. There is the slightest hint of Frank Robbins in the facial expressions of the Andrax characters, but that is where the likeness ends, as Bernet has a powerful style all his own.

Andrax has proved extremely popular. Besides being featured in *primo*, the series also appeared in *Action Comic* albums, in the digest-sized *Super Action*, and in 1975 became one of three series alternating in the revamped *Action Comic*, a continuation of *primo* after that comic book was discontinued in 1974. The feature ended in 1981, some time after Rolf Kauka had sold his company.

W.F.

ANDREASSON, RUNE (1925-   ) Rune Andreasson, Swedish writer/artist, born August 11, 1925, in Lindome, is now living in Göteborg-Viken. After graduation from high school, Andreasson attended theater school in Göteborg for three years. But, after several roles in the theater and films, he started working mainly on comics. He had been working as a self-educated comic strip artist ever since he was in high school, his earliest strip, *Brum*, being published in the weekly *Allers*, starting in January 1944.

Andreasson's best-known feature, *Lille Rickard och hans katt* ("Little Richard and his Cat"), began in Stockholm's evening newspaper, *Aftonbladet*, on December 23, 1951, and has since been exported to other countries. Like all of his comic strip work, *Lille Rickard och hans katt* is chiefly aimed at children. The idea for this strip dated back 10 years to a time in high school when, during English lessons, Andreasson read a story titled "Dick Wittington and his Cat." Andreasson had drawn some 80 pictures inspired by the story. They served him well when he created his own boy hero who roams the world, his tiny cat at his side.

Also for children, Andreasson created the little bear, Bamse, and Pellefant, the blue-skinned kid elephant. *Bamse* was very successfully transplanted to television in 1973. Since then a new series of *Bamse* films has gone into production, and *Bamse* is also available in albums, coloring books, etc. Pellefant started appearing in his own monthly comic book in 1965. Pellefant is a small, blue toy elephant with a tiny orange mouse as his best friend. They live in a world of living toys, acting out their humorous little adventures to their young readers' delight. With a little bit of their own magic they usually succeed in outsmarting an evil wizard who occasionally tries to make short work of Pellefant because he cannot stand his good nature.

Pellefant, like all of Andreasson's work, is distinguished by a clear style with firm lines and enough uncluttered space for perfect color reproduction. Andreasson, who, by his own admission, has been influenced by the work of Walt Disney and Charlie Chaplin, has devoted his time to writing and drawing mainly for the youngest readers. He has also freelanced for Swedish television as a writer.

W.F.

ANDRIOLA, ALFRED (1912-1983) American cartoonist, born in 1912 in New York City. In 1935, after dropping out of the Columbia University School of Journalism, Alfred Andriola started working in the studio of Noel Sickles and Milton Caniff as secretary and man Friday (not as an assistant, as often stated). In October 1938, with the help of Caniff and Sickles (who assisted on the writing and drawing respectively), he started his first comic strip, *Charlie Chan*, based on the famous detective created by Earl Derr Biggers, for McNaught Syndicate. After the demise of the strip in March 1942, he took over *Dan Dunn*, which he drew and scripted for one year.

In 1943 Andriola created *Kerry Drake*, an original detective strip, for Publishers Syndicate. Under the pseudonym of Alfred James, and in collaboration with Mel Casson for the drawing, he created in 1957 the short-lived girl strip *It's Me Dilly*. Andriola died of cancer on March 29, 1983, in New York City. One of the most articulate practitioners (some would say exploiters) of the newspaper syndicate system, he succeeded in creating four different strips for which he received credit without hardly ever having worked on any of them. After his death it was learned that he had not drawn a speck or written a line in decades; *Kerry Drake*, the feature he had promoted exactly 40 years earlier, survived him by only a few weeks.

M.H.

ANDY CAPP (G.B.) On August 5, 1957, a truculent little layabout, cloth cap too big for his head, was kicked out of the Boilermaker's Arms and landed in the new Northern Edition of the *Daily Mirror*. The single-panel cartoon, signed Smythe (Reginald Smythe), came to the National Edition less than a year later (April 14, 1958), and shortly after spread to the *Sunday Pictorial* (May 8, 1960). This little Northerner, with his cigarette, his beer, his bets on the dogs, his mate Chalky, and his long-suffering missus Florrie, not only touched a chord common to Cockneys and Scotsmen alike, but soon touched the world. Russia printed him in *Izvestia*, the Swedes put him in a monthly comic book called *Tuffa Viktor*, and the Americans not only syndicated him in his daily strip form, they asked for a colored Sunday strip too! He appears in 34 countries in 13 dif-

"Andy Capp," Reginald Smythe. © *Daily Mirror Ltd.*

ferent languages, and if Andy himself isn't surprised, his creator, who became Britain's richest strip cartoonist, is.

Smythe was born in Hartlepools, Yorkshire (1917), son of a boat builder. He left Galleys Field School at the age of 14 to become a butcher's boy, and then enlisted in the army as a regular soldier. A machine gunner during WWII, he joined the post office after demobilization and began freelancing single gags to *Reveille* and the *Mirror*'s joke page. The first "Andy" was little more than an extension of this daily gag cartoon, given a semblance of character continuity. Reprints include the hardback *Cream of Andy Capp* (1965), regular paperback series from 1958 to date (32 books by 1974), and the *Laugh Again with Andy Capp* reprints series (1968). Andy's son is featured in the children's comic *Buster* (May 28, 1960, to date). Having now reached the 40th anniversary mark, *Andy Capp* is still going strong on both sides of the Atlantic.

D.G.

ANGEL, THE (U.S.) When Timely published *Marvel Comics* number one in November 1939, most eyes were focused on the trail-blazing *Human Torch* and *Sub-Mariner* features, although Paul Gustavson's *The Angel* also made its debut there. The feature was unique in several ways: The Angel sported an almost-never-seen mustache; he had no appreciable superpowers, save the ability to cast an angel shadow as he disappeared victorious; and he had no secret identity, being known only as The Angel in or out of costume. On the other hand, he did have a yellow and blue superhero suit, incongruously topped by an outstretched eagle emblazoned upon his chest attire.

The feature began as a direct steal from Leslie Charteris' Saint character, and the first story was unabashed plagiarism of *The Saint in New York*. The Angel soon became involved in a series of "weird" tales, however, which made him one of the first heroes to prowl the supernatural beat. Because of these aberrations, it was also an offbeat strip: The Angel, sometimes in uniform, sometimes in a business suit, would battle some eerie menace with only his physical prowess, would be ultimately victorious, and would then cast that curious angel shadow as he disappeared. If nothing else, these stories were a change-of-pace diversion from the more standard fare offered by the *Human Torch* and *Sub-Mariner* features.

Artistically, Gustavson handled the strip in his fast-paced, no-nonsense style. Most of his panels were long shots, Gustavson having no use for frills or tricky layouts. He handled the feature until 1942, but George Mandel (1941), Al Avison (1941), Simon and Kirby (1940), and Carmine Infantino (1945-1946) also drew stories.

The Angel appeared in the first 79 issues of *Marvel Mystery* (formerly *Marvel Comics*) until December 1946, and in the first 21 issues of *Sub-Mariner* (Spring 1941 to Fall 1946). The character was briefly revived from 1985 to 1987 in Marvel's *X-Men* line of comic books.

J.B.

ANGLO, MICK (1916-   ) British cartoonist, writer, editor, and publisher, born Maurice Anglo in Bow, London, on June 19, 1916. Educated at the Central Foundation School, he then studied art at the John Cass Art School in the city. He did professional artwork, fashion sketches (1936), then freelancing in commercial art to 1939, when he was conscripted into the army. He drew his first cartoons for *Seac*, the official army newspaper for South East Asia Command (1942), and then for Singapore papers (1945). Upon demobilization, being seven years behind the times, he abandoned designing for advertising agency work. Anglo began writing fiction and created *Johnny Dekker*, a detective story in the style of Damon Runyon, whom he greatly admired. He drew the cover for *The Siamese Cat*, whereupon the publisher, Martin & Reid, suggested that he try strips for their children's comics. After a few pages signed "Mick," he was given a complete comic to draw: *The Happy Yank* (1948).

An admirer of the American school of comic art as well as of crime fiction, he soon abandoned his primitive humor style for frankly imitative superheroes. After a short period with a comic art agency run by Eric Souster and Jack Potter, he became editor of the comics put out by Paget Publications. To their weeklies *Premier* and *Comic Wonder* he added *Wonderman*, featuring *Captain Justice*, a *Superman* figure, which ran for 24 issues between 1948 and 1951.

When Martin & Reid expanded comic publication in 1949, he took on their editorial work, opening his own studio in Gower Street, and soon the "Gower Studios" imprint began to appear on a long list of independent comics. His best productions here were the full-color photogravure series, *Frolicomic* and *Jolly Western* (1949), and cartoonists working at Gower included Bob Monkhouse and Denis Gifford. Clients included Barrett Publishing (*The Sheriff, Bumper Comic*) and Timpo Toys (*Pioneer Western*). When Paget discontinued publishing, L. Miller & Son became clients, then separate clients, as Arnold Miller left his father to set up the Arnold Book Company (ABC Comics). For Arnold, Anglo created the monthly *Ace Malloy* (1951) and the weekly *Space Comics* (1953), featuring *Captain Valiant*, a character who caught on sufficiently enough to warrant heavier merchandising. For Miller, Anglo took over a number of established American titles, continuing (with English and Spanish artists) series such as *Jim Bowie, Annie Oakley*, and *Davy Crockett*. When Miller, who was the British agent for Fawcett Publications, had to cease publication of the weekly *Captain Marvel Adventures*, Anglo replaced this with *Marvelman*, who quickly became the number one British superhero. *Young Marvelman* replaced *Captain Marvel Junior*, and *Marvelman Family* replaced *The Marvel Family*. These were Anglo's most successful comic books, running from 1954 till 1963.

Under "Anglo Comics," he published his own series of comic books, mostly revised versions of earlier Miller strips—*Gunhawks, Battle, Captain Miracle*, and *T.V. Heroes* (1960-61)—then continued the American Gilbert on *Classics Illustrated* for Thorpe & Porter. From 1967-68 he edited his best weekly, *T.V. Tornado*, which ran 88 issues for City Magazines. Next he served as editor of *Look & Cook* magazine, as a compiler of cookbooks and *Striker Annual*, and as a ghostwriter to comedian Tommy Cooper, while continuing to work in comics as editor of several Picture Library series of war comics, translated from the Spanish. He retired during the 1980s.

D.G.

ANIBAL 5 (Mexico) *Anibal 5* was created on October 1, 1966. Although lasting a total of only six comic books, it represented in its time a major renovation of the Mexican comic. Its greatest contribution came from the scriptwriter, Alexandro Jodorowski, writer, draftsman, actor, and stage and movie director, who produced stories filled with innovations in the fields of fantasy and science fiction. His illustrator was Manuel Moro, an artist with traditional style, a fine line, and a taste for the erotic.

Anibal 5 was a cyborg, a human being who had miniature electronic devices inserted into him, making him an exceptional being. His arms were rifles, his pupils television cameras, and his ear lobe concealed a receiver. His mortal enemy was Baron de Sader, and in this titanic struggle, Anibal 5 was pitted against mule-women, killed on five separate occasions, reincarnated in several animals, imprisoned inside a woman's womb, and witness to the invasion of the world by mummies.

Expressive inventions thrived in the strip, such as lipstick that allowed the wearer to launch kisses into space, or the resurrection of the incomplete remains of Attila, Hitler, Napoleon, Genghis Khan, and Al Capone. (Anibal 5 was modeled after movie actor Jorge Rivero.)

L.G.

ANITA DIMINUTA (Spain) *Anita Diminuta* ("Tiny Anita") was created on April 2, 1941, in the first issue of the girl's weekly *Mis Chicas*, where it remained until 1950. Its author was the illustrator Jesus Blasco (who also wrote the scenarios), and the 12 very long adventures of *Anita* that he published in *Mis Chicas* made his little heroine into the mascot of the magazine.

Anita was a little blonde orphan girl who lived in Illusion Land with her old grandmother and her teddy bear Mateo. Her friends were the Genies of the Woods; Soldatito (who introduced himself as "Andersen's little lead soldier"); Payasito the clown; and the cat Morronguito, with whom she fought Carraspia the witch and the wizard Caralampio, as well as assorted sorcerers, pirates, and spell-casters. Her wanderings blended traditional fairy tales and Oriental magic stories, thereby

"Anita Diminuta," Jesus Blasco. © Chicos.

conjuring an imaginary world in which Anita, dressed like a modern little girl, blissfully moved, oblivious of the anachronisms that surrounded her. Her adventures were at once tender and cruel; on occasion she found herself in terrifying circumstances from which she would always escape with the help of her friends. The tenderness was mostly obvious in the episodes published in the annual almanacs, while the strip took on a decidedly humorous character in the pages published by the magazine *Gran Chicos*.

Anita Diminuta's success was such in Spain and Portugal that its author published two *Anita* books, a doll was named after the character, and it was made into a radio program.

On October 1, 1974, *Anita Diminuta* was revived in *Chito* magazine, where it was set in modern times in a series of "hippie" comic strips. It ceased publication in the 1980s.

L.G.

ANMITSU HIME (Japan) *Anmitsu Hime* ("Princess Anmitsu"), created by Shōsuke Kuragane, made its first appearance in the May 1949 issue of the Japanese monthly *Shojo*. The strip was born out of the creator's concern for the children of Japan, most of whom were deprived of food, clothes, or parental affection (because of the losses suffered in World War II). Kuragane wanted to show these children that these deprivations were only temporary and that Japan would one day return to the old days of plenty.

Anmitsu Hime was therefore set in the Edo era, and all the characters' names related to food items: Anmitsu (boiled beans, bean paste sweetened with syrup), her father Awano Dangonokami (dango is a Japanese-style dumpling), her mother Shibucha (astringent tea), her English teacher Kasutera (sponge cake), her little friend Manjū (a kind of Japanese jelly cake), her page Amaguri-nosuke (amaguri is a sweet roast chestnut), her maids Anko (bean paste), and Kinako (bean flour), etc.

Anmitsu was a tomboy whose pranks enlivened the castle of Amakara (amakara means sweet and pun-

"Anmitsu Hime," Shōsuke Kuragane. © Shōjo.

gent), where she lived with her parents and entertained her friends with all kinds of festivities during which they were served the utmost delicacies and where the guests wore the most gorgeous clothes. It was a simple but romantic and optimistic fairy tale, which enchanted the young readers (and their parents) and made them forget the rigors of the day.

As Japan steadily recovered from her postwar prostration, there was no need for *Anmitsu Hime*, and the strip was finally discontinued in April 1954. During its lifetime it had proved popular enough to inspire several motion pictures as well as a TV series.

H.K.

APARTMENT 3-G (U.S.) Beginning daily and Sunday publication on May 8, 1961, *Apartment 3-G* was the product of author Nicholas Dallis; Harold Anderson, head of Publishers Syndicate; and artist Alex Kotzky.

The main characters are three young career women (3-G is an obvious derivative of "three girls"): Lu Ann Powers, schoolteacher; Tommy Thompson, nurse; and Margo Magee, secretary. Lu Ann married in the strip, but her husband, Gary, was and remains an MIA in Viet Nam, which provides ongoing suspense and pathos.

The girls' neighbor, Professor Papagoras, is a college professor, a dead ringer for Ernest Hemingway, and as the girls' best friend, trusted advisor, and sometimes protector, he provides a counterpoint personality. Other characters are short-term: those moving in and out of the apartment building, workmates, or would-be boyfriends.

Kotzky's art is slick and breezy, and his characters are handsome without being academic, as in other story strips. Likewise, Dallis' stories flow easier than in his other efforts, *Rex Morgan, M.D.*, and *Judge Parker*. *Apartment 3-G* concentrates on the characters and their personalities, rather than emphasizing heavy plot developments. In this way, *3-G* appears less substantial than other story strips, but its characters are definitely more human than their counterparts in the other straight strips. Humor is also frequently introduced as a plot element.

The space crunch in newspapers has forced Kotzky's rendering to include more close-ups; this has been a coincident advantage to *3-G*'s scheme of accentuating character identification. (The title of the strip was briefly changed to *The Girls of Apartment 3-G*.)

R.M.

Due to protests from women's groups, the strip reverted to its original title in 1977. Dallis died in 1991, and Kotzky assumed complete authorship of the feature, which he maintained on an even keel, with very few changes. After his death in September 1996, it was taken over by his son, Brian Kotzky, who had been assisting his father since the early 1990s. *Apartment 3-G* is now being distributed by King Features.

M.H.

A. PIKER CLERK (U.S.) Clare Briggs (later famed for *Mr. and Mrs.* and *When a Feller Needs a Friend*) was just beginning his cartooning career on the new Hearst *Chicago American* and *Examiner* papers in 1903 as a sports, feature, and editorial cartoonist when editor Moe Koenigsberg decided that a continuing sports-page comic strip might keep the fickle afternoon newspaper audience of the time buying the *American* rather than seesawing back and forth between that paper and its

"A. Piker Clerk," Clare Briggs.

chief rival, the afternoon *Daily News*. The final sports edition of the *American* was the edition to be moved by this innovative device, and so Koenigsberg and Briggs devised a feature about a fanatically dedicated horse player named A. Piker Clerk, to be prominently featured in the sports section of that edition.

This much seems to be agreed upon by published sources and by reference to the *American* of the time. From this point, however, written accounts and the actual files seem to disagree. Koenigsberg, for example, states in his 1941 autobiography, *King News*, that he and Briggs started the strip in 1904, while the San Francisco Academy of Comic Art files of both the *American* and *Examiner* for 1903 contain episodes of the *Clerk* feature. Koenigsberg states that he innovated the idea of a day-to-day comic strip years before Bud Fisher launched *Mutt and Jeff* in the *San Francisco Chronicle* of 1907, yet the Academy files of the *American* and *Examiner* show only two *Clerk* runs of even three successive days in all of 1904, while gaps of three days to a month between episodes are frequent. (*Mutt and Jeff*, on the other hand, ran six days a week every week from its initial appearance.) It is apparent that Koenigsberg grasped the idea of using a weekday comic strip to bring readers back for the next day's paper, but since the strip's "suspense" was based on whether or not Clerk's hot horse tip would pay off in the next day's race (actual racing horses in actual races were used), the strip tended to be published only during major track seasons. The strip probably died of public apathy, although Koenigsberg claims that Hearst himself suppressed the strip as "vulgar" shortly after it had been launched and had given an upwards boost to the *American's* circulation. This is a good story, but obviously untrue, since *A. Piker Clerk* was published for over a year and a half in a straggling, desultory manner before it was finally dropped on June 7, 1904, with Clerk making a farewell appearance as a minor figure in a general Briggs sports cartoon of that date. *Clerk*, then, was not "the first daily strip," as has been claimed, nor was it in any way a strip novelty in its

time except in its advocacy of horses for gamblers, being a true "first" in that limited field. It is not even an important Briggs work (although it is possibly his most curious undertaking), nor a memorable strip in any other way. No book collection exists, and—of course—it ran only in the *Chicago American* and *Examiner* during 1903 and 1904. It is, perhaps, best left there.

B.B.

APPLE MARY   see Mary Worth.

AQUAMAN (U.S.)   *Aquaman* was created by writer Mort Weisinger and artist Paul Norris and made its first appearance in November 1941's *More Fun* number 73. The character was National's response to Timely's phenomenally popular *Sub-Mariner*.

Aquaman was the son of a marine scientist who had discovered the secrets of underwater living. He was also the leader of the lost continent of Atlantis. His duties, as described in his premiere adventure, were to "swim forth to keep the freedom of the seas in tropic and arctic waters alike."

Aquaman lasted in *More Fun* through January 1946's 107th issue and then moved to *Adventure* comics starting with April 1946's 103rd issue. During this time, Aquaman used the secret identity of Arthur Curry. This cover didn't last long, however, and Aquaman now appears solely as the sea monarch.

Despite a horde of authors, *Aquaman* was never a fascinating feature. The addition of Aquaman in *Adventure* number 269 did little to help, and the feature was dropped from *Adventure* after the 284th issue. The strip was finally given its own title in January 1962, and it was only there that the strip began to take on several interesting aspects. Mera was introduced in Aquaman 11 and Aquaman married her in issue 19, one of the infrequent comic book marriages. A child was born in the 23rd issue, aptly christened Aquababy. The series ended after the March 1971 issue of *Aquaman* number 56. The character is a charter member of the Justice League and has also appeared on television in animated cartoon form. The first series of *Aquaman* comic books ended in 1978. The title was briefly revived by DC Comics in 1986, and again in 1989. A second monthly series was attempted in 1991, but it only lasted for 13 issues. Undaunted, in 1994 DC Comics launched a third series, which has managed to survive so far.

J.B.

ARABELLE LA SIRÈNE (France)   Jean Ache (Jean Huet) created *Arabelle la Sirène* ("Arabelle the Mermaid") on May 2, 1950, for the French daily newspaper *France-Soir*.

Arabelle, the last representative of the legendary race of mermaids, is discovered in the course of a marine expedition by the American professor H. G. W. Bimbleton. After a surgical operation that gives her two (shapely) legs, Arabelle becomes indistinguishable from the host of other pretty comic strip girls, except in the water, where she is capable of accomplishing the most extraordinary stunts. Jean Ache makes generous use of Arabelle's aquatic abilities in his strip, sending her to find sunken treasures, to rescue floundering ships, or to fight a band of undersea pirates. In the course of her adventures Arabelle is accompanied by her pet monkey Kouki and by her boyfriend Fleur Bleue (Blue Flower), who often has to rescue the adventurous mermaid from the clutches of her enemies.

Arabelle was discontinued by *France-Soir* in 1962 but made her reappearance in the short-lived *Illustré du Dimanche*. After a long absence, *Arabelle* surfaced again in the pages of the Belgian weekly *Tintin* in 1972 but, after only two adventures, the strip was dropped the next year. The little mermaid surfaced again in 1976 in a new adventure in *Tintin-Selection* but only lasted into 1977. She was used in a number of commercials, however, until the creator's death in 1985.

Arabelle la Sirène was not without a pixieish charm, in spite of the conventionality of its plots and its unimaginative drawing style. In the 1950s its popularity ran high, and a number of the strip's episodes have been reprinted in book form by Denoël.

M.H.

ARAGONÉS, SERGIO (1937-   ) Mexican-American comic book and magazine cartoonist, born in 1937 in Spain. At the age of six months, because of the Spanish Civil War, the family relocated to a French refugee camp and, several years later, moved to Mexico City. Aragonés grew up as a compulsive doodler, creating endless streams of cartoons for his friends. In 1953, one of these friends sent some to the Mexican humor magazine, *Ja Ja*, which bought them, beginning the appearance of Aragonés' work in various Mexican magazines, including a weekly page in *Mañana*. Aragonés went to architectural school and enrolled later in a mime workshop set up under French pantomimist Marcel Marceau. For a time, Aragonés worked as a clown, and he credits his mime training as a major influence on his cartooning, most of which consisted of wordless gags.

In 1962, with very little money, Aragonés went to America and made the rounds of New York publishers, trying—and failing—to sell his cartoons to small magazines. Advised to start at the top, Aragonés went to *Mad* magazine and had no trouble selling a two-page spread of astronaut cartoons. The feature, which ran in *Mad* number 76, marked the beginning of Aragonés' affiliation with *Mad*, and he quickly became one of its star artists. In addition to various cartoon features, Aragonés did "marginal" cartoons, which *Mad* printed in the corners of pages throughout each issue. Aragonés also began contributing to other magazines, illustrating books and designing storyboards for cartoon specialties.

In 1967, Aragonés began doing work for National Periodical Publications (DC). He drew pages of his pantomime cartoons, which ran as comedy relief in DC's ghost comics, worked on some stories for those books, and collaborated on the scripts for a short-lived western strip, *Bat Lash*.

Sergio Aragonés is probably the fastest cartoonist in the world. He works directly in ink, with rarely any preliminary pencil work, using a fountain pen to put down his visual ideas. His specialty is large mural-cartoons, which generally consist of immense crowd scenes, filled with countless gags, and he is constantly trying to top himself on these. His work remains very cartoony, virtually always in pantomime, and is highly regarded by most for its range of subject matter and expression.

M.E.

Aragonés created his most popular character, Groo the Wanderer, in the pages of *Destroyer Duck* in 1982. One of the innumerable parodies of *Conan*, *Groo* soon gathered a vociferous coterie of fans, and the title has managed to stay afloat to this day, despite sophomoric humor and ham-handed writing, on the strength of the artist's very funny and appealing drawing style.

M.H.

ARCHIE (U.S.) *Archie* was created by artist Bob Montana and made its first appearance in December 1941 in the 22nd issue of MLJ's *Pep*. The strip was an instant success and eventually became one of the most famous comic features in the world. By the next winter, *Archie*

"Archie," Dan DeCarlo. © Archie Publications.

number one had been published, and MLJ knew its future lay with *Archie* and not with its superhero line. The MLJ group was eventually retitled Archie Publications, dozens of spin-off magazines appeared, and *Archie* was soon a syndicated newspaper strip as well.

Archie was and is the consummate American humor feature: it portrays the teenagers of the day, as the adults apparently see them. Stereotypes abound and multiply. First and foremost, there is Archie Andrews himself, the "typical high school student." Then there are the dozens of narrowly defined supporting characters: Jughead, who loves hamburgers more than girls; Reggie, Archie's rival, complete with slick black hair; Betty and Veronica, Archie's girlfriends who vie for his attention; Moose, the dim-wit football hero; and dozens of others too numerous to mention.

It is impossible to judge the influence the *Archie* feature has on its young audience. Aimed at juveniles, the strip has never strayed from the "basic" American principles, whatever they may be. And it has only minutely changed to fit the drastically altered mores of an American civilization 50 years removed from the strip's first appearance. For this reason—their "wholesomeness" to parents of American children—*Archie* and spin-offs have always been the most consistently high-selling comic books on the market. In short, they are a tremendously saleable anachronism.

Naturally, this high-powered appeal has not been lost on the publishers, and *Archie* has made appearances in every possible form. In addition to a whole line of *Archie* comic books—*Jughead* (1949), *Betty and Veronica* (1950), *Pals and Gals* (1951), and *Joke Book* (1954) are just a few of dozens—there have been paperback books, religiously oriented comic books, toys, games, merchandising material, and just about every other conceivable commercial gimmick. There has been one sort of Archie cartoon program or another on television since 1968. When the series peaked in 1969, comic book sales on *Archie* alone surged over a million copies a month while the other best-sellers barely managed 300,000. There was even a "bubble-gum" rock-and-roll group from the program called the Archies, and they recorded several hit songs. This television success matched the earlier radio success—when the *Adventures of Archie* ran for nine years after World War II.

Archie, like *Batman, Superman*, and a small handful of others, has transcended comic books into pure Americana. There will, it often seems, always be an Archie. It is as inevitable as death and taxes.

J.B.

King Features Syndicate started distributing *Archie* as a newspaper strip in 1947. The cast of characters and setting remained virtually unchanged from the comic book version, but the relatively greater freedom enjoyed by newspaper features has allowed Bob Montana to go beyond the mere teenage antics of Archie and his gang into somewhat more believable situations.

Following the creator's death in 1975, Dan DeCarlo, who had been working on the comic-book version since 1961, wrote and drew the *Archie* newspaper strip until 1993. Since that time it has been done by Henry Scarpelli, later joined by Craig Boldman. Archie is still going strong in 1997, both in comic books being published under the banner of Archie Comics and in news-

"De Argonautjes," Dick Matena. © PEP.

paper strips (with Creators Syndicate having taken over from King Features).

M.H.

ARGONAUTJES, DE (Netherlands) *De Argonautjes* ("The Little Argonauts") is one of the comic series that ushered in a new era of the Dutch comic strip. The introductory episode appeared in 1968 in the Dutch comics weekly *Pep*, in issues number 3 through 23. *Pep* began publication on October 6, 1962, but had mainly featured foreign comic material, especially Walt Disney strips and features from the pages of *Tintin*. In 1964 strips from *Pilote* were added. But in 1968 *Pep* decided to bring in more Dutch comic art. That was to the advantage of Dick Matena, who had received a thorough schooling in comic art at the Mart en Toonder studios, and who was already successful with *Polletje Pluim*, an animal strip published in the women's magazine *Prinses*. *De Argonautjes*, written by L. Hartog van Banda and drawn by Matena, immediately established Matena as one of the foremost artists among the new school of Dutch comic artists.

Strongly influenced by *Astérix* and the Belgian school, Matena displays an energetic style with good layouts, the right amount of animation, a firm, flowing line, a balance of black and white, and considerable care for detail. *De Argonautjes* takes the reader back to the times of the ancient Greeks, when two young argonauts do their best to make short work of Greek mythology—for example, by involving King Tantalus in a tantalizingly funny tale, having a run-in with Hypocrite during the Olympic games, or trying to beat each other and a lot of curious people to open Pandora's box.

While continuing work on *De Argonautjes*, Matena started alternate series to provide for a change of pace in the pages of *Pep*. In 1969 he started *Ridder Roodhart* (scenario by L. Hartog van Banda) and in 1970 turned writer/artist for *De Grote Pyr* (retitled *Peer Viking* for publication in Germany), before also starting to write scenarios for Dino Attanasio's *De Macaronis*.

Pep's change of policy went one step further in 1969 when it was decided that Geillustreerde Pers, the publishers of *Pep*, should have their own stable of comic artists. *De Argonautjes* was only one of the harbingers of new things to come out of the Netherlands.

W.F.

ARMAN EN ILVA (Netherlands) The innovative science-fiction strip *Arman en Ilva* was created in 1969 by scriptwriter Lo Hartog van Banda and illustrated by artist The Tjong Khing. Hartog van Banda and Khing had previously collaborated on *Iris* (1968), which con-

"Arman en Ilva," The Tjong Khing. © Marten Toonder.

stituted an introduction to *Arman en Ilva*. Distributed by Marten Toonder Studio, the strip was widely published in daily newspapers all over Europe.

In an eerie and disturbing world of the future where wars between planets are continuous and existence a constant peril, the young Arman and his blonde girlfriend Ilva serve as troubleshooters for Earth. Along their way they meet mad potentates, crazed rulers, ruthless space pirates, and a slew of seductive secret agents of both sexes who invariably (but in vain) try to kill them when they cannot seduce them.

Banda's scripts—ambiguous, ironic, searching—were well served by Khing's unique style, a harmonious blend of action-packed composition and a decorative, sinuous Oriental line. The teamwork of Banda and Khing assured the success of *Arman en Ilva*, but early in 1975 it was learned that Khing had been replaced on the strip by Gerrit Stapel, a competent, but uninspired, draftsman. In his hands the strip did not survive the decade.

M.H.

ARRIOLA, GUS (1917-   ) With a Mexican rooster perched sadly on his oversized military cap, the lean, hungry-looking guy with curly black hair cradled a chihuahua against his chest with one arm, looked straight out of the comic strip panel at a million readers, and said a dolorous farewell to each and every one. Gustavo Montano Arriola, born in July 1917, was an eminently draftable 26 years old in the fall of 1942, and he had been tagged by Uncle Sam for immediate service. His new daily comic strip, *Gordo*, launched one year earlier, was being shot down in flames. Arriola had to put in his basic training, and there would be no time for strip work. So Arriola drew himself woefully engulfed in his new uniform in the last panel of an episode dated October 28, 1942—which would be the last panel of the daily *Gordo* for the duration—surrounded himself with the characters he had created over the two years of the new strip (from the sveltely plump Gordo himself and the bosomy Widow Gonzales to Gordo's elfin-eared nephew Pepito and the strange mountain of flesh called Goblin), blew a plume from

Gordo's cocked hat out of his way, and thanked his *nuestros buen amigos*, "each one," for their "eenterest," and promised to "be back real soon." He also sounded a topical note in knocking "that dorty jork—Heetler!!"

Arriola was speaking in the *patois* English of his characters—much subdued in later years—but what he said was correct. He was back "real soon," with a Sunday half page on May 2, 1943, never to leave the comic strip scene again. What the young draftee was doing, of course, was managing to do a weekly strip and his military duties as an animator in the air force. (After his discharge in 1946, he resumed the daily strip as well.) Circumstances were varied for strip artists drafted in wartime; Fred Lasswell, working on *Leatherneck Magazine*, managed to find the time to draw both the daily and Sunday *Barney Google*, for example. Arriola, however, was unique in World War II in closing down a major new strip completely until he was able to get it under way again.

Born in Arizona, Arriola moved to Los Angeles at an early age and grew up in the shadow of the great animation studios. From high school he moved into the MGM cartoon story department in the mid-1930s. Other animation work followed, and then Arriola sold the concept for *Gordo* to United Features in 1941. The local color and folk pageantry of Mexico had had very little exposure on the comic page, and it proved a natural for strip use as handled by the young artist. Moreover, Arriola drew funny; his character and situation ideas were fresh, and grew naturally out of the setting and populace of Mexico. Despite the wartime break in continuity, the strip's popularity mounted through the 1940s, until *Gordo* became one of the most widely published and read strips in the country. The author decided to retire in 1985.

A winner of numerous awards in his field, Arriola moved to the Monterey peninsula, where he periodically advertised (via the *Gordo* strip) his fabulous recipe for beans with cheese and pursued artistic interests beyond his strip work. He occasionally still departs for explorative trips into Mexico with his wife, Mary Frances, and son Carlin, where they presumably at least touch base with a drink at Pelon's before driving to Monterey or flying down to the Hotel of Parrots in Yucatan.

B.B.

ASHITA NO JOE (Japan) *Ashita no Joe* ("Joe Who Aims to Win Wonderful Tomorrow") was created by Asao Takamori (script) and Tetsuya Chiba (drawing) in January 1968 for the weekly magazine *Shōnen*.

The protagonist of the strip, Joe Yabuki, was a lonely boy in a strange land. One day Joe met former boxer Danpei Tange, and it changed his whole life. Tange trained Joe as a professional boxer, and the strip took a realistic and even naturalistic turn as it followed Joe's career. Unlike American boxing strip heroes, Joe did not always win and was even knocked out on occasion. But he doggedly fought on, finally meeting his old reformatory school rival, Tooru Rikiishi, who knocked Joe out after an especially vicious grudge fight. Rikiishi, however, died from the weight loss he had sustained in order to be able to meet Joe in his category. After Rikiishi's death, Joe went into a slump and lost his title to Tiger Ozaki.

Coming out of his depression, Joe started to fight again, winning match after match, until he got a chance to fight the world bantamweight champion Jose

"Ashita no Joe," Tetsuya Chiba. © Shōnen.

Mendoza. Mendoza proved too strong for Joe, who exhausted himself and died in the ring. Joe's death also signaled the end of the strip (May 1973).

Joe's popularity had been very great but was eclipsed by that of his hated rival Tooru Riikishi. After the latter's death, a farewell ceremony was held in his memory in the Kodansha boxing hall on March 24, 1970. A gong sounded the count of 10, after which a minute of silent prayer was observed. During the prayer people could be heard sobbing from all corners of the hall.

Ashita no Joe has also inspired a series of animated cartoons.

H.K.

ASPIRINO Y COLODION (Spain) Alfonso Figueras created *Aspirino y Colodion* on June 6, 1966, in issue 234 of the comic magazine *El Capitan Trueno*, from which it passed the next year to the weekly *DDT*.

With *Aspirino y Colodion* the author paid homage to the old comedies of the silent cinema and to the American humor strips of the 1920s, by successfully reconstructing a whole atmosphere long since lost, but not forgotten. The two protagonists are a pair of inventors: Aspirino, ancient and bearded, and Colodion, young and completely crazy. They both devote their time to inventing the most extravagant devices, and to complicating each other's life, in a constant struggle to top each other, with innocence on the part of the older savant, with sly goofiness on the part of the younger. They come up with the most outrageous inventions, to the great amazement of Adolfo, the guard who vainly tries to restore a little sanity into the relations between the crazy pair.

In this humor series falls and fights are rife, punctuated with onomatopoeias, and, when the two inventors get involved in one of their interminable quarrels, they disappear under clouds of smoke, re-creating the spirit, grace, and subtlety of such comic masterpieces

as *Krazy Kat* and *Happy Hooligan*. It is no longer being published, but the characters live on in reprints.

L.G.

ASSO DI PICCHE (Italy) The immediate postwar period saw a proliferation of Italian masked avengers dressed in close-fitting tights. One of those was Asso di Picche ("Ace of Spades"), whom his creator Hugo Pratt modeled after Eisner's *Spirit*. Written by Mario Faustinelli and published in the collection "Albi Uragano," *Asso di Picche* first appeared at the end of 1945.

The newsman Gary Peters is in actuality the "Ace of Spades," a mysterious justice-fighter and the nemesis of evildoers everywhere. Dressed in tights and a yellow cloak complete with his emblem, an ace of spades, the hero fights in the company of his fiancée, Deanna Farrel and his assistant, the Chinese Wang. The Ace of

"Asso di Picche," Hugo Pratt. © Editrice Sgt. Kirk.

Spades' most dangerous enemies were the Gang of the Panthers, and the Club of Five, a sinister organization plotting to take over all the world's resources. The Ace of Spades' last adventure, against an organization of Nazi criminals, was unfortunately interrupted by the disappearance of *Asso di Picche* in 1947.

The stories were well plotted and well written, with the emphasis more on suspense than violence. Hugo Pratt's style, still heavily influenced by the American comic strip and comic book artists, was to gradually come into his own, and foreshadows his later creations.

In addition to *Asso di Picche*, the "Albi Uragano" published many other comics in the three years of their existence and revealed to the public the talents of such authors as Alberto Ongaro, Dino Battaglia, Damiano Damiani, Giorgio Bellavitis, and Mario Leone.

Some of the adventures of the Ace of Spades were reprinted in 1967-69 in the monthlies *Sgt. Kirk* and *Asso di Picche*.

G.B.

ASTÉRIX (France) Created by René Goscinny (text) and Albert Uderzo (art), *Astérix le Gaulois* ("Asterix the Gaul") appeared for the first time in issue number one of the French comic weekly *Pilote* (October 29, 1959).

Astérix is a diminutive, moustached Gaul who lives in a little village in Armorique (the ancient name for Brittany), the last holdout in a country overrun by the Romans. Made invulnerable by the drinking of a magic potion concocted by the druid Panoramix, Astérix, helped by his loyal companion, the dim-witted but strong Obélix, and by his fellow villagers, is able to keep Julius Caesar's Roman legions at bay. (The Romans are invariably depicted as dumb, cowardly, rapacious, and gullible.)

Starting from this basic premise, the authors soon were enlarging on the theme by having the duo of Astérix and Obélix travel to Cleopatra's court, to the Olympic Games, and to Britain, without departing from the belief that everything is better, more beautiful and more rational in Gaul (i.e., France). The heroes' constant refrain: "Ils sont fous, ces Romains!" ("They're crazy, those Romans!"—or Britons, or Teutons, as the case may be) gives some indication of the author's smug assertion of xenophobic superiority.

There are a few good things in *Astérix* (the clever use of balloons, drawing that is clean and uncluttered, and some genuinely funny situations), but the basic plot is tiresome, and Goscinny's endless stream of bad puns and chauvinistic asides make this quite unpleasant as a strip. *Astérix* was incredibly popular in the France of the 1960s (at the height of de Gaulle's *politique de grandeur*), so much so that even the respected newsweekly *L'Express* had a cover story on the strip, but its decline in the 1970s was as precipitous as its rise had been meteoric. Following Goscinny's death in 1977, Uderzo continued to produce *Astérix* solo (averaging one adventure a year). He has toned down some of its more egregious faults, and the series, now published by the author under the Albert René imprint, remains extremely popular in France and in Europe to this day.

Astérix has been reprinted in book form by Dargaud, and the success of the books has also been phenomenal (although not in the United States, where they failed both as hardcover books and as paperbacks). Two feature-length animated cartoons, *Astérix le Gaulois* and *Astérix et Cléopatre*, were produced in the 1960s

"Astérix," René Goscinny and Albert Uderzo. © Editions Dargaud.

and early 1970s by Belvision. An Astérix theme park opened with great success near Paris in 1989.

M.H.

ATLAN (Germany) *Atlan* is to Perry Rhodan what Spock is to Captain Kirk. Yet, Atlan is not just another member of the cast of the *Perry* comic book or the *Perry Rhodan* novels; he is also the star of his own line of novels and for some time was the backup feature of *Perry Rhodan—Bild* (Numbers 1 to 27) and of *Perry* (Numbers 1 to 36). These stories gave the history of Atlan from around 8000 B.C. to his meeting with Perry Rhodan in 2040 A.D. Although interesting enough in plot, *Atlan* was not very artistically stimulating at the time. This was drastically changed when *Perry* expanded to 48 pages with No. 106, once again to share the spotlight with *Atlan* in his solo adventures. Now the visually pleasing artwork was done by Massimo Belardinelli from the Giolitti shop in Rome, Italy. Belardinelli, who also has drawn some of the backgrounds for Alberto Giolitti's artwork on *Turok Son of Stone* and *Star Trek*, did a magnificent job of putting the scripts of Dirk Hess into striking pictures. The fact that Belardinelli seems to favor the John Buscema style of drawing comics has no doubt helped the strip's popularity but accounts only for part of the feature's fascination.

Atlan, a native of the planet Arkon and admiral of the space fleet of Arkon, is stranded on Larsaf-III (Earth) when the Druuf, a fifth-dimensional warrior race, wipe out the Arkon colony on Atlantis. Atlan is given a cell activator by the Immortal of Wanderers to endow him with immortality. Seeking refuge in the only base left to him, a bubble-house on the bottom of the Atlantic Ocean, Atlan rests in suspended animation awaiting spaceships from Arkon or ventures forth to speed up the progress of humanity, the sooner to be able to leave Earth for his home planet. Thus he becomes witness to and aide in humanity's struggle from the Stone Age to modern civilization.

Time and again he is confronted by alien beings who are out to destroy or conquer humanity, yet Atlan always succeeds in averting disaster and in speeding up progress. Picking up ideas expounded by von Däniken, Charroux, et al., *Atlan* turns them into a kind of feasibly realistic "sword and sorcery" saga from Earth's past, with technological explanations for whatever "sorcery" occurs. The demise of the *Perry* comic book in 1975 also stopped the further exploits of *Atlan*.

W.F.

ATOM, THE (U.S.) National's original feature entitled *The Atom* was a long-lived but rather pedestrian strip created by artist Ben Flinton and writer B. O'Connor for October 1940's *All-American* number 19. Actually five-footer Al Pratt, The Atom, had an unusually powerful body and, as was the custom of the day, used it to fight crime. He donned his almost mandatory costume in his second appearance, and it was the most unique facet of the feature. It had short leather trunks, leather wrist bands, a blue mask and cape, and a yellow tunic open to the navel.

The story line was never particularly inventive, as the Atom spent most of his time beating up criminals startled by the great strength in his tiny body. Most of these macho scripts were written by O'Connor (until 1942) and Ted Udall (1942-1946). Artistically, Ben Flinton was sloppy and uneven, and he had an unfortunate "talent" for drawing incredibly ugly women. He handled the artwork until 1942, passing it on to the more competent Jon Kozlak (1946-1948) and Paul Reinman (1947-1949).

The Atom survived in *All-American* until April 1946's 72nd issue and appeared with the Justice Society in *All-Star* from Winter 1941's third issue to March 1951's 57th issue. The feature also made sporadic appearances in *Flash, Comic Cavalcade*, and several other titles.

National launched a second Atom character in October 1961's *Showcase* number 34. This Atom was scientist Ray Palmer, who, finding white dwarf star material, constructed a device that allowed him to change his size and alter his weight.

The stories—mostly by John Broome and Gardner Fox—concentrated on scientific plots and subplots. The writers concentrated heavily on the Atom's ability to transport himself through telephone lines. There were several well-received "time pool" stories, and Chronos, the strip's major villain, was also scientifically based. Almost all of the artwork was handled by penciller Gil Kane and inkers Side Greene and Joe Giella. Kane's artwork was tight and clean, just a notch below his stellar material for the *Green Lantern* strip.

The *Atom* feature got its own book in July 1962, and it lasted 39 issues before merging with *Hawkman* and then finally folding in November 1969. The character also appears regularly in the Justice League of America.

J.B.

In 1983 the Atom was brought back to comic books by Gil Kane and Jan Strnad in the *Sword of the Atom* miniseries. The character again came back in 1988 for a somewhat longer run in *Power of the Atom*, which lasted for 18 issues into 1989.

M.H.

AVENGERS, THE (U.S.) *The Avengers* was created by writer Stan Lee and artist Jack Kirby and made its first appearance in Marvel's *The Avengers* number one for September 1963. Originally consisting of Thor, Iron Man, The Wasp, The Hulk, and Ant-Man, there was almost immediate upheaval when The Hulk went his own way. But in the fourth issue, Captain America was revived and joined the group; for a long while, the newly revived Captain dominated the action. By the 16th issue, however, there were further upheavals: the remaining original members resigned and Captain America re-formed the group around Hawkeye, Quicksilver, and the Scarlet Witch. Over the years, there were more switches and identity changes, most often in Henry Pym, who was Ant-Man, then Giant-Man, then Goliath, then Yellowjacket.

Artistically, many fine illustrators handled the strip over the years. Jack Kirby produced the first eight issues and Don Heck drew the next few dozen, followed by John Buscema, Sal Buscema, Gene Colan, and Bob Brown. All did credible jobs, most notably John Buscema. Three writers have handled the bulk of *The Avengers* stories. Editor Lee handled almost all of the group's first three dozen issues; he was followed by Roy Thomas, who scripted 70 consecutive stories. Next, Steve Englehart took over as the writer.

Because of the large number of cast changes and frequent artist switches, the feature has gone through several different periods, many not resembling that which had gone before. However, the unquestionable peak of the series came with five 1972 issues. Written by Thomas, who had just become the book's editor, and drawn by Neal Adams, a long serial was started. Involving dozens of characters invented by Stan Lee over the years, Thomas consistently wrote top-notch stories with a most unusual sidebar: The Scarlet Witch had fallen in love with The Vision, a red-skinned humanoid, much to the chagrin of her brother, the quick-footed but slow-witted Quicksilver. Artist Adams' dazzling pencils and superb layouts are among the best work of his illustrious career.

J.B.

In the last 20 years the series has experienced a number of ups and downs, and its quality has varied widely, depending on the teams that were working on the title at the time. It fared best at the hands of John Byrne, Sal Buscema, and George Perez.

M.H.

AWAY, CAESAR *see* Caesar, Kurt.

AYERS, RICHARD (1924-) American comic book artist born in Ossining, New York, on April 28, 1924. After service in the Army Air Corps during World War II and attending the Cartoonists and Illustrators School, Dick Ayers began his comic book career in 1947 as the pencil artist on M.E. Comics' *Funnyman* feature. From that feature, the young Ayers worked on a number of diverse strips, including the comic book version of comedian Jimmy Durante. But his major work at M.E. was production of several Western features: the white-outfitted *Ghost Rider, Bobby Benson and the B-Bar-B Riders* and the *Calico Kid*. He also worked on one of the few important superhero strips of the 1950s, *The Avenger*, the first superhero feature initiated under the comics code. Ayers remained with M.E. until 1956, and during this time also drew for Charlton (1953-1955, humor strips), Prize (1951), and St. John (1956).

But the bulk of Ayers' comic book work came for the Timely/Atlas/Marvel group, which he joined in

1951 as an inker for the newly revived *Human Torch* strip. Most of his work with Marvel during the 1950s was done on Western material. Utilizing a clean and uncluttered style, which made him equally competent as a penciller or an inker, Ayers worked on such Marvel Westerns as *Rawhide Kid, Outlaw Kid, Wyatt Earp* and *Two-Gun Kid*. None of them were well written, but Ayers' art was always above average, especially for the often-inferior Atlas line.

When Marvel ushered in the Stan Lee-Jack Kirby "Marvel Age of Comics," Ayers worked on the whole range of creations. Over the years, he has pencilled and inked such diverse strips as *Captain America, Hulk, Combat Kelly, Rawhide Kid* (a revived and revised version of the earlier feature), and *Ka-Zar*. In addition, Marvel started a new *Ghost Rider* feature—one that bore only a superficial relation to M.E.'s earlier strip—and Ayers again handled the art. Undoubtedly, however, Ayers' best work in the 1960s came in conjunction with inker John Severin on the *Sgt. Fury*

war book. A title that alternately ranged from the sublime to the ridiculous—one month's release portrayed Fury as a torn-shirted superman seemingly impervious to harm and the next brought a superhuman, superfallible character—Ayers' and Severin's artwork was consistently top-notch. Both were masters at portraying some of the horrors and pain of war, something that was rare for comic books.

Ayers has made only one foray into syndicated strip art; in 1959 and 1960, he inked Jack Kirby and Wally Wood's *Skymasters* space feature.

J.B.

Ayers confirmed his position as the foremost Western artist with his illustrations for *Jonah Hex* in the early 1980s. He has also taught at the Joe Kubert School of Cartoon and Graphic Art and given classes at the Guggenheim Museum. After an absence of several years, he returned to comic books in 1996 with *Dr. Wonder*, a thriller.

M.H.

BABY SNOOKUMS *see* Newlyweds, The.

BACKER, HENK (1898-1976) Henk Backer, Dutch comic artist and illustrator, was born December 15, 1898, in Rotterdam. For five years he studied at the Academie voor Beeldende Kunsten en Technische Wetenschapen (Academy of Fine Arts and Technical Sciences). In 1921 it was he who started the tradition of Dutch comic strips.

Comic strips and picture stories had been well known in the Netherlands thanks to imported materials. The newspaper *De Telegraaf* published *Jopie Slim en Dikkie Bigmans* (an English import) when, in 1920, Backer offered them his services without success. Backer had more luck in 1921 when he offered his own strip to the *Rotterdamsch Nieuwsblad* ("Rotterdam News"). On April 1, 1921, Backer's first strip, *Yoebje en Achmed* ("Yoebje and Achmed"), appeared. The strip is generally considered to be the first Dutch comic strip, despite persistent rumors that there might have been earlier Dutch efforts to enter the comics field. Done in the European tradition of child-oriented comic strips, *Yoebje en Achmed* presented the narrative below the pictures. The second strip by the 22-year-old Backer started that same year in *Voorwaarts* ("Forward"), the Social Democratic party newspaper. The strip was called *Hansje Teddybeer en Mimie Poezekat* ("Johnny Teddybear and Mimi Pussycat"), and reprints in book form started appearing in 1922. While obviously written (by Jet van Strien) and drawn for juvenile readers, adults also enjoyed the strips.

After becoming staff artist for *Rotterdamsch Nieuwsblad* in 1923, it did not take long before Backer started a new comic strip, *Tripje en Liezebertha*. Backer continued doing this strip until he retired in December 1963. *Tripje en Liezebertha* charmed the public, and many persons stood in line to buy the first *Tripje* book published in 1924. The strip's popularity was used to endorse a number of products.

While continuing *Tripje en Liezebertha*, Henk Backer also did a number of other comic strips, such as *Adolphus* (in 1930), for *Rotterdamsch Nieuwsblad*. Henk Backer's seemingly simple style breathed an amazing life into dolls and toys, making for comic strips ideally suited for children while also charming the young-at-heart with their dreamy fantasies. He died in Eemness, the Netherlands, on June 5, 1976.

W.F.

BAKER, GEORGE (1915-1975) Born in Lowell, Massachusetts, on May 22, 1915, George Baker, creator of the famed *Sad Sack,* was raised in a middle-class merchant's family, who moved to Chicago in time for Baker to attend Roosevelt High School before he took on the usual budding cartoonist's variety of jobs: truck driver, cleaner and dyer assistant, salesman, office clerk, etc. Finally he landed his first art job: drawing pots and pans for an advertising artist at $7.00 a week.

His cartooning ability improved, and in 1937 he contacted the Walt Disney Studios in Burbank for a job. Hired after he completed the usual Disney trial mail assignment, he left Chicago for good, taking the train to California and a career in animation.

After four years with Disney, he was inducted into the army in June 1941 and quickly developed—through experience—his basic concept of the browbeaten little infantry private he called the Sad Sack (based on the old army term for a worthless soldier: "a sad sack of s--t"). S. Sack, as Baker's hero dolefully signed himself, became an almost instant hit when his weekly, black-and-white strip adventures (related in double rows of unmargined panels) began to appear in *Yank,* the U.S. Army service magazine, in May 1942. (In fact, the *Sad Sack*—already a widely reprinted winner of a commercial contest for soldier cartoonists a few months earlier—was the first permanent feature selected for the still unpublished magazine in the spring of 1942.)

The Sack's fame ballooned; he shared G.I. pinup space beside Ann Sheridan and Betty Grable; he forced chuckles from second lieutenants and guffaws from generals; he was read by the hundreds of thousands of copies in his first book, *The Sad Sack,* a collection of the *Yank* strip episodes published by Simon & Schuster in 1944, and reprinted as an Army Overseas Edition; and finally he made the U.S. newspaper syndication scene when Consolidated News Features, Inc., began to circulate the *Yank* episodes as a limited daily series in February 1945.

Phased out in *Yank* by the end of the war in 1945, *The Sad Sack* was launched as a newspaper comic strip through Baker's own organization on May 5, 1946, becoming the basis for a movie starring Jerry Lewis in 1960 and the focus for a series of comic books that still appear (drawn by other hands). Baker, who had become a sergeant by the time of his army discharge, moved to Los Angeles in 1946 and formed Sad Sack, Inc., through which he merchandised Sad Sack artifacts

George Baker, "The Sad Sack." © *George Baker.*

of all kinds. Hospitalized at the Alhambra Medical Center on the campus of the University of California at Los Angeles for cancer, Baker died there on May 8, 1975, a few days short of his 60th birthday.

B.B.

BALD, KENNETH (1920-   ) American comic book and comic strip artist, born in 1920 in New York City. Kenneth (Ken) Bald graduated from Pratt Institute in New York and immediately started working in the comic book field. He was first with the Binder shop, then moved to the Beck-Costanza studio. His credits for this period (1941-43) include, either under his own name or under the pen name "K. Bruce": *Captain Marvel* and *Bulletman* for Fawcett; *Doc Strange* for Pines; *Doc Savage* for Street & Smith; *Black Owl* for Prize; and *Captain Battle* for Gleason.

In 1943 Bald was called to serve in the Marine Corps. He fought in New Guinea and New Britain and served as an intelligence officer in Okinawa and Peking before being discharged with the rank of captain in 1946.

Back in civilian life, Ken Bald resumed his career as an advertising and comic book artist, drawing romance comics for Marvel and doing illustration work. In 1957 King Features Syndicate asked him to draw the newly created *Judd Saxon*, about a young executive on his way up in the business world. In 1963 he abandoned *Saxon* to illustrate the comic strip version of *Dr. Kildare*, which was then a hit television series. In 1971, in addition to his work on *Kildare*, he took up the drawing of *Dark Shadows* (also based on a TV show), but the strip was dropped the following year. After *Dr. Kildare* was discontinued in 1984, he went into retirement in Florida, briefly resurfacing in 1996 to write the preface for the reprint book of *Dark Shadows* newspaper strips.

M.H.

BALLATA DEL MARE SALATO, UNA (Italy) Hugo Pratt's *Una Ballata del Mare Salato* ("A Ballad of the Salty Sea") made its appearance in the first issue (July 1967) of the comic monthly *Sgt. Kirk*. After *Sgt. Kirk* folded in 1970, the strip went on to *Il Corriere dei Piccoli*.

The story relates the adventures of two adolescents, Cain and Pandora, who are brother and sister searching for their father among the islands of the Pacific Ocean. The action takes place during World War I, and the two youngsters are confronted with German submarines, British spies, and, most dangerous of all, the dreaded old pirate Rasputin and the faceless "Monk." They also meet an enigmatic adventurer, Corto Maltese, who puts them under his protection. (Corto Maltese later became the hero of another of Pratt's comic creations.)

In a climate reminiscent of Robert Louis Stevenson's and Jack London's novels of the South Seas, Pratt succeeds in telling a superb story, at once dramatically gripping and visually exciting.

M.H.

"Banana Fish," Akimi Yoshida. © Akimi Yoshida.

"Una Ballata del Mare Salato," Hugo Pratt. © Editrice Sgt. Kirk.

BANANA FISH (Japan) Moving swiftly from the steamy jungles of Vietnam to the asphalt jungle of Manhattan, *Banana Fish* is one of the more entertaining thrillers to come out of the Japanese *manga* tradition. The work of Akimi Yoshida (a woman), it blends the conventional manga style with the West's more illustrative comic-book line. Taking as its starting point the words "banana fish" uttered by an American G.I. gone berserk, it centers on a conspiracy involving the Mafia, America's military establishment, and some of its political leaders, all related to a potent, mind-altering drug called banana fish.

The hero of the piece is a young street punk turned avenging angel who goes by the name of Ash Lynx. Spurred by the drug wars going on all around him and enraged by the fact that his brother (who happens to be the run-amok soldier we meet at the beginning of the tale) has been rendered useless by the drug, he takes on all comers, from a female Chinese gang leader to the homicidal head of the Corsican Mafia, Papa Dino (coincidentally his former homosexual lover). Ash Lynx is helped in his monumental task by a few honest New York City cops and by a young visitor from Japan named Eiji. The story takes place in a nightmarish New York, much inspired by Yoshida's repeated viewings of 1940s American *films noirs*; it is, as Fred Schodt notes in his study *Dreamland Japan*, "a hard-boiled action thriller filled with killings and blood."

Yoshida's blood-curdling saga (it runs to more than 3,000 pages) was serialized in (of all places) the girl's magazine *Shojo Comics* from 1985 to 1995. *Banana Fish* remains unpublished in the U.S., but excerpts have appeared in Europe.

M.H.

BANANA OIL (U.S.) Milt Gross's first really popular comic page feature, *Banana Oil*, began as a daily gag sequence of four panels in the *New York World* in late 1921. Not a strip, the feature had no continuing characters; its daily anecdotes were linked by the climactic, mocking cry of disbelief uttered by an observing figure in each: "Banana oil!" In a typical example, a timid little man is shown assiduously reading a text on jujitsu, which tells him of various simple systems of leverage that will render an opponent "helpless and entirely at your mercy." Immediately thereafter he is depicted cornered in an alley by an enormous holdup man brandishing a large gun. The little guy glances shrewdly at his encouraging text—and in the following panel is deep in his grave, from which a mournful but sarcastic "Banana oil!" is heard.

Picked up by a number of the more sophisticated metropolitan dailies around the country, *Banana Oil* was a popular hit, and the term itself moved into gen-

eral usage for the better part of the decade, dying in the 1920s, together with such other popular phrases of that epoch as "hootch," "flapper," and "bathtub gin." (Oddly, it remains unmentioned in the three volumes of H. L. Mencken's *American Language*.) A softcover book collection of *Banana Oil* appeared in the mid-1920s and went into several printings, while a number of lapel pins and other artifacts celebrated the phrase.

In 1926 *Banana Oil* became a Sunday feature, running as a four-panel gag across the top of the new Gross weekly strip, *Nize Baby*, while Gross undertook a new daily strip, *The Feitlebaum Family* (which became *Looy, Dot Dope* a few months later). Continuing in the top-strip position when the Sunday *Nize Baby* was replaced by *Count Screwloose of Tooloose* in early 1929, *Banana Oil* was finally dropped in 1930 when Gross left the *New York World*'s Press Publishing Company for King Features.

B.B.

BANCKS, JAMES CHARLES (1895-1952) Australian cartoonist, born in 1895 at Hornsby, New South Wales, the son of an Irish railway worker. On leaving school at the age of 14, he worked for a finance company as a clerk/office-boy/lift driver. Unhappy with the drudgery of his job, Jimmy Bancks decided to become an artist, and his first drawing was accepted by *The Arrow* in 1914. This encouraged Bancks to submit drawings to *The Bulletin*, which not only accepted them but also offered him a full-time job at $16 per week. He accepted the offer and remained with *The Bulletin* until 1922. During this period he took art lessons from Datillo Rubbo and Julian Ashton and began supplying freelance cartoons to the *Sydney Sunday Sun*. In 1921 the veteran editor Monty Grover suggested that Bancks draw a strip about the adventures of *Gladsome Gladys*, under the title of *Us Fellers*. It didn't take very long for Bancks to tire of *Gladys* and, in its place, to create a strip based on one of the minor characters, *Ginger Meggs*—which was to become Australia's best-known and most-loved comic strip.

"Banana Oil," Milt Gross. © Milt Gross.

Around 1923, Bancks created the first Australian daily strip, *The Blimps*, for the *Melbourne Sun*, but the strip was dropped when this paper was swallowed up in a Murdoch-Fink takeover in 1925. At the suggestion of Sir Keith Murdoch, Bancks drew a single daily panel called *Mr. Melbourne Day By Day*, for the *Melbourne Sun-Pictorial*, which ran for many years under the pens of Len Reynolds and Harry Mitchell.

Apart from writing the book for a musical comedy, *Blue Mountain Melody*, in 1934 and several newspaper columns in 1939, Bancks devoted most of his time to *Ginger Meggs*, which, as well as appearing all over Australia, had become the first Australian strip to be syndicated overseas and was appearing in England, France, South America, and the U.S. There was a large demand for *Ginger Meggs* material and merchandise. In 1924 the first colored annual was produced, and these volumes continued to be published annually for the next 35 years. There were *Ginger Meggs* dolls, badges, school blotters, calico wall decorations, and many other items. *Ginger* even became the subject of a stage play and a pantomime.

In February 1951 Bancks repudiated his $160 per week contract with Associated Newspapers Ltd. (*Sunday Sun*) on the grounds that they had violated his contract by failing to run *Ginger Meggs* on the front page of the comic section. The resultant Equity Court decision ruled in favor of Bancks and, as the result of a new contract with Consolidated Press Ltd., *Ginger Meggs* became a permanent feature on the front page of the comic section of the *Sunday Telegraph*.

Jimmy Bancks was noted for his kindness and good humor, as well as for the scholarship he established to assist young black-and-white artists to study overseas. While his drawing ability improved with maturity, his draftsmanship and fidelity of line never reached the same high level as many of his contemporaries—yet his humor and wit-without-cruelty placed him in a class of his own. His sudden death from a heart attack on July 1, 1952, left a void that has never been filled.

J.R.

BANDE DES PIEDS-NICKELES, LA *see* Pieds-Nickeles, Les.

BANGER, EDGAR HENRY (1897-1968) British cartoonist Edgar Henry Banger was born in Norwich, Norfolk, on February 27, 1897. His father ran a photographic studio and his uncle was an art teacher. He was educated at Cambridge House but had no formal art training. He drew sports cartoons for *Eastern Daily Press* before doing full-time freelance work in children's comics. His first strips were published in *Chips*, *Butterfly*, and *Comic Cuts* during 1926, and his first full page was a red/black serial *Tubby & Trot* on the back of *Crackers* in 1927. In 1933 he began contributing to the new group of weeklies published in Bath, edited by Louis Diamond, eventually becoming their top artist. For them he did *Rattler* (1933), *Dazzler* (1933), *Chuckler* (1934), *Target* (1935), *Rocket* (1935), *Sunshine* (1938), and *Bouncer* (1939). With their abrupt discontinuation, Banger joined D. C. Thomson and created the colored cover strip *Koko the Pup* for their new weekly *Magic* (July 22, 1939). When paper shortages finished this comic, he joined the new independent publisher Gerald G. Swan and created many characters in two-page and even four-page episodes, a departure from the traditional 6 to 12 panels that were the average for Brit-

ish strips. He also tried an adventure series, *Rockfist the Jungle Ruler* (1940), but was better with a touch of humor, as with his serial secret agent *Slicksure* (1940). When Swan changed format from comic book to "traditional" after the war, Banger drew strip covers for all titles and returned to his happiest style, the "nursery" comic, with *Kiddyfun* (1945). He remained outside Amalgamated Press for the rest of his career, working on J. B. Allen's *Sun* (1947), the *Fido* series (1950), and dozens of Paget titles, including one he drew entirely himself, *Surprise*. His last work was *Funny Folk of Meadow Bank*, detailed panels in color that filled the center spread of *Sunny Stories* (1955). Although he signed his strips "Bang," he pronounced his name "Bainjer." He died in 1968, aged 71.

His characters include: 1926: *Curly Crusoe*; *Willie Write*; *Enoch Hard*. 1927: *Boney & Stoney*; *Dinah Mite*; *Cheekichap the Jap*. 1929: *Diary of a Bad Boy*. 1930: *Stanley the Station Master*. 1931: *Oggle & Woggle*; *Bob Stay*. 1932: *All Sorts Stores*. 1933: *Teddy Turner & his Television*; *Percival the Perky Page*. 1934: *Jimbo the Jungle Boy*. 1935: *Dudley Dudd the Dud Detective*; *Boney Prince Charlie*. 1936: *Freddie & His Flying Flea*. 1937: *Sandy Cove*. 1938: *Fatty Fitt*. 1939: *Sheriff Sockeye*. 1940: *All at Sea*; *Coal Black Jones*; *Exploring*; *Over There*; *Baffels*; *Stoogie*; *Chubb & Tubb*; *Tornado Tom*. 1945: *Lollipop Gnomes*; *Kiddyfun Circus*. 1946: *Tip & Topper*. 1947: *Addy*. 1948: *Rollicking Ranch*. 1950: *Tropical Tricks*. 1951: *Wanda the Wonder Girl*. 1955: *Funny Folk of Meadow Bank*.

D.G.

BARA *see* Herzog, Guy.

"Barbarella," J. C. Forest. © J. C. Forest.

BARBARELLA (France) Jean-Claude Forest created *Barbarella* for the French *V-Magazine* in 1962. This tale of a scantily dressed (when dressed at all), sex-loving blonde astronaut met with instant success (as well as with the ire of the French authorities, who banned the book version). Of this same book version the reviewer for *Newsweek* was later to write: "Cruising among the planets like a female James Bond, Barbarella vanquishes evil and rewards, in her own particular way, all the handsome men she meets in outer space. And whether she is tussling with Strikno the sadistic hunter or turning her ray gun on weird, gelatinous monsters, she just cannot seem to avoid losing part or all of her skin-tight space suit."

The ballyhoo generated by *Barbarella* should not obscure its merits. The first outstanding space-heroine of the comics since Godwin's Connie, Barbarella went through a string of harrowing adventures, from her sexual encounters with assorted weirdos (including a robot) to her explorations of bizarre worlds, all of them told with tongue-in-cheek relish by J. C. Forest. Forest's line is elegant, perhaps too elegant, and somewhat brittle, but he remains a master at the evocation of disquieting places (the city of Sogo, for instance) and of haunting faces (Barbarella herself, the Black Queen.)

As mentioned above, *Barbarella* was reprinted in book form, by the French publisher Eric Losfeld, in 1964. In turn, the book was translated into an American version by Grove Press in 1966. In 1968 Roger Vadim directed a screen adaptation of *Barbarella* with Jane Fonda in the title role. Following the release of the movie, Forest tried unsuccessfully to revive *Barbarella* several times (in France in 1969, in Italy in 1970). In 1981 Barbarella made a comeback of sorts in the pages of the humor monthly *L'Echo des Savanes*; in this episode Forest wrote only the script, leaving the drawing to Daniel Billon. It did not meet with great success, and the liberated heroine has not been heard from since that time.

M.H.

BARBIERI, RENZO (1940-   ) Italian writer, editor, and publisher, born March 10, 1940, in Milan. Renzo Barbieri decided on a writing career very early in life: at the age of 15 he had his first story, "La Perla Nera" ("The Black Pearl"), published in the *Dick Fulmine* comic book. Then for Dardo he wrote a number of Western stories, which were published in the comic books *Ranch* and *El Coyote*. He also assumed the writing of the successful strips *Nat del Santa Cruz, Sciuscia,* and *Il Piccolo Sceriffo* ("The Little Sheriff"), created by Tristano Torelli and continued by Bubi Torelli and Giacomo Dalmasso. For the Genoan publisher De Leo, Barbieri authored a number of stories published in the monthly *Avventure Western* and other publications.

Barbieri's first novel, *Vitellini in Citta,* was published in 1954 by Maccari. From 1956 to 1966 he wrote short stories for the magazine *La Notte* while continuing his collaboration with a number of Milanese publishers. Then, for Dardo, he wrote the scripts for a number of comic books: *Tornado,* drawn by Giuseppe Montanari; *Billy Rock,* by Sandro Angiolini; and *Timber Jack,* by Pietro Gamba.

Meanwhile, in partnership with Gino Casarotti, Barbieri had founded his own publishing house, Edizioni del Vascello, but his attempt was unsuccessful; some time later he tried again with Editrice Sessantassei, specializing in comics for adults. His first creations were *Isabella* and *Goldrake,* drawn by Sandro Angiolini and Giuseppe Montanari, and both were huge popular successes. A year later, in 1967, he took a partner and changed the name to Edizioni RG, while substantially adding to the two previous collections. In 1972 he left RG, and during the next year he established Edifumetto and GEIS, two publishing firms. One specializes in comics for adults, the other in comics for children, thus

covering the whole spectrum. For his adult publications, Barbieri wrote racy adaptations of famous fairy tales, the best of these being *Biancaneve* ("Snow White"), drawn by Leone Frollo.

In addition to his involvement in comics, Renzo Barbieri has written regularly for the fiction page of the *Corriere d'Informazione* and is the author of 10 published novels. He is still active in both fields, although his output has somewhat diminished.

G.B.

BARKS, CARL (1901-   ) Long the anonymous artist and author of the *Donald Duck* pages in *Walt Disney's Comics and Stories* (between April 1943 and March 1965), and creator of the renowned Uncle Scrooge McDuck, Carl Barks was born in 1901 in Oregon. Randomly educated, he held a variety of jobs, from cowboy to logger, steelworker to carpenter, until he decided to make use of his long-noticeable ability as a cartoonist to freelance in that area. After six years of this, he signed on as an apprentice animator at the Walt Disney Studios in Burbank in the mid-1930s, shortly after Donald Duck himself had gained public prominence through his animated cartoon success. After six months in animation, Barks was transferred to the studio story department, where he sketched in panel outline narrative ideas for the animated cartoons. He had the good luck to be assigned to outline the story for a projected Donald Duck feature-length movie in the late 1930s, to be called *Donald Duck Finds Pirate Gold* (or possibly just *Pirate Gold*). Knocked out of the running by the spectacular success of *Snow White* and *Pinocchio* (which turned Disney's fancy to other prepublished film sources at the time), the Donald feature was salvaged in part by being utilized as the basis for a one-shot, 64-page comic book printed by Dell Publishing Co., Disney's non-newspaper comic strip outlet. Drawn by Barks and a Disney artist named Jack Hannah (each doing successive pages), the *Donald Duck Finds Pirate Gold* comic book of 1942 was a considerable success—so much so that when Barks left the Disney studios in late 1942, tired of studio pressure and routine, he was made an offer by Dell (also known as Western Publishing Co., and K. K. Publications) to draw an original *Donald Duck* feature story in strip form for *Walt Disney Comics and Stories.*

Prior to 1943, the bulk of the *WDC&S* content had consisted of reprinted newspaper comic strips featuring Mickey Mouse, Donald Duck, and other Disney characters. Now these were running short, and the editorial decision was made to fill the pages with original stories and art. Accordingly, Barks was given story control of his continuing *Donald Duck* feature and 10 pages of six panels each per monthly issue. At about the same time, Barks was asked to do another *Donald Duck* 64-page one-shot for 1943, this one to be entirely Barks' work. Called *Donald Duck and the Mummy's Ring,* this work convinced Barks' Dell bosses that they had a considerable talent on their hands. So did the reader response to the *Mummy's Ring* issue and the *Donald Duck* strips in the monthly magazine.

Barks' assignments mounted through the years, until he was doing a number of complete magazine stories and lead stories for Disney character books together with his monthly *Donald* stint every year. In December 1947, he capped his previous success by inventing Uncle Scrooge McDuck, as a character in a *Donald Duck*

Barks, Carl

feature magazine entitled *Christmas on Bear Mountain*. Scrooge was reintroduced as a regular character in Barks' *Donald Duck* work, and in March 1952 he appeared as the lead character in his own feature magazine: Uncle Scrooge in *Only a Poor Old Duck*. From then until his retirement from active drawing in 1965, Barks' Duck comic work won thousands of devoted fans, who finally ferreted out his identity from Disney studio and Dell publishing secrecy (their policy was to use only the Disney name for all published material featuring Disney characters) and bombarded him with appreciative letters. In response to this acclaim, Barks began to produce a series of remarkable oil paintings for his fans, based on familiar scenes and covers from his Dell Duck artwork of the past. At the same time, repeated pleas from Dell persuaded Barks to write scripts for other artists on the magazine staff, a task he gave up in 1973 to devote himself to personal pursuits and art interests.

He retired to Goleta, California, not far from the sea upon which he once sent Donald Duck in high adventure, and from which he received such deserved critical and popular success.

B.B.

Barks came out of retirement in the mid-1970s at the urging of his many admirers. In the last 20 years he has been turning out numerous paintings based on his comic-book covers and has even written and/or drawn an original story or two for the anthologies of his work that have kept appearing since that time.

M.H.

"Barnaby." Crockett Johnson (David Leisk). © Crockett Johnson.

BARNABY (U.S.) *Barnaby* was created by Crockett Johnson (David Johnson Leisk) for Marshall Field's experimental New York newspaper *PM*. After the strip's debut in April 1942, Field's Chicago Sun-Times Syndicate distributed the strip.

Carl Barks. "Uncle Scrooge." © Walt Disney Productions.

Barnaby is a youngster graced with a fairy godfather, but the makings of a cute nursery tale are irretrievably shattered as the character of the fairy godfather manifests himself. Mr. O'Malley is, simply, a cross between Little Nemo's Flip and W. C. Fields; even on the rare occasions when he makes a concerted effort to work his magic for good (instead of good mischief), he leaves an incredible wake of disaster, confusion, and trouble—all from which he walks away contentedly, usually benignly lecturing Barnaby on a totally unrelated and often irrelevant subject.

The boy is a blonde towhead who manages to elude the frustrations of living neither in the real, nor in the fairy, world totally. He can, on the one hand, befuddle gangsters, but he can never convince his perplexed parents that Mr. O'Malley really does exist. There are many times when a meeting almost takes place, but O'Malley inevitably and absentmindedly misses each opportunity.

Also in the strip are Barnaby's parents, the Baxters, who can never fully resign themselves to the fact that their son lives matter-of-factly in the fairy world, and so seek counsel with an endless string of child psychologists. Aunt Minerva is a brief visitor who readily believes in Barnaby's friends. Those friends include a sandman who always sleeps late; Gus the Ghost, afraid of his own shadow; Davy Jones, a nautical shade in 1890's bathing suit; and Gorgon, the talking dog.

Barnaby was an instant hit in critical terms, but it never enjoyed widespread sales. It shared the fate of other intellectual-appeal strips—it was cherished by an influential and loyal few.

Johnson's emphasis in the strip was clearly literary rather than artistic, and shortly before his death he listed to this author his major inspirations and influences: Robert Benchley, Dorothy Parker, Donald Ogden Stewart, Max Beerbohm, the old *Life* magazine, the *New Yorker* humorists, and films such as those of Frank Capra. He admitted to no special fondness for any other comic strip in his life.

His concern with *Barnaby* was to "tell a rather brighter story"; and to further his zany but reserved stories he decided to typeset the lettering "to allow for 60 per cent more words." The neat machine lettering fit in well with the stark, simple, unshaded drawing of the strip. The virtual lack of action accentuated its literary emphasis.

In spite of the critical acclaim and the artistic success of *Barnaby*, a waning concentration and other interests led Johnson to turn the strip over to others in late 1946. Jack Morley, a commercial artist, copied Johnson's style closely, and Ted Ferro, a writer for radio's comic soap opera *Lorenzo Jones*, were able to approximate the flavor of the feature until its demise in 1952 (when Johnson returned to write the concluding continuity).

In mid-passage *Barnaby* shifted syndicates from the Sun-Times to Bell. Henry Holt published two books—*Barnaby* and *Barnaby and Mr. O'Malley*—the first of which has been reprinted by Dover. An ill-fated attempt by Johnson and the Hall Syndicate in 1962 to revive *Barnaby* with the same characters and even the same early sequences (the Hot Coffee Ring was updated to the Hot Credit Card Ring) was a disappointment. Peter Wells worked on the art, but the project died after a few episodes. (Also short-lived was a *Barnaby* Sunday page around 1950.)

In spite of the troubles incumbent upon any effort that avoids broad appeal in strips, *Barnaby* was an artistic masterpiece. It contained some of the cleverest and most literate writing in comics and was extremely engaging. In the best tradition of comics since Opper, Johnson created a clever situation—a device, a basic conflict—and worked variations upon it. His characters were real, his humor very much in the tradition of his idols Benchley and Capra: zany but never out of hand, broad but always sophisticated. This experimental presentation was so unique and appropriate that it has never been employed since by any other artist.

Minor merchandising ventures included Mr. O'Malley dolls and a television cartoon. Johnson maintained that the best of the *Barnaby* strips never saw light of re-publication; the "lost" strips are surely classics of strip art that fans can look forward to with anticipation.

R.M.

"Barney Baxter," Frank Miller. © King Features Syndicate.

BARNEY BAXTER (U.S.) Frank Miller's *Barney Baxter in the Air* (later *Barney Baxter*) appeared as a daily strip on December 17, 1936, followed by a Sunday version on February 21, 1937. The feature was distributed by King Features Syndicate. (A local version of the strip had been running in a Denver newspaper since 1935.)

Barney Baxter represented the quintessence of the pilot-turned-adventurer in the tradition of the thirties—clean-cut, fair-haired, and freckle-faced, he was forever ready to hop into his plane and answer the latest call of adventure. Thus we find him successively fighting kidnappers in North America, rescuing the heir to the throne of Bronzonia from the clutches of foreign agents, and helping the police capture a gang of bank robbers. In the course of a forced landing in Alaska he meets Gopher Gus, a grizzled gold prospector who will become his trusted assistant and the strip's comic relief. Together they go adventuring to the far corners of the earth, leaving behind Barney's long-suffering sweetheart Maura.

With the coming of World War II Barney and Gus enlist in the RAF, later transferring to the U.S. Air Force. In 1942 they bomb Tokyo, just days ahead of General Doolittle. By the end of 1942, Miller having enlisted in the Coast Guard, *Barney Baxter* passed into the hands of Bob Naylor, who turned the strip into one of the most racially stereotyped of the war comics: yellow-skinned, fang-toothed Japanese were forever torturing war prisoners and blonde, white-skinned female civilians while shouting "Banzai!" By 1948 the strip's appeal had declined so severely that Frank Miller was called back to salvage it. In a misguided attempt to bring it up to date, Miller tried to turn *Barney Baxter* into a science-fiction strip, but he did not succeed and the strip folded in January 1950.

While it never had the quality of *Scorchy Smith* or the renown of *Tailspin Tommy*, *Barney Baxter* was still one of the more interesting aviation strips of the 1930s and 1940s, because of solid draftmanship and the flair for accurate detail.

M.H.

BARNEY GOOGLE (U.S.) *Barney Google* was born of a love affair between Billy De Beck and the American sporting scene. Originally, Barney had nothing to do with sports, or even the name he later made famous. He emerged out of De Beck's inkwell as one of several harassed spouses featured in a daily and Sunday strip De Beck was doing for the *Chicago Herald* in 1916. Called *Married Life*, this feature, without continuity or even regular characters, focused on the bickering between men and their wives. But one lean, cadaverous figure appeared more often than any other. With his bulbous nose and bushy moustache, he went under a number of names at first, such as Willis and Thomas (never a last name); finally he came to be called Aleck. His wife, whose physical appearance changed frequently, had no permanent name before Pauline was casually used in 1917. By this time, De Beck had dropped the other married couples to concentrate on Aleck and Pauline, and *Married Life* acquired a fairly large syndicated following.

When the *Herald* was sold to Hearst in 1918, De Beck and *Married Life* went along. But De Beck gained an additional plum: the new *Herald-Examiner* sports page, where his first sports cartoon appeared on May 7, 1918. *Married Life* continued to run on the *H-E* comic page every day, but it was plain that De Beck's heart was in his sports work. His cartoons here for the next year are graphically and humorously among the finest sports cartoons of all time. *Married Life* was finally dropped, with the last episode appearing March 13, 1919. De Beck's sports work continued for a few more months and then—on the *Herald-Examiner* sports page for June 17, 1919—the first daily sequence of a strip called *Take Barney Google, For Instance* appeared.

Changed the following week to *Take Barney Google, F'Instance*, the new strip featured the old Aleck of *Married Life* under the Google moniker; married to a woman markedly different from the Pauline of *ML*, and named Lizzie; and with a daughter named Gwennie. The theme was entirely sports-oriented. Barney was

almost totally uninterested in family life, spending most of his time around prize fighters, race track touts, horses, baseball diamonds, et al. Still tall and lean, Barney was carefully shortened by three feet over two years as De Beck began to develop the comic potential in his new character. At the same time, his wife's stature increased, until by 1920 she was literally the "wife three times his size" of the Billy Rose "Barney Google" song. At this time Barney devoted all his interest to a racehorse named Spark Plug (carefully draped with a blanket so his knock knees wouldn't show), and lost his unhappy home. Although Barney's wife, the "Sweet Woman," took him back more than once afterward, De Beck's pint-sized hero was never again to know routine domestic horror; he had taken his horse to the road forever, to become the comic strip's first picaresque figure.

Barney's popularity increased in the 1920s. The public was delighted by the exploits of the feisty, top-hatted little guy—especially the readers of the nation's sports pages, where *Barney* usually ran, and was quite different than the standard comic page fare. Over the next 15 years, Barney won and lost fortune after fortune (and Sparky himself); tried other horses (Pony Boy, etc.); raced an ostrich named Rudy; managed a prizefighter named Sully; wooed heiress after heiress; became involved in murders, hijackings, flagpole-sitting, rum-running, secret societies, and opportunistic trips to Cuba and Europe; and finally undertook a flight from the law deep into the Kentucky woods in 1934, which introduced readers to Snuffy and Lowizie Smith (or Smif) and effectively closed Barney's stage-center career on the comic page.

Snuffy, originally somewhat more rambunctious and obnoxious than the milder fellow of Fred Lasswell's present-day strip, captivated the public as much as Barney had done a decade earlier, running away with the strip and De Beck until his hitch in the service during World War II (he was one of the first comic characters in uniform). In 1942 De Beck died, and assistant Fred Lasswell took over the strip. Barney was eventually reduced to the status of a visitor to Snuffy's hill home, and this is how he appears in the strip today. Spark Plug is gone, with Sully, Rudy, and the rest, although all are unforgotten and unforgettable.

In the 1920s Barney Google was the subject of a hit song, "Barney Google with the Goo-Goo-Googly Eyes" by Billy Rose and Con Conrad, and the hero of a series of movie shorts. In the 1960s he was adapted to the television screen in animated form.

B.B.

"Barney Google," Billy DeBeck. © King Features Syndicate.

Dan Barry, "Flash Gordon." © King Features Syndication.

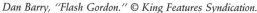

Lasswell has successfully continued the strip (now officially called *Barney Google and Snuffy Smith*) to this day, adding new characters such as Little Tater, Elviney, Lukey, and the hound dog Ol' Bullet along the way. A *Barney Google and Snuffy Smith* anthology was published in 1995 by Comicana Books and Kitchen Sink.

M.H.

BARRY, DANIEL (1923-1997) American comic strip and comic book artist, born July 11, 1923, in Long Branch, New Jersey. Daniel (Dan) Barry attended Textile High School and the American Artists' School, where he studied under Ralph Soyer and Osato Kuniyushi.

In 1941 Dan Barry met cartoonist George Mandel, who started him on a comic book career. Among other features, Barry drew *Airboy* for Hillman, *Blue Bolt* for Novelty, and *Doc Savage* for Pines; he also wrote some of the *Blue Beetle* stories for Holyoke. In 1943 he was drafted into the air force, and while on duty did *Bombrack*, a comic strip for the 20th Air Force magazine. He was discharged in 1946. Barry immediately resumed his comic book career, freelancing for Fawcett (*Commando Yank, Captain Midnight*), Gleason (*Daredevil, Crimebuster*), Hillman (*The Heap*), Marvel, and National, among others. At the same time he did advertising work, and in 1947-48 he drew the *Tarzan* daily strip.

In 1951 he was asked by King Features Syndicate to revive the *Flash Gordon* daily strip (after a seven-year hiatus). At the end of 1967, following Mac Raboy's death, he took over the *Flash Gordon* Sunday strip, leaving the dailies to his former assistant Ric Estrada. He left *Flash Gordon* entirely in 1990. Afterward he worked mainly in comic books; his contributions to the many *Indiana Jones* titles published by Dark Horse were particularly notable. He died in late January 1997.

Dan Barry was a versatile artist who, in addition to his work in the comics, had exhibitions of his paintings both in the United States and abroad. A dependable artist, smooth and polished, he seemed to lack the spark of true creativity, however.

M.H.

BARRY, LYNDA JEAN (1956-   ) A cartoonist who has helped broaden and deepen the range of comic art, Lynda Barry brings to her work a unique vision. The trenchant blend of pathos and humor in her *Ernie Pook's Comeek*, exploring, as she has written, "the torments, dreams, and awakenings of childhood," has been described in the *Washington Post Book World* as "almost literature—literature that culminates in an unbearably poignant insight."

Raised in Richland Center, Wisconsin, in a racially mixed working-class neighborhood, Barry grew up with a sense of social disorientation, which provided a rich source for her creative work. From 1974 to 1978 she studied art at the progressive Evergreen State College in Olympia, Washington, where she began drawing a strip entitled *Spinal Comics*, which depicted men as horny cacti in pursuit of women. Published in the school newspaper, which was edited by her schoolmate Matt Groening, of *Life in Hell* and *The Simpsons* fame, the strip went on to appear in other college and alternative newspapers for several years.

A technically accomplished artist, Barry supported herself as a painter and illustrator after her graduation from college, winning a Seattle Design and Advertising Silver Award for illustration in 1985, while continuing to draw cartoons. In 1980 a mention of her work in an article written by Groening brought her to the attention of the editor of the alternative weekly newspaper *The Chicago Reader*, who offered her a slot for a strip then called *Girls & Boys*. A collection, *Girls & Boys*, was later published in Seattle.

As Barry's strip, renamed *Ernie Pook's Comeek* in 1984, appeared in an increasing number of papers (winning an Excellence in Journalism Award for Cartooning in 1986 and published in more than 60 weekly papers by 1990), it broadened its cast of characters and the range of painful topics it addressed, incorporating parental infidelity, romantic betrayal, homosexuality,

Lynda Barry, "Boys and Girls." © Lynda Barry.

and teenage drug addiction, alcohol abuse, and sex into its ongoing story. Published collections include *Big Ideas* (1983), *Everything in the World* (1986), *The Fun House* (1987), *Down the Street* (1988), *Come Over, Come Over* (1990), and *My Perfect Life* (1992).

In 1984 Barry created a coloring book of female nudes accompanied by a text in which an adolescent girl bitterly examines the impossible male ideal of female beauty; entitled *Naked Ladies! Naked Ladies! Naked Ladies!*, it enraged both puritans and feminists but found a large audience. Barry's novel *The Good Times Are Killing Me*, published in 1988, dealt movingly with the problems of teenage friendship between races and brought its author a new and larger audience. Described in the *New York Times* as "a funny, intricate and finally heartbreaking story [that] exquisitely captures an American childhood," it became a play that ran successfully in Chicago and New York.

Fame as a novelist, playwright, and National Public Radio commentator has not diminished Barry's reputation as a cartoonist. Drawn in a deliberately crude style befitting its adolescent narrative voice, *Ernie Pook's Comeek* enjoys popularity among the adult as well as adolescent audiences.

D.W.

BARRY McKENZIE (G.B.) This strip is the modern version of the innocent abroad, Australian style. Barry McKenzie, broad-beamed and broad-brimmed Australian from the outback, arrived in London in 1967 as a two-bank strip in the weekly satirical paper *Private Eye*. The strip, written by Australian comedian and female impersonator Barry Humphries, is seen by some as a modern *Pilgrim's Progress* of Swiftian satire and venom; others see it as crudely drawn and worthless. (The artist is Nicholas Garland.) Barry McKenzie's attitude may be gauged by his cover comment on the first collection of his strips published in paperback: "Jeez! If you poor old Poms read this you'll flaming well read anything!" The book contains a useful dictionary of Australian

slang terms as used in the strip, *Glossary of McKenzie-isms*. This includes such classics as "Technical or Yawn" (one of 10 terms for being sick) and "Point Percy at the Porcelain" (translated as "to drain the dragon"). The first book, *The Wonderful World of Barry McKenzie* (1968), was followed by *Bazza Pulls It Off* (1972), and the strip was turned into a feature film *The Adventures of Barry McKenzie* (1972). Humphries scripted and also played Barry's aunt, Edna Everidge, and Barry Crocker played Barry McKenzie. The anti-hero still pursues his raucous adventures to this day.

D.G.

BARRY, SEYMOUR (1928-   ) American artist and brother of Dan Barry, born March 12, 1928, in New York City. Seymour (Sy) Barry studied at New York's School of Art and Design and upon graduation went to the Art Students League while working as an assistant to his brother Dan.

In the late 1940s and early 1950s Sy Barry freelanced, mainly as an inker, for such comic book companies as Gleason, Marvel, and especially National, where he worked on such features as *Johnny Peril, Rex*, and *Phantom Stranger*. He also did commercial illustrations for various companies and dabbled in watercolors. In the late 1950s he again assisted his brother with the inking of *Flash Gordon*. This put him in contact with the King Features editors, who asked him to take over *The Phantom* after Wilson McCoy's death in 1961. After drawing the adventures of the Ghost-Who-Walks for over 30 years—longer than any other artist—he retired in 1995.

Sy Barry has a clean, flowing line and a flair for composition, and his work on *The Phantom* has earned him much praise.

M.H.

BATEMAN, HENRY MAYO (1887-1970) British cartoonist, caricaturist, and illustrator, Henry Mayo Bateman was born in Australia on February 15, 1887. Brought to England almost immediately, he was educated at Forest Hill House, studying art at Westminster and New Cross Art Schools under Frederick Marriot, and in the studio of Dutch painter Charles Van Havenmaet.

Of a humorous bent, he "studied" comic drawing by copying from *Comic Cuts* and *Ally Sloper's Half-Holiday*, and sold his first cartoon to *Scraps* at age 16 (1903). He graduated to *The Tatler* the following year, then moved to *Punch*. Influenced by the clean lines of Phil May and Tom Browne and the purely visual strip cartoons of the Frenchman Caran d'Ache, Bateman evolved a totally new style in 1911. "Going mad on paper," he called it, drawing people as they felt, rather than as they looked. Thus, the embarrassment in his famous cartoon *The Guardsman Who Dropped It on Parade* was the ultimate of embarrassment, and the behavior of *The Boy Who Breathed on the Glass at the British Museum* (1916), wherein a breath led to arrest, trial, jail, and a defiant last, aged gasp upon the sacred glass, was the ultimate in revenge. This strip took 31 pictures to tell. It was something completely new to English magazines, and old volumes of *Punch* spring to life as his spreads come into view—the day in the life of *The One Note Man* that takes 58 pictures to tell; the 48 pictures that illustrate the tragedy of *The Plumber*; then, in contrast, great double-page spreads in full color for some single

Henry M. Bateman, "The Men Who Broke the Tube." © H. M. Bateman.

moment of life, such as *The Man Who Dared to Feel Seasick on the Queen Mary*.

Bateman died in February 1970, fortunately living to see, and contributing a lively sketch to, Michael Bateman's book celebrating his work, *The Man Who Drew the 20th Century* (1969). Bateman's own collected works and books include: *A Book of Drawings* (1921); *More Drawings*; *A Mixture*; *Rebound*; *Brought Forward*; *Burlesques*; *Colonels*; *Suburbia Caricatured*; *Adventures at Golf*; *Considered Trifles*; *Himself* (1937); and *The Evening Rise* (1960).

D.G.

"Batman," Bob Kane. © National Periodical Publications.

BATMAN (U.S.) When National Comics realized their success with *Superman*, editor Whitney Ellsworth

assigned artist Bob Kane to create a new hero. Working with writer Bill Finger, Kane created *Batman* for the May 1939 issue of *Detective Comics* number 27. Unlike his predecessor, The Batman had no super powers—he was just a normal human being with a keen mind and strong body. He traveled the alleys of Gotham City by night, striking fear into the hearts of criminals with his unique, batlike cape and cowl. In his civilian identity, The Batman was millionaire Bruce Wayne, who, as a child, vowed revenge on all criminals because of the murder of his parents. Wayne soon took a ward, Robin, The Boy Wonder, a young circus performer named Dick Grayson who was also orphaned.

The earliest *Batman* stories were among the most unique in comics. The Batman was portrayed as a relentless manhunter dedicated to the eradication of crime. He would play on criminals' fear of the night and exploit his batlike appearance. He could be vicious—he shot more than one man—and his amazing abilities overwhelmed the common hoodlum. In short, The Batman was an avenging vigilante. He was never depicted as the *bon vivant*, talk-of-the-party crime fighter; rather, the early *Batman* strips presented him as a slightly unsavory character.

This dark, mysterious mood was greatly cultivated and well portrayed in the 1940s and early 1950s. The writing was handled by top-notch scripters like Gardner Fox, Jack Schiff, Bill Woolfolk, Otto Binder, and especially Bill Finger. Artistically, the bulk of the stories fell to Bob Kane's assistant, Jerry Robinson. His version quickly became definitive and the character soon began to appear in a variety of National books, including *World's Finest*, *All Star*, *Batman*, and others. This early *Batman* also produced some of comicdom's most remembered villains. First and foremost, there was Robinson's pasty-faced Joker, the homicidal "clown prince of crime." Also in the parade of unique, inventive adversaries were The Penguin, an overstuffed, umbrella-toting snob; The Riddler, a crazed criminal who gave clues before he attacked; the murderous Two-Face, an insane former district attorney with a deformed visage; The Catwoman, a feline lover who fell in love with The Batman; The Scarecrow, a schoolteacher gone mad; and the incomparable Tweedledee and Tweedledum, two emigrants from Lewis Carroll's *Alice in Wonderland*.

But during the mid-1950s, many of the original creators left the strip, and this ushered in a low point in the *Batman* feature. Saddled with new and outlandish characters like Bathound, Batwoman, Batgirl, and Bat-Mite, and crippled by poor science-fiction scripts about monsters, robots, aliens, time travel, and crackpots, *Batman* quickly slumped in sales and popularity. In 1964, however, editor Julius Schwartz and artists Carmine Infantino and Murphy Anderson concocted The Batman's "New Look." The change in art style and the new, more detective-oriented editorial direction returned much of the character's flavor. By 1966, however, the *Batman* television program brought in a new series of changes, all of them "campy" and in complete disregard of the character's former traits. The camp look disappeared by 1970, and artists like Frank Robbins, Neal Adams, Jim Aparo, and Walt Simonson provided interesting new variations on the "Dynamic Duo."

Batman also reached into other media, too. There were two movie serials in the 1940s, *Batman* and *Batman and Robin*, starring Lewis Wilson and Douglas

Croft. There have also been two *Batman* newspaper strips (1943 and 1966), a radio program, and a 1971 Crown anthology, *Batman from the Thirties to the Seventies*. In 1966, ABC-TV premiered *Batman*, starring Adam West as Batman and an array of major stars as villains, including Burgess Meredith (Penguin), Cesar Romero (Joker), Frank Gorshin (Riddler), and Victor Buono (King Tut). This program unleashed a torrent of *Batman* material, including two paperback novels, a cartoon collection, and literally thousands of novelties.

J.B.

The notoriety of the title attracted a number of outstanding practitioners to the Batman banner, and those have included (among the artists) John Byrne, Walt Simonson, Gene Colan, and Berni Wrightson, and such writers as Jim Starlin and Alan Moore. It was Frank Miller, however, who as artist/writer introduced in 1986 a new, older Batman, self-doubting and disillusioned, in *The Dark Knight Returns*. This "dark and gritty" interpretation has been followed almost slavishly by those who came after Miller and has become as much of a worn-out cliché as the dashing crime fighter of yore.

The media has been very good to the Batman mythos in the last 10 or so years. There was the phenomenally successful 1989 *Batman* movie, with Michael Keaton in the title role, followed (to date) by three popular sequels: *Batman Returns* (1991), *Batman Forever* (1995), and *Batman & Robin* (1997). There has also been a third *Batman* newspaper strip (1989-91), and an animated version was produced for television by the Fox network in 1992.

M.H.

BATTAGLIA, DINO (1923-1983) Italian cartoonist, born in 1923 in Venice. Dino Battaglia was a member of the team who established the famed periodical *Asso di Picche* ("Ace of Spades") at the end of 1945. For *Asso di Picche* (which was the first Italian magazine of the post-war period) Battaglia produced the *Junglemen* strip (after an introductory page by Giorgio Bellavitis), which was later taken over by Hugo Pratt. After *Junglemen*, Battaglia created the sea-adventure strip *Capitan Caribe* for an Argentine publisher.

In the early 1950s Battaglia drew a few episodes of *Pecos Bill* (with texts by Guido Martina), and for Edizioni Audace he did a series of adaptations from the classics, as well as the Western *El Kid* (1955), later continued by Calegari and D'Antonio with scripts by Bonelli. Around that time Battaglia hit his full stride, producing illustrations for English publishers and creating a number of adventure strips for *L'Intrepido* and the Catholic weekly *Il Vittorioso*.

Starting in 1962, Battaglia became one of the most active contributors to the *Corriere dei Piccoli* and later to the parent *Corriere dei Ragazzi* as well. There he successively created *La Pista dei Quattro* ("The Trail of the Four," a Western, 1964), *Ivanhoe* in 1966, and his two most famous creations, both of them science-fiction strips, *I Cinque della Selena* ("The Five of the Selena," 1966) and the sequel *Cinque su Marte* ("The Five On Mars," 1967). He also did illustrations, mostly for juvenile stories and novels.

In February 1968 the illustrated monthly *Linus* published Battaglia's strip adaptation of a short story by Fabrizio Gabella. Starting in August of the same year, Battaglia did his famous series of adaptations from tales by Matthew Shiel, Edgar Allan Poe, Herman Melville,

H. P. Lovecraft, and others, which won Battaglia wide acclaim. Also looming very large in the Battaglia corpus are his 10 interpretations of the Devil, which he drew for the essay *Il Diavolo*. Battaglia also contributed to the *Messaggero dei Ragazzi*, notably *Frate Francesco* ("Brother Francis"), which he produced in collaboration with his wife Laura (1974).

Dino Battaglia was awarded the Phénix (France) for "best foreign artist" in 1969, and the Yellow Kid (Italy) for "best Italian artist" in 1970 at Lucca. He died in Milan on October 4, 1983.

G.B.

BATTAGLIA, ROBERTO (1923-) An Argentine cartoonist of Italian origin, Roberto Battaglia was born in Buenos Aires in 1923. Battaglia, about whose early life little is known, is famous for his comic creation *Mangucho y Meneca*, started in 1945 (under the title *Don Pascual*) in the children's magazine *Patoruzito*.

A draftsman with a fine sense of design and a supple line, and endowed with a very personal sense of humor, Battaglia is the creator of other comic strips, all done for the publisher Dante Quinterno: *María Luz*, *Martín a Bordo*, and *Orsolino Director*.

L.G.

BAXENDALE, LEO (1930-) British cartoonist Leo Baxendale was born in October 1930 in Whittle-le-Woods, Lancashire. He received a grammar school education; as an artist he was self-taught. His first job was at the Leyland Paint and Varnish Company designing paint labels. After national service in the Royal Air Force as a catering clerk (1949-1950), he worked on the art staff of the *Lancashire Evening Post*, where he drew sports and editorial cartoons, designed advertisements, and wrote and illustrated his own series of articles.

Inspired by his own reading of *Beano* as a boy, he tried his hand at some strips for that weekly comic and was immediately accepted. His first original character was *Little Plum Your Redskin Chum* (October 10, 1953), followed by *Minnie the Minx* (December 15, 1953). This latter character was intended as a female counterpart to *Dennis the Menace*. His specialty appeared to be mischievous kids, cemented by his creation of a large panel of riotous mayhem in the style of *Casey Court* called *When the Bell Rings* (February 13, 1954). This became a full-page strip, and its name was changed to the more familiar *Bash Street Kids* (December 1, 1956). Later it became a two-page color spread. A similar gang of juvenile delinquents was created for a new D. C. Thomson comic, *Beezer*, and was christened *The Banana Bunch* (January 21, 1956). A determination to extend himself became clear with a new strip, *The Three Bears*, which began in *Beano* on June 6, 1959. These voracious beasts, Pa, Ma, and Teddy, developed from the zany bears that had popped up in Little Plum's neck of the woods.

Although all the strips thus far mentioned are still running in Thomson comics, Baxendale himself has not drawn any since 1963. He abandoned them to create an entire weekly comic for Odhams Press, *Wham* (June 20, 1964). For this he devised the characters, modeled them, scripted their adventures, and drew and colored the main ones: *Eagle Eye Junior Spy*, *The Tiddlers*, and *General Nitt and His Barmy Army* (all two-page spreads). Other characters included *Danny Dare*, *Biff*, *Georgie's Germans*, and *Footsie the Clown*. The comic was as revolutionary as *Eagle* had been in the 1950s, and a com-

Leo Baxendale, "Little Plum." © D.C. Thomson.

panion, *Smash*, was launched (February 5, 1966). For this he provided *Grimly Feendish, Bad Penny*, etc.

When I.P.C. absorbed Odhams and Fleetway, Baxendale joined them and created such characters as *The Pirates* (1967), *Mervyn's Monsters* (1968), *Big Chief Pow Wow* (1969), *Sam's Spook* (1970), *Nellyphant* (1972), *Sweeny Toddler* (1973), and *Snooper* (1974). He stopped working for British comics in 1975 and stopped drawing altogether in 1992, due to what he characterized as "wonky eyesight."

The most imitated artist in British comics today, Leo Baxendale is the modern equivalent of Roy Wilson in the 1930s and Hugh McNeill in the 1940s.

D.G.

B.C. (U.S.) Cartoonist Johnny Hart's *B.C.* was refused by five major syndicates before finally being accepted by the Herald-Tribune Syndicate (later absorbed by Publishers-Hall Syndicate). The first daily strip appeared on February 17, 1958, followed by a Sunday version on October 19 of the same year.

Around the strip's titular "hero" (B.C., the "average caveman," not far removed from the typical suburban-dweller, meek, gullible and unimportant) a weird assortment of prehistoric characters endlessly mope around, passing their time in mindless errands or on subtle speculations about the world's progress and the future of civilization. Their discussions are often fuzzy, carried out, as they are, by such creatures as Wiley, the dirty, one-legged poet; Thor, the inexhaustible (but befuddled) inventor; Peter, the rhetorician of the absurd; Clumsy Carp, the happy blunderer; and Curls, the suavely sarcastic sophist; not to mention an existentialist anteater and a couple of peace-loving dinosaurs. (Despite this abundance of talents, however, B.C.'s world doesn't seem to be in any better shape than ours.) Johnny Hart later added to his *dramatis per-*

sonae the barely human Grog, a hirsute, macrocephalic freak, and Hart's idea of the "missing link."

By renovating the conventions of the humor strip, *B.C.* became the graphic prototype of the modern sophisticated comics. To express the passing of time, the relativity of space, Hart makes use of all the signs and symbols of the earlier cartoonists but places them

"B.C." Johnny Hart. © Field Newspaper Syndicate.

in a shifting context where, by their presence, they add an element of uncertainty. (*Krazy Kat* had earlier used such devices, but the effect was mainly circumstantial; in *B.C.* the changing moon and the moving rocks are at the heart of the matter and the objects of the cavemen's fascinated incomprehension.)

Hart's drawing is accordingly functional, linear, and elemental. Even the characters are drawn in conformity with geometrical patterns, which freeze in a same perspective living creatures and inanimate objects. The prehistoric setting is not just a source of gags but a dimension of the action. By going back to the dawn of time, Johnny Hart shows the permanence of human nature (this would seem to be in contradistinction to the widely held—but unsubstantiated—notion that *B.C.* is an "existential" strip).

In spite of the seriousness of its intent, *B.C.* is studded with rib-splitting slapstick, hilarious dialogue, and a delightful sense of the absurd, which make it a masterpiece of light comedy and an irrepressible parody all rolled into one starburst of a comic strip.

B.C. has been reprinted in paperback form by G. P. Putnam and by Fawcett and was made into an animated cartoon for ABC-TV.

M.H.

BEA, JOSÉ-MARIA (1942-) Spanish cartoonist and illustrator, born in Barcelona in 1942. José-Maria Bea attended the School of Art of Barcelona, studying design, sculpture, and drawing for six years. These studies strongly influenced his future career as a cartoonist and gave him the opportunity of meeting and exchanging artistic ideas with the noted painter Francese Artigau. In the first stage of his development Bea worked for the comic syndicate Selecciones Illustradas and produced a great many romance comic stories designed for the English market.

In 1962 Bea moved to Paris and enrolled in the Academie Julian, a well-known art school, and started experimenting with color, alternating between painting and book illustration. He later went back to Spain and opened his own art studio in Barcelona. There, under the influence of Esteban Maroto, he resumed his cartooning career. In 1971, in collaboration with Luis Vigil for the texts, he created the horror strip *Sir Leo* for the comic magazine *Dracula*. The feature attracted the attention of American publisher James Warren, who put the artist under contract. Beginning in 1973 Bea collaborated for the Warren magazines, notably *Creepy*, *Eerie*, and *Vampirella*.

L.G.

Bea wrote and drew his acclaimed series of science-fiction tales, *Historias de la Taberna Galactica* ("Stories from the Galactic Tavern"), for the Spanish magazine *1984*; started in 1979, the series ended in 1981 with the closing of the tavern on account of financial difficulties. Among his later works, mention should be made of *En un lugar de la mente* ("In a Place of the Mind," 1981-82), *La Muralla* ("The Wall," 1983) and *Siete Vidas* ("Seven Lives," 1984), the last two in the form of animal strips, with the cat Gatony as the protagonist. Bea is also the author of several how-to books on cartooning, and since the late 1980s he has adapted a number of his stories for television.

J.C.

BÉCASSINE (France) In 1905 Maurice Languereau, publisher of the children's weekly *La Semaine de Suzette*, imagined the adventures of a naive young peasant girl as a simple filler story for his magazine. Drawn by cartoonist Jean-Pierre Pinchon, the story met with immediate success and a sequel was eventually concocted, followed in short order by an entire series named *Bécassine* (from the French word *bécasse* meaning a scatterbrain).

Annaik Labornez ("Bécassine"), a native of Brittany, was a maid in the affluent household of the Marquise de Grand-Air, in the little town of Clocher-les-Bécasses. Loyal and well-meaning, she would commit the worst blunders out of a kind heart and an easily abused credulity. Later on, however, she became somewhat wiser, and even made a contribution to the victory of the Allies in World War I. After Pinchon's death in 1953, the series passed into the hands of Jean Trubert (with scripts contributed by various authors), who tried, without success, to jazz up the character of the little Breton girl.

Bécassine never was (and is still not) a genuine comic strip. The written text (quite good) takes up a disproportionate amount of the total allotted space. The drawings themselves are not interconnected but instead serve as illustrations to the narrative, which can be read separately. In fact *Bécassine*, in tone and in structure, is a picture-story more in the tradition of the 19th-century *Bilderbogen* and *histoires illlustrées* than in the form of the modern comic strip. Unlike its contemporary *Les Pieds-Nickelés* (1908), *Bécassine* never developed into a major feature.

In spite of these drawbacks, *Bécassine* enjoyed tremendous popular success before and immediately after World War I. It was reprinted in over 30 hardbound volumes from 1913 onwards, adapted to radio, and celebrated in song and records; and in 1939 Pierre Caron directed a movie version, with Paulette Dubost in the title role. While no original *Bécassine* story has been produced in the last two decades, the little maid continues to live in endless reprints of her old adventures more than 90 years after her debut.

M.H.

BECK, CHARLES CLARENCE (1910-1989) American comic book artist, born June 8, 1910, in Zumbrota, Minnesota. After studies at the Chicago Academy of Fine Arts and the University of Minnesota, C. C. Beck broke in as a humor illustrator for Fawcett's pulp magazines in 1933. In 1939, Fawcett comic book editor Bill Parker created the *Captain Marvel* strip and assigned Beck to design the character. Using American motion picture actor Fred MacMurray as a model, he created the character and drew the first 13-page adventure.

In 1941, the strip became the best-selling feature on the American market, and Beck was promoted to chief artist. That same year he formed his own comic book studio in New York City; most of the work was for *Captain Marvel*, but his studio later drew for Fawcett's *Spy Smasher* and *Ibis, The Invincible* strips. As the *Captain Marvel*–related features continued to expand in the mid-1940s, Beck also became de facto editor and applied his rigid personal standards to scripts as well as artwork. His shop, which was managed by fellow artist Pete Costanza, later took on advertising work and Beck created *Captain Tootsie*, a single-page advertising comic strip for the Tootsie Roll candy company.

Beck opened a second studio in Englewood, New Jersey, in 1944, but when Fawcett folded their comic book line in 1954—partly due to lagging sales and partly due to National Comics' celebrated copyright infringement lawsuit against *Captain Marvel*—he closed his shops and moved to Florida. He eventually formed his own studio of art and design and even sold a text story to *Astonishing Science Fiction* magazine.

Beck returned to the comic book industry briefly in 1966 when Milson Publications, a combine of old *Captain Marvel* artists, writers, and editors, convinced him to draw *Fatman, The Human Flying Saucer.* It lasted only three issues before the company went bankrupt. He made a second and equally short return in 1972 when National Periodical Publications—the company that had originally helped drive *Captain Marvel* into obscurity—revived the character in their *Shazam!* book. Beck was hired to draw the character he made famous, but left after nine issues in a bitter dispute over the feature's editorial direction. His last years were spent writing opinionated articles on the subject of comics and contributing an irregularly published column, *Crusty Curmudgeon*, for comics fanzines. He died at his Florida home on November 22, 1989.

Beck's artistic style remains one of the cleanest ever used by a comic book artist. The stories he drew were told simply and humorously, and he disliked portraying violence. "Let the readers imagine the violence," he said, and it was not uncommon for him to draw only the scenes before and after a punch rather than the punch itself.

As chief artist on *Captain Marvel*, Beck was meticulous in his control of the strip's other illustrators. Everyone was made to conform to his clear, crisp, fast-moving style, and the artists who draw the feature today still utilize and emulate C. C. Beck's classic simplicity.

J.B.

BECK, FRANK HEM (1894-1962) Frank Beck, one of the most skilled and amusing of the strip cartoonists who built their fame and fortune on funny drawings of boys and dogs (and made his particular hit with the dog strip *Bo*), blinked into the light of day in Tacoma, Washington, on March 17, 1894. Brought up in a rural, middle-class family, Beck underwent routine childhood schooling in the Northwest, then went to Chicago to study cartooning at the Art Institute there. He found a job on the art staff of the *New York Tribune*, where he drew a general panel series with individual titles, commenting on the current scene. Beck later drove an ambulance on the western front in World War I, and then returned to draw such popular daily series as *Hem and Amy, Down the Road, All in a Lifetime,* and *Gas Buggies*, all based on men's and boys' relationships with cars, women, and dogs; most were syndicated by Beck himself. In the late 1920s, Beck bought an English bloodhound and became so enchanted with the dog's antics that he developed the daily and Sunday strip that is today most associated with his name: *Bo*. Bo, however, was anything but a thoroughbred of any breed; he was a tumbling, stumbling composite of every big, long-legged dog that ever lived, with a lolling tongue and a black patch of fur over one eye.

Like many cartoonists, Beck went to the West Coast to live after his success with *Bo*. He died in San Diego on March 21, 1962, at the age of 68. *Bo*, distributed by McNaught Syndicate, did not survive its creator.

B.B.

Franziska Becker wishing a happy New Year to readers of a comics fanzine—in typical character and style.

BECKER, FRANZISKA (1949-   ) Franziska Becker was born on July 10, 1949, in Mannheim, Germany. She studied to become an art teacher, but her career took another turn when, in 1977, she started to work for *emma*, the premiere feminist magazine in Germany, founded by Alice Schwarzer. She has since become the quintessential female cartoonist in Germany.

Becker, whose favorite artist and influence is Wilhelm Busch (her favorite Busch character is "pious Helen"), has drawn spot cartoons and comic strip pages for *emma*, and she has become popular among feminists as well as the general public. She emphasizes the female view of life, but she does it with so much versatility that men are also able to see the humor in her stories. Her comics deal with feminist issues, women's views on men, fitness, and pop culture; they include indispensable tips for a multitude of situations.

Collections of her work were first published in 1980 with *Mein Feministischer Alltag* ("My Everyday Feminism"), and continue to appear. In 1992, her comic album *Feminax und Walkürax* was published as a feminist answer to the new *Asterix* album *Asterix and Maestria*.

In addition to the more feminist cartoons she produces as house artist for *emma*, Becker also creates cartoons for weekly magazines, including *stern*. Freelancing offers her a means to explore the humorous antics of both genders. Today, because of her intrinsic humor and her simple but effective style, Becker, along with Claire Brétecher, is considered one of the most important female artists in Europe.

BEEP BEEP THE ROAD RUNNER (U.S.) The characters of the Road Runner and Wile E. Coyote were created for Warner Brothers animated cartoons by director Charles M. ("Chuck") Jones with the help of story man Michael Maltese. The duo first appeared in the film *Fast and Furry-ous* in 1948, which was followed by a successful series under Jones' direction until 1964, when Warner Brothers closed the cartoon department and subcontracted the work to DePatie-Freleng. In July 1958, Western Publishing Company named the Road Runner "Beep Beep" and added him and the Coyote to its line of Dell comics starring the Warner Brothers characters. *Beep Beep* first appeared in a special issue of the Dell Color Comics series, number 918. Two more tryout issues followed before the first issue of *Beep Beep the Road Runner* was issued in 1959.

The comic books followed the same basic format as the animated cartoons: The Road Runner raced about the desert, avoiding the schemes and elaborate inventions of Wile E. Coyote. The Coyote had a maniacal obsession with catching and eating the Road Runner and this, coupled with his vast overestimation of his own brainpower, inevitably caused his machinations to backfire. In the cartoons, the Road Runner never spoke, his dialogue being limited to "Beep beep!" (The Coyote spoke in only one film—a 1951 Bugs Bunny short called *Operation: Rabbit*.) For the purposes of the comic book, both were given the powers of speech and it was designated that all road runners speak in rhymed dialogue. The Road Runner was clearly a male in the comic books, there having been some question previously. (Some publicity material on the cartoons gave the Road Runner's name as Mimi.) The comic book Road Runner was given three identical, unnamed sons who followed him about and, on occasion, a female road runner named Matilda who was featured as Beep Beep's wife.

Dell's comic book version proved very popular, and after 14 issues, Western Publishing Company continued it under the Gold Key company logo, starting the numbering over. A wide selection of writers handled the scripting over the years, including Michael Maltese, Jerry Belson, Lloyd Turner, Vic Lockman, Don Christensen, Jack Cosgriff, Cecil Beard, and Mark Evanier. Most of the artwork was handled by Pete Alvarado, Jack Manning, or Phil DeLara.

Beep Beep the Road Runner and Wile E. Coyote were the subjects of hundreds of merchandising items, including games, children's books, dolls, puzzles, jewelry, and even an automobile, "The Road Runner," produced by the Chrysler Motor Company. Both characters appeared in Gold Key comics of other Warner Brothers characters, including the revived *Looney Tunes* comic (1975), *Golden Comics Digest, March of Comics* and a cover-featured "guest stars" spot in some issues of *Daffy Duck* (1972-1973).

BEETLE BAILEY (U.S.) Created by Mort Walker and bought by King Features in 1950, *Beetle Bailey* was the last comic introduced by that firm for several years; it was also the last comic personally approved by William Randolph Hearst. Debuting on September 3, 1950,

"Beetle Bailey," Mort Walker. © King Features Syndicate.

Beetle soon became one of the most popular of comic strips. It is still among the five most popular strips.

The cast of the army strip, based at Camp Swampy, is one of the largest in the comics. For more than 45 years of turbulent history, the camp has remained untouched by any disturbance, domestic or foreign. By resisting temptations to localize or inject issues into the strip, Walker's aloof world has fared better than George Baker's *Sad Sack* and Bill Mauldin's *Willie and Joe*.

Beetle Bailey, whose eyes (like those of his magazine-cartoon prototype, Spider) have never been seen from under hats and helmets, is Mort Walker's Everyman. He resists authority, seeks easy ways out, and was, like Walker, a reluctant draftee.

Sergeant Orville Snorkel, the authority figure, is Beetle's eternal antagonist. He relishes food as much as ordering his men, is very shy around the girls, has only one real friend (his dog, Otto, one of the funniest dogs in the comics) and, in spite of the constant battle with Beetle, maintains a covert affection for the hapless private. Every year Beetle brings Sarge home on leave.

Other characters include Gen. Halftrack, the elderly symbol of inept authority; Chaplain Staneglass, utterly ineffectual but lovable; Beetle's chum Killer Diller, the self-appointed ladies' man; chubby Plato, the intellectual; and Zero, a village idiot who is always trying and absolutely never succeeding at doing good. Lt. Sonny Fuzz, a punky upstart, was in fact inspired by Walker's own regrets about his swelled head when he attained that rank; Lt. Flap is an Afro-coiffed black officer who seems to run his own army; and Miss Buxley, Gen. Halftrack's secretary, is a bosomy blonde who takes over the gags for weeks at a stretch.

The gags in this stylized, slick strip rely almost exclusively on the interplay of personalities; virtually no outside characters or locales are introduced.

Beetle Bailey appears in approximately 1,300 papers around the world and has inspired dozens of games, toys, puzzles, and patches. A dozen paperback books have appeared, as well as a series of animated cartoons, which were artistic and commercial failures.

R.M.

Beetle Bailey has continued virtually unchanged through the Vietnam War, the Cold War, and the Gulf War, without its soldiers ever leaving Camp Swampy. It is a tribute to Walker's talent and sense of timing that the strip's popularity has never flagged in all this time.

M.H.

BEKER, ŽARKO (1936-   ) The talented cartoonist Žarko Beker lives in Zagreb, Croatia, where he was born on December 2, 1936. Besides soccer, he liked drawing very much, and was happy to have the famous academic artist Željko Hegedušić for his art teacher. Unfortunately, Beker's father read an unhappy biography of van Gogh and decided not to allow his son to be an artist. Therefore Beker turned to architecture, but he never graduated.

His first comic strip, produced under Disney's influence, was published in 1951 by *Pionir* magazine. After that, while pursuing his schooling, he continued to illustrate some magazines until 1956, when he involved himself in the cartoon film field. For three years he worked as an animator on seven films and, in 1968, became a regular collaborator to *Plavi Vjesnik* magazine in Zagreb. Then he began a long series of comic strips; *Pavel Biri, Bint el Hadra, Zaviša, Mak Makić, Operacija palac, Suparnici, Špiljko, Demonja,* and *Magirus* were only a few of them. But most popular of all was *Zaviša,* written by Zvonimir Furtinger, which only lasted for four episodes. Beker collaborated with Furtinger on all of his comics except for two, which were based on his own scripts. One of them was *Špiljko,* a parody of prehistoric life, and another was *Magirus,* about a super-hero. With superheroes appearing all over the world, even Yugoslavia had to have its own,

Žarko Beker, ''Magirus.'' © Žarko Beker.

but *Magirus* lasted for only one episode. Unlike Superman, who could fly, Magirus lived and worked in the sea.

Beker developed his graphic style based on that of Frank Bellamy, but in *Magirus* and in the last episode of *Zaviša,* he copied directly from Alberto Breccia's Western strip *Roy Renk.* Nobody knows why Beker imitated, because he is really a very talented cartoonist and commercial artist.

After he stopped working on comics, Beker became art director of Vjesnik's Marketing Agency in Zagreb.

E.R.

BELINDA BLUE EYES (G.B.) Brave, big-hearted *Belinda Blue Eyes,* who would lose her slightly embarrassing ''surname'' with the war, came into the *Daily Mirror* on September 30, 1935. She was a cross between Shirley Temple and *Little Orphan Annie,* with the mop of curls of the former and the big, blank eyeballs of the latter. She also had Annie's philosophical bent, which kept her cheerful through many a misery, as she wandered waiflike through the world. ''I reckon there's nothin' like good honest work to make you ferget ya troubles, Mrs. Frizzle!'' she smiled bravely as she sweated over the hot fat in the chip shop. She had a dog (like Annie), a Scottish terrier that faded away in 1944, and an equivalent to Daddy Warbucks, Daddy Pilgrim, forever turning up in time to end an episode, then departing in time to start another. In a close survey of 10 months of the strip made during 1943 by Margot Bennett, Belinda offered 19 pieces of advice, performed 28 courageous actions, and said ''Gee!'' 139 times and ''Gulp!'' 11 times.

Belinda's boyfriend—and staunch supporter—was Desmond Dare, one of the Bomb Alley Kids dating from 1944. But among readers her favorite supporting players were the bad girls, teenage Spitfire Kitty, Mrs. Frizzle's sporty daughter, and especially saucy Suky Schoolgirl, rebel of Magdala House. And when Daddy Pilgrim was not around, which was often, who better to go to for comfort and cuddles than bosomy Mrs. Bounty?

Originally drawn by the pseudonymous ''Gloria,'' the strip was taken over by Steve Dowling, then by Tony Royle from 1943 to the end on October 17, 1959. Reprints include: *Belinda and the Bomb Alley Boys, Belinda in Shooting Star,* and a monthly comic book published in Australia.

D.G.

BELL, STEVE (1951-   ) This left-handed lad from Walthamstow, where he was born on February 26, 1951, is one of the few ''adult'' cartoonists to come up from the ranks of children's comics—and in a very short time he established himself as one of the up-and-coming artists. He began to draw for three I.P.C. weeklies, *Whoopee, Cheeky,* and *Jackpot* in 1978, and by 1979 was drawing the satirical anti-Tory strip cartoon, *Maggie's Farm* (Maggie, of course, being Prime Minister Margaret Thatcher) for *Private Eye,* the radical comic fortnightly. Two years after that he started his own cruel daily strip, *If . . . ,* for the *Guardian* newspaper, where it has run ever since.

Educated at Slough Grammar School, Bell studied art at the Teeside College of Art, graduated in Fine Art from Leeds University in 1974, and began a career as an art teacher in Birmingham in 1977. He started strip cartooning in that same year as a freelancer, turning

Steve Bell, an affectionate tribute to Leo Baxendale's "Little Plum." © Steve Bell.

full-time in no time. After a year on the comics, he began to appear in the political press, including the *New Statesman* and *New Society*. His first comic strip was the left-wing series *Good God Almighty* in the Socialist weekly *The Leveller* (1978). Always busy, he took up animation and joined Bob Godfrey in making adult cartoon films for Channel Four Television and the BBC. He was voted Humorous Strip Cartoonist of the Year 1984 by the Cartoonist's Club of Great Britain.

Among his books are: *Maggie's Farm* (1981), *Further Down on Maggie's Farm* (1982), *If* (annual series from 1983), *Waiting for the Old Uptown* (1986), *Maggie's Farm: The Last Roundup* (1987), and *Funny Old World* (1991).

D.G.

BELL, WALTER (1893-1979) Walter Bell was one of those cartoonists whose work for children's comics was both prolific and unoriginal. Able to impersonate almost any of his contemporaries, his talents were used by editors at the Amalgamated Press to fill in for other artists' regular characters during the artists' holidays or illnesses. However, as a freelancer working from an art studio, and later running a studio himself, he was able to create several successful heroes of his own.

Walter Bell was born in Newcastle upon Tyne, England, on January 23, 1893, and died in 1979. He was still cartooning in his eighties: in 1976 he worked on the revival of *Ally Sloper*, Britain's first strip cartoon hero and the cartoon Bell cut his teeth on back in 1920.

Fresh from a distinguished army career in World War I (where he was an officer in the cavalry and won the Military Medal), Bell bought a copy of the cartoonists' bible, *The Writers and Artists Year Book*, and armed with his portfolio of work samples, began to call on every agency in the book. He met with Ralph Hodgson at Byron Studios on Fleet Street, which was then the world's center for newspaper publishers. Hodgson had once drawn *Airy Alf and Bouncing Billy* under the pen name "Yorick." This strip, originated by the genius of British comics, Tom Browne, had served as the model for Walter Bell's style, and so Bell and Hodgson became lifelong friends and collaborators.

Bell's first published cartoon appeared in the *Daily Chronicle*, substituting for W. F. Thomas, the *Ally Sloper* artist who, at the time, was drawing a daily thumbnail cartoon for the newspaper. While working in the studio, Bell was given the opportunity to draw some Tom Browne creations, titled *Weary Willie and Tired Tim*, for Amalgamated Press. His substitute front page for their weekly vehicle, *Illustrated Chips*, impressed the art editor, Langton Townley. He offered Bell the chance to take over *Casey Court*, the back-page panel of pranks that inspired a young Charlie Chaplin. Bell drew the cartoon weekly for 10 years.

Now well established in the comics world, Bell soon had a roster of characters to draw each week: *Mat the Middy* for *Merry Moments*; *Lottie Looksharp* for *The Golden Penny*; *The Sporty Boyees* for *The Monster Comic*; and *Sonny Shine the Page Boy* for *The Jolly Jester*. These were all independent comics, but by 1922 Bell was working exclusively for the Amalgamated Press chain. He drew *Geordie Brown* in *Funny Wonder*, and many characters for the Nursery Group, which was aimed at younger readers, including *Children of the Forest*, an early picture serial, for *Bubbles*; *Fun and Frolic in Fairyland* for *Playbox*; *Bobbie and his Teddy Bears* in *Sunbeam*; *Redskin Chums* in *Bo-Peep*; and *Snow White and Her Friends* in *Happy Days*.

In 1930 the rival firm of George Newnes and C. Arthur Pearson invented the idea of a seasonal comic and launched *The Seaside Comic*, published that summer. Bell illustrated the entire 12-page color tabloid. It was a great success with children on vacation, and Newnes-Pearson followed it a few months later with *Christmas Comic*, then *Holiday Comic*, *Spring Comic*, *Summer Comic*, and other annual titles, all illustrated by Bell. Amalgamated Press expressed its displeasure with Bell's defection to Newnes-Pearson by reducing the amount of work offered to him. Undeterred, Bell found further work outside Amalgamated's near-monopoly as national, and later local, newspapers began to publish comic supplements of their own. Bell's parade of characters now included *Molly the Messenger*, in the *Daily Mail Comic* and *Jolly Jenkins* in the *Daily Express Comic*.

Bell moved from the comics to the boys' weekly story department at Amalgamated, where he drew *Mike, Spike and Greta* for *The Pilot*, *Mustard and Pepper* for *The Ranger*, and *The Professor and the Pop* for *Detective Weekly*. His full-blown return to A.P. Comics came with the sudden death of George W. Wakefield, who had just begun drawing the weekly adventures of Bud Abbott and Lou Costello for *Film Fun*. Bell completed the first unfinished page and from that took over the series. He later worked for many of the one-shot comic books, most of which were published by P.M. (Phillipp Marx) Productions, with such titles as *Starry Spangles* and *Jolly Jack-in-the-Box*, and his final series, *Flipper the Skipper*, which appeared in 1954 in the A.P. weekly, *Jack and Jill*. In his retirement, Bell drew single cartoons for his local newspaper, the *Barnet Press*, until his death in 1979 at the age of 86.

D.G.

BELLAMY, FRANK (1917-1976) Frank Bellamy, British cartoonist, was born in Kettering, Northamptonshire, in 1917. On leaving school in 1933, he became junior assistant in a local art studio. During his six-year stay there, he painted and designed display boards and cutouts for films showing at the Regal Cinema, Kettering. He was conscripted into the army in 1939, where he spent six months painting every known aircraft for an Aircraft Recognition Room. After the war he returned to the art studio, where he remained until 1948, when he went to London to look for work. Taken on by the first studio he showed his samples to (Norfolk Studio), he was soon designing advertisements for the *Daily Telegraph*. This led to freelance work through the International Artists agency, love story illustrations for *Home Notes* magazine and story illustrations for *Boy's Own Paper, Lilliput, Men Only*, etc.

Bellamy's first strip was *Commando Gibbs*, an advertisement for Gibbs Toothpaste; it was published in *Eagle*, a portent of things to come. *Mickey Mouse Weekly* gave him the chance to take over the adventure strip *Monty Carstairs*, created by R. MacGillivray, and his serial *Secret in the Sands* began on July 25, 1953. This led to his first full-color strip, a version of *The Living Desert*, to which he was required to add the signature "Walt Disney!" Now fully freelance, he drew for *Swift*, a weekly comic for younger readers: *Swiss Family Robinson* (1954), *King Arthur* (1955), *Robin Hood* (1955), all scripted by Clifford Makins, who later edited *Eagle*. Bellamy's first work on *Eagle* was a serial strip biography of *Winston Churchill* (1956), in which he pioneered his unique use of splash panels and contrasting color techniques, together with deep research, working from photographs, for example. The complete serial was reprinted in book form by Hulton Press, and Sir Winston was presented with a leatherbound copy. Then came *The Shepherd King* (1958), a Bible strip; *Marco Polo* (1959); and the ultimate *Eagle* accolade, *Dan Dare* (1960). After redesigning the Space Fleet uniforms, spaceships, etc., he abandoned the strip after a year for *Frazer of Africa* (1960), *Montgomery of Alamein* (1962), and the acme of his comic achievement, *Heros the Spartan* (1962-1966). This two-page center spread, painted in full color, took Bellamy five to six days a week to complete. It was scripted by Tom Tully. In 1967 Bellamy changed publishers to draw the strip version of the television series *Thunderbirds* for *TV Century 21*. His last comic page was published September 11, 1969, in the third issue of the combined comic, *T.V. 21 and Joe 90*.

He began to change directions toward newspapers in 1967 with an Edgar Allan Poe story as a strip for *Sunday Extra*, the comic section of *Sunday Citizen*. Later came illustrations in comics technique for *Sunday Times Magazine* and *Radio Times* (1970), the first time strips had appeared in such adult publications. This drew the interest of the *Daily Mirror*, and from December 7, 1971, Bellamy took over the daily fantasy strip *Garth*. A reprint of his strips, entitled *Daily Mirror Book of Garth*, was published in September 1974. He died on July 5, 1976.

Bellamy was considered by many to be the top British comics artist (Best Foreign Artist Award, American Academy of Comic Book Arts, 1972). His work was in the tradition of his early idols, Hal Foster and Burne Hogarth, and the line originated by Frank Hampson.

D.G.

BERG, DAVID (1920-   ) American comic book artist and writer, born June 12, 1920, in Brooklyn, New York. After studies at the Pratt Institute, the Art Students League, and Cooper Union—all in New York— Dave Berg broke into the comic book business as the writer and artist of Quality's *Death Patrol* strip; his first material on the adventure series appeared in the

Dave Berg, "Summer Resorts." © Mad magazine.

November 1941 issue of *Military Comics*. Besides his early Quality work (which also included work on *Uncle Sam*), Berg worked for many comic book producers during 1941 and 1942. For Ace Publications, he wrote and drew the Captain Courageous adventure character; at Fawcett, he worked briefly on *Captain Marvel, Sir Butch* and several others; at Fiction House he drew and wrote *Pvt. Pippin*; and at Western, he wrote and drew the *Jinx* feature.

Most of his comic book work during the 1940s and 1950s was done for the Timely/Marvel/Atlas group edited by Stan Lee. Between 1941 and 1958, Berg produced a wide range of stories for whatever type of books were then in vogue, whether horror or humor features. His most notable work came as a writer/artist/editor on Marvel's *Combat Kelly* war feature, which Berg handled sporadically between 1945 and 1957. During the 1950s, he also contributed to the Archie group (1951-1955), EC (1952), St. John (1953), and Ziff-Davis (1952).

But it was not until Dave Berg moved to *Mad* magazine in 1956 that his work was recognized. Under the direction of Al Feldstein, Berg started "The Lighter Side" series that eventually expanded from its two-page premiere to a five-page mainstay in the *Mad* lineup. The feature's premise was simple enough: Berg selected a common topic (like "love," "television," or "automobiles") and drew a series of gags about the ironies of American society in that context. Using a clean, straightforward, and realistic approach to drawing, Berg commented that he often sketched at cocktail parties and always carried a pad with him to capture the foibles of American life. Rather than being roughly satirical, however, "The Lighter Side" was more often slanted toward humorous observations and good-natured ribbing.

Over the years, Berg began utilizing set characters in his issue-by-issue vignettes. One of his favorites was his boss, publisher William M. Gaines, whom he drew as the rotund, bearded neo-hippie that he was. More often, however, Berg injected himself into the strip, meticulously rendering himself with ever-present pipe,

glasses, silver-grey hair, and sport jackets with patches at the elbow.

Berg's "The Lighter Side" feature became one of the most popular series in *Mad*, and the writer/artist has published seven paperbacks under the Mad imprint. They are under the general title of "Mad's Dave Berg Looks At . . ." and do essentially the same observatory work as his magazine series. He also had two paperbacks ostensibly about "God," entitled *My Friend God* and *Roger Kaputnik and God*. In 1996 he marked his 40th anniversary of working for *Mad*.

His wife, Vivian Lipman Berg, was a writer/artist/editor in comic books during the 1940s.

J.B.

BERGDAHL, GUSTAV VICTOR (1878-1939) Gustav Victor Bergdahl, Swedish illustrator, painter, and graphic artist, was born December 12, 1878, in Osteråker. He died in Stockholm on January 20, 1939. As a youth, Bergdahl worked as a seaman but, after an accident in 1899, gave up the sea to devote himself to a career in art. At first his main source of income was from editorial cartooning and newspaper illustration. Then, in 1915, Bergdahl conquered a new medium—animated cartoons. Bergdahl, a Swedish pioneer of animated cartoons, also transformed one of his cartoon characters, *Kapten Grogg* ("Captain Whiskey"), into a comic strip version between the World Wars.

Well known for his work in daily newspapers and humor weeklies, Bergdahl was so impressed by Winsor McCay's animated cartoons that he wanted to try his hand at it, too. With no one to teach him the art of animated cartooning, Bergdahl attempted to devise his own method. He tried selling motion picture producers on his ideas, without much luck. Finally, in 1915, he was able to go ahead on production of his first animated cartoon, *Trolldrycken* ("The Magic Brew"), which premiered in November 1915. The public and the critics liked the feature, so Bergdahl continued producing animated cartoons centering on circuses. Finally, he returned to his first love, the sea, with *Kapten Groggs underbara resa* ("Captain Whiskey's

Wonderful Voyage"). The adventures of Kapten Grogg were continued in a number of episodes that were also popular outside Sweden because they were well made and, most importantly, funny. Bergdahl continued producing animated cartoons until his death in 1939.

The success of Kapten Grogg's adventures led to their publication in book form in 1923 under the title *Kapten Grogg och Kalle* ("Captain Whiskey and Kalle"). In 1937 *Kapten Grogg* was included in the first comics magazine published in Sweden, *Musse Pigg-Tidningen* ("Mickey Mouse Newspaper"). Eight issues appeared in 1937, 15 in 1938. It is only thanks to Sweden's comic fandom that Bergdahl's pioneering work in animated cartoons and comic strips has been rediscovered.

W.F.

"Bernard Prince," Greg and Hermann. © Editions du Lombard.

BERNARD PRINCE (Belgium) *Bernard Prince* was created for the Belgian weekly magazine *Tintin* by Hermann (Hermann Huppen) as artist, and Greg (Michel Régnier) as writer, on February 17, 1966.

Bernard Prince is a former Interpol agent turned adventurer and soldier of fortune. Aboard his yacht *The Cormorant* and in company of his loyal crew—the hirsute and hard-drinking Barney Jordan and the teenaged Djinn—he has traveled to the wilds of Amazonia, the deserts of Central Asia and the "jungles" of Manhattan.

An adventure strip in the classic tradition, *Bernard Prince* has introduced its readers to some colorful villains: the sinister Kurt Bronzen, international agitator and criminal mastermind; the bloodthirsty captain of a band of assassins, General Satan; the mad dictator Mendoza; and other smaller fry that Prince and his companions would usually round up after a festival of gunfights, chases, and assorted mayhem. Hermann's drawings are bold and powerful, filled with restless energy, and excellently complementing the whirlwind proceedings of the strip.

Bernard Prince has been reprinted in book form by Editions du Lombard, and one of the early adventures

has been published in the American magazine *Wonderworld*.

After Hermann left the series in 1977, it was turned over to Dany (Daniel Henrotin), who managed to carry it to the end of the decade. It was revived in 1992, with Greg still writing the continuities and Edouard Aidans providing the artwork.

M.H.

BERNDT, WALTER (1899-1979) American cartoonist, born November 22, 1899, in Brooklyn, New York. At age 16 Walter Berndt, a high school dropout, took a job in the *New York Journal* art department as an office boy for the likes of famed cartoonists Herriman, Gross, McCay, Segar, and Sterrett. After closely studying their techniques and giving them an occasional hand when they had trouble meeting a deadline, Berndt had, within five years, risen to full-fledged cartoonist status. As early as 1915 he was doing sports cartoons and occasional fillers, and in 1916 he took over the gag panel *And then the Fun Began* from the overworked Milt Gross.

In 1920 Berndt left the *Journal* to create his own comic strip; entitled *That's Different*, it lasted only a little over one year. He then went to the *New York World* to create a feature based on his reminiscences, *Billy the Office Boy*. Fired for insubordination after a couple of weeks, he took the strip to Captain Patterson, who changed its name to *Smitty* and distributed it through the Chicago Tribune-New York News Syndicate in 1922. From then on Berndt's time was devoted to *Smitty* (and its companion strip *Herby*, which came along in 1930), which he drew and wrote until his retirement in 1973. He died in 1979.

Walter Berndt was not an outstanding cartoonist, but his work exhibits an infectious charm and an obvious love for the medium. As the artist stated: "Drawing was really never work for me," and his enthusiasm and dedication can be seen shining through his lifework of over 50 years.

M.H.

BERRILL, JACK (1923-1996) Jack Berrill was an American cartoonist born in Brooklyn, New York, in 1923. Following service in the air force during World War II, Berrill went to work for Eastern Color Printing Company on their comic book line, including *Famous Funnies*. After many of their titles were discontinued in the mid-1950s, Berrill became an assistant on Martin Branner's *Winnie Winkle*. The job proved to be a stepping stone to better things when he sold a comic strip of his own creation, *Gil Thorp*, to *Winnie Winkle*'s distributor, the Chicago Tribune-New York News Syndicate; the first release was dated September 8, 1958.

Gil Thorp was a clean-cut, earnest sports coach at fictional Milford High. In addition to his professional duties, he had to cope with problems ranging from rock-and-rolling and hot-rodding in the early years of the strip to teen pregnancy, drug abuse, and the AIDS epidemic in later episodes. Gil also had a series of mild romances with a string of nubile maidens, but those never amounted to much or contributed anything to the overall action of the strip.

Berrill drew *Gil Thorp* in a pleasant, unobtrusive style, and his plots were leisurely played out over weeks, or even months, in routine soap-opera fashion. He turned out the feature daily and Sunday for almost four decades, making it into one of the longest-running sports strips of all time until illness forced him to leave the drawing board late in 1994. Berrill died of cancer at his home in Brookfield, Connecticut, on March 14, 1996.

M.H.

BESS, GORDON (1929-1989) American cartoonist, born in 1929 in Richfield, Utah. Gordon Bess followed his parents from mining camp to mining camp throughout the West. After high school (where he had already displayed a talent for cartooning and caricature) he joined the Marine Corps, with which he spent 10 years, including one year in Korea. During his service with the Marines, Bess produced illustrations for the Corps Training Aid Section, and in 1954 he became staff cartoonist for *Leatherneck*, the Corps magazine.

In 1957 Gordon Bess left the service, married, and got a job as art director for a greeting card company in Cincinnati, with which he remained for over 10 years. At the same time he contributed cartoons to various magazines around the country. In 1967 he created *Redeye* for King Features Syndicate, a rollicking humor strip about a screwball tribe of comic-opera Indians. The success of the strip allowed him to return to the West, in this case to Boise, Idaho, where Bess devoted his spare time to hunting, fishing, and skiing. He died of cancer at his Idaho home in December 1989.

Gordon Bess belongs to the post-*Pogo* and *Peanuts* school of humor cartoonists. Unassuming, and even modest about his accomplishments, he nonetheless succeeded in maintaining the high tradition of American comic art.

M.H.

BESSY (Belgium, Germany) *Bessy*, created by Flemish writer/artist Willy Vandersteen in 1951 for publication in *La Libre Belgique* (Free Belgium), then picked up by *Belang van Limburg* and *Gazet van Antwerpen* before being published in album form, is today largely produced in comic book format for German audiences.

After having created a number of funnies, Vandersteen felt it was about time to enter into the field of realistic comic strips and did so with *Bessy*, a comic strip starring a collie dog much in the *Lassie* vein with the added interest of a Wild West setting. The success of the strip, especially in Germany, proves that Vandersteen did not miscalculate reader interest. Spreading out with an ever-increasing number of newspaper strips and comic books also led to the founding of the Studio Vandersteen in 1951 where gagmen, scriptwriters, and artists helped to create a line of diversified strips. Thus, the earliest *Bessy* strips were signed Wirel, a contraction of the names of artists Willy Vandersteen and Karel Verschuere. Later on, the artwork on *Bessy* was left completely to Verschuere, with other artists like Frank Sels filling in when the workload grew heavier.

In 1962 the stories of *Bessy* were exported to Germany, where they appeared as one of the features in *Felix*. Some of the stories were also published in giveaway customers' magazines. It was publication in *Felix*, however, that made *Bessy* a success in Germany. Broadcasts of the perennial *Lassie* on German television may have boosted reader enthusiasm, which finally resulted in a 32-page *Bessy* comic book that started publication in May 1965. It was published monthly for the first five issues only, then was stepped up to biweekly and, with number 58, turned weekly.

"Bessy," Willy Vandersteen. © Bulls Pressedienst.

Bastei Verlag, the publishers of the *Bessy* comic book in Germany, put the character in digest-sized comics as well. The feature was also dramatized for records. After spreading out into various forms of publication, the regular weekly comic book ended after 992 issues in 1985. The weekly format, by that time, had already downgraded the artwork, giving it a hurried, industrialized look. Sometimes the painted covers by German illustrator Klaus Dill were the only redeeming factor of the books.

Reprints of classic *Bessy* comics were issued by various publishers starting in 1989. Bastei Verlag, which shut down its comic production almost entirely in 1995, has picked up the feature once again for a new reprint series.

W.F.

BETTY (U.S.) *Betty* was the *New York Herald*'s entry into the girl-strip sweepstakes. Spurred on by the success of Hearst's *Polly and Her Pals*, in 1914 the *Herald*'s editors came up with their own idea about a working girl whom they named Betty. They turned the drawing of the Sunday page over to a young staff artist named Russell Westover. Westover (who was already doing the daily *Fat Chance*) does not seem to have taken on the added burden with much relish. When the *Herald* merged with the *Tribune* in 1918, he left the paper.

Betty was taken over by the noted illustrator Charles Voight, with whom it is most often associated. Voight remade the feature into a model of the new, crisp style of illustrated strip. Except for Betty's grotesque suitor Lester de Pester, all the characters were drawn straight, the girls being especially depicted with loving care. However much admired and imitated (the strip gave rise to a number of rivals, *Connie* and *Jane Arden* being the most notable), the feature was rather dull. It was more like a succession of well-turned-out vignettes

"Betty," Charles Voight. © New York Tribune.

"Betty Boop," Max Fleischer. © King Features Syndicate.

than a full-blooded comic strip. The readers must have felt the same way, for *Betty* never reached any heights of popularity, and finally folded in June 1943.

M.H.

BETTY BOOP (U.S.) Betty Boop, the earliest representation of the "French doll" figure in animated films, made her first appearance in the 1931 Max Fleischer cartoon short "Betty Co-Ed." It was a fair success and Fleischer decided to initiate a series of Betty Boop cartoons. Betty's falsely angelic face was modeled after that of the famous singer Helen Kane (who sued the Fleischer studios to no avail) and her figure patterned after that of Mae West (who had sense enough not to sue). Betty's success continued to grow, and a catchy title tune added to her popularity.

In 1935 King Features decided to distribute *Betty Boop* as a Sunday feature: drawn by Bud Counihan, it was given only second-class status and in New York ran in the *Mirror* (a sure-fire indication that the strip occupied a very low position in the Hearst pecking order). The feature was not without merit, nonetheless, although King toned down its more blatant sex suggestions (on the screen Betty was nothing if not a flirt, throwing kisses and hearts at the audience, and demurely batting her long eyelashes).

In the strip Betty worked in the movies, and there were some good satirical takeoffs on Hollywood. Around 1937, however, the spotlight shifted to Betty's overwhelming Aunt Tillie and her midget lover Hunky Dory. The charm of the screen original never really worked in the strip version, and when attacks from the bluenoses began to mount against the Betty Boop animated cartoons, King—always one to play it safe—quietly dropped the feature (1938). The animated films went on for a while longer, until Max Fleischer too decided to throw in the towel with one last cartoon defiantly titled "Yip, Yip, Yippy" (1939).

Three decades later, Betty Boop's underground fame grew, with revivals of her cartoons playing to packed houses in Europe and the United States; and a collection of *Betty Boop* comic strips was published in paperback form by Avon in 1975.

Betty's enduring popularity prompted King Features to resurrect the character in the comic pages. Under the title *Betty Boop and Felix*, the animated screen vamp costarred with the little black feline in a newspaper strip that made its debut in November 1984 and was turned out by four of Mort Walker's sons. The new feature failed to catch fire, however, and Felix made his exit in 1987. The strip, now rechristened *Betty Boop and Friends*, lasted only through January 1988.

M.H.

BEVÈRE, MAURICE DE (1923-   ) Belgian cartoonist, born December 1, 1923, in Courtrai. At 20 Maurice de Bevère was already working as an artist in an animation studio specializing in short features and screen commercials. In 1945, with the studio floundering, de Bevère joined the Belgian magazine *Le Moustique,* for which he contributed over 300 cover illustrations. In 1946, under the pen name "Morris," he created *Lucky Luke*, a humorous Western strip that started appearing as a regular feature in the comic weekly *Spirou* the following year.

In 1948, in order to perfect his knowledge of the American West, de Bevère left for the United States. During his six-year stay (in the course of which he continued to draw *Lucky Luke* for *Spirou*) he met American cartoonists such as Harvey Kurtzman and Jack Davis. In New York he met René Goscinny, with whom he was to start a long collaboration.

De Bevère returned to Belgium in 1954, with Goscinny as his scriptwriter on *Lucky Luke*. In 1968 he left *Spirou* for the French weekly *Pilote* (of which Goscinny was then editor), a decision that proved unfortunate. In 1971 de Bevère, in collaboration with Goscinny and Pierre Tchernia, produced a feature-length animated cartoon of *Lucky Luke* for Belvision. After Goscinny's death in 1977, he continued to turn out the strip with the help of a number of writers and assistants. In 1987 he started *Ran-Tan-Plan*, a *Lucky Luke* spin-off, and in 1990 he established his own publishing company, Lucky Productions.

Maurice de Bevère has received a number of European awards and distinctions for his work on *Lucky*

Luke. His graphic style, flowing and clean, parodic without being caricatural, has been widely imitated by scores of aspiring cartoonists in Europe and elsewhere. In 1993 a vast retrospective of his work was mounted by the Comic Strip Museum in Angouleme, France.

M.H.

BIB AND BUB (Australia) Created by author-cartoonist May Gibbs for the *Sydney Sun News* in 1925, the strip was adapted from her own book, *Gumnut Babies*, which was first published in 1916. The strip appeared as a weekly and adopted the European comic strip format of no speech balloons and placing the text below each panel. For many years, the doggerel verse text was hand-lettered by Gibbs, but in time this gave way to typesetting.

Bib and Bub has a unique place in the history of Australian comic strips, as it was the most successful of any strip (local or imported) aimed at very juvenile readers. Despite its unprecedented long run and undoubted popularity, the strip was not an honest translation of the delightful, fairytale world of Gibbs' books. In her books, Gibbs was able to express her many-sided originality with her loving treatment of the bush creatures and to contribute her messages of kindliness.

At her bidding, the gumnut babies, wattle blossom elves and creatures of the bush, came tripping forward to assist Bib and Bub play out their fantasy adventures. The kookaburra, wattle sprite, beetle, Christmas-bell baby, and butterfly gambolled in an atmosphere of gum leaves, golden sunshine, and gossamer. Like all good children's fantasies, the stories followed a simple plot that contained elements of danger or apprehension.

As a comic strip, *Bib and Bub* did not contain the unique quality of the books. Each strip was complete in itself, and the restrictions imposed by panel limitations did not allow Gibbs to develop characters and plots and weave the same patterns of fantasy as she had done in her books. May Gibbs tried to counter this by giving the comic strip a separate identity. Bib and Bub took up residence in Gumnut Town, where they lived with Mr. & Mrs. Wuzzy Bear. More often than not, Bib and Bub were relegated to the roles of spear-carriers as they observed the antics of Bill Bandicoot, Dad and Mum Platypus, Mrs. Roo, Lizzie Lizard, and other birds, animals, and reptiles that inhabited the town. While this formula proved successful, the downgrading of the contribution of Bib and Bub, the transfer of the locale to a pseudo-village, and the almost total elimination of danger robbed the strip of the opportunity of duplicating the charm and appeal of Gibbs' books. The comic strip also introduced anomalies in the form of elephants, giraffes, monkeys, llamas, and other animals not indigenous to the Australian bush—but their presence helped, rather than hindered, the strip.

While many strips were reprinted in their latter years, *Bib and Bub* was the longest-running strip by one artist to appear in Australia. The strip survived mergers with the *Guardian* (1929), the *Sunday Sun* (1931), and the *Sunday Herald* (1953), and the last strip appeared in the *Sunday Sun-Herald* in September 1967.

J.R.

BIBI FRICOTIN (France) Louis Forton created *Bibi Fricotin* in October 1924 for the French comic weekly *Le*

"Bibi Fricotin," Louis Forton. © SPE.

Petit Illustré. Partly autobiographical, *Bibi Fricotin* chronicles the bittersweet adventures of a lonely young boy who learns how to survive in a cruel world the hard way. Bibi is an orphan and at first something of a juvenile delinquent. But Forton later changed him into a world-wise youngster, smart-alecky and resourceful, with a quick wit and a golden heart, the very epitome of the Parisian *gavroche*. His most famous adventure involves a round-the-world odyssey in which he manages to come out ahead of friend and foe alike.

Following Forton's death in 1934, *Bibi Fricotin* passed into the hands of Callaud. After a wartime interruption from 1940 to 1948, the strip was revived by Pierre Lacroix, who drew it in a style reminiscent of Forton's until 1988, when the series came to an end. The hero's character had changed by then, however: Bibi had become less rebellious, more conventional—a typical good boy, closer to Hergé's Tintin than to Forton's original conception of the character.

Less original than Forton's more famous series *Les Pieds-Nickelés*, *Bibi Fricotin* nonetheless occupies a respected position among European strips. It has been reprinted in book form and was made into a movie in 1950.

M.H.

BIG BEN BOLT (U.S.) *Big Ben Bolt* was created for King Features Syndicate in 1949 by Elliot Caplin, no doubt in response to the success of the premier boxing strip, *Joe Palooka*. Caplin sought the services of illustrator John Cullen Murphy, who had done fine boxing sketches for *Collier's* magazine. The samples were accepted (*Big Ben Bolt* was the second-to-last strip bought by William Randolph Hearst himself) and was first released to newspapers in February of 1950.

The strip concerns Bolt, heavyweight champion of the world (although the title has been won from him several times) and his adventures, most of them out of

"Big Ben Bolt," John Cullen Murphy. © King Features Syndicate.

the boxing world. He lives with his kindly aunt and uncle on Beacon Street in Boston. The other continuing character is Bolt's manager, Spider Haines; the rest of the cast (including a string of non-steady girlfriends) changes with each episode of mystery, murder, romance, and adventure revolving around the rough but kind fighter.

Murphy's art was tense, cinematic, and highly illustrative, surviving the crippling onslaught of newsprint shortages and strip reductions. The strip was voted "Best Story Strip" by the NCS for 1971.

R.M.

After 1971 Murphy spent less and less time on *Ben Bolt* to devote himself to *Prince Valiant*. In 1975 the Sundays were discontinued, while a succession of artists worked on the daily strip, including Al Williamson, Angelo Torres, and Gray Morrow. Neal Adams brought the feature to an end, with the hero shot down by an assassin in April 1978.

M.H.

BIG BOY (U.S.) So popular was the medium of comic books in the 1940s and 1950s that a multitude of these publications were printed to be given away free in the furtherance of a variety of political, religious, or educational causes. A majority of these giveaways, however, served to publicize commercial enterprises, and in this field none was as active as the Big Boy family-restaurant chain.

To advertise their double-decker hamburger, the Big Boy (a precursor of the Big Mac), the restaurant chain brought out their corporate mascot, a burly 10-year-old in checked overalls, and featured him as the hero of a monthly comic book that started its run in 1956. *Adventures of Big Boy* (later *Adventures of the Big Boy*) was the brainchild of Manfred Bernhard, who approached Stan Lee of Timely Publications with the offer to write the first year's worth of stories, which were then illustrated by such artists as Bill Everett and Dan De Carlo. Compared to the superhero fare Timely (the predecessor of today's Marvel Comics) was turning out at the time, Big Boy's adventures were rather tame. Big Boy, his girlfriend Dolly, and his dog Nugget would go exploring a cave in the surrounding countryside in search of treasure, or Big Boy would straighten out the school bully, even foil a robbery attempt. Each five-to-

seven-page story ended with a moral homily, often mouthed by Big Boy's Grandpa.

After the first year, Bernhard took charge of the production, employing a variety of artists and writers, often well-known names, sometimes using rank amateurs or pulling former artists out of retirement. Given away free at each of the chain's restaurants, the *Big Boy* comic book, usually 16 pages thick and consisting of puzzles and games in addition to the stories, was meant to entertain the children. It enjoyed an astounding run of 40 years. Its farewell with issue number 466 in August 1996 (it was replaced by a series of activity books) not only signaled the end of a era but also confirmed the sad fact that comic books were no longer a surefire attraction, not even for children. The activity books came out in 1997, and they contain comic stories done by Craig Yoe.

M.H.

BILAL, ENKI (1951-   ) A French cartoonist, illustrator, and filmmaker born in Belgrade, Yugoslavia, on October 7, 1951, Enki Bilal moved to France with his parents when he was 10 years old. After studying at the Paris School of Fine Arts, he started his career in 1972 with several short stories that were published in the weekly comics magazine *Pilote*. Beginning in 1975 with *La Croisière des Oubliés* ("The Cruise of the Forgotten"), he illustrated the cycle "Today's Legends," which had been initiated by scriptwriter Pierre Christin. This uncertain attempt at a longer story was followed by increasingly more skillful artwork in each succeeding narrative: *Le Vaisseau de Pierre* ("The Ship of Stone," 1976); *La Ville qui n'Existait Pas* ("The Town That Didn't Exist," 1977), which American publishers called "a docufantasy about a small town saved from disaster and pushed into utopia"; and the 1979 *Les Phalanges de l'Ordre Noir* ("The Ranks of the Black Order"), the authors' first openly political tale. Bilal's most impressive achievement of the decade, however, had come in 1978 with *Exterminateur 17*. With a script by *Métal Hurlant* editor Jean-Pierre Dionnet, this innovative graphic novel successfully mixed elements of science fiction and theological musings in almost equal measure.

In 1980 Bilal released his first solo comic, *La Foire aux Immortels* (released as "Gods in Chaos" in America), a disturbing story set in a dystopian Paris of the near future. It was well received by the public and critics alike, but was eclipsed several years later by *Partie de Chasse* ("The Hunting Party"), with a script written by Christin. The authors' second foray into political allegory, this "historical fantasy," as Bilal termed it, related the chilling schemes of Soviet bloc oligarchs hunting for wild game and for one another. Bilal followed this with two solo sequels to *La Foire*, *La Femme-Piège* ("The Woman Trap," 1986) and *Froid Equateur* ("Cold Equator," 1992). From the 1980s on, the artist devoted an increasing amount of his time to other media, notably cinema, designing the sets of Alain Resnais's 1982 film *Life Is a Novel*, and even directing his own feature film, *Bunker Palace Hotel*, in 1989. He directed a second movie, *Tykko Moon*, which came out in 1997.

Bilal has been the recipient of many honors and awards, not only in his adopted country, but in many other parts of the world. In the United States, *Publishers Weekly* called him "one of the great comics artists working today"; and in 1997 the San Francisco Cartoon Art Museum organized a 25-year retrospective of his work.

M.H.

BILBOLBUL (Italy) Bilbolbul, created by Attilio Mussino, was the first Italian character to appear in the pages of the *Corriere dei Piccoli*, the weekly supplement of the daily newspaper *Corriere della Sera*. This took place in the very first issue (December 27, 1908) of the supplement. Bilbolbul was also the character most popular with the young readers and he accordingly appeared with a greater frequency than any other of the *Corriere's* creations (this was a time when a number of features would rotate instead of a few of them appearing weekly).

True to tradition and stereotype, Bilbolbul was a half-naked, mean little black savage who, at the end of each episode, would meet his well-deserved punishment. In the illustrations (accompanied by verse captions in the tradition of the *Corriere dei Piccoli*) there was a mixture of paradoxical and metaphoric happenings finely drawn by Mussino's clever brush strokes. The poor child underwent punishments so realistic that they became frightful, while Mussino built his metaphors to the point where they turned into paradoxes. Bilbolbul actually became "green with rage," his eyes really "burned with fire," his tongue would truly "hang out," and so on.

Bilbolbul's transformations no doubt fascinated the children, but they also frightened them. In a conservative country such as Italy was at the beginning of the century, such a novelty could not be tolerated for long. In spite of *Bilbolbul's* success, Mussino was advised by his editors in 1912 to turn his talents to more sedate creations—one of which was to be an imitation of *Little Nemo*—but those were all short-lived. (Besides the moral reasons for *Bilbolbul's* cancellation, there was also a political one: the recent annexation by Italy of Cyrenaica and Tripoli made the environment of the strip look out of place.)

Bilbolbul made a few fleeting appearances after World War I, still in the pages of the *Corriere dei Piccoli*, but only in recent years has its status as a pioneering comic strip been recognized in Italy and abroad.

G.B.

BILLY BIS (Italy) The word *playstory* usually means a series of interrelated adventures with several protagonists. The concept was thought up by scriptwriter Antonio Mancuso for Universo's two comic weeklies, *L'Intrepido* and *Il Monello*. These stories mix a touch of romance with a heavy dose of crime and suspense, and always end up in a clinch.

One of these stories, *Billy Bis*, was conceived by Mancuso in 1966 and drawn by Loredano Ugolini. Billy Bis is an eccentric U.N. secret agent who sports long hair and casual attire. He usually drives an Isotta Fraschini, and his adventures take place in a typically American environment, from the beaches of Florida to the skyscrapers of Manhattan. In the background lurk America's social problems: racial strife, the consumer revolt, political infighting, the clash between old ideals and pressing social needs.

Billy Bis is officially engaged to the beautiful Dorothy Matson, but he is not always faithful to her; contrary to tradition in this kind of story, Dorothy does not just sit up waiting for him, but has her own adventures in which she is the heroine.

The feature has been warmly received by its readers because it presents all types of crime stories and offers gripping suspense, with a few glimpses at social life and frequent romantic interludes, spiced with a bit of sex and violence.

The success of *Billy Bis* as a magazine feature prompted the publishers to issue a monthly comic book called *Billy Bis Super*; at first a reprint of old stories, the comic book later contained only original material drawn by Ugolini, with the frequent help of Ferdinando Corbella. It ended in the 1980s.

G.B.

"Billy Bunter," Frank Minnitt. © Knockout Comic.

BILLY BUNTER (G.B.) This strip is the classic example of survival by transference from the printed word to the picture story. William George Bunter, Billy to his pals, the "Famous Five" of the Remove Form of Greyfriars School, was created by Frank Richards (real name: Charles Hamilton), prolific author of school stories, in the first issue of *The Magnet Library*, dated February 15, 1908. Billy, known as "the Owl of the Remove," was by no means the first "Fat Boy" in British school stories, but he is certainly the most famous and, thanks to comics, the longest-lived. His talents (greed, petty larceny, lying, and cheating) have remained unchanged for almost 70 years.

The first *Magnet* illustrator to depict Bunter was Hutton Mitchell, and the last was C. H. Chapman, and it was Chapman who first tried his hand at a Bunter strip, a half-page, six-panel item in *Magnet*. This was a trial balloon for a full two-page picture story by Chapman, which ran from the first issue of *The Knock-Out Comic* (March 4, 1939). This weekly duly absorbed *Magnet* from May 25, 1940. Chapman did not stay long as illustrator, however; perhaps his style proved too detailed for slicker comic strip work. *Billy Bunter* was soon taken over by Frank Minnitt, not tremendously talented as an anatomist but the possessor of an old, rounded style suited to his subject. Minnitt continued the Frank Richards characters of teacher Mr. Quelch and gatekeeper Gosling, but added a supporting stooge of his own, the diminutive, studious Jones Minor (1942). The strip remained at two pages for some years, but expanded to 24 panels in the space of the original 12. In 1950 the strip was printed in two colors (red/black) instead of one, and soon another idea was tried: a serial strip, *Nobody Wants Billy Bunter*.

After the death of Minnitt, other artists were tried, including Reg Parlett, Arthur Martin, and Les Barton. The best was A. T. Pease, under whose slapstick style *Billy* expanded to fill a five-page weekly strip, including the full-color cover and the actual title of the comic: *Billy Bunter's Knockout* (June 10, 1961). When his comic was discontinued, Bunter lived on, transferring to *Valiant* (February 23, 1963), where he outlived artist Pease. Both he and the strip, however, did end in the late 1970s.

D.G.

BILLY PACK (Japan) *Billy Pack* was created by Mitsuhiro Kawashima and made its first appearance in the October 1954 issue of the Japanese monthly *Shōnen Gahō*. Billy Pack is a private detective, the son of an American, Professor William Pack, and his Japanese wife Tokiko. Professor Pack was arrested on the charge of spying by Japanese policemen, at the start of the Pacific War. He was shot to death along with his wife, who had tried to protect him.

After the war, Billy was adopted by his paternal uncle in the U.S. but could not dispel the memories of his native Japan and the image of his mother; and after completing a detective-school course he went back to his native country.

Billy Pack started his career as a private eye in Tokyo. Always wearing a striped hunting cap and a double-breasted coat, the tall and handsome Billy and his friendly rival, Chief Investigator Onihara Sōsa Kachō, make up a dynamic pair, responsible for the apprehension of an endless number of malefactors. The detection scenes alternate with episodes of violent action in a constantly inventive story line.

After Kawashima's untimely death at the age of 30 on March 19, 1961, the strip was taken over by his former assistant Riichi Yajima. *Billy Pack* has been adapted to radio, and later, to television. The TV dramas were introduced in the United States by CBS without success. *Billy Pack* made its last appearance in the June 1962 issue of *Shōnen Gahō*.

H.K.

BINDER, JACK (1902-198?) American comic book artist, born in Austria-Hungary on August 11, 1902. Binder immigrated to the United States in 1910. He attended fine art courses at the Chicago Art Institute and later studied under the renowned illustrator of the Edgar Rice Burroughs novels, J. Allen St. John. After stints as a commercial artist, pulp illustrator, and animator, he joined the Harry "A" Chesler comic shop in 1937 as the group's art director. In 1940, he left the Chesler studio and formed his own shop, producing thousands of pages of comic book art for companies like Fawcett, Pines, Street and Smith, New Friday, and Marvel. After three years of high-paced work, most notably on the secondary line of Fawcett characters, Binder closed his shop and became the sales manager for C. C. Beck's studio—the company that produced the bulk of Fawcett comics. He resigned in 1946 to continue his personal art career.

Jack Binder's own talents as a draftsman and storyteller were just average. Although his work was always slick and clean, his material lacked the stylized excite-

ment of a Jack Kirby or the sharp realism of a Lou Fine. And even though his material was well drawn and technically flawless, he never utilized the cinematic techniques that Will Eisner did. His stories were usually composed of standard medium-range shots and static poses that lacked significant drama or impact.

In earlier years, Binder had drawn several minor superhero and adventure strips for MLJ (*Press Guardian, Scott Rand*) and Marvel (*Destroyer, Flexo*), but while he ran his own shop and worked for Beck's, he rarely had much drawing time. His most notable work in that period were two Fawcett features, *Mr. Scarlett* and *Mary Marvel*. Producing the former in *Wow* from 1941 through 1947, Binder drew the red-clad Batman imitation in a clean, refreshing style, and, though the strip lacked a novel gimmick or particularly innovative story line, Binder managed to keep the feature readable. With *Mary Marvel*, however, which he drew from 1943 to 1950, he had the advantage of well-written scripts and the natural Marvel Family appeal. The strip carried Binder's best artwork, and while not as classically simple as C. C. Beck's *Captain Marvel* or as flamboyantly beautiful as Mac Raboy's *Captain Marvel Jr.*, Binder's drawings were finely done and well conceived.

Jack Binder, whose brother Otto was a famous comic book writer, retired from the comic book industry in 1953 and returned to commercial art. He will be remembered more for his organizational skills than his artwork. His shops pioneered the technique of breaking down comic pages into eight areas, each of which could be handled piece-by-piece by a specialist. And during the hectic, high-pressured "Golden Age" of the 1940s, that achievement was a key innovation in the still embryonic comics industry. He reportedly died at the end of the 1980s.

J.B.

BINDER, OTTO O. (1911-1974) American comic book writer and brother of Jack Binder, born August 26, 1911, in Bessemer, Michigan. Between the years 1932 and 1942, Binder spent the bulk of his time writing short stories, books, articles, and pulp novels in collaboration with his brother Earl under the pen name "Eando" Binder. He began his comic book career in 1939 as a writer for the Harry "A" Chesler shop, and later began writing for his brother Jack's shop in 1941; there he came in contact with Fawcett's Marvel Family of comic books.

Binder was a workhorse—and he showed this best as the main scripter for *Captain Marvel Adventures* and other books. Historian/artist James Steranko once estimated that he "wrote a staggering fifty-seven per cent of the entire Marvel saga." And while producing fast-paced, enjoyable stories for the Captain occupied the bulk of his time—he wrote 451 of the possible 618 stories, according to Steranko—he also helped create some of the other Marvel features, including *Mary Marvel, Marvel Family*, and the *Jon Jarl* text feature. In addition, he created many of the superb Marvel Family supporting cast: Tawky Tawny, a phenomenally popular talking tiger; Mr. Mind, the evil worm who almost defeated Captain Marvel many times; and The Sivana Family, arch-enemies of the Marvel Family. And this is not to mention his scripts for other already-established Marvel characters like *Captain Marvel Jr.* and *Hoppy, The Marvel Bunny*.

In a comic book career that spanned 32 years, Binder wrote stories for 18 major comic book publishers and well over 200 features, among them *Blackhawk* (1942, 1943), *Captain America* (1941-1946), *Superman* (1953-1969), *Spy Smasher, Bulletman,* and *Hawkman*. He also created dozens of other characters, including The Young Allies (Timely), Uncle Sam (Quality), and Captain Battle (New Friday). Binder also showed tremendous flexibility, writing all types of stories, from science fiction and horror tales for E.C.'s "New Trend," to humor stories for *Campy Chimp* and Fatman, to straight superhero material for *Dollman, Steel Sterling, Spy Smasher,* and *Captain Midnight*, to spin-offs of established features. "Comics," he once said, "were like a drug," and he did not retire from active comic book writing until 1969.

Binder's career as a writer also had great success outside the comic book industry. After he dropped the pen name "Eando"—"E" for his brother/collaborator Earl, and "O" for Otto—he began writing material under his own name. Binder has dozens of science-fiction novels to his credit, was an editor of *Space World* magazine, and wrote for the National Aeronautics and Space Administration among dozens of other writing projects.

Binder died on October 13, 1974.

J.B.

BINET, CHRISTIAN (1947-   ) French cartoonist, born in Tulle in central France on March 27, 1947. Christian Binet showed an early disposition for cartooning, selling his first drawings to *Humour Magazine* at age 14, before going on to art school in Paris. Prior to and after military service, he embarked on a career as a magazine cartoonist, working for such national publications as *Top, France-Dimanche,* and *Plexus*.

Binet made his first foray into comic strips in 1969 with a number of humorous creations, notably the children's strip *Poupon la Peste* ("Poupon the Pest," 1975), followed by *Kador* in 1977. Kador was a thinking dog, capable of reading Kant's treatises in the original German, whose intellectual brilliance, however, proved no match for Poupon's terrible pranks.

These early cartoons were to lead directly to Binet's most famous comic feature, *Les Bidochon*. The Bidochon couple, Robert and Raymonde, were initially Kador's masters but soon graduated to a series of their own. As obtuse as their pet is bright, they find themselves confronted by the myriad frustrations and vexations of a society with which they can barely cope. They are badgered by bureaucrats, harassed by their neighbors, snubbed by their relations, and gypped by their local shopkeepers. So popular did the couple become that their misadventures were brought to the stage in 1990 and made into a movie in 1995.

Throughout the years, Binet has widened his targets to include the Roman Catholic hierarchy (*L'Institution*, 1981) and the political establishment (*M. le Ministre*, 1989), but *Les Bidochon* remains his undisputed masterpiece.

M.H.

BIRO, CHARLES (1911-1972) American comic book writer, artist, and editor, born in New York in 1911. After studies at the Brooklyn Museum School of Art and the Grand Central School of Art, Biro became the writing and artwork supervisor of the Harry "A" Chesler Shop in 1936, a post he held until 1939. That year he moved over to a similar job at MLJ Comics, drew and wrote some stories, and even created the *Steel Sterling* strip.

But not until he joined the Lev Gleason (also known as Comic House) group in 1941 did his real talent become known. If Jack Kirby was the most important artistic force in comics during the 1940s, Biro certainly proved to be the finest editor and writer. While others were providing escapist fantasy in their comic books, Charles Biro decided his books would be different and better. He even dubbed them "Illustories," but the name never caught on. Throughout his 16-year stint as editorial director and chief writer at Lev Gleason, Biro proved to be the most innovative and certainly most advanced writer in the comic book field.

Christian Binet, "Les Bidochon." © Christian Binet.

His most miraculous job was possibly on the *Daredevil* feature, Gleason's top seller and a fine superhero concept in its own right; it was created in 1940 by Don Rico and Jack Binder. Biro assumed immediate control over the strip and wrote, drew, and edited for the book throughout the strip's life. In 1942, he introduced the Little Wise Guys, four youngsters who started as Daredevil's sidekicks. His third Little Wise Guys strip became a classic as he killed off Meatball in a gentle and heroic story rarely matched since. The strip took a similarly surprising turn in 1950 when Biro simply wrote Daredevil out of the strip—his own strip in his own book—and allowed the Little Wise Guys to carry the feature.

In 1942, Biro and coeditor Bob Wood created Chuck Chandler in the *Crimebuster* strip. Appearing in *Boy Comics*, Crimebuster was just that, a boy. A hero, yes, but first a boy who had a delightful monkey side-kick named Squeeks. The strip remains arguably the best-handled boy's adventure feature ever to appear in comics.

Biro's third innovation in 1942 was changing the superhero-oriented *Silver Streak* comic into *Crime Does Not Pay*. Usually regarded as the comic book industry's first crime title, it brought on an almost mind-boggling number of imitators, all of them vastly inferior. Throughout its run, *Crime Does Not Pay* was always the best-written, best-illustrated, and best-edited crime title, and it was always the best-selling title, as well. And although its imitators were gory and excessive, and eventually brought on a ruinous round of censorship of comics, the stellar title was the last book to succumb.

Perhaps the best indicator of the obvious popularity of Biro's material was the fact that for several years during the late 1940s and early 1950s, *Boy, Daredevil,* and *Crime Does Not Pay* were the three best-selling titles in a comic field of over 400 competitors.

Biro also had other highlights in his comic book career: his marketing of the first adult comic book, *Tops*, a 1949 experiment in full color and standard magazine size; his *Poppo of the Popcorn Theatre*, an outstanding but virtually ignored humor book of the 1950s; and his creation of Hillman's *Airboy*.

The artist/writer/editor left the field for television in 1962. He died on March 4, 1972.

J.B.

BLACK CAT (U.S.) When the superhero craze seized the comic book industry in the early 1940s, it was only natural that the publishers experimented with all types of formats. Men dominated the scene, but women eventually appeared, and the Black Cat was one of the longest-lasting women heroes. Created in August 1941 for Harvey's *Pocket Comics* number one, the Black Cat was really movie actress Linda Turner; she had no superheroic powers, but did have an intricate knowledge of karate.

Text-wise, *Black Cat* was never particularly appealing. Apart from riding her motorcycle, the character was shown fighting and capturing criminals while giving detailed karate lessons on the side. *Black Cat* was primarily a visual feature. Creator Al Gabriele gave the movie actress a tight, skimpy costume and illustrated her adventures until the end of 1941. Art Cazeneuve (1942) and Alex Schomburg (1944) also handled the strip before Joe Kubert took over in 1945 and 1946. Kubert jazzed up the red-haired Black Cat and exaggerated the anatomy. But the strip reached its artistic "height" when Lee Elias handled it between 1946 and 1951. He meticulously drew the Black Cat as a beautiful, sexy creature, someone sure to attract the young and mostly male comic book audience. It was this aspect that kept the strip in print for 11 years.

The strip also gained some notoriety when Dr. Frederic Wertham attacked it in his 1953 *Seduction of the Innocent*. He was particularly disturbed by what he claimed were zealous efforts to emphasize the karate aspects of the strip. He said that the lessons, which were dispensed at every opportunity, could cause children to hurt each other. Twenty years later, Juanita Coulson noted in *The Comic-Book Book* (Arlington House, 1974) that, "In these days of militant Women's Lib groups chanting, 'Rape is not a party—learn karate,' *Black Cat* would seem a bit tame. She never taught the reader how to *really* cream a male assailant."

In all, *Black Cat* appeared in four issues of *Pocket* (through January 1942), in *Speed* 17 through 38 and 44 (April 1942 to January 1947), and in 29 issues of *Black Cat* (June 1946 to June 1951).

J.B.

BLACK CONDOR, THE (U.S.) Some comic book features deserve mention in any history of the comic medium solely on the strength of their artwork. *The Black Condor*, graced with the superb artwork of Lou Fine, was just such a strip.

Writing under the pen name of Kenneth Lewis, Fine introduced the strip in Quality's *Crack Comics* number 1 (May 1940). But throughout the feature's 31-issue run (ending with the October 1943 issue of *Crack*), the story line was mediocre. It told the story of an infant named Richard whose parents were killed by raiders. He was raised by a flock of black condors and eventually simulated their power of flight. Meeting an old, hermetic missionary, who was also later killed by raiders, the grown Richard decided to use his aerial abilities to aid mankind. He adopted the identity of the Black Condor and wore a black costume that incorporated a pair of glider-like wings, which stretched from the wristband to the torso.

Eleven issues into the series, the Black Condor adopted the guise of Senator Tom Wright, a murdered legislator who looked remarkably like him. He also inherited the late senator's fiancée, Wendy, but his impersonation was known only to Wendy's father, Dr. Foster. Fighting an assortment of run-of-the-mill villains and lackluster adversaries was Richard's fate both in his Black Condor role and in his political duties.

But Fine's artwork was never deterred by the inconsequential stories. Although early issues were rather tame as Fine used a straightforward style with 12 panels per page and then 9, as the series progressed, Fine's work developed. He began to use *The Black Condor* as a showcase for his anatomic genius and a variety of shading and stippling techniques.

The work excelled when Fine began drawing expansive flying scenes. The Black Condor in flight often took up a half-page by himself, and the best issues were replete with panel after panel of aerial shots shown close up and in great detail. Besides Fine's amazing photographic accuracy, his artwork had a quality of weightlessness and ease of execution that made the flight scenes workable. The Black Condor was always swooping and diving and maneuvering in uncanny poses never seen before or since in the comic book medium.

When Fine abandoned the strip in 1942, a less talented group of illustrators, including Rudy Palais, Charles Sultan, and Gil Fox, could not match the technical excellence of Fine's work.

J.B.

BLACKHAWK (U.S.) *Blackhawk* was created for the first issue of Quality's *Military Comics* in August 1941, and while no one can claim exclusive credit for the feature's creation, Chuck Cuidera was the strip's prime mover and first artist. *Blackhawk* was different from the standard superhero fare of the early 1940s. While the majority of strips were steeped in fantasy and utilized outlandishly costumed supermen, *Blackhawk* was conceived for the World War II era, complete with grim, mercenary characters. In fact, the only differentiation between the methods used by the *Blackhawk* team and their Fascist enemies was that they were fighting for good and not against it. In its early years, *Blackhawk* was a violent strip with a heavy emphasis on military escapades, soldier-of-fortune ethics, and a vigilante-like method of dealing out justice. Blackhawk was one of the few comic book characters to carry a pistol.

The feature and its characters went through many changes in the early issues of *Military*, but seven men eventually became *Blackhawk* regulars: Hendrickson, a stereotyped anti-Nazi German and weapons expert; Chuck, a young American communications specialist; André, a French ladies' man and Blackhawk's second-in-command; Olaf, a Swedish gymnast; Stanislaus, a physically massive Pole driven from his homeland after the 1939 German invasion; and Blackhawk himself, a grim, expatriate American who was the leader. For comic relief, there was Chop-Chop, a roly-poly pony-tailed Chinaman who wielded a meat cleaver and screamed, "Yippee! Me make hamburger." Flying scenes and realistic scripts were the most important factors in the early strip, and the group was usually depicted as ready to jump into their planes and fly into battle at any moment.

"Blackhawk," Reed Crandall. © Comic Magazines, Inc.

Blackhawk's greatest years were from 1941 to 1953. Designed for that time period, the stories didn't require much "willing suspension of disbelief." These were grim, violent tales of war and death. There could never be a Superman—everyone knew that—but there could have been a Blackhawk, an Andre, or a Chuck. And for many years, most notably while artist Reed Crandall and writer Bill Woolfolk were in control, the strip relied heavily on realism. Crandall's fine line and Woolfolk's fast-paced scripts made *Blackhawk* one of the best-known features ever produced. The Blackhawks outlasted most of their "Golden Age" compatriots and, unfortunately, it was their longevity that eventually destroyed them.

At the end of the Korean War, the team had no one left to fight. Created to fight wars that had already been won, they were forced to surpress revolutions in two-bit banana republics and combat the "Red Menace." Their fatalistic, men-of-their-time image began to fade. As the 1950s progressed and Quality sold the feature to National Periodicals, *Blackhawk* became littered with outlandish gimmicks, super-duper aircrafts, demagogic patriotism, and mushy science fiction. The group that had once fought tyrants like Hitler was now fighting mad scientists, crazed super-animals, and common, garden-variety thieves. Changes in the strip came quickly. Chop-Chop, who once rated his own strip, went from a fat, buck-toothed Chinaman to a hip Oriental. The fatalistic, semi-militaristic atmosphere became passé, and the group's oft-moved hideout, Blackhawk Island, began to look more and more like a playground. In the 1960s, innovations like "Lady" Blackhawk, Blackie the mascot, and the "Tom Thumb" Blackhawk robbed the strip of its old glory. Finally, their utilitarian, Gestapo-like blue uniforms were phased out in favor of garish green and red outfits. Writers even advanced the theory that André was secretly afraid of women! As the feature began its final years, the once-proud men were turned into CIA-employed superheroes with another set of uniforms—all in a vain effort to boost sales. When that too failed, new editor Dick Giordano returned the Blackhawks to their former posture and uniforms. But the Blackhawks had lost their following, and the feature was cancelled in 1969.

Blackhawk remains one of the greatest comic strips of all time, and it lasted through 243 issues of its own book as well as 102 issues of *Military* (later *Modern*) *Comics*. At the height of its popularity in 1952, Columbia produced a movie serial with Kirk Alyn as Blackhawk. There was also a short-lived radio drama during the mid-1940s.

J.B.

Ever loath to waste a character, the editors at DC brought Blackhawk back to life again and again. He resurfaced first in 1976, lasting into the next year, then was revived in 1982, 1984, 1988, and 1989-90. His last appearance to date was in *Blackhawk Special* (1992).

M.H.

BLACK HOOD (U.S.) *Black Hood* was created in October 1940 by MLJ editor Harry Shorten and made its first appearance in *Top-Notch* number nine. Quickly becoming one of MLJ's most popular creations, "The Man of Mystery" soon began appearing in *Jackpot* (Spring 1941), and then in his own magazine (starting with issue number nine, Winter 1944).

Shorten concocted a melodramatic motif for the character, and for a long time, Black Hood ran into one misfortune after another. "The Dark Knight" was actually New York patrolman Kip Burland, who had been attacked by a villain called the Skull, who looked like a skeleton. The Skull not only dazed Burland, but made it appear as if he had looted a jewelry store, too. Instantly discharged from the force, Burland set out to capture the Skull; however, it was he who was captured, and his body was riddled with bullets and thrown into a river. But Burland survived because of an old man called The Hermit, who had also been framed by the Skull. The Hermit saved his life and trained him as The Black Hood. After another long series of mishaps, all spread out over several issues of *Top-Notch*, everything was set right and The Black Hood concentrated on catching criminals.

Artistically, *Black Hood* was handled briefly by Charles Biro (1941) and *Archie* artist Bob Montana (1942). But Al Camerata and Irv Novick handled most of the stories. Novick, who drew the strip between 1943 and 1946, was more stylistic; Camerata, an underpublicized artist who drew the strip sporadically throughout its tenure, portrayed more action and adventure.

Black Hood appeared in *Top-Notch* (later called *Top-Notch Laugh*) until April 1944's 44th issue. It also appeared in *Black Hood* until Summer 1946's 19th issue, and made its last showing in *Pep* 60 (March 1947). The character was revived in MLJ's "camp superhero" drive of 1965, but was back in mothballs the following year.

J.B.

BLACK TERROR (U.S.) *Black Terror* was created by writer Richard Hughes and artist D. Gabrielsen in May 1941 and made its first appearance in Better's *Exciting Comics* number nine. The character became Better's (later Nedor and Standard) top superhero, appearing in more than 170 stories.

The Black Terror was really meek druggist Bob Benton, who developed a super potion that gave him extraordinary physical powers. He donned a primarily black costume and domino mask, and a skull and crossbones was emblazoned upon his chest. As the strip continued, Tim Roland, Benton's assistant, and Jean Starr, secretary to the mayor, became the primary supporting characters.

Editorially, the strip was never exceptional, although the stories were always well handled and fast-paced. Before the war, *Black Terror* stories dealt mainly with street crime. As with many of his costumed compatriots, World War II found the character battling the Axis, and the postwar period saw the Black Terror back on the police beat. Cocreator Hughes handled most of the scripts in 1941 and 1942, but he later gave way to Edmond Hamilton, who began scripting in 1941 and lasted through 1945.

Alex Schomburg, an underrated draftsman and illustrator, handled the bulk of the series' stories from 1943 through 1949. As the strip began to fade, however, George Tuska and Mort Meskin also contributed outstanding material to the feature.

The Black Terror outlasted many of the more-heralded superheroes and remained in *Exciting* through September 1949's 69th issue. The character also appeared in 27 issues of his own magazine, from 1942 to June 1949. He also was featured in *America's Best* for the first 31 issues, running from February 1942 through July 1949.

J.B.

BLAKE ET MORTIMER (Belgium) Edgar P. Jacobs created *Blake et Mortimer* for the first issue of the Belgian weekly *Tintin* on September 26, 1946.

Captain Francis Blake (from British Intelligence) and Professor Philip Mortimer join forces in a series of powerful adventures in which mystery, suspense, and even archaeology are cleverly woven into the overall science-fiction theme. In his strip, Jacobs has dealt with some of the most important themes of post-World War II science fiction: survival after a nuclear holocaust ("The Secret of the Swordfish," "The Diabolical Trap"); the horrors of mind-control ("The Yellow Mark"); the strangers among us ("The Enigma of Atlantis"); the dehumanization wrought by a techonology-mad society ("The Diabolical Trap"); and the callous unleashing of unknown cosmic forces ("S.O.S. Meteors"). Very often the enemies of our two heroes are the blind emissaries of a science gone mad (like the demented Professor Septimus) or the willing agents of (totalitarian) darkness best personified by the demoniacal and sinister Colonel Olrik, one of Jacobs' most powerful creations.

In all of Jacobs' stories there can be found the same currents of humanistic concern and passionate commitment to truth as in the works of Ray Bradbury, Arthur C. Clarke, and Richard Matheson.

The graphic excellence of the strip is not as readily apparent as its spellbinding plot and subtle characterization. *Blake et Mortimer* nonetheless constitutes one of the high points in visual storytelling. In epic sweep, in breadth and scope of imagination, in sheer imagery power, *Blake et Mortimer* often equals, and sometimes surpasses, *Buck Rogers*, *Brick Bradford*, and even *Flash Gordon*.

Eight *Blake et Mortimer* adventures have been published so far (all of them later reprinted in book form). Next to *Tintin* and *Asterix* they are probably the best-sellers among French-language comic strips. Jacobs' series has also been adapted to radio-plays and records.

One last episode, "Professor Sato's Three Formulas," left incomplete at the author's death in 1987, was finished by his former assistant Bob de Moor in 1990. An entirely original Blake and Mortimer adventure, written by Jean Van Hamme and drawn by Ted Benoit, came out in 1996.

M.H.

BLASCO, JESUS (1919-1995) Acknowledged as the best artist of the Spanish comics, Jesus Blasco was born November 3, 1919, in Barcelona. Entirely self-taught, Blasco started his cartooning career in his teens with a series of comic strips for various comic weeklies of the time, such as *Mickey, Boliche* (where he created the first version of *Cuto* in 1935), and *Pocholo*. Later he became a member of the staff of the juvenile magazine *Chicos*; in its pages Blasco revived *Cuto*, and it became his most popular success. Simultaneously he drew *Anita Diminuta* in *Chicos'* sister magazine, *Mis Chicas* (1941).

Other important works in Blasco's early career include: *La Escuadrilla de la Muerte* ("The Death Squadron," 1941), *El País del Oro Negro* ("The Land of Black Gold"), *El Planeta Misterioso, Los Tres Inseparables* ("The Inseparable Three," 1943), a series of war comic books, *Episodios de Guerra* ("Tales of War"), and the humor

"Blondie," Chic Young. © King Features Syndicate.

strips *Chispita* (1946), *Kul-Hebra* (1949), *Tontote y Cia* ("Tontote and Cy"), and *Rabituerto*. Mastering further his style with each new creation, Blasco produced *El Condor y el Bebé* ("The Condor and the Baby"), *Una Aventura en la India, Dan Jensen* for *Alcotan* magazine, *Jim el Terrible* ("Jim the Terrible"), *Wild Batson*, which he did along with another Western, *Smiley O'Hara* (1950), and *Dos Hermanos* ("Two Brothers") for *El Coyote*. At the same time he created the adventures of two little girls, *Marcela y Kiki*, for the girl's magazine *Florita*.

The eldest son in an artistic family that includes the illustrators Pili, Alejandro, Adriano, and Augusto, Jesus Blasco formed a partnership with his brothers Alejandro and Adriano for the production of comic features designed for the French, English, Portuguese, Belgian, and Spanish markets. During this international phase Blasco produced, among his more important titles, *Billy the Kid, Wyatt Earp, Buffalo Bill, Blackbow*, and *Shot Basky*, all Westerns, as is his masterwork, *Los Guerrilleros*, published in *Spirou, Chito*, and other magazines since 1968.

The most prolific among Spanish cartoonists, Blasco has also created *Montezuma's Daughter, Miss Tarantula, The Indestructible Man, The Slave of the Screamer, Phantom of the Forest*, and, foremost, *The Steel Claw*, for the English market. In the tradition of English picture stories with captions, he produced the whimsical *Edward and the Jumblies*, and illustrated a lovely series of children's tales, among which his version of *Alice in Wonderland* stands out. Jesus Blasco, a master of the *chiaroscuro*, has been able to endow his pictures with great dynamism and action by using the brush exclusively. Among his later contributions to the comics, mention should be made of *The Return of Captain Trueno* (1986) and *El Chacal de Bir Jerari* ("The Jackal of

Bir Jerari," also 1986). He died at his home in Barcelona on October 21, 1995.

L.G.

BLONDIE (U.S.) *Blondie* was created for King Features Syndicate on September 15, 1930, by Murat (Chic) Young. Blondie Boopadoop was, in the beginning of the strip, a bird-brained flapper pursued by Dagwood Bumstead, a rather ineffectual playboy and the son of a railroad tycoon. On February 17, 1933, Blondie married Dagwood, who was promptly disinherited by his father. Since that time the strip has assumed the look and the character it retains to this day, midway between the humor strip and the family series.

Blondie became a devoted wife and affectionate companion, as well as the actual head of the Bumstead household. While losing none of her charm, she acquired solid virtues of pluck and level-headedness, and often has to rescue Dagwood from the many jams he gets himself into. In 1934 a son, Alexander, joined the family, followed in 1941 by his sister Cookie. There are many colorful characters revolving around the Bumsteads, the most important being their neighbors Herbert and Tootsie Woodley; Mr. Dithers, Dagwood's irascible boss; the harried mailman, Mr. Beasley; not to mention Daisy the family dog and her five pups. This little world is in a state of perpetual agitation, and this provides *Blondie* with most of its gags as well as its hectic, loony atmosphere.

The simplicity of the series and its happy, optimistic outlook have won a remarkable international popularity for *Blondie*. It has been for a long time the most widely circulated comic strip in the world, translated into most languages and with an international audience reaching into the hundreds of millions. It has inspired 28 movies from 1938 to 1951 (Penny Singleton played

"Bloom County," Berke Breathed. © Washington Post Writers Group.

Blondie and Arthur Lake, Dagwood) as well as a TV series and a novel. The strip has also given rise to countless imitations in the United States and abroad. There is also a *Blondie* comic book drawn by Paul Fung, Jr.

After the death of its creator in 1973, the strip was taken over by Chic Young's two former assistants, Jim Raymond (brother of the late Alex Raymond) and Chic's own son Dean. They have managed to keep the strip's original look, and *Blondie* has so far lost none of its appeal. In 1984 Stan Drake took over the drawing, which he carried on until his death in 1997.

M.H.

BLOOM COUNTY (U.S.) While attending the University of Texas, Berke Breathed published from 1978 to 1979 in the school newspaper a comic strip entitled *Academia Waltz* that served as the origin of *Bloom County*. Set in a fictional town deep in the American heartland, it was syndicated by the Washington Post Writers Group and first appeared on December 8, 1980.

Initially, the strip was populated mostly by human characters; Milo Bloom, the irreverent blond-haired 10-year-old boy who worked as a general assignment reporter for the *Bloom Beacon* (sometimes called *Picayune*). His favorite target was Senator Bedfellow, whom he loved to photograph in embarrassing situations and whose statements he would always distort. His best friend, Michael Binkley, a "nincompoop" so lacking in virility that he asks Santa Claus for "machismo," is full of anxieties, feeling nothing in the world has been right since Marie Osmond's divorce. Not even his love for Blondie, a cool girl from Los Angeles, can possibly save him. Oliver Wendell Jones is an African-American boy genius on the cutting edge of science (he discovered that cat sweat stimulates hair growth).

The recurring adults are Cutter John, a paraplegic Vietnam vet, who loves to race around in his wheelchair/starchair "Enterpoop." When not riding with his Star Trek companions, he is heavily engaged with

Bobbi Harlow, a dark-haired beauty and elementary school teacher who loves his reckless *joie de vivre*, if not his hooked nose. She is constantly pestered by a self-centered, clothes-conscious, shallow young lawyer by the name of Steve Dallas. That this unenlightened "elitist boob" (her words) became ashamed of defending murderers and other criminals and is now a feminist and a man in touch with his feelings (he cries during *Bambi*) is not at all surprising in light of the fact that the young Binkley's ultra-conservative gun-loving father had himself metamorphosed into an ultra-liberal Democrat filled with guilt for hating Bill Cosby and his pudding commercials.

To earn a living, Steve becomes manager of the heavy-metal band "Deathtöngue," renamed "Billy and the Boingers" under pressure from sanctimonious censors. The band's members are Bill the Cat (on tongue), Opus the bow-tie adorned penguin (on tuba), and Hodge-Podge the rabbit (on drums). In fact, animals had invaded Bloom County earlier and soon took over the strip. Opus came first, a refugee of the Falklands war, whose mother had been abducted in 1982 by Mary Kay Cosmetics "commandos" ("Even their Uzis are pink."). Just like his human friends, Opus enjoys TV, car rides, Diane Sawyer's good looks; at the newspaper, he works in various positions from classified ad-taker to film critic, not to mention as Bill's vice-presidential candidate in 1988, in a hilarious send-up of presidential politics. Opinionated, but in a gentle way, he pronounces the final moral on human foibles and stupidity.

Bill wanted to be a comic-strip cat, not unlike Garfield, whose merchandising empire he envies and resents. Unfortunately for his dreams of fame and fortune, he drinks too much and takes too many drugs to ever achieve his goal. Even a presidential campaign run does not bring him happiness, despite lots of dirty tricks and illegal contributions. Perhaps his "Ack!" exclamations explain his disgusted view of life. The grumpy woodchuck Portnoy, Hodge-Podge the sharp-tongued rabbit, Rosebud the basselope (part basset hound, part antelope), and Milquetoast, Milo's pet cockroach, round out the menagerie.

Bloom County attacked liposuctions, cable TV, home shopping networks, and other wonders of the universe. In fact, there are few sacred cows in this wickedly funny strip, as it satirizes creationism, the moral majority, and football, and is not afraid to name names; Carl Sagan and his "biiillyuns of years," the British royal couple and their bratty son, William, the no less bratty Sean Penn and Madonna, the publicity-hungry Lee Iaccocca, Jim and Tammy Faye Bakker, members of the press, and politicians ("Bozos," in Opus's opinion).

The humor is pointed but not wounding, and the art clean, simple, and imaginative, favoring profiles. The strip won the Pulitzer Prize for editorial cartooning in 1987 and has been reprinted in a number of best-selling collections. However, wishing to go on to his next project, *Outland*, Breathed stopped the daily *Bloom County* strip on August 5, 1989, and the Sunday page the following day.

P.H.

BLOSSER, MERRILL (1892-1983) American cartoonist, born in Napanee, Indiana. After graduation from high school, Merrill Blosser attended Blue Ridge College in Maryland for one year, and then went on to the Chicago Academy of Fine Arts. Blosser started his professional career in 1912, when he sold his first cartoon to the *Baltimore American*. Thus encouraged, he decided to pursue his avocation, working variously for *Motor-Cycling* magazine in Chicago, and with the Denton Publishing Company in Cleveland, contributing political cartoons to the *Wheeling* (West Virginia) *Register* and sports cartoons to the *Cleveland Plain Dealer*.

In 1915, "tired of drifting" as he himself put it, Merrill Blosser joined NEA Service and, later that same year, started *Freckles and His Friends* in both daily and Sunday form. The strip, which recounts the various exploits of an enterprising youngster and his no-less-adventurous pals, met with great success (at one time it was carried in over 700 newspapers around the country). Blosser drew and wrote *Freckles* for more than 50 years (it was then taken over by Henry Formhals). He later retired to California, where he died in 1983.

Merrill Blosser is the perfect example of the old-style journeyman cartoonist whose entire life was devoted to the drawing and writing of one strip. Blosser's creations may have been humble and his penmanship short of graphic perfection (but with a bite of its own, nevertheless), but he was among the last in a breed faced with extinction, in a time of fast-changing popular tastes and short-sighted syndicate policies.

M.H.

BLOTTA, OSCAR (1918-   ) An Argentine cartoonist born in 1918, Oscar Blotta studied at the National Academy of Fine Arts in Buenos Aires. After working as a freelance cartoonist for a number of publications, he started his comic strip career in the 1940s with two humor features produced for the publisher Dante Quinterno: *El Gnomo Pimentón* ("Hot Pepper the Gnome"), published in the children's magazine *Patoruzito*, and *Ventajita*, which appeared in *Patoruzú*.

The titular heroes of these two strips inspired the first feature-length animated cartoon ever produced in Argentina: *Upa en Apuros*. Blotta collaborated in a decisive

way in the production, while simultaneously doing illustrations for children's books. He retired in the 1980s.

L.G.

BLUE BEETLE (U.S.) *Blue Beetle* was created by Charles Nicholas and made its first appearance in Fox's *Mystery Men* number one for August 1939. One of the earliest superheroes, the character quickly merited his own book (Spring 1940), and *Blue Beetle* became one of the most intriguing strips of all time.

The origin most often cited reveals that rookie policeman Dan Garrett was given his superhuman powers from a vitamin known as "2X." He also wore an almost invisible suit of blue chain mail. Almost all of this changed over the years, however, and the uniform rarely looked like actual mail armor. Inconsistencies aside, the strip became immensely popular, and the character was soon appearing on radio and in an ill-fated newspaper strip. He even picked up a sidekick named Spunky in 1943, but this character did not last long. In fact, the only regularly featured supporting characters were Mike Mannigan, Garrett's police partner, and Joan Mason, the ever-present love interest.

The strip was never outstanding, either editorially or artistically. Illustrations were crude and stories infantile, yet the feature remained popular. Besides creator Nicholas—who drew *Blue Beetle* between 1939 and 1942 and received the syndicated strip byline—Jack Kirby, Don Rico, Alex Blum, and Allan Ulmer contributed to the feature. Overall, during this initial run, *Blue Beetle* appeared in all 37 issues of *Mystery Men* until its discontinuation in February 1942. He also appeared in 60 issues of *Blue Beetle* from Winter 1939 to August 1950. Oddly enough, the issues between numbers 17 and 26 were published by Holyoke and not Fox. He also appeared in *Big Three* and other books.

Charlton purchased the rights to the strip and produced a new series of *Blue Beetle* comics, but the series lasted less than a year—November 1954 to August 1955. Charlton made another attempt in 1964 and 1965, but these 10 issues are among the worst comics ever produced. Notable, however, is the fact that Roy Thomas began his career here.

The strip finally got superior writing and drawing when Charlton revived it again in 1967. Handled primarily by artist Steve Ditko, the feature was gutted of all its previous affiliations. The Blue Beetle was now a duo-toned, gadget-minded hero known in civilian life as Ted Kord. A scientist, Kord was originally suspected by police of killing the Dan Garrett Blue Beetle, but this story line eventually became overworked and was dropped. Ditko's rendition was easily the best *Blue Beetle* ever produced, but poor sales dictated its cancellation after five issues (June 1967 to November 1968). A sixth Ditko *Beetle* tale, produced in 1968, was finally published in the *Charlton Portfolio* in 1974. A new version was published by DC in 1986–88.

J.B.

BLUE BOLT (U.S.) *Blue Bolt* was created in June 1940 by Joe Simon and made its first appearance in *Blue Bolt* volume one, number one, published by Novelty Publications.

The Blue Bolt was really Fred Parrish, a football star struck by lightning during practice. Almost immediately after, he crashed his private plane into a lost valley and was saved only by massive doses of radium administered by a Dr. Bertoff. The doctor also supplied

Parrish with his blue costume, a crash helmet and a lightning gun—all of which Parrish was supposed to take back to civilization. For a long while, however, the character remained in the lost valley and battled a lady known as the Green Sorceress, one of the best-remembered villains of the 1940s.

Artistically, *Blue Bolt* is significant because it was the first collaboration of Joe Simon and Jack Kirby. And although they did not begin their partnership until a year later, Simon and Kirby handled the strip during 1940. After the pair jumped to Timely, George Mandel (1941-1942), Dan Barry (1943), and others began illustrating the character.

Despite his relatively unique lightning bolt motif, Blue Bolt began faltering, and Lois Blake was given a similar costume and powers in volume two, number seven. But by volume three, number four, Blue Bolt abandoned his costume and spent the rest of his career in civilian garb. *Blue Bolt* ended after September 1949's volume 10, number two. The feature lasted exactly 100 issues. The company began a *Blue Bolt* reprint title in 1950, but it ended after a few issues.

J.B.

BLUE SEA AND RED HEART (China) This tale of heroism was adapted from an original story by Liang Hsin into a comic book published in 1965 by the People's Art Publications in Shanghai. The script was by Wan Chia-ch'un and the artwork by Hsü Chin.

Blue Sea and Red Heart recounts in some detail the exploits of Captain Hsiao Ting of the People's Liberation Army during the reconquest of Hainan in 1949. The script reads like an adventure movie in its single-mindedness and high purpose: there is not one dramatic device missing, from the daring raid on enemy headquarters to the obligatory rescue of a comely, if headstrong, damsel in distress. It all ends with Hsiao Ting maneuvering his explosive-laden junk onto the enemy flagship and blowing it up. The last panel (looking suspiciously like a shot from *The Sands of Iwo Jima*) shows Hsiao Ting in a heroic posture, leading his men onto the beaches, while the caption reads: "At dawn, our army has already set foot on the northern shore of Hainan. Hsiao Ting at the head of his troops pushes fearlessly forward. The island of Hainan is liberated at last!"

Childish as the narrative may sound, *Blue Sea* provides a good example of comic book art. Hsü Chin is an accomplished craftsman; his drawings are detailed without being cluttered, his line is simple and effective. Best of all are his compositions: brooding, suspenseful, and functional. On the strength of this one example, Hsü Chin's artistry is far superior to that of any number of American cartoonists currently doing comic book work.

Blue Sea and Red Heart was reprinted (as "Bravery on the High Seas") in *The People's Comic Book* (Doubleday, 1973).

M.H.

BLUEY AND CURLEY (Australia) Created by Alex Gurney for the *Herald and Weekly Times Ltd.* in 1940, the strip appeared briefly in *Picture News* magazine before transferring to the *Sun-News Pictorial* on February 1, 1941, as a daily strip. Soon the strip was appearing in all Australian states and servicemen's newspapers and later was syndicated in New Zealand and Canada.

The strip accurately reflected the Australian soldier's vision of himself as a fighting man without peer but more interested in his beer and gambling; resenting all military authority (and later, all forms of authority); a confidence man with the ability to laugh at himself and a ready disciple of the "You can't win" attitude. More than any other strip, *Bluey and Curley* gave civilians an insight into the hardships of army life and the slang expressions of the period. It also projected the mood of envy directed towards the more highly paid U.S. soldiers. Still, all subjects were handled in a gentle, smile-provoking manner—for, while Gurney was not particularly subtle, he was never cruel. His handling of "fuzzie-wuzzies" or "boongs" and their Pidgin English were classics. The strip perpetuated traditional back-block humor, and the army cook was often the butt of jokes and situations, previously reserved for the shearer's cook.

Bluey had a protruding nose, long jaw, and straight red hair (hence the traditional Australian nickname of Bluey) and, with a cigarette hanging from his bottom lip, was usually a foil for his more exuberant mate. Curley had a baby-face, small up-turned nose, and curly, blonde hair and was the ladies' man of the team, with a girl in every town. Their dialogue was purely Australian, right down to the cursing and swearing, which only lacked the great Australian adjective, 'bloody,' to make it fully authentic. They wore their slouch hats at a jaunty angle, pushed back off their foreheads as an added mark of their disrespect for authority. Yet, despite their rebellious attitude, they were never to be seen drunk or A.W.O.L.—points raised by Gurney when the strip was dropped from an army newspaper as setting a bad example for the service. An immediate protest by the soldiers assured that the strip was reinstated.

Bluey and Curley was a very nationalistic strip that covered all facets of Australian humor. It was at its peak of popularity during the 1940s but tended to lose some of its punch and individuality when it made the transition to civilian life. The common enemies of army life were then missing.

When Gurney died of a heart attack in December 1955, the strip passed on to Norm Rice, who died in a car accident less than 12 months later. The strip was then taken over by Les Dixon, a former *Smith's Weekly* artist and art editor. Dixon gradually altered the art style and added new characters (e.g., a swaggie Jazzer; an old reprobate Trotters), assisting the strip's continued popularity—but it is Alex Gurney's wartime adventures of *Bluey and Curley* that made this strip a household name. The strip finally ended in July 1975.

J.R.

BOBBY THATCHER (U.S.) George Storm's second adventure strip, entirely his own and one of the most popular ever drawn, the daily *Bobby Thatcher* began publication with the McClure Syndicate in a number of papers between March and August, 1927. Since the *Thatcher* episodes carried numbers rather than dates (as did those of many adventure strips to follow), papers could begin the strip months after its original release date and still run the full continuity. Not as exciting at the outset as Storm's earlier, bloodier, and grimmer (but premature) seafaring strip, *Phil Hardy*, *Thatcher* possessed elements that appealed more to the public of the time. An attractive, 15-year-old tow-headed kid (physically similar to Chester Gould's Junior Tracy sev-

"Bobby Thatcher," George Storm. © McClure Syndicate.

eral years later), Thatcher was often on the road in a peaceful, rural American locale immediately recognizable to millions of readers. A public highly partial to *Little Orphan Annie* was more than ready to welcome a well-done male equivalent, and that was what the McClure Syndicate meant to provide.

But *Bobby Thatcher* (which moved to the Bell Syndicate with episode 1013 on June 6, 1930) was more than an *Annie* imitation. Storm's charming narrative imagination, skilled sense of pace, and stunning graphic style followed their own highly individual course in combining to produce an adventure strip that stood second to none but *Annie* and *Wash Tubbs* at the close of the 1920s. At first slow to develop permanent characters, Storm established several close friends for Bobby by 1931, such as Marge Hall, Bobby's longed-for but elusive girlfriend; Lulu Bowers, his "regular" girl; and Ulysses "Tubby" Butler, Peewee Nimmo, and Elmer Bowers, three of his juvenile companions. All these characters are inhabitants of rural Jonesboro, where Bobby, his sister, Hattie, and his Aunt Ida Baxter live for much of the central continuity of the strip. The most powerful character of Storm's *Thatcher*, however, was introduced somewhat later: the tough-hewn, Popeyesque sailor, Hurricane Bill, with whom Bobby is involved in a shipboard struggle against the hulking, brutal Captain Bottlejohn in 1935. This story, featured in the only *Bobby Thatcher* book reprint, was a Whitman Topline paper-covered book of that year.

Storm tired of strip work in 1937, however, hired a full-time ghost (Sheldon Mayer), and abruptly closed down *Thatcher* with a publisher's printed farewell to the readers on various dates in 1938 (depending on the point at which subscribing papers ran out of *Thatcher* continuity). Storm went on to draw other strips of brief duration, largely for comic books, through the 1940s,

but *Thatcher* remains his unique triumph, a major comic strip work of its period, richly deserving of reprinting in full.

B.B.

BOB MORANE (France/Belgium) The Belgian writer Henri Vernes created the character of Bob Morane in a series of best-selling novels published since 1955 by Editions Marabout in Belgium. In 1958 Bob Morane was adapted into the comic strip medium by Dino Attanasio in the pages of the women's magazine *Femmes d'Aujourd'hui.*

Bob Morane is a modern-day adventurer who performs his exploits in all parts of the world. He is clean-living and crew-cut in the best tradition of the 1950s, and he is more than a little on the dull side. The color is supplied by his inseparable companion, the red-haired Scottish giant Bill Ballantine (a chicken farmer in his spare time), whose earthy humor and lively shenanigans make him the favorite of readers. Among the many enemies that Morane and Ballantine encounter—saboteurs, mad scientists, master spies, and other miscreants—the most implacable is the cruel Mister Ming, also known as "the Yellow Shadow," whose niece, the enigmatic Tania, is the hero's secret love. Science fiction and fantasy agreeably mix with derring-do and suspense in Vernes's well-plotted tales.

In 1960 Attanasio was succeeded by Gerald Forton, who drew the feature in a more up-to-date style; in turn, in 1967 Forton left the drawing of the strip to William Vance, who proved himself as the series' definitive artist. (In addition to his work for *Femmes d'Aujourd'hui,* Vance has also done a few *Bob Morane* episodes for *Pilote.*) In 1979 Vance handed the art chores over to his assistant (and brother-in-law) Francisco Coria; and in 1993 Forton came back to draw *Bob*

Morane for the second time after a quarter-century absence.

Bob Morane has been reprinted in book form by Editions Dargaud in France. In 1970 it also inspired a French TV series with Claude Titre in the title role.

M.H.

BŌKEN DANKICHI (Japan) *Bōken Dankichi* ("The Adventures of Dankichi") was created by Keizo Shimada, a pioneer in the field of children's comic strips, and made its first appearance in the Japanese monthly *Shōnen Kurabu* ("Boys Club") in April 1934.

Dankichi was a little Japanese boy who went fishing one fine day along with his pet mouse Kari-kō; while fishing they fell asleep and drifted to sea. Landing on a South Seas island inhabited by ferocious cannibals, they managed by cunning to defeat the island's chief, and Dankichi ascended to the throne. Under Dankichi's wise leadership, and with the assistance of Kari-kō, the island became a haven of peace and serenity, which did not fail to attract interlopers. Dankichi fought against a crew of pirates intent on seizing the island. His army (consisting of hippopotami used as submarines, vultures serving as dive-bombers, elephants substituting for tanks, and the like) defeated the pirates. Other perils loomed, however, and Dankichi had to fight again until May 1939 when the strip was temporarily discontinued.

Bōken Dankichi reappeared after the war in several monthlies: *Yōnen Book, Shōgaku Ichinensei,* and *Norakuro.* The strip tried to explain the rules of the American military administration and the new ways of Japan to its readers.

"Bōken Dankichi," Keizo Shimada. © Shōnen Kurabu.

In spite of the simplicity of its story lines and the bareness of its drawings, *Bōken Dankichi* enjoyed the highest popularity of any strips in its day, and it is one of the longest-lasting strips in Japan.

H.K.

BONELLI, GIOVANNI LUIGI (1908-   ) Italian writer, editor, and publisher, born December 22, 1908, in Milan. Bonelli's entire output was directed at a juvenile public. He started as a contributor to the *Corriere dei Piccoli* in the late 1920s with a series of poems, which were followed by some articles for the *Giornale Illustrato dei Viaggi.* At the same time he wrote two adventure novels: *Le Tigri dell'Atlantico* ("The Tigers of the Atlantic") and *I Fratelli del Silenzio* ("The Brotherhood of Silence").

In the mid-1930s Bonelli entered the comics field as writer, and later as managing editor of the comic weeklies *Primarosa, Robinson, L'Audace, Rintintin,* and *Jumbo,* published by SAEV in Milan. His stories were illustrated by artists of the first rank, such as Franco Chiletto, Rino Albertarelli, and Walter Molino. When *L'Audace* was taken over by Mondadori, Bonelli stayed on as editor until 1939, when he bought out the magazine and started publishing it himself. He decided immediately to change the format of the publication, from tabloid to comic-book size, foreshadowing the change in illustrated magazines in Italy by some six years.

When the war broke out, Bonelli resumed his writing career, mainly for small publishers, until 1947, when he joined forces with Giovanni De Leo to launch several ventures, including a Western magazine with no illustration and the adaptation of a string of comic books produced in France by Pierre Mouchot.

In 1946 Bonelli wrote a short story, *La Perla Nera* ("The Black Pearl"), and in 1947 *Ipnos.* In 1948 Bonelli initiated a long and successful series of Western strips, starting with the popular *Tex Willer* and *La Pattuglia senza Paura* ("The Fearless Patrol," the adventures of two brothers, Alan and Bob Gray, drawn by Guido Zamperoni and Franco Donatelli). Among his other creations, there are: *Il Vendicatore del Oeste* ("The Western Avenger"); *Yuma Kid* (both 1948); *El Kid* (drawn by Dino Battaglia, most notably); *Davy Crockett* (1956); and *Hondo* (1957). In 1962 Bonelli took over *Un Regazzo nel Oeste* ("A Boy in the West"), which had been originated by Nolitta, and he brought this long saga to an enjoyable end. He retired in the early 1980s, leaving his flourishing publishing house in the hands of his son Sergio.

G.B.

BONER'S ARK (U.S.) Mort Walker, under his real first name Addison, created *Boner's Ark* for King Features Syndicate on March 11, 1968.

Boner is the skipper of an ark that wanders the world's seas aimlessly—never sighting land more than postage-stamp size. On Boner's Ark the animals are not in pairs, although each is accompanied by a singular psychosis or bit of nuttiness that keep an essentially limited basis for gags always fresh and funny.

Boner himself is a gentle, victimized, and sometimes befuddled human. The short skipper briefly sported a blonde mustache in the strip. In 1974 his bushy-haired wife Bubbles was introduced (she was found drifting on a raft). She is flaky, wears tennis shoes, and

"Boner's Ark," Addison (Mort Walker). © King Features Syndicate.

unleashes as much madcap terror on the ark as the wildest of the animals.

The animals include Cubcake, a lovable koala bear; first mate Arnie Aardvark, Boner's blasé sidekick; Priscilla Pig, who stretches a little bikini to its limits and fantasizes about herself as a beauty queen sought after by suitors; Sandy Ostrich, a pal of Priscilla; Dum-Dum, a large, strong, and very stupid gorilla; Duke, the suave penguin in a tuxedo; Spot the dog, a perpetual flunk-out from obedience school; Rex the dinosaur, the hippopotamus, and the giraffe—large-size vehicles for gags about their weight and height problems; and, perhaps the funniest, the trio of the nameless hyena, bear, and mouse, eternal mutineers.

The interplay of the personalities provides ample room for latitude in the strip, which is consistently fresh. Another factor that helps the flow of ideas is Walker's "factory" of gagmen—Ralston Jones, Bob Gustafson, and Jerry Dumas, chiefly—who devote every Monday to conferences on *Boner*. Since 1971 the indefatigable Frank Johnson has pencilled and inked the strip.

The artwork is particularly engaging and individualistic, closer in originality to *Sam's Strip* than Walker's other post-*Beetle Bailey* pastiches, *Hi and Lois* and *Mrs. Fitz's Flats*. The style is sketchy but firm, and simplicity is the hallmark. Panoramas of the ark on the horizon, with an enormous drop of water or two at the crest of a wave, achieve almost a poster effect. The strip, which runs daily and Sunday, has maintained its level of about 145 papers for several years.

R.M.

Frank Johnson, who had been assisting Walker since 1971, finally got to sign *Boner's Ark* in 1982. Despite multiple false sightings, the ark's inmates are as far from land in 1997 as they ever were since the strip's inception.

M.H.

BONVICINI, FRANCO (1941-1995) Italian cartoonist, born March 31, 1941, in Modena, Italy. After attending classes in several universities without getting any degree, Franco Bonvicini decided upon a career in animated cartoons. He entered the comics field in 1969, creating his first strip, *Sturmtruppen*, about a batallion of inept German storm troopers in World War II, which immediately gained wide acclaim in critical circles as well as from the public. *Sturmtruppen* won a contest organized by the Roman daily *Paese Sera* where it was published, then went on to the short-lived weekly *Off-Side*, and later to the *Gazzetta di Parma*; it now appears in the monthly *Eureka* and in the illustrated weekly *Corriere dei Ragazzi*. A number of *Sturmtruppen* episodes were collected in two hardbound volumes and in two paperbacks. (All are signed with the pen name "Bonvi.")

Along with his *Sturmtruppen*, Bonvi produced several other features for the magazine *Giorni* and the *Gazzetta*

Franco Bonvicini, "Cattivik." © Bonvi.

di Parma, as well as a series of strips drawn for the publications of Edizioni Alpe, the most notable being *Cattivik* ("The Baddie") and *Posapiano* ("Slowpoke"). He also contributed short stories to the monthly magazines *Psycho* and *Horror*.

In 1972 Bonvi created *Nick Carter* (a parody on the fabled detective) in cooperation with Guido de Maria for a TV series called *Gulp! Comics on TV*. The character was an immediate success and the films enjoyed a number of reruns. It was announced that, beginning in 1975, Nick Carter would be the leading character in *Supergulp!* (a spin-off from *Gulp!*). Bonvi and de Maria also produced another series for television, *Saturnino Farandola*, a science-fantasy story based on a novel by Albert Robida. As for Nick Carter, he also appeared in a short series of comic books as well as in the *Corriere dei Regazzi* and in several foreign publications.

In 1973, in collaboration with Mario Gomboli, Bonvi created *Milo Marat* for the French weekly *Pif*. In the meantime *Sturmtruppen* had inspired a stage play, and a movie was also announced. Bonvi succeeded in creating a school around him, made up of some excellent artists, and this strongly contributed to the success (and to the multiplicity) of his comic creations. In the last 20 years of his life he devoted himself more and more to the field of animated cartoons. He died in a car accident on December 9, 1995.

Bonvi was the recipient of a number of awards, including the "Saint-Michel" (Belgium) in 1973, and the "Yellow Kid" (Italy) in 1974.

G.B.

BONZO (G.B.) Bonzo, a happy, laughing, pudgy pup with one black ear, a couple of black spots, and a stump of a tail, was created by George E. Studdy. Bonzo's birthday is unknown, as is his form of origin. He appeared in almost every popular medium during the 1920s and 1930s: picture postcards, cigarette cards, pictures, posters, children's picture and story books, magazine illustrations, stuffed dolls, toys, souvenirs, ashtrays—and all before he appeared in comic strips! He was even the star of the only successful series of animated cartoon films made in Britain during the silent film era. The *Bonzo* cartoons, 26 of them, were produced by his creator in conjunction with animator William A. Ward and scriptwriter Adrian Brunel (1924). A *Bonzo* daily strip appeared briefly around the late 1920s, but seems to have been published abroad rather than in Britain. This is also true of a syndicated Sunday strip page that Studdy drew for King Features in 1930-1931. Bonzo was also featured in color on the cover of *Toby*, a monthly magazine for children, and in an inside strip (1927). The daily strip was reprinted in *Bonzo: The Great Big Midget Book*, published by Dean (1932), the British equivalent of the famous *Big Little Book* series. In addition, Dean published a *Bonzo Annual* each year, with full-color plates by Studdy. After the

"Bonzo," G. E. Studdy. © Studdy.

artist's death, others took over and the annual continued into the 1950s. The early Bonzo material is widely collected today, but the character himself and his artist are almost totally forgotten.

D.G.

BOOB McNUTT (U.S.) *Boob McNutt*, the one considerable and long-lived comic strip Rube Goldberg was to draw, appeared only as a Sunday page during its entire 20-year span. It was Goldberg's second Sunday color feature (the first was a short-lived *Mike and Ike* half-page in the old *New York World* in 1907) and first appeared in the *New York Evening Mail* in May 1915. It did not receive notable national distribution until the growing popularity of Goldberg's daily multititled sports-page gag miscellany (copyrighted by the artist but distributed by the *Mail*) led Hearst's Star Company to contract with the *Mail* for distribution of both the daily panel and the Sunday *Boob* on June 9, 1918. Once the public at large saw *Boob*, primarily in Hearst newspapers, the strip's popularity grew a bit, and when the *Mail* folded in 1924, Goldberg negotiated a new, personal contract with the Star Company, which continued until Goldberg ended *Boob* on September 30, 1934.

Initially, *Boob McNutt* was a weekly gag strip, in which the red-headed, sharp-nosed hero with the tiny green hat and the spotted pants was asked by some trusting person to aid in a minor or major undertaking (from lifting a statue off a roof to piloting a Mars rocket)—and brought about total disaster instead. This

"Boob McNutt," Rube Goldberg. © King Features Syndicate.

Keystone formula was not very different from what was happening in *Happy Hooligan* and a dozen other strips, and though the public liked *Boob* well enough, it was not a wildfire sensation. However, when Boob began to court a flapper named Pearl in early 1922 and managed—usually by dumb luck—to survive the murderous attacks of his rival, Major Gumbo (aided and abetted by Pearl's father, Toby), the public interest in the strip grew. And when the complications that followed on the appearance of a new and richer rival, Shrimp Smith, led to a sudden cross-country trek by Boob, Pearl, Shrimp, and Toby and the creation of genuine week-to-week narrative suspense, more and more readers turned to *Boob* first every Sunday to see what would happen next to this preposterous quartet. Noting this, Goldberg exercised his developing talent for anecdotal narrative during the tense summer of 1924, when attempt after attempt by Boob to marry Pearl went maddeningly awry. Finally, again by dumb luck, the two made it to the altar on September 24, 1924—only to tumble into fresh trouble in a shipwreck on an ocean isle inhabited by such comic-page innovations as ostrich-legged ikmiks and grass-eating biffsniffs.

Plot was intrinsic to *Boob McNutt* now, and narrative development brought fresh characters into the strip. First was Bertha the Siberian cheesehound (with her engaging dialogue of "ipple gopple zuk," "gifke nok wup," and the like), bought by Boob as a gift for Pearl on January 24, 1925, but who remained Boob's dog for the rest of the strip. (Later, on January 9, 1926, Bertha became the star of *Bertha*, a companion fifth-of-a-page strip for the Sunday *Boob*, which ran until July 11, 1926. A gag strip, it had no narrative connection with the main page.) Next, as the climax of a months-long search in mid-1927 for the long-lost twins of his adopted parents, Boob discovered the missing twins were the old sawed-off Goldberg characters, Mike and Ike, performing as tramp trapeze artists with a circus, on August 14, 1927. Their compulsive explanatory refrain—"I'm Mike." "I'm Ike."—quickly became a schoolyard catch phrase, while their derby-topped, scraggly-bearded moon faces became a nationally recognized double image.

The strip's permanent adventure team was now complete, and Boob, Pearl, Mike, Ike, and Bertha proceeded to follow Goldberg's imagination into the wildest escapades yet. Sea piracy, foreign intrigue, kidnapping—all made the Sunday page an area of animated excitement amid the surrounding placid sea of domestic gag strips like *Elmer, Polly, Tillie*, and others. Then Goldberg recalled the public's enthusiastic response to the earlier desert island ikmiks and biffsniffs and decided to populate the strip with an almost limitless array of fantastic creatures in 1931 and '32: flying goppledongs, horn-billed zoppuluses, darting ploffs, and bomb-headed bambams—all being rounded up by Boob and his gang on a crippled dirigible from a stormy sea. This was the beginning of the gorgeously inventive era of *Boob* most readers of the time remember best, and it was followed by more fabulous beasts when a nutty scientist, Dr. Zano, enlarged reptiles and insects to a ghastly size and unleashed them onto a flabbergasted world in 1933. Eventually, Boob and a considerable part of the local constabulary licked this zoological challenge on December 31, 1933, after months of intensive strip action—and then, as if Goldberg could think of nothing wilder for Boob to do, the

strip stumbled into a short series of tired narratives and collapsed for good at the end of September 1934.

For all of its heady imaginative content in its last years and skillful narrative pace, *Boob* was badly marred by the careless, slapdash comic style Goldberg affected at every point, and perhaps fatally flawed by the characterless void where the hero should have been. For, far in the wake of the public's eagerly recalled fantastic animals, the lookalike twins Mike and Ike, and Bertha the mutt straggled the *zilch* hero who was literally nothing more than his name indicated: a boob. The flaw was Goldberg's: talented at creating memorable supporting characters in all of his strips, he could never evoke a gripping central protagonist—and yet just such a vital figure, from Popeye and Paw Perkins to Krazy Kat and Dick Tracy, was essential to the creation of a great strip. But *Boob* remains good reading in spite of this, thanks to its narrative pace.

A third-rate gag strip called *Bill* occupied a third of the Sunday page space Goldberg used for *Boob* between July 18, 1926, and September 30, 1934. There is little to be said in favor of this space-filler: its gags are tired, its story tiresome, and its hero even more of a nullity than Boob himself: the narrative of an ambitious young soda jerk with an empty face and a shock of black hair, *Bill* is probably the nadir of Goldberg's strips, including the ill-fated *Doc Wright*.

B.B.

BOOTH, WALTER (1892?-1971) British cartoonist and illustrator, born in Walthamstow, London. He was educated at Samuel Road School before studying art at Walthamstow Art School. He then joined the staff of Carlton Studio (1908), drawing general commercial work until trying his hand at strips for the James Henderson & Son publishing house in Red Lion Square. His extremely clean style, detailed and neat, yet occasionally extruding beyond the frames, seems fully formed from the start (1911) and hardly changes throughout the 60 years of comic work that followed.

His first strip was *Private Ramrod* (1911) in *Comic Life*, echoed by *Ram and Rod* (1914), more soldiers, in *Sparks*. He created his most famous comic character, *Professor Potash*, in 1915 for *The Big Comic*, continuing him in *Lot O' Fun* in 1919. In this same year he deserted the knockabout comic for the nursery comic with *Peggy and Peter in Toyland*, a series for *Sparks*. When that weekly changed its title to *Little Sparks*, which suited its nursery policy, he created *Jumbo* (1920).

The year 1920 was the year that the powerful Amalgamated Press bought out the Henderson comics, and Booth was welcomed to the higher-class fold. He was brought aboard *Puck*, the leading A.P. color comic weekly, and for this paper he created the first dramatic picture serial in British comics, *Rob the Rover*, in 1920. He took over the full-color front page in 1930 with his *Jingles' Jolly Circus*, a return to humor, but continued to exploit the new picture story field. This expanding productivity was made possible by taking on the young Stanley White as assistant. Booth's serials included *Orphans of the Sea* (1930), *Cruise of the Sea Hawk* (1936), and *Captain Moonlight* (1936), all for *Puck*; *The Adventure Seekers* (1926) in *Lot O' Fun*; and *The Pirate's Secret* (1939) in *Happy Days*.

With the discontinuation of *Puck* in 1940, the war years proved to be lean ones for Booth, but he drew some good strips for *Merry Maker* (1946), a small comic started by his old pupil, White. This led to strips for

"Boots and her Buddies," Edgar Martin. © NEA Services.

Scion comics in their *Big* series of one-shot titles, and eventually, despite living in far-off Wales, he managed a full comeback, drawing for the new nursery comic printed in photogravure, *Jack and Jill*. His *There Was an Old Woman Who Lived in a Shoe* (1954) was a large, action-filled picture that covered the center spread. This transferred to *Harold Hare's Own Paper* in 1964, and proved to be his last contribution to comics. He died in February 1971.

D.G.

BOOTS AND HER BUDDIES (U.S.) Cartoonist Edgar Martin created *Boots and Her Buddies* (the name is almost a play on *Polly and Her Pals*) for NEA Service on February 18, 1924.

Boots was a girl strip, and it followed on the heels of such established staples of the genre as *Tillie the Toiler* and *Winnie Winkle*. Boots was a vivacious, eye-pleasing blonde whose charms moved Coulton Waugh to lyrical heights in his study *The Comics*: "Ah, Boots! Sexy Boots! Curvaceous plump one . . . when she stretches out a long rounded leg with those very small feet, we . . . we had better put on our pince-nez again. How can that girl be both thin and plump at once?" Since 1924 Boots pursued her career undisturbed by outside events, going from naive coed to married woman to mod mother without ever losing her cool. Boots' buddies have included her own brother Bill, always handy for a buck or a piece of advice, her kind-hearted lodgers, Professor Stephen Tutt and his prim wife Cora, her fellow students, the disorganized Horace and his fat girlfriend Babe (who later married and got a strip of their own), not to mention her numerous suitors and admirers.

Boots reached the height of its popularity in the 1930s and 1940s when her adventures were followed by millions of readers. As Boots settled into domestic bliss in the later 1940s, the strip became indistinguishable from the host of other married strips cluttering the comics pages, and went steadily downhill. After being

taken over by Les Carroll for a few years, it disappeared in the late 1960s.

M.H.

BORING, WAYNE (1916-1987) American comic book and comic strip artist, born in 1916. He attended the Chicago Art Institute and the Minnesota School of Art. Boring, sometimes working under the name Jack Harmon, became a comic book artist in 1937, working on detective strips like *Slam Bradley* and *Spy* for National. But the overwhelming bulk of material Boring produced during his 30-year association with National was for *Superman*. Along with Paul Cassidy, he was one of the first ghosts to work on the strip, and he was with creators Siegel and Shuster when they opened their first studio in 1938.

And it was Boring's rendition of the "Man of Steel" that eventually became definitive. Whereas Joe Shuster's *Superman* art was crude and plodding, Boring's work was infinitely tighter and more polished. Influenced by Frank Godwin's work on the *Connie* syndicated strip, he remade Superman's squat and chunky figure into a massive, rippling, muscular body. His Superman always sported bulging chest and thigh muscles, never stood or flew in anything but the most classic poses, and always looked the part of the world's mightiest creature. Boring also excelled in expressive faces, every character flawlessly rendered for the best dramatic effect. But many save their highest praise for Boring's city scenes. When editor Mort Weisinger tried to make the *Superman* feature more futuristic, he resorted to gimmicky science fiction plots, but Boring's backgrounds achieved a futuristic look simply by ingenious uses of vertical lines. Unlike Carmine Infantino's prettier, more rounded, and lower cities in *Adam Strange*, Boring created captivating masses of stylized, rectangular skyscrapers.

Boring finally left National and *Superman* for syndicated strip work in 1968, spending four years assisting Hal Foster on *Prince Valiant* and Sam Leff on *Davy Jones*.

"The Born Loser," Art and Chip Sansom. © NEA.

He returned to comic books in 1972, drawing Marvel strips like *Captain Marvel* and *Gullivar of Mars*. He gave up drawing comics in 1991. He was working as a night watchman when he died on February 20, 1987, in Pompano Beach, Florida.

J.B.

BORN LOSER, THE (U.S.) After working for two decades as a bullpen cartoonist drawing several story features for the Newspaper Enterprise Association, Arthur B. Sansom Jr. added a refreshingly new strip to his syndicate in 1964. Dubbed *The Born Loser*, the new humor strip was one of the more sophisticated features to emerge during the 1960s. The beleaguered subject, Brutus P. Thornapple, is a typical, middle-aged Everyman who is beset by fate and family. His towering wife Gladys delivers smug remarks and derogatory support to her husband, while his seven-year-old son Wilberforce usually gets the upper hand in most situations. Neighbor Hurricane Hattie O'Hara is a formidable opponent, particularly for Brutus—a seven-year-old smart aleck specializing in aggravation, while sardonic mother-in-law Ramona Gargle and lethargic pet mutt Kewpie finish off the dysfunctional domestic cast. The discouraging nature of Brutus's existence is mirrored outside the home, in his dealings with discourteous store clerks, persistent beggars, and obnoxious drunks. His boss, Rancid W. Veeblefester, is a towering menace who belittles and berates his employees during putting practice in his executive suite of an office.

Launched by NEA as a daily on May 10, 1965, and on the following June 27 on Sundays, *The Born Loser* contributed significantly to the modern minimal drawing style now common, with only slight movement indicated in the static, generally verbal sequences. Consistently funny, Sansom managed to instill an accommodating slant to his incisive creation, entertaining audiences in 1,300 newspapers in over two dozen countries.

Sansom's son Chip began apprenticing in 1977, gradually rising from gag writer to artist as well. The two have shared a byline since the mid-1980s, even though the strip has been done entirely by Chip Sansom since Art's death on July 4, 1991. Four book collections of *The Born Loser* have appeared since 1975, and the National Cartoonist Society named it Best Humor Strip for 1987 and 1990. A classic, *The Born Loser* is on par with most of the industry's other great

strips, making Brutus P. Thornapple the winningest loser in the comics.

B.J.

BOTTARO, LUCIANO (1931-   ) Italian cartoonist, born November 16, 1931, in Rapallo, Liguria. After dropping out from a technical college, Luciano Bottaro entered the field of comics in 1949 with a few pages he drew for the magazine *Lo Scolaro*. In 1950 he created his first strip, *Aroldo*, a pirate story that started publication two years later. After military service, Bottaro worked for Edizioni Alpe, producing a number of humor strips, among them *Tim, Pepito, Baldo, Marameo*, and *Whisky e Gogo*. At the same time Bianconi published two more of his comic creations: *Pik Pok* and *Papi Papero* ("Daddy Duck").

In 1951 Bottaro started working for the Italian branch of Walt Disney Productions and in short order became one of the more noted and imaginative artists on *Donald Duck*. When Faisani released the comic monthly *Oscar* (1959), Bottaro contributed a number of strips, all endowed with a special graphic lyricism: *Lola, Nasolungo* ("Bignose"), and the Western parody *Maiopi*. *Pinko e Ponko* of the same period were early forerun-

Luciano Bottaro, "Nel Paese dell'Alfabeto." © C. d. P.

ners of Hanna-Barbera's *The Flintstones*, while his tender strip about a little mushroom, *Pon Pon*, was regarded as one of the most imaginative creations in Italian comics. Two of Bottaro's other strips, *Pepito* (1951) and *Redipicche* (1969) are also his most successful. Collaborating with Bottaro on almost all of his strips has been the scriptwriter Carlo Chendi. In 1982 Bottaro realized a new adaptation of *Pinocchio* in comics form. He has also been very active in computer graphics throughout the 1990s.

Bottaro's characters have been widely utilized in merchandising, while a gift shop in San Remo currently uses the name Pon Pon.

G.B.

BOUCQ, FRANÇOIS (1955-   ) French cartoonist, born November 28, 1955, in Lille in northern France. After art school studies, François Boucq started his professional career in 1974 as a political cartoonist for such publications as *Le Point, L'Expansion*, and the daily *le Matin*. The following year he contributed his first, tentative comic strips to the humor magazine *Mormoil*; but it was only in 1978, with *Les Cornets d'Humour* ("Humor Scoops") for *Pilote*, that his talents in the field came to be recognized nationally. For a long time he restricted himself to turning out humor strips, particularly for the comic magazine *Fluide Glacial*, in whose pages he created in the early 1980s *Rock Mastard* (a spoof of superheroes) and *Les Leçons du Professeur Bourremou*, about the ramblings of a zany pedagogue.

Boucq took a job at the comics magazine *A Suivre* in 1983, publishing short, humorous stories, but soon turned his attention to more ambitious fare. In a collaboration with the noted American novelist Jerome Chayrin, he realized two highly original graphic novels. The first, *The Magician's Wife* (1985), set in Saratoga Springs in the shady world of jockeys, race touts, and crooked gamblers, was a thriller with fantastic overtones. *Bouche du Diable* ("Billy Budd, KGB") followed in 1989; it again mixed elements of suspense, mystery, and the fantastic, as it records the fateful progress of a Soviet spy from the KGB's training school in the Ukraine to the streets of New York City.

With these and the equally innovative stories that have come out from his brush in the 1990s, the most outstanding being *Face de Lune* ("Moon Face," 1991) with a story line by famous screenwriter Alexandro Jodorowsky, Boucq has joined the front ranks of international comics creators.

M.H.

BOY COMMANDOS (U.S.) Of all the kid groups comic books that World War II produced during the 1940s, Joe Simon and Jack Kirby's *Boy Commandos* was undoubtedly the most popular and distinctive. Created just three months after their *Newsboy Legion* feature, the four-boy, one-adult combine premiered in National's *Detective Comics* number 64 in June 1942. The group was ethnically balanced—like the adult *Blackhawk* group before it—and showcased one kid from each country fighting the Germans.

America was represented by a tough, swaggering Brooklynite who talked like Jimmy Cagney and dressed in a green sweater and garish red derby; from France, Pierre Chavard joined the group to fight the "Boche," and eventually changed his name to Andre; Jan Haasen came from Holland to help defeat the Nazis because they killed his parents; and finally, there was the

English child, Alfy Twidgett, who battled the "Jerries" mostly with his cockney accent. Leading this brigade of children was Captain Rip Carter, the group's mentor and teacher. He trained the boys for one purpose only: to battle and defeat the Axis and make the world safe for democracy.

Throughout the war years, the *Boy Commandos* did fight the enemy everywhere possible, to the apparent vicarious glee of the readers who eventually helped the group into their own book in the winter of 1942. Their popularity was such that besides the score of imitators that were to follow, Harvey Comics introduced the "quartette of fighting queens" called the Girl Commandos. As the war ended, however—and Simon and Kirby moved elsewhere—the strip slowly began to degenerate. Jan and Alfy were dropped, and in their stead came Tex, an uninteresting cowboy character who was of little value either as an action figure or an ethnic figure. The group was also forced to return to America and fight more common crooks, and without the menace of Nazis and Japanese, *Boy Commandos* became just another comic book strip.

In all, *Boy Commandos* was a durable strip and lasted until *Detective* number 150 and *Boy Commandos* number 36 before disbanding in December 1949. In 1973, however, National reprinted two issues of *Boy Commandos* for a seemingly uninterested audience.

J.B.

BOZZ *see* Velter, Robert

BRAMMETJE BRAM (Netherlands) A creation of Belgian artist Edouard Ryssack (with Piet-Hein Broenland as writer), *Brammetje Bram* is a fast-paced, humorous strip about pirates in the early 19th century. It first appeared in 1970 in the Dutch comic weekly *Sjors*. Its star, of course, is Brammetje Bram, a red-haired boy wearing red pants and a red striped shirt. Brammetje does not get into the story until page eight of the first episode, well after the stage has been set by introducing his antagonist, the terror of the seven seas, the pirate captain Knevel de Killer. While walking along the street, Brammetje comes across a striped cat pursued by a butcher. Together with the cat he escapes the butcher by running aboard a ship, which turns out to be that of the pirate captain, who has agreed to take the king's daughter to her Prince Charming. The pirate, of course, secretly plans to hold the princess for ran-

"Brammetje Bram," Edouard Ryssack. © Eddie Ryssack.

som. These plans, however, do not work out after Brammetje Bram and the cat (who had fallen asleep) are discovered as stowaways far out at sea. Brammetje Bram is hired as cabin boy and turns out to be the one person who can ward off the attacks of fleets of other pirates. It is also he who causes a happy ending.

Besides Brammetje and the captain there is a strong cast of supporting characters, all acting in the best of the (animated) cartoon tradition. Besides being a visual delight with its sense for movement and visual gags, *Brammetje Bram* is also well written. In a way, the series also is an allegory of the constant struggle of Good against Evil. Whatever evil the pirate captain may plan is held in check and eventually turned into good by Brammetje, without the slightest semblance of moralizing.

W.F.

BRANDOLI, ANNA (1945-   ) Italian illustrator and cartoonist, born July 27, 1945, in Milan. Anna Brandoli began her career as a cartoonist drawing the medieval story *La strega* ("The Witch"), written by Renato Queirolo and published in the monthly *Alter Alter* in 1977.

In 1979 she illustrated the comics adaptation of L. Frank Baum's *The Wizard of Oz* for the weekly *Corriere dei Piccoli*. During the 1980s, working with scriptwriter Queirolo, she drew the as-yet-unfinished trilogy *Testamenti di Sant'Ambrogio* ("Saint Ambrose's Testaments/Wills") of which only the first and second episodes, *Rebecca* and *Scene di caccia* ("Hunting Scenes"), appeared in the monthly *Orient Express*. The trilogy follows the gypsy Rebecca through her wanderings in Northern Italy in the year 1492, which, though considered the beginning of modern times, still marked an era of intolerance and prejudices.

Brandoli's next work was *Alias*, another unfinished adventure written by Queirolo and set in 17th-century Netherlands. It was published in 1987 in the monthly *Comic Art*, which also published *Cuba 1942* (1991) and *Il gigante italiano* ("The Italian Giant," 1993), both written by Ottavio De Angelis. Since then Brandoli has given up drawing comics and has devoted herself to book illustration. This is a real loss to the comic book world, since her powerful graphic style, with expressionist overtones based on violent contrasts between black and white, has left a mark on the Italian comics world. Most of Brandoli's stories have been reprinted in book form. Brandoli was awarded a Yellow Kid in Lucca in 1984.

G.C.C.

BRANNER, MARTIN (1888-1970) American cartoonist, born December 28, 1888, in New York City. Martin Michael Branner was educated in the New York public schools. In 1907, with his 15-year-old bride, Edith Fabrini, he started a song-and-dance act and met with some success on the vaudeville circuit. After service during World War I, he sold his first comic strip, *Looie the Lawyer*, to the Bell Syndicate in 1919. A short time later he started a second Sunday feature, *Pete and Pinto*, for the *New York Sun*. The success of *Looie*, meanwhile, had brought Branner's work to the attention of Arthur Crawford, general manager of the New York News-Chicago Tribune Syndicate. In September 1920, *Winnie Winkle, the Breadwinner*, Branner's most enduring creation, made its debut (later to be joined by *Looie* as its bottom strip). Martin Branner retired from the comic strip field in 1962, leaving *Winnie Winkle* in the hands of his assistant Max van Bibber. Branner died on May 19, 1970, after a long illness.

While he was not an outstanding cartoonist by any means, Branner possessed sufficient charm, originality, and freshness to leave a durable imprint on the history of the comics.

M.H.

BRECCIA, ALBERTO (1919-1993) A resident of Argentina for many years, the Uruguayan cartoonist Alberto Breccia was born in Montevideo in 1919. In 1936 he started his collaboration to Buenos Aires publications with a number of comic strips: in this youthful period only *Mu-fa, un Detective Oriental* (1939) stands out. In 1941 Breccia moved to Brazil but came back to Buenos Aires, where he drew *Vito Nervio* from 1947 to 1959. In this period he also produced *El Vengador* ("The Avenger") for the magazine *El Gorrion*, and *Jean de la Martinica* for *Patoruzito*. His latter works include *La Ejecucion* ("The Execution"), written by Hector Oesterheld, the scriptwriter of other Breccia creations such as *Richard Long, Pancho Lopez* (published in the magazine of the same name), and *Sherlock Time*, which he created in 1958 for *Frontera* magazine. With the latter, Brecia initiated his most ambitious and complex cycle, opening fresh vistas and blazing new trails.

During a long European trip starting in 1960, Breccia was contracted by Fleetway Publications of London and he worked on a number of their publications. Back in Argentina in 1962, Breccia resumed his career with *Mort Cinder* the same year. In 1968 he took over the drawing of *El Eternauta* and created his very personal *La Vida del Che* ("The Life of Che [Guevara]") which was subjected to the rigors of the censors. Soon after, he devoted most of his time to a long-cherished project, the pictorialization of H. P. Lovecraft's difficult and controversial stories, *Los Mitos de Cthulhu* ("The Myths of Cthulhu").

In 1984 he started a new, long-running science-fiction series, *Perramus*, which proved to be his valedictory. He died in Buenos Aires on November 10, 1993.

L.G.

BREGER, DAVID (1908-1970) Born in 1908 into a Russian immigrant family in Chicago, the future coiner of the famed term "G. I. Joe" (in a comic panel series of the same name) was called Dave from the moment he entered a Chicago grammar school. Educated fitfully between stints working with his father in the sausage industry in his teens, the young Breger encountered the Chicago gangsters of the 1920s more than once. (On one occasion, he was actually shot at by a protection racket hoodlum, saving himself only by moving a door between himself and the bullet and catching it miraculously on the metal lock.) In the 1930s, he developed his cartooning talent with serious professionalism and began to sell gag panels to the big slicks (*Collier's, Liberty*, etc.). Entering the army as a buck private in the year before America's entry into World War II, Breger created a comic panel series based on his basic-training experiences as a rookie, selling it to King Features Syndicate under the title *Private Breger*.

Shortly after its appearance in 1941, it caught the eyes of the men who were preparing the publication of an official entertainment and historical magazine for the American forces, to be called *Yank*. They wanted Breger's self-caricature series in *Yank*, but since the

Dave Breger, "Private Breger." © *King Features Syndicate.*

new magazine would be entirely filled by the work of enlisted men done for the magazine, the syndicated strip could not be used. Breger agreed to do a separate weekly panel for *Yank*, under a new name. In thinking of this new name, Breger came up with *G. I. Joe* (for Government-Issue Joe), and sold the *Yank* people on it. Within a week of the first *G. I. Joe* panel in the first *Yank*, on June 17, 1942, the term was on everyone's lips in the services, and a week later it was being heard everywhere in the country, as if it had always been in existence. G. I. Joe had a reality beyond that of Breger's character: it had replaced "Yank" as the popular term for an American foot soldier.

A book collection of Breger's *G. I. Joe* panels appeared in 1945, and was a best-seller for months, being read avidly by the same people who treasured their collections of *The Sad Sack* and Mauldin's *Joe and Willie* panels. Breger's King Features panel had its title changed after Breger's discharge at the end of the war to *Mr. Breger*, and a Sunday half-page was added, in comic strip format. *Mr. Breger*, however, was not the universal hit Breger's military life feature had been, for his highly individual wit and acid view of humanity in private life was not to everyone's taste. The strip and panel continued with reasonable success, however, into the 1960s, when the panel was dropped and the Sunday strip continued alone. At this time, Breger wrote what many consider a basic reference work, his *How To Draw and Sell Cartoons* of 1966. (In 1954 he had also written a very funny and revealing exposé on cartoon censorship, *But That's Unprintable!*)

A large, full-faced man who did not look in the least like the bespectacled, shrimpish Private/Mr. Breger, Dave Breger lived most of his postwar life on an estate in South Nyack, New York, where he died (in a nearby hospital) after a long illness on January 16, 1970, at the age of 61. His highly individual strip died with him.

B.B.

BRENDA STARR (U.S.) *Brenda Starr* was born on June 30, 1940, as a Sunday page, from the pen of Dalia (Dale) Messick, despite the misgivings of Captain Joseph Patterson of the Chicago Tribune-New York News Syndicate, which distributed the feature. The captain's fears were ill-founded as it turned out: *Brenda* went on to become a steadily growing success, and a daily strip was added in October 1945.

Dale Messick wanted to make her heroine a woman-bandit, but settled for a girl reporter on the advice of her editor, Mollie Slott. Brenda is always flying to the far corners of the earth on assignments for her newspaper, *The Flash*, and is always impeccably dressed and coiffured, even in the unlikeliest of situations. Her love life is as restless as her career: relentlessly pursuing her lover, the elusive Basil St. John, who suffers from a "secret disease" and sends her black orchids from afar; and being pursued in turn by every male character in the strip. Her problems are not made any easier by her gruff managing editor Livwright, her homely female colleague Hank O'Hair, or her overbearing cousin Abretha Breeze, from Pinhook, Indiana.

Romance dominates the events in *Brenda Starr*, which has remained popular over the years in spite of its outlandish characterization and the ludicrousness of most of its situations. The strip (which eventually was produced by a team of specialized artists under the direction of Miss Messick) seems to appeal mainly to younger female readers who tend to identify with the heroine and relish her stormy and doomed love affairs. A movie serial, *Brenda Starr, Reporter*, was produced by Columbia Pictures in 1945.

"Brenda Starr," Dale Messick. © *Chicago Tribune News Syndicate.*

Messick retired from the strip in 1980. The writing was then taken over by Linda Sutter, who turned over the scripting chores to Maria Schmich in 1985. After a 15-year stint drawing *Brenda Starr*, former comic-book artist Ramona Fradon resigned in 1995. The feature is now being illustrated by June Brigman.

M.H.

BRICK BRADFORD (U.S.) *Brick Bradford* was the product of the collaboration between writer William Ritt and artist Clarence Gray. Appearing as a daily strip on August 21, 1933, and as a Sunday page in November 1934, *Brick* was distributed first by Central Press Association and then by King Features Syndicate.

In 1949 Ritt stopped writing the story lines, and Gray became his own scriptwriter. Illness forced him to abandon the daily strip in 1952, but he continued to draw the Sundays until his death in 1957. During Gray's tenure Brick enjoyed his own comic book (done by Paul Norris) in the 1940s and 1950s; and in 1948 Spencer Gordon Bennett and Thomas Carr adapted *Brick Bradford* into a movie serial.

Having taken over the dailies and later the Sundays from Gray, Norris managed to pilot Brick through time and space in his own laborious, plodding way for almost twice as long as his predecessor. Under his guidance *Brick Bradford* lasted until 1987, the dailies ending on April 25, and the last Sunday appearing on May 10.

Brick himself is a hero devoid of neuroses and ambiguities. He represents the tradition of an earlier, more optimistic era. In his actions he is motivated by nothing more than his curiosity and love of adventure, which draw him into the most unlikely situations in alternating tales of exploration, suspense, and science

"Brick Bradford," William Ritt and Clarence Gray. © King Features Syndicate.

fiction. It is to the latter genre that *Brick Bradford* belongs most firmly, and while it possesses neither the futuristic vision of *Buck Rogers* nor the epic grandeur of *Flash Gordon*, *Brick Bradford* displays the undeniable qualities of fantasy, poetry, and imagination that put in on a par with its better-known rivals. Brick Bradford's exploration into the atoms of a copper penny and his adventures in the center of the earth were particularly spectacular.

Aside from the hero himself, few memorable characters emerged out of *Brick Bradford*; Kalla Kopak, Brick's scientist companion, and Bucko O'Brien, his loud-mouthed, ill-tempered sidekick, were the only exceptions.

M.H.

BRIEFER, RICHARD (1915-1982?) American comic book artist and writer, born in 1915. He attended New York's Art Students League and entered the comic book business in 1936 as a member of the S. M. "Jerry" Iger studio. Dick Briefer's earliest work appeared in Helne's *Wow* in 1936, one of the first comic books to carry original material. Over the next several years at the lger studio, Briefer produced material for Fiction House (1938-1941, *Hunchback of Notre Dame, Flint Baker*, others), Fox (1939-1941, *Rex Dexter of Mars*), Worth (1940), Marvel (1940, *Human Top*), and others.

In 1940, however, Briefer approached the Prize group with a proposal to adapt Mary Shelley's 1818 *Frankenstein* to comics. The artist/writer's version, which premiered in *Prize* number seven for December 1940, had Victor Frankenstein creating his monster during an experiment in 1940 Manhattan. The doctor sees his monster begin a crusade against humanity, and in a repentant mood, vows to care for an orphan named Denny; the boy eventually catches up with Frankenstein and puts him into the care of Dr. Carrol for rehabilitation.

Drawing the strip under the painfully obvious pen name of "Frank N. Stein"—much of Briefer's other work was signed "Richard Norman" or "Remington Brant"—Briefer handled the strip poorly. His work was crude, his layouts loose and lackadaisical, and his execution juvenile. It was, in fact, comedic. But after the monster's rehabilitation, Briefer cashed in on his own style and began playing the strip for laughs with great results. His artwork was ideally suited for this twist: his whimsical Frankenstein interpretation was appealing and his scenes and drawings were pleasantly humorous. He relocated the monster in "Mippyville," and this humorous, often underrated version of Frankenstein became a financial success, and a *Frankenstein* title was added to his *Prize* appearances. After six years of good fortune, however, the *Frankenstein* series ended with February 1949's 17th issue, and Briefer returned to serious drawing.

After some horror work for Atlas, Briefer then moved to the romance line in a two-year stint with Hillman on *Rosie Romance*. But Prize recalled him in March 1952 to revive *Frankenstein*. Unfortunately, however, it was the serious version and the artist/writer was obviously bored with the whole concept. His stories were poor and hackneyed, his artwork sloppy. This revival mercifully died in November 1954.

Briefer left the comic industry shortly thereafter to concentrate on advertising artwork, and then in 1962 turned his attention to portrait painting. He reportedly died in the spring of 1982.

J.B.

BRIGGS, AUSTIN (1908-1973) American cartoonist and illustrator, born September 8, 1908, in Humboldt, Minnesota. After studies at the Detroit City College and the Wicker Art School, Briggs moved to New York City in the early 1930s; there he worked for an advertising agency and freelanced for various magazines while attending classes at the Art Students' League. He started his comic strip career as Alex Raymond's assistant in 1936, then took over the *Secret Agent X-9* strip from 1938 to 1940. On May 27 of the same year he created (uncredited) the *Flash Gordon* daily, and in 1944, following Raymond's enlistment, started drawing the Sunday pages (also including *Jungle Jim*) as well. He also worked briefly on the *Spy Smasher* comic book in 1941.

Chiefly known as an illustrator, Austin Briggs also left his mark as a comic strip artist. As Alex Raymond's successor on both *X-9* and *Flash Gordon*, he showed talent, style, and imagination, proving himself Raymond's most worthy rival.

In 1948 Briggs left the comic strip field to devote himself fully to magazine illustration. A cofounder of the Famous Artists School and a member of the Society of Illustrators' Hall of Fame, Briggs was also the recipient of countless awards. On October 10, 1973, Austin Briggs died of leukemia in Paris, where he had retired.

M.H.

BRIGGS, CLARE (1875-1930) American artist, born in Reedsburg, Wisconsin, on August 5, 1875. When Briggs was nine, his family moved to Dixon, Illinois, where the youngster drew his first sketches, and later

to Lincoln, Nebraska, where he attended Nebraska University. His first published cartoons appeared during this time in *The Western Penman*.

At age 21, Briggs went to work for the *St. Louis Democrat* as a $10-a-week sketch artist, depicting news events in the days before widespread photographic reproduction. Two years later, in 1898, he switched to the *St. Louis Chronicle* as an editorial cartoonist. He played the Spanish-American War for all it was worth, but when the war ended so did his subject material and Briggs was out of a job.

He then traveled to New York City and failed in various jobs peripheral to the art world: sign-painting, show cards, catalog illustration, etc. He returned to Lincoln in 1900 and married Ruth Owen. Another "invasion" of New York was more successful: Briggs became a sketch artist for the *New York Journal*. A perceptive editor told Briggs he was meant to be a cartoonist, and William Randolph Hearst assigned the penman to his Chicago properties, the *American* and *Examiner*.

Here Briggs shone and became a celebrity (no mean feat in a city dominated by John McCutcheon). For the *American* he pioneered daily strips with the short-lived *A. Piker Clerk*. In 1907 Briggs was lured away by McCutcheon's Chicago *Tribune*, and his humorous panel cartoons earned him a national reputation.

In 1914 he returned to New York at the invitation of the *Tribune*; here he stayed until his death.

Briggs succeeded in producing the synthesis of various newspaper cartoon genres emerging in the early years of the century. His panel creations spanned sports, suburban life, nostalgia, and the kibitzer-vignettes creates by Tad. His series ran to dozens of titles: *When a Feller Needs a Friend, The Days of Real Sport, Movie of a Man, Golf, Someone's Always Taking the Joy Out of Life, There's at Least One in Every Office, Ain't it a Grand and Glorious Feelin'?*

Briggs' humor seldom failed; he was, simply, a genius at recognizing and chronicling human emotion—a boy and his dog at the swimming hole, frustrations on the golf course, or marital squabbling. Perhaps his greatest series is one least remembered—significantly, because it dealt with things in life also seldom noticed: *Real Folks at Home*. Here Briggs glorified the commonplace, visited the homes of ordinary people—streetcleaners, bakers, cab drivers—and imagined the small talk. No funny endings, no glamour—just a brilliant insight into the soul of the common people and a contrast to the flashiness and celebrity addiction of the rest of the newspaper.

Briggs produced several strips besides *A. Piker Clerk* in his Chicago days—Sunday features—and his *Mr. and Mrs.* color page for the Herald-Tribune Syndicate was a funny, realistic picture of the never-ending bickering between Vi and Joe Green.

Briggs' style was breezy and informal, a solid familiarity with anatomy hiding handsomely behind economy of line, abbreviated strokes, little detail or background, and masterful blocking and spotting of blacks.

He died in New York on January 3, 1930, after a long illness; pneumonia followed lung problems and he was bothered by troubles with the optic nerve (drawing was difficult during his last year). He divorced his wife in 1929; she and a common-law wife made headlines as they fought over the estate.

Clare Briggs, "Danny Dreamer."

Briggs' kid cartoons were put on the screen in 1919, and *Mr. and Mrs.* became a radio serial in 1929. The latter feature was continued, very badly, by a succession of artists, into the 1960s.

R.M.

BRIGGS, RAYMOND (1934-) British cartoonist Raymond Briggs was born on January 18, 1934, in Wimbledon, London, the son of a milkman. He attended the Rutlish School, Merton, and studied at Wimbledon School of Art and at The Slade for two years. His career began in 1957 when his illustrations appeared in magazines and children's books. In 1966 he won the Kate Greenaway Medal for his illustrations in *The Mother Goose Treasury*. Convinced that he could write better stories than the ones he was illustrating, he wrote and drew *Father Christmas*, his first full-color book, in 1973, for which he won his second Kate Greenaway Medal. He based his refreshingly down-to-earth, no-nonsense *Father Christmas* on his father and modeled Santa's house on his parents' home. The sequel, *Father Christmas Goes on Holiday*, was published in 1975.

Having humanized the sugar-coated cliché of Father Christmas, Briggs took on his next project, exploring the hilariously disgusting world of slimy monsters in *Fungus the Bogeyman* in 1977, upsetting some parents but delighting children. The next year, after this detailed and complex book, he switched to a much simpler, completely silent strip book, *The Snowman*. This tells the story of a boy's snowman who comes to life, capturing the beauty of winter landscapes and the comfort of home in evocative drawings done in colored pencil. The book has become a classic and was adapted into an animated film.

In 1980 Briggs introduced Jim and Hilda Bloggs, trusting elderly English pensioners battling the forces of law and society in *Gentleman Jim*. Two years later they returned in his masterpiece, *When the Wind Blows*. Briggs felt passionately about the government's inadequate and misleading contingency planning in the event of a nuclear attack. The early scenes of the Bloggs' simple life are told in small, cheerful panels, interrupted by huge two-page illustrations of the escalating war. These climax in two white pages, when the bomb is dropped. Briggs then shows the couple following the advice of the government, which utterly fails in dealing with the true horror of the situation. The Bloggs hope for the best, but radiation sickness rapidly erodes their health and leads to their deeply moving deaths. The book was discussed in the House of Commons and adapted into a play and an animated feature film in 1987.

Briggs' anger at the lives lost and damaged in the Falklands War inspired *The Tin-Pot Foreign General and the Old Iron Woman*, published in 1984. A political picture book, it contrasts savage political caricatures with haunting pencil drawings of the dead and injured. In recent years, Briggs has created several successful children's illustrated books, starting with *Unlucky Wally Twenty Years On*, which was published in 1989, but so far he has not returned to the complete comic strip format.

P.G.

BRIGMAN, JUNE (1960-) Born in Atlanta, Georgia, in 1960, comic strip artist June Brigman grew up reading *Brenda Starr* in the *Atlanta Journal*. Her other favorite strip was *The Phantom*. Brigman studied art at the University of Georgia and Georgia State University.

She freelanced at many different art jobs, including a summer stint working as a quick portrait artist at a Georgia amusement park. In 1982 she sent samples of her work to Marvel Comics in New York City, where she was offered a job. At Marvel she teamed up with writer-editor Louise Simonson to create the *Power Pack* series. *Power Pack* was a group of children, two boys and two girls, ages 6 to 12, who had been given super powers by a friendly alien.

Brigman went on to draw a wide range of comic books, including *She Hawk* for Marvel, *Supergirl* and *Teen Titans* for DC Comics, and a four-book miniseries of *Star Wars* for Dark Horse Comics. Brigman's last comic book work was drawing *Barbie* for Marvel Comics. She also drew illustrations for the children's book *Choose Your Own Adventure* and the comic strip *Where in the World Is Carmen Sandiego?* for National Geographic Society's children's magazine.

After hearing from a friend that Ramona Fradon, the cartoonist who was drawing *Brenda Starr*, was retiring, Brigman contacted Tribune Media Services, submitted samples of her work, and was hired. On November 6, 1995, Brigman became the third female cartoonist to draw *Brenda Starr*. The comic strip about the star reporter for *The Flash* newspaper was created in 1940 by Dalia (Dale) Messick for the Chicago Tribune-New York News Syndicate. Copying neither Messick's nor Fradon's style, June Brigman has successfully kept the traditional *Brenda Starr* look and mood of the strip, while initiating a very clean line style. The future of *Brenda Starr* looks bright with the professional team of June Brigman and Mary Schmich.

B.C.

BRINGING UP FATHER (U.S.) When George McManus created *Bringing Up Father* for the Hearst organization, he was already a cartoonist of high repute. *Bringing Up Father*, which first appeared in the dailies in 1913, was only one of a number of strip ideas that McManus had played around with. It was sometimes missing for weeks at a time, and only in 1916 did it become definitively established (with the Sunday version following on April 14, 1918).

The most striking feature of *Bringing Up Father* is its theatricality. Inspired by William Gill's 1893 play *The Rising Generation* (which McManus saw as a child), the strip, in the neat unfolding of each of its episodes, resembles a skit or playlet, loaded with witty dialogue, nutty characters, and outlandish happenings. The underlying theme of the strip is quite simple (as in all great creations): Jiggs, a former mason, and his wife Maggie, an ex-washerwoman, have suddenly become wealthy by winning the Irish sweepstakes. But while Maggie, the epitome of ugliness, snobbishness, and egotism, seeks to forget her social origins, Jiggs' only wish is to meet his buddies at Dinty Moore's tavern for a dish of corn beef and cabbage and a friendly game of pinochle. Most of the strip's hilarious events derive from this basic situation.

The luxurious setting of the action, an astounding mixture of rococo architecture, Art Nouveau furnishings, and weird-shaped curios, form the appropriate backdrop for this battle of the sexes, in which the immaculately dressed Jiggs is forever ducking out of the house (while ducking Maggie's rolling pin at the same time). These almost ritual proceedings are refereed by

"Bringing Up Father," George McManus. © King Features Syndicate.

Maggie's and Jiggs' stylish daughter Nora, and sometimes upstaged by the outrageous shenanigans of the scores of secondary characters who blissfully wander in and out of the plot.

Bringing Up Father is one of the very few comic strips in which all strata of society are represented in an astounding gallery of portraits ranging all the way from the upper crust to the lower depths: genuine and false princes, captains of industry, social climbers, petty-bourgeois, dim-witted cops, shiftless workingmen, querulous maids, smart-alecky errand-boys, loafers, moochers, small-time grifters, and bums of every type and description, who all take part in the great parade.

After McManus' death in 1954, *Bringing Up Father* was written by Bill Kavanagh and the Sunday page was drawn by Frank Fletcher, while Vernon Greene drew the daily strip until his death in 1965, when he was succeeded by Hal Campagna (signing "Camp"). As of 1996 Frank Johnson was doing both versions of the feature.

Bringing Up Father was the first comic strip to enjoy worldwide fame. It has been reprinted in book form, translated into most languages, adapted six times to the screen, and made into animated cartoons. During the war Jiggs was the official emblem of the Eleventh Bombardment Squadron. In the 1920s a stage play, *Father*, toured the United States and Canada, and McManus himself appeared as Jiggs in some of the productions. Several other plays based on McManus' comic strip were also produced in later years.

M.H.

BRINKERHOFF, ROBERT MOORE (1880-1958) American cartoonist and illustrator, born May 4, 1880, in Toledo, Ohio. R. M. Brinkerhoff's father, R. A. Brinkerhoff, was a cofounder of the *Toledo Post*, which later merged into the *Toledo News-Bee*. Brinkerhoff *fils* developed an early liking for the arts and started studying music at the Cincinnati Conservatory before going on to the Art Students League in New York City. After a brief stay in Paris, he returned to Toledo and became a political cartoonist on the *Blade* before moving to the *Cleveland Leader* and the *Cincinnati Post*.

In 1913 Brinkerhoff moved to New York, where he joined the staff of the *Evening World* and became a successful painter and illustrator. In 1917, at the urging of fellow cartoonist Will B. Johnston, he created his first (and only) comic strip, *Little Mary Mixup*. The tale of this mischievous little girl, drawn in an airy and graceful style, was slight but Brinkerhoff made it enjoyable as well as believable. Conceived first as a little devil with innocent blue eyes and girlish blonde curls, Little Mary eventually grew up and in World War II even

joined the fight against the Nazis. The strip could have reached greater heights of popularity had Brinkerhoff devoted his full time to it. Certainly he was an artist of outstanding talent, but he never gave poor Little Mary more than casual attention. Brinkerhoff had many other interests: he painted, illustrated stories and books, and wrote several books himself. But his real passion was the sea: he owned several yachts—on which he went several times around the world—and even owned an island—Brinkerhoff-Island—in Maine. After a long and productive life, R. M. Brinkerhoff died in Minneapolis on February 17, 1958.

(Brinkerhoff's son, Robert Jr., an advertising artist, also tried his hand at cartooning: he drew the short-lived *Hagen, Fagin and O'Toole*, a comic strip about a Great Dane, a Siamese cat, and a parrot.)

M.H.

BRISTOW (G.B.) "In the Chester-Perry Building/Massive Chester-Perry Building/Was an office known as Buying/Buying was their occupation/And their names were Jones and Bristow." That was Frank Dickens writing/drawing (his drawing is so basic and speedy it is almost writing) one of his popular parodies in *Bristow*, the first British newspaper strip to follow the non-art tradition begun by James Thurber. The quoted poem continues with references that set Bristow firmly in his milieu: "All the phoning, all the filing/All the dreary dreadful filing/Nine to five for just a pittance/So they hated Chester-Perry/Hated him with all their being/And they lived for going-home time. . . ."

Actually, the "lovely, glorious going-home time" is not all that lovely and glorious to Bristow, who loves his daily routine and encounters with the incredibly badly drawn pigeon, Mrs. Purdie the Tea Lady, his lunch lovingly prepared by Mr. Gordon Blue, master chef of the Chester-Perry canteen, the Blondini Brothers ("scaffolding to the gentry"), the shouting Mr. Fudge, the letter to Messrs. Gun and Fames and the ensuing fun and games, and the rejection slip for the great Bristow novel from Messrs. Heap and Trotwood.

Created and written by Frank Dickens (born 1932), who was fortunately allowed to return to his own handwrought lettering after a period of unsuitable legibility, *Bristow* grew out of *Oddbod*, his first strip for the *Sunday Times* (1960), and the picture stories in his book, *What the Dickens* (1961). It began in the *London Evening Standard* in 1962 and is syndicated by Dickens himself to many provincial British newspapers, as well as to the *South China Morning Post*, the *Sydney Morning Herald*, the South African *Eastern Echo*, and papers in New Zealand and Brazil. Bristow's name varies, even in England. The *Lancashire Evening Post* acted on complaints from a Mr. Bristow and changed his name to Dickens! There is an original book, *Bristow*, published by Constable in 1966, and several reprints of the strip: *Bristow!* (1970); *Bristow* (1972); *More Bristow* (1973); *Bristow Extra* (1974). Dickens was voted cartoonist of the year four times by the Cartoonists Club of Great Britain, has transferred *Bristow* to the stage, and, shortly, hopes for a film and television series. After 35 years of existence, *Bristow* is still going as strong as ever.

D.G.

BRONC PEELER (U.S.) In 1934 Fred Harman created his first comic strip, *Bronc Peeler*, which he syndicated himself, as both a daily and a weekly feature, to a few newspapers (including the *San Francisco Chronicle*).

Bronc was a young ranch hand who fought cattle rustlers and bank robbers, saved innocent young girls from swarthy seducers, and once even worked as an undercover agent for the F.B.I. When he was not out riding through the Rockies or along the Rio Grande, Bronc could usually be found in the company of his sweetheart—blonde, energetic Babs—or with Coyote Pete, his grizzled, slow-witted sidekick. *Bronc Peeler's* locale was New Mexico, and unlike *Red Ryder*, it took place in modern times: Bronc could be seen riding a car or even flying an airplane.

Fred Harman once made a statement to the effect that his early strip was now completely forgotten, and justly so—but he was wrong on both counts. While the artwork in *Bronc Peeler* was sometimes clumsy, it also displayed vigor and zest; the plots were quite imaginative and well handled visually ("The Lost Valley of the Aztecs" is a good example). As to the first point: by some yet unexplained fluke, *Bronc Peeler* was published in France, where it enjoyed wider circulation (and

greater popularity) than in the United States—and in recent years fond reminiscences of the strip have appeared in a number of French (and Belgian) publications.

M.H.

"Broom Hilda," Russ Myers. © Chicago Tribune-New York News Syndicate.

BROOM HILDA (U.S.) *Broom Hilda* was created by Russell Myers in 1970 for the Chicago Tribune-New York News Syndicate.

Situated in an undetermined country and at an indeterminate time (possibly the Middle Ages), the strip tells of the adventures—or misadventures—of a rather ineffectual witch. Despite her repulsive aspect and her greenish complexion Broom Hilda is a rather tame and even endearing creature. Her black magic often misfires on her, her spells, more often than not, do not work, and even her pet buzzard Gaylord seldom heeds her commands. In her rare moments of triumph, however, she is capable of flying through the air, of shuttling back and forth in time, and of unleashing lightning and thunder. She uses her awesome powers (such as they are) to satisfy her whims and peeves more than to spread terror in the hearts of her (generally) unbelieving cohorts.

As a counterpart to Hilda's self-aggrandizement, Myers has created the hirsute, uncouth troll Irwin, whose mindless antics seem to mock the witch's attention-getting shenanigans.

Obviously inspired by *The Wizard of Id*, *Broom Hilda* is nonetheless one of the best and funniest comic strips to come out of the 1970s. It has continued to entertain readers, daily and Sundays, for more than 25 years now.

M.H.

BROOS, PIET (1910-1964) Piet Broos, Dutch artist and cartoonist, was born on December 16, 1910, and died on July 9, 1964. Broos studied art at the Den Haag Academy of Art in hopes of making it his career. In 1939 he debuted as a comic strip artist with *Professor Pienterbult*, a strip done for *Roomsche Jeugd*, a magazine for young people. From the start, *Broos* tended to com-

"Bronc Peeler," Fred Harman. © Fred Harman.

Piet Broos, "Tommie's Avonturen." © *Piet Broos.*

plete tales in order to start another one or more with different characters. At times he revived earlier characters either with new stories or by completely redrawing old ones. Thus, *Professor Pienterbult* reappeared in 1948 in the newspaper *Onze Krant*, and in 1954 the character graced the pages of *Maas en Roerbode*, another newspaper.

In 1940 the Flemish comics magazine *Zonneland* published his *Avonturen van Knobbeltje Knop* ("Adventures of K.K."); in 1941 *Tommie's avonturen* appeared in *Panorama*, a newspaper with a weekly children's supplement titled *Sjors*, which had started on January 2, 1936. (*Sjors* is the Dutch version of Martin Branner's *Winnie Winkle* Sunday page. In 1938 an originally Dutch version of *Sjors*, written by Lou Vierhout and drawn by Frans Piet, replaced the original.)

After World War II Broos's first comic strip was *Professor Snip Snap*. It appeared in *St. Antoniusalmanak* in 1946. That same publication published his *Avontuur van Pinkeltree* (1948) and *Keesje Slim* (1949). In 1946 he also created characters like *Daniël* and *Okkie en Knokkie* for the newspaper *Onze Krant* and *Jan Pierewiet* for *Maas en Roerbode*. *Jan Pierewiet* also appeared in *Credo* from 1962 to 1964.

While *Kuif de onverschrokkene* ("Kuif the Intrepid") was the last strip he did for *Onze Krant* in 1948, Broos continued working for *Maas en Roerbode* with features like *Stroppie* (1948), *Streken van Reintje de Vos* ("Pranks of Reinecke Fox," 1950), *Toon Okkernoot* (1950), *Kwikkie Kwiek* (1952), et al. From 1948 to 1964 he drew *Avonturen van Brom, Ping en Ming*, and other features for *Kinderkompas*, a life insurance company's children's magazine. His *Ali Baba* appeared in *Okki* from 1956 to 1964, and he contributed various strips regularly to *Hartentroef* (1957-1964) while working for a number of other magazines and papers. He was nearly omnipresent, making him one of the best-known Dutch comic artists.

W.F.

BROWN, BERTIE (1887-1974) British cartoonist Albert Thacker ("Bertie") Brown was born in 1887 in Epsom, Surrey. Educated at council schools in Sutton and Brockley, he won an art scholarship to the Slade School of Art, but was unable to take it up because of the poverty of his large family. He started work at Elliott's of Lewisham in the blueprint department while studying the strips of Tom Browne in the halfpenny comics. He visited Browne on his sickbed and was encouraged to try submitting joke cartoons.

His first published work appeared in Henderson's *Scraps*. He submitted specimens to Harmsworth's *Illustrated Chips* and was immediately offered a staff job by editor Langton Townley, which he accepted, remaining with that publisher for 50 years, from 1908 to 1958. During this time he drew perhaps a million frames (for many years he drew five full front pages a week, each with 12 panels). His early work closely followed Tom Browne and G. M. Payne, whose characters he often took over. Later he developed a hasty style that nevertheless retained considerable detail, and his eye for contemporary types and backgrounds makes his comic work an important reflection of the social life of his period. He was also particularly adept at capturing a caricatured likeness, and from his creation of the *Charlie Chaplin* strip for *Funny Wonder* (August 7, 1915), Bertie (originally nicknamed "Buster"), drew many stage, screen, and radio celebrities in comic form. He died in February 1974 at the age of 87.

His first original character was *Homeless Hector* (1908), a dog who hunted bones in *Chips* right to the last issue on September 12, 1953. His strips include: 1911—*John Willie's Jackdaw; Nibby Nugget; Peter Parsnips;* 1912—*Marmaduke Maxim; Coffdrop College;* 1913—*Herr Kutz; Cyril Slapdab;* 1914—*Willy & Wally; Ragged Reggie; Brownie Boys* (long run in *Rainbow*); 1915—*Angel and Her Playmates; Gussy Goosegog; Sally Cinders; Charlie Chaplin;* 1916—*Corny Cachou;* 1917—*Rushing Rupert;* 1918—*Dandy and Dinky;* 1919—*Our Kinema Couple* (long run in *Funny Wonder*); 1920—*Pimple; Moonlight Moggie; Annie Seed;* 1921—*Harry Weldon; Wizzo the Wizard; Piggy and Wiggy;* 1922—*Pa Perkins and Percy* (long run in *Chips*); *Billy and Buster;* 1923—*Abie the A.B.;* 1924—*Jessie Joy;* 1925—*Merry Boys of Dingle School;* 1926—*Smiler and Smudge* (long run in *Butterfly*); 1928—*Skinny and Scotty;* 1930—*Jolly Uncle Joe;* 1931—*Snappy Sammy,* 1933—*Nelson Twigg,* 1934—*Kitty Ken and Koko,* 1935—*Captain Skittle,* 1936—*Will Hay;* 1937—*Kitty & Ken;* 1939—*Ping the Panda;* 1940—*Richard Hassett; Little Teddy Tring;* 1941—*Pinhead and Pete; Troddles and Tonkytonk; Vic Oliver;* 1945—*It's that Man Again; Petula Clark; Jimmy Durante;* 1946—*Charlie Chester;* 1948—*Gracie Fields; Derek Roy;* 1949—*Joy Nichols and Dick Bentley;* 1950—*Sid Field; Reg Dixon; Arthur English;* 1952—*Mustava Bunn;* 1953—*Red Skelton; Beverley Sisters; Diana Decker;* 1954—*Martin & Lewis;* 1956—*Frankie Howerd; Shirley Eaton;* 1957—*Harry Secombe;* 1959—*Jimmy Durante.*

D.G.

BROWNE, DIK (1917-1989) American cartoonist, born August 11, 1917, in New York City. Richard (Dik) Browne started as a newsboy on the *New York Journal* and made the customary climb up the ladder to newspaper cartoonist in a few years. In 1941 he joined *Newsweek* magazine as an illustrator but was drafted the following year.

Upon his return to civilian life, Dik Browne resumed a career as book illustrator and advertising artist with the Johnstone & Cushing agency (where he designed the Chiquita Banana cartoon character for the United Fruit Company and the Campbell Soup Kids, among other things). In 1954 he met cartoonist Mort Walker and together, with Walker writing and Browne drawing, they produced *Hi and Lois*, a gentle, genuinely warm and funny family strip. In 1973 Dik Browne created his own strip, *Hagar the Horrible*, the rollicking saga of a comic-opera Viking band of plunderers.

Dik Browne received a number of awards, including the Reuben and the Silver Lady, and served as president of the National Cartoonists Society from 1963 to 1965.

In the late 1970s he moved to Sarasota, Florida, where he continued to work on *Hagar* and *Hi and Lois* with the help of his two sons, Chris and Chance. He died on June 4, 1989.

M.H.

BROWNE, TOM (1870-1910) British cartoonist, illustrator, poster designer, and painter, born in 1870 in Nottingham of "humble parents." He was educated at St. Mary's National School and became a milliner's errand boy in 1882. Apprenticed without pay to a local lithographic printer until 1891, he eked out his living by freelancing cartoons to London comic papers. His first strip was published in *Scraps* dated April 27, 1880: "He Knew How To Do It," which was a prophetic title. For the eight panels he was paid 30 shillings. The boom in comic papers begun by Alfred Harmsworth's *Comic Cuts* (1890) opened the ideal market for Browne's humorous line, and from the close-hatched style of the time he developed a clean approach with bold blacks, ideal for the cheap printing of the halfpenny comics. His work was so much in demand that, once out of his apprenticeship, he became a full-time comic artist, moving to London and setting up a studio in Wollaton House at Westcombe Park, Blackheath. From here he turned out six or more full comic pages per week, together with story illustrations for boys' papers, joke cartoons, illustrations, and full-page features for *Graphic* and other national magazines, full-color postcards in series, huge posters for the theater (particularly pantomimes), and watercolors. He joined the Langham Sketch Club, then seceded to form the London Sketch Club, and was made an R.I. (Royal Illustrator). An avid bicyclist, he rode from London to Paris and to Gibraltar across the Pyrenees, toured Holland, and visited New York, drawing his adventures for newspapers. He established his own color printing

business in his hometown and joined the Territorial Army. When he died in 1910 at the early age of 39, after an operation for an internal illness, he was buried with military honors at Shooters Hill.

Browne's characters in comics were many, ranging from the immortal *Weary Willie and Tired Tim*, who continued in comics 40 years after his death, to their bicycling blood-brothers, *Airy Alf and Bouncing Billy* (1897). He was also responsible for *Doings at Whackington School* (1897), *Dan Leno* (1898), *Don Quixote de Tintogs* (1898), *Robinson Crusoe Esquire* (1898), *The Rajah* (1898), *Little Willy and Tiny Tim* (1898), *Mr. Stankey Deadstone and Company* (1898). He published several editions of *Tom Browne's Christmas Annual* (1904-5?) and is the only British comic artist to be treated in a serious study: *Tom Brown R.I.* by A. E. Johnson, in the *Brush Pen and Pencil* series (Black, 1909).

The first true comic strip artist in Britain, he set the style and standard of the British comic paper, and his influence may be traced through to the present day.

D.G.

"Bruce Gentry," Ray Bailey. © Post Syndicate.

BRUCE GENTRY (U.S.) Ray Bailey, a former assistant to Milton Caniff, created *Bruce Gentry* for the Robert Hall Syndicate on March 25, 1945.

Bruce Gentry and a small group of friends have started a small airline in South America. Using surplus fixed-wing airplanes, they ply the Andes, carrying the mails and supplies to remote points of the continent. Powerful competitors are watching, however, and soon Bruce finds himself in the role of flying troubleshooter, always putting out fires before they have time to spread.

In 1947 Bailey told Coulton Waugh he felt that "readers are tired of battles, hence he has none." The times weren't ripe for peace and harmony just yet, however, and soon Bruce got involved in some rough fights against smugglers, pirates, and foreign agents, in an effort to retain the strip's readership. But to no avail—it folded early in 1952.

Bruce Gentry was one of a number of aviation strips that sprung up during the war and soon thereafter; it was among the best and deserves to be ranked alongside *Buz Sawyer, Johnny Hazard* and *Steve Canyon*. The art was uniformly excellent, but on the writing side, Ray Bailey could not compete with Crane, Robbins, or Caniff. *Bruce Gentry* lacked that special touch of indi-

Tom Browne, "Robinson Crusoe Esq."

viduality which might have made it into a success. In 1946 the indefatigable Spencer Gordon Bennett and Thomas Carr directed a movie serial of *Bruce Gentry, Daredevil of the Skies*.

M.H.

BRUNO BRAZIL (Belgium) *Bruno Brazil* was created in 1967 by scriptwriter Louis Albert (pseudonym of Michel Régnier) and cartoonist William Vance for the comic weekly *Tintin*.

Bruno Brazil was the leader of a commando group, the "Cayman Commando," assigned to desperate missions, mostly espionage. The recruits for the commando were a motley crew of several men and one woman with unsavory pasts who were whipped into shape by the hard-driving, no-nonsense Bruno Brazil. A cross between *The Dirty Dozen* and *Mission: Impossible*, the strip was filled with exciting characters, weird happenings, and outrageous derring-do. In addition to Brazil, the principal protagonists were the strong-willed "Gaucho" Morales and "Whip," the sexy, lash-wielding heroine. There was a good deal of violence, blood-letting, and mayhem in the commando's encounters with master spies, would-be dictators, and Mafia chieftains; death occurred quite frequently and occasionally struck members of the group.

The stories were carefully plotted and enjoyably written by the veteran Régnier, while Vance's graphic style, vigorous and dynamic, kept the action moving at a neck-breaking pace.

Bruno Brazil has been reprinted in book form by Editions du Lombard in Brussels. The feature ended its run in 1983.

M.H.

BUCK DANNY (Belgium) *Buck Danny*, the poor man's *Terry and the Pirates*, made its first appearance in the pages of the Belgian comics magazine *Spirou* on January 2, 1947, drawn by Victor Hubinon and written by Jean-Michel Charlier. Indeed, with the very first episode evocatively titled "Les Japs Attaquent!" ("The Japs Are Attacking!"), *Buck Danny* sounded like a delayed echo of the war's *Terry*. Buck Danny and his comic sidekick Sonny Tuckson (looking a lot like Caniff's Hot-shot Charlie) were pilots with the U.S. Navy

"Buck Danny," Victor Hubinon. © Editions Dupuis.

and took part in the battles of Midway and the Coral Sea. The battle scenes were straight out of old war movies, as was most of the dialogue. After the Pacific War, Danny and Sonny became flying adventurers on dangerous assignments from Arabia to Borneo. Then came the Korean War and the Cold War, and our two heroes reenlisted in the U.S. Air Force (at times *Buck Danny* could sound more bellicose than even *Steve Canyon* or *Buz Sawyer*).

In recent years the war angle has been considerably played down, and the team (now up to three members with the addition of Tumbler, in the strong, silent type tradition) is getting involved more in counterespionage, one of their enemies being the leggy, alluring master spy known as Lady X.

Buck Danny first suffered an interruption in 1979, following Hubinon's death. It was resumed in 1983, with Francis Bergèse supplying the artwork in a very illustrative, dynamic style. A second interruption occurred in 1989, when Charlier died. But the series was picked up again in 1993 on continuities written by various scribes.

Buck Danny is the oldest European aviation strip in existence. While definitely not on the same level as Caniff's *Terry* or *Steve Canyon* at their best, it never got as bad as Wunder's *Terry* at its worst. The adventures of Buck Danny and his friends have been reprinted in book form by Editions Dupuis.

M.H.

BUCK ROGERS (U.S.) The first American science-fiction strip appeared on January 7, 1929. Adapted by Phil Nowlan from his own novel *Armaggedon 2419 A.D.*, drawn by Dick Calkins, and distributed by John F. Dille Co., it was first called *Buck Rogers in the Year 2429 A.D.*, later *Buck Rogers in the 25th Century*, then simply *Buck Rogers*.

Awakening from a five-century-long sleep, former U.S. Air Force lieutenant Buck Rogers finds himself in a devastated America overrun by Mongol invaders. With the help of young and pretty Wilma Deering (who was to become Buck's constant companion), our 20th-century hero almost single-handedly defeats the Mongols and liberates America. But his labors are far from over as new enemies appear on the horizon: the tiger-men of Mars; the pirates from outer space; and most dangerous of all, Buck's arch-foe Killer Kane, and his seductive accomplice Ardala Valmar. Aided by the scientific genius of Dr. Huer, Buck will triumph over all enemies and overcome all perils.

The *Buck Rogers* daily strip has known a long series of artists and writers of varied merit. After Calkins there was Murphy Anderson (1947-49), then Leon Dworkins (1949-51), Rick Yager (1951-58), again Anderson (1958-59), and finally George Tuska, who drew the strip until its final demise in 1967. On the writing side, creator Nowlan was replaced by Calkins himself (1940-47), and the strip was later written by Bob Barton (1947-51), Rick Yager (1951-58) and a variety of other writers, including noted science-fiction author Fritz Leiber.

The Sunday *Buck Rogers* (which first saw publication on March 30, 1930) had a double particularity: it was never drawn by Calkins, who signed it, and for a long time the titular hero never appeared in it. Instead it was given over to Wilma's kid brother Bud Deering and his girl companion Princess Alura from Mars. Their adventures were quite creditable, very imaginative and

"Buck Rogers," Dick Calkins and Phil Nowlan. © National Newspaper Syndicate.

always enjoyable. In later years Buck Rogers took back the Sunday page from his younger stand-ins, and the page was again filled with Buck's space-opera pyrotechnics until the feature was finally discontinued in 1965 (two years before the daily strip).

The most noteworthy contributors to the Sunday version were Russell Keaton (1930-33), Rick Yager (1933-58), Murphy Anderson (1958-59), and George Tuska (1959-65) for the drawing; and for the writing Phil Nowlan (1930-40) and Rick Yager (1940-58).

For a long time *Buck Rogers* was the most popular science-fiction strip, challenged only by *Flash Gordon*. It had its own comic book version (with Frank Frazetta among the contributing artists) and was adapted into a highly successful radio series. In 1939 veteran serial director Ford Beebe directed a movie version of *Buck Rogers* with Buster Crabbe in the title role. In 1969 (the year of the first moon landing) Chelsea House published a hardcover anthology, *The Collected Works of Buck Rogers in the 25th Century* (with a preface by Ray Bradbury), which was followed by *Buck Rogers 1931-32* (Ed Aprill, 1971) and *Adventures in the 25th Century* (Funnies Publishing Company, 1974).

Following on the heels of the *Buck Rogers* theatrical movie and television series (both starring Gil Gerard), the newspaper strip was revived on September 9, 1979, in a new, more streamlined version drawn by Gray Morrow and written by Jim Lawrence. Cary Bates took over the scripting chores in 1981, and the next year Jack Sparling became the titular artist of the series. Distributed by the amateurish New York Times Syndicate (which was not even able to sell any of its strips to its parent newspaper), the feature was never a conspicuous success, and it petered out in the fall of 1983. (From 1979 to 1983 there was also a parallel *Buck Rogers* comic book carried under the Gold Key banner.)

M.H.

BUCK RYAN (G.B.) Buck Ryan, amateur sleuth, receives a cryptic cable from New York: Silas Craig, millionaire, wants him to meet his ward, Sonia Dell, at Southampton. With youthful assistant Slipper by his side, Buck motors down to the docks. The heiress steps down the gangplank: "What a peach!" Then a pistol pokes into his spine: "Move and I'll plug you!" In four whirlwind panels, readers of the *Daily Mirror* were swept into a world of murder, mystery, and mayhem that lasted for 25 years. From March 22, 1937, to July 31, 1962, Jack Monk's seldom signed, never bylined strip hardly changed: guns, girls, Yankee chat, and action. Only Slipper, the kid assistant cast in the traditional Sexton Blake-Tinker mold, disappeared. He was replaced by Zola Andersen, blonde and beautiful, who

"Buck Ryan," Jack Monk. © Daily Mirror Newspapers Ltd.

could lick any man (or woman)—a crooked lady who reformed for Ryan.

Ryan was created as a stopgap replacement for *Terror Keep*, a serial strip adapted from Edgar Wallace's *Mr. Reeder* novel, when an American syndicate claimed all rights to Wallace. Harry Guy Bartholomew, editor, asked for a character in the style of America's successful *Dick Tracy*. "Buck," close to Dick and inspired by cowboy star Buck Jones, was one of the names on a list circulated by artist Monk and writer Don Freeman among the *Mirror* staff. The most popular combination came out as Buck Ryan—but soon after the strip was published, letters came in from readers asking if there was any connection between the character and the old established London chain of shops, Buck and Ryan! The name stayed.

Many popular characters emerged from the strip. Zola became the pinup girl of a minesweeper, an anti-aircraft battery, a Wellington bomber, and the submarine *Tally-ho*, all in pinups drawn by Monk. The most popular question from readers was: "When will Buck and Zola marry?" Bartholomew answered for Monk: "Never, never!" Outbidding even Zola in the popularity polls was Twilight, the glamorous girl crook, a brunette with a peekaboo bang. This obscured half of her face, the side scarred by acid. The tease was kept going until she finally had a skin graft operation, and her full beauty was revealed. Under a new writer, James Edgar, Twilight reformed her evil ways and replaced Zola as Ryan's helpmate. Monk's second-favorite character was Ma-the-Cache, an old biddy who smoked a pipe and lived on a barge on the River Thames. On the side of the law was Inspector Page of Scotland Yard.

Monk, famous for his authenticity of detail, went to Canada in November 1945-January 1946, on a sketching "holiday" that attracted much Canadian attention and resulted in an excellent series with authentic settings.

Reprints of *Buck Ryan* include: *The Case of the Broken Thistle*, a *Mirror* paperback comic of a 1945 adventure; a number of pocket-size paperbacks in the *Super Detective Library* series; and a monthly comic book published in Australia.

D.G.

BUFALO BILL (Italy) William Frederick Cody (nicknamed "Buffalo Bill" for having killed over 4,300 buffaloes in the course of 18 months) was a hunter, explorer, Indian scout, and show-biz entrepreneur.

Very early in his life, writers got hold of his legend and completely altered the historical character of Colonel Cody. The first was E.Z.C. Judson, who wrote a string of dime novels devoted to the mythical Buffalo Bill for Street and Smith in the 1870s. Their sales were extraordinary and worldwide, and they spawned a multitude of Buffalo Bill stories in every conceivable medium. The comics were not long in following suit, and the fabled sharpshooter was soon the hero of strips from Japan to Argentina (in the U.S. his fame was never so great; let us mention, however, *Young Buffalo Bill*, later retitled *Broncho Bill*, by Harry O'Neill). Among the many Italian versions, the most popular remains the one written by Luigi Grecchi and illustrated by Carlo Cossio. This series differs from the others not only by the missing "f" in the title, but also for its long life.

Conceived in 1950, *Bufalo Bill* made its appearance in 1951 in the weekly *L'Intrepido* when the publication changed from tabloid to comic book format, and it remained there until the mid-1960s. "Silver Cody is killed by Juarez Alvarando, the cowboy boss, who mistook him for a cattle rustler. William, his son, leaves his home and his mother to track down the killer. . . ." Thus begins *Bufalo Bill* in a vein not unlike other Western sagas such as *Il Piccolo Sceriffo, Kansas Kid,* and *Capitan Miki.* These adventures were made more entertaining, thanks to the secondary characters introduced into the strip, like Old Toby and Susy, the nice young girl. Carlo Cossio's artwork, usually hurried and superficial, is much more detailed here and fits well with Grecchi's tangled plots. The stories were obvious and larded with rhetorics, but they impressed the readers with their air of authenticity and sophistication.

Other *Buffalo Bill* strips (all spelled with two "f's") have appeared in the Italian market, from an earlier version written by Amilcare Medici and drawn by Lina Buffolente (1945) to a more recent one produced by Armando Bonato (1965). In 1975 an erotic Buffalo Bill made his appearance in a saga called *Zora*, written by Renzo Barbieri and drawn by Balzano and Micheloni.

G.B.

BUFFALO BILL (Germany) *Buffalo Bill* is one of a number of Western comics that, to a degree, are a staple product of the German comics market. The character of Buffalo Bill, known in Germany since the times of the original William F. Cody and made famous through pulps and his Wild West show, was kept alive in postwar Germany by reprints of the Fred Meagher syndicated strip in a *Tom Mix* comic book that appeared from 1953 to 1954 and in a *Buffalo Bill* comic book reprinting of French and/or Italian strips.

Buffalo Bill took a well-earned rest until July 29, 1968, the day the first issue of *Lasso-Sonderheft* ("Lasso Special") was published. The 68-page comic books, which at the time starred Arturo del Castillo's *Randall*, featured *Buffalo Bill, Reno Kid, Lederstrumpf* ("Leatherstocking"), et al. The initial adventures of *Buffalo Bill* were reprints of a series originating in the Willy Vandersteen stable, written by Rik Dierckx and drawn by Karl Verschuere in a style influenced by Vandersteen and Alberto Giolitti. The Vandersteen material ran only to several books, so the German publishers asked Hansrudi Wäscher to work on the strip.

Reno Kid, one of the features in *Lasso-Sonderheft*, took over the regular 32-page *Lasso* comic book with issue number 82 (September 23, 1968). In order to publish *Lasso* weekly, the specials ended with number 17, and *Buffalo Bill* invaded the regular *Lasso* comic book with number 116 (January 12, 1970), continuing in all of the even-numbered issues, up to number 376 in 1974. *Reno Kid* appeared every other week in the issues with uneven numbers. Still alternating from week to week, *Lasso*, starring *Reno Kid* and *Buffalo Bill*, received individual numbering with issue 377. In 1970 both series were produced by the Giolitti studio in Rome from scripts written by Dirk Hess, with Hansrudi Wäscher doing some of the *Buffalo Bill* stories. In 1971 *Buffalo Bill* was turned over to Studiortega of Barcelona, Spain, with artists like Sola, Andres, and Rojo, and, of course, to Wäscher. Studio Giolitti continued doing *Reno Kid*, which has also been exported to other European countries. While most of the stories of either series make good use of the Western formula, some of the artwork is substandard. If not for Wäscher and some foreign artists of considerable talent, *Buffalo Bill* might not have endured so long.

W.F.

BUFFOLENTE, LINA (1924-   ) One of the few women cartoonists in Italy, Lina Buffolente was born October 27, 1924, in Vicenza. She moved to Milan with her family, where she attended the Brera Academy, but her studies were interrupted by the war. She began her career with a series of adventure comic books without a permanent cast of characters for Edital in Milan (1941), while at the same time assisting Professor Giuseppe Capadonia, one of the most prolific Italian comic strip artists of the prewar period.

In 1942 Buffolente began work with Edizioni Alpe, realizing in collaboration with Leone Cimpellin *Petto de Pollo* ("Chicken Breast"), a humorous comic book. A collaboration ensued, which was to last for the whole period of the war and beyond, during which time Lina Buffolente signed the sagas of *Piccolo Re* ("Little King," no relation to Otto Soglow's character), *Frisco Jim, Colorado Kid, Hello Jim,* and *Calamity Jane*. In 1948 she drew the comic books *Tom Bill* and *Tom Mix* for Casa Editrice Arc, and *Furio Mascherato* ("Masked Fury"), a superhero comic book, for Edizioni Audace. In the same year she drew a series of adaptations of the classics (*Les Misérables, The Mysteries of Paris*, etc.) for the publisher Ventura, for whom she also created the character of Nadia in his bilingual magazine *Per Voi/For You*. Also in 1948, Lina Buffolente began a very fruitful collaboration with Casa Editrice Universo.

In addition to many episodes in the "Albo dell'Intrepido," *la* Buffolente took over the long-running western saga *Liberty Kid*, created by the painters Toldo and Albanese in *L'Intrepido*, and *Fiordistella* ("Starflower"), a soap opera started by Cesarina Putato in the pages of *Il Monello* (1961). In addition to her work for Casa Editrice Universo, she did occasional works for other publishers: *Mosqueton, Rouletabille* (a detective strip based on Gaston Leroux's famous character), and *Nick Reporter*, published in France by Editions Aventures et Voyages; a revised version of *Sciuscia* for Edizioni Sepim; a few episodes of *Reno Kid* for a German publisher; and the adventures of *Zembla, Ivan il Veggente* ("Ivan the Seer"), and *Gun Gallon* for Editions Lug in Lyons, France.

At the present, Lina Buffolente's time is almost completely absorbed by the production of *Il Piccolo Ranger* ("The Little Ranger"), yet another Western, created by Andrew Lavezzolo and now written by Decio Canzio. In the early 1990s she also drew several episodes of *Il Commandante Mark* and *River Queen*.

G.B.

BUGS BUNNY (U.S.) The *Bugs Bunny* comic books and strip were based on the character in animated cartoons produced by Leon Schlesinger. The creation of the wise-cracking rabbit was done in stages, with contributions by many studio employees. The genesis was in a *Porky Pig* film, "Porky's Hare Hunt," directed by Ben "Bugs" Hardaway and Cal Dalton, based on a story by Bob Clampett. The hare, which was quite unlike the final Bugs, proved popular and warranted another film. "Hare-um Scare-um" was done by the same directors, featuring a remodeled version of the rabbit. Another version appeared in "Presto Change-o," directed by Chuck Jones. In 1939, when it was apparent that the rabbit was becoming a star, two

"Bugs Bunny." © Warner Bros.

more films were assigned: "Elmer's Candid Camera," directed by Jones; and "A Wild Hare," directed by Fred "Tex" Avery. It was in "A Wild Hare" that the character most closely resembled the definitive version and used his famous catch phrase, "What's up, doc?" Upon completion of the film, suggestions were solicited from around the studio for a name for the bunny. "Bugs," inspired by Hardaway's nickname, was chosen.

A long series of *Bugs Bunny* cartoons and comic books followed. The cartoons were released (and later produced) by Warner Brothers until 1969. The bulk was directed by Avery, Clampett, Jones, Fritz Freleng, Robert McKimson, and Frank Tashlin, featuring voices by Mel Blanc. The cartoons have been perennial television favorites and Bugs has been the subject of hundreds of toys, records, books, and other merchandise.

Bugs Bunny's affiliation with Western Publishing started in 1941 when he joined the other Warner characters in the first issue of *Looney Tunes and Merrie Melodies*. The comic ceased publication in 1962 and resumed again in 1975.

The *Bugs Bunny* comic book began as part of the Dell *Four-Color* series and appeared in 27 intermittent issues, many by Chase Craig, before beginning regular publication in 1953 with issue number 28. The feature also appeared in dozens of specials, including issues of *Golden Comics Digest, March of Comics*, and *Super Comics*, in addition to Bugs' guest-starring in other Warner comics, especially *Porky Pig* and *Yosemite Sam*. Among the writers involved in *Bugs Bunny* stories were: Lloyd Turner, Don Christensen, Sid Marcus, Carl Fallberg, Tom Packer, Cecil Beard, and Mark Evanier. Artists have included Wyn Smith, Tom McKimson, Phil DeLara, Ralph Heimdahl, and John Carey. The series was discontinued in 1983 but was revived 10 years later.

The *Bugs Bunny* newspaper strip began in 1942, starting as a Sunday page only. The first few were by Chase Craig, and the strip, syndicated by NEA, was produced by Western Publishing under the supervision of Carl Buettner and, later, Al Stoffel. A great many writers and artists worked on the strip, most notably Fallberg, Stoffel, McKimson, Roger Armstrong, Jack Taylor, and Heimdahl. In 1948, a daily version of the strip was begun, written at first by Taylor and drawn continuously by Heimdahl. Eventually, Heimdahl also assumed the Sunday page and Stoffel handled the writing of both on a regular basis. The newspaper feature was closed down in 1993.

M.E.

BULANADI, DANNY (1946-) Danny Bulanadi was born in Tondo, Manila, Philippines, on February 9, 1946. He started working for comic books at the age of 18, after he graduated from high school. His first art job was for *Romansa Komiks*, and for many years he worked as an assistant to Tony Zuñiga. He did pencilling and inking on various Zuñiga assignments, but his first big break was with Craf Publications, where he illustrated short stories for *Theme Song*.

He then collaborated with Mars Ravelo and did graphic-novels for *Bulaklak*. In 1973 he drew for a government-sponsored publication. He did the visual sequences on the feature *The Many Fascinating Islands* and illustrated a historical account of *Jose Rizal*, the national hero of the Philippines.

On June 21, 1974, he teamed up with Ric Poblete to do *Gloria Sagrada*, a fantasy novel that appeared in Top Star. It ran for 32 chapters. Later he joined Pablo Gomez, who wrote *Katakumba*, which was published on August 2, 1974. The story became a success and was made into a movie.

One of Bulanadi's most popular works is *Ako Si Abraham* ("I am Abraham"). It was written by Carlo J. Caparas and appeared in *Philipino Komiks* starting on September 3, 1974. This long, visual-novel was also made into a motion picture.

While doing individual assignments, Bulanadi has also maintained his position as Zuñiga's assistant. He worked on many of the American series that Zuñiga handled, such *as Jonah Hex, Black Orchid, Phantom Stranger, Dr. 13*, and other strips for National Periodicals. He also worked on the Marvel characters Ka-Zar and Conan.

Just before he left the Philippines, Bulanadi had the opportunity to work with Nestor Redondo, learning from one of the most influential artists in the comic book medium. He has recently arrived in the United States. He plans to pursue his career as a freelancer and to continue his work as a comic book artist.

O.J.

BULLETJE EN BONESTAAK (Netherlands) *Bulletje en Bonestaak* ("Fatty and Beanstalk"), which first appeared in the newspaper *Het Volk* ("The People") in 1921, is one of the earliest Dutch efforts in the field of comic strips. Written by Adrianus Michael de Jong

"Bulletje en Bonestaak," G. A. Van Raemdonck. © Het Volk.

(1888-1943) and drawn by George van Raemdonck (1888-1966), from the start *Bulletje en Bonestaak* had a different approach to the comics medium than the earlier *Yoebje en Achmed* by Henk Backer. Although both are humorous, *Bulletje en Bonestaak* is drawn in the more realistic, down-to-earth style that makes the difference between a fairy-tale strip and a kid strip. As their names suggest, Bulletje is the little fat boy and Bonestaak the big thin boy. They are inseparable while journeying around the world, going from one adventure to the next. *Bulletje en Bonestaak* even provided one of the earliest crossovers of comic strip characters when, during one of their journeys, the two visit London and meet Jopie Slim and Dikkie Bigmans, whose adventures were reprinted in the Dutch newspaper *De Telegraaf* as early as 1920.

In 1924 *De wereldreis van Bulletje en Bonestaak* ("Fatty and Beanstalk's Journey Round the World") was the first in a long series of book editions of the comic strip. These books are still reprinted, despite the end of the series in *Het Volk* in 1934. Earlier reprintings deleted scenes in which invalids of World War I appeared, but a 1968 edition included these scenes once again.

Bulletje en Bonestaak, like so many early European comic strips, separated pictures and narrative, but because it was included in a newspaper, it did not have to be printed on a strip of paper. Nevertheless, one such series did exist in early Dutch comics history. These stories were printed on strips of paper two meters long and rolled up for safekeeping in a round box. This strip, by artist W. Heskes and with verse by C. J. Kievit, pictured stories centered on two characters called *Flip en Flop* ("Flip and Flop").

W.F.

BÜLOW, BERNHARD-VIKTOR VON (1923-) Loriot, whose real name is Bernhard-Viktor von Bülow, is a German cartoonist and writer/artist, born November 12, 1923, in the city of Brandenburg, 60 kilometers west of Berlin, Germany, the son of an army officer turned police officer. The Bülow family always had a penchant and secret admiration for acting, which in a way influenced young Bernhard-Viktor, who grew up and went to school and high school in his hometown and in Berlin. He left high school with a makeshift graduation to join the army, fighting in World War II as an officer.

When the war ended, von Bülow worked two years doing odd jobs like woodcutting. Then he returned to school for a regular high school graduation before taking up his studies at the Academy of Art in Hamburg, Germany. Having finished his studies, he started working as a graphic artist, his first cartoons getting published in the short-lived magazine *Die Strasse* ("The Road") in 1950. He moved on to the weekly *Stern* in the early 1950s, where he debuted with *Auf den Hund gekommen* ("Gone to the Dogs"), a series of cartoons reversing and parodying the relationship between humans and dogs. These cartoons also were the first to be reprinted in book form by the Swiss publishing house Diogenes. This series of cartoons sent von Bülow well on his way toward having his pen name, Loriot, become a household word.

Never using speech balloons, Loriot entered the realm of the comic strip with the furiously funny *Wahre Geschichten erlogen von Loriot* ("True Stories Made Up by Loriot") and with *Reinhold das Nashorn* ("Reinhold the Rhinoceros"), which originally was scheduled to appear for six consecutive weeks in the mid-1950s but actually ran 15 years in the pages of *Stern*. For legal reasons, the comic strip was signed Pirol (which is the German equivalent to the French "Loriot," the name of a blackbird species). Reinhold das Nashorn and his son Paul were as enjoyable as Loriot's other work. Each episode of four pictures was complemented by verse within the pictures.

In 1966, Loriot got his own TV show, *Cartoon*, which ran until 1972, attesting, among other things, to Loriot's considerable acting talent. A dog used in a 1971 cartoon in *Stern* became his best-known animated cartoon character, the lovable Wum in 1972.

The antics of Wum and his friend, the naive and stubborn elephant Wendelin, who were occasionally visited by a little UFO complete with a green-skinned pilot, were the highlight of a long-running quiz program aimed at collecting funds for charity. The five-minute cartoons usually were made so the characters seemed to be engaged in dialogue with the shows' (real live) host. The cartoons were produced by Loriot, who was also the voice of all the characters. The comedic aspects of the stoic Loriot persona as depicted in cartoons and television shows led to a number of very successful German motion pictures written by and starring Loriot.

W.F.

"*Bulletman,*" Ken Battefield. © Fawcett Publications.

BULLETMAN (U.S.) Early in their publishing history, Fawcett experimented with formats. One of their books, *Nickle Comics*, was a five-cent biweekly, about half the size of a normal color comic. Although the book didn't last long, *Bulletman* premiered in May 17, 1940s first issue and later became a Fawcett staple. Created by artist Jon Small with an origin similar to that of The Batman, Bulletman was really policeman Jim Barr. An orphan dedicated to wiping out crime because of his parents' murder, Barr studied chemistry and became a ballistics expert. He developed a secret serum that gave him tremendous physical and mental powers. He then perfected a bullet-shaped "gravity regulating helmet," which provided the power of flight.

When *Nickle* folded after eight issues in August 1940, *Bulletman* began a regular series in October 1940's *Master* number seven. In the 30th issue, Susan Kent became his partner, Bulletgirl. Together they fought all kinds of crime, perpetrated by crooks, spies, madmen, murderers, and crazed lunatics. Although none of the strips were as good as Fawcett's Marvel Family, *Bulletman* developed several outstanding villains. The Black Rodent, Dr. Mood, the Black Spider, and Dr. Riddle were all constant enemies of the duo, who soon came to be called "The Flying Detectives." Most of the scripts were written by Otto Binder, Fawcett's workhorse, in a snappy, fast-paced style that left no room for humor.

Bulletman had a long series of artists, starting with the crude, almost primitive material of creator Jon Small. Jack Binder eventually handled the bulk of stories between 1941 and 1946 in a straightforward, no-nonsense manner. However, artists like Jack Kirby and Joe Simon (1941), C. C. Beck (1940), and Winsor McCay Jr., son of *Little Nemo* creator Winsor McCay, all did outstanding work. Mac Raboy, who later illustrated Fawcett's *Captain Marvel Jr.*, also drew some of the finest *Bulletman* adventures during 1941 and 1942.

Over the years, the feature has appeared in *Master*, *Whiz*, *America's Best*, and other normal-sized comics. But it was also placed in a wide range of Fawcett's experimental books, including the book-sized *Bulletman Dime Action*, a pocket-sized *Bulletman Miniature*, and even *Gift*, *Xmas*, and *Holiday*, the company's oversized Christmas specials. There were also 16 issues of *Bulletman* comics, beginning in 1941 and ending in fall 1946. The feature was finally discontinued in September 1949 after its story in *Master* number 106.

J.B.

BUNGLE FAMILY, THE (U.S.) The finest, most inventive, and socially critical of the family strips, Harry Tuthill's *The Bungle Family* first emerged under its original title, *Home, Sweet Home*, as part of a miscellany of staggered daily strips also by Tuthill in the *New York Evening Mail* late in 1918. Before the end of 1919, however, only *Home, Sweet Home* remained as a nationally syndicated daily. Anecdotal for the whole of its five-year life, the strip featured a quarreling married couple initially named George and Mabel, but by the end of 1919 renamed George and Jo (for Josephine). Living in a city flat with their in-laws, George and Jo suffered endless tribulations with their landlord and neighbors.

When the *Evening Mail* was sold in January 1924, Tuthill took George and Jo to the McNaught Syndicate, gave his strip a new name and his team a last name at the same time, and added a grown daughter to the

"The Bungle Family," Harry Tuthill. © McNaught Syndicate.

menage. Peggy Bungle served as the focus for the continuing story structure now utilized in the new *Bungle Family* strip, and her on-again, off-again affairs with the con man and adventurer Hartford Oakdale led George Bungle, a small-time opportunist and harried householder, into a series of scrapes and escapades that ultimately took him to Africa, outer space, and forward in time. With the addition of a gripping narrative (and a hilarious Sunday page in 1925), the public took sharper notice of the strip, and within a few years it became one of the most widely read and printed features of the time.

Aside from George, Jo, Peggy, and Oakdale, the cast of characters was evanescent but ultimately came to include world rulers, gnomes, invisible animals, a super-strong slob beloved by women, magicians, hypnotists—and an endless, horrendous array of scurvy, aggressive, brutal neighbors; outraged and stone-hearted landlords; and cold-faced, nightstick-prodding policemen.

Tuthill himself decided to close down the strip for reasons never fully disclosed, and he ended it with the daily episode of August 1, 1942, after Peggy had married Oakdale and the current story had been wound up. Then, unexpectedly, he revived the strip on May 17, 1943, apparently for the Bungles to do their part in the national war effort. With the close of World War II, however, Tuthill again folded *The Bungle Family* on June 2, 1945. This time the closing was permanent, Tuthill politely refusing the endless requests of readers for revival of the strip.

Only one book publication of *The Bungle Family* is known: a collection of the early anecdotal episodes under the *Home, Sweet Home* title, by M.S. Co. in 1925. The strip was reprinted in early issues of *Famous Funnies* as well, but not prominently or for long.

B.B.

BUNKER, MAX *see* Secchi, Luciano.

BUNKY (U.S.) A Sunday third-of-a-page strip (later a half-page), Billy De Beck's *Parlor, Bedroom and Sink* began on May 16, 1926, replacing a short-lived Sunday gag strip accompaniment of *Barney Google* named *Bughouse Fables* (which became a daily gag panel series). The new strip opened with the marriage of Bunker and Bibsy Hill to a shower of shoes and rice and the discovery of the disillusioned bride that far from getting a honeymoon in Paris, the young Bunker was taking her to a cheap hotel, where he signs for a "parlor, bedroom, and sink" (the cheapest family accommodations of the time). Bunker (whose nickname is Bunky) has a third-rate office job and barely makes ends meet; his financial problems serve as the comic nexus of the strip for the ensuing few months.

Gradually, however, De Beck introduces a new dimension to the strip: continuity based on comic melodrama. Bunker Hill is arrested for robbing his own wife after she has become a newly hailed movie star, is reduced to stark poverty, etc., all in a close satire on the popular newspaper serial stories of the time. However, De Beck makes this garish nonsense oddly suspenseful. De Beck, it is apparent, is a master of comic narrative.

By May of 1927, Bunker and Bibsy are reconciled, still broke, and in the midst of new troubles acquire a child: Bunker Hill, Jr., first seen in the strip on November 13, 1927. Bunky, the baby, grows rapidly and turns out to be preposterously and hilariously precocious, speaking words of world-weary philosophy while still in baby clothes and lace cap. All at once, it dawns on the reader, as the young Bunky is plunged into a dark netherworld of crooks, prostitutes, and dope pushers, where his steadfast morality shines fierce and true against all odds, that De Beck is doing a full-length satire on Harold Gray's *Little Orphan Annie*. In keeping with this aspect, the young Bunky takes over the strip *in toto* by late 1928, and has his name added to the title: *P, B & S, Starring Bunky* (one of the longest strip titles on record). Meanwhile, on February 5, 1928, the nefarious Fagin the Viper enters the strip, attempting to train Bunky in a life of crime (*a la* the Dickens character). Bunky's resultant and oft-repeated cry of outraged alarm: "Fagin, youse is a viper!" became a hallmark of the strip and of an era. During the remainder of the 1920s, through the 1930s, and well into the following decade, Bunky and Fagin meet and part in an endlessly engaging series of sordid or plush backgrounds, the story remaining as absorbing as ever, even when taken over by De Beck's successor, Fred Lasswell. Outright fantasy is often introduced into *Bunky* (as, to a much lesser extent, it was in *Barney Google*), and it is one of the great works of comic strip imagination. It was, unfortunately (in view of Lasswell's ability to maintain the quality of the strip), folded in 1948 by King Features.

B.B.

BUN LOUR SARN (Thailand) In Thailand, Bun Lour Sarn is a name synonymous with comic books. Founded in 1953 by Bun Lour Utsahajit, the company is the oldest and, by far, the country's largest publisher of comics, with a dozen or more titles in its fold.

Bun Lour Sarn titles are humorous, often containing one gag after another in cartoon or story format. Some books are published in two versions—one the size of

American comic books, and one pocket-sized edition. As many as 13 panels are sometimes stacked on a page in the pocket versions. The drawings are black and white, and simple in their execution, characterized by bold and dark strokes.

Bun Lour Sarn's best sellers are *Kai Hua Lok* ("Laughter for Sale"), and *Maha Sanuk* ("Super Fun"), with hundreds of thousands in print. The earliest titles, *Baby* and *Nuja* ("Little Baby"), were first published in 1957 and 1958. Other books include *Ai Tua Lek* ("Little One"), *Konulawang* ("Mess Up"), *Yornsorn* ("Reversed Arrow"), *Pean* ("Fanatic"), *Bakropsuit* ("Completely Mad"), *Parade*, and *Mitti Pisawang*. Bun Lour Sarn's policy is to have a new issue of one of its monthly comics on the market every five days.

Although the company has closed some of its divisions, such as feature film production, it has continued to expand its comics production. By the mid-1990s, four to five new humor titles were in the works, with plans to distribute Chinese, Indonesian, and Japanese language versions of *Kai Hua Lok* overseas.

J.A.L.

BUNNY See Schultze, Carl Edward

BURGON, SID (1936-   ) Sid Burgon is a good example of a latecomer to cartooning who succeeded as a gag artist, then transferred his talents to comic strips, and remained happily in children's comics for the rest of his career.

Sidney William Burgon was born in Berwick-on-Tweed, England, on October 3, 1936. His father was a gardener, his mother a housemaid with a natural artistic talent. She taught young Sid the elements of sketching. In 1950 he left school to become a mechanic in a local garage, a job he had for 13 years. He would occasionally display his sketches at work, and his coworkers persuaded him to pursue his talent. He took classes at the London Art School and Percy V. Bradshaw's Press Art College.

Burgon's first success, after years of sending pencil cartoons to various newspaper editors, came when *The Weekly News*, a national newspaper published in Scotland, published one of his cartoons. Burgon signed his drawing "Swab," a name created from his initials, plus his wife Annie's "A." This success led to more of his work being published, and he made the unusual decision to submit only finished artwork to newspapers. Fortunately, this was not much more difficult than only submitting sketches—so simple was his style.

In 1963 he stopped working as a mechanic and began freelancing as a cartoonist. His drawings appeared in many publications, including the *Daily Mirror*, the *Sunday Express*, and *Weekend* magazine, all of which ran plenty of gag cartoons at the time. His mechanic experience paid off as well: he became a staff cartoonist at *Motor World* magazine and supplied a regular motoring cartoon to the *Daily Telegraph* newspaper.

In 1970, at the urging of cartoonist friend Colin Whittock, Burgon sent a strip to the editor of the new comic *Whizzer & Chips*. His work was accepted and his substitution for "Hot Rod," a dragon drawn by the comics' art editor, Alf Saporito, was published. In 1971 he created *Joker* for another new comic, *Knockout*, which was a revival of an old title, but not of the comic itself. Scripted by Roy Davis, *Joker* was designed to be a rival to D.C. Thomson's *Dennis the Menace*, and was

a great success, continuing elsewhere after *Knockout* folded. Burgon's later characters took on the "comic horror" style popular at the time: *The Haunted Wood* in *Knockout*, *The Invisible Monster*, a two-page series for *Monster Fun* (1973), and *The Little Monsters*, a large panel series in the style of Fred Robinson's *Gremlins*. Later still came *The Toffs and the Toughs* (*Whizzer*), which had been created by Reg Parlett; *Milly O'Nare and the Penny Less* (*Jackpot*, 1979); and their male clones, *Ivor Lott and Tony Broke* (*Buster*). Other series Burgon worked on included *Biddy's Beastly Bloomers*, *Shiver & Shake*, *Lolly Pop* (*Whoopee*), and *Bookworm* (1984) for the same comic. In 1982 Burgon won the Society of Strip Illustration Best Comic Artist Award for his long-running series *Joker*.

D.G.

BURGOS, CARL (1920?-1984) American comic book artist and writer, born in New York City; although both Steranko's *History of Comics* and the *Who's Who of American Comic Books* pinpoint Burgos' birthdate as 1917, the artist/writer claims he was born April 18, 1920. After one year at the National Academy of Design, Burgos eventually joined the Harry "A" Chesler shop in 1938 before moving to Lloyd Jacquet's Funnies, Inc. studio. He remained there until drafted for service in World War II in 1942. When he returned, Burgos entered City College and spent most of the next 25 years in advertising art.

But his early work included the creation of one of comic books' most important strips, *The Human Torch*. Burgos had spent most of 1938 and 1939 producing material for the Centaur group, writing and drawing features like *Iron Skull* and *Stoney Dawson*. When he moved to the Jacquet shop, however, he and Bill Everett began working on Timely's *Marvel Comics* number one (November 1939), and while Everett created the aquatic *Sub-Mariner* strip, Burgos created the flaming android known as the Human Torch. Despite his merely adequate scripting and even poorer artwork, Burgos' fiery character caught on and was appearing in his own book by autumn 1940. Burgos' own art style—which was straight-forward and uninspiring, notable only because he refused to "swipe" from other artists—never appreciably improved. He left the strip and comics in 1942.

Burgos made only three brief reappearances in color comics: in the mid-1950s he drew several horror stories for Atlas; in 1964 and 1965, he handled some *Giant-Man* and *Human Torch* stories for Marvel; and in 1966, he created Country-Wide's short-lived version of *Captain Marvel*. Later that year, he assumed the editorship of Country-Wide's line of black and white "horror" titles, poor imitations of Warren's *Creepy* and *Eerie* books. He died in April 1984.

J.B.

BUSCEMA, JOHN (1927-   ) American comic book artist, born in New York City on December 11, 1927. After studies at the High School of Music and Art and Pratt Institute, Buscema broke into the comic business in 1948 with the Marvel/Timely/Atlas group. From that time until 1950, he worked on a wide variety of strips, mostly in the love, crime, and Western genres.

In 1950, he went to work for the Orbit group, where he continued to work on the same type of features he had done for Marvel. He left the firm in 1955, and, after a very brief stint at Charlton, began concentrating on work for Western (Gold Key), which he had been contributing to since 1953. Buscema again worked on a wide range of comic book story types, but he began concentrating on Western's movie adaptations and the *Roy Rogers* book. Although his work was not outstanding or particularly unique, it was clean and realistic, and this made him a perfect choice for the movie books, which always tried to closely parallel their motion picture counterparts.

Between 1958 and 1966, Buscema worked mainly for the ACG group, mostly on forgettable features and in the lucrative advertising art field. He returned to Marvel in 1966, however, about the time editor Stan Lee began a major expansion. Buscema has remained at Marvel ever since, and his uncluttered style became a Marvel mainstay. Along with John Romita and Jack Kirby, Buscema set the Marvel house style, mainly emphasizing straightforward storytelling and bigger-than-life, majestic heroes with staggering drawbacks. Over the years, he has drawn nearly every Marvel superhero and fantasy character, including the much-footballed *Hulk* (1966-1967), *Sub Mariner* (1968-1970), *Captain Marvel* (1969), *Thor* (1970), *Warlock* (1972), *Ka-zar* (1971-1972), *Fantastic Four* (1971-1973), *Black Widow* (1970), and many others. He also had a long, highly successful run on the *Avengers* strip, which he drew more or less regularly between 1967 and 1973.

Despite his herculean effort, Buscema did manage to make two particular strips totally his own. Both of them, strangely enough, had been previously handled by highly stylized artists, and most observers thought Buscema was the sacrificial lamb. When he began drawing the *Silver Surfer* in 1968, he succeeded Jack Kirby, who, along with writer Stan Lee, had elevated the strip to a level where it had a rabid cult following. Nevertheless, he handled the feature until 1970, and his pleasing, steady style and plausible storytelling methods brought him much acclaim. Similarly, when artist Barry Smith—a young Briton with a fascinating and ornate, if not perfect, style—abandoned *Conan* at the height of its cult popularity in 1973, Buscema was expected to generate little excitement. But even though he was saddled with what seemed to be a different inker for every story, he drew *Conan* in a pristine but exciting style that began accumulating a cult following all its own.

J.B.

From the 1960s to the 1990s Buscema has proven to be the ideal Marvel artist, working on every major title put out by the company, from *Savage Sword of Conan* to *Tarzan*, from *Wolverine* to *Punisher*, and returning to *The Avengers* in the 1980s. So valued is his talent that he was chosen as the main illustrator on the *How to Draw Comics the Marvel Way* manual.

M.H.

BUSCH, WILHELM (1832-1908) German poet, artist, and cartoonist, born April 15, 1832, in Wiedensahl (near Hannover, Germany), the first of his merchant parents' seven children. At the age of nine, Busch was sent to his uncle, the pastor of Ebergötzen, who was to educate him so he could enter secondary school. In 1845 they moved to the parish of Lüthorst. At the age of 16 Busch was accepted by the Polytechnic School of Hannover. He stayed in Hannover for about four years, and there made the acquaintance of a painter who suggested that he study at the Academy of Düsseldorf.

From there he went to Antwerp, Belgium, and got to know the paintings of Rubens, Brouwer, Teniers, and Frans Hals, which influenced his own paintings, most of which were not displayed until after his death (and are now valued at about $10 million).

After Antwerp it was back to Wiedensahl, then to Lüthorst, and finally on to the Academy of Munich, Germany. Here, he became a member of the "Künstlerverein" (artists' club), which led to the first publication of his caricatures in the weekly *Fliegenden Blätter* ("Flying Leaves," or "Looseleaves") in 1859. He continued working for them and for the *Münchener Bilderbogen* until 1871, even after he returned to his native Wiedensahl. Busch's first picture story, not unlike "pantomime" comic strips of today, was published in the *Fliegenden Blätter* in 1860. It was titled "Die Maus oder die gestorte Nachtruhe. Eine europäische Zeitgeschichte" ("The Mouse, or Sleep Disturbed. A European Story of the Times"). Busch's picture stories, predecessors of the modern comic strip, were later collected in the books *Schnaken und Schnurren* ("Wit and Drollery") and *Kunterbunt* ("Pell-Mell").

The best-known creation of Wilhelm Busch appeared in 1865. It is, of course, *Max und Moritz*, on which the *Katzenjammer Kids* were based. Actually, the publisher who had printed Busch's earlier picture books *Bilderpossen* ("Pictorial Farces"), *Der Eispeter* ("Icy Peter"), *Katze und Maus* ("Cat and Mouse"), among others, rejected *Max und Moritz*. Nevertheless, the book was published and, because of its grim moral, was harshly criticized by pedagogues. It is not surprising, then, that comics met with similar criticism while their predecessor had long since become a children's classic.

In the 1870s Busch became fed up with having to grind out picture stories week after week for humor

Wilhelm Busch.

magazines and turned to writing and illustrating books, living a hermit's life in Wiedensahl. In 1898 Busch moved to Mechtshausen, where he continued writing prose and verse, illustrating, and painting until his death on January 9, 1908. Busch's narrative figuration still holds up well. His wit, precise line drawing, and humorous verse live on. They have also been of some influence in the development of what is called the comic strip. Maybe art critic Arsene Alexandre sums it up best in his obituary in the Paris *Figaro*: "Wilhelm Busch was one of the most surprising inventors of comic syntheses who ever lived. . . . Many makers of 'simplified' drawings have borrowed from him. Unfortunately they have not borrowed his depth of observation."

W.F.

BUSHMILLER, ERNEST (1905-1982) Ernest Paul Bushmiller was born in 1905 in the Bronx, New York, and went to work at 14 as copy boy on the old New York *World* as soon as he was out of grammar school. At the time, many of the great strip artists drew every day at their desks at the paper (working at home and sending your strips to the syndicate by mail was almost unheard of), and the young Ernie hobnobbed with many of his idols, such as Rudolph Dirks, H. T. Webster, Milt Gross, and others. He spent two of his teen years studying after work at the National Academy of Drawing, and then got his first break as a cub artist in the "comic room"—the strip artist's domain.

A few years later, he sold his first comic strip to United Features: *Fritzi Ritz*, a working-girl feature with more zest than most. *Phil Fumble* was added to the *Fritzi* Sunday page and replaced in 1940 by *Nancy*. Later the instantly popular *Nancy*, a simple gag strip about a young girl (Fritzi's niece), replaced *Fritzi* first as a daily and then as Bushmiller's sole Sunday feature. It is as the creator of *Nancy* that he is widely known today, and *Fritzi* (to say nothing of *Phil Fumble*) is largely forgotten, although both were funnier and better drawn than most of *Nancy*.

The excellent visual comedy of *Fritzi Ritz* led Harold Lloyd to invite Bushmiller to Hollywood in the 1920s, where the Bronx cartoonist spent nearly a year inventing gags and narrative for Lloyd films, managing to

draw *Fritzi* at the same time. He died in Stamford, Connecticut, on August 15, 1982.

B.B.

BUSTER BROWN (U.S.) R. F. Outcault's second great strip, *Buster Brown*, first appeared in the color Sunday section of the *New York Herald* on May 4, 1902, where it replaced Outcault's minor *L'il Mose* page. In sharp contrast to the slum grubbiness of the artist's earlier Yellow Kid, Buster Brown was the markedly well-dressed 10-year-old scion of a well-to-do suburban family, literate enough to write weekly, tongue-in-cheek "Resolutions," which reflected temporary contriteness at having been punished for another of the recurrent pranks he played with savage ingenuity on family and friends. Always accompanied by a toothily grinning evil muse of a bulldog named Tige, Buster—who appeared only in the Sunday pages for the duration of his nefarious career, aside from a few scattered, irregular daily appearances in the early 1910s—plagued the family maids, the deliverymen, policemen, his juvenile peers, and parents with explosives, paint, infuriated cats, wrecked cars, sunken boats, and a multitude of other devices that Outcault seemed able to inexhaustibly invent.

The strip soared to instant, nationwide popularity, provoking William Randolph Hearst to hire Outcault for the second time—the first was when he was drawing *The Yellow Kid* for the *New York World*—and once more put him and his character to work on Hearst's *New York American* Sunday page, where Buster first appeared on January 14, 1906 (after making his last Outcault bow in the *Herald* on December 31, 1905). The dismayed *Herald* reprinted a couple of old, 1902 *Buster* pages, then hired a miscellany of artists to keep its version of the strip going. In a court battle, it was decided that Outcault could keep the characters but not the strip name, while the *Herald* could use both the characters and the name. The public wasn't fooled, of course, but the *Herald* stubbornly kept its ersatz *Buster* running, finally as a half-page, until late into 1910.

Outcault's own *Buster*, appearing weekly under a different descriptive title every Sunday in the Hearst papers, ran merrily on through World War I, with Buster doing his devastating part, and finally retired from comic page action (after Outcault had felt forced

"Buster Brown," R. F. Outcault.

by waning inspiration to repeat more than one earlier sequence in slightly differing context) on August 15, 1920, when the work of other hands on the strip was already evident. But Buster's fame, like that of his dog, Tige, and vigorous feminine aide-de-vamp, Mary-Jane, was far from exhausted, and these characters continued a career already established in newspaper and magazine advertising pages, promoting clothing of all kinds (as a result of the public's early fascination with Buster's outfits), notably the still-popular Buster Brown shoes. Outcault drew or supervised much of the earlier advertising; later work was done by other artists.

A number of books reprinting or based on the *Buster Brown* strip appeared during the first two decades of the century: *Buster Brown's Pranks, Buster Brown and Mary-Jane, Buster Brown's Resolutions, Tige—His Story,* etc., to be echoed many years later by a giveaway *Buster Brown Comics* from the shoe company in the 1940s. There were also minor stage and vaudeville adaptions of the strip, radio ads, and some early short films based on the characters. Curiously, there were fewer Buster Brown toys of all kinds than there had been Yellow Kid artifacts, but the strip itself was much more widely popular and longer lasting. It has been recently reprinted in an inexpensive edition by Dover (*Buster Brown*), and will probably, deservedly, see more extensive textual revival in the future.

B.B.

BUTSCHKOW, PETER (1944-   ) Peter Butschkow was born on August 29, 1944, in Cottbus, Germany, but two months later his family moved to what would later become West Berlin. There he went to elementary school and then studied at a private art school for four semesters, followed by a yearlong apprenticeship as a typesetter. This was followed by nine semesters at the State School for Graphics. While preparing for his career, he was also a drummer in a rock band for nearly eight years.

Butschkow had decided to pursue a career as a graphic designer, and was employed at a Berlin advertising agency before leaving for a 10-year stint as a freelance graphic designer. He had started drawing gag cartoons for the satirical magazine *pardon*, and left Berlin—and advertising—in 1979, intending to continue working with only gag cartoons, comics, and illustrations. It took him almost five years to make a success of this transition.

In 1983 he moved to Hamburg and shortly after had his first collection of cartoons published. Since then, more than two dozen books of his cartoons have been published. Butschkow's work has appeared in numerous magazines and newspapers, as well as on television. His most popular work, however, is published regularly in the weekly magazines *stern* and *Hör zu*. For the latter, Butschkow has created a comic strip titled *Siegfried*. This strip, which began in 1985 and has been running ever since, depicts the very funny antics of a dragon named Siegfried living in a Neanderthal Stone Age world. While making the best of an occasional atrocious pun, the gags about dragons and Stone Age characters have kept readers in stitches ever since inclusion of the strip in the magazine. Unlike Reinhold Escher, Butschkow is not under exclusive contract to *Hör zu*. Therefore, he creates his ever-popular funnies not only for other magazines and newspapers but also for competing television programs.

W.F.

BUTZE OLIVER, GERMAN (1912-   ) Mexican cartoonist and illustrator German Butze was born February 11, 1912, in Mexico City. He studied painting and drawing at the San Carlos Academy in Mexico and later worked under the noted portrait painter Ignacio Rosas.

Butze started his career as an advertising artist, creating many ad characters that were to become famous. In the mid-1930s he turned to comic strip work with such features as *Memo Migaja* and *Pinito Pinole*. His most famous comic creation, *Los Supersabios* ("The Supersavants"), followed in 1936 in the pages of the magazine *Novedades*. The feature was so successful that it soon appeared in daily strip form as well as a weekly page. Later it also appeared in *Mujeres y Deportes* and was carried in the newly created periodicals *Chamaco Grande* and *Chamaco Chico*. Butze also did a strip for the magazine *Pepin* called *Pepe el Inquieto* ("Pepe the Worrier").

For a period, Butze devoted his time exclusively to *Los Supersabios*, which was published in the form of a twice-monthly comic book for a long time by Publicaciones Herrerias before being converted to a weekly format. Serious cardiovascular problems forced him to cease working in the early 1980s. (His older brother Valdemar was also a cartoonist.)

M.H.

BUZ SAWYER (U.S.) Roy Crane's *Buz Sawyer* was one of a number of armed-services strips kindled into existence by the development of World War II. Its first episode, published at the height of war on November 2, 1943, by King Features (followed by the Sunday half-page on November 23) and depicting the launching of the aircraft carrier *Tippecanoe*, from which Naval Lieutenant (J. G.) Buz Sawyer and his gunner, Roscoe Sweeney, were to fly sorties against the Japanese enemy, reflected the openings of other new military strips between 1941 and 1945. The difference between nearly all of those and *Buz Sawyer* is that Crane's strip lasted.

The reason is simple. *Sawyer* was planned over a long period of time by Crane as a means by which the cartoonist could gain control of his own creative work, enabling him to leave his contracted employment with NEA. If the conditions of war hadn't served as a launching pad for the new strip, Crane would have used something else. But essentially it was Crane's

"Buz Sawyer," Roy Crane. © King Features Syndicate.

superb graphic, narrative, and character-creating abilities that built *Sawyer* into a major, and now classic, comic strip.

Buz Sawyer was a clean-cut American boy, just out of flight school, with an apple-pie family in a small American town and a girl named Christy Jameson waiting for him. His gunner, Roscoe Sweeney, a comic-relief character, was older than Buz, and without any home. But the real characters in the strip at the outset were the war, Sawyer's aircraft carrier and crew as a unit, and the fighter planes that filled panel after panel with exciting, authentic air action (for Crane had researched his material thoroughly, even making tours with navy authorization to check details and foreign scenes). Nevertheless, Crane wrote continuously gripping adventure narratives involving his two heroes and their war activity, stories so imaginative that today they seem wholly undated by their war content. (The Sunday material, on the other hand, put more direct emphasis on G. I. humor, via Sweeney and his kooky pals, and consequently does not hold up so well.) The end of the war, of course, reopened the world to adventure, and Crane was prompt to plunge Buz into the kind of goofy, slam-bang, exotic escapades he liked best to write and draw, while he literally farmed Sweeney into exclusive appearance in the Sunday half-page gag sequences (where for the next three decades Sweeney and his sister, Lucille, plagued occasionally by cousinly horrors called Swatleys, tended their farm).

After Buz's discharge in October 1946, the postwar *Sawyer* daily strip got seriously under way. Chili Harrison, a wartime flyer buddy of Buz's (who was a somewhat more realistic equivalent of Mort Walker's Killer—he calls Sawyer "Buzzo," for example), gets Buz involved in a New York skyscraper intrigue, which is at once grisly and comic: Buz's fiancée, Tot Winter, is shoved off a balcony dozens of floors above the street by a woman gang leader's pet tiger, and Tot's death is blamed on Buz by the law. From that point, events simply get wilder and woolier, involving high peril in all parts of the world, man-eating plants, mad Russian exiles on glaciers, and Malay pirates, among others. Buz confronts a fabulous assortment of unique villains: the Tiger of Hong Kong; the phony American named Jerome Pomphrey, who is apparently concealing Hitler himself in an African hideout; Don Jaime of Mexico; and, Harry Sparrow and Gool. Buz himself had a number of tentative occupations, most relating to private investigation and government work, and finally married his wartime girl, Christy.

But *Buz Sawyer* continued, with Crane actively interested in the story line and art, although personal health made it increasingly difficult for him to work directly on the strip, and Ed Granberry began to do the nominal script and Harry Schlensker the bulk of the drawing. Growing taboos against violence in strips since the 1950s cut down much of the range and impact of *Sawyer*, while decreased size in syndicated comics reduced the graphic scope possible in individual panels. As a result, the strip, although still striking in art and intelligence of story line, became but a hearty shadow of the *Buz Sawyer* of the first two decades.

B.B.

Crane's death in 1977 did not signal any marked changes in either style or content. While the Sunday page had been discontinued in 1974, the daily strip continued in the hands of Schlensker and Granberry.

John Celardo guided *Buz Sawyer* in its twilight years from 1983 until the strip's demise in October 1989.

M.H.

Guido Buzzelli, "La Rivolta dei Racchi." © Buzzelli.

BUZZELLI, GUIDO (1927-1992) Italian cartoonist and illustrator, born July 27, 1927, in Rome. The son of a painter, Guido Buzzelli always showed more predilection for the comics than for painting; and at the age of 18 he joined the staff of the illustrated weekly *Argentovivo*. In the period immediately following the war, he produced a few covers for comic books. After drawing the adventure strip *Zorro* for the publisher Gabriele Gioggi of Rome and a multitude of covers for the Italian versions of *Flash Gordon, Mandrake,* and *The Phantom,* he started working for the British Daily Mirror Syndicate, later moving to London, where he illustrated the *Angélique* series based on Serge and Anne Golon's popular string of novels.

In 1965 Buzzelli returned to Italy and decided to follow in his father's footsteps, producing a number of paintings that were later exhibited. But he missed comic artwork and in 1969 drew a comic story for the catalogue of the Lucca Comics Convention, *La Rivolta dei Racchi* ("The Revolt of the Racchi"), a wildly surrealistic strip that won him critical acclaim. He was then dubbed "a master of the comics," a title that he confirmed with a series of highly innovative comic strips: *The Labyrinths, Zilzelub,* and *Annalise and the Devil* (these stories were first published in the French monthly *Charlie* and later introduced in Italy in the pages of *Linus* and *Alterlinus*). For a short while Buzzelli authored a series of pornographic parodies (based on comic characters, not unlike the "Tijuana bibes") for the satiric monthly *Menelik*. In the last 15 years of his life he divided his work almost equally between French and Italian publishers. He died in Rome on January 25, 1992.

Buzzelli was awarded the Yellow Kid in 1973 as best comic author, and his works have been exhibited at the Louvre in Paris.

G.B.

BYRNE, JOHN (1950-   ) Born on July 6, 1950, in Walsall, England, but raised in Canada, John Byrne burst onto the comics scene in the late 1960s with his

John Byrne, The Incredible Hulk. © 1998 Marvel Comics.

contributions to *Monster Times* and other fanzines. A graduate of the Alberta College of Art, Byrne made his professional debut in the early 1970s drawing for Charlton Comics on such titles as *Doomsday + 1*, *Space: 1999*, and *Emergency!*

In 1978 the big time beckoned to Byrne when he began work on a variety of titles for Marvel Comics, including *Iron Fist*, *Fantastic Four*, *The Incredible Hulk*, *Spider-Man*, *Daredevil*, and *The Avengers*. He is best remembered, however, for his work on the *X-Men* group of titles, for which he created Alpha Flight, which received its own title in 1983. In addition to his pencilling and scripting duties on these and other titles, he also drew close to 200 covers for Marvel.

Attracted by his innovative style and his newfound star status, DC Comics hired him away from Marvel in 1986 to revive its faltering Superman line of comics. This Byrne did, earning even more kudos in the process. During his two-year stint at DC Comics, he also worked with marked success on *Batman* and *Green Lantern*.

Returning to Marvel Comics, he turned his attention to *The West Coast Avengers* and *The She-Hulk*, but the comic-book-buying public's tastes had changed, and Byrne, whose work had been considered "hot" a scant 12 months before, now met with only a lukewarm response, prompting him to leave Marvel Comics for the second time. Since 1993 he has been published by Dark Horse, working on its own titles, *John Byrne's Next Men* and *Critical Error*, and drawing occasional issues of outside comics such as *Aliens* and *Judge Dredd*.

John Byrne's career can be considered a prime example of the fickleness of comic book fans and of the precariousness of the star system in the comics universe. His fall from grace between the mid- and the late 1980s proved as precipitous as his rise had previously been meteoric. Yet his solid craftsmanship and polish endure, and he will be heard from long after some of today's hotshots are gone.

M.H.

BYRNES, EUGENE (1889-1974) American cartoonist, born on Manhattan's West Side in 1889. After graduation from high school, Gene Byrnes embarked on a promising sports career which was unfortunately cut short at the age of 22, when he suffered a broken leg in the course of a wrestling match. During his stay at the hospital, Byrnes spent his time first copying Tad Dorgan's cartoons, then drawing cartoons of his own, which he sent to various newspapers. His first cartoon series, *Things That Never Happen*, was published as a two-column panel in a California newspaper in 1915.

Later that year, Byrnes met Winsor McCay, who got him a job as sports cartoonist on the *New York Tele-*

Gene Byrnes.

gram, for which Byrnes also created his famous humor panel *It's a Great Life If You Don't Weaken* (whose title became the slogan of the American Expeditionary Force in World War I). As a complement to *It's a Great Life*, Byrnes in 1917 began a two-column companion panel, *Reg'lar Fellers*. The new creation was all about a high-spirited gang of kids whose names, "Jimmy Dugan," "Pudd'n Head," "Aggie," soon became household words. Impressed by the success of their new feature, Byrnes' publishers shifted *Reg'lar Fellers* to their more prestigious parent publication, the *New York Herald*, in the form of a full-fledged comic strip (it appeared first as a Sunday page to which a daily version was later added).

Gene Byrnes' influence as a cartoonist was at its peak from the 1920s to the 1940s. His drawing style, detailed, precise, and almost academic, and his lively but gentle humor proved a distinct departure from the slam-bang school of cartooning prevalent during his time.

Byrnes reinforced his preeminent position as a guiding light for cartoonists with the publication of a number of professional textbooks that he wrote and edited himself, starting with *How to Draw Comics and Commercial Art* (New York, 1939) and continuing with *A Complete Guide to Drawing, Illustration, Cartooning and Painting* (New York, 1948), *A Complete Guide to Professional Cartooning* (Drexel Hill, Pa., 1950), and *Commercial Art* (New York, 1952).

Gene Byrnes retired from professional life in the 1960s. On July 26, 1974, he died of a heart ailment.

M.H.

CAESAR, KURT (1906-1974) Italian cartoonist and illustrator of German origin, born in 1906 in Montigny, Lorraine, when it was part of the German Empire. After starting his career as a journalist for the Ulman News Agency in Germany, Kurt Caesar decided to settle in Italy in the mid-1930s. There he began his new activity as an illustrator, signing his pages with the pen name "Caesar Away" (or "Avai"). His first published works appeared in the weekly *La Risata*, which in 1936 published *I Due Tamburini* ("The Two Drummer-Boys") and *Cristoforo Colombo*. Now and then he would contribute to other big-circulation weeklies, such as *Topolino* and *L'Intrepido*, with illustration work and comic features. In 1938 he produced his most famous creation, *Romano il Legionario* ("Romano the Legionary"), about an Italian pilot whose adventures took place during the Spanish Civil War. (Later, Romano would be able to contribute to a bigger conflict, World War II.)

Although heavily influenced by Alex Raymond as far as his characterization was concerned, Caesar cast a new and very personal element, which is apparent in the perfect technical rendering of machines and flight scenes. The intricate detail of his drawings has earned him the appellation of "master craftsman of the comics," a very apt description. Caesar's ability to faithfully reproduce machines and aircraft led him into more war stories, all widely popular at the time, such as *I Moschettieri del Aeroporto Z* ("The Musketeers of Airport Z"), *Will Sparrow*, and *Il Mozzo del Sommergibile* ("The Cabin-Boy of the Submarine"). Caesar's favorite fields of operation were the pages of the Catholic weekly *Il Vittorioso*, where his big illustrations of war machines were always well received.

After the war, Caesar published a few more stories in *Il Vittorioso* and in *Il Giornalino*, but devoted most of his time to illustration work, producing a good number of covers for *Urania* (a monthly science-fiction magazine published by Mondadori) and drawing many pages for Fleetway Publications in Britain, all of them with a war or science-fiction angle. In the 1960s Caesar drew the first episodes of the new science-fiction strip *Perry Rhodan* for a German publisher, and he also contributed grandiose and intricate double-page spreads for the *Messaggero dei Ragazzi* of Padua.

Kurt Caesar died at Bracciano, where he had been living and working for the previous two decades, on July 12, 1974.

G.B.

CALKINS, RICHARD (1895-1962) American artist and writer, born in 1895 in Grand Rapids, Michigan. Richard (Dick) Calkins studied at the Chicago Art Institute and soon became a cartoonist for the *Detroit Free Press*. In 1917 he joined Hearst's *Chicago Examiner* as a sports cartoonist and illustrator. During World War I he was commissioned a lieutenant in the U.S. Air Force

but the war ended before he saw any action (for a long time afterwards he would sign "Lt. Dick Calkins").

Discharged from service in 1919, Calkins went back to the *Chicago Examiner*, where, in addition to his other duties, he originated a weekly panel, *Amateur Etiquette*; later he joined the John F. Dille Co. When Dille decided to launch a daily science-fiction strip based on a Phil Nowlan novel that he had retitled *Buck Rogers 2429 A.D.*, Calkins became the first artist on the feature, which debuted on January 7, 1929. That same year Calkins created, in collaboration with another former pilot, Lieutenant Lester J. Maitland (who did the writing), *Skyroads*, an aviation strip.

Calkins was to draw *Buck Rogers* till November 29, 1947; after Nowlan's death in 1940 he also assumed the writing duties. (On the other hand, the Sunday feature, while credited to Calkins, was actually ghosted by his assistants, Russell Keaton and Rick Yager.) In 1947 Calkins left *Buck Rogers* after a bitter dispute with his employers.

In the latter part of his life, Calkins worked mostly in comic books, chiefly in a writing capacity. He scripted a good many stories for the *Red Ryder* comic books published by Western in the late 1940s and early 1950s. Calkins died on May 13, 1962, in Tucson, Arizona.

Calkins' work as an illustrator looks outmoded and clumsy today, but he had a flair for depicting spaceships and other far-out gadgets in a detailed and almost naturalistic fashion. His visual inventiveness never flagged, his drawings and compositions fired the imagination of his adolescent readers, and (as Ray Bradbury, among others, has testified) his influence on future science-fiction writers proved decisive and enduring.

M.H.

CALVIN AND HOBBES (U.S.) The most innovative and delightful comic strip to come out in the last decade was sprung on an unsuspecting public on November 19, 1985. Distributed by Universal Press Syndicate, it was called *Calvin and Hobbes*, and the perpetrator was a 27-year-old cartoonist named Bill Watterson.

The keynote was struck in the very first daily with the introduction of six-year-old Calvin and his pet tiger Hobbes, whom he had captured with the lure of a tuna sandwich. From the outset the relationship between the crabby, querulous, manic Calvin and the suave, laid-back Hobbes proved to be the heart of the matter. The good-natured tiger added a dash of sophistication and a whiff of wisdom as a willing participant in Calvin's many escapades. These adventures took place unbeknownst to the boy's parents and to the world at large, for whom Hobbes appeared to be a normal, stuffed toy tiger.

"I don't think of Hobbes as a doll that miraculously comes to life when Calvin's around. Neither do I think of Hobbes as the product of Calvin's imagination," Watterson once declared, suggesting that Hobbes, the

"Calvin and Hobbes," Bill Watterson. © Bill Watterson/UPS.

flesh-and-blood tiger, might have been the secret identity of Hobbes, the stuffed animal (a kind of ironic twist on the Superman/Clark Kent gambit). In any case, the tiger soon became Calvin's favorite—and often only—companion, accomplice, and alibi. When the boy came back with his clothes filthy and in tatters from a wild ride through the woods in his wagon, he would blame it on Hobbes' lack of driving skill; and when asked by his parents for his school report card, he could announce with a straight face that his "tiger ate it."

The strip's main protagonists were given a very limited cast of characters with whom to interact. There were Calvin's unnamed parents—Dad, a sarcastic, somewhat remote figure; Mom, the disciplinarian and nurturer whom Calvin imagined in his more resentful moments as his "evil arch-enemy—Mom-Lady." At school his nemesis was Moe, the schoolyard bully who periodically shook down the cowering Calvin for his lunch money; and his persistent suitor, the straight-A student Susie Derkins, with whom he entertained a love-hate relationship. (He once kidnapped her doll, Binky Betsey, for ransom, but he also sent her hate-mail valentines every year.) Miss Wormwood, his much put-upon teacher, and Rosalyn, the tough (and justifiably well-paid) babysitter, rounded out the strip's list of characters.

To relieve the tedium of school or the routine of home life, the hyperactive Calvin would cast himself as "Spaceman Spiff," the interplanetary pioneer; "Tracer Bullet," the unflappable private eye; or "Safari Al," the indomitable jungle explorer. His more sedate pursuits led him to found the "Get Rid of Slimy Girls" Club, or GROSS for short, and he declared himself its Supreme Ruler and Dictator for Life; in most instances a sarcastic Hobbes would bring his high-flying companion back to earth with some barbed remark. The interplay between boy and tiger, in turn joyful and introspective, complicitous and antagonistic, gave the strip its peculiar charm along with undertones of pathos and poignancy.

Calvin and Hobbes represented a welcome oasis of superlative (if understated) draftsmanship, luminous composition, and graceful design. Watterson often returned to the wellspring of the form, drawing inspiration from the medium's greats—George Herriman, Winsor McCay, Walt Kelly—whom he emulated but never copied. This painstaking attention to detail produced inevitable burnouts for Watterson, during which times the strip would go into reruns. (These elicited almost no protest from the readers, since *Calvin and*

Hobbes reprints were still wittier and better drawn than many other comics.)

Calvin and Hobbes enjoyed unprecedented popularity from the start. The strip ran in every major newspaper market to great acclaim, and its many book reprints invariably topped the *New York Times* bestseller lists. Amid all this adulation Watterson abruptly decided to discontinue the 10-year-old feature, citing a variety of reasons (fatigue, disgust at the ever-shrinking space allotted to comics on the newspaper page, disputes with his syndicate over the artist's adamant refusal to allow merchandising of his characters). The last release appeared on December 31, 1995.

Calvin and Hobbes was to its multitude of fans an endless freshet of inspiration and charm, and its passing was felt by many like a death in the family. Watterson is still young, and the advent of the new millenium may well bring the second coming of *Calvin and Hobbes.*

M.H.

Edmond-François Calvo, "Le Centaure Vezelay." © SPE.

CALVO, EDMOND-FRANÇOIS (1892-1958) A
French cartoonist and illustrator born in 1892 in Fleury-sur-Andelle, a little town in Normandy, Calvo, who liked to draw even in early childhood, had the usual cartoonist's training, working on one publication after another. After World War I (when he saw service) his career stabilized somewhat and he started contributing cartoons and illustrations to nationally distributed publications.

Calvo came into the comic strip field late in life. His earliest recorded work in this area is *La Vengeance du Corsaire* ("The Privateer's Revenge," for the comic weekly *Junior* (1938), followed in 1939 by the excellent *Le Centaure Vezelay* ("The Vezelay Centaur") on a script by Robert Mazières, a historical strip set at the time of the French Revolution. Then came the flood: an adaptation of the Errol Flynn movie *Robin Hood* (also 1939), the Western *Tom Mix* (1940-1942), and the gag strip *Croquemulot*, only a few of the many titles contributed by Calvo from 1939 to 1943. Then in 1944-1945 he produced what many consider his masterwork: a two-volume comic strip allegory of World War II, *La Bête Est Morte* ("The Beast Is Dead"). In this animal transposition closely paralleling historical events as they were then known, the Germans were presented as wolves, the British were bulldogs, the Russians bears, the Japanese monkeys, etc. Calvo followed this with another excellent creation in 1946, *Rosalie*, about the comic tribulations of an old jalopy.

Aside from a few forays into advertising art and illustration, Calvo devoted the rest of his life to comic strip work. Among the innumerable features he created or worked on, the most worthy of mention are *King Kong* (1948); *Cricri Souris d'Appartement* ("Cricri Apartment Mouse"), a charming animal strip written by Marijac and drawn by Calvo from 1948 to 1955 (his most popular series, it was reprinted *ad nauseam* long after the cartoonist's death); *Babou* (1952); *Captain Gin* and *Moustache et Trotinette* (started in 1957, this seems to be Calvo's last creation).

In the mid-1950s Calvo (while continuing with his drawing) retired to his native town of Fleury. There he opened a hostelry where, as his friend Marijac stated, "he was the best customer." Calvo died in 1958, almost without notice.

Calvo's position is difficult to assess: his talent is indisputable but he never created—aside, perhaps, from the offbeat *La Bête Est Morte*—any enduring work. He remains, however, an important figure in the French comic strip field of the 1940s and 1950s.

M.H.

CANALE, ANTONIO (1915-1991) Antonio Canale was born in 1915 in Monza but grew up in Milan, where he lived all his life. He started his career in the early 1930s as an illustrator; but only the comic strip gave him the opportunity to fully realize his talents. Before World War II Canale drew some beautiful stories for the comic weeklies *L'Audace* and *Il Vittorioso*. Between 1939 and 1940 he produced several comic features, first for *L'Audace*, then for *Topolino*, where he

Antonio Canale, "Vecchia America." © Canale.

created his first recognized masterpiece, *Il Solitario dei Sakya* ("The Long One of the Sakya"), on a text by Federico Pedrocchi. Unfortunately Canale was drafted into service before he could complete the story, which was continued by Bernardo Leporini.

Immediately after the end of the war, in 1945, Canale reached an important stage in his artistic development with a relatively short-lived feature, *I Dominatori dell'Abisso* ("The Rulers of the Abyss"): by eschewing etch marks and relying chiefly on contrasting masses of blacks and whites, he was able to renew and refresh his drawing style. His new comic strip style was further emphasized in such works as *Yorga* (1945) and in the series *Amok, il Gigante Mascherato* ("Amok, the Masked Giant," 1946). Also in 1946, for *Topolino*, Canale drew one of the best episodes of *Virus*, "Il Signore del Buio" ("The Master of Darkness").

Then, after many years of drawing uncounted war and espionage stories for London's Fleetways Publications, Canale made a comeback on the Italian comic strip scene around 1960 with his drawing of Hiawatha's adventures in the *Corriere dei Piccoli*, on a text by R. D'Ami. In these stories Canale succeeds in blending a subtle mixture of the grotesque and the realistic, an approach perfectly suited to old legends and ballads. This stylistic innovation is further refined in his "Stories of Old America," which Canale did in 1963 but which were only recently published.

Canale seemed to be going more and more in that direction, and his next venture was being awaited with much anticipation. In his later years, however, he turned more and more to illustration. He died on October 15, 1991.

G.B.

CANIFF, MILTON (1907-1988) American cartoonist and writer, born February 28, 1907, in Hillsboro, Ohio. He attended high school in Stivers, Ohio, and graduated from Ohio State University in 1930. While still in school Caniff successively worked on the *Dayton Journal*, the *Miami Daily News*, and the *Columbus Dispatch*. In 1932 he moved to New York City and joined the Associated Press, for which he created in 1932 *The Gay Thirties*, a weekly panel; and *Dickie Dare*, a daily adventure strip, in 1933. In 1934 his work was brought to the attention of Captain Joseph Patterson, publisher of the *New York News*, who was then looking for a feature "based on a blood-and-thunder formula, carrying a juvenile angle, and packed with plenty of suspense." The answer to the captain's prayer turned out to be *Terry and the Pirates*, which Caniff debuted as a daily strip on October 22, 1934, and as a Sunday page a few weeks later.

During the war, while continuing *Terry*, Caniff created *Male Call*, a strip especially designed for the G.I.s. Due to contractual difficulties, Caniff abandoned *Terry* in December of 1946 (it was taken over by George Wunder) to start his own strip, *Steve Canyon*, for Field Enterprises (January 1947).

A cartoonist of unequalled qualities (who has often been referred to as "the Rembrandt of the comic strip") and a first-rate storyteller, Milton Caniff is one of a small group of artists who succeeded in raising the comic strip to the level of art. Caniff's mastery of drawing, his subtle sense of composition, his skillful use of characterization and dialogue, have all made him justly famous in and out of his profession. He has influenced a whole school of cartoonists who have heavily borrowed from his techniques.

In addition to his comic strip work Caniff also did book and magazine illustration, wrote many articles about his work and comic art in general, and lectured extensively on the subject. His awards, civil and military, are too numerous to mention. He was one of the original founders of the National Cartoonists Society in 1946, and served as its president in 1948-49.

A man fiercely devoted to his work, Caniff continued to write *Steve Canyon* in its entirety and to draw it with the assistance of Norman Rockwell's nephew Dick Rockwell; not even ill health and advancing age could keep him away from the drawing board. He died in New York City of lung cancer on April 3, 1988; his strip survived him only by a few weeks.

M.H.

CAPITAINE FANTÔME, LE (France) This highly unusual comic strip was created by writer Jacques François (actually Jacques Dumas, better known as Marijac) and artist Raymond Cazanave in issue number 10 of the French illustrated magazine *Coq Hardi* (April 1946). Set in the 18th century, *Le Capitaine Fantôme* ("Captain Phantom") is a story of violence and horror the likes of which were rarely (if ever) seen in the pages of European comic papers of the time. Murder, torture, and rape are among its more subdued moments, and its mood of unrelieved psychological terror is a far cry from the wholesome fun offered by the rest of the *Coq Hardi* pages.

During an ocean crossing to Europe from South America, Don Juan Cavalaros' ship is attacked by pirates. Don Juan is left for dead and his daughter Juanita is abducted. A young Frenchman, De Vyrac, swears to deliver Juanita, who is to be sold as a slave. He joins the pirates, led by a peg-legged, mysterious figure known as "Captain Phantom" and his sinister henchman, Pater Noster, a hunchbacked monster. After many fights, plunders, and other pleasantries, De Vyrac saves Juanita and Pater Noster (who turns out to be the girl's lost father, whose body and spirit have broken down under Indian torture). Mad with rage, Captain Phantom sets fire to his own ship and massacres the entire crew before he is himself stabbed to death by the demented Pater Noster. At the end of the episode (June 1947) only Juanita, Pater Noster, and De Vyrac are left alive.

The authors had probably planned to conclude on this note, but the insistence of their readers forced them to hastily concoct a sequel, which started appearing in *Coq Hardi* 88 (November 1947). In this episode, titled "Le Vampire des Caraïbes" ("The Vampire of the Caribbean"), Captain Phantom reappears as a specter who must drink human blood in order to keep his human appearance (shades of Dracula!), and there is the usual quota of mayhem and mischief going on before De Vyrac and Juanita are finally allowed to marry each other. A third episode, "Les Boucaniers" ("The Buccaneers"), has the couple battling to save their estate from Juanita's greedy uncles, but Captain Phantom does not appear in this one. The series finally ended on something of an anticlimax on September 26, 1948.

Le Capitaine Fantôme seems to have been inspired largely by Russell Thorndyke's *Dr. Syn* novels, with which it shares its black mood, supernatural happenings, ghoulish characters, and unruly passions. The nar-

"Le Capitaine Fantôme," Raymond Cazanave. © Coq Hardi.

rative is well served by Cazanave's style, sinister and brooding, and his compositions of ominous black splashes and blinding whites, unrelieved by any shade of gray. As it is, *Le Capitaine Fantôme* is an oddity in the French comic strip, like one of those black monoliths sometimes found in sunny Southern landscapes.

M.H.

CAPITAN L'AUDACE (Italy) *Capitan l'Audace* ("Captain Fearless") was the longest-running Italian costume adventure strip. Its chief character was a corsair clearly derived from Salgari's novels, and a worthy successor to that author's Black Corsair. Written by the prolific Federico Pedrocchi and drawn by the brilliant Walter Molino, *Capitan l'Audace* made its first appearance in the pages of the comic weekly *L'Audace* on April 20, 1939.

With his faithful lieutenants Barbanera ("Blackbeard") and Spaccateste ("Headbreaker"), Capitan l'Audace fights against the sinister Baron Armando di Torrerossa, who plans to marry his attractive cousin, the Countess Vera, in order to lay hands on the young girl's estate, which had been willed to her by her father, Count Stefano di Coldrago. Of course, after innumerable bloody battles, hairbreadth escapes, and suspenseful chases, victory finally belongs to the bold captain, who marries the beautiful Vera.

After the Captain's wedding, unfortunately, the story loses its incisiveness and originality, a fact further precipitated by Molino's departure from the strip and his replacement by Edgardo dell'Acqua and Bernardo Leporini. (At the same time as it changed artists, *Capitan l'Audace* also changed magazines, while still remaining in Mondadori's fold—transferring first to *Paperino* and then to *Topolino*, where it remained until its demise in 1946.)

A few episodes of *Captain l'Audace* were reprinted in the series "Albi d'Oro" (1948).

G.B.

CAPITAN MIKI (Italy) In the 1950s the teenage hero (usually no more than 16 years of age) was a popular staple of Italian comic books, with titles numbering in the dozens. *Capitan Miki* was different from other such

"Capitan Miki," Essegesse. © Editrice Dardo.

"El Capitan Misterio," Emilio Freixas. © Freixas.

features because it presented less-tangled plots and combined mystery with adventure and humor.

Capitan Miki was produced by Essegesse (a collective label combining the names of authors Sinchetto, Sartoris, and Guzzon) and appeared for the first time in publisher Dardo's *Collana Scudo* on July 1, 1951. Miki is a 16-year-old boy whose guardian, Clem, was killed by a band of outlaws; along with his loyal companion Doppio Rum ("Double Rum"), he enlists in the "Nevada Rangers." After he has unmasked the killer and accomplished a multitude of other hair-raising exploits, Miki rises to the rank of captain (thus justifying the title of the strip).

The daughter of the fort commandant, Susy, is Miki's girlfriend. She leads a lonely life, with her fiancé always away on dangerous missions in the company of his two sidekicks, Doppio Rum and Dr. Salasso ("Bloodletting"), a pair of characters cut out of a different cloth from the hero. While Miki is a teetotaler with a brave and honest heart, his companions are inveterate drinkers, troublemakers, and swindlers, and no paragons of courage either. They often disrupt the hero's earnest undertakings with their uninhibited shenanigans. (*Capitan Miki*'s straight narratives are also often enlivened by freckle-faced Susy's scenes of jealousy.)

With *Miki* the authors hit on a winning formula that they later utilized in other titles such as *Grande Blek* ("Big Blek"), *Alan Mistero,* and *Commandante Mark.* After Essegesse left the strip in the early 1960s, the feature was continued by artists Franco Bignotti and Nicolino Del Principe on scripts by Amilcare Medici. *Capitan Miki* was published in two of Dardo's comic books, *Collana Prateria* and *Collana Freccia.* It came to an end in the 1980s.

G.B.

CAPITAN MISTERIO, EL (Spain) *El Capitan Misterio* was created by the illustrator Emilio Freixas on an idea and script by Angel Puigmiquel. The first episode was published in the comic book collection *Mosquito* in 1944; the following year the feature transferred to the

magazine *Gran Chicos*, where it ran uninterruptedly from October 1945 to July 1948. In 1949 it was being published in the magazine *Historietas* and in the comic weekly *Chicos*, where it ended its career later in July of that year.

Capitan Misterio was a masked justice-fighter of the Far East, with strong athletic and hypnotic powers and indomitable spirit and courage. In his most imaginative adventure he discovered the lost city of Tanit located on one of the Pacific islands, where Queen Nerea fell in love with him. Misterio's companions, the gigantic mulatto Pancho Tonelada and the youthful Balin, helped him in his fights against mad scientists with exotic names and Nazi faces who were always trying to conquer the world. To conceal his real identity (of which nothing is known except that the hero is blond and is named John), Misterio covers his face with a purple hood decorated with a skull—a sign with which he marks his enemies. As one can easily see, *El Capitan Misterio* has more than a passing resemblance to *The Phantom* (with elements of *Jungle Jim* and *Mandrake* thrown in).

In this feature, which unfolded in the course of four episodes, Emilio Freixas had recourse to his usual technique made of a conventional panel layout and a line at once fine and powerful, to emphasize his main strengths: the drawing of animals—in which he is a master—and the skillful depiction of the human body. A talented anatomist, Freixas made Capitan Misterio into his most perfect hero, while giving us at the same time a model of feminine beauty in the person of the queen of Tanit.

L.G.

CAPITAN TERROR (Germany) *Capitan Terror*, as the name suggests, is a pirate captain born on Spanish soil. He was created by Peter Wiechmann, editorial director of the Kauka comic book line, in cooperation with the Bardon Art Studios of Barcelona, Spain. The first adventure was drawn by noted comic artist Esteban Maroto in a somewhat restricted style that helps tell the story and avoids drowning it in graphic experimentation. *Capitan Terror* first appeared in *primo* number

"Capitan Terror," Sola. © Rolf Kauka.

9/1974. As expected, readers liked this additional entry to the line of Kauka adventure comics.

Capitan Terror is the story of Captain Javier Aguirre, who, after refusing to enter the military services of the dictatorial Catalonian governor, finds his ship attacked and sunk. His wife and crew are killed in the incident; Aguirre and the boy Chico are the sole survivors. With vengeance in his heart, Aguirre arrives on the island of Ibiza, a pirate hangout. He is accepted into their ranks, no little thanks to Cuchillo "Knife," the red-haired daughter of the pirate chieftain El Diablo.

Terror enlists the aid of Samurai, "Black Powder" the ace cannonier, the French pistolero Guy, the evenly matched fighters Ramirez and Yogi, and strongman Turco. This motly international group takes up the fight against the tyrant Carlos Fernando on Cuchillo's ship "Flecha" (Arrow), which is rechristened "La Venganza" (Revenge) after some alterations that are to make it maneuverable even in the slightest of breezes.

Capitan Terror stands in the classic tradition of a hero driven into the life of an outlaw by extremity. Nevertheless, he stays true to a standard of morals, a code of conduct that permits him to shape his crew to his ideals and that gives him the necessary strength to fight a dictator who does not care whether his subjects live or die. The stories are fast-paced, well written and drawn, the artwork having been taken over by Sola after Maroto's episode. There is also the additional interest of the growing relationship between Terror and Cuchillo. Although largely escapist literature, *Capitan Terror*, by reflecting on the hero's actions, makes interesting reading. The strip was carried over into *Action Comic* when *primo* was discontinued in December 1974. When Rolf Kauka sold his company, Peter Wiechmann continued writing the feature at Comicon, a company he founded in Barcelona, to be closer to the artists he works with. When Rolf Kauka merged with Springer and took over *Zack* magazine, the feature moved along and was also published in *Zack* albums.

The feature ended in 1981 when production of the *Zack* line of comics ended.

W.F.

CAPITAN TRUENO, EL (Spain) One of the most famous features of the post-World War II Spanish comics, *Capitan Trueno* ("Captain Thunder") was created by Victor Alcazar (pseudonym of Victor Mora) as scriptwriter, and Ambros (pseudonym of Miguel Ambrosio Zaragoza) as illustrator, in June 1956.

"El Capitan Trueno," Victor Mora. © Editorial Bruguera.

A contemporary of Saladin and Richard the Lion-Hearted, Capitan Trueno was a man of action and a defender of the traditional ideals of chivalry, which he upheld against the encroachments of tyrannical authority. His vast cultural knowledge did not prevent him from being a fearless warrior, nor did his wealth inhibit him in his defense of the weak. In spite of his valor, Capitan Trueno was often overwhelmed by his numerous enemies and was subjected to the most terrible tortures, which he bore with courage and fortitude.

In his adventures Trueno had two constant companions, his squire Crispin and Goliath, the big-hearted giant. The trio wandered around the world in search of adventures, which often pitted them against monsters of every description, the succession of which undoubtedly constitutes one of the most important bestiaries in Spanish comics. Humor was alternated with action, romance with fighting, and idyllic interludes with brutal scenes of mayhem and torture.

El Capitan Trueno's long saga ended in March 1968 after no fewer than 618 comic books, 417 issues of its own magazine, and a 232-issue run in the weekly *Pulgarcito*. Not long after its demise, the feature went into three successive reprintings, the last of them in full color. In its first period it was one of the most enjoyable of adventure strips, thanks to Mora's inventive scripts and Ambros' dynamic renderings, but it later fell into mediocrity, without losing, however, the public's favor. The two original authors were succeeded by a swarm of lesser lights, among whom mention can be made of Acedo, Cassarell, and Ortega (as scriptwriters), and of Beaumont, Marco, Martinez Osets, Fuentes Man, Casamitjana, and Comos (as illustrators).

El Capitan Trueno was adapted into novels, anchored several advertising campaigns, and has inspired a number of toys and cut-outs. It made a brief return in 1986, drawn by Jesús Blasco.

L.G.

CAPLIN, ELLIOT (1913-   ) American writer, younger brother of Al Capp, born in New Haven, Connecticut, on December 25, 1913. The young Caplin moved a lot with his family and attended Ohio State University and Yale, receiving a B.A. from the latter institution in 1935.

He went to work for the old rotogravure *Midweek Pictorial* of the *New York Times*, and, in succession, *Judge* magazine, *Parents'* magazine, and Toby Press, where he edited several magazine titles.

Always interested in comics, a fairly inevitable proclivity, Caplin's first effort was authoring *Hippo and Hookey* for artist John Pierotti; King Features bought the ill-fated strip on the phone.

In short order, however, Caplin-scripted strips were appearing everywhere. *Abbie an' Slats*, conceived by Al Capp, was written for a "trial week" by Caplin—a week that lasted 23 successful years. Another United Features strip, *Long Sam*, was written by Caplin on a basic theme by his brother; Raeburn van Buren and Bob Lubbers were the two very competent artists engaged, respectively, for the two strips.

His first successful strip for King Features was *Dr. Bobbs*, followed by a host of others, notably *The Heart of Juliet Jones*, *Big Ben Bolt*, and *Dr. Kildare*. He has also created and authored a bevy of strips for other syndicates through the years, many running simultaneously.

Caplin has a genius for continuity writing that seems to sustain half the industry. Some titles show the effect of formula production, and his handling of *Little Orphan Annie* (with another brother, Jerry) after Harold Gray's death in 1968 until 1973 was at best neglectful and at worst malevolent.

But the art of the comic strip owes much to Caplin—in terms of sheer volume and quality of production. His versatility is remarkable; one day's comic section could include the folksy humor of *Abbie an' Slats*, the soap-opera doings of *Juliet Jones*, the stilted moralizing of his version of *Orphan Annie*, the Herriman-like craziness of another of his creations, and many more just as diversified—all from the same typewriter.

Some have argued—including King Features comic editor Sylvan Byck—that the decline of the story strip is due as much to decline in quality as other factors of reproduction, competing entertainment media, etc. Caplin must share the praise or blame for the state of the business that he, to a large extent, dominates. But his value to the development of the art is clear and ongoing; Caplin continues to both write and develop new comic features. In his entry to the 1996 *National Cartoonists Society Album* he modestly noted that he had been "employed by King Features since 1937 as a writer."

R.M.

CAPP, AL (1909-1979) Alfred Gerald Caplin, creator of *Li'l Abner*, was born in New Haven, Connecticut, on September 28, 1909, to a father with a silver pencil in his hand. The elder Caplin used the pencil to draw comic strips for the family's amusement (using family members as characters), and entranced the young Alfred. Finding himself talented as well, the son ignored university work and went to a number of art schools, landing a job with Associated Press doing a strip called *Col. Gilfeather* in 1927 at 19. When Caplin left to tackle New York, the strip was turned over to a young Milton Caniff. In New York, Caplin was persuaded to ghost the *Joe Palooka* strip by its creator, Ham Fisher, who made him exaggerated promises of fame and fortune in the immediate future.

Caplin made the *Palooka* prize-fighting strip into a hilariously attractive work by his renovative art and his fanciful rendering of such presumed Fisher characters as Senator Weidebottom, women athletes, Russian boxers, and—above all—the hillbilly menage of Big Leviticus and his Mammy and Pappy, with which the strip reached its all-time heights of art and humor in 1933 and 1934. But Caplin was feeling his ink by now, and he had become thoroughly tired of making millions for Fisher while Fisher paid him in castoff artboard—a situation he later satirized in a July 1950 Sunday sequence of *Li'l Abner*. The 26-year-old cartoonist took his own strip idea to the syndicates, where (after being tempted to change his strip idea wholly to one syndicate's specifications in return for a fat contract) he found United Feature willing to try *Li'l Abner* as Caplin had prepared it.

In mid-1934 the first daily episode was released, and Caplin made use of his now-famous abbreviation (initially "Al G. Cap"). In early 1935, the Sunday *Abner* page was released, together with a third-page feature by Capp called *Washable Jones*. This weekly continued fairy tale (about a hill boy of 12 or so who pulls a ghost out of a fishing hole and gets involved with a Granny Groggins, a Squire Grunch, a monstrous horror named Zork, sneezing Beezars, talking trees, and a li'l girl named Majorie) was charming, unaffected, and wholly entertaining. It lasted only 16 weeks, unfortunately.

Li'l Abner quickly became a hit. By 1935, the daily and Sunday strip were being syndicated in most major American cities. Part of the reason was the topical response: the jobless or short-houred readers of the depression were being given portraits of impoverished hillbilly characters far worse off than they were—yet apparently able to enjoy it. The lift to morale that this daily look at such people gave in the 1930s is hard to estimate now, but it must have been considerable. The prime reason for Capp's immediate success, however, was his own tremendous imagination, humor, and obvious desire to break fresh ground in strip narrative and gag content. For years, the Capp strip looked fresh, new, and different—mainly because it was.

Capp's later life was one of large personal and financial success: his gain of effective control of *Li'l Abner* and its adaptive uses (he headed Capp Enterprises in Boston for this purpose); his defeat of an attempt by a disgruntled Ham Fisher to railroad him into jail on forged evidence of obscenity in *Li'l Abner* in the 1950s; his establishment of a Disneyland-like amusement park in Kentucky called Dogpatch, U.S.A.; his weathering, both with the strip and personally, a legal hassle involving alleged seduction of college women (an accusation possibly evoked more by dislike of Capp's right-wing politics and campus-stumping for them than his actual bedroom manner), etc. Capp adequately demonstrated his abilities as a humorous writer and critic in numerous articles (for the *Atlantic Monthly* and elsewhere), books, and a cantankerous syndicated column of comment. Once the darling of liberally inclined individuals, Capp was (as the result of his liberal-denouncing political reorientation of the 1950s) able to observe how much of the once-ample liberal praise given his art and story in *Abner* was the result of his political stance at the time, rather than of any objective viewing of the worth of the strip itself. Individuals who enjoyed good strip art, regardless of political slant, however, relished *Abner* both before and after Capp's change of viewpoint, although many of them came to regret the disappearance of the once-suspenseful, relatively serious daily story line of the 1930s and early 1940s and its total replacement by the surreal narratives of the 1950s and later, enjoyable as these often were in their own right. Capp brought *Li'l Abner* to an end in 1977; he died two years later, on November 5, 1979, in Cambridge, Massachusetts.

B.B.

CAPRIOLI, FRANCO (1912-1974) Italian cartoonist, born in Rieti into a wealthy family on April 5, 1912. Franco Caprioli started his career as a fresco painter in a Benedictine abbey, before moving to Rome, where he exhibited his paintings and etchings. Caprioli entered the comics field in 1937, working for the illustrated weeklies *Argentovivo* and especially *Il Vittorioso*, in whose pages he created *Gino e Piero* and *Pino il Mozzo* ("Pino the Cabin-Boy") in 1939. In 1940 he worked for *Topolino* (producing several *Mickey Mouse* stories), and in 1943 he illustrated *Le Aquile de Roma* ("The Eagles of Rome") for Edizioni Alpe. Toward the end of the war, his works also appeared in the *Corriere dei Piccoli* and in *Giramondo*.

After the war, Caprioli resumed his prolific career, contributing *Mino e Dario* (1947), *I Pescatori di Perle* ("The Pearl-Divers," 1950), *Dakota Jim* (1954), *Wild Yukon*, as well as a good number of educational panels, to the Catholic weekly *Il Vittorioso*. For the Mondadori weekly *Topolino*, Caprioli produced several adventure stories, the most notable being *I Tigri di Sumatra* ("The Tigers of Sumatra," 1948).

In 1970 Caprioli joined the staff of the newly formed Catholic weekly *Il Giornalino*, for which he illustrated adaptations of novels by such writers as Jules Verne and Mark Twain. Caprioli also illustrated books for children, the most famous being an adaptation of *Moby Dick* for Mondadori.

Franco Caprioli was known as "the artist with the dots" because of his peculiar graphic style, closely derived from the *pointillisme* of such painters as Seurat and Pissaro. A special element is common to all his stories: the sea, which he loved so much and which he represents in every detail with graphic faithfulness; an imaginary sea, romanticized and idealized by a native of the mountains.

Franco Caprioli was awarded the distinction of "Best Italian Cartoonist" at the Genoa Comics Festival in 1973. He died in Rome of heart failure on February 8, 1974.

G.B.

CAP STUBBS AND TIPPIE (U.S.) The beginnings of *Cap Stubbs and Tippie* are clouded in mystery. Edwina Dumm, the strip's author, has always contended that she was asked to undertake the feature at the behest of George Matthew Adams a few months after she got her diploma from the Landon Correspondence Course. As Dumm was born in 1893, that would place the start of *Cap Stubbs* somewhere in the mid-1910s. The earliest recorded date of any *Cap Stubbs* strip, however, is

1918. The latter date seems more likely, as it is probable that Edwina (as she signed her work) might have indulged in some innocent fibbing about her age to later interviewers. A Sunday page simply called *Tippie* was added in 1934.

Adams reportedly asked for a strip about a boy and a dog, and that was what he got. Cap Stubbs is the boy—a nice, well-behaved, clean-cut, if high-spirited, little man. His pranks are quite innocent, although they always seem to upset in some way his equally nice and concerned Grandma Bailey. The dog is, of course, Tippie, a bedraggled mutt who always manages to be in the way.

In retrospect it takes time to understand all the praise heaped upon the strip: the plots are minimal, the gags slight, yet it all comes together in the end. Coulton Wugh justly wrote: "Edwina's work succeeds through a delicate balance of factors; she stops at that point in human interest and warmth before sentiment begins to rot the idea. She draws straight, natural people doing natural things."

Dumm left the daily strip in 1966 and the Sunday page some time later. She has since been sorely missed.

M.H.

CAPTAIN AMERICA (U.S.) *Captain America* was created in March 1941 by Jack Kirby and Joe Simon and made its first appearance in Timely's *Captain America* number one. Garbed in a dazzling red, white, and blue flag-inspired costume, Captain America quickly became one of the foremost manifestations of American patriotism during World War II. A bigger-than-life all-American, Steve (Captain America) Rogers soon epitomized all that the country claimed to be fighting for.

The character's origin, which has been told and retold dozens of times, explained how scrawny Steve Rogers, previously rejected for military service, drank a secret potion that turned him into a superhuman. The government planned to create a whole army of Captain Americas, but the creator was immediately assassinated by Nazis and the secret died with him. Adopting the guise of Captain America, Rogers and his sidekick Bucky spent the war attacking and conquering horde after horde of Axis enemies. But, as the war ended, *Captain America* began to falter. Created to capture the emotions of the wartime American public, the Captain simply could not make the postwar transition from Nazis and Japanese to garden-variety criminals. And despite frantic attempts to keep the strip from folding—Bucky was dropped in favor of Golden Girl, and the magazine was retitled *Captain America's Weird Tales*—the Captain's adventures ceased after May 1949's 74th issue.

When Timely's successor, Atlas Comics, reentered the superhero market in May 1954, *Captain America* was one of the returnees. But it was a short-lived revival, and the strip appeared in only two issues of *Men's Adventures* and three more issues of *Captain America*.

The character was revived again in the *Avengers* number four (March 1964). Although saddled with a hokey explanation of his 15-year absence—he was supposedly trapped in an iceberg—the Captain caught on again and the strip began appearing in *Tales of Suspense* (beginning with October 1964's 58th issue). It was finally awarded a new *Captain America* magazine (beginning with number 100) in April 1968. During the

"Captain America," Jim Steranko, © Marvel Comics Group.

subsequent years, changes came in rapid-fire succession: a new Bucky was added but eventually dropped; The Red Skull, the quintessential opposite of Captain America, was revived; Steve Rogers became a spy, then a cop, then a drifter, and finally a neurotic introvert who considered himself an anachronism; the Falcon, a black, crime-fighting ghetto-dweller, was brought in as the Captain's partner; and, in the strangest quirk, the 1950s Captain America was revealed as a reactionary fraud.

There have been close to 100 artists and writers on the feature, but Jack Kirby is clearly the definitive artist. His version is legendary and is often praised as the best comic book work ever produced. Handling the first three dozen stories in the 1940s and several years' worth of adventures in the 1960s, Kirby used stylized, highly detailed, and action-laden artwork to make the character a legend in its own time. He elevated *Captain America* from comic book strip to Americana. Stan Lee, who authored and edited material on the strip from its conception to 1972, is considered the definitive writer.

Besides dozens of comic book guest appearances, *Captain America* has also been published in paperback, drawn in animated cartoons, depicted in a 1943 Republic movie serial, and shown up in dozens of other items.

Over the years, *Captain America* has always mirrored the American psyche: in the 1940s, he was the superpatriot; in the 1950s, he was the reactionary; in the Vietnam era, he was the unsure giant. He is America.

J.B.

In the last two decades Cap, as he is familiarly called, has known a somewhat checkered career. For two years in the mid-1970s Kirby came back to draw the character again. He was followed by a legion of artists, Jim Steranko, Sal Buscema, Gene Colan, John Byrne, and Frank Miller being the most notable of the bunch, with every succeeding illustrator changing Cap's appearance. The writers working on the series also altered the character to suit their inclinations or prejudices, recasting him up and down the line from rabid jingo to liberal do-gooder. All these changes did not help the hero's image, and neither did two disastrous movie versions (in 1979 and 1992). *Captain America*, however, limps on, with Rob Liefeld cast by Marvel in 1995 in the unlikely role of the title's savior. Liefeld has since left the strip.

M.H.

CAPTAIN AND THE KIDS, THE (U.S.) After the celebrated court decision that gave him the right to use his *Katzenjammer Kids* characters, Rudolph Dirks wasted no time in starting a new strip for the *New York World*. The first Sunday page appeared on June 14, 1914; in the beginning the strip had a different caption every week followed by the words: "by Rudolph Dirks, Originator of the Katzenjammer Kids," and it

"The Captain and the Kids," Rudolph Dirks. © United Feature Syndicate.

was not called *Hans and Fritz* until May 23, 1915. In June 1918, in response to anti-German feelings, the title was dropped, and the strip was rechristened *The Captain and the Kids* on August 25, 1918. (There was a panel explaining that Hans and Fritz were actually Dutch and not German!)

Dutch or German, Hans and Fritz are of course none other than the terrible Katzenjammer Kids (minus the surname). Dirks also retained the cast of characters that had done yeomen's service in his earlier strip: der Captain, as irascible and bumbling as ever; and his foil der Inspector; the long-suffering Mama; not to forget "Chon Silver" and his crew of comic-opera pirates—all the above-mentioned and many more still being the unwilling butts of the Kids' destructive shenanigans. From time to time Dirks tried to introduce new permanent characters into the cast, often relatives, such as der Captain's explorer brother and die Mama's twin sister, but none of them clicked with the public. (At the same time Hearst, who had retained the right to the title, entrusted *The Katzenjammer Kids* to Harold Knerr, and a lively competition resulted between the rival strips.)

In 1930 the *World* went out of business, and *The Captain and the Kids*, along with other *World* features, was taken over by United Feature Syndicate. In 1932 a daily strip was added, but later that same year Dirks left, following a contractual dispute (both the dailies and the Sunday were taken over by Bernard Dibble). Dirks returned in 1937, taking charge of the Sunday page again. (The daily strip remained in Dibble's hands but lasted only a few more months.)

Rudolph Dirks' son John started assisting his father as early as 1946, and he gradually took over the strip when illness kept his father away from the drawing board. After his father's death in 1968, *The Captain and the Kids* was officially signed by John Dirks.

Dirks Jr. preserved the unique flavor and charm of the strip, often taking his juvenile heroes into the fields of science fiction and fantasy. In the 1960s and '70s John Dirks went back to the more basic plot and theme of the strip, often re-creating with loving and nostalgic care the situations and settings of his father's early pages.

The Captain and the Kids has often been reprinted in comic book form; in the 1940s and 1950s it had its own comic book, with John Dirks contributing most of the artwork and continuity of the original stories. *The Captain and the Kids*, unfortunately, did not enjoy the circulation that its reputation and quality warranted, and in the 1970s it could be seen only in a handful of newspapers across the country. It was terminated by the syndicate in May 1979.

M.H.

CAPTAIN EASY *see* Wash Tubbs.

CAPTAIN MARVEL (U.S.) When Fawcett decided to enter comics publishing in 1939, writer Bill Parker was chosen to spearhead the drive. Together with artist C. C. Beck, he created *Captain Thunder* for *Whiz* number one. Written and drawn solely to secure copyrights, the issue never appeared publicly, but the feature was retitled *Captain Marvel* and published in February 1940's *Whiz* number two. Modeled after motion picture actor Fred MacMurray, Captain Marvel was really a homeless orphan named Billy Batson who was taken to see the old wizard Shazam. When Billy spoke his name, he was magically transformed into "The Big Red Cheese"—complete with orange-and-gold superhero suit.

Artist Beck's visualization of the strip was the cleanest and most straightforward yet to appear in comics. Often devoid of backgrounds, stories were easy to read and children doubtlessly identified with the young Billy Batson. *Captain Marvel* became a phenomenal success and was soon outselling all the competition. In short order there was a Mary Marvel, a Captain Marvel Jr., an Uncle Marvel, three Lt. Marvels, and even a feature called *Hoppy, The Marvel Bunny*. The lure of simply yelling "Shazam"—which stood for *Solomon's* wisdom, *Hercules'* strength, *Atlas'* stamina, *Zeus'* power, *Achilles'* courage, and *Mercury's* speed—and becoming the "World's Mightest Mortal" was so enticing to readers, *Captain Marvel Adventures* was soon selling over a million copies every two weeks. A serial, *The Adventures of Captain Marvel*, was released by Republic in 1940, and Captain Marvel soon began appearing in dozens of comic books.

To keep pace with the tremendous demand for stories, many artists were employed under the strict supervision of chief artist C. C. Beck. Even Jack Kirby produced material—he drew the first issue of *Captain Marvel Adventures*. There were also many writers on the feature, but Otto Binder emerged as the strip's major architect in 1941. His gently satirical stories set the style for secondary writers like Ron Reed, Bill Woolfolk, and Bob Kanigher. Editors Bill Parker, Ed Herron, Ron Reed, Will Lieberson, and especially Wendell Crowley, the last editor, kept the strip on an even keel. Everyone worked to make *Captain Marvel* the most consistently entertaining feature produced during the 1940s.

The strip's downfall came primarily from a long, oppressive lawsuit. Soon after *Whiz* appeared, *Superman* publisher National Comics filed a celebrated copyright infringement suit against *Captain Marvel*. The features showed circumstantial similarities, Fawcett readily admitted, but they claimed the heroes were both unique. But after several time-consuming trials and National's dogged determination—they even engaged famed Louis Nizer as Superman's counsel—Fawcett decided not to continue the costly defense. They voluntarily killed not only *Captain Marvel*, but the complete Fawcett comics line.

The *Captain Marvel* feature appeared in 155 issues of *Whiz* and 150 issues of *Captain Marvel Adventures* before the ax fell after January 1954's *Marvel Family* 89. Dozens of toys and novelties had also spun off from the World's Mightiest Mortal in its 13-year history. And many outstanding subsidiary characters were developed, including Mr. Mind, the evil genius of a worm; Mr. Tawny, the talking tiger with urbane pretentions; Dr. Sivana, the mad-scientist-you-loved-to-hate whose family was the arch-enemy of the Marvel Family; and a long series of inventive criminals like Ibac, Black Adam, and Captain Nazi. Ironically, *Captain Marvel* was revived in February 1973's *Shazam* number one. The publisher was National Comics, the people who originally put the feature out of business!

Captain Marvel is part of Americana. "Shazam" became part of the English language as an interjection expressing surprise or astonishment. He was and is the classic example of America's naivete, cheerfulness, and undying optimism. He's a Horatio Alger in superhero tights. The new version lasted only for 35 issues, to

"Captain Marvel," C.C. Beck. © D.C. Comics.

mid-1978, although it was revived in a 1987 mini-series.

A second Captain Marvel character was introduced in *Captain Marvel* number one, published in April 1966 by Country-Wide comics. An obvious attempt to capitalize on the now-legendary name, this Captain Marvel had the ability to parcel his body into five parts by yelling the magic word "Split!" The short-lived feature suffered an obscure death in November 1966 after five issues.

A third *Captain Marvel* feature was introduced in the 12th issue of Marvel Comics' *Marvel Super-Heroes* (December 1967). In an original story written by editor Stan Lee and illustrated by artists Gene Colan and Frank Giacoia, "Captain Mar-vell" was an officer from the Kree Galaxy sent to scout Earth. The feature was given its own book in May 1968 and the origin, motivation, and costume of Captain Marvel changed continually. The title was dropped in August 1970, but was later revived in September 1972. Late in 1973, writer Al Milgrom and artist Jim Starlin brought to

Captain Marvel the stability and respectability it needed to compete side-by-side with the original *Captain Marvel* feature.

J.B.

CAPTAIN MARVEL JR. (U.S.) The phenomenal success of *Captain Marvel* caught the Fawcett company off-guard, and it was almost two years before they added a spin-off feature to their line. It was finally introduced in *Whiz* number 25 for December 1941, created by writer and editor Ed Herron. Drawn by Mac Raboy, Captain Marvel Jr. was a boy-turned-superboy and a natural companion for Captain Marvel, a boy-turned-superadult. The readers appreciated the difference, and the feature immediately began a regular series in February 1942's *Master Comics* number 23. *Captain Marvel Jr.* comics number one premiered in November of the same year.

Captain Marvel Jr. was really crippled newsboy Freddy Freeman. Viciously attacked by a villain named Captain Nazi, an old enemy of Bulletman, Freddy was near death until Billy (Captain Marvel) Batson took him to Old Shazam, the wizard who'd originally endowed Captain Marvel with his abilities. Unfortunately, Shazam said only Captain Marvel could help, so when Freddy spoke the words "Captain Marvel," he was miraculously transformed into the blue, gold, and red-suited Captain Marvel Jr. Ironically, for all the new powers granted to his alter ego, Freddy Freeman was still crippled. And it was never explained why Billy Batson became a super*man* and Freddy Freeman became a super*boy*!

Writer Otto Binder, who scripted the bulk of all the Marvel Family tales, also directed the fortunes of the *Captain Marvel Jr.* series. But for all his excellent, fast-paced stories starring villains like Captain Nippon and The Piped Piper, Binder never developed the strong secondary characters for Junior as he had for the Captain himself. There were never characters as ingenious as Mr. Tawny, the talking tiger, or Mr. Mind, the evil worm, in *Captain Marvel Jr.* The feature limped along with mundane and pedestrian supporters like landlady Mrs. Wagner and banker Mr. Davenport.

The strip did have some outstanding artistic moments, however. Mac Raboy, who handled almost all the stories drawn in 1942 and 1943, was more illustrator than cartoon artist. Unlike the simple, almost comedic style set by C. C. Beck for *Captain Marvel*, Raboy handled *Captain Marvel Jr.* far more realistically. A disciple of *Flash Gordon* artist Alex Raymond, Raboy made his stories brilliantly detailed, with anatomically perfect characters and a lavishness strange for comic books. His covers, drawn almost at the printed size, looked more like rich, expressive poster art than comic book drawings. When he left the strip in 1944, artists like Bud Thompson and Joe Certa worked especially hard to maintain the style he had established.

Captain Marvel Jr. continued until April 1953—just months before Fawcett folded their complete comic book line. The character was revived in 1973 when National Periodicals began republishing all the Marvel Family heroes in *Shazam!* comics. He vanished again, along with *Shazam!* comics, in 1978.

J.B.

CAPTAIN MIDNIGHT (U.S.) The Captain Midnight character was created by radio writers Willfred Moore and Robert Murit and premiered in his own radio show on September 30, 1940. His first comic book appearance was in Dell's *The Funnies* number 57 in July 1941. After eight issues, the *Captain Midnight* feature moved

"Captain Marvel, Jr.," Mac Raboy. © D.C. Comics.

"Captain Midnight." © Fawcett Publications.

to Dell's *Popular Comics* in June 1942, but it was not until Fawcett Comics purchased the character that *Captain Midnight* became a major comic book feature. He made his first Fawcett appearance in September 1942's *Captain Midnight* number one.

As set out in his radio program, Captain Midnight was really aviator Captain Albright, a crack flyer assigned to defeat Nazi mastermind Ivan Shark before midnight. If he failed, the Allied cause would be defeated. Despite the herculean proportions of his task, Albright accomplished the mission at exactly midnight, hence the name Captain Midnight. He later added a group of assistants known as the Secret Squadron.

In his 11 Dell stories, *Captain Midnight* followed the radio adventures closely. He wore a brown leather jacket and aviator's cap, goggles, and the ever-present Captain Midnight emblem—a winged clock with both hands at 12. And, as in the radio program, Captain Midnight was heavily assisted by the Secret Squadron. But when Fawcett assumed the strip's direction, Captain Midnight was decked out in a colorful new costume (primarily bright red and gray), operated almost totally independent of the Secret Squadron, and added a sidekick, Ichabod Mudd (a Secret Squadron member who often called himself "Sgt. Twilight"). The Fawcett series, written primarily by Otto Binder, also equipped the Captain with a wealth of gadgets, including blackout bombs, a "swing spring," and a "doom beam" torch.

The strip lasted until September 1948's *Captain Midnight* number 67. Comic books were never the feature's strong suit, however, and Captain Midnight's radio show was constantly more popular than the comic. He also appeared in a Columbia movie serial starring Dave O'Brien (1942), had a short-lived newspaper strip, was published by Whitman as a "big little book" hero, and had a sought-after series of radio premiums and giveaways.

J.B.

CAPTAIN WINGS (U.S.) Fiction House was one of the companies that switched from pulp magazines to comic books in the late 1930s and early 1940s. One of their comic titles, *Wings*, was simply a compilation of old Fiction House pulp stories with drawings added. But in the 16th issue, the company decided to develop a "lead" strip entitled *Captain Wings*. It premiered in December 1941, though the credits for the strip's creation are unclear: the story, as did all future *Captain Wings* adventures, carried the byline "Major T. E. Bowen," but that was probably a pen name. Likely creators include Gene Fawcette, who drew the Captain Wings cover for *Wings* 16; interior artist Artie Saaf; art studio head S. M. "Jerry" Iger; and pulp-writer-turned-comic-scripter Joe Archibald. Company president Thurman Scott probably suggested the name Captain Wings.

In reality, Captain Wings was really Captain Boggs, an efficient but hard-hearted commander who gave orders but never took the risks his fliers did. Unknown to the fliers who hated him, however, after he had issued the often-suicidal orders, Captain Boggs snuck into his plane and joined them as Captain Wings. None of his fliers knew Boggs and Wings were one and the same—"a man with two faces, two souls, two names," as the scripts said—which reflected little intelligence on their part since neither Wings nor Boggs wore a mask at any time. Captain Wings eventually dropped the

Captain Boggs ruse and led the Captain Wings squadron into action.

The stories themselves centered on the Captain and his P-51 Mustang—painted black and white to look like a huge eagle—and his adventures fighting Nazi and Japanese aces. Scantily clad women were strip staples—as they were in all Fiction House titles—and after the war, Wings fought those Axis pilots who refused to believe that the war had ended. Among later villains of this type were Mr. Atlantis and Mr. Pupin.

Besides artists like Artie Saaf and Ruben Moreira, who handled some early stories in 1942 and 1943, *Captain Wings* had two major artists: Bub Lubbers, who drew the strip from 1942 to 1943, and again from 1946 to 1948; and Lee Elias, who handled the strip from 1944 to 1946 while Lubbers was in the service.

Lubbers' stories were highly action-oriented and featured the obligatory bare-legged and barely clad females. Elias, on the other hand, was an expert at drawing planes, and his stories tended to feature long dogfights between Wings and his adversaries.

The air ace could fight unconvinced enemy pilots for only so long, and the strip finally ended in 1952. *Captain Wings* appeared in all issues of *Wings* between 16 and 113, and then appeared in three later issues before disappearing.

J.B.

CAREY, ED (d. 1920) Ed Carey, virtually forgotten today, was one of the most popular and prolific comic strip artists of his time.

His first major works can be found in the pages of the old *Life* magazine at the turn of the century and the following two decades. His work matured from tight line drawings to exaggerations to comical wash renderings. Carey contributed infrequently—only several panels a year—but the quality of both his art and gags compensated for the "dry spells" in between. His major occupation at this time was drawing color comic strips, and it was in the Sunday supplements that Carey made his mark.

Many of that era's most published comic artists are forgotten today—the Hearst stable had big-city clout, reaching influential readers and surviving to modern syndication. On the other hand, artists with the early preprint houses faded from sight when the major syndicates took over around 1920, unless they were snapped up by Hearst, as were Herriman, Carl Anderson, C. H. Wellington, and others.

Ed Carey is perhaps the foremost example of a big name who never made it to the history books because he didn't draw for a major paper or syndicate. But in 1905 he was the highest-paid comic strip artist of his day, earning $500 for one page of *Simon Simple*.

Carey's first strip was a spoof on the Conan Doyle rage of the day: *Sherlock Holmes*. Other early strips were *Jack Webster's Dictionary* and *Brainy Bowers*, a tramp comic he inherited from R. W. Taylor.

In 1905 we find his *Simon Simple* distributed by T. C. McClure. Simon was one of the great early comic characters. He was a red-haired simpleton—an early Boob McNutt—whose collars and ties were as enormous as his pants and whose swallow-tail jackets were always too small.

Simon was a victim (in the already-familiar comic strip convention) of a society that seemed to conspire against him. He had luckless experiences with girlfriends, cops, strangers. Among the regular characters was a half-pint black boy whose success in each page contrasted with Simon's bad luck. Simon for a while has a pet tiger, and in 1908 the strip, then distributed by Otis F. Wood, was called *Simon Simple and Ben-Gal.*

In 1907-8 Carey illustrated the very popular *Dickenspiel Stories* on comic pages. These were German dialect tales (Dickenspiel was a Teutonic Mr. Dooley) written by George V. Hobart. Originally Frederick Opper had illustrated the first collection of these columns from the *New York Journal.*

Carey's last published work was *Pa's Family and Their Friends* for the new McClure Syndicate in 1915; he succeeded C. H. Wellington, who carried on the characters in *Pa's Son-In-Law* for the *New York Tribune.* Carey also introduced the character of Charlie Chaplin into the strip (it would also be done by Elzie Segar and others in other features). Chaplin was the rage across America in the mid-teens and Carey's strip fared well, although not with the verve of earlier efforts, until 1918. After that his work disappeared from sight, and reports list his death around 1920.

If he had done the same work, but had moved to New York and major syndication with some of his coworkers from the early distribution houses, Carey's name and work would need little introduction today.

R.M.

CARLSON, WALLACE A. (1884-1967) American cartoonist, born March 28, 1884, in St. Louis, Missouri. In 1905 W. A. Carlson moved with his family to Chicago and started his career as a copy boy for the *Chicago Inter-Ocean*, where he soon had several sports and humor cartoons published at the age of 11. When the *Inter-Ocean* folded in 1914, Carlson turned to animation, single-handedly producing in 1915 a five-minute animated cartoon. He later joined the Essanay studio, where he spent two-and-a-half years. In 1919 he founded the Carlson Studios, releasing through Metro-Goldwyn-Mayer. When later that year Paramount decided to animate Sidney Smith's *The Gumps*, they called on Carlson to oversee the animation. The series was a flop, but during the course of production, Carlson met Sol Hess, who was then writing *The Gumps'* continuity. Later, when he was approached to do a new family strip, Hess remembered Carlson, and together they created *The Nebbs* (May 22, 1923).

W. A. Carlson drew *The Nebbs* (along with its top strip *Simp O'Dill*) until 1946, when it was finally discontinued. After *The Nebbs'* demise, Carlson created a gag strip, *Mostly Malarkey*, about the shenanigans of a bumbling office worker. W. A. Carlson died in 1967 on the West Coast and left behind a long record that still has not been fully evaluated.

W. A. Carlson was one of those cartoonist boy prodigies whose talents for some reason never fully blossomed. His drawings for *The Nebbs* have an endearing charm, which gave him at least modest fame in the history of comic art.

M.H.

CARPANTA (Spain) Created in 1947 for the weekly *Pulgarcito, Carpanta* was the brainchild of Josep Escobar, who was also the author of a number of animated cartoons produced at that time. The word "carpanta" means ravenous hunger, but it was not widely used until Escobar made it famous in his comic strip.

Carpanta the tramp is characterized by his insatiable hunger, epitomized by his daydreams of people with inaccessible barbecued chickens (the zenith of his aspirations), from which nothing can distract him. He enbodies the widespread hunger suffered by the people in this period, the difficult years following the Spanish Civil War, with its obsession for food and its daily struggle for survival. These were the years when barbecued chicken was the symbol of wealth and well-being.

Carpanta is a gag feature unfolding in one or two pages. Its bum hero is a lovable vagabond, clean despite his poverty, whose attire, with its neat black hat and high collar, parodies that of a banker. He makes his home under a bridge and each morning he sets out, confident that some bright idea will, if not get him out of his poverty, at least provide him with a hot meal. His failures, as inevitable as taxes, serve only to reinforce Carpanta's stoical attitude and his lonely life, only shared by his friend Protasio.

The strip, besides giving rise to a number of Carpanta toys and dolls, also inspired a TV series at a time when this medium was still in its infancy in Spain. It is no longer being published.

L.G.

CARR, EUGENE (1881-1959) American cartoonist, born in New York City on January 17, 1881. Born into a very poor family, Eugene (Gene) Carr had to go to work at an early age. At nine he was an errand boy for the *New York Recorder,* where he liked to hang around the art department and learn the tricks of the trade. At 15 he launched his prolific cartooning career. During the course of his life, he was to work at one time or another for the *Herald*, the *World*, and the *Evening Journal* in New York; the *Times* in Philadelphia; and McClure and King Features Syndicates. The comic strips that he either created or took over are innumerable, although only a few attained any popularity. There was *Lady Bountiful*, a modern fairy tale that he created for the *Herald*, in 1904; *Nobody Works Like Father* (1906, in the *World*), which Coulton Waugh dismisses as "a comic which was too reminiscent of the ancient days of Dickens and Cruikshank to last long in a modern world," but which today has a period charm; *The Bad Dream That Made Billy a Better Boy* (a forerunner of *Little Nemo*, which Carr had taken over from William Steinigans); and a host of others whose titles will suffice: *All the Comforts of Home, Buddy, Uncle Crabapple, Phyllis, The Jones Boys, Father, Romeo, Willie Wise, Reddy and Caruso,* and *Flirting Flora.*

In 1913 Carr took over the famous panel *Metropolitan Movies*, which had been created by Rollin Kirby, and he did a creditable job; *Metropolitan Movies* was to become Carr's most noted feature, and it was popular enough to be reprinted in book form under the title *Kid Kartoons.*

Gene Carr represents the quintessential cartoonist of the start of the century: restless, experimental, and highly prolific. Had he stayed with one feature instead of rolling around like the proverbial stone, he might have become one of the more respected names in comic art. He died of a heart attack at his home in Walpole, New Hampshire, on December 9, 1959.

M.H.

CARREÑO, ALBERT (1905-1964) American comic strip and comic book artist, born in Mexico City in 1905. Albert (Al) Carreño's father was a bank manager who was once abducted by Pancho Villa but managed to escape, and he lived to the ripe age of 96. Carreño Jr. attended the University of Mexico and was expected to follow in his father's footsteps; but his love was art, not banking, and he moved to the United States in the mid-1920s to make his mark as a cartoonist. Working first as a caricaturist on the *Chicago Daily News*, he later went on to New York, where he became the roommate of Miguel Covarrubias and contributed cartoons and illustrations to various national magazines.

In 1935 Carreño, while working for United Theater Advertisers turning out movie ads and posters, was contacted by the George Matthew Adams Service to do a comic strip for an eight-page tabloid comic section they planned to offer to client newspapers. The result was *Ted Strong*, an atmospheric and lovingly rendered Western, one of the better efforts in the genre. Unfortunately the service's comic section (which featured such other obscure strips as Paul H. Jepsen's *Rod Rian of the Sky Police*) picked up only scant circulation and was dropped after a few years.

From there Carreño went on (as do many other disappointed strip artists) to comic book illustration (*Ted Strong* had appeared in reprints as early as 1937), working variously at Fox, Fawcett, Marvel, National, Pines, Prize and Ziff-Davis throughout the 1940s and 1950s. He turned out love, horror, superhero, and Western stories by the bushel. His best efforts were on the *Ibis*, *Red Gaucho*, and *Captain Marvel Jr.* titles for Fawcett, and on *The Blue Beetle* for Fox. In the 1950s he also became active in the National Cartoonists Society and became NCS membership chairman. Al Carreño died in September 1964.

Carreño is one of a number of obscure laborers in the comic vineyards whose work deserves to be re-examined in a new light.

M.H.

CARTER, AUGUSTUS DANIELS (1895-1957) The cartoonist father of Mush Stebbins and Fatso Dolan—*Just Kids*—known by millions of newspaper readers as Ad Carter, was born Augustus Daniels Carter near Baltimore in 1895. He claimed later that two school friends at Baltimore's Donaldson School were the originals for Mush and Fatso (Mush, he said, died on the western front in World War I, while Fatso went on to success in the insurance field). Orphaned at 11 by the death of his mother, Carter missed much of the childhood fun he created for his kid characters, and had to go to work as soon as he could, where he could. Until he could market his talent, Clare Briggs, then established as one of the foremost panel cartoonists in the country, got Carter a job as a reporter on the *Brooklyn Times*. After a stint on the *Brooklyn Eagle* as well, Carter had his strip idea shaped up and submitted it, again with the encouragement and assistance of Briggs, to King Features Syndicate in 1922. The King Features people liked Carter's kids and gave the strip an old King Features title that had been used on and off in its Sunday supplement since the 1890s.

Popular from the outset, Carter's *Just Kids* was always a King Features second-string Sunday strip, never appearing for any prolonged time in *Puck*, but running in many other papers around the country. Daily, however, it ran in most Hearst afternoon papers and was published widely beyond these. Perhaps the best-known accomplishment of the strip was its emphasis on children's safety. Carter introduced the Just Kids Safety Club into the daily and Sunday feature

in 1927, then augmented the idea with a separate series of panels focusing on commonsense ways for kids to avoid injury and danger, which ran in many papers not subscribing to the strip as well as all those that did.

In the late 1920s, Carter added *Nicodemus O'Malley* to his Sunday page; this was another kid strip that ultimately developed a theme of pure fantasy with the addition of a whale in the 1930s. Fathering three children of his own, the rotund Carter lived on a broad estate at Mamaroneck, New York, until his death there from a heart attack on June 26, 1957, at the age of 62. *Just Kids* was interred with its creator.

B.B.

CARTER, REG (1886-1949) Reginald Arthur Lay Carter, also known as Reg, was born on December 6, 1886, in Southwold, East Suffolk, England. His earliest published works were the many colored comic postcards he drew in the early 1900s, following the craze created by Tom Browne and others. Carter's style was distinctive: his urchins wore large berets, his adults wore cloth caps with peaks, beads of sweat flew everywhere, and most of all he pioneered squared-off speech balloons with cutaway corners. Radiating from people's heads were descriptive words such as "Rage!" or "Wrath!" when they were angry, and he also added the word "Throw!" when one of his characters threw something. He continued to use this same style when he began to create children's comics in 1920.

His earliest strip was of the comedian Oliver Hardy, who appeared in a full-page strip in the new comic *Film Fun* (1920), under the popular sobriquet of "Babe Hardy." This was many years before the comedian paired up with Stan Laurel to form their famous duo. In 1921 he drew the adventures or, as they were called, *Astonishing Stunts* of Ernie Mayne, a bulbous Music Hall comedian, for *Merry-and-Bright*, a penny comic. No further real-life characters came from his pen, despite his obvious ability as a caricaturist, but a string of alliterative heroes ensued for the next 20 years. There was *Priceless Percy* in *Sports Fun*; *Wireless Willie and Bertie Broadcast* in *The Monster Comic*; *Horace Horseradish* and *Ferdinand the Fire Fighter* also appeared in *Monster*; while *Nathaniel Nodd* and *Benjamin Beetroot* starred in that comic's companion, *Golden Penny*.

A slew of working-class heroes came next, beginning with *Daniel Dole and Oscar Outofwork* in *Tip Top*; *Oswold the Odd Job Man* in *Up-to-Date*; *Filleter Fish and Jack Sprat* in *Sunny*; and *Gussy the Gas Meter Manipulator* in *Happy*. In 1936 the new comic *Mickey Mouse Weekly* was started, and Carter found a new venue with such series as *Bob the Bugler*, about an army cadet, and the unusual strip *Sea Shanties*, which was set beneath the ocean. In 1938 he found a new home and his best showcase with *The Beano*, a new comic launched by the Scottish publisher D.C. Thomson. He won the full-color front cover of *The Beano* with his carefully drawn adventures of Big Eggo, an ostrich in search of his egg. Eggo ran on the cover for 10 years, a record for that comic. His final features, also for *The Beano*, were *Freddy Flipperfeet* (1947), about a comic seal, and *Peter Penguin* (1948). Carter died on April 24, 1949.

D.G.

CASEY COURT (G.B.) On May 24, 1902, a large single panel depicting the opening of the Casey Court Rowing Season appeared on the back page of the pink

"Casey Court," Charlie Pease. © CHIPS.

comic paper *Illustrated Chips*. On September 12, 1953, a larger single panel depicting the Casey Court Funny Face Contest appeared on page nine of the pink comic paper *Chips*. Little had changed in the interim. The original cartoonist was Julius Stafford Baker, the last cartoonist "Charlie" Pease. In between, M. C. Veitch, Louis Briault, and others have drawn the weekly escapades of this gang of back-street urchins in much the same crowded manner, with the boys bossed about by Billy Baggs, the girls in the charge of Sally Trotters, and the usual background signs of "Boots Mendid" and "Washin Dun Ere." In all there were 2,385 episodes (including a few reprints).

J.S. Baker was clearly inspired by the single-panel happenings featuring the American *Yellow Kid,* and his early urchins all had that monkey-faced look that popularly suggested the Irish. But his ideas were British, for he quickly established a pattern. Whatever was topical, the Casey Court "Nibs" would stage, build, or construct their own version. Be it a fireworks display, tennis at Wimbledon, racing at Ascot, the Lord Mayor's Show, or even the threatened invasion of England, the Casey Court Kids were ready with their homemade answer.

The only British comic characters to take to the vaudeville stage, *Casey Court* toured the music halls from 1905 with Will Murray as Mrs. Casey. The 1906 tour had young Charlie Chaplin as Billy Baggs!

D.G.

CASEY RUGGLES (U.S.) Unquestionably the finest Western adventure strip yet created, Warren Tufts' *Casey Ruggles* first appeared in a number of Sunday papers around the country as a half-page United Features release on May 22, 1949, with the daily starting on September 19, 1949. Subtitled *A Saga of the West,* Tufts' impeccably researched, grippingly cast, brutal, bloody, and fast-moving strip stunned readers of the early 1950s as it single-handedly lifted the possibilities of serious strip drama several daring notches—only to

find that no one followed. Casey himself is an army sergeant serving with Fremont in California who is eager to get in on the California gold rush. He returns to the East to pick up his fiancée, Chris, only to become entangled with Lilli Lafitte, the daughter of pirate Jean Lafitte. Although some of the strip action takes place in the East, the general narrative locale is California, featuring the gold-rushing Americans, native Spanish, and Indians (a later major character is Kit Fox, an Indian boy).

With its narrative themes including graphically portrayed rape and torture, the strip tended to be published only in the Sunday and daily papers of the more sophisticated cities, and it was subject to recurrent waves of protest even there. Tufts' trampling on the genteel traditions of the earlier Western confections in strips and films anticipated the same steps later taken by Sergio Leone in *A Fistful of Dollars* and other films, although the public was not ready for this in the early 1950s. Although no specific data is available, as Tufts does not discuss his strip work, syndicate requests that he "tone down" his material seem to have led him to abandon the *Casey Ruggles* property to United Features (which continued it for a while with an inept ghost) on Sunday, September 5, 1954 (he had dropped the daily on April 3 of the same year), while he prepared *Lance*.

If any recent strip deserves a memorial reprinting in full, daily and Sunday, it is *Casey Ruggles*. Gripping, colorful, exciting, and mature, the strip should be packaged and sold as a graphic novel of several volumes.

B.B.

CASPER (U.S.) *Casper the Friendly Ghost,* which later became the keystone feature of the Harvey Comics line, debuted in animated cartoons in 1946. The debut film, *The Friendly Ghost,* was produced by Famous Studios (formerly Fleischer) based on an unsold children's book conceived by Joe Oriolo and written by him and Sy Reit. Oriolo, a Famous Studios animator, had invented the character two years earlier and collaborated with Reit on the book, which dealt with a meek little ghost who desires only to make friends—a difficult task when his transparent appearance frightens everyone off. In 1946, on an impulse, Oriolo and Reit submitted their story to Famous and the cartoon, intended as a one-shot, blossomed into an entire series. Casper and other Famous Studios characters were licensed for comic book use to Jubilee in 1949, which issued Casper number one in the fall of that year.

The comic book was not successful, and after a year, Jubilee allowed its contract to lapse, whereupon it was taken over by St. John, which issued a new Casper number one in 1950. As was the case with St. John's comics based on Paul Terry's characters, the comic book company worked closely with the New York animation studios, employing many studio employees to write and draw the comic books. A roster of supporting characters developed in the St. John issues, based upon characters who had appeared in the cartoons. When the Casper series switched over to Harvey Publishing Company, these characters, who included Wendy the Good Little Witch, Nightmare the Ghost Horse, Spooky, and the evil Ghostly Trio, graduated to star status and their own features.

Harvey's association with Casper began with a new number one issue in 1953, the third numbering for the comic. A number of companion comics, featuring Casper and his co-stars, soon followed with titles like Casper's Ghostland, Casper and Spooky, Casper and Wendy, Casper and the Ghostly Trio, Casper and the Cub Scouts, Casper and Nightmare, Casper and Richie Rich, TV Casper and Company, plus several magazines starring Wendy and Spooky. Since 1986 Harvey Publications has been issuing a digest-size Casper magazine in addition to their regular line of comic books.

The Casper series and its spin-offs soon became the cornerstone of the Harvey line, and when Famous Studios ceased production, the parent company, Paramount Pictures, sold Harvey all rights to the characters, including television rights to the cartoons. The films were retitled with a "Harveytoons" logo and subsequently enjoyed great popularity, which in turn bolstered the sales of Harvey comics. Through judicious use of reprints, Harvey managed to keep an ample supply of Casper adventures on the newsstand, much to the delight of younger comic book readers.

As with most Harvey features, Casper artists received almost no recognition for their work. Only Dom Sileo—whose works hang in the Brooklyn Museum's Community Gallery—is generally known for his participation.

M.E.

CASSON, MELVIN (Ca. 1920-) Mel Casson was born in Boston on a date he refuses to divulge. He grew up in New York City, attended the Art Students League on scholarship, and studied under George Bridgman and Kunyiosha.

Casson always wanted to be a cartoonist and was no doubt inspired by his talented father, a "Sunday artist." While in art school, he sold his first magazine cartoons. At 19, he sold to the Saturday Evening Post and became the youngest artist in the magazine's history to sign a first-refusal contract.

He saw bitter action in World War II and was wounded as an infantry captain in the European theater. He returned to the U.S. with a Bronze Star and two Purple Hearts and took another plunge into the magazine gag field. Casson was the first Secretary of the American Society of Magazine Cartoonists.

His first strip was Jeff Crockett for the Herald Tribune Syndicate, about a small-town lawyer. Casson strained for a satirical slant; the editors wanted straight laughs and the feature died after a modest five-year run (1948-1952).

Next came Sparky, a little kid panel for Publishers Syndicate, and Angel, a baby panel for the same distributor, which fared well and ran from 1953-1966 with merchandising and a series of books. With Alfred Andriola (under the name of Alfred James) he created It's Me, Dilly! for the Hall Syndicate; it ran from 1958-1962.

Dilly was a bright, smart, and funny glamour-girl strip that might have been more successful a decade later. After this strip, Casson coedited a cartoon book with Andriola, Ever Since Adam and Eve, and worked in advertising, books, and TV writing and production.

In November 1972, Casson and veteran gag cartoonist William F. Brown created Mixed Singles, a trendy strip about young adults. Brown, one of the best funnymen in comics, also had credits in Julius Monk's off-Broadway revues and was responsible for the book of Broadway's The Wiz.

Mixed Singles achieved moderate success through United Features. It starred an array of hip, square, sexy, and troubled singles, with sophisticated gags and sharp, poster-effect art (both partners wrote and drew the strip). The slick style was achieved by the use of rapidograph pens. In early 1975, in an effort to revitalize the strip, which had leveled off in sales at around 150 papers, it was renamed Boomer, after the lead character, who married shortly thereafter.

Casson's art through the years has mirrored the style in vogue. He is an accomplished draftsman and dedicated worker in cartoonists' causes.

In 1973, he and Brown won the Philips Award from the 24th Festival of International Humor in Italy.

R.M.

The Sunday version of Boomer was discontinued on April 29, 1979; and on August 1, 1981, the daily strip also came to an end. From 1990 on, Casson has been drawing the Redeye newspaper feature on texts by Bill Yates.

M.H.

CASTELLI, ALFREDO (1947-) Italian writer and editor, born June 26, 1947, in Milan. Alfredo Castelli began his career drawing and writing a filler, Scheletrino, in the pages of the popular Diabolik comic book. In 1966 he started writing the scripts of well-established features: Diabolik, Pedrito El Drito, Cucciolo, Tiramolla, and Topolino (Mickey Mouse Italian style), for different magazines. In 1969, with a group of friends, he edited Tilt, an Italian Mad magazine; it published parodies of established comics (both American and Italian), such as Peanuts, The Wizard of Id, Valentina, and Feiffer, and spoofs of movies, as well as satires on contemporary subjects. This was the first attempt to establish the Mad type of humor in Italy, and it failed.

In 1969 Castelli founded and coedited Horror, a fine magazine devoted to horror and the supernatural, for which he wrote a number of stories, illustrated by leading Italian artists (Dino Battaglia, Sergio Zaniboni, Marco Rostagno, Sergio Tuis, et al.). For Horror he also created the humor strip Zio Boris ("Uncle Boris"), the story of a mad scientist and his friends:—a vampire, a werewolf, and a ghoul. *Zio Boris*, drawn in the beginning by Carlo Perini and later by Daniele Fagarazzi, was published in many Italian newspapers and magazines and has been translated in a number of European and Latin American countries. At the same time, Castelli wrote the stories of *Van Helsing*, about a vampire turned detective, and other *Tilt*-type series.

In 1972 Castelli became a member of the editorial staff of the leading Italian weekly *Corriere dei Ragazzi*, for which he continued the *Zio Boris* and *Tilt* series; created a humor strip, *Otto Kruntz*; and created two adventure series, *L'Ombra* ("The Shadow") drawn by Mario Cubbino, and *Gli Aristocratici* ("The Aristocrats") drawn by Fernando Tacconi. (The latter strip relates the exploits of a gang of British gentlemen-thieves. It has been widely reprinted throughout the world.) Alfredo Castelli has also written stories about famous characters of lore and legend (Aladdin, Sinbad, Gulliver, etc.) for the French weekly *Pif*, and his prolific career also includes writing TV commercials and magazine stories. In 1978 he created the highly successful *Martin Mystère* comic strip, and most of his efforts since that time have focused on developing this very lucrative property.

G.B.

CATHY (U.S.) "Cathy" was born on November 22, 1976, and quickly came to represent the prototypical busy modern woman who tries to balance career and relationships with parents, friends, and lovers while she struggles (unsuccessfully) with weight gain and constantly changing fashions. Created by her namesake Cathy Guisewite, the comic strip's heroine takes on the world alternately with anger and resignation, as when she rants against Valentine's Day for having become "capitalism at its worst" or when she lists all the things she should have done but didn't for one reason or another, except "Wanted to eat cake. Ate cake," concluding with a self-indulgent smile, "The only time I ever live in the moment is when it has to do with chocolate."

Other characters include Cathy's parents, Mr. and Mrs. Andrews. Whereas Mr. Andrews is ineffectual but properly sympathetic to his daughter's situation, the mother works on Cathy by indirection, ladling equal portions of advice (what she calls "wisdom") and guilt on subjects as diverse as how to follow a recipe, shop-

ping for food or clothes, Cathy's single status, or life in general. Regardless of Cathy's avowed desire for independence, ultimately she still needs the advice and support of her family—much to her mother's delight. Rounding out the cast of characters in Cathy's world are Mr. Pinkley, her manipulative boss; her coworkers with a mob mentality; lying salespeople working on commissions; a dog who understands her too well; her insensitive boyfriends; and female friends to pal around with but who are also rivals for the insensitive men they complain about.

However, in spite of insecurities fostered not only by her mother but also by countless advice columns, self-help books, and ad campaigns, Cathy knows that deep down she is not a brainless young woman programmed by clearance sales and fashion magazines, with low self-esteem and a craving for male affection. Thanks to her deprecating sense of humor, often directed at herself, she remains an optimist about life, love, family, and friends, even after setbacks: "I've given up my quest for perfection and am shooting for five good minutes in a row."

Drawn in a simple, almost caricature style, *Cathy* is distributed by Universal Press Syndicate and runs daily and on Sundays in over 1,200 newspapers worldwide. The strip, which has been reprinted in numerous paperback collections, received the Reuben Award from the National Cartoonists Society in 1993, and its characters appear on sundry merchandise. In 1987, Guisewite won an Emmy Award for the first of several animated television cartoons based on Cathy's amusing, though frustrating, travails.

P.L.H.

CAT-MAN, THE (U.S.) 1—The first strip entitled *The Cat-Man* appeared in Centaur's *Amazing Man* numbers five (September 1939) and eight (December 1939). The strip was created by writer and artist Tarpe Mills, and was a rather pedestrian feature starring Barton Stone as The Cat-Man.

2—The second strip entitled *The Cat-Man* was created by Charles Quinlan for Holyoke (Helnit) Publications and made its first appearance in number one for May 1941. This Cat-Man was really David Merrywether, the sole survivor of a caravan of Americans attacked by bandits in Burma. Merrywether was reared, educated, and cared for by a tigress—just as

cathy®  **by Cathy Guisewite**

"Cathy," Cathy Guisewite. © Universal Press Syndicate.

Tarzan was cared for by apes—and eventually adopted all the traits of the cat family. He had great strength, was extremely agile, was able to see in the dark, and had tremendous leaping ability. As was the custom in comic books of the 1940s, Merrywether came to America, adopted the Cat-Man identity, and set out to save the world from crime. His costume was an orange tunic with a "C" emblazoned on the chest, red gloves, boots, cape and hood, and bare legs. He also sported a pair of catlike ears.

Most of the material was produced by Quinlan, who was not a stellar artist or writer. (He created another animal-inspired character for Fox, *The Blue Beetle*.) In the fifth issue, a female sidekick was added. Katie Conn, dubbed The Kitten, was orphaned when her parents were killed in a train wreck. She joined The Cat-Man to fight crime because she was a trained acrobat—just as Dick Grayson, alias Robin, was a trained acrobat and joined Batman to fight crime—and had the ingratiating habit of calling Merrywether "Uncle David." She later appeared in another strip, *Little Leaders*, another of the 1940s group of "sidekicks banded together to fight crime without the aid of their mentors."

In all, *The Cat-Man* contains just about every comic book cliché of the 1940s—Holyoke was a house known for producing just such characters. It lasted until *Cat-Man Comics* folded after August 1946's 32nd issue.

J.B.

CAVAZZANO, GIORGIO (1947-   ) Italian cartoonist, born on October 9, 1947, in Venice. As an assistant to Romano Scarpa, the famous Italian illustrator of Disney characters, Giorgio Cavazzano inked a Donald Duck adventure that appeared in the Italian magazine *Topolino* ("Mickey Mouse") in 1962. His first pencil and ink work was published in the same magazine in 1967. Since then his contribution to the Italian Disney production has been vast and important: it totals more than 250 stories involving Donald Duck,

Mickey Mouse, and other Disney characters. He has also drawn several other comic characters: *Oscar e Tango* (1974) for the magazine *Messaggero dei Ragazzi*, and *Walkie & Talkie* for the weekly *Corriere dei Pioccoli*, both written by Giorgio Pezzin. In 1975 he drew *Altai & Jonson*, written by Tiziano Sclavi, for the weekly *Corriere dei Ragazzi* and later for the magazines *Il Mago* and *Orient Express*. Cavazzano's body of work also includes *Smalto & Jonny* (1976), written by Pezzin, for the monthly *Il Mago*; *Captain Rogers* (1981), written by Pezzin and later by François Corteggiani, for the weekly *Il Giornalino*; *Silas Finn* (1985), written by Sclavi, for the magazine *Messaggero dei Ragazzi*; and *Timothy Titan* (1991), written by Corteggiani for *Il Giornalino*. In all of his series, he merges humor with adventure, and his artwork is marked by the realism of the settings and the caricatural drawings of the characters, both of which are drawn with a thick and supple line. Several of these adventures have been reprinted in book form.

Cavazzano has also drawn the French animal strip *Pif*, and he coordinated the art production for *Pif* magazine from 1988 to 1991. *Timothy Titan* has been reprinted in the German magazine *Zack!* under the name *Peter O'Pencil*. Cavazzano's talents have also been displayed on illustrated posters, booklets, and other promotional materials for various advertising campaigns. In 1992 he was awarded a Yellow Kid prize in Lucca, Italy.

G.C.C.

CELARDO, JOHN (1918-   ) American artist, writer, and editor, born in Staten Island, New York, on December 27, 1918. Celardo attended public schools in Staten Island (he has remained there all his life) and later enrolled as a student in the Arts Students League and the New York School of Industrial Arts. His ambitions were to be a painter and illustrator.

Celardo's first professional work was doing sports cartoons and spots for Street and Smith publications in 1937. From there he graduated to comic books and worked for Eisner and Iger. When Quality Comics

Giorgio Cavazzano and Tiziano Sclavi, "Altai & Jonson." © the authors.

gathered its own staff and raided the Iger shop, Celardo was one of the artists; there he worked on *Dollman, Wonder Boy, Uncle Sam, Paul Bunyan, Espionage, Hercules, Old Witch,* and *Zero* comics. He sometimes signed his work John C. Lardo.

In 1940 Celardo also worked for Fiction House (only to be interrupted by the draft in the next year). There he drew *Hawk, Red Comet, Powerman, Captain West,* and *Kaanga;* after the war, from 1946-49, he rejoined Fiction and worked on the *Tiger Man, Suicide Smith,* and other titles.

After a short stint with Ziff-Davis in 1950, Celardo freelanced until landing the position of artist on the *Tarzan* newspaper strip, succeeding Bob Lubbers. His first daily strips appeared in 1953 (Sunday in 1954), scripted by Dick van Buren (son of Raeburn van Buren of *Abbie an' Slats*) and others.

In 1960 Celardo took over the writing chores and had control over Tarzan. His drawing was stiffer and heavier than other Tarzan artists, and Tarzan was taken to meet Red Chinese spies and various new antagonists in and out of the jungle.

In 1967 he left United Features to take over *The Green Berets* at Chicago Tribune-New York News Syndicate from Joe Kubert. This assignment lasted until the strip died in 1969, at which time Celardo found himself back at United finishing the career of *Davy Jones,* which had been created by Sam Leff and Alden McWilliams. *Jones* sank in 1970.

In 1968 and thereafter Celardo freelanced the comic book market again, drawing *Believe It or Not* for Western and miscellaneous work for National. In 1973 he was hired as a comics editor at King Features and soon bowed out of the drawing-board side of the business. He returned, however, to draw the *Buz Sawyer* newspaper strip from 1983 to its end in 1989.

R.M.

CELLULITE (France) *Cellulite* was created by female cartoonist Claire Bretécher in the French magazine *Pilote* of June 19, 1969.

Claire Bretécher conceived Cellulite as the antithesis of the stereotyped fairy-tale princess: she is ugly, with dull hair and a blotched face, sniveling, sex-starved, avaricious, mean, and stupid. In spite of her rank, she has been unable to find a husband, although she spares no effort in this endeavor—from booby-trapping the highway leading to the castle in the hope that some prince will get caught, to blackmailing her father's counsellor. If Cellulite is grotesque, the strip's male characters fare no better, confirming the cynical judgment of the misbegotten princess that, "while women aren't much, men are nothing at all." Her father the king is a feckless, self-absorbed moron, a certified coward and an unabashed lecher; the knights are conniving flunkeys, and the peasants a bunch of uncouth louts well deserving of their lot.

The resemblance to *The Wizard of Id* is inescapable; but, if anything, Bretécher is even more pessimistic than Hart about the worth of the human race. *Cellulite* is often very funny, yet the laughs always leave a bitter aftertaste—perhaps because they hit too close to home. The misadventures of Cellulite have been reprinted in book form by Dargaud. Bretécher definitively abandoned *Cellulite* in 1977, after which time she restricted her cartoon work almost exclusively to the pages of the newsweekly *Le Nouvel Observateur*.

M.H.

"Cellulite," Claire Bretécher. © Editions Dargaud.

CEREBUS (Canada) In the mid-1970s barbarian comics, spurred by the success of *Conan* comic books, were all the rage. A young Canadian cartoonist named David Sim decided to design a Conan parody starring—of all creatures—an aardvark. With his wife Deni Loubert he self-published a black-and-white comic book titled *Cerebus,* whose first issue hit the newsstands in December 1977.

Described as being "five hands high, with a lengthy snout, a long tail, and short grey fur," Cerebus, the unlikely protagonist, mimicked everything Conan was doing at the time in the Marvel comics. Soon, however, he evolved a personality and a history of his own, helped by such supporting characters as the female barbarian Red Sophia, the ineffectual wizard Elrod the Albino, not to mention Lord Julius, who looked, behaved, and presumably talked like Groucho Marx. In the course of his adventures in the pre-industrial human world of Lower Felda, the "mean and lethal aardvark" has battled such worthy opponents as the Moon Roach (a malevolent version of Batman) and the Woman-Thing, was appointed prime minister of the mythical country Iest, and even managed to get crowned pope.

Well drawn and humorously plotted, *Cerebus* has enjoyed growing popularity since its inception. The series has been regularly reprinted in 500-plus-page anthologies, the so-called "telephone books"; it has also received its share of controversy, because of Sim's frank depiction of sex and rape scenes, his long disquisitions on the war between the sexes, and his occasional racial allusions. At the outset Sim vowed to complete the saga in 300 issues; at the rate of 12 issues a year coming out like clockwork, this should put *finis* to the whole enterprise sometime in the year 2002.

M.H.

CÉZARD, JEAN (1925-1977) A French cartoonist born in 1925, Jean Cézard started his prolific cartooning career in 1946 with a humor strip, *Monsieur Toudou,* published in the children's magazine *Francs-Jeux.* This was followed by more comic creations: *Pilul* (1946-1948), a series of humorous adventures; *Les Mirobolantes Aventures du Professeur Pipe* ("The Out-of-

"Cerebus," Dave Sim. © Dave Sim.

Sight Adventures of Professor Pipe," 1949); *Jim Minimum*; and three adventure features, *Brik* (a pirate strip), *Yak* (about a superhero), and *Kiwi*, his most famous creation in the action genre (1952).

Cézard is best noted, however, for the hilariously funny strip that he created for *Vaillant* (now *Pif*) in 1953, *Arthur le Fantôme Justicier* ("Arthur the Justice-Fighting Phantom"). This saga of a mischievous little ghost always in search of wrongs to redress is one of the funniest strips to come out of post-World War II France. Along with *Arthur*, Cézard produced several short-lived strips for *Vaillant-Pif*: *Les Rigoius et les Tristus*, a comic fable in the manner of Rabelais, and *Les Facéties du Père Passe-Passe* ("The Pranks of Pop Legerdemain").

Jean Cézard was awarded the First International Prize in the comic strip category at the Brussels Humor Salon of 1968. He died on April 8, 1977.

M.H.

CHAI RACHAWAT (1941-) Thai cartoonist, born in 1941. Chai Rachawat did not start out as a cartoonist; in fact, he was college-educated as a bookkeeper. Cartooning was a hobby he practiced while working as a bank bookkeeper in the early 1970s. By 1973 he landed his first full-time cartooning position with Bangkok's *Daily News*, where his antigovernment vitriol quickly drew the attention of the authorities. Inevitably, Chai landed on the government's blacklist, and in 1976, he sought refuge in the United States, settling in Los Angeles, where he worked in a variety of menial jobs for two years. In 1978 he returned home and joined Thailand's largest and most influential daily newspaper, *Thai Rath*.

Chai has been voted by readers as Thailand's most popular cartoonist. He is easily recognized in Bangkok's popular culture scene and appears frequently on television talk shows. His major strip in *Thai Rath*, *Poo Yai Ma Kap Tung Ma Muen*, described as Thailand's

Chai Rachawat, a typical Chai strip. © Chai Rachawat.

Doonesbury, has been made into a full-length film and featured in television commercials, many articles, and a graduate-school dissertation. The two major characters, Poo Yai Ma, a village headman, and Ah Joy, his spunky deputy, are symbolic of the government and the common people and are used by Chai to express his strong opinions about political and social issues. Chai has survived various authoritarian regimes despite his hard-hitting style; at times, he has been forced to abandon his career. In the politically turbulent times of May 1992, he stopped drawing altogether for fear of possible retribution and as a tribute to the hundreds of pro-democracy demonstrators killed or injured in anti-government riots. Even then he seemed to have the upper hand, vowing not to resume his drawing until the dictators were removed from office, and in the last published sequence of his strip, he turned the once lively fictional village into a wasteland.

Along with the *Thai Rath* comic strip, Chai draws other cartoons and strips for weeklies and monthlies and for advertising agencies. He also presides over his own television production company, where he scriptwrites a weekly talk show, handles numerous land investment interests, and teaches the first cartooning course in Thailand at Silpokorn University.

J.A.L.

CHALAND, YVES (1957-1990) Inarguably one of the more brilliant representatives of the much-touted Franco-Belgian school of comics, Yves Chaland was in the process of transcending this artistic concept and attitude that had become somewhat outdated when his

career was tragically cut short in its prime. Born in Lyon, France, on April 3, 1957, he started contributing to various comic fanzines while still in high school, and after studying at the School of Fine Arts in Saint-Etienne in central France, he made his professional debut in the magazine *Métal Hurlant* in 1978. There he produced a series of masterly spoofs of the Belgian comics of the 1950s that had charmed him since childhood, while at the same time he denounced the subtle racism, chauvinism, and sense of superiority inherent in most of these stories.

In the pages of *Métal Hurlant* Chaland also created in 1980 the first of his many comic characters: Bob Fish, a Belgian private eye in the mold of Humphrey Bogart, living precariously in a Brussels of the future occupied by the Chinese. Following hard on the heels of Bob Fish, Adolphus Claar made his appearance the next year. A citizen of the 23rd century, Claar reflected ironically on the lunacies of our own times. In 1982 Al Memory, better known as *le jeune Albert* ("Young Albert"), formerly a sidekick of Bob Fish, was promoted to his own series, a succession of cruel vignettes in which the artist expressed his revulsion at the cruelties and hypocrisies of contemporary society. His most famous creation, however, remains *Freddy Lombard*, about a go-getting teenager and his two inseparable companions, a boy and a girl; set in the artist's favorite time and place—Brussels in the 1950s—it satirized not only many of the Belgian cartoonists of the period (Hergé, Jijé, Franquin, et al.) but also slyly subverted the values they stood for.

Yves Chaland, "Bob Fish." © Humanoides Associés.

"Chanoc," Angel Mora. © Publicaciones Herrerias.

Chaland was slowly emerging from the shadow of his elders and developing an exciting style of his own, as his posthumously published sketches and drawings demonstrated, when he was killed in a fiery car crash on a French highway on July 18, 1990.

M.H.

CHANOC (Mexico) Created on October 16, 1959, as a comic book by cartoonist Angel José Mora and scriptwriter Martin de Lucenay, *Chanoc* soon became the best sea-adventure feature in Mexico, with its clever blend of humor and pathos.

Chanoc, who lives in the village of Ixtac, earns his living as a fisherman, although, through his experience and curiosity, he has become a respected zoologist and an eminent oceanographer. An accomplished athlete who has mastered many skills, and a courageous man, Chanoc devotes his life to the preservation of wildlife and the fight against injustice. As in the case of *Alma Grande, Chanoc* develops over many adventures without chronological consistency. As a humorous counterpoint to the hero, the authors have created the character of the ancient and bewhiskered Tsekub, as excitable as his companion and of incredible physical strength in spite of his age. Chanoc's extensive love life is characterized by a healthy and youthful eroticism: well-endowed and liberated females are as abundant in the strip as the sports events in which the two friends can shine.

With the assistance of Javier Robles, Antonio Hernandez, and his brother Ulises, Angel José Mora has continued drawing the adventures of Chanoc to this day, while de Lucenay was later succeeded by the equally excellent Pedro Zapiain. Chanoc, the hero of no fewer than six movies, has been used to introduce a brand of chocolate into the Mexican market.

L.G.

CHARLIE CHAN (U.S.) Alfred Andriola created *Charlie Chan* as both a daily strip and a Sunday page for the McNaught Syndicate. Based on Earl Derr Biggers'

famous Chinese detective, the *Charlie Chan* strip appeared from October 1938 to May 1942.

Graphically, Al Andriola modeled his hero after actor Warner Oland (who played the title role in many of the *Charlie Chan* movies). In the course of his investigations Inspector Chan of the Honolulu police fights crooks, international conspirators, spies, and saboteurs in many parts of the world. He is very ably assisted in his endeavors by Kirk Barrow, a handsome, tall adventurer in the tradition of the 1930s, and by Kirk's actress sweetheart, the lovely and enterprising Gina Lane.

"Charlie Chan," Alfred Andriola. © McNaught Syndicate.

Characterized by witty dialogue and brisk plotting, *Charlie Chan* figures among the best comic strips of the "Caniff school" and is highly entertaining as well as excellently drawn.

In comic books, *Charlie Chan* has known a slightly longer, if checkered, career. Prize Publications issued a series of nine *Charlie Chan* comic books in 1948-49 (among its contributing writers and artists were Joe Simon and Jack Kirby). From 1955 to 1959 the character was run by Charlton (under the title *The New Adventures of Charlie Chan*) and then by National. In 1965-66 it was briefly revived by Dell.

M.H.

CHARLIE CHAPLIN'S COMIC CAPERS (U.S.) Drawn by several artists, *Charlie Chaplin's Comic Capers* was introduced early in 1915 by publisher James Keeley into his newly purchased *Chicago Record-Herald and Inter-Ocean* (later the *Chicago Herald*.) A Sunday and daily strip based on the screen character of Charles Chaplin, it attained nationwide syndication within six months through the publisher's J. Keeley Co. Keeley, whose *Herald* was the first paper to discover the talents of such later famed cartoonists as Frank Willard and Billy De Beck, had noted the popularity of comic strips based on screen personalities in England (where Chaplin, Fatty Arbuckle, and others were featured in comic magazines), and decided to try the same thing stateside in his new paper. The immensely popular figure of Chaplin (released for strip use to Keeley by Essanay Films in 1915) sold the strip; the art and narrative, contributed by a number of now-unknown *Herald* staff cartoonists (some of whom signed themselves only as "Bud" or "Aurie," etc.), varied from poor to terrible. Once subscribing papers realized this, the strip was frequently dropped, and its run in a given paper was unlikely to be longer than a year at most.

Yet to a newcomer to strip cartooning in 1916 like Elzie Crisler Segar (later creator of *Popeye*), the Chaplin epic looked like a royal chance to make a major public bow. R. F. Outcault, realizing this, persuaded Keeley's staff to give the ambitious young man a chance on *Capers*. The job didn't pay much (and what it did pay was cut considerably when Keeley dropped the daily *Capers* in 1917), but Segar was eager, and he published his first Chaplin page on March 12, 1916.

The humor of the strip picked up at once, although Segar's style at the time left much to be desired. The ambitious cartoonist added a comic companion for Chaplin, a shrimp named Luke the Gook (later kidded as a strip figure by Segar himself in his *Thimble Theatre* of the mid-1930s), but generally followed the story content of the Chaplin shorts of the time. Segar made his only sharp departure from the films when he put Chaplin into the European war in mid-1917, with a new buddy named Brutis (Luke the Gook having been dropped earlier).

When Chaplin left Essanay to sign with the Mutual Company in February 1916, Essanay's deal with Keeley was apparently continued by Chaplin's business manager of the time, his brother Sydney. After Chaplin contracted for film release with the First National Circuit in 1917, however, he or his brother seemed to feel a need to call a halt to the strip, for it ended abruptly in the *Herald* of Sunday, September 16, 1917. Segar remained with Keeley another year, but the *Capers* strip was finished—and with it any real prospect of a widespread use of screen stars in the Ameri-

can comic strip (although Charlie McCarthy was featured much later in his own newspaper strip, and W. C. Fields was utilized as a character named The Great Gusto in *Big Chief Wahoo*, for example).

B.B.

CHARLIER, JEAN-MICHEL (1924-1989) One of the most prolific and successful of European comic strip writers, Jean-Michel Charlier was born in Liège, Belgium, on October 30, 1924. After studies at the University of Liège law school, he started working for different newspapers. In 1945 he met cartoonist Victor Hubinon and together, with Charlier writing and Hubinon drawing, they created *Buck Danny* (1947), an aviation strip. The success of *Buck Danny* prompted Charlier to write scenarios for a number of other strips: *Kim Devil, Marc Dacier, Jean Valhardi, Tiger Joe*, etc.

After a stint as a professional pilot for Sabena Airlines, Charlier moved to Paris, where he became coeditor of the newly formed comic weekly *Pilote* in 1959. In addition to his editorial duties, Charlier contributed a number of well-crafted scripts to the paper: he created, among others, *Le Démon des Caraïbes* ("The Demon of the Caribbean"), a pirate story drawn by Victor Hubinon, and *Michel Tanguy*, an aviation strip, first drawn by Albert Uderzo, both in 1959; and in 1963 he created a Western with Jean Giraud, the widely acclaimed *Fort Navajo* (later *Lieutenant Blueberry*.)

Charlier was coeditor of *Pilote* until 1972, and he brought the weekly to unprecedented heights of popularity. While continuing to provide scripts for his comics series, he also wrote a number of adventure novels for the French publisher Hachette. In the 1970s he increasingly turned to television as an outlet for his creative talents: he adapted his own *Michel Tanguy* as a successful television series and produced numerous documentaries for French television on subjects ranging from the St. Valentine's Day massacre to the development of the Concorde airplane. He was working on a script for a projected *Blueberry* theatrical movie when he died in Paris on July 10, 1989.

Charlier was the recipient of many distinctions and awards, including the Order of the Crown of Belgium and the French Medal for Arts and Letters.

M.H.

CHARTIER, ALBERT (1912-) Canadian cartoonist, born June 16, 1912, in Quebec. After studies at Mont Saint-Louis, the Montreal School of Fine Arts, and Chicago's Meyer Both, Albert Chartier started his career as a cartoonist in the 1930s with a daily strip, *Bouboule* (written by René Boivin), for the Québec newspaper *La Patrie*. In 1940 he went to New York, where he stayed for two years, drawing a humor panel for Columbia Comics Corporation. During World War II Chartier worked at the Information Office in Ottawa as an editorial cartoonist whose drawings were published in English-speaking countries around the world.

In 1943 Albert Chartier created what is now the oldest Canadian comic strip in existence, *Onésime*, for the obscure *Bulletin des Agriculteurs* ("Farmers' Bulletin"). Recounting the adventures and misadventures of a middle-aged Québécois of that name, *Onésime* is today credited with upholding the tradition of French-Canadian comic art at a time when Canadian newspapers were inundated with American imports. (In 1974 a collection of the best pages of *Onésime* was reprinted with the subtitle: "The adventures of a typical Québe-

Albert Chartier, "Onésime." © Editions de l'Aurore.

cois.'') For the same publication Chartier produced another comic strip from 1950 to 1968, *Séraphin*, with Claude-Henri Grignon as scriptwriter.

In addition to his work as a comic strip artist, Chartier has also drawn many illustrations and covers for the French-Canadian magazines *Le Samedi* and *La Revue Populaire* from 1945 to 1960, a number of panels and cartoons for the *Montreal Star* and *Weekend Magazine* (1950-1965), as well as a good deal of advertising cartoons for the McKim agency, Vickers & Benson, and others. From 1945 to 1960 he also did a number of editorial cartoons and illustrations for *Le Petit Journal*. In 1968 Chartier created a bilingual strip for the Toronto Telegram News Service, *Les Canadiens* ("The Canadians''), which took place at the time when Canada was a French colony, in an effort to promote bilingualism.

Albert Chartier, whose work has long been neglected even in his native province, is now regarded as the dean of French-Canadian cartoonists. His style and humor are typically Québecois and often accurately reflect the views and attitudes of the French-Canadian community. He retired in the mid-1980s.

M.H.

CHATILLO Y FEDERICO (Spain) The first episode of *Chatillo y Federico* was published in issue 73 of the weekly *Chicos* (July 26, 1939), with later episodes issued in book format, on scripts credited to José Maria Huertas Ventosa, and with illustrations by Emilio Freixas. Chatillo is a busboy at a military officers' club, and Federico is the nephew of Colonel Bustamente, a Phalangist soldier, agent of the Information Service. In the first stories, uncle and nephew are wearing the blue shirt of Franco's Phalangists, while Chatillo dresses like any other young boy of the period.

In the course of their first adventure, the two young heroes explore a hidden country in the recesses of a hollow mountain where they are pitted against a Soviet agent. In successive episodes they discovered a medieval kingdom and faced a hostile sect of assassins

in what was then French Indochina. Coinciding with this third episode, their adventures were simultaneously published as a straight narrative in the monthly *Chiquitito* (April 1942). When this publication disappeared in 1943, these illustrated tales were taken back to the pages of *Chicos* where they were born, with scripts by Antonio Torralbo Marin. Fantasy was abandoned in favor of action and espionage.

The main characteristic of this first stage in the history of *Chatillo y Federico* is the absence of speech balloons. These were replaced by a straight narrative that inserted itself between the panels of irregular sizes and shapes. Years later, in 1954, the cartoonist Borne revived the feature in the pages of *Chicos*, this time as a traditional comic strip, blatantly plagiarizing Emilio Freixas' earlier drawings and illustrations. This version did not last long.

L.G.

CHAYKIN, HOWARD (1950-) American comic-book artist and illustrator, born October 7, 1950, in Newark, New Jersey. Of his education, Howard Chaykin admitted that he received "precious little," but learned much from his apprenticeship with such masters as Wally Wood and Gil Kane. After turning out a Wood-inspired erotic Western, *Shattuck*, for an army publication, followed by a passage at Neal Adams' studio, Chaykin started work at Marvel Comics in the mid-1970s; there, in 1977, he attracted critical notice with his artwork on the *Star Wars* comic-book adaptation.

It was for his work for independent publishers, however, that he really made his mark. After his profusely illustrated adaptation of Alfred Bester's *The Stars My Destination*, he returned to comic books with *Cody Starbuck* (1978). A space-opera of uncertain merit, it was mostly notable for Chaykin's restless line and unconventional compositions. But it was with his next project, *American Flagg!*, that he finally came into his own as an artist and writer. Created in October 1983 and published by First Comics, the title became an overnight sensation.

A dystopian science-fiction tale set in the year 2031 in an America that had been ravaged by thermonuclear warfare and was now run by a gigantic conglomerate called Plex-USA, it unfolded in a district of Chicago "nameless, lawless, and devastated by sexually transmitted diseases." In this urban jungle, scene of incessant combat between such gangs as the Genetic Warlords and the Ethical Mutants, Reuben Flagg, former video star Plexus Ranger, tried to restore some semblance of order with the help of Raul the talking cat and a robot named Luther Ironheart, not to mention the liberal use of the euphoria-inducing drug Somnambutol, nicknamed "the tender riot-ender." An amalgam of Aldous Huxley's *Brave New World* and George Orwell's *1984* with comic-book boilerplate and a generous dose of eroticism, it was innovative, fast-paced and highly entertaining.

Chaykin turned out another science-fiction series, involving time travel, *Time²*, for First Comics. When that company started to falter, he worked for DC Comics briefly, doing a Batman tale and working on the miniseries of *The Shadow* (1986) and on the first issues of the revived *Blackhawk* comic book (1988). He then returned to his earlier specialty, erotic fantasy, in a violent story of murder and sex titled *Black Kiss*, later *Thick Black Kiss*. In recent years he has only occasionally contributed to the comic-book field, preferring to concentrate on illustration and on television work; he was the executive script consultant on the *Viper* and *The Flash* television series.

M.H.

CHENDI, CARLO (1933-   ) Italian comic strip writer, born in 1933 in Ferrara. Carlo Chendi had a passion for comics since childhood; at 14 he moved to Rapallo, where he began to work variously as an electrician, cheese salesman, etc. In the meantime he met Luciano Bottaro, then an accounting student, and like himself a comic fan.

In 1952 Bottaro, who had begun to draw two years before, asked Chendi to write some stories for him. A year later Chendi decided to become a professional comic writer. Besides writing Bottaro's strips, such as *Baldo*, *Pepito*, *Pik e Pok*, and *Papi Papero*, Chendi contributed texts for *Cucciolo*, *Tiramolla*, and *Il Sceriffo Fox*. In 1957 he began a long and fruitful collaboration with the Italian branch of Walt Disney Productions, for which he contributed stories featuring Donald Duck, Mickey Mouse, and Uncle Scrooge. These stories, drawn by Luciano Bottaro, G. B. Carpi, Romano Scarpa, and Giorgio Rebuffi, are considered classics and have been reprinted in 25 countries (excluding the United States).

Chendi was one of the founders of Studio Bierreci, along with Bottaro and Rebuffi, and has contributed scripts for *Big Tom*, *Vita di un Commesso Viaggiatore* ("The Life of a Traveling Salesman"), *Whisky e Gogo*, and *Vita col Gatto* ("Life with the Cat") for the magazines *Redipicche* and *Whisky & Gogo*. Some of his stories, drawn by Bottaro and Rebuffi, have been anthologized in two volumes published by Cenisio, *Un Mondo di Fumetti* 1 and 2.

Besides being a scriptwriter, Carlo Chendi is also a student of comic art. In 1956, along with Bottaro, Rebuffi, Nino Palumbi, and Guiseppe Greco, he organized a conference on the comics in Rapallo. He was responsible for public relations at the Comics Festival in Genoa, and was the organizer of the International Comics Conventions held in Rapallo in 1973 and 1975. He is now planning a museum of comic art in Rapallo.

Carlo Chendi also finds time for writing, notably for Bottaro's *Pon Pon* and *Il Paese dell'Alfabeto* ("Alphabet Land"), and for the Disney productions in Italy. "I still write stories," he declared in 1996, "and carry out new comic-magazine projects for the Walt Disney Company Italy with the same enthusiasm as ever."

G.B.

CHEVALIER ARDENT (Belgium) François Craenhals created *Chevalier Ardent* ("Knight Ardent") in 1966 for the comic weekly *Tintin*. Ardent is a young nobleman of the Middle Ages, full of chivalrous ideals, youthful dreams, and righteous ardor (hence his name). Inheriting the estate of Rougecogne, he must fight to reclaim it from a murderous bunch of cutthroats (whose chiefs later become his friends and retainers in feudal fashion). Having thus established his manhood, Ardent becomes a knight at the court of King Arthus (the author's spelling), where he promptly falls in love with Arthus' own daughter Gwendoline. Later, for the greater glory of King Arthus and for the love of Gwendoline, Ardent will fight robber barons and renegades all over Europe, and will even venture as far as the Holy Land in quest of the mysterious Lady of the Sands.

The plot sounds familiar, but Craenhals makes it all seem fresh, mainly through his well-plotted adventures and his flair for the period. The drawing is vigorous and full of dash, and the depictions of tournaments, pageants, and battles are not unworthy of comparison with some of the best *Prince Valiant* scenes. Starting in the 1980s, Craenhals also introduced fantastic and supernatural elements into his story lines.

Chevalier Ardent is one of the few historical strips of note, and it has enjoyed a solid, if not overwhelming, success from its inception. A number of episodes have been reprinted in book form by Casterman in Belgium.

M.H.

CHIBA, TETSUYA (1939-   ) Japanese comic book artist born January 11, 1939, in Chiba. When Chiba was a senior in high school he decided to become a comic book artist and at 17 made his professional debut with the 1956 publication of *Fukushū no Semushiotoko* ("The Hunchbacked Avenger"). In 1958 his strip *Odettojō no Niji* ("The Rainbow of Odetto Castle")

"Chevalier Ardent," François Craenhals. © Editions du Lombard.

began publication in the girls' monthly *Shōjo Kurabu*. More famous strips were to follow: *Mama no Violin* ("Mama's Violin") in 1958; *Rina* (a story about a young girl by that name) in 1960; *Chikai no Makyū* (Chiba's first boy's strip) in 1961; *Shidenkai no Taka*, a highly popular Japanese war strip, in 1963; *Yukino Taiyō* ("Yuki's Sun") in 1963; *Harisu no Kaze* ("The Whirl-wind Boy of Harisu School") in 1965; *Ashita no Joe* (a noted boxing strip) in 1968; *Ore wa Teppei* (another boy's strip) in 1973; *Notari Matsutaro* (Chiba's first strip for young adults, also in 1973), and more.

Most of Chiba's strips met with great success. Because he thought highly of the comic art field, he devoted much care to his drawings and stories. Once the top girl's-strip artist, he became bored with the formula and switched to more action-oriented series.

Chiba's graphic style is delicate and charming, his compositions as warm as his stories. Chiba's strip protagonists are ordinary people rather than superheroes, and so his characters are popular because one can easily identify with them. Chiba has influenced a whole school of young artists, including his younger brother Akio Chiba, Tashiya Masaoka, Sachio Umemoto, and Shin Ebara.

Chiba's strips (with the exception of his early efforts) have all been reprinted in book form, and he is currently the highest-paid of all boy's comic strip artists. *Ashita no Joe* ended in 1973, and *Ore wa Teppei* in 1980, and since that time the artist has branched out into even more exotic sports, such as kendo, sumo, and even golf.

H.K.

CHIEF WAHOO *see* Steve Roper.

"Chikaino Makyū," Tetsuya Chiba. © Shōnen.

CHIKAINO MAKYŪ (Japan) *Chikaino Makyū* ("The Miracle Ball of Great Promise") was created by writer Kazuya Fukumoto and artist Tetsuya Chiba. Soon after its first appearance in the weekly *Shōnen* magazine (January 1961), *Chikaino Makyū* became the foremost sports strip of its time.

Hikaru Ninomiya was an ace pitcher at Fuji High School, and he would throw miracle balls (his first miracle ball jumped in front of the batter); he became known as the miracle pitcher. He was soon spotted by a baseball scout named Yagi, who hired him as pitcher for the Yomiuri Giants. Hikaru's friend Tagosaku Kubo later joined him on the team as catcher. His miracle

balls continued to prove effective until the day his ball was hit by Henry Nakagawa, a half-breed player on the Taiyo Whales team.

Hikaru worked out a new miracle pitch (in which the ball would spin so violently that the batter thought he saw several balls) with his coach Aikawa. Only Kubo could catch this ball. With this pitch he won the "most valuable player" award and entered the Nihon Series (the Japanese equivalent of the World Series); but his ball was hit by Ichiro Otawara of the opposing Hanshin Tigers, and again Hikaru felt despondent. He soon recovered, however, and mastered a third pitch: the vanishing miracle ball, which disappeared before the batter's very eyes, which was taught to him by a mysterious old amateur pitcher.

During the deciding match between the American and Japanese top teams, Hikaru bedeviled his opposition with three miracle balls. Because of the strain put on his shoulder by his efforts, however, he was badly hurt and had to leave the Yomiuri Giants as a result. Turning to coaching, Hikaru brought the team of his old high school to victory.

Chikaino Makyū was the pioneer of baseball strips and exercised a strong influence on *Kyoshin no Hoshi*, which was soon to surpass *Chikaino* in popularity. The strip's last appearance was in December 1962.

Chikaino Makyū was Tetsuya Chiba's first boy's strip, and it made him into the most noted artist of the genre. Chiba did not know the first thing about baseball when he started work on the strip; but he studied the game and soon became a baseball nut, to the extent of creating a baseball team called the Whiters.

H.K.

CHIP *see* Bellew, Frank.

CHLOROPHYLLE (Belgium) On December 1, 1953, in the pages of the Belgian weekly *Tintin*, Raymond Macherot revitalized the tradition of the European animal strip with *Chlorophylle et Minimum* (later called simply *Chlorophylle*).

Chlorophylle and Minimum are a couple of field mice, the former brave, resolute and resourceful, the latter troublesome and loud-mouthed, but loyal and ingenious, and their adventures, in the company of

"Chlorophylle," Raymond Macherot. © Editions Dargaud.

other animals or in the land of the humans, are always mixed with a large dose of humor and more than a touch of poetry. The first episode involved our two diminutive heroes in a long struggle against a pack of black rats who tried to take over their territory. Led by the dreaded and cunning Anthracite, the black rats almost won the day, and Chlorophylle had to enlist the help of more allies: Sybilline the mischievous mouse, Verboten the tenacious hedgehog, and Torpille the unstoppable otter. Representing the forces of justice and fair play, Chlorophylle and his friends never give up, even in the face of overwhelming odds; and in the end their perseverance defeats the deviousness of the villains, be they Anthracite (who had usurped the throne of Croquefredouille), or the bloodthirsty Croquillards, a gang that terrorizes the country in their homemade tank.

In 1963 Macherot left Chlorophylle, which was taken over first by Guilmard and Hubuc, and later by Dupa and Greg. Since 1985 the title has been drawn by Willi (André van der Elst) on scripts by Bob de Groot and later by Michel de Bom.

Chlorophylle is not only an entertaining strip of humorous adventure (in the illustrious tradition of *Felix the Cat, Mickey Mouse,* and *Popeye*), but also an excellent parody of human foibles and follies and a satire of modern civilization.

The adventures of Chlorophylle and his gang have been reprinted in book form by Dargaud. They are now published by Editions du Lombard.

M.H.

CHIMEL, PAPCIP *see* Chmielewski, Henryk Jerzy.

CHMIELEWSKI, HENRYK JERZY (1923-) Polish cartoonist born in 1923 near Warsaw. After studies at the Warsaw Academy of Fine Arts, from which he received a degree in graphic art, Henryk Chmielewski started working for *Swiat Modlich*, a scouting publication, in whose pages he published such now-classic comic strips as *Tytus, Romek* and *Tomek*, under the penname "Papcio Chimel." These are the oldest comic series still in existence, and they have been reprinted in a number of books since 1966. (The latest volume of his comics, the twenty-second, was published in May 1996.)

A pioneer of postwar Polish comics, Chimel (as he is better known) has seen his efforts in the field finally recognized in the early 1990's. Since 1992 he has been producing and editing comics for the prestigious Prusynski i S-ka publishing house. His graphic style, an harmonious blend of old-time cartooning and straight illustration, has been widely imitated in his native country. His work during the 1940's signaled a revival of comic art activity in Poland.

K.R.

CHRISTMAN, BERT (1915-1942) American cartoonist born May 31, 1915 at Fort Collins, Colorado. Bert Christman displayed artistic qualities at an early age, and he began his career (while in high school) as a department store artist. After graduation from Colorado State College as an engineer, he came to New York in 1936, and became a staff artist for the Associated Press. Christman, whom a fellow worker was later to describe as "a nice quiet kid" got his first break, after only a few months, as Noel Sickles' successor on the *Scorchy Smith* daily strip. Christman did a creditable

job on *Scorchy* (after the initial awkward period of "breaking in") and he might have gone on to become one of the top adventure strip artists, but he was restless (and A.P. was notoriously cheap towards their cartoonists) and so, after 18 months of drawing the strip, he left. He then briefly worked for the newly emerging medium of comic books: on the super-hero feature *The Sandman* at National, where he later created *The Three Aces* (1939) described as: "three winged soldiers-of-fortune, sick of war and tragedy, who pledge themselves to a new kind of adventure."

Christman must have heeded the same call for "a new kind of adventure": in 1940 he became an air cadet at the Naval Air School in Pensacola, and later joined Clare Chennault's fabled "Flying Tigers" in Burma. On January 23, 1942, during a heavy Japanese raid over Rangoon, Christman's P-40 plane was shot down; Christman himself bailed out but was machine-gunned to death by a Japanese strafing plane while hanging helplessly in the parachute harness (his death was to inspire one of the most memorable sequences in Howard Hawks' 1943 movie *Air Force*).

Even during his service with the American Volunteer Group (as the Flying Tigers were officially called) Bert Christman never stopped drawing. In a letter to Coulton Waugh, Zachary Taylor, comic editor of the Associated Press, recounting the circumstances of Christman's death, added this postscript: "Not many weeks ago, his effects reached his mother at Fort Collins, Colorado. Among them was his scrapbook of sketches of Burma, flying pals, insignia designs."

M.H.

CHRISTOPHE *see* Colomb, Georges.

CHU, RONALD *see* Chu Teh-Yung.

CHU TEH-YUNG (1960-) Taiwanese cartoonist Chu Teh-Yung was interested in drawing from the age of four, and by the time he was a film student at the World Junior College of Journalism in Taipei, his cartoons were appearing in campus publications. However, it was during his two-year, compulsory military duty in the mid-1980s that he created the strip that made him famous—*Shuang Hsiang Pao* ("Double Big Guns," also known as "The Couple"). To evade military harassment and censorship while in the army, Chu drew many of the strips under a blanket while holding a flashlight. He would then cut up the four panels and mail them one by one to his father, who relayed them to the *China Times*. He had no idea how successful the strip had become until he left the military and was offered a full-time position drawing for the *China Times*.

Shuang Hsiang Pao is Taiwan's longest-running newspaper comic strip; it now appears in *China Times Express*. Its immense popularity has led to book compilations that have sold hundreds of thousands of copies in Taiwan, Hong Kong, and South Korea. The plot of *Shuang Hsiang Pao* revolves around the domestic life of a nameless couple in their sixties who constantly berate and put each other down. The wife is bug-eyed, mean-spirited, and domineering; the husband is spindly and hen-pecked, but capable of retaliating in their constant bouts of verbal abuse.

In 1989, Ronald Chu (as he is professionally known) created *Chu Liu Chu* ("Wayward Lovers"), a strip in the *China Times* that lampoons Taiwan's unmarried yup-

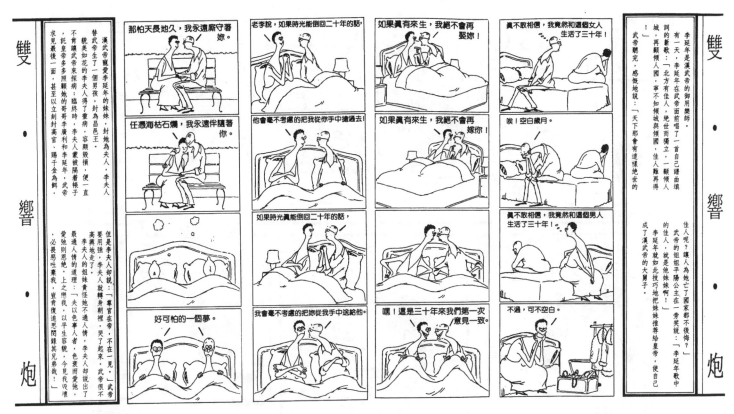

Chu Teh-Yung ("Ronald Chu"), "The Couple." © Ronald Chu.

pies. Less slapstick than *Shuang Hsiang Pao*, the strip is just as sarcastic and derisive as its predecessor. It too has been compiled into best-selling books. Other Chu strips include *Capitalists* for *Commercial Daily* and *Bitter Olive* for *Liberty Times*.

Chu's strips offer up large doses of sardonic wit and are universally appealing. They are fondly reminiscent of the comic art prevalent in the United States before the days of political correctness.

J.A.L.

CHUPAMIRTO (Mexico) During the winter of 1925-1926 the daily newspaper *El Universal* sponsored a contest aimed at discovering fresh Mexican comic strip talent. Among the artists thus discovered was Jesus Acosta Cabrera, who that same year created one of the most popular comic strips in Mexican history, *Chupamirto*.

Chupamirto (literally "myrtle sucker," a synonym for hobo) was a disheveled, unshaven little tramp who always wore a snap-brimmed hat and whose tongue perpetually hung out. His wanderings took him to all parts of Mexico, thus giving Acosta the opportunity of satirically depicting many of Mexico's social shortcomings. Chupamirto's persona is said to have inspired the screen characterization of Cantinflas, Mexico's most renowned comedian.

Chupamirto enjoyed tremendous success in Mexico until it was discontinued in 1963, following its creator's death.

M.H.

"Chupamirto," Jesus Acosta. © Jesus Acosta.

CICERO'S CAT (U.S.) From its first appearance on the *Mutt and Jeff* Sunday page on December 3, 1933, the weekly *Cicero's Cat* was the work of Al Smith, who had then just begun his ghosting of Bud Fisher's signed work. The cat of the title, Desdemona, was the pet of Mutt's son, Cicero, and the bulk of the action in the color feature concerned the cat (often humanized in hat and coat) in various domestic, backyard, and neighborhood adventures with other cats and dogs (the humans of the *Mutt and Jeff* strip being only infrequently involved). Some of them were extremely humorous—Smith having a competency with comic animals that his work with the older Fisher human characters often lacked. (In an amusing corollary, Desdemona's humanized escapades were rarely as effective as her purely catlike sequences, where Smith's pen was most inspired.)

A single strip of a few panels at the top of the Sunday Fisher page at the start (*Cicero's Cat* took over an untitled space long given to a separate Sunday gag

"Cicero's Cat," Al Smith. © Bell Syndicate.

sequence also featuring Mutt and Jeff above the main narrative layout), the Smith cat opus was abruptly and startingly switched to a full half-page of three rows with several panels each on August 26, 1934, while the *Mutt and Jeff* portion of the page was correspondingly reduced to a companion half-page, reflecting the general reshaping of Sunday pages going on in the early 1930s. In following episodes, however, the *Mutt and Jeff* half-page appropriated a row of panels from *Cicero's Cat* and turned it into a one-panel logo for the main strip, while *Cicero's Cat* became and remained a two-row, third-page feature below *Mutt and Jeff* for the next 12 years. With the new division of Sunday page space in the late 1940s, however, *Cicero's Cat* and *Mutt and Jeff* both often ran as third-page features, sometimes separated by several pages in the same Sunday section. As a separated second-fiddle feature, Smith's *Cat* strip suffered frequent omissions from papers when advertisements were run, and it steadily lost circulation until it was eased into limbo in the early 1960s, survived by the Smith *Mutt and Jeff* feature. Initially distributed by H. C. Fisher, Inc., *Cicero's Cat* was later a Bell Syndicate property till its demise.

B.B.

CIFRE, GUILLERMO (1922-1962) In the course of his short but extraordinarily fecund career, Spanish cartoonist Guillermo Cifre produced a great many comic strips of quality, most of them for Editorial Bruguera's children's publications. His most popular creation remains the hilarious *El Reporter Tribulete que en Todas Partes se Mete* ("The Reporter Tribulete who Meddles in Everything"). Another successful strip was *Don Furcio Buscabollos* (literally "Don Furcio Troubleseeker"), about an Italian knight in medieval times; the series inspired a number of popular expressions with its peculiar Hispano-Italian jargon and the fabled conversations held between Don Furcio and his mare, Isabelita.

For many years Cifre also drew numerous cover illustrations (mostly of well-endowed females) while ceaselessly turning out weekly comic features, among which mention should be made of *Amapolo Nevera, El Sabio Megaton* ("Megaton the Scientist"), *Golondrino Perez,* and *Don Tele.*

Guillermo Cifre died in 1962 at the age of 39.

L.G.

CIMPELLIN, LEONE (1926-   ) Italian cartoonist, born June 6, 1926, in Rovigo. Leone Cimpellin moved to Milan while a child; there he started his cartooning career some years later as assistant to Lina Buffolente. His first works were adventure series. The imitation of Alex Raymond's *Rip Kirby* was obvious, but Cimpellin added a touch of the grotesque, which was later to find its full utilization in *Johnny Logan.*

After continuing the Italian version of Warren Tufts' *Casey Ruggles,* written by Giovanni Bonelli, Cimpellin created *Pultos* in 1949, a masked-avenger strip for Edizioni Audace, and *Il Tamburino del Re* ("Drummer of the King") for Edizioni Alpe. In 1953 he joined the art staff of the weekly *Corriere dei Piccoli,* where his talents as a humor cartoonist first flowered. In the *Corriere* he created *Papero Grosso e Fiorello* (1954), about a fat peasant and his little pig; *Codinzolo,* about a little faun; and *Gibernetta,* a hilarious parody of army life (1958). In 1961 Cimpellin created *Charlie Sprint,* the adventures of a racing-car enthusiast, written by Guglielmo Zucconi, and in 1966 he produced *Tribunzio* in collaboration with Carlo Triberti (the latter strip recounted the tragicomic adventures of a Roman legionary). In 1967 there was *Gigi Bizz,* a newspaper satire.

Leone Cimpellin, "Johnny Logan." © Editrice Dardo.

"Cinco por Infinito," Esteban Maroto. © Selecciones Illustradas.

Meanwhile Cimpellin, hesitating between a realistic and a "big-foot" style, again tried his hand at adventure with *Oklahoma* (1952), a Western written by Guido Martina, and diverse series for other publishers. Only in 1972 did Cimpellin find his niche with *Johnny Logan*, his weird depiction of the antihero created by Romano Garofalo for Edizioni Dardo. Since the early 1990s he has illustrated a number of *Martin Mystere* stories.

G.B.

CINCO POR INFINITO (Spain) *Cinco por Infinito* ("Five for Infinity") started in September 1967, vaguely inspired by Jean Hougron's novel *The Sign of the Dog*. The team responsible for this series was initially made up of Esteban Maroto, who wrote the scripts and pencilled the pages; Ramon Torrens, who drew the female characters; Adolfo Usero, who did the male protagonists; and Suso (pen name of Jesus Paña), who did the backgrounds. The first three episodes were done in this way; the fourth was the work of Usero and Maroto, after which Maroto remained in sole control of the 26 remaining episodes.

The protagonists are five earthlings who help Infinito, the survivor of an extinct extraterrestrial race, to keep order in the cosmos. Each of the five possesses special abilities that complement those of the rest of the team. Aline, the woman doctor, is endowed with exceptional mental powers, Sirio enjoys great agility and keen reflexes, Orion has herculean strength, Altar is gifted with vast intelligence, and Hidra, who has been incorporated into the team by accident, is extremely beautiful.

The special quality of the feature is the conception of each page as a whole, in which panel limitations are ignored in favor of a fusion of the images into one single baroque composition. Maroto was then in search of his style, and it is easy to discover in this work the stages of his graphic evolution, the excellence of his draftsmanship, and the influences that were at work on him over the course of the years. Initially intended to be reproduced in black and white, the feature was later printed in color, which gave it an added dimension, but which also eliminated Ben Day and hatchings; negative images and floral motifs, so decorative in black and white, lost their qualities with the imposition of color.

L.G.

CIOCCA, WALTER (1910-   ) An Argentine cartoonist and illustrator born in 1910, Walter Ciocca studied architecture, majoring in urban projects. He became interested in comic art in the 1940s. Drawing his inspiration from Argentine folklore and the legends of gaucho life in the pampas, he produced a series of daily strips for the newspapers of Buenos Aires, all drawn in his energetic and austere style. The first was *Hilario Leiva*, created in 1948, followed by *Santos Vega*, *Hormiga Negra* ("The Black Ant," 1950), and *Fuerte Argentino* ("Argentine Fort"). Since 1954 he has been devoting himself to his most famous comic creation, *Lindor Covas*, subtitled *"El Cimarrón"* ("The Untamed").

Walter Ciocca is famous for his virile and unsentimental depiction of Indian and gaucho life. His graphic style is forceful, direct, and minutely realistic.

L.G.

CIRCUS SOLLY *see* Slim Jim.

CISCO KID, THE (U.S.) The character of the Cisco Kid (from O. Henry's story "The Caballero's Way") was made famous in a series of Fox movies, the first of which was *In Old Arizona* (1929) starring Warner Baxter, who won an Oscar for his interpretation of the Kid. The success of the Cisco Kid in movies (and later in television) prompted King Features Syndicate to make a comic strip version, which was entrusted to the talented Argentinian artist José-Luis Salinas (for the drawing) and to Rod Reed for the writing. *The Cisco Kid* made its debut on January 15, 1951, as a daily strip (there never was a Sunday version).

Like his *compadre* Zorro, the Cisco Kid is a Mexican righter of wrongs, an indefatigable fighter against the crime and corruption afflicting the territory of New Mexico at the turn of the century. Impeccably attired in a richly embroidered black outfit and wearing a huge sombrero, he is one of the legendary figures of the American West. In the company of his comic sidekick, the potbellied and crafty Pancho, his rides often take him—in the best tradition of the Western—far from his usual field of operations. His specialty seems to be damsels-in-distress whom the Kid invariably woos in the most stereotyped Latin fashion, with flowery phrases and large sweeps of the sombrero.

In spite of a creditable story line, some good characterization, and Salinas' lyrical evocation of the limitless vistas and the magnificent scenery of the West, *The Cisco Kid* never fared well with the public, and it was finally discontinued in August 1968.

M.H.

"The Cisco Kid," José-Luis Salinas. © King Features Syndicate.

CLASSICS ILLUSTRATED (U.S.) The comic-book medium has been used mostly for entertainment, as everyone knows, but occasionally it has served educational purposes. Such has been the case with *Classics Illustrated*.

Albert L. Kanter conceived the idea of introducing children to the classics of literature via comic books in 1941. In October of that year the first issue of what was originally called *Classic Comics* was published; it was an adaptation of *The Three Musketeers*. Scores upon uplifting scores of new titles would follow, mixing literature high and low in almost equal doses, such as *Macbeth* and *The Prisoner of Zenda, The Iliad* and *King of the Khyber Rifles*, or *Crime and Punishment* and *Swiss Family Robinson*. The first three titles in the series were issued under the Elliot Publishing imprint, and the rest of the titles were released by Gilberton Publications; with issue number 35, *The Last Days of Pompeii*, the series acquired its familiar Classics Illustrated logo.

The first 20 or so adaptations were characterized by uneven artwork, ranging from the barely adequate to the impersonally professional. In 1944 Jerry Iger took over production of the series, bringing in a number of excellent artists from his shop, including Alex Blum, Henry Kiefer, and Matt Baker. The demise of the E.C. Comics line in 1954 resulted in many former E.C. artists moving to *Classics Illustrated*, and the series soon boasted artwork by the likes of Joe Orlando, George Evans, and Graham Ingels.

The original *Classics Illustrated* series ended in the spring of 1969 with issue number 169. An offshoot of the original, titled *Classics Illustrated Junior*—a series for the very young (sporting titles like *Jack and the Bean-*

stalk and *The Ugly Duckling*)—lasted for over 70 issues from 1953 to 1971. The end of the original *Classics Illustrated* was not the end of the story, however, as new titles continued to be published in Europe. In addition, reprints of the original *Classics* were issued throughout the 1970s and 1980s.

Early in 1990, First Publishing, in association with Berkley Books, acquired the rights to the Classics Illustrated name and released a new series of Classics with original art by such outstanding talents as Gahan Wilson, Kyle Baker, and Mike Ploog. A noble experiment, it lasted for only 27 issues, coming to a close in the fall of 1991.

Undaunted by First Publishing's experience, Acclaim Comics started reprinting some of the old *Classics Illustrated* in December 1996, recoloring the original artwork and reformatting the titles to digest size (approximately 5¼ by 7½ inches). Calling the new series "your doorway to the classics," a press release averred that, "Featuring essays on the author, background, theme, characters, and significance of the work . . . these editions make perfect study guides." Time will tell whether this latest effort will prove successful.

M.H.

CLIVE (G.B.) On January 8, 1968, a mop-haired teenager introduced himself to readers of the *Evening Standard*: "I'm Clive. Clive Bravo. Clive Genet Marat-Sade Bravo. Of course, my parents didn't call me Genet Marat-Sade, but that's typical of parents. No thought for others!" He scorns his "Aged Parents" (his father is 41!), and when his sister Augusta demands a bedtime story, he reads her *The Forsyte Saga*. At his parent's

"Clive," Dominic Poelsma. © Evening Standard.

party he discusses "Flagellation, le vice Anglais" with the wife of his father's chairman, Sir Reginald Bull, and recommends *The Naked Lunch* to the vicar's wife. Actually, Augusta isn't much better: her nighty-night question to Mummy is "Do you think Rodney Harrington's on pot?" Clive, in quest of fame and fortune, joins Imperial Imperials and gets his first girlfriend, Enid, secretary to the secretary's secretary of Sir Percival Hubbard Browne's secretary. He winds up as lift boy and gives up commerce for school. More adventures in the same wacky vein have been going on for over two decades now.

A daily gag strip, *Clive* is written by *Standard* columnist Angus McGill and drawn by Dominic Poelsma. Reprints include *Clive* (1968), *Clive in Love* (1970), and *Clive and Augusta* (1971).

D.G.

COCCO BILL (Italy) *Cocco Bill* started on March 28, 1957, in the pages of the *Giorno dei Ragazzi*, the weekly supplement of the Milanese daily *Il Giorno*, and it turned out to be the most hilarious comic strip parody ever concocted by Benito Jacovitti. During his long career, this cartoonist (whose distinctive trademark is a fishbone) had already shown a marked taste for the mock Western epic. This predilection is easy to see in the many strips he produced, from the first, *Il Barbiere della Prateria* ("The Barber of the Prairie," 1941), to the more recent *Pippo Cow Boy* (1946) and *Tex Revolver* (1955). But with *Cocco Bill* Jacovitti summoned all the resources of his sarcastic mind to demolish the myths and legends of the Old West.

The hero, Cocco Bill ("Soft-hearted Bill"), whose name has become a byword of the Italian language, is a heavy drinker of chamomile tea and a teetotaller. Otherwise he has all the requisite qualities of the Western hero: flawless marksmanship, fists of steel, herculean strength, gift of gab (especially with the Indians); all these are used by the author to satirize the godlike figure of the traditional hero.

The text is not contained only in the balloons: Jacovitti's most scathing lines can be found here and there in the middle of the large crowds who so often fill up his panels. These pithy aphorisms can be found on walls, on the bellies of cows, on the backsides of his characters. This characteristic, coupled with the screwball dialogue (often on a topic wholly unrelated to the action), makes *Cocco Bill* one of the most outrageously funny Italian strips. The same approach can be found in the surrealistic and chaotic drawings in which the characters elbow their way among the panels disposed any which way, and directly address the reader.

"Cocco Bill," Benito Jacovitti. © Jacovitti.

Cocco Bill and his faithful horse Trottalemme (Slowpoke) have been the heroes of a great number of stories, first in *Il Giorno dei Ragazzi*, then, after it ceased publication in 1968, in the *Corriere dei Piccoli*, and finally in *Il Corriere dei Ragazzi* (1972). Since 1980 *Cocco Bill* has appeared in the pages of *Il Giornalino*.

Eldorado, a confectionery manufacturer, used Cocco Bill to advertise its ice creams in newspapers and on television. The ad campaign was produced by the Pagot brothers.

G.B.

COCKING, PERCY (1881-1964) Percival James Cocking was perhaps the widest-known, yet unknown, comic artist in the British Empire: in a cartooning career that lasted well over half a century, his signature appeared just once. The rest of the huge volume of his weekly work was anonymous, save for his waning years when he signed his work with the pen name "Jack Daw."

Percy Cocking was born in London on March 10, 1881. He grew up less than a mile from the home of Amalgamated Press, where he would work for most of his life. The exact date when he began to draw for children's comics is unknown, but he was known well enough in the industry to be given an entire tabloid page in *The Jester & Wonder* under the heading "Our Artist's Page" on June 25, 1903. This was the only time his name appeared on one of his cartoons.

His drawing style, like so many cartoonists of the period, imitated that of Tom Browne, the father of British comics. In 1908 Cocking took over Browne's famous tramp characters *Weary Willie and Tired Tim* for *Illustrated Chips*. He continued to draw this 12-panel series until the last issue of *Chips* on September 12, 1953—a record run of 45 years, give or take a week or two when he was ill or on vacation.

From 1903 his work, recognizable mainly through his characteristic lettering and extremely neat and precise style, included *Sunbeam and the Innocent*, a "good little girl" character in *Illustrated Chips*, and two unusual series set on a street of shops and buildings, *Racketty Row* in *Jester* (1906) and *Mulberry Flats* in *Comic Cuts* (1906). In 1910 he created *Tom the Ticket of Leave Man* for *Comic Cuts*, a full front page series starring a well-meaning ex-convict. In a later, clean-up-the-comics campaign, Tom was turned into *Jolly Tom the Menagerie Man* (1917), which in turn became the adventures of *Jackie and Sammy* (1931), twins to whom Jolly Tom was a sort of guardian. These cartoon kids continued to be published with variations for several years.

Cocking worked on many other series, totaling 40 in all, including *Happy Hambone* (*Funny Wonder*), *Constable Cuddlecook* (*Jolly Jester*), *Hip Pip and Hoo Ray* (*Butterfly*), *Oliver Twister* (*Jester*), *Doctor Doodah* (*Joker*), *Tinwhiskers the Pirate* (*Chips*), and the cinema stars Joe E. Brown and Old Mother Riley in *Film Fun* during World War II. In 1949, by now considered too old by the Amalgamated Press, Cocking began working for the independent publisher Gerald G. Swan and began producing series for *Slick Fun*, *Comicolour*, and *Cute Fun*. These series included *Puny Peter Pieface*, *Fuller Gusto*, *Ossie Oddsocks*, and *Konko the Clown*. Cocking died at St. Francis Hospital on January 17, 1964, and his widow died just three weeks later. It is a cruel irony that a cartoonist who spent his lifetime making millions of children laugh should be denied any acknowledgement by Amalgamated Press, the publisher to whom he devoted his talent and most of his life.

D.G.

COLAN, EUGENE (1926-) American comic book artist, born September 1, 1926, in New York City. With art training from his years at George Washington High School and the Art Students League, Gene Colan broke into the comic book field in 1944 and has since become one of the industry's most durable contributors. Often using the name "Adam Austin," he has worked for a dozen companies here and abroad and is also an illustrator and commercial artist.

Colan's first work in comic books appeared in 1944 and 1945 on Fiction House strips like *Wing Tips, Clipper Kirk,* and *Suicide Brigade.* All were airplane adventure strips, and Colan used a clean illustrative style that he has continued to improve over the years. Throughout his career, he has also worked for Ziff-Davis (*Ken Brady*), Dell (illustrating two television spin-off titles, *Burke's Law,* which starred Gene Barry, and *Ben Casey,* which starred Vincent Edwards), Quality, St. Johns, Charlton, Ace, EC, and Warren. Colan also worked sporadically for National between 1947 and 1965; there he illustrated all types of stories (romance, science fiction, war, weird, adventure). His flexible style was best utilized on two diverse strips at National, however; he drew the *Hopalong Cassidy* Western strip for several years during the early 1950s, and then contributed some finely rendered material to the *Sea Devils* adventure feature during the early 1960s.

Undoubtedly, Gene Colan's finest material has been done for the Timely/Atlas/Marvel group edited by Stan Lee. Throughout his many years there—he began in 1948—he has contributed to hundreds of features of all kinds. Although he has drawn mostly for Marvel's war, horror, and romance departments, his most recognizable work has been in the superhero field. Colan draws incredibly handsome figures in majestic poses, and this fits perfectly with editor Lee's concept of the "noble-bearing" hero. His most productive years were between 1965 and 1972, when he handled the *Sub-Mariner* and *Daredevil* strips concurrently. On the former, he is perhaps the best-known artist after creator Bill Everett. Like most of the other illustrators who assumed *Sub-Mariner* after Everett, Colan's handling differed radically from the creators; but only Colan's material can stand on its own and compare favorably to the uniqueness of Everett's. He had even more success with *Daredevil.* Preceded by such top-notch artists as Everett, Wally Wood, John Romita, and Joe Orlando, Colan went on to become the feature's definitive artist. His handling of the blind-lawyer-cum-superhero was tastefully direct, and his well-paced stories did much to keep Lee's often confusing plot lines believable. Colan finally abandoned both features, illustrating *Sub-Mariner* between 1965 and 1971 and *Daredevil* between 1966 and 1972.

Also at Marvel, Colan has contributed work to *Captain America, Dracula, Silver Surfer,* and many others. In recent years, however, ill health forced him to give up drawing mainstream comics, and he has been working mainly (and episodically) for independent publishers; his latest efforts can be seen on Dark Horse's *Predator* (1997).

J.B.

COLE, JACK (1918-1958) American comic book artist, writer, and editor born in New Castle, Pennsylvania, on December 14, 1918. Although his only formal art training was the Landon Correspondence Course, Cole was a natural-born "bigfoot" comedy artist and began drawing humor features for the Harry "A" Chesler Shop in 1937. Using the pen name "Ralph Johns," he turned out comedy strips like *Peewee Throttle* and *Officer Clancy* until he became the editor of the New Friday Comics group in 1939. There he wrote and drew adventure strips like *Silver Streak* and *Daredevil* in a tight, realistic style that caught the eye of Quality Comics publisher "Busy" Arnold.

Joining Quality in 1940, Cole quickly began producing outstanding superhero and adventure features like *Quicksilver, Midnight, The Barker,* and the tongue-in-cheek *Death Patrol.* But August 1941 brought *Police Comics* number one and Jack Cole's *Plastic Man*—a superb, highly inventive strip that propelled him to the top of the comic book humor field. Utilizing a judicious and tasteful mix of his realistic and bigfoot art styles, Cole made the unpredictable and zany "Indian Rubber Man" an instant best-seller. His *Plastic Man* material was unique, using breathless storytelling and a refined, semi-slapstick type of humor—all of it showing influences of George McManus and Elzie Segar. Assisted by Woozy Winks, his roly-poly assistant of dubious character, "Plas" laughed, stretched, and gimmicked his way through crime fighting, all the time allowing Cole to gently poke fun at superhero strips that took themselves too seriously. The *Plastic Man* feature soon merited its own book in 1943 and even a short-lived syndicated strip.

Cole continued creating his goggled crime fighter until 1950 and then began a full-time freelance cartooning career. Over the years he had become a highly successful magazine illustrator who frequently contributed cartoons to *Collier's Judge* and *The Saturday Evening Post,* and by 1955, *Playboy* began featuring his *Females by Cole,* a cartoonist's view of the modern feminine mystique. His sophisticated and beautifully rendered full-color cartoons were also well received, and they remain among the finest cartoons ever printed in *Playboy.*

In 1958, the Chicago Sun-Times Syndicate commissioned Cole to create a new feature, *Betsy and Me,* a humorous look at American family life. But, on August 15, 1958, only months after the strip had started, Jack Cole shot himself to death with a .22 caliber pistol. At the height of his career, Cole ended it with his own hand. No one ever learned why.

J.B.

COLOMB, GEORGES (1856-1945) French artist, writer, and teacher, born in 1856 in Lure (Haute-Saône) in northeastern France. After graduating from the prestigious Ecole Normale in Paris, Colomb taught natural history, but his passion for drawing prompted him to become a contributor to various illustrated magazines. Using the pen name "Christophe," a play on words derived from his surname (Christophe Colomb is French for Christopher Colombus), he created in 1889 what some consider the first modern comic strip, *La Famille Fenouillard* ("The Fenouillard Family"), followed in 1890 by *Les Facéties du Sapeur Camember* ("The Antics of Sapper Camember") in the tradition of service comedies, and *L'Idée Fixe du Savant Cosinus* ("The Fixed Idea of Dr. Cosinus"), about an

Gene Colan, "Daredevil." © Marvel Comics.

absent-minded professor who is thwarted by cruel fate in all his efforts to get out of Paris (1893). Two lesser series, *Plick et Plock* (1894), about the doings of two mischievous gnomes, and *Le Haut et Puissant Seigneur Baron de Cramoisy* ("The High and Mighty Lord Baron of Cramoisy"), begun in 1899 but left unfinished, and a natural history textbook in comic strip form complete Christophe's *oeuvre* as a comic strip artist.

In 1903 Colomb, abandoning the comic field, devoted himself entirely to his academic career and later became director of the botany laboratory at the Sorbonne. He died in 1945.

Colomb never used balloons but inserted a text (of excellent literary quality) under his pictures. Far from being an outmoded pioneer, however, he contributed a number of important stylistic innovations, such as action depicted from odd angles, and accelerated narratives, thus foreshadowing techniques that would later become hallmarks of the comic strip. In his delineation of action and in his use of motion to link different pictures together, Colomb was also far ahead of his time, and he accordingly deserves to be ranked among the major contributors to the then-nascent art of the comics.

M.H.

"Colonel Pewter," Arthur Horner. © Associated Newspapers.

COLONEL PEWTER (G.B.) Col. Hugo Pewter (retired), late the Duffs (Bull's Foot) and Pewter's Pike, resides at "The Chukkas," a half-hidden mansion among the bandanna trees and dense placebos that outskirt the village of Much Overdun (turn right at Great Twittering, along the narrow road through Wits End and Dipping Hemline), outside the Market Town of Quirk, beyond the County Town of Whimchester, in the County of Whimshire (which in turn, bounded to the north by Nossex, nestles between John's End and Land o' Groats).

The Colonel lives quietly with his great-nephew Master Martin and housekeeper Mrs. Aspic, when he is not busy in his pottering shed with a tea-cozy on his head ("It's to keep my brain simmering, my boy!"), inventing the Pewter Rotor-Bike Mark One. This foot-powered helicycle bears man and boy through the clouds to the Lost City of Ironicus, complete with Chloe the Cat asleep in the saddlebag. King Leo XXXVII turns out to be a talking lion. A later adventure, "Dog Star," introduces Sirius the Wonder Dog, a thoughtful part-Salmanian Putschound and

part-Spacedog, expert at telepathy, telekinesis, and teleportation, much to the distress of Glub, the Colonel's man, who has been quick-frozen in a pothole since Palaeolithic Times.

Created and written by Arthur Horner in 1956 as the *News Chronicle's* answer to *Flook, Colonel Pewter* was the replacement for *Japhet and Happy.* This daily strip for children (but more for their parents) moved to the *Daily Mail* upon the *Chronicle's* demise (October 18, 1960), then moved again to *The Guardian* on May 24, 1964, an unprecedented double crossing. But, surprisingly, the rarer air of that classier newspaper did not prove conducive, and Horner was obliged to replace it with a more overtly adult strip. This was ingenious from a different angle: *The Thoughts of Citizen Doe* (1970) made readers the heroes by depicting everything from their point of view. It, too, disappeared, overtaken by John Kent's sexy *Varoomshka.*

Reprints of the strip include *Colonel Pewter in Ironicus,* a large paperback with an introduction by Christopher Fry, and *Sirius Dog Star* (1972), a hardback.

D.G.

COLONEL POTTERBY AND THE DUCHESS (U.S.) Chic Young started *Colonel Potterby and the Duchess* in 1934 as a top to *Blondie,* along with *The Family Foursome,* with which it alternated and eventually replaced.

Colonel Potterby is an amiable, bemoustached, jolly old gentleman, always attired in coat-and-tails and opera hat. His only goal and occupation in life seems to be the wooing of "the Duchess," an angular, homely spinster who fights the colonel's amorous advances with all and every means at hand. Never daunted, the colonel displays the utmost (if crackbrained) inventiveness in order to get the Duchess to marry him, but he is thwarted week after week by the Duchess' obsessive chastity.

Colonel Potterby was probably conceived by Young as a relaxation from the domesticity of Blondie: the humor there is looser and more fanciful, and there is no attempt at realism, sentimentality, or even verisimilitude. Because of this, *Colonel Potterby* is a delightful little strip, unpretentious, whimsical, and very funny.

It is doubtful whether Young himself worked on the strip after the 1940s. From that time on *Colonel Potterby* steadily declined in both interest and readership, and it finally folded in November 1963.

M.H.

COLQUHOUN, JOE (1927-1987) Joseph William Colquhoun (pronounced "ca-hoon") "was not just one

"Colonel Potterby and the Duchess," Chic Young. © King Features Syndicate.

of the best comic artists Britain has ever produced—he was the best!" Praise indeed. This quote came from Barrie Tomlinson, Joe's last editor at the Amalgamated Press/Fleetway comics empire. Among the many heroes Joe created there, one still survives; *Roy of the Rovers*, a popular football hero whom Joe first drew for the first issue of *Tiger* weekly in 1954, which was scripted by Frank S. Pepper.

Joe was born in 1927, and as a boy was more interested in the illustrations that accompanied the stories and serials in the "Tuppenny Bloods," the popular boys' story weeklies of the 1930s. His early influences were Steve Chapman, who drew for *Triumph*, and R. Simmons, who drew for *Champion*. Curiously, both artists illustrated stories written by the same Frank Pepper (who scripted *Roy of the Rovers*), who was using the pen name "Hal Wilton" at the time. An American influence was Alex Raymond, who drew *Flash Gordon*, which was being reprinted in *Modern Wonder*.

After attending art school, Colquhoun enlisted in the navy in 1943 and returned to art college in 1947, upon his discharge from the navy. Colquhoun saw a newspaper advertisement for comic-strip artists and sent samples of his work to the new studio, formed by two ex-GIs and financed with their army severance pay. King-Ganteaume was in the business of packaging 28-page comic books for various small publishers, such as L. Miller and Son and the United Anglo-American Book Company, under whose trade name, Streamline, *Masterman Comics* (1952) was published. Colquhoun tried his hand at scripting and wrote a four-part serial entitled *The Naval Stowaways* for *Lion* (1952), his first encounter with the Amalgamated Press. In the same year he joined the freelance artists on *Champion*, one of his favorite prewar papers. Colquhoun drew a long-running series entitled *Legionnaire Terry's Desert Quest*, which ran for 44 weeks, followed by *Biff Benbow* and *Wildfire*, published through 1953.

Roy of the Rovers first appeared on September 11, 1954, and after the fourth strip Colquhoun took over the scripting and continued the strip, somewhat unhappily, until 1959. "Writing never came terribly naturally to me, compared with drawing," he said. In 1959 he moved to *Lion Comic* to draw the adventures of the World War II fighter pilot *Paddy Payne* through 1964. Many other series followed, usually two-page spreads, plus a return of *Roy of the Rovers* in 1965. Titles included *Saber, King of the Jungle* (Tiger, 1967), *Football Family Robinson* (Jag, 1968), *Adam Eterno*, (Thunder, 1970), *Kid Chameleon*, (Cor, 1970), *Zarga, Man of Mystery*, (Buster, 1972), the television comedians *The Goodies* (Cor, 1973), *Zip Nolan* (Valiant, 1974), and a 64-page comic book, *Flash Point*, in the monthly series *Air Ace Picture Library* (1961). Colquhoun's most popular and arguably best series was, however, *Charley's War*, a long saga about a soldier serving in World War I. It ran for seven-and-a-half years, which was three-and-a-half years longer than the war itself. Scripted by Pat Mills, it was later reprinted as two books by Titan Publishing. It was also reprinted in the original *Battle Action* series (1979) in both *Battle* and *Eagle*, but the reruns were heavily censored for a younger audience.

Colquhoun retired from full-time comic drawing in 1986, but died shortly thereafter of a heart attack on April 13, 1987.

D.G

"Comanche," Greg and Hermann. © Editions du Lombard.

COMANCHE (Belgium) The team of Hermann and Greg, already responsible for the brilliant *Bernard Prince*, conceived a new adventure strip in 1971, *Comanche*, also for *Tintin*.

Comanche is a conventional but solid Western about a ranch hand named Red Dust, his comic sidekick Ten Gallons, and Comanche, the young and pretty ranch owner they work for. Comanche manages her ranch with a firm hand and a level head, Red Dust is strong and silent as befits a Western hero, Ten Gallons is the fabled crotchety old man with a heart of gold, and Clem is the callow youth who drinks at Dust's feet, not to forget the Western's latest wrinkle, the black cowboy (in this case his name is Toby and he is, of course, courageous, tolerant, and wise).

The stories are well researched and well written but, as in the case of so many European Westerns, they are somewhat disappointing, refusing to strictly conform to the mythology of the West, but never quite succeeding in giving us a genuine sense of the time and the place either (but Greg is *trying*).

Hermann's style is bold and powerful, his compositions visually striking, although he tends to overload his imagery with too much detail. *Comanche* tries hard to emulate *Lieutenant Blueberry* in realism and color, and in sheer skill Hermann is often the equal of Gir, but lacks his narrative skill and sense of pace. Yet *Comanche* must be ranked as one of the more interesting creations of the 1970s adventure-strip genre.

Editions du Lombard have been reprinting the adventures of Comanche and Red Dust in book form since 1972. In 1983 Hermann abandoned the feature, sending it into a prolonged hiatus, which ended in 1989 when Michel Rouge picked up the series on continuities still written by Greg.

M.H.

"Come on, Steve!", Roland Davies. © Sunday Dispatch.

COME ON, STEVE! (G.B.) "A lovable, usually stupid, occasionally artful animal." This was Steve the cart horse, in the words of Charles Eade, editor of the national newspaper *Sunday Dispatch*, in his introduction to a collation of the weekly *Come On, Steve!* strips, entitled *Adventures of Steve* and published in 1947 as a

P. J. Press paperback. Steve galloped into the *Dispatch* in 1939, a few months before the outbreak of the war. He survived Adolf Hitler by some years, despite the paper shortage that reduced his strip to a pocket-sized two panels. In fact, *Steve* lived longer than his 10 years in the *Dispatch*, for he had come there from an earlier existence in a rival newspaper, the *Sunday Express*. Such a radical change of venue was unheard-of in British newspaper strips of the 1930s.

Steve was created by Roland Davies and was the very opposite of all Davies loved: speed and power. A cartoonist and illustrator obsessed with racing cars and aircraft, Davies christened his stolid old cart-horse, almost an anachronism in the 1930s, Steve, after the catchphrase shouted by crowds at the racetrack when Steve Donoghue, champion jockey, came roaring in to win: "Come on, Steve!" Davies tried his strip, a pantomime gag, as a daily for the *London Evening Standard*, but they turned it down, and so he then tried the *Daily Express*. Arthur Christiansen, the bright assistant editor, took it in to John Gordon, editor of the Sunday edition, who snapped it up immediately to commence the very next Sunday. Within a few years Steve was so popular that Davies taught himself animation, set up a studio in his kitchen, and with a stop-frame camera costing 18 shillings spent seven months making an animated cartoon. He showed it to Butcher's Film Distributors and secured a contract for six sound cartoons. With some professional animators and local talent from the Ipswich Art School, the films were made. *Steve Steps Out* (1936) was crude, but *Steve of the River* (1936), a burlesque of Edgar Wallace's *Sanders of the River*, was good. Story books were published using drawings from

Didier Comés, "Silence." © Casterman.

the films. After the *Dispatch* discontinued the strip, Davies retained his copyright and produced an excellent series of full-color picture books lithographed by Perry's Colourprint: *Steve Goes to London* (1946); *Steve and the Little Engine* (1947); *Steve's Christmas Holiday* (1947); *Steve on the Farm* (1948); *Steve's Dream* (1948); *Steve and the Burglar* (1949); *Steve and the Racing Car* (1949). There were also *Come on, Steve!* annuals in 1947 and 1950.

D.G.

COMÉS, DIDIER (1942-   ) Belgian cartoonist and illustrator, born December 11, 1942, in Sourbrodt, in that part of eastern Belgium that was annexed by the Germans during World War II; given the name Dieter at birth, Comés was rechristened Didier after Belgium's liberation in 1944. Following studies at a vocational art school, he became an industrial designer, working in that capacity from 1959 to 1969.

His career as a professional cartoonist started in earnest in the early 1970s, when Comés contributed several short comic stories to Belgian and French publications, such as the daily *Le Soir* and the comic weeklies *Spirou* and *Pilote*. In the pages of the latter he published his first long-breathed creation, *Ergun l'Errant* ("Ergun the Wanderer"), in 1973. It was the saga of a space traveler, in which arresting images and imaginative layouts counterpoint a rather conventional script.

Having refined and simplified his style in *L'Ombre du Corbeau* ("The Shadow of the Raven," 1976-77), a nature story blending the commonplace with the fantastic, Comés unfolded what turned out to be his masterpiece, *Silence*, from 1979 to 1981. A legend-drenched graphic novel full of mystery, magic, and yes, silence, set amidst the forests, the ponds, and the mists of the artist's native region, it brought a welcome breath of fresh air to the claustrophobic Franco-Belgian comics scene. He followed this up with more gripping tales of magic realism, *La Belette* ("The Weasel," 1981-82), *Eva* (1985), and *Iris* (1990). From 1985 to 1986 he also produced *L'Arbre-Coeur* ("The Heart-Tree"), the romantic adventure of a female reporter returning from assign-

ment in Afghanistan. In his narratives as in his compositions, Comés has shown himself to be a highly original talent, the poet of the eerie, the magical, the unspoken.

M.H.

COMMISSARIO SPADA, IL (Italy) Few Italian mystery writers have ever made it big under their own names: the almost single exception is Giorgio Scerbanendo, who acquired fame and honors toward the end of his long career. On the other hand, many other writers had no trouble selling their works by using an Anglo-Saxon pseudonym. The shibboleth that a good mystery story had to be written by an Englishman or an American carried even to the characters, who had to have English-sounding names, and to the locale, which had to closely resemble an American metropolis. This prejudice held true not only in novels and stories, but in comic strips as well.

Il Commissario Spada ("Commissioner Spada") was the first exception to the rule. It was created on April 19, 1970, by Gian Luigi Gonano (writer) and Gianni DeLuca (artist). Spada is the commissioner of the Squadra Mobile (mobile squad), and he is often engaged in everyday cases full of human interest, all of them cleverly told and solved by Gonano. DeLuca, in his turn, cinematically translates the suspenseful action into comic strip terms, focusing not only on the athletic commissioner but also on his subordinates and adversaries, who are all realistically drawn with broad strokes.

The themes of the stories are those of everyday life, and the problems Commissioner Spada has to face are not only professional but also personal (Spada is a widower with a young son named Mario). *Commissario Spada* appeared in the pages of the widely circulated Catholic weekly *Il Giornalino* (whose editor, Gino Tomaselli, physically resembled the hero—and not by coincidence). The series ended in the early 1980s.

G.B.

CONAN (U.S.) For years, the late Robert E. Howard's *Conan* series had seen many editions in paperbacks.

"Il Commissario Spada," Gianni DeLuca. © Ed. Paoline.

...AS THE GLEAMING FANGS OF THE *BEAST* HEAD, WHICH IS SURELY *DEATH* ITSELF, *GNASH* AND *CHAMP*!

THE EYELIDS OF THE *OTHER* HEAD...*SLEEP,* IT MUST BE... ARE *CLOSED* IN EERIE TRANQUILITY.

TO AWAKEN THEM, THEN--TO SEE *THOSE* EYES OPEN, AND THE BEAST'S *CLOSE*-- BUT *HOW*??

"Conan," Gil Kane. © Marvel Comics Group.

Graced with cover artwork by illustrator Frank Frazetta or others of equal note, the barbarian from mythical Cimmeria had occasional revivals and celebrations. But the comic book industry, never receptive to, or willing to experiment with, sword and sorcery material of the Howard/Conan ilk, ignored the character and its attendant popularity like a plague.

But then Marvel Comics purchased the rights to the Howard stories and planned to issue a *Conan the Barbarian* comic book. Roy Thomas was assigned to write the title, and young Barry Smith to illustrate, even though Thomas had publicly indicated a preference for John Buscema, who was unavailable. The first issue of the full-color *Conan the Barbarian* was issued in October 1970, and it immediately became that rare kind of title: a book hailed by the critics that sold well to the general comic-buying public. As issues progressed, Thomas managed to balance Conan's essentially violent nature—Howard had characterized him as a barbarian in the true sense of the word; he was mean, cruel, ruthless, unmannered, and mercenary, with a conscience guided only by personal survival—and the restrictions of the oft-condemned comics code. But perhaps more amazing was that the talented Thomas even managed to save Conan from becoming just another Marvel character. Whereas most of Marvel's minions were standard types—usually noble-bearing, upright, considerate, and more often than not, gifted with superhuman powers but normal intellect—Thomas maintained Conan as a demigod fighting unnatural phenomona with none of the strictures inherent in the Marvel world of superheroes with problems.

Writer Thomas, who also edited the book, relied mostly on adaptations of Howard stories, and later adapted unfinished Howard manuscripts. Still later, when the volume of Howard material was exhausted and the Conan work by writers such as De Camp, Carter, and Nyborg was contractually unavailable, Thomas turned to adapting sword-and-sorcery work by writers like Edgar Rice Burroughs and Gardner F. Fox. Under his constant tutelage, the *Conan the Barbarian* book has won a score of comic art awards from fans and professionals alike.

Artistically, the book has gone through many changes. Young Smith developed quickly, and although his Conan was not nearly as brutal-looking as described by Howard, his characterizations gained a quick following. His material was heavily laden with intricate designs—at times bordering on ornate, art deco-like scenes and backgrounds—and eye-pleasing page composition and layout; his coloring was delicate and compatible. But, by early 1973 differences between Smith and Marvel came to a boil and he left the strip. After several fill-in issues by Gil Kane, John Buscema, Thomas's original choice, assumed the strip in April 1973. His Conan was even less vicious-looking, but Buscema's design and execution were excellent and two quite diverse factions developed, some favoring Smith and others preferring the Buscema version, which was inked by Ernie Chua, among others. Neal Adams and Esteban Maroto also rendered the character.

The Conan character was also highly saleable and has appeared in many of Marvel's newer formats. A second Conan title, a one-dollar black-and-white book entitled *Savage Sword of Conan*, premiered in August 1974.

J.B.

In the late 1970s Thomas's increasingly sloppy writing almost doomed the barbarian in a way his enemies had not been able to do. The title was rescued by the two movies based on the character, the 1981 *Conan the Barbarian* and the 1985 *Conan the Destroyer*, both starring Arnold Schwarzenegger in the title role. Despite this shot in the arm and the contributions of some good artists (Howard Chaykin, Walt Simonson), the title continued to falter, and it was discontinued in December 1993. Several spin-offs (*Conan the King, The Conan Saga*, etc.) that had sprouted in the meantime proved to be short-lived. Since August 1995 the barbarian's adventures have been carried in the black-and-white *Conan the Savage* magazine.

M.H.

CONNIE (U.S.) Frank Godwin's *Connie* is, along with Noel Sickles' *Scorchy Smith* and Burne Hogarth's *Tarzan*, one of the causes célèbres of comic strip scholarship. Distributed by the obscure Ledger Syndicate from 1927 to 1944, it ran in only a few newspapers (including the *Brooklyn Eagle*) and was completely ignored by the early historians of the medium. Even as late as 1974 Jerry Robinson's *The Comics* does not mention it (an unjustifiable omission, since the earlier *History of the Comic Strip* and *75 Years of the Comics* not only discussed the strip but also reprinted illustrations). Yet a close study of *Connie* reveals it as one of the most fascinating strips of the era.

"Connie," Frank Godwin. © Ledger Syndicate.

In the early years of the strip, Connie was a pretty blonde living with her parents and going to picnics and masquerade parties in the company of eligible young men with such names as Percival Llewellyn-Smith and Clarence Dillingworth. Then came the depression and Connie turned out to be a girl with a social conscience; she helped her mother with her charity work and often visited the men on the breadlines (one of the very few instances where the depression was graphically depicted in a comic strip).

In 1934 Connie went to work, first as a reporter, then as the operator of a detective agency (a kind of female Sam Spade). Her assignments led her to all parts of the United States and as far as Mexico and South America. Her most unusual adventure took place in Russia, where she helped foil a plot against the Soviet regime (certainly an oddity in comic strips of the 1930s). Then, to top it all, Connie joined an interplanetary expedition headed by another woman, Dr. Alden, and her son Hugh. Connie's explorations of the solar system—which were to last over two years—is one of the most remarkable sequences in the history of the adventure strip, and in the power of its imagery and suspense, it can be ranked alongside the best episodes of Raymond's *Flash Gordon*, Caniff's *Terry,* and Foster's and Hogarth's *Tarzan*.

The narrative, good as it often is, is overshadowed by the personality of the heroine and her chaste, cool beauty. Connie is a liberated woman: intelligent, self-reliant, at ease in all situations. Holding her own against any man, she would certainly have made a better representative for the women's movement than the masochistic, dull-witted Wonder Woman.

Connie was sparsely reprinted in comic books and was never adapted to radio or the screen. The strip was rescued from total oblivion only through the efforts of dedicated lovers of the medium. *Connie* is a constant visual delight, even when the narrative falters, and it deserves to be exhumed from dusty library archives into the light of print.

M.H.

CONTI, OSCAR (1914-1979) Oscar Conti (better known as "Oski") was born in Buenos Aires in 1914. After studies at the Buenos Aires Academy of Fine Arts, Conti became a poster designer. In 1942 he started his collaboration as a humor cartoonist with Carlos Warnes, who used the pseudonym "César Bruto." A man of great culture, obsessed by the oppression exercised by Latin American dictators, concerned about the life of the Indians, the inventions of mankind, and the re-creation of the old didactic texts from world literature, Conti transferred his deep knowledge of these subjects into his thematic treatment.

Conti edited many collections of his graphic work gathered from magazines from many countries. With his comic strip *Amarrotto*, published in the comic magazine *Rico Tipo*, he influenced many cartoonists who later become his disciples. At the same time he wrote the daily *Versos y Noticias de César Bruto* ("Rhymes and Notes of César Bruto").

Conti's fertile creativity led him to combine many of his hobbies into one: he repaired pocketwatches, put in a new setting, and decorated them in his own masterly style. He died in Buenos Aires on October 30, 1979.

L.G.

CORBEN, RICHARD VANCE (1940-   ) American comic book and underground artist and animator, born October 1, 1940 in Anderson, Missouri. Rich

Richard Corben, "Rowlf." © Richard Corben.

Corben—or "Gore" Corben as he often signed his work—was educated at BFA, Kansas City (Missouri) Art Institute.

Corben is one of the groundbreakers of comic art, but also extremely unique. His first experience with comics was with Calvin productions in Kansas City, where he worked in the animation department from 1963 to 1972. His first published comic work in printed form appeared not in a professional magazine, but in a fanzine—*Voice of Comicdom* number 12 (1968). He moved into the underground market in mid-1970 when his first story, "Lame Lems Love" appeared in *Skull* number two. His first traditional, "above-ground" comic book work appeared in the November 1970 issue of Warren's *Creepy* black-and-white magazine (number 36). Since that time, he has continued to work in all three veins, becoming at one time the best fanzine artist, the most-respected underground horror artist, and the best horror artist in the black-and-white mainstream magazines.

Most of Corben's appeal and popularity—which grew steadily and has recently reached cult proportions—comes from his highly stylized, completely individual approach to a comic story. Much of his style developed from his animation work. Corben's anatomy is always grossly exaggerated: his men are unbelievably muscular and his women abnormally well-endowed. His figures are sometimes amazingly three-dimensional, other times agonizingly two-dimensional. Most of his panels have highly developed foreground action with just the barest detail in the background. He often works in color—both in the underground and with special sections of Warren's black-and-white books—and his work there is exceedingly vibrant, eerie, and always well conceived.

Corben usually develops three distinct types of stories with repetitive trends and ideas. His sword-and-sorcery work was done mostly for a vast number of out-of-print and hard-to-find fanzines. His neo-EC, gory horror tales are usually found in underground comix like *Skull*, *Death Rattle*, and *Weird Fantasies*. Science fiction is Corben's other major theme and these stories are found in undergrounds like *Fever Dreams* and *Slow Death* and fanzines like Mike Barrier's outstanding *Funnyworld*. Corben uses all three types of stories in his above-ground work, but they are considerably more sedate and sexually demure than his underground and fanzine work.

Perhaps his best-known work is *Rowlf*, which originally appeared in fanzines and was republished as an underground in 1971. It is a strange tale about a woman named Maryara, her dog Rowlf, and their eerie devotion to each other.

Corben has racked up several awards in a relatively short professional career in comic books. In addition, one of his animated films—*Neverworld*, a completely Corben animation-and-line action film—has won three awards.

J.B.

The last 20 years have been extremely productive for Richard Corben. *Bloodstar* (1976), *Neverwhere* (1978), and *New Tales of the Arabian Nights* (with Jan Strnad, 1979) strengthened his reputation as a master storyteller. It is in *Den* and *Den II* (both 1984) that all of the artist's narrative strands—heroic fantasy, speculative fiction, horror play—came together, building up to what is perhaps the author's most representative work.

With *Werewolf* and *Edgar Allan Poe* Corben explored further the twin themes of horror and madness that run through his oeuvre as a scarlet thread. While continuing the saga of Den, in the late 1980s and early 1990s he also touched upon more science-fictional and even metaphysical themes; at the same time the more openly erotic aspects of his work have found since 1994 their ideal vehicle in *Penthouse Comix*. Corben has also evidenced great strength as an animator, especially in the "Den" segment of the *Heavy Metal* theatrical feature.

M.H.

"Corentin," Paul Cuvelier. © Editions du Lombard.

CORENTIN (Belgium) Started as *Les Aventures de Corentin Feldoë* in the first issue of the comic weekly *Tintin* (September 26, 1946), the strip was the brainchild of cartoonist Paul Cuvelier and writer Jacques van Melkebeke (who also happened to be *Tintin's* first editor).

Corentin Feldoë was a young Breton orphan of the 17th century who was sent to join his uncle in India. There he was to experience many adventures in the company of the young Indian boy Kim, whom he had befriended, and his two pet animals, Belzebuth the gorilla and Moloch the tiger (as one can see, in the beginning at least, the series was strongly influenced by Rudyard Kipling's tales). Later Corentin traveled to China, North America, Arabia, and anywhere else under the sun. Very often magic and the supernatural played an important role in the series, which was consistently well plotted and always exciting. Corentin grew up over the years into a handsome adolescent; his appearances in *Tintin*, however, became fewer and farther between, due to the author's preoccupations with other series (such as *Line*, a circus strip) and with other pursuits (painting, sculpture). Following van Melkebeke's departure as scriptwriter after two episodes, *Corentin* was written by Greg, Jean van Hamme, and Cuvelier himself. Cuvelier died in 1978, and *Corentin* died with him.

Corentin is probably one of the best adventure series to come out of the immediate postwar years. The situations and plots are very imaginative, the characters interesting and colorful, and the backgrounds lovingly detailed. Cuvelier's graphic style helped in no small measure the success of the strip: clean, uncluttered, and very dynamic, it is the classic style of the adventure strip of the 1930s, but brought up to date, with a dash of European sophistication and flair.

M.H.

Jayme Cortez, "Sergio Amazonas." © Jayme Cortez.

"Corto Maltese," Hugo Pratt. © Pratt.

CORTEZ, JAYME (1926-1987) Brazilian cartoonist and comic strip artist of Portuguese origin, born in Lisbon in 1926. Jayme Cortez started his career as a disciple of E.T. Coelho, working for the weekly *O Mosquito*, where he drew such series as *Os Dois Amigos* ("The Two Pals"). In 1947 he moved to Brazil, where he produced a number of comic strips for the São Paulo daily *O Diario da Noite*, notably *Caça aos Tubaroes*, a jungle strip, and *O Guarany*, a saga of Indian life. He married a Brazilian woman in 1948 and became a permanent resident of the country. He worked alongside veteran cartoonist Messias de Melho in *A Gazeta Juvenil* and *A Gazeta Esportiva*, and he drew the covers for the horror comic-book title *O Terror Negro,* published by Editora La Selva. When horror comics were banned in the United States in the mid-1950s, La Selva hired Brazilian cartoonists to keep the market going. From the late 1950s through the 1970s Cortez drew *Dick Peter*, a detective story, as well as *Zodiac* for the Italian market.

In 1951 Cortez, along with Syllas Roberg, Miguel Penteado, Reynaldo de Oliveira, and Alvaro de Moya, organized the first international exhibition of comics; rare originals by George Herriman, Milton Caniff, Alex Raymond, Hal Foster, and other American cartoonists were displayed alongside the work of Brazilian and European artists. Cortez was the inspiration for a whole generation of Brazilian cartoonists, especially Mauricio de Souza. He authored three how-to books on drawing and cartooning. He received the Caran d'Ache Lifetime Achievement Award in Italy and had a retrospective exhibition of his work organized by the Museu de Arte de São Paulo, the most important art museum in Latin America. He died in 1987, a few months before the publication of an anthology of his horror stories titled *A Saga do Terror*.

A.M.

CORTO MALTESE (France and Belgium) One of the most popular of French-language strips, *Corto Maltese* is the work of an Italian, Hugo Pratt, who created it as a spin-off from one of his earlier efforts, *Una Ballata del Mare Salato* ("A Ballad of the Salty Sea"). *Corto* first appeared in the French weekly *Pif-Gadget* on April 1, 1970.

Corto Maltese is a sea captain without a ship and, by all appearances, without a country. The action takes place around 1910, when there were still worlds to conquer, treasures to discover, and causes to fight for. There is a heavy atmosphere in these tales full of sound and fury, in which magic and witchcraft play a large part.

In adventures that lead him from South America to Europe (where he takes part in the fighting of World War I) to North Africa, Corto always sides with the rebels and the oppressed. He fights alongside the Indians against the military and the settlers, with the Irish revolutionaries against the British, and with the Arabs against the Turks. A host of secondary characters lend color and relief to the action, like the old pirate captain Rasputin, the dypsomaniacal professor Steiner, Banshee the fiery Irish lass, and the voluptuous adventuress Venexiana Stevenson, among others.

In 1974 Pratt left *Pif* for the Belgian *Tintin*, where the adventures of Corto Maltese appeared in full color (they were published in black and white in *Pif*). New *Corto Maltese* episodes continued to appear like clockwork over the years, up to the time of the author's death in 1995.

In the space of a few years, *Corto Maltese* has risen to the top of the list of adventure strips. All the episodes have been reprinted in book form and translated into a halfdozen languages. *Corto Maltese* has also been adapted (in animated form) to the television screen. Several book-length studies have been devoted to the seafaring adventurer, the most notable being Michel Pierre's *Corto Maltese Memoires* in 1988.

M.H.

CORY, FANNY YOUNG (1877-1972) American cartoonist and illustrator born in Waukegan, Illinois, in 1877, Fanny Young grew up in Montana and started her art studies at age 14 in Helena, then went to New

York. She sold her first drawing in 1896 to *St. Nicholas* magazine. She then became very much in demand, with contributions to *Life*, *Scribner's* and the *Saturday Evening Post*. In 1901 she went back to Montana, married the next year, and settled on a 1,800-acre ranch near Helena. She became a noted illustrator of children's books (her illustrations for Frank Baum's novels are best known, along with *The Fanny Cory Mother Goose*).

In 1928 Fanny Cory created a one-column panel, *Sonnysayings*, for the Philadelphia Ledger Syndicate. Encouraged by her first foray into the newspaper field, she then decided to become a comic strip artist. After a few false starts, she finally came up with *Babe Bunting*, an orphan strip, in 1934. *Babe* was successful enough for King Features to take notice, and the following year, Cory left *Babe Bunting* to create *Little Miss Muffet*, another little girl adventure strip, for King. The feature enjoyed reasonable success and Cory continued it until 1956.

Fanny Cory's comic strip style was delicate and clean, perhaps a little too elaborate for the simple stories she was given to illustrate. While not outstanding, her contribution (usually ignored in comic strip histories) is worthy of mention. She died on her Montana ranch in 1972.

M.H.

COSSIO, CARLO (1907-1964) Italian cartoonist, born January 1, 1907, in Udine. Along with his younger brother Vittorio (born in 1911), Carlo Cossio moved to Milan during childhood. He started his career as a decorator but in 1928 became interested in animation. Around this time he did a number of advertising cartoons in collaboration with his brother (Carlo Cossio was among the first Italian animators to draw directly on animation "cells") and also drew a number of magazine illustrations and book covers. In 1932 the Cossio brothers produced their first commercially successful animated cartoon, *Zibillo e l'Orso* ("Zibillo and the Bear"), and thereafter went on to create more cartoons.

Carlo Cossio's most famous creation, however, was not an animated cartoon but a comic strip, *Dick Fulmine*, which he created in 1938 for the illustrated weekly *L'Audace*. Centering on the extraordinary adventures of a muscular superhero, *Dick Fulmine* ("Lightning Dick") enjoyed a tremendous success, and Cossio worked on the feature almost uninterruptedly until 1955.

In 1940, after a series of run-ins with Mussolini's Ministry of Popular Culture (the infamous "Minculpop"), Carlo Cossio judged it prudent to leave the comics field for a while, and returned to the animated cartoon with *Pulcinella nel Bosco* ("Punch in the Woods"). His exile did not last long, however, and he made his comeback later that same year with *X-1 il Pugile Misterioso* ("X-1 the Mysterious Prizefighter"), about a boxer-turned-crimefighter, which he left to his brother Vittorio after a few episodes. (Under the title of *Furio Almirante*, it was to have a great career and almost eclipsed *Dick Fulmine* at one time.)

During and after the war, Cossio created a number of other comic strips: *Franca* (about a youthful and spirited heroine), *Tank* (a superhero after the fashion of American comic books), *La Freccia d'Argente* ("The Silver Arrow," 1941, depicting the exploits of another justice-fighter), and *Bufalo Bill* (1950; an entertaining, if

spurious biography of the legendary American scout, which he drew for the weekly *L'Intrepido*).

All the while Carlo Cossio had been working on *Dick Fulmine* (with the assistance of his brother Vittorio on some episodes). It is therefore not surprising that he suffered a complete breakdown, which forced him to leave the field in 1955. He tried to make a comeback unsuccessfully in 1963, and he died (of cancer) in Milan on August 10, 1964.

Carlo Cossio was made famous by *Dick Fulmine* and was perhaps the victim of his own success. Working hastily and at times mindlessly (he once boasted of having drawn an entire 16-page episode in one night), he was never able to display his undeniable graphic talents to their best advantage. He left behind a legacy of dubious achievements, with a few diamonds sparkling brightly amidst heaps of rubbish.

M.H.

"Count Screwloose," Milt Gross. © Milt Gross.

COUNT SCREWLOOSE OF TOOLOOSE (U.S.) One of the most fondly remembered, quoted, and described of all departed U.S. comic strips, Milt Gross' weekly *Count Screwloose of Tooloose*, which began on Sunday, February 17, 1929, with the *New York World*'s syndicate, was partly prefigured by a wild scene in a madhouse involving the characters of Gross' immediately preceding strip, *Nize Baby*, early in 1927. For the springboard of the early *Screwloose* adventures was a madhouse—an institution called Nuttycrest, to which the chronic escapee, Count Screwloose, was always glad to return after a weekly experience in the outside world that convinced him that the asylum was a far saner place. The Count (whose nobility, with his appropriately misspelled notion of an aristocratic place of origin, the French city of Toulouse, was his only delusion) was a shrimpish, balding, daffily cross-eyed brunette dressed neatly in fedora and vest. His closest asylum companion and later co-escapee, a black-collared, cross-eyed, humanized mutt in a Napoleonic hat, named Iggy (not seen in the strip until the third episode, of March 10, 1929), and who appears as first a white, then yellow, and finally an orange dog over the run of the strip, was the Count's steadfast welcomer back to Nuttycrest in the early years of the feature, and Screwloose's admonitory, last-panel refrain of this period, "Iggy, keep an eye on me," became a widely used term for professed dismay at someone else's foolishness.

After two years with the *World*, Gross took *Count Screwloose* to Hearst's King Features in early 1931, which began national distribution of its new acquisition on March 1, 1931. Now sharing the Sunday page with a new page-top Gross feature, *Babbling Brooks* (about a fat fellow who talks himself into weekly disasters), *Screwloose* continued as before—but with the "of Tooloose" dropped from the title—until June 1931, when the strip was moved into the page-top space (*Babbling Brooks* being discarded) and was replaced below by a new feature, *Dave's Delicatessen*. In its new, smaller Sunday spot, *Screwloose* dropped the weekly escape-and-return routine, and focused on the Count and Iggy as edgy but continuing denizens of the outside world, fearful of being found out and returned to the asylum, but managing by nervy inventiveness to make out.

In early 1933, a single-panel feature called *That's My Pop* cut down the size of *Screwloose* even more, until its space was turned over entirely on June 24, 1934, to a new strip featuring two penguins, while the Count himself, who had entered the *Dave's Delicatessen* strip below in December of the previous year, continued there as a close companion of that strip's hero, Honest Dave. The new comic team joined the Foreign Legion in November 1934, for a prolonged stint of comic adventure in the course of which the *Dave's Delicatessen* strip was retitled *Count Screwloose* (January 20, 1935). In June 1938, a third of the *Count Screwloose* half-page space was given over to a new Gross gag panel called *Grossly Xaggerated,* which ran there through October 1938. *Count Screwloose* continued to run (by now almost exclusively in the *Mirror*) until Gross was forced in 1945 by a heart attack to refrain from further comic strip work.

A great strip in its early years, but of declining quality after 1934, *Count Screwloose* remains one of the most continually funny, inventive, and sophisticated comics of all time.

B.B.

COYOTE, EL (Spain) El Coyote's adventures were first published as a series of novels in the collection "Oeste," starting in December 1943. The aim of the publishers was to establish a hero similar to the protagonists of the American pulps; the success of the hero created by the novelist José Mallorqui was so widespread that his novels were translated into several foreign languages and inspired adaptations in all mass media.

In 1946 *El Coyote* started its long career as a weekly comic book with illustrations by Francisco Batet, who had previously drawn the hundreds of Coyote novels. El Coyote, whose first adventure took place during the Mexican-American War, is in actuality the young César de Echague, who conceals his identity under a mask and a curious disguise, in order to fight with impunity the "yanquis" and brigands who devastate his lands. His life is far removed from that of the traditional American West, closer to the traditional ways of the Spaniards of California: he is a caballero who has known struggles, loves, and marriages; he has created

"El Coyote," Francisco Batet. © Ediciones Cliper.

a dynasty, represented in the persons of his children, in the course of the hundreds of comic books depicting his adventures. Batet's version was unfortunately afflicted by lengthy and meandering dialogues and a verbose narrative that considerably choked up the action. Batet's style was very individual, fine and light, without any research or innovation, but effective in its preservation of the Coyote myth, then at the height of its popularity. When Batet left for France and a new career in the early 1950s, he was succeeded by the less inspired José Ramon Larraz. The character managed to survive in his and other artists's hands into the 1980s.

El Coyote was made into three motion pictures, was adapted to the stage, and inspired a musical comedy as well as several records. A fan club further helped to maintain its popularity, and there were also many Coyote toys and costumes.

L.G.

CRAENHALS, FRANÇOIS (1926-) Belgian cartoonist, born November 15, 1926, at Ixelles, near Brussels. After studies at the Brussels Royal Academy, Craenhals started his cartooning career with a series of caricatures (which he signed "F. Hals") for the Belgian magazine *Vrai*.

In 1948 Craenhals entered the field of comic art with *Druka*, a medieval adventure strip strongly influenced by *Prince Valiant*, for the weekly *Le Soir Illustré*, where it ran from July to October. Craenhals originated a new feature, *Karan*, also short-lived, for *Heroic-Albums* in 1950, the same year that he started his long collaboration with the comic weekly *Tintin*, first as an illustrator, and later as a comic strip artist. For *Tintin* Craenhals was to create a number of features over the years: *Rémy et Ghislaine* (1951); *Pom et Teddy*, a kid adventure strip that started in 1953; *Luc Tremplin*, an adventure tale (1962); and more importantly *Chevalier Ardent* ("Knight Ardent"), a story of adventure in King Arthur's time (1966). Craenhals has also drawn a daily gag strip, *Primus et Musette*, for the newspaper *La Libre Belgique* (1958-1961), and is, since 1965, the illustrator of *Les 4 As* ("The 4 Aces"), yet another kid adventure strip written by François Georges (George Chaulet). While continuing his work on *Chevalier Ardent*, he also

MAMA'S BOYZ®   BY JERRY CRAFT

Jerry Craft, "Mama's Boyz." © King Features Syndicate.

drew *Fantomette*, a teenage mystery strip, for Editions Hachette from 1982 to 1983; and in the 1990s he turned out a number of short stories for foreign (mainly German) publishers.

A cartoonist with a versatile and free style, François Craenhals is somewhat underrated in Europe, where his traditional outlook and introverted personality do not attract as much attention as the flashier idiosyncrasies of some of his colleagues. Yet he is an artist of solid and noteworthy accomplishment.

M.H.

CRAFT, JERRY (1963-) Cartoonist Jerry Craft was born in New York City on January 22, 1963. He graduated from the School of Visual Arts in 1984. Currently a staff artist at King Features, his strip *Mama's Boyz* is part of a weekly package distributed by King Features to over 1,500 newspapers in the United States.

The main characters in *Mama's Boyz* are Pauline Porter, a widow, and her teenage sons Tyrell and Yusuf. The Porters own a bookstore featuring a large selection of African-American books, and they live in an apartment above the store. The strip's setting, extended family, and friends are all true-to-life and believable, which adds to the appeal of the strip set in a large city. Jerry Craft has designed *Mama's Boyz* to specifically bring African-American family experiences and humor to the general public. Craft has volunteered the characters for use by the American Diabetes Association to educate readers about diabetes and its impact on those who have the disease. In the strip, diabetes was the cause of the father's death.

Prior to having his work syndicated, Craft worked on *New Kids on the Block* for Harvey Comics and *Sweet 16* for Marvel Comics. His work has been published in the *Village Voice, Ebony* magazine, *Street News*, and *Jewish Weekly*. A Sunday-page comic, *Mama's Boyz* is a regular feature in the *City Sun*, a New York City African-American-owned newspaper. It is one of the leaders in the next generation of African-American comic strips, which include such big names as *Curtis, Herb & Jamal*, Jump Start, and *Where I'm Coming From*.

Craft's clean, distinctive style, family humor, and ability to keep up with the latest trends among teenagers, as well as the fact that he presents a pair of African-American young men coping with the teenage years, make his strip a good alternative for newspapers looking for an African-American strip besides the current big four.

B.C.

CRAIG, CHASE (1910-) American comic book and strip writer, artist, and editor, born August 28, 1910, in Ennis, Texas. Following study at the Chicago Academy of Fine Arts, Craig moved to California in 1935 and joined Walter Lantz's animation studio. In 1936, he switched over to Warner Brothers to work as an animator and story man in Fred (Tex) Avery's unit, followed two years later by a stint drawing a short-lived comic strip, *Hollywood Hams*, for the *Los Angeles Daily News*. While the strip never achieved national syndication, Craig did. V. V. McNitt of the McNaught syndicate saw the strip and liked it, and so Craig and his collaborator, Carl Buettner, were hired to take over the Charlie McCarthy newspaper strip based on Edgar Bergen's popular character. Originally, Craig was to function as Buettner's art assistant, but he soon assumed most of the scripting duties. Buettner, a former contributor to *Capt. Billy's Whiz Bang* and a Disney veteran, subsequently joined Western Publishing Company, where he worked on various comic books in addition to supervising, writing, and illustrating many "Little Golden Books."

After *Charlie McCarthy* folded in 1940, Craig worked with writer Fred Fox on another daily strip, *Odd Bodkins* (Esquire Syndicate), which was probably the first parody of *Superman*. He also began freelancing for Western, writing and drawing the first *Porky Pig* stories for the *Looney Tunes* comic book and many of the early *Bugs Bunny* one-shots. Also for *Looney Tunes*, Craig took a cartoon mouse (Sniffles) from the Warner Brothers films, added a heroine named after Mrs. Craig, and thus launched the very popular strip *Mary Jane and Sniffles*. Craig also wrote and drew the first few *Bugs Bunny* Sunday newspaper pages. The strip was sold to NEA Syndicate in 1942, about the time *Odd Bodkins* ended and Craig went into the navy.

In 1945, after leaving the service, he returned to freelance writing for Western. He did thousands of scripts for various Western comics, including *Looney Tunes, Bugs Bunny, Porky Pig*, and the various Walt Disney comics. In 1950, he joined the firm as an editor, subsequently becoming managing editor and then executive editor. He supervised the stories and artwork of many different comics, ranging from *Tarzan* to various television-based titles to the Disney books, such as

Mickey Mouse and *Donald Duck*. He also created many originals for the line, such as *The Little Monsters, Baby Snoots, The Jungle Twins,* and *Magnus, Robot Fighter.* In each of these comics, he worked closely with his staff of writers and artists to maintain the highest possible standard of quality.

M.E.

CRAIG, JOHN (1926-   ) American comic book artist, writer, and editor, born April 25, 1926, in Pleasantville, New York. After training at the Art Students League, Johnny Craig broke into the comic book industry in 1938 as an assistant to National Comics artist Harry Lampert, who was then illustrating *The King.* He later lettered for Sheldon Mayer's *Scribbly* strip. When World War II erupted, Craig joined the Merchant Marine and then the U.S. Army and fought in Germany.

After the war, Craig spent 1947 and 1948 drawing for the old Fox, ME, and Lev Gleason lines. He then joined the EC group, which was producing nondescript love, crime, and adventure titles. However, when editor and publisher Bill Gaines ushered in the "New Trend" EC line in 1950, Craig immediately became a mainstay and drew outstanding covers and stories for virtually all the horror, crime, and suspense titles. He later became the chief writer and editor of *Vault of Horror* and *Extra!* from 1953-1955.

While Craig was a notoriously slow worker and Gaines once commented that he drew the "cleanest" horror stories he had ever seen, the artist's work drew an inordinate amount of public scrutiny for its alleged violent excesses. His cover for *Crime SuspenStories* 20—showing a close-up view of a hanging victim—was reproduced in *Seduction of the Innocent,* Dr. Frederic Wertham's highly controversial 1953 study of comics and violence. And his cover drawing for *Crime Suspen-Stories* 22—depicting a man holding a bloodied ax and a severed head—sparked a celebrated encounter between Gaines and Tennessee Democratic Senator Estes Kefauver, chairman of the Senate Judiciary Committee's 1954 hearings on comic books. On the other hand, comic art critics consider Craig's 1953 adaptation of Ray Bradbury's *Touch and Go* a comic book classic.

When E.C. folded, Craig left the field and became a commercial artist. He was later an art director and then vice president of a Pennsylvania advertising agency. He made several brief reentries into the comic book field in the 1960s. After drawing stories for the now-defunct ACG group and Warren's black-and-white magazines, Craig illustrated for National in 1967 (*Batman* and *Hawkman*) and Marvel (*Ironman* and others, from 1968 through 1970). He now maintains a commercial art studio in Pennsylvania.

J.B.

CRANDALL, REED (1917-1982) American comic book artist, born in Winslow, Indiana, on February 22, 1917. After studies at the Cleveland School of Art (1935-1939), Crandall began his career in 1940 as an editorial cartoonist for the NEA Syndicate, later moving to the Eisner-Iger shop, where he produced top-notch material for Fiction House and Quality comic books.

"Reed was a real problem for Iger," fellow shop artist Gerry Altman once said. "His stuff was so great, everytime he came into the shop we all stopped to look at his stuff. Iger eventually had to tell him not to come to the office with his pages." When Quality publisher "Busy" Arnold saw Crandall's fine-line draftsmanship, he hired him exclusively in 1941, and over the next 12 years, Crandall turned out several dozen features, including *Uncle Sam, The Ray, Capt. Triumph,* and *Dollman.* But he did his greatest work on Quality's top-selling feature, *Blackhawk.*

Created by artist Chuck Cuidera in *Military* (later *Modern*) *Comics, Blackhawk* was a difficult strip to draw. It required an intricate knowledge of guns, tanks, and planes, as well as an exceptional ability to draw exciting "group" shots. Crandall, whose fine art training led him to be influenced by the likes of N. C. Wyeth, Howard Pyle, and James Montgomery Flagg, was one of the few who could draw the feature. His stories were amazingly realistic, leaning more toward classic illustration than cartooning; and aided by Crandall's acute attention to details and his great anatomical skill, *Blackhawk* quickly became one of the most popular strips ever created. Crandall was the feature's main artist from 1942 through 1944, and after a short stint in the Army Air Force, he returned to *Blackhawk* in 1946 and continued to draw it until 1953.

After leaving Quality in the 1950s, Crandall applied his fine-line technique to several highly acclaimed EC "New Trend" and "New Direction" stories, features for the educational *Treasure Chest,* and material for Charles Biro's ill-fated *Tops*—a forerunner of today's black-and-white magazines.

In the 1960s, Crandall collaborated with George Evans to produce several outstanding *Classics Illustrated*

Reed Crandall, "Jungle Jim." © King Features Syndicate.

comics, and he later drew for Gold Key's *Twilight Zone* (1961-1965), for Tower's *Thunder Agents* (1965), and for the comic book version of *Flash Gordon* (1965, 1969). His best later comic book work was for the black-and-white magazines of the Warren Publishing Company. Unfettered by the poor coloring and smaller page size of standard comic books, Crandall's work for Warren during the middle and late 1960's was outstanding in its detail. Always superbly drawn and flawlessly shaded, his horror and "weird" stories were among the best supernatural tales ever produced.

Crandall also drew a lavish, highly acclaimed series of illustrated Edgar Rice Burroughs books for Canaveral Press in the 1960s. Using pen and ink, dry brush, and wash techniques, Crandall's renditions of the Burroughs characters have become classics in a field dominated by artistic giants like Frank Frazetta, J. Allen St. John, Hal Foster, and Burne Hogarth. In later years ill health forced him to give up drawing; he died in 1982.

J.B.

CRANE, ROYSTON CAMPBELL (1901-1977) Roy Crane, whose *Wash Tubbs* daily strip did much to revolutionize graphic and narrative content in the American comic strip, and whose *Captain Easy* Sunday page was one of the half dozen finest color-strips, was born Royston Campbell Crane in Abilene, Texas, on November 22, 1901. Digging oilfield pipelines and jerking sodas while he went to school, the young Roy drew continuously as he grew up in nearby Sweetwater. Stints at the University of Texas and Hardin-Simmons bored him, and Crane struck out for adventure in the Southwest, rail-riding, panhandling, and even working now and again; then he went to sea. Finally he settled in New York, after taking a correspondence course in cartooning, and landed a job as assistant to H. T. Webster on the old *New York World* in the early 1920s. Trying a gag panel series called *Music to the Ear* with United Features, he sold it to two small papers at a dollar each—and went over to the local NEA office to take another flyer. Here the visiting syndicate head turned out to be the same man who managed the correspondence course Crane had taken—and was not averse to hiring a former pupil. He liked a strip notion Crane had built around a curly-headed little fellow named George Washington Tubbs II, and told Crane to shape the character up a bit and put him to work in a grocery store, perhaps, so the working public would like the strip. Crane was too delighted to do more than murmur that the young hero of NEA's *Salesman Sam* strip was also working in a grocery store, but his new boss failed to see why a good idea shouldn't be used twice, and that was that: the *Wash Tubbs* strip was born, and the first episode, a splash layout about Wash, appeared in many NEA papers on April 21, 1924.

By 1929, the popularity of *Wash Tubbs* (and Harold Gray's *Little Orphan Annie*, also a pioneer in bloodcurdling suspense) had sparked numerous imitators, from *Tailspin Tommy* to *Bobby Thatcher*, and Crane had to hustle to keep up his lead. Then Crane launched his stunning display of technical and imaginative virtuosity, the *Captain Easy* Sunday page, on July 30, 1933. The Sunday *Easy* capped Crane's work, and it has never been surpassed for sheer graphic verve and narrative movement, although Alex Raymond's early *Flash Gordon* equalled it for a while. Easy, based on the face and easy movement of Crane's brother-in-law, was

Roy Crane, self-caricature.

never as nationally famed as he should have been, because of the syndication policies of NEA, which preferred to move its strips in packages to small-town dailies, often lacking Sunday editions. So, when Crane moved to Orlando, Florida, in the summer of 1938, he was already considering the line of action that resulted in his outright ownership of his own strip and its appearance in the largest-circulation Sunday papers in the country.

This strip was *Buz Sawyer*, a swift-paced, wartime story of a navy aviator, which Crane launched (owning all rights) via King Features on Monday, November 2, 1943. The Sunday half-page started on November 23, focusing on Sawyer's gunner, Roscoe Sweeney. (NEA kept *Tubbs* and *Easy* going with Crane's understudy, Leslie Turner.) Within a few weeks, it was obvious that Crane had another hit—one that would keep going in hundreds of newspapers for more than four decades. In the 1960s an ulcer condition forced Crane to give up most of the *Buz* work, so that the strip of this period lacked much of the pictorial and narrative zest that characterized it through its first 20 years. But the story line remained entertaining, and the art retained the fundamental characteristics of Crane's work, and it continued to be one of the nation's outstanding adventure strips.

Full of accomplishments, honors, and awards (winner of both a Reuben and a silver plaque from the National Cartoonists' Society; the U.S. Navy Gold Medal for Distinguished Service; U.S. Navy War Correspondent Citation; the Silver Lady award for Outstanding Cartoonist of the Year, 1961, etc.), Crane lived in the lake area of Orlando on an estate of several acres, working with Ed Granberry, creative writing instructor at Rollins College, on the *Buz* story line, and the talented Harry Schlensker on the strip's art. He died on July 8, 1977, in Orlando, Florida.

B.B.

Guido Crepax, "Anita." © Crepax.

CRAVERI, SEBASTIANO (1899-1973) Italian cartoonist, born March 30, 1899, in Turin. His middle-class family sent him to study the classics, but when Italy entered World War I, Sebastiano Craveri was drafted into the army. After the war he worked at a publishing house but quit after a short time to devote himself fully to painting and newspaper reporting; from 1930 to 1934 he contributed humorous sketches to the weekly magazine *Radiocorriere*. In 1931 the first of his humanized animals appeared in the color pages of the *Giornale dei Fanciulli*; in 1932 he also drew a comic feature for the publication *Doposcuola, Porcellino* (whose hero was a little pig that had previously appeared in the *Giornale*). When this publication folded, Craveri, under the pen name "Pin-Tin," edited, wrote, and drew *Quidi*, a magazine for young children published by SEI (1935).

In 1937 Sebastiano Craveri started his long collaboration with the Catholic weekly *Il Vittorioso*, for which he created a great number of animal strips: *Zoo Film, Zoolandia*, the comic adventures of *Pinco Pallino, Giraffone, Tony*, not to mention uncounted stories without permanent characters, fables, and topical illustrations. In 1939 he created a weekly feature for *L'Aspirante* titled *Avventure di Spinarello, Moccolino e Zaratustra*.

In addition to his work for *Il Vittorioso* (which lasted until 1962) Craveri also wrote and drew for the weekly *Corrierino*, in which he created more animal strips: *Buffo, Orsetto* ("Little Bear"), and *Pentonino* (1946-49); for *La Bussola* of Turin (1946); *Famiglia Cristiana* (1953), *Il Giornalino* (1955-66), and others.

During his long career Craveri also illustrated books, worked in advertising, and designed stage plays. His works were all directed at children, for whom he wrote very simple stories illustrated with strongly delineated drawings.

In 1969 a grave illness consigned Craveri to absolute immobility, and he died in Rome on October 25, 1973. His drawings, collected by the "craverian" Mario Giubbolini, are now being reprinted in totality by Camillo Conti.

G.B.

CREPAX, GUIDO (1933-   ) Italian artist and illustrator, born in 1933 in Milan. After high school, Guido Crepax attended the School of Architecture of the University of Milan, from which he graduated in 1958, while supporting himself in the meantime as an illus-

trator of book covers and record jackets. Crepax started his cartooning career in 1959 with drawings for the medical magazine *Tempo Medico*. In 1965 he was one of the first contributors to the newly created comic monthly *Linus*, with a fantastic strip called *Neutron*, about an artist with superhuman faculties. From the strip there evolved Crepax's most celebrated creation, *Valentina* (Valentina was at first a girl-reporter playing a secondary role in *Neutron*).

Valentina brought Crepax fame and recognition, and he embarked on new strip creations: *L'Astronave Pirata* ("The Pirate Spaceship," 1968), a strip midway between science fiction and satire, which was published in book form by Rizzoli; *La Casa Matta* ("The Mad House," 1969), a sadomasochistic fantasy published in the magazine *New Kent*, about a young girl in a nightmarish universe; *La Calata di Mac Similiano* ("The Fall of Mac Similiano," also in 1969), a war story and an allegory on American intervention in Viet Nam; the epic *Alexandre Newski*, and two other series about victimized young girls (a theme evidently dear to Crepax's heart): *Belinda* and *Bianca* (the latter an elaborate reworking of the themes of *La Casa Matta*).

At the same time Crepax has been able to pursue his career as an illustrator for books and magazines, and in 1970 he successfully branched out into animation with a series of animated cartoons for Italian television.

Called by some "the Raphael of the comics," Guido Crepax is one of the most controversial, as well as one of the most fascinating, comic strip artists. His universe is unmistakably and uniquely his own, a universe of violence and sex, where innocence is constantly outraged and vice often rewarded. Crepax's line is a model of elegant decadence, and his inspiration places him in the ranks of the "écrivains maudits," alongside the Marquis de Sade and Baudelaire.

While sporadically continuing to draw the adventures of Valentina, Crepax in the last 20 years has devoted much of his time to illustrating the classics of erotic literature, from the Marquis de Sade's *Justine* and *Juliette* to Pauline Réage's *Story of O* by way of Sacher-Masoch's *Venus in Furs*. He has also given a decidedly erotic treatment to such works as *Dr. Jekyll and Mr. Hyde* and *The Turn of the Screw*. The artist has become quite popular in the United States in recent years, and many of his works have been translated into English as well as other languages.

Widely imitated, although never equalled, Guido Crepax has proved himself, within the space of a few years, as not only one of the great masters of the comic idiom, but also as an innovator whose experiments have already revolutionized the comic form, both in structure and in content.

M.H.

CRIMEBUSTER (U.S.) One of the strangest ironies of American comic books of the 1940s was that although the overwhelming majority of readers were children, the overwhelming majority of characters they read about were adult heroes. The few "kid" heroes that did appear were stereotyped: the "Kid Group" of diverse racial background and social status (i.e., the Boy Commandos and Daredevil's Little Wise Guys); the "kid" spin-off of the adult hero (i.e., Captain Marvel Jr.); or the ingratiatory sidekick who was forgettable (i.e., Robin or Bucky). Two features broke away from the mold, however. Street and Smith had great success with *Supersnipe*—which told the story of Koppy McFadden, the boy with the most comic books in the world (all Street and Smith titles, of course)—and Lev Gleason was phenomenally successful with *Crimebuster*.

Created by artists/writers/editors Charles Biro and Bob Wood for the April 1942 issue of *Boy Comics* (number three), *Crimebuster* told the story of Chuck Chandler, an orphan whose parents had been killed by Iron Jaw, the head of all Nazi agents in America. Vowing revenge—it was the thing to do in the 1940s—Chuck adopted the Crimebuster identity, complete with red and white costume and a delightful monkey sidekick named Squeeks. (Only the *Star Spangled Kid*, a National strip, sported a kid hero and an adult sidekick.)

Almost all the stories in the series were written by the innovative and unpredictable Charles Biro. His stories were sometimes overwritten, but they always exuded a tremendous amount of reality and social concern. *Crimebuster* was not a strip about a midget masquerading as a child hero; Chuck Chandler was a child hero and the readers apparently accepted and liked the concept. Artistically, the strip was graced with many fine illustrators. Besides the flexible Biro (who handled art chores sporadically between 1942 and 1956), Joe Kubert (1955), George Tuska (1954-1955), Dan Barry (1947-1948), Frank Bolle (1953), Bob Fujitani (1950), and Norman Maurer (1943-1953) also contributed to the feature.

Crimebuster outlasted many of his older costumed compatriots, appearing in *Boy Comics* until March 1956's 119th issue. The last nine issues carried the name *Chuck Chandler, Crimebuster* because the character had abandoned his costume. The Crimebuster character also appeared in text stories in the *Daredevil* book from 1942 until 1952.

J.B.

CRIME SMASHER *see* Spy Smasher.

CROSBY, PERCY LEO (1891-1964) When Percy Leo Crosby was the age and size of the 10-year-old hero of his famed *Skippy* comic strip, he used to sit on the curb of a street in the Brooklyn neighborhood where he was born on December 8, 1891, and draw comic pictures in the summer dust with a crooked branch. He forgot little of his boisterous, lower-middle-class Irish boy-

hood, and much of it surfaced for decades in the ragamuffin kid strips he drew from the first moment a newspaper editor let him sketch out an idea of his own. This happened on the old *New York World*, where he received his first job as a strip cartoonist after he had finished high school and gotten work on two other papers briefly as a news artist at 19. Gifted with a great natural talent for easy handling of line and mass, and an amusing if often quirky sense of humor, the young Crosby quickly discovered on the *World* that the kid antics that amused him also delighted his editor and the paper's readers, and he moved from one child-oriented strip to another, fielding such titles as *Babyettes*, *Toddles*, and *Beany and the Gang* in the early 1910s. In 1915, the McClure Syndicate hired him to do a new strip, *The Clancy Kids*, one of whose title characters, Timmie Clancy, was the prototype of Skippy. Crosby turned out this strip with increasing success until World War I intervened, and he went overseas with the American Expeditionary Force.

Returning to active cartoon work in 1919, Crosby freelanced for many markets, notably the old *Life* humor magazine, where he sold a comic strip called *Skippy* by one-page installments. This first-rate showcase for Crosby's talents got him many newspaper offers, and he began his own syndication of *Skippy* in the mid-1920s. The strip's popularity led Hearst to make him several offers, and finally Crosby accepted King Features distribution of his daily and Sunday feature in 1928.

Skippy, like *Peanuts*, was much more than a kid strip, however, and it often reflected its creator's ardent right-wing political biases in amusing ways. More eccentric and strident statements appeared over Crosby's signature in full-page newspaper advertisements in New York and elsewhere, however, as well as in a series of bizarre books he published himself, such as *A Cartoonist's Philosophy* (1931) and *Three Cheers For the Red, Red, and Red* (1936). Needless to say, the sales of these curious works were minor compared to those of Crosby's illustrated *Skippy* novels and strip collections (such as *Skippy, Always Belittlin'*, etc.) in the 1930s. An adaptation of the strip for film starring Jackie Cooper (*Skippy*, 1931) made Cooper a star and *Skippy* an even

Percy Crosby.

more widely known character than Crosby's strip had made him.

Crosby developed his artistry in many mediums, from watercolor to oil painting to sculpture, and he had many acclaimed exhibits of his wide talents in the 1930s and 1940s. In 1942, however, Crosby's health began to fail, and he had increased trouble in maintaining control of his lines (a difficulty strikingly apparent in a number of his last published episodes). Refusing to hire a ghost for the strip, he withdrew it from King Features and formally retired from commercial work in 1943. Married three times, he lived in continuing ill health with his third wife of 1940, Carolyn, until she died in 1960. Finally death came to Crosby too, in New York City on his 73rd birthday, 1964. (According to Jerry Robinson's biography *Skippy and Percy Crosby*, he had spent the last 15 years of his life in a mental institution.)

B.B.

CROSS, STANLEY GEORGE (1888-1977) Australian cartoonist, born in 1888 in Los Angeles, California. His English parents, who had married in Australia, returned there in 1892 and settled in Perth. A brilliant schoolboy scholar, Stan Cross left school at the age of 16 and joined the Railways Department as a cadet clerk and, a few years later, enrolled for an art course at Perth Technical School. In 1912, he resigned from his job to spend a year in London studying art at St. Martins School and other studios—during which time his cartoons were accepted and published by *Punch*. He returned to Perth, where he contributed freelance drawings to the *Western Mail* and the *Sunday Times*.

In 1919, Robert Clyde Packer, the managing director of *Smith's Weekly*, induced Cross to join the staff of the new newspaper being founded in Sydney. For *Smith's*, he originated Australia's first and longest-running newspaper strip, *The Potts* (originally called *You and Me*), which he handled from 1919 until late 1939, when the strip was taken over by Jim Russell. For the same paper he created *Smith's Vaudevillians* in 1928, which also passed to Russell. He also drew a huge volume of single-panel cartoons—one of which ("For godsake stop laughing—this is serious!") has been hailed as the most famous in the history of Australian comic art. During his 20 years with *Smith's*, Stan Cross earned the reputation of the finest draftsman ever to work on that paper and produced a great deal of the work that made him the leading black-and-white cartoonist in Australia.

In 1940, Stan Cross received an offer from Sir Keith Murdock of the *Melbourne Herald* to leave *Smith's* and create a new daily strip. He accepted, but the new domestic strip, *The Winks*, was not successful. Cross then transferred two of the characters from this strip and featured them in a new daily, *Wally and the Major*, which proved to be an outstanding success. He continued to draw this strip until his retirement in 1970, when the strip was inherited by Carl Lyon, who had been his assistant for a number of years. It was during his stay with the *Melbourne Herald* that Stan Cross became the highest-paid journalist in Australia. He died in June 1977.

Stan Cross was the pioneer of the Australian comic strip. His work reflected his superb comic sense, while his expressions and characterizations were always perfect for the never-ending variety of types that inhabited his drawings. His bold and distinctive pen style showed great skill in building up his forms and tones.

His work was influenced by the artists of both *The Bulletin* and *Smith's Weekly* eras—including Cecil Hartt, whose traditional humor he admired, and Norman Lindsay, whose excellence in comic art he came close to equalling during the 1930s. Over the years, he made himself an authority on such subjects as economics, social credit, soil conservation, and grammar—the latter interest being responsible for an almost total absence of slang in his *Wally and the Major*.

J.R.

CROWLEY, WENDELL (1921-1970) American comic book writer and editor, born September 1921. After attending the University of Oklahoma, Crowley began his comic book career in 1941, when he took a summer job as a "gofer" in Jack Binder's art studio. He quickly moved up to writing, however, and began turning out scripts for books the Binder studio packaged for comic publishers. Among Crowley's stories was material for *Captain Battle* (Lev Gleason), *Black Owl* (Prize), *Flying Dutchman* (Hillman), and the whole range of Fawcett features like *Captain Marvel* and *Bulletman*. Crowley eventually became the shop's editor, a position that entailed considerable business work and art directorial decisions. In 1943, however, he moved over to become the editor of the Beck-Constanza studios, which was then primarily responsible for the Captain Marvel family of books.

In 1944, Crowley elected to go with Fawcett as their general editor and assumed control of not only Captain Marvel and family, but of the whole Fawcett line of comics. But his best work was done on the Marvel family, and he is regarded as the best of the Captain's many editors. "He was totally committed to the comic medium," artist/historian Jim Steranko wrote in 1972. "His enthusiasm showed in his work."

Indeed, much of the finest material in the Marvel lore appeared under Crowley's hand. He was instrumental in the creation of the "Society of Evil" serial that eventually brought about the creation of the delightful but deadly Mr. Mind, the world's evilest villain, who just happened to be an intelligent worm from another planet. And Crowley was editor when Mr. Tawny, the talking tiger, was introduced. Crowley was also financially good for Fawcett, as *Captain Marvel Adventures* garnered its best sales reports with him as editor. Crowley finally left as Fawcett's editor during 1950, and Captain Marvel and company faded away several years later.

Crowley made only one brief return to comics. In 1967, he teamed up with longtime *Captain Marvel* writer Otto Binder and artist C. C. Beck to create *Fatman, The Human Flying Saucer*. It was an unabashed and nostalgic imitation of *Captain Marvel*, and Crowley functioned as the editor, but the title lasted only three issues.

Crowley died in February 1970.

J.B.

CRUIKSHANK, GEORGE (1792-1878) English cartoonist, illustrator, and engraver, born in London on September 27, 1792, into a highly artistic family. George's father, Isaac Cruikshank (1756-1810), was a renowned caricaturist, and his older brother Isaac Robert (1790-1856) was at one time more famous as an illustrator than the younger George. A sister, Eliza, and a nephew, Percy, also added artistic distinction to this extraordinarily gifted family.

George Cruikshank.

George Cruikshank was the last cartoonist of note to follow in the footsteps of Rowlandson and Gillray, and provided the link between the 18th-century school of violently contrasted etchings and the realistic style of *Punch* wood engravings. He started his career as a cartoonist for the satiric monthly *The Scourge* and also illustrated several newspaper serials. In 1823 he became equally famous as a book illustrator, but his style remained rooted in caricature. He was called the perfect illustrator for Dickens (and the appeal of his illustrations contributed in no small measure to the novelist's popular success), but he also illustrated *Don Quixote, Robinson Crusoe, John Gilpin's Ride,* and the brothers Grimm's fairy tales. Cruikshank added painting to his already numerous activities in 1853, and he remained creative until his death on February 1, 1878.

George Cruikshank continued and consolidated the work of the early English cartoonists, contributing further innovations to the medium, such as the dynamic use of balloons (he is particularly noted for his invention of the interlocking balloons to mark a rapid-fire exchange of repartees and *bons mots*—a convention still widely used in satiric strips, vide *Mad* magazine). This alone should give Cruikshank a place in the pantheon of the patron saints of the comic medium, somewhere between Rowlandson and Töpffer.

M.H.

CRUMB, ROBERT (1943-   ) In any compendium of this nature, there is always someone who does not fit the strictures of the established pattern. Robert Crumb is such a writer and artist. One hesitates before writing anything about him or his characters, mainly because so much of his work consists of raw, uncensored, unfettered fantasies drawn and written on paper. None of Crumb's work was done for "art's sake," and most of it was done simply for fun, and not to make money. Additionally, Crumb the human being is as elusive as his work. As Mark Estren writes in his underground comix history, "no two people come away from him with the same impression—he seems to change his opinion of himself almost every hour."

Born in Philadelphia on August 30, 1943, Crumb never had any formal art training, and as a teenager, he and his brother began drawing a series of single-copy comic books, usually relying heavily on funny animal material. It was here he developed Fritz the Cat, one of his most important characters, a con-man cat who more resembled humans than the humans Crumb would later depict. In 1962, Crumb moved to Cleveland and began drawing for the American Greeting Card company. In 1964, he married and began traveling and contributing to other outlets. He did several pieces for *Help!*, an offbeat humor book published by James Warren and edited by Harvey Kurtzman. He also began contributing heavily to the blossoming underground newspaper market, which was headed by *Yarrowstalks* (Philadelphia) and the *East Village Other*. He settled down in San Francisco in 1966, about the time the city's Haight-Ashbury section was becoming the home of the "hippie" movement. But, while Crumb might have wanted to be a hippie, he was not. He was an introvert, different not only from the flower children who were his neighbors, but also from the flock of other underground cartoonists who were making the Bay area a hotbed of underground publishing.

Although the underground comix business had "officially" started when Jack Jaxon published *God Nose* in Texas in 1963, it was Crumb's *Zap #0* and *Zap #1* (1967) and his two issues of *Snatch* (1968) that began the modern movement as it was now known. Crumb never published his own books, however; Don Donahue and Charlie Plymell were instrumental in the distribution and publishing of the *Zaps* and *Snatchs*, and after that, Crumb went from underground publisher to underground publisher. His main concern was never money; it seemed he was more interested in working out his fantasies ("The pleasure is ours, folks!" Crumb told his audience in *Snatch* number two, "we really like drawing dirty cartoons!"), having fun, and giving his readers enjoyment. Over the years, Crumb's work has been in dozens of underground publications, including *Uneeda; Big Ass;* and *Motor City Comics,* among many others.

The body of Crumb's work can be divided into two distinct groups. The first is his overtly sexual work. Often indulging every possible fantasy, Crumb's work was shockingly explicit for the late 1960s. Each and every story centered around lovemaking, or kinky variations of it. Crumb pictured himself as an unabashed sex craver who would do anything for any woman. This sexual material was roundly criticized by some (mainly by feminists who complained that almost all his women were stereotypic sex objects; they were right, and even Lenore Goldberg, Crumb's feminist character, eventually was shown to be a closet "Jewish mother"). Crumb was censored by others (Viking Press' *R. Crumb's Head Comix* was unusually explicit for the book market, but they drew the line at Crumb's singing vagina and censored that panel). And occasionally his work led to criminal prosecution (Crumb's celebrated incest story in *Zap* number four caused it to be prosecuted in New York before Judge Joel Tyler in the famed "Zap Obscenity Trial").

Many famous characters came out of Crumb's sexual lore, however: Whiteman, a typical sexually repressed man of modern-day America; Angelfood McSpade, an African amazon, who was a totally sexual and unthinking child of nature; and the "yetti," another Amazonian, hair-covered "woman" who

Snarf #6 cover, Robert Crumb. © Robert Crumb.

eventually captured Whiteman and took him for her lover.

Crumb's other school of work was more philosophical, although not without a healthy dose of sexual fantasy. Out of those works came characters like Mr. Natural, the con-man guru who became a symbol of the younger generation; Flakey Foont, Natural's repressed, hung-up disciple who will probably grow up into Whiteman; Schuman the Human, and many more.

Crumb's art style has traces of many of the old masters, including Segar, Wolverton, Barks, and Herriman. It is sometimes sloppy, rarely cinematic, but always

natural and powerful. It totally changed the traditional standards of "good comic art," and eventually became an art style as recognizable as Peter Max's or Art Déco.

In short, Crumb, a living anachronism in personal life, an introvert outdone only by Howard Hughes, completely changed American mores in the 1960s and early 1970s. He has since sharply curtailed his art production and moved to a secluded farm in California.

J.B.

In the 1980s Crumb edited his own magazine, *Weirdo*, to which he contributed a number of original stories. He also wrote and drew numerous autobio-

Howard Cruse, "Death." © Howard Cruse.

graphical anecdotes of diminishing wit and interest for different publications. The already shaky underground press almost collapsed at the end of the decade, and in 1990 the artist moved to France with his wife Aline Kominsky. The couple was the subject of a 1995 award-winning documentary tersely called *Crumb*. His last work of note has been the 1996 *Kafka*: in it writer David Mairowitz adapted a number of the Czech author's most famous stories (including *The Trial* and *Metamorphosis*), some of which Crumb simply illustrated and others he told in comic-strip fashion.

M.H.

CRUSE, HOWARD (1944-   ) An American cartoonist and illustrator, born on May 2, 1944, in Birmingham, Alabama, Howard Cruse, the son of a Baptist minister, was fascinated by the comics from earliest childhood. "When he was 6 years old," Clarke Stallworth wrote in the *Birmingham News*, "the preacher's son drew his first comic book. It was an adaptation of *Alice in Wonderland,* and little Howard Cruse showed the crude drawings to his parents Clyde and Irma Cruse." With the encouragement of his parents

Cruse continued to draw comics in his spare time, while pursuing a more conventional career as a staff artist and illustrator.

In the 1970s Cruse's comic-strip work started appearing regularly in the pages of underground comic publications such as *Yellow Dog, Snarf,* and *Dope Comix*; he gained national recognition with *Barefootz*, a strip about a naive (and, of course, barefoot) Southern boy, which appeared from 1973 to 1979 in a number of underground and college newspapers. Moving to New York City in 1977, he enjoyed a brief stint as art director of the science-fiction magazine *Starlog*. He came into his own as a comics creator in *Gay Comix* (of which he was the founding editor) with such stories as "Billy Goes Out" which, he said in 1985, "got more response . . . than anything else I've done." From there he went on to develop more features in the same vein, including *Wendel*, which appeared in the pages of the gay magazine *The Advocate* from 1983 to 1989.

Cruse has also contributed a number of comic strips, cartoons, and illustrations to magazines as diverse as *Playboy, Heavy Metal,* and the *Village Voice*. It was with the publication in 1995 of *Stuck Rubber Baby*, a poi-

"Cucciolo," Rino Anzi. © Edizione Alpe.

gnant coming of age (and coming out of the closet) graphic novel set in the South against the backdrop of the civil rights struggle, that Cruse garnered his greatest critical acclaim, along with many commendations and awards.

M.H.

CUBITUS (Belgium) *Cubitus* was created in 1968 for the weekly magazine *Tintin* by the Belgian cartoonist Dupa (Luc Dupanloup).

Looking somewhat like a huge ball of down, Cubitus is a dog who lives in a dilapidated house—in the company of a moth-eaten retired sailor named Semaphore. Cubitus' life would be idyllic were it not for a number of nuisances like the neighbors' cat Senechal; a bothersome (and sports-crazy) phantom who had decided to take up residence in Semaphore's beaten-up motorcycle; and the mysterious Isidore, whose elusive presence sometimes disturbs the canine's generally placid digestion.

"Cubitus," Dupa (Luc Dupanloup). © Editions du Lombard.

When left to himself, Cubitus turns out to be a daydreamer (not unlike Schulz's Snoopy), but his dreams display a peculiar, put-down quality. Whether impersonating Humphrey Bogart or James Bond, Cubitus always manages to remain true to his old self. The most hilarious gags, however, have Cubitus reinterpreting old fairy tales such as "Red Riding Hood" or "Puss in Boots" in a devastating parody usually ending in mayhem.

Dupa's humor, which is unpredictable, fast, and loony, coupled with his easygoing but accurate drawing line, made *Cubitus* into one of the best European gag strips of recent years. It has been reprinted in paperback and hardbound form, and there has also been a *Cubitus* animated cartoon. In 1989 the roly-poly dog even got his own magazine; and in 1990 a series of animated *Cubitus* shorts made in Japan aired on French television.

M.H.

CUCCIOLO (Italy) Around 1940 publisher Giuseppe Caregaro and cartoonist Rino Anzi got together and conceived two new characters: Cucciolo and Beppe. In the beginning these were two little dogs in the Walt Disney tradition. At the end of World War II Cucciolo and Beppe were completely altered and became fully human. This operation proved successful; after a trial balloon the publisher decided to issue a pocket-size comic book featuring the lead character. On December 22, 1951, the first issue of *Cucciolo* (dated January 1, 1952) hit the newsstands.

Some stylistic changes had also taken place in the meantime: in the late 1940s Giorgio Rebuffi had taken over the feature and given it its current graphic line. Some other talented cartoonists assisted Rebuffi over the years: Umberto Manfrin, Tiberio Colantuoni, Motta, etc. Starting in 1959 Pugacioff the steppe wolf (wolfski!) was one character that became very popular with the reader, and in the 1960s he eclipsed Cucciolo as the star of the show.

The *Cucciolo* comic book has also revealed a number of other outstanding cartoonists. For instance, Luciano Bottaro's *Pepito* first appeared in *Cucciolo*, as did Egidio Gherlizza's *Serafino*; Rebuffi also created *Il Sceriffo Fox* (continued afterwards by Colantuoni and Maria Luisa Uggetti), and Antonio Terenghi produced two series, *Gionni e Geppina* and *Caribu*, in the pages of the comic book. Among the writers working for the publication were Roberto Renzi, Attilio Mazzanti, Carlo Chendi, Franco Frescura, Roberto Catalano, and Giorgio Rebuffi.

Cucciolo continues, strong as ever. At first monthly, it was changed to a fortnightly, but it is once more issued on a monthly basis. A good many of the *Cucciolo* features have been published in other European countries, especially France.

C.B.

CULLIFORD, PIERRE (1928-1992) Belgian cartoonist, born in Brussels on June 25, 1928, of a Belgian mother and an English father. After a brief stay at the Brussels Academy of Fine Arts, Pierre Culliford started working at the age of 17 in an animated cartoon studio, alongside such future luminaries of the comic strip as Franquin, Jije, and Morris. In 1947 Culliford created *Johan* (under the nom-de-plume Peyo), his first comic strip, about a young page in medieval times, for the Belgian daily *La Derniere Heure*; it was followed the next year by *Pied Tendre* ("Tender Foot"), the story of a little Indian, which he did for the Boy Scouts' publication *Mowgli*.

In 1954 Peyo (to give him his chosen name) started his long collaboration with the comic weekly *Spirou*, to which he brought his first creation, retitled *Johan et Pirlouit* (Pirlouit was Johan's bumbling companion). From this strip evolved *Les Schtroumpfs* (1957), Peyo's most durable and endearing creation. In 1960 *Benoit Brisefer* made its appearance, written by Peyo and drawn by Will—about a little boy endowed with superhuman strength—followed a few years later by *Poussy* (a kitten), which Peyo created for the women's magazine *Bonnes Soirees* (eventually *Poussy* also ended up in the pages of *Spirou*).

In the 1960's Peyo assisted on the series of animated cartoons adapted from *Les Schtroumpfs*, and he has also done illustration and advertising work. Peyo is the recipient of several cartooning awards, mostly for his work on *Les Schtroumpfs*.

One of the most original of European cartoonists, Pierre Culliford is also a storyteller full of imagination and fancy. His work sets him apart from his contemporaries, and while his style has been widely imitated in Europe, he is one of the few European creators who has been able to construct an entirely original comic strip vision of the world.

In the 1980s the Schtroumpfs enjoyed phenomenal worldwide success, especially in the United States, where they became known as the Smurfs. Animated cartoons, comic books, dolls, toys, and other merchandise soon followed, and in later years Peyo devoted most of his time to overseeing his growing corporate empire. After his death in Brussels in 1992, his son Thierry Culliford took over the family interests.

M.H.

CUORE GARIBALDINO (Italy) Like every other Italian publication, the comic weekly *L'Intrepido* had to close down all its American features (which included *Connie* and *Gordon, Soldier of Fortune*) on orders from the Fascist government in 1938. The publishers, the brothers Del Duca, then decided to concentrate their reinforced national production on one theme: the melodramatic story, of which they became the acknowledged masters.

One such novel was *Cuore Garibaldino* ("Garibaldian Heart"), a title full of patriotic and nationalistic connotations, Garibaldi being Italy's foremost independence hero. Begun in 1939, the story, subtly propagandistic, was written by Ferdinando Vichi and illustrated by Carlo Cossio.

The narrative opens in 19th-century South America where Leardo Stigli, a Garibaldi supporter and foreign agent, falls in love with the beautiful Italian immigrant girl, Stella Natoli. Their love is thwarted by the cruel and unfaithful Carmensita and by the despotic governor of the colony in which they live. The Austrian Captain Stern aids and abets them in their vicious deeds.

These patriotic adventures unfold at length, generation after generation until the present day, with every melodramatic device milked in the process. After the Italian capitulation, the grandchildren of Leardo and Stella make a quick about-face and, as the dialogue indicates, they now stand ready to fight "the Teutonic invaders and their Fascist henchmen."

The saga ends with the inevitable triumph of true love. While a terrible strip, *Cuore Garibaldino* is a fascinating document for anyone interested in understanding Italy's troubled modern history.

G.B.

CURLEY HARPER (U.S.) Started as *Curley Harper at Lakespur* on March 31, 1935 (and later shortened to *Curley Harper*), this strip replaced *The Kid Sister* as the top piece to *Tim Tyler's Luck*. It was distributed by King Features Syndicate and signed by Lyman Young (who had several "ghosts" working on it).

Curley Harper was first an athlete at Lakespur College who constantly won championships and other distinctions for his alma mater, often thwarting the schemes of shady game-fixers and corrupt managers in the process. This clean-cut and clean-living all-American later became an investigative reporter, fearlessly exposing graft in high places and fighting rackets and corruption.

During the war Curley found even better use for his talents as the nemesis of German spies, fifth columnists, and Axis saboteurs. After the war he tried to reconvert himself into an insurance investigator, but the kind of hero he personified had gone out of fashion, and his adventures ended in the mid-1940s.

In spite of its limitations, *Curley Harper* is quite an entertaining strip, always competently drawn and well plotted. In its lack of sophistication it is most revealing of some of the American dreams, prejudices, and fears of the 1930s and 1940s.

M.H.

CURLEY KAYOE see Joe Jinks.

CURTIS (U.S.) A carefully crafted daily and Sunday comic strip about an inner-city African-American family, *Curtis*, by Ray Billingsley, began syndication by King Features on October 3, 1988. This strip followed on the heels of another humor strip by an African-American artist also syndicated by King Features. From mid-1970 until 1988, *Quincy*, a strip about an 11-year-old boy living with his grandmother, was drawn by Ted Shearer. Two years after the death of Shearer and the end of *Quincy*, *Curtis* appeared.

As a 12-year-old living in New York City's Harlem area, Ray Billingsley came to the attention of an editor

"Curtis," Ray Billingsley. © King Features Syndicate.

at *Kids* magazine and worked as a cartoonist from then on. Born in 1957, Billingsley graduated from New York City's High School of Music and Art and was awarded a full scholarship to the School of Visual Arts in New York. He also completed a Walt Disney animation internship. At age 21 his first feature, *Lookin' Fine*, was syndicated for a time by United Features Syndicate. Between *Lookin' Fine* and the first appearance of *Curtis*, Billingsley did extensive freelance work.

As an African-American who grew up in an urban environment, Billingsley draws on his own childhood experiences for inspiration for the characters in *Curtis*. His own parents are models for Greg and Diane Wilkins. Rounding out the family are Curtis and his nosy eight-year-old brother Barry. Like most 11-year-olds, Curtis's life revolves around home, family, school, and a series of inner-city perils not found in family comic strips situated in the suburbs.

Billingsley has stated that his goals in *Curtis* are to make his readers laugh, to present a realistic day-to-day view of urban African-American family life, and to encourage inner-city children. He has succeeded in all three goals. Living in a rented apartment in the city, the Wilkins family is hardworking and religious. Two neighborhood fixtures, the church with Reverend Woodward and the local barbershop with proprietor Gunther, are prominently featured.

At home Curtis and his father constantly bicker over Curtis's love of loud rap music and his father's love of cigarettes. Barry, the devilish brother, does his best to get Curtis in trouble, but it is evident that deep down the brothers love one another. Curtis's mother is the glue that holds the family together.

At school, Curtis has yet to appreciate his teacher's message of the importance of education. He is wrapped up in a puppy love triangle. He longs for the spoiled, aloof Michelle, who knows that she is way too cool for Curtis, while fending off the advances of tomboy Chutney. His best friend is Gunk, a white boy in a student exchange program from Flyspeck Island, part of the northeastern tip of the Bermuda Triangle. Derrick, the school bully, represents the underbelly of inner-city life.

In his standard four-panel dailies, Billingsley uses as much situational humor as gags. Situations involving drug abuse, crime, and the problems of the inner city are handled in a realistic fashion. *Curtis* is a funny strip, but it mixes in hard social commentary with great success.

B.C.

CUTO (Spain) The most famous character in the history of Spanish comics saw the light of print in 1935, in the pages of the comic magazine *Boliche*, under the title of *Cuto, Gurripato y Camarilla*; it was a series of gag strips, without continuity, and its success was scant (it was discontinued after a short run). Its creator, Jesus Blasco, in this first comic strip effort, decided to revive the character, this time without his battery of friends, for the comic weekly *Chicos* (November 27, 1940). With its small boy-hero and a style that was to improve with each passing year, *Cuto* soon became the main staple of the magazine, reaching unheard-of heights of popularity. A newspaper-boy in his first adventure, he converted soon afterwards into a roving adventurer, who lived adventures in the Orient, the American West, the Pacific Islands, and the Egypt of the pharaohs. He was equally at ease among the New York skyscrapers or the snowfields of Alaska.

Cuto's appearance also changed with the years, and he went from young boy to young man, remaining always an adolescent afterwards. With increasing frequency he could be found in the company of his girlfriend Mary, with whom he shared soft drinks and

"Cuto," Jesus Blasco. © Chicos.

adventures. He was always characterized by his wit, thanks to which he got himself out of the most perilous situations that could be concocted by Jesus Blasco. The author had recourse to all the conventions of the comics to enhance the suspense of his strip. *Cuto* is a highly personal work in which the author never stopped experimenting from the start of the feature, playing with color schemes, innovating in the layouts, and sometimes succeeding in making Cuto a genuine masterpiece.

Cuto was made into a radio program and adapted into novel form and a series of short stories. Beginning in the 1970s, the character appeared in the Portuguese magazine *Jornal do Cuto* and in the Spanish comic weekly *Chito*. It is now no longer published, but the character lives on in countless reprints of the earlier adventures.

L.G.

CYBORG 009 (Japan) *Cyborg 009*, created by Shotarō Ishimori, made its first appearance in the Japanese weekly *Shōnen King* in July 1964. Featuring the exploits of Cyborg 009 and his colleagues (Cyborgs 001 through 008), it soon became the most popular science-fiction strip in Japan.

Initially a half-caste juvenile delinquent who had escaped from prison, Joe Shimamura was captured by the evil Black Ghost, the leader of the world's Merchants of Death, who subjected him to experiments aimed at making him into the perfect soldier of future wars. Reborn as a cyborg, 009 could run at speeds higher than Mach 3, had the strength of a hundred men, and could jump over 100 feet. Cyborg 009 and his colleagues, also endowed with special powers, rebelled against the Black Ghost and blew up his secret base with a nuclear device. The battle between the cyborgs and the Black Ghost then started in earnest.

After having vanquished the Black Ghost, Cyborg 009 and his colleagues found many more enemies to combat: Cyborg 0012 (who was as big as a brick mansion), Cyborg 0013 (who controlled a huge robot by means of brain waves), not to mention the Robot Monster, the One-Eyed Robots, the human Bombs, the Skull, the Giant Monsters created by a mad scientist, and the Giant Warriors. Cyborg 009 and his companions also fought against a human race of the future, and even against the gods themselves.

"Cyborg 009," Shotarō Ishimori. © Shonen King.

Ishimori's most popular and longest-lasting work, *Cyborg 009* was published in *Shōnen King*, of the weekly *Shōnen* magazine, and in the monthly *Bōkenō*, before going on to the monthly *Com*, where it appeared for the last time in November 1970.

Cyborg 009 has inspired a series of TV animated cartoons, as well as a full-length animated feature.

H.K.

DAFFY DUCK (U.S.) *Daffy Duck* was created by Fred ("Tex") Avery for a 1936 *Porky Pig* cartoon, "Porky's Duck Hunt," produced by Leon Schlesinger and released by Warner Brothers. The character was originally called "that darnfool duck" but was named Daffy for his second appearance a year later in "Daffy and Egghead." He quickly became a regular in the Warner Brothers stable of characters, often appearing with Bugs Bunny or Porky Pig in cartoons directed by Frank Tashlin, Robert McKimson, Chuck Jones, Fritz Freleng, and others. In 1951, he joined the other W.B. characters in the *Looney Tunes* and *Merrie Melodies* comic book produced by Western Publishing Company under the Dell logo.

Previously, a duck resembling Daffy had guest-starred in some stories in that comic and a duck named Daffy (but not resembling him in appearance or actions) had appeared in some one-page gags. In 1951, however, the Daffy Duck of the cartoons joined the magazine, guest-starring first in the *Henery Hawk* strip and later as permanent guest star of the *Elmer Fudd* strip, beginning with the November issue of that year. In December 1954, Daffy took over the *Elmer Fudd* strip and began a popular series in *Looney Tunes* until it was discontinued in 1962. Daffy was featured as a zany, crazy duck who delighted in mooching free meals off Elmer Fudd and, later, Porky Pig and Yosemite Sam.

In 1953, Dell also issued a one-shot test issue of *Daffy* in the Dell Color Comics series, number 457. It proved so popular that two more followed before the first issue of *Daffy*, released in April 1955. In 1959, the title was expanded to *Daffy Duck*, and in 1963 the magazine made the transition when Western Publishing Company shifted its books from the Dell logo to Gold Key. The character appeared in all other magazines based on Warner Brothers characters, including a number of *Bugs Bunny* giant specials, *Elmer Fudd, The Tasmanian Devil and his Tasty Friends, Golden Comics Digest, March of Comics*, and the revived *Looney Tunes* book (1975).The *Daffy Duck* comic book ended its run in 1983.

Scripts for *Daffy Duck* were supplied by, among others, Lloyd Turner, Don Christensen, Bob Ogle, Jerry Belson, and Mark Evanier. Most of the artwork was done by Phil DeLara until his death in 1973. Other artists include Jack Manning, Joe Messerli, and John Carey.

M.E.

DAIHEIGENJI (Japan) *Daiheigenji* ("A Boy of the Western Plains") was created by Shigeru Komatsuzaki and made its first appearance in the June 1950 issue of the monthly *Omoshiro Book*.

The strip featured the exploits of Daiheigenji Jim, a 15-year-old western scout whose parents had been killed by the King Hell Gang. Brought up by his father's friend Petousu, Jim became an expert marksman and horse rider. Mounted on his white stallion Bright Moon, Daiheigenji fought against the Apaches, the King Hell Gang, the Wolf Girl, and Red Bear (both of them King Hell's accomplices), with the assistance of Tomahawk Morgan, the mysterious chief of the Chit-supetsu tribe whose weapon was a golden tomahawk, and of the beautiful Cherio. There was also a heroine named Jane who had a mole in the form of a butterfly on her left arm and was a missing person with a prize on her head.

The main theme of *Daiheigenji* was the American pioneer spirit of the frontier. In addition to the excellent stories, *Daiheigenji*'s greatest charm resided in Komatsuzaki's graphic style. His drawings were realistic and minutely documented; his compositions powerful and dramatic. Komatsuzaki made especially good use of the double-page center spread. *Daiheigenji* was the first Western strip born in the postwar era, and its popularity was due in great part to Komatsuzaki's art.

Daiheigenji last appeared in October 1952.

H.K.

DALLIS, NICHOLAS (1911-1991) American psychiatrist and author, born in New York City on December 15, 1911. Dallis' family moved to Glen Cove, Long Island, when he was a young boy, and he was educated in public schools there and at Washington and Jefferson College in Washington, Pennsylvania. He graduated from Temple School of Medicine in 1938 and became a general practitioner near Reading, Pennsylvania. Dallis decided to become a psychiatrist and completed four years of residency at Henry Ford Hospital in Detroit before setting up private practice in Toledo, Ohio.

Dallis always loved comics and drew cartoons for his college newspaper. He developed the idea for a "doctor strip" in 1948, and with the help of Allen Saunders, a Toledo acquaintance, took the concept to Publishers Syndicate. Two artists were engaged: Marvin Bradley and Frank Edgington, and the product, *Rex Morgan, M.D.*, debuted on May 10, 1948.

With its success, Dallis and publishers developed another story-strip, this time based on the legal profession—*Judge Parker*. Dan Heilman was the first artist, succeeded upon his death by his assistant, Harold LeDoux. Further success led to a third collaboration, *Apartment 3-G*, with the art supplied by Alex Kotzky.

Dallis abandoned his psychiatric practice in 1959 as the pressure of writing necessitated the abandonment of medicine. Before his work in comics, Dallis had edited his college newspaper and written periodically for pulp magazines.

The trio of Dallis and his friends Allen Saunders and Elliot Caplin account for the major portion of contemporary story strip production. Dallis exemplifies the conversion of the straight strip from adventure to domestic, soap-opera continuity. His story lines were solid and respectable, although rarely exacting. Dallis' characterizations could be interesting (especially in 3-*G*) but were seldom as mature and never as versatile as Elliot Caplin's. He died on July 6, 1991, in Scottsdale, Arizona, where he had retired.

It should be noted that Dallis' three strips are relatively healthy survivors in the days of the twilight of the story strip, when many of their straight neighbors are dying.

R.M.

DAMONTE TABORDA, RAUL (1939-1987) An Argentine cartoonist born in Buenos Aires in 1939, Raul Damonte Taborda (better known as "Copi") started his cartooning career in the 1950s in the humor magazine *Tía Vicenta*. He then went to the satirical publication *Cuatro Patas*, before moving to Paris in 1961. There he worked with great success, contributing to such publications as *Bizarre* and *Le Nouvel Observateur*; soon his cartoon pages made him famous throughout Europe.

Copi's distinctive graphic style, his wiggly line, and the situations in which he put his characters became a trademark. His famous chicken, his woman sitting on a chair, and his questioning little girl became known in France, the United States, Italy, and Spain and helped him win the Prize of Black Humor.

In addition to his magazine work, Copi made several animated cartoons and wrote several plays (in which he also acted): *El Día de una Soñodora* ("The Day of a Girl Dreamer"), *Té Inglés* ("English Tea"), *Navidad en Ia Isla de los Pacíficos* ("Christmas on a Pacific Island"), *El Caimán, La Cola del Pescado* ("Fish Tail"), and the comedy in drag, *Eva Perón*. He died of AIDS in Paris on December 14, 1987; his last play, *La Visite Inopportune*, was staged after his death.

L.G.

DAN DARE (G.B.) Daniel MacGregor Dare, Colonel O.U.N. Interplanet Space Fleet, was awarded the Order of the United Nations for leadership in the Venus Expedition of 1996. Born on February 5, 1967, in Manchester, England, and educated at Rossall, he finished Cambridge and Harvard Universities and became a Class 3 Space Pilot by the time he was 20. Two years after a Planetary Exploration Course on the moon, he became Chief Pilot of the I.S.F. at the age of 30. His hobbies are cricket, fencing, riding, painting, and model-making.

The official biography differs slightly from the real one. *Dan Dare*, created by Frank Hampson and the Rev. Marcus Morris, was born on the first and second pages of *Eagle* number one, April 14, 1950. His subtitle, *Pilot of the Future*, narrowly missed being *Chaplain of the Future*; it was first intended as a Christian comic of limited sales. However, publisher Edward Hulton took up the idea and helped Morris and Hampson launch the weekly comic that changed the face of British children's publications.

Dare, with his lightning-jagged eyebrows, was pure invention, but Sir Hubert Gascoine Guest, Marshal of Space, K.C.B., O.M., O.U.N., D.S.O., D.F.C. (born 1943) was modeled on Hampson's father. Dare's faithful companion and batman was Spaceman Class 1 Albert Fitzwilliam Digby ("Dig" for short), born Wigan. Others in the regular crew were Professor Jocelyn Mabel Peabody ("Prof"), expert on nutrition, agriculture, and botany, and honorary Pilot/Captain;

"Hank," Pilot/Captain Henry Brennan Hogan of Houston, Texas, red-tape hater; and "Pierre," Pilot/Major Pierre August Lafayette from Dijon, an analytical mathematician whose hobby was gastronomy. There was also Dig's Aunt Anastasia, after whom a two-seater spaceship was named in recognition of the old lady's part in the overthrow of the Mekon of Venus, oppressor of the green Treens, in 1996. (The Mekon was Dare's archenemy.)

Writers of *Dan Dare* after Hampson included Alan Stranks, David Motton, and Eric Eden. Artists who worked on Hampson's pencilings or, later, in his style were Harold Johns, Donald Harley, Bruce Cornwell, Desmond Walduck, Frank Bellamy, and Keith Watson. Harley drew the weekly newspaper strip that ran in *The People* on Sundays (1964).

At the height of Dare's fame, a daily radio serial sponsored by Horlick's was broadcast over Radio Luxembourg. Dan was played by the former *Dick Barton* (actor Noel Johnson). There was considerable merchandising, apart from special appearances in *Eagle Annual* and *Dan Dare's Spacebook*: Dan Dare ray guns, wrist compasses, card games, filmstrips and viewers, inflatable rings, telescopes, periscopes, bagatelle, uniforms (playsuits), Lifebuoy soap stamps, etc. A Dare fanzine, *Astral*, official journal of the International Dan Dare Club, was published through Volume 3, Number 12.

Eagle was taken over from Hultons by Longacre Press/Odhams on March 19, 1960, but the rot began to set in. Clifford Makins took over the editorship, printing changed from color gravure to litho, and Frank Hampson left, disillusioned. *Dan* was reduced to monochrome reproduction in 1962, but restored to the front page in 1964. In 1966 it was down to a single page. Reprinting began in 1967 under the title *Dan Dare's Memoirs*. I.P.C. took over the comic in 1969 and killed it on April 26 (issue 991). For a while the title continued as part of another comic, *Lion and Eagle*, with Dan relettered and redrawn from the originals. By 1971 even that subtitle had gone. However, a happy revival occurred in September 1973, when *Dan Dare Annual* was published, reprinting *Red Moon Mystery* and *Safari in Space* in full color and in their entirety. A "modernized" Dan Dare series started in the all sci-fi comic *2000 AD* (1977) drawn by Dave Gibbons; and later still the original *Eagle* was revived as a part-photo, part-comic magazine in 1982. Once again Dan was reborn with further "modernization," all of which upset the original Dan fans. Finally a book publisher brought out the entire original run of *Eagle* strips in a series of facsimile volumes. Of the many plans to make television and cinema films of Dan's adventures, the only one to reach the screen has been a commercial.

D.G.

DAN DUNN (U.S.) Norman Marsh's imaginative, well-paced, but stiffly drawn and ill-plotted detective strip, *Dan Dunn, Secret Operative 48*, began daily on October 16, 1933, and Sunday the following week, with the daily and Sunday narrative continuous for many years. Created for Publishers' Syndicate as an inexpensive alternative to *Dick Tracy*, *Dan Dunn* featured a detective hero who was in the U.S. Secret Service, as the subtitle indicated. Dunn had a pet "wolf dog" (apparently a German shepherd) named Wolf, who frequently attacked a hood or two. Later, Dunn befriended an adopted orphan girl named Babs. Babs

"Dan Dunn," Norman Marsh. © Publishers Syndicate.

and Wolf pal around together during much of the continuity, thus making the strip a competitor with *Little Orphan Annie*. Dunn also acquired a fat, comic assistant named Irwin Higgs, who appeared in a number of routine Sunday-page gag sequences in the late 1930s, as well as bumbling about in the daily narrative. With many of its plot devices borrowed straight from the pulp magazines of the day, *Dan Dunn* provided a wilder and stranger story mix than *Dick Tracy* much of the time. It featured such master villains as a Fu Manchu parallel named Wu Fang and a death-ray wielder (who operated a dirigible from a mysterious island) named Eviloff.

Popular until Marsh began to dilute the fearsome story lines with more routine criminal material (and featured in several 1930s Big Little Book reprints), *Dan Dunn* declined sharply in readership after 1940, chiefly because subscribing papers decided to go the higher price and buy *Dick Tracy*. Marsh himself enlisted in the Marine Corps in 1942 after wangling a commission, and the strip was continued by a Paul Pinson, then by Alfred Andriola. The latter's slicker art did not help, and *Dan Dunn* finally folded obscurely in the pages of a handful of small newspapers before the close of the war (1943).

Marsh went to King Features on his return and immediately undertook a direct imitation of his own *Dan Dunn*, complete with Irwin, called *Hunter Keene*, which lasted a year, from April 15, 1946, to April 12, 1947. This was followed by a second strip named *Danny Hale*, a pioneer epic, which was similarly short-lived. Perhaps the "pulpiest" of the 1930s crime strips—in fact, the strip itself was the basis for a briefly extant dime novel pulp called *Dan Dunn*, which ran for two issues in the fall of 1936—*Dan Dunn* deserves at least partial reprinting as an often amusing record of the taste in strips during its time.

B.B.

DANNY DINGLE (U.S.) Certainly the most obscure of the really memorable strips of the 1920s and 1930s, Bernard Dibble's *Danny Dingle* is difficult to pinpoint as to its beginning and ending dates. Launched in early 1927 by King Features as a bottom-string strip, *Danny*

Dingle began as a daffy romantic comedy with rapid-fire continuity, unlike anything else in print. Wildly slapstick and hilariously drawn—Dibble's art here, as elsewhere, is infectiously funny—the new strip was too unusual and insufficiently exploited by an obviously dubious King Features to catch on. When Dibble was hired by United Features to ghost *The Captain and the Kids* for Rudolph Dirks (and actually byline the strip for a short period in the early 1930s), he renewed *Danny Dingle* with the new syndicate, this time with larger success. Accompanied by an anecdotal Sunday page (where the companion half-page, a weird extravaganza involving slobbish and hirsute men with little, mockingly angelic wings on their backs, was called *Dub-Dabs*), *Danny Dingle* ran from the early 1930s until the latter part of the decade, being reprinted regularly in *Tip-Top Comics*, and even appearing in a comic book collection of its own in 1939.

Notable in the *Dingle* cast were Danny himself, a "lemon-haired" youth; Pa Dingle, Danny's father and most frequent companion; Ma Dingle; Nellie Maloney, Danny's girl; and Otto Maloney, her father. Intermixed were a variety of crackpot inventors, men from outer space, political revolutionaries, gangsters, corrupt politicians, etc., all done with a fresh and ingenious touch. After 1940, when Dingle disappeared as a strip and when Dibble was ghosting much of *Fritzi Ritz*, as well as drawing *Iron Vic* in *Tip-Top Comics*, the cartoonist took over *Looy Dot Dope* from Johnny Devlin (who had originally carried the strip on after its creator, Milt Gross, left it), and continued it in much the same manner as *Danny Dingle*, actually carrying over Pa Dingle (renamed Dilbury) as Looy's buddy. Dibble's *Looy* ran for several years in the 1940s, largely as a reprint feature in *Tip Top Comics*, then vanished as abruptly and unascertainably as *Danny Dingle*. One of the great comic narrators and artists of the strip form, Bernard Dibble reached his creative peak in *Danny Dingle* and its *Looy Dot Dope* appendage—yet went largely unseen and unappreciated because of his offbeat content and his syndicate's inadequate understanding of the worth of his work. Needless to say, this area of Dibble's work should be reprinted in full, as soon as an adequate and reproducible run has been assembled.

B.B.

DAREDEVIL (U.S.) 1—Even though Siegel and Shuster's *Superman* didn't start the costumed hero boom until 1938, by 1940 the comic book industry was already overrun with "superheroes." But Don Rico and Jack Binder combined to create one of comic book's most unique strips, *Daredevil*, in the September 1940 issue of *Silver Streak* (number six); it was published by Comic House (later Lev Gleason). Even the character of Bart (Daredevil) Hill was innovative: not only didn't he have any powers, but he also used a boomerang, perhaps the only hero of his time to do so; instead of the standard cloth belt, Daredevil used a spiked steel one; and rather than some pedestrian superhero jumpsuit, Daredevil sported a suit that was blue on the left and red on the right.

The earliest *Daredevil* stories were fast-paced, but relatively standard: Daredevil and his constant companion/fiancée Tonia Saunders locked horns and eventually defeated some tremendous menace to the country. The paramount menace was the evil Claw, a particularly malevolent villain who flitted from Lev Gleason title to Lev Gleason title to battle the book's paramount superhero. In July 1941, this mix of action and intrigue merited Daredevil his own book, which was first entitled *Daredevil Battles Hitler*, and then simply *Daredevil*.

The year 1941 brought a new editor, Charles Biro, who proved to be one of the most innovative artist/writer/editors in the field. In *Daredevil* number 13 (October 1942), Biro introduced the Little Wise Guys and then very quickly moved into the spotlight, eventually easing Daredevil out of his own feature. And it was here Biro shone, as his Little Wise Guys became the most popular kid group in comics. As it happened, the group was formed when one of them, Meatball, ran away from his orphanage and met up with Scarecrow, another runaway. Meanwhile, Jocko (later called Jock) saves Pee Wee (who adopted the name Slugger) from a beating, and the four meet in a barn and declare their friendship for one another. Shortly after, the group is saved by the millionaire playboy Daredevil, and he and the Wise Guys begin a long series of adventures together.

Writer Biro was a gutsy, innovative scripter, and tradition was broken when Biro killed off Meatball and replaced him with Curly, an unsavory-looking convert from a street gang called the Steamrollers. Even more gutsy was Biro's totally shocking decision to write Daredevil out of his own strip and let the Wise Guys carry the ball. He last appeared in *Daredevil* number 69 (December 1950), but the boys carried on for five years without him.

Over the years, *Daredevil* showcased many fine artists, too, including Biro himself (1941-1943 and covers until 1950), coeditor Bob Wood (1941), Dan Barry (1947-1948), Norman Maurer (1943-1948), cocreators Rico and Binder (1940-1941), and later Tony DiPreta. In all, *Daredevil* appeared in *Silver Streak* until December 1941's 17th issue, in 134 issues of *Daredevil* (the last issue dated 1955), and in text stories in Boy comics sporadically during the 1940s.

2—The second *Daredevil* strip was created by writer/editor Stan Lee in June 1964 and premiered in the first issue of Marvel's *Daredevil*. In reality a lawyer named Matt Murdock, Daredevil was blind but compensated for that fact by increased hearing, strength, and radar senses. The strip was more action-oriented than most Marvel features, but also had strong supporting characters like Matt's partner Foggy Nelson; his first love interest, Karen Page; and even a bogus brother Matt, invented to allay suspicions that he was Daredevil. Later in the series, after Karen Page was written out, The Black Widow, a Communist spy-turned-American-superheroine, became Daredevil's love interest and partner.

Over the years, *Daredevil* has had a group of good artists, including Bill Everett, Joe Orlando, Wallace Wood, Jack Kirby, John Romita, and definitive illustrator Gene Colan. Among the writers were Lee, Colan himself, Gerry Conway, Tony Isabella, and definitive writer Roy Thomas.

J.B.

The character received a makeover at the hands of Frank Miller, who arrived on the scene in 1979; starting as a penciller on the series, he also took over the writing chores in 1981. During his tenure Daredevil engaged in a grim battle against the almost invincible Kingpin and the female assassin (and the hero's former lover) Elektra. After Miller's departure in 1983, the strip, despite some occasional flashes of brilliance, turned mostly into just another humdrum superhero comic book.

M.H.

DATELINE: DANGER! (U.S.) Writer Allen Saunders's son John and artist Alden McWilliams teamed up to

"Daredevil." © Marvel Comics Group.

"Dateline: Danger!" John Saunders and Al McWilliams. © Field Newspaper Syndicate.

Dateline: Danger! is not, as some have claimed, the first "integrated" strip (there has been Mandrake and Lothar; the Spirit and Ebony White) but it is the first one to represent black and white heroes on an equal footing.

Although not on a par with the adventure classics of the 1930s and 1940s, *Dateline: Danger!* is among the very few worthwhile action strips to come out of the adventure-starved 1960s. It was discontinued in 1974.

M.H.

DAUNTLESS DURHAM *see* Desperate Desmond.

DAVE (U.S.) David Miller's comic strip *Dave*, about the life of a twentysomething single guy, was first syndicated by Tribune Media Services in 1992. The strip focuses on relationships, using them to provide both humor and insight. As a member of Generation X straddling the space between his college years and a more responsible adult life, Dave claims that he detests everything Yuppies stand for, "everything . . . except the part about owning all that neat stuff!!!"

Miller first drew a precursor to *Dave* as an undergraduate at the Rhode Island School of Design. Following his graduation and a turn as an automobile designer, Miller settled on cartooning as his career choice. His timing was good, and *Dave* became Tribune Media's offering to appeal to not only twentysomethings, but also to men and women of a variety of ages.

Of great importance in Dave's life is his relationship with his childhood sweetheart, Darla. The relationship does not always go smoothly, and Dave and Darla have broken up on occasion. At work, where he is a mid-level office worker, Dave's relationship with his boss has more of the personal Dagwood Bumstead overtones rather than the alienated relationship *Dilbert* has with his boss. Miller combines the realism of a

produce *Dateline: Danger!* in November 1968 for Publishers Hall Syndicate.

The strip introduces Danny Raven, a black man and former football hero, currently a reporter for the Global News Co., and his white colleague Troy (short for Theodore Randolph Oscar Young). Danny and Troy are also U.S. undercover men on the side, and their adventures take them from Africa to Europe to South America, where they cover (and uncover) riots, coups d'etat, and other assorted upheavals and conspiracies (the overall idea was obviously inspired by the then-popular TV show *I Spy*).

Closer to home, Danny, along with his sister Wendy and his younger brother Lee Roy, often has to foil the plots hatched by black extremist Robin Jackson, publisher of the underground newspaper *The Revolt*.

"Dave," David Miller. © Tribune Media Services.

bachelor's life with politically incorrect moments with humorous results.

For example, in a strip that showed Dave double-dating at a restaurant, Miller has the women at the table thinking, "I'd like something fattening, but I'll probably have a salad." Simultaneously both men look at the waitress and think, "That waitress was hot. She probably wants me!"

David Miller is a mountain-bike enthusiast and has successfully worked his interest in the sport into the strip. He uses brisk, clean lines with little crosshatching or benday in drawing the strip. As often happens as a strip evolves, Dave's appearance has changed to a chubbier fellow with a more filled-out face in the years the strip has been in syndication. Darla, who initially was a full-figured young woman with a head of wild hair, has been toned down with a more slender figure and a simple ponytail hairstyle.

A contemporary strip for the 1990s, *Dave* has many story lines to continue to develop. Will he drift from Generation X to Generation Next as a commitment-challenged bachelor? Will he marry Darla or another woman and become a family man? As always in David Miller's *Dave*, relationships will be key to the future and the humor of the strip.

B.C.

DAVE'S DELICATESSEN (U.S.) Milt Gross's least-remembered major strip, *Dave's Delicatessen*, a wildly fanciful work, was begun for King Features in June 1931 as both a daily and Sunday strip. Usually called "Dave," "Davey," "Honest Dave," or (by his employees) "Mr. Dave," but otherwise unnamed, Dave operates a zany, down-at-the-heel delicatessen in a middle-sized town, with the bumbling assistance of a nephew named Chester. The imaginative range of the strip is extensive, however, quickly involving Dave and Chester with spies, racketeers, labor thugs, and locals over a good part of the globe. Both Sunday and daily strips involved ongoing continuity interspersed with one-episode gags, with the Sunday strip more inclined toward the latter, but the tone of both was lunacy and absurdity.

In December 1933, Count Screwloose joined Dave in his concern with the movie career of Dave's dalmatian, J. R. (known as *The Spotted Wonder*, he was featured briefly in a daily strip of the same name in late 1933), and became engaged in Hollywood-scene escapades on and off the movie lots, reflecting Gross's own script-writing background of the time.

During a later adventure of Dave and the Count in the French Foreign Legion, the title of the Gross King Features strip was changed (on January 20, 1935) from *Dave's Delicatessen* to *Count Screwloose*. The daily *Dave's Delicatessen* had already been dropped in 1934. Thus the strip of that name was effectively ended, although Dave himself continued as a central character in the newly named strip for a short while.

B.B.

DAVIES, ROLAND (1910-198?) British cartoonist, animator, illustrator, and painter, Roland Oxford Davies was born at Stourport, Worcestershire, on July 22, 1910. Educated at Hanley schools, he studied art at Ipswich Art School from 1926-28. For seven years he was a lithographic artist and designer of cinema posters at a printer in West Drayton. He first freelanced cartoons to *Motor Cycle* magazine, and gags in the form of

a strip. Always obsessed by cars, planes, and speed, he freelanced illustrations to *Autocar* and *Modern Boy* weeklies. Curiously, the antithesis of these drawings was the inspiration for his first newspaper strip: *Come On, Steve!*, which described in a weekly pantomime gag the adventures of a horse and cart! The strip moved from the *Sunday Express* to the rival *Sunday Dispatch*, where it continued for another 10 years. While on the *Express* group, he drew his first comic page, *Larry Leopard*, for the colored cover of the weekly comic supplement, *Daily Express Children's Own* (1933-34). Also for the *Sunday Express*, he did a weekly sports cartoon and the strip *Percy the Policeman*. Signing himself "Pip" he drew a daily pocket cartoon for the *Evening News*, and *Bessie*, a weekly strip featuring a charlady, in the green-paper Saturday Magazine of the *News Chronicle*.

Davies taught himself animation in 1936 and produced his own series of cartoon films starring *Come On, Steve!*, opening a studio in Ipswich. Six cartoons were made in all, but the venture failed through lack of financial support. He drew strips for D. C. Thomson's new weekly comic *Beano* (July 1938), *Whoopee Hank*, and *Contrary Mary*; the latter strip, featuring Mary the Moke (a close relation to Steve), was reprinted years later in *Weekly News* as *Neddy the Cuddy*. He then drew *Charlie Chasem*, a speed cop, in *Knockout* (1939), and joined the staff of the *Sunday Dispatch* as topical/political cartoonist throughout the war.

He returned to comics in 1949 by taking over the long-running serial *Sexton Blake* in *Knockout*, beginning with *The Red Rapier* series on December 10, 1949. He also did the comic series *Old Phibber* and *Sparks & Flash* in 1950, adapted the film *Ambush* in *Knockout*, and then changed publishers for the *T.V. Comic* series: *Norman and Henry Bones* (1953), *Jack & His Baby Jet*, and a super-hero, *Red Ray, Space Raynger* (1954), who grew popular enough to have his own club and badge. Also in 1954, he did *Roddy the Road Scout* and *Topple Twins* in *Swift*. *Snowfire* (1959) in *T.V. Comic*; *Pete Madden* (1961) in *Knockout*; *What's Cooking* (1962) in *Girl*. He took over *Sally* in *School Friend*, and *The Trolls* in *Princess*, and he drew the British version of *Beetle Bailey* in *T.V. Comic* (1965). He did children's series (panels) in *Woman's Realm*: *Pedro* and *Sheepy*; and also drew in full color many episodes of Walt Disney's *Jungle Book*, *Peter Pan*, *Winnie the Pooh in Disneyland* (1971), and war strips: *Victor* (1974).

Books: *Steve Steps Out* (1937); *Steve of the River* (1937); *Great Deeds of the War* (1941); *Knights of the Air* (1943); *Steve Goes to London* (1946); *Adventures of Steve* (1947); *Come On, Steve! Annual* (1947); *Steve's Xmas Holiday* (1947); *Steve on the Farm* (1948); *Steve's Dream* (1948); *Steve and the Little Engine* (1947); *All About Engines* (1948); *Daily Mail Speedway Book* (1949); *Steve & the Burglar* (1949); *Steve & the Racing Car* (1949); *Daily Mail Motorcycling Book* (1949); *Come On, Steve! Annual* (1950); *Ace Book of Speed* (1952); *Famous Trains* (1953). Retiring from the weekly grind of strip cartooning, Davies took up painting in his late years. With former comic-book publisher Alan Class as his agent, he staged several successful exhibitions before his death in the late 1980s.

D.G.

DAVIS, JACK (1926-) American comic book and comic strip writer and artist, born in 1926 in Atlanta, Georgia. After studies at the University of Georgia, Davis went north in 1951 and entered the comic book field as a writer and artist for the fledgling "New

Jack Davis, comic book illustration. © E.C. Comics.

Trend" line of William Gaines' EC comics. His unique, personalized art style made him an instant favorite and his work stands as some of the finest to come from the EC era of 1950-56.

In the serious vein, although Davis did some work on the EC crime and science-fiction titles, his best work came under the direction of Al Feldstein's horror titles and Harvey Kurtzman's war and Western line. His horror work was always extremely effective because of its contrast; while Feldstein was writing heavy tales of gore and retribution, Davis was illustrating in an almost comic style. His characters were always common-looking, but almost always depraved and disheveled. Many consider his finest horror tale "'Taint the Meat, It's the Humanity," a grotesque story of a crooked butcher during the rationing days of World War II. After killing his own child with poisoned meat, he is hacked to death by his wife, who displays the dismembered butcher's body in his display cases. In another story, "Foul Play," Davis rendered several controversial panels in which a ball player is ripped apart and used as baseball equipment.

Under the direction of Harvey Kurtzman, Davis produced some absolutely breathtaking war, Western, and adventure stories, but the best was probably "Betsy," a Western tale written and sparklingly illustrated by Davis. But Kurtzman and Davis' collaboration reached fruition in Kurtzman's *Mad*, perhaps the finest American satire and parody book ever produced. Collaborating with other fine humor talents—Wallace Wood and Will Elder among others—Davis helped contribute to the cluttered *Mad* style. Besides his zany figures, always in motion and exaggerated to humorous extremes, Davis crammed his panels with dozens of sight gags, funny people, and crazy illustrations.

When Kurtzman left *Mad*, Davis followed him to *Trump*, *Help!* and even *Playboy*'s lush *Little Annie Fanny*, but also eventually returned to *Mad* and remains one of its most talented and prolific contributors.

When the bulk of the EC line folded in 1956, Davis made a brief attempt to continue work in serious comics at Atlas, but his stylized and innovative humor work led him into the illustrating field. Within several years, he became the most sought-after advertising artist in the country and has worked in almost every

advertising medium. Davis developed into a top-notch cartoonist as well as a cover artist (*Time*, *TV Guide*, and many others), and he may well have been the best-known and most often seen artist of the 1970s.

Davis has also worked on several syndicated strips, including *The Saint* and *Beauregard*, in addition to the *Superfan* strip for *Quarterback* magazine. In 1973, Nick Meglin wrote an excellent chapter on Davis' humor work in his Watson-Guptill book, *The Art of Humorous Illustration*. In the last 20 years Davis has become famous for his album covers, illustrations, humorous ads, and work for such high-circulation magazines as *TV Guide*, *Esquire*, and *Time* (for which by his own count he has drawn over 30 covers to date). He was the subject of a book-length study, *The Art of Jack Davis*, published in 1987.

J.B.

DAVIS, JIM (1945-   ) Creator of the most famous cat in newspaper comics, cartoonist Jim Davis was born on July 28, 1945, in Marion, Indiana. Surrounded by nearly 25 cats while growing up on a farm near Fairmont, Indiana, he became aware of their mystical appeal and instinctive behavior. While he was kept indoors often due to his asthma, his mother provided him with pencil and paper, prompting Davis to focus his boyhood imagination on drawing funny animals. In 1963 Davis entered Ball State University as an art and business major, followed by two years as a pasteup artist with an advertising agency. For nine years beginning in 1969, Davis was assistant to Tom K. Ryan on the Western humor strip *Tumbleweeds*, providing backgrounds, borders, and speech balloons. In addition to rendering freelance commercial art and copywriting at this time, he also developed his first strip, *Gnorm Gnat*, which was rejected by syndicate editors because of its insect characters. Davis noticed that there were virtually no felines in contemporary comics and developed *Garfield*, about a curmudgeon of a cat with a sardonic sense of humor but a heart of gold. United Feature Syndicate accepted the idea and launched the feature in 41 newspapers in 1978. Perfectly suited in concept and appearance to both cat lovers and those who appreciated *Garfield*'s wit, the strip quickly flourished.

In the beginning, Valette Greene assisted Jim Davis on the strip, while now dozens are employed at his company—Paws, Incorporated—which develops and manages the media and merchandising industry the strip has spawned. In 1986 the cartoonist saluted his rural roots with the publication of his short-lived strip *U.S. Acres*, a comic that featured the zany escapades of farm animals, aimed exclusively at younger readers.

Recognized by the National Cartoonists Society with its Best Humor Strip, Reuben, and Elzie Segar Awards for unique and outstanding contributions to the comics field, Jim Davis has helped redefine the modern humor strip by adhering to his philosophy that "the only legitimate reason for a comic strip to be is to entertain." He lives with his family in Albany, Indiana.

B.J.

DAVIS, PHIL (1906-1964) American cartoonist and illustrator, born March 4, 1906, in St. Louis, Missouri. Phil Davis studied at the Washington University Art School while working as a commercial artist for the local telephone company. In 1928 he started work on the *St. Louis Post-Dispatch* as an advertising artist while at the same time contributing illustrations and covers for various magazines. In 1933 he met writer Lee Falk and together they created *Mandrake the Magician* for King Features Syndicate. *Mandrake* appeared as a daily on June 11, 1934, and as a Sunday feature in February of 1935.

During the war Davis was drafted as art director of the Curtiss-Wright aircraft company; as such he edited and partially illustrated the instruction manual for the A-25 bomber. At about the same time his wife Martha (a talented fashion designer in her own right) joined him to work on the drawing of *Mandrake*. Phil Davis died of a heart attack on December 16, 1964.

Davis' ability to create subtle moods and tones with a few simple lines, the right placement of objects and characters, and a touch of shading, has earned him the admiration of many artists and filmmakers, such as Alain Resnais and Federico Fellini.

M.H.

DE BECK, BILLY (1890-1942) Billy De Beck, the comic strip poet of America's big-city and sporting life of the Jazz Age and depression, was appropriately born in Chicago, on April 15, 1890. He grew up in middle-class surroundings and attended the city's prestigious Academy of Fine Arts, graduating in 1910. After some early success on a local paper, he returned to the academy in 1918 to head a cartoon school for a short time.

De Beck landed his first job as a cartoonist on the Youngstown (Ohio) Telegram in 1910. In 1912, he left the *Telegram* to do political cartoons for the *Pittsburgh Gazette-Times* until 1914, when he obtained his first Chicago opportunity on the old *Herald* and launched his first two comic strips: *Movies Featuring Haphazard Helen* (an anonymously drawn Sunday-page takeoff on film melodrama), and *Married Life* (a daily and Sunday gag strip featuring a number of argumentative married couples, one of which would later serve as prototypes for the early Barney Google and wife). De Beck also did a panel on the daily sports page for the *Herald*, which ran under various topical titles. When the *Herald* was done in by the *Chicago Tribune's* infamous newsprint-cornering tactics in 1917, De Beck and his *Herald* strip peer, E. C. Segar, found jobs on the two Hearst Chicago papers: De Beck taking the sports cartoonist's seat on the old *Examiner*.

After a few months there, De Beck introduced *Barney Google* as a quasi-daily strip, reviving the last of the *Married Life* squabble teams as the stars. The story line

focused on husband Barney's attempts to sneak out to the racetrack without his wife finding out. *Examiner* readers loved it and howled for more; Hearst took note, and abruptly De Beck found himself in New York, on the great *American* comic strip staff, doing *Barney* as a nationally syndicated sports page feature. Barney's 1922 acquisition of the horse Spark Plug cost him his home, of course, but gained him nationwide fame. A Sunday page was slow in coming, but by 1923, *Barney* was running in full color weekly almost everywhere. In 1925, De Beck added a subtle takeoff on *Little Orphan Annie* to the Sunday *Barney* page, entitled *Parlor, Bedroom, and Sink, Starring Bunky*, whose most famed character, aside from the diminutive, night-capped Bunky, was the despicable Fagin. In 1934, after racing an ostrich as well as Spark Plug and other horses, and managing a prizefighter named Sully, who was as preternaturally strong as Popeye, De Beck's Barney took to the Kentucky hills and met the hillbilly duo of Snuffy and Lowizie Smith (or Smif), who became so enormously popular that they took over the strip by the early 1940s.

When De Beck died in 1942, after a full and active life of travel, golf, and exhaustive socializing (his assistant from 1933, Fred Lasswell, often remarked on how much of the world he got to see with De Beck: Havana, Lake Placid, New York, etc.), his strip was continued by Lasswell, with the emphasis increasingly on Snuffy Smith, as it is today. This De Beck classic, easily one of the 10 greatest American comic strips of all time, was marked by its stunning graphic imagery from the outset, its often hilarious visual and verbal comedy (De Beck coined such once-famed comic terms as "Sweet Mama," "the heebie-jeebies," "horse feathers," "OKMNX," "Osky-Wow-Wow," and "So I took the $50,000"), and a rare mastery of narrative suspense and intrigue—the latter evidenced in the daily strip of the 1920s and in the Sunday *Bunky*, and often overlooked by students of the genre.

B.B.

DELAČ, VLADIMIR (1927-1969) A Yugoslav cartoonist born in Slavonski Brod, on October 13, 1927, Vladimir Delač graduated from grammar school in Zagreb and in 1946 sold his first cartoon for 200 dinars to the humorous paper *Kerempuh*. The subject of his cartoon was the United Nations. Very soon he became a member of the *Kerempuh's* editorial staff and eventu-

Vladimir Delač, "Marina." © Vladimir Delač.

"*Delta 99*," Carlos Gimenez. © IMDE.

ally published over 1,500 cartoons in that paper. In 1950, together with Walter Neugebauer and Borivoj Dovniković, he produced the first Yugoslav cartoon film, *Veliki miting* ("The Big Meeting"). In 1952 Delač finished his own cartoon film, *Revija na dvoristu* ("The Review on the Yard").

Comic strips were Delač's great love, and in 1950 *Ornladinski borac* published his first comic strip, *Vuna Kićo orasi Mićo*. In the following years he published many comic strips in *Vjesnikov zabavni tjednik, Petko,* and *Miki strip*. His most popular character, *Svernirko*, was born in 1957 and started appearing in the *Globus* magazine, but in 1959 Delač moved his little hero from outer space to the pages of *Plavi vjesnik*, where his gags were published for almost 10 years. Delač's other characters—*Ivica Bucko, Viki and Niki, Marina, Davor, Tramvajko, Toma Vank,* and others—were also very popular in Yugoslavia, thanks to his fine style and original humor.

During the last months of his life, Delač was very ill, but Svemirko and Davor did not leave the pages of *Plavi Vjesnik* and *Arena* until their creator died in 1969. Delač's very last gags were done standing near the drawing board on long winter nights, because he was unable to sit down or to sleep.

E.R.

DEL CASTILLO, ARTURO (1925-1992) Chilean cartoonist and illustrator Arturo Del Castillo was born in Concepción in 1925. Del Castillo started his professional career as a commercial artist. Following in the footsteps of his brother, Jorge, also an illustrator, he moved to Buenos Aires in 1948. There he got a job as a letterer on the comic weekly *Aventuras*. A year later he started his collaboration with *Intervalo* magazine with a series of comic strips, and he quickly became famous among comic strip scholars for his incredibly skillful and detailed penwork, an artistic mode in which he is an acknowledged world master.

In the late 1950s Del Castillo worked for Fleetway Publications, contributing a number of comic strip adaptations of Alexandre Dumas's novels, such as *The Three Musketeers* and *The Man in the Iron Mask*. His most famous creation, however, remains *Randall*, a Western he brought to life in 1957 on a script by Hector Oesterheld; in *Randall* Del Castillo refined his graphic style even further, drawing his backgrounds with a fine network of pen lines that imitated benday and gave his work a highly personalized look. Other important works by Del Castillo followed: *Garret* (1962), published in the magazine *Misterix*, with scripts by Ray Collins (pseudonym, E. Zappietto); *Larrigan* and *Ringo* (both 1964); two more Westerns, *Dan Dakota* and *Los Tres Mosqueteros en el Oeste* ("The Three Musketeers in the West"); and *El Cobra* (also written by Ray Collins), which is currently being published in the Buenos Aires review *Skorpio*. In his later career he worked mainly for an Italian publisher and for the Argentinian Ediciones Record until his retirement in 1989. He died in Buenos Aires in January 1992.

L.G.

DELTA 99 (Spain) *Delta 99* was created by cartoonist Carlos Giménez in 1968, on a script by Flores Thies, and it lasted for 30 complete episodes, each published separately.

The locale of *Delta 99* is a faraway galaxy from which the titular hero is sent to Earth on a peace mission by the confederation of planets to which he belongs. Intelligent, but without any super power or herculean strength, Delta 99 is a curious character, at once sensuous and cold. He lives with a wealthy woman pirate named Lu, who maintains, spoils and adores him at the end of each adventure.

In a second stage, after Giménez had left and the illustration work had passed into the hands of Usero, Mascaro, Nebot, and especially Manuel Ferrer, and with new scripts by Roger (the pseudonym of series producer José Toutain) and Victor Mora, Delta 99 was changed from a sex-hunting extraterrestrial being into a secret agent with a lively sense of humor. In his new adventures (in which could now be found a number of

Gianni De Luca (and William Shakespeare), "Ofelia." © De Luca.

private jokes) he eschewed the woman-robots of his first exploits to tangle with female adventurers and ballerinas.

Created in black and white, *Delta 99* was later reprinted in its entirety in color, with new texts by novelist José Maria Mendiola.

L.G.

DE LUCA, GIANNI (1927-1991) Italian artist and cartoonist, born January 25, 1927, in Gagliano (Catanzaro); died June 6, 1991, in Milan. While studying architecture, Gianni De Luca started drawing comics for the Catholic weekly *Il Vittorioso*. After his comic book *Anac il distruttore* ("Anac the Destroyer," 1946) was published, he drew *Il Mago da Vinci* ("The Wizard from Vinci," 1947-48), which highlighted some aspects of the artist Leonardo da Vinci's life. Then came a succession of remarkable adventures set against historical backgrounds: *Prora vichinga* ("The Viking Prow," 1949),

L'impero del sole ("The Empire of the Sun," 1949), *La Sfinge nera* ("The Black Sphynx," 1950), *Il tempio delle genti* ("The Peoples' Temple," 1950).

In 1951 he published *Gli ultimi della Terra* ("The Last Survivors on the Earth"), the story of the tragedy of those who have survived an atomic disaster. De Luca's elegant and impressive style is enriched by the use of unusual shading to counterpoint the emotions of the characters and by the different psychological expressions he gives his characters.

In 1957 De Luca left *Il Vittorioso* and started collaborating with the other Italian weekly, *Il Giornalino*, for which he produced several illustrated series on the Bible and the history of the Catholic Church. In 1969 the weekly's content was revised and its graphics were updated. Beginning in 1970, De Luca illustrated a new series of comics written by Gian Luigi Gonano, *Il Commissario Spada* ("Commissioner of Police Spada"), a character who deals more with the social implications of criminal cases than with solving the crime. Here De Luca experimented with his technique. In the years 1975-76 he reached the peak of his creative graphic invention with the so-called Shakespearean trilogy: *La Tempesta* ("The Tempest"), *Amleto* ("Hamlet"), and *Romeo e Giulietta* ("Romeo and Juliet").

In these comic adaptations of the plays, De Luca begins to employ, instead of the single panel, the entire page as a basic graphic unit. The page, which has a single setting, is divided into panels to advance the narration through the images of the characters in action. Instead of dividing the page into geometrical and artificial panels, he utilizes the natural (e.g., a tree) or architectural (e.g., a column) elements of the single setting to divide the successive stages of the narration. Later on he eliminated all divisions within the single setting, instead depicting the characters in different successive positions in order to describe the action, with a final strobe effect.

In the following years De Luca drew several covers for the Comic Art reprints of American vintage comics, which were done in album form. He continued to draw the *Il Commissario Spada* series and other stories for *Il Giornalino*, including *Il giornalino di Gian Burrasca* (1983), an adaptation of Vamba's humorous novel for children, *Paulus* (1987), *Avventura sull'Orinoco* ("Adventure on the Orinoco River," 1988), and *La freccia nera* (1988), an adaptation from R. L. Stevenson's *The Black Arrow*. With the graphic novel *Paulus*, De Luca carried on his research in graphic style. Here he tells on parallel planes, on the same page, two stories: one set in the distant past, dealing with Saint Paul's conversion and the spread of Christianity; the other of the science-fiction genre, set in the distant future.

De Luca worked up to the end of his life: the story *I giorni dell' impero* ("The Days of the Empire") was published posthumously in 1990-91 in *Il giornalino*. In 1977 he was awarded a Yellow Kid prize in Lucca.

G.C.C.

DÉMON DES CARAÏBES, LE (France) An enjoyable sea-adventure story created by Jean-Michel Charlier (script) and Victor Hubinon (art), *Le Démon des Caraïbes* ("The Devil of the Caribbean") ran in *Pilote* magazine from the first issue (October 29, 1959) until September 1967.

The titular hero (or antihero) is the one-eyed, red-bearded pirate, Barbe-Rouge, who sails the Spanish Main aboard his ship, the *Black Hawk*, spreading slaughter and terror in his wake. He is assisted by his adopted son, Eric, who follows his father out of a sense of loyalty, and by his two henchmen, the gigantic black Baba and the lame and devious Triple Patte ("Triple Paw").

A healthy dose of humor, good draftsmanship (Hubinon's improvement is quite impressive when compared to his shaky start on *Buck Danny*), and hearty adventure made *Le Démon des Caraïbes* into a quite entertaining strip. After Hubinon's death in 1979 the series was sporadically continued by Joseph Gillain and his son Laurent (who signed "Lorg"); Patrice Pellerin and Christian Gaty have carried on from 1982 to this day.

M.H.

DENNIS THE MENACE (G.B.) Not to be confused with the American *Dennis the Menace*, the British character who bears the same name has little in common with his Yankee cousin other than a love for mischief. Actually his is more a mania for mischief, and so the British Dennis is closer to those practical jokesters, the Katzenjammer Kids, than to Hank Ketcham's lovable moppet.

The late David Law created Dennis for D. C. Thomson's weekly *Beano*, drawing him in a style that got looser and wilder through the years. Dennis's first appearance was on March 17, 1951, in a half-page strip headlined "Look! Here's a new pal you'll enjoy—He's the world's wildest boy!" When Dennis persists in walking on the park grass, his dad puts him on the leash instead of the dog! On September 8 Dennis moved to the red and blue of page two, mowing down fences with a homemade steamroller made from a garden roller and a soapbox.

On March 7, 1953, the strip increased to a full page of 15 panels, and on February 13, 1954, it moved to the full-color back page. Dennis celebrated by taking over a railway engine! In 1969 he was joined in his escapades by an incredible mess of black hair and teeth, a dog called Gnasher. So popular was this beast that the title was changed to *Dennis the Menace and Gnasher* in 1971. The ultimate triumph came on September 14, 1974, when Dennis and Gnasher took over the front page of *Beano*, moving the previous occupant, *Biffo the Bear*, to the inside!

"Dennis the Menace," David Law. © Beano.

Law created a female counterpart to Dennis, *Beryl the Peril*, and other descendants of his original include *Minnie the Minx*, by Leo Baxendale, and *Roger the Dodger*, by Ken Reid. An annual reprint, *Dennis the Menace Book*, began publication in 1959.

So well established is this British Dennis that Ketcham's American character had to be rechristened *The Pickle* for his British reprint. In the 1990s Dennis became the first British children's comic character to be animated, and a series of half-hour cartoons was released to television and for home-screen viewing as *The Beano Video* (1994). In support were other *Beano* comic heroes, the Bash Street Kids, the Three Bears, and Ivy the Terrible. They were produced by Flicks Films and directed by Terry Ward. The credits included 58 names, but nowhere were the original cartoonist-creators mentioned.

D.G.

DENNIS THE MENACE (U.S.) Hank Ketcham's *Dennis the Menace* appeared for the first time, as a single-panel daily, on March 12, 1951, and soon became so popular that the Hall Syndicate, which distributed the feature, added a Sunday page a year later.

With *Dennis the Menace* Hank Ketcham proved that the kid strip was not yet dead (as many syndicate editors then believed). His tiny hero is a tousle-haired, enterprising tot whose counterfeit innocence, unflattering candor, and joyous vandalism are in delightful contrast to the docile conformity of the adult world. Dennis (who was inspired by the cartoonist's own four-year-old son) is the terror of his suburban neighborhood, whose quiet he disrupts with his devilry and high jinks: his targets are often his harassed parents, Henry and Alice Mitchell, who usually stare in helpless wonder at their son's irrepressible shenanigans.

"Dennis the Menace," Hank Ketcham. © Field Newspaper Syndicate.

The Mitchells' next-door neighbor, the grouchy and miserly Mr. Wilson, also figures high on the list of Dennis's hapless victims. Margaret, a precocious prig often at odds with Dennis, Joey (Dennis's inseparable friend and accessory in mischief), and Ruff (his idiot dog possessed of an irrational fear of cats), complete the merry cast of characters.

Ketcham's scripts for his Sunday page are always funny and refreshingly acerbic, while his daily one-line gags often display a barbed point. His graphic style is unobtrusive in its appearance, yet highly effective in its purpose. Since the late 1980s Ketcham has left most of the artwork to his assistants, Ron Ferdinand and Marcus Hamilton.

Dennis the Menace has been consistently popular for close to 50 years: its very title has become a household word. It has been reprinted in hardcover by Holt and in paperback by Fawcett (over 20 titles published to date), and has its own Dell comic book. In the 1960s a long-running television series starring Jay North as Dennis was broadcast by CBS. A live-action *Dennis the Menace* movie, with Mason Gamble in the title role and Walter Matthau as Mr. Wilson, came out in 1993.

M.H.

DERICKSON DENE (G.B.) *Derickson Dene Super Inventor* can lay claim to being the first British superhero strip. Although its heroes possess no physical superpowers, their fantastic adventures qualify the strip for the distinction. It was certainly the first British strip to follow the American comic book format. The captionless strip, with dialogue carried purely through speech balloons, was considered so revolutionary by the traditional Amalgamated Press that they billed the strip as "A Thrilling Story You Don't have to Read!" The comic book technique was also imitated in that Dene's strip formed a four-page detachable center section to a weekly story paper, *Triumph*, although in later issues the space was somewhat reduced.

Dene, working on a detector device to protect London's banks, was kidnapped by flying batmen and taken to the hideout of the Vampire, who sought his collaboration on a Planet-Rocket. They arrive on an unknown planet where they are attacked by Giant Rhamdhorns, Medusa Snakes, and Apemen. Dene's metal-melter saves the day.

The first serial ran from July 8 to July 29, 1939, when *Dene* was replaced by the first British reprint of *Superman.* But popular demand brought him back, and on September 23 *Derickson Dene in the Valley of Frozen*

"Derickson Dene," Nat Brand. © Triumph.

Monsters began. Still marooned in space, Dene took an ice-car to the realm of the Snow-Mammoths and tunneled his way to a tropical jungle where Dryptosaurs threatened and Basilisks flew. In November came a new saga, *Sabotage and War*, which took Dene under the sea to Marshland. This scenario concluded with his rocket return to Earth on February 17, 1940. However, that proved to be Dene's farewell appearance, although a new serial was trailered: *The Nazi Spy Ring*.

Dene was written and drawn by Nat Brand, who modeled his hero, and his drawing style, on Alex Raymond's *Flash Gordon*. His artwork improved considerably during the series, but the "Yankee" style was frowned upon by A.P. and Brand found no more work. He turned to the minor publisher A. Soloway and created some excellent serial heroes for their comic books: *Crash Carew* (Daredevil of the Stratosphere) in *Comic Adventures*; *Argo Under the Ocean* in *All Star*, which also featured *Dandy McQueen* (of the Royal Mounted); *Halcon* (Lord of the Crater Land) in *Comic Capers*; and *Bentley Price* (Scientific Detective). These ran approximately quarterly throughout 1940-49. Brand later created *Steve Samson* (Strongman of Sport) for the Mans' World Comics series, but seems to have drawn remarkably little for so promising and exciting a talent.

D.G.

DE SOUZA, MAURICIO (1936-   ) Brazilian cartoonist, born October 7, 1936, in Santa Isabel, a city near São Paulo, but raised in Mogi das Cruzes. At age 17, Mauricio De Souza moved to São Paulo and worked for the daily newspaper *Folha de S. Paulo* as a crime reporter. He often submitted daily comic strips to the newspaper, until the editors accepted one entitled *Bidu and Franjinha* about a boy and his dog. In 1959, he quit his reporting job and dedicated his career to the comics. He married and had a daughter, Monica, who was the inspiration for one of his strips: *Monica and her gang*. De Souza started creating strips with male characters inspired by boys he knew from childhood: *Cascão*, a boy who hated baths, and *Cebolinha*, a boy with only three strands of hair. He developed a gallery of children characters: *Penadinho*, about a small phantom; *Chico Bento*, a hillbilly; *Astronauta*, *Nico Demo*, a demon boy; *Anjinho* ("Li'l Angel"); and *Horacio*, a dinosaur orphan. His strips were distributed in the small newspapers in Brazil. A food company bought the rights to one of his characters, a green elephant, to use in a television campaign, and the character was a hit. In 1970, Editora Abril launched a full-color monthly magazine,

Monica, and eventually other De Souza characters were given their own titles. The sales of these monthly magazines were good, and once he moved to the Editora Globo, which was owned by the TV Globo group, sales of his magazines reached the millions each month, surpassing Disney publications. Today De Souza makes feature films for theatrical release, animates cartoons for television and home video, shows, theme parks, theater, CDs, CD-ROM, phone answering services, and the Internet. He has become the most successful cartoonist in the Brazilian comics industry. He was awarded Italy's Yellow Kid.

A.M.

"Desperate Dan," Dudley Watkins. © Dandy.

DESPERATE DAN (G.B.) "Desperate Dan was born in the town of Tombstone, and all the natives of that town are tough, but Desperate Dan was the toughest of them all." So begins the official biography of this famous comic hero as published in *The Wizard Midget Comic*, a one-shot giveaway dated September 11, 1954. It continues: "His Paw was a quarry-man at the granite quarries. When Dan was six months old his Paw used to bring home useless hunks of granite too hard for making tombstones, for his baby to chew. That helped his teeth to come through the gums." The extraordinary mixture of British and American lore that gives this strip so much of its charm comes in the following paragraph, which describes how 12-year-old Dan loved playing cricket and hit every ball a mile out of town! Cactusville, where Dan settled, is noted for its quaint British lampposts and, from time to time, its trams and gasworks!

Dan's real birthday was December 4, 1937, and his birthplace was number one of *Dandy*, the first weekly

Mauricio De Souza, "Monica." © Mauricio De Souza.

comic published by the Scots firm of D. C. Thomson. His three rows of pictures on page two expanded to a full page of five rows in 1940, and he fills a similar page to this day.

Created by Dudley D. Watkins, Dan has been drawn in his style ever since. Originally something of a bad hat, Dan mellows to use his super-strength on the side of law and order. He lives with his Aunt Aggie, who bakes him cow-pie (with the horns in) for supper, and the bane of his life is Desperate Danny, his tough little nephew, who came on a visit on June 4, 1949, and is still around—so is niece Katey, who arrived in 1957. A hardback reprint, *The Dandy's Desperate Dan*, was published in 1963.

D.G.

DESPERATE DESMOND (U.S.) The young Harry Hershfield's first comic strip for the Hearst papers was a direct imitation of C. W. Kahles' popular *Philadelphia Press* Sunday half-page, *Hairbreadth Harry*. Unlike *Harry*, Hershfield's new *Desperate Desmond* strip was daily, although it ran only six times in the first month of its appearance in the *N.Y. Journal*, where it began on March 11, 1910. Its popularity grew rapidly, and it ran regularly in Hearst dailies and other papers around the country for the next few years.

Hershfield's *Desmond* copied Kahles' early *Harry* format in featuring a stalwart hero and his betrothed lady-love faced with a fiendish villain in a top hat and tails, and by running a largely redundant narrative text beneath each panel. Hershfield's strip, however, was named for its villain rather than its hero and showed greater ingenuity and wit from the outset than did the more labored Kahles work.

The burlesque melodrama content of Desmond lent itself to suspenseful continuity from episode to episode. It was the first daily strip after *Mutt and Jeff* to utilize this device. The first episode, for example, opens with Desmond trying to throw lovely Rosamund from a high tower of the Brooklyn Bridge, from whence she is rescued by Claude Eclair, the hero, who has

tightrope-walked a cable to save her in the nick of time, and closes with Claude trussed loosely by Desmond to the minute hand of a huge tower clock, from which he will fall 900 feet at 5:27.

On July 12, 1912, Hershfield gave Desmond, Claude, and Rosamund an announced "vacation," effectively ending their adventures after 28 months, in order to do a political burlesque with the strip—to Hearst specifications, of course. The new version featured Rosamund Election, Desmond Prohibition, and three heroes: Claude Taft, Claude Roosevelt, and Claude Wilson. This hastily conceived epic was switched to the editorial page, where it ran intermittently over the election months, while Hershfield introduced *Homeless Hector*, his old pre-Hearst strip, to the *Journal* comic page.

By 1913, the political nonsense was over, and Hershfield replaced Hector on January 22 with a new daily strip called *Dauntless Durham of the U.S.A.* This strip, minus the subpictorial text of *Desmond*, followed the same basic pattern (adding a touch of English caricature), with a hero, Durham, a heroine, Katrina, and a dark-eyed villain, Lord Havaglass, who was a moustached Englishman accompanied by a valet, Watkins. By March 12, 1913, Lord Havaglass had become the president of Mexico and Desperate Desmond was reintroduced as the primary heavy. Desmond and Durham went at each other for the remainder of the year, and then on January 31, 1914, Durham wed Katrina, Desmond retired to home life (he had a wife and three kids all the time), and the Desmond odyssey ended for good. It is all entertaining to read even today, and deserves reprinting.

B.B.

DETEKTIV SCHMIDTCHEN (Germany) *Detektiv Schmidtchen* ("Detective Smitty") may have been the only daily newspaper adventure strip to come out of postwar Germany. The series was created and initially written by Frank Lynder, who hoped to raise a German comics emporium of Disney dimensions, but the project never came off, allegedly because of a lack of German comic artists. *Detektiv Schmidtchen* was drawn by Friedrich-Wilhelm Richter-Johnsen, who had moved to Hamburg in 1954 to work for the Springer newspaper chain. It was in the largest of the Springer newspapers, *Bild-Zeitung* (Picture-News), that *Detektiv Schmidtchen* started on May 6, 1954. When Lynder's idea of a large-scale comics production did not work out, he went on to other journalistic pursuits, even abandoning his comic strip creation. The strip had to continue, however, so Richter-Johnsen, while continuing to draw the strip, also started to write it. The strip continued in *Bild* until March 26, 1962. It was killed off not because of lack of reader interest but because it was so decreed by the new editor-in-chief, who disliked comic strips. Since then *Bild*, which at times could boast national sales of almost five million copies per day because of its blood-and-guts sensationalism, has used strips like *Bugs Bunny* and *Sesame Street* as a kind of TV tie-in, but they are usually discontinued after very short runs.

Detektiv Schmidtchen is a very unusual type of detective; he is a tiny white mouse. Schmidtchen is the pet of the elderly, kind, and energetic Kommissar Schmidt ("Police Commissioner Smith"). Schmidt carries his pet along wherever he goes and this is only natural since the pet, whose beady eyes uncover even

"Desperate Desmond," Harry Hershfield. © International Feature Service.

the tiniest of clues, provides his master with a perfect record of solved crimes. Schmidtchen's incentive may be the special ration of milk and crackers the commissioner offers to him whenever a crime is solved. It goes without saying that Schmidtchen has scared his share of females during Schmidt's investigations.

While never boring, the strip had an aura of calmness, largely due to its artwork of a somewhat academic realism. This was a welcome change in a newspaper of *Bild's* kind of sensationalism. It is regrettable that in Germany editors put their dislike of the strip medium above reader interest.

W.F.

"Diabolik," Angela and Giulana Giussani. © Astorina.

DIABOLIK (Italy) *Diabolik* was created by two sisters from Milan, Angela and Luciana Guissani, in the winter of 1962.

Diabolik is a supercriminal, an athletic antihero. He is cast in the usual hero mold of being both brave and clever. He is also a master of disguise who not only changes his facial features (by the use of plastic masks of his own invention) but also has gadgets that can transform his physical appearance. He is a modern-day version of the fabled rogue Arsene Lupin or the infamous Fantomas, in that he doesn't fight on the side of the law, as do traditional heroes, but against it, for his own amoral purposes. Theft and murder are his *modus vivendi*—but he pursues both with the skill and the intelligence of a master chess player.

While the reading public acclaimed *Diabolik*, the strip was immediately accused by puritans of "exalting crime and violence." Because of this the feature has been nicknamed "fumetto nero" (black comic strip); but Diabolik does not symbolize evil in every respect—one should not grant him total immorality. He is a superman (in the Nietzschean sense), and for him the morality of the average man is irrelevant. Stealing and killing does not ease his conscience, however—for he has a conscience and has demonstrated it many times. His own morality keeps him from breaking his monogamous relationship with Eva Kant, his beautiful and inseparable companion, and an essential figure in the story. Diabolik's code also compels him to come to the help of those loyal to him. On the other hand, Diabolik would destroy those who betray or deceive him, and likewise would eliminate those who might cross his path, not because of blood lust, but for the same reason one might crush an irritating insect.

Diabolik respects only those who are not afraid of him, or those who oppose him with a conviction equal to his. His main opponent is Ginko, a policeman who is Diabolik's double—perhaps an alter ego who has chosen good over evil. The stories in *Diabolik* present the encounter between two equally pure consciences who have deliberately chosen different and opposing paths.

The feature, though now written and drawn by a variety of ghosts, is still under the firm control of the Guissani sisters, who personally supervise the art assignments. The present staff consists of Flavio Bozzoli, Alarico Gattia, Sergio Zaniboni, Franco Paludetti (pencils); Glauco Cretti and Enzio Facciolo (pencils and inks); Paolo Ongaro, Lino Jeva, and Saverio Micheloni (inks).

Diabolik has given rise to a phenomenon of great importance in the Italian comics—the "fumetto nero" or "per adulti" (for adults only). Despite public outcry, political and media denunciation, and even condemnation from the Church, the amoral antihero has been pursuing his nefarious career for over 35 years now.

G.B.

DIAMOND, H. LOUIS (1904-1966) Henry Louis Diamond, British cartoonist, editor, and publisher, was born in 1904 in Bath, Somerset, where he died on October 13, 1966, at age 62. He worked on the *Daily Herald* and began freelancing strips to children's comics published by Fleetway Press. *Sweet Hortense* (1924) in *The Monster Comic* led to his drawing the full front page of *The Golden Penny* from their Hundredth Celebration Number: *High Jinks at High School* (1924). He replaced this with the extraordinary strip *Pot T. Pot and his Pet Patient, Piecan* (1927). Early strips for Amalgamated Press include *Ginjar the Turk* (1926) in *Butterfly*. After A.P. bought out the Fleetway comics, he drew for *Frolix* and *Rover*, the D. C. Thomson boys' paper, but was quick to join a local Bath firm, Provincial Comics, when they tried comic publishing in 1931.

He drew *Micky the Merry Midget* on the front of *The Merry Midget* and *Alfie, Auntie & Annabel* for *The Sparkler*, soon taking over editorial control of these weeklies. The venture failed within six months but, enjoying

H. L. Diamond, "Chuckle Our Own Clown." © Ovaltiney.

the experience, Diamond enlisted another Bath printer and set up Target Publications. After a trial run with two weekly story libraries, *Target* and *C.I.D.*, he brought out his first pair of comic weeklies, *Rattler* and *Dazzler* (August 19, 1933). The first issues were bumper 16-page affairs for one penny, but he soon settled down to 12 pages. Thus, although the artwork was generally lower than A.P. standards (Diamond paid half-a-crown [12-1/2 p; 25 cents] per panel), to indiscriminating children they were a bargain buy, having four more pages for the price than their A.P. counterpart.

Diamond followed with *Chuckler* (1934), *Target* (1935), *Rocket* (1935), *Sunshine* (1938), and *Bouncer* (1939), plus the giveaway *Ovaltiney's Own Comic* (1935), all with artwork by the same team: E. H. Banger, Bert Hill, S. K. Perkins, G. Larkman, and Diamond.

Target publications sold out to A.P. in 1939, and all the titles were immediately discontinued. Diamond was not given the editorial post he had been promised, but returned to freelance drawing for A.P.'s *Jester* and *Crackers*. There was an immediate improvement in his work (*Buster Button*, etc.), which had grown very hasty at Target. During the war he worked for the Admiralty at Lansdown, Bath, freelancing his first adventure strips, *Caleb King's Mine*, etc., to *Comic Capers* (1943) and other Soloway Publications.

He became freelance editor of Martin & Reid's comics in 1947 (*Jolly Western*, etc.) while working as an income tax officer. His last drawings appeared in *Fizz* (1949). Although his style was considered below standard by the major publishers, it was simple and clean and amused undiscerning children.

D.G.

DICK BOS (Netherlands) *Dick Bos* ("*Dick Bush*" is one of the possible translations) is one of the earlier adventure strips to come out of the Netherlands. The strip's creator, Alfred Mazure (born September 8, 1913, in Nijmegen, Netherlands) had already done another private detective comic strip, *De Chef* ("The Boss"), in 1932. The adventures of private eye Dick Bos started on July 20, 1940, with a story entitled "De geval Kleyn" ("The Kleyn Case"). With World War II in progress, it did not take German occupation forces long to discover Dutch comic strips and try to convert them into a propaganda tool. Allegedly it was the Berlin publishing house Ullstein Verlag that offered print runs of one million copies of *Dick Bos* comic books for distribution among the Wehrmacht, if Mazure went along with their plans to change Dick Bos into a Nazi spy. Mazure, an active member of resistance groups at the time, refused to cooperate, and *Dick Bos* was barred from publication. Thus the first run of *Dick Bos* comic book reprints (of nearly square format) ended in 1945. *Dick Bos* shared this fate with a number of Dutch strips.

Dick Bos was back in the private eye business in his "beeldroman" ("picture novel") world after World War II ended. The picture novel became the pattern for a number of books, like *Tarzan*, *Bob Crack*, and *Lex Brand*. The books not only had a tendency toward the same kind of style, more often than not they also sported similar plots. The new series of *Dick Bos* comic books started with reprints of earlier books in a somewhat edited form, then continued with new material until 1964.

Dick Bos started out as a tough guy with whom crooks had to reckon. He not only cleared up crimes but meted out justice as well, much in the tradition of classic private eyes of the day. While his first case hinted at his having killed a criminal, the character was toned down in later years, when he used guns only to shoot other guns out of criminals' hands. *Dick Bos* was done in a style consisting of firm lines with a well-balanced use of black, gray, and white spaces.

W.F.

DICKENSON, FRED (1909-1989) American newspaperman and writer, born in Chicago on January 18, 1909. After studies at the University of Illinois, Fred Dickenson began his career with the Chicago City News Bureau and, as one of his first assignments, covered the St. Valentine's Day Massacre on February 14, 1929.

In subsequent years Dickenson worked as a reporter, rewrite man, and editor for a number of newspapers throughout the country, and for the Associated Press. He covered many of the most important crime stories of the era, including the Winnie Ruth Judd murders, the search for John Dillinger, the murder of Arthur Flegenheimer (alias "Dutch Schultz"), and the capture of Bruno Hauptman, kidnapper of the Lindbergh baby.

Fred Dickenson joined King Features Syndicate as an associate editor in 1943, while continuing to write stories for newspapers and magazines, and a mystery novel (*Kill'em With Kindness*, 1950). In 1952 he began writing the continuity for *Rip Kirby*, the detective strip created by Alex Raymond in 1946.

Fred Dickenson's knowledge of crime, the criminal world, and police procedures was a contributing factor in *Rip Kirby*'s enduring success. Following Alex Raymond's sudden death in 1956, Dickenson worked harmoniously with Raymond's successor, John Prentice. He continued to write the strip, despite ill health, almost until the time of his death in 1989.

M.H.

DICK FULMINE (Italy) In 1938 Mussolini banned all American comic strips from Italian newspapers (with the exception of *Mickey Mouse*), and the unhappy Italian publishers frantically scrambled to replace them with homemade products. *Dick Fulmine*, drawn by Carlo Cossio and written by Vincenzo Baggioli, was

"Dick Fulmine," Carlo Cossio. © Vulcania.

one of these newly minted strips, making its appearance that same year in the illustrated weekly *L'Audace*.

Dick Fulmine (whose name means "lightning") was initially an Italian-American adventurer, vaguely affiliated with an imaginary international law enforcement agency, whose exploits carried him to all corners of the world. Unabashedly modeled after the "giant of Sequals" Primo Carnera, whose popularity was then at its peak in Italy, Dick was a broad-shouldered, square-jawed, thick-boned athlete who used his fists as his most powerful weapons in preference to his guns (or his brains, unfortunately). He could be seen, at least four or five times per episode, ritualistically rolling up his sleeves, while taunting his enemies to a fight with such verbal incitements as: "Don't be afraid, my little turtledoves, I'll take good care of you!" before flattening them with a few well-directed blows from his powerful arms.

Among Fulmine's many enemies were the herculean black Cuban Zambo, the only man able to stand up to Dick for more than a few seconds; the underhanded White Mask, a master criminal who used a gas-filled gun to overcome his opponents; the South American adventurer Barerra; and the mighty hypnotist Flattavion. Try as they might, however, in the end they could never quite measure up to Dick's simple justice.

During World War II our hero became simply Fulmine, and his adventures took a decidedly bellicose turn: he fought on the African and Russian fronts, and even helped the Japanese in the Pacific; after the war he resumed his free-booting ways. When Carlo Cossio retired (for reasons of health) in 1955, his creation disappeared with him.

Dick Fulmine was undeniably Cossio's strip. Others might have at times written some of the scripts (Baggioli, A. Martini, Carlo's brother Vittorio) or even drawn a few of Fulmine's adventures (Vittorio Cossio again, Giorgio Scudellari, Sinchetto), but the strip remains permeated with Carlo Cossio's unique style, a mixture of slapdash (but effective) draftsmanship and breathless showmanship. Cossio had a flair for the colorful pose, the bravura stance, the fast pacing of action, and these qualities made *Dick Fulmine* into one of Italy's most popular strips, and a favorite with many foreign readers as well.

In 1967 Editoriale Corno started reprinting the complete and unexpurgated collection of Fulmine's adventures, and this caused an outcry in Italy, with many critics leveling charges of fascism and racism against the strip. The furor died down, however, and *Dick Fulmine* has now taken its place among the classic Italian comic strips.

M.H.

DICKIE DARE (U.S.) *Dickie Dare* was created by Milton Caniff for Associated Press Newsfeatures in July 1933.

Dickie was a bright young lad with a yen for adventure and a vivid imagination, who would daydream his way into any book that fired his enthusiasm. The first episode involved Dickie and his dog Wags on the side of Robin Hood and his Merry Men; he later fought alongside Jim Hawkins against Long John Silver and even rescued Robinson Crusoe!

The readers, however, did not take overwhelmingly to Dick's imagination, and early in 1934, Caniff remodeled *Dickie Dare* into a slam-bang adventure strip, adding Dan Flynn, a swashbuckling soldier of fortune, as

"Dickie Dare," Milton Caniff. © AP Newsfeatures.

Dick's companion and mentor. The new *Dickie Dare* strip attracted the notice of Colonel Patterson, of the Chicago Tribune-New York News Syndicate, who asked Caniff to create a new action feature for his syndicate (it turned out to be *Terry and the Pirates*, in which Caniff used the same combination of manly hero and boy companion).

Upon Caniff's departure in October 1934, *Dickie Dare* was taken over by Coulton Waugh, who, in the course of his 10-year stewardship over the strip, retained much of Caniff's flavor and added a few personal touches of his own. Unlike Caniff's *Terry*, Waugh's *Dickie Dare* was to remain a strip of pure adventure. Dickie and Dan sailed the seven seas aboard Dan's yacht, getting involved with brigands, gunrunners, international spies, and power-mad potentates along the way (one 1939 episode had Dan and Dickie foiling the evil designs of an Arabian sheik in one of Waugh's most entertaining and exciting stories).

In the spring of 1944, Coulton Waugh was succeeded by his former assistant (and future bride) Mabel Odin Burvik (she signed her name simply "Odin"), who managed to keep the strip on its course for a while; but times had changed, and after a slow decline, *Dickie Dare* was finally dropped in the late 1950s.

Dickie Dare is remembered today chiefly for Caniff's contribution. Yet one should not forget Coulton Waugh, who managed, in his easygoing, winning style, to establish *Dickie Dare* as the most entertaining and agreeable kid-adventure strip of the period.

M.H.

DICK'S ADVENTURES IN DREAMLAND (U.S.) King Features Syndicate's *Dick's Adventures in Dreamland* was created at the express direction of William Randolph Hearst himself. In December of 1945 Hearst sent the following message to J. P. Gortatowsky, then president of KFS: "I have had numerous suggestions for incorporating American history of a vivid kind in the adventure strips of the comic section. It seems to me that something (sic) which told the youthful life of our American heroes and how they developed into great men and their great moments might be interesting." The editors took the hint and on January 12, 1947, *Dick's Adventures* finally saw the light as a Sunday feature written by Max Trell and drawn by Neil O'Keefe.

A FEW MOMENTS LATER THEY ARE AT WHARFSIDE! HERE A BUSTLING CROWD OF STEVEDORES IS ALREADY LOADING A THIRD SHIP! "LOOK," CRIES DICK, "WE'RE ALMOST READY TO SAIL!"

"Dick's Adventures in Dreamland," Neil O'Keefe. © King Features Syndicate.

"Dick Tracy," Chester Gould. © Chicago Tribune.

Utilizing the dream device (in a manner more reminiscent of *Dickie Dare* than of *Little Nemo*), Dick traveled back in time in the company of some of the most illustrious names in American history. He fought alongside George Washington at Valley Forge, sailed the oceans with John Paul Jones, and even witnessed the invention of the cotton gin by Eli Whitney. The successive episodes did not flow naturally into one another but were arbitrarily tied together by Dick's waking up from one dream to relapse into another, a kind of oneiric fade-out fade-in. Dick was slowly dreaming his way toward World War I when, the gimmick having worn thin (and Hearst having died in the meantime), the series was discontinued in October 1956.

Didactic strips have never been popularly accepted, and *Dick's Adventures* was no exception. The strip was not without merit, however. O'Keefe's style is airy and atmospheric, with none of the clutter that many draftsmen feel obligated to bring to the "historical" feature, and one can occasionally learn something from the earnest but pedestrian text.

M.H.

DICK TRACY (U.S.) In 1931 Chester Gould, after several unsuccessful attempts, submitted a strip to Joseph Patterson, editor of the Chicago Tribune-New York News Syndicate, about a Chicago detective tentatively named "Plainclothes Tracy." Patterson accepted the proposed feature but changed the name, and so *Dick Tracy* was born on Sunday, October 4, 1931. The daily strip soon followed, on Monday, October 12, of the same year.

In the first daily episode, Dick Tracy was the powerless witness to a holdup in the course of which his sweetheart, Tess Trueheart, was kidnapped and her father murdered. In revulsion Tracy joined the police force and unrelentingly tracked down the criminals responsible for the act.

Tracy's first adversaries, Ribs Mocco, Larceny Lu, Stooge Viller, Boris Arson, Shirtsleeve Kelton, and Whip Chute, were the conventional villains of pulp and movie fiction—racketeers, killers, kidnappers, bank robbers, counterfeiters, mob lawyers, etc. Gradually these were replaced by a rogues' gallery of grotesque criminals with appropriate faces or mannerisms for their names. One of the first was Frank Redrum, alias "the Blank," who hid his face behind a featureless mask. The Blank was soon followed by Jerome Trohs, a midget with a giant ego and a criminal brain; "the Brow," a master spy whose forehead was a mess of creases and wrinkles; the aptly named Pruneface; Shaky, who must kill in order to steady his shattered nerves; Mr. Bribery, collector of roses and shrunken heads; and many more in this grisly circus of horrors. Most of them met ends as horrible as their deeds. They were shot through the head, impaled on flag poles, buried alive, scalded, hanged, frozen to death.

Tracy's career has also had its vicissitudes; he has been shot countless times, blinded by acid, tortured, stabbed, maimed, and crippled. Not that his personal life has been any quieter. His adopted son, Junior, was kidnapped and beaten on several occasions, his fiancée Tess, a moody and unpredictable lady, jilted him at regular intervals before they finally got married in 1949, and their daughter Bonny Braids was also kidnapped. Tracy's only support has come from his superior, Chief Brandon, and from his associates, Pat Patton, Sam Catchem, and Lizz the policewoman. But the eagle-nosed, square-chinned Tracy has always pursued his relentless crusade against crime.

Dick Tracy was the first realistic police strip. Violent, brutal, often cruel, it has played an important role in the history of American comics by breaking many taboos. Its influence, due both to its massive, dark appearance, and the tightness of its scripts, has been noticeable not only on other detective strips, but also on the whole field of action comics, which have borrowed heavily from its plotting and its techniques.

Dick Tracy was the subject of over a half-dozen movies from 1937 to 1947 (Ralph Byrd played the detective in most of them), a radio program in the forties, a television series in the fifties (starring Ralph Byrd again), and a number of animated cartoons in the sixties. He also inspired Al Capp's parody, *Fearless Fosdick*. In 1970 Chelsea House published a hardbound anthology of his adventures, *The Celebrated Cases of Dick Tracy*, with an introduction by Ellery Queen. A new Dick Tracy movie was released in 1990, with Warren Beatty directing himself in the title role.

Gould retired from the strip at the end of 1977, while still retaining a byline on the feature. Rick Fletcher, who had been Gould's assistant, took over the artwork, and mystery writer Max Allan Collins wrote the scripts. Collins imparted a less grim, more modern tone to the square-jawed detective's adventures, which prompted protests from the creator, who withdrew his name from the strip in 1981. Fletcher's death in 1983 further complicated matters: as his replacement, the syndicate picked editorial cartoonist Dick Locher. In 1992 Collins was abruptly replaced by Michael Kilian, in the latest chapter of the real-life *Dick Tracy* saga.

M.H.

DIEGO VALOR (Spain) In October 1953 the Spanish radio network SER started a daily program devoted to the adventures of Keith Watson's hero Dan Dare under the title of *Diego Valor*. A little later the producers decided to drop the original British scripts in favor of a purely Spanish treatment, which no longer had anything to do with its initial inspiration. The program reached the record number of 1,200 broadcasts before being discontinued in June 1958.

One year after its birth on the air, *Diego Valor* was adapted into comic book form (June 20, 1954). With issue number 10, the comic book version was entrusted to its original creator, the writer Jarber (pseudonym of Enrique Jarnés Bergua), who gave it its definitive characteristics, with the help of his illustrators, Buylla and Bayo (Braulio Rodríguez). With issue 168 (March 1958), the comic book ceased publication, while *Diego Valor* was revived for one short year as a color page in the children's supplement of the magazine *La Revista Española* (1963).

Diego Valor was a Spanish commandant born in the year 2000 and regarded by his fellow men as the great-

"Diego Valor," Buylla. © Editorial Cid.

est hero in the history of the world, no less! At the head of his team, he visited the planet Venus and a satellite of Jupiter named Kelos, where he fought a race of extraordinarily old beings who wanted to conquer the world. Valor's main collaborator and friend was Beatriz Fantana, a shining example of future womanhood, the equal of any man. The scenarios of *Diego Valor* were bellicose and triumphalistic, the drawings simple and without great quality, but the rapid-fire action made up for any artistic deficiency. With the double advantage of a daily radio program and a weekly comic book, *Diego Valor* was, in its time, a phenomenal success. There were several stage adaptations, a television serial, and countless collections of records, color cards, and toys.

L.G.

DILBERT (U.S.) More than 30 years after William H. Whyte Jr. published *The Organization Man,* an engineer with an MBA from Berkeley named Scott Adams created *Dilbert* for United Feature Syndicate, which began its distribution on April 16, 1989.

Dilbert, an engineer and corporate denizen, is the bespectacled, white-shirt-and-tie-wearing, unheroic protagonist working at a company on the proverbial cutting edge of technology. He spends his eight-hour-plus workdays combating the incompetence of his dismissal-proof manager, who, with two spikes of hair on either side of his head reminiscent of the Devil's horns, is too interested in the latest management fads to learn the basics of his job. Dilbert is inundated with meaningless and contradictory memos while forever

DILBERT

"Dilbert," Scott Adams. © United Feature Syndicate.

Ding Cong, a typical pose from a 1985 strip. © Ding Cong.

attending meetings and pre-meetings and reading mission statements from upper management, "visioning" documents from consultants, and team-building morale reports from facilitators.

Fans of the comic strip see a faithful reflection of their own professional world, with its maze-like layout of cubicles, corporate jargonistic gobbledygook, and double-talk (for example, "We have to be more competitive" means "Say goodbye to salary increases," or "We're market driven" means "We blame customers for our lack of innovation"), not to mention outright lies such as "Your input is important to us" and "We reward risk takers."

Dilbert's colleagues share his experiences. Although the frizzy-haired Alice may work 80-hour weeks and donate bone marrow to the company's biggest customer, she receives a 2% raise because her performance for the year "meets expectations." Tina, the public relations person, must put a positive spin on a product that "causes hallucinations and sterility"—not without tiny pangs of conscience, however. For his part, Wally gets a white T-shirt for his 10 years of service to the company, but since he does so little around the office, he gratefully acknowledges his employer's generosity.

Catbert, the evil Human Resources director, aptly portrayed as a cat, enjoys his unlimited pink-slip power as he plays cat-and-mouse games with the employees. Constantly inventing new ways of demeaning them, he shrinks cubicle sizes (the "Densification Project") or orders that employees wear smaller shoes (the "Footsizing Program") to reduce wear and tear on the carpeting: "We must do this to be competitive," he gleefully concludes one of his E-mail nastygrams.

Only Dogbert, Dilbert's potato-shaped sidekick and canine master-of-all-trades, views the world clearly: Stupidity, ignorance, morning breath, selfishness, lust, fear, money, and luck—in that order—are the ruling forces of the universe. To him, people (including Dilbert) are morons and prove his theory again and again. He believes people are in desperate need of "a leader whose vision can penetrate the thick fog of human incompetence"—in other words, himself!

What the strip lacks in artistic development, it more than compensates for by its satirical bite and true-to-life workplace situations and characters. This explains the strip's tremendous success—more than 1,000 newspapers carry the strip, while Dilbert and Dogbert have graced the covers of *Newsweek* and *TV Guide*—and the exploding market for *Dilbert* merchandise. In addition, Scott Adams wrote two illustrated, wonderfully funny books, which appeared in 1996 and which were both immediate best-sellers: one, based on Dilbert's life in "cubicle hell," *The Dilbert Principle*, and the other, a highly useful compilation of management wisdom by Dogbert, *Dogbert's Top Secret Management Handbook*.

P.L.H.

DING CONG (1916-   ) Ding Cong's father, Ding Song, was a well-known cartoonist in China in the 1920s who did not want his son to be an artist like himself. Desiring an easier life for Ding Cong, the cartoonist refused to teach him to draw. The only professional training the self-taught Ding Cong had was one semester at the Shanghai Fine Arts Institute. Once he started publishing cartoons at the age of 17, he never stopped creating, with the exceptions of the period from 1957 to 1960 when he was not allowed to publish cartoons after being wrongly accused as a "rightist"; and later during the Cultural Revolution when all cartooning in China ceased for 10 years from 1966 to 1976. His cartoons have brought him fame as one of the best cartoonists in China. He is known not only for his speed in creating his works, but also for the fine drawing and outstanding humor and satire in his comics.

In addition to Ding's single cartoons, his best-known cartoon series includes a comic titled *Reflection of the Society*, which was created in early 1945 during the Sino-Japanese War. Another one of Ding's collections is *Wit and Humour from Ancient China: 100 Cartoons by Ding Cong*, published in 1988 in both English and

Chinese. In this collection, Ding's jokes are inspired by Chinese history, biographies, novels, and anecdotes dating from the third century B.C. to the 17th century A.D. With wit and humor, Ding ridicules stupid government officials and pokes fun at the follies and pretensions of people.

During his more than 60-year career in cartooning, Ding Cong has drawn cartoons, illustrated stories, and designed for many different publications. Although he is an older man, he always signs his work with the name "Xiao Ding" (Little Ding), which indicates his childlike heart with an optimistic, energetic, and diligent spirit.

H.Y.L.L.

DINGBAT FAMILY, THE (U.S.) An oblong, upright strip of six panels, with a separate, illustrated logo, *The Dingbat Family* started in the *New York Journal* on June 20, 1910. Its cast of five was lined up and labeled in the opening logo as "Ma" Dingbat; the family kids named Imogene, Cicero, and Baby; and their father, E. Pluribus Dingbat. Beside the Dingbats, two unnamed family pets, a cat and a dog, were shown, although neither took part in the first episode. (They were to become, after some permutations, two of the stars of the ultimate strip: Krazy Kat and Offisa Pupp.)

The Dingbat Family from the outset was a raffish, knockabout farce about an underpaid, middle-aged office clerk, his lumpish wife, and their difficult prog-

"The Dingbat Family," George Herriman. © King Features Syndicate.

eny. It does not seem to have been too successful, and by July 9, 1910, Herriman had apparently been urged to dump the family conflict and focus on Dingbat, for a series of strips simply titled *Mr. Dingbat* began on that date. On July 26, 1910, however, Herriman had one of those bursts of inspiration that are the prerogatives of genius, and produced an episode titled "Mr. Dingbat Demands His Rights from the Family Upstairs." The action took place in Dingbat's apartment and involved the irritating behavior of an unseen family living in the apartment directly above. This family, which continued in subsequent episodes to keep out of the Dingbats' sight without ceasing to harass them, had become Herriman's focal point. The Dingbats became obsessed with the desire to find out who the upper tenants were, and to get them out of the building—always without success. Readers were fascinated and absorbed, and the Herriman strip (which underwent its second title change in six weeks, this time to *The Family Upstairs* on August 1, 1910) became a *Journal* institution and a feature in Hearst afternoon papers across the country.

On November 15, 1911, Herriman surprised everyone by ending the *Family Upstairs* mystery with the total destruction of the Dingbat apartment building, after which, on November 22, 1911, the Dingbats returned in a strip once again called *The Dingbat Family*. Herriman continued with the feature, drawing it in tandem with *Krazy Kat* (which was given its own berth on October 28, 1913) until the older strip wearied its creator, and he replaced it with a new daily feature, *Baron Bean*, on January 5, 1916.

B.B.

DINGLE, ADRIAN (1912-1974) Born in Wales of Cornish parents in 1912 and brought to Canada at the age of three, Adrian Dingle launched his adult working career as an insurance company employee in Oakville, Ontario, near Toronto, but soon began serious work as a painter, gaining critical attention in the early 1930s. During this period he turned to commercial art to finance his artistic endeavors. In 1941 Dingle created a comic strip called *Nelvana of the Northern Lights* for Triumph-Adventure Comics, an independent "Canadian white" established that June by the Hillborough Studio in Toronto. In 1942 Triumph Adventure, its name pared down to Triumph, was absorbed by Bell Features and Publishing Company, Toronto. Beginning in September 1941 with one publication—Wow Comics—in the wake of a Canadian government embargo on U.S. comic books, it grew to include Dime, Active, Joke, Commando, and Dizzy Don as well as Triumph.

Dingle joined Bell and carried on with Nelvana, a semi-mythological heroine who received fantastic powers from the Aurora Borealis. In addition, he created *The Penguin*, about a crime fighter in birdlike mask, white tie, and tails; *The Sign of Freedom*, the tale of an RCAF pilot turned Underground hero; and *Nils Grant, Private Investigator*.

During his years with Bell, doubling as its art director, Dingle also succeeded other artists on such strips as *Active Jim*, *Rex Baxter*, *Clift Steele*, and *Guy Powers Secret Agent*, the last two done under the pen name Darian. Eventually, Dingle also took on the task of drawing the majority of Bell's color covers, either under his own name or the Darian pseudonym, after the principal cover artist, Edmond Good, left to take over the *Scorchy Smith* comic strip in the United States.

With the reappearance of U.S. comic books on Canadian newsstands near the end of World War II, Canadian publishers geared up for full-color printing. When the changeover came, Dingle continued *Nelvana* and *The Penguin* (which was renamed *The Blue Raven*). Competition from the U.S. was too stiff, however, and Canadian comics faded from the scene by the late 1940s, although publishers kept their presses busy by printing Canadian editions of U.S. titles. By the early 1950s, even this industry had disappeared.

Dingle had kept at his painting through the war years and, with the demise of the Canadian comic book industry, decided to pursue it as a full-time career. Over 25 years he developed into one of Canada's foremost landscape and semi-abstract artists, traveling and painting in France, Italy, Spain, England, Portugal, Ireland, New England, and Canada's Atlantic Provinces, before his death in 1974.

P.H.

"*Dinglehoofer und His Dog Adolph*," Harold Knerr. © King Features Syndicate.

DINGLEHOOFER UND HIS DOG ADOLPH (U.S.)

Harold Knerr created *Dinglehoofer und His Dog Adolph* in 1926 as a top to his celebrated *Katzenjammer Kids*. Obscured by the fame of its dazzling companion strip, *Dinglehoofer* has remained almost totally unresearched in spite of its undeniable qualities.

Dinglehoofer ("Mr. Dingy") was a small, dumpy middle-class German-American (he spoke in a Teutonized version of English, not too far removed from the Katzenjammers' jargon) who lived with a young boy named Tad and a feisty little bulldog named Adolph. Tad was a good fellow, high-spirited but helpful, mischievous but nice, a far cry from Hans and Fritz. In this strip it was the dog who got the others involved in a variety of escapades. As another (and far more threatening) Adolph arose in the 1930s, Dinglehoofer traded his dog Adolph for a basset named Schnappsy, and the strip retained all of its quality.

Dinglehoofer's humor always remained quiet and serene, a counterpoint to the thunder and lightning of the hectic *Katzenjammers*. The adventures of the Dinglehoofers were in the same low-key mode (Adolph—or Schnappsy—digging up the bones of a prehistoric animal, or befriending a pair of burglars, etc.) and often were continued from week to week. While not on a par with *The Katzenjammers*, *Dinglehoofer* was nonetheless a minor gem of gentle and engaging fun. *Dinglehoofer* survived its creator's death in 1949 by a few

years. It was continued by Doc Winner until it was finally dropped in 1952.

M.H.

DIRKS, JOHN (1917-   ) American cartoonist, son of Rudolph Dirks, born November 2, 1917, in New York City. He graduated from Yale University in 1939 with degrees in English and fine arts. He started selling cartoons to *Collier's* and the *Saturday Evening Post* while he was still an undergraduate. Drafted during World War II, he was sent to the European theater and was demobilized as a captain in 1945.

Soon after the end of the war, John Dirks returned to illustration and cartooning. He started assisting his father on *The Captain and the Kids* in the mid-1940s and took over the strip in 1958 without altering its original character and spirit.

Since 1960 John Dirks has acquired growing recognition as a metal sculptor as well as a cartoonist. He is particularly noted for the water fountains that he designs and sells all over the world. After *The Captain and the Kids* was discontinued in 1979, he did some drawings of the Kids for promotion and advertising purposes.

M.H.

DIRKS, RUDOLPH (1877-1968) American cartoonist, born in 1877 in Heinde, Germany. The son of a wood-carver, Rudolph Dirks came to Chicago with his immigrant parents at the age of seven. By 1894 he was already selling cartoons to *Judge* and *Life*. In 1897, at the height of the newspaper war between Hearst and Pulitzer, he joined Hearst's *New York Journal*. Rudolph Block, the *Journal's* editor, was then looking for a feature that could compete with the highly successful *Yellow Kid*, the rival *World's* star attraction. He asked the young Dirks to create an original Sunday strip and sug-

Rudolph Dirks.

gested Wilhelm Busch's *Max und Moritz* as a model. On December 12, 1897, *The Katzenjammer Kids* first appeared.

In 1912 Dirks wanted to leave for Europe to devote himself to painting, with the result that Hearst took *The Katzenjammer Kids* away from him. A celebrated court battle ensued, and Dirks won back the right to draw his characters (but not the right to use the title, which went to Hearst), which he did, in 1914, for the *World* under the title of *Hans and Fritz* (later changed to *The Captain and the Kids*).

In addition to his work as a cartoonist, Rudolph Dirks did paintings and engravings. He was associated with different art movements, including the "Ash Can School," and he cofounded the artists colony at Ogunquit, Maine. In 1958 he retired and relinquished *The Captain and the Kids* to his son John. Dirks died in New York City on April 20, 1968.

One of the "founding fathers" of the American comics, Rudolph Dirks has left a permanent imprint on all facets of the medium, which he helped to develop. His themes and style were widely imitated and shamelessly plagiarized in the United States and in Europe; his creative use of balloons and dialogue revolutionized the technique and format of the picture-story; while his legal battle with Hearst created the precedent on which most of the jurisprudence relating to the comic strip is based.

M.H.

DISNEY, WALT (1901-1966) American artist and businessman, born in Chicago on December 5, 1901. Walter Elias Disney, born into a very poor family, studied first in Kansas City, then at the Chicago Art Institute. After a short stint as an ambulance driver on the European front during World War I, Walt Disney started working for an advertising agency in Kansas City. In 1923, in partnership with his brother Roy, he opened a small motion-picture animation studio in Hollywood. After having created two ephemeral series, *Alice in Cartoonland* in 1925 and *Oswald the Rabbit* in 1927, Walt Disney, with the assistance of Ub Iwerks, produced in 1928 the first cartoon of Mickey Mouse, perhaps the most beloved cartoon character ever conceived. Dozens upon dozens of inspired creations followed: the *Silly Symphonies*, *The Three Little Pigs*, *Donald Duck*, *Snow White*, *Pinocchio*, *Dumbo*, and many others. Most of these creations were later adapted into comic strips and comic books with great success (notably *Mickey Mouse* and *Donald Duck*).

Though not a comic strip artist himself, Walt Disney had great impact on the field, either directly through his creations or indirectly through the many cartoonists who served their apprenticeships in his studios—among them Carl Barks, Floyd Gottfredson, and Walt Kelly.

Walt Disney died in Hollywood on December 15, 1966.

M.H.

DI 13 (Philippines) The June 14, 1947, premier issue of *Pilipino Komiks* featured the strip *DI 13* ("DI Trese"). The series was written by Damy Velasquez, the brother of Tony Velasquez, and illustrated by Jesse Santos.

DI 13 was one of the longest-running dramatic features ever to appear in the history of Philippine comic

"DI-13," Tony Velasquez. © Pilipino Komiks.

books. It was also the most popular detective strip in the country.

DI is the abbreviation for the Detective Bureau of Investigation. Trese, the main character, is a James Bond-type of individual—sure of himself, dashing, suave, brave, debonaire, daring, intelligent, and tough. Though he has a regular girlfriend named Sally, he is not averse to tangling with members of the opposite sex.

The tempo of the series varies, depending on the type of story being told. At times the setting is quiet, but there is always a feeling of suspense in the air. In the case of very puzzling crimes, Trese's approach is methodical in order to cope with the perplexity and intricacy of the mystery. Intellect rather than force is used. Then there are other moments when everything is moving at high velocity—cycles dashing about, roaring through the countryside, and cars careening in the city streets, knocking down everything in sight and then exploding into a million fragments. There are also situations in which the hero has to rely on his quick wits and fast reflexes to subdue a swift and tricky assailant, to parry the cobralike lunges of a villainous knife-wielder, or to escape the clutches of a strong and murderous fiend. And when the only thing that separates Trese from certain death is the instinct to survive, though battered and bleeding, he pulls through by sheer tenacity and courage—which almost leaves the reader gasping from the exertion.

The locale is often changed to add variety to the script. Humor is interjected at the right moments to add relief from the suspense and to break the seriousness of a situation. The series combined well-written stories with excellent artwork and lasted into the 1960s.

O.J.

DITKO, STEVE (1927-) American comic book artist, born November 2, 1927, in Johnstown, Pennsylvania. He was educated at the Cartoonist and Illustrators School, where he was heavily influenced by renowned comic artist Jerry Robinson. Even Ditko himself is not sure where his first strip appeared—"It was so small," he once said, "I can't even remember the name"—but his material was appearing as early as

Steve Ditko, "Collector's Edition." © Warren Publications.

1953 in horror comics published by Farrell, Prize, Charlton, and St. John. In 1956, Ditko began drawing horror and supernatural stories for Atlas (later Marvel).

After a short stint on Charlton's ill-fated *Captain Atom* and *Gorgo* books, Ditko got his first major superhero assignment in 1962—drawing the *Spider-Man* strip in Marvel's *Amazing Fantasy* number 15. It quickly became a phenomenal success, due mainly to a strong story line and Ditko's unique, almost grotesque renderings of Spider-Man and alter ego Peter Parker. Slightly paranoid and always guilt-ridden, *Spider-Man* was a perfect vehicle for Ditko's exciting but simple style. Ditko also began writing and drawing the *Dr. Strange* feature in 1963, which, unlike the realistic *Spider-Man*, afforded him the opportunity to introduce intricate, eerie worlds of mysticism and intrigue. And although he left both strips in 1966—precipitated by a disagreement with editor Stan Lee—his versions remain the definitive ones.

Immediately following his abrupt departure from Marvel, Ditko produced outstanding material for Warren, Tower, Dell, National, and other groups. But his best work during 1966 through 1968 was done for Charlton, where he received two old superheroes, *Blue Beetle* and *Captain Atom*, and created *The Question* strip.

Originally designed as a backup feature in *Blue Beetle*, *The Question* quickly became the most provocative feature on the market. Based on *Mr. A*, a character he created, wrote, and drew for Wally Wood's *Witzend* magazine, *The Question* dealt with the tremendous philosophical battles between the diverse elements of American society. The character's world was a narrow one: there were "black" or evil forces; there were "white" or good forces; but there were no "gray" forces of compromise. *The Question* saw any compromise as an acceptance of evil that could not be tolerated. The quintessential display of the character's philosophy was exhibited in *Mysterious Suspense* number one (Summer, 1968). It consisted of a 25-page battle between the thinly veiled forces of "good" and "evil," and many critics consider the strip one of the best commercial comic books ever published.

After Charlton dropped their superhero titles in 1968, Ditko created two short-lived features for National that same year. Entitled *The Hawk and The Dove* and *The Creeper*, both were less successful ver-

sions of *The Question*. An illness forced Ditko off both strips shortly after their inception, and both were discontinued within a year. When he returned to drawing in late 1969, it was for Charlton's horror and supernatural titles.

Ditko was intent on pursuing the philosophical comics he pioneered, however, and he revived *Mr. A* for many limited-edition magazine appearances. Two collections of his philosophy comics have appeared, *Mr. A* (1973) and *Avenging World* (1974).

J.B.

In 1979 Ditko returned to Marvel, working notably on such titles as *Rom*, *Captain Universe*, and *Indiana Jones*. He left the comic-book field in the mid-1980s but made a much-publicized comeback in February 1997 with the cumbersomely named *Steve Ditko's Strange Avenging Tales*.

M.H.

Guillermo Divito, "Fulmine". © Rico Tipo.

DIVITO, GUILLERMO (1914-1969) An Argentinian cartoonist and illustrator born in Buenos Aires in 1914, Guillermo Divito owes his early fame to the grace and style with which he depicted the female figure, his famous "Divito girls," tall and luscious beauties with incredibly narrow waists and exaggerated and generous bosoms.

Divito started his career in 1931 in *Paginas de Columba*, and some time later he began his collaboration with Dante Quinterno, producing such comic strips as *El Enemigo del Hombre* ("Man's Enemy") and *Oscar Dientes de Leche* ("Milk Teeth Oscar"), both published in the comic magazine *Patoruzu*. Starting in 1944 he devoted himself to the launching and success of the humor magazine *Rico Tipo*, which he founded. He also inspired a whole school of cartoonists, not only in Argentina but also in Spain. His creations, typically

"Dixie Dugan," John Striebel and J. P. McEvoy. © McNaught Syndicate.

Argentinian, include *Bombolo*, *Pochita Morfoni*, *El Doctor Merengue* (his first big success in 1942), *Fulmine* (about a black-hearted villain), and his most popular work, *Fallutelli* (1944).

Guillermo Divito was killed in a car crash in 1969.

L.G.

DIXIE DUGAN (U.S.) The history of *Dixie Dugan's* conception is complicated and in a sense exemplary, as it explains the many factors (artistic, financial, commercial) that go into the making of a syndicated strip.

Artist John Striebel and writer J. P. McEvoy had been friends since boyhood, and when McEvoy sold *Liberty* the serialization rights to his novel *Show Girl*, he insisted that Striebel be the illustrator. Later the novel was adapted to the stage and made into a movie. This prompted the McNaught Syndicate to ask McEvoy and Striebel for a comic strip version, and it made its appearance in October 1929. The strip did not sell, and the editors decided to change the title from *Show Girl* to *Dixie Dugan*, to get the heroine out of show business. A new salesman, aspiring cartoonist Ham Fisher, took the strip on the road and promptly sold it to 30 newspapers. (His success, incidentally, led Fisher to sell his own strip, *Joe Palooka*, the same way a few months later.)

The object of all this maneuvering seems in retrospect not worth the effort. *Dixie Dugan* was never a very distinguished strip, even when judged by the low standards of its genre. The drawing is just adequate and the situations trite. Dixie's countless run-ins with her bosses and relatives and her flirtations with an endless string of suitors are as tiresome as her eternal optimism. *Dixie Dugan's* success represents a greater tribute to Ham Fisher's salesmanship than to the authors' talent or originality.

Dixie Dugan, which died a slow death in the 1960s, was brought to the screen in 1943 by 20th Century Fox (Lois Andrews was Dixie).

M.H.

DIXON, JOHN DANGAR (1929-   ) Australian cartoonist, born at Newcastle, New South Wales, in 1929, the son of a school principal. After completing his education at Cooks Hill Intermediate School, he joined a soft-goods company as a trainee window dresser. On finishing his course he became interested in art and obtained a position as an advertising artist with the same company. Pursuing his artistic career, he went to Sydney in 1945 and took a series of jobs with department stores and advertising agencies. An agency acquaintance suggested that he try the comic book field, and so he commenced a long association with the H. John Edwards publishing company—one of the newer postwar publishers. In 1946 he created *Tim Valour Comics*, which was to run through three series and over 150 issues. The same year he created *The Crimson Comet Comics*, which also had a long run—but Dixon handled less than 50 issues as he was busy producing other comic features for the company. *Tim Valour*, in particular, allowed him to indulge his passion for airplanes and served as an excellent training ground for his future newspaper strip.

Dixon created a "new" *Catman Comics* for Frew Publications in 1958 and *Captain Strato Comics* for *Young's Merchandising* the same year. His last major comic book work was done in 1959 when he created *The Phantom Commando Comics* for Horwitz Publications. For many months he had been developing a newspaper strip and on June 14, 1959, the Sunday version of *Air Hawk and the Flying Doctors* appeared in the *Sydney Sun-Herald*.

Despite the absence of any formal art training and the obvious crudeness of his early work, Dixon's basic technique had always been reasonably sound. The formative years of *Air Hawk* exhibited many of the slick techniques and treatments used in comic books, but it was obvious that the left-handed Dixon was constantly striving to lift the standard of his work. The introduction of the daily *Air Hawk* strip, in May 1963, seemed to give him added impetus, and by the late 1960s he had polished and refined his technique to the point where it was comparable with that of any comic strip artist in the world.

His careful spotting of black gives his panels great depth and assists in presenting his panel-to-panel continuity dramatically—particularly when he chooses to eliminate all words from the panel and allow the illustration to tell its own story. While impressed by the work of Raymond, Foster, and Caniff, only the latter influenced his art to any noticeable degree, in the early years. With maturity, this influence vanished and the distinctive John Dixon style took over. In the 1970s *Air Hawk* literally took flight, being published in Europe, the United States, and throughout the world; since that time Dixon has largely devoted his time and energies to the production and distribution of his strip.

J.R.

DJON DOMINO (Indonesia) *Djon Domino*, in its many manifestations, has blanketed Indonesian print media since 1970. Created by Johnny Hidajat, Djon was sculpted from a long-nosed, shadow play character known and loved by all Indonesians. The popularity of the strip has been enhanced from the beginning by the numbers Hidajat includes in each sequence; they are used by readers as tips for the national lottery. In describing *Djon Domino*, Hidajat said he has "no special message; he can be a judge, a lawyer, a criminal, a doctor, a bad guy. He changes regularly, day to day." In fact, Djon is a schizophrenic character, appearing under varying names in different media—*Djon Domino* in *Pos Kota* (a daily); *Djon Tik* in *Waspada* (a daily); *Djon Kaget* in *Pos Film*; *Si Djon* in *Terbit*; and *Djon Teremol Ngook* in *Humor Magazine*. Each variation is designed for a specific audience; for example, *Djon Teremol*

"Djon Domino," Johnny Hidajat. © Johnny Hidajat.

Ngook, which is the Indonesian word for conglomerate spelled backward, deals with big business. Hidajat has little trouble cranking out multiple versions of his character; he is both prolific and flexible. From 1970 to 1975, he worked at a breakneck pace, drawing 60 to 75 three- or four-panel strips every day. He said he drew everywhere all the time—in restaurants, the car, at home, or in the office. The leeway he affords himself with Djon's name, personality, and opinion enables him to fit the character to the editorial stances of the periodicals to which he contributes.

J.A.L.

DOBRIĆ, MILORAD (1924-1991) Yugoslav cartoonist, editor, and writer Milorad Dobrić was born in Belgrade on August 18, 1924. Dobrić studied architecture, but his beloved hobby was cartooning. In 1945 it became his profession. His first comic strip was influenced by Louis Forton's *Les Pieds-Nickelés*. Even the characters were drawn in the same way as Forton's, but the strip involved Yugoslavs whose adventures were influenced by events of World War II.

In 1950 Dobrić got a job as political cartoonist on the humor weekly *Jež* in Belgrade. His cartoon comments were inspired by everyday life. It was the time of his professional growing up, and very soon he became one of the top cartoonists in his field in Yugoslavia.

In August 1951 Dobrić wrote and illustrated his first published comic book, *Veliki turnir* ("The Big Rivalry").

The same year he used chessmen as characters in a comic strip written by Yugoslav poet Andra Franićević. In 1952 *Pera Pešak* ("Pera the Pedestrian") became a very popular comic strip. Pera was used as a symbol on three-way traffic lights to signal pedestrians as to when to cross the street. A pantomime gag strip, *Ljuba Truba*, was created in 1954 for *Jež*. The amazing drunkard of the strip still appears there.

Dobrić is also the author of a few comics with animal characters. From 1954 to 1968 Belgrade's newspaper *Borba* published Dobrić's daily comic strip, *Kurir Fića*, which later became a regular daily cartoon panel and is well known today in that format. From 1961 to 1967 Dobrić was editor-in-chief of the comic magazine *Mali Jež*, where he had two very successful comic strips: *Slavuj Gliša* and *Inspektor Žuća*. He returned to *Jež* in 1968 and became that magazine's cartoon editor.

This very prolific and outstanding Yugoslav cartoonist, who won several international and national prizes for his work, was syndicated by Strip Art Features. He died in Belgrade on June 10, 1991.

E.R.

DOC SAVAGE (U.S.) 1—Street and Smith was one of the preeminent pulp magazine publishers of the 1930s, having both *The Shadow* and *Doc Savage* in their stable. The company decided to enter comic books with their features, and the *Doc Savage* strip made its first appearance in March 1940's *The Shadow* number one; it graduated to its own book in May 1940. Unfortu-

Milorad Dobrić, "Ljuba Truba." © Strip Art Features.

"Doc Savage." © Street and Smith.

nately, the series was an artistic disaster. A superman of sorts, who had five assistants, the Doc Savage character never established a firm comic book foothold. He was a weak imitation of his former pulp self. The comic book writers could not inject the excitement that Lester Dent and others had brought to the 181 pulp stories, and comic artists like Jack Binder, Joe Certa, Henry Kiefer, and Bob Powell simply could not match pulp illustrator Edd Cartier.

In all, *Doc Savage* lasted 20 issues until October 1943, and the strip appeared sporadically in *The Shadow* until 1949.

2—Doc Savage made a one-shot appearance in a Gold Key book in 1966 with art by Jack Sparling.

3—Bantam Books began reprinting the *Doc Savage* pulp novels in the 1960s, and more than 20 million copies of over 75 paperback titles have been circulated. Warner Bros. and George Pal began producing a *Doc Savage* movie, and Marvel revived the *Doc Savage* comic in 1972. It was also uninspired, and the feature has been fighting off comic book obscurity although both a black-and-white and color version have apparently been failures.

J.B.

4—Over the years many attempts were made to bring the Man of Bronze back to comic books. First came Marvel (1972-74; 1975-77), then DC Comics (1987-90), Millenium Publications (1991-92), and lastly Dark Horse (which paired Doc with the Shadow in 1995). All these efforts were half-hearted and ultimately unsuccessful.

M.H.

DR. FATE (U.S.) *Dr. Fate* was created by writer Gardner Fox and first illustrated by Howard Sherman for National's *More Fun* number 55 for May 1940. The strip was as colorful as it was inconsistent. Unlike many of his more subdued magical predecessors, the doctor sported a shimmering blue and gold superhero suit, complete with gold amulet and epaulets. In early adventures, he also sported a gold cape and full-face helmet. But, by the strip's end, Dr. Fate had no epaulets, no cape, and only half his original helmet.

The character's origin was just as changeable. One story had the magician placed on earth by elder gods long before the dawn of civilization. Another claimed he was archeologist Kent Nelson, who happened to find the temple of Nabu the Wise. According to this story, Nabu, who came from the planet Cilia, taught Nelson the magic and gave him the costume. Dr. Fate's powers were just as confusing. Often he was portrayed as omnipotent, but at times he couldn't fly, couldn't break out of bonds, or wasn't invulnerable. In fact, the only thing in *Dr. Fate* that remained stable was his secret lair—an ominous, doorless, and windowless brick tower in Salem.

Artistically, Sherman (1940-43) handled the strip competently, though not innovatively. Joe Kubert (1944) and Stan Asch (1941-42) were other contributors. *Dr. Fate* appeared in *More Fun* through January 1944—the 98th issue. The character also appeared as a member of the Justice Society in *All-Star* from issue number three (Winter 1941) through issue number 21 (Summer 1944). The character made two brief appearances in *Showcase* during 1965 as *Hourman*'s partner. *Doctor Fate* is also a member of the revived Justice Society.

"Dr. Kildare," Ken Bald. © King Features Syndicate.

After years of lurking in the shadow of the superheroes' comic books, the mystic hero finally got his own title in 1988. The series, however, lasted only until 1992, after which it was back to the salt mines for the ill-fated Dr. Fate.

J.B.

DR. KILDARE (U.S.) The character of Doctor Kildare was created in 1938 by the prolific writer Max Brand in his script for the MGM film *Interns Can't Take Money*, but it was firmly established by the movie *Young Doctor Kildare*, with Lew Ayres and Lionel Barrymore. Its success was so great that no fewer than nine sequels followed in the period from 1939 to 1947 (as well as a spin-off series based on Kildare's mentor Dr. Gillespie). In 1960, *Dr. Kildare* started its long TV career, and this seemingly inexhaustible success prompted King Features to release a comic strip version of *Dr. Kildare*. Drawn by Ken Bald, it made its daily debut on October 15, 1962, and was followed by a Sunday version on April 19, 1964.

The plot is well known by now: young, idealistic intern Dr. Kildare (modeled after the TV Kildare, Richard Chamberlain) is entirely devoted to his calling, sometimes with a too-youthful élan but moderated by crusty, wise Dr. Gillespie. Kildare's medical and romantic adventures take place in the mythical Blair General Hospital, and there is never a scarcity of attractive young women around, be they nurses or patients. Dr. Kildare, however, shuns any permanent entanglement, always preferring medicine to love.

The comic strip version of *Dr. Kildare* was as good (and sometimes better) than anything that the movies or television was in the same genre. And Ken Bald's enjoyable artwork was always a relief from the well-worn clichés that too often afflicted the script. The feature outlasted the TV series by many years, ending in 1984.

M.H.

DOCTOR MERENGUE, EL (Argentina) First appearing as *El Otro Yo del Doctor Merengue* ("Doctor Merengue's Other Self") in 1942, the feature was created by cartoonist Guillermo Divito as a series of gag strips

"El Doctor Merengue," Guillermo Divito. © Rico Tipo.

"Dr. Merling," Knud Larsen. © Bulls Pressedienst.

without continuity. It was successively published in the magazines *Rico Tipo*, *El Hogar*, and *Dr. Merengue* (a monthly comic magazine whose star attraction it was), and as a daily newspaper strip.

At the beginning of the strip, Dr. Merengue was a middle-aged gentleman, bald-headed and mustachioed. But he had the rare ability of pulling his stomach in, a neat trick he would use with increasing frequency in the course of his life, with the result that his silhouette was to look more stylized with each passing year. A lustful quinquagenarian always attired in a black suit and a hat to match, he had delusions of being a lady-killer, and would parade down the street with his nose held up high. The only bright note in the doctor's attire was a white handkerchief that stuck out ostentatiously from his breast pocket.

Married to a dumpy and benighted woman, Dr. Merengue earns his living as a general practitioner, though he could be seen at times dressed as an explorer or settled in an executive role. He leads a comfortable life, employs a majordomo named Abel, but likes to give himself airs and spends his life faking, because he is a repressed, libidinous, lying, cheating, and hypocritical philanderer. He has a double identity, and this "other self" is the one that always appears in the last panel of each strip, where it tells the truth with an overabundance of gestures and poses. But Dr. Merengue goes on his merry way, seemingly unfazed by the revelations spoken in pure Buenos Aires dialect by his other image. Having survived the death of its creator in 1969, the feature lives on without its former luster.

L.G.

DR. MERLING (Denmark) *Dr. Merling* (also known as Dr. Merlind) was created, written, and drawn by Knud V. Larsen, a Danish artist now living in an old schoolhouse deep in the forests of Småland, Sweden. Albert Merling, the hero of this comic strip that was published in newspapers as renowned as the *Berlingske Tidende* of Copenhagen, Denmark, is the alter ego of the artist, who is also an amateur illusionist performing magic tricks. Although created as far back as 1963, *Dr. Merling* did not see print before 1970.

Just like Larsen, Dr. Merling is an illusionist, a magician. Dr. Merling tours Europe, together with his fam-

ily, in the 1870s, an epoch of scientific advancement that was still surrounded by mysticism and an atmosphere of expectation; in short, the epoch of Jules Verne. True and false ghosts and monsters, magic, mesmerism, hypnotism, and the occult pitted against and/or controlled by Dr. Merling meet the new mysticism of the 20th century halfway and are in line with the flowering of occultism in literature and comics. Depending on the case at hand, *Dr. Merling* shows humorous undertones or is played out for the sheer dramatic effect.

Although largely escapist fantasy, *Dr. Merling* nevertheless was based on Larsen's actual experience combined with the necessary amount of fantasy, according to the artist. This and research into the 1870s made for a genuine atmosphere correctly flavored for the delighted perusal of the modern reader.

The hero of the strip was not a superman but rather a reasoning, more or less normal protagonist who, through insight and learning, was able to master even the craziest situations he encountered. In comics, his type is relatively rare. His adventures, unfortunately, are no longer being published.

Knud V. Larsen, who had a thorough professional education as an artist, employed a bold, very personal style in *Dr. Merling*. Using a special technique, he incorporated details from engravings and illustrations of the 1870s into his artwork in order to add to the aura of authenticity that helped him pull off the fantastic and outlandish occurrences met by his hero.

W.F.

DR. MID-NITE (U.S.) *Dr. Mid-Nite* was created by writer Charles Reizenstein and artist Stanley Aschmeier (Stan Asch) and first appeared in National's *All-American* number 25 in April 1941. One of the most unique characters to appear as a National backup feature, Dr. Mid-Nite was actually blind surgeon Dr. Charles McNider. During the day he saw with the aid of infrared glasses, but at night, his eyesight increased tremendously. His only weapon was a blackout bomb, a pellet that spread a blanket of blackness over the doctor's quarry. Dr. Mid-Nite also sported one of the most original costumes of the 1940s superheroes—black tights, a red blouse, a cape and cowl, goggles, and yellow quarter-moon crescents on the cowl and blouse.

Despite Reizenstein's conceptual overkill (with his goggles and a blackout bomb, Mid-Nite was sharper than most sighted persons), his scripts were always crisp and fast-moving. And while the doctor was usually confined to the standard street crime gambit, his blackout bombs were constant fun. Artistically, Asch stayed with *Dr. Mid-Nite* until 1947. His work was never outstanding, but it was competent and the feature worked well. He was succeeded by Bernard Sachs, Alex Toth, and several others.

Overall, *Dr. Mid-Nite* appeared in *All-American* until October 1948's 102nd issue. As a member of the Justice Society of America, however, he survived in *All-Star Comics* from issue eight (December 1941) through issue 57 (February 1951). He was revived in the mid-1960s and has made several cameo appearances in *Flash* comics.

J.B.

DOCTOR NIEBLA (Spain) Adapted from a series of popular novels written by Rafael Gonzalez, *Doctor Niebla* ("Doctor Fog") appeared for the first time as a mystery strip in issue number 17 of the magazine *El Campeón* (November 1948). After this first publication, the feature was to appear in other publications put out by Editorial Brughera, such as *Superpulgarcito*, *Almanaques de Pulgarcito*, and *Supplemento de Historietas del DDT*, usually in the form of isolated two-page episodes, before disappearing definitively in 1959.

Rafael Gonzalez was soon succeeded as scriptwriter, first by Silver Kane (pseudonym of F. Gonzalez Ledesma) and Victor Mora. *Doctor Niebla's* only illustrator was Francisco Hidalgo, who succeeded in re-creating, in his use of black and white, the mood of American gangster films of the 1930s and the atmosphere of London and New York, the two cities where most of the action took place.

Dr. Niebla was a man in his thirties who did not deny his admiration for Sam Spade, Dashiell Hammett's private eye hero, and who wore a trench coat, sunglasses, and an ample scarf. A skilled violinist like Sherlock Holmes, a man of refined tastes, and somewhat of a stickler for niceties, he would leave a note of explanation for the police after each case he would solve, along with a small bouquet of heliotropes. In the course of each investigation, Dr. Niebla would take time out to telephone his girlfriend, the newswoman Alice Stark, whom he would scrupulously keep informed of his discoveries and without whose collaboration and patient devotion his life would probably hold no inducement. More than his fight against mas-

ter criminals, Alice's admiration was what kept the hero going through his paces.

Some *Doctor Niebla* stories were printed in two colors, but Hidalgo, like Caniff and Robbins, was at his best in black and white.

L.G.

DOCTOR STRANGE (U.S.) Less than two years after Marvel's *Fantastic Four* premiered in 1961, editor Stan Lee had built a stable of strips that included *Spider-Man*, *Thor*, and *The Hulk*. He added a fifth strip, *Doctor Strange*, in July 1963. Created by artist Steve Ditko and Lee, this master of the occult made his debut in *Strange Tales* number 110.

Doctor Strange was really prominent surgeon Stephen Strange, a selfish, rather callous man who had abandoned the spirit of the Hippocratic oath. As fate would have it, he was injured in an auto accident and could never operate again. He searched in vain for a cure, finally coming upon "The Ancient One," keeper of the forces of white magic. After some initial reluctance, Strange became his willing pupil and was taught the old one's powers. He also inherited a horde of evildoers bent on using magic to destroy Strange and the forces of good. Among them were Baron Mordo, the Ancient One's original pupil and Strange's most persistent enemy, the "dread" Dormammu, Nightmare, Umar, and many others of mystic persuasion.

The doctor lived in Greenwich Village, wore an oriental-like costume and cape, possessed the mystic amulet, the power to separate his spirit from his body, and a rich vocabulary that included phrases like "By the hoary hosts of Hoggoth" and "The all seeing eye of Agamotto." *Doctor Strange* was one of the first strips Lee drifted away from, however, and over the years,

"Doctor Niebla," Francisco Hidalgo. © Editorial Bruguera.

"Doctor Strange," Frank Brunner. © Marvel Comics Group.

Don Rico, Roy Thomas, Denny O'Neil, Jim Lawrence, Ray Holloway, Steve Englehart, and even artist Ditko wrote the feature. Unfortunately, no one could capture Lee's flair and the strip never regained its early mystique. For a while, Doctor Strange was even made into a superhero, complete with long johns.

Artistically, Steve Ditko remained on the strip until 1966, creating heretofore unseen fantasy worlds. Most noted for his realistic, "everyman" artwork on *Spider-Man*, Ditko's *Doctor Strange* work was a fantastic trip into the occult. After his departure, Bill Everett, Marie Severin, Dan Adkins, Gene Colan, and others handled the feature with varying degrees of success, but only Frank Brunner's short-lived 1974 rendition ever matched Ditko's inspired originality.

The feature continued in *Strange Tales* until the book was dubbed *Doctor Strange* beginning with June 1968's 169th issue; it folded after November 1969's 183rd issue. After many subsequent guest appearances and a regular spot in *The Defenders* feature, *Doctor Strange* began a new book in June 1974.

J.B.

In the hands of capable artists (Rudy Niebres, Frank Miller, Frank Brunner, etc.) and of writers who involved the hero with such mythical figures as Dracula and Lilith, the revived series fared reasonably well, lasting to 1987. The character was brought back in 1988, given a nifty moniker ("Sorcerer Supreme"), and under this new guise *Doctor Strange* managed to hang on until 1996, when it was finally discontinued (but perhaps not for good).

M.H.

DODD, EDWARD BENTON (1902-1991) American cartoonist and author, born November 7, 1902, in La Fayette, Georgia. Ed Dodd attended the Georgia Institute of Technology and later the Art Students League in New York, where he studied under the noted animal painter and sculptor Daniel Beard. In 1926 his love of the great open spaces took him to Wyoming, where he managed a cattle ranch; he later went on to become a guide and mule packer in Yellowstone National Park. All during this time he kept drawing and sketching people, animals, and scenes around him.

In 1930 Dodd started a nature panel for United Feature Syndicate, *Back Home Again*, which he drew until 1945. In 1946 he created *Mark Trail* for the Hall Syndicate, a strip into which he poured all of his love and knowledge of nature, his feelings for the open spaces and the free life. Dodd won a multiplicity of distinctions in different fields, from the Sigma Delta Chi award for cartooning to an award from the National Forestry Association for his contribution to conservation. He was also the author and illustrator of a nature book, *Mark Trail's Book of North American Mammals*, as well as other books also concerned with the great outdoors and wildlife.

Dodd retired from *Mark Trail* in 1978, although his doctor continued to appear on the strip for some years thereafter. Along with his wife Rosemary he established the Mark Trail-Ed Dodd Conservation Foundation and was active in environmental issues. He died in Gainesville, Georgia, in May 1991.

M.H.

DOLL MAN (U.S.) *Doll Man* was created by Will Eisner and made its first appearance in Quality's *Feature*

"Doll Man," Reed Crandall. © Comic Magazines, Inc.

Comics number 27 in December 1939. Using more traditional methods of transformation, Darrel Dane simply willed himself into Doll Man, a change that made him shrink from his normal height to Doll Man's five-inch stature.

Wearing a simple blue uniform and red cape, Doll Man spent over 12 years fighting a wide assortment of villains, all of whom were much bigger than he. But because he retained his normal strength at his minuscule height, Doll Man rarely had trouble with foes, though many of the feature's best moments came when Doll Man went searching for a means of transportation. Over the years, he traveled in pockets, on a roller skate, or in briefcases. As the years progressed, he also enlisted the aid of a dog and later a miniplane. Doll Man hid behind inkwells, in books, and in drawers. As the strip began to falter in the 1950s, Doll Girl was added. She was Darrel Dane's fiancée, Martha Roberts, and she made her first appearance in December 1951's *Doll Man* number 37.

Many of Quality's best artists worked on the strip, including Eisner (1939-41) and Reed Crandall (1942-43). But Al Bryant, who drew the feature between 1943 and 1946, became the definitive artist. Although he was not as creative as other Quality artists, his material was always clean and straightforward.

Doll Man continued to appear in *Feature Comics* until the 139th issue in October 1949. The character was also given his own book, starting in autumn 1941 and lasting until October 1953 through 47 issues.

J.B.

DONALD DUCK (U.S.) Donald Duck, a major Walt Disney Studios animated cartoon star, appeared in two major comic strips, one drawn by Al Taliaferro from August 30, 1936, and the other by Carl Barks from April 1943. The bad actor who was to become the biggest hit in the history of animated films initially appeared dancing a hearty hornpipe on the deck of his

nephews were the magic mixture that made the strip a solid hit.

Donald, Daisy, and the nephews next appeared in comic book form in *Walt Disney's Comics and Stories* for April 1943, as drawn by cartoonist Carl Barks. For a long time, the Disney magazine had been reprinting the Taliaferro *Donald*, but the immediate supply was running low, and the magazine editors wanted more Donald up front right away. The answer was to keep reprinting Taliaferro, but to add new material in the form of monthly 10-page Barks stories. For the first time in comic form, Donald burst the bounds of daily and Sunday gag strip limitations and became involved in longer, more elaborate narratives written by Barks. The readers loved it and wrote in increasing numbers for more. Barks branched into book-length *Donald Duck* narratives published as 64-page comic magazines by the Disney people under titles such as *The Pixilated Parrot*, *Voodoo Hoodoo*, and *The Sheriff of Bullet Valley*. The effort, which earned Barks the magazine Duck assignment, was a 64-page magazine adaptation of a projected Donald Duck feature film in 1942.

Donald as an adventurer intrigued readers as much as Donald the daily gagster, and the magazine feature became as strong a hit as the newspaper strip. Barks introduced some original characters into his work, such as Gladstone Gander and Uncle Scrooge McDuck (who later starred in his own comic books by Barks), while Taliaferro stuck to new studio characters such as Gus Goose and Grandma Duck. Both versions of *Donald* are still appearing: the Barks magazine stories are reprinted each month, and the newspaper strip by a new, less capable Disney hand, although Donald has virtually disappeared from the screen except on occasional TV reruns of his old cartoons. The major *Donald Duck* strip work appears to be in the past, although it will live on in reprint and memory, thanks to the fine work of Al Taliaferro and Carl Barks.

B.B.

Since Taliaferro's death in 1969 Donald has known a bewildering succession of artists, including Frank Grundeen, Frank Smith, and Peter Alvarado; while the writing, done by Bob Karp from the feature's inception to 1974, has been continued by, among others, Bob Foster and Larry Meyer. The strip still appears daily and Sundays (as *Walt Disney's Donald Duck*) to this day. The comic book title meanwhile continued with diminished fortune until 1984, when it was discontinued by Whitman. In 1986 Gladstone Publishing revived the title, carrying on to the present (with a brief interlude in 1990-93 when it was published by the ill-starred Disney Comics).

M.H.

"Donald Duck," Floyd Gottfredson. © Walt Disney Productions.

rural scow in a Disney short called *The Wise Little Hen* in 1934. The Disney animators liked working with the new character, and since public response to the first short had been good, Donald was given a supporting part in a Mickey Mouse cartoon, *The Band Concert*. The raucous, popcorn-peddling duck completely stole the show, and his stardom was assured.

Donald's popularity was delayed a bit in the comic strip arena. Although Donald made his initial strip appearance in the first Sunday episode of a strip version of *The Wise Little Hen*, published in the *Silly Symphony* third-page portion of the *Mickey Mouse* page on September 16, 1934, which ran until December 16, 1934, his impact was not comparable to his screen smash. Given minor roles in *Mickey Mouse* daily and Sunday strip continuity of the time by Floyd Gottfredson (first daily *Mickey* appearance was as a newsboy on March 15, 1935; first Sunday, a little earlier, was as a tough neighborhood kid in the *Mickey* for February 10, 1935), Donald did not receive a major role in the comics until Sunday, August 23, 1936. Then, in the last panel of a *Silly Symphony* page otherwise devoted to the closing episode of a Three Little Pigs story, an aggressive-looking Donald, tilting his hat drakishly, glared out at the audience while black and red letters behind him announced: *Next Week*: DONALD DUCK!

Sure enough, next week a full half of the Sunday *Mickey Mouse* page was shared by a new strip titled *Silly Symphony Featuring Donald Duck*. Signed by Walt Disney but drawn by Al Taliaferro, the gag sequence displayed Donald demolishing a wall in his house to blast a mosquito with a shotgun. The new screen legend had come in full bloom to the comic page. The daily *Donald* strip, which started a bit later, was also drawn by Taliaferro and, like the Sunday, featured individual gags with little inter-episode continuity. Goofy, Horace Horsecollar, Pluto, and other *Mickey Mouse* regulars appeared in the new *Donald* strip from the outset. Daisy Duck, Donald's girlfriend, appeared a bit later. The real bombshell of characterization hit the strip on October 17, 1937, when Donald's tormenting nephews, Huey, Louie, and Dewey, appeared, on a visit from Donald's cousin, Della Duck. They stayed, to the delight of millions of readers, for Donald and his

DON BERRINCHE (Spain) Created in 1948 in the magazine *El Campeón*, *Don Berrinche* moved the following year to *Pulgarcito*, another Bruguera publication, while, as was customary with most features distributed by this publishing house, it also appeared in the comic weeklies *DDT* and *Ven y Ven*. The author of this gag strip was Peñarroya, a prolific and talented cartoonist.

Don Berrinche was in the beginning a bitter little man, an irascible curmudgeon, incapable of controlling his temper, who would roam the streets wielding an enormous club surmounted by a nail. The most frequent target of Berrinche's temper was the hapless Gordito Relleno, a slow-witted and good-natured milquetoast, who suffered with resignation all of Berrinche's indignities. The latter would scream, get mad, and end each episode wildly flaying his arms while letting out terrible curses.

With the passing of time, Don Berrinche's character softened considerably, underwent a radical mental transformation, and became a quiet middle-class citizen. He went to work as a company manager, enjoyed a higher standard of living, and got fat; his face did not look as angry, and his eyes were more peaceful. He traded his club for a cane, and for screams and curses he substituted unctuous platitudes. While earlier he was impulsive, he became calculating, hypocritical, and coldly cruel: the very epitome of the petty bourgeois. Don Berrinche continued for some time after José Penarroya's death in 1975, ending when Bruguera closed its doors in the mid-1980s.

L.G.

DONDI (U.S.) Launched on September 25, 1955, *Dondi* was the joint effort of Gus Edson and Irwin Hasen for the Chicago Tribune-New York News Syndicate. Coming at the end of a large number of GI adoptions of war orphans, Dondi was an Italian boy (with a dead American GI father) whose first great battle was attempting to enter the United States over immigration restrictions.

This first continuity was a master stroke on the part of Gus Edson, the author, as it created a national sensation and a great deal of real anxiety about the comic character's fate.

Dondi became enmeshed in a long-running tug-of-war over his guardianship in the States—between rich, matronly Mrs. McGowan, mother of one of Dondi's GI buddies in Europe, and Ted Wills, one of the GIs. The other major characters were Katje, Ted's wife (they would become his parents in Midville, a typical small town); Pop Fligh, Dondi's new "grandfather"; friends Baldy and Web in their Explorer's Club; and Dondi's dog Queenie.

In 1966 Gus Edson died and Hasen assumed the continuity. When Dondi's family affairs were straightened out, much of the pathos left the strip, and it then revolved around incidents with his club members and weird characters who came and went. The strip outlasted such competitors as *On Stage* in the syndicate's flagship papers.

"Dondi," Irwin Hasen. © Chicago Tribune-New York News Syndicate.

Dondi, with its basic appeal formulated for all age groups, was made into a feature movie, with David Janssen, Patti Page, and David Cory in the title role, in 1962. Other spin-offs have included comic books, clothing accessories, and a TV pilot. *Dondi* was awarded the NCS Best Story Strip Award in 1961 and 1962. It ended in June 1986.

R.M.

DON DIXON AND THE HIDDEN EMPIRE (U.S.) *Don Dixon and the Hidden Empire* resulted from the collaboration of writer Bob Moore and artist Carl Pfeufer. The feature (with *Tad of the Tanbark* as a top) ran in the *Brooklyn Eagle* from October 6, 1935, to July 6, 1941.

Don Dixon, his companion Matt Haynes (soon to disappear from the strip), and Dr. Lugoff enter the unknown country of Pharia in the course of their explorations. There Don fights against giants and pygmies, witches and sorcerers; leads the revolt against Karth, who has usurped Pharia's throne; and frequently rescues Princess Wanda from a fate worse than death. After a brief trip back to civilization, Don, Lugoff, and Wanda return to Pharia, where the princess is finally restored to her throne.

"Don Dixon," Carl Pfeufer. © Brooklyn Eagle.

Don Dixon was probably the best of all the *Flash Gordon* imitations. Don looks very much like Flash and Dr. Lugoff is an obvious reference to Dr. Zarkov. Pfeufer's style was at first reminiscent of the early Raymond but it later acquired authority and dash and is not without merit. Bob Moore's stories were imaginative, with a good plot. This evocation of "the hidden empire" is quite enjoyable, even today, and it deserves an honorable mention among science-fiction strips.

M.H.

DON FULGENCIO (Argentina) The humor strip *Don Fulgencio o el Hombre que no Tuvo Infancia* ("Mr. Fulgen-

"Don Fulgencio," Lino Palacio. © La Razón.

cio, or the Man Who Had No Childhood") was created in 1935 by cartoonist Lino Palacio. It was first published in the Buenos Aires daily *La Opinión*, moved in 1939 to *La Prensa* and later to *La Razón*.

In the 60 years of his existence, Don Fulgencio has changed little in his physical appearance. He is still the same middle-aged, black-attired man with a cucumber-shaped head surmounted by a minuscule derby. Bald and short-sighted, he has gotten a little more jowl in the face with the years, but his character has not changed one iota. Well-mannered, indecisive, good-natured, and shy, he goes through life in an optimistic daze.

Like so many men who had to work hard to succeed, it is presumed that Don Fulgencio had to earn a living at a tender age, which is why he never had toys, or a genuine childhood, or had ever been mischievous. Now that he enjoys a good station in life, having money in the bank and servants, all he wants is to drop out of life, chuck everything, and play. If he finds his house empty, he dresses like Tarzan and swings from the dining room chandelier; if his neighbors invite him for a snack, he asks to be given a second helping of cherry pie; if he misses the streetcar, he goes home on a skateboard. Such is Don Fulgencio, more temperamental, impudent, mischievous and childish at 50 than he ever was at 5. The unique adult's toy that he cherishes is his record player on which he plays the songs of his lost love: Shirley Temple!

Don Fulgencio lives in the world of dreams. In recent years he has been saddled with a cheeky nephew whose attitude is opposite to that of his uncle: he wants to be an adult, and he'd rather wear a suit much too large for him than allow Fulgencio to buy him more suitable attire in the children's department. In the *Don Fulgencio* daily strip, as well as in the accompanying *Ramona* strip (about Fulgencio's maid), Palacio has created a whole score of secondary characters such as Tripudio, Pochito, Pototó, Liberato, and Radragaz, who have gotten strips of their own in the magazine *Avivato*.

Don Fulgencio, the most popular Argentine strip in and out of its country of origin, has been adapted to the screen and radio. Among Palacio's assistants on the strip have been cartoonists who later became famous, such as Toño Gallo, Guerrero, Atilio, Montes, Pereda, Haroldo, and Flores.

L.G.

DON PANCHO TALERO (Argentina) *Don Pancho Talero* was created by the pioneering Argentinian cartoonist Arturo Lanteri, for the magazine *El Hogar*, where it ran without interruption from 1922 to 1944.

It is a family strip, deeply rooted in Argentine middle-class life, although Don Pancho Talero himself bears more than a passing resemblance to Jiggs (but only in appearance). A sailor by profession, Talero, when at home, is dominated by his energetic wife, a stout and sturdy woman, who is fond of awaiting her philandering husband, concealed behind a curtain with a bottle in her hands. The household includes Pancho's mother-in-law, his children, his daughter's fiancé, his loafer brother-in-law, and a maid of formidable aspect, an immigrant from Vigo whose peculiar accent contrasts sharply with the typically "porteño" (from Buenos Aires) dialect and mannerisms of the Talero family.

Lanteri started his comic strip career in 1916 with *El Negro Raul*, but *Don Pancho Talero* met with greater popularity, thanks to its familiar roots and to the male readers' easy identification with the main character, whose only preoccupation is to escape this home where everybody screams, and seek refuge in the company of his friends inside a friendly café.

The first talking picture ever produced in Argentina was released in 1931: directed by Lanteri himself, it dealt with Talero's adventures in Hollywood.

L.G.

DON WINSLOW OF THE NAVY (U.S.) The idea for *Don Winslow* came to Lt. Commander Frank V. Martinek when Admiral Watson T. Cluverius, then commandant of the Ninth Naval District and of the Great Lakes Naval Training Station near Chicago, complained of the difficulties of navy recruiting in the Midwest. Martinek started a series of novels with a young naval officer, Don Winslow, as the hero. Colonel Frank Knox, Secretary of the Navy, became interested and helped in selling the concept to the Bell Syndicate. Written by Martinek himself, drawn by Lieutenant Leon A. Beroth, USN, assisted by Carl Hammond, and approved by the Navy Department, *Don Winslow of the Navy* premiered on March 5, 1934.

Commander Don Winslow of navy intelligence, helped by his partner Lieutenant Red Pennington, pursued a long and successful struggle against various espionage and subversive groups that threatened the welfare and security of the United States. His chief opponent in the thirties was the crafty and ruthless "Scorpio," head of the worldwide spy network known as "Scorpia." During World War II Don and Red turned their attention to the Japanese and Germans, and their domestic allies and supporters. From time to time Don Winslow was allowed a rest in the arms of his eternal fiancée, Mercedes Colby, daughter of Don's commanding officer, Admiral Colby.

From 1940 to 1942, Ken Ernst assisted on the strip. In 1942 Hammond was drafted and replaced by Ed Moore, then Al Levin. In the fifties *Don Winslow's* appeal steadily waned, and the strip was discontinued July 30, 1955.

Don Winslow was more a mystery strip than a sea-adventure story. Competently written and carefully

Don Winslow of the Navy

263

"Don Winslow," Frank Martinek and Leon Beroth. © Bell Syndicate.

"Doonesbury," Garry Trudeau. © G. B. Trudeau.

drawn, it held its own in the crowded adventure field and was popular for over a decade. Commander Winslow's adventures were published in book form, broadcast on the radio, and carried in a series of comic books issued by Fawcett. Two movie serials were also released, *Don Winslow of the Navy* (1941), directed by Ford Beebe and starring Don Terry, and *Don Winslow of the Coast Guard* (1943), also with Don Terry.

M.H.

DOONESBURY (U.S.) Garry Trudeau, then a Yale undergraduate, created a strip called *Bull Tales* in 1968 for the *Yale Record*; from there it went to the *Yale Daily News* in 1969, where it attracted national press coverage. In the following year the strip, retitled *Doonesbury*, started syndication. It was distributed by Universal Press Syndicate; the first issue date was October 26, 1970.

Doonesbury is a C-minus college student—and a minus in most other enterprises as well. He never quite succeeds in asserting himself, or winning an argument with fellow students, or scoring with campus coeds. His friends are almost as hapless as he is—B.D. (inspired by Yale quarterback Brian Dowling) fancies himself a football hero and big man on campus; Mark Slackmeyer (alias Megaphone Mark) is a self-styled campus revolutionary who tries to upset the establishment with the help of his trusted megaphone through which he utters the well-worn clichés of the radical left. Not surprisingly, Mark has lately become a disc jockey on station WBBY.

Obviously inspired by the sophisticated strips of the 1950s and 1960s (Feiffer) *Doonesbury* often rises to the level of genuine satire. Trudeau is unsparing in his parodies: the coeds are depicted as a bunch of neurotic girls, as pathetic as their male counterparts; the police, as a mob of sadistic bullies whose greatest enjoyment

in life is cracking students' skulls. Political figures are not spared either, and Trudeau did a running commentary on the Watergate situation. A comic strip sensation almost from the first, *Doonesbury* has been reprinted in book form by Holt, Rinehart.

Trudeau received the Pulitzer Prize for cartooning in 1975 for *Doonesbury*. Following marriage (to TV personality Jane Pauley) and fatherhood, he became the first cartoonist in modern times to take a sabbatical from his strip. The feature went on hiatus in January 1983 (subscribing newspapers were supplied with reruns). When it came back in September 1984, it was a changed strip, hovering uncertainly between satire and soap opera. Consequently, it started losing papers, and in order to maintain his income, Trudeau branched out to merchandising *Doonesbury*, a practice he had previously declared he would never resort to.

M.H.

DORGAN, THOMAS ALOYSIUS (1877-1929) "Tad" Dorgan was born Thomas Aloysius Dorgan to laborer parents in San Francisco on April 29, 1877. Erratically schooled and a part-time factory worker before his teens, Dorgan lost the last three fingers on his right hand in a factory machine accident at age 13. Recuperating, he was urged to develop a latent cartooning talent as manual therapy. He became enthusiastically involved and landed his first job at 14 as staff artist on the *San Francisco Bulletin*, where he illustrated news events, did classified-ad-page filler art, and drew visiting celebrities. By 1895 his weekly illustration for the *Bulletin*'s continued children's stories revealed his capacity for arresting humorous art, and within a few years he had been hired by the city's most prestigious paper, the *Chronicle*, as general artist, where he was assigned his first comic strip work, a weekly color-page

called *Johnny Wise*, which ran for several months in 1902. Able as ever to spot talent in the pages of rival papers, W. R. Hearst hired Dorgan away from the *Chronicle* in late 1902 and put him to work as a sports-page cartoonist on his *New York Journal*, where he flourished both as a personality able to almost instantly become close friends with virtually every sports celebrity of the period, and as an extremely able sports cartoonist, drawing action poses of boxers and other sports figures so accurately that they are still reprinted as textbook records.

In the lax periods between the major sports seasons, Dorgan began to develop characters out of his own fancy and put them through anecdotal and narrative paces. Most of these were canine figures with human attributes and problems, from Silk Hat Harry, a dog about town with a revengeful wife; through Curlock Holmes, a bulldog detective; to Judge Rummy, Tad's central character. Despite Tad's inconsistent narrative and often flat jokes, the public adored his non-sports work, and particularly relished his relaying of contemporary big city street argot and sports slang into both his strips and his handwritten prose column of wit called *Daffydills*, which accompanied them on the *Journal* sports page. So wide was the popular response to

his innovative terms, such as "drug-store cowboy," "the storm-and-strife" (for wife), "Dumb Dora," "Yes, we have no bananas," etc., that many have entered the American idiom permanently.

Dorgan's comic dog continuity eventually acquired a continuing name, *Silk Hat Harry's Divorce Suit*, a name that became one of the half-dozen most popular daily strips of the 1910s. A panel gag series called *Indoor Sports* (poker, dice, pool, etc.) ran concurrently and continued after Dorgan dropped Judge Rummy and the others in the early 1920s. Suffering from recurrent ill health, particularly after his last out-of-town sports assignment—the Dempsey-Miske bout in 1920—Dorgan went into enforced retirement at his Great Neck, Long Island, estate, where he continued his sports-page art until his premature death from a relatively minor case of pneumonia at his home on May 2, 1929.

Hearst papers across the country turned over what amounted to entire editions to commemorate his passing and immediately undertook a reprinting of his *Indoor Sports* panel and boxing history features, which continued for years. Lean and angular, and a familiar figure to his readers through his frequent self-caricatures, Dorgan was remembered as much as a personal friend by his followers as he was a cartoonist. A significant personage of his time, Dorgan deserves the comprehensive memorial biography and collection of his work he never received.

B.B.

DOT AND CARRIE (G.B.) Dorothy and Caroline, dubbed "Dot and Carrie" after the shorthand typist's catchphrase, "Dot and carry on," brought the working girl into British newspaper strips. They were created by J. F. Horrabin, already writing and drawing *Japhet and Happy*, at the request of Wilson Pope, editor of the London evening newspaper *The Star*. He wanted a daily strip in the American mold of *Somebody's Stenog*, and Horrabin obliged. The early credit was "By the Horrabin Brothers," as J. F. drew the scripts written by his brother-in-law, H. O. Batho. The strip, which began on November 18, 1922, was American in style, but soon settled into a more native and individual form. The cast was Dot, the pretty blonde who felt sure she was born for movie stardom; Carrie the plain and bespectacled spinster; their boss, bald and fiery Henry Spilliken (Motto: "Work like Helen B. Gloomy"); the handsome Junior Partner; Adolphus the cheeky office boy; Carrie's rotund boyfriend, Aubrey V. DuPois; and Mrs. Mopps, the cheery cockney charlady. Once a year they would abandon their daily gags for continuity in

the form of the Office Pantomime. The strip did not end until Horrabin died, having survived an absorption of *The Star* by the *Evening News*, in which paper it ran from October 18, 1960, to March 2, 1962. The final strip bore the serial number 11,735.

Only three books of *Dot and Carrie* strips were published: *Dot and Carrie* (1923); *Dot and Carrie (and Adolphus)* (1924); *Dot and Carrie (not forgetting Adolphus)* (1925).

D.G.

DOTTOR FAUST, IL (Italy) Wolfgang Goethe's *Faust*, that masterpiece of German literature, seemed in 1939 to be a fit subject for adaptation into comic strip form. Its cultural credentials and high moral tone would put it past the censors without a hitch; and the propaganda value it would give to Italy's ally, Germany, was a further consideration in view of Mondadori's strained relations in the past with the Fascist authorities.

Of course, for a work of such distinction an exceptional talent had to be found, and the publishers picked Gustavo Rosso, who was not a cartoonist but a painter and illustrator of children's books. Rosso (using the pen name "Gustavino") set to work, and on July 20, 1939, the first page of *Il Dottor Faust* appeared in the comic weekly *L'Audace*, following the strip adaptation of Federico Pedrocchi. Unfortunately Rosso fell ill after having completed only four pages, and the publication was suspended.

Mondadori had not given up on his pet project, however, and in 1941, *Il Dottor Faust* was revived by Rino Albertarelli for another one of Mondadori's comic weeklies, *Topolino*. If Rosso's pages had been technically flawless, Albertarelli's artwork proved just as remarkable. His architecture was grandiose or sinister, according to the plot; the backgrounds were exquisitely detailed; the pace was unrelenting; and the color work was matchless. But the artists who continued Albertarelli's work after 1943, the painters Chiletto and Maraja, were markedly inferior.

In the end, the original figure of Doctor Faust, a religious man tormented by his sins, was changed into

that of a mindless fop, a portrayal that did not fit either the place or the character. His antagonist Mephistopheles soon became the principal character, owing to the author's sympathetic treatment and, more significantly, to his popularity with the readers; so much so that the second episode of *Il Dottor Faust* was actually devoted to the doctor's fiendish enemy.

G.B.

Borivoj Dovniković, "U Zemlji Lijepog Nogometa." © Dovniković.

DOVNIKOVIĆ, BORIVOJ (1930-) Born in 1930, Borivoj Dovniković today is known as one of the best Yugoslav cartoon filmmakers. He lives in Zagreb and works for "Zagreb film." His childhood was filled with comics—Walt Disney and Harold Foster were his idols.

Dovniković's first comic strip, *Udarnik Ratko*, was published in *Glas Slavonije*; it was the first realistic strip published in Yugoslavia after World War II. After that Dovniković worked at the first Yugoslav cartoon film studio, "Duga film," but when the firm was liquidated in 1952, he and Walter Neugebauer came back to their mutual love—comic strips. From there Dovniković started his collaboration with the new comic magazine *Horizontov Zabavnik*, where he created his most popular strip, *Velika utakmica* ("The Big Match"), which he drew on the verses of Neugebauer's brother, Norbert.

For the Zagreb magazine *Plavi Vjesnik* he drew three episodes of a realistic soccer strip, the scripts for which were written by famous Yugoslav sports journalist Ljubomir Vukadinović. For the same magazine he did a longer comic strip series, *Mendo Mendović*, based on a very popular children's TV series. The strip was discontinued along with the TV series, and it was the last one done by Dovniković. He is now occupied producing cartoon films and sometimes does cartoon illustrations for the TV magazine *Studio* in Zagreb. His hobbies are going to the movies and photography.

E.R.

DOWLING, STEVE (1904-1986) Stephen P. Dowling was born in 1904 in Liverpool. Educated at Liverpool Collegiate, he studied art at the Liverpool School of Art, continuing at the Westminster School of Art in

"Il Dottor Faust," Gustavino (Gustavo Rosso). © Mondadori.

London. Upon graduating in 1924, he did freelance drawing and advertising work for the Charles W. Hobson Agency. After two years in various art studios, he set up his own in 1927, and in 1928 was made assistant art director of the Dorland Advertising Agency. He drew his first strip, *Tich* (November 21, 1931), for the *Daily Mirror*, a pantomime gag written by his brother, Frank Dowling, who was also an advertising man.

His first successful daily strip was *Ruggles*, at first a daily gag, again by Frank Dowling, but soon becoming a continuity strip. *Ruggles* ran from March 11, 1935, to August 3, 1957. He also took over *Belinda Blue Eyes* for the same paper, and drew both strips daily from 1936 to July 24, 1943, when he started *Garth*. Meanwhile, he did freelance advertising work, notably the Roses Lime Juice series featuring Hawkins the Butler, and served as a captain in the British Home Guard.

After the war he joined the *Daily Mirror* staff, assisting Bill Herbert, the strip editor, continuing *Garth*, visualizing *Jane*, and creating the new daily, *Keeping Up With the Joneses* (March 9, 1960) in conjunction with the paper's city editor. Required to retire at the age of 65 in 1969, Dowling became a full-time farmer, market gardener, and riding-school proprietor in Pett, near Hastings, Sussex. The most prolific British newspaper strip artist, Dowling's style and characters were both popular and influential. He died on March 19, 1986, at the age of 82.

D.G.

DOWN HOGAN'S ALLEY *see Yellow Kid, The.*

"Drago," Burne Hogarth. © Burne Hogarth.

DRAGO (U.S.) Soon after he left *Tarzan* for the first time in 1945, Burne Hogarth created a Sunday page for the *New York Post*. Called *Drago*, it ran for a year, from November 4, 1945, to November 10, 1946.

Physically and psychologically Drago looks pretty much like Tarzan's kid brother, in his dark and athletic good looks. The locale is Argentina instead of Africa, but the universe of violent landscapes and sinister shadows favored by the author are quickly rediscov-

ered. In the two episodes that make up the entire strip Drago and his comic sidekick Tabasco fight Baron Zodiac, a sinister Nazi with a plan to destroy the world, and foil a plot aimed at discrediting Drago and his father.

Despite its brief existence, *Drago* remains one of the adventure strips most deserving of study, as well as the one most revealing of its author. Hogarth's baroque imagination enjoys free play in the opulence of the women's costumes and in the phantasmagoric atmosphere of the plot. Never before did Hogarth's talent rise to such expressionistic fury as it did in the violent depiction of the action. A song, aptly titled *The Song of Drago the Gaucho*, was composed, to which Hogarth contributed the lyrics, but without much success.

M.H.

DRAKE, STANLEY (1921-1997) American artist, born in Brooklyn on November 9, 1921. Stan Drake moved with his family to New Jersey and grew up in River Edge and Hackensack. In 1939 he attended the Art Students League and studied under the great anatomist George Bridgman. Before and during his training there he was a pulp illustrator, starting with *Popular Detective* and *Popular Sports* at age 17.

Also as a youngster, he drew for early comic books beside Bob Lubbers and Bob Bugg—writing, drawing, and lettering at seven dollars a page. He also worked for Stan Lee before entering the service in August 1941. Discharged in February 1946 after wartime action in the Pacific theater, he immediately went to Madison Avenue and drew for many advertising accounts of the Perlowin Studios. Soon Drake transferred to the training ground for a generation of strip artists—Johnstone and Cushing. Drake successfully opened his own studio, with Bob Lubbers and John Celardo, and had a staff of 12 before exhaustion overtook him.

At the suggestion of Lubbers, Drake decided to draw a newspaper strip, and Gill Fox introduced him to Eliot Caplin. Together they filled King Features' need for a romantic soap opera. *The Heart of Juliet Jones* has been a leader in the story-strip field ever since they created it in 1953.

Drake's strongest influences came at the start of this strip. He moved to Connecticut and became friendly with the inhabitants of the artists' colony around Westport, including Al Parker, Al Dorne, and Robert Fawcett. Drake sought a definite illustrative flavor and a liberation from the comic-book conventions for *Juliet*.

His two goals have been well met. He preserved his integrity in the strip format changes, and his strip lasted in the days of the dying story strip.

Drake's art is strong and his bold men and winsome women vibrate with character and emotion. The attraction of his art lies in the use of benday as a wash, and the pioneering of a confident pen (as opposed to brush work). For the last 13 years of his life he contributed the artwork to *Blondie*. He died at his home in Westport, Connecticut, on March 10, 1997.

R.M.

DRAYTON, GRACE (1877-1936) American cartoonist and illustrator, born in Philadelphia on October 14, 1877. The daughter of Philadelphia's first art publisher, Grace Gebbie married Theodore E. Wiedersheim Jr. in her twenties and, under the name G. Wiedersheim, created the series *Bobbie Blake* and *Dolly Drake* for the *Philadelphia Press*. She also illustrated nursery rhymes

Grace Drayton, "Dimples." © Grace G. Drayton.

"The Dream of the Rarebit Fiend," Silas (Winsor McCay).

written by her sister Margaret G. Hayes, with whom she created, in 1909, *The Terrible Tales of Captain Kiddo*. In 1911 she divorced her first husband and married W. Heyward Drayton III (whom she was subsequently to divorce in 1923). Using the name Grace (Gigi) Drayton she illustrated a number of children's books and created several comic features: *Toodles* (around 1911), *Dolly Dimples* (1915), *The Campbell Kids*. In 1935 she started the series she is best remembered for, *The Pussycat Princess*. She died on January 31, 1936.

Grace Drayton was probably the first and certainly the most successful of American female cartoonists, and her position in the history of the comic strip is unique. As an artist, however, her work is overly cute and mannered, and her creations designed only for younger children.

M.H.

DREAMS OF THE RAREBIT FIEND (U.S.) Winsor McCay's first acknowledged masterwork and first exposition of the oneiric theme was *Dream(s) of the Rarebit Fiend*. It made its appearance in the *New York Evening Telegram* in 1904, signed with McCay's pseudonym "Silas."

In 1907 McCay gave this explanation of the genesis of the unusual strip: "The Dream of the Rarebit Fiend is an evolution of a drawing I made for the New York Telegram two years ago (sic) . . . You know how a cigaret fiend is when he gets up in the morning and can't find a dope stick? Well, I drew a picture once showing a fiend at the north pole without a cigaret and about ready to die. I introduced some other characters who happened to have paper and tobacco and a match, but the only match went out before they got a light. Then I had to frame up a finish and I made it a dream. My employer suggested that I make him a series of pictures and make them as rarebit dreams and you know the result."

The Rarebit Fiend is especially remarkable as a dry run for the later *Little Nemo* and as an earnest effort at exploring the depths of the unconscious—and doing it one year before the publication of Sigmund Freud's *The Interpretation of Dreams*. During the "fiend's" nightmares, caused by his inordinate, manic craving for Welsh rarebits, he encounters situations and themes that examine the nature of a man's fears. Topics include nudity and the taboo that is attached to it, masks, transvestism, the fear of castration, the fear of going insane, and the obsession of impotence. More than in *Little Nemo*, where it is rationalized and sublimated, the dream quest appears here in its naked, spontaneous immediacy.

The Rarebit Fiend appeared with weekly regularity from 1904 to 1907, until McCay became more absorbed elsewhere and the strip appeared intermittently. When McCay joined the Hearst organization in 1911, the Herald Co. (publisher of the *Telegram*) started syndicating reprints of *The Rarebit Fiend* that were hand colored by McCay. Hearst's International News Service tried to compete with a new version variously titled "A January Day Dream," "Midsummer Day Dream," etc. Both versions disappeared in 1914.

Dreams of the Rarebit Fiend enjoyed notable success, presumably due more to the strip's imaginativeness and artistry than to its theme. In 1905 a total of 61 of the fiend's dreams were reprinted in book form by Frederick A. Stokes; they were reprinted by Dover in 1973. In 1906 the American movie pioneer Edwin S. Porter produced a film adaptation called *The Dream of a Rarebit Fiend*, which is widely acknowledged as a masterpiece of the early cinema. In 1916 Winsor McCay himself made an animated version of the strip under the title *The Adventures of a Rarebit Eater.*

M.H.

DROPOUTS, THE (U.S.) Howard Post launched *The Dropouts* in 1968 as a daily strip for United Feature Syndicate, and a Sunday version followed a year later. At first the feature was little more than a one-joke strip. Two young men, the stringy, conceited Alf and the diminutive, naive Sandy, were literally "dropouts," having been washed ashore on a desert island after a shipwreck. Their inept, harebrained attempts at adapting to their new situation provided most of the gags, but they became tiresome after a while.

Post quickly realized he was painting himself into a corner, and in 1969, he transferred his dropouts to another island, inhabited this time by a host of nutty characters. Not only did Alf and Sandy rediscover mankind, mankind came back at them with a vengeance. There were, in addition to the natives, Harbinger, the professional hippie and prophet of doom; the drunkard Chugalug; and an assortment of weird female characters from selfish debutantes to affectionate old maids to shrews. The animal and vegetable kingdoms also played a part in the strip, with such (rare) specimens as Irving the playful gorilla, Elliott the dancing frog, and a horrible carniverous plant.

The Dropouts is in the tradition of the modern sophisticated humor strip (it is close to Johnny Hart's *B.C.* both in intent and treatment). A number of *Dropouts* strips have been reprinted in paperback form. But Post's downbeat humor proved unfortunately at odds with the go-go spirit of the Reagan years, and the Dropouts dropped out of the comic pages for good in 1984.

M.H.

DRUILLET, PHILIPPE (1944-   ) French artist and illustrator, born in Toulouse on June 28, 1944. Philippe Druillet spent his childhood in Spain, returning to France in 1952. After his high school studies, Druillet worked as a photographer. In 1965 he met French publisher Eric Losfeld, for whom he created *Lone Sloane*, a science-fiction strip published in book form in 1967. Druillet also illustrated a number of science-fiction stories and novels, and his work earned him some recog-

Philippe Druillet, "Lone Sloane." © Druillet.

nition. In 1970 he joined the art staff of *Pilote*, for which he revived the adventures of Lone Sloane. In 1973, also for *Pilote*, he created a new feature, *Yarzael ou la Fin des Temps* ("Yarzael or the End of Time") from a scenario written by science-fiction author Michel Demuth. Since the late 1970s he has virtually eschewed comics in favor of painting, sculpture, and set designing.

Philippe Druillet is probably the most overrated of all European cartoonists. He has received an impressive number of prizes at various gatherings of comic art fans, and his publishers keep promoting him with persistent, if misguided, zeal. The trouble with Druillet is that he has been judged more on his professed intentions than on his actual performance. His strips have been few in number and, while high in graphic excellence, they are lacking in narrative construction and in conceptual clarity and do not constitute a truly impressive body of work.

Some have hailed Druillet as a genius, while other observers remain unconvinced. Certainly Druillet's inability to draw the human face does not exhibit a high degree of psychological insight, just as his sterile delineation of character does not show any great enthusiasm for moral examination.

M.H.

DU JIANGUO (1941-   ) Born in Guangdong but raised in Shanghai, Chinese cartoonist Du Jianguo worked as a high school art teacher for about 10 years before he became an art editor at the Children Journals Publishing House in Shanghai. Beginning in 1958 he published cartoons in newspapers and journals and also illustrated and made decorative designs for books. His artwork received more than 20 awards in national and regional competitions. A member of the Chinese Artist Association, the Chinese Animation Society, and the Chinese Cartoon Art Commission, Du has been named one of the best comic artists in China.

Since 1960, Du has concentrated on comics for children. His well-known strips are *Xiaotu Feifei* ("The Little Rabbit Feifei"), *Xiang Gege* ("The Brother Elephant"), *Xiao Moli* ("The Little Jasmin"), *Quan Buzhi* ("The Not-Know-It-All"), and *Xiaoxiong he Xiaoxiaoxiong* ("The Little Bear and the Littler Bear"). His strips are usually not continuous but independent stories in each issue of the children's journals. Among them, "The Little Rabbit Feifei" and "The Brother Elephant" have been adapted to animated television series.

H.Y.L.L.

DUAN JIFU (1935-   ) Before he was sent to study art at Tianjin Art Academy, Duan Jifu worked in a bank as an accountant for three years and then as a public relations person for four years. His first cartoon was published in Tianjin in 1956, and he has continued to create cartoons since then. In 1958 he became an art editor for *Tianjin's Daily*, and since 1981 he has worked at the Xin Lei Publishing House in charge of children's reading material.

He has created numerous cartoons, comics, and illustrations—some of which have received national and international awards. He has been a board member of the Chinese Artist Association Tianjin Branch and vice president of the Tianjin Cartoonist Association.

Duan's comic strip entitled *Lao Ma Zheng Zhuan* ("Old Ma's Adventures") appeared for the first time on

Duan Jifu, "Lao Ma's Adventures." © Duan Jifu.

December 18, 1984, in *Jinwan Bao* (Tonight News). It has been published weekly without interruption since it began. Readers find similarities between their own lives and the adventures of Lao Ma, which is the main reason for the strip's popularity and its status as the longest-running comic strip still in existence since the founding of the People's Republic of China. To date, 600 stories of *Lao Ma's Adventures* have been created, some of which were published in three collections.

"Lao Ma" has a double meaning: it is a common family name in China and older men are often called "Lao Ma." At the same time, "Lao Ma" also means "old horse." The double meanings in the stories of Lao Ma reflect the double meanings in the lives of its readers. The strip is done in a four-panel format, and some strips include simple dialogue.

Duan has also published several dozen comic books on other topics. In 1995, his Lao Ma Adventures was chosen to be adapted into a series of animated films by Tewei Humorous Animation Center of Shanghai Xiejin-Hengtong Film and TV Company Limited.

H.Y.L.L.

DUMAS, GERALD (1930-   ) Born in Detroit in 1930, Jerry Dumas went through schooling, including an English degree from Arizona State University in 1955, with very little art training, even though his love of cartoons and comics was an obsession. He cartooned for school, service, and neighborhood publications until he broke the New York gag market in 1955.

In that year, desiring to move closer to the magazines than Arizona, he contacted an acquaintance, Frank Roberge, who had been assisting Dale Messick on *Brenda Starr, Reporter*.

The postcard reached Roberge as he was leaving Mort Walker to draw *Mrs. Fitz's Flats*. Roberge had told Walker of this "kid from Arizona" with a sense of

humor and "bigfoot" drawing style. The rest is history and Dumas continues to assist on all of Walker's creations in lettering, penciling, inking, and gag writing.

His most important contribution was *Sam's Strip*, a joint venture with Walker, in which Dumas did the art. The cast was the roster of all classic comic strip characters, which Dumas drew in styles closely resembling the originals. The ill-fated classic died too soon, running only from 1961 to 1963. Since then Dumas has remained active in Walker's factory, and published children's books, an autobiographical *Afternoon in Waterloo Park* for Houghton Mifflin, and a collection of children's verse, and has done occasional cartoons for the *New Yorker*, among others.

R.M.

In 1977 Dumas and Mort Walker revived *Sam's Strip* (as *Sam and Silo*). In addition to his work for Walker, Dumas has also written several short-lived comic strips, including *Rabbits Rafferty* (with Mel Crawford, 1977-81), *Benchley* (with Mort Drucker, 1984-86), and *McCall of the Wild* (again with Crawford, 1988-90).

M.H.

DUMAS, JACQUES (1904-1994) French cartoonist, writer, editor, and publisher, born in Clermont Ferrand in 1904. After a variety of odd jobs (errand boy, window cleaner, handyman, commercial artist), Jacques Dumas started his cartooning career (under the soon-to-become famous pseudonym "Marijac") with the Catholic weekly *Coeurs Vaillants* in 1934. His first comic strip was *Jim Boum*, a Western so terribly clumsy that it is endearing. The strip enjoyed a fair success due to the excellence of its scripts. At the same time Dumas did a series of comic books with a variety of characters, some humorous, some realistic.

Drafted during World War II, Dumas was taken prisoner by the Germans, escaped, and later joined the

Resistance movement in Auvergne. There he created an underground newspaper, *Le Corbeau Déchaîné* ("The Unleashed Crow"), which gave birth to the first French comic magazine of the postwar era, *Coq Hardi* (1944). Dumas remained the editor of *Coq Hardi* until its demise in 1957. In it he created many comic features, both as a cartoonist and scriptwriter (the best remembered is probably *Les Trois Mousquetaires du Maquis*, "The Three Musketeers of the Maquis"). After 1957 Dumas went on to create more boys' and girls' magazines, such as *Mireille, Frimousse,* and *Nano Nanette*. After suffering a heart attack in 1970, he went into retirement. He died in 1994.

Dumas is best known as Marijac, the inexhaustible purveyor of comic fun. When asked during a 1973 interview to name some of his comic creations, he ticked off in rapid-fire succession: *Jules Barigoule, Jim Boum, Joe Bing, Rouletabosse, Flic et Piaf, Les Trois Mousquetaires du Maquis, Onésime Pellicule, Rozet Cochon de Lait, Capitaine Brisquet, Capitaine Barbedure, Patos Enfant de Ia Brousse, Costo Chien Policier, Césarin, Sidonie en Vacances, Jim et Joe, Baptistou le Lièvre, Marinette Cheftaine, Line et Zoum, Jim Clopin Clopan, Bill de Clown,* and *François Veyrac l'Emigrant*. He added that he had also been the scriptwriter for over 300 different strips illustrated by such luminaries of French comic art as Poïvet, Forest, Liquois, and Le Rallic.

M.H.

DUMB DORA (U.S.) Feeling a need for another flapper strip in 1925, despite its ownership of *Tillie the Toiler, Hotsy-Totsy,* etc., King Features assigned Chic Young to begin a feature built around a college-age brunette named Dora Bell. Starting first as a Sunday page, fielded by the King affiliate, Premier Syndicate, and then as a daily as well, *Dumb Dora* dealt with boy and girl dating and related college activities. Dora was nicknamed "Dumb Dora," although the nickname is not notably used in the strip dialogue, and always had a thick-witted boyfriend, whom she continually passed up (a la Tillie, et al.) for handsomer, brighter, but less permanent boys. Dora's earliest boyfriend, simply named Ernie, didn't last past 1926. A bespectacled, old-looking oaf, he was quickly replaced by the rotund,

"Dumb Dora," Milton Caniff (ghosting for Bill Dwyer). © King Features Syndicate.

straw-hatted Rodney Ruckett, who stayed on as Dora's steady for a number of years. The strip's famed payoff line, used to the point of inanity in the Sunday page, but much less often in the daily strip, was "She ain't so dumb!", and was usually muttered, shouted, or sobbed by the misused Rodney in the last panel.

Young gave the daily strip an engaging narrative, with a certain amount of wit and character skill, which foreshadowed his later, more mature work on *Blondie*. When Young left the strip in April 1930 to work on *Blondie*, it was turned over to the talented King Features stringer Paul Fung, who did an excellent job in continuing the strip in Young's style and content. Fung kept Rod as Dora's boyfriend until 1932, when he turned the strip over to Bil Dwyer, who gave Dora a new love interest named Bing Brown. Dwyer did away with the old payoff line and drew a fresh, witty, well-scripted strip, but the day of the flapper had gone with the 1920s, and the strip died in the middle 1930s, distributed obscurely by King Features to a few outlets until it ended.

B.B.

DUMM, FRANCES EDWINA (1893-1990) Edwina Dumm was born in Upper Sandusky, Ohio, in 1893, the daughter of newspaperman Frank Edwin Dumm, whose father also ran a newspaper. Printer's ink turned to India ink in the veins of the daughter, though, and she pursued an interest in cartooning. Upon "graduation" from the Landon Correspondence School, she secured a position drawing editorial cartoons for the *Columbus* (Ohio) *Daily Monitor*. In 1916 Edwina Dumm was the only member of her sex to hold such a job in the United States (although female cartoonists were common enough, including Rose O'Neill, Grace Wiedersheim (Drayton), Fay King, Albertine Randall, Bertha Corbett, Kate Carew, and Barksdale Rogers).

She drew a strip for the *Monitor* called *The Meanderings of Minnie,* about a little girl and her dog. The feature caught the eye of syndicate wizard George Matthew Adams in New York, and Edwina was offered a contract to do a dog strip, for Adams was not convinced a little girl was the proper companion. When the offer coincided with the folding of the Ohio newspaper, Edwina moved to New York.

In 1921 the result of her work with Adams debuted: *Cap Stubbs and Tippie* was about a little boy and his dog. The combination was perfect, and although the strip never achieved great heights in terms of syndication, it had widespread appeal and popularity spanning two generations.

Her early work on the strip was engaging, although it sharpened noticeably the first years; two major influences were courses in anatomy under George Bridgman at the Art Students League (for human study), and the drawings of Robert L. Dickey, premier dog cartoonist, in *Life*.

In later years, for a healthy run into the 1960s, Dumm drew *Alec the Great*, little dog drawings (Alec looked just like Tippie) with four-line verses written by Edwina's brother, Robert Dennis.

Edwina's other work in cartooning was also dog-oriented. She illustrated the songsheets for songs written by Helen Thomas in honor of the Edwina dogs: "Tippie and the Circus" (1944); "Tippie's Christmas Carol" (1946); and "Tippie's Hallowe'en Serenade" (1950), recorded by Buffalo Bob Smith. Book illustrations included *Two Gentlemen and a Lady* by Alexander

Edwina Dumm, "Tippie." © Adams Service, Inc.

Woolcott, Burges Johnson's *Sonnets from the Pekinese*, and others.

The drawings for Woolcott's book caught the attention of the editors of the old *Life* magazine, and by the mid-1920s Edwina's full-page dog strips in wash were among the most popular things in the magazine. The puppy star was named in a reader contest: "Sinbad/ Was in bad/ From Trinidad to Rome/ And Edwina's Dog/ 'S in bad/ Wherever he may roam." Ultimately two hardcover collections of *Sinbad* strips were published. And Gluyas Williams noted to Edwina that the London *Tatler* was reprinting the cartoons without her knowledge or *Life*'s; soon, by arrangement, her drawings were a regular fixture in that sophisticated English journal.

Edwina's dog and kid cartoons are among the warmest and friendliest in all of cartooning. She had an uncanny ability to portray the world of a little boy, the relationships of kids, and, especially, the unique bonds between a boy and his dog. Few of her strips are knee-slappers in terms of humor, but that type of laugh would be out of place in the gentle, homey world observed, examined, and so definitively captured by Edwina. The Sunday pages of *Tippie* (distributed by King Features because Adams lacked color distribution and production facilities) allowed greater exposition of the dog's character. But the dailies were charming glimpses into the antics and observations of Tippie, the boyhood pranks of Cap Stubbs, and the fussy exterior but lovable essence of Grandma.

Edwina is a genius; the utter simplicity and sketchiness of her pen lines are as deceptive as the homey themes she mastered. There is a cult of Edwina fans, especially among cartoonists. A smattering of her work was published in 1975 by Ideals, and will hopefully be followed by more collections. She died in April 1990 in New York City.

R.M.

DWIG *see* Dwiggins, Clare Victor.

DWIGGINS, CLARE VICTOR (1874-1959) By far the greatest of the American comic strip's lost and forgotten talents was the late Clare Victor "Dwig" Dwiggins, of *School Days, Tom Sawyer and Huck Finn, Nipper,*

Ophelia, and many other strips. Dwiggins was born in Ohio on June 16, 1874, and was educated in country schools. He apprenticed as a draftsman with an architectural firm, then went into cartooning in 1897, producing gag drawings and panels for newspapers. Dwig's subject was simple and basic—the vanished past of boyhood in rural America between 1870 and 1920. The artist also did some earlier daily and Sunday strips, of which only one is worthy of extended comment.

J. Filliken Wilberfloss, Leap Year Lizzie, Them Was the Happy Days were typical titles among Dwig's pre-1920 work. The exceptional strip was the Sunday feature *School Days*, of the 1910s, a markedly different work from the later panel series of the same name. These Sunday half-pages were usually one large panel, filled with schoolkids involved in mischief inside the one room of a rural schoolhouse or the schoolyard outside, while their lovely, unconcerned schoolmarm was courted by various local gentry in the background. Central to the majority of these panels were elaborate devices cooked up by the kids to carry out various pranks, such as mechanisms of pulleys, wires, and wholly absurd connective parts such as dogs who have to lap up the contents of water buckets so that the emptied buckets will permit a weightier part of the device to lower, and so forth. In short, they were Rube Goldberg inventions before Rube Goldberg drew any inventions.

Interesting as these were, however, Dwig's finest sustained work lies in the daily panel series also called *School Days* (1917-32) with its continuing cast of kid characters and its lovely, sharply etched visual comments on the past these kids knew.˙ Against the wooded hills and riversides that once surrounded or bisected so many American small towns, along the dirt streets and picket fences and haystack-sided barns, in the forest swimming holes and spotless Victorian parlors of their parents, Dwig's children spoke and adventured with stunning authenticity.

Dwig's Sunday pages, such as *Nipper* and *Tom Sawyer*, retained much of the atmosphere of the daily panels, but syndicate requirements for broad gag situations on Sunday too often took Dwig into slapstick and blunted the haunting, ethereal quality of his best work.

Dwig later tried an adventure strip, *The Adventures of Bobby Crusoe*, without success. In 1945 he went back to book illustration, which he had also done in his early career, and worked on that until his death in 1959.

B.B.

DYLAN DOG (Italy)   About 35 years old, handsome, tall, a vegetarian, agnostic, claustrophobic, with a phobia of heights (he never flies), former policeman, rehabilitated alcoholic, clarinet player, miniature galleon builder, and womanizer. These are the main physical and moral characteristics of *Dylan Dog*, the character created in 1986 by Tiziano Sclavi and drawn by Angelo Stano, intentionally copying the features of the British movie actor Rupert Everett.

Sclavi, born in 1953, has contributed to many Italian magazines and dailies as a journalist, novelist, and comic scriptwriter and has created several comic characters: *Altai & Jonson* (1975) and *Silas Finn* (1978), both drawn by Cavazzano; *Agente Allen* and *Vita da cani* ("A Dog's Life"), drawn by Gino Gavioli; *Roy Mann* (1987), drawn by Micheluzzi; and many more.

In 1981 Sclavi started to write scripts for some of the many series of the publisher Sergio Bonelli, and in 1986 *Dylan Dog* inaugurated a new monthly black-and-white comics series in book form. *Dylan Dog*, officially baptized "Nightmare Investigator" because he tries to solve dreadful and supernatural phenomena, began as a sort of horror and splatter comic strip echoing the horror movies of Argento, Romero, Carpenter, and Craven. Soon the plots went beyond the traditional figures of the horror domain—vampires, werewolves, and zombies—and started to present monsters of contemporary society such as serial killers and others who inflict pain and oppression on people. With the passing of time, the *Dylan Dog* saga has dealt with more romantic, fantastic, and psychological problems, which are troubling nonetheless in daily life.

In *Dylan Dog* the borderline between good and evil, the normal and the abnormal, is quite uncertain. There is always a benevolent attitude toward the "monsters" of society and an attempt to understand why these people have become what they are. *Dylan Dog* has been an unexpected success and became a cult hero among male and female Italian teenagers of the 1980s. At the beginning of the 1990s the series sold half a million copies a month, plus another half million of two monthly reprints. The series has also been reprinted in hardbound books and has been extensively merchandised. The success of the strip is due in part to its appeal to the younger generations, to their curiosity of the mysteries of life, and to the questions that trouble our society, which *Dylan Dog* explores in detail. Young readers frequently write to their hero for advice on a variety of problems, from the trivial to the personal. The character has been used in several advertising campaigns for social and humanitarian issues.

In his fight against evil *Dylan Dog* is supported by his assistant Groucho, who, like his namesake Groucho Marx, is garrulous and humorous to compensate for the dark thoughts and silences of his master. They live in a house in London where the doorbell howls instead of ringing. Other characters in the strip include Inspector Bloch of Scotland Yard, a father figure, and *Dylan Dog*'s parents, Dr. Xabaras and Morgana.

Since its inception, many hands have helped Sclavi make *Dylan Dog* a success: scriptwriters Claudio Chiaverotti and Luigi Mignacco; artists Giampiero Casertano, Corrado Roi, Carlo Ambrosini, Luigi Piccatto, Gianni Freghieri, Bruno Brindisi, Montanari & Grassani, and Piero Dell'Agnol. *Dylan Dog* has been published in many European countries and in Brazil, where it failed to find a large readership. Sclavi was awarded a Yellow Kid in Lucca in 1990 for the series.

G.C.C.

DZJENGIS KHAN (Netherlands)   *Dzjengis Khan* ("Genghis Khan") or "De strijd om het bestaan" ("The Fight for Survival") is one of the most interesting new comic series to come out of Holland since the Dutch comic weekly *Pep* (1962) decided to cut back on comic imports in 1968 and build its own stable of Dutch comic artists. This new policy was initiated by the editor-in-chief, Hetty Hagebeuk. It was also her idea to ask Jos Looman, who had already done some short features for *Pep*, to do a strip about the life of Genghis Khan from a script by Anton Kuyten. Thus, in the early 1970s a historic figure was given new life on the comic page.

Looman had to get acquainted with the character and the period before starting work on *Dzjengis Khan*. He did so admirably, the result being an ideally complemented epic sweep of Anton Kuyten's scenario that could have been a motion picture script. The comic strip epic of *Dzjengis Khan* in all probability has a greater semblance to reality than any wide-screen motion picture super-production could ever hope to achieve without spending millions of dollars.

The epic contains everything necessary to hold reader attention: sweeping landscapes, drama, and a strong cast of characters. Whatever Genghis Khan may have meant to history, he also had a personal history. Thus, the reader gets to follow the growing up and coming into power of Temoedzjin Khan (Temujin Khan). The reader is presented with the picture of an epoch, the lives and loves of another time, and their decisions and decision making.

Although bigger than life, Dzjengis Khan is not blown up to superhero proportions in this Dutch comic strip. The strip avoids the pitfall of becoming overly "talky," while making good use of page layouts and composition. Marianne Veldhuizen's colors top off the work on *Dzjengis Khan*. It is comics like this that make up for some of the shortcomings of certain aspects of the history of comics.

W.F.

ED, CARL FRANK LUDWIG (1890-1959) The man who first celebrated the juvenile teens in a comic strip, *Harold Teen*, Carl Ed (rhymes with "swede"), was born Carl Frank Ludwig Ed in Moline, Illinois, on July 16, 1890. Ed's father, a working man, died when the boy was 13, causing him to leave high school in his freshman year and go to work. Ed continued his studies when and where he could, and later attended Augustana College in Illinois, getting a job as a sports writer on the Rock Island (Illinois) *Argus* at 20. From there, his cartooning ability got him a job as sports cartoonist on the Chicago *American* in 1912. The World Color Syndicate of St. Louis enabled him to try a strip when it circulated his daily feature for a number of years in the 1910s.

His talent was noted by Joseph Patterson, then co-publisher of the *Chicago Tribune*, who hired him to undertake the nation's first strip about a boy in his teens in 1918. Booth Tarkington's minor classic, *Seventeen*, had appeared in 1916. Called *The Love Life of Harold Teen* at the outset, Ed's new daily and Sunday strip was a hit in both the *Tribune* and Patterson's new New York tabloid, the *Daily News*. Aimed at newspaper readers between the ages of 12 and 20, *Harold Teen* was read widely by teenagers of the 1920s because of the wide-eyed Harold's reflection of their lifestyle, from the jalopies to the soda fountain socializing. Among the terms Ed popularized nationally with the kids of the 1920s were "lamb's lettuce" (for a girl) and "fan mah brow" (for surprise). "Panty-waist," a term for a juvenile "sissy," has lasted until the present.

In the grim 1930s, some of the appeal of *Harold Teen* ebbed, and by 1941, Harold was not only in uniform, but also a government spy, and the strip had been given a sharp twist toward melodrama. This was not all that well done, however, and public interest slipped further, not returning even when Ed renewed his teenage content in the post-war years. The strip's peak was reached when a silent film was made of it in 1928 and remade as a talkie in 1933. A few *Harold Teen* strip collections were published in the late 1920s and early 1930s.

Living in Skokie, a Chicago suburb, in his later years, Ed continued drawing his strip until 1959, when an acute illness took him to the Evanston, Illinois, Hospital, where he died a short time later on October 10, 1959, at the age of 69. The strip was laid to rest with its creator.

B.B.

EDSON, GUS (1901-1966) Gus Edson, creator of *Dondi* and continuer of *The Gumps* from 1935, was born in Cincinnati, Ohio, on September 20, 1901. Leaving high school at 17 to join the Army just as World War I ended, he served in the U.S. After his discharge, Edson studied art at the Pratt Institute in New York. He landed a job as a sports cartoonist on the sleazy *New York Graphic* in 1925. When that paper collapsed, Edson went in fast succession from the Paul Block newspaper chain to the *New York Evening Post*, and from there to King Features Syndicate as a standby ghost, and finally landed on the *New York Daily News* in the early 1930s, again on the sports page.

After Sidney Smith's tragic death in 1935, a desperate News-Tribune Syndicate contacted, without success, all major cartoonists from Rube Goldberg to Stanley Link to ask them to continue Smith's *The Gumps*. Gus Edson, still with the *Daily News*, was finally tapped to continue the popular Smith strip. With no previous strip experience and no evident talent either as an artist or an author, it is little wonder that he ran the brilliant *Gumps* strip into the ground in less than a decade, making millions wonder what they had ever seen in the once-popular feature.

After the propped-up corpse of *The Gumps* finally embarrassed even the executives of the *News* and the *Chicago Tribune* (which were about the only papers still carrying it), a decision was made to allow Edson to undertake a new strip with the artistic aid of Irwin Hasen in 1955. The new strip, called *Dondi*, appalled even the most astute supporters of the comic strip as an art form with its doe-eyed hero and its wholly insipid sentiment and callow melodrama, while the public loved it. *Dondi* ran in many papers until Edson's death in Stamford, Connecticut, on September 27, 1966, wealthy but little famed (for even the public that adored *Dondi* hardly noticed the name of its author). His only other major attempt at creativity was a script for a film version of *Dondi*, which was a box office

Gus Edson.

bomb. *Dondi* was drawn by Irwin Hasen until 1986, when the strip was discontinued.

B.B.

EDWINA *see* Dumm, Frances Edwina.

"Eek and Meek," Howard Schneider. © NEA Service.

EEK AND MEEK (U.S.) Howie Schneider created *Eek and Meek* in 1965 for NEA service. It was another one of the fables in which creatures in animal form were supposed to reveal the wisdom of the ages to us. In this case the action, or rather what there was of it, took place among mice. Meek, as his name implies, is a rather bland individual, eternally put upon by Eek, the unshaven and discreditable cynic, and eternally put down by Monique, the object of his unrequited love. There are also a couple of teenage mice, a female named Freaky, and a male named Luvable (a misnomer) who indulge in all the activities (protests, marches, sit-ins) once deemed fashionable by their human counterparts.

With the limited *dramatis personae* at his disposal, Howie Schneider bravely tried to make some meaningful statements, although he never managed to sound convincingly original. The trouble with *Eek and Meek* was that it plowed much the same ground previously, and more successfully, worked by *Peanuts, Pogo, B.C.,* and others. To come up with that kind of strip in 1965, complete with stick figures, settings without background, and contemporary situations showed a marked lack of originality. Yet one has to give Schneider the benefit of his intentions, and granted that, he succeeded reasonably well. Several collections of *Eek and Meek* were reprinted in pocket-book form by Paperback Library.

In 1977 Schneider decided to turn his rodent characters into human beings (or their approximation); the metamorphosis took place gradually and was only completed in 1982. Eek and Meek in human guise behave no differently than their former animal personas, but the strip has benefitted from the change and has substantially increased in readership in recent years.

M.H.

8-MAN (Japan) *8-Man* was created by artist Jirō Kuwata and scriptwriter Kazumasa Hirai (now one of the most famous authors of Japanese science fiction).

The strip made its debut in the weekly *Shōnen* magazine in April 1963.

8-Man was the reincarnation of Detective Rachiro Azuma, who had been killed by the Mukade gang. Dr. Tani remade him into a super-robot, giving him Azuma's memory and cool brains as well as his human appearance. Under his identity of Private Detective Azuma, 8-Man worked out of his office with his two assistants, Ichiro and Sachiko, who did not know his secret. Only Chief Tanaka of the Japanese Metropolitan Police Board knew Azuma's real identity.

8-Man could change his facial appearance at will, due to the special properties of his artificial skin (one of his favorite ploys was to assume the identity of his enemy's girl); he could run a thousand times faster than any human being; he had a small atomic reactor in his body, and concealed strength tablets (in the form of cigarettes) in his belt buckle.

8-Man fought against criminals, and came to the help of people in distress. His enemies have included: Dr. Demon; the Satan brothers, chiefs of a gang of kidnappers; Machine-gun Geren; 007, a powerful but dull-witted robot; Kitō, the boss of an international ring of criminals; Chōnenten, a master of magic and Kung Fu; the knife-wielding Apache; a huge electric brain called Superhuman Saiba; the super-robot 005; Dr. Yūrei, chief of an international spy organization known as "the Black Butterfly"; a witch with extrasensory perception; and superhuman beings trying to conquer the earth.

In spite of the fact that he was a machine, 8-Man had human feelings, and even problems, after the fash-

"8-Man," Jirō Kuwata and Kazumasa Hirai. © Shōnen.

ion of the Marvel superheroes. 8-Man soon became the idol of the comic-book-reading public, and must be ranked as one of the most famous superheroes in the history of Japanese comics.

The strip gave birth to a series of animated cartoons and was the inspiration for a whole line of metamorphic superheroes, such as Ultra Man, Ultra 7, Ultra Man Leo, and Kamen Rider. 8-Man made his last appearance in February 1966.

H.K.

EISELE UND BEISELE (Germany) It is doubtful whether *Eisele und Beisele*, originally titled *Des Herrn Baron Beisele und seines Hofmeisters Dr. Eisele Kreuz- und Querzüge durch Deutschland* ("Baron Beisele and His Private Tutor Dr. Eisele's Trips Through Germany"), should be termed comic strip characters. However, they *are* comic characters. Created by Caspar Braun, one of the founders of the *Fliegenden Blatter* and the *Münchner Bilderbogen*, Eisele and Beisele are two innocents journeying through Germany, later on through various countries. The two characters, who first appeared in the late 1840s, enjoy the distinction of being among the first recurring characters in cartoon history.

While Caspar Braun sometimes had Eisele and Beisele appear in sequential pictures and a sort of narrative figuration, they started out in cartoon illustrations loosely connected by narration that usually commented on some problem. The *Fliegenden Blatter* appeared weekly as a humor magazine with many illustrations by the same artists who also drew the *Münchner Bilderbogen*, most notably, of course, Wilhelm Busch.

What makes *Eisele und Beisele* of interest for the comic historian, however, is the fact that, in addition to being early—if not the first—continued cartoon characters, they have the distinction of being the first cartoon characters involved in litigation over "merchandising" products. At the height of their popularity, the characters were put on cakes and other sweets. This irked Caspar Braun, particularly because the Munich bakeries who used the characters had never asked for his permission.

W.F.

EISNER, WILL (1917-   ) American cartoonist, writer, and businessman. Born March 1917 in New York City, William Erwin Eisner wanted at first to become a stage designer, but upon graduation from high school he studied under George Bridgeman at the New York Art Students' League; this led to a staff job

"Eisele & Beisele," Caspar Braun, 1850's.

on the *New York American*. In 1936 he produced his first comic book work for the short-lived *Wow, What a Magazine*. In 1937, in collaboration with Jerry Iger, he founded his own studio where, along with a number of other beginning cartoonists, he turned out comic strips, games, and cartoon material. Under his own name or pseudonyms such as "Willis Rensie" and "Will Erwin," Eisner created such features as *Muss'em Up Donovan* (a detective strip), *The Three Brothers* (a foreign legion tale), *K-51* (a secret agent strip) and, most noteworthy of all, *Hawk of the Seas*, a beautifully delineated and hauntingly atmospheric tale of pirates and buccaneers.

On June 2, 1940, Eisner created and produced a comic book insert to be carried by Sunday newspapers along with their regular comic section. The 16-page insert, sized as a regular comic book, contained three features: Nick Cardy's *Lady Luck*, Bob Powell's *Mr. Mystic*, and Will Eisner's own *The Spirit*.

In 1942 Eisner was doing *The Spirit* both as a Sunday comic section and as a daily strip (as of 1941) when he was called to service. He was stationed in Washington, D.C., where he contributed, among other things, the character of Joe Dope for the instruction magazine *Army Motors*.

Demobilized in 1946, Eisner went back to *The Spirit*, which he was to draw until 1950. In the meantime, he had founded the American Visual Corporation, which published a host of official manuals and magazines (often in comic book form). Will Eisner's influence on the art and development of the comic book has been tremendous and lasting. He has received a number of awards and citations (including the title of "best comic book artist") both in the United States and in Europe.

Eisner's pedagogical propensities have been very much in evidence in the two books he has devoted to the comics medium, *Comics and Sequential Art* (1985) and *Graphic Storytelling* (1996). In the past 20 years he has also published a number of graphic novels and stories, many of them of an autobiographical nature, such as *A Contract with God*, *The Dreamer*, and *To the Heart of the Storm*. His most ambitious project to date has been the 176-page *Dropsie Avenue*, in which the author chronicled in comic-book form the history of a New York City neighborhood from the time of the Dutch colonization to the present.

M.H.

ELDER, WILLIAM W. (1922-   ) American comic strip and comic book artist born September 22, 1922, in the Bronx, New York. After studies at the High School of Music and Art and the Academy of Design in New York City, "Will" Elder began his comic book career in 1946, writing and drawing the *Rufus DeBree* humor feature for Orbit's *Toy Town* book. In 1947, Elder, Harvey Kurtzman, and Charles Stern formed an art studio, and after doing work for the Prize and Pines groups between 1948 and 1951, Elder joined the E.C. group in 1951.

The E.C. group was launching their vaunted "New Trend" books, and Elder worked on crime, horror, and science fiction stories. Unfortunately, his work on those was stiff. He did better material for the war books—*Frontline Combat* and *Two-Fisted Tales*—but there he was overshadowed by John Severin, whose work he frequently inked. It was not until his friend Harvey Kurtzman began E.C.'s *Mad* in November, 1952, that Elder's style developed and flowered. Under Kurtzman's aegis, Elder cut loose and began filling his panel backgrounds with designs, humorous characters, and outrageous gags. He is credited with developing the early *Mad* style—a panel cluttered with gags and sharp one-liners. When friend and mentor Kurtzman left *Mad* in 1956, Elder went with him to draw for a string of Kurtzman-edited black and white humor books. He continued developing his zany style through the regrettably short lives of *Trump* (1957-1958), *Humbug* (1958-1959), and *Help!* (1960-1962).

When Kurtzman created *Little Annie Fanny* for *Playboy* in 1962, Elder was the logical choice to illustrate the feature. But because the strip was printed in full-process color—the first American strip to be printed so lavishly—Elder was forced to simplify the cluttered style so as not to muddy and darken the rich colors. Instead, he concentrated on understated cleverness and slickness, and with the aid of Kurtzman and humor specialists Allan Jaffee and Jack Davis, Elder's *Annie Fanny* became the most complex and impressive comic material produced in America. Every panel was a painting, and a four-page strip often took several months to complete.

In addition to his comic book and strip work, Elder has also done considerable amounts of commercial art and book illustrating. His *Little Annie Fanny* work was exhibited in a 1974 Brooklyn Museum show, and his paintings have merited several one-man shows. After a brief return to *Mad* in 1985-87, he definitively retired from professional activities in 1988.

J.B.

ELEUTERI SERPIERI, PAOLO (1944-   ) Italian painter, scriptwriter, and cartoonist, born February 29, 1944, in Venice. In 1975 he started drawing comics for the Italian weekly *Lancio Story*, and several years later he distinguished himself as an excellent illustrator of Western adventures written mainly by Raffaele Ambrosio. Many of these Western stories, which were drawn during the 1970s for *Lancio Story* and the first half of the 1980s for the monthlies *L'Eternauta* and *Orient Express*, were reprinted in book form by the publishing house L'Isola Trovata from 1982 to 1987. In this period Serpieri illustrated some episodes of the French *Histoire du Far West en B.D.*, written by Jean Ollivier.

Serpieri's artwork of the Old West is noteworthy because it is rich in references to the works of photographers and painters of the Frontier and it reflects the spirit of the plots, both fictional and biographical. The powerful composition of the figures and the harsh hatching give a sense of crude realism to the strips. In Serpieri's West there is no room for myth.

After contributing artwork to the French collective work *Decouvrir la Bible* (Larousse, 1983-1985), Serpieri devoted himself to a new character of his own and at the end of 1985 his story *Druuna*, and later *Morbus Gravis* ("Serious Disease") appeared in the Italian monthly *L'Eternauta* and in the French *Charlie*.

In a far distant future, after an atomic catastrophe has destroyed the Earth, the last human beings are living aboard a spaceship where life is controlled by the supercomputer Delta. Druuna, the main character, is plunged into a world of depravity and horror, and Serpieri's powerful artwork helps to remind the reader of the possibilities of a technological, dull future, of the fear of losing our lives through atomic catastrophe, and the presence of hidden powers at work.

So far Serpieri has published five long versions of the series in Italy and France: *Morbus Gravis*, *Morbus Gravis 2-Druuna*, *Creatura*, *Carnivora*, and *Mandragola*. In 1982

Paolo Eleuteri-Serpieri ''L'indiana bianca.'' © Editoriale l'Isola Trovata.

Serpieri was awarded a Yellow Kid in Lucca, and he has received many other prizes at home and abroad.

G.C.C.

ELFQUEST (U.S.) Wendy Fletcher always had a fascination for drawing and for fairy tales; eventually she joined the ranks of organized comics fandom, one of the female fans in an otherwise male-dominated field. (Indeed she met her husband, Richard Pini, through their common love of the comics.) All the elements of fairy tale fantasy and comic book imagery coalesced into *Elfquest*, a project the Pinis tried unsuccessfully to sell to every major and minor comic book company. After encountering only rejection and disappointment from all quarters, they decided to form their own publishing company, which they defiantly called WaRP—a name with a definitive science-fiction tinge that also stands for *Wendy and Richard Pini*. The first *Elfquest*

''Elfquest,'' Wendy Pini. © WaRP Graphics.

story (drawn and plotted by Wendy with writing assistance from Richard) appeared in WaRP's *Fantasy Quarterly* in the spring of 1978; it was given its own title in August of that year.

Outwardly *Elfquest* is the story of a clan of elves, the Wolfriders, in their suspenseful search for a new home after their ancestral grounds have been invaded by human barbarians; but it also serves as a metaphor for the eventual triumph of the spirit over brute force. It is also an allegorical projection of the Pinis' inner life and personal turmoil. *"Elfquest* is almost a symbolic autobiography of mine," Wendy told an interviewer. "Many of the incidents that happen in *Elfquest* are symbolic representations of things that have happened to me or to me and Richard. Quite literally some of the dialogue has been spoken by either Richard or me at certain times. We draw from our life experience and translate it into this beautiful fantasy."

When the last of the 21-episode saga was printed in February 1985, it was the culmination of a success story that had resulted in numerous reprintings, several paperback anthologies, and a host of merchandising. Between August 1985 and March 1988 Marvel, under its Epic imprint, reissued in color the stories that had originally appeared in black and white. Since 1987 the Pinis have also published a number of parallel series and miniseries, each under its own subtitle ("New Blood," "Siege at Blue Mountain," "Kings of the Broken Wheel," etc.)

M.H.

ELIAS, LEOPOLD (1920-   ) American comic book and comic strip artist born in Manchester, England, on May 21, 1920. After studies at the High School of Music and Art (with Israel Epstein) and Cooper Union, both in New York City, "Lee" Elias began his comic book career with the Fiction House group in 1943. Perhaps his most remembered work at this "pulp group turned comic house" was as Bob Lubbers's successor on the *Captain Wings* feature.

Appearing in *Wings Comics*, one of the foremost comic-aviation titles of the 1940s, Elias immediately upgraded the strip's treatment of airplanes. While Lubbers was an excellent anatomy artist, his technical work was poor and Elias's lovingly rendered airplanes were among the finest of the time. On the other hand, Elias, whose black-oriented work and economy of line often makes his work resemble that of Alex Toth and Frank Robbins, was not an outstanding figure artist. His characters lacked maturity and the rugged masculinity of the better artists of the time. His women were not particularly beautiful or voluptuous. Nevertheless, Elias also handled features like *Suicide Smith*, *Firehair*, and *Space Rangers* for Fiction House in the 1943-1946 period.

From there, Elias began a long career of journeyman work and illustrated for Western (*Terry and the Pirates*, 1948), Harvey (*Black Cat*, *Green Hornet*, 1946-1958), National (*Black Canary*, *Green Lantern*, 1947-1948), Hillman, and Marvel.

During the 1950s, however, Elias spent most of his time doing comic strips. After a two-year stint as an assistant on Al Capp's legendary *Li'l Abner*, he went on to cocreate with author Jack Williamson the *Beyond Mars* strip. One of a slew of aerospace strips spurred by the country's technological advances, the feature was well written and drawn, but it was as ill-fated as the genre and had a short run.

Elias returned to National and comic books in 1959 and drew for a large number of books. He is probably best remembered for his dark illustrating on the *Green Arrow* series, but he also did some fine work for both the *Cave Carson* adventure feature and the *Eclipso* strip. During 1959-1968 Elias also drew sporadically for the *Adam Strange*, *Ultra*, and *Automan* features, as well as doing a group of science fiction and horror work. In 1972, he once again rejoined National, concentrating almost entirely on the horror work. His last comic book work was on *The Rook* (1980).

Throughout his career, Elias has had great success as a commercial illustrator and has had several painting exhibitions, including one at the New York Metropolitan Museum of Art. In the 1980s he taught at the School of Visual Arts in Manhattan and at the Joe Kubert School of Cartoon and Graphic Art in New Jersey.

J.B.

ELLA CINDERS (U.S.) Originally one of the most popular strips of all time, and the only one to have been printed despite being damaged by fire, from coast to coast, Bill Conselman and Charlie Plumb's *Ella Cinders* began as a daily strip on June 1, 1925, and as a Sunday page on January 1, 1927. The Sunday pages followed the daily continuity. Created by a writer and artist team in Los Angeles, California (Conselman was editor of the *Los Angeles Sunday Times*; Plumb a cartoonist from nearby San Gabriel), *Ella Cinders* was the first strip to focus on the Hollywood scene as its principal locale and theme and involved a Cinderella heroine (toiling, of course, for her selfish mother and sisters) who won a filmland studio contract. Distributed by the Metropolitan Newspaper Service at the outset, *Ella Cinders* was a hit within its first year, and was made into a major studio film starring Colleen Moore by mid-1926.

Drawn with great comic style by Plumb, *Ella Cinders* was witty and fast-paced from the beginning, with imaginative publicity spinoffs from time to time which maintained public involvement beyond the story line level (for example, there was a 1929 request for readers to write in and advise Ella whether to marry or follow a career; there was also a $500 contest for the best letter telling Ella how to spend a million dollars in 1932).

In 1930 Conselman wrote a book-length novel for the Stratford Company of Boston called *Ella Cinders in Hollywood*, based on the early episodes of the strip; in September of the same year, a mail plane carrying a week's originals of *Ella* (October 6-11) from Los Angeles to New York crashed in flames at Warren, Ohio, charring the outside edges of the episodes to a depth of an inch and a half or more. Rushed to the syndicate by the post office, proofs made from the burned originals were sent out to the subscribing papers barely in time for publication and they appeared exactly as rescued from the ruins of the plane: flame-eaten dialogue balloons, panel details, and all. Luckily, enough remained of the episodes to make continuity sense; the publicity engendered for the strip was incalculable.

Built around such memorable characters as Ella herself; her close friend and brother Blackie Cinders; her devoted adventurer-father Samuel Cinders; her domineering mother Mytie Cinders; her two step-sisters, Prissie and Lotta Pill; her dumb but faithful admirer, the powerful Waite Lifter; her Hollywood director, Phil M.

"Ella Cinders," Charles Plumb and Bill Conselman. © United Feature Syndicate.

Waister; her co-star, Fluffy Frizelle; and her arch-enemy, producer O. Watters Neek, *Ella Cinders* reached its imaginative and popular peak in 1929-1931. At this point, however, her creators decided to glamorize Ella, drop the Hollywood setting, and pursue an outright romantic story line on the order of that in *Winnie Winkle* and *Boots and Her Buddies*. The now-comely heroine surrounded by handsome boyfriends in the daily strip, while being actually married to a mystery-man named Patches and plagued by jokebook gags in the Sunday episodes, *Ella* steadily lost its original appeal and its following in the 1930s, moving to a new syndicate, United Features, on January 1, 1933. (A Sunday companion strip, *Chris Crusty*, was added on July 5, 1931. Featuring a spectacularly nervy lead, the strip was often funnier than the main page by the mid-1930s.)

Despite an attempt to return to more imaginative story lines in the late 1930s and 1940s, *Ella Cinders* remained a second-string strip, without any noticeable improvement when the story line was taken over by Fred Fox in the 1950s after the death of Bill Conselman. The strip plummeted in circulation when Plumb's art was lost a few years later and replaced by that of Roger Armstrong. Nevertheless, for its first half-dozen years, *Ella Cinders* was a glittering, absorbing body of

comic strip work, graphically outstanding and both amusing and gripping as a narrative.

B.B.

ELMER (U.S.) *Elmer*, the boyhood strip creation of A.C. Fera in 1916, is one of the few strips which achieved its early fame under a different name than the one most contemporary readers know it by. In fact, as long as Fera drew the strip (until 1925), it was titled *Just Boy*, and it was Fera's successor as artist and narrator on the strip, Charles H. (Doc) Winner, who changed the name to *Elmer*.

Just Boy was first released under Hearst syndication on a trial basis as a full weekly Saturday page in the *San Francisco Call* on May 6, 1916; it was not released in other Hearst papers until some time later. Fera's Elmer Tuttle was a tall, lean boy of about 13, growing up in a semirural community. His parents, Clem and Ella Tuttle, were solid, middle-class types; Clem Tuttle apparently held down an office job in the city. The family had a black maid, and a close acquaintance with the local beat cop, Officer Nolan (largely because of Elmer's shenanigans).

Fera had a deep, rich awareness of the lore of American boyhood in the 1910s and 1920s, and his *Just Boy* is as excellent a treatment of that subject as Booth Tarkington's *Penrod* of a slightly earlier period. His

"Elmer," A. G. Fera. © King Features Syndicate.

death in 1925 was a distinct loss to the art of the comic strip. The *Just Boy* feature, by then widely circulated, was continued by Hearst interests under a new title, *Elmer*, and drawn by Hearst cartoonist Doc Winner. The first Winner *Elmer* was released on October 4, 1925, and made a sound attempt to maintain the Fera quality of narrative and art. (By now, Elmer had become the short, rotund kid readers knew in the 1920s and later.)

Winner's *Elmer* speedily became the standard boy and dog gag strip found in a dozen features of the time, however, and its earlier wide appeal faded. By the mid-1930s, it had become a distinct second-string King Features strip, usually running as a Sunday half-page, accompanied by an even more obscure Winner upper half-page, *Alexander Smart, Esq.*, about a henpecked householder in his 50s. Always a Saturday or Sunday page feature from its inception, *Elmer* was folded with Winner's death, the last episode appearing on December 30, 1956. All or most of the Fera *Just Boy* portion of the strip calls for reprinting.

B.B.

ELWORTH, LENNART (1927-   ) Lennart Elworth is a Swedish writer, cartoonist, illustrator, and graphic artist, born February 5, 1927, in Surahammar, Sweden. After finishing public school, Elworth started working in an industrial office. From there he moved on to a technical bureau where he was to draw nuts and bolts, but he soon realized he was not cut out to be an engineer. Then, while serving in the army, he decided to study art. When he returned to civilian life, he started studying commercial art at the Bergh's school of advertising, earning his way through as a jazz musician. Having completed his studies, he started working as an illustrator on work ranging from editorial cartooning to illustrating children's books. In recognition of his work, he received a cultural scholarship from the city of Stockholm in 1968.

One year earlier, in 1967, Elworth had started the comic strip *47:an Löken* (which freely translates into "Soldier 47, Chowderhead") in *Lektyr*. *47:an Löken* is in the Swedish tradition of humorous army series, started in 1932 with Rudolf Petersson's *91 Karlsson* and with Torsten Bjarre's *Flygsoldat 113 Bom* ("Air Force Pvt. 113 No-hit") in the 1940s. There are some similarities to *91 Karlsson* because of the subject matter of the strip and Elworth was not at all convinced that it was a good idea to go up against a strip as well established as *91 Karlsson*, but the editors of *Lektyr* talked him into going ahead on the project.

With the success of the feature came the realization that he need not have worried. His anecdotal comic strip is modern in approach, with a cast of characters that fits in well with this comic strip sitcom. The character of Löken is more or less Elworth's alter ego. Kapten Kruth ("Captain Gunpowder") is based on Elworth's father, and most of the other characters are also based on real people. Elworth worked in an easygoing style, rarely ever using closeups. His style was in the tradition of Swedish comics as represented by Knut Stangenberg's *Fridolf Celinder* or Axel Bäckmann's *Påhittiga Johansson* ("Imaginative Johansson"), according to the Swedish fanzine *Thud*. Elworth created the strip *Thudor* for *Thud* and made good use of the man-stranded-on-an-island situation. With the discontinu-

ance of his strips in the 1980s he disappeared from the comics scene.

W.F.

EMBLETON, RONALD S. (1930-1988) British cartoonist, illustrator, and painter, born 1930 in London. He studied art at the South East Essex Technical College and School of Art under the painter David Bomberg. He entered a commercial art studio for six months, during which period he drew his first strips for Scion, a London publisher of one-shot comics. To their *Big* series he contributed dozens of two-page, 24-panel adventure strips, including *The Black Lion* (Africa) in *Big Noise*; *The Ranger* (Canada) in *Big Boy*; *Sahara* in *Big Idea*; *Litening* (superhero) in *Big Flame*; *Black Hawk* (Western) in *Big Win*; climaxing in a complete eight-page comic of his own, *Big Indian* (1949). His signature, "Ron," was a familiar one when his comic career was interrupted by national service in the British Army in Malaya, which meant he was unable to continue the character *Ray Regan* in the Modern Fiction comic book of the same title.

Returning to London in 1950, the comics scene had changed and the style was now the American type of comic book. Forming a team with cartoonists Terence Patrick and James Bleach, Embleton provided Scion with a sequence of sixpenny comic books: the *Gallant* series (*Gallant Adventure, Gallant Detective, Gallant Science, Gallant Western*), and while his style had improved he remained as prolific as ever, contributing to *Buffalo Bill, Five Star Western*, and the science fiction comics *Jet* and *Star-Rocket* (1953). He also advanced into the higher-quality comics published by Amalgamated Press, and drew the weekly serials *Forgotten City, Mohawk Trail*, and *Tom o' London* for *Comic Cuts* (1951-52); and *Black Dagger* and *Into Strange Lands* for *Wonder* (1952).

As the traditional British comic paper faded out, Embleton's interest in color work increased. And he became a member of the Royal Institute of Oil Painters in the 1950s, and of the National Society of Painters and Sculptors in the 1960s, eventually holding exhibitions in Australia, Canada, and the United States. His strip work moved out of the comics and into the adult field: he drew *Johnny Carey* for *Reveille* (weekly), and *The Life of Ben Hogan* for Beaverbrook Newspapers (daily).

In 1957 he combined his two techniques, painting and strips, by producing his first painted strip. This was *Wulf the Briton*, a serial saga in *Express Weekly*, printed full color gravure. His special interest in history continued to show in such superbly painted serials as *Wrath of the Gods* in *Boy's World* (1963) and the feature strips *Rogers' Rangers, Marco Polo*, etc. in *Look and Learn* magazine. Then came a reversal in his career, a switch to science fiction, adapting the television series *Stingray* and *Captain Scarlet* for *TV Century 21* (1967). Later he concentrated on historical paintings for books, prints, etc., but returned to strips with *Wicked Wanda*, an adult sex-cum-satire strip for *Penthouse* (1972). In 1978 he added the drawing of the science-fiction strip *Trigan Empire* to his workload. He died suddenly on February 13, 1988, in Bournemouth.

D.G.

ENGHOLM, KAJ (1906-   ) Kaj Engholm, a Danish comic and graphic artist, was born 1906 in Copenhagen, where he grew up and went to school. To his own surprise he made it through final exams at Copenhagen's commercial college, where he met his future wife. Having been interested in drawing since childhood, he paired his interest and education by working and drawing in the advertising business. He handled advertising campaigns for Carlsberg and Tuborg (oil) and C.W. Obel (tobacco) among others.

In 1942 Engholm's wife mailed some of the drawings he had done for fun to a contest in a Copenhagen newspaper. This led to the start of Engholm's comic strip *Gnidén* that same year. Mr. Gnidén was a miser; A symbolic skinflint representative of a human phenomenon usually occurring in well-to-do countries. This might help explain the fantastic success of *Gnidén* in Denmark and Sweden; the Dutch, however, did not see the humor of Mr. Gnidén's escapades.

During the war, Engholm introduced a character named W. Kirkehøj to the *Gnidén* comic strip. (W. Kirkehøj is a literal translation of Winston Churchill in Danish.) One episode showed Gnidén lamenting about the amount of postage due to send Kirkehøj a Christmas card. This resulted in lots of letters sent in by readers sending stamps for Gnidén's card to Kirkehøj, who was very popular with most readers, Germans excepted.

In 1947 Engholm started a second daily strip, *Far till fyra*, a domestic comedy strip. Nine movies based on this comic strip were produced. Of these, the first three starred Ib Schönberg as *Far* ("Father"). After this, Engholm added the weekly comic strip *Kon Rosa* to his two daily strips.

He is now retired.

W.F.

ERIC DE NOORMAN (Netherlands) *Eric de Noorman* ("Eric the Norseman"), created by Hans G. Kresse, one of the big-three of Dutch comic artists, started in the Flemish newspaper *Het Laatste Nieuws* on June 6, 1946, and was picked up by Marten Toonder's weekly *Tom Poes Weekblad* in 1947. Some 66 episodes, at times written in collaboration with Dirk Huizinga, then Jan Walin Dijkstra, appeared until Kresse, in 1964, discontinued the strip, which at the time appeared in *Het Vaderland*. However, September 10, 1966, saw the return of the Norse hero in *Erwin*, a strip appearing in the weekly comics magazine and featuring the adventures of Eric's son.

When Kresse was accepted for work in the studio of Marten Toonder after submitting artwork at the age of 23, he had an idea about a Nordic comic hero named Leif. Toonder suggested that he rename the hero Eric, and he also suggested that Kresse draw a science fiction epic about Atlantis, based on a Toonder idea. Kresse felt ill-at-ease with Atlanteans and ray guns. Thus Atlantis was completely destroyed, with Eric and his wife, Winonah, the only ones to escape the holocaust. Kresse's art improved significantly when he changed from pens to brushes after the first few episodes. The stories also improved when, after a run-in with the Romans, Eric departed for his home country, there to depose the usurper who had assassinated Eric's father, Wogram, the rightful king. To achieve victory and revenge, Eric had to enlist the aid of a magician, who in turn wanted payment in gold. The victory was won and Eric departed for a seven years' journey taking him to South America, Australia, Hawaii, and China. Finally, Eric returned to Norway, the gold having been lost and recovered again on the way. He stayed in Norway for several episodes to reestablish peace before again roaming the world, the most famous of his quests being the search for the invincible sword of Tyrfing, stolen from him.

Taking on more and more work in addition to *Eric* resulted in Kresse having a nervous breakdown in 1954, but he soon was back on the job, sending his hero first to Britain, then to Iceland and North America. Finally, Eric passed his crown on to his grown son, Erwin, before going to Britain to help King Arthur fight the Saxons, and then encountering the Huns in Europe.

In 1964 Kresse abandoned *Eric* to work on other comic features. But in September 1966 his hero returned in *Erwin*, the story of Eric's son. When Erwin was accused of being a pirate, Eric began dominating the strip in order to clear his son. Like Prince Valiant, Eric also was aged enough by his creator to become one of the few heroes who are grandfathers. In 1972 Kresse's interest moved to doing a comic strip about the history of Native Americans.

While the Dutch version of the strip used narrative below the pictures up to 1964, foreign editions often were done in the more usual way of putting narration and dialogue in captions and speech balloons. *Erwin* is done in speech balloon version only, despite Kresse's preference for the more literary and original way. In *Eric* good writing and excellent art were merged into a quality strip that later enjoyed success in newspapers and strip reprints in the Netherlands, Belgium, and a number of other countries.

W.F.

"Eric," Hans G. Kresse. © Marten Toonder.

"Ernie," Bud Grace. © King Features Syndicate.

ERNIE (U.S.) The zany, farcical and frenzied comic strip *Ernie* by Bud Grace was launched on February 1, 1988, by King Features Syndicate. Deemed "a comedy of low manners," it portrays the absurd doings of affable bachelor Ernie Floyd and a diverse cast of loony and expedient characters.

Ernie is an assistant manager at a repugnant squid restaurant, playing a benign foil to the grotesque cast fictitiously set in Bayonne, New Jersey. Doris Husselmeyer is his nebbish girlfriend, whose juvenile brother Spencer is better adjusted than his deranged guardians. Ernie's miscreant uncle Sid Fernwilter is the feature's most developed personality, a bamboozling con man and manager of the fraternal Piranha Club, whose cold-blooded mascot Earl would prefer to devour them all. Landlady Effie Munyon provides the leeching Sid with incredibly disgusting meals, while his friend Enos Pork operates an equally odious medical practice. Rounding out the primary company are the felonious Wurlitzer brothers and the lecherous yet simple-minded Arnold Arnoldski.

A former atomic physicist, Bud Grace began to draw magazine panel cartoons as a freelancer in 1979, and soon after left his research and teaching position at Florida State University. Noticeably influenced by underground cartoonists Robert Crumb and Kim Deitch, *Ernie* currently appears in over 200 domestic papers and in 25 countries. It is very popular in Scandinavia, and numerous book collections have appeared there, eclipsing the sales of the two paperbacks and the comic book released in the United States. Manic, uncouth, and humorously outrageous, the strip's highly developed troupe of characters were inspired by the cartoonist's divergent interests and anomalous associations, consequently raising the work above the usual syndicated fare.

On occasion Grace has caricatured himself into the strip, creating a rare and self-satirical portrayal not seen since Al Capp's cameos in *Li'l Abner*. Drawn in a solid, sketchy style, the comic was acclaimed as the "Best Newspaper Comic Strip" for 1993 by the National Cartoonists Society, and has received numerous international awards. Although not suited to everyone's taste, the well-defined humor and personalities in *Ernie* make it one of the finest examples of the contemporary style in comic strips.

B.J.

"Ernie Pike," Hugo Pratt. © Editrice Sgt. Kirk.

ERNIE PIKE (Argentina) Hector Oesterheld created *Ernie Pike* in 1957 in the magazine *Hora Cera* and entrusted the drawing to Hugo Pratt, who gave its protagonist the features of Oesterheld.

The figure of Ernie Pike was based on the real-life Ernie Pyle, an American war correspondent killed in Okinawa in 1945 and made into a legend by William Wellman's movie *The Story of G.I. Joe*. Burgess Meredith played the role of Pyle in the film with notable humility and patriotic fervor.

Hugo Pratt gave the character a different outlook, avoiding patriotic speeches to project only the image of a decent human being, lost amid the clamor of war, without regard to the cause for which it was fought. Resorting to a somber and austere drawing style, unpretentious and fast, Pratt succeeded in pushing the war heroics into the background to concentrate on the men struggling in the muck and mire of everyday military life. His Pike, in the company of photographer Tony Zardini (himself patterned after the real-life cameraman Robert Capa), moves from one theater of war to the next in order to tell the world of the tragedy of war.

The *Ernie Pike* episodes drawn by Hugo Pratt were widely reprinted in Italy, while in Argentina the feature had passed into the hands of Guzman, who drew it in the early 1960s. Years later, *Ernie Pike* was revived in the magazine *Top*, with the Vietnam War as the background this time: Oesterheld was still the scriptwriter, while the drawings were contributed by Nestor Olivera. In 1976 *Ernie Pike* was taken over by Francisco Solano Lopez, but the feature only lasted for a few more years.

L.G.

ERNST, KENNETH (1918-1985) American artist born in Illinois in 1918. Kenneth (Ken) Ernst studied at the Chicago Art Institute, but started his career as a magician. In 1936 he joined the "A" Chesler studio, and worked for a number of comic book publishers, including Western, for whom he did *Buck Jones* and *Clyde Beatty*, and National, where he drew *Larry Steele* (1939-40).

In 1940 Ken Ernst moved into the newspaper strip field as assistant on *Don Winslow of the Navy* before being asked by Publishers Syndicate to take over the drawing of *Mary Worth's Family* (1942). Together with writer Allen Saunders, Ken Ernst gave the feature (shortened to *Mary Worth*) the look it still retains.

Ernst was one of the more gifted practitioners of what had come to be called the "Caniff school." His drawings were elegant and uncluttered, and he always displayed in his layouts and compositions solid qualities of taste and craftsmanship. He continued working on *Mary Worth* until his death in Salem, Oregon, on August 6, 1985.

M.H.

ERNSTING, VOLKER (1941-   ) Volker Ernsting, German cartoonist and writer, was born in Bremen on May 4, 1941, the son of a bank clerk. He grew up, went to school and high school, and then went to the Hochschule für Gestaltung (college of design), all in Bremen. Ernsting's earliest work (1962) appeared in *Pardon,* a German monthly progressive satirical magazine. Ernsting contributed illustrations, political cartoons and cartoon portraits, and comics to *Pardon* in the 11 years he was closely associated with that magazine. The comic satire he produced for *Pardon* included a series of "pop classics" like "Don Giovanni" or "Odysseus," the latter appearing on the occasion of the military takeover in Greece. "Ballermann" was a satire on neo-Nazis. In 1970 he drew Jesus comics.

Also in *Pardon* were his *Köter & Co.* ("Cur & Co."), animal comics with topical contents, and illustrated fictitious reports about military maneuvers, sex, etc. Among the best of Ernsting's work for *Pardon* is an eight-page comics spoof done in the form of a comic supplement and poking fun at *Superman, Batman, Phantom, Rip Kirby, Tarzan,* and *Astèrix.* This satire, written by Gerhard Kromschröder, appeared in the October 1970 issue of *Pardon.* From 1966 to 1971, Ernsting had a regular column in *Pardon,* titled *MoPS,* which is short for M*onatlicher* P*resse* S*piegel* ("monthly review of the press"), and is at the same time a pun, as a *mops* (pug) is a dog.

Starting in 1966, some Ernsting cartoons appeared in book form: *Hals- und Beinbruch* (an equivalent of "Happy landings!" meaning literally "Break your neck and leg!" which is quite appropriate for doctor cartoons), *... und läuft und läuft und läuft* (a Volkswagen satire), *Goldrausch* ("Gold Rush," olympic cartoons). 1971 saw Ernsting's super production *Sherlock Holmes und das Geheimnis der blauen Erbse* ("Sherlock Holmes and the Secret of the Blue Pea"), a highly individual comic strip satire of television mystery programs fea-

turing far in excess of 100 TV personalities. Appropriately enough this comic strip satire appeared in *Hör Zu,* Germany's largest television weekly, before being published in book form. For many years, starting in 1972, Ernsting drew one *Mike Macke* story per year for *Hör Zu.* He also worked on ad campaigns for *Hör Zu* and for the city of Bremen. When *Mike Macke* was discontinued, Ernsting continued working in advertising and also did occasional cartoons.

W.F.

ERWIN, WILL   *see* Eisner, Will.

ESCHER, REINHOLD (1905-1994)   Reinhold Escher, German artist and cartoonist, was born April 12, 1905, in Hamburg. At the age of 10 he drew his first picture stories—strips in the true sense of the word, as they were drawn on paper strips several yards in length. They came from rolls of silk and were provided by a milliner, a relative of the family. These early stories told of wars and Indian fights.

Escher grew up and went to school in Hamburg. There, he also studied painting and decorating at the Landeskunstschule (county art school). Following his studies, Escher did illustrations and cartoons. During an extended stay in Switzerland, he busied himself with rustic painting.

In the 1930s Escher first got a chance to draw fullpage animal stories for the Sunday edition of the paper *Hamburger Anzeiger.* His first strip, *Peter mit dem Mikrophon* ("Peter with the Microphone"), appeared in the paper's insert *Der kleine Genossenschafter.* He also found employment with the renowned illustrated weekly *Hamburger Illustrierte,* for which he wrote and drew the strip *Hein Ei* ("Hennery Egg").

After World War II Escher first worked for Swiss magazines. Then, back in Hamburg, Escher illustrated several picture books, worked in advertising and for *Hör Zu* ("Listen In"), a large circulation radio and television weekly. Eduard Rhein, first editor-in-chief of *Hör Zu,* acquired the rights to *Mecki,* a cute hedgehog well known because of the films of the Diehl brothers. For *Hör Zu* the animated dolls of the Diehl films were transformed into a comic strip by Reinhold Escher. He created a number of additional characters, like Charly Pinguin or the Schrat (a troll), to widen the story potential beyond the rather domestic humor of the original animated films. *Mecki,* having the status of editorial talisman, occupied a full color page in all issues of *Hör Zu* from 1951 to 1972. Up to 1971 the stories used a running narrative within the picture frames, and in 1971 speech balloons were added to give the strip a more modern look. The strip, as conceived by Escher, was put on hiatus in 1978 when Hans Bluhm, second editor-in-chief of *Hör Zu,* was looking for new attractions.

Most of the stories of differing length and an innumerable number of single-page gags were written and drawn by Escher, with some of the writing done in cooperation with his wife. Escher was influenced by Wilhelm Busch, Lawson Wood, and the Disney productions, as well as by Buster Keaton, Charlie Chaplin, and Harold Lloyd. His stories had a warm, human quality, and there was a penchant toward adventure, especially in the continued stories. The success of the strip led to some 15 *Mecki* books published annually. They usually told a *Mecki* novel, with each page of text facing a page of art. Of these, only the first one was illustrated by Escher. Escher died in Switzerland on May 9, 1994.

W.F.

ESPIÈGLE LILI, L' (France) One of the longest running French comic strips, *L'Espiègle Lili* ("Mischevious Lili") saw first publication in the French weekly *Fillette* on October 21, 1909. It was the creation of Jo Valle for the text and Andre Vallet for the drawings.

Lili d'Orbois was a precocious seven-year-old girl whose tricks and escapades frustrated her parents. Sent to the boarding-school of the Poupinet sisters, she led her companions into innumerable scrapes and generally proved herself a worthy cousin of the Katzenjammers and Buster Brown.

Well before Frank King used the same device, Valle and Vallet had their heroine mature in the strip. During World War I Lili did her bit for the Allies, and in 1923 she married her aviator fiancé, bringing the strip to a temporary end.

In 1925 *Lili* came back, drawn by René Giffey. She was again the terrible little girl of her earlier life. Interrupted by World War II, the strip was revived in the late 1940s by Alexandre Gérard (who signed AL G). Gérard made Lili into a typical teenager with new friends, a family, a fiancé, etc. During its third life (which extended until 1972) the strip was first written by B. Hiéris, then by Paulette Blonay. Seemingly indestructible, the character was resurrected by Jacques Arbeau (signing his work Jacarbo) from 1978 to 1986.

L'Espiègle Lili enjoyed a solid success and was probably the most popular of European girl strips. A number of Lili's adventures were reprinted in book form and for a short while in the early 1920s she gave her name to an illustrated weekly, *Le Journal de Lili.*

M.H.

ETERNAUTA, EL (Argentina) The prolific Argentine scriptwriter Hector Oesterheld (author of the comic strip scenarios of *Ticonderoga, Verdugo Ranch, Bull Rocket, Indio Suarez,* and many others) created *El Eternauta* for the monthly magazine *Hora Cero* in 1957. The premise of the strip is one of the weirdest in the history of comics: a comic strip writer receives a visit from an extraterrestrial being who claims to be a 21st century philosopher, a navigator of time and traveler of eternity who had already lived over 100 lives. Tired of wandering and reincarnation, this "eternaut" came to Earth in order to take human form for the last time.

In the beginning, the feature was drawn by cartoonist Solano Lopez, and this version inspired an animated film produced by Hugo Gil and Mario Bertolini in 1968. But the strip took on added dimension when Alberto Breccia took over in the late 1960s and brought out the strip's potential. Breccia eschewed the conventional techniques of comic drawing to innovate on each page. He used an imaginative layout complemented by a very individual graphic style, and techniques in which he is a master: use of benday, scratch lines, chromatic experimentation, and other devices (unfortunately often lost in reproduction) in order to create an oneiric atmosphere which has contributed to making *El Eternauta* one of the most unusual comic strips of its time. This second version met only with incomprehension in Argentina, but was very successful in Europe, especially in Italy where a comics magazine in 1980 took the name *L'Eternauta* as a tribute to the pioneering

"Etta Kett," Paul Robinson. © King Features Syndicate.

series. Francisco Solana López is now turning out the series.

L.G.

ETTA KETT (U.S.) Cartoonist Paul Robinson produced *Etta Kett* for King Features Syndicate in 1925. It was initially intended as a panel for teaching good manners to teenagers (hence the pun on the word etiquette). It proved an impossible task, however, and *Etta Kett* soon turned into a typical teenage girl strip.

Etta Kett was a vivacious, curvaceous young lady who never got involved in anything more compromising than forgetting the money for the dress she had just bought or holding hands with some pimply boy in a soda parlor. Paul Robinson was very effective in keeping Etta and the other characters in the strip up-to-date on the latest fads and fashions, but the setting and psychology remained Squaresville, USA, in the 1940s. The fact that the strip survived until November 1974 is a testimonial to the endurance of the myth of American innocence right into the self-examining and cynical 1970s. As such, *Etta Kett* is probably more exemplary than other staples of the genre, such as Hilda Terry's *Teena* or Harry Haenigsen's *Penny.*

M.H.

EVANS, GEORGE (1920-) American comic book and comic strip artist born February 5, 1920 in Harwood, Pennsylvania. His first professional work appeared in pulp airplane magazines when he was 16. After studies at the Scranton Art School, Evans entered the army and served in World War II. He later enrolled in the Army Extension Correspondence Course. He began his comic art career in 1946 with the now-defunct Fiction House group, where he drew several of their minor features (*Air Heroes, Tigerman,* and others).

In 1949 he began working for the Fawcett group and drew strips such as *When Worlds Collide* and *Captain Video.* During this time he was also attending night classes at New York City's Art Students League. Evans joined E.C. Comics in 1953 and turned out superior work for all of the group's legendary horror, science fiction, war, and crime titles. But he did his greatest work in 1955 when he wrote and drew stories for the group's "New Directions" *Aces High* title. An avowed airplane fan, Evans' work on the short-lived (five issues) book's "flying" stories is among the best ever produced in comics. He also contributed artwork to E.C.'s abortive "Picto-Fiction" black and white magazines.

After E.C. folded in 1956, Evans began drawing for Gilberton's *Classic Comics*, illustrating the comic book adaptations of Shakespeare's *Romeo and Juliet* and *Julius Caesar*, Conrad's *Lord Jim*, Hugo's *Hunchback of Notre Dame*, Dumas's *Three Musketeers*, and other major literary works. He continued with Gilberton until 1962. During the early 1960s, Evans also worked for Western (Gold Key) and drew for such varied titles as *Twilight Zone* and *Hercules Unchained*. During 1964 and 1965 he contributed to Warren's *Creepy* and *Eerie* black and white magazines. In 1968 he began working for National Comics and contributed to their supernatural and humor books. He also drew for the war titles, illustrating an occasional "flying" story.

In 1960, Evans made his first foray into syndicated newspaper strips when he began ghosting George Wunder's *Terry and the Pirates*. Although he worked on the feature until 1972, he never received a byline. Throughout his career, (which has been highly influenced by the work of Alex Raymond and Hal Foster), Evans has done considerable advertising work. He is a member of the National Cartoonist Society. In 1980 he took over the syndicated *Secret Agent Corrigan* newspaper strip, which he drew until the feature's demise in 1996.

J.B.

EVERETT, BILL (1917-1973) American comic book artist and writer born May 18, 1917, in Cambridge, Massachusetts. After studies at the Vesper George School of Art in Boston, Everett went through a variety of commercial art jobs and finally landed with the Lloyd Jacquet Comic Shop in 1939.

Working under his own name and pseudonyms like "William Blake" and "Everett Blake," he created *Skyrocket Steele* and *Dirk the Demon* for Centaur. His best strip for that company was a unique superhero feature called *Amazing Man*. Between 1940 and 1942, he also produced a series of minor features for Novelty, including *Chameleon*, *Sub-Zero*, and *White Streak*.

Everett's greatest achievement came in 1939 when he invented *The Sub-Mariner*. Created out of the Jacquet shop, along with Carl Burgos' *Human Torch*, the character made his first appearance in *Marvel Comics* number one. Everett's undersea antihero quickly became a major success. And although his work was not technically perfect, it was highly stylized, and

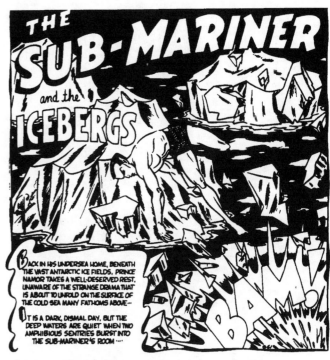

Bill Everett, "The Sub-Mariner." © Marvel Comics Group.

Namor's triangular head and arched eyebrows became the character's trademark.

In 1940, Everett created an imitation of his character for Eastern Color and called it *Hydroman*. Back at Timely he created still another water hero called *The Fin*. During the early 1940s he also worked on features like *The Patriot* (Timely), *Conquerer* (Hillman), and *Music Master* (Eastern). After a stint in the armed forces, Everett returned to Timely in 1947. He began handling *Sub-Mariner* again and drew still another aquatic feature, *Namora*, in 1948. She was another spin-off of the Namor series. He later produced a large volume of horror material for Atlas (nee Timely) in the early 1950s.

After another stint on *Sub-Mariner* from 1953 to 1955, Everett left comics and worked in commercial art until 1964. He then returned to Marvel (the newest Timely name) and worked on most of their superhero strips. During this time, he made one final return to *Sub-Mariner*. After several contributions to the strip in the 1960s, he was reassigned to the feature in 1972 and immediately revitalized the series.

Just as the public was becoming reacquainted with Everett's material, the artist took ill and died February 27, 1973. He was so well-liked by his colleagues that the Academy of Comic Book Arts formed The Bill Everett Fund for Indigent Artists in his honor.

J.B.

FABULAS PANICAS (Mexico) Alexandro Jodorowski created his most personal work, *Fabulas Panicas* ("Panic Fables"), after completing his collaboration as scriptwriter of *Anibal 5*. Starting in 1967, this strip appeared in the form of a color page in "Heraldo Cultural," the Sunday supplement of the daily *El Heraldo de Mexico*. This time Jodorowski had complete control over the scenarios, the drawing, and the coloring. The author—founder with Juan Arrabal and Roland Topor of the "panic theater" movement—expressed in these simple pages, purportedly addressed to children, his own philosophy, inspired by his hippie-like attitude toward life. Jodorowski caricatured himself as the protagonist, with his kinky hair and tunic, who listened to or argued with the "Master," a kind of blonde god, bewhiskered and loving, who had two nearsighted and querulous children, a boy and a girl.

Jodorowski's style, informal and similar to the experiments of the American "underground," used color in a psychedelic fashion. The author utilized montages of old prints and caricatures, or hatchings, to narrate the questions put to the Master and his answers, or to have the fingers of one hand talk to one another. When the characters felt at a loss for words, or were too bored to talk, they employed blank balloons. At other times they limited themselves to groans, or to an exchange of onomatopeias. Sometimes machines would talk (foreshadowing the future world that Jodorowski would present years later in his movie *The Holy Mountain*), with meditations which lend consistency to these new fables.

L.G.

FABULOUS FURRY FREAK BROTHERS, THE (U.S.) Gilbert Shelton, whose cartooning career had begun with *Wonder Wart-Hog* in 1961, began his second series of outstanding material in 1967. Completely different in orientation from his superhero parodies in *Wonder Wart-Hog*, the *Freak Brothers* feature was a humorous look at what was then the emerging drug and youth culture of the 1960s. In truth, however, Shelton's stories were usually just exaggerations of real-life happenings among the youth of the time.

Shelton began *The Freak Brothers* for the *L.A. Free Press*, but its appeal was so universal that it soon began being syndicated to most of the underground newspapers beginning to flourish throughout the rest of the country. Along with Crumb's *Fritz the Cat* and *Mr. Natural*, *The Freak Brothers* became the best-known strip to emanate from the underground press. The feature made a smooth transition into underground comix book in 1968, in *Feds and Heads*. In their own title, which began in 1971, they became the most-read underground feature, with a circulation well over 100,000 copies.

Several factors account for the phenomenal success of *The Freak Brothers*: Shelton is generally regarded as the most professional of all the underground artists; the strip was meant to entertain more than to proselytize; and it was amazingly true to life and readers could identify with the antics of the three dope- and sex-hunting heroes. Perhaps most importantly, the characters were strong in themselves. Fat Freddy, Freewheelin' Franklin, and Phineas Freak were identifiable characters in the late 1960s. They were funny and crazy, and, occasionally, philosophical. In fact, Freewheelin' Franklin's utterance that "Dope will get you through times of no money better than no money will get you through times of no dope" became as widely quoted as Crumb's reintroduction of "Keep on Truckin'," and it was probably more germane to its readers.

On the artistic level, Shelton never allowed his position as chronicler of the times to interfere with his attempts to make the feature a showcase for the absurd. He parodied other strips—*Little Orphan Annie* became Little Orphan Amphetamine, the brothers' "favorite 14-year-old runaway"; *Dick Tracy* became Tricky Prickears, the "blind, deaf cop" who spouted enforcement codes in "Crimestompers Meinkampf"; and Mell Lazarus' Momma even made an appear-

"Fabulas Panicas," Alexandro Jodorowski. © El Heraldo de Mexico.

"The Fabulous Furry Freak Brothers," Gilbert Shelton. © Gilbert Shelton.

ance—and mercilessly exploded both the establishment and the counterculture's greatest myths.

As the strip developed, Shelton even borrowed a trick from George Herriman's book. Back in the 1910s, while Herriman devoted most of his time to *The Dingbat Family*, he ran *Krazy Kat* along the bottom of the daily strip. Shelton did likewise, and *Fat Freddy's Cat*, featuring an orange tomcat with a penchant for relieving himself in the most annoying places, began to appear at the bottom of the *Freak Brothers* pages. The strip-within-a-strip even developed its own characters: mice who constantly fought with Fat Freddy's Cat.

Since the brothers most consistently appeared in the *Free-Press*, most adventures are only a single tabloid-sized page long; however, there have been several longer stories drawn for the underground books. The best of these were collected in the 1974 *Best of Rip Off Press, Vol. II* anthology. The brothers have also appeared in a movie—something of a classic at comic conventions since it is too sex-oriented to be shown in regular theaters. In January 1975, they appeared in dazzling color in a multi-page story in *Playboy*.

J.B.

After Shelton left for Europe in the late 1970s, the brother's appearances in American comic books were more and more sporadic, despite the creator working in tandem with associate Paul Mavrides, who had remained in California. So scarce had the Freak Brothers made themselves that in 1985 the publisher of Rip-Off Press could announce only half-facetiously that the two cartoonists had set a record by managing to produce two issues of the title within the year.

M.H.

FACÉTIES DU SAPEUR CAMEMBER, LES (France)
Christophe's second masterpiece, *Les Facéties du Sapeur*

Camember ("The Pranks of Sapper Camember"), appeared for the first time in 1890 in the pages of the weekly *Le Petit Français Illustré*.

Camember was an enlisted man in the French Army of the Second Empire. His simplicity and guilelessness made him an easy target for any sharpies in his outfit, and Camember would often end up in trouble with his sergeant or his officers as a result of his often self-defeating "pranks." The series ended in 1896 on a note of pathos: Camember took part in the Franco-Prussian War of 1870 and saw his colonel killed in front of him, but he wiped out the enemy platoon. Old and covered with decorations, he retired to his native village.

La Sapeur Camember, like *La Famille Fenouillard* before it, did not use speech balloons. Unlike *La Famille Fenouillard*, however, it did not contain weekly continuity (except in the very last episodes); it was a series of gag stories of military humor typical of the period. It gave rise to many other service comic strips, and can even be seen as a remote ancestor of *Beetle Bailey*.

Le Sapeur Camember has been kept in continuous print by Armand Colin, which issued many editions of Christophe's picture-story over the years; it has also been reprinted in paperback form by Hachette. In the 1960s it inspired a French television series that mixed animation and live action.

M.H.

FALK, LEE (1905-   ) American writer, born in 1905, in St. Louis, Missouri. From his days in high school, when he edited the school's paper, and throughout his adult life, Lee Falk felt a compulsion to write. He wrote stories, articles, and poems for his college newspaper and, after graduation from the University of Illinois, went to work as a copywriter for a St. Louis advertising agency. There he met artist and fellow Missourian Phil Davis, with whom he was to create *Mandrake the Magician*, his first attempt at comic strip writing.

After a stint as a producer-writer for a local radio station, Lee Falk went to New York to make the rounds of the syndicates, and in 1934 he succeeded in selling *Mandrake* to King Features. The success of the feature was such that two years later Lee Falk originated *The Phantom*, again for King.

In addition to writing the scripts for *Mandrake* and *The Phantom*, Lee Falk is the author of several theater plays; one of these, *Eris*, was staged in Paris in 1968, and revived in 1973 by a French repertory company. Since 1962 Lee Falk has been writing (or at least plotting) the *Phantom* paperback novels published by Avon Books. Falk received a special award for his work as a comic strip writer at the Lucca, Italy, Comics Conference in 1971. Now in his nineties, he is still actively writing the continuities of both *The Phantom* and *Mandrake*; in 1996 he was featured in a special on the A&E network celebrating the 60th anniversary of *The Phantom* and the theatrical release of the Phantom movie.

In a medium dominated by graphic artists, Lee Falk stands out as the creator of two successful features and as a fiction writer of great skill and imagination, whose characters and stories have been popular throughout the world for over six decades.

M.H.

FALLUTELLI (Argentina) The noted gag cartoonist Guillermo Divito, who had founded the humor magazine *Rico Tipo* in 1944, created *Fallutelli* the following year in the pages of his own magazine. Fallutelli is an Italianized version of a Buenos Aires slang word meaning "phony," and no other term can better define the protagonist of this humor strip.

Fallutelli is an office clerk; short, ridiculously attired with false and garish elegance, with bulging eyes and buck teeth, a fine moustache, and a narrow-brimmed hat. A servile flatterer of his superiors, scheming and pushy, capable of deceiving even his best friends in order to climb the social ladder, he displays his anxieties to little advantage and has remained in the same obscure position he occupied at the start. *Fallutelli* is a classic example of the Argentinian humor strip in which a simple and basic situation is milked to the limit, while succeeding in remaining fresh all the while.

When everyone else had abandoned him, Fallutelli would seek refuge in the house of his tall and attractive girlfriend Doris. To her alone he would confide his worst fear: that his coworker Escolasio would be promoted ahead of him. This typical obsession of the average bureaucrat would soon become reality, and Escolasio (who started initially as a secondary character on the strip) was to gain in time a more important position than Fallutelli. Escolasio, a womanizer, gambler, con artist, and professional survivor, became the star of the strip. The feature survived Divito's death in 1969 by more than a decade.

L.G.

FAMILIA BURRON, LA (Mexico) In 1937 the writer and cartoonist Gabriel Vargas created for the Mexican magazine *Pepín* a humor strip entitled *El Señor Burron o Vida de Perro* ("Mister Burron, or A Dog's Life"), which later became a color comic book under the definitive title of *La Familia Burron*.

The strip's direct antecedent was another series by the same author, *Los Superlocos* ("The Supercrazies"), in

which he created the character Jilemon Metralla y Bomba. The Burron family has as its titular head Don Regino, the barber-owner of the "Golden Curl" beauty salon, a good-natured and meek little man incapable of standing up to his wife, the jovial Borola. A female counterpart of the above-mentioned Jilemon, Borola runs the household, leads the family—and soon becomes the real star of the strip. A female figure carved all of a piece, Borola is as bold as she is aggressive and assertive. She takes chances in all and every conceivable enterprise, ready to make use of every trick without scruple or remorse, sure as she is that every conceivable way for advancing the fortunes of her children must be good. Social status is her ultimate goal: thrifty, protective of her children, she thrives and prospers under all conditions. Nothing seems too good for her children, her son Reginito, her daughter Macuca (a much sought-after girl with two boyfriends), and her adopted son, Foforito, who reflects all the virtues that are conspicuous by their absence in her natural children.

This long-lived series' greatest merit lies not in the drawings of Vargas and his successors, Miguel Meji and Gutu (pseudonym of Agustin Vargas), but in its implicit social criticism, as valid today as it was in 1937. Regarded as the most famous Mexican humor strip, *La Familia Burron* is characterized by the colorful language spoken by the protagonists, sometimes derived from that used by street people, and sometimes invented, or even on occasion picked out of old dictionaries of obsolete idioms.

L.G.

FAMILIA ULISES, LA (Spain) Created in 1945 by cartoonist Benejam on the back cover of the Spanish children's weekly TBO with texts by Joaquin Buigas, *La Familia Ulises*, which depicts a typical Catalan family, is the best example of a satirical comedy of manners in the Spanish comic strip. Throughout its run it met with enormous success.

The author was able to narrate the events of more than 30 years as reflected in the doings of his family. Señor Ulises is an average man who has been successful enough to own his automobile, go for a vacation every year, and send his older son Lolin to a private college. He is a peaceful conformist. His wife is anxious to keep up with the times, his other children are too young to have a well-defined personality: the one who revolts is the grandmother, a cantankerous oldster who stubbornly refuses to enjoy the rewards of technology. She is a woman of the people, distrustful of newfangled inventions, who gets carsick, hates air conditioning, and spurns the good uses of the Spanish language to boot. Her conversation is filled with Catalan locutions and her most typical pose is that of the old woman with a black shawl over her shoulders sitting on a cane chair and nodding her head. So much does she shun reality (at least the social reality of post-Civil War Spain) that she still sleeps as in her youth, on a cot with a handkerchief fastened to her hair.

The success of the strip (written since 1949 by Carlos Bech) gave rise to a multitude of toys and dolls, as well as to a series of records. After the death in 1975 of Marino Benajam, the series was continued for some time by other hands; *La Familia Ulises* is no longer, but it lingers in memory through many reprints.

L.G.

"La Famille Fenouillard," Christophe (Georges Colomb). © Armand Colin.

FAMILLE FENOUILLARD, LA (France) Christophe (Georges Colomb) on August 31, 1889, published in the comic weekly *Le Petit Français Illustré* a short picture-story called *La Famille Fenouillard à l'Exposition* ("The Family Fenouillard at the Fair") on the occasion of the 1889 Paris World Exposition. The success was such that *Le Petit Francais Illustré* started issuing *La Famille Fenouillard* as a regular feature.

Agénor Fenouillard and his imposing spouse Léocadie are a couple of small-town shopkeepers, blessed with two quarrelsome daughters, Artémise and Cunégonde, and a pretension to culture and sophistication. Their consciousness having been raised by their experiences at the Fair, the whole family decides to leave their native Saint-Rémy-sur-Deule and see the world.

In a devastating parody of Jules Verne's *Around the World in Eighty Days*, the Fenouillards first find themselves by mistake aboard a ship bound for New York, and then in short order journey through the States on a train that is attacked by Sioux Indians. They cross the Bering Strait on an ice floe, are shipwrecked on a Pacific island where Agénor is made king, and go through a series of madcap adventures before finally reaching home.

La Famille Fenouillard (like all of Christophe's creations) did not make use of balloons but had the text running underneath the pictures. It was the first French comic feature to reach a wide public, and it introduced a variety of new themes and novel techniques into the formerly bloodless picture-story.

Armand Colin published *La Famille Fenouillard* in book form in 1893; the book has gone into countless reprints in hardcover and in paperback and has been in print ever since. In the 1960s a movie version of *La Famille Fenouillard* was directed by Yves Robert, with Jean Richard as Agénor and Sophie Desmarests as Léocadie.

M.H.

FAMILY UPSTAIRS, THE *see* Dingbat Family, The.

FANTASTIC FOUR (U.S.) When Atlas editor Stan Lee decided to reenter the superhero field, he renamed his company Marvel and together with artist Jack Kirby created the *Fantastic Four* in *Fantastic Four* number one (November 1961). Using themes that would constantly recur in all their future superhero features, Lee and Kirby gave birth to a group of four individuals endowed with superpowers who were constantly beset with personal difficulties while they fought crime. The title immediately became Marvel's keynote feature. There Lee and Kirby perfected the "superhero with problems" concept and introduced dozens of fascinating characters in their books. Lee and Kirby set what could be called the Marvel style, a style so different it revolutionized the comic book industry.

The Fantastic Four themselves are Reed (Mr. Fantastic) Richards, an intellectual scientist with stretching abilities; Sue (Invisible Girl) Richards, Reed's flighty wife with the powers of invisibility; Johnny (Human Torch) Storm, Sue's quick-tempered younger brother, who can burst into flame at will; and Ben (The Thing) Grimm, a tough but lovable man who became a monstrous orangy being with phenomenal strength. The quartet had endless flaws: Reed was often insensitive and oafish, Sue was immature, Johnny was simply too young, and Ben suffered tremendous insecurity because of his hideous looks. Together, the group fought epic villains while trying to keep their own lives from crumbling around them.

Writer-editor Stan Lee handled the feature for 11 years and juggled the characters' idiosyncrasies magnificently. His realistic and poignant characterizations stand out as possibly the most outstanding achievement of the 1960s in the comic book world. Artist Jack "King" Kirby turned the feature into a pleasing maze of exaggerated muscles, complicated gadgetry, and innovative and exciting layouts. Joe Sinnott began inking Kirby's pencils in 1965, and he made Kirby's work more subtle and cleaner than it had ever been. Both Lee and Kirby abandoned the strip in 1971, however, and despite the best efforts of talented creators like John Buscema, Roy Thomas, and John Romita, the strip faltered.

It would be impossible to catalog the many intriguing supporting characters Lee and Kirby developed in *Fantastic Four*, but Dr. Doom and the Silver Surfer rate particular attention. Doom is a schizophrenic eastern European monarch whose scientific powers surpass even those of Reed Richards. He wears an iron mask to hide a damaged face, and he is perhaps the most popular villain (or antihero) to develop in the 1960s. His complex psyche has fascinated scholars. On the other hand, the surfboard-riding Silver Surfer is a neo-Christ, a sort of perfect being chained to this imperfect and violent world. Many have called Lee's characterization of the Surfer the most mature and developed in comics.

Lee and Kirby produced the first 102 issues of *Fantastic Four*, and they are undoubtedly among the greatest group of commercial comic books ever assembled.

J.B.

A host of artists and writers have worked on *Fantastic Four*, since the departure of Lee and Kirby. Most notable have been John Byrne, who gave new life to the tired feature in 1980-84, and Walt Simonson, who was responsible for some enjoyable stories in 1990. Other artists of merit who have drawn the title include Art Adams, Barry Smith (for one issue), George Perez, and Paul Ryan. In recent years there have also been a number of spin-off comic books, such as *Fantastic Four*

Unlimited, Fantastic Four Unplugged, and *Fantastic Four 2099.*

M.H.

FANTOMAS (Mexico) At the initiative of Alfredo Cardona Peña, Editorial Novaro, on March 1, 1966, started the publication of the first *Fantomas* comic book, which bore the number 103 in the collection "Tesoro de Cuentos Clasicos." This series of full-color comic books has the same format and characteristics as American comic books, except that its illustrators and writers are all Mexican. The drawing of the first comic book was entrusted to Rubén Lara Romero, assisted by his brother, Jorge, who did the backgrounds.

This initial adaptation was quite conventional and followed an earlier version done by Alfredo Valdés in the Mexican magazine *Paquín* (1936-1937). Fantomas' dress was modeled after the covers of the first French edition: the master criminal created by French novelists Pierre Souvestre and Marcel Allain traditionally wore high tails and hat, a scarlet vest, white gloves and ample cape, and a walking stick. Lara Romero's graphic style, with his primitive look and coarseness of line, was in perfect keeping with dime novel illustration. This team was to produce a few more episodes of *Fantomas* until 1969, when the favorable reception the protagonist received from the public prompted the publisher to issue a twice-monthly *Fantomas* book, under its own title.

The new title was greeted with a tremendous popular response, and a team had to be set up to ensure the smooth functioning of the collection. Up till then Cardona Peña had closely supervised the scripts written by Guillermo Mendizabal; when Mendizabal left in 1969, Cardona Peña took over the writing, assisted by a number of collaborators. The drawings were signed "Equipo Estudio Rubens," which was composed of José S. Reyna, Fermin Marquez, and Agustin Martinez, with Luis Carlos Hernandez and Jorge Lara as background men.

In this second version, the character of Fantomas was considerably altered. He became a young man, athletic, powerful, full of vitality, who wore a white mask that showed only his eyes and ears. While he went on committing misdeeds and burglaries, his aims were altruistic, he proclaimed himself a supporter of universal brotherhood and progress, and in general he shunned the unwholesome characteristics of the ruthless antihero he had been in the original novels. He used the latest gadgets provided by science and was helped in his endeavors by Professor Semo and a whole army of secret agents. Fantomas lived surrounded by antiques and paintings, which contrasted with his taste for well-endowed and somewhat *déclassé* women.

It should also be noted here that *Fantomas* had enjoyed a much earlier comic strip adaptation in the short-lived French comic weekly *Gavroche* (1941).

L.G.

FATTY FINN (Australia) Originally called *Fat and his Friends,* this strip was launched by Syd Nicholls on September 16, 1923, in the *Sydney Sunday News.* It was created at the instigation of the managing editor, Sir Errol Knox, as a means of competing against *Us Fellers/Ginger Meggs,* which had been running in the *Sunday Sun* for the previous two years. Fat was a corpulent, almost bald, nasty schoolboy after the style of *Billy Bunter* and was, more often than not, the butt of his friends' jokes. On August 10, 1924, the title was changed to *Fatty Finn,* and this heralded a gradual change in the strip's direction and the role of the main character. Over the next few years, Fatty lost considerable weight as well as gaining a Boy Scout uniform, a dog (Pal), a goat (Hector), and supporting characters such as Headlights Hogan, Lollylegs, and Mr. Claffey the policeman. Fatty adopted a more heroic role and the strip moved closer to the standard "kid" strip formula, with a distinct Australian flavor. In 1927, a motion picture called *Kid Stakes* was made with Fatty and Hector as the stars.

By the late 1920s, *Fatty Finn* had become the country's most visually pleasing strip. Nicholls' excellent draftsmanship and experimentation with long, sweeping frames and tall, column-like panels were complemented by vibrant coloring. In 1928, a new dimension was added when Nicholls introduced an adventure theme by involving Fatty in fanciful tales of pirates, cannibals, and highwaymen. While Fatty was still drawn in the traditional cartoon style, the other characters were depicted in a realistic manner—like a combination of animation and live-action films. Nicholls was, in fact, pioneering the adventure strip, which was to lead to his creation of *Middy Malone,* in 1929. That same year, the *News* merged with the *Guardian,* but when that paper merged again, with the *Sunday Sun* in 1931, *Fatty Finn* was dropped.

Fatty Finn emerged in May 1934 in its own tabloid-sized comic paper, *Fatty Finn's Weekly,* but faded by the

"Fantomas." © *Editorial Novaro.*

"Fatty Finn," Syd Nicholls. © Nicholls.

middle of 1935. From 1940 to 1945, it appeared in many of the comic books that were published by Nicholls, and from 1946 until 1950 Fatty appeared in his own monthly, *Fatty Finn's Comic*. He returned to the newspaper comic sections in October 1951, in the pages of the *Sydney Sunday Herald*. When that paper merged with the *Sunday Sun* (the paper that had originally dropped him) in October 1953, *Fatty* made a successful transition and continues to appear in the pages of the Sunday *Sun-Herald*. It now appears only episodically, however.

Although the passage of time has made *Fatty Finn* somewhat anachronistic, the strip is a constant reminder of the happier, less complicated childhood life of yesteryear. Fatty was the only serious rival to *Ginger Meggs*, but there was not a great deal of similarity between the two strips. *Ginger* was a humorous strip with a far greater appeal to adults looking back on their childhoods. *Fatty* tended to rely more on sight gags, was infinitely superior in art, and had a greater appeal for children. Had *Fatty Finn* not suffered so much editorial indifference over the years, it would have been Australia's longest-running comic strip that was created and drawn by the same artist.

J.R.

FAZEKAS, ATTILA (1948-   ) Hungarian cartoonist and writer, born July 25, 1948, in Keszthelyen, Hungary. After his final secondary-school examinations Attila Fazekas burst upon the Hungarian comics scene in the mid-1970s with his first strip, *Adventure in Ujvar*, which displayed a realistic, spectacular, detailed, and dynamic artistic presentation. As a result, by the 1980s he had become the most popular cartoonist in Hungary. His work appeared in the magazines *Pajtas* and *Fules* and in the daily political newspaper *Népszava*. He is equally at home working in science fiction and in humorous stories. He has turned out about 150 graphic novels and over 3,000 pages of comics. In addition, he has illustrated books, including 10 Tarzan novels, and has scripted an animated film.

The publishing of independent comic books was forbidden for a long time in Hungary. A breakthrough occurred when Fazekas was asked by a Hungarian publishing house to draw a comic-book adaptation of *Star Wars* in the late 1970s. After that he adapted many more films into comic-book form, including *Ben Hur* and *Alien*.

Fazekas was the first cartoonist to publish his own comic magazine, from 1988 to 1993, with all features drawn and written by himself. *Botond* was a humorous strip about a valiant warrior from the age of Hungarian conquests in the mold of Astérix who fought for truth in modern-day Hungary as well. His other major comic-strip character is Captain Perseus, who fights against robots and fantastic creatures in a distant future. (It is interesting to note that the artist drew himself as the hero.) He was also the first to publish a sex-comic magazine in Hungary: called *Szexi*, it features a buxom heroine named Tunde; and since 1989 his erotic illustrations have also become very popular.

K.R.

FEARLESS FOSDICK (U.S.) Al Capp's often hilarious strip-within-a-strip, *Fearless Fosdick* (an irregular continuity feature appearing sporadically in the *Li'l Abner* strip), is an affectionate parody of Chester Gould's *Dick Tracy*. It first appeared in the Sunday *Abner* episode of November 22, 1942, with a profile of Fosdick in a very Tracyesque pose in the *Abner* title logo (startling New York readers who found apparent Tracys looking at them from the covers of *both* of New York's highly competitive tabloid Sunday papers: the real Tracy on the *Sunday News,* and Fosdick on the *Sunday Mirror*). The initial *Fearless Fosdick* episode filled half of the *Abner* continuity. Fosdick, we learned, was not only Abner's favorite "comical paper" character, but also his heroic "ideel." (Fosdick, of course, hates women—to the despair of Daisy Mae.) In his first appearance, Fosdick does little but escape from a murder attempt in which he is tied to a quantity of high explosives with lit fuses; the kicker is that Pappy Yokum has torn part of the page away to smoke cornsilk behind the woodshed, and the torn part contains Fosdick's escape device. Abner is desperately trying to figure out how his hero got loose—and so has himself tied into the same trap by the agreeable Scragg Brothers. He, of course, can't escape and is blown up—to find out in another copy of the paper that Fosdick was having a bad dream and simply woke up. Weak as this gimmick was, the public liked the Fosdick concept, and Capp returned with the character on the Sunday page of May 30, 1943, this time as a full-length takeoff on *Dick Tracy*, complete with artist's byline (Lester Gooch) and eccentric adversaries (Bomb-Face, Stone-Face, etc.).

"Fearless Fosdick," Al Capp. © United Feature Syndicate.

"Feiffer," Jules Feiffer. © Jules Feiffer.

Gooch himself is introduced in the sequence as a small, bespectacled, moustached, mouse-like fellow, and there is much fun had with the Flattop-type of Gould villain.

By now, Capp was enjoying the Fosdick continuity as much as his readers (and presumably, Chester Gould), and he introduced a third, longer Fosdick narrative into the daily strip on June 16, 1944. The Fosdick character and continuity was in *Li'l Abner* to stay, and in a short time Capp had developed a separate cast of characters within *Fosdick*, such as Prudence Pimpleton, Fosdick's frustrated and aggressive girlfriend; Fosdick's sadistic Chief; and a superb array of comic villains, from Rattop (who sports the head of a snarling rodent) to Fosdick's archenemy, a brilliant and fiendish parrot named Sydney.

In later years there was little *Fosdick* in *Abner*, possibly for the reason cited above—or simply because Capp had so little real interest in or close supervision of the *Abner* continuity from his residence in London. But the dozens of *Fosdick* sequences printed remain an impressively funny body of work, and deserve reprinting in part. One *Fearless Fosdick* collection, with that title, was published in 1954.

B.B.

FEIFFER (U.S.) Jules Feiffer started a weekly series of comic strips satirizing current events for the *Village Voice* in 1956. Soon he branched out into a more general approach, relating his strips to each other and setting up a gallery of permanent characters. For lack of a better title he called his creation *Feiffer*. In 1958 several of the strips were published in book form under the title *Sick, sick, sick*; his work was then brought to the attention of Robert Hall, who started syndicating *Feiffer* that same year.

Feiffer's universe is the blackest and most depressing ever to be found in a comic strip. Spineless and craven men, neurotic and poisonous women occupy the center stage, pouring out plaintive accounts of their frustrations and misfortunes. A number of protagonists appear in the strip, but the most representative and

best known of these wretches is the abject Bernard Mergendeiler, a psychological wreck devoured by tics and complexes.

The atrocious repetition and the terrible banality of these confessions succeed in creating a vortex in which people, language, and concepts are swallowed up and destroyed. A parody of a bitter parody, *Feiffer* is not as much related to the classic comic strip as it is to the work of the "absurdist" playwrights, such as Adamov, Pinter, or Albee.

It is as a political strip that *Feiffer* is best known, however. It has lampooned every president since Eisenhower, although the author reserved his strongest venom for Nixon. After the collapse of the Soviet Union in 1991, the strip's Marxist undertones have become increasingly irrelevant; now distributed by Universal Press Syndicate to a very short list of newspapers (including the *Village Voice*, which is now a free sheet), it sounds as a distant echo of the 1960s, growing fainter with each passing week.

The *Feiffer* strips have been reprinted in both hardbound and paperback forms; following *Sick, sick, sick* there have been *The Explainers, Passionella, Feiffer's Marriage Manual*, and *The Unexpurgated Memoirs of Bernard Mergendeiler*. Feiffer's comic strip antiheroes also appeared in a play, *The Explainers*, staged at Chicago's Playwrights Cabaret in 1961.

M.H.

FEIFFER, JULES (1929-   ) American cartoonist and writer, born January 26, 1929, in the Bronx, New York. After a "miserable four years" at James Monroe High School, Jules Feiffer attended the Art Students League in New York. From 1947 to 1951 he studied at the Pratt Institute while working as an assistant on Will Eisner's *The Spirit*; in 1949 he created his first comic feature, *Clifford*, as part of the *Spirit* comic section.

In 1951 Feiffer was drafted into the Signal Corps doing animated cartoons. Returning to civilian life, he worked on different jobs before starting his long association with the *Village Voice* in 1956 with a weekly social and political commentary in comic strip form, which he simply called *Feiffer*. (Later *Feiffer* was to be syndicated by Publishers-Hall Syndicate.)

In addition to his work as a cartoonist, Feiffer has written a novel, *Harry the Rat with Women* (1963); a one-act play, *Crawling Arnold*, which was staged at Spoleto's Festival of Two Worlds in 1961; and a musical comedy, *Little Murders* (which was later adapted to the screen). He is the creator of *Munro*, an animated cartoon about a four-year-old mistakenly drafted into the army (which won an Academy Award in 1961), and the screenwriter of the award-winning film *Carnal Knowledge* (1971). Feiffer has also compiled an anthology of comic book stories, *The Great Comic Book Heroes*, published by Dial Press in 1965.

Jules Feiffer's work has been widely acclaimed and he has influenced many young cartoonists in both the comic strip and editorial cartoon fields. His sparse and desiccated style of drawing, so in tune with the times, has also given rise to numerous imitators. He wrote the script for the thoroughly unpleasant 1980 *Popeye* movie; and in 1986 he received the Pulitzer Prize for editorial cartooning.

M.H.

FEIGN, LARRY (1955-   ) Larry Feign was born in Buffalo, New York, in 1955 and grew up in California, where, contrary to his mother's plans, he dreamed of a cartooning career. He started a degree in folklore at the University of California-Berkeley, but quit after two years and hitchhiked across the country, working at menial jobs along the way. Later, he finished his degree at Goddard College, after which he went to Hawaii, drawing caricatures of tourists on the beach while pur-

suing a master's degree at the University of Hawaii. He returned to California after marrying a native of Hong Kong and worked briefly at DIC Studios, where he drew *Heathcliff the Cat* for television.

His career took a giant step forward when he settled in Hong Kong in 1985. His first work was a light-hearted introduction to the Cantonese language titled *Learn Cantonese the Hard Way*, which appeared in the *Hong Kong Standard*. Salvaging choice characters from this cartoon, Feign created *The World of Lily Wong* in November 1986, which for most of its life, ran six times a week in the *South China Morning Post*. The plot revolved around the sassy, self-confident, Hong Kong-born Lily, her gweilo (American) boyfriend Stuart Farnsworth, her lazy brother Rudy, her xenophobic father, and other characters. Originally, the strip emphasized Stuart's culture shock and experiences with the daily life of Hong Kong, but gradually, with a nudge from the *Post* management, the strip took on political nuances, becoming, in the eyes of some, one of the government's few critics in the press.

By the 1990s Feign had become the colony's most popular and controversial newspaper cartoonist. His strip won awards and was reprinted in at least six anthologies, in the daily *New Straits Times* of Malaysia, and on the Internet. At the same time, Feign increasingly used the strip to lash out at things that annoyed him—ineffectual bureaucrats; the British, who, in Feign's mind, sold Hong Kong down the river; the Hong Kong Legislative Council; and mainland China. In May 1995, at the peak of its popularity, *The World of Lily Wong* was dropped by the *Post*. The media throughout the world saw the move as a political

Larry Feign, "The World of Lily Wong." © Larry Feign.

maneuver on the part of the new *Post* owner, who had strong ties to the Chinese government in Beijing, and as an indication of what could be expected when Hong Kong reverted to Chinese rule in 1997. Feign remains in Hong Kong, although he has abandoned cartooning, disillusioned by his recent experiences.

J.A.L.

FEININGER, LYONEL (1871-1956) American painter and graphic artist, born July 17, 1871, in New York City. Lyonel Feininger's parents were both professional musicians and in 1886 they sent him to Germany to study music. Feininger soon shifted his interests toward art, and he studied in Hamburg, at the Berlin Art Academy, and at the Colarossi Academy in Paris. In 1894 Feininger started on a long and fruitful career as a cartoonist and illustrator for a number of German, French, and American magazines.

In 1906 James Keeley of the *Chicago Tribune* asked Feininger to create two strips for his newspaper, which appeared that same year under the signature "Your Uncle Feininger": *The Kin-der-Kids*, a fantastic round-the-world odyssey featuring an enterprising group of youngsters, and the wistful, lyrical *Wee Willie Winkie's World*. Following a dispute with his publishers, Feininger quit after a few months, and his two creations were left unfinished. The *Tribune* would have had trouble replacing Feininger, even if they had tried.

Feininger went on to a long and successful career as a painter and fine artist. His work was exhibited widely in Europe and the United States, and he taught at the famed *Bauhaus* school until it was closed down by the Nazis in 1933. In 1937 Feininger went back to the United States, teaching at Mills College in Oakland and exhibiting his paintings.

Although Feininger's career as a comic strip artist lasted for less than one year, his contribution to comic art is far from inconsequential. As Ernst Scheyer stated in his book *Lyonel Feininger: Caricature and Fantasy*, "Feininger's achievement as a cartoonist lies there like an erratic rock on the plains of the American comic strip."

Toward the end of his life Feininger would nostalgically go back to his comic creations. He carved small wooden figures of the *Kin-der-Kids* characters for his children and laid out the plans of a fantastic city ("the city at the edge of the world") directly out of *Wee Willie Winkie's World*. On several occasions Feininger expressed the desire to bring the *Kin-der-Kids* to conclusion. He died on January 13, 1956, before he could realize that dream.

M.H.

FELDSTEIN, ALBERT (1925-   ) American comic book artist, editor, and writer, born October 24, 1925, in Brooklyn, New York. After studies at the High School of Music and Art, the Art Students League, and Brooklyn College, Al Feldstein broke into the comics industry in 1941 with S. M. "Jerry" Iger's comic book shop. Working at the shop through 1946, he drew a multitude of strips for many companies, including Fiction House (*Sheena*, *Kayo Kirby*, and others), Quality (*Dollman* and others), Fox, and Aviation Press.

After a stint in the air force during World War II, Feldstein joined the E.C. group in 1947 and drew love, crime, and Western strips until the beginning of the "New Trend" in 1950. When the "New Trend" started, Feldstein quickly blossomed as an artist, writer,

and illustrator. But when he assumed the editorship of the line in late 1950, he almost totally abandoned his drawing board for the typewriter. Heavily affected by Bradbury and other contemporary writers, Feldstein produced almost all of the now-legendary E.C. crime, horror, science fiction, and suspense tales from 1951 through 1955. The first writer to utilize the O'Henry-like "snap ending" in comic strips, his scripts were among the most heavily worded and descriptive ever to appear in comic books.

Though he restricted himself to only an occasional science-fiction cover, his fine, clean renderings quickly became classics. His depiction of "static horror"—freezing a single action in time—has never been successfully duplicated in comics. After Harvey Kurtzman launched the fabulously successful *Mad* for E.C., managing editor-publisher Bill Gaines and Feldstein invented *Panic*, an imitation of their own title. Later, when the "New Trend" titles folded because of adverse public opinion and poor sales, Feldstein helped launch the short-lived "New Direction" series and the abortive "Picto-Fiction" black-and-white magazines.

When Kurtzman and Gaines parted company over the direction of *Mad* in 1956, it was Feldstein who was called in to edit the magazine. Having already made the transition from 10-cent color-comic to 25-cent magazine, *Mad* became an American institution with Feldstein at the controls. And while some critics complained that the magazine became more juvenile than it was when Kurtzman controlled it, circulation climbed to over two million copies per issue with Feldstein at the helm. After an almost 20-year absence from the comic-book scene, he came back in 1997 to draw covers for the newly minted comic-book series *Tomb Tales*, published by Cryptic Comics.

J.B.

FELIX (Denmark) *Felix*, a creation of Jan Lööf, is one of the highly individual comic strips to come out of Sweden in the 1960s and '70s. Having studied art in Stockholm, Lööf did his first picture book for children, *En trollkarl i Stockholm* ("A Wizard in Stockholm"), in 1965. This was followed by two more the following year. These books convinced the people of P.I.B., a press service based in Copenhagen, Denmark, that Lööf might be ideally suited to do a comic strip along the lines of his books. Jumping at the chance, Lööf came up with *FiffigeAlf* ("CunningAlf"), a 15-year-old boy falling from one adventure into another. By the time the first episode saw print in 1967 in *Politiken*, a newspaper in Copenhagen, Denmark, the strip had been rechristened *Felix*. Having moved to southern France at the time, Lööf worked ahead of schedule, assisted by his brother-in-law, Krister Broberg.

Felix is about a 15-year-old boy, bespectacled, five feet tall, who wears all kinds of different hats and caps. The fondness for hats has since worn off, but Felix still finds adventure wherever he turns. *Felix*, with its independent child-hero, is well in the tradition of *Tintin*, *Little Orphan Annie*, and a host of others. But *Felix* is more progressive than either of these, both in style and content. *Felix* is drawn in a seemingly simple, naïve style that is a cross between picture-book illustration and underground comix. Lööf makes good use of black and white in the composition of his art, which, despite its cartoon simplicity, comes alive with a feeling of three-dimensionality.

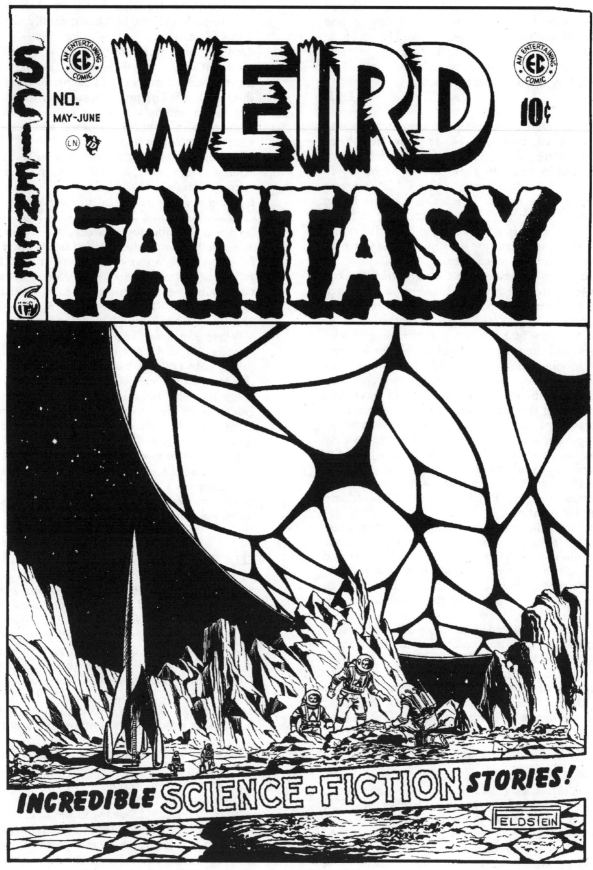

Albert Feldstein, comic book illustration. © E.C. Comics.

It is not only the art of *Felix* that appeals to young and older readers alike. The stories also appeal. The first episode has Felix help Captain Karlsson fight a power-crazed Latin dictator named Lurifaxus. Closer inspection of this seeming stereotype shows that Lööf never fails to add a new twist, testing the reader's memory. In fact, Lööf spices adventure with satire. Felix meets with heroes and crooks of radio, television, films, and comics, while also commenting on politics.

Returning to Sweden, Lööf produced *Felix* animated cartoons for television, finally abandoning *Felix* in 1972. The strip, which had been picked up by 20 Euro-

"Felix," Jan Lööf. © PIB.

"Felix the Cat," Pat Sullivan. © King Features Syndicate.

pean newspapers, was continued by Danish artist Werner Wejp-Olsen, whose first work had been a humorous detective series, *Peter og Perle* ("Peter and Perle"), in 1966. Continuing *Felix* was his breakthrough into the comics world. Wejp-Olsen toned down the political and socially critical elements of *Felix*. He stayed with the feature until 1976. It was then handed over to other writers and artists, among them Ole Munk Rasmussen and Per Sanderhage. The strip ceased publication in 1987.

W.F.

FELIX THE CAT (U.S.) Australian-born cartoonist Pat Sullivan created the character Felix the Cat in an animated cartoon produced in 1917. Its success was so great that Sullivan was to produce over 100 more animated cartoons of Felix before his death in 1933 (including the first sound cartoon and the first televised cartoon, in the historic NBC broadcast of 1930). In 1923 King Features Syndicate approached Pat Sullivan with an offer to adapt the character into a comic strip. Thus *Felix the Cat* made its debut as a Sunday page on August 14, 1923, and a daily strip followed on May 9, 1927.

Although the *Felix* strips were signed Pat Sullivan for a long time (at his death in February 1933, the original Pat Sullivan was succeeded by a nephew also named Pat), it is doubtful whether Sullivan, uncle or nephew, ever did any of them. There have been many conjectures and conflicting claims as to *Felix*'s actual authorship (Bill Holman is alleged to have ghosted the strip from 1932 to 1935, for instance), but it is likely that Otto Messmer (who was an early collaborator of Sullivan's and who signed his name to the strip starting in 1935) had been drawing—or at least directing—*Felix*

from its inception until he relinquished it to Joe Oriolo in 1954. The strip was then done by a variety of ghosts working for Joe Oriolo Productions (which also produced *Felix the Cat* animated cartoons for TV).

Felix is said to have been inspired by Rudyard Kipling's "cat who walks by himself." The little black feline is one of the great creations of comic art: his loneliness, his sense of alienation, and his obstinate fight against fate, the elements, hunger, cold, and an uncaring and callous humankind, mark him as an early hero of the absurd in animal guise. Under Messmer's inspired pen, Felix was to live his most memorable adventures—in the land of Mother Goose, in a mechanized civilization of the future, on the planets of the solar system, among the savages of Africa—drenched in a fantastic mood hovering midway between daydream and fantasy. And always the star-crossed Felix found himself on the outside, spurned by his love light Phyllis, kicked out of his master's house, or pursued by unrelenting enemies. Messmer also experimented with the formal contents of the comic medium, probably reflecting his training as an animator: having Felix use his speech balloon (after having blown away all the lettering inside) to parachute down to earth from Mars, for instance; or providing his hero with a weapon in the form of the exclamation mark suspended over his head.

In the 1920s and 1930s *Felix* displayed a poetry and a lyricism not unworthy of that other legendary cat strip, *Krazy Kat*. *Felix* has always been better known and appreciated in Europe than in the United States. In 1954 French Academician Marcel Brion wrote in a famous essay: "Felix is not a cat; he is the Cat. Or better to say yet, he is a supercat, because he does not fit in any of the categories of the animal kingdom."

Many of the *Felix* episodes were reprinted in Popular Comics; Felix also had his own comic book published by Toby in the 1940s and 1950s (some of the original stories were done by Messmer, but most were the product of uninspired hacks). And, of course, Felix lived on bravely on the television screen.

Indeed it was the durability of the screen Felix that induced King Features to bring back the little feline, along with his screen contemporary Betty Boop, in a newspaper strip called *Betty Boop and Felix*. The new feature was done by the Walker brothers (Neal, Morgan, Brian, and Greg, sons of Mort) and only lasted from November 1984 to the summer of 1987 (Betty lingered a little while longer).

M.H.

FENG ZIKAI (1898-1975) A well-established writer, literature critic, art teacher, calligrapher, and translator, Feng Zikai was also considered the founder of modern cartoons in China after his *Zi Kai Man Hua* ("Cartoons of Zikai") was published in 1924. Since then the term "Man Hua" is used to describe modern cartoons by Chinese cartoonists.

Feng's numerous published cartoons fall into four categories: children's cartoons based on his own children's behavior; cartoons displaying a deep love of the beauty of nature; cartoons showing a hatred of the dark side of society; and cartoons demonstrating his profound knowledge of classical literature, especially poems, which were often found in Feng's cartoons.

Feng graduated from the First Zhejiang Normal College in 1919 and studied music and art in Japan in 1921. While teaching high school a year later, Feng began his cartooning. His typically Chinese traditional style, characterized by its simplicity, was heavily influenced by a Japanese artist named Takehisa. After the People's Republic of China was founded, Feng was made a board member of the Chinese National Artist Association, chair of the Shanghai Chinese Artist Association, and president of Shanghai Chinese Art Academy.

Hu Sheng Hua Ji ("Collections of Drawing on Life Protection") were created between 1927 and 1973 during his 50-year-long career as an artist. The six collections reflect the deep friendship between Feng and artist Li Shuong (1880-1942). Li was a famous artist, teacher, and pioneer for his introduction of Western culture—music, opera, arts—to contemporary China. Feng was Li's best student at the Normal College during the 1910s. In 1918, Li unexpectedly became a monk, and in 1927, Li proclaimed Feng a Buddhist in a ceremony during the same period they decided to create *Hu Sheng Hua Ji* with the purpose of "advocating humanitarianism in art form."

All the creations in the collections followed Feng's style, and each picture was accompanied by a poem written by Feng in collections one, two, and six. In collections three, four, and five, the poems were copied by Ye Gongzhuo, Zhu Youlan, and Yu, respectively. The collections contained a total of 450 drawings, and although each was treated independently, the theme of "protecting life" was clearly evident in each drawing.

The first volume, completed in 1928, contained 50 works of art celebrating Li's 50th birthday. Thus, every 10 years thereafter, the number of art pieces in each volume increased in accordance with Li's age. Li died in 1942 at the age of 62, but Feng continued this practice until the final volume contained 100 pieces of artwork.

During the Cultural Revolution (1966-76) all cartoon drawing was curtailed by the government. Along with most of the other Chinese intellectuals and artists, Feng was accused of subversive activity; he was labeled one of the "Shanghai ten most important targets for criticism," so it was very dangerous for Feng to openly paint or draw. He kept his promise to Li and secretly continued working on the collection, however, with the last volume completed in 1973, two years before Feng's death. Long after he died, after the Cultural Revolution was over, collections of Feng's essays and cartoons have been republished and are still popular with the Chinese public.

H.Y.L.L.

FERD'NAND (Denmark) *Ferd'nand*, a comic strip that came out of Denmark, fits in with the kind of Scandinavian comic strips traditionally exported to the United States. Created in 1937 by Danish artist H. Dahl Mikkelsen, *Ferd'nand* followed a European form of pantomime comic strips that is easily understandable the world over. Like *Adamson*, by Swedish artist Oscar Jacobsson, and *Alfredo*, by Danish artists Jørgen Mogensen and Cosper Cornelius, *Ferd'nand* is a strip of universal appeal, combining European and American ideas in a calm, quietly humorous family strip.

Ferd'nand is published in newspapers all over the world in daily comic strip and Sunday-page versions. Reprints have appeared in a number of comic magazines, books, and annual albums. This does not come as a surprise, considering the constant quality of this pantomime strip. To a degree, pantomime strips are more difficult to do than strips incorporating speech balloons because the point to be made is put across by illustration alone. "Reading" *Ferd'nand* is like watching a silent movie. The full meaning is arrived at by watching action, gestures, and facial expressions. While no word is spoken, writing on signs, for example, "To trains," appears whenever necessary to identify a certain location. And, of course, onomatopoeic words are used when the need arises.

The "hero" of this humorous strip is Ferd'nand, a round-headed, big-nosed, wide-eyed, somewhat plump, middle-aged, middle-class husband. He usually sports a cone-shaped hat to hide the bald spot on his pate. Even his little son (of kindergarten age) is never

"Ferd'nand," H. Dahl Mikkelsen (Mik). © PIB.

seen without similar headgear. Neither father nor son seems to have a mouth but, in the case of the elder Ferd'nand, the mouth might be hiding behind his tiny, black mustache. Ferd'nand's wife is nearly as tall and wide as her husband. The Ferd'nand family has a shaggy dog for a pet.

Ferd'nand depicts all kinds of humorous situations that might happen to a middle-class family living in the suburbs of American or European cities. Mikkelsen has a knack for evoking smiles with the little things of life. This is one aspect of *Ferd'nand* that explains the strip's success. Another is Mikkelsen's admirably clear and expressive style.

W.F.

FERD'NAND (U.S.) The American distribution of Henning Dahl Mikkelsen's 1936 creation, *Ferd'nand*, was begun by United Feature Syndicate on November 10, 1947, in dailies and on April 4, 1948, for the Sunday page. Already an established favorite in Europe, Mik's silent little man caught on quickly in the Western Hemisphere and still remains a favorite.

The hero of this pantomime strip wears a Tyrolean hat and is whatever occupation a particular gag requires. Ferd'nand has a wife and son who have never needed the names they don't have, and the hero has no surname.

Mik lived in his native Denmark during World War II, when the German occupation government let *Ferd'nand* continue happily in the Danish press. Later he moved to California, where he engaged in several lucrative real estate deals.

Since late 1970 veteran cartoonist Al Plastino (*Hap Hooper, Barry Noble, Abbie an' Slats*, much D.C. work) has been drawing *Ferd'nand* with the same delightful, cozy style and humor. He signs his work "Al Mik." In 1993 Henrik Rehr took over the feature, which is now closing in on the half-century mark of publication in American newspapers.

R.M.

FERNANDEZ, FERNANDO (1940-   ) Spanish cartoonist and illustrator, born February 7, 1940, in Barcelona. Immediately following his high-school studies Fernandez embarked on an artistic career by drawing science-fiction stories for a French comic-book publisher and romance and war comics for a British publisher from 1956 to 1965. He later veered away from purely commercial considerations; since 1972 he has imparted a spirit of poetry and humanism that immeasurably adds to the visual spectacle of his compositions.

His stories in black and white, which were published between 1972 and 1975 in the American magazine *Vampirella*, are rich in lyrical expression that transcends the simple graphic lines. In *L'Uomo di Cuba*, for the Italian publisher Sergio Bonelli, the beauty of the illustrations overwhelms the narrative thread of the comic. With great literary and artistic conviction Fernandez undertook *Zora* (1980-81), a series first published in the Spanish magazine *1984* and later translated in the United States in the pages of *Heavy Metal*. In *Zora* the artist brought out the full panoply of his graphic, narrative, and illustrative talents in a vast display of spectacular effects.

In 1982 Fernandez, who had already used color in *Zora*, produced a pictorial version of Bram Stoker's novel *Dracula*. "Fernandez's most personal expression

Fernando Fernandez, an extract from one of his science-fiction stories. © *Fernando Fernandez.*

in *Dracula* resides in his composition, his sense of line, and his use of color," Maurice Horn wrote in his preface to the book. "The painter's touch is apparent at every step, and the painter's eye recognizable in each frame." At the same time he was using his skills as a painter, Fernandez, however, was reverting back to a more traditional method of storytelling, with his use of a grid consisting of rectangular panels, in contrast to the curvilinear structure of *Zora*. The story was thus told in predominantly cinematic terms, and the color tones all had a deep narrative function. More than any other Spanish comics artist perhaps, Fernandez realizes how much the intelligent staging of narrative sequences can contribute to the art of the comics.

Fernandez's next comic series, *La leyenda de los cuatro sombras* ("The Legend of the Four Shadows," 1983), based on a script by the Argetine writer Carlos Trillo, was a fantasy on a medieval theme. In the early 1990s he turned out a science-fantasy series titled *Lucky Starr*. Since that time he has alternated drawing for comics and working as a highly prized illustrator.

J.C.

FERRIER, ARTHUR (1891-1973) Arthur Ferrier was a British cartoonist and painter, who was born in Scotland in 1891 and died on May 27, 1973, at 82. The son of an organist, he qualified as an analytical chemist, and while working in Glasgow he freelanced cartoons to the *Daily Record*. When the editor, William McWhirter, came south to London as editor of the *Sun-*

Arthur Ferrier, *"Spotlight on Sally."* © News of the World.

day *Pictorial*, he sent for Ferrier to redraw the topical strip cartoons by their aged staff artist, G. M. Payne.

Once in London, Ferrier began to draw joke cartoons for *Punch* (April 1918), *London Opinion*, *The Humorist*, *Passing Show*, and other weekly magazines. By the 1920s his cartoons were appearing in five Sunday newspapers, and Sir William Carr offered him an exclusive contract for his *News of the World*. Always interested in show business, Ferrier began a weekly composite cartoon feature devoted to whatever show or play had opened that week, and this panel ran from 1922 to the 1950s. As his contract allowed him to continue to draw for magazines, he started a similar showbiz spot in *Everybody's Weekly* in the 1930s, quickly augmenting this with *Ferrier's World Searchlight*, a similar composite featuring topical gags, and his first weekly strip, *Film Fannie*.

Fannie, although not the first "glamour girl" strip (q.v. *Jane*), was Ferrier's first. He was the pioneer of the glamour girl cartoon in Britain, and his leggy lovelies, stripping off over some forgettable wisecrack, were star attractions in magazines through the 1930s and, especially, the war-torn 1940s, when the armed forces magazine *Blighty* regularly ran his pinup fun.

When his newspaper contract ended, he created another regular girl, a panel spot called *Our Dumb Blonde* (1939), in his old home paper, *Sunday Pictorial*. This ran for seven years until the *News of the World* once again signed him exclusively. George Davies took over the Dumb Blonde, and Ferrier started a new strip, *Spotlight on Sally* (1945). His only attempt at a daily strip, *Eve*, ran in the *Daily Sketch* from November 23, 1953, to January 21, 1956. Over the years the models for Ferrier girls included Anna Neagle, Lillian Bond, Mirian Jordan, Renee Gadd, Elsie Randolph, and Dodo Watts; all became film stars. His oil portraits of celebrities are collectors' items. His books include *Arthur Ferrier's Dumb Blonde* (1946).

D.G.

FIGHTING YANK (U.S.) *Fighting Yank* was created by writer Richard Hughes and artist Jon Blummer and made its first appearance in Nedor's *Startling* number

10 in September 1941. The character quickly became popular and was appearing in his own title by September of the next year.

The Fighting Yank was really Bruce Carter III, a rather mild-mannered young man who happened to stumble upon his ancestor's bulletproof cloak. Somehow, the cloak also gave him great strength, and Carter set out to save America from crime. Billed as "America's Greatest Defender," the Fighting Yank sported a costume in the colonial motif: three-sided hat, an American flag chest emblem, and square-buckled boots. Additionally, whenever he needed that little bit of extra inspiration to defeat an enemy, the spirit of old Bruce Carter I would appear to instill the needed bits of confidence and, of course, patriotism.

The strip was never particularly well written, although *Fighting Yank* did boast some exceptional artists during its run. Jack Binder (1942-43) is the most remembered illustrator, but Alex Schomburg (1943-49), Jerry Robinson (1947-48), and Mort Meskin (1948-49) all worked on the feature.

While most of *Fighting Yank*'s superheroic competitors were felled by the end of the war, the character held on in *Startling* until the 48th issue (January 1949). His own magazine even lasted until August 1949's 29th issue, and he also appeared in *America's Best* from April 1944 until February 1948.

J.B.

FIGUERAS, ALFONSO (1922-   ) A Spanish cartoonist born near Barcelona on October 15, 1922, Alfonso Figueras started his apprenticeship with the printing plant of Editorial Bruguera in 1939, working as a letterer and a layout man. From there he graduated to cartoonist on the magazines *Chicos, Nicolas, Leyendas Infantiles, Cubilete, Paseo Infantil*, and others published by Editorial Bruguera.

A man of ample culture and an expert on American humor strips, as well as dime novels, science fiction, and the horror film, he has devoted his professional life to the production of such humor strips as *Dedalito, Hércules Paput* (about a comical private eye), *Loony*, and *Patoflor* (whose hero seems to be a relative of Chico Marx's), all for *Nicolas*. For *Cubilete* Figueras has drawn *Rubin Rut* and *Tonty*. He is also the creator of *Rody, Aspirino y Colodíon, Mysto*, and the daily newspaper strips *Don Placído* and *Topolino*. His latter creations have included *Don Terrible Banuelos* and *El bon Jan* ("Good John"); beginning in the early 1980s he published his reminiscences of the Spanish comics scene in a number of magazines and fanzines.

Figueras's dozens of comic creations are bathed in a sentimental and preposterous humor that marks him as a master of nonsense.

L.G.

FILS DE CHINE (France) *Fils de Chine* ("Son of China") saw the light of print in the Communist-controlled French comic weekly *Vaillant* on October 8, 1950, at a time when China was still within the fold of orthodox communism (and, not coincidentally, about to strike in Korea). The feature was written by *Vaillant*'s chief scribe, Roger Lécureux, and drawn by the talented Paul Gillon.

Set at the time of the Long March, the strip re-created the hardships, vicissitudes, and ultimate triumph of the Communist troops in their struggle against the forces of Chiang Kai-shek. The story revolved around Tao, a young farmer who joined the Communists through a mixture of idealism and class conviction. Although heavy on political propagandizing at times (especially in the beginning), the strip made an effort at historical accuracy while telescoping events of many years into a few months. The Communist leaders made a few discreet appearances, but their contributions were usually played down. The strip finally ended in March 1962, at a time when China was about to be written out of the world Communist movement.

Fils de Chine is worthy of study on at least two counts. From an artistic viewpoint it remains one of Gillon's best contributions (far superior to the daily *13 rue de l'Espoir* strip, which he was doing at the same time for *France-Soir*); a few pages were drawn by Pierre Legoff and Pierre Dubois, but Gillon's rendition remains supreme, with a number of images of sheer lyric beauty. The strip also provides an ironic footnote to the history of international communism in recent times.

M.H.

FINE, LOUIS (1914-1971) American comic book artist, born in 1914 in New York City. His major art training was from New York's Grand Central Art School, but he also studied briefly at the Art Students League and Pratt Institute. He joined the Eisner-Iger comic book shop in 1938 and quickly became, with Eisner himself and Reed Crandall, one of the shop's best artists.

Producing a horde of comic strips under house names like "Jack Cortez" and "Basil Berold," Lou Fine won immediate praise for his excellent draftsmanship and tremendous knowledge of the human anatomy in motion. For the Eisner-Iger shop he drew parts of *Jumbo* and *Sheena* comics (Fiction House) and also produced several adventures of *The Flame* (Fox) and later *Rocketman* and *Master Key* for Harry Chesler's Dynamic Comics group.

Fine's most prolific and creative comic book period was from 1939 through 1943, when he was the major artist for "Busy" Arnold's Quality Comics group. He produced *Black Condor* for *Smash Comics*, *Stormy Foster* for *Hit Comics*, and various adventures of *Uncle Sam*, *Quicksilver*, and other Quality features. He also drew an outstanding array of covers for Quality comics like *Hit*, *Smash*, *National*, *Uncle Sam*, *Police*, and *Blackhawk*. Fine also ghosted a substantial portion of *The Spirit* newspaper strip when Will Eisner joined the armed forces.

One particular feature, however, was to make Lou Fine a major force in the comic book field. Looking for a new feature for *Smash*, Arnold assigned Fine to create a strip, and he developed *The Ray* (*Smash* number fourteen, September 1941). *The Ray* had all the prerequisites for a superhero strip: a hero with an offbeat origin, a colorful costume, an alter ego, a gimmick, and even a sidekick named Bud. But it was Fine's spectacular renderings that made the strip a success. Although he drew only about half the feature's 26 stories, his work contained some of the most impressive and stylized material in the comics. Despite the fact that all strips of *The Ray* are signed by "E. Lectron," Fine's work is easily recognizable—his heroes were classically featured, and his backgrounds were highly detailed with cross-hatches, stipples, and every conceivable comic technique. As drawn by Fine, *The Ray* became a minor classic, and much of it has been reprinted in *Special Edition Comics* number two (Alan Light, 1974).

Fine left the comic book industry in 1944 and concentrated for most of the next 25 years on commercial art and magazine illustrating, most notably his material for the now-defunct *Liberty*. He made several minor attempts at comic strips, the best of which, *Peter Scratch* (1965), was highly acclaimed but short-lived. Lou Fine died of a heart attack on July 24, 1971, and was eulogized by Will Eisner in *Graphic Story World*: "Lou Fine was one of the greatest draftsmen I have ever known," he said. "His consummate skill may never be equalled. What can one say at the death of a giant?"

J.B.

FINGER, BILL (1917-1974) American comic book writer, born February 8, 1914, in New York City. After studies at De Witt Clinton High School in Manhattan, he and artist Bob Kane created two minor adventure strips for National Comics in 1938: *Rusty and His Pals* and *Clip Carson*.

But Finger's greatest achievement was his collaboration with Kane on *The Batman*, the quintessential costumed mystery feature in comic books. Premiering in the 27th issue of National's *Detective Comics* (May 1939), the strip became fabulously successful and spawned many less inventive imitations. Although Finger was instrumental in the design of the character and his costume, only Kane's name went on the strip. He never signed his stories either. Consequently, it is only recently that Finger has been receiving recognition for his integral part in the *Batman* legend.

Finger's *Batman* scripts were far and away the best of the character's "golden age" period of 1940 through 1947. His stories were always moody, mysterious, and somber, and when the strip became more gimmick-oriented, Finger's scripts were always the most inventive. He is considered the definitive writer of *Batman*, despite a horde of talented successors.

Although Finger produced some material for the Timely, Fawcett, and Quality groups in the mid 1940s, most of his scripts were done for National. During the period between 1938 and 1967, he produced hundreds of stories for every genre of National comic—superhero, mystery, crime, adventure, science fiction.

He died in February 1974, and when National reprinted the first *Batman* comic book later that year, publisher Carmine Infantino dedicated the book to Finger's memory.

J.B.

FISHER, HAMMOND EDWARD (1901-1955) The tragically vain creator of *Joe Palooka*, Hammond Edward Fisher was born in Wilkes-Barre, Pennsylvania, in the fall of 1900, the son of a middle-class businessman. Fascinated by comic strips from the age of five, Fisher worked every spare moment at his cartooning ability through high school, then skipped college to enlist in the army during World War I, just in time for the armistice. Back in Wilkes-Barre, he landed his first job on the local *Herald* as editorial and sports cartoonist in 1919, then moved on to the *Wilkes-Barre Times-Leader* a year later in the same capacity. Going into local politics, he stayed with his newspaper work in order to keep cartooning. As early as 1920, however, Fisher had drawn his first *Joe Palooka* episodes, and tried them out on every syndicate in the business—to no avail. In 1925, Fisher started his own newspaper in

INSTEAD OF A SELF PORTRAIT I HAD PALOOKA DRAW ME!

Ham Fisher.

Wilkes-Barre, until a minor depression wiped out his capital and forced him to fall back on his *Palooka* idea again. Going to New York in 1927, he took a temporary job with the advertising department of the *New York Daily News* and started around the syndicate circle once more. This time he found real interest in Charles V. McAdam, general manager of the McNaught syndicate, who took on *Palooka* for a 1928 release.

Fisher decided to promote the strip himself, going on the road to visit a number of large newspapers around the country and taking the promotional material for another new McNaught strip, *Show Girl* (later *Dixie Dugan*) with him. Emphasizing *Show Girl* first, Fisher placed the strip with some 30 papers in 40 days, a syndicate record. Tackling his own *Palooka* next, Fisher sold it to 20 papers in three weeks, and returned to New York to find McAdam almost more interested in making Fisher the McNaught sales manager than in publishing *Palooka*. Fisher, however, true to his early ambition, stuck with the strip.

Fisher promptly used his sales technique to acquire sharper artistry for his strip, and he beat the Manhattan bushes for young talent on its way up. Among the first such cartoonist he signed up was Al Capp, who later berated Fisher for the fast talk and low pay (plus hard work) Fisher gave him. (After Capp, Moe Leff did the bulk of the work on the strip.)

Fisher's real contribution to his own strip was the story line. The *Palooka* readership had gone into the tens of millions by World War II, and Fisher's early plunging of Joe into the war sent the circulation soaring even higher. For a time Fisher was on the top of the comic strip world. Then came the first slow, and finally precipitous, collapse.

Fisher was fundamentally concerned with his public image as a great cartoonist and princely fellow. Al Capp, his old ghost, began to erode that image—at least in Fisher's eyes. Capp wrote articles for *The Atlantic Monthly* in the late 1940s (one was called "I Remember Monster") in which he excoriated Fisher, though not in name, for his treatment of the young artist a decade before, and he pilloried him in the *Li'l Abner* strip as a savagely vicious strip artist. Fisher grew increasingly paranoid, until he destroyed himself by going to court to accuse Capp of public obscenity, using faked examples of the *Li'l Abner* strip he had prepared himself. It took Capp no time at all to disprove the charge (he simply showed copies of newspapers carrying the actually printed episodes), and the dis-

gusted members of the National Cartoonists Society expelled Fisher from membership. As a result, Fisher committed suicide at the New York studio of a friend on December 27, 1955. It was a petty, tragic, unnecessary end for a man who had started out so adroitly and risen so high with such good reason. His strip continued in Moe Leff's hands, but the spirit was gone forever.

B.B.

FISHER, HARRY CONWAY (1885-1954) Harry Conway Fisher, who was to draw the world-famed *Mutt and Jeff* strip as "Bud" Fisher, was born on April 3, 1885, in a Chicago rebuilding from its great fire. Precociously talented, Fisher had left the University of Chicago in his third year to take a job as a triple-threat cartoonist (theater, sports, and general news) on the *San Francisco Chronicle* in 1905. Here, in the wake of the San Francisco fire, he persuaded the sports editor to let him draw a page-wide daily comic strip, imitative of Clare Briggs' *A. Piker Clerk*, to be called *A. Mutt*, and (like the Briggs work) to deal with a chronic horseplayer's hunches, wins, and losses. Drawn like Briggs' chinless Clerk, Mutt was simpler and funnier and made a great hit with San Francisco pony players. He also sold papers—so many that the *Chronicle*'s rival, Hearst's *San Francisco Examiner*, hired Fisher for more money a few weeks later. Here Fisher's star met his short pal, Jeff, the two going into national circulation when Fisher was shunted to Hearst's *New York American* in 1909. A Sunday page was added around the time the strip got its permanent title, *Mutt and Jeff*, but Fisher wanted greener pastures and took the strip to the Wheeler Syn-

BUD FISHER AS SEEN BY HIMSELF

H. C. (Bud) Fisher and friends.

dicate at the close of his Hearst contract in 1915, receiving $1,000 a week for just six strips. (Later a Sunday page was added by Wheeler, for more money.)

By now Fisher was established as the richest and most famed strip cartoonist in America. He had proven that readers would buy a daily paper for an outstanding strip, but only if they were sure it would be there every day. By the time he transferred to the Bell Syndicate in 1921, he was well on his way to making his top salary of $4,600 a week. He now owned a string of racehorses himself, including a number of outstanding winners, loved the racing life and the international set, and grew less and less interested in the daily mechanics of drawing *Mutt and Jeff*. Accordingly, he hired Billy Liverpool to do most of the drawing on the strip. Liverpool was a talented Hearst cartoonist originally assigned to draw *Mutt and Jeff* for Hearst after Fisher's departure in 1915, until Fisher won a lawsuit for the rights to his own characters.

This freed Fisher to follow the life of a bon vivant as he wished. Loving well but unwisely (his marital squabbles with two wives gave the still-rancorous Hearst papers good scandal copy), Fisher often made more newspaper copy than his actor and writer friends of the 1920s and 1930s. But he was never far from his creations in mind, and timely gag and continuity ideas reached Liverpool's drawing board from Fisher and made the strip arrive at its peak of art and wit between 1919 and 1934. But then Liverpool left the strip, and a new aide, Al Smith, took over. Then, for some reason, much of the old fantasy and high jinks drained out of the strip, and it became little more than a routine gag strip, as it is today.

Aside from his apparent loss of interest in the strip after 1934, Fisher continued to enjoy life but managed to squander most of the wealth *Mutt and Jeff* had made him before his death on September 7, 1954.

B.B.

FIVE FIFTEEN, THE *see* Sappo.

FIX UND FOXI (Germany) *Fix und Foxi* ("Fix and Foxi") started out as a feature in Rolf Kauka's comic book *Eulenspiegel*, which began early in 1952. At the time Kauka probably didn't know he would soon have one of the hottest comic properties in Germany, second only to Walt Disney's *Micky Maus* ("Mickey Mouse"). With issue No. 10 of *Eulenspiegel*, Fix and Foxi became the stars of the book. Fix and Foxi, two clever little foxes, characters that could be found in German fairy tales and fables, started out as relatively naturalistic anthropomorphic animals but, in time, the art became more stylized so changes of artist would not be too apparent. Over the decades the art on *Fix und Foxi* has been handled by artists Werner Hierl, Ludwig Fischer, Walter Neugebauer, Branco Karabajic, Vlado Magdič, Ricardo Rinaldi, V. Kostanjsek, Franz Roscher, and Florian Julino.

Fix and Foxi eventually got their supporting cast of Lupo, the roguish wolf, Grandma Eusebia, Uncle Fax, Cousin Lupinchen, and Professor Knox, the absent-minded inventor.

In 1953-54 expansion set in after a setback over the initial press run had occurred. The *Fix und Foxi* comic book always had a policy of including backup features. Thus comics like *Hops und Stops; Tom und Klein Biberherz* ("Tom and Little Beaverheart"), later retitled *Tom & Biber; Mischa* (Mike); and *Pauli*. The latter started in

"Fix und Foxi," Rolf Kauka. © Rolf Kauka.

1954 and since 1963 was done almost exclusively by Branco Karabajic. Despite a loyal following, *Pauli*, a mole, never got his own book. As some of the animal characters were defined more clearly, they stopped crossing over into each other's series. Funnies featuring human characters like *Tom und Biber* (a Western) or *Mischa* (science fiction) did not lend themselves to crossovers anyway.

Fix and Foxi stories, in general, are either sitcoms or comedy-adventures. The artistic style has been largely influenced by Walter Neugebauer, who, as art director, also drew style sheets that had to be adhered to by other artists. Neugebauer's style, influenced by his Yugoslav experience, has become exemplary for a new "German" style of comics.

If anything, Rolf Kauka and his writers have bent over backwards to represent a humorous intact world. Allegations of reactionary or nationalistic tendencies have never been proved for the bulk of the Kauka comic books but have been inferred after the *Asterix* fiasco in *Lupo*.

Fix und Foxi and their supporting cast have seen quite a commercial success. Besides the weekly comic book there have been specials, annuals, digest-sized comics, and some 18 comic books with accompanying record. There have also been dolls, puppets, cups, puzzles, games, bubble gum cards, iron-ons, stick-ons, rub-offs, coloring books, cut-outs, calendars, T-shirts, wallpaper, some 10 records, etc. In 1972, Fix and Foxi appeared in a first cartoon short, "Synfonie in Müll" (Symphony in Trash), taking up the ecology theme. It was presented together with Kauka's feature-length animated cartoon of the fairy tale "Maria d'Oro."

By 1970 Kauka's artists grew restless, with some leaving to return later. In 1972 Walter Neugebauer broke with Rolf Kauka over copyright and financial arrangements that had been smoldering since production of *Maria d'Oro*. This did not hurt the Kauka magazines, however. In fact, Kauka enlarged his operations by collaborating with a British company and with

Springer Verlag. In a series of shrewd deals, Kauka sold his company but retained copyrights to his features.

In his deals, he usually kept the *Fix und Foxi* comic book as a separate entity. But, ultimately, he sold out on his creations and retired to the United States. In the 1990s the magazine's sales stagnated, and when the magazine's editors decided to include editorial matter aimed at teenagers in 1994, Kauka was so appalled that, out of retirement, he used his copyright ownership to suspend publication of the magazine until the decision was rescinded. In October 1994 the magazine ceased publication after more than four decades on the market. The characters remain popular in numerous reprints, as a merchandising property, and in advertising.

W.F.

FLAMINGO (U.S.) *Flamingo* was one in the line of daily comic strips fielded by S.M. "Jerry" Iger's newly created Phoenix Features in February 1952 (others were George Thatcher and Jack Kamen's *Inspector Dayton*, Thorne Stevenson's *South Sea Girl*, Rod Maxwell and R.H. Webb's *The Hawk*, and Iger's own *Bobby* and *Pee Wee*). *Flamingo's* scripts were written by Ruth Roche, and the artwork was supplied by Matt Baker.

Flamingo was a dark-haired, full-bodied, and sexy Gypsy dancer who got involved in all kinds of romantic and dangerous adventures while traveling the European roads with her caravan. When danger lurked she was always ready to lend a hand, whether to foil the plot of some scheming impostor bent on talking an innocent lad out of his inheritance, or to rescue the kidnapped heir to a throne. She was vigorously assisted in her endeavors by her tribe of fellow Gypsies led by her grandfather, Old Pepo the mask-maker. Most of the men who crossed Flamingo's path fell madly in love with her, although the alluring Gypsy remained fiercely faithful to her boyfriend, Joe, an American.

The story line sounds conventional, but the strip came to life under the expert handling of Matt Baker, who displayed superior draftsmanship and a sense of mood and composition. The action moved at a fast pace, punctuated by large, detailed panels in which the fiery figure of Flamingo burned bright. Following Baker's untimely death at age 33, John Thornton took over the daily strip on July 3, 1952 (a Sunday feature was added a few weeks later). A competent craftsman, Thornton had little of Baker's brilliance and vibrancy, and the strip steadily lost most of its appeal. It was finally discontinued on March 21, 1953; the last strip ended with Flamingo's wedding to Joe.

Despite the brevity of its run, *Flamingo* created a strong impression on its readers (especially the episodes drawn by Matt Baker). Had Baker not died so soon after the strip's inception, it may have gone on to become a success. (Baker had also prepared two stories for a planned *Flamingo* comic book before he died. They were never published).

M.H.

FLANDERS, CHARLES (1907-1973) American comic strip artist, born in 1907 in Mayville, New York. Flanders' father was a painter and encouraged his son's early artistic efforts. While attending high school, Flanders spent all of his spare time drawing and studying art. After graduation, he took a job in the art department of a silk-screen company in Buffalo and at the same time attended classes at the Allbright Art School. Later he became an instructor in another Buffalo art school.

In 1928 he came to New York, where he worked as a freelance artist, an assistant art director in an advertising agency, and a magazine illustrator before joining the staff of King Features Syndicate in 1932. There he served his apprenticeship by working on any strip that came his way, from *Tim Tyler's Luck* to *Bringing Up*

"Flamingo," Matt Baker. © S. M. Iger.

Father. In 1935 Flanders got his big chance at KFS when he was asked to draw the only feature he ever created, *Robin Hood*, a Sunday page depicting the adventures of the legendary outlaw of Sherwood Forest. The strip was not a success and was retired from circulation after only three months.

This setback did not discourage either Flanders or the editors at King Features. When, later that same year, Alex Raymond abandoned *Secret Agent X-9*, the strip was turned over to Flanders, who was to draw it until April of 1938. In addition, early in 1936, Flanders took over the Sunday page of *King of the Royal Mounted*; in April 1938, Flanders became sole artist on *King*, drawing both the Sunday and the dailies until one year later, when he was assigned to draw *The Lone Ranger*, a Western strip created by Fran Striker.

With *The Lone Ranger*, Flanders had finally found his niche and his style, and he was to draw the feature until the syndicate decided to discontinue it in December 1971. On January 10, 1973, Charles Flanders died in Palma-de-Mallorca, where he had retired.

Flanders was never a remarkable artist. Unlike some of his more gifted colleagues, he had to overcome obscurity by sheer effort, hard work, and staying power. He always managed to do a creditable, if unexalted, job, with a solid, craftsmanlike, and earnest attention to the task at hand. In his love for the comic strip medium, Flanders represents the quintessence of the journeyman strip artist.

M.H.

FLASH (U.S.) *Flash* was created by writer Gardner Fox and first illustrated by Harry Lampert in January 1940. It made its first appearance in National Comics' *Flash* number one. The Flash was really Jay Garrick, who, when bathed in the fumes of hard water, became the fastest man alive. He adopted a red, blue, and yellow costume, boots, and wing-adorned steel helmet.

The character was never handled as imaginatively as he could have been. He spent most of the time running or catching bullets, and the most enjoyable parts of the *Flash* were the inventive and offbeat villains. The best of this evil lot was The Fiddler, who often plagued the speed monarch. Looking like a virtuoso conductor gone astray, The Fiddler had a magical Stradivarius that could force others to do his bidding. One of the best-known villains of the comic book's golden age, he was one of the first to be revived in the 1960s.

Artistically, E. E. Hibbard drew the bulk of *Flash* from 1940 to 1949, although his material was always too linear and static for such an action-oriented character. Many of the later artists, including Lee Elias, Joe Kubert, and especially Carmine Infantino, handled the feature with considerably more style and verve.

Flash appeared in all 104 issues of *Flash* until its demise in February 1940. The character also appeared in all 32 issues of *All-Flash* from Summer 1941 to January 1949, and also made appearances in *All-Star* and *Comic Cavalcade*.

The revival of the Flash in October 1956's *Showcase* number four is officially regarded as the beginning of the second "golden age" of superheroic comics. This time Flash was police scientist Barry Allen, who became the super speedster after being doused by chemicals. Unlike his predecessor, this new Flash wore a more standard superhero costume—a skin-tight red and yellow suit and cowl, which sprung to full size from a special ring.

"The Flash." © National Periodical Publications.

The Flash was eventually reinstated in his own title in March 1959, and the book began with number 105. The definitive creators of this Flash were two veteran *Flash* artisans, writer John Broome and artist Carmine Infantino. Broom's scripts were fast-paced and tightly organized, and Infantino's pencils, aided by inkers Joe Greene and Joe Giella, set the pattern for the illustration of super-speed characters. Over the years, Broome created a rogues' gallery of exciting villains, including Grodd, a super-gorilla; Mirror Master, a felon with a reflection fetish; and Captain Cold, who controlled ice and frost with a cold gun. Broome and Infantino made *Flash* the quintessential superhero strip of the 1960s.

At the same time, Gardner Fox was using *Flash* to develop his Earth-one and Earth-two theory, which conveniently allowed National to revive all their old 1940s characters by claiming that they existed on Earth-two. In short, while Broome was using *Flash* for character development, Fox was using *Flash* for character revival.

Flash fell on hard times late in 1967. Infantino left to become a National executive, and his artistic replacements did not match up to his outstanding achievements. Both Broome and Fox began to falter, and both were gone by the end of 1969. Since then the strip has been handled by many people, none of whom were able to recapture the Fox-Broome and Infantino-Greene-Giella magic.

J.B.

In 1982 Infantino returned in an attempt to bolster the character's faltering fortunes. He was unsuccessful, as were Rich Buckler, Frank Robbins, and Mike Grell, who were among the artists who succeeded Infantino. The Flash was killed off in 1985, but he was resurrected in a different guise in a new *Flash* comic book (June 1987) that continues to this day.

M.H.

FLASH GORDON (U.S.) Alex Raymond created *Flash Gordon* on January 7, 1934, as a Sunday page (with *Jungle Jim* as its top) for King Features Syndicate. In the opening sequence (inspired by Philip Wylie and Edwin Balmer's novel *When Worlds Collide*) three earthlings, Flash Gordon, "renowned polo player and Yale graduate," his female companion Dale Arden, and a scientist, Dr. Hans Zarkov, set out in Zarkov's spaceship to the alien planet Mongo, which threatened to destroy Earth. In the strange world they entered, Flash and his companions found themselves locked in a death struggle with Ming the Merciless, the dreaded emperor of Mongo. Amid the grandiose landscapes, in the futuristic cities and the forsaken regions of the planet (Queen Undina's undersea kingdom, the land of the tuskmen, Queen Fria's ice kingdom), Flash, the defender of justice, helped by Ming's daughter Aura and her husband Barin, the king of Arboria, clashed swords with Ming until final victory and the liberation of Mongo (June 1941).

After a brief return to Earth, Flash again returned to Mongo in 1942 (along with Dale and Zarkov), but his fight against the tyrant Brazor no longer had the same dash as his earlier exploits. In February 1944 Raymond joined the Marines and abandoned his creation (his last page appeared on April 30, 1944).

In the meantime a daily *Flash Gordon* strip had appeared (May 27, 1940), drawn by Raymond's former assistant Austin Briggs. Thus Briggs was the logical choice to succeed Raymond on the Sunday page, and he did a creditable job in sustaining the epic inspiration and the grandiose imagery of his predecessor.

After Briggs (who left *Flash Gordon* in July 1948) there came Mac Raboy (1948-67), succeeded by Dan Barry, who took over the Sunday page, with the help of a number of assistants (his brother Sy, Al Williamson, Frank Frazetta, Ray Krenkel, Ric Estrada, and others) beginning December 31, 1967. The daily strip, meanwhile, had been discontinued from June 1944 to

November 1951, but was revived by the same Barry who left it to his former assistant Ric Estrada in 1967. In the hands of Barry and Estrada, Flash became just another space adventurer working for an intergalactic police force of the future. After Barry left the strip in 1990, he was followed by a bewildering array of artists, including Ralph Reese, Gray Morrow, and Tom Warkentin. The daily strip was discontinued in 1993, while the Sunday is now being done by Jim Keefe.

The first episodes of *Flash Gordon* were written by Raymond himself, but he soon had to call upon Don Moore to relieve him of the writing burden. Moore proved a skillful scriptwriter and was to work on *Flash Gordon* until the late 1940s, when he was replaced by a succession of staff writers, Fred Dickenson notable among them.

Flash Gordon met with immediate success, establishing itself as the supreme science-fiction strip (over *Buck Rogers*). Alex Raymond's style, imagery, and composition were widely imitated (but never equaled), and the strip has been held ever since as the epitome of the adventure story. In 1936 an original novel, *Flash Gordon in the Caverns of Mongo*, credited to Alex Raymond (who, in all probability, did not write it), was published by Grosset & Dunlap. That same year, a memorable movie serial, with Buster Crabbe as Flash and Charles Middleton as Ming, was made of *Flash Gordon*, followed by *Flash Gordon's Trip to Mars* (1938) and *Flash Gordon Conquers the Universe* (1940), both with the same cast. *Flash Gordon* was also made into a radio program in the 1930s and 1940s, and into a television series in 1953-54. A new version of *Flash Gordon* was produced by Dino de Laurentiis in 1980, with Sam Jones in the title role, and with Ornella Muti, Max von Sydow, and Topol in supporting roles. There has also been a *Flash Gordon* telefilm in 1982, as well as a series of animated cartoons, also in the 1980s.

Flash Gordon had a number of comic books from 1930-70 variously published by King, Harvey, Charlton, and others. Among its many contributing artists, mention should be made of Paul Norris, John Lehti, Reed Crandall, and especially Al Williamson (1966-67), Alex Raymond's most faithful imitator. Raymond's early episodes have been reprinted by Nostalgia Press in two hardbound volumes: *Flash Gordon—In the Ice*

"Flash Gordon," Alex Raymond. © King Features Syndicate.

Kingdom of Mongo (1967) and *Flash Gordon—Into the Water World of Mongo* (1971).

M.H.

FLEISCHER, MAX (1885?-1972) An American cartoonist and animator born in Vienna, Austria, in 1885 (other sources say 1888), Max Fleischer was taken to the United States at the age of four. After studies at the New York Evening High School, the Mechanics' and Tradesmen's School, the Art Students League, and the Cooper Union, he finally got a job as photo-engraver on the *Brooklyn Eagle*. In 1915 he started doing research in animation, turning out the first *Ko-Ko the Clown* cartoon with his brother Dave.

After seeing service in World War I, Max and Dave Fleischer worked for pioneer animator J. R. Bray before forming their own partnership in 1921 called Out-of-the-Inkwell Films, Inc. During the 1920s the Fleischer brothers turned out many cartoon films. Their fame came with the advent of sound, however: in 1931 the first full-fledged *Betty Boop* cartoon was released. The success was immediate; more Betty cartoons followed, and in 1933 the Fleischer brothers scored an even bigger hit with the animation of Segar's *Popeye the Sailor*. In 1934 King Features, which syndicated *Popeye*, adapted *Betty Boop* to comic strip form.

In 1937, Max Fleischer decided to move his studios from New York to Miami. There he produced several feature-length cartoons and the acclaimed *Superman* series. But financial success did not follow, and Fleischer had to sell his studios to Paramount in 1942. After several tries at a comeback in motion pictures and TV, Max Fleischer finally retired in the 1960s. He died on November 12, 1972.

Max Fleischer is mentioned here not only for his creation of *Betty Boop*, but also for his contribution to the mythography of two of the most legendary comic characters—Popeye and Superman.

M.H.

FLETCHER, FRANK (1919-   ) American artist, born in St. Louis, Missouri, on November 26, 1919. Fletcher's early interests were drafting, engineering, and aviation, and his first artwork appeared in the newsletters of a local power and light company. At the University of Missouri, Fletcher earned spare money through commercial art when his studies permitted. After graduating with a degree in engineering, Fletcher joined the air force in late 1940 and served in combat intelligence, once again employing drafting talents.

After the war, Fletcher went to New York City as an art director with the Hearst organization and served as art director on two newspaper magazine supplements, *Pictorial Review* and *Saturday Home*. From there he transferred to King Features' "tragic art"—as opposed to comic art—department, and did staff and promotional work for five years.

An opening in King Features' comic art department and Fletcher's budding talents in that area led to a drawing board assignment, alongside the other artists who worked under Frank Cilino there: incomplete strips were finished, benday laid in, Sunday pages reworked for format changes, and special artwork drawn to order.

In 1954 George McManus died, and Fletcher, who had shown a special feeling for McManus's techniques, was given a shot at the *Bringing Up Father* Sunday page. He won the assignment, and Vern Greene drew the dailies. Bill Kavanaugh wrote, and continues to write, the gags for *Father*.

Fletcher's background in the engineering arts and drafting boards served him well in an unusual way when the *Father* assignment came along, for Fletcher draws with a pen in one hand and a straightedge in the other; very few of his lines, including those for clothing, are drawn freehand. Thus Fletcher succeeded in capturing McManus's precision and restrained exactitude.

Likewise the characteristic architectural backgrounds of McManus's fancy were approximated by Fletcher. He strove, consciously, for the combination of the comic and the illustrative that he sensed in McManus.

The drawing in the latter-day *Bringing Up Father* has definitely continued close to McManus's style; if the zip has left the strip, it too can be traced to the continuum, for McManus's later work had lost much of its earlier genius and life. Fletcher retired from the strip in the late 1980s.

R.M.

FLINDERS, EVELYN (1910-   ) One of the few female strip cartoonists, Evelyn Flinders was another of the British artists who were forbidden by their publishers to sign their names to their work. Nevertheless, her style was recognized by her many loyal fans, who particularly adored her long-running serials about *The Silent Three*, three very ladylike public school girls, Joan, Peggy, and the Unknown Number One, who attended St. Kit's and donned masked cloaks to right the wrongs of the world that cropped up with surprising regularity. The trio were the front-page stars of *School Friend*, one of the earliest comics designed solely for circulation among schoolgirls, which first appeared on May 20, 1950. For its first two years, *The Silent Three* was the most popular feature among *School Friend*'s readers, and was consistently popular for a run of more than 370 weeks, ending in 1957.

Evelyn Flinders was born in London in 1910. She demonstrated unusual artistic promise and was permitted to enter Hornsey Art School at the early age of 15. She studied there for over three years, then met an art

Max Fleischer.

agent who gave her a children's story to illustrate. Flinders' goal was to work for the Amalgamated Press, the London-based publishers of almost every comic and story-paper for children. "I just kept badgering them and worrying them," she later said. "I can't think how I dared!" Her first break came with *Schooldays*, a new weekly that began with promise in 1928. The two female editors gave Flinders "little nick-knacks to copy for articles." The weekly was not a success and was incorporated into another, more popular paper, *Schoolgirl*.

By the time she was 21 years old, Flinders was illustrating stories for virtually all the A.P.'s girls' weeklies and also the Christmas annuals. The advent of World War II brought paper shortages to England, and *Schoolgirls' Weekly* folded in 1939, and soon only the *Girls' Crystal* was left. Flinders was given a serial to illustrate, and the occasional cover drawing for the monthly *Schoolgirls' Own Library*, but this was not enough to live on. She took a job making shell cases in a munitions factory for four years. After the war, Flinders was back in the A.P. family, illustrating annuals, libraries, and the new *School Friend*. A total of 15 picture serials came from her pen before she retired in 1959. There were six serials of *The Silent Three*, plus such titles as *Rivals at the Alpine School*, *The Riding Mystery at Moorland School*, *The Masked Ballerina*, and *Rozana, Schoolgirl of Mystery*. In retirement she continued to illustrate books for girls, including several stories by Constance White, and various girls' books for Dean Publishers.

D.G.

FLOOK (G.B.) Originally titled *Rufus* after its red-headed hero, a boy in search of a pet, renamed *Rufus and Flook* as the pet's part grew in proportion, and finally renamed *Flook* in honor of his takeover, this strip started on April 25, 1949. It celebrated its silver jubilee in 1974, and shows no sign of flagging. This is partly due to a changing line of celebrated scriptwriters who keep a highly contemporary line of social comment running throughout their plots, but mainly due to the excellent and individual artwork of its cartoonist.

The man who signs himself "Trog" is actually Canadian-born Wally Fawkes, jazz bandleader and clarinetist, who took his pseudonym from one of his groups, The Troglodytes. Trog's artwork has remained consistent, while his writers have changed around him. Douglas Mount created the strip on instructions from the editor of the *Daily Mail*, who wanted a children's strip in the style of the popular American strip *Barnaby*. Robert Raymond took over and was followed by Sir Compton Mackenzie, for a sequence set in Scotland, then Humphrey Lyttelton (another jazz-man-turned-cartoonist), George Melly (a writer-turned-jazz-singer), Barry Norman (a television personality), and radio writer and panel game chairman from *Sounds Familiar*, Barry Took.

Rufus, who lived with an oppressive Victorian uncle, met Flook during a prehistoric dream. He and Flook fell out of the dream balloon and into reality in strip number 21. Flook (so called because, originally, he could say nothing but that sound) was a magical creature able to turn himself into whatever might be required, but gradually he lost that convenient ability. The friends' earliest opponent was Moses Maggot, abductor of Sir Cloggy Bile's daughter Ermine. The voyage to Volcano Island was fraught with peril: pirates turned out to be actors for a film directed by Orson Kaart!

"Flook," Trog (Wally Fawkes). © Associated Newspapers Ltd.

Then there was Lucius Phiz, Shakespearean ham, and a sojourn at Blackwoods Academy under Dr. Beebe and the introduction of the memorable Bully Bodger and his sister, Lucretia, who was exposed as a witch! Both reappear from time to time, but not so frequently as Sir Montagu Ffolly, Bart. Then there was another upper-class twit, Scoop, of "Instant Sludge" fame. But the cast list is endless. In 1999 Flook will celebrate his golden jubilee.

Reprints of the strip in paperback form include: *The Amazing Adventures of Rufus & Flook*; *Rufus & Flook v. Moses Maggot*; *Rufus & Flook at School*; *Flook by Trog*. There is also an "autobiography": *I, Flook* (1962).

D.G.

FLORITA (Spain) In 1949 cartoonist Vincent Roso created *Florita* as the standard-bearer of the Spanish girls' magazine of the same name.

Florita is a young girl with an abundant mane of hair who wears dresses more appropriate for an older woman. But Florita plays at being adult because she was conceived as an example to be followed by the readers. If the other characters of the magazine could be cheeky and mischievous, Florita always showed contrition after her rare strayings from strict morality. She would offer advice to her readers not only in her comic strip, but also in other parts of the publication as well, where she recited verses and gave lessons in crafts, cooking, and etiquette. One of her comic sequences, "Andanzas de Florita revoltosa" (The Wanderings of Florita the Mischievous) was discontinued because it might have tarnished her image. Florita's closest friend was the blonde Gildita, much shorter but of equal priggishness. Her boyfriends were named

Oscar and Fredy, and they would escort her on her shopping trips and her excursions to the beach. Weak, sugar-sweet and sad-looking, they set a pitiful example for Spanish boys to emulate. The scripts, anonymous with the exception of a few signed by Sebi, were written in a florid language whose extreme correction was itself a manual of good manners.

Florita was the last "good girl" to appear in Spanish comics, the heiress to a long tradition of children's literature and a cousin to the legendary Nino Juanito. After Roso left the magazine, *Florita* was drawn by anonymous cartoonists, among whom Perez Fajardo is the only one to stand out. In France, *Florita* was published by the indefatigable Marijac, and, under the new name of *Mireille*, the strip was to enjoy even greater success than in Spain. A relic from the Franco era, *Florita* managed to survive into the 1980s.

L.G.

FLUTTERS, THE (G.B.) The Flutters, Mr. and Mrs., lived at "The Fluttercote" on the back, or sports page, of the *Daily Mirror,* and as their name and station might indicate, they were interested in a gamble. Their lodger, Bert Cert, not only spoke in rhyme ("My name is Bert, though I lost my shirt, I hope and pray that later today, my shirt's back and wid me, protectin' my kidney!") but also had a talking shirt that lisped! ("I wesisted till he bwoke my buttons!")

To add to this wacky whimsy, the Flutters later adopted the milkman's horse (it talked, of course) and trained it to race in the Whalemeat Stakes. Bert rode Incognito ("Sire Unknown, Dam Doubtful") to win, and the strip was a winner too, once it whittled away the more outrageous fantasies of writer Ian Gammidge. (A cartoonist himself, he drew the weekly *Gammidge's Bargain Basement* for the *Sunday Pictorial*.) The artist was "L.G." in the 24 years of the strip's life.

The strip started as a thrice-weekly serial on July 7, 1947, then went daily, and eventually ended happily with a marriage for Bert Cert and the overweight

Brenda on February 27, 1971. *The Flutters* were replaced by another family strip, this time from the North: *The Fosdyke Saga.*

D.G.

FLYIN' JENNY (U.S.) Aviation features were in full flower in 1939 when veteran cartoonist Russell Keaton (who was still drawing the *Skyroads* strip at the time) proposed the idea of an aviatrix as the heroine of a new series; Bell Syndicate liked the notion and bought the feature, called *Flyin' Jenny* (the name was inspired by the JN-40 training plane of World War I). It started as both a daily and a Sunday page in October 1939.

Jenny Dare was a blonde and sexy bombshell who flew all kinds of planes in all kinds of weather. Like her male counterparts, she was always fighting one menace or another when she did not take part in hair-raising air competitions. She also met a number of eligible bachelors who invariably fell in love with her, but she professed not to notice. To her friend (and rival) Wanda—who once wistfully observed, "You really are a beautiful brat, Jenny! I can't say I blame Rick for being crazy about you!"—Jenny demurely replied, "Tut! He admires my flying ability! I taught him, you know!"

At first Keaton both wrote and drew the strip. Later he turned to former navy pilot and Hollywood scriptwriter Frank Wead for the text. In 1941 Wead was recalled to service and Glen Chaffin (former scriptwriter of *Tailspin Tommy*) succeeded him. In 1943 Keaton himself became a flying instructor, and he turned over the drawing of the Sunday page to his assistant, Marc Swayze; when Keaton died of a sudden illness in 1945 Swayze took charge of the daily as well.

Flyin' Jenny was a winsome strip, beautifully drawn and entertainingly written by a much-improved Chaffin. Chaffin and Swayze kept on turning out the strip for a dwindling number of newspapers until it finally ended with a whimper in 1952.

M.H.

FOOTROT FLATS (New Zealand) Murray Ball, a farmer and amateur cartoonist, had been living and working on his ranch near Gisborne on the eastern coast of New Zealand's North Island for some time when it occurred to him that he might use his experiences as the basis of a comic strip. He sent samples of his proposed feature to local publications. In 1976 the strip, called *Footrot Flats*, made its appearance in several New Zealand newspapers, where it was seen by Sol Shifrin of Inter Continental Features, resulting in wide syndication in Australia, beginning in 1977.

As befits a feature set in the outback, *Footrot Flats* has a limited cast of characters. Wallace (Wal) Footrot, from whom the strip derives its name, is an unmarried sheep rancher of dubious abilities who lives on a secluded farm with his redoubtable Aunt Dolly, an old spinster with strict morals. (She once washed Wal's mouth out with soap after hearing him call his dog's inamorata a no-good bitch.) His closest neighbor is Cooch Windgrass, a dirt farmer and animal lover extraordinaire. His lady love is Cheeky Hobson, a buxom blonde working as a beautician in a nearby town.

Animals play a large part in the goings-on in Footrot Flats. Wal's sheepdog, variously going by the names "Dog" and "the Big Black Brute," herds sheep by

"The Flutters," Len Gamblin. © Daily Mirror Newspapers Ltd.

"Footrot Flats," Murray Ball. © Murray Ball.

throwing them over the fence. His pet peeves are Major, Cooch's hunting dog, and Prince Charles, Aunt Dolly's pampered corgi; and his nemesis is a colossal cat called "Horse" whose greatest delight is grabbing the hapless dog by the neck and throwing him out of the house.

Australian comics historian John Ryan characterized the strip as "mirroring the humorous side of farm life in New Zealand." So far the barnyard humor has included jokes about golf balls lost in cow dung, humans finding themselves in bed with goats, birds dropping on Aunt Dolly's wash, dogs in heat, and, of course, footrot. Reasonably well drawn and written in a colorful vernacular, *Footrot Flats* is an amusing, if not quite delightful, strip.

M.H.

FOR BETTER OR FOR WORSE (U.S.) Canadian-born Lynn Johnston has been drawing her comic strip, in which she mixes humor and drama, since September 9, 1979. It is internationally distributed by Universal Press Syndicate to about 1,700 newspapers.

Using her own family as models, Johnston presents the relationships among the fictional members of the Patterson household, while she shares with her readers the ups and downs, trials and tribulations, joys and sorrows of everyday life in and out of the family circle. The family of five includes John Patterson, a dentist by profession, who in a welcome change from other domestic humor entries is not the usually harried father and henpecked husband. Neither is Elly, the wife and mother, a harebrained and cutely silly woman. In fact,

an early strip shows her vacuuming in her old robe and curlers while she hears a song on the radio advising housewives to be beautiful and perky when their husbands come home after a hard day at work. Her reaction is a very modern one: she smashes the radio to bits.

The Patterson children are Michael, a college student; his sister Elizabeth, a high schooler; and April, the youngest, a first grader. The Pattersons had a dog, Farley, who, unhappily, died in 1995 shortly after he rescued April from drowning. Edgar, a lovable mutt, has recently been introduced and has his own share of typical (mis)adventures. The strip's main focus is on how the Pattersons interact with one another and with extended family members and friends. Whether April is testing her mother by saying vulgar words, or Michael is regurgitating little-understood Freudian theories, or Elizabeth is interfering with Mike's phone call with the current love of his life by posing—loudly—as his girlfriend ("That's for all the times you've called me 'Lizardbreath' "), it is all acutely depicted, as is the relationship between husband and wife ("for better or for worse"). In the end, one knows of course that they all love and respect each other.

Like the Wallets in Frank King's *Gasoline Alley*, Johnston's characters are allowed to age, albeit in comic-strip time. This not only gives the strip a realistic feel but also provides for discussions of contemporary, even controversial, topics. The March 26-April 24, 1993, episode concerning Lawrence, the son of Elly's friend, was an example of this. The sequence dealt poignantly with the teenager's revelation that he was

"For Better or For Worse," Lynn Johnston. © Universal Press Syndicate.

gay; although a number of newspapers decided not to run it, it elicited a wide positive response from readers who appreciated the honesty, sensitivity, and complete absence of moralizing in Johnston's work.

For Better or For Worse is drawn in an easy, illustrative style (after art school in Vancouver, Johnston had worked in animation and medical illustration), with special emphasis on the treatment of the protagonists' hair, which adds to their liveliness and recognition. Regularly reprinted in paperback collections and the subject of a number of animated TV cartoons, the strip received the Reuben Award from the National Cartoonists Society in 1986. Additionally, in recognition of her work, Lynn Johnston was elected the Society's first woman president (1988) and in 1997 was the first woman to be inducted into the International Museum of Cartoon's Hall of Fame in Boca Raton, Florida.

M.B.C.

FOREST, JEAN-CLAUDE (1930-   ) French comic strip artist and illustrator, born in 1930 in Le Perreux, a suburb of Paris. At 17, while still at l'Ecole des Arts et Métiers in Paris, J. C. Forest produced his first comic strip, *La Flèche Noire* ("The Black Arrow"), adapted from R. L. Stevenson. In 1952 he joined the staff of the French weekly *Vaillant*, for which he contributed two comic strip creations: *Pour la Horde* ("For the Horde"), a tale set in prehistoric times; and *Copyright,* about a fantastic animal.

In 1955 Forest's career really took off. He started designing magazine covers, took over the new version of *Bicot* (*Bicot* had been the French title of Branner's *Winnie Winkle*) and re-created *Charlot* (one of the countless comic strips based on the famous Charlie Chaplin tramp character), both for Offenstadt. In 1959 he contributed a number of comic strip serializations to the daily *France-Soir*. Forest's most famous creation, *Barbarella*, appeared in 1962 in the quarterly *V-Magazine*. He conceived the adventures of the scantily dressed female space explorer as a kind of *divertissement,* and he was taken aback by the strip's unprecedented success. (*Barbarella* was reprinted in hardbound form in 1964, and in 1968 it was made into a movie, which Forest himself designed.)

J. C. Forest, "Mystérieuse Matin, Midi et Soir." © J. C. Forest.

In 1964 Forest was asked to edit the newly created (and short-lived) comic magazine *Chouchou,* in whose pages he created *Bebe Cyanure* ("Baby Cyanide"), a girl strip, and for which he wrote (under the pseudonym Jean Valherbe) *Les Naufragés du Temps* ("The Shipwrecked Men of Time"), a science-fiction strip. In 1965 he created a series of animated cartoons for French television, *Marie Math,* a toned-down teenage version of *Barbarella*.

Since the mid-1960s Forest's career has been mostly downhill. He exhibited his paintings and illustrations in various French galleries without much success. In 1969 he tried (again unsuccessfully) to revive *Barbarella*. Discouraged, he went back to illustration before trying his hand again at a comic strip, *Mystérieuse Matin, Midi et Soir* ("Mysterious Morning, Noon and Night") using once more the well-worn formula of adventure with sex. *Mystérieuse* first appeared in *France-Soir* before winding up in *Pilote*. Other strips of interest created by Forest have been *Contes de la Barque Saoule* ("Tales of the Drunken Boat," 1977), *La Déchéance du Professeur Adamus* ("Professor Adamus's Downfall," 1979), *La Jonque Fantome Vue de l'Orchestre* ("The Ghost Junk Seen from the Orchestra," 1980), and *Enfants, c'Est l'Hydragon Qui Passe* ("Children, Here Comes the Hydragon," 1982). In recent years he has mostly confined himself to writing scripts illustrated by others, including one last Barbarella story.

Jean-Claude Forest deserves to be remembered for more than *Barbarella's success de scandale*. As it happened, however, Forest could not maintain the self-discipline and integrity required by any serious artist, and he chose instead to succumb to facility and formula, trying to repeat endlessly (and futilely) the success of *Barbarella*. He is the classic example of a great talent gone to waste due to a lack of direction or purpose.

M.H.

FORTON, LOUIS (1879-1934) French cartoonist, born March 14, 1879, in Sées, a small town in Normandy. Forton's life reads like the scenario of one of his own strips. The son of a horse trader, he was "almost born on horseback." He never received a formal education or learned to draw but was successively stable-boy, jockey, and racetrack tout. Fittingly enough, he met his future publishers, the brothers Offenstadt, at the racetrack in Vincennes. The Offenstadts owned a string of magazines, and Forton soon started contributing to most of them, under his own name or various pseudonyms. Drawing from his own experiences, he created *Les Aventures de Seraphin Laricot* ("The Adventures of Seraphin Laricot") about a bum he once knew, in 1907, and *Les Exploits d'Isidore MacAron and Anatole Fricotard*, relating the escapades of two con artists, in 1908. That same year Forton's most famous creation appeared: *La Bande des Pieds-Nickelés* ("The Nickel-Plated-Feet Gang"), depicting the unsavory doings of a trio of unredeemable rogues. The success of the new series was immediate and overwhelming, and Forton was to draw and write it (with minor and major interruptions) until his death.

Forton is also the creator of a number of other comic strips of note: *La Carrière Militaire d'Onésime Baluchon* ("The Military Career of Onesime Baluchon"), which in 1909 anticipated *Beetle Bailey* by some 40 years; *Les Cent Vingt-Six Métiers de Caramel* ("The 126 Jobs of Caramel"), about a born loser in 1920; and, in 1924, his second most popular strip, *Bibi Fricotin*, a nostalgic look at his childhood.

Forton retained his interest in horses throughout his life; he was also a dandy, an inveterate gambler, a pillar of café society, a convivial host and bon vivant—all of which left him scant time for drawing. (This explains why *Les Pieds-Nickelés* was interrupted for months and sometimes years at a clip.) On February 15, 1934, Forton died at 55 of cirrhosis of the liver.

Forton is most famed as a writer and creator of types (he has been compared to Francois Villon, LeSage, and Balzac). As a cartoonist he was no innovator. He inserted a printed narrative underneath the pictures and used the balloon only sparingly. The success and popularity that he enjoyed stimulated many cartoonists around him and contributed to making France a major center of comic strip creation, second only to the United States.

M.H.

47:AN LÖKEN (Sweden) *47:an Löken* (literally, "The 47 Onion"; freely translated, "Soldier 47, Chowderhead") was created in 1967 by Swedish comic artist and illustrator Lennart Elworth for the newspaper *Lektyr*. The strip stands in a Swedish tradition of humorous army strips, which was started in 1932 by Rudolf Petersson with *91 Karlsson* and continued in the 1940s by Torsten Bjarre with *Flygsoldat 113 Bom* ("Air Force Pvt. 113 No-hit"). Elworth had not quite liked the idea of entering the comic strip ring with a feature that would have to stand up against something as well established and popular as *91 Karlsson* (also known as *91:an* in the comic book version). But the editors of *Lektyr* talked him into it, and Elworth never rued the day he signed his contract.

The army being a kind of society within society with a certain set of rules and rank, it does not come as a surprise that there should be some parallels

"47:an Löken," Lennart Elworth.

between *47:an Löken* and *91 Karlsson*. Both soldiers have their costars: 47:an's best friend is 69:an, and 91 Karlsson has 87 Axelsson for a friend and sometimes antagonist. Karlsson and Axelsson fight each other to win the favor of Captain Berån's buxom daughter Elvira. Löken and friend have an eye out for the shapely WACs frequenting their garrison's sauna and bathing facilities. Finally, there are generals and other officers to be made fun of and, of course, the privates' efforts to avoid having to go on cross-country hikes.

The anecdotal episodes of *47:an Löken* are in a way Elworth's memories of his own time in the army. Or rather they are an amalgam of having to bow to the necessities of army life and trying to make the best of it by not succumbing to a military outlook on life. The humor and the stereotypes are one way of taking the sting out of military life. The stereotypes, characterized by their names, have their roots in real persons. Thus, Kapten Kruth ("Captain Gunpowder") has certain of Elworth's father's character traits.

47:an is played strictly for the fun of it. The strip is modern in approach, makes use of some very fresh humor, and is drawn in a zesty, flowing style. The comics are now drawn by various artists.

W.F.

FORZA JOHN (Italy) In recent years it has become a trendy gimmick to insert a cheap gadget within the pages of comic magazines in order to attract the younger readership. The practice, however, is not so new. At the end of World War II Cino and Domenico Del Duca resorted to the same idea of giving out something for nothing by enclosing a small comic book (of the kind that sold for 10 or 15 lire on the newsstands) within the pages of their comic magazine, *L'Intrepido*. They succeeded in increasing their circulation and gave birth to two worthwhile features to boot: *Forza John* and *Rocky Rider*.

Forza John (that could be translated as "Come On John") first appeared in late 1949, became self-selling and, starting with issue number 100 on August 28, 1951, enjoyed its own weekly comic book until April 14, 1953, when it was transferred to the pages of the comic weekly *Il Monello*; there it remained for over 10 years, winning the appreciation of a wide public.

Forza John, written in the beginning by Luigi Grecchi and drawn by Erio Nivolo (later replaced by Lino Jeva), had as its leading character a strapping, fair-haired, blue-eyed air cadet named John Graham. He was cast in the youngish heroic mold of many of the boy-heroes of the time (Capitan Miki, Piccolo Sceriffo, Sciuscià, etc.). After accomplishing several suicide war missions, John worked as a secret agent, battling outlaws, drug smugglers, saboteurs, and spies. His adventures, often very involved, made up a picaresque novel filled with interesting characterizations. There was Linda, a typical Italian girl, faithful and family-loving, who joined the WACs in order to be beside her fiancé, John; other characters included the wise and loyal Dr. Sam; the athletic and shrewd Captain Conterios and his wife; the scrawny and nearsighted newspaperman, Palissandro Giacinto Livingston, nicknamed "Pal"; and the thinking parrot, Geremia, who added a touch of welcome slapstick to the stories.

G.B.

FOSDYKE SAGA, THE (G.B.) "A kind, cussed, but totally endearing family, name of Fosdyke (raised in

Lancashire, weaned on tripe), will be moving, lock, stock and black pudding, into the *Daily Mirror*, starting Monday." With these words, a full-page article by Donald Zee, *Mirror* columnist, introduced the new daily strip, *The Fosdyke Saga*. It began on Monday, March 2, 1971, with an epic scene. Josiah Fosdyke, a coal miner from Insanitary Cottages, Griddlesbury, a grimy mining town in Lancashire, is caught in a cave-in in No. 3 shaft. Brought up alive, just able to walk, he is promptly chucked out of town, coal nuggets raining on his bald head, for blacklegging his mates: "Strike Now for Tuppence a Week." To keep his family ("We need luxuries like bread and dripping") Jos goes cap-in-hand to his wife Rebecca's rich brother, Bloody Tod Olroyd of the Black Pudding Factory. "Lend us two shillin's for train fare to Manchester. I'll have my solicitors draw up a contract with the children as security!" (Jos and Becky had three offspring, Tom, Victoria, and Albert, plus Little Tim, brought on by the mine hooter!) and so the saga was under way. As of 1997 it was still going strong.

The strip was treated by Bill Tidy (born 1932), a big Northerner from Southport, as his low-class answer to the middle-class Galsworthy serial, then running on BBC Television: "When I saw *The Forsyte Saga* I thought the working classes ought to have their own. Their lives, thoughts and dreams have been neglected for years. I hope the Fosdykes will fill the gap." Helping them to fill it were their prominent noses, a Tidy trademark: "I believe in the Duke of Wellington's dictum that strong characters go with big hooters."

Tidy, a postwar phenomenon in British cartooning, was a major provider of "singles," or one-gag drawings, to *Punch* and other periodicals, before taking to strips. His weekly strips include *Grimbledon Down* (1970) in *New Scientist* and *The Cloggies* (1969), the saga of an everyday Northern clog-dancing team, in *Private Eye*.

The Fosdyke Saga has been reprinted in annual paperback collections since 1972. Bill Tidy has become a television personality with his appearances on *Quick On the Draw* and other shows, and he was named Cartoonist of the Year in 1974.

D.G.

FOSTER, HAROLD (1892-1982) American artist, born August 16, 1892, in Halifax, Nova Scotia. In 1906 Harold R. Foster moved with his family to Winnipeg, Manitoba. At age 18 he quit school to support his family, trying his hand as a prizefighter, a guide in the wilds of Manitoba, and a gold prospector. In 1921 Foster travelled to Chicago on a bicycle to attend classes at the Art Institute. From there he went to the National Academy of Design and the Chicago Academy of Fine Arts.

After his studies Foster worked as an illustrator and advertising artist and soon gained a solid professional reputation for his illustration and poster work. In 1928 Joseph H. Neebe, a literary agent who had acquired the rights to adapt Edgar Rice Burroughs' *Tarzan* into comic strip form, approached Foster (after J. Allen St. John had turned him down) and asked him to take the job. Foster agreed to draw only the first *Tarzan* episode (January-March, 1929), then went back to advertising. In September 1931 he did finally come back, and then only to draw the *Tarzan* Sunday page.

In 1937, tired of illustrating someone else's stories, Foster created *Prince Valiant*, the tumultuous saga of a knight in King Arthur's court. In 1944-45 Foster gave *Prince Valiant* a companion strip, *The Medieval Castle*, another tale of the Middle Ages; he also found time to do some illustration work. But the main object of his attentions remained *Prince Valiant*, on which he worked as much as 50 hours a week. In the 1960s the overworked and aging Foster left more and more of the work to his assistants, and in 1971 he finally ceased drawing *Prince Valiant*, while continuing to submit pencil layouts to his successor, John Cullen Murphy, until 1980. He also wrote most of the story lines at least until the mid-1970s, and he kept his interest in his creation up to the time of his death on July 25, 1982, in Florida, where he had retired.

Harold Foster's reputation as one of the foremost artists of the comics is secure. He never made use of balloons but instead enclosed his text within the frame of the image (a throwback to earlier European usage), but as an illustrator rather than a cartoonist he brought to the comic strip a number of new techniques as well as a knowledge of anatomy and a sense of space. As Coulton Waugh wrote in 1947, "Foster possesses also the true illustrator's passion for periods and authentic detail. He is a remarkable figure among comic artists and his place in strip history is unique."

Foster has exercised a decisive influence on the following generation of comic strip artists, from Clarence Gray and Alex Raymond to his successor on *Tarzan*, Burne Hogarth. He was also the recipient of a number of cartooning awards (the Reuben among them), but in view of his achievements, these seem rather trivial.

M.H.

FOX AND THE CROW, THE (U.S.) *The Fox and the Crow* was created by Frank Tashlin, who directed the first *Fox and Crow* cartoon for Screen Gems, a division of Columbia Pictures, in 1941. This cartoon, *The Fox and the Grapes*, inspired by Aesop's fable "The Crow and the Fox," introduced the two friendly enemies who later made their comic book debut in *Real Screen Funnies* number one (Spring 1945) published by National. The magazine, renamed *Real Screen Comics* in the second issue and changed to *T.V.-Screen Comics* shortly before its demise in 1960, featured characters licensed from Columbia. These included *Tito and His Burrito* and *Flippity and Flop*.

Despite the mild success of the animated films and Columbia closing down its cartoon operation in 1948, bringing the *Fox and Crow* cartoons to a halt, the characters remained popular in comic books. In 1948, *Comic Cavalcade*, a National comic that had previously featured superheroes, converted to the "funny animal" material and lasted until 1955, featuring *The Fox and the Crow* in the lead spot. In April 1950, *The Fox and the Crow* was awarded its own comic book of the same name and continued for 108 consecutive issues until 1968.

At first, the stories and artwork for the Columbia-licensed comic books were done by an art "shop" composed of men from the animation studio, including Jim Davis, Bob Wickersham, Howard Swift, Paul Sommer, Hubert Karp, Warren Foster, and Cal Dalton. Wickersham was the primary artist on early *Fox and Crow* stories. In 1948, he decided to concentrate on the *Kilroys* comic for the American Comics Group, so Jim Davis began drawing *Fox and Crow* and working directly for National. Davis employed a former story man and animator from Columbia and Disney, Cecil Beard, to help with some of the inking. Hubert Karp, also a Disney alumnus, supplied the stories and refined the format. Most stories involved only two characters—Fauntleroy F. Fox and Crawford C. Crow—and the untiring efforts of the latter to cheat the former out of food, money, and/or personal dignity. The Crow employed an array of costumes and schemes, usually appealing to the Fox's incurable vanity.

In 1953, Karp died, and the stories were handled for a time by Davis and Beard, until Beard finally took over the entire writing chore with the help of his wife, Alpine Harper. Except for brief art fill-ins by Owen Fitzgerald and Karran Wright, Davis handled the artwork until the end. Many covers were done by Mort Drucker.

In 1968, a backup feature entitled *Stanley and His Monster* took over the *Fox and Crow* comic book, bringing to an end a series that had spanned 20 years and over 500 stories. Seven issues later, *Stanley and His Monster* was canceled. It resurfaced briefly in 1993 in a four-issue miniseries.

M.E.

FOX, FONTAINE TALBOT, JR. (1884-1964) Born March 3, 1884, in Louisville, Kentucky, Fontaine Talbot Fox Jr. drew from his grammar school days, kept it up through high school, and then went to work in the *Louisville Herald* as a reporter and part-time cartoonist. Among the local subjects he caricatured was the Brook Street trolley line, noted in Fox's youth for its haphazard schedule and prolonged nonappearance in rain or snow. His cartoons were popular with readers, and when Fox made enough to go to the University of Indiana, the paper asked him to draw them a cartoon a day on current subjects while away. The strain of studies and cartoon work proved too much after two years, however, and Fox dropped out to follow his obvious profession. Now the *Louisville Times* wanted him for more money, so Fox carried on his daily gag miscellany for them, and then for the *Chicago Post*, until the Wheeler Syndicate gave him national distribution in 1915.

For several years, Fox developed his small-town characters (it is not recorded when he first hit on the town name of Toonerville), basing many of them on people he had known in suburban-rural Louisville. His own father was the source of the Terrible-Tempered Mr. Bang, for example. At first, he used the Toonerville Trolley and its Skipper (based on his memories of the Brook Street line and another in Pelham Manor, New York, which he saw while visiting a friend), and its popularity grew, the avalanches of letters letting him and the syndicate know they had a hit. Thereafter, the Trolley was in at least once a week.

A Sunday page was added in 1918, where the Trolley appeared with increasing frequency. In 1920, he went to the McNaught Syndicate, then after a few years to Bell, finally gaining contractual control of his own work, which he retained to his death.

Fox, an accomplished golfer, won various tournaments, belonged to over six golf and art associations, and was the author of several books and articles, including one series that ran in many papers based on his narrow escape in 1939 from war-torn Europe. During the war, he was a member of the Division of Pictorial Publicity.

In February 1953, Fox (aware of the replacement of trolley lines by buses) converted a wrecked Toonerville Trolley into a new Toonerville Bus, still driven by the Skipper. But he relented three months before he retired, in November 1954, and restored the Trolley to service. He formally retired in February 1955 and folded his strip and characters away for good. He died in Greenwich, Connecticut, on August 10, 1964.

B.B.

FOX, GARDNER (1911-1986) American comic book writer, born in May 1911 in Brooklyn, New York. Scripting more than 50 million words in his career, Fox is considered the quintessential superhero and science-fiction comic book writer.

After securing a law degree from St. John's University, Fox opted for writing short stories for pulp magazines. He moved to National Comics in 1937 and produced a horde of noncostumed adventure features like *Steve Malone*. From there he went on to write literally dozens of National superhero strips, including *Starman, Zatara, Dr. Fate, Batman, Spectre, Flash, Hawkman,* and others. He also produced a line of minor strips for Columbia in 1940 and 1941, most notably *Skyman*.

But Fox's greatest achievement during the 1940s was his stories for the *Justice Society of America*, a National superhero group feature that appeared in the pages of *All-Star Comics*. Populating his stories with offbeat villains and well-researched scientific information, Fox's scripts were always among the best-handled in the comics' golden age. The adventures of the Justice Society, which at one time or another featured about 25 heroes, remain among the most-sought-after comics from the 1940s.

As the emphasis shifted away from superheroes during the late 1940s and early 1950s, Fox changed too. After producing material for ME, Avon, and EC, he returned to National and began churning out an exciting series of science-fiction tales for books like *Strange Adventures* and *Tales of the Unexpected*. Fox's scientific bent made the stories believable. One of these science-fiction titles, *Mystery in Space*, showcased what many believe to be Fox's greatest effort, *Adam Strange*. An earth-bound scientist, Strange was struck by a strange beam and transported to the planet Rann. Falling in love with a Rann woman and the Rann civilization, Adam Strange eventually became a permanent resident and the planet's greatest defender. Aided by Carmine Infantino's outstanding artwork and Fox's most fantastic flights of scientific fancy, the strip became a phenomenal success and lasted from 1959 to 1965.

When superhero comics took a new upturn in early 1960, Fox and John Broome became editor Julie Schwartz's mainstays, and Fox turned out a string of fine superheroic stories for *Hawkman, Atom, Green Lantern, Flash,* and several others. He was instrumental in reviving many of the golden age heroes and making the 1960s the "second golden age." His finest work in the period was done on a superhero group strip, this time called *Justice League of America*. Fox turned the feature into a showcase for his scientific knowledge and tight scripting. Several of his human interest stories, including "Riddle of the Robot Justice League," "Man, Thy Name Is Brother," and "Indestructible Creatures of Nightmare Island," predated the "relevance" craze of the early 1970s. He died in Princeton, New Jersey, on December 24, 1986.

Despite his fantastic comic book success, Fox also found time to write over 100 novels in all fields under the pen names "Jefferson Cooper" and "Bart Sommers." He also scripted a popular series of fantasy titles under his own name.

J.B.

FOXWELL, HERBERT (1890-1943)   One of the best "nursery school" artists to work in British comics, Herbert Foxwell was famous for taking over two characters created earlier by other cartoonists and making them almost immortal. The first was *Tiger Time*, created by Julius Stafford Baker, and the second was *Teddy Tail*, created by Charles Folkard. Foxwell was also famous because he insisted on signing his strips, first with his initials, "H.S.F.," and later simply as "Foxwell"; he was one of the few British comic strip artists granted this privilege.

Herbert Sydney Foxwell was born in Camberwell, South London, in 1890. Although virtually nothing is known about his early years, he arrived on the children's comic paper scene in 1912 when he was 22 years old. His first known strip was entitled *Jumbo and Jim* and appeared in *The Penny Wonder*, an Amalgamated Press publication. He would stay with this prolific publisher until 1933, when he was their top juvenile artist and was lured away to draw the front pages of two newspaper comic supplements, *The Boys and Girls Daily Mail* and *Jolly Jack's Weekly*, the supplement to the *Sunday Dispatch*.

His early work involved adult characters such as Harold Hazbean in *Comic Cuts* (1913), Artie Artichoke in *The Favorite Comic* (1913), and others. In 1914, Foxwell began to work for *The Rainbow*, a nursery comic edited by William Fisher. First he drew *Sam the Skipper*, a jolly old seadog, and then *The Dolliwogs' Dolls' House*, an unusual strip depicting the inhabitants of a three-story dollhouse. His success led to an offer to take over the front-page heroes *Tiger Tim and the Bruin Boys* from Julius Stafford Baker, whose style was considered too cartoony for juvenile consumption. Foxwell introduced his highly decorative style to the series, and especially wonderful were his "specials," such as the Seaside Holiday Numbers, Christmas Numbers, Grand Boat Race Numbers, and Fireworks Numbers.

The popularity of Foxwell's work among both the children readers and their parents who were buying the comics soon shot *The Rainbow* into the top sellers list, and legend has it that one copy was delivered to the Royal Family inside the daily copy of the king's *Times*. This legend was noted in one issue's headline, "The Comic for Home and Palace!" New series of publications followed, *Tiger Tim's Tales* (1919) with *Pauline and Patsy* by Foxwell, whose title changed the following year to *Tiger Tim's Weekly*, to which Foxwell contributed *Goldilocks, Tinklebell Tree*, and *The Tiny Toy Boys*. Soon he was also drawing the front color page of *Bubbles* (1921) and *Mrs. Bunty's Boarding House*, which featured humans for a change, but it was back to animals when *The Playbox* began in 1925. Foxwell created clones of the entire Tiger Tim brood. Throughout this prolific output of comics, which included a real-life strip, the adventures of Hollywood star Lloyd Hamilton in *Kinema Comic* (1920), plus *Merry Merlin* in *Children's Fairy* (1919) and *Mr. Croc's School* in *Bubbles*, never once did Foxwell's line falter or any picture or page seem slapdash.

In 1933, when the boom in free comic supplements for younger readers began in the British press, Associated Newspapers—once part of but now a rival to the Amalgamated Press—lured Foxwell away to illustrate their *Boys and Girls* section, best remembered as the *Teddy Tail Comic*. Foxwell also drew *Rollicking Rollo*, a pirate, *The Gay Goblins*, and *The Happy Family* (1935), as well as *Chubby and Lulu, Professor Simple, Toby and Tinker*, and the cover characters for *Jolly Jack's Weekly* for the *Sunday Dispatch*.

This prolific period was all too short. Foxwell joined the army during World War II. He was made a captain in the Royal Army Service Corps and was killed in action in 1943. No one ever replaced him, despite the attempts of several cartoonists to revive Teddy Tail after the war.

D.G.

FOXY GRANDPA (U.S.)   The least-rewarding of the great classic titles from the early days of comic strips, C. E. Schultze's *Foxy Grandpa* opened the 20th century by first appearing on the front page of the *New York Herald* Sunday comic section on January 7, 1900. The charming, simply rendered art of the new strip, together with its easy, unelaborated switch on *The Katzenjammer Kids* theme—in which the kid-plagued parent cleverly turns the tables on the trick-playing kids (two 10-year-old boys, blonde and brunette, never named)—captivated the public of the time and made the strip an overnight success.

Soon after joining Hearst's *New York American* for its 1902 Sunday section, Schultze continued *Foxy Grandpa* as a half-page, second-fiddle strip inside a four-page color section opened and closed by Opper, Dirks, and Swinnerton full pages. Public interest in the dully repetitive strip swiftly waned, however, so Hearst's editors omitted *Foxy Grandpa* entirely from the comic section within a few years, running it only when space permitted on the back of the Sunday *American Weekly* magazine section. Since other subscribing papers outside the Hearst group were few, *Foxy Grandpa's* renown faded. Only a few readers noticed or cared when the strip left Hearst at the end of the decade and moved to the *New York Press*, where it continued sporadically as a full page once again until 1918, when *Press* owner Frank Munsey's repeated amalgamations of the paper with other New York dailies squeezed it into oblivion.

Within a few years, Schultze revived Foxy Grandpa as the narrator of a daily series of animal and nature narratives for children, each accompanied by a small drawing of Grandpa and a younger boy named Bobby observing the subject of the day's 500-word piece. Titled *Foxy Grandpa's Stories* and distributed by Newspaper Feature Service, the series ran in many papers in the early 1920s, without any specific opening or closing date (they were sold in yearly sets), but generally dropped from sight by 1929. Published in several book collections of the Sunday strip in the early 1900s (*Foxy Grandpa and the Boys, Foxy Grandpa's Surprises*, etc.), the feature has had no other publication in any form (aside from examples in texts) since 1930.

B.B.

FRANKENSTEIN (U.S.)   The most successful attempt to put Mary Shelley's Frankenstein Monster into a regularly scheduled comic book feature was made by artist and writer Dick Briefer. Combining aspects of Shelley's 1818 novel and some popular features of contemporary horror movies, Briefer premiered the *New Adventures of Frankenstein* in Feature's *Prize* number

André Franquin, "Modeste et Pompon." © Editions du Lombard.

seven for December 1940. Briefer's version, done under the name "Frank N. Stein," had Victor Frankenstein creating his monstrosity in 1940 Manhattan. He immediately saw his creation begin a crusade against humanity; meanwhile, the repentant Dr. Frankenstein cared for a boy named Denny, whose family had been killed by the monster. The youth subsequently became "Bulldog Denny" and set out after the monster. The creature is eventually caught and put in the care of Dr. Carrol for "rehabilitation."

This was the turning point of the series. Briefer's art, which had always been loose and comical, was quickly becoming a lampoon. His monster was now more whimsical than horrifying. By the end of 1943, the strip was simply being called *Frankenstein* and played strictly for laughs. The monster was even given a home in "Mippyville." This comical Frankenstein got his own book in 1945, and Briefer's humor was appealing; the humorous interpretation became extremely popular in the mid-1940s, but the string eventually ran out. Already having been dropped from *Prize* after March 1948's 68th issue, the humorous series ended with the publication of February 1949's *Frankenstein* number 17.

When horror made an upswing in the early 1950s, Briefer was called in to revive the *Frankenstein* title. Beginning with March 1952's 18th issue, Briefer again resurrected the character, but this time he was once more the snarling, raging monster of the earlier years. This third interpretation was Briefer's weakest, however. His forte was not serious material, he was obviously bored, and he relied heavily on stories rewritten from old plots. This series ended in Frankenstein number 33 (November 1954).

Between Briefer's humorous monster and the 1952 reincarnation, the ACG group published the lackluster *Spirit of Frankenstein* series in *Adventures Into the Unknown*. Appearing only sporadically between June 1949 and February 1951, the stories totally ignored the Shelley novel.

After a 1963 adaptation of the 1931 Universal film, Dell comics introduced a new *Frankenstein*: a superhero with a red costume, a crewcut, and the secret identity of Frank Stone. It was a financial and artistic disaster and made only three appearances between September 1966 and March 1967.

Tom Sutton (under the name Sean Todd) began a series called *Frankenstein Book II* in the third issue of Skywald's black-and-white *Psycho* magazine in May

1971. The series began where the Shelley novel left off, but Sutton's weak writing doomed the series after three appearances.

In January 1973, Marvel comics began publishing another series set in 1898. Originally drawn by Mike Ploog, the strip bears little resemblance to recognized Frankenstein lore.

Early in 1973, National introduced the *Spawn of Frankenstein* series, a backup feature in *Phantom Stranger*. Set in the present, the strip boasted artwork by Mike Kaluta and Bernard Baily, but folded in April 1974 after eight appearances.

Additionally, the Frankenstein monster has appeared as a character (usually a villain) in hundreds of stories from many publishers; these one-shot appearances rarely had anything to do with the cast of characters in the original novel. There was also a chapter on Frankenstein in comic books in *The Comic-Book Book*, published in 1974 by Arlington House.

J.B.

Mary Shelley's monster was brought back to life again (and again) in *Frankenstein, or The Modern Prometheus*, a one-shot published in 1994 by Caliber Press, and in 1995 he was confronted by Bram Stoker's vampire in Topps Comics' *The Frankenstein/Dracula War*. Mention should also be made of Berni Wrightson's lavishly illustrated version of the 1980s.

M.H.

FRANQUIN, ANDRÉ (1924-1997) Belgian cartoonist, born in 1924 in Brussels. After high school André Franquin studied art at the Académie St. Luc near Brussels for only one year. In 1945 he was, along with Jijé, Morris, and Peyo, one of the animators in a cartooning studio that closed down the following year. Franquin then joined the staff of the comic weekly *Spirou*, where in 1946 he succeeded Jijé on the drawing of the title strip. Franquin was to draw *Spirou* until 1969, and he is universally regarded as the definitive artist on the strip as well as its most innovative contributor.

In 1948, along with his inseparable companions Morris and Jijé, Franquin left for a long journey of discovery to the United States and Mexico. Upon his return to Belgium in 1955, and following a contractual dispute with his publisher, Franquin created for *Tintin* a new strip, *Modeste et Pompon*, about a boy and a girl and their (nonromantic) adventures, which he drew until 1959. Meanwhile he had settled with his publishers and resumed drawing *Spirou* in 1956—one of the rare cases of a European cartoonist working for two rival publications at once, without benefit of a pseudonym.

Within the framework of the *Spirou* strip, Franquin created a number of secondary characters, two of whom were to gain strips of their own: Gaston Lagaffe, a befuddled, blundering copyboy; and the fantastic animal known as the Marsupilami. (*Gaston* debuted as a strip in 1957, and *Le Marsupilami* in 1968). Beginning in 1969 Franquin devoted most of his time to these two features. He occasionally found time, however, for outside projects. He wrote a few episodes of Will's *Isabelle* in the 1970s; and in 1978 he wrote *Ernest Ringard*, a satirical strip drawn by Frederic Jannin. His last attempt at an original creation, *La Chroniqu des Tifous* ("The Chronicle of the Li'l Imps," 1989) met with scant success and lasted only a few months. He died on January 5, 1997.

André Franquin was one of the foremost European cartoonists, the head of what has come to be called the "Marcinelle school" (from the city where *Spirou* magazine is published) and the inspiration of scores of comic strip artists. One of his colleagues defined him as "a realistic draftsman among humor cartoonists." Indeed Franquin's style, in the attention paid to details, and verisimilitude, is a far cry from the broad "big foot" traditions of the gag cartoon. Franquin was honored with a number of awards and distinctions in the course of his long career, not only in his native Belgium, but in most European countries and in the United States as well.

M.H.

FRAZETTA, FRANK (1928-   ) American comic book and comic strip artist, born February 9, 1928, in Brooklyn, New York. After studies at Brooklyn's Academy of Fine Arts under the Italian artist Michael Falanga, "Fritz" began his career at age 16 as the assistant to science-fiction artist John Giunta. His first comic book work, a character called Snowman, appeared in Baily Comics' *Tally Ho* number one (December 1944).

Throughout the rest of the 1940s, Frazetta drew a multitude of minor characters for many comic houses, including Toby, Pines, Fawcett (notably *Golden Arrow* in 1949), Prize, Fiction House, Standard, and Avon. His first major assignment came in 1949 when he began drawing the *Shining Knight* feature for National's *Adventure Comics*.

Frazetta was later praised for *Ghost Rider* and *Tim Holt* comics of the M.E. group, and in April 1952, he produced what many critics consider his best comic book work, M.E.'s *Thun'da* number one. Written by Gardner Fox, the book contained four flawlessly drawn jungle tales. The book was so popular that it was reproduced as a 10-dollar, limited collector's edition (Russ Cochran, 1973). Also during the early 1950s, Frazetta produced other superb comic book work. His Buck Rogers covers for *Famous Funnies* are among the best-loved and most-reproduced pieces of comic book work ever published. During 1953 and 1954, Frazetta drew some particularly excellent material for comics like *Personal Love*. The stories were mediocre at best, but Frazetta's artwork, especially where the female figure was concerned, reached great heights. He also contributed a small amount of steller cover and interior work for E.C.'s "New Trend" books, mostly in collaboration with Al Williamson. "Squeeze Play," his only solo story (*Shock SuspenStories* number 13, March 1954), was so well drawn that it appeared in the *E.C. Horror Library* (Nostalgia Press, 1972). It was this material that solidified Frazetta's reputation as one of the best illustrators in the field.

Frazetta made his first foray into syndicated strips in 1952 when he drew a short-lived feature called *Johnny Comet* (later titled *Ace McCoy*). When this was dropped in 1953, Frazetta spent several weeks ghosting Dan Barry's *Flash Gordon* and then joined Al Capp's *L'il Abner* staff. He left Capp nine years later to begin a career as a freelance illustrator.

Although he started slowly (most of his early work was done for "girlie" publications), he soon blossomed as one of the most-sought-after cover artists in the book field. After creating a memorable series of covers for Ace's *Tarzan*, he illustrated several outstanding *Conan* covers for Lancer. In recognition of his superlative work in the science-fiction and fantasy field, Frazetta was awarded sci-fi's highest honor, The Hugo Award, in 1966.

Preferring to spend his time drawing more lucrative assignments (like book covers and movie posters), Frazetta has produced little recently in the way of comic art. He contributed several drawings to Kurtzman and Elder's *Little Annie Fanny*, but his only sub-

Frank Frazetta, "White Indian." © Frank Frazetta.

"Freckles and his Friends," Merrill Blosser. © NEA Service.

stantial work has been an occasional cover painting for Warren's black-and-white magazines. His material was so impressive, however, that publisher James Warren named a corporate award in his honor—and then bestowed several of them upon him.

Although Frazetta has chosen to concentrate on fields outside the comic book and comic strip, and even though his volume of work is meager in comparison to workhorses like Gil Kane and Jack Kirby, his work has always been so outstanding and visually excellent that he is considered one of the major artists ever to work in comics. Many successful artists—Jeff Jones, Berni Wrightson, Mike Kaluta, and others—began by imitating Frazetta's unique style.

J.B.

FRECKLES AND HIS FRIENDS (U.S.) Merrill Blosser's classic boyhood strip, *Freckles and His Friends,* one of the earliest continuing daily strips circulated by NEA Syndicate, first appeared in most newspapers in mid-1915. A Sunday page was added in the early 1920s. Like Frank King's Skeezix, Freckles McGoosey was a comic strip boy who grew up, although much less smoothly and logically than Skeezix (a freckle-faced, buck-toothed eight-year-old in 1915, Freckles was the same age, minus the buck teeth, in 1927). Initially introduced with an older sister and younger brother (Elsie and Tagalong), as well as a small spotted dog, Jumbo, Freckles had lost Elsie by the early 1920s but added four new boy pals, Alek, Slim, and a pair of twins named Ray and Jay. By the end of the 1920s, only two other major kid characters had been added to Freckles' gang: Oscar, with his huge bow tie engulfing his mouth, and Patricia Penelope Fitts, a plain neighbor girl who plagued Freckles and the boys.

In the 1930s, however, Freckles shot up into young adolescence and acquired a whole new troupe of bud-

dies and girlfriends, such as June Wayman, his best girl; Lard Smith, his closest friend; Nutty Cook, boy inventor; Hilda Grubble, Lard's girl; Hector, Hilda's obnoxious kid brother; and other assorted kids such as Pepper, Fuzzy, and Kenny. Tag, Freckles' brother, had grown to Freckles 1920's size in the meantime, while Freckles' old buddy Oscar had not aged at all, and became Tag's friend. Oddly enough, all of this worked in the context of the strip, and since one only glimpses at certain of the characters before and after Freckles' worldwide adventures and travels (he left his hometown, Shadyside, about once a year on some junket or other), their growth or lack of it was not too noticeable.

During World War II, Blosser defied the nearly universal trend elsewhere in the strips and ignored the war almost altogether. Freckles did not surge to age 18 and enlist; he stayed sanely 16 and kept on with his adolescent activities and buddies. The result was a refreshing consistency of content through the 1940s. In the 1950s and 1960s, too, Freckles remained the same age and retained the same crowd of friends, although the wilder sort of 1930s adventuring involving plane crashes in the wilderness, ship mutinies, African safaris, etc., largely disappeared from the strip. Beginning in the mid-1960s the strip was ghosted, and signed, by Henry Formhals under Blosser's supervision, with considerable thematic and graphic similarity to the Blosser original. *Freckles and His Friends* ended its long run in 1973.

B.B.

FRED BASSET (G.B.) Alex Graham was drawing basset hounds in his joke cartoons for some years before it occurred to him to transfer the dog to strip cartoons. The result, *Fred Basset,* started in the *Daily Mail* on July 9, 1963, and managed to stay ahead (hold his lead, one might say) despite the heavy cartoon canine opposition: *Snoopy* appears in the same newspaper!

Fred, subtitled "the hound that's almost human," cannot talk—aloud, that is. But he can think, and it is his very human thoughts that make the fun, floating out of his head in traditional "thought balloons," such as the time he smilingly studies his master posing for a seaside snap. As his mistress lowers the camera, Fred thinks: "You can relax. Stop pulling in your stomach!" Many of his comments are addressed directly to the reader, with a smile or a quizzical pucker over the outward-looking eyes. Fred's little world is highly domesticated suburbia: home, car, pub, and golf club, the latter venue reflecting his Scots creator's private mania.

Alex Graham, born in Glasgow in 1915, won portrait painting prizes at the Glasgow School of Art and started submitting "singles" (gag cartoons) to the Scots papers of D. C. Thomson. His first strip was *Wee Hughie* in the *Weekly News*, followed by *Our Bill* (1946) and *Willy Nilly* in *Sunday Graphic* (1947). He raised his sights to the society weekly *Tatler* with *Briggs the Butler* (1949), who served tea, scones, and jokes for 17 years! Later came *Graham's Golf Club* in *Punch*.

Reprints of *Fred Basset* in paperback collections were published regularly, having reached 17 volumes by 1974. Other strips appeared among the gags reprinted in his many collections, of which *Oh Sidney Not the Walnut Tree* (1966) was the first. Graham was such a great professional that after his sudden death on December 3, 1991, his newspaper had so many unpublished *Fred Basset* strips in hand that the series continued with new gags for more than a year. (It is now done by anonymous staffers.)

D.G.

FREDERICKS, HAROLD (1929-   ) American comic book and comic strip artist, born in Atlantic City, New Jersey, on August 9, 1929. Harold (Fred) Fredericks was educated at the Atlantic City Friends School, where he was art editor of the school paper. From 1947 to 1949 he worked for the *Atlantic City Press*. After joining the Marine Corps in 1950, Fredericks became a cartoonist on the *Camp Lejeune Globe*, where he drew *Salty Ranks*, a military comic strip. Discharged in 1953, Fredericks attended classes at the School of Visual Arts and drew a number of historical strips and panels, including *New Jersey's Patriots* (syndicated throughout the state from 1957 to 1960), *The Late Late War*, and *Under the Stars and Bars* (the latter two originated in 1960.)

In 1960, Fredericks started his career as a comic book artist with Dell and Gold Key, working on such titles as *Daniel Boone*, *The Munsters*, *Mister Ed*, *King Leonardo*, and *The Blue Phantom*. His work attracted the attention of Lee Falk, who was looking for an artist to succeed Phil Davis on *Mandrake the Magician* after Davis's death in 1964. Fredericks tried for the job and was accepted by the syndicate. His work on the *Mandrake* Sunday page and daily strip started appearing in 1965. Since that time he has devoted most of his career to drawing the feature, aside from a brief foray back into comic books in the late 1980s, inking such Marvel titles as *The Hulk* and *Captain America*.

While his illustrations for *Mandrake* cannot compare with those of Davis, Fred Fredericks has nonetheless remained faithful to the spirit of the strip. Ironically, his competent but hardly innovative artwork seems as

"Freelance," Ted McCall and Ed Furness. © Anglo-American Publishing Co.

well suited to the dull *Mandrake* of today as Davis's stirring pen line was to the golden *Mandrake* of yesteryear.

M.H.

FREELANCE (Canada) Written by Ted McCall and illustrated by Ed Furness, Freelance, a daring guerrilla battling the Axis powers, appeared during the war years in his own black-and-white comic book published by Anglo-American Publishing Company of Toronto. During a wartime embargo on the importation of American comic books, Anglo-American offered black-and-white versions of such Fawcett heroes as Captain Marvel, Bulletman, Captain Marvel Jr., Spy Smasher, and Commando Yank. Sometimes the original American artwork, *sans* color, was used, but for much of the time, the strips were redrawn by Canadian artists. Along with these reprints such Canadian creations as *Freelance*, *The Crusaders*, *Commander Steel*, *Dr. Destine*, and *Sooper Dooper, Mighty Man of Yesterday* appeared. Head and shoulders above them all stood *Freelance*.

Furness's initial artwork on *Freelance* can only be described as crude, but issue by issue he evolved a dramatic style to suit McCall's well-rounded scripts, which, within context, were relatively sophisticated for the time and generally took a realistic approach to war. True, Freelance always won out against the Axis, but it was often at great cost and physical and mental effort. An example of one such endeavor centered on Allied attempts to sink a heavily defended German battleship while it was tied up for repairs. Using a high-explosive mine dropped by an RAF bomber, Freelance, with the assistance of his powerful aide Big John Collins, managed to fasten it to the side of the battleship and set it off under cover of a diversionary air raid. The Nazis believed the battleship's destruction was due to a powerful new type of bomb dropped by the British and therefore did not take reprisals against French civilians for an act of sabotage.

In his book-length adventures, Freelance operated all over the map—in France, Italy, Yugoslavia, Belgium, Portugal, Switzerland, North Africa, and Southeast Asia—giving the Axis all kinds of problems and always leaving his trademark, a tiny stick figure jauntily waving from its perch on a flying lance, a symbol similar to that of Leslie Charteris's The Saint. Freelance's nationality was never clearly established in any of the stories, although in issue number 2 (July-August 1941) he is described as a "valiant champion of freedom's cause who fights alone for Britain—and doomed by fate to hide his true self from his own people."

Of all the Canadian wartime comic books, the Anglo-American titles were the most cheaply produced. The covers were newsprint, printed in black and white and one other basic color and, the interior pages, of course, were black and white throughout. But, when Anglo-American converted to full color at the end of the war, its product became thoroughly professional in appearance. However, U.S. competition was too tough, and within two years, Freelance had disappeared. With him went any hope for a viable Canadian comic book industry.

P.H.

FREYSE, BILL (1898-1969) One of the most skillful and enthusiastic imitators of a major strip artist's feature characters, Bill Freyse has been equaled in this difficult art only by F. O. Alexander (who continued Kahles' *Hairbreadth Harry*), Leslie Turner (Crane's *Captain Easy*), Paul Fung (Young's *Dumb Dora*), and a bare half-dozen others, out of the many who have tried. Freyse's task was to continue Gene Ahern's widely read *Our Boarding House* for NEA after Ahern decamped to King Features in 1936. Born in 1898 in Detroit, Freyse graduated from Detroit's Central High School and took his youthful talent to the *Detroit Journal*, where he did editorial cartoons until the *Detroit Times* took him on as entertainment page cartoonist. From there he went into commercial cartooning, doing advertisements, billboards, etc., until he went to work for NEA in the 1930s. His big break came when NEA turned Ahern's pompous Major Hoople and his rooming-house ménage over for daily and Sunday continuation. Freyse saw no point in tampering with Ahern's perfect formula for the strip, nor with his effective style, and he closely followed both in going forward with the strip. Freyse's comic inventiveness was the equal of Ahern's, and there was no perceptible difference in the art or content of the strip from the time Ahern left it until Freyse's death in 1969, after which the strip was continued by NEA in new and notably less adept hands. Freyse lived in Tucson, Arizona, for most of his active career with NEA. His *Our Boarding House* moves as briskly and hilariously from panel to panel as did Ahern's, and would make a fine series of reprints in book form.

B.B.

FRIDAY FOSTER (U.S.) *Friday Foster* made its debut on January 18, 1970. Written by Jim Lawrence and drawn by the Spanish artist Jorge Longaron, it was distributed by the News-Tribune Syndicate.

Friday Foster is a black American woman, beautiful and sophisticated, who comes to New York to start a professional career as a photographer. Her assignments for agencies and newspapers bring her into contact with many diverse characters, both glamorous and shady. From New York to Hong Kong she always maintains her cool and her remarkable qualities of understanding and good humor.

The scripts, frequently devoted to Friday's sentimental complications, sometimes lightly delve into racial problems. It is evident from the reading of the strip that Lawrence (or his editors) tried hard not to offend anyone (in the most hallowed tradition of syndicate editors) and thus defeated the stated purpose of the strip.

Longaron's remarkable artwork could not compensate for the blandness and aseptic quality of the scripts. *Friday Foster* started floundering after the first few years. At the beginning of 1974 Longaron left the strip, to be succeeded by Gray Morrow, who was unable to stem the downward slide, and *Friday Foster* finally expired in May of the same year.

Friday Foster is worthy of interest purely on an artistic level and as another example of a doomed collaboration between American scriptwriter and foreign artist, a combination that has never proved successful in the history of the American comic strip.

M.H.

FRISE, JAMES LLEWELLYN (1891-1948) A self-taught Canadian cartoonist-illustrator born on a farm on Scugog Island, Ontario, in 1891, Jimmie Frise created one of the enduring institutions of the Canadian popular arts—*Birdseye Center*, a weekly black-and-white strip that was the comic realization of everyone's dream of small-town life, but with a gentle touch of satire and slapstick humor. Until the age of 19, Frise helped out on his father's farm and then, in 1910, headed for Toronto to pursue a career in drawing. He got a job with an engraving company, Rolph, Clark, Stone, ruling squares on Canadian Pacific Railway immigrant-settlement maps of Saskatchewan. Six months later, when the map project was completed, Frise was let go and almost immediately, on the strength of a cartoon submitted on speculation, was hired by the *Toronto Star*'s art department.

In 1916, Frise moved to Montreal to work for another engraving firm, but after a few months left that job to enlist in the Canadian Field Artillery. During overseas service, he lost part of his left hand (not his drawing hand) when an enemy shell landed so close to him that it killed two packhorses he was using to deliver ammunition to his battery. After the war, Frise returned to the *Toronto Star* and, in a few months, was a full-time cartoonist-illustrator for the *Star Weekly*, the *Star*'s separate weekend publication that included features, fiction, comics, and rotogravure sections.

In 1921 Frise began a weekly panel called *Life's Little Comedies*, which, by 1922, evolved into *Birdseye Center*. Regular characters developed over the next 25 years, including Pig-Skin Peters, Archie, Eli and Ruby, Big Jack the Giant Jackrabbit, Hector the Pup, the Police Chief, and the Captain of the Noazark, a tiny lake steamer.

"Friday Foster," Jorge Longaron. © News-Tribune Syndicate.

Frise left the *Star Weekly* in 1947 to join the *Montreal Standard*, which offered him the opportunity of doing the strip in color. The *Star Weekly* retained the *Birdseye Center* title, so Frise's strip became *Juniper Junction* in the *Standard*, which began syndicating it to the U.S., initially in Pennsylvania and New Jersey. Frise's death 18 months later cut short his promising new career.

In 1965, a hardcover collection of Frise's *Birdseye Center* panels was published by McClelland & Stewart Ltd., Toronto, and in 1972 the 43rd Battery Association published a collection of his wartime drawings.
P.H.

FRITZ THE CAT (U.S.) Perhaps the best-known of the "underground comix" features is writer/artist Robert Crumb's *Fritz The Cat*. Paradoxically, however, only the last Fritz story was created with the underground comic book market in mind, all the others being drawn for Crumb's own amusement. Even more ironic was the fact that although *Fritz The Cat* didn't begin to reach the public eye in significant quantities until 1968 and 1969, all but two of the stories were drawn before 1965.

The definitive Fritz the Cat character—complete with human dress, human foibles, wiseacre dialogue, and upright posture—was apparently first drawn for one of Crumb's numerous one-copy comics, *Crumb Brothers Almanac*, which Robert and brother Charles Crumb produced and dated October 15, 1959. This book—which, like all the other Crumb brothers books

before it, did not call the character Fritz by name, and which featured a more feline Fritz prototype—was meant only for Crumb's friends and relatives. From then on, Robert Crumb produced many pencil and pen-and-ink Fritz stories, almost none of them being publicly presented. In fact, the first general-public appearance that Fritz made was in the "Fred the Teenage Girl Pigeon" strip in *Help!* magazine in 1965. In this James Warren-published, Harvey Kurtzman-edited magazine, Fritz is not called by name, but the escaping rock star that eventually eats the girl pigeon groupie is definitely Fritz. Another story done around this time, which recounts Fritz's journey around the world and his return to seduce his sister, finally appeared in 1969, in a pamphlet entitled *R. Crumb's Comics and Stories*.

Most of the 1959-1965 stories that Crumb produced were lost, but the dozen or so stories that eventually surfaced produced a mass of publicity for Crumb and the character. *Head Comix*, an outsized paperback book published by Viking Press in 1968, showcased some of the finest Fritz material. Again, all of this work was first done in 1960-65 and was just being published. In 1969, two more old *Fritz The Cat* stories were published for the first time by Ballantine. A third story, *Fritz the No-Good*, was drawn specially by Crumb for the book in 1968, almost three years since his last Fritz effort, and he has said that he produced it simply to fill out the book.

Fritz The Cat is essentially a phony, and the fact that he is a cat is arbitrary. He is quite human, in fact more human than many of the people Crumb was to draw later in his career. He is a con man, a sex maniac, and totally incorrigible. Artistically Crumb handled the strip with a fixed "camera" angle: there were no innovative storytelling approaches, most of the panels consisting of simple, medium-range shots. And generally, Crumb's work here is more sexually subdued than his later, more explicit material. Some critics contend that the bulk of the Fritz material was Crumb's "wish fulfillment": Fritz was glib, Crumb was not; Fritz was a ladies' man, and Crumb did not see himself as such. Crumb denies such a relationship, but in any event, he dropped the character in 1965. His original Ballantine strip, as mentioned, was done only to fulfill a commitment.

His only other strip done after 1965 was drawn in 1972, and he did it simply to kill off Fritz the Cat. Crumb was moved to do this new strip—which was the only one prepared expressly for underground comic books and appeared in *People's Comics*—because of the forthcoming *Fritz The Cat* animated motion picture. In 1969, Crumb met with Ralph Bakshi and Steve Krantz to discuss a possible *Fritz The Cat* motion picture. Crumb says he never "really" agreed to the film, but production went on haltingly and the X-rated film was released in 1972. Crumb hated it, took the producers to court to have his name removed from the film, and drew the story that eventually appeared in *People's Comics*. In the story, Crumb showed a new Fritz: a playboy movie star who is becoming a "fatcat" establishment type along with cohorts "Stevie" and "Ralphie." Crumb kills Fritz by having a rejected female ostrich split his skull with an icepick. In this way, the enigmatic Crumb rids himself of a character he had outgrown years before it ever appeared publicly, and also disassociated himself from any further Fritz movies.

A second Fritz movie, *The Nine Lives of Fritz The Cat*, was produced in 1974 without Crumb or Bakshi, and unlike its predecessor, this film was both financially and artistically a disaster.

J.B.

FUCHS, ERIKA (1906-   ) German writer, translator, and editor, born in Rostock, Macklenburg. Erika Fuchs, née Petri, was the only girl to attend the boys' secondary school emphasizing the study of Latin and Greek in Belgard an der Passante, in Pomerania. Intending to become an art dealer, she studied the history of art, archaeology, and ancient history at the Universities of Lausanne, London, and Munich from 1926 to 1931. She received her PhD—magna cum laude—for her dissertation "Johann Michael Feichtmayr—a Contribution to the History of the Rococo." In 1932 she married Günter Fuchs, an engineer and inventor.

Living in her husband's native Schwarzenbach/Saale after World War II, she freelanced, translating articles for the German edition of *Reader's Digest* in Stuttgart. While visiting there, she met a representative of Walt Disney Productions who was looking for four Germans who would collaborate on a German edition of *Mickey Mouse*. Her husband's arguments that there were some pedagogical aspects to the job contributed to her decision to become editor-in-chief of *Micky Maus*.

The first issue of *Micky Maus* appeared in September 1951 and was a smash success, no little thanks to Mrs. Fuchs, whose linguistic artistry enhanced the success of Carl Barks' *Donald Duck* and of the other Disney features in the comic book that was made up of material from *Walt Disney's Comics and Stories*. At first, *Micky Maus* was published monthly, then specials were added on a monthly basis until the book turned to biweekly. Finally, in December 1957, *Micky Maus* turned weekly.

The day Mrs. Fuchs accepted her editorial job on *Micky Maus* was a very lucky one indeed for German children. This brought them not only the wit of the likes of Carl Barks and Paul Murry but also the wit and witticism of a highly literate lady (with a penchant for the works of Jane Austen, George Eliot, and Henry James) whose translations have a flavor all their own that, in its creativity, has yet to be surpassed by other writers. Despite allusions to literature, her dialogues are never bookish, and those who have grown up with

"Fritz the Cat," Robert Crumb. © Robert Crumb.

"Fuku-chan," Ryūichi Yokoyama. © Asahi.

her version of Disney comics fondly cherish the gems of her genial wit.

Erika Fuchs met Carl Barks for the first time in 1992. While she retired from her position as editor-in-chief of the *Mickey Maus* comic long ago, at age 90 she is still at work translating Barks's stories that have not yet been published in Germany. Fuchs has probably been the strongest influence on the German language in the past four decades. Her lines are quoted like those of the literary geniuses of the past and Internet-speak abounds in her vernacular.

W.F.

FUKU-CHAN (Japan) On January 25, 1936, Ryūichi Yokoyama created *Edokko Ken-chan* ("Ken from Eddo") for the *Daily Asahi*. Fuku-chan was only a secondary character, but, as often happens in comic strips, his popularity soon grew larger than that of Ken-chan, the titular hero, and as of October 1, 1939, the strip's title was changed to *Fuku-chan*. From this time, and for the next 35 years, Fuku-chan became the hero, and his popularity remained constant through the years, not only in newspapers, but also in magazines. On January 1, 1956, the strip transferred to the *Daily Mainichi*, where it appeared until its demise on May 31, 1971.

Fukuichi Fukuyama, alias Fuku-chan, was a five-year-old boy, bright and lovable, always wearing a college cap, wooden clogs, and a short kimono. His name was derived from that of a cartoonist friend of Yokoyama's, Fukujirō Yokoi, as were the names of most of the others characters in the strip: Konkichi Shimizu, alias Kon-chan (inspired by cartoonist Kon Shimizu); Kiyoshi Shimizu, alias Kiyo-chan; and Namiko Shimizu, all little friends of Fuku-chan. There were also Arakuma the moocher (whose name came from a comic book) and Fuku-chan's grandfather Fukutarō Fukuyama. (The latter two were the most famous characters in the strip, after Fuku-chan himself.)

The stories, genteel and simple, retraced the daily adventures of the little hero, his friends, and his family. At one time *Fuku-chan* was as popular in Japan as *Blondie* was in the United States. (Their humor was not that dissimilar.) It remains the longest-running daily strip in the history of Japanese comic art.

The masterpiece of Ryūichi Yokoyama, *Fuku-chan* has been beloved by intellectuals as well as by the general public. It has also influenced many cartoonists. Fuku-chan himself has become the mascot of Waseda University during their yearly baseball match with the rival Keiō University.

H.K.

FULLER, RALPH BRIGGS (1890-1963) An American artist born in Michigan in 1890, R. B. Fuller's first work in a major market was a drawing sold to *Life* magazine in 1910. It was incredibly crude and out of place in that journal, but editor J. A. Mitchell obviously had a sixth sense about latent talent: Charles Dana Gibson's first drawing for *Life* in 1886 was also embarrassingly crude.

In short order Fuller was the most published cartoonist in American magazines. His panel cartoons filled the pages of *Puck, Life,* and *Judge,* as well as *Collier's, Harper's,* and, later, *Liberty, Ballyhoo, College Humor,* and occasionally the *New Yorker.*

His work was so popular that in the early 1920s *Judge* devoted a standing feature—*Fuller Humor*—to his work, an honor afforded few others.

The early cartoons, even when Fuller was published everywhere, were always slightly crude and stiff, just as was the work of his contemporary, Percy Crosby. Just after the war, however, Fuller's work matured and he mastered anatomy and his tools; the inevitable pen-and-ink cross-hatching gave way to a handsome use of washes. Unlike many of his fellows, he wrote all his own gags and was one of the funniest of the breed that launched *Ballyhoo* and brought lunacy to *Judge* magazine in the mid-1920s.

With cartoon markets drying up in the Depression years, Fuller turned his creative talents to the strip form and sold *Oaky Doaks* to Associated Press Newsfeatures. It debuted in October 1935. Into this strip, one of the classic historical comedies in all of stripdom, Fuller poured his long experience, excellent artistic capabilities, and a pleasantly surprising knack for writing continuities. He immediately adapted to the strip format; *Oaky Doaks* has some of the greatest inane adventures in comics. His funny characterizations of sappy men and brassy women were inimitable.

Fuller was bitter when the AP folded its comic operation in 1961. His strip was appearing in few papers then, but was still witty and stood far above its few fellow survivors in the AP stable, such as the poorly drawn *Scorchy Smith* by John Milt Morris. Fuller reluctantly laid down his pen, for he enjoyed drawing the strip.

An accomplished watercolorist, Fuller lived for years in the artists' colony around Tenafly and Leonia, New Jersey. He died on August 16, 1963, while vacationing in Boothbay Harbor, Maine.

R.M.

FULTON *see* Lazarus, Mel.

FÜNF SCHRECKENSTEINER, DIE (Germany) *Die Fünf Schreckensteiner* ("The Five Schreckensteiners"), by the artist Barlog, graced the pages of the *Berliner Illustrirte* (Berlin Illustrated) from 1939 to 1940. The *Berliner Illustrirte* had already had experience with the comics medium in the form of the very successful *Vater und Sohn*. The five Schreckensteiners are the ancestors of the modern-day owners of Castle Schreckenstein (which might be translated as Scarystone). They are depicted on three paintings hanging on the castle's walls. A large rectangular one shows the three early seventh-century gentlemen, the brothers Schreckenstein. A smaller oval painting holds the ancestress in

Restoration dress. A small square picture with a little boy is there, too. At the stroke of midnight the five Schreckensteiners step out of their paintings to haunt the castle for one hour. They are very playful ghosts whose pranks never fail to leave butler Johann or the castle's owner with open-mouthed consternation. One very cold night they step out of their paintings shivering with cold. They step over to the fireplace to warm up. Finally, at the stroke of one A.M., the butler is flabbergasted to see that the paintings have moved from their wall to a spot above the fireplace.

The *Schreckensteiners* were done with a kind of humorous realism that looks a bit like cute picture-book illustrations. They used speech balloons sparingly. In one 1940 episode they commented on the war effort, admonishing their offspring not to hoard. Apart from that they remained true to their prankish nature and kept out of politics during their run of 51 episodes, 46 of which were reprinted in book form at the end of 1940.

Artist Barlog, before doing the Schreckensteiners, had already been known for his comic strip work in *Der heitere Fridolin* ("Cheerful Fridolin"), a biweekly children's magazine that was started in 1921. For it Barlog had drawn *Laatsch and Bommel*, a Mutt-and-Jeff-type pair, and *Professor Pechmann* ("Professor Badluck"). Some of Pechmann's inventions, like TV, have since become reality. *Pechmann* combined pictures and verse much like the traditional Bilderbogen. *Der heitere Fridolin* also featured *Benjamin Pampe* by Schafer-Ast, who put his hero on a new job in every episode. There was also *Onkel Toldi* ("Uncle Toldi") with his dog Schlupp. They are practically forgotten nowadays, and their tradition, by and large, has been replaced by the traditions imported (and reimported) with foreign comics.

W.F.

FUNG, PAUL (1897-1944) Born in 1897 in Seattle into the family of a Baptist minister of Chinese origin named Fung Chak, Paul Fung started school in Portland, Oregon, and was then sent by the Reverend Fung to secondary school in China, where he studied art in the traditional Chinese mode. His father, however, sent him the American Sunday comic sections in packages from home every month, and the young Fung, more excited by these than by the fan painting of his instructors, developed an expert comic strip style—to the dismay of his conservatively raised classmates and teachers. Back in Seattle, the boy finished Franklin High School and prepared for Stanford (from which his father had been an honorary graduate). The unexpected death of his father left Fung on his own, and the boy managed to get a position on the *Seattle Post-Intelligencer* as a sports and news cartoonist in 1916. There, on March 1, his first comic strip, *Innocent Hing* (about a young Chinese boy in traditional clothes facing problems in an American city) appeared, but was short-lived, as the editors obviously preferred Fung's talents in sports commentary.

In the early 1920s, the *Post-Intelligencer* became a Hearst newspaper, and Fung a Hearst employee. His talents caught the eye of his new boss, and before long Fung was turning out such popular Hearst strips and panels as *A Guy from Grand Rapids*, *Bughouse Fables*, and others. When Chic Young left *Dumb Dora* in April 1930 to start *Blondie*, Fung was assigned to continue the popular strip both daily and on Sunday, which he did in fine style. He then went to work as assistant to the

great Cliff Sterrett on *Polly and Her Pals* later in the 1930s. Fung died on October 16, 1944, and was survived by his talented cartoonist son, Paul Fung Jr., whose active career in comedy began as a six-year-old Warner Brothers film star named One Long Hop (the name being his father's invention). Highly skilled, Paul Fung Jr. has drawn the *Blondie* comic book for many years and today lives in Greenwich, New York, on a "116-acre chop suey farm."

B.B.

FUNKY WINKERBEAN (U.S.) Appearing in some 400 newspapers, Tom Batiuk's strip was syndicated in 1972, first by Publishers-Hall, then by Field Enterprises, and now by North America Syndicate. It takes place in and around Westview High School and presents the goings-on of the students and their teachers in mildly amusing fashion.

As a high school student, Funky Winkerbean is an average teenager, more interested in girls than in trigonometry. Other characters in the strip include Bull Bushka, the gridiron star, whose low football scores match his IQ; the bespectacled Les Moore, a nerd as inept at sports (he was once a bowling goalie) as with pretty coeds. Grown-ups, mostly teachers and coaches, are not any smarter or more dedicated than the students. Mr. Dinkle, the band director, always in his glittering uniform, is apt to lead his charges down the field in a freezing rain, compose some silly ditty for Earth Day assembly, push yet another candy sale fund-raiser on an unwilling student body, or celebrate the first anniversary of the Rock and Roll Hall of Fame by playing "A Hundred Bottles of Beer on the Wall . . ." on the sax.

Besides the talking computer or the copying machine with an attitude, the strip's other personnel include Cliff the security guard, who enjoys Sundays, since the students are not in attendance; Dr. Schoentell, a superintendent who lacks vision for the future, in contrast to Westview's principal, who cannot wait for the 21st century so he can *finally* retire. With a team named the Scapegoats, Coach can only be the losingest man in the school's football history.

As the pizza-parlor proprietor, Tony Montoni is the only adult who understands and empathizes with the kids. Never one to lecture, he teaches his young clients by example and by the genuineness of his concern for them.

Over the last few years, many of these students have graduated: Les is now an English teacher, a soon-to-be published author (he wrote a novel on the murder of talk-show host John Darling), and the husband of perky Lisa Crawford (wedding reception *chez* Montoni and honeymoon in Niagara Falls); he seems to have taken over the entire strip, even if Funky appears every so often as a worker in Tony's pizzeria. Following Coach's final humiliating defeat and subsequent retirement, Bull takes over at the helm of the Scapegoats, although the team probably won't win soon under his direction either.

During all of this character development, Batiuk has dealt with some important social and adolescent problems, ranging from underfunding of schools to teenage smoking and drug abuse. A June 1995 sequence, for instance, showed in a compassionate manner how Susan Smith, an A+ student and a lovely girl, had attempted suicide over her unrequited love for Les, her English teacher.

FUNKY WINKERBEAN

THERE'S A PICTURE OF FUNKY WHEN HE WAS IN HIGH SCHOOL!

THAT'S YOU!?

CHECK OUT THE FLANNEL SHIRT! VERY PRE-SEATTLE, DON'T YOU THINK?

"Funky Winkerbeam," Tom Batiuk. © Batom Inc.

The anecdotes are drawn in a pleasant, unencumbered style suitable to the daily happenings at good old Westview High.

P.L.H.

FURIO ALMIRANTE (Italy) The comic weekly *L'Audace* was purchased in the early months of 1940 by Casa Editrice Idea of Gianluigi Bonelli, who transformed it completely in content as well as in format. He called in the most able Italian writers and artists of the period, and after a few months he changed the magazine (which until then had published a whole series of continuing strips) into a comic book featuring a complete story devoted to a different character each issue, foreshadowing the postwar editorial trend.

Among the most successful characters, there was Furio Almirante, conceived by Bonelli himself with illustrations by Carlo Cossio. Furio's psychology was very close to that of Cossio's very popular Dick Fulmine, and Furio was soon nicknamed "the steel-fisted man" for his great ability in the ring. First called *X-1 il Pugile Misterioso* ("X-1 the Mysterious Prizefighter"), the strip was soon rechristened *Furio Almirante*. In February 1941 Carlo Cossio turned over the feature to his brother Vittorio.

Furio had thick, raven-black, curly hair and was exceptionally strong; he exterminated the hoodlums who tried to muscle in on the boxing business as well as the racketeers who preyed on the poor Italian immigrants of whom Furio became the defender. Thanks to his job, which took him from Africa to Central America and from Australia to Canada, Furio was able to help a host of expatriate Italians victimized by unscrupulous foreigners.

In 1942, when the war propaganda was at its peak among comic strip heroes, Furio (whose adventures were now produced by Franco Donatelli and Enrico Bagnoli) did his duty in a number of battles in every conceivable theater of war. When the speech balloons were later abolished from the strip, *Furio* looked more like a propaganda tract than a story meant to entertain.

After the war, the strip was revived with appropriate modifications and was presented in a new version drawn by Franco Bignot: it was met with indifference, however, and lasted but a few months.

G.B.

FURTINGER, ZVONIMIR (1912-   ) A Yugoslav writer, journalist, radio editor, good historian, expert technician, passionate sailor, constant researcher—in short, a man who is interested in everything and who knows about everything—Zvonimir Furtinger was born in Zagreb on November 12, 1912. The world crisis of 1929 interrupted his schooling, and he had to take care of his mother and himself. Furtinger worked as a gravedigger, magician, musician, singer, clerk, and technician and studied military science, history, and linguistics. His life's wish was to be a naval officer. However, today he sails only his own yacht. He has published several science-fiction novels and monographs on Schliemann and Karl May.

In the 1950s Furtinger started writing for comics. His first product was a science-fiction strip drawn by Walter Neugebauer and titled *Neznanac iz svemira* ("An Unknown from the Universe"). After that he met Jules Radilović, and they collaborated on many comic strip series together. The most popular ones were *Herlock Sholmes*, *Kroz minula stoljeća* ("Through the Past Centuries"), and *Afričke pustolovine* ("The African Adventures"), which they produced for *Plavi Vjesnik* magazine in Zagreb, and later for *Strip Art*, Sarajevo.

Furtinger also collaborated with Žarko Beker and Zdenko Svirčić, also cartoonists of the *Plavi Vjesnik* group. Furtinger is now an editor at Zagreb Radio Station and the author of several radio and TV dramas.

E.R.

FUSCO BROTHERS, THE (U.S.) The innovative and wacky strip *The Fusco Brothers* was developed by J.C. Duffy for Lew Little Enterprises and began distribution by Universal Press Syndicate in August 1989.

An illustrator as well as cartoonist, J.C. Duffy attended Temple University's Tyler School of Art and contributes drawings to the Philadelphia *Daily News*. His drawings have appeared in such publications as *Esquire* and *TV Guide*. He has designed greeting cards distributed by Recycled Paper Greetings since the early 1980s.

His strip depicts the lives of Rolf, Al, Lars, and Lance Fusco, who live in Newark, New Jersey, with their pet dog Axel. Axel, who thinks of himself as a wolverine, uses word balloons, not thought balloons, to speak with the other characters. In essence, he is the fifth brother, sharing the family physical trait of a large nose. Occasionally Ma Fusco visits the brothers. She leaves the impression that the never-seen Pa Fusco is a career criminal. Asked why she now lives in Nebraska, Ma responds that she wants to be close to Mr. Fusco, who used to make license plates in New Jersey and now makes them in Nebraska.

While each brother has a distinct personality, it is difficult to tell them apart. This may be the reason why

THE FUSCO BROTHERS

LARS, WHY DON'T WE HAVE A LITTLE CONTEST...LET'S SEE HOW LONG IT TAKES ME TO GET A DATE. THEN LET'S SEE HOW LONG IT TAKES YOU TO GET A DATE.

MAYBE WE SHOULD SYNCHRONIZE OUR WATCHES.

MAYBE YOU SHOULD SYNCHRONIZE YOUR CALENDARS.

"The Fusco Brothers," J.C. Duffy. © Universal Press Syndicate.

Duffy often has the brothers address each other by name. Although they are all in the strip together quite often, the four do not equally share the spotlight. It is usually Lance and family dog Axel who carry the strip. Al is the easily contented, not-too-bright optimist. Lars is quiet, and Rolf considers himself a classy individualist, although others consider him neither. Lance has a live-in girlfriend named Gloria, but he shirks from commitment. Gloria often bests Lance with rapier comebacks to his comments. While reading *Gray's Anatomy*, Lance grabs Gloria's arm and bites her elbow. "I'm trying to keep the humerus in the relationship," he explains. "A little knowledge is a terrible thing," Gloria retorts, inspecting her bleeding elbow.

Theirs is a strange love, but *The Fusco Brothers* is a strange strip and therein lies its charm. Even though the strip has no action drawings, Duffy has fun with his artwork. In one daily, "Al has an out-of-drawing experience," only Al's feet and his shadow on the floor are seen in the frame as his word balloon shouts "Help!" Rolf looks up from reading the newspaper to comment to Axel, "Gosh, You don't see this kind of thing in *Beetle Bailey*." Axel, with martini in hand, responds, "With good reason, perhaps." *The Fusco Brothers* have been called "nerds for the nineties." Duffy blends wild, hip writing with artwork that uses strong cross-hatching and dots, and solid black areas to keep the strip varied and visually interesting.

B.C.

FUSHIGINA KUNI NO PUTCHĀ (Japan) Fukijiro Yokoi's *Fushigina Kuni no Putchā* ("Putchā in Wonder World") made its first appearance in the Japanese monthly *Shōnen Kurabu* in 1947.

Putchā, the son of a Japanese scientist, and his companion, the robot Perii, met Dr. Banbarun, who had invented an electric wave that allowed people to levitate in the skies. Dr. Bunbarun tried out his invention on Perii, and it worked; Perii, however, was spirited away by Bunbarun's arch-rival, Torahige, in his black plane. After many chases and adventures, Putchā, with the help of Dr. Banbarun, rescued his robot companion.

After this episode, Dr. Banbarun, Putchā, and Perii started a long journey through the universe in the year 2047. They discovered a new element, X-nium, capable of neutralizing atomic power (a big concern in Japan at the time) on the moon, then traveled to Mars, where they met with the Martian president who, gave them a seven-color light wand with supernatural powers.

The feature was a blend of comic strip and illustrated story, using both balloons and narrative under the pictures. After Fukijiro's death on December 5, 1948, the strip was taken over by Tetsuo Ogawa. It lasted only for a short time longer.

Fushigina Kuni no Putchā was the star strip of its time, and it is credited for the renewed interest in science fiction as a source for comic art in Japan.

H.K.

FŪTEN (Japan) Created by Shinji Nagashima, *Fūten* made its first appearance in the April 1967 issue of the monthly magazine *COM*. It related the doings of those young boys and girls who had dropped out of general society (they were called "fūten" and were the Japanese equivalents of the American hippies). *Fūten* soon became a favorite of young people, and Nagashima's

作・構成
永島慎二

"Fūten," Shinji Nagashima. © Shinji Nagashima.

most famous creation, along with *Mangaka Zankoku Monogatari* ("The Cruel Story of a Cartoonist").

There was no one hero in the strip. The main characters were Hinji Nagahima (a cartoonist, and the creator's alter ego), Coat-san (a clever fūten who always wore a coat), Minori (a vagabond fūten), Akira (a former trumpet player), and Sanchi. Midorikawa, the only one of the little band holding down a job, and Shachō, a company president turned fūten after he had met Nagahima and his companions, were also in the strip.

Nagashima graphically depicted the reasons why all these people had dropped out of society, and he pictured their lives filled with decadence and suffering, but also with joy and fulfillment. The creator tried to answer the questions: "What is life?" and "What is the meaning of youth?", drawing on his own experience as a fūten.

The strip was the second in a trilogy titled *Kiiroi Namida* ("Yellow Tears"); the first had been *Mangaka Zankoku Monogatari* (1961), and the third was *Usura Retsuden* (1971). *Fūten* last appeared in June 1970 in the twice-monthly magazine *Play Comic*.

Fūten has been reprinted twice in book form—first as a large-run paperback, and second as a deluxe limited edition.

H.K.

FUTUROPOLIS (France) In 1937 the readers of the French comics weekly *Junior* were treated to a new series of hitherto unprecedented violence (at least in a French comic strip): *Futuropolis* by René Pellos.

Futuropolis is a subterranean city of the remote future dominated by a tightly knit oligarchy—"the Sages"—who rule their subjects with the help of a heartless technology and an arid science. The masters of Futuropolis, upon learning that on the earth's surface there still remains a race of men that have gone back to the Stone Age, decide to send one of their henchmen, Rao, and his female companion, Maia, to destroy the "barbarians." Rao, however, befriends the primitive but honest and loyal stone-men and leads a revolt against the masters of Futuropolis. The struggle soon involves not only what remains of mankind but also the animal and vegetable kingdoms, and even the primeval forces of nature, all uniting in a final Götterdämmerung that engulfs the whole planet.

In *Futuropolis* the text (there are no balloons) is tightly enclosed in the surrounding images. Pellos's style, an epitome of kinetic tension and restless motion, prefigures Hogarth's. His compositions, chaotic and forceful, sweep away all semblance of normality in a whirlwind of jarring images and distorted perspectives. The characters, tense with excitement or braced for danger, never seem to know peace and are in constant turmoil.

Futuropolis is at once an outstanding example of comic art at its most powerful, and an almost desperate cry against the civilization of the machine (a theme dear to the French science-fiction writers of the time). It is now justly regarded as a classic comic, on a par with *Buck Rogers* and *Flash Gordon*.

M.H.

GAI LURON (France) On September 30, 1962, French cartoonist Marcel Gotlib created a new feature in the pages of the *Vaillant* comic magazine, *Nanar et Jujube*, about the young boy Nanar and his pet fox Jujube, who were later joined by a little girl, Piette. Only with the arrival some months later of the unseemly mutt Gai Luron did the feature assume its definitive character: one by one the other protagonists left the strip, which was successively retitled: *Nanar, Jujube et Piette, Jujube et Gai Luron*, and finally (in 1966) *Gai Luron*.

Gai Luron (his name meaning "jolly fellow" is a misnomer) is a canine philosopher whose hangdog face reflects all the vicissitudes of a world-weary life. Disabused and sarcastic, he comments on (in a uniform, slightly disparaging tone) and reacts to (with a visible reluctance of effort) the various indignities that an uncaring world keeps throwing at him. There are few supporting characters: Belle Lurette, Gai Luron's girlfriend and a mimicking mouse, who are the only ones capable of cheerfully accepting Gai Luron's definitely morose attitude.

In 1970 Gotlib relinquished the strip to his former assistant Dufranne. While the drawing style remained essentially the same, Dufranne was not able to maintain the original tone and wit of *Gai Luron*, which was

"Gai Luron," Marcel Gotlib. © Vaillant.

subsequently downgraded from two weekly pages of gags to only one in 1973. Gai Luron faded out of the comic pages in 1976, only to be revived by his creator 10 years later in the humor monthly *Fluide Glacial*. More disabused and as cynical as ever, the hangdog canine has now become embroiled in a number of political and sexual escapades.

A number of *Gai Luron* episodes drawn by Gotlib were reprinted in book form by Editions Vaillant.

M.H.

GAINES, WILLIAM M. (1922-1992) American comic book editor and publisher born on March 1, 1922, in New York. The son of M. C. Gaines, celebrated as the father of comic books, "Bill" Gaines inherited his father's flagging company, E.C. Publications, in 1947.

He made several attempts at love, Western, and funny animal books with little success. In 1950, however, Gaines decided to try horror comics. The genre took hold, and he and editor Al Feldstein ushered in the vaunted E.C. "New Trend" line of horror, science-fiction, war, crime, and humor stories. Written mostly by editors Feldstein, Johnny Craig, and Harvey Kurtzman, the stories were unique in comics, several cuts above anything else then produced. In addition, Gaines lined up a bevy of the finest artists available; among them were Frank Frazetta, Al Williamson, George Evans, Reed Crandall, Bernie Krigstein, Jack Davis, Will Elder, Wally Wood, John Severin, and Graham Ingels. In 1952, Kurtzman invented *Mad*, perhaps the zaniest and most offbeat comic ever to appear. It quickly became an unbelievable success story. Gaines' 11 titles—*Haunt of Fear, Crypt of Terror, Vault of Horror, Crime SuspenStories, Shock SuspenStories, Weird Science, Weird Fantasy, Two-Fisted, Frontline Combat, Mad,* and *Panic*—were all artistic and financial successes. Imitations flourished profusely, and Gaines became a wealthy man.

But the bubble burst in 1953. Excesses of gore and violence in imitators' titles—and later Gaines' books—led to heavy public scrutiny. Magazines and newspapers lobbied against comics, and Fredric Wertham's 1953 book, *Seduction of the Innocent*, claimed crime comics were a cause of juvenile delinquency. The adverse publicity mounted quickly and was highlighted by Gaines' appearance on national television before The Kefauver Senate Subcommittee hearings on crime. Distributors began shying away from comics in general and Gaines' books in particular. By 1954, his empire had collapsed, and after two ill-fated attempts at survival, Gaines gave up the ghost in 1956.

All that remained was Kurtzman's *Mad*. Gaines transformed it into a 25-cent, 48-page black-and-white magazine. It was even more successful than the comic book version, survived Kurtzman's departure, absorbed Feldstein as editor, and now sells over two million copies per issue. Gaines made *Mad* his sole publication, and it has made him fabulously wealthy. He later sold

"The Cosmic Ray Bomb Explosion" (Featuring publisher Bill Gaines and editor Al Feldstein). Illustrated by Al Feldstein.
© William M. Gaines, Agent, Inc.

the magazine to the Kinney conglomerate, but he has stayed on as the autonomous publisher.

Lyle Stuart, Inc. published his biography, *The Mad World of William M. Gaines*, in 1972. Gaines died in his sleep at his Manhattan home on June 3, 1992.

J.B.

GAKI DEKA (Japan) Created by Tatsuhiko Yamagami, *Gaki Deka* ("The Boy Policeman") made its first appearance in the weekly *Shōnen Chambion* in September 1974. Soon *Gaki Deka* became immensely popular, and it is now the topmost boy's strip.

Komawari-kun (nicknamed "Gaki Deka") is a pupil at Sakamuke elementary school. He always wears a police officer's cap, a long and extra-wide polka dot necktie, has extraordinarily swollen cheeks, a wild look in his eyes, a snub nose, an extremely wide mouth and a very dirty mind. He is also impudent, undependable,

filthy, stupid, and vulgar. As one can see, Gaki Deka is hardly a credit to the human race.

Regarding himself as a policeman, Gaki Deka indulges in the weirdest acts. He once fought against a dog and put handcuffs on him; later he arrested himself and handcuffed himself. To stay away from school he purposely created a traffic accident; at another time (while late for school) he entered his classroom after breaking the windows. Other shenanigans included tearing a girl's panties with his bare hands (he pretended to be a crab), practicing for the broad jump with a photograph of a nude girl in front of him, and fighting with aquarium sea lions for fish.

The other characters in this unusual strip include Komawari's classmate and rival Sai jō-kun, Sai jō's girlfriend Momo-chan and her younger sister Junchan, Kamawari's parents, and the teacher, Miss Abe.

Gaki Deka became the most talked-about strip of the moment, and its hero's ritualistic poses (such as the "death penalty pose" in which Komawari simulates shooting an enemy) were widely imitated among Japanese youth. *Gaki Deka*, a revolutionary strip in its own way, completely renewed the tradition of Japanese humor strips by introducing absurd and nihilistic elements into its story line. In 1981 Yamagami abruptly decided to terminate the strip; he abandoned comics altogether, in favor of writing short stories and novels.

H.K.

GAMBOLS, THE (G.B.) George and Gaye Gambol made their debut in the *Daily Express* on March 16, 1950. Gaye, clearing up the paper muddle at the end of the football season, encounters George bearing armfuls of more paper muddle for the start of the racing season. She promptly goes home to mother!

Fortunately, she does not stay; fortunately for readers of the *Express* and for creators Barry Appleby and his ex-schoolgirl sweetheart Dobs, long Mrs. Appleby. She writes the scripts, he draws. As implied by their first gag and by the pun of their name, the Gambols

"Gaki Deka," Tatsuhiko Yamagami. © Shōnen Chambion.

"The Gambols," Barry Appleby. © Daily Express.

began as gamblers, which suited their venue, the sports page. They evolved from a daily "single" gag panel and became a daily strip on June 4, 1951; before then they had made thrice-weekly appearances on "big paper days." By 1956 they expanded to the *Sunday Express* as well, and boosted to three banks of strips to suit overseas syndication. The Gambols toned down to a cozy domestic scene, occasionally enjoying an outing to the races, an echo of their past obsession. To expand their appeal, a ready-made family was introduced through two children, Flivver (nephew) and Miggy (niece). This was deemed preferable to Gaye becoming pregnant at her age. Flivver and Miggy come and go during school holidays, making things conveniently cozy for Christmas.

Barry Appleby, born in Birmingham, learned to draw through Percy V. Bradshaw's Press Art School course, to which he subscribed by post in 1930. By 1937 he had a cartoon in *Punch*, by 1938 a daily panel in the London evening *Star*, and by 1940 had entered comics by taking over *Skit, Skat and the Captain,* and *Pinky Green* from the conscripted Basil Reynolds in *Mickey Mouse Weekly*.

The first paperback collection of *The Gambols* was published in 1952 (the 1953 edition reproduces examples of Appleby's "roughs"), and since then many volumes have appeared. Appleby's style, always very ordinary, has improved over the years since he eliminated all background detail from his panels.

Tragically Appleby lost his wife and collaborator Dobs, but his cartoon characters continued to supply a daily laugh to his readers. After Barry's own unexpected death, the strip was carried on for some time using the stock in hand; and in fact it continues to be published under the title *Barry Appleby's Gambols*, with drawings by Roger Mahoney.

D.G.

GARFIELD (U.S.) Currently the most widely syndicated comic strip in history, Jim Davis's *Garfield* was first launched into 41 newspapers by United Feature Syndicate on June 19, 1978. Reportedly born in the kitchen of Mama Leone's Italian Restaurant, the corpulent, self-indulgent feline is joined by Odie, a witless, slobbering pooch, and cartoonist Jon Arbuckle, their unassertive, nerdy owner.

During the strip's first years, a nondescript housemate, Lyman, shared the spotlight but was soon omitted. Infrequent appearances by Garfield's love interest Arlene, his teddy bear Pookie, and rival Nermal, "the world's cutest kitten," help diversify the otherwise limited ensemble. Creator Davis was previously an assistant on *Tumbleweeds*, and modeled much of Garfield's pacing and sharp delineation on T.K. Ryan's work.

Consciously avoiding any social or political commentary, the feature centers primarily on the cynical cat's pursuit of creature comforts; food, sleep, television, and full control of his domestic domain. Davis's command of direct, universal esprit and low comedy create an aura of slapstick and general silliness, giving the work a broad appeal. All action is presented front and center with few words of dialogue, making it effortless to read and easily translatable into the many languages used in its worldwide circulation. The consistency of clean artwork and honed script is due much to the talented assistants Gary Barker, Valette Green, Brett Koth, and Jeff Wesley, in addition to the dozens of others who oversee the generation of a countless number of licensed products.

Since 1980, the entire strip has been chronicled in book form, with seven titles listed simultaneously on the *New York Times* best-seller list in 1982. That same year the first of thirteen prime-time television specials was aired, and in 1988 the animated show *Garfield and Friends* made its debut on Saturday mornings.

The fat cat has been a float in the Macy's Thanksgiving Day parade and has a permanent exhibit in the Muncie Children's Museum in Indiana. The National Cartoonists Society awarded it the Best Humor Strip for 1981 and 1985, and four years later honored it with the coveted Rueben Award.

Now syndicated by Universal Press, the strip that started as a simple premise has blossomed into an epic phenomenon of pop culture, and it is sure to continue its popularity in the years to come.

B.J.

GARFIELD AND FRIENDS (U.S.) Jim Davis's *Garfield* had been a hit for almost 10 years in newspapers when CBS decided to add an animated version of the strip to its Saturday-morning lineup of cartoons. The show, called *Garfield and Friends*, premiered on October 15, 1988, with the author supervising the production.

All the familiar characters from the comic strip are there going through their usual paces. Garfield plays all kinds of underhanded tricks on his favorite foil, Odie the dog, and runs circles around his putative master, the cartoonist Jon Arbuckle. The plots revolve around the smug feline's love of food and sleep. Although limited, the animation is nicely done, and the series exudes a charm and freshness too often absent from most "kidvid" fare.

The "Friends" promised by the title are Orson the piglet, the four-legged hero of Davis's short-lived *U.S. Acres* comic strip, and his cohorts. These include Roy the rooster, who uses a bugle to wake up the neigh-

Jim Davis, "Garfield." © United Feature Syndicate.

borhood; Booker the chick, who believes Orson is his mother; and Orville, Sylvia, Woodrow, and Fred, the early worms Booker is constantly (and vainly) trying to catch. These animals cavort in separate segments of the series, and the off-the-wall humor of these small vignettes often makes them funnier than the main feature.

In advance of the regularly scheduled program, there had been a number of *Garfield* animated specials, many of which won Emmy Awards, including the first one, *Here Comes Garfield* (1982). Produced by Lee Mendelson and directed by Bill Melendez, the team responsible for the *Peanuts* cartoons, it went on to spawn many sequels. In contrast to the serenity of most of the *Peanuts* shorts, the *Garfield* episodes were filled with action and movement. In one of them the gutsy cat fought against ghosts and goblins; in another adventure he had a run-in with unfriendly natives on a tropical isle. In these specials Garfield often played a variety of tough characters, including Cave Cat, Space Cat, and the no-nonsense private eye, Sam Spayed. In all of the cartoons, the cat's thoughts are voiced by Lorenzo Music, while Tom Hoge and Greg Berger play the other regulars.

M.H.

GARTH (G.B.) "Whence did Garth come! The answer may be forever unknown. For Garth is not as other men. He is a powerful, mysterious, fascinating figure; moving at will through the maze of Time, lending his mighty strength to the cause of Right." Thus reads the foreword to *Garth, Man of Mystery*, a reprint of his first series of daily strips written and drawn by Steve Dowling for the London *Daily Mirror*. The still-continuing

saga began on July 24, 1943, with the body of the blond giant drifting on a raft. He is washed ashore and revived by Gala, the first of many girls to fall in love with this handsome giant. The amnesiac hero was frankly created as a British answer to *Superman*, but beyond his abnormal strength, Garth quickly evolved along more original lines (although for one story he did don a cloak to fly the sky in the best *Superman* manner.)

In his first adventure Garth, hailed as Son of Mor, thwarts an evil High Priest and sails off by barrage balloon to find his destiny! A dark girl, Ola, has become Gala's rival, a pattern which crystallized in the long-running feud that traversed many ages between Dawn, the bare-breasted cavegirl, and Karen, the dark sorceress. Garth's earthbound controller through his far-

"Garth," Steve Dowling. © Daily Mirror Newspapers Ltd.

ranging adventures is Professor Lumiere, the scientific genius of Carter Island, who calls everyone "mon ami"; Garth's key word for a safe return during a crisis is "Karma." In 1948, en route to the Olympic Games, he found himself running in the original games in the lost land of Olympia. In 1957 an encounter with Dr. Baal and his Black Magic brought Garth true love in the shape of Lady Astra, who turned out to be the goddess Venus! Perhaps his strangest metamorphosis occurred on December 7, 1971, when Garth was suddenly and utterly revitalized by a new artist: Frank Bellamy had taken over from John Allard (who had replaced Dowling in 1957).

The strip has been reprinted in several paperbacks: *Garth Man of Mystery*; *Garth in the Last Goddess* (1958); *Daily Mirror Book of Garth* (1974). There was also a *Garth* comic book published in Australia.

After a 54-year career, the longest in British newspaper strip history, *Garth* was suddenly discontinued on Saturday, February 8, 1997, at the end of an adventure entitled "Dam Drivers." The last cartoonist on the feature was Martin Asbury, a storyboard artist for cinema films.

D.G.

GASCARD, GILBERT (1931-   ) Belgian cartoonist born October 28, 1931, in Marseilles, France. Gilbert Gascard moved with his family to Brussels while a child, and exhibited a marked predilection for drawing and caricature during his high school studies. At age 18 he started his cartooning career in the Belgian magazine *Heroic-Albums*, in which he created (under the pseudonym "Tibet") *Dave O'Flynn*, an adventure strip, in 1950. The following year, Tibet transferred to the weekly *Tintin*, where he originated a string of short-lived series: *Yoyo, Jean-Jean et Gigi, Titi et Tutu, La Famille Petitou*, while creating his first continuity strip, *De Avonturen von Koenrad* ("The Adventures of Conrad") for the Flemish-language *Ons Volkske*. In April 1953, Tibet created his first successful comic strip, *Chick Bill*, a parodic Western starring the intrepid Federal Marshal Chick Bill and his faithful Indian boy-companion Petit-Caniche ("Little Poodle," a transparent allusion to Red Ryder's Little Beaver), and featuring the quick-tempered Dog Bull, the sheriff, and his inept deputy Kid Ordinn. The success of *Chick Bill* was such that it was transferred from *Ons Volkske* (where it had first appeared) to the more important *Tintin* a few years later.

In the wake of *Chick Bill*, Tibet followed (between 1953 and 1957) with a string of strips of varying merit: *Globul le Martien* ("Globul the Martian"), *Pat Rick, Alphonse* (with scripts by René Goscinny), and others.

His best-known feature appeared in March 1955 when he created, together with scriptwriter A. P. Duchateau, the detective strip *Ric Hochet* for *Tintin*. In 1958, Tibet tried his hand at another comic strip, *Junior*, with Duchateau and Greg as his writers, but it did not last, and since that date, he has been devoting most of his career to *Chick Bill* and *Ric Hochet*. Tibet has also contributed a number of covers to *Tintin*, as well as a series of caricatures spoofing celebrities, from Barbra Streisand to Chairman Mao. In 1992 he succeeded the late Bob de Moor as art director of the Belgian publishing firm Editions du Lombard.

Tibet has received a number of awards over the years, in his adopted Belgium as well as in his native France. His graphic style is loose and relaxed, with few innovations or flashes of brilliance, but well-suited to the youthful readers who make up the bulk of Tibet's public.

M.H.

GASOLINE ALLEY (U.S.)   Frank King's *Gasoline Alley*, which first appeared on Sunday, November 24, 1918, in the *Chicago Tribune* (the daily strip commencing on August 23, 1919, in the *New York Daily News*), was the first comic strip to develop a self-serving realization of its open-ended temporal potential. By the close of the 1910s, it was as apparent to Frank King as anyone else that successful strips could go on almost forever—as *The Katzenjammer Kids* and *Happy Hooligan* had aptly demonstrated by that time—but only King saw that there was no reason why a comic strip character shouldn't have as long a *growing* life as an actual human, and age accordingly, day by day, on the comic page.

This is what Skeezix Wallet, adopted foundling son of *Gasoline Alley's* initial hero, bachelor Walt Wallet, did over the 21 years between 1921 and 1942, and later, in front of the amused eyes of fifty million plus American newspaper readers. His baby brother and sister, Corky and Judy (the first born to a married Walt Wallet in 1928; the second another foundling of 1935), did the same, as did all of Skeezix's childhood friends. Only the original adult characters of the strip in 1918, Walt, his married Alley buddies, Doc, Avery, and Bill, and their wives, remained relatively static as far as age.

The spectacle of first one, then three normal, typical American kids (by general prevailing standards of the time) going through all of the vicissitudes of growing up on a daily basis delighted the average newspaper reader, and the strip, which at first gained only limited if amused attention by its focus on a motley group of suburban car enthusiasts, soon riveted public involvement from the moment fat, bumbling Walt Wallet

"Gasoline Alley," Dick Moores. © Chicago Tribune-New York News Syndicate.

found a basketed Skeezix on his womanless doorstep in the daily *Gasoline Alley* episode of February 14, 1921. King and *Tribune* publisher Joe Patterson (who suggested the introduction of a child to enlarge the interest of woman readers for the strip) chose Valentine's Day for the memorable event, and this later became Skeezix's "birthday."

The story line in *Gasoline Alley* was as wandering and ramshackle as life itself: the characters had parties and spats, took trips and were sick, went to school and played hookey, but for the most part nothing out of the ordinary happened. King was not as inventive or comfortable with melodrama as his *Tribune* conferee, Sidney Smith, and his one major attempt at the lurid vein, when a mysterious Mme. Octave claims Skeezix as her child, is only mildly diverting as told in the strip between May 2, 1922 to June 17, 1924; in fact, it barely affects the continuingly slow meandering of the characters' lives. Realizing his indifferent ability in this area, King wisely returned afterward to his simple, realistic, day-to-day manner of storytelling, touching only occasionally on the Mme. Octave threat and letting the normal events of childhood life dictate the story and anecdote content.

There were a surprisingly large number of relatively memorable characters in *Gasoline Alley*, perhaps because King fashioned so many of them to be like someone the reader was likely to know. In addition to the original Alley gang and Skeezix's kid brother and sister, there was Rachel, the black cook Walt hires to keep house for him and Skeezix; Phyliss Blossom (Skeezix's "Auntie"), whom Walt marries on June 24, 1926; Squint the cowboy; Mr. Wicker; Nina Clock and Trixie, two of Skeezix's earliest girlfriends (he later married Nina, on June 28, 1944); Spud, Whimpy, and Gooch, Skeezix's boyhood pals; his Army buddies, Tops, Sissy, and Wilmer; Mrs. Nosey, and many more.

Since Skeezix was fortuitously 18 in 1939, he was among the first comic strip characters to serve in the Armed Forces, and his wartime experiences filled much of the strip's continuity between 1942 and 1945: like the strip itself, they were carefully low-keyed and routine, much of what the average GI encountered in England and Europe during the war. As an adult in the postwar years, he did the dutiful, expected things: went into business, had a child (Chipper), took vacations, etc. And so the strip continued until Frank King died in June 1969. Bill Perry, who took over the Sunday page in 1951, and Richard Moores, who worked carefully and closely with King in the 1960s on the daily strip, both kept *Gasoline Alley* a going concern after King's death, with Moores gradually guiding it away from close involvement with Skeezix, Walt, and the old characters, and into emphasis on a fresh batch of individuals, with whom the continuing strip is chiefly concerned today. After Moores died in 1986, the feature passed into the hands of his assistant, Jim Scancarelli.

Much of the popularity that *Gasoline Alley* earned derived from its commonplace presentation of life as it was for many middle-class Americans of this century, and it is accordingly an invaluable pictorial record of America's general way-of-life in our times. Its actual book republication record is poor, however: a single collection of early strips from Reilly & Lee in 1929; several picture-and-text children's books from the same publisher based loosely on the strip; a Big Little Book in 1934; and a few comic book reprints of the strip in the late 1930s and 1940s. (There were a wide variety of Gasoline Alley artifacts and toys, however; a Columbia film of 1951 named for the strip and starring Scotty Becket; and a short-lived radio show of the early 1940s.) It is evident, therefore, that *Gasoline Alley* is a neglected and important American work of art calling

"Gaston Lagaffe," André Franquin. © Editions Dupuis.

for republication in full to be made generally accessible for social study in institutions of learning.

B.B.

GASTON LAGAFFE (Belgium) *Gaston Lagaffe* was created by André Franquin as a panel feature in issue 985 of the Belgian weekly *Spirou* of February 28, 1957. *Gaston* became a full-fledged strip on December 5, 1957; it then appeared as a half-page from September 24, 1959, until 1966, when it finally graduated to full-page status, and has remained there ever since.

Gaston (who had previously appeared in Franquin's earlier strip *Spirou*) is an aggravating, bumbling, and incompetent newspaper office boy whose antics and flights of fancy are the despair of his boss Monsieur de Mesmaeker (in actuality the real name of Franquin's assistant Jidehem) and of his coworkers: Prunelle the harassed editor, Boulier the slightly dilapidated accountant, and Lebrac the resident artist. Even M'oiselle Jeanne, de Mesmaeker's secretary, whose love for Gaston is as hopeless as it is unrequited, does not escape the slings and arrows of mischievous fortune unleashed by the irrepressible object of her admiration.

Gaston's talents, moreover, are as varied as they are obnoxious. He is an inventor (whose experiments more often than not result in chaos and mayhem), an artist (his portraits of M'oiselle Jeanne are justly infamous), a sports enthusiast (who would not let such things as office routine stand in the way of his training as bicyclist or javelin thrower), a musician (he plays a variety of instruments, including the gaffophone, of his own invention). His greatest avocation, however, is that of animal lover, and he keeps a veritable menagerie around him, such as mice in file drawers, turtles in the paper basket, goldfish in the water cooler, not to mention a laughing seagull, a hedgehog, and several species of wildcats. All this contributes, of course, to the hectic pace and lunatic atmosphere for which the strip is famous. In the 1980s Gaston lent his goofy presence to a number of Spirou episodes. Franquin ended the series in 1996, shortly before his death.

Since 1960 Editions Dupuis in Belgium has reprinted a number of Gaston's adventures and misadventures. Since 1985 his adventures have been reprinted in their near-entirety by Rombaldi in hardcover, and in paperback form by J'Ai Lu BD.

M.H.

GEKKŌ KAMEN (Japan) Created by Jirō Kuwata (artist) and Yasunori Kawauchi (scriptwriter), *Gekkō Kamen* made its debut in the Japanese monthly *Shōnen Kurabu* (May 1958). When the *Gekkō Kamen* television series started the next year, the strip was also published as a newspaper feature.

Gekkō Kamen (the Moonlight Mask) is the secret identity of detective Jurō Iwai. Wearing a white cloak, white suit, yellow gloves, yellow boots, and a white mask with a moon symbol, Gekkō Kamen spreads terror in the hearts of his enemies, with the help of his trusted assistant Gorohachi. Mounted on his white motorcycle and firing from both his guns (which he never uses for killing) Gekkō Kamen seems to materialize from nowhere in his relentless pursuit of evildoers. Among the more picturesque villains against whom Gekkō has pitched his powers are Satan no Tsume, Yūreitō (the Ghostly Gang), Dragon no Kiba (Dragon's Fang) and the fittingly named Mammoth Kong.

The strip, filled with action, thrill, and speed, was one of the most popular ever to appear. Gekkō Kamen himself became the most famous superhero in Japan, as well-known there as Superman and Batman are in the United States. On October 1961 he made his last appearance in the pages of *Shōnen Kurabu*.

Gekkō Kamen was also the hero of a number of animated films and of a number of live-action movies. His adventures were collected in a series of seven hard-bound volumes which rapidly became bestsellers. The theme song from the TV show *Gekkō Kamen wa Dare-deshō?* ("Who is Gekkō Kamen?") also enjoyed great popularity in the heyday of the strip.

H.K.

GHOST RIDER (U.S.) The name *Ghost Rider* has appeared on three different U.S. comic book features, two of them westerns of a supernatural flavor.

1—In 1950, Magazine Enterprises introduced its *Ghost Rider*, about a Western avenger cloaked wholly in white to give a ghostly appearance and strike terror in the hearts of bandits. The identity of the strip's author is unknown, but Dick Ayers did all of the interior art. Some of the covers on the *Ghost Rider* comic book were by Frank Frazetta. The first issue of *Ghost Rider* was dated 1950 (no month given) and it—and all subsequent issues—were sub-numbered as issues of the company's *A-1* comic book. Each issue of *A-1* was actually an issue of a different comic book. (*Ghost Rider* number one was *A-1* number 27; number two was *A-1* number 29 and so forth.) There were 14 of these *Ghost Rider* issues in all, plus appearances of the strip in *Tim Holt Comics* (some with Frazetta covers), *Red Mask*, in all 12 issues of *The Best of the West*, and in *Bobby Benson's B-Bar-B Riders*.

2—In February 1967, the Marvel Comics Group issued a new number one of a new *Ghost Rider*, identical in appearance to the first one and also drawn by Dick Ayers. The book lasted only seven issues but was revived in reprints in 1974. The reprints were retitled *Night Rider* so as not to conflict with another *Ghost Rider* which Marvel had brought out in the interim.

"Ghost Rider," Dick Ayers. © Marvel Comics Group.

3—In 1972, Gary Friedrich (who had authored Marvel's Western hero of the same name) and artist Mike Ploog brought out a new *Ghost Rider*, this one about a motorcyclist set in the present. Otherwise known as Johnny Blaze, this Ghost Rider was a daring trick-cyclist who called upon Satan for a bargain to save the life of his longtime friend, Crash Simpson. In the deal, Johnny lost his soul and was later transformed into a creature with a flaming skull for a head. The character first appeared in *Marvel Spotlight* number five (August 1972) and, after six more issues, went into his own comic, beginning with number one (September 1973). Following Friedrich, stories were by Tony Isabella who moved the strip away from the supernatural angle, towards superheroics. Succeeding Ploog on the art were Tom Sutton, Jim Mooney, Sal Buscema, Frank Robbins, George Tuska, and Bob Brown.

M.E.

4—The third Ghost Rider series ended in 1983. In May 1990 Marvel revived the title character, giving him a new costume and persona and teaming him with many of the other superheroes (Spider-Man, Dr. Strange, Wolverine, et al.). Among the artists working on this latest series mention should be made of Al Williamson, Andy and Joe Kubert, and Jim Lee. A spin-off, *Ghost Rider 2099*, ran briefly from 1994 to 1996.

M.H.

GIARDINO, VITTORIO (1946-   ) Italian illustrator, scriptwriter, and cartoonist, born December 24, 1946, in Bologna. In 1978 his first short stories appeared in the weekly *La Citta Futura*. In 1979 Giardino quit his job as an electronic engineer to devote himself entirely to comics. In the same year he started to write and draw for the magazine *Il Mago* (1979-1980) the black-and-white adventures of the contemporary private investigator *Sam Pezzo*, which moved to the monthly *Orient Express* in 1982-1983. Pezzo's adventures are in the tradition of the *roman noir,* where the urban social environment and the troubled existence of the main characters is more important than solving the mystery.

In 1982 the same magazine published Giardino's first long, color spy story *Rapsodia ungherese* ("Hungarian Rhapsody"), followed in 1985 by *La Porta d'Oriente* ("Orient Gateway"), published in the monthly *Corto Maltese*. The protagonist of both adventures set in the late 1930s is the Jewish Frenchman, Max Friedman, who tries in vain to prevent the disaster of the impending war.

Little Ego is Giardino's series of dreamlike erotic short stories with humorous implications, which appeared in *Glamour International Magazine* in 1983 and 1985, and later in the monthly *Comic Art*. This magazine has also printed his series *Vacanze fatali* ("Fatal Holidays"), a crime story with a final humorous surprise at the end. Giardino has contributed cover illustrations to several comic magazines and has done illustrations for dailies such as *L'Unita*, *Il Messaggero*, *La Repubblica*, and the weekly *L'Espresso*.

Giardino is not a prolific author, but certainly one of the most learned, elegant, and sophisticated of the Italian cartoonists. His crime and spy stories are accurately plotted, the dialogues are literary and relevant, the characterization is accurate, and the settings are well documented. His main characters do not share the traits of conventional heroes; they are fallible, emotionally unstable, and have mood swings. His artwork offers rich and deep insights, thanks to its painstaking detail. In his black-and-white stories, the light and shade effects are stronger than in the color stories, where the narrative and rhythm are expressed through the combination and contrast of different colors.

Giardino's present work in progress is *Jonas Fink*, of which only the first of a three-volume set was published in 1994 in Belgium and France titled *L'Enfance* ("Childhood"). This trilogy narrates the life of a Czechoslovakian boy whose father has been accused of being an enemy of the people by the Communist regime.

Almost all of Giardino's works have been reprinted in book form by different publishers and have been translated in 18 countries. He has been awarded several prizes in Italy and abroad, including a Yellow Kid

Vittorio Giardino, "Sam Pezzo." © Vittorio Giardino.

in Lucca in 1982, and Alfred in Angouleme, and a Saint Michel in Brussels.

G.C.C.

GIBBS, CECILIA MAY (1876-1969) Author-cartoonist born in Surrey (England) in 1876. May Gibbs came to Australia aboard the *Hesperus* in 1880 and eventually settled near Harvey, W.A. She began drawing as a small child and was instructed and encouraged by her father, who was a gifted amateur artist. She soon developed her love for the Australian bush and its animals, and often invented stories about them to entertain younger children. After completing her education at the Church of England Grammar School, Perth, she journeyed to London around 1896 with her mother—the first of many such trips. She spent eight years studying art at Cope & Nichol School, Chelsea Polytechnic, and the Henry Blackburn School of Black and White Art. The poverty, cruelty, and richness of London made a deep impression on her, causing her to write and illustrate her first book, *About Us*, which was published in Bavaria about 1901.

On returning to Australia, she settled in Sydney and by 1914 was earning money by doing quick sketches of soldiers departing for WWI. In 1916, she produced her best-known book, *Gumnut Babies*, published by Angus and Robertson. This was followed by such books as *Snugglepot and Cuddlepie* (1918), *Little Ragged Blossom* (1920), *Little Obelia* (1921), and a host of others over the next 45 years. In 1925, she adapted *Gumnut Babies* to a Sunday comic page, which was titled *Bib and Bub*. The strip first appeared in the *Sydney Sunday News* and continued to run until September 1967—surviving three newspaper mergers in the process.

In her unique style, May Gibbs immortalized the Australian bush and its creatures, and recorded the faery lore of the continent. Her clean, crisp line drawings and soft watercolors were accurate and instructive and drawn for the juvenile reader. While her artwork generally tended to be charming and gentle, the lingering impressions of her London visits made her quite capable of producing some rather frightening characters (e.g., The Banksia Men).

She became Cecilia May Ossoli Gibbs Kelly when she married at the age of 40. She was quoted as once saying, "I think you can influence children through books. You can teach them to be thoughtful and kind to animals, and to love the bush." When she died on November 27, 1969, May Gibbs had no children of her own—but she had won the love of generations of children with her books, illustrations, and comics. And she remembered children in her will; leaving her estate to be auctioned with the proceeds going to UNICEF, The Spastic Centre, and Crippled Children. She was awarded an M.B.E. for her services to children's literature.

J.R.

GILLAIN, JOSEPH (1914-1980) Belgian cartoonist and illustrator born January 13, 1914 in Gedinne. After two years of studies at the Royal Academy of Fine Arts and a job painting church murals, Joseph Gillain started a career in comics in 1939 when he was asked to join the staff of *Spirou* magazine. That same year Joseph Gillain (using the pseudonym Jijé, under which he was to become famous) produced *Freddy et Fred*, a humorous adventure series strongly influenced by Herge's *Tintin*, and *Trinet et Trinette*, which depicted the tribu-

lations of two young children, a brother and a sister; also in 1939, Jijé created *Blondin et Cirage* ("Blondin and Shoe-Polish"), yet another humor-adventure strip, for the comic weekly *Petits Belges* (it was later tranferred to *Spirou*): This feature—Jijé's first popular success—retraced the adventures of a pair of bright-eyed young boys, one white, the other black.

By the early 1940s Jijé seemed to be producing the whole magazine almost single-handedly; not only did he continue to draw all the above-mentioned features, but he also assisted Rob Vel on the title strip, *Spirou*, and in 1941 he created (with the help of Jean Doisy as scriptwriter) *Jean Valhardi*, an adventure strip with an insurance investigator as hero (Jijé drew it straight). To top it all he also took complete control of the *Spirou* strip in 1944.

In 1950, tired and overworked, Jijé decided to leave on a long trip to the United States (as early as 1946 he had already begun to turn over his vast production to other artists), where he was later joined by fellow cartoonists Franquin and Morris. The trio wandered around the North American continent, from New York to California, and from Canada to Mexico. Coming home in 1954, Jijé, inspired by his travels, started a Western, *Jerry Spring*, for *Spirou* (it is now regarded as his masterwork). Difficulties with his publishers led Jijé to enter into a contract with the competing *Pilote* magazine: in 1966 he took over the drawing of the *Michel Tanguy* aviation strip from Albert Uderzo, and the next year he abandoned *Jerry Spring*. Jijé's love of the Western led him in 1970 to create (with his brother Philippe writing the scenario) *Le Specialiste* ("The Specialist"), another horse-opera, for the short-lived *Johnny* magazine; and in 1974 he finally rejoined *Spirou* where he revived *Jerry Spring*. In 1979 he also drew two stories for the swashbuckling strip *Barbe-Rouge*, in collaboration with his son Laurent (who signs "Lorg"). He died in Versailles, France, on June 20, 1980.

In addition to his comic strip work, Jijé has also illustrated the biographies of famous figures: Don Bosco, Christopher Columbus, Baden-Powell, and did a respectful treatment of the life of Christ. However, his name is forever connected with the European adventure strip, of which he is a pioneer and an innovator who has influenced a whole generation of cartoonists. In 1974 Jijé summed up his artistic credo in these words: "The main thing is to tell a story. One must be readable, understandable, simple. This is a tendency that I strive not to lose. . . ."

M.H.

GILLRAY, JAMES (1757-1815) The most eminent of English caricaturists was born 1757 in Chelsea, supposedly of Irish descent, the son of a church sexton. Like William Hogarth, James Gillray started his career as a letter engraver but soon escaped apprenticeship to join a company of strolling actors. Returning to London he became a student of the Royal Academy where he perfected his skills as a designer. He attained remarkable proficiency, as evidenced by a number of plates he engraved after his own designs, notably two subjects from Goldsmith's "Deserted Village" (1784), "The Wreck of the Nancy Packet" (1785), and two portraits of William Pitt.

It is as a caricaturist and cartoonist that Gillray is best known. The caricatures he turned out during his lifetime are said to number over 200, among which

Carlos Gimenez, "Bandolero." © Carlos Gimenez.

some are particularly famous. In 1792 he engraved a very funny illustration of "John Bull and his family landing at Boulogne," which is generally regarded as his first great work as a cartoonist. (The first cartoon attributed to him is the mediocre "Paddy on Horseback" of 1779.) Among his famous political cartoons are the "Anti-Saccharites" (1792), the "Fatigues of the Campaign in Flanders" (1793), a savage satire on the Duke of York and his way of conducting war from a safe distance, "The Consequences of a Successful French Invasion," in which the horrors to be expected are depicted with acerbic wit, and more significant "The King of Brobdingnag and Gulliver," published in 1803 and 1804 on the subject of an imaginary confrontation between King George III and Napoleon Bonaparte.

Gillray's nonpolitical cartoons (often having a social bite) include: "A Pic Nic Orchestra," "Blowing Up Pic Nics," and the three remarkable series which he executed from 1800 to 1805: *Cookney Sportsman*, *Elements of Skating*, and *The Rake's Progress at the University*, a further takeoff on Hogarth's celebrated character and a bitter denunciation of the unsavory goings-on at England's most exalted seats of learning. The last known Gillray cartoon is dated 1811. Soon afterwards Gillray sank into a state of mingled delirium and early senility. He died in London in 1815.

Gillray's cartoons were highly popular and widely circulated not only in Britain, but also throughout Europe, and they have been credited with introducing the English style and format of the cartoon to the Continent. Gillray made ample (and often innovative) use of the balloon and pioneered in frame continuity, thus bringing his work up to the very threshold of the comic strip.

M.H.

GIMENEZ, CARLOS (1941-   ) Spanish cartoonist and writer born on March 6, 1941, in Madrid. After an apprenticeship at a porcelain factory, Carlos Gimenez started his art career in 1959 at the studio of illustrator Manuel Lopez Blanco. From there he went on to comics, at first only drawing, then, beginning in 1974, also writing the scripts. In the 1960s and early 1970s he drew comics on demand, many of them for the foreign market. His contributions in this period include *Drake & Drake*, *Gringo*, *Delta 99*, and *Dani Futuro*, an enjoyable science-fiction series by Victor Mora.

From 1974 on, his work took on a more original character. Taking his inspiration from a Brian Aldiss novel, he started work on a very personal story, *Hom*. The titular hero came first under the domination of a parasitic fungus, then fell prey to a pseudo-prophet, until the final annihilation of both dictators. Only after Fransisco Franco's death could this thinly veiled allegory be published in Spain.

Gimenez's autobiographical saga opened with *Paracuellos* ("Daredevils" 1976). The strip's different episodes, short and self-contained, refer directly to the author's childhood and include deeply lyrical sketches about an unusual juvenile world subjected to the cruelties of a dictatorial regime. The author continued his bitter reminiscences in *Auxillo social* ("Social Assistance"); in the meantime he had published recollections of his adult life in several interrelated series of short duration, *Barrio* (1977) and *La saga de los Menendez* (1978).

Gimenez used the same formula to retrace his career as an artist at Josep Toutain's art agency in his long-running series begun in 1982. In it there are many humorous allusions to Spanish artists and to Toutain himself. In addition to his more personal work, Gimenez has produced a number of stories dealing with sexual problems, including *Espana Una, Espana Grande*, and *Espana Libre!* He has also adapted the works of famous authors such as Stanislaw Lem and Jack London into comic-book form. In 1987 he started a new strip, *Bandolero*, based on the memoirs of the 19th century Spanish highwayman Juan Caballero.

Gimnenez is better known in other European countries and known even better in the United States than in his homeland. Most of his creations during the 1990s, such as *Amor Amor!!* and *Coco, facho & co* ("Commie, Fascist and Co.") have been published first in France.

Unlike many of his Spanish colleagues, Gimenez does not display any spectacular grahpic abilities. The artist's style is based on a slightly cartoony line, with emphasis on the scripts first and foremost. There exists in the artist a burning desire to express his passionate conviction, which fully comes out in his work.

J.C.

GIMENEZ, JUAN (1943-   ) Spanish cartoonist and illustrator of Argentinean origin born on November 26, 1943, in Mendoza, Argentina. After studies at the Universidad Nacional de Cuyo in Mendoza, Juan Gimenez worked as an art director, and later, owner, of an advertising agency from 1966 to 1978. Since 1975, he has devoted most of his time to the creation of comics, although he is an illustrator and a designer for promotional and animated films. He worked on *Heavy Metal*, the 1981 animated feature, and on the live-action movie *El caballero y el dragon* ("The Knight and the Dragon" 1985). His clients have included many

Spanish publishers and corporations, but it is for his highly original comic stories that he is best known.

Gimenez's most frequent scriptwriter has been Richard Barreiro, whose radical ideas regarding sociology and politics surface, though subdued, in his war and para-scientific stories. These collaborations first gained recognition with *As de Pike*, an aviation series published in the Argentine comic magazine *Skorpio* (1975-1979), followed by *La Estrella Negra* ("The Black Star") about a neutron star inhabited by zombies revived by magnetic storms and under the control of warrior-monks. Then came *Ciudad* (1982) also scripted by Barreiro and published in *Comix Internacional*; another Argentinean, Carlos Trillo, wrote the texts of *Basura* ("Garbage"), a science-fiction tale serialized in *Zona 84* (1985-1986), and published the following year in the U.S. magazine *Heavy Metal*. Barreiro, Trillo, and several other scriptwriters collaborated with Gimenez on a series of short stories, some of which were later compiled in the books *El extrano juicio a Roy Ely* ("The Strange Life of Roy Ely") and *La fabricas*. Gimenez himself wrote the tales that make up the volume *Cuestion de tiempo* ("A Matter of Time" in the United States, 1985).

In recent years Gimenez has written and illustrated two comic-strip series in the Sunday supplement of the Madrid daily *ABC*, titled respectively *Lem Dart* and *Leo Roa* (1986-1988). *Leo Roa* ran until the end of the decade. Gimenez also drew and scripted *El cuarto poder* ("The Fourth Power," 1988). In the 1990s he has divided his time between drawing illustrations and comic strips. Among the most notable has been *La caste des metabarons* ("The Caste of the Meta-Barons"), a long episode in the John Difool series (1992-1993), scripted by Alejandro Jodorowsky.

J.C.

GIMPEL BEINISH THE MATCHMAKER (U.S.) Samuel Zagat created *Gimpel Beinish the Matchmaker* for the Yiddish-language daily *Warheit* in 1912.

As his title indicates, Gimpel was in the business of arranging marriages (for a fee), a profession popularized in more recent times by one of the hit songs in *Fiddler on the Roof*; a bearded little man sloppily attired in black coat and striped pants, he went about his business unperturbed by the idiosyncrasies, pretensions, and foibles of his prospective customers. Scheming widows, self-deluded spinsters, and desperate mothers all found an attentive ear in Gimpel, who would attempt to match the most unlikely of twosomes with amiable but firm persistence. While admittedly not on a par with Sholem Aleichem, Samuel Zagat nevertheless paints a loving but truthful portrait of Jewish life in the New York of the 1910s. Unlike many other ethnic comic strip artists, he never tried to homogenize his characters and settings for general consumption, and his strip remains a sociological document virtually untainted by parochial self-consciousness.

Gimpel Beinish was dropped by *Warheit* in 1919 when Zagat left the paper to become the editorial cartoonist and illustrator of the *Jewish Daily Forward*, a position he retained until his death in 1964. Zagat was an artist of great, if unrecognized, comic talent and, like McManus, Opper, and a few others, had the knack of making his characters always look funny. *Gimpel Beinish* can thus be enjoyed even without any

Juan Gimenez, "Cuestion de Tiempo." © *Juan Gimenez.*

knowedge of Yiddish (the text was always printed in captions unobtrusively kept away from the pictures).

M.H.

GIM TORO (Italy) Very few of the comic strip characters created after World War II lasted more than five years; and even fewer have been reprinted or revived. Rarest of all are those characters still recalled with affection by other than comic fans: and of all of those none is more fondly remembered than *Gim Toro*.

The long saga of Gim Toro (literally "Jim Bull") started on May 12, 1946, and lasted for a total of 332 comic books published by Gino Casarotti, the last of which appeared on the newsstands on February 22, 1959.

Gim Toro—a name chosen by the publisher to symbolize the hero's strength—was a globe-girdling adventurer whose first exploits took him to the wilds of the Matto Grosso. Later Gim was confronted by his most deadly opponent: a Chinese gang, "the Hong of the Dragon," whose hideout was located in the subterranean depths of San Francisco. With the help of his companions, the muscular Greek Bourianakis, and the

scrawny Kid, Gim Toro finally wipes out the sinister band, not, however, without plenty of fights and perils. In the course of his mortal struggle against the "yellow peril," our hero meets for the first time his most beautiful opponent, Lilyth Howard, nicknamed "the blonde viper," whom he would later convert to the good cause and who would become his faithful life-companion. After final victory over the Chinese gang, our heroes bring justice to other countries from Latin America to the Middle East.

The adventures of *Gim Toro* were written by Andrea Lavezzolo and most of its pages drawn by the painter Edgardo Dell'Acqua. A number of specials—"I Gimtorissimi"—were realized by other artists, among them Cappadonia, Cossio, Ferrari, Perego, and Canale. Very popular in Italy, the *Gim Toro* stories have also been translated in several European countries (especially in France, where the hero was depicted as French) and in South America.

G.B.

GINESITO (Spain) One of the rare Spanish features to be produced by a team, *Ginesito* came out in comic

"Gim Toro," Andrea Lavezzolo and Edgardo Dell'Acqua. © Editrice Dardo.

book format in 1944. The scripts were the product of various authors working under the supervision of playwright Adolfo Lopez Rubio, including Pipo, José Laffond, and Gordillo. The illustrations were done by a number of cartoonists who alternated and shared the work: some of them went on to become famous, like Victor de la Fuente, José Laffond, J. Fernandez, Lodial, and Perellon. At the start of the series, not anticipating the incredible success awaiting their creation, the authors had called their hero Satanas; when the feature became popular, however, the censorship authori-

"Ginesito," Adolfo López Rubio. © Editorial Rialto.

ties, ever vigilant, demanded that this diabolical name be changed, and thus the feature became *Ginesito* (which was the name of the real young boy who served as model to the cartoonists, and who later had a role in the movie *Lecciones de Buen Amor*).

Ginesito is probably the ugliest character in Spanish comics: his head is very big and he wears double-focus glasses, but each of his comic books, in which he goes through one complete episode, contains thrills galore. Ginesito has fought against the invisible man, against the Amazons, has traveled to the country of the dwarfs, and to the center of the earth. *Ginesito* was a typical product for consumption, without any pretense, and it enjoyed a tremendous success among young boys for a short period, superseding foreign comic books for a time. It inspired a movie, in which puppets were used alongside live actors, in the last year of its run (1946).

L.G.

GINGER MEGGS (Australia) Originally titled *Us Fellers, Ginger Meggs* was created for the Sydney *Sunday Sun* by Jimmy Bancks on November 13, 1921. *Ginger*, along with *Weary Willie and the Count de Main* by D. H. Souter, was Australia's first Sunday comic strip; the first major strip to occupy a full newspaper page printed in color; the first to be syndicated overseas and the most popular local strip ever published. Initially, Ginge (as he was affectionately known) was only a supporting character to the strip's star, Gladsome Gladys—but it wasn't long before the lovable, red-headed, eternal schoolboy became the lead character. Bancks had an instinctive feeling for his urchin and was able to capture all the warmth, charm, character, and innermost feelings of a small Australian boy, almost from the beginning; and it was these traits blended with Bancks' natural humor that allowed the strip to transcend the rather poor draftsmanship of the early years.

Whether winning or losing, Ginge's homespun philosophy and observations on life were a sheer delight.

He exuded monumental self-confidence in his own abilities as a sportsman and all-around "good feller" and was almost devoid of modesty—yet, his bragging was done with such style that it was impossible not to admire his youthful swagger. Always the opportunist, *Ginge* was quick to take advantage of any given situation, even if it meant a complete reversal of his previously stated principles. For such a small boy, he was involved in a remarkable number of fights—many of them violent. His bitter enemy was Tiger Kelly, an uncouth ruffian some years older than Ginge, who took a constant delight in battering Ginge insensible on sight unless Ginge outsmarted him by splattering Tiger's face with a rotten tomato or rendering him unconscious with the assistance of some outside source.

He often crossed gloves with Eddie Coogan, his rival for the affections of the red-headed Minnie Peters—but generally, his encounters with this rival were based more on belittling than on mayhem. Minnie spent most of her life in the same dress, carrying a muff, and trying to lead Ginge to church or Sunday school and getting him to become a gentleman. His constant companions were his young brother, Dudley; a monkey, Tony; a dog, Mike; and his mate, Benny. Ginge lived with his parents who, despite their stern exterior, admired his spirit and often succumbed to his silver-tongued flattery. Next to Ginge, the down-to-earth, hard-working, plump Sarah Meggs was the most important character in the strip. Doomed to spend her entire life in the same dress, she was an excellent foil for Ginge and was responsible for her own subtle brand of humor. Nationalistic in flavor, the strip exhibited a resentment of authority which appealed to the Australian taste. When Bancks died, suddenly, in July 1952, the strip passed into the hands of Ron Vivian, who tried to be faithful to the original concept but never captured its unique flair. After Vivian's death in 1974, the strip was handled by a number of ghost artists who have only assisted in its decline. Lloyd Piper drew the strip for a while. It is now in the hands of James Kemsley, who marked the 75th anniversary of the venerable feature in November 1996.

J.R.

GINO E GIANNI (Italy) The Italian version of Lyman Young's *Tim Tyler's Luck* met with extraordinary success not only among the readers, but also among comic strip writers; and soon a whole host of youthful adventurers (all looking like Tim and Spud) were born. They always worked in pairs and helped each other out of various scrapes and perils: there were *Gianni e Luciano* by Fancelli and Guido Moroni-Celsi; *Marco e Andrea* by Sandro Cassone and Mario Tempesti, *Mario e Furio* by Federico Pedrocchi and Edgardo dell'Acqua, and so on.

Gino e Gianni, whose heroes were two young African colony settlers, were drawn by Rino Albertarelli. The strip first appeared on October 13, 1938 in the pages of the comic weekly *Topolino*; only later was the name of the scriptwriter revealed: Federico Pedrocchi (followed in 1942 by Amedeo Martini).

In the first episode titled "The Raiders of the Guardafui—Adventures in Somaliland, 1918," the two young friends were called in to put an end to the raids against Italian shipping off Cape Guardafui, perpetrated by Somali rebels led by the Greek adventurer Pandelidas. The story (now retitled *I Grande Caccie di Gino e Gianni*—"The Big Hunts of Gino and Giani") moved

from there to more typical adventures in which Gino and Gianni, together with white hunter Bracchi, were hired by American millionaire Clink to capture a white lion. Albertarelli displayed his drawing abilities and pictorial sense to the fullest, making this the best period of *Gino e Gianni*, with beautifully laid-out pages rich in adventures. Unfortunately the strip was ruined early in 1942 by a heavily propagandistic text and did not survive the defeats suffered by Italy the following year.

G.B.

GIORDANO, RICHARD (1932-) American comic book artist and editor born July 20, 1932 in New York City. After studies at the School of Industrial Art, "Dick" Giordano began his comic book career in 1951, working on Fiction House's *Sheena* for the Jerry Iger Studio. In 1952, he began a 17-year relationship with Charlton, working on the group's complete range of comic titles, including Western, war, crime, science fiction, love, and horror. He was the group's assistant editor (1957-1959) and editor (1966-1967).

As a Charlton artist, Giordano's best strip was undoubtably his artwork on the adventure-oriented *Sarge Steel* strip. While his storytelling was weak—it was apparent he was not concerned with the story's flow—his draftsmanship and illustrations were superb. When Giordano assumed the group's editorship in 1966, he began a series of well-received superhero titles, among them Steve Ditko's *Blue Beetle* and *The Question* strips. While Charlton always had a deserved reputation for inferior material, Giordano's short tenure as editor allowed them to produce some of the finest material in the otherwise depressed late 1960s. Unfortunately, the line was not financially successful, and was cancelled, and the last titles appeared in summer 1968.

Giordano moved to National as an editor in 1968. Again he instituted a whole new line, among them the well-done but short-lived *Creeper, Hawk and Dove,* and the *Secret Six.* He also gave established books like *Aquaman* and *Blackhawk* notable, if short, creative boosts. He was also instrumental in bringing talents like writer/artist Steve Ditko, writer Denny O'Neil, and artists Jim Aparo and Pat Boyette to National. He resigned in 1970, after most of his titles—perhaps too advanced for the comic books' younger readership—had been cancelled.

After his resignation from National, Giordano resumed his art career, primarily as an inker. His style—which had become more lucid since his *Sarge Steel* days—made him one of the most respected and prolific inkers in the field, and he and Neal Adams eventually opened a studio to produce comic books and advertising work. During his career, Giordano has also worked for Dell (1964-1966), Archie (1974), Lev Gleason (1955), Marvel (1970-1975), and others. His brother-in-law, Sal Trapani, is also a comic book artist. Giordano came back to DC as managing editor in 1980. He had risen to the rank of vice-president and editorial director by the time he resigned in 1993 to resume a freelance career. (In 1994, for example, he illustrated an original *Modesty Blaise* graphic novel.)

J.B.

GIR See Giraud, Jean.

GIRAUD, JEAN (1938-) A French cartoonist and illustrator born 1938 in Paris, Jean Giraud—or "Gir" as he is better known—displayed a love of comics at the earliest age, copying comic features before he even went to school. Later he attended the Technical School of Applied Arts, where he studied home furnishing and decorating crafts. In 1954, while still at school, he produced his first comic strip, a Western called *Les Aventures de Franck et Jéremie* ("The Adventures of Franck and Jéremie") for *Far West*, one of the many comic magazines edited at one time or other by Marijac. That same year Gir met Jean-Claude Mézières, also a comic strip fan, who introduced him into the Catholic publication, *Coeurs Vaillants*; there Gir illustrated a number of realistic and didactic stories. After two years he was drafted into the army, but continued to draw for the military magazine *5/5*.

Discharged in 1960, Gir became assistant to Joseph Gillain (Jijé) on *Jerry Spring*; as he himself admitted, this proved to be the best art school he ever attended. In 1961 he left Jijé to work for Studio Hachette (again on an introduction by Mézières) until 1963, when he created (with scriptwriter Jean-Michel Charlier) a Western strip titled *Fort Navajo* (which became *Lieutenant Blueberry* the next year for the comic weekly *Pilote*.)

In addition to his work on *Blueberry*, Gir has produced a number of other comic strips under the pseudonym "Moebius" for such publications as the satirical monthly *Hara-Kiri* and the cartoonist-run *L'Echo des Savanes*; he has also done illustration work for science-fiction novels and stories published by Editions Opta.

Gir is widely—and justly—regarded as one of Europe's top comic strip artists; his *Lieutenant Blueberry* has been a popular, as well as a critical, success since 1964. And Gir himself has been the recipient of countless awards, including one as "best foreign artist" awarded him by the Academy of Comic Book Arts in the United States.

Since 1975 Giraud has led a double life. As Gir he has continued to turn out the *Blueberry* series, adding the writing to his drawing chores after Charlier's death in 1989. Along with supervising *La jeunesse de Blueberry* ("Blueberry's Youth") drawn by Colin Wilson, he has also been scripting since 1991 *Marshal Blueberry* on illustrations by William Vance.

At the same time, under his Moebius *nom-de-plume*, he was one of the founders of the trailblazing *Métal Hurlant* magazine: it was there that he published some of his most acclaimed creations, beginning with the fantasy tale of *Arzach* realized entirely with visuals, *sans* text or dialogue. Other notable stories to stumble out of his facile pen have been *Le garage hermétique* ("The Airtight Garage," 1976-77), midway between science fiction and tall tale; *The Long Tomorrow* (on a script by Dan O'Bannon, 1976); and an episode of *The Silver Surfer* written by Stan Lee (1988-89). Some of his more memorable narratives have been done in collaboration with *avant-garde* filmmaker Alejandro Jodorowsky, who supplied the scripts: *Les yeux du chat* ("The Eyes of the Cat," a 1977 exercise in terror); *John Difool* (the extraordinary adventures of a detective of the future) from 1981 to 1989; and *Le coeur couronné* ("The Crowned Heart," 1992).

In addition he has also been very active in the field of animation. In 1978 he drew the storyboards of René Laloux's *Les maitres du temps* ("Time Masters"); followed by his doing the storyboards and backgrounds for Disney's *Tron* (1982); and in 1985 he did the same

for the Japanese *Little Nemo*. He is currently working on animated versions of some of his works. Among the many distinctions and honors bestowed upon him, Giraud was made a Knight of Arts and Letters by the French Minister of Culture.

M.H.

"The Girl from the People's Commune," Ho Yu-chih.

GIRL FROM THE PEOPLE'S COMMUNE, THE (China) Adapted from an original short story by Li Chun, *The Girl From the People's Commune* was published in comic book form in 1965 by the People's Art Publications in Shanghai. The narrative was written by Lu Chung-chien, and drawn by Ho Yu-chih.

The Girl From the People's Commune is a good example of the didacticism and homespun philosophy often explicit in Chinese comic books. In this simple tale of a young, uneducated peasant girl, Li Shuang-shuang, who is able to reform not only her whole commune but also her non-reconstructed husband, the traditional values of Chinese life are subtly interwoven with the teachings of Chairman Mao (although his name is never mentioned). The pace in this tale of edification is slow, and nothing much happens. Actually the story is often boring and were it not for the unmistakeable Socialist message, one might easily confuse *Girl* with any number of *Treasure Chest* homilies about the rewards of hard work and clean living.

The artwork is not very distinguished, although it always remains craftsmanlike. As in most Chinese comic books, the layout is uninspired (four panels of equal size to a page), and speech balloons are only sparsely used (befitting peasant people, as the characters do not talk much). All in all, *The Girl From the People's Commune* is of interest only to historians, sociologists, and Sinologists.

The Girl From the People's Commune was reprinted (under the title "Li Shuang-shuang") in the collection of Chinese comics published by Doubleday (*The People's Comic Book*, 1973).

M.H.

GIRLS IN APARTMENT 3-G *See* Apartment 3-G.

GLASS, JACK (1890-1970) Although the artwork of Jack Glass was striking and recognizable immediatly to any young reader of the comics and boys' weeklies published by D.C. Thompson from the 1920s to the 1960s, he was another cartoonist who was refused the right to sign his own work. Among his credits is the first American-style superhero in British comics, *The Amazing Mr. X,* who first burst into action in *The Dandy Comic* on December 23, 1944.

John Glass was a Scotsman, born in Edinburgh in the late 1890s. He joined the art department of D.C. Thompson Company in the late 1920s. In the early years of his career he specialized in drawing what were known then as "the heading blocks," the title illustrations which decorated every story series and serial published in the Thompson "Big Five:" the boys' story papers *Adventure, Rover, Wizard, Hotspur,* and *Skipper.* Glass adapted his style to any story, from western to epics of the Empire, school stories, and early science-fiction sagas. He also drew many of the full-color covers, the best remembered of which was *Wilson the Wonder Man* (1943), a black-cloaked athlete around 100 years old who came out of nowhere to break every record at the Olympic games.

Glass's career as a picture story and serial artist began in 1937 with the first issue of *The Dandy Comic* (1937), Thompson's first weekly comic for children. His two-page strip, *The Daring Deeds of Buck Wilson,* starred a cowboy. The strip's format set Glass's style for the rest of his comic art life: no lettering or speech balloons, but lengthy captions teling the story in eleven or more lines under every panel.

Later characters included *Never Never Nelson, the Circus Scout Who Never Fails; Cracker Jack, the Wonder Whip Man* (both 1938); *Young Strongarm, the Axe Man* (*Beano,* 1939); *Wildfire, the War Horse* (*Dandy,* 1940); *The Prince on the Flying Horse* (*Beano*); and *Boomerang Burke, the No-Gun Mountie* (*Dandy,* 1941). He also adapted some of the story paper heroes into strip serials, including *The Iron Teacher,* a prewar serial, returned as a strip to *The Hotspur* in 1951, and in the same paper a masked cowboy called *Leatherface* had four adventures from 1951 to 1956. Among the fantasies drawn by Glass were *Little Master of the Swooping Monster* (*Dandy,* 1953), *The Iron Fish* (*Beano,* 1958), and *South with the Hover-car* (*Dandy,* 1967). His last serial was *Gunsmoke Jack* (*Dandy,* 1968), after which he drew several single episode items for *New Hotspur,* and the complete adventure, *Randall's Vandals* for the *Dandy Annual* (1969). He then retired, and died not long after in the early 1970s. His style, bold, harsh, some might say crude, but always action-packed and distinctly his own, died with him.

D.G.

GLOBI (Switzerland) *Globi,* created by J. K. Schiele and Robert Lips (1912-1975), is one of the few comic characters that grew out of an advertising campaign. When the Swiss department store Globus's 25th anniversary was to be celebrated in 1932, J. K. Schiele, head of the advertising department, invented the parrot Globi, who was to head a two-week children's festival in all of the five Globus stores in Zurich, Basel, St. Gallen, Chur, and Aarau. On August 24, 1932, Globi made his first newspaper appearance in a comic strip advertising campaign announcing the big event. Emerging from his egg clothed with checkerboard pants, Globi immediately left the Sahara to fly north, where he discovered all the festivities at hand and invited children to join him in the fun. The art was by Robert Lips, who hit the spot with his clean, witty style. The name "Globi" was given to the parrot by Heinrich Laser.

"Globi," Robert Lips. © Globi Verlag.

The festival, personal appearances of Globi included, was immensely successful. There were Globi ads in Swiss newspapers during its duration. The character was too good to be wasted in a one-time advertising campaign. Thus, J.K. Schiele started *Der Globi,* a children's magazine that featured Globi comics, poems, stories, puzzles, contests, etc. The magazine was available at the Globus stores and after specials in 1933 and 1934, was published monthly starting in January 1935. Also in 1935, J.K. Schiele had the first *Globi* book published, but it was not overly successful. It was decided that future books should be printed on other than slick paper so it would be easier for children to color the comic strips. It was also decided to add verses, and these were written by Alfred Bruggmann. They are now being written by Jakob Stäheli.

The second book, *Globi junior,* introducing the first of the Globi kids, was published in 1938, and this new format worked. Since then, a total of 42 *Globi* books have been published, the latest one drawn by Swiss cartoonist Werner Büchi. Total sales in Switzerland alone up to 1975 have totalled some four million books. Over the years there have been numerous foreign editions, in France, Belgium, Holland, Norway, Brazil, Japan, and in 1948 *Globi* came to the United States in the monthly *Story Parade.* *Globi* books were exported into Germany and Austria after World War II for some time. They have been introduced there in pocket book editions in 1973. There have been many Globi toys, and a television program is being prepared.

Renowned cartoonist Werner Büchi only produced two *Globi* books. His style did not mesh with the *Globi* universe. Since 1980 new stories have been written and drawn successfully by Swiss cartoonist Peter Heinzer. (Born in 1945, Heinzer is one of the few Swiss who did not get to read *Globi* as a child.) Heinzer's stories are put into verse by Guido Strebel. In 1988 a female version of Globi was introduced, *Globine,* drawn by Anne Christiansen. A baby Globi, *Globeli,* was introduced in 1992 by Brigitte Conte. In 1994 another relative was introduced, the Scot McGlobi. The McGlobi comic (with speech balloons instead of rhymed narrative) was written by Jan Marek and drawn by Heiri Schmidt. After more than 60 years, Globi is still a successful merchandising character and has appeared on a number of products as well as on television.

W.F.

GLOOPS (G.B.) Gloops is the original lisping cat, born years before Warner Brothers's cartoon cat, Sylvester. He first appeared in May 1928, in the *Sheffield Evening Telegraph,* a four-panel daily strip in the Children's Corner run by "Uncle Nick." His original artist signed himself "Ken," later "Cousin Ken," and then a remarkably

"Gloops." © *Weekly Telegraph.*

similar artist took over in 1934, "Cousin Toby." (Around the same time "Uncle Nick" gave way to "Aunt Edith.") The strip then appeared in the *Yorkshire Telegraph* and *Weekly Telegraph*, and in 1939 transferred to *The Star*, an evening paper. Dropped for some years, both the character and his Gloops Club were revived by *The Star* in November 1972, when the old strips were reprinted in a new weekly supplement for children, *Junior Star*. An actor in a specially made Gloops Suit made personal appearances and promoted the newspaper at children's hospital parties, etc.

Gloops ("Thummer time ith over, it'th my turn to get breakfatht!") is a large white cat who lives with twins Burford and Belinda, Granpa, and their maid, Emmer. There is the odd visit from Aunt Snork, and the odder visit from cat Ginger. The format is a daily joke, with occasional continuity, and Gloops's ability to speak is taken for granted by all.

The strip was reprinted in thirteen thick paper comic books between 1930 and 1939, beginning with *The Christmas Book of Gloops* (1930) and ending with *Gloops*

Christmas Annual (1939), including a special *Jubilee Number* (1935).

D.G.

GODWIN, FRANCIS (1889-1959) American cartoonist, illustrator, and painter born October 20, 1889, in Washington, D.C., Francis (Frank) Godwin's father, Harry R. Godwin, was city editor of the *Washington Star*, and the young Godwin started his art apprenticeship on that paper around 1905. He later went to study at the Art Students' League in New York, where he became friends with James Montgomery Flagg, with whom he shared a studio at one time. Thanks to Flagg's friendship, Godwin started contributing to the major humor magazines of the day (his earliest recorded work, a two-line cartoon, appeared in *Judge* in 1908). From then on, he became one of the most prolific cartoonists and illustrators of the time, whose work (signed and unsigned) appeared regularly in every major (and not so major) magazine in the country. His illustrations (notably for *Collier's*, *Liberty*, and *Cosmopolitan*) display a craftsmanship that few other illustrators could equal. He also did a great deal of advertising work (his ads for Prince Albert tobacco in *Life* are as good as anything he did in straight illustration) and in the 1930s he took up painting—the murals he did for the Kings County Hospital in Brooklyn show him as a vigorous and accomplished practitioner of the art.

By his own account, Godwin felt no special inclination toward the comic strip and, like Harold Foster, he entered the field at a relatively late age. In 1927 he started *Connie* for the Ledger Syndicate: a girl strip at the beginning (not unlike Charles Voight's contemporary *Betty*), *Connie* soon became a sophisticated action feature worthy of comparison with the best production of the period. Unheralded and almost unnoticed during the time it ran from 1927 to 1944, *Connie* is now regarded as one of the most vibrant, innovative, and lyrical creations ever to grace the comics page. (In the early to middle 1930s the Sunday *Connie* was accompanied by a bottom strip, *The Wet Blanket*, a weak gag feature saved only by Godwin's superlative penwork.)

Frank Godwin's talent was soon noticed by the *Ledger* editors and he found himself turning out most of the illustration strips distributed by this unfortunately obscure syndicate. Most of Godwin's prodigious output for the *Ledger* remained unsigned, but his mark (composed of a network of fine crosshatchings and a cursive line, as distinctive as a signature) can clearly be

"Rusty Riley," Frank Godwin. © *King Features Syndicate.*

seen on such disparate features as *Babe Bunting* (the adventures of a little girl, created by Fanny Cory and later credited to Roy L. Williams); *Eagle Scout Roy Powers* (a Boy Scout strip bylined by Paul Powell); and the anonymous *War on Crime* (a comic strip pictorialization of the careers of notorious criminals, on which each and every *Ledger* artist and writer seems to have taken turns). Just before and after *Connie* folded, Godwin worked sporadically in comic books (on *Wonder Woman* for National in 1943-45, and for various Lev Gleason publications from 1945-48). That same year he produced *Rusty Riley*, a luminous strip of youth and the outdoors, for King Features Syndicate. He died of a heart attack in his home in New Hope, Penn. on August 5, 1959. A few weeks earlier he had abandoned the drawing of *Rusty Riley*.

Frank Godwin has always received greater recognition as an illustrator than as a cartoonist (he was vice-president of the Society of Illustrators and a member of its Hall of Fame). Yet his work in the comics field, underrated as it is, deserves the higher praise. *Connie* is an undisputed masterpiece of draftsmanship, composition, and design, and *Rusty Riley* is not too far behind. Even *Babe Bunting* and *Roy Powers* are worthy of study. It has been Godwin's misfortune that the bulk of his work was carried by a syndicate so obscure as to be virtually invisible; and that his latter and better-known effort (*Rusty Riley*) was saddled with an inane story line and a restrictive editorial policy. Unlike Harold Foster's, Alex Raymond's and Burne Hogarth's, Frank Godwin's *oeuvre* is still waiting for a comprehensive, scholarly evaluation: when this study finally comes, he will be found to be one of the undisputed giants of the field.

M.H.

GOHS, ROLF (1933-   ) Rolf Gohs, born 1933 in Esthonia, lived and grew up during World War II in Poland, from there fleeing to Germany, then to Austria, and finally coming to live in Sweden in 1947. He finished school there and at the age of 16 started working for Centerförlaget, the first Swedish comics publisher. His earliest illustrations were destined for covers or as illustrations for cowboy novels. His first chance to do a comic feature came along when the artist of *Kilroy* died and the 19-year-old Gohs took over the strip, which was published in Sweden in *Seriemagasinet*. Later, the strip was continued by Spanish artist Francisco Cueto, while Gohs drew the science-fiction comic *Mannen från Claa* ("Man from Claa") and the mystery strips *Bomben* ("Bombs") and *Dödens fågel* ("Bird of Death"). These appeared in *Seriemagasinet* between 1956 and 1958. Also in 1958 he concentrated on illustration, photography, and film. For some time he even became chief illustrator for *Levande Livet* ("Live Life"). In 1958 he won a prize with *Statyetten* ("Statuettes"), one of his movie shorts. Another of his films shown on Swedish television was a short about war comics, *Pang, du ar dod* ("Bang, You're Dead").

While working mainly as a photographer and on movies, in the 1960s Gohs started working for Semic Press, another Swedish comic book publisher, doing covers for *Fantomen* ("Phantom") comic books. At the same time he also helped Börje Nilsson draw a daily strip version of *Pelle Svanslös* ("Pelle No-Tail"), a humor strip about an adventurous anthropomorphic cat without a tail.

In 1969, Rolf Gohs and comic editors Per Anders Jonsson and Janne Brydner started their own publishing house—Inter Art, which produced two comic books, *Kilroy*, a revival of the *Seriemagasinet* feature now written by Swedish writers and drawn by Spanish artists, and *Mystiska 2:an* ("The Mystic Two" or "Sacho and Stefan"), an original Gohs creation. When financial difficulties developed, the group sold out to Semic Press, and *Mystiska 2:an* was continued. Gohs himself is now largely out of the comics scene.

The Gohs style depends largely on sharp contrasts of light and dark. It is a photographic style influenced by Gohs's other career in photography and by Hal Foster, Burne Hogarth, and Alex Raymond, favorite comic artists.

W.F.

GOLDBERG, REUBEN LUCIUS (1883-1970) Born July 4, 1883, Reuben Lucius Goldberg was the second-born of three sons of Hannah and Max Goldberg. As the son of a well-to-do moneylender and land speculator, and possessed of a competent talent as an artist, the young "Rube" had a great time at the University of California at Berkeley, cartooning for the campus humor magazine and yearbook. Deciding to work on newspapers, Goldberg went to the *San Francisco Chronicle* after graduation in 1904, and made a fair hit with readers with a series of amusing sports cartoons. From there, he went to the *S. F. Bulletin*, covering the raucous boxing and football scene of the period. By then he felt ready to tackle the big city, and went to New York in October 1907, in the wake of a series of *Mike and Ike* Sunday half-pages (dealing with identical twin shrimps in slapstick situations) he had sold to the World Color Printing Co. comic section. But the company appears to have reported minimal reader response to the early, crude pages upon Rube's arrival, and he had to resort to considerable street-tramping to land a job as sports-page cartoonist on the *N.Y. Evening Mail*. Starting at $50.00 a week, Rube made some impact with his drawings on *Mail* readers, and shortly found his work appearing back in San Francisco (in the *Call*) and elsewhere on a semi-syndicated basis. The popularity of his sports cartoon work with the *Mail* made the paper give Goldberg a Sunday page in 1915, which he called *Boob McNutt*. Quickly syndicated by Hearst, this strip led to much of Rube's later national recognition (as did the nutty comic-strip string, pulley, and fire-bucket inventions with which the public credited him), and after a stint as creator of other, lesser strips, a job as political cartoonist for the *N.Y. Sun*, notable accomplishments as a comic sculptor, and acclaim as an after-dinner speaker, Goldberg died, full of fame and friendship, on December 7, 1970.

After *Boob McNutt* was launched, Goldberg revived his early Mike and Ike characters in his daily *Mail* strip in 1917 as occasional gag sequence figures. By then, his daily sports-page feature had developed such publicly popular running gag items as *Foolish Questions, I'm The Guy* (source of one of the first song hits based on newspaper cartoon work, in 1912), and *Boobs Abroad* (based on Rube's 1913 trip to Europe). Rube had found time to go into vaudeville in 1911 as a stand-up funnyman, cartoonist, and fortune-teller. It was not until 1928 that he finally gave up his daily miscellany strip (which never had a standard running title) and launched his first daily continuity strip (probably the best sustained work he ever did) called *Bobo Baxter*, about a middle-aged, balding man who stumbles in and out of fantastic adventures suited to the more stalwart kind of hero,

COOLING DEVICE FOR BUSY OFFICE-WORKER

IRANIAN PREMIER **MOHAMMED MOSSADEGH(A)** WEEPS AND FAINTS DURING SPEECH, FALLS ON PIANO **(B)** AND MUSIC STARTS **BARBARA HUTTON** AND **BARON GOTTFRIED VON CRAMM(C)** DANCING —

BARON KICKS OVER BOTTLE OF **GROMYKO'S** VODKA **(D)** WHICH DROPS IN **JOE E. BROWN'S** MOUTH**(E)** — HE PATS SELF ON BACK WITH HAND**(F)** TO STOP CHOKING —

LEVER **(G)** STARTS **EDDIE ARCARO (H)** TESTING NEW **CENTRAL PARK** MERRY-GO-ROUND **(I)**, TURNING AUGER **(J)** WHICH BORES HOLE IN LARGE CAKE OF ICE **(K)** —

PIECES OF ICE DROP DOWN NECK OF OFFICE WORKER **(L)** GIVING REFRESHING COOLING EFFECT — **HE DRIES SELF WITH HANDY DESK BLOTTER.**

Rube Goldberg, gag cartoon.

which Goldberg unfortunately dropped in 1930 to return to the miscellany format. On January 28, 1934, he again tried continuity in a disastrous stab at a serious, soap-opera strip called *Doc Wright* (distributed, like all of his post-1918 work, by Hearst syndicates), which folded its story about a doctor and his troubled patients a year later. On September 20, 1936, he started a daily *and* Sunday comic strip narrative called *Lala Palooza* for the Frank Markey Syndicate, having left Hearst distribution with *Doc Wright* in 1935. This, too, had a mediocre public response—Rube's image of a Mae West-shaped, chocolate-munching heiress as heroine and her ne'er-do-well brother, an imitation of Segar's Wimpy, did little to spark reader fancy—and was dropped in 1939 with little notice and no regret. His last strip effort, a 1939 Sunday miscellany page called *Rube Goldberg's Sideshow*, distributed by the Register and Tribune Syndicate, featured one minor continuity strip, *Brad and Dad*, part of which was as amusing as anything Rube ever did, but was tucked away in 1941. (Unlike most cartoonists, his wealth, inherited from his father, permitted him to indulge his whims in this high-handed fashion with no financial worries.) After *Sideshow*, Rube turned to editorial cartooning (for which he won a Pulitzer prize in 1948), augmenting this work with the occasional magazine article and book writing which he had done throughout his career, and developed his skills as a sculptor. He also found time to do important work in organizing the National Cartoonists' Society in 1945, (becoming its first president the next year), and filled out his time with toastmaster stints and travels.

Goldberg's cartooning style, compared to that of his equally famed peers, was not attractive or memorable. It was sloppy and imprecise, and often betrayed his sometimes excellent conceptions, which were more than his faulty style could handle adequately. Striking comic notions and humorous narrative suspense were his real talents, yet when he hit his stride with a good strip concept, as he did with the later *Boob McNutt* and *Bobo Baxter*, he didn't seem to know it, and tired of these works as readily and abruptly as he did of his less

effective efforts. He engaged the public interest with simple gimmicky running features (such as the *Foolish Questions*) and reaped enormous general fame as a result (much as did the MCs of the *Professor Quiz* and *People Are Funny* radio shows at a later date). His foolishly complicated inventions, which gained him dictionary entry (for "Rube Goldberg contraption," etc.), appealed to the same broad audience base, even though it was not his unique idea. W. Heath Robinson had developed fanciful inventions of his own in various cartoon series for English magazines and newspapers in the 1910s, while the American strip cartoonist, Clare Victor Dwiggins, introduced devices very similar to those of Goldberg's in a *New York World* Sunday page called *School Days* of the 1900s, which Goldberg must have read before he ever drew any of his own comic contraptions, since his early *Mike and Ike* ran in the same comic section. A curious case of a strip cartoonist better known to the public than any of his characters (except possibly Mike and Ike), Goldberg did some memorable work in spite of all his defects, and is one of the major strip artists.

B.B.

GOLGO 13 (Japan) Golgo 13 was created by Takao Saitō for the monthly (later twice-monthly) *Big Comic* and made its debut in January 1969.

Golgo 13 is a super-efficient killer whose real name, race, nationality, and personal antecedents are all equally unknown. He has thick eyebrows, sharp eyes, a long nose, crew-cut hair, and steel-like muscles. He never expresses his feelings, laughs, or cries. He always accomplishes his murders with the utmost professionalism and detachment, whomever his clients may be (these have indifferently included the C.I.A., the K.G.B., the F.B.I., Arab guerrillas, and American gangsters). Golgo's victims have been equally eclectic, ranging from mafia chieftains to neo-Nazis to spies to highjackers, and none has ever escaped the implacable fire of his guns (his favorite one being a custom-crafted M-16 rifle). Golgo 13 has also been the target of other

わすことに全力を注げ.

"Golgo 13," Takao Saitō. © Big Comic.

killers, detectives, and sharp-shooters, none of whom could match his steely resolve and machine-like precision.

Golgo 13's name is a combination derived from "Golgotha" and the unlucky number 13. The protagonist himself is clearly beyond law and morality. His activities have taken place all over the world, in North and South America, Europe, Africa, the Middle East, etc.

Golgo 13's scriptwriters have been Takao Saitō himself, Kazuo Koike, K. Motomitsu, Kōtarō Mori, Tsutomu Miyazaki, Kyōta Kita, and Masaru Iwasawa. Soon after the strip's inception, Golgo 13 became the new kind of hero—cool, cruel, nihilistic—and widely imitated by other comic book artists. *Golgo 13* has also appeared in magazines and in book form. His books have been best-sellers and have been reprinted many times. *Golgo 13* was also adapted to television (but with considerable alterations) and was made into a movie. After a record 25 years of serialization, the series ended its run in 1994.

H.K.

GOMEZ, PABLO S. (1931-   ) Pablo Gomez is a Filipino cartoonist born on January 25, 1931, in Manila. He was the seventh child in a family of 14. His greatest ambition was to become a good writer and a publisher. Both his goals have long been fulfilled. His brother, Dominador, is also a comic book writer.

Pablo Gomez started out in 1950 as a proofreader for one of the comic companies in the Philippines. At that time he was also developing his craft as a writer. Eventually he was promoted to assistant editor, then editor, for *Pilipino Komiks* and *Hiwaga*, two of the foremost comic books in the country.

As a writer, his dramatic and moving portrayal of people trapped in the web of circumstances beyond

their control was immensely popular. His graphic novels had solid plots and excellent characterizations. His sensitive handling of emotional scenes and his ability to create the proper mood and feeling in his comic strips made his work readily applicable to the performing arts of stage, motion pictures, and television. Many of his stories have been adapted into film.

Through the years Gomez has teamed up with many of the finest comic artists in the field to produce memorable graphic stories. Some of the artists he worked with were Nestor Redondo, Alfredo Alcala, Noly Panaligan, Jesse Santos, Alex Niño, Hal Santiago, and Tony Caravana.

In 1963 he formed his own company, P.S.G. Publications. Along with his art director, L. S. Martinez, Gomez produced a variety of movie and rock music magazines as well as songbooks. His line of comics included *United Continental, Kidlat* ("Lightning"), *Universal,* and *Planet.* Among the contributing writers and artists for his comics have been Francisco Coching, Jun Bordillo, Ruding Mesina, Frank Redondo, Jorge Peñamora, Alcabral, Steve Gan, Rico Rival, Abe Ocampo, Fred Carillo, Deo Gonzales, and Vir Aguirre.

Recently Gomez was the recipient of the highest award the Philippine publications industry has to offer. He has also been awarded by the film industry for his writing. His most popular works are *Gonzales, Kalik Sa Apoy* ("Kiss of Fire"), *Odinah, Pagbabalik Ng Lawin* ("Return of the Hawk"), *Santo Domingo, Esteban,* and *Biyak Na Bato* ("Broken Stone"). In the 1980s he went to work for Philippine television, notably with his own series, *Panohon;* he has also written well over 100 novels, many illustrated by Nestor Redondo.

O.J.

GONICK, LARRY (1946-   ) American cartoonist and author born on August 24, 1946, in San Francisco. Larry Gonick forsook an early love of drawing for a foray into mathematics at Harvard University, where he received both his B.A. and M.A. He later returned to drawing, however, and he later averred, "I dropped out of mathematics graduate school and into cartooning because I wanted to abandon the estoteric for the accessible and popular."

Gonick's efforts at enlightening the masses initially took the form of comic books, which he turned out for Rip Off Press from 1978 to 1985 under the general title *The Cartoon History of the Universe.* These proved reasonably successful and became best-sellers several years later. Encouraged by his success, Gonick followed up with *The Cartoon Guide to U.S. History* (1987-1988). In the meantime he had also penned *The Cartoon Guide to Genetics* (in collaboration with Mark Wheelis), *The Cartoon Guide to Computer Science,* and *The Cartoon Guide to Physics* (with Art Huffman). His latest venture in this vein has been *The Cartoon Guide to (Non) Communication* (1993), which is a revised version of an earlier work he turned out for a Belgian publisher, *New Babelonia.*

Gonick treats his serious subjects with a light, even facetious, touch. A chapter of U.S.history is titled "In which happiness is pursued, with a gun," while a chapter dealing with Julius Caesar is called "Caesarian Section." In his overview of the institution of slavery in the South, he writes, "Race mixing was illegal—which only proves that not all laws were enforced 100%." Compared to the writing, the drawing is primitive, even crude, and only serves as humorous counterpoint.

His works are more like comic treatises with doodles than *bona fide* comic books, but they are very entertaining, as well as highly informative in a light-hearted way. Gonnick may have found the key to every educator's dream—making learning fun.

M.H.

GOODWIN, ARCHIE (1937-   ) American comic book and comic strip writer born September 8, 1937, in Kansas City, Missouri. Goodwin's first comic art material began appearing in 1959 and 1960, when he assisted Leonard Starr on *On Stage*, drew a comic art page for *Fishing World*, and was an assistant art director and spot illustrator for *Redbook* magazine. Harvey's *Hermit* strip was his first comic book work, and it appeared in October, 1962's *Alarming Adventures* number one.

After another stint at *Redbook*, Goodwin became an associated editor/writer for Warren's black-and-white comic magazines, and it was there that he wrote for the landmark *Blazing Combat* title. At a time when the American citizenry was still supporting their country's involvement in Vietnam, *Blazing Combat* was an early, outspoken, consistent critic of all types of war; in this regard Goodwin's scripts surpassed even the Kurtzman stories from a decade before. This novel editorial stand doomed the book to a short, four-issue history (October 1965 to July 1966). Goodwin remained at Warren until 1970, scripting for the usually nonpolitical horror magazines.

In December 1966, Goodwin teamed up with Al Williamson to produce King's *Secret Agent Corrigan* syndicated strip. And while the contemporary spy features were heavily-influenced by the then-popular James Bond "gimmick" movies, Goodwin's material was more mature and intelligent than the standard fare. It might well have been the best adventure strip of the time, and he and Williamson still do the strip. Goodwin also ghosted King's *Captain Kate* feature from 1966 through 1969.

Goodwin made his first considerable foray into the comic book market in 1968, when he joined the Marvel group and began writing the whole range of Marvel superheroes, including *Iron Man, Sub-Mariner,* and *Dr. Strange*. While many of his contemporaries were indulging in gimmicks and campiness to bolster the faltering "Marvel Age of Comics," Goodwin emerged as the company's premier adventure writer. While Roy Thomas, Marvel's other young star of the period, concentrated on personalities and interaction, Goodwin wrote Marvel's most intelligent and believable action

stories. Rarely was there a lacklustre or skimpy Goodwin script. In 1972 he moved to National as an editor, and while his National war material fell short of his *Blazing Combat* work, he was responsible for helping *Batman* regain the aura of mystery and intrigue that was once its trademark. He and artist Walt Simonson created the unique *Manhunter* adventure feature, and it earned Goodwin two ACBA "Shazam" awards for best dramatic writer and best short story.

Goodwin also ghost-wrote, under the pseudonym "Robert Franklin," two of the era's most experimental features, both drawn by Gil Kane: *His Name is Savage* magazine (1968) and the *Blackmark* paperback (1971).

J.B.

In 1980 Goodwin took over the editorship of *Epic Illustrated*, a comics magazine published by Marvel. In addition to his considerable comic-book writing, he also continued to turn out scripts for newspaper strips; besides *Secret Agent Corrigan*, which he left in 1980, he also wrote again on illustrations by Al Williamson for the *Star Wars* strip from 1981 to 1984.

M.H.

GORDO (U.S.) Gus Arriola started *Gordo* for United Feature Syndicate on November 24, 1941; the strip was suspended from October 28, 1942, to June 24, 1946, as a daily but the Sunday page followed on May 2, 1943.

The Widow Gonzales is a very determined woman, and she has to be. For better than 30 years now she has schemed, stolen, defrauded, and all but murdered in order to obtain in marriage her conception of a small Mexican town's most eligible bachelor. The shrinking bachelor of Del Monte is a one-time local farmer (now the driver of a marginally profitable tourist bus that he owns himself) named Gordo, who is more interested in following his roving eye in pursuit of women in general than in settling down with one: marriage is a state he views with mortal terror. It would mean no more tippling at Pelon's grape juice lounge, no more batching around with such close buddies as Juan Pablo Jones or Poet Garcia (himself married now and only infrequently in view), no more driving young female tourists around in El Cometa Halley, no more lounging in bed with Senor Dog, Senor Pig, Popo the rooster, Poosey Cat, Senor Owl, and tousle-headed nephew Pepito, until all hours of the *mañana*.

So over the decades Gordo has valiantly warded off the most fiendish efforts of the determined Widow to wed him, avoiding her subterfuges of witchcraft, interstellar science, a mammoth carniverous plant called the Widow's Weed, a teleporter, a dormitutor, a double, etc., by hairbreadth degrees each time. In the long intervals between the wealthy Widow's onslaughts, however, Gordo has enjoyed himself immensely with his cronies, greedy or hapless American tourists, strange local characters, and various inanimate and/or animal aspects of the Del Monte scene. Poet Garcia's love affair and marriage with the American girl, Rusty Gates, occupied a long and amusing story, as did the visit by freckle-faced 12-year-old Mary Frances Sevier to Rusty and Garcia (followed by her amorous pursuit of Gordo's nephew, Pepito). The attempt (and failure) by an American tourist car collector to buy Gordo's 1912 Michigan Mateor for $70,000 or more is still a local legend around Del Monte. And the curious appearance and behavior of such local phenomena as Shocking Pedro, Goblin, and Little Coronado with his

"Sinner," art and story, Archie Goodwin. © Archie Goodwin.

"Gordo," Gus Arriola. © United Feature Syndicate.

bottomless bag of tricks enlivened the strip over the years. Among the inanimate characters featured were the philosophic crackpots of Del Monte; while the least visible but perhaps most noted creature of the city is Bug Rogers, the hip and hungry spider with his splendidly designed webs (not to mention the drunken earthworms who make whoopee in the wee smalls of the Mexican night).

Gus Arriola is a weaver of strip legend and a creator of comic characters in the best tradition of E. C. Segar, Billy De Beck, and Charles Schulz. Unfortunately, Arriola developed a tendency to neglect the narrative adventures that once sharpened and defined his characters so well, and too many of his Sunday episodes became little more than eye-pleasing designs built around a simple verbal gag. Following the last assault by the Widow Gonzales (it was a masterpiece!), there was no prolonged story of any worth in *Gordo*. But Arriola had, in any event, accomplished enough in over three decades of *Gordo* to do with the strip as he pleased: he created a classic among the best in his field. Eight paperback reprints of the *Gordo* comic strips were published by Nitty Gritty Productions in 1972. The strip ended in 1985, the Sunday in February, the dailies in March.

B.B.

GORDON FIFE AND THE BOY KING *See* Gordon, Soldier of Fortune.

GORDON, SOLDIER OF FORTUNE (U.S.) Created in October 1935 (under the title of *Gordon Fife and the Boy King*, later changed to *Gordon, Soldier of Fortune*) as a daily strip for the *Brooklyn Eagle* by Bob Moore (script) and John Hales (drawing). In December 1936, Carl Pfeufer (who was already doing *Don Dixon and the Hidden Empire*, also scripted by Bob Moore) took over the drawing of *Gordon* as well. In August 1940, *Gordon*

started as a Sunday feature (replacing *Tad of the Tanbark* and sharing the page with *Don Dixon*). Both daily and Sunday were discontinued a few months later, in July 1941.

Gordon Fife is an American adventurer who gets himself involved in the intrigues of the mythical Central European kingdom of Kovnia. In an atmosphere reminiscent of Anthony Hope's *The Prisoner of Zenda*, Gordon, with the help of his faithful Hindu partner Ali, foils assassination plots, coups d'etat, and other assorted conspiracies directed against young King Nicholas and his sister, regent of Kovnia and Gordon's light-of-love, Princess Caroline. His most constant adversaries are the scheming prince Karl of neighboring Livonia, and the subversive organization known as "the Markala."

Gordon was not by any means among the topmost adventure strips of the 1930s, but it was unpretentious and entertaining. Today it seems to reflect with great accuracy some of the fears, hopes, and concerns of the period.

M.H.

GOSCINNY, RENÉ (1926-1977) French writer and editor born in Paris in 1926. When René Goscinny was two, his parents emigrated to Argentina, where the young boy received his schooling; he also developed a love for cartooning in his schooldays. After his high school graduation he worked briefly as a bookkeeper, but in 1945 he left Argentina to join an uncle in the United States, with the secret ambition of becoming a cartoonist for Walt Disney. He never made it but instead worked in various jobs in New York; in the early 1950s he worked in the *Mad* magazine offices, where he was spotted by Morris, the creator of *Lucky Luke*, then on a trip around the United States.

In 1954 Goscinny went back to Europe with Morris, and in 1955 he became the scriptwriter on *Lucky Luke*. Under Goscinny's guidance, this parodic Western started incorporating real figures from the old West into its *dramatis personae*. While writing the continuity for *Lucky Luke*, Goscinny also contributed scripts for many other features then appearing in *Spirou* magazine: from *Blondin et Cirage* to *Jerry Spring*, rare is the series in which his name did not appear at one time or another. Not content with his work for *Spirou*, Goscinny produced a number of strips for other publications: *Le Docteur Gaudeamus* (drawn by Coq) for *Jours de France* in 1954; *Signor Spaghetti* (a gag strip illustrated by Dino Attanasio) for *Tintin* in 1958; and, also for *Tintin* in 1958, *Oumpah Pah le Peau-Rouge* ("Oumpah Pah the Redskin"), the comic tale of a gigantic Indian during the French and Indian War. *Oumpah Pah* was drawn by Albert Uderzo, who had already teamed up with Goscinny one year earlier on the short-lived *Benjamin et Benjamine*.

In 1959 Goscinny cofounded the comic weekly *Pilote* (later sold to Editions Dargaud). In the first issue of the new magazine, Goscinny and Uderzo created *Astérix*, about a diminutive Gaul in the time of Caesar's conquest. In a short while *Astérix* was so extravagantly successful that it made its authors millionaires several times over.

Along with *Astérix*, Goscinny has created a number of lesser-known series in recent years: *Le Petit Nicolas* ("Little Nicholas" with Sempé); *Haroun El Poussah* (with Jean Tabary), and *La Fée Aveline* ("Aveline the Fairy") with Coq.

René Goscinny is certainly the best-known, as well as the highest-paid, comic strip writer in recent history. With the income derived from *Astérix* he bought a large share of Editions Dargaud stock, and for a long time he guided the destinies of *Pilote*, a responsibility which he wisely relinquished in 1974. Goscinny has been the recipient of countless awards and honors; in 1967 he was made a Chevalier of Arts and Letters by the Minister of Culture, André Malraux. He died of a heart attack in Paris on November 6, 1977.

M.H.

GOTTFREDSON, FLOYD (1905-1986) Floyd Gottfredson, uncredited artist and interpretative author of the daily *Mickey Mouse* newspaper strip from its fourth month on, was born on May 5, 1905 in the railroad station of Kaysville, Utah, the grandson of the town station agent. As a youngster entranced by the comics (his early favorites were Walter Hoban's *Jerry on the Job*, *Krazy Kat*, *Barney Google*, and *Wash Tubbs*, among others), he took a number of correspondence courses in cartooning and won a prize in a cartooning contest. Then a projectionist in Utah, he saw no reason why he couldn't work as a projectionist in Hollywood and see what he could do about making a career out of his cartooning talent, so he went to Los Angeles in the late 1920s.

News that Walt Disney was about to go to New York to hire more animators for his burgeoning Hyperion studio prompted the young Gottfredson to try his luck at landing a job with Disney, with hopes that the experience might lead to strip work at a later date. Disney hired him at $18.00 a week as an apprentice animator (a considerable cut from his $65.00 a week salary as a projectionist, particularly since he was then married), but Gottfredson managed to survive by doing freelance cartooning on the side for an automotive trade journal. Within eight months, however, his salary had increased considerably, the freelancing was no longer necessary, and when an opening for an artist occurred in April, 1930, on the four-month-old *Mickey Mouse* daily strip then being drawn by studio personnel for King Features distribution, Gottfredson was tapped for a two-week fill-in stint, even though he had now gotten to like animation work and wasn't greatly interested in tackling a strip of any kind.

Comic strip work proved so swiftly engaging and rewarding to Gottfredson, however, that when Disney forgot about the two-week stint, the young artist did nothing to remind him. Originally grudgingly scripted by Disney in his spare time, the *Mickey Mouse* strip was quickly turned over to the eager Gottfredson for both art and story in mid-May of 1930, after which he drew and scripted it until late 1932. By then the strip was felt important enough to be handled by group discussion, with new plot ideas being threshed over by Gottfredson and several story men, after which one of the latter would be assigned to do a general action layout script, which would then be adapted panel by panel and balloon by balloon by Gottfredson in a penciled strip, and turned over for inking to a number of artists, most notably Ted Thwaites (between late 1932 and 1940). In January, 1932, Gottfredson was also assigned to write and draw the *Sunday Mickey* page, which was then just being launched via King Features distribution, a welcome job which he continued (with the later aid of the same group of story outliners and inkers he had on the daily strip) until mid-1938, when the Sunday page was turned over to another artist to permit Gottfredson to undertake more elaborate illustrative techniques in the daily strip.

The *Mickey Mouse* strip which Gottfredson drew and effectively wrote between 1930 and 1950 remains as a two-decade monument to one man's graphic and narrative genius, and nothing which followed it can change that accomplishment. In terms of all the conceivable elements that go into the making of a great narrative comic strip: unforgettable characterization, sharp and apposite dialogue, graphic delineation enhancing character and action, inborn story sense, skillfully handled narrative pace, effectively maintained comedy, and an indefinable infusion of uniqueness that can come only from the personality of the artist himself (if it is there), Gottfredson's Mickey Mouse is an obvious masterpiece. Read today, it seems as fresh as if it were just published, a sure test of fundamental quality in any work a quarter-century or more old. The urge to keep reading, once begun, is irresistible. He retired in 1975 and died on July 22, 1986, at his South California home.

Whatever time and syndicate policy have imposed on Floyd Gottfredson's once free-flowing genius, or studio policy has tried to deny him by scrawling a "Walt Disney" signature upon every one of his 15,000-plus episodes for 45 years, then, is effectively negated by the living miracle of his unfettered work at the peak of his talent. One of the half-dozen finest strip talents of the 1930s, Floyd Gottfredson will always be mentioned in the same breath with Milton Caniff, Al Capp, Will Eisner, Walt Kelly, and Alex Raymond—now that he is at last known by name as well as accomplishment.

B.B.

GOULD, CHESTER (1900-1985) American artist born November 20, 1900 in Pawnee, Oklahoma. His father was publisher of the *Advance-Democrat*, a Stillwater, Oklahoma newspaper but wanted his son to become a lawyer. Gould went to Oklahoma A and M College for two years and at the same time worked as a sports cartoonist for the *Oklahoma City Daily Oklahoman*. From there he went to Northwestern University in Chicago and graduated in 1923.

Soon after graduation he started working for Hearst's *Chicago American*, where he created *Fillum Fables*, a takeoff on Hollywood movies, in 1924. In 1931 he sold one of his comic strip ideas about a hard-nosed plainclothes detective to Captain Joseph Patterson of the Chicago Tribune-New York News Syndicate. The strip, rechristened *Dick Tracy* by Patterson, started running as a Sunday page on October 4, 1931, and as a daily strip a week later.

Since 1931 Chester Gould has been devoting most of his life to *Dick Tracy*, in which can be found the author's personal views and philosophy. In this connection Gould's research into police rules and procedures has been painstaking. His "Crime Stoppers," small vignettes he inserts near the title of the Sunday page, are designed to draw the reader's attention to some small facet of police procedure or crime prevention. Gould still spends a great deal of time with the Chicago police as well as in the crime laboratories of Northwestern University, and he has received a number of awards and commendations from police departments and law enforcement agencies all over the country.

Chester Gould's position in the comic strip world was just as impressive. While he was never personally the kind of guiding influence on younger cartoonists that Milton Caniff or Alex Raymond were, his work permeated many aspects of the comic book as well as the newspaper strip. In recognition of his pioneering research in the field, Gould received a number of professional awards and citations, including the Reuben award.

Gould retired from the strip in 1977, and it was taken over by Rick Fletcher (art) and Max Alan Collins (writing), with the creator retaining a byline. Dissatisfied with the direction *Dick Tracy* was taking, Gould asked his name to be removed from the feature in 1981. He died a few years later, on May 11, 1985.

M.H.

GOULD, WILL (1911-1984) American cartoonist and illustrator born 1911 in the Bronx, New York. Will Gould (no relation to Chester Gould) started his cartooning career while still in high school. In 1929 he was sports cartoonist at the *Bronx Home News*, for which he also contributed a humor strip with a sports angle, *Felix O'Fan*. From there he went to the *New York Graphic*, again as a sports cartoonist, creating a racing strip along the way: *Asparagus Tipps* about a black waiter always ready with a tip for the morrow's races (along the lines of Ken Kling's *Joe* and *Asbestos*).

In 1930 Will Gould, along with his entire family, moved to California. He then freelanced as a sports and feature cartoonist variously for the McNaught Syndicate (whose outlet in New York was the *World Telegram*), Kay Features, and King Features (Gould's work appearing in the *New York Mirror*). In 1933 Gould competed (unsuccessfully) for the drawing job on the planned *Secret Agent X-9* strip, and then attracted the notice of the ever-vigilant W. R. Hearst. A few months later King Features approved a new police strip submitted by Gould, *Red Barry*, which started publication on March 19, 1934 as a daily (and on March 3, 1935 as a Sunday).

Almost from the start Gould had difficulties with the syndicate: his editors wanted (Will) Gould's *Red Barry* to compete with (Chester) Gould's *Dick Tracy* but could not abide the violence (a contradiction of purposes!). In 1940, after years of running arguments with his editors, Gould left *Red Barry* (which was dropped) and went on to a scriptwriting career for motion pictures and radio. Drafted in 1942 at Fort McArthur, Gould was given the task of creating the camp's paper, which he called *The Alert* and on which he worked as editor, reporter, and cartoonist. At the end of the war he went back to scriptwriting and also worked as reporter for various newspapers. After 1963 Gould was the cartoon editor of *Writer's Forum* and drew a cartoon series, *The Schnoox*, for the Writers' Guild's monthly newsletter. He died in 1984 in a Los Angeles home for senior citizens from burns sustained while smoking in bed.

Will Gould's career as a comic strip artist was brief, but his contribution to the art is undisputable. *Red Barry* had a pulsating, restless energy about it, a driving spontaneousness caused in great part by the artist's free-flowing, almost slapdash brush technique. "Pencilling was never in great detail," confided Will Gould in a 1974 interview, "The time was always fleeting. I knew what I wanted, looked at the clock and slapped it in." Will Gould has received increasing rec-

ognition (as usual, the movement started in Europe), and we can only hope, therefore, that some of the old *Red Barry* adventures will be reprinted in book form as they have already been in Europe.

M.H.

GRAFF, MEL (1907-1975) American cartoonist born 1907 in Cleveland, Ohio. Mel Graff's father was a small lumber mill operator who was wiped out by the Depression. As a child, Graff liked to draw, and while attending West Technical High School in Cleveland he became a cartoonist on the school paper, *The Tatler*. Dropping out of school in his teens, he worked at odd jobs in and around railyards and roamed the country on freight trains.

In the early 1930s, Graff got a small job in the commercial art department of NEA. Transferred to New York in 1933, he came under the influence of noted cartoonist George Clark, and in 1934 started drawing *The Adventures of Patsy* for Associated Press. A little girl strip in the beginning, *Patsy* turned more and more toward adventure. One of Mel Graff's strokes of luck came in 1939 when he got his former AP colleague Noel Sickles to ghost *Patsy* for him: the result was so eye-catching that King Features hired Graff the next year to succeed Austin Briggs on *Secret Agent X-9*.

Mel Graff's tenure on *X-9* proved disastrous. Not only was his drawing barely adequate but, following the departure of Max Trell (who had been writing the *X-9* scripts since 1936 under the pen name Robert Storm), he took up the writing chores as well, emasculating in no small measure the character of his G-man hero. In the 1950s Mel Graff, who was suffering from the strain of a weekly deadline, had a series of breakdowns and was finally eased out of the strip in 1960. He moved to Orlando, Florida, and lived in semi-retirement there, doing a variety of small illustration and advertising jobs.

Mel Graff was probably one of the most pathetic examples of the mindlessness of the King Features system. Despite a lackluster performance and a serious health problem, he was allowed to plod along in mediocrity and run the strip into the ground because of the editors' misguided sense of loyalty. He is only remembered today because of his 20-year-long association with the *X-9* strip and for his undisputed, if minor, contribution to *Patsy*. Graff died on November 2, 1975.

M.H.

GRAY, CLARENCE (1901-1957) American cartoonist and illustrator born in Toledo, Ohio, on November 14, 1901. During his grammar and high school days Clarence Gray (when he was not playing hooky) concentrated on art courses. After his high school graduation he was deciding what art school to attend when he was offered a job on the art staff of the *Toledo News-Bee*. Gray accepted the offer and throughout the 1920s he drew editorial and sports cartoons for the newspaper.

In addition to his newspaper career Gray had become a contributor to various national magazines, and he was spotted by Hearst in 1933. In August of that year he started *Brick Bradford* (on continuity by William Ritt) for the Hearst-owned Central Press Association of Cleveland. An adventure strip at the beginning, *Brick* soon veered toward science fiction (especially after the addition of a Sunday page in November 1934). For a brief period in 1935 Gray also drew a companion piece to *Brick, The Time Top* (again written by Ritt). When Ritt stopped writing for Brick in 1952, Gray abandoned the daily strip to Paul Norris to concentrate on the Sunday page, which he wrote and drew until his untimely death at 54 on January 7, 1957.

Gray's draftsmanship helped make *Brick Bradford* into one of the most exciting adventure and science-fiction strips of the 1930s and 1940s. His graphic style—elegant and unambiguous—radiated a warm poetry and a youthful élan often absent from other strips in the genre. *Brick Bradford* still continues in the hands of Paul Norris.

M.H.

GRAY, HAROLD (1894-1968) Unlike many strip cartoonists, who become bored in later years with the characters they once made famous and hire "ghosts" to do the bulk of the continuing strip work (usually with adverse results, which only the unperceptive general readership fail to notice), Harold Gray remained as vitally concerned with the creations of his imagination as a great novelist would from the day he began work on his *Little Orphan Annie* until the day he died. Gray was one of the few natural comic strip artists and authors: a man who took to the new strip medium as readily as a poet to verse, and who was as creatively fulfilled in it as Shaw was playwriting. He was also one of the most gifted storytellers of our time.

Born in Kankakee, Illinois on January 20, 1894, the young Gray got his first newspaper job in Lafayette, Indiana, in 1913, while he was attending Purdue University. Graduating in 1917, he enlisted in the army and served as a bayonet instructor, ending up as a second lieutenant. Always interested in cartooning, he got a job on the *Chicago Tribune* art department after his discharge, but left to do the lettering on Sidney Smith's *The Gumps* between 1921 and 1924. In mid-1924, Gray approached J. M. Patterson with an idea for a News-Tribune strip called *Little Orphan Otto*. Paterson thought the boy looked slightly effeminate, suggested to Gray that he make her a girl, and give her the name of the once-famous James Whitcomb Riley poem, *Little*

Harold Gray.

Orphan Annie, a *Tribune* property, which the paper was periodically reprinting. The first episode of the new *Annie* strip appeared on August 5, 1924, in the *New York Daily News*, where it was given a trial run. After making a hit with the *News* readers, the strip was added to the *Chicago Tribune* roster a short time later, and the first Sunday *Annie* page appeared in both papers on November 2, 1924.

The strip was a growing success in the mid-1920s, soon appearing in syndication from coast to coast. Gray moved to the east coast, residing in New York and Southport, Connecticut and eventually buying a California home at La Jolla. He added a long-lived Sunday gag strip named *Maw Green* to the *Annie* page on January 1, 1933 (Maw having been a character in *Annie*), after experimenting for two years (1931-32) with humorous social commentary in a Sunday quarter-page called *Private Lives* (*Private Life of a Hat, Private Life of a Doormat*, etc.). On Sunday, May 3, 1933, Gray's sole *Annie* assistant, a cousin, Ed Leffingwell, launched a weekly half-page strip in the *Tribune* and *News* featuring a youngster growing up in a part of the contemporary west that was still old-fashioned cattle ranch country, which was called *Little Joe*. Gray was always involved in shaping the narrative and characters of *Joe*, and by the mid-1930s was drawing the human figures in the strip, while Leffingwell concentrated on the western backgrounds: perhaps the only instance in strips where a major, successful cartoonist was vitally and regularly concerned with the minor strip of an aide over so many years. (Later, Ed's brother, Robert, took over *Little Joe* after Ed's death, and drew the entire strip, Gray returning full-time to *Annie*.)

Gray loved his strip work, preferring it to almost anything else. He spent long hours writing, drawing, and researching both *Annie* and *Joe*, and travelled little outside of the United States, where he enjoyed driving around back-country roads alone in the less populous states of the west and midwest.

With only minor flagging in his narrative invention toward the end, Harold Gray closed 45 years of continuous work on *Little Orphan Annie* and other strips with his death on May 10, 1968. Attempts to continue his strip by other hands have proven monumental failures, and the News-Tribune syndicate was finally forced to turn to direct reprinting of the old strip for current syndication.

B.B.

GREEN ARROW (U.S.) *Green Arrow* was created by writer Mort Weisinger and artist George Papp and made its first appearance in National's *More Fun* number 73 for November 1941. A rather pedestrian archery strip, the character's only innovations were a quiver's worth of trick arrows and the Arrow Car. His partner, Speedy, was added in the March, 1943 issue of *More Fun*.

The Green Arrow was really industrialist Oliver Quinn, another in National's long line of playboy heroes, and his partner's name was Roy Harper. Without a particularly fascinating storyline—most adventures consisting of a character being defeated by a barrage of Green Arrow's arrows—the feature was continually bouncing from book to book. After being dropped from *More Fun* after February 1946's 107th issue, he began a long run of more than 100 issues of *Adventure* and *World's Finest*. He also appeared in the

"Green Arrow," Bob Fujitani. © National Periodical Publications.

first 14 issues of *Leading* (Winter 1942 to Spring 1945) as a member of the ill-fated *Seven Soldiers of Victory* strip, a poor imitation of the *Justice Society*.

After his series in *Adventure* expired, Green Arrow did not have a regular feature, and his only appearances came as a member of the Justice League. The character was finally handed to artist Neal Adams who totally revamped him in the September 1969 issue of *The Brave and the Bold* (number 85). Stripping Oliver Quinn of his wealth, he gave the character a beard and a vicious, self-righteous disposition. He became the outspoken and impatient champion of the oppressed. When the *Green Lantern* strip was nearing extinction in 1970, editor Schwartz allowed writer Denny O'Neil and artist Adams to team up the two heroes in the now classic *Green Lantern/Green Arrow series*.

Given outstanding art and story for the first time, the character became a tireless—though often erratic, pompous, and ignorant—hero of the downtrodden. His bursts of self-righteous indignation became classic. Two highly acclaimed issues cast Speedy as a junkie, and both Green Arrow and Speedy's reactions became comic history. Unfortunately, due to flagging sales and artistic conflicts, the *Green Lantern/Green Arrow* book was discontinued after May 1972's 89th issue.

J.B.

In the 1980s DC starred Green Arrow in two miniseries: the first one, in 1983, was unsuccessful. The second one, however, *Green Arrow: The Longbow Hunters* (1987), scripted by Mike Grell, clicked with readers and led to an ongoing comic book series, starting in February 1988. Grell wrote the continuities for the first 80 issues and also did some of the artwork. Other artists of note on the revived title have included Denys Cowan and Frank Springer.

M.H.

GREENE, VERNON VAN ATTA (1908-1965) American artist born September 12, 1908 in Battle Ground, Washington. Vernon Greene grew up in Battle Ground, and attended the University of Toledo. He studied art with Dong Kingman and Henry G. Keller. His first work in cartooning was for the Port-

land, Oregon *Telegram* doing sports cartoons from 1927 to 1929; he also drew sports cartoons for the *Toledo Blade*, (1930 to 1932) and the *New York Mirror* (1934-1936).

Green drew editorial cartoons for Hearst's Central Press from 1932 to 1942, for the *New York Mirror* (1935 to 1937) and for the *Portland Oregonian* (1945 to 1950).

Greene broke into the pulp and comic book field in 1940, illustrating the *Shadow* and *Masked Lady* for Street and Smith; *Perry Mason* for McKay in 1946; various titles for Western in the 1940s and 1950s; and a good deal of freelance work from 1938 to 1954.

The versatile Green—he worked, at different times in his career, in every branch of cartooning except animation—from 1935 onward illustrated children's books, magazine stories, medical articles, and advertising comics, including Dentyne, Chiclets, Woolworth's, etc.

In the Air Force in World War II, he graduated from medical photography to cartooning; two service-related features were *Charlie Conscript* for *Pic Magazine*, 1941 to 1944, and *Mac the Med*, a comic strip. His first work in comic strips consisted of a few ghost panels for *Bringing Up Father* in 1935, six masterful years ghosting *Polly and Her Pals* (1935 to 1940), the *Shadow* from 1938 to 1942 for the Ledger Syndicate, and *Bible Bee*, a panel for the Register and Tribune Syndicate from 1946 to 1954.

Upon the death of George McManus in 1954, Greene was engaged by King Features to pick up *Bringing Up Father* when negotiations with McManus' assistant Zeke Zekely fell through. He continued with Jiggs and Maggie until his death in 1965.

Vern Greene was one of the warmest and friendliest men in the cartooning profession. His services to the NCS, other groups, and his young fans were remarkable. He did a creditable job with Jiggs, very conscious of McManus' style and conventions. He was an officer in the National Cartoonists Society, organized major comic strip exhibits in 1942 and at the 1964 World's Fair and won the prestigious Silver T-Square from the NCS in 1964. He was the host of the syndicated radio show, "The Cartoonist's Art," during which he proved to be a knowledgeable, sympathetic, and polished interviewer.

Greene adapted well to any genre he tackled; certainly the style of Sterrett's *Polly* and the *Shadow* were at the opposite ends of the artistic pole, but he handled both splendidly and simultaneously. The ever-active Greene seemed always engaged in half a dozen projects; in his last years he was drawing, attending to NCS duties, doing USO shows, hosting his radio program, and earning a degree in philosophy from Columbia University. He was a talented and unselfish lover of his profession and is sorely missed.

R.M.

GREEN HORNET (U.S.) 1—Like many radio heroes, pulp stars, and other media heavies, The Green Hornet's career in comic books was spotty and unimpressive. Shortly after the character made the successful transition from radio star to serial star—there were two Universal Green Hornet serials in 1940, both utilizing Keye Luke in the role of Kato—Holyoke introduced the first issue of *Green Hornet* in December, 1940. Like previous versions, the green avenger was really newspaper publisher Britt Reid who fought crime outside the law with the aid of his gas gun and his limousine, The

Black Beauty. Naturally, he was assisted by his Japanese assistant, Kato. When WWII erupted, Kato was hastily transformed into a Filipino, and his original Japanese heritage was never mentioned again. The stories in the comic version were hackneyed and pedestrian, saved only by the then-unique gimmick that the Green Hornet was wanted by the police because they frowned on his extra-legal crime fighting. Most of the stories were drawn by Irwin Hasen and Irv Novick, but the book died after August 1941's sixth issue.

2—The following year, Harvey (Family) comics began publishing the *Green Hornet* comic book beginning with the seventh issue (dated June 1942). The character was somewhat more successful here, however, and managed to survive until September, 1949's 47th issue. The writing continued in a facile vein, but the feature did have artwork by Art Cazeneuve (1942), Al Avison (1947), and Jerry Robinson (1946). The strip also appeared in two issues of Harvey's *All New* comics in 1946 and 1947.

3—Dell Publications issued a one-shot *Green Hornet* strip in 1953 as issue number 496 of their *Color* series.

4—When The Green Hornet made its move to television in 1966, Gold Key put out three issues of *Green Hornet* from November 1966 to August 1967.

J.B.

5—The character was revived once more by Now Comics. This was a politically correct version, in which Kato shared equal credit with his boss (he even briefly enjoyed his own comic book, *Kato of the Green Hornet*). Started in November 1989, *The Green Hornet* lasted until December 1994.

M.H.

GREEN LANTERN (U.S.) *Green Lantern* was created by artist Martin Nodell and writer Bill Finger and made its first appearance in National's *All American* number 16 for July 1940. Sporting a loud black, red, green, purple, brown, and yellow uniform, Alan Scott became Green Lantern by charging a "power ring" which gave him almost omnipotent qualities. Most *Green Lantern* stories were lighthearted, often concentrating on Doiby Dickles, an overweight, Brooklyn-born, tough cabbie. The more serious stories became predictable, however, because writers continually used the power ring's inefficiency against wood as the central theme of an adventure.

Like *Flash, Green Lantern* had a horde of interesting villains, the best being the Harlequin. Alan Scott's secretary in real-life, the Harlequin wore an equally outrageous costume and frequently fought the Green Lantern. She eventually became a government agent.

Artistically, *Green Lantern* wasn't particularly noteworthy. Literally dozens of artists, including Carmine Infantino (1948), Joe Kubert (1948), and Irwin Hazen (1941-1948), handled the strip in a relatively pedestrian manner. The character's best illustrator, Alex Toth, handled stories between 1947 and 1949 and was inventive with both layouts and pacing. Alfred Bester, a renowned and award-winning science fiction author, scripted stories between 1943 and 1945, aiding National staffers like John Broome and Bob Kanigher.

In all, *Green Lantern* appeared in *All-American* through October 1948's 102nd issue. A member of the legendary Justice Society of America, the character appeared in 48 stories in *All-Star Comics* between fall 1940 and March 1951. *Green Lantern* also appeared in *Comic Cavalcade* from winter 1943's number one through November 1948's number 29 and 38 issues of its own magazine from fall 1941 through June 1949.

When National made a general revival of superhero characters in the 1960s, Green Lantern was revived as a member of the Justice Society. Several months after National revived *The Flash*, they opted to revive *Green Lantern*, in October 1959, under the direction of editor Julius Schwartz, writer Gardner Fox, and artist Gil Kane. Introduced in *Showcase* number 22, this Green Lantern was test pilot Hal Jordan who had assumed the Green Lantern mantle from a dying, red-skinned alien. His powers, including the almost invincible power ring, were the same as the 1940 version, except that his ring was inoperative against yellow. This latest Green Lantern wore a more conservative green and black jumpsuit, which underwent only a modest change over the years. The feature was given its own book in August 1960.

Gardner Fox made the feature an amazing sample of scientific fantasy. This Green Lantern was cast as only one of hundreds, all from different planets, and all under the guidance of the blue-skinned Guardians of the Universe. Tomar Re, an orange, bird-faced Green Lantern, was the most often used alien, and the two Lanterns shared several interesting adventures. Fox also created a series of Green Lantern-in-the-future stories where the character became the leader of 58th century Earth, and a fascinating world-within-a-power-ring series. Along with these interesting, if far-fetched concepts, Fox also had strong supporting characters: Pieface, an Eskimo mechanic and Green Lantern's sidekick; and Carol Ferris. Hal Jordan loved her, but she loved Green Lantern, and the relationship developed into a Superman-Clark Kent-Lois Lane triangle. To complicate matters, she was Hal Jordan's boss and was often hypnotized into becoming Star Saffire, one of the character's toughest opponents. Sinestro, a fallen Green Lantern with red skin and a yellow power ring, was Green Lantern's most dangerous enemy and appeared often.

Artist Kane quickly made the strip into one of the best drawn in the 1960s. His style lent itself favorably to Fox's fast-paced material, and his work was always flawlessly rendered. Kane garnered a great deal of respect from *Green Lantern*, and it opened many new avenues for his unique abilities. He eventually became one of the most inventive and outspoken creators in the comic medium.

Green Lantern took a sharp downturn around the 50th issue—mainly due to the demise of the romantic menage-a-trois and Fox's and Kane's increasing boredom with the feature—and began a headlong artistic and financial decline.

Just before its cancellation, the feature was handed to artist Neal Adams and writer Denny O'Neil. What evolved is the already legendary Green Lantern/Green Arrow series. Starting in April 1970's 76th issue, the two superheroes made comic book's first significant excursion through the real world. Handling topics like racism, politics, religion, cultism, and contemporary social problems—including two highly publicized drug abuse stories—O'Neil and Adams and editor Schwartz revamped comic history. These dozen team-up issues are already collector's editions. Unfortunately, *Green Lantern* ended after the 89th issue (May 1972) amidst universal praise, discouraging

357

Green Lantern. © DC Comics.

sales, and increasingly antagonistic relationships between the creative trio.

A member of the Justice League of America, Green Lantern has appeared in the group's book since its inception. He was recently returned to his 1960s science-fiction bent, and now appears as a strictly adventure-oriented character in *Flash*.

J.B.

DC brought back the title with issue number 90 (August-September 1976), picking up where it had left off four years earlier. Mike Grell's gritty writing and graceful artwork ensured the success of the revived series. After Grell's departure a number of talented artists worked on the feature, including George Perez, Gil Kane, and George Tuska; the writing, however, was not on par with the drawing, and after turning into *The Green Lantern Corps*, the series was cancelled in 1986. A fourth series began in 1990 and is ongoing.

M.H.

GREG *see* Régnier, Michel.

GRIFFITH, BILL (1944-   ) American cartoonist Bill Griffith was born in Brooklyn, New York, on January 20, 1944. He attended the Pratt Institute of Technology in New York in the hopes of becoming a fine artist. He turned to cartooning in 1967, and in 1970 moved to San Francisco, which was then the Mecca of underground artists. There he contributed to a number of "comix" publications, including *Yellow Dog, Real Pulp,* and *Yow.*

"My first character," Griffith told an interviewer, "was Mr. ('The') Toad, a rather mean-spirited amphibian dressed in a tight-fitting tweed suit." Mr. Toad was a tough customer, always spoiling for a fight with neighbors, coworkers, and the world at large. Among his hangers-on were the Toadettes, a bad-girl trio of singing (or croaking) batrachians. The artist's first hit came with *Young Lust*, a hilarious parody of 1950s romance comics, in which his fondness for bringing real-life figures into his plots initially surfaced. In its pages he created the modern couple of Randy and Cherisse who were patrons of shopping malls and after-hours bars, and spend a great deal of time in therapy.

Zippy the Pinhead, Griffith's most famous character, was created almost as an afterthought, in a story characteristically titled "I Gave My Heart to a Pinhead and He Made a Fool Out of Me." Originally known as Danny, the character evolved into his Zippy persona in 1971 as a sidekick to Mr. Toad. Dressed in a polka-dot clown suit, wearing an idiotic grin, and uttering his famous catchphrase, "Are we having fun yet?", he soon gained a loyal following among college students

and amateurs of the bizarre. In the early 1980s, King Features started syndicating a daily and Sunday *Zippy* comic strip to a small but growing list of newspapers. While considerably toning down his creation for general consumption, Griffith still indulges his penchant for raucous humor and biting satire, best evidenced in his devastating attacks on our media-saturated and celebrity-obsessed society.

Zippy has been reprinted in numerous anthologies and has been the subject of serious analysis in *People* magazine, the *New York Times*, and the *San Francisco Examiner*, among other publications. Asked to comment on his creation's popularity, Griffith replied, "Possibly, Zippy provides a kind of release valve for all the pressure, all the information we're bombarded with every hour of the day." As the tempo of modern life accelerates, Zippy's brand of wise foolishness appears more timely than ever.

GRINGO (Spain) A Western created in 1963 by Carlos Giménez, *Gringo* was the literary brainchild of scriptwriter Manuel Medina, although a few episodes were authored by Miguel Gonzalez Casquel and Carlos Echeverria.

Under the nickname of Gringo, Syd Viking is a young, fair-haired American who devotes his life to the defense of oppressed people, whether Mexican or Indian. A foreman on the ranch where he has lived most of his years, he turned the pejorative-appellation of "gringo" from a term of contempt into a synonym of justice and chivalry. A man with a nervous trigger-finger, but never one to shoot first, he has become a homeless wanderer since taking up the cause of justice. He is a misogynist, and women have only played minor roles in his adventures, while Conchita, his original girlfriend, did not come back later. In turn, Gringo can on occasion be seen in the company of a pig-headed and ridiculous young girl with whom he sings *rancheras* accompanying himself on the banjo.

The seeds of Giménez's later graphic excellence can already be found in *Gringo*, such as his love for whimsical compositions, his taste for twisted trees and branches, and his frequent touches of humor. His work was later continued by Domingo Alvarez Gomez, and

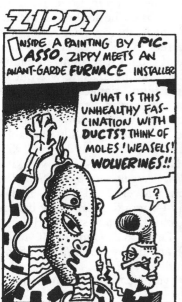

Bill Griffith, "Zippy." © Bill Griffith.

by "Suso" (pseudonym of Jesus Pena Rego) who has been the cartoonist best able to understand and follow the trail blazed by Giménez. Like many comics of the Franco era, *Gringo* was terminated in the 1980s, but it lives on in countless reprints.

L.G.

GROSS, MILTON (1895-1953) Milton (Milt) Gross, born above the Bronx pushcarts in New York City in 1895, was one of the best things to ever happen to the comic strip. He began drawing in the sixth grade at the age of 12 (while attending classes with a kid who grew up to be Dutch Schultz, the gangster famed for his Joycean deathbed babble). He did little but draw throughout his single year of high school in Kearney, New Jersey, from which he fled to get his first job—a position that gave him more time to cartoon than school did. After about 16 other menial jobs, he took his first newspaper stint as copy boy on the *New York American* while still in his teens. Here the editors paid attention to his cartooning ability, and by the time he was 20, Milt was not only assisting the famed Tad Dorgan as sports cartoonist for the *American's* companion afternoon paper, the *New York Journal*, but was also turning out his first comic strip (in May 1915): a sports-page feature about a sporting fanatic named George Phan called *Phool Phan Phables* (initially spelled with "F's"). This was followed by other brief strips and features, such as *Izzy Human* (1915), *Amateur Night* (1915), *Kinney B. Alive* (1916), *Sportograms* (1916), and *And Then The Fun Began* (1916). In early 1917, Gross quit Hearst to try animation work at New York's Bray Studios, and from there enlisted and served with the U.S. Seventh Division in France in 1918. After his return, he worked for Hearst again, doing a short-lived daily continuity strip called *Frenchy*, then took a better-paying job with the *New York World*, where he did such occasional strips and panels as *Banana Oil* and *Help Wanted* in the early 1920s, but made his big hit with a weekly column of prose and cartoons called *Gross Exaggerations*.

It was in this column that Milt first introduced the Yiddish-dialect humor, distilled from the accents of first-generation Jewish immigrants, which made his initial fame. A book collection of 1926 based on some of these columns, *Nize Baby*, was a best-seller. In the same year, Gross and the *World* decided he was ready for a sustained Sunday page effort, and *Nize Baby* was launched across the country on January 7, 1927. Gross' *Banana Oil* gag strip ran in an untitled single row of panels across the top of the *Nize Baby* Sunday page.

More books appeared in short order from Gross' facile pen: *Hiawatta Witt No Odder Poems* in 1926, *De Night In De Front From Chreesmas* (1927), *Dunt Esk* (1927), *Famous Fimmales Witt Odder Ewents From Heestory* (1928), and, above all, his superb parody of woodcut narratives in pictures masterfully undertaken in a 1930 volume titled *He Done Her Wrong* (Dell paperback reprint, 1971).

Gross, like his brother cartoonist Rube Goldberg, was rarely content with one idea or set of characters for long: on February 17, 1929, he replaced *Nize Baby* with a new Sunday page, *Count Screwloose of Tooloose*, but continued the *Banana Oil* strip until he was hired away from the *World* by Hearst in 1931; continuing *Count Screwloose* for the Hearst papers, but replacing *Banana Oil* with a quarter-page top strip, *Babbling Brooks*. By June 1931, *Babbling Brooks* was gone,

replaced by *Count Screwloose* at the top of the Sunday page, while Gross introduced a new feature in the primary space: *Dave's Delicatessen*, which also appeared daily. In June 1934, Gross usurped the *Count Screwloose* Sunday space for a pair of penguins named *Otto and Blotto*, while Screwloose dropped down to join Dave in the main Sunday strip. In January 1935, the penguins were replaced by *That's My Pop!* while *Dave's Delicatessen* was retitled *Count Screwloose*, with Dave and the Count featured together. In mid-1935, *That's My Pop!* became the primary feature, and in 1936, the two Sunday strips were altered in format to a half-page each, and ran in this form until the late 1940s, with ghost Bob Dunn taking over much of the work from Gross.

In the meantime, Gross himself continued with his books, with film scripting in Hollywood, with a new prose column and art for the *New York Mirror* called *Grossly Exaggerated* (which also ran as *Grossly Xaggerated*), another feature titled *Joe Runt*, and ultimately a daily news cartoon—all in the first half of the 1930s. *Pasha the Persian* (1936), *What's This?* (1936), and other books appeared, while Gross supervised a radio show based on *That's My Pop!* in the early 1940s. Also in the 1940s, Gross—by now a nationally acclaimed personality, famed magazine writer, scriptwriter, radio show guest, master of ceremonies, etc.—authored a new illustrated prose narrative feature for the Hearst papers called *Dear Dollink*, which appeared in book form in 1944. All this activity took its toll, unfortunately, and in 1945, Gross suffered a heart attack, after which he was forced to cut down his workload. Another, last book appeared: *I Shoulda Ate the Eclair* (1946), about a family named the Figgits, together with a short-lived cartoon feature for a curious comic book of 1946 called *Picture News*. Milt Gross did little of public note after that, and he died suddenly of a second heart attack at 58 while he was returning from a Hawaiian vacation aboard the liner *Lurline* on November 28, 1953.

B.B.

GUARDINEER, FREDERIC (1913-) American comic book artist and writer born October 3, 1913, in Albany, New York. After acquiring his fine arts degree from Syracuse University in 1935, Guardineer came to New York and drew for several pulp magazines before joining the Harry "A" Chesler Shop in 1936. There he drew adventure features for the Chesler books, including *Lobo* and *Dan Hastings,* before beginning his freelance comic book career in 1938. Over the years, Guardineer became one of the most recognized names in the fledgling comic book business, as he was one of the few artists who consistently signed his work. His appealing and unique art style was also easily recognizable and the artist's ability to turn out great amounts of work made his material readily available.

After a stint with Centaur between 1937 and 1939, Guardineer moved to National (1937-1940, working mainly on the *Zatara, Pep Morgan,* and *Speed Saunders* strips and covers), then Marvel (1941), New Friday (1941), Quality (1941-1944, working primarily on the *Tor, Merlin, Quicksilver,* and *Marksman* strips), Hillman (1946-1947), Eastern, Pines, Gleason (1946-1953, mostly on crime stories), and finally Me (1952-1955, on *Durango Kid*) before retiring at 42.

Of all his work, however, Guardineer's three magical strips made him most important to comic book history. While they were all heavily reliant on the *Mandrake* formula developed in the newspaper strips by Falk and Davis, they were all original in their own right. Consistently, *Zatara*, Guardineer's magical character for National, and *Merlin* and *Tor*, his Quality features, all spoke their mystical spells backwards. Even the simplest of tasks required the reversing of English, a gimmick which made the Guardineer strips fun to read.

About his art, much has been said in several comic art histories, but little of it is clear. Unlike many of his "golden" age contemporaries, Guardineer never illustrated with flashy design or spectacular drawings. His material was always presented in as straightforward a manner as possible. Drawings and narration were simple, backgrounds and foregrounds were divided by sharp contrasting uses of colors, and his anatomy was not realistic. On the other hand, all the individual panels in the artist's work, although they were drawn with an extremely heavy line and a self-styled technique, were the scenes one could have portrayed with a photograph. If nothing else, Guardineer was literal; he drew what the caption and dialogue called for. His characters may have been uniformly rounded and designed, but they followed the script explicitly. Many of his followers attempted to copy Guardineer's literal style, but his work always excelled beyond any imitators.

Guardineer left the comic book industry in 1955 to work as a government employee, but continued to draw for many publications generating from around his Long Island home.

J.B.

GUERILLEROS, LES (Belgium) Created in 1968 by Spanish cartoonist Jesus Blasco, *Les Guerilleros* ("the Guerilla-fighters") was produced for publication in the Belgian comic magazine *Spirou*. The initial idea came from the scriptwriter, illustrator, and movie director, José Larraz, who also wrote one of the episodes (others were written by Miguel Gusso and Blasco himself). In this work, Blasco tried to elaborate on a theme that was dear to him. His very personal vision of the American West had already inspired him to do one of his masterworks: *En los Dominios de los Sioux* ("In the Domains of the Sioux"), as well as a number of striking watercolors. The protagonists are: the American, younger than his companions and endowed with all the virtues found in Blasco's heroes, from Ta' Tanka to Wild Batson and Smiley O'Hara; Yuma the second guerillero, an Apache Indian integrated into the little group; and the colorful character of Pedro de Guzman. The latter (much beloved by the readers) is a coarse, shabby, cheating, gambling, and thieving little man; his major defect also turns out to be his greatest virtue: he is an inveterate liar. His lying, while often landing him and his friends in trouble, also just as often gets them out of delicate situations. Pedro adds a touch of humor and common humanity to the strip, in contrast to the earnestness of Yuma and the chivalry of Ray, both of whom are afflicted with all the virtues of conventional heroes.

L.G.

GUERRE À LA TERRE (France) The second science-fiction strip to appear after the end of World War II, *Guerre à la Terre* ("War to Earth") debuted in issue number 10 of the comic magazine *Coq Hardi* (April 1946); the illustrations were by Pierre Liquois and the

continuity was supplied by the magazine's inexhaustible editor, Marijac.

The starting point of the series is as old as H. G. Wells's *War of the Worlds*: the inhabitants of the planet Mars, after having subjugated the other peoples of the solar system, plot to invade and conquer Earth. They find a willing Fifth Column in the Japanese, still seething with dreams of revenge (World War II was not far away), and start on their plan of conquest. In their strange, spherical spaceships they take over Siberia, then move on to Europe, before being crushed by the forces of the United Nations and their ace special agent, the Frenchman, Veyrac.

Moving at such a fast pace, the story left the readers breathless. There was no time for characterization, but the images were genuinely gripping (such as the Martian warships landing in the serene landscapes of Southern France, or the UN defenders checking the Martian advance along the tracks of the Paris subway). Of course, *Guerre à la Terre* ended in victory for the people of Earth (in July 1947).

In November 1947 a sequel was tacked on. This second round of the duel between Mars-Earth, no longer illustrated by Liquois, was taken over by Marijac's protégé, Duteurtre, a capable cartoonist who lacked in brilliance. *Guerre à la Terre* ended finally in July 1948.

Seemingly naïve by today's standards, *Guerre à la Terre* was a worthwhile series, strongly plotted and well written; had Marijac not changed illustrators in midstream, it would probably have gone on to a longer run than it enjoyed.

M.H.

GUERRERO DEL ANTIFAZ, EL (Spain) The most popular Spanish adventure strip of the postwar period was typical of a time when there was only scant competition from other mass media: radio had not yet conquered the imaginations of young people with *Diego Valor,* television did not exist, while, on the other hand, a publication like *El Guerrero del Antifaz* ("The Warrior with the Mask") offered, at a small cost, adventures galore to be continued each and every week. The feature debuted in October 1944; when it was finally discontinued in 1966, the *Guerrero* weekly comic book had reached number 668. Text and illustrations were the work of Manuel Gago, who achieved success with the feature.

The Masked Warrior was a noble son of the Count of Roca, whose adventures took place in the Spain of the Catholic Kings, before the conquest of Granada. The ferocious Ali Khan, who was later the Warrior's most deadly enemy, had abducted his pregnant mother and kept her in his harem. The child was born there, believing he was the son of the abductor; when he learned the truth he fled the palace, wearing a mask so as not be be recognized. He then devoted his life to fighting Ali Khan and his assassins, and later found a family and had a son.

If one was to define the author's style in one word, it would be action. Each page was filled with roaring fights and drawn sabers, the narrative unfolding its multiple plots and counterplots without a break. Gago was later succeeded by Matias Alonso (as illustrator) and Pedro Quesada and Vicente Tortajada (as scriptwriters), but his was the definitive version of the strip.

The value of the formula devised by Gago proved once again irresistible, when a new edition of the Warrior's adventures—this time in color—started success-

"El Guerrero del Antifaz," Manuel Gago. © Editorial Valenciana.

ful publication in 1974. The series ended with its creator's death in 1980.

L.G.

GUMPS, THE (U.S.) Sidney Smith's *The Gumps* (which first appeared daily on February 12, 1917, and Sunday on June 29, 1919, on both occasions only in the *Chicago Tribune*) was certainly the most famed and widely read comic strip of the 1920s, and its author was the F. Scott Fitzgerald of the newspaper reader. Like Fitzgerald, Smith mirrored the ambitions and appetites of his readers, accepting them himself as natural and rational elements of life; and like Fitzgerald, he died when the halcyon time he loved was over, from excessive indulgence in the good things of that lost age.

Yet *The Gumps* was intended only to chronicle the doings of a typical lower middle class family in Chicago when *Tribune* publisher Joe Patterson assigned the strip art and story to Sidney Smith in 1917, at a time when the *Tribune* was publishing no regular daily comic strip. The first episode, in which the Gump menage was introduced, portrayed Andrew (Andy) Gump (then with a round, stubby nose and a general James Finlayson appearance) as paterfamilias with cane and derby; Minerva (Min) Gump as "family brains" and an obviously dedicated housewife with purse and umbrella; Chester Gump, their son, about seven, with hoop and stick, described as a hellion; and two family pets: a cat named Hope, and a dog named Buck. Mentioned in a box on the main panel is the data that "the Gumps have a daughter in college and a son in the navy."

A good part of that information was probably Patterson's idea, to make the Gumps patently average and typical. Smith, however, was concerned almost entirely with the principal family trio: Andy, Min, and

Chester: the dog and cat were seldom seen in the following months, and then disappeared completely; the grown son and daughter were never mentioned again. Moreover, Smith was fascinated with money and cars, and communicated these desires to his characters early in the strip, giving Andy and Min the hopes of riches through the grace of an Australian billionaire relative, Uncle Bim Gump.

Aside from his compelling subject matter of imminent riches, Smith possessed a remarkable storytelling ability, with a love for the soap-opera frills of melodrama which the public, then as now, adored. With the gifted wit of Chicago jeweler Sol Hess to aid him with dialogue for a time, and the graphic skill and imagination of Stanley Link at the helm in the Sunday page continuity (which sent Chester Gump into one exotic adventure after another) through the early 1930s, Smith managed an unbeatable team for the time, and fielded what was certainly the most attractive strip in existence for the general reader.

Smith was not, oddly enough, a great creator of characters (aside from his central figure, Andy Gump himself). His comic and melodramatic actors, such as the Widow Zander, Mama De Stross and her daughter Millie, Carlos, Old-Timer, etc., etc., were superbly adequate for the parts they played in the Gump epic, but did not loom as fascinating and memorable figures in themselves. Uncle Benjamin (Bim) Gump is probably the strip's most sizable character after Andy, but he is only a richer physical and psychological duplicate of Andy himself. (Ching Chow, a Chinese adventurer, who achieved some popularity beyond *The Gumps* itself, was a Sunday strip creation who never took part in the principal daily narrative.)

Smith's Gump figures were everywhere: on lamp shades, penny banks, playing cards, games, curtain material, dolls of all sizes, mechanical toys: the list is almost endless. Screen comedies and animated films were made of the characters, while reprint comic books of *The Gumps* were large sellers (Smith even wrote and illustrated an autobiography of his hero, in *Andy Gump: His Life Story*, Reilly & Lee, 1924).

Some of the steam went out of the public identification with *The Gumps* as the Great Depression of the early 1930s deepened, but readers were still fascinated with the dramatic complications of the daily strip, and the Sunday page continued on the front pages of hundreds of comic sections. Then, abruptly in 1935, it all ended with the automobile crash which killed Sidney Smith after he had just signed the biggest contract of his life for the continuation of *The Gumps*. The syndicate panicked; after desperately trying to find someone (Link, Rube Goldberg, etc.) to continue the strip at its Smith level of humor and invention, they finally settled on a man who proved to be one of the worst choices possible: Gus Edson. Edson's strip became dull and predictable, and after coasting a number of years on the afterglow of Smith's stunning work, it was folded in 1959, with a bare dozen newspapers in its roster.

In 1974, Scribner's published a collection of Sidney Smith's *The Gumps*.

B.B.

GUNNIS, LOUIS (1864-1940) Louis Gunnis, who began his art career as a painter and illustrator, became one of the first comic artists in England to work in the picture story field, later known as adventure strips, although his work was limited to the more straightfor-

"The Gumps," Sidney Smith. © The Tribune Company.

ward serials published in the "Nursery School" comics, such as *Tiger Tim's Weekly* and *My Favorite Comic*.

Gunnis was born in Windsor in 1864 of a professional family. His father was Musician-in-Ordinary to Queen Victoria, and his grandfather was a musician in the Royal Marines Band. At age fifteen Gunnis was apprenticed to an engraver. He continued his art studies at Lambeth Art College where, in 1888, he won the Cressy Prize for his painting, 'Tilting at the Ring.' He exhibited his paintings at the Royal Academy from 1887 to 1897, while contributing black-and-white and color illustrations to monthly magazines including the famous *Strand*. His illustrations for the series, *How the Other Half Lives* for the *English Illustrated Magazine* were donated to the Victoria and Albert Museum, where they were exhibited.

When his wife died in 1905, leaving him with three young daughters, Gunnis decided to concentrate on more commercial illustration work for the popular but cheaper magazines. He had already contributed the occasional cartoon to the adult comic weekly, *Scraps*, and the publisher Edward Hulton hired him as a staff artist for his magazine chain.

In 1914, Gunnis joined the staff of the Amalgamated Press and developed the idea of picture stories in weekly episodes, and in 1920 his earliest-traced story appeared in *Tiger Tim's Weekly*. It followed the adventures of a young boy, *Bobby Dare*, and was followed by

The Baby and *Poor Peggy* in 1921, and a serial for *Bubbles* comic in 1922, *The Adventures of Matt. Our Bobbie* began in *Tiger Tim's* in 1924, followed by the more adventurous *School on the Island* (1925), *Mystery Wood* in *Puck* (1927), and *Little Jim from Nowhere* (1929). He moved to the new weekly, *My Favourite Comic*, in 1929 with *The Ivory Elephant*. Then came *Uncle Jonathan's Will* (1930), *Poor Little Lone Girl* (1932), *Children of the Mayflower* (1933), and *Chums of the Circus* (1934).

When *My Favourite Comic* folded, so did much of Gunnis' regular work, now considered old-fashioned by younger editors. He returned to painting, and his oversized painting of the 1937 Coronation was accepted by the Royal Academy. Disappointingly, the picture was too large for exhibition. He died, it is said, brush in hand as a bomb from a German airplane scored a direct hit on his house in August 1940.

D.G.

GURNEY, ALEXANDER GEORGE (1902-1955)

Born at Portsmouth (England) in 1902, Alex Gurney was the son of a Naval Petty Officer, who died when Gurney was 5 months old. His Australian mother brought the boy back to Hobart, Tasmania. Completing his education at Macquarie Street State School at the age of 13, he worked for a short period as an ironmonger. He then joined the Hydro Electric Commission and served a seven-year apprenticeship as an electrician. During this period he commenced art training by attending night classes at the Hobart Technical School and started selling cartoons to the *Tasmanian Mail, Melbourne Punch, The Bulletin,* and *Smith's Weekly.*

In 1926, he published a book, *Tasmanians Today,* comprised of caricatures of notables. This brought Gurney to the attention of mainland newspapers, and he was given a position with the *Melbourne Morning Post.* When this paper disappeared down the maw of the *Herald,* Gurney went to Sydney. Here he freelanced for *The Bulletin* and developed Australia's first strip based on actual personalities. The strip, *Stiffy & Mo,* was based on the exploits of the well-known vaudeville team of the same name, created by Nat Phillips (*Stiffy*) and Roy Rene (*Mo*), and appeared in *Beckett's Budget* in 1927. During 1928-29 he worked for the *Sunday Times,* and in 1931 he joined first *The Guardian* and then the short-lived Labour paper, *The World.* When that paper folded in 1932, he went to the *Adelaide News* and in 1933 found a permanent position with the *Melbourne Herald* as a sporting cartoonist.

In October 1933 Alex Gurney was asked to design a daily strip based on the *Gunn's Gully* letters written by C. J. Dennis. These letters presented a countryman's humorous views, particularly on city life. Gurney created *Ben Bowyang* (called *Gunn's Gully* in some States), which later passed on to such artists as Mick Armstrong, Keith Martin, and the very competent Alex McRae. That same year, Sam Wells elected to go to England, and Gurney took his place as leader page cartoonist.

On Wells' return, in 1940, Gurney set about creating his delightful humor strip about army life, *Bluey and Curley.* The strip, which was to make Gurney famous, first appeared in the magazine, *Picture News,* and then transferred to the Melbourne *Sun* as a daily. To get an authentic view of army life and humor, Gurney visited many army camps all over Australia and, in 1944, took his sketchbook to Port Moresby, Ramu Valley, Lae, and other points in New Guinea where Australian troops were fighting. A legacy of this visit was a bout of malaria in August 1944, resulting in *Bluey and Curley* being published only 3 times per week, until Gurney returned from the hospital.

His outstanding sense of humor was backed-up by very detailed panels, which contained a great variety of angles and well-balanced figures. Acknowledged as one of Australia's finest cartoonists, his particular strength was his ability to capture the flavor of the Australian character, as seen by the Australian. Alex Gurney died of a heart attack on December 4, 1955.

J.R.

GUSTAFSON, PAUL (1916-1977) American comic book artist born in Aland, Finland on August 16, 1916. He moved with his family to America in 1921, and "Gustavson" eventually studied surveying and engineering at New York City's Cooper Union. Using the pen-name "Paul Earrol" as well as his own, he joined the Harry "A" Chesler and Funnies, Inc. comic shops in the late 1930s and proceeded to unleash a torrent of comic strips. Always a clean and meticulous worker, Gustavson rarely attempted to stylize his work. It was straightforward and fast-paced, certainly competent, and never too frilly or gimmicky. His forte was volume. At the comic shops, he produced material for several companies. For Centaur he drew or helped create superheroes like *The Arrow* (1938-1941), *Black Panther* (1941), and *A-Man*; he created and drew *The Angel* for Timely in 1939, and it was probably the only superhero strip to feature a mustache-wearing hero; and he helped create Novelty Press' Twister character in 1941.

But Gustavson produced his best material as a member of Busy Arnold's Quality comics stable. Working side-by-side with the likes of Lou Fine, Jack Cole, Reed Crandall, and other greats, Gustavson drew *Quicksilver* (1941-1942), *Magno* (1941), *The Human Bomb* (1941-1946), and *Midnight* (1942-1946), all superheroes of one sort or another. *The Jester,* a strip he invented in 1941, probably contains his best work.

Gustavson spent most of 1942-1945 in the Air Force, but returned to Quality after his discharge. After the war, however, Gustavson began concentrating on Quality's ever-expanding humor line, especially *Will Bragg,* a well-drawn feature about a perenially poverty-stricken braggart. He remained with Quality until owner Arnold sold the company to National in 1956. After a short stay at the ACG group, again drawing humor features, Gustavson left the field entirely to begin a career as a surveyor and engineer. His brother, Nils, also worked in the comic book industry during the 1940s. Paul Gustafson died in 1977 in upstate New York, where he had been working as a surveyor for the state.

J.B.

Alex Gurney, "Bluey and Curley." © The Herald and Weekly Times Ltd.

HAENIGSEN, HARRY (1900-1990?) American cartoonist born 1900 in New York City. After brilliant studies in high school, where he developed a flair for drawing and caricature, Harry Haenigsen was contemplating a career in engineering—he even applied for, and was granted, a scholarship at Rutgers University—but his love for drawing prevailed and in 1918 he joined the Bray animation studio as an assistant. In 1919 Haenigsen enrolled at the Art Students League while supporting himself on a weekly salary of $7 as an art assistant on the *New York World*.

Haenigsen's first comic strip, created for the *World* in 1922, was *Simeon Batts*. It was about the zany doings of a radio buff and the havoc he caused with his attempts at building crystal sets out of kitchen utensils and office furniture. In 1929 Haenigsen developed a cartoon panel commenting on the day's news which the *World* ran until its demise in 1931. Transferring to the *Journal*, Haenigsen revived his panel (which he then called *News and Views*). Along with his career as a cartoonist, Haenigsen pursued a successful occupation as an illustrator, doing numerous drawings for magazines, books, and advertising (his illustrations for *Collier's* won him special notice).

In 1937 Haenigsen left the newspaper field briefly for a short stint as story editor for Max Fleischer Studios. Returning a year later to the comic strip, Haenigsen created *Our Bill* on March 6, 1939, for the Herald-Tribune Syndicate. This was a teenage strip with more energy than charm which ran until 1966. Haenigsen's most memorable creation came a few years later, on June 20, 1943, when he originated *Penny* as a replacement for Charles Voight's *Betty*, which the *Tribune* had just dropped. *Penny* was one of the first bobby-soxer strips. Penelope Mildred Pringle (Penny), her best friend Judy, and the members of the Pringle family were well-characterized, the plots reasonably funny, and the language up to date. But Haenigsen's graphic treatment was too elaborate, and his close-ups, angle shots, and scale distortions were too much of a distraction for what was essentially a simple premise. In 1970 Haenigsen discontinued *Penny* and went into semiretirement. He died at his home in Lambertville, New Jersey, in late 1990 or early 1991.

Harry Haenigsen's undisputed talents never found a satisfactory outlet. His creations, likable though they were, never caught the public's fancy or the critics' eye. Haenigsen will be remembered chiefly for his elegance of line and his understated and warm humor.

M.H.

HÄGAR THE HORRIBLE (U.S.) The creation of Dik Browne, who somehow resembled the title character, *Hägar the Horrible* invaded comic pages in February of 1973 and achieved the most notable success of a new comic in the art form's history: within two years it was carried in more than 600 papers worldwide—a rank near the top among a field of veterans.

Both critically and commercially *Hägar* has been a success. Browne almost instantly achieved a comfortable mix of "bigfoot" art and sophisticated design; slapstick gags and social commentary; broad humor and sympathetic characterizations.

The hero is a plunderer, sacker, and looter by profession, but not very far below the Viking exterior is a softie akin to Jackie Gleason's Ralph Kramden—or even Browne himself. Hägar may invade Gaul, but he takes a Paris shopping list from his wife. In one revealing Sunday page, Hägar tried on crowns on the sly—fantasizing like a little boy.

The family of this ninth-century Viking is cut from a different pattern as well. Wife Helga is more the warrior. Physically she is as ample as Hägar and is more consistently ferocious. Hamlet is the young son who continually embarrasses his parents: he refuses to grow his hair long, go without baths, or lust after conquest—he even reads books and aspires to dentistry! Daughter Honi is a 16-year-old beauty, almost an old maid, who, as a protean women's libber, dreams of accompanying her father on raids. Her major suitor, Lute, is a minstrel as sappy and unkempt as Honi is assertive and pretty.

One of the most inspired characters is Lucky Eddie, Hägar's amazingly chinless sidekick. He has a justifiable persecution complex, bungles the most simple tasks, and provides great slapstick relief in the strip.

Hägar's name was inspired by an incident in Browne's household: his sons Chris and Bob were having an animated debate one afternoon when the elder Browne came bounding down the stairs, lobbying for an atmosphere conducive to napping. "Well, if it isn't Hägar the Horrible," said one of the boys in a wisecrack out of the blue that later named this great comic figure.

"Hägar the Horrible," Dik Browne. © King Features Syndicate.

Dik Browne was named "Cartoonist of the Year" by NCS in 1974 for his work on Hägar. After his death in 1989, his son Chris, who gained a name as an underground comic book artist and also assisted his father on Hägar for many years, took over the strip.

R.M.

HAGIO, MOTO (1949-   ) The second of four children born to a white-collar mine worker in Fukuoka Prefecture, Japan, Moto Hagio began to show artistic talent at a very young age (one drawing assignment she submitted led her first-grade teacher to believe an adult had drawn it for her), and became an avid reader of both literature and comics. In her second year of high school, inspired by Osamu Tezuka's relatively unknown *Shinsengumi* (1963), Hagio decided to become a *manga* ("comic") artist.

In 1969, shortly after graduating from fashion design school, Hagio made her professional debut in *Nakayoshi*, Kodansha Publishing's popular comics magazine for girls, with the short story *Ruru to Mimi* ("Lulu and Mimi"). Lured to Shogakukan Publishing by innovative girls' comics editor Junya Yamamoto, she produced a string of short stories for the magazines *Bessatsu Shōjo Komikku* ("Special Edition Girls' Comic") and *Shūkan Shōjo Komikku* ("Weekly Girls' Comic"), culminating in 1971 with the groundbreaking *Jūichigatsu no gimunajiumu* ("November Gymnasium"), the first girls' comic to feature only boys and the first to overtly suggest same-sex love, thereby giving birth to a genre of girls' comics—stories of love between boys or young men—that remains popular to this day. In 1974, Hagio developed this story into the longer *Tōma no shinzō* ("The Heart of Thomas"), a work widely recognized as a classic of Japanese comics.

Hagio is a prominent member of a loosely defined group of women artists known as the *Hana no nijūyonen gumi* ("Magnificent 24-Year Group") because many were born in the year Showa 24, or 1949. Before these "Forty-niners," *shōjo manga* ("girls' comics") were generally dismissed by male comics fans as sappy melodramas and romances, but this group, which includes Yumiko Ōshima, Keiko Takemiya, and Ryōko Yamagishi, helped create a boom in girls' comics in the 1970s and brought the genre critical attention it had never enjoyed before.

In 1976, Hagio was awarded the Shogakukan Comics Award (Girls) for her science fiction classic *Jūichinin iru!* ("They Were Eleven," 1975), and her epic tale of two adolescent vampires, *Pō no ichizoku* ("The Poe Clan," 1972-76). The two-part *Hagio Moto sakuhinshū* ("Collected Works of Moto Hagio") spans 34 volumes, and since its publication she has produced more than 20 additional volumes, including the four-volume sci-fi masterpiece *Marginal* (1985-87) and her critically acclaimed drama of child sexual abuse, *Zankoku na kami ga shihai suru* ("A Cruel God Reigns," 1992 to present, nine volumes as of this writing).

M.A.T.

HAIRBREADTH HARRY (U.S.) In 1906 C. W. Kahles, already a veteran cartoonist at 28 with over a half-dozen comic strip creations to his credit, produced the feature that was to make him justly famous. Named *Hairbreadth Harry, the Boy Hero* (later simply *Hairbreadth Harry*) it was published as a Sunday half page (and later as a full page) first by the *Philadelphia Press*, then by T. C. McClure, and finally by the Philadelphia Ledger Syndicate.

Harold Hollingsworth (alias "Hairbreadth Harry") was forever outwitting villain Rudolph Rassendale and rescuing Belinda Blinks the beautiful boilermaker from his clutches in this witty cartoon burlesque of dime novels and movie melodramas of the period. In the beginning, Belinda was a head taller than the "boy hero" and although described as "a ravishing creature of dazzling loveliness," Kahles made her look pretty homely in his drawings, which made the whole thing all the funnier. Harry however, kept growing and sometime around 1916, he assumed a normal man's size, when he and Belinda became true sweethearts.

In relentless pursuit was Rudolph, the typical storybook villain, complete with black dress suit, top hat, handlebar mustache, and flashing teeth. He regularly concocted wild plots which Harry foiled no less regularly. Thwarted at every turn, Rudolph would shake his fist, exclaiming: "Curses on you, Harold Hollingsworth!" and vow terrible vengeance—and the triangle chase would resume, as funny and furious as before.

In 1923 the Philadelphia Ledger Syndicate acquired the distribution rights to *Hairbreadth Harry* and immediately asked Kahles to add a daily strip to his Sunday feature. Kahles carried both the *Hairbreadth Harry* daily and Sunday, practically unassisted, until his death in January 1931. The feature then passed to F. O. Alexander, who tried his best to maintain the strip's original flavor while attempting at the same time to accommodate it to the changing tastes of the 1930s, but the readership kept dwindling and *Hairbreadth Harry* was finally discontinued in 1939.

Hairbreadth Harry was the first strip to make systematic use of week-to-week suspense in order to hold the reader's attention, and as such it spawned a multitude of imitators (*Desperate Desmond* is probably the best-known of these). It was very popular in the 1910s and 1920s, and around 1925 six movie comedies were produced by West Brothers Happiness Comedies for Artclass Pictures Corporation in Long Island City. Some of these two-reelers were later released for television. Several attempts were made to revive *Hairbreadth Harry* in the 1940s and 1950s for radio, television, and newspapers, but none of these were very successful.

M.H.

HAKABA NO KITARŌ (Japan) Hakaba no Kitarō ("Kitarō of the Graveyard") was created by Shigeru Mizuki and made its first appearance in a comic book titled *Yurei Ikka* ("The Ghost Family") in 1959. Mizuki did a number of *Kitarō* stories, but the books were not widely circulated. Only in August 1965, when *Hakaba no Kitarō* started appearing in *Shōnen*, the most famous boys' weekly magazine in Japan, did the strip attain popular acceptance.

Kitarō was not a human being but a ghost with a grotesque face. He had use of only his right eye; his left eye, concealed behind a lock of hair, was the dwelling of his ghostly father. Kitarō was friendly to man and wore the traditional *chanchanko*, the Japanese vest, filled with the spirits of his ancestors. Kitarō could disembody his hands and project them on independent missions; he also had antennas concealed in his hair.

The storyline mainly related Kitarō's many battles against a host of monsters: La Seine, a vampire; Hangyojin, the sea monster; Gyūki, half-bull, half-spider monster; Ungaikyō, the mirror monster; as well as

"*Hakaba no Kitarō*," Shigeru Mizuki. © *Shōnen*.

assorted witches, werewolves, and demons. At one time or another, Kitarō took on every monster made famous by literature or film, from Dracula to Frankenstein. In his adventures, he had two assistants: his father and a mischievous and dirty old ghoul called Nezumi-Otoko. Kitarō also held sway over toads, spiders, lizards, and scorpions, and they would join in a song of praise (the *Ge-ge-ge no Uta* or "ge-ge-ge song") at the end of each story.

The prototype of *Hakaba no Kitarō* was *Hakaba Kitarō* (1933-1935, by Masami Ito), a story of horror and revenge. This was one of the most famous *kamishibai,* a kind of picture-show with drawings presented in sequence to the audience.

Kitarō was one of the weirdest Japanese comic strip heroes. His stories are imaginative, fantastic, and tinted with irony.

Hakaba no Kitarō inspired a series of animated TV cartoons before being discontinued in March 1969.

H.K.

HALF-HITCH (U.S.) Hank Ketcham's *Half-Hitch,* distributed by King Features as a daily and Sunday comic, began in early February 1970. It was originally intended to be a panel, but Ketcham disagreed with his own syndicate and went to King with a strip that gave the naval locale a more appropriate showcase. Ketcham designed all the characters and sought out Dick Hodgins, Jr., then an Associated Press staff artist (and later an editorial cartoonist for the *New York News*). Hodgins was engaged for the artwork and Bob Saylor

(no pun), a gagman on *Dennis the Menace,* worked on the story line. The characters, sailors on the aircraft carrier *Clagmire,* formed a little community on what was practically a floating city. In addition, shore leaves took the crew to all parts of the world.

The title character was based on the *Collier's Magazine* panel of the same name (although he was much changed in appearance and was no longer a mime) from Ketcham's gag days. He was, naturally, short; a fairly successful wolf; and was journalist third class on the ship's newspaper. Poopsy, a talking sea gull, was a major character who offered commentary, advice, and gibes to the crew. His speech was in lowercase lettering. Fluke was a country boy, new to big-city and foreign-port ways, but not as dumb as he looked.

Other major characters included: Zawiki, Hitch's big, dumb pal who worked in the sick bay; Flip Feeney, a hip disk jockey on the ship's radio station; Marji, his women's lib companion; gruff and lantern-jawed Capt. Carrick; Ensign Sweet, a prissy and inept foil of Poopsy; wise guy Haw Haw McGraw; the gourmet Chinese chef Ding Chow, who managed to raise exotic foods in every part of the ship; and a bevy of pretty females assigned to the *Clagmire.*

The combination of talent and research made the artwork in *Half-Hitch* something to behold; silhouettes, stylized shading, and panel experimentation made the strip, especially in Sunday format, a handsome piece of work. Unfortunately, the gags scored much less often and the strip, clever in conception and beautiful in visual execution, often lacked the narrative punch that could have lifted it to greater heights. *Half-Hitch* was discontinued in 1975.

R.M.

HAMLIN, VINCENT T. (1900-1993) American cartoonist born 1900 in Perry, Iowa. V. T. Hamlin, like so many other cartoonists, displayed an early flair for caricature which he put to use by lampooning his high school teachers. When World War I came, he enlisted in the Army at the age of 17 and was sent to France with the American Expeditionary Force. Returning to Perry in 1918, he finished high school, and then studied journalism at the University of Missouri. Out of the university, Hamlin worked as a reporter in Des Moines, Iowa, for the *Register and Tribune,* and later for the *News.*

In the early 1920s Hamlin moved to Texas, where he held jobs as photographer, reporter, and cartoonist at the *Fort Worth Record* and the *Fort Worth Star Telegram.* In 1927 he quit newspapering and went to work in the oil fields as layout man, poster designer, and mapmaker. It was then that the idea of a prehistoric comic strip developed in Hamlin's fertile mind, according to his own account. He started developing his idea upon his return to the art department of the *Register and Tribune* in 1929. The process was slow and painstaking, as Hamlin later recalled: "I first put a modern rough family into the cave-dwelling days. I worked on that idea for a year, then destroyed the strips. I tried another idea in caveman style for another six months and dropped that. Then I got the idea for *Alley Oop.*"

Hamlin sold his new strip to NEA, which brought it out on August 7, 1933, as a daily (and on September 9, 1934, as a Sunday). Hamlin worked on *Alley Oop*—while pursuing his hobbies of playing football, fishing, and driving race cars—until his retirement in 1971

367

(Dave Graue and Jack Bender are now turning out the strip). He died in Brookville, Florida, on June 14, 1993.

Hamlin's career was unobtrusive, but fecund and rewarding. He was never self-assertive and was therefore passed over for cartooning awards in favor of lesser but pushier artists. Yet his stature as a fine humor strip artist and a master of the absurd has quietly grown among comic art critics, and it is likely that V. T. Hamlin's career will be reevaluated in light of his achievements as a comic innovator and storyteller.

M.H.

HAMPSON, FRANK (1918-1985) British cartoonist and illustrator, born at Audenshaw, Manchester, on December 21, 1918. He was educated at King George V School in Southport, leaving in 1932 to become a telegraph boy for the post office. His first cartoon was published in *Meccano Magazine* and he became its joke illustrator (1932-1935). He then became a civil servant and attended Southport School of Arts in the evenings, studying life drawing. He freelanced his first strips to the post office magazine, *The Post* (1937), but resigned from the post office in 1938 to become a full-time art student, then joined the Territorial Army in 1939. During the war he served as a driver in the Royal Army Service Corps, being commissioned in 1944. Despite passing the test for RAF aircrew training, he was refused a transfer. He was demobilized in 1946 with a grant to continue his art studies.

Hampson freelanced illustrations for *The Anvil* (1947), a religious monthly published by a local Anglican, the Rev. Marcus Morris. With Morris he designed and planned an ambitious new comic weekly for boys, which was christened *Eagle* by Mrs. Hampson. His dummy was accepted by Hulton Press, and the new paper, the most important landmark in postwar British comics, was launched on April 14, 1950. Hampson wrote and drew *Rob Conway*, *Tommy Walls*, *The Great Adventure*, and the two-page cover feature that became nationally famous, *Dan Dare, Pilot of the Future*. To cope with the weekly output, he set up a studio, with writers, art assistants, and models, both human (for the characters) and artificial (for the space ships, cities, etc.). Hampson acted as chief artist and designer for *Eagle* until 1960, when Hulton sold out to Odhams Press, and Marcus Morris resigned editorship to join National Magazines. Although Hampson had not drawn *Dan Dare* for some time, his style stamped the strip, the *Eagle*, and the companion comics that he and Morris had created: *Girl*, *Swift*, and *Robin*. Eventually all the titles were killed, but Hampson's influence remains, particularly in science fiction strips and the work of Frank Bellamy.

After a period of illustrating the educational color books for young children published by Ladybird, Hampson contracted cancer of the trachea in 1970. Recovering after treatment, he joined Ewell County Technical College as a graphics technician. His work on *Eagle* remains ahead of its time, and it is still unequalled in British comics. He died in Epsom on July 8, 1985.

D.G.

HANGMAN, THE (U.S.) MLJ comics did something rare in the July 1941 issue of *Pep* (number 17)—writer Cliff Campbell engineered the death of a minor superhero called the Comet. The Comet's brother, Bob Dickering, swore to avenge his death and adopted the role of the Hangman. He also inherited the Comet's spot in *Pep* as well as his brother's girlfriend, reporter Thelma Gordon. Garbing himself in a darkly colored costume with a ropelike belt, the Hangman was appearing in his own book by the winter of 1941. (The book had started as *Special* comics and the Hangman didn't have the book named after him until the second issue.)

Throughout its tenure, *The Hangman* had superior stories, mostly scripted by comic veterans Bill Woolfolk (1941-1942) and Otto Binder (1943-1944). Both writers kept the mood dark and ominous, and the Hangman apparently had no qualms about actually hanging transgressors. He also had an array of interesting villains. One of them, Mother Goose, committed all her crimes using nursery rhymes as clues; another, Captain Swastika, actually overpowered the Hangman. When he lost one of his many battles it was because of stupidity or carelessness, and he didn't die until he was inadvertantly stabbed with an ice pick by one of his own henchmen.

Artistically, the feature began poorly because George Storm, an excellent humor artist, simply couldn't handle adventure strips properly. In later years, however, Irv Novick (1941-1943) and Bob Fujitani (1942-1944) both handled *The Hangman* with the necessary verve and style.

The Hangman strip lasted in *Pep* through March 1944's 47th issue. The last issue of *Hangman* (number eight) was published in the fall of 1943. The Hangman was unsuccessfully revived as a villain in 1965 by MLJ.

J.B.

HANS AND FRITZ see Captain and the Kids, The.

HAPPY HOOLIGAN (U.S.) Fred Opper's classic Irish tramp with the tin-can hat, Happy Hooligan, made his first comic-page appearance in a single row of four colored panels in Hearst's Sunday comic sections in New York and San Francisco on March 26, 1900. This began a series of Sunday episodes called *The Doings of Happy Hooligan*, the first of several running titles under which the Hooligan strip would appear between 1900 and 1932.

Hooligan, first portrayed with a distinctly ruddy nose and a blue can for a hat (later changed to a permanent red, sometimes with a blank label), was the simple innocent whose impulsive undertakings nearly always landed him in the hands of the law (played, in these early years, by a heavily mustached policeman with a stout club and a Keystone Cop hat). Despite this continual bad luck, Hooligan lived up to his name by remaining always optimistic, and his enormous smile became a quick symbol of the new comic strip art form to millions of readers.

Soon a half page, then frequently a full front or back page feature in the four-page Hearst Sunday comics, Opper's *Doings of Happy Hooligan* often dropped its running title for a one-time episode caption, like "The Unfortunate Gallantry of Happy Hooligan." Originally short and rotund, Hooligan was already his leaner, taller self of later years when he met the first of several continuing characters in the *Hooligan* strip: his "long-lost" brother, Gloomy Gus, on April 20, 1902. Gus, as long-faced as Happy was jolly, experienced exactly the reverse of Happy's bad luck—whenever Happy ran afoul of the law, his disaster almost inevitably left Gus with a fine meal, a sack of diamonds, or some other

"Happy Hooligan," F. B. Opper. © King Features Syndicate.

such windfall. A bit later, Gus (of the ankle-length brown or yellow coat and battered top hat) was with Happy when the strip's hero acquired his pet dog, the black-spotted white mongrel, Flip, on March 15, 1903. (In an unusual episode of June 22, 1902, Happy and Gus dine with their parents, a brother-in-law, and Happy's three young nephews, of whom only the nephews are seen again in the strip.) Before long, on February 14, 1904, Happy meets a third brother, a monocled, Anglophilic tramp in ragged cutaway, spats, and tails, named Montmorency, with whom he eventually makes a very funny trip to England.

By 1914, the Hooligan strip was a full page running every Sunday under the fixed title of *Happy Hooligan*. By mid-1916, however, reflecting events in the strip, the regular title had become *Happy Hooligan's Honeymoon*, changing back in late 1918 to *Happy Hooligan* once more. In early 1919, however, Happy had joined forces with a scraggly mustached little fellow in a plaid hat named Mr. Dubb, for whom Opper renamed the Sunday page *Mr. Dubb*. In the spring of 1921, Dubb left the strip, and the locale changed to the farm home of Si, Mirandy, and Maud the mule together with a strip title switch to *Down on the Farm*.

After a period of rural adventures with Happy and (of all people) Alphonse and Gaston, the strip name was changed back, with the beginning of a world tour by Happy and Gloomy, to *Happy Hooligan* again in mid-1923. In the summer of 1925, however, Happy was dropped altogether for a time, the focus of the Sunday strip was switched to Mr. Dubb once more, and the title altered again to *Mr. Dough and Mr. Dubb*. (Mr. Dough, seen in the strip briefly in 1920, was Mr. Dubb's portly employer.) Happy reentered the strip by December 1925 as a night watchman (then a janitor) for Mr. Dough, and he and Dubb were a team for the remainder of the titular sequence until the strip name returned permanently to *Happy Hooligan* in January of 1927.

By the end of 1910 and thereafter, *Happy Hooligan* had become an involved continuity strip, with narratives running for many weeks and frequently involving cliffhanger episode breaks, with the simple weekly theme of Happy's bad luck long since dropped. In the early 1920s, a daily *Hooligan* strip, called both *Mr. Dough and Mr. Dubb* and *Happy Hooligan* ran rather obscurely and erratically in some Hearst papers at various times; it seems to have been short-lived, however, since Opper's weekday efforts were almost always political cartoons done for the Hearst chain of papers,

and *Hooligan* remained an essentially weekly strip from start to finish.

In the mid-1920s, when all Sunday Hearst strips were adding second weekly features at the top of the page, Opper first revived an old strip of his from the 1900s called *Our Antediluvian Ancestors* to run above *Mr. Dough and Mr. Dubb* as a single row of panels on January 17, 1926. He changed this for one week to a two-row, eight-panel strip called *The Optimist* on May 16, 1926, then reanimated *Maud* the following week for his permanent Sunday cofeature with *Hooligan*.

Hooligan was a popular figure in a number of fields beyond the comic page: he appeared in several stage productions in the 1900s, was featured in a song by Stillman and Vogel in 1902, starred in a number of animated cartoons released through Hearst's International Film Service circa 1917 (*Happy Hooligan at the Zoo*, etc.), and was reprinted in several books from the turn of the century on. These included *Happy Hooligan*, *Handy Happy Hooligan*, *Happy Hooligan's Travels*, *Happy Hooligan Home Again*, *The Story of Happy Hooligan*, etc. Most were published by Frederick Stokes & Co. before 1910, although the last work dates from 1932.

Drawn by Opper until he was in his mid-70s, *Happy Hooligan* finally had to be abandoned by its creator in 1932 (the strip last appeared in most papers on August 14, 1932) because of his failing eyesight. It deserves extensive reprinting, preferably in full, as a major classic work of the American comic strip.

B.B.

HARGREAVES, HARRY (1922-   ) British cartoonist, animator, and illustrator, born in Manchester in 1922. Educated at Chorlton High School, he then trained as an architect and engineer. In 1939 he joined the art staff of Kayebon Press, a Manchester agency, and assisted Hugh McNeill with his strips for D. C. Thomson. His first comic work was *Pansy Potter* in *Beano*, "ghosting" for McNeill. He turned down an offer from Thomson to do full-time freelance work on their comics, preferring a job with Rolls Royce working on the Merlin engine. He volunteered for the Royal Air Force Signals branch in 1942 and served four years in the Far East. During this time, he drew the Christmas airgraphs for RAF Ceylon and illustrated unit magazines. In 1946, he returned to engineering at Simon's of Stockport, then applied for an aptitude test with Gaumont British Animation, a new unit set up by David Hand, a Disney director. Taken on as trainee, he became an animator on the *Animaland* and *Musical Paintbox* series, until the unit was disbanded in 1949.

The Disney-style training both inspired and aided Hargreaves, and his new style quickly found strip work in children's comics: *Scamp*, a dog in *Comet* (1950); *Harold Hare* (1950) and *Ollie the Alley Cat* (1951) in *Sun*; *Don Quickshot* (1952) in *Knockout Fun Book*; *Terry the Troubadour* (1954) in *TV Comic*. He then joined the "Dutch Walt Disney," Marten Toonder, in Amsterdam to draw the newspaper strip version of his film character *Panda*, syndicated to 150 European papers and the *London Evening News*. Returning home in 1959, he settled in the West Country, where his love for animals combined with his animator's technique and interest in the strip form to originate a series of pictorial narratives featuring a small bird. This *Punch* series (1958) quickly caught on, and the reprinted episodes filled four books: *The Bird*; *The Bird and Others*; *It's a Bird's Life*; and *Bird for All Seasons*. From 1962 he drew cartoons for a local television series, *Discs a Go Go*, and then the weekly strip *Budge & Co* for Reveille (1966), and the advertising strip *Sammy Squirrel* (1968). His daily strip *Hayseeds* started in the *Evening News* in 1969 and ran until the mid-1980s. His other cartoon books include *How's That*; *Not Out*; *Googlies* (all about crickets); and two reprints of *Hayseeds*. After his strip was discontinued, Hargreaves went into retirement.

D.G.

HARISU NO KAZE (Japan) Created by Tetsuya Chiba, *Harisu no Kaze* ("The Whirlwind of Harisu") made its first appearance in the weekly *Shōnen* magazine in April 1965. *Harisu no Kaze* was a Gakuen Manga (the equivalent of the English public school story) and it soon rose to the top position in that genre.

Kunimatsu Ishida, the strip's diminutive hero, had been transferred to Harisu Gakuen (Harisu High School) from another school. As soon as he arrived at Harisu, he started acting like a whirlwind. Ishida was small, but bold, fearless, and a hater of injustice. He excelled in all sports, and was a friendly sort of fellow, but he was weak in his academic studies and his fondness for girls often landed him in trouble. Ishida soon established himself as a sports winner: he led the Harisu team to victory in the interscholastic baseball tournament, won the national fencing title, and insured his team's victory in the Tokyo soccer tournament by scoring the decisive goal. Ishida was also a peppery fighter, winning against all comers in fencing, boxing, and judo. Soon after he entered the school, Ishida became the hero of Harisu, as well as a very popular character in the history of Japanese comics.

Aside from Ishida, the main characters in the strip were: Yōko Asai, alias Ochara, the hero's classmate and the editor of the school paper; his teacher Gōzō Iwanami; A-bo, Ishido's younger brother; and Koyama, the captain of the new boxing club.

Harisu no Kaze was a very human story, full of laughter, emotion, friendship, and vitality. It was very popular with the readers and inspired a series of animated cartoons. The strip made its last appearance in November 1967.

H.K.

HARMAN, FRED (1902-1982) American artist born February 9, 1902, in St. Joseph, Missouri. Fred Harman, while still an infant, was taken by his parents to Pagosa Springs in Colorado, near the New Mexico border, where his father owned a ranch. There he grew up in the wilds of Colorado and northern New Mexico, learning the hard life of a ranch hand. In 1915 the Harmans moved to Kansas City, where Fred started a short-lived cartooning career on the *Star* in 1920. In 1921 he worked at the Kansas City Film Ad Company, a small animation outfit, alongside two other fledgling cartoonists, Walt Disney and Ub Iwerks.

In 1924 Harman shuffled around the country, doing illustrations in his native St. Joseph and trying different ventures in California, Minnesota, and Iowa, before settling in Hollywood in 1930. In 1934 he produced his first comic strip, a Western called *Bronc Peeler* which he syndicated himself, but the returns were meager and he abandoned it early in 1938.

Harman then went to New York, where he tried unsuccessfully to succeed Allen Dean on *King of the Royal Mounted*. (His agent, Stephen Slesinger, also represented Dean and *King's* creator, Zane Grey). Discouraged, he was about to leave when, through his agent, he met Fred Ferguson, president of the Newspaper Enterprise Association, who asked him to do another western strip for NEA. On November 6, 1938, *Red Ryder* was born.

In 1940 Fred Harman returned to Pagosa Springs where he developed the "Red Ryder Ranch" and could be seen parading around dressed-up as his comic strip hero. He became a painter of western scenes and one of the founders of Cowboy Artists of America. In the 1960s Harman moved to Albuquerque, New Mexico. He died in Phoenix, Arizona, on January 2, 1982.

Fred Harman received a number of distinctions over the years, but as a western artist rather than as a cartoonist. He was made Man of the Year in Colorado and an honorary citizen of Texas, and he received many other awards and trophies. A number of Fred Harman's works were reproduced in Ed Ainsworth's excellent study *The Cowboy in Art* (World, 1968) and an anthology of his pictures was published in 1969 by Sage Books under the title *The Great West in Paintings*.

M.H.

HAROLD TEEN (U.S.) One of the additions to the *Chicago Tribune's* new comic section of May 4, 1919, was Carl Ed's *The Love Life of Harold Teen*. A bright page of nine panels, it presented its dark-haired juvenile hero in a straw skimmer and red jacket, learning from a teenage crony named Buck that there is a new "queen" in town. The queen (1919 teen slang for girl) was named Mae Preston, and she was to be Harold's love interest for several months to come. (His longer-lived love, Lillums Lovewell, first appearing on March 28, 1920, was still in the future.) A weekly gag strip without continuity—aside from the love affair—*The Love Life of Harold Teen* was an invention of the Tribune's copublisher, Joseph Patterson, who felt that the public would like a teenage comic, in view of the success of Booth Tarkington's *Seventeen* two years before. Ed did a fast, amusing job with the Patterson character, and within five months was asked to start a daily version for Patterson's new tabloid, the *New York Daily News*. The first daily episode, still bearing the long title, appeared in the *News* on Thursday, September 25, 1919, and was an introductory panel listing the early characters of the strip—none of whom were retained in the later, 30-year cast of the comic, except for Harold's "Moms," his "Pa" (Thomas Teen), and his kid sister, Josie (here given her full name of Josephine). Immedi-

"Harold Teen," Carl Ed. © Chicago Tribune.

ately after the introduction, the daily strip (not introduced into the *Tribune* for some time) continued with
the Sunday page story of Harold's difficult romance
with Mae Preston. (We also learn Harold's exact age
here for the first time—it is, of course, 17.)

The teenage populace of America took to the *Harold
Teen* strip (its long title was quickly trimmed) because
of Ed's awareness of the current teen vogues in speech
and dress. Harold's use of popular terms like "Sheba"
(for a girl), and "lamb's lettuce" (as an endearment)
wowed the juvenile set of the time, and the strip
served as a bridge to carry the latest city slang and
doings to the laggard countryside. Given his head by
Patterson, Ed now developed and introduced his own
characters, such as Lillums Lovewell; her father Lemuel
Lovewell; the shrimpish Shadow Smart; Pop Jenks and
the Sugar Bowl soda parlor gang, Horace, Beezie, and
the others; the swinging Aunt Pruny, and many more
characters relished by the comic readers of the 1920s
and 1930s.

By the wartime 1940s, however, Ed assumed his
readers would be out of sympathy with a self-
indulgent teen set and moved Harold into the service
of his country as an espionage agent. Ed was not particularly good at the melodrama this entailed, however,
and his dramatics were more often ludicrous than
effective. An attempt to return to the old Sugar Bowl
ways after the war didn't work well, either, and the
once-large circulation of *Harold Teen* began to dwindle,
until by Ed's death in 1959 the strip was appearing primarily in its original newspaper birthplace. The strip
was folded after Ed's death—the era that it represented
so memorably was then as long gone as F. Scott
Fitzgerald and Texas Guinan.

Several *Harold Teen* strip collections were published,
and two film versions were made of the strip: the silent

one of 1928 starring Arthur Lake (later of *Blondie* fame),
and the sound film of 1933 featuring Rochelle Hudson
as Lillums.

B.B.

HART, JOHNNY (1931-) American cartoonist
born in Endicott, N.Y., on February 18, 1931. Graduating from Union-Endicott High School in 1949, Johnny
Hart joined the U.S. Air Force one year later and was
sent to Korea, where he drew cartoons for the Pacific
Stars and Stripes. Discharged in 1953, Johnny Hart and
his wife, Mary (whom he had married two years
before), went to live at her mother's farm in Georgia.

In 1954 Hart sold his first cartoon to the *Saturday
Evening Post* and gradually established himself as a cartoonist, contributing regularly to the *Post, Collier's,* and
Bluebook. In 1956 the Harts moved to New York City,
and Johnny went to work for two years in the art
department of General Electric. After several unsuccessful attempts, Hart finally persuaded the Herald-
Tribune Syndicate to accept his first comic strip
creation, *B.C.,* a far-out feature about a weird assortment of cavemen, talking plants, and animals. The first
B.C. daily strip appeared on February 17, 1958.

In 1964 Hart developed a new strip idea and teamed
up with cartoonist Brant Parker (whom Hart had
known since the time they were both residents in
Endicott) to produce *The Wizard of Id*, the hilarious saga
of a ludicrous monarch and his equally grotesque subjects.

Johnny Hart is capable of dazzling humor and hilarious originality, and is also a thoughtful author who
tries to impart his vision of the modern world, seen
through the reducing lens of faraway (and purely imagined) historical periods. He has been the recipient of a
great number of prizes for his work, including the

Reuben Award, which he received in 1968 in a tie vote with the editorial cartoonist Pat Oliphant. Other honors have included the NCS's Elzie Segar Award in 1981 and the Silver Plaque for best newspaper comic strip in 1989.

M.H.

HARTOG VAN BANDA, LO (1916-   ) Lo Hartog van Banda, one of the busiest and most prolific of Dutch comic writers, was born November 11, 1916, in Den Haag, Netherlands. Hartog van Banda did not emerge as a comic writer until after World War II. He wrote *Fabulus de klokkendokter* ("Fabulus, Clock Doctor") for a clockmakers' trade journal in 1947. In 1952 he was hired as a staff writer in the Marten Toonder Studios. He wrote some of the episodes of *Panda*, the first of the *Kappie* episodes for Toonder, *Kappie en het drijvende eiland* ("Cappie and the Floating Island"), and *De ondergang van Ur* ("The Destruction of Ur"), an episode for the strip *Aram*, normally written by Waling Dijkstra and drawn by Piet Wijn.

Most importantly, however, he plotted and wrote all of the *Tom Poes* episodes for the weekly version of that strip which appeared in *Week in beeld, De Avrobode, Revue*, and *Donald Duck*. Apart from the weekly version of *Tom Poes*, which incorporated speech balloons, he also suggested some of the plots used in the daily *Tom Poes* strip, talking them over and developing them with Marten Toonder, who always wrote the finalized version to be put under the strips. He also created some of the characters to appear in the strips plus new comic features. For several years he even added Toonder's *Koning Hollewijn* to the strips he was writing. In 1966, after 14 years with the Toonder Studios, Hartog van Banda left the world of comics to enter that of advertising. It was only two years later that he returned to writing comics, this time casting off the cloak of anonymity, working under his own name on eight different series.

Working with The Tjong Khing, he wrote *Iris* in 1968. That same year he also started writing scenarios for *De Argonautjes* ("The Little Argonauts"), drawn by the very talented Dick Matena, expanding this collaboration the following year by writing *Ridder Roodhart* ("Knight Redheart"). In 1969 he started working with several other artists: with Cideon Brugman on *Ambrosius*, a strip about the wild adventures of elderly Professor Ambrosius; with John Bakker on the superhero parody *Blook*; and with artist The Tjong Khing on *Arman en Ilva* ("Arman and Ilva"). In 1970, among other things, he started writing the semifunny science fiction series *Arad en Maya* ("Arad and Maya") for artist Jan Steeman. With the discontinuance of most of his strips in the mid-1980s, he went into retirement.

W.F.

HASELDEN, W. K. (1872-1953) Regarded as the father of the British newspaper strip, William Kerridge Haselden was born in Seville. As a 30-year-old insurance clerk, he walked into the office of the newly revamped *Daily Illustrated Mirror* on Tuesday, January 5, 1904, a portfolio of sample cartoons under his arm. Editor Hamilton Fyfe was so impressed that he published one the very next morning: *Only Waiting for the Torch*. Haselden did not leave the Mirror until 1940, for 36 years their staff cartoonist. Very soon his daily panel evolved from a single joke to a series of small comments on a single topic, not a new idea in itself but

W. K. Haselden, "Big and Little Willie." © *Daily Mirror Newspapers Ltd.*

new to newspapers. His first cartoon in this prototype strip style was published January 15, 1904: *The Bourchier-Walkeley Episode in Four Scenes*. Gradually characters began to recur and by the summer of 1908 a form of serial developed: *Mr Simkins On His Holiday*, which ran for 16 days. Other running characters he included from time to time were Burlington Bertie the Knut with a K; Miss Joy Flapperton, the sweet young thing; and Colonel Dugout, departmental beureaucrat.

His most famous creations first appeared on Friday October 2, 1914, under the title *The Sad Experiences of Big and Little Willie*. These were caricatures of Kaiser Wilhelm of Germany and his son, the Crown Prince. The public so loved these ludicrous representations of England's enemy that they became running characters and were reprinted in a sumptuous art paper book by Chatto & Windus (1915). When a *Daily Mirror* reporter interviewed the captured Kaiser at the end of the Great War, he confessed that the cartoons were "damnably effective."

Haselden's 100 best cartoons were collated each year into annual paperbacks titled *Daily Mirror Reflections*, the first being dated 1908, the last (Vol. 31) 1937. Other books illustrated by Haselden included: *Accidents Will Happen* (1907), *The Globe 'By The Way' Book* (1908), and *America As I Saw It* (1913). He also illustrated drama reviews for *Punch*. He died in 1953 at the age of 81.

D.G.

HASEN, IRWIN (1918-   ) American cartoonist born July 8, 1918, in New York City. Irwin Hasen attended the National Academy and the Art Students League. He started his cartooning career in the late 1930s by drawing sports cartoons and doing advertising artwork. In 1940 he went into comic books, working for various publishers on such features as *The Green Hornet* (1940), *The Fox* (1940-42), *Green Lantern* (1941), *The Flash* (1943), and creating the short-lived *Citizen Smith, Son of the Unknown Soldier* for Holyoke in 1941.

Drafted into the Army, Hasen became the editor of the Fort Dix Reception Center newspaper. Discharged in 1946, he went back to more comic book work, almost exclusively for National Periodicals, where he drew, among other features, *Johnny Thunder*, *The Justice League of America*, and reprised both *The Flash* and *Green Lantern*. He also tried his hand at his first newspaper strip (for the *New York Post*); this was *The Goldbergs*, based on a top-rated radio program of the time, but it folded after a few months.

In the 1950s Hasen became active in the National Cartoonists Society and while on a NCS tour in Europe he met Gus Edson; this resulted in their collaboration (with Edson writing and Hasen drawing) on a new comic strip, *Dondi*, which first appeared in September of 1955. After Edison's death in 1966 Hasen also took over the writing of the strip. In 1986 *Dondi* was discontinued, and Hasen has been occasionally working in comic books again.

A competent and solid craftsman, Irwin Hasen is one of the many unsung cartoonists who have managed to carry on the best traditions of comic art in an unobtrusive and yet praiseworthy way.

M.H.

HATANOSUKE HINOMARU (Japan) *Hatanosuke Hinomaru*, created by Kikuo Nakajima, made its first appearance in 1935 in the comic monthly *Shōnen Kurabu*.

Hatanosuke was a boy samurai: he wore a sun-crested kimono (*hinomaru* means "sun" in Japanese) and a striped hakama. He was brave and witty; as a lord's squire he was adviser to the lord's son. His activities were boundless—not only did he give wise advice, he took part in its implementation, arresting thieves and thwarting conspiracies. Hatanosuke was a master at swordplay (which he learned from Musahi Miyamoto, Japan's most famous swordsman) and a skilled practitioner of lasso throwing. He was a brilliant warrior and a loyal vassal to his lord.

Hatanosuke Hinomaru was created in answer to Japanese militarism; it faithfully toed the official line, stressing loyalty, obedience, duty, and military prowess. Very nationalistic and bellicose, it did not resist Japan's defeats in the Pacific and was discontinued in 1943. (After World War II it was revived, but lasted only four more years.)

The strip's artistic style and story line were equally simple and did not display any great inventiveness. It was fairly popular, however, and presumably served its purpose of psychologically preparing Japanese youths for war. When the war did come, *Hatanosuke Hinomaru* inspired a song (with words by the author himself) that was sung by children in school. A record of Hatanosuke's adventures was also made at about the same time.

H.K.

HATLO, JAMES (1898-1963) The madcap cartoonist who tipped his hat in thanks to the thousands of readers who suggested theme after theme for his daily panel, *They'll Do It Every Time*, James "Jimmy" Hatlo, was born in Providence, Rhode Island, in 1898, the son of a printer. Moving with his family to California the following year, Hatlo attended school in Los Angeles, developing a natural aptitude for cartooning. But he approached his later newspaper fame as a cartoonist through an odd back door: his first press job, following

a trek to San Francisco in 1918, was with the old *San Francisco Bulletin* as automobile news editor at a time when newspapers were just beginning to devote considerable Sunday sections to autoing events and advertising. Leaving the *Bulletin* for the *Call* a few years later, Hatlo (an inveterate sports fan and game attendee) whipped up a football cartoon for the *Call* sporting section. Delighted, the editor demanded more and soon Hatlo became the new *Call* sports cartoonist. Hatlo quickly developed a mythic setting for the local football players in an annual seasonal series which ran under the title of *Swineskin Gulch* for many years.

Early in 1929, in response to a *Call* feature editor's request for a small filler panel gag on the comic page, Hatlo drew his first *They'll Do It Every Time* cartoon. He never stopped drawing it. The public guffawed and wrote letters agreeing with Hatlos points and suggesting their own. The *Call*, sensing a hot property, switched the panel to the sports page, where it garnered an even more enthusiastic following and a King Features syndication a few years later (1936).

Aside from a year-long series of advertising panel cartoons for Standard Oil in 1933 and 1934 called *Give It a Whirl*, and a 1943 Sunday half-page titled *Little Iodine* (from a character developed in the daily panel), *They'll Do It Every Time* remained Hatlo's prime outlet for almost 40 years. Married in May 1937 to Eleanor Dollard, who met him while asking for an autograph, the Hatlos lived in San Francisco and New York (the latter for four months a year "so as not to stagnate"). He gave the last tip of the Hatlo hat to his millions of

Jimmy Hatlo, "They'll Do It Every Time." © King Features Sydicate.

readers on December 1, 1963, when he died in New York City, mourned by more devoted readers than any other sports page cartoonist since Tad Dorgan, whose mantle Hatlo had inarguably acquired.

B.B.

HAWKMAN (U.S.) *Hawkman* was created for National Comics by writer Gardner Fox and was first drawn by Dennis Neville. Making its first appearance in January 1940s *Flash* number one, *Hawkman* was one of the earliest comic book strips to utilize the old flying-man legends. The character sported a massive hawk headgear and a huge pair of furry, birdlike wings. Through the years, the headgear underwent constant change and there were over a dozen variations.

In reality, Hawkman was Carter Hall, a reincarnation of the Egyptian Prince Khufu. His flying powers came from an antigravity belt made from a substance known as "ninth metal." He was also able to communicate with birds, and eventually added a partner, Hawkgirl, in *Flash* number 24. As the strip matured, the team became more deeply involved in pseudo-Egyptian culture, and their fighting arsenal included crossbows, maces, axes, shields, spears, and anything vaguely resembling ancient weaponry. The feature also showcased an array of colorful villains, the most notable one being the Ghost, an exotically attired apparition.

During the strip's career, Fox handled most of the scripts, although Bob Kanigher contributed several outstanding tales during the 1947-1949 period. Artistically, *Hawkman* was graced with two outstanding illustrators. The first was Sheldon Moldoff, who assumed the strip from Neville and drew it from late 1940 to early 1945. He was an excellent draftsman and his work showed the influences of Alex Raymond and Hal Foster. In late 1944, the young Joe Kubert began taking control and he used unique layouts and heavy blacks to give the strip a pleasing and appropriately moody look. He handled the strip until its demise in 1949.

Hawkman was one of National's major supporting features and lasted through all 104 issues of *Flash*, the last published in February 1949. The character also appeared in *All-Star Comics* from the first issue (Summer 1940) through the last, March 1951's 57th issue. He was a member of the Justice Society of America.

When the superhero feature began to sell again, *Hawkman* was revived in March 1961's *Brave and Bold* number 34. Hawkman was still Carter Hall, but this time he was cast as a visiting policeman from the planet Thanagar. Much of the ancient weaponry was returned, even though this Hawkman had his headquarters in an orbiting spaceship. *Hawkgirl* was also revived and the artist was once again Joe Kubert. After several more tryout issues of *Brave and Bold*, the character was given a regular feature in *Mystery In Space*, starting with the 87th issue (November 1963). He lasted there through the 91st issue, and began his own title beginning in April 1964. By this time, however, Kubert had been replaced by Murphy Anderson. And, as had happened in the 1940s, *Hawkman* again developed two outstanding artists. Anderson's slicker, more pristine renditions also suited the character well.

As the second superhero era faded, however, *Hawkman* folded after September 1968's 27th issue, and the feature lasted several final months in a hybrid book entitled *Atom and Hawkman*. The character still appears, however, as a member of the Justice League of

"Hawkman." © DC Comics.

America, a group which he joined in the 31st issue of *Justice League of America*.

The post-1970s history of *Hawkman* gets a bit complicated. A second *Hawkman* series came about in August 1986, but it lasted only to December 1987. In 1989 a miniseries titled *Hawkworld*, retracing the history of Thanagar, Hawkman's home planet, enjoyed sufficient success to warrant the issuance of a *Hawkworld* monthly series in June 1990; this in turn led to a third (and still ongoing) *Hawkman* series, starting in September 1993.

J.B.

HAWKSHAW THE DETECTIVE (U.S.) In 1913, when Gus Mager, who had just taken his *Sherlocko the Monk* to the *New York World*, was threatened with a lawsuit by A. Conan Doyle's representatives in the United States, he decided to turn for inspiration to a 19th-century detective play, *The Ticket-of-Leave Man*, by Tom Taylor, with its famed sleuth, Hawkshaw (a detecting name as widely known as Sherlock, but safely out of copyright). Accordingly, the new feature appeared in bright colors on the first page of the *New York World* Sunday comic section for February 23, 1913, (with obvious corrections in the dialogue balloons to eliminate the "Sherlocko" and "Watso" references and replace them with new names) as *Hawkshaw the Detective*. Hawkshaw and his aide, the Colonel, had now lost all "monk" resemblances, although they still encountered their old associates, Groucho, Nervo, Bookkeepo, et al. (A curious daily strip Mager now undertook for the *World*, called *Millionbucks and Kandykiddo*, featured a team which looked exactly like Sherlocko/Hawkshaw and Watso/the Colonel, but who were presented as eccentric millionaires in slapstick situations.)

The strip folded in time, and Mager concentrated on the Sunday page. This continued until mid-1922, when Mager dropped *Hawkshaw* as a full page and replaced it with a new small town life strip called *Main Street*, ghosted by someone in close mimicry of George McManus' style. Mager himself devoted his talents to developing a semiserious continuing daily strip once more called *Sherlocko*, which he distributed to a number of papers in 1924 on his own. The venture was unfortunately short-lived, since the Doyle representatives did indeed move against the strip and closed it down in 1925.

Mager's detective surfaced one last time, however, on December 13, 1931, again as *Hawkshaw the Detective* for United Feature Syndicate, as a top for Dirks' *Captain and the Kids*. Mager, who had left the *World* and had been working for Dirks, drew the first five months of the new feature himself, then turned it over to Bernard Dibble for a year and a half (as Dirks did his kid strip), taking it up again, under the pseudonym "Watso," after 1933. Mager continued with it as a companion piece to *The Captain and the Kids* until the late 1940s, when he retired to paint on his estate in Newark, New Jersey. Only two collections of Mager's strip work appeared: *The Monk Joke Book* (N.Y. American, 1912), and *Hawkshaw the Detective* (Press Publishing Co., 1916).

B.B.

HAXTUR (Spain) With a name perhaps derived from that of Ambrose Bierce's shepherd-god, and also utilized by Chambers and Lovecraft, *Haxtur* was created by Victor de la Fuente for the Spanish magazine *Trinca*. It lasted 14 episodes, the first of which saw publication on May 15, 1971, and the last appeared on January 1, 1972.

Haxtur was a character of heroic fantasy, but with a difference. He was a guerrilla fighter, not unlike Che Guevara, whose exploits also took place in the jungle; fighting against the forces sent to defeat him by the government he had only his anachronistic medieval sword as a weapon. The four horsemen of the Apocalypse had condemned him to wander through space and time in search of his destiny, until death brought him ultimate liberation in the last episode: this end adds an epic dimension to the feature, the first in the history of comics in which the principal hero dies.

The place of the action is a neverland where everything is possible, where we do not know whether the protagonist dreams or remembers, or whether his memories are recalled by his slow agony. Haxtur rides along the road, meeting beings and people who wander in and out of his life. The comic was rendered with a fascinating technique: the action took place on three different time levels, which were presented to the reader by means of flashbacks all coming together at the same time. The reading is not easy, and one must discover (or imagine) the time frame for himself, as in an Alain Resnais movie or in Carlos Saura's *La Prima Angelica*. The colors, masterfully overlaid, do not help comprehension, but do fulfill an aesthetic function. A

difficult work of great merit, *Haxtur* was widely translated abroad.

L.G.

"The Hayseeds," Harry Hargreaves. © Daily Mirror Newspapers Ltd.

HAYSEEDS (G.B.) The Hayseeds were an amiable crowd of country-dwellers who happened to be animals. They talked and occasionally walked like humans, but despite these characteristics they were amazingly close to the real creatures they represented. Harry Hargreaves, their creator, is an animal artist and lover, and was careful to keep his cartoons, animated as they are, as similar to nature as he could. Inspired by the American animal strip *Pogo*, but lacking even Walt Kelly's scraps of clothing, *Hayseeds* soon developed along its own line, reflecting human behavior in the animal world. Toby the Badger, the nearest thing *Hayseeds* had to a regular hero, was central to the strip. But even he left the stage for days at a time while Hargreaves pursued stories with another of the strip's cast. This included, in no pecking order, Braithwaite the water-wading Bird, Homer the Snail, Ern the Owl, Entwistle the Mole, Lizzy Lizard, a pair of shrews called the O'Toofs, and a Frog, a Squirrel, a Hedgehog, a Worm, a Rabbit, a Snake, a Bat, a religious Bird and on occasion, a Great Spotted Twit.

The strip commenced July 1, 1968. A paperback reprint, *Hayseeds*, was published in 1971. It was dropped September 14, 1974, when the *Evening News* changed from broadsheet to tabloid, but restored by readership demand on November 20, 1974. *Hayseeds* was dropped again in the 1980s.

D.G.

HE YOUZHI (1922-) From 1952 to 1980, He Youzhi created more than 30 comic books. The best-known stories and plays were *Chao Yang Gou* (the name of a village), *Li Shuangshuang* (a woman's name), *Lou Ah Shu* (a classical drama named after the main figure in it), *Shan Gou le de Nu Xiou Cai* ("A Woman Scholar in the Remote Mountains"), *Hua Tuo* (name for a medical doctor in ancient China), *Lian Sheng San Ji* ("Promoted Successfully Three Times"), and *Shan Xiang Ju Bian* ("Great Changes in a Mountain Village," which is based on a long novel). Some of his works are made in traditional Chinese painting style with brush and color ink, others are drawings with full-page backgrounds, and some have a blank background. He tries to make vivid drawings that reflect the original stories. "Every figure drawn should be of a live person, but not the illustration of an autopsy," He Youzhi believes.

In *Chao Yang Gou*, when the city girl Yin Huan is traveling to the countryside to visit the family of her fianceé, Shuan Bao, for the first time, Shuan Bao's younger sister rushes into the house to tell her mother, "Ma, she is here! My sister-in-law! Ma, this time she has really come!" The artist purposefully let Shuan Bao's father forget to take the hoe from his shoulder, which creates an expression of the excitement from this simple, honest old peasant.

In *Li Shuangshuang*, after Shuangshuang and her husband, Xi Wang, had a big fight, Xi Wang left home. Soon, he realized he was wrong but he was ashamed to return home, so Shuangshuang came to him to make peace. She whispers, "This family will never dismiss you," and in order to represent the love expression of a typical Chinese wife in such a circumstance, the artist depicts the couple's young daughter handing Xi Wang the key to the family home. *Lian Sheng San Ji* is color-inked with brush. Both paintings and text are humorous. The story is about a rich, stupid young man of ancient times who gets a high-ranking position by tricks and sheer luck.

He Youzhi is a self-taught comic artist; he learned to draw in 1952 at age 30 when he was assigned to work in the Shanghai New Art Publishing House. His comic book *Shan Xiang Ju Bian* won the first award in the National Comics Contest in the 1960s.

H.Y.L.L.

HEAP, THE (U.S.) The Heap character was created in December 1942 by writer Harry Stein and artist Mort Leav for an appearance in the *Sky Wolf* feature in Hillman's *Air Fighters* number three. Originally introduced as a villain, the Heap was once World War I flying ace Baron Eric von Emmelman. And though his origin was retold and revised constantly over the years, the most often cited "facts" claimed that von Emmelman had been shot down in a dogfight over Poland, survived the ensuing crash into a swamp, and somehow evolved into the hairy, brownish-green brute called the Heap.

After two additional appearances as a foe of Sky Wolf (February 1945 and May 1946), the Heap was awarded his own feature beginning in the October 1946 *Airboy* number 32. And, as the emphasis of *The Heap* series evolved from airfights and Nazis to sociology and almost religious allegories, the Heap was given a young sidekick, Rickie Wood. Ironically, *The Heap* outlasted *Sky Wolf* and was not discontinued until *Airboy* number 111 (May 1953). Over the years, many outstanding artists like Leonard Starr, Carmine Infantino, Bernard Sachs, and Dan Barry produced stories, but none handled it with the grace and style of Mort Leav. His visualization of Stein's character, which was drawn while he was employed by the Jerry Iger shop, remains the definitive version, even though Leav drew only the character's first story.

On the other hand, writers Bill Woolfolk and creator Harry Stein made *The Heap* the most perplexing

"The Heap," Mort Leav. © Hillman Periodicals.

feature of the era. As the strip continued to grow in popularity and respect, Woolfolk transformed the Heap from a snarling, raging behemoth into a puzzling and misunderstood paradox. Created by Stein strictly as a wartime villain, the character was revamped by Woolfolk who used concepts from classic horror creatures such as Frankenstein and Dracula. By the end of the strip's run, the Heap was cast as a victim of our insane and corrupt society. He became more a symbol of man's inhumanity to man than a hulking, crime-combatting hero-villain. He even developed many of the traits later found in the cinematic antiheroes of the late 1960s.

A new *Heap* feature began in *Psycho* number two (March 1970), a black-and-white comic magazine published by Skywald. Greatly inferior to his namesake, this Heap was also a pilot—a test pilot who fell into a vat of chemicals and emerged as a gelatin-like mass of glop. Although the stories were generally vapid, artist Tom Sutton produced one outstanding story in *The Heap* number one (a one-shot, standard-sized color comic published in September 1971). Drawing heavily on the hero-as-victim-of-society motif of the original *Heap*, this singular story displayed both emotion and sensitivity—rare qualities for this second *Heap* series.

J.B.

HEART OF JULIET JONES, THE (U.S.) One of the few outstanding strips of its genre, *The Heart of Juliet Jones* was the happy collaboration of Stan Drake's desire to draw a strip, Eliot Caplin's desire to write a romantic strip, and King Features's desire to develop high-quality competition to *Mary Worth*, the leading soap-opera strip of the time. The strip began in dailies in March 1953 and in Sundays a year later.

Bob Lubbers had suggested strip work to the commercial artist Drake, and Gill Fox had introduced him to Eliot Caplin. Ironically, in a conference between comics editor Sylvan Byck and Caplin, each insisted he had the perfect artist—and eventually realized they were both talking about Drake.

Margaret Mitchell, of *Gone with the Wind* fame, had been developing a love strip for King at the time of her death, so when *Juliet Jones* came along the syndicate was satisfied that it could enter the field. An advance sales push sold *Juliet Jones* to almost 90 papers before the start of the strip, a record at that time.

"The Heart of Juliet Jones," Stan Drake. © King Features Syndicate.

The major characters live in Devon, a small town. Juliet Jones, originally a girl in her early 30s, is a smart, attractive, and conservatively stylish woman who served a term as mayor of her town. In the course of the strip—how long could an attractive young lady have romance after romance without A) getting married or B) being suspected of one of several character defects?—Juliet married Owen Cantrell, a major criminal lawyer, and they lived in an apartment in a New York-type city while Eve, Juliet's vivacious blonde sister, in her early 20s, carried the romance of the strip. However, Cantrell was murdered in the 1970s and Juliet and Eve now live at home with their father, wise old Howard "Pop" Jones, a retired lumber company executive. He counsels and scolds as the perfect story strip father should. Other characters are recurring rather than major (people of the town) and new episodes bring temporary casts.

Drake and Caplin combined to make *Juliet Jones* an exciting strip with one of the most sophisticated story lines and outstanding artwork. The scripts ran the gamut from ethereal happiness to intense loneliness to profound tension. And Drake's art attempted great things and achieved them; there was frequent experimentation in visual techniques, shading, and mood. Where other straight artists use models and photographs to work from, Drake far surpassed his fellows in utilizing bold angles and cinematic blocking. Only Leonard Starr is perhaps his equal in their particular branch of strip art: romantic, breezy, and sophisticated.

At its peak, Juliet Jones had over 600 papers—a major showing. The strip was the recipient of the NCS Best Story Strip award in 1969, 1970, and 1972. Drake left *Juliet Jones* in 1989 to devote his full time to drawing *Blondie*, and he was replaced on the strip by Frank Bolle.

R.M.

HEATH, GEORGE (1900-1968) British cartoonist and illustrator, born 1900 in Tonbridge, Kent. Considerable aptitude at drawing while at school led him to study art at the Goldsmith College, then to train as an art teacher at the Regent Street Polytechnic in London. He taught art at the Teddington Art School in Middlesex until it closed down in the early 1930s. He then abandoned teaching for commercial art, entering an agency in London. His work interested Stanley J. Gooch, controlling editor of a comics group at Amalgamated Press, and a few story illustrations led to a picture story assignment for the back page of a penny comic. He quickly became the top artist for these full-page serials, drawing with a firm line, attention to setting and detail, and dramatic action. These serials were a new departure for the penny comics, which up to the 1930s featured nothing but humor strips. They reflected the trend to adventure strips begun in the American newspaper funnies a few years earlier and were more dynamic than the picture serials already running in the twopenny comics, such as *Rob the Rover* (q.v.). Later, Heath introduced the American style of speech balloon and caption to replace the typeset narrative that ran underneath his panels.

His first serial strips were *Forest of Fear* in *Funny Wonder* and *Young Adventurers* in *Larks* (both 1932), changing to *Sacred Eye of Satpura* (*Funny Wonder*) and *Two Little Wanderers* (*Larks*) in 1934. That year he added a third serial, *Red Man's Gold*, in *Jester*. In 1935 he introduced *Fortune in the Desert* (*Funny Wonder*), and in 1936 *Call of the West* (*Jester*). Also in 1936 came a new departure, the depiction of famous film stars in adventure strips: *Tim McCoy* (*Funny Wonder*), and *James Cagney* (*Larks*). This trend continued in 1938 with *Clark Gable* in *Radio Fun*, followed by radio stars *The Western Brothers,* and *Bebe Daniels* and *Ben Lyon*, his first attempts at humorous strips (1941); *Felix Mendelssohn and his Hawaiian Serenaders* (1946); *Stewart McPherson* (1947); and *Anne Shelton* (1949). Moving to *TV Fun*, he drew *Jack Warner* (1953). His other serials were *Two True Friends* (1938) in *Crackers*; *Happy Bob Harriday* (1947) and *Rivals of the Spanish Main* (1948) in *Tip Top*; *Outlaw Trail* (1949), *Land of Silent Perils* (1951), and *Cowboy Charlie* (1952) in *Jingles*; *I Vow Vengeance* (1954) and *Family Theatre* (1958) in *TV Fun*. But his best remembered character is *The Falcon*, a detective character whom he converted into a flying superhero. *The Falcon* ran in *Radio Fun* from 1947 to 1960.

Despite an enormous body of excellent work, Heath never signed a single strip, and it is said by his son, cartoonist Michael Heath, that he disliked his job. He died in Brighton in 1968.

D.G.

HEATH, RUSSELL (1926-) American comic book and comic strip artist born September 29, 1926, in New York City. Russ Heath's first work came at 16 on Holyoke's *Hammerhead Hawley* strip in 1942, and in 1946 he moved to Timely and began drawing a full range of strips. His best work was on Westerns, however, and his material for *Arizona Kid* and *Kid Colt Outlaw* stands as some of the finest Western work ever done in comic books. It was amazingly realistic and Heath's ability to draw the "nuts and bolts" aspects of costumes, scenery, and weapons was unsurpassed. Comic writer Archie Goodwin once commented that his work was "filled with convincing grit."

Also during this time, Heath was working for Lev Gleason (love), St. John, Quality (*Plastic Man*), Avon (science fiction), E.C. (*Mad* and *Frontline Combat*) and National. Joining the latter in 1950, he became a mainstay and drew the full range of comic book features. His *Silent Knight* and *Golden Gladiator* stories, which ran in *Brave and Bold* in the late 1950s and early 1960s, are among the best ever produced in the sword-and-sorcery genre. Again, it was Heath's flair for accuracy and realism that excelled. His storytelling style was straightforward and direct, never stooping to gimmicks or frills.

After some dazzling work on National's *Sea Devils* adventure book, Heath assumed the *Sgt. Rock* strip from editor Joe Kubert. Although he had already done outstanding war material for Warren's *Blazing Combat* book in 1965 and 1966, it went generally unnoticed. But Heath outdid himself on *Sgt. Rock*, and utilizing Goodwin's "convincing grit," turned the feature into a war comics clinic. His chronicles of the adventures of Rock and his Easy Company was always as good or better than the finest cinematic interpretation.

In addition to his comic book work, Heath assisted George Wunder on *Terry and the Pirates*, Dan Barry on *Flash Gordon*, and Kurtzman and Will Elder on *Playboy* magazine's *Little Annie Fanny* feature.

Heath finally got to sign a newspaper strip when he was asked by the New York Times Syndicate in 1981 to draw the revived version of *The Lone Ranger* on texts by Carey Bates; the venture unfortunately lasted only until 1984. Aside from a few comic book assignments, he has devoted most of his time to animated cartoons.

J.B.

HECKLE AND JECKLE (U.S.) Heckle and Jeckle debuted in a cartoon produced by Paul Terry in 1946, "The Talking Magpies." The two identical, zany birds were created by Terry's story department and the first film was written chiefly by Tom Morrison, although in later years Terry was known to claim credit for the characters' inception. Whatever their origin, Heckle and Jeckle appeared in a series of cartoons and quickly joined the other Paul Terry characters in *Terry-Toons Comics*, published by Timely (later known as Marvel).

When the license on the Terry properties passed to the St. John company, *Heckle and Jeckle* went along. The feature was never an overwhelming success and its future was linked to the more popular Terry strip *Mighty Mouse*. The two magpies appeared frequently in the *Mighty Mouse* book and, beginning in 1949, in a *Heckle and Jeckle* comic, the first issue named *Blue Ribbon Comics*. The magazine lasted ten years and 34 issues, well into the period when the Terry license was assumed by the Pines company.

The St. John and Pines issues were amusing, though never outstanding. Both companies drew upon New York animation studios (especially Terry's) for their writers and artists and so the Terry strips passed through many hands, often adapting the cartoons into comic book format. Many of the stories were surrealistic in their humor, paralleling the animated films' format of having Heckle and Jeckle defying all laws of science. The two were completely unrestrained, not even by what is considered "possible" and "impossible." Some of the comic book stories had Heckle and Jeckle discussing the fact that they were comic book characters; other tales had them playing strange—and often cruel—tricks on a variety of opponents, including Dimwit Dog.

Heckle and Jeckle appeared in a number of Pines's *Mighty Mouse* giant specials before Western Publishing Company assumed the licence and featured them in three issues of *New Terrytoons* (1960-1961) and two issues of a new *Heckle and Jeckle* comic (1962). These were under the Dell Comics banner. When Western shifted its book to the Gold Key company name, it issued four issues of *Heckle and Jeckle*, beginning again with number one in 1963. They also began anew with *New Terrytoons*, which was published intermittently from May 1963 on, starting and stopping but always

featuring *Heckle and Jeckle* in the lead position. The new version of the strip lacked the surreal brand of humor but was rather successful nonetheless. Although companies had always bought the rights to the Paul Terry characters to acquire *Mighty Mouse*, at Western the *Heckle and Jeckle* feature outlived the *Mighty Mouse* comics. A *Heckle and Jeckle 3-D* comic book was issued by Spotlight Comics in 1987.

M.E.

HELD, JOHN JR. (1889-1958) An American illustrator and cartoonist born on January 10, 1889, in Salt Lake City, John Held sold his first cartoon to *Life* magazine in 1904. Encouraged by this initial success, the young boy sold more cartoons to various national magazines. After dropping out of school in 1905 he became sports cartoonist on the *Salt Lake City Tribune* and received his only art training from sculptor Mahonri Young. He moved to New York in 1910 and took a job with the *Collier's* agency. In the years preceding World War I he contributed his first cartoons to *Vanity Fair* under the pseudonym "Myrtle Held."

In 1918 John Held started drawing the flat-chested, angular girls that became the flappers of the 1920s. His full talent flowered in the pages of the *New Yorker*, where he depicted with a caustic, if indulgent, pen the ludicrous goings-on of America's silliest decade. It was inevitable that Held would attract the attention of William Randolph Hearst. In the late 1920s, Held did a panel, *Oh! Margy!,* which blossomed in 1930 into a full-fledged comic feature called *Merely Margy*, with *Joe Prep* as a companion piece. The flapper era was over by then, however, and John Held's complacent depictions of the fatuous antics of racoon-coated, hare-brained college boys and their vacuous girl friends did not quite fit the mood of the Depression. By 1935 *Margy* was gone. John Held tried again with *Rah! Rah! Rosalie*, about a pompom girl, but it flopped instantly.

Discouraged, Held went back to illustration, turned to sculpting in 1939, and later became artist-in-residence at Harvard University and the University of Georgia. He died on March 2, 1958.

M.H.

HENRY (U.S.) Carl Anderson's *Henry* started on March 19, 1932, as a series of weekly cartoons for the *Saturday Evening Post*. At first the bald-headed little hero spoke a few lines of dialogue, but later Anderson had him express himself strictly in pantomime. The cartoon series was so popular that it was often reprinted abroad; a German version drew the attention of the ever-vigilant William Randolph Hearst, who decided there and then that it should be distributed by his own syndicate, King Features. *Henry* started its career as a full-fledged daily strip on December 17, 1934, and was followed by a Sunday version on March 10, 1935.

Drawn in a sketchy, "cartoony" style, Henry is neither a Katzie-like childish demon nor a "reg'lar feller" like most other comic strip kids of the time, from Perry Winkle to Mush Stebbins. He is a loner, and his muteness (its cause is never explained) keeps him all the more estranged from the society around him. This estrangement is reflected in Henry's almost unlimited freedom: he does not seem to have strict parents or a real home or to go to school often. He is a creature of impulse who does whatever strikes his fancy; when his whims are challenged he is quite capable of hitting back at his tormentors. There are no memorable characters in the strip besides Henry himself—the secondary figures who recur from time to time are only there as foils to this diminutive hero of the absurd.

In 1942 Anderson was forced by ill health to turn *Henry* over to assistants Don Trachte, who drew the Sundays, and John Liney, who did the dailies. Trachte and Liney were reasonably successful in preserving the feature's flavor, and *Henry* remained the most popular strip of the dying pantomime genre. At Liney's death in 1979 the dailies devolved to Jack Tippit, who drew them until his own death in 1983. From that time, Dick Hodgins has been turning out the daily strip, while the Sundays are still done by Trachte.

M.H.

HERB & JAMAAL (U.S.) The very existence of *Herb & Jamaal*, by African-American cartoonist Stephen R. Bentley, was prompted by a letter sent in the late 1980s to cartoonists and syndicates from the *Detroit Free Press*. This newspaper, in a city with an African-American majority population, wanted to see more blacks in newspaper comics. It is not conicidence, therefore, that the start dates for King Features's *Curtis*, Tribune Media Services's *Herb & Jamaal*, and United Feature Syndicates's *Jump Start* are, respectively, 1988, 1989, and 1990.

Stephen Bentley is a cartoonist who paid his dues prior to the success of *Herb & Jamaal*. Born in Los Angeles, California, in 1954, Bentley joined the U.S. Navy after graduating high school. During his military service, he drew a panel titled *Navy Life* for his base newspaper. After leaving the navy, Bentley attended Pasadena City College in California and began a freelance career. He drew artwork for the Los Angeles Dodgers baseball team, including the feature *The Tenth Player*.

Bentley's freelance cartoon career prospered. In 1983, his comic strip *Squirt*, about a female firefighter (then a radical concept), was briefly distributed by Weekly Features Syndicate. His cartoon *Hey Coach* was a regular feature in Swimming World magazine. For three years prior to *Herb & Jamaal*, he drew weekly humorous ad layouts for Quinn's Natural Food Centers that appeared in the *Los Angeles Times*.

After hearing about the *Detroit Free Press* letter from fellow cartoonist Ed McGeean, Bentley was introduced to *Motley's Crew* creators Ben Templeton and the late Tom Forman, who were trying to collaborate with an African-American cartoonist on a feature for Tribune Media Services (TMS). Ultimately, *Herb & Jamaal* was created, and TMS quickly decided it should be written and drawn exclusively by Bentley.

Herb & Jamaal centers on two high-school pals who meet at a reunion and decide to go into business together, opening what was first an ice cream parlor and has become a soul food restaurant. The lanky bachelor Jamaal, a former pro basketball player, finances the business. Herb had previously worked for the gas company. He's married to Sarah Louise, and the couple has a son, Ezekiel, and a daughter, Uhuru, named in honor of the Nichelle Nichols' character in the original *Star Trek* television series. Herb's mother-in-law, Eula, is a Trekkie.

This is family humor done in a style distinctive to Bentley. His theory is that a cartoonist must entertain but can still get a message into the start of a daily if he has a good punch line for the last panel. The charac-

ters are also involved in their community, although this aspect of the strip is not as hard-edged as the inner-city life shown in *Curtis*. Both *Herb & Jamaal* and *Jump Start* focus more on pure family humor.

B.C.

HERCULES (U.S.) 1—The first comic book character to capitalize on the mythological name "Hercules" was Timely's *Hercules* which made only two appearances, in issues three and four of *Mystic* (January 1940 to August 1940). Known only as the "son of Dr. David," the character and premise were as short on imagination as on longevity.

2—The second comic book *Hercules* appeared in MLJ's *Blue Ribbon* comics from June 1940 to January 1941 (issues four through eight). Probably created by writer Joe Blair, this Hercules was sent back to earth by Zeus to rid the planet of gangsters, mobs, and the like. Alternately costumed in a blue business suit or white trunks with red boots, this Hercules occasionally returned to Olympus for advice.

3—The next use of the Hercules name came in Quality's *Hit* number one. Created by artist Dan Zolnerowich and writer Gregg Powers in July 1940, this strip featured Joe Hercules, a blond and superpowered character who wore a relatively standard superhero suit and cape. But despite the hackneyed plots and villains, *Hercules* managed to be handled by a few of Quality's fine artistic stable, including Reed Crandall, Lou Fine, Matt Baker, and George Tuska. The feature last appeared in the April 1942 issue of *Hit* number 21.

4—Marvel introduced their version of Hercules in a 1967 issue of *The Avengers*. Still a man-god from Olym-

"Hercules," Lou Fine. © Comic Magazines, Inc.

pus, this Hercules was also saddled with the stereotypic superhero-with-problems theme plaguing every Marvel character, but he only appeared sporadically.

5—In 1963, Gold Key produced two issues each of the *Adventures of Hercules* and *Mighty Hercules*. The first was a serious comic book, the second a funny adaptation, but neither were financially or artistically successful.

6—Charlton Comics produced the only serious adaptation of the Hercules mythology in 13 issues of *Hercules* produced between October 1967 and September 1969. Written by Joe Gill, the stories were only adequate and suffered from poor research. A black and white reprint of the eighth issue was produced, but its almost invisible distribution has made it somewhat of a collector's item.

7—Additionally, Dell Comics produced two comic versions of *Hercules* movies in their *Color* series and they were numbered 1006 and 1121. The latter contains art by Reed Crandall.

Naturally, over the years, the name Hercules has been used in various comic books as a moniker for both hero and villain, but any complete listing of its uses would clearly be impossible. Mention should be made, however, of the *Hercules Unbound* comic book series published by National in 1975-77, and of the two *Hercules* miniseries (1982 and 1984) released by Marvel.

J.B.

HERGÉ *see* Rémi, Georges.

HERLOCK SHOLMES (Yugoslavia) *Herlock Sholmes, the Master of Disguise,* later simply called *Herlock Sholmes,* was created in 1957 by Jules Radilović and Zvonimir Furtinger, but appeared ten years later in the Yugoslav comic weekly *Plavi Vjesnik.*

If Sir Arthur Conan Doyle had been alive he would have read with great pleasure the adventures of Herlock Sholmes, an obvious adaptation of his popular detective, because in this series the detective is presented in an entirely new kind of adventure. He finds no difficulty in transforming himself into a horse, a stove, a dog, a palm, or even into a signpost if need be, if only he has his indispensable makeup case at his side. The indefatigable Sholmes jumps from one incredible adventure to another, always in the company of his good-natured and faithful friend, Doctor Waston. The strip is a fascinating creation, full of delightful humor, suspense, and hilarity.

With this series Furtinger and Radilović presented themselves as masters of the many sides of any subject which could be used in comics. In his adventures Herlock Sholmes often met Pinkerton agents or Scotland Yard detectives, who frequently asked him for help. In the first episode Sholmes searched for the gorilla-thief Anastasia; in the third episode he was in the Wild West saving a kidnapped girl; and the fourth episode, which bore the title "The Ghost of Baskervil," abounded in humor and strange events in a Scottish castle. In the fifth episode, Sholmes met his rival in the art of disguise—Prince Nana—and in the sixth episode he was a guest at the court of King Arthus. In the seventh he journeyed into the wilderness of the African jungle and there met the real Tarzan.

Radilović suspended the series in the late 1970s after he began working for several foreign publications.

E.R.

"Herlock Sholmes," Julio Radilović. © Strip Art Features.

HERMANN *see* Huppen, Hermann.

HERNAN EL CORSARIO (Argentina) Argentine cartoonist José Luis Salinas created the adventure strip *Hernan el Corsario* ("Hernan the Privateer") in one of the first issues of the comic magazine *Patoruzú* (November 1936). The strip's historic value is notable because it represents the first attempt by an Argentine cartoonist to produce a nonhumor feature of quality. Considering that this was Salinas's first work of this type and that he was then learning the rudiments of his art, one must concede that *Hernan el Corsario* was a memorable creation. With this strip, one of the author's masterworks, Salinas gave birth to his unforgettable graphic style, and many of the qualities that can be found in the later *Cisco Kid* are already present in these pages. Each panel could be compared to a film frame, never static, but full of motion.

When Salinas's publisher decided to launch a new comic magazine called *Patoruzito,* he again selected *Hernan el Corsario* for the first issue (October 11, 1945). The new version was smaller in format and Salinas made use of speech balloons where previously he had used only captions; it retained, however, all its flavor and its masterly quality. It was discontinued on August 20, 1946, with Salinas going on to greater triumphs.

L.G.

HERRIMAN, GEORGE (1880-1944) Born 1880, in New Orleans of African heritage, George "Garge" Herriman, creator of *Krazy Kat* and the foremost comic strip artist, was the son of a baker who moved to Los Angeles while he was growing up. While in high school, Herriman drove the family bread wagon and helped with the baking. Never happy with his parents, he played pranks on them, such as salting several hundred doughnuts and burying a dead mouse in a loaf of bread—the last trick getting him thrown out on his own. Herriman then got a job on the old *Los Angeles Herald* as an office boy. He put all of his spare time into his cartooning ambitions, sending work off to such magazines as *Life* and *Judge*, where much of it sold. Unable to persuade his *Herald* bosses to upgrade him to staff cartoonist, he rode the rails to New York at 20 and took a sustaining job as a salesman, while he spent most of his time selling himself—hopefully—to New York newspaper editors. Finally he landed a job as staff artist on the *New York World* in 1901, where he did daily art and Sunday full and half comic pages in color (some reprinted in Philadelphia and elsewhere), but did not undertake an actual comic strip.

Seeing little future with the *World*, Herriman tried a short-lived half-page Sunday strip (his first), with the McClure Syndicate, called *Lariat Pete* (about a rough-and-tumble cowhand visiting relatives back East), of which only seven episodes appeared between September 6, 1903, and November 15, 1903; then he turned to sports-page work on the Hearst *New York Journal*, where he shared cartooning honors with the *Journal's* famed Tad Dorgan (and in fact drew a large number of the cartoons signed by Dorgan at that time). Unable to interest his Hearst editors in his strip ideas, Herriman sold three series in 1905 to the World Color Printing Co. of St. Louis (which circulated a four-page color strip section to many newspapers): *Major Ozone's Fresh Air Crusade, Rosy-Posy—Grandma's Girl,* and *Bud Smith. Major Ozone* was a wildly fanciful strip and some of its freewheeling pages resemble those of the later *Krazy Kat* in unbridled imagination, about a contemporary Don Quixote obsessed with clean air; *Rosy-Posy* was a simple gag strip about an eight-year-old girl, and *Bud Smith* focused on a slightly older boy. On the strength of the income from these strips, Herriman left the *Journal* and returned to Los Angeles. Recalled by the *Journal* in 1907, he traveled back to New York to do general cartooning and launch a short-lived daily strip called *Baron Mooch* (essentially continued in his later *Baron Bean*). He followed this in June 1910 with the extraordinary daily strip, *The Dingbat Family*, in which his talents fully flowered in the creation of his most famed characters: the crew of humanized animals who populate the mythic fantasy land of *Coconino County* in *Krazy Kat*. (*Krazy Kat* appeared as a strip of its own in October 1913, to which a Sunday page was added in 1919.)

By January 1916, however, Herriman had dropped *The Dingbat Family* and replaced it with the daily *Baron Bean*, a very funny fantasy strip which ran until December 31, 1918. Herriman followed with two relatively short-lived and unimportant daily strips: *Mary's Home From College,* which ran for the first four months of 1919 and was replaced by *Now Listen, Mabel* (following a love-sick lad yearning for a fickle girl named Mabel Malarkey) which ended at the end of 1919. From this point, Herriman worked only on *Krazy Kat* until December 4, 1922, when he opened *Stumble Inn*. A continuing comedy strip about a Mr. and Mrs. Stumble who run a ramshackle hotel, their bumbling

house detective, and the series of weird guests they entertain, *Stumble Inn* was a major comic strip hit of the 1920s and was nearly made into a live-action film. It folded in April 1925, after which Herriman started his last strip independent of *Krazy Kat, Us Husbands*. A Sunday gag strip about married conflict, *Us Husbands* started on July 3, 1926, and ran for little more than half a year, as did its weekly companion piece, *Mistakes Will Happen*, a gag feature without continuing characters. After this page was dropped, Herriman concentrated on *Krazy Kat*, doing only a daily panel called *Embarassing Moments* for a few years in the late 1920s.

In the meantime, Herriman had moved to Los Angeles in 1924 and built a Spanish-style house in the Hollywood hills, where he lived with his wife, children, and dogs until his death. He liked poetry, especially the comic poetry of Don Marquis, whose three *Archy and Mehitabel* books he illustrated with stunning effect in the 1920s. But Herriman's classic work, *Krazy Kat*, speaks more for his fundamental graphic and literary genius than any other undertaking, and any episode from that magnum opus is enough to tell the reader that he is looking at the work of a master in the field of comics. Time eventually ran out for Herriman in Los Angeles on April 26, 1944, and he died quietly in his sleep after a short illness.

B.B.

HERRON, FRANCE EDWARD (1916-1966) American comic book writer and editor born 1916 in New York City. Eddie Herron broke into the comic book business at Fox in 1939, and after a short stint at the Harry "A" Chesler shop, became an editor at Fawcett on October 10, 1940.

Herron's Fawcett assignments came as a result of several excellent *Captain Marvel* scripts he had submitted. In addition to his tightly knit scripts and editing, Herron was responsible for the first of many *Captain Marvel* spin-offs when he and artist Mac Raboy created the *Captain Marvel Jr.* feature for December 1941's *Whiz* number 25. Earlier that year, he and artist Jack Kirby developed the *Mr. Scarlet* strip in *Wow* number one (Spring 1941). Herron was dismissed as Fawcett editor March 1, 1942, for purchasing scripts he had written under a pen name.

While he was still editor at Fawcett, however, Herron freelanced for other companies. Along with artist Al Plastino, he created *The Rainbow* for Centaur, a colorful—if short-lived—superhero who made his sole appearance in *Arrow* number three (October 1941). He also created *The Red Skull*, perhaps the most famous comic book villain. The malevolent super-Nazi made his first appearance in Timely's *Captain America* number one (March 1941).

After serving in the armed forces during World War II, Herron returned to comics and wrote several outstanding stories for Quality's *Blackhawk* feature. He later moved to National and scripted stories for *Batman* and *The Boy Commandos*, but then turned his attention to short story writing. He continued working sporadically for National (*Challengers of the Unknown, Blackhawk, Tomahawk*) and on syndicated strips (*Bat Masterson, Davy Crockett*) until his death on September 2, 1966.

J.B.

HERSHFIELD, HARRY (1885-1974) Next to James Swinnterton the longest-lived of the great comic strip

Harry Hershfield.

artists, Harry Hershfield was born of newly arrived Russian immigrants in Cedar Rapids, Iowa, on October 13, 1885. Like many of his peers of the time, Hershfield roamed about the country with his cartooning talent from an early age, doing newspaper sports and feature-story comic art first on the *Chicago Daily News* in 1899 at the age of 14 (where he drew his first strip, *Homeless Hector*, about a big-city street mutt), moving to the *San Francisco Chronicle* in 1907, then to the Hearst *Chicago Examiner* in late 1909 (where he created another dog strip, *Rubber, the Canine Cop*), and finally to the *New York Journal* to begin his first major strip in 1910, *Desperate Desmond*. Later, Desmond, a silk-hatted villain, was switched to another, similar strip called *Dauntless Durham of the U.S.A.,* where his adventures ended in January 1914. Hershfield then immediately began his most successful and longest-lasting strip, *Abie the Agent,* for the same paper, running it both daily and Sunday at various times until 1940, when this notable ethnic comedy finally and lamentably folded. While drawing and writing *Desmond, Durham,* and *Abie,* Hershfield periodically reintroduced *Hector* to readers, for the last time as a Sunday strip accompaniment to *Abie* in the 1920s. During a legal disagreement with the Hearst interests circa 1933-35, Hershfield worked for the *New York Herald-Tribune,* where he drew a Sunday half-page called *According to Hoyle,* about a well-to-do, elderly, walrus-moustached New Yorker named Hugo Hoyle and his modish wife, Hannah.

Hershfield quickly developed a marked reputation as a humorous writer and raconteur quite apart from his repute as a strip artist. For a number of years in the late 1910s, Hershfield wrote weekly short comic pieces, presumably narrated by Abie, under such titles as "Abie on Conversation," "Abie on Summer Snapshots," etc., which ran on the editorial and feature pages of newspapers, many of which did not carry the *Abie* strip at all. In 1932, he became a columnist ("My Week") for the *New York Daily Mirror,* and, later, in the 1930s, began to broadcast theatrical criticism, scripted for Hollywood studios, and joined the radio cast of *Can*

You Top This? a 1940s show tailored for comic raconteurs. His ethnic dialect stories, largely about Irish, Jewish, and German types, were marked by wit and good taste. A toastmaster who was always in great demand, Hershfield also authored such books as *Laugh Louder, Live Longer* (Grayson, 1959), a title which seems to have been happily prophetic in his case. He died on December 17, 1974, in New York City.

B.B.

HERZOG, GUY (1923-   ) A Belgian cartoonist born July 11, 1923, in Riga, Latvia, Guy Herzog spent his childhood in a number of foreign countries. A member of the Belgian diplomatic service, Herzog's father returned his family to Belgium in 1940.

In 1945 Herzog founded the arts and letters weekly *Le Faune,* which folded the next year, carrying away all of the young man's savings. From 1946 to 1949 he held a variety of jobs as an advertising man, lathe operator in a plant manufacturing car engines, sports writer, designer, and cartoonist. In 1949 he became editor-in-chief of the weekly publication *Vivre.* In 1950 he moved to Paris and contributed a great many cartoons (under his pseudonym "Bara") to various French publications.

In 1955 Bara created the pantomime strip *Max l'Explorateur* (later simply called *Max*). Syndicated by P.I.B. of Copenhagen, the strip appeared for the first time in the daily *France-Soir* on March 1, 1955; it was later published in newspapers throughout Europe. In addition to his work on *Max,* Bara designed stage sets from 1960 to 1963.

Returning to Belgium in 1963, Bara produced a continuity strip featuring *Max* for the comic weekly *Spirou.* From there he went to *Tintin* in 1969. At *Tintin* he resumed the drawing of *Max* and later did another gag strip, *Ephémère,* about a star-crossed traveler. In 1973 he produced *Cro-Magnon,* featuring a zany tribe of prehistoric cavemen. Bara was also the founder, publisher, and editor of a monthly magazine aimed at the medical profession, *L'Oeuf,* which ran from 1971 to 1973. After leaving *Tintin* in 1977, he contributed to a number of European periodicals, notably *Zack* in Germany, for which he created *Sigi the Frank* (1978), about a feckless warrior of the Middle Ages. His mainstay, however, remains *Max,* which has now passed the 40-year mark.

Bara is one of the most versatile and talented gag cartoonists in Europe. With a few lines and a simple background he is able to create a hilarious situation that he then presents in all of its variations, transformations, and implications. Bara is, without a doubt, the supreme pantomime strip artist, far ahead of even Carl Anderson or Dahl Mikkelsen.

M.H.

HESS, SOL (1872-1941) American comic strip writer born October 14, 1872, on a farm in Northville Township, Illinois. When Sol Hess was eight years old, his parents moved to Chicago; the next year his father died and Sol went to work as an errand-boy for a wholesale jewelry company. Hess eventually became a salesman for the firm and traveled the western United States with a line of watches and jewelry. He did so well that he founded, with two partners, the watch and diamond firm of Rettig, Hess, and Madsen.

Sol Hess's involvement in comics came late and quite by accident. His office was located a block from

Stilson's, a favorite hangout of newspapermen. John Wheeler, former head of the Bell Syndicate, recounted in his memoir *I've Got News For You*: "Sol Hess was a Chicago jeweler who liked to associate with newspapermen and pay the tabs, so he was welcome. Among those he met in this rendezvous were Ring Lardner, Clare Briggs, John McCutcheon, and a struggling cartoonist, Sid Smith."

Sol Hess became a close friend of Sidney Smith, who had just started to draw *The Gumps*, and before long he was supplying most of the dialogues for the strip as a labor of love. When Smith got his famous million-dollar contract in 1922, he asked Hess to stay with him as his ghost-writer for $200 a week. Feeling insulted Hess broke with Smith and proposed a brand-new idea for a family strip to Wheeler, who promptly accepted. For the drawing Hess then turned to W. A. Carlson, with whom he had previously worked on a short-lived series of *Gumps* animated cartoons. In May of 1923 Hess and Carlson finally brought in the new strip, called *The Nebbs* (to which was later added a companion strip, *Simp O'Dill*, about a sap-headed coffee-house owner).

The Nebbs did so well that Sol Hess was able to quit the jewelry business in 1925. A generous, friendly, and much-beloved man in and out of his chosen profession, as well as a creator of small but solid achievement, Sol Hess was greatly missed when he died on December 31, 1941.

M.H.

"Hi and Lois," Dik Browne and Mort Walker. © King Features Syndicate.

HI AND LOIS (U.S.) The quintessential suburban family strip, *Hi and Lois* has climbed steadily but quietly in circulation and popularity since its inception in 1954; it remains one of the most popular comics.

Mort Walker, with three years of a successful *Beetle Baily* under his belt, suggested the story idea to King Features after introducing a sister and brother-in-law on some of Beetle's visits home. He and comic editor Sylvan Byck developed the names and basics and began looking for an artist.

In one of those coincidences that luckily frequent the annals of comic history, Byck noticed Dik Browne's *Tracy Twins* in *Boy's Life* magazine during a dentist visit; Walker saw a candy advertisement of Browne's, one of many for the Johnstone and Cushing agency. Browne topped both their lists and was offered the job of drawing *Hi and Lois*. The first strip appeared in October of 1954.

The family has not changed since inception except for a more sophisticated personality on the part of Trixie, the baby who doesn't walk or talk but thinks and dominates half of the strips. The parents, Hi and Lois Flagston, are typical suburbanites; Hi goes to the Foofram offices every morning and Lois is inevitably cleaning or shopping. She is more of a real housewife than Blondie.

Chip, the early-teen eldest son, is mop-haired, lazy, and at the inevitable awkward age. Nobody but his friends quite understand him. The twins, Dot and Ditto, are first-graders whose main interest in life seems to be outshining—or outmaneuvering—each other. And Trixie, the baby, has been given to thoughts and "conversations" with sunbeams that seem to be the most popular feature of the strip today.

Other incidental characters and settings have become more incidental through the years: Thirsty Thurston, the next-door souse; Hi's boss Mr. Foofram; the Abercrombie and Fitch; neighborhood garbagemen.

The gags are gentle and real (perhaps the strip's most endearing quality) and the art simple and clean. After Dik Browne's death in 1989, his son, Bob "Chance" Browne, took over the drawing duties. Mort's sons, Brian and Greg Walker, are now in charge of the writing.

R.M.

HICKS, REGINALD ERNEST (1915-   ) Born in Kent, England, in 1915, Reginald Ernest Hicks's parents brought him to Melbourne, Australia, in 1921. At the age of 14, Reg Hicks obtained a job learning color stencil designing in a soft goods factory, where he spent the next four years learning his trade and ending up in charge of the art department. During that time he began to study music and learned to play violin. On leaving the factory, he taught violin and attended art training at the National Gallery School under Napier Waller and John Rowell. Hicks became an exhibiting member of the Victorian Artists Society as well as doing freelance caricatures, cartoons, and interviews for various magazines.

In 1934 he produced Australia's first adventure strip of any consequence. This was an adaptation of Erle Cox's *Out of the Silence*, which ran in the *Melbourne Argus* from August 4 to December 21. At the same time he was drawing a single column children's feature, *Kitty's Kapers*; like much of his early comic work these features were signed "Hix." In the following six years he created a multitude of strips for both the *Argus* and the *Age*, including *Robinson Crusoe* (1936), *The Deerslayer* (1936), *Willy and Wally* (1937), *Betty and Bob* (1936-37), *The King's Treasure* (1938), and *The Space Patrol* (1938-40). During this period, he created *The Adventures of Larry Steele,* which ran in the *Age* from October 2, 1937, to October 30, 1940, and became the first Australian adventure strip to prove popular with readers and establish any reasonable lifespan. Reg Hicks had a tremendous capacity for work—while his strips were running in the *Age* (sometimes as many as two dailies and two weeklies at the same time) he was still freelancing as well as working as a story reader for the Australian Broadcasting Commission and doing commercial radio work.

In 1940, Hicks became a member of naval intelligence but was released from service after nine months. He joined Associated Newspapers and created *Tightrope Tim*, which appeared in the *Sydney Sunday Sun* on

Reg Hicks, "Jungle Drums." © The Herald and Weekly Times Ltd.

August 3, 1941. This adventure strip ran until May 29, 1949, setting a record for the genre which wasn't beaten until the advent of *Rod Craig* (1946-1955). He also created a daily domestic strip, *Family Man*, which ran in the *Sydney Sun* for over 12 years. Again, Hicks kept up his frantic outside activities, freelancing for *Rydges*, the *Sydney Morning Herald*, and various advertising agencies, and still found time to produce four *Kid Koals* comic books.

When he left Associated Newspapers in 1958, he became involved in a number of commercial enterprises, including kitchen utilities, plastics, fiberglass, and pottery, yet he still found time to create a strip called *Debbie* for *The New Idea* as well as writing and drawing stories for overseas children's annuals and drawing book covers for Hodders. He is a life member of the A.J.A., an Associate of the Royal Society of Art, and served as vice president of the Adelaide Art Society. Reg Hicks is a remarkably versatile and prolific artist who can rightly lay claim to instigating and popularizing the adventure strip in Australia. He retired in 1977.

J.R.

HIDALGO, FRANCISCO (1929-   ) Spanish cartoonist and French photographer born in Jaen, Spain, on May 7, 1929. Self-taught in art (although he later studied at the School of Fine Arts in Paris to perfect his skills), Francisco Hidalgo was an avid reader of the comics from the earliest age. "I don't know when I started to get interested in drawing," he said. "I believe I was born a cartoonist." At any rate, he soon developed his own idiosyncratic style, and at age 17 began to see his creations published in the Spanish comics magazines of the period. The influence of American comics is evident even in the titles of these early stories, such as *Skilled* and *Dick Sanders*.

It was in 1948, with *Dr Niebla* ("Dr. Fog"), that Hidalgo achieved his greatest success. Based on a series of paperback novels written by Rafael Gonzalez, *Dr. Niebla* was in the tradition of mysterious defenders of justice ("No one has ever seen his face. He appears and disappears in the mist"), and his adventures took him from London to New York and throughout the entire world. The artist fleshed out the character, giving him presence and motivation far beyond the conventionality of the scripts (first written by Gonzalez himself, later by Victor Mora). His use of black and white was masterful, and his compositions succeeded in re-creating the atmospheric settings of the *film noirs* of the period. *Dr. Niebla* is now regarded as one of the classics of the Spanish comic strip.

In the 1950s, Hidalgo settled in Paris, where economic circumstances were more favorable for cartoonists than in his native Spain. He soon began contributing a great number of comics to many French magazines, while continuing to draw *Dr. Niebla* until 1959. Among his most notable French contributions were *Bob Mallard* (which he signed "Yves Roy"), an interesting aviation series, and *Teddy Ted*, a Western in which the artist's knowledge of and love for American films served him well. He was equally at ease with the handling of machines, horses, and human characters, and his sense of composition remained as sure as ever.

At the same time, Hidalgo had become fascinated with the medium of photography, and in the mid-1960s, he abandoned the comics (*Pat Patrick* in 1964 was his final contribution to the field) in favor of his new vocation. As a photographer, he has become world famous and he has exhibited widely and received many honors. Yet, as he has often said to interviewers, the comics remain "his one enduring love."

M.H.

HILDEBRANDT, GREG AND TIM (1939-   ) The fraternal twin brothers Greg and Tim Hildebrandt are best known for their work illustrating J.R.R. Tolkien's *Lord of the Rings*, painting a series of 64 Marvel superheroes for trading cards, and reviving *Terry and the Pirates* in March 1995 for Tribune Media Services.

Francisco Hidalgo, "Teddy Ted." © Editions Vaillant.

Born in Detroit, Michigan, in 1939, at age three the Hildebrant brothers sat on their grandfather's knees as he read them the Sunday funnies. As kids, *Prince Valiant*, *Tarzan*, *Tim Tyler's Luck*, *Dick's Adventures in Dreamland*, and *Terry and the Pirates* were their favorites. The first movie they ever saw was Walt Disney's *Pinocchio* when they were five years old. All through childhood, the twins drew their own comic books, made animated flip books, built models and puppets, and loved anything having to do with cartooning and art.

After a six-month stint at Mienzienger Art School in Detroit, at age 19 Greg and Tim were hired by Jamhandy Company of Detroit, at the time the largest industrial film production house in the world. During their four-year stay at Jamhandy, they progressed to doing storyboards and more advanced work. During this time, they also worked as freelancers illustrating some religious children's books that were published by Franciscan monks in New Jersey. This project brought them to the attention of Bishop Fulton J. Sheen, who had a nationally syndicated weekly television show.

At the time, Dik Browne, of *Hi and Lois* and later *Hägar the Horrible* fame, was the house artist for Bishop Sheen. However, Sheen hired the Hildebrandts to make 16mm documentary films depicting world poverty, which he would use on his television show to educate his viewers about the world beyond the United States. The Hildebrandts traveled to Africa, Asia, and South America, and did very little artwork during this seven-year period. However, constant exposure to the despair of the Third World took its toll,

and they left to pursue a career as a freelance illustration team.

They gained a reputation for always making their deadlines and being able to imitate any style. They drew children's books for Western Publishing's Golden Books, record album covers, and drawings for a myriad of publishers from Doubleday to Random House. Then, on the back of the 1975 Tolkien calendar they noticed a request for artists who would like to draw a *Lord of the Rings* calendar for Ballantine Books. To their surprise, the Hildebrants were the only professional artists to submit work, and they received the job. In all, the Hildebrandts did three calendars for Ballantine, a total of 40 paintings, and they also wrote and illustrated their own fantasy epic, *Ursurak*. Nothing they had done previously equalled the fame the Tolkien paintings brought. Their reputation grew further when they created the original movie poster for *Star Wars* in 1977.

In the early 1980s, after working as a team for their entire lives, Greg and Tim split up. Each pursued independent careers as artists. During that period, Tim drew all the artwork for Parker Brothers' *Clue* games. They merged their talents again in 1992 and continued doing commercial art and paintings of fantasy and comic book heroes. In 1994, Michael Uslan, a driving force behind the successful *Batman* movies, approached the Hildebrandts about a new 1990s version of *Terry and the Pirates*.

The original *Terry* had been continuously syndicated from October 1934 until February 1973. Tribune Media Services launched the second version in March 1995 with characters redesigned by the Hildebrandts and scripts by Uslan. Although newspaper feature editors did not respond well to the new *Terry*, Uslan's stories were sassy, sexy, and action-packed, and the Hildebrandts' drawings of the Dragon Lady, Burma, and Pat Ryan were creative successes. However, the punk-influenced Terry, with his thin face, earring, severe haircut, and backward baseball cap, did not meet with success. Tim and Greg continued drawing the strip for over a year, but not enough newspapers subscribed to justify the Hildebrandts' efforts. Comic book veteran Dan Spiegle took over the artwork and Jim Clark the scripts, and the twins returned to painting and illustration.

B.C.

HILL, ALBERT (1901-1986) British cartoonist Albert Hill was born in Guernsey in the Channel Islands on December 1, 1901. He left school at 13 to become a trainee projectionist at the Electric Cinema, where he became fascinated by the "Lightning Sketch" films of G. E. Studdy, Hy Mayer, and other cartoonists. These films showed the artists' hands quickly sketching cartoons, that then became animated. Always top at art in school and interested in the comic papers, Hill decided to try his hand at cartoons. When the Electric Cinema closed down in 1917 he joined a printing firm as an apprentice and was encouraged by his employer to submit his cartoons to mainland publishers. His first acceptance was a joke drawing for *Merry & Bright*, executed in 1919 but not published until June 5, 1920.

Over the next few years his "singles" appeared in most of the penny comics, and his first strip, a five-panel "one off," was published in *Larks*, on March 9, 1929. When Provincial Comics of Bath published their first weekly, *The Midget Comic* (June 5, 1931), Hill submitted his samples and was immediately given the front-page character, *Sammy Spry*. When the comic changed its format to tabloid and its title to *Merry Midget* (September 12, 1931), Hill moved inside with an additional strip called *Frolics in the Far West*, and was given the large front page of a new companion comic, *Sparkler* (September 12, 1931) on which appeared *Breezy Moments on Wurzel Farm*. This rapid success prompted Hill to think of going freelance, but, unfortunately, Provincial Comics collapsed, leaving Hill

unpaid for several strips. He returned to the printing trade as a typesetter.

In 1933 he was contacted by Louis Diamond, the former editor of Provincial Comics, with an offer to contribute to two new comics Diamond was about to publish from Bath. Taking the chance, Hill was soon launched on a cartooning career that quickly enabled him to freelance. Both comics had Hill strips on the front pages, *Crazy Kink the Goofy Gangster* in *Rattler*, and *Charlie Chuckle* in *Dazzler* (both August 19, 1933). These were later replaced by *Willie Wart & Wally Warble* and *Squirt & Squib*.

The comics were such a success that companions were launched, with Hill drawing for them all. *Chuckler* (March 31, 1934) had *Tommy Trot the Tudor Tramp* and *Grizzly Gus the Tricky Trapper*. *Target* (June 15, 1935) had *Tom Tip & Tim Top the Tramps* and *Western Willie the Cowboy Coughdrop*. *Rocket* (October 26, 1935) had *Freddie Freewheel*. *Sunshine* (July 16, 1938) had *P. C. Copperclock the Desert Cop*. *Bouncer* (Fetruary 11, 1939) had *Willie Scribble the Pavement Artist*. These and his other characters were killed when the comics were bought out by Amalgamated Press. Hill made the transfer to Amalgamated, and after taking on a number of strips by other artists, including *The Chimps* (Ray Bailey) and *Will Hay* (Bertie Brown), he created *Puckville Pranks* for *Puck* (1939).

World War II was a bigger setback for Hill than any of the publishers' crises: Guernsey was occupied by the Germans. Affer the war, Hill was quickly in print with the official Liberation cartoon; he then drew *Larry and Len*, a children's strip, for the *Guernsey Star* (1946). He settled in Chichester, England, in 1947, and sent some samples of his work to the minor comic book publisher Gerald G. Swan. He was immediately taken on, and drew *Inspector Slop the Plain Clothes Cop* for *Colored Slick Fun* (January 1949), *Mike the Mule* for *Cute Fun*, and *Betty & Brian* for *Kiddyfun*. His slapstick style was as firm and funny as ever, stronger now that the prewar style of captioned strips had gone. His best work appeared in *Kiddyfun Album*, an annual hardback for which he also painted the covers.

When Swan collapsed in 1951, Hill returned to his printing trade and after retirement took up show-card lettering. He worked in that capacity until his death on October 22, 1986, at age 84.

D.G.

Albert Hill, "Bobby Bubble." © Guernsey Star.

HI NO TORI (Japan) *Hi no Tori* ("The Phoenix," also spelled *Hinotori*), created by Osamu Tezuka, made its first appearance in the January 1967 issue of the monthly *COM* magazine.

Hi no Tori was a legendary bird who lived in a volcano; when a man drank of its blood he became immune to aging and death. No one could kill *Hi no Tori*; it could only burn to death through its own will (later to rise again from the ashes). *Hi no Tori* could understand the language of man and communicate with human beings through telepathy, and it was a symbol of eternity and eternal life.

In his strip, Tezuka tackled the eternal questions: the meaning of life and death and of man's existence and purpose. This was a gigantic theme that challenged the creator and made him rise to new heights of artistry and pathos. The story unfolded freely without regard to the requirements of time and space: moving fron ancient times to the future, and from earth to the farthest recesses of the universe. The main thread con-

"Hi no Tori," Osamu Tezuka. © COM.

necting the stories were the humans who came into contact with Hi no Tori and how this phoenix affected their lives.

In the episode titled *Reimei-hen* ("The Chapter of Dawn") for instance, the old queen of Yamatai, Himiko, wanted to drink the blood of Hi no Tori to achieve eternal life and ordered her soldiers to bring the phoenix to her. Hi no Tori was shot down and brought to Himiko, but before the queen could drain its blood, life ran out for her as the phoenix burned before her eyes. When the queen had died, Hi no Tori was reborn from its ashes and flew away. The theme of this particular episode was the deadly peril man places himself in when he tries to challenge the mystery of eternity.

Hi no Tori was conceived by Osamu Tezuka as his life work. It was unfortunately left unfinished when *COM* folded with the August 1973 issue, although two additional installments were published, in *Manga Shōnen* between 1976 and 1980, and in *Yasei no Jidai* in 1986-88. Many mourned the passing of this strip, the most ambitious work undertaken by Tezuka. "Of all the series Tezuka created in his lifetime, *Phoenix* is the only one he referred to as his *raifu waaku*, or his 'life work,'" Fred Schodt wrote in *Dreamland Japan*. "He began drawing it in 1954, and he was still drawing it 35 years later when he died in 1989."

H.K

HIRATA, HIROSHI (1937-) A Japanese comic book artist born February 9, 1937, in Itabashi, Tokyo, Hiroshi Hirata became interested in cartooning when he met Masahiro Miyaji, who was drawing four-panel cartoons for his junior high school. He had to drop out of school to carry on the family business, however, when his father died. When he turned 20, he met Miyaji again, who advised him to draw comics: Hirata followed the advice and in 1959 published a short strip, *Aizo no Hissatsuken*, a samurai revenge story for *Mazō*, a rental library comic book. A little later he decided to leave his business and fully devote himself to comic art.

Hirata has published a great number of comic books, the most famous including *Jaken Yaburetari*, the story of a swordsman, in 1959; *Tsunde ha kuzushi*, a revenge story, in 1961; *Hishū no Tachi* ("The Pathetic Sword") and *Musō Ogidachi*, a tragic samurai tale, both in 1963; a host of short-story and novel adaptations from 1966-67; *Soregashi Kojikini Arazu* ("I Am Not a Beggar") in 1970; and *Kubidai Hikiukenin* in 1973. Since the 1980s, he has devoted himself to depicting the bloody tales of Bushido (the samurai code of honor) set in medieval Japan.

Hiroshi Hirata wrote and drew stories for a wide audience and was very popular with boys and young adults in the 1960s. In the early days, his line was very schematic and sketchy, but his style acquired more and more realism and detail. He is probably one of the best illustrative artists in Japan today. His work belongs to the Jidaimono genre (the Japanese equivalent of the American Western) in which he likes to depict samurais of the lower class as miserable, cheerless, and dispirited.

Hiroshi Hirata has influenced a number of young Japanese cartoonists, among them Ken Tsukikage, Shinzō Tomi, Masami Ishii, and Mito Tsukiyama. His younger brother is also a comic book artist.

H.K.

HISTOIRES EN ESTAMPES (Switzerland) The Genevan Rodolphe Töpffer had to renounce his ambition to become a painter because of poor eyesight; instead he became a noted lecturer, scholar, and writer. However, he never abandoned his artistic dreams and illustrated his own humorous accounts of his trips to the Swiss mountainside. For his personal pleasure Töpffer drew a series of illustrated stories which he called "dramas in pictures;" over the years, from 1827 until his death in 1846, he produced eight of them. These are (in chronological order): *Les Amours de M. Vieuxbois* ("The Loves of Mr. Oldwood"), *Les Voyages et Aventures du Docteur Festus* ("The Travels and Adventures of Doctor Festus"), *Monsieur Cryptogame, Histoire de M. Jabot* ("The Story of Mr. Jabot"), *La Veritable Histoire de M. Crépin* ("The True Story of Mr. Crépin"), *L'Histoire d'Albert, M. Pencil*, and *L'Histoire de Jacques*. Töpffer was inspired (as he himself stated) by the cartoon sequences of Hogarth and Rowlandson (whose *Dr. Syntax* was the direct model for Töpffer's own *Dr. Festus*) but his stories were fresh and vibrant, and Töpffer had the uncanny ability to weave a brilliant graphic narrative around his humorous (but largely redundant) text.

In 1844 Töpffer's picture-stories came to the attention of Goethe, who waxed enthusiastic and advised the author to have them published. The first two stories had a limited run of 500 and 800 copies, respectively. In 1845 a German edition was released. The renown of Töpffer's illustrated narratives kept growing by leaps and bounds, and the important French publisher Garnier decided to release all the tales in a collective edition in two volumes that appeared after Töpffer's death (1846 and 1847). This edition (its success was immediate and universal) bore the title by which Töpffer's picture-stories became famous: *Histoires en Estampes* ("Stories in Etchings").

So great was the fame of these stories throughout the 19th century that John Grand-Carteret, in his monumental study *Les Moeurs et la Caricature* ("Mores and Caricature," 1885) simply stated that Töpffer's work was too well known to require illustration.

Ellen Wiese, in her helpful essay on Töpffer, *Enter the Comics* (1965), claims for the author the distinction of having invented the new art form which later came to be called the comics. On the face of it, the claim seems exaggerated, however; Töpffer's work, inspired as it undoubtedly is, is still too overloaded with extraneous literary preoccupations. It signals not the birth of a new form, but the brilliant end of an already outmoded artistic concept.

Töpffer's *Histoires* went through several American editions (all of which are out of print today). The aforementioned *Enter the Comics* reprinted *M. Crépin*, along with the amusing *Petit Essai de Physiognomie* ("Little Essay on Physiognomy").

M.H.

HOBAN, WALTER C. (1890-1939) The strip artist whose fey talent gave birth to *Jerry On The Job* and *Needlenose Noonan* was born Walter C. Hoban in Philadelphia in 1890, into the family of the director of the Philadelphia Municipal Department of Purchases and Supplies—which itself sounds like a comic invention of Hoban's. Raised in a very strict Catholic family—his father, Peter J. Hoban, was a founder of *The Catholic Standard and Times*—the young Hoban attended Catholic schools, graduating from St. Joseph's College and going on to the Philadelphia School of Industrial Art. A precocious student, Hoban was still young when he took his first job as office boy on the Philadelphia *North American*, hoping to become a reporter.

Curiously, he had no special ambitions to be a commercial cartoonist, although he entertained the older reporters with his drawings and as a result was often invited to accompany them to local ball games. At one of these, he made his usual "fun" sketches—and had one of them used on the sports page when it was discovered that no photographs existed of an important aspect of the game. The response to Hoban's cartoon was immediate and enthusiastic, and his sketches became frequent treats in the paper.

Now convinced that his true future lay with his art, Hoban accepted an invitation to join the staff of the Hearst *New York Journal* in 1912, where he ultimately created his best-known strip, a daily and Sunday feature called *Jerry On The Job* for King Features (taking some time off in 1917-18 to serve in Europe as a second lieutenant of artillery). *Jerry On The Job* featured a precocious kid—like Hoban—who was a ticket seller, porter, and jack of all trades at a suburban railway terminal. From the start, the strip was notable for a zany kind of background detail that foreshadowed the later work of cartoonists like Bill Holman (*Smokey Stover*), although the gags themselves were generally routine.

Hoban's strip was never enormously popular with the public—it remained from the start a second-string King Features comic—but his fellow artists enjoyed it greatly, and one, Cliff Sterrett, used Jerry and his train station as elements in his own *Polly and Her Pals* strip, later elaborating upon Hoban by using visually weird settings in his stunning *Polly* Sunday pages of the late 1920s. By the 1930s, however, the public seemed to have lost all interest in *Jerry*, and Hoban undertook a new feature for the new Hearst daily and Sunday *Mirror* tabloid in New York in 1932: *Needlenose Noonan*. *Noonan* was an outright fantastic strip about a rookie cop and his big city predicaments, and Hoban accompanyied it on Sundays with a smaller feature called *Discontinued Stories*, in which various humans and animals meet obvious disasters in the undrawn weekly climaxes. This page was popular in the *Mirror*, and appeared briefly in *Puck* in the early 1930s, but it was not a national success and Hoban turned to commercial art, reviving *Jerry* and his train station for a number of nationally printed advertisements in the late 1930s.

He lived in Port Washington, New York, in later life and fathered two daughters. Suddenly becoming ill in the fall of 1939, Hoban was taken to the Post Graduate Hospital in New York where he lingered for two months, visited by dozens of his old cartooning colleagues, and died on November 22, 1939, at the age of 49.

B.B.

HOEST, BILL (1926-1988) American cartoonist born in Newark, New Jersey, on February 7, 1926. Upon graduation from high school, Hoest enlisted in the U.S. Navy; discharged in 1946, he went on to study art at the Cooper Union in New York. His first art job was as a greeting card designer for Norcross from 1948 to 1951. He left to engage in freelance work and was soon contributing cartoons to such publications as the *Saturday Evening Post*, *Collier's*, *Playboy*, and the *Ladies Home Journal*.

Walter Hoban, "Jerry on the Job." © Int'l Feature Service.

Hoest's career as an inexhaustible purveyor of comic-strip fare began in the 1950s with the sale to the Chicago Tribune-New York News Syndicate of *My Son John*, a teenage strip that didn't last. He clicked, however, with *The Lockhorns*, distributed by King Features as a daily panel beginning in September 1968 and as a Sunday page from April 1972. Featuring the bickerings of a childless couple, the philandering Leroy and his querulous wife, Loretta, *The Lockhorns* proved a hit with readers.

Hoest followed this initial success with another panel series, *Bumper Snickers*, a string of loosely connected gags about cars and their bumptious drivers, for the *National Enquirer* in 1974. In 1977, he created the daily and Sunday strip *Agatha Crumm* for King. The titular character, a spunky old lady who runs her business empire with an iron hand, is perhaps his most original creation. In 1979 he became cartoon editor for *Parade* magazine; there he produced *Laugh Parade*, a weekly gag feature, in 1980, followed the next year by *Howard Huge*, about a friendly, if overbearing, St. Bernard. *What a Guy!*, a newspaper strip about a young executive on the make, syndicated by King in 1987, turned out to be his last comic strip creation.

A versatile and prolific cartoonist, Hoest varied his graphic style according to the tenor of the strips. *The Lockhorns*, for example, was drawn in a well-rounded, cartoony line, while *Agatha Crumm* was rendered with angular, spindly strokes. He died from cancer at the height of his success, on November 7, 1988. After his death, his widow, Bunny, took over production of the Hoest-originated features in collaboration with her husband's former assistant, John Reiner.

M.H.

HOGARTH, BURNE (1911-1996) American artist and educator born in Chicago on December 25, 1911. Hogarth displayed artistic inclinations as a child and later studied art history and anthropology at Crane College and Northwestern University in Chicago and at Columbia University. He learned to draw at the Chicago Art Institute, the breeding ground of many American artists.

At the age of 15 he became an assistant cartoonist at Associated Editors Syndicate while pursuing his studies at the same time. He was not yet 16 when the syndicate asked him to draw his own panel, *Famous Churches of the World*, and to illustrate two sports features. In 1929 he created his first comic strip, *Ivy Hemmanhaw*, for Bonnet-Brown Company, without success. The following year he started a panel entitled *Odd Occupations and Strange Accidents* for Leeds Features.

In 1935 he was hired by the McNaught Syndicate to draw *Pieces of Eight*, a pirate story written by noted author Charles Driscoll. Hogarth's big chance came in 1936. After Harold Foster announced his decision to leave *Tarzan*, which he had been drawing for United Features Syndicate, Hogarth, among many others, applied for Foster's place. He was accepted on the strength of the sample drawing he had submitted. The first *Tarzan* page signed by Hogarth appeared May 9, 1937.

More than any other artist, Hogarth gave *Tarzan* the mark of his own talent. In 1945, unhappy with the restrictions imposed upon him by United Feature Syndicate, Hogarth left *Tarzan* and gave the Robert Hall Syndicate an original creation, *Drago*, which made its first appearance in November of the same year. How-

ever, *Drago* lasted little more than a year, and in 1947 he went back to *Tarzan*, but not before he had obtained more advantageous conditions, including the freedom to write his own scenarios. At the same time, Hogarth created (also for United Feature Syndicate) the short-lived *Miracle Jones*, his only attempt at a humor strip.

A new conflict soon arose between the artist and the syndicate over the foreign rights to *Tarzan*, so when his contract expired Hogarth declined to renew it. He left *Tarzan* and the comic strip field to devote his time to the School of Visual Arts that he had founded with Silas Rhodes in 1947. (It is today one of the most comprehensive centers of art training in the United States.) In 1970 Hogarth retired from the School of Visual Arts in order to devote himself fully to painting, drawing, and writing.

Hogarth produced a number of drawings, paintings, and etchings which have been exhibited in galleries all over the world. He also authored three books of art instruction, *Dynamic Anatomy, Drawing the Human Head*, and *Dynamic Figure Drawing* for Watson-Guptill Publications. Hailed as "the Michelangelo of the comics" in Europe and Latin America, Hogarth's fame was slow in coming in the United States. His renown and influence have grown tremendously in recent years, however.

In 1972 Burne Hogarth went back to *Tarzan* with a totally new pictorial version of Edgar Rice Burroughs's novel *Tarzan of the Apes*, also for Watson-Guptill. His second book based on Burroughs's stories, *Jungle Tales of Tarzan*, came out in 1976.

At an age when most people entertain thoughts of retirement, Hogarth kept pursuing his multifaceted activities at a frenzied pace. He served as president of the National Cartoonists Society in 1977-79, taught art classes at the Parsons School of Design in New York City, and, after his move to California in 1981, taught

Dynamic Anatomy Demonstration, Burne Hogarth. © Burne Hogarth.

at the Otis Art Institute in Los Angeles and the Art Center College of Design in Pasadena. He also published two more art instruction books, *Dynamic Light and Shade* (1981) and *Dynamic Wrinkles and Drapery* (1992).

Hogarth received many distinctions and honors during the last two decades of his life. He was named Artist of the Year at the Pavilion of Humor in Montreal in 1975, received the Lifetime Achievement Award in Lucca, Italy, in 1984, and was the recipient of a special award at the International Festival of Comics and Illustration in Barcelona, Spain, in 1989. He was on his way back from a comics convention in France, where he had been the guest of honor, when he died of a heart attack in Paris on January 28, 1996. At the time of his death he had been working on the concept of a pacifist superhero named Morphos.

M.H.

HOGARTH, WILLIAM (1697-1764) English painter, engraver, and cartoonist born in London, in Ship Court, Old Bailey, on December 10, 1697. William Hogarth's father, Richard Hogarth, had been a schoolmaster in Westmoreland before moving to London, where he worked as a journalist. From his earliest days William Hogarth had a predilection for drawing and he was apprenticed, at his own request, to a silversmith. On the expiration of his apprenticeship he turned to engraving. His first works seem to have been engravings for shop bills and letters for books (1720). In 1726 he became known in his profession with his plates for Samuel Butler's *Hudibras*, and in 1728 he turned to oil painting.

In 1729 William Hogarth eloped with Sir James Thornhill's only daughter, whom he subsequently married. This was followed by a period of intense artistic activity and creativity. This period marked the culmination of Hogarth's fame, with such works as *A Harlot's Progress* (a series of six oil paintings and a corresponding series of six engravings, 1735) and *A Rake's Progress* (a series of six engravings, 1735). Due to pirating of these two works, Hogarth obtained in 1735 an act which vested artists with the exclusive rights to their own designs and restricted their use by others (this act is regarded by law scholars as the first of the modern copyright laws).

William Hogarth is the first artist to whom the term "cartoonist" can be legitimately applied. He was the first artist to draw humorous scenes without recourse to caricature or physical deformities. The backgrounds and details were sufficient to bring out the humor of his compositions; Hogarth's effects were primarily dramatic (and not graphic) and his drawings can be acknowledged as the first direct forerunners of the comic strip. As Alan Gowans perceptively noted in his study *The Unchanging Arts*: "Adapting the theatrical principle of 17th-century Baroque painting, he created distinctive little stage sets, immensely detailed, busy with gesticulating actors, all making a different and distinct contribution to the complex whole." These are, of course, some of the principles later adopted and put to good use by American comic strip artists (notably Outcault and Opper).

William Hogarth died in Chiswick on October 26, 1764.

M.H.

William Hogarth, "The Laughing Audience."

HOGG, GORDON (1912-1973) Born in London in 1912, Gordon Hogg won an art scholarship at the age of 14. He studied art with Ruskin Spear for three years, then became a commercial artist. His first cartoon, a topical gag, appeared in the *Daily Sketch* in 1938, and a series evolved featuring a little man with one big ear listening to wartime whispers.

During World War II he was an official war artist to the Indian Army under General Auchinlek. After the war, he rejoined the *Daily Sketch* as an editorial cartoonist. In 1945, after the retirement of J. Millar Watt, Hogg (who signed "Gog") took over the famous *Pop* daily strip, but later reduced it from four panels to one single picture, which took away the original's special appeal. One book of Gog's *Pop* comics was published, and the cartoon ran for 15 years, concluding January 23, 1960, in the *Daily Mail* after the newspapers merged.

"Gog" then begame "Gay Gordon," the racing tipster, with a daily cartoon tip for readers of the *Sun*, and finally turned to children's comics with *Pop Parade* in *Sunday Extra* (1965), *Glugg* in *Wham* (1966), and *Ronnie Rich* in *Smash* (1966). He died in March 1973.

D.G.

HOKUSAI, KATSUSHIKA (1760-1849) Japanese Ukiyo-e artist born September 23, 1760 in Edo (later called Tokyo).

In 1778 Katsushika Hokusai became a student of the popular Ukiyo-e artist Shunshō Katsukawa and he made his artistic debut in 1779. In 1793 he became a pupil of Yūsen Kanō but soon left him for reasons unknown. In 1794 he was expelled from the Katsukawa family and became acquainted with Tourin Tsutsumi. In addition to Ukiyo-e, he studied many other schools of art such as Yamato-e paintings, Chinese (Kan) painting, and Western painting. In 1778 he took the pen name under which he is most famous: Hokusai (he had earlier used the name Souri).

Jim Holdaway, "Romeo Brown." © *Daily Mirror Newspapers Ltd.*

Hokusai gained fame with his book illustrations after 1806 (he was especially active in this field from 1807 to 1809). His illustrations, full of monsters and violence, were rendered in a highly dramatic style. In 1812 Hokusai produced his first drawing manual, *Ryakuga Hayaoshie*; and in 1814 the first volume of his monumental *Hokusai Manga* ("The Hokusai Cartoons") appeared. A veritable encyclopedia of Hokusai's art, the *Manga* displayed Hokusai's awesome ability in its drawings of people engaged in every possible activity—of faces, manners, animals, fish, insects, natural scenes, monsters, etc. The 15th and final volume of the *Hokusai Manga* was not published until 1878, long after the artist's death. Other famous works by Hokusai are *Hyaku Monogatori* ("The 100 Tales," 1830), *Fugaku Sanjūrnkkei* ("36 Scenes of Mt. Fuji," 1831), *Shokoku Meikyō Kiran* ("Famous Waterfalls in Various Provinces," 1834), *Fugaku Hyakkei* ("100 Scenes of Mt. Fuji," 1834), and *Ehon Musha Burui* (1841).

Hokusai is probably the most famous of Ukiyo-e artists. He drew every conceivable subject—from landscapes to genre compositions to action scenes. He gave fresh impetus to the lethargic tradition of book illustration with his bold and striking compositions. Hokusai was also a pioneer in landscape Ukiyo-e. His works are full of life, vitality, and elan, and display a great inventiveness in composition as well as a keen sense of color. Hokusai has influenced countless numbers of Japanese artists (among his many students were Gyōsai Kawanabe, Kuniyoshi Utagagawa, Yositushi Tsukioka, and others), and his works were introduced in Europe where they exercised a great influence on the Impressionists. He can also be credited with bringing the tradition of the European cartoon to Japan, and thus paving the way for the later acceptance of the Western-style comic strip in Japanese publications.

Hokusai died on April 18, 1849.

H.K.

HOLDAWAY, JAMES (1927-1970) British cartoonist, born at Barnes Common, London, in 1927. He was educated at New Malden Secondary School, winning an art scholarship to the Kingston School of Art. In 1945 he was called for military service in the East Surrey Regiment, serving in Italy, Austria, and Greece, and returning to art school in 1948 on an ex-service grant.

His first professional artwork was designing shoe advertisements in France, and he then worked as a rubber engraver for the Reed Paper Group in Brentford. While there (1950) he began freelancing cartoon work.

In 1951 he joined the art staff of Scion Ltd., a publisher in Kensington, London, that specialized in one-shot comics and science-fiction paperbacks. Here he drew all types of artwork, from comic pages to illustrations, advertisements, and full-color book jackets. As Scion changed their style of comics from the typical British "funny" format of eight pages in two colors to the American style comic book format of 24 pages with full-color covers, Jim Holdaway began to draw more comics. An admirer of the American comic book style, he modeled his technique on Will Eisner, Milton Caniff, and other masters. His first full-length picture stories were for *Gallant Detective* (1952): *Inspector Hayden* in issue number one, *Lex Knight* in number two.

In 1953 he went freelance, working from home for the new independent Sports Cartoons, a division of Man's World Publications. He contributed individual episodes of such regular heroes as *Captain Vigour*, *Dick Hercules*, and *Steve Samson*, as well as strips for *Football Comic*. Then came more adult strips for the pocket-size "library" comic books, *Tid-Bits Science Fiction Comics*, and a weekly Western featuring the stage and radio cowboy Cal McCord for *Comic Cuts* (1953). *Cal McCord*, his first page for better-class comics, led to *Cliff McCoy* (1955), *The Red Rider* (1956) in *Swift*, and an excellent full-color page in *Mickey's Weekly* adapted from Walt Disney's *Davy Crockett* (1956).

His first daily newspaper strip was *Romeo Brown* in the *Daily Mirror*, which he took over from Albert Mazure and quickly made his own. Suddenly, Jim Holdaway had became Britain's top "girlie" cartoonist! This strip marked his first association with writer Peter O'Donnell, and together they later created the superlative *Modesty Blaise* (1963) for the *London Evening Standard*. Tragically, Jim died in February 1970, but his style lives on in the modern *Modesty*.

D.G.

HOLLANDER, NICOLE (1939-   ) The single girl has had her spokesperson in the comics since Russ Westover's Tillie became a Toiler in 1921, but it was not until Nicole Hollander created the acid-tongued *Sylvia* more than half a century later that the middle-aged woman really had a voice. It isn't a strident voice, but it cuts through the hypocracy and absurdity of modern life as trenchantly as that of any of the younger heroines in comics. Sylvia is today's woman. She is not concerned about diet or failed relationships; her answer to "feminine protection every day" is "use a hand grenade," and one of her answering machine messages is, "I can't come to the phone right now. When you hear the beep, please hang up."

With a Bachelor of Fine Arts degree from the University of Illinois and a M.F.A. ("Master of Feisty Arts," Hollander jokes) from Boston University, Hollander left school expecting to be a painter. She settled for becoming a graphic designer in California, where she styled matchboxes "and other projects of significant social value." After returning to her native Chicago, she worked as an art teacher and art director. She also tried illustrating textbooks and children's books, but, she recalls, people found her illustrations "too weird." It was a job redesigning the Chicago-based national feminist magazine *The Spokeswoman* that led to a career she

Nicole Hollander, "Sylvia." © Sylvia Syndicate.

describes as "cartoonist by surprise." *Sylvia's* first tart observations on popular culture and the status of women appeared in *The Spokeswoman* in 1976. Boldly drawn, in a manner more influenced by German expressionism than by traditional cartoon style, *Sylvia's* astringent dialogue appears without balloons, sprawling throughout the panels like the clutter of its heroine's apartment.

Sylvia was refused by Universal Press Syndicate in 1979 (described by one of its less-perceptive editors as "deep but narrow"), and was taken on by the Toronto Sun Syndicate in Canada. The strip went to Field Enterprises two years later, but Hollander found their promotion of it so lackluster that she took its syndication over herself and soon doubled *Sylvia's* readership. By 1997 it was running in over 80 daily and weekly papers, including the *Boston Globe, Chicago Tribune, Los Angeles Times, Detroit News,* and *Seattle Times.* The first collection of *Sylvia* strips, *I'm in Training to be Tall and Blonde,* was published by St. Martin's Press in 1979; since then a flood of volumes (15 by 1997) have appeared from St. Martin's, Random House, Avon Books, and Dell; all, after the first few, were composed of original work created for book publication.

Hollander also has a line of greeting cards and calendars, provides illustrations for the *New York Times Book Review, Mirabella,* and other magazines, has illustrated two children's books, and does a regular political cartoon for *Mother Jones.* In 1992 her musical comedy, *Sylvia's Real Good Advice,* coauthored with Arnold Aprill and Tom Mula, had an extended run in Chicago and San Francisco, and articles by Hollander have appeared in the *New York Times.*

The audience of *Sylvia* crosses lines of both gender and generation. In *Print* (1988), Tom Gross described the strip as an example of a new genre of comics that are intermediate between the underground and the mainstream. "While they remain well within the mainstream of comic strip sensibility," he wrote, "they represent the leading edge of a more sophisticated and personal perspective."

D.W.

HOLMAN, BILL (1903-1987) An American cartoonist born in 1903 in Crawfordsville, Indiana, Bill Holman exhibited a flair for caricature and the outrageous at an early age. In 1919 he moved to Chicago, where he studied at the Academy of Fine Arts under Carl Ed, and the next year he took a job as copy-boy on the *Chicago Tribune.*

Bill Holman's first comic strip, an animal parody called *Billville Birds,* was released by NEA Service in 1922; it lasted only a few months. Undaunted, Holman

Bill Holman.

went to New York in search of his fortune. His first years there are only fuzzily recorded, but by the late 1920s he was drawing *G. Whizz Jr.* for the Herald Tribune Syndicate and self-syndicating another strip, *Wise Quacks,* about a duck (what else?) giving silly answers in the form of puns to questions asked by readers. Both were failures, however, and Bill Holman turned to the magazine field, contributing innumerable cartoons to *Collier's,* the *Saturday Evening Post, Life, Judge,* and *Everybody's Weekly* in London.

Holman's ceaseless efforts finally found their reward in 1935 when he signed a contract with the News-Tribune Syndicate. On March 10, 1935, *Smokey Stover,* a Sunday feature depicting the antics of a pair of zany firemen, appeared, accompanied by *Spooky,* about a loony cat, and followed by a daily panel called *Nuts and Jolts.*

Bill Holman, whose lifestyle was only slightly less frenzied than that of his fireman hero, once said, "I like to draw firemen because I think they are funny." Holman's art (if it can be called art) was the closest the comics came to burlesque since the days of Opper and Herriman. His devices were the outrageous pun, the raucous aside, the grotesque composition, and the devastating punchline. This is a skill of a special kind that should not be slighted.

Holman served as president of the National Cartoonists Society in 1961-63. He retired after *Smokey Stover* came to an end in 1973, but continued to entertain at charity functions until his death in New York City on February 27, 1987.

M.H.

HOLMES, FRED (1908-   ) One of the best-liked adventure strip artists in British comics, Frederick T. Holmes was born in Linsdale, Buckinghamshire, on November 12, 1908. As with most comic strip artists, he began drawing at an early age. He fondly recalled his love for the full-color cover illustrations of the Aldine series of *Buffalo Bill* novels that he studied and copied long before he was able to read the semiadult stories of life in America's Wild West. In 1923, at the young age of 15, Holmes began to send small sketches into the Children's Page of the *Birmingham Weekly Post*, and five years later he was good enough to illustrate the fiction pages.

While working as an artist for the weekly edition of the *Post*, Holmes improved his artwork by joining the British and Dominions School of Drawing. By the late 1930s he was working full time for the *Post*, drawing cartoon jokes, comic strips, and story headings as well as illustrations. However, he eventually decided his *Post* work was trivial and, deciding to put his talent to a more worthwhile purpose than mere entertainment, took a position as staff artist for the religious publisher Drummonds of Stirling (Scotland). The firm, delighted with his drawing, gave Holmes a lifetime contract; however, it went bankrupt in the post-World War II slump of 1951.

The next year, Holmes's father-in-law found a copy of *Advertiser's Weekly*, and Holmes applied to an advertisement for an artist. He was accepted immediately and asked to illustrate a serial in *Fun Film* titled *Life in Hand*. This led to a commission for another comic magazine, *Comet*. Holmes's *Comet* series, *Claude Duval, the Laughing Cavalier*, started September 19, 1953, and ran until the magazine folded in 1959 (however, later episodes of the series had been drawn by Eric Parker and Patrick Nicolle).

By the mid-1950s, Holmes was illustrating *Buffalo Bill* (his favorite boyhood hero) in *Comet*, *Billy the Kid* in *Sun*, *The Gay Gordons* for *Playhour*, and his longest-running serial, *Carson's Cubs*, a football story, for *Lion*. Holmes drew *Cubs* from 1957 to 1975. From 1960-63, he also drew *Roy of the Rovers*, the front-page football star of *Tiger*. His best work, however, appeared in the 64-page pocket-size monthlies *Thriller Comics Library* and *Tiger Sports Library*, including *Rob Roy*, *Robin Hood of Sherwood*, *Dick Turpin, King of the Highway*, and *Claude Duval and the Traitor Cavalier*.

Holmes was never a strong man—he suffered from bad asthma much of his life—and he was forced to retire in the mid-1970s after 20 years of comic work.

D.G.

HOLROYD, BILL (1919-   ) Bill Holroyd was one of the most prolific strip cartoonists for the Scottish comic publisher D. C. Thomson, working exclusively for Thomson from 1947 until his retirement in 1986. His work always showed good humor, even when he developed his line from pure comedy to adventure serials.

Born in Salford, Lancashire, on March 21, 1919, Holroyd showed an interest in artwork at a young age and developed his abilities at Salford Technical College and Hornsey Art College. His first job was with an advertising agency in Manchester in 1937. Two years later, when World War II broke out, he enlisted in the Royal Artillery and remained in the military until 1946.

Holroyd made his first contact with Thomson toward the end of the war, writing from Italy to ask if there was room for a comic artist on the staff. However, there were no open positions, and after his discharge from the army Holroyd joined the David Hand Studio in Cookham, which had been set up as J. Arthur Rank's film cartoon company. While with David Hand, Holroyd began freelancing in his spare time and had his first series, *Alf Wit the Ancient Brit*, published in the Thomson comic *Beano* on February 22, 1947. He also provided strips for many smaller independent publishers around this period, contributing *The Petrified Valley* to *Sun* (1948), *Big Game Gannon* to *Big Flame*, *Rescue from the Roundheads* to *Big Slide*, *Post Atom* to *Oh Boy* (Paget), *Puppet Land* to *Children's Rocket* (1949), and *Rollo the Gypsy Boy* to *Merry-Go-Round*. The latter series were for J. B. Allen.

But it was with the *Dandy* and *Beano* comics that Holroyd soon found a permanent home. *Plum MacDuff, the Highlandman Who Never Gets Enough*, about a fat fellow with an enormous appetite (a Scottish variation on the popular strip *Hungry Horace*), began in *Dandy* in 1948, followed by *Wuzzy Wiz, Magic is his Biz* (1949). For *Beano*, Holroyd created *Have a Go Jo, Wandering Willie*, and *Ding Dong Belle*. Belle, a tough female sheriff, was notable in a period when female comic strip protagonists were rare.

A touch of the fantastic could be found in Holroyd's serial strips, which began with *Danny Longlegs* (*Dandy*, 1950), about a very tall boy. This was followed by *Tick Tock Tony*, about a robot boy; *The Iron Fish*, about a boy with an incredible one-person submarine; *Tommy's Clockwork Brother*, another robot series; and *Nobby the Enchanted Bobby*, a magical policeman. There was also an experimental series, *Big Hugh and You*, in which the reader of the strip participated in the adventure.

One serial that stands out was *The Fighting Frazers*, which appeared in *Topper* from the first issue (1953). Many years later, Holroyd met a member of the production team for the science fiction movie *Alien*, who told the artist how the strip inspired him in creating the creature from space. Never underestimate the power of a children's comic!

D.G.

HOT ON THE TRAIL (China) This comic book story was published by the People's Art Publications of Shanghai in 1965. Adapted by Hsin Sheng from a short story by An Chung-min and Chu Hsiang-chun, it was drawn by Hao Shih.

The story opens like a classic thriller: in the purse of an old woman who has come to Canton from Hong Kong to visit relatives, a bomb mechanism is found. There follows an investigation conducted by security agent Li Ming-kang and Inspector Hsia Huang of the Canton police. The two men patiently retrace the old lady's path until they come to a likely suspect: a mysterious traveler by the name of Chien Chia-jen. After more detection work the two protagonists unmask

"Hot on the Trail," Hao Shih.

(mixing speech balloons with a narrative under the panels) comes closer to that of the English comics of the 1920s than to contemporary American strips. All in all, however, it is quite an entertaining and enlightening experience.

Hot on the Trail was among the comic strips reprinted in *The People's Comic Book* (Doubleday, 1973).

M.H.

Chien, who is actually a foreign agent assigned to blow up the Canton power plant.

The action is remarkable on several counts: first as a straight spy thriller, complete with shadowy characters, strange happenings, and a general atmosphere of suspense and expectation. The authors make use of every narrative device, including the obligatory chase scene (in this case aboard a motorboat in Canton harbor). Second, there is absolutely no trace of propaganda. Nowhere in the story is there mention of the foreign country for which Chien is working, nor is there any denunciation of class enemies or foreign interlopers. In fact *Hot on the Trail* could have been authored by any number of comic book writers from the United States or Western Europe, with only a few name changes.

The drawings of *Hot on the Trail* are not very remarkable, but are adequate, and the total effect of the strip

HOWARD THE DUCK (U.S.) In the pages of *Adventure Into Fear* issue 19 (December 1973), a Marvel comic book title, Steve Gerber introduced a cantankerous, cigar-chomping duck that had strayed from another dimension into our world, as a kind of Superman-meets-Daffy Duck pastiche. The foul-tempered fowl proved a surprise hit with many readers, so much so that in January 1976 he gained his own comic book, also published by Marvel.

It turned out that Howard (as the palmipede was called) was a denizen of the planet Duckworld, where ducks had evolved instead of humans. Howard was the possessor of a high I.Q., had a sarcastic turn of mind, and could speak fluent English. Fleeing from his arch-nemesis, the monstrous Thog, he landed (of all places) in Cleveland, Ohio, where he saved a comely model named Beverly Switzler from the clutches of the malevolent accountant Pro-Rata. He eventually shacked up with the grateful damsel now out of distress, a case of interspecies miscegeneation that boggles the mind. Setting himself up as a fighter for justice, Howard confronted such menaces as the giant Gingerbread Man, the clangorous Dr. Bong, and the radioactive Morton Erg, all of whom he defeated with the help of Quack-Fu, a lethal form of martial art taught only on Duckworld.

At first the comic book spoofed the absurdities and lunacies of the superhero genre, especially as it was

"Howard the Duck," Steve Skeates and Gene Colan. © Marvel Comics Group.

practiced at Marvel, but soon Gerber cast a wider net, venturing into the sphere of social criticism with his attacks on racial discrimination and political corruption. Following in the footsteps of Pogo Possum, Howard even ran for president in 1976 as a protest candidate on the All-Night Party ticket. All the while, the *Howard the Duck* comic book benefitted from the superlative artwork of such luminaries as Val Mayerik, Gene Colan, Brian Bolland, John Buscema, and Walt Simonson, all of whom seemed to have a good time drawing the strip.

Despite the character's popularity (which caused a *Howard the Duck* newspaper strip to be added in the mid-1970s), and for reasons that are disputed to this day, Gerber and Marvel had a falling-out. In order to recover the rights to the character he had created, Gerber took Marvel to court, subsequently winning the case. During the legal proceedings, however, the object of contention—Howard himself—had quietly expired (1981). He was revived in 1986 in a truly awful movie by George Lucas (with Marvel responsible for the comic book adaptation), after which nothing further has been heard from the crotchety bird.

M.H.

HOWARTH, F. M. (ca. 1870-1908) F. M. Howarth is an important name in comic strip history; his series of strip drawings in *Puck* in the 1890s no doubt paved the way and heightened public acceptance for cartoons in strip form.

Howarth's drawings surfaced in the pages of *Puck*, *Judge*, *Life*, and such lesser humor magazines as *Truth* and *Tid-Bits* in the late 1880s. He was then still a talented amateur and his work looked no different than that of the young T. S. Sullivant and James Montgomery Flagg. But in a few short years he found a truly individualistic style and was engaged by *Puck* as a staff artist.

Howarth was the first *Puck* cartoonist who didn't double as an editorial artist; by the 1890s the magazine was toning down its partisan flavor. Howarth's drawings were almost always in sequence, with narration and dialogue underneath.

His two contributions were this narrative innovation—it had been employed by others infrequently before and frequently after Howarth—and a painfully exact stylization. Howarth's characters had enormous heads with exaggerated features (particularly popping eyes), but otherwise everything else in the panels was drawn realistically. Nothing was left to chance; in a day when photoengraving and the heliographic process were permitting cartoonists greater freedom, Howarth achieved success through rigid exactitude.

He drew continuing sequences for *Puck*, but without characters that continued from week to week. This curious fact is contrasted to cartoonists who copied his format but introduced regular weekly characters: James Montgomery Flagg with *Nervy Nat* in *Judge* and Louis Glackens with *Hans* in *Puck*.

In 1903 he had such an opportunity, however, when William Randolph Hearst hired Howarth to work for his Sunday supplement. *Lulu and Leander* was the result, and it quickly became a standby in Hearst's *American-Journal-Examiner* comic sections. (By coincidence, his page-mate was *Foxy Grandpa* by Carl Schultze—the cartoonist who more than any other tried to ape Howarth's style back in the 1890s. By the Hearst days Schultze had settled on his own style.)

Howarth occasionally drew other features, notably *A Lad and His Lass*, which was really no more than a medieval *Lulu and Leander*. By 1907, Hearst and/or the public had tired of Howarth's precisely drawn pictorial narratives, and *Lulu and Leander* was dropped from the Hearst pages. Soon Howarth emerged in the *Chicago Tribune* comic section, doing *Ole Opey Dildock—the Storyteller* in his familiar fashion. This strip about a teller of tales didn't last long—at least with Howarth as artist, for he died in 1908. An artist named Wells continued the strip for the *Tribune*.

Howarth, a man who pioneered the narrative form, ironically never used balloons.

R.M.

HUBERT (U.S.) *Stars and Stripes* was in its earliest stages, a weekly paper published in Ireland, when Dick Wingert submitted his first cartoons. Having just been transferred to Ireland with the U.S. Army and already an aspiring artist stateside, Wingert was able to get in on the ground floor with the army publication. This was in 1942, and when *Stars and Stripes* went to London, so did Wingert.

His earliest cartoons were one-shot gags without a central or continuing character. As cartooning was new to him, he recalls having to copy from the previous week's drawing for his style and format. Soon, however, he introduced a regular character, a short, big-nosed, brash oaf who was named Hubert (by vote of Wingert's buddies).

Hubert, in panel format, became one of the great comic characters of WWII, not as front-line as Mauldin's *Willie and Joe*, but bawdier than any, including Sansone's *Wolf* (a famous gag has two well-dressed Parisian girls saying, as Hubert walks down the street, "Don't look now, but here comes old 'Couchez Avec' again!").

With General Patton's army in France, Wingert met Bill Hearst, who promised to syndicate the feature after the war. So in 1945 *Hubert* changed into his civvies for a daily panel and Sunday page. The transition, consid-

"Hubert," Dick Wingert. © King Features Syndicate.

ering the rakish and freewheeling character Pfc. Hubert had been, was remarkably smooth and successful. He married a pretty blonde named Trudy, battled an impossible mother-in-law (merely a fat, feminine substitute for his previous antagonistic superiors), and had a daughter named Elli who was just starting school, and a large, lazy sheepdog, Freddy, that always got in the way of things. Also in the cast were Charlie the Milkman; Hubert's boss Dexter L. Baxter; and the secretary at the office.

Hubert remained the half-pint, big-nosed bag of seed that he always was, but slightly less grotesque as a suburbanite rather than a serviceman on leave. And his nemeses became crabgrass, broken hammocks, jammed lawnmowers, and nagging motorbikes.

Wingert's art and gag style are one: broad, basic slapstick. For this reason his gags were always more successful in Sunday-page format, where there is more room for development and animation. Even in the daily panel, King Features suggested a novel change—slice the panel in two and let papers run it in strip format. Many chose that option, but this proved less successful with other panels such as *Trudy and Hazel*.

The old slapstick, albeit heavy-handed, managed to survive in the Sunday page, despite the inhibition of spatial restrictions, until 1994.

R.M.

HUBINON, VICTOR (1924-1979) Belgian cartoonist born 1924 in Angleur, near Liège. Upon graduation from high school, Victor Hubinon entered the Liège Academy of Fine Arts where he studied decoration, painting, etching, and drawing, while contributing cartoons and caricatures to several Belgian newspapers and magazines. During the German occupation of Belgium, Hubinon fled to England and enlisted in the Belgian section of the Royal Navy. After the liberation of his homeland, he joined the newspaper *La Meuse* as an advertising artist.

In 1946 Hubinon met Jean-Michel Charlier, who introduced him to the comic weekly *Spirou*. After doing a number of illustrations for *Spirou*, Hubinon created *Buck Danny* in collaboration with Charlier as script-

writer. The story of a U.S. Air Force pilot in the Pacific War, the first episode of *Buck Danny* appeared in January 1947. (With *Buck Danny*, Hubinon found his métier; at first he left the drawing of airplanes to Charlier, a former pilot, but he later earned his own pilot's license and went on to become an aviation expert.)

In addition to *Buck Danny*, Hubinon took over Jijé's *Blondin et Cirage* for a couple of years (1950-52), and did a number of illustrated biographies (Surcouf, Mermoz, Stanley) for *Spirou* in the 1950s. In 1959, again with Charlier writing the scenarios, he produced *Le Démon des Caraibes* ("The Demon of the Caribbean," title later changed to *Les Aventures de Barbe-Rouge et d'Eric*) for *Pilote*; this excellent sea-adventure strip lasted until 1967. Hubinon also contributed illustrations and cartoons to such publications as *Moustique, La Libre Belgique, Pistolin,* and *Junior. La Mouette* ("The Seagull"), the tale of a female pirate written by Gigi Marechal (who also served as a model for the heroine), was his last comic-strip creation. He died suddenly of a heart attack at his drawing table in January 1979.

Hubinon is not regarded as one of the foremost innovators of the European comics. His early drawings were strongly influenced by Caniff, but he later came into his own agreeable and undemanding graphic style. He occupies a comfortable and honorable position in European comic art.

M.H.

HULK, THE (U.S.) Shortly after the phenomenal success of *Fantastic Four*, Marvel editor Stan Lee was faced with creating a second feature to cash in on the burgeoning Marvel market. His solution was *The Hulk*, which premiered in its own book in May 1962. The script was by the irrepressible Lee and the art was by staff king Jack Kirby.

Early issues by Lee and Kirby exhibited heavy influences of Mary Shelley's *Frankenstein*, but *Hulk* tales also borrowed liberally from *Dr. Jekyll and Mr. Hyde* and *The Hunchback of Notre Dame*. As the original story explained, Doctor Bruce Banner created a highly powerful gamma-ray bomb for the United States government. Shortly before its testing, however, Banner ran

"The Hulk," © Marvel Comics Group.

to the test site to rescue a trespassing youth, Rick Jones. In doing so, he was bathed in the rays of the exploding bomb and turned into the snarling, raging, green-skinned (originally gray) Hulk, and like Jekyll and Hyde, changed character at regular intervals; like Frankenstein's monster, he was never understood, always mistaken for evil even when he was simply frightened.

Added to this classical mixture were several strong supporting characters: Rick Jones, the Hulk's only friend although he eventually went on to team up with Captain America and then Captain Marvel; Betty Ross, Banner's lover, who later scorned him for Major Talbot and then shuttled back and forth between the two with fickle regularity; and "Thunderbolt" Ross, Betty's father and Banner's boss, a general who instantly became the Hulk's prime enemy. Lee handled this melange of plot threads and characters until 1969, when he gave way to Roy Thomas, who added even a larger cast and story lines. Archie Goodwin, Gerry Conway, science fiction writer Harlan Ellison, Gary Friedrich, Steve Englehart, and Chris Claremont took turns scripting *The Hulk*, and together they made the feature too complex, inconsistent, and muddled.

Artistically, *The Hulk* did not fare much better. After Kirby and his Frankenstein-like version disappeared, Steve Ditko, Gil Kane, John Buscema, Marie Severin, and finally Herb Trimpe took turns at the strip. Trimpe became the definitive artist, and his mellow, sketchy version appeared regularly for many years in the late 1960s and early 1970s.

The Hulk book lasted only six issues until March 1963, but the feature then began in the 59th issue of *Tales To Astonish* (August 1964). The title was changed to *The Hulk* with April 1968's 102nd issue.

The success of the 1978-82 *Hulk* television series considerably boosted the fortunes of *The Incredible Hulk* (as the comic book was by now officially named). It attracted a number of talented artists to its stable, notably John Byrne, Frank Miller, Todd McFarlane, and Walt Simonson. It also gave rise to a number of spin-offs; to date, these have included *The Savage She-Hulk*, *The Sensational She-Hulk*, *The Rampaging Hulk*, and *Hulk 2099*.

J.B.

HUMAN TORCH, THE (U.S.) *The Human Torch* was created in November 1939 by Carl Burgos and made its first appearance in Timely's *Marvel Comics* number one. (The title of the book was eventually changed to *Marvel Mystery*.) The character quickly became a fantastically successful hero and Timely's first major superheroic strip. By the fall of 1940, *Human Torch* number one had been published, and the strip soon began appearing in *Captain America*, *All Winners*, and several other Timely titles.

In actuality, the Human Torch wasn't human at all. He was an android, a "synthetic man," created by the visionary Professor Horton. Unfortunately, as soon as Horton released the creation from its protective beaker, it burst into flame and had to be encased in concrete. The fire-man quickly escaped, however, and after accidentally killing his creator and inadvertently operating in a protection racket, the Torch learned how to control and harness his flaming prowess. After learning how to fly and devising techniques to hurl fireballs and control all types of flame, he became a blue (later red) costumed crime fighter. For a while he even

"The Human Torch." © Marvel Comics Group.

adopted the secret identity of Jim Hammond, but the alter-ego was soon dropped and the Human Torch operated in character throughout the rest of his career. Toro, an orphaned circus performer with an immunity to fire, was eventually introduced as the Torch's sidekick and partner. As the years progressed and the strip continued to grow in stature, the character became more and more human until no further mention was made of his android heritage. He became just another man—albeit a man who could set himself and others ablaze.

The best of the *Human Torch* stories came in three early issues of *Human Torch* (numbers five, eight, and ten). There he was locked in exciting and memorable combat with Timely's water-based character, the vindictive, half-human/half-Atlantean Sub-Mariner. Given the natural dramatic elements inherent in conflicts between fire and water, the epic battles are among the best-remembered stories of the 1940s. Artistically, the strip was never more than average, and after Burgos left for the armed forces in 1942, a long procession of illustrators, including Carmine Infantino, Syd Shores, Don Rico, Mike Sekowsky, and Alex Schomberg, produced the feature.

The Human Torch was another superheroic victim of the post-war comic book bust, however, and the feature's own book folded after the 35th issue (March 1949). By June of that year, the character made its last appearance in *Marvel Mystery* number 92. Atlas Comics Group, Timely's successor, attempted a brief revival of the strip in 1953. After his initial appearance in *Young Men* number 24 (December 1953), the Torch also appeared in several other titles, including his own; by September 1954's *Captain America* number 78, however, *The Human Torch* was again retired.

And although he was one of Timely's high-powered 1940s triumvirate (*Captain America* and *Sub-Mariner* were the other two), he was the only character not totally revived during the superhero boom of the early 1960s. Instead, Marvel Comics gave his powers to Johnny Storm, a teenaged member of the Fantastic Four. This Human Torch was human, however, even if

Hermann Huppen, "Comanche." © Editions du Lombard.

his age made him more akin to Toro than to the original Human Torch. The old-time hero, however, put in one last appearance in *Saga of the Original Human Torch* (1990).

J.B.

HUPPEN, HERMANN (1938-   ) Belgian cartoonist born July 17, 1938, in Beverce, in the disputed Eupen-Malmédy region of Belgium. After graduation from high school and a short stay in Canada, Hermann Huppen tried his hand at different jobs: furniture designer, draftsman, architect's assistant, and decorator. In 1963 he drifted into the comic strip field with a few stories done for a second-rate publisher, and started signing his work simply "Hermann."

In February 1966, Hermann and scriptwriter "Greg" (Michel Régnier) originated an adventure strip, *Bernard Prince*, for the weekly magazine *Tintin*; it was a success and in 1967 *Bernard Prince* became definitively established. Concurrently, he started a historical feature, *Jugurtha*, but it was short-lived. Hermann had more luck in 1971 when, in collaboration with Greg again, he created his acclaimed Western, *Comanche*, also for *Tintin*. In addition to his comic strip work, Hermann is noted for the many illustrations and covers he has contributed to *Tintin* and other publications.

In 1978, Hermann authored his first series, *Jeremiah*, a Western set in a postnuclear world that proved he could write as well as he could draw. After turning out a children's story, *Nic* (1980-83), in 1984 he produced his most celebrated comic series, *The Towers of Bois-Maury*, a medieval fantasy that showed his artistic powers at their peak. All through the 1980s and 1990s he also worked as a book illustrator, poster designer, and movie storyboarder.

A highly regarded cartoonist, Hermann is also a scrupulous and painstaking artist whose work always displays the utmost professionalism, even when his inspiration sometimes flags. Hermann has been the recipient of a number of awards in the cartoon field from organizations in Belgium, France, and Italy.

M.H.

HURTUBISE, JACQUES (1950-   ) Canadian cartoonist born November 5, 1950, in Montreal. It was in the course of his studies toward an engineering degree at the University of Montreal that Jacques Hurtubise first became interested in the problems of the comics. Along with a group of schoolmates, and with a grant from the University, he produced the first issue of a French-language comic magazine, *L'Hydrocéphale Illustre* ("The Illustrated Hydrocephale") in November 1971. After a short study trip to Paris, Hurtubise became more convinced than ever of the need to develop an indigenous French-Canadian comics industry; his efforts and a grant from the Quebec government led to the establishment in 1973 of a cooperative of French-Canadian comic artists, Les Petits Dessins ("The Little Drawings"). In 1974 Les Petits Dessins signed an exclusive contract with the newly founded Montreal daily *Le Jour* for the production of the paper's daily strips.

Among the six new features appearing in *Le Jour* on February 28, 1974, was Hurtubise's own creation, *Le Sombre Vilain* ("The Black-Hearted Villain"), signed with the pseudonym "Zyx." *Le Sombre Vilain* depicts the various schemes of a comic-opera conspirator whose goal is nothing less than the total destruction of the world. Hurtubise's graphic style, very stylized and modern, and his caustic sense of humor put *Le Sombre Vilain* in the forefront of French-Canadian comics. As Jacques Samson noted: "Hurtubise has managed to achieve a synthesis between text and image possibly unique in French-Canadian comic art."

In addition to his work as a cartoonist, Jacques Hurtubise continues to be active in the promotion of comics made in Quebec. In 1975, along with Pascal Nadon and Pierre Huet, he was one of the driving forces behind the First International Comics Festival of Montreal. Two years later, Hurtubise and Huet founded the humor magazine *Croc*. In 1983, Hurtubise created a publication of his own, *Titanic*; however, it only lasted a few issues. In recent years, his career has been devoted mainly to illustration and advertising.

M.H.

IANIRO, ABEL (1919-   ) Argentine cartoonist, born in Buenos Aires in 1919. After a career as a caricaturist of political and show business personalities, Abel Ianiro started his collaboration with the magazine *Leoplan* in the early 1940s. There he created his most famous comic strips: *Tóxico y Biberón*, the hilarious saga of a couple of drunks, and *Purapinta*. With this latter creation, the story of a typical bully of the outskirts of Buenos Aires who lives for his depredations but who is at heart a coward, Ianiro reached his major fame. The strip was published for a long time in the humor magazine *Rico Tipo*, run by fellow-cartoonist Guillermo Divito. For *Rico Tipo* Ianiro also contributed a number of caricatures of famous movie actors, a genre in which he was an undisputed master.

L.G.

IBIS THE INVINCIBLE (U.S.) Created by writer/editor Bill Parker in February 1940, *Ibis the Invincible* first appeared in Fawcett's *Whiz* number two. Nattily attired in a black suit and blazing crimson turban, Ibis was one of literally dozens of comic book magicians proliferating during the industry's "golden age." To creator Bill Parker's credit, however, *Ibis the Invincible* was one of very few that did not take their major inspiration from Lee Falk's syndicated *Mandrake* strip. The feature was original in most respects, and that may account for its longevity.

Ibis had two, somewhat related origins, but the one most cited was written by Otto Binder and appeared in *Ibis the Invincible* number one (1942). A captive of the evil Black Pharaoh, Prince Amentep (Ibis) was soon freed by a magic wand called the "Ibistick." Invincible against anything except other magic forces, the stick helped Ibis kill the Pharaoh, but only after the hero's love interest, Taia, had been put to sleep for 4,000 years. Lover that he was, Ibis put himself to sleep for 4,000 years, too. Upon awakening, he freed his beloved, and in the 1940s, they embarked on a war against evil.

Most *Ibis the Invincible* stories were horror tales, and Ibis and Taia were constantly battling vampires, werewolves, winged demons, and all sorts of supernatural creatures. Scenes depicting human sacrifices, rotting corpses, and all types of evil occurrences were not uncommon. But paramount in all the stories, even over and above the skimpy, revealing halter top worn by Taia, was the Ibistick. It could do almost anything—a sort of wooden Superman. Most of the stories were written by Fawcett workhorse Otto Binder, but Bill Woolfolk and Manly Wade Wellman also contributed heavily to the series. Mac Raboy, Carl Pfeufer, Kurt Schaffenberger, and Alex Blum handled the bulk of the artwork, which was always consistent, almost never poor, but not really above ordinary.

Ibis the Invincible appeared in all 155 issues of *Whiz* comics, which was discontinued in June 1953. The feature also had six issues of its own magazine (from 1943 to 1948) and made appearances in many of Fawcett's other magazines.

J.B.

IDÉE FIXE DU SAVANT COSINUS, L' (France) The last part of Christophe's picture-story trilogy, *L'Idée Fixe du Savant Cosinus* ("Learned Cosine's Fixed Idea") is, in many ways, also the funniest. This comic saga started, like Christophe's earlier *La Famille Fenouillard* and *Le Sapeur Camember*, in the pages of *Le Petit Français Illustré*, where it ran from 1893 to 1897.

Zéphyrin Brioche (nicknamed "the learned Cosine") was the prototype of the absentminded professor whose head is always in the clouds. He was leading a sedate life filled with abstruse research and algebraic formulas until the day he learned of his cousin Fenouillard's round-the-world exploits and subsequent fame. Bitten by jealousy, he decided to circle the globe in his turn (his "fixed idea"). Plagued by misfortune, he never made it out of Paris. Cosinus's attempts to start on his journey, on foot and by train, bicycle, horse carriage, and in a variety of outlandish contraptions of his own invention, always ended in abject failure. On this basic theme Christophe wove the most hilarious variations involving the professor's hapless efforts and the implacable quirks of fate that thwarted him at every step.

Le Savant Cosinus has been reprinted in hardbound form by Armand Colin, and in paperback by Hachette.

M.H.

IGAGURI-KUN (Japan) Created by Eiichi Fukui, *Igaguri-kun* ("Mr. Crewcut") made its first appearance in the March 1952 issue of the monthly *Bokeno*, and it grew rapidly in popularity as a judo strip.

Igaguri-kun's real name is Kurisuke Igaya. He is the son of a barber—like Charlie Brown!—but unlike the hapless Charlie he is tall and strong, the captain of his high school's judo team, which he brings to victory over all opponents (again unlike Charlie Brown), finally becoming champion.

The strip's popularity increased by leaps and bounds, and Fukui drew more and more pages as the demand increased. On June 26, 1954, he died suddenly of a heart attack, and the strip passed first into the hands of Ippei Doya, then to Asakazu Arikawa.

Igaguri-kun's success ushered in the boom of sports comic strips (*Daruma-kun* by Yoshiteru Takai, *Inazuma-kun* by Chohei Shimoyama, *Bokutō kun* by Yoshiteru Takano, to name a few). It also inspired a radio program. The strip, however, is no longer being published.

Fukui's work on *Igaguri-kun* was fast-paced, visually striking, and very impressive. If he were alive today Eiichi Fukui could have challenged Osuma Tezuka for the title of "king of the Japanese comic strip" on the strength of his work on *Igagura-kun* alone.

H.K.

IGER, SUMUEL MAXWELL (1903-1990) American comic book and comic strip artist, writer, and editor, born August 22, 1903, in New York City. "Jerry" Iger had no formal art training, but broke directly into the field as a news cartoonist for the *New York American* in 1925. During the late 1920s, he also did advertising artwork for New York Telephone (with Rube Goldberg) and several other companies. In the early 1930s, he began working for Editors Press Service, for which he created features like *Sheena, The Flamingo,* and *Inspector Dayton*. He also formed his own syndicate, Phoenix Features Syndicate, during this time.

Iger became one of the very first people involved in the comic book business. Three of his strips, *Bobby, Peewee,* and *Happy Daze,* appeared in Eastern's *Famous Funnies* in 1935; it is among the first ever produced especially for comic books. In 1936, he was the editor of Herle's *Wow Comics* and published the first work of two later-prominent cartoonists: Bob Kane and Will Eisner. In 1937, he formed the S. M. Iger Studios (in partnership with Eisner, 1937-40) and began packaging material for the slew of new comic book publishers. One of his earliest jobs was Fiction House's *Jumbo,* an oversized comic featuring his Sheena feature (drawn by Mort Meskin). Iger was also Fiction House's feature editor from 1940-55.

Many talented artists passed through the Iger studios over the years (his was the second shop created primarily to package comics); among its best talents were Lou Fine, Reed Crandall, Al Feldstein, Mort Meskin, Will Eisner, Mort Leav, and the underpublicized Mart Baker. His shop contracted and produced work for many of the publishers of the 1940s: Fox, Quality, Harvey, MLJ, Holyoke, Crown, Farrell, EC, and others.

Certainly one of the comic book's earliest pioneers, Iger finally closed his studio in 1955 and became Ajax's art editor until 1957. He then taught art and produced commercial artwork for advertising. He died in a New York City nursing home on September 5, 1990.

J.B.

INDIO, EL (Philippines) *El Indio* ("The Indio" or "The Indian") is not a novel about an Indian of the Old West or an inhabitant of India. The word *Indio* also applies to the non-Spanish inhabitants of the Philippines. The Spaniards who were searching for the Indies mistakenly called the Malayan populace "Indios."

El Indio, written and illustrated by Francisco V. Coching, appeared in *Pilipino Komiks* in 1953 and ran for over 30 chapters. The story is part of a series that featured Barbaro, even though he does not play the main role in this particular tale.

The main character of the novel was Fernando, a constant problem to the Spanish colonists who ruled the Philippines with an iron hand. Using guerrilla tactics, Fernando harassed and attacked his enemies. He was extremely elusive because of his shrewdness and his ability as a horseman. He was equally skilled with a sword as with a dueling pistol.

The other leading characters in this dramatic adventure novel were Victoria, Fernando's girlfriend; Kapitan Castillo, the archenemy; and Blanquita, Fernando's mother and also Castillo's lover.

Fernando's sworn enemy, unknown to him, was his own father. Kapitan Castillo was aware of his son's identity but was powerless to prevent the chain of events that led to the capture and imprisonment of his son and to his eventual facing of the firing squad.

One of the most suspenseful turns of events occurred when Kapitan Castillo faced his son in a duel. The novel was filled with such gripping sequences and emotional scenes. Coching handled each situation with finesse and mastery, qualities that are seldom seen in the comic book medium, where sensationalism and gimmicks have been the tools used by lesser individuals to hide their inability to portray and convey subtle and delicate moments. Coching has the judgment, taste, and control that make him one of the true masters in the comics field. *El Indio* is one of his many contributions to that field.

O.J.

INFANTINO, CARMINE (1925-) American comic book artist, born May 24, 1925, in Brooklyn, New York. After studies at the School of Industrial Arts, the Art Students League, and other institutions, Infantino broke into the comics in 1942 as the illustrator of Timely's *Jack Frost*. After working for a handful of other companies, he landed at National in 1946, illustrating the *Ghost Patrol* adventure feature.

Impressed with his material—mostly done in collaboration with Frank Giacoia—National editor Shelly Mayer assigned work to Infantino on a horde of strips, including *Flash, Johnny Thunder, Green Lantern,* and *Black Canary*. Much of this work was angular and rough, showing heavy influences of the Chester Gould and Harold Gray styles. In the 1950s, however, Infantino refined his style radically, and his work began to show better design and drawing. Strongly influenced by the fine-line illustrations of pulp artists Edd Cartier and Lou Fine, Infantino's work on dozens of science-fiction and Western tales began to show increased maturity and style.

But Infantino's finest career effort was the revived version of *The Flash*. Beginning with its first appearance in *Showcase* number four in October 1956, Infantino guided the strip artistically for 11 years. During that time, although his anatomy drawing was often lacking, his inventive maneuvers to simulate speed became industry standards. During the same time, however, Infantino was also drawing the highly acclaimed *Adam Strange* science-fiction series. There, his tightly knit illustrations and impeccable Hal Foster-inspired layouts were highlighted by some of the most beautiful cityscapes ever to appear in comics. In 1964, Infantino and *Adam Strange* inker Murphy Anderson were called in by Julius Schwartz to revamp the *Batman* strip. The resulting "new look" Infantino brought to the strip reversed the character's 10-year decline, and *Batman, Flash,* and *Adam Strange* all became comic book classics.

Infantino abruptly left the drawing board in 1967 and became National's editorial director. He experimented extensively with the National line and included two Steve Ditko titles; a feature from the 1950s *Bomba* movies, illustrated by comic strip artist Howard Post; *Bat Lash,* a highly acclaimed Western strip by Nick Cardy and Sergio Aragones; and many others. Most of the titles were financially unsuccessful, however. Infantino was appointed publisher in 1971 and continued to experiment. Under his leadership, National revived *Captain Marvel, The Shadow, The Avenger,* and others, introduced the dollar-sized comic, produced the highly acclaimed *Green Lantern-Green Arrow* series, secured the

"DC Special," Carmine Infantino. © DC Comics.

services of Jack Kirby, acquired the comic book rights to *Tarzan,* and issued hardbound and softbound reprints of landmark comic books.

Infantino won several fan awards and was given the National Cartoonist Society award in 1958. He and Stan Lee were instrumental in the founding of The Academy of Comic Book Arts (ACBA), the comic book's equivalent of the NCS.

J.B.

By all accounts Infantino's tenure at DC was a disaster, and he was forced to resign in the late 1970s. Since that time he has had a checkered career, working for Marvel Comics and Warner Publications, then going back to DC in 1982, working principally on *The Flash.* In recent years he has been living in semi-retirement, only occasionally drawing for comic books.

M.H.

INGELS, GRAHAM (1915-1991) American comic book artist, born June 7, 1915, in Cincinnati, Ohio. After several years as a commercial artist, Ingels joined the navy and had his first comic material published in a 1946 issue of Eastern's *Heroic Comics.* After his discharge in 1947, Ingels illustrated for the pulps briefly before joining the Standard group as an editor.

At Standard, which was also known as the Better and Nedor groups, Ingels concerned himself mainly with plotting and scripting, but he did manage to turn out several outstanding cover illustrations for *Startling Comics.* He returned to freelance comic illustrating in 1948 and did some work for the M.E. and Fiction House groups before joining the E.C. group. There he illustrated Western, crime, and love stories in a clean and competent manner.

But it was not until editor and publisher Bill Gaines instituted the E.C. "New Trend" horror line in 1950 that Ingels began to hit his artistic peak. Illustrating horror and crime stories for a wide range of the new titles—including *Crypt of Terror, Vault of Horror,* and *Haunt of Fear*—Ingels made it apparent that he was becoming the definitive Gothic-horror comic illustrator of the day. Adopting the pen name "Ghastly," Ingels began drawing a series of highly regarded covers and stories for the already high quality E.C. line.

Though he was competing with E.C.'s other talents, such as Reed Crandall, Al Williamson, Frank Frazetta, and Jack Davis, it was Ingels's sympathetic handling of gory horror tales that became E.C.'s most popular material. Writer Al Feldstein once commented that "when we did an Ingels script, we did gothic, gooky, horror stories . . . we didn't set limitations . . . we encouraged him to develop his own screw-ball hairy black and white style."

Much of that "screw-ball" style was lost on the color comics. Ingels's horror material was complex and sharp and contained tremendous amounts of fragile line-work. But, at the same time they were evoking nerve-shattering horror, his stories would also show brilliant flashes of whimsy, understanding, and even comedy. Some of his best material has been included in the five issues of *E.C. Portfolio,* a large, black-and-white art magazine published by E.C. fan Russ Cochran.

After the E.C. "New Trend" line was scuttled by adverse publicity in late 1954, Ingels spent several years illustrating for *Treasure Chest, Classics Illustrated,* and several of the later E.C. titles. He retired from comic books in 1959 and became a painting instructor in Florida. A born-again Christian, he repudiated his

AND SO, AS HOWLING WINDS SHRIEK THROUGH OPEN MAUSOLEUMS... AS TOTTERING REMAINS OF EVIL STUMBLE TOWARD THE SPOT... AS CREATURES OF THE NIGHT LEER FROM BEHIND TOMBSTONES... AS FOUL ODORS OF DECAY AND ROT WAFT THROUGH THE NIGHT AIR... ELICIA AND ZORGO ARE WED! THE MOANING OF THE DEAD THEIR ORGAN MUSIC... THE SCREAMING OF BANSHEES THEIR CHOIR...

Graham Ingels, "A Little Stranger." © William M. Gaines, Agent, Inc.

former horror work as "satanic." He died in Florida on April 4, 1991.

J.B.

INSPECTOR DAN, EL (Spain) Created in 1947 by the writer Rafael Gonzalez, *El Inspector Dan de la Patrulla Volante* ("Inspector Dan of the Mobile Squad"), as it was first called, enjoyed a long life in the pages of the Spanish weekly *Pulgarcito*, as well as in comic books and newspaper strips produced for the foreign market. The first episodes (there were 38 of them) were drawn by Eugenio Giner, who endowed the character with life and zest and who marked the series with his personal style. Along with the scriptwriter Francisco Gonzalez Ledesma, Giner contributed the best moments of this feature, which cultivated a genre up to then only slightly successful in Spanish comics: the tale of terror.

Dan was a Scotland Yard inspector who was sent on the most dangerous assignments by his superior, Colonel Higgins; he was assisted in his investigations by Inspector Simmons and his beautiful deputy Stella. The locales were the slums of London, filled with fog and teeming with criminals; the British Museum, where mummies sprang back to life; Chinese opium dens; and castles inhabited by mad scientists. Giner's drawings were rendered with care and were very detailed, always effective, with backgrounds lovingly pencilled in. His successors, Macabich, Vivas, Costa, Henares, and Pueyo, did not succeed in re-creating the atmosphere of terror called for by the story line. In the months preceding *El Inspector Dan*'s demise in 1963, Victor Mora wrote the scenarios.

L.G.

INSPECTOR WADE (U.S.) In 1934 King Features Syndicate decided to add yet another entry to its already abundant line of detective strips (*Secret Agent X-9, Radio Patrol,* and *Red Barry*). A deal was arranged with the estate of Edgar Wallace to adapt the late British novelist's thrillers into a daily comic strip. The writing was entrusted to Sheldon Stark, Lyman Anderson was hired to do the illustration, and the first release of the *Inspector Wade* feature was scheduled for December 1934. A hitch developed, however; the *London Mirror* was running a strip called *Terror Keep*, based on Edgar Wallace's *Mr. Reeder* stories, and King moved to suppress it. After some legal and business finagling, the *Mirror* dropped the feature, and *Inspector Wade* made its American debut on May 20, 1935. (While King was waiting for the legal dust to settle, its European representatives sold the strip to Mondadori in Italy, where

"Inspector Wade," Lyman Anderson. © King Features Syndicate.

it appeared on May 1, 1935, almost three weeks ahead of its American release.)

The pipe-smoking, tweed-suited Wade of Scotland Yard was a suave gentleman-detective who, with the help of his assistant, the bowler-hatted Donovan, solved the most baffling mysteries. His assignments often took him far afield—for instance, to Arabia, where he put an end to the depredations of a terrorist group—but his usual beat was the teeming streets of London or the peaceful English countryside.

Lyman Anderson drew the strip in a casual way that was not without charm, but failed to grip the reader. He was succeeded on July 4, 1938, by Neil O'Keefe, who changed the mood of the feature to one of suspense and foreboding. The action picked up in pace and violence, and *Inspector Wade* came closer to the hard-boiled school of American gangster movies than to the urbane criminality of Wallace's novels. In spite of O'Keefe's talent, *Inspector Wade* continued on its downward slide, and the daily strip (there never was a Sunday version) finally came to a halt on May 17, 1941, after a six-year run.

M.H.

IN THE LAND OF WONDERFUL DREAMS see Little Nemo.

INVISIBLE SCARLET O'NEIL (U.S.) *Invisible Scarlet O'Neil*, distributed by the now-defunct Chicago Times Syndicate, was the creation of former *Dick Tracy* assistant Russell Stamm, and it debuted in June 1940.

Touted in press releases as "America's new superheroine," Scarlet O'Neil was a shapely redhead who had suddenly become endowed with invisibility powers after she was accidentally exposed to "a weird looking ray" in her scientist-father's laboratory. (She was also able to make herself visible again by pressing a nerve in her left wrist, and to revert back to invisibility by the same process.)

Scarlet's early adventures, which were on the mournful side (perhaps in a bid to attract female readership), involved crippled children, kidnapped ingenues, and doe-eyed orphans, but this proved to be a passing phase. By 1944, when Stamm went into military service and left the strip to his assistants, the invisible heroine was fighting foreign agents, subversive organizations, and conspiracies on an international scale. After Stamm's return in 1946, the stories changed once again and became more and more whimsical, even sarcastic, as Stamm appeared to be poking fun at his heroine and her improbable escapades. In 1952 a new character was introduced into the strip (now simply called *Scarlet O'Neil*): Stainless Steel, a Texas swashbuckler with iron fists and a sense of humor. Stainless soon stole the show, and the feature was retitled *Stainless Steel* in 1954, only to disappear two years later.

Russell Stamm drew Scarlet in a loose, broad style with only touches of the tough, *Dick Tracy* treatment. The trouble with the feature was that it was always too cartoony for a straight adventure strip, but not quite funny enough for a parody. What is surprising is that it lasted as long as it did.

M.H.

IRON MAN (U.S.) *Iron Man* was created by Stan Lee and debuted in the March 1963 issue of *Tales of Suspense* (number 39). The origin story, scripted by Lurry

Lieber and illustrated by Don Heck, introduced Tony Stark, a wealthy industrialist and munitions builder. While in Vietnam on government work, Stark stumbled across a land mine. He wound up in the clutches of Red Terrorists, having sustained a severe chest injury. The Communists put the American inventor to work on their behalf, working with an elderly physicist, Professor Yinsen. Together, Yinsen and Stark built a suit of invincible armor, equipped with weaponry, flying jets, and devices to keep Stark's injured heart beating. Stark escaped in the suit but Yinsen died. Thereafter, Stark refined the suit and, as Iron Man, devoted himself to fighting tyranny and assorted evils.

Early *Iron Man* adventures, drawn by Heck, Jack Kirby, and Steve Ditko, usually involved Communist villains. Eventually, a Fu Manchu-type named The Mandarin became his major foe. The stories, written by Berns and Lee, centered on Stark's American factory and the various threats to its top-secret work. Stark never completely recovered from his heart injury, and he endured only because of the energy fed into his metal chest plate.

For a time, Heck was the principal artist and Iron Man's outfit was continually being redesigned. In 1966, Gene Colan took over as regular illustrator, and with Stan Lee's scripting, the strip became particularly heavy on "soap opera" aspects, notably in a love triangle involving Stark; his secretary, Pepper Potts; and his sidekick, Happy Hogan. In addition to his health problems, Stark continually faced legal and business problems that his bodyguard, Iron Man (that was the cover

"Iron Man," © Marvel Comics Group.

story for Iron Man's nearness to Stark) couldn't help with. No one suspected that the foppish playboy Tony Stark actually was Iron Man.

In 1968, after a one-shot appearance in a double-feature comic with *Sub-Mariner, Iron Man* began its own magazine. Number one started in May, and by this time, Archie Goodwin had become the regular scripter of the feature. Johnny Craig illustrated a few issues before George Tuska became the regular artist for the strip. A number of temporary artists interrupted Tuska's run on the feature, and after Goodwin left in 1970, several writers handled the chore before Gerry Conway and, finally, Mike Friedrich took over.

Iron Man appeared, as a guest star, in many of Marvel's other magazines, including a regular role as a member of *The Avengers*.

M.E.

Iron Man was put through the wringer in the 1980s: he lost the use of his legs, was elbowed out by an impostor, and turned into an alcoholic, among other vicissitudes. His physical and mental health stabilized somewhat in the 1990s. Among the artists who have worked on the series in this period, mention should be made of John Byrne and Steve Austin.

M.H.

IRVING, JAY (1900-1970) American cartoonist, born in New York City on October 3, 1900. Jay Irving's father, Abraham Rafsky, was a police captain, as his grandfather had been. After studies at Columbia University, Irving shifted from one newspaper job to another, then became police reporter for the *New York Globe*, and later a sports cartoonist. After a stint with the Universal wire service, Irving created a sports strip for King Feature Syndicate, *Bozo Blimp* (1930), which sank with hardly a trace.

Discouraged, Irving went into advertising work for two years before joining (in 1932) *Collier's Weekly*, with which he was to remain for 13 years, doing a weekly panel, *Collier's Cops*, and contributing occasional covers. During World War II, Irving was attached to the Marine Corps as a war artist for *Collier's*.

In 1946 he created a new comic strip, *Willie Doodle*, about a lovable and cuddly police officer, for the Herald-Tribune Syndicate; it did not last long. Then Irving tried to syndicate a TV cartoon show that he had created with Mel Casson, but the project did not succeed either. Finally, in May of 1955, Irving tried his hand at another comic police strip for the Tribune-News Syndicate, *Pottsy*, whose hero was a chubby, cherubic city cop with a penchant for humor and poetry that often put him on a collision course with the police brass.

Irving had been collecting police memorabilia since the 1930s, when his father had given him his own shield and presentation stick, and owned more than 5,000 items related to police work or folklore. He was such an authority on police matters that he was often consulted on the subject by the New York Historical Society and the Museum of the City of New York. Irving was also an honorary member of the New York Police Department, and of more than 200 other departments throughout the country. His stature as a cartoonist, unfortunately, was never as exalted, although with *Pottsy* he made an agreeable, if minor, contribution to American comic art.

Jay Irving.

Jay Irving died of a heart attack in his apartment in New York City on June 5, 1970, and *Pottsy* was discontinued shortly afterward.

M.H.

ISABELLA (Italy) On April 2, 1966, the so-called "fumetti per adulti" ("comics for adults only") underwent an abrupt turnaround with the introduction of their first heroine: Isabella. Considering the tastes prevailing among the comic-book-reading public, it seemed at first a gamble to thrust *Isabella* into this slightly disreputable genre. The new feature clashed violently with the traditional depictions of murder, violence, masked fiends, and assorted evildoers and sadists who were populating the adult comic books. Isabella, on the other hand, was created as a far more complex character, full of courage but also full of apparent contradictions, even flaws.

The new strip, however, made a favorable impression on the public, either because of its very incongruities, or because in the titular heroine it was easy to recognize another very similar feminine firebrand: Anne and Serge Golon's Angélique, who was then enjoying wide popularity in books and movies. No man could dominate Isabella, no woman could outdo her in boldness or passion. Her love was completely free, as was her heart: a passionate heart, or an icy one, according to the situation or the men who came in contact with her. She was an extremely modern heroine, in revolt against the aristocratic caste to which she belonged. Drenched in a splendid, touching, and romantic atmosphere, Isabella stands out from every other female character in the world's comic literature.

Isabella was created by scriptwriter Renzo Barbieri (on the basis of an apocryphal manuscript, "Les Memoires d'Isabella de Frissac") and adapted by Giorgio Cavedon. The artwork was done first by Sandro

Angiolini, who was succeeded by Sergio Rosi (pencils) and Umberto Sammarini (inks), assisted by draftsmen of the Rosi studio in Rome. Released in the beginning through Edizioni RG, *Isabella* moved to Ediperiodici in Milan. It ended in 1976.

G.B.

ISHIMORI, SHŌTARŌ (1938-   ) Japanese comic book artist, born January 25, 1938, in Nakata-machi (Miyagi prefecture). During his years in high school, Shōtarō Ishimori made his debut in *Manga Shōnen* with the work *Nikyu Tenshi* ("Second-Class Angel") in 1954. After his graduation from high school, Ishimori went to Tokyo in the hope of becoming a novelist. Unfortunately, he could not break through, and in order to make a living, he turned again to comic strips. In 1959, he created his first successful strip, *Kaiketsu Harimao,* an adventure story, which was followed by a succession of other creations: *Yureisen* ("The Ghost Ship," 1960), *Mutant Sabu* (1961), *Shōnen Dōmei* ("The Boys' League," 1962), and *Cyborg 009* (1964) All were science-fiction strips. In 1965 Ishimori tried his hand at his first gag strip, *Bon Bon,* but it was not terribly successful and he returned to science fiction with *Genma Taisen,* which traced the epic battles fought by a group of heroes endowed with extrasensory perception against alien creatures who tried to conquer the world (1967).

Shōtarō Ishimori is an extraordinarily versatile artist who has drawn literally hundreds of comic strips of all types for children, young adults, and adults. He has mastered every conceivable genre with dexterity and incredible speed. Under his full name, Ishinomori (of

Shotaro Ishimori.

which Ishimori is a contraction), and in an altogether different register he published in 1985 *Manga Nihon Keizai Nyumon* ("A Comic Strip Survey of the Japanese Economy"), translated with great success in the United States as *Japan Inc.,* and since 1989 he has been working on a monumental history of Japan told in comics form, *Manga Nihon no Rekishi.*

Like most Japanese artists, Ishimori was under the influence of Osamu Tezuka during his formative years, but he has developed a style of his own, which is fluid and airy, even sparse, especially in his gag strips.

H.K.

ISHINOMORI, SHŌTARŌ *see* Ishimori, Shotaro.

JABATO, EL (Spain) *El Jabato* was created by Francisco Darnis in 1958, at a time when adventure comic books were entering their decline, yet it succeeded in gaining an impressive readership in the course of its 381 comic books, published until 1966.

El Jabato was born as a feature designed to emulate the success of *El Capitan Trueno*, which is why the publishers chose Victor Mora, who was already *Capitan Trueno*'s scriptwriter. Ancient Rome provided the background (the so-called peplum films were then in their heyday, with such heroes as Hercules and Maciste), and the hero's companion was named Taurus, like one of those screen hefties. El Jabato was an Iberian warrior enslaved by the Romans, who took him to the capital of the empire and trained him as a gladiator. Not coincidentally this stage of his apprenticeship was similar to that of the historical Spartacus. In Rome El Jabato met his two most loyal admirers, the young Roman girl Claudia, and the stringy poet Fiedo Mileto, who was drawn with such caricatural exaggeration that he clashed with the dominant style of the feature.

The success of *El Jabato* was such that it led to the creation in 1962 of a magazine that bore his name, and his adventures were also being published in other weekly magazines of the same publisher, such as *Ven y Ven*, *Suplemento de Historietas del DDT*, *El Campeón*, and *El Capitan Trueno Extra*. In 1965 and 1969 the strip was reprinted, the second time in color.

Francisco Darnis, whose vigorous and personal style did much to establish the series, was helped or succeeded in his weekly labors by Luis Ramos, Martinez Osete, Carregal, and others.

L.G.

JACOBS, EDGAR-PIERRE (1903-1987) Edgar-Pierre Jacobs was probably the most secretive of all European cartoonists. Even his official biographies fail to divulge his exact date and place of birth; however, a close study of his career and several clues provided by the artist himself in his reminiscences lead to the conclusion that he was born in 1903 in Brussels or one of its suburbs.

Jacobs himself stated that "he could not remember a time when he did not draw." In the company of his childhood friend, Jacques van Melkebeke, he haunted Brussels museums and galleries. While preparing for his admission exams for the Royal Academy of Fine Arts, Jacobs did all sorts of small art jobs, from lace design to illustration of mail-order catalogs. Yet Jacobs had another avocation: he was an opera singer. Endowed with a rich baritone voice, he decided to enroll in the Conservatory of Music while pursuing his art studies at the same time! For a while bel canto prevailed as Jacobs graduated with top honors from the Conservatory and promptly found a position with the Lille Opera in France. There he sang all the baritone roles of French, Italian, and German opera. The outbreak of World War I put an end to his promising career, however.

Back in Brussels and penniless, with no further hope of pursuing an opera career, Jacobs decided to go back to drawing. After contributing many cartoons and illustrations to such publications as *Bimbo*, *Stop*, *A.B.C.*, and *Lutin*, in 1942 he joined the staff of the comic weekly *Bravo*, which was still publishing a number of American comic strips, including old pages of Raymond's *Flash Gordon*. By the end of 1942 *Bravo* was running out of Raymond pages, and Jacobs was commissioned to bring the current episode to a logical end. His work was of such high quality that the editors asked him to create an original science-fiction feature to replace *Flash*. Thus *Le Rayon U* ("The U-Ray") began to appear in February 1943. In 1944 Jacobs became assistant to Hergé on *Tintin*, which marked the beginning of a long-lasting friendship between the two artists.

In 1946, at the recommendation of Hergé, Jacobs became one of the first artists on the newly created *Tintin* magazine. There he produced his most famous comic strip creation, the universally acclaimed science-fiction adventures of *Blake et Mortimer* (September 1946). In addition to his work on the strip, Jacobs also did many illustrations for *Tintin* (his illustrations for H. G. Wells's *War of the Worlds* are especially worthy of mention).

E. P. Jacobs's reputation as an artist and storyteller stands second only to that of Hergé among European cartoonists. He received a multitude of awards and honors, his works are continuously reprinted, and in 1973 he was the subject of a book-length study titled *Edgar-Pierre Jacobs: 30 Ans de Bandes Dessinées* ("Edgar-Pierre Jacobs: 30 Years of Comic Strips").

In 1977 Jacobs released the first part of the long-awaited Blake and Mortimer album, *Les Trois Formules du Professeur Sato* ("Professor Sato's Three Formulas"). He was laboriously working on the second (and last) part of the story when he died in Brussels on February 21, 1987. (The unfinished project was later completed by Bob de Moor.)

M.H.

JACOBSSON, OSCAR (1889-1945) Oscar Jacobsson, Swedish artist and cartoonist, was born on November 7, 1889, in Göteborg, and died in Solberga on December 25, 1945. Jacobsson's first newspaper illustration was published in 1918 in Naggen. It was only two years later that Hasse Zetterström of *Söndags-Nisse* ("Sunday Troll") suggested that Jacobsson create a comic strip for that humor weekly. The resulting comic strip, *Adamson*, premiered in *Söndags-Nisse* number 42/1920 of October 17, 1920. *Adamson* caught on and became immensely popular because of the title character's funny misadventures.

Adamson is a stout little man, bald-headed except for three hairs growing on his head. Rarely is he seen without his cigar dangling from his lips. This offers Adamson the chance to be literally fuming whenever he gets caught in a fix of his own making, like gradually sawing off a chair's legs to keep it from tilting or cutting off loose ends of thread after having sewn a button to a coat and the button's falling off again.

Besides working on *Adamson*, Jacobsson, in the grip of an incurable illness before he turned 60, created *Abu Fakir* for the newspaper *Vi* ("We"). *Abu Fakir* is a strip about a magician, much in the tradition of *Mannen söm gor vad som faller honom in*. The strip was reprinted in album form in 1945. During his career, Jacobsson also worked for newspapers like *Dagens Nyheter, Exlex,* and *Lutfisken*, and exhibited his paintings in Gummeson's art hall in Stockholm in 1930. A memorial exhibition was shown in 1946 in Göteborg, where Jacobsson was a member of the artists' club. Göteborg's museum of art is one of many that exhibits Jacobsson's work.

W.F.

JACOVITTI, BENITO (1923-   ) Italian cartoonist, born March 9, 1923, in Termoli, in the district of Campobasso. At age 15 Franco Benito Jacovitti moved with his family to Florence. He was still a high school student when his first cartoons appeared in the satirical weekly *Il Brivido*. In issue 40 (October 5, 1940) of the weekly *Il Vittorioso*, Jacovitti's most famous character, Pippo, appeared in an episode titled "Pippo e gli Inglesi" ("Pippo and the English"). Later Pippo would be joined by his two inseparable friends, Pertica and Palla, to form the hilarious threesome known as the "three P's."

In addition to *Pippo* (which was published from 1940 to 1967), Jacovitti produced innumerable comic features, such as *Il Barbiere della Prateria* ("The Barber of the Prairie," 1941), *Chicchirichi* (1944), *Raimondo il Vagabondo* ("Raimondo the Tramp," 1946), *Giacinto Corsaro Dipinto* ("Giacinto the Painted Corsair," 1947), *Pasqualino e Pasqualone* (1950), and *Jack Mandolino* (1967). Jacovitti also adapted such enduring works of literature as *Ali Baba* and *Don Quixote* into comic strip form, and drew many parodies of American comic strips, among which *Mandrago il Mago* ("Mandrago the Magician") and *L'Onorevole Tarzan* ("The Honorable Tarzan") are the best known. (A great number of Jacovitti's stories were reprinted in *Albi e Almanacchi del Vittorioso*.)

In 1957 Jacovitti created for the weekly supplement of the Milanese newspaper *Il Giorno* a riotous, nonsensical Western parody, *Cocco Bill*, which appeared on March 28 of that year. For the same publication Jacovitti later produced *Gionni Galassia* ("Johnny Galaxy," a science-fiction parody, 1958) and *Tom Ficcanaso*, about the exploits of a nosy reporter aptly named "nose-sticker" (1957).

After the expiration of his contract with *Il Giorno*, Jacovitti transferred *Cocco Bill* to the *Corriere dei Piccoli* (1968), and in the same year he produced *Zorry Kid*, a clever parody of the famed masked hero Zorro. In 1973 he revived *Jack Mandolino* and *Cip e Zagar* for the *Corriere dei Ragazzi*.

Jacovitti was under exclusive contract to the *Corriere*, while in the past he contributed not only to *Il Vittorioso* and *Il Giorno*, but also to a lesser extent to Taurinia Publications (1940-41); *Intervallo* (1945); *Albi Costellazione*, for which he created the very funny *Ghigno il Maligno* ("Grimace the Evil One") in 1946; *Il Travaso; Il Piccolo Missionario; L'Automobile; L'Europeo;* and *Linus*. In 1980 he transferred most of his creations, including *Cip, Cocco Bill*, and *Zorry Kid*, to the weekly *Il Giornalino*.

Benito Jacovitti (who often signs his work simply "Jac") is probably the best-known Italian satirical cartoonist. His works have been reprinted in hardcover by Milano Libri and Edizione Piero Dami and have appeared in Rizzoli's famous BUR collection. Jacovitti now lives and works in Rome.

G.B.

JAFFEE, ALLAN (1921-   ) American comic book and comic strip artist and writer, born March 13, 1921, in Savannah, Georgia. After studies at New York's High School of Art and Design, Al Jaffee began his comic book career in 1941 as the writer/artist of Quality's *Inferior Man* feature. He moved to Marvel in 1942 and began producing funny animal and humor features, all of them rather standard comic book fare.

In 1955, while packaging two teenage humor books for Marvel, Jaffee produced his first work for Harvey Kurtzman's *Mad*. Intrigued with the possibility of expanding his humorous horizons, Jaffee decided to drop his Marvel titles and concentrate on *Mad*. By that time, however, Kurtzman had left as the magazine's editor, and Jaffee followed him through stints at two highly acclaimed—but short-lived—new humor books, the Playboy-published *Trump* and the artist-owned *Humbug*. Although both books were financial disasters and lasted a total of 13 issues, and although Jaffee had signed on with Kurtzman at about half his old Marvel rate, it was his first real opportunity to develop his humorous abilities. His writing was sharp, snappy, and brilliantly satiric. His artwork was direct, with little emphasis on anatomic perfection, but with considerable time devoted to humorous effect. The two unsuccessful magazines propelled Jaffee into humor's inner circle, and he became recognized as one of the most inventive artists in the field.

Shortly after *Humbug* faded in 1958, Jaffee entered the advertising field, returned to *Mad*, and began the *Tall Tales* syndicated panel. All three were financially and artistically successful. His advertising work is among the most unique and effective in the industry, prompting the NCS to award him its 1973 plaque as the best "Advertising and Illustrations" artist. He soon became one of *Mad*'s most prolific and easily recognizable contributors. In 1964, he invented the "Mad Fold-In," an inside back cover feature that entailed the reader's folding an intricately written and drawn scene into thirds, thus producing an entirely different scene with an always-satiric bite. He has also had many *Mad* paperbacks published, most notably several collections of his "Snappy Answers to Stupid Questions" feature. The *Tall Tales* panel lasted until 1965, and Jaffee went on to write *Debbie Deere* (1966) and *Jason* (1971).

Jaffee continues to produce considerable amounts of advertising work and children's illustrations, has worked on *Little Annie Fanny* (1964-66), and was written about in Nick Meglin's *Art of Humorous Illustration* (Watson-Guptill, 1973). "I did my first job for *Mad* magazine in 1955," Jaffee wrote in 1996, "and have been with it ever since."

J.B.

JAMES, ALFRED   see Andriola, Alfred.

JAMES BOND (G.B.) James Bond, the secret agent with the most famous number in the world—007 ("Licensed to Kill"), was created by the late Ian Fleming. Among the most successful popular novels in lit-

Mad *fold-in*, Al Jaffee. © Al Jaffee.

erary history, they were adapted by the *London Daily Express* as a serial strip. The first novel, *Casino Royale*, began picturization in 1957. It was adapted by an *Express* staff writer, was drawn by John McLusky, and ran for 139 days. *Live and Let Die* followed, and then, in order of adaptation, *Diamonds Are Forever, From Russia with Love, Dr. No, Goldfinger, Risico, From a View to Kill, For Your Eyes Only, On Her Majesty's Secret Service,* and *You Only Live Twice*. These were adapted by Henry Gammidge. During the run of the strip, McLusky changed his conception of Bond to fit the likeness of Sean Connery, who had begun playing the role in films, beginning with *Dr. No* in 1962. The strip was

dropped in 1963 when the current supply of novels was exhausted.

The strip resumed in 1964 with an adaptation of *The Man with the Golden Gun*. There was a new artist and a new writer: James Lawrence, an American author of strip stories for *Joe Palooka, Captain Easy,* and *Buck Rogers*. Lawrence proved so successful that, by arrangement with the Fleming Trust, he was permitted to originate Bond stories for the strip. The only non-original in the sequence of stories beginning with *The Living Daylights* (1965) was *Colonel Sun*, the Bond novel written by Kingsley Amis. The new artist was Yaroslav "Larry" Horak. A Russo-Czech born in Manchuria

"James Bond"(promotion piece).

"Jane," Norman Pett. © Daily Mirror Newspapers Ltd.

and naturalized in Australia, he started his art career as a portrait painter, then turned to magazine illustration. In Sydney he began to write comic books, draw them, and finally produced them. He turned to newspaper strips in the *Sydney Morning Herald*, creating an outback adventure feature called *Mike Steel*. McLusky is currently drawing *Laurel and Hardy* in *T.V. Comic*. James Bond's career in British newspapers ended in the 1990s, but the suave secret agent can still be seen in a number of American comic books published as *James Bond 007*.

D.G.

JANE (G.B.) The most famous British newspaper strip, and the first heroine to take the name of her medium literally—strip!—was born out of a true incident that happened to cartoonist Norman Pett's wife. Mrs. Pett received a telegram asking her to look after a dignified visitor from the Continent who spoke no English. "Count Fritz von Pumpernickel" turned out to be a red dachshund! Inspired, Pett drew the incident as a strip and sent it to the *Daily Mirror*. Editor Harry Guy Bartholomew, eager to establish British strips in the American manner, saw the potential immediately, and on December 5, 1932, *Jane's Journal, the Diary of a Bright Young Thing* was opened. For some years it ran as a daily gag, with a hand-lettered text spotted among the pictures to give it the effect of a diary. At the time that panelling was introduced to replace the single landscape box (December 1938), Bartholomew suggested a switch to continuity, and Don Freeman, a writer, came in on the stories.

Always a girl to show a leg, Jane was originally posed by Pett's attractive wife. Other models came in as her clothes were shed more frequently, and during the war Jane toured the music halls with a striptease act. The actress was Christabel Leighton-Porter, and it was she who played the role in a film version, *The*

Adventures of Jane, which was made by New World Films in 1949. Her appeal in the war years was tremendous, especially in the armed services. She actually made page-one headlines in *Roundup*, the U.S. Army newspaper in the Far East: *Jane Gives All* commemorated the great day when she finally stripped to the blonde buff!

Jane always topped *Mirror* surveys of readership of their strips: 86 percent in 1937; 85 percent in 1939; 90 percent in 1946; 80 percent in 1947; 79 percent in 1949; 77 percent in 1952. Michael Hubbard, Pett's assistant on backgrounds and male characters, took over the entire strip on May 1, 1948. Pett left to create a similar stripteaser, *Susie*, in the *Sunday Dispatch*, and also drew some rather glamorous strips for the children's comics. Hubbard's version of *Jane* lacked the lightness and fun of Pett's line, and the series became a soap opera. Finally, on Saturday, October 10, 1959, Jane and her beloved Georgie Porgie sailed off into the sunset.

There was an immediate and surprising (to the *Mirror*) outcry, as other national newspapers published articles and obituaries. She was replaced by a teenager, *Patti*, a more "with it" character drawn by Bob Hamilton. *Patti* lasted from October 12, 1959, to April 8, 1961. Then came *Jane Daughter of Jane*, drawn by Albert Mazure, but this, too, failed to last, running from August 28, 1961, to August 30, 1963. *Jane* was irreplaceable.

Norman Pett's *Jane* appeared in several reprints and special paperbacks; *Pett's Journal*, *Jane's Journal*, and *Another Journal* all have special artwork and full color. *Jane's Summer Idle* (1946) reprints a 1945 series; *Jane on the Sawdust Trail* (1947) is a colored reprint of the 1946 series. *Farewell to Jane* (1960) reprints a selection of strips published between 1944 and 1953. There was also a monthly reprint comic book *Jane*, published in Australia.

D.G.

JANE ARDEN (U.S.) *Jane Arden* debuted on November 26, 1928, in the Des Moines *Register and Tribune,* the brainchild of that paper's Henry Martin. The author of the strip was Monte Barrett, and the first artist was Frank Ellis; the strip was among the first sold by the newspaper syndicate operation.

Jane is a newspaper girl, sometime detective, and war correspondent. She is in her early twenties, leggy and predictably attractive. She never marries, but is married to her reporting job on a big-city paper.

The only other permanent character in this early-day *Brenda Starr* is Tubby, the office boy, a comic foil. The bosses change as frequently as do real-life managing editors.

After a few years the syndicate had trouble with artist Ellis; he suddenly disappeared and did not send his drawings in. Russell Ross was recruited from the art department of the newspaper. He had drawn another strip based on a Zane Grey story, *Bullet Benton,* later called *Slim and Tubby,* the latter character switching to become the office boy in *Arden* (the Western feature was continued by Jack McGuire, who was doing the Sunday *Arden*).

Succeeding Ross as artist was Jim Speed, a Toledo cartoonist; a briefly appearing artist from Florida; and finally Bob Schoenke. When Schoenke joined the strip, Walt Graham, who was the writer after Barrett died, retired.

When Schoenke took over the strip, *Jane Arden* underwent a strange transformation. Schoenke had drawn a strip called *Laredo,* and, under his direction, *Arden* became *Jane and Laredo.* It seemed that one day Jane came upon her family history and discovered that her mother was a reporter on a small-town Western paper. Strangely, the strip became one long flashback. Jane became her mother, the time became the 1880s, and Jane Arden and Sheriff Laredo Crockett rode off into the sunset. The strip died in the late 1950s.

The high point of the strip was during the 1940s, when wartime intrigues combined with Ross's attractive blend of the comic and straight styles for a very

interesting strip. Ross kept his lines simple and details to the minimum, and he boldly shifted angles and settings. His work had a slick, uncomplicated look that should put many modern artists to shame.

For years *Lena Pry*, a humorous top strip about a hillbilly gal, and Jane Arden fashion cutouts accompanied the Sunday page.

R.M.

JANKOVIĆ, DJORDJE (1908-1974) Serbian artist Djordje Janković was born on April 25, 1908, in the village of Jazak, some 30 miles north of Belgrade. After secondary school, Janković moved to Belgrade and started to work at illustration. He was the staff illustrator for the daily newspaper *Vreme* ("Time"). His first comic strip, *Tajne abisinskih gudura* ("The Secrets of Ethiopian Ravines"), appeared in installments in Serbia's most respected comics magazine of the interwar period, *Mika Miš,* beginning with number 80 (March 16, 1937). The artwork was stiff and somewhat amateurish. Three more strips followed; all, like his initial effort, were realistically rendered adventure strips and were clearly the work of a beginner. But the last of this group, *Džungla Ved* ("Jungle Ved"), shows the influence of Foster's *Tarzan* and Raymond's *Jungle Jim.* With *Put oko sveta* ("Journey Around the World"), based on the popular novel of the Serbian humorist Branislav Nusić, Janković's work begins to assume its mature form, especially in the grotesque drawing that goes with the comic text. Interestingly, with the exception of this text, which was adapted by Branko Vidić, Janković wrote the scenarios for all of his comics.

By early 1938, Janković had become a solid comic artist, adept in the art of the adventure genre. Of his works that year, two were outstanding: *Mysterious Driver No. 13* and a humorous comic titled *Kića.* After discontinuing *Džungla Ved,* Janković devoted himself fully to humorous strips, first *Aga od Rudnika* ("Aga of Rudnik Mountain"), then *Tri bekrije* ("Three Chums"). He reached the apex of his creativity with his last five comics before the German invasion of Yugoslavia on April 6, 1941. The first was an adaptation of another classic Serbian humor novel, *Pop Ćira I pop Spira* ("Reverend Cira and Reverend Spira"), written by Stevan Sremac. The adventures of two Orthodox Christian village priests, it is still popular today. The remaining four were a series of stories about what may be the first Serbian antihero in comics, the loser Maksim. Publication began in *Mika Mis* on December 12, 1939.

During the war, he stopped producing comics, but he did illustrate some fairy-tale books for children. After the war, many Serbs tried to publish their own comics magazines. One such enterprising publisher was Živko V. Rajković, who launched his magazine *Vrabac* ("Sparrow") just before Christmas 1945. All five comics in the premiere issue, four realistic and one grotesque, were written and drawn entirely by Janković. They show continued improvement on his prewar work, and with the grotesque strip, *Nasradin Hodža,* Janković first uses elements of Disney style (smooth soft line, rounded human body and extremities, reduced number of fingers, etc.). Unfortunately, he never got to finish these stories and we will never know how his work would have further developed. After *Vrabac*'s third issue, in January 1946, Communist authorities banned all comics as "capitalist machination." The ban lasted until 1950, when a few comics appeared in youth magazines. In 1951 comics maga-

"Jane Arden," Monte Barrett and Russell Ross. © Register and Tribune.

zines were again legalized; all were strictly state-owned and controlled by the Communist party, but they did present the world's most important comics to their readers. This relaxation, and a general turning toward Western art and culture, was the result of the great ideological schism between Tito's Yugoslavia and Stalin's Soviet Union in 1948.

Unfortunately, Janković did not stay in Yugoslavia long enough to benefit from these changes. In 1950 he slipped illegally across the border and escaped to the West. He remained in Italy, where he changed his name to George Jacoby. From 1951 to 1957 he lived in Rome and only painted, and in 1957 he moved to South Africa. He died in Johannesburg on November 24, 1974, only two days before the opening of a major retrospective of his work.

S.I.

JANSSON, LARS (1928-   ) Finnish artist and writer Lars Jansson was born on October 8, 1926, the younger brother of Tove Jansson. Like her he was endowed by their mother, Signe Hammarsten-Jansson, one of Finland's best-known artists, with a love for literature and art. Having finished his studies, Lars Jansson worked as a freelance writer and artist before joining his sister in producing the extraordinary *Mumin* ("Moomin") comic strip. By 1957 Tove Jansson felt that *Mumin* was too much of a full-time job, keeping her from other art projects, so she assigned her brother the writing duties in 1958. In 1961 he also started drawing the strip and continued to do so until 1974.

Mumin being the highly individual comic strip it is, it was all the more fantastic that Lars could take over the strip without anybody knowing the difference. To be sure, he had had three years in which to get acquainted with the *Mumin* characters by writing their exploits. Nevertheless, this is one of the rare instances in which the artwork continued to have the same fairy-tale quality established by the strip's originator. Free to do what he wanted on the strip, he always ended up doing *Mumin* the way Tove Jansson would have continued it. Although the Mumin trolls were always a bit behind times, Lars Jansson managed to weave into the strip such modern concerns as ecological problems, the youth revolt, and the trials of city life. Throughout the strip's long run, Lars Jansson remained true to its motto. As he put it, "the essential message of the *Mumin* strip is that people should be kind to each other. It sounds terribly naive, but that's the way it is. All members of the Mumin family must be allowed to go their own ways and do what they like, but they still remain interested in each other and follow what the others are doing."

When copyrights went back to Tove and Lars Jansson after the newspaper strip ended, numerous Mumin products were merchandised. The characters appeared in various TV series (in both limited and full animation) over the years. A children's comic and activity magazine—based on the animated series—started being published in the Scandinavian countries in 1991 with stories written and drawn by various Scandinavian artists.

W.F.

JANSSON, TOVE (1914-   ) Tove Jansson, a Finnish painter, artist, and writer, was born on August 9, 1914, in Helsinki. The daughter of artist parents, she readily took to a career in art. She studied art at the academies of Helsinki, Stockholm, and Paris. As it turned out, she was successful both as an artist and as a writer. The first of her novels, *Kometjakten* ("Comet Quest"), was published in 1945, but had been written as early as 1939. Aimed largely at a young readership, the book featured trolls in animal form, the Mumin trolls. Tove Jansson once credited the name of Mumin troll to her uncle, who had used it to warn her not to raid the pantry. The book's success encouraged her to continue in the same vein of illustrated books starring the Mumin family. This resulted in books written in Swedish, such as *Trollkarlens hatt* ("The Wizard's Hat," 1949) and *Muminpappans Bravader* ("Muminpapa's Bravado," 1950). She was awarded the *Svenska Dagbladet's* literary prize in 1952, the Nils Holgersson plaque and the Finnish State's literary prize in 1953.

In 1953 Associated Newspapers of London asked Tove Jansson to do a *Mumin* comic strip to be published in the *Evening News*, the world's largest evening newspaper. Despite warnings from a comic artist friend not to sign a long-running contract, Tove Jansson signed a seven-year deal, and the *Mumin* strip began in 1954. In 1956 Associated Newspapers started an international drive that ultimately resulted in the strip's being published in some 20 languages. All the while Tove Jansson continued writing and illustrating Mumin novels, and raking in awards for her exceptionally fine work. She received the H. C. Andersen diploma in 1956, 1958, 1962, and 1964, and was awarded the Hans Christian Andersen Medal, a kind of Nobel Prize for fairy-tale writers, in 1966, making her the only other female Scandinavian writer besides Astrid Lindgren to win the coveted award.

Tove Jansson continued drawing the *Mumin* strip until 1960, but turned the writing over to Lars Jansson, one of her brothers, in 1958. In 1961, when the contract was renewed, Lars also took over the drawing of the strip. Tove continued working on the books and other art projects.

W.F.

JAPHET AND HAPPY (G.B.) *The Adventures of the Noah Family* began in the *Daily News* in 1919. Originally a serial story in text and illustrated by a single panel, it gradually developed into a four-panel strip, dropping text in favor of balloons. The writer and artist, identified by the single letter "H," eventually appended the flowery signature "Horrabin." He was James Francis Horrabin, illustrator, diagram- and mapmaker, and ultimately artist for another popular daily strip, *Dot and Carrie*.

The Adventures of the Noah Family was based on a traditional children's toy, the wooden Noah's Ark. Mr. and Mrs. Noah, wooden peg dolls, lived at "The Ark" on Ararat Avenue with their sons Ham, Shem, and the bad boy of the family, bespectacled Japhet. Oddly, the animals of "The Ark" were all "real": Polixenes the Parrot, Horatio the Horse (known as "Raish" for short), and Happy the Bear. This chubby little cub, smiling and speechless, arrived somewhere around strip number 2,000 and promptly stole the show. Soon the strip was called *Japhet and Happy*, although for a time it was also known as *The Arkubs*, after the children's club formed by the newspaper; Happy was featured on the badge. When the *Daily News* combined with the *Daily Chronicle* in 1930, the strip continued in the *News-Chronicle*. For a while (1935-39) it expanded to a double

"Japhet and Happy," J. F. Horrabin. © News Chronicle.

"Jean des Flandres," Marcel Moniquet. © Heroic-Albums.

bank of strips, but was reduced to three small panels during the war. It ended in the 1950s.

The first reprint in book form, *Some Adventures of the Noah Family*, was published in 1920; it was followed by *The Noahs on Holiday* (1921); *More About the Noahs & Tom Tossett* (1922); *The Japhet Book* (1924); *About Japhet & the Rest of the Noah Family* (1926); *Japhet & Co.* (1927); *Japhet & the Arkubs* (1928); *Japhet & the Arkubs at Sea* (1929); *Japhet & Co. on Arkub Island* (1930); *Japhet & Happy Book* (1931); *Japhet & Happy Annual 1933* (1932). The latter became the regular title until 1951. In addition, there was a paperback comic annual, *The Japhet Holiday Book* (1936-40); a *Japhet & Happy Painting Book* (1949); cutout "shape books," *Mr. Noah* and *Japhet & Fido* (1922); and sheets of colored transfers, postcards, cutouts, and wooden mascots.

D.G.

JEAN DES FLANDRES (Belgium) The series of cheap comic books published in Belgium under the catchall title of "Heroic-Albums" has usually elicited only disdain from comic strip scholars. Yet, amid the generally squalid tenor of the series, a few features stand out: one such is *Jean des Flandres* ("John of Flanders"), created in February 1950 by the prolific Belgian novelist and illustrator Marcel Moniquet.

Jean des Flandres was a young Flemish nobleman raised by the Countess of Hainaut in what was then (1563) the Spanish Low Countries. The action begins in Spain, where Jean delivers the pure and beautiful Doña Flor Della Torres from the clutches of the villainous Don Cesar Blasco de Lopez, and brings her back to

his native Flanders. There our hero becomes one of the leaders of the rebellion against the Spanish crown; with his faithful retainer Claas Platzak and his band of guerrillas, he succeeds in holding back Don Blasco and his henchmen, who were sent from Spain to crush him. Following an abundance of ambushes, fights, massacres, and chases throughout Europe and as far away as North Africa, Jean des Flandres and Doña Flor (whom he had married in the meantime) finally enjoy some peace after 52 action-filled episodes (May 1955).

Jean des Flandres is better enjoyed for its plots, full of twists and turns, than for Moniquet's graphic style. The strip also gives us a fanciful but entertaining re-creation of one of the most eventful periods in European history.

M.H.

JEFF HAWKE (G.B.) Squadron Leader Jeff Hawke, R.A.F. test pilot, took off in the *Daily Express* on February 15, 1954. He flew the experimental X.P.5, the fastest aircraft in the world, which was not quite fast enough for his target, a flying saucer! Rescued from his crashing craft by tentacled aliens, he revived 3,000

"Jeff Hawke," Sydney Jordan. © Sydney Jordan.

miles beyond the moon, where the Lords of the Universe, responsible for the crash, offered him a choice: safe return to Earth with memory erased, or life as the First Citizen of the Space Age. He opted for the latter, and for 20 years widened the horizons of his readers with his fantastic science-fiction adventures. His partner in many of these adventures was Commander Maclean ("Mac"), from Canada; his worst enemy, Chalcedon, avowed foe of His Excellency the Overlord of the Galactic Federation. Hawke's unexplained disappearance from the *Express* on April 18, 1974, was as fantastic as any of his other adventures, and drew many protests from readers. He was replaced by a sexy instruction strip, *Isometrics*. *Jeff Hawke* wouldn't stay grounded for long, however; the strip was picked up by London Features Syndicate, which distributes it throughout Europe, to Australia, and even in the United States.

Jeff Hawke, Space Rider, to restore its original title, was created by Sydney Jordan of Scotland, who had cut his comic teeth on *Dick Hercules* and other Man's World publications. His original concept was for a comic book hero, Orion, in the space-opera style of *Flash Gordon*, but his hero was renamed by the *Express* editor, who wanted an R.A.F. connection. Assisting, and later taking over the writing, was Willy Patterson, who was responsible for the quirky humor in many of the stories. The early strips were redrawn for *Junior Express* starting on September 4, 1954, changing into a full-color gravure spread in *Express Weekly* from February 18, 1956.

D.G.

JERRY ON THE JOB (U.S.) Walter C. Hoban's best-known comic strip, the daily and Sunday *Jerry on the Job*, began as a rather tentative daily strip in the *New York Journal* on Monday, December 29, 1913. Jerry, a tow-headed, husky kid of about 17 (he is made to appear younger as the strip develops), applies for a job as an office boy in the opening episode with a suave, moustached employer named Frederick Fipp, and immediately tumbles into the sort of office-gag situations used again almost a decade later in *Smitty*. Luckily, Hoban, who had been doing the sports-page cartoons for the *Journal* with Tad Dorgan at the time, had a fey twist to his imagination and a graphically saucy way with his routine figures and backgrounds, which captured the reader's attention virtually on sight.

In a few months, *Jerry* had become one of the *Journal's* standard daily features, going into national distribution with Hearst chain papers. A regular cast of characters had been introduced: Fred Blink, a young rival for Jerry's job; Jerry's younger brother, Herman; a stenographer named Myrtle; and an effeminate bookkeeper (with an odd, rectangular nose) named Pinkie McJunk, who with Jerry and his boss comprised the active figures in the strip. (Within his second month, on February 17, 1914, Hoban introduced 30-panel movie parodies in strip form into the daily continuity of *Jerry*, with such titles as "The Dog Hero," "Jake the Scout," and—written by Jerry himself—"The Country Youth," anticipating the later use of the same idea by Merrill Blosser of NEA and Hearst's Ed Wheelan in his *Midget Movies*.)

Not content with this amusing initial cast and setting, Hoban transferred Jerry after a year or so to a job in a railroad station as a combination ticket-seller, fountain clerk, newsdealer, baggage-smasher, and sweep-out boy, where he worked for a white-haired,

"Jerry on the Job," Walt Hoban. © King Features Syndicate.

middle-aged man named Mr. Givney, and was regularly plagued by passengers and packages all going to a location called New Monia. This final job set the regular format for the strip as it appeared thereafter—except for a vacation in 1917-18, when Hoban was in the armed forces—until its end in 1932. Hoban added a Sunday *Jerry* page in 1921, which ran until 1932, becoming, however, only the page-topper to a new Hoban Sunday strip in 1931 called *Rainbow Duffy* (which featured a young bank clerk and physical culturist). Dropped as a page-topper in 1932, *Jerry* was replaced by an animal gag feature named *Discontinued Stories*, which topped a new strip supplanting *Rainbow Duffy* called *Needlenose Noonan* (narrating the slapstick problems of a comic cop), both running (as Sunday strips only) from 1932 until 1935, when Hoban left King Features to do advertising and other work.

Jerry on the Job is, in its low-keyed way, one of the most graphically innovative and appealing of all humorous comic strips; much of its gag humor is of the "wow-plop" variety, on the level of *Smokey Stover* (another visually inventive strip), but a small part, especially in the earlier years, is sparkling and witty. This latter body of work richly deserves reprinting for contemporary readers.

B.B.

JERRY SPRING (Belgium) Joseph Gillain (who signs his work Jijé) created *Jerry Spring* for the comic weekly *Spirou* in 1954.

Jerry Spring is the Western's equivalent of the knight-errant, the fearless and indomitable figure of lore and legend. With determination and righteousness as his only baggage, and his trusted Colts on his side, he wanders endlessly on the western plains, often sleeping under the stars, always going his own way and being his own man. It is to Jijé's credit that he could take the hackneyed theme of countless horse-operas and make it into a work of significance and even grandeur.

Under Jijé's pen, the magnificent vistas of the West came to life, the action scene took on an added dimension and meaning, and the characters rose from stereotypes to incarnations of myth. The strip, transcending the limitations of plot and situation, became an allegory of life and death centering on the friendship between the dour, inflexible Jerry Spring and his youthful Mexican companion, the cheerful, pragmatic Poncho.

Jerry Spring from the outset caused quite a stir in European comic art circles and was at the center of the revival of the Western strip in Europe. The scenarios for the strip were written by Jijé himself, as well as by his brother Philippe, Lob, Acquaviva, and René Goscinny.

Jerry Spring—which was discontinued in 1967—has been reprinted in book form by Editions Dupuis in Belgium. It was revived in June 1974, again in *Spirou*. It lasted only into 1977, but was resumed again, after Jijé's death, by José-Louis Bocquet (text) and Franz Drappier (drawing) in 1990.

M.H.

JIJÉ *see* Gillain, Joseph.

JIM BOUM (France) One of the first French Western strips, *Jim Boum*, was created in September 1934 in the

"Jerry Spring," Jijé (Joseph Gillain). © Editions Dupuis.

Catholic weekly *Coeurs Vaillants* from the prolific pen of cartoonist Marijac (Jacques Dumas).

Jim Boum was a Galahad of the plains in the tradition of the 1930s. He went through a series of stock situations with the cool aplomb and steely resolve required by the genre. At one time or another, he dutifully rid the range of a gang of cattle rustlers, led a wagon train safely through countless perils and Indian attacks, saved a schoolmarm by stopping her team of runaway horses, and tracked a bunch of desperadoes all the way to Mexico. All these adventures were well plotted and entertaining, in spite of Marijac's inability to draw horses (admittedly a strong handicap for a Western strip).

Marijac may have finally realized his own shortcomings, or he may have tired of the Western scene, for, in 1939, he catapulted his hero all the way to Africa. At the outbreak of World War II, Jim Boum, remembering that he was of French origin, enlisted in the air force and started battling Germans with the same gusto he had previously exhibited fighting outlaws. The French defeat of June 1940 interrupted Jim Boum's war adventures, and he went back to the West, where he remained until 1944 (this was all the more surprising since the German occupation forces were frowning on anything even remotely American).

"Jim Boum," Marijac (Jacques Dumas). © Marijac.

After France's liberation, Jim Boum reappeared in the first issue of *Coq Hardi* (October 1944) as a pilot with the American forces in the Pacific. He later went back to the West, but his best adventure took place on the planet Mars, where Jim had to battle prehistoric monsters and bloodthirsty Martians. *Jim Boum* disappeared from the comic pages in 1950, but some of the earlier episodes were periodically revived in one form or another.

The most striking feature about *Jim Boum* was Marijac's almost total lack of draftsmanship; yet, after a while, the clumsy rendering of characters and the imprecise delineation of action take on an almost endearing quality. On the other hand, the scenarios and situations, trite as they may today appear, were extremely well conceived and brilliantly written. Marijac is a true Western buff (in the 1940s he was made an honorary member of the Blackfeet tribe), and in *Jim Boum* he handled the mythology of the West with integrity and deep affection. These two qualities accounted, more than anything else, for the long-lasting success of the strip: all its episodes were reprinted in softcover albums, and a variety of Jim Boum toys and novelty articles were successfully merchandised over the years.

M.H.

JIM ERIZO (Spain) A humor strip created by Gabriel Arnao (who signs his work "Gabi"), *Jim Erizo y su Papá* ("Porcupine Jim and his Daddy," as it was first called) made its appearance in issue 433 (April 20, 1947) of the comic weekly *Chicos*. Jim Erizo had well-defined characteristics: enormous, with the face of a retired prizefighter, his physical appearance was that of a boy who grew up too fast, and his mental state that of a hapless if lovable moron. His adventures—in which he was accompanied by his father, the Señor Pop, a shrimp of a man who made his first appearance as the father of another protagonist of the magazine, the boxer Rak Tigre—lasted only for the space of four very long episodes, coming to an end in the early 1950s. Jim Erizo, his father, and his father's twin brother, the equally dwarfish Señor Jules Pas, fought witches, criminals, and sadists; most of all, though, they were pitted against the gang called "the intermittently resurrected ones."

In this work, Arnao pursued his experiments in the field of nonsense humor, where language plays an essential role, ahead of the drawing. He also paid great attention to the layout and color, with a cinematic treatment of the panels, which stood out all the more because of the originality and grace of his drawing style, stylized and loose. He later widened these experiments to include the lettering of the onomatopeias and the speech balloons, by which he broke with accepted conventions.

L.G.

JIM HARDY (U.S.) In 1935 Dick Moores, then assistant to Chester Gould on *Dick Tracy*, imagined a tough-guy crime strip which he tentatively called "Jim Conley." Mailing samples to various newspaper syndicates, he got a favorable response from United Feature, which eventually bought the strip and rebaptized it *Jim Hardy*. After a series of false starts, the feature, considerably altered and toned down, finally appeared in print in May 1936.

Jim Hardy was at first an ex-convict trying to make it back into straight society. He later underwent several changes of profession, finally settling for that of a newspaper reporter. As such he was a crusader, exposing corrupt politicians, nailing down racketeers, and

"Jimmy das Gummipferd," Roland Kohlsaat. © Kohlsaat.

clearing the names of falsely accused men. *Jim Hardy* was drawn in a graphic style that could only be called a hand-me-down *Dick Tracy*, but it exuded an earthy, rustic charm; and the stories, as neatly done as any in *Tracy*, never displayed the viciousness and self-righteousness of Moores's model. This was probably the strip's undoing, as the readers did not seem to take to medium-boiled detective fiction. At any rate Jim Hardy, as a character, was judged a liability, and he was eased out by a cowboy named Windy and his racehorse, Paddles. *Windy and Paddles* (as the strip was then named) itself disappeared in October 1942.

M.H.

JIMMY DAS GUMMIPFERD (Germany) *Jimmy das Gummipferd* ("Jimmy the Rubber Horse") was created in 1953 by Roland Kohlsaat, who wrote and drew this comic strip published exclusively in the children's supplement *Sternchen* (Starlet) of the renowned German weekly newsmagazine *Stern*. In a readership analysis this popular feature boasted some incredible numbers: 30 percent of all adult readers regularly followed it—besides the youngsters that it was aimed at.

The basic premise of *Jimmy das Gummipferd* is fantastic enough. The gaucho Julio's horse is made of inflatable rubber, yet Jimmy also lives and breathes and carries his master through numerous adventures. It is no small wonder that Julio and Jimmy's adventures more often than not border on science-fantasy and science fiction, despite—or maybe because of—their home on the pampas. It may even be argued, that, wherever Erich von Däniken's high-flying "chariots of the gods" arrived, Julio and Jimmy had already been there, thanks to the inexhaustible fantasy of their creator. Kohlsaat's tongue-in-cheek heroes seem to find lost temples, secret tunnels, vanished civilizations, and flying saucers at every corner of their "pop odyssey" (as Kohlsaat called it), in their never-ending quest to solve all types of intriguing mysteries.

In Kohlsaat's fantasyland everything is believable, even a living horse made of rubber. In fact, his world of dreams would burst like a bubble, were Jimmy not made of rubber. Thus, Kohlsaat managed to spin a fantastic yarn simply by putting a dream on paper. His lit-

erary and artistic styles blended to perfection, and narrative and illustration balanced well. Calm and serenity prevailed, counterbalancing the climactic suspense. The fine-line drawings with their washed-in gray tones—the strip was published in black and white—were graphically satisfying as they blended humoristic and realistic elements. This ruled out graphic spectaculars but seemed to be the ideal way to maintain the special magic of this comic strip.

Jimmy das Gummipferd, which later on was aptly retitled *Julios abenteuerliche Reisen* ("Julio's Adventurous Voyages"), despite continued success for almost a quarter-century, was never reprinted in its entirety in book form. Fan interest generated some book editions, however. The feature ended December 23, 1976, as Roland Kohlsaat was slowly being incapacitated by illness.

W.F.

JIMMY OLSEN (U.S.) "Superman's Pal" Jimmy Olsen was created by producer Bob Maxwell for the *Superman* radio show and did not make his first comic book appearance until the November 1941 issue of National's *Superman* (number 13). For years the red-haired and bow-tied Olsen was a cub reporter for the *Daily Planet*. His freckles set him apart from the other, more serious characters of the *Superman* tableaux, and for a long time, he was the feature's only bit of comic relief.

When gadget-minded Mort Weisinger began directing the "Superman Family," Jimmy Olsen got one of the first gadgets: an emergency signal watch, which sounded whenever Olsen deemed Superman's presence necessary. He was also paired off with Lois's sister, Lucy Lane, and the two carried on a platonic and antiseptic love affair over several years. The character also maintained a Superman trophy room, which supposedly housed much Superman memorabilia.

Jimmy Olsen was finally given his own title in September 1954, and it was here that the character began to develop as an individual. Jimmy Olsen became the Elastic Lad in issue 31, and he would sporadically readopt the guise to foil criminals. He also became a hero in the bottled Kryptonian city of Kandor and was elected an honorary member of the Legion of Super-Heroes.

When Jack Kirby was lured to National in late 1970, *Jimmy Olsen* was his first assignment. He immediately made Olsen the leader of the Newsboy Legion, and he swiftly began severing the Superman/Jimmy Olsen relationship. It was also in this book that Kirby made most of his changes in the Superman mystique, including the introduction of Morgan Edge and the destruction of the *Daily Planet* globe. The *Jimmy Olsen* title was changed to *The Superman Family* in 1974; it ended in 1982.

J.B.

JIMPY (G.B.) On January 5, 1946, Jimpy was thrown out of the Royal College of Magic and into the strip page of the *Daily Mirror*. He had failed to pass his Magiculation Certificate and, despite a fair run of six years, failed to pass the readers' popularity polls. He was thrown out again, this time of the *Mirror*. A low 33 percent liked him from the start; his highest point came in 1949 with 36 percent; and he dropped to 29 percent in 1952. "That was the year Jimpy died," writes Hugh Cudlipp coldly in his biography of a newspaper, *Publish and Be Damned* (1953). He calls Jimpy "the favourite of the intellectuals," and perhaps he was, by *Mirror* standards, but certainly he never reached that sophisticated audience that was delighted by *Flook*. However, he undoubtedly entertained those readers for whom he was intended, the children who had not had a strip of their own in the paper since *Pip Squeak and Wilfred* retired for the war. Indeed, one feels that Jimpy's strip may have been a victim of opinion polls, for the figures Cudlipp quotes are for men and women; he never mentions children.

Hugh McClelland set Jimpy in a medieval world of magic, magic that usually goes wrong or backfires, thanks to his failed sorceror's apprenticeship. He told his story in square panels, with boxed narrative in the present tense; there were no speech balloons. His second adventure, *Jimpy and the Kind Hearted Dragon*, was a great improvement on the first, and introduced the rival knights Sir Clueless and Sir Binder (names derived from the slang of McClelland's old service, the R.A.F.). Later adventures found Jimpy in an Arabian Nights' setting, crossing Merlin the Magician in the court of King Bonedome, and in 1948 meeting Poco the Llama, who would become his faithful companion and transport. Almost immediately they were transported to Old Spain to meet Christopher Columbus in *Jimpy, Poco and the Admiral of the Ocean Sea*, an adventure that introduced McClelland's wackiest running gag. From here on, at the unlikeliest times, Don Abba de Dab would float by on his umbrella crying, "Beware of the Fiddlygubs!"

Reprints included hardbacks with color, *Jimpy 1952* and *Jimpy Paintbook* (1953); also an Australian monthly comic book.

D.G.

JODELLE (France) The Pop Art movement, which owed so much to the iconography of the comics, in turn inspired a novel in comic strip form, *Jodelle*, illustrated by Guy Pellaert on a script by Pierre Bartier and published by Eric Losfeld in 1966.

Jodelle is a young beauty who gets herself involved in a series of fantastic adventures. The action takes place in an ancient Rome suspiciously resembling New York and Las Vegas (with Cadillacs drawn by horses, neon signs inviting the people to come see Christians tossed to the lions, and toga-clad majorettes). The main characters (aside from Jodelle herself) are the sadistic and scheming Proconsuless, who plots the overthrow of Emperor Augustus, depicted as an effeminate fop; and the lesbian head of the women-spies, always surrounded by a bevy of available young women (among whom Jodelle has infiltrated).

Jodelle was an incredible hit when it came out. The book was translated in many countries (in the United States by Grove Press). Pellaert went on to do a similar opus: *Pravda* (1968), but by then the novelty had worn thin. Pellaert's style, a mixture of Pop Art mannerism, decadent line, and clashing colors, proved a flash in the pan.

M.H.

JODLOMAN, JESS M. (1925-) Like many of the comic artists in the Philippines, Jesús Jodloman is self-taught. Born on February 5, 1925, he started to draw at the age of 16. He admired the *Tarzan* and *Prince Valiant* strips done by Hal Foster and the *Flash Gordon* series drawn by Alex Raymond.

Jodloman, who started out as a portrait artist, illustrated a school book for Abive Publishing House. His first break in the comic field was in 1954, when he illustrated a short story for Terry Cinco, publisher of *Luz-vi-minda Klasiks*. It was written by Flor Afable Olazo and was titled *Ang Rosas na Itim* ("The Black Roses").

On January 4, 1955, he wrote and illustrated the heroic epic *Ramir*. It appeared in *Bulaklak*, a weekly comic-oriented magazine written in the Tagalog dialect. The series ran for 83 chapters until August 28, 1957. *Ramir* was so popular that it was made into a movie.

Jodloman has also done cover and interior artwork for such diverse publications as *Hasmin, Paraluman, Maharlika, Top Komiks, Zoom Komiks*, and *Pilipino Komiks*. He has written and drawn other fast-paced visual novels, one of the most popular being *Los Pinta-*

"Jimpy," Hugh McClelland. © Daily Mirror Newspapers Ltd.

dos ("The Painted Ones"). He collaborated with the well-known Tagalog novelist Clodualdo del Mundo (who is also the head of the Philippine comics code) to do a science-fiction story about a Filipino astronaut called Brix Virgo.

In addition to his work in the comic medium, Jodloman has done costume and set designs for movie productions, advertising layouts, calendar painting, and biblical illustrations. He did short stories for DC's mystery titles and *Kull* for Marvel comics (both in the United States).

His illustrations are strong and rugged with an earthy feeling about them. His characters, male and female alike, are sensual and endowed with great physical attributes. His heroes are extremely muscular, surging with power and vitality. His heroines are hightly voluptuous, possessing feline grace and independence. He has a loose and detailed rendering style that is very effective for the type of stories he likes to do.

A family man, Jodloman resides in Quezon City with his wife and seven children. His younger brother, Venancio Jr., is also involved in the comic industry.

O.J.

JOE AND ASBESTOS (U.S.) One fine day in the summer of 1925, Ken Kling, then assistant to cartoonist Bud Fisher, accompanied his boss to the Saratoga races. It was Kling's first day at the racetrack, and at the urging of his employer, he bet his whole bankroll on Fisher's horse Cartoonist, which unfortunately finished fourth. There and then Kling decided to create a new comic strip character, Joe Quince, who would perennially bet (and perennially lose) all his money at the racetrack.

Kling's new strip appeared for the first time in the *Baltimore Sun* and used the names of real horses in local races as a gimmick. As the horses started to win (to the cartoonist's amazement) and the circulation of the *Sun* soared, *Joe Quince* was picked up by an increasing number of newspapers (in New York it was carried by the *Mirror* for 25 years, then by the *News* for three more). In 1926 Ken Kling added a new character to the strip, a black stable boy named Asbestos, and changed the name of the feature to *Joe and Asbestos*. When his contract expired later that year, Kling took a year's vacation. Upon his return to New York he started a new strip, *Windy Riley* and revived *Joe and Asbestos* (1928).

Because of the nature of the strip, *Joe and Asbestos* could not be widely syndicated, but Kling's clientele, made up mostly of large metropolitan newspapers, was nonetheless a highly rewarding one (in 1947 his yearly salary was said to be over $100,000). When he decided to discontinue the strip in 1966, Kling retired a millionaire. He died in New York City on May 3, 1970.

Joe and Asbestos was not an outstanding or highly innovative strip. The gags, always revolving around horses and horse races, were slight, the penmanship competent but unremarkable, and the dialogues of the Amos 'n' Andy variety. Yet, as the most successful of American racing strips, it deserves a place all its own: it is a tribute to the appeal and versatility of the medium that Kling was able to sustain so successfully and for so long a feature based on the skimpiest of plots and the most hackneyed of themes.

M.H.

JOE JINKS (U.S.) The ill-starred feature best known as *Joe Jinks* was born *Joe's Car*, the 1918 *New York World* creation of Vic Forsythe.

As the title implied, *Joe's Car* was about automobiles and the passion that they aroused in the hearts of otherwise sedate and meek little men, a theme not unlike that of Frank King's early *Gasoline Alley*. *Joe's Car*, how-

"Joe Jinks," Henry Formhals. © United Feature Syndicate.

ever, never developed the subtle delineation of place and character that King was able to bring to his strip.

From motoring, Joe went on to aviation, and then on to become a cigar-chomping fight manager, the role for which he is best known. In the early 1930s Forsythe left the strip to do *Way Out West* for King Features (he came back a little later). Sports cartoonist Pete Llanuza carried on until 1936. Then came Moe Leff (the best artist on the strip), who drew both the dailies and the Sunday; he was followed by Henry Formhals on the Sunday, while the dailies saw, in quick succession, Harry Homan (creator of the Sunday *Billy Make Believe*) until 1939, then George Storm, Al Kostuk, Morris Weiss, and Al Leiderman. This sorrowful roll call ended in 1944 with Sam Leff (Moe's brother), who soon introduced to the strip its most popular character, a fair-haired young fighter named Curly Kayoe. On the last day of 1945 the daily strip was officially renamed *Curly Kayoe* (the Sunday continued to be called *Joe Jinks* for a while). The feature perked up briefly, then went down without a murmur in the 1950s.

Never a remarkable strip, *Joe Jinks* deserves mention for its long and checkered career.

M.H.

JOE PALOOKA (U.S.) Ham Fisher's famed boxing strip, *Joe Palooka*, began at staggered dates in early 1928 in some 20 newspapers, all of them personally sold on using the strip by Fisher himself. The early episodes, lacking specific release dates, could be started at any time, and were. Most of the first Palooka runs in print were under way by mid-1928, but the strip did not attain any great reader attention until the widely circulated *New York Mirror* took on the feature on January 1, 1931.

Since boxing as a sport had a bad editorial reputation with many papers until the early 1920s (largely because of the Jack Johnson championship and the absence of a "Great White Hope," a strip featuring a prizefighting champion was really only possible at the time when Fisher managed to get his into print. (Some earlier strips, such as *Moon Mullins* and *Smitty*, had touched favorably on boxing, but not as a steady theme.) Fisher's schmaltzy story line and Palooka's naive charm—which subtly controlled the worse excesses of his outwardly tough and cynical manager, Knobby Walsh—caught on big, once readers began to pay prolonged attention to the rather ill-drawn strip, and the ultimately vast popularity of *Palooka* (the *Dondi* of its day) began to take form.

Sharper readers of the strip, rather taken at various times with such amusing Fisher characters as Senator Weidebottom, the French-Canadian Bateese ("by tam, Joe, I keel you!"), Humphrey, and even Jerry Leemy, thought Palooka by far the worst thing in the feature, dreading even glancing exposure to his terrible sweetness and semiliterate platitudes about home, mother, and fair play. The public reaction was, of course, just the reverse: to the general reader, Palooka was the whole strip, and his tepid, unendurable affair with Ann Howe (Joe's totally colorless girlfriend) was endlessly gripping to them, with Joe's ultimate marriage to Ann in 1949 one of the major events of their time.

Fisher's hired art often made up for much of the sentimental and sappy story line: Al Capp and Moe Leff (who had earlier drawn a boy-adventure strip of some merit, *Peter Pat*, for United Feature Syndicate) did the

"Joe Palooka," Ham Fisher. © McNaught Syndicate.

bulk of the work from the early 1930s; they were accomplished draftsmen and graphic storytellers. (Capp even developed a group of hillbilly characters—Big Leviticus and his Mammy and Pappy—while working on *Palooka* who were so amusing that he used them in launching his own strip, *Li'l Abner*, in 1934). But it was Fisher's story and dialogue that held the strip's basic popular appeal, a fact demonstrated by the strip's sharp decline in the hands of its artist for almost two decades, Moe Leff, after Fisher's suicide in 1955. Moe Leff's continuation of *Palooka* did it little good, but it reached an even keel, on a minor level of popularity, with Tony DiPreta's intelligent work on the strip, which extended from October 1959 to the strip's close in November 1984.

Made into a feature film (with Jimmy Durante as Knobby Walsh and Stuart Erwin as Joe) in 1933, and into a series of two-reel comedy shorts in the 1940s, *Joe Palooka* was also a radio program in the 1930s (and later a TV series), and was featured in a long-running comic book series in the 1940s.

B.B.

JOE'S CAR *see* Joe Jinks.

JOHNNY HAZARD (U.S.) At the end of 1943 Frank Robbins, then at the height of his popularity as the artist of *Scorchy Smith*, was asked by King Features Syndicate to create a new strip; Robbins jumped at the chance, and in June 1944 *Johnny Hazard* was born.

In the opening episode, American pilot Johnny Hazard escaped from a German POW camp and rejoined the Allied lines (but not without first inflicting heavy losses on the enemy). With typical comic strip—or military—logic, he was then shifted to the Pacific front (Robbins, like any other armchair strategist, thought that the war in Europe was coming to an end), where he fought an assorted array of Japanese spies and saboteurs, not to mention some of the leading aces of the Imperial Air Force. After the war Johnny became a commercial pilot and the director of a private airline, exercising his talents in the four corners of the world in the rediscovered tradition of *Scorchy Smith*.

This was all changed by the coming of the Cold War (and then the Korean War), which gave Johnny an ill-defined role as a secret agent in a bewildering succession of missions ranging from spy cases to information gathering to rescue operations, from Paris to Rio, and from Greenland to China. Johnny was sometimes accompanied by second bananas like Snap the brassy reporter or Gabby Gillespie the garrulous navigator, but mostly he operated alone. A James Bond before James Bond, Johnny Hazard followed his dangerous calling unfazed by the (countless) beauties who invariably threw themselves at his feet—blondes, brunettes, and redheads with interchangeable faces and evocative feminine names: Brandy, Gloria, Ginny, Maria, and the fittingly named Lady Jaguar.

In the 1970s Johnny shifted gears again, turning into an airline troubleshooter and investigator. In these changing times he looked more and more like an anachronism, and in August 1977 his adventures finally came to their conclusion. *Johnny Hazard*'s passing also marked the end of Robbins's 40-year career in newspaper strips, as he perforce had to return to doing comic books.

"Johnny Hazard," Frank Robbins. © King Features Syndicate.

Robbins's artwork on *Johnny Hazard* had been exemplary. A cartoonist's cartoonist, he never ceased to display his awesome technical skills, even when commercial success (or the lack of it) did not warrant such a superfluity of effort (toward the end of its run, the strip was carried by a mere handful of newspapers). The writing, however, did not keep pace with the times, and that probably was the feature's main weakness. Be that as it may, *Johnny Hazard* remains one of the outstanding adventure strips of the postwar era and one most deserving of study and preservation.

M.H.

JOHNNY-ROUND-THE-WORLD (U.S.) One of King Features' perennial attempts at educating their readers, *Johnny-Round-the-World* came out (as a Sunday page only) in February 1935. The feature was purportedly written by William LaVarre, Fellow of the Royal Geographical Society, and was illustrated (in a straight, unimaginative style) by anonymous artists from the King bullpen.

The titular hero was a teenage boy taken along by his father, Major Jupiter, on a scientific expedition into the jungles of (then) British Guiana and Surinam. The action (or what there was of it) unfolded leisurely as the reader was treated to the sight of native dancers, flash floods, a couple of forest fires, and a number of animal battles, all depicted with actual black-and-white photographs (presumably taken by Johnny's "zoom camera") and with a pontificating, pedestrian text. The strip's comic relief was supplied by Johnny's dog Peppy, who constantly got into trouble, and by the native carriers whose comments often indicated that they did not take the Major's, or his son's, earnest endeavors all too seriously.

This rather wearisome travelogue did not last long: by 1938 it was gone. Its passing was much lamented by the advocates of cultural uplift in the comics. "It seems strange that the public is so exceedingly scared of anything that might add to its knowledge or stretch its mind a notch," bemoaned Coulton Waugh. But the public knew better and recognized *Johnny* not for the genuine attempt at enlightenment that it pretended to be, but for the patronizing bore it actually was.

M.H.

JOHNNY THUNDER (U.S.) Perhaps one of the strangest "superhero" strips ever to appear was National's original *Johnny Thunder* feature. Making its debut in *Flash* number one in January 1940, it was created by writer John Wentworth and artist Stan Asch as a parody of the already-flourishing, deadly dull superhero features of the era.

As described in his initial appearance, the green-suited Johnny Thunder had a "pet thunderbolt working for him." Colored pink with a triangular head perched atop a jagged thunderbolt, it was of Badhnisian origin and Johnny never quite knew what to make of it (him?). "All Johnny knows," the story continued, "is that when the power is on (and it lasts an hour at a time) he can make everything obey his slightest wish. The secret words which Johnny must say to get control of his thunderbolt are 'cei-u'!" To complicate matters, however, Johnny never realized this, and the thunderbolt appeared whenever he accidently uttered the phonetic equivalent "say you."

Given Johnny's admittedly absurd "power" and his own outrageous ignorance, the strip was fairly success-ful as a parody, but only rarely was it sophisticated or intentionally satiric. Usually the bumbling Johnny fumbled around through an adventure until bailed out by the thunderbolt. Drawbacks aside, however, *Johnny Thunder* was a delightful strip when compared with National's dour *Superman* and its grim and ghastly *Spectre*. Asch and Wentworth plotted the strip's course until 1947, and then gave way to writer Bob Kanigher and artist Carmine Infantino. By that time, however, the Black Canary had already been introduced, and Johnny was soon eased out of his own feature.

Johnny Thunder appeared in all *Flash* issues until January 1948's 91st issue. (It was entitled *Johnny Thunderbolt* in its first 10 strips and *Johnny Thunder and The Black Canary* in its last two.) He was also the Justice Society's comedic relief, appearing in most issues of *All-Star* between 2 (Fall 1940) and 39 (March 1948).

When National exhumed its 1940s characters in the mid-1960s, Johnny and the thunderbolt were revived, too. And while Johnny had gotten a somewhat better grip on himself and his "power," he was still a hopelessly lovable fumbler. His thunderbolt, however, had gained a personality. Writer Gardner Fox—who used the pair in several *Justice League* tales—made him a snappy comic who was infinitely smarter than his master. Their interplay became simultaneously burlesque spoofery and satire.

National premiered a second *Johnny Thunder* strip in *All American* number 100 in August 1948. Created by writer Bob Kanigher and artist Alex Toth, this Western strip was notable only for Toth's rapidly maturing and well-conceived artistic execution. This unrelated feature was short-lived, but three issues of a *Johnny Thunder* reprint title appeared in 1973.

J.B.

JOHNSON, CROCKETT *see* Leisk, David Johnson.

JOHNSON, FERD (1905-1996) An American cartoonist born on December 18, 1905, to middle-class parents in Spring Creek, Pennsylvania, Ferd Johnson was cartooning before he was in high school. Johnson won a cartoon contest in the *Erie* (Pa.) *Dispatch-Herald* at 12, then earned a gold watch for cartoons he drew for a railroad station agent's magazine at 13. After graduating from the Corry, Pennsylvania, High School in 1923, he attended the Chicago Academy of Fine Arts that fall, only to spend more time hanging around the strip cartoonists' desks at the *Chicago Tribune*. Tired of the eager kid looking over his shoulder, Frank Willard finally handed him a *Moon Mullins* Sunday page to color after it had been statted. Willard liked what he did and had him hired as a Sunday page colorist at $15 a week. Johnson's cartooning talent was so evident, however, that Willard soon engaged him as a full-time assistant, and in late August 1925, Johnson undertook his own Sunday page, called at first *Texas Slim*, concurrent with the *Tribune*'s expansion of its Sunday comic section from four to eight pages. *Texas Slim* was a popular strip where it appeared, but it had to compete for space in the nation's then-small comic sections with other already well-established *Tribune* strips, and Johnson was forced to drop it after two and a half years. Continuing to work with Willard, Johnson married Doris Lee White and began a second Sunday half-page in 1932: *Lovey-Dovey*, with *Texas Slim* as a minor gag appendage at the bottom. After this short-lived strip venture folded, Johnson undertook a sideline

Lynn Johnston, "For Better or For Worse." © Universal Press Syndicate.

series of advertising strips for subscribing auto dealers, which ran for years in the 1930s.

Johnson's major break came with the *Tribune*'s second revival of *Texas Slim and Dirty Dalton* in 1940. Read by a mass audience across the country, the cowboy comedy strip had suspenseful continuity and was enthusiastically acclaimed for 18 years until Willard's death in 1958. Johnson then took over *Moon Mullins* as his own. Living in Beverly Hills, California, Johnson, his wife, and son Tom moved down the coast to Corona del Mar in 1969 to escape the smog of Los Angeles. Here Johnson and his son worked on the daily and Sunday *Moon Mullins*. The feature was unhappily retired in 1991, and Johnson went into retirement. He died in Irvine, California, on October 14, 1996.

B.B.

JOHNSTON, LYNN B. (1947-   ) Canadian cartoonist and writer Lynn Johnston was born on May 28, 1947, in Collingwood, Ontario. Her family later moved to Vancouver, British Columbia, where her father was a jeweler and watchmaker and her mother produced calligraphy and illustrations for her grandfather's stamp business.

Early on, Johnston was inspired to draw and create by her mother's artistic ability, her father's humor, and her grandfather's intense interest in newspaper comics. She studied the intricate art of classic comedy by watching the films of Charlie Chaplin, Abbott and Costello, and the Three Stooges and by reading the comic-book work of John Stanley and Carl Barks. Later, the editorial cartoons of the *Vancouver Sun*'s Len Norris and the sarcastic wit of *Mad* magazine appealed to her rowdy, impulsive nature.

As a student at the Vancouver School of Art, she leaned toward commercial illustration and left the school in 1967 to animate Hanna-Barbera's *Abbott and Costello* television series at Canawest Films. At McMaster University Medical Center in Hamilton, Ontario, she spent five years as a medical illustrator, preparing audiovisual graphics for student training. She then obtained a layout position at a packaging firm.

During her first pregnancy she created numerous panel cartoons about her parturient condition for her obstetrician, which led to three books on child rearing, the first of which was published in 1974. The books were *David, We're Pregnant!*; *Hi, Mom! Hi, Dad!*; and *Do They Ever Grow Up?* Universal Press Syndicate's Jim Andrews discovered the series of books and was anx-

ious to add another female creator to the syndicate following the success of Cathy Gusewite's *Cathy*.

Johnston signed a contract in 1978 to originate her masterwork *For Better or For Worse*. Debuting on September 9, 1979, it portrayed the modern family from a woman's viewpoint. With its richly developed characters, artwork, and plot lines, *For Better or For Worse* soon reached the zenith of contemporary humor-story strips. Johnston bases much of the feature on personal experience and emotional retrospect. The strip's fictitious Patterson family loosely mirrors the activities and tribulations of the cartoonist's own kin.

A former president of the National Cartoonists Society, Johnston was given the society's coveted Reuben for 1986 and its Best Newspaper Comic Strip Award in 1991. The International Museum of Cartoon Art inducted her into its Hall of Fame in 1997—making Johnston the first woman to be so honored. Johnston and her family currently live in Corbeil, Ontario, where she continues to produce *For Better or For Worse*.

B.J.

JONAH HEX (U.S.) For some unknown reason a boomlet in Western titles developed among comic-book companies in the late 1960s and early 1970s. Marvel launched *Mighty Marvel Western* in 1968, and in 1970 DC Comics (then called National) resuscitated one of its old titles, *All Star Western*.

At first the *All Star* comic books were, like the rival *Mighty Marvel*, filled chiefly with reprint material; however, because National had a smaller backlist of Western stories than Marvel, original material began to creep in. There was a weak version of *Billy the Kid*, along with *El Diablo*, a good tale of a Zorro-like masked rider by Gray Morrow. But the star of the series was to make its entrance in issue number 10: *Jonah Hex*.

Jonah Hex was an embittered ex-officer of the Confederacy who had had the right side of his face blown away by gunfire in the last days of the Civil War. Since that time, he had been roaming the West, torn between good and evil, each personified by a different side of his face. Hex could sometimes be callous, but he was never intentionally evil. At one point he allowed a woman to be hanged despite the entreaties of his sidekick, Redeye Charlie; but his wrath would habitually turn against the clever crooks, high-placed manipulators, and corrupt lawmen who were forever crossing paths with the disfigured rider. Hex's nemesis was the Yellow Mask Gang, against which he waged an unrelenting and deadly guerrilla war.

The artwork on *Jonah Hex* had been entrusted at the outset to a stable of talented foreign cartoonists: first came the Filipinos Tony de Zuniga and Noly Panaligan, followed by the Latin Americans George (Jorge) Moliterni and José Luis García López. The most notable writer on the series was unquestionably Michael Fleisher, who imparted a dark, despairing tone to the tales.

In 1977 the antihero of the West was given his own comic-book title. While Fleisher remained as the principal writer, other artists came to work on the series, notably Dick Ayers, Gray Morrow, and Joe Kubert. *Jonah Hex* as a title ended in August 1985; the next month the protagonist reappeared in a world that had been devastated by thermonuclear war, with the name of the comic book changed to simply *Hex*. This revamped version didn't take hold, however; it lasted for only 18 issues, to February 1987. DC tried to revive the original character again in two separate miniseries published in the Vertigo line, one in 1993 and the other in 1995.

M.H.

JUDGE, MALCOLM (1918-1989) Cartoonist Malcolm Judge was born in Glasgow, Scotland, in 1918. He began contributing to the newspapers and magazines of D.C. Thomson & Co. while in his twenties, during World War II. When paper shortages were over and the Dundee-based newspaper *Weekly News* expanded, he submitted the idea of a panel gag built around a football-crazy hero named "Saturday Sammy," although the local Scottish edition of the paper preferred to spell his name "Sattorday Sanny." *Saturday Sammy* first appeared on January 5, 1946, and it has yet to miss a week since, despite the artist's death. Judge signed his work with the pen name "Mal."

Mal decided to try his hand at Thomson's comic strips in 1948; he was given the retired *Meddlesome Matty*. This strip, featuring a thoroughly nosy schoolgirl, was first published in *The Dandy* in 1937, when it was drawn by veteran cartoonist Sam Fair. Although *Matty* was fairly popular, it would not be until 1960 that Mal's cartoon career really took off, in the pages of Thomson's new weekly comics tabloid, *The Beezer*. Mal created a gang of three inept crooks called Boss, Fingers, and Knucklehead, collectively Known as *The Badd Lads*. They began their criminal career in *Beezer* number 210 (January 23, 1960). That same year, Mal started in *Beano* (October 15) *Colonel Crackpot's Circus*, which chronicled the Colonel's attempts to keep control over a crazy company of circus performers.

Within the next three years came Mal's two best-loved and most-memorable series, *The Numskulls* in *Beezer* (1962) and *Billy Whizz* in *Beano* (1963). The Numskulls were minute creatures that lived inside a man's head, running such departments as his nose, his eyes, his ears, and his mouth. Billy Whizz was less incredible, despite his phenomenal speed. Some years later Mal added to his comic creations *Ali and His Baba*, a magic strip (*Sparky*, 1970), and *Hop, Skip, and Jack* (*Buzz*, 1973). *Ball Boy* joined *Beano* in 1975, and *Square Eyes* was in *Topper* from 1981. Although his contributions began to taper off, Mal was still drawing *Ball Boy*, *Billy Whizz*, and *Square Eyes* at the time of his death in Bournemouth on January 17, 1989. Many of his characters continue still, penned in the simple style of their

creator by anonymous cartoonists, a tribute to Mal's creativity.

D.G.

JUDGE DREDD (G.B.) The most successful character to emerge from the hard-edged British science-fiction comic *2000 AD*, Judge Dredd was featured every week since he premiered in the second issue, dated March 5, 1977. Modeled after Clint Eastwood in the motion picture *Dirty Harry*, Dredd is essentially one-dimensional in his total dedication to the law. Dressed in black leather and an eyeless helmet that he never removes, he was created by writer John Wagner and artist Carlos Ezquerra and developed by them with contributions from writers Pat Mills and Alan Grant and artists Mike McMahon, Brian Bolland, Ian Gibson, and Ron Smith, among others. The "Lawman of the Future," who hunts down criminals on his LawMaster motorbike, is the toughest in the army of Judges dispensing instant justice through the barrel of a gun. His turf is the gigantic Mega-City One, a 22nd-century conurbation spread across the whole of North America's eastern seaboard.

Dredd was the first British comic character to be exported to and licensed in the United States in his own comic books, at first in reprints from 1983, then in new episodes from 1994 from DC Comics. In 1985 he was awarded his own daily newspaper strip in the *Daily Star*, and from 1990 he also starred in his own title, *Judge Dredd: The Megazine*. In 1991 he had his first encounter with Batman, illustrated by Simon Bisley. In 1995 Dredd was played by Sylvester Stallone in a Hollywood movie, but most of the series' distinctly British irony was lost in the translation, and despite impressive special effects, the film flopped.

Nevertheless, *Judge Dredd* has maintained its popularity in British comics and has grown into a complete, complex future world, adding fresh characters such as the terrifying Judge Death, to whom all life is a crime, and Psi-Judge Anderson, a female psychic. At their best, the stories operate on multiple levels, balancing straight action-adventure and black comedy with satirical commentary on current issues, exaggerated for effect, from food scares and fashion crazes to human rights and world politics. It is no coincidence that Dredd first became popular in Britain during the punk revolution and the rise of Thatcherism. The character has an ambiguous appeal to both ends of the political spectrum. To some readers, he symbolizes the worst excesses of a police state and the erosion of civil liberties; to others, his brand of no-nonsense law enforcement seems to offer the perfect solution to escalating crime and social disorder.

P.G.

JUDGE PARKER (U.S.) *Judge Parker*, which debuted in November 1952, was the product of author Dr. Nicholas Dallis and artist Dan Heilman. It was distributed by Publishers Syndicate of Chicago. It is now distributed by King Features.

Dallis had moved to Toledo, Ohio, where he struck up a friendship with comic strip artist Allen Saunders and created *Rex Morgan, M.D.* four years previously. The title character was based on a progressive juvenile-court judge in Toledo, Dr. Paul Alexander, whom Dallis had come to know during his service as a consulting juvenile psychiatrist. His interest in aspects of the legal

"Judge Dredd," John Howard and Brian Bolland. © IPC Magazines Ltd.

profession in general and Judge Alexander's actions in particular led to the creation of Judge Allan Parker.

Parker, approximately 50 years old, was a widower in the early days of the strip but has since remarried. He has a more youthful look today than when the strip began. Parker has become almost a minor character, with more of the action generated by handsome young attorney Sam Driver. In his mid-thirties, Driver is a moral, aggressive hero who carries the infrequent physical action in the strip. He has a pretty girlfriend, Abbey Spencer, the daughter of wealthy parents.

Other characters come and go with the cases. The strip, though relatively sophisticated, has steered clear of social issues; an exception is a 1975 continuity dealing with ethics in the law profession.

Through the years, *Judge Parker* has come to seem like a continuing series of *Perry Mason* reruns. For the actual and infrequent technical references to the legal profession, author Dallis subscribed to law journals and consulted friends and relatives in the profession. Dan Heilman's art was an easy, straight style that fit well with Dallis's easy, sometimes taut story. Heilman also had a cinematic visual sense.

Upon Heilman's death in July 1965, Harold LeDoux, assistant on the strip since its first year, took it over full-time; his style is less polished and more abrasive— also more stylized—than that of his former boss.

"Judge Parker," Dan Heilman. © Field Newspaper Syndicate.

Woody Wilson has been writing the script since Dallis's death in 1991.

A sturdy item in Publishers' stable of story strips, *Judge Parker* is as predictable as the long-running soap operas on afternoon TV, which it approximates in quality and appeal.

Parker has received awards from the American Bar Association, the Freedom Foundation, and other organizations.

R.M.

JUDGE WRIGHT (U.S.) Try as they might, United Feature Syndicate never succeeded in fielding an even moderately successful mystery strip. In 1945 they tried again with *Judge Wright*, written by Bob Brent and illustrated by Bob Wells.

Wright was a magistrate who spent more time solving crimes than judging cases. In one way or another he got involved with various investigations, and he often had to bring the criminals to justice himself, hampered as he was by the skeptical district attorney on the case (this was probably the same D.A. who, under another name, kept losing to Perry Mason). Judge Wright's adventures, however, were far from the ordinary, as he tracked down desperate wife-killers, murderous nightclub operators, and corrupt politicians, or unraveled complicated conspiracies and bizarre intrigues. A host of characters were always popping in and out of the strip, which was written in a circuitous, almost cryptic, tone and drawn in a hard-edged, black style.

In spite of its good points (entertaining mysteries, varied motivations, and fine suspense), *Judge Wright* did not take hold. In 1947 the syndicate replaced Bob Wells with comic book artist Fred Kida, with no appreciable result. George Roussos was subsequently called in, but he fared no better, and the strip was finally dropped in 1949.

M.H.

JUKES, JOHN L. (1900-1972) John Jukes, a British cartoonist, was born in Birmingham in 1900. After some years in Australia he returned to England and contributed single-joke cartoons to the Amalgamated Press comic papers. His first strips with original characters appeared in 1931: *Merry Mike's Ice Cream Bike* and *Heap Big Beef* in *Comic Cuts*; *Jim Jam* in *Joker*; *Jollity Farm* in *Funny Wonder*. From the start his work was clean and bold, with a firmer line than many of his contemporaries, well in the tradition of Roy Wilson and other mainline masters.

In 1932 came *Ben & Bert the Kid Cops* in *Funny Wonder*, and in 1933 *Dutchy & Dolly* for *Comic Cuts* and *The Wonder Zoo*, a large panel, for *Funny Wonder*. In 1934 he contributed some strips to the comic section of the *Bristol Evening World*, which prompted A.P. to give him more important work; in addition to *Sam Scatterem* and *P. C. Easy*, which he created for *Comic Cuts*, he took over the front page of *Joker*. This popular strip, *Alfie the Air Tramp* (created by Charlie Pease), had been running since 1931, but it is Jukes's image that is recalled today: the rotund Alfie, his "Flying Flea" one-man plane, and his pet pup Wagger, who acted as a rudder.

Especially good were Jukes's full-page designs at Christmas and other special occasions. Oddly, his other best-remembered character was also a "takeover"; Roy Wilson created *George the Jolly Gee Gee* for *Radio Fun*, but Jukes continued it, moving the hayseed horse across to *Funny Wonder*. Another series featuring a horse, *Mike Spike & Greta*, was also given to Jukes, who made it also his own. This Western comic page began on the colored front of *Pilot* (1937) and continued in *Knockout* (1939).

After the war Jukes freelanced for the *Big* series of comic books published by Scion, and then got busier at *Radio Fun*, drawing *Tommy Trinder* (1945), *Archie Andrews* (1949), *Norman Wisdom* (1952), and other radio and film stars. Work dwindled in 1957 as the traditional British style fell from editorial favor, and Jukes took a job with the North Atlantic Treaty Organization drawing instructional material in strip form. He retired to the southern coast of England and was brought back to freelance a weekly page in *Whizzer & Chips* (1971)—*Dinah Mite*, which, curiously, was yet another "takeover." He died in Looe, Cornwall, on October 31, 1972.

D.G.

JULES *see* Radilović, Julio.

JULIOS ABENTEUERLICHE REISE *see* Jimmy das Gummipferd.

JUMPSTART (U.S.) Begun on October 2, 1989, Robb Armstrong's *JumpStart* depicts a young married couple, Joe and Marcy Cobb, in their respective careers of police officer and nurse; at home, where they vainly try to keep up with their baby girl, Sunny; or out and about with friends. The middle-class Cobbs are an average American family. That they are African American is not a central issue but only one detail among many that describes them as they pursue the American dream.

At work, Joe's observations on the human condition resonate: from the one-woman crime wave victim who recognizes everyone in the lineup—plus all the mug shots—as former criminal transgressors but, ironically, can't identify any as her purse snatcher to Joe's own oversensitivity in accusing his curmudgeonly white partner Crusty of a racial remark in referring to four young men as "Hootie and the Blowfish," only to learn that they really are the musical group, the full array of humanity is affectionately represented.

Circumstances in the hospital are no different. Whether it's the patient who grumbles about the food only to discover after Marcy crams a spoonful into his mouth during a tirade that it's actually tasty or the HMO newsletter bigger than the federal budget, there is no respite from human folly. Nor is this environment free from racially based assumptions or blind spots, as when Marcy expresses surprise that an Asian-American colleague has no interest in *The Joy Luck Club*, only to be reminded by a white colleague that she responded identically when he assumed she admired Spike Lee.

The most endearing strips revolve around home and family, with the proud, protective parents either overloading the baby-sitter with cautions or boring the teacher into a trance with their endless commentary on Sunny's talents. With witty glances at sexually explicit films (they ultimately opt for a Barney video) and husband-wife sparring (Joe must scramble when Marcy asks his opinion of another woman's figure, while Marcy has to trick Joe into getting a physical checkup), the Cobbs are a typical couple. As for Sunny, she cries over playtime "wounds" only in sight of her mother,

"JumpStart," Robb Armstrong. © United Feature Syndicate.

exhausts her parents trying to ready her for day care, and at bedtime makes her dad choose between reading *War and Peace* or the Bible or else so befuddles him with questions that she tells her little pals, "My daddy is having difficulty reading."

The strip's panels, with their combination of thick, rounded edges or no borders at all, together with similarly configured balloons (which are sometimes overlaid or with edges whimsically connected or only partially complete), mixed with free-floating dialogue, provide extra appeal. Armstrong's sure handling of his material, gentle character treatment, and generous worldview make his strip the most popular by a black American cartoonist. *JumpStart* is distributed seven days a week by United Feature Syndicate to about 250 newspapers, and selections have been reprinted in *JumpStart: A Love Story* (1996).

M.B.C.

"Jungle Jim," Alex Raymond. © King Features Syndicate.

JUNGLE JIM (U.S.) Alex Raymond created *Jungle Jim* on January 7, 1934, as the companion strip to *Flash Gordon*. Just as *Flash* was King Features Syndicate's answer to *Buck Rogers*, *Jungle Jim* was designed as competition to Foster's *Tarzan*, which was then dominating the straight adventure field.

"Jungle Jim" Bradley was at first an explorer and animal trapper (in the tradition of Frank Buck's *Bring'em Back Alive*), but he was soon to take up the role he is best remembered for, that of a professional adventurer. His field of operation is the vast and undefined region known as "east of Suez," where Jim, aided by his faithful companion Kolu, fights brigand chiefs, international agitators, and pirates of every description. In 1935 he meets (and reforms) the shady lady who was later to become his constant companion, Lil' de Vrille, known in her trade as "Shanghai Lil." (The name and the type are obvious borrowings from Josef von Sternberg's 1932 film *Shanghai Express*.)

Alex Raymond's inspired pen endowed Jungle Jim's action-packed adventures with a striking elegance of line, a fine delineation of atmosphere and background, and a visual excitement that gave the strip a highly polished gloss. While it did not succeed in topping *Tarzan*'s popularity, Alex Raymond's *Jungle Jim* remains one of the highest-rated adventure strips, and its tone and style were widely imitated all through the 1930s and 1940s.

In the early 1940s, Raymond worked less and less on *Jungle Jim*, leaving the feature in the hands of uninspired "ghosts" (among whom can be found Alex's brother Jim). In May 1944, following Raymond's enlistment in the Marine Corps, *Jungle Jim* (along with *Flash Gordon*) was taken over by Austin Briggs, who did a highly creditable job. After Briggs's departure in May 1948, the strip was given to Paul Norris (who had been doing the comic book version until then) until its final demise in 1954.

Jungle Jim had his own comic book and was the hero of a radio serial. The strip was also made into a movie serial in 1937. In the 1940s and 1950s Johnny Weissmuller had the role in no fewer than 10 *Jungle Jim* pictures for Columbia, and later in a television series.

M.H.

JUNGLE TATEI (Japan) *Jungle Tatei* ("Jungle Emperor"), created by Osamu Tezuka, made its first appearance in the October 1950 issue of the monthly *Manga Shōnen*.

"Jungle Tatei," Osamu Tezuka. © Manga Shōnen.

Leo, the white lion, was the son of Panja, the first Jungle Emperor, but Pancha was killed by white hunters and Leo's mother, Raga, was shipped to the London zoo in a cage, where she gave birth to the white lion. Set free by his mother, Leo escaped on a ship, was adopted by a Japanese boy named Kenichi, and grew up among human beings.

Later returned to Africa, Leo was torn between his animal instincts and his almost-human stirrings. As king of the animals, he tried to fashion a civilized society among the jungle beasts in order to stop the encroaching waves of hunters and other humans trying to despoil the animal kingdom. Within this theme Tezuka wove a variety of subplots involving the animals and parties of explorers who were after the mysterious Moonlight Stone, an extraordinary source of inexhaustible energy.

With *Jungle Tatei*, Tezuka broke sharply with the static, one-dimensional, and slow-paced tradition of old-style Japanese comic strips as he introduced new and exciting cinematic techniques into his strip. *Jungle Tatei* was Osamu Tezuka's first successful magazine feature and ran until April 1954.

Jungle Tatei was adapted into animated form: it was the first color cartoon series produced for Japanese TV. *Jungle Tatei* was awarded the Silver Lion at the International Children's Film Festival held in Venice in 1967.

H.K.

JUST BOY *see* Elmer.

JUST JAKE (G.B.) It was on Saturday, June 4, 1938, that the British newspaper strip finally came to full fruition and found its first true native hero—not "Jake," the titular hero of the strip, but its villain. "Our Grand New British strip character" heralded the *Daily Mirror*'s introduction to *Just Jake*, by Bernard Graddon, but before long this hayseed hero vanished from the scene, off to fight for king and country at the call of war, leaving the scoundrelly, scurvy squire, all chin and bent cigar, to take over the strip. But he could not win the apple-cheeked, melon-chested Hazel Nutt, the heroine;

she remained true to her tradition as a country maiden, and to her swain, ploughboy Jake.

Captain A.R.P. Reilly-Ffoull, G.G., F.F.I. and bar (a name full of allusions: Air Raid Precautions, Galloping Gertshires, Free From Infection), the Squire of Arntwee Hall, Much Cackling, Gertshire, was present right from the first strip. He was awakened by a large crash. "By carbonate of zodiac!" he cried. Equally aroused were Titus Tallow, his greasy bailiff ("Suffering subpoenas!") and Eric or Buttle by Bottle the scrub-jawed serf ("Lumme! Oozat?"). It was none other than Jake the Hero, returning from Old Australy on his mobile sheep-dipper. In the offing lurked a third member of the Arntwee Hall household, gritty old Maida Grannitt,

"Just Jake," Bernard Graddon. © Daily Mirror Newspapers Ltd.

of the flying hairpins and the broad brogue: "May the awfu' consequences be upon ye'r pesky pates, ye black-hairted bogles!"

Drawing aside, which was brilliant, the dialogue of artist/writer Bernard Graddon has never been equaled this side of *Li'l Abner*: "Stap me sideways, serf, you've snuffled a snozzleful!" Eric could but reply, "Cor!"

Steve Dowling, who worked on the *Mirror* during *Just Jake*'s reign, called Bernard Graddon "a bloody genius but, alas, a drunken one." Dowling had to step in and draw the strip when Graddon was too gone in his cups to ink straight. Often he would disappear in the middle of a serial and another hand had to take over. Ron Gibbs and Tony Royle could work from Graddon's synopsis. But the spark was gone. Graddon died in the night from pneumonia contracted after a particularly sodden office party to celebrate Christmas 1951. The strip ended on April 14, 1952.

A paper-covered reprint of the 1945 saga *Educating Eric* was published by the *Daily Mirror* under the title *The Sly Sinister Scurvy Adventures of Captain Reilly Ffoull*, and the first history of British newspaper strips was named after his classic expletive and dedicated to his memory: *Stap Me! The British Newspaper Strip* (1971).

D.G.

JUST KIDS (U.S.) In 1922 cartoonist Ad Carter, with the encouragement of Clare Briggs, submitted a new child strip to King Features Syndicate. The new feature, named *Just Kids* by KFS, made its appearance on July 23, 1923, as a daily strip, followed by a Sunday page on August 20 of the same year.

Ad Carter filled the strip with characters and reminiscences of his own childhood. Mush Stebbins and his pals, the voracious Fatso Dolan and the far-from-inscrutable Pat Chan, were involved in all the pranks of boyhood and what was essentially high-spirited but harmless mischief. The little band never got involved in anything more dangerous than cutting classes (much to the chagrin of truant officer Bluenose) or wheedling Mr. Trumbull, the soda parlor owner, out of some free chocolate malteds.

The action centered on the suburban town of Barnsville, where the other characters of the strip resided: Mr. Branner, the club-juggling cop; the song-loving street cleaner; the skating oldster; and some other nuts and oddballs. There was never much happening, and the little band of youngsters provided most of the action.

Suddenly, in the mid-1930s, *Just Kids* completely changed character (at least in the daily version). Mush

"Just Kids," Ad Carter. © King Features Syndicate.

and his friends got involved in sinister plots and violent adventures, which were as suspenseful as they were unpredictable. There were secret societies and masked outlaws, and the kids took it all in stride, as if they were playing cops-and-robbers. This probably marked the high point of *Just Kids'* career: from the late 1940s on it was mostly downhill and the strip finally disappeared, without fanfare or notice, following the author's death in 1957.

Just Kids had a crude, even primitive look, and much of its appeal resided in its atmosphere and story line. It enjoyed only middling readership and success, and was never made into a movie; nor did it have its own comic book. Today the strip exhales a nostalgic charm redolent of suburban *Gemütlichkeit* and of quixotic boyhood dreams.

M.H.

JUSTICE LEAGUE OF AMERICA (U.S.) When it became apparent to National that superheroes were again going to be big sellers, editor Julius Schwartz, writer Gardner Fox, and artist Mike Sekowsky combined to create the *Justice League of America* (*JLA*), a group feature that starred Flash, Green Lantern, Aquaman, Wonder Woman, J'onn J'onzz, Superman, and Batman. Certainly influenced by his earlier experience with the 1940s' *Justice Society of America* (Fox eventually revived this group and wrote an annual two-part super-team-up), Fox's group made their first appearance in February 1960's *Brave and Bold* number 28. They were awarded their own title in October of that year.

Over the years, the membership has changed considerably. Green Arrow, Black Canary, Elongated Man, Sargon, and The Phantom Stranger have all joined; Hawkman joined and then resigned; Wonder Woman resigned and then rejoined; J'onn J'onzz returned to his Martian homeland; and Metamorpho declined entrance altogether. But it was never the "roll call" that made the *JLA* stories among the best produced in the 1960s. Writer Fox had a wide scientific grasp and an empathy for superheroes and used them to create some amazingly poignant stories. "Man, Thy Name Is Brother" is considered by many to be the best antidiscrimination story ever published in comics, and "The Creatures of Nightmare Island" and "The Riddle of the Robot-Justice League" are two of the most subtle stories ever written for a hero feature. When Fox left the feature toward the end of the 1960s, the strip took a sharp downhill slide despite the best efforts of Len Wein and Denny O'Neil, two of the more talented young replacements.

Artistically, the much-maligned Mike Sekowsky handled the first 50 *JLA* tales in a fast-paced and beautifully taut manner. Even panels overcrowded with heroes and villains were well done, and Sekowsky received excellent inking help. His work declined dramatically in the later issues, however, and he was eventually replaced by Dick Dillin and Dick Giordano.

Like the Justice Society before them, the Justice League fought some of the most original villains of their time. Among them were Felix Foust, a wizard of sorts, and the Royal Flush Gang, a group of thugs who dressed like playing-card characters.

J.B.

To revive the fortunes of the group, which had fallen on hard times, National brought in old Fawcett characters it had just acquired—namely, Bulletman,

"Justice League of America." © *National Periodical Publications.*

Spy Smasher, and even Captain Marvel. Initially, it didn't help, and, in quick succession, a bewildering array of writers (Denny O'Neil, Mike Friedrich, Len Wein, Cary Bates, et al.) were ushered in, to no avail. In 1987 the title was changed to simply *Justice League* (it recovered its original appellation a couple of years later). It finally turned around in the late 1980s and became one of the most popular superhero titles of the 1990s, even spawning such spin-offs as *Justice League Europe* and *Justice League International*.

M.H.

JUSTICE SOCIETY OF AMERICA (U.S.) *The Justice Society of America (JSA)* was created by editor Sheldon Mayer and writer Gardner Fox and made its first appearance in National's *All-Star* number three for Winter 1940. The group started a new trend in comic books—the grouping of a company's heroes in a single adventure. Imitators followed in droves, and the group concept is still going strong today. The group began with eight members: Flash, Green Lantern, Hawkman, Hourman, Sandman, Dr. Fate, Spectre, and Atom. Over the years, however, many others have entered and left the convocation. Batman and Superman made their first joint appearance here, and Black Canary, Dr. Mid-Nite, Johnny Thunder, Mr. Terrific, Red Tornado, Starman, Wildcat, and Wonder Woman all became members or made brief cameo appearances.

Gardner Fox wrote 35 of the 57 adventures single-handedly. The format for dealing with so many characters became formularized out of necessity: the heroes gathered for an introductory chapter, were each defeated by their enemies in an individual chapter, and finally reunited to defeat the villains in the last chapter. As patterned as the stories were, however, they were among the finest ever produced, championing democracy, brotherhood, and tolerance. With the 19 tales scripted by John Broome and Bob Kanigher, the series is perhaps the most sensitive and idealistic produced in the 1940s.

The feature boasted a long line of fine illustrators. Among those contributing material to the strip were: Irwin Hasen (1947-49), Alex Toth (1947-48), Carmine Infantino (1947-48), Jack Burnley (1942), and Frank Giacoia (1950-51).

The feature outlasted many of the characters' individual strips, continuing through the 57th issue of *All-Star* (February 1951). The title was then changed to *All-Star Western*.

When the second superhero boom began in the 1960s, it was inevitable that Fox would also reincarnate the *JSA*. The group was revived in the 21st issue of *Justice League of America* (August 1963) and now appears in an annual team-up with the Justice League. The group made a brief return in its own title in 1991-93.

J.B.

KAHLES, CHARLES WILLIAM (1878-1931) American cartoonist born in Lengfurt, Germany, on January 12, 1878. C. W. Kahles came to the United States at the age of six with his immigrant parents. Settling in Brooklyn, Kahles studied art at the Pratt Institute and the Brooklyn Art School. His career in journalism began at the age of 16 as staff artist for the *New York Recorder* and the *New York Journal*. In 1898 he joined Pulitzer's *New York World* and contributed a great number of comic features. The first of these was *The Little Red Schoolhouse* (1899), followed in rapid succession by *Butch the Butcher's Boy* and *Clarence the Cop* (1900), *The Perils of Submarine Boating* (1901), *Sandy Highflier, the Airship Man* (1902), *Billy Bounce, Pretending Percy*, and *The Merry Nobles Three* (all in 1905), *Clumsy Claude* (1906), *Optimistic Oswald* (1912), and *The Kelly Kids* (1919). In addition, Kahles was a regular contributor to *Life* and *Judge* (where he created *Captain Fibb* in 1905) and did a fair amount of book illustration.

In 1906 Kahles started the feature he is chiefly remembered for, *Hairbreadth Harry*, for the *Philadelphia Press*. In 1923, he began the daily strip of *Hairbreadth Harry* that he drew in addition to the Sunday page, and he discontinued all his other strips. He died of a heart attack on January 21, 1931.

C. W. Kahles was a great innovator, leaving to others the dull task of fully developing his discoveries. As his most constant exegete, his own daughter, Jessie Kahles Straut, wrote: "As a pioneer in American comic art, C. W. Kahles contributed many firsts. Among them were the first suspense serial and the first superhero, *Hairbreadth Harry*, 1906; the first serial story about a policeman, *Clarence the Cop*, 1900; the first comic strip about an aviator, *Sandy Highflier, the Airship Man*, 1902; and the first strip about undersea adventure, *The Perils of Submarine Boating*, 1901."

The sheer number of strips he produced has somewhat obscured Kahles's qualities as a draftsman and a storyteller, but there has been a renewal of interest in his work.

M.H.

KALENBACH, DIETER (1937-) Dieter Kalenbach is a German comic artist and graphic artist born August 29, 1937, in Düsseldorf. Having shown a talent for drawing, he decided to develop it further at the Hamburg College of Commercial Arts and Crafts. After concluding his studies there, he worked for various companies and freelanced as a graphic artist, decorator, and scene painter for stage and television. Every

C. W. Kahles, "Clarence the Cop."

now and then Kalenbach interrupted his professional career by extensive traveling. Several times his travels took him to the Balkan countries and to Africa for months. He returned from a voyage to the Arctic regions with an idea for a comic strip about Laplanders, the last nomads of Europe. Their closeness to nature fascinated him. Thus, together with writer Erka, *Turi and Tolk* was created in 1973. The stars of this series are Turi, a young Laplander, and his eagle Tolk. Turi's grandfather, Pavva-Troms, also figures prominently in the stories.

Turi und Tolk appeared in *Zack* magazine when it started including original German material in 1973. The feature ended with the demise of *Zack* in 1981. The magazine did not meet the expectations of the Springer conglomerate managers, who had hoped it would bring in money quickly. Instead, after much criticism at the magazine's inception and a Yellow Kid Award as best foreign comic book at Lucca, Italy, in 1973, sales had leveled off. Despite good licensed and original matter like *Turi und Tolk*, and despite a loyal following of regular buyers, the magazine was axed. With no other publishers wanting original material at the time, Kalenbach more or less left the comic field.

W.F.

KALUTA, MICHAEL WM. (1947-) American comic book artist and illustrator born August 25, 1947, in Guatemala to U.S. citizens. As a child of the 1950s, Michael Kaluta was part of a wide-eyed audience of American boys, pencil in hand, watching TV art instructor Jon Gnagy give a weekly drawing lesson. The practice in the fundamentals of drawing gleaned from those TV shows—particularly perspective drawing—poured forth onto the comic pages years later, and to this day Kaluta still mentions Gnagy as his first artistic influence.

Kaluta studied fine arts at the Richmond Professional Institute (now Virginia Commonwealth University). Much to the dismay of his instructors, who were immersed in the Abstract Impressionism trend of the day, Kaluta turned to the comic page for artistic expression. Arriving in New York City in 1969, Kaluta's first published comic book assignment was a three-page story in *Flash Gordon* number 18 (January 1970). His early comic book work, primarily for National Comics (now DC), consisted of filler stories and cover art for many of their horror and fantasy titles. A significant part of his early work illustrated the fantasy stories of Edgar Rice Burroughs, particularly the *Carson of Venus* series. Along with the story work, Kaluta created an impressive number of comic book covers for both DC and Marvel comics. A few of the notable titles that had extended runs with Kaluta covers include *House of Mystery*, *House of Secrets*, *Batman*, *Detective*, *Conan the King*, and more recently, *Vampirella* and *The Books of Magic*. The original artwork for these covers is highly sought after by art collectors today.

In 1972 DC Comics revived *The Shadow*, a crime-fighting character who originally enjoyed popularity in the 1930s. Kaluta was selected to re-create the character, and his run on the series was brief but brilliant. His artwork manifested a smoky mood and atmosphere. From his art studio on the Upper West Side of Manhattan, Kaluta had every dark alley of Hell's Kitchen, dusty street of Chinatown, and architectural wonder of the city within his reach to cast in The Shadow's world. His sketchbook-style realism gave *The Shadow* an urban feel that evoked the 1930s but looks fresh and inventive even today. Deadlines conflicted with Kaluta's detailed style, and after five issues and eight covers he left the series. *The Shadow* has become the most notable comic character associated with Kaluta. After the DC series, he brought the character back for several publishers, including Marvel and Dark Horse. In 1994 Kaluta contributed to production of the Universal Pictures film *The Shadow*. Kaluta created illustrations over photos of Alex Baldwin, the film's star, to help develop the makeup design for the Shadow in the movie.

In 1976 Kaluta and two close friends, comic artist and illustrator Bernie Wrightson and painter Jeff Jones, formed an art studio with British comic artist and illustrator Barry Windsor-Smith. Kaluta, Wrightson, and Windsor-Smith all lived in the same apartment building when they first arrived in New York in the late 1960s. A close look at some of Kaluta's and Wrightson's early 1970s comic book work reveals hints of "midnight hour collaborations" as the artists helped each other meet tight deadlines. Each of the studio artists had made contributions to the comic art form in the 1970s but their studio works represented an evolution in illustration and painting for posters, books, and limited-edition prints. Kaluta produced some of his most imaginative work during this period.

The *Starstruck* comic series, which appeared in 1981, was based on an off-Broadway play created by Elaine Lee. The comic book series, which was created by Kaluta and Lee and illustrated by Kaluta, has been published under several imprints, including Marvel's Epic line and most recently at Dark Horse. *Starstruck*, a science fiction satire with feminist overtones, gave Kaluta a fresh vehicle to display his mature drawing and design talents and features some of his most original work in the comic book field. Visually, *Starstruck* is pure Kaluta, with a drawing style that has matured beyond his original comic artist influences. Throughout the 1970s Kaluta's work affectionately reflected his early artistic influences, particularly the virtuoso trio of Frank Frazetta, Al Williamson, and Roy Krenkel. These three brilliant draftsmen created—together and individually—many of the science-fiction comic classics of the 1950s and later reintroduced impeccable draftsmanship and style to the comics at the Warren comic magazines in the 1960s.

Throughout the 1990s, Kaluta has created new works for *The Shadow* and *Starstruck* for various comic publishers. Most recently, he enjoyed a long run of cover designs for DC Comics's Vertigo title *The Books of Magic*. His modern fantasy interpretations of the title, reminiscent of the antiquarian children's illustrators Rackham, Robinson, and Dulac, have been a welcome relief from the ultraviolent and nihilistic subject matter that pervades comic books in the 1990s.

Perhaps Kaluta's most important contribution to the comic field has been his blending of classic visual design and illustration styles within the comic page. Kaluta integrates classical graphic design motifs influenced by the Art Nouveau works of Aubrey Beardsley and the Art Deco patterns of Alfons Mucha—bringing a welcome new look to the comics. Kaluta's comic work represents one of the underappreciated links to the great illustrators and designers of the early part of this century. Perhaps Kaluta can best be described as

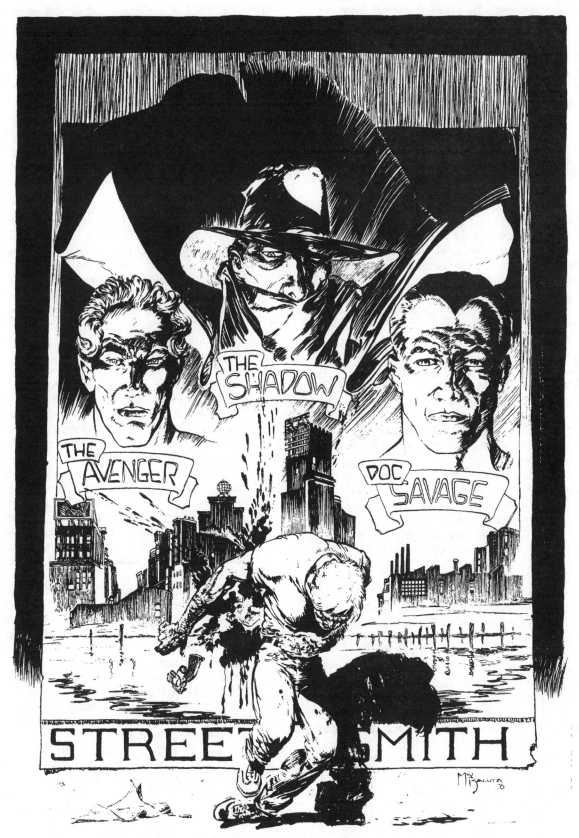

"The Avenger, The Shadow, Doc Savage," Michael Kaluta. © Conde Naste Pub.

an antiquarian-futurist who visually romances the future with the lyrical lines of the past.

Currently working in the digital media, Kaluta is designing characters and environments for several video games, often with famed British designer and illustrator Roger Dean. Hopefully, his love for the art form will continue to draw him back to the pages of comic books in the years ahead.

R.G.

KAMUI DEN (Japan) *Kamui Den*, created by Sanpei Shirato, made its first appearance in the December 1964 issue of the comic monthly *Garo*.

This long-lasting strip depicted the dramatic history of a number of characters during a 20-year period from about 1640 to 1662. The scene was laid mostly in Hioki, and many characters appeared in the strip, from samurais to *hinin* (persons of the lowest class). The main characters were Kamui, son of Yasuke, a hinin who became a ninja spy in order to escape from his class, and his friend, the rebel peasant leader Shousuke, who later became Kamui's brother-in-law. These two were later joined by Ryūnoshin Kusaka, a samurai who wanted to avenge the death of his father and his whole clan at the hands of the wicked lord of Hioki.

Many others appeared in this chronicle of life in the feudal society of the Edo era. Shirato exposed the fundamental conflict besetting this society and he particularly denounced the *Mibun Sida* ("class system") whereby a handful of samurais could oppress the masses of people. The strip also related the wars between the peasants and the samurais, the peasants' uprising (the so-called Ikki) and their defeat under the samurais' superior military power and tactics.

Planned as a trilogy, *Kamui Den* part one ended in July 1971. Part two was published from 1982 to 1987; and in 1988 Shirato started work on the third and final part. A magnificent work of fiction, *Kamui Den* is also the product of painstaking historical research. *Kamu Den* has been reprinted in book form and sold over four million copies.

H.K.

KANE, GIL (1926-) American comic book artist and publisher born Eli Katz on April 6, 1926, in Riga, Latvia. Coming to America at the age of three, he broke into the comic book field at age 16. His earliest work began appearing in 1942 while he was with the Binder shop; he also had a short stint in the Baily shop (1944) before turning to freelancing. Throughout the 1940s, Kane worked for all the major comic houses: for MLJ he produced the *Scarlet Avenger* (1941-43); for Street and Smith he backgrounded *Blackstone the Magician* (1942); he drew *Red Hawk, Vision,* and *Young Allies* for Timely (1943-44); produced the *Candy* humor feature for Quality in 1944; produced *Sandman* and *Wildcat* for National (1947-48); and, under pen names like "Scott Edward," "Gil Stack," and "Al Kame," drew material for Fox, Holyoke, Aviation, Hillman, Eastern, Fawcett, Prize, and Avon. As the 1950s brought hard times for superhero strips, Kane spent most of his time producing war, crime, and horror stories for Atlas, and science fiction and mystery comics for National.

It was not until the second superhero boom of the 1960s that Kane was able to cast off the workhorse role. Concentrating on two of National's major features, *Green Lantern* and *The Atom,* Kane refined his style considerably. While most of his work throughout the previous two decades had been rushed and sloppy, these two features were detailed, cleanly illustrated, and sported fast-paced layouts.

Kane's increasing fame and skill also fired his wandering spirit and, by 1967, he was drifting away from the strips. He began a short stint at Marvel illustrating *The Hulk* (1967), drew stories for Warren's black and white horror titles, produced *Flash Gordon* for King in 1967, and contributed stories to Tower's *Thunder Agents* and related strips (1965-67). Kane finally left standard comics in 1968 and published his own black and white adventure comic magazine under the "Adventure House" label. Entitled *His Name Is Savage,* the book lasted only one issue, but presaged the black and white comics boom by several years. Kane returned to Marvel in 1970, producing outstanding material for *Conan, Spider Man,* Marvel covers, and many secondary features.

In 1971, Kane drew a unique feature called *Blackmark,* which was published by Bantam in paperback form. One of the finest sword-and-sorcery strips ever conceived, *Blackmark* was plagued by poor distribution and was financially unsuccessful. But Kane had outpaced the comics establishment once again, and several years later sword-and-sorcery became a saleable product.

Gil Kane came back to newspaper comics with *Star Hawks,* a science fiction strip he drew from 1977 to 1981 on scripts by Ron Goulart. In the mid-1980s, he moved to southern California and went into television animation, working on the *Superman* cartoon and others. After drawing the adaptation of Richard Wagner's *The Ring of Nibelung* (1989-90) for DC Comics, he went on to illustrate *Jurassic Park* for Topps Comics (1993). He has also worked sporadically in recent years on a number of monthly DC titles.

Kane was awarded the NCS's 1971 comic book award and the 1973 Reuben Goldberg Award for Outstanding Achievement in a Story Comic Book. He is considered one of the most articulate and thoughtful comic book artists.

J.B.

KANE, ROBERT (1916-) American comic book and comic strip artist born October 24, 1916, in New York City. After attending Cooper Union and the Art Students League, Bob Kane entered the comic book field in 1936 as a staff artist in Jerry Iger's studio. Concentrating primarily on humor features, Kane's first comic book work appeared in *Helne's Wow,* edited and packaged by Iger. This 1936 *Hiram Hick* feature was followed by similar attempts for Fiction House from 1937 to 1939. Titled *Peter Pupp, Jest Laffs,* and *Pluto,* they were all typical "bigfoot" humor types, but studio owner Iger once insisted that Kane "could have been one of the finest humorists of our time if he'd stayed with it."

But by 1938 Kane went out on his own and attempted several adventure strips at National Comics, after creating more humor features like *Gumshoe Gus* and *Jest a Second.* Collaborating with writer Bill Finger, Kane drew two rather pedestrian thrillers, *Rusty and his Pals* and *Clip Carson.* But the times were calling for more *Superman*-types, and, in 1939, National editor Whit Ellsworth assigned the duo the job of finding a suitably costumed companion to cash in on *Superman's* popularity. They developed the quintessential creature of the night: *The Batman.*

Kane drew the original sketches and created the characterizations, but his concept borrowed too heavily from Superman, so Finger suggested the bat-ears and cowl. Thus was born The Batman, a midnight avenger who stalked criminals by preying on their fears, superstitions, and insecurities. Artistically, however, much like Joe Shuster's *Superman* work, Kane's drawing of the strip was amateurish. The backgrounds were nonexistent, characters were stereotypic, usually lifted from the Cagney-Robinson-Bogart genre of crime movies, and the anatomy was still and lifeless. Still, much like the unrealistic and blocky artwork Chester Gould used on the *Dick Tracy* comic strip, Kane's *Batman* work was frighteningly effective. Scenes were eerily quiet, always belying some hideously evil purpose, and shadows were used with unusual success. Finger's stories always utilized the most unsavory of characters, all of whom Kane would render unflatteringly. Batman, on the other hand, although as stiff as the other characters, was drawn to most effectively capitalize on the seedy scenes.

The Batman strip began in *Detective* number 27 (May 1939). It quickly spread to several other titles and a comic strip, and Kane immediately began hiring assistants, the first and best of them being Jerry Robinson. Over the years, Kane did less and less of the artwork, but his byline remained on every story until 1964 and Kane claims to have worked actively on the strip until 1968.

In recent years, however, Kane has spent most of his time in other fields. He created the *Courageous Cat* animated television show in 1958, the *Cool McCool* animated series in 1969, and has also created several motion picture formats. Kane's serious paintings were first shown at his 1969 one-man show at New York's Gallerie Internationale. He published his autobiography, *Batman and Me*, in 1984, and was involved with the 1989 *Batman* movie.

J.B.

KANIGHER, ROBERT (1915-   ) American comic book writer and editor born 1915. Bob Kanigher began his long comic book career in 1940 at Fox, where he wrote for the *Blue Beetle* and *Samson* adventure strips; *Samson* was a totally forgettable filler, but Kanigher's work on *Blue Beetle* was excellent, even though the character had never been either particularly well-drawn or written throughout its long life. Also during his career, Kanigher wrote for Fawcett (*Captain Marvel*), Marvel (*Iron Man*), MLJ (*Steel Sterling, The Web*), Skywald (*Horror* and *The Heap*) and Pines.

But it was for National that Kanigher did the great majority of his comic writing and editing. He wrote regularly for the company after 1943, and was an editor from 1945 to 1967 and from 1972 until his retirement in the 1980s. He worked in every genre from love to superhero to war to fantasy to adventure.

Strangely enough, there are few specific characters of his that come to mind instantly. Kanigher is known mainly for his outstanding work in two genres: war and Western. Among the many war features he has been acclaimed for are *Sgt. Rock and Easy Co.*, probably the preeminent war strip of all time in the comics; *Enemy Ace*, an affecting series about a good man on the "wrong" side of the war; *Capt. Storm*; *Balloon Buster*, one of the more unique war strips in comics; and *The Haunted Tank*. In the Western group, some of the many strips Kanigher worked on include *El Diablo*, an offbeat and well-received strip; *The Outlaw*; *Johnny Thunder*, where Kanigher did excellent material in collaboration with artist Alex Toth; *Tomahawk*, and later, *Son of Tomahawk*; and many others.

As an editor, he had a reputation as a taskmaster, especially with artists. One of the premier visual storytellers in the medium, Kanigher was once described by a comic-artist-turned-art-director as an editor "who would eat up artists and spit them out for breakfast."

Kanigher has also done extensive amounts of freelance writing, and has published several books, including a 1943 Cambridge House book entitled *How to Make Money Writing for Comic Magazines*. He retired in the 1980s and his contributions to the field since then have been limited to an occasional article or reminiscence.

J.B.

"Kapitein Rob," Pieter-Joseph Kuhn. © Het Parool.

KAPITEIN ROB (Netherlands) *Kapitein Rob* ("Captain Rob"), one of the best-known and cherished Dutch daily adventure strips, started on December 11, 1945, in the newspaper *Het Parool*. Captain Robert van Stoerum lived through some 72 adventures, a total of 5,420 individual strips, before the series came to a sudden end with the untimely death of its creator and artist, Pieter Joseph Kuhn, on January 20, 1966. The first adventure, "De Avonturen van het zeilschip De Vrijheid" ("The Adventures of the Sailing Vessel Freedom"), did not quite live up to Kuhn's own expectations of his abilities as a writer. Therefore, he started a cooperation with Evert Werkman, a Dutch journalist, who wrote most of the exploits of *Kapitein Rob*. Although originally an adventure strip with narrative printed below the pictures, some of the many foreign editions put the narrative and dialogue into captions and speech balloons. The strip worked both ways and Dutch reprints in book form sold by the millions.

Kapitein Rob was written and drawn in the best of adventure traditions. The hero was an adventurer sailing the seven seas, accompanied only by his faithful dog, Skip. His good ship, *De Vrijheid* ("Freedom"), took him to exotic places and faraway lands where the relatively simple and one-dimensionally unalterable character of the Captain was met by unexpected situations and dilemmas. Although the Captain married in 1954 and had a son in 1955, his family, as with Tarzan, rarely figured in the stories. With the addition of Professor Lupardi early in the strip's history, science fiction was added to romanticism. A tunnel under the sea, a trip around the moon, a time machine, or the discovery of a "lost" continent all were made possible and plausible by the very realistic art work of Pieter Joseph Kuhn, himself a sailing enthusiast and the model for his hero. Whenever possible, he traveled to the places Kaptein Rob was to visit. This and extensive research helped to lend the strip an atmosphere and a special flavor that made Kuhn one of the "big three" among Dutch comic strip artists.

W.F.

KAPPIE (Netherlands) Kappie is immediately characterized by his name as a diminutive captain in a humor strip. *Kappie* is one of the many successful strips created by Marten Toonder, possibly the most influential personality in Dutch comics. At one time or another some 80 percent of all Dutch comic artists and writers have worked either as staffers or as freelancers for Toonder's studios. Among those working on the *Kap-*

"Kappie," Marten Toonder. © Marten Toonder.

pie strip were artist Piet Wijn and writer Lo Hartog van Banda, himself as prolific as Toonder and on the Toonder staff for 14 years. "Kappie en het drijvende eiland" ("Cappie and the Floating Island") was the first of the *Kappie* episodes written for Toonder by Hartog van Banda when the latter took over the writing of this strip. *Kappie* was started in 1946, along with Toonder's *Panda*. The strip presented 140 adventures before it ended in 1972. As was usual with most of the earlier Dutch comic strips and with many of the Toonder productions, *Kappie*'s narrative and dialogue was printed below the pictures.

Kappie offered the reader adventures in all kinds of exotic places. In a way this made *Kappie* a cartoon version of Pieter J. Kuhn's adventure strip *Kapitein Rob*. As with Toonder's other strips, money was the driving factor behind the good captain's voyages across the seven seas. Kappie, who, except for a white moustache which lent him added dignity, might have been a relative of *Bugs Bunny's* Elmer Fudd in looks and stature, was aided and abetted by his somewhat stereotyped helmsman and first mate, who followed his every whim to guide the good ship *De Kraak* to wherever the moneymaking mission was to take place.

In outlook and appearance, *Kappie* was more geared for a younger readership than most of Toonder's other work which, like *Tom Poes*, developed an adult appeal over the decades. Like other strips by Toonder, *Kappie*'s comic strip adventures were reprinted in a number of comic books.

W.F.

KAS *See* Kasprzak, Zbigniew.

KASPRZAK, ZBIGNIEW (1955-) Cartoonist born May 31, 1955, in Zielona Gora, Poland. During his studies at the Krakow Academy of Fine Arts (1973-80), Zbigniew Kasprzak (who signs "Kas" for obvious reasons) started contributing to the comics magazine *Relax*. After he won a competition sponsored by the magazine, he became a frequent contributor. At the same time, he explored new methods of expression in painting, graphics, and satirical drawing, for which he won a prize at the Lodz Satirical Drawing Triennial in 1980.

In the 1980s, during the difficult period of military emergency in Poland, *Relax* and many other periodicals had to close their doors, so Kas devoted his time to painting because of the lack of opportunity in the comic field. When the situation improved and some houses resumed publishing, he turned out many book and cover illustrations and posters, in addition to the comics he contributed to the magazine *Kaw* and to the Sport y Trystika publishing company. He wrote more than 10 comic stories, mainly on history and science fiction themes.

His big break came in 1988 when he was invited to the International Comics Festival in Sierre, Switzerland. There he met Grzegorz Rosinski, who had already made a name for himself in Western Europe. Rosinski was then drawing both *Thorgal* and *Hans*, and he recommended to his publisher, Brussels-based Editions du Lombard, that Kas take over drawing *Hans*. After being accepted, Kas moved to Brussels with his family. In addition to drawing *Hans*, a postnuclear tale scripted by André-Paul Duchateau, he has also recently started a new series, *Les Voyageurs* ("The Travelers"), of which two volumes have been issued to date.

K.R.

KATO, YOSHIROU (1925-) Japanese cartoonist born June 25, 1925, in Tokyo. Under the influence of such childhood readings as *Norakuro*, *Bōken Dankichi*, and other comic strips, Yoshirou Kato decided very early in life to become a cartoonist. In 1938 he started to work at Komagome Hospital while going to night school. At 14 years of age, he sold his first cartoon to *Asahi Graph*; after this he became a frequent contributor to several magazines.

In 1943 he entered Kawabata Academy and took up a new job with the Defense Ministry. Drafted into the army in 1944, Kato departed for the North China front, but was demobilized the next year. Upon his return to civilian life, Kato contributed cartoons, illustrations, and etchings to the cartoon magazine *Manga* while holding an eight-to-five job. In 1947 he became a regular cartoonist for *Manga Shūdan*, and the next year he quit his job, determined to earn his living with cartoon work. Gradually Kato became one of the most prolific cartoonists of the day, contributing to every major publication in Japan. In 1951 he tried his hand at several newspaper strips, but these did not click. Only in 1954 did Kato create a successful comic strip: *Mappirakun*, for the daily *Mainichi*. Many other comic creations then followed: *Onboro Jinsei* (1954); *Ojisama Daimiyō* and *Ore wa Obake dazo* ("I Am a Monster"), both in 1959; *Gejigeji Tarō Gyōjōki* (1961), *Motemote Ojisan* (1963), *Senbiki no Ninja* ("A Thousand Ninjas," 1964); *Benben Monogatari* ("The Story of Benben," 1965); and others.

Yoshirou Kato's comic world is full of fantastic images and far-out concepts. He was the first to break the taboo against showing excrements and filth in comics. While challenging these and other taboos, he created comic strips of interest and high graphic quality, and became famous not only as a comic strip artist, but also as a magazine cartoonist and TV personality. He is still active in the field of comics, although his output has slowed considerably since the 1980s.

H.K.

KATZENJAMMER KIDS, THE (U.S.) Rudolph Dirks created *The Katzenjammer Kids* on December 12, 1897,

"The Katzenjammer Kids," Harold Knerr. © King Features Syndicate.

for the American Humorist, the famed Sunday supplement of the *New York Journal*. Inspired in part by Wilhelm Busch's *Max und Moritz*, *The Katzenjammer Kids* depicts the guerilla war conducted by the twins Hans and Fritz (the Katzenjammer Kids, also called "the Katzies") against any form of authority and indeed against society itself. Their more popular targets include Mama (the mother of the Katzies), the Captain (a former shipwrecked sailor acting as their surrogate father) and the Inspector, (representing school authorities). All these and other assorted characters resort to an Anglo-German pidgin, the effect of which is nothing short of devastating.

In the hands of Rudolph Dirks *The Katzenjammer Kids* became a genuine tale of destruction incarnated in the twin person of Hans and Fritz for whom, in the apt words of the Inspector, "society iss nix."

In 1912 Dirks decided to leave the *Journal* for the *World* and wanted to take *The Katzenjammer Kids* with him, a move fought by William Randolph Hearst in the courts. After much legal maneuvering the case was finally decided in appeal; Dirks retained the rights to the characters while Hearst kept the title.

After an absence of two years *The Katzenjammer Kids* reemerged in 1914, drawn by Harold Knerr. (Dirks started his own strip in the *World*, first titled *Hans and Fritz*, later changed to *The Captain and the Kids*.) During World War I, due to anti-German feelings, Knerr's strip changed its title to *The Shenanigan Kids*, but it reverted back to the original title in 1919.

Knerr not only retained the original flavor of the strip, he also contributed several additions to its cast of characters: the hypocritical little girl Lena, the priggish Miss Twiddle, and the foppish Rollo, whose cunning often proved a match for the Katzies' diabolical inventiveness.

After Knerr's death in 1949, *The Katzenjammer Kids* passed first to Doc Winner, then in 1956 to Joe Musial, while its quality and appeal went steadily downhill. At Musial's death in 1977 it passed into the hands of Joe Senich, who was succeeded in 1981 by Angelo DeCesare. It was then taken over by Hy Eisman, who took the venerable feature to the century mark in December 1997.

The oldest comic strip still in existence, *The Katzenjammer Kids* was adapted to the stage in 1903, and has been the subject of countless animated cartoons. The critic Kenneth Rexroth has hailed it as "one of the two American contributions to modern mythology."

M.H.

KAUKA, ROLF (1917-   ) German writer, editor, and publisher born in Leipzig on April 9, 1917. The Kauka family can be traced through several centuries of Finnish history. Rolf Kauka's great-grandfather had left his village near Vasa, where he had been a kalavala-

singer (a sort of storytelling entertainer in a pretelevision era), in order to move to Germany in 1890.

Rolf Kauka grew up in Leipzig, attending grammar school and high school there. At the age of 17, while still in senior high, he earned some money selling cartoons to the newspapers *Leipziger Neueste Nachrichten* and *Weissenfelser Tageblatt*.

He was three semesters into economic studies when, late in 1937, he was drafted into the German Army. He remained in the service until May 8, 1945, when World War II ended in German capitulation. After the war Kauka found himself in Munich, where he wrote some legal books and a reference work for the police. Finally, in 1950, he started his own publishing house, at first reprinting the romances of Hedwig Courths-Mahler in dime-novel format. Also around this time, with publisher Heinz Ullstein, Kauka got the idea to produce animated cartoons for distribution in the United States, and he planned to keep the cartoon artists busy between films by producing comic books.

Spring of 1952 saw the first issue of *Eulenspiegel*, based on the German folk character. The book was written by Kauka and drawn by Dorul van der Heide. The comic book also featured two characters that became its main attraction with issue number 10, Fix and Foxi, two clever anthropomorphic little foxes. Kauka felt the story potential of the *Eulenspiegel* character would quickly be depleted and had to be replaced. Thus, the perennial *Fix und Foxi* was born. Sales picked up and in time the comic book, now published weekly, was the second most popular comic in Germany, behind *Micky Maus* ("Mickey Mouse").

Fix and Foxi was drawn by various artists, at first almost true to nature, finally in a stylized version. Kauka wrote all the storied and created a great number of additional characters and comic series, but never actually drew them, although it was popular belief that he did because all of the material was published with only his byline and copyright.

Kauka's line of comics expanded over the years, finally including adventure stories which Kauka never really liked. Rolf Kauka sold his publishing company in 1973 but retained control of his characters. In 1975 he founded the Kauka Comic Akademie. This school trains artists and writers to draw and create comics.

In 1972 Kauka turned film producer for the feature-length animated cartoon *Mario d'Oro* and the lead-in cartoon short featuring Fix and Foxi. His earlier efforts in animated cartooning had been *Tom & Biber* and *Baron Münchhausen*.

Kauka's adventure strips ended in 1982 with the demise of *Zack* magazine, which he had taken over. Kauka's funnies continued being produced by the publishing company that had originally just been his distributor, and Kauka left the comic business to retire to a plantation in Georgia. However, in 1994 he was so irked by the noncomic editorial content of the floundering *Fix und Foxi* comic book (especially a photo of pop star Madonna) that—as copyright owner—he filed a court request to suspend publication of the magazine, which was granted. Kauka's characters survived these theatricals, because the quibbling over what was to be in the magazine did not scare off advertisers who wanted to make use of the property. The Kauka comics continue in various types of reprint editions and with more merchandising available than ever before.

W.F.

KAWANABE, GYŌSAI (1831-1889) Gyōsai Kawanabe was a Japanese print artist born in Koga, Shimofusa (now Ibaragi), on April 7, 1831. When he was seven years old, Kawanabe became a pupil of the famous master Kuniyoshi Utagawa. Later he also studied under Douhahu Kanō and Hokusai, and learned Chinese art and Western painting techniques.

Kawanabe used pen names such as Shōjō Kyōsai ("Crazy Orangutan") and Shuransairaisui ("Drunken Bum"), but changed his name to Gyōsai after being thrown in prison because of his cartoons in 1870.

Kawanabe is famous not only for his prints but also for his cartoons. He worked as a staff artist on the cartoon magazine *Eshinbun Nipponchi* from 1874 until his death. He liked to depict the monstrous and the grotesque in such works as *Hyakki Yakō Byōbu* ("The Nightly Walks of the 100 Monsters"), *Gaikotsu no Buyō* ("The Skeleton Dance"), *Namakubi* ("The Freshly Cut-Off Head"), and others. Many of his works were anthologized in book form (*Gyōsai Gadan, Gyōsai Donga,* and *Gyōsai Suiga,* among others). In his later years Kawanabe had as his pupil the English architect J. Condre, who later changed his name to Gyōei in admiration of his teacher. After Kawanabe's death on April 26, 1889, Condre collected the artist's works into an anthology titled *Gyōsai Gashū* ("Gyōsai's Art Collection"), released in 1911.

H.K.

KEATON, RUSSELL (1910-1945) American comic strip artist born 1910 in Corinth, Mississippi. Like so many youngsters who loved to draw, Russ Keaton left his hometown after graduation from high school and moved to Chicago, where he enrolled at the Academy of Fine Arts. When Dick Calkins started the daily *Buck Rogers* and *Skyroads* strips in 1929, Keaton, just out of school, was his first assistant. His draftsmanship was so superior to the mediocre Calkins's that he was asked to ghost the *Buck Rogers* Sunday from its inception in 1930. Eventually Keaton got to sign *Skyroads* and continued with the strip into the 1940s, giving it an airy, elegant look.

In 1939 Keaton decided to get his pilot's license and launch his own strip at the same time. In October of that year both ambitions were realized: he graduated from flying school and saw his *Flyin' Jenny* (an aviation feature starring a toothsome, blonde daredevil) get off the ground. For the first few months Keaton both wrote and drew the *Jenny* daily strip and Sunday page, but he later relinquished the scripting chores to Frank Wead, who was succeeded by Glen Chaffin. In 1943 he became a flying instructor and had to turn over the drawing of the Sunday to his assistant, Marc Swayze. Early in 1945 Keaton, feeling ill, entered the hospital for tests; the illness was diagnosed as an acute form of leukemia. On February 13, 1945, Russ Keaton was dead at age 35.

With Russ Keaton's untimely death the comic strip field lost one of its most brilliant craftsmen. Keaton had an instinctive feeling for space, action, and speed, and a sense of drama and style. Both *Skyroads* and *Flyin' Jenny* displayed a genuine air of excitement and expectation. Had his talent been allowed to mature further, Keaton might have gone on to take his place alongside such other greats as Caniff and Sickles.

M.H.

KELLY, WALT (1913-1973) American cartoonist Walter Crawford Kelly Jr. was born August 25, 1913, in Philadelphia. His family moved to Bridgeport, Connecticut, when Walt was two years old. Walt's father was a theatrical scenery painter and taught the boy how to draw. In high school Walt Kelly edited the school paper and after graduation, went to work as a reporter and cartoonist for the *Bridgeport Post*.

In 1935 Kelly went to Hollywood and became an animator for Walt Disney Studios (he worked notably on *Dumbo* and *Fantasia*). Six years later he returned east in the aftermath of the strike at the studios in 1941. He then did comic book work for Western Printing & Lithographing, creating in 1942 *Bumbazine and Albert the Alligator*, about a young boy (Bumbazine) and his pet alligator in the Okefenokee swamp, which was to become the genesis for *Pogo*.

During the war years, Kelly worked as a civilian employee of the Army's language section, illustrating language manuals. In 1948 he became art editor of the short-lived *New York Star*, where *Pogo* first appeared as a daily feature. When the *Star* folded, *Pogo* was taken over by the *New York Post*.

In addition to his work on *Pogo*, Kelly delivered hundreds of lectures, reviewed and illustrated books, drew editorial cartoons, and wrote several thoughtful articles (in one of these, paraphrasing Pogo, he coined the now-famous phrase: "We have met the enemy and he is us.") Kelly also wrote the nonsense verse and some of the music, as well as sang some of the songs on the record "Songs of the Pogo." In 1952 he was named Cartoonist of the Year, and he was elected president of the National Cartoonists Society in 1954.

Walt Kelly, who liked to call himself "the oldest boy cartoonist in the business," was uncompromising in the opinions that he often expressed in his strip. His influence on the so-called "sophisticated cartoonists" has been publicly acknowledged by such artists as Johnny Hart and Mel Lazarus.

Walt Kelly died in Hollywood on October 18, 1973, of complications from diabetes.

M.H.

KENKOY (Philippines) The most popular cartoon character to appear in the Philippines began in Liwayway publications in 1929. It was created by Tony Velasquez, who is considered the father of the Philippine comic industry.

Kenkoy is a typical Filipino male and the series dealt with his life and times as he coped with the prevailing conditions of his environment. The strip underwent several stages as Kenkoy, starting out as a carefree bachelor, went through the agonies of growing up. During this period he got involved with the usual teenage preoccupations—sports, dances, school, and girls (not necessarily in that order).

One of the highlights in the development of the feature was the courtship of Rosing, Kenkoy's eventual wife. Tony Velasquez created many humorous situations and incidents showing the intense rivalry between Kenkoy and the various suitors who vied for Rosing's attention. These episodes kept the readership laughing for many years.

Another interesting and memorable event in the series was the marriage of Rosing to Kenkoy, and their attempts afterwards to solve the numerous problems relating to newlyweds. The strip evolved as the couple produced their first child and eventually became the parents of a large family. The names of some of the children are Junior, Julie, Tsing, Nene, and Etot. One of the really fascinating and unforgettable characters to appear in the feature is Tsikiting Gubat, the non-speaking, wooly-haired, perennial child. As the members of the household grew and matured, Tsikiting remained the same through the years. He is as stubborn as a mule, but cute and lovable.

To this day *Kenkoy* remains the favorite comic creation in the Philippine Islands. Offshoots and imitations often try to duplicate the formula that made the series successful. A movie was made and many *Kenkoy* products emerged, such as comic books and T-shirts.

Despite the tremendous following of the feature, Tony Velasquez had to give up illustrating the escapades of the Kenkoy family due to his heavy commitment to other aspects of the medium. He was chief editor of several publications as well as the writer for other features and strips. The drawing chores were taken over by Celso Trinidad, who later illustrated the series *Mga Kuwento Ni Kenkoy* ("The Stories of Kenkoy") for *Pinoy Komiks*. After all these years, *Kenkoy* is still going strong in the 1990s.

Tony Velasquez has received the full range of awards in the comic and publication fields. The Citizens Council for Mass Media paid tribute to his many contributions by awarding him the CCMM trophy, the highest honor in Philippine mass communications.

O.J.

KEN PARKER (Italy) Nicknamed "Long Rifle" for his habit of using an outdated muzzle-loading Kentucky rifle, this character is the most peculiar Western hero (better, antihero) made in Italy in a long time. Created by Giancarlo Berardi and drawn by Ivo Milazzo, *Ken Parker* was launched by Bonelli Publishing in 1977 through a series of black and white comics in book form. These enjoyed a sudden success.

In this series, the whole epos of the American frontier is revisited with modern sensibility and critical attitude according to the lesson derived from new and unconventional Western movies such as *Soldier Blue* (1970), *Little Big Man* (1970), and *Jeremiah Johnson* (1972). The genocide of the natives is not the only drama *Ken Parker* dealt with. Many other issues, such as racial prejudice, labor and social conflict, capital punishment, and emancipation of women, have been brought to the attention of the readers through captivating adventures.

Ken Parker has married an Indian woman, Tecumseh; adopted an Indian child, Theba; and roams the West earning a living through different activities: trap-

"Ken Parker," Ivo Milazzo and Giancarlo Berardi. © Edizione Cepim.

per, army scout, detective, actor, lumberjack, and eventually, novelist. For a long time, he was wanted for killing a policeman in self-defense during a strike, but he eventually was imprisoned and paid his debt to society.

The West where Ken wanders is declining and melancholy, and the strip shows how difficult it is to live in the wilderness when an industrial revolution is taking place. Ken lives from day to day, trying to fulfill his ideals with consistency. He is romantic, tenderhearted, and disenchanted, but he never gives up.

Berardi, born in 1949, has written several comic series and has created interesting characters for strips such as *Tiki* (1976), *Welcome to Springville* (1977), *Marvin il detective* (1983), and the graphic novel *L'uomo delle Filippine* ("The Man of the Philippines," 1980). All of these have been drawn by Milazzo, who was also the graphic creator of *Ken Parker*, although the strip has also been drawn by other artists, such as Calegari and Giorgio Trevisan.

The first *Ken Parker* series ended in 1984 with issue 59, but the hero's adventures continued in the comic magazines *Orient Express* and *Comic Art*, and from 1992 to 1996 in the *Ken Parker Magazine*. The old adventures now appear in the bimonthly *Ken Parker Magazine* and the new ones in the semiannual *Ken Parker Special*. Also worth mentioning is a *Ken Parker* graphic novel in four episodes, entitled *Il respiro e il sogno* ("The Breath and the Dream," 1984), with no text and completely based on pantomime. In 1995 Berardi was awarded a Yellow Kid.

G.C.C.

KENT, JACK (1920-1985) American artist and writer born in Burlington, Iowa, on March 10, 1920. John Wellington Kent grew up in various parts of the country, spending his formative years in Chicago and living in different parts of Texas, where he finally settled. He had no formal art training and dropped out of high school to practice commercial art locally. While still in his teens he sold magazine gags to *Collier's* and other publications.

Kent volunteered for service during World War II and saw action with the army in Alaska and the South Pacific; after his discharge he was a partner in a printing plant and worked at nearly every job in the factory. In 1950 his long-cherished dream of producing a comic strip was realized when the McClure Newspaper Syndicate bought *King Aroo*. It first appeared, daily and Sunday, in November 1950.

The strip, like *Krazy Kat*, appealed to a broad but select group of people; it was an "intellectual" strip. Contractual difficulties arose when Bell merged with McClure and the strip was terminated until the newly formed Golden Gate Syndicate of San Francisco took over distribution. In 1965, *King Aroo* died.

Fans of Jack Kent lost touch with him for a while—it was reported that he was driving trucks—but he soon resurfaced drawing greeting cards for Hallmark and others, writing and illustrating children's stories, drawing cartoons for markets from *Humpty Dumpty* magazine to the *Saturday Evening Post* to *Playboy*, and producing children's books.

The children's books brought Kent the acclaim and recognition that was denied him when he was a strip artist. His first, *Just Only John*, won the Chicago Graphics Award and sold over 400,000 copies. Other titles included *Nursery Tales* for Random House, *Mr.*

"Kerry Drake," Alfred Andriola. © Field Newspaper Syndicate.

Elephant's Birthday Party (a reworking of some *King Aroo* gags) for Houghton-Mifflin, and others for Parents Magazine Press, Putnam, McKay, and Golden Press.

Kent's drawing style was incredibly loose—a testament, perhaps, to his lack of formal training—full of broad, wiggly brush lines. In *Aroo*, his panels were free-floating and filled with rolling hills, flowers, and little stars studding the skies. As a writer, Kent produced some of the slickest nonsense in the funnies—literate, absurd, and gay. He died of leukemia on October 18, 1985, in San Antonio, Texas.

R.M.

KERRY DRAKE (U.S.) Fresh from having drawn two police strips in succession, *Charlie Chan* and *Dan Dunn*, Alfred Andriola again picked a detective as the hero of *Kerry Drake*, the new comic strip that he created for Publishers Syndicate on October 1, 1943.

Kerry Drake was a likable, earnest city detective whose adventures were closely related to daily life. Kerry was not a super-cop like Dick Tracy or an accomplished criminologist like Rip Kirby; he did his job with an honest dedication and a dogged determination that ultimately won the day. In the course of his investigations he was helped (and sometimes hampered) by his pretty wife, Mindy, to whom he remained unwaveringly faithful despite all the women (with such evocative names as Pussycat, Ermine, and Cricket) who constantly threw themselves at him. There was a great deal of documentation in *Kerry Drake*, and the atmosphere was suspenseful and violent. While *Kerry Drake*'s gallery of villains was not a match for *Dick Tracy*'s, it did contain some colorful characters like the sadistic Stiches and the warped Mr. Goliath.

Andriola's style on the strip was incisive, somewhat linear, and almost aseptically clean, and Kerry Drake became so popular that a comic book version was printed in the 1940s and '50s. Unfortunately, as time went on Andriola did less and less work on the feature, leaving it almost entirely in the hands of his assistants, and the writing was frequently ghosted by others (most notably Allen Saunders). *Kerry Drake* accordingly (and deservedly) declined in popularity; when the strip was discontinued in March 1983 following Andriola's death it was only being carried by a handful of newspapers.

M.H.

KETCHAM, HENRY KING (1920-   ) American cartoonist born March 14, 1920, in Seattle, Washing-

"Kevin the Bold," Kreigh Collins. © NEA Service.

ton. Hank Ketcham attended the University of Washington in 1938, but soon tired of formal studies and started a career in animation, first with Lantz Productions of Universal Studios (until 1940), then with Walt Disney Productions, where he worked on *Pinocchio, Fantasia,* and the Donald Duck shorts.

From 1941 to 1945 Ketcham served as chief photographic specialist with the United States Naval Reserve in Washington, D.C., where he created his first comic strip, *Half Hitch,* about a zany sailor, for a service newspaper. After his return to civilian life, he settled in Westport, Connecticut, and freelanced cartoons and illustrations for magazines and advertising agencies. In 1948 Ketcham moved to Carmel, California, where his most famous creation, *Dennis the Menace,* was conceived. The first daily panel was released by Hall Syndicate on March 12, 1951; its success was so immediate that it earned Ketcham the Billy DeBeck Award the following year. Ketcham devoted most of his professional life to *Dennis,* which he drew with an irreverent yet affectionate pen.

In 1960 the peripatetic Ketcham moved to Geneva, Switzerland. It was there that he decided to revive his old service comic strip *Half Hitch;* written by Ketcham and drawn by Dick Hodgins, the feature was distributed by King Features Syndicate from 1970 to 1975. Hank Ketcham also wrote a book, *I Wanna Go Home* (McGraw-Hill, 1959), based on his experiences during a tour of the Soviet Union.

Hank Ketcham is a facile cartoonist whose drawings and lines flow easily across the comic page. *Dennis the Menace* made him very wealthy, letting him indulge his hobbies: golf and travel. After the 1980s, however, Ketcham left most of the work to his assistants, Ron Ferdinand and Marcus Hamilton. He officially retired in October 1995 and the dailies are now done entirely by Hamilton under Ketcham's signature.

M.H.

KEVIN THE BOLD (U.S.) NEA's *Kevin the Bold* page, which began on October 1, 1950, was created by Kreigh Collins. *Kevin* was a spin-off from another Collins Sunday feature for NEA, *Mitzi McCoy,* which began November 7, 1948, and was used as a Christmas service feature for NEA in December 1949.

Kevin was an Irishman in the days of Henry VIII, a special agent for the king and a troubleshooter whose assignments took him around the globe. His sidekick was a big, strong Spaniard named Pedro who was married to a beauty named Maria. Kevin's young squire,

Brett, provided an outlet for more youthful adventures as Kevin dealt with big-boy troubles and (too infrequently) big-boy romance.

Kevin's adventures took him throughout Europe and into the New World. The strip featured much sailing flavor, a strong dose of history, and passable continuities that nonetheless conveyed a sense of adventure and some sea salt. *Kevin the Bold* was discontinued in 1972.

Collins's art in the 1950s was more exciting than his later work, with broad panoramas and some historical facsimiles. *Kevin* was an obvious answer to King Features's *Prince Valiant,* and, despite other shortcomings, Collins's Irish heroes managed to look Irish. *Kevin the Bold* had a companion piece, *Up Anchor;* this was also a tale of adventure, set on the seven seas.

R.M.

KEWPIES, THE (U.S.) Rose O'Neill's impish, curly-topped cupids, which she nicknamed Kewpies on their first appearance in print in the *Ladies' Home Journal* in 1905, were first corralled into newspaper page form on December 2, 1917. Copyrighted and distributed by the artist herself, the *Kewpies* page—not a comic strip—consisted of a weekly set of verses and drawings with individual titles, without balloons. These early *Kewpies* (unlike Palmer Cox's self-sustaining *Brownies,* on which they were partly based) were generally portrayed dancing and playing pranks around the children and old people to whom their attentions, amused and helpful, seemed to be centered. Some minor identity was given to certain Kewpies (a Wags, a Cook, and a Booky were prominent), but by and large these Kewpies were little more than a wildly tumbling array of small background figures. (O'Neill also distributed a daily *Kewpie* panel at this time; usually only one Kewpie appeared in a panel, along with a cheery slogan or motto.)

This first page and panel lasted barely a year; distress with the American losses in 1918 was said to have caused her to end the feature. Returning to magazine work, O'Neill did not undertake a newspaper feature again until 1935, when she decided once more to copyright and circulate a Sunday page—this time a true comic strip called *The Kewpies.* First appearing in Hearst papers across the country on February 3, 1935, the new strip introduced a jammed roster of characters immediately involved in a complex, continued narrative. Booky, the Information Kewp, survived the years from the first feature; with him were such new figures as Kewpidoodle, Uncle Hob Goblin, Johnny and Katy

Kewp, Frisky Freddie (a frog), Gus the Ghost, Squabby (a duck), and Scoodles Tourist (a human four year old touring Kewpieville). Aside from Scoodles, there were no humans around, and the Kewpies were the whole show.

O'Neill's lovely facility with comic images was the substance of the strip; her stories were often charming and amusing, but rarely more than that (she was not a Kelly or a Johnson), and it was the unfailing delight of her art, her eye into elfland, that sustained attention over weeks of practical jokes, pratfalls, and alarums among the Kewpies. The Hearst papers dropped *The Kewpies* in mid-1937, about the time Rose O'Neill retired from active social life in New York and withdrew to her Ozark Mountain estate to paint and write. No evidence of any continuation of the strip has been found in other papers of the period, and it must be assumed that she ended it at that time.

B.B.

"Keyhole Kate," Allan Morley. © Dandy.

KEYHOLE KATE (G.B.) Keyhole Kate was the first of her kind, an obsessive person whose obsession rebounded to make the reader laugh. She was also that rare species—a comic strip heroine. With her eagle beak, her horn-rimmed spectacles, her twin plaits, her gym-slip, and holes in the knees of her black stockings, Kate arrived complete with keyholes in the first issue of D. C. Thomson's first weekly comic, *Dandy*, on December 4, 1937. She remained in a six-panel strip during her whole career, save once when, perhaps through some editorial crisis, she made the front page in full color, replacing *Korky the Cat*. Every week Kate's snoopy obsession with keyholes proved no problem to her creator, Allan Morley. When forced by Uncle to read a book, she came back from the library with *Keyhole Topics* by O. Howie Peeps! When Cousin Cuthbert took a snap of her yawning, Kate's open mouth came out shaped like a keyhole! Morley's unique neat style never varied, and small oblong panels were his ideal format. He was particularly good with obsessed characters, and drew *Nosey Parker* in *Rover* and *Hungry Horace* in *Dandy* for many years.

Kate's last appearance in *Dandy*, playing a keyhole-shaped triangle, was on September 17, 1955. She returned on January 23, 1965, in number one of *Sparky*, all togged out in a new dress decorated with keyholes. Little else had changed, save the cartoonist. Between her revival and August 1974 when she retired

again, several hands drew the strip, including Drysdale and Brian White, but *Keyhole Kate* was never quite the same.

D.G.

KHALID, MOHAMED NOR (1951-   ) Mohamed Nor Khalid was born in Kota Baru, a *kampung* ("village") in northern Malaysia. His professional career began at age 13 when his cartoons were published in *Majallah Filem* and *Movie News*; while still in his teens, his first comic book, *Tiga Sekawan*, and regular comic strips saw print. One of these strips, *Si Mamat*, has appeared weekly in *Berita Minggu* for nearly 30 years. However, "Lat" (as he signs himself) was not placed in the art department of the *New Straits Times*, the top English-language daily, when he was hired after graduation; instead, he was made a crime reporter. The *Times* did not take note of his artistic talent until a regional magazine published one of his cartoons in 1974. That same year, Khalid was named editorial cartoonist of the *Times*, and his wildly popular *Scenes of Malaysian Life*, a one-panel depiction of the nation's multicultural society, has appeared on the editorial page since then, even after he left the paper in 1984 to become a freelancer.

Called the Chekhov of the Kampung, Lat often concentrates on the simplistic and humorous aspects of the rural life of his youth, and with more than a touch of nostalgia he laments its loss to the modern day. Because his images and messages are universal, Lat's cartoons have been reprinted widely and translated into other languages. In addition to compiling his strips into books that are issued annually, Lat has written and drawn four stories especially for the book market. His *Kampung Boy* (1979) has sold more than 100,000 copies.

Lat strongly denies any political motives, claiming he makes social commentary, not political cartoons. Yet his satirical works, benefitting from his eagle eye, sharp wit, and societal astuteness, have taken swipes at usually off-limit subjects such as the Malaysian establishment and Singapore's Lee Kuan Yew.

Few cartoonists anywhere have achieved the exposure and status of Lat. A movie, musical play, 13-part animation series, many commercials, all types of merchandise, and even a McDonald's "Kampung-burger" have sprung from his works. Respected by his colleagues, he was elected president of the Malaysian cartoonists association in the 1990s. His many achievements were crowned with the awarding of the Malaysian honorific "datuk" in 1994.

J.A.L.

KIBAŌ (Japan) Kibaō ("King Kiba"), adapted from Yukio Togawa's famous novel *Kibaō Monogatari*, was created by Kyūta Ishikawa for the weekly *Shōnen* magazine in April 1965.

Kiba was born of a male dog called Tetsu and a she-wolf named Devil in the rugged foothills of Daisetsuzan in Hokkaido. While still a cub he fell prey to Gon, the one-eyed bear, but was rescued by a party of hunters. Taken to the Hidaka ranch, the little wolf-dog was raised by Sanae, a young girl who taught him the ways of humans.

When Kiba was grown he was taken on a bear hunt, but his wild instincts returned and he ran away to the mountains. In time he became Kibaō, the King of Daisetsuzan, succeeding his mother, Devil. Hunted

SCENES OF MALAYSIAN LIFE By LAT

THE PAHANG GOVERNMENT will consider the idea of using rock music to frighten off wild elephants from plantations....

Mohamed Nor Khalid ("Lat"), "Scenes of Malaysian Life." © Lat.

down by trappers, Kibaō was finally captured and sent to zoos, but he managed to escape and eventually was reunited with Sanae. Happy days ensued but these were brutally interrupted when Sanae was clawed to death by Gon. Enraged by Sanae's death, Kibaō raised a pack of wolves and stray dogs and they hunted down Gon, whom Kibaō himself killed. Then the wolf-king left civilization forever and returned to the wild.

Ishikawa faithfully retained the flavor of the original novel. The top animal artist of Japan, he also adapted many of Ernest Thompson Seton and Yukio Togawa's animal novels, and he created a number of original animal strips. *Kibaō*, his most famous animal strip, ended in February 1966.

H.K.

KIDA, FRED (1920-) American comic book and comic strip artist born December 12, 1920, in Manhattan. After attending New York's Textile High School, Fred Kida broke into the comics as an inker and background artist in the Iger Studios in 1941. From there, he moved to Quality (*Phantom Clipper*, 1942-43), MLJ (pencilled *Hangman* strip that was inked by Bob Fuji, 1942), and finally landed at Hillman Publications in 1942. There he produced work on strips like *Iron Ace*, *Boy King*, and *Gunmaster*, but he did not attain much artistic acclaim until he moved over to the Hillman lead

feature, *Airboy*, in 1943. At first he only inked the pencils of Dan Barry—who he later assisted on the *Flash Gordon* newspaper strip in the 1960s—but Kida eventually assumed both the pencilling and inking.

Created by Charles Biro in late 1942, *Airboy* had quickly been relegated to a gimmick strip with most of the emphasis on Davy "Airboy" Nelson's magnificent flying machine, Birdie. But when Kida finally became the strip's artist, he completely reversed the direction of the feature. Whereas Airboy had been subordinate to his plane in earlier adventures, Kida made Davy Nelson a teenaged adventurer and soldier-of-fortune. Birdie was still there, to be sure, but it was for Airboy that people began buying the book. "In Kida's best stories," artist/historian Jim Steranko wrote, "Airboy became a kind of flying Pat Ryan—less a boy aviator in a man's world, more a youthful adventurer with a sophisticated veneer."

To achieve this effect, Kida used simple and tasteful drawings and an amazingly straightforward and direct page composition. His exciting action scenes—both on the ground and in aerial shots—were always busy and utilized an illustrative approach rather than a comic style. Additionally, Kida probably used more blacks in his stories than any other comic artist of the time, and his strips always appeared morose and suspenseful.

After finally leaving the *Airboy* feature in 1948, Kida began to split his time between Charles Biro's crime books and the Atlas line. At the Biro-edited Gleason line, the artist produced several dozen fine crime strips for *Crime Does Not Pay* before leaving in 1953. At Atlas, Kida concentrated on the sometimes-exceptional Western *Ringo Kid*, but also found time to draw some horror and war stories and some fine sword-and-sorcery stories for the Black Knight feature. He left Atlas and comic books in 1959 and his last comic art work was on the *Flash Gordon* daily strip.

J.B.

KIM SONG HWAN (1932-   ) Kim Song Hwan was born October 8, 1932, in Kaisong City (located in what is now North Korea). His fascination with art was evident from early childhood, when he covered the floors of his home with drawings. During his final year at Kyongbok Middle School in 1949, *Yonhap Shinmun* published his *Mongtongguri* ("Fool") in 15 issues, a long life span for a strip in those days. After graduation, he contributed to *Hwarang* magazine and worked as a reporter for the weekly *Cartoon News* magazine.

The conceptualization of *Old Kobau* ("High, Sturdy Rock"), which made Kim Song Hwan a household name for nearly half a century, occurred in 1950 as he was hiding to avoid conscription in the People's Army. In the beginning, *Kobau* was four to twelve humorous panels dealing with family life, but on December 30, 1950, *Kobau* gained a separate identity in a cartoon meant for soldiers of the Republic of Korea. The character was revived in 1954 in four-panel cartoons for the magazines *Huimang* and *Shinchonji*, and the following year it became a fixture in the daily *Dong-A Ilbo*, where it remained for 26 years before shifting to *Chosun Ilbo*. *Kobau* found its current home in *Munwha Ilbo* in October 1992.

Kim is recognized as a pioneer in Korean newspaper cartooning. He was the first to create an enduring four-panel strip and drew the earliest one-panel political cartoons. More importantly, however, he helped make strips and cartoons, which had previously been for children only, adult fare. Kim can take credit for teaching most major Korean cartoonists the elements of approach and presentation, and can take pride in making *Kobau* (and four-panel strips generally) the most read feature of dailies. (When it was published in *Chosun Ilbo*, the one-inch advertisement directly under *Kobau* was the most expensive space in the entire newspaper.) Through *Kobau*, Kim also fought against a series of authoritarian regimes, for which he suffered censorship, surveillance by the Korean Central Intelligence Agency, torture, and imprisonment.

Kim and *Kobau* have been given many honors. One of the most recent was the issuance of a sheet of postal stamps featuring the bald, bespectacled character.

J.A.L.

Kim Song Hwan, "Kobau." © Chosun Ilbo.

KIN-DER-KIDS, THE (U.S.) The famous painter and illustrator Lyonel Feininger created *The Kin-der-Kids* at the request of James Keeley of the *Chicago Tribune*. The title was suggested by Keeley (as an obvious takeoff on *The Katzenjammer Kids*) but the inspiration was all Feininger's. The Sunday page (signed "Your Uncle Feininger") started on April 29, 1906.

The Kin-der-Kids were a motley crew of enterprising youngsters made up of Daniel Webster, the precocious whiz-kid always flanked by his funereal-looking dachshund Sherlock Bones; Pie-Mouth, the ravenous ne'er-do-well; Strenuous Teddy, the group's athlete,

who could lift the most enormous weights; and Little Japansky, the "clockwork waterbaby" whom the little band had adopted as mascot.

To escape from the clutches of the sinister Aunt Jim-Jam and the hypocritical Cousin Gussie, the Kin-der-Kids embarked on a fantastic round-the-word odyssey aboard the family bathtub. Against a comic-opera background of pointed church steeples, vertiginous staircases, and cobbled meandering streets, the Kids met a host of picturesque characters: Mysterious Pete the outlaw; the sorrowful Mr. Pillsbury, the pill manu-

Frank King, "Gasoline Alley." © Chicago Tribune-New York News Syndicate.

facturer, and his five homely daughters; and Kind-Hearted Pat the Irish chimney sweep.

Aunt Jim-Jam and Cousin Gussie's pursuit, rich in ludicrous events, was not destined to reach a conclusion: following a contractual dispute with his publishers, Feininger abandoned the strip and it was left unfinished. The last page appeared on November 18, 1906.

M.H.

KING, FRANK O. (1883-1969) Frank O. King, whose *Gasoline Alley* family feature was faithfully read by half a nation for 50 years, was born into a middle-class family on June 11, 1883, in Cashton, Wisconsin. The family moved to nearby Tomah in Wisconsin's Kickapoo Hills (source of the name of Al Capp's Kickapoo Joy Juice in *Li'l Abner*) shortly thereafter, and King developed his early cartooning ability through grammar and high school, absorbing local color and family behavior that was reflected later in *Gasoline Alley*. He got his first cartooning job on the old *Minneapolis Times* in 1901 at 19, through the aid of a traveling salesman who saw a comic sign King drew for a Tomah bootblack and mentioned his skill to the *Times* editor. After working four years at the *Times*, King left to study for a year at the Chicago Academy of Fine Arts, then took a new job briefly with Hearst's *Chicago American*, switching later after some advertising agency work to Hearst's other Chicago paper, the *Examiner*. Here he did general cartooning and art work without arousing much attention for three years—except at the *Chicago Tribune*, which was then (1910) developing its own staff of comic strippers and cartoonists and liked the look of King's work. The *Tribune* hired King and put him to work in its Sunday comic supplement (the *Tribune* then had no daily strips) doing such quarter-page and half-page features as *Tough Teddy, The Boy Animal Trainer, Here Comes Motorcycle Mike!*, and *Hi Hopper* (a strip about a frog).

King's first real strip break came on January 31, 1915, when the first episode of his Sunday feature *Bobby Make-Believe* (spelled *Bobbie* in the first episode only) appeared in the *Tribune*. This feature was widely syndicated, and King's income improved considerably. His son, Robert Drew King, on whose behavior his famous Skeezix's childhood antics were largely based, was also born in 1915.

While turning out *Bobby Make-Believe*, King also drew another Sunday feature in black and white for the *Tribune* editorial section's front-page. Nameless as a whole, this page was divided into two half-pages. The upper half was always occupied by a large single panel containing a graphic observation of Chicago life in some form, called *The Rectangle*. The lower half-page was divided into a group of varying-sized panels featuring continued characters (Private Hoozus, etc.), and themes ("Our Movies," "Rubber Stamp," "Is This Your Little Pet Peeve," etc.). As a new addition to this lower group of panels, King introduced *Gasoline Alley* on November 24, 1918, in a panel titled: "Sunday Morning in Gasoline Alley," and subtitled: "Doc's Car Won't Start."

The new panel grew in popularity, and ultimately received more mail than *Bobby Make-Believe*. Accordingly, Joe Patterson of the *Tribune* started King on a daily version of *Gasoline Alley* in August 1919 (starting first in Patterson's *New York Daily News* and beginning in the *Tribune* almost immediately). *Bobby Make-Believe* folded in November 1919, and King's first color Sunday-page *Gasoline Alley* appeared on October 24, 1920.

By his late 30s King was already a wealthy man, and his prosperity increased with the spreading circulation of *Gasoline Alley*. (Essentially an American strip, King's family narrative had little publication outside of the U.S. and Canada.) The owner of two estates, one in Illinois and another in Florida, King spent what spare time the strip left him working at his hobbies: sculpting, collecting old maps, and raising amaryllis bulbs on his Florida property. He retired from the Sunday page in 1951, turning it over to a protege named Bill Perry, then began grooming an artist named Richard Moores to understudy him on the daily strip. Moving at last to the Florida estate near Lake Tohopekaliga at Winter Park, King, the gentlest and most domestic of strip cartoonists, died there of unreported causes at the age of 86 on June 24, 1969. Perry and Moores continued *Gasoline Alley*, which is still appearing today.

B.B.

KING AROO (U.S.) The McClure Newspaper Syndicate introduced *King Aroo* in November 1950 in daily and Sunday versions. The artist was Jack Kent, a high school dropout with no formal art training.

The 1950s was one of the periods in comic history when a new breed seemed to debut almost at once; at that particular time men like Mort Walker, Charles Schulz, Hank Ketcham, Bill Yates, and others entered the scene. Most were college graduates, had drawn for their school papers, and had slick styles. Kent was an exception. Self-taught and wildly individualistic, he quickly carved a niche for himself in comic history.

"King Aroo," Jack Kent. © McClure Syndicate.

King Aroo most certainly belongs in the uncrowded class of such creations as *Little Nemo, Krazy Kat, Barnaby, Pogo, Peanuts,* and *Calvin and Hobbes*: an "intellectual" strip not aimed at any particular age or readership group but cherished by cults in varied categories. Kent quickly created his own world where logic and illogic battled happily to irrelevant ends.

Some of the most literate and sophisticated nonsense in the funnies appeared in *King Aroo*. In one page, as the King learns of the earth's rapid revolution, the wind blows hard against him. A friend informs him that everything is proper, except that the earth revolves in the other direction, whereupon the gales blow from behind. Mixed in with every episode there was a heavy dose of joyful playing with literalism, puns, the consistencies and inconsistencies of the real world, and philosophical satire.

The cast starred King Aroo, a short monarch, the ruler of Myopia. He was an unassuming fellow, almost a child in grownup guise. Yupyop, his companion in a business suit, was the opposite: cynical and authoritative. The King may have had a fatherly image, but Yupyop proclaimed himself the "uncle-type." Professor Yorgle was the expert on everything; Mr. Pennipost was an early satire on the postal service—he was always late and has a coat with pockets like Harpo Marx's; and Wanda Witch, like the King, was the antithesis of everything her job description called for. She was very unwitchlike and none of her spells or tricks quite worked.

Kent freely admitted to inspiration by Herriman, whom he met. If the visual influence was slight, the spiritual bond was there. Kent's art was breezy, with the loosest of brush strokes and the suggestive but heavy indications of sparse backgrounds—hilly horizons, trees, bushes, and flowers—often bordering on surrealism, but the stylistic opposite of the mannered Sterrett.

The strip was carried with moderate success by McClure until it merged with Bell Syndicate. Contractual difficulties arose and Kent decided to surrender his contract. One client paper, however, refused to let the King abdicate; Stanleigh Arnold of the *San Francisco Chronicle* agreed to buy the strip as long as Kent would draw it. Encouraged by soundings from other local fans, Arnold eventually used an inheritance to found a small syndicate operation, Golden Gate Features, principally to distribute *King Aroo*.

Did insufficient promotion do *King Aroo* in? Each syndicate was noted for its very modest sales pushes.

Or was the strip destined to share the fate of most of its select counterparts? The appeal of the intellectual strip is almost always limited to small, albeit loyal, audiences. For whatever reason, *King Aroo* died in 1965. A book of collected strips was published in 1952, and several others were printed in the 1970s and '80s, after the strip's demise.

R.M.

KING OF THE ROYAL MOUNTED (U.S.) King of the Royal Mounted was created in February 1935 as a Sunday page for King Features Syndicate by the noted Western author Zane Grey (from one of his novels) and artist Allen Dean. In March 1936 a daily strip was added with drawings by Dean, who relinquished the Sunday strip to Charles Flanders. In April 1938 Flanders assumed the drawing of the Sunday page as well until April 1939, when Jim Gary took over the feature. *King* was discontinued in March 1954.

A Western with a different touch, *King* took place in Canada. The locale gave it a foreign quality that didn't have to be explained away as in *Red Ryder* or *The Lone Ranger*. At the same time its themes were easily recognizable and never strayed from the tried-and-true conventions of the genre. From the snow fields of the Yukon to the endless plains of Saskatchewan, Sergeant King, true Mountie that he was, always got his man. In his fights against fur thieves, cattle rustlers, smugglers, and assorted miscreants, he was helped by his loyal sidekick Pilot Laroux, his eternal sweetheart Betty Blake, and her brother, Kid.

King of the Royal Mounted does not rank as one of the best adventure strips but its qualities are simple and direct. It was a clean, fast-paced action strip with straightforward dialogue and characterization. The artists who worked on the strip were all good craftsmen (although Dean must be ranked above the other two). *King* was a fairly popular strip in the 1930s and 1940s, and it was made into a movie serial in 1942.

M.H.

KINOWA (Italy) In the jungle of Western comic books crowding the newsstands between the late 1940s and the early 1960s, there are few worthy of mention either for originality of story line or excellence of draftsmanship. Although it did not last long, *Kinowa* is among the features that are worthy. Written by the skilled scriptwriter Andrea Lavezzolo and drawn first by the group Essegesse (Sinchetto, Sartoris, and Guzzon), and later by Pietro Gamba, *Kinowa* appeared in the early months of 1950 as a monthly comic book.

The opening story did not seem to announce anything new; there was the usual Indian ambush of a wagon train, followed by the burning of farms by intoxicated savages, wild chases, and so on. Suddenly, however, a new element was added: an avenger completely different from the others, a being utterly fiendish and evil—or so it appeared to the terror-stricken Indians. Actually the demon was a human being, the long-bearded Sam Boyle, who, in order to wreak vengeance on the Indians who had scalped him when he was a youth, wore a demon mask made all the more terrifying by the light of a campfire or the shining of the moon. The easygoing Sam completely changed his personality once he donned the costume of Kinowa the avenger; he became cruel and ruthless, showing no pity for his fallen enemies.

Called the Spirit of Evil by his Indian foes, Sam was accompanied in his mission of vengeance by his son, even though he was born of an Indian mother. The adventures of Kinowa, which lasted only a few years, were very sophisticated and imaginative. The artwork of the Essegesse group—heavily inspired by Alex Raymond—was characterized by a sharp and firm line and a fine attention to detail.

G.B.

KIRBY, JACK (1917-1994)   American comic book and comic strip artist, writer, and editor born in New York City on August 28, 1917. Perhaps the most accomplished of all comic book creators, he is recognized as the comic book king. Jack Kirby began his career in 1935 as an illustrator for Max Fleisher's animation studio, producing material for cartoons like *Betty Boop* and *Popeye*. He moved to Lincoln Newspaper Syndicate in 1936 and produced a horde of short-lived newspaper strips, including *Black Buccaneer, Socko the Seadog,* and *Abdul Jones.* Joining the Eisner-Iger comic shop briefly in 1939, he also produced work for Novelty's *Blue Bolt* and Fox's *Blue Beetle*; in 1941, he drew the first issue of *Captain Marvel Adventures.*

Kirby began his famed partnership with Joe Simon in 1941. Together they created *Captain America* for Timely that year. With this comic Kirby developed his artistic style and garnered the most fame. Instantly becoming an American idol, the Captain remains Kirby's most brilliant character. Kirby drew him like a superhuman, complete with a fluid and exaggerated anatomy, and Captain America soon became the country's morale-boosting anti-Nazi. Kirby invented the full-page and double-page comic spread here, and although he handled only 35 stories, his *Captain America* work during 1941 and 1942 is considered among the best ever produced.

Simon and Kirby moved to National in 1942 and produced four strips, including *Boy Commandos* and *Newsboy Legion.* These became the prototypes for all the "kid" comic books to follow. After a stint in the army, Kirby returned to comics and his partnership with Joe Simon in 1945. They immediately created three new titles for Harvey Comics, including *Boy's Ranch,* one of the few Kirby excursions into the Western genre. After originating *My Date,* their first romance comic book for Hillman in 1947, they produced a short-lived line of titles for Crestwood, and then created *Fighting American,* a parody of their own *Captain America,* for Headline in 1954. Simon and Kirby formed Mainline Comics in 1954, but the company folded and their five titles were sold to Charlton.

They dissolved their partnership in 1956, and Kirby began collaborating with Dick, Dave, and Wally Wood on the *Skymasters* newspaper feature in 1957. During this time, Kirby also found the opportunity to create *Challengers of the Unknown* for National (1958) and help ex-partner Simon launch *The Fly* and *Private Strong* for Archie.

Kirby returned permanently to comic books in 1959, joined the Marvel Comics Group, and teamed up with writer-editor Stan Lee. In 1961, they created *Fantastic Four,* a superhero strip Kirby used to further his artistic genius. When he began drawing *Thor* in *Journey Into Mystery* in 1962 and the revived *Captain America* in 1964, Kirby once again captured the comic book market. Kirby, Lee, and Marvel rose to the top of the industry and many claim they completely revamped the comic book world. A festering disagreement with Lee led Kirby to return to National as a writer/editor/ artist in 1970. He created nearly a dozen titles— including several interrelated books and two black-and-white comic magazines—but none were as aesthetically or as financially successful as his Marvel work had been.

Kirby went back to Marvel in the mid-1970s, working on such titles as *The Eternals* and *2001: A Space Odyssey* (both 1976) and turning out a few more Cap-

"King of the Royal Mounted," Allen Dean. © King Features Syndicate.

Jack Kirby, "Fantastic Four." © Marvel Comics.

Jack Kirby, "The Silver Surfer." © Marvel Comics.

tain America stories. In 1981-83 he drew *Captain Victory and the Galactic Rangers* and *Silver Star* for Pacific Comics. He briefly returned to DC in 1985 to work on *Super Powers*. His later years were darkened by his dispute with Marvel over the company's refusal to return his original artwork to him; thanks to fan pressure he finally received partial satisfaction. He died in Los Angeles in February 1994.

In his 50-year career, Jack Kirby produced every conceivable type of comic book work. Many of the field's most successful concepts are his creations and he has been responsible for more comic book sales than any other artist, writer, or editor. "Without him," artist-historian James Steranko said in 1970, "there may not have been comics to write about."

J.B.

KITAZAWA, RAKUTEN (1876-1955) Japanese cartoonist born 1876 in Omiya, Saitama. After learning Western-style painting at the art institute run by Yukihiko Ono, Rakuten Kitazawa joined the magazine *Box of Curios*, where he became influenced by the Australian cartoonist Frank A. Nankivel. Nankivel taught Kitazawa the art of political cartooning, and soon Kitazawa was working as a cartoonist for *Box of Curios*, the only Japanese cartoonist on the staff of the magazine. His talent was recognized by Yukichi Fukuzawa, a famous enlightenment thinker, founder of the Keio Gijuku university, and president of the Jiji Shinpou company. Soon Kitazawa was working for *Jiji Manga*,

the Sunday supplement of the daily *Jiji Shinpou*, where he generalized the term *manga* as meaning both cartoon and comic strip in Japanese.

In addition to his satirical, political, and social cartoons, Kitazawa also drew a number of comic strips, including *Togosaku to Mokubē no Tokyo Kenbutsu* ("The Tokyo Trip of Togosaku and Mokubē," 1901), *Haikara Kidoro no Shippai* ("Fancy Scenes at the Theater," 1901), and *Chame to Dekobo* ("The City Slicker and the Hayseed," 1905). Kitazawa's early comic strips were strongly influenced by the work of American cartoonists such as Outcault, Dirks, and Opper.

In 1905 Kitazawa started the first Japanese cartoon magazine, *Tokyo Puck* (the title was derived from the American *Puck* of which Nankivel was then a cartoonist). *Tokyo Puck*, at first a bimonthly, was soon changed into a weekly due to its enormous success. Kitazawa drew a great many humor and editorial cartoons for *Tokyo Puck* until his departure from the magazine in 1911. The next year he started the bimonthly *Rakuta Puck* (by then the word "Puck" had come to mean any kind of illustrated magazine), and in 1918 he founded the Manga Kourakukai, an association of Japanese cartoonists. In 1929 Kitazawa went on a long journey to America and Europe. In Paris he had a one-man show of his works and was awarded the French Legion of Honor. A complete edition of his works was started in Japan in October 1930, but was never brought to fruition (only seven books were published). After 32 years of working in the Jiji Shinpou Co., Kitazawa left in

1932 (his salary when he left was the highest paid in Japanese newspaper work).

After leaving the company, Kitazawa started his own school, where he taught a new generation of cartoonists and artists. In 1948 he retired to his native Omiya, where he led a peaceful and contented life until he died of a heart attack on August 25, 1955.

Rakuten Kitazawa was the pioneer of Japanese comic art. His greatest merit was the establishment of the modern comic strip in Japan. His influence on the succeeding generation of cartoonists has been tremendous (His disciples included Jihei Ogawa, Outen Shimokawa, Batten Nagasaki, Tetsuo Ogawa, and Tatsumi Nishigawa, to name but a few.) In commemoration of Rakuten Kitazawa's accomplishments, his native city of Omiya inaugurated the City Museum of Cartoon Art in 1966.

H.K.

KIT CARSON (Italy) Rino Albertarelli was the artist who transposed, in a very unconventional and personal fashion, the figure of the legendary frontier hero and guide for John Carles Fremont to the comic strip. *Kit Carson* was the first Italian Western strip, and its titular hero was not some young cowpuncher but a wizened old man, bald and heavily mustached, yet with a determination and an ability that could match those of any man 30 years younger.

Carson, the last representative of a dying era, offered his services and experience to the fight for justice and the redress of wrongs. As a kind of Don Quixote of the West, he had his Sancho Panza in the person of the lazy Uncle Pam, a very funny character who enlivened the strip with his shenanigans. Although old enough to draw a pension, Kit Carson never let his age interfere with his adventures, filled with chases, fights, duels, and challenges. His was an idealized figure, that of the old pioneer in a fast-disappearing frontier. Albertarelli drew his inspiration from a book by Truslow Adams, and his *Kit Carson* appeared in the pages of *Topolino* from July 15, 1937, until October 1938.

The sequel to the adventures of Kit Carson, written by Federico Pedrocchi and drawn by Walter Molino, was quite different. The Old West had vanished and Kit Carson moved his operations to Mexico, where he fought assorted outlaws and adventurers such as the despicable Carvajan or the power-mad Tuerto. In these later adventures, which appeared in the weekly *Paperino* from July 6, 1939, to August 15, 1940, he was aided by the mysterious "White Amazon," a female Zorro. At the end of the strip, Kit Carson was depicted as a very old man who would tell of his adventures to an audience of his grandchildren. (In the 1950s Gianluigi Bonelli added the character of Kit Carson to the *dramatis personae* of his *Tex Willer*.)

A classic of the Golden Age of Italian Comics, Rino Albertarelli's *Kit Carson* was reprinted in book form by Milano Libri. The episodes drawn by Molino were published in the deluxe anthology *Le Grandi Firme del Fumetto Italiano*.

G.B.

KITCHEN, DENIS (1946-   ) American underground comics artist, writer, editor, publisher, and entrepreneur born August 27, 1946, in Milwaukee, Wisconsin. A graduate of the University of Wisconsin at Milwaukee's School of Journalism, Kitchen says, "none, thank God," when asked about his art training.

Unlike many of his underground compatriots who sprung up as part of the alternative "comix" movement of the late 1960s, Kitchen never restricted himself strictly to the underground. He was one of the few who accepted commercial assignments, worked for "straight" magazines, and contributed to other usually taboo ventures.

Kitchen made his first appearance in an underground comic of 1969 which he wrote, drew, published, and distributed himself. Mainly a melange of sometimes-funny, sometimes-not vignettes about Milwaukee, *Mom's Homemade Comics* number one sold its complete run of 4,000 copies and was later reprinted by one of the then-existing underground publishers.

However, being a Milwaukee-based cartoonist, Kitchen found it impossible to deal with the flighty, often-incompetent San Francisco/Berkeley-based underground publishers, and he formed Kitchen Sink Enterprises in 1970. In the years since then, Kitchen Sink has published hundreds of titles, including *Bijou Funnies*, *Home Grown*, *Bizarre Sex*, and *Snarf*. Kitchen contributed to many of these with a simple, cartoony style. *The Crow*, another Kitchen comic, was very popular and two movies based on the comic were filmed in the 1990s. Kitchen Sink has also published reprints of classic comics such as *Li'l Abner* and *Alley Oop*. Kitchen's company produced 78 rpm records by underground cartoonist Robert Crumb, ran an underground comic syndicate which serviced the burgeoning underground newspaper market of the late '60s, operated a cartoon art studio, and produced a variety of underground-oriented novelties that were usually comic-related. In 1970, Kitchen helped found the *Milwaukee Bugle-American*, an underground newspaper for which Kitchen drew a strip in his now-familiar bigfoot style. The paper lasted for a couple of years.

When the alternate comix movement began to flounder in 1974, Kitchen made a deal with Cadence Industries—Marvel Comics"s conglomerate parent company—to edit *Comix Book*, which was ostensibly meant to be an underground comic book for audiences and general distribution. Despite Kitchen's best efforts, all three issues published were both financial and artistic disasters. Many of the top underground cartoonists

Denis Kitchen, "Ingrid the Bitch." © Kitchen Sink Enterprises.

refused to cooperate, citing their traditional reluctance to participate in straight ventures. Distribution was spotty and usually inept.

In the last 20 years Kitchen has devoted all his time to his publishing venture under the name Kitchen Sink Press. It has become one of the more important publishers of books in comic form.

J.B.

KLOTJOHAN (Sweden) Klotjohan was the name of one of those beings from northern mythology that never seem to fail to reach an enthusiastic public when they are handled by Scandinavian creators. The prefix "klot" in this particular troll's name means "ball," and it aptly described the little tyke's looks. Klotjohan's body was a round, black, furry ball. His unkempt head was a bit on the oval side, with a roundish nose and saucer eyes holding pupils as black as coal. For good measure this troll was endowed with comparatively large hands and feet and a tail that was almost twice as long as the little fellow stood tall.

This lovable little creature was a creation of Swedish cartoonist Torvald Gahlin, a staff member of the Swedish newspaper *Dagens Nyheter*. By means of his sharp wit Gahlin also became a radio personality. *Klotjohan*, for much of the strip's 36 years, appeared in *Dagens Nyheter*, after having been created for the weekly *Vårt Hem* ("Our Home") in 1935. Two years earlier, Gahlin had created another comic strip, *Fredrik*, well known and cherished for the "f" alliterations of the funny feature's star. *Fredrik* was started and remained loyal to *Göteborgs Handels-och Sjöfartstidning*. During the last three years of *Klotjohan's* existence, from 1968 to 1970 when Gahlin decided to end the feature, that strip appeared in a farmer's trade journal.

"Klotjohan," Torvald Gahlin. © Torvald Gahlin.

Torvald Gahlin, one of the pioneers of the Swedish comic strip, displayed an original cartoon style from the very start—unmistakable roundish noses and very thin arms and legs—in a conscious effort to have his work differ from the American comic imports then appearing in the weekly press of Sweden. While trying to be different, *Klotjohan* also was a parody on all kinds of children's strips, Klotjohan being a Chaplinesque troll constantly colliding with modern society. Gahlin was awarded the Adamson (the Swedish comics' Oscar) for both *Fredrik* and *Klotjohan* in 1970.

W.F.

KNERR, HAROLD H. (1882-1949) American cartoonist born September 4, 1882, in Bryn Mawr, Pennsylvania, into a family of German descent. During his Pennsylvania schooldays Harold H. Knerr enjoyed something of a "Katzenjammer Kid" boyhood, sliding down roofs, doctoring automobile engines, and playing pranks on his elders, before realizing his dream of becoming an amateur balloonist. "Then I spent my two years raising hell in a Philadelphia art school," confided Knerr in 1942. "My first newspaper work was drawing pictures of gravestones atop the oldest graves in a local cemetary for the *Philadelphia Record*."

Still in Philadelphia, Knerr went to work for the *Ledger*, where he drew an animal strip of uncertain merit, *Zoo-Illogical Snapshots*; in 1902 he joined the staff of the *Inquirer*, where he created no fewer than four kid strips. Two of these are noteworthy: *Scary William*, about a young daredevil not unlike the one he himself had been, and *The Flenheimer Kids*. *The Flenheimer Kids* (which starred two hellraising twins and a peglegged sea captain) was, in terms of quality of style and wit, several notches above the other *Katzenjammer Kids* imitations which were appearing at the same time, and when Hearst had to look for a new artist to continue the adventures of the Katzies he immediately selected Knerr.

From 1914 on Knerr's fame merged with that of the *Kids*. Knerr did create another strip in 1926, the tender and funny *Dinglehoofer und His Dog*, and in the early 1920s he illustrated a series of humorous articles, "This Dumb World," written by comics editor Bruno Lessing. Through all this the Katzies remained the object of his constant care. An innovator in his own right, Knerr brought to the strip a better organization but faithfully preserved its hectic pace and diabolical inventiveness. As critic Jim Walsh observed, "Certainly no one ever accomplished a more brilliant feat of continuing another man's original conception than did Knerr during the 36 years that he drew the *Katzenjammer Kids*."

Knerr also maintained the characters' inimitable speech, sprinkling it with tongue-in-cheek quotes from Shakespeare ("Lay on, MacStuff!"), the Bible ("Der Flesh iss veak!"), and fairy tales ("Vot do you see from der turret, sister Ann?").

Knerr, who was a shy, bald, bespectacled man, never married. His only passion—aside from cartooning—was flying private airplanes, which he continued to do despite the heart ailment which darkened the last years of his life and to which he finally succumbed. On July 8, 1949, Harold Knerr was found dead on the floor of his apartment in the Blackstone Hotel in New York City, leaving behind him the legacy of a comic genius on a par with that of Dirks, Opper, and McManus.

M.H.

KNIGHT, CLAYTON (1891-1969) American cartoonist, illustrator, and writer born 1891 in Rochester, New York. After graduating from the Chicago Art Institute, Clayton Knight enlisted in the Lafayette Escadrille, saw much action over France during World War I, and was once shot down and gravely wounded. After the war he resumed his career as an illustrator and writer, authoring many books and articles on aviation and air warfare, often in collaboration with his illustrator-wife, Katherine Sturges Knight. Clayton Knight's illustrations for *Collier's* drew the attention of the editors at King Features, who asked Knight to draw the illustrations for *Ace Drummond*, an aviation strip just created for them by World War I air ace Eddie Rickenbacker (1934).

Featuring the predictable team of youthful pilot-adventurer Ace Drummond and his grizzled, cynical mechanic Jerry, the strip was not too distinguished as it involved the two heroes in a series of disjointed adventures from China to South America. In spite of Knight's soaring depiction of flight scenes and limitless skies, which were his forte (he never bothered much with characterization or continuity), the strip never caught on and was dropped in the late 1930s (in 1936 a movie serial of *Ace Drummond* was produced by the team of Ford Beebe and Clifton Smith).

Somewhat longer-lasting was *Ace*'s companion feature on Sundays, *The Hall of Fame of the Air*, which extolled the lives and times of aviators from all parts of the world (although after the start of World War II it restricted itself chiefly to the exploits of Allied pilots).

Soon after the outbreak of hostilities in Europe, Clayton Knight started the Clayton Knight Committee to help American pilots enlist in the Royal Canadian Air Force (for this work he received the Order of the British Empire). In 1942 he was one of the founding members of the Wings Club, and later was named official historian of the 8th, 11th, and 20th Air Forces. In this capacity he was present at the Japanese surrender ceremonies aboard the U.S.S. *Missouri* in 1945.

Clayton Knight is more famous as an illustrator and painter than as a cartoonist. His contributions to the literature of aviation are also considerable: *Hitch Your Wagon* (with Robert C. Durham, 1950), *The Story of Flight* (1951), *Lifeline in the Sky* (1957), and *Plane Crash* (1958).

During his lifetime Clayton Knight received more distinctions, civilian as well as military, than can be mentioned here. He died of a heart ailment in Danbury, Connecticut, on July 17, 1969.

M.H.

KOBAYASHI, KIYOCHIKA (1847-1915) A Japanese print and woodcut artist born August 1, 1847, in Tokyo, Kiyochika Kobayashi studied photography with Renjo Shimooka, and traditional Japanese printmaking with Gyōsai Kawanabe and Zeshin Shibata. Kobayashi's love for cartooning developed under the influence of Charles Wirgman, a correspondent for the *London Illustrated News* and the founder of the illustrated monthly *Japan Punch* in 1862, who taught him Western-style painting. Mixing photography, Japanese print techniques, and Western painting, Kobayashi developed his own distinctive style in a series of prints which he did from 1876 to 1881 called *Kōsenga*. These depicted scenes of Tokyo in the early days of the Meiji era.

From 1882 to 1893 Kobayashi created a great many historical prints. From 1894 to 1905 he devoted himself to war prints of the Sino-Japanese and the Russo-Japanese conflicts. He also worked as a cartoonist (again influenced by Charles Wirgman), creating many cartoon series for the satirical weekly *Maru Maruchinbun*: *Kiyochika Punch* (1881), *Shinban Sanju ni Mensō* (1882), *Hyakumensō* (1883), *Hyakusen Hyakushō* (1894-85), and *Kyoiku Iroha Tango* (1897), among others.

Kobayashi became a staff artist for the *Niirokushinpo* and contributed many cartoons. He also drew many illustrations for newspapers and magazines and founded his own art school, Kyochika Gajuku, in 1894. He influenced a number of cartoonists such as Yasuji Inoue and Beisaku Taguchi.

Kiyochika Kobayashi spent his later years in obscurity until his death on November 28, 1915.

H.K.

KOHLSAAT, ROLAND (1913-1978) German artist and writer born May 24, 1913, in Hamburg. The son of a merchant, Roland Kohlsaat attended public school and secondary school in Hamburg. At Kunstgewerbeschule Hamburg (the Hamburg College of Arts and Crafts) he studied under Professor Wohlers. After graduation he worked as a painter of portraits, horses, and landscapes. It was not until after World War II that he started working for the press, doing illustrations, cartoons, and comic strips.

His first comic strip was an adaptation of Erich Kästner's famous novel *Emil und die Detektive* ("Emil and the Detectives"). It appeared in *Funkwacht*, a weekly radio guide that, in time, transformed into *TV*, a weekly television guide. In the early 1960s he returned to *TV* for some time with two strips, *Plisch und Wisch* and *Tele Wischen* (pronounced television). *Tele Wischen* was very well received by the public but not by the new editor-in-chief of *TV*, which had merged with another television weekly. The discontinuation of the comic strip drew lots of reader protest, but it was then Roland Kohlsaat who refused to revive the feature after the new editor-in-chief begged him to do so. Kohlsaat did continue to write and draw *Plisch und Wisch* for *TV* for several years.

It was in 1953, however, that Kohlsaat created his most famous comic strip, *Jimmy das Gummipferd* ("Jimmy the Rubber Horse"). This strip began one night in 1953 when the editors of *stern* contacted him to develop a comic feature for their children's supplement *sternchen* by the next morning. About half an hour later, he had conceived the basis of a comic strip that would run for nearly 24 years. The feature was retitled *Julios abenteuerliche Reisen* ("Julio's Adventurous Voyages") in the late 1960s, and was discontinued in 1976 when Kohlsaat became incapacitated and could no longer continue working. The editors of *stern* felt the feature was so much Kohlsaat's brainchild that they discontinued the strip even though some basic ideas and outlines for a continuation may have existed.

While the feature lasted, Kohlsaat maintained a high-spirited story line, writing and drawing fantastic stories full of artistic verve. Kohlsaat also did a regular full page of gag cartoons for the weekly *Das Neue Blatt*. These cartoons usually featured some very curvaceous ladies. Kohlsaat's artwork was also known to help increase the sales of a number of books that he worked for as illustrator. Roland Kohlsaat died February 1, 1978.

W.F.

KOJIMA, GOSEKI (1928-) Japanese comic book artist born November 11, 1928, in Yokkaichi, Mie. After graduation from high school, Goseki Kojima (no relation to Koo Kojima) worked as a billboard painter. In 1950 he went to Tokyo in the hope of becoming an illustrator, but he worked instead as a *kamishibai* artist, creating short illustrated stories which he narrated himself to an audience of children.

In 1957 Kojima started to draw comic stories for a company specializing in producing comic books for rental libraries (these books were not sold on newsstands); his output was enormous. A few of his best or more popular works are: *Onmitsu Yūreijō* ("an illustrated story," 1957); *Yagyū Ningun* (1959); *Chōhen Dai Roman* (a series of adaptations from great novels and kabuki stories done from 1961 to 1967); and many ghost stories which were later published in magazines. In 1964 Kojima was voted the most popular artist in his field by the readers.

Starting in 1967 with *Doninki*, Kojima then worked for comic magazines, creating successively *Oboro Jūninchō* (1967), *Akai Kagebōshi* (a comic strip adaptation of Renzaburō Shibata's famous ninja novel, 1968), *Kozure Okami* ("A Wolf and His Cub," Kojima's most famous creation, 1970), *Guremono* ("Delinquent Youth," 1974), and many others.

With *Kozure Okami* (scripted by Kazuo Koike), Kojima became one of the most highly praised artists in Japan; he is regarded as the top *Jidaimono* artist (Jidaimono is a popular Japanese genre set in ancient times) along with Sanpei Shirato. After ending *Kozure Okami* in 1976, he went on to draw *Kawaite Soro, Tatamidori Kasajin, Hanzo Nomon,* and *Bonachi Bushido.* All of these were bloody tales of samurai warfare.

Goseki Kojima's graphic style is realistic and he can render his characters' most subtle emotions. His line, at first very delicate, became firmer with time. Kojima uses both pen and brush in his drawings, making for a warm and personal touch. He has influenced many comic book artists in Japan (Ryōchi Ikegami, Takami Nagayasu, Tsuyako Nishimura, Haruo Koyama, to name but a few). Regarded as the ideal comic strip artist for adult stories, Kojima has also done many illustrations for books and magazines. His sense of composition and his detailed draftsmanship have placed him in the forefront of Japanese artists.

H.K.

KOJIMA, KOO (1928-) Japanese cartoonist and illustrator born March 3, 1928, in Tokyo. Koo Kojima decided to become a cartoonist at age 15. He studied at the Kawabata School of Fine Arts and later at the Taiheiyo School of Fine Arts. Along with his fellow students Giichi Sekine, Kouji Nakajima, and Tatsuo Baba, Kojima organized the Dokuritsu Mangaha ("the unknown cartoonists' group") in 1947. At the start of his career Kojima produced many magazine cartoons, panels, and etchings, but his name became famous as a creator of adult comic strips such as *Sennin Buraku* (1956), *Miss Doron Ototo* (1957), and *Kuroneko Don* ("Don the Black Cat," 1958).

More adult comic strips followed, with an emphasis on melodrama, after his first venture into the humor strip in 1959 with *Chūsingura*. A simple listing will suffice to show Kojima's extraordinary creativity: *Oretacha Rival Da!* ("We are Rivals!," 1960); *Ahiruga Oka 77* (which inspired a series of Japanese television cartoons) in 1961; *Uchi no Yomehan* ("My Wife") and *Nih on no*

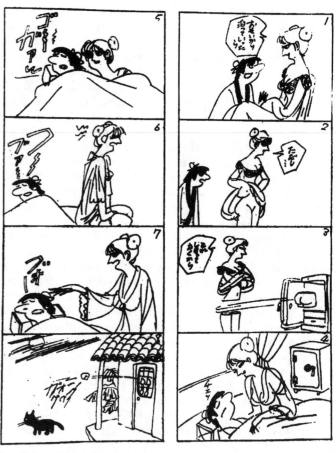

Koo Kojima, "Sennin Buraku." © Kojima.

Kaāchan ("Japanese Wives") in 1966; *My Name Is Natsuko* (1968); *Tama no Kashi Monagotari* (1969); *Oumaga Tsuji* (1971); *Ano Eka Kūn* (1975); and others.

Kojima has also drawn a great many cartoons, magazine and book illustrations, and covers. In this aspect of his work he is most noted for the more than 100 covers that he did for the weekly *Manga Sunday.* His stories since the late 1970s have been published mostly in *Big Comic Original,* a comics magazine that, according to Fred Schodt, "serializes many long-running, popular works by older and famous artists."

Kojima is famous for the beautiful and glamorous women whom he lovingly draws into all his work. His girls have large, dewy eyes, generous lips, thin and long noses, and sensuous bodies. If one word was to define Koo Kojima's art, it would be eroticism. His stories are as erotic as his girls are, and his line is very elegant and sinuous. As a matter of fact, when Kojima took over Kon Shimizu's *Kappa* after the latter's death in 1974, he turned this fantasy series into an erotic strip.

H.K.

KÖNIG, RALF (1960-) Ralf König was born in 1960 in Soest, Westphalia, where he grew up, attended school, and completed an apprenticeship as a carpenter. But working with wood was not exactly what he had in mind for a career. König may not have thought he would become an internationally known comic strip artist when his first comics were published when he was 19. These first comics were a creative way he could come to terms with being gay, and showed the humorous side of problems he was experiencing. Friends who read his work found it true to life and

Ralf Konig, "Muttersorgen" ("A Mother's Worries"). © Ralf Konig.

encouraged him to carry on—which he has, with success among both homosexual and heterosexual readers.

Ever since he first began writing and drawing comics, König's material was published either by gay magazines or by book publishers in either paperback editions or comic albums. While developing his simplistic style and realistic dialogue, König studied at the State Academy of Art in Düsseldorf from 1981 to 1986. In 1988 he received the first award for his comics work, the Joop Klepzeiker Prize, in Amsterdam. He was awarded a Best German Comic Artist at a comics salon in Grenoble in 1990 and won best German Comic Artist and Best International Comic Artist in Erlangen and in Barcelona, respectively, in 1992. In 1996 he was nominated for best international comic strip at the salon in Angoulême.

König is best known for his comic albums *Lysistrata, Der bewegte Mann* ("Man on the Move"), *Pretty Baby, Kondom des Grauens* ("Killer Condom"), *Beach Boys*, and *Bullenklöten* ("Cop's Balls"). In 1993 he started a series of albums titled *Konrad und Paul*, centered around the exploits of two young homosexuals, Conrad and Paul. Here, like in other books before, Konig no longer deals exclusively with gayness but with general themes, while the protagonists of his stories are obviously gay and live in a gay world. *Konrad und Paul* has a cast of supporting characters that had appeared off and on in earlier works.

König, because of the frankness of his language and of his caricatures, has also been fairly successful in raising the hackles of conservative critics. In fact, there have been efforts to ban some of his comics, like *Bullenklöten*, for reasons of obscenity and morality. How-

ever, these efforts have been unsuccessful so far. This in part may be due to the fact that König's readership does not only consist of gays. His stories contain some hilarious humor for both homosexuals and heterosexuals.

König is respected as an artist in addition to becoming a commercial success, with some of his works transformed into motion pictures. *Der bewegte Mann* hit the screen in 1994 and was so successful that, in 1995, it received the Golden Screen Award with an Asterisk, a German Motion Picture Industry prize for films that are box-office hits. With 6.5 million tickets sold, *Der bewegte Mann* was the most successful film of the year. The film version of *Kondom des Grauens*, however, did not live up to expectations. Arguably the film would have been better as a filmed version of the puppet play based on the original comic. The latest project is a 26-episode animated series of *Konrad und Paul* for television and for movie theaters.

Comics of Ralf König so far have been translated into 11 languages and have appeared in 17 countries. Total print run for his book editions is in excess of 5 million copies.

W.F.

KONING HOLLEWIJN (Netherlands) *Koning Hollewijn* ("King Hollewijn") is one of the many comic strips created by the very prolific and successful Marten Toonder, whose studio's comic strips and animated cartoons netted him the public's admiration and praise, and led to his title: the Dutch Walt Disney.

Koning Hollewijn was created in 1954 and was published as a daily strip in the newspaper *De Telegraaf/ Nieuws van de Dag*. With over 5,000 episodes under its

"Koning Hollewijn," Marten Toonder. © Marten Toonder.

belt, the strip started strongly commenting on Dutch politics in 1971. A number of the exploits of *Koning Hollewijn* were reprinted in book form. The strip ended in July 1972.

Koning Hollewijn's story concept was fairly unusual for a comic strip; the hero was a bald, white-bearded, bespectacled old King who was an introvert. Constantly busy at self-analysis, the good King lost all touch with reality while his court remained busy trying to get him to face "real life." His shapely secretary, Wiebeline Wip, a lively extrovert, usually succeeded in interesting him in the situation at hand and in making sure that her employer did not fall for any tricks. The pathetic hero and the sparkling heroine were the backbone of this Toonder strip that used humans (although in caricature) instead of the anthropomorphic animals of so many Toonder successes.

Given the large number of strips produced by the Toonder studios, it would be asking the impossible to expect all of them be done by Toonder. In fact, probably 80 percent of all of the Dutch comic artists got their start in or were associated with the Toonder studios at one time. Thus, *Koning Hollewijn* for some time was drawn by Ton Beek (a Dutch comic artist born August 18, 1926), who was with the studios from 1946 to 1959 before he moved to his own comic series, most notably *Birre Beer*, published in *Handelsblad* and first reprinted in album format in 1964. Beek has since been doing *Yogi Bear* and *Huckleberry Hound* comics that in Holland are leased by Geillustreerde Pers. Like so many others, Beek is proof that Toonder did not merely employ artists he felt could work in his style. After a period of learning, they could very well make it on their own if they so desired.

W.F.

KOTZKY, ALEX (1923-1996) American artist born September 11, 1923, in New York City. After a public school education, Kotzky attended the Art Students League on a scholarship in 1941. His intention was to become an illustrator and he studied under George Bridgman, the greatest of contemporary anatomy artists.

While an art student, Kotzky penciled for DC Comics (started August 1940) and drew backgrounds for Will Eisner's *Spirit* comics (starting November 1941).

After wartime service from September 1943 to February 1946, he returned to the comic book field, working on the *Plastic Man, Doll Man,* and *Black Hawk* titles for Quality from 1946 to 1951. In 1951, Kotzky joined the Johnstone and Cushing Agency, the foremost comic strip advertisers; he handled the Ford, Dodge, and other auto accounts. By 1954, Kotzky was freelancing and doing illustrations for medical magazines; he was also periodically ghosting *Steve Canyon, Juliet Jones,* and *Big Ben Bolt,* as well as drawing the Sunday advertising comic strip *Duke Handy* for Phillip Morris cigarettes.

In the late 1950s Harold Anderson, head of Publishers Syndicate, contacted Kotzky about a new strip idea submitted by Nick Dallis, author of *Rex Morgan* and *Judge Parker.* The strip that developed was *Apartment 3-G,* which debuted on May 8, 1961, and has remained a solid fixture of Publishers-Hall's battery of story strips.

Kotzky's art retained its basic slick realism with a strong infusion of lightness and humor. The artist claimed that the newsprint crunch of the 1970s actually worked to his advantage; because of space and format strictures, he was forced to concentrate on faces—bringing an emphasis to characterization. Kotzky's style was confident and comfortable but not outstanding, a perfect marriage with Dallis's respectable story line. After Dallis died in 1991, Kotzky took over the writing of the strip until his own death on September 26, 1996, in New York City.

R.M.

KOZURE OKAMI (Japan) *Kozure Okami* ("A Wolf and His Cub") was created by Kazuo Koike (script) and Gōseki Kojima (art) for the comic weekly *Manga Action.* It first appeared in August 1970.

Kozure Okami is a period strip set in the Edo era and features the adventures of Ittō Ogami, former high executioner of the realm, and his son, Daigorō. Ittō was the target of assassins hired by the powerful Yagyū family; he escaped assassination but his wife, Azami, was killed, and he vowed vengeance on the Yagyū clan. Giving up his life as a samurai, he and his son became paid assassins. Soon people were calling father and son the "wolf and his cub."

In the long saga that then unfolded Ittō and Daigorō, escaping ambushes and traps set by their enemies, succeeded in slaying Retsudō Yagyū's four sons and his daughter; Retsudō himself lost an eye in one of their encounters. In 1974 a new enemy came into the story: the ambitious and murderous Kaii Abe, who opposes both Yagyū and the Okamis.

Kozure Okami was a revenge story filled with violence and passion, but it also depicted with rough tenderness the relationship between father and son, stressing the family loyalties and ties which have become loosened in modern Japan. When reprinted in book form the strip became an instant best-seller (over five million copies sold) and inspired several motion pictures, a television series, and a number of records. It ended its long run in 1976 after more than 8,400 thrill-packed pages.

H.K.

KRAAIENHOVE (Netherlands) *Kraaienhove* ("Raven Manor"), a fascinating and intelligent combination of horror and adventure genres with wit and parody, was a creation of the very gifted Dutch comic artist Willy Lohmann. Lohmann, born May 7, 1936, in Zutphen,

"Kozure Okami," Gōseki Kojima. © Manga Action.

Netherlands, was only 24 when, in 1960 after a thorough education, he started the comic strip *Bazurka en Jampie Hoed* in the newspaper *Algemeen Dagblad*. Two years later he moved on to even greater things, creating *Kraaienhove*, which started in the newspaper *Het Parool* on December 21, 1962.

The stage was set in the first episode, entitled "Het eerste verhaal" ("The First Tale"). In it a vegetable dealer approaches an old manor that might have come straight from a horror movie set. The house gives him the shivers, as do its owners, Lucius and Grizelda. The exquisitely counterbalanced blacks and whites of the artwork create a moody atmosphere that befits a Gothic tale and seems to explain the vegetable dealer's (and all the neighbors') fears. At the same time the reader's mind is eased by a cartoony touch and by the presentation of Lucius and Grizelda as harmlessly eccentric, if surrounded by an air of mystery.

Lucius is perfectly impractical but superintelligent; his wife, Grizelda, is a parapsychological marvel. Lucius is the embodiment of the mad scientist, forever experimenting to find the explanation for everything. To him, knowledge is power, yet he would never dream of using this power for his gain. (Besides, the way some of his experiments turn out, there is not much to be gained by them anyway.) His counterpoint is magical, mystical Grizelda who more than once proves that ambition and intuition may be more powerful than science.

Kraaienhove has developed by leaps and bounds over the years, always staying true to its special flavor but going off more into the direction of detective mystery at one time or becoming more of a parody at another. The result, because of the strip's extraordinary graphics, is always pleasing. This has also led to the strip's

"Kraaienhove," Willy Lohmann. © Willy Lohmann.

"Krazy Kat," George Herriman. © King Features Syndicate.

"Krazy Kat," George Herriman. © King Features Syndicate.

being added to the lineup of features published in the Dutch comic weekly *Pep*, with stories done especially for that magazine and coloring perfectly blended in with the strip's mood.

W.F.

KRAZY KAT (U.S.) Universally acclaimed as the greatest comic strip, George Herriman's *Krazy Kat* began inauspiciously as a minor part of Herriman's first strip for the Hearst papers, the quasi-daily *Dingbat Family* which opened in the *New York Journal* on June 20, 1910.

As a kind of comic tailpiece to the human action in *The Family Upstairs* (which had become the *Dingbats'* new title as of August 1, 1910) Herriman involved the family animals (a cat and a bulldog) in a nether side-show at their feet: in effect, a separate little gag going on within the main strip. Later a mouse was introduced into the floor level drama and was shown sneaking in to sock the cat with a stone. The little animal byplay delighted the public and by August 17, 1910, the miniscule action had been encased in its own Lilliputian set of panels (at that date, the disgusted mouse first uses the disparaging term "Krazy Kat!'"). Minus a title, this separate section of *The Family Upstairs* strip ran with the *Dingbat* saga until July 1, 1911, when the first wholly individual and titled cat-and-mouse strip appeared in the temporary absence of *The Family Upstairs*. Titled *Krazy Kat and Ignatz*, the new feature was reincorporated into *The Family Upstairs* on July 18, 1911, where it resumed its previous untitled run.

For two more years, the wonderful little cat and mouse vaudeville team remained locked into the *Dingbat* opus, until a general page widening in the Hearst evening papers permitted the addition of a vertical, page-high, six-panel strip beside the five horizontal strips already running. On October 28, 1913, the first episode of what was at last to be a continuing *Krazy Kat* strip appeared in this space in the *New York Journal*.

The separate *Krazy Kat*, even in its odd vertical format, was a considerable hit at the time, and Hearst was sufficiently impressed to start Herriman on a Sunday *Krazy Kat* page, the first of which appeared on April 23, 1916. It was in these early Sunday pages that Herriman's graphic and poetic fancy first flowered to their fullest, dazzling the handful of readers (including Hearst) who were able to grasp the wonderful things Herriman was doing in the visual and narrative arts: pulling apart backgrounds in every panel, fluidly shifting scenes to fit mood and dialogue, utilizing the stark, angular shapes of the great American deserts to offset the colorful grotesqueness of his animal characters and their Byzantine interplay. What had been simplistic vaudeville in the plain, bare daily strips of the 1910s turned to operatic grandeur of concept and execution in the Sunday pages.

Before long, Krazy, Ignatz, and their brick-plagued romance had reached and gripped the attention of intellectuals and artists, from John Alden Carpenter, who wrote a full-length ballet based on *Krazy Kat* in 1922, to Gilbert Seldes, otherwise an indifferent and crotchety critic of the popular arts, who was moved to virtually deify *Krazy Kat* in print in his watershed work of 1924, *The Seven Lively Arts*.

Delighted with the response of intelligent readers, Herriman and Hearst enlarged upon the sparse content of the daily strip in the early 1920s, and transformed it into the daily version of the Sunday extravaganza that it remained for the next two decades. It was then that the great Herriman cast of characters, already partly developed in the seminal Sunday pages, were fully rounded into their complex roles in the ceaseless flow of the *Krazy Kat* drama. Offisa Bull Pupp, at first a very infrequent figure in the daily *Kat* of the early 1910s (who might turn up as a mailman or a baker as well as a kop), hit his characteristic club-wielding stride in the initial Sunday pages, then his full imaginative integration into the *Kat* theme after 1921. Developing beside him were such perennials as Mrs. Kwakk-Wak, Joe Stork, Kolin Kelly (the brick baker), Don Kiyote, the Krazy Katbird and the Krazy Katfish, Ignatz's wife and kiddies ("Mizzuz Mice" and Milton, Marshall, and Irving), Sancho Pansy, Mock Duck, Bum Bill Bee, Walter Cephus Austridge, Dr. Y. Zowl, Mimi, Kiskidee Kuku, Mr. Meeyowl and his son Gatita, and many, many, more.

It is part of the record, however, that the strip made no money for the syndicate after the 1920s, and that its continued appearance was due to Herriman's lifetime contract and Hearst's personal affection for *Krazy Kat*. It was folded on Herriman's death in 1944 quite simply because there was no profit left in it.

It is understandable in this context why only one minor publisher risked a book based on *Krazy Kat* during Herriman's lifetime (Saalfield, *Krazy Kat and Ignatz*, 1934), and why only two book collections of the strip (Henry Holt's *Krazy Kat* of 1946, and Nostalgia Press/Grosset & Dunlap's *Krazy Kat* of 1969) appeared after his death; together with a Herriman-illustrated pamphlet edition of the Carpenter ballet score, they constitute the only referential record of this major strip. (There were a number of animated cartoons based on the *Krazy Kat* strip; the first and best were the Herriman-supervised Hearst-Vitaphone releases of 1916-17; those which followed from other studios are only related to the Herriman work by the borrowed title.)

B.B.

KRESSE, HANS G. (1921-1992) Hans G. Kresse was a Dutch comic artist and writer, born December 3, 1921, in Amsterdam. Self-educated in art, Kresse's first comic strip was published in *De Verkenner*, the monthly magazine of the Dutch scouts, when he was 17. The strip was *Tarzan van de apen* ("Tarzan of the Apes") with obvious Hal Foster influences. Like Foster's first *Tarzan*, Kresse put the text below his comic strips in many cases. Also for *De Verkenner*, Kresse did *De Avonturen van Tom Texan* ("Adventures of Tom Texan") from 1940 to 1941. At the age of 23, he was one of the first artists to join the Marten Toonder studios. While there, he did strips like *Per Atoomraket naar Mars* ("To Mars by Atomic Rocket") and, for the newspaper *Trouw*, the daily strip *Robby Robijn* (1945-46). The Toonder influence on Kresse's work started showing strongly in *Robby Robijn*.

In 1946 the first episode of *Eric de Noorman* ("Eric the Norseman") was published in the Netherlands. In both plot and art it showed strong Toonder influences, the first adventure being a compromise between a Toonder suggestion of Atlantean science fiction combined with Kresse's concept of a historic hero. The series reached its climax around 1952 in the "Sword of Tyrfing" cycle, and continued in more routine fashion until 1964 in a number of newspapers and book reprints. In 1951, the

Hans G. Kresse, "Eric de Noorman." © Kresse.

Flemish newspaper *Het Laatste Nieuws* included the strip in its pages and started the weekly magazine *Pum Pum* (named after a character of the *Eric* strip). The first page of the magazine featured a serialized novel with large-sized illustrations of Eric's youth.

In addition to *Eric*, Kresse also created *Matho Tonga*, a Western for *De Kjeine Zondagsvriend* that was later continued in *Pep*, the Dutch weekly comics magazine founded in 1962. After withdrawing from comics for some time, Kresse returned to the medium with *Zorro* (1964), *Vidocq* (1965), and *Erwin* ("Son of Eric," 1966), all published in *Pep*. In 1972 Kresse started a historic series about North American Indians in the time of the Spanish invaders.

Despite his own inclinations as a writer, Kresse had to introduce speech balloons into his artwork in the 1960s. The addition of color to his artwork lent a new dimension to his already superb handling of black and white effects.

Kresse died March 12, 1992. As his health had been failing for some time and he wanted some control over who continued his prestigious series on the Native Americans, he had a clause added to his contract with the publisher that, if the series was to be continued after his death, the artwork should be handled by Dick Matena.

W.F.

KRIGSTEIN, BERNARD (1919-1990) American comic book artist born March 22, 1919, in Brooklyn, New York. Primarily a painter and illustrator, Bernie Krigstein entered the comic book field to earn extra money for his family before serving in the army during World War II. Most of his prewar work was uninspired superhero material for MLJ. After he returned from the war, however, Krigstein's interest in the field as an art form increased and he had short stints with Novelty (1947, on the *Bull's Eye Bill* Western strip), Fawcett (1948, on the Western *Golden Arrow* and jungle *Nyoka* features), and several other groups (Pines, National,

Hillman) before landing with Atlas in 1950. He was used there mainly on crime, horror, and science fiction stories. They were all second- and third-rate stories, but editor Stan Lee gave Krigstein considerable artistic freedom and he used these tales to experiment with the makeup and panel breakdown of the comic book page. And although some of the material was interesting, little of it matched the material he began producing for E.C. in 1953.

Krigstein joined E.C. in the last years of its vaunted "New Trend" and was one of the final arrivals in a stable that already included talents like Kurtzman, Davis, Crandall, Ingels, and others. But Krigstein was undoubtedly the most artistically talented—and the hardest to handle from the conformity standpoint. He was interested in expanding the formats of the comic page, and he used the three dozen or so stories he produced for E.C. to accomplish that goal, much to the chagrin of editors Bill Gaines and Al Feldstein. Whereas Feldstein wrote stories to fit E.C.'s relatively standard seven-panel page, Krigstein constantly altered the page layouts to suit his purposes. The captions that Feldstein wrote to explain what he visualized as one large panel were more often than not chopped up and spread across several of Krigstein's smaller ones. Krigstein was redesigning the comic book page along his own lines, and in the process produced some of the most powerful, innovative, and sophisticated storytelling techniques ever seen in comic books. His best known story is undoubtedly *Master Race*, and its 1955 appearance in *Impact* made it perhaps the most advanced graphic

Bernard Krigstein, "The Flying Machine." © William M. Gaines, Agent, Inc.

story of its time. The story was eventually reprinted in Nostalgia Press's 1971 *E.C. Horror Library*.

E.C.'s color books folded in early 1956, and after contributing material to the short-lived Picto-Fiction series and more stories for Atlas, Krigstein turned to commercial illustration. He eventually devoted his career to painting, concentrating primarily in oils, watercolors, and pastels, and became an accomplished painter with several awards and many one-man and group shows to his credit. He died on January 8, 1990, at his upstate New York home.

J.B.

"Kriminal," Luciano Secchi and Roberto Raviola. © Editoriale Corno.

KRIMINAL (Italy) The first comic book to feature an antihero as protagonist in the wake of *Diabolik*'s success, *Kriminal* appeared for the first time in August 1964.

Kriminal, who was dubbed the King of Crime, was a character of unusual cruelty and wickedness. The very first issue introduced very strong elements of sex and sadism, and this raised an immediate outcry from a number of civil groups, which denounced *Kriminal* as an "immoral publication." There began a long series of lawsuits and seizures that by then involved many other titles from different publishers attracted by the lucrative market for sex-cum-violence comic books. Finally the publisher of *Kriminal*, Andrea Corno of Editoriale Corno, became tired of the controversy and threw in the towel, radically altering the personality of the antihero. To put it succinctly, *Kriminal* became in short order the ex-King of Crime and switched from his antisocial status into the position of occasional defender of the law. The period of his fights with his nemesis, Commissioner Milton, of his surrealistic car flights, of his pitiless and senseless killings, was definitively over.

Married now, *Kriminal* became a suave gentleman-burglar in the tradition of Arsène Lupin, and his adventures, in the company of his trusted Oriental assistant Shan-Ton, had toned down considerably. One of the most famous creations of the *fumetto nero* ("black comic strip"), *Kriminal* was first published as a monthly, then as a fortnightly, and finally as a weekly (the only one of its kind). *Kriminal* was the product of a smooth-

working team signing "Magnus and Bunker" (in actuality Luciano Secchi and Roberto Raviola) who gave *Kriminal* an unsurpassed excellence of themes, mingling social and political satire with the killings, and an undeniable graphic quality. Unfortunately, the feature passed into the inept hands of mindless scriptwriters and mediocre draftsmen and the comic book finally folded after nearly 400 issues in 1973.

G.B.

KRÜGER, HANS MARTIN (192?-198?) Hans Martin Krüger (*nom de plume* Hans Martin) was born in the Sachsen-Anhalt region in the 1920s (the exact date of his birth is not known, at the artist's insistence). He grew up in the Harz mountain region in the 1930s and developed a love for drawing cartoons in school. Nevertheless, he decided to study natural science but in the 1940s he was handed a rifle and sent to war. Several shell splinter wounds and years as a prisoner of war changed his outlook on life. He had to work in the dismantling program, then worked on farms and as a gardener, and finally as a dramatic adviser.

He started a self-education program in order to develop his earlier penchant towards drawing, aiming towards the styles of Uderzo and Mordillo. In 1956 he started getting regular work from the cartoon pages of *TV-Fernsehwod* and *Neue Post*. In 1960 he drew his first comic strips for *Bild und Funk*, a radio and TV weekly. This strip starred Mufti, a toy donkey, and his friends in fairy tale adventures written by Karl-Heinz Barth. The series ended in 1968 despite the fact that 80 percent of children and 50 percent of adults regularly read the stories. Also with Karl-Heinz Barth as writer, Krüger drew comics for *Wochenend* for several years. These were adaptations of fairy tales like "Ali Baba."

In 1969, Krüger began drawing comic strips for *Hör Zu*, another radio and TV weekly. The first of these was *Jak-ki und Paff*, the fantastic story of a little boy and his rotund friend, the flying dragon Paff. The story was written by Jörg Ritter. This was followed up by the more substantial adventures of *Die Unbesiegbaren* ("The Invincibles"). This comic strip dealt with the adventures and misadventures of medieval knights in a completely humorous vein. The first two stories were reprinted in book form, and three records based on the comic strip were released. In 1975 the strip was revived, after a change in editorial policy had almost crowded comics out of *Hör Zu*. However, trouble developed over who actually owned the series, so it was axed again and not revived. Krüger died in the 1980s, with the date of his death as uncertain as he had wanted the date of his birth to be.

W.F.

KUBERT, JOE (1926-   ) American comic book and comic strip writer, artist, and editor born in Brooklyn, New York, during 1926. Kubert broke into the comic book business while still a student at New York's High School of Music and Art; in 1939, according to the artist, Harry "A" Chesler took him into his comic book shop at five dollars a week. Kubert says Chesler told him, "I can't use your work, but you show some talent. How about coming up here after school every day for a couple of hours. Just sit up here and draw. I'll have the other guys come and kind of critique your stuff."

After that unorthodox initiation, Kubert eventually began to publish work with the Holyoke group in

1942, drawing adventure strips like *Volton*, *Flag-Man* and several others. Also during the 1940s, Kubert drew for many other groups: at MLJ (1942-43), he drew *Boy Buddies* and *Black Witch*; at Quality (1942-43), he drew *Phantom Lady* and *Espionage*; at National (1943-49), he worked on many strips, including *Johnny Quick*, *Zatara*, *Newsboy Legion*, *Hawkman*, *Dr. Fate*, and *Flash*; and he also worked sporadically for Timely, Avon, Harvey, Fiction House, and others.

Artistically, Kubert's early work was crude but promising. Influenced mainly by Hal Foster and Alex Raymond, and later by comic book artist Mort Meskin, Kubert began to develop into a highly stylized craftsman, his work always utilizing stark blacks, heavy shading, and dynamic design and composition. His figures were not always anatomically correct, but they were fine studies of figures in action.

Perhaps Kubert's finest work came during the 1950-55 period when he was an editor at the St. Johns group on a short-lived prehistoric strip called *Tor*. The group's enterprising publisher, Archer St. John, allowed artists to package the complete book, so Kubert was given the opportunity to own, write, edit, draw, letter, ink, and color the *Tor* feature. Over its short-lived run, *Tor* carried much of Kubert's most brilliant drawings and most inventive stories. The strip became a comic book legend, so much so that National eventually allowed Kubert to revive the feature in 1975.

After the productive St. John period, Kubert continued to freelance, but most of his work was for National. He began to concentrate on war strips, and he and writer Bob Kanigher collaborated on two fine war features, *Sgt. Rock* and *Enemy Ace*. In particular, *Enemy Ace* was outstanding; a strip which took the

Joe Kubert, "Tarzan." © Edgar Rice Burroughs, Inc.

enemy point of view—in the form of World War I flying ace Baron Von Richthofen—the feature became a showcase for fine aerial artwork, sensitive and humanistic characterizations, and Kubert's consistently interesting layouts and page compositions. But throughout the 1950s and 1960s, Kubert also worked on other strips, most notably the excellent *Viking Prince* sword-and-sorcery strip, the revived *Hawkman*, and several others.

During 1966 and 1967, Kubert left comic books and drew the *Green Berets* syndicated newspaper strip for the Chicago Tribune-New York News Syndicate. Although it was an interestingly drawn feature, it was done during a time of increasing hostility towards war features, and Kubert returned to National as an editor in late 1967. He handled many features but the most notable was the National renditions of *Tarzan*. His work on the strip during the 1970s has garnered considerable acclaim for its "classic interpretation."

Since 1976 Kubert has devoted most of his time to the School of Cartoon and Graphic Art that he founded in Dover, New Jersey. The school has turned out such talent as Rick Veitch, Steve Bissette, Tom Yeates, and Timothy Truman. He has kept his hands at comics and illustration at the same time, briefly drawing the *Winnie Winkle* newspaper strip in the 1980s and contributing illustrations and covers to many comic books. In 1996 he published *Fax from Sarajevo*, a harrowing account of the civil war in Bosnia.

J.B.

KUDZU (U.S.) Doug Marlette used his southern roots and his years as a prizewinning editorial cartoonist for the *Atlanta Constitution*, the largest newspaper in Georgia, to shape the world of *Kudzu*, about a skinny young man with aspirations of being a writer and a desperate need to leave his tiny rural hometown of Bypass, North Carolina.

Kudzu began syndication on June 15, 1981. Some 16 years later, he's still stuck in Bypass working for a beer-bellied, redneck good ol' boy, Uncle Dub, at the family garage. It's Kudzu's desire to move to New York City and write for the *New Yorker*. (Marlette himself moved to New York to become editorial cartoonist for *Newsday*, Long Island's largest newspaper.)

In addition to good writing and art, Marlette's terrific cast of characters keeps *Kudzu* consistently funny. Over the years, the fundamentalist evangelist Rev. Will B. Dunn has come to rival Kudzu as the leading character of the strip. Rev. Dunn is the wildest preacher in comics since *Li'l Abner*'s Marryin' Sam. Dressed all in black, a homage of sorts to country singer Johnny Cash's man-in-black image, he's as interested in becoming a powerful televangelist as he is in saving souls. The good reverend has a passion for watching soap operas (no doubt to see sin in action so he can recognize it) and winning the church league basketball trophy. One is left with the impression Rev. Dunn has often bet the collection plate offering on the game. He is one of the funniest rogues in all comics.

Rev. Will B. Dunn, more than the other characters, allows Marlette to use his editorial cartoonist skills in *Kudzu*, which varies from gag-a-day to short continuity format. In one daily he's shown interviewing spiritualist Bhagwan Hasheesh (a name Al Capp of *Li'l Abner* fame would have been proud of) about his message. After learning the message is just "have a nice day," Rev. Dunn proclaims it dumb. Bhagwan

Hasheesh asks him if he owns a fleet of Rolls Royces, and Dunn ends the strip saying, "Have a nice day!"

Still, Kudzu himself is the heart of the strip. He's surrounded by traditional Southern "steel magnolia" women. His manipulative mother blackmails him emotionally to keep him in Bypass. The love of his life, blonde cheerleader-goddess Veranda, knows he exists but rarely admits it in public. For Veranda, watching the Miss America beauty pageant on television takes on religious significance. She and her talking mirror both know she has the potential to cause even the President of the United States a "major bimbo eruption." Kudzu's intellectual soulmates are Doris, his mute pet parrot whose thought balloons tell volumes, and Maurice, an African-American man his age who shares many of his interests but is much more realistic about life.

The strip can swing from Kudzu being introspective in a quietly humorous way to Rev. Will B. Dunn having a manic hellfire-and-brimstone conflagration of out-of-control riotous humor.

B.C.

KUHN, PIETER JOSEPH (1910-1966) Pieter Joseph Kuhn, a Dutch writer, comic artist, and graphic artist born May 22, 1910, joins Marten Toonder and Hans G. Kresse as one of the three biggest names in Dutch comics. Kuhn received art schooling at the Kunstnijverheidschool "Quellinus," which was followed by a course in lithography with the Senefelder printing office. He received his lithographer's diploma in 1929 and applied his artistic talent to advertising drawing. During World War II he created *Kapitein Rob* ("Captain Rob"), a daily adventure strip with running narrative below the pictures that first appeared in the newspaper *Het Parool* on December 11, 1945. *Kapitein Rob* lived through 72 adventures in *Het Parool* before the series suddenly ended when Kuhn died on January 20, 1966. The story "Rendezvous in Jamaica" was never completed in *Het Parool*. The Dutch fanzine *stripschrift* reprinted the last episode up to its untimely end, some 60 episodes beyond the last one appearing in *Het Parool*. Quite apparently, Kuhn had worked two months ahead of publication.

The first story, "De Avonturen van het zeilschip de Vrijheid" ("The Adventures of the Sailing Vessel *Freedom*"), was written and drawn by Kuhn as "a tale for boys, based on reality, in order to enlarge their maritime, geographic, and general knowledge." However, the first adventure's texts fell short of Kuhn's own expectations. Therefore, he started a cooperation with Dutch journalist Evert Werkman, who wrote most of the exploits of Captain Robert van Stoerum.

Kuhn, a sailing enthusiast, identified with his character, who sailed around the world in search of adventure. Whenever possible, Kuhn visited the places his hero was to visit. If traveling was out of the question, Kuhn pursued extensive research so his facts would be correct. Thus the strip had an overall realism that was responsible for the success of *Kapitein Rob*. With the addition of Professor Lupardi, the inevitable mad scientist, the comic strip took a turn toward science fiction.

Practically all of the captain's adventures were reprinted in book form. Foreign editions were published in England, Finland, Denmark, Germany, France, Italy, Spain, Poland, Brazil, and other countries. Some of these editions used speech balloons instead of the narrative below the strip.

W.F.

KULAFU (Philippines) One of the very first Filipino artists to illustrate *Tarzan* was Johnny Perez. His work appeared in *Bannawag*, a periodical written in Ilokano, in 1934. Appearing in the same publication was another jungle hero called *Kulafu*, the Filipino Tarzan, and it was drawn by Francisco Reyes (the elder).

The works of Rudyard Kipling and Edgar Rice Burroughs, as well as the myths and legends of feral children, have influenced many variations of the jungle hero theme. In 1934, Francisco V. Coching drew *Marabini*, the jungle girl, for *Liwayway*. During the late 1940s and the early 1950s he wrote and illustrated the *Tarzan*-inspired jungle strip, *Hagibis*, which also appeared in *Liwayway*. For *Pilipino Komiks* he created *Dumagit* in 1953.

Nestor Redondo, whose *Tarzan* illustrations have been published by various American publications, drew *Diwani* in the 1950s. It is considered by many to be the most beautifully rendered jungle novel to appear in comic books, rivaled only by *Rima*, which was also done by Redondo for DC Comics (U.S.). In 1963 he teamed up with Mars Ravelo to do *Devlin* for *Redondo Komix*. He also did *Tani*, which was later drawn by Vic Catan.

Larry Alcala did a hilarious strip containing *Tarzan*, and Alfredo Alcala did a satire on *Tarzan* for his humorous feature *00 Ongoy*, about a simian private eye. One of the most popular of the *Tarzan*-type strip heroes was *Og*. The strip was drawn by Jess Ramos and was eventually made into a movie starring Jesus Ramos.

On October 21, 1971, the weekly comic book *Nora Aunor Superstar* serialized *Tarzan and the Brown Prince*. It was illustrated by Franc Reyes (the younger). It ran consecutively for 16 chapters until February 14, 1972. This feature was made into a movie starring Steve Hawkes as Tarzan and Robin Aristorenas as the Brown Prince. Later on, Franc Reyes illustrated *Tarzan of the Apes* for National (U.S.).

The first artist in the Philippines to work on the syndicated Sunday *Tarzan* feature was Alex Niño. He also drew *Korak, The Son of Tarzan* for DC (U.S.). But before working on any American jungle strips, he illustrated, in the various *Tagalog Komiks*, many jungle series such as *Sargon, Tsannga Rannga, Gruaga*, and *Mga Ma tang Naglilivab* ("The Eyes That Glow"). Niño stopped doing *Korak* when he left the Philippines to visit the United States, and the strip was turned over to the capable Rudy Florese.

Virgilio Redondo contributed to the long list of tree-swingers by writing and illustrating the exciting jungle adventure *Buntala*. This was drawn in a format reminiscent of Hal Foster's *Tarzan*. Elpidio Torres visualized the stirring experiences and the romantic escapades of *Robina*, the jungle maiden.

Other artists who have drawn *Tarzan* for various publications are Jesse Santos, Frank Magsino, Edna Jundis, Pit Capili, Seg Belale, and Danny Bulanadi. The following individuals have illustrated *Tarzan*-type characters for foreign publications—Steve Gan, Sonny Trinidad, Tony Zuñiga, and Noly Zamora.

O.J.

KUMA (Germany) *Kuma* was Germany's very own jungle boy strip in the time-honored Kipling vein. It might very well be argued that *Kuma* was a Spanish strip as the artwork was done by Spanish artist Rafael Mendez. However, as the comic series was produced originally for a German readership, just as many American comic books are now produced in Spain or in the Philippines, Kuma definitely was a German comic strip.

When, in April 1971, the comic book *prima* (soon retitled *primo*) was started, it contained funnies and reprints of the *Prince Valiant* strip. Issue number 22 of 1972 introduced Arturo del Castillo's excellent Western *Randall*, and the first issue of 1973 featured material from the now defunct *Trinca*. The trend toward adventure comics had been set. Issue 18 of that same year contained the first original entry to the Kauka line of adventure comics: *Kuma*.

Kuma was a sandy-haired boy who grew up among the animals of the African jungle. His best friend was Sharim the wolf. Kuma spoke all of the animal languages; this came in very handy in the first story, when Kuma was captured by a native tribe and put into a hut where a cobra was supposed to finish him off. With a glowing description of what the freedom of the jungle outside meant, Kuma convinced the deadly snake not to waste its poison on him and to help in the escape effort.

In order to justify the introduction of this adventure strip, much care was given to add a decidedly educational touch by depicting in true-to-life (almost academic) delineation as many animals as could be fitted into the stories without detracting from the dramatic structure of the story. This was slightly overdone, however, as it turned the animals into actors with quite a bit of dialogue. This may have accounted for the fact that *Kuma* did not turn into the success that had been hoped for. The formula was much more readily accepted in foreign countries, but in Germany the feature was discontinued after several continued stories in *primo*, in the *Action Comic* albums and in the digest-sized *Super Action*.

This series will be remembered for its hints of Wayne Boring in the depiction of humans.

W.F.

KURTZMAN, HARVEY (1924-1993) American comic book and comic strip artist, writer, and editor born October 3, 1924, in New York City. After studies at the High School of Music and Art and at Cooper Union, Kurtzman's first comic book work appeared in 1943 on Ace's *Magno* and *Unknown Soldier* adventure features. In 1945, he produced an aviatrix strip, *Black Venus*, and then drew *The Black Bull* for Prize. Also during this time, Kurtzman created *Silver Linings*, an acclaimed but rare strip, for the Sunday supplement of the *Herald-Tribune*. He moved to Timely and several other groups in 1945 and produced humor features and gags, most notably *Hey Look*, a one-page gag strip.

In 1950, Kurtzman moved to E. C. and produced several fine science fiction stories for the burgeoning "New Trend" line. Within six months, he was editing a war/adventure book called *Two-Fisted Tales*. *Frontline Combat* followed immediately, and Kurtzman wrote and drew pencil layouts for almost all of the two books' tales. Perhaps the best description of his totally unique and refreshing material came from artist Gil Kane. Kurtzman "had a feeling for humane things, a

Harvey Kurtzman, "Air Burst." © William M. Gaines, Agent, Inc.

feeling for profundity. There was a reek of death, a sense of futility about war that just never occurred in anything else I've read in comics," Kane said.

Kurtzman also began E.C.'s *Mad* in November, 1952, and the book immediately became an American phenomenon. It is impossible to adequately describe all of Kurtzman's innovations here, but among them were his introduction of popular humorists to comic books; parodies of every facet of American life, including comics, movies, television, magazines, and advertising; development of the humor talents of Wood, Elder, and Davis; and his supervision of *Mad*'s transition from color comic book to black-and-white magazine.

Kurtzman left *Mad* in 1955, but *Playboy*'s Hugh Hefner hired him in 1957 to staff his new humor magazine, *Trump*. Thanks to a lavish budget and great talent, the book was an artistic success. But it was a financial disaster, and folded after two issues. Kurtzman then headed an artists' syndicate that published *Humbug*, a 15-cent black-and-white comic that lasted only 11 issues. Despite its short stay, however, Kurtzman—who was limiting himself to writing and editing—produced some of his sharpest, timeliest, and most impressive satire here. He and publisher Jim Warren then became partners in a low-budget humor magazine called *Help!* Kurtzman's "Public Gallery" introduced some of the earliest work by underground cartoonists Jay Lynch, Robert Crumb, and Gilbert Shelton.

Shortly before *Help!* folded, Kurtzman and Elder launched *Little Annie Fanny*, a sexual pollyanna and parody of *Little Orphan Annie*, in the October 1962 issue of *Playboy*. It was the most lavish comic strip ever produced in America. And keying off the exploits of *Annie*, Kurtzman wrote some of the 1960s and '70s most mature and biting satire. In the 1970s, he also drew underground material for *Bijou* and produced four paperbacks of original material, most notably *The Jungle Book*, which contained four stories written and drawn by Kurtzman.

From 1980 to 1985 Kurtzman turned out a comic strip titled *Betsy's Buddies*, in collaboration with his former student Sarah Downs. He also briefly published *Nuts!*, a humor magazine in paperback format. In his later years he wrote two books of memoirs, *My Life as*

a *Cartoonist* (1988) and *Harvey Kurtzman's Strange Adventures* (1991). He died in Mount Vernon, New York, on February 21, 1993.

J.B.

KUWATA, JIRŌ (1935-   ) Japanese comic book artist born April 17, 1935, in Osaka. At the age of 13, while he was still a first-year student in junior high school, Jirō Kuwata had his first comic strip published. The strip was *Kaiki Seidan*, a science-fiction story that Kuwata created under the influence of Osamu Tezuka's *Tarzan no Himitsukichi* ("Tarzan's Secret Base"). At 15, Kuwata created a new strip, *Daihikyō* ("The Big Unexplored Lands"), which was published serially in *Tanteiō*. From then on, Kuwata devoted himself entirely to comics, drawing *Rocket Tarō* for the monthly *Omoshiro Book*, *Maboroshi Kozō* for *Shōnen Gahō*, and *Tantei Gorō* ("Goro the Detective") for the monthly *Bokura* (1955-56).

In 1957 Kuwata's first popularly acclaimed strip, *Maborashi Tantei*, a detective feature, appeared in *Shōnen Gahō*. The next year he created his greatest comic strip, *Gekkō Kamen* ("The Man with the Moonlight Mask," also a detective strip). *Gekkō Kamen* met with great success and was followed by a number of other comic features: *8-Man* (about an android detective) and *Android Pini* (a science-fiction story), both in

Jirō Kuwata.

Konstantin Kuznjecov, "Three Lives". © Konstantin Kuznjecov.

1960; *Mao Dangā* and *Chōken Leap* ("Leap the Super Robot Dog"), both in 1965; *The Time Tunnel* in 1967, and many others.

Kuwata's line and art style are icy-cold and metallic, well-suited for science fiction and similar stories. The influence of the American comic strip masters can be found in Kuwata's love for contrasted compositions, but he has evolved a style of his own. In turn he has influenced a number of young Japanese artist such as Takahuru Kusunoki, Haruo Koyama, and Yū Matsuhisa. In the 1980s Kuwata had an epiphany and converted to Buddhism; since that time he has been doing religious comic books devoted to the life of Buddha and to Buddhism's doctrine and precepts.

H.K.

KUZNJECOV, KONSTANTIN (1895-19??) Serbian comic artist between two world wars. Of his education and private life, little is known. Konstantin Kuznjecov was Russian, born in Saint Petersburg on May 3, 1895. After the Bolshevik Revolution, he moved to Serbia, living first in Pančevo then in Belgrade, where he began to work in applied art.

Kuznjecov had a permanent job painting advertisements in the large department store Mitić, and he also illustrated books, magazines, and daily newspapers, and drew caricatures. Before World War II, he published about 30 comics. His first comic was *Majka* ("Mother"). It started in installments on January 4, 1937, in the 61st issue of the comics magazine *Mika Miš*. *Majka* featured "romanticized historical events from Serbian past," and with his second comic endeavor, *Kraljević Marko* ("Prince Marko"), and some of his subsequent comics, such as *Knjaz Miloš* ("Duke Miloš"), constituted one thematic circle of Kuznjecov's work. In fact it was a genre; knowledge of Serbian his-

tory, literature, folklore, and epic tradition were necessary to understand these comics.

Kuznjecov adapted several world-famous novels, primarily Russian, into comics, including: *Hadži Murat* (1937-38) by Leo N. Tolstoy, *Stenyka Razyn* (1940) and *Christmas Eve* by Nikolay V. Gogol, *Don Quxote* (1940-41) by Cervantes, and three works of Aleksandar S. Pushkin: *The Queen of Spades* (1940), *Fairytale about Tzar Saltan* (1940), and *Fable about Little Golden Rooster* (1940). Around this time, he also created comics based on the Arabian Nights and other fairytales: *Sinbad the Sailor* (*Mika Mis*, 1938), *Aladin and His Magic Lamp* (1938), *Ali Baba and 40 Thieves* (1938), and *The Magic Flute* (1940-41).

Between 1937 and 1938, three related comics appeared in *Mika Miš*: *In the Kingdom of Apes*, *In the Wild West*, and *The Shipwrecked*. All three featured two anthropomorphic chimpanzees, Sony and Tony, who were, by stylization and ambiance, neighbors of Mickey Mouse and Donald Duck. The fifth circle are classic adventure stories: *Mysteries of Chicago* (1937-38), *Orient Express* (1938), and two episodes about Ben Kerigan, an Intelligence Service agent ("Descendant of Ghengis Khan" and "Green Dragon," 1937-38).

Kuznjecov's most effective comics were his stories of mysticism, most successfully *Grofica Margo* ("Duchess Margot"), *Baron vampir*, and *Tri života* ("Three Lives"). These comics, first published in *Mika Miš* between 1938 and 1940, unrolled in elegiac and picturesque landscapes, dark forests, stilled swamps, abandoned greenfields, quiet graveyards, and lonely castles. In the stories, Kuznjecov attempted to create an atmosphere mixing Gothic novels and the horror movies that were popular between the two world wars.

The erudition of this author is best shown by the fact that he wrote all but five of the scripts for his approximately 40 comics. The quality of his work showed in its success abroad, mostly in France.

Evidently, until World War II he worked for only two magazines, *Mika Miš* and *PZ*. When Belgrade was bombarded and occupied by Germans in April 1941, Serbian publishers stopped publishing their magazines. Suddenly word got around, from sources unknown, that Kuznjecov was working for S Department, in charge of propaganda for the occupational German military command of Serbia. This rumor was true. He designed and illustrated posters, booklets, leaflets, and other propagandic materials for the Nazis and was also the caricaturist of the satirical-humorous magazine *Bodljikavo prase* ("Porcupine"), published also by S Department. The crescendo of this activity was the starting of *Mali Zabavnik* ("Little Entertainer") magazine on December 1, 1943. Of the staff, only the editor was named on the masthead; authors, artists, and writers all remained anonymous, fearing the retaliation of their neighbors and the Resistance movement. Five comics appeared in the first issue; at least two can be ascribed to Kuznjecov (the style is obvious): *Between Love and Fatherland* and *Frog Prince*.

After World War II, Kuznjecov managed to escape into the West; to Austria, according to some hints. It seems that he continued with drawing and illustration there. The year of his death is not known.

S.I.

KYOJIN NO HOSHI (Japan) *Kyojin no Hoshi* ("The Star of the Giants"), created by Ikki Kajiwara (script) and Noboru Kawasaki (artwork), made its debut in the May 1966 issue of *Shōnen* magazine.

The story related the growth of Hyūma Hoshi (Hyūma is derived from the word "humanism"), the son of Ittetsu Hoshi, once a famous ballplayer on the Kyojin team whose career had been cut short by the war. Ittetsu wanted his son to be a player with the Kyojin (the most famous baseball team in Japan) and trained him from childhood for this purpose. After a promising start as a pitcher for his high school team, Hyūma was scouted by 11 different professional teams (but not the Kyojin!) and he turned down all offers. Training intensively, he finally passed the test of the Kyojin and was accepted into the club.

The rest of the strip followed Hyūma as he experienced the vicissitudes of the competitive life, winning some, losing some. A father-son rivalry developed when Ittetsu was hired as coach for the rival Chūnichi Dragons. Ittetsu coached the powerful black batter Armstrong Ozma to defeat his son. Hyuma won the first challenge but lost to Ozma on the second. He then developed a new pitching method with which he

"Kyojin no Hoshi," Noboru Kawasaki. © *Shōnen.*

defeated Ozma decisively, but the effort had been strenuous and Hyūma tore his arm muscles. On this mixed note of victory and sorrow the strip ended, as Hyūma left the Kyojin and baseball to the plaudits of his fans (March 1971). *Kyojin no Hoshi* was more than a simple baseball strip; its central theme was a young man's coming of age and the ambiguous relation between son and father. The strip was published in book form (19 books selling over 5 million copies) and inspired a series of animated cartoons as well as a stage play and several novels. It also extended the vogue of the comic strip from children to young adults.

H.K.

LABORNE, DANIEL (1902-1990) French cartoonist Daniel Laborne was born in Verneuil sur Avre, in Normandy, on October 6, 1902. Upon graduation from vocational high school, he started his career as an industrial draftsman; when the Great Depression hit France in 1930 and he was laid off, he turned his drawing abilities to illustration and cartooning. His humorous drawings and caricatures soon appeared in a number of French magazines, including the venerable *Chat Noir*, to which he was one of the last contributors. Later he extended his freelance activities to the daily press, and his sports illustrations were published as early as 1938 in the Paris evening paper *Ce Soir*.

It was in the pages of another Paris daily, *Le Petit Parisien*, that he created in 1939 his first comic strip, the famous *Lariflette*, which was to last for almost half a century. The title character, Désiré Lariflette, was a typically French "little man," bent on his comfort, his leisure, and his meals. Perpetually wearing a collapsed cylinder hat and a puzzled expression, he tried to cope with the multifarious vagaries of life, the nagging of his formidable wife Bichette, and the pranks of his young son Tatave.

After a two-year hiatus during World War II, *Lariflette* resurfaced in 1945 in the children's weekly *Coq Hardi*, and a little later in syndication to French and foreign newspapers. The character grew to even greater popularity in the immediate postwar period and gave rise to two spin-offs, *Polop le Caïd* ("Polop the Toughie"), featuring the exploits of his wiseguy pal, and *Tatave*, which starred his unruly son. Laborne drew the daily adventures of Lariflette until ill-health finally forced him to abandon the character in 1988; he died two years later at his home in Argenteuil, near Paris.

Laborne received a number of distinctions during his lifetime, but he was proudest of having been deputy-mayor of Montmartre. He was a conscientious and unassuming craftsman whose talents were recognized by French historians only after his death.

M.H.

LANCE (U.S.) Warren Tufts' self-syndicated *Lance* (distributed by Warren Tufts Enterprises to start on Sunday, June 5, 1955) was one of the last full-page Sunday strips, intended to be reproduced in the *Prince Valiant* manner. It was certainly the best of the page-high adventure strips undertaken after the 1930s, although inferior to Tufts' own preceding half-page daily, *Casey Ruggles*. Like *Ruggles* (which Tufts abandoned to United Features in order to have complete control over his own work), *Lance* was a historically oriented strip, taking place around the Kansas and Missouri area in the 1840s rather than in California during the gold rush days.

The hero, Lance St. Lorne, is a second lieutenant in the U.S. 1st Dragoons, serving at Fort Leavenworth, Kansas. The Dragoons are fighting the Sioux, and the strip narrative develops from this situation, introducing later on—as with *Casey Ruggles*—a number of actual historical figures, including Kit Carson. Again as in *Ruggles*, Tufts is a forceful, realistic storyteller for adults: blood flows copiously where necessary, and the extramarital sexual relationships among the characters are related frankly. Tufts' raw, hard-bitten style and content strikes a sharp contrast with Harold Foster's bland art and cheerful narrative of the period in his *Prince Valiant*.

The strip audience of the time was no more ready for *Lance* than they had been for *Casey Ruggles*, however, and newspaper editors began to feel that the relatively tepid public response did not justify a full page for Tufts' strip. Tufts was forced to supply a half-page, then a third-page version. Some papers dropped the strip before it had run a year, and its original distribution was not extensive. Others carried it into its third year and then cut it. Because Tufts never had much interest in discussing the details of his work, it is impossible to pinpoint the date of the last Lance strip distributed, but the last episode printed in the several subscribing newspapers available for review was on

QUAND FAUT Y ALLER...

– Allons, Lariflette, réveillez--vous !

– Je sais que vous êtes bien ici !

– Mais la loi le veut : votre tour est venu...

...de connaître les joies des vacances !

Daniel Laborne, "Lariflette." © D. Laborne.

May 12, 1957. Like *Ruggles*, *Lance* deserves the time and effort of a full reprinting.

B.B.

THIS IS THE WORST PART OF THE HOLIDAY... WAITING FOR THE AIRPORT BUS!

"The Larks," Jack Dunkley. © Daily Mirror Newspapers Ltd.

LARKS, THE (G.B.) *The Larks* is a gag-a-day family situation strip introduced in the *Daily Mirror* on August 5, 1957. First scripted by the radio comedy writing team of Bill Kelly and Arthur Lay, then by Robert St. John Cooper, it was written by television scriptwriter Brian Cooke since 1963. Cooke, himself no mean cartoonist in his prewriting days, brought the characters of the Lark family out of the working class and into the middle class. A typical balloon of 1961 has the wife and mother, Sal Lark, addressing her little lad Stevie thus: "You keep your thievin' cake-'ooks off these, young Stevie, or there'll be dead trouble!" In the strip's later years, apart from the occasional "flippin'," Sal's speech became more refined. Sam Lark, the breadwinner, worked in a white coat at the local supermarket, run by tightfisted Mr. McCreep. The other Lark child was Susie, and for a few years the children were allowed to grow up naturally within the strip. Once Stevie had started work and Susie started school, however, their ages were frozen, as were those of the Newley family next door, with their young twins, Nicholas and Louise. A running gag was Sam Lark's attempts to teach Mike Newley to drive. Other regulars included Milkie the Milkman and the Larks' cat, So-so. The latter is believed to be the only cartoon cat who thinks in rhyme!

The Larks was drawn by Jack Dunkley in his familiarly flexible line. It is no longer being published.

D.G.

LARSEN, KNUD V. (1930-) Knud V. Larsen, Danish comic artist born in Copenhagen on May 3, 1930, now lives in Småland, Sweden. He has been drawing ever since he can remember; he started practicing magic tricks at age 8 and got interested in hypnotism at age 16. All of these interests came in handy years later, when he decided to create a comic strip of his own, *Dr. Merling*. The main character of the strip,

Albert Merling—an illusionist by profession—is the alter ego of Knud V. Larsen, who derived the name from King Arthur's wizard Merlin and used it when performing his own magic tricks. Larsen tried to sell the comic strip as far back as 1963, but at the time most Scandinavian newspapers were buying comics from foreign markets. So the strip did not start until 1970. It is now carried by, among other papers, *Berlingske Tidende* of Copenhagen and *Helsingin Sanomt* of Helsinki. Reprints have also appeared in the Swedish comic book *Serie-Pressen*.

Before turning his alter ego into a comic strip based in the 1870s, Larsen took time to study graphic art from scratch. In 1951 he finished his studies in painting and decorating, and up until 1954 he taught art at the technical school of Frederiksberg, Denmark, while at the same time perfecting the magic tricks he performed.

He worked up to the position of art director in an advertising agency and, under four pseudonyms, did book illustrations and newspaper cartoons. He always dreamed of doing a comic strip, and his perseverance finally paid off. His knowledge of human psychology, which he acquired through performing magic tricks, may have been of additional help.

Larsen's imagination never fails to produce interesting reading, thanks to plots bordering on the fantastic and occult. He is recognizably fascinated by the age of Jules Verne, and his bold and very personal style employs a special technique to include details from illustrations of the 1870s; his style also evokes the necessary mood for making this type of strip a success.

W.F.

LARSON, GARY (1950-) The creator of the unique panel *The Far Side* was born on August 14, 1950, in Tacoma, Washington. He particularly liked *Mad* magazine and Gahan Wilson's *Playboy* cartoons during his adolescence, even though he displayed no particular inclination then toward the cartooning profession. After graduating from Washington State University with a communications degree in 1973, he moved to Seattle. Employed as a music store clerk, he created six animal cartoons and submitted them to the nature magazine *Pacific Search* in 1976. All were accepted, and after Larson got a job with the Humane Society, his panel, now titled *Nature's Way*, was promoted to the *Seattle Times*. When his feature was canceled by that paper two years later, the cartoonist impressed the *San Francisco Chronicle*'s reticent editor with his twistedly funny panel, which resulted in a five-year syndication contract with Chronicle Features. Given its permanent title, *The Far Side*, by the syndicate, the panel officially debuted on January 1, 1980. Universal Press Syndicate began distributing it four years later, allowing Larson a 14-month sabbatical starting in late 1988. Upon his return, new releases were reduced to five days a week, allowing more opportunity for the development of increased merchandising, color features in his best-selling books, and animated projects handled by his company, FarWorks.

Since abruptly retiring *The Far Side* on the first day of 1995, the private artist has kept busy developing new projects, in addition to studying jazz guitar and writing a children's book.

B.J.

"Voila! . . . Your new dream home! If you like it,
I can get a crew mixing wood fibers and saliva
as early as tomorrow."

Gary Larson, "The Far Side." © Universal Press Syndicate.

LASSWELL, FRED (1916-   )   As an eight-year-old tyke leaving Gainesville, Florida, for Tampa, Fred Lasswell may well have been whistling and singing "Barney Google, with his goo-goo-googly eyes" (the hit song of 1923), without the remotest inkling that he'd be drawing the adventures of Billy De Beck's shrimp-sized hero under De Beck's supervision in another 10 years. But that, of course, is exactly what happened.

Born in 1916 in Kennett, Missouri, (not far from the Kentucky homeland of the Snuffy Smith ménage, which he was later to guide to continuing fame after their creator's death), Lasswell and his parents moved to Gainesville when he was six. In Tampa two years later, he attended Hillsborough High School, from which he graduated into a job as sports cartoonist for the *Tampa Daily Times* circa 1928. A devotee of the pen and ink work of Charles Dana Gibson, Lasswell developed his comic techniques on the *Times* until a poster he had done for a golf tournament at the nearby Palma Ceia Club in 1933 attracted the eye of the golfing rover Billy De Beck. De Beck, who had reached the age where he wanted to groom a younger man to help him with the *Barney Google* strip, saw in Lasswell's skillful lines just the potential talent he wanted.

He called Lasswell at the *Times* and asked if he wanted to go to work on *Barney*. Lasswell accepted, and for the next nine years until De Beck's death in 1942 he worked and traveled with De Beck constantly, until his style was virtually identical to that of his mentor. Lasswell's continuation of *Barney* was—in its early years, at least—one of the most successful prolongations of a major comic in strip history. (Lasswell's work on the Sunday *Bunky* was even more effective, though the strip was dropped in the early 1950s.) Later, when Lasswell was forced, by a King Features' edict prohibiting continuity in the syndicate's humorously drawn strips, to drop narrative for day-to-day gags, the fine edge of the strip was dulled. Lasswell's artistry, however, has not flagged, and the daily and Sunday *Barney Google and Snuffy Smith* remains a visual pleasure on any comic page it graces.

Lasswell himself is a remarkable man of many accomplishments: a flight radio operator in World War II; creator of a major wartime strip, *Hashmark*, for *Leatherneck Magazine;* inventor of a successful citrus fruit harvester; member of the American Society of Agricultural Engineers; developer of a technique to enable the blind to read comic strips on their own; and winner of many strip awards, including the Reuben in 1964. Snuffy would remark that Lasswell was "tetched in the haid"—with genius of a very memorable sort.

B.B.

Lasswell, affectionately known to all as "Uncle Fred," has kept remarkably active at an age when most people dream of retiring. In addition to turning out *Barney Google and Snuffy Smith* daily and Sundays, he has produced a number of *Draw and Color with Uncle Fred* videos and developed his own web page on the Internet. He received the National Cartoonists Society's Elzie Segar Award for outstanding contribution to the art of cartooning twice, in 1984 and 1994. The only surviving charter member of NCS, he celebrated 50 years with the society in 1996.

M.H.

LAT *see* Khalid, Mohamed Nor.

LAVADO, JOAQUIN (1932-   ) An Argentine cartoonist born in Mendoza on July 17, 1932, to Spanish immigrants, Joaquin Lavado (better known under his pseudonym "Quino") displayed drawing abilities at an early age. One of his maternal uncles, Joaquin Téjon, was a commercial artist, and he often would draw to amuse his nephew (who was to recall years later: "To me it was a thing of magic; that is when I decided to become a cartoonist"). Quino studied at the Buenos Aires Art Institute, contributing hundreds of cartoons and humor pages to Argentine publications all the while. In this phase of his career Quino distinguished himself as a graphic historian and critic of his time and his people, with his keen political perceptions and his depictions of television and its myths. In 1963 an anthology of his best cartoons, *Mondo Quino*, was published with great success in Buenos Aires.

In 1964 Quino created his great comic strip *Mafalda*, at first as a Sunday page, and, starting in 1973, as a daily strip. This humorous saga of a precocious and argumentative little girl was greeted with universal acclaim. Quino is regarded as the foremost Argentine cartoonist, and his work is being published throughout the world. Since discontinuing *Mafalda* in 1973, he has devoted his talents to illustration and humor cartooning.

L.G.

LAVINIA 2.016 (Spain) Enric Sío's first work as an independent and original cartoonist was *Lavinia 2.016 o la guerra dels poetas* ("Lavinia 2016, or the War of the Poets"), which first appeared in issue 68 (January 1968) of the Catalan-language monthly *Oriflama* and continued until issue 76 (October 1968).

The script, by Emili Teixido, described life in a city of the future, easily recognized as Barcelona, under a

"Lavinia 2.016," Enric Sío. © Enric Sío.

matriarchal regime where words are prohibited and the image triumphs (a theme similar to that of Ray Bradbury's *Fahrenheit 451*). The poets revolt and decide to use words once again, for which they are jailed and prosecuted. Starting from this premise, Sío opened on a parodic style not too well defined at first, but his graphic evolution was so swift that before long he had achieved the very personal style that he was later to utilize on *Sorang* and *Nus*, the other two works corresponding to the first stage of his artistic development.

A political work in code, where the symbols are very elementary, *Lavinia* presented, in humorous and caricatural guise, well-known personalities of the Catalan cultural left: singers, writers, playwrights, and poets, who mingled freely and interacted with comic strip characters like Snoopy, mythic figures like Bonnie (of Bonnie and Clyde), reminiscences of childhood readings, images from advertising, and toys and montages of news pictures.

L.G.

LAZARUS, MEL (1927-   ) American cartoonist, born in Brooklyn, New York, on May 3, 1927. Mel Lazarus was educated in public schools and hated the whole process ("I even flunked art in high school," he revealed proudly in 1964). After high school he freelanced for magazines, then became assistant on Al Capp's *Li'l Abner* (he was later to recount these experiences in a novel entitled *The Boss Is Crazy, Too*). In the early 1950s he created two weekly panels, *Wee Women* and *Li'l One*, both about precocious children.

In February 1957, Mel Lazarus (under the pseudonym "Mell") launched his first full-fledged comic strip, *Miss Peach*, about a classroom full of rebellious kids. It met with instant success. In 1966, in collaboration with artist Jack Rickard and under the pseudonym "Fulton," he produced the short-lived *Pauline McPeril*, a tongue-in-cheek adventure strip taking off on Pearl White's cliff-hanging serial *The Perils of Pauline*. Mel (or Mell, as he prefers to spell his first name) Lazarus was to be more successful with *Momma*, a rollicking strip that he created in November 1970, based on the "Jewish mother" stereotype.

An avowed admirer of Walt Kelly and Charles Schulz, Lazarus is a member of that small group of cartoonists who helped revive the humor strip in the 1950s and 1960s. His creations, while not on a par with *Peanuts* or *Pogo*, occupy nonetheless an honorable place in what has come to be called "the sophisticated school" of comics.

In 1973 and again in 1979 Lazarus was named Best Humor Strip Cartoonist by the National Cartoonists Society; and in 1982 he won the coveted Reuben Award. Very active in his profession, he served as a board member of NCS in the 1980s and was its president from 1989 to 1993.

M.H.

LEAV, MORT (1916-   ) American comic book artist, born in New York City on July 9, 1916. Leav's only art training came in WPA-sponsored adult education courses during the Great Depression. By 1936, however, he was handling daily and Sunday strips, along with sports and editorial cartoons for Editors Press Service, a South American syndicate based in New York. He broke into comic books in 1941 when he joined the S. M. Iger shop and began drawing a minor feature called *ZX-5, Spies in Action* for Fiction House.

He later drew *Doll Man* and *Uncle Sam* for Quality and *The Hangman* for MLJ while still with Iger.

In 1942, the shop began packaging books for Hillman, and it was then that Leav designed his most famous character. Writer Harry Stein had invented a supporting character called The Heap, and while most other artists laughed Stein's idea off, Leav visualized a hulking, brutish, eight-foot-tall green and brown swamp monster covered with hair. His eerie, illustrative approach to The Heap's first appearance (which came in the *Skywolf* strip in *Air Fighters Comics*) helped create one of the slickest and most original stories produced at the time.

Leav also began working for Busy Arnold's Quality group in 1942 and became a staff artist on features like *Blackhawk* and *Kid Eternity*. Always underrated throughout his career, Leav's work was never artistically overshadowed, even though Quality boasted recognized talents like Lou Fine, Jack Cole, and Reed Crandall. Forced to leave Quality when he was drafted in 1943, Leav turned his attention to illustrating army magazines. His work is probably best noted for his devastating caricatures of Adolf Hitler as a hairy, unkempt petty tyrant.

After the war, Leav did several *Captain America* tales for Timely and several love stories for Ziff-Davis before becoming art director and chief artist at Orbit Publications in 1946. For eight years, he drew almost all the covers and lead stories for books such as *Wild Bill Pecos*, *Wanted*, and *Patches*. Leav left Orbit in 1954, and after two years as a freelance commercial artist, he joined the prestigious Benton and Bowles Advertising Agency. There he drew some of the first television storyboards and became the agency's "TV art director." He is now retired.

J.B.

LECTRON, E. *see* Fine, Louis.

LEE, JIM (1964-   ) American comic-book artist Jim Lee was born in Seoul, South Korea, on August 11, 1964. He came to the United States as a youth and received most of his education at American schools. Lee graduated from Princeton University with a degree in psychology; he is largely self-taught in art. His love of art and of comics triumphed over his formal studies, and he got his first job in the field in 1987 at Marvel, where he worked as one of the artists on *Alpha Flight*. It was his work on the *Punisher War Journal* the next year that brought him to the attention of fans. After that he went from strength to strength, capping his career at Marvel with the second series of *X-Men*, which he pencilled; its first issue was published in five

Jim Lee, "X-Men." © Marvel Comics.

different editions with a total print run of 8 million copies.

That same year, 1991, saw Lee and other Marvel artists form their own company, Image Comics. At Image he created *WildC.A.T.S. Covert Action Teams* in 1992 and *Stormwatch* in 1993. These both came under his own Wildstorm Productions imprint, which also publishes *WetWorks* and *Team 7,* along with the highly successful *Gen 13*, released initially as a miniseries in 1994, and the next year as a regular monthly series. In 1996 he was contracted by Marvel to produce new stories for *Iron Man* and *The Fantastic Four*.

He is known for his attention to detail and for the sense of motion and excitement he imparts to his compositions. He is the most talented and creative of the Image Group, and not coincidentally the most self-effacing (his release of the first issue of *Gen 13* with 13 variant covers can be chalked up to youthful exuberance). If the comic-book universe undergoes an irreversible implosion, as many predict, Jim Lee is the most likely to succeed in some other artistic field.

M.H.

LEE, STAN (1922-   ) American comic book and comic strip writer, editor, and publisher, born Stanley Lieber in 1922 in New York City. As a youth, Lee won the *New York Herald Tribune* essay contest for three consecutive weeks; at 17, he entered the comic book industry as an assistant editor and copywriter for the Timely comics group owned by Martin and Arthur Goodman. At the time, Joe Simon and Jack Kirby were the group's editors, but when the pair moved to National in 1942, Lee was promoted to editor. He held that post as the company changed names from Timely to Atlas and finally to Marvel, and only relinquished his editorship in 1972 when he was promoted to publisher and editorial director.

During the 1940s, most of Lee's writing was done for the Timely superhero groups. His best work probably came on the *Captain America* and *Young Allies* strips, but he also wrote stories for superhero strips like *The Witness, The Destroyer, Jack Frost, Whizzer,* and *Black Marvel*. As editor, he was also responsible for producing material for the Timely group's war, crime, funny animal, and humor books. When William Gaines' E.C. group turned comic book publishers' attention to horror, war, and science-fiction titles during the 1950s, Lee led the Atlas group through several tough years. Although the group offered some fine artwork—including material by Basil Wolverton, Jack Kirby, Joe Maneely, Al Williamson, Joe Orlando, and many others—Lee's scripts were always rushed and usually below par. In fact, the Atlas years were prolific but artistically vapid for Stan Lee the writer.

It was not until 1961 that he began producing outstanding comic book stories and formats. Together with artist and compatriot Jack Kirby, he formulated the Marvel group of superheroes, starting with *The Fantastic Four* and *Spider-Man* and later expanding to *Dr. Strange, Thor, The Hulk, Sub-Mariner, Daredevil, Iron Man,* and many others. But all the features were founded on one basic premise: that even though the character was a hero with some sort of superhuman ability, he had human failings, emotions, and foibles the teenaged reader could identify with. Spider-Man, for example, had girl problems, a doting grandmother, and not much of a personality. Johnny Storm, the Human Torch, was erratic and unreliable, and all of

Lee's other creations had similar character defects. Strangely enough, however, with the exception of Ditko's early *Spider-Man* renditions, Lee had all the characters portrayed as noble in bearing and majestic, often belying their essential, albeit sometimes adolescent, humanity.

Lee's material catapulted the Marvel line to pop-culture status throughout the 1960s, and sales responded in a like manner. Lee was celebrated as the savior of the comic book, the great innovator, and his personal reputation kept pace with his characters' popularity. He went on lecture tours to college campuses, made broadcast media appearances, and even held an "Evening with Stan Lee" at Carnegie Hall in 1972. Comic book fans bestowed on him six consecutive "Alley" awards between 1963 and 1968. He was instrumental in the formation of the Academy of Comic Book Arts (ACBA), and Simon & Schuster published his *Origins of Marvel Comics* in 1974.

Over the years, Lee has also worked on several syndicated comic strips, including *My Friend Irma* (1952), *Mrs. Lyons' Cubs* (1957-1958), and *Willie Lumpkin* (1960).

J.B.

In 1972 Stan Lee became Marvel's publisher, and in 1978 he moved to California to supervise the operation of its film and television arm, where his performance has been less than stellar. Aside from his writing of the *Amazing Spider-Man* newspaper strip (started in 1977) and an occasional comic-book story, he has now almost totally abandoned creative activities. Furthermore, his record as a publisher has also come under fire of late: his egomaniacal insistence on taking credit for every story Marvel ever published ("Stan Lee Presents . . .") and his shabby treatment of Jack Kirby, Steve Ditko, and others of his most talented collaborators have drawn special criticism from fans and historians alike.

M.H.

LEHNER, RENÉ (1955-   ) A Swiss comic artist born April 3, 1955, René Lehner grew up with comic books and began drawing while he was still quite young. Although he never pursued formal art training, he continued to doodle and draw, and in 1974 he cofounded *Comixene*, the first German comics fanzine. Around the same time, he sold some of his cartoons and gag strips to various publishers. After leaving *Comixene*, he also began publishing his cartoons on his own. In 1981 he moved to Spain with his family; later he lived in Hamburg before returning to his native Switzerland.

Finally an idea took form that Lehner pursued with a vengeance. He created Bill Body, a sports enthusiast with an egg-shaped head and a penchant for getting into all kinds of predicaments. In addition to developing the *Bill Body* comic strip, Lehner began producing animated cartoon shorts of his character in the "comic factory" he cofounded with Rinaldo Schweizer. At first these cartoons were just short sight gags and blackouts used as fillers between advertising segments on privately owned German commercial television, which was then in its infancy. Eventually production was stepped up so that Bill Body could appear in 15- and 30-minute programs on German commercial TV and state-owned Austrian public TV.

While originally influenced by the Franquin school of drawing, Lehner, who signs his work simply

René Lehner, self-portrait
. . . and his best-known character, Bill Body

JA, JA, LACHEN SIE NUR...

"René," has developed a style and concept of his own for the lovable and highly marketable *Bill Body*.

W.F.

LEHNER, SEBASTIJAN (1921-1945) Born in 1921 in Osijek (now in Croatia), Sebastijan Lehner traveled to Belgrade in the autumn of 1938 to pursue a career in comics. Incredibly, when the Belgrade comics magazine *Paja Patak* ("Donald Duck") launched its inaugural issue on October 3, 1938, the 17-year-old Lehner was represented with three realistic serials. The magazine, owned and edited by Djuradj M. Jelicic, featured Serbian translations of popular American comics like *Radio Patrol*, *Felix the Cat*, and *Little Orphan Annie*, along with original Serbian comics by such artists as Zika Mitrovic, S. Petkovic, Marijan Ebner (pseudonym of Dragan Kalmarevic), and J. Uhlik. In such company,

young Lehner's comics, although clearly the work of a beginner, showed great promise, which was confirmed in later issues. Despite their weaknesses, his *Mysterious Island in the Pacific*, *Inhabitants of Planet Monip*, and especially *Dzarto, Prehistoric Hero* gained a loyal readership. Titles defined genre affiliation unerringly. Lehner's main characteristics were clearly visible even then: strictly visual stylization; inclination toward monumentality and long, epic adventure serials; and a determination to write all his texts himself.

After *Paja Patak* folded following its 24th issue, Lehner was hired by Milutin S. Ignjacevic to work on his new magazine *Mikijevo carstvo* ("Mickey's Domain"). For the first issue, published on February 23, 1939, Lehner drew *Gospodar sveta* ("Master of the World"), which was based on Jules Verne's *Maitre du monde*. He also did the serial *Dzarto, sin Sunca* ("Jarto, Son of Sun"), a tale subtitled "Hero of Prehistoric Era." In August 1939 Lehner's other well-known serial, *Sigfrid*, inspired by the medieval German saga of the Nibelungen, started. It belonged to a genre (adventure-fantasy) and subgenre (epic sword-and-sorcery) that Lehner liked best. His third serial, *Princ Bialco*, started ambitiously in 1941 but was never finished. In April the Nazis rolled into Serbia, and Serbian publishers ceased producing newspapers and magazines.

On December 1, 1943, during the third winter of the German occupation, there appeared a new Belgrade magazine, *Mali zabavnik* ("Little Entertainer"), which contained five comics. Contributors were anonymous so that the resistance forces couldn't retaliate against them for collaborating with the Nazis. People quickly recognized Kuznjecov's style, but only in 1995 was it discovered that a certain Vsevolod Guljevic, about whom virtually nothing is known, also worked on the magazine. Lehner's comics appeared too, now titled *Nibelunzi* and subtitled *Zigfrid*, clearly a continuation of the prewar *Sigfrid* serial. Set in pencil probably by Lehner, it was inked probably by Guljevic or Kuznjecov. It certainly seems to have been a collective effort.

The circumstances of his death have never been officially confirmed, but very soon after the Germans' defeat in Serbia, Lehner was killed. Most likely he was executed by partisans for collaborating with the Nazi occupation forces.

S.I.

LEHTI, JOHN (1912-   ) American artist, born in Brooklyn, New York, on July 20, 1912. Lehti grew up in Brooklyn and studied at some of the finest art schools in the nation: the Art Students League (under George Bridgman, Frank Dumond, and Nicholaides), the National Academy, the Beaux Arts Institute, and Grand Central Art School under Harvey Dunn, probably the greatest influence on his art and approach to work.

In 1935 Lehti's first published work appeared in pulps; his dry-brush drawings ran in Street and Smith and Double Action group magazines. Within three years the pulp market had narrowed and the rarer illustration assignments were going to the top artists only.

Fortunately for Lehti and other pulp illustrators, comic books were emerging as a new market—for artists as well as readers. He joined the staff of Detective Comics and worked on four titles: *The Crimson Avenger*; *Sgt. O'Malley of the Redcoat Patrol*; *Steve Conrad, Adventurer*; and *Cotton Carver*. During this time, just before split assignments, Lehti and others wrote, drew, inked, and lettered their own titles.

During the war Lehti served in Europe, collecting a Bronze Star, a Purple Heart, and four bronze Battle Stars. Returning to the United States, he was offered the position of art editor with Leigh Danenberg's Picture News, a comic-book-format hodgepodge with everything from news angles developed by the legendary Emil Guvreaux (Bernard McFadden's editor on the *New York Graphic*, who, among other achievements, launched Walter Winchell) to Milt Gross cartoons, among the last drawn by the comic genius, from his hospital bed.

Picture News lasted approximately six issues, evidently neither beast nor fowl to readers; in the spring of 1946 Lehti sold a comic strip to King Features—*Tommy of the Big Top*—which ran until 1950. With the strip's demise he returned to Detective Comics for one year to do pencils for *Big Town* (crossing paths, coincidentally, with Dan Barry, whose place he took; Barry had left to work for King Features). For a while, in 1949, he also worked on *Tarzan*.

This time it was the comic book industry that was hit by relatively hard times—in the early 1950s—and Lehti switched to Western, where he worked on several titles until 1954, including *Lassie, Space Cadet*, and *Flash Gordon*.

In 1954 Lehti sold *Tales from the Great Book* to Publishers Syndicate. It was a Sunday feature, dramatizing the most exciting and heroic parts of the Bible. Stories were continued, and what was lacking in historical precision was compensated for by a great sense of drama—a legacy, no doubt, of Harvey Dunn's classroom lectures. *Tales* was a natural Sunday feature for many newspapers and had a healthy run, to 1972. Lehti later returned to Detective Comics and worked on *Sgt. Rock* and *The Loser*.

Lehti's art is that of a very competent craftsman—never outstanding in the sense of setting trends or breaking ground, but ahead of many contemporaries in technical accuracy and capturing moods. From 1967 to 1970 he headed a production team of animators working on 13 animated Tales from the Great Book; earlier experience in animation included storyboard work on the television cartoon *The Mighty Hercules* in the early 1960s. After self-syndicating a weekly panel again based on biblical stories, he retired in the 1980s.

R.M.

LEISK, DAVID JOHNSON (1906-1975) An American artist born in New York City on October 20, 1906, he was better known as "Crockett Johnson." Johnson grew up on Long Island and returned to New York for art courses at Cooper Union. His first job had him doing advertising work in the art department of Macy's Department Store. He also did freelance magazine art, mostly of the design variety.

In the early 1940s, Johnson drew a little weekly comic strip for *Collier's Magazine. The Little Man with the Eyes* became the unofficial title of this nameless feature; as the major action consisted of the face's moving eyes, the captions carried the concept.

This feature overlapped with a newspaper comic strip he created in 1942 for New York's experimental newspaper *PM. Barnaby*—a whimsical strip about a boy's fairy godfather, the latter's weird assortment of ghostly friends, and the boy's unbelieving parents. The

strip was destined to become one of the classics of comics history.

In addition to creating one of the few "intellectual" strips in the *Little Nemo–Krazy Kat–Pogo* fraternity, Johnson introduced an innovation to the form of the comic strip: machine-lettered balloons. Interestingly, however, there has been virtually no follow-up by other artists to this innovation.

The typeset dialogue, Johnson maintained, was to ensure the maximum amount of space for the continuity—a fact that illustrates his primary concern with story over art in *Barnaby*. Eventually other interests became more important than *Barnaby* itself and he turned the strip over to Jack Morley and Ted Ferro.

Reportedly he kept close tabs on the strip (indeed, he returned to write the farewell episode when the strip folded in 1952), but Johnson was interested in other things. He wrote several children's books alone and with his wife, Ruth Kraus (*Harold and the Purple Crayon* was their most memorable collaboration), and then turned to oil and acrylic painting; he characterized his painting style as "non-objective, mathematic and geometric."

This man who remembered no great fondness for comic strips as a child and to whom *Barnaby* was only a passing episode in his life nevertheless remains one of the giants of comic history. His strip was an inspired creation, striking in originality of conception and presentation. He died in Norwalk, Connecticut, on July 11, 1975.

R.M.

LEONARD, FRANK (1896-1970) Born in Port Chester, New York, on January 2, 1896, Frank E. Leonard (later to be known as "Lank" Leonard, creator of *Mickey Finn*) went from high school to the Eastman Gaines Business College in 1914. In the army in 1917 and 1918, Leonard became a traveling salesman in the early 1920s, then did animation with Bray Productions in 1926. He finally landed a syndicate sinecure between 1927 and 1936 with a sports-personality and news feature distributed by the George Matthew Adams Service, doing magazine sports art on the side. Leonard's real fame and fortune began in 1936, when he created his new strip concept, *Mickey Finn*, and it was accepted by McNaught Syndicate for major promotion and sale.

Mickey Finn was the first and almost the only strip to deal sympathetically with the police foot patrolman in a large city. (The comparative glamour of the earlier *Radio Patrol* is evident.) Leonard opted for humor and character over crime and violence, however (although there was plenty of the latter at points in the narrative), and the public seemed to like the theme and creative combination. This led to a wide circulation of *Finn* in its first few years, especially when the real focus of the strip turned from Mickey's exploits to those of his knockabout Irish uncle Phil Finn. (The emphasis in the Sunday page was on Uncle Phil almost from the outset.)

A professional basketball player after high school, Leonard became an ardent golfer in later years. Hiring the very capable Morris Weiss to continue *Finn* while he went into semi-retirement a year and a half before his death, Leonard took a novel step for a strip cartoonist in asking his readers to vote on whether or not Phil Finn should marry a much younger sweetheart named Minerva Mutton. The readers voted 30 to 1 that he should, and Leonard saw them married on the newspaper pages a few days before his death at Miami Shores on August 1, 1970.

B.B.

LEWIS, BOB   *see* Lubbers, Robert.

LIAO BINGXIONG (1915-   )   After a difficult childhood, Chinese cartoonist Liao Bingxiong graduated from Guangzhou Normal School at age 17, in the midst of World War II. That year his anti-Japanese comic strips began to appear in newspapers. The strips, which would eventually total 27, gave Liao's view of why the Chinese would eventually defeat the Japanese invaders.

During the war years, Liao also began drawing *Spring and Autumn in Cat Kingdom*, the general title for 100 color cartoons with animal characters that would make his reputation as one of China's greatest cartoonists. The cartoons, which were exhibited successfully in 1946 in Chongqing, openly attacked the political and economic abuses of China's Nationalist government, which was then battling the Communists. Wanted by the government for the criticism he expressed in his cartoons, Liao changed his name and fled.

After the Communist victory and the establishment of the People's Republic of China, Liao returned from Hong Kong and became vice president of the Chinese Artists Association, Guangdong Branch; he also worked as director of the Guangzhou Literature Federation Publishing Department. But he continued to criticize government wrongdoing in his cartoons, and in 1957 he was denounced as a "rightist" and removed from his positions. For 20 years he was forbidden to draw cartoons and forced to work in various positions, including as a physical laborer. When the Cultural Revolution finally ended in 1976, he resumed cartooning.

Liao's artistry has been recognized both in his homeland and internationally. Many exhibitions of his work have been organized around the globe. Two of his cartoons, one from the earlier *Cat Kingdom* series and the other, "Self-portrait," an acknowledged masterpiece from his later years, are in the permanent collection of the International Cartoon Art Museum in Florida.

H.Y.L.L.

LIBERATORE, GAETANO (1953-   )   An Italian cartoonist and illustrator born on April 12, 1953, in Quadri, Liberatore is better known as Tanino, which is short for Gaetano. After graduating from an art school, he moved to Rome, where from 1974 to 1978 he worked for advertising agencies and drew record covers. In 1978 he started contributing to the newly

Gaetano Liberatore, "Ranxerox." © Gaetano Liberatore.

Liao Bingxiong, "Spring and Autumn in Cat Kingdom." © Liao Bingxiong.

launched lampoon magazine *Cannibale*, which printed his black-and-white short stories *Tiamotti*, *Saturno contro la Terra*, and *Folly Bololy*. Also appearing in the pages of that magazine were the first adventures of *Rank Xerox*, written by Stefano Tamburini and drawn by Pazienza and Liberatore. For the biting satire magazine *Il Male* (1978-82) he created short stories, illustrations, and several covers.

In 1980 Liberatore contributed to the opening issue of the magazine *Frigidaire* with the new and muscular version of *Ranxerox* (renamed under pressure from the famous producer of photocopiers), based on an idea and a script by Tamburini. Ranxerox is an android built by a student during a campus protest. The android, whose circuits are crossed, escapes the police after they kill his master and mates with an amoral teenager, Lubna, who becomes his mistress. Together they live some shocking adventures amid the urban decay and moral degeneration of an indeterminate metropolis that combines features of Rome and New York. More than the plot, it is the violence and hyperrealism of many scenes—depicted with powerful and colorful graphic style—that bear witness to contemporary moral and social squalor.

The sudden success of *Ranxerox* made Liberatore internationally popular. His hero's adventures were printed in France, Spain, Greece, Canada, the United States, and Japan. Many young artists drew inspiration from his style. In 1982 Liberatore moved to Paris, where he worked mainly on painting and illustration for posters and magazine and disk covers (for example, for Frank Zappa's *The Man from Utopia*). For some time he was also active as a fashion stylist for the Italian TV program *Mister Fantasy*.

Ranxerox adventures have been reprinted in three books released between 1981 and 1997. Illustrations and drawings by Liberatore have also been collected in *Plasmando* (1992). Liberatore and Tamburini are the protagonists of the comics adventure *La leggenda di Italianino Liberatore* ("The Legend of Little Italian Liberatore," 1995), written and drawn by Pazienza.

G.C.C.

LIBERTY KID (Italy) On November 13, 1951, in the pages of the new, pocket-sized comic magazine *L'Intrepido*, published by the brothers Del Duca, *Liberty Kid* started its checkered career. The feature was drawn first by the painters Toldo and Albanese, then taken over by Lina Buffolente, who carried it until its demise early in 1960.

As his name implied, Liberty Kid was a lover of freedom. He was a Southerner who could not countenance the practice of slavery, and for this reason he left his father's home to join the Union army. The tall, fair-haired hero fought bravely on all fronts and helped the Union achieve victory. The Civil War over, he became President Ulysses Grant's favorite secret agent; sent to all parts of the Western Hemisphere, Liberty Kid saw to it that justice and democracy prevailed.

Liberty Kid was more of a soap opera than an adventure strip (the same applies to most of the Del Duca productions). The hero's exploits were often a gimmick meant to introduce old people or harmless black children molested by unscrupulous louts. The story line complacently depicted white-haired mothers looking for their dead sons amid the rubble of the battlefield, or bereaved wives waiting in vain for the return of their lost husbands. Yet, in the midst of all the pathos, a good story would occasionally be told, with flashes of inspiration and some good, zestful artwork.

G.B.

LIEFELD, ROB (1967-   ) The wunderkind of American comics, Rob Liefeld was born October 3, 1967, in Orange City, California. His only training consisted of some art courses during his high school years. He started contributing to fanzines while still in his early teens, and he had his artwork professionally published for the first time in the mid-1980s in the short-lived *Megaton* comic book.

His work soon attracted the attention of the two major publishers in the field. In 1988 he freelanced for DC, working most notably on *Warlord*; and the following year he went to Marvel, where he created the character Cable for *The New Mutants*. In 1991 the first issue of *X-Force*, which boasted Liefeld's cover and interior art, sold an astonishing 3 million copies. Later that same year Liefeld, dissatisfied with working conditions at Marvel, left to cofound Image Comics with five other Marvel defectors, Jim Lee and Todd McFarlane among them. *Youngblood*, his first creation at Image, sold 700,000 copies of its first issue (April 1992), a number never before realized by any independent comic-book publisher. Amid much acrimony and a flurry of lawsuits, however, he broke with his partners at Image in 1996. While continuing to publish *Youngblood* under his own Maximum Press imprint, Liefeld that same year contracted with Marvel to produce a number of issues of *The Avengers* and *Captain America*.

There has been much bashing of Liefeld in the fan press and on the Internet, where he has been accused of (among other sins) bad writing and slapdash draftsmanship. The critics miss the point, however: Liefeld's appeal has little to do with art or creativity; rather, it resides in his ability to titillate the adolescent minds of his fans with depictions of brawny heroes wielding gigantic weapons and big-busted women sporting skimpy outfits. With this caveat in mind, he could more aptly be compared with Madonna than with Jack Kirby.

M.H.

LIEUTENANT BLUEBERRY (France) In 1963 writer Jean-Michel Charlier and artist Jean Giraud (signing simply "Gir") created the adventures of Lieutenant Blueberry for the French magazine *Pilote* in a story called "Fort Navajo." (When the story branched out into a highly successful series, it became known as *Lieutenant Blueberry*.)

Lieutenant Blueberry was the most vigorous, exciting, and authentic Western to come along since the early *Red Ryder*. Lieutenant Mike S. Blueberry, a somewhat disillusioned soldier bearing a strong resemblance to French actor Jean-Paul Belmondo, was drawn with a sure hand by Gir. An officer with the mythical Seventeenth Regiment of the U.S. Cavalry, he is headquartered at Fort Navajo, an army encampment in the New Mexico territory. More often than not, however, Blueberry seems to be pursuing his own private wars, whether against gunrunners or marauding Apaches, quite independently from any official authority. In his adventures he finds help and succor from his inseparable companion Jimmy McClure, whose fondness for whiskey is only equaled by Blueberry's partiality to fighting and gambling.

and his use of color nothing short of inspired. From its inception in 1954 *Lieutenant Blueberry* was been a revelation and a treat to those who appreciated the comics primarily for their graphic and plastic qualities.

Excellent as it was, however, the strip could have been made even better had Gir been allowed to write his own scenarios. Unfortunately he was saddled with Charlier, who, for all his other virtues, did not have a genuine feel for the Western mythos. Furthermore, Charlier was so eager to show off his textbook knowledge of the American West that he could never pass up an opportunity to cram every irrelevancy or cliché into his text. Yet *Lieutenant Blueberry*, thanks to Gir's brilliant artwork, remained one of the masterpieces of the European comics. *Lieutenant Blueberry* has had numerous book reprints, all of them published by Dargaud.

In the 1970s Gir devoted more and more of his time (as Moebius) to other, more cutting-edge projects, and Blueberry's appearances became increasingly sporadic. In 1985 Colin Wilson took over *La jeunesse de Blueberry* ("Blueberry's Youth"), a spin-off title retracing the hero's adventures prior to his enlistment in the army; and in 1991 William Vance started drawing the main series on scripts supplied by the creator. A number of *Blueberry* episodes drawn by Gir have been reprinted in the U.S. by Marvel and other publishers.

M.H.

"Lieutenant Blueberry," Gir (Jean Giraud). © Editions Dargaud.

All the characters in the series, from the hero down to the lowest walk-on, are highly individualized—their faces look lived-in. Gir's depiction of action is masterful, his delineation of background sharp and assertive,

LIFE IN HELL (U.S.) As a child, Matt Groening dreamed of becoming a writer; he showed little artistic ability. The incisive portrayals of contemporary angst in his *Life in Hell* grew out of a series of crudely drawn doodles Groening began producing in 1977. The reflections and experiences of a rabbit named Binky (an image chosen because it both represented the helplessness of the character and was the only recognizable

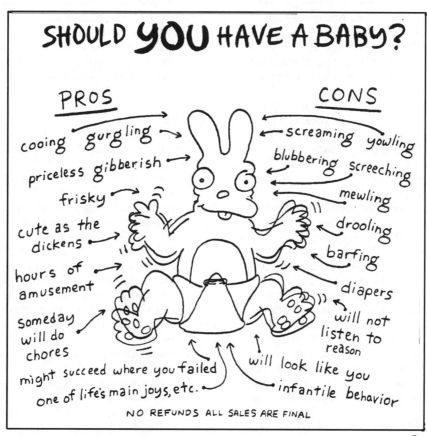

"Life in Hell," Matt Groening. © Matt Groening.

"Li'l Abner," Al Capp. © United Feature Syndicate.

animal Groening could draw), they dramatized human alienation with savage humor.

In 1978 the new-age graphics publication *Wet* published several of Groening's cartoons. The next year, the leading alternative weekly in the area, the *Los Angeles Reader*, picked the strip up, and in April 1980 *Life in Hell* became a regular feature. An employee of the *Reader*, Groening self-syndicated his work, and by 1983 it was appearing in about 20 college and alternative newspapers. In 1984, *Reader* coworker Deborah Caplan independently published a collection entitled *Love Is Hell*, which sold out its edition of 20,000 almost immediately, and the next year Caplan took over the syndication of the series, forming the *Life in Hell* Cartoon Company and the Acme Features Syndicate with Groening. The two, who were married in 1986, now distribute the strip and license use of its images on such products as posters, T-shirts, and greeting cards.

In his first year, Binky changed from a confrontational character to a victim, and his popularity increased exponentially. "The more tragedies that befell this poor little rodent," Groening reports, "the more positive response I got." Although the strip has remained minimally drawn, reflecting the influence of such Groening favorites as James Thurber and Charles Schulz, its range of topics and characters has increased. It now includes Binky's girlfriend Sheba; his even more beleaguered illegitmate son Bongo, graced with only one ear to distinguish him from Binky; and two plump little humans, Akbar and Jeff, who wear identical Charlie Brown sweaters and tasseled fezzes and who operate a series of sleazy businesses such as the Liposuction Hut.

In addition to *Love Is Hell*, which was reissued as a trade book in 1985 by Pantheon, *Life in Hell* has given rise to several successful collections, including *Work Is Hell* (1986), *School Is Hell* (1987), *Childhood Is Hell* (1988), and *The Big Book of Hell* (1990). But Groening's animated television series *The Simpsons*, begun in 1989, "makes the *Life in Hell* Company look like a drop in the bucket," the author admits. Nevertheless, the audience of the shrewdly iconoclastic newspaper feature continues to grow as the strip continues to address the universal themes of "the hellishness of most people's jobs and love lives and fear of death."

D.W.

LI'L ABNER (U.S.) *Li'l Abner*, drawn from the outset by Al Capp (Alfred Gerald Caplin), began as a daily strip on August 20, 1934, with the Sunday page following on February 24, 1935. Released initially by United Features, the strip has been distributed since June 1964 by the New York News Syndicate. Aside from the relatively unimportant World War II bond-selling Sunday half-page, *Small Change* (initially *Small Fry*), and a Sunday third-page companion strip with which the Sunday *Abner* began publication (and which lasted 16 weeks) named *Washable Jones*, *Li'l Abner* has been the only strip bylined by Capp. He did the unsigned story line and art on *Joe Palooka* (nominally by Ham Fisher) in 1933 before starting *Abner*; and while his *Fearless Fosdick* (a takeoff on *Dick Tracy*) has been a strip-within-a-strip of great popularity, it has always been signed Lester Gooch, to kid the Tracy creator, Chester Gould. Capp's signature in the early daily *Abner* episodes was "Al G. Cap," the second "p" being added only with the 25th episode. A similar early confusion can be noted in the Sunday page bylines.

Readers took a careful, interested look at the new daily strip from the moment the 19-year-old, six-foot-three Li'l Abner Yokum was depicted chest-deep in a Kentucky mountain pool of 1934 thinking about dinner back in his parents' log cabin. The artistry was eye-catching, the concept amusing, and the setting novel. (Only Capp himself had used contemporary hillbilly characters and settings in comic strips before, when he was ghosting *Joe Palooka*.) And the public chuckled gleefully when Abner upset New York society scions while visiting his sophisticated and wealthy Aunt Bessie Bopshire in the big city during the first daily story, a situation in which Abner played the cherished American folk-hero image of the noble and naive backwoodsman to the hilt. Readers were delighted, too, with the antics of Abner's "mammy," Pansy Yokum, and her spavined, browbeaten husband, Lucifer Ornamental Yokum. They howled as the strip's other comic characters entered the scene, such as the red-nosed and pompous-bellied Marryin' Sam, sweating on a 1935 Sunday page in an elaborate histrionic attempt to swindle Mammy Yokum out of " 'fo' dollahs." But they were driven to bite their nails during a weekend wait when a swindler named Payne Morland closed a 1935 Saturday episode by firing an automatic pistol bullet into Abner's stomach at point-blank range.

And so the strip went during its initial decades: surprise upon chuckle upon suspense, reflecting such highlights as the first appearance of Sir Cecil Cesspool, with a cigarette holder as long as a Fu Manchu fingernail dripping ashes on the majestic bosom of Lady Cesspool as he schemed to snare the Bopshire billions; the strange and final exit of one of the strip's early major characters, Abijah Gooch, galloping in tandem muleback over a hill with the shotgun of a murderous mountaineer at his head; the flesh-and-blood Garden of Paradise called the Schmoo, in his proliferating millions; the nefarious, deep-cavern skullduggeries and discoveries of Hairless Joe and Lonesome Polecat, not the least of which was the powerful, steaming Kickapoo Joy Juice; etc., etc.

The prompt, far-flung fame of *Li'l Abner*, which put it on the front pages of innumerable Sunday comic sections from Philadelphia to Los Angeles by the late 1930s, led to a filming of the strip by RKO Studios in 1940, with an unimportant but skillfully made-up cast. Later, it was produced as a major Broadway musical comedy in 1957 (hit song: *Jubilation T. Cornpone*) featuring such stars as Julie Newmar, Stubby Kaye, and Jerry Lewis, some of whom also starred in the 1959 Paramount color film version. A series of animated cartoon shorts featuring the inhabitants of Abner's hometown, Dogpatch, and produced in color by Dave Fleischer for Columbia were released in the mid-1940s, while Dogpatch itself serves as the name of a contemporary Disneyland-style amusement park in Kentucky based on Capp characters. (A short-lived soft drink called Kickapoo Joy Juice was marketed for a time in the 1950s, but it failed because of poor marketing techniques.) A number of paperbacks, comic books, and one hardback (prefaced by John Steinbeck) have featured reprints of the Abner strip since the 1930s, and its characters have served as the basis for many artifacts and toys.

Li'l Abner abandoned some of its focus on Abner and his family in later years, to cover the adventures of other associated characters for weeks at a time; Fearless Fosdick was long delayed in reappearing: the taut, gut-twisting narrative suspense of the first years of the strip vanished almost completely, but *Abner* remained a graphically delectable strip, with still-surprising and bizarre characters and events—one of the daily and Sunday treats of any newspaper. *Li'l Abner* ended on November 13, 1977.

B.B.

"Lilla Fridolf," Torsten Bjarre. © Torsten Bjarre.

LILLA FRIDOLF (Sweden) *Lilla Fridolf* ("Little Fridolf"), written by Rune Moberg and drawn by Torsten Bjarre, had its origins in Swedish radio. The funny adventures of the little, plump man had been a popular radio series that made the transition into comic strips in 1957. The series having long since ended, Lilla Fridolf continues to entertain readers in comic annuals that were started in 1958 and in a comic book that was started in 1960.

Lilla Fridolf, however, seems an unlikely choice for a comic strip character. Who would believe that a stout, small, henpecked husband could work out in a series of his own? Readers in Sweden know the answer, for they are well entertained by the exploits of Fridolf and his domineering wife Selma. Both Fridolf and Selma are over 50 years of age, they already have grandchildren, and Fridolf is working in an office while Selma takes care of their house in the suburbs. For the most part, *Lilla Fridolf* is sheer situation comedy spiced with marital bickering. Drawn in a clear cartoon style similar to that of American comics, it nevertheless differs from American comics in the way family life is depicted. With all the bickering going on and the many odd situations Fridolf gets into, *Lilla Fridolf* is a very entertaining and enjoyable comic feature.

It is therefore not too much of a surprise that Torsten Bjarre won the 1971 Adamson, the Swedish comics award given annually by the Swedish Comics Academy, for his work on *Lilla Fridolf* along with his work on *Oskar* and *Flygsoldat 113 Bom* ("Air Force Private No. 113 No-hit"), all of which have established him as a comic artist emulated by younger colleagues.

W.F.

LILLE RICKARD OCH HANS KATT (Sweden) *Lille Rickard och hans katt* ("Little Richard and his Cat"), created, written, and drawn by Swedish artist Rune Andreasson throughout its 22-year run, was one of a rare breed: the Swedish daily comic strip.

Andreasson, a self-educated comic artist who graduated from high school and Göteborg's theater school, has dedicated most of his work to the entertainment of young readers, finding an ideal tool for this task in the comic strip and comic book media. He got the idea for *Lille Rickard och hans katt* about 1940 while a student studying English. Andreasson's class was reading a story titled "Dick Wittington and His Cat," and the youth was inspired to draw 80 pictures illustrating the tale. Some 10 years later, the memory of Dick Wittington sparked life into Andreasson's boy-hero, Lille Rickard, who is never without his cat while roaming the world in search of adventure.

Lille Rickard och hans katt started in Stockholm's evening newspaper, *Aftonbladet*, on December 23, 1951; it proved one of the nicest Christmas gifts imaginable. In the first strips Rickard leaves his hometown together with his tiny pet cat, forever to stumble into new adventures until the final curtain call in 1973. Swedish daily comic strips, which started in 1929 with Ruben Lundqvist's *Herr Knatt* ("Mister Little") and were continued in 1933 with Torvald Gahlin's *Fredrik*, have always been few and far between. Most daily strips in Swedish newspapers have been foreign imports. The weekly magazines became the seedbed of Swedish comic art much more easily, although they too started out with foreign comic imports. It is therefore quite an achievement to have produced for 22 years an indigenous comic strip that held its own against British and American strips.

At the time he started *Lille Rickard och hans katt*, Andreasson had already had comic strip experience, having done *Brum* for the weekly *Allers* since 1944. While working on *Lille Rickard*, Andreasson also created *Bamse* (about a bear) and *Pellefant* (about a very much alive toy elephant). Through syndication *Lille Rickard* has become Andreasson's best-known work, inside and outside Sweden. *Pellefant* has also been exported; it won him the Adamson, the Swedish Comic Academy's top honor, in 1969.

W.F.

LINDOR COVAS (Argentina) Walter Ciocca created *Lindor Covas el Cimarron* ("Lindor Covas the Untamed") as a daily strip for the Buenos Aires paper *La Razón* in 1956.

"Lindor Covas," Walter Ciocca. © La Razón.

Lindor Covas is part and parcel of the tradition of *gaucho* literature, alongside the famous epic *Martín Fierro*. Its hero is a gaucho, a South American horseman who lives on the pampas, along with his tough companions or with the women who drift in and out of his at times brutal sex life, like Sisina the prostitute or Rita the half-breed. Full of the fatalism characteristic of gaucho tales, Lindor's wanderings are a succession of misfortunes and mishaps, and the hero suffers tribulations parallel to those of Martín Fierro, although he lives in a later period and sometimes experiences happy moments, such as the creation of the tango. The language of *Lindor Covas* is that of the people, and it's so thick with gaucho expressions that on occasion the author feels compelled to include a translation into modern-day Spanish.

Before *Lindor Covas*, Ciocca had written and illustrated a number of stories for *La Razón*, including *Juan Cuello* (1949); *Santos Vega* (1951); *Hilarion Leiva* (1953); and foremost, his two previous successes, *Hormiga Negra* ("Black Ant," 1953) and *Fuerte Argentino* ("Fort Argentina," 1954). Ciocca's style imitates the quality of the wood engravings that illustrated the first editions

"Lille Rickard och hans katt," Rune Andreasson. © Bulls Pressedienst.

of *Martín Fierro*, with a technique that frequently uses chiaroscuro to add power to the images.

In 1962 Carlos Cores directed and interpreted a motion picture based on three episodes of *Lindor Covas*.

L.G.

LINK, STANLEY J. (1894-1957) Stanley Link was one of the few strip artists who stayed put. Born in 1894 in Chicago to a lower-middle-class laboring family, Link (whose *Tiny Tim* was a household name for 20 years) never left the Chicago area until he moved to his final home in nearby Long Beach, Indiana. As a teen, he attended night school and took a correspondence course in cartooning while working full-time at a number of jobs. Finding his first cartooning job with a Chicago-based animated-cartoon company at the age of 16, Link soon developed his natural facility through the repetitive work of endlessly drawing animation frames. Joining the navy in 1917, Link used his cartooning ability in presenting chalk talks on military subjects to groups of sailors while the young Benny Kubelsky (later Jack Benny) played the fiddle for background effect. After freelancing for a time in the early 1920s, Link was hired by Sidney Smith as an assistant on *The Gumps*, and he created the character Ching Chew for the Sunday adventure continuity featuring Chester Gump; he also drew the bulk of that continuity from 1923 until Smith's death in 1935.

In the meantime, Link introduced the popular, philosophical panel *Ching Chow* as a daily feature for Smith's syndicate, the News-Tribune group, and began his own strip, a Sunday feature about a boy shrunk to minuscule size, *Tiny Tim*, in 1933. This latter half-page feature became a great favorite, especially with children, which is not surprising, as it was one of the few newspaper comics deliberately aimed at youngsters. But Link got into serious trouble with his syndicate when he refused to continue *The Gumps* after Sidney Smith's sudden death in 1935, believing that an artist's creation should die with him and not be picked up by other hands. The strip was then at the height of its nationwide popularity, and as a master of the Smith style and story line, Link was the syndicate's obvious choice to carry on. Link refused to budge, however.

In the end, the syndicate held a contest for a *Gumps* artist (after desperately courting such artists as Rube Goldberg for the job), which the late Gus Edson won. Link, in bad grace with the syndicate, found much of his *Tiny Tim* continuity now rejected, his rewriting criticized, and his long-range plans for developing the strip arbitrarily changed in directions he was known to dislike. Link was never able to establish deliberate sabotage of his work, but he sensed it strongly, and this demoralized him and adversely affected much of his later *Tiny Tim* continuity. Eventually the strip was folded in the postwar period, and Link undertook a semi-autobiographical family strip called *The Baileys* for the News-Tribune Syndicate, which he continued until shortly before his death in Long Beach, Indiana, on December 24, 1957, at the age of 63. An extremely amusing and inventive cartoonist and continuity writer at his best, as he was while working on *The Gumps* and the early *Tiny Tim*, Link seems to have precipitated his own creative demise in mid-career by his very questionable decision not to continue *The Gumps*, which he could almost undoubtedly have rendered nearly as well as Smith himself. The sincerity of his conviction, how-ever, cannot be questioned, and his later difficulties can only be regarded as tragic and unjustifiable.

B.B.

LITTLE ANNIE FANNY (U.S.) *Playboy* publisher Hugh Hefner and *Mad* creator Harvey Kurtzman produced two issues of a slick satire magazine called *Trump*, but *Playboy*'s financial empire being weak at the time, the magazine folded. But the pair reunited and Kurtzman and Will Elder premiered *Little Annie Fanny* in the October 1962 issue of *Playboy*.

The feature is an American comic-art landmark simply because it exists. As Hefner puts it, the strip had "an expensive birth. Instead of flat, fake color . . . we decided *Little Annie Fanny* should be rendered in full color, just as the commercial artist does for a magazine illustration, and then reproduced in the same elaborate, expensive four-color separation and process printing as we use for . . . the rest of the magazine." In short, *Little Annie Fanny* was the ultimate comic strip, production-wise. Every panel was a full-color painting.

The story line was simple: Little Annie, beautiful and zaftig, is a sexual Pollyanna. And from there, Kurtzman took off, lampooning everything. He satirized liberals, conservatives, woman's libbers, unions, Ku Klux Klanners, the FBI, and anything else pompous or overblown. And if his stories weren't as spontaneously hilarious as his early *Mad* work, they showed an unprecedented satiric maturity and development. By comparison, his *Mad* work was sophomoric.

Artistically, Will Elder handled the feature with anatomically exaggerated completeness. And while the art too lacked the *Mad* zaniness, it also showed an increased awareness of what is visually funny. Over the years, many other fine illustrators worked on *Little Annie Fanny*. Jack Davis' and Al Jaffee's wild backgrounds added the most to the feature, while Russ Heath's and Frank Frazetta's drawings blended well with the prevailing Kurtzman-Elder style.

The strip also featured several outstanding supporting characters, including Sugardaddy Bigbucks, the Daddy Warbucks imitation and obvious big-business scion; Wanda Homefree, Annie's idealistic girlfriend; and Solly Brass, the slick press agent with the pie-in-the-sky schemes.

A collection of *Annie Fanny* adventures, *Playboy's Little Annie Fanny*, was published in book form.

J.B.

The heroine pursued her free-spirited career through the 1970s and well into the 1980s. She got to meet a number of personages in the news at the time, from the Ayatollah Khomeini to Marcello Mastroianni, in a series of zany encounters. Among the artists who worked on the feature, additional mention should be made of Arnold Roth, Terry Austin, and underground cartoonists Gilbert Shelton and Robert Crumb. The last *Little Annie Fanny* episode appeared in the September 1988 issue of *Playboy*.

M.H.

LITTLE ANNIE ROONEY (U.S.) King Features' *Little Annie Rooney*, an adventure strip about a 12-year-old girl, drawn by five artists and scripted from the start by Brandon Walsh, first appeared in 1927. The Hearst syndicate's competitive reply to *Little Orphan Annie*, Walsh's *Rooney* strip was first drawn by Ed Verdier in a sharp, simple style similar to that of Ernie Bushmiller. He signed himself, cryptically, Verd. The same name

"Little Annie Rooney," Darrell McClure and Brandon Walsh. © King Features Syndicate.

was supplied by King Features for the printed byline. On May 11, 1929, a second, unknown cartoonist, working in a cruder style, took over the strip. Verd's signature vanished, but his byline was retained. The third Rooney artist began work on the strip on July 22, 1929. This was Ben Batsford, who took over the famed *Doings of the Duffs* strip in the mid-1920s and went on to author and draw *The Doodle Family* (later *Frankie Doodle*) through the 1930s. Batsford was the first to draw Walsh's principal *Rooney* character (after the heroine herself), the orphan-asylum head, Mrs. Meany. Batsford's temporary stint was completed on October 6, 1930, when King Features finally located an artist they felt was ideal for the strip: Darrell McClure, who began his long-lived association with *Annie Rooney* on that day.

The 27-year-old McClure, earlier the creator of King Features' *Vanilla and the Villains*, also began to draw the Sunday half-page, which first appeared on November 30, 1930. McClure's style quickly became much more realistic and detailed than those of his three predecessors on the strip, but he made no essential change in the appearance of Annie Rooney herself: the short black bangs, patched dress, black sandals, and white socks remained the same. McClure did change Annie's dog, Zero; early in 1931, he shortened the dog's muzzle considerably, gave him a black button nose, and reduced his size. Mrs. Meany was also altered markedly from Batsford's concept, but chiefly in the direction of collective small details of face and dress.

The McClure strip had genuine eye-appeal and exciting graphic movement. For the first time, Walsh's rather sophisticated script and story line had art that complemented it. But the work on both the daily strip and Sunday half-page (especially when the latter was

enlarged to a full weekly page) was more than the meticulous McClure could handle, and a fine adventure-continuity artist, Nicholas Afonski, was commissioned to draw the Sunday strip after 1932. With Afonski, Walsh developed a new boy-hero for the Sunday page, Joey Robins (whose parents had adopted Annie), and a new feature character, an Oriental adventurer named Ming Foo. Annie was absent for long periods from the new Sunday page in the 1933-35 period, while Joey and Ming Foo went adventuring around the world; then the two were given their own Sunday space in a strip called *Ming Foo* beginning March 17, 1935, which shared *Annie Rooney*'s page thereafter. Annie, of course, continued her escapades in the McClure and Walsh daily strip, and resumed them in the Afonski and Walsh Sunday strip after March 1935.

Curiously, for someone who had gone on the record (in King Features' *Famous Artists and Writers* for 1949) as having accepted the authorship of *Little Annie Rooney* to "write a strip under my own name," Brandon Walsh waited long enough to do it: his first printed byline on *Rooney* appeared on Sunday, August 25, 1935 (although he had been given a handwritten byline on an early Sunday Rooney page-topper called *Fablettes*, a weekly gag sequence with nonrecurrent characters replaced by *Ming Foo*). Earlier, only the drawing artists' signatures had appeared on the daily or Sunday strip, and the daily strip was still being bylined Darrell McClure late into the 1930s. King Features' records, and Walsh himself, however, attest that Walsh wrote *Annie Rooney* from the start.

After Walsh's death in 1954, *Little Annie Rooney* continued in its role as King Features' leading second-string strip for another decade. With McClure at the helm until the end, the Sunday page folded on May 30, 1965, and the daily strip on April 16, 1966. Only two obscure reprints of the strip appeared, in the 1930s.

B.B.

LITTLE BEARS AND TYKES (U.S.) The first publication of James Swinnerton's *Little Bears and Tykes* in anything that could be called a comic strip format appeared in the *San Francisco Examiner* on June 2, 1895. This was a small square filled with black-and-white bear cubs saying and doing various amusing things with a common theme. Previously, Swinnerton had drawn his cubs (called, in occasional *Examiner* captions, the Little Bears) in humanized postures for special spot art, including daily weather announcements in a small box on the editorial page, from 1893 on. Now, as features multiplied in the *Sunday Examiner*, the Swinnerton bears panel was added to the new children's page. When Swinnerton added a few kids to the bears' antics on Sunday, the paper's caption writer referred to the "Little Bears and Tykes," a term that somehow became distorted over the decades and emerged half a century later in some texts on comic strips as "Little Bears and Tigers," a work that never existed.

The Swinnerton bear cubs lacked individuality and had no separate names in his panel series for the *Examiner*. There was no continuity of action within the panel, either: each cub was engaged in a small spot gag with a caption. (Although some of this was in dialogue form, none of the cubs' remarks were rendered in balloons.) In essence, the cub panel differed little from such earlier character panel sequences as the early English *Ally Sloper*: The drawing was the crucial element, while the dialogue was incidental and largely disposable. There was, accordingly, little in the Swinnerton panel series to anticipate the comic strip art form that was soon to emerge in New York.

However—and this is a vital point—the *Little Bears and Tykes* panel was the first regularly repeated original character cartoon series in a newspaper. It made a portion of the reading public aware that a newspaper could bring them a familiar set of figures on a given day (Sunday) with fair regularity, and that augmented newspaper sales.

Swinnerton carried on the *Little Bears* (dropping the Tykes) in the added 1897 color comic section of the *Examiner*, then took them to New York with him when he joined Hearst's strip artists in that city. They appeared there sporadically until 1901, when the last one or two *Little Bears* appeared as comic section half-pages. It seems apparent that Swinnerton thought of the *Little Bears* as a strip of essentially regional appeal (the bears being derived from the California state flag and seal emblem), and best replaced with his newer, New York work, such as *Mount Ararat* and *Little Jimmy*.

B.B.

LITTLE IODINE (U.S.) Little Iodine started her obnoxious career as a recurring character in Jimmy Hatlo's humor panel *They'll Do It Every Time*; the readers grew so fond of this juvenile monster that, in 1943, a Sunday color half-page titled *Little Iodine* was added to the *They'll Do It* panel.

Iodine is a contrary-minded, stubborn, and grudge-bearing little pest whose pranks, deceptions, and connivings are the bane of her suburban neighborhood. Her favorite target is her own father, the meek and petty Henry Tremblechin, whose dreams of getting a

"Little Iodine," Jimmy Hatlo. © King Features Syndicate.

raise or a promotion from his boss, the foul-tempered Mr. Bigdome, are always thwarted by his progeny's diabolical inventions and her implacable (if contrived) candor. Iodine's mother, Effie Tremblechin, gets scarcely better treatment from her flesh and blood, whose greatest pleasure is aping her mother's one-upmanship and social pretenses. When she grows tired of bedeviling her parents, Iodine, often aided and abetted by her boyfriend Sharkey, exercises her nefarious talents against the world at large, in the form of broken windows, false police alarms, and a superb contempt for the rules of accepted behavior—all of which contribute to making Little Iodine a female counterpart to the Katzenjammer Kids.

Jimmy Hatlo drew his strip in a skillful, if somewhat cluttered, way, and his characters were always depicted in a very funny vein. After Hatlo's death in 1963, *Little Iodine* was taken over by former assistant Bob Dunn (in 1967 Dunn turned over the drawing of *Little Iodine* to Hy Eisman, while continuing to write the stories). Their collaboration proved harmonious and fruitful, lasting for almost 20 years, until the strip's discontinuation in 1986.

Little Iodine has appeared in comic books and was also reprinted in paperback form. In 1946 it was made into a movie, without apparent success.

M.H.

LITTLE JIMMY (U.S.) James Swinnerton's *Little Jimmy* (first titled just *Jimmy*) opened in the Hearst Sunday comic sections on February 14, 1904, in an episode titled "Jimmy—He Goes for the Milk." Jimmy, an eight- or nine-year-old boy with a round head and button nose, was sent out to buy milk for the family dinner, but he managed to get so entangled in street events on the way that he was hopelessly late, showing up with a broken milk pot as well. This became the theme of most of the early *Jimmy* episodes, as the strip moved from its initial inside half-page position to full, front-page spread. Appearing sporadically at first, *Jimmy* had become a regular weekly page by the 1910s, running by then in the second-string Hearst Saturday comic sections.

"Little Jimmy," James Swinnerton. © King Features Syndicate.

Jimmy Thompson, to give the boy's full name (his first name, of course, was Swinnerton's own nickname), expanded his range of activities in the second decade of *Jimmy*, and added a child friend, the baseball-cap-wearing Pinkie. (Pinkie owned a bulldog named Buck, which was the prototype of Beans, the dog Jimmy himself would later own.) The Sunday *Jimmy* page was dropped for a time at the close of the 1910s, then revived in early 1920 as *Little Jimmy*, with a strong emphasis on the Nevada and Arizona desert regions, which Swinnerton had come to love over the past 15 years. (The Thompson family went there on vacation.) In 1922, Jimmy acquired the first of his several pets, the bulldog Beans. This was followed by a small bear cub in the summer of 1924 (who bore little resemblance to the Swinnerton cubs of the 1890s), which Jimmy called "Lil Ole Bear," and by a Mexican fighting rooster named Poncho in early 1928. (By this time, Jimmy had been shipwrecked on a fantastic island with a drooping-moustached Mr. Batch, an earlier strip creation of Swinnerton's; traveled to Mexico; been to Hollywood; and generally gotten around.) A return to the American Southwest in the late 1920s was permanent, however, and it was here that Jimmy met the last of his regular kid companions, a Navaho canyon kid, borrowed from the popular Swinnerton *Good Housekeeping* color page of the 1920s and 1930s, *Canyon Kiddies*. A knowledgeable older Indian brave named Somolo also entered the strip at this time; Somolo was able to talk to animals, and he involved Jimmy and his pals and pets in numerous funny or weird desert experiences.

Little Jimmy began as a daily strip on July 24, 1920, with Jimmy's daily experiences paralleling those in the Sunday pages for the most part. The daily was dropped in the late 1930s (last date in most Hearst papers was October 25, 1937), while the Sunday page was replaced for a few years in the 1940s by Swinnerton's *Rocky Mason*. Revived in 1945, the Sunday page continued until April 27, 1958, when Swinnerton retired from comic strip work to devote himself to painting his famed desert-scapes. Often charming, enormously informative in its later years about Navaho Indian life and desert wildlife in general, and a particular delight for younger children, *Little Jimmy* deserves selective reprinting. (It should be mentioned that considerable stretches of the daily and Sunday strips were ghosted by Doc Winner in the 1920s and 1930s; these were always left unsigned by Swinnerton.) *Little Jimmy* was reprinted many times in collections and paperbacks from the 1900s to the 1940s.

B.B.

LITTLE JOE (U.S.) One of seven new Sunday half-page strips added to the *New York News* and *Chicago Tribune* family of comics on October 1, 1933, Ed Leffingwell's *Little Joe* was the first major syndicate strip to be set wholly in the contemporary cattle ranch West. Joe, a chapped and booted kid of about 13, lives with his widowed mother on a ranch managed by an old cowhand (and probably gunfighter) named Utah. Utah and Joe quickly come to dominate the narrative, which is an admixture of single-episode gag-finish pages and continuing series or semi-humorous stories of varying lengths. At the outset, the strip seems to have been entirely drawn by Leffingwell, Harold Gray's cousin, letterer, and background aide of the time. The story and dialogue seem to be largely Gray's, however, and by 1936, most of the human figures are clearly his, to remain so through the mid-1940s. Effectively, *Little Joe* must be regarded as an additional Gray strip from its inception in 1933 to at least 1946, when the strip returned primarily to weekly gags and the artistry of Leffingwell and (after his death) that of his brother, Robert, also a later Gray aide.

The combination of Leffingwell's background style (his handling of the western landscape, especially the rocky gorges and mountainsides of the cattle states, is stunning) and Gray's lively figure work made *Little Joe* one of the most visually attractive strips of the 1930s and 1940s. Its wide popularity in syndication seems to have reflected this appeal, as much as it did the amusement and suspense afforded by Gray's mature, cynical, and hard-bitten narrative.

Until American's involvement in World War II, the *dramatis personae* of *Little Joe* consists of wise and just Indian tribes (Gray felt strongly that the American Indian had gotten a very dirty deal from the white man), brutal gunmen, conniving rival ranchers, rustlers, an occasional eastern tenderfoot, gigantic bears, and—in the late 1930s—the comic figure of a Mexican general whose rank and stature at any given time depend on the political complexion of his native country. When out of power, Ze Gen'ral, as he calls himself (and is called in a small companion strip to *Little Joe* that ran in the 1940s), hangs out on Joe's mother's ranch and goes adventuring with Joe and Utah for a long period of time. After 1941, wartime comes to the West of *Little Joe*, and even a submarine-landed invading party of Japanese saboteurs (whom Utah captures and quietly puts to work on his shorthanded ranch as convenient slave labor for the duration) is introduced. Ze Gen'ral takes command of a Mexican division in the war, the ranch characters suffer through rationing, gun down saboteurs, torment draft dodgers, and undergo the general narrative dislocation of most strip characters during the war. Afterwards, Gray seems to have felt he had exhausted the potential of *Little Joe*, and he returned full-time to *Annie*. The Leffingwell brothers continued the strip as a Sunday gag filler until the late 1950s, after which its distribution by the News-Tribune syndicate is obscure, since it was dropped by both parent papers.

Between its gag periods, *Little Joe* could be an intelligently written, well-drawn, and gripping strip. It is definitely a minor classic and merits reprinting in permanent form.

B.B.

LITTLE KING, THE (U.S.) Making its premiere appearance in Sunday comic sections on September 9,

"The Little King," Otto Soglow. © King Features Syndicate.

1934, *The Little King* succeeded the artist's similar page, *The Ambassador*, and the earlier magazine version in the pages of the *New Yorker*. *The Ambassador* was a stopgap feature that ran between Hearst's signing of the talented Soglow and the expiration of the contract with the *New Yorker* for *The Little King*.

Soglow was a magazine panel cartoonist whose drift to strip ideas was manifested in the *King* pages, one of those rare, spontaneously popular features that burst onto the scene full-blown.

Curiously, although the character was a favorite in comic pages and in Max Fleisher-Paramount animated cartoons for 35 years, the king had no name. Likewise, his kingdom was never named, and the queen and their comely daughter (who appeared with less frequency through the years) were also nameless. But these facts meant little to the understanding of the strip.

Soglow's kingdom was zany and unpredictable—sometimes almost surrealistic—and presided over by a consistently unconventional king. The Little King outraged stuffy ambassadors, surprised dignified ladies, interrupted official functions for childlike games, and, all in all, was the king of the common, uninhibited, playful, irreverent folk. As such he is one of the classic comic creations, strikingly original in broad conception and endearing in individual shenanigans.

King Features' chief Joe Connelly's suggestion to populate the strip with more characters resulted in such figures as Ookle the Dictator (six months in 1940), but few new faces lasted long; they were superfluous.

In the days of top strips, *Sentinel Louie*, a half-pint palace guard with a generous torso, carried on his antics in evidently different neighborhoods of the same kingdom. And *Travelin' Gus* was a short-lived Sunday feature about an inveterate bus rider's trips to strange neighborhoods, presaging some of Mr. Mum's travels and echoing Soglow's *New Yorker* days.

After more than 40 years with King Features, *The Little King* had become one of the most familiar of comic creations: the shrimpy stature, the pointed beard, and the ever-present crown (in bed and swimming pools!). He never spoke, and indeed Soglow's world was almost always silent. The occasional dialogue appeared without benefit of balloons in keeping with Soglow's stark, simple artwork. There was no shading, backgrounds were scarce, and the figures were really glorified stick figures.

Continuing quietly in the 1970s, *The Little King* lost some of its pizzazz and much of its earlier surrealistic flavor. The feature ended on July 20, 1975, a few months after its creator's death.

R.M.

LITTLE LULU (U.S.) *Little Lulu* first appeared in June 1935 as a single-panel gag cartoon by "Marge" (Marjorie Henderson Buell) in the *Saturday Evening Post* magazine. In 1945, Western Publishing Company obtained the rights to the feature for its *Dell Four Color* and *Color* series of specials, commencing with number 74 in June 1945. Nine more "one-shot" issues of *Little Lulu* followed, and in January 1948 the first regular issue was published, beginning a long and successful series.

Marge was not responsible for any of the stories or artwork in the comic book or the subsequent newspaper strip. For some 14 years, the comic book was written by John Stanley, whose storyboarded scripts were then adapted into the artwork. Stanley did finished art on the covers. The newspaper strip, produced for the Chicago Tribune-New York News syndicate by the staff of Western Publishing, ran from 1955 to 1967. It was a daily strip done first by Woody Kimbrell, and, for its last six years, by writer Del Connell and several

"Little Lulu," Marge Henderson. © Marge.

artists, including Roger Armstrong. Both Stanley and Kimbrell developed and/or created a number of supporting characters who peopled Little Lulu's neighborhood.

From the start, *Little Lulu* was a strip about childhood and childhood fantasies, dwelling on the title character, a little girl in a typical urban neighborhood. Along with the other neighborhood kids, especially her "boyfriend," Tubby Tompkins, Lulu Moppet would get into endless dilemmas, often the products of overactive youthful imaginations. Superb characterization made even the most minute crisis funny, and for that reason the *Little Lulu* comics by Stanley are nostalgic favorites among collectors, many of whom consider it the best "kid strip" of all time.

Based mainly on the popularity of the comic books, *Little Lulu* was in demand for merchandising, including dozens of story and activity books produced by Western's book division and a series of animated cartoons produced by Famous Studios.

During the 1950s, Western's comic book division produced a great many giant specials with names like *Little Lulu and Tubby Halloween Fun* and *Little Lulu and Tubby at Summer Camp.* Many of these spotlighted a charming series by Stanley in which Lulu, as babysitter to little Alvin, would ad-lib fairy tales about the evil Witch Hazel and a small apprentice witch, Little Itch. In addition, Tubby had his own comic book for 49 issues from 1952 to 1962.

In 1972, Western Publishing assumed full ownership of the feature and Marge's byline was dropped. *Little Lulu* continued to appear in its own magazine and in various issues of *Golden Comics Digest* and *March of Comics.* The title came to an end in April 1984.

M.E.

LITTLE NEMO IN SLUMBERLAND (U.S.) Winsor McCay founded his masterpiece *Little Nemo in Slumberland,* which first appeared in the pages of the *New York Herald* on Sunday, October 15, 1905, on a very simple premise: each night Little Nemo is carried in dream to Slumberland, and each morning he is brought back to earth by the rude shock of awakening. In the course of his nightly wanderings, Little Nemo enters a little deeper into his dream-world, meeting along the way the characters who become his guides and companions: Flip, the green, grimacing dwarf; Impy the cannibal; Slivers the dog; the quackish Dr. Pill; and Morpheus, king of Slumberland, and his daughter the Princess (whose name we will never learn).

Doggedly, Winsor McCay proceeds with his methodological exploration of the dream. Lovingly he details its transpositions, its visions, its transformations. Graphically and pictorially, he re-creates its sensations, the sense of free fall, of flight, the feeling of dizziness, of estrangement. Like Freud, and with a similar purpose, he explores the depths of the unconscious. From the evidence of McCay's letters there can be no doubt that these explorations were in part autobiographical, and in part cautionary. McCay gave shape to his dreams in order to exorcise his demons.

Yet there has never been so luminous a treatment for so Faustian a theme. Slumberland is a country of no

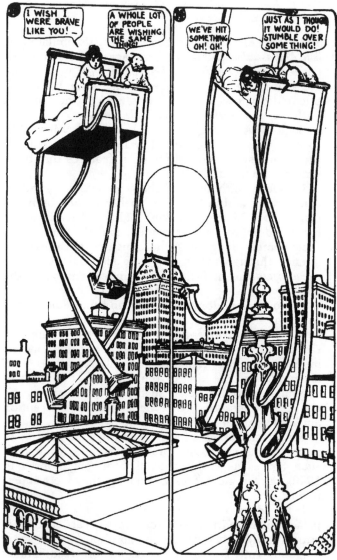

"Little Nemo in Slumberland," Winsor McCay.

"Little Orphan Annie," Harold Gray. © Chicago Tribune-New York News Syndicate.

shadows, and its light is the vibrant light of the early Renaissance painters. The grace of baroque composition and the freedom of Art Nouveau design touch its storybook palaces, its fairy-tale landscapes, the dress and poise of its characters. In this brightly lit universe, if the protagonists look shadowy (although there is a definite psychological progression as the action advances) it is because the hero is subordinate to the vision.

The last *Nemo* page appeared in the *Herald* of April 23, 1911. In the meantime McCay had gone over to Hearst (as so many other cartoonists had done before him), where he blissfully continued Little Nemo's adventures (under the title *In the Land of Wonderful Dreams*) from April 3, 1911, to July 26, 1914. Then, after a 10-year absence, *Little Nemo* was revived by the *Herald* from 1924 to 1927, after which it disappeared, this time for good.

Little Nemo's success had been immediate. In 1908 it was made into a musical (with a score by Victor Herbert); in 1909 McCay himself animated it (it was his first film cartoon). Greeting cards in the likenesses of Nemo, the Princess, and Flip were printed in England. Then there was a 20-year silence from 1927 to 1947. In 1947 Robert McCay (Winsor's son and his model for Little Nemo) tried to syndicate the old *Little Nemo* pages, but he was unsuccessful. Only in the late 1960s and early 1970s was interest in *Little Nemo* rekindled. In 1969 Garzanti published in Italy a hardbound collection of *Little Nemo* pages, and an American version appeared in 1972, issued by Nostalgia Press.

M.H.

LITTLE ORPHAN ANNIE (U.S.) According to legend, Captain Joseph Patterson of the *New York News* received a submission from *Gumps* assistant Harold Gray in 1924, performed a sex change on the strip, and thus gave *Little Orphan Annie* to the world. Whatever the circumstances of her birth, the little red-haired orphan girl soon developed into one of the truly classic figures of comic strip—and indeed, of American pop-culture—history. The strip debuted on August 5, 1924.

The first few years saw Annie in vaguely humorous, often sentimental, continuities—similar to *The Gumps*, another story strip long before the commonly acknowledged birth of story strips. In the early years the *Annie* Sunday page was an entity unto itself and complete within each day's page.

The feisty, curly-haired heroine—who, like all her fellow characters, was drawn with blank eyes—fended for herself in the early days against bratty playmates and bossy protectors. Her only true friends were her dog Sandy and her doll Emily Marie. About the time that the doll left the strip as a prop, "Daddy" Warbucks entered.

With the evolution of Warbucks from a henpecked member of the idle rich (his wife disappeared from the strip in short order) to an adventurous soldier of fortune, international businessman, and the richest man in the world, the strip took on its special meaning.

But more than novels in strip form (thus epitomizing the unique art form that is the comic strip), Gray's tales were morality plays. They were parables, folktales, told with Bunyan-like simplicity, allegory, and characterization.

Thus Gray wrote tales that gripped, that were at once fanciful and glaringly real. Characters were easily identified by their names: Warbucks was originally a munitions manufacturer; Mrs. Bleating-Hart a hypocritical do-gooder; Fred Free a wandering, kindly soul; J. Preston Slime a cynical, two-faced reformer. In time Warbucks (and more so his Oriental associates Asp and Punjab) assumed supernatural powers. These men were always present in the nick of time, dispensing justice arbitrarily, ruthlessly, and quietly.

Gray's art is not to be overlooked and is as important a factor as his writing; his drawings are simply as dramatic—and as suspenseful and pregnant—as the text. In his reserved, heavy lines, Gray created a world that was his own. Seldom have plot and art been so perfectly fused as in the integrated, very personal statement that was *Little Orphan Annie*.

Criticism has been harsh through the years against Gray for his (conservative) political views and his alleged propagandizing, but in the end, Gray needs no posthumous defense. *Annie* was one of the five top strips for decades; at its height it was the basis for two movies, a long-running radio serial, and countless merchandising items.

When Gray died in 1968, his syndicate did the unforgivable: farming out *Annie* to a succession of artists and writers who understood nothing of Gray's fragile creation save the most superficial—and erroneous—stereotypes. In early 1974 a youngster was given the strip with the intention of transforming art and story: Annie was to become a with-it kid. A barrage of complaints and cancellations brought back the Annie of her prime, via reprints starting with the classic Jack Boot murder story of 1936.

R.M.

Following the success of the Broadway musical (and later movie) *Annie* based on Harold Gray's characters, the syndicate decided to do a relaunch of the strip, with original stories this time. In December 1979 *Annie* (as the feature was now renamed to capitalize on the Broadway and upcoming Hollywood versions) made its appearance, drawn and written by Leonard Starr, who had been doing *On Stage* up to that time. Starr remained remarkably faithful to the original: he did bring a more contemporary look and feel to the feature, but otherwise his interpretation has been uncannily respectful to Gray's creation, without being slavish. Now approaching the third decade of its existence, *Annie* has proved the only successful revival of a classic comic strip to date. (*Little Nemo*, *Pogo*, and *Buck Rogers* all failed on their second go-round; the jury is still out on *Terry and the Pirates*.)

M.H.

LITTLE PEOPLE, THE (U.S.) When Walt Scott relinquished the Sunday *Captain Easy* in February 1952, he began his own *Huckleberry Hollow*, a Sunday comic featuring the doings of talking animals. It debuted on February 24, 1952.

The NEA comic, possibly created in answer to the success of *Pogo*, soon took second billing to *The Little People*. This new Sunday strip first appeared on June 1, 1952, based on characters that Walt Scott had drawn for a special NEA Christmas series of strips the previous year. Solely a Sunday page, *The Little People*, with *Huckleberry Hollow* as a top strip, continued until Scott's death; the last page appeared on September 6, 1970.

Scott, a former Disney artist and versatile cartoonist, packed a lot of charm into *The Little People*. The little folks are forest dwellers, the friends of friendly animals and fearful of bigger people and fiercer animals. They have enormous heads with floppy ears and impish expressions, and enormous feet.

In the beginning the little ones lived in a big log and made toys for Santa, but the Christmas theme soon vanished and the happenings in the Valley of the Small People became simple humorous situations on a cuter, smaller scale. Among the regular cast of little people were Cork, Chub, Wembly, Woosh, Weesh, Loop, Jink, and Old One.

R.M.

LOBAČEV, JURIJ (DJORDJE) (1909-   ) One of the most important Serbian comics authors, Jurij Lobačev was born on March 4, 1909, in the city of Skadar (then under Turkish control, now in Albania). His father, Pavie Lobačev, was a Russian diplomat. A month after Jurij's birth, he was transferred to Centinje, the second-largest city in Montenegro. From 1912 to 1914 the family lived in a succession of places: first Serbia, then Macedonia, Italy, and Crete. In 1916 Pavie Lobačev was promoted to consul general in Thessaloniki (Greece). But after the Russian Revolution toppled the czarist regime, the Lobačevs decided not to return to their native country. Instead, they settled after World War I in the newly created nation of Yugoslavia, which consisted of the former kingdoms of Serbia and Montenegro along with territories that used to be part of the Austro-Hungarian or Turkish empires.

Jurij Lobačev took the first name Djordje at this time; it was a name he would keep until being exiled from Yugoslavia in 1949. In 1922 he moved to Belgrade, where seven years later he finished secondary school and became a student of the Philosophical Fac-

Djordje Lobačev, "Hajduk Velijko." © Djordje Lobacev.

ulty. He eventually graduated from the Department of the History of Arts.

In 1934, after losing his job as a clerk in a building firm, Lobačev devoted himself completely to the new medium of comics. He published his first comic, *Krvavo nasledstvo* ("A Blood-smeared Inheritance"), under the pseudonym George Strip in installments in the Belgrade weekly magazine *Panorama*, beginning March 23, 1935. His scriptwriter for this initial and rather naive work was a close friend, Vadim Kurganski. Their second collaboration, *Zrak smrti* ("Death Ray")—based on the Alexei Tolstoy novel *Hiperboloid of Engineer Garin* and published in the magazine *Strip* beginning April 10, 1935—was only slightly better. Up until Yugoslavia became involved in World War II, Lobačev published some 30 long comics. For all but five of them he wrote the script himself. The most successful of them was *Princeza Ru*, which was published in France, Italy, and elsewhere.

During the war Lobačev worked as a technical editor for the illustrated magazine *Kolo*, which was published in Nazi-occupied Belgrade. He published only one comic during the war, *Biberce* ("Pepper-sized Boy"), in the magazine *Kolo*. The comic, based on a Serbian folktale about a small boy who defeats an evil giant, was banned by the Germans after the 10th installment. Nevertheless, a small Serbian publisher quietly printed the entire story as a comic book. In 1942 Lobačev became active in the resistance movement, and when Belgrade was liberated by Soviet and partisan forces in October 1944, he joined the advancing Allies, fighting all the way to Vienna, where he was wounded. After recovering, he returned to Belgrade in 1945.

In 1949, after a rift had developed between the Soviet Union and Yugoslavia, Lobačev, like many other Yugoslav citizens of Russian origin, was deported to the U.S.S.R. There he created *Hurricane to the Rescue*, which was probably the first Russian comic ever; in 1967 it began to be published in installments in the magazine *Kostyor*, which was based in Leningrad. However, after just a few installments, the regional committee of the Soviet Communist Party ordered publication of the strip to cease, declaring that comics were harmful to youth. However, Lobačev managed to publish his work in Serbia. For *Pegaz* magazine he completed an adaptation of *The Wizard of Oz*. He also drew comics inspired by Serbian folk traditions, drew a new version of *Baron Munchausen*, and created, in 1991, *Bajke A. S. Pushkina* ("Fairy Tales of A. S. Pushkin").

As of 1997 he was still doing new artwork for Belgrade comics publishers and visiting the city once a year.

S.I.

LOCHER, RICHARD (1929-   ) A Pulitzer Prize-winning editorial cartoonist for the *Chicago Tribune* in 1982 and the cartoonist for the *Dick Tracy* comic strip since that year, Dick Locher was born in Dubuque, Iowa, on June 4, 1929. He studied art at the University of Iowa, the Chicago Academy of Fine Art, and the Art Center of Los Angeles. He also served as a pilot in the U.S. Air Force. Working in a freelance art studio in Chicago, Locher met *Dick Tracy*'s creator, Chester Gould, in 1957. Gould asked him to be his assistant and Locher agreed, working for Gould for four years before starting his own advertising firm. Among other jobs, he was part of the team that developed the design of

Ronald McDonald and other characters representing the fast-food chain. Locher credits Gould for informing him of an opening for an editorial cartoonist at the *Chicago Tribune*. That was in the 1970s, and before then Locher had never done any editorial cartooning; now it's his passion.

With his experience as a former assistant to Gould on *Dick Tracy*, Locher was the logical choice to take over the artwork when Rick Fletcher, the artist who had succeeded Gould on the strip, died. Locher was teamed with scriptwriter Max Allan Collins, who had written *Dick Tracy* since Gould's retirement in December 1977. Then in 1992, Collins was abruptly fired by Tribune Media Services, the syndicate that owns *Dick Tracy*. He was replaced by Mike Kilian.

Locher readily admits that while he enjoys his comic-strip work, editorial cartooning is his preference. His editorial cartoons can be brilliant. While adequate, his artwork for *Dick Tracy* lacks the verve of both Gould's and Fletcher's work on the strip. It continues to maintain the stark black-and-white look with ample use of the classic Tracy profile and other stylistic elements created by Gould. Although the strip scored an increase in readership in 1990 when the Warren Beatty *Dick Tracy* movie was released, Locher has been fighting an uphill battle against comics editors' preference for humor over story strips. He has also suffered from scripts that for a time during the end of Collins's tenure depended too much on nostalgia and on bringing back old villains. The Kilian era of scriptwriting has not brought glory to America's most famous detective either.

Still, *Dick Tracy* may survive another decade of syndication. Locher has the talent, as his tight yet ornate editorial-cartooning style, replete with biting, dead-on caricatures, proves. However, he needs stories that excite him to take Tracy from the flatfoot cop he is today to the premier detective of yore.

B.C.

LOIS LANE (U.S.) Lois Lane is, amazingly enough, as old as Superman himself. She made her first appearance in National's *Action* number one for June 1938, the issue that introduced the *Superman* strip. She has been Superman's major love interest ever since.

Lois Lane, because she was part and parcel of the first comic book superhero feature, became the model for all future comic book love interests. And because creators Siegel and Schuster included a woman in *Superman*, most superhero imitators included one, too.

As originally conceived by the creators, Lois Lane was nothing more than a bitch—a conniving, self-serving, egotistical reporter with few ethics and fewer morals. She was not your typical girl-next-door, apple-pie woman. Perhaps the greatest example of her viciousness was her hatred of Superman's alter ego, Clark Kent. She rarely missed an opportunity to degrade or humiliate him.

This led to the classic comic book love triangle—Superman–Clark Kent–Lois Lane. It too became a prototype for almost all comic book superhero love affairs. It has also been scrutinized by psychiatrists and psychologists, and school-aged child throughout America recognize Lois Lane as Superman's girlfriend.

As the years went on, however, her character changed subtly and she finally made the transition from repulsive bitch to curious scatterbrain. Although not as aesthetically pleasing, this characterization made Lois Lane all the more saleable.

After appearing virtually everywhere Superman appeared, Lois Lane, National finally decided, was ready for a solo feature. After two appearances in *Showcase* in 1957, she was finally awarded her own title in March 1958. In that book, Lois Lane handled just about every possible situation: at one time or another she married virtually everyone in the "Superman family," from Superman himself to Clark Kent to Batman and Lex Luther; she fought and won a bitter rivalry for Superman's affection with Lana Lang, Superboy's sweetheart; and she became any number of superheroines and developed and subsequently lost any number of super powers. All this while she remained a reporter for the *Daily Planet*.

Kurt Schaffenberger, who worked on *Captain Marvel* and other adventure strips, is most often cited as the definitive artist. Lois also had a sister, Lucy, a former airline stewardess who sometimes doubled as Jimmy Olsen's love interest.

Noel Neill is most often remembered as the television incarnation of Lois Lane (from the *Superman* television series starring George Reeves), and Neill even conducted a college lecture tour concentrating on her Lois Lane career.

J.B.

Superman's Girlfriend Lois Lane (as the comic book was officially titled) came to an end in October 1974. It was briefly revived (as simply *Lois Lane*) in 1986. As for Lois herself, she came back with a vengeance in *Lois & Clark* (based on the television series) in 1994.

M.H.

LONE RANGER, THE (U.S.) In 1938 the editors at King Features decided to adapt Fran Striker's hit radio program, *The Lone Ranger*, into a comic strip; written by Striker himself, the new feature debuted on September 10, 1938, and was at first drawn by Ed Kressy, who was replaced by Charles Flanders early in 1939.

The Lone Ranger (whose identity is kept secret) is the sole survivor of a band of Texas Rangers cowardly gunned down in an ambush by a gang of outlaws circa 1890. Vowing to avenge his fallen comrades, he dons a mask and starts a career of fighting alone against crime. Mounted on his faithful white horse Silver, and accompanied by his loyal Indian companion Tonto (who had earlier rescued him from the clutches of the Cavendish gang), he is the scourge of the numerous evildoers plying the West. The Lone Ranger overcomes them all, leaving on the scene the existential trace of

his passage in the form of a silver bullet, before uttering his famous victory cry "Hi-Yo, Silver!" and riding into the sunset.

The Lone Ranger was one of the longest-running Western strips, disappearing finally in December 1971. Its popularity was greatest in the 1940s, when it gave rise to its own comic book (drawn by Tom Gill most notably, and written first by Striker, and later by Paul Newman). There were also Lone Ranger novels, and in 1938 William Witney and John English produced a stirring screen version of the strip, which was followed by three more movies and by a long-running television series (with Clayton Moore as the Lone Ranger and Jay Silverheels as Tonto).

A jazzed-up movie version, *The Legend of the Lone Ranger*, starring Klinton Spilsbury, briefly came (and went) in 1981; it prompted the New York Times Syndicate to attempt a revival of the newspaper strip that same year. Despite eye-pleasing graphics by Russ Heath and atmospheric writing by Cary Bates, the feature lasted only from September 1981 to April 1984.

M.H.

LONG SAM (U.S.) The brainchild of Al Capp, who created it and wrote its earliest sequences, *Long Sam* debuted on May 31, 1954, for United Feature Syndicate. The artist was Bob Lubbers, journeyman cartoonist who had been doing *Tarzan* and was later to draw *Secret Agent X-9* (under the name Bob Lewis) and *Robin Malone* and assist on *Li'l Abner*.

Long Sam was a hillbilly strip, built on the clever device of a sexy young girl who had never seen, or been allowed to see, a man. Sam was incredibly leggy and naive, her good looks and innocence getting her into many scrapes. Her constant companion and "protector" was Mammy.

Unfortunately but inevitably the device did not last forever; Sam just had to run into a man eventually. It was a one-gag or, rather, a one-theme strip; and it turned into a routine hillbilly feature. In many ways it was a copy of *Li'l Abner* instead of the reversal of it. It last appeared on December 29, 1962.

But during its run *Long Sam* showed much quality. Capp's original continuities were interesting, as were the tales after the original theme was discarded; Capp's brilliant brother, Elliot Caplin, supplied the scripts. Lubbers's art was always exciting—supple, full of motion, with a command of composition and anatomy. His style had much verve and deserved a better fate than a succession of near-great features throughout the years.

R.M.

LÖÖF, JAN (1940-   ) From his earliest years, Jan Lööf, a Swedish illustrator and comic book artist born in 1940 in Trollhättan, showed a fascination with drawing. Thus, it comes as no surprise that he started studying art in Stockholm in 1959. His main interest centered on drawing three-dimensionally, to create an illusion of space in his pictures. In 1965 he undertook the first steps that led to comic strips; he worked on picture books for children. The first of these, *En trollkarl i Stockholm* ("A Wizard in Stockholm"), was followed the next year by *Morfar är sörövare* ("Grandpa Is a Pirate") and *Den flygande hunden* ("The Flying Dog"). His publisher felt that his style would also be suited to a comic strip. Lööf jumped at the chance and came up

"The Lone Ranger," Charles Flanders. © King Features Syndicate.

with *Fiffige Alf* ("Cunning Alf"), an adventure strip with a cartoony, simplified style.

Together with his wife and brother-in-law, Krister Broberg, Jan Lööf moved to southern France to start drawing well ahead of publication. It was the newspaper *Politiken* of Copenhagen, Denmark, in which *Fiffige Alf* debuted in 1967, after having been retitled *Felix* by the syndicate. The deliciously simple style of *Felix*, a cross between picture-book and underground comix style, appealed to both children (for which the strip was originally intended) and grown-ups (for which the strip added more intellectual food in time). Lööf's comic strip art no doubt was also influenced by his favoring Wilson McCoy of *The Phantom* fame and cartoonist Saul Steinberg.

After several years in France, Lööf returned to Sweden and started working on animated cartoons of *Felix* for television, a medium in which he apparently felt quite at ease. In 1972 the weekly *FIB/Kulturfront* asked Lööf to do a somewhat different strip. The resulting *Bellman* was a strip about an old man from Stockholm's slums. However, Lööf abandoned the strip very soon. He also withdrew from *Felix* in the autumn of 1972 to devote his time to television. *Felix*, appearing in some 20 European newspapers, is being continued by a Danish artist.

W.F.

LOOK-ALIKE BOYS, THE *see* Mike and Ike.

LOOMAN, JOS (1941-   ) Jos Looman, a Dutch graphic artist, illustrator, and comic artist, was born on November 20, 1941, and grew up in Haarlem, Holland. In school he displayed a knack for drawing. Thus, after serving in the army, he started working for a company doing interior decorations. After six years, Looman moved to the United States to work for an advertising agency. Returning to the Netherlands one year later, he started looking for assignments. He had already drawn a number of book covers and several short comic features for *Pep*, the Dutch comic weekly, when it decided to develop its own stable of artists in 1968. Hetty Hagebeuk, then editor in chief of *Pep*, asked Looman to do a comic series about the life of Genghis Khan, which was being written by Anton Kuyten.

Looman agreed to try his hand at the task, experimenting a bit and studying the character and the times to get a feeling for this comic strip epic. It would have to have an air of believability in order to become a success. The resulting comic strip, *Dzjengis Khan—De strijd om het bestaan* ("Genghis Khan—The Fight for Survival"), with its strong characters and its flair for drama and adventure, turned out to be one of the most interesting comic strips created by the new school of Dutch comic artists.

Looman's talents were also tapped for *Jacht naar geluk* ("Pursuit of Happiness"), a combination horror/science-fiction comic feature written by Jan van Erp, which appeared in the first issue of *Baberiba*, a comics magazine with a more adult appeal than that of *Pep*. Looman, who showed an artistic maturity in this feature and in *Dzjengis Khan*, in which he experimented with his medium's layouts, continuity, and style, left the comics field after *Dzjengis Khan* was discontinued in the mid-1980s.

W.F.

LORD SNOOTY AND HIS PALS (G.B.) "Son of a Duke but always pally—with the Beezer Kids of Ash-Can Alley": thus ran the headline that introduced Lord Mamaduke (Snooty to you!) and his gang in number one of *Beano* (July 30, 1938). It was his young lord-

"Long Sam," Bob Lubbers. © United Feature Syndicate.

"Lord Snooty and his Pals," Dudley Watkins. © Beano.

ship's birthday, and Aunt Matilda, looking through her lorgnettes, informed her noble nephew that Algeron, Percival, and Vernon Tootle were on their way with a gift of a dog-cart. "Huh, those three Tootle guys give me a pain in the neck!" said Snooty, hopping through the bathroom window, slipping into his patched alter ego suit, and popping down to Ash-Can Alley. His gang had a similar birthday gift in store, a soap-box cart pulled by Gertie the Goat! The youthful Earl of Bunkerton Castle was off on a full page of fun that has continued to the present day.

Created by Dudley D. Watkins, Snooty's original "Pals" were Rosie, Hairpin Huggins, Skinny Lizzie, Scrapper Smith, Happy Hutton, and, of course, Gertie. Then came the terrible twins Snitchy and Snatchy, two toddlers in long johns who arrived in 1939. The gang remained unchanged until the series was suspended on July 30, 1949. When Snooty returned in the Christmas edition of *Beano*, December 23, 1950 ("by popular demand"), the Pals were slightly reconstituted: Rosie, Scrapper, Snitchy, and Snatchy remained, and the rest were recruited from past *Beano* characters: Big Fat Joe, Swanky Lanky Liz, Doubting Thomas, Polly Wolly Doodle and her Great Big Poodle, and Contrary Mary the Moke. As the quality of the artwork declined, fewer pals appeared in each episode, and the title was eventually reduced to *Lord Snooty.* Following Watkins's death in 1969, the feature has been drawn by a variety of artists, the most noteworthy being Robert Nixon.

D.G.

LORIOT *see* Bülow, Bernhard-Viktor von.

LUBBERS, ROBERT (1922-   ) American comic strip and comic book artist, born in 1922. After graduation from high school, Bob Lubbers attended the Art Students League, and like many of his fellow students, freelanced for pulp magazines and comic book compa-

nies, notably Centaur, for which he worked on *Reef Kincaid, Liberty Scout,* and *The Arrow.* From there Lubbers went to Fiction House in 1942 (where he would become art director from 1945 to 1950), working at one time or another on practically all of their features, including *Captain Wings, U.S. Rangers, Captain Terry Thunder, Rip Carson, Commando Ranger,* and *Firehair.*

After 1950 Bob Lubbers's career was almost exclusively devoted to syndicated strips. He joined United Feature Syndicate the same year that he took over the *Tarzan* daily strip and Sunday page, which he drew until 1954; he then went on to do his own strip, *Long Sam,* the story of a sexy hillbilly girl written by Al Capp (1954-58). Leaving United Feature, he went to King Features, where, after assorted chores as an assistant, he drew *Secret Agent X-9* (under the pen name Bob Lewis) from 1960 to 1967. In 1968 he tried a new strip for NEA, *Robin Malone* (about an alluring young widow), which lasted only a year. Beginning in 1970 he ghosted Al Capp's *Li'l Abner.* After *Li'l Abner* ended in 1977, he went to work in advertising as a specialist in animatrics (the animation of inanimate objects). He retired in 1989.

Bob Lubbers' motto seems to be *cherchez la femme.* Throughout his career he has been noted for his complacent renderings of the female figure, a penchant for which his graceful and somewhat cloying drawing style is well suited. Otherwise, his work has been competent, with few surprises, either up or down, along the line.

M.H.

LUCKY LUKE (Belgium) *Lucky Luke* was created by Morris (Maurice de Bevère) in 1946 as a one-shot for the *Almanach de Spirou,* but its success was such that it became a regular feature in the weekly *Spirou,* starting on June 12, 1947.

"Lucky Luke," Morris (Maurice de Bevère). © Editions Dupuis.

Following Goscinny's death in 1977, Morris turned to a number of writers for *Lucky Luke*. These have included notably Bob de Groot, Lo Hartog van Banda, Guy Vidal, and Xavier Fauche. Spurred on by the continued popularity enjoyed by his hero, he started in 1987 *Ran-Tan-Plan*, which starred the lonesome cowboy's hapless dog in a succession of pratfalls. He left Dargaud in 1990 and is now publishing his works under his own imprint, Lucky Productions. In the late 1970s and early 1980s there also was a *Lucky Luke* newspaper strip.

M.H.

"Lulu and Leander," F. M. Howarth.

Lucky Luke began as an affectionate takeoff on movie Westerns of the period. Lucky himself was the traditional pure-of-heart cowboy, always ready to bring justice to the Wild West before riding into the sunset. Lucky Luke rapidly became famous along with his trusted horse Jolly Jumper and his slightly self-deprecating refrain: "I'm a poor lonesome cowboy."

In 1955 the overworked Morris, while continuing the drawing of *Lucky Luke*, entrusted the writing to René Goscinny, and the strip became more and more realistic as it incorporated into its *dramatis personae* authentic figures from the history of the West. Thus Judge Roy Bean ("the law west of the Pecos"), Calamity Jane (depicted as an ugly, toothless harridan), Billy the Kid (represented as a nasty and precocious teenager), and Jesse James all locked horns (to their chagrin) with Lucky Luke. At the same time some colorful imaginary characters also came to the fore: the cousins Dalton, Joe, William, Jack, and Averell, outlaws of increasing size and diminishing intellect and Lucky's most persistent foes; and the cowboy's dog Ran-tan-plan (an obvious dig at Rin-tin-tin), the most hapless and cowardly canine on any side of the Mississippi. (In 1968 Morris and Goscinny transferred *Lucky Luke* from *Spirou* to *Pilote*.)

One of the best of the European humor strips, *Lucky Luke* has enjoyed from the beginning a well-deserved success. All the adventures of the lonesome cowboy have been reprinted in book form, first by Dupuis in Belgium, later by Dargaud in France. *Lucky Luke* has also inspired a song, been adapted into records, and been made into a musical comedy. In 1971 Belvision produced a feature-length Lucky Luke animated cartoon.

LULU AND LEANDER (U.S.) Created in 1903 for the Hearst comic sections, *Lulu and Leander* was the brainchild of F. M. Howarth, a 15-year veteran of magazine cartoons, principally for *Puck*.

Lulu and Leander was a one-gag strip: Leander was Lulu's suitor and, though he always kept Lulu, he usually got the worst of some weekly mishap in front of Lulu and her Mommer and Popper (none of the principals ever had last names). Among Leander's competition were Charley Onthespot and Lieutenant Shrapnell, clean-shaven dandies against whom Leander perpetually plotted. Leander himself was a slick-haired, mustachioed young man with the inevitable Howarthian oversized head. He was obviously well-to-do. Lulu was an attractive, shapely (wasp-waisted, at any rate) young lady who never had a hair out of place. As a matter of fact, it might have been the precise, sterile drawing of Howarth that led the public to tire of *Lulu and Leander*. To revive interest, Lulu and Leander got married on August 16, 1906, in a rare full page.

The format that worked for *Blondie* and later strips failed *Lulu and Leander*; shortly after their marriage, the strip was dropped by Hearst. Howarth moved on to the *Chicago Tribune* and died in 1908, just one year after the demise *of Lulu and Leander*.

R.M.

LUPO (Germany) Lupo is the roguish antagonist of Rolf Kauka's *Fix und Foxi*. As the name suggests, Lupo is supposed to be a wolf; however, his looks are only slightly reminiscent of one. Lupo is a friend of Fix and Foxi's, yet he is also their somewhat crooked opponent, an egomaniac who is always trying to outwit others with his get-rich-quick schemes. Of course, he never fails to get the short end of his deals. The lovable rogue was featured in solo adventures in *Fix und Foxi* before he became the star of his own comic book in 1965 after more than a decade of playing second fiddle to Fix and Foxi.

The *Lupo* comic book was soon retitled *LUPO modern* and given a very diversified lineup of features, ranging from original comics to translations of Belgian and French comics to reports on movie and record stars. *LUPO modern* earned a certain notoriety, not for its lead character but because of one of its backup features, the translation of the French comic series *Astérix*. Retitled *Siggi und Babarras*, it was this version of *Astérix* that became largely responsible for allegations of nationalistic tendencies in Kauka comic books. Here, *Astérix* no longer was a Gaul fighting Romans but a West German opposing East Germans. The Kauka group had felt that the French chauvinism in *Astérix* would not be palatable to a German readership; hence, they introduced a kind of West German chauvinism to the strip instead. The creators of *Astérix* were appalled, canceled their contract, and signed a new one with Kauka's competitors, whose faithful translations have since been sold by the millions.

The *Siggi und Babarras/Astérix* fiasco was just the culmination of ultraconservative or even reactionary tendencies in the Kauka line of comics. While it is not clear just who was responsible for these tendencies, they must somehow have been condoned by Mr. Kauka. The strange thing is that this type of not-so-palatable humor, which has been analyzed in various articles, seems to have occurred mostly in comic material not originated by the Kauka staff. Kauka's original funny animal heroes, living in a fairy-tale country, by and large stayed away from touchy subjects and politically incorrect language.

LUPO modern changed to *TIP TOP* in 1967 when Lupo was crowded out of the book by translations of foreign comics. Several title changes later, and the book became a digest-sized comic. In a way, *LUPO modern* paved the way for *primo*, the comic book that featured the first regular Kauka adventure comics.

W.F.

LUPO ALBERTO (Italy) For some time the most popular Italian comic character, Lupo Alberto was created and drawn by Silver, the pen name of Guido Silvestri. Silvestri, born in 1952 in Modena, served as Bonvi's assistant while in his late teens. In the early 1980s he worked as a political and satirical cartoonist for the daily *L'Occhio*.

Lupo Alberto ("Albert the Wolf") appeared for the first time in 1975 in the weekly *Corriere dei Piccoli*; the following year the strip began in the monthly *Eureka*. In 1983 the character gave birth to his own monthly, also titled *Lupo Alberto*, which was published by, successively, Corno, Glenat Italia (1985), ACME (1989), and Macchia Nera (1991).

Lupo Alberto's minimalist adventures take place on the fictional McKenzie farm, where many other characters enliven the action in the humorous strip. Among them are Marta, the hen who reciprocates Alberto's love; Enrico, the outspoken mole, and his wife Cesira; Alcide the pig; the cock Omar; Lou-Lou, a sexy pussycat; and the upstanding hedge sparrow Silvietta. All of these characters are portrayed physically as animals, but they speak, think, and act like human beings, although each also shows a bit of his or her animal instinct.

In the beginning, the strip was simply comical, but soon it started to deal with more complex situations and societal issues. Over the years, the graphic format has also evolved from a strip to a page.

Lupo Alberto has had a great impact on teenagers in particular, some of whom write the character for advice on all manner of personal problems. For this reason Alberto has been used in public-interest ad campaigns—for example, promoting the use of condoms and educating about the danger of AIDS. *Lupo*

"Lupo," Rolf Kauka. © Rolf Kauka.

"Lupo Alberto," Guido Silvestri ("Silver"). © Silver.

"Lurchis Abenteuer," Heinz Schubel. © Salamander Shoe Co.

Alberto adventures have been published in both hardbound and paperback books, and the character is widely used in merchandising. In 1996 some European TV stations began producing an animated cartoon serial, and a contract has been signed with United Feature Syndicate for its world distribution.

G.C.C.

LURCHIS ABENTEUER (Germany) In 1937 the advertising department of the Salamander shoe factory in Kornwestheim, Germany, decided that the company logo, a spotted salamander, might make for an interesting character in a pictorial giveaway to children. Thus were born the character Lurchi and the 12-page comic books titled *Lurchis Abenteuer* ("Lurchi's Adventures"). Five issues appeared up to 1938, then publication was suspended because of World War II.

In 1951 Salamander Shoes reissued the first five books. With the books' original artist missing, Heinz Schubel got the contract to rewrite and redraw the first books in an eight-page format and to continue the series. Schubel took Lurchi and his friends—Hopps, Mäusepiep, Igelmann, and Unkerich (frog, mouse, hedgehog, and toad)—and put them into a fairy-tale world that charmed generations of children and parents. Some of the stories drew on actual events, as when Lurchi went into space or visited the 1972 Summer Olympics in Munich. The Olympics also marked the end of Schubel's work, with issue number 52.

Some of the following 13 issues were done by anonymous artists; issues 57 through 63 were drawn by Angela Hopf. The series returned to a more distinctive style and continuity with isssue number 64. It is now being drawn by Georg Nickel and Peter Krisp, who alternate on the art chores. Reprints of the first 76 issues have been published in four volumes. Meanwhile, the series has passed number 100, with three issues published annually. By 1997 a remarkable 250 million copies of *Lurchi Abenteur* had been distributed since the inception of the series.

Although narrative is put into rhyme under the pictures, the stories are nevertheless split into individual panels that tell the stories almost like a pantomime strip. The early and recent artwork is full of detail and has a certain fairy-tale charm. While always adventure-oriented, some of the more recent stories deal with ecological themes. Entertainment is the main focus, but the advertising character is not completely forgotten. For one thing, Lurchi and some of the other characters wear Salamander shoes. And one way or another, the shoes often end up helping to solve a problem.

The books are still given away free, though the reprint collections are not. They can be purchased in the Salamander Shoe stores, where the Lurchi characters also are available as toys, dolls, and figures. They have also recently been used on records, in games, and on stickers and postcards.

W.F.

LYNCH, JAY (1945-   ) American underground comix book artist and writer, born January 7, 1945, in Orange, New Jersey. "Jayzey" Lynch, as he frequently signed his strips, has been cartooning since childhood. Some of his earliest artwork appeared in fanzines like *Wild* and *Jack High*. While he was studying art at the Art Institute in Chicago, he was working for *Aardvark* and *Charleton*, two legendary college humor magazines that were frequently the target of censors. Around this time (1963), Lynch was also a writer for *Cracked*, an imitation of *Mad*, and, in 1964 and 1965, he began appearing in the "public gallery" section of Harvey Kurtzman's *Help!* magazine.

Lynch's first major comic work came in 1967, however, when he introduced *Nard n' Pat* in the *Chicago Seed*, an underground newspaper that got sporadic national distribution. Undoubtedly, *Nard n' Pat* has been Lynch's most successful vehicle, and when he decided to start his own underground comix book, *Nard n' Pat* was one of its stars. The new underground book, *Bijou*, first appeared in the summer of 1968, with Lynch as its editor, publisher, and guiding light.

In *Nard n' Pat* Lynch adopted a unique style that fused the old "big-foot" style of humor drawing with heavily detailed renderings to produce a highly stylized page. Although he rarely, if ever, used backgrounds, his painstaking cross-hatchings, shadings, and zip-a-tones showed a heavy investment of time that comes only with a labor of love.

The plots usually revolved around Nard, a prudish Milquetoast who bears a remarkable resemblance to Andy Gump, and Pat, a wiseacre, smart-alecky "kitty kat." Pat's penchant for mechanics, easy sex, and inventiveness—not to mention a nostalgia for old rock-and-roll songs like "Duke of Earl"—makes him more human than Nard, who is funny because of his outrageously anachronistic opinions and actions. Unlike Snoopy, the beagle who constantly dreams of being human in Charles Schulz's *Peanuts*, Pat the cat does everything his human master will not, and does it with humorous results.

And although *Nard n' Pat* and some of Lynch's other underground work have made him one of the foremost underground cartoonists in America, he says he "has never made much of a living in comix." Nevertheless, Lynch poured considerable amounts of energy into the underground field. He edited *The Best of Bijou Funnies*, a 1975 anthology of the best *Bijou* material, taught comic art at his old art school, and even found time to draw a complete book of *Nard n' Pat* adventures, which appeared in 1974. He is currently producing sketches and sticker albums, using comic characters.

J.B.

LYNDE, STAN (1931-   ) American cartoonist, born in 1931 in Lodge Grass, Montana (by some accounts in Billings, Montana). Lynde's father was a cattle rancher, and the young Stan became familiar at an early age with the rough western life. Lynde's mother, who was artistically inclined, encouraged her son to draw; Lynde kept sketching the scenes around him and practiced his drawing by doing a comic strip for his high school paper. Later he studied art and journalism at Montana State University.

In 1951 Lynde went into the navy and was stationed on Guam, where he drew a comic strip titled *Ty Foon* for the base newspaper. Discharged in 1955, he briefly tried ranching, then went to work on a Colorado Springs newspaper before moving to New York in 1956.

In New York, Lynde worked for the *Wall Street Journal*, attending art classes at night. In 1958, after several unsuccessful attempts, he sold *Rick O'Shay*, a humorous Western strip, to the Tribune-News Syndicate. Dissatisfied with the lack of promotion it was receiving, Lynde left *Rick O'Shay* in 1977 (the strip was continued by other hands until 1981). In 1979 he created for Field Syndicate *Latigo*, another Western strip, which lasted only until 1983. Since the late 1980s he has been reissuing old episodes of *Rick O'Shay* and *Latigo* (along with some new stories) under his own Cottonwood Graphics imprint.

Lynde has been living on a 160-acre ranch near Billings, Montana, since 1962. There he attends to his herd of black Angus cattle (all branded RIK in honor of his most famous comic-strip creation), and he continues sketching the people and landscapes of Yellowstone and Big Horn counties, which helps keep the flavor of the real West in his publishing ventures.

M.H.

Stan Lynde.

MACACO (Spain) *Macaco* was specially created as the star attraction of the weekly comic magazine to which it gave its name, appearing in the first issue (January 29, 1928) as a gag strip. When *Macaco* magazine was discontinued in November 1930, the feature transferred to the succeeding publication *Macaquete*, this time (and until its demise on May 31, 1931) as a continuity strip.

Macaco was a little man with an inclination for rest and sleep. He lived in a surrealistic universe where anything could happen (and usually did), in which he calmly witnessed the most absurd situations, while watering (with a waterless sprinkling can) the beautiful cloth flowers of his garden. His kid brother Macaquete always walked by his side; an infant dressed in a red woolen suit from which hung a sucker, he was far more awake than his older brother, and his consciousness was also superior. The incidents would multiply because of Macaquete, although he himself would show no emotion.

In this historic creation, the clean and simple graphic style of K-Hito (pseudonym of the cartoonist Ricardo García López), *Macaco*'s creator, stands out, while the sparse text (also written by K-Hito) accentuates the action. The skillful use of color further contributes to the impression of fantasy that emanates from this work, with its warm tones and unbroken masses of solid color.

L.G.

McBRIDE, CLIFFORD (1901-1951) Clifford McBride was born in Minneapolis, Minnesota, in 1901. The son of a purchasing agent for a threshing machine company, McBride moved to Pasadena, California, in 1910, and drew assiduously through his school years. In fact, he was expelled (and later reinstated) twice for artwork in the high school paper that upset the principal. He graduated from Pasadena High School in 1920, having already sold an editorial cartoon to the *Los Angeles Times* in 1917. Just out of Occidental College in 1923, McBride was given his first newspaper job on the *Times*, where he drew a series of pantomime gag strips until he was offered a job through the mail by the *Chicago Tribune* in 1924. Illustrating humorous fiction for the *Tribune* (and its new magazine, *Liberty*) was not to McBride's liking, however, and he was delighted when the McNaught Syndicate offered to syndicate his pantomimic strip gags nationally in 1925, thus permitting him to return to Pasadena.

McBride's 8-to-12-panel weekly gag pages lacked recurrent characters until he introduced a roly-poly, middle-aged man who was remotely based on McBride's rotund Wisconsin uncle, Elba Eastman. McBride used him in his gag situations every third or fourth week. Readers seemed to like the character, so McBride gave him a name—Uncle Elby—and decided to involve him with a monstrously oversized mutt for the sake of a few gags in May 1929. Before long, most of McBride's mail demanded more of Elby and the dog—named Napoleon to counterpoint his uncle's name—and the artist decided to try a daily and Sunday strip featuring the pair for the Arthur J. Lafave Syndicate of Cleveland, Ohio. The new feature *Napoleon*, launched initially as a daily-only in June 1932, was an immediate hit, and McBride's fortune was made.

Moving to nearby Flintridge, California, with his wife, Elizabeth, McBride purchased a Saint Bernard even larger than his comic strip namesake, and pursued his hobbies of boat racing, swimming, performing magic, playing the piano, and voracious reading. Plagued by heart trouble and the loss of his wife, McBride aged quickly but did remarry. He died of a heart disorder on May 22, 1951, at the age of 50. His wife, Margot Fischer, continued to author the *Napoleon* strip for some time after his death.

B.B.

McCAY, WINSOR (1869-1934) American artist born in Spring Lake, Michigan, on September 26, 1869. McCay never completed grade school, but he received some rudimentary art instruction from an Ypsilanti teacher named Godeson. He then went to Chicago at age 17, drawing posters and taking more art lessons. In 1891 McCay moved to Cincinnati, where he designed the murals for the Vine Street Museum. McCay started his long newspaper career in 1897, first with the *Cincinnati Times-Star*, then with the *Commercial Tribune*, and finally with the *Enquirer*, where he created in 1903 his first comic strip, *Tales of the Jungle Imps*.

At the invitation of James Gordon Bennett, head of the New York Herald Co., McCay came to New York at the end of 1903 to work on the *Evening Telegram*. For the *Telegram* McCay created (under the pseudonym

Winsor McCay, "Gertie, the Trained Dinosaur."

Silas) a number of strips, including *Dull Care, Poor Jake*, and, best of all, *Dreams of a Rarebit Fiend* (1904), about the nightmarish encounters experienced by a voracious rarebit eater.

Under his own name for the parent *New York Herald*, McCay contributed more comic creations: *Little Sammy Sneeze*, about the cataclysmic sneezes of the little Sammy of the title (1904), *Hungry Henrietta*, about a ravenous little girl (1905), *Sister's Little Sister's Beau*, and others. Finally, with the stage all set for its appearance, *Little Nemo in Slumberland* made its first appearance on October 15, 1905.

In 1911 McCay went over to Hearst, for whom he continued Little Nemo's dream adventures (under the new title *In the Land of Wonderful Dreams*) until 1914, but mainly did editorial cartooning. From 1924 to 1927 he went back briefly to the *Herald* with a revised version of *Little Nemo*, then went back to Hearst, drawing more cartoons and large lifeless allegorical illustrations for editor Arthur Brisbane's editorials.

In 1909, meanwhile, McCay had started a parallel career in animated cartoons, producing in that same year *Little Nemo* (based on the strip), *How a Mosquito Operates*, and *Gertie, the Trained Dinosaur* (the complete title), which created a sensation when McCay released it. In 1917 McCay produced the first feature-length film cartoon, *The Sinking of the Lusitania*, and in 1920 his last work in the animation field, *The Flying House*, was released.

Among his other activities, McCay also did advertising and commercial work, and toured the vaudeville circuit, doing chalk talks and showing his animated cartoons, which he accompanied with a commentary of his own. (In New York he once shared the bill with Houdini and W. C. Fields.) Winsor McCay died on July 26, 1934. A few years earlier, in a letter to fellow cartoonist Clare Briggs, he had written his own epitaph: "Simply, I could not keep myself from drawing."

McCay's achievements are impossible to summarize in a few lines. He is an acknowledged pioneer in the field of animation and, by universal consent, the foremost master of the art of the comics (as well as one of the giants of American 20th-century art, as museums and critics everywhere are belatedly realizing). Yet it has been said of McCay that he left no disciple, founded no school—but this is true only in the most literal sense. Certainly the scale and sweep of his vision, the magnitude of his accomplishments, awed his fellow cartoonists and discouraged imitation. But McCay's merit lies in another direction: by liberating the comic strip from outmoded conventions of styles and limited choices of inspiration, he blazed new trails and paved the way for the bold and unceasing experimentation that was to take place in the comics for the next three decades.

M.H.

McCLELLAND, HUGH (1912-198?) South African cartoonist and illustrator, born in Roodeport, Transvaal, on November 21, 1912. Educated at Klerksdorp Hoer School, he studied art at the Johannesburg School of Art. He then joined the art department of the *Cape Times* in 1930. In 1933 he moved to England and began work for the *Daily Mirror* on September 5. It was a time of radical change for that newspaper, hitherto aimed at women, and as designer, with Basil Nicholson as publicity manager, he reconstructed the paper. The new editor, Harry Guy Bartholomew, was inspired by

American newspaper methods and anxious to introduce more strips. McClelland's first was an adaptation of *Love Me Forever*, a novel by Netta Muskett, into a daily strip of photographs: the first British *fumetto*. He became the first head of the expanding strip department, and under his aegis *Ruggles* (1935), *Belinda Blue Eyes* (1935), *Buck Ryan* (1937), and *Just Jake* (1938) were originated.

He created his first strip in 1937, a Western parody named after its sheriff hero, *Beelzebub Jones*. It ran from December 28, 1937, to December 28, 1945. Jones was modelled on McClelland's father, a farmer with a wooden leg. Extremely productive, McClelland's work method was to pencil 20 weeks worth of strips, writing dialogue as he went, then ink them, and then fill in blacks. This way he was able to continue *Jones* through his war service as sergeant instructor on the Link Trainer in the Royal Air Force.

He created several new strips after the war, starting with *Dan Doofer*. This strip, inspired by *Moon Mullins*, failed, running from December 29, 1945, to July 20, 1946. *Sunshine Falls*, a strip set in his native South Africa, replaced *Doofer*, but this too failed to click, running from July 22, 1946, to July 19, 1947. But his third strip, *Jimpy*, met with instant success and ran from January 5, 1946, to August 23, 1952. A revival of *Pip, Squeak and Wilfred* followed, but modernization of this traditional strip did not work.

Hugh McClelland, "Beelzebub Jones." © Daily Mirror Newspapers Ltd.

McClelland then moved to a rival newspaper, the *Daily Sketch*, where he produced his best-drawn strips: *Scott Lanyard* (1955) and *Jimmy Gimmicks* (1957). Unfortunately neither caught on. He then emigrated to Canada, and found work on the *Toronto Telegraph*. He reportedly died in the 1980s.

D.G.

McCLURE, DARRELL (1903-1987) American cartoonist and illustrator born February 25, 1903, in Ukiah, California. When Darrell McClure was nine, his parents moved to San Francisco. McClure, who later asserted that, "from the age of six, I never once swerved from the ambition to be a newspaper strip artist," was encouraged in his artistic endeavors by his mother. In 1917 and 1918 he studied at night in the California School of Fine Arts, and later attended a cartooning school, working variously as lumberjack, cowhand, and sailor. In 1920 he got his first professional job as a tracer in a small Los Angeles animation studio; when the studio folded, he went back to San Francisco and worked as a commercial animator. When this also failed McClure went to New York on a freighter, via the Panama Canal, and tried unsuccessfully to land a job at one of the newspaper syndicates. Discouraged, he went back to sea, plying the North Atlantic as a seafarer.

In 1923, a chance reunion with fellow Californian Jimmy Swinnerton led to McClure taking a job at King Features Syndicate as an apprentice artist. After five years of ghosting for a number of King Features cartoonists, McClure was finally given the go-ahead to create his own strip, *Vanilla and the Villains*, which debuted on September 10, 1928. After little over a year, the strip folded and, after an attempt to do *Hard Hearted Hicky*, McClure in 1930 went on to take over Brandon Walsh's faltering *Little Annie Rooney* daily strip (October 6), and to draw the newly minted *Annie Rooney* Sunday half-page (November 30).

In 1933 McClure relinquished the Sunday *Annie Rooney* to Nicholas Afonski (or Afonsky) in order to create a Sunday page of his own, *Donnie*, about the sea adventures of an enterprising teenage boy (not unlike Walsh's and Afonski's contemporary *Ming Foo*). Debuting in 1934, *Donnie* met with scant success despite its evocative qualities and McClure's loving knowledge of the sea, and the artist went back to the *Annie Rooney* Sunday page (1937). McClure drew the daily and Sunday adventures of the spunky little waif and her dog Zero until the strip's demise in 1966. During World War II McClure produced his last comic strip creation, *Ahoy McCoy*, for *All Hands*, the U. S. Coast Guard magazine. He retired in the late 1960s to his California hometown, where he died on February 27, 1987.

Darrell McClure will be chiefly remembered as the definitive artist on *Little Annie Rooney*, a strip he served well despite the lunacies of the plot, and as the creator of two charming, if underrated features: *Vanilla and the Villains* and *Donnie*.

M.H.

McDOUGALL, WALTER HUGH (1858-1938) American artist born in Newark, New Jersey, on February 10, 1858. The young McDougall entered and quit a military academy in 1874—learning more about life on the streets of Newark and about his early love, art, from his father, a painter.

Shortly thereafter McDougall broke into the growing field of illustrated journalism when he was hired by the *New York Graphic*, the first illustrated daily paper in America. Here, and on *Harper's Weekly*, where he sold sketches and cartoon ideas, he met many of the great early illustrators and cartoonists: A. B. Frost, C. J. Taylor, Gray-Parker, Theodore Wust, W. A. Rogers, and of course, Thomas Nast.

In the early 1880s he sold some drawings and ideas to *Puck* magazine; one favorite for years afterward was a comment on the watering of milk—a dairy farmer being startled by a cow, not knowing what it was.

And on October 30, 1884, he made history with his front-page cartoon in the *New York World*, "The Royal Feast of Belshazzar Blaine and the Money Kings," an exposé that is credited with losing New York—and the presidential election—for James G. Blaine to the benefit of Grover Cleveland.

McDougall scored a first on May 21, 1893, when his cartoon "The Possibilities of the Broadway Cable Car" became the first printed in color in an American newspaper. And on Feb. 4, 1894, in the same *New York World* pages, his collaboration with magazine cartoonist Mark Fenderson, "The Unfortunate Fate of a Well-Intentioned Dog," became the first color comic strip in an American newspaper.

During this period McDougall was also drawing full-page editorial cartoons in color for the *World*, and illustrating Bill Nye's weekly column for the American Press Association of Col. Orlando Jay Smith, making McDougall the first syndicated cartoonist.

In 1898 he drew probably the largest single-panel cartoon in color in an American newspaper—a double-page affair for the *New York American*—and once had front-page drawings in color in New York's *Herald*, *World*, and *American*, all on the same Sunday!

Among his Sunday features for the *Philadelphia North American* were *Fatty Felix*, *Peck's Bad Boy*, *The Wizard of Oz* (with continuity by Baum), and *Handsome Hautrey*. For the Western Newspaper Syndicate, and later T. C. McClure, he drew the long-running *Hank the Hermit and His Animal Friends*. His daily comic strips into the 1920s included *Absent Minded Abner*, *Teddy in Africa*, *Gink and Boob*, and *The Radio Bugs*.

Other projects in his long career included a play, *The Summer Boarder*, written with Henry Guy Carleton; the short-lived *McDougall's Magazine;* and an animated campaign cartoon for the Democratic National Committee in 1912.

McDougall was indeed in the forefront of several movements in the comics, and the graveyard of yesterday's titles is crowded with dozens of his minor strips. His friendship with the famous in art, journalism, and politics would seem to imply as strongly as study of his work that much of McDougall's success must have been due to personal contacts and camaraderie. His drawings were stiff and awkward, though full of a certain earthy and crude humor. He never matured to a facile style, and there was a direct correlation between the anatomical accuracy of his figures and obvious laboring at the drawing board. Ralph Pulitzer refused to rehire McDougall to do strips at the *New York World* because he "didn't like his style."

Nevertheless McDougall was a pioneer; if not as polished as Frost, facile as Opper, funny as Dirks, or inspired as the early Herriman, he was prolific and influential and was there when it all started.

McDougall committed suicide in 1938.

R.M.

McEVOY, JOSEPH PATRICK (1895-1955) Creator of *Dixie Dugan* and a noted novelist and humorist, Joseph Patrick McEvoy was born June 27, 1895, in New Burnside, Illinois, where he went to school. He attended the Christian Brothers' College in St. Louis, Missouri, and the University of Notre Dame. While attending the latter, he obtained his first newspaper job as office boy on the *South Bend* (Indiana) *News*. Later a reporter for the same paper, he parlayed his writing talent into a position as humor writer for the *Chicago Tribune*, where he wrote a series of comic poems called *Slams of Life* (these were collected into a book of the same name, with illustrations by Frank King, in 1919). In the early 1920s he did a weekly account of the doings of a typical Midwestern American family called *The Potters*, with illustrations by John H. Striebel, also for the *Chicago Tribune*. With a hit Broadway play based on this series (printed in book form with a dust jacket by Striebel in 1923), *The Potters* carried McEvoy into New York theatrical writing, where he authored such hits as *The Comic Supplement* (a revue based on the comic strips of the 1920s), *Americana*, and the *Ziegfeld Follies* of 1924 and 1926 (aside from the W. C. Fields skits).

Transferring *The Potters* to the Hearst papers in 1924, McEvoy saw the play adapted as a feature film with W. C. Fields in 1926. His first novel, *Show Girl*, which featured Dixie Dugan, was serialized in *Liberty* in 1928, then published in several printings by Simon & Schuster the same year. Dixie reappeared in two later novels as well: *Hollywood Girl* (1929) and *Society* (1931). A remaining major novel of the period, *Mister Noodle* (1931), was subtitled "A Novel of the Comic Strips" and dealt hilariously with the newspaper strip syndicate world of the time. It was drawn in large part from McEvoy's own experiences scripting *Show Girl*, the comic strip based on his Dixie Dugan novels.

With art by Striebel, *Show Girl* was begun in various subscribing papers on October 21, 1929, and emphasized the "fast," sensational Hollywood and Broadway show business life of the time (Flo Ziegfeld himself was caricatured—as Flo Zigfold—in the first week of the new strip). But with the Depression souring American life, the frivolous theme of *Show Girl* was felt to be hampering the new strip's potential circulation. The strip title was changed to *Dixie Dugan* in the mid-1930s, and Dixie was eased out of show business and into a mainstream working-girl existence: her strip became one of the most widely read in America.

In the mid-1940s, McEvoy left the scripting of *Dixie Dugan*, turning that task over to his son, Renny, who continued the strip with Striebel until the late 1960s. Famed for film script work in the 1930s, columns for the Hearst newspapers, and a long series of engaging articles for *Reader's Digest*, McEvoy died in 1955.

B.B.

McFARLANE, TODD (1961-   ) American comic book artist born April 16, 1961, in Calgary, Canada. After attending Eastern Washington University, where he earned a bachelor's degree in graphic design, Todd McFarlane went to work for Marvel in 1985 as a penciler on the *Coyote* title for their Epic Comics imprint. That same year he crossed over to DC Comics, drawing for the Infinity Inc. line of comic books.

It was with *The Incredible Hulk* and *The Amazing Spider-Man*, however—two of Marvel's flagship titles that a burned-out Stan Lee and a succession of second-stringers had allowed to go stale—that McFarlane rose to fame. Starting in 1987, his dramatic rendering of these two superheroes, coupled with a kinetic sense of visual storytelling, rescued the venerable features from the doldrums, and in 1990 he was allowed to write his own stories. The McFarlane-scripted *Spider-Man* number one broke all previous sales records for a single comic-book issue.

McFarlane was among the Marvel defectors who founded Image Comics late in 1991. "When I quit Marvel, I was the top-paid guy and I couldn't spend all the money they were paying me," he later declared in an interview. In May 1992, under his own Todd McFarlane Productions imprint, the first issue of *Spawn*, written and drawn entirely by the author, came out and sold over one million copies, a record for an independent comic book title. While visually dynamic and fast-moving, the early issues of *Spawn* had laughable dialogue and desultory plots—weaknesses McFarlane remedied by bringing in talented wordsmiths such as Alan Moore and Neil Gaiman to write the scripts. The title has been a constant top-seller since its inception and has given rise to a number of spinoffs as well as to several action figures marketed by Todd McFarlane Toys. In May 1997 the animated *Todd McFarlane's Spawn* debuted on HBO, and a live-action *Spawn* movie was released in August 1997.

M.H.

McLOUGHLIN, DENIS (1918-   ) British cartoonist and illustrator born April 15, 1918, at Bolton, Lancashire, and educated at Dearden's Private School and Sunninghill School prior to winning a scholarship to Bolton School of Art in 1932. His first professional work was done for Ward and Copley Studio in Manchester, drawing realistic illustrations for John Noble's Sixit Club Catalogue (1934). His first cartoons were for Atlas Stores and he entered the comics field by drawing three covers for Sunday supplements imported from the United States for market sales (1938). He was called into the Royal Artillery (1940) and during his service he painted 50 humorous and pinup murals for Woolich Depot. Freelancing in his spare time, he drew the book jacket for *Navy Colt* by Frank Gruber, the first of 700 of this type. In 1944-45 he drew three complete cartoon books: *Laughter for Home and Front*, *New Laughs for All*, and *Laughter Parade*—the publisher, Kangaroo, changed his name to David McLoughlin. The same publisher issued his first complete comic book, *Lightning Comics* (1946), which included a Western and a science-fiction strip, two fields in which he would excel.

In 1947 he was exclusively contracted by T. V. Boardman, a prolific publisher of novels and comics, and created their house style. His many book jackets and paperback covers belong to this period, as does creation of the famous trademark, the Boardman Bloodhound, that he also sculpted for a trade exhibition. For the Boardman comics, 12-page booklets printed in excellent two-tone gravure, he created the detective *Roy Carson*, the spaceman *Swift Morgan*, and the covers for such U.S. reprints as *Blackhawk*. He also took over the *Buffalo Bill* series, formerly a reprint of the Swiss strip by Lennart, improving it considerably with his expertise in the Old West, while drawing and compiling 13 *Buffalo Bill Annuals* (1949-1961).

After Boardman's retirement from publishing, McLoughlin wrote and drew the book *Derek the Tor-*

George McManus, "The Whole Blooming Family." © King Features Syndicate.

toise (Dean), and compiled the *Encyclopedia of the Wild West* (Doubleday, 1973). In between he drew the serial strips *Saber* and *Big Hit Swift* for *Tiger* (1967), *Fury's Family* for *Thunder* (1970), and *Power the Danger Ranger* and *Terror in the Tall Tower* for *Wizard* (1974). He continues to be a forceful contributor to British comics, working in the American style, which he much admires. Although he slowed down in the 1990s, he still draws an occasional war comic book.

D.G.

McMANUS, GEORGE (1884-1954) American cartoonist born in St. Louis on January 23, 1884. At 16, George McManus became cartoonist (and later fashion editor) for the *St. Louis Republic*, where he published his first comic strip. Of that effort, *Alma and Oliver*, McManus later said, "It was a terrible mess and wouldn't get by high school editors today."

In 1904 McManus went to New York and started a long association with Joseph Pulitzer's *World*. Over the years he contributed a variety of comic features in the hope that one (or more) would click. They were: *Snoozer*; *The Merry Marcelene*; *Panhandle Pete*, one of the first in a long line of comic strip bums; *Nibsy the Newsboy in Funny Fairyland*, an unabashed but beautiful imitation of *Little Nemo in Slumberland*; *Cheerful Charley*, about a stone-faced Indian; and *Let George Do It* (a phrase that was to become famous). But the most popular and best of McManus's strips for the *World* was *The Newlyweds* (1904), the first of his family strips.

In 1912 McManus moved to William Randolph Hearst's *New York American*, transferring *The Newlyweds* with him, under several alternate titles (*Their Only Child, Baby Snookums*, etc.). But McManus was still not satisfied artistically and he started experimenting again with several ideas in the period from 1913 to 1918,

George McManus, "Their Only Child." © King Features Syndicate.

simultaneously creating *Rosie's Beau*, a humorous girl strip; *The Whole Blooming Family*, about a much put-upon husband and father; and *Spareribs and Gravy*, a take-off on scientific explorers; as well as the feature for which he was to receive world acclaim, *Bringing Up Father*.

McManus also worked on animated cartoons (producing notably the *Snookums* series with Emile Cohl) and contributed occasional illustrations to magazines, but he remained first and foremost an artist of the comics. His elegance of line and elaborate mise-en-scène have been widely imitated but never equalled; every cartoonist has, at one time or another, borrowed some of McManus's pungent aphorisms, but none has ever matched his impeccable timing and delivery.

McManus's popularity was as great as his artistry. Countless awards from art groups and civic organizations were heaped upon him. On the occasion of *Bringing Up Father*'s 25th anniversary a Congressional dinner was held for him in Washington, and he continued to receive innumerable fan letters from simple citizens and government leaders alike until his death in Santa Monica, California, on October 22, 1954.

M.H.

McNEILL, HUGH (1910-1979) British cartoonist and illustrator, born in Manchester of Scottish parents on December 13, 1910, Hugh McNeill received a secondary school education and attended Manchester School of Art evening classes from 1925 to 1927. He became a four-year apprentice at Kayebon Press, a Manchester advertising studio. His first published drawing was a gag cartoon in *Topical Times* (1927).

McNeill tried comic strips in response to an advertisement in a local newspaper by D. C. Thomson, which was seeking artists for its new comic publications, *Dandy* and *Beano*. His first original character, *Ping the Elastic Man* (July 30, 1938), in *Beano*, was an indication of the special kind of wild whimsy that would make his comic work stand out. Then came *Simple Simon* (1938) for *Dandy*, and McNeill's most enduring character, *Pansy Potter*, for *Beano* (1938). Comic strip work suited his sense of humor and proved more rewarding to his employers than advertising work. They extended him to the main comic publisher, Amalgamated Press, and he created *Simon the Simple Sleuth* (March 4, 1939) for the new comic *Knockout*, and *Professor P. Nutts* and *Binky & Granpop* (both March 18, 1939) for the revamped *Jolly Comic*. His style so suited *Knockout* that he rapidly took over, creating *Deed-a-Day Danny* for the colored front page and making the already-established *Our Ernie* conform to his own wacky wit.

Unhappily, war curtailed his burgeoning career and he was conscripted into the Royal Army Service Corps. He continued to draw his *Knockout* characters, and, when posted overseas in 1943, he drew his *Danny* pages on air letter forms that were the same size as reproduction.

Hugh McNeill, "Deed-a-Day Danny." © Knockout.

After demobilization McNeill returned to *Knockout* with *One Eyed Joe* and *Two Toof Tom* (1946) and others, then showed a new side to his art by taking on an adventure strip, *Tough Tod & Happy Annie* (1947). He expanded this style further with *Deadshot Sue* (1949), *Highway Days/Dick Turpin* (1951), adaptations from films (such as *King Solomon's Mines*) in *Sun*, and the superhero *Thunderbolt Jaxon* (1949) in *Comet*.

A third change of direction occurred on February 27, 1954, when A.P. launched the gravure weekly *Jack and Jill* for younger children. McNeill not only drew these front page children, he also revived Harry Hargreave's *Harold Hare* from *Knockout*, but with his own new nursery style, plus a touch of his old fantasy. The character was virtually reborn. Harold grew so popular that he was given a weekly comic of his own, *Harold Hare's Own Paper* (November 14, 1959), and a newspaper strip in the *Sunday Pictorial* (1960).

In 1961 McNeill took on the adventures of the son of Andy Capp, Buster, in the comic of the same name, and from February 25, 1967, he drew *The Trolls*, a two-page strip adapted from the familiar little dolls, for *Tina*, a girl's comic. Meantime, he created and drew many characters and strips, all with the great humor and charm that has marked his work from the start.

"Hughie," as his friends called him, died on November 22, 1979, in Sussex, on the eve of being presented with the Ally Sloper Award for a lifetime devoted to comics. He never knew he was going to receive the award.

D.G.

McWILLIAMS, ALDEN (1916-1993) American artist born 1916 in Greenwich, Connecticut. A graduate of the New York School of Fine and Applied Arts, Al McWilliams started his career in pulp magazines before becoming one of the pioneering comic book artists in 1935.

For Western (his most constant comic book employer from 1935 to 1942) McWilliams contributed both writing and artwork (with a strong leaning to science fiction) to such diverse features as *Captain Frank Hawks*, *Gangbusters*, *Space Cadets*, *Stratosphere Jim*, and *Flash Gordon*. During the same period he also worked for Centaur (*Skid Davis*, 1939) and Quality, where his forte from 1940 to 1942 was war stories (*Spitfire*, *Atlantic Patrol*, *Captain Flag*, *Destroyer 171*).

After three years in the army during World War II, McWilliams was discharged in 1945 and promptly resumed his comic book career, developing *Steve Wood* for Quality and *Young King Cole* and *Sergeant Spook* for Novelty, as well as a number of crime stories for Gleason. Al McWilliams is best noted, however, for his newspaper strip work which began in 1953 with the science-fiction daily *Twin Earths*, written by Oskar Lebeck and distributed by United Feature Syndicate. When *Twin Earths* folded in 1963, McWilliams went on to draw *Davy Jones* (a sea adventure strip that he had originated with writer Sam Leff in 1961). Later came *Dateline: Danger!* (1968-1974, for Publishers-Hall Syndicate), an excellent spy adventure strip with scenarios by Allen Saunders. In his later years he drew the *Star Trek* and *Buck Rogers* strips, and assisted John Prentice on *Rip Kirby*.

Al McWilliams also did a great deal of advertising work and never stopped working for comic books. (*Man From UNCLE* and *I Spy* were two of the titles he contributed to in the 1960s.) A talented and unassuming craftsman, Al McWilliams always managed to make a distinguished contribution to every feature on which he worked. He died in March 1993.

M.H.

MADAM AND EVE (South Africa) A comic strip about a "wannabe liberal" white housewife and her street-wise black maid, *Madam and Eve* satirizes the new South Africa through one of society's oldest and closest—yet most distant—interracial relationships. Gwen Anderson and her assertive maid Eve Sisulu verbally tangle about household matters, while also commenting in rather critical terms about changes in postapartheid South Africa.

Madam and Eve's tremendous success can be attributed to its understated irony and to the fact that its two lead characters are given almost equal chances to come out on top. Madam does so through her dominant position and use of blunt force, while Eve employs a more conniving and subtle style. Playing off current events, the strip also pokes fun at the high-and-mighty and society at large, paying no attention to rank, color, or class. It aims to make South Africans laugh at themselves, while also making them squirm a bit.

Madam and Eve was started in 1992 by Harry Dugmore, Stephen Francis, and Rico Schacheri, three non-South African-born transplants from Botswana, New York, and Austria. They have worked together since 1988, first on the satirical magazine *Laughing Stock*, and then in another branch of the parent publishing company. The first newspaper to pick up the strip in its original 12-panel format was the *Weekly Mail and Guardian*. The four-panel version was first introduced in the *Johannesburg Star*; seven dailies and three magazines now carry *Madam and Eve*, and efforts are being made to syndicate it abroad.

American influences, such as the one-two gag punch of Johnny Hart, the political humor of *Doonesbury*, and the philosophical style of Bill Watterson, are acknowledged by Dugmore. According to him, *Madam and Eve* uses "cynical humor which people love. Sometimes we are hard-hitting, but we also bring a certain warmth to the strip." Dugmore, who has a Ph.D. in history, is very much aware of the wide berth *Madam and Eve* has been given by the authorities, as it has held up for ridicule, without incident, the few scandals that have blemished the Mandela administration. Government largesse and inefficiency were targeted in the daily strips for weeks on end, as well as in *All Aboard the Gravy Train* and *Somewhere over the Rainbow Nation*, two of the four bestselling *Madam and Eve* collections that have been published.

J.A.L.

MAFALDA (Argentina) Created first as a weekly page for the Buenos Aires magazine *Primera Plana* on September 29, 1964, *Mafalda* soon became a daily strip as well, published for the first time in this format in March 1965 by the newspaper *El Mundo*.

With a highly individual and simple graphic style, its creator Quino (pseudonym of Joaquin Lavado) humorously related the adventures of Mafalda, an argumentative little girl who refused to be integrated into the adult world. Her extraordinary insight and precociousness allowed Mafalda to understand, better than her elders, the situations of the world at the time. From the mid-1960s to the mid-1970s (when Quino decided to abandon his strip) the author seemed to share his character's astonishment in the contemplation of a world bent on its own destruction. This work mirrored the contradictions of the thinking man, when confronted with mindless individuals merely intent on existing, through the mediation of a little girl.

"Madam and Eve," Harry Dugmore, Stephen Francis, and Rico Schacheri. © Rapid Phrase Entertainment.

"Mafalda," Quino (Joaquin Lavado). © Quino.

Mafalda and her little friends—Felipe the idealistic dreamer; Susanita the already adult little girl, obsessed, like her mother, with boys and money; Manolito the future businessman, and others—with their deep psychological insights, judged the world in which they live. For this reason, the strip transcended the concrete Argentine situation which gave rise to it, and reflected the universal anxieties, obsessions, and preoccupations of the time.

Mafalda was published in book form (1968), translated into six different languages, and distributed widely throughout Europe and Latin America. Its success, like that of *Peanuts*, led to its rapid commercialization, with hundreds of toys, dolls, and gadgets of every description, and a series of animated cartoons for television.

L.G.

MAGER, CHARLES AUGUSTUS (1878-1956) Creator of the famed *Monks* strip series of 1904-1913, and the later *Hawkshaw the Detective*, Charles Augustus "Gus" Mager was born 1878 in Newark, New Jersey. Growing up in Newark, the son of middle-class German immigrants, Mager went through the old-world comic humor magazines sent to his parents by relatives in Germany as he attended grammar and high school in his hometown, basing much of his emerging cartoon style on the work of Wilhelm Busch and others. Getting his first newspaper job with the Hearst papers in New York at 20, Mager had already sold a number of spot gag cartoons to the American cartoon magazines of the time, and provided the same sort of material for Hearst's *New York American* and *New York Journal*, from which they were sent to other Hearst papers for reprinting. Mager's early talents leaned toward humorously drawn animals, and his gag cartoons emphasized this element, particularly African jungle fauna such as tigers and monkeys. Before long, Mager's gags had a running title for their occasional daily appearance: *In Jungle Land* (sometimes also *In Jungle Society*).

From this springboard, the young, just-married Mager launched his first gag sequence about a separately named animal, *Knocko the Monk*, which first appeared in the *Journal* on April 25, 1904. The public loved *Knocko*, and Mager gave them a continual series of *Knocko* episodes for the rest of the year. He made a brief stab at another kind of strip (with humans), *Everyday Dreams*, then turned back permanently to his monkey characters, introducing a *Rhymo the Monk*, then reintroducing *Knocko*, and adding fresh figures every few months: *Henpecko the Monk*, *Groucho the Monk*, etc. Finally, in 1910, he created *Sherlocko the Monk*; this became his most popular figure and eclipsed public interest in the earlier *Monk* strips. Most of his subsequent work focused on Sherlocko and his involvements with the other *Monk* characters, and it was the Sherlocko character (a close parody of Doyle's Sherlock Holmes) that he took with him when he left Hearst and joined the staff of the *New York World* to create *Hawkshaw the Detective*, a humanized version of the old *Sherlocko* strip, on February 23, 1913. Mager continued with *Hawkshaw* (aside from a brief attempt in 1922 at a small-town family-type strip, largely ghosted for him by another artist, called *Main Street*, and to circulate a renovated *Sherlocko* strip on his own in 1924) for the rest of his life, adding it to Rudolph Dirks's *Captain and the Kids* page in 1931, and continuing with it there until his retirement in the late 1940s.

Living continually in Newark, Mager had built a sizable home there and now took up his lifetime hobby of serious painting in earnest, selling paintings to the permanent collections of the Newark Museum and the Whitney Museum in New York, among others. A devoted naturalist, as his early strip work suggested, Mager also drew a feature page titled *Games and Gimmicks* for *Outdoor Life Magazine*. He published only two small books (aside from comic book reprints in *Tip Top Comics* and elsewhere) in his lifetime, and died on July 17, 1956, at the home of his son, Robert, in Murrysville, Pennsylvania, where he had been ill.

B.B.

MAGER'S MONKS (U.S.) Charles A. Mager's series of interrelated and simultaneously running daily *Monk* strips (*Knocko the Monk*, *Rhymo the Monk*, *Sherlocko the Monk*, etc.) that ran in the first two decades of this century and were the direct source of the Marx Brothers' acting names, first appeared in Hearst's *New York Journal* on April 25, 1904, in the form of a *Knocko the Monk* ("He Always Says What He Thinks") episode. Earlier, Mager had done spot animal gags for the morning and evening Hearst papers, incorporating these after a time into an editorial page feature called *In Jungle Land*, or, alternatively, *In Jungle Society*, which ran through 1903 and 1904. Like its predecessor gag feature, *Knocko the Monk* appeared every second or third day on the *Journal* editorial page, alternating with other quasi-daily strips of the period, such as *Johnny Bostonbeans* and *Mr. E. Z. Mark*. Mager dropped *Knocko* at the end of 1904 and turned to human characters in a short-lived strip called *Everyday Dreams*. The public didn't care for this, demanded more Mager Monks, and by mid-1905 Mager had satisfied them by introducing *Rhymo the Monk*, which ran in the *Journal* through the rest of the year.

Mager's early simian characters were small apes, with a multiplicity of facial hair and baggy human clothing. Gradually, as his strips continued, his monks became more humanized and their settings became contemporary houses and cities. Each of his title characters had a quirk or obsession reflected in his name,

"Mager's Monks," Gus Mager.

and as these strips increased in variety of titles after 1905, running intermixed in the *Journal* as the already mentioned *Knocko* and *Rhymo*, *Tightwaddo the Monk*, *Groucho the Monk*, *Nervo the Monk*, *Hamfatto the Monk*, etc., their layout became standardized as an upright, oblong set of six panels per episode.

The popularity of the *Monk* strips was enormous, and various vaudeville comics of the 1910s adapted Mager's titular idea for themselves, so that Hickos, Sharpos, Plumpos, *et al*, flourished for a while. This fad died down with the closing of most of Mager's *Monk* strips in the early 1910s, but it was recalled by a vaudeville monologuist named Art Fisher who improvised the names of Groucho, Chico, Harpo, and Gummo for four of the five Marx brothers during a 1918 poker game.

Mager's future was settled, however, when he introduced *Sherlocko the Monk* in the *Journal* for December 9, 1910. The first *Sherlocko* was a lovely take-off on A. Conan Doyle's *Sherlock Holmes* detective stories, complete with an admiring aide named Dr. Watso, and a neat six-panel mystery-and-solution involving Tightwaddo the Monk. Before long Mager was drawing just the one title for Hearst, and felt he deserved a Sunday page. Hearst had no place for Mager in his already jam-packed four-page Sunday section, and Mager began to shop around. He found a sympathetic ear at the *New York World*, and left Hearst's *Journal* (where the last *Sherlocko* ran on February 23, 1913, followed by one or two old *Monk* strips the *Journal* still had on hand) to undertake a Sunday *Sherlocko* for the *World*.

In the meantime, Doyle's representatives in the United States had gone to court to suppress Mager's *Sherlocko* title as an infringement of copyright. (Worried, the *World* asked Mager to find new names for his two principals, which he did, but this is another story that can be found in the entry for *Hawkshaw the Detective*.)

B.B.

MAGGIE AND JIGGS see Bringing Up Father.

MAGSINO, FRANK (1937-   ) Frank Magsino was born on December 3, 1937, in San Jose, Occidental, Mindoro, an island in the Philippines famous for its wild buffalo, the tamaraw. Frank Magsino attended the University of Santo Tomas and majored in art, but left school when he was offered a job working for Araneta University doing a variety of art chores. From there he went on to work for Hontiveros Associates Incorporated, doing layouts, illustrations, and advertisements for Pepsi Cola. He also did a stint with Adver Incorporated in commercial art.

From 1961 to 1968, Magsino worked as a freelance artist doing covers and interior art for several magazines such as *Women's World* and the comic-oriented publications *Liwayway* and *Bulaklak*. He illustrated many short stories and novels that appeared in these Tagalog comic magazines.

He continued his education in the United States, receiving a Bachelor of Arts degree from the San Francisco Academy of Art. Galleries in Europe, the Philippines, and the United States have sold many of his works in oil, acrylic, tempera, and watercolor. Though much of his art was done in the classical manner, dealing with traditional subjects, his later endeavors were varied and eclectic in approach. Ventures into the fields of surrealism and fantasy brought further acclaim to his works.

Despite his heavy commitment to painting, Magsino experimented with a variety of strips and did some cartoon features, as well as some artwork for Marvel's *Conan* comic book (U.S.) in the early 1970s. He is no longer much involved with comics.

Being ambidextrous, Magsino drew and painted with his right hand and did his lettering with his left. He was one of the very few individuals who used a brush to do his lettering.

O.J.

MAIN STREET (U.S.) Decidedly the flattest and least interesting Gus Mager strip, and a very minor strip in its own right, *Main Street* was created by Mager as a

Sunday page for the *New York World* shortly before his popular *Hawkshaw* page folded in mid-1922. It appeared first in nationwide syndication by the *World's* Press Publishing Company on April 22, 1923.

A bad mistake as a strip, *Main Street* attempted to present too many ill-defined characters at once (the residents along a middle-sized town's Main Street). Its style, an odd mixture of Mager faces and ghosted torsos done in a pseudo-McManus manner, was not captivating. Although some of the individual weekly gags and situations were good, the lack of strongly defined central figures ultimately sank the strip and ended Mager's career with the *World*.

By the extent of his more frequent appearances, Henry Meek, a henpecked husband, might be said to have been the strip's main character, but other families and individuals such as the Millers, the Ticks, and the Smithers shared the confused scene. Within a few months, *Main Street* had been dropped by most of the subscribing papers initially attracted by the Mager name and the reputation of *Hawkshaw*, and it disappeared from the *World* itself late in 1924.

B.B.

MAISON IKKOKU (Japan) In *Maison Ikkoku*, artist Rumiko Takahashi pursues the male fantasy of the hopeless slob who gets the perfect woman. What separates *Maison Ikkoku* from other such stories, however, is the fact that Takahashi is herself a woman. Serialized in the weekly magazine *Big Comic Spirits* from November 1980 to April 1987, *Maison Ikkoku* was the first title by a woman to become a popular hit in a Japanese men's comics magazine. (Another well-known work of hers, *Urusei yatsura*, was the first title by a woman to be a popular hit in a Japanese boys' comics magazine, and ran more or less concurrently with *Maison Ikkoku*.)

The hero of this charming romantic comedy is young Yusaku Godai, a resident of the dilapidated Maison Ikkoku apartments who failed to pass the college entrance exams on his first try and, as the story opens, is preparing to take the exams again a year later. Yusaku is indeed a slob, and, like most men his age, has his share of impure thoughts, but he falls genuinely in love with the Maison Ikkoku's new superintendent, the young and beautiful widow Kyoko Otonashi.

An awkward love-quadrangle quickly forms, as Yusaku must deal with Kozue Nanao, who has declared herself to be his girlfriend, and vie for Kyoko's attention with Shun Mitaka, another young man who is not only older, better-looking, wealthier, and better mannered, but is also a nice guy. Shun seems to have everything going for him, and Yusaku seems to have nothing going for him but his sincerity. Fortunately for Yusaku, Kyoko turns out to be more than a pretty face: she is strong-willed, stubborn, sometimes short-tempered, surprisingly witty, often silly, and eccentric enough to be more attracted to Yusaku than to Shun. Double entendres, slapstick humor, and Takahashi's trademark puns abounded, as did hilarious and poignant plot twists.

When Viz Comics translated *Maison Ikkoku* into English, it skipped several of the early episodes and changed the plot somewhat, feeling that English-language readers might be confused by the motif of the college entrance exams.

Takahashi's other works include *Ranma 1/2*, *The Mermaid Saga*, *One Pound Gospel*, *Rumic World*, and *Inu Yasha*.

M.A.T.

MAL *See* Judge, Malcolm.

MALAYA (Philippines) The word *malaya* means "freedom" in the Tagalog dialect; it is also the name of the most intriguing Filipino underground cartoonist. No one knows for sure whether this pen name applied to an individual or to a group of artists. However, there are many who speculated that Malaya was actually a group of individuals illustrating under one name to protect themselves from political pressures that could be brought upon their families, relatives, friends, or themselves. This theory is plausible because of the variety of styles and approaches that the work bore.

Malaya submitted comic strips, editorial cartoons, political illustrations, and humorous features to conservative and radical publications alike. Adding to the mystery, many of the envelopes that contained these works were mailed in various segments from different localities.

According to some individuals the earliest known appearance of Malaya's work was sometime in the 1950s, but definite documentation of these strips is difficult to obtain because of the rarity and obscure nature of the publications.

From January 3 to April 1, 1963, a daily strip titled *Dili Ako Mahadlok* ("I Am Not Afraid") appeared in the now-defunct newspaper *Leyte Express*. It was written in Cebuano, one of the many dialects of the Visayan region, and dealt with the atrocities perpetrated by rich landlords and their spoiled offspring against the hapless tenants of the vicinity. Many of the sequences in the strip were actual incidents, thus bringing forth the wrath of the landlords. All copies of the paper were confiscated and destroyed, but the elusive Malaya seemed to disappear into thin air. Many of the inhabitants later denied the existence of the publication for fear of the consequences.

In 1967, after a heavy typhoon, an airplane appeared out of the blue skies in the area of Bago Bantay in Quezon City. The plane dropped leaflets containing several comic strips concerned with the excessive power of the Church over the populace. On the last page of the pamphlets the name Malaya was scribbled. This led to a rumor that Malaya was an eccentric millionaire who crusaded against wrongdoers; after all, only someone extremely rich could afford to use a plane and print thousands of leaflets.

In 1971, a new publication, *Kalayaan International*, appeared on the scene. No one knew who published it. Copies were available in various Filipino stores throughout the San Francisco Bay Area in California, as well as in the lobby of the International Hotel located on Kearney Street, a block away from the tourist-infested Chinatown area. In the February/March issue of the newspaper (volume 1, number 6) there appeared several editorial and political cartoons signed by Malaya. The *Kalayaan* quickly disappeared, and Malaya has not been heard of since.

O.J.

MALE CALL (U.S.) Milton Caniff created *Male Call* (one of his more lighthearted contributions to the war effort) for the Camp Newspaper Service in 1943. The

"Male Call," Milton Caniff. © Milton Caniff.

year before, Caniff had been drawing another strip for the GIs with Burma (one of the sexy leading ladies of *Terry and the Pirates*) as its heroine, but the Chicago Tribune-New York News Syndicate had objected to the use of the character, which led Caniff to produce an altogether original strip. Named *Male Call* by the staff of the Camp Service, it had as its heroine the fondly remembered Miss Lace.

Miss Lace was a pretty, scantily clad, not overly shy brunette whose relations (usually innocent, as it turned out) with soldiers on every arm (whom she invariably called "general" or "admiral") constituted the gist of the strip's weekly gags. Miss Lace enjoyed a quite deserved popularity with the GIs and ranked as one of the major pinups of the war years, alongside Rita Hayworth and Betty Grable.

Caniff lavished as much care on the done-for-free *Male Call* as he did on *Terry* (for which he was highly paid), and some of his best work of the period can be found in the strip. He certainly enjoyed throwing in risque lines and situations which he could not have done with the relatively more inhibited *Terry*. The last weekly *Male Call* strip appeared on March 3, 1946, signaling the end of the war era.

A collection of *Male Call* strips appeared in 1945, and in 1959 Grosset & Dunlap reissued the entire feature as it had originally appeared during its three-year run.

M.H.

MALLARD FILLMORE (U.S.) In 1994 the people of the United States proved conservatism still had appeal by voting in a Republican Party majority to both houses of Congress for the first time in 40 years. That same year, King Features recognized the lack of a true politically conservative syndicated comic strip and successfully launched Bruce Tinsley's *Mallard Fillmore*. Mallard's namesake is Millard Fillmore, who served as

the 13th President of the United States from 1850-53. (As a member of the Whig party, Millard Fillmore would have considered today's Republicans the lunatic liberal fringe.)

Cartoonist Bruce Tinsley has done conservative-inspired editorial cartoons for a number of years. He claims that *Mallard* is drawn for the average person—the forgotten American taxpayer who is sick and tired of a liberal media and cultural establishment that acts like he or she doesn't exist.

The premise is that Mallard Fillmore, recently fired from his job on a newspaper, is forced to find work at a television station, WFDR. He's hired not because he is a good journalist, but because he is "an amphibious American." Mallard is continuously at odds with his ultraliberal news director. Physically, Mallard is a duck whose squat body is squeezed into a tweed jacket. He also favors a fedora with press passes stuck in the band and regimental-stripe neckties. If Mallard resembles any prior cartoon ducks physically, it's neither Donald Duck nor Uncle Scrooge, but Marvel Comics's now-defunct Howard the Duck.

For Tinsley, the ethically challenged administration of President Bill Clinton has been fodder for endless gags. Both gag-a-day and brief continuity concepts have been used. In the spring of 1996, the strip portrayed President Clinton and Sen. Edward Kennedy of Massachusetts taking a road trip to attend college spring-break parties in Florida. For more than a week, Bill and Teddy drove south in a convertible, bantering back and forth about booze, babes, and partying. In another episode, Mallard, unable to sleep, decided to do something "really mind-numbing . . . like counting Veep: one Al Gore, two Al Gores, three Al Gorezzz . . ." And President Clinton has been shown on his knees seeking spiritual guidance from the divine Elvis. The King of Rock and Roll tells the President, "You even look a little like me in my, uh, mature years. Watch out for the Big Macs, Bill."

Mallard Fillmore is a brilliant example of niche marketing by King Features. The newspaper business is competitive, and papers are anxious to keep readers. *Mallard Fillmore* allows King Features to offer a counterpoint to *Doonesbury*. A good number of papers publish *Mallard Fillmore* and *Doonesbury* together on the editorial or op-ed page seven days a week. Because knowledge of American politics is critical to enjoyment of the strip, *Mallard Fillmore*'s popularity is an American phenomenon.

B.C.

MANARA, MAURILIO (1945-   ) Italian cartoonist and illustrator born September 12, 1945, in Luson (Bolzano) and better known as Milo, short for Maurilio. As a student in architecture and at the academy of arts in Venice, he painted and sculpted, and then to earn his living decided to exploit his vocational drawing ability.

He started in 1962 drawing pocket-size criminal and erotic comics that became very popular in Italy at the time: the series *Genius, Jolanda de Almaviva*, and a few episodes of the series *Terror* and *Cosmine*. He also drew 15 issues of the monthly *Telerompo* (1973-75), lampooning Italy's state-controlled television system. In 1974 he started drawing some adventures, and then some episodes of the series *Il fumetto della realta*, for the *Corriere dei Ragazzi*; in 1975 he was asked by the same magazine to draw the artwork for a series written by

Milo Manara, cover illustration for Glamour International. © Edizione Glamour.

Mino Milani, *La parola alla giuria* ("The Verdict of the Jury"). In this series, a famous historical figure (for example, Nero, Oppenheimer, Custer, or Helen of Troy) was brought to trial, letting the readers judge if he was guilty or not guilty. During this experience Manara's graphic style changed completely.

In 1976 Manara drew for *Corrier Boy* three episodes of the new character *Chriss Lean*, written by D'Argenzio, and then started contributing to the monthly *Alter Linus* with the story *Lo scimiotto* ("The monkey," 1976-77), written by Silverio Pisu. It was the adaptation of a famous 15th-century Chinese novel that tells the wanderings and adventures of a monkey that epitomizes man in search of wisdom and freedom from all kind of submission. The author's political interpretation transformed the monkey into a symbol for China's president, Mao Tse-Tung. Manara contributed to some collective works printed by the French publishing house Larousse, illustrating five episodes of *L'histoire de France en B.D.* (1978), and some episodes of *L'histoire de Chine* (1979).

Manara was extremely prolific in 1978. He illustrated some episodes of Enzo Biagi's *Storia d'Italia a fumetti*, drew the adventure *L'uomo delle nevi* ("The Snowman") written by Alfredo Castelli and set in Tibet, and began to write and draw for the French magazine *A Suivre* the black-and-white series *HP e Giuseppe Bergman*. While working on this peculiar graphic novel, the author himself toured the world in search of adventure and eventually met Hugo Pratt (HP), who became in the novel adventure personified.

In 1981 Manara wrote and drew for the Italian magazine *Pilot* a western adventure titled *L'uomo di carta* ("The paperman"), and in 1983 he published his first erotic story, titled *Il gioco* in the Italian magazine *Playmen*, and named *Le Declic* in the French *L'Echo des Savanes*. His superb skill in rendering the glamour of the female figure and the daring sexual situations depicted made Manara famous as an erotic author. Making the most of his talent as an erotic illustrator, over the years Manara drew *Il profumo dell'invisibile*

parts one (1985) and two, *Candid Camera* (1988), and *Il gioco* parts two (1991) and three.

His friendship with Pratt gave birth to two graphic novels written by Hugo and drawn by Milo. The first, *Tutto ricomincio con un estate indiana* ("It all Started Again with an Indian Summer") was printed during 1983-85 in the magazine *Corto Maltese*. This graphic novel, set in 17th-century New England, described in critical terms the puritanical attitude of the American colonial period through a dramatic story illustrated in a masterly way. The second, *Il gaucho*, which started in 1991 in the Italian magazine *Il Grifo* and then shifted to the French *A Suivre*, is an adventure set in 19th-century Argentina. Also in 1991 Manara drew the colored book *Cristoforo Colombo* based on Biagi's script. Because of his admiration for Federico Fellini, with whom he was on good terms, Manara was authorized to draw two short stories based on film ideas the movie director could not shoot: *Viaggio a Tulum*, published in the magazine *Il Grifo* (1991). Manara also illustrated the posters of two of Fellini's movies, *Intervista* (1987) and *La voce della luna* (1990).

Manara over the years has produced several portfolios, including *Erotique* (1984), *Le Declic* (1984), *Nubinlove* (1985), and *Un' estate indiana* (1987). He has also illustrated several books by Wilbur Smith, Richard Allen, Pedro AlmoDovar, and other writers, and has created artwork for advertising campaigns.

Most of Manara's works has been reprinted in book form by many publishers. Manara was awarded a Yellow Kid in Lucca (1987) and has received many other prizes abroad. The movie *Declic* (1985), shot by French director Jean-Louis Richard and inspired by Manara's homonymous comics story, was a flop mainly because it lacked the joyful eroticism and the sarcastic remarks against bourgeois moral prejudices of Manara's erotic stories.

G.C.C.

MANDRAKE THE MAGICIAN (U.S.) Author Lee Falk and artist Phil Davis joined forces to create *Mandrake the Magician in 1934. Distributed by King Features Syndicate, *Mandrake* appeared first as a daily strip on June 11, 1934, and then as a Sunday page in February 1935.

In his coat-and-tails suit, opera hat, and black-and-red cape, Mandrake is the quintessence of all the music-hall magicians Lee Falk admired as a child. (It is interesting to note that Mandrake, with his neatly parted hair and trim moustache, was modelled after Falk himself.) In the beginning Mandrake was an actual magician endowed with supernatural powers but later he took on a more human, more believable, persona. As a master of hypnotism and illusion (skills he learned in Tibet) Mandrake uses only his superior faculties of intelligence, resourcefulness, and courage to triumph over his enemies. These have included masters of black magic pitting their power against Mandrake's white magic, mad potentates, and invaders from outer space.

In the course of his exploits, Mandrake is assisted by his faithful companion Lothar, king of a faraway African tribe, whose Herculean strength often wins the day where Mandrake's magic has failed. He also met his match in the person of Princess Narda, who tried to do him in on several occasions before settling into what seems to have become a morganatic union of sorts. In later years Mandrake's twin brother Derek and his younger sister Lenore were also introduced into the strip. Today, Mandrake leads an existence of comfort and ease on his secluded country estate, Xanadu, in the company of the ever-faithful Narda. He occasionally leaves his placid lifestyle, however, to engage in secret missions for the good of world peace on instructions from the UN-related organization Inter-Intel.

Lee Falk's writing was pithy and literate, his scenarios very imaginative, ranging from straight adventure to mystery story to science-fiction, and the story line was ably complemented by Phil Davis's elegance of line (at least before illness forced Davis to rely more and more on his assistant-wife). After Davis's death in 1964, the drawing was taken over by Fred Fredericks, who is still doing it today.

Mandrake met with immediate success from the outset and spawned a host of imitators, especially in the comic books of the 1940s and 1950s. It was made into a movie serial in 1939.

M.H.

MANGUCHO Y MENECA (Argentina) A long-lasting humor strip, *Mangucho y Meneca* was created in 1945 by Robert Battaglia (initially under the title *Don Pascual*, then changed to *Mangucho con Todo*, before assuming its most recognizable name). The series unfolded its gags (usually with continuity from week to week) in the pages of the comic magazine *Patoruzito*. It ended in 1977 when *Patoruzito* ceased publication.

Mangucho y Meneca's protagonists were the resourceful Mangucho and his girlfriend Meneca. Mangucho, a chubby boy always wearing an oversized cap, had a large bag of tricks that he used to get out of every conceivable predicament. He worked for a shopkeeper in a Buenos Aires suburb, Don Pascual, a gullible and easily frightened little man. Other popular characters in the strip included the megalomaniacal and slightly crazy inventor Agustín, Mr. Naña, and the dim-witted Taraletti.

L.G.

MANI IN ALTO! (Italy) Tea Bonelli's Edizioni Audace, which had offered so many imitations of *Tex Willer*, came up in 1952 with an original and welcome interlude: *Mani in Alto!* ("Hands Up!"). It was very different from their usual, run-of-the-mill productions in both style and content. The story featured not one, but several leading characters. Eventually the snappy

"Mandrake the Magician," Lee Falk and Phil Davis. © King Features Syndicate.

young Sergeant Teddy Starr emerged as the strip's most popular protagonist, but the others were so well portrayed as to vie with him for attention. Foremost among them was the old boozer, Cherry Brandy, whose name was fitting: hot-tempered and clownish, he was the comic sidekick so often depicted in American movies. Cherry Brandy's effervescent personality won him his own comic book some time later. Another star of the series was Cora, a beautiful, long-haired brunette, who often embarked on her own independent adventures. In recognition of his large cast, Rinaldo D'Ami (who wrote and drew the feature under the pen name Roy D'Amy) presented on the cover the faces of his characters, each of them enclosed in a star design: Teddy, Cherry, Cora, Little Svetola, Chinese Yo-Yo, and Corporal Cicoria.

In addition to adventures in which all the characters participated, there were individual escapades that ranged from the dramatic to the humorous, depending on the character. D'Ami, who was trained in the Venetian School of Asso di Picche, combined realistic drawings with caricatural or stylized figures.

Mani in Alto! was often reprinted in various formats, and, in spite of its short-lived career, is most deserving of mention.

G.B.

MANNEN SOM GÖR VAD SOM FALLER HONOM IN (Sweden) *Mannen som gör vad som faller honom in* ("The man who does whatever comes to his mind") is a creation of Swedish cartoonist and comic artist Oskar Andersson, best known by his initials O.A., which also served as a pseudonym. O.A. started selling his cartoons to *Söndags-Nisse* (Sunday Troll), a Swedish humor weekly of the time, at the age of 20 in 1897. He was employed as a regular contributor to *Söndags-Nisse*, whose editors realized the fantastic talent they

had found. Their faith in O.A. was well founded, as he became one of the best-known Swedish cartoonists.

O.A. read all that he could find of the American comic strips of his day, and in 1902 created his *Mannen som gör vad som faller honom in*, a comic strip of which some 20 episodes graced the pages of for *Söndags-Nisse* until 1906. The man who is following his each and every whim is a sour-faced libertarian living out his free will against morals and mechanization. He is also a deeply pessimistic being, reflecting the inner essence of O.A. An episode in which the man pulls a folded car out of his coat pocket, and then drives away in it seems harmless enough. Even the man's disposal of his opened umbrella after it has stopped raining seems innocent, but cutting off his fingers after shaking hands with a person he dislikes, or watching a dynamiting site at close proximity while others warn the man from a safe distance, strongly hints at O.A.'s pessimism and morbid concern for self-destruction. It is a pessimism of life, a reflection of death foreshadowing O.A.'s suicide in 1906. Thus, more than anything else, *Mannen* was a kind of self-portrait of O.A., as was much of his other work, consisting of comic strips, cartoons, and book illustrations.

The dark side of O.A. was obscured, however, by satire and humor, and by precise pen-and-ink rendering of his subjects. O.A. wanted his headstone to read simply "Here rests O.A." He no doubt was aware of the irony of this inscription, as he has been kept very much alive through reprints of his work, which has long been internationally known.

W.F.

MANNING, RUSSELL (1929-1981) American comic book and comic strip artist born in Van Nuys, California, in 1929. After graduation from high school, Russ Manning enrolled in the Los Angeles Art Institute. After a short stint as a comic book artist, he was drafted in 1950 and sent to Japan, with the prospect of being shipped to Korea. This did not happen, however, and Manning's duties, such as mapmaking and drawing cartoons for the base newspaper, remained peaceful.

Discharged in 1953, Manning met Jesse Marsh, who was then drawing the *Tarzan* comic book for Dell Publications. On Marsh's recommendation Manning joined the Dell art staff, working on their entire line of comics at one time or another. In 1965 Manning succeeded Marsh on *Tarzan* and his work was hailed by comic fans everywhere. This prompted ERB, Inc. and United Feature Syndicate to assign the *Tarzan* daily strip to Manning in 1967, and the Sunday the next year. While Manning's work continued to be critically acclaimed, the feature itself was a commercial failure. In 1972 Manning left the daily *Tarzan* strip (which went into reprints) to concentrate on the Sunday and to draw *Tarzan* comic books especially designed for the European market.

When the Los Angeles Times Syndicate decided to launch a *Star Wars* newspaper strip in 1979, the editors asked Manning to take charge of the artwork. He drew the feature until ill health forced him to relinquish it to Alfredo Alcala in 1981. He died on December 1 of that year in Long Beach, California.

Russ Manning has been hailed in the United States and in Europe as *Tarzan*'s third great comic strip artist (along with Hal Foster and Burne Hogarth). His work

"Mannen som gör vad som faller honom in," Oskar Andersson.

has proven as enduring as that of his illustrious predecessors.

M.H.

MANOS KELLY (Spain) Created in 1970 in the Spanish magazine *Trinca, Manos Kelly* was the work of cartoonist Antonio Hernandez Palacios.

Manos Kelly was a Spanish explorer who served as a guide to General Scott at the time of the Guadalupe treaty of 1848. With his companion in adventure, Siglo, he lived a multitude of experiences in the age of the gold rush, the Californian missions, and the wagon trains. A defender of the oppressed Indians and a man who went his own way without regard to prejudice or material gain, Kelly was one of the most singular heroes in the already crowded mythology of the American West.

To produce his strip, Hernandez Palacios made use of a highly personal technique in which he energetically etched out the figure of his robust hero and played with shadows and light in a style that was never one-dimensional. The quality of chiaroscuro, here rendered in full color, contributed a new dimension to the feature. The light that enhanced the images was bright and fiery, always done in warm tones, with the foregrounds remaining monochromatic. The whites were thus given additional value, directing the reader's attention, and accentuating the fast pace of the narrative.

Palacios, the author of another comic strip with similar qualities, his very personal version of *El Cid*, drew the last *Manos Kelly* story in 1984.

L.G.

MARC, RALPH *See* Marcello, Raffaelo Carlo.

MARCELLO, RAFFAELO CARLO (1929-   ) Italian cartoonist and illustrator born November 16, 1929, in Ventimiglia, near the French border. After art studies in local schools, Marcello sent samples of his work to a number of publishers in Italy and France. After being accepted at SAGE, a French publisher of comic books, he decided to settle in Paris in 1948. His first series (which he signed Ralph Marc) were *Loana*, a jungle strip starring a blonde bombshell lording it over the natives in Africa (an obvious ripoff of *Sheena, Queen of the Jungle*), and *Nick Silver*, detailing the exploits of a justice-fighting private eye.

In 1950 Marcello embarked on a long and extraordinarily prolific career as a newspaper-strip illustrator, while continuing to work as a comic book artist. Working for Opera Mundi, the largest press syndicate in France, he drew hundreds of stories, usually adaptations of popular novels such as *Ben-Hur, Oliver Twist*, or *Jane Eyre*. Since most of these adaptations comported a copious text running under the pictures and no balloons, they were not authentic comic strips, except for their presentation in horizontal rows of panels and their publication in daily newspapers. Switching to the rival Mondial-Presse in 1956, the artist continued turning out innumerable series, including such classics as Stendhal's *The Charterhouse of Parma* and *The Red and the Black*, and Henry Fielding's *Tom Jones*.

In 1971 Mondial-Presse folded, and Marcello began freelancing full-time for comic books and comic weeklies. Again the sheer volume of his output proved astonishing. Contributing to every possible publication in the field, he illustrated Westerns (*Buffalo Bill, Daniel Boone*), science-fiction tales (*John Parade, Space Patrolman*), romance stories (*Mylene, Star Ballerina*), costume epics (*The Unknown Rider*), and of course adaptations from novels (*The Quest for Fire, The Black Tulip*). His most notable creation during this time was *Docteur Justice*, which he drew on original scripts by Jean Ollivier for the weekly magazine *Pif* from 1970 to 1977. Benjamin Justice, a flying doctor working for the World Health Association, practiced expeditive justice against gun runners, drug traffickers, and despoilers of the wilderness more than he practiced medicine.

An artist of great facility, gifted with a supple line, he was always proficient and craftsmanlike; but being without personal style or originality, he made no lasting contribution to the medium. He deserves mention, however, for his massive presence in all facets of comics production. Possibly exhausted by the crushing workload he had imposed on himself for the previous 40 years, in 1989 Marcello returned to his hometown where he now lives in semiretirement, drawing an occasional story for such popular Italian comic books as *Tex Willer* and *Zagor*.

M.H.

"Manos Kelly," Antonio Hernandez Palacios. © Trinca.

Rafael Marcello, "Ben-Hur." © Opera Mundi.

MARI AGUIRRE (Spain) On April 14, 1968, the young cartoonist Juan Carlos Eguillor started *Mari Aguirre* in the magazine *El Correo Español-El Pueblo Vasco*.

Mari Aguirre was a young and pretty girl living in the mythical city of Bilbania (a transparent parody of the Basque city of Bilbao, where her comic strip adventures were published) in a world dominated by money, social stratification, and the love of material comfort. Rebellious and energetic, Mari tried without success to escape from her family and her native city. She continually encountered characters from advertising and comic strip heroes such as the Phantom, as well as real human beings. In the first incarnation of the strip she worked for a spy organization and had a number of adventures in which she fought her most famous enemy, the villainous Valmaseda. On December 28, 1968, Mari was killed and buried with full honors.

On August 29, 1970 *Mari Aguirre* was resurrected in the pages of the magazine *Mundo Joven*, and then taken back by the publication in which she lived her first adventures. Although the stories previously occupied an entire page, the second version of *Mari Aguirre* was published in the space of only one or two strips. The strip has since been discontinued.

Eguillor's style was very individual, a little naïf, elementary and simple, and his drawings were infested with weird cultural onomatopoeias which, instead of phonetically reproducing noises, rang out the names of philosophers or singers.

L.G.

MARIJAC *see* Dumas, Jacques.

MARKOVIĆ, MOMCILO-MOMA (1902-1977) The author of one of the most popular Serbian comics between two World Wars, Momcilo-Moma Marković was born in 1902 in Belgrade. Marković was among several authors who modernized Serbian comic art and illustration and harmonized it with international comics methods.

Marković studied in Paris at Ecole Nationale des Arts Decoratifs. After he had graduated, around 1933, he returned to Belgrade and worked as a book illustrator and painter. From 1932 to 1935 he was the editor and illustrator of the Belgrade magazine *Jugoslovenče*. Between 1935 and 1941 his comics were published in the most popular youth magazine of that time, *Politikin Zabavnik*, as well as in the best Serbian satiric magazine, *Ošišani Jež* (after World War II this magazine was renewed as *Jež*). His two most popular strips were *Rista Sportista* ("Rista The Sportsman"), which appeared in *Politikin Zabavnik*, and *Stojadin*, which was popular in *Ošišani Jež*. The stories for both series were written by Mica Dimitrijevic and famous Belgrade actress Ljubinka Bobic.

Rista Sportista was about boys from Belgrade who were chasing a soccer ball and often found trouble and adventures. *Stojadin* was a witty comic about a common Serb who lived in Belgrade. The author defined him in these words: "You meet Stojadin everywhere: in the life, in the street, in politics, while shopping, in coffee bars . . . everywhere. He is our typical 'common man,' witty and cheerful, always an optimist and opportunist."

During World War II, after the occupation of Belgrade, the Nazis sent Marković to a concentration camp in Austria. After several unsuccessful attempts to run away from the camp, finally he succeeded and moved to territory liberated by the Allies in Italy. For some time, he worked in the Royal Air Forces Service as an editor of the RAF magazine. Toward the end of the war, he was moved to the British Army Headquarters, which published the soldier magazine *Union Jack*. After the war he did not want to return to communist Yugoslavia and emigrated to Canada in 1951. It was then that a family tragedy occurred: his son Mirko, who had stayed in Belgrade during the war, was killed in an attempt to cross the border illegally and join him. Marković's wife suffered a nervous breakdown and was hospitalized, and this tragedy affected his career. Although he tried to continue his art in Canada, he had little enthusiasm and a poor mental condition. Eventually, having lost the will to create, he accepted employment at the Department of Highways of Ontario County, where he worked until his retirement. He was awarded a medal for his professional contribution to the development of railways.

Moma Marković never integrated into Canadian society. He never published any comic there, and his works were never exhibited during his lifetime. He is not even in the Catalogue of the National Gallery in Ottawa. In 1980, three years after his death, his paintings (not his comics) were exhibited during the Anniversary of the Railways Development in Ontario. After the exhibition had closed the paintings were returned to the Ministry offices.

S.I.

MARK TRAIL (U.S.) In 1946 Ed Dodd, a journeyman cartoonist who had drawn the nostalgic *Back Home*

Again for United Feature, sold *Mark Trail* to the *New York Post*.

It was an unlikely matchup; the *Post* was perhaps the nation's most decidedly urban newspaper and the new comic strip dealt with outdoor, nature themes. But within four months the fledgling New York Post Syndicate had sold *Mark Trail* to 50 newspapers, and by 1950 the new Post-Hall Syndicate under Bob Hall had doubled that client list.

Mark is the archetypal outdoor person—although in modern garb, not an old backwoodsman. He is a handsome, pipe-smoking conservationist and wildlife expert. His girlfriend, Cherry, is one of the comics' most patient female leads. She is a demure, dark-haired beauty without much passion, who is always awaiting Mark's return. Scotty is Mark's young friend, a recent college graduate with degrees in biology and wildlife management. He works for an international wildlife concern. Doc is Cherry's gentle father, whose main function in the strip is to chaperone Mark and Cherry—when they can manage some time together. Rounding out the cast is Mark's trusting, lovable Saint Bernard, Andy.

Mark Trail is notable for the trails it blazed; it predated the ecology movement by decades. When nature lore was still esoteric to the masses, it was common stuff in *Mark Trail*. Through the years the strip has received many awards and recognitions. Dodd's philosophy in the strip was to take his readers outdoors and tell them of the fun and beauty of nature. There is a heavy dose of education but little pedantry.

The characterizations of the strip are strong. Incidents showcase emotions rather than vice versa, and the continuity moves at a brisker pace than many of its fellow story strips. The art is solid, somewhat heavy but not stiff or lacking in action. Naturally, the animal world is depicted with painstaking accuracy. Dodd and his assistants—animal artist Tom Hill and journeyman cartoonist Jack Elrod—produced an informative, well-paced action, adventure, and romance strip. Elrod took official credit for the strip upon Dodd's retirement in 1978.

For years the Sunday *Mark Trail* has been given to nature notes. A daily panel, also distributed now by Field Newspaper Syndicate (the successor to Hall), is *Mark Trail's Outdoor Tips*. The strip is now distributed by King Features.

R.M.

MARMITTONE (Italy) *Marmittone* was created in the pages of the *Corriere dei Piccoli* on January 29, 1928, by Bruno Angoletta, an illustrator of children's stories and a former caricaturist for *L'Asino*.

Marmittone (whose name can be loosely translated as "rooky") is derived from the "marmitta," the huge pot out of which soldiers' rations are ladled; the term is applied to a novice and simple-minded soldier, and the protagonist of the strip was true to his name. Marmittone compulsively saluted any man in a uniform, including movie ushers and hotel bellmen; on his first day of training, he was so eager to fall in that he bumped into the captain and fell on him. Because of his bewildered incompetence he spent most of his days in the stockade.

At first *Marmittone* unfolded its six panels on a half-page of the magazine, but it was later increased to 12 panels covering a full page, a sure sign of the success encountered by the hero (or rather antihero). This success was justified because *Marmittone* was read by thousands of soldiers for whom the army (and later the war) was only a silly game they were forced to play. The years went by and, despite all the bellicose propaganda spewed out by other Italian comic heroes, *Marmittone* continued to violate every military regula-

"Mark Trail," Ed Dodd. © Field Newspaper Syndicate.

"Marmittone," Bruno Angoletta. © Corriere dei Piccoli.

tion in the book. In 1940, however, Italy went to war, and a caricature like Marmittone could no longer be tolerated; he was eliminated in 1942. It is interesting to note that, while Marmittone usually ended up in jail in the last panel of each strip, in the final episode he was thrown in prison in the very first panel.

G.B.

MAROTO, ESTEBAN (1942-   ) Esteban Maroto is a Spanish artist born in Madrid. He served his apprenticeship in comic drawing as an assistant to Manuel López Blanco on the adventure series *Las Aventuras del F.B.I.* in the early 1960s. Together with Carlos Gimeénez, he began an independent artistic career a little later, with such strips as *Buck John* and *El Príncipe de Rodas* ("The Prince of Rhodes"). In 1963 he worked in Garcia Pizarro's studio, which was producing comic features for the English market. He then joined the group of Selecciones Illustradas in Barcelona, where he drew *Alex, Khan y Khamar, Beat Group,* and *Amargo.*

Maroto definitively established his strong personality and mastered his unique graphic style with his long series *Cinco por Infinito* (1967); this was followed by *La Tom ba de los Dioses* ("The Tomb of the Gods") and by two exceptional heroic-fantasy stories, *Wolff* (1971), and *Manly.* In the 1970s he devoted his talents to illustrating and developing comic stories for Warren Publications.

Probably the most remarkable draftsman in Spanish comics today, Maroto has received numerous awards from amateur and professional organizations in Spain, Europe, and the United States.

L.G.

It was Warren that contributed most to Maroto's appreciation in the U.S. through its magazines *Eerie, Creepy, Vampirella,* and *1984* (later changed to *1994*), for which the artist drew numerous short stories. Among his works in the 1980s, mention should be made of *Prison Ship* and of *Manhuntress,* a science-fiction series scripted by Bruce Jones. In the latter part of the decade Maroto devoted himself exclusively to illustration; he came back to comics in 1993, drawing *Zatanna* for DC Comics and later working on a number of titles published by Topps.

M.H.

MARRINER, WILLIAM (ca. 1880-1914) Billy Marriner stands as one of the most talented and influential, but most forgotten and tragic stories in the comics.

Details of his early life are obscure—obituaries dealt with the circumstances of his death and omitted biographical data—but his first major work appeared in the pages of *Puck* magazine in the late 1890s. His signature then was an elongated "Marriner" in contrast to the compact signature of his later career. But his drawings also were stretched out, and he is notable in the musty pages of old issues of *Puck* for the unorthodox formats of his panels.

Also his drawing style differed from those of its neighbors: Marriner was definitely of a new wave of comic artists in a day when Gibson imitators still dominated. A. Z. "BB" Baker, Gus Dirks (the brother of Rudy), and Henry "Hy" Mayer were technical cousins of Marriner. Their styles were loose and free. Marriner's, in particular, was delicate and wispy—his rambling drawings would include essential lines that would become decorative tools. Smoke wound around the panel; horizon lines grew into borders; his signa-

ture itself, often in a sea of white space, would serve as a balance in the total effect.

He touched on all subjects, but soon kid cartoons predominated his drawing board. Gags with adults inevitably contained a gratuitous kid or two. He became so popular in this genre that *Puck* began heralding Marriner's kid cartoons.

And inevitably—given the flux in the comic industry at the turn of the century—he joined Opper, Howarth, and other *Puck* cartoonists into the funny pages. As with all funny-paper comic artists in those days who were not under contract to Hearst or Pulitzer, Marriner had many outlets and generally freelanced.

From 1902 to 1905 he worked for the *Philadelphia Enquirer,* the *New York World* (briefly), and T. C. McClure Syndicate. It was with the latter organization that he formed a permanent association.

His first comic was *Foolish Ferdinand,* which, like all the features for McClure and other early syndicates, gave Marriner and his fellows greater circulation in America than Hearst artists. *Mary and Her Little Lamb* was a longer-running feature, and *Sambo and His Funny Noises* ran until Marriner's death. The latter strip concerned the efforts of two white boys to wreak mischief on little black Sambo. But, in a manner that predated *Gerald McBoing-Boing* by generations, Sambo was able to confound his tormenters with strange sounds.

Marriner's most enduring and engaging effort, however, was *Wags, the Dog that Adopted a Man.* It concerned what the title implied: the harried pet-hater made it his life's effort to rid himself of the pup which had decided on him ("My Nice Man") as an owner. *Wags* ran from 1905 to 1908, with reprints years thereafter by boilerplate syndicates.

Wags was the only strip among Marriner's many that regularly featured an adult. His kids—indeed all his characters—had enormous heads, larger-than-normal feet and hands, button eyes, and Opperesque upper lips. The world in which they moved was Marriner's traditionally wispy and slightly distorted universe.

Marriner's personal life is in contrast to the innocent world of children that he drew. Clare Victor Dwiggins, with whom he worked on the *Enquirer,* remembered that Marriner, a little fellow, liked big women. Ernest McGee remembers Jimmy Swinnerton's theory that Marriner was drunk when he died in a house fire.

Swinnerton's suspicion is confirmed by contemporary reports. Marriner in 1914 was working for *Cosmopolitan* magazine and owned a house in Harrington Park, near Closter, New Jersey. He was on one of his frequent benders, during which time his wife inevitably packed herself and their son off to New York City until he dried out. On this occasion, after a visit to nearby Westwood, Marriner swore to a neighbor, "If my wife doesn't come home tonight I'm going to burn down this house and the whole village!"

Early on the morning of October 9, Marriner died in a fire that consumed his home. Early reports suggested a burglary mishap as the real cause; a gunshot report was never explained.

This tragedy nipped in the bud one of the most promising careers in the story of the comics. Billy Marriner was in his early 30s and his work was enjoyed by an entire nation—and many of his fellow cartoonists—when he took himself from their midst.

R.M.

MARSTON, WILLIAM MOULTON (1893-1947)

When comic books first became a medium for original material, there was considerable scrambling for the right formats. National struck first with *Superman*, and literally dozens of companies followed suit. Seriously lacking in the infant industry, however, was a female hero, and it remained for non-comics writer W. M. Marston to create one—Wonder Woman.

Born in Cliftondale, Massachusetts, on May 9, 1893, Marston had discovered the lie detector in 1915. By 1919, he was a member of the Massachusetts state bar, and by 1921 had secured a psychology doctorate from Harvard. During the 1920s and 1930s, he lectured at many universities, served on government study groups, was vice president of an advertising agency, wrote books on several topics, and syndicated psychology articles to newspapers and magazines.

In 1941, he turned to comics and created *Wonder Woman*; the strip made its first appearance in *All-Star* number eight (December 1941). Using the pen name Charles Moulton, Marston used the strip to express his latest theories on the psychology of the male-female relationship. Aided by the stolid, linear artwork of H. G. Peter, the feature was an instant success and was soon appearing regularly in *Sensation* and in its own magazine.

Next to the archetypal *Superman*, Marston's work is the most scrutinized in comics. Today's feminists claim it was years ahead of its time, with Wonder Woman doing everything a man could do and more. They see it as a story of a woman fulfilled. On the other hand, detractors find lesbianism, bondage, and sadomaso-chism. In his 1953 attack on comics, Dr. Fredric Wertham singled out *Wonder Woman*, calling it "one of the most harmful" crime features on the market. But despite the relatively recent, and outré, interpretations placed on the strip, there is little to indicate that Marston's young readers were particularly aware of the feature's psychological implications. In fact, since the strip continued without Marston and his theories for over 25 years, it appears readers never treated *Wonder Woman* as anything more than just another comic book story.

Marston wrote all the *Wonder Woman* stories—and the short-lived 1944 syndicated strip—until his death on May 2, 1947. Regardless of one's opinion of the feature, however, Marston's work is easily the most thought-provoking and unique ever produced for comic books. *Wonder Woman* continues to be published 50 years after its creator's death.

J.B.

MARTIN, EDGAR EVERETT (1898-1960)

American artist born in Monmouth, Illinois, in 1898. Abe Martin's father was a college biology professor, and Martin later said his first drawings were of bugs in his father's laboratory. Hooked on art, the young Martin left college in his junior year to study at the Chicago Academy of Fine Arts. Although there is no record of his having taken the Landon correspondence course, he must have done so, because he joined NEA Service in Cleveland just about the time other graduates were also signing up; Landon himself had just been named art director.

After a few immediate failures with strips, *Boots* was introduced in 1924 as a daily strip and caught on with the service's subscribing newspapers. The Sunday page did not fare as well; it was originally a top strip for the *Our Boarding House* page, running from 1926 to 1931. Martin then began a full Sunday page of his own—*Girls*—on Oct. 11, 1931, but by 1933 (on July 30, to be exact) the popular blonde Boots popped up as a character and on Sept. 9, 1934, the title was changed to *Boots* for the Sunday comic.

Although *Boots and Her Buddies*, as it came to be called, was an obvious takeoff on *Polly and Her Pals* right down to the alliteration, the resemblance soon

William Moulton Marston, "Wonder Woman." © National Periodical Publications.

Edgar Martin, "Boots and her Buddies." © NEA Service.

stopped. Boots was a flapper, who, like Blondie, eventually married and settled down. She was often sexy, but was she plump or thin? Martin's art was often confusing—encompassing clever design devices, but awkward composition. The lettering was annoyingly backhanded and the square balloons so angular that they detracted from the art.

Nevertheless, *Boots* through the years had qualities, such as inclusion of the latest fashions, that attracted a loyal set of fans. Martin gave the top strip to a pudgy couple from the main strip, Babe and Horace, and featured Boots, Babe, and other girls in popular paper cutouts on the Sunday pages. Martin's art, with all its visual distractions heightened, was continued by his assistant, Les Carroll, on a Sunday page after Martin's death on Aug. 31, 1960.

R.M.

Menny Martin, "Ayos!" © Pinoy Komiks.

MARTIN, MENNY EUSOBIO (1930-   )

Menny Martin was born on February 2, 1930, in Manila, Philippine Islands. He started to draw at the age of 13 and realized that he had a natural knack for cartooning. Two of his brothers, Jess Torres and Elpidio Torres, were well known in the field of art, so his artistic ability might well have been inherited.

In 1950 Martin started to work for *Pilipino Komiks*. He did his first comic character, *Kelot*, for *Tagalog Klasiks*. In 1951 he won first prize for his work in *Pilipino Komiks*. Later he attended the University of the East and in 1955 he finished his schooling in the field of commerce. He continued to do cartoon strips and won another major award in 1956 for his work on *Little Hut*. In 1958 he became an editor of *Espesyal Komiks*.

Through the years Martin has created and illustrated numerous cartoon characters for the many comic publications in the Philippines.

Creative, imaginative, and gifted with a great sense of humor, Martin is one of the most popular cartoonists in his country. His work has a uniquely Filipino touch and flavor, and he has the ability to capture and portray the foibles and idiosyncracies of his fellow countrymen and to use this effectively in his continuous array of jokes, gags, puns, and comedy situations.

Among his favorite subjects are mothers-in-law and sexy women.

O.J.

MARTIN MYSTERE (Italy)

Originally titled *Martin Mystere, Detective of the Impossible*, the comic created by Alfredo Castelli made its first appearance in the magazine *Supergulp* in 1978. Since 1982 the series has been published monthly in book form by the publisher Sergio Bonelli, and so far nearly 20,000 comics pages of *Martin Mystere* have been produced.

Martin Mystere is a peculiar detective who does not investigate criminal cases but mysteries concerning the world's great enigmas from the distant past to the present: old civilizations, monsters and mythical creatures, legendary heroes, long lost books, historical figures, secret societies, unexplainable events, imaginary worlds, impossible inventions, powers of the mind and magic, UFOs, and aliens. Born in America but raised in Europe, Martin Mystere is knowledgeable in many fields, from archeology and anthropology to history and computer sciences. He possesses a large personal library and huge archives stored in his personal computer; these are a valuable source of information for his adventurous explorations, for writing books, and for his own TV show *Martin's Mysteries*.

Martin lives in New York City, but he is perennially traveling in search of mysteries and their solutions. This wandering life disturbs his relationship with his fianceé, Diana Lombard, in spite of her calm patience, sense of irony, and deep feminine wisdom. Martin's most loyal and devoted friend, always at his side, is Java, a representative of the Neanderthal race, born in Mongolia and now an American citizen. Java communicates by gestures and grunts, but posesses an acute intelligence, completely different than that of modern man, that allows him to sense by instinct all kinds of dangers and to communicate mentally with animals. The many differences in character between Martin and Java only complement their partnership, based on trust and mutual understanding.

Some of the many villains who try to prevent Martin from unraveling the mysteries of the world are recurrent: the powerful Men in Black, who shape the course of history by targeting and eradicating beliefs, ideas, and opinions that might disrupt the accepted view of world history (for example, evidence that UFOs exist or that highly developed civilizations preceded our own); Martin's archenemy Sergej Orloff, the wealthy leader of a group that shares Martin's interests, but for evil purposes rather than for learning; Mr. Jinx, an expert in computer sciences who grants men's secret and forbidden desires at a Mephistophelean price; and an ineffable trio of scoundrels among whom the deliciously sexy Angie stands out.

Martin's stories are fictional but extremely well-grounded in fact. Informative elements are woven throughout the narrative, allowing the reader to be entertained while at the same time learning about history, current events, geography, science, the arts, language, mythology, and cultures past and present. Spinoff series of *Martin Mystere* have appeared since 1992 in the magazine *ZonaX* and also some stories with Dylan Dog have been published.

So far, Castelli, the main scriptwriter of the series, has been assisted in his task by 21 collaborators, including Vincenzo Beretta, Andrea Pasini, and Carlo Recagno. The artwork, originally produced by Gian-

"Martin Mystere," Alfredo Castelli and Leo Filippucci. Martin Mystere is greeted in New York by all his Italian friends from the comics.

carlo Alessandrini, the graphic creator of the character, has been carried on over the years by 37 artists, including Giampiero Casertano, Franco Devescovi, Lucio Filippucci, Esposito Bros., Paolo Morales, Guiseppe Palumbo, and Rodolfo Torti. *Martin Mystere's* adventures are scheduled for publication in the United States under the name *Martin Y* in 1997 by Dark Horse.

G.C.C.

MARVELMAN (G.B.) Recluse astroscientist Guntag Barghelt, while working in his secret laboratory on an island in the Mississippi, finds the keyword to the Universe: "Kimota!" When uttered, this dynamic word endows the speaker with all the natural power that exists. Seeking a young lad of honesty and integrity to use this power only against evil, Barghelt is saved from young thugs by crew-cut Micky Moran, copyboy on the *Daily Bugle*. After subjection to atomic treatment, Micky is able to save his benefactor from the evil Herman Schwein by shouting "Kimota!" At the magic keyword atomic power crashes down and immediately Micky becomes Marvelman, Mightiest Man in the Universe.

Born more of necessity than ingenuity, the *Marvelman* comic book weekly began at number 25 (February 3, 1954); number 24 was the last British edition of the American comic book *Captain Marvel*. The changeover was devised to continue the sales of its predecessor, which had suddenly ceased upon the filing of the famous lawsuit brought by National Comics against Fawcett Publications in America. *Captain Marvel* became *Marvelman*, Billy Batson became Micky Moran, Station Whiz became *Daily Bugle*, "Shazam" became "Kimota," and Dr. Sivana became Dr. Gargunza.

On the same day *Captain Marvel Jr.* was re-created as *Young Marvelman*, while Freddy Freeman became Dicky Dauntless, not a crippled newsboy but a messenger boy in the Transatlantic Messenger Service. And

"Marvelman," Don Lawrence. © Marvelman Family.

from October 1956 *Marvel Family* comic book became *Marvelman Family*, with *Mary Marvel* replaced by *Kid Marvelman*. Publisher Leonard Miller (of L. Miller & Son) was the impresario behind what became Britain's longest-lived and most popular superhero.

The architect of this venture was cartoonist Mick Anglo, with editors W. A. Knott, Anthony Miller, and later D. W. Boyce. Artwork was originally shared by King-Ganteaume Productions and Anglo's Gower Studios. Cartoonists on the series included R. Parker, Don

Lawrence, Norman Light, James Bleach, Stanley White, Denis Gifford, George Parlett, Leo Rawlings, and Ron Embleton. The last issue, number 370, was published in February 1963. There was also an annual for both characters.

Nearly 20 years later, Dez Skinn, a British comics-buff-turned-publisher, acquired the revival rights to *Marvelman* and reintroduced him to a new young audience in the monthly comic *Warrior*. The artist this time around was Garry Leach. The original run was from 1982 to 1985. Skinn then interested a small American publisher and so introduced *Marvelman* to the States. When mighty Marvel Comics stepped in and claimed infringement on their registered copyright name, the publisher changed *Marvelman's* name to *Miracleman*. What the British publisher Top Sellers thought is not known—for the record, they published a monthly *Miracle Man* back in the 1950s.

D.G.

MARY MARVEL (U.S.) Flushed by the success of *Captain Marvel Jr.*, the first spinoff of the monumental *Captain Marvel*, Fawcett decided the time was right for a lady Marvel. Otto Binder subsequently created *Mary Marvel* in *Captain Marvel Adventures* number 18 (December 1940). The next month it began appearing regularly in *Wow* and then in *Mary Marvel* comics in 1945. Otto's brother, Jack Binder, was the strip's major artist.

Mary Marvel's origin was a strange one. Unlike orphans Billy (Captain Marvel) Batson and Freddy (Captain Marvel Jr.) Freeman, Mary Bromfield was living a comfortable childhood with a well-to-do family. But Billy later learned that she was his long-lost twin sister, and he saved her just before she was kidnapped. Billy scoffed at the thought of Old Shazam giving his

"Mary Marvel," Jack Binder. © Fawcett Publications.

magic powers to a girl, but when Mary yelled the magic word (Shazam) in a crisis, she was immediately transformed into Mary Marvel. Her reaction was to exclaim "My! What a lovely costume!" And except for the short sleeves and a demure miniskirt, hers were the same gold-and-orange togs worn by Captain Marvel himself.

The *Mary Marvel* feature was one of the best produced in the 1940s, but it was the weakest of the Marvel Family troika. Although Binder had the foresight to revise the meaning of the magic word for her—Shazam now stood for Selena's grace, Hippolyta's strength, Ariadne's skill, Zephyrus' fleetness, Aurora's beauty, and Minerva's wisdom—Mary Marvel was never treated like a girl. In fact, she was almost always treated like just another Marvel. Despite all his talents, Otto Binder only rarely managed to imbue Mary with any real female characteristics. And even though girls were buying hordes of romance comics, Mary Marvel never had the slightest hint of a romantic interest!

Artistically however, Jack Binder handled the strip with a verve and style rarely seen in his work. Known more for his organizational talents rather than his artwork, Binder constantly produced clean, pretty, and interesting interpretations. His backgrounding and panel details struck an aesthetic balance between C. C. Beck's cartoonish *Captain Marvel* and Mac Raboy's illustrated *Captain Marvel Jr.*

In *Wow* number 18, the Binder brothers created still another Marvel, the lovably fraudulent Uncle Dudley Marvel. Claiming to be related to Mary Batson Bromfield, he wanted to organize Shazam, Inc. to profit from the Marvel Family powers. A W. C. Fields lookalike, he wore a tattered imitation of the majestic Marvel costume and had absolutely no powers—even though he claimed all the family prowess. He was eventually proven to have a "heart of gold" and was made an honorary Marvel—the family even humored his superpowered delusions! Never more than a supporting character, he added much to *Mary Marvel* and the whole Marvel cadre.

Mary Marvel continued to appear in *Marvel Family* until 1953, but she stopped appearing on a regular basis after *Wow* and *Mary Marvel* were discontinued in 1948. She was revived by National Periodicals in 1973, but only made occasional appearances in *Shazam!* comics from 1973 to 1978.

J.B.

MARY PERKINS see On Stage.

MARY WORTH (U.S.) In 1932 Mary Orr (niece of *Chicago Tribune* editorial cartoonist Carey Orr) created *Apple Mary* for Publishers Syndicate. The title character was a middle-aged woman who had been reduced to selling apples on street corners by the market crash. (She was no doubt inspired by a Damon Runyon character of the same ilk named "Apple Annie"—herself the heroine of the successful 1933 Capra movie *Lady For a Day* and its later remake *A Pocketful of Miracles*.) The series met with instant success in the bleak 1930s but, as the United States was slowly getting out of the Depression, the worthy but indigent Mary became more and more irrelevant.

In 1940 Martha Orr left *Apple Mary*, and the strip, rechristened *Mary Worth's Family*, was entrusted to writer Allen Saunders and female cartoonist Dale Conner (their byline was "Dale Allen"). The strip was

"Mary Worth," Ken Ernst and Allen Saunders. © Field Newspaper Syndicate.

considerably revamped and Mary, along with her new surname, acquired a less shabby, more dignified persona. The metamorphosis was hastened by Kent Ernst, a cartoonist of the new school of no negligible talent, who had succeeded Dale Connor in 1942 and who now endeavored to remove from Mary any vestige of her earlier slightly déclassé existence. Further shortened to *Mary Worth*, the strip seems today almost exclusively peopled with artists, actresses, promising executives, and other glamourous types to whom Mary dispenses motherly advice with deadpan impartiality.

The seeming conventionality of the series can be attributed not so much to either Allen Saunders (whose scripts were often excellent) or Ken Ernst (who made imaginative use of framing and composition) as to the inevitable limitations of the soap opera genre.

Saunders retired in 1979 and the scripting of the feature passed into the hands of his son, John Saunders. When Ernst died in 1985 he was succeeded by his longtime assistant, Bill Ziegler, who had to quit in 1990 due to illness. *Mary Worth* is now drawn by Joe Giella and distributed by King Features Syndicate, which in 1996 characteristically wrote of the heroine that "this confidante of the comics dispenses kindness and wisdom to all who enter her life."

A few *Mary Worth* episodes were reprinted in paperback form by Dell in 1964 and by Avon in 1969.

M.H.

MASTER OF KUNG FU (U.S.) In the early 1970s the martial-arts craze (fueled mainly by Bruce Lee's movies) was sweeping the country. It was therefore inevitable that a comic book on the theme would come out sooner or later—which it did right on cue in issue number 15 (December 1973) of *Marvel Special Edition*, an oversized line devoted to movie adaptations.

The hero (or antihero) of the piece was Shang-Chi, reportedly the son of that archfiend of Oriental menace Fu Manchu. Trained in all the martial arts, and particularly in kung fu, the youth was sent by his cunning father to fight Fu's nemesis, Sir Denis Nayland Smith of the British Intelligence Service, and his associate Dr. Petrie. When he realized how evil his father really was, Shang turned against him, but like most do-gooders he only found himself the target of both opposing forces.

On this premise writer Steve Englehart built an intriguing tale of suspense and derring-do; he was ably abetted in his efforts by Jim Starlin, who provided a

kinetic visual flow to the fast-paced stories. The series turned out to be so popular that *Marvel Special Edition* changed into *Master of Kung Fu* with issue number 17 (April 1974). Additionally, a black-and-white comics magazine, *Deadly Hands of Kung Fu*, came out on the same date.

The original team soon departed, however, and the title experienced a number of ups and downs, faring well under capable artists and writers (Doug Moench with Paul Gulacy or Gene Day, for instance), going dismally down in the hands of time-serving hacks. At any rate the kung fu craze was played out by the beginning of the 1980s in favor of the kickboxing fad, and *Master of Kung Fu* was discontinued in June 1983 (*Deadly Hands* had only made it to February 1977, but for the record it should be noted that the title was revived for an issue in 1991).

M.H.

MATENA, DICK (1943-   ) Dutch comic artist born April 24, 1943, in Den Haag (The Hague), where he grew up and went to school. In school he enjoyed a certain notoriety for the charicatures he made of his teachers. After leaving school he became assistant in a photo shop, tried several other jobs, and finally landed a job that afforded him a chance to display his artistic talents painting and drawing window displays for a huge department store. Realizing Matena's talent, his boss suggested that he apply for a position in the Toonder Studios. Marten Toonder, whose studio does everything from cartoons to graphic design, gave young Dick Matena a chance.

Matena stayed with the Toonder Studios from 1961 to 1968, working on a freelance basis for four of these years. He received intensive training for work on the Toonder strips. In 1966 he drew his first comic strip, *Polletje Pluim*, an animal strip, that was published in the women's magazine *Prinses*. This led to *De Argonautjes* ("The Argonauts"), on which he started working with writer Lo Hartog van Banda in 1967. The feature first appears in 1968 in the Dutch weekly comics magazine *Pep*, founded in 1962. It was soon followed by the humorous adventures of the knight *Ridder Roodhart*, starting in *Pep* in 1969. Once again the writer was Lo Hartog van Banda.

Dick Matena turned writer/artist in 1970 for *De Grote Pyr*, a comic strip that quickly caught on. It was an exceptionally funny comic series in the vein of *Asterix*, seasoned somewhat by a grain of Jacovitti. The hero of this series, a Viking chieftain, was very

Dick Matena, "De Zoon van de Zon." © Marten Toonder.

worried about his son, who would rather sing than fight despite his superb build. Nevertheless, it was usually the son who solved all of the Norsemen's troubles.

In ensuing years Matena turned to realistic artwork. The science-fiction epic *Virl*, published in 1977, marked the definitive change. He impressed readers with his literary adaptations and comic biographies of famous people like Mozart and Edgar Allan Poe. One of the highpoints of his current work was titled *Alias Ego*. In 1992 Matena started a series of comic albums about an adventurer, *Flynn*, and also revived *De Grote Pyr*.

Matena knows how to give the comic page just the right amount of animation. His firm line, balance of black and white, care for detail, and storytelling prowess make his stories highly entertaining.

W.F.

MATSUMOTO, REIJI (1938-   ) Japanese comic book artist born January 25, 1938, in Tokyo. Reiji Matsumoto started drawing at an early age and while still in high school he sold his first strip, *Mitsubachi no Bōken* ("The Adventures of Honeybee"), to the monthly *Manga Shōnen* in 1954; the following year it was picked up by the Western edition of the *Mainichi Shogakusei Shin bun Seibuban*, a daily newspaper for schoolchildren.

After graduation Matsumoto created *Kuroi Hanabira* ("Black Petal," a girl strip) for the monthly *Shōjo* (1957). Many more creations were to follow: *Denkō Ozma*, a science-fiction strip, in 1961; *Zero Pilot*, a war strip, in 1962; *Gohikino Yōjimnō*, a Western strip, and *S no Taiyō*, a girl strip, in 1967. In 1968, three new Matsumoto titles were published: *Akage no Hitotsu* (which told of the friendship between Hitotsu, a big red bear, and Yuki, a young girl); *Sexaroid*, and *Kōsoku Esper* (both science fiction). After this, Matsumoto created such titles as *Yojigen Sekai* ("The Four-Dimensional World," 1969); *Mystery Eve* (a science-fiction strip, 1970); *Otoko Oidon* (one of his most famous creations, 1971); *Gun Grontier* (a Western, 1972); *Uchū Senkan Yamato* ("Space Battleship Yamato," 1974), which inspired a series of animated cartoons; and others. In 1977 he produced the very successful *Captain Harlock*; Harlock and his other creations have kept him busy (and rich) up to this day.

Matsumoto is a versatile artist who has created comic strips for boys, girls, and adults with equal ease. He is noted for the wide range of his undertakings, from humor strips to war tales, and he is especially good at depicting alluring young ladies, animals, weapons, machines, and insects (his predilection). In his early strips, Matsumoto was greatly influenced by Osamu Tezuka (like every other young Japanese cartoonist) but he quickly came into his own with a style full of zest and vitality.

Reiji Matsumoto, "Otoko Oidon." © Reiji Matsumoto.

Matsumoto is also known as an avid comic book collector. His wife, Miyako Maki, is a famous illustrator of women's comic books.

H.K.

MATTOTTI, LORENZO (1954-   ) Italian cartoonist, illustrator, and painter born January 24, 1954, in Brescia. While a student in architecture in Venice, Lorenzo Mattotti turned to comics. His first short works were printed during 1975 in the Italian magazines *La Bancarella* and *King Kong*, and in the French publications *Biblipop* and *Circus.* In 1977 he contributed to *Eureka* and drew *Alice brum Brum*, written by Jerry Kramsky (Fabrizio Ostani) and printed in book form by the publisher Ottaviano. In 1978 he drew *Tram Tram Rock-Tram Tram Waltz*, written by A. Tettamanti, for the magazine *Secondamano*, and *Huckleberry Finn*, adapted by Tettamanti from Mark Twain's novel and printed in book form by Ottaviano. In 1979 he drew *Agatha Blue* for the magazine *Canecaldo*, and *Mandrie*

sulla sabia, written by Ostani, for a supplement of the magazine *Eureka.*

In 1980 Mattotti started collaborating to the monthly *Linus* with the story *Ale tran tran*, written by Tettamanti, and contributed to other magazines such as *Nemo in blue, Panorama*, and *Satyricon.* In 1981 he developed other short works for different magazines and drew for the monthly *Alter Alter* the story *Incedenti*, written by Tettamanti and dealing with social ostracism. The following year he drew for *Secondamano* the weekly strip *Jazzamentos*, based on a Kramsky script, and for *Alter Alter* he drew *Il Signor Spartaco* (to which Kramsky added the text after the artwork was done), a tale which does not narrate any action, but the protagonist's interior evolution.

In 1983 Mattotti joined in Bologna Giorgio Carpinteri, Igort, Marcello Jori, and other artists in founding the group Valvoline which gave birth to an insert for the magazine *Alter Alter.* There Mattotti published the story, based on a Kramsky script, *Dottor Nefasto*, about a mad doctor who wants to conquer the world. In the

Lorenzo Mattotti, © Lorenzo Mattotti.

same year Mattotti started drawing the series for children *Barbaverde*, written by Ostani, printed in the *Corriere dei Piccoli* and continued up to 1988.

In 1984 Mattotti began contributing to the fashion magazine *Vanity* with covers and illustrations. In the same year he worked for different magazines but, above all, he wrote and drew the story *Fuochi* published by installments in *Alter Alter*. The plot is quite simple: a battleship has the task of destroying a little island, but one of the sailors, attracted by the colors and creatures of the island, tries to prevent his companions from doing it. What is fascinating in this story is the artwork midway between realism and abstractionism, and the existing narrative tension among words and colors. With *Fuochi* Mattotti's reputation grew considerably on an international scale. In the following years he contributed increasingly with short comics stories and illustrations to many foreign magazines. In the United States Mattotti's contributions appeared in the magazine *La Dolce Vita* in the years 1987-88, and *L'uomo alla finestra* ("The man at the window") a long poetic and melancholy story based on a script of Mattotti's former wife L. Ambrosi, and printed in book form in the same year 1992 in Italy, France, Germany, Holland, and Finland. Many of Mattotti's comics stories have been reprinted in book form in several countries.

Mattotti's graphic activity has also included illustrations of books (worth mentioning is Collodi's *Pinocchio* in 1990), book and CD covers, calendars, portfolios and serigraphies, posters, and advertising campaigns. Mattotti received a special prize in Lucca (1986), a Caran d'Ache in Rome (1995), and other prizes abroad.

G.C.C.

MAURICIO *see* De Souza, Mauricio.

MAUROVIĆ, ANDRIJA (1901-199?) The history of Yugoslav comic strips began in 1935 when Andrija Maurović decided to create the comic strip *Vjerenica mača* ("The Sword's Fiancée") for the first Yugoslavian comic magazine, *Oko*. The father of Yugoslav comic strips was born in Kotor in 1901, and during his career Maurovič drew over 150 comic strip episodes. He lived very modestly for years in his very poor Zagreb home, alone, without any financial help, except for his small pension. Years ago Maurović was the highest-paid art-

Andrija Maurović, "Grucka Vjestica." © Andrija Maurović.

ist in Yugoslavia, earning a lot of money very quickly, but spending it even faster. He reportedly did not possess a single page (printed or original) of any of his comics. He was also unable to remember more than four or five titles of his own comics or his characters. He said that he was turning out comics so quickly that he never found time to look at them after he had finished drawing, or after they were printed.

The fact remains, however, that Maurović was the most important and most productive of all Yugoslav cartoonists. His Western series *Stari Mačak* ("The Old Cat"), published in 1937, was the most popular. Thirty years later Maurović wanted to make a comeback with *Stari Mačak*, and in 1968 *Plavi Vjesnik* published his *Povratak Starog Mačak* ("The Return of the Old Cat"), but the venture proved unsuccessful. It was the last strip drawn by Maurović.

Maurović was a very original, an inimitably realistic artist, and in his drawings no other artist's influences can be found. He has also done some comics directly in color, and these were very much appreciated by readers and art critics. Only one criticism can be made of Maurović. That is that he never used any archives in all his work. Also he never took any long trips, and all the people, animals, costumes, countries, or arms in his comics "were always coming from his head," as he used to say.

Maurović was thrown out of the Yugoslav Republic Society of the Fine Arts when they complained that he had not been paying his membership fees regularly. However, he believed that his colleagues were envious of his art mastery and that the society liked neither comic strips nor cartoonists. He reportedly died in the early 1990s.

E.R.

MAUS (U.S.) The seminal inspiration for *Maus* came in 1972 in a three-page comic book story that Art Spiegelman published in *Funny Aminals* (sic) number 1. In it a little mouse named Mickey was told by his father at bedtime of the holocaust that had been perpetrated against Jewish mice by "Die Katzen," the German cats. It was a simple tale, devoid of rhetoric and highly affecting.

In 1980 when he began to publish his own magazine, *Raw*, Spiegelman decided to amplify and personalize the tale, retaining the cat-and-mouse analogy. The now grown-up mouse Art enticed his father, Vladek, into telling him of his life before and during the Second World War as a Jew living in Poland. There unfolded a horrifying story of persecution and genocide endured by the Jewish mice at the hands (or paws) of the Nazi cats with the tacit complicity of the Poles (portrayed as pigs). Although the use of an animal fable did not in itself trivialize the Holocaust story, naming the Germans the Katzies (with its echo of the pranks played by the comic-strip Katzenjammer Kids) was unfortunate. Furthermore, as many have pointed out, genocide is a policy of extermination whereby killers and victims are members of the same species, which cats and mice definitely are not. At any rate the story ended six years later with Vladek and his wife, Anja, being shipped to Auschwitz (or Mauschwitz, as it is called here).

Later in 1986 all the different chapters were collected into book form by Pantheon with the title *Maus: A Survivor's Tale*. The volume received thunderous critical acclaim and became a bestseller; a few demurs from

"Maus," Art Spiegelman. © Art Spiegelman.

some in the Jewish press and elsewhere were quickly drowned by the drumbeat coming from the amen corner. Encouraged by this response and with a grant from the Guggenheim Foundation, Spiegelman set to work on a sequel picking up the story in 1944 and bringing it up to the present. Completed in 1991, it was again published by Pantheon, as *Maus II; From Mauschwitz to the Catskills*, and again there were generally favorable reviews and good sales.

Viewed in its totality *Maus* revealed not only a highly complex structure but also some disturbing flaws in its narrative thrust. While Vladek's story is as grippingly told in the second volume as in the first one (and even more horrifying), many of the exchanges between father and son (and Art's later expostulations upon them) seem contrived to accord with the author's politically correct ideology. In particular Art's attempts to take away the mantle of victimhood from his father's shoulders to wrap it around himself makes Vladek look even more heroic in comparison to his son, who comes out as a mean-spirited, self-pitying weasel (to continue the animal analogy). The interpolated four-page episode "Prisoner on the Hell Planet" wherein Art, accoutered in concentration-camp garb, seems to accuse his mother of having killed herself in order to make him feel guilty, is very revealing in this regard.

Maus remains an important work, although it is neither the literary ("on a par with Kafka") nor the artistic ("comparable to Goya") achievement its more rabid admirers have claimed. In 1996, when minds had had time to sober up and to more lucidly weigh the work on the scales of art and literature, Pantheon issued a special 10th anniversary edition of *The Complete Maus*. It flopped.

M.H.

MAX (Belgium) *Max* is a typical example of the internationalism of today's European comic strips. Conceived by the Belgian cartoonist Guy Herzog (under the pseudonym "Bara") in 1955, it was distributed by the Danish syndicate P.I.B. and appeared for the first time in French (as a daily strip) in the Paris newspaper *France-Soir*. It was later picked up by the Belgian weekly *Spirou* (1963) and, in 1968, by another Belgian weekly, *Tintin*.

Max is an explorer but his methods and attitudes would have made Stanley and Livingstone turn in their graves. He would shoot down maharaja-carrying elephants, make fun of African witch-doctors, bait chest-thumping gorillas, and get into arguments with Mexican taxi-drivers, all to his ultimate chagrin. There is more than a hint of the absurd in Max's character as he imperturbably went on to race Indian fakirs on flying carpets, or rescue mermaids lost on land. The surreal atmosphere was very close to Irving Phillips's

"Max," Bara (Guy Herzog). © Bara.

Mr. Mum (a strip that *Max* predated by some five years).

Max is a pantomime strip and relies chiefly on its drawing style to make its points. Bara's line, deceptively simple in appearance, is actually highly stylized and sometimes almost abstract. With a few strokes of his pen, the author could suggest a whole atmosphere of Oriental bazaars or African jungles, as he could in a few panels (usually three) dissect a whole scene. Max himself was very funny, with his toothbrush mustache, his perpetual grin, and his eyebrows arched high over his pith helmet. There are no other permanent characters in the strip; Max is the entire cast and crew.

For years *Max* was the most widely syndicated European strip (appearing at one time in over 20 newspapers). It was also reprinted in paperback form (by the Editions Dupuis in Belgium). In the late 1960s, however, it started getting repetitive, or perhaps the author was tiring of it, and it was discontinued by *Tintin* in 1972. It continued, however, in the daily press, where in 1994 the strip numbered 10,000 appeared. *Max* has also been reprinted in nine albums to date.

M.H.

MAXON, REX (1892-1973) American artist born in Lincoln, Nebraska, on March 24, 1892. His family moved to St. Louis where Maxon studied at the St. Louis School of Fine Arts and worked on the staff of the *St. Louis Republic*. He moved to New York in 1917 and contributed drawings to a number of New York newspapers, including the *Globe*, the *World*, and the *Evening Mail*. In March 1929, succeeding Harold Foster, Rex Maxon started drawing the daily strip of *Tarzan*, a task that he would carry on (with the exception of a short interruption in 1937-38) for the next 18 years. He was called upon to draw the newly created *Tarzan* Sunday page in March 1931, but this proved too much for his abilities and he turned it over to the returning Foster in September of the same year.

After his departure from *Tarzan* in 1947, Maxon worked mainly in comic books as an illustrator of cowboy stories. In 1954, in collaboration with Matt Murphy, he created for Dell *Turok, Son of Stone*, which he drew until his retirement in 1960. For a while he lived in London before settling in Boston, where he died on November 25, 1973.

Maxon's main claim to fame rests upon his long association with *Tarzan*. His work on the strip, however, was unremarkable and a far cry from the brilliance of Harold Foster and Burne Hogarth, who were drawing the Sunday page during the same period of time.

M.H.

MAX UND MORITZ (Germany) *Max und Moritz* may well be the most famous creation of German artist/writer Wilhelm Busch. It has been an important influence in the development of the comic strip, and in fact, may be counted among the earliest comic strips.

After having produced a large number of full-page funny picture stories for the humor weekly *Fliegenden Blätter* and for the *Münchener Bilderbogen* since 1859, Wilhelm Busch started doing picture-books in 1864 that were published by a Dresden publisher. These books did not turn into an immediate smash success, and so the publisher rejected *Max und Moritz* in 1865 as unsuitable for publication. Busch sent it to Munich explaining that it could be used as a continuous children's story in the *Fliegenden Blätter* and, with slight changes of text, might be reprinted in the *Bilderbogen*. The publisher liked what he got; the rest is history.

Max und Moritz as a story with a story with a cast of continuing characters told in pictures and text that are interdependent, filling most, if not all, of the classic requirements that define a comic strip. Sound effects, for that matter, are not lacking either; "Rickeracke! / Rickeracke! / Geht die Mühle mit Geknacke," (As the farmer turns his back, he / Hears the mill go "creaky! cracky!"). *Max und Moritz* was even met by the same teachers' resentment that confronted comic books in the 1950s.

The most obvious influence of *Max und Moritz* is the pattern it set for *The Katzenjammer Kids*, which is regarded as one of the first genuine comic strips. But *Max und Moritz* and Busch's other work also set a trend that was followed by artists like Carl Spitzweg, Eduard Ille, Adolf Oberländer, Lothar Meggendorfer, Emil Reinicke, and Franz Stuck, who also worked for the *Fliegenden Blätter*. Some of them, like Spitzweg, are better known for their paintings, which proves that "fine art" and "comic art" are not incongruous. It should also be noted that the *Fliegenden Blätter* had a continuing character that was done by different artists: the Bavarian Lion (stepping into the comic pages from the Bavarian coat-of-arms).

The masterful strokes of Busch's art were also copied by the comic supplements of German newspapers in the 1880s and 1890s. His method of telling stories in verse stayed with most German picture stories up to the 1940s. Although designated as literature for children, Busch's work, because of its social satire and biting sarcasm, was also aimed at adults. Nevertheless, comics were simply regarded as kid stuff in Germany up to the late 1960s. This attitude, besides being a gross insult to Busch's wit, consciously denies any such thing as a German comic tradition.

W.F.

MAYER, SHELDON (1917-1991) American comic book writer, artist, and editor born April 1, 1917, in New York City. Shelly Mayer's first comic artwork came when he was an assistant for several New York newspaper cartoonists between 1932 and 1935. In 1935, he became one of the earliest contributors to comic books when he wrote and drew *J. Worthington Blimp* and *The Strange Adventures of Mr. Weed* for the early books of Major Nicholson. Mayer joined the McClure syndicate in 1936, producing editorial odd jobs which including ghosting George Storm's *Bobby Thatcher*. At the same time, he was also editing Dell's fledging comic line.

Mayer resigned both posts in 1939 to assume the editorship of publisher M. C. Gaines' All-American comic book line. That group and the National (DC) line were jointly owned by Gaines and by Jack Leibowitz and Harry Donnenfeld, but the two groups maintained separate staffs and offices until 1945. Under the A-A logo, Mayer was responsible for the direction of *Flash*, *All-Star*, *Green Lantern*, *Wonder Woman*, and several other titles, all among the best selling comic books of the early 1940s.

In addition to his editorial duties, Mayer scripted the *Ultra-Man* superhero strip from 1939 to 1944. *Scribbly*, a feature he wrote and drew, was a delightfully whimsical strip about a boy who wanted to be a cartoonist.

Mayer drew the strip in All-American comics between 1939 and 1944, and then in its own title—Mayer calls it a "novel in comic book form"—between 1948 and 1950.

Mayer resigned as editor in 1948, but continued to write for National. He wrote and drew dozens of children's comics and funny animal books, most notably *Sugar and Spike*, a feature about two children who can walk but can't talk. In 1973, he turned his attention to mystery strips and created *The Black Orchid* for Adventure comics. He had to abandon drawing in 1977 because of eye trouble; he died on December 21, 1991.

J.B.

MECKI (Germany) Mecki was originally the star of the animated puppet films of the Diehl brothers. Eduard Rhein, first editor-in-chief of *Hör zu*, acquired the rights to use *Mecki* as editorial talisman and as a comic strip. For this, the more domestic atmosphere of the original hedgehog in Mecki's films had to be expanded upon. This task was given to Reinhold Escher, who created a number of supporting characters like Charly Pinguin or the Schrat. *Mecki* appeared in *Hör zu* from 1951 to 1972. Up to 1971 a running narrative was included in the picture frames. For the last two years speech balloons were added. The strip was cancelled when Hans Bluhm, the second editor-in-chief of *Hör zu*, was looking for a new attraction, but a revamped version of *Mecki* appeared in October 1975.

During the 21 years of its first run, *Mecki* lived through some 21 continued stories and a large number of single-page gags. Most of these were written and drawn by Reinhold Escher, who was sometimes assisted on the writing by his wife. Some of the stories were drawn by Professor Wilhelm Petersen and Heinz Ludwig. But of these, it is only Escher's art that is slightly reminiscent of Lyonel Feininger's stylistics in *The Kin-der-Kids*.

The star of this strip, of course, was Mecki, a hedgehog with a wife and children. He was both father figure and adventurer, mastering every situation with wit and cunning. His "crew cut" appearance led to a German word for crew cut, *Mecki-Schnitt* ("Mecki cut"). Charly Pinguin, the penguin friend of Mecki, was the wise guy of the group. His high-flying plans were usually wrecked by his own shortcomings, and more often than not by his choleric temperament. The Schrat was a kind of ape-like sloth whose utmost goal seemed to be being lazy. It was only his good nature that motivated him occasionally to act—say, if one of his friends was in a pickle—but even then he was soon overcome by sleep. The stories were sheer escape into an anthropomorphic world of fun and suspense that held reader interest for over two decades because of excellent storytelling, art, and color.

The success of the strip led to books that were published annually and the production of cuddly toys of Mecki and the Schrat. However, the full-page comic strips that appeared until 1978 were not reprinted in book form. After a hiatus of some seven years, *Mecki* was revived in 1985 as a comic strip. It is now a two-tier strip published weekly in *Hör zu*, written and drawn by Volker Reiche, who originally was an underground comic artist before drawing *Donald Duck* for the Dutch Disney magazines. The strip has become a family affair with humorous pranks and gags. Popularity of the characters is still high; an animated series was developed and produced for television in 1995. The series is loosely based on the original puppet animation films and does not make use of additional characters appearing in the comic strip.

W.F.

MEDIEVAL CASTLE, THE (U.S.) Harold Foster created *The Medieval Castle* as a companion feature to *Prince Valiant*. Conceived as a three-picture strip, usually placed at the bottom of the page, *The Medieval Castle* ran from April 1944 to November 1945.

This slight tale of two young English squires, Arn and Guy, in the time of the First Crusade, is remarkable mostly for its graphic qualities and the minute realism of its details. Into it Foster poured all his knowledge of medieval lore and his love for the period in an abundance of painstakingly detailed vignettes about the lifestyles and mores of the times. In many ways Foster used *The Medieval Castle* as a sketchboard and idea-board for his main feature, *Prince Valiant*. One of the young heroes, Arn, served as the model for Prince Valiant's elder son, also named Arn.

In 1945 a color version of the strip was published by John Martin's House under the title *The Young Knight: A Tale of Medieval Times*, and in 1957 Hastings House again reprinted the strip (in black and white and a slightly altered format) under its original title.

M.H.

MELOUAH, SID ALI (1949-   ) A native of Algiers, Algeria, where he was born on September 23, 1949, Sid Ali Melouah is the foremost cartoonist and comics artist of his country. He exhibited a love of drawing from an early age, and as an outlet for his budding talents he cofounded the first Algerian comics magazine, *M'Quidech*, in 1968. After graduation from the Academy of Commercial Art in Copenhagen, Denmark, he embarked in earnest on a career as a cartoonist, illustrator, and journalist, notably working for the dailies *El Moudjahid* and *Horizons* and for the weekly *Algérie-Actualités*. Equally fluent in the French and Arabic languages, he was instrumental in the creation of the first Algerian magazines of satirical humor, *El Manchar* and *Baroud*.

Melouah has so far divided his comic strip production almost evenly between children's and adult comics. In the former category he has contributed to many international children's magazines, especially in Middle Eastern countries such as Saudi Arabia and Kuwait; he has released a graphic album, *Le grand trésor* ("The Big Treasure") under the auspices of the United Nations. His most significant work, however, has been geared to an adult audience, notably two well-received graphic novels, *La cité interdite* ("The Forbidden City") and *La secte des Assassins* ("The Sect of the Assassins") on themes of Oriental history and legend. His latest effort in this vein was *Pierrot of Bab El Oued*, about a *pied-noir* (literally "black foot," the nickname given to European settlers in Algeria) returning to his native country after 30 years of independence. For the Algerian Department of the Environment he also produced a series of comic strips featuring a bemused (and disgusted) member of the nomadic Touareg tribe confronted with the depredations of modern civilization.

In his dual capacities as an internationally renowned journalist and cartoonist, Melouah has incurred the wrath of the Moslem fundamentalists who are trying to

Sid Ali Melouah, "The Touareg." © Algerian Department of the Environment.

overthrow the Algerian government. After several attempts on his life, he had to go underground, and as he wrily stated in a recent letter to the editor of this encyclopedia, "Due to threats on my life, my comics production has become very sporadic of late." He now lives in France.

M.H.

MESKIN, MORTON (1916-1995) American comic book artist born May 30, 1916, in Brooklyn, New York. After studies at Brooklyn's Pratt Institute and New York's Art Students League, Mort Meskin broke into comics in 1938 when he illustrated Fiction House's *Sheena* strip as a member of the S. M. "Jerry" Iger studio. The next year he joined the Chesler shop and produced strips for MLJ like *Bob Phantom, Mr. Satan, Shield*, and *Wizard*, among others. Concentrating on the superhero and adventure strips, Meskin was considerably more polished than recognized geniuses like *Superman*'s Joe Shuster and *Captain America*'s Jack Kirby. Drawing under the pen name "Mort Morton Jr." and several others, his work was illustrative and detailed rather than expressive and gaudy.

In 1941, Meskin joined National and produced probably the best work of his career. Again concentrating

on superhero features like *Vigilante, Wildcat*, and *Starman*, Meskin was an early proponent of the cinematic technique. His stylized drawings and flowing panels seem inspired by the motion pictures of the day. His finest work in the 1941-48 National period came on a minor strip, *Johnny Quick*. Initially a variation of National's already successful *Flash* strip, *Johnny Quick* featured cameraman Johnny Chambers as a crime fighter who gained super speed simply by uttering the magic formula "3X2(9YZ)4A." Never an outstanding strip textually, Meskin's cinematic approach to depiction of speed made the strip a landmark. Unlike a sketched series of speed lines utilized by the *Flash* artists of the 1940s or the strobe technique applied later by Carmine Infantino, Meskin drew a series of fully drawn figures per panel. This, of course, gave the impression that *Johnny Quick* was everywhere.

While he was working for National, Meskin also managed to handle work for Marvel (Timely), Gleason, Spark, and several others. Between 1947 and 1949, he and *Batman* artist Jerry Robinson drew some fine material for Nedor's *Black Terror* and *Fighting Yank* strips. Both features were past their prime editorially, but the Meskin-Robinson team's work on the features was the best the strips ever had. In 1949, Meskin moved on to

Prize and drew a whole range of features until 1956. Between 1952 and 1958 he drew weird and horror stories for the Atlas group, and, in 1956, he returned to National. Remaining there until 1965, Meskin drew some fine war, science-fiction, and love tales, but the *Mark Merlin* adventure strip was the finest work he produced in the last part of his comic book career. He was also a member of the Simon and Kirby shop between 1949 and 1955, where he helped create the *Black Magic* book.

Later Meskin became an illustrator and art director for an advertising agency. He retired in 1990 and died in July 1995, but artists like Steve Ditko, Joe Kubert, and Jerry Robinson continue to produce material heavily influenced by his innovative artwork of the 1940s.

J.B.

MESSICK, DALE (1906-   ) American comic strip artist and writer born 1906 in South Bend, Indiana. Dalia Messick's father was a sign painter and her mother a vocational-school teacher. After flunking most of her subjects in high school, Dalia Messick finally graduated at age 20 in 1926. Her only art training came that same year when she enrolled at the Chicago Art Institute for one summer.

In 1927 she was designing greeting cards for a company in Chicago and changed her name to Dale because of the prejudice against women cartoonists among art editors. The Depression found her in New York where she managed to land another job as a greeting card designer at $50 a week. All the while she was haunting comic syndicate rooms trying to find employment as a cartoonist. Some 30 years later she bitterly remembered her experiences: "It was always the same story. They couldn't believe I could draw because I was a woman. They would just put my samples away and say, 'Come on, honey, let's go out and talk things over.'" The final blow came in 1939 when she was turned down by the News-Tribune Syndicate. Mollie Slott, then assistant to Joseph Medill Patterson, liked her work, however. Together, Slott

Dale Messick.

and Messick laid out the premises of a new girl strip whose heroine Dale Messick wanted originally to be a lady bandit. Mollie Slott thought that a newspaper girl was more appropriate; thus, on June 30, 1940, *Brenda Starr, Reporter*, appeared as a Sunday page (in October 1945 a daily strip was added).

With the help of a large and specialized staff, Dale Messick was able to turn *Brenda Starr* into one of the topmost features, with scant regard to verisimilitude ("Authenticity is something I always try to avoid," she once confessed). She retired in 1980, leaving the strip in the hands of Linda Sutter (writing) and Ramona Fradon (drawing).

The success of *Brenda Starr* was a puzzlement to many. Messick's stories were chaotic, to say the least, and her drawing was less than adequate. In a field where women have never been conspicuously successful, however, Dale Messick's prosperous career shines especially bright.

M.H.

MÉZIÈRES, JEAN-CLAUDE (1938-   ) Jean-Claude Mézières is a French cartoonist born September 23, 1938, in Paris. After graduation from high school Mézières, who had shown a marked inclination for drawing, sold his first illustrations to *Editions de Fleurus* at age 17; contributions to *Spirou* magazine followed. In 1957-58 Mézières's first comic strip, a clumsily rendered Western, appeared briefly in the children's magazine *Fripounet*.

Drafted into the army in 1959, Mézières spent 28 months cut off from his professional contacts. Upon his return to civilian life, he became a staff illustrator at the Hachette studio in Paris and later worked for three years in an advertising agency. During his stay with the agency, Mézières was asked to illustrate a short comic strip written by his friend, Pierre Christin, for *Total Journal*, an oil company comic book giveaway. Later he became a member of *Total Journal's* editorial board. In 1965 Mézières took a pilgrimage to the United States in order to perfect his art and to observe American cartoonists' working methods. The trip lasted a year and a half—well into 1966.

Back in France Mézières resumed his collaboration with *Total Journal* and began to contribute illustrations and cartoons to *Pilote*. For *Pilote* he illustrated *L'Extraordinaire Aventure de Monsieur Faust*, a modern parody of the Faust legend written by Fred (Othon Aristides), in 1967. The strip was not a success, but later that same year, with Pierre Christin (signing "Linus"), he produced the popular science-fiction feature *Valérian*, also for *Pilote*. The strip is still going strong. While still working on *Valérian*, Mézières and Christin have also been producing *Canal Choc* ("Shock Channel") since 1990. In addition to his work as a comics artist, Mézières did the backgrounds and design of Luc Besson's 1997 movie *The Fifth Element*.

Jean-Claude Mézières is among the "new wave" of European cartoonists. While not as revolutionary as some of his colleagues, he nonetheless displays a pleasant—and sometimes striking—graphic style, as well as a keen sense of composition and suspense.

M.H.

MIAO DI (1926-   ) During his childhood, Miao Di became interested in his mother's paper-cuttings for window decorations; this became a lifelong love of and interest in art. While a university student, he was not interested in medicine and education, his majors, and so he switched to study art at North China University and Central Art Academy in the late 1940s. He has worked for the *People's Daily* as art editor since the 1950s. In 1979, *Humor and Satire*, a supplement to the *People's Daily*, was founded, and Miao Di worked there as editor until his retirement in 1990.

His comic strips *Grandpa and Grandson*, created in the early 1960s, and *Xiao Hou's Adventures*, created in the late 1970s, are Miao Di's best-known works and the ones that brought him fame. Each story was told in a four-panel comic strip; the themes were commonly shown with little words and the punchlines were often unexpected.

In his retirement, he has been cartooning actively, especially doing cartoons in brush and ink, traditional Chinese painting techniques, and four-panel comics. He is a member of the China Cartoon Art Commission of the Chinese Artists Association, is advisor to the Chinese News Media Cartoons Research Society, and is a member of the board of directors of the Shenzhou Painting Institute (affiliated with the *People's Daily*). Collected works include *Miao Di Cartoons Collection*, *Cartoon Selection of Miao Di*, *Social Satire Cartoons*, a volume in a series of Chinese cartoons, and *Comic Strip Collection*.

H.Y.L.L

MICHEL (Germany) *Michel* was created by Franz Roscher and published in the Munich newspaper *tz* from September 18, 1968, to December 8, 1969. The rotund Michel is based on the character Deutscher Michel, who, in editorial cartoons, stands for Germany, just as John Bull symbolizes England or Uncle Sam means the United States. Besides the trials and tribulations of Mr. and Mrs. Average, *Michel* also offered comments on local, national, and international politics.

A rather simplistic, yet well-rounded style was one of the faults, and yet one of the charms of this humorous comic strip that sometimes bordered on editorial cartooning. *Michel* had been in *tz* from the day the paper was launched, but a change of editor-in-chief ended this singular German experiment in editorial comic strips while it was still far from its peak of perfection and popularity. The fact that *Michel* was published in only one newspaper did not help to create a sizeable following in cities other than Munich. This says nothing about the success and potential of *Michel* but rather about the state of recognition that German newspapers give to comic strips.

Writer/artist Roscher had an agreement with *tz* to distribute *Michel* nationally, but this effort was never undertaken. When *tz* refused to pay more for the exclusive use of *Michel* and when a new editor-in-chief with a dislike for comics came along, *Michel*'s comic strip life ended. Franz Roscher moved on to other comics but would still revamp the strip for national syndication. *Tz*, after more editorial changes, reintroduced comics to its weekend television supplement, starting out with a Disney Sunday page. The Disney material has since been replaced by *Prince Valiant*.

Miao Di, "Xiao Hou's Adventures." © Miao Di.

"Michel," Franz Roscher. © tz.

"Michel Tanguy," J. M. Charlier and Albert Uderzo. © Editions Dargaud.

Michel was one of a rare breed: the German daily comic strip. It may very well have been the last of its kind for some time to come.

W.F.

MICHEL TANGUY (France) *Michel Tanguy*, France's answer to *Steve Canyon*, was created by writer Jean-Michel Charlier and illustrator Albert Uderzo in the first issue of *Pilote* (October 29, 1959).

Lieutenant (and later Captain) Michel Tanguy of the French Air Force was a hero in the traditional mold; unselfish, courageous, and clean-living, his sole aim in life was to enhance the prestige and power of the French tricolor. At the head of his formation of Mirage fighters, the "Stork Squadron," he was often called upon to impress by his aerial prowess the head of some foreign state in order to gain for France an advantageous political position or simply a large order for French planes (this was during the height of De Gaulle's "politique de grandeur" and Charlier was just doing his bit for "la patrie"). Michel Tanguy often had to fight foreign agents after French secrets, or foil sinister plots designed to show the French Air Force in a bad light (in all fairness it should be noted here that Charlier didn't do anything that Caniff wasn't doing in spades with *Steve Canyon*).

Tanguy, as is usual in adventure strips, had his comic side-kick, Lieutenant Ernest Laverdure, whose bumbling heroics and short temper often landed him in all kinds of trouble from which Tanguy had to rescue him. The adventures of Tanguy and Laverdure, always fast-paced and entertaining, took place all over the planet, from Greenland to Central Africa and from South America to the Pacific.

Charlier, a former pilot himself, gave a good account of the techniques of flight and although his plots sometimes needlessly meandered, he knew how to keep the suspense going. In this he was ably assisted by his artists: first Uderzo, who handled the feature with a deft, light, and even humorous pen until his workload (he was also drawing *Astérix* at the same time) forced him to quit in 1966; then Jijé (Joseph Gillain), who gave the

strip an austere, almost somber look, decried by some, lauded by others, but always interesting to look at.

Michel Tanguy is an adventure strip in the classic tradition, and an aviation strip as worthwhile as any currently done in the United States. All of Tanguy's adventures were reprinted in book form by Editions Dargaud; in the late 1960s it was made into a television series under the title *Les Chevaliers du Ciel* ("Knights of the Sky").

Jijé's death in 1980 interrupted the series in mid-adventure; the story was completed by Patrice Serres, who would illustrate the strip (now called *Tanguy et Laverdure*) until 1988. That same year French television broadcast a new series of *Les Chevaliers due Ciel*, with Christian Vadim and Thierry Redler in the principal roles. Alexandre Coutelis was the last artist to work on the feature (for the length of one episode), as Charlier's death in 1989 also spelled the end of his most notable creation.

M.H.

MICHEL VAILLANT (Belgium) Cartoonist Jean Graton introduced his Michel Vaillant character in a series of short comic strip stories published in *Tintin* magazine during 1957. Their success prompted the editors to establish a regular *Michel Vaillant* feature the next year.

Michel Vaillant is an automobile racer, the standard-bearer of the Vaillante team and the son of the cars' manufacurer. Young, athletic, and clean-cut, he is cast in the mold of the conventional comic strip hero—self-assured, brave, and unimaginative. His first adventure pits him (on the race circuit) against the American champion Steve Warson; in the course of the strip Vaillant and Warson constantly compete against each other (but always in a gentlemanly way), losing and winning in turn before they finally team up on and off the raceway against unscrupulous promoters and dishonest drivers. Most of the action takes place in and around speedways, and Graton is not averse to plugging brands of tires, gasoline, or oil lubricants as a lucrative sideline.

The strip hero's close companionship with his teammates brought on accusations of latent homosexuality,

"Michel Vaillant," Jean Graton. © Editions du Lombard.

been reprinted in many albums). *Michel Vaillant* has also appeared on the television screen and in a number of annuals devoted to more of his adventures.

After jumping from publisher to publisher with his creation in the late 1970s, the author has been releasing *Michel Vaillant* himself, under the imprint Editions Jean Graton, since 1982.

M.H.

MICHELUZZI, ATTILIO (1930-1990) Italian cartoonist and illustrator born August 11, 1930, in Umago (Istria) and died September 20, 1990, in Naples. After graduating with a degree in architecture, Attilio Micheluzzi worked for many years in different African countries; eventually, upset by various coups d'état, he returned to Italy. Because he could not stand the politics connected with licensing public buildings, he devoted himself to comics. In 1972, under the pen name Igor Artz Bajeff, he started drawing short historical stories and biographies for the weekly *Corriere dei Ragazzi*. In 1974, his first comic character, *Johnny Focus*, appeared in *Corriere*, and in 1976 he carried on the drawing of *Capitan Erik*, written by Claudio Nizzi and created by Giovannini, for the same weekly. In 1977 his second creation appeared: *Petra Chérie*, an aristocratic female pilot who lived in Holland and operated as a secret agent against Germany during World War I.

After this he wrote and drew two historical graphic novels: *L'uomo del Tanganyka* ("The Man from Tanganyka," 1978), set in Africa during the First World War, and *L'uomo del Khyber* ("The Man from Khyber, 1980), set in 19th-century India. Between these he adapted Mark Twain's *Prince and the Pauper* to the comics.

In 1980, his third creation appeared in the monthly *AlterAlter*: *Marcel Labrume*, a pleasure-loving and politically indifferent young Frenchman, who in 1940 decides to uphold the honor of his country against the Nazis. In 1982 he illustrated *Molly Manderling*, a long graphic novel written by Milo Milani that examined the political intrigues of a small German court in the 19th century. His next two series were *Rosso Stenton*, about the adventures of an American sailor in China during the 1930s, and *Air Mail*, devoted to the first experiments in air mail service in the United States during the 1920s.

so Graton decided to have Vaillant marry in 1973. The hero continues, however, to shun all semblance of domestic life for the more exciting action in the arena.

Graton possesses one of the most detestable styles in contemporary comics: all his characters look alike, their faces are locked in an expressionless, vacant stare. Only the cars seem alive, and it is they that have assured the phenomenal success of the strip (which has

Attilio Micheluzzi, "Johnny Focus." © Editoriale l'Isola Trovata.

In the second half of the 1980s, features that Micheluzzi wrote and drew included *Bab El Mandeb* (1986), a war adventure set in Africa during the Ethiopian war of the 1930s; *Roy Mann* (1987), the dreamlike adventure of a young American; and a very long adventure in the *Dylan Dog* series (1988). His last work, *Afghanistan*, was published posthumously (and unfinished) in the magazine *Comic Art*.

Micheluzzi's extensive knowledge of history, and his fluency in German, French, and English, allowed him to create competent and accurate stories in different social and historical contexts. With elegant scriptwriting, intelligent characters, and a polished graphic style, Micheluzzi's stories were pleasant to read and epitomize the spirit of comic art.

Micheluzzi received many prizes, including an Alfred (1984) in Angoulême and a Yellow Kid (1990) in Lucca.

G.C.C.

MICKEY FINN (U.S.) Lank Leonard's sympathetic, lightly humorous strip about a big city beat cop, *Mickey Finn*, was released by McNaught Syndicate as a daily on April 6, 1936, and as a Sunday page on May 17, 1936. At the opening of the strip, Mickey (named Michael Aloysius Finn in full) was the working son of a widowed woman who lived with her brother, Mickey's Uncle Phil. A young trial employee at the Schultz Soap Company, Mickey lost his job through a comic catastrophe, but rescued a runaway steer in the street with his bare hands on his way home. Offered a chance to take a police physical as a result, Mickey did, and made the grade. From that point (May 26, 1936), Mickey was a beat patrolman, undergoing continuity escapades in the daily strip and comic escapades in the Sunday page.

At first serio-comic melodrama, the daily narratives gave way in a few years to mildly farcical stories centering on Mickey's Uncle Phil, who was something of a wayward Romeo and con man (though more often conned himself). Early teamed with another patrolman named Tom Collins, and frequently involved with the antic activities of a reporter named Gabby, Mickey found an on again-off again romance with a girl named Kitty Kelly. Other regulars were Clancy the bartender; Sergeant Halligan, Mickey's immediate superior; Mr. Houlihan, Uncle Phil's nemesis; Flossie Finn, Mickey's niece; and Red Fedder, a baseball player.

Sports were central to Lank Leonard's life; he did the sports-page cartoon for over a decade on the *New York Sun* before launching *Mickey Finn*, and he occasionally introduced actual sports personalities into the strip, particularly the Sunday page. Lou Gehrig, Joe Louis, Jack Dempsey, and others appeared over the years. This was a notable aspect of Ham Fisher's *Joe Palooka* strip as well (although the noted figures there tended to be politicians and show people), and for that reason, as well as the teamed appearance of the two strips in many papers (in the *New York Sunday Mirror* they were the front and back page strips for some time), many readers linked the strips in their minds. The personalities of their two heroes assisted in this linkage, of course: both were sweet simpletons with enormous strength and comic companions—Uncle Phil and Knobby Walsh.

Mickey Finn was very much a one-man strip, and it effectively died with the passing of its creator in 1970. The strip was continued, however, by Morris Weiss;

"*Mickey Finn,*" Lank Leonard. © McNaught Syndicate.

the Sunday page was dropped in late 1975, with the dailies coming to an end on July 31, 1976.

An amusing record of certain aspects of Irish social city life in the 1930s, *Mickey Finn* deserves a more permanent record than the handful of comic book reprints it incurred in the 1940s, and should be collected into at least one well-selected volume.

B.B.

MICKEY MOUSE (U.S.) With a sensational new animated film star named Mickey Mouse dancing across the theater screens of America in 1929, it struck a King Features executive as important that the mouse star appear in a comic strip as well. Walt Disney Studios, which had launched the smash box office hit in a short called "Steamboat Willie" a short time earlier, agreed with the executive, and put its artists to work on a daily strip featuring Mickey, the first episode of which appeared in a dubious handful of newspapers on the grim depression date of January 13, 1930.

Scripted haphazardly in odd moments by Walt Disney himself, and drawn by two different artists in its first few months (one of whom was Ub Iwerks; the other a man named Win Smith), the strip was doing a fair job of reproducing the quality of the animated cartoons of the period, but little more. Then by what was little more than a lucky accident, when Smith asked to leave the strip Disney appointed a new studio animator he recalled once having mentioned an interest in strip work, Floyd Gottfredson, to the Mickey comic. The work suited Gottfredson perfectly, and he took to the strip like Donald Duck to a fight. Within a few months the strip began to take on a character and quality of its own, edging away from the broad surrealism of the film cartoons toward a realism consistent with the more straightforward narrative line Gottfredson had introduced, and it was apparent that the strip had

"Micky Mouse," Walt Disney. © Walt Disney Productions.

the creative basis to maintain reader interest and stick around awhile.

More papers took note of the daily strip and added it to their rosters as Gottfredson's story line gathered momentum and suspense from Mickey's cross-country battle with the archvillains Pegleg Pete and Sylvester Shyster, Minnie Mouse in desperate tow. By late 1931, King Features felt that a Sunday page was called for, and after a draft layout was done for the first episode by an artist named Earl Duvall, the new feature was also given to the devoted Gottfredson, the first episode by Gottfredson appearing a week after Duvall's on January 17, 1932. Gottfredson's adept handling of his cast of characters, largely derived and developed from their sketchier film counterparts such as the already-mentioned Pete and Shyster team and Minnie Mouse, but also including the redoubtable Horace Horsecollar, Clarabelle Cow, Pluto, and Minnie's uncle, Mortimer Mouse (bearing the name originally intended for Mickey himself), made the essentially anecdotal Sunday page as enjoyable as the daily narrative. (Later, Gottfredson was able to introduce superb adventure continuity to the Sunday page from time to time as well, and these comparatively rare sequences stand up with the best of the daily stories.) Finding the Sunday page ultimately burdensome, however, Gottfredson dropped it in mid-1938 for good.

Studio developments were in no way reflected in the Gottfredson strip. Here, in a splendid world of his own, an adventuring Mickey continued to fight pirates, fly fighter planes against armed dirigible cities in the air, rescue friends from the hypnotic rays of mad scientists, pursue desert bandits in bat costumes on horseback, match a fighting kangaroo against a gorilla, and other-

wise involve himself hazardously with such friends as Captains Dobermann and Churchmouse, Dippy Dawg (later Goofy), Donald, Gloomy, detectives Bark and Howell, and others, and such devoted enemies as Captain Vulture, the Phantom Blot, the Bat Bandit, Eli Squinch, and the aforementioned Pete and Shyster duo. There was no effective letup until well into the 1940s, when a slowing-down of realism went hand-in-hand with a sophisticated fantasy which, while engaging in itself, was a silk-gloved betrayal of the hard-core action-adventure elements that had made the earlier strip so consistently gripping and delightful.

Then the stories ceased altogether. By the early 1950s, the strip had bowed to a King Features edict which eliminated action-adventure in humorous strips. Against Gottfredson's own recorded preference, the daily strip turned to spot gags, an area in which it did not particularly shine. A certain rare talent, such as a Mort Walker or a Johnny Hart possesses, can transform the dreary joke-book gag format into a paragon of characterization and wit—but Gottfredson's talent simply did not lie in that direction. The popularity of the strip with its old and dedicated readers nosedived immediately and permanently—a situation in which it is hard to perceive King Features's gains from the change of content. (It should be noted that, starting in late 1939, Gottfredson's contribution had become less and less, as he was edged out by such as Al Levin, Bill Walsh, and Roy Williams.)

In any event, the greatness of Gottfredson's *Mickey Mouse* strip during its 20-year heyday cannot be denied, and it is hoped that the good fortune of many Europeans in having countless reprints of all of Gottfredson's early narratives available in bookstores everywhere, as a permanent testament to his genius, will one day be duplicated for Americans.

B.B.

Mickey has had a checkered career in comic strips in the last 20 years. Roman Arambula became the titular artist on the dailies after Gottfredson's retirement in 1975. In 1983 he also took over the Sundays, which Manuel Gonzales had been drawing from 1938 to 1981 (the interim period had been filled in by Tony Strobl, Daan Jippes, and Bill Wright). From 1989 to 1993 the artwork was assured by Rick Hoover. The *Mickey Mouse* newspaper strip now only appears in reprints of old episodes.

M.H.

MIGHTY MOUSE (U.S.) In 1945, a strip based on the *Mighty Mouse* animated cartoons debuted in *Terry-Toons Comics* number 38, published by Timely (later known as Marvel). The magazine showcased charac-

"Mighty Mouse," Art Bartsch. © Paul Terry.

ters from the cartoons produced at the Paul Terry cartoon studio where the first *Mighty Mouse* film, "The Mouse of Tomorrow," was made in 1942. The character, conceived as a parody of *Superman* and originally called *Supermouse* for three films, was the idea of a story man and animator, Isidore Klein, although Paul Terry himself often claimed credit for the idea, as he did with most of his characters. *Mighty Mouse* quickly became the most popular of Terry's cartoon properties and a successful series of films were made, culminating in 1955 when Terry sold his operation to the Columbia Broadcasting System which began the *Mighty Mouse* television program.

The history of *Mighty Mouse* in comic books is a checkered one. The strip's debut in *Terry-Toons Comics* boosted periodical sales such that the first full issue of *Mighty Mouse* was issued in the fall of 1946. Two years later, Timely (then called Atlas) lost its license to the Paul Terry characters and the St. John company took over publication of *Mighty Mouse* and of *Terry-Toons Comics*, which was later changed to *Paul Terry Comics* and finally, for its last issue (number 127), to *The Adventures of Mighty Mouse*. St. John also issued a wide range of specials and giants, including two 3-D editions of *Mighty Mouse*.

The St. John comics were produced in close cooperation with the Paul Terry studios, often employing moonlighting Terry staffers. Many of the covers were drawn by Tom Morrison, a longtime Paul Terry story man and the voice of *Mighty Mouse* in the animated films. Most *Mighty Mouse* adventures were set in Terrytown, a city inhabited solely by mice who were forever at the mercy of invading herds of cats. It was always up to the town hero, the ultramuscled, flying Mighty Mouse, to fend off the invaders.

The same format was followed when the Terry characters shifted to the Pines Company which published *Mighty Mouse* beginning with number 69. In 1958, Dell/Western (later Gold Key) took over *Mighty Mouse* and Pines replaced it with *Supermouse*, based on an imitation previously published by Standard Comics. Charlton also published an imitation called *Atomic Mouse*. From time to time, other superpowered "funny animals" have appeared, but none could match the popularity of *Mighty Mouse*, which finally folded in 1968 under the Gold Key banner. It was unsuccessfully revived twice: by Spotlight Comics in 1987 and by Marvel in 1990-91.

M.E.

MIKE AND IKE (U.S.) These famed derby-hatted twin brothers of Rube Goldberg's initiated his comic-page career when they first appeared nationwide in the four-page Sunday color comic section distributed to many papers by the World Color Printing Co. of St. Louis on September 29, 1907. They weren't called Mike and Ike then; Goldberg—who apparently freelanced the strips to the St. Louis syndicate from San Francisco and/or New York (accounts differ on where he may have been in the fall of 1907)—named the duo Tom and Jerry, and called his strip, *The Look-A-Like Boys*. The World Color Printing feature, which ran until March 22, 1908 (although not every week), was a half-page, six- to eight-panel strip, which appeared in two colors. Tom and Jerry were ne'er-do-well tramps, who panhandled themselves into trouble with everyone from washerwomen to magicians.

Goldberg abandoned the strip when he began his sports-page work for a regular salary in New York, and later seemed to have almost forgotten his first comic strip altogether, never mentioning it (except vaguely) in interviews, autobiographical sketches, or the like. The two derbied twins turned up sporadically in Goldberg's daily miscellany strip for Hearst in the late 1910s, however—and this time as Mike and Ike. The bewhiskered pair of shrimps did minor vaudeville turns in the Army, the Navy, Europe, or wherever Goldberg put them for the sake of a short gag sequence included with other panels and short narratives from day to day, and they made a considerable public hit.

Goldberg did little more with them, though, until he introduced them as regular characters in his long-running continuity Sunday strip, *Boob McNutt*, on August 14, 1927, as the long-lost sons of a farmer couple, for which Boob had been desperately and ham-handedly searching for several months (they are found by Boob performing as acrobats at a circus). From that point on, Mike and Ike remained in the *Boob McNutt* strip until it folded on September 1934. Their joint refrain, identifying themselves to anyone in sight, and sometimes to no one at all except each other, was "I'm Mike," "I'm Ike," which caught on nationally on the schoolyard level for a number of years.

Mike and Ike appeared in no other Goldberg strip, and never appeared solely in a strip of their own (although some papers did run the episodes included in the Goldberg miscellany strips of the 1910s and 1920s as if they were independent material, perhaps under the title *Mike and Ike*). No *Mike and Ike* book exists, nor has there been a cinematic adaptation, either as separate characters or as part of the *Boob McNutt* gang.

B.B.

MIKE MACKE (Germany) *Mike Macke*, created, written, and drawn by Volker Ernsting, was one of the comic strips that replaced the humorous adventures of the hedgehog, *Mecki*, in Germany's largest television weekly, *Hör zu*, when the editors were looking for new attractions.

The first *Mike Macke* story appeared in *Hör zu* on December 23, 1972, and ended after 15 full-page episodes on March 31, 1973. It was a follow-up to an earlier Ernsting comic strip appearing in *Hör zu* in 1972, *Hein Daddel*, about a dune detective and his zany friends working on the seashores of Northern Germany. Still included in *Mike Macke*, Hein Daddel and friends were dropped for *Mike Macke und der Piratensender* ("Mike Macke and the Pirate Station," November 17, 1973, to February 2, 1974) and *Mike Macke: Das Erbe von Monte Mumpitz* ("The Estate of Monte Humbug," October 19, 1974, to May 10, 1975). They were replaced by Airwin, Mike's pet dog, who ran around in Batman costume performing incredible feats.

Hein Daddel was already geared for the readership of a television weekly, but despite zany madcap adventures, it lacked an attractive hero. Thinking back to his television satire, *Sherlock Holmes und das Geheimnis der blauen Erbse* ("Sherlock Holmes and the Secret of the Blue Pea"), which featured more than 100 television celebrities, Ernsting found a blueprint for a hero in Mike (Mannix) Connors. Of course, Mike Macke (which loosely translates into Mike Daft) is a very dis-

"Mike Macke," Volker Ernsting. © Hör zu.

tant relative of Mannix, stepping from one improbable situation into the next while being furiously funny, quoting and misquoting, or simply making fun of clichés or getting involved in slapstick routines. Never, however, does he forget that there also is a story that needs telling. In addition to a little help from his dog, this sleuth also has his special gun which shoots rubber tipped arrows with a line tied to them, obviously to facilitate the tracking down of elusive crooks.

Ernsting's satirical comic strip may be unorthodox at times, but it never failed to get its readers laughing. It evoked such strong and favorable response that it alternated with other *Hör zu* features. It was even reprinted in book form. When editorial policies were changed once again, and full page comics like *Mike Macke* were axed in favor of a full page of comics (*Mecki, Mafalda,* and *Siegfried,* the latter depicting the adventures of a Stone Age dragon), Ernsting continued doing gag cartoons for the magazine for some time.

W.F.

MILLER, FRANK (1898-1949) American cartoonist born in Sheldon, Iowa, on October 2, 1898. Frank Miller attended school erratically in South Dakota, Colorado, and California, while showing artistic ability at an early age. Yet his career first took a very unartistic turn. After graduating from Harvard Military School in Los Angeles, he took a position as bookkeeper in a bank. From there he went successively to cattle ranching, accounting, sheep ranching, and mapmaking, among other pursuits; at the same time that he was restlessly shifting from job to job he never lost his taste for drawing. In 1919 he sold his first cartoon and slowly built up his professional reputation. By the mid-1920s Miller decided to make cartooning his full-time profession, working first for the *Denver Post* and the *Rocky Mountain News,* and later joining the art staff of the Scripps-Howard chain of newspapers.

In 1936 Frank Miller went over to King Features Syndicate, creating *Barney Baxter,* an aviation strip, in December of that year. In 1942 he left the strip to Bob

Naylor and joined the U.S. Coast Guard. When the war ended, Miller, instead of going back to his comic strip work, settled on his ranch near the town of Craig in Colorado and turned to painting. His watercolors depicting the life of cowhands and Indians of the Rockies, were critically recognized, and Miller had a number of his works exhibited in galleries and museums.

In 1948, with *Barney Baxter* faltering, KFS called on Miller to take his feature back, which he did. Frank Miller alternated his work between *Barney* and his paintings, just as he alternated his residence between his ranch in Colorado and his home in Daytona Beach, where he suddenly died of a heart attack on December 3, 1949 (*Barney Baxter* was discontinued after his death).

M.H.

MILLER, FRANK (1957-   ) American comic book artist not to be confused with the creator of *Barney Baxter,* to whom he bears no relation. This Frank Miller was born in Olney, Maryland, on January 27, 1957, almost eight years after the other Miller's death. He grew up in New England, where he received his education; coming to New York in the late 1970s, he got his first job in comic books in 1978, working for Gold Key. His big break came the next year when he succeeded Gene Colan on Marvel's *Daredevil;* working first as a penciler, he later also wrote the scripts and made the title into a fan favorite.

Transfering to DC Comics in 1983, Miller created *Ronin,* a manga-style comic-book mini-series set in medieval Japan. In 1986 he conceived *Batman—The Dark Knight,* which depicted an aging and weary Caped Crusader in a Gotham City of the near-future. For the next six years he devoted most of his time to scripting, notably writing *Daredevil: Love and War* and *Elektra Assassin* on illustrations by Bill Sienkiewicz for Marvel and *Batman: Year One* with art by David Mazucchelli for DC. In the early 1990s, he wrote two series for Dark Horse Comics: *Give Me Liberty,* which was graced by Dave Gibbons's outstanding artwork, and *Hard Boiled,* excellently illustrated by another British artist, Geoff Darrow. Only in 1992 did he come back to drawing with *Sin City,* a dark tale of the outer fringes and the lower depths, which he also wrote.

While Miller has proven himself a writer of great ability, his status as an artist is more difficult to nail down. He was strongly influenced by Neal Adams in his work on *Daredevil* and *Batman,* his *Ronin* was clearly inspired by Goseki Kojima's Lone Wolf and Cub, while *Sin City* is a take on José Munoz's dramatic black-and-white rendition of *Alack Sinner* (even the two titles sound similar). So will the real Frank Miller please stand up?

M.H.

MILLER, SYDNEY LEON (1901-198?) Cartoonist born 1901 at Strathfield, N.S.W., Australia, the son of a news agent. After completing his education at Fort Street High School in 1916, he worked briefly at a pharmaceutical importer before becoming a trial apprentice in the Process Engraving Department of the *Bulletin.* Being surrounded by the best black-and-white technique artists of the day inspired Miller to further his interest in art by attending night classes at the Royal Art Society for a short period. In 1917, he joined Harry Julius, who had returned from the U.S. to start *Filmads,* and they produced the first animated cartoons made in Australia. He also did freelance work, selling cartoons to the *Bulletin, Aussie,* and, in 1920, *Smith's Weekly.* Later that same year, he was given a contract with *Smith's* and drew political, sports, and general cartoons, in addition to writing and illustrating film and stage critiques. He resigned in 1931 to freelance with Sun Newspapers and the J. Walter Thompson agency.

During the 1930s he ran a weekly strip feature, *Curiosities,* in the *Melbourne Herald,* and *Nature Notes* in the *Daily Telegraph.* In 1938, he created a half-page adventure strip, *Red Gregory*—one of Australia's earliest adventure strips and certainly the best-drawn strip of that genre of that time. The same year, he created *Chesty Bond* in conjunction with Ted Moloney of J. Walter Thompson. Possibly the first five-day-a-week advertising strip, Miller handled it until 1945 when it was relinquished to a series of artists (Mahony, Reilly, Linaker, and Santry) who carried the strip through until 1958. The inclusion of Bob Hope in a wartime sequence of *Chesty Bond* brought the threat of a $200,000 lawsuit, but it was averted.

From 1942 to 1946, Miller published many comic books containing his own characters (*Red Gregory, Molo the Mighty, Red Grainger,* and others) as well as the work of aspiring comic artists such as Len Lawson, Albert De Vine, and John Egan. In July 1945 he created a daily strip, *Sandra,* for the *Melbourne Herald* that was syndicated in England and ran until November 1946. This strip was immediately followed by *Rod Craig,* which appeared daily until November 1955—the longest run of any daily adventure strip up to that time. *Rod Craig* was syndicated in Jamaica, Paris, and Buenos Aires, and became the first Australian thriller strip to be adapted to radio. Starting in 1948, his single column comic spot, *Animalaughs,* was also appearing in England, Scotland, and South Africa. It was unprecedented for an Australian artist to have two strips being syndicated overseas at the same time.

In December 1955 Miller started a new daily, *Us Girls,* which ran until he resigned in 1957 to enter a partnership in the production of television animation and sound-slide films. He remained in this field until retiring to his painting and copperwork. He died in the 1980s.

Syd Miller was possibly the most prolific and versatile of Australian comic artists. Miller's style was influenced by Norman Lindsay and David Low at the *Bulletin* as well as by the animals of Harry Towntree (England), the dry brush drawings of Bert Thomas (England), and the split-brush technique of Dan Smith (U.S.). Apart from his undoubted skills as an illustrator, Syd Miller helped enrich the field of comic art by his encouragement of Australian artists and writers.

J.R.

MILTON, FREDDY (1948-   ) Freddy Milton is one of the most important representatives of the modern Danish comic artists. Starting in 1975 he acquired a reputation as one of the best funny animal artists of Europe when he drew *Donald Duck* stories for the Disney comic book published by Oberon in the Netherlands. Like Daan Jippes, Milton is one of the modern interpreters of the adventures of the indomitable duck, and his artistic style is based on that of Carl Barks. Milton's Disney work was inspirational for other European artists who wanted to enter the Disney field. Germans Volker Reiche, Jan Gulbransson, and Gabriel

"Tschap" Nemeth are among those his work inspired to knock, successfully, on Disney's doors.

Milton has not concentrated solely on Disney material, however. He also offered his version of *Woody Woodpecker* in two comic albums published in 1978 and 1979; these were very successful. In 1983 Freddy Milton created a funny animal series of his own, *Gnuffen* ("The Gnuffs"), the whimsically funny adventures of a dragon family. The stories, however, do have a penchant toward social criticism. In the United States, *The Gnuffs* were published in *Critters* magazine.

Milton's social criticism has become stronger over the years, and was particularly visible in his semifunny albums for adult readers, like *Villiams Verden.* He has drawn entertaining comics for Danish toy producer Lego, and has also done social satire in comic form which is highly critical of efforts to achieve a European Union. Another of Milton's ambitious projects is an interpretation of the Ten Commandments—in comic form, of course.

W.F.

MING FOO (U.S.) One of the most oddly appealing of adventure strips, *Ming Foo,* by Brandon Walsh and Nicholas Afonski (signing Afonsky), started on March 17, 1935, as a Sunday top piece to Walsh's already-established *Little Annie Rooney.* (Actually the titular hero of the strip and his boy companion, Joey Robins, had first appeared on the *Rooney* Sunday page as early as 1933, and their popularity on the strip prompted King Features to give them their own berth.)

Ming Foo was an Oriental adventurer with inexhaustible patience and unlimited resourcefulness. He was also given to phrase-mongering such as: "It has been truly said: He who could see two days ahead would rule the world!" and "It is written: Even the gods will not help a man who loses opportunity." Joey, on the other hand, was a typical American kid of the "gee-golly" variety. Together with an old sea-captain whom they had met in the course of their wanderings, Ming and Joey went adventuring aboard the captain's yacht, the *Sea Swallow* (the captain did not seem to ever need a name: he was always referred to as "Captain"). Our friends (as Walsh was fond of calling them) met with no paucity of action: pirates along the China coast, cannibals in Borneo, revolutionaries in South America, and other toughs always managed to make life interesting for them.

Afonski's faintly grotesque style was ideally suited for the strip: a little redolent of old book illustration, it gave *Ming Foo* the right humorous touch to match the levity of the storyline. (During the middle 1930s Afonski illustrated another Sunday half-page, *Heroes of American History,* a straight and earnest series of weekly history lessons fortunately—if unintentionally—made impossible to take seriously by Afonski's peculiar line and rendering.) As for Walsh's storytelling, it was positively brilliant, suspenseful, and involved without being overplotted. As Bill Blackbeard noted (referring to Walsh's scripting of *Little Annie Rooney*): "The *Ming Foo* spinoff of the 1930s, however, was first-rate: one of the great adventure strips of all time, suggesting that Walsh's real talent, lay elsewhere than with fleeing and helpless orphans."

Everyone may not agree with Blackbeard's glowing assessment of the strip, but *Ming Foo* was certainly entertaining and was missed by the few readers who

OH, THAT'S WHAT THE TWO NATIVE MESSENGERS WERE FOR!

IT IS TRULY WRITTEN, FOOLS WATCH ROBBERS EATING STOLEN FISH -- WISE MEN WATCH THEM ON THEIR WAY TO THE EXECUTIONER!!

1935, King Features Syndicate, Inc., Great Britain rights reserved.

"Ming Foo," Nicholas Afonsky and Brandon Walsh. © King Features Syndicate.

saw it (it had a pitifully low circulation) when it disappeared early in the 1940s.

M.H.

MINNITT, FRANK (1894-1958) Although the name of *Billy Bunter* is still well known and loved in the United Kingdom some 90 years after his creation in 1908, the name of the cartoonist whose comic strip interpretation of the "world's fattest schoolboy" delighted millions of children for a long period remains unknown. This is the continuing tragedy of British comics, where publishers refuse their artists the right to sign their work.

Frank John Minnitt was born in New Southgate, London, on September 3, 1894. A completely self-taught cartoonist, he attended the Hugh Middleton School, where his twin interests, art and boxing, were first developed. In 1914 he enlisted in the Coldstream Guards and soon found himself at war. During action in Flanders he was gassed and buried alive by a shell explosion for three days. The effects of the mustard gas would remain with him for the rest of his life. After his release from the army, he married and found work welding the headlights onto taxicabs. The family moved to Leigh-on-Sea, where the clean air helped the respiratory problems caused by the gas. In Leigh, he began to freelance joke drawings to newspapers, magazines, and comics. By 1927 he had successfully taken over several other artists' strips in the penny comics and was given the chance to draw characters of his own creation. These included *Pat O'Cake* in *Butterfly*, *Breezy Ben* in *Comic Life*, *Darkie and Dick* in *Golden Penny*, and *Jack O'Spades* in *Chips*. Usually short strips of four, or occasionally six panels, they continued with *Nanny the Nursemaid* in *Monster* (1928), *O'Doo and O'Dont* in *Joker* (1929), and from 1930 a string of characters in *Butterfly*.

In 1930, Minnitt tried his luck with the Dundee-based company D.C. Thompson, drawing *Peter Pranky*, *Smiler Smutt*, and *Jimmy and Jumbo* for the boys' weekly *Adventure*. These would all be reprinted (without renumeration for the artist, another typical gambit of British publishers) in the *Sunday Post Fun Section* (1939) under the new titles *Billy Banks*, *Nickum the Nigger*, and *Wee Eck and his Elephant*.

Unlike a contemporary, Allan Morley, Minnitt decided to stick with the Amalgamated Press Comics, which paid slightly better than Thompson. His luckiest editorial encounter was with the A.P. boys' weekly *Pilot*, to which he contributed two "real life" strips about popular stars: *Stainless Stephen*, about a radio comedian, and *Will Hay*, the top British comedy movie star (1937). Minnitt later contributed four unusual strips: *Kiddo the Boy King*; *Ali Barber, the Whisker Wizard of Old Bagdad*; *Bob's Your Uncle*; and *Merry Margie the Invisible Mender*. More interesting than his earlier characters, these strips became so popular that Minnitt soon took over the two-page *Billy Bunter* strip, the top feature in *Knockout*. This strip made Minnitt's reputation.

When the paper shortage of World War II cut down the size of *Knockout* from 28 to 16 pages, *Bunter* became a single page, so Minnitt promptly increased his picture quotient from six to 12 per page, then to 15. After the war, an editorial change resulted in a major crisis. The new editors in charge of the magazine didn't care for what they called Minnitt's "old-fashioned" style, and he found himself out of work.

He was able to find work in the many one-shot and minor comics published in the postwar 1940s, and single-page adventures of all manner of characters flowed from his nib. Beginning with a page in Swan's *Comicolour* (1946), he contributed to nine new titles in 1947, 36 new titles in 1948, and 34 new titles in 1949. He was frequently asked to draw the front covers, as many publishers were proud to have a former top A.P. cartoonist decorating their small eight-page books. He also drew much of the top-class *Frolicomic*, published in full-color photogravure by Martin & Reid. Although Amalgamated Press occasionally provided him some work, it was often embarrassing. He was not asked to draw the special long strips of *Billy Bunter* for the annual *Knockout Fun Book*; instead, he would draw the figure of Bunter while other, more "modern," artists drew the rest of each picture.

His later years were unhappy; he and his second wife spent their days addressing envelopes for a pittance, and he wrote pathetic letters to all the editors he knew pleading for work. Very little came. He died on May 12, 1958.

D.G.

MINUTE MOVIES (U.S.) Ed Wheelan's 1921 creation *Minute Movies* is widely credited as being the first suc-

"Minute Movies," Ed Wheelan. © George Mathew Adams Service.

cessful continuity strip. It is not, but it is an important early factor in the development of the story strip.

Based on Wheelan's earlier prototype, *Midget Movies*, *Minute Movies* was frankly designed for continuity, but its heavy dose of satire makes it confusing, in retrospect, to determine whether its main intent was to parody movie serials or to bring the daily continuity to the comic strip idiom. No matter: in short order *Minute Movies* had a large following; Wheelan had a personal product filled with inside comments and chatter to the readers; and the characters themselves had large fan clubs. The feature wonderfully combined the best magic of the movies—vignettes, titles, synopses—with the freedom and pliability of the comic strip.

The stars were stereotypical: Dick Dare was the dashing hero, Ralph McSneer was the villain, Blanche Rouge the femme fatale, and Hazel Deare the Mary Pickford heroine-type; the rest of the regular cast of characters were also unabashedly lifted from the movies. And so were the plots, which ran in a two-row strip format every day. After a few mysteries, melodramas, and romances, Wheelan followed with shorts, travelogues, and even trailers for upcoming episodes. Much of the charm left the strip—although acclaim from educators was forthcoming—when Wheelan abandoned his own imaginative scripts to pictorialize the classics in the early 1930s. Outlandish satire was replaced with conventional lightness in *Ivanhoe* and *Hamlet*; the strip was also assertedly aimed at children, to the dismay of adults who had thrived on the farce and inside jokes of the earlier *Minute Movies*. The art changed, too, and it is easy to recognize the hand of ghost Nicholas Afonsky, whose work was neater and funnier.

In Wheelan's own private melodrama, he became convinced that William Randolph Hearst exercised a personal vendetta against him when Afonsky was lured away to do the Sunday *Little Annie Rooney*.

Minute Movies left the comic pages in the mid-1930s and resurfaced in *Flash Comics* in the late 1930s and early 1940s.

R.M.

MISS FURY (U.S.) One of the few female cartoonists successful in the action genre, Tarpe Mills started *Black Fury* (soon to be changed to *Miss Fury*) on April 6, 1941, as a Sunday feature for the Bell Syndicate.

Tarpe Mills served her apprenticeship in comic books, working on such titles as *Mann of India*, *Daredevil Barry Finn*, and *The Purple Zombie*. From her comic book work she acquired a very direct, forceful style. Violence, action, and thrills were the hallmarks of the *Miss Fury* Sunday page, along with a sadistic streak that only grew larger after America's entry into World War II. The implied or actual use of the whip was a recurrent theme, as were branding irons, spiked-heel shoes, vicious women fights, clawing, and eye-gouging. In this respect the heroine gave as much as she received at the hands of ruthless gangsters or evil-looking Nazi spies.

The plot was also derived from comic books. *Miss Fury* was, in actuality, wealthy socialite Marla Drake, who donned a black leopard-skin costume to fight crime and subversion in her own way. Tarpe Mills liked to show her heroine's luscious body in various states of undress, but otherwise sex was only implied. *Miss Fury* made her exit from the comic pages at the end of the 1940s, and her passing was much deplored by aficionados of the bizarre.

M.H.

MISS PEACH (U.S.) Mell Lazarus created *Miss Peach* for the *New York Herald-Tribune* on February 4, 1957. The background of the strip is occupied by a mythical establishment of learning called the Kelly School where the children are always one up (or better) on their teachers. The adults of the strip—from the young and pretty Miss Peach, the teacher and titular star of the feature, to her colleague, the homely and pedantic spinster, Miss Crystal, and the harried and frustrated Mr. Grimmis, the principal—are upstaged at every turn, and out of turn, by their clamoring and unruly charges.

In a 1963 interview Mell Lazarus declared, "As a kid I hated school. This strip is my way of getting even."

"Miss Peach," Mell Lazarus. © Field Newspaper Syndicate.

"Mr. and Mrs.," Kin Platt. © New York Tribune.

And indeed the inmates of the Kelly School—the over-bearing Marcia, the craven Ira, the uncouth Arthur, and the rest of this ill-mannered and loudmouthed horde—hit back at the school system with a vengeance: they interrupt classes with incongruous questions and irrelevent asides, cheat on exams, misplace books and papers, and generally make a shambles of the whole education process.

One of the funniest of contemporary strips, *Miss Peach* has been reprinted several times in paperback form. It was adapted into several TV specials in the 1980s and it helped Lazarus win the Reuben Award in 1982.

M.H.

MR. ABERNATHY (U.S.) The collaboration of two magazine panel cartoonists, Ralston "Bud" Jones and Frank Ridgeway, *Mr. Abernathy* was launched by King Features Syndicate in October 1957.

A conversation on submission day at the *Saturday Evening Post*'s offices led to the effort by writer Ridgeway and artist Jones. The former's original title was *Mr. Moneybags*, but comic editor Sylvan Byck suggested the change. The Sunday page started about a year after the dailies, which was a King practice in those days.

Abernathy is the typical half-pint multimillionaire, a debonair ladies' man with yacht and servants—the kind of fellow that, by design, virtually no readers would identify with. He is head of Abernathy Enterprises, a nebulous industry engaging in something or other. Always playful and never autocratic, Abernathy lives in studied opulence just as a kid would live in a tree house. His friend is Admiral Asterbloom, who joins him in upper-class pastimes—including girl-chasing, as there are the inevitably pretty girls at every elbow. On the staff are Dudley, the butler; Hilda, the maid; Flossie, Abernathy's secretary; and Monty, his playful dog.

The collaboration worked well; Ridgeway, living in California, wrote the gentle and chuckle-provoking gags, and Jones's art never slipped into the "bigfoot" school as many of his fellows had. He drew *Abernathy* in a modern, stylized, firm pen-line manner, utilizing broad spaces—whites, blacks, Ben Day—effectively, making it a pleasant gag strip.

Jones resigned from the strip in the late 1970s, and Ridgeway carried on alone until his death in 1994. It is now being done by syndicate staffers.

R.M.

MR. A. MUTT *see* Mutt and Jeff.

MR. AND MRS. (U.S.) Clare Briggs's Sunday page strip *Mr. and Mrs.*, dealing with an eternally bickering middle-class couple, began in the *New York Tribune* on April 14, 1919, shortly after he left the *Chicago Tribune*, where he had drawn such once-famed Sunday pages as *Danny Dreamer*, *Danny Dreamer, Sr.*, and *Sambo Remo Rastus Brown*. Unlike such similar but heavily populated strips as *The Gumps* and *The Bungle Family*, Briggs's *Mr. and Mrs.* rarely featured any characters other than the title figures, Joe and Vi, and their son, Roscoe, who occasionally asks wistfully, like an idiot Greek chorus, "Mamma love Papa?" There is no doubt that *Mr. and Mrs.* accurately reflected a large segment of domestic life as it was in America: it did so with such adamant realism and unadornment that the strip is unrelentingly dull and obvious from start to finish. There is little real humor and invention, and it is hard to believe that *Mr. and Mrs.* was a product of the same pen that created the witty and sharply observant daily panel features such as *It Happens in the Best Regulated Families*, *Tedious Pastimes*, and *How To Start the Day Wrong*.

The last *Mr. and Mrs.* page drawn by Briggs appeared on January 26, 1930, but the strip continued with a text by Arthur Folwell and art by Kin Platt for almost two more decades—duller and more obvious, if possible, than the Briggs original. This latter pair added a daily *Mr. and Mrs.* strip in the early 1930s in place of the daily panel gags that Briggs drew, and which were reprinted for a time. This was a daily gag strip with no continuity and it ran about as long as the post-Briggs Sunday page. Bad as it was, however, it cannot be argued that the public did not find a familiar and welcome note in the original Briggs strip. As a social record of the times, it has its undoubted value.

B.B.

MR. BREGER (U.S.) Dave Breger's immensely popular World War II panel series, *Private Breger*, about the training and warfare experiences of a shrimpish, bespectacled GI, was first distributed to newspapers by King Features on October 19, 1942, and had its name changed to *Mr. Breger* on October 22, 1945, to reflect its hero's return to civilian life. A Sunday half-page in strip form was issued on February 3, 1946. Originally created as a new weekly panel character series for the *Saturday Evening Post* on August 30, 1941, *Private Breger* caught the fancy of enlisted men at once. Reflecting on the woes of newly drafted men in the peacetime armed forces, its sharply mocking view of officer pomp and ceremony and wryly sympathetic portrait of the put-upon private soldier struck responsive chords. Asked to do a similar panel and strip feature for the new army magazine *Yank*, Breger eagerly agreed, but because the *Private Breger* name was already in copyright use by the *Post* and was being considered for syndication by King Features, he felt he had to coin a new title for his work. He came up with *GI Joe*, shortly to become the most widely used term of reference for the American enlisted man.

As *Private Breger* in the American press and *GI Joe* in the weekly *Yank* and daily overseas army paper *Stars and Stripes*, Breger's freckle-faced little hero was as universally known as Baker's *Sad Sack* and Mauldin's *Willie and Joe*. Mustered out of the service along with his creator in late 1945, *GI Joe* appeared in a farewell book collection of the same name, while *Private Breger*, already celebrated in a book titled *Private Breger's War* in 1944, continued as a civilian newspaper panel character. Its hero now married (to Dorothy Breger), and the father of a son, Harry, *Mr. Breger* carried much of the same wit and comedy into middle-class American life that had made the wartime strip so enjoyable. Too subtle and satirical for many readers, however, and lacking the kind of identification tags the public relishes (such as Dagwood's sandwiches and Snoopy's doghouse), *Mr. Breger* never enjoyed a wide circulation outside the Hearst press (indeed, many ex-GIs never knew the post-1945 strip existed). Partly because of its poor income and partly because Breger owned the rights to his character, King Features folded the panel and strip with its creator's death, the last episode appearing on March 22, 1970.

B.B.

MISTERIX (Italy) *Misterix*, Italy's second masked hero feature, made its appearance in the comic publication *Albi le Più Belle Avventure* on December 12, 1946, only a few months after *Asso di Picche*.

Paul Campani, the artist, and Max Massimino Garnier, the scriptwriter, chose the United States as the locale for their strip. Their graphic style was close to that of Caniff's *Steve Canyon*, while the mood was more inspired by *Batman*. Campani, however, unlike most of his colleagues who were content to depict an imaginary America, was very attentive to authentic detail; instead of the bland treatment usually associated with this kind of feature, he depicted a cruel metropolis similar to the locales of countless gangster movies of the 1940s.

Misterix was in reality John Smith, a reporter for the *Globe* (a cover similar to that of Superman), and the inventor of a special rubber suit powered by nuclear energy. This suit endowed its wearer with extraordinary strength and exceptional powers; unfortunately, as all machines do, it often went haywire (this usually happened at the most critical moment so as to build up the suspense). Misterix's enemies were many, but the most dreaded of all was the evil Takos, a ruthless gang leader who turned out to be the hero's lost brother.

The struggle with Takos unfolded throughout 15 comic books and these episodes were reprinted many times. The most imaginative and enjoyable of Misterix's adventures, however, were those done by Campani for the Argentine market. So successful was the hero in Argentina that in 1948 Editorial Abril of Bue-

nos Aires launched a weekly comic magazine titled *Misterix*. Along with the hero's adventures, it published a host of other strips, most of them by Hugo Pratt.

G.B.

"Mr. Jack," James Swinnerton. © International Feature Service.

MR. JACK (U.S.) One of the most fondly remembered of early American comic strips was James Swinnerton's *Mr. Jack*, which first appeared as a separate strip (it developed from a strip series about humanized lynxes that Swinnerton was drawing at the time) on November 2, 1902, in a half-page Sunday episode titled, "No Friend of Hers." Several more episodes featuring Mr. Jack (a girl-ogling young and married cat-about-town who inevitably lost out with the fancy women he pursued) appeared over the next few months, separately captioned and without a specific name for the lead character. Finally, on November 1, 1903, it received the title, *Mr. Jack!*, from which point on the strip ran almost weekly until February 7, 1904, when it was abruptly dropped from the Hearst Sunday comic section for good, being continued some time later as an occasional daily strip called *The Troubles of Mr. Jack* from 1912 to 1919.

Again abandoned by Swinnerton, *Mr. Jack* was revived under that title as the companion page-topper for the Sunday *Little Jimmy* on February 7, 1926, first as a single row of four panels, then in a few weeks as a double-rowed strip of eight to ten panels. It continued as such until June 5, 1935, when the last episode appeared (drawn, incidentally, by Swinnerton's frequent ghost, Doc Winner), the Sunday space being filled the following week by a new Swinnerton feature, *Orvie* (later *Lil Ole Orvie*), about a very young, round-headed, and pop-eyed kid.

Mr. Jack seems to have worried Hearst syndicate executives as a character. Initially a married and humanized cat, his hot pursuit of show girls, sometimes thwarted by his wife, apparently seemed too risqué for the juvenile audience of the Sunday comics, and he was shunted to the editorial pages of the daily Hearst papers. When he returned as a Sunday character in 1926, his amorous proclivities were as much in evidence as before, but he was no longer married. Despite this, the vulgarity of the Mr. Jack character, above a page essentially intended for young readers, seems to have gotten him scuttled again in 1935, when the innocent *Orvie* was introduced. One of the best-

"Mr. Kiasu," Johnny Lau. © the Kuppies.

drawn and most amusing of the humanized animal strips, *Mr. Jack* is a minor but memorable feature of its time. (In all likelihood, the character inspired Robert Crumb's *Fritz the Cat* some 50 years later.)

B.B.

MR. KIASU (Singapore) *Mr. Kiasu* was an unusual phenomenon in 1990s Singapore. First of all, it proved to be popular and lucrative in a country not known for comics; second, it made its mark by exploiting negative characteristics of Singaporeans.

Derived from the disparaging Hokkien term meaning desire to be number one at anyone's expense, "kiasu" was often used to refer to brash, obnoxious, and selfish bargain hunters and freebie seekers. The character that goes by that name was created by architect/cartoonist Johnny Lau, with help from James Suresh, Eric Chang, and Lim Yu Cheng, in time for exhibition at the 1990 Singapore Book Fair. From the beginning, Lau and his coentrepreneurs, calling themselves the Kuppies, approached *Mr. Kiasu* in a businesslike way, marketing a slew of products simultaneously with the character's first appearance and self-publishing and using the alternative distribution means of introducing the book at the fair. The latter assured a greater take of profits and retention of all rights by the Kuppies.

The formula worked, for although only one book appears each year *Mr. Kiasu* is known far and wide, with spinoffs including a radio show, a compact disc, music videos, cartoon shows, and other comics titles, as well as arrangements with fast food, travel agencies, and hotel businesses, and merchandising of about two dozen products such as watches, cereals, and school bags. The books have also been translated into other languages for sale in Hong Kong, Indonesia, and Japan.

Mr. Kiasu is a nerdy, bespectacled young man with an insensitive disposition and vulgar behavior. The humor, according to Lau, is a workable blend of the East and West—satire influenced by *Mad* magazine and slapstick comedy emanating from an old Asian comic, *Old Master Q*. Suresh described *Mr. Kiasu* in this way: "His philosophies in life are: to win all the time; bor-

row but never return; cheap is good; pay only when necessary."

J.A.L.

MR. MUM *see* Strange World of Mr. Mum, The.

MR. NATURAL (U.S.) Of all the characters created by Robert Crumb, undoubtedly the most famous of all the "underground" comix artists, Crumb's *Mr. Natural* is easily the most vexing, hardest to interpret, and most subtle.

Since Crumb himself has those characteristics also, he is often cast as Mr. Natural; this, however, is probably not the case. But because *Mr. Natural* as a strip and as a character does run so far afield, it is easy to see why many look upon Crumb and Mr. Natural and find them similar.

Mr. Natural, a white-bearded guru-type in white gown and sandals, began to appear in print late in 1967 in *Yarrowstalks*, an underground paper published in Philadelphia by Brian Zahn. At about the same time, Zahn commissioned Crumb to produce complete books of Mr. Natural and his *Yarrowstalks* characters—which were also appearing in the *East Village Other* and many of the other underground tabloids beginning to emerge. Crumb responded by completing two issues of *Zap*. Zahn disappeared with some of the art, however, and neither book saw print until Crumb moved to San Francisco and teamed with Don Donahue and printer Charles Plymell. The books subsequently appeared as *Zap* number one and *Zap* number zero.

As for the character of the *Mr. Natural* strip itself, perhaps the simplest description is to say that it is a vehicle through which all of Robert Crumb's ideas have flowed. The historical basis for the existence of any real-life Mr. Natural has been bandied about frequently—he has been pegged as a legendary Afghanistian, a parody of an infamous San Francisco guru popular during the time of *Mr. Natural's* creation, and even a reincarnation of a Dr. Von Naturlich—but it really has little bearing on Crumb's *Mr. Natural*.

At best, this fluffy-bearded pragmatist can be called a lovable old fraud who dispenses wisecracks and occa-

"Mr. Natural," Robert Crumb. © Robert Crumb.

sional sage advice on life to a horde of not-quite-convinced followers. At worst, Mr. Natural epitomizes all the ripoffs and dangerous mindwarping that stemmed from the "hippie" movement during the late 1960s. Probably, however, the inconsistencies in Mr. Natural's character came from Crumb's own ambivalence about the "movement," which drew Crumb and other followers to HaightAshbury in San Francisco. If anything can be firmly stated about this capitalistic cross between Santa Claus and a confidence man, it is that he was infinitely wiser and more realistic than any of his followers. The best-known of his subjects were Flakey Foont, a neurotic city-dweller constantly obsessed with sex and life's true meaning who was never quite sure why he took all the abuse Mr. Natural heaped upon him, and Shuman the Human, a bald truth-seeker whom Crumb often used to poke fun at the latest religious fad.

Mr. Natural, besides appearances in many undergrounds—including two bearing his name—is a favorite merchandising gimmick for those looking to cash in on Crumb's popularity. He has appeared on just about every type of merchandise trying to appeal to the young. Crumb, however, rarely authorized the bastard editions and was paid royalties on them even less often.

J.B.

MR. SCARLET (U.S.) Early in the 1940s, the National and Fawcett groups locked horns over two alleged imitations of the *Superman* feature, and National eventually sued Fawcett, claiming their *Master Man* and *Captain Marvel* strips were plagiarisms. While critics still argue the merits of both cases—National won settlements—National certainly missed attacking another, more vulnerable, Fawcett property, *Mr. Scarlet*, a close imitation of *Batman*. Created by writer Ed Herron and artists Jack Kirby and Joe Simon, *Mr. Scarlet* first appeared in *Wow* number one (Spring 1941), and borrowed many of *Batman*'s major concepts. Although Mr. Scarlet was actually prosecutor Brian Butler and not a playboy, he and Batman were both nonsuperpowered crime stoppers. And just like Batman, Mr. Scarlett was cast as a mysterious figure of darkness, prowling the city streets in the dead of night. (His blood-red and silver-trimmed costume quickly scuttled that aspect, however.) And, again like Batman, he used a gun (two, in fact) in early stories, and shortly added a kid sidekick (Pinky Butler).

Unlike Batman, however, Mr. Scarlet sported a moustache, and his entry into crime fighting was based on his desire to bring to justice "those who escape the law through its loopholes." A noble desire, indeed, and writers Herron and Otto Binder kept the strip teeming with cops-and-robbers clichés. Simon's and Kirby's artwork on the strip was pleasant, complete with strange angles and interesting composition, but they were restricted by the standard nine-panel page. The Binder shop handled the artwork in 1942, and Mac Raboy (1941-1942), Harry Anderson (1942-1944), and John Jordan (1944-1948) drew the strip afterward.

Mr. Scarlet appeared in *Wow* for 69 consecutive issues (until Fall 1948), and also appeared in *America's Greatest* from issue one (1941) to issue seven (May 1943).

J.B.

MR. TERRIFIC (U.S.) Along with the premier episode of *Wonder Woman* in *Sensation* number one (January 1942), National introduced a costumed hero backup feature entitled *Mr. Terrific*. Created by writer Charles Reizenstein and artist Hal Sharp, the strip was pedestrian and uninspired, but Mr. Terrific was blessed with a garishly colorful outfit: scarlet tights and face mask, green tunic, yellow gloves, black boots, and a brown waist girdle. Escaping the use of the normal superheroic chest emblem, Mr. Terrific chose to sport a yellow chest patch that righteously promoted "Fair Play."

In reality he was child prodigy Terry Sloane, who was so successful in sports, academics, and business that he was bored by life, and so Mr. Terrific became a crime fighter simply to shake off his boredom. In his first effort, he delayed his planned suicide long enough to don his costume and turn a group of youthful thugs into fine, upstanding young Americans. He also changed their name from the "Purple Dagger Gang" to—as one might expect—the "Fair Play Club." Naturally, he then found a purpose in life and applied his genius to thwarting crime. Most of the scripts by Reizenstein and replacement Ted Udall were similarly simplistic.

Sharp's artwork was flat and linear, but Mr. Terrific's loud costume helped him stand out against the sparse background. Sharp turned the artistic chores over to Stan Asch in 1944, and the versatile Asch handled the feature until its 1947 demise.

Mr. Terrific appeared in *Sensation* until March 1947's 63rd issue, and the character made a cameo appearance with the Justice Society in 1945. He was revived by National, along with their other 1940s heroes, in the mid-1960s for several appearances.

J.B.

MIZUKI, SHIGERU (1924-   ) Japanese comic book artist born March 28, 1924, in Sakaiminato (Tottori prefecture). Shigeru Mizuki attended Musashino Art University but dropped out in 1949 and became associated with Koji Kata. He then started a career as a *kamishibai mangaka* (an artist who specialized in drawing stories in pictures for exhibitions), but the genre's popularity was then at a low ebb and Mizuki went to Tokyo in order to work on comic books.

His first comic book creation, *Rocket Man*, a strip combining elements of horror with a science-fiction theme, was published in 1957. For the next eight years Mizuki became a *kashibonya yō mangaka*, an artist working for comic books circulated in special rental libraries (a peculiarly Japanese institution). Among his works during this period, mention should be made of the following: *Yūrei Ikka* ("The Ghost Family," 1959); *Kappa no Sanpei* (a monster story, 1963); *Akumakun* (about a magician who can conjure Mephistopheles with the help of King Solomon's flute, 1964); *Hakaba no Kitarō* ("Kitarō from the Graveyard") and Mammoth Flower (both 1965); and *Renkin Jutsu* (a tale of alchemy and black magic, 1967).

Shigeru Mizuki is the most talented artist working in the horror/terror genre in Japanese comics today. His ghoulish creations are always tempered, however, with a generous touch of civilized irony. The most striking feature of his unique art is the blending in the same panel of realism and distortion. This imbalance allows him to strike for even greater effects of horror and dread.

Mizuki has also written a number of hardbound horror novels with illustrations by himself. His works have inspired a number of animated cartoons (*Hakabano Kitarō*) and have been adapted to the television screen (*Akumakun, Kappa no Sanpei*).

In an altogether different vein, Mizuki completed his monumental series *Komikku Showa-shi* ("A Comics History of the Showa Era"), about the controversial reign of Emperor Hirohito, in 1994. He was awarded the Japanese Medal with Ribbons in 1992.

H.K.

MIZUNO, HIDEKO (1939-   ) Hideko Mizuno knew from the time she was in third grade that she wanted to be a comics artist. In middle school, she began sending samples of her work to Osamu Tezuka, the undisputed leader of Japanese comics artists, and Tezuka recommended her to the editor of Kodansha Publishing's girls' magazine, *Shojo Club*. She soon began doing small illustrations and four-panel strips for the magazine, and in 1956, at the age of 15, she was asked to create a short story. This debut story, *Akakke ponii* ("Red Pony"), was a Western that featured a free-spirited tomboy who bore no resemblance to helpless-but-pretty little heroines of the melodramas that were the standard fare for Japanese girls' comics—all created by men—at the time. That same year, Mizumo was given her first serial, *Gin no hanabira* ("Silver Flower Petals), a medieval adventure tale of a horse-riding, sword-wielding princess. It was an enormous hit that shattered stereotypes of what Japanese girls wanted to read.

Mizuno made her debut at more or less the same time as two other women, Masako Watanabe and Miyako Maki, and the three became the first women to create narrative comics (as opposed to humor strips) in Japan. All three were tremendously popular, but whereas the other two more or less continued the tradition of domestic melodramas featuring little girls, Mizuno, who was more influenced by the dynamic work of Tezuka than by earlier girls' comics, always pushed the envelope, and her stories, like her lines, were bold. One of her best-known works, *Hoshi no tategoto* ("Star Harp," 1960), was a mythic epic in the style of Wagner that was the first girls' comic to feature romantic love between a woman and a man.

Mizuno again broke new ground in 1969 with *Fire!* ("Freedom!"), a passionate story of a juvenile delinquent's rise to rock stardom, and his encounters with sex, drugs, and rock 'n' roll along the way. Although the theme of *Fire!* may seen corny today, it captured the feelings of the youth of the day, and Mizuno's exquisite technique still shines. *Fire!*, which was published in the teen-oriented weekly magazine *Seventeen*, earned Mizuno the 1970 Shogakukan Comic Award.

Mizuno proved to be a major influence on the subsequent generation of women artists, particularly the innovative artists known collectively as the *Hana no nijuyonen gumi* ("Magnificent 24-Year Group") because many were born in the year Showa 24, or 1949.

Most of Mizuno's better-known work is now available in soft-cover collector's editions, and in 1981 her adventure comedy *Hanii Haniino sutekina boken* ("Honey-Honey's Wonderful Adventures") was made into an animated television series.

M.A.T.

MIZUSHIMA, SHINJI (1939-   ) Japanese comic book artist born April 10, 1939 in Niigata. Mizushima, who dreamed of becoming a cartoonist since his grammar school days, started work as a fishmonger as soon as he finished junior high school. In 1959 he made his debut as a cartoonist, working for the famous Kashibon Manga Kage, a comic company specializing in the publication of comic books for rental libraries.

Working on all of Kage's releases from number 17 to 120, Mizushima created many features, including *Ore wa Yaru* ("I'll Kill You," 1959), *Thrill o Ajiwan Otoko* ("The Man Who Craved Thrills," 1960), *Muteki Dump Guy* (a story about a stock car driver, 1961), *Idaten Santa* (a humor strip, 1962), *Heno Heno Moheji* (a story about a boy who loved a scarecrow, 1963), and *Botchan*, a 1964 comic book adaptation of a famous work of Japanese literature.

In 1965 Mizushima produced his first magazine strip, *Takaou*, which was followed by *Ushitsuki* (an animal strip, 1966) and *Left wa Shinazu* (a boxing strip, 1969). After this, Mizushima specialized in baseball strips, with four consecutive creations in this field: *Ace no Jōken* (1969); *Otoko Doahou Koushien* (1970); *Yakyūkyō no Uta* (1972); and *Abu-san* (1973). These and later sports comics made their author very rich, and since 1978 he has regularly made the list of the highest income-earners in Japan.

Mizushima is now a famous and popular comic book artist. Greatly influenced by the work of playwright Kobako Hanato, his stories are full of warmth and drama. He created so many baseball strips because he is a baseball fan himself.

H.K.

MODESTY BLAISE (G.B.) The official biography of Modesty Blaise reads as follows: Origins: Date of birth unknown. Place of birth unknown. Age, approximately 26. Education: Self-acquired. Excellent. Occupation: Retired. Previous Occupation: Suspected head of "The Network," international crime syndicate based in Algeria. Financial category: Very rich. Present address: London W. 1. Close friends: Only one—William Garvin soldier of fortune (retired). Hobbies: Sculpting precious stones. Future Plans:?????

The strip biography tells of a small female child, a war refugee, her memory erased through shock, who escaped from a prison camp in Greece to a displaced persons camp in Persia. She saved an old professor from a thief, and in return he educated her and named her Modesty. Her surname she took from Merlin's tutor. She buried the old man and entered civilization, spinning a roulette wheel in Tangier.

In two years she had taken over her late employer's gang; in two more she was boss of the international crime syndicate "The Network." It was in Saigon that she first saw Willie Garvin, Thai-style fighter, gutterbred. She bought him out of jail without strings, and from then on he called her "Princess." Partners in crime, they retired to England where Sir Gerald Tarrant, head of British Intelligence, appealed to them for their help in a mission requiring an intimate knowledge of the underworld. Bored with the luxury life, they became unpaid agents for Britain.

The third biography is the correct one: *Modesty Blaise* is a daily newspaper strip created by writer Peter O'Donnell and artist Jim Holdaway. Intended for the *Daily Express*, it was rejected at the last moment, on the grounds that the life of a "fallen woman" was unsuitable to a family newspaper. The *Evening Standard*, another Beaverbrook newspaper, took it on immediately, starting on Easter 1963, and soon the strip was syndicated to 76 newspapers and magazines in 35 different countries.

A major movie was made from the strip in 1966, starring Monica Vitti as Modesty, Terence Stamp as Willie, and Harry Andrews as Sir Gerald. It was directed by Joseph Losey. O'Donnell's first novel, *Modesty Blaise*, was published in 1965. When Holdaway died in 1970, the strip was taken over by the Spanish cartoonist Romero. Thirty-four years after its inception, the strip is still doing well internationally with Peter O'Donnell and Enrique Romero firmly at the helm.

D.G.

MOEBIUS *see* Giraud, Jean.

MOLINO, WALTER (1915-   ) An Italian cartoonist and illustrator born November 5, 1915, in Reggio Emilia, Walter Molino moved with his family to Milan in 1920. There the young Molino went to high school and, upon graduation, entered the University of Milan. Molino, whose father was an art teacher, exhibited an early talent for drawing but decided to follow in the footsteps of his older brother, Antonio, a noted short-story writer (later killed in the Mathausen concentration camp). In 1934 Molino's first drawing was published in the student newspaper *Libro e Moschetto*, on the occasion of Arnaldo Mussolini's death. This was followed by a series of short-lived comic strips for the brothers Del Duca's publications, *L'Intrepido* and *Il Monello*, and a brief stint as an advertising artist.

In 1935, at the formal request of Mussolini and in collaboration with Mario Sironi, Molino originated a series of political and satirical cartoons, published first in *Libro e Moschetto*, and later in *Il Popolo d'Italia*. He also contributed fashion drawings to such publications as *Per Voi, Signori*, and *Arbiter*. In 1936 the humor magazine *Il Bertoldo* was founded, and Molino became one of its most talented contributors. But Molino's talent shone brightest in the series of comic strips starting in 1937 that editor and scriptwriter Federico Pedrochhi asked him to illustrate. "Aside from my work at *Il Bertoldo*," Molino later reminisced, "all I did was draw comic strip after comic strip." During this golden period he drew *Virus, il Mago della Foresta Morta* ("Virus, the Magician of the Dead Forest"), a masterly science-fiction thriller (1938); *Capitan l'Audace* (1939), a tale of intrigue and violence set in 16th-century Italy; the moody Western, *Kit Carson*, which Molino took over from Rino Albertarelli in 1939; the parodic *Don Antonio della Mancia*, about a modern-day Don Quixote; and many others.

In 1941 Molino started his 25-year collaboration with the *Domenico del Corriere*, contributing cartoons, illustrations, and double-page spreads. In 1946, using a clever combination of wash and photographic techniques, he created the spectacularly successful *Grand Hotel*, the soap opera to end all soap operas, an outrageous display of all the clichés the genre has to offer (many of Molino's former fans have yet to forgive him to this day).

In the 1960s Molino retired from comic strip work, concentrating on illustration and cartooning. His work has been amply reprinted and anthologized, as indeed it deserves to be. In 1984 a large retrospective of his works was organized by the Academia d'Arte and later traveled through Italy.

M.H.

MOMMA (U.S.) Thirteen years after launching the acclaimed *Miss Peach*, Mell Lazarus created another very amusing comic strip, which he affectionately named after the meddlesome heroine. *Momma* thus appeared on October 26, 1970, and was immediately recognized as the archetype of so many put-upon, self-sacrificing (though not silent), and unappreciated mothers.

Mrs. Sonya Hobbs is a widowed lady whose three children seldom meet her expectations—or maybe they meet them all too well. Thomas, her 42-year-old son, a successful professional, married and father of one, is still not treated as an adult by Momma. Neither, for that matter, is his wife Tina, "the person my Darling Son saw fit to pick as a wife," whom Mother Hobbs bombards with constructive criticism and unwanted advice, usually regarding raising little Chuckie or performing household duties to more demanding standards.

At age 22, Francis is a failure in her eyes—perhaps justifiably so, particularly when compared to other people's sons. Forever unemployed, always about to get married to some new girl, and always shamelessly sponging off his white-haired mother, he endures her nagging with equanimity while she suffers his ungrateful behavior with dismay. Daughter Marylou, 18, has a different boyfriend every other day, much to her mother's consternation—and pride.

Mrs. Hobbs never read Dr. Benjamin Spock. Her method of bringing up children, regardless of their age,

"Momma," Mell Lazarus. © Creators Syndicate.

rests instead on large quantities of food (since food *is* maternal love, and vice versa) and especially on larger quantities of guilt. Therefore, she tests their love constantly ("minimum daily requirement"), checks to see that her phone is indeed working, and reminds them how sorry they will be when she dies of worry, sorrow, abandonment, or heartbreak. Yet, despite all her aggravations, Momma will admit in some unguarded moment that she does have "fine children, a nice home, warm memories, friends, security, [and] health."

Momma is drawn in the same caricatural style as Lazarus's *Miss Peach*: foreshortened characters with distinguishing features, such as Francis's big jaw and flowing black hair, Marylou's skinny figure and stringy hair, or Mrs. Hobbs's protruding eyes. Its popularity, however, comes from its on-target observations and sophisticated wit. The National Cartoonists Society awarded joint honors to the two series in 1973, 1979, and 1982.

First distributed by Field Newspaper Syndicate and since 1988 by Creators Syndicate, the strip has been reprinted in a number of paperback editions, including *The Momma Treasury* (1978), which also has a funny introduction by the author's mother.

P.L.H.

MONK, JACK (1904-197?) British cartoonist John Asthian Monk was born in Bolton, Lancashire, in 1904. He was educated at a council school, leaving in 1918 with an art scholarship to join Tillotson's Process Engraving as an office boy. He supported himself by doing retouching for catalogues and other publications, while attending evening classes at Bolton School of Art. His first published cartoons were sports drawings freelanced to the *Bolton Evening News Buff*, a Saturday sports edition. He was then invited to join the art staff of Allied Newspapers in Manchester, where he drew fillers, caricatures, and maps for the *Evening Chronicle*. He moved to the northern edition of the *Daily Express* and created a fact strip, *Can You Beat It?*, and *The Funny Side of Northern Towns* (both in 1934).

In July 1936 Monk moved south to Richmond, Surrey, to freelance for the *Daily Mirror*. His first daily strip was an adaptation of the Edgar Wallace novel *Terror Keep*, scripted by Don Freeman. Unfortunately, although rights had been cleared with Wallace's estate, the American syndicate producing the daily *Inspector Wade* claimed prior rights and the strip had to be ended. But Guy Bartholomew, the *Mirror* editor and champion of strips, liked Monk's style and asked him

to create an original detective. The result was *Buck Ryan*, which began on March 22, 1937, and ran for 25 years.

On the side he drew advertising strips for Phillips Stickasoles, and served part time as an auxiliary fireman during the war. At the end of his *Mirror* run Monk turned to comic work, beginning with *Commander Cockle* (1962) in *Lion*, then a number of series for D. C. Thomson's comics, including *Wee Tusky* (1965) in *Sparky*, *Inspector Jellicoe* (1963) in *Hornet*, and *Million Pound Mutt* (1973) in *Debbie*. None of these, however, had an impact similar to that created by his famous detective hero. He died in the late 1970s.

D.G.

MONKHOUSE, BOB (1929-) British cartoonist, editor, comedian, actor, and writer, Bob Monkhouse was born in Beckenham, Kent on, June 1, 1929, and educated at Dulwich College, where he drew the amateur magazine, *Modern Mag* (1943), and freelanced his first strips, *Bobby Brain* and *Professor Poosum*, to *All Fun* (1944). He contributed many different characters to this and the other Soloway Publications, which he followed by two comic painting books for R. & L. Locker, *Bimbo Goes to the Moon* and *Chubby & the Christmas Star* (1946), and the weekly newspaper strip *Just Judy* in the *South London Advertiser* (also 1946).

He passed the aptitude test for trainee animators at Gaumont British Animation and worked on the *Animaland* and *Musical Paintbox* series at the Cookham Studio until his conscription into the Royal Air Force in 1947. In the same year he edited and produced his first complete comic book, *Smasher Comics*, for Tongard Trading. He also wrote and pencilled strips for editor/artist John R. Turner to ink for *Okay*, *Ripping*, and *Winner* comics (1948). He became freelance editor for Martin & Reid comics in 1948, taking over existing titles (*Merry Go Round*, *Merry Maker*, *Funny Tuppeny*, *Jolly Chuckles*, etc.) and creating new titles: *Crash Comics* (1948), in the American superhero style, and *Super Star* (1949).

While his humorous work was much influenced by the animated cartoon style of the American funnies, he also admired the superhero style and created *Oh Boy Comics* (1948) for Paget Publications, drawing the super-adventures of *Tornado*. After four issues the comic was taken over by Mick Anglo, and continued with different artists for some while.

His last strips were for *Amazing and Modern Comics* (1949), published by Modern Fiction and edited by his schoolmate, Denis Gifford. Gifford brought Monkhouse back to cartooning in 1974, after many years as a star comedian and scriptwriter, to chair the first television panel game for cartoonists, *Quick on the Draw*. He also illustrated the book, *The A to Z of Television* (1971), which he coauthored with Willis Hall.

Bob Monkhouse is still very active in the field of comics.

D.G.

"Monsieur Poche," Alain Saint-Ogan. © Alain Saint-Ogan.

MONSIEUR POCHE (France) Alain Saint-Ogan, then at the height of his fame, created *Monsieur Poche* (literally "Mister Pocket") for the weekly *Dimanche Illustré* on October 14, 1934, where it ran as a full page.

Monsieur Poche is a solid citizen, of advanced middle age and ample proportions. Free of money worries (we certainly never see him trying to earn a living) he also feels free to stick his big red nose into everybody's business, ever generous with unsolicited advice, or ready to loudly assert his rights. During a conversation he never lets anybody else speak; in social gatherings he tries to upstage everyone (with usually disastrous results). He is also smug, vainglorious, cowardly, stingy, and loud-mouthed; the portrait, scarcely caricatural, of the typical small-town bore.

Monsieur Poche, a bachelor, was served (not always too well) by his elderly housekeeper, who didn't seem to take her boss's whims or orders too seriously. He was often accompanied by a young boy named Ratafia who is not adverse to taking advantage of Poche's credulity on occasion. Poche's constant companion, a kangaroo named Salsifi, made his appearance one full year after the inception of the strip (on October 28, 1935). A gift from Poche's Australian uncle, Salsifi was an unusual animal whose unpredictable behavior very often lands his master into the most screwy incidents. In 1937 *Monsieur Poche* ended its run in *Dimanche Illustré*. In December of that year it was revived in the pages of *Cadet-Revue* (where it had been preceded by *Zig et Puce*), which often simply reproduced the old *Dimanche Illustré* episodes. In 1940 the feature disap-

peared for good (in the interim Librairie Hachette had reprinted four volumes of *Monsieur Poche*'s adventures).

While not as famous as *Zig et Puce*, *Monsieur Poche* is a good example of Saint-Ogan's humor, made of subtle little touches and an unfailing eye (and ear) for the ridiculous. The characters of Poche and Salsifi are certainly among the author's most felicitous creations.

M.H.

MONTANA, BOB (1920-1975) American comic book and comic strip artist and writer born in Stockton, California, on October 23, 1920. After studies at the Phoenix Art Institute, the Art Students League, and the Boston Museum School of Fine Arts, Bob Montana broke into comic art as Bob Wood's assistant on Novelty's *Target Comics* in 1940. In 1941, he moved to MLJ and drew a slew of superhero features, including *Black Hood*, *Fox*, and *Steel Sterling*, and, between 1942 and 1945, drew material for Lev Gleason's superhero and crime books.

Without a doubt, however, Montana's greatest comic art contribution came in the 22nd issue of MLJ's *Pep* (December 1941). Almost unnoticed behind the superhero features, he created *Archie*, a teenage humor strip based on the then-popular Henry Aldrich radio show. With Montana at the helm, the strip soon became the most saleable humor strip feature on the market, was the basis for dozens of comic titles, a comic strip, all sorts of merchandising, a radio show, and several television programs.

The *Archie* concept has been roundly criticized because it has never accurately depicted teenage life, but Montana's creation has survived and profited mightily. The artist added a curious collection of stereotyped supporting characters: Archie Andrews's brunette girlfriend, the rich and spoiled Veronica Lodge,

Bob Montana, "Archie." © Archie Comics.

"Moomin," Tove Jansson. © Bulls Pressedienst.

was modeled after motion picture star Veronica Lake; the blond, middle-class Betty was based on one of Montana's old girlfriends; and Mr. Wetherbee, Riverdale High's harried principal, and Miss Beasley, the spinster schoolteacher, were developed from people Montana met during his Manchester, New Hampshire school days. Strangely enough, he created the lovable-but-inept Jughead on the drawing board. "I never knew him," Montana once said.

In 1947, an *Archie* comic strip was started under Montana's byline, and he soon abandoned the comic book line to concentrate on the dailies and Sundays.

Throughout his 35-year stint on *Archie*, Montana never varied his art style. It was always straightforward, uncluttered and unembellished, usually relying on the situation gag and one-liners rather than sight jokes. Montana died of a heart attack near his Meredith, New Hampshire, home on January 4, 1975.

J.B.

MOOMIN (Finland, G.B.) Moomintroll, to give him his full name, has a full figure: a sort of cuddly hippo who walks on two legs and loves something similar called Snorkmaiden. The full Finn Family Moomintroll, to use the title of one of their many books, is headed by Moominpappa, who may be recognized by his top hat and cane; or is more likely headed by Moominmamma, who may be recognized by her apron and handbag. Otherwise, Moomins are much the same, but very lovable in it. They all live in Moomin Valley in Moominland, a Nordic paradise spoiled only by doomladen Fillyjonks and horrifying Hattifatteners.

Their creator, the artist and author of many children's books, is Tove Jansson, who turned the Moomins into a daily strip at the request of her English publishers and the *London Evening News*. The series began on September 20, 1954, to the instant joy of millions, children and adults alike. The decorative linework, slender yet curvaceous, was something new in strips, and so was the whimsical humor. From 1957 her brother, Lars, wrote the stories for her. At the end of her contract, she gave up completely and let Lars draw the strip, too. He continued until the *News* dropped it on June 29, 1968. Tove Janssen, beset by requests to commercialize her creations, refused, and reacted by writing them into a final, despairing novel, *Moominland*

Midwinter. An excellent hardback volume of *Moomin* from the first strip was published under that title in 1957.

D.G.

MOON MULLINS (U.S.) Moon Mullins (and his earliest strip crony, Mushmouth) arrived on the comics scene by box, being dumped off a delivery van in Jack Dempsey's training quarters at Shelby, Montana, in the first daily episode of Frank Willard's new *Chicago Tribune* strip of June 19, 1923 (the first Sunday page appeared September 9, 1923). In training for his July 4, 1923, fight with Tom Gibbons, Dempsey (shown in this first *Moon Mullins* episode in a dressing gown lavishly decorated with pre-Hitler swastikas) was prominently featured in the sports news of the time, and his presence must have attracted many eyes to the new strip. Moon's idea, once inside the compound, was to rent his own fighter, Mushmouth (whom he calls Wildcat) to Dempsey as a great "punching bag," or spar-

"Moon Mullins," Frank Willard. © Chicago Tribune-New York News Syndicate.

ring partner, but Dempsey has both Moon and Mushmouth thrown out of the camp, minus their box.

This opening episode (badly printed in many papers because of a damaged proof) characterized both the small-time opportunism of the new strip's hero, and the rowdy, slam-bang narrative that was to follow. Essentially, Willard's *Moon Mullins* was *Tribune* publisher Joe Patterson's competitive reply to the success of Hearst artist Billy De Beck's *Barney Google*; and it looked for a few weeks as if Willard was going to develop the boxing world as a strip theme much as De Beck had developed horse racing. Willard veered away from that limited area shortly, however, and never returned: Moon's natural habitat, it turned out, was the circus, the neighborhood pool parlor, and any ritzy mansion he could bluff his way into for a free meal or two.

Moon's full first name was "Moonshine" (given to him by Patterson with an eye on the popular Prohibition term for bootleg liquor), and he had a markedly prognathous, Popeyesque jaw in the early weeks of the strip, which Willard rounded off gradually. Joining a carnival, he met the next regular character in the strip, his love-light, Little Egypt, in the daily episode for July 30, 1923. Losing Egypt for the time being, Moon wanders to a strange town where he moves into a rooming house run by the scrawny, elaborately coiffeured Emmy Schmaltz (March 3, 1924), where the strip took on the general shape it maintained over the next 50 years. Emmy, it turned out some time later, is ardently pursuing the reluctant, plump, and nobly moustached Lord Plushbottom (who resisted her charms until their marriage in 1934). Kayo, Moon's bratty little brother, turns up, as does Mamie, a cook hired by Emmy who turns out to be the estranged wife of Moon's Uncle Willie, the last regular character to enter the strip, in a Sunday episode for May 29, 1927. From that date, the continuing *dramatis comicae* of *Moon Mullins* was complete.

While there was little or no continuing narrative in the anecdotal *Mullins* Sunday page, the daily strip was one of the most intricately-plotted and imaginatively-developed continuing narratives in the comics. Willard and his assistant, Ferd Johnson, mastered the difficult art of maintaining cliff-hanging continuity while mustering a neat daily gag each and every day almost from the outset of the strip. Much of the compelling story pace of the strip and the narrative imagination of the strip's first 15 years ebbed in the early 1940s for some reason, however, and was never effectively regained, although the quality of many of the daily and Sunday gags remained relatively high.

Willard's only *Moon Mullins* companion strip was the four-panel Sunday feature called *Kitty Higgins*, involving the escapades of a young female playmate of Kayo's, which began in early 1930 and was dropped in the 1960s. A number of *Moon Mullins* episodes were reprinted in book form, but no complete daily narratives were published as they originally appeared until a few from the late 1930s were obscurely reprinted in comic books of the period. A comprehensive book is still needed.

Following Willard's death in early 1958, Ferd Johnson took over the *Moon Mullins* strip, which he continued until its demise in June 1991. Johnson's Mullins-Plushbottom menage was much more amiable and clean-scrubbed than the old Willard bunch: the derbies Moon and Kayo both sported disappeared, as did the other antisocial rough edges of the original crew. But there was a marked humor and charm in the latter strip that was very much Johnson's own, and it held the attention of a new generation of readers.

B.B.

MOORE, ALAN (1953-   ) British artist born in November 1953 in Northampton, England. Dropping out of school at age 17, Alan Moore started writing, under the pseudonym "Curt Vile," for the rock magazine *Sounds*. After trying his hand at cartooning with *Maxwell the Magic Cat*, he went back to scripting, working notably for the comic magazines *2000 AD* and *Warriors*. His break came in 1982 with *V for Vendetta*, a tale about a British society of the near-future laid waste by war and ruled by a Fascist government; illustrated with great sensitivity by David Lloyd, *V for Vendetta* was very well received by readers and critics alike.

This success drew the attention of the editors at DC Comics, who brought Moore over to the U.S. in 1983. He made an acclaimed debut writing some of the most suspenseful *Swamp Thing* episodes; then in 1986 came *Watchmen*, illustrated by Dave Gibbons, which definitively established him as one of the modern masters of comic-book storytelling. Two more remarkable stories followed in 1988: a *Superman* tale ("Happy Birthday, Superman!," again with Gibbons) and a *Batman* episode ("The Killing Joke," with art by Brian Bolland).

Back in Britain by the end of the decade, Moore turned out a number of personal projects (some of a political nature), including *Big Numbers* (illustrated by Bill Sienkiewicz), the tale of a small English town disrupted by the opening of a shopping mall; and *From Hell*, one more version of the Jack the Ripper murders, with art by the Australian Eddy Campbell. Since 1996 he has been writing *Supreme* for Rob Liefeld's Extreme Studios, and he is currently at work on the *Judgment Day* miniseries. The recipient of many honors and awards, Alan Moore has also lectured extensively on the subject of comics.

M.H.

MOOSE MILLER (U.S.) A standard King Features-style "bigfoot" humor strip, *Moose Miller* celebrated its 30th year of international syndication in September 1995. Considering the attrition rate of newspaper comic strips, this is a notable accomplishment for *Moose*'s creator, Bob Weber Sr.

Moose Miller was King Features's answer to the instant success of *Andy Capp*, the British import about a drunken but funny lout, that was syndicated in the United States by Publishers Syndicate beginning in September 1963.

Weber's *Moose Miller*, unlike *Andy Capp*, is a devoted family man. With wife Molly, son Bunky, daughter Blip, and a mini-zoo of family pets, from Grits the dog to goats and parrots, it's the type of family you'd wish to be anybody's neighbors but your own. The Miller family's neighbors in the strip, Chester and Clara Crabtree, are often the butt of the Miller's low-rent behavior, such as stealing food from their barbecue.

Fat and extremely lazy, Moose Miller works at not working. He's the kind of guy who gives white trash a bad name. Until the arrival of the cartoon family in Bud Grace's feature *Ernie* in 1988 and Matt Groening's animated family sitcom *The Simpsons* in 1989, the *Moose Miller* clan held the prize as cartooning's most physically unattractive characters.

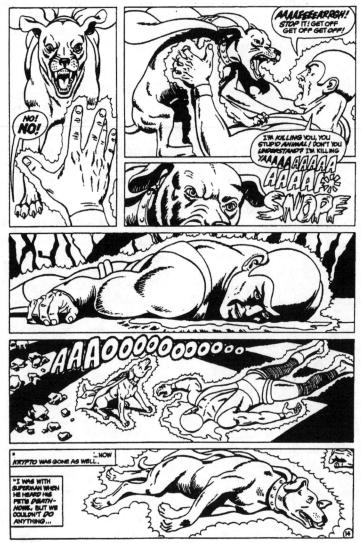

Alan Moore and Curt Swan, "Superman." © DC Comics.

With sight gags, broad burlesque, slapstick, and old-fashioned bigfoot-style fun, *Moose Miller*, in Bob Weber Sr.'s competent hands, continues the King Features tradition of humor strips. Weber's son, Bob Jr., assisted his father on *Moose Miller*, prior to creating his own feature for King, *Slylock Fox*.

One of a legion of cartoonists who attended the School of Visual Arts in New York City, Bob Weber Sr. credits magazine cartoonist Orlando Busino for getting him to leave technical illustration for cartooning. A raconteur with endless stories about cartooning, Weber has taught cartooning to children all over the northeastern United States for many years.

B.C.

MORDILLO, GUILLERMO (1933-   ) An Argentine cartoonist born in Buenos Aires in 1933, Guillermo Mordillo started his cartooning career in animation and advertising. In 1955 he moved to Lima, going from there to New York, where he got a job as a greeting card designer for the Hallmark Company. In 1966 the peripatetic Mordillo settled in Paris, where he produced books of extraordinary cartoons without captions, such as *Crazy Cowboy*. He also designed posters, greeting cards and merchandising material, all of which bore the stamp of his unmistakable style.

At the same time Mordillo experimented with the comic strip form, laying out his humor pages in rows of panels and creating his series of unforgettable characters, such as the giraffe, the little Tarzan, Superman, and the inflatable woman. These pages were published all over the world in magazines such as *Lui*, *Oui*, and *Bocaccio*, making Mordillo the most widely published cartoonist of the 1970s. In the last 20 years he has worked almost exclusively in humor and children's illustration.

L.G.

MORONI-CELSI, GUIDO (1885-1962) Italian artist born 1885 in Rome. Guido Moroni-Celsi began his professional career as a portrait artist and humor cartoonist with a series of sketches called *L'Album di Pippo* ("Pippo's Sketchbook") published in *Il Messaggero dei Piccoli*. Under the pen name "F. Sterny," he contributed a number of cartoons to the humor magazines *Il Mulo* of Bologna and *Ma chié* of Naples. In 1926 he started his first comic strip, *Bonifazio*, partly inspired by Swinnerton's *Little Jimmy*, for the juvenile weekly *Il Novellino*, and the same year also contributed to the *Domenica dei Fanciulli*. In 1929 he alternated with Rino Albertarelli in producing the center-spreads of the *Cartoccino dei Piccoli*.

Only in 1930 did Moroni-Celsi do drawings and illustrations in a straight style: these were hunting, battle, and sport scenes for the magazine *Viaggi e Avventure* (Albertarelli, Ballerio, and Rivolo also worked

Guido Moroni-Celsi, "Le Tigri di Mompracem." © Mondadori.

on these pages). In 1934, for the *Corriere dei Piccoli*, he created *Grillo il Balillino* (the "balillas" were Fascist youth), a politically motivated strip featuring the brave deeds of a blackshirted young man.

In 1935, for Mondadori's *I Tre Porcellini*, he produced *Ulceda*, a Western whose title character was the daughter of the Great Hawk of the Prairie. Once again the hero was an Italian—Vittorio Ranghi—who married the beautiful Ulceda at the end of the story. In 1935-36 he published his only science-fiction story, *S.K. 1*, in the weekly *Topolino* (it was reprinted in 1970 by Sansoni); but his best-remembered work remains his illustrated version of Salgari's jungle novels (*I Misteri della Giungla Nera*, *La Conquista di Mompracem*, etc). Published between 1936 and 1941 (when he was succeeded by Franco Chiletto) in the pages of *Topolino*, they tell in vivid and memorable fashion of the adventures of Yanez, Tremal Naik, and the pirates of Mompracem.

After the war, Moroni-Celsi faded from public favor. He died in Naples in 1962 in utter obscurity, but he was later resurrected as one of "the fathers of the Italian adventure strip."

G.B.

MORRIS *see* Bevère, Maurice de.

MORTADELO Y FILEMON (Spain) The Spanish cartoonist Francisco Ibañez created his comic strip hit in 1958 in the weekly *Pulgarcito* under the initial title *Mortadelo y Filemon, Agencia de Informacion* ("Mortadello and Filemon, Information Agency").

This information agency is made up of a pair of private eyes, Filemon, the boss, and his clever assistant Mortadelo, who is capable of disguising himself as a butterfly or an earthworm. Mortadelo's skill at outlandish transformations and the latent sadomasochism in the duo's relations constitute the main attractions of the strip. The stories are rich in absurd interludes, fist and club fights, madcap situations, and the introduction of the surreal into the mundane world of small-time hoods and scientists as crazy as the two investigators. In a second stage of their adventures, the pair met Doctor Bacterius, an inventor who used them as guinea pigs in his experiments, and they later joined the secret agency TIA (*TIA* in Spanish means "AUNT," a parodic pun on both the fictitious organization UNCLE and the real CIA), which allowed them further scope in their hare-brained exploits around the world.

The adventures of Filemon and Mortadelo were so popular that, in addition to their publication in *Pulgarcito*, they gave rise to two new publications, *Mortadelo*

and *Super Mortadelo*, in which the pair were the star attractions. After Ediciones Bruguera, owners of *Pulgarcito* and *Super Mortadelo*, went out of business in 1986, the pair continued their exploits under the banners of different Spanish publishers.

The success of the strip is so enormous that it can only be compared to that of *Asterix* in France. It soon spawned toys, books, gadgets of all kinds, advertising campaigns, animated films, and publications in numerous foreign countries, garnering the sort of acclaim aimed only at internationally-recognized hits.

L.G.

MORT CINDER (Argentina) *Mort Cinder* was created by Argentine cartoonist Alberto Breccia in 1962; written by Hector Oesterheld, it unfolded over a total of 206 pages in the comic magazine *Misterix*. The protagonist is a criminal with a wide knowledge of neurosurgery; having already lived a series of lives, he is resurrected by the antiquarian, Ezra Winston, who gives him work and studies his history, along with that of Hilaire Belloc.

A masterpiece of the chiaroscuro technique, *Mort Cinder* is bathed in the nightmarish atmosphere of foreboding and terror favored by the author and carried to its limits in *Los Mitos de Cthulu*. Each of the strip's episodes is treated in the author's unique style, always unified by his visual experiences, from the expressionist cinema of Fritz Lang to the films of Ingmar Bergman.

L.G.

MOSLEY, ZACK (1906-1994) American artist born in 1906 in the Indian Territory of Oklahoma. Zack Mosley displayed an early interest in drawing, but

"Mort Cinder," Alberto Breccia. © Editorial Abril.

"Mother Goose and Grimm," Mike Peters. © Grimmy Inc.

spent his youth in nonartistic pursuits such as cotton picker, cowboy, and soda jerk.

His interest in comic strips, manifested by incessant copying of newspaper strips, led him to schooling at the Chicago Academy of Fine Arts, the Chicago Art Institute, and under Carey Orr, the great editorial cartoonist of the *Chicago Tribune*. Mosley claimed that during his student days he assisted in the artwork of *Buck Rogers* and *Skyroads*.

The aviation strip was a natural for Mosley, who loved planes as much as comic art. When he was 11 years old an army Jenny was forced down on the Mosley ranch and Zack instantly fell into a lifelong love affair with aviation. He took up flying, got a pilot's license and earned himself a reserve commission.

In 1933 he sold a strip to the Chicago Tribune-New York News Syndicate, *On the Wing*, one of seven that debuted simultaneously that year. Walter Berndt, creator of *Smitty*, was asked by Captain Patterson of the *News* to make a final decision on the seventh strip between a now-forgotten effort and Mosley's strip. Berndt, with the prearranged vote of editorial cartoonist C. D. Batchelor, picked *On the Wing*.

The strip was short-lived under this name. The main characters were Mack, his pal Bumpy, girlfriend Mary Miller, Steve the flying instructor (who, in the promotional material, was a "thoroughly good scout who will win the heart of every boy"), Pinfeathers, a kid who, like the young Mosley, hung around airports, and Dart, "the villain of the piece. See them moustaches?" A moustache was to reappear immediately on the face of the hero in Mosley's second effort, *Smilin' Jack*. This strip met with greater success and ran as a daily and Sunday page until April 1, 1973.

Mosley retained several assistants, including Ward Albertson, during the duration of *Smilin' Jack*; his research into the latest aviation developments was enormous and Mosley continued to fly a great deal. He owned nine planes and flew to many spots around the world, flew on Civilian Air Patrol antisubmarine flights

during World War II, and through the years he designed insignias, posters, and program covers for many aircraft-related events and organizations. Upon the cancellation of *Smilin' Jack* he retired to Stuart, Florida, where he died in January 1994.

Mosley's artwork actually had a handsome naiveté in the early years of *Wing* and *Jack*. His aircraft was, of course, authentic and his girls ranged from pretty to sexy. In later years, many readers saw a mannered crudeness (almost ugliness) in the artwork which, perhaps, as part and parcel of the adventure themes, was appropriate.

R.M.

MOTHER GOOSE AND GRIMM (U.S.) Created by Pulitzer Prize-winning editorial cartoonist Mike Peters, *Mother Goose and Grimm* first appeared on October 1, 1984, as a zany and irreverent takeoff on fairy tales and popular culture—from Snow White and the Magnificent Seven to Mrs. M&M accusing her husband of melting in someone else's hands.

The strip, however, soon focused on the madcap actions and thoughts of Grimm, Mother Goose's dog, and his entourage of animal friends: a pig who adores food, a goldfish named Lassie, and an assortment of various pooches, including the RCA Victor dog. Most of his attention, of course, is directed at Attila the cat, whom he persecutes mercilessly—without ever laying a paw on him. Yet the result is always terrified eyes and raised fur, sometimes even broken bones. Other Grimm favorite targets are the paperboy and the postman, or at least his truck, as Grimm likes to puncture the tires. When the dog catcher's truck and the mail van crash into each other, he jubilantly exclaims, "Is this a great country or what?" For fun, he enjoys chasing cars, raiding garbage cans, playing poker (his wagging tale gives him away), going for rides, watching Carl the Wonder Poodle on TV, and sleeping. In short, he is Everyman's Dog.

For her part, Mother Goose is an old lady with an acerbic viewpoint. While she often indulges her pets and speaks to them (Attila in particular) in baby talk, which makes her seem doddering in Grimm's opinion, she is quite sharp-eyed and sharp-tongued about the world, and herself, as when she sits down to a seven-course dinner—"a pizza and a six-pack"—or confides that the most important thing that she looks for in a man is "a pulse."

Although mostly about these characters, the strip still makes many references to fairy tales (Pinocchio afraid of termites), literary allusions (Frankenstein's monster playing hide-and-seek with the Invisible Man), and current events ("When Euro-Disney fell on bad times, the commissary started serving chicken-dumbo soup"). In addition, Mike Peters loves visual and word plays: 40-year old bald eagles sporting wigs; light bulbs watching a slide of an electric plug approaching the outlet in sex education class; one fly whispering to another, "Your human's open"; a shark ordering a manwich; the wicked witch asking for the children's menu; or Sarge, Dagwood, Nancy, Hägar, Dennis, and Grimm playing "strip poker."

Peters draws in the modern caricatural style that has made him famous as a political cartoonist: thick lines, exaggerated features, and no unnecessary details. Widely distributed by Tribune Media Services, *Mother Goose* was also a television cartoon and has been reprinted in numerous albums and merchandised. It even has its own web site on the Internet (http://www.grimmy.com). For his work, Peters was named Cartoonist of the Year by the National Cartoonist Society in 1992.

P.L.H.

MOTLEY'S CREW (U.S.) In 1996 Tribune Media Services's *Motley's Crew* celebrated its 20th anniversary of syndication. Sadly, its writer, Tom Forman, also died that year. Since becoming a writer/cartoonist team in 1975, Tom Forman and Ben Templeton had been responsible for a string of syndicated panel and comic strips for TMS. In 1975, Foreman had contacted Templeton with the idea of a strip called *Super Fan* about a blue-collar sports fanatic. TMS liked the idea but wanted to broaden the appeal to humor beyond sports. Forman who earned a degree in government from California State University at Los Angeles found politics and family humor in a factory town dominated by Drudge Industries the perfect stage for his gag writing.

Ben Templeton earned a graphic design degree from the University of California-Los Angeles and had been an advertising art director prior to teaming up with Tom Forman. After *Super Fan* was turned into *Motley's Crew* and successfully launched September 6, 1976, the pair turned their interest in sports into the daily panel plus Sunday *The Sporting Life* which was syndicated in the 1980s.

As with all comic strips, the characters change physically over time. Mike Motley was squat, beer-bellied, and a bit grungy in 1976. Now he's taller, thinner, and the hard blue-collar edge has been elevated to almost middle-class sensibilities. Promotional material from 1976 has Motley saying, "Remember class people bring their own six-pack," or seen in a sleeveless T-shirt turning on the TV, saying, "If there ain't no game on we'll catch the reruns of celebrity bowling."

"Motley's Crew," Tom Forman and Ben Templeton. © Tribune Media Services.

Contemporary themes such as the Olympics, Super Bowl, baseball's World Series, and elections have been a staple for *Motley's Crew*. Since 1977, when President Jimmy Carter visited the Motley family to find out about a real slice of American life, every current American president has been in the strip.

The core characters include Motley's wife Mabel and son Truman who's married to the beautiful Tacoma. Motley's boyhood pal Earl, with Elvis-style sideburns, is a fellow worker at Drudge Industries. Cigar-loving Earl would rather be exercising his elbow at Dolly's Bar than be either at work or home with his wife Abigail. His favorite hiding place in the Drudge factory's warehouse was discovered when he accidentally left behind his copy of *Chicks & Ammo* magazine. Motley explained to a fellow worker it wasn't the photos of women in tiny bikinis but those of guns that turned Earl on. "In high school Earl's locker pin-up was a Model 94 Winchester lever action with an octagonal barrel," he noted. *Motley's Crew* needs an unapologetic politically incorrect working guy to be true to its original premise.

In forays into foreign affairs, Forman and Templeton introduced Yuri Gregorvich Linov, Motley and Earl's guide on their cultural-exchange tour of Russian factories. Later Yuri defected from communist tyranny dressed in drag in a size 48 tutu. Motley got him a job at Drudge Industries but after the fall of communism, Yuri answered the call for expatriates to return to Mother Russia. He now owns a gambling casino in Moscow.

Comic strips are a blend of writing and art. The loss of writer Tom Foreman has put this veteran strip at a crossroads. Only time and reader reaction will in the end determine if a slowly gentrified Motley is as funny as the hard-edged blue-collar guy for whom the good life meant a fresh beer and a good-looking woman to leer at.

B.C.

"Muggs and Skeeter," Wally Bishop. © King Features Syndicate.

MUGGS AND SKEETER (U.S.) Originally billed as one syndicate's answer to Percy Crosby, *Muggs and Skeeter* ironically wound up in the same stable as *Skippy*, outlived it, and went on to become one of the longest-running strips in comic history.

It was introduced in 1927 by Virgil V. McNitt of the McNaught Syndicate, but was released by McNitt's Central Press Association of Cleveland. The following year, Hearst bought the Central Press and Muggs McGinnis (the strip's featured character and original title) was in the same Hearst family as Crosby. Coincidentally, Crosby entered the newspaper world similarly; his drawings first appeared for the Editor's Feature Service of CP. The return of Wally Bishop, *Muggs*'s artist, to Hearst completed another cycle: he had tried (and failed) several strip efforts previously, including *The Golf Bug*.

Originally *Muggs* was an imitation of *Skippy*—the cast included scrappy kids, who were never quite as tough as Crosby's. But eventually the gang grew more domesticated and Bishop's style became his own—rather stiff but quaint and, to the end, old-fashioned. Skeeter, a pal of the young Muggs, was found on a train about eight years after the strip's debut and soon shared the billing.

Other members of the cast included Grandma and Grandpa, with whom the kids lived; Effie Mae, a hillbilly kid in the neighborhood; Beauregard, another friend; and several dogs through the years, including the popular Junior, a dachshund.

Muggs and Skeeter, which never ran as a Sunday page, ran continuities in the adventurous decade of the 1930s, but never to the extent that other strips did; Bishop's thin storylines averaged about a week apiece.

The strip was ended short of a half-century in February 1974. In its prime, it appeared in comic book format and Bishop, who claims to have been the youngest syndicated cartoonist of his day (at 17), eventually wound up subbing for Percy Crosby on occasion.

R.M.

MUÑOZ, JOSÉ (1942-   ) Spanish cartoonist and illustrator of Argentine origin born October 7, 1942, in Buenos Aires. While still in his teens José Muñoz began collaborating on publications put out by the legendary publishing house Frontera, then run by Hector Oesterheld. His first important work was a police serial written by Ray Collins (Eugenio Zappietro) and titled *Precinto 56*, first published in the magazine *Misterix* in 1963. Muñoz pursued his career in relative obscurity until he decided to move to Europe in 1973 and started his fruitful collaboration with the scriptwriter Carlos Sampayo, a fellow Argentinian. In 1975 the duo initiated *Alack Sinner*, which is at the origin of most of their later creations; since that time their collaboration has been continuous and has resulted in an enormous output, in which they have transcended the traditional relationship between artist and writer.

In *Alack Sinner* stories and characters constantly stand at the confluence of past and present, in a world peopled with memories and torn by all the contradictions of society. Influenced by Alberto Breccia and George Grosz, Muñoz dramatically accentuates the private sufferings of his characters, expressionistically voicing their innermost feelings. It is as though Muñoz and Sampayo share a common secret: how to tell, in heartrendingly lyrical accents, stories of love and friendship, of fear and melancholy, of solitude and solidarity, in an atmosphere reeking of cruelty and injustice, chaos and violence, misery and death. The artist's line, pushing to their limits the contrasts between black and white and between light and dark, shapes with righteous anger a world condemned to the torments of social anomie and iniquity. The stories read like a documentary of the lower depths, a travelogue from hell, transfigured in the course of its sordid journey into a demented pictorial fantasy.

Muñoz and Sampayo have also produced a collection of independent stories dealing with South American problems, later published in book form in France as *Sueurs de Métèques* ("Spics' Sweat," 1984). Muñoz has also collaborated on occasion with other scriptwriters, such as Luis Bustos in *Rayos y centellas* ("Rays and Sparks," 1992). Most of Muñoz's stories have been translated in the United States, where they have wielded tremendous influence on a number of American comic book artists.

J.C.

MURPHY, JAMES EDWARD (1891-1965) American cartoonist born November 20, 1891 in Chicago, Illinois. James Edward "Jimmy" Murphy Jr. spent one year at Creighton University in Nebraska. From June to December of 1906 he was a cartoonist for the *Omaha Examiner* and he was about to get a job on the *Omaha Bee* at 16 when a new editor vetoed his prospects.

After the *Bee*-stung bubble, the young Murphy (who was as inclined to move about the country to improve his prospects as did his furniture-dealing parents) went to Spokane, Washington, where he began his career as

José Muñoz and Carlos Sampayo, "Alack Sinner." © Muñoz and Sampayo.

an editorial cartoonist on the *Spokane Inland-Herald* in 1910. A year later he was in Portland, doing editorial drawings for the *Oregon Journal*. By 1915 he had reached San Francisco, where he did editorial cartoons for the *San Francisco Call* (which were also carried in the companion Hearst California evening paper, the *Los Angeles Herald*). His work impressed Hearst, who invited him to come to New York and join the art staff of the *New York Journal* in 1918. It was there that Murphy, intrigued by the processes of drawing comic strips in the offices adjoining his, did his first samples of *Toots and Casper*—and obtained King Features's approval on the strip.

Toots and Casper, daily and Sunday from the outset in a number of the Hearst coast-to-coast papers in 1919, was a bit slow in catching on. Considered a Hearst second-string strip, it ran only as a filler or as a Saturday color comic in Hearst evening papers. But the delightfully zany appearance of Murphy's married team and their baby, Buttercup (who never grew up during the 30 years of the strip), caught many eyes and aroused amusing comments, and before long *Toots and Casper* was a permanent daily and Sunday feature in Hearst's showcase newspaper, the *New York American*. Noting the success of humor-tinged soap opera in *The Gumps* and *The Nebbs*, Murphy altered his content from family gags to involved continuity on a neighborhood problem level—and the public loved it. In a very short time, *Toots and Casper* became one of the most avidly followed strips in the country. A live-action comedy series was filmed in the mid-1920s, but oddly, no book collection was ever published.

In 1926, Murphy added a second Sunday-page strip, *It's Poppa Who Pays*, and in 1934 he introduced the Sunday comic section idea of comic character stamps, which took the public by storm, and spread to strips

Jimmy Murphy, "Toots and Casper." © *King Features Syndicate.*

from virtually all other syndicates. King Features reportedly gave Murphy a bonus for this wildfire promotional idea, and he moved his family (including his wife, Matilda Katherine, whom he used as a model for Toots) to the West Coast as a result. Here he developed his interests in golf and driving long distances to sightsee, while *Toots and Casper* continued to enjoy great popularity.

Murphy retired from his strip in 1958 as the result of a debilitating illness. He recovered somewhat during the next several years, but did not revive the strip, and died in Beverly Hills, California, on March 9, 1965. His strip, closed down by his earlier decision, died with him.

B.B.

MURPHY, JOHN CULLEN (1919-   ) American illustrator and cartoonist born May 3, 1919, in New York City. As a youth he moved with his family to Chicago and studied at the Chicago Art Institute when he was nine years old. In 1930 the Murphys moved to New Rochelle, New York, where he became friends with Alex and Jack Raymond (later cartoonists themselves) and worshipped the work of neighboring illustrators Norman Rockwell and the Lyendecker brothers.

While in high school he studied at the Grand Central Art School and received a scholarship to the Phoenix Art Institute, where he studied under Franklin Booth. His artistic training then continued at the Art Students League under George Bridgman and Charles Chapman.

Murphy's first professional work was sports cartooning for Madison Square Garden promotions in 1936, followed by covers for *Columbia* and *Liberty* magazines. During World War II he drew on-the-spot war sketches for the *Chicago Tribune* and, while serving on the staff of Gen. Douglas MacArthur, painted portraits of MacArthur and many other military figures.

After the war Murphy worked on Hollywood movie promotions and illustrated for *Esquire, Holiday, Colliers,* and *Look* magazines. In 1949 Elliot Caplin conceived an idea for a boxing strip and contacted Murphy, whose reputation as a sports artist was established through magazine work. *Big Ben Bolt* made its appearance through King Features Syndicate in February 1950.

A supreme compliment to Murphy's talent was the request by Harold Foster in 1971 that Murphy assist on *Prince Valiant*, a task Murphy accepted without sacrificing *Big Ben Bolt*. Since that year he has drawn the Sun-

day feature from script and comprehensive roughs. (He finally had to abandon *Big Ben Bolt*, however, in 1977.)

Murphy's work has been highly regarded by other members of his profession as well. The recipient of the National Cartoonists Society award for story strips in 1971, Murphy has kept the illustrative quality of his strips at a high level, sacrificing neither detail nor visual sophistication.

R.M.

MUSIAL, JOSEPH (1905-1977) American cartoonist born 1905 in Yonkers, New York. Joe Musial attended Yonkers High School and then enrolled at Pratt Institute in Brooklyn. After graduation from Pratt he studied for a year at the Sorbonne.

Back in the United States in 1929, Musial got his first professional job as assistant on Billy De Beck's *Barney Google*. In 1932 he joined the staff of King Features and was assigned a variety of strips to work on. The strips he ghosted at one time or another included: *Thimble Theatre, Bunky, Tillie the Toiler, Pete the Tramp, Elmer, X-9, Little Iodine,* and *Toots and Casper*. In 1956, following "Doc" Winner's death, KFS picked Musial to do *The Katzenjammer Kids* (a very unjudicious choice, to put it mildly).

Being more literate and better educated than most of his colleagues, Musial proved a better choice as King's education director. In that position he was responsible for *Dagwood Splits the Atom*, a comic book explaining nuclear fission; another one on mental health with Blondie as spokeswoman this time; and a flag-waver called *This Is America*. He earned a Congressional citation for each of these publications. Musial also was the author of *The Career Guide for Cartoonists* and lectured extensively as a spokesman for the newspaper strip industry. He died on June 6, 1977, at his home in Manhasset, Long Island.

Impressive as his extraartistic achievements were, Joe Musial will ultimately go down in comic strip history as the man most responsible for the mindless emasculation of *The Katzenjammer Kids*.

M.H.

MUSTER, MIKI (1925-   ) Miki Muster is a Yugoslav cartoonist and cartoon filmmaker born in Murska Sobota, on November 22, 1925. From his earliest childhood Muster liked to draw, and his parents encouraged him in that direction. He wanted to be a cartoonist and to produce cartoon films, admiring the work of Walt Disney very much. After grammar school Muster acquired a diploma as a sculptor at Ljubljana s Academy of Plastic Art.

In June 1952 a new magazine for children, *PPP*, was launched in Ljubljana, featuring a few comics. Since a Walt Disney comic strip that had been ordered did not arrive in time, the editor asked young Muster to draw his own comic strip. It was then that *Zvitorepec*, one of the longest running Yugoslav comics, was born. Since *Zvitorepec* was so very popular among its readers in the Republic of Slovenia (where it started to appear), the publishing house Delo decided to launch a comic weekly titled *Zvitorepec* in 1965. *Zvitorepec*, about a talking rabbit, was influenced by Walt Disney. However, this popular character and his friends, Trdonja and Lakotnik, lived in Slovenian magazines and newspapers for over 20 years, and were reprinted only in *Novi List*, in Trieste, Italy.

Miki Muster, "Zvitorepec." © Miki Muster.

He is no longer involved with comics. Muster's favorite hobby was the cinema, and it eventually became his profession. He produced successful animated commercials for television, as well as for several German firms.

E.R.

MUTT AND JEFF (U.S.) The first continually published, six-day-a-week comic strip, Bud Fisher's *A. Mutt* (later given its more famed title *Mutt and Jeff*) was introduced to an unsuspecting audience on the sports page of the *San Francisco Chronicle* for Friday, Novem-

ber 15, 1907, under the title "Mr. A. Mutt Starts In To Play the Races." (Mutt himself had first appeared in a page-wide racing cartoon by Fisher on the November 10, 1907, sports page, together with Mrs. Mutt.) The idea for the strip was clearly derived from Clare Briggs' horse-touting *A. Piker Clerk*, for the action in Fisher's first episode simply relates how a fanatic bettor (Mutt) gets tips and places bets on three nonfictitious horses running the same day at the local track.

Fisher's born loser, with his scraggly moustache and slept-in clothes, had enormous visual appeal and soon thousands of nonhorseplayers were reading Fisher's witty dialogue and following Mutt's fretful search for the big money. Within a month, the *Chronicle*'s circulation had increased measurably against that of its morning rival, Hearst's *Examiner*. In the meantime, Fisher had informed the readers about Mutt's first name, Augustus, on November 18, 1907, in a panel also portraying Mrs. Mutt, Cicero, and his cat. And, by the end of November, a real plot line had developed within the strip. It was apparent that there was much more to Fisher's strip than the communication of horse tips, and by the beginning of the next month, Fisher (having shrewdly copyrighted his strip title and idea before leaving the *Chronicle*) had been hired by the rival *Examiner* to continue his feature there. (Fisher's last *Chronicle* episode was dated December 10, 1907; his first *Examiner* episode appeared the following day. The *Chronicle* hired Russ Westover to continue *A. Mutt*, starting December 12; Westover's work ran until June 7, 1908, when Westover actually killed Mutt off in the final episode.)

Fisher was not long at the *Examiner* before Hearst had his new talent shipped off to New York—not before, however, he had introduced the character who was to become Mutt's shrimp-sized partner, Jeff, on

"Mutt and Jeff," Bud Fisher. © H. C. Fisher.

March 27, 1908. (Jeff is a lunatic who imagines himself to be James Jeffries, the prizefighter, and is encountered casually by Mutt amid several other asylum denizens in the same episode.)

The first formal *Mutt and Jeff* designation appeared on the pioneer Fisher strip collection, *The Mutt and Jeff Cartoons* (1911), but the title was not used in newspapers until Fisher left Hearst for the Wheeler Syndicate in 1915, the first specific *Mutt and Jeff* logo appearing on September 15, 1916. The first full-page color Sunday *Mutt and Jeff* did not appear, however, until Wheeler distributed it coast to coast on August 11, 1918.

It was not until Fisher had effectual control of his own strip under Wheeler that most of the other characters for which the strip would be famed emerged—Sir Sidney (who met Mutt and Jeff in the trenches during the first World War); Gus Geevum; Jeff's twin brother Julius; and Mutt's brother's Ima—to say nothing of the debauched members of the infamous Lion Tamers' Club. This was also the period when Fisher hired the gifted Billy Liverpool (earlier known only for an obscure strip called *Asthma Simpson, the Village Queen*) who had briefly ghosted Hearst's attempt to continue his own version of *Mutt and Jeff* after Fisher's departure. Fisher's instinct was right: Liverpool's raucously comic drawings made *Mutt and Jeff* probably the most visually funny strip of the 1920s.

By this time, *Mutt and Jeff* had become one of the half dozen best known and most widely read strips in America. *Mutt and Jeff* reprint books proliferated; *Mutt and Jeff* musicals toured the country; animated cartoons starring the duo appeared throughout the 1920s; there was even a ballet and a song (called *The Funny Paper Blues*) which became a hit in 1921.

Some of their popularity declined in the 1930s and 1940s, possibly because of Al Smith's inferior handling of the strip gags and graphics after Liverpool's departure in late 1933. Nevertheless, a major, multiissued series of comic book reprints of the daily and Sunday Smith strip appeared throughout the 1940s, introducing the team anew to millions who had not seen it in their local papers.

Distributed later by the Bell Syndicate, and then by the Bell-McClure Syndicate (until it merged into United Feature Syndicate), *Mutt and Jeff* did not keep abreast of the tone of the times, either in Smith's hands, or in those of the men working on the strip with him. Accordingly, it lost most of its vast outlet of newspapers, and appeared only obscurely here and there, usually in the daily format, for the next 40 years. For most readers, the strip's fund of imaginative vitality faded rapidly in the 1940s, to vanish almost altogether by 1950. Drawn by George Breisacher in the last two years of its existence, it was finally discontinued in November 1983; but as a major strip landmark for all time, *Mutt and Jeff* will never die.

B.B.

MUTTS (U.S.) Every so often a new strip comes along that proves there are still areas of cartooning left to be explored. In American newspaper cartooning *Calvin and Hobbes* set the cartoon world on fire in 1985. Now *Mutts*, launched by King Features on September 5, 1994, is doing the same thing. In fact, with *Calvin and Hobbes* ceasing syndication in 1995 at the wish of its creator, Bill Watterson, *Mutts* became a

major beneficiary of the space this opened on many comic pages.

Mutts is the creation of Patrick McDonnell, a 1979 graduate of the School of Visual Arts in New York City. A skilled illustrator, his work has been published in everything from the *New York Times* to *Sports Illustrated* to *Reader's Digest*. McDonnell is also a cartoon historian and coauthor of *Krazy Kat: The Art of George Herriman* (Abrams, 1986). His monthly cartoon *Bad Baby* has been published in *Parent's* magazine for over a decade.

The stars of *Mutts* are Earl, a small white dog with black ears and a patch on his back, and Mooch, a black cat who talks with a lisp. In an *Editor & Publisher* magazine interview, McDonnell said that art is really important. "It's what draws you into a strip. Comics are a visual medium." Thus it is not surprising that *Mutts* is visually exciting. McDonnell is one of the few strip cartoonists to use prescreened Crafting paper to give his crosshatching a different look. Simplicity rules, but it is not the simplicity of a neophyte artist, but that of a trained professional.

Mutts alternates between gag-a-day humor and continuity stories. Sunday pages let McDonnell experiment with layout and color and he takes full advantage, even with the horrific restrictions that space limitations in comics sections dictate today.

Earl, who looks like a dog that has been a feature of McDonnell's illustrations for years, lives in his own comic strip world, not present-day reality. There he and his feline pal Mooch deal with life's basics, such as survival, the weather, their relationship with their owners (who are neighbors), and with other pets, including a large bulldog and Sid the fish, who is tired of life in a fishbowl.

Hip but not cynical, the writing of the strip can be as goofy as the drawings are funny. Earl's owner, Ozzie, and Mooch's owners, Millie and Frank, are integral parts of the humor, as who is more important in the lives of pets than their owners?

Mutts is a comic strip with worldwide appeal that may well earn the pedigree of "classic." McDonnell was awarded Germany's Max and Moritz Prize for best international comic strip artist in 1996. However, the greatest prize may have been when Charles Schultz, of *Peanuts* fame, wrote in the introduction to the first collection of *Mutts* (published by Andrews and McMeel) that Patrick McDonnell keeps coming up with ideas that Schultz wished he'd thought up himself.

B.C.

MYERS, RUSSELL (1938-   ) American cartoonist born October 9, 1938, in Pittsburg, Kansas. After graduating from the University of Tulsa in 1960, Russell Myers joined the Hallmark Company, illustrating and writing contemporary greeting cards. In 1970 he started *Broom Hilda*, a comic strip relating the half-baked exploits of a most unspooky witch, for the News-Tribune Syndicate.

Russell Myers's drawing style—broad, simple, and seemingly easy—and his tongue-in-cheek approach to characterization and situation place him in the tradition of the sophisticated strip. Myers himself is prompt to acknowledge his debts to his famous elders, Charles Schulz, Johnny Hart, and Brant Parker.

Russell Myers, like many cartoonists of his generation, has a genuine love for his medium: he collects original comic art, is knowledgeable in the history of

"Myra North," Charles Coll. © NEA Service.

the form, and he has been a familiar figure in comics conventions throughout the country.

After more than a quarter-century *Broom Hilda* is still going strong; asked in 1996 to comment on his successful career, Myers tersely replied, "Cartooning is fun."

M.H.

MYRA NORTH (U.S.) *Myra North, Special Nurse* (later simply *Myra North*), drawn by Charles Coll and written by Ray Thompson, was created for NEA Service as a daily on February 10, 1936, and as a Sunday on June 12 of the same year.

Myra North was a pretty blonde and, as the title implied, a special nurse whose talents took her far afield from the nursing profession. In one of her first adventures, she traveled to Urbania, "a small African kingdom," to foil the evil designs of a group of conspirators plotting war. In another episode she engaged in a battle of wits with the mad scientist Dr. Zero, who had invented an invisibility process. But her most constant foe was the sinister and ubiquitous Hyster, an egomaniacal and evil mastermind, whose goal was nothing less than total world domination (a popular pursuit among villains of the period). Myra's most famous encounter with Hyster came in a 1937 adventure which took place in "a country ravaged by civil war," obviously Spain transparently disguised under the name of "Morentia."

In some of her other exploits, Myra solved several murders, a kidnapping involving the crown prince of another European power, had a movie role in Hollywood and, in the main, tried her level best to emulate Frank Godwin's *Connie*. In her adventures she was often accompanied by her (innocent) love interest Jack Lane, an insurance investigator.

The adventures of Myra North were inventive and entertaining, and Coll's drawing style barely adequate but pleasing nonetheless. *Myra North* was one of the few girl-adventure strips around, and deserved a longer run than the one it actually enjoyed. For the record, the daily strip ended on March 25, 1939, while the Sunday page was discontinued not too long afterward, on August 31, 1941.

M.H.

MYSTISKA 2:AN (Sweden) *Mystiska 2:an* (*Mystiska Tvåan*, "The Mystic—or Mysterious—Two"), a Swedish adventure comic, was created and drawn by Estonian Rolf Gohs, who has been living in Sweden since 1946. The series, mostly written in cooperation with Janne Lundström, first appeared in 1970 in its own comic book published by Inter Art, of which Gohs was a founder. When Inter Art folded, Semic Press continued the comic book with two issues per year, arriving at number seven in 1973 before starting the book over with a different concept and a new numbering. In order to step up the frequency of publication, *Det Okända* ("The Unknown," meaning The Twilight Zone) was added to the book. Before this change occurred, there also appeared a continued story of *Mystiska 2:an* in numbers 16 to 26 (1972) of the biweekly *Fantomen* comic book. The series was also remounted in the daily strip format for inclusion in the comics page of the newspaper *Expressen*.

Mystiska 2:an stars two boys, Sacho Taikon and Stefan (whose last name is never told), whose story is told in the classic tradition of boyhood friends as it is represented in the novels of Sivar Ahlrud or Enid Blyton,

"Mystika 2:an," Rolf Gohs. © Rolf Gohs.

for example. Sacho is a gypsy boy whose family lives a Swedish lower-middle-class life. It is quite by intention that Gohs depicts him as any normal boy from any normal Swedish home. Stefan seems to have a well-to-do background; he is intelligent, a logical thinker. Sacho is naive and impulsive. Yet, Sacho is the star of the strip, possibly because he is a "foreigner" like Gohs and shares a number of similar interests (like photography and music) and character traits. With number seven (1973), a girl, Carina, enters the boys' lives.

The adventures of *Mystiska 2:an* take place in and around Stockholm and, as the name suggests, are usually in the mystery and horror vein. The two boys often get involved in intrigue, pitting them against unscrupulous reactionary or fascist groups. They are usually up against the mysterious and the unknown.

In 1987 Rolf Gohs took what must be considered a daring step for a series aimed at readers the age of his youthful heroes: in an episode of soul-searching, Sacho discovers that he is gay and falls in love with an older man. The theme was handled matter-of-factly and without much ado. However, the publishers were not happy with this development. They would have preferred the youthful hero to go on living a straight life of adventure.

The stories, printed in black and white, have the appearance of stark realism and a constant atmosphere of suspense because of the very graphic Gohs style that makes excellent use of black-and-white contrasts. Good writing, excellent art, and social commentary make *Mystiska 2:an* extraordinarily worthwhile reading.

W.F.

NAGAGUTSU NO SANJŪSHI (Japan) *Nagagutsu no Sanjūshi* ("The Three Musketeers with Boots on Their Heads") was created by artist Suimei Imoto and scriptwriter Taisei Makino. It made its first appearance in book form in August 1930.

Nagagutsu featured the exploits of Denko Denyama, a modern and brave girl; Tonkichi Hesoyama ("a lion at home and a mouse abroad"); and Saru, a monkey who had once been a vassal of Momotarō (the hero of a famous Japanese tale who had conquered the ogre Oni). The trio embarked on a long journey in a Zeppelin, but it crashed in a storm. On the island of Oni the ogre they tried to steal the ruby of life but were caught by Oni, who sentenced them to wear boots on their heads (hence the title). In vain efforts to get rid of the boots, the trio tried standing on their heads and hanging from tree branches, but all was useless. So they went back to school and their schoolmates' taunts.

One sunny spring day, the trio discovered a strange bamboo shoot in which was concealed Princess Kaguya (a famous fairy-tale heroine); from Kaguya the trio learned that their boots would disappear only if they found Murasaki-Zukin ("The Purple Mask"). After one month's training at swordmanship by the American teacher Douglas Farebunks, they set out on their journey. After many adventures in which they encountered a number of fairy-tale characters (the woman who lived in a shoe, the fabled swordsman Isamu Kondo, etc.) the three musketeers finally came upon Murasaki-Zukin, who tried to trick them; but, by luck and pluck, they finally got rid of the boots, which were later enshrined as a tribute to their exploits.

Nagagutsu was more a picture story than a comic strip. There were no speech balloons, but text under the panels. The pace, however, was very brisk, with no redundant panel or sentence. The artwork was simple but effective; the storyline fantastic and highly fanciful. The strip itself enjoyed only moderate success, but it is now considered a classic of Japanese comic literature.

H.K.

NAGAI, GŌ (1945-) Japanese cartoonist born September 6, 1945, near Tokyo. After formal studies, Gō Nagai burst upon the comics scene with *Harenchi Gakuen*, which began serialization in *Shōnen Jump* in 1968. *Harenchi Gakuen* ("Shameless School") was exactly what its name denoted: the students cavorted in the nude, the teachers played mah jong during class hours, and the assistants drank beer. "*Harenchi Gakuen* was a fantastical school of bedlam," noted Japanese comics scholar Fred Schodt wrote, "where the main preoccupation of both male students and teachers was not study but catching glimpses of girls' underwear or contriving to see them naked." The series ended (1972) in a set battle, complete with guns, tanks, and missiles, that culminated in the school being razed to the ground.

The same year, Nagai started *Devilman*, a tale of the supernatural involving demons, ghouls, monsters, and a teenaged hero determined to stop them, in *Shōnen Magazine*. He also came out with *Mazinger Z* in *Shōnen Jump*, about a gigantic warrior-robot controlled by yet another teenager (the author knew how to play his public). *Mazinger Z* enjoyed unprecedented popularity on three continents; in 1974 an animated cartoon series began, followed by toys, games, and assorted merchandising.

In the 1980s the enterprise mushroomed into a business empire, and to control it Nagai formed his own corporation, Dynamic Productions, with himself at the helm. Employing more than 50 people, including 13 studio assistants and Nagai's two brothers as corporate executives, Dynamic was to become the prototype of the assembly line comics workshops that have sprouted all over Japan in recent years, with a resulting loss of creativity that is deplored by all observers of the form.

M.H.

NAGASHIMA, SHINJI (1937-) Japanese comic book artist born in Tokyo on July 8, 1937. Shinji Nagashima decided very early in life to become a cartoonist. As a schoolboy he particularly cherished two comic books, Osamu Tezuka's *Shin Takarajima* ("New Treasure Island") and Tetsuo Ogawa's *Pikadon Hakase no Dai Hatsumei* ("The Great Invention of Dr. Pikadon"), which he reread many times. At the age of 14, Nagashima decided to drop out of school and go to work while pursuing his dream of becoming a comic book artist. He studied in his spare time by himself, but did not go to art school. In 1952, at the age of 15, he made his professional debut.

In 1961 he created his best work, *Mangaka Zankoku Monogatori* ("The Cruel Story of a Cartoonist") for the Japanese magazine *Deka*. The strip met with great success and was followed by a number of other creations: *Fūten* (about a Japanese hippie) in 1967, the *Minwa* series (adaptations of Japanese folktales) and *Wakamonotachi* ("Young Men") in 1968, and *Dōyō Sanbusaku* (a trilogy of children's songs) in 1971. From 1963 to 1965 Nagashima also worked as an animator at the famous Mushi Productions studio.

Among the major influences on his work, Nagashima lists Osamu Tezuka, André François, Raymond Peynet, and Ben Shahn. He is currently working on a new strip, *Tabibito-kun* ("The Boytraveller") strongly influenced by Schulz's *Peanuts*. *Tabibito-kun* and shorter stories done by the author in the course of the past 20 years have been published mainly in *Big Comic Gold*.

Shinji Nagashima tells his stories warmly and poetically. His art style is not realistic but it has flavor and bite. Regarded as the artist who gave fresh stimulus to the Japanese strip in the 1960s, Nagashima has influenced a great number of Japanese comic book artists

Shinji Nagashima.

such as Eiichi Muraoka, Manabu Ōyama, Tsuguo Kōgo, Hisao Hayashi, and Kazuhiko Miyaya.

H.K.

'NAM, THE (U.S.) In one of their periodic forays into gritty realism, the editors at Marvel came up with a comic book series that would retrace the experiences of ordinary grunts in Vietnam, much as such contemporary movies as *The Deer Hunter, Full Metal Jacket,* and *Platoon* have done. The idea was proposed to Marvel in the early 1980s by Doug Murray, a Vietnam war veteran, and after some hesitation it was accepted. *The 'Nam* first appeared in *Savage Tales* in 1985 before getting its own independent title in December 1986.

The story followed the fortunes of enlisted man Ed Marks: his induction into the U.S. Army, his training during boot camp, and his orders to serve in Vietnam. Once Marks was in the field, Murray's narrative line became even more realistic—and controversial for some readers, as Murray described incompetence at high levels and corruption and malingering in the ranks, showing, for instance, how noncoms doled out cushy assignments at headquarters to those privates who could come up with a bribe. Firefights, ambushes, the burning of villages, and other perils of guerilla warfare were also depicted with unusual candor and a marked lack of romanticism. Murray's scripts were brilliantly complemented by Michael Golden's artwork, which seemed to mesh seamlessly with the author's vision.

The Marvel editors eventually became uneasy with the uncompromising tone of the feature, and early in 1990 Murray was replaced by a string of lesser scriptwriters, including Chuck Dixon and Herb Trimpe, who introduced such incongruous Marvel heroes as the Punisher into the storylines. This only served to trivialize the series further, and it finally bowed out in September 1993.

M.H.

NANCY (U.S.) Nancy appears to be a small girl, about eight, who is imitating a chipmunk with a case of mumps—but it is precisely her endless cheekiness that much of the mass comic-reading public seems to like. Bright-eyed, chirpy, and simple, Nancy was perhaps the most widely followed strip character of the 1950s and early 1960s; attempts by exasperated feature editors to dump her daily and Sunday gag strip were met with outraged public cries. Among other things, every newspaper executive's mother-in-law seemed to love *Nancy* avidly, along with people with influence generally.

What was it in *Nancy* that brainy people hated and the broad middle-aged public loved? Probably the same thing: incredibly simple points which could be grasped at a glance, acted out by a minimal and unconfusing cast of cute kids, drawn with stark plainness against an unadorned background. (Someone once started the unkind rumor that *Nancy* was turned out by a guy with *Joe Miller's Joke Book* and a set of rubber Nancy and Sluggo stamps; a few episodes of the strip read in succession makes one wonder if it was really a rumor.)

Ernie Bushmiller, the strip's creator, was certainly not to be blamed. When he decided to try a kid strip, and the new strip became an almost overnight gold mine, he is hardly at fault for giving the huge public that loved Nancy more of what it wanted, including closing down his daily *Fritzi Ritz* strip and turning its characters over to *Nancy*. Not that Nancy herself was all that new; she had been appearing as Fritzi's niece in the *Fritzi Ritz* strip since the 1920s but was always in tandem with Fritzi herself in an adult-kid gag sequence. Somehow, putting Nancy on her own, with a pseudo-

"Nancy," Ernie Bushmiller. © United Feature Syndicate.

"Napoleon," Clifford McBride. © LaFave Newspaper Features.

tough slum kid named Sluggo, made an electrifying difference to many readers.

Originally, Nancy's Aunt Fritzi was a brighter-than-average flapper when the *Fritzi Ritz* strip began in the early 1920s. She did a number of adventurous and amusing things in the continued daily strip: driving cross-country at a time when highways were unknown; making the Hollywood scene; getting involved with grisly crime mysteries. All these stories were done with great verve and humor by the young Bushmiller, who had a real gift for quality comic continuity. (It is easy to see the elements that Harold Lloyd noted and liked in Bushmiller's work when he invited the cartoonist to come West to work on his film comedies.) The Sunday Bushmiller page was well drawn, with fine comic touches, and sound, often novel, pay-off gags, both in its top half (*Fritzi*) and its bottom section (*Phil Fumble*, about a ne'er-do-well boyfriend of Fritzi's who went his own bumbling way each week.)

Nor did their quality lag as the strips proceeded into the 1930s. More and more newspapers, however, were dropping halves of Sunday pages in favor of a remaining half, to accommodate ads and more comics, and Bushmiller realized that *Fumble* was a weak property in this situation. Deciding to try a fresh feature gambit, he replaced Phil's domain with Nancy's simple-minded world—with results that we all know.

In the late 1970s, Bushmiller became seriously ill and left most of the artwork on *Nancy* to his assistants, Will Johnson and Al Plastino. After Bushmiller died in 1982, the strip was briefly done by Mark Lansky until his own death a year later. Jerry Scott then took it over, giving it a jazzier, less stereotypical look. After he left in 1995, brothers Guy and Brad Gilchrist have been carrying it in close imitation of Bushmiller's tone and style.

Bushmiller's work is best read from his early days until 1940, when *Nancy* began. The remainder will always be on tap at an institution or two for the stalwart and devoted research student; the rest of us would be happier forgetting it.

B.B.

NAPOLEON (U.S.) Easily the finest comic strip built around a man and a dog, Clifford McBride's *Napoleon* began on May 5, 1929, as an episode in an untitled irregular weekly series about a fat, jovial fellow named Uncle Elby. (McBride drew a weekly panelled gag feature about various unnamed individuals, in which Uncle Elby reappeared frequently as the only named character.) The first episode involving Napoleon, the gaunt, huge, ungainly black and white mongrel so familiar on comic pages for a quarter of a century, was titled "Uncle Elby Befriends a Lonesome Dog." The dog struck a popular chord, and reappeared with Uncle Elby on May 12 and again on June 23, 1929. Before long, man and dog were an inseparable pair in the McBride Sunday feature, so popular that the Arthur J. LaFave syndicate urged McBride to highlight them in a regular, titled comic strip.

The first episode of the new daily strip, named *Napoleon and Uncle Elby*, appeared in the *Boston Globe* and other papers on June 6, 1932. Phasing out his Sunday feature on April 2, 1933, McBride opened the Sunday *Napoleon* page in the *Denver Post* and elsewhere on March 12, 1933. Based in part on the antics of a 210-pound St. Bernard named Napoleon that was owned by Clifford McBride's Uncle Elby Eastman (on whom the strip character was largely based), the *Napoleon* strip was essentially an episodic gag feature, although some highly fantastic continuity involving finned mermen and other fabulous narrative elements, in which Elby and Napoleon accompany a grizzled old sailor named Singapore Sam, ran in the Sunday pages of 1933. Unfortunately, the public seemed to want Elby and the dog in more mundane surroundings, and the fantasy element was dropped. Widely distributed, the Sunday page dropped to a half-page in 1944, then to a third a year later, losing appeal as the aging McBride redrew more and more of the old strip episodes in the later 1940s. Carried on by several artists after his death, and bylined by his wife, the daily and Sunday *Napoleon* strips finally dropped from publication in 1960.

Several book collections of the strip were published between 1930 and 1950, notably a Big Little Book-type pair from Saalfield (*Napoleon and Uncle Elby* in 1938, and *Napoleon and Uncle Elby and Little Mary* in 1939); and a comic book collection of the early Sunday pages from Eastern Color in 1942 named for the strip. Delightfully drawn and often hilariously funny, much of the McBride strip calls for republication in permanent form.

B.B.

NARCISO PUTIFERIO (Italy) Narciso Putiferio ("Narcissus Rumpus"), a shop clerk at Stevens General Stores, learns of the death of his grandfather Filippone, an old pirate who left him a huge legacy in his will. Upon receiving the news, Narciso leaves on his grandfather's ship, the *Mermaid of the Seas*, and sails for the Island of Mirages to claim his inheritance. After overcoming the dreaded pirate Skipper Shark in combat and freeing an Indian princess, Narciso again sets sail to find new treasures hidden in the Sargasso Sea that he has learned about from an old parchment.

Thus begins *Narciso Putiferio*, a very original and funny series created in 1954 by Ferdinando Corbella, a clever cartoonist who always filled his work with weird contraptions, paradoxical situations, and an assortment of highly individualized characters made even funnier by his easy and free-flowing line. Corbella, one of the first artists to use the stipple technique in his adventure strips (*Rolan Aquila* chief among them), displayed the best of his comic talents in this feature, in which the individual panels stand out sharply.

The adventures of *Narciso Putiferio* ended abruptly in 1962, after having enthused a whole generation of young readers, when the new editors of the comic weekly *Il Monello* (where *Narciso* had been appearing) made the decision to change the editorial policies of the magazine, forcing Narciso and his mates (Gambadilegno, Occhiodilince, and Uncino among others) to retire.

G.B.

NATACHA (Belgium) In the late 1960s the editors of the weekly comics magazine *Spirou* felt the need for a female protagonist to add to their lineup of all-male heroes. They turned to Francois Walthéry, who was then working in the Peyo studios and had a knack for drawing sexy-but-nice young women. *Natacha* made its debut on February 26, 1970, on a script by Roland Goosens.

Natacha was a stewardess working for an international airline company, and this allowed the spunky, toothsome blonde heroine to roam the globe in search of wrongs to redress, villains to combat, and new thrills to experience. She has gone through hair-raising adventures in India ("Natacha and the Maharajah") and Japan ("Double Flight"), on a mysterious island ("The Island Beyond the World"), and even under the seas ("The Thirteenth Apostle"). The enemies she has faced and conquered include arms smugglers, diamond thieves, skyjackers, and a horde of panting lechers, and there have been plenty of crash landings, car chases, and gun fights to keep the story moving at a brisk pace.

Walthéry often writes his own scripts, but to keep the stories from getting stale he has called on many of his colleagues at *Spirou* to lend a hand in the writing department. Others have helped with the backgrounds. As the author himself declared, "It's a team effort." Walthéry retains overall direction, however, and there

has been great consistency of style and tone from episode to episode.

Mixing suspense and adventure with a welcome dose of humor, designed for adults without talking down to children, and never preaching or overreaching itself, *Natacha* is one of the more winsome creations to come out of the French-Belgian school of comic storytelling in the last quarter-century.

M.H.

NATHAN NEVER (Italy) This peculiar science-fiction series, created in 1991 by the so-called "Sardinian Trio" (Michele Medda, Antonio Serra, and Bepi Vigna) is published in black-and-white book form by the Sergio Bonelli publishing house. In an environment dated 2097, which is clearly reminiscent of *Blade Runner*, the official police forces are inadequate to keep order, so citizens must turn to private organizations for help. Nathan Never is a special agent of Alfa Agency, an organization that guarantees security for a fee. Monstrous aliens are absent from this sci-fi narrative set in the near future where people are dressed up in modern ways and are living in Megalopolis, the architectural structure of which looks like that of the present's most modern buildings.

The world of *Nathan Never* has undergone deep geographic transformations owing to a catastrophe caused by man. The Earth's axis has a new inclination, the sea level is increased, the continents are shaped differently, and Megalopolis has a seven-level structure. In the lower levels live mutants, originally artificial beings expressly created for manual jobs that were later outlawed and left to their own destiny. These mutants, now ostracized, often struggle against humans. The social and political organization of this huge city is undermined by corruption, crime, tensions, and fights; these are the background of many of *Nathan Never*'s plots. Other adventures take place in the colonies orbiting the Earth or in the radioactive desert originated by the wild pollution produced by man.

Nathan Never's stories are made up of many characters that are harmoniously blended. On his missions Nathan is accompanied by a team of colleagues, including Legs Weaver (who, thanks to her success, has given birth to a spinoff series), Sigmund Baginov, an expert in computer sciences, Edward Reiser, the boss of Alfa Agency, and many others. The most interesting feature of Nathan Never is his deeply humane attitude that makes him a very peculiar hero—some of his decisions are mistaken, but he pays for them.

The original "Sardinian Trio" has been supported by other scriptwriters, and the team of drawers counts 24 artists, among whom are Claudio Castellini, Robert De Angelis, Nicola Mari, Germano Bonazzi, Stefano Casin, Mario Alberti, Ivan Calcaterra, and Dante Bastianoni.

G.C.C.

NAUSICAÄ OF THE VALLEY OF WIND (Japan) Any but his most dedicated fans would be hard-pressed to name another comic created by Japan's most popular animator, Hayao Miyazaki, but the one comic he is known for, *Nausicaä of the Valley of Wind*, is without a doubt one of the most important comics ever produced in Japan, and it has generated more than a little controversy.

The story is set a millennium in the future, hundreds of years after survivors of the Seven Days of Fire dragged themselves out of the rubble of industrial civi-

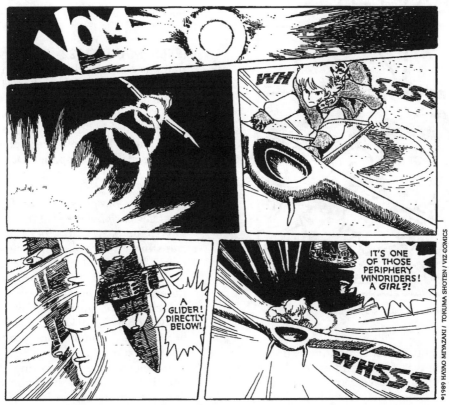

"Nausicaä of the Valley of Wind," Hayao Miyazaki. © Tokuma Shoten.

lization and began to scratch a meager existence from what little usable soil remained on the face of the Earth. In this postapocalyptic world, humanity huddles in villages and kingdoms, coexisting uneasily with the enormous (and growing) Sea of Corruption, a forest of overgrown molds spewing poisonous gases and inhabited by giant insects.

The heroine is Nausicaä, a teenaged girl who seems to be a savior prophesied in ancient writings. Nausicaä, the daughter of the chieftain of a peaceful agricultural community known as the Valley of Wind, struggles to end a war that breaks out between three major powers. In the process, she discovers that the feared Sea of Corruption is in fact cleansing the Earth of a millennium of industrial and military pollution, and that the giant insects are the Earth's ecological conscience.

Nausicaä of the Valley of Wind began as a straightforward environmental cautionary tale, and Miyazaki's hugely popular 1984 animated version was indeed little more, but the comic developed into a complex, often brooding discourse on hubris and moral relativity. Nausicaä, all but flawless in the animated film, becomes a character wracked by doubt and, occasionally, rage or depression.

Nausicaä became controversial when it was revealed that it had been a source of inspiration (one of many, actually) to the Aum Divine Truth cult that was responsible for the tragic sarin gas attack on a Tokyo subway line in 1995. Critics implied a connection between the terrorism and such popular media as comics, animation, and video games, and although no coherent connection was ever made, *Nausicaä's* previously pristine image has been indelibly tarnished by this tenuous link to infamy.

The feature-length animated version was introduced to English-speaking audiences as the notorious *Warriors*

of the Wind, a heavily edited version that still invokes anger in those familiar with the original. *Warriors* led creator Miyazaki to adopt a far more cautious approach to granting licenses for foreign-language editions of his films. The first four volumes of the English edition of the comic were translated by Studio Proteus for Viz Comics, and the remaining three volumes were translated by Viz Comics.

M.A.T.

NAYLOR, ROBERT (1910-   ) American cartoonist born February 15, 1910, in New York City. After art studies at the C. N. Landon School, Bob Naylor worked in animation with the Stallings-Nolan studio. He first entered the field of comics as an assistant at King Features Syndicate in 1928 and ghosted for a number of King Features artists, including George Herriman. In 1935 Naylor was promoted to staff artist for advertising, and he later became one in a stable of cartoonists on whom King Features regularly called to take over a strip left vacant by the death or departure of the previous artist.

Bob Naylor received his first byline as the successor to Frank Miller on *Barney Baxter*, an aviation strip that Miller had created in 1935. From 1942-48, Naylor drew and wrote the feature with such ineptitude that the ailing Miller had to come back to try and save the faltering strip. In 1948 Naylor took over Walt Hoban's old gag strip *Jerry on the Job* and promptly ran it down. Nothing daunted, he was given the task in 1954 of continuing Les Fosgrave's anemic strip *Big Sister*, with which he finally found a niche for his modest talents. *Big Sister* was discontinued in 1972, and Naylor retired to Monroe, New York, in the mid-1970s.

Bob Naylor was another sad example of King Features' seniority system at work. His most conspicuous quality (if such it can be called) was blandness; it was

BARNEY BAXTER

Bob Naylor, "Barney Baxter." © King Features Syndicate.

hard to find any personality or conviction in his drawing style, and his writing was a compendium of clichés (his race epithets in *Barney Baxter* were particularly offensive, even for the times). Nevertheless Naylor deserves mention because of his long career in the field and his association with at least two noteworthy features.

M.H.

NEBBS, THE (U.S.) Sol Hess, who had previously written most of the continuity for *The Gumps*, created *The Nebbs* (whose name, Hess once confided to Martin Sheridan, comes from the Jewish "nebbich," meaning a poor sap) for the Bell Syndicate. The strip, written by Hess and drawn by W. A. Carlson, first appeared on May 22, 1923.

In the introductory strip Hess himself described his intentions in the following words: "In presenting the Nebb family, I will try to portray from day to day, in a humorous, human way, the things that happen in everyday life. The Nebbs are just a little family like thousand of other families. While they have their differences, they are good wholesome people and I hope you like them much."

In spite of its stated intentions, *The Nebbs* was an unusual family strip in many ways. Instead of being the stereotyped henpecked husband of comic strip folklore, Rudolph Nebb, in addition to being a troublesome resort hotel operator, was also an unyielding *pater familias* and a confirmed martinet. He bullied and nagged and thundered, running his household in dictatorial (though fully ineffectual) fashion. His wife, the chubby and angelic Fanny, stoically smiled through her husband's tantrums and never as much as talked back. His daughter, the teenaged Betsy, and his son, Junior, obediently listened to their father's homilies while doing their own thing on the sly. The only man who could stand up to Rudy's constant badgering was the rambunctious Max Guggenheim (named after Hess's real-life next-door neighbor), the Nebbs' unofficial adviser and *eminence grise*.

Following Sol Hess's death on the last day of 1941, his daughter and her husband, Stanley Baer, took over the continuity, but they did not possess the creator's

spark and *The Nebbs* slowly lost its popularity, finally disappearing in 1946.

M.H.

NEELS, MARC (1922-   ) Marc Sleen (whose real name is Marc Neels), a Flemish writer, artist, and cartoonist, was born December 31, 1922, in Gentbrugge, and had always felt an urge to write and draw. Therefore, he studied at the Sint Lucasinstituut in Gent in order to find his own style. He finished his studies in 1944 and in the same year debuted as an editorial cartoonist in the newspaper *De Standaard*. In 1947, he started editing the comics magazine *'t Kapoentje*. During the next two years he did three strips for *'t Kapoentje—Stropke en Flopke, De Lustige Kapoentjes,* and *Piet Fluwijn en Bolleke*—all the while continuing to draw newspaper strips. In 1949 the weekly magazine was transformed into a supplement for *Het Volk*. It was edited by Marc Sleen until he left *Het Volk* in 1965.

Sleen created some short-lived comic strips before his enduring *De avonturen van detektief Van Zwam* ("The Adventures of Detective Van Zwam") was published on October 3, 1947, in the Brussels newspaper *De Nieuwe Gids*. Roughly one year later, on September 8, 1948, he started the fourth adventure in this series, but now with former supporting character Nero the star and title of the strip. *Nero* appeared in *De Nieuwe Gids* and, after a merger, in *Het Volk* until 1965.

In 1965 Sleen moved the strip to *De Standaard*, with *Nero* being introduced to the newspaper by "The Story of Nero & Co.," drawn by the Studio Vandersteen. Apart from this one instance, Marc Sleen has done all of his writing and drawing without the help of assistants.

Sleen's ever popular *Nero* strip is reprinted in four albums per year. *Nero* is quite successful because of the wild situations he gets into and because of the spicing of satire to be found throughout the strip. Still a master at cartooning, Sleen sometimes includes caricatures of politicians in his strips. He has tapped a number of adventure genres for the parodistic uses to which they can be put. *Nero* regularly takes part in photo safaris in Africa, just as Sleen does. Since the late 1960s Sleen has devoted all his professional time to *Nero* and all of his extracurricular activities to his African travels; as a board member of the World Wildlife Fund he has had many of his film documentaries broadcast on the Flemish-language programs of Belgian television. And, for all of its long run, the *Nero* strip is still fresh because of good writing, good characterization, and a continued standard of art befitting a humorous strip.

W.F.

NEGRO RAUL, EL (Argentina) Started as *Las Aventuras del Negro Raul* ("The Adventures of Raul the Black Man"), the strip was created by pioneer cartoonist Arturo Lanteri in the pages of the Buenos Aires magazine *El Hogar*, in which it appeared in 1916. Raul lived a life of continuous frustration in a hostile and racist city, where all his efforts were bound to fail. To compensate for the existence of poverty and deprivation which was his real lot, Raul dreamed up a life of princely splendor.

In this work Lanteri did not make use of balloons, but inserted a long text under each panel, usually ending on a morality lesson similar to those in *Buster Brown*. Unlike those in *Buster Brown*, however, Raul's moralities were not funny but as bitter as his life. A

"El Negro Raul," Arturo Lanteri. © El Hogar.

"Nelvana," Adrian Dingle. © Triumph Comics.

nonintegrated and daydreaming character very modern in his predicament, *El Negro Raul* ended his career in the early 1920s when his creator went on to other endeavors such as *Pancho Talero*.

L.G.

NELVANA OF THE NORTHERN LIGHTS (Canada)

Nelvana of the Northern Lights was created by artist Adrian Dingle for an independent wartime Canadian comic book, *Triumph-Adventure*, established in June 1941 by the Hillborough Studio of Toronto. The black-and-white book was absorbed in 1942 by Bell Features and Publishing Company of Toronto and was renamed simply *Triumph Comics*. At the end of World War II, when a Canadian government embargo against the importation of U.S. comic books was lifted, Canadian publishers switched to full-color printing to meet the renewed competition. *Nelvana* then appeared in a new book called *Super Duper Comics*, which was later taken over by F.E. Howard Publications of Toronto. It became the only Canadian comic book title ever to appear under the imprint of three different publishing companies.

Nelvana was a semimythological heroine who received superhuman powers from Koliak, the King of the Northern Lights. Initially her efforts were aimed at thwarting Nazi plans to invade Canada's Arctic regions, but in issue number eight of *Triumph* (by then under the Bell trademark) *Nelvana* began a seven-part serialized adventure in the subterranean world of Glacia, a modernistic city that she finds frozen in a state of suspended animation when she is sent by Koliak to learn the Glacians' secret of undying life. The light of the North Star shining down a deep crevasse and magnified by a great glass dome over Glacia brings life back

to the inhabitants after five million years of frozen sleep.

Nelvana later became involved in a running battle between King Rano and his son Targa on one side and, on the other, Vultor the Villainous, who hoped to usurp the Glacian throne. Eventually Vultor was beaten and then, midway through the seventh installment, the narrative abruptly left Nelvana and switched to a Japanese plot to occupy the Arctic.

Nelvana was absent from the strip during the next two installments as Dingle changed his focus to the adventures of Spud Jodwin, an engineer on the Alcan Highway project. It was he who discovers the Japanese plot. Nelvana eventually returned and, in another change of direction for the strip, adopted an alter-ego, that of secret agent Alana North, most of whose adventures took place in the civilized world and not in the frozen north.

After a five-part series called "The Ice-Beam," dealing with efforts of enemy agents to steal plans for a secret weapon, the strip returned to a fantasy theme with Earth facing the threat of war with the Ether People who claimed, as justification for a planned invasion of the world, that man's radio broadcasting was driving them insane. Nelvana journeyed to the world of Etheria and discovered that Vultor the Villainous was masterminding this latest threat to Earth. Using the powers given to her by Koliak, Nelvana defeated Vultor and the great Etherian fleet once and for all. The last chapter of the strip appeared in the third issue of *Super Duper*, dated May 1947.

P.H.

"Nero," Marc Sleen (Marc Neels). © Marc Sleen.

NERO (Belgium) *Nero* is the most popular and most successful creation of Flemish comic artist Marc Sleen. Originally a humorous detective strip titled *De avonturen van detektief Van Zwam* ("The Adventures of Detective Van Zwam"), it started on October 3, 1947, in the Brussels newspaper *De Nieuwe Gids*. As a detective, Van Zwam worked wonders, but his near-perfect character was not very funny. He had a very human assistant, however, whom readers immediately liked. Thus it was that Nero, originally a supporting character, took over the title and the starring role in the fourth adventure, "Het Rattenkasteel" ("The Rats' Castle"), starting on September 8, 1948.

After the merger of *De Nieuwe Gids* and *Het Volk*, four *Nero* albums reprinting his adventures were published per year. In 1965 the strip moved on to yet another newspaper, *De Standaard*, with the first tale to appear there "De Geschiedenis van Nero en Co" ("The Story of Nero and Co."), drawn by the Studio Vandersteen. Apart from this fill-in story, Marc Sleen has worked alone on his strips.

Nero is a globetrotter, following any cue to beckoning adventures and leaving his wife at home. Nevertheless he is a father figure, confronted by the generation gap in the form of his highly talented son, Adhemar. *Nero* also represents strong elements of Flemish folk character without permitting them to become stereotyped. His adventures make humorous use of a number of adventure genres, like fantasy, science fiction, or mystery, as Marc Sleen has tapped almost all sources that lend themselves to parody. He even adds topical material and real-life politicians in order to enable Nero to expound his wishes for world peace. Since 1962, when Sleen started regularly going on photo safaris in Africa, Nero is often seen searching out an African setting for his adventures.

The witty *Nero* comic feature is extremely well written and has a strong cast of characters to add to its enjoyment. This strip tries to teach readers to face each day with a smile. It is still going strong after 50 years of existence.

W.F.

NEUGEBAUER, WALTER (1921-1992) Walter Neugebauer was a German comic artist, born March 28, 1921, the son of German parents, in Tuzla, Bosnia (Yugoslavia). Neugebauer grew up in Zagreb, Yugosla-

via, and got his public and secondary schooling there. He interrupted his studies at the Academy to work full time for the press.

At the age of 12 his cartoons were published in a catholic parish paper; at age 14 he drew the children's page of the newspaper *Novosti* which featured stories and poems (mostly written by his older brother, Norbert, born June 9, 1917). He drew his first comic strip, *Gusarsko Blago* ("Pirate Treasure"), in 1935-36 and, at the same time, started *Nasredin Hodža* for *Oko* ("The Eye"). At 17, together with the journalist Franjo, he founded *Mickeystrip*, the first Yugoslav comic magazine. The title was derived from *Old Mickey*, a Western serial. Here he drew and wrote *Bimbo Bambus*, the humorous story of an African and his white hunter friend.

He continued on *Mickeystrip* until he finished secondary school in 1940, then founded his own magazine, *Veseli Vandrok's* ("The Happy Wanderer"). This magazine contained more funnies and his first attempts at realistic comics: The humoristic *Nasredin Hodža*; the funny snails *Puž and Pužek*, a scouting story; and the realistic Western adventures of *Winnetou*. Text features included a serialized version of "Huckleberry Finn." The magazine folded when Yugoslavia entered the war in 1941. The war years led to some narrow escapes and occasional comic work. After the war, he started working as a cartoonist for the satirical *Kerempuh*. While working there from 1946 to 1948 he became interested once again in animated cartoons. This interest was sponsored by the blossoming *Kerempuh* and finally led to the 21-minute animated cartoon *Veliki Miting* ("The Big Meeting") which told about a meeting of frogs and toads. It was a very successful film that was withdrawn from public showing 10 years later because of Albanian-Yugoslavian quibbling over borderlines.

The film led to the financing of Duga-Film ("Rainbow-Film") which folded in 1952 because of a financial crisis. In 1952-53, Neugebauer introduced the first postwar comic strip to *Pionir*, a children's magazine. The strip told of the adventures of a rabbit and a bear and was called *Priča s Rubašume* ("Tales from the Edge of the Forest"). Next came adaptations of Jules Verne yarns for *Plavi Vjesnik* ("Blue Herald"), a magazine that changed to tabloid size and eventually introduced American and British strips.

In 1954 Neugebauer was back in animated cartoons, working for *Interpublik*, an advertising agency with animated cartoon facilities. While working there, contact between Rolf Kauka and Walter Neugebauer was established. Neugebauer started freelancing for Kauka's *Fix und Foxi* comic books and in 1958 produced a *Munchhausen* cartoon for Kauka, who featured the legendary Baron in his comics of the time. In the following years, Neugebauer helped develop, cocreate, or draw Kauka features like *Fix und Foxi*, *Tom und Biber*, *Mischa*, and *Bussi Bär*.

From 1958 to 1972 Neugebauer held the position of art director at Kauka, although not continuously. In 1970 Neugebauer and Kauka started quarreling over finances and copyrights. The argument was mainly fueled by production of the animated cartoon feature Maria d'Oro. It ultimately led to Neugebauer's breaking with Kauka and leaving the company to freelance for various others, Kauka's fiercest competitor just one of these. Neugebauer drew cover illustrations for Ehapa's *Micky Maus* comic book and, more importantly, produced some 100 animated cartoons for television ads for *Micky Maus*. The 20-second spots usually showed some funny happening that ultimately became the cover issue of the weekly *Micky Maus* magazine.

Neugebauer was known for the speedy delivery of his animated cartoons. Together with six assistants he could crank out two such spots in one week while others took six weeks just to produce one. For a while Neugebauer's studio was the busiest animated cartoon studio in Germany.

Despite his speedy delivery, Neugebauer had a mature, slick style, although it sometimes looked simplistic. On the whole, however, his funny and realistic comic art was always polished and original, and showed his devotion to his two professional loves: comics and animated cartoons. Neugebauer died May 31, 1992, in Geretsried, near Munich, Germany.

W.F.

NEUTRON *see* Valentina.

NEWLYWEDS, THE (U.S.) George McManus tackled the family theme that was to become his hallmark for the first time in *The Newlyweds* (also known as *The Newlyweds and Their Baby*), a Sunday feature which he created in 1904 for Pulitzer's *New York World*.

The plot was simple: Mr. and Mrs. Newlywed (whose first names we never learn, as they are unusually fond of calling each other by such endearing terms as "dovey" and "precious") are inordinately proud and protective of their only child, a rather dull-looking baby. The infant (later christened Snookums) was prone to temper tantrums, and in order to assuage him the Newlyweds would go to any length, such as renting a movie house to show the brat the same Charlie Chaplin picture over and over again, getting Caruso to reprise one of his arias, or having a bum repeatedly kicked out of a saloon, all to the baby's drooling enjoyment.

When McManus left Pulitzer in 1912 to join the Hearst organization, he took *The Newlyweds* with him, mining the same theme again and again in a new version rebaptized *Their Only Child* until the definitive

"The Newlyweds" ("Snookums"), George McManus. © King Features Syndicate.

establishment of *Bringing Up Father* on the Sunday page in 1918.

After a 25 year absence, the Newlyweds and their baby made a comeback in yet another version called *Snookums* in November 1944, as a top to *Bringing Up Father* (replacing *Rosie's Beau*). This third serving of the same theme (which was never as imaginative as the earlier ones) survived its creator by two years, disappearing in December 1956.

The Newlyweds (to use the title by which the strip is best known) was McManus's most popular creation prior to *Bringing Up Father*. A musical comedy, titled *The Newlyweds and Their Baby*, was staged in 1909, and a few years later George McManus collaborated with the famous French animator Emile Cohl to produce the *Baby Snookums* series of animated cartoons based on his strip (1912-1914).

M.H.

NEWMAN, PAUL S. (1924-   ) Paul S. Newman (no relation to the movie actor) bills himself as King of the Comic Book Writers, and he may well be right. Born in Brooklyn, New York, on April 29, 1924, he attended Dartmouth College, majoring in 17th- and early 18th-century drama, before seeing service in World War II. Aspiring to become a playwright, he wrote a number of plays while he was still in his 20s, but none of these were ever produced. In 1947 he received an introduction to National Periodicals (now D.C. Comics) and it wasn't long before he had wrangled his first writing assignment; from then on, there was no stopping him.

Newman's first comic book script was for *A Date With Judy*, based on a then-popular radio show. Thus encouraged, he branched out. "Within three years I was working for 12 different publishers," he relates. His credits during these years included scripts for *Patsy Walker*, *Crime Detective*, *The Two-Gun Kid*, and *Hopalong Cassidy*.

His Western stories finally led to assignment to the title Newman is best remembered for, *The Lone Ranger*. In 1951 he succeeded Fran Striker, the creator of the series, as the main writer on the title, a position he would keep for the next quarter-century. Newman milked every plot and cliché from the Western genre; North and South, from the Canadian border to the Painted Desert, his masked rider and faithful companion Tonto proved the scourge of every lawbreaker who ever rode the West. The stories were always interesting, sometimes gripping, and they earned him the scriptwriter's spot on the *Lone Ranger* newspaper strip in 1961.

In addition to his work on *The Lone Ranger*, he continued to turn out scripts for every possible comic book company. Among the more than 350 titles he contributed to were such now-classic names as *Airboy*, *Archie*, *Captain Marvel*, *G.I. Joe*, *Roy Rogers*, *Superman*, and *Zorro*; he received no credit on any of these. "In the world of comic book writing," Greg Metcalf stated in the *Journal of Popular Culture*, "chances are that Anonymous is Paul S. Newman."

Only in 1976 did he finally receive a credit in an issue of *Turok, Son of Stone*, a title he had been writing for the previous 20 years. Next to *The Lone Ranger*, *Turok* is Newman's most notable achievement. For 27 years he scripted every single issue of the continuing saga of Turok and Andar, two 19th-century Native Americans lost in a primitive world of cavemen and dinosaurs. In the course of a career that has already spanned half a century, Newman has also written plays, children's stories, radio skits, song lyrics, and newspaper comics (notably *Tom Corbett, Space Cadet* and *Robin Malone*, in addition to *The Lone Ranger*).

Recognition has finally come to the author in the 1990s. He has been interviewed and profiled in several publications, and in 1993 comic book historian Robin Snyder was able to document the fact that to date Newman had written over 4,000 comic book stories for 350 different titles. This incredible fact alone would make him worthy of special mention, had not his writing abilities, solid craftmanship, and sense of humor already earned him a privileged place in the history of the medium.

M.H.

NEW MUTANTS, THE (U.S.) *The New Mutants* were a group spun off from the *X-Men*, and first appeared in a Marvel graphic novel of that title in 1982. The new-comers enjoyed enough popularity in their first solo outing to warrant a comic book line of their own the following year.

The New Mutants were teenage heroes who had acquired their superpowers genetically (instead of get-ting them from external sources). They formed a het-erogeneous phalanx of justice-fighters from diverse social, religious, and ethnic backgrounds who all shared the common bond of being persecuted for their "otherness." They had been brought together for train-ing and mutual support by Professor X, the head hon-cho of the X-Men. While going through the rigors of a martial education, they also found time to fight a wide assortment of villains and alien menaces.

Chris Claremont created this team of teenaged won-ders and endowed the story of their growing together into a close-knit unit with genuine pathos and humor. When *New Mutants* went into a regular monthly title a year after its initial appearance, he created some com-pelling narratives; consequently, the comic book enjoyed instant, if short-lived, success. The title also had the great luck of attracting top artistic talent to its banner, including John Buscema, Bill Sienkiewicz, Rob Liefeld, and Todd McFarlane. It also had some good writing from Claremont, who produced a clever varia-tion on the tired superhero theme, but after a couple of years he seemed to grow tired himself. After its initial rocket-like takeoff, *The New Mutants* started to come down steadily; it ended neatly with issue number 100 (April 1991).

M.H.

NEWSBOY LEGION (U.S.) After Joe Simon and Jack Kirby launched the first of all comic book kid groups at Timely during the summer of 1941, they moved to National to create their second kid group in April 1942. Beginning in *Star-Spangled* number seven, the *Newsboy Legion* was the first of two superior kid groups the pair invented for National, the other being *Boy Commandos*. The Newsboy Legion was comprised of four ghetto youths: Big Words, the brains of the group; Tommy, the closest of all to the middle-class ideal; Gabby, and Scrapper. They were aided (or monitored) in their exploits by the Guardian, who was really slum police-man Jim Harper.

The strip's origin chronicles the sad tale of rookie policeman Jim Harper, who, during his off-duty hours from the "Suicide Slum" beat, was severely beaten.

Instead of taking the message to cooperate with the powers-that-be of the ghetto, the zealous Harper declared the attack "the last straw," spirited himself into a nearby costume shop and gathered up a blue and gold superhero suit complete with a badge-shaped shield. (Naturally, Harper left payment behind.) Dub-bing himself the Guardian, the cop caught his attacker and meted out punishment he could not have employed as a crimefighter within the law.

Later in the original story, Patrolman Harper arrested the Newsboy Legion in the midst of their theft of tools (meant to build their clubhouse), but saved them from a reformatory school by agreeing to be their guardian. Thus, the group and its protector are formed, and, for the next five years, they combated crime blithely. The kids weren't supposed to know that Patrolman Harper, their legal guardian, and the cos-tumed Guardian were one and the same, but they were not easily fooled. They discovered the dual-identity straightaway, but proceeded to keep that fact from Jim Harper throughout the group's career.

The *Newsboy Legion* ran through the 63rd issue of *Star-Spangled* (January 1947) before disappearing with many of its crimefighting compatriots. But when Jack Kirby returned to National in 1971, the second genera-tion *Newsboy Legion* group was introduced in *Jimmy Olsen*. Androids genetically produced from body tissue of the original Legion, the revived group was used as another component of Kirby's complicated "Third World" series.

J.B.

NIBSY THE NEWSBOY (U.S.) A short-lived but very impressive early Sunday strip by George McManus, *Nibsy the Newsboy* (which ran in the *New York World* from April 1905 to July 29, 1906) was originally based on one of the *World*'s street newshawkers that McManus had once seen and liked. Nibsy was a skinny, felt-hatted, shock-haired kid of about 14 who quickly found himself involved in the affairs of a fan-tasy kingdom he was able to enter as easily as Nemo could dream himself into Slumberland. In fact, it was easier, because Nibsy did not have to dream his way into what McManus called Funny Fairyland, but found

"Nibsy the Newsboy," George McManus.

it around almost any corner of a downtown New York street.

McManus's strip, most often titled in full as *Nibsy the Newsboy in Funny Fairyland*, was a genial takeoff of Winsor McCay's *Little Nemo in Slumberland*, with McManus jovially vulgarizing many of the imaginative elements McCay treated fancifully in his own strip. The boy hero meets a fairy king's daughter turned into a donkey, who is uglier than the donkey when she is retransformed into herself; he uses a magic sword to conjure up an army for the fairy king, but the army falls to fighting among its own members and manages to get the king into the slugfest as well. The king is even able to return Nibsy's visits, as he does in the final episode of the strip, to be trampled in the mob leaving a New York baseball game and run down in automobile traffic. Deliberately crude devices were used to kid McCay's subtle concepts, and McManus continued to draw *Nibsy* at the peak of his graphic imagination. As a result, the strip is one of the high points of comic strip art and vitally in need of reprinting in full, preferably in color.

The troublesome thing about McManus strips like *Nibsy* (and *Panhandle Pete, Spareribs and Gravy,* and others) with their highly colorful narrative, superb comic figures, and constantly inventive graphics that make every large panel an individual visual delight, is that his later successful and more long-lived works like *Their Only Child, Rosie's Beau,* and *Bringing Up Father* seem dull in comparison. One rather resents them for usurping the imagination which might perhaps better have been allowed to continue romping in Funny Fairyland with Nibsy and the ugly enchanted princess.

B.B.

NICHOLLS, SYDNEY WENTWORTH (1896-1977)
Cartoonist born 1896 at Frederick Henry Bay, Tasmania, with the surname of Jordan. After his mother remarried, he adopted the name of his stepfather in 1908. Because his stepfather worked on railway tunnels, Nicholls was educated in a number of schools throughout New South Wales and New Zealand. On leaving school in 1910 he attended art classes until he was 21, the last four years being spent at the Royal Art Society, Sydney. His first published art appeared in the *International Socialist* in 1912, and by 1914 his cartoons were accepted by *The Bulletin*.

One of his cartoons for *Direct Action* caused the magazine's editor, Tom Barker, to be jailed for 12 months for publishing material prejudicial to recruiting. In 1917 he began designing art titles and posters for motion pictures and stayed in this field for the next five years. During this time he was responsible for titles and posters for *The Sentimental Bloke* and many Snowy Baker films. He joined the staff of the Syndey *News* and in 1923, as senior artist, was invited to produce a colored Sunday strip to compete with *Ginger Meggs/Us Fellers,* which was proving very popular in the *Sunday Sun*. The result was *Fatty Finn,* first called *Fat and his Friends,* which debuted on September 16. The strip became popular and in 1927 a motion picture, called *Kid Stakes,* was produced using the characters from Nicholls's strip. Three colored *Fatty Finn Annuals* were published during 1928-30. In 1931, the *News* merged with the *Sunday Sun* and *Fatty Finn* was dropped.

Nicholls went to New York where he tried to sell his adventure strip, *Middy Malone*. Developed in 1929, *Malone* was one of the world's first adventure strips

created for newspapers. Late in 1931, Nicholls ghosted a number of weeks of Ad Carter's *Just Kids*. Unable to sell his strip, he returned to Australia in 1932. In 1934 he began publishing a tabloid-size comic, *Fatty Finn's Weekly,* but by 1935 he was back designing for the motion picture field, where he stayed until 1940. In 1941 he produced the first of a series of colored books devoted to *Middy Malone,* as well as commencing production on a series of comic books featuring the work of other Australian artists as well as his own.

He founded his own comic line in 1946 which ran until 1950. In 1951, after an absence of 20 years, *Fatty Finn* returned to newspapers when it appeared in the *Sunday Herald*. Following a merger, the strip transferred to the *Sun-Herald* in October 1953 where it continues to appear.

In his formative years, Nicholls was influenced by the work of Will Dyson, Norman Lindsay, Alf Vincent, Dan Smith, and *The Bulletin* school—yet he developed a very distinctive and personalized style of fine line art. His figures generated movement and his detailed linework on sailing ships was not only effective but accurate. His book *About Ships—from the Egyptian Galley to the Queen Elizabeth* is an outstanding work in this area.

Because of his strong antisyndication beliefs, Syd Nicholls and the characters he created were seldom received sympathetically by newspaper managements. He was the first to produce all-Australian comics and, in company with Syd Miller, did more to foster the cause of local artists and writers than any other publisher. He was a former president of the Australian Journalist's Club. Sydney Nicholls died on June 3, 1977.

J.R.

NICK DER WELTRAUMFAHRER (Germany)
Nick der Weltraumfahrer ("Nick the Spaceman") was the response of Lehning Verlag, a German comic book publishing house, to the sputnik shock of the late 1950s. Science fiction had been one of the staples of dime novels before the first rocket putting a satellite in orbit had been launched. But until then science fiction in comic books was relatively rare in Germany, most of the material being imported. Sputnik came just in time to help launch a science-fiction comic series created, written, and drawn by a very prolific German, Hansrudi Wäscher.

Nick der Weltraumfahrer started on his journeys through space in January 1958 in the piccolo (or Italian) format of $2^7/_8 \times 6^7/_8$ inches so favored by Lehning Verlag. This first series of books ended after 139 issues in September 1960. This did not ground Nick, however, as the daring black-haired hero had already started additional adventures in a color comic book of more standard proportions in January 1959. This book was titled *Nick. Pionier des Weltraums* ("Nick. Pioneer of Space") and enjoyed a run of 121 books, ending in July 1963. The last 10 books reverted to the title of the original piccolo series but added the subtitle "space magazine." *Nick* reprints appeared in a *Tarzan* comic book in the early 1960s, in *Harry,* in a "piccolo giant" series, and in a *Nick* special.

By and large, Nick was a hero of the late 1950s and early 1960s. He became slightly outdated when his crewcut became obsolete. His disappearance may also have been connected with a growing sophistication in science-fiction stories, something *Nick* was not geared

"Nick," Hansrudi Wäscher. © Hansrudi Wäscher.

for because its space-opera format used the usual threats-of-strange-environments plot (but seemingly took care to avoid the bug-eyed monster routine). The strip held up while it lasted, making many readers devoted fans of science fiction and of the Wäscher style which, although effective telling a story, lacked the visual extravaganza that would have helped to turn the series into a classic.

A first set of reprints was published in 1976. The entire *Nick* material of piccolo-sized comics and regular-sized comic books was again reprinted in 1982. A new series of *Nick* comics also features stories that are not illustrated by Hansrudi Wäscher.

W.F.

NICKEL, HELMUT (1924-   ) Helmut Nickel was born in 1924 in a small village south of Dresden where his father worked as school principal. As a kid he liked visiting the zoo and the Museum of History in Dresden, as well as the museum of German novelist Karl May in Radebeul. There he liked to copy some of the exhibits. Drawing came to him naturally; his only study was an evening course when he was 15.

After graduation from high school, Nickel wanted to become a veterinarian and work in a zoo. Instead he was inducted into the army, spent three years serving in Russia during World War II, and another three years as a prisoner of war. When he returned home to what was now East Germany, he stood no chance of receiving permission to study because he came from a bourgeois family, so he worked in advertising for movies and illustrated children's books.

When he heard that a Free University was being founded in West Berlin, he left the East. Again, however, he could not study to become a veterinarian because there was no faculty of natural sciences at the university, so he studied the history of art. In order to pay for his studies he started working as a freelance graphic designer on the side. This led to contacts with comics publishers in 1952.

The first comic book he wrote and drew was *Die drei Musketiere* ("The Three Musketeers," 1952). He

went on to do various other comic books, working for the Western comic book *Hot Jerry* (with scripts by Fritz Klein), and writing and drawing *Don Pedro*, the science-fiction adventures of *Titanus* (the first issue was 3-D), as well as comic features *Francis Drake* and *Peters seltsame Reisen* ("Peter's Strange Voyages"). *Peters seltsame Reisen* was a serialized comics parody along the lines of "The Secret Life of Walter Mitty" that featured a youthful hero, Peter, stumbling through all kinds of comic adventures by meeting comic book heroes like Nick the astronaut or Akim the jungle hero, and later meeting characters from literature. Nickel also created cover illustrations for a *Tarzan* comic book and for a number of pulp novels, and wrote and drew several issues of *Winnetou*, based on the novels of Karl May.

Nickel left the comics field in the early 1960s to take a position with a museum in Berlin. He also earned his doctorate in history. After this he took a position as curator for arms and armor with the Metropolitan Museum of Art in New York, where he worked until he retired in 1988. Although Nickel looks back fondly on his work in the comics, much of which has been reprinted, he never regretted his decision to move to New York. While this move may have been in the best interest of both Helmut Nickel and the Metropolitan Museum, it was a loss for comics published in Germany.

Helmut Nickel always managed to instill into his comics a sense of historic reality and reliability. His heroes, although quite adventuresome, were never musclebound, and his pen-and-ink artwork always stood out because of an intrinsic elegance. Publishers did not always appreciate the amount of talking Nickel's heroes sometimes did, but he always had so much story to tell—and historic background to explain—that he felt he sometimes had to put all the necessary information into dialogue balloons and captions. What made Nickel's comics special were a dose of wry humor and a tendency toward caricature, especially in supporting characters.

W.F.

Helmut Nickel, "Titanus." © Helmut Nickel.

NICK KNATTERTON (Germany) *Nick Knatterton* (one possible literal translation of the name would be "Nick Rattlesound") was created one autumn night in 1950 by Manfred Schmidt in order to satirize *Superman.* Anton Sailer, cartoon editor of the German weekly illustrated paper *Quick,* accepted the adventures of the pointy-headed detective for publication. He felt the feature would not last eight weeks unless it contained lots of well-proportioned females—which it did.

Nick Knatterton was an instant success. Manfred Schmidt had intended to make fun of the comics and, because of the success of the feature, ended up drawing an extremely successful comic feature for ten years. At one time he retired the hero by marrying him off. But his pipe-smoking creation returned to haunt him for some more years until, after more than 500 weekly episodes, Schmidt definitely killed the feature.

In addition to satirizing the likes of *Superman, Dick Tracy,* and *Sherlock Holmes, Nick Knatterton* also offered political satire that was sometimes quoted in the Houses of Parliament of the Federal Republic of Germany. Schmidt used the strip as a vehicle for political

satire after the initial idea of satirizing comics had become routine. For much of his work on *Nick Knatterton* Schmidt depended heavily on his cool witticism instead of the brilliance of his art.

The adventures of Nick Knatterton the super sleuth were reprinted in seven album-size comic books and, in 1971-72, in two hardcover volumes. Foreign editions of the strip underwent some surprising changes. In the Netherlands edition in the Amsterdam paper *Volkskrant,* the well-rounded girls had to trim their shapely figures on the altar of chastity, whereas in the Turk paper *Millyet* an artist had to add to the girls' measurements. *Nick Knatterton* was even reprinted in Iron Curtain countries.

The *Knatterton* success led to a movie that was well received by the critics and the public. Based on the *Knatterton* story "Der Raub der Gloria Nylon" ("The Kidnapping of Gloria Nylon"), the motion picture added some comic climaxes like a bar brawl in which Nick Knatterton fights and downs two dozen gangsters to the tune of Mozart's *Kleine Nachtmusik* coming from a jukebox.

Knatterton dolls, card games, coloring books, masks, decals, schnapps, and even orange wrappers turned *Nick Knatterton* into an even bigger commercial success. Manfred Schmidt, after killing off *Knatterton,* continued writing humorous articles for *Quick,* illustrating them in his seemingly simple style.

When the strip's creator had spread out into the field of animated cartoons for advertising he was promptly asked to do his original strips as animated cartoons. Despite some initial misgivings, Manfred Schmidt did start doing *Nick Knatterton* again. The animation actually had the feel of the original strip, because Schmidt's studio did the cartoons, and with Schmidt supplying the narration himself, the animated cartoons have an added dimension the original strips never had: the ironic and sarcastic voice of the feature's creator. The *Nick Knatterton* cartoons were originally made to be aired with continuity, like the original strip. The animated *Nick Knatterton* has since been made available on videocassette.

"Nick Knatterton," Manfred Schmidt. © Manfred Schmidt.

For a comic strip that was originally intended as an anticomic strip, *Nick Knatterton* helped popularize comics in Germany while turning itself into a classic example of the possibilities the comic form offers to satire.

W.F.

"91 Karlsson," Rudolf Petersson. © Rudolf Petersson.

91 KARLSSON (Sweden) *91 Karlsson*, or simply *91:an* ("Soldier No. 91") in the comic book version, is Sweden's most popular comic strip. It was created in 1932 by Swedish artist Rudolf Petersson for the weekly *Allt för Alla*, which had already premiered a number of Swedish strips like Axel Backman's *Burre Busse*, Petter Lindroth's *Jocke, Nicke och Majken* (1921), and Elov Persson's *Kronblom*. The trend had been started by *Allt för Alla* in 1912 with Knut Stangenberg's *Fridolf Celinder*. When *Allt för Alla* merged with *Vårt Hem* in 1933, all strips except *91 Karlsson* were kept. *91 Karlsson* moved on to *Lefvande Livet*. Today, the strip is published in *Året Runt* and has been drawn since 1960 by Nils Egerbrandt. The strip survived its creator, Petersson, who died on April 24, 1970, aged 73. In 1965 Petersson had received the first Adamson, the annual comics Oscar awarded by Svenska Serieakademin, the Swedish Comics Academy. Annuals of *91:an* have been published since 1934; the *91:an* comic book started in 1956.

91 Karlsson started out with a simple farmer's son, Mandel Karlsson, being drafted to serve in the army and, at first, rather realistically showed the troubles he was having adapting to army life in the Halmstad garrison. The strip's creator knew well enough what he was writing about and drawing as he, too, had been in Halmstad during World War I. But after a few years the strip concentrated more on the private aspects of soldiers' lives.

Considerable space was devoted to Karlsson's courting of Elvira, Captain Berån's girl. 91 Karlsson had to compete with his friend and costar, 87 Axelsson, in trying to win Elvira's favors, however. Not unexpectedly,

91 Karlsson is nice, if a bit dense, whereas 87 Axelsson is mean and smart.

The characters of *91 Karlsson* are well rounded and made additionally attractive because of the different stylized dialects which highlight individuality and believability. It is the characterization and the very civilian humor of this parody of army life that ensures continued success for *91 Karlsson* and the *91:an* comic book, as well as for other Swedish strips like *47:an Löken*, which takes up army life in a humorous vein.

W.F.

NINJA BUGEICHŌ (Japan) *Ninja Bugeichō* (subtitled "The Life of Kagemaru") was created by Sanpei Shirato and made its first appearance in a comic book published in December 1959. Seventeen books of *Ninja Bugeichō* were published (its last appearance was in March 1962). *Ninja* soon became the top-selling *kashibonya manga* (comic books published for the exclusive use of lending libraries) of its day; however, these had only a small run and were known only to patrons of the lending library. In 1966 *Ninja Bugeichō* made a reappearance in a series of small comic books published by an important company; it soon became their best seller as well (it was the first time that *Ninja* appeared in a mass-circulation comic book).

The action of the strip took place during Japan's Age of Wars (1560-1588) when the peasants and the ruling samurais were locked in a merciless class war. Kagemaru was a leader of the peasant revolts who enjoyed a charmed life; his invulnerability was due to a dummy created in his likeness, called Kage Ichizoku, that gave him special powers. Kage Ichizoku was destroyed by a female spy, however, and Kagemaru himself was executed by the samurai chieftain Nobunaga, who subsequently made himself master of the realm.

In this long strip Shirato depicted battle scenes with realistic detail, as well as gruesome scenes of death

"Ninja Bugeichō," Sanpei Shirato. © Sanpei Shirato.

(individual or of whole masses of people). The bloody sequences were moderated by romantic interludes. The strip's success was phenomenal, and Shirato achieved a fame comparable to that of Osamu Tezuka.

At the time when *Ninja Bugeichō* was a success as a *kashibon manga* it gave rise to countless imitations (*Ninja Zankokushou* was only one of them). *Ninja Bugeichō* was also made into a motion picture.

H.K.

NIÑO, ALEX N. (1940-   ) Filipino cartoonist born May 1, 1940, in Tarlac. As a child Alex Niño spent many hours just outside of his home drawing on the ground. When he finished, he would erase the drawing and start all over again. He loved to draw, and one of his boyhood dreams was to become a comic book artist. After much perseverance and tribulation, he finally got his chance to work for some of the more obscure titles in the Philippines. Unfortunately, not all of them paid him, but he was happy to be published.

In 1965 he teamed up with Clodualdo del Mundo to do *Kilabot Ng Persia* ("The Terror of Persia") for *Pilipino Komiks*. This was an adventure novel reminiscent of the Arabian Night fables. Later he joined Marcelo B. Isidro to work for *Redondo Komix*. They did *Dinoceras*, a story about a prehistoric creature surviving in modern times. Then in 1966, for *Pioneer Komiks*, he illustrated his own feature, *Gruaga—The Fifth Corner of the World*. This fantasy epic gave Niño a chance to use his fertile imagination and display his artistic ability. During that same period he combined with Virgo Villa on *Tsannga Rannga* for *Espesyal*, and with Amado S. Castrillo, who wrote *Maligno* for *Redondo Komix*.

Eventually Niño began to illustrate for *Alcala Komix*. His stint with this publication produced many memorable artistic achievements. He drew *Mga Matang Nagliliyab* ("The Eyes that Glow in the Dark"), a serialized novel written by Isidro. This title contains some of the most beautiful graphics to ever appear in the comic medium. It combined technical virtuosity with innovative layouts and storytelling. At this stage he developed a calligraphic drawing style that gave his illustrations a rhythmic and flowing quality.

Despite numerous assignments for *Redondo* and *Alcala Komix*, Niño continued to freelance for other companies, among them PSG Publications. At PSG he did a series of short stories dealing with Bruhilda Witch. These short mystery and horror tales enabled him to elaborate and experiment, resulting in some unique visual effects. Because Pablo Gomez's forte was dramatic stories, Alex Niño did many novels in the usual, straightforward manner, but even then he managed to use several drawing styles to add individuality to each story. When many of his collaborations with Gomez were made into motion pictures, Niño started to do movie ads in the realistic mode.

Not content working only for local publishers, Niño also drew for various American publications such as D.C., Gold Key, Peterson, Educational Classics, and Marvel. He pencilled the first *Black Orchid* story for National and inked some of the Sunday *Tarzan* strips for United Feature Syndicate. For D.C. he handled *Captain Fear*, *Korak*, *Space Voyagers*, and many mystery and horror stories. He did *Conan*, *Man-Gods*, and the unique short story *Repent Harlequin, Said the Tick Tock Man* for Marvel comics.

Alex Niño, magazine illustration. © Orvy Jundis.

Alex Niño has received numerous awards in the Philippines and the United States. In 1974 the International Science-Fantasy Society, in cooperation with the Philippine Comic Archives and the Philippine Science-Fantasy Society, sponsored Niño on a visit to the United States to attend the World Science Fiction Convention. Unlike many of his compatriots, Niño chose to remain in the United States, where he has enjoyed a solid if unspectacular career. In 1983 he and Trevor Von Eeden created *Thriller* for D.C. Comics; since then he has worked for virtually every U.S. comic book publisher on such titles as *House of Mystery, House of Secrets, Valeria the She-Bat, Bold Adventures,* and *Star Reach Classics.*

O.J.

NIPPER (G.B.) *The Nipper* (who later lost his "The") was created by Brian White as a daily pantomime strip. Rejected by the *London Evening Standard*, it was immediately accepted by the *Daily Mail*, where it ran nationally from August 30, 1933, to July 1947, with a break of a few years during the war.

Nipper, a small boy in frock and diapers, grew slightly older over the years, allowing for a companion to join him in mischief. Called Nobby, this bald baby with but a single hair became Nipper's brother, but was originally a neighbor's child. The other regulars in the strip were Nipper's proud but suffering father and his distraught mother. The gag-a-day format was occasionally varied to permit continuity and the use of speech balloons.

Nipper's popularity rose rapidly as parents recognized in his adventures a genuine humor. In fact, White

"Nipper," Brian White. © Associated Newspapers Ltd.

based Nipper on his own "nipper," his young son John. A weekly page, *Nipperisms*, was added to his output, and the strips were reprinted annually in a thick paperback, *Nipper Annual*. The first was published on December 7, 1934, the last (dated 1942) in 1941. Altogether there were eight annuals, several with full-color, 16-page sections. (The last two were in reduced format due to wartime paper shortages.) Other spin-offs included *Nipper* postcards in color for valentines, a series of color booklets in the *Merry Miniatures* giveaway comics (1937-39), *Nipper* dolls by Merrythought, *Nipper* figures in china by E. C. Hales, and *Nipper* brooches.

In the postwar period White revived *Nipper* for his own publishing company, having retained the copyright of the character. He reprinted some of the strips in painting books and comic books, and drew new adventures for Road Safety propaganda called *Careful Nippers*. He also produced *Nipper* film strips for home viewers. From March 7, 1959, he drew *Nipper* weekly for *Woman's Day*, until that magazine folded in 1961.

D.G.

NIXON, ROBERT (1935-   ) Bob Nixon, one of the few modern comic artists permitted to sign his comic pages for the Scottish publisher D. C. Thompson, has a delightfully recognizable style of rounded figures in rapid action; his *King Arthur and the Frights of the Round Table* (1974) for *Whoopee* is masterly in its combination of period and traditional comic style.

Robert T. Nixon was born about 1935 in Southbank, the son of a steelworker. He went to the local Secondary Modern school, where his teachers encouraged his artistic interests, and Bob eventually won a scholarship to Middleborough Art College. He was forced to leave Middleborough after three months because of his father's death, however, and took a job in a printing factory's art department, where he was apprenticed to a lithographic artist. After 10 years, Bob decided to try freelancing to children's comics and sent some samples to *Beano*. Harry Crammond, then the editor, let Bob try his hand at a *Little Plum Your Redskin Chum* strip (created by Leo Baxendale). It was successful enough to warrant a few more fill-ins, and in 1965 Bob decided to freelance full time.

Bob's *Beano* work really began in earnest with *Roger the Dodger*, which he would draw for eight years. Then he took over *Lord Snooty and His Pals* after the death of Dudly Watkins, the strip's creator. Although he succeeded quite well, imitation of another artist's style did not suit Bob's development as an original. Other Thompson work included *Grandpa* for *Beano*, and *Esky Mo* and *Captain Cutler* for *Sparky*.

In the 1970s, Bob moved to the London comic publisher IPC and took over two Reg Parlett series, *Hire a Horror* and *Ivor Lott and Tony Broke*, in *Cor*. Comic horrors suited Bob and he began to specialize in these popular strips for editor Bob Paynter. His work included *Soggy the Sea Monster* (in *Shiver and Shake*), *Frankie Stein* (Bob's favorite character, created by Ken Reid), and *Kid Kong*, about a childlike monster gorilla, based on the Edgar Wallace film, that became the front page star for the *Monster Fun* comic (1975). Soon he was drawing six pages of comic strips per week, as well as special features for the Christmas annuals, summer specials, and other publications. His work included *Kid King* (*Jackpot*), *The Buy-tonic Boy* (*Whizzer & Chips*), *Stage School* (*Whoopee*), *Gums* (a parody of the film *Jaws*,

Claudio Nizzi and Lino Landolfi, "Occhio di Luna." © Nizzi and Landolfi.

in *Monster Fun*), and many others. In addition, he drew cartoon greeting cards, illustrated children's paperbacks, and drew a daily newspaper strip, *The Gems*, for the *Sun*, beginning in 1976.

D.G.

NIZE BABY (U.S.) Milt Gross's first Sunday color page, the funny and inventive *Nize Baby* (1927-29) first appeared in national syndication through the *New York World* on January 2, 1927. It was based on characters Gross had lovingly created more than half a decade earlier in his *Gross Exaggerations* (an illustrated column of comic narrative); these characters had also just appeared in a book based on the column, the bestselling *Nize Baby* (1926).

The comic strip, like the column, featured a first-generation Jewish family of New York called the Feitlebaums. The strip family included the title character, a nefarious infant simply called "Nize baby" by his loving mother; the mother herself, variously called Momma, Mama, and Mom Feitlebaum; her husband, Morris; and Baby's brothers, the six-year-old Isadore and the near-grown Looy Dot Dope. (In the column and book, these people were divided into three different families, living on successive floors of an apartment house; in joining them into one family and dropping various parents here and there, Gross retained only one other family head from the column for occasional use in the strip, Mrs. Yifnif of the second floor.)

Basically, the comedy of the strip evolved out of the hilarious interrelations of the family members, rather than from the ethnic humor and dialogue emphasized in the column and book. Mr. Feitlebaum's failure to persuade the distracted Isadore to take Baby off his hands at vital moments led to slapstick disaster of Keystone dimensions; Looy Dot Dope's brash stupidity led to the collapse of houses and major train wrecks, while Baby's disastrous antics had to be read to be believed. This strip, which would have been a lifetime success for a lesser cartoonist, was dismissed in favor of fresher conceptions by Gross a bare two years after it had been launched, to be replaced by *Count Screwloose of Tooloose* on February 17, 1929. The hundred or so *Nize Baby* pages remain as funny today as ever, and are a major accomplishment in the history of the American comic strip.

B.B.

NIZZI, CLAUDIO (1938-   ) One of the most prolific Italian scriptwriters and comics character creators, born September 9, 1938 in Setif, Algeria. Working as a technician in a tractor factory, in 1960 Claudio Nizzi started contributing short novels to the weekly *Il Vittorioso*. Two years later his first comic adventure, *Il segreto del castello*, appeared, followed by *Safari*, a long series set in Africa and drawn by Renato Polese, which continued up to 1966 when the weekly ceased publication.

For the next three years he wrote novels and short stories that were printed in popular women's magazines such as *Novella*, *Grand Hotel*, *Confidenze*, and *Bella*. In 1969 he went he back to comics and started collaborating with the catholic weekly *Il Giornalino*, for which he created characters such as *Piccolo Dente* (1970) and *Il Colonnello Caster Bum* (1970), both drawn by Lino Landolfi; *Larry Yuma* (1971), drawn by Carlo Boscarato and later by Nadir Quinto; *Capitan Erik* (1972), drawn by Ruggero Giovannini and later by Attilio Micheluzzi; *Il tenente Marlo* (1977), drawn by Sergio Zaniboni; *Rosco & Sonny* (1981), drawn by Giancarlo Alessandrini and later by Rodolfo Torti; *Nicoletta* (1981), drawn by Clod; and others. Nizzi has also adapted in comics form several classic tales like Jules Verne's *The Mysterious Island* and *Un capitano di 15 anni,* Charles Dicken's *Oliver Twist*, Victor Hugo's *Les Miserables*, Robert Louis Stevenson's *Treasure Island*, Lewis Carroll's *Alice in Wonderland*, and Mark Twain's *The Adventures of Tom Sawyer*, as well as *Robin Hood* and *The Adventures of Ulysses*. In 1981 Nizzi began his collaboration with the publisher Sergio Bonelli, for whom he wrote stories for the *Mister No* and *Tex* series, created the criminal series *Nick Raider* (1988), and wrote short novels. At present, he is the official scriptwriter of the western series *Tex* (born in 1948); it is the oldest Italian comic still in existence and one of the most popular.

G.C.C.

NOBODY WANTS BILLY BUNTER   *see* Billy Bunter.

NONKINA TOUSAN (Japan) Nonkina Tousan ("Easygoing Daddy"), created by Yutaka Aso, made its first appearance in the *Sunday Hochi* in October 1923. The motivation of the strip was to give hope and comfort to the people of the Kanto district in Japan who had seen their homes destroyed by the great earthquake of September 1, 1923. And indeed the strip did succeed in lifting the spirits of many of its readers.

Nonkina Tousan, a middle-aged, bespectacled man always wearing a splash-pattern kimono and a black Japanese coat, was a kind and cheerful person. Indefatigable, he would crisscross the streets of Tokyo and do his bit for the reconstruction of the city, spreading hope and good cheer in his wake. The strip met unprecedented success, and several books of Nonkina's adventures were published, rapidly becoming bestsellers.

Nonkina Tousan is also credited with bringing the modern daily strip (consisting of four panels across) to Japan. Its debut as a daily took place in January 1924 in the daily edition of Hochi, where it continued until October 1925. After that date, Nonkina Tousan was carried by a number of Japanese magazines. It folded in 1950.

Nonkina Tousan also inspired several motion pictures, Tousan dolls, and a song, Non Tou Bushi, which was very popular in the 1920s.

H.K.

NORAKURO (Japan) Created by Suihou Tagawa, Norakuro made its first appearance in the January 1931 issue of the monthly Shōnen Kurabu as Norakuro Nitohēi ("Private Second Class Norakuro").

Noraini Kurokichi ("Kurokichi the stray dog"), alias Norakuro, was a parentless, homeless little dog; but Norakuro had pledged to become a world-famous general and to this end he joined the Mōken Rentai

("fierce dog regiment") under the command of Buru the bulldog. At first Norakuro made repeated mistakes, but he later rescued regiment commander Buru and his captain Mōru from the enemy Yamazaru ("mountain monkeys"), and saved the battle flag from the pig army. With the passing of time, Norakuro earned his bars and became a professional soldier. Losing all personality, he became the perfect soldier, was promoted to lieutenant, and was twice decorated. The militarism rampant in Japan at the time greatly influenced the development of the strip.

After rising to the rank of captain, Norakuro retired from the army and became a continental pioneer (a euphemism for colonial settler) in Manchuria and Mongolia. He made his last appearance in the December 1941 issue of Shōnen Kurabu.

After the war an attempt to revive Norakuro in the pages of Shōnen Kurabu proved unsuccessful; the feature fared better in the monthly war comic magazine Maru, where it has been flourishing since 1958. Norakuro also appeared in the monthly Manga Gekijo in 1963, and was given his own comic book in 1964. Before the war a series of Norakuro hardcover books sold over a million copies; a new series of books was released after the war, starting in 1969. Norakuro has also inspired a series of animated cartoons, several motion pictures, and a number of records.

Norakuro is the most famous prewar comic strip, and also the oldest and longest-running feature in the whole history of Japanese comics: Suihou Tagawa and others have been drawing the strip for over 65 years.

H.K.

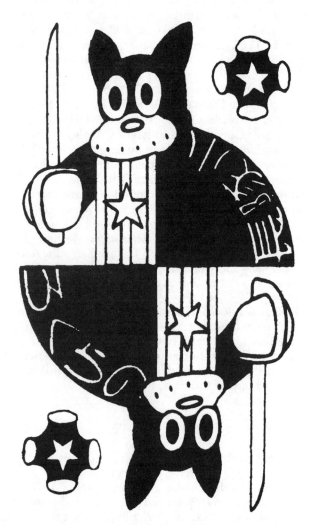

"Norakuro," Suihou Tagawa. © Shōnen Kurabu.

NORRIS, PAUL (1914-) American cartoonist born April 26, 1914 in Greenville, Ohio. Paul Norris studied journalism and art at Midland College in Fremont, Nebraska, and then went on to the Dayton (Ohio) Art Institute. In the late 1930s he started working as an illustrator and cartoonist for the Dayton Daily News, before moving to New York in 1940.

In New York, Norris started a career in comic books, first with Prize Publications, where he created and drew Power Nelson, Futureman (1940-42), and Yank and Doodle (1941-42); from there he went on to National, notably creating (with Mort Weisinger) Aquaman in 1941 and working on many other features, including The Crimson Pirate, The Sandman, and TNT. Norris drew his first newspaper strip in 1942 when he was asked to take over Vic Jordan for the New York daily PM.

Norris was drafted in 1943 and spent three years in the armed forces. After his return to civilian life, he was hired as a staff artist for King Features Syndicate, drawing the Jungle Jim and Flash Gordon comic books. Norris's big break at King Features came in 1948 when he was given the Jungle Jim Sunday feature. In 1952 he assumed the drawing of the Brick Bradford daily strip, and he started drawing the Sunday page in 1957. In the late 1950s Norris also sporadically ghosted Mel Graff's Secret Agent X-9. He went into retirement following the demise of Brick Bradford in 1987.

A cartoonist of limited artistic range, Paul Norris is one of the most glaring examples of the kind of second-rate workhorses KFS keeps throwing at an unwary public. In Norris's case the offense was compounded by the fact that he was asked to succeed such comic art luminaries as Alex Raymond and Austin Briggs (on Jungle Jim) and Clarence Gray (on Brick Brad-

ford), thus doing an injustice to both the creators and the readers.

M.H.

NOWLAN, PHILIP (1888-1940) American writer born 1888 in Philadelphia, Pennsylvania. After graduation from the University of Pennsylvania in 1910, Phil Nowlan embarked on a newspaper career in Philadelphia, where he worked successively on the *Public Ledger*, the *North American,* and the *Retail Ledger*. At the same time he started writing for science-fiction magazines (many of his published stories were signed by the pen name "Frank Phillips").

In the August 1928 issue of *Amazing Stories*, Phil Nowlan published a short novel, *Armaggedon 2419 A.D.*, about a 20th-century American pilot named Anthony Rogers who was overcome by toxic gas and reawakened five centuries later. The story was so popular that Nowlan wrote a sequel, *The Warlords of Han* (March 1929), that, together with his earlier story, was later published as a two-part novel under the umbrella title *Armageddon 2419 A.D.* The story also attracted the attention of John F. Dille, who convinced a skeptical Nowlan to adapt it into comic strip form; Dille also changed the hero's name from Anthony to Buck and hired former pilot Dick Calkins as the artist on the strip. *Buck Rogers 2429 A.D.* made its first appearance on January 7, 1929.

In subsequent years Phil Nowlan wrote a few more science fiction stories (for *Amazing* and *Astounding* among others) but his main contribution to the genre was the scenarios of *Buck Rogers*, which he continued to write until his death in Philadelphia on February 1, 1940.

Phil Nowlan was never regarded as a science-fiction author of note (none of his short stories were ever anthologized) and his fame rests solely upon the memories conjured up by the comic strip which he had been so reluctant to originate.

M.H.

NUS (Spain) The weekly collection of comic books published by Salvat Editores under the title "Vector 1"

featured on its back cover, *Nus y el Atleta* ("Nus and the Athlete") by Enric Sío, the stylistic counterpart to *Sorang*. It began in October 1968.

Nus aspired to show a double perception of reality: one formed by the apparent, "official" aspect of things; the other "intuitive," consisting in the deductions of truth from appearance. Nus (from the Greek word meaning intellect)—a seer endowed with extra-sensory perception—is capable of divining or intuiting the truth that lies buried under the conventions of normal life.

One day he discovers that his friend, the athlete Quim Fibla, has been abducted by a madman. The pages present panels entirely rendered in black and white, projecting a phantasmic reality, as befits a dream world; this world was re-created from "real" elements, with the utilization of effects produced by the pseudosolarization of photographic negatives, a device previously used by Robert D. Routh and Giovanni Rutelli. When Nus, the protagonist, intuits the truth, this is graphically rendered by means of a color panel. But Sío's treatment is equally phantasmic, aiming at illustrating the mental images picked up by the hero, but not by those surrounding him. In these cases, color—always solarized—stands out all the more from the rest of the page illustrated only in black.

The plot of the strip started with a typical mystery story premise, enriched with connotative references to pop art, photography, posters, movies, and television.

Its plasticity was a forward step in relation to *Sorang*: the violent contrast between color and black-and-white has also been used by Sío for the illustration of record jackets and a Cortázar tale. The incorporation of analytical montages, slow motion, simultaneous representation of several levels of reality—visible, intuitive, etc.—into the narrative language of the comics, the conception of each page as a significant unit (or better, as a macrounit), were at the time absolutely new concepts introduced by Sío.

L.G.

OAKY DOAKS (U.S.) *Oaky Doaks* was launched in 1935 by the Associated Press, and drawn by veteran magazine cartoonist Ralph Briggs Fuller. Although it never forged the comic paths being charted at the time by AP companions Noel Sickles and Milton Caniff, *Oaky Doaks* was a solid entry—genuinely funny, superbly drawn, and well written.

Oaky, an honest, muscular, thickheaded, handsome medieval knight, was the hero, and his Sancho Panza was Cedric—chubby, lazy, bald, and bespectacled. The king, Corny, was a skinny crank, and Oaky's horse, Nellie, rounded out the regular cast; Nellie was trustworthy, often the smartest being in miles, and sometimes capable of supernatural feats.

Almost every episode (beginning in the 1940s) saw Oaky involved with the plight of a pretty maiden, a fringe benefit of knighthood and a great device for establishing bases for continuity and adding some glamour to the strip. Fuller's stories were always well spun and contained a delightful mix of real danger and action with all types of humor—visual, sophisticated, sarcastic, slapstick, and sometimes even topical. His women wisecracked the latest slang and generally—earthy as they were—were more logical and determined than the men in the strip. Each episode averaged four months in the dailies and two to four weeks in the Sundays.

Fuller's art was a thing to behold. For all its comic touches it seemed basically realistic, so accurate was his use of anatomy and composition. He also had a unique sense of action and could heighten that quality by the simple device of splitting up a movement—a sock to the jaw or a jump from a balcony—into two panel frames. His oafs (such as Oaky) were oafish, his women handsome, his villains comically menacing. In all, it was an immensely attractive strip until its demise, along with the AP Newsfeatures service, in 1961.

Oaky's adventures, which retained their strongest traits of witty characterizations and breezy, chummy self-kidding on the part of Fuller, are still enjoyable today. His classic strip was only dropped because the syndicate folded, and Fuller, who died two years later, sincerely wished to continue drawing it.

Oaky Doaks' motto was the pig-Latin "Onay Aday without a Oodgay Eedday," and Fuller's wonderful efforts were indeed a good deed a day to many fans.

R.M.

OBERLÄNDER, ADOLF (1845-1923) Adolf Oberländer, a German painter and cartoonist, was born October 1, 1845, in Regensburg and died on May 29, 1923, in Munich, Germany. After completing public and secondary schools he went to Munich to study art at the academy as a student of Piloty, a fact blissfully unnoticeable by his paintings and cartoons. Oberländer's interest turned toward satire and humorous cartoons. He completed his studies in the heyday of the

Fliegenden Blätter, and it was only natural that he should join the ranks of that satirical magazine's staff, eventually becoming a kind of "house artist" and, with Wilhelm Busch and Edmund Harburger, one of the *Fliegenden Blätter*'s Big Three. Incidentally, he was not only a "house artist" because he regularly contributed to the magazine, but also because he lived in the house that harbored the offices of the magazine.

The *Fliegenden Blätter*, founded by Kaspar Braun and started on November 7, 1844, was the first German satiric magazine of renown to achieve about a century of regular publication. Published in Munich, the magazine could draw upon the best of the artist colony of Munich to fill its pages with witty cartoons and the best illustrations to be had. Well-known artists like Count Pocci, Moritz von Schwind, Carl Spitzweg, and Eduard Ille were among the regular contributors who questioned the artificial division of art into fine arts and graphic and/or comic arts.

The *Fliegenden Blätter* and similar magazines laid the foundation for the comic strip. Some of the material included in the pages of the *Fliegenden Blätter* no doubt must be counted among the earliest comic strips or, at least, as among the closest predecessors. This can be seen in the work of Busch and Oberländer. In layout and style, much of Oberländer's work looked like later comic strips. Oberländer made use of the German family's foibles and of anthropomorphic animals. He was also one of the artists to use a recurring strip character, the Bavarian Lion. From 1879 to 1901 the work of Oberländer was reprinted in 12 splendid albums. His *Schriebheft des kleinen Moritz* ("Copy-book of Little Moritz") offered humorous highlights of schools of the time.

W.F.

OESTERHELD, HECTOR GERMAN (1919-1977) The medium of comics has had its geniuses and its mountebanks, its noblemen and its toadies, occasionally its heroes, but very rarely has it had its martyrs, which makes Hector Oesterheld perhaps unique in the field. Born in Buenos Aires in 1919, he graduated with a degree in literature and began a writing career in the early 1940s, publishing short stories in the daily *La Prensa* and children's tales for the publishing house Codex. His real calling, however, only became apparent in 1950, the year he joined Editorial Abril, then one of the most important comics publishers in Argentina.

At Abril, Oesterheld worked with some of the most notable artists residing in Argentina at the time. He wrote scripts for Francisco Solano Lopez (*Uma-Uma*, a tale of the Andes, 1953), Carlos Freixas (*Indio Suarez*, another example of his fascination for Indian life and lore, also 1953), and Daniel Haupt (*Hazañas de Tarpon*, a sea adventure, 1954). It was with the transplanted Italian cartoonist Hugo Pratt that he created some of his most notable series, starting in 1952 with *Sargento Kirk*, an anti-Western starring a deserter from the U.S.

Hector Oesterheld and Alberto Breccia, "El Eternauta." © Editorial Frontera.

Cavalry who had joined the Indians. This sweeping epic lasted until the end of the decade.

In 1957, in association with his brother Jorge, Oesterheld set up his own publishing company, Ediciones Frontera. Working principally with Pratt, he created *Ticonderoga* (a tale of the French and Indian wars) and *Ernie Pike*, about an American war correspondent modeled after the actual Ernie Pyle. Among the innumerable series he gave birth to as the editor of Frontera, mention should be made of *Randall*, a more conventional Western; *Capitan Caribe*, a tale of piracy; and especially a number of fascinating and unusual science-fiction stories such as *El Eternauta*, *Sherlock Time*, and *Mort Cinder*. To provide outlets for his abundant production, he founded a number of comics magazines (*Hora Cero*, *Frontera*, *Hora Cero Extra*) and employed the top talent in the business (Alberto Breccia, Arturo Del Castillo, and Carlos Roume, among others).

Following a severe recession in 1968, Oesterheld was forced to close Frontera's doors. He then turned to the Chilean market, turning out a number of potboilers but also some politically sensitive projects, such as a biography of Ché Guevera, the Argentinean revolutionary and brother-in-arms of Fidel Castro. Drawn by Enrique and Alberto Breccia, this comic-strip series appeared in 1968. Among his more conventional creations of the period were *Guerra de los Antartes* (science fiction), *Roland el Corsario* (sea adventure), *Tres por la Ley* (crime stories), and *Kabul de Bengala* (adventures in India).

In the mid-1970s the military took power in Argentina, and every independent spirit in the land became a suspect. On April 21, 1977, Oesterheld was arrested at his home, taken away, and nothing more was heard of him (his four daughters shared the same fate). Alberto Ongaro, an Italian journalist inquiring about his fate during a visit to Argentina in 1979, received the chilling reply, "We did away with him because he wrote the most beautiful story of Ché Guevara ever done."

M.H.

OGON BAT (Japan) *Ogon Bat*, one of the most famous superhero strips in Japan, had a checkered career. Created in 1930 by scriptwriter Ichirō Suzuki and artist Takeo Nagamatsu as a *kamishibai* (comic strip for public narration), it soon became famous and lasted until 1935. Ogon Bat (whose name came from a popular brand of cigarette) was a justice fighter who wore a golden hood and a red cape and could fly in the air. At its peak of popularity (1930-34) *Ogon Bat* inspired a host of imitators. After the Pacific War (1946) *Ogon Bat* again reappeared as a *kamishibai* done by Kouji Kata; Nagamatsu recreated his own version of the character in 1947. Four comic books of Nagamatsu's *Ogon Bat* were published from November 1947 to March 1949. From July 1948 to May 1950 it also appeared in the comic monthly *Bōken Katsugeki Bunko* (later *Shōnen Gaho*).

The new Ogon Bat wore a skull-mask, a broad-brimmed hat, and a musketeer costume. The story was a parable of good and evil as Ogon Bat (who was a demigod rather than a mere human being) and his allies, the private detective Oki, Queen Shima, and the great scientist, Dr. Mōguri, battled the forces of darkness led by Kuro Bat ("the Black Bat"), later rechristened Nazo. Ogon Bat's most terrifying weapon was his sardonic laugh, which instilled fear in the hearts of his enemies when they heard it.

Nagamatsu's style, a cross between the American comic book and the illustrated story, was an oddity in Japanese comics of the time. *Ogon Bat* was made into a series of animated cartoons. In 1967 it was revived briefly in *Shōnen Gaho* and *Shōnen King*, and two *Ogon Bat* comic books appeared in May 1975.

H.K.

OHSER, ERICH (1903-1944) German artist/cartoonist born March 18, 1903, in Untergettengrun near Plauen, Saxony, where he grew up. He studied in Leipzig and started drawing cartoons for the *Sächsische Sozialdemokratische Presse* (Saxon Social Democratic Press) in 1928, and continued cartooning for the newspapers *Vorwärts*, *Wahrer Jakob*, *Querschnitt*, and *Neue*

Erich Ohser, "Vater und Sohn." © Südverlag Constanz.

Revue until 1933. In 1934 he came up with *Vater und Sohn* ("Father and Son"), which was published in the *Berliner Illustrirte*. This magazine, like *Das Reich*, also published Ohser's editorial cartoons. At that time Ohser was better known by his pen name E. O. Plauen, derived by adding the name of his hometown to the initials of his real name. Ohser's way to Berlin had been paved by Erich Kästner, world famous for his children's books. From the end of the 1920s, Ohser had been Kästner's satirical brother-in-arms, illustrating Kästner's books.

Ohser's *Vater und Sohn* enjoyed tremendous success. The strip was loved and cherished by millions. It was reprinted in Africa, America, and Australia, and there were even Chinese editions. Exporting *Vater und Sohn* to foreign countries was not much of a problem, as it was a pantomime comic strip in a clearly drawn, easily understandable cartoon style.

In addition to *Vater und Sohn*, the *Berliner Illustrirte* also published another comic strip, *Die fünf Schreckensteiner* ("The five Schreckensteiners," 1939-40) by Barlog, who also did a number of comic features for department-store giveaway children's magazines. These strips in a way prove that the Wilhelm Busch tradition of comic art never died out in Germany. The fact that, with the exception of *Vater und Sohn*, these comic strips are virtually unknown today sheds an interesting light on the kind of esteem Germany has for her comic and cartoon art. After 1974, some of the material reappeared in collectors' circles.

Erich Ohser, despite being adored by his readers, was not treated too well by Third Reich Germany. Following a denunciation for "defeatist remarks in an air-raid shelter," Ohser was arrested, together with a friend, by the Gestapo. This drove him to commit suicide in his cell in March 1944 before he could be brought to trial. His friend was executed.

W.F.

OKAMOTO, IPPEI (1886-1948) Japanese cartoonist and writer born June 11, 1886, in Hakodate, Hokkaidō. After graduation from the Tokyo School of Fine Arts in 1906, Ippei Okamoto took a job as stage painter for one year under Professor Wada.

In 1912 Okamoto made his debut as a cartoonist, working for the newspaper *Asahi*. His talent as a prom-

ising cartoonist was recognized by the famous Japanese writer Sōseki Natsume, after the publication of his first work, *Kuma o Tazunete* ("A Visit to the Bear") that same year. Soon Okamoto displayed great creative activity, and his comic stories for magazines and newspapers were being reprinted in book form as quickly as he could turn them out: *Tanpō Gashu* (his first published work, 1913); *Kanraku* ("Surrender," 1914); *Match no Bou* ("Matchstick," 1915); *Monomiyusan* ("The Sightseeing Picnic," 1920); and *Nakimushi Dera no Yawa* (his most famous story in comic form, "Night Tales at Nakimushi Temple," 1921).

In 1921 Okamoto started on a round-the-world journey that lasted over one year and took him to the United States, England, France, Germany, Italy, and other countries. During his travels he met with foreign cartoonists, visited the offices of *Punch*, and put down many of his observations on paper. Upon his return, he introduced popular American strips, such as *Mutt and Jeff* and *Bringing Up Father*, to the Japanese public. The account of his journey, which appeared in *Asahi* and in *Fujokai* magazine, was released in book form in 1924.

More of Okamoto's works continued to appear: *Yajikita Saikou* ("The Resurrection of Yajikita," 1925); *Ippei Zenshū* (a 15-volume anthology of Okamoto's greatest works, published in 1929-30); and *Shin Mizu ya Sora* (Okamoto's masterwork, a collection of caricatures, 1929) are probably the most famous. Around the same time Okamoto published his famous novel *Fuji wa Sankaku* ("Mt. Fuji is Triangular," 1927).

Ippei Okamoto was the greatest cartoonist of the Taishō era (1912-1926) and the early Shōwa era. He produced many comic strips, humor cartoons, and illustrations; he was also a noted author who wrote several novels and essays. His cartoon creations were dignified and a bit stuffy, but his writings were light and humorous. He contributed mightily to raise the social status of cartoon art, and he was also a pioneer in the use of comics in advertising. He influenced many Japanese cartoonists, such as Shigeo Miyao, Kon Shimizu, Yukio Sugiura, Hidezō Kondō, and others.

Ippei Okamoto's wife, Kanoko Okamoto, was also a famous writer, and his son, Tarō Okamoto, was a noted contemporary painter. Ippei Okamoto died in October 1948.

H.K.

O'KEEFE, NEIL (1893-198?) American cartoonist and illustrator born April 19, 1893, in Galveston, Texas. His father, Colonel John O'Keefe, retired when Neil was still a child and took his family to St. Louis, where the young O'Keefe attended St. Margaret's School, McKinley High, and Washington University. O'Keefe went to work in the art department of the *St. Louis Post-Dispatch* in 1913, going on to the *Chicago Tribune* one year later. In 1918 O'Keefe moved to St. Paul, Minnesota, as a writer for the *Daily News*, also occasionally doing a sports column, *As I Saw It*.

O'Keefe's cartooning really took flight in 1921 when he succeeded such luminaries of the art as Rollin Kirby and Gene Carr on *Metropolitan Movies*. Around the same time he started doing illustrations for the pulp magazines, quickly becoming one of the most noted, and one of the most prolific, pulp artists.

Called in by King Features to replace Lyman Anderson on *Inspector Wade* in July 1938, O'Keefe stayed with the syndicate for the rest of his career. After *Wade* was dropped in 1941, he became one of King's staff cartoonists, moving up to art director of Hearst's Sunday supplement, the *American Humorist*, in 1944. Along with writer Max Trell, O'Keefe created *Dick's Adventures in Dreamland* in 1947. A rather tepid account of great events in American history, it died in 1956. After some more years of illustration, O'Keefe retired in the 1960s. He reportedly died some time in the 1980s.

One of King Features's unsung journeymen artists, O'Keefe deserved better than the second-string features he got. Certainly, he would have made a better *X-9* or *Jungle Jim* artist than either Mel Graff or Paul Norris. His work had the bittersweet quality of a talent deserving of better things.

M.H.

OLD DOC YAK (U.S.) Sidney Smith's *Old Doc Yak* (which ran from March 10, 1912, to June 22, 1919, as a Sunday page) was one of the three foremost pioneers of the humanized animal strip (with James Swinnerton's *Mr. Jack* at the turn of the century and Dok Hager's *Dippy Duck* of the 1910s), and easily the most successful of its time.

From an early date, Smith had included a goat caricature as a signature accessory or speaking character in many of his sports and political cartoons. By 1908, when he was working on the *Chicago Examiner*'s sports page, Smith elevated the goat to stardom in his first serious attempt at a comic strip, and named him with the strip: Buck Nix. Appearing daily only, Buck moved in a world of other humanized goats and became involved in a series of suspenseful continued adventures, among the first in daily comics (rescuing girlfriend Nanny Millionbuck from kidnappers, etc.), most of which revolved around money and the need for money—vis: the hero's name—and the sporadic, grim advice of an old goat in black spectacles and frock coat called The Old Man of Mystery. Highly imaginative, funny, and enormously entertaining when read today, the popular *Buck Nix* led to Smith's being hired away from the *Examiner* by the *Chicago Tribune*, where he was asked to continue his strip under a new name. To avoid legal problems with the *Examiner*, Buck was changed from a goat to a yak, and the new strip, to be run as a Sunday page feature only, was titled *Old Doc Yak*.

Old Doc Yak was an even more sensational success than *Buck Nix* in Chicago, and gained Smith nationwide syndication, running for eight years in the *Tribune* until the greater impact of Smith's *The Gumps* closed it down after the introduction of the Sunday *Gumps* page in 1919. Smith added other animal characters to his original all-goat cast: hippos, monkeys, tigers, all in a very humanized world centered on Doc Yak's love affair with his sports car (which bore a huge license plate number that became as famous as the strip: 348). Doc Yak also acquired a young son named Yutch, and a recurring rival and enemy in the form of a hairy-eared black bear given several names (Greisheim and Metzler, to name just two) during the course of the strip. Several of Doc Yak's Sunday adventures were as suspenseful and fantastic as the daily escapades of Buck Nix, later narratives being satirically tied into World War I.

Old Doc Yak was revived by Smith on December 7, 1930, as a four-panel Sunday companion strip to *The Gumps*, dealing largely with Doc Yak's verbal and fistic encounters with the bear. It was folded with the last Sidney Smith-signed Sunday page on December 8, 1935.

Old Doc Yak was made into a movie in April 1916.

B.B.

OLD GLORY STORY, THE (U.S.) In May 1953 the Chicago Tribune-New York News Syndicate debuted a Sunday-only strip that paired the creative team of history writer Athena Robbins and *Chicago Tribune* staff artist Rick Fletcher.

The Old Glory Story focused on the history around the different flags flown in America, beginning with the colonial period. Initially the strip proceeded chronologically through the European settlement of America, the Indian wars, the American Revolution, the War of 1812, and so on. While often featuring military conflict, *Old Glory* also did extended stories on the mountain men of the West and such developments in the East as the Erie Canal. However, more often than not, armed conflict, even if on the level of cowboys and Indians, was deemed necessary to keep this comic strip history lesson lively and interesting.

The strip benefitted by the centennial of the American Civil War (1961-65). The title was modified, to *Old Glory at the Crossroads*, and Sunday after Sunday a wonderful cartoon history of the Civil War was presented. Because of the great interest in the Civil War, circulation of the strip reached its peak during this period. Ironically, once the centennial ended and *Old Glory* returned to a cowboys-and-Indians type story of westward expansion, the strip soon ended, not even finishing out 1965. This might be due in part to Rick Fletcher having become the lead assistant to Chester Gould on *Dick Tracy* beginning in 1963.

Fletcher's representation of the Civil War was definitely a tour de force. Returning to less dynamic subject matter, as *Old Glory*'s circulation slipped, must have seemed anticlimactic. For Fletcher, the relationship with *Dick Tracy* continued until the cartoonist's death in 1983. During that time, Fletcher, who inherited the strip in late 1977 when Gould retired, was instrumental in bringing many technological advances to Tracy's police technique. These current police procedures and techniques were lost from the strip after he died.

The format for *Old Glory* featured illustration with text underneath. Word balloons were not used. Although created in the "politically incorrect" days of telling only one side of America's westward expansion, the scripts still hold up as basic history. Fletcher's research on costumes, uniforms, and the moods of different time periods was as excellent as his artwork. Comics are a visual medium, and *Old Glory*, which has rarely been reprinted, remains a visual treat.

B.C.

OLD TIMER, THE *see* Snake Tales.

O-MAN (Japan) *O-Man* was created by Osamu Tezuka for the Japanese comic weekly *Shōnen Sunday* in August 1959.

O-Men were higher creatures than human beings who inhabited an underground city in the Himalayan glaciers. O-Men were descended from squirrels and had a vestigial tail. Rickie was a young O-Man who had been brought up by a Japanese man named called Chikara, and who opposed the evil designs of Daisokān ("the Archbishop"), a leader of the O-Men who dreamed of wiping out the whole human race and taking over the earth. Wanting to make Tokyo his first outpost for conquest, Daisokān unleashed his dreaded Electric Freezing Machine and froze the whole world by error.

Rickie, with the aim of stopping the machine, returned to the O-Men's world, and was befriended by Daisokān's daughter Reeze. After many adventures, a closed-door conference between humans and O-Men, and a raid on the Freezing Machine, Rickie succeeded in stirring up the O-Men against the rule of Daisokān; a revolution ensued and the evil leader was overthrown.

Daisokān did not give up his ambitions, however; while in exile he entered into league with a group of cutthroats whose aim was also world domination. Internal strife brought about their downfall in the end.

O-Man is regarded as one of Tezuka's masterpieces, along with *Tetsuwan-Atom, Jungle Taitei,* and *Hinotori.* The drawings had the brooding, fragile quality of all of Tezuka's creations, while the storyline continually surprised and enchanted with its twists and turns and its inexhaustible inventiveness.

O-Man was reprinted many times in both hardcover and paperback form.

H.K.

O'NEAL, FRANK (1921-1986) American cartoonist born in Springfield, Missouri, on May 9, 1921. Frank O'Neal received a desultory education in schools from Arkansas to California, following his traveling father. After service in World War II, O'Neal attended art classes for three years with noted cartoonist Jefferson Machamer. In 1950 he sold his first cartoon to the *Saturday Evening Post.* Thus encouraged, he decided to embark on a full-time cartooning career, and became a contributor to many national magazines and publications.

In 1956 Frank O'Neal took a job drawing storyboards for television but quit in 1958 when his strip *Short Ribs* (depicting the outlandish doings of a host of nutty characters) was accepted by NEA Service. He worked on the strip for the 15 years until, due to diminishing financial returns, O'Neal abandoned *Short Ribs* to his assistant, Frank Hill, in 1973. He devoted the rest of his life to advertising and commercial art, and died in Pacific Groves, California, on October 10, 1986.

Frank O'Neal ranks higher as a keen observer of the absurdities of life and as an inventive and witty humorist (both in his dialogues and in his situations) than as a cartooning innovator. His drawing style, clean and functional, was perfectly suited, however, to his Martini-dry wit.

M.H.

O'NEIL, DENNIS (1939-) American comic book writer and editor born May 3, 1939, in Clayton, Missouri. After a short stint as a Marvel assistant editor in 1965, Denny O'Neil moved to Charlton and wrote for editor Dick Giordano under the pen name Sergius O'Shaugnessey. He worked on a variety of superhero and adventure books, but his best work was *Children of Doom,* a chilling postnuclear holocast tale, and it presaged a long string of O'Neil's later "social consciousness" stories.

When Giordano moved to National in 1968, O'Neil went along and scripted dozens of stories for superhero

titles like *Creeper, Justice League, Atom, Hawkman,* and several others. But, like his previous Charlton work, O'Neil's best material came on comic books that later came to be called "relevant." Along with editor Julie Schwartz and artist Neal Adams, O'Neil began producing the *Green Lantern/Green Arrow* series in 1970, and the title became an instant classic due to his sharp, hard-hitting scripts and Adams's inspired artwork. O'Neil took on all the subjects previously taboo in comic books; he did stories on political repression, cultism, Jesus-freaks, slumlords, racism, and many other "touchy" topics. Two highly publicized O'Neil stories cast Green Arrow's sullen young assistant, Speedy, as a heroin addict. Unfortunately, the series folded after two years amidst high praise, low sales, and increasingly antagonistic relationships between the creators.

O'Neil continued to write superhero, mystery, and adventure stories for National, and also became an editor. Quickly becoming one of the most respected writers in the field, he was subsequently asked by National to revamp *Superman* (as a writer) and *Wonder Woman* (as writer/editor); when National revived *Captain Marvel,* O'Neil became the top writer, and he edited and wrote the revived *Shadow* title for National in 1973. Quite different from much of his earlier material, *Shadow* afforded O'Neil an opportunity to create mood and period pieces, and he and artists Mike Kaluta and Frank Robbins produced several outstanding issues despite artistic conflicts and flagging sales. In the course of his decades-long career at DC (formerly National), O'Neil worked on many of the company's titles, but he remains best noted for his contributions to *Batman* in the 1970s and 1980s.

J.B.

O'NEILL, DAN (1942-) Dan O'Neill is an American underground comix artist and writer born in 1942. A former Catholic seminarian, O'Neill began his underground career in 1967 when he began producing a strip titled *Odd Bodkins* for the *San Francisco Chronicle.*

Dan O'Neill, "Dan O'Neill's Comics."

Odd Bodkins was different from strips running either in the "straight" newspapers or in the underground newspapers that were beginning to flourish at the time. Basically, it concerned itself with two characters named Hugh and Fred, neither of whom looked the same from one panel to another. Fred had what passed as a beak of sorts, and Hugh was a little taller than Fred, but those were about the only definitions the characters retained. In fact, the whole strip was odd. Characters and backgrounds were always in transition and color came and went in an apparently capricious manner.

The strip itself had a philosophical bent, but most critics and readers found it hard to consistently decipher O'Neill's meanings. One example, a strip entitled "God is a Rock," concerned a repartee between Fred, Hugh, and Lulu the garter snake. Fred tells Hugh that God is everywhere; Hugh therefore decides God must be under a nearby rock because he is everywhere. Under the rock, Hugh finds Lulu the snake, thinks she is God, and then ponders the "fact" that both God and Lucifer are snakelike. In another strip, "100% American Dog in Magic Cookie Land," Hugh decides all he has learned from a long, color-laden adventure is that "Life can be a picnic . . . only if you accept the ants."

O'Neill produced *Odd Bodkins* off and on for the *Chronicle*—and for about 350 underground papers that carried it via the Underground Press Syndicate—until 1969, when he left after a censorship hassle. He later redrew some of the strips for the underground comix market under the title, *Dan O'Neill's Comics and Stories*. Three issues were published by Company and Sons in 1971 and *Odd Bodkins* was also released as a series of Glide books in large, paperback format.

During the *Odd Bodkins* fun, O'Neill infused parodies of Walt Disney characters throughout. Mickey and Minnie Mouse and many others frequently appeared, because, like many cartoonists, O'Neill had been greatly influenced by the old Disney movies and comic strips. In 1971, O'Neill and several other artists produced two comic books—*Mickey Mouse Meets the Air Pirates* and *Air Pirates* number two—that took this Disney parody to its logical conclusion. In short, the books were Walt Disney characters grown up, and some depicted sexual scenes, including a celebrated tableau in which Mickey Mouse and Minnie performed sex acts.

The Disney empire was incensed, of course, and quickly moved to block publication of the third issue. It then sued O'Neill and his associates, Ted Richards, Bobby London, Ron Turner, and Gary Hallgren, for $700,000. The latter two eventually settled out of court, but O'Neill, London, and Richards remained adamant; the trial finally began in August 1975. In the interim, O'Neill garnered considerable publicity from the case and the two issues of *Air Pirates* became collectors' items.

J.B.

In July 1976 the three holdouts issued a four-page illustrated pamphlet, *Walt Disney versus the Air Pirates*, explaining their position and asking for donations to their legal defense fund. Despite this last-ditch effort they eventually lost the case. Outside of an occasional story, O'Neill has largely remained inactive in the field of comix since that time.

M.H.

O'NEILL, ROSE CECIL (1874-1944) Rose O'Neill, the woman who had the genius to give the common choirloft cupid a nickname and who drew her famed *Kewpies* as a comic strip for over a quarter of a century, was born Rose Cecil O'Neill in Wilkes-Barre, Pennsylvania, in 1874. Her father, a merchant, moved his family shortly afterward to Omaha, where his daughter attended the Sacred Heart Convent and won an art competition sponsored by the *Omaha Herald* at the age of 13, drawing a series of weekly cartoons for the paper as a result. By 1889, when she was 15 and the family had moved to New York, Rose O'Neill had sold cartoons and drawings to such major magazines as *Puck, Judge, Life, Truth,* and *Harper's*. Her first, brief marriage at 18 was to a Gray Latham, who died five years later. Four years after his death, she had married the editor of *Puck*, Harry Leon Wilson, later to be famed as the author of *Merton of the Movies*, and illustrated his early novels, such as *The Spenders* (1902) and *The Lions of the Lord* (1903). In 1904, she wrote and illustrated her own first novel, *The Loves of Edwy*. After a trip to Italy and her divorce from Wilson, the writer and artist became a full-time freelancer. She drew her first group of clustered cupids, with curly topknots borrowed from Palmer Cox's popular Brownies, to illustrate some children's verses which she printed in the *Ladies' Home Journal* in 1905. She called them Kewpies, and their public impact was sensational.

Before six months had passed, she was being bid for by the top magazines in the country. *The Woman's Home Companion* paid a small fortune to obtain her Kewpie drawings in 1910, then *Good Housekeeping* paid more. In 1913, George Borgfeldt & Co. of New York manufactured the first of the famed Kewpie dolls that circled the globe in millions over the next two decades. By 1917, Rose O'Neill had drawn, copyrighted, and syndicated a Sunday comic page devoted to verses and drawings of the Kewpies, with a different title each week; it lasted a year and was widely printed, as were her daily *Kewpie* panels of the same period.

Fifteen years later, she was persuaded by King Features to renew her feature, this time as a weekly Sunday page with dialogue balloons and continuity; it appeared early in 1935 and ran until late in the decade. In 1937, however, she retired and left New York to live on a farm in the Ozark Mountains that she had purchased earlier, after an active and Bohemian social life of many years. Here she continued her painting and drawing, but fell into ill health and moved in with nearby relatives in Springfield, Missouri, where she died on April 6, 1944, at the age of 69.

Curiously, no animated cartoons were made of the Kewpies, and only a few books based on them were published, mostly paper-doll and coloring books in paper covers. Two somewhat more substantial titles were *The Kewpies, Their Book* (1911) and *The Kewpie Primer* (1916), but all are now very rare. A contemporary collection of the strips is long overdue.

B.B.

ON STAGE (U.S.) Artist-writer Leonard Starr created *On Stage* for the Tribune-News Syndicate on February 10, 1957.

On Stage's heroine, Mary Perkins, was in the beginning a naive small-town girl who had come to New York to seek her big chance on Broadway. In the first year of the strip she was "discovered" by a deranged stage director, chosen on a bet by star photographer

"On Stage," Leonard Starr. © Chicago Tribune-New York News Syndicate.

Pete Fletcher, picked for an ingenue role in summer stock, lured to Hollywood by a megalomaniacal movie producer, saved from his clutches by a friendly gangster, and was back on Broadway without so much as a missing eyelash.

After that Mary slowed down somewhat, married Pete Fletcher, and went on to make her mark on the stage and in movies. She still kept right on meeting outlandish characters, from the enticing and venomous Morganna D'Alexias to Maximus, "the man without a face," a Phantom-of-the-Opera type. But she matured considerably in the course of the strip and became able to face any situation with cool and aplomb.

On Stage was a stage opera with something extra. The atmosphere, settings, and characters were realistically rendered without excluding humor and even poetry. Starr excelled in the depiction of subtle emotions, furtive expressions, and revealing gestures. Incisive plotting, literate writing, and elegant drawing were some of *On Stage*'s hallmarks, making it one of the best of contemporary comic strips.

Despite its graphic and narrative excellence, *On Stage*, like all story strips, suffered in the 1970s from the growing disaffection of the public toward continuing series, and its circulation slowly eroded. Starr finally abandoned his creation in the fall of 1979, after he had been asked by the syndicate to take charge of the born-again *Annie* strip.

M.H.

OOR WULLIE (G.B.) "Oor Wullie," translated into English, is "Our Willie." He is the scrub-headed star of a Scottish dialect strip that appears on the front page of *Fun Section*, the pullout and foldover comic supplement to the *Sunday Post*, a weekly newspaper published in Scotland by D. C. Thomson. *Oor Wullie*, created by Dudley D. Watkins (who also drew the other full-page dialect strip, *The Broons* ("The Browns"), has appeared continuously since the first issue of the supplement on March 8, 1936.

Wullie begins and ends each adventure sitting on an upturned bucket, and his catchline "Oor Wullie, Your

"Oor Wullie," Dudley Watkins. © Sunday Post.

Wullie, A'body's Wullie" ("anybody's Willie") describes his character, as does the verse that introduces one of his book appearances (to the tune of *Comin' Thro the Rye*): "Gin a body meet a laddie, Fower an' a half feet high./Towsy-heided, rosy-cheekit, Mischief in his eye./Patchit breeks an' bulgin' pockets. Fu' of spirit forbye,/Then like as no' ye've met Oor Wullie, Scotland's fly wee guy."

Wullie divides his time between house and home, one of these being a shaky structure scrawled with the words "Wullie's Shed." In this structure lives his wee moose ("mouse"), Jeemy ("Jimmy"). Friends and acquaintances include Fat Bob, Soapy Soutar, Wee Eck, and P. C. Murdoch, not to mention a particularly human Ma and Pa. He also has very deep pockets in his dungarees, only slightly less capacious than Harpo Marx's, which can be relied upon to provide almost anything in an emergency.

The strips have been reprinted in annual collections since October 1940. They are still running as of 1997.

D.G.

OPPER, FREDERICK BURR (1857-1937) The famed creator of *Happy Hooligan, Maud, Alphonse and Gaston,* and other immortal comic characters, Frederick Burr Opper was born on January 2, 1857, to Austrian immi-

F. B. Opper, magazine cartoon.

"Yes, Willie, this is a rubber toy to amuse you and Teddy. It represents the Working Classes. See how Papa pulls its leg."

F. B. Opper, political cartoon.

grant parents in Madison, Ohio. A prospering craftsman, Opper's father, Lewis, was the brother of the once-noted newsman Adolphe Opper, who wrote under the name De Blowitz as Paris correspondent of the *London Times* in the 1880s. The young Fred, aware of his considerable cartooning talent, cared little for formal schooling and left high school to go to work on the *Madison Gazette* when he was 14. Eager for recognition, he mailed cartoons to notable magazines of the time; his art was often purchased, and appeared in such titles as *Scribner's*, *The Century*, and *St. Nicholas*. Encouraged, he left for the east coast before he was 20 and almost at once found a staff artist job on a now-forgotten magazine called *Wild Oats* (managing to make eating money at a dry-goods store job at the same time).

Meanwhile, he continued to freelance work to other magazines, including *Puck* and *Harper's Bazaar*, where Colonel Frank Leslie, publisher of *Leslie's Magazine* (a news publication), saw the young man's work and hired him as a news correspondent, cartoonist, and artist. After three busy years with *Leslie's*, Opper found a better-paying position as *Puck's* leading political cartoonist, a job he held for many years, until William Randolph Hearst hired him in 1899, when Opper was 42, to do weekly humor cartoons for Hearst's American Humorist section of the *New York Journal*. Here the now famed cartoonist and book illustrator (his works included *The Hoosier Schoolmaster*, Bill Nye's *Comic History of the U.S.*, Eugene Field's *Tribune Primer*, and several Twain stories collected in book form) drew additional readers to the Hearst papers in New York and San Francisco—especially when a plump, ragged little tramp with a blue tin-can hat named Happy Hooligan made his first appearance on March 26, 1900. The public loved the tramp, and although Opper tried other characters from time to time, such as a comic farmer named Uncle Si and a practical joker named Mr. Henry Peck, it quickly became obvious that the readers primarily wanted as much Hooligan as possible. They got him almost every week in the Hearst comics, and in a succession of popular reprint collections through the early 1900s. By this time, Opper had fully grasped the potentials of the new comic strip medium and was introducing still more widely popular characters, such as Alphonse and Gaston, and Maud the Mule, all of

whom began appearing in their own strips concurrently with *Hooligan* (often appearing together in the same Sunday section) and in books of their own as well.

In the meantime Opper's competence as a political cartoonist had not gone unnoticed by Hearst, and Opper put in a major daily stint doing topical cartoons for the daily Hearst press from the turn of the century on, a task which delighted Opper, and which he continued side by side with his strip work for the rest of his life. Opper's bloated oil industry tycoons, porcine capitalists, and shrewdly caricatured politicians from Bryan through Hoover were as widely recognized comic figures among the general public as Opper's own strip characters; and he often organized the former into strip sequences with running titles, such as "Mr. Trusty," "The Cruise of the Piffle," and "The Free-neasy Film Co. Presents," which Hearst ran daily on his papers' editorial pages.

Opper did little daily strip work, doing a few spot gag sequences now and again, and attempting a brief daily version of *Happy Hooligan* in the early 1920s. In the Sunday comic section, however, he did as many as three separate full- and half-page episodes a week during the 1900s and early 1910s, finally falling back on a single weekly page dealing with Hooligan, but into which he would periodically reintroduce such popular figures as Maud, Si, Alphonse and Gaston, Gloomy Gus, and others. By the end of the 1920s, he had become recognized as the Dean Emeritus of American strip artists because of his fame, competence, and comparative maturity in years.

Forced by failing eyesight to give up his weekly strip and daily political cartoons in 1932, Opper went into semiretirement, managing to do a bit of special cartooning now and again, at his estate in New Rochelle, New York, where he died of heart trouble on August 28, 1937. His claim to fame is self-evident.

B.B.

ORLANDO, JOE (1927-) American comic book artist and editor born April 4, 1927, in Bari, Italy. He and his family immigrated to the United States in 1929, and Orlando first became acquainted with comic art by reading *Tarzan* in the Italian language daily *Il Progresso*. Orlando attended the High School of Art and Design—classmates were comic book artist Rocco Mastroserio and singer Tony Bennett—and then served in Europe as part of the U.S. Army's occupation. When he returned, he attended the Art Students League, and about this time began his comic book career by illustrating the *Chuck White* adventure strip in the educational *Treasure Chest* comic book.

In 1950, he and Wallace Wood opened an art studio and began producing science-fiction material for Avon, Youthful, Charlton, and Ziff-Davis. When Wood moved to E.C., Orlando briefly went his own way but soon joined E.C. when they were looking for someone to draw in Wood's style. He was assigned to the horror and science-fiction titles, and while publisher Gaines said he was "a little stiff with his interpretations," he was more than adequate. He drew most of his material in a clean, unpretentious, and straightforward manner, and it would have been conspicuously excellent at any other comic group of the 1950s; but at E.C. Orlando had to take a back seat to the likes of Crandall, Ingels, Frazetta, Wood, Williamson, and many others.

When E.C. folded in 1956, Orlando moved on to work for the horror and science-fiction comics published by Stan Lee's Atlas group, and then began drawing for *Mad*. By the end of the decade, however, Orlando was concentrating almost entirely on advertising art and painting, but when James Warren began his black-and-white comic magazine line with *Creepy* in 1964, Orlando was one of the heaviest and best contributors. His artwork had become more stylized and intricate, but it was still amazingly well-paced and fluid; his storytelling and page composition remained deceptively simple.

In 1966, National elevated artist Carmine Infantino to editorial director and Orlando was one of the first new wave of artist/editors he hired. His best book was *Swamp Thing*, a stellar horror title written by Len Wein and drawn by Berni Wrightson. Orlando was named vice president at DC in the late 1970s; he retired in 1996.

J.B.

ORMES, JACKIE (1915-1986) Jackie Ormes holds a special place in the history of American newspaper cartooning as the first African-American woman to create, write, and draw a comic strip that became nationally syndicated. Her strip, *Torchy Brown, From Dixie to Harlem*, was first published by the *Pittsburgh Courier*, a black-owned newspaper, in 1937. The strip was syndicated to other black newspapers. It was not until 1991, when Universal Press Syndicate began to distribute Barbara Brandon's *Where I'm Coming From*, that an African-American woman cartoonist was syndicated by a major mainstream syndicate.

Ormes's romantic adventure strip, featuring sexy black heroine Torchy Brown, predated the debut of Dale Messick's *Brenda Starr* by three years. It is fair to note that while Messick had to battle sexism in her rise to become a mainstream syndicate star, Jackie Ormes had the double whammy of sexism and racism working against her break into the big time.

Torchy Brown's adventures took her from the rural South to the Apollo Theater in New York City. Mixed in with all the romance was a realistic portrait of African-American culture in the 1930s. However, the revenues from the strip were disappointing, and Ormes dropped *Torchy Brown* in 1940, turning to magazine and advertising art to make a living.

In the 1940s Ormes was a newspaper reporter and cartoonist for the black-owned *Chicago Defender*. Her single-panel strip *Candy* starred an African-American maid. *PattyJo 'n Ginger* was a single panel created by Ormes at the request of Smith-Mann Syndicate in 1950. The humor panel, featuring a young African-American girl as its star, even sparked the merchandising of a PattyJo 'n Ginger doll that is now an expensive collectible. Also in 1950, Torchy Brown returned to newspapers, with the feature renamed *Torchy Brown Heartbeats*. It was published through 1955.

The character of Torchy was always a bit more risqué than her white contemporary, Brenda Starr. While Dale Messick used pinups of Brenda to catch the eye of male readers, Jackie Ormes often let her heroine's voluptuous charms be seen in lingerie. Although both Torchy and Brenda shared many heartbreaks, Torchy's boyfriends were always more rough-and-tumble and more sexually aggressive. However, a more significant difference was that while *Brenda Starr* remained basically soap opera fluff, *Torchy Brown* showed in stark realism the problems of racism, bigotry, and even environmental pollution. It would be almost 40 years before mainstream soap-opera strips could even come close to the realism and passion that Ormes presented in these themes.

Jackie Ormes is truly an unsung heroine of American cartooning. During her lifetime her success was unfortunately limited because *Torchy Brown* was only printed in black-owned newspapers and not in a wider market. Still, in Torchy Ormes created a proud, strong African-American heroine, not just the one-dimensional character seen in so many soap-opera strips.

B.C.

OSCAR (Italy) When Oscar was created by Luciano Bottaro in 1959, he was then named Nasolungo ("Bignose"), and slated to appear, along with a host of other characters, in the new monthly publication planned by publisher Angelo Fasani. The name of this comic monthly was to be *Il Musichiere*, also the name of a popular television show of the time. Just as the magazine was due to come out, however, the TV show was dropped, and Fasani decided to change the name of the new publication to *Oscar*. As there was no character by that name in the scheduled features, Bottaro and his scriptwriter Carlo Chendi were asked to write a story in which their Nasolungo character would acquire the nickname "Oscar."

Oscar's first issue came out in 1960. It featured the works of cartoonists G.B. Carpi, Giulio Chierchini, Franco Aloisi, Giancarlo Tonna, and others. Luciano Bottaro, busy as usual, left the drawing in the hands of one or another of his assistants after the 10th episode. The scripts were mostly written by B. Torelli, Carlo Chendi, and Bottaro himself. In the stories—which took place in the African bush country—Nasolungo (alias Oscar) was a professional game warden and an amateur actor in his spare time. Oscar's constant antagonist was Gambacorta ("Shortleg"), a scheming mouse always trying by hook or by crook to kidnap the jungle animals and sell them to some zoo. The series was also enhanced by a rich assortment of characters: an opera-singing hippopotamus afflicted with a terrible-tempered wife; a cowardly octopus; a raven detective; and a worm with a superiority complex, among others.

In the summer of 1961, Oscar was reprinted in a splendid four-color gift album, an unusual occurrence in Italy at the time (the practice later became standard among publishers of comics). In this album were also featured two other Bottaro creations: Piper Maiopi (about a comic-opera sheriff) and Lola and Otello. Oscar has also been published in France, in the pages of the magazine Bravo.

During the publishing crisis of the mid-1960s, Angelo Fasani retired, leaving his publishing house in the hands of his son Franco, who proved to be more interested in adult magazines than in comics, and he soon ended Oscar.

G.B.

OSHIMA, YUMIKO (1947-) Yumiko Oshima made her professional debut in 1968 in Shueisha Publishing's popular weekly girl's comics magazine Margaret with the short story Pora no namida ("Paula's Tears") while still at student at a two-year college. Although her first story was a melodrama that was typical of the genre of Japanese girls' comics, or shojo manga, at the time, Oshima soon carved out an utterly singular niche for herself. In 1970 she stunned readers and gained the attention of critics with Tanjo ("Birth," also published in Margaret), a story of a teenage girl's pregnancy that probed the most basic questions of existence. In 1973, the ordinarily cliquish Japan Comic Artists Association, Nihon Mangaka Kyokai, presented the young Oshima with their Excellence Award, Yushusho.

Oshima is best known for her only multi-volume work, Wata no kunihoshi ("The Country-Star of Cotton"), which tells the story of Chibi, a kitten who believes she will one day grow to be a human being. With a heroine (the kitten) portrayed as a little girl with a kitten's ears and tail wearing a frilly dress, this work is often dismissed as simply "cute," but a close reading reveals serious themes: the fear of becoming physically mature, maternal rejection (a recurring Oshima theme since her debut work), and the inevitability of death. For Wata no kunihoshi, Oshima was awarded the Kodansha Comic Award in 1979.

The vast majority of Oshima's work, however, is short stories, a fact which, in the Japanese comics industry, all but precludes popular success. It is a testimony to the power of her work that, in spite of this fact, she is one of the most beloved and influential members of a loosely defined group of groundbreaking women artists known as the Hana no nijuyonen gumi ("Magnificent 24-Year Group") because many were born in the year Showa 24, or 1949. (Other "Forty-Niners" include Moto Hagio, Keiko Takemiya, and Ryoko Yamagishi.)

Oshima's power stems from her uncanny talent for exploring the most profound themes through characters, settings, and storylines that seem whimsical: on the first page the reader is laughing, on the last, weeping. There is a dreamlike surrealism to her stories, but never a hint of the irony or cynicism that many in the West consider to be the sine qua non of "artistic" works.

The Oshima Yumiko senshu ("Selected Works of Yumiko Oshima") spans 16 volumes to date. Two of Oshima's stories, Shigatsu kaidan ("April Ghost Story") and Mainichi ga natsu yasumi ("Every Day Is Summer Vacation"), were made into feature films, and another, Akihiko kaku katariki ("Thus Spoke Akihiko") was made into a movie for television.

M.A.T.

OSOMATSU-KUN (Japan) Osomatsu-kun (which can be loosely translated as "the Osomatsu Clan") was created by Fujio Akatsuka and made its first appearance in April 1962 in the pages of the weekly Shōnen Sunday.

Osomatsu was one of sextuplets (his five brothers were Choromatsu, Ichimatsu, Jūshimatsu, Karamatsu, and Todomatsu). They were children of a working family, and all exhibited the same characteristics of idleness, uncouthness, and naughtiness embodied in their collective personality called "Osomatsu-kun." The Osomatsu kids had two principal enemies: Chibita, a sneaky, hateful, and gluttonous little boy; and Iyami, a sissified, disagreeable, and cunning prig (modelled after the Japanese actor Tony Tani) who always gave out a little cry, "Shē," when he was surprised by some of the boys' pranks (the cry started a fad among youngsters in Japan at the time).

Some of the other characters included Dekapan (a middle-aged and simple-minded man who always wore oversized drawers); Totoko, the beautiful girl on whom all the sextuplets, as well as their rival Chibita, had a crush; not to mention two weird characters named Dayōn no Ojisan and Hatabō, and the sextuplets' hapless parents. One of the reasons for Osomatsu-kun's continued success was Akatsuka's skill in depicting secondary characters. Another reason was the continually inventive situations that Akatsuka contrived for his characters.

Osomatsu-kun was one of the longer-lasting Japanese humor strips (it was discontinued in August 1969). Although a boys' strip, it was enjoyed by many adults as well. Osomatsu-kun was adapted (in animated form) to the television screen in the 1960s.

H.K.

OTOMO, KATSUHIRO (1954-) Japanese cartoonist born in Miyagi Prefecture on April 14, 1954. After high school studies, Katsuhiro Otomo began his artistic career in 1971 as an illustrator for an educational television program. His first comic strip work was Jusei ("The Gun Report," 1973), a very loose adaptation of Prosper Mérimée's novella Matteo Falcone. After publishing a series of brief, self-contained stories in the mid-1970s (later anthologized in a volume fittingly titled Short Pieces), he created several longer narratives, notably the apocalyptic Sayonara Nihon ("Farewell Japan"), the science-fictional Fireball (1979), and most especially the work that some critics regard as his masterpiece, Domu ("A Child's Dream," 1981). A suspense-filled thriller with Hitchcockian overtones, Domu opened with a series of suspicious deaths occurring within the same apartment complex. These turned out to have been the work of an embittered old man who used his parapsychological powers to cause his victims to commit suicide; in the end his nefarious designs were thwarted by a child endowed with equally awesome powers.

Otomo delved further into the paranormal with the long-running Akira, serialized in Young Magazine from

Katsuhiro Otomo, "Domu." © Katsuhiro Otomo.

1982 to 1992. Set in the megalopolis of Neo-Tokyo in the 21st century, it was a dark, dystopian tale involving motorcycle gang wars, a mysterious force codenamed Akira ("more powerful than a thousand nuclear bombs"), a sinister government conspiracy, and a cold-blooded, ruthless avenger. *Akira* caused a sensation as soon as it came out in Japan; its success was so great that the author had to form his own studio to supervise the increased production. This was topped in 1987 by the feature-length *Akira* animated film, which was shown in Europe and the United States and resulted in a comic book version that was published around the world. (In the United States it has appeared since 1988 in a colorized version issued by Marvel under its Epic banner.) After *Akira*'s conclusion, Otomo released *Megamex* in 1995, on a script by noted filmmaker Alejandro Jodorowsky.

Otomo, termed by Fred Schodt "the artist who created a revolution in clean-line realism" in Japan, eschews the cartooniness usually associated with *manga* and draws in an illustrative, cursive style much influenced by the French *bande dessinée*. He seems to have bridged the aesthetic gap that has existed between Japanese *manga* and Western comics, a feat not even Osamu Tezuka ever accomplished.

M.H.

OUR BOARDING HOUSE (U.S.) Major Amos Barnaby Hoople was a Fieldsian figure before W. C. Fields himself had developed (via Ziegfeld and the hit play, *Poppy*) his classic con-man character. Hoople, as presented by Gene Ahern in an innovative daily panel strip of 1923, was a short, sag-bellied man of middle age with a lantern jaw and drooping moustache, whose wife, Martha Hoople, presided militantly over the boarding house which was Hoople's sole continuing source of support. Hoople himself did little or nothing to keep the rooming house going, except what he was forced to do by Mrs. Hoople's badgering. Normally he occupied himself with the grandiose development of self-enriching schemes of an almost endless variety—from the ultimate failure or collapse of which he was rescued by either his own good fortune, an accidental element in the scheme which he had overlooked, or by the vigilant and long-suffering Martha and her carefully guarded boarding-house income.

As the strip developed in the early 1920s, Hoople's moustache shortened to a Grouchoesque smear behind his expanded, now-bulbous nose, and his long chin lifted to meet his nose in a near-Popeye profile. Some of the early boarders, such as a Mrs. Church and a prizefighter named Kid Portland, were dropped as the years went by, but a set of basic characters remained: three bachelor boarders named Buster, Clyde, and Mack (whose background comments provided a kind of cynical Greek Chorus for the Major's escapades); the Major's obnoxious 12-year-old nephew, Alvin; and his perennially reappearing black-sheep brother, Jake Hoople. Jake, unlike the Major, was a genuine, unscrupulous con-man who frequently went to jail, and about as frequently got the Major involved in really criminal undertakings—from which the Major, however, normally squeaked out with his usual luck.

The Sunday *Our Boarding House* was a weekly gag page, lacking the continuity of the daily panel, and was for years featured as the front page of the NEA Sunday comic section distributed by many small-town newspapers. Above the main *Boarding House* strip after 1932, Ahern drew a quarter-page weekly feature called *The Nut Brothers: Ches and Wal*. This remarkable strip was

"Our Boarding House," Bill Freyse/Gene Ahern. © NEA Service.

"Our Ernie," Hugh McNeill. © Knockout Comic.

pure fantasy, preceding the similar but better-known *Smokey Stover* in nutty, surrealistic background. Usually a comic point was made in the successive panels, but the madly shifting backgrounds and their contents were the real focus of attention.

In 1936, Ahern left his NEA strip to begin a new feature for King Features called *Room and Board*, very similar to *Our Boarding House*, with a Sunday companion strip named *The Squirrel Cage*, which paralleled *The Nut Brothers* in content. NEA appointed a talented cartoonist named Bill Freyse to take over the *Boarding House* feature, which he did with great zest and aplomb—so well that very few readers could have been aware of the shift in artists. Ahern's signature vanished, but there was no other sign of his absence until Freyse's signature appeared many years later. The Major's daily adventures continued as before, just as funny with the same basic characters, and the Sunday features followed suit.

After Freyse's death in 1969, the *Boarding House* daily and Sunday strip was continued by other hands. Although the old Ahern-Freyse style was noticeably different, the fundamental characters of the strip continued as before: American institutions as familiar and comfortable as the Major's slippers and fez. Drawn by Les Carroll since 1971, the Sundays ended in March 1981 and the dailies came to a close in December 1984.

B.B.

OUR ERNIE (G.B.) *Our Ernie*, subtitled "Mrs. Entwhistle's Little Lad," was one of the funniest strips to appear in British weekly comics. It was created by a cartoonist named Holt for the first issue of *Knockout* (March 4, 1939), and the first adventure set the theme. Ernie, fishing for kippers near Blackpool Tower, was crunched up in the cogs of a crane. Clearly inspired by the famous ballad *Albert and the Lion*, long a part of Stanley Holloway's repertoire, *Our Ernie*'s caption writer took the adventures even closer with his versified libretti: Ma and Pa picked up their little son/All kinked and bent, but still in one/Said Ma, "I'm glad that you were saved/But I'm blowed if I like you per-

manent waved!" Pa Entwhistle says the line that became his regular last-panel catchphrase, "Daft, I call it!" Our Ernie responds with his classic "famous last words," "What's for tea, Ma?"

The strip established several "firsts" in comics: the first northern hero, the first comic use of an already-established radio gimmick, the repeated catch-phrase, and the first time a strip hero continually wound up in some incredible predicament.

After a few weeks, Hugh McNeill took over the strip and made it even zanier, particularly after he added a typical touch, a companion for Ernie—Charlie the Caterpillar. Charlie's corner comments added an extra level to the fun. When McNeill went to war, A. J. Kelly arrived to draw even wilder adventures. Kelly's untimely death did not affect *Ernie*, save in inspiration, for the strip continued under Reg Parlett, Denis Gifford, Fred Robinson, Frank Lazenby, and many other hands, until it disappeared in 1960.

D.G.

OUTCAULT, RICHARD FELTON (1863-1928) Richard Felton Outcault was born at the height of the Civil War on January 14, 1863, in Lancaster, Ohio, the son of well-to-do parents. Considered highly talented from early childhood, Outcault majored in art at McMicken University in Cincinnati, Ohio, then returned home to marry Mary Jane Martin on Christmas Day 1890. Moving to New York to pursue an art career, Outcault settled in Flushing, Long Island, and worked as a freelance illustrator, doing work initially for such publications as the *Electrical World*, but quickly discovered that his bent for humor gave him a market for the immediate sale of virtually every gag cartoon he drew and submitted to *Life* and *Judge*. As the *New York World* also provided a lucrative cartoon market, Outcault placed a few cartoons there and found an interest in some back-alley studies of Manhattan urchins he had been doing as a sideline. Initially named for various slum area streets and courts, the series quickly became known by its *Hogan's Alley* title. Once he was permanantly employed by the *World* in 1894, Outcault found increasing fame for the small, nightshirted figure of a bald child the artist usually placed among his juvenile figures. This latter figure became the "Yellow Kid"—so named by the public and later by William Randolph Hearst when he hired Outcault away from the *World*, although Outcault never adopted the name—and he soon starred as the central character of Outcault's slum series.

The hearty vulgarity of Outcault's *Hogan's Alley* kids charmed the readership of the *World* as much as it alarmed the self-appointed keepers of the big city's proprieties, and nothing seemed worse to the latter group than Hearst's upstart sensational paper, the *New York Journal*, which acquired Outcault's services in 1896. The combination of Hearst journalism and his widely flaunted *Yellow Kid* feature created an outpouring of acrimony from New York's elite establishment—an outpouring that had its effect on Outcault himself. Much as he relished the money the Kid was bringing, the notoriety of the legal squabble between the *World* and the *Journal* over the rights to the Kid was socially embarrassing to him, and as soon as he conveniently—and economically—could, Outcault left Hearst and introduced a new, more subdued character, *Poor Li'l Mose*, for the *New York Herald* in 1901. This new feature reflected Outcault's interest in black children as subjects of caricature—an interest carried to its extreme in a series of drawings he did at about the same time for *Judge* called *Shakespeare in Possumville*—but it failed to hold much appeal for the public, and in 1902 Outcault introduced his immensely popular *Buster Brown* to *Herald* readers.

This time the mixture of juvenile hell-raising and propriety was exactly right for the public palate. Although there were still angry noises from certain church and school groups about "bad examples," most people found the wealthy background of the young prankster, Buster, either familiar or something to which they aspired, and so not as frightening or repulsive as many had felt the *Hogan's Alley* locale was. Buster himself was an ordinary healthy boy of the times, exaggerated enough to make for hilarious reading in the Sunday papers (and Outcault never drew any daily continuity strips), and dressed in a manner that made him very attractive to parents, who garbed an entire generation of boys in "Buster Brown" clothing of all kinds.

Again lured by Hearst money, Outcault left the *Tribune* and returned to the *Journal* in 1905, continuing *Buster Brown* there. Because Outcault controlled the rights to his character, he was making more by this time from clothing and artifacts based on *Buster* than

R. F. Outcault.

from the strip itself. A wealthy man by 1910, the artist continued the Sunday *Buster* almost as a hobby, finally dropping it for good in 1920 (although reprints were circulated to many papers as late as 1926) in order to retire to pursue his basic love, painting. The Outcault Advertising Company of Chicago, which he formed to merchandise his Buster Brown figure, was also relinquished at this time to his son, Richard F. Jr., who became the firm's new president.

The author of several prose works on his characters, as well as of serious articles on cartoon art for various journals, and the compiler of a number of *Yellow Kid* and *Buster Brown* reprint volumes, Outcault enjoyed more than one major exhibit of his paintings, and was free to travel as well, a widely respected figure in American art. Taken unexpectedly ill in the summer of 1928 at his Flushing home, Outcault lingered for nearly ten weeks, suffering from a variety of ailments, but died on September 25, 1928, at the age of 65.

B.B.

OUTLAND (U.S.) Having abandoned *Bloom County* the preceding month, on September 3, 1989, Berke Breathed brought out *Outland*. As a Sunday-only distributed by the Washington Post Writers Group, it hadn't been planned as a sequel to the former strip, but it turned out that way anyhow.

The star of the piece was originally a little African-American girl named Ronald-Ann who sought solace from her bleak ghetto life in escapist dreams and ego-boosting fantasies. When asked to read her American history paper at school, for example, she averred that Columbus was "a black man named Nabutu Bubu . . . who built three ships from the African baobab tree." The former denizens of *Bloom County* started dropping in, however, beginning with Opus the penguin in search of his mother, followed by Bill the Cat, Steve Dallas, Milo Bloom, Oliver Wendell Jones, and all the others, displacing the hapless Ronald-Ann from her own strip.

The characters behaved pretty much as before, but at a hyperkinetic pace. Their tribulations ranged from the puzzling to the esoteric. Steve Dallas decided to write *The Bridges of Bloom County* (subtitled "A Romance for Men"), banging out at his typewriter the opening sentences of chapter one: "Francesco . . . gazed upon the barren dust of his farm, his marriage, and his life. Suddenly, a pickup stopped before him. The door opened and out stepped [pause] three stewardesses." ("Six," whispered Opus, who was sitting at his elbow.) In other vignettes, Milo uncovered the skeletons in his closet (unfortunately they kept asking for Michael Jackson or the President); and troopers from the Information Highway Patrol came to arrest precocious hacker Oliver Wendell Jones for making "an illegal left turn into the White House international memo network."

In an extended narrative Steve turned into "the lawyer lost in time," meeting Calamity Jane in the Old West, filing a claim for a caveman in 10,000 B.C., visiting the site of the Hindenburg dirigible disaster, and dropping in on an underground bunker in 1945 Berlin ("I'm a victim too," Hitler whined). These arcane references, coupled with compositions that grew more and more abstract, disconcerted a great number of readers, and newspapers started cancelling the strip left and right. Breathed bowed to the inevitable and in

January 1995 announced he was dropping *Outland*; the last installment appeared on March 26 of that year.

M.H.

OUT OF THE SILENCE (Australia) Based on a novel of the same name by Erle Cox (1873-1950), *Out of the Silence* appeared as a daily strip in the *Melbourne Argus* from August 4 to December 21, 1934, and was drawn by "Hix" (Reg Hicks). It was the first Australian adventure strip of any consequence and followed the earlier comic strip format of no speech balloons and typeset text below each panel. As much of the original novel was based on lengthy dialogues and static situations, this format allowed the strip to remain basically true to the theme. By contemporary standards, the artwork, though stiff and unpolished, was adequate.

Silence told the story of a huge sphere discovered by Alan Dundas, buried on his property. The sphere contained records of the accumulated knowledge of a great civilization that had perished 27 million years ago. It also contained the body of the remarkably beautiful Earani—a veritable superwoman, placed in a state of suspended animation and committed to remaking the world in the image of her own civilization. The story follows the attempts of Dr. Richard Barry to forestall the plans of Earani and the infatuated Dundas for world domination.

Cox originally wrote *Silence* between 1913 and 1916 but was unable to find a publisher upon its completion. As a part-time contributor to the *Argus*, Cox submitted the story to that paper, which published it in weekly episodes between August and October 1919. The following six years saw a steady stream of inquiries from both Australia and overseas and, in 1925, the book was published by Edward A. Vidler of Melbourne. The same year a British edition was published by John Hamilton Ltd. of London and in 1928 an American edition was brought out by Rae D. Henkle Co. of New York. Both French and Russian translations have been reported and further Australian editions were published by Robertson & Mullens of Melbourne in 1932 and 1947. Over the past half century, *Silence* has come to be regarded as a science-fiction classic.

While *Silence* was the first adventure strip per se, the first adventure strip using original material and speech balloons was *The Adventures of Larry Steele* (1937-40) by Reg Hicks. Despite the trail-blazing performance of *Silence*, Australia has produced very few strips of the science-fiction genre. Only a handful (*Space Patrol, Silver Starr, Captain Power*) would qualify. No doubt, the space devoted to overseas strips in the Australian press (*Flash Gordon, Buck Rogers, Brick Bradford, Twin Earths, Jeff Hawke*, and others) has deterred local growth in this area.

J.R.

OUT OUR WAY (U.S.) At once one of the richest sources of memorable strip characters and the most individually structured of daily strips, J. R. Williams's *Out Our Way* first appeared in NEA Syndicate distribution on November 22, 1921, in a one-panel format. Eye-catching from the outset, with its homely realism of style and content and invested with an almost unfailing wit and originality of concept, *Out Our Way* quickly began to develop a series of characters who recurred at irregular intervals of a few days each in panel episodes of their own. Each of these series within a strip carried its own running title, and before long,

"Out Our Way," J. R. Williams. © NEA Service.

narrative continuity between these individual series episodes was added. (In one such 1924 narrative with a Western setting, Williams presented the first realistically dead bodies ever seen in a comic strip.) So sharply perceived and individualized were the Williams characters and narratives that none of his episodic shuffling confused his enthusiastic and growing public in the least.

Among the early series with the *Out Our Way* title were, "The Crossing Watchman," "Why Mothers Get Gray" (the panel that introduced the Willits family), "Heroes Are Made, Not Born" (with the Worry Wart), "Elf Dakin," "Wash Funk," and others. Other series featured a number of characters within their framework, but carried no running titles as such; among these were the cowboy group, which covered a broad range of memorable individuals, all interrelated, over its three-decade-plus run, including Smoky, Spuds, Cotton, Wes, Chuck, the School Marm, Soda, Jiggin' Jack (a horse), and others; and the machine shop set, sometimes run under the recurrent title, "Bull of the Woods," referring to the shop foreman, in which many characters figure, instantly recognizable by face and manner but largely unnamed.

A Sunday page titled *Out Our Way* but largely based on the Willits family of the "Why Mothers Get Gray" series, was released by NEA in the early 1920s. Aside from keeping an eye on the story line, Williams had little to do with the weekly page, and most of the continuity was drawn by Neg Cochran, who also continued drawing the Willits panel series after Williams died in 1957, running these between selected Williams reprints for several years. Paul Gringle carried on the Sunday strip for a time, and was later replaced on it by Ed Sullivan. The feature was discontinued in 1977.

A major part of the American experience for those who grew up with it, Williams's *Out Our Way* daily panel was one of the richest sources of popular lore and authentic records of how a wide variety of Americans lived, looked, felt, and thought from the turn of the century to the 1950s. A good cross-section of Williams's work is found in a fine series of volumes published by Charles Scribner's Sons between 1943 and 1947, under such titles as *The Bull of the Woods, Kids Out Our Way,* and *Cowboys Out Our Way.* A permanent collection of his daily work is needed.

B.B.

OVERGARD, WILLIAM THOMAS (1926-1990)

American artist born in Los Angeles on April 30, 1926. William Overgard grew up and attended public schools in Santa Monica, California. He graduated from high school and joined the U.S. Navy in 1944; he served for two years and saw action at Okinawa. After discharge from the service he attended Santa Monica City College, where he took art and art history courses.

His big push toward the comics started when he was 12 years old and wrote a fan letter to Milton Caniff. This began a longtime relationship during which Caniff became young Overgard's mentor and teacher. Even in the service Overgard would send strips and samples of his work to Caniff and receive tips and encouragement in return; Caniff advised Overgard to seek a profession in cartooning.

After the war, Caniff introduced his "pupil" around the industry. Overgard went to New York and joined Lev Gleason comic publishers under editor Charlie Biro. He worked on the *Boy* and *Daredevil* titles and wrote and drew *Black Diamond* Western comics. He soon moved to Western Publishing (Dell) and composed complete books of *Jungle Jim, Ben Bowie,* and others. During this time Overgard ghosted Caniff's *Steve Canyon* on occasion and wrote and drew two *Steve Canyon* comic books, as well as *Crime Buster* comics from 1950-53.

Also during this period—into the Wertham era—Overgard was constantly submitting strips to syndicates, particularly Publishers and United Features. *Gay Honor,* about a crusading woman lawyer, was one of many ill-fated efforts. Finally, early in 1952, Harold Anderson of Publishers Newspaper Syndicate contacted Overgard about a problem with *Steve Roper*: The foreground figure man had quit and Elmer Woggon's cartoony backgrounds were out of character with the adventure theme that had overtaken what used to be *Big Chief Wahoo.*

Overgard was engaged (Milton Caniff advised acceptance of the offer) and his first strips appeared in April of 1952.

Overgard's slick art, combined with writer Allen Saunders's maturing story-adventure script, brought *Steve Roper* new popularity. It picked up papers and soon became one of the leading story strips. Overgard

used the camera extensively and often posed himself as the model to achieve the realism he sought (and succeeded in capturing).

In later years Overgard spent several years living in Mexico and wrote a novel, *Pieces of a Hero,* a satirical adventure bought by 20th Century Fox. Other fiction efforts included a sequel, *Once More the Hero,* and a paperback, *Moonlight Surveillance.* Pop art master Roy Lichtenstein lifted an Overgard panel for his famous "I Can See Into the Room." Overgard left *Steve Roper* in 1982 to create *Rudy,* a gag strip about a talking gorilla, but it lasted only a little over a year. He died May 25, 1990, in Stony Point, New York.

R.M.

OVER THE HEDGE (U.S.)

When suburban sprawl hits the border of the wilderness, some critters retreat further into the woods; others, like *Over the Hedge's* R. J. the raccoon and Verne the turtle, adapt. While the animals have lost the theoretical purity of nature, they have become the most consumer-driven, junk-food-crazed creatures of any syndicated comic strip.

Over the Hedge began international distribution by United Feature Syndicate on June 12, 1995, and was aggressively marketed. It successfully filled the spot left vacant in many papers when *Calvin and Hobbes* ended syndication. *Over the Hedge* was created and is written by Michael Fry and drawn by T. Lewis, who met because they shared the same artist's representative in Houston, Texas. Fry also writes and draws the panel *Committed* for United Feature, about being married with children, that began syndication in 1994. *Committed* has been described as "*Family Circus* meets *The Far Side.*"

Fry's offbeat sense of humor has developed over the years as he has had several strips almost, but not quite, make it. *Scotty* was a popular local comic strip published by the Houston Press from 1984 until 1991. His first syndicated strip, *Cheeverwood,* was distributed by the Washington Post Writers Group from 1985 to 1987. Then King Features distributed *When I Was Short,* which he did with Guy Vasilovich from 1989 to 1992. Fry has also written for the *Mickey Mouse* syndicated comic strip for King Features and the Walt Disney Company. His collaborator on *Over the Hedge,* Lewis, a fellow Texan, had been one of the cartoonists drawing *Mickey Mouse.* Lewis is also an illustrator of children's books, with over 15 published.

Fry and Lewis first worked on a strip idea they were unable to sell called *The Secret Life of Pigs,* which had a rural setting. Pigs were turned into a turtle and a raccoon, and the setting changed to suburbia, and *Over the*

"Over the Hedge," Michael Fry and T. Lewis. © United Feature Syndicate.

Hedge was born. It clicked with the syndicate and editors of major U.S. newspapers.

R. J. (alias Fur Boy, the Masked Malcontent, or the Racoonerator) and his philosophical pal Verne (alias Mr. Sensitive or the Terribly Taciturn Terrapin) bear a resemblance to Pogo and his fellow critters only in that they are funny animals. While social commentary abounds, *Over the Hedge* does not have political commentary. Also, R. J. and Verne, because of their constant contact with humans, make Pogo and friends look like hicks from the Okefenokee Swamp.

R. J. and Verne have taken a liking to watching a big-screen television through the living room window of their neighbors, Norene and Nathan Furkin, and eating the garbage that the Furkins carefully cover. But what's a trash can with a lid on it to a critter crazed for a junk food sugar rush.

"Nathan, I'm kind of shy about this with the curtains open," complained Norene in their darkened bedroom in one strip. "Norene, this is the last house on the block," answered Nate. "Nobody's out there except a few fuzzy critters, and they've got their own problems." The final panel showed 11 animals on wooden bleachers watching the couple, with R. J. complaining to Verne, "The popcorn's stale again." In a later strip, Norene became pregnant, and the "Boys in the Wood" monitored the pregnancy with the same curiosity that the act of conception engendered.

R. J. is smitten with Dolly, a pampered pooch whom Verne notes is "domesticated, spoiled," and, after she trips over her own ears, "highly inbred." However, Luby, the lady raccoon with long eyelashes and a polkadot bow, thinks R. J. is neat, even if he does have to be approached with "tongs." Verne the turtle has a girlfriend of sorts in a fellow terrapin, Velma.

Over the Hedge definitely is humor with a late 1990s edge. The critters not only love watching *The X-Files* on television, they'd probably qualify to be the subject of an investigation. It will only get funnier with the addition of Norene and Nate's baby.

Lewis's artwork has a contemporary look and does not copy the funny animal style of Walt Kelly or others. As the strip is new, expect the characters to change as time goes by. *Over the Hedge* features the bad boys of the animal world, and it would appear they are just getting warmed up for a long and successful syndicated run.

B.C.

OZARK IKE (U.S.) A baseball strip, the first of its kind to achieve success and one of the few sports strips to survive, *Ozark Ike* was sold to King Features Syndicate by sports cartoonist Ray Gotto. The first strip appeared in November 1945.

The hero was Ike, a lanky left fielder for the Bugs baseball team. He was something of a hick, and most

"Ozark Ike," Ray Gotto. © King Features Syndicate.

certainly a bad baseball player. His girlfriend, a blonde beauty with a Veronica Lake hairstyle, was named Dinah. Bubba Bean was the second banana of the strip; like Ike, he was tall, thin and ignorant. J. P. Moran, a harried and bristling "fat cat," was owner of the team.

Gotto's drawing style, unlike many strip artists and certainly unlike many sports cartoonists, was precisely mannered and almost mechanically rendered. Shading was meticulously laid in with careful lines, and the impression of overbearing stylization was just saved by Gotto's grasp of anatomy, composition, and action.

Unfortunately, a baseball strip, even a good one, would expect to have a rough opening season and *Ozark Ike* was no exception. But Gotto's effort managed to become a moderate success for King; its art stood out on the comic page, and the humor, though seldom outstanding, was stronger than the continuities. What caused Gotto to leave the strip in 1954 was a contractual disagreement with Stephen Slesinger, the so-called "producer" of the strip; he was, in fact, a kind of agent and acted in a similar capacity with other strips, notably *Red Ryder*.

The strip was enough of a success for King to find another artist (Bill Lignante) to continue it; it failed after a couple of years (in 1959), as did Gotto's rival effort for General Features, *Cotton Woods*, another sports strip but in a straighter vein.

R.M.

PAI, ANANT (1931-   ) Anant Pai was born September 17, 1931, in Karkala, Karnataka, India. Although his college degrees were in chemistry, physics, and chemical technology, Pai developed a lifelong passion for publishing, comics, and literary activities. From 1954 to 1967 he worked successively as an editor and publisher of a magazine, freelance writer, publishing house representative, partner in a book export/import company, and junior executive in the Times of India Books Division. While at the latter, he helped conceptualize one of India's first comics, *Inkrajal*, which led to his 1967 launch of the very successful *Amar Chitra Katha* ("Immortal Picture Stories") series of educational comics.

Pai said the inspiration for this venture came while listening to Indian children spout knowledge about Western civilization but remain mute about their own culture. He set out to remedy this shortcoming, offering to do a set of comic books, each devoted to a person or event in Indian history, religion, and mythology. He finally sold the idea to India Book House, which, during the next 24 years, brought out a total of 436 different titles. Pai conceptualized all of the books and wrote many of the scripts.

Amar Chitra Katha was both a financial and educational success. By the 1990s more than 79 million copies of the English-language edition were sold, and more in a number of other language editions worldwide. The books impressed government officials, who allowed federal funds to be used to purchase them for school use, and overall, helped comics gain a moderate rate of respectability in India.

Additionally, Pai started one of India's first comics and cartoons syndicates, Rang Rekha Features, in 1969, and the monthly children's magazine *Tinkle* in 1980; he has also authored novels in Hindi and Kannada, and four volumes on personality development.

J.A.L.

PALACIO, LINO (1904-198?) An Argentine cartoonist born in Buenos Aires in 1904, Lino Palacio, a graduate of the School of Architecture, taught drawing for many years and held a variety of municipal positions in the city of Buenos Aires. He initiated his career as a caricaturist under the pseudonym "Flax," and he was for a long time cover designer of the children's magazine *Billiken*. His most famous comic creations included *Ramona* and *Doña Tremebunda*, both about opinionated women; *Don Fulgencio*, his first popular success (1935); *Tripudio*; and, most famous of all, Avivato (1946), which inspired a movie of the same name and gave birth to a magazine, also titled *Avivato*.

All the Palacio strips were carried on, after their creator tired of them, by anonymous cartoonists working in a style imitative of their master, who died in the late 1980s.

L.G.

PANDA (Netherlands) *Panda* is one of the many successful creations of Marten Toonder, sometimes called the Dutch Walt Disney because of the large number of funny comics and cartoons produced by his studio. *Panda* was created in 1946 and, as the name suggests, is a strip about a cute little panda bear. The strip appears in a number of Dutch newspapers, all of which are subscribers of GPD, a press service that distributes the comic feature. *Panda* is also exported to a number of foreign newspapers and magazines, and two versions of the feature are in existence: the more traditionally Dutch version of a strip with narrative below the pictures, and the more international format of the story told in captions and speech balloons. More than 120 adventures with lengths between 40 and 100 strips have appeared since the strip was created.

Panda is a kind of morality play in which innocence forever wins out over a crooked trickster. Little Panda, of course, is the innocent. His antagonist is the sly fox Joris Goedbloed (George Goodfellow, in English versions) who, from the very first episode that has Panda picnicking under a tree, has tried to outwit Panda, but he inevitably fails. Panda's motto is *"Ik moet nu zorgen dat ik vooruit kom in de wereld"* ("I must strive to get ahead in the world"). Thus, money and rewards play an important role in Panda, his honesty even helping him to become a millionaire. A somewhat static figure, Panda does not go into action by himself; he usually has to be forced to go into action by Goedbloed, who spends his fantasies and energy on get-rich-quick schemes. When success seems within reach, Panda waits in the wings to straighten things out and preserve the status quo. Nevertheless, Panda never turns Goedbloed over to the authorities as he probably has a secret, romantic admiration for the gentleman rogue.

Panda is a character readers identify with since he gets involved in the stories the same way they do, by watching the goings-on. By proving that innocence cannot be corrupted, *Panda* provides the reader with a vehicle that mirrors—and tests—his morals.

W.F.

PANHANDLE PETE (U.S.) An early and often hilarious strip by George McManus, *Panhandle Pete* (which began in the *New York World* in April 1904 and ended there late in 1910) was one of the major Sunday page pioneers in extending narrative over many weeks. Initially a weekly gag page (or half-page) about a very grubby and tattered tramp with a pot belly and an unshaven chin, Panhandle Pete had turned by 1905 to world exploration in long continued sequences, attempting to reach the south pole—not once, but twice; on the second time finding and coming back with the "pole" itself—conquering cannibal kingdoms, making rocket and balloon ascensions, etc., etc. Aided by a thin bum named Cecil and a fat one who remains nameless (as well as by a pugnacious goat called Bill),

"Panhandle Pete," George McManus.

"Pansy Potter," Blackaller. © D. C. Thomson.

Pete swindles and connives his way from port to port, even taking over an entire African kingdom by fraud. (McManus's native blacks probably represent the extreme of comic page racism: he represents them as being hatched from eggs!)

Pete's vocabulary has an independent fascination: he speaks of vazzes (vases), "J. Pinpoint Morgan," and so on, while his fat tramp buddy smokes what must be the most remarkable (and smelly) pipe on record: it is in the shape of a small wood-burning kitchen stove, and he belches endless quantities of smoke. The goat, Bill, is as personable as the three humans, and frequently makes comments on the action in spoken balloons (although he is not humanized, and never converses directly with the others).

McManus's stunning comic draftsmanship is as sharply in evidence here as in any of his work, but he has a good deal more to work with, in terms of exotic settings, strange animals, etc., than before or later (except for the fantastic *Nibbsy the Newsboy* and *Spareribs and Gravy*—the latter being a re-creation of *Panhandle Pete* in 1911, again featuring traveling tramps in strange parts of the world). It is a strange, funny, and gorgeous strip, well worth collecting in a single memorable volume.

B.B.

PANSY POTTER (G.B.) *Pansy Potter the Strong Man's Daughter* made its debut in the Christmas number of *Beano*, 1938. "Welcome to the *Beano, Pansy*," said a caricature of the editor of that weekly comic in her first six-panel adventure, but he was soon saying "Ow! Leggo!" (just like one of his comic characters), when the daughter of the World's Strongest Man shook his hand.

Pansy was created by Hugh McNeill, but her corkscrew curls and Popeye arms have been drawn by many cartoonists since, the best being Blackaller, who adopted an unusual (for *Beano*) "animated cartoon" style. Pansy, whose name was changed by a last-minute editorial decision from the original *Biff Bang Bella*, really got cracking once war was declared: her

favorite pastime was sinking Hitler's U-Boats—by hand!

She moved into two-color printing in 1942 and over to the back page on April 21, 1945. She was reduced to six panels again on page two from June 15, 1946, then dropped after a paper cut reduced the size of the comic on January 10, 1948. However, she returned to the fray with renewed strength on August 13, 1949, when *Pansy Potter in Wonderland* was a serial strip that filled the entire back page, in full color. This became a complete weekly episode, and ran until February 6, 1954, after which, displaced by *Dennis the Menace*, she retired. However, a good Strong Man's Daughter is hard to keep down, and publisher D.C. Thomson revived her for their new comic, *Sparky*, on January 30, 1965. She ended her career in the late 1980s.

D.G.

PANTERA BIONDA (Italy) In April 1948 there appeared in newsstands all over Italy the first issue of the fortnightly collection "La Jungla" ("Jungle") published by Casa Editrice ARC. The flagship of the series was *Pantera Bionda* ("The Blonde Panther"), about a well-endowed jungle-woman, which introduced a not unwelcome touch of sex into the world of Italian comics, until then rather straitlaced. With an eye toward the male public, the publisher thought that a female Tarzan might do nicely. While there had been a few instances of similar characters in American comic books (Sheena, Camilla), this was an absolute novelty in Italy.

With scripts by Gian Giacomo Delmasso and drawings by Enzo Magni (who signed "Ingam"), the blonde heroine swung into a 16-page king-size comic book priced at 30 liras. Pantera Bionda lived in Borneo, fought against cruel and treacherous Japanese soldiers, and had only two friends: the serene Lotus Leaf, an old Chinese woman, and her pet chimpanzee, Tao. She also had a boyfriend in the person of an American explorer named Fred, who was to play second fiddle for a long time.

The scantily clad heroine soon attracted the ire of the prude and the righteous, who accused the publishers of pornography. In order not to disturb the supposedly innocent minds of their youthful readers (and to continue to publish in the process) the artists had to lengthen the heroine's hemline, and cover her too revealing breasts. In spite of *Pantera Bionda*'s enormous

"Pantera Bionda," Gian Giacomo Dalmasso and Enzo Magni. © SEAT.

success (100,000 copies of each issue were reportedly sold—a record for the Italian market), the publisher grew tired of the many lawsuits and seizures brought on by the enraged pillars of the community and decided to stop publication after two years and devote himself exclusively to educational comics; thus was born *Il Piccolo Centauro* ("The Little Centaur").

G.B.

PARKER, BRANT (1920-   ) Brant Parker was an American artist born in Los Angeles on August 26, 1920. Parker attended public schools in Los Angeles, as well as the Frank Wiggins Trade School and the Otis Art Institute—which provided the closest, he has said, to cartooning instruction that he could get.

Ultimately he joined the Walt Disney Studio and, after the mandatory training in the animation school, went straight to the animation department. He aspired to the story department but was assigned to "in between" animation, working on miscellaneous shorts before entering the Navy in late 1942.

After his discharge in 1945, Parker worked for Disney another year and a half ("Make Mine Music" was a major credit) and then moved East to settle with his new bride, Mary Lou, in her hometown of Endicott, New York. He got a job drawing political cartoons and staff art for the *Binghamton Press*. After another hitch in the Navy, Parker returned to work for IBM in the Binghamton area. He rose from technical illustration to advertising and promotion, being transferred to the greater Washington, D.C., area in the process.

While still in Endicott, cartoonist Parker judged an art show that included work by a local high school student named Johnny Hart. A friendship began that manifested itself in the early 1960s in a phone call by Hart (then successful with *BC*) to Parker concerning a new strip.

The strip, ultimately, was *The Wizard of Id*, as classic a strip as *BC* or any other in comic history. Parker and Hart sold the strip to the executives of the Herald Tribune Syndicate in a conference in a New York City hotel and, with an initial list of about 50 papers, launched *Wizard* on Nov. 9, 1964.

Parker's *Wizard* has remained consistently outstanding, his deceptively loose drawing style one of the medium's most painstakingly executed and the gags first-class lunacy (written in equal parts by Parker and Hart).

Appreciation of *The Wizard of Id* has been accorded by the National Cartoonists Society, which awarded it the Best Humor Strip award, LUCA 8, and other organizations. On behalf of NCS and USO, Parker has made several tours of Army hospitals and bases.

Parker, incidentally, must have one of the most unlikely influences on anyone's future career in cartooning: Jack Webb, the producer and star of the television detective series *Dragnet*. Webb was student body president at Parker's high school and cartoonist for the school newspaper. Impressed by the ability to draw, the thrill of publication, and the recognition received, Parker was inspired to become a cartoonist.

Parker's consistent quality and exacting personal standards for his strip make him one of today's most notable professionals and one of the comic art form's greatest exponents.

Brant Parker, in association with artist Bill Rechin and writer Don Wilder, created *Crock* in 1975. A newspaper strip starring Vermin P. Crock, the heartless commander of a hapless French Foreign Legion troop, it spoofs such old-time movies as *Beau Geste* and *Outpost in Morocco*. Parker also continues to draw *The Wizard of Id*, for which he received a Reuben Award in 1984.

R.M.

PATORUZÚ (Argentina) Patoruzú is a Pampa Indian who made his first appearance in 1928 as a secondary character in Dante Quinterno's humor strip, *Don Julian de Monte Pío* (started in 1926 in the daily newspaper *La Razón*). In 1931 Patoruzú gave his name to a new strip,

"Patoruzito," Dante Quinterno. © Dante Quinterno.

"Patoruzú," Dante Quinterno. © Dante Quinterno.

"Patsy," Mel Graff. © AP Newsfeatures.

also by Quinterno. From *La Razón*, *Patoruzú* passed to *El Mundo* in 1935, the year that also saw the birth of Quinterno's publishing empire patterned after the American syndicate system, an enterprise without precedent in the Spanish-speaking countries. From that time *Patoruzú* not only appeared as a daily strip but as a weekly color page as well, published in *Mundo Argentina* and in the comic weekly to which it gave its name in 1936. On October 11, 1946, *Patoruzú* also appeared in Quinterno's second comic magazine, *Patoruzito*, with scripts by Mirco Repetto. In the United States *Patoruzú* was published by the New York newspaper *P.M.*, starting in August 1941.

Patoruzú represents the myth of the good Indian confronted by civilization. Endowed with Herculean strength and an elemental, but practical, mind, he is the most outstanding member of a family of Patagon people, of the Tehuelche tribe. Patoruzú discovers Buenos Aires in the course of his wanderings, a place so different from his native land, where he meets his cousin Isidoro, who has already been corrupted by the big city. Other family members include the little Patoruzito and Upa, Patoruzú's brother, as guileless as he is big. Like Astérix and other heroes, Patoruzú gets help from a magic source, in this case a flute given him by the chief of a North American tribe. The strip ended its long run on April 30, 1977.

In 1942 Dante Quinterno produced a *Patoruzú* animated cartoon in which he used a new chromatic system named "Alex-color," developed by Connio Santini and Rosiano.

L.G.

PATSY (U.S.) Started by Mel Graff in 1934, *The Adventures of Patsy* (simply called *Patsy* by most newspapers carrying the strip) had a checkered career fairly typical of most comic features distributed by Associated Press.

Conceived at first as a little-girl fantasy strip (a kind of modern-dress *Alice in Wonderland*) *Patsy* took place in

the fairy-tale lands of Odd Bodkins and King Silhouette, where the little heroine tangled with witches, giants, and monsters from whom she was often rescued by the Phantom Magician (who turned out to be her uncle Phil Cardigan). In mid-1935 Patsy and her guardian were back in the real world, and in December 1936 arrived in Hollywood where Patsy got a role in the movies.

Mel Graff's graphic treatment of *Patsy* was at first sketchy and uncertain. In 1936 he came under the influence of his AP colleague Noel Sickles and his style firmed up, becoming more airy and impressionistic. Graff was a very slow worker, however, and always had trouble making deadlines; in 1939 he hired the out-of-work Sickles to ghost for him. This was to be the high point of Patsy's career, which came to an end in 1940 when Graff was hired to do the *X-9* strip.

Upon Graff's departure, the strip was taken over by Charles Raab, who did a creditable job before leaving in 1943 to create the ill-starred *Foreign Correspondent*. Raab was succeeded by George Storm (of *Bobby Thatcher* fame) who lasted only until 1945; then came Richard Hall (who took Patsy back to the stage and screen); followed in 1946 by Bill Dyer, who drew *Patsy* in a caricatural style until the demise of the strip in the early 1950s.

Like most other AP features, *Patsy* suffered from the indecisiveness of its editors, who could not quite make up their minds whether it should be a fantasy tale, a little-girl story, or a straight adventure strip; accordingly, it did not succeed in any of these genres. The strip is still fondly remembered today, chiefly because of the contributions of Graff, Raab, and the uncredited Sickles.

M.H.

PATTERSON, RUSSELL (1894-1977) American cartoonist and illustrator Russell Patterson was born December 26, 1894, in Omaha, Nebraska. Patterson's father, a railroad lawyer, took his family to Newfoundland soon after the boy was born, then to Toronto and later to Montreal where Patterson was educated at St. Patrick's School. After one year of studies at McGill University, Patterson started his cartooning career with the weekly *Standard* (he was fired after a few weeks), then went to the French daily *La Patrie* where he originated his first comic strip, *Pierre et Pierrette*. In 1914

Patterson tried to join the Canadian Army but was turned down; so he went to study at the Chicago Art Institute, working meanwhile as a designer for Carson, Scott, Pirie, then as a decorator for Marshall Field.

After four years of interior decorating, Patterson became bored and left for France. From 1920 to 1925 he stayed in Paris where he studied under the aging Impressionist master Claude Monet and painted oils (mostly landscapes). Back in Chicago after his Parisian fling, Patterson embarked on a career in illustration, where he practically created the flapper. His popular success prompted him to go to New York where he worked for all the important magazines: *Redbook*, *Harper's Bazaar*, *Cosmopolitan*, *College Humor*, the old *Life*, and *American Magazine*. He also designed costumes for the Ziegfeld Follies and for George White's Scandals. When the Depression signaled the end of the flapper era, Patterson moved to Hollywood where he designed movie sets and costumes.

In 1951 Patterson again tried his hand at a comic strip, the stylish *Mamie* for United Feature Syndicate. *Mamie* featured some of Patterson's most striking designs and compositions (as well as a bevy of fashionably dressed females), but the public was not receptive to the artist's slightly dated elegance, and the strip folded in 1956. He died in Brigantine, New Jersey, in 1977; a retrospective of his works was organized by the Delaware Art Museum in June of that year.

As Stephen Becker noted in 1959: "He [Patterson] is not primarily a comic artist at all; but he is a great illustrator, and his style has been imitated by more currently successful comic artists that would like to admit it." Russell Patterson was the recipient of many awards over the years, including the Academy of Design Gold Medal and the silver plaque for best cartoonist in advertising and illustration (1957). He was one of the founders of the National Cartoonists Society and served as its president from 1952 to 1953.

M.H.

PAUL TEMPLE (G.B.) The daily strip *Paul Temple* began in the *London Evening News* on November 19, 1951, and ran a 20-year span to May 1, 1971. The hero, however, a crime novelist turned private detective, was created many years earlier by the playwright Francis Durbridge. Temple first appeared in a six-part radio serial called *Send For Paul Temple*, broadcast by the B.B.C. in 1938. Hugh Morton played Temple, and the serial accumulated a record amount of fan mail. Naturally, other serials followed: *Paul Temple and the*

Front Page Men; *Paul Temple Intervenes*, and so on, and the character was brought to the cinema in four Paul Temple films made during the 1940s.

Durbridge wrote the screenplays from his radio plays and also adapted his first serial into novel form. The character's continuing popularity on radio and successful transfer to television prompted Julian Phipps, the Associated Newspapers strip editor, to develop a strip version. Francis Durbridge wrote the original continuity, retaining all the regular characters: Paul, his wife Steve, and Sir Graham Forbes of Scotland Yard.

The original artist was Alfred Sindall, who left the strip in 1954 to create a more adventurous one, *Tug Transom*. *Temple* was taken over by Bill Bailey, but eventually settled down with John McNamara, who drew it until the end. It was McNamara who had to change Paul's likeness to that of his television persona, Francis Matthews.

Reprints of the strip were published in pocket-size comic books, *Paul Temple Library*, the first issue being *The Magpie Mystery*.

D.G.

PAYASO (Philippines) *Payaso* ("The Clown") is a comic book novel written and illustrated by Noly Panaligan, one of the most respected names in Philippine comics. It appeared in *Tagalog Klasiks* during 1953. The novel is about the adventures and escapades of Ariel, the impish and talented young clown.

Ariel becomes the ward of a palace after he saves a young princess, Flordelisa, from the clutches of a band of soldiers who tried to abduct her. He is groomed to become the future court jester of the king. His training is supervised by Gino, the current court entertainer. At the beginning, Gino resents the young upstart but eventually becomes fond of the young rascal, realizing that he is worthy of becoming his eventual replacement. Amidst the laughter and the social carryings-on in the palace, treachery is brewing, and it is up to the young Ariel to prevent any harm from befalling the pretty princess.

"Paul Temple," John McNamara. © Evening News.

"Payaso," Noly Panaligan. © Tagalog Klasiks.

One of the villains in the story is Kasan, who continuously tries to kidnap the princess. His attempts are always thwarted by the child-clown who happens to be at the right place at the opportune moment. The constant battle of wits between the older and seasoned warrior against the youthful and clever Ariel provides an entertaining and humorous aspect of the novel. Kasan, raging with fury, invariably becomes a victim of one of Ariel's shrewd maneuvers with hilarious results. But it takes more than a bag of tricks for Payaso to sustain himself from the dangers and intrigues of the royal court.

This serialized novel is set in Europe during the days of heraldic pageantry and knighthood. This particular series became the reference source for many young, aspiring Filipino artists who wanted to do some research on medieval architecture, costumes, weapons, and designs.

Payaso is considered the best work of Noly Panaligan, who has done a tremendous amount of work for the Philippine comic book industry. He is also well-known for his commercial and motion picture work. The 1950s is considered the Golden Age of Philippine comic art, and one of the persons most responsible for the high quality of the art produced then is Panaligan.

O.J.

PAYNE, CHARLES M. (1873-1964) An American artist, Charles M. Payne was born in Queenstown, Pennsylvania, in 1873. Payne was seven when his father died and the family moved to his grandmother's farm. In 1894 Payne hung around the offices of the *Pittsburgh Post*, suggesting cartoon ideas, and two years later he was offered a job on the art staff. He became a popular personality in that city and the trademark of his cartoons was a little raccoon—adopted later by Billy DeBeck when he drew editorial cartoons in Pittsburgh.

The little mascot became a regular in Payne's first comic strip, a Sunday feature called *Coon Hollow Folks*. Soon his other comics, such as *Bear Creek Folks, Scary William,* and *Yennie Yonson,* drawn for papers in Pittsburgh and Philadelphia, were picked up by the early boilerplate syndicates. When national popularity and a steady income were assured, Payne gave up his editorial cartoons in Pittsburgh and moved to Hollywood, California, with his family. From there he sent *Honeybunch's Hubby,* a thrice-weekly early married strip, to the *New York World*.

While on a prospecting trip in Death Valley, he sent a new feature idea to the *World*, and it soon caught the fancy of New York and the nation. He gave up life in the West and miscellaneous freelance jobs to draw the new hit, *S'Matter, Pop?* The year was 1910, and the wildly loose and very funny adventures of Pop, Willyum, Desperate Ambrose, and others were to continue for 30 happy years in the *World* (until 1917), and on and off via the Bell Syndicate. The revived *Honeybunch's Hubby* shared Sunday slots as the top strip and occasionally the major Sunday page.

After the demise of *S'Matter, Pop?*, Payne attempted to develop new comics, including *G.I. Daddy,* a hillbilly strip similar to his earliest comics, and a high-schooler strip with the latest slang—all efforts to no avail. Payne gradually grew poorer and dropped from the public eye. But around Christmastime 1962, an item appeared in the New York papers about a poor old man in a dingy apartment building who was mugged by three assailants—his jaw broken in four places: the attackers escaped with less than a dollar in change.

The man was Charlie Payne, and the tragedy was all the greater because of the life the octogenarian was leading in spite of his poverty. He was always active, lively, and full of humor, a ladies' man to the end and an agile dancer. The late Vernon Greene had been drawing Payne out of his seclusion and bringing him to meetings of the National Cartoonists Society, where he became a great favorite. The vicious assault broke his pride and spirit worse than the injured parts of his body, and "Popsy" Payne ("the girls away back in 1923 always called me that," he wrote to this writer) died soon thereafter.

If Payne was never quite a major figure in comics, he was certainly one of the most unique and individualistic. His style was consistent throughout his career and, like Fontaine Fox, he took only casual notice of the strict comic strip conventions of his times.

His pages were decorative statements taken in the whole; panels would drop, circles would replace them, figures would stand outside of panel lines, horizon lines would disappear, colors would be used boldly. If the figures were sketchy, the shading was seemingly careless—broad, free brush dabs.

But there was a homely quality, a friendly, informal humor and a familiarity to his work that could never be denied. There was a touch of Sterrett in his incidental props, and the dialogue, especially Desperate Ambrose's, was involved, stagey, flowery, and full of glorious malaprops and pretensions.

Payne's work was always a very personal statement—of his humor and his own unique sense of composition and design. His comics are delightful little glimpses into the nonsense world of scheming kids, indulgent fathers, and light fancy.

R.M.

PAYO, EL (Mexico) With the descriptive subtitle "A Man Against the World," *El Payo* started in 1966 as a weekly pocket-size comic book published by Editorial Senda. The scripts were by Guillermo Vigil and the artwork was supplied by Fausto Buendía, Jr., in a style similar to that of Angel-José Mora, although not of equal quality. Buendía was later succeeded by a string of other staff artists.

El Payo and his girl companion, Lupita, live in the Mexican town of Vilmayo, although the hero's adventurous existence leads him to the most distant places. In any locale in which he chances to be, El Payo encounters adventure as well as passionate women, in a skillful blend of violence and sex, in the best tradition of this type of public-oriented publication.

El Payo has inspired three motion pictures: *El Payo* (1971), *El Fantasma de Mina Prieta* (1973), and *Los Caciques de San Crispín* (1973).

L.G.

PAZIENZA, ANDREA (1956-1988) An Italian cartoonist and illustrator, Pazienza was born in S. Menaio (Foggia). After graduating from art school, Pazienza attended university for some years and was active as a painter. Pazienza drew cartoons and short comic strips for the satirical graphic magazine *Il male.* In 1978 he cofounded, along with Filippo Scozzari, Stefano Tamburini, Massimo Mattioli, and Tanino Liberatore the lampoon magazine *Cannibale,* to which Pazienza contributed cartoons and comic strips.

"El Payo," Guillermo Vigil. © Editorial Senda.

the anxieties of an Italian juvenile protester of the late 1970s. His subject matter came from his own experiences; his drawing style hovered between realism and caricature.

In 1980, Pazienza cofounded the magazine *Frigidaire* with Scozzari, Tamburini, Mattioli, and Liberatore. Among Pazienza's other contributions appeared the stories *Zanardi* (1983), *Alter Alter* (1987), and *Pompeo* (1985), the moving drama of a young drug addict.

Throughout his career, Pazienza contributed to a variety of other magazines as well, including *Frizzer, Tango, Zut*, and *Glamour*. Additionally, he produced artwork for disk covers, publishing houses, a film poster (for Fellini's *La città delle donne*, 1979), and an advertising campaign. In 1988 Pazienza disappeared suddenly. Many of his works have been reprinted in book form by several publishers.

G.C.C.

PEANUTS (U.S.) The most shining example of the American success story in the comic strip field began inauspiciously in 1950 when a timid young cartoonist with the unlikely name of Charles Monroe Schulz started making the round of comic syndicates with a new feature which he wanted to call "Li'l Folks." After being turned down by a half-dozen syndicates, Schulz's brainchild was finally accepted by United Feature Syndicate editors who rechristened the strip *Peanuts*. Schulz resented the syndicate-imposed title (and still does) but went along with the change. On October 2, 1950, *Peanuts* made its debut as a daily strip.

Building slowly from an initial list of seven newspapers, *Peanuts* was carried by 35 papers in October 1951, and by 45 papers in October 1952 (by which time a Sunday page had been added, starting on January 6, 1952). As Schulz himself stated: "It took a long time to develop . . . in fact the next twenty years saw a basic evolution of the strip." Be it as it may, *Peanuts* was not long in hitting its stride, and by the early 1960s its success had already become phenomenal, and continued to grow until, as John Tebbel noted in a 1969 article,

In 1976 he collaborated again with Filippo Scozzari to produce comic strips for the magazine *AlterLinus*, using the art name/art mark "Traumfabrik." From 1977 to 1981 he wrote and drew (in his own name) the series *Le straordinarie avventure di Penthotal* for *Alter Alter*. In this strip and his next, *Zanardi*, Pazienza depicted

Andrea Pazienza, "Finzioni." © Milano Libri Edizione.

"Peanuts," Charles Schulz. © United Feature Syndicate.

"the total income from the strip, including that of its twenty-one licensed subsidiaries, has been estimated at $50,000,000 a year." Today *Peanuts* is probably the most successful comic strip of all time: the *Peanuts* reprint books (handled by no fewer than seven different publishers) cover two full columns of *Contemporary Authors*; there has been (at last count) 16 *Peanuts* cartoons produced for CBS-TV, as well as two feature-length animated films for National General Pictures; a musical comedy adaptation, *You're a Good Man, Charlie Brown*, arrived in 1967 (and has since been seen all around the world); and the strip has been exegesized at length in evangelist Robert Short's two books, *The Gospel According to Peanuts* (1965) and *The Parables of Peanuts* (1968).

Yet the theme of *Peanuts* is the great American unsuccess story. The strip's meek hero, Charlie Brown, has proved himself so far unable to kick a football, fly a kite, or win a baseball game, to name a few of his more conspicuous failings. Charlie Brown's chief tormentor is a scowling, sneering child-bitch named Lucy van Pelt. Linus, Lucy's brother, is a precocious, fragile intellectual who goes to pieces without his security blanket. Schroeder, whose only passion is to play Beethoven on his toy piano, the rough but generous Peppermint Patty, the dirty Pigpen, Franklin, the bespectacled black boy (a relative newcomer to the strip) and a few others, complete the human cast of *Peanuts* (in which no adult is ever seen).

Of course Snoopy, Charlie Brown's beagle, occupies a place of his own in the strip; he is (if only in fantasy) the total antithesis to Charlie Brown: a great writer, great athlete, great lover, the owner of the most palatial doghouse in the world, as well as being the most celebrated World War I ace pilot in all history ("Some day, I'll get you, Red Baron!"). In 1969 NASA picked Snoopy as the name for the Lunar Excursion Module on the *Apollo 10* flight to the moon, a fitting tribute to the venturesome beagle.

These children who reason and act like adults, the situations in which comedy is but a thin veil thrown over underlying sadness, the cruelty hidden under laughter, all this endows *Peanuts* with a bittersweet quality and a subtle ambiguity which are often disconcerting. There is in *Peanuts* a cry of despair almost Kirkegaardian in its accent, and thoroughly modern in its pretense.

In 1997, after almost 50 years of existence, *Peanuts* still ranks among the five top newspaper strips in America and is distributed in more than 70 countries, a remarkable record. The feature and his creator have mellowed in the last two decades, but only to an extent. The most telling evidence of this "softening" came on March 30, 1993, when Charlie Brown was finally allowed to score a home run (the pitcher later confessed he had actually tossed him a grapefruit). Like the Lord, Schulz giveth, and he taketh away.

M.H.

PECOS BILL (Italy) The school of Italian comic strip artists that formed in Mondadori and Vecchi's magazines in the mid-1930s reached a very high level of proficiency in graphic excellence as well as in storytelling ability. Few features were produced but they were of high artistic value and could hold their own against the comics imported from the United States. After World War II, when the number of magazines grew, the increased demand for material led to a decline in quality. The only creation worthy of the prewar Italian production was *Pecos Bill*.

Pecos Bill was written by Guido Martina and drawn by Raffaele Paparella and Pier Lorenzo De Vita, with the assistance of Dino Battaglia, Leone Cimpellin, Gino D'Antonio, and others. The feature appeared in the *Albi d'Oro* comic books published by Arnoldo Mondadori from 1949 to 1955. The story opens at a cowboy campfire with the participants telling of the legendary exploits of Pecos Bill. Then the action moves to Pecos

"Pecos Bill," Piero Gamba. © Edizioni Alpe.

Bill himself, an athletic horseman with parted blond hair and traditional dress made of a blue shirt, leather armbands, leather jacket, neckerchief, and red pants. The hero does not carry a gun or a rifle; his only weapon is the lariat, which he uses with masterful versatility. Mounted on his black horse, Turbine ("Whirlpool"), whose help is often welcome, Pecos Bill roams the West, ever ready to do battle with rebel Indians or white outlaws, to defend the oppressed, and to right every conceivable wrong. His sweetheart, a blonde girl named Sue, welcomes him back after each adventure. Pecos Bill's heart, however, is throbbing for a more aggressive and dynamic woman: the former outlaw Calamity Jane, whom our hero had been able to reform. Together they fight against all odds in a bond made of mutual respect and admiration.

In 1956 there was a new, short-lived version of *Pecos Bill* drawn by Piero Gamba for Edizioni Alpe. In 1960 the old episodes were reissued, followed and continued by a third series (this time for Torelli) done by a number of artists, among whom were Armando Bonato and Cimpellin (1964-1966). An attempt to revive the series with new episodes only lasted from 1978 to 1980.

G.B.

PEDRITO EL DRITO (Italy) An amusing parody of the Western genre, *Pedrito El Drito* has been recounting the tragic-comic vicissitudes of its title hero ever since it first appeared in the pages of the comic weekly *Rocky Rider* in 1948. Born as a strip, the saga of Pedrito developed into a gag page (published by the weekly *Albo dell'Intrepido*) and then back into a continuity strip in the weekly *Il Monello.* In these three comic books (all published by Universo) *Pedrito* has managed to last for over 25 years: it was the last series to appear in *Rocky Rider* and, when this publication folded, it went to *Il Monello* where it remained until the weekly replaced all of its humor features with adventure strips (1972). Since then, *Pedrito* has been featured weekly on the back cover of *Albo dell'Intrepido*, a publication which has already passed the 1,500-issue mark.

Pedrito, the sheriff of Tapioca City, is an inveterate drinker and a chronic gambler. His vices are scarcely toned down by the admonitions—reinforced by a few strokes of the familiar rolling pin—of his wife, Paquita, who vainly tries to bring her husband back to the straight-and-narrow. The good sheriff, whose work does not seem to bother him unduly, spends most of his time in fights with Paquita and in elaborate schemes designed to elude her and get him to the town saloon.

This series (more than slightly reminiscent of *Bringing Up Father*) is the creation of the prolific cartoonist Antonio Terenghi, who is also the author of many other comic features, including *Piccola Eva* ("Little Eva"), *Tarzanetto* and *Poldino* (which is published in France by Sagédition). It ended its ample career in 1975.

G.B.

PEDROCCHI, FEDERICO (1907-1945) Federico Pedrocchi was an Italian journalist and writer born 1907 in Buenos Aires, Argentina, of Italian parents. In 1912 Pedrocchi was brought back to Italy by his parents. His father died a few years later and Pedrocchi had to go to work as soon as possible, drawing during his free time.

In 1930, after a short stint in advertising, he started writing short novels, which he also illustrated, did book covers, and contributed, both as writer and cartoonist, to a number of magazines such as *Domenica del Corriere, Corriere dei Piccoli, Jumbo,* and *Tempo.* He made his comic strip debut in 1935 with a colonial story, *I Due Tamburini* ("The Two Drummer-boys"), for Mondadori. This was followed by a number of other contributions by Pedrocchi, and in 1939 he became editor for all of Mondadori's children's magazines, a position that he was to hold until 1942, when he was inducted into the army.

Pedrocchi's "Mondadori years" were his most productive; there he wrote the continuities for some of the most remarkable among Italian strips: *Kit Carson,* a Western strip about the legendary explorer and Indian fighter; *La Compagnia dei Sette* ("The Company of Seven") about a gang of high-spirited adolescents; *Virus, il Mago della Foresta Morta* ("Virus, the Mage of the Dead Forest"), one of the more successful forays into science fantasy; *Zorro della Metropoli* ("Zorro of the Metropolis"), *Gino e Gianni,* and others.

Discharged at the end of 1943, Pedrocchi became editor of the Carroccio publishing house, writing four novels for them based on his own comic strip narratives. At the same time he kept his ties with Mondadori and continued his career as a comic strip writer. In January 1945 Pedrocchi was killed when the train in which he was riding was strafed by English planes.

Federico Pedrocchi made a sterling contribution to Italian comics in the difficult period of the late 1930s and early 1940s. Helped by a remarkable group of artists whom he was able to assemble around him (Rino Albertarelli, Cesare Avai, Giovanni Scolari, and Walter Molino, among others) he was the leading figure in what has been termed "the Italian comic strip renaissance."

M.H.

PEKKA PUUPÄÄ (Finland) *Pekka Puupää* ("Peter Blockhead"), the famous Finnish comic strip, was created in 1925 by the Finnish cartoonist Ola Fogelberg (1894-1952), who was also known by his pseudonym "Fogeli," and was launched in the cooperative maga-

"Pekka Puupää," Ola Fogelberg. © Kuluttajain Lehti.

zine *Kuluttajain lehti* ("Consumers' paper"). Fogelberg made cartoons, illustrated gags, magazine illustrations, book illustrations, and calendars and worked as illustrator and publicity manager of a big Helsinki cooperative from 1918 to 1945. It was therefore no surprise that he should also try doing a comic strip for the cooperative's *Kuluttajain lehti*. Besides, he had already done another comic strip during the winter months of 1917 to 1918, before the Finnish civil war. This had been a strongly allegorical satire on the political life of the time, entitled *Janne Ankkanen* ("Jimmy Duck"). *Janne Ankkanen* was written by the famous Finnish satirist Jalmari Finne and was published in *Suomen Kuvalehti*, a big pictorial.

As in *Janne Ankkanen*, there was a decidedly ideological commitment in the *Pekka Puupää* comic strip, appearing in a consumers' paper propagating cooperative and leftist ideas. However, the comic strip also exposed human weaknesses in general. *Pekka Puupää* is drawn in a relatively simple, cartoony style, with text and dialogue printed below the pictures.

In 1945 Fogelberg turned to freelance work and started publishing his *Pekka Puupää* series in book form. With these annually published books, the series reached its peak of popularity, selling about 70,000 copies per year.

Soon after Fogelberg's death in 1952, a film based on the *Pekka Puupää* comic strip was produced by a big Finnish movie mogul, T. J. Särkkä. Over the next decade, a total of 13 films was produced. The films were mainly aimed at juvenile audiences. They are counted among the most popular Finnish films ever made. As happens so often, the movie version eclipsed the artistically subtle original. Nevertheless, the tradition of *Pekka Puupää* annuals was carried on after Fogelberg's death by his daughter, Toto Fogelberg-Kaila.

W.F.

PELLOS, RENÉ (1900-   ) A French cartoonist and illustrator born in 1900 near Lyons, René Pellos never received any formal art education, although he remem-

bers drawing from the age of five and filling his notebooks with sketches and caricatures. After dropping out of school, Pellos held all kinds of jobs—advertising artist, lithographer, book designer, stage decorator, and pianist (in 1919-1920). In the 1920s Pellos's career stabilized when he became sports cartoonist for the important Paris daily *L'Intransigeant*, while contributing cartoons and illustrations to other newspapers, doing sports panels for *Le Miroir des Sports*, and drawing covers for *Match* magazine.

Pellos's comic strip career started inauspiciously in 1935 with *Riri, Gogo et Lolo*, a kid strip that even its creator prefers to forget. Then came the dazzling *Futuropolis* (1937), a tale of anticipation in which Pellos displayed all his talents as an artist and designer. In quick succession there followed *Jean-Jacques Ardent* (a sports strip turned war strip at the outbreak of World War II), *Monsieur Petipon* (a humor strip not without merit), *Moustique* (a kid strip), and *Electropolis* (Pellos's second attempt at science fiction, unfortunately interrupted by the German invasion in June 1940).

During the German occupation, Pellos, while working as a sports cartoonist and illustrator and continuing some of his series (notably *Monsieur Petipon*), took

René Pellos, "Atomas." © Mon Journal.

an active part in the French Resistance. In 1944, following France's liberation, he resumed his professional career with contributions to such publications as *Record, Sporting,* and *Le Petit Echo de la Mode* (a woman's magazine). In 1946 he came back to the comic strip with *Durga-Râni* (on a script by Jean Sylvere), a kind of secondhand *Futuropolis* with a muscular young heroine instead of the obligatory male hero. In 1948 another science fiction strip, *Atomas* (on the well-worn theme of the power-mad scientist) followed. In the meantime Pellos had met Georges Offenstadt, who suggested that the cartoonist revive Forton's classic comic strip, *Les Pieds-Nickelés.* At first reluctant, Pellos finally accepted the offer, and his new version of the strip appeared in 1948.

Since then Pellos has devoted his career almost exclusively to *Les Pieds-Nickelés* (with an occasional foray into magazine or book illustration). A genuine artist who has excelled in all facets of his profession, he is especially noted for the innovations (and the breath of fresh air) which he brought to the anemic French comic strip of the prewar years. Since the death of Alain Saint-Ogan in 1974, René Pellos has been cast (somewhat diffidently) into the role of the grand old man of French comic art. In 1981 he left *Les Pieds-Nickelés* and went into retirement, although he continued to turn out an occasional drawing and give a number of interviews to the press.

M.H.

PENG GUOLIANG (1940-   ) As many others, Peng, from his childhood, liked art and especially cartoon art. But he was assigned to work as a photogra-

pher in a publishing house in Beijing at the beginning of his career. From 1979 to date Peng has worked as an art editor for *Young Children Pictorial,* a monthly journal published by the Chinese Children and Juvenile Publisher, in Beijing.

Among other comic strips for young children, Peng's *Little Dog Guaiguai* is one of the most popular strips that has been carried by *Young Children Pictorial* and other similar journals since 1986. Each story is narrated in about 30 color drawings in a two-page spread. The hero of each story, Little Dog Guaiguai (*guaiguai* in Chinese means "obedience") is a clever dog but does not always prove to be obedient. The disobedient dog, however, learns his lesson at the end of the story, which is intended to be of educative value to the young readers. For example, the little dog dislikes washing his head, as many children do in reality. After the little dog goes through all the troubles caused by being dirty, he learns that not washing his head is no good.

Little Dog Guaiguai was adapted into a 120-program series by a Beijing television station in the early 1990s, after ten years of being broadcast every month. These 120 stories in more than 6,000 drawings were also published in five volumes by Beijing Normal University Press in 1996.

In addition, Peng has created many other comic strips for children, including *Little Taotao, Little Pals, Little White Rabbit and Big Grey Wolf, Doggy Officer, Good Friends, Small Fox with Big Feet,* and others. Among them, *Doggy Officer* is an officer dressed in ancient-time uniform; the strip functions as a metaphor of life today.

H.Y.L.L.

Peng Guoliang, "The Little Dog Guaiguai." © *Peng Guoliang.*

PENGUIN, THE (Canada) Not to be confused with the villain of the same name in Batman and Detective Comics in the United States, the Canadian crimefighter and counterspy known as the Penguin made his debut in 1943 in issue number 15 of *Wow Comics*, one of six titles launched by Bell Features and Publishing Co., Toronto, after a wartime embargo wiped U.S. comic books off Canadian newsstands. The first issue of *Wow* (September 1941) appeared in full color; issues 2 to 8 in two colors, and thereafter in black and white with full-color covers.

Created by Adrian Dingle, later one of Canada's foremost painters, *The Penguin* featured a debonair crimefighter who wore a birdlike mask, white tie, and tails. And, like the majority of Bells's adventure strips, it was serialized. One of Dingle's gimmicks was to conceal the Penguin's real identify from the reader, never showing his face. Another break from comic-hero tradition was Dingle's readiness to have the Penguin unmasked by a criminal or ally. In Wow number 16, for example, Lugar, the fiendish master spy, unmasks the captive Penguin who says, "Those who peer under the mask don't live long." Eventually, of course, his warning comes true. In *Wow* number 18 the Penguin meets a good-natured American named Simon Snurge who accidentally learns his identity and then helps him break up a ring of gasoline ration coupon counterfeiters.

When Bell converted to full-color printing at the war's end to counteract the reappearance of U.S. comic books, Dingle continued the feature under the title, *The Blue Raven*, presumably because Bell was planning to try and crack the U.S. market with his color product and foresaw a conflict with National Periodical Publications over its right to the Penguin name. *The Blue Raven*'s flight was short-lived, however, and ended in the disintegration of the Canadian comic book industry in the face of U.S. competition.

P.H.

PENSION RADICELLE, LA (France) Eugène Gire is one of the unsung heroes of the French humor strip. He was one of the first to transplant the crazy humor of the Marx brothers to France, and he honed the lowly pun to a fine point of accuracy long before René Goscinny was cutting his teeth as an office boy at *Mad* magazine. As one of the pillars of the comic weekly *Vaillant*, he contributed innumerable series to the publication, from *R. Hudi Junior* to *Kam et Rah, les Terribles*. His masterpiece (if such it can be called) remains, however, *La Pension Radicelle* ("The Radicelle Boarding-House"), which unfolded its merry compendium of absurdities in July 1947.

In the boarding-house run by the big-hearted and elderly Mrs. Radicelle, a joyous band of youngsters led by the high-spirited, devilishly inventive Saturnin, spreads good-natured mischief in the region. When the kids run out of pranks to play on their neighbors, they elect to live in a deserted village, which they turn into a kind of pranksters' paradise. Then they leave for an African island (the resemblance with the Katzenjammers is evident) only to come back to their village.

La Pension Radicelle was a funny, nonsensical strip. Had Gire made up his mind whether he wanted it to be a chronicle of weekly gags or to turn it into a tale of humorous adventure, the feature would have probably gone on forever, so inexhaustible was the author's imagination. As it turned out, *La Pension Radicelle* ended its long career in *Vaillant* (now called *Pif*) on February 23, 1968.

M.H.

PEPITO (Italy) The protagonists of the rollickingly funny strip *Pepito*, while not well-known in their own country, are very popular abroad. Pepito, Ventoinpoppa, Hernandez De La Banane, Admiral Debath O'Lavoir, and the pirate Schiacciasassi were all created by the prolific cartoonist Luciano Bottaro in 1951. Carlo Chendi writes the scripts for this series which has been published in France since 1954, first as a fortnightly, then as a king-size monthly, by Sagédition. The French publishers have also issued several annuals, one-shots and hardbound volumes of *Pepito*. In Germany the strip has been published by Kauka Verlag since 1972. Under the name *Corchito*, it has also been translated into Spanish and Portuguese in several

Latin American countries. In Italy, on the other hand, after being initially published by Edizioni Alpe, it went out with hardly a murmur.

As happens quite often in the comics, the main protagonist of the strip is not the title character but a side-kick who had become popular with the readers. In this case it is Hernandez De La Banane, the governor, who appeared in the first episode of *Pepito*, but only on the sidelines. He later acquired his full personality as a petty colonial tyrant: two-faced, cheating, conniving, and deceitful, but ingratiating nonetheless. He is surrounded by a colorful entourage of wizards and sooth-sayers, admirals and inventors, noble ladies and witches. "His Ventripotence," as his subjects call him, pressures the people with all kinds of imaginative taxes, which he usually pockets. When a shortage is discovered by some zealous auditor, the governor arranges to have his ship scuttled by a crew of accommodating pirates.

Pepito and his corsairs, on the other hand, fight against the Spanish Crown and try to right the injustices committed by the governor.

The *Pepito* strip, on the strength of its popularity abroad, finally came back to Italy in paperback form published by Editrice Cenisio (1975). More than 40 years after its inception it is still going strong in Italy and abroad, especially in France where it is being reprinted over and over again.

G.B.

PERERA, CAMILLUS (1945?-   ) "Camillusge" is the prefatory signature to the titles of various Sri Lankan strips created and drawn by Camillus Perera and published in periodicals of his corporation, Camillus Publications. There are at least 15 major characters and eight periodicals, two of the latter, *Sathsiri* and *Rasika*, devoted entirely to comics.

Perera's strips are among the longest surviving and most popular in Sri Lanka; *Camillusge Don Sethan* dates to May 1, 1966, and *Camillusge Gajaman Samaga Sathsiri* to August 1972. These strips appeared in scattered comics papers (for example, *Gajaman* debuted in the country's first comics paper *Sathuta* and switched to *Sittara* and then *Sathsiri*, both Camillus papers) before Perera pulled them together under one corporate structure.

Three special magazines done by Perera in 1984 to 1985 formed the basis for Camillus Publications. In April 1984 Perera did *Camillusge Gajaman*, full of cartoons about the Sri Lankan New Year, followed by *Camillusge Samayan* and *Camillusge Gajaman 2* in December 1985. Sales of 200,000 to 300,000 prompted Perera to form the company.

Camillus comics take on a number of genres, such as love and romance (the most popular), historical fiction, jungle adventure, and humor. A typical issue of *Sathsiri* or *Rasika* consists of 16 pages with one story per page. Fourteen stories are done by almost as many different freelance artists; the fifteenth is the humor strip by Perera. Almost all stories emanate from Perera who commissions freelance artists to draw them; most are serialized, with some running for years.

As comics papers faced stiff competition from television and video in the 1990s, Perera was seeking other avenues, particularly animation.

J.A.L

"Le Père Ladébauche," Albéric Bourgeois. © La Presse.

PÈRE LADÉBAUCHE, LE (Canada) The character of Père Ladébauche (which could be translated as "Pop Debauchery") was created in 1879 by the prolific newspaperman, cartoonist, and writer Hector Bertelot. On March 5, 1904, this picturesque figure was adapted to the Sunday comic page by J. Charlebois for the newspaper *La Presse*. But it was only with the arrival of Albéric Bourgeois, who took over *Le Père Ladébauche* on February 11, 1905, that the feature really took off.

Père Ladébauche was a colorful rogue: bald, bewhiskered, with a twinkle in his eye, he had a fondness for liquor, gambling, and a pretty skirt. His adventures took place at first in the restricted locale of the province of Quebec, but he soon launched his ne'er-do-well career around the globe, which he circled several times, always coming back to Montreal to brag about his world-wise experiences. When he took over *Le Père Ladébauche*, Bourgeois was already in control of his drawing style: his line was elegant and humorous, his characters portrayed with a deft hand. Although he owed some of his techniques to the early American cartoonists (notably Richard Outcault and Charles Schulz from whom he borrowed his graphic treatment of children) Bourgeois was much his own man, and his style is highly individual. Thanks to his talent, *Le Père Ladébauche* became the best-known Canadian feature of the time, and it fended off the assaults of more famous (and cheaper) American imports for more than 50 years. The only survivor of the entire comic strip line of *La Presse* in 1910, *Le Père Ladébauche* was to pursue its long career until 1957, when Bourgeois retired from active life.

Le Père Ladébauche is indisputably the most important Canadian comic strip in the French language. After years of obscurity, it is now being studied by young

French-Canadian cartoonists conscious of their artistic heritage.

M.H.

PERISHERS, THE (G.B.) Maisie, Marlon, and Baby Grumpling were the original kids called *The Perishers*, a strip dreamed up by Bill Herbert, strip editor of the *Daily Mirror*, for the northern edition. It replaced *Hylda Baker's Diary*, a failure to adapt into strip form the popular radio comedienne. Artist Dennis Collins, then signing himself "Kol," was retained; writer Denis Gifford was replaced by Ben Witham.

The strip started on February 10, 1958, a shadow of the *Daily Sketch*'s popular *Peanuts*. Herbert brought in a new writer, advertising artist Maurice Dodd, and moved Witham to caption for Jack Greenall's panel, *Useless Eustace*. Dodd revived the absent Wellin'ton, the kid in a deerstalker who lives in a drainpipe, and fitted him out with Boot, a great big lovable lion of an Olde English Sheepdog. Then came Plain Jane, Fiscal Yere (B. H. Calcutta, failed), Tatty Oldbit, a beetle, a delinquent caterpillar, a Teutonic tortoise, assorted crabs and other scuttling things which "festoon the bottom of the strip like barnacles on a barge" (Dodd).

In July 1962 *The Perishers* moved to larger premises, a solo position out of the gallery where the rest of the *Mirror* strips lived. Their panels grew larger in size, upwards: the first day the little denizens solved the problem by taking to the air on stilts! They crossed the border to the Scottish edition of the *Mirror* in 1966, and currently appear in full color in that part of the world. Rod McKuen took them to the United States and published a hardback, *Old Boot's Private Papers* (1970), and

"The Perishers," Dennis Collins. © Daily Mirror Ltd.

regular paperback reprints began in 1962, the sixteenth arriving in 1974 together with an anthology, *The Perishers Omnibus*.

After Collins retired, Maurice Dodd took over the drawing chores but eventually found the daily grind too much of an imposition. Currently the strip is illustrated by Bill Mevin, a former children's comic artist with a number of television cartoon characters to his credit. *The Perishers* have also been animated into a successful television series.

D.G.

PERONI, CARLO (1929-) Carlo Peroni is an Italian cartoonist born on November 24, 1929, in Senigallia. After his art school studies, Peroni first devoted himself to the restoration of old paintings, then to frescoes and mural paintings in churches. This did not pay well, however, and he moved to all kinds of odd jobs—clerk, mechanic, warehouse guard, barrel-maker, songwriter—before going on to stage design. From there the step to comics was an easy one. In 1948 he moved to Milan and began contributing to *Vispa Teresa* magazine as an editor and artist. At the same time he ghosted for several comic artists, setting the pattern for his very personal and funny style.

In 1949 Peroni started working for the Catholic magazine *L'Aspirante* where he created *Lillo, Lallo e Lello*. Moving to Rome in 1952 he continued his collaboration with Catholic magazines, especially *Il Giornalino*, where he published centerspreads, illustrations, and comic strips, among which Brick is the most notable (1954). Brick was a puppetlike creature who often lived wild adventures in the company of movie stars (Frank Sinatra and Claudio Villa) or comic strip heroes (Dan Dare or Superman).

In 1959, in the pages of the pocket-size comic book *Capitan Walter*, Peroni produced a number of short-lived comic creations: *Grama Gramelloni, Gambalesta* ("Rubberlegs"), *Veneziano Telegtammi*; of longer duration, more than 100 episodes, was his comic saga, *Gervasio*, later continued in *Jolly*. After a stint as a layout man and a television graphic artist, Peroni went back to the comics in 1961, trying his hand at adventure with such features as *Sand e Zeos* and *Gorin e Obi*. Both were produced for the Communist Party weekly, *Il Pionere*, as was his zany *Gigetto, Pirata Picoletto* ("Gigoletto, the Diminutive Pirate").

More comic creation followed from Peroni's prolific pen: *Ping e Pong* (1961); *Teddy Sprin* (a Western parody, 1963); *Zio Boris* a pastiche of horror movies written by Alfredo Castelli; and *Van Helsing*, about a screwball vampire, on texts by Castelli and Baratelli (both in 1969); *Lumak* (1971), from which a book, *Mondo Lumace*, was produced; and in 1973, *Gianconiglio* ("John Rabbit"), a very successful strip which now absorbs all his time. Among his latter creations mention should be made of *Spugna* (1976) and *Gipsy* (1984). He is also among the staff that draws the *Sherlock Holmes* comic stories and the Hanna-Barbera characters.

Carlo Peroni has also enjoyed a successful career as an animator, working on such series as *Calimero, Ferrarella, Gatto Silvestro* ("Sylvester," the cat created by Warner Bros. studios), *Braccobaldo, Coccobill,* and others.

G.B.

PERROTT, REG (1916?-1948?) A British cartoonist born in Charlton, London, Reg Perrott joined the Morley Adams and Henry Fidler Agency as a staff artist in 1934, contributing strips and illustrations to the newspaper features and comic sections syndicated by that concern. At first he drew humorous strips: *Benny & Buster* in the *South Wales Echo, Bobbie & Bertie Bruin* in the *Scottish Daily Express, The Imps* in the *Yorkshire Evening News* (all 1933). In 1934 he continued this style with *Buster & Bones* (Y.E.N.), *A Hair Raising Voyage* (S.W.E.), and *Roly & Poly*, a daily strip in the *London Evening Star*. During that year he suddenly switched styles with a dramatic picture serial called *Luck of the Legion* for the *Bristol Evening World*.

It was the birth of a new talent, and Perrott rapidly rose to the forefront of British adventure artists with his succeeding series for the same newspaper: *The Archer Highwayman* (1934) and *Targa the Tiger Man, Land of the Lost People*, and *Code of the Northland* (1935). In 1935 he left Adams & Fidler to freelance for the Amalgamated Press. Whirling Round the World on the back page of *Joker* visualized a voyage in a new design of autogyro. *Wheels of Fortune* (March 3, 1935) on the back of *Jolly* featured young Bob Dean as the driver of Lord Tom's new racing car, the Red Flash. The Young Explorers (October 17, 1936) brought thrills aboard the school ship *Sea Foam* to *Puck*.

A new opportunity arose when Walt Disney Productions launched *Mickey Mouse Weekly* in 1936. Perrott contributed a tremendous historical serial, *Road to Rome*, then went into full color for the first time with a Western, *White Cloud*. He followed this with the superb color serial, *Sons of the Sword*, and a complete story for the *Mickey Mouse Holiday Special* called *Secret of the Manor*.

Perrott began 1937 with another Western, *Golden Arrow. Puck* presented this strip as if it were a film; it was the first time this children's weekly had broken with tradition. Instead of captions in type beneath the pictures, Perrott lettered captions and balloons within the panels of the strip. He also varied the size and shape of his panels as required by the situation. Another 1937 departure was his serial *Golden Eagle*, a two-color (black and orange) saga of Ace Eagle and his experimental aircraft, on the back of *Golden* (October 23, 1937). The title was later changed to *Kings of the Air*. The year ended with *Crusader's Christmas*, another complete strip for *Mickey Mouse Holiday Special*.

In 1938 Perrott was back in *Mickey Mouse Weekly* with another flying serial, *Wings of Fortune*, and he did another complete strip, *Rescuer's Reward*, for the *Holiday Special*. His best strip began on October 8, 1938, in the first issue of *Happy Days*. In full-color gravure, this historical saga was called *Song of the Sword*, and in it he used long cinemascopic panels for battle scenes. His last major work was the Western serial *Red Rider* in *Jolly*, another two-tone (red and black) job (March 18, 1939).

Perrott enlisted in the Royal Air Force Regiment in 1939. Discharged, he was made art editor of *Mickey Mouse* (by now a fortnightly). In 1944 he drew a small comic serial, *Sir Roger de Coverlet*, followed by *White King of Arabia* (1945). Replaced when Basil Reynolds returned, he freelanced *Spaceship to the Moon* to a one-shot comic, *Look & Laugh* (1948?), and illustrated the book, *King Harold's Son* (1946). His early death robbed British comics of perhaps their best adventure artist.

D.G.

PERRY (Germany) Perry is the comic book version of *Perry Rhodan*, the most successful science fiction hero to come out of postwar Germany. Perry Rhodan, the practically immortal Terran Overlord, first started in the comic realm with *Perry Rhodan im Bild* ("Perry Rhodan in Pictures") in 1968. Twenty-seven issues later, in 1970, the title of the book was changed to *Perry*, the numbering starting once again from 1. Whereas *Perry Rhodan im Bild* had stayed fairly close to the original novels, *Perry* started a new line of stories that made use of a somewhat streamlined cast of characters. This change was made so that the comic book would be more appealing to readers not yet initiated by the novels.

Since No. 37, *Perry* is being written by Dirk Hess. From the very beginning, the artwork was provided by the Studio Giolitti. Some of the earlier issues were by German-born artist Kurt Caesar, who occasionally worked for the Giolitti shop in Rome, Italy. With *Perry* No. 37, a change was made to make the book more visually stimulating. Giorgio Gambiotti, another artist from the Giolitti stable, had devised a new style that was inspired by pop art and Marvel Comics. The futuristic flavor was further enhanced by doing away with most of the women's wear. Rectangular and square

"Perry," Studio Giolitti. © Moewing Verlag.

"Peter Piltdown," Mal Eaton. © Herald-Tribune Syndicate.

panels were given up for full-page compositions with interlocking pieces. This was toned down in time to make the stories less puzzling. The new style showed a strong penchant toward the art of John Buscema. Thus, cameo appearances of The Thing and the Silver Surfer or of the changeling computer from one *Star Trek* episode may have been meant as inside jokes.

To be sure, *Perry* doesn't exactly come as a revelation to either comics or science fiction fans. Yet, besides giving glimpses of shapely females accompanying the hero through space, *Perry* is keeping the sci-fi format alive in Germany and, thanks to the new style initiated with No. 37, foreign language reprints in France, Italy, and Israel have been made possible.

The *Perry* comic book did not remain the only spin-off of the Perry Rhodan novels. In 1967 to 1968 Rhodan was put on film—a fact much deplored by disgruntled fans—and, for some years thereafter, some of the Rhodan space operas have been marketed as stereo dramas on long-playing record albums.

In its heyday, *Perry* made a comic strip guest appearance in *Bravo*, a weekly magazine for the teenage movie, television, and pop music fans. Early in 1975, however, the *Perry* comic book ceased publication with No. 129, a victim of ever-increasing production costs. Due to a sales method of regional distribution and redistribution, that last issue did not go on sale in some parts of Germany until late in the summer of 1975.

W.F.

PETER PILTDOWN (U.S.) Leading caricaturist Mal Eaton introduced his unique stone-age comic strip *Peter Piltdown* to the *New York Herald-Tribune* Sunday section on August 4, 1935. Each week his group of motley urchins created havoc and slapstick adventure with their mischievous pranks in the tradition of *Buster Brown* and *The Katzenjammer Kids*.

Peter was an artful figure supported by more developed innocents and meddlers, such as Charlie Cro-

Magnon, Oofty, and the guiltless girl Inna-Minnie. The situations Eaton created were usually manic and full of hilarious slapstick. Minus a handful of parental appearances, the strip's sole adult, bearded hermit Mr. Shadrack, stumbled into the feature in 1940, adding a classic personality and perfect comic foil to the cast. Ever spouting tall tales of fictitious valor, he was often the victim of capers prompted by the unruly imps or any of the limitless species of animals that populated their primeval world. Kiltie the scottie, Bolivar the octopus, Artie the dinosaur, and other members of the menagerie shared equal importance with their human companions and paved the way for the eclectic cast of Johnny Hart's *B.C.* some years later. In 1940 he also added Pookie, a carrot-top simpleton whose naive charm made her another target and the strip's most endearing figure. By 1943 the prehistoric aura was diluted with less frequent sightings of dinos, while contemporary dress replaced animal skins.

Eaton's drawing style was loose and physical, capturing well the activity in fluid simplicity and the varying environs in rich textures. On December 15, 1946, the strip ceased, replaced for a short time with *Pookie*, a daily-sized Sunday filler. In the early 1950s it reappeared as *Rocky Stoneaxe* within the comics section of *Boy's Life* magazine, retitled after its only new character. The feature appeared monthly until finally disappearing in 1973, and it is forgotten today. Eaton's strip should be recalled for its consistent humor and unique treatment of classic comic formulas.

The strip's name was clearly inspired by the "Piltdown Man," the skeleton of a purported prehistoric man discovered near Piltdown in England. The "discovery" was exposed as a hoax in the 1950s, but it held credibility for a long time: as late as the 1970s it led Australian cartoonist Donald Langmead to create *Piltdown—the Almost Human*, which ran from 1973 into the 1980s.

B.J.

PETER RABBIT (U.S.) Harrison Cady's adaptation to the Sunday comic page format of Thornton W. Burgess's children's animal narratives, *Peter Rabbit*, began in the *New York Tribune* on August 15, 1920. Cady, the noted illustrator of the highly popular Burgess books, was the effective scripter of the comic strip, but soon departed sharply from the story and character lines of the Burgess works, within a few months after beginning the strip. Domesticating Burgess's bachelor hero of many stories, Cady made Peter Rabbit a cozily married bunny with two twin boys, either or both of whom responded to the name "Petey," while the Cady-created Mrs. Rabbit was named "Hepsy." Cady also quickly abandoned the many Burgess characters and introduced such regular figures of his own as Old Mr. Bear and Mr. (or "Professor") Possum.

Leaning heavily on wild, rambunctious slapstick rather than on the mildly poetic subtleties of the Burgess books, Cady swiftly shaped a strip which generally pleased the 6-to-10-year-olds at whom it was aimed over the 30-plus years of its existence. Never carried in a large number of papers, and reprinted only infrequently in comic books between 1937 and 1950, *Peter Rabbit* was essentially an institution of the *New York Herald-Tribune* until Cady retired on July 25, 1948. After the few remaining Cady Sunday pages were run, Vincent Fago took the strip over with disastrous effects (a worse artist would be hard to imagine in any context), and it was omitted from even the *Herald-Tribune*'s pages after a few years in 1956.

B.B.

PETE THE TRAMP (U.S.) In the late 1920s C. D. Russell had created the character of a seedy, weather-beaten tramp who appeared in a series of gag cartoons in the magazine *Judge*. Hearst, always looking for new talent, spotted Russell's tramp cartoons and had him signed up by King Features Syndicate. Russell's creation *Pete the Tramp* appeared for the first time as a Sunday feature on January 10, 1932. (There briefly was a *Pete* daily strip as well, starting in February 1934 and lasting till June 1937.)

Pete and his yellow mutt, Boy (who later had his own strip titled *Pete's Pup*), roam the streets and parks of the city in search of food, shelter, and companionship, most often rebuffed, sometimes beaten up, but never disheartened. In the sad little tramp's breast hope springs eternal, and he concocts the wildest

"Pete the Tramp," C. D. Russell. © King Features Syndicate.

schemes to mooch a meal or swipe a fat cigar. There is more than a bit of pathos in Pete's small triumphs, and in the bitter years of the Depression the humor must have rung as true as it did funny.

Pete's only support is the cook Linda who often bakes a pie or prepares a meal for the little tramp; and his nemesis is O'Leary, the fat cop who delights in waking up poor Pete and rousting him off his park bench with a blow of his nightstick. Later Pete was also to acquire an adopted infant as sad-looking as himself.

After the 1940s *Pete*'s tramp humor began to wane, and the gags often seemed repetitious and forced. *Pete the Tramp* finally folded on December 12, 1963, shortly after the creator's death.

M.H.

PFEUFER, CARL (1910-1980) Carl Pfeufer is an American comic strip and comic book artist born September 29, 1910, in Mexico City. In 1913 the Pfeufer family moved to New York where the young Carl grew up and went to high school, majoring in commercial art. After graduation he went on to Cooper Union, studying freehand drawing (he won first prize three different times), to the National Academy of Design (where he unsuccessfully competed for the Prix de Rome), and to the Grand Central Art School. Toward the end of the 1920s Carl Pfeufer started work with the McFadden publications doing layouts, spot illustrations, and editorial cartoons.

In the mid-1930s Pfeufer was working as a staff artist for the *Brooklyn Eagle* when he created with writer Bob Moore a Sunday comic page comprised of two features: *Don Dixon and the Hidden Empire*, a science fiction strip, and *Tad of the Tanbark*, a jungle story (both started on October 6, 1935). In December 1936 Pfeufer took over *Gordon, Soldier of Fortune* from John Hales. All three features were initially distributed by the *Eagle* itself, but were later farmed out to the Watkins Syndicate. *Tad* folded in 1940; *Gordon* and *Don Dixon* lasted a while longer, until July 1941.

Like so many other unemployed comic strip artists, Pfeufer turned to comic book work, at first for Marvel (*The Human Torch, Submariner*) then (from 1943) for Fawcett, where he enjoyed an enduring career. His credits there include *Ibis the Invincible, Commando Yank, Don Winslow*, and a host of Western titles (*Hopalong Cassidy, Ken Maynard, Tom Mix*, and *Gabby Hayes*). In 1955, following Fawcett's wholesale discontinuance of their comic book line, he shifted to Charlton, working on many of their titles, notably *Charlie Chan*. (In the meantime Pfeufer had tried his hand at newspaper strips again with such short-lived creations as *Bantam Prince* for the *Herald-Tribune* and *Chisholm Kid* for the *Pittsburgh Courier*.) From Charlton he went to Dell, working on many television comic titles, and in the 1960s he quit comic book work altogether.

Making his home in Texas, Pfeufer devoted the last years of his life to turning out paintings and sculptures for galleries around the world. He died in 1980, and his passing went more or less unnoticed.

M.H.

PHANTOM, THE (U.S.) 1—In the wake of *Mandrake*'s success Lee Falk brought out another adventure strip for King Features, *The Phantom*. First appearing as a daily strip on February 17, 1936 (with a Sunday page added in May 1939), the feature was originally drawn

"The Phantom," Lee Falk and Ray Moore. © King Features Syndicate.

by Ray Moore. Moore, however, suffered a grave injury in 1942, and his assistant Wilson McCoy took over gradually. From 1947 to 1961 (the date of his death) McCoy alone assured the drawing of *The Phantom*, which then passed for a few months into the hands of Bill Lignante. Sy Barry took over in 1962 and is still drawing the feature today.

A mysterious, hooded figure of justice, the Phantom carries on a long tradition of crime fighting begun in the 16th century and passed on from father to son. He is, therefore, not just a man but a legend, "the ghost-who-walks," believed to be invincible and immortal. Like all legendary figures he has his symbol—"the sign of the skull"—whose simple mention instills fear in the heart of the most callous criminal. In his fight against crime, the Phantom is assisted by Guran, the crafty leader of the dreaded Bandar pygmies and by Devil, his faithful gray wolf. But the Phantom is also human: a great part of his time is spent in the pursuit of his fiancee, Diana Palmer.

After the war the Phantom changed his base of operations from the Bengal region of India to a mythical country, part African, part Asian. He was also a naturalized American under the name of Kit Walker (in the earlier episodes he was English, the 20th descendant of Sir Christopher Standish) and now had a whole organization, "the Jungle Patrol," working for him. The Phantom and Diana finally were married, after many a mishap and contretemps, in December 1977, and in the spring of 1979 twins were born to the happy couple: Heloise and Kit, Jr., thus ensuring that the legend of the ghost-who-walks would go on for at least another generation.

Skillfully playing on this aura of myth and mystery, Lee Falk has been able to raise *The Phantom* above the customary level of the adventure tale into the realms of the fable and the parable.

Ever since its beginning, *The Phantom* has been among the half-dozen or so top adventure strips. It is especially popular overseas and is being translated and read in some 60 countries. There have been countless imitations of the character in the United States and abroad. *The Phantom* was adapted to the screen in 1943, and a series of paperback novels (purportedly written by Lee Falk) are now being published by Avon. A theatrical movie version of *The Phantom*, starring Billy Zane, was released in 1996.

M.H.

2—Despite its great success in the syndicated newspaper field, *The Phantom* feature has had a less successful and generally nondescript career in comic books. Its first half dozen appearances came between 1939 and 1949 in David McKay Publishing's *Feature Books*, which were simply reprints of *The Phantom* comic strip in comic book format.

And while the feature's second series—less than a dozen stories in *Harvey Hits* and *Harvey Comics Hits* between 1951 and 1960—did utilize new material, the stories and artwork left much to be desired.

The latest Phantom comic book series began in November 1962; Gold Key comics published 17 issues before abandoning the title. Not wishing to see their character lose the comic book market, however, King Features began publishing the book beginning with number 18 (September 1966). And while the King version was considered the best of the comic book lot—it featured art by Wallace Wood, Jeff Jones, Al Williamson, and also *Flash Gordon* back-up stories in many issues—the company gave up the ghost with the 28th issue in December 1967. In February 1969, Charlton Comics purchased the comic book rights from King and resumed publication of *The Phantom*. And although the Charlton series used material by artists like Steve Ditko and Jim Aparo, not everyone was happy. "Lee Falk was complaining about how we were handling his creation," editor George Wildman was quoted as saying, and Charlton began using translations of Spanish and Italian *Phantom* stories in June 1974. There were a few short-lived attempts at reviving the character in the late 1980s and early 1990s.

J.B.

PHANTOM LADY (U.S.) 1—*Phantom Lady* was a minor back-up feature, which made its first appearance in Quality's *Police* number 1 for August 1941. Created by artist A. Peddy, Phantom Lady was really Sandra Knight, daughter of a U.S. senator. Her adventures were pedestrian at best, but her greatest asset was her costume: a revealing halter and tight, short pants. The character never merited any considerable financial or artistic attention, but the Quality version is best remembered for a one-liner uttered during comic books' high-pitched patriotic days. "America comes first," explained Phantom Lady, "even before Dad." *Phantom Lady* appeared in *Police* through the 23rd issue (October 1943).

2—When Fox decided to return to comic publishing, they immediately exhumed the Blue Beetle—in a way. He rarely appeared on the cover—he narrated crime stories on the inside while a long-legged girl in underwear adorned the cover. When Fox acquired the rights to *Phantom Lady*, much the same thing happened. She would appear on the cover—breasts jutting seductively forward, just barely covered by her tight halter—and then simply narrate crime stories on the inside.

And while this reincarnation lasted only between August 1947 and April 1949, one of the worst of the covers eventually appeared in Dr. Fredric Wertham's *Seduction of the Innocent*, a 1953 attack on comic books, The *Phantom Lady* cover (April 1948) showed a large-breasted, scantily clad Sandra Knight tied to a wooden post; Wertham claimed it represented "sexual stimulation by combining 'headlights' with the sadist's dream of tying up a woman." Whether he overreacted or not, the cover has come to be regarded as an example of the seamier aspects of comic book publishing.

3—A third *Phantom Lady* feature, published by Ajax, appeared briefly between December 1954 and June 1955. A more reasonable anatomy and a less-revealing costume were used in this four-issue series, however.

J.B.

PHILÉMON (France) *Philémon* was created in 1965 by Fred (pseudonym of Othon Aristides) for the French comic weekly *Pilote*. The first two episodes (dating back respectively to 1965 and 1966) were not yet clearly defined, hovering between parodic adventure and satirical fantasy, with Fred not quite making up his mind about which way he wanted to go. With the third sequence, however, "Le Naufragé du 'A'" ("The Stranded Man of 'A'"), Fred finally hit his stride, making *Philémon* into one of the most exciting comic strip creations in recent times.

With *Philémon*, we squarely step over the fine line between science fiction and fantasy. Philémon, Fred's stringy farm-boy hero, accidentally crosses into a parallel world, landing on one or another of the letters of the words "Atlantic Ocean" in the mythical Sea of Maps. Along with the old well-digger Barthélemy, the stranded man of the title whom he meets there, he runs into countless perils, which include sinking into a mirage, fighting a deadly grand piano, and having to answer a Sphinxlike riddle asked by a giant mousetrap. After overcoming all the dangers of "A," Philémon and Barthélemy succeed in getting back to the everyday world; but they will try and try again to rejoin the fantasy world they have known, made each time more inaccessible.

The stories of *Philémon* are always imaginative and fresh, with unpredictable turns and twists, and Fred's universe is full of weird creatures, magical landscapes, and surreal vistas, reminiscent of *Krazy Kat*. In the

"Philémon," Fred (Othon Aristides). © Editions Dargaud.

1980s Fred started parallel careers as scriptwriter for television and children's book illustrator and publisher; as a result, new *Philémon* adventures have become few and far between.

One of the high points of the modern European comic strip, *Philémon* has been translated in several languages, and all its episodes reprinted in hardbound form by Editions Dargaud.

M.H.

PHIL HARDY (U.S.) The first 100-percent, all-out, concentrated adventure comic strip, and one of the best, was George Storm's sadly short-lived *Phil Hardy*, which began distribution by the Bell Syndicate on November 2, 1925. Nominally scripted by the byline-credited "Edwin Alger, Jr." (Jay Jerome Williams), *Phil Hardy*, dealing with a boy adventurer of 15, was overwhelmingly infused with artist Storm's stunning stylistic pace, narrative visualization, and prolongation of suspense and violence at every opportunity. (Williams's own normal, dull narration is best perceived in its correct perspective in his later *Bound To Win*, or *Ben Webster's Career*, one of the tritest, flattest strips ever published.) Filled with brutally dispatched corpses and a swashbuckling atmosphere of derring-do within the first few weeks of continuity, *Phil Hardy* presented at full-length what such other early adventure epics as *Wash Tubbs* and *Little Orphan Annie* could then only hint at.

Unfortunately, this rapid and uncompromising strip (derived from such rousing boys' adventure fiction as *Treasure Island* and *Tom Cringle's Log*) was too sharp and sudden an innovation for editors and many readers, and both its distribution and thematic influence were minimal at the time. As a result, *Phil Hardy* lasted barely 11 months, to be replaced by the much milder and more conservative narrative strip, *Bound To Win*, which Williams—initially using Storm's art—undertook for the same syndicate. Storm, however, departed shortly to begin his own highly successful adventure strip, *Bobby Thatcher*, for McClure. With its initial rousing cast of characters from Phil himself to old Jason Royle, the gun-wielding ship's cook, through such rough customers as Ghost Hansen, Baldy Scott, and Captain Eli Bent, *Phil Hardy* was strong stuff for its time, although the syndicate warily slackened its forceful pace several months before the strip closed on September 29, 1926. Brief and memorable, the landmark, *Phil Hardy*, should be reprinted complete in a compact volume.

B.B.

PHOEBE ZEIT-GEIST (U.S.) An American attempt at duplicating *Barbarella's succès de scandale*, *Phoebe Zeit-Geist* appeared for the first time in 1966 in the pages of *Evergreen Review* as a comic feature written by Michael O'Donoghue and drawn by Frank Springer.

Phoebe Zeit-Geist, the lovely 24-year-old heroine, is drugged and abducted during a party in Antwerp; she is then to know a series of ordeals comparable only to those suffered by Sade's Justine: she is violated (a number of times), whipped, branded, suspended from a flying helicopter, raped by a giant iguana, and so on. The authors were evidently trying for satire and social criticism (with references to Vietnam, the Congo, the race problem), but their approach was ham-handed and far from the mark. Springer's drawings were adequate but did not quite fit the point of the story. The whole enterprise was singularly lacking in conviction and looked like the put-on that it indeed was.

Phoebe Zeit-Geist was reprinted (in both hardbound and paperback forms) by Grove Press, the publishers of *Evergreen*.

M.H.

PICCOLO SCERIFFO, IL (Italy) Just after World War II the regular comic book was replaced by a so-called "strip book" of five inches by four inches in size. This product allowed for greater sales because it could be sold very cheaply. From the 10 lire which it cost at the beginning, it went up to 12, then 15, and stayed at 20 lire for several years. The later increase in page number and in price (which reached 50 lire) led to its disappearance in the early 1960s. However, during its 15 years on the market the "strip book" made the fortune of several publishers, chief among them Tristano Torelli who, after the success of *Sciuscia*, issued *Il Piccolo Sceriffo* ("The Little Sheriff") in 1950 with illustrations by Dino Zuffi.

Kit, the son of Sheriff Hodgkin, took the place of his father who had been killed by outlaws. With the help of his sister, Lizzie, his fat sidekick, Piggie, and his girlfriend, the beautiful Flossie, he fought for more than 20 years to bring law and order to the Wild West. His enemies were sometimes a ruthless band of criminals, sometimes Indian rebels. Kit's youth—he was 16—won him the loyalty of young readers who identified with him. The lively and buoyant character of the hero made up for any holes in the plots—of which there were many—as well as for the mediocrity of Zuffi's draftsmanship.

Once the strip book closed down, the adventures of the little sheriff—which were by then called *Il Nuovo Sceriffo* ("The New Sheriff"), since the hero had grown up in the meantime—were published first in pocket book format and then in a giant comic book. Over the years there have been reprints of the series in the original as well as book formats.

The strip's writer, Giana Angissola, authored a novel based on the little sheriff's adventures in 1951, with illustrations by Ferdinando Tacconi. A movie was also produced in 1950.

G.B.

PICHARD, GEORGES (1920-   ) The dean of French erotic cartoonists, Georges Pichard was born January 17, 1920, in Paris. Following studies at the School of Applied Arts, he embarked on a traditional advertising career, later setting up his own ad agency in 1946. After contributing a number of cartoons to the humor magazine *LeRire*, in 1956 he signed his first comic strip for the very staid girl's weekly *La Semaine de Suzette*; a conventional teenage girl tale titled *Miss Mimi*, it in no way foreshadowed his creations to come, although his knack at drawing pretty girls was already in evidence.

In 1964 he met Jacques Lob, who was to become his most constant scriptwriter. After turning out a number of superhero parodies (*Tenebrax*, *Submerman*, etc.), the duo came up in 1967 with their first overtly erotic creation, *Blanche Epiphanie*. A spoof of turn-of-the-century dime novels, the feature was notable for showing the well-endowed heroine in various states of distress and undress. Pichard followed in the same vein in 1970 with *Paulette* (on a script by fellow cartoonist Georges Wolinski), detailing the progress of a voluptuous redhead who went through all sorts of harrowing ordeals, of which rape was the least objectionable. He later sounded much the same theme with *Caroline Choléra* (1976), but perhaps due to the fact it was written by a woman—Danie Dubos—it provided an interesting twist to the proceedings. Caroline experienced the whole gamut of kinky sex out of sheer feminine curiosity.

Pichard crowned his already notorious career with *Marie-Gabrielle* (1977-1981), in which he pulled out all stops in a horrendous tale of a buxom, dark-haired beauty subjected to every conceivable form of torture and torment—in full color and minute detail. Perhaps as a take on one of the Marquis de Sade's most famous anthology pieces—wherein Justine and her companions are victimized by an order of monks—he had his Marie-Gabrielle and her cellmates tormented by nuns who kept piously reciting the catalog of tortures visited upon Christian saints and martyrs all the while meting out the most barbarous treatment to their helpless charges.

Like most of his colleagues in the same line of work, he also illustrated in the 1990s a number of classics of erotic literature, notably Guillaume Apollinaire's *Memoirs of a Don Juan* and the *Kama-Sutra*. In a related but somewhat more acceptable vein he has produced a highly intriguing version of the *Odyssey*, *Ulysses* (in 1968, with Lob), an entirely uncanonical adaptation of *Carmen* (1981), as well as a tongue-in-cheek tale of evolution gone mad, *Bornéo Joe* (with Dubos, 1982-1983). In addition Pichard has turned out countless book and magazine illustrations, humor cartoons, and lithographs in his 40-plus-year career.

M.H.

Georges Pichard and Georges Wolinski, "Paulette." © Editions du Square.

PIEDS-NICKELÉS, LES (France) *La Bande des Pieds Nickelés* ("The Nickel-Plated-Feet Gang"), later simply called *Les Pieds-Nickelés*, was created by Louis Forton on June 4, 1908, for the French comic weekly *L'Epatant*. Drawn from real life, the long-nosed Croquignol, the one-eyed Filochard and the bearded Ribouldingue (calling themselves the "Pieds-Nickelés") are a trio of swindlers, impostors, and con artists whose exploits, at first rather tame, were gradually to rise to cosmic proportions. Forton used the strip to direct his savage humor and barbed wit at well-known personalities (depicted under their real names) and at established institutions. In 1911, for instance, Croquignol, Filochard, and Ribouldingue became, by hook and by crook, first deputies, then cabinet ministers, before kicking out (literally) the President of the French Republic Armand Fallières and taking over the government. For sheer impudence this episode represents some kind of high-water mark in the history of comics.

In 1921 the Pieds-Nickelés went to America, and Forton took some more potshots at prohibition, racial segregation, the electoral process, Hollywood, and President Harding. After an interruption from 1924 to 1927, the Pieds-Nickelés resurfaced in France, still as crooked as ever, but less anarchistic and somewhat more world-weary.

After Forton's death in 1934, the strip was taken over by Aristide Perré, and then by A. G. Badert who drew it from 1938 to 1940, when it was interrupted by the war. *Les Pieds-Nickelés* came back in 1948, drawn by René Pellos. Pellos introduced the exclusive use of balloons to the strip (instead of a printed narrative) but otherwise plot and characterization have changed little to this day.

In 1981, at age 80, Pellos retired from the strip. After a one-year interim by Jean-Louis Pesch, the series was taken over by Jacarbo (a.k.a. Jacques Arbeau). Since 1987 the feature has been done alternately by Jacarbo, Gen-Clo, and others.

A classic of French comic art, *Les Pieds-Nickelés* is the oldest existing European strip (and the second oldest in the world—after *The Katzenjammer Kids*). In France it has achieved the status of an institution. (In 1949, when a law prohibiting the glorifying of "criminal characters" in the comics was passed, the *Pieds-Nickelés* were specifically exempted from this proscription.) Les Pieds-Nickelés has also inspired a series of novels, a

"Les Pieds-Nickelés," Louis Forton. © SPE.

string of animated cartoons (by noted animator Emile Cohl), several motion pictures and a musical comedy.

M.H.

PIER CLORURO DE' LAMBICCHI (Italy) The inventor whose inventions turn against him had been a figure of folklore ever since the Sorcerer's Apprentice, when the Italian cartoonist and painter Giovanni Manca decided to adapt him into comic strip form in 1930. The result was *Pier Cloruro De' Lambicchi,* which appeared in the pages of the *Corriere dei Piccoli.*

Pier Cloruro De' Lambicchi (whose name literally means "Peter Chloride of Stills") was a bald and dignified gentleman-scientist who had devoted his life to his never-ending experiments. One day in his laboratory he discovered the formula for "arch-paint," a substance with the incredible property of bringing photographs and still pictures to life: a few brush-strokes of arch-paint were enough to animate paintings and drawings. The invention had its drawbacks in the fact that the subjects thus brought to life were often not too happy with the situation and took their frustrations out on the hapless professor. They would break and destroy his possessions, beat people up, and generally make the poor inventor very sorry about the whole situation. (Sometimes the arch-paint would be used by some innocent bystander which would make things even worse!)

Every week the tragi-comic adventures of De' Lambicchi would be repeated in their ineluctable unfolding, with the unrepentant inventor ready to resume his comic-opera experiments in the next installment.

After World War II (which saw the temporary suspension of *Pier Cloruro*) the feature was revived for more than ten years in the comic weekly *Il Monello;* and later in the weekly supplement of the Milanese newspaper *Il Giorno* (1967).

G.B.

PIËT, FRANS (1905-) Frans Piët, a Dutch comic artist, was born February 17, 1905, in Haarlem, the Netherlands. After his schooling he picked a career in art, studying at the Press Art School in London, England, taking lessons from Herman Moerkerk, and also studying at the Free Academy Montparnasse in Paris, France. Finally, in the 1930s he drifted into comics, first doing *De luchtrovers van Hoitika* ("The Air Pirates of Hoitika"), then embarking on the strip *Wo Wang en Simmie* ("Wo Wang and Simmie") in 1932. This strip was successful enough to be reproduced in book form in 1936.

The year 1938 brought a big change for Frans Piët: he took over writing and drawing the strip, *Sjors,* on which he was to continue working until 1970, when he retired. Actually, *Sjors* was an American comic strip, *Winnie Winkle* (Sunday pages only) by Martin Branner. *The Sjors Weekblad* had started two years earlier, in 1936, as a children's supplement of the newspaper, *Panorama.* This supplement had three pages of editorial matter plus one page of the *Sjors* strip. While Branner changed his Sunday page, which originally was a kid strip, the Dutch public craved for more of the same. That is when Frans Piët came in. He continued the strip in the original vein, ever so slowly enlarging on the original premise. World War II put an end to the supplement in 1941. It was revived in 1947. (In the meantime Piët drew *Jossie Jovel* for *Panorama.*) There were some title changes over the next few decades; the comic book, which became an independent publication, was called at various times *Rebellenclub* ("Rebels' Club"), *Sjors van de Rebellenclub* ("George of the Rebels' Club"), and finally, simply, *Sjors.* Most importantly, however, the strip became *Sjors en Sjimmie,* adding a black costar. For some time Piët collaborated with writer Lou Vierhout.

Sjors was created in America, but Piët, while retaining some of the original characters, created the strip anew, making it into a different strip that has long since transformed the original into a dim memory. The many *Sjors* adventures have been reprinted in album format since 1936. When Piët retired in 1970, the strip was continued by Jan Kruis until Jan Steeman took over.

W.F.

PIF LE CHIEN (France) The genesis of *Pif le Chien* ("Snoozle the Dog") is such a beautiful instance of a real-life cat-and-dog story that it bears relating in some

"Pif le Chien," Claude Arnal. © Editions Vaillant.

detail. For years, the French Communist Party newspaper *L'Humanité* had been running *Felix the Cat* (one of the editors' personal favorites) when, after the start of the Cold War, the Party hierarchy decided that the King Features strip was too glaring an example of American enterprise to be tolerated any longer in the pages of their official publication. Accordingly, they turned to Claude Arnal (José Cabrero Arnal) who was then doing the successful *Placide et Muzo* animal strip for the communist-financed comic weekly *Vaillant*; and in 1950 *Pif le Chien* was thus launched on its long career.

Pif was a rather cheerful mutt, with a perpetual grin and an oversize nose (hence his name), in the humanized tradition of Walt Disney's animals. His adventures were pedestrian and a far cry from the inspired tribulations of Felix. The outside world might at times frustrate or infuriate him, but it was never heartless or cruel. Pif's main adversary was the cat Hercule, whom he loved to outwit at every turn. The drawing was latter-day Disney and a bit cloying in its slavish imitation of the master's style.

Whether Pif was popular with the readers of *L'Humanité* remains a well-kept secret; at any rate in 1952 he went on to *Vaillant* where he was given an entire page in which to pursue his harmless pranks. In 1955 the overworked Arnal (he was also doing the *Placide et Muzo* feature for *Vaillant*, and another animal strip, *Roudoudou*, for the magazine of the same name) relinquished *Pif* to René Mas, who was in turn succeeded in 1970 by Louis Cance, without significant improvement in either drawing or story line.

Pif le Chien has been so popular that it added a spin-off in 1964: *Pifou* (Pifou is Pif's pup) by René Mas; and in 1965 it gave its name to the newspaper in which it was appearing (which became *Le Journal de Pif*, later changed to *Pif-Gadget*).

Due to age and illness (he died in 1982), Arnal left more and more of the drawing to other hands in the 1970s, notably those of Roger Mas and Giorgio Cavazzano. In 1992, after more than four decades, *Pif* was scuttled along with the weekly that bore its name, but the strip can still be seen in reprints.

M.H.

PINCHON, JOSEPH PORPHYRE (1871-1953) Joseph Porphyre Pinchon was a French cartoonist, illustrator, and painter born in Paris in 1871. After graduating from the School of Fine Arts, devoted himself to painting and illustrating. Around the turn of the century he became an illustrator for the various magazines published by Gauthier-Languereau. In 1905 in the girl's weekly *La Semaine de Suzette* Pinchon illustrated a filler story written by one of the publishers, Maurice Languereau, under the pseudonym "Caumery." The story was "Bécassine" and it proved an immediate hit. For the rest of his life Pinchon devoted the best of his talent to the drawing of further adventures of the little Breton maid nicknamed Bécassine.

In addition to *Bécassine* Pinchon contributed a number of other picture-stories (none of them could be called comic strips in the strict sense): *La Vie des Hommes Illustres* ("The Lives of Famous Men"), *La Famille Amulette* and *Patatras* (inspired by *Gasoline Alley*) in the 1920s and 1930s; and *La Vie des Grands Fauves* ("The Life of the Big Cats") in the weekly *Fanfan la Tulipe* from 1941 to 1943.

Pinchon never stopped painting and he was for a long time the president of the National Society of Fine Arts. He died in 1953.

M.H.

PINKERTON, JR. *see* Radio Patrol.

PINKY RANKIN (U.S.) In 1942 the editors of the *Daily Worker*, the newspaper of the Communist Party U.S.A., decided to create their own comic strip hero who would compete with the bourgeois representatives of the commercially syndicated adventure strips. The result was *Pinky Rankin* drawn by Dick Floyd and scripted by the paper's staff writers. (The *Daily Worker* did have another home-grown product, *Lefty Louie*, but its hero was judged too tame for the purpose.)

Pinky was a proletarian hero who took part in the struggle against the Nazis as an underground fighter in the occupied countries of Europe. When he was not busy blowing up bridges, derailing trains, and killing off lines upon lines of advancing German storm troopers with witheringly accurate machine-gun fire, he could be counted on to deliver stern lectures on the role played by American Communist workers in the struggle against fascism, and on the necessity for a second front. The strip was one of the most brutal of the war years, and graphically depicted scenes of torture, rape, and slaughter perpetrated by the German soldiers who were portrayed as sadistic brutes and sexual degenerates. The end of the war in Europe and the onset of the Cold War contributed to the decline of *Pinky Rankin* and its subsequent demise occurred around 1948.

Dick Floyd's graphic style, while never very distinguished, was adequate. The texts, however, were far-fetched, even by the standards of the time, and cannot

"Pinky Rankin," Dick Floyd. © Daily Worker.

"Les Pionniers de l'Espérance," Roger Lécureux and Raymond Poïvet. © Editions Vaillant.

be taken today without a large dose of salt. *Pinky Rankin* is included here as an oddity rather than for any outstanding qualities of its own. It also serves to illustrate the point that, for philosophical reasons, it is very difficult to create a credible hero of the Left (a problem which Chinese comics have had to grapple with ever since Mao Tse-Tung's accession to power).

M.H.

PIONNIERS DE L'ESPÉRANCE, LES (France) *Les Pionniers de l'Espérance* ("The Pioneers of the Hope"), written by Roger Léureux and drawn by Raymond Poïvet, first appeared in the French comic weekly *Vaillant* on December 14, 1945.

The *Hope* is a spaceship whose crew is made up of men and women of different nationalities: Professor Wright, an English naturalist; Maud, the American woman doctor; Tsin-Lu, a Chinese woman chemist; Tom (later called Tangha), a filmmaker from Martinique; Rodion, a Russian physicist; and Robert, a French engineer and the designer of the vehicle.

Since 1945, when they embarked on their first interplanetary expedition, the pioneers of the Hope have lived through an incalculable number of adventures, some of them in outer space, some of them right here on the planet Earth. The first episode, which took place on the alien planet "Radias," was clearly inspired by Alex Raymond's *Flash Gordon*, but the strip later acquired its own distinctive look and flavor.

In the 1950s Léureux and Poïvet introduced their readers to all kinds of different universes, some natural, some artificial, peopled by menlike creatures, by machines, and even by crystallike thinking molecules; they also refined their themes away from conventional space-opera and into the more sophisticated patterns of classical science fiction. It ended its run as a weekly feature in 1973, but a number of independent stories appeared in the late 1970s and early 1980s.

Les Pionniers de l'Espérance has always been highly imaginative in conception and execution; where it is weakest is in the creation of memorable characters (even the protagonists blur after a while), but remains nonetheless one of the best and most popular of the European science fiction strips.

M.H.

PIPPO (Italy) *Pippo*, which first appeared in the Catholic magazine *Il Vittorioso* in 1940, is probably Benito Jacovitti's most famous comic creation.

At first Pippo was only an emblematic figure, dispensing to the readers the moral advice and beliefs of the editors. He was a good boy, always ready to help his neighbors whenever his assistance was needed. He was born during the war years and his first adventures pictured him fighting the British. Then he gradually went on to satirize the Fascist government; in his latter exploits Pippo was politically nonaligned.

Jacovitti has thrust Pippo into the most desperate predicaments in the most remote places: in the American West, Africa, India, or in some imaginary kingdom. Pippo's sworn enemy is Zagar, the symbol of evil, always attired in black tights, in what seems to have been a spoof of *Diabolik* many years ahead of its time! After a period of time Pippo has acquired two comic allies, Pertica and Palla, and a normal dog (at least insofar as any man or beast can be called normal in Jacovitti's weird world) named Tom. Pertica ("Bean Pole") is a lanky and absentminded fellow who always gets in trouble because of his gullibility; on the other hand Palla ("Ball") is chubby, astute, and spunky. They both play as foils to Pippo.

It is impossible to get bored with the adventures of Pippo and his friends (the "three P's" as they are affectionately called), not only because of the very funny satire but also for the outlandish situations in which the heroes find themselves—from 16th-century France to ancient Rome, from Cleopatra's Egypt to the America of today. They now live mostly in reprints of their old adventures.

G.B.

PIP, SQUEAK AND WILFRED (G.B.) The most famous and popular children's strip in British newspa-

"Pip, Squeak and Wilfred," A. B. Payne. © Daily Mirror Ltd.

pers, *Pip* (a dog), *Squeak* (a penguin), and *Wilfred* (a rabbit) began quietly. On Monday, May 12, 1919, the *Daily Mirror* launched their postwar revival of their prewar children's corner, *The Children's Mirror*. It was edited and written by journalist Bertram Lamb, who called himself "Uncle Dick," and in his first "letter" he introduced his pets, Pip and Squeak. They were so named in honor of Lamb's former Army batman, who had been nicknamed "Pipsqueak." A small illustration drawn by A. B. Payne, a Welsh cartoonist who worked on the children's comics, accompanied the text.

There was an immediately favorable response, and by the end of the month the single panel had become a four-panel strip. The following year Pip and Squeak found a baby bunny and christened it Wilfred (February 7, 1920). The trio was complete. Wilfred, who could say only "Gug" (because he was a baby) and "Nunc" (meaning "uncle"), stole everyone's heart, and ultimately (on January 3, 1927) the Wilfredian League of Gugnuncs was inaugurated, with badges, songs (The Gugnunc's Chortle), and a climactic rally of 87,000 members in the Royal Albert Hall (April 14, 1928).

Payne's daily strip had expanded to six panels a day, with an edition in *Sunday Pictorial*. All this in turn expanded into a pull-out weekly comic supplement to the *Mirror* called *Pip & Squeak* (October 15, 1921, reducing to a single page by 1925), and another supplement, *Children's Own Sunday Pictorial* (August 6, 1933, reducing during 1934).

The first reprint of the strips was published as a book in November 1920, and *Pip and Squeak Annual* appeared every Christmas from 1923 to 1939. This was supplemented by *Wilfred's Annual* from 1924 to 1938 and *Uncle Dick's Annual* (1930). Lancelot Speed animated a series of cartoon films called *The Wonderful Adventures of Pip, Squeak and Wilfred* for Astra National Films in 1922.

Payne introduced a supporting cast of fascinating characters: Auntie, the shaggy old penguin who had not learned to talk English ("Oomsk! Oogle!"); Peter, the Dalmatian pup; Stanley, the baby penguin; Wttzoffski, the anarchist, and his pup, Pop ski. The strip was concluded on June 14, 1940, and revived on January 18, 1947, again drawn by veteran Payne. This time the strip was published weekly, on Saturdays.

After Payne's retirement the characters were revamped and given a modern look by Hugh McClelland, who dressed the hitherto naked animals in dungarees and skirts. Despite a revival of *Pip, Squeak and Wilfred Annual* (1953-1955), the "new" characters did not really catch on. They were discontinued on March 9, 1955, transferred to the weekly newspaper for children, *Junior Mirror*, and then dropped. But old Gugnuncs still greet each other with their secret password: "Ick-ick! Pah-boo!"

D.G.

PISTOL JIM (Spain) The Western strip *Pistol Jim* was created in the first issue (October 1945) of the comic magazine *Gran Chicos* by Carlos Freixas. The feature had an eventful career in the course of its five episodes, which were published not only in the aforementioned magazine, but also in the weekly, *El Coyote*, in the comic book collection "Mosquitó," and in the Argentine publication, *Aventuras*.

Pistol Jim was a hero always attired in black (not unlike Hopalong Cassidy) and always wearing his emblem, a six-shooter, on his chest. The weapon sym-

"Pistol Jim," Carlos Freixas. © Carlos Freixas.

bolized the hero's spirit of justice, which often led him to uphold the law by means of a quick draw. In the course of his cleaning out the West, Pistol Jim was assisted in his labors by the freckle-faced Nick, a jujitsu expert and the Spanish idea of American boyhood as pictured in countless Hollywood movies. In addition to his task of policing the West, Pistol Jim also had the delicate duty of choosing between the love of his childhood sweetheart—the rich ranch owner Nelly Cayo—and the seductions of the alluring saloon singer, Belle Smith. *Pistol Jim*'s scripts were simple and straightforward, but Carlos Freixas (son of the master, Emilio Freixas) displayed an elegance of line and an energy that made the strip more than a simple recital of fist and gun fights.

L.G.

PITCH AND TOSS (G.B.) *Pitch and Toss*, subtitled *The Nautical Nuts*, was cast in the classic mold of all British comic double acts: fat and thin, tall and short. They were first sighted in *Lot-O-Fun* on April 3, 1920, where Joe Hardman drew them upsetting their punt at the Boat Race. But it was a false start, and after an early retirement they were reenlisted by the editor of *Funny Wonder*, who gave them to Don Newhouse to draw. Newhouse passed them on to his young assistant, Roy Wilson, and the result, with its brand-new subtitle, *Our Saucy Shipwrecked Mariners*, floated onto page five of *Funny Wonder* number 449, dated October 28, 1922. They anchored in this weekly for 22 years. After much drifting on their raft, they hove to on the back page as a full 12-panel strip. There they shipped aboard the good ship *Saucy Sal*, and proceeded to make life miserable for the skipper, Cap'n Codseye (who labeled his cabin "No admish without permish"), not to mention Clarence the Cookie and the noble owner, Lord Topnoddy.

In the 1930s came another move, which proved out their enormous popularity: they up-anchored for the front page of *Funny Wonder*, where Bertie Brown's strip of *Charlie Chaplin* had reigned supreme since 1915. Charlie continued on an inside page, while *Pitch and Toss* grew stronger and stronger. Wilson added two newcomers to the crew, Pengy the Penguin and Occy the Octopus, and from April 26, 1941, color was added, a two-tone effect in red and black. The merry mariners were finally pensioned off in 1944, and Wilson replaced them with a soldier, *Private Billy Muggins*.

D.G.

PITT, STANLEY JOHN (1925-   ) Born at Rozelle, N.S.W., Australia, in 1925 the son of a plasterer, Stanley Pitt became attracted to drawing when he was a young boy. Educated at the Marist Brothers, he was

Stanley Pitt, "Flash Gordon." © King Features Syndicate.

constantly in trouble for drawing instead of pursuing his studies. By the time he left school in 1940, he had fallen under the spell of Alex Raymond, through the Flash Gordon pages appearing in the *Sydney Sunday Sun*. Raymond's sense of the heroic and romantic, coupled with his proportions, anatomy, and crisp, fine line left an indelible impression on Pitt—and all his future artistic efforts were directed at emulating Raymond's efforts. While working as a milkman in 1942, he sold his first comic to *Consolidated Press: Anthony Fury*.

In 1943, he began to sell four-page comics to Frank Johnson Publications, which allowed him to rub shoulders with such artists as Cecil "Unk" White Rhys Williams, Carl Lyon, and Emile Mercier. This was invaluable experience as Stanley Pitt was never to take a formal art lesson in his life. In 1945, he began producing comic strip advertisements for Colgate-Palmolive, which lead to being placed under contract by *Associated Newspapers Ltd.* to produce a science fiction adventure strip. The resultant *Silver Starr in the Flameworld* appeared in the *Sunday Sun* in November 1946 replacing *Flash Gordon*. The following two years saw Pitt set a new standard in realistic-style comic art, and *Silver Starr* became a household name. Due to a dispute about the printed size of the strip, Pitt left the paper and the last *Silver Starr* appeared on November 14, 1948.

Almost immediately, Pitt was approached by the *Sunday Herald*, for whom he created another Sunday color strip, *Captain Power*. Dissatisfied with the story line (provided by a journalist) and his salary, Pitt left the paper in late 1949 and returned to the comic book field. With the assistance of his brother, Reginald, Paul Wheelahan, and Frank and Jimmy Ashley, he produced 32 issues of *Yarmak Comics* for Young's Merchandising. In the early 1950s, with his brother, he attempted to get two strips, *Lemmy Caution* and *Mr. Midnight*, syndicated in the United States. When these attempts failed he joined the *Cleveland Press* in 1956 to produce new *Silver Starr* comics and, when the comic industry folded, to produce covers for Western paperbacks.

The magnificent artwork on his unpublished strip, *Gully Foyle*, became legendary in the late 1960s. Samples of this work were responsible for Pitt being asked to produce comics for *National Periodical Publications* and *Western Publishing* as well as ghosting an 11-week sequence of *Secret Agent Corrigan* in 1969, and a further four weeks in 1972. Because of his detailed style and perfectionist approach, Stanley Pitt has not been a prolific producer of comic art—yet, combining dedication with integrity, he has become recognized as a leading illustrator of science fiction, and the finest comic artist in the classic tradition that Australia ever produced.

J.R.

PLACID ET MUZO (France) *Placid et Muzo* (the names of the characters can be broadly translated as "Placid and Mug") started in issue 56 of the comic weekly *Vaillant* (as *Muzo et Placide*) on May 16, 1946. Its creator was the Spanish cartoonist Claude Arnal (pseudonym of José Cabrero Arnal).

The story relates the rather innocuous adventures of two animal friends, Placid the slow-witted bear and Muzo the sly fox. They frolic and gambol amid pasteboard scenery and cardboard animal caricatures. Arnal's drawings are an obvious imitation of the Disney style, just as his animal characters are directly derived from countless cartoons turned out by the Disney studio. Indeed, *Placid et Muzo* is so inane in its story line and sugary in its psychology that it may well be called a "sillier symphony." As it was, however, it met with fair success among *Vaillant*'s young readers, who made up the bulk of its audience and was promi-

nently featured on the first page of the magazine until it was later dethroned by the author's next and equally bland creation, *Pif le Chien*. (It should be noted that the scenarios of the first few years were written by Jean Ollivier, who often used doggerel verse—thus accenting the resemblance with Disney's *Silly Symphonies*.)

In 1958 *Placid et Muzo* passed into the hands of cartoonist Nicolaou and is ploddingly pursuing its career toward the 30-year mark. Still in the hands of Nicolaou it has now passed the half-century milepost.

M.H.

PLASTIC MAN (U.S.) Created by humor artist and writer Jack Cole in August 1941, *Plastic Man* made his first appearance in Quality Comics' *Police* number 1. An unabashed parody of all the existing superhero strips, the feature handled crime fighting with tongue-perennially-in-cheek, allowing "Plas" and Woozy Winks, his maladroit assistant who was added in *Police* number 13, a full range of zany antics, outrageous situations, and offbeat villains.

Plastic Man wasn't your run-of-the-mill superhero, either. He eschewed the almost mandatory cape and cowl, opting instead for sunglasses and a red jumpsuit. Even Woozy was strangely attired, always wearing the same straw hat, polka-dot shirt, and green trousers in all his appearances. The team also had origins which were less than superhero pristine: Plastic Man was once a petty crook named Eel O'Brien, who gained his stretching power after being thrown into a vat of acid; Woozy, on the other hand, was well-known as a notorious jail breaker who went straight only after Plastic Man allowed him to become his partner. In short, the pair were two characters who didn't fit the mold, and that made their adventures refreshingly different from the glut of deadly serious crimefighters prevalent in the 1940s.

Plastic Man was handled by creator Cole with tremendous verve and style, always striking a wholesome balance between antic slapstick and sophisticated humor. From the strip's inception, Cole knew *Plastic Man* wouldn't follow in the steps of *Batman*, *Superman*,

"Placid et Muzo," Claude Arnal. © Editions Vaillant.

"Plastic Man," Jack Cole. © Comic Magazines.

and the like. The strip was to be played strictly for laughs, and Cole's judicious mixture of "bigfoot" and realistic artwork made the feature one of the best ever to appear in comic books. Novel villains like sad-faced Sadly Sadly and beautiful temptresses like the Figure allowed Plastic Man to assume outrageous shapes to combat evil. At times he was a lightning bolt, or a steamroller, or a glider, or a bull's-eye, or dozens of other objects, all allowing Cole to exploit every possible satiric angle.

Plastic Man also appeared in his own magazine as well as in 102 issues of *Police*. The *Plastic Man* comic book began as a one-shot in 1943 and continued until November 1956. Unable to handle the story load by himself, Cole had some outstanding artistic help, including Bernie Krigstein, Lou Fine, and Chuck Cuidera; after Cole left the strip in 1950, Russ Heath took over as the main artist. Novelist Mickey Spillane also scripted several of the character's tales in the mid-1940s.

National Periodicals produced a second series of Plastic Man adventures, albeit without Woozy Winks, starting in December 1966. A greatly inferior version, however, it lasted only ten issues and ceased publication in June 1968. A revival was attempted from 1976 to 1977, and a *Plastic Man* miniseries appeared in 1988 to 1989.

J.B.

PLAUEN, E. O.   *see* Ohser, Erich.

POGO (U.S.)   In 1943 Walt Kelly, fresh out of the Disney studios, imagined the adventures of a little boy living in the (Okefenokee) swamp in company of an alligator. *Bumbazine and Albert the Alligator* first appeared in issue number 1 of Animal Comics. In subsequent years the little boy Bumbazine faded out of the strip, which was rechristened *Albert and Pogo* (Pogo was Albert's opossum friend). Unfortunately the *Albert and Pogo* comic books lasted but a few issues.

A few years later (1948) Kelly transferred his creation to the *New York Star* of which he was art editor, under the title *Pogo*—but the *Star* folded in January 1949. Undaunted, Kelly persuaded the Hall Syndicate to distribute (and the *New York Post* to run) the strip which soon became a success.

In the loose social structure of the Okefenokee swamp, where everybody and anybody tries to impose their idiosyncrasies, there throbs a teeming population composed of all animal (and social) classes: worms, insects, birds, reptiles, herbivores, and carnivores cohabit in more or less peaceful harmony, in pursuit of their variegated goals. Dr. Howland Owl, his head surmounted by a wizard's cap, indulges in obscure and crack-brained experiments; P. T. Bridgeport the bear tries to promote his mind-boggling schemes; Beauregard, the retired bloodhound, epitome of war veterans everywhere, never tires of relating his former exploits; Churchy-la-Femme the turtle pokes his beak into everyone else's business, while Porky the porcupine vainly attempts to keep his from everyone else. (Politi-

"Pogo," Walt Kelly. © *Walt Kelly.*

cal figures—under animal guise—make their appearance from time to time in the swamp; one could recognize the late Senator McCarthy, Castro, Khrushchev, etc., but this is a minor, if overplayed, aspect of the strip.)

Pogo the little opossum, sagacious, modest, tolerant and generous, and Albert the alligator, anarchistic, nihilistic, egotistic, and vain, dominate this little world. With his wild flights of fancy, his sudden impulses, his unbridled imagination, Albert is the perfect incarnation of the poet whom Plato wanted to run out of the city. It is Pogo's role in the strip to reestablish the order and harmony of the society, which Albert does his best to disturb.

The privileged relationship between Albert and Pogo has been analyzed in detail by critics and researchers. Reuel Denny has compared Pogo to Socrates confronting Albert the Sophist. Some psychologists such as Kenneth Fearing have seen in Pogo and Albert the symbolic representations of the Ego and the Id. Whatever interpretation one chooses to give it, *Pogo* is undeniably the most self-analytical and self-reflective strip in the whole history of the comics—of which Walt Kelly gave the following definition in a famous 1959 *Pogo* page: "A comic strip is like a dream . . . a tissue of paper reveries . . . it gloms, an' glimmers its way through unreality, fancy an fantasy."

In the 1960s Walt Kelly became increasingly ill and left more and more of the drawing to others; since his death in 1973 the strip has been taken over by his widow, Selby, and his son, Stephen, with the help of several assistants.

Simon and Schuster have published close to a score of *Pogo* books in hardcover, as well as a remarkable anthology, *Ten Ever-Lovin' Blue-Eyed Years with Pogo*, compiled by the artist himself. A Pogo animated cartoon was shown on television in 1969.

Pogo was discontinued on July 20, 1975. Almost a decade and a half later, an attempt was made to bring the strip back to life. Written by Larry Doyle and drawn by Neal Sternecky, a new version started appearing on January 8, 1989, under the title *Walt Kelly's Pogo*. In February 1991 Doyle left the strip and Sternecky carried on alone for about a year; he was replaced by two of Kelly's children in March 1992, but they only managed to carry the strip into 1993, when it ended.

M.H.

POÏVET, RAYMOND (1910-   ) A French comic strip artist born in Paris, Raymond Poïvet made a brief passage at the School of Beaux-Arts in Paris. After this Raymond Poïvet served his apprenticeship with several French artists and sculptors. In the 1930s he designed a number of war monuments but also executed the decoration for several Paris nightclubs, and made a name for himself as a decorator and designer.

Poïvet started on his comic strip career in 1941 with a rather fanciful adaptation of Daniel Defoe's *Robinson Crusoe*. This was followed by a number of pseudo-historical comic strips such as *Christophe Cofomb* ("Christopher Columbus"), *Marion Delorme*, *La Reine Margot* ("Queen Margot"), and other regrettable (albeit entertaining) distortions of historical figures.

In 1945 Poïvet, in collaboration with Roger Lécureux, created *Les Pionniers de l'Espérance* ("The Pioneers of the Hope"), his masterpiece and a trailblazer in the field of graphic science fiction. Poïvet was later to pro-

duce two other science fiction strips, *Marc Reynes* (1946) and *Mark Trent* (1959), but both were short-lived.

Poïvet has over the years contributed a number of other comic creations: *P'tit Gus* ("Li'l Gus"), a comic strip mixing fantasy with realism; *Colonel X*, a tale of French resistance during the German occupation; *Minouche*, about the adventures of a teenage girl; and *Guy Lebleu*, a mystery-adventure series, none of them very successful.

Upon leaving *Les Pionniers* in 1973, he created *Tiriel*, a tale of heroic fantasy that ran until 1983. In addition to contributing a number of comic strips to a variety of publishers, he also illustrated several didactic works on French history, science, the Bible, and so on. His most notable works in this cultural context have been his adaptations of famous operas such as *The Magic Flute* and *Faust*. He is now semiretired.

Raymond Poïvet's style has been compared to Alex Raymond's although it probably comes closer to Austin Briggs's. After years of relative obscurity, Poïvet has finally been recognized as one of the foremost French comic artists of the last quarter century.

M.H.

POLLY AND HER PALS (U.S.) Cliff Sterrett's 40-year-long masterpiece of comic narrative and innovative graphic art called *Polly and Her Pals*, which began daily on December 4, 1912, and Sunday on December 28, 1913, is perhaps the most remarkable example of artistic legerdemain in the history of the comic strip.

Polly and Her Pals was foreshadowed by a 1911 strip (run as a Sunday feature by some papers) called *For This We Have Daughters?*, which Sterrett drew for the New York Telegram and Herald Co. and in which the basic four characters (a soundly middle-age father and mother called Maw and Paw, a ubiquitous family cat, and a college-age daughter named Molly) were ringers in manner and appearance for the *Polly and Her Pals* cast to come. It is difficult, in fact, to tell from the published strips (titles and copyrights aside) at what point *Daughters* ends and *Positive Polly* (the first title of the classic strip Sterrett was hired by Hearst to draw for his National News Company) begins.

Positive Polly first appeared in the *New York Evening Journal*. The cumbersome title was dropped within six weeks, however, and replaced by the familiar *Polly and Her Pals* on January 13, 1913. (The Hearst Sunday page, launched a year later, was originally titled *Here, Gentlemen, Is Polly!*, then retitled *Polly!* for a time, then simply *Polly*, which remained the Sunday title until November 7, 1925, when the *Polly and Her Pals* title of the daily strip was finally adopted by the Sunday page.)

The title in all its variations was misleading from the outset, since Sterrett always focused the primary attention of the strip on the activities of Maw and Paw (Samuel and Susie) Perkins, and on the hilarious comic menage which surrounded them in the Perkins home, rather than on the distinctly minor theme of Polly and her collegiate suitors. The Dickensian household figures included Paw's scapegrace nephew, Asher Earl Perkins; the family butler, Neewah; a malignant brat named Angel and her doting mother, Maw's Cousin Carrie; a scrawny cat who is Paw's constant shadow, named Kitty; and many others who moved on and off the Perkins scene over the years. Polly herself was

"Polly and Her Pals," Cliff Sterrett. © King Features Syndicate.

chiefly occupied with her constant string of boyfriends, foreshadowing such later comic heroines as Blondie (before her marriage, of course) and John Held's Margy.

Sterrett began to introduce graphic and thematic fantasy into his strip as early as 1918, gradually increasing the level of pictorial strangeness and novelty (with frequent heady incorporation of elements of cubism, surrealism, and even Dadaism) through the 1920s and well into the 1930s, then relaxing these elements in the later, closing years of the strip. Sterrett himself stopped drawing the daily *Polly* on March 9, 1935, after which it was ghosted by Paul Fung and others. He continued with the Sunday page, however, until his retirement in 1958, the last Sunday page appearing on June 15 of that year.

Curiously, only very minor reprint volumes based on Polly have been published: a Saalfield-Big-Little-Book style title in 1934, and a coloring book reprint of some of the 1935 daily strips constituting the total. No film or stage adaptations of the strip were even undertaken.

Polly and Her Pals, in terms of narrative and graphic wit and inventiveness, as well as inspired characterization and a rich sense of comedy, is one of the most memorable works of comic art yet created.

B.B.

PONCHO LIBERTAS (France) *Poncho Libertas* appeared in the very first issue (November 20, 1944) of the comic magazine *Coq Hardi*, the creation of cartoonist Le Rallic and the magazine's editor, Marijac (pseudonym of Jacques Dumas).

Poncho Libertas was a horse-opera of a different color: it took place in Mexico and glorified the exploits of a daring band of rebels led by the dashing Poncho Libertas. The hero's persona owed as much to the French Resistance fighters of World War II as to Pancho Villa, on whose legend he was obviously based. The plots were tight and filled with hair-raising exploits, breathless horse rides, and villainy and heroism a-plenty. Le Rallic's stiff style was more than offset by his brilliant depiction of horses and the limitless Mexican vistas.

Poncho Libertas ended its run on December 30, 1948. Some of its episodes have been reprinted in fan publications.

M.H.

POP (G.B.) The first classic in British newspaper strips, Pop was created by John Millar Watt, who signed with the occasional cryptic initials J. M., for the *Daily Sketch*. *Pop* first appeared on Friday, May 20, 1921, under the title *"Reggie Breaks it Gently."* Pop, the rotund paterfamilias, "something in the city" with his waistcoat, his top hat, his striped trousers, was at first both mustachioed and pince-nez'd, the bald, put-upon papa henpecked by wife and family: a middle-class variant of *Bringing Up Father*, the American strip which was, curiously enough, currently running in the same newspaper. However, Pop always rose above the daily drag with a snappy retort, a verbal crack that Watt echoed in his printed caption, a sort of secondary wisecrack. To the verbal pranks Watt added a visual twist, often using his fourth and last panel as a silent comment or

"Pop," J. Millar Watt. © Associated Newspapers Ltd.

punctuation mark. Another visual gimmick he originated was to set his complete strip against a single continuing landscape or setting, divided into equal portions by the borders of his panels, while his figures carried action along from frame to frame.

The cast of players included Pop's queen-size wife Mag, daughters Phoebe (elder) and Moreen (schoolgirl), son Johnny (schoolboy) and baby Babs. Pop's principal opponent was the Colonel, tall and distinguished. During the war years Pop was reduced from four to three panels, and apparently enlisted in every known branch of the services! An extra strip was added for the *Illustrated Sunday Herald* in 1924, and a special feature on his 25th anniversary was run in the *Daily Graphic* (his newspaper was suffering a temporary name change), including tributes from Sir Alfred Munnings, Chic Young, David Low, and Strube. On Watt's retirement the strip was taken over by Gordon Hogg, who signed himself "Gog." The strip was finished on January 23, 1960, after it failed to survive a reduction to a single gag panel.

Pop was one of the few British strips syndicated in the United States (by Bell Features), and appeared each year in *Pop Annual* (originally a hardback), in 24 editions between 1924 and 1949.

D.G.

POPEYE *see* Thimble Theater.

PORKY PIG (U.S.) Porky Pig made its comic book debut in *Looney Tunes* and *Merrie Melodies* number 1 published by Western Publishing Company in 1941. This was some six years after the character first appeared in animated cartoons produced by Leon Schlesinger for Warner Brothers Studios. The rotund, stuttering pig first appeared in "I Haven't Got a Hat," a musical cartoon emulating the Hal Roach "Our Gang" comedies of the day. The film, directed by Friz Freleng, and based on an idea by Bob Clampett, launched a successful series of films, two of which—"Porky's Duck Hunt" and "Porky's Hare Hunt," introduced the characters who soon evolved into Daffy Duck and Bugs Bunny. *The Porky Pig* cartoons were made until the late 1960s, their directors including Frank Tashlin, Fred ("Tex") Avery, Norman McCabe, Ub Iwerks, Bob Clampett, Chuck Jones, Art Davis, and Robert McKimson.

Like the other Warner Brothers cartoons, the *Porky Pig* films made their character very much in demand for merchandising items such as books, records, toys, and, of course, comic books. After his initial appearance in *Looney Tunes*, Porky returned in every issue thereafter until the book was dropped in 1962. It resumed in 1975 with Porky in guest-star status. The earlier *Porky Pig* stories were by Chase Craig and Roger Armstrong, among others, although, like the other early W.B. stories, they carried the byline of Leon Schlesinger (who was neither a writer nor an artist). In 1943, the first comic devoted exclusively to *Porky Pig* was issued, a special in the Dell Four Color series (number 16). Twenty-five specials followed until the first regular issue of *Porky Pig*, number 25, was issued in November of 1952. After issue number 81, the book suspended publication and resumed in 1965 under Western Publishing's Gold Key banner with a new numbering system. *Porky Pig* also turned up in issues of *March of Comics*, *Golden Comics Digest* and in guest-starring roles, the character has appeared in the comics featuring

other Warner Brothers characters and vice versa. The series ended in July 1984.

Most *Porky Pig* stories deal with coping with life in a suburban setting. The crises that confront Porky range from romantic spats with his girlfriend, Petunia (created for the cartoons by Frank Tashlin), to adventure stories that find Porky and his ward, Cicero, in grave peril. Scripts have been supplied by many writers including Lloyd Turner, Vic Lockman, Don Christensen, Bob Ogle, Tom Packer, Don Glut, and Mark Evanier. *Porky Pig* artists have included Phil De Lara, John Carey, and Lee Holley.

In addition, Porky, Petunia, and Cicero were made regulars in the *Bugs Bunny* newspaper strip (NEA) almost from its inception in 1942.

M.E.

POSITIVE POLLY *see* Polly and Her Pals.

POTTS, THE (Australia) Originally entitled *You and Me, The Potts* was created by Stan Cross for *Smith's Weekly* in 1919. The main characters were Pott and Whalesteeth and, initially, the strip was political, commenting on bread-and-butter issues that affected the average citizen. With the introduction of Mrs. Pott, the strip assumed something of a domestic flavor even though the humor was based on frank, uninhibited low comedy. Constant bickering, cursing, and marital squabbling typified the humor of this strip until Stan Cross left the paper in late 1939. The strip passed into the hands of Jim Russell, who recast the tone of the strip but retained the general flavor of domestic cat-and-dog fights. In the process of altering the strip, the name was changed to *Mr. & Mrs. Potts*.

When *Smith's Weekly* ceased publication on October 28, 1950, the strip was accepted by the *Herald and Weekly Times Limited*, for syndication in all Australian states. Because the adult-male humor of *Smith's* was not acceptable to the more respectable, conservative daily newspapers, the basis of the strip's humor had to be toned-down considerably. Pott, the former star, became almost a "straight man"; Mrs. Pott received most of the punchlines and the name of the strip was changed to *The Potts*.

For 30 years, the Potts had no children—when Russell decided to give the strip a new dimension by suddenly materializing a daughter, Ann; son-in-law, Herb; and grandchildren, Mike and Bunty. In the quest for respectability, a new character was added in the form

"The Potts," Jim Russell. © *The Herald and Weekly Times Ltd.*

of Uncle Dick; a genteel scrounger who became an increasingly important contributor to the strip's humor and who shares top billing with *The Potts* in the Sunday page. With Uncle Dick gradually eliminating the original character, Whalesteeth, the strip assumed the mantle of a conventional domestic strip.

By 1958, *The Potts* had become an international strip appearing in 35 U.S. dailies as well as New Zealand, Turkey, Canada, Finland, and Ceylon, with an estimated daily circulation of 15 million.

Australia's first newspaper strip, *The Potts* has become something of an institution, having been blessed with consistently good art; a reasonably high level of humor (not always typically Australian), and an ability to adapt to topicality. The latter is assisted by many strips being drawn on location of major events such as the Coronation, Olympic Games, and so forth, and involving *The Potts* family in these events. As of 1996 Russell had been drawing the strip (now called *The Potts and Uncle Dick*) for 56 years, arguably a world record.

J.R.

"Powerhouse Pepper," Basil Wolverton. © Basil Wolverton.

POWERHOUSE PEPPER (U.S.) When artist and writer Basil Wolverton decided to create comic book humor features, he joined the Timely group and introduced *Powerhouse Pepper* in *Joker* number 1 in April 1942. Powerhouse himself was possessed of tremendous physical strength, and in that sense, was a superhero of sorts. On the other hand, he was also cast as something less than a mental giant. Early in the feature's history, Powerhouse had a somewhat belligerent attitude, but this soon disappeared. In fact, if it's at all possible to define his character, Powerhouse could only be described as "lovable," replete with the clichéd "heart of gold." He never had a steady job, although he was often cast as a cowboy or prizefighter.

Wolverton invented a unique—and as yet uncopied—textual device: beginning with the strip's third appearance, all the characters in *Powerhouse Pepper* spoke in rhymes and alliteration. This technique became so popular, Wolverton eventually used it on all his other humor strips, too. But it was always best handled in *Powerhouse Pepper*, perhaps the quintessential usage coming in *Joker* number 9 when Powerhouse is rejected for Army service because no helmet would fit him:

Pepper: "You mean I'm in, doc, old sock?"
Doctor: "No, you're out, sprout, because it's hopeless to hang a helmet on a head like yours!"
Pepper: "Isn't my bean clean?"
Doctor: "It's too lean, if you know what I mean! See? A helmet teeters down over your cheaters, and there's no way to clap a strap under your map!"
Pepper: "Fap! I must look like a sap!"

It went on continuously in all Powerhouse stories, rarely appearing strained or tiresome. Wolverton occasionally would leave a rhyme incomplete or dangle a string of alliterations, but, more often than not, Powerhouse would simply exclaim: "Madam! Don't tan your man with that pan!", the woman would refrain: "Out of my road, toad!", and Wolverton would move on.

Artistically, the strip was totally without precedent, although Wolverton would occasionally borrow a technique from Elzie Segar. The strip featured tight line work, fine detailing, and elaborate shading. Wolverton populated the strip with outrageously exaggerated anatomy and cluttered backgrounds with off-beat sight gags. It was not uncommon for him to draw signs like "Fighters: don't mope on the rope" and "Don't pile in this aisle" into the background of a prize-fighting scene.

Powerhouse Pepper appeared in *Joker* through issue 31 (April 1942 to Spring 1948), five issues of *Powerhouse Pepper* (1943 to November 1948), five issues of *Gay*, and nine issues of *Tessie the Typist*.

J.B.

PRAN KUMAR SHARMA (1938-   ) Pran Kumar Sharma (Pran) was born on August 15, 1938, in Kasur (now Pakistan). With the partition of the subcontinent in 1917, he crossed over to India with his family, settling in Madya Pradesh. He earned a university masters in political science and studied fine arts as a nonresident student at the J.J. School of Art, Bombay.

His career began in 1960 on an Urdu newspaper in Delhi, *Milap* ("Togetherness") where he did a comic strip and a front-page pocket cartoon. At the time, Indian newspapers used American and European syndicated strips exclusively, so that Pran's strip, *Daabu*, the adventures of a teenage boy and a science professor, was unique. Pran takes credit for not only doing the first Indian comic strip, but also for starting the comics syndicate, as *Daabu* appeared in three other periodicals besides *Milap*. As newspapers and magazines called for other characters, Pran created them. In 1969, he started *Chacha Chaudhary*, the story of a wise and simple man, who with his hefty alien sidekick, Sabu, solves people's problems without the use of superman powers or miracles. Used originally in the humor magazine, *Lodpot* ("Laugh"), *Chacha Chaudhary* went on to become the most popular and longest lasting of comics personalities in India. The second most popular Pran title among the more than 295 comic books he has done is *Shrimatiji*, a humorous strip built around a middle-age housewife; others are *Billoo*, *Pinki and Uncle Sulemani*, *Raman and Bhagat Ji*, and *Daabu and Dangerous Capsoul*.

Pran works with three assistants in a studio in his home, drawing daily strips that he self-syndicates through Pran's Features to 20 newspapers and magazines throughout India. Later, the strips are compiled into books produced and sold by Diamond Comics in seven language editions. Pran estimates the readership of his comics at more than 10 million and believes his success results from doing straight and simple humor based on a number of gags.

J.A.L.

PRATT, HUGO (1927-1995) Hugo Pratt was an Italian comic strip artist and illustrator born near Rimini on June 15, 1927. As a child Pratt acquired a taste for travel as he moved along with his parents, first to Venice, then to Ethiopia (when it became an Italian colony) before coming back to Venice in 1942, after Italy's defeat in Africa.

In 1945, while attending the Venice Academy of Fine Arts, he created, in collaboration with Mario Faustinelli and Alberto Ungaro, *Asso di Picche* ("Ace of Spades") about a hooded justice fighter in the best comic book tradition; this was followed in 1946 by *Junglemen*. Opportunities for a burgeoning cartoonist in postwar Italy weren't good, however, and in 1950 Pratt accepted an invitation to work in Argentina, first for the publisher Cesare Civita, then for Editorial Abril in Buenos Aires, and later for Hector G. Oesterheld, editor of Editorial Front era. It was there that he created some of his most important strips: *Sgt. Kirk* (1953), a Western in the new, revisionist mode; *Ernie Pike* (1956), the story of a war correspondent (inspired by the real-life Ernie Pyle); *Anna della Jungla* (1959), about a young girl in darkest Africa; *Wheeling*, an adventure tale set in colonial America, and many others.

For a while during his South American period Pratt went to San Paulo, Brazil, and taught at the Escuela Panamericana de Arte. He returned to Argentina in 1959, then resumed his peripatetic career, working in London in 1964 for the *Daily Mirror* and the *Sunday Pictorial*, and for Fleetways Publications, went briefly back to Argentina where he edited the magazine *Mister X*. In 1965 he settled back in Italy, working for the *Corriere dei Piccolo* in Milan, then in 1967 for the newly created monthly *Sgt. Kirk* to which, in addition to the title strip, he contributed *Capitan Cormorand*, a pirate story, *Luck Star O'Hara*, a detective strip, and foremost, *Una Ballata del Mare Salato* ("A ballad of the Salty Sea"), a brooding tale of the South Seas worthy of Conrad or London. When *Sgt. Kirk* folded in 1970, Hugo Pratt created *Corto Maltese* (based on one of the characters in *Ballata*) for the French comic weekly *Pif*. In 1973 he went over to the Belgian *Tintin*, where he created *Les Scorpions du Désert*, a war story set in North Africa; and continued the adventures of Corto Maltese.

At first an obvious imitator of Milton Caniff, Pratt in the 1960s and 1970s evolved his own striking style, at once more calligraphic and less documentary than Caniffs. Not as boldly innovative as his equally celebrated compatriot Guido Crepax, Hugo Pratt is also less esoteric, which accounts for his greater popularity—a popularity which has made him the best-known European cartoonist of the last decade.

In addition to pursuing the *Corto Maltese* cycle, bringing the adventurer up to the mid-1920s, Pratt also created a number of independent comic strip series in the last 20 years of his life. Most notable were *Cato Zulu* (1984), a tale of the colonial wars in South Africa; *West of Eden*, an adventure set in the wilds of East Africa; and especially *Jesuit Joe*, subtitled "The Man of the Far North" (1978-1984). He also wrote the scripts for two outstanding graphic novels illustrated by Milo Manara, *Indian Summer* (1983) and *The Gaucho* (1991).

In addition he found time to write several prose novels as well as a book of memoirs. He was working on a new episode of *Corto Maltese* when he died of cancer at his home near Lausanne, Switzerland, on August 20, 1995.

M.H.

PRENTICE, JOHN (1920-   ) An American artist born in Whitney, Texas, on October 17, 1920, John Franklin Prentice moved with his family to a variety of small towns in Texas during his boyhood as they followed work on oil fields. He obtained his early education in public schools, followed immediately (1940) by six years with the Navy during World War II.

Prentice was exposed to major illustrators and comic strip artists for the first time during his years in the Navy; although he had followed the works of Raymond, Caniff, and Crane as a boy, he now discovered the magazine work of Al Parker, Austin Briggs, Peter Helck, Harold von Schmidt, and Noel Sickles. He enrolled at the Art Institute of Pittsburgh in 1946 and left after 10 months to handle layout and design work with Industrial Publications of Hazleton, Pennsylvania, for the same amount of time.

In New York in late 1947, Prentice succeeded in breaking into the popular art field, handling advertising and magazine illustration before entering the comic book market. His work in comic books included *Buckskin Benson* for Hillman, *House of Mystery* and other titles for National; and work for the Simon & Kirby and Ziff-Davis studios. Most of his work was penciling and inking.

On September 6, 1956, Alex Raymond was killed in an auto crash. It was suggested to Prentice by veteran inker and background man Philip (Tex) Blaisdel to apply for the job of continuing Raymond's *Rip Kirby*. Unbelievably enough, Raymond drew only ten days in advance of publication so King Features Syndicate was desperate for an artist.

Prentice competed with a host of other straight artists and on the basis of one sample strip and his portfolio of illustrative work (Alex Raymond had been an early influence of his), he got the awesome nod to fill the shoes of one of the art's greatest visual masters.

Prentice, by all accounts, succeeded well. The taut story line continued—Fred Dickinson doing the continuity—and the artwork was so close to Raymond's that King Features challenged editors to discern when Raymond stopped and Prentice began. In fact, *Rip Kirby* picked up papers after Raymond's death, an unusual occurrence with any strip.

John Prentice's art has remained in Raymond's slick *Kirby* style, with only subtle stylistic changes. He employs a variety of cinematic angles and cross hatches which, respectively, lend a rich maturity and visual excitement to the comic strip. His style remains one of the smoothest and least tacky of the story strips, a genre increasingly taken over by formula art, fashion-drawing clichés, and unimaginative uniformity.

To the regret of both Prentice and fans, the recent paper crunch has led to strictures in *Rip Kirby* and all other strips. He has met the challenge with more close-ups and less rendering. Prentice has employed, at various times, some of the most talented assistants in the business, which, under his direction, has kept the quality of *Kirby* high: Al McWilliams, Al Williamson, Frank Bolle, Angelo Torres, and Gray Morrow.

Rip Kirby by John Prentice was voted three times the Best Story Strip by the National Cartoonists Society.

R.M.

PRICE, CYRIL (1905-1970) Cyril Gwyn Price, who drew under the several pen names of "Gwynne," "Kim," and "Spike," was one of the few Welsh cartoonists to work in Great Britain, and perhaps the only one to rise to national success in both children's comics and adult newspapers.

Price was born in Penrhiwfer, Glamorgan, Wales, in a coal miner's cottage on February 8, 1905. The family moved to Abertridwr where he was educated at the village school. Showing early signs of artistic aptitude, Price was encouraged by his headmaster and won a place at the Caerphilly County School, then the equivalent of a modern grammar school. The poverty of his family, however, forced him to go to work at the age of 14, and he was sent down Windsor Colliery. Here he lost the tip of one finger, which luckily had no effect on his artistic ability. After ten years down the pit, the closing of many Welsh coal mines caused widespread unemployment, and Price was forced to leave his homeland in search of work.

Price went to the city of Bristol, and while there began to accompany his uncle, a well-known amateur athlete, to various athletic meetings. His uncle introduced Price to several newspaper reporters and, encouraged by them, he began to submit caricatures of local athletes to the newspapers, all of which had special sporting editions published every Saturday. These were published and as his cuttings mounted, the newly confident Price approached the largest paper in the area, the *Bristol Evening World*, with some specimen cartoons. His talent was immediately recognized and the paper's publisher, the large national company of Northcliffe Newspapers, signed him on.

The *Evening World*, one of the first newspapers in the country to introduce a colored comic supplement for children, was a perfect venue for Price and an ideal place in which to develop the cartooning side of his talent. From 1932 he drew *Junior and Happy*, then *Smash and Grab* (1933), *Fitz and Startz* (1934) as well as the large front-page cartoons for the comic.

In 1934 Price tried his hand at drawing strips for the London comic publisher, Amalgamated Press, and drew *Chimp and the Imp* for *Joker* and *Private Potts* for *Chips*. By 1935 he was drawing *Komedy Kids* in *Butterfly*, *Tomato Khan* for *Comic Cuts*, and *Susie Snaffle* for *Joker*. His success, with a style clearly inspired by the A.P.'s top cartoonist, Roy Wilson, caused his abandonment of the provinces and a move to London, where a regular flow of work from A.P. kept him fully employed.

Price's politics were, as with many with his background, left-wing and during the 1940s he supported Russia and the communists by art-editing a series of children's comic-style one-shots for the Junior Press. At the same time he ran the harmless *Screwy Scrapbook with Pop Cornish*, a joke page for *Knockout Comic* (1943).

In 1948 he joined the *Daily Graphic* (later *Daily Sketch*) to draw their daily children's corner. This was *The Whiskers Club*, the first postwar return to prewar-style children's corners , and featured *Whisk the Squirrel* and his animal pals. Later becoming a strip, this

series, which ran for some years, revealed Price's wondrous ability for depicting humanized animals. The best strips were published every Christmas in a delightful run of children's annuals and were signed "Gwynne," the first of Price's pen names. The Whiskers eventually wound up in the weekly *T.V. Comic* (1957), where Price had found a second home drawing television favorites like Tusker and Tikky and Coco the Clown. At the same time he was drawing a newspaper strip for the *Daily Sketch* featuring a "silent" character called Harry. This one was signed Kim, another pen name.

By 1970 he was back with Fleetway Publications, the successor to the Amalgamated Press, drawing *Georgie's Germs* for *Pow* and *The Spooks of St. Luke's* for *Thunder*. He died of a heart attack on September 17, 1970, at age 65.

D.G.

PRINCE ERRANT (U.S.) H. C. (Cornell) Greening, a longtime cartoonist for *Judge* magazine and an early Sunday supplement comic strip artist, created *Prince Errant* for the *New York Herald* in 1912.

Greening was a versatile artist whose style ranged from crude exaggeration in the late 1880s to restrained starkness in the 1920s. But granting that, *Prince Errant* was still a remarkable work—both in relation to his other work and intrinsically.

First, it was one of the first strips to have its time frame in another age (F. M. Howarth did a strip for Hearst also based in medieval times—*A Lad and His Lass*); it ran without balloons; and artistically was several cuts above other comics (and even Greening's other work).

The Prince was a young lad whose adventures and misadventures were gently humorous. *Prince Errant* always ran a full page and the continuity underneath the panels gave the strip a respectable narrative air that befitted its artistic maturity. The strip was definitely in a class with *Little Nemo*, Peter Newell's *Polly Sleepyhead*, Palmer Cox's *Brownies* and Lyonel Feininger's pages—all comic pages wherein artistic quality and sophistication of story line combined to transcend the level of the average color comic.

Greening gave up the doings of the luckless Prince, after a short stint in 1914. Perhaps he could not sustain the high level demanded by *Prince Errant*; *Percy the Mechanical Man—Brains He Has Nix*, and other Greening creations ran concurrently. Perhaps *Errant* suffered by comparison with a strip it followed, *Little Nemo*. In any event, Greening's notable work should be remembered at least because the tale of a medieval prince in such a format obviously—if unknowingly—presaged *Prince Valiant* by a generation.

R.M.

PRINCE VALIANT (U.S.) *Prince Valiant* was created by Harold Foster for King Features Syndicate on February 13, 1937. As early as 1934 Foster had proposed the idea to United Feature Syndicate (his then current employer) which had turned him down—to their everlasting regret, presumably.

Carefully plotted and laid out far ahead of time, the scenario of *Prince Valiant* is not a collection of unrelated episodes arbitrarily woven around the central character, but an organic whole reflecting the vicissitudes and joys of the hero's life as well as the (legendary) times and society around him—which is the strip's greatest

"WE WON! WE WON!" CRIES EDWIN GLEEFULLY, BUT
AT THE SIGHT OF VAL'S SET FACE, HIS SMILE FADES.

"YOU CAUSED A GAP TO BE LEFT IN OUR LINE, THROUGH
WHICH MOST OF THE ENEMY ESCAPED TO THEIR SHIPS,
TO RAID OUR LAND ONCE MORE!" AND VAL ADDS CRUELLY,
"RECKLESSNESS WILL WIN APPLAUSE ON THE TOURNA-
MENT FIELD; IT IS A HINDRANCE IN BATTLE."

FORTUNATELY THE BATTLE HAS TURNED, AND THE SAXONS
ARE MORE INTENT ON ESCAPE. SO EDWIN IS SAVED, BUT AT
THE COST OF LEAVING A GAP IN THE LINES.

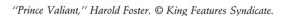

"Prince Valiant," Harold Foster. © King Features Syndicate.

narrative achievement. The action however, moves slowly, due partly to Foster's rather weighty text, partly to the static composition of his pictures (a fault most apparent in the last two decades).

The son of the exiled king of Thule, Valiant attaches himself as squire to Sir Gawain before becoming a full-fledged knight of King Arthur's Round Table. Brave and sometimes reckless, he will fight for the glory of the king and for his own renown against the Saxons and the Huns who have come to invade Britain. He will roam the globe, all across Europe and to the Holy Land, and as far away as the jungles of Africa and the forests of the New World in search of glory or in pursuit of Princess Aleta, "queen of the Misty Isles" whom he will finally marry in 1946, and who will give him four children. Having thus become a *pater familias* Valiant will gradually fade out of the strip which has become of late the playground of his elder son, Arn.

Prince Valiant is clearly in the tradition of the novels of chivalry, and only unthinking critics can talk of Foster's historical authenticity and accuracy: his is the Europe of legend and folklore and not the Europe of historians (this in no way detracts from Foster's formidable achievements as an interpreter and chronicler of medieval lore). *Prince Valiant* is awesome as a work of illustration and fiction, but lacks rhythm and pacing, and thus fails to be a trailblazer of the same magnitude as Foster's earlier *Tarzan*.

In 1971 Foster relinquished the drawing of the Sunday page (there never was a *Prince Valiant* daily strip) to John Cullen Murphy—which only accelerated the feature's steady decline of the last decades. In the more than 20 years of his tenure, Murphy has turned *Prince Valiant* into a family affair, with his son, Cullen Murphy, writing the scripts and his daughter, Meg Nash, doing the lettering and coloring.

A series of seven novels faithfully adapted from *Prince Valiant* and illustrated with a profusion of drawings from the strip have been published by Hastings House, and there were also a number of *Prince Valiant* comic books. In 1953 noted movie director Henry Hathaway adapted *Prince Valiant* to the screen with Robert Wagner in the title role and Janet Leigh as Aleta.

M.H.

PRINCIPE AZZURRO, IL (Italy) It is a common tradition to call "Principe Azzuro" (literally "Blue Prince," although better rendered as "Prince Charming") the future husband for whom every young girl prays. He was usually portrayed as a long-haired, blue-eyed blond knight with a regal bearing. Nowadays this figure is not as common, but it was everywhere evident in the 1930s. Therefore, the publishers speculated, a comic strip featuring such a hero would appeal to women who until then had spurned the comic magazines.

Principe Azzuro was introduced on April 9, 1938, in the pages of *L'Intrepido*, the comic magazine published by the brothers Del Duca. The strip, signed "Tredi" (Domenico Del Duca who wrote the text and Antonio Salemme for the art), told of the adventures of Selim, "handsome as the sun." In the very first page Selim saved the life of Bubi, Princess Aurora's greyhound, and love instantly blossomed between the two young people. It was a stormy and much-contraried love whose incidents kept thousands of young girls breathless. A trio of evil characters—Princess Orchidea (Orchid) seeking revenge on Selim, who had scorned her; Raja Karval, Aurora's father who wanted the Blue Prince out of the way for reasons of state; and "Milord," his scheming and hateful English counselor—stood in the way of the lovers.

The feature, which lasted until the suspension of *L'Intrepido* during the war in 1943, is the most outrageous example of a production concocted by greedy publishers in order to cash in on the-less-educated strata of the population. It is also important because it was at the origin of a new kind of publication: the photonovel weekly, with the start in 1948 of *Grand Hotel*, now an illustrated magazine, but at the beginning made up only of comic stories in the soap opera genre.

G.B.

PRIVATE BREGER   *see* Mr. Breger.

PROCOPIO (Italy)   Short, stubby, and bald, Procopio is one character who did not rely on his looks to win over his readers. Yet he has been immensely successful and draws a lot of fan mail. *Procopio* was created by the talented cartoonist Lino Landolfi and first appeared in the Catholic weekly *Il Vittorioso* in 1951, passing recently into the pages of *Il Giornalino* (1974).

In fact there is not one Procopio but a multitude of Procopios!—indeed as many as the ancestors of our "Procopio," a dumb but gentle American cop who tells of the adventures of his ancestors to please his grandchildren; or who relives in his nightmares some of their most perilous encounters. In the scores of stories so far published, "Procopio" has assumed many guises: a caveman; a knight of the Middle Ages; a seventh-century Scot; an opponent of Cardinal de Richelieu; or a pioneer of the American West.

Procopio has been drawn in a bold, personal style by Landolfi, in a break from the traditional "big foot" school of cartooning. While it is drawn in a grotesque line, *Procopio* is also filled with minute, realistically rendered technical details, which are hard to find even in straight adventure strips. *Procopio* often poked fun at the adventure heroes' ethos, as in a devastatingly funny "metaphysical" spoof of the popular Ace of Spades entitled "Procopio and the Ace Poker."

For years *Procopio* has been produced as a continuity strip, never as a comic book; yet it was so successful that it won a radio contest in 1958—eliminating in the process scores of other characters from the movies, comics, and literature. This led to a short-lived series of animated cartoons for television, as well as to a best-selling record (1959). Landolfi's death in 1988 brought the character to an end.

G.B.

PROFESSEUR NIMBUS, LE (France)   One of the innumerable heirs to the tradition of the absentminded professor, Nimbus appeared in 1934 in a daily newspaper strip called *Les Aventures du Professeur Nimbus* ("The Adventures of Professor Nimbus"). His creator was French cartoonist André Daix.

Nimbus was a middle-aged, sad-faced little man: he was entirely bald except for one hair growing over his pate in the form of a question mark, which made him look like a wizened version of Carl Anderson's Henry; like *Henry, Nimbus* was a pantomime strip. At the beginning the titular hero justified his professorial status by coming up with the most outlandish contrap-

tions designed to solve the problems of gravity or perpetual motion. Later on, however, he could be found in various guises (as an explorer, a navy captain, a magician, etc.) and in the most exotic climes, from Africa to the North Pole.

After the hiatus caused by World War II the strip made its reappearance in the late 1940s under the shortened title *Le Professeur Nimbus*, signed by Darthel (this might have been a pseudonym). Darthel's style was a faithful imitation of that of his predecessor, but the formula had by then worn thin, and Nimbus's increasing irrelevance to modern problems led to the gradual disappearance of the strip in the late 1960s (it now runs only in a few provincial newspapers). There was a resurgence of sorts after Robert Velter had taken over the character in 1973; when he quit in 1977 he was replaced by Michel Lefort and in 1981 by Pierre LeGoff, who brought the series to an unlamented close in 1991. During all that time the strip kept carrying the signature "J. Darthel" (except at the very end when LeGoff was finally allowed to sign his own name).

Le Professeur Nimbus is not a very original or artistic creation; it owes its importance to the fact that it was the very first French daily newspaper strip. As a novelty it thus enjoyed a fair success in the 1930s, being reprinted several times in book form, and even inspiring a few animated cartoons.

M.H.

PROFESSOR PI (Netherlands)   *Professor Pi,* the work of Dutch artist Bob van der Born, debuted in the newspaper *Het Parool* on January 2, 1955, and for more than a decade enthralled readers with its insight, wit, and unbounded imagination.

Bob van der Born, born October 30, 1927, in Amsterdam, Netherlands, received his formal art training at the Kunstnijverheidschool (School of Arts and Crafts) department of art teachers. When Van der Born started doing his *Professor Pi* in 1955, the business end of the deal was handled by the Swan Features Syndicate, founded by Mr. De Zwaan, who undertook this project after leaving his managerial position at the Marten Toonder Studios in 1953; this makes him one more person of the Netherlands comics scene to have been associated at one time or other with the seemingly omnipresent Mart en Toonder who, because of his many humorous strips and animated cartoon studios, is sometimes called the Netherlands's own Walt Disney.

Professor Pi originally started out as a pantomime gag strip that usually had three pictures per strip. The star of the strip was an almost run-of-the-mill egghead professor stereotype. But in time the strip's individual pictures merged into one oblong illustration, thus straddling the narrow line between cartoon and comic strip. The feature, nevertheless, belongs more in the realm of the comic strip, as each episode narrates a story that must be "read" from left to right with a sweep of the eyes if one is to understand the point of the episodes. In a way *Professor Pi* makes perfect use of the split-panel technique dividing one large background into several segments, with the action partitioned by the segments. *Professor Pi*, one is tempted to say, uses the split-panel technique without the seams showing (for example, the professor's meeting another explorer, read from left to right, first informs us that we are witnessing an explorer's hike, next we learn that the professor is walking through a vast expanse of even terrain and, finally, that he is meeting another explorer

"Le Professeur Nimbus," André Daix. © Opera Mundi.

"Professor Pi," Bob van der Born. © Swan Features.

hacking away at imaginary jungles). *Professor Pi*, with modernistic style, bizarre gags, and enjoyable wit, has also been made available in the more lasting form of book reprints.

W.F.

PROTHEROE, GLYN (1906-   ) Welsh cartoonist Glyn Protheroe, who frequently signed his artwork "Glynne," was born in Swansea on July 3, 1906. He studied art under Walter Fuller from 1923 to 1926, thereafter coming to London to live. He worked in a commercial art studio in Southampton Row and later moved to a different one in Shaftesbury Avenue. Full of amusing ideas, he was successful in contributing gag cartoons to many popular magazines of the period, including *The Leader, The Sporting News*, and *The Sports Post*. He was helpful to younger aspiring cartoonists, and gave a helping hand to many, including George Chatterton, who would be forever grateful.

Glyn's hobby was to breed canaries and study and draw wild birds, and this brought him F.Z.S. (Fellow of the Zoological Society) after his name and eventually the editorship of a bird fanciers' magazine, *In Your Aviary*. However, it is his comic work that interests us, and this began during the war when the barrow-boy turned publisher, Gerald G. Swan, launched his chain of comic books, the first in Britain. From his home in Mount Pleasant, Swansea, whither Protheroe had returned to avoid the London Blitz, he submitted an adventure strip entitled *Jakun of the Jungle*. This was immediately published in Swan's *War Comics* (1942). Glyn followed through with *Castle of Terror* (*Topical Funnies*), and then he got lucky with several series for Swan's rival, A. Soloway and his group of four irregular comic books. He ran several series beginning with *Scoop Smithy*, a reporter (*Comic Capers*), 1943. Then came *The Man from the Past* (*All Star*), a Western, *The Kansas Kid* (*Comic Adventures*), *Richard Venner, M.D.*, an unusual theme for those days (*Comic Capers*), *Dude Dawson* (*All Fun*), plus many comic pages.

In those wartime days of paper shortages, the independent publishers issued many one-shot eight-pagers, and Glyn drew five complete comics in this format for Philipp Marx (P.M. Productions) through 1944 to 1945: *Merry Comics, Midget, Bantam, Mighty*, and *Monster*. He also drew some paperbacks, pictorial pocketbooks of facts and puzzles. His clean, perhaps repetitive style, easily understood by young readers, did not suit the major publishers, however, and early postwar he left comics to concentrate on his bird illustrations.

D.G.

Salvador Pruneda,*"Don Catarino."* © Salvador Pruneda.

PRUNEDA, SALVADOR (1895-198?) A Mexican cartoonist born November 3, 1895, in Veracruz, Salvador Pruneda is the son of noted painter Alvaro Pruneda. Salvador Pruneda took part in the Mexican revolution, alongside his father and his two brothers, Alvaro and Ernesto.

Pruneda's first cartoons were published in the magazine *El Jacobino* as early as 1907. He then worked in most countries of the American continent, including the United States. In 1921 *El Heraldo de Mexico* asked him to come up with the idea for a daily strip: the result was the hilarious *Don Catarino*, which Pruneda created on texts by Fernández Benedicto. The strip passed later to *El Demócrata* and from there went to *El Nacional*.

Salvador Pruneda is a founder of the National Union of Newspaper Editors, the Association of Press Photographers, the Mexican Press Club, and the Workers' Union of *El Nacional*. He has written three books: *Estampas* ("Etchings"), *Huellas* ("Traces"), and *La Caricatura como Arma Politica* ("Caricature as a Political Weapon"). He is also the recipient of numerous awards and honors, both for his cartooning work and for his civic and professional contributions. He died in the late 1980s. (His son Alvaro was also a cartoonist.)

M.H.

PUSSYCAT PRINCESS (U.S.) Grace G. Drayton (she drew under her married name of Wiedersheim before her second marriage) drew perhaps the most "cutesy"

"The Pussycat Princess," Ruth Carroll. © King Features Syndicate.

of all the children's cartoon features, including Rose O'Neill (*The Kewpies*) and Bertha Corbett (*Sunbonnet Babies*). She was certainly the most active female cartoonist involved in children's comics, followed closely by Fanny Y. Cory.

Drayton created the Campbell Soup Kids (continued in advertising a generation later by the young Dik Browne) and drew a Sunday page in the early 1910s, *Dolly Dimples and Bobby Bounce*. Eventually this kid comic was picked up by Hearst and run with coloring pictures as a top-strip feature.

The Pussycat Princess was picked up when *Dolly* was retired. The first appearance of the Sunday-only comic was on March 10, 1935, with art by Drayton and text by Ed Anthony, an editor and executive with Crowell-Collier Publishers. Soon after the start of the strip, Ruth Carroll took over the art.

The strip, described by Waugh as cuddly, was casted by kittens—the Princess herself, different ladies in waiting, knights, and, strangely, everyday contemporary cats with contemporary problems and concerns. Puns on anything feline were abundant.

The Pussycat Princess was last run on July 13, 1947—something less than a cat-astrophe; few papers outside the Hearst chain ever carried the strip, and Hearst's own papers went through a decline themselves during this decade.

R.M.

PUTZKER, RONALD (1962-   ) Ronald Alfred Alexander Putzker was born September 13, 1962, in Wiener Neustadt, Austria. He grew up in the Tyrol. He drew his first comic books at age 5 and sold them to his grandmother. He started going to high school in Innsbruck but dropped out after five years, started a six-year stint as rock musician while also becoming an apprentice cook at the suggestion of his father, a surveying engineer and official. Putzker never got his diploma but moved to Vienna instead where he started taking courses at a graphic designer school. Finally he

tried his hand at studying to become a bookseller. At the time he discovered the comics store of Heinz Pollischansky, who also was a publisher of comic books and collector of original art.

Upon seeing an album by Milo Manara his childhood interest in comics was reawakened. He produced a 46-page photo comic entitled *Linda Denim*. It was later published under the new title of *Eva Sedlitzky* in a comics fanzine. This led to a job as bookseller in the comic store of comics fanzine publisher Wolfgang Alber. Putzker soon started to do the graphic design for the fanzine, then at the suggestion of the late Markus Tschernegg, a devoted Austrian comics fan, translator and journalist, started drawing comics. Putzker created *Inspektor Burnadz*, the name allegedly a combination of Burenwurst, a Viennese fast-food sausage, and an Austrianized transcription of the word "nuts," as in "being nuts."

The first album had a print run of some 35 copies, which he gave away as Christmas presents. This got Wolfgang Alber to suggest he start drawing comics for his fanzine *Comic Forum* in 1984. Thus Putzker's career as comic artist got underway. His work was published in Alber's *Comic Forum* and in German fanzines. At the time the coincidence of a stuffed-up drain got Putzker to meet writer Erich Nussbaumer who then started writing scenarios for Putzker.

The incredible happened. Offers started coming in. Another series, *Aglaya*, was conceived for publication in album form in 1987 in Germany. This series was followed by *Anna Stein* in 1989, also in Germany. Then, finally, Putzker achieved the realization of a dream: working on a newspaper strip, *Kolumbus*. This strip, published in 1991 to 1992, was conceived for publication in the weekly Austrian newspaper *Die ganze Woche* but with the idea of making it into a 52-page comic album afterward. Now foreign publishers started showing interest in his work.

From that time on the indomitable Alfred Putzker has continued to produce comic stories and albums

Ronald Putzker, "Inspektor Burnadz." © Ronald Putzker.

together with writer Erich Nussbaumer or, alternatively, with Günter Brödl. He is also busy working as illustrator for the Austrian newspapers. Putzker's comic style, although influenced by Milo Manara, is usually looser than Manara's, and instead of hatching he uses solid blacks. Putzker's career may seem unorthodox.

But then who said there was an orthodox way of becoming a comic artist in Austria?

W.F.

QUADRATINO (Italy)

QUADRATINO (Italy) In a short period, 1908-11, *Il Corriere dei Piccoli* became the most successful Italian publication for children with the highest circulation among weekly magazines; it was recommended by educators and read in every middle-class Italian home. This success was due, in no small measure, to the generous amount of good illustrations published in the magazine. In turn, the *Corriere*'s style was established by two of the great Italian masters of illustration: Attilio Mussino and Antonio Rubino, who filled the pages of the *Corriere* with the adventures of scores of characters they had created. These artists each created a comic feature that they are often associated with; *Bilbolbul* was created by Mussino, *Quadratino* ("Little Square Head"), which first appeared in 1910, is Rubino's most unforgettable creation.

Quadratino owed his name to the shape of his head, which was a perfect square. He was a relative of Scientific Knowledge; Geometry was his mother, Mathematics his grandmother, and Algebra was his aunt. Quadratino, however, was not too happy with his stern relatives, and he played pranks any time he could. As a result he very often got his head out of shape, and his relatives, with perfect, rational, and scientific formulas, had to return his head to its normal form.

This symbolic conflict between science (or reason) and fantasy (or just normal childhood) was most often solved in favor of the age-old traditional lifeview, but Rubino sometimes managed to make it clear that he disagreed with this tradition-bound method of educating children. The strip ended in the 1940s.

A selection of *Quadratino* episodes was anthologized by Garzanti in their collection, *The Golden Age of the Comics*.

G.B.

QUINCY (U.S.)

QUINCY (U.S.) In 1970 King Features Syndicate, prompted by the growing success of Morrie Turner's *Wee Pals*, decided to produce an "integrated" strip of its own. Jamaica-born cartoonist Ted Shearer was promptly contacted, and on June 17, 1970, *Quincy* made its debut.

Again, as in *Wee Pals*, readers were confronted with a lively and lovable bunch of youngsters. Some were black, like Quincy himself, the bright-eyed enterprising title character; his sloppy kid brother, Li'l Bo; and his flirtatious and self-assertive girlfriend, Viola; others were white, like the ravenous Nickles, Quincy's best friend (a twist on the old-line disclaimer: "some of my best friends are"). Over the tightly knit little group (whose doings were quite sedate by modern, or any other, standards) hovered the kindly presence of Granny Dixon, sandwich-maker, pants-mender, and ego-booster extraordinare.

There was great topicality in *Quincy*, and much hip talk, but the ethnic humor sounded forced somehow, as if Shearer did not quite believe in the goings-on. The drawing was competent, but no more, and the kids' fires seemed, for the most part, to have been banked. All in all, this King Features contribution to interracial understanding was—like so many other "do good" efforts in the fields of art, literature, cinema, or the comics—more an embarrassment than a help.

Since 1976, however, there has been a reappraisal of the strip and its place in newspaper comics history (or at least in black newspaper comics history). In *100 Years of American Newspaper Comics*, Bill Crouch wrote, "*Quincy* is blessed with artwork of strong design and a creative use of zip tone." Whatever the strip's charms, Shearer's creation started faltering in the late 1970s and it was discontinued by the syndicate in 1986. A *Quincy* paperback was released by Bantam Books in 1972.

M.H.

QUINO   *see* Lavado, Joaquin.

"Quincy," Ted Shearer. © King Features Syndicate.

RAAB, FRITZ (1925-) Fritz Raab, German journalist and writer, was born April 2, 1925, the son of a pediatrician in Siegen. Raab's high school education was interrupted when he was drafted into the Luftwaffe, the German air force, from 1943 to 1945. He returned to secondary school for his final exams after the war. He then became an editor from 1948 to 1949, and then finally a freelance journalist and author.

Raab has written some 200 radio plays for the educational programs of the North and West German radio authorities, NDR and WDR. He has also authored 50 radio plays, 20 scripts for television dramas, and eight novels for children. In 1959 he created the popular comic strip *Taró*, published in the weekly illustrated magazine *stern* ("star") from June 13, 1959, to March 3, 1968. Raab was fascinated by the comic medium ever since he had first seen "genuine" comics as a private in occupied France. Therefore, he was delighted to be offered the chance to create a comic strip of his own. He worked much in the vein of Karl May, the prolific German adventure novelist, unknowingly using the same method of carefully researching geographic and ethnographic data for his stories.

Taró is the story of a highly educated Latin American Indian working as an inspector in the Indian Protection Agency in the Mato Grosso area. The exoticism of the locale and the characters, paired with an unending number of plot twists and the very graphic art of F. W. Richter-Johnsen made for an extraordinary comic strip. Raab usually wrote four episodes at a time, much in the form of a movie script. He handed them over to the editors of *stern*, who in turn handed them to artist Richter-Johnsen. The writer and the artist of *Taró* only met four times during the nine years that the strip lasted. *Taró* was canceled because of a reduction of *stern*'s children's supplement, *sternchen* to just two pages of the magazine itself. In a way, the comic strip was saved the disgrace of being disproved by atrocities of the Indian Protective Agency of Brazil that were headlined 17 days after the strip ended. Nevertheless, *Taró* will be remembered for its careful writing and art that created mood and atmosphere, strong characters and fascinating stories. Raab's work is also positive proof that adventure and excessive violence in comics need not be synonymous. When *Taró* ended, Raab returned to writing novels, some of which were made into movies for television.

W.F.

RABOY, EMANUEL (1914-1967) Emanuel Raboy was an American comic book and comic strip artist born April 9, 1914, in New York City. After attending government-funded drawing classes, "Mac" Raboy became a work-project artist and several of his wood engravings from this era remain in the permanent collection of New York's Metropolitan Museum. He entered the comic book field in 1940 as an artist for the Harry "A" Chesler shop and quickly began producing well-drawn material for Fawcett features like *Mr. Scarlett* (1941), *Ibis* (1942), and *Bulletman* (1941-1942). But his biggest opportunity came when Fawcett editor Ed Herron created *Captain Marvel, Jr.*, and recognizing Raboy's talents from his previous Fawcett superhero work, assigned him to visualize the strip.

Heavily influenced by the outstanding *Flash Gordon* work of Alex Raymond, Raboy created *Captain Marvel, Jr.* in its image. His figures were lithe and majestic, tightly rendered and classically posed. Like Raymond, Raboy avoided the heavy use of blacks and all of his work on *Captain Marvel, Jr.* was bright and exciting. The anatomy and draftsmanship was always perfect. Another outstanding point of his two-year term on the feature—which soon outgrew its origins in *Master Comics* and expanded into its own book—was his superlative cover work. Unlike most of his colleagues, Raboy did not draw his covers "twice-up" (or double the size of the printed page). Instead, he opted for a size almost as small as the printed cover. The result was a static, poster-type illustration, an almost serene still-life rendering, completely different from the hectic, active covers gracing most contemporary superhero books.

Raboy left *Captain Marvel, Jr.* in 1944 to draw the adventures of Spark Publications' *The Green Lama*, a pulp-hero-turned-comic-book-superhero. The strip became a minor classic, but it never sold enough. After the book folded in early 1946, Raboy spent most of 1946 and 1947 as a commercial artist.

He returned to the comic art field in the spring of 1948, however, when King Features signed him as the new artist on his idol's old strip, *Flash Gordon*. Producing the strip's Sunday pages, Raboy made a creditable showing on the feature, but the highlight of his comic art career remained his short-lived but brilliant period as the definitive artist on *Captain Marvel, Jr.* He continued illustrating *Flash Gordon* until his death in December 1967.

J.B.

RADILOVIĆ, JULIO (1928-) The first Yugoslav cartoonist to have his work syndicated throughout the world by Strip Art Features (and thus published in France, Germany, Spain, Brazil, the United States, and other countries), Julio Radilović, like many Yugoslav cartoonists, is equally competent with both realistic and humor comics. His mastery of details can be seen in each of his drawings. Radilović was born in Maribor, on September 25, 1928. When he started to read, his uncle sent him American papers regularly. It was his first contact with comics and Radilović liked them. However, cartooning soon became more than a hobby for Radilović and therefore he never finished secondary school. His brother worked at the Studio for Animated Films in Zagreb and helped him to find his first job on a comic strip in 1952.

In 1956 Radilović met noted scriptwriter Zvonimir Furtinger and they realized a dozen episodes of the comic strip *Izumi i otkrića* for the German publisher, Rolf Kauka. In the same year Radilović and Furtinger started the production of one of the longest historical strips in Yugoslavia. The strip had more than 160 pages, was titled *Kroz minula stoljeca* ("Through the Past Centuries") and was published by *Plavi Vjesnik*. The strip was discontinued in the spring of 1959 when Radilović became ill. A Yugoslav motion picture became very popular in the early 1960s and Radilović produced four episodes of *Kapetan Leši*, using the movie characters in the strip. In the spring of 1962, after he read Edgar Wallace's novel, *Sanders of Africa*, Radilović got an idea for a strip and together with Furtinger realized three episodes of *The African Adventures for Plavi Vjesnik*. Their other realistic and humor comics were also very popular, especially the Western series, but their most popular comic strip remains *Herlock Sholmes*.

Radilović is a master of color and has produced cover pictures and illustrations for many publications, including a complete set of Tarzan books. Since the late 1970s he has worked mainly for foreign publishers, notably turning out *Jaimie McPheters* for the British market and *Die Partizanen* for the Dutch magazine *Eppo*.

E.R.

RADIO PATROL (U.S.) In 1933, responding to many requests from their readers, the editors of the *Boston Daily Record* assigned two of their staff people, Eddie Sullivan the night city editor and Charles Schmidt, to produce a detective strip with an urban setting. In August of the same year *Pinkerton Jr.*, written by Sullivan and drawn by Schmidt, made its appearance; its success was such that Joseph Connolly, editor of King Features Syndicate, decided to give it national distribution. A revamped version thus appeared under the title of *Radio Patrol* (and later *Sergeant Pat of the Radio Patrol*) starting as a daily strip on April 16, 1934, followed by a Sunday page on November 11 of the same year. (Like most strips of the 1930s, *Radio Patrol* had a top, *Public Enemies Through the Ages*;—a kind of "Who Was Who In Crime"—it didn't last long.)

The basic appeal of the strip was founded on a recent police innovation, the radio patrol car. In this case the car was occupied by two Irish cops, the red-haired, ruggedly handsome Pat and his elephantine partner Stutterin' Sam. In the course of their assignments, which included from time to time busting a gang of racketeers, infiltrating the ranks of truck hijackers, or putting the arm on safe-crackers, kidnappers, bank robbers, and assorted miscreants, Pat and Sam were often assisted by their young pal Pinky (the Pinkerton Jr. of the earlier version) and his faithful Irish setter named (what else?) Irish. The romantic interest was supplied by female police officer Molly Day, a beautiful slip of an Irish lass, and a sharp crime-solver in her own right.

In spite of hot competition from other police strips (*Dick Tracy* chief among them) *Radio Patrol* enjoyed honorable, if not spectacular popularity for over a decade. The postwar years, however, proved fatal to the feature's mix of ethnic corn and righteous pow, and *Radio Patrol* soon faded into oblivion (the Sunday page in October 1946, the daily strip in December 1950).

A *Radio Patrol* radio program was regularly broadcast in the 1930s, and in 1937 Ford Beebe and Clifton Smith directed a movie serial, with Grant Withers as Pat and Adrian Morris as Sam.

M.H.

RAHAN (France) Rahan (subtitled "the son of the grim ages") was started on February 24, 1969, in the comic weekly *Pif-Gadget*; the prolific Roger Lécureux was the scriptwriter, and André Chéret the illustrator.

Rahan is a caveman, a member of "those who walk erect" and roam the prehistoric world, going from tribe to tribe, never settling with any one group: it can be said that he was the first citizen of the world. In those faraway ages of ignorance and superstition, he keeps an open and searching mind and possesses uncanny powers of insight and observation: these lead him from one momentous discovery to another (such as fire and

"Radio Patrol," Charlie Schmidt and Ed Sullivan. © King Features Syndicate.

"Rahan," André Chéret. © Editions Vaillant.

the throwing spear). Ever generous, Rahan shares his discoveries with all of mankind. (Mankind does not always pay him back with kindness, however, and his fellow-men prove at times as much of a deadly threat as the savage beasts he has to fight to keep alive.)

If Rahan's adventures often recall Tarzan's, and Chéret's compositions sometimes resemble Hogarth's, the major merit of the strip lies in the evocation—at once naturalistic and fabulous—of these distant times. Lécureux's scenarios are imaginative and thoughtful, Chéret's line firm and assertive. After a slow start, Rahan now figures at the top of European adventure strips, and has been reprinted several times in book form.

The character also appeared in the pages of an eponymous magazine published irregularly between 1971 and 1984. Because of this added workload Chéret left many episodes to be drawn by other artists, Enrique Romero and Guido Zamperoni most notably. After Editions Vaillant ceased publication in 1992, *Rahan* went into very successful reprinting in chronological order. The series was also adapted to animated cartoons seen on television in 1987.

RAPELA, ENRIQUE (1911-1978) An Argentine cartoonist born in Mercedes in 1911, Enrique Rapela started his cartooning career in 1937 with a series of illustrations published in the magazine *El Tony*. His comic creations, for which he is best known, are all inspired by the folklore and the characters common to his native land; these include *Cirilo El Audaz* ("Cirilo the Bold"), a daily strip originated in 1940 in the newspaper *La Razón*, *El Huinca*, and *Fabián Leyes*.

Rapela is also famous for his series of illustrations for books depicting Argentine folklore and customs. He died on February 9, 1978.

L.G.

RASMUS KLUMP (Denmark) *Rasmus Klump* is a cute little teddy bear living in a world of fantasy especially designed for younger readers. *Rasmus Klump* is the very

"Rasmus Klump" ("Petzi"), Vilhelm Hansen. © Vilhelm Hansen.

successful creation of Danish artist Vilhelm Hansen, who originated the charming little tyke and his entourage in 1951 for syndication as a daily strip. Until 1959, captions were printed below the pictures. Since 1959 *Rasmus Klump* and friends have been talking in speech balloons and continue to do so in about 75 daily newspapers and magazines in Denmark, Sweden, Norway, Finland, Iceland, Holland, Belgium, France, Spain, Italy, Japan, Great Britain, Austria, Switzerland, Germany, Ghana, and South Africa. Thus far, more than 8,000 individual strips have been produced, also some 25 children's books which have been translated into 12 languages (including Japanese). After starting the feature on his own, Hansen has enlisted the help of his wife, Carla, in the production of the strip.

The title, *Rasmus Klump*, besides being the name of the strip's star, does not tell much about the strip itself, except maybe suggesting the strip's modern fairy tale contents, which are done in a style very close to children's book illustrations. (This is a fitting style, as the *Rasmus Klump* books are primarily aimed at a young readership.) The alliterative German title of the strip, *Petzi, Pelle, Pingo*, immediately suggests a strip with anthropomorphic animals—a little bear, a pelican, and a penguin. These three stars of *Rasmus Klump* are aided in their funny adventures by a large cast of other animals who play out stereotypes and roles.

Of the three main characters, the pelican is the most interesting. He is the wise bird, coming up with solutions for everything and always carrying around all kinds of tools in his pelican's beak, fitting them in the same way Mary Poppins fits all of her belongings into her carpet bag. What boy would not wish for pockets as large and magical as the pelican's beak to hold all of his treasures? It is the wish fulfillment capacity intrinsic to the *Rasmus Klump* strip that makes it such a success with children.

The feature, which is reprinted *ad infinitum* enjoys great popularity especially in Europe and in Japan. In the 1980s the adventures of Rasmus Klump and friends were also produced as animated cartoons for television.

W.F.

RAVIOLA, ROBERTO (1939-1996) Roberto Raviola is one of the most prolific and peculiar Italian cartoonists. Raviola signed his artwork with the pen name "Magnus" (the beginning of the Latin expression *Magnus pictor fecit*—"A great painter did it"). Born in Bologna July 31, 1939, Raviola started to draw the series *Kriminal* (1964), a negative hero, then *Satanik* (1965), a criminal heroine, and *Agent SSO18* (1965), an international spy, and finally *Gesebel* (1966), a science fiction heroine. Magnus's style, based on the very effective contrast between black and whites, helped to lend more fascination to these characters, a fact which, along with *Diabolik*, launched a new genre called "black comics." With the series *Maxmagnus* (1968) and *Alan Ford* (1969), Magnus showed his ability in comical and grotesque styles as well. All the previous series were written by Bunker (Luciano Secchi) and printed in black and white pocket-size book form by publisher Corno.

In 1975 Magnus divorced from Bunker and Corno but went on writing and drawing an impressive number of comics adventures inspired by two somehow different standards: the first is a kind of realistic storytelling with some grotesque graphic aspects; the sec-

Roberto Raviola, "I Briganti." © Edizione l'Isola Trovata.

ond is a comical and humorous storytelling quite grotesque in style. Samples of the first genre are the series *Lo sconosciuto* ("The Unknown," 1975), which portrays the dramatic adventures of a former soldier of fortune who now fights alone and all over the world against crime, injustice, and political totalitarianism. *Lo sconosciuto* is moved by progressive ideals, and the setting of the adventures, though fictional, is well documented and marked by crude realism. The series *I briganti* ("Brigands," 1978), is a long saga inspired by a Chinese medieval novel that tells of a people's revolt against the authoritarian central government. The series *Milady* (1980) is a peculiar science fiction adventure where the heroine is engaged to do justice. And later on is *L'uomo che uccise Ernesto "Che" Guevara* ("The man who killed Ernesto Che Guevara"), a violent and detailed account of the death of the famous guerrilla.

Examples of the second genre are the series *La Compagnia dell Forca* ("The Gallows Company," 1978), which narrates the funny vicissitudes of a shabby company of mercenary troops wandering through medieval Europe and the Near East. The series *Necron* (1981, written by Ilaria Volpe) is a screwball comedy where a mad female doctor gives life to a monstrous human creature of whom eventually she loses control. *Le 110 pillole* ("110 Pills," 1988) and *Le femmine incantate* ("Enchanted women") are two long, polished stories of extreme graphic elegance inspired by Chinese erotic novels.

During the last years of his existence Magnus illustrated some books, wrote and drew some short stories, but mainly devoted himself to illustrating with extreme accuracy *La valle del terrore* ("The Valley of Terror"), a long adventure of the Italian Western hero Tex, written by Nizzi and printed after the author's death on February 5, 1996. Many comics stories by Magnus have been reprinted in book form. In spite of his great popularity and probably because of it, he did not enjoy a full critical appraisal, especially on the side of the comics criticism that confuses comic art with political engagement, seriousness, and incommunicability, and has thus completely misunderstood Magnus's work inspired, with reference to the different genres he has produced, by a great familiarity with Asian culture and art, a political anarchist attitude, and a real popular comic spirit.

G.C.C.

RAWHIDE KID (U.S.) The creation of writer and editor Stan Lee, the *Rawhide Kid* debuted in the comic book of the same name published by Atlas (later known as Marvel) in March 1955. Issue number 1, illustrated by Bob Brown with assistance from Joe Maneely, told the story of the young gunslinger whose reputation preceded him across the West. The Rawhide Kid boasted the fastest gun around and wielded a bullwhip, employing both with brutal results. The violence was tempered, however, with the second issue, the first under the Comics Code seal.

Within a year, the format was altered further with the Kid abandoning his bullwhip and buckskin costume to become a rancher. Randy Clayton, a young protégé from the first two issues, returned to the strip as "Kid Randy," whose relationship to the Rawhide Kid was never made clear. The two of them lived on a ranch near Shotgun City and their stories, drawn by Brown and Dick Ayers, dealt with cattle rustlers and outlaws disrupting the peace of the town. The ranch-owner format proved unsuccessful and the book folded with number 16, September 1957.

In 1960 the comic book was resurrected with Ayers inking the pencil art of Jack Kirby. The origin issue, number 17, introduced a different Rawhide Kid in the person of Johnny Bart. Johnny was an orphan adopted by Ben Bart, a retired Texas Ranger who taught Johnny his fast-gun skills. When Johnny reached 18, his mentor was gunned down by outlaws. Johnny avenged the death and set out to protect the West from similar terrorists. In subsequent issues, he encountered a variety of Western outlaws and early American super-villains. Following Kirby on the art chores were Jack Davis, Dick Ayers, and Jack Keller before Larry Lieber took up both scripting and penciling duties in 1964. Lieber continued on a regular basis in stories that found the Kid roaming the West, encountering gunslingers out to gain reputations by outdrawing the famous Rawhide Kid. Occasional art fill-ins were done by Ayers, Paul Reinman, and Werner Roth.

In October 1968, publication of *Mighty Marvel Western* began, a title reprinting stories of three Marvel Western strips: *Two Gun Kid, Kid Colt,* and *Rawhide Kid.* In 1970 reprints began appearing frequently in the *Rawhide Kid* comic book and, in 1973, edged out the new material completely. Stories of *Rawhide Kid* also appeared in two one-shot books: *Rawhide Kid Special,* 1971 and November 1973. *Rawhide Kid* ended in May 1979 but reappeared briefly in 1985.

M.E.

RAYMOND, ALEX (1909-1956) Alex Raymond was an American cartoonist and illustrator born October 2, 1909, in New Rochelle, New York. After studies at Iona Preparatory School in New Rochelle and at the Grand Central School of Art, Alexander Gillespie (Alex) Raymond served out his apprenticeship first with Russ West (creator of *Tillie the Toiler*), then with Lyman Young (*Tim Tyler's Luck*), from 1930 to 1933. In 1932 and 1933 he ghosted both the daily strip and the Sunday page of *Tim Tyler*.

Toward the end of 1933 Raymond was asked by King Features Syndicate to create a Sunday page made up of two features: *Flash Gordon* (a space strip) with *Jungle Jim* (an adventure strip) as its top piece. In addition Raymond was to draw the daily *Secret Agent X-9,* a police strip scripted by Dashiell Hammett. All three creations started publication in January 1934. By the end of 1935 the load was too much for Raymond, who abandoned the drawing of *X-9* to lavish all his care on his Sunday features. Under his pen they became world famous (especially *Flash Gordon*).

In May of 1944 Raymond relinquished *Flash Gordon* and *Jungle Jim* to his former assistant Austin Briggs and joined the U.S. Marine Corps. He was commissioned a captain and saw action in the Pacific aboard an aircraft carrier in the Gilbert Islands. Demobilized as a major in 1946, Alex Raymond created in March of that same year *Rip Kirby*, a daily police strip, which soon became another popular and critical success. Alex Raymond died at the top of his fame, on September 6, 1956, after a car accident near Westport, Connecticut.

Of all the comic strip creators, Alex Raymond unquestionably possessed the most versatile talent. His style—precise, clear, and incisive—was flexible enough to enable him to master every kind of strip at which he tried his hand. His influence on other cartoonists was considerable during his lifetime and did not diminish after his death.

One of the most celebrated comic artists of all time as the creator of four outstanding comic features (a feat unequaled to this day), Alex Raymond received many distinctions and awards during his lifetime for his work, both as a cartoonist and as a magazine illustrator. He also served as president of the National Cartoonists Society in 1950 and 1951.

M.H.

RAYMONDO O CANGACEIRO (Brazil) Unlike what could have been expected from a country of its size, Brazil never developed a national comic industry of any importance. The early comic newspapers such as the fabled *O Tico Tico* carried only American features. After World War II European and South American strips partially replaced the American production. Only in the 1950s did Brazil produce some worthy features of its own: one such strip was *Raymondo o Cangaceiro*, by José Lanzelotti.

The *cangaceiros* have always been a popular literary subject in Brazil. Bandits who roamed the *serta'* of Northeast Brazil in the first decades of the century, they have been glorified in the Brazilian media much as the Western desperadoes have been in the United States. They have inspired several novels and movies, including Lima Barreto's *O Cangaceiros*, which won a prize at the 1953 Cannes Festival. That same year also saw the first of Lanzelotti's series of comic books devoted to the adventures of Raymondo the Cangaceiro. As depicted in the strip, Raymondo is a bush Robin Hood who, with the assistance of his band of rebels, rights the wrongs committed against helpless *peones* by corrupt government officials and greedy landowners. Lanzelotti's graphic style was quite good, with many accurate details of Brazilian life, and the stories were entertaining, if loosely plotted.

Raymondo o Cangaceiro enjoyed fair success until the 1960s, when its subject became politically objectionable and it was discontinued.

M.H.

Giorgio Rebuffi, "Lo Sceriffo Fox." © Edizioni Alpe.

"Red Barry," Will Gould. © King Features Syndicate.

REBUFFI, GIORGIO (1928-   ) Giorgio Rebuffi, one of Italy's most famous cartoonists, was born November 6, 1928, in Milan. He began to draw while attending the university and created *Sceriffo Fox* in 1949 for Edizioni Alpe. This series met with great success and convinced Rebuffi to embark on a cartooning career. In 1950 he took over *Cucciolo e Beppe*, originally a strip about two little dogs, also for Alpe. Rebuffi changed the characters into human beings and gave the strip its contemporary graphic look.

Among Rebuffi's innumerable creations mention should be made of *Lupo Pugacioff* ("Pugacioff the Wolf," 1959), *Grifagno Sparagno* (1963), and *Professor Cerebrus* (1967). He also created the popular humor strip *Tiramolla* in 1952 in collaboration with scriptwriter Roberto Renzi. In recent times Rebuffi has been responsible for *Romeo Lancia* (1969), about a lackadaisical playboy, *Vita di un Commesso Viaggiatore* ("Life of a Traveling Salesman," also 1969), *Vita col Gatto* ("Life with the Cat," 1970), and *Esopo Minore* (1970), on which Rebuffi does everything, including the lettering. The last two are the pillars of the comic books published by Alpe, along with *Redipicche* and *Whisky & Gogo*.

In addition to his work for Edizioni Alpe, Rebuffi has also drawn *Donald Duck* and *Mickey Mouse* stories for Walt Disney Productions and produced two more strips: *I Dispettieri* ("The Spiteful Ones") for *Il Corriere dei Piccoli* in 1974, and *Volpone Dulcamara* ("Bittersweet the Fox") for Editrice Cenisio in 1975. From 1989-1992 he was one of the many cartoonists to draw the French series *Pif le Chien*.

Giorgio Rebuffi is one of the few Italian cartoonists who has been able to make a personal statement through his graphic and narrative undertakings. When he is not drawing or writing scripts, he snorkels and devours science fiction novels.

G.B.

RED BARRY (U.S.) *Red Barry* was one of a quartet of police strips fielded by King Features Syndicate against *Dick Tracy* in 1934; drawn and written by Will Gould (no kin to Chester Gould), it made its first appearance on March 19 as a daily strip, followed by a Sunday version a year later.

Will Gould made *Red Barry* into a disturbingly accurate synthesizing of a Warner Bros. gangster movie of the period. The atmosphere is dark and oppressive, the lighting violent and contrasted, the dialogues fast and tough. Red Barry himself physically resembles James Cagney, with his red hair and sullen expression. He is an "undercover man" for a big-city police force (the city is not named but the feel and backgrounds are unmistakably New York's), and his main beat seems to be Chinatown. He is alternately advised, cajoled, and scolded by his superior, Inspector Scott, loved by the blonde, wistful girl reporter Mississippi, and sometimes assisted by the street urchin Ouchy Mugouchy and his "terrific three," a juvenile trio straight out of the *Dead End Kids*.

Among the villains Red meets and subdues in these fast-paced tales of mystery and suspense, one can mention the mysterious "Monk," head of a gang of murderous thieves; the Eurasian adventuress "Flame," and Judge Jekyll, a former magistrate turned killer after going underground (this episode was obviously inspired by Judge Crater's real-life disappearance).

In 1938, frightened by readers' mail protesting *Red Barry*'s blackness and violence, King Features tried to change the format of the strip. It reappeared in 1940 as an eight-page comic book insert (after the fashion of Will Eisner's *The Spirit*) that never saw print.

Red Barry occupies an honorable position among detective strips, somewhere between *Dick Tracy* and *Secret Agent X-9*; it is regrettable that Will Gould was not allowed to develop the feature into what might have become one of the most exciting action strips of the era.

An ironic footnote should be added: the strip was adapted into a 1938 movie serial starring Buster Crabbe and featuring an unknown actor, Donald Barry, who henceforth was to be known under the screen name of "Red" Barry long after the original had become a memory.

M.H.

RED DETACHMENT OF WOMEN, THE (China) The story which inspired this Chinese comic book is among the most famous and best-known works of fiction in the People's Republic of China. First published as a short story by the noted author Liang Hsin, *The Red Detachment of Women* was soon adapted to the stage and later became a staple of the Peking Opera (a movie of the ballet was made in 1970). In 1966 the scriptwriter Sung Yu-chieh adapted the famous story to the medium of the comics, and Lin Tzu-shun did the artwork; the comic book faithfully follows the plot and

"The Red Detachment of Women," Sung Yu-chieh and Lin Tzu-shun.

action (even in the exact reproduction of colors) of the opera version.

The action takes place in 1930 on the island of Hainan. Wu Chiung-hua, a slave-woman in the household of the warlord Nan, succeeds in escaping and later joins the Red Army, setting up a detachment composed uniquely of young women like herself. Under Wu's leadership and the guidance of Hung, the political commissar attached to the outfit, the Red Detachment fights against land-owners, foreign capitalists, and other class enemies until they reach final victory.

The plot and narrative of the strip (written entirely in text underneath the pictures—there is no balloon, a rarity among Chinese comic books) are representative of the "socialist realism" prevalent in mainland China. If one discounts the political elements, however, *The Red Detachment* reads like a good adventure story: there is plenty of action; fights, escapes, and ambushes abound; the authors provide a good deal of suspense and even a slight hint of sex.

The intrigue is clear and competently handled, and the drawing style strikes a happy medium between traditional Chinese design (such as can be found in 19th-

century scrolls) and Western composition (there are even some interesting camera angles). The page layout, however, is monotonous, with each picture neatly enclosed within the same rectangular frame (obviously rhythm and pacing have been sacrificed to the needs of indoctrination). In spite of its orthodox line, the book was nonetheless attacked during the Cultural Revolution for "bourgeois tendencies" and "revisionism."

The Red Detachment of Women is a very popular comic book in China. In 1967 it was translated into English and circulated in Hong Kong (and probably other Far Asian countries as well). *The Red Detachment* also figures among the collection of Chinese comics published in the United States by Doubleday in 1973.

M.H.

REDEYE (U.S.) Gordon Bess started *Redeye* for King Features on September 11, 1967, as a daily and on September 17 as a Sunday strip.

Redeye is the somewhat eccentric sachem of a no less bizarre tribe of Indians living on the borderline of white "civilization" in a state of half-war, half-peace. Grouped around him are some of the most incompetent, befuddled, and outrageous braves ever to wear a feather headdress—always ready to run in the opposite direction when the sachem orders a charge, or to get drunk on smuggled firewater. Tanglefoot in particular is an albatross around the sachem's neck: not only can't he tell a herd of buffaloes from an oncoming train but his persistence in trying to marry Tawney, the sachem's lovely daughter, gives Redeye a special pain. (Nor are these the sachem's only trials: he is poisoned by his wife's cooking, badgered by his young son Pokey, outsmarted by the medicine man, and constantly thwarted in his dreams of military glory by his faint-hearted mustang Loco.)

In this gem of a comic strip Gordon Bess tellingly but unobtrusively commented on a number of topical subjects: conservation, the ecology, and the ethics of business, without the ham-handed approach of many other "relevant" strips. He made his point lightly and humorously, always leaving a laugh at the end. He also put his firsthand knowledge of the West (Bess lived in

"Redeye," Gordon Bess. © King Features Syndicate.

Idaho) to good use, and scenery, customs, and animals were depicted with a sure if satirical hand. He died in 1989, and the strip passed into the hands of Bill Yates for the writing and Mel Casson for the drawing.

Redeye is one of a few hilariously funny strips to come along in a long time and it is no doubt headed for a long career.

M.H.

REDIPICCHE (Italy) *Redipicche* ("King of Spades") appeared for the first time, and simultaneously in Italy and in France, in the spring of 1969 in the bimonthly magazine bearing its name. The idea for the characters was much older, however, and was concretely formulated, albeit in a less sophisticated form, as early as 1950.

Written and drawn by Luciano Bottaro, the series deals with the vicissitudes of Redipicche and the three other kings, each representing a suit in the traditional deck of cards: hearts, clubs, and diamonds. The biggest play is given to the antagonism between Redipicche, a petty tyrant who is choleric and inept, and Redicuori (King of Hearts), a peaceful and fun-loving monarch. Some other characters weave their schemes around the two protagonists, such as Barone Catapulta (Baron Catapult), the arms manufacturer, and the bloodthirsty Generale Falco (General Hawk).

Redipicche's aggressive disposition seems due to a variety of frustrations, including a liver ailment and a nagging mother-in-law. So he fights against his neighbors but finds the going rough, with such enemies as the witch Filippa; Filippone da Todi, the forest archer, and the Alchemist of Hearts, conjurer of terrible nightmares with which he plagues the hapless monarch.

Redipicche did not meet with overwhelming success at first, but it was picked up some years later by the established weekly *Corriere dei Piccoli* where it became extraordinarily popular with the younger readers. The surprised (but delighted) author then decided to play down the satirical aspects of the strip in favor of the fantasy elements already present in the original version. It has now become one of Bottaro's most popular

series, and from the mid-1970s on it has been published in France, Germany, Sweden, Mexico, and Brazil.

In complement to *Redipicche* in the *Corriere dei Piccoli*, Bottaro has been drawing *Il Paese delAlfabeto* ("Alphabet Land"). This series (written by Carlo Chendi) is a fantasy involving the letters of the alphabet and is bathed in an atmosphere not unlike that of the older strip.

G.B.

RED KNIGHT, THE (U.S.) Cartoonist Jack W. McGuire and scriptwriter John J. Welch (who had previously collaborated on an ill-starred adventure strip called *Slim and Tubby*) started *The Red Knight* for the Register and Tribune Syndicate in June 1940.

The Red Knight was the laboratory creation of Dr. Van Lear, who exclaimed at the end of his experiment: "Finished! My scientific masterpiece! A man who through chemical process will become all-powerful in body and mind!" Thus charged with the doctor's secret formula (which he called "Plus Power"), the Red Knight could perform all kinds of superhuman feats from tearing down buildings to turning invisible. The only hitch was that Plus Power wore off quite rapidly, and the Red Knight had to get back each time to be revitalized. Welch played on the conceit theme awhile, but not too successfully; the Knight's adventures, a pale echo of the Superman exploits, were not quite suspenseful or gripping enough to hold the reader. Even McGuire's excellent (if hurried) artwork could not save the feature, which folded in 1943.

The Red Knight was not a very remarkable strip—albeit pleasant in a mindless way—but it featured the first superhero especially created for the newspaper page and, as such, deserves mention.

M.H.

REDONDO, NESTOR (1928-1995) Filipino artist Nestor Redondo was born in Candon, Ilocos Sur, Philippines on May 4, 1928. After attending high school Redondo studied to be an architect. His elder brother

"*Redipicche*," Luciano Bottaro. © Bierreci.

"Red Ryder," Fred Harman. © NEA Service.

Virgilio, who is an artist and a novelist for the comics, influenced the younger Redondo to take up his trade. The older brother became the better writer while Nestor became a better artist. The two teamed together and became a formidable duo. Nestor first achieved success with a superheroine feature named *Darna* by Mars Ravelo, one the Philippine's foremost comic book novelists. In the 1950s it became apparent that Nestor was the most popular artist in the comics. He had a great influence on other artists and many tried to copy his style. Someone once described his drawings as "pleasing to the eye." His heroes were always rugged and handsome, while the heroines were always beautiful. On many occasions he received fan mail from girls requesting to meet the models he used for his heroes, but Nestor never used a model.

Like many artists of his time, Nestor Redondo was influenced by Alex Raymond and Harold Foster. But he was also influenced a great deal by American magazine illustrators such as Jon Whitcom, Albert Dorn, Robert Fawcett, Norman Rockwell, and Dean Corneal. Nestor would usually draw in the evening, far into the early hours of the morning. He used a Chinese brush and hardly ever a pen. On tight schedules he used assistants. When not drawing for the comics (which was rare), he dabbled in oil painting and was an avid chess player.

In the 1960s Redondo published his own comic book in the hope that he could produce the kind of high standard and quality-oriented comic he always dreamed of, but inflation and the high costs forced him to fold and go back to drawing for the other publishers. In the early 1970s one of the biggest comic book publishers, D.C. National, saw the potential that Nestor had to offer and they hired him. It was not long before his popularity soared to a level where the publishers gave him a book all his own. This was *Rima*; followed by *The Swamp Thing*. He was also commissioned to do a series in a giant-size comic book on the Bible. Until his death on December 31, 1995, Nestor Redondo had a studio where he trained and taught young, aspiring artists for the comics.

M.A.

RED RYDER (U.S.)   Fred Harman's *Red Ryder* was first distributed as a Sunday feature by NEA Service on November 6, 1938; a daily version was added on March 27, 1939.

The action of *Red Ryder* takes place in the 1890s after the last of the Indian wars but before the advent of the automobile. Near the little town of Rimrock, Colorado, Red Ryder owns a ranch, which he manages with the help of his aunt, the Duchess. Ranch life is carefully and lovingly depicted by Harman, himself a rancher. But oftentimes Red must come to the help of old Sheriff Newt; he then puts on his boots and his beat-up Stetson and with the aid of Little Beaver, the Navajo orphan he has adopted, he rides into the wilderness, ranging far and wide, from the northern Rockies to Old Mexico, in pursuit of some stagecoach robbers or cattle rustlers.

Red Ryder's enemies have included (among the more notable) the sinister gambler and hired assassin Ace Hanlon, Banjo Bill the music-loving killer who would hide his gun in his instrument, Donna Ringo, the seductive head of a gang of train robbers, not to mention a gang of circus freaks operating out of a traveling tent show. Among other things, Red has also brought peace to ranchers and farmers, settled disputes between miners and cattlemen, and between whites and Indians, ridden shotgun on stagecoaches, and prospected for gold in the desert.

In 1960 Fred Harman left the comic strip field to devote himself to painting. *Red Ryder* lingered a while longer under the uninspired pen of Bob McLeod, before disappearing in the late 1960s.

The most popular of all Western strips, *Red Ryder* was adapted into comic books (among the contributing writers was Dick Calkins, of *Buck Rogers* fame) and to the screen (no fewer than 22 times!). It was also voted "favorite comic strip" by the Boys' Clubs of America. *Red Ryder* may also have been the first comic strip to achieve transatlantic cross-media recognition: in 1947 a play called *Les Aventures de Red Ryder* was staged in a theater in Brussels.

M.H.

RED SONJA (U.S.) "Know also, O prince, that in those selfsame days that Conan the Cimmerian did stalk the Hyborian kingdoms, one of the few swords worthy to cross with his was that of Red Sonja, warrior-woman out of majestic Hyrkania. Forced to flee her homeland because she spurned the advances of a king and slew him instead, she rode west across the Turanian Steppes and into the shadowed mists of legendri." So stated Robert E. Howard's *Nemedian Chronicles*. In 1972 the fiery-haired Sonja crossed into comic books, making a couple of appearances in Marvel's *Conan the Barbarian*. She later starred in *Marvel Features* before finally getting her own title toward the end of 1975.

Dubbed "the she-devil with a sword," the well-endowed heroine took up pillaging as her trade and crossed swords with Conan along with a myriad of other male opponents. Because of the double standard then prevailing in comic books, she was never allowed (unlike Conan) to enjoy triumphs in the bedroom as well as on the battlefield, on the convenient pretext of a vow of chastity. She came close at times to losing her virtue, but her otherwise scanty chain-mail bikini provided too great an obstacle to the awestruck males who came into bodily contact with her.

Red Sonja owed much of her initial success to the artistry of Frank Thorne, whose depiction of the fierce-tempered amazon remains the definitive one. Thorne uncannily captured her fiery sexiness as well as her more contemplative side. He also managed to re-create with a great measure of accuracy the landscapes, trappings, and flavor of the original Howard novels. On the other hand, Roy Thomas scripted the texts and dialogues in a flat, mindless variation on Howard's pseudo-archaic prose, his writing falling miles short of Thorne's excellence of drawing.

Thorne left Sonja in 1978 to create his own warrior heroine, Ghita of Alizzar. In the early 1980s Thomas departed in his turn, to be replaced by Tom de Falco, while Mary Wilshire assumed most of the artwork. The title steadily declined in the course of the decade and, despite high expectations, was not helped by the *Red Sonja* movie, with Brigitte Nielsen in the lead role, which was released in 1985: the comic book was canceled the next year.

M.H.

REGGIE (Philippines) Reggie is the pen name of a well-known, young Filipino artist. Along with Malaya, he is the most underground of underground artists. His biting and caustic political cartoons are vivid commentaries on the inequities and injustices of the social conditions in his homeland.

Some of his earliest works appeared in *Ang Bali tang Pilipino* (the "Filipino News") and in the literary publication, *Kapatid*. In 1971 he collaborated with the well-known Filipino poet Serafin Syquia, to do a humorous comic strip called *Flip*.

A highly accomplished etcher, Reggie captures and conveys the agony and suffering of the oppressed. He likens himself to Goya and Daumier—artists who portray the realities of the human condition. His graphic works are dramatic statements dealing with the brutalities and excesses of war, as well as historical documentations of the physiological and psychological manifestations caused by the painful, degrading, and humiliating experiences brought on by fear, poverty, ignorance, greed, hunger, and corruption.

Reggie, "The Demonyo Made Me Do It." © *Reggie.*

His most popular work is the comic book publication titled *The Demonyo* ("Devil") *Made Me Do It*. It is a satirical account of the colonialization of the Philippines by the Spaniards who used religion as their main tool for subjugating the populace. It also deals with the coming of the Americans and their relationship with the inhabitants. It was published by Pilipino Development Associates, Inc., in 1973.

Stylistically, Reggie's cartoons are deceptively simple but powerful in their visual impact. By means of allegory and personification he weaves a seemingly innocent tale that actually contains several levels of interpretations.

Reggie is the most respected of the younger Filipino artists, along with Ed Badajos, who did the unique *Filipino Food*, an innovative sequential visualization of the "now" generation.

A gifted painter, Reggie has won awards for his scenic paintings of the Philippines. Among his favorite subjects are the nipa huts that are still found in the provinces of Luzon, Mindanao, and the Visayan Islands.

O.J.

REG'LAR FELLERS (U.S.) *Reg'lar Fellers* began in the latter days of World War I as an adjunct feature to Gene Byrnes's popular *It's a Great Life If You Don't Weaken*. The title of the major comic strip became a slogan of the day and because of it, Byrnes gained a national reputation. These and other creations were the mainstays of the fledgling *New York Telegram* and its syndicate operation; a Sunday comic, *Wide Awake Willie*, was distributed into the 1920s by the parent company of Byrnes's paper, the *New York Herald*.

Shortly after its introduction *Reg'lar Fellers* became a sensation; Byrnes had a particular talent for portraying the world of kids. The *Herald* itself picked it up and the comic soon became one of the most popular in the nation. (*Wide Awake Willie* continued for a few years as a Sunday feature, but with virtually the same cast of kid characters.)

In the *Fellers* cast were Jimmie Dugan, Pudd'nhead and his little brother Pinhead, Aggie, Bump, various parents, Flynn the cop (who wears a Keystone Kop uniform), neighborhood adults like Heinbockle the Baker, and Bullseye the dog-a copy (or vice versa) of the dog from the *Our Gang* movies.

The Fellers' neighborhood was in the suburbs or residential outskirts of a city. They played in fields but also in lots. The Fellers were less conniving than Ad Carter's *Just Kids* (no doubt created by Hearst to answer Byrnes's success) and less than the philosopher-urchins of Percy Crosby; the Fellers' struggles with ontology never left the realms of boyhood perspectives. The kid life affectionately portrayed was, therefore, very real and sympathetic and, to many, the truest of the comics' many depictions of kid life.

The ups and downs of the feature illustrate the problems that often stem from the lack of syndicate ownership and management. Byrnes eventually left the *Herald-Tribune* and was handled by an early mentor, John Wheeler of the Bell Syndicate. But later he sought to distribute the comic himself, and it suffered the fate of such other ventures as *The Bungle Family*: uneven distribution, the loss of major markets, disappearance and resurfacing. The *Reg'lar Fellers* comic died in 1949.

During its decline, however, Byrnes kept it alive in different forms: a *Reg'lar Fellers* radio show replaced Jack Benny in the summer of 1941; a book, *Reg'lar Fellers in the Army*, was published during World War II with many propaganda photographs interspersed with some colored cartoons by Byrnes; and the title was lent to *Reg'lar Fellers Heroic Comics*, blood and guts stuff published by Famous Funnies during the war. Earlier, a series of hard- and softcover reprint books were published by Cupples and Leon. Hollywood filmed a series of six-reel comedies based on the characters.

Byrnes shared an innovation with his one-time Bell stablemates Fontaine Fox and Charlie Payne: Sunday pages were often composed in unorthodox, asymmetrical ways, dropping panel lines and employing circles instead of boxes.

For years Byrnes had two talented ghosts—"Tack" Knight, whose style was inalterably identical, and G. Burr Inwood, once among the funniest gag cartoonists on *Judge* and *Ballyhoo*.

R.M.

RÉGNIER, MICHEL (1931-   ) Belgian cartoonist, writer, and editor born May 5, 1931, at Ixelles, near Brussels. Michel Régnier was attracted to drawing and writing at an early age and he edited several school newspapers during his student days. After graduation from college, he became a copywriter for a rather tacky newspaper agency grandiosely named Internationale Presse. There he met other fledgling authors and cartoonists: Albert Uderzo, Jean-Michel Charlier, Eddy Paape, René Goscinny, and contributed innumerable stories and drawings to the agency comics, under his pen name of "Greg" (by which he is best known).

In 1960 Greg was given the opportunity to enlarge his public when he published his Western parody, *Rock Derby*, in the comic weekly *Tintin*. This was followed in 1963 by a re-creation of *Zig et Puce*, Alain Saint-Ogan's classic comic strip (also for *Tintin*), but the results were disappointing and Greg dropped the feature in the late 1960s. In 1963, however, (in the pages of the comic magazine *Pilote*) Greg's *Achille Talon* began, the hilarious tale of an egotistical petit-bourgeois, which met with instant success.

On January 1, 1966, Greg became *Tintin*'s editor and its driving force for over eight years. He changed *Tintin*'s rather staid formula, infused new blood into the magazine, and launched a whole raft of new features to which he very often contributed the scripts. Indeed it seemed at times that the whole publication was being written by Greg from cover to cover! Among the memorable series he created, let us mention: *Bernard Prince* (1966), an adventure strip, and *Comanche* (1971), a Western, both superbly drawn by Hermann; *Bruno Brazil* (1967), another adventure strip (which he signs "Louis Albert") drawn by William Vance; *Olivier Rameau* (1968), a fantasy strip illustrated by Dany (Daniel Henrotin); *Les Panthères*, a girl strip with Edouard Aidans as illustrator (1971); and *Go West!*, a humorous Western illustrated by the Swiss cartoonist Derib (Claude de Ribeaupierre).

Greg has also written the dialogues and/or scripts of many of the animated films produced by Belvision in Brussels, including those for *Tintin et le Temple du Soleil* and *Tintin et le Lac aux Requins*. In September 1974 Greg left *Tintin* after a contractual dispute and is now working for Editions Dargaud in Paris.

In 1983 Greg set up Dargaud International in the United States to promote and distribute Dargaud's comics production. The enterprise ended in failure after a few years, however, and he returned to France. Since that time he has written several crime novels and a number of telescripts in addition to his comics.

M.H.

REICHE, VOLKER (1944-   ) Volker Reiche, one of the new breed of comic artists in postwar Germany, was born May 31, 1944, in Belzig near Brandenburg but grew up in the area of Frankfurt am Main. He studied law but, despite his diploma, never followed a career in law as his love for drawing got in the way. For his first comic album, *Liebe* ("Love"), he had to become his own publisher in 1979 as German comic book publishers had no intention of publishing newcomers at the time.

From 1978 to 1981 Reiche worked sporadically for the satirical monthlies *pardon* and *Titanic* as well as for *Hinz und Kunz*. The latter was a magazine published on their own by aspiring comic artists. In the German language the names *Hinz* and *Kunz* used in conjunction are meant to signify just about anyone. Hence the magazine's pages were open to just about anyone and not only to established artists and writers. One of

Volker Reiche, "Willi Wiederhopf." © Volker Reiche.

Reiche's stories published there was titled *"In Biblis ist die H'lle los"* ("Hell broke loose in Biblis"). It depicted in comic strip form the protest movement against building a nuclear power plant near the town of Biblis and police reaction to the protests.

Reiche's early work in theme and art showed that he was obviously influenced by American underground comics. However, Reiche did not intend to become known as an underground artist only. He therefore developed a more commercial style. This end of his work was helped along by his love for the work of Carl Barks on *Donald Duck*. Once again, his efforts to draw *Donald Duck* were futile in Germany. However, the Dutch publishing group Oberon, which had permission to create their own Disney material, bought half a dozen of his stories right away and helped him with artistic suggestions.

Reiche created a comic character of his own in the early 1980s, *Willi Wiedehopf* ("Billy Hoopoe"). The first comic album of his series appeared in 1984. He also started drawing for animated cartoons for television. Then along came the chance of a lifetime. After a seven-year hiatus, the popular mascot of the television weekly *Hör zu* was to be revived in 1985. Reiche was asked to do the new series of *Mecki* comic strips for weekly publication in a strictly funny comic format. He took the character of Mecki and the group of characters added by Reinhold Escher and put them into a family situation comedy making good use of the storytelling hints he had gotten while doing *Donald Duck*. The cheerful stories that always are good for a chuckle or a hearty laugh have been published ever since. On the side, Volker Reiche has started painting oils.

W.F.

REID, KEN (1919-1987) *Fudge the Elf*, a long-running provincial newspaper strip for children, and *Jonah*, an even longer-running crazy page in *The Beano* comic, were perhaps two of the most famous series created by Kenneth Reid, a meticulous and wacky-minded cartoonist whose funny artwork appeared in some of Britain's best comics.

Reid was born in Salford on December 18, 1919, the son of a manufacturing chemist. Always an artist, at the age of nine he was confined to bed with a tubercular hip and whiled away his time with sketchbook and pencil. Eventually returning to school, he won a scholarship to the Salford Art School when be was 13 and in 1936 set up his own freelance art studio. His father helped him contact clients, including the art editor of the *Manchester Evening News*, who was contemplating beginning a daily feature for the children of his readers. Reid submitted some ideas and six weeks later was contracted to supply the daily adventures of *Fudge the Elf* as a serial of three pictures per day. From Fudge's first appearance on April 7, 1938, Reid wrote and drew 11 serials before he was called into the Royal Army Service Corps in 1940. In his three years of life Fudge had become so popular that Fudge Dolls were produced and several compilations of the strip were published as books by Hodder & Stoughton and the London University Press.

After the war Reid returned home and the *Evening News* restarted the strip. This time Fudge had a longer run: from 1946 to 1963, when Reid had an illness that stopped him working for a while. His first contact with children's comics came in 1952 when he contacted the editor of *Comic Cuts*, a weekly paper that had been published by the Amalgamated Press since 1890. The comic was seeking to modernize itself and introduced Reid's semianimated style with great hopes. He drew *Super Sam*, a Superman burlesque, and *Foxy*, an animated animal, followed in 1953 by Billy Boffin, a boy inventor. However the comic was destined to fold and when it did so in 1953, Reid's brother-in-law, the comic artist Bill Holroyd, introduced Reid's work to his own editor at *The Beano*.

Reid's first series for D. C. Thomson, the Scots publisher of *Beano*, was *Roger the Dodger*, about a naughty boy in the already classic mold of *Dennis the Menace*. He followed with *Grandpa*, a mischievous old man; *Little Angel Face*, a female version of *Roger*, and *Bing Bang Benny*, a kid cowboy (1956). In 1958 came the debut of Reid's first comic classic, *Jonah*. This cursed sailor had virtually only to look at a ship to sink it, and was greeted with cries of "It's 'im!" by terrified nauticals. The full-color back pages, designed for 12 pictures, often reached as many as 36 under Reid's crazy pen. Later characters included *Ali Haha* (*Dandy*, 1960) and *Jinx* (*Beano*),which was Reid's last for Thomson.

Reid now moved south to the higher-paid pages of Odhams Press, where his characters took a left turn into the macabre. *Frankie Stein*, frequently verging on the truly horrific, started in *Wham* (1964), followed by *Jasper the Grasper*, a mean old miser (1965), and *Queen of the Seas*, a revamped variation on *Jonah* for *Smash*. *Dare-a-Day Davy* (1967) was the star of *Pow*, Odham's third comic, but the company was bought by IPC, who also now owned the Amalgamated Press.

Reid's final switch, to the IPC Group, was crowned by his creation of *Faceache* for *Jet* (later *Buster*) in 1971, a boy who could pull any kind of face, man or beast! Later came *Hugh Fowler* and *Soccer Spook* for *Scorcher & Score*, a sporting comic (1972), *Creepy Creations*, a truly repulsive full-page cartoon series for the comedy horror comic *Shiver & Shake* (1973), and the similar *World Wide Weirdies* for *Whoopee* (1974). More macabre creations were seen in his *Martha's Monster Makeup*, in which a girl turned herself into monstrosities, in *Monster Fun* (1975).

Reid's final series was the science fictional funny *Robot Smith* in *Jackpot* (1979) He died on February 2, 1987, of a sudden stroke suffered while drawing his last comic page. Ken Reid's books include *The Adventures of Fudge the Elf* (1939), *Frolics with Fudge* (1941), *Fudge's Trip to the Moon* (1947), *Fudge and the Dragon* (1948), *Fudge in Toffee Town* (1950), *Fudge Turns Detective* (1951), *Adventures of Dilly Duckling* (1948), and *Fudge in Bubbleville* (1949).

D.G.

RÉMI, GEORGES (1907-1983) Georges Rémi was a Belgian cartoonist known as Hergé born May 22, 1907, near Brussels. Hergé (his pen name is the phonetic rendering in French of the initials of his name, R. G.) was raised in les Marolles, a working-class neighborhood of Brussels whose dialect was later to find its way into his writings.

Hergé's first contribution to comic art was *Totor de la Patrouille des Hannetons* ("Totor of the June Bug Patrol") for a boy-scout newspaper in 1926. In 1929, encouraged by Alain Saint-Ogan, he created his world-famous feature *Tintin* in the weekly supplement of the Belgian daily *Le Vingtième Siecle*. In 1930 the first Tintin book, *Tintin in the Land of the Soviets*, was published, followed in succession by 21 more books, the most notable being: *The Blue Lotus* (1936), *King Ottokar's Scepter* (1939), *The Crab with the Golden Claws* (1941), *The Secret of the Unicorn* (1943), *Prisoners of the Sun* (two tomes, 1948 and 1949), *Explorers on the Moon* (two tomes, 1953 and 1954), *The Calculus Affair* (1956), *The Red Sea Sharks* (1958).

Hergé is also the creator of a series of juvenile adventures, *Jo, Zette et Jocko*, and of *Quick et Flupke*, a gag strip depicting the tribulations of two Brussels street urchins. Also of note is a satirical animal strip in book form *Popol et Virginie ou Pays des Lapinos* ("Popol and Virginie in the Land of the Lapinos").

Hergé is the most famous of all European cartoonists. His influence has been immense; he has created around himself and his studio of collaborators a whole school of cartooning sometimes referred to as "the Brussels school," and has spearheaded the post-World War II renaissance of European comic art. He has received wide acclaim around the world as well as countless awards and distinctions.

Hergé published his twenty-third (and last) *Tintin* album, *Tintin and the Picaros*, in 1976. He died on March 3, 1983, after a long illness: the Tintin story he had been working on for more than two years—which would have taken his hero into the world of art counterfeiting—was left unfinished and, according to the creator's express wish, will never be completed.

M.H.

RENE *see* Lehner, René.

RENSIE, WILLIS *see* Eisner, Will.

REX BAXTER (Canada) Most of the adventure strips that appeared in the World War II era comic books known to collectors as "Canadian whites" differed in one major respect from their American counterparts: the Canadian strips were serialized. Perhaps the best example of all is *Rex Baxter*, a *Flash Gordon*-type feature created by artist Edmond Good for Bell's *Dime Comics*. The initial Baxter adventure, subtitled "The Island of Doom," began in the premiere issue of *Dime* in February 1942, and ran for a total of 13 episodes, each with a cliffhanger ending.

Baxter is introduced as an "adventurous young soldier of fortune returning aboard the *S.S. Luxor* to enjoy a well-earned rest from duty with the British army in northern Africa." A Nazi U-boat torpedoes the *Luxor*, and Baxter and a shipboard acquaintance, Gail Abbott, are set adrift. They land on a tropical island where they encounter two strange men aboard a flying metal sphere, Captain Zoltan and Tula, who take them underground to the lost cavern empire of Xalanta, the setting for a curious mixture of futuristic inventions and ancient buildings.

Shortly after their arrival, Riona, queen of Xalanta, is dethroned by her adviser, Lerzal, who sets himself up as dictator and, upon learning of the existence of the surface world, embarks on a plan to become master of that world by unleashing germ warfare. Rex, Gail, Queen Riona, and Zoltan escape to carry on the fight against Lerzal and—after a series of adventures in the cavern world of Xalanta, right prevails.

With issue number 14 of *Dime Comics*, Adrian Dingle took over the strip, Edmond Good having left to do the *Scorchy Smith* newspaper strip in the United States. Dingle introduced a new series called *Xalanta's Secret*, which took Rex and Gail to the South Pacific in search

of Zoltan, their Xalantan friend who had been missing since the flying sphere bringing them back to the surface world crashed at sea and sank. A subsequent serialized adventure by Dingle was entitled *Rex Baxter, United Nations Counterspy*, a postwar story in which Baxter was assigned to track down Adolf Hitler, a quest taking him to the undersea kingdom of Mu. *Rex Baxter* did not survive the subsequent transition by Bell to full-color comics, although the *Dime Comics* title eventually became, for a brief period, a catchall for reprints of minor U.S. strips such as *Captain Jet Dixon of the Space Squadron*, *Rocketman*, and *Master Key*.

P.H.

REX MORGAN, M.D. (U.S.) Begun on May 10, 1948, *Rex Morgan, M.D.* was the brainchild of author Nicholas Dallis, a psychiatrist, and artists Frank Edgington, a background man, and Marvin Bradley. Dallis, who sold the strip to Publishers Syndicate in Chicago with the help of Allen Saunders, based *Morgan* on his own experiences in the medical profession.

The title character is the hero of the strip, about 40 years old, and a bachelor. The nurse at his office is June Gale, who is secretly in love with her boss; in return she receives appreciation and respect from Morgan. The third major character is Melissa (she has never been given a last name), an elderly cardiac patient. She comforts June, scolds Rex, and assumes the role of the matriarch of this "family." These are the only major characters.

Although the minor characters come and go like epidemics, which keeps the story line very fluid, most stories are related to the hero's profession, unlike the companion strip, *Judge Parker*. *Morgan* is one of the best examples of soap opera in strip form, relying as it does upon dramatic and tangled plots and strong characterization.

The artwork, which continues to be done by its original team, however, is merely competent and never exciting. It is more static than Dallis's other strips and too often appears mired in its own conventional stereotypes.

"Rex Morgan," Nicholas Dallis and Marvin Bradley. © *Field Newspaper Syndicate.*

Following Marvin Bradley's death in 1984, Tony DiPreta took over the drawing of *Rex Morgan*, and for a time spruced up the strip's tired look. When Dallis died in 1991, Woody Wilson took charge of the scripting. The new team imparted a more relaxed tone to *Rex Morgan*, even allowing the good doctor and his devoted nurse to marry on August 3, 1996.

R.M.

Basil Reynolds, "Skit and Skat." © Willbank Publications.

REYNOLDS, BASIL (1916-) British cartoonist and illustrator Basil Hope Reynolds was born on December 22, 1916, in Holloway, London. He was the beneficiary of a tremendous artistic heritage: His grandfather, Warwick Reynolds, drew cartoons for *Ally Sloper's Half Holiday*, and others, while his father, Sydney, drew a famous advertising poster for Nugget Boot Polish; his uncles Percy, a comic artist, Ernest, a political cartoonist, and Warwick, a boy's story illustrator and famous nature painter, shared an interest in art with Reynold's two elder brothers, who were also artists.

He was educated at Holloway County School, studied art at evening classes, and joined the Adams and Fidier Agency in 1933. Morley Adams, a designer of newspaper features, had convinced several newspapers of the viability of a weekly comic supplement and was producing complete comics, drawn mainly by staff artists. Reynolds joined Stanley White, Reg Perrott, Tony Speer, Wasdale Brown, and others and became possibly the youngest cartoonist with strips in national newspapers: *Our Silly Cinema* in the *South Wales Echo & Express* (1933) and *Septimus and his Space Ship* in the *Scottish Daily Express* (1934). He added a daily strip in 1935, *Billy the Baby Beetle* in the *Daily Sketch*, his first work in the Walt Disney style. When the Disney organization opened up in Britain with *Mickey Mouse Weekly* on February 8, 1936, Reynolds was on the staff, creating *Skit, Skat* and *the Captain* and writing and illustrating *Shuffled Symphonies*, a serial incorporating all the Disney characters.

After his war service Reynolds returned to *Mickey Mouse* as art editor, painting full-color covers, then drawing *Bongo* (1948), *Li'l Wolf and Danny the Lamb* (1949), *True Life Adventures* (1953), and others. He joined the staff of Amalgamated Press as art editor of *Jack and Jill*, *Playhour*, and *Tiny Tots*, color gravure weeklies for the nursery age. He drew *Peter Puppet* (1955) for *Playhour* and became the last editor of *Tiny Tots* (discontinued on January 24, 1959). He created *Bizzy Beaver* (1962) for *Robin* and took over *Nutty Noddle* from Hugh McNeill.

He returned to his favorite Disney characters for *Disneyland* (February 27, 1971), painting the cover spreads and drawing *O'Malley's Mystery Page* for *Goofy* (October 20, 1973). This puzzle feature started a new trend for him, and he currently specializes in devising puzzle books and games featuring Disney characters.

D.G.

RIC HOCHET (Belgium) *Ric Hochet* was created in March 1955 for the comic weekly *Tintin*, the product of the collaboration between cartoonist Tibet (Gilbert Gascard) and the scriptwriter André-Paul Duchateau.

Ric Hochet is a rather conventional police strip. The hero, Ric Hochet, is a young private detective, son of a retired police official, who gets involved in all kinds of mysteries, which he always manages to solve one step ahead of the police, as represented by the grumpy, middle-age Commissaire Bourdon.

Tibet's draftsmanship, terrible in the beginning, has steadily improved over the years, and is today adequate, and even agreeably refreshing. His compositions have also evolved from the simplistic, one-dimensional pattern of the strip's beginning, and are now well-conceived and expertly handled.

The greatest part of the credit should go, however, to A. P. Duchateau, who was already a noted author of detective fiction when he started on the strip. The action is suspenseful, the mysteries always enjoyable (in the great tradition of the writers of classic crime fic-

"Ric Hochet," Tibet (Gilbert Gascard) and A. P. Duchateau. © Editions du Lombard.

tion), and the characters entertaining and often offbeat. Duchateau has taken his hero into the worlds of finance, cinema, and espionage with the same attention to detail and the same concern for verisimilitude that have characterized his noncomic writings. These qualities have enabled *Ric Hochet* to become one of the most successful of contemporary European strips (in the past eight years, it has consistently classed first in the referendums organized among *Tintin*'s readers).

Since 1963, Ric Hochet's adventures have been reprinted in hardcover form by Editions du Lombard in Brussels. To mark the release of the fiftieth title in the series, in 1991 the publisher issued *Dossiers Ric Hochet*, retracing the history of the feature and adding an original tale.

M.H.

RICHTER-JOHNSEN, FRIEDRICH-WILHELM (1912-)

F. W. Richter-Johnsen, German painter, graphic and comic artist, was born April 23, 1912, in Leipzig. He grew up and went to public and secondary schools in Leipzig, finally studying philosophy at the university there, but soon giving that up for studies at the Academy of Graphic Arts and Printing Trade. He studied under H. A. Müeller and Tiemann, then continued his studies under Gulbransson in Munich, Germany, before returning to Leipzig for additional studies in wood engraving.

After World War II, Richter-Johnsen earned money as a railway worker and house painter before being able to freelance in art jobs like drawing portraits of American troops occupying Germany. This also brought first contact with American comic books, which he viewed with "amused dismay." Richter Johnsen soon moved on to stage painting and freelance editorial cartooning for *Weserkurier* and *Bremer Nachrichten* (both are Bremen newspapers). In 1954 he moved to Hamburg and started working for the Springer newspaper chain. This led to the creation of *Detektiv Schmidtchen* for *Bild*, a large circulation daily newspaper published by the Springer chain. *Detektiv Schmidtchen*, for the eight years of its run, may have been the only daily newspaper comic strip of German origin. The series was created and written by Frank Lynder, who wanted to raise a German comics emporium of Disney dimensions, a project that never materialized because of a lack of artists. When Lynder went on to other things, Friedrich-Wilhelm Richter Johnsen took over writing *Detektiv Schmidtchen*. The adventures of the kindly police commissioner who had a white mouse for a pet ended when *Bild* got a new editor-in-chief who disliked comic strips.

While working on *Detektiv Schmidtchen*, Richter-Johnsen was contacted by the editors of the weekly illustrated *stern*, who wanted him to do the art on a comic strip created and written by Fritz Raab. Thus *Taró* came into being, to fascinate readers from June 13, 1959, to March 3, 1968. This script ended when the children's supplement of *stern* became just two pages of the magazine. Besides painting, Richter-Johnsen has continued illustrating for newspapers and magazines. He has also used comic techniques in advertising campaigns for various companies. Earlier in his career he had done a large number of loose-leaf giveaway comic strips for a margarine company. These giveaways had a wide thematic range, giving Richter-Johnsen a chance to display his talents and techniques.

Richter-Johnsen does most of his illustrative work (and did all of *Taró* and *Detektiv Schmidtchen*) on textured illustration board, that allows for both solid blacks and grainy grays and helps prevent the somewhat mechanical look of acetate overlays. His work is rich in precision and realism as well as in mood. The action is relatively subdued, giving the strips an aura of calm.

While still working for newspapers and magazines, Richter-Johnsen has refrained from doing more comic work.

W.F.

RICK O'SHAY (U.S.)

Stan Lynde's *Rick O'Shay* was created for the Chicago Tribune-New York News Syndicate; the Sunday page appeared on April 27, 1958, followed by a daily version on May 19 of the same year.

Rick O'Shay occupies a unique position midway between humor and adventure. The action takes place in the mythical ghost town of Conniption where, at one time or another, several colorful characters have chosen to take permanent refuge: first there was Deuces Wilde, the gambler who elected himself mayor of the town and appointed his likable partner Rick O'Shay as marshal. They were later joined by Hipshot Percussion, the gunslinger; Gaye Abandon, saloon singer and Rick's heartthrob; Basil Metabolism, M.D.; the Mexican cowpoke Manual Labor, and others. From time to time, Horse's Neck, the crafty chief of the neighboring Kyute Indians, and General DeBillity, the befuddled commandant of nearby Fort Chaos, also drop in.

All is not sweetness and light, however. Undesirable characters also drift into town and invariably try to take it over. Then Rick, Hipshot, and the other worthy citizens of Conniption have no other recourse than to shoot it out in the best tradition of the Old West (at first Lynde had placed the action in modern times, but in 1964 he shifted it to the 1890s).

When Lynde created *Rick O'Shay*, the popularity of the cowboy strip was already on the wane. Since the demise of the Lone Ranger in 1971, *Rick O'Shay* remains the only Western strip with any sizable following; it is also the most authentic since the early *Red Rider*. It is to Stan Lynde's credit that he continues his work with talent and integrity at a time when other cartoonists have either given up or turned to slapstick and caricature.

Unfortunately Lynde left in 1977 after a contractual dispute with his syndicate. Alfredo Alcala (artist) and Marion Dern (writer) carried the strip into 1981, when it was discontinued. In an ironic twist, Lynde later bought back the rights to *Rick O'Shay*, which he has been releasing with great success in high-quality paperbacks under his own imprint, Cottonwoods Graphics. In 1992 he even started turning out new Rick stories for an ever-growing public.

M.H.

RIP KIRBY (U.S.)

Rip Kirby was created by Alex Raymond upon his return to civilian life, on an idea suggested by King Features editor Ward Greene. The first daily strip (there never was a Sunday version) appeared on March 4, 1946.

Kenneth Rexroth once wrote that all adventure stories can be reduced to two prototypes: the *Iliad* and the *Odyssey*. Alex Raymond, whose Flash Gordon was cer-

"Rick O'Shay," Stan Lynde. © Chicago Tribune-New York News Syndicate.

tainly the Achilles of the comic strip, wished to create its Ulysses with Rip Kirby. Kirby is a criminologist, a former Marine Corps major (like Raymond himself). He has none of Flash Gordon's driving fixations, but displays a worldly wisdom, a superior intellect, and a brilliant wit that were too often absent from Raymond's earlier creations. The whole atmosphere is changed, morally and spiritually, more relaxed, less action-ridden, as if Raymond had decided to poke gentle fun at everything Flash Gordon stood for.

Unrelenting, violent physical action is not the keynote in *Rip Kirby* (as it was in *Flash Gordon*). There is no paucity of fist- and gunfights, but Kirby does not rely primarily on his athletic prowess to solve the difficult cases handed to him. He wears glasses, smokes a pipe, plays chess, and can appreciate the complex harmonies of modern music as well as the aroma of a fine French brandy.

In his investigative methods Kirby often follows his hunches (or calculated guesses) based on solid criminological foundations, with a sprinkling of extralegal gambits, and a dash of violent action. He is, in short, a combination Philo Vance and Philip Marlowe. His assignments are usually vague: locate a missing wife, trace a fortune in stolen diamonds, stop a blackmailer, but the plot soon thickens and takes on flesh.

Around the hero there lurks a netherworld of two-bit hoodlums, blackmailers, gigolos, shyster lawyers, trigger men, and other seedy characters who are depicted with a high sense of realism as well as of drama. Whatever the dangers he faces, Rip Kirby can count on the unswerving loyalty of his majordomo Desmond, a reformed burglar who plays Watson to his master's Sherlock, and on the love of Honey Dorian, the blonde fashion model who is Rip's inamorata.

Alex Raymond made the strip famous from the start. Bold and striking, his style can also be gentle and soft,

"Rip Kirby," Alex Raymond. © King Features Syndicate.

even subdued, as he closely parallels the action. Away from the brilliant colors of the Sunday page, Raymond proved that he could be a master of the black-and-white technique as well.

After Raymond's accidental death in 1956, the strip passed into the hands of John Prentice, who proved worthy of the succession. Prentice's style has a clarity, vigor, and precision especially suitable to the requirements of the detective strip. Prentice is also a master of compositions made up of alternating masses, of elaborate chiaroscuros and daring visual effects. A good share of the credit for *Rip Kirby*'s continuing success should also go to Fred Dickenson, who has been writing the continuity since 1952. In 1996 *Rip Kirby* celebrated its fiftieth anniversary with Prentice still drawing and now also writing the feature.

Rip Kirby had a comic book version in the 1940s and 1950s, but in spite of its popularity, was never adapted to the screen, although the unflappable, world-wise Rip should have been a natural for a television series.

M.H.

RITT, WILLIAM (1901-1972)   An American newspaperman and writer born in Evansville, Indiana, on December 29, 1901, William Ritt grew up in Evansville and after graduation from high school worked on the staff of local newspapers. In 1930 he moved to Cleveland where he worked for the *Press*. In 1933 the Cleveland-based Central Press Association (later incorporated into King Features) asked him to create an adventure strip for distribution to the midwestern papers served by the association. In collaboration with Clarence Gray he produced *Brick Bradford*, which saw the light of print on August 21, 1933. Ritt's imagination, nurtured on mythology tales and Abraham Merritt's stories, and Gray's superior draftsmanship contributed to make *Brick* into an exciting tale of adventure and science fiction. In 1935 Ritt also wrote the short-lived companion strip to *Brick*, *The Time Top*.

Fired by the success of *Brick Bradford*, Ritt tried his hand at writing another action feature in the mid-1930s, *Chip Collins, Adventurer*, which did not last long. He then went back to writing the continuity for *Brick Bradford*, but left the strip in 1952 for reasons never made clear. Returning to his job on the *Cleveland Press*, Ritt did a number of articles and feature stories, and contributed a regular column to the paper, *You're Telling Me*. He also wrote short stories, as well as nonfiction, and contributed a chapter on the Kingsbury Run torso murders for a book on Cleveland murder cases. He died on September 20, 1972.

M.H.

ROBBINS, FRANK (1917-1994)   Frank Robbins was an American artist born September 9, 1917, in Boston, Massachusetts. Robbins displayed amazing artistic qualities at an early age, won several art scholarships at nine, painted great murals for his high school at 13, and received a Rockefeller grant at 15. All this happened, however, in the midst of the depression years and Frank Robbins, moving along with his family to New York, had to look for work, foregoing a college education. This setback, painful as it may have felt at the time, did not prove altogether baneful. As Robbins later wryly remarked: "I can attribute my success today to two scraps of paper. My high school and college diplomas . . . or rather the lack of them! Without them, I went to work at fifteen . . . with them I might have

accepted a job as a bank president and gone through life . . . a failure!"

After an apprenticeship as an errand boy in an advertising agency, Robbins was noticed by the well-known muralist Edward Trumbull, who was then working on the Radio City project, and Robbins drew the sketches for the murals of the NBC building. In 1935, having dropped out of the project because of poor health, Robbins did promotion and poster illustrations for RKO Pictures, painting in the meantime and winning a prize at the National Academy show that same year. In 1938 he flirted briefly with the comic book medium and, the following year, was asked by Associated Press to take over the *Scorchy Smith* daily strip which had been floundering ever since Sickles had departed from it in 1936.

Under Robbins's aegis the strip flourished, so much so that a Sunday page was added in the 1940s. King Features then took notice and asked Robbins to produce an aviation strip for them: it turned out to be *Johnny Hazard* (1944). The new strip met stiff competition in the changed atmosphere of the postwar years, and in the 1960s Robbins was forced to go back to comic books (while continuing his work on *Hazard*). He has worked almost exclusively for National, writing for such titles as *Batman, The Flash*, and *The Unknown Soldier*, and doing occasional artwork on *The Shadow*.

After *Johnny Hazard* ended in 1977, Robbins again went back to comic books, working for Marvel that time. There he labored briefly on such titles as *Captain America* and *Ghost Rider*. Discouraged by the cold reception his work was receiving from comic book readers, he quit comics altogether and retired to Mexico, where he took up full-time painting and sculpture. He died in San Miguel de Allende, Mexico, shortly before Christmas 1994.

Frank Robbins is an artist of almost awesome powers. In addition to his comic artwork, he has done illustrations for such publications as *Life, Look*, and the *Saturday Evening Post*. His paintings have been exhibited at the Corcoran Gallery, the Whitney Museum, and the Metropolitan Museum. The number of awards and distinctions he has received is staggering, but he never attained the fame that his undisputed talent should have brought him. Perhaps his very versatility is the cause of his undeserved obscurity; at any rate a reevaluation of Robbins's work seems to be now in order.

M.H.

ROBBINS, TRINA (1938-)   An American cartoonist and writer, Trina Robbins was born in Brooklyn, New York, on August 17, 1938. After attending Cooper Union in New York City ("expelled after one year," she states), she moved to California, where she designed clothes for such rock stars as David Crosby, Donovan, Mama Cass, and Jim Morrison, and later went back to her first love—drawing comics. "Trina in 1966 gave up six years of marriage and Los Angeles to return to New York to do an underground strip for *The East Village Other*," Ronald Levitt Lanyi wrote in the *Journal of Popular Culture*. "This work was followed by strips for the comics tabloids *Gothic Blimp Works* (New York) and *Yellow Dog* (San Francisco)." These and other creations established Robbins as the preeminent woman cartoonist on the underground scene in the late 1960s and the 1970s.

Trina Robbins and Chris Browne, "Crystal Sett." © Robbins and Browne.

Among the many comic books Robbins contributed to, mention should be made of the underground *After Schock*, *Girl Fight Comics*, and *San Francisco Comic Book*. For mainstream publishers she illustrated and/or wrote *Meet Misty* (Marvel, 1986), *Wonder Woman* (DC, 1986), *Barbie* (Marvel, 1990-1993), and *The Little Mermaid* (Marvel/Disney, 1994-1995). She is the author of *The Silver Metal Lover*, a graphic novel originally published by Crown in 1985. She also edited the first all-women comic book, *It Ain't Me Babe*, in 1970, and she later established, along with other female cartoonists, the longer lasting *Wimmen's Comix*. In addition she has been a frequent contributor of cartoons and illustrations to magazines as diverse as *Playboy*, *National Lampoon*, *High Times*, and *Heavy Metal*.

Starting in the mid-1980s Robbins evidenced a knack for study and research into neglected areas of the comics field. In 1985 she coauthored (with Cat Yronwode) *Women and the Comics*, a book about the lives and works of women cartoonists. This she later updated and expanded into *A Century of Women Cartoonists* (1993), and in 1996 she published the self-explanatory *The Great Superheroines*. For her endeavors in and out of comics, Robbins has received many distinctions, from the Inkpot Award for Excellence in Comic Art to the NOW Outstanding Feminist Activist Award.

M.H.

ROBERTO ALCAZAR Y PEDRÍN (Spain) *Roberto Alcazar y Pedrín* was created, in the form of a weekly comic book, by cartoonist Eduardo Vaño. Juan B. Puerto was the first scriptwriter of the series (it is currently being written by Tortajada).

In the first episode titled "The Air Pirates," Roberto Alcazar is a newspaperman who is sailing to Buenos Aires aboard the liner *Neptunia*. He has been assigned to watch over the five fabulous "Gypsy" diamonds. It

"Roberto Alcazar," Eduardo Vaño. © Editorial Valenciana.

"Robin Hood and Company," C. R. Snelgrove. © Toronto Telegram.

is during this crossing that he meets the stowaway, Pedrín, a Portuguese ragamuffin of about 14 who becomes his inseparable companion in adventure.

In the course of their adventurous and action-packed career, Roberto Alcazar and Pedrín have helped put away innumerable malefactors. In return the "fearless Spanish adventurer" and his "little pal" (as they are dubbed) have received countless citations from the authorities, as well as large quantities of reward money which they have either given to poor children or deposited in the boy's savings account "for when he is grown up." It is likely, however, that Pedrín, like Peter Pan and Joselito before him, will never grow to be 15. The series ended in the mid-1980s when its publisher went out of business. It still can be seen in reprints, however.

L.G.

ROBIN HOOD AND COMPANY (Canada) Of all the heroes of lore and legend none has had a more diversified career in comic strips than the outlaw of Sherwood Forest. Robin's adventures have been pictorialized not only in England, but also in the United States (at least twice), France, Italy, and Spain, and probably in other countries as well. In 1935 one of the more entertaining versions, *Robin Hood and Company*, made its appearance in the comics page of the *Toronto Telegram*, written by Ted McCall and drawn by *Telegram* staff artist Charles R. Snelgrove.

The Robin of the strip was true to the character of legend: brave, cocky, and fleet-footed, he was always on the side of the weak and the oppressed, laughing when cornered, generous when triumphant. Around him gathered the gallant band of merrymen whose names have become famous through countless retellings: Little John, Friar Tuck, Scarlett, and others. Robin's adventures did not follow the exploits ascribed to him by legend (as the later Robin Hood movie version was to do) but were original stories. Thus we could find the outlaw fighting robber barons such as the dreaded Red Roger, helping restore King Richard to his throne, defeating the Norsemen who had come to invade England, and even being taken to North Africa by Barbaresque slave traders.

Robin Hood and Company was one of the few epics to last for any length of time in the comic strips. This was primarily due to McCall's deft writing, inventive plots, and earthy humor. (Snelgrove's drawing was ade-

quate—and probably better than that of any other Canadian comic strip artist of the period—but certainly not outstanding.) The strip (which disappeared in the mid-1940s) enjoyed a good deal of success in Canada and in Europe (it doesn't seem to have appeared anywhere in the United States).

M.H.

ROBINSON (Germany) *Robinson* is one of a number of long-running and often underrated comics to come out of Germany. Robinson seems to be only a distant relative of the Robinson Crusoe of literature, who has lived his adventures in a series of 222 comic books published between December 1953 and May 1964. Robinson did emerge from the same mold, however, sailing the seven seas on his trusty ship, *Sturmvogel* ("Storm Bird"), and accompanied by Xury, a native boy sporting a huge turban. The shipwreck in the first issue of the *Robinson* comic book is not much more than a token recognition of the character's literary origins, which serve as a starting point for high adventure.

The comic book started out as a full-color comic book, slightly smaller than the standard comic book format, but for most of its run it was reproduced very cheaply in black and white on newsprint. Despite the seemingly substandard appearance, the *Robinson* strip, usually filling a bit more than half of each comic book and continued in the best of serial traditions, is endowed with remarkably good writing. The plots are very imaginative and make use of a number of subplots, one of them centering around the Portuguese girl, Gracia, accompanying Robinson on many of his voyages. There also is the confrontation of the Christian and Islamic religions as the backdrop for some of the action and as characterization of protagonist and/or antagonist. This is handled in the best tradition of the novels of Karl May.

Yet another surprise is the exceptionally good art of most of the books. Credit for this goes to Helmut Nickel, who has elected to stay anonymous and has since abandoned comics for another career. The

"Robinson," Helmut Nickel. © Druck-u. Verlagsanstalt.

anatomy of Nickel's figures is perfect, and the artist has a knack for adding a cartoony touch to some of the characters, thus providing the comic relief that so often is the frosting of the cake in adventure stories. The first 125 issues of *Robinson* were reprinted in a 32-volume book series in 1979-1980. During the initial run of the comic book the material from issue 126 on was all reprints. While *Robinson* had been initiated by artist Willi Kohlhoff, it was turned into a Nickel creation upon his taking over as artist and writer.

W.F.

ROBINSON, FRED (1912-198?) British cartoonist Fred Robinson was born in Walthamstow, London, October 20, 1912. He left school at 14 to become office junior at Cambridge University Press, studying art in the evenings at Bolt Court Art College. His first art job was in the studio of Sir Joseph Causton & Sons advertising agency. In 1930 he joined the studio of C. Arthur Pearson publishing company, illustrating *Pearson's Weekly*, and others. His first joke cartoons were published in *The Scout*.

After four years with Pearson, Robinson joined the Amalgamated Press, contributing strips on a retainer. In 1934 he took over Terry Wakefield's *Quackie the Duck* for *Tiny Tots*, and this area of cartooning—simple comedy for the nursery-age group—became his specialty, despite occasional forays into slapstick. His first original characters, *Ambrose and Al*, two monkeys based on Laurel and Hardy, appeared in *Butterfly* (1935). His first color work was the full-page serial *Crasy Castle* in *Happy Days* (October 8, 1938), the pioneering gravure comic.

During the war Robinson took over *Our Ernie* and created his best-remembered characters, *It's the Gremlins* (1943), based on the famous Royal Air Force myth. When Amalgamated Press took over *Sun* and *Comet* in 1949, he did much work on them and was made that company's first art editor on the new gravure comic *Jack and Jill* (February 27, 1954). In 1966 he joined Polystyle Publications to paint full-color strips of television characters: *Sooty and Sweep* (1967) in *Playland* and *Chigley and Trumpton* (1973) in *Pippin*. This excellent

artwork is only excelled by his color pages in these comics' annuals.

His strips include: *Pecky the Penguin* (1935); *Star Struck Sam* (1936); *Bruno Lionel* and *Percy Thggins* (1937); *Andy Benjamin* and *Chick* (1938); *King Toot* (1939); *The Kitties* (1940); *Scoop* (1949); *Dotty and Scotty* (1951); *Flipper the Skipper* (1954); *Peter Puppet* (1957); *Noah's Ark* (1958); and *Musical Box* (1966). He died in the 1980s.

D.G.

ROBINSON, JERRY (1922-   ) Jerry Robinson is an American comic book and comic strip artist, writer, and critic born in New York in 1922. In 1939, at 17, Bob Kane hired him as an art assistant on the newly created *Batman* strip Kane was doing for National Comics. In reality, even though he was officially Kane's assistant, he was a better artist, and his material was easily recognizable. It was usually better detailed, more imaginatively designed, and better crafted than the work Kane was producing.

Robinson assumed the complete *Batman* art assignment in 1941 when Kane moved on to other features. And although Robinson was the major artist on the strip until well into the late 1940s—not only was he drawing *Batman* stories, he was also drawing the covers for *Batman* and *Detective* and *Alfred*, Batman's butler, the back-up feature—he never received bylines. In fact, Kane's byline was the only one to appear on the feature until well into the 1960s.

Besides the anatomical improvement and drafting crispness Robinson lent to the strip, he was instrumental in the creation of two of *Batman's* major supporting characters. Together with writer Bill Finger, Robinson injected both Robin, the Wonder Boy, Batman's ward, and the Joker, Batman's arch-villain, into the feature in 1940. The Joker was probably the paramount Robinson creation: sardonic, absolutely insane, and possessing green hair, ruby lips, and a white face. The Joker became the greatest villain in the comics and eventually got a book of his own (1974).

Robinson also did considerable work for other strips during his comic book career, which extended through 1963. He worked on *Green Hornet* (Harvey, 1942-1943), *Atoman* (Spark, 1944), *Fighting Yank* and *Black Terror* (with Mort Meskin, for Nedor from 1946-1949), *The Vigilante* and *Johnny Quick* (again with Meskin, for National from 1946-1949), *Lassie, Bat Masterson, Rocky and Bullwinkle*, and *Nancy Parker* (for Western, 1957-1963). Over the years he also drew and wrote for Timely (1950-1955) and Prize (1946-1949).

In 1955 Robinson turned to the newspaper strip with *Jet Scott*, for the New York Herald-Tribune Syndicate, which lasted four years even though it was only a mediocre science fiction feature. In 1963 Robinson began his *still life* daily panel for the NewsTribune Syndicate. In addition he also does *Flubs and Fluffs*—a Sunday strip for the *Daily News*, which illustrates children's bloopers—and *Caricatures by Robinson*, a weekly feature which takes off on people in the news.

In the 1970s Robinson created *Life with Robinson*, a satirical panel feature that he syndicated himself. This eventually led to the establishment of the Cartoonists and Writers Syndicate, which is now distributing the work of more than twoscore cartoonists worldwide. The success of his syndicate paradoxically forced the overworked Robinson to abandon *Life with Robinson* in 1996.

Robinson has also been active as a book author and illustrator and has over 30 books to his credit. In 1974 G. P. Putnam published his *The Comics: An Illustrated History of Comic Strip Art*. Robinson is also a former president of the National Cartoonists Society (1967-1969).

J.B.

ROBOT IMPERIUM (Germany) This comic about a Robot Empire is the first European comic ever to be produced entirely on a computer (an Atari 520). It was the creation of Michael Götze who had started publishing comics in fanzines in 1973 and finally moved on to a professional career with seven *The Flintstones* albums for a German publisher in 1974. In 1976 he was taken on by another publisher for whom he drew all kinds of action and funny comics. Apart from his mass production stuff, Götze also started his own series *Voltfeder, ufo,* and *Commander Mantell* beginning in 1979. Götze's *Vorg* was a barbarian along *Conan* lines.

In 1984 Götze's previous comics were put aside for an idea he was obsessed with: creating comics with the help of a computer. First he took a course in computer programming, then it took him some two years to program his computer, translating his designs of machines and landscapes into his computer. The most complicated thing to program was the human anatomy with some 20,000 single points. Finally, in 1986, the result of his efforts—which combined computerized artwork as well as artwork drawn with the help of a mouse and computer "colored" with shades of gray—was presented at the Frankfurt Book Fair: the first volume of *Robot Imperium*. It was fascinating to look at, even to read. A number of European publishers immediately grabbed at the novelty production; and Götze followed up this herculean effort by a second volume, which had the added dimension of computer coloring.

While interest in Götze's robot empire was high, the effort invested was a bit much for one person to handle since the artist continued producing mass-market comics like the *Masters of the Universe* series and doing covers for German editions of Marvel comics.

W.F.

ROBOT SANTŌHEI (Japan) *Robot Santōhei* ("Private Robot") was created in 1952 by Koremitsu Maetani. It appeared first in comic book form (six books were released in all) and then made its reappearance in the June 1958 issue of *Shōnen Kurabu*.

Santōhei was a funny little robot created by the scientist Dr. Toppi. At the end of the Pacific war Santōhei joined the army where he soon became one of the worst goofs this side of Beetle Bailey. Artist Maetani had been a soldier during the war and hated the experience, vowing never to make war again. His sentiments were reflected in the misadventures of his creation (officially, at least, the army represented in the strip was not the Japanese Army). Nevertheless *Robot Santōhei* represented the common soldier in the grip of an idiotic and unfeeling organization, and leveled many barbed criticisms against the military.

Santōhei was an imperfect robot in that he had feelings (these had been instilled in him by an angel, not Dr. Toppi) just like a human being. *Robot Santōhei* was not just a service comedy (like *Beetle Bailey*), it was also a satire on war, and the artist quite freely expressed his bitter views on war and militarism.

Robot Santōhei made its final bow in the December 1962 issue of *Shōnen Kurabu*.

H.K.

"Rob the Rover," Walter Booth. © Amalgamated Press.

ROB THE ROVER (G.B.) The first dramatic serial strip in British comic history, *Rob the Rover* came floating in from the sea on May 15, 1920, 23 years before *Garth* did the same thing. Rob was found by grizzled old Dan the Fisherman, who became his close companion and father-figure during a search for identity that lasted for 20 years. When the weekly comic paper *Puck* folded suddenly during the war (May 11, 1940), Rob roved over to *Sunbeam*, but unhappily that comic, too, folded two weeks later (May 25, 1940), leaving Rob stranded in mid-rove.

Rob was created and drawn by Walter Booth, hitherto a "comic" man, with occasional adventures done by Vincent Daniel when Booth was busy launching other serials. The style of the strip was very much British traditional, with storybook-type illustrations over seven-line typeset captions. Later strips were printed in black and red, but English readers never saw Rob in full colors. This privilege was reserved for the Danes, who had Rob's rovings reprinted in full color in one of their magazines.

"The picture story of a Brave Boy who was All Alone in the World" (the regular subtitle) took Rob to fight an octopus on a desert island (1921), with a film company to the North Pole (1922), to a Lost City in the jungle (1930), to the Valley of the Lost Kings (1931), to an underwater temple (1932), to save an Indian Rajah's jewels (1933), to the mysterious Veiled Lady (1935), and, especially, on a trip aboard Professor Seymour's secret submarplane, the *Flying Fish* (1936). In his last adventure Rob saved his girl chum, Joan, from the Leopard Men.

D.G.

ROB-VEL *see* Velter, Robert.

ROCKY RIDER (Italy) *Rocky Rider* first appeared in 1951 and, like *Forza John* before it, it originated as a free comic book insert offered by *L'Intrepido* to its readers. It had the added advantage of being partly in color and having more pages than similar publications regularly sold on newsstands.

Rocky Rider (the name is clearly inspired by Harman's Red Ryder) is a sheriff who lives in a somewhat unrealistic West. He is very fast with his gun and his lariat and, true to tradition, he stands ever ready to fight for law and justice. His adventures involve him with rum-runners plotting to spur an uprising by selling liquor to the Indians, or with swindlers trying to con gullible prospectors out of their gold. Rocky Rider is a friend to cowboys and Indians alike, and he is determined to see that both obey the law. In compliance with the editorial policy of *L'Intrepido*, romantic and soap opera elements are always present in the story line. For this reason the handsome sheriff spends a good portion of his time looking for kidnapped or runaway children. The strip also never loses an opportunity to offer the reader a few tears wedged in between gunfights.

In his struggle for the triumph of justice Rocky Rider is helped by the brawny trapper Moses and by a freckle-faced boy named Golia ("Goliath").

In 1953 *Rocky Rider* was transferred to the pages of *Il Monello*. The strip has been written by a variety of authors; Alfredo Castelli has been writing many of the scripts in recent times. In the early 1960s it was drawn by the talented Mario Uggeri, who was later replaced by Loredano Ugolini. The strip ended in the late 1960s but there has been a number of reprints since then.

G.B.

ROD CRAIG (Australia) Created by Syd Miller for the *Melbourne Herald*, the strip first appeared in November 1946 and ran daily until November 1955. In a country with a built-in aversion to using local adventure strips to compete with imported strips, *Rod Craig* set a standard in art, story line, and longevity that proved Australian continuity strips could be a viable proposition. As well as appearing in a number of Australian papers, the strip was syndicated in Jamaica, Paris, and Buenos Aires—and became the first Australian adventure strip to be adapted to radio.

Originally intended to follow Craig's adventures as a charter boat owner servicing the Pacific Islands, the story line soon became centered on the Australian mainland and took on the general theme of a detective strip. *Rod Craig* was an excellent example of comic strips that reflect the thoughts and attitudes of a particular era. The postwar preoccupations with large black-market operations, Nazi war criminals cloaked by a veneer of respectability, secret political organizations, gun-running, and so forth, can all be found in the strip. Because Miller was greatly influenced by current trends and events, Rod Craig was constantly on the move and—with some stories as short as six weeks—it was obvious that certain plots were finalized quickly to allow the strip to be diverted in the direction of Miller's latest inspiration. The strip's topicality was assisted by the emphasis placed on melodrama and suspense.

Although Rod Craig was the nominal hero of the strip, his rather conservative, stereotyped personality was overshadowed by the myriad of supporting characters who vied for space in the strip. There was Geelong, a gentle giant and former circus strongman

"Rod Craig," Syd Miller. © The Herald and Weekly Times Ltd.

who stayed on and replaced Cal Rourke as Craig's Man Friday; the curvaceous Lacey, stage assistant to the crooked nightclub owner, Cherub Bim, and later Geelong's girlfriend; Indigo, the scarred-face former R.A.A.F. Squadron Leader, pilot of the remarkable "Stingray" aircraft and employed by Head, the crippled dwarf of the One-World Government organization—to mention but a few of the colorful characters that contributed to the advancement of the strip. Perhaps the most constant of these characters was Carlina, the female villain. She first appeared in October 1947, and continued to cross Craig's path over the years—always chasing easy money. Initially presented as a willowy, thin-lipped, hard-faced woman, she blossomed with the passing years into a well-proportioned, attractive lady. Even more attractive was Anna (first called Leeanna), Craig's blonde girlfriend, who made her debut in the first story as the White Goddess. Most of the women in the strip were wide-eyed, well-fleshed beauties who reflected Norman Linday's influence on Miller.

The strip abounded in the use of Australian towns, cities, and locales and these, along with a good proportion of colloquial expressions, assisted in giving the strip a distinct Australian flavor. Miller used many different styles in illustrating the strip—delicate fine line, intricate hatching, stark black spotting, drybrushing, halftones—with each style calculated to assist the mood.

Rod Craig was concluded because of Miller's wish to attempt another type of strip. It is a tribute to Syd Miller's skill and versatility that he was immediately able to follow *Rod Craig* with a daily humor strip, *Us Girls*, which ran until 1957 when Miller left the field of comic art.

J.R.

RODRIGUEZ, EMILIO D. (1937-   ) In the Philippines, where many of the finest comic illustrators and cartoonists are self-taught, Emilio Rodriguez holds the distinction of being one of the few individuals who received a full range of academic education in the field of art.

Born on October 15, 1937, in Sorsogon, Rodriguez finished high school as the valedictorian at the Sorsogon School of Arts and Trades, and later attended the University of the Philippines, receiving the degree of Bachelor of Fine Arts (cum laude). He also studied at the Cranbrook Academy of Art, Michigan, as a

Fullbright/Smith Mundt scholar, and obtained a masters degree in fine arts. He taught at the University of the Philippines College of Fine Arts and Architecture.

Apart from Federico Javinal, "Emile" Rodriguez is the foremost exponent of the Francisco Coching style of comic illustration. This style is characterized by bold strokes, exuberant and dynamic action scenes, effective use of dramatic angles, good composition and design, and, foremost, the ability to make one scene flow smoothly into another. The rendering is loose but controlled and accurate.

Not satisfied with just emulating the works of Coching, Emile Rodriguez developed his own individual artistic approach. His work is distinguished by his imaginative use of negative space. When a script calls for a classical approach to the subject matter, his work is a joy to behold. His highly decorative rendering and flourishes are done in good taste, just enough that the panels are not overdone or crowded. And when the story requires a simple but effective style, he readily adjusts to the conditions and makes his work come to the point. He excels in calligraphy; his comic book logos are among the most beautiful in the field.

He has worked with many well-known writers in the Philippines, among them are Virgilio Redondo, Nemesio Caravana, and Angel Ad Santos. He illustrated the popular graphic novel *Carlomagno* for *Liwayway*, did short stories for Ace Publications, and biblical adaptations for *Kenkoy Komiks*.

In 1963 Rodriguez collaborated with Gemma Cruz, the former Miss International beauty queen, to produce the prize-winning children's book, *Makisig, The Little Hero of Mactan*. The book deals with the invasion of a Malayan province in the Visayan Islands. The invaders fail due to the heroic exploits of a child who is able to warn the great *Datu* ("Chief") Lapu-Lapu, the first Asian to repel European intrusion.

Emile Rodriguez was one of the first Filipino artists to work for American comics when he illustrated short stories for Treasure Chest comics.

O.J.

ROLAND EAGLE (Italy) After World War II the comic weekly *L'Intrepido* changed its editorial policy. New comic features were created and, while they did not temper the sentimentality that was *L'Intrepido's* trademark, they gave more play to action, adventure, and even eroticism (without allowing them to get out of hand). This process (still continued to this day) is best represented in *Bufalo Bill* and *Roland Eagle*, both created by Carlo Cossio in 1951.

In *Roland Eagle* in particular the erotic element is very strong in the figure of Jasmine, the savage girl turned into a civilized woman for love. Unlike most other comic strip heroines, whose main functions seem to be getting into some kind of trouble so that the hero can rescue them, Jasmine can take care of herself and fights with the courage of a lioness. Raised by the members of a Dayak tribe, she is actually the daughter of a Malay princess and a white man. Her mysterious origins have always fascinated the readers who like to speculate on who her father might be.

Roland Eagle, on the other hand, is an uncomplicated young man, skipper of the schooner *Eagle of the Seven Seas*. His adventures are filled with Malay princes and princesses (Jasmine is only one of them), slave-traders and mad scientists who want to rule the world. The action takes place in modern times (one of the

early episodes involved him and his boat in a secret mission against the Japanese) and it is full of storms, shipwrecks, and other catastrophes. Around Roland are his boss, Machete, who takes care of him like a father, Lady Barbara, and her sweet daughter, Lili, whose life Roland saved, and many others.

Cossio was later succeeded by Ferdinando Corbella on the strip, which lasted into the 1960s.

G.B.

ROMANO IL LEGIONARIO (Italy) After only one year of publication, the Catholic weekly *Il Vittorioso* paid its dues to the Fascist regime with the creation of one of the most jingoistic and propagandistic comic features ever produced in Italy: *Romano il Legionario*, written and drawn by the German-Italian Kurt Caesar (under the pen name "Cesare Avai") in 1938.

In the first months of his adventures, Romano, piloting his Fiat CR 32 fighter, fought against the "Reds" during the Spanish Civil War. Then, after Franco's victory, he came back to Italy and resumed his duties as a civilian pilot. Not for long however: hours after he had heard Mussolini's voice on the radio announcing to the Italian people that Italy was at war against France and England, Romano left his humdrum job—and his new bride, Isa, a Red Cross nurse—to offer his services to the fatherland. Romano fought in all of Italy's battles—in Africa, in Greece, in Russia—until the fateful day when Italy was knocked out of the war and nothing was left to legionaries like him but to fade into the shadows.

If on one hand *Romano* was excellent for the quality of its images and the wonderful technical rendering of the realities of combat, on the other hand it was pitifully shortsighted as to Italy's actual potentialities and oppressively blinded by its own propaganda, which Romano compulsively spouted in his balloons and which Caesar further reinforced in his captions.

The technical details were originally conceived and laid out with an almost photographic precision. The characters, however, owed much to Alex Raymond, whom Caesar faithfully and almost slavishly copied. Romano, in particular, is very close in conception and make-up to Flash Gordon: they share a common moral

"Romano il Legionario," Kurt Caesar. © Nerbini.

affinity, and are similarly endowed with the qualities of courage, loyalty, and duty, and possess the ability of rising to every occasion to an exceptional degree.

G.B.

ROMITA, JOHN (1930-   ) American comic book artist born January 24, 1930, in Brooklyn, New York. After studies at the School of Industrial Arts and the Phoenix School, Romita spent a year in commercial art and then began drawing all types of stories for Stan Lee's Atlas group in 1949. Concentrating mainly on horror and romance stories—the romance titles were particularly terrible, he once said, because he "had never drawn a girl before"—he also had a short stint on the short-lived, 1954 *Captain America* revival. He also drew several war, crime, and Western features, most notably the *Western Kid* strip.

When Atlas faltered in 1957, Romita was unceremoniously released in the middle of a Western story. Turning to National, he was rejected by the superhero and Western departments, and refused to even try the war group because he said editor Bob Kanigher "ate" artists "and spit them out for breakfast." He eventually drifted into the romance department; he spent eight anonymous years there, never signing his work, even though he penciled and inked at least six stories a month and all the romance covers. And although his work was consistently the most dynamic in the romance field, it was ignored.

Consequently, when National's romance line faltered in 1965, Romita was dismissed and had to return to Lee, who was then riding herd on Marvel's increasingly popular superhero group. He began by inking the *Avengers*, then moved to penciling *Daredevil*, before gaining Marvel's most important feature, *Spider-Man*. Original illustrator Steve Ditko, whose intriguing presentations had garnered considerable admiration, left the strip after a dispute with Lee, and Romita was handed the assignment in September 1966.

In complete contrast to Ditko's individual handling of the feature, Romita brought *Spider-Man* in line with the rest of Marvel's handsomely illustrated titles: Ditko's homely women gave way to Romita's voluptuous girl-next-door types; Ditko's "everyman" Peter Parker yielded to Romita's smashingly dashing Parker; and the overall appearance of the strip went from "common man" to "superheroic." Whereas Ditko's *Spider-Man* was populated by everyday people, Romita's *Spider-Man* was populated by noble-bearing and majestic-looking characters. Under Romita's and Lee's guidance, the character became the quintessential antihero of the late 1960s and early 1970s.

Romita began easing off *Spider-Man* in 1971 to assume greater responsibility for Marvel's artistic direction, and was appointed art director in October 1972. When the *Spider-Man* newspaper strip started syndication in 1977, Romita was entrusted with the artwork. He drew the feature with his customary artistic flair and dynamic line until 1982, when he was promoted to an executive position at Marvel. His son, John Romita, Jr., is also a talented comic book artist.

J.B.

ROOM AND BOARD (U.S.) In the late 1920s, a minor cartoonist named Sals Bostwick was hired by King Features to draw a daily panel series to compete with NEA's successful *Our Boarding House* by Gene Ahern. Named *Room and Board*, the panel ran obscurely in a few Hearst papers, failed to catch on with general readers (drawn in a nondescript style vaguely similar to Frank Willard's, the strip had no memorable characters to attract attention), and was dropped in due time. But Hearst did not give up. By 1935, he solved the competitive problem by hiring Ahern himself to draw a revived *Room and Board* for King Features. Peopled with all-new characters created by Ahern, the new daily and Sunday strip was very similar in cast, narrative, and format to his famous *Our Boarding House* (which was adeptly continued by Bill Freyse for NEA).

The feature character, a fat braggart whose wife runs a boarding house to bring in the bread, is named Judge Homer Augustus Puffle (he is, of course, as much a judge as Major Hoople was an Army officer). His wife, Nora, takes care of a 12-year-old nephew (named Duncan in this case), and the same Greek chorus of bachelor boarders (Snoff, Steve, etc.) comments on the Judge's bumbling gambits for fame and fortune. There is no equivalent of Jake Hoople in *Room and Board*, but the Judge is plagued by the recurrent appearances of a Two-Gun Terry, a mildly dangerous lunatic who fancies himself a lawman of the Old West and shoots up the boarding house on occasion. A maid named Delia is another minor variation from the *Our Boarding House* format.

Physically, Judge Puffle simply reverses Major Hoople (except in the vast belly). Puffle's nose is small, his mustache is less pronounced, his chin is normally proportioned—in sum, he is a much less striking comic figure. His background seems to be more southern than the Major's: his speech, especially in placating his tyrannical wife, is somewhat more flowery. But the differences are minor; essentially Judge Puffle and *Room and Board* are duplicates of Ahern's earlier inventions, so that fans of one at the time could "double their pleasure, double their fun" with both, by reading Ahern's King Features imitation of *Our Boarding House* together with Bill Freyse's exact continuation of the original feature for NEA—at least until *Room and Board* ceased publication with Ahern's death in 1960.

B.B.

ROSCHER, FRANZ (1928-   ) German cartoonist and graphic designer, born May 26, 1928, in Aussig, in the then German Sudeten, Franz Roscher went to school and high school there. While in school, his artistic talent was discovered and encouraged by an understanding teacher.

Wanting to pursue a career in the arts, Franz Roscher took the qualifying examinations at the Academy of Arts in Prague after leaving high school. He had already been accepted by the Academy's standards when World War II ended and his family fled west to Southern Germany. There he found work painting and drawing for a club entertaining Americans only.

More or less self-educated in the graphic arts, he also started working as a decorator and doing posters before attending the Blochauer school of graphics in order to further his means of artistic expression.

While working for U.S. troops, Franz Roscher also got to know American comic books and was thoroughly impressed and influenced by them. This experience gave him a penchant for the comics medium. He kept his fondness of comics, carrying it over into his advertising work by using the comics format whenever possible.

"Rose Is Rose," Pat Brady. © United Feature Syndicate.

He then got several chances to put his fondness of comics to the test by actually doing comic book work for several German publishers. In the 1960s this culminated in his two-year appointment as studio head of Rolf Kauka productions. This position involved watching over artistic continuity in the *Fix und Foxi* comic book according to the style of the book by Walter Neugebauer. The style influenced Roscher's later freelance comic book work for other publishers.

Roscher created *Plop*, a multicolored troll, that was featured in *Max und Molli* before being awarded its own comic book which folded after about a year. Then Roscher created *Michel*, a daily comic strip published by the Munich newspaper *tz* from September 1968 to December 1969. The antics of Michel, a German Mr. Average, ended after the newspaper had a change of editor-in-chief. The clear, well-rounded style of Franz Roscher has since been used largely in his advertising work (sometimes in the form of comic strips) while plans for new comics led to Roscher's starting to create comic strips for Catholic children's and youths' publications for which he is also doing numerous illustrations.

W.F.

ROSE IS ROSE (U.S.) The huge success of *Rose Is Rose* by Pat Brady proves there will always be a place in American syndicated cartooning for upbeat family strips full of love, humor, fantasy, and imaginative artwork. *Rose Is Rose* began syndication by United Feature Syndicate in 1984 with 30 newspapers subscribing. It now is way over 400 newspapers and growing. However, cartoonist Brady has seen the downside of syndication. His first syndicated comic strip *Graves, Inc.* lasted only three years and dwindled to a scant 12 subscribers.

In a warm mix of fantasy and reality, *Rose Is Rose* presents the just regular-folks Gumbo family. Rose is proud to be a stay-at-home mom. She and husband, Jimbo, a decent Neanderthal type who works as a handyman, still have white-hot heat between them. Their son, Pasquale, began in the strip only being able to gurgle baby talk, which Rose had to interpret: now he's in kindergarten. Other characters include Pasquale's infant cousin, Clem, a neighbor, Mimi, and an engaging cut-yet-cagey kitten, Peekaboo. Pasquale's ever-present guardian angel, who changes size and demeanor at any perceived threat to his charge, features in many dailies and Sundays. Cartoonist Brady claims that daydreaming is an important part of his thought process in developing gags and short continuities for *Rose Is Rose*. Hence everybody from Rose to the kitten has out-of-body daydream sequences.

It's implied by Pasquale's guardian angel that he'll grow up to be an astronaut. Jimbo dreams of traveling with a Shaolin priest and Kung Fu master. Rose's alter ego wants to ride a big Harley motorcycle through Paris wearing her jacket, miniskirt, and cycle hat all of black leather. Her regular eyeglasses become cool, dark glasses. She sports a rose tattoo (what else?) on her thigh. The sweet, sexy Rose has become in her own fantasy one of the hottest women in all syndicated comics. Cartoonist Brady claims he has no political agenda. His goal seems to be to present the upbeat side of love, marriage, and raising children. Not that *Rose Is Rose* is lacking its pensive moments.

At a time in syndicated cartooning when good drawing is less important than good writing, *Rose Is Rose* displays both. Pat Brady's treatment of artistic perspective is innovative and extraordinary in today's comics, especially in his Sunday pages where he is one of the few cartoonists to make full use of the color palette. On Sundays, Brady's drawings are ones that readers seek out to see what he's tried next. In one, a colorful kaleidoscope shows in the intricate design first the Gumbo house, then trees, then Pasquale, then his face, and finally the snowflake that lands on his nose.

Love rules in *Rose Is Rose*. Although Brady denies the characters are autobiographical, he tends to favor dressing in the baseball cap, plaid shirt, and jeans that are Jimbo's uniform. Several newspaper stories have also noted that Rose is physically very similar to his wife, showing that brunettes with glasses can have lots of fun.

A classic *Rose Is Rose* gag has Rose telling Jimbo, "I found an old leftover kiss that I never used. Do you want it?" When he responds in the affirmative, she puts a Louisiana-liplock on him that literally has his hair standing straight up, his shirt all rumpled. Jimbo sputters, "It tasted fresh!" Assuming a modest pose, Rose answers, "I think my sweetness acts as a preservative!"

Sure it's cute and lovey-dovey, but *Rose Is Rose* is a beautifully crafted strip that readers look for, and it ultimately does its job of entertaining and selling newspapers.

B.C.

ROSIE'S BEAU (U.S.) A Sunday strip of long duration by George McManus, *Rosie's Beau* first appeared as a full-color page in the Hearst weekly comic sections on October 29, 1916, where it replaced the short-lived McManus Sunday feature, *The Whole Blooming Family*. Running for a little over a year and a half, *Rosie's Beau* was replaced in its turn by *Bringing Up Father* on April 14, 1918. It then dropped from sight until it was resurrected by McManus as a companion page-topper to the *Bringing Up Father* Sunday strip on June 13, 1926,

where it supplanted a minor gag strip called *Good Morning, Boss* and ran for almost two decades.

Rosie was a typically lovely young girl of the comic pages, courted by a typically foolish and ardent young office-worker of the funnies named—in this case—Archie (or Archibald, as Rosie often calls him). Archie, based physically on McManus, was fat and double-chinned, but shone as a Paladin in armor to his beloved Rosie. The two lovers, much to the disgust of Rosie's father (who is later, in the 1920s, Archie's boss as well), continually exchange the soppiest possible *mots d'amour*. Surprisingly, McManus managed to get enormous comic strip mileage out of this seemingly limited and cloying subject, keeping the little Sunday strip fresh and amusing until November 12, 1944, when he finally replaced it with a new strip called *Snookums*. Archie was in the army at the time (amusingly, he was turned down for the army in World War I), but no nearer marriage with Rosie.

No book collection of *Rosie's Beau* was published; it had only brief comic book reprinting in the late 1930s, and there was no film or radio adaptation.

B.B.

ROSINSKI, GRZEGORZ (1941-   ) Belgian cartoonist and illustrator Grzegorz Rosinski was born in Stalowa Wola, in southeastern Poland, on August 3, 1941. Rosinski was first exposed to Western-style comics as a child reading *Vaillant*, a French Communist children's weekly that was widely distributed in Poland. He drew his first comic strip for his high school newspaper. After studies at the Warsaw School of Fine Arts, from which he graduated in 1967, he devoted himself to drawing and writing comics as his life occupation.

From the late 1960s to the mid-1970s he turned out a great number of comic books, mostly adventure and mystery stories, along with several epic and science fiction strips for the Warsaw magazine *Relax*. The excellence of his drawings attracted the attention of the editors of the Belgian magazine *Tintin*; and in 1976 Rosinski was invited to Brussels. In that year his long professional involvement with Editions du Lombard (publishers of *Tintin* magazine) began. He contributed a few short comic stories for *Tintin*, as well as a fantasy strip for the rival publication *Spirou* (on that occasion he used the alias "Rosek" and greatly simplified his sophisticated graphic style).

In 1977, on scripts by Jean Van Hamme, he started in *Tintin* what was to turn into his masterwork, *Thorgal, Fils des Etoiles* ("Thorgal, Son of the Stars"). A sweeping tale of heroic fantasy, it has majestically unfolded over 30 episodes to date. Endowed with super- and extra-sensory powers, Thorgal had been adopted by a band of Vikings who found him lying unconscious on the ocean shore and gave him the name of Aegirson, son of Aegir, the sea god. In adventures that took him over the seas and into unknown lands, Thorgal is not without resemblance to Prince Valiant. Furthermore, Rosinski's graphic style, in its meticulous renderings and compositions, has undoubtedly been inspired by Harold Foster's. Be that as it may, *Thorgal* is withal a gripping historical saga and a masterly tale of sword-and-sorcery.

In addition to his long-term commitment to *Thorgal*, Rosinski has found the time to turn out several other comic book series, the most notable being *Hans*, a post-

"Rosie's Beau," George McManus. © King Features Syndicate.

nuclear war tale scripted by André-Paul Duchateau, which he illustrated from its outset in 1980.

M.H.

Really Gentlemen if you gaze on me in this manner you will put me quite to the blush?

Thomas Rowlandson, "A Lump of Innocence."

ROWLANDSON, THOMAS (1756-1827) English cartoonist and engraver born July 1756 in the Old Jewry, London. Thomas Rowlandson attended Dr. Barrow's Academy in Soho and distinguished himself by the caricatures he made of his fellow-students and school teachers. In 1772 he went to Paris at the invitation of his Uncle Thomas's French widow. There he made rapid advances in the study of the human figure (so one of his biographers tells us, perhaps with unconscious humor) and upon his return to London he registered at the Royal Academy to which he had been admitted before his visit to Paris.

In 1775 Rowlandson exhibited at the Academy with a number of allegorical scenes. From 1778 to 1781 he devoted himself to painting portraits, several of which were also exhibited at the Academy. Rowlandson was veering away from serious art to caricature, and his first cartoons began appearing in 1784, among them "An Italian Family," "Vauxhall," and "The Serpentine River." During this time Rowlandson was supported by his aunt's liberalities and when the lady died in 1788 she left him several thousand pounds besides other valuable property. Rowlandson was now free to indulge his penchants for women and gambling, losing not only his legacy but sinking further and further into debt; this situation left him no alternative but to turn back to drawing, which he called "my only left resource." He was a prolific worker and frequently produced two finished cartoons a day. *The Miseries of Life, The Comforts of Bath, The Cries of London* were among

the remarkable cartoon series which he then produced (they were later collected into books). But Rowlandson's most celebrated creations were produced under the prodding (and with the generous assistance) of his long-time friend, the book and print-seller Ackermann. *The Tour of Dr. Syntax in Search of the Picturesque* (with accompanying text in verse by William Combe) appeared first in Ackermann's *Poetical Magazine* in 1809, was reprinted in book form in 1812, and was followed by two more *Tours of Dr. Syntax* books (*In Search of Consolation*, 1820; *In Search of a Wife*, 1821).

Rowlandson's narrative sequences (especially *The Tours of Dr. Syntax*) provide a direct link between the 18th-century picture story and the modern comic strip (they only lack dialectic motion to qualify as full-fledged comic strips). Along with his contemporary, James Gillray, Rowlandson also pioneered in the use of the balloon as a dramatic device. Thomas Rowlandson died in 1827.

M.H.

ROY, YVES *see* Hildago, Francisco.

ROY TIGER (Germany) *Roy Tiger*, a creation of the editorial staff of Bastei Verlag, came into being in collaboration with a group of Spanish artists including Esteban Maroto, Carlos Gimenez, L. Garcia, A. Usero, Lopez Ramón, et al. By and large this ensured a high standard of illustration for this comic series taking place in the exotic jungles of India. However, as so often happens, Bastei Verlag did not fully realize the art potential of the series and ruined some of the books by heavy-handed "improvement" drawing of the same kind that had helped wreck the style of Arturo del Castillo's Western, *Kendall*, Joseph Gillain's *Jerry Spring*, or Raymond Poïvet's *Les pionniers de l'Espérance*. The exotic flair of *Roy Tiger* nevertheless escaped destruction and allowed for its publication in 79 issues in a period of some two years.

Roy Tiger first saw print on April 15, 1968, in *Lasso*, number 63. *Lasso*, a Western comic book featuring *Kendall* at the time, should have been the most unlikely title in which to try out a series taking place in India. Nevertheless, it was done. In fact, the Wild West had to turn over four more complete issues to mysterious India before *Roy Tiger* was allowed to continue on its own as a biweekly comic book. For awhile the book was even stepped up to weekly status. The series ended in June 1970 after a reshuffling of the Bastei comic lineup. It may also have ended because Spanish artists involved in the production of *Roy Tiger* moved on to other projects.

Spanish readers had a chance to follow some of the *Roy Tiger* material in *Trinca*. At the time *Roy Tiger* was published, Bastei Verlag sold their comics nationwide at the same date of sale. The books not sold by the time the next issue rolled around were then returned to be bound in volumes for later sales. Since then Bastei's system of distribution has changed in order to reduce the number of leftover books. This was achieved by selling according to the six Nielsen areas of Germany, six regions defined by infrastructure as separate marketing areas. What is not sold in one Nielsen area is collected for shipment to the next and so forth.

Roy Tiger, while the book lasted, told the story of Roy Tiger, the sandy-haired son of a Caucasian doctor; Khamar, an Indian of the Kalong tribe; Paki, the orphaned Kashmiri native boy; and their animal friends, Shumba the python, Sheeta the black panther, and Shimmy the monkey. Occasionally they were also aided by an elephant named Lahani. Between them they saved the Indian subcontinent from some major catastrophes and helped put their share of criminals behind bars. Roy Tiger's parents rarely entered the scene, making the comic strip ideal wish-fulfillment for the young readership for whom the feature was intended.

W.F.

RUBINO, ANTONIO (1880-1964) Italian cartoonist born 1880 in Sanremo. Antonio Rubino started his career as an advertising artist and book illustrator; in 1907 he entered the field of children's illustrations with contributions to the *Girnalino della Domenica*. In 1908 he became one of the most important contributors to the newly created *Corriere dei Piccoli*: it was Rubino who dreamed up the idea of replacing the speech balloons in the Italian version of such famous American comic strips as "Fortunello" (*Happy Hooligan*), "La Checca," (*And Her Name Was Maud*), "Bibi e Bibo" (*The Katzenjammer Kids*), and "Arcibaldo e Petronilla" (*Bringing Up Father*) by captions in verse (this was to become the hallmark of the Italian comics).

In addition to his editorial duties, Rubino created a myriad of different titles for the *Corriere*, most of them only ephemeral features that appeared and disappeared from the pages of the magazine without any seeming regularity or pattern. In the course of his long tenure (1908-1927) it is possible to distinguish a few creations which proved longer-lasting or more noteworthy than the others: *Quadratino* ("Little Squarehead," 1910), *Pino e Pina* (a kid strip, also 1910), *Lola e Lalla* (1913), the hilarious and long-lasting saga of *Il Collegio 1a Delizia* ("The Delight Boarding-School," 1913), *Italino e Kartoffel Otto* (the Italian comic strip's contribution to World War I, 1915), *Pierino e il Burattino* ("Peter and the Puppet," 1921), *Rosaspina* (1922), *Pippotto ed il Ca prone Barbacucco* ("Big Joe and Barbacucco the Billy-Goat," 1924), *Lionello e Nerone* (1926).

During World War I Rubino also contributed to the army magazine *La Tradotta* for which he created a host of memorable characters like Corporal C. Piglio, always ready with advice, the handsome hero Muscolo Mattia, Apollo Mari the troublemaker, along with the grotesque figures of the rulers Cecco Beppe, Guglielmone, and Carletto.

In 1927 Rubino was invited to contribute to the Fascist Youth's magazine *Il Balilla*: during the short time he worked for that publication his most notable contribution was a pictorialization of Aesop's fables. In 1931 he started his long collaboration with the publisher Mondadori, becoming in 1934 the editor of the comic weekly *Topolino*, in whose pages he used speech balloons for the first time (he always maintained that captions were educationally superior to balloons in stories for children). In 1942 *Rubino* added to his activities that of animator, producing *Il Paese dei Ranocchi* ("The Land of the Frogs") which won the award in the animated cartoon category in that year's Venice Biennial.

After the war, Rubino devoted himself to painting, but when he was called back to the *Corriere dei Piccoli* he could not resist one last fling at comics. His stories no longer appealed to the public, however, and he retired in 1959.

Antonio Rubino's style was a combination of geometric design and floral pattern, with a sinuous line

akin to Art Nouveau. He was also a master of color and must be regarded as the chief architect of *Corriere dei Piccoli*'s success during the two decades of his tenure. Then, in the 1930s, the American comics established themselves and Rubino's conceptions became more and more obsolete. Antonio Rubino died at Sanremo on July 1, 1964.

G.B.

RUDI (Germany) Rudi, a very human dog, is the main comic hero of a number of comic albums produced by writer/artist Peter Puck, a native of Heidenheim where he was born July 23, 1960. The name Peter Puck, incidentally, is not a pseudonym. Puck studied history of art and literature and is a self-educated comic artist whose style was strongly influenced by that of Carl Barks's.

Rudi was first published in May 1985 in the Stuttgart magazine *Stuttgart live* and later on continued in the Stuttgart magazine *lift*. The full-page strips published there have been collected in a number of comic albums since 1987 and have gone through numerous printings. The stories that straightforward Rudi and his anarchic friend Fred get involved in are social satires of life in Germany with all kinds of people and happenings straight from everyday life. As a Stuttgart newspaper once put it: "Rudi is a better guide through German subculture and youth culture than the most alternative city guide. . . ."

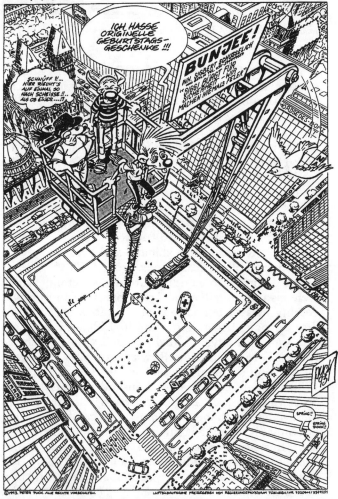

"Rudi," Peter Puck. © Peter Puck.

Puck depicts his world in realistic backdrops filled with cartoon characters. In fact, Puck may be one of the funny-animal artists with the most realistic background drawings. Puck's material has become so popular in Germany that he was nominated twice for best German comic artist at the Erlangen Comic Salon. In 1994 his large format originals were also presented in an exhibit at the Erlangen Salon.

Puck gave up his academic studies to devote himself entirely to creating comics and to produce advertising using funny comic elements. While his artwork certainly is one of the reasons for the success of *Rudi*, the writing is at least as important. While sometimes speech balloons are filled with lots of dialogue they only appear text-heavy. Actually, dialogue is as much a necessary tool as is the artwork for Puck to create his aura of visual and verbal verisimilitude necessary to make for a functional and witty satire.

W.F.

RUFUS *see* Flook.

RUGGLES (G.B.) John Ruggles and family (wife Gladys, teenage daughter Maisie, young son Herbert, and the mother-in-law) were the first working-class family in British newspaper strips. A step down the social scale from city gent *Pop*, they reflected the readers of the *Daily Mirror* and quickly caught on. The first strip appeared on March 11, 1935, signed "Blik" (Steve Dowling on art, Frank Dowling on script), and was a simple gag strip. Domestic jokes were the routine until continuity was introduced during 1937. Interest immediately increased and caught 74 percent of the readership in the first Mirror strip poll. This rose slightly by 2½ percent in 1946, but dwindled to 51 percent in 1949, a year after the strip had taken an unprecedented turn.

For years the serial ran as a soap opera tinged with humor; Ruggles in bowler and raincoat rising above domestic troubles and unlikely romantic entangle-ments with glamorous Greta, while Maisie had married boyfriend Julian Balham and borne a child, and Herbert had taken up with teenaged Elsie Watson, a fellow architecture student. Suddenly, in 1948, Ruggles turned to face his readers and said, "Look out for us on page two. We're taking a trip to Margate on the *Royal Eagle* and we're going to see if you're aboard!" For the first time a cartoon hero stepped into reality—or vice versa—and the real life Mrs. Pearson and family found themselves featured in a strip! Although Ruggles's "meet the people" was a new idea, and certainly worked for a while, the actual readership appreciation fell, and the strip was killed on August 3, 1957. The last writer was Ian Gammidge, while the artist remained Steve Dowling.

D.G.

RUPERT (G.B.) Rupert is an endearing little bear cub in his checked trousers, jumper, and scarf, who lives in Nutwood with Mummy and Daddy. (If not the original Three Bears, then certainly the originals as far as British newspaper strips go.) Not strictly a strip, *Rupert*'s panels have never exceeded two per day (for some years reduced to one), with his story carried in text or verse beneath, but he has also appeared in strip form in the *Daily Express Children's Own* (May 20, 1933), a pull-out comic, and is currently reprinted in strip form and in full color in *Pippin* (1974), a weekly nursery comic. The panels also take on strip form in the annual reprints in color, *Rupert Annual* (1945-   ).

With successful children's strips running in the *Daily Mirror* and *Daily News*, R. D. Blumenfeld, editor of the *Daily Express*, asked his night news editor to look for something similar. Herbert Tourtel told his wife, Mary, no mean artist and writer, and within days she had come up with *The Little Lost Bear*. It commenced on Monday, November 8, 1920, ran its course, and was replaced by a different story. But readers wrote in demanding more adventures of Rupert Bear, and so Mary obliged with a sequel. Soon other stories were dropped altogether, and by the 1930s Rupert had a full-blown club, The Rupert League, and regular reprints in book form.

"Ruggles," Steve Dowling. © Daily Mirror Ltd.

"Rupert," Alfred Bestall. © Beaverbrook Newspapers Ltd.

Rupert's regular playmates include Bill Badger, Algy Pug, and Edward Trunk the elephant, and his adventures always have a fairy-tale touch of fantasy, landing him safely home in Nutwood. Mary Tourtel retired in 1935 when her eyesight failed after drawing 105 stories. She died in Canterbury in March 1948, aged 74. The strip was taken over by Alfred Bestall, illustrator and *Punch* cartoonist. His first story, *Rupert and the Smugglers*, commenced June 28, 1935. After 30 years he too retired, and Alex Cubie took over the drawing, while Frederick Chaplain, a former comic editor from Amalgamated Press, took on the writing. Rupert celebrated his fiftieth anniversary (1970) by expanding his activities. He was turned into a puppet film series for television—and also appeared pornographically in the underground paper *Oz!*

In 1984 pop stars Paul and Linda McCartney financed a fully animated cartoon film, *Rupert and the Frog Song*. The film was produced, directed, and animated by Geoff Dunbar, but plans to expand it into a feature collapsed, and the film was released as a short.

D.G.

RUSSELL, CLARENCE D. (1895-1963) Clarence Russell was an American cartoonist born in 1895 in Buffalo, New York. C. D. Russell studied at the Chicago Art Institute and, after freelancing cartoons to magazines around the country, he came to New York City in 1915. When World War I rolled around he enlisted in the Marines, became sports editor of *The Leatherneck*, the Corps' publication, and was sent overseas with the American Expeditionary Force.

Back in the United States in 1920, Russell worked for different New York newspapers, notably the *Evening Mail* and the *Evening Post*. At the same time he contributed regularly to *Judge* (legend has it that the editors of *Judge* had him signed under exclusivity in 1927 to keep him out of *Life*). Around that time Russell developed the character of a peppery little tramp who appeared with increasing frequency in the pages of *Judge*. Eventually the cartoonist was contacted by King Features Syndicate and drew the little tramp into a new comic strip, *Pete the Tramp*, which first appeared in January 1932.

For the rest of his life Russell stayed with King, contributing a number of other strip creations as companion pieces to *Pete*. *The Tucker Twins* (a pale imitation of the Katzies) and *Pete's Pup* were not remarkable either in style or content; *Shorty*, about a shrimpish bum even seedier than Pete, did have some merit but basically it was only more of the same. In 1946 Russell helped form the National Cartoonists Society of which he became the first secretary. He died of cancer at Kings Bridge Veterans Hospital in the Bronx on October 22, 1963, and *Pete the Tramp* died with him.

The possessor of a very remarkable graphic talent, C. D. Russell never knew how to develop his potential to the fullest. Fresh and imaginative when it came out in the 1930s, *Pete* soon floundered on the shoals of irrelevance and repetitiveness. With all its shortcomings, however, it remains the only work for which Russell deserves to be remembered.

M.H.

RUSSELL, JAMES NEWTON (1909-   ) Australian cartoonist born at Campsie, N.S.W., Australia, in 1909, the son of a council plumber, who was killed in an accident when Russell was six years old. On complet-

ing school at Lewisham Christian Brothers, in 1924, he became a copy boy on the *Sydney Daily Guardian* and soon transferred to *Smith's Weekly*. With no prospects of advancement and because his drawing ability had not reached the standard required for publication, Russell drifted into a series of jobs in leather and steel factories and worked as a junior in the office of Sydney Stadium, where he also became a preliminary boxer for a brief period. During this time he improved his drawing skills by sketching notable boxers, which were published in the Sydney papers. In 1926, the head artist of Fox Films offered to tutor Russell in the fundamentals of art if he paid $200 and worked for two years without pay. Russell accepted the offer and by the time he left Fox Films he had become a capable artist.

He joined the *Sydney Evening News* in 1928 and became the youngest political cartoonist in Australia. When the paper folded in 1931, Russell became a sports caricaturist with the *Referee* and soon transferred back to his original paper, *Smith's Weekly*. Here he was to spend almost two decades in handling single-block cartoons as well as strips. When Stan Cross left *Smith's* to join the *Melbourne Herald*, in 1940, Jim Russell not only inherited the strips *Smith's Vaudevillians* and *You and Me* but also took over the position as art editor. He altered the tone of *You and Me* and changed the name to *Mr. & Mrs. Pott*. During the war years, Russell was responsible for two satirical strips, *Adolf, Hermann* and *Musso* and *Schmit der Sphy*, which not only delighted his readers but were rumored to have put Russell on a blacklist, if the Allies lost the war.

In 1950, when *Smith's* folded, Russell was able to sell a further modified version of *Mr. & Mrs. Pott* (retitled *The Potts*) to the *Herald & Weekly Times Ltd.* for national and, eventually, worldwide syndication. While influenced by artists of *The Bulletin* and *Smith's Weekly* schools, Russell developed a slick caricature technique that is closer in origin to the U.S. style of humorous cartooning than any particular Australian style. His international rather than national approach to both art and humor would appear to be the basis of the wide acceptance of *The Potts*, rather than any unique qualities inherent in the strip.

Jim Russell is a writer, tennis administrator, radio and TV personality, publisher of dancing and music magazines, President of the White City Club, Sydney, and finds time to run two travel agencies. In his biographical entry for the 1996 *National Cartoonists Society Album* he also lists himself as the NCS representative for Australia.

J.R.

RUSTY RILEY (U.S.) Frank Godwin's last creation, *Rusty Riley* saw the light of print as a daily strip on January 26, 1948, and was followed by a Sunday version on June 27 of the same year. The feature was distributed by King Features Syndicate, and Rod Reed wrote the daily continuity, while the Sunday page was authored by Frank Godwin's brother Harold.

In the first episode, Rusty, a bright, attractive lad of about 14, flees in the company of his fox terrier Flip, the orphanage where he had been confined since the accidental death of his parents. In the course of his wanderings he comes upon the estate of Mr. Miles, a wealthy race-horse owner, where he works as a stable boy, and later as a jockey, bringing his trusted horse, Bright Blaze, to victory in the Kentucky Derby.

"Rusty Riley," Frank Godwin. © King Features Syndicate.

The horse-racing scenes alternate with stories of detection in which Rusty and Patti Miles, Mr. Miles's teenage daughter, often foil the plots of robbers or racetrack fixers. Slowly romance blooms between the two young people, but this aspect of the strip was cut short by the sudden disappearance of Rusty Riley in the summer of 1959, a few weeks before its creator's own death.

Rusty Riley is a work of old age (Godwin was 60 when he started it), but it carries with it the luminescence of youth, a youth certainly romanticized and idealized, but as vital and vibrant as Godwin's art. The trite story line is irrelevant; Rusty Riley was always purely an artist's strip, and it should be enjoyed as such by all those who appreciate elegance of line, artistry of execution, and sheer graphic excellence.

M.H.

RYAN, TOM K. (1926-   ) American cartoonist born June 6, 1926, in Anderson, Indiana. Tom K. (T. K.) Ryan grew up in small Indiana towns, and later studied at Notre Dame University and the University of Cincinnati. Ryan, who always wanted to become a cartoonist, started his career as a commercial artist (he designed the football helmet emblems of the Green Bay Packers and the New York Giants). He was bored, however, and started reading Western literature. ("It was kind of an escape for me as well as a hobby," he was later to confide.) In turn, his reading led him back to cartooning and he decided to try a new "hip" idea, which would combine, in his words, "the Old West with a hip approach."

T. K. Ryan's brainchild, *Tumbleweeds*, was thus launched in September 1965. Distributed by the small Lew Little Syndicate, it was later picked up by the Register and Tribune Syndicate (and eventually by King Features Syndicate). Today *Tumbleweeds* is carried by more than 300 newspapers around the country. Originally Ryan had intended *Tumbleweeds* to be a gag strip, but later he went more and more deeply into continuity, keeping a sharp eye on the 30-odd characters in the cast.

Ryan's style is simple, even basic, harking back to the caricatural line and slapstick situation of the early comic strip artists. His humor is pointed, but never offensive, and though he keeps his dialogue up to date, it is still literate. T. K. Ryan, a somewhat shy artist who never joined a professional society and seldom appears in public, lives and works in Muncie, Indiana. His dedication to *Tumbleweeds* is total, and it shows in the high narrative and graphic quality of the strip. In one of the rare interviews that he granted (to Beth Slocum of the *Milwaukee Journal*), Ryan expounded his artistic philosophy in simple terms: "I believe strips should be relevant and attuned to modern times and language, but not message oriented." In the case of *Tumbleweeds*, of course, the medium itself is the message.

The growing success of his strip in the 1970s persuaded Ryan to join the National Cartoonists Society. Still shunning the limelight, he devotes the greatest part of his time turning out *Tumbleweeds*, now in its fourth decade. His recognizable line and brand of humor have inspired many later cartoonists, including Jim Davis, who was his studio assistant from 1969 to 1978, prior to creating *Garfield*.

M.H.

SABAKU NO MAŌ (Japan)

Sabaku no Maō ("The Devil of the Desert") was created by Tetsuji Fukushima for the comic monthly *Bōkenō* where it first appeared in April 1949. (*Bōkenō* is now the only monthly comic magazine for boys left, as all the others—*Shōnen, Mangaō, Bokura*, etc.—having gone out of existence.) Earlier in 1949, in the first issue of *Bōkenō*, Fukushima created *Daiya Majin* ("Diamond Devil") which served as the prologue and the springboard for *Sabaku no Maō*.

Inspired by the legend of Aladdin and the magic lamp, *Sabaku no Maō* featured the adventures of a genie and his enterprising young master, Boppu. Sabaku had sprung out of an incense burner when Boppu had inadvertently let it burn out: he wore a scarlet cape, a huge sword, a white turban, and long boots. This costume occurred to Fukushima while he was reading an issue of the *National Geographic* magazine about an old African regal ceremony. Sabaku unquestionably obeyed the orders of the master of the lamp, as he was invincible: no weapon known to man, whether arrow, spear, gun, or cannon, could bring him down. Thanks to the large ruby embedded in his turban (the Hikōseki, or "flying stone") he could fly through the air.

Sabaku no Maō soon became one of the more successful boys' strips. The highlight of each story was Sabaku's obligatory battle scene with armies mounted against him. Fukushima's dynamic composition and arrangement of glittering colors led the readers into a fantastic and enchanting story world. *Sabaku no Maō*'s last appearance was in the February 1956 issue of *Bōkenō*.

H.K.

SADHÚ (Spain)

A jungle strip created by Emilio Freixas on scripts by José Canellas Casals, *Sadhú* started in issue 326 of the comic weekly *Chicos* (November 1, 1944). The first episode was titled "The Tiger of Sambar" and was followed by "The Seven Altars of Sapta Mata," published in *Chico*'s 1948 annual. Many years later, after Freixas's temporary retirement from the comic field, this feature helped him make a comeback. Again written by Canellas, this new version of *Sadhú* appeared in the first issue of the magazine *Chito* (October 1, 1974). It lasted only a few years.

Sadhú is a grown-up Mowgli: like Kipling's hero he is a friend of animals. He also has a certain resemblance to Bomba, the jungle boy. Freixas's mastery in the rendition of animals, along with his exotic and baroque backgrounds, help him to re-create accurately the locale and atmosphere in which his hero finds himself.

L.G.

SAD SACK, THE (U.S.)

The creation of ex-Disney animator and striker George Baker, *The Sad Sack* debuted in the pages of *Yank* magazine, the army weekly, in 1942. He was, according to Baker, an average soldier, steeped in psychological, if not actual, reality and reflected the soldiers' state of mind: resigned, tired, helpless, and beaten.

The Sack, a classic variant of the Little Man, became one of the most popular characters to come out of the war, surpassing *Yank*'s other star, Private Breger (G.I. Joe). The *Sack* cartoons were always in strip form and in pantomime. He saw action, during his over three and a half years with *Yank*, in every theater of the war and on every front.

The Sack's tormentors were many usually master sergeants, but often, a la Happy Hooligan, Charlie Chaplin, Robert Benchley, and others in the tradition, his troubles were simply a natural function of his existence in the harsh world around him. The world seemed to conspire against the Sack: He never got the girl, regulations foiled his sincerest efforts, superiors inevitably took advantage of him. In keeping with the elements of the classic comic figure, he was designed to reflect the frustrations of the common man but at the same time became something for the common man to look down on. *The Sad Sack* was enormously popular.

He was too popular to die with the armistice. The ever-alert John Wheeler, near the war's end, arranged for the republication of the best of the *Sack* strips in stateside papers through his Bell Syndicate. After the war the Sack lived on in a Sunday page distributed by Bell; it debuted on May 5, 1946. But in civvies the Sack was a fish out of water. That and Bell's traditionally poor promotion and sales caused *The Sad Sack* Sunday page to dwindle to nothing. It was discontinued in the early 1950s.

Elsewhere, however, back in uniform, the Sack happily suffered his persecutions. The original cast of the

"The Sad Sack," George Baker. © George Baker.

Sack, a growling Sarge and ever-changing faces, was beefed up to include the General, the K-9 Muttssy, the ugly WAC Sadie Sack, and others in the pages of a wide range of titles for Harvey. Many artists have worked on these books, most recently Joe Dennett, but Baker continued to draw all the covers until his death in May 1975.

Merchandising was also heavy, with many Sad Sack ash trays, pieces of jewelry, glasses, and other items. He also came to life on the screen when Jerry Lewis played the title role.

Baker had one of the great comic drawing styles. His Disney training stood him in good stead, although there were no traces of the cutesy, animator style that was popular in the postwar years. There was a great deal of movement, expression, and very basic humor in the drawings. Baker varied the angles in his panels; the view was always slightly from above and employed the classic comic strip conventions: beads of sweat, symbols of pain and consternation, clouds of dust. Pot bellies were everywhere, every pant leg bagged absurdly at the knee, the feet were the biggest since Zim, and, all in all, *The Sad Sack*'s adventures were presented in a most agreeable, old, slapstick style.

R.M.

SAGA DE XAM (France) Spurred on by the heady praise heaped on two of his previous ventures, *Barbarella* and *Jodelle*, the indefatigable Eric Losfeld released in 1967 yet another comic strip novel, *Saga de Xam*, written by Jean Rollin and illustrated by Nicolas Devil.

Saga is a beautiful young woman from Xam, a distant planet of our galaxy. Xam, inhabited exclusively by women, is threatened with a terrible alien invasion. Not used to violence and war, the inhabitants of Xam send Saga to learn the ways of evil and destruction from the people of earth. Saga then starts on a space and time odyssey which takes her to the Middle Ages, in among the Vikings, to ancient Egypt, China, and the United States. Upon her return to Xam she will have the opportunity to apply her newly acquired knowledge....

Saga has been highly praised by some, yet, to most, it remains a sophomoric exercise, dull and derivative, a sterile attempt at being original at all costs, without regard to the niceties of good storytelling and accomplished draftsmanship.

M.H.

SAINT-OGAN, ALAIN (1895-1974) Saint-Ogan was a French cartoonist, journalist, and writer born in Colombes, near Paris, on August 7, 1895. His father was a newspaper editor, and the son decided very early in life to become a press illustrator. He studied at l'Ecole Nationale des Arts Decoratifs in Paris and had his first drawings published in 1913. He enlisted during World War I and was sent to the Balkans. After the war he resumed his career as a cartoonist and newspaperman. In 1925 he created his first comic strip, *Zig et Puce*, about two venturesome youngsters, for the French weekly *Dimanche Illustré*. The series met with instant success and was followed by a number of other comic features: *Mitou et Toti* (more kids, brother and sister this time; 1932), *Prosper l'Ours* ("Prosper the Bear") in 1933; *Monsieur Poche* (1934), a gag strip about a fat and stuffy French bourgeois; and *Touitoui* (an elf) also in 1934.

Alain Saint-Ogan.

At the same time Saint-Ogan wrote and drew for a number of newspapers and magazines. In 1941 he became editor of the children's weekly *Benjamin* (where he created *Trac et Boum*, yet more kids) and he was also active in the Resistance. From 1950 to 1958 he was cohost of a radio show and later became a television producer. Saint-Ogan has also illustrated a number of books and was the author of several novels and two books of memoirs. He toned down his activities in the 1960s. Alain Saint-Ogan died on June 23, 1974, of circulatory trouble.

Alain Saint-Ogan is widely regarded as the artist who gave fresh impetus to the French strip in the 1920s and 1930s. His greatest merit was to introduce the art deco look (of which he is one of the foremost representatives) to the comic strip. He has influenced countless numbers of European cartoonists (including Hergé, who owes his cartooning start to Saint-Ogan). Saint-Ogan was the recipient of a number of awards and distinctions. In 1967 he became the first cartoonist to have a medal coined in his effigy by the French Mint, and a retrospective exhibition of his works was organized by the Bibliotheque Nationale in 1971.

M.H.

SAITŌ, TAKAO (1936-) Japanese comic book artist born in Osaka on November 3, 1936, Takao Saitō wanted to be an illustrator; he studied toward that goal during his high school years. One day, however, he discovered by chance the work of Osamu Tezuka (particularly *Shin Takarajima*, "The New Treasure Island") and there and then made up his mind to become a comic strip artist.

In 1954 Saitō produced his first comic strip, *Kūki Danshaku* ("Baron Kuki"), which strongly showed Tezuka's influence. Later he drew many more comic strips for Kage, one of the most important and durable of the *kashibonya yō manga* (comic book companies that did not distribute through dealers but circulated their publications through rental libraries) as well as for Machi and Deka.

13 in 1994 after a record-breaking run of 25 years, he went on to produce a number of shorter works.

Saitō's art style, at first very simple and even caricatural, grew more realistic with time. Saitō is widely regarded as the artist who gave fresh impetus to the Japanese comic strip in the 1960s. His work, which has influenced a whole new generation of Japanese cartoonists (Takeshi Kanda, Yuzuro Saitō, Fumiyasu Ishikawa, Saburō Takemoto, to name a few), is representative of contemporary Japanese comic art, with its emphasis on speed, thrills, and sex.

H.K.

SALINAS, JOSÉ LUIS (1908-1985) Argentinean cartoonist and illustrator born in Buenos Aires on February 11, 1908, Salinas broke into illustration in 1929 without the benefit of formal art studies. He worked for such magazines as *El Tony* and *Paginas de Columba* in his native country before embarking on a career as a designer and advertising illustrator for the Exitus agency.

His first contribution to the comics was *Hernán el Corsario* ("Hernán the Privateer"), a sea adventure story set in the 1600s, which he wrote and drew for the magazine *Patoruzu* from 1936 to 1938, and again from 1940 to 1946. It was on this strip that Salinas honed his skills as a master craftsman and graphic storyteller. In the same period he also adapted a number of famous novels, such as Jules Verne's *Michel Strogoff* and Alexandre Dumas's *The Three Musketeers*, into comic strips for the magazine *El Hógar*.

By the end of the 1940s his fame had spread far beyond his native Argentina, and he went to the United States in search of more lucrative employment than he could find in his country. His contacts with

Takao Saitō.

Among his most successful comic strips are: *Taifu Goro* (a detective strip, 1960); *Bugei Kikou* (a samurai story, 1962); his 007 series (which he adapted from the Ian Fleming novels for the monthly *Boy's Life Magazine* in 1965); *Muyōnosuke* (the story of a one-eyed professional prize-fighter in the Edo era) for the weekly *Shōnen* magazine; and *Golgo 13*, about a professional killer, for the bimonthly *Big Comic*. After ending *Golgo*

José Luis Salinas, "Hernán el Corsario." © *José Luis Salinas.*

King Features proved fruitful, and in 1951 *The Cisco Kid*, a Western based on an O. Henry story and starring a flamboyant Mexican righter of wrongs, debuted in American newspapers: drawn by Salinas on texts by Rod Reed, it lasted until 1968 and received much critical acclaim. The artist, who in the meantime had settled in the States with his family, then returned to Argentina.

He kept up his contacts with King, however, and in 1973 made a comeback with *Gunner*, a detective strip set in the milieu of professional sports. In 1975 he abruptly left the strip and abandoned comics for good. He died in Buenos Aires on January 10, 1985, having devoted the last years of his life to illustration again and to painting.

Called by Franco Fossati "a superlative artist of the comics," Salinas, more than any of his contemporaries, helped develop the style and look of Argentine comics in the last half-century. His son, Alberto Salinas, is also a renowned cartoonist.

M.H.

SALLY FORTH (U.S.) King Features Syndicate touts *Sally Forth* as "every working mother's story" and has carved out a niche of more than 600 subscribers for this comic strip about a woman who juggles marriage, a child, and a full-time job outside the home. In 1995 *Sally Forth* took a quantum leap in popularity expanding its subscriber base by 25 percent. Part of the reason is that *Sally Forth* delivers an audience to newspapers desperate to reach two-income families. Women in particular like *Sally Forth*; the strip is often published in the "Style" (a.k.a. women's) section of newspapers just as Universal Press Syndicate's *Cathy* is.

With more than 70 percent of all women who have school-age children working outside the home, Sally's trials and tribulations have a ready audience. Editors publish *Sally Forth* because they know she reflects the lifestyle of most married women, albeit not all are in middle management like Sally.

Sally Forth was originally developed by Field Syndicate and debuted January 4, 1982. Since then Field has been absorbed by King Features. Just signed "Howard," many readers have been surprised to discover their beloved Sally was created by a man, Minneapolis attorney Greg Howard. A partner in a law firm with more than nine years of litigation experience, he left that career to become a cartoonist. Greg Howard has always considered writing his strength. He

himself has called his artwork "crude" and has struggled to improve to "mediocre."

Although Howard's poor drawing style did keep *Sally Forth* out of a number of newspapers initially, it was the concept of the script and the writing that sold it, not pretty art. The same might be said of Universal Press's *Cathy*.

Sally puts up with a demanding boss, Ralph, and a husband whom she often gets to help her with "women's work" around the house. Sally is not a wimp, but her ever-so-politically-correct husband is, in the opinion of many male readers. When asked by Sally, who is running late, to iron her blouse for her, Ted raises his arms and shouts, "Yes! 1,000 husbanding points!" When she changes her mind, he whines, "Rats. That would have been enough points to last me a whole month."

Sally and Ted Forth's eight-year-old daughter, Hillary, rounds out this nuclear family. With Hillary the challenges of raising a precocious, upscale child are ever present. She's also expert at dropping lines such as, "I'll ask Dad. It's probably men's work anyway." When Sally jumps to fix her bicycle, Hillary notes to herself and the reader, "A friend of mine taught me that trick for getting fast action."

Because of cartoonist Howard's limited drawing ability the action of *Sally Forth* was until 1991 limited to Sally's office and the kitchen, living room, and bedroom at the Forth's home. At the office, the strip has the same type of corporate culture satire that's a proven success in *Dilbert*. When the new voice mail system is installed, Sally comments, "Nothing that comes with a 78-page manual is going to make my life easier."

In November 1991 *Sally Forth* and Greg Howard experienced the "artwork incident." Recognizing his own limits as an artist and successful enough to hire an assistant, Howard changed the drawing style of the strip. Specifically, he brought in Craig MacIntosh, editorial cartoonist for *The Minneapolis Star* and cocreator with Steve Sack of the kids' comic strip *Professor Doodle's* for Tribune Media Services. MacIntosh was to draw and Howard would write. It proved to be a disaster with *Sally Forth* fans. Suddenly Sally was too thin and curvy. The characters' faces were too angular. The stiffness of Howard's drawings, which readers interpreted as calm, was gone. All hell broke loose. More than 1,000 irate fans called up King Features, and that was just the beginning. Recognizing his mistake,

"Sally Forth," Craig MacIntosh and Greg Howard. © King Features Syndicate.

"Sam's Strip," Jerry Dumas. © King Features Syndicate.

Howard worked with MacIntosh to only slightly modify the original drawing style. However, MacIntosh's skill as an artist has permitted *Sally Forth* to improve as a strip. (With all the publicity the strip picked up 40 new subscribers.)

As *Sally Forth* continues to gain popularity, it's an anomaly that Greg Howard's *Sally Forth* isn't cartooning's first *Sally Forth*. Blonde, buxom, given to wearing little or nothing, Wallace Wood's *Sally Forth* was first published and copyrighted in the late 1960s in the independent civilian-owned *Overseas Weekly* newspaper, sold at military bases in Europe and Asia.

Wood's *Sally Forth* was the antithesis of Howard's. She started as an "R-rated" *MAD* magazine-style parody and ended her career in porno comics that Wood drew shortly prior to committing suicide in 1981.

Wood himself reprinted his *Overseas Weekly Sally* stories between 1976 and 1978. When Field Syndicate launched Greg Howard's *Sally Forth* in 1982, one of Wood's publishers wrote Steve Jehorak, then president of Field to inform him of the double Sallys. He received no response. Naughty *Sally Forth* reprints are still readily available at comic conventions. Her existence, which predates Greg Howard's *Sally Forth*, will remain in cartoon history just one more twist of life for modern working mom Sally to handle with grace, wit, and humor.

B.C.

SAM AND SILO *see* Sam's Strip.

SAM'S STRIP (U.S.) This short-lived burst of brilliance was the comic fan's comic strip. *Sam's Strip* starred Sam (no last name) and his assistant (who never had any name) and a cast of thousands. The supporting players were great comic strip characters of the past.

The genre of the strip was the biggest prop; forms and conventions were discussed matter-of-factly; characters longed for days off; panels became the literal stage as backgrounds would be erased; old-time figures such as Happy Hooligan and Krazy Kat would reminisce about the old days; comic strip character conventions were periodically held.

Mort Walker conceived the idea with Jerry Dumas; both were comic fans since childhood, the former did the lettering, the latter the drawing, and both men cooked up the ideas.

In the context of the forms of the comic strip, *Sam's Strip* was surreal and high camp. Beginning in early October 1961, it died in June of 1963 with 48 papers after peaking at 60 papers and never graduating to a Sunday page.

A collection of *Sam* strips was published privately by Mort Walker in 1968. In 1977 the strip came back in a new incarnation as *Sam and Silo*. Sam and his sidekick (now bestowed the name of Silo) are now the entire constabulary of a small town and find themselves confronted, in a series of mildly humorous gags, with petty crooks and an ornery citizenry, not to mention the feckless town fathers. Turned out by Jerry Dumas, the feature now only appears daily (the Sunday version was discontinued in 1995).

R.M.

SANDMAN (U.S.) *Sandman* was created by artist Bert Christman and writer Gardner Fox and made its first appearance in National's *Adventure* number 40 in July 1939. The original Sandman dressed inconsequentially in superheroic terms. He wore a simple, snap-brimmed hat, a green suit and cloak, a yellow gas mask, and a gas gun. In civilian life, he was playboy Wesley Dodds, and many of the adventures centered around the caprices of his girlfriend, Diane Belmont. Most of the early stories also cast the character as an outcast wanted by the police. His only real method of attacking criminals, however, was his somewhat dubious sleep-inducing ability.

This *Sandman* format didn't last too long, despite the best efforts of artists like Gill Fox and Craig Flessel. So, beginning in December 1949 with *Adventure* number 69, a new Sandman was born. Created by the already well-known team of Jack Kirby and Joe Simon, this Sandman sported a yellow and purple supersuit and cowl. Simon and Kirby even added a young sidekick, Sandy Hawkins. And although he never became a major hero, *Sandman* lasted until *Adventure* number 102 in February 1946. He also made appearances in *World's Finest, All-Star,* and *World's Fair.*

When the superhero boom of the 1960s brought about a general revival, the original *Sandman* was rejuvenated as part of the Justice Society. And although he was never awarded a strip of his own, he was an interesting character in the Justice League/Justice Society format. When Jack Kirby and Joe Simon were again working for National, they created a one-shot entitled *Sandman* number 1. Published in January 1974, but drawn in early 1973, this *Sandman* was still another rendition, resembling neither the Green Hornet-ish Sandman of 1939 or the first Simon and Kirby Sandman.

DC brought back the character in 1989 in a new version scripted by Neil Gaiman, who provided a number of well-crafted story lines and original situations to the title, as well as bringing forth some imaginative supporting characters, such as Death (an angelic-looking young girl). The excellence of the writing attracted many talented artists to *Sandman*, including Sam Kieth, Kelley Jones, Clive Barker, Chales Vess, and Todd McFarlane. It received consistently good notices and even inspired a spin-off, *Sandman Mystery Theatre*, in 1993. Two years later Gaiman decided it was time for him to move on to different things, and he retired from the series.

J.B.

SANDY HIGHFLIER *see* Airship Man, The.

SAN MAO (China) San Mao is a teenage boy known to adults and children in China from 1947 up to today. *San Mao* ("Three Hair") first appeared in Shanghai, where he was living in the streets. The boy is an orphan with a soft heart, always willing to help others in trouble, although his own life is full of misfortune. His good intentions are often rewarded by others, especially the rich. To make a living, San Mao has tried baby-sitting, polishing shoes, apprenticing in a printing shop, and performing in a circus; he has even tried to sell himself. With a bitter humor, readers often shared in San Mao's sufferings in every story: In one strip San Mao was sleeping in a street covered by some newspapers, which caught fire when a cigarette butt was thrown from a car ("The cover caught fire"). In another, San Mao and his friend were hungry and freezing in the streets while a rich-family boy, the same age as San Mao, was eating ice cream, sweating from sitting in an overheated room ("Two worlds"). Hungrily, San Mao ate bark peeled off a tree. He was beaten and chased away by a policeman who was protecting the trees along the street ("Eating tree bark is forbidden").

Usually by means of a four-panel cartoon, San Mao's life was told successively in Shanghai's *Da Gong* newspaper every day in the late 1940s. People, especially children, in Shanghai eagerly waited to see *San Mao*'s next episode of fortune and misfortune. Some children sent money, clothing, and shoes, and often wrote letters to Zhang Leping, the cartoonist who drew *San Mao*, expressing their concern for and desire to help San Mao. This imaginary San Mao was so popular that one family in Shanghai even named their seven children Da Mao ("Big Hair"), Er Mao ("Two Hair"), and so on, until the last child, called Qi Mao ("Seven Hair"). When San Mao suffered from hunger and cold in the strip, these children tried to save food and offer their sweaters to San Mao via the newspaper editorials. When San Mao was beaten by his boss because he broke a glass bottle, Wu Mao ("Five Hair") in this family immediately found a bottle and wanted to "pay it to the boss of San Mao" in order to spare San Mao from being further punished.

The *San Mao Liu Lang Ji* ("San Mao the Homeless") collection has been republished since 1959 with more than 16 million copies sold up to 1990. In another collection, *San Mao Can Jun* ("San Mao Joined the Army"), which was first published in 1947 and repub-

lished in 1990, the cartoonist described the misfortunes of San Mao when he became an underage soldier. In all of the stories, which lasted into the 1950s and 1960s, the title hero never grew older.

Zhang Leping (1910-1992), known as "Father of San Mao," was born in a poor family whose father was a teacher in a village school. As a child Zhang began to draw by first helping his mother who was trying to make extra money to support the family of six by doing tailoring and embroidery. Zhang learned his art from copying and cutting the paper designs. He learned drawing in elementary school, but at 15 he had to quit school and work in various jobs: as an apprentice in a lumber company, in a printing shop of an advertising company, and in a studio making calendars. Some of the stories of *San Mao* were based upon Zhang's own teenage life. After the People's Republic of China was founded Zhang continued to create children's cartoons, and most of them were carried on the children's pictorial series *Xiao Peng You* ("Little Friends") since 1956. All of them emphasized teaching children good behavior and helping needy people, of which a collection of 72 cartoons created in the 1950s and 1960s was published by the Children Publishing House, entitled *Wo Men de Gu Shi* ("Our Stories") in 1990.

One of Zhang's storytelling characteristics was that most cartoons were told by drawings without words except a title, which made them easier to be understood by almost everyone, especially young children. *San Mao* has been popular through generations not only in mainland China but also in Taiwan. A well-known woman writer in Taiwan named Chen Ping wrote a letter in August 1988 to Zhang in Shanghai. She stated that she read *San Mao* when she was three years old. Because she liked it so much, she used "San Mao" as her pen name when she became a famous writer. In 1989, she came to mainland China and handed to Zhang the *San Mao the Homeless* book reprinted in Taiwan. Since then she called Zhang "father" (until she committed suicide in Taiwan in the early 1990s).

H.Y.L.L.

SANTOS, JESSE F. (1928-   ) As far back as he can remember Jesse Santos has always been drawing. When he was 10 years old, the Filipino cartoonist, born June 24, 1928, in Teresa, Rizal, did a mural that was placed in front of the town church. At the age of 15 he embarked in the field of professional art. He did portraits of American GIs and Japanese soldiers who occupied his hometown. Filipino guerilla fighters also sought out his services to draw and embellish *antingan-tings* (talismans) on their clothing.

While working as a sidewalk portrait artist he was discovered by Tony Velasquez, the well-known cartoonist. In 1946 Santos illustrated his first comic book feature, *Kidlat* ("Lightning"), for *Halaklak*, the first comic book to be published in the Philippines. When Pilipino Komiks appeared on the scene Santos teamed up with Damy Velasquez to do *DI 13*, which became the most famous detective strip ever to appear in the country. This series continued until the 1960s when Santos left for greener pastures. The strip was so popular that offshoots appeared, such as *DI Jr*, which Santos also illustrated. The best cartoonist in the country, Larry Alcala, did a series called *13½*, which was a spoof on *DI 13* and on Santos. *DI 13* was also made into a movie.

Santos attended the University of Santo Tomas but quit when his services as an artist became more in demand. He was the chief artist for *Paraluman* magazine, staff contributor for Gold Star publishing company, and a permanent staff contributor for *Liwayway*, *Ace Publications*, *Graphic Arts Inc.*, and *G. Miranda & Sons Publishing Co.*

Despite a hectic schedule doing magazine and book illustrations, covers, movie ads, and portraits, he somehow found time to collaborate with Mars Ravelo, Pablo Gomez, Greg Igna De Dios, Mauro Cabuhat, and Larry Tuazon to produce many comic book serials such as *Inspirasiyon* ("Inspiration"), *Boksingera* ("The Girl Boxer"), *Dambanang Putik* ("Altar of Mud"), *ROTC*, *Paula*, *Tomador*, and *Dar Aguila*.

For many years Santos served as a member of the board of the Society of Philippine Illustrators and Cartoonists (SPIC) and was elected vice president several times. In 1965 he won a SPIC award for his published works. He is also a member of the National Press Club of the Philippines.

Santos came to the United States in 1969. In 1970 he started to work for Western Publications doing the book illustrations for *Davy Crockett*. Currently he has been doing the art chores for Gold Key's *Brother of the Spears*, *Dagar*, *Dr. Spektor*, and *Tragg*. He also worked for *Mystery Digest* and *Red Circle Comics*.

He has contributed artwork for literary publications such as *Kapatid* and the Pilipino-American anthology *Liwanag* ("Light"). His paintings have been exhibited by the Society of Western Artists, and he has won the best of show award. His fine art paintings have been exhibited at international art shows, galleries, universities, museums, and in private collections. He is a senior advisor of the Philippine Comic Archives and a member of the Philippine Science-Fantasy Society. In the 1980s he worked on *Mystery Digest*, a pocket-size anthology of weird tales; he has devoted his efforts of late to painting murals and drawing record covers.

Santos's works in the comics have a lifelike quality to them. This is due to his many years experience in the portraiture field. He excels in utilizing cartoon techniques such as exaggerations and distortions and in using them effectively in a realistic manner.

O.J.

SANTOS, MALANG (1928-) A Filipino cartoonist and painter born in Manila on January 20, 1928, Malang, as he is most widely known, joined the *Manila Chronicle* as a staff artist in 1947. He created a captionless character called Kosme the Cop, which the *Chronicle* carried daily. His was the first and only local strip to appear along with the well-known American strips. At an early point in his career, Malang was sued by the Manila police department for one of his prizewinning cartoons satirizing the practice of bribery among the members of Manila's finest. After several months Malang retired Kosme from the force and the strip has been known since then as *Kosme the Cop (Retired)*. Malang also created a cartoon character, Chain Gang Charlie, and a third one, Belzeebub, was featured in *Pageant* magazine. However, it is Kosme the Cop (Retired), the henpecked husband with an endless stock of ways-out, with which Malang is most associated.

Malang also became very popular for his ads depicting barrio scenes, which he did for a well-known cola drink. Soon there was a great demand for his illustra-

tions by the advertising agencies in the country. Using tempera, a medium he has mastered as a commercial artist, as well as colored ink, his paintings are owned by the former First Lady of the Philippines and by prominent publishers in the United States. He has been commissioned to do murals as well.

From a lowly cartoonist in 1947 to one of the highest paid painters in the country, Malang's success has encouraged other artists similarly employed (working in newspapers or ad agencies) to raise their art to a serious plateau.

M.A.

SAPPO (U.S.) E. C. Segar's fourth comic strip, the satiric science-fantasy work called *Sappo*, began as a daily strip named *The Five-Fifteen* in Hearst's *New York American* on December 24, 1920. Initially, the six small panels of each episode told a simple daily gag about a resident of suburban Despaire named John Sappo, emphasizing his tribulations in riding the 5:15 a.m. Funkville-City train to his office job, and occasionally involving his wife, Myrtle. By February 24, 1923, when the strip's name was changed to *Sappo the Commuter* in the *American*, and simply to *Sappo*, in other Hearst papers, long continuity had become a mainstay, with a story about Sappo's twin brother, Jim, being the most amusing of this period.

The Sunday *Sappo* began on February 28, 1926, about a year after the daily strip had folded on February 17, 1925. The revived *Sappo* returned to the early gag format for a time, then resumed continuity on March 18, 1928, with Sappo and Myrtle taking up oil painting in bitter rivalry. Once Segar got his narrative gears in action, *Sappo* became hilariously gripping, and before long Segar had introduced a series of ingenious and hugely comic devices invented by Sappo.

These inventions became the keynote of *Sappo* from 1930 on. And after May 8, 1932, when the arrival of Professor O. G. Wottasnoozle added the strip's greatest character to its limited cast (the Professor taking up residence with the Sappos), no limits of any kind were set on the imaginative range of the *Sappo* narrative; and Segar's dauntless characters traveled more than once to the outermost reaches of the solar system, probed the recesses of the most minute particles, and casually but satirically toyed with invisibility, robotics, hypnosis, and hyperpilosity.

Sappo reached its imaginative peak between the enlargement of the strip to its final, full size of three rows of panels on August 16, 1931, and its close with Segar's death on September 18, 1938. (Its continuation by inferior hands, such as those of Bela Zaboly and Bud Sagendorf, is hardly worthy of comment.) Surprisingly little has been reprinted since the strip appeared as one small book, *Sappo*, in 1935, and ran for a time in the reprint magazine, *King Comics*, in the 1930s. One of the most continually amusing and absorbing comic strips ever created, *Sappo* needs to be reprinted in full for the fresh appreciation of a new generation of readers.

B.B.

SASUKE (Japan) Created by Sanpei Shirato, *Sasuke* made its first appearance in the September 1961 issue of the monthly *Shōnen*. Sasuke was a boy-*ninja* (a peculiar caste of Japanese warriors, almost raised to superhuman status through the mastery of their secret art called *ninjutsu*), the son of the great ninja, Ōzaru. The strip detailed the process of Sasuke's growing up under

"Sasuke," Sanpei Shirato. © Shōnen.

the guidance of his father, who intended that his son become a great ninja. Sasuke mastered the ninjutsu but also learned many other things as well, such as the importance of life and the severity of the ninja code.

Going out into the world Sasuke met with a host of troubles and had to fight many enemies: some were rival ninjas such as Hanzō Hattori, the chieftain of the ninja warriors of the Tokugawa shogunate, and his daughter, who was responsible for the murder of Sasuke's mother. Others were swordsmen and brigands trying to thwart Sasuke's progress. When the hero was in a tight situation, he was indirectly helped by his father, but his feats of arms were his own. Part one of this long saga ended with the death of Sasuke's father, Ōzaru, along with Ōzaru's new wife and daughter, in an ambush set by Hattori.

Part two spelled more trouble for Sasuke and his baby brother, Kozaru. Fights, intrigues, and treachery abounded, with Sasuke getting out of every trap set for him. Kozaru, however, was not so lucky: he was killed in a riot. The strip ended with Sasuke roaming the fields in a mad search for his brother's body.

Gōseki Kojima assisted Shirato on some parts of *Sasuke*, which ended in March 1966. The strip has inspired a series of animated cartoons, and in 1968 the weekly *Shōnen* Sunday started reprinting the old episodes of *Sasuke* in their entirety.

H.K.

SATONAKA, MACHIKO (1947-   ) Born January 24, 1947, in Osaka, Machiko Satonaka knew by the seventh grade that she wanted be a manga artist. She wasted no time in fulfilling that dream. By age 16, whe made her debut with *Pia no Shōzo* ("A Portrait of Pia"), for which she was awarded the Kodansha prize for new artists. A year later she dropped out of high school, moved to Tokyo, and launched a professional career that made her, by age 30, one of the most popular and best comics creators for young girls and women.

Satonaka's stories concentrate on romance and melodrama, although she has dabbled in other genres. She explained, "I wanted to do everything, children's kindergarten, romance, crime stories for high school students, female adult, historical, and classical themes." Many of her works take novel twists, incorporating social commentary themes such as the Nazi persecution of Jews, the Vietnam War, and racial discrimination. In *Watashi no Joni* ("My Johnny"), published in 1968, she portrayed love in a southern U.S. town between a white woman and a black man.

The amount of work Satonaka puts out is prodigious. While still "young and healthy" she did eight titles simultaneously, a number of which were major works stretching to more than a thousand pages each. Since the 1980s she has been doing two series monthly for *Kodansha* and one monthly for *Shogakan*, a total of 150 pages. Some of her series, averaging 40 to 60 pages each, have lasted for a year, one for more than a decade.

Among her early titles were *Lady Ann* (1969), *Manayome Sensei* ("Teacher Bride," 1971), *Ashta Kagayaku* ("Shining Tomorrow," 1972), and *Hime Ga Yuka* ("Hime Goes Forth," 1973). The latter two won her the 1974 Kodansha Shuppan Bunka award (children). In recent years, Satonaka has catered primarily to young male readers with *Pandora*, *Akiko*, and *Atom's Daughter*, all of which provide advice on how to deal with women.

Besides setting high standards for *shōjo* (comics for young girls) and lending skilled draftmanship to all her works, Satonaka has been the spearhead behind movements to protect and advance manga generally. She has organized campaigns to block manga censorship, to exchange cartoonists internationally for the enhancement of global understanding, and to protest against Disney for lifting parts of Osamu Tezuka's *The Jungle Emperor* in the making of *Lion King*.

J.A.L.

SATURNO CONTRO LA TERRA (Italy) In 1934 American adventure strips started appearing in the more popular Italian comic weeklies, such as *L'Audace* and *L'Avventuroso*: among them *Flash Gordon* became the most successful feature of the genre. Several Italian publishers then sought to emulate *Flash*'s formula; among the more successful attempts was *Saturno Contro la Terra* ("Saturn Against the Earth") conceived by Cesare Zavattini (later Federico Fellini's most constant

"Saturno Contro la Terra," Giovanni Scolari. © Mondadori.

screenwriter) and written by Federico Pedrocchi. On December 31, 1937, the strip appeared in the pages of *I Tre Porcellini*, and then moved to the more widely circulated *Topolino*, where it remained until 1943 and where it was revived from 1945 to 1946.

The artwork of *Saturno* was entrusted to Giovanni Scolari, who was a master of background and technical details: his weapons and machines were especially well-rendered. Scolari's line, however, left something to be desired, and while *Saturno* tried to emulate *Flash Gordon* in spirit, it came closer to *Buck Rogers* in realization. This long saga told of the adventures of Rebo, the terrible chief of the Saturnians, and of his burning dream to conquer earth and the whole solar system. Rebo was opposed by the 80-year-old Italian inventor, Marcus, and his youthful son-in-law, Ciro, in the classical combination of brain and brawn. The strip was complete with old-time unabashed nationalism: for instance, the meeting of all the powers of earth took place in the Po valley. Aside from political restrictions, however, *Saturno* displayed a good deal of character and suspense, and it gave a few novel twists to the hackneyed plot.

One of the most highly entertaining of the science-fiction strips, *Saturno Contro la Terra* has been widely translated abroad: in the United States it appeared (with color added) in the ephemeral Future Comics of the 1940s. Several episodes of *Saturno Contro la Terra* were also reprinted by Milano Libri in 1969.

G.B.

SAUNDERS, ALLEN (1899-1986) An American comic strip writer born in Indiana on March 24, 1899, Allen Saunders learned to draw by taking the Landon correspondence course and attending classes at the Chicago Academy of Fine Arts. He graduated from Wabash College in 1920 and taught French there for the next seven years. At the same time he freelanced as both a cartoonist for humor publications and a detective story writer for pulp magazines. He even acted in stock for one season.

In 1927 Saunders quit teaching and joined the *Toledo News-Bee* as a reporter and cartoonist. He became its drama critic a few years later. In 1936, in collaboration with Elmer Woggon for the drawing, Saunders produced a comic strip about a hard-blowing medicine man, *The Great Gusto* (later changed to *Big Chief Wahoo*, later still to *Steve Roper*) for Publishers Syndicate. At about the same time Saunders also created a humor panel, *Miserable Moments*, which he both wrote and drew, but this attempt was short-lived.

In 1940, when Martha Orr announced her decision to quit *Apple Mary*, which she had created in 1932, the syndicate called upon Saunders to take up the continuity while female cartoonist Dale Connor assumed the drawing. (The strip, retitled *Mary Worth's Family*, was signed Dale Allen until 1942 when Ken Ernst took over the drawing and the strip's name was further shortened to *Mary Worth*). A third strip bearing Allen Saunders' byline appeared in 1968, *Dateline: Danger*, an adventure strip drawn by Al McWilliams. In addition to being a writer, Saunders is also editor at Publishers-Hall Syndicate. He served as chairman of the Newspaper Comics Council in 1958. Saunders stopped writing for comics in 1979, when he officially retired, but he kept an eye on his features, now being scripted by his son John. He also wrote his memoirs (published only in excerpts in fan magazines) and continued to participate

in various promotional activities. He died in Maumee, Ohio, on January 28, 1986.

Next to Lee Falk, Allen Saunders is probably the best-known as well as the most dramatically gifted of comic strip writers. His scripts are sophisticated and his dialogues literate without being stuffy.

M.H.

SAZAE-SAN (Japan) *Sazae-san* was created by female cartoonist Machiko Hasegawa. Machiko Hasegawa conceived the characters of the strip while she was vacationing at the seaside resort of Momoji: she then gave all the characters names related to the sea. Thus there was Sazae herself (*Sazae* means "propeller"); her father, Namihei ("wave"); her mother, Fune ("boat"); her younger brother, Katsuo ("bonito fish"); and her younger sister, Wakame ("seaweed"). The family name was Isono ("beach"), and thus Namihei Isono meant waves rolling on the beach. Hasegawa carried this idea further by having Sazae marry Masuo Fugata ("trout") by whom she had a son, Tarao ("codfish").

Sazae-san first appeared in May 1946 in the Fukunichi evening newspaper. Toward the end of 1949 it transferred to the Asahi evening paper. *Sazae-san* was the top newspaper strip of the postwar years and a perfect example of the kind of domestic strip pioneered by *Blondie* in the United States. Sazae-san was a cheerful, simple, carefree housewife, married to a working man of limited means. The Fugatas lived with Sazae's parents and had only mild adventures. In the beginning Sazae was tall and graceful, but after her marriage she became smaller and dumpy.

Sazae-san was one of the longest-running newspaper strips in Japan; it was discontinued in 1975 but was revived the next year and lasted up to the time of Hasegawa's death in 1992. Sazae herself was the most famous strip character for young and old alike. The feature was reprinted in book form a number of times (it was a million-seller), and has inspired a television series, a series of animated cartoons, as well as a stage play.

H.K.

SCARTH (G.B.) Readers of the renovated *Sun*, a new tabloid version of the former companion newspaper to the *Daily Mirror* under the control of Australian magnate, Rupert Murdoch, saw a near-naked blonde passing out in the path of a speeding auto. This was their first glimpse of Scarth, a cross between Jane and Garth:

"Scarth," Luis Roca. © The Sun.

a science-fiction stripper! They would see more of her in the future: she became the first full frontal nude female in British newspaper strips.

Scarth not only lost her flimsy G-string, she also lost her long tresses. A brain transplant, which revived her from her death on the superway, also gave her the cute crewcut that remained her trademark for the rest of her life. Set 200 years in the future, the first episode appeared on November 17, 1969; the last exactly three years later. She was finally killed, not by another accident, but by an incoming newspaper executive who disliked the permissive tone of the strip. It had introduced a hermaphrodite, Rudolf Quince, a bearded lady married to an army captain. Despite its demise, the strip continues in world syndication, although it has lost its subtitle: *Scarth A.D.2170*.

Scarth was created by Les Lilley, a scriptwriter whose work includes *Better or Worse*, which was later retitled *Jack and Jill*, and then *Bonnie*. The artist was Luis Roca, a resident of Barcelona whose decorative art had previously graced many romantic comic books for girls. Roca is no longer working in newspaper strips, but Lilley is currently scripting other strips.

D.G.

SCHAFFENBERGER, KURT (1920-   ) Kurt Schaffenberger is an American comic book artist born in Germany on December 15, 1920. His family moved to America in 1927, and Schaffenberger eventually attended the Pratt Institute in Brooklyn, New York. Joining the Jack Binder shop in 1942, he produced strips for many publishers, including work on *Captain Marvel, Bulletman, Fighting Yank, Captain America*, and many others. He was inducted into the army in 1943, and, on his return to comic books in 1945, produced material on a freelance basis for Fawcett, publishers of the Marvel Family.

Although C. C. Beck was the recognized star and chief artist on the Marvel Family, Schaffenberger's work also gained considerable respect. While Beck championed the more cartoony illustrations, Schaffenberger's work was heavily influenced by Alex Raymond and Hal Foster and always leaned to realism and straight adventure.

When Fawcett discontinued their comic book line in 1953, Schaffenberger did work for Timely and others before drifting into commercial artwork. He returned as the artist for National's newly created *Lois Lane* feature in 1958; his 11-year stint and his clean, uncluttered renditions made him the feature's definitive artist. While he was producing material for *Lois Lane*, he also created a horde of commercial comic strips for Custom Comics, and under the pen name of "Lou Wahl," invented the *Nemesis* and *Magic Man* features for ACG comic.

When National revived the Marvel Family in 1972, Schaffenberger was slated for only spot duty but took over the bulk of the work when C. C. Beck resigned over a jurisdictional dispute. From that time on he worked on virtually every DC title until the early 1990s. He now occasionally draws comics for advertising.

J.B.

SCHEUER, CHRIS (1952-   ) An Austrian comic artist born in 1952 in Graz, Chris Scheuer stems from an artistically inclined family. With one grandmother a sculptor, the other one a jazz pianist, one grandfather

a sculptor, and his father a restorer of paintings, it seems only natural that Chris Scheuer should become interested in art. He discovered comics in the 1970s and liked their way of telling stories in a combination of words and pictures.

He popped into view as a comic artist in 1982 when a first collection of comic short stories was published in Austria; some of his stories were published in *Schwermetall*, the German version of *Heavy Metal*. He teamed up with the late Markus Tschernegg, computer specialist, comic fan extraordinaire, and writer, for a comic feature that was published in *Comic Forum*, the Austrian comics fanzine and center for a line of comic publications. But their plan for a comic album to be published in Germany did not work out. Instead, Scheuer's first comic album, *Sheshiva*, was published in 1983 in Austria. Scheuer's career went ahead at dizzying speed with the 1984 Max und Moritz Award at the Erlangen Comics Salon as best German-language artist.

While this award did not entice German publishers to dare produce an album by Scheuer right away, he was asked by Dargaud to work for *Charlie Mensuel*, and later on for *Pilote* and *Charlie*. The first story he did for them with a scenario by French writer Rodolphe was *Marie Jade*. Scheuer then moved to Hamburg for four years to cooperate with writer Wolfgang Mendl on an album for Carlsen Verlag, *Sir Ballantime* (1990), and to create a large number of comics and illustrations for advertising. While in Hamburg, Scheuer also worked out storyboards for television ads, drew posters and magazine advertisements, and worked under contract to create posters for the Hamburg Opera. For some time Scheuer collaborated with Matthias Schultheiss and colored René Lehner's *Bill Body* strips. Scheuer has a very distinctive style with very distinctive, well-endowed girls. They pop up in various European countries, including his native Austria to which he has since returned to continue producing comics, paintings, and portfolios of his work.

W.F.

SCHMIDT, MANFRED (1913-   ) German cartoonist, journalist, and writer born in Bad Harzburg on April 15, 1913, Schmidt grew up in Bremen where he also went to school. While most of his high school teachers praised the joy and beauty of fighting and dying for home and fatherland, an art teacher who had returned from the battlefields of World War I, a convinced pacifist, opened his class's eyes with his description of the sordid mess that war inevitably is. Thus Schmidt no longer put heroic images on paper and started cartooning. At the age of 14 the newspaper *Bremer Nachrichten* published the first cartoon he had sent in.

After his final exams he had to choose between the careers of art teacher, musician, pastor, dentist, or movie director. He decided to go into the motion picture business. Starting from the bottom, he had to lug around the heavy gear at minimal wages, so he returned to drawing. However, he had to forget about his career for four years of fighting in World War II. He lived through several retreats at various fronts. While the troops retreated from Russia he drew cartoons for *Panzer Voran!* ("Forward, Tanks!"), a soldiers' newspaper that kept its title during a retreat of over one thousand miles.

Returning to civilian life and cartooning, Schmidt got hold of a *Superman* comic book and immensely dis-

Chris Scheuer, a page from an adventure graphic novel. © Chris Scheuer.

liked it. He decided to do a satire of the superhero by creating Nick Knatterton, a cross between *Superman*, *Dick Tracy*, and *Sherlock Holmes*. In the autumn of 1950 the first episode of *Nick Knatterton* appeared in the German weekly illustrated paper *Quick*. It met with unprecedented success. Schmidt's simplistic, yet effective style is one of many individual styles that could be termed to be in the German tradition of cartooning.

After killing off the *Knatterton* strip, Schmidt wrote a great many articles and humorous books, aptly illustrated with cartoons. He also wrote and produced

several travel features and animated cartoon advertisements for television.

With his animation studio Schmidt was himself "forced" into producing *Nick Knatterton* as an animated cartoon program that first ran as a continued feature to loosen up advertising time blocks for *Westdeutscher Rundfunk*. The feature was picked up by other stations, with some splicing them together and broadcasting them as complete stories. These cartoons are now also available on videocassette. As Schmidt produced the films himself, they are true to the original comic strip

"Les Schtroumpfs," Peyo (Pierre Culliford). © Éditions Dupuis.

spoof in contents and in artwork. The narration is supplied by Schmidt himself, giving the films an additional sarcastic note.

Despite Schmidt's aversion to regular comics he was lured into hosting a 13-episode half-hour program about the history and the genres of comics scripted by Wolfgang J. Fuchs and Reinhold Reitberger in 1976. While he strayed from the scripts to inject some of his criticism of comics in the narration, sometimes in an ironically entertaining way, the series nevertheless managed to be quite informative and presented original animation of some comic strips that up to then had not had their own television show.

W.F.

SCHTROUMPFS, LES (Belgium) Peyo's *Les Schtroumpfs* evolved as a spin-off from his earlier comic strip creation, *Johan et Pirlouit*. In 1957 Johan and his companion Pirlouit came upon the fabulous country of the Schtroumpf little people who were so friendly and endearing that they soon received a strip of their own in the pages of the weekly magazine *Spirou* (1960).

The Schtroumpfs are a race of gentle, civilized, and utterly charming elves whose ingenuity triumphs over all the mishaps that often befall their sleepy village. Identical in appearance and costume, but each with his own personality, the Schtroumpfs form a microcosm of society under the wise and enlightened guidance of the Grand Schtroumpf. The strip is drenched in a poetic atmosphere directly derived from European folklore, and its landscapes are often reminiscent of *Little Nemo*'s fairy-tale settings. Peyo's style, subdued and simple as are his stories, is never too cute and mannered, despite the temptations of the genre.

Peyo (Pierre Culliford) has been throwing his little people into the most diversified adventures, inventing for them menaces and enemies of all kinds, whether external like the brigands who try from time to time to steal their treasure, or internal like the would-be dictator who once sprang from their midst and declared himself *schtroumpfissimo*. All of these mishaps have a happy ending, and the Schtroumpfs go back to their happy-go-lucky life of singing and dancing.

Les Schtroumpfs' happy mixture of fantasy and adventure, delightful drawing and clever narrative have made the strip into a favorite of European readers (in

recent years Peyo has left more and more of the writing to Yvan Delporte, who has managed to maintain the strip's unique poetry and appeal). *Les Schtroumpfs* has gone through numerous reprints in both hardcover and paperback form; they have been made into toys and used for advertising. In the 1960s there was a series of nine *Schtroumpfs* animated cartoons produced by Eddy Rissack and Maurice Rosy with more than a passing assist by Peyo.

In the United States the Hanna-Barbera studios brought the *Smurfs* (as the little blue elves are known here) to NBC-TV in 1981. In parallel with the weekly show, which ran until 1990, there were a number of specials and one theatrical feature. After Peyo's death in 1992, his son, Thierry Culliford, took over the characters.

M.H.

SCHUITEN, FRANÇOIS (1956-   ) Belgian cartoonist born in Brussels on April 13, 1956, François Schuiten, the son of architect parents, had his first comic strip story published in *Pilote* at age 17. While studying art at the Institut St. Luc in Brussels, he contributed to the art magazine published by the school. In 1977 he decided on a career as a freelance artist, and his work (sometimes done in collaboration with his brother, Luc) started appearing in the major French and Belgian comics magazines of the time.

His break came in 1980 when *Aux Médianes de Cymbiola* ("At the Medians of Cymbiola"), a tale of mysticism and initiation entirely rendered in pencils, saw print in the pages of the comics magazine *Métal Hurlant*. After a brief stint as art director on Just Jaeckin's 1983 movie *Gwendoline*, he finally realized a long-deferred project when, again in collaboration with his brother, he published *La Terre Creuse* ("The Hollow Earth," 1984), a complex story mixing elements of science fiction with sociological musings.

In the meantime he had begun the work he is best noted for, the cycle he calls *Les Cités Obscures* (meaning both "dark" and "obscure") on scripts by Benoit Peeters. Started in 1983 with *Les Murailles de Samaris* ("The Walls of Samaris"), this monumental saga has unfolded to date over three more titles: *La Fièvre d'Urbicande* ("Fever at Urbicande," 1985), *La Tour* ("The Tower," 1987), and *Brusel* (1992). In all of the titles the characters are dwarfed by the futuristic, tentacular, recondite cities which, perhaps reflecting the artist's parental heritage, are the real protagonists of the tales. Schuiten has also written and illustrated a string of more conventional prose stories related to the cycle.

In addition to his work on the "Cities" cycle, Schuiten is also the author of a number of unrelated comics stories, sometimes on texts by others. He has also realized sculptures, serigraphs, and lithographs, and has overseen the decoration of the Luxembourg Pavilion at the 1992 World Exposition in Seville. He is only in his early forties and even more should be heard from him.

M.H.

SCHULTHEISS, MATTHIAS (1946-   ) One of the new breed of German comic artists, Schultheiss was born July 27, 1946, in Nuremberg but grew up in Hamburg. He spent four years at a country boarding school in Franconia; the first action of the new principal was to confiscate Schultheiss's cornet. After high school and a stint in the army he was taken into the High School for Graphic Design and allowed to skip the first four semesters because of above-average talent. His hopes to get the artistic education he craved was not fully realized at this school, so he went on to educate himself by copying comic strips like *Rip Kirby*. He left school after only three semesters in 1969 with the grudging admission that he had enough knowhow to make it professionally—which he did. For

Matthias Schultheiss, "Trucker," © Matthias Schultheiss.

about ten years he worked in advertising as a freelance artist.

During this time he worked on his storytelling technique and developed comic strips of his own, which he offered to Bull's Pressedienst, the German affiliate of King Features Syndicate. A series about the St. Pauli district of Hamburg did not meet with much interest, but Bull's picked up his strip about a trucker done in a style that perfectly copied the style of the British *Modesty Blaise* strip. However, the series was never sold to a newspaper. In 1977 he was asked to do comics about historic events. Once again, the finished product did not see print.

Schultheiss's interest in comics did not diminish. He decided to try his truck driver story once again and offered the series to *Zack* magazine. The publishers picked up an option on the series, but for publication in color, everything had to be redone completely with fewer black areas. Hence he prepared *Trucker*, the story of a truck driver going the length and breadth of the United States and getting into all kinds of adventures. To do so he gave up his advertising work to devote himself entirely to comics. Then he was informed that the editors felt his material was not aimed at a general mass market, and his comic story was axed.

Trucker was published in 1981 in *Comic Reader*, a book printing work by German comic artists not published by regular comic publishers. Schultheiss had the last laugh, as *Zack* magazine folded soon after. Schultheiss for a time worked shifts as a loader at the airport to forget about the frustrations of trying to do comics in Germany. But finally, due to his interest in literature and his penchant for exceptional stories, he got permission to adapt several stories of Charles Bukowski into comic album format. These met with critical acclaim although they were not published by a comic book publisher but by a "normal" publishing house. The German market was still slow in giving him more comic work.

In the mid-1990s Schultheiss had some of his own comic short stories published in *Special USA* and in *L'Echo des Savanes* in France. The most interesting comic novels produced by Schultheiss since then are *Le Théorème de Bell* ("The Truth about Shelby") and *Le rêve du requin* ("The Sharks of Lagos"). They were highly dramatic and graphically satisfying comic novels. When they turned out to be a success in France as well as in the United States they were picked up for publication in Germany.

Schultheiss is the epitome of the saying that the prophet isn't thought to be worth anything at home. For while his comic debut was published in Germany and his literary adaptations were well received, there simply wasn't anyone daring enough to want to risk publishing comics by a German artist at first. Only when Schultheiss's qualities had been recognized by French publishers was he reimported for publication at home. When these books proved successful on the German market, he was finally asked to do comic albums that were to premiere in Germany. Still, Schultheiss was not completely happy with German comic publishers and left for the United States in 1993, having conceived comic projects for publication in America and in Japan.

W.F.

SCHULTZE, CARL EDWARD (1866-1939) Carl Edward Schultze, creator of the widely popular turn-of-the-century strip, *Foxy Grandpa*, was born in Lexington, Kentucky, on May 25, 1866, into a lower-middle-class German immigrant family. As the family prospered, Schultze was sent from Kentucky to study in German schools during his teens, where he perfected his simple but fetching comic style sufficiently to obtain a job on the *Chicago News* at $16 a week in the late 1880s. Among his colleagues of the time were such later famed figures as R. F. Outcault and George Barr McCutcheon. After a number of years doing general newspaper art and cartoon work, Schultze moved to the *New York Herald*, where in the early heyday of comic strips he was asked to develop a strip, and introduced his initial concept of a shrewd old man who turns the tables on the Katzenjammer-type pair of kids who plague him. Schultze just called the old man Grandpa, but an assistant editor of the *Herald*, William J. Guard (later press agent for the Metropolitan Opera), said he was foxy, and suggested the full name for the strip, which Schultze used. Introduced as the leading strip in the Sunday *Herald* comic section for January 7, 1900, *Foxy Grandpa* was an almost immediate hit with the paper's readers.

Like other popular comic strip artists of that period, Schultze was hired away from the *Herald* by William Randolph Hearst for his *New York American* and *Journal* combine. In the powerful Hearst Sunday array, however, the mild and repetitive Schultze strip did not shine notably, and Schultze, although well-paid and a notable New York figure with a Park Avenue home and a string of saddle horses for most of the first two decades of the century, was dropped by Hearst and moved at a lower income to the *New York Press*, where *Foxy Grandpa* was folded as a regular comic strip in 1918.

Trying other approaches, Schultze fielded a nature story series in prose, with a daily one-panel drawing accompanying the text (usually featuring *Foxy Grandpa* and a bunny enlarged from Schultze's bunny signature trademark of the *Foxy Grandpa* strip with a variety of animals), to newspapers in the 1920s, but this did not do noticeably well, and was folded in a few years. After this, Schultze, plagued with debts and personal problems accentuated by the death of his wife of many years, dropped from sight, to reappear in January 1935

Carl Schultze, "Foxy Grandpa."

at the offices of the Association for Improving the Condition of the Poor (AICP), in New York. This organization, responding to his desperate appeal for help, got him a WPA position working on a government reading-materials project at $95 a month. Here he illustrated school books, one of the most popular of which was titled *Julia and the Bear*.

Now an aging man, Schultze lived in a $4 a week room at 251 West 20th Street in New York, popular with neighborhood kids for whom he would draw pictures of Foxy Grandpa and his other characters and other nearby inhabitants, but apparently forgotten by the newspaper publishing world and his old cartoonist conferees. Here he died of a heart attack near the door of his room on January 18, 1939. He was buried in Ward Manor Cemetery, in Dutchess County, near New York City, through the aid of one of his West 20th Street neighbors and the AICP.

B.B.

SCHULZ, CHARLES MONROE (1922-   ) An American cartoonist born November 26, 1922, in Minneapolis, Minnesota, Charles Sparky Schulz graduated from a St. Paul high school and took art lessons from a correspondence course offered by Art Instruction, Inc., of Minneapolis. He was drafted in 1943, served in France and Germany, and was discharged in 1945 as staff sergeant.

After the service, Schulz returned to St. Paul, where he got a job lettering cartoons for a religious publication. Later he became an instructor at Art Instruction where he met his first wife, Joyce Halverson. At the same time he freelanced and had his cartoons published in the *St. Paul Pioneer Press* and the *Saturday Evening Post*. In 1950 he started making the rounds of newspaper syndicates with a child feature tentatively called *Li'l Folks*. After a number of rejections, the strip was finally accepted by United Feature Syndicate, and made its debut on October 2, 1950, under the new title of *Peanuts*. The rest is comic strip history: unnoticed at first, *Peanuts* was to become the most successful comic feature of all times. For the material of his strip, Charles Schulz has been drawing on childhood memories (Charlie Brown, the leading figure in *Peanuts*, has a barber for a father, just like Charles Schulz), and from his raising of five children. Schulz has made many disclaimers about the philosophical content of the strip, such as stating that his chief purpose is to "get the strip done in time to get down to the post office at five o'clock when it closes"; yet he was to comment on another occasion: "It has always seemed to me that the strip has a rather bitter feeling to it, and it certainly deals in defeat." It is clear that the ambivalence in the man is reflected in the curious ambivalence of the strip, which makes *Peanuts* one of the most fascinating creations in American comic literature.

Charles Schulz is also the coauthor (with Kenneth F. Hall) of a child study, (*Two-by-Fours: A Sort of Serious Book About Small Children* (Warner, 1965); and he has illustrated a few books by others (notably Art Linkletter's *Kids Say the Darndest Things*), but most of his career has been devoted to the *Peanuts* strip (on which he does everything himself, including the lettering) and to *Peanuts*-related material. His personal life (except for his divorce and remarriage in 1973 to a woman much younger than himself) has been uncommonly stable. Charles Schulz has received the Reuben award twice, in 1955 and 1964, the Peabody and Emmy awards in 1966, and many other distinctions too numerous to mention. A documentary on Charles Schulz was produced for CBS-TV and broadcast in 1969. He was made a Knight of Arts and Letters by the French government in 1990.

M.H.

SCHWARTZ, JULIUS (1915-   ) American comic book editor born June 19, 1915, in the Bronx, New York, Schwartz was a science-fiction fanatic. He and Mort Weisinger founded *The Time Traveller* (1932), the first generally distributed science-fiction fanzine. Later, the duo founded the Solar Sales Service, in which they served as agents for the work of such science-fiction writers as Ray Bradbury, Robert Bloch, Edmond Hamilton, Alfred Bester, Otto Binder, and H. P. Lovecraft to pulp magazines.

When the pulp field collapsed, Bester introduced Schwartz to National and he began editing comic book stories in 1944, and was later instrumental in introducing many science-fiction writers to the comic book market. During this time, Schwartz was editing stories in many titles, including *Sensation, All-Star, Flash,* and *Green Lantern*. In the 1950s, Schwartz's major work came on two science-fiction titles, *Mystery in Space* and *Strange Adventures*. There he helped writers like Gardner Fox, Binder, Hamilton, and John Broome produce some of the finest science-fiction tales in comic books. Sy Barry and Carmine Infantino were his top artists. Infantino, Murphy Anderson, and Fox teamed up with Schwartz to produce *Adam Strange* in *Mystery in Space*, perhaps the best sci-fi hero strip ever to appear in comic books.

In 1956 it was Schwartz and his writers and artists who revived the superhero concept by revamping the defunct *Flash* feature for *Showcase*; they later helped launch what is commonly known as The Second Heroic Age, and it was under Schwartz's guidance that Fox wrote the landmark "Flash of Two Worlds" story, which lead to the revival of many 1940s superheroes. The flagging sales of two of National's mainstay books, *Batman* and *Detective*, both of which featured the Batman character, precipitated moving Schwartz in as editor in 1964. He immediately initiated the New Look with Infantino and Anderson, and this revamping eventually led to the *Batman* television series and its attendant camp style that Schwartz personally detested, but which catapulted National to unheard-of sales heights.

Schwartz eventually moved on to edit the highly acclaimed *Green Lantern/Green Arrow* series of relevant stories, a short-lived series that garnered favorable press but no appreciable sales boost. In recent years, he was also handed the major *Superman* family books, which he also revamped after his friend Weisinger resigned. It was Schwartz who presided over the national revival of the original *Captain Marvel* in 1973. Since his retirement in 1982 he has been a popular fixture at comic conventions throughout the country.

J.B.

SCIUSCIÀ (Italy) After the success encountered by *Il Piccolo Sceriffo*, publisher Tristano Torelli tried his hand again with a product which, while seemingly different, was actually similar to his earlier ones—it featured the same size publication, same editorial formula, same basic topic. The new feature got its theme (and its name) from Vittorio De Sica's 1947 film, *Sciuscià*. As in the movie, the hero was a juvenile waif, one of the numerous war orphans then roaming the streets who were called *sciuscià* by American soldiers (a deformation for the term for shoe shine).

The sciuscià, Nico, was a 15-year-old boy and a fugitive from a little town in southern Italy. He had been chosen by Captain Wickers of the American Secret Service to bring a coded message to Rome, which was still occupied by the Germans. Nico's adventures went on from there. He was accompanied by the ever-present Fiametta, his fiery girlfriend, and by Pantera, his loyal lieutenant. After the war ended (in comic books), Nico traveled to Burma, China, Africa, and Canada.

The first *Sciuscià* comic book came out on January 22, 1949, drawn by Ferdinando Tacconi and Franco Paludetti. In a matter of months its circulation had doubled. The reasons for this success are not too clear; it could not have been for the artwork, which was primitive or for the stories, which were stereotyped. It must have been due to giving its readers a dose of cheap escapism. At any rate a flood of comic books featuring the exploits of brave young boys hit the newsstands, and Torelli himself issued a kindred product in 1951: *Nat del Santa Cruz*, drawn by the ubiquitous Tacconi.

The publication was discontinued in the late 1950s but resumed again in 1965 with Lina Buffolente as the artist; it did not last long. *Sciuscià* was reprinted in the short-lived publication *Evviva* (1973) and is now being republished by Edizioni De Miceli of Florence. In 1952 Giana Anguissola and Tristano Torelli authored a novel based on the strip.

G.B.

SCORCHY SMITH (U.S.) *Scorchy Smith* was Associated Press News's most exemplary comic strip. It was one of the original group of strips and the only memorable one fielded by A.P. in March 1930; it suffered the checkered career and miserable direction characteristic of all A.P. comic features, and it finally folded along with the entire line of A.P. comics (or what was left of it) in 1961.

Scorchy Smith was the creation of John Terry, brother of famed animator Paul Terry, and himself a former animator and editorial cartoonist. Modeled after Charles Lindbergh, whom he was supposed to resemble, Scorchy had an uncertain personality and identity, somewhere between that of an earnest aviation pioneer and a devil-may-care barnstormer. Terry's line did not help the often muddled plot: the faces were chiefly blurs, and the action depicted with such incredible sloppiness that a lengthy narrative was

always needed just to keep the readers informed of the goings-on. With all its faults, *Scorchy* was A.P.'s best-selling strip.

In 1933 Terry became sticken with tuberculosis and a young staff artist, Noel Sickles, was called upon to ghost the strip (after Terry's death the following year, Sickles was allowed to sign his own name, starting in December). Sickles literally turned the strip inside out, making it into one of the most sophisticated features of the time, with his airy brushwork, his atmospheric effects, his perfect setting of mood and action, using only a few simple lines and impressionistic shading. The plot and dialogue (ghost written by Milton Caniff with whom Sickles shared a studio at the time) also became wittier and more suspenseful. Scorchy was now a soldier-of-fortune always ready to leap into his plane in order to thwart bloodthirsty revolutionaries from taking over some South American banana republic, or to save an heiress from the hands of her kidnappers. Under the combined leadership of the Caniff-Sickles team, *Scorchy* reached new heights of popularity and readership; yet when Sickles asked for a raise he was turned down and, disgusted with it all, he abandoned the strip in October 1936.

Succeeding Sickles was Bert Christman, another young A.P. staffer. The strip remained artistically praiseworthy (Christman's depiction of planes was especially striking) and narratively entertaining. In April 1938, however, Christman decided to leave in his turn, and the strip was handed over first to Howell Dodd (who drew it for only a few months), then to Frank Robbins, early in 1939.

Robbins had served out his apprenticeship briefly with an aviation strip of uncertain merit called *Flying To Fame* (a blatant misnomer) and he turned out to be *Scorchy*'s most remarkable artist, next to Sickles. His line was forceful, virile, and quite heavy, his drawing done in masses of solid, ominous blacks. He endowed the strip with a striking reality and a palpable solidity. The popularity of *Scorchy* was so great that, early in the 1940s, a Sunday page was added, wherein Robbins was able to demonstrate that he could handle color with as much assurance and aplomb as black and white.

When Robbins left the strip in 1944, he was succeeded by Edmond Good, followed in 1946 by Rodlow Willard, one of the most hapless of comic strip illustrators, who, in the course of his eight-year tenure, mightily contributed to the strip's downfall. Limp drawing, trite situations, and insipid intrigues by John Milt Morris marked the last years of *Scorchy*'s career; when A.P. finally decided to discontinue the feature in 1961, it was less a case of murder than mercy killing.

"Scorchy Smith," Noel Sickles. © AP Newsfeatures.

Scorchy Smith is one of the great forgotten illustration strips; despite its unpromising beginning and lamentable end, it deserves to be exhumed from the dust of private archives into the light of print if only for the brief period from 1934 to 1944 when it was one of the most innovative and vibrant features of the era.

M.H.

SCOTT, JERRY (1955-   ) Jerry Scott, an American cartoonist, was born in Elkhart, Indiana, on May 2, 1955. After briefly attending Arizona State University, Scott became a freelance graphic artist in 1974, working in this field for a few years. In January 1981 he took over George Crenshaw's *Gumdrop*, a gag panel presenting the precocious mischievousness of children and the subsequent befuddlement of their parents. Two years later, United Feature Syndicate proposed that, in addition, he bring *Nancy*, the Ernie Bushmiller classic, back from its continuing decline during the 1970s and early 1980s.

This Scott did remarkably well while he maintained the strip's original spirit and gentle humor: under his pen, the characters are more sharply defined and subtle and speak in a modern voice, and the situations are more true to contemporary life and ways of thinking. He continued to write and draw *Nancy* until 1995 when, its mounting popularity notwithstanding, he decided to quit and devote his creative talents to a new and very funny child strip, *Baby Blues*, which he signs with Rick Kirkman and which made its debut in late 1995. It is distributed by King Features Syndicate.

P.L.H.

SECCHI, LUCIANO (1939-   ) Luciano Secchi is an Italian newspaperman, writer, and editor born in Milan on August 24, 1939. After studies in Milan, Secchi freelanced for different publications, contributing short stories, articles, and reviews. In 1963 Secchi (under the pseudonym "Max Bunker") and with the help of Antonio Raviola (signing "Magnus") for the drawing, created his first comic strip *Kriminal*, in the

Luciano Secchi.

tradition of the Italian *fumetto nero* (black comics), followed the next year by *Satanik*, a female variation on the same theme of the antihero fighting against the blind repressive forces of society. Both of these strips enjoyed great success and earned Secchi a considerable reputation as a scriptwriter.

In 1968 Secchi created (again in collaboration with Raviola) the burlesque *Maxmagnus* about the predatory king of a mythical European kingdom. Secchi is also the author of a number of other strips, notable among them *Virus Psik*, an experimental series with drawing by Chies, and the recent *Fouche, un Uomo nella Revoluzione* ("Fouche, a Man in the Revolution"), an ambitious attempt at depicting in comic strip form the turbulent era of the French Revolution (the drawings are by Paolo Piffarerio). Also significant is *Alan Ford*, Secchi's greatest success to date.

Luciano Secchi has also been the editor of the Italian comic magazine *Eureka* since its inception in 1967. In this capacity he has greatly contributed to the appreciation of comic art in Italy; he has been instrumental in the Italian publication of *Terry and the Pirates*, *Steve Canyon*, and the Marvel stable of superheroes. He has received numerous distinctions, including top awards at the International Salon of Humor in Bordighera and the comics festival in Genoa. In addition to his achievements in the field of comic art, Secchi has also had published several of his novels as well as anthologies of his short stories, and he is a regular contributor to *Storia Illustrata*, the most important history magazine in Italy.

In 1982 Secchi left Corno to found his own company, Max Bunker Productions (now Max Bunker Press), which published all six titles of the *Alan Ford* saga and produced the first full-animation cartoons of the character as well as a few feature films. In the meantime he continued to write mystery novels with Ricardo Finzi as the protagonist.

In 1990 he started the short-lived comics magazines *Bhang* and *Super Comics*. That same year he also created *Angel Dark*, about a hard-boiled detective, that lasted only for ten issues. In 1994 another experiment, *Kerry Kross*, involving a lesbian investigator, caused the feminist press to launch a campaign against the character; the title was discontinued after 11 issues, but there are plans to revive it in 1997. In 1995 the indefatigable Secchi launched a new title written by his son Ricardo, *Gabriel*, about a nun with superpowers.

M.H.

SECRET AGENT CORRIGAN *see Secret Agent X-9.*

SECRET AGENT X-9 (U.S.) *Secret Agent X-9* made its first appearance (with much preceding and accompanying fanfare) on January 22, 1934; written by famous author Dashiell Hammett and drawn by up-and-coming artist Alex Raymond, it had been slated as King Features' answer to *Dick Tracy*.

In spite of the syndicate editors' mindless tamperings with the original script, the first four episodes (written by Hammett) remain by far the best. They established the character of the secret agent as a lone wolf, an implacable foe of crime who mingles in the midst of the underworld, adopting its habits, its jargon, and even its methods. In the first episode, the hero asks to be called Dexter ("it's not my name but it'll do") but later relinquishes even that alias to keep only his cryptic code number. X-9 moves swiftly but warily in the metropolitan jungle inhabited by gigolos, racketeers,

"Secret Agent X-9," Alex Raymond. © King Features Syndicate.

did a creditable job of continuing the feature until its unfortunate demise in the spring of 1996.

Because of syndicate mishandling *X-9* misfired badly; it never even came close to rivaling *Dick Tracy* in popularity. It did inspire a radio program and two (bad) movie serials (1937 and 1945). Its influence on other strips (even police strips) has been negligible; but on the screen the dazzling and inflexible persona of the hero created by Dashiell Hammett and Alex Raymond has left a durable imprint, from James Cagney's 1935 role in *G-men* to Robert Stack's characterization in *The Untouchables* in the 1960s to Kevin Costner in the movie version of the 1980s.

M.H.

SECRET OPERATIVE DAN DUNN see Dan Dunn.

SEEKERS, THE (G.B.) "The Seekers" is the name given to a kind of Missing Persons Bureau run by Una Frost. It consists of Suzanne Dove, brunette and beautiful, and Jacob, blond and beautiful. This take-on-anything (and also take-off-anything) team was created in the image of the highly successful *Modesty Blaise* strip by writer Les Lilley and artist John Burns. Intended for the *Evening News*, the strip was sidetracked into the *Daily Sketch* via strip editor Julian Phipps, and began on May 2, 1966. After that paper's demise it continued in syndication and concluded on May 10, 1971. One of the first strips to reflect the permissive age, heroine Suzanne went one up on Modesty by regularly appearing naked. This happened whenever she took off her dress, for she wore no underclothes!

John Burns drew *The Seekers* in a style very close to that of the late Jim Holdaway. Born in Wickford, Essex, Burns had no formal art training, yet he has emerged as one of today's finest sex-and-violence illustrators. He joined Doris White at Link Studios as an apprentice at the age of 16, and worked on strips for such weekly comics as *Girl's Crystal*, *School Friend*, and *Boy's World*. For *Wham* he drew *Kelpie* (1964), then the fantastic color serial *Wrath of the Gods* (1964) for *Eagle*. His first newspaper strip was *The Tuckwells* (1966), a weekly serial in *Sunday Citizen*. In 1971 he adapted the television series *Countdown* for the comic of the same title,

molls, kidnappers, and extortionists, amidst the trappings of a luxuriant and decadent society and in an atmosphere of cynicism and amorality. So strong was Hammett's characterization and so stunning Raymond's artwork that this is the image of *X-9* that remained in the reader's mind, long after the creators had abandoned the strip, within a few months' interval from each other, in 1935, (Hammett in April, Raymond in November).

Raymond was succeeded by Charles Flanders, the first in a bewildering array of artists and writers (who included Leslie Charteris of the *Saint* fame). Flanders tried to remain in the line of his predecessor but, although he did a creditable job, he could not sustain the character over the long haul, and he left in 1938, to be followed first by Nicholas Afonski (who drew *X-9* in a broad, grotesque style) and then by Austin Briggs.

Briggs's work on *X-9* (from November 1939 to May 1940) rivals even Raymond's in sheer brilliance. In his capable hands *X-9* became once again the enigmatic G-man of whom little is known. Aided and abetted by his talented scriptwriter Robert Storm (who had taken over from Charteris in 1936) Briggs re-created a world of shadows and menace, of bizarre intrigues and dark deeds, of dangerous and desperate men, and sultry and driven women.

When Briggs left the strip to create the daily version of *Flash Gordon*, he was followed by Mel Graff who, after 1942 (when Storm left as scriptwriter), was to betray the spirit of the strip to a considerable extent. Graff saddled *X-9* with an official name, Phil Corrigan, a family life, and even a fiancée. In 1960 Bob Lewis (pseudonym of Bob Lubbers) succeeded Graff and his cute and overmannered style drove *X-9* deeper into mediocrity. The strip would have probably gone under (it carried very few papers at that point) had it not been for Al Williamson who took over in January 1967. Williamson (helped by his able scriptwriter Archie Goodwin) restored *X-9* (now rechristened *Secret Agent Corrigan*) to something resembling its erstwhile splendor. In 1980 it was taken over by George Evans, who

"The Seekers," John M. Burns. © Associated Newspapers Ltd.

and did a similar strip adaptation of *Mission Impossible* (1973) for *T.V. Action*.

D.G.

SEGAR, ELZIE CRISLER (1894-1938) Elzie Crisler Segar, tragically short-lived creator of the immortal Popeye and Wimpy in his *Thimble Theater* strip, was born in Chester, Illinois, on December 8, 1894, to Amzi Andrews and Erma Irene Crisler Segar. Amzi Segar was a housepainter and paperhanger, and Chester, Illinois, was a long way from anywhere in the horse-and-buggy days of the turn of the century. Yet the Sunday papers from Chicago and Indianapolis reached even there, and the young Elzie was as familiar as any city kid with *Happy Hooligan, The Newlyweds, The Kin-Der-Kids,* and *Old Doc Yak.* More important, he was stirred to draw himself. He soon realized that his talent was minimal, yet his will to make it as a cartoonist kept him at his youthful drawing board into the small hours of night. A correspondence school course helped, and when he went to Chicago to try his luck on the papers there, his work showed enough verve to impress R. F. Outcault, creator of the seminal *Yellow Kid* and an idol of Segar's, who got him a job working on the hackneyed *Charlie Chaplin's Comic Capers,* a daily and Sunday strip running in the old *Chicago Herald.*

Segar's first *Chaplin* appeared on Sunday, March 12, 1916, and he continued with the strip until its syndicate owner, James Keeley, broke with Chaplin and scuttled the feature on April 16, 1917. The following Sunday, Segar got a crack at a strip of his own, a weekly page called *Barry the Boob* (about a young, nitwit soldier in an unnamed army on the European battlefields). *Barry* lasted a year, folding when the *Herald* was purchased by the Hearst *Chicago American* and *Examiner* combine, in April of 1918. Segar went with the *Herald's* assets, and started his first really successful feature on June 1, 1918, in the evening *American.*

The first *Looping The Loop,* a column of small cartoons satirizing downtown Chicago (the loop district) and its theater and film attractions, was a considerable hit, and its regular appearance on the paper's theater page for the next year built the *American's* circulation considerably. Hearst's New York syndicate officials noted the newcomer with interest, and trained him to go to Manhattan in late 1919 to start work on a comic strip for the Hearst chain. This new feature, called *Thimble Theater,* and similar in format and content to Ed Wheelan's popular *Midget Movies,* which Hearst had just lost to another syndicate, dealt with melodramatic stage themes and figures in daily gag routines. The first episode ran in the evening *New York Journal* on December 27, 1919. Public response was favorable, if not sensational, and the new feature continued, with Segar quickly shucking the stage drama trappings and concentrating on developing his own individual characters, such as Olive Oyl, her brother Castor, and her boyfriend, Ham Gravy. Drawn simply, in six small daily panels, the early *Thimble Theater* resembled Charles Schulz's *Peanuts* in style and gag structure. The strip also had the virtue of fitting into odd corners on daily comic pages, so that Segar was asked to start a companion daily strip of the same size for the Hearst morning *New York American,* to appeal to the new breed of suburban office commuter, and to be named (for a commuter train) *The Five-Fifteen.* Segar created a new character for this miniscule epic named John Sappo,

E. C. Segar, "Thimble Theater." © King Features Syndicate.

gave him a nagging wife, Myrtle, and set readers to chuckling from the outset, on December 24, 1920. (He also gave Sappo a son named Archie, mentioned in the opening episode, but never seen or mentioned again in the strip.) By the early 1920s, the Hearst syndicate felt Segar was ready to do a *Thimble Theater* Sunday page, and the first full-color page appeared in the Saturday comic section of the *New York Journal* on April 18, 1925. *The Five-Fifteen,* renamed *Sappo,* was added as a single strip of panels to the color page on March 6, 1926, and increased to an upper third on July 10, 1926.

Meanwhile, Segar himself, once he felt secure as a cartoonist, took his wife (named, like Sappo's, Myrtle) and left New York for Los Angeles, where he settled at a nearby beach city called Santa Monica for the rest of his life. It was there that he conceived the first character to give him international fame and personal fortune when he introduced Popeye the sailor into the *Thimble Theater* daily strip on January 17, 1929. Popeye took the nation by storm wherever Segar's strip was published, and within a year, orders were pouring into King Features from newspapers everywhere demanding local publication rights. Yet in the midst of this acclaim, Segar, already ill for some time, died on October 13, 1938: one of the most untimely deaths in strip history.

The earliest strip cartoonist mentioned by name in a major popular dictionary (*Webster's Collegiate,* Fifth Edition, 1941, in which he is credited with adding the words *jeep* and *goon* to the language), Segar was a devoted sports fisherman and a long member of the Santa Monica Rod and Reel Club; he loved to do carpentry of all kinds, and had his work covered in articles in such magazines as *Mechanix Illustrated;* but above all, he was one of the most naturally gifted artists and writers the strip medium ever afforded drawing board space to, and one of the major creative geniuses of the century.

B.B.

SEGRELLES, VICENTE (1940-   ) Spanish artist born in Barcelona on September 9, 1940, Vicente Segrelles apprenticed with the ENASA truck manufacturing company while attending night school at the School of Arts, where he specialized in advertising art. He eventually rose to the position of project draftsman, and at the same time freelanced as an illustrator with assignments that included *The Iliad* and *The Odyssey.* After his military service he devoted himself fully to advertising work as an illustrator and designer. In 1970

Vicente Segrelles, "El Mercenario." © Vicente Segrelles.

he left advertising to freelance as an illustrator, mostly in the field of popular science books (some of which he wrote himself) and of magazines, where he gained a solid reputation as a cover artist. Only in 1980 did he turn to comics with his series *The Mercenary*, currently published in over a dozen countries, including the United States.

A characteristic feature of Segrelles's work, which applies equally to his illustrations and to his comics work, is fantasy. He naturally chose fantasy as the main theme of his series, with some additions of sword-and-sorcery elements and a good dose of science fiction. He develops his stories in a way that allows him to display his talents as an illustrator to best advantage, composing each panel as a separate picture and maximizing its visual impact through his use of color. The adventures of the Mercenary (no name is given to the taciturn hero) have been published from their inception in the magazine *Cimoc* and later collected in book form. In the United States they have appeared in *Heavy Metal* and in a series of hardbound volumes.

In addition to *The Mercenary*—whose success from the outset was international and whose imagery was greatly admired by Federico Fellini—Segrelles has also over the years authored a number of shorter stories, most on heroic fantasy or sword-and-sorcery themes, some of which were later anthologized in *Historias Fantasticas* (1992). At the same time he never abandoned the illustration field and he has worked for many European and American publishers (notably Tor, Warner, Bantam, and New American Library).

J.C.

SERAFINO (Italy) Egidio Gherlizza created *Serafino* in 1951 in the pages of the *Cucciolo* comic book as a filler intended for the younger readers of the publication. Serafino is a cute little dog always attired in a bizarre costume made of a pair of too-short pants held by huge black suspenders, a red sweater, yellow shoes, and a soft hat sandwiched between his large ears. Serafino is

"Serafino," Egidio Gherlizza. © Edizioni Alpe.

ready to do anything to earn himself the sumptuous dinner of which he is always dreaming. To date he has worked as a truck driver, gardener, night watchman, fruit picker, potmaker, pantmender, and in any number of other odd jobs. His goofiness invariably gets him in hot water but his persistent good fortune always allows him to get out of it. At the end of each episode he can be seen seated with fork in hand in front of a big roast chicken.

Gherlizza has introduced into his strip good surrealistic touches that brighten and enliven the simple story line. The feature has been so well received over the years that *Serafino* was given its own monthly comic book in 1973. It lasted into 1985.

G.B.

"Sgt. Fury." © Marvel Comics Group.

SGT. FURY (U.S.) *Sgt. Fury and His Howling Commandos* debuted in its own comic book by writer and editor Stan Lee and artist Jack Kirby in May 1963. Issue number 1 introduced the gruff sergeant and his World War II platoon of Howlers such as Dum Dum Dug and bugler Gabe Jones, Dino Manelli, and Izzy Cohen. The lineup of the platoon changed from time to time but always featured a cross section of ethnic groups. The men frequently bickered over petty matters but always rallied together when confronted with the Nazi menace, usually depicted in typical B-movie tradition. A frequent antagonist was the bald, monocled Baron Strucker.

Kirby drew the feature, incorporating some of his own wartime experiences, for seven issues, returning later for issue number 13 when Fury met Captain America. Though Kirby continued to do covers for several years, the feature soon became identified with penciler Dick Ayers. Apart from occasional fill-in issues by John Severin, Tom Sutton, and Herb Trimpe, Ayers handled all the penciling. Various inkers did the strip but the issues embellished by Severin are generally considered the best in terms of art.

Scripting was done by Lee until 1966 when Roy Thomas took over for a year, followed by Gary Friedrich. The stories gravitated from gritty emotion to super heroics with Fury, his shirt perpetually in shreds, dodging a barrage of Nazi bullets. Eventually, Marvel

began a superspy strip, set in the present day, entitled *Nick Fury, Agent of SHIELD.*

Apart from the superhero influence, *Sgt. Fury* was also influenced by trends in the other Marvel books. The constant bickering among Fury's men was obviously inspired by the fights that divided groups like the *Fantastic Four* and the *Avengers.* Some issues, attempting to make a negative statement about war, depicted Fury as a frail, very human man in direct opposition to his usual image as a cigar-chewing superman.

Marvel attempted two spin-off imitations of *Sgt. Fury. Captain Savage and his Leatherneck Raiders* began in 1968 and lasted four years. After it ceased publication, Marvel tried *Combat Kelly and the Deadly Dozen,* which lasted a year. Both followed the *Sgt. Fury* format of a lead character commanding a team of various ethnic characters. Both imitations employed much the same creative team as *Sgt. Fury,* also.

Sgt. Fury appeared in seven annual specials (1965-1971), some featuring new material. In the 1970s, the *Sgt. Fury* comic began to fluctuate in quality with a variety of writers and inkers. Frequent reprint issues disrupted the comic's continuity and soon took over completely. Reprints also ran in *Special Marvel Edition* (1972-1973) and *War Is Hell* (1974). The series was finally canceled in 1981.

M.E.

SERGEANT PAT OF THE RADIO PATROL *see* Radio Patrol.

SGT. ROCK (U.S.) *Sgt. Rock* was the creation of writer and editor Robert Kanigher as the first recurring feature in National's line of war comics. The series began in *Our Army at War* number 81 (April 1959) with a story drawn by the team of Ross Andru and Mike Esposito. The title character, however, was a composite of several from earlier Kanigher stories, most notably the sergeant from *The D.I.* and the Sand Fleas in *G.I. Combat* number 56, dated January 1958.

In the first *Our Army at War* appearance, the character was named Sgt. Rocky, nicknamed "The Rock of Easy Company." Within a few issues, he evolved into the more conventional platoon leader, Sgt. Rock, and

"Sgt. Rock," Joe Kubert. © DC Comics.

was illustrated by the artist most closely identified with the strip, Joe Kubert. Other artists who relieved or followed Kubert on *Sgt. Rock* include Jerry Grandenetti, Irv Novick, Russ Heath, George Evans, and John Severin. Kanigher remained the principal writer.

The origin of Sgt. Frank Rock, as told by Kanigher and Kubert, ran in *Showcase* number 45 (August 1963). The story introduced Rock as an army private who enlisted in the early days of World War II. He subsequently rose to the rank of sergeant when he held Easy Company's position on a hill despite a Nazi onslaught that killed the other men in his unit.

The various members of Easy Company were introduced in issues of *Our Army at War* and included such supporting characters as Ice Cream Soldier, Bulldozer, Wild Man, and one of the comics' first nonstereotyped black characters, Jackie Johnson. The *Sgt. Rock* stories were mainly set in the European theater of operations, dealing with the men of Easy, their battle against the enemy, and the personal strains that each found themselves confronting in the face of war. The stories were introduced and told in the first person by Sgt. Rock, and many of them concentrated on the tremendous mental anguish endured by men in wartime.

Rock teamed with the characters of two other National war strips, the *Haunted Tank* and *Johnny Cloud*, in *The Brave and the Bold* number 52 (March 1964). He later teamed up with *Batman* in that same magazine for several stories that found Rock alive in the present-day army, still with the rank of sergeant. For a brief period, National attempted a spin-off with a series in *Our Fighting Forces* detailing the exploits of Rock's lieutenant brother, Larry. The *Lt. Larry Rock* strip achieved neither the popularity nor the longevity of the *Sgt. Rock* feature.

The comic book was officially renamed *Sgt. Rock* in 1977. Joe Kubert was again the mainstay of the series, but other talented artists, including Ric Estrada and Doug Wildey, also worked on the title. It was discontinued as a monthly in 1988 but continued as a quarterly until 1992.

M.E.

SEVERIN, JOHN POWERS (1921-   ) American comic book artist, writer, and editor, John Powers Severin was born December 21, 1921, in Jersey City, New Jersey. Although he had no academic art training, Severin began drawing cartoons for the *Hobo News* in 1932 and continued until 1936. He did not enter the comic book field until November 1947, however, when he illustrated a crime story for the Simon and Kirby team, then working at Crestwood. Severin then went to work directly for the Crestwood/Pioneer group and became the writer/editor of *Prize Western* comics, and also drew Western strips like *Lazo Kid*, *Black Bull*, and *American Eagle*. The first strip, *Lazo Kid*, was about a Mexican character and wasn't outstanding, but Severin's work on *American Eagle* was. A great fan of realistic Western tales, his work on the feature was one of the few serious, relatively unbiased handlings of the American Indian in comic books. Done in collaboration with Will Elder and Colin Dawkins, the strip remains unpublicized. When you get the feeling of realism, Severin once said in an interview, when *American Eagle* wasn't just tomahawks and cavalry sabres, it was about then I began taking a hand. Severin remained with the feature and Crestwood until its 1953 demise.

It was about that time he began working for William Gaines's EC group. Concentrating mainly on Westerns and wars under the direction of editor Harvey Kurtzman, Severin began developing his realistic, illustrative approach. He spent considerable time on detail and accuracy, and he once said he didn't draw comic book people, rather he drew people as they were. Some of Severin's finest work came in the last three issues of the *New Two-Fisted Tales*, for which he edited, wrote, and drew. Again concentrating on Western tales, the Severin-edited issues are among the best of the EC years, but they too folded when EC garnered too much negative publicity in 1953 and 1954. He also drew some outstanding, if somewhat static, material for the early issues of Kurtzman's *Mad*.

After EC folded in 1955, Severin began working for the Charlton and Harvey groups and began working more often for Stan Lee's Atlas group. There again he concentrated mainly on Western strips, but when Lee began the Marvel group in 1961, Severin went on to contribute fine material for the full range of Marvel comics, including *The Hulk* and a successful collaboration with Dick Ayers on *Sgt. Fury*, a war strip.

Over the years, Severin has also worked for Nedor (1948-1950), Skywald, Seaboard, National, and several others. He also contributed fine work to Warren's black-and-white magazines during the middle and late 1960s, particularly on the short-lived but excellent *Blazing Combat* title. Throughout his career, he has also contributed to Major Magazines, mostly for *Cracked*, a *Mad* imitation. Some of his noteworthy contributions in the 1980s have been *Bold Adventures* (1984) and the Marvel graphic novel *Conan the Reaver* (1988).

His sister, Marie, is also in the comic book business, and they collaborated at Marvel for a short time as the artist-inker team on the ill-fated *King Kull* book (1973).

J.B.

SEXTON BLAKE (G.B.) Britain's second greatest fictional detective (some say first; others brand him the office boy's Holmes), Sexton Blake, was created by hack writer Harry Blyth, under one of his pen names, "Hal Meredyth." Blake first appeared in a long novelette, *The Missing Millionaire*, published in Alfred Harmsworth's weekly for boys, *The Halfpenny Marvel*, on December 13, 1893. He appeared in similar stories for some 80 years, via such papers as *Union Jack*, *Detective Weekly*, and his own *Sexton Blake Library*.

He had already appeared in a number of films, silent and sound, when Percival Montagu Haydon, an Amalgamated Press editor, decided to include Blake in his new weekly children's comic, as a picture story. And so in number 1 of *The Knockout*, dated March 4, 1939, *Sexton Blake and the Hooded Stranger* began. "My word, this is a grand change from work," commented Blake's boy assistant, Tinker, in panel one. But then a car roared past their picnic. The man in that car is the Hooded Stranger, the most dangerous crook in Europe! cried Blake, and Pedro the Bloodhound was hot on the trail. A haystack camouflaged a lift, and down they all went to a Giant Underground Stronghold packed to the rivets with armored tanks! The game was afoot. Within weeks the strip had expanded from two pages to three, virtually unprecedented in British comics, and the villain behind the scenes turned out to be General Bomgas, dictator of Etland. (He was not the Hooded Stranger, however; his identity remained unknown.)

"Sexton Blake," Alfred Taylor. © Amalgamated Press.

The first artist to draw Blake as a strip hero was Joe (Joseph) Walker, a long-time illustrator of adaptations of Western movies starring Buck Jones and Tim McCoy for *Film Fun*. But he soon switched for Alfred H. Taylor, who continued the series until January 1, 1949. Taylor created the saga's best-remembered gimmick, the Rolling Sphere, invented by Chinese scientist Hoo Sung, and a handy thing to have during *Sexton Blake on Secret Service* (1942), when General MacRobert had to be rescued from Malaya. Then came *Sexton Blake and the Golden Lion* (1944), *Sexton Blake and the Threat of Kwang Shu* (1945), *Sexton Blake and the Atom Eggs* (1946), and so on.

Taylor was suddenly reduced to the status of lettering artist on January 8, 1949, when the artist who had done so much to establish Blake's original character and appearance in the old story papers took over the strip. This was Eric R. Parker, long a strip artist on *Knockout* for *Patsy & Tim* and other serials. The artwork took a decided leap upwards as Parker plunged his old favorites into *The Secret of Monte Cristo*, but he lasted only 14 weeks. Then the strip was given to R. C. W. Heade, then to R. MacGillivray, until Roland Davies took over from December 10, 1949. By 1954 Heade was back, but the episodes were complete each week. They stayed this way to the end (1960), with Taylor still doing lettering.

When television took up the rights to the character in 1967, *Sexton Blake* was revived as a strip in *Valiant*, the weekly comic that had, meanwhile, absorbed *Knockout*. The hawk-nosed detective was remodeled to match his television image, actor Laurence Payne. A large paperback reprint was published called *Valiant Book of T.V.'s Sexton Blake* (1968). But when the television series was dropped, so was the strip.

D.G.

SHADOW, THE (U.S.) 1—*The Shadow*, alias Lamont Cranston, first appeared in a Street and Smith pulp story called "The Living Shadow" (*The Shadow Magazine* number 1) in April 1931. Written by Walter Brown Gibson under the pen name "Maxwell Grant," the feature introduced the mysterious, crime-fighting Shadow and his equally inscrutable crew of helpers. Running concurrently with *The Shadow* radio show, the character became one of the most popular figures of the 1930s, and when comic books began making strides later in the decade, it was only a matter of time before *The Shadow* made an appearance.

In March 1940, Street and Smith issued the first *Shadow* comics, and the once invisible creature of the night became a gnarled face peering out from between a blue, low-brimmed hat and blue cloak. Most of the stories were signed by Gibson's pen name, but it is a virtual certainty that he did not write them. Artistically, most of the early stories were produced by the Jack Binder shop, but Bob Powell (1947-1949) and under-publicized pulp illustrator Ed Cartier contributed some excellent material in later years. But despite its scrupulous adherence to *Shadow* traditions and its first-rate production, the strip never matched the pulp or radio popularity the character enjoyed. *The Shadow* lasted in comic books until November 1950—a total of 107 appearances.

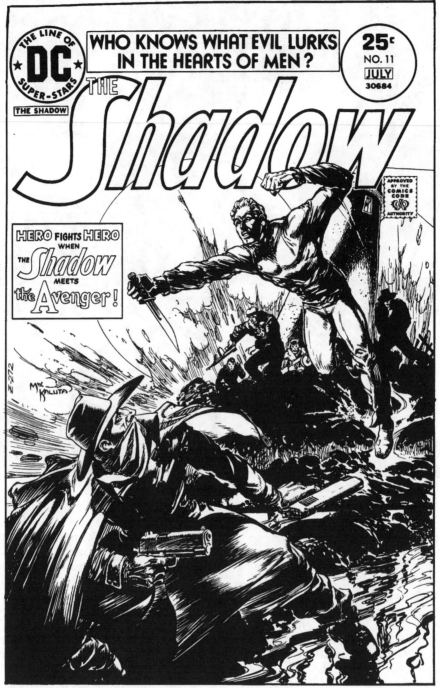

"The Shadow," Vernon Greene. © Ledger Syndicate.

2—During the superhero resurgence of the 1960s, the Archie group released a new *Shadow* series beginning in August 1964. And although this Shadow also claimed to be Lamont Cranston, the strip bore absolutely no resemblance to the old Shadow. He was a superhero, complete with green and blue tights and campy, juvenile dialogue. Doug Murray, comic writer for *The Monster Times*, counted it among the ten worst comic strips ever published. It died in September 1965 after eight issues.

3—National Comics announced plans to reissue the old *Shadow* series in early 1973 and Denny O'Neil was chosen as writer and editor. But the strip, which premiered in November of that year, has had tremendous artistic problems. Recognized talents like Berni Wrightson, Alex Toth, and Jim Steranko all quit before the first issue was published; however, young Mike Kaluta handled the first three issues and he was widely

acclaimed for his sensitive treatment and the 1930s mood of decay he portrayed. Frank Robbins began illustrating the book with the fourth issue and his version was completely different, mainly concentrating on action and adventure.

J.B.

4—*The Shadow* also enjoyed a brief newspaper career from 1938 to 1942 in a strip drawn by Vernon Greene and distributed by the Ledger Syndicate. The newspaper version was close to the original conception of the pulps, both in mood and execution. Greene proved to be a surprisingly effective action artist, and his somber and disquieting compositions, full of foreboding and menace, mark his Shadow as a forerunner of Will Eisner's Spirit.

The Shadow has known a checkered career in comic books (see above). The first version appeared in 1940, done by Greene. From 1942, when he was drafted to the end of the *Shadow Comics* run in 1949, came Jon Blummer, Jack Binder, Charles Coll, and Bob Powell, among others. *The Shadow* was brought back in the 1960s, 1970s, and 1980s, without success every time. Dark Horse Comics is currently trying to revive the crime fighter's fortunes by pairing him with other pulp heroes such as Doc Savage.

M.H.

SHAW, ERNEST (1891-197?) British cartoonist, writer, illustrator, and game creator Ernest Shaw was born in Hull, Yorkshire, on January 21, 1891. He was educated at Day Street School, leaving in 1905 to become errand boy to a printer. He studied art by copying the strips of Tom Browne from the halfpenny comics, then took a postal course with Percy V. Bradshaw's Press Art School. He sold his first cartoon to *Puck* (1910), then freelanced to his local weekly newspaper, *Hull & Yorkshire Times*. He joined the staff as general artist, drawing sports cartoons and caricatures of local celebrities, moving to the *Hull Daily Mail*, *Evening News*, and *Sports Mail* group as sports and political cartoonist.

He volunteered for war service in the Royal Army Medical Corps in 1914, and drew cartoons for the service magazine, *The Ration*. He also devised a *Lightning Cartoon* act to entertain convalescent soldiers. His sketches of details of operations on wounded soldiers as performed by surgeon Major J. L. Joyce were printed in *The Lancet*.

After demobilization Shaw raised his sights to the London market and began to submit his work to Amalgamated Press. He began with sports cartoons for *All Sports* (1919), but Tom Webster was by then king of this field. Very attracted to the American newspaper

strips *Mutt and Jeff* and *Bringing Up Father*, Shaw was determined to develop in this area. He began with *Clarence* and *Cyril the Sporty Scout* in *Sports Fun* (1922), and *First Aid Freddie* and the extraordinary crazy strip *Ikeybod & Tinribs*, both in *Champion* (1923). His big break came when he was given one day in which to take over a full-page weekly composite cartoon, *The Gay Goblins* for *Family Journal*, upon the sudden death of its creator, Lewis Higgins. He succeeded and continued the feature from 1926 until the last issue. An even longer run came with *Mr. and Mrs. Dillwater*, a weekly domestic strip, which he drew for *Answers* magazine from 1923 to 1948.

Other strips include *Hector in Wireless* (192?); *Sandy in People's Journal* (193?); *Dr. Gnome of Gnomansland*, which ran for 21 years in *Woman's Illustrated*; *The Wee Macs* in *Sunday Mail* (1940); *Sammy the Scout* (1938) in *Liverpool Daily Post*; *Gingham & Polkadot* (194?) in *Home*. From the 1940s Shaw concentrated on the juvenile market and created *The Dingbats*, a group of pixies who appeared in strips, puzzle books, painting books, story books, *Dingbats Comic* (1948), and three *Dingbats Annuals* (1949-1951). He devised card and board games, including *Menuette*, and syndicated his own puzzle panels, *Tantalising Teasers* and *Problematics*. His books include *Pocket Brains Trust* (1943), *Believe It All Rot* (1945), *Daily Deeds of Sammy the Scout* (1948), *Jolly Jokes for Juvenile Jokers*, *Dr. Gnome's Annual* (1953), and the primer, *How to Be a Successful Cartoonist* (1946).

In 1973 Shaw was rediscovered by Denis Gifford, and as Britain's oldest working cartoonist appeared as a panelist on the television series *Quick on the Draw*. An honorary member of the Cartoonists Club of Great Britain, Shaw died in the late 1970s.

D.G.

Ernest Shaw, "Mr. and Mrs. Dillwater." © Answers.

SHEENA, QUEEN OF THE JUNGLE (U.S.) Because of the plethora of fine artists it has had, Edgar Rice Burroughs's *Tarzan* remains the definitive jungle comic strip. It dominated both the newspaper strip and comic book jungle market. In fact, the only worthy comic book competition was *Sheena, Queen of the Jungle*, a strip with healthy doses of sex, sadism, and items surely aimed at arousing prurient interests. S. M. Iger and Will Eisner created the feature for the Editors Press Service in 1937, but the character did not make its first American comic book appearance until artist Mort Meskin and writer William Thomas produced it for Fiction House's *Jumbo* number 1 (September 1938). There it became fabulously successful and lasted 167 issues until March 1953. The character also had 18 issues of her own title from Spring 1942 until Winter 1953.

Unlike *Wonder Woman*, which featured material aimed at a girls' audience, *Sheena* was aimed at young boys. Sheena was a beautiful blonde with an outrageous figure. She wore only the skimpiest fur-and-leopard-skin costume, certainly more than enough to attract boys just reaching the point of sexual awareness. Sheena would swing through the pages Tarzan-style, Juanita Coulson wrote in *The Comic Book Book* (Arlington House, 1974), her long blonde hair flying and her fur bikini plastered to her 42-23-34 figure. I'm sure it brought the drooling male reader back for more. And it probably did, because the feature had many imitators, including *Nyoka* (Fawcett) and *Jann of the Jungle* (Atlas).

But Sheena was always the leader. Her companion was a hapless man named Bob who functioned in

"Sheena," Mort Meskin. © Fiction House.

much the same way Lois Lane operated in *Superman*: Bob would always be caught or captured by some African interloper and Sheena was pressed into service to defeat Bob's captors and rescue her assistant.

Sheena's popularity reached into other media, as well. She made many pulp magazine appearances and there was even a short-lived *Sheena* television series starring Irish McCalla. A movie version, starring Tanya Roberts in the role of Sheena, was released in 1984.

J.B.

SHELTON, GILBERT (1940-   ) While Robert Crumb and his creations are unquestionably the best-known of the underground comix society, Gilbert Shelton certainly ranks on a comparable level. His creations, *The Fabulous Furry Freak Brothers* and *Wonder Wart-Hog*, have become ingrained in the American consciousness, and probably say more about the readers they cater to than Robert Crumb's sexual fantasies. Whereas Crumb took readers to the outer levels, and some say the basest and most chauvinistic fringes, Shelton's features reflected things as they were and as they probably would continue to be. While it was Crumb who opened the sexual vistas and broke many of the old taboos, it was Shelton who went beyond the pioneering and made the later strides.

Born in June 1940, Shelton produced his first major strip, *Wonder Wart-Hog*, in December 1961. Written by Bill Killeen, the strip made its first appearance in the University of Texas magazine, *Texas Ranger*. Both Shelton and Killeen were studying there, and, for several months, the duo continued to work together on the strip. *Wonder Wart-Hog* himself was always the sex-crazed parody of *Superman* and the whole superhero mystique. In his secret identity as reporter Philbert Desenex, an outrageous and sharp parody of Superman's alter ego Clark Kent, the Hog of Steel destroyed just about every superheroic cliché, and, in the words of one critic, virtually destroyed any validity the superhero concept claimed.

Shelton soon assumed the complete writing and drawing of the strip, but when Killeen began *Charla-*

tan, another college humor magazine, Shelton was there with *Wonder Wart-Hog*. The strip eventually found its way into *Help!*, the Harvey Kurtzman-edited magazine. Unfortunately, *Help!* folded shortly after *Wonder Wart-Hog* began, but the feature survived in car magazines like *Hot Rod Cartoons* and *Drag*.

By 1968, however, Shelton began to branch out. He had already created the *Freak Brothers* for the *L.A. Free-Press* the year before, and, when his first underground comix book, *Feds and Heads*, appeared, it was apparent Shelton was ready to move on from *Wonder Wart-Hog*. Although the Hog of Steel made several sporadic appearances throughout the rest of the 1960s and early 1970s, it was the *Freak Brothers* that became Shelton's main vehicle. Unlike *Wonder Wart-Hog*'s dogged parodies of the antiquated superhero myths, the Freak Brothers were sex-seeking, dope-hungry revolutionaries of sorts, who accurately reflected the emerging youth culture of the late 1960s. While *Wonder Wart-Hog* mirrored past values, Frankling, Fat Freddy, and Phineas were contemporary characters entertaining contemporary audiences with contemporary humor. In the late 1970s Shelton took up residence in Europe, whence he continued to send material to Rip-Off Press until the late 1980s.

As an artist, Shelton never had the effect on styles and accepted standards of quality as Crumb did. His work was always clearly done and pleasingly presented, but it was not as earth-shaking or revolutionary. While his peers were busy shaking the trees of established art worlds, Shelton continued to entertain. As a result, Kurtzman, who is seen by some as one of the guiding lights of the underground movement, called Shelton the pro of the group.

J.B.

SHENANIGAN KIDS *see Katzenjammer Kids, The.*

SHEN PEI (1934-   ) Originally named Shen Peijin, Shen Pei graduated in 1954 from Central Art Academy, East China Branch (which at present are Zhejiang Art Academy and Chinese Art Academy). Until he moved and settled in Hong Kong in 1980, Shen had been a member of the Chinese Artist Association and worked as art editor for the *Xin Shaonian Bao* ("New Juvenile Journal"), which later became *Zhongguo Shaonian Bao* ("Chinese Juvenile Journal") and for the People's Art Publication House.

In June 1958, Shen started his long comic strip for children, *Xiaohuzi* ("Little Tiger"), published with the *New Juvenile Journal* (later with the *Chinese Juvenile Journal*). The hero in the comics, whose name was "Little Tiger," was a cartoon figure known by every young reader, even every adult, in China. In the first issue, "Little Tiger" was telling the readers: "My name is Xiaohuzi, and from now on I will be your friend. You should learn from me when you see what I am doing is good, and criticize me when you find what I am doing is wrong." Hoping to guide children to better behavior Xiaohuzi was established in Shen's comics as a good boy who was honest and warmhearted, loving, and caring of his peers, protecting the young and respecting the elderly, and was a hard-working pupil. In one such episode, Xiaohuzi gives the smaller pear to his younger brother. At the end, the unhappy younger brother realizes that Xiaohuzi is a good big brother who keeps the bigger but worm-eaten pear to himself.

Shen Pei, "Dividing Pears." © Shen Pei.

In order to make his strip even better, Shen visited many schools and talked with teachers, even disguised as a school janitor, and observed children by making friends and playing with them. After Shen left for Hong Kong, *Xiaohuzi* was continued by other artists.

It is now the oldest comic strip in China, having run for almost forty years. Since he settled in Hong Kong, Shen has published cartoons with the *Hong Kong Business News* under the pen name "Wei Chi Heng." Although they are still light, humorous cartoons in both content and style, they are quite different from his previous works.

H.Y.L.L.

SHERLOCK LOPEZ (Spain) Every country, it would seem, must have its comic strip spoof of A. Conan Doyle's *Sherlock Holmes* tales. In the United States it is *Sherlocko the Monk*, in Yugoslavia *Herlock Sholmes*; *Sherlock Lopez y Watso de Leche* (to give it its original title) is the Spanish parody of the British detective and his assistant, and first appeared in issue 229 of the magazine *Flechas y Pelayos* (April 25, 1943). The strip's author is cartoonist Gabriel Arnao (who uses the pseudonym "Gabi"), one of the best representatives of Spanish humor, a specialist of the absurd and the creator of other popular features of the 1940s and 1950s, such as *El Señor Conejo* ("Mr. Rabbit," 1944), *El Pequeño Professor Pin y su Ayudante Freddy* ("Little Professor Pin and his Assistant Freddy," 1944), *Jim Erizo y su Papá* ("Porcupine Jim and his Daddy," 1947), *Pototo y Boliche* (1948), and *Don Ataulfo Clorato y su Sobrino Renato* (1948).

After having lived numerous outlandish adventures in Flechas y Pelayos, *Sherlock and Watso* have been recently resurrected in the pages of the comic weekly *Trinca*, where they carry on in a style and an atmosphere reminiscent of a now-vanished era. The new series ended in 1982.

L.G.

SHERLOCKO THE MONK *see* Mager's Monks.

SHIELD, THE (U.S.) Comic books were fighting World War II long before Pearl Harbor, and one of the first super-patriots was *The Shield*, created by artist Irv Novick and writer Harry Shorten. Making his first appearance in MLJ's *Pep* number 1 in January 1940, the character predated *Captain America* and became one of the most popular heroes of the 1940s. There were two origins, but the most often cited appeared in the first issue: Joe Higgins, his father killed by foreign agents, vowed to spend his life fighting to protect the American way of life and constructed a shieldlike costume which gave him superpowers and invulnerability.

The Shield feature also included several outstanding supporting characters. Two of them, Ju Ju Watson and Mamie Mazda, were among the earliest attempts to inject humor into a straight superhero adventure strip. But Dusty, the Boy Detective, the Shield's youthful sidekick, eventually became the major supporting character. His 1941 premiere also predated the introduction of Bucky in the *Captain America* feature.

The strip underwent several drastic changes toward the end of 1942. Novick, an outstanding artist of rare maturity, left the strip in less capable hands; then, after a minor costume change, the Shield was stripped of all his powers and cast as an everyman champion of the people. But neither change was to help the strip fight off the postwar superhero malaise, and a once-obscure back-up humor feature called *Archie* knocked *The Shield*

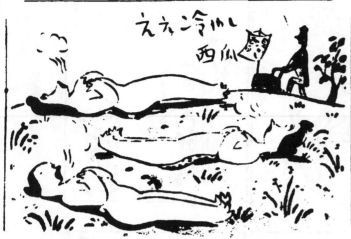

Kon Shimizu, "Kappa Tengoku." © Kon Shimizu.

from its lead position; *The Shield*'s last appearance was in the January 1948 issue of *Pep* (number 65). The character also appeared in 13 issues of *Shield-Wizard* comics between Summer 1940 and Spring 1944. There was also a Shield G-Man Club, but that too was soon changed to the Archie Club.

The Shield was revived in 1965 when the MLJ (now Archie-Radio) group attempted to exhume several of their characters as high camp during the mid-1960s *Batman* craze. In this new version, the Shield was a hopelessly destitute drifter who couldn't hold down a job because his crime-fighting interfered with his work. The whole line faded the next year, but not before Belmont issued a *High Camp Superheroes* paperback written by *Superman* co-creator Jerry Siegel. The title was briefly revived in 1983 by Archie Comics.

J.B.

SHIMIZU, KON (1912-1974) A Japanese cartoonist born September 22, 1912, in Nagasaki, Shimizu's parents died when he was seven and he was brought up by his grandmother. At Nagasaki Commercial School, Shimizu became famous for his caricatures of teachers and schoolmates. After graduation, he decided to become an artist and left for Tokyo in 1931 in order to enter the School of Fine Arts. His ambition was not realized, however, and Shimizu became a sidewalk artist in order to survive.

In 1933, through the intervention of a friend, Shimizu began working for the Bungeishunjii Publishing Company, contributing illustrations, fillers, and cartoons. That same year he joined the Shin Mangaha Shudan, the cartoonists' group founded by a band of young and iconoclastic artists, led by Ryūichi Yokoyama. In 1935 he produced a comic strip for the daily *Shinseinen, Tokyō Senichi ya Monogatari* ("The Tales of 1,001 Tokyo Nights"), noted for its new and fresh style (later inspiring a movie).

Soon after the Pacific War, Kon Shimiza became the political cartoonist for the daily *Shinyūkan*; his cartoons were so popular that in 1948 he was hired away by the much more prestigious *Asahi*. In 1951 he created his famous comic strip *Kappa no Kawatarō* ("Kowatarō the Kappa") about a merry band of river imps (called *kappa* in Japanese). The strip was so successful that it was made into a television series and gave rise to countless sequels: *Kappa Tengoku* ("The Kappas' Paradise," the most famous title in the series, 1952); *Sen-*

goku Zouhyō ("Soldiers of the Sengoku Era," 1961); *Kappa Houdai* ("The Fancy-Free Kappa," 1964); *Kappa Furai* ("The Wandering Kappa," 1966); and others.

Kon Shimizu also illustrated a number of books and magazines. He wrote several picture books and short stories but was most famous for his kappas. The kappas had a traditional representation in Japanese folklore, but Shimizu, instead of slavishly following tradition, gave his own rendition of these uncanny creatures in a tender and lovely style. His female kappas were especially sexy and alluring. Shimizu's creations were used as the trademark of Kizakura sake (wine), and in television, magazine, and newspaper advertisements.

Kon Shimizu had been influenced by the works of Ippei Okamoto from his high school days. His comic universe was depicted with restraint and taste but with a fine sense of humor. He used only the brush in his drawings, with a light and expressive touch that perfectly matched the mood of the story. In addition to being a great cartoonist, Shimizu also displayed his talents as a portrait artist, illustrator, book designer, and picture book artist. He died on March 27, 1974.

H.K.

SHIRATO, SANPEI (1932-) Sanpei Shirato is a Japanese comic book artist born February 15, 1932, in Tokyo. Shirato's father was a proletarian artist and his son, soon after graduation from junior high school, started working as a *kamishibai* artist (showing and narrating sequences of cartoons which he had drawn himself). In 1952 he also concerned himself with the puppet show company, Tarōza, for which he did stage design. In 1957 he made his debut as a *kashibon manga* (a cartoonist who draws stories for rental comic books) with his work, *Kogarashi-Kenshi*.

Many more creations followed from the pen of Sanpei Shirato: *Kōga Bugeichō* (a ninja story, 1957), *Onikagejo Hishi* (1959), *Fūma Ninpūden* (1959), *Ninja Bugeichō* (the strip that made him famous, 1959), *Kaze no Ishimaru* (his first feature for a magazine, 1960), *Ōkami Kazō* ("Wolf Boy"), *Seton Dōbutsuki* (an adaptation of Seton's novels), and *Sasuke*, all in 1961; *Shinigami Shōnen Kim* (a Western) and *Haiiroguma no Denki* (an adaptation of Seton's novel, *The Biography of a Grizzly*), both in 1963; *Kamui Den* (1964); *Watari* (1965); *Fūma* (1965); and *Tsuri* ("Fishing," 1967).

"Shoe," Jeff MacNelly. © Tribune Media Services.

Shirato created a number of ninja strips, and he is most famous for those. A ninja is a superhuman being who is able to use the special abilities which he has developed into an art (called ninjutsu). But Shirato's ninjas are not simple superhuman beings: their ninjutsu is scientifically substantiated. Shirato is also famous for the violence contained in his works: scenes of battle and uprisings, depictions of cruelty and malevolence. Setting his work in the past, Shirato also severely castigates the injustice and cruelty present in modern society. His major creation, however, remains *Kamui Den*, which he picked up again in 1982 and on which he has been working ever since.

Shirato's early style was simple and basic like that of Tezuka, but it became gradually more and more realistic. His works have been reprinted often, and they have influenced a whole school of comic book artists: Haruo Koyama, Shōhei Kusunoki, Yashiharu Tsuge, Seiichi Ikeuchi, and others.

H.K.

SHŌCHAN NO BŌKEN (Japan) *Shōchan no Bōken* ("The Adventures of Shōchan") was created by artist Tōfujin and scriptwriter Shousei Oda for the illustrated weekly *Asahigraph* where it first appeared in January 1923.

Shōchan was a clever and courageous little boy who loved adventure and was always accompanied by a pet

"Shōchan no Bōken," Tōfujin (Katsuichi Kabashima). © Asahigraph.

squirrel. *Shōchan no Bōken* was a fantasy strip not unlike the fairy tales of old, in which monsters, demons, and other assorted creatures played an important role. After the great earthquake of 1923, Shōchan moved to the daily *Asahi* (November 1923) and became a very popular feature (around this time the *schōchan-bou*, a white woolen cap with a pom-pom on top, worn by the hero enjoyed a great vogue among Japanese youngsters). The strip ended in 1925 when Tōfujin left the *Asahi* staff.

Actually Tōfujin was the pen name of Katsuichi Kabashima (1888-1965), a noted and talented Japanese illustrator, who taught himself art by copying the ink illustrations of the *National Geographic* magazine. After he left the *Asahi* offices, Kabashima worked as a magazine illustrator for the Kōdansha publishing house. He drew many illustrations for books, especially for the war novels of Minetarō Yamanaka. His graphic style was very realistic and highly detailed (his drawings almost looked like photographs). He particularly enjoyed drawing ships and earned the nickname "Fune no Kabashima" ("Kabashima of the Ships").

Kabashima's artwork on *Shōchan* was not realistic, however, but simple and sharp, showing a fine eye for humorous detail.

H.K.

SHOE (U.S.) Jeff MacNelly was already an award-winning editorial cartoonist when *Shoe*, his comic strip on the trials and tribulations of the avian staff of the east Virginia newspaper the *Treetops Tattler-Tribune*, began in September 1977. It is syndicated by Tibune Media Services who also syndicates this thrice-weekly editorial cartoons and his panel *Pluggers*, which began in 1992. One of the first of the modern wave of editorial cartoonists to draw syndicated humor strips as well as their editorial cartoons, MacNelly had won the Pulitzer Prize in 1972 for his work at the *Richmond News-Leader*.

Shoe was an instant success. The antics of P. Martin "Shoe" Shoemaker, editor-in-chief, and his sloppy but lovable ace reporter and columnist "Perfesser" Cosmo Fishhawk had great appeal to the feature editors who buy comic strips. It didn't hurt that MacNelly won a second Pulitzer Prize for editorial cartooning in 1978.

In 1978 his editorial cartoons also won him the coveted Reuben for Best Cartoonist of the Year voted by the National Cartoonists Society (NCS). So highly did his peers think of *Shoe* that in 1979, MacNelly won a second NCS Reuben statue for *Shoe*. (Jeff MacNelly is the only cartoonist to ever win back-to-back NCS Reuben awards.)

MacNelly, who was born in 1947, is an alumnus of the University of North Carolina—Chapel Hill, where he drew cartoons for the student newspaper. He then worked for *The Chapel Hill Weekly*. His editor there was Jim Shumaker who taught journalism at the university, smoked cigars, and wore high-top black sneakers to work. His nickname was "Shoe," and MacNelly named the strip in his honor.

As an editor, the *Tattler-Tribune*'s Shoe is of the old school. He chomps a cigar, likes a drink now and then, and will occasionally bet on the horses. His counterpoint, Cosmo Fishhawk, is a dedicated writer who can't find anything on his incredibly messy desk; is constantly on a diet; procrastinates; and has an eye for the women.

While drawn as birds, the characters are human in every other way. The supporting cast includes Skyler, who's Cosmo's 12-year-old nephew; Roz, a tough old bird who runs the local diner; Loon, the wacked-out newspaper delivery bird; Muffy Hollandaise, a very preppy cub reporter; and U.S. Senator Battson D. Belfry, who's a laughable semi-scoundrel drawn as a caricature of former House of Representatives legend Tip O'Neill.

MacNelly is one of the funniest editorial cartoonists published. *Shoe* allows him to use gags to comment on the state of everything from popular culture to politics in America. For example, Cosmo is watching an ad on television for a tabloid talk show that hypes a program about "men who sleep with daughters of their mothers-in-law." When Sen. Belfry encounters Shoe and Cosmo at Roz's diner he claims he's visiting his constituents to see what they think. Shoe responds, "Actually, we were just thinking how nice it was that you were there and we were here."

The drawing in the strip is full of detail and wild crosshatching in a style MacNelly has made his own. He acknowledged his debt to Walt Kelly by writing an introduction to *Pogo Even Better* in 1982. However, MacNelly never copied but broke new ground in the use of talking animals as he created his own cartoon world.

Big business and government and many of the subjects of his editorial cartoons appear as targets of his humor in *Shoe*. However, he also can indulge in his love of sports as nerdy Skyler is shown playing baseball, football, and basketball and even being accidentally sent through marine boot camp on summer vacation.

A cartoonist who loves to draw and loves the newspaper business, MacNelly has seemingly endless energy. He illustrates the weekly syndicated Dan Barry humor column and in 1992 Tribune Media Services debuted his cartoon panel *Pluggers*. *Shoe*, which celebrated its twentieth year of syndication in 1997, is published in more than 1,000 newspapers.

B.C.

SHŌNEN OJA (Japan) *Shōnen Oja* ("The Boy King") was created by Soji Yamakawa in 1948 and was first published in book form in the *Omoshiro Bunko* series (issues 1 through 4); when the magazine *Omushira Book* was founded, *Shōnen Oja* was among the first features that it published.

Shingo Makimura, alias Shōnen Oja, was a jungle boy brought up by Mera the gorilla in Africa. His father was a Japanese missionary who had discovered a mys-

"Shōnen Oja," Soji Yamakawa. © Omoshiro Bunko.

terious green stone, the cure for an incurable disease, but later disappeared. With his father missing and his mother killed by tropical fever, Shingo was carried away while still a baby by Mera who had saved him from the claws of a lion. Shingo grew up strong and hardy, and he battled many enemies, including the Red Gorilla, the Big Crocodile, the Monster Tree, the cannibalistic Gara-zoku tribe, Ura the Devil, not to mention a brontosaurus. When he was faced with mortal danger and no hope of triumphing by himself, Shingo was saved by the timely intervention of a mysterious stranger Amen Hoteppu (who, in fact, was none other than Yuzō Makimura, Shingo's father, who had escaped from the clutches of his enemies and was hiding under a secret identity).

Shōnen Oja was clearly inspired by E. R. Burroughs's *Tarzan* but it succeeded in creating a flavor all its own and is probably one of the more inspired variations on the ape-man theme. *Shōnen Oja* was not, *stricto sensu*, a comic strip but an illustrated story with text under the pictures, but it exerted a great influence on the post-World War II Japanese comics. Along with such other celebrated features as *Sabaku no Maō*, *Daiheigenji*, *Chikyu S.O.S.* and *Shōnen Kenya*, *Shōnen Oja* represents the Golden Age of Illustrated Stories in Japan.

H.K.

SHORT RIBS (U.S.) Frank O'Neal created *Short Ribs* as a daily strip for NEA Service on November 17, 1958, and it was quickly followed by a Sunday version on June 14, 1959.

Short Ribs is not the usual run-of-the-mill comic strip. The action (or what there is of it) takes place on several levels, spatial and temporal: one day in a castle of the Middle Ages, the next in Dodge City, and the one after that in ancient Egypt. There are accordingly several sets of characters who keep reappearing at intervals (although they never meet, after the fashion of John Dos Passos's novels), and who constitute the weirdest assortment of oddballs ever assembled in one comic strip. Those include a feisty witch ("fastest wand in the kingdom"), an insecure king and his nagging wife, a soft-hearted hangman, a pair of hot-tempered duelists ("I dare you to step over this line"), two self-examining Soviet commissars ("Why do they keep call-

"Short Ribs," Frank O'Neal. © NEA Service.

ing it the Party? Who's having any fun?") and an inept sheriff ("still the slowest gun in the West").

Like the contemporary *Mr. Mum*, *Short Ribs* utilized the incongruous, the absurd, and the nonsensical. Visual puns abound as do inside jokes (an Egyptian reading a comic strip on a pyramid wall comes upon the inscription: "to be continued on next pyramid").

Short Ribs was never been able to achieve the success it deserved, probably because of the very wealth of the artist's imagination. There was something compulsive, almost manic, in O'Neal's inexhaustible inventiveness and in his staccato but deadpan delivery; and one can well understand the bewilderment of many a reader coming for the first time upon this unorthodox comic strip. Yet *Short Ribs* is a rich lode to mine for the connoisseur who can easily find in it the inspiration for such disparate strips as *The Wizard of Id*, *Sam's Strip*, *Tumbleweeds*, and *Broom Hilda*.

In the 1960s Gold Medal reprinted a number of *Short Ribs* strips in pocket-book form. In 1973 O'Neal left the comics field in search of more lucrative pursuits, and his assistant Frank Hill took over the feature. In his hand *Short Ribs* lost much of its freshness and spontaneity, often degenerating into a patchwork of tired clichés and bad puns. It steadily lost circulation until it finally came to an end in May 1982.

M.H.

SHUSTER, JOE (1914-1992) Joe Shuster was an American comic book and comic strip artist born July 10, 1914, in Toronto, Canada. Shuster's family moved to Cleveland, Ohio, in 1923, and it was there that he met writer Jerry Siegel. Together as teenagers the pair began publishing science-fiction fan magazines. In one of the issues, they reviewed Philip Wylie's novel, *Gladiator*, and it was the basis for their biggest creation, *Superman*, which was conceived in 1933.

At the same time, Shuster was studying art and attended John Huntington Polytechnical Institute and the Cleveland School of Art. In 1936, Siegel and Shuster broke into the comic book business with New Fun Comics, Inc., later to become Detective Comics,

Joe Shuster, "Slam Bradley." © National Periodical Publications.

and later National Periodicals by drawing lacklustre adventure strips *like Dr. Occult, Henri Duval, Spy, Federal Men, Radio Squad*, and *Slam Bradley*.

In 1938, however, the company purchased the first *Superman* story from them for $130. Making its first appearance in June's premiere issue of *Action Comics*, the feature was an immediate success, and since then Superman has gone on to become the best-known adventure character in the comics.

Shuster's art was primitive, blocky, even crude, but it was beautifully designed and well conceived. For the most part, Shuster's simple work became the style of the earliest adventure comic books, but his work was generally better and more inspired than the horde of imitative artists who followed. He worked mostly in long shots which presented a full look at the character; Shuster's art was never pretentious or fancy. Instead, he settled for straightforward narrative work that critic and artist James Steranko once likened to the style of editorial cartoonists.

Although Siegel and Shuster made a considerable amount of money on a superficial basis from *Superman* (The *Saturday Evening Post* estimated their 1940 income at $75,000) they owned no part of the character. And even though they opened a shop to produce the ever-burgeoning amounts of work being requested by National and Wayne Boring was probably the best of the shop workers, they never had any rights to the character. Although Shuster drew the character through 1947 both in comic books and for the McClure Syndicate comic strip he was left with nothing.

After a stint with the Bell Syndicate on the Siegel-scripted *Funnyman* strip, Shuster left the industry completely. While Siegel continued to work sporadically in the field and kept his name in the public eye by waging a long-running court battle with National over the rights to *Superman*, Shuster vanished. According to most reports, Shuster was now almost blind in a California nursing home, and the information for this entry was obtained through the intercession of Siegel, who convinced his former coworker to respond after what Siegel called these years of seclusion. In 1977 Shuster, along with his partner Jerry Siegel, won a lifetime annuity from DC Comics, the owner of the *Superman* franchise. He died in Los Angeles on July 30, 1992.

J.B.

SHWE MIN THAR (1932-   ) Shwe Min Thar has been drawing Burmese comics since 1958, contributing both gag and strip cartoons to various magazines and newspapers since the early 1960s. He also has drawn political cartoons, although for almost all of his career, Burma has been under oppressive governments. Thus, his cartoons usually deal with social, rather than political, issues.

For three years, Shwe Min Thar studied at the State School of Fine Arts, where he won top honors; afterward he continued to learn as a student of Pagyi U Thein Han. His paintings have also been popular in Burma, having sold regularly over the years.

Since the 1990s Shwe Min Thar has been doing much caricature, newspaper, and magazine cartoons, and also produces covers of comic books and humorous novels. Like his fellow cartoonists, he works as a freelancer and self-publishes his comic books. Shwe Min Thar's work is characterized by simply executed drawings that use firm but not very bold lines, omit all backgrounds, and pertain mainly to gags.

J.A.L.

SICKLES, NOEL (1910-1982) Noel Sickles was an American cartoonist and illustrator born 1910 in Dayton, Ohio. Sickles received his only formal art training (aside from drawing lessons in high school) from a correspondence course. He started his career in the late 1920s as a political cartoonist for the *Ohio State Journal*. In 1933 he moved to New York and got a job as a staff artist for the Associated Press at $45 a week. At AP, Sickles renewed his friendship with fellow Ohio-born Milton Caniff, who was then doing *Dickie Dare* and, before long, the two men were sharing a common studio. Early in 1934, when John Terry, creator of the aviation strip *Scorchy Smith*, became too ill to work on the feature, AP called on Sickles to ghost the strip (when Terry died later that year, Sickles was allowed to sign his name to the feature).

Noel Sickles's tenure on *Scorchy* was nothing short of revolutionary. As Henry C. Pitz, himself a noted illustrator, stated in a 1949 article: "At the end of six months the technique had changed from sketchy conventional line to much more positive and realistic type of rendering; and the next step introduced light and shade, bringing the pictures into the realm of solid, pictorial, flesh and blood illustration." Soon this new method of drawing caught on like wildfire among adventure strip cartoonists, starting with Milton Caniff who had just shifted from *Dickie Dare* to *Terry and the Pirates*. By 1935 Caniff and Sickles were working closely together. At times, Sickles would pencil a whole sequence of *Terry* while Caniff would write the continuity for *Scorchy*. (In addition they were collaborating, under the pen name of "Paul Arthur" on the *Mr. Coffee Nerves* ad strip for Postum.)

In view of the soaring success of the *Scorchy Smith* strip, Sickles in 1936 asked for a raise on his $125 a week salary. When he was turned down, he quit AP and the comics field, and retired to upstate New York in order to, in his own words, meditate. He was back in New York City in 1939, however, briefly working with Caniff on *Terry* again and ghosting *Patsy* for Mel Graff. In 1940 he returned to illustration and did a series of war drawings for *Life*. These attracted the attention of the War College in Washington, and Sickles was commissioned to do instructional illustration for the armed services. Later he transferred to the Navy Department where he worked on highly classified assignments in which his skills as a draftsman were needed.

At the end of the war, Sickles went back to freelancing for magazines and advertising agencies, doing illustrations and full-color paintings for *Life*, *The Saturday Evening Post*, *Reader's Digest*, *This Week*, and other publications.

Noel Sickles has been honored many times for his work as an illustrator; yet his comic strip career, short as it was, may prove just as significant. With the possible exception of Milton Caniff, no other realistic strip artist has had as much impact on the profession as Sickles. He once summed up his artistic method in these words: "Rather than work in minute detail all over my drawing, I have found that if I take pain to use careful and exact detail in the right places . . . I can handle the balance of my drawing in a broad fashion. The eye will infer a complete statement from such indication."

Sickles retired in the late 1970s and devoted his time to painting Western scenes and landscapes in and around Tucson, Arizona; he died on October 3, 1982. It is a tribute to his stylistic brilliance that the technique he had introduced in the mid-1930s is still

"Il Signor Bonaventura," Sto (Sergio Tofano). © Corriere dei Piccoli.

widely used and emulated more than a decade after his death.

M.H.

SIEGEL, JEROME (1914-1996) Jerome (Jerry) Siegel's first comic book creation was *Superman*, the quintessential comic book character and granddaddy of thousands of superheroes that have since overrun the medium. Siegel's career was haunted by the character ever since its conception in 1933 and its first publication in *National's Action* number 1 in June 1938. Siegel and artist Joe Shuster, a childhood friend, sold the character for $130 and received little else since. In fact, Siegel spent a good portion of his adult life vainly attempting to regain some rights to what is unquestionably the most lucrative character ever to appear in comic books.

Born in Cleveland, Ohio, on October 17, 1914, Siegel loosely based his *Superman* concept on Philip Wylie's 1930 novel, *Gladiator*. *Superman's* origin has been enshrined in Americana, of course, and hundreds of imitations followed. In retrospect, however, Siegel's *Superman* was unique because it featured a superpowered being adopting the guise of a mild-mannered reporter, Clark Kent. Superman's contemporaries were usually normal humans transformed into superheroes. The psychological implications of Siegel's juxtaposition have been studied for years.

But despite its now eminent position, the *Superman* strip was originally rejected by every major newspaper-strip house of the time. Subsequently, Siegel's first published comic work appeared in an advertising supplement for the *Cleveland Shopping News* in 1936. His first comic book work began appearing shortly thereafter. Written mostly for the law-and-order oriented *Detective Comics*, it consisted of pedestrian cops and robbers and adventure material.

In 1938, the publishers of *Detective* purchased the rights to *Superman*, published it, and Siegel and Shuster's character immediately took off. Siegel continued to work on the character until 1948, his tales con-

sisting of little morality plays and his characterization of *Superman* being more sedate than that of later writers. Litigation surrounding the ownership of the character followed almost immediately.

Although Siegel constantly claimed that he was blackballed from the comic book industry as a result of the suit, his list of credits is as long as any in the field. But many industry observers find it strange that none of his later creations were ever successful over long periods. Many believe that while Siegel may not have been blackballed, he may have been consistently punished for his attempts to regain *Superman*.

Over the years, Siegel worked on many newspaper strips, including *Superman, Funnyman, Reggie Van Twerp, Ken Winston, Tallulah*, and others. He also was Ziff-Davis's first comic book director.

Siegel had little of his comic book writing published in his later years. Until 1975, in fact, he lived a reclusive life in West Los Angeles before he began publically commenting on his many fights with National: he wrote an article on the litigation in the fourth issue of *Inside Comics*, an industry magazine, and attended his first comic convention in San Diego, where he received the conclave's Inkpot Award. Yielding to public pressure, DC (successor to National) awarded Siegel (along with his partner Joe Shuster) a lifetime annuity. He lived quietly in Los Angeles until his death on January 28, 1996.

J.B.

SIGNOR BONAVENTURA, IL (Italy) A playright, an interpreter, and finally a cartoonist, Sergio Tofano (better known as "Sto") produced one of the most celebrated characters in Italian comics for the readers of the *Corriere dei Piccoli*; a character who has been beloved by at least three generations of readers: il Signor Bonaventura. Tofano's simple line and elementary message were the main ingredients in Bonaventura's popularity for more than 50 years, during which time hundreds upon hundreds of whimsical stories were turned out.

Il Signor Bonaventura ("Mister Bonaventura"), starring a dapperly attired, clownish-looking little man, first appeared in October 1917, and ran every single week until 1955; it was again revived in 1970. An optimistic counterpart to the luckless Happy Hooligan (whose adventures also ran in the Corriere dei Piccoli), Bonaventura, whatever the calamities that befell him in the course of the story, always ended up winning the big reward (in the form of a one-million lire bill, later increased to one-billion, due to inflation).

In the course of his wanderings in search of some good deed to perform, Bonaventura is always accompanied by his very small and elongated basset hound. His son, Pizziri, always gets into trouble playing with the millions his father has won, while many other colorful characters populate the strip, such as the handsome bar-fly Cecè, the ever-present Barbariccia, Comissar Sperassai, the lugubrious Crepacuore, the meek Omobono, and many others equally as funny. Every Bonaventura episode starts with the characteristic verse: Qui comincia l'avventura/ Del Signor Bonaventura ... ("Here begins the adventure/ Of Mister Bonaventura...") and then winds its merry way to a crescendo of lightheadedness and optimism, regardless of time, place, or situation.

In 1927 and again in 1953, Tofano adapted his own comic strip to the theater. In 1942 he directed a film of Il Signor Bonaventura starring Pablo Stoppa. In 1966 Bonaventura appeared again on stage with Paolo Poli in the title role. Since Sergio Tofano's death in 1973, the strip has been drawn by Carlo Peroni and others.

G.B.

SIGURD (Germany) Sigurd is a genuinely German comic book feature with a young blond knight errant as its hero. The name and saga of the original Sigurd is almost identical to that of Siegfried. The comic book Sigurd, despite the fighting prowess and seeming invincibility of its hero cannot boast an impenetrable skin like Siegfried's, however.

Sigurd was created by Hansrudi Wäscher and first published in 1953 by Walter Lehning's comics group as the fifth series put on the market in the Italian or piccolo format of 6⅝ × 2⅞ inches. Each issue had 32 pages printed in black and white on newsprint plus a color cover. The books were published weekly and ran continued stories much in the manner of American movie or radio serials with an unavoidable climax and questions about how the hero could possibly escape his latest cliff-hanging predicament to ensure the sale of next week's issue which, of course, starts out with a recapitulation of the goings-on.

The adventures of Sigurd are shared by Bodo, a suave, Gawain-type knight. They were soon joined by Cassim, an orphaned boy Sigurd had saved from a house set afire by pillaging Viking pirates. The daring trio embarked on a journey with damsels in distress, crooked knights, dragons in the form of dinosaurs, and the like, waiting at each and every turn of the road. Like the original Siegfried and/or Sigurd of legend and myth, the comic book Sigurd has a run-in with Etzel (Attila the Hun).

Except for the first 40 issues, Hansrudi Wäscher wrote all the stories he drew. Although his graphic style is relatively simple (a consequence of having to draw to the same scale as the book page), even stiff or wooden, it never failed to attract a large following, for

"Sigurd," Hansrudi Wäscher. © Hansrudi Wäscher.

Wäscher managed to tell exciting stories. Wäscher's style is still emulated by up-and-coming fan artists.

The first run of Sigurd piccolos ended with number 324 and was followed by 87 reprint issues. Earlier, a full-sized color comic book, reprinting three of the piccolo pages to one page, had been started. With number 125, this Sigurd comic book switched to original material and continued to issue number 257. Sigurd's life ended when the Lehning group folded in 1968. The feature had a seven-issue comeback in 1971, but production was stopped when problems arose over the estate of Walter Lehning. The death of publisher Lehning brought about the end of a line of comics that is still fondly remembered as one of the uniquely German entries in the history of comic books. Sigurd may have been the most popular of this line of comics, as it was also reprinted in Harry, a magazine combining comics and text features. For some time, Harry even carried a specially produced Sigurd comic strip. And, in 1964, a Sigurd special containing an illustrated novel was published.

In 1976 a first short-lived series of Sigurd reprints was published. Finally in 1980 publisher Norbert Hethke, devoted to reprinting 1950s comic books, started reprinting the entire Sigurd material. Thanks to good contacts with Hansrudi Wäscher, new material was added. Some of the reprints have been done as deluxe editions.

W.F.

SILAS see McCay, Winsor.

SILLY SYMPHONIES (U.S.) A Sunday strip created by artists of the Walt Disney Studios (Al Taliaferro most notably) and published in the 1930s, Silly Symphonies was named for a Disney series of musical animated shorts of the period, and first appeared together with the first Mickey Mouse Sunday page on January 10, 1932.

The Silly Symphonies strip consisted of several different narratives featuring unrelated characters, sometimes based on studio releases of the time, and running for widely varied periods of time. The first and longest Silly Symphony story carried no subtitle (as did the later narratives), and featured the sometimes epic adventures of a ladybug complete with antenna, whose wings had been stylized into a natty spotted jacket, named Bucky Bug. The opening Bucky Bug saga ended on March 4, 1934, with Bucky's marriage to June, and

A Silly Symphony: "The Practical Pig," Al Taliaferro. © Walt Disney Productions.

on March 11, 1934, the second *Silly Symphonies* narrative, *Birds of a Feather,* began. The Bucky Bug story was partly reprinted in a *Big Little Book* of 1934, titled: *Mickey Mouse Presents a Walt Disney Silly Symphony.*

Birds of a Feather was followed (with a one-week break for a full *Mickey Mouse* page) by *Peculiar Penguins* on July 1, 1934. Next were: *The Little Red Hen* on September 16, 1934 (in which Donald Duck made his first strip appearance on the same date); *The Boarding-School Mystery,* with Max Hare and Toby Tortoise (in which the prototype of Bugs Bunny, Max Hare, appeared) on December 23, 1934; *Ambrose the Robber Kitten* on February 24, 1935; *Cookieland* on April 28, 1935; *Three Little Kittens* on July 28, 1935; *The Life and Adventures of Elmer Elephant* on October 27, 1935; *The Further Adventures of the Three Little Pigs* on January 19, 1936; and *Donald Duck* on August 30, 1936. Beginning with *Donald Duck,* the *Silly Symphonies* feature carried a weekly subtitle for the first time, appearing as *Silly Symphony Featuring Donald Duck,* while, also for the first time, the rhyming dialogue was abandoned.

In July, 1937, the *Mickey Mouse* Sunday companion feature became simply *Donald Duck,* and the *Silly Symphony* was abandoned. (Later in 1939, it was revived for a short time as part of the title of a *Pluto* half-page, which had been running earlier as *Mother Pluto,* and then as simply *Pluto the Pup*: the elongated title was *Silly Symphony Featuring Pluto the Pup,* which ran from September 3, 1939, until November 10, 1940, when a new strip titled *Little Hiawatha, A Silly Symphony,* began and ran until November 16, 1941.) After the *Donald Duck* title addition, the single Sunday Disney page added further weekly half-pages: from 1937 on, as many as five or six different Disney-bylined half-pages could be found running at the same time, such as *Mickey Mouse, Donald Duck, Pluto, Jose Carioca,* and an animated feature serial (such as *Snow White, Pinocchio,* etc.). *Silly Symphonies,* as a strip title, got lost in the shuffle, disappearing after *Little Hiawatha.* (The Three Little Pigs, revived as strip characters in *The Practical Pig* on May 1, 1938, and Elmer the Elephant returned in *Timid Elmer* on December 4, 1938, but both ran without the *Silly Symphony* title.)

Physically, *Silly Symphonies* opened as a narrow, page-topper Sunday strip, enlarging to a full half-page on September 22, 1935, in the middle of the Three Little Kittens story. *Birds of a Feather, The Little Red Hen, Peculiar Penguins, Ambrose, Three Little Kittens,* and *Elmer*

all appeared as *Silly Symphonies* animated cartoons in the 1930s. One other *Big Little Book* collection based on the strip: *Walt Disney's Silly Symphonies Stories* was published in 1936. This included *The Little Red Hen, Birds of a Feather,* and some more *Bucky Bug* adventures.

B.B.

SILVER ROY (Spain) *Silver Roy* (subtitled "The Lone Commando") saw the light of print in the first issue of the revived comic magazine, *Pulgarcito* (1947). The strip was also published in various annuals, as well as in the magazine *Super Pulgarcito* from 1949 until its demise in 1951.

The strip's creator was Bosch Penalva, who later left the comic field to devote himself to cover illustration for juvenile novels, a genre in which he excelled with his flair for color and his facility of line.

His hero, Roy Silver, was an agent for the United Nations, stationed first in the waters of the China seas, later in the jungles of India. The strip was bathed in an atmosphere of Asian intrigue and opium dens very reminiscent of *Terry and the Pirates* and *Jungle Jim.* The hero was characterized by the pith helmet which always covered his head, and by his anti-Japanese feelings, both typical of an era influenced by American war movies in which the Japanese were the villains.

L.G.

SILVER STARR IN THE FLAME WORLD (Australia) Created by Stanley Pitt, the strip first appeared in the *Sydney Sunday Sun* on November 24, 1946. Initially, the strip was given the entire tabloid centerspread and the result was breathtaking. This allowed Pitt a freedom of layout that was closer to comic books than newspaper strips. Pitt utilized this freedom by presenting sweeping panoramas; long, towering panels down the side of the page or large central panels that dominated those surrounding it. Pitt's beautiful artwork was complemented by delicate pastel tones and shades, tastefully administered by a master colorist. The sheer beauty of the early *Silver Starr* pages has never been equalled in Australia.

Silver Starr was Pitt's tribute to *Alex Raymond* and *Flash Gordon* and there is no denying that he borrowed heavily from that strip for his inspiration. Silver was an Australian soldier who had returned from the war to join an expedition into the earth's interior. Though their backgrounds were different, Silver and Flash were the same kind of dynamic hero. The trip to the earth's core was lead by a scientist, Onro, the counterpart of Dr. Zharkov. Another member of the team was Dyson, whose features were based on those of Errol Flynn. (Over the years, Flynn's features found their way into many Pitt illustrations.) As this trio ground their way through the earth's crust in a rocket-type ship with a great drill on the bow, their radar-television threw up an image of a beautiful, red-haired girl who was surrounded by lashing tongues of bluish flame. This was the lovely Pristine (De Solvo) Queen of the Flameworld and Pitt's compliment to *Dale Arden.* This was the setting for a series of thrilling adventures that was to earn *Silver Starr* a permanent place in the history of Australian comic art.

While the story line never reached the imagination heights of *Flash Gordon,* it was entertaining and provided Pitt with exotic locales on which to employ his talents. Under Pitt's deft handling, the underground caverns and rock formation scenes came to life; as did the scenes of seas of molten lava and the ship winding its way through rock and water. The earth's interior was peopled by a race of giants, with massive heads, and a race of scaly Ape-men all of whom made ideal subjects for Pitt's fertile imagination. The one weakness of the strip was that it never produced an antagonist of the calibre of *Ming the Merciless*. The sequence of villains Ungra, Tarka, and Gorla were stereotypes, who were always overshadowed by the personality of Silver.

Silver Starr suffered a series of reductions in the printed size and when it was, eventually, reduced to 6 × 6½ area, Pitt left the paper. The final *Silver Starr* strip appeared on November 14, 1948.

During the early 1950s, there were six reprint comic books published by Young's Merchandising. Starting in 1958, Cleveland Press reprinted these stories, again, along with another four original *Silver Starr* stories. Although it had only a short life and a comparatively limited circulation, the impact of *Silver Starr* was sufficient to establish the reputation of Stanley Pitt for all time.

J.R.

SILVER SURFER (U.S.) When writer and editor Stan Lee and artist Jack Kirby created the *Fantastic Four* strip in 1961, neither was aware of the fantastic following the feature and subsequent creations would garner among older teenagers and college students, a market rarely, if ever, reached by comic books. They eagerly accepted Lee's moralizations, his often sophomoric rationalizations, and even his disorganized and inconsistent theories on humanity. In response, he continued creating stranger and more confusing civilizations and races, all of them used to grind out the Lee line on civilization as we know it. There was the Watcher, a sort of intergalactic storyteller; there were the Inhumans, a race of superhumans who lived apart from humanity; there were the Kree and Skrull galaxies, two more superhuman races who constantly battled over long-contested racial differences; and there was even Galactus, characterized almost godlike by Lee.

And from Galactus came the Silver Surfer, the former's herald and top henchman. A native of another of Lee's super galaxies, the Silver Surfer was extremely powerful: his body was covered by a coat of silvery galactic glaze which would protect him from anything in the universe; he had an atomic surfboard that he used for instantaneous transport; and, to make him complete, he was almost limitlessly powerful. Premiered in *Fantastic Four* number 48 (March 1966), the character became instantly successful and Lee made him his own, personal Jesus Christ-surrogate. "I do my most obvious moralizing in the *Silver Surfer*," the writer/editor once said.

At first an occasional guest star in the *Fantastic Four* strip, Lee eventually revealed that the Surfer had been sentenced to earth permanently by Galactus for showing too much concern for humans, whom the Surfer rarely understood and always pitied. For several appearances in the *Fantastic Four*, the Surfer traveled the earth, constantly trying to be of help, constantly misconstruing a situation, constantly fighting against his will. Almost every story ended with his moralizing about his unfair imprisonment on earth and earthlings' inhumanity to him and other beings. A galactic crybaby of embarrassing proportions, comic critic Dwight Decker once complained, claiming the feature was for those looking for spoon-fed moral instruction.

Nevertheless, the *Silver Surfer* became phenomenally popular, prompting Lee to launch the character in his own title, *The Silver Surfer*, which premiered in August 1968 with artwork by John Buscema. The book was immediately hailed by most critics as the finest and most sensitive strip of its time, although there remained a vocal minority who complained of its facile philosophizing and childish ethical values. But the strip won fan-issued Alley awards in 1968 and 1969 for best full-length stories, and the character was voted most popular in 1968. Buscema's artwork, unlike the controversial stories, was universally hailed as brilliant and innovative.

After 18 issues, however, *The Silver Surfer* folded due to poor sales, Lee blaming its demise on the general comic-reading public's inability to handle more mature features. The character has since appeared sporadically as a guest in many Marvel strips. He reappeared briefly in his own title in 1982, and again in 1988 to 1989.

J.B.

SIMMONDS, POSY (1945-) British cartoonist Rosemary Elizabeth "Posy" Simmonds was born August 9, 1945, in Cookham Dene, near Maidenhead, Berkshire. A farmer's daughter, she was educated at Queen Mary's School, Caversham, and studied fine art and French at the Sorbonne in Paris and graphic design at the Central School, London. After illustrating for *The Times*, she began her first regular daily cartoon feature, *Bear* in *The Sun* on November 17, 1969. In 1972 she moved to *The Guardian* as an illustrator. From May 1977, while John Kent, creator of *The Guardian*'s weekly strip *Varoomschka*, was away in America for six months, her idea for a replacement was accepted. Recalling one of her childhood favorites, she started by showing what had happened to "The Silent Three," a schoolgirl mystery originally drawn in the 1950s by Evelyn Flinders in *School Friend*. This soon developed into a contemporary comedy of manners centered around long-suffering Wendy Weber and her family and friends.

Posy Simmonds pinpoints the everyday crises among suburban liberals, reflecting and satirizing *The Guardian*'s own readership. In 1981 she produced *True Love*, an original graphic novel, exposing the alluring fallacies of British girl's romance comics. She left the newspaper strip to create children's books in color strip form, including *Fred* about the secret nighttime stardom of an ordinary domestic cat, which was adapted into an animated film in 1996. She has also written film scripts and television documentaries. In 1997 she completed a graphic novel to be serialized in *The Guardian*.

She is ambidextrous and has invented her own distinctive lettering font, jokingly called "Anal Retentive." She was voted Cartoonist of the Year in Granada Television's awards in 1980 and in the British Press Awards in 1981.

P.G.

SIMON, JOSEPH (1915-) American comic book writer, artist, editor, and publisher, Joseph Simon was born October 11, 1915, in Rochester, New York. Joe Simon began his comic book career in 1940 as an artist/writer/editor on the *Blue Bolt* adventure strip. He also helped create some of Novelty's minor features like *Hillman* and *Gunmaster*. About the same time, however, he was an editor at Fox comics and worked on their major strip, *Blue Beetle*.

In 1941, Simon and Jack Kirby began their famed partnership and created the legendary *Captain America* feature. Much has been said about the working relationship of the pair, many claiming Simon was the business genius while Kirby handled the creative end, but it was obvious that Simon had a considerable hand in creating the red, white, and blue character that made Timely a major force in the comic industry of the time. The pair also created the *Fiery Mask* and *Young Allies* strip for Timely.

They next moved to National in 1942 and created a horde of adventure features, including *Boy Commandos* and *Newsboy Legion*. They also handled characters like *Manhunter, Robotman*, and a revamped *Sandman*. Simon is credited with creating the *Real Fact* book. Harvey was the next stop for the team, and, in 1945, Simon and Kirby created the stellar *Boy's Ranch* Western feature. After Harvey, there came books for Hillman and Crestwood before the pair formed their own outfit, Mainline, with Simon as publisher. Formed in 1954, the company folded the next year, and, in 1956, Simon and Kirby split their long partnership.

In the years immediately following the breakup, Simon spent most of his time with the Archie group as an artist, editor, and writer. During his tenure, he created two superhero books of note, *Private Strong* and *The Fly*. Neither were outstanding, but they were Archie's only two nonhumor books of the period.

Simon eventually returned to National in 1968 to write, draw, and edit a new book entitled *Brother Power, The Geek*. Attempting to cash in on the peace movement of the time, the Geek was a hippie sort who was really just an animated dummy. Although it was a rare opportunity to see Simon's artwork and storytelling ability without Kirby's influence, the book was badly done and lasted only two issues. In 1973 in the midst of America's Watergate presidential crisis Simon launched *Prez*, an unlikely tale of a teenager made president with the help of an unscrupulous machine politician. Another attempt to capitalize on the political state of the nation, the book was a dismal failure and folded the next year. In the late 1970s he moved on to advertising.

Over the years, much has been said of the Kirby half of Simon and Kirby, most critics simply assuming Simon did little or none of the team's creative work. This has not been proven, however, and it may still be some time before Simon's contributions to the creative efforts of Simon and Kirby are fully known.

J.B.

SINNOTT, JOE (1926-   ) American comic book artist born in Saugerties, New York, on October 16, 1926, Sinnott, joined the navy after high school and served in the Pacific. After his discharge, he worked three years in a cement factory and finally entered the Cartoonists and Illustrators School in 1949. While there, he published his first comic book work, *Trudi*, a five-page filler for St. John. Tom Gill, one of his instructors, then hired him as an assistant for his Dell and Timely work. Sinnott began working directly for Timely in March 1951, penciling and inking everything from crime to horror to humor to superhero strips. He also produced material for Dell, Charlton, Treasure Chest, and Classic Illustrated before limiting himself to Timely/Atlas/Marvel in 1959.

One of the most outstanding inkers in comic book history, Sinnott began producing his best work when he and Jack Kirby began working together on a regular basis in November 1965. Starting with *Fantastic Four* number 44, Sinnott became Kirby's regular inker on the strip. Perhaps the greatest comic artist of all time, Kirby had a big, brawling style which highlighted exaggerated anatomy, gadgety panels, sprawling layouts, and general mayhem. Sinnott tightened Kirby's pencils considerably, smoothing out his occasional rough spots and weaknesses. He also added slickness and more blacks than Kirby had previously utilized. The *Fantastic Four* became a showcase of graphic excellence, and when Kirby abandoned the feature in late 1971, it was Sinnott who was given the task of maintaining continuity. In rapid-fire order, John Romita, John Buscema, and Rich Buckler all attempted to fill Kirby's spot, but Sinnott remained the inker and kept the strip as Kirby-esque as possible.

Sinnott remained at Marvel until 1992, working on every major title, from *The Avengers* to *X-Men*. He also illustrated the one-shot *Life of Pope John Paul II* in 1983. After his departure from Marvel he inked some *Zorro* comic books and illustrated several stories from the Bible.

J.B.

SIOPAWMAN (Philippines) What superhero can boast of having the largest nose, the most rotund body, the softest muscles, the least amount of hair on the head (without being completely bald), and buck-teeth? No one else but, Siopawman!

On July 9, 1963, *Siopawman* began in the first issue of *Alcala Fight Komix* and has been appearing for that publication every other week. This laughable, well-meaning, super-misfit was the brainchild of Larry Alcala, who devotes much of his spare time to writing, lettering, and illustrating *Kalabog en Bosyo, Tipin, Congressman Kalog, Laber Boy, Dr. Sabak en his Monster, Mang Ambo*, and a slew of other features and editorial cartoons for newspapers, magazines, and comic books. Alcala spends the rest of the time as a professor at the University of the Philippines.

Siopawman originally came from the planet Siopaw. Somehow, his big nose and unusual shape irritated the rest of the inhabitants and he was unceremoniously shipped out to the planet earth. Coincidentally, *Siopaw* is also the name of a Chinese pastry that is quite popu-

"Siopawman," Larry Alcala. © Alcala Fight Komix.

lar in the Philippines. Needless to say, the hero bears a strong resemblance to this exotic delicacy.

Siopawman can withstand the hail of bullets as well as the most devastating blows that his arch-enemies can lay upon his fat-laden body; he is as invulnerable as Superman. And like Superman he has an *S* on his uniform. He also wears a cape (to hide the patch on his shorts). His hostile opponents are among the most wickedly ingenious in the annals of comic history. Alcala's fertile imagination created a bizarre array of villains who are just as wacky as his main character. Among them are vegetable creatures, space aliens, local crooks, berserk geniuses, and the pulsating, quivering, Jello-Man! Siopawman gives no sign of slowing down after 35 years of ordeals and tribulations.

A fascinating aspect of the series is Larry Alcala's clever use of American and Filipino words, with his inventive puns and play on words, to convey a multiplicity of meanings. Alcala is also an entertaining and innovative storyteller with a great sense of humor.

His ability to control the continuity and the flow of movement in his strips, and the masterful manner in which he visualizes his ideas make him one of the foremost experts in sequential storytelling. The economy of his linework and the simplicity of his approach underlies his sophisticated understanding of the medium. He has gained the admiration of the readers and the respect of the industry and has distinguished himself in the field of education and communications. He is the recipient of the much coveted CCMM (Citizens Council for Mass Media) award.

O.J.

SI YEOO KI (China) *Si Yeoo Ki* ("The Westward Pilgrimage") was written by Wu Tcheng-en in the 16th century: an allegorical novel of fantasy and the supernatural, it has long since become a classic of Chinese literature. Its hero, Souen Wu-kong the monkey, became, through arduous training, a super-being capable of reaching up to the heavens and digging down to the center of the earth. Proclaiming himself the equal of the Celestial Emperor, he brought toil and turmoil to the kingdoms of earth and the skies. Exceeded, Buddha himself had the meddlesome monkey chained to the Mount of the Five Elements (there is a striking similarity with Prometheus). Five hundred years later, having converted to Buddhism, Souen Wu-kong escorted the monk Santsang in his westward pilgrimage in search of the sacred Buddhic scriptures.

Si Yeoo Ki is an account of this long and perilous journey in which Souen Wu-kong accomplished the most brilliant feats, fought spirits and demons, and finally achieved the ultimate goal. In their quest Santsang and Wu-kong are joined by two more of the monk's disciples: Tchou Pa-kie the pig, and Ho-chang the bearded warrior. The four travelers constitute the allegorical personifications of four different attributes of man: *Santsang* the mind, *Wu-kong* the heart, *Pa-kie* the appetites, and *Ho-chang* brute force. The Chinese theater has maintained and reinforced this tradition by giving the stage protagonists masks through which their primal attributes are expressed.

The People's Republic of China has kept these old legends alive, taking away their more metaphysical connotations. In the 1950s and 1960s a series of comic books illustrating the different stages of the westward journey were issued by the People's Institute of Art and Culture in Peking. The most interesting episode, titled

"Si Yeoo Ki," Tchao Hong-pen and Tsien Siao-tai.

81 Adventures, which tells of the pilgrims' encounters with the skeleton witch, was adapted by Wang Sunpei and drawn by Tchao Hong-pen and Tsien Siao-tai. The book proved so popular that it was translated into English and French in 1964 (with a second printing in 1974) for distribution abroad.

The drawings of the comic book version of *Si Yeoo Ki* are in the traditional Chinese manner, there are no balloons, and each panel (with a printed text running underneath) fills an entire page, making it more an illustrated book than a comic book as we know it. The story is nonetheless fascinating in its minuteness and detail. (The tale has been widely known outside China, especially in Japan where a comic strip parody, *Shifumai Yamana's Songoku*, appeared as early as 1930.)

M.H.

SJORS EN SJIMMIE (Netherlands) *Sjors en Sjimmie* ("George and Jimmy") stars two boys, one white and one black, in humorous adventures. Originally titled simply *Sjors*, it starred a boy and his friends in the tradition of *Our Gang*. *Sjors*, it must be noted, was actually named *Perry Winkle* and was the star of the *Winnie Winkle* Sunday page for a number of years. The Sunday *Winnie Winkle* enjoyed a large success in Europe in the 1930s and was published under a number of different titles in France, Germany, and (among others) the Netherlands. *Sjors* appeared in *Sjors Weekblad* ("George's Weekly"), which was first published on January 2, 1936, as a children's supplement of the newspaper *Panorama* and continued until October 31, 1941, when it became a casualty of World War II.

At the time *Sjors* was an original Dutch comic strip and had been so since 1938 when Frans Piët had taken over writing and drawing the strip when Branner was changing the tone and lineup of his Sunday page. Owning the rights to their title, the Dutch were able to continue the strip on their own, subtly changing it over the years so that its origins are nothing more than a

"Skeets," Dow Walling. © Herald-Tribune Syndicate.

long-forgotten memory today. The never-aging *Sjors* is more than six decades old.

There was a six-year hiatus from 1941 to 1947, however. But by then the weekly supplement of *Panorama* was back in print, ultimately becoming an independent publication with considerably more pages than the original four, of which *Sjors* had been the only comic feature. From 1951 to 1954 the comic book was titled *Rebellenclub* ("Rebels' Club"), from 1954 to 1968 *Sjors van de Rebellenclub* ("George of the Rebels' Club"), and since 1968, once again simply *Sjors*. By that time the strip itself had been rechristened *Sjors en Sjimmie*, incorporating Sjors' black costar, Sjimmie.

Sjors en Sjimmie was continued in 1970 by artist Jan Kruis who later on turned the artwork over to Jan Steeman, noted for also having done the semifunny science-fiction comic *Arad en Maya* ("Arad and Maya") for the *Sjors* magazine. Other originally Dutch series published in *Sjors* over the decades include *Tommy's Avonturen* ("Tommy's Adventures") by Piet Broos, *Monki* by B. J. Reith, *Olaf Noort*, *Cliff Rendall*, and other strips by Bert Bus, plus *Brammetje Bram* by Eddy Ryssack. *Sjors* and other strips serialized in the magazine have been reprinted regularly in album-sized books.

W.F.

SKEETS (U.S.) Former King Features cartoonist Dow Walling created his gentle strip about a young boy, *Skeets*, in 1932, debuting on May 1. Syndicated by the *New York Herald Tribune* as a Sunday strip only, it depicted the simple premise of the innocent boyhood adventures of Skeets, his passive parents, pals Button-Nose, Whiffle, cousin "Eggy" Hanty, Pudge Willikins, and others.

Owing much influence from and noticeable imitation of Percy Crosby's *Skippy*, the mischievous antics of the neighborhood boys mirrored a Norman Rockwell portrayal of baseball, skating, fishing, dips in the pond, and trips to the candy store. Occasionally, spirited dream sequences, visits to Santa, and poignant episodes of youthful reflection hinted at Walling's aesthetic range, but most of the time the feature remained dedicated to commonplace, domestic hijinks. Walling never developed the characters' personalities to any degree, relying primarily on formulaic, situational humor. His semicrude artistry simplified notice-

ably during the late 1940s, yet his earlier work displayed unique and innovative attention to environmental detail not seen in other strips of the genre. The strip was reprinted in the 1940s in *Peter Rabbit* comic books.

Childless himself, the cartoonist drew the charming exploits of his fictional boy with the pillbox hat until its last appearance on July 15, 1951. Walling was a charter member of the National Cartoonists Society.

B.J.

SKIPPY (U.S.) In 1919 Percy Crosby, fresh out of World War I, started his long collaboration with the humor magazine *Life*. In the pages of the old *Life* there appeared, with increasing frequency, a 10-year-old curbstone philosopher named Skippy who soon became so popular with readers that Crosby decided to syndicate his adventures to interested newspapers in the middle 1920s. In 1928 King Features took over the distribution of both the daily strip and Sunday page of *Skippy* (while Crosby wisely retained ownership).

"Skippy," Percy Crosby. © Percy L. Crosby.

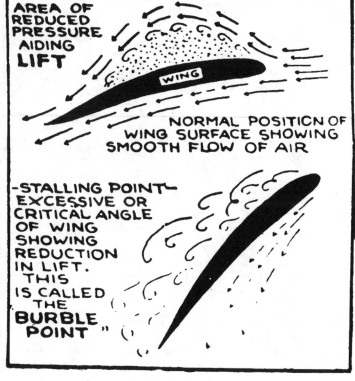

"Skyroads," Dick Calkins. © National Newspaper Syndicate.

Skippy Skinner, floppily attired in a nondescript checked hat, oversize jacket, and short pants, held forth on the neighborhood curbside, flanked by the fawning court of his pals, Sooky Wayne the slob, Sidney Saunders the schemer, and a few other wide-eyed life observers. Skippy was not a nice kid (even by comic strip standards), he had none of the spontaneousness of Perry Winkle or the high spirits of the Katzenjammers. His view of the adult world was bitter and disenchanted, and there was a viciousness in his attitude to others. He was forever calculating the odds, pitting his wits against the institutions, and manipulating his little companions for his own purposes. In short, he was a fully developed adult with the appearance of a kid.

There was great humor in *Skippy*, but it was always tinged with sadness, even pessimism. More often than not it dealt in humiliation, defeat, and alienation, thus offering the readers a foretaste of the themes that Charles Schulz would later develop in *Peanuts*. Crosby's drawing style (closer to straight illustration than to the cartoon) has been praised to the skies by some critics, but it was probably a bit too academic for the purpose. (In the 1920s and all through the 1930s, a top piece, *Always Belittlin'*, was tacked on to the Sunday *Skippy*: also a child strip, it reflected even more strongly the author's misanthropy in its depiction of small tots busily engaged in putting one another down.)

Percy Crosby became seriously ill in 1942 and was soon unable to continue drawing the strip. In 1943 he formally withdrew *Skippy* rather than have it ghosted by somebody else (a rare occurrence in a profession not particularly noted for its high ethical standards). While it lasted (and with the exception of the last painfully shaky episodes) *Skippy* was a well-crafted and thoughtfully written feature, but it somehow fell short of the mark, and its potential was never fully realized. (In 1971 the old *Skippy* daily strips were being resyndicated by Windy City Features.)

Percy Crosby's strip has inspired two movies: the 1931 *Skippy* (which launched the career of kid actor Jackie Cooper) and the less successful *Sooky* (1932). The 1931 film won an Oscar for best direction (Norman Taurog).

M.H.

SKYROADS (U.S.) *Skyroads* was created in 1929 by two former World War I pilots, Dick Calkins and Lester J. Maitland, for the John F. Dille syndicate. Calkins, however, was already overburdened with the drawing of *Buck Rogers* and he turned the artwork over to his two assistants, Zack Mosley and especially Russell Keaton.

The first strip opened with a stirring address by Maitland, the first paragraph of which might be useful to quote in its entirety: "Since the beginning man has struggled to conquer his environment. The lands of the earth and the waters of the sea have come under his dominion. The air alone remained unchallenged. Earthbound man has gazed fascinated at the limitless blue above him, yearning to ride the ocean of the air. This generation has seen the age-old yearning realized."

After that soaring announcement, the basic plot of the strip (as given in the next panel) must have seemed to many a reader as something of a letdown: Ace Ames and Buster Evans find themselves owners of a new biplane. They form a partnership, Skyroads, Unlimited. In a nutshell this represented the predicament of the early aviation strips: the discrepancy between the lofty aims and the pedestrian plot. In the case of *Skyroads*, the authors tried to alleviate the situation by inserting at least one didactic panel in each strip, explaining the importance of wind factors and detailing the workings of wing flaps; this practice, however, had the disadvantage of slowing down the action considerably, without appreciably enlightening the reader, and it was soon discontinued.

Over the years, *Skyroads* featured several teams of actors playing in alternance, as it were: Ace Ames and Buster Evans disappeared around 1933 (along with Maitland) and were succeeded by *Hurricane Hawk*, a dashing and resourceful air devil. At this point Russell Keaton was the sole author of the strip (even signing his name to it) and some of the adventures he concocted were excellent in the quality of their suspense and the clarity of their drawing. The episode pitting Hurricane against a hooded legion of air pirates led by a malevolent dwarf known as the Crimson Skull was particularly memorable. In 1939 Hurricane was replaced by Speed McCloud, then by another hero, Clipper Williams. With the assistance of a score of young boys and girls known as the Flyin' Legion he cleaned the skies of foreign agents and saboteurs. Around 1942 the strip vanished into the wild blue yonder for the last time.

After the first couple of years, *Skyroads* turned into one of the better-drawn aviation strips, with Russell Keaton firmly at the controls. It cannot be ranked among the top strips of the decade but it certainly deserves some recognition for its high spirits, unflagging action, and flavorful plot.

A few of the early episodes of *Skyroads* were reprinted in paperback form by Edwin Aprill, Jr. (Ann Arbor, 1966).

M.H.

SLIM JIM (U.S.) One of the most popular of all early American comic strips, *Slim Jim* is also notable for showcasing some of the most original, though virtually forgotten, comic strip art. The feature began as *Circus Solly*, originally a daily strip in the *Chicago Daily News*. Distributed in Sunday format by the World Color Printing Co. of St. Louis in September 1910, dozens of rural papers soon carried the strip under its new title, *Slim Jim and the Force*. The artist was George Frink, an authentically funny cartoonist who is hardly remembered today; he also illustrated two Peck's *Bad Boy* books: *Peck's Bad Boy and the Circus* and *Peck's Bad Boy and the Cowboys*.

Frink's style was sketchy and filled with native humor. His art was original but reminiscent of McCutcheon, Joe Donahey, and early Herriman. There was free movement in his panels and as much slapstick as in *Opper*.

Slim Jim was an outrageously tall and thin character. His three eternal pursuers, the force, were comical constables and therein is the basic plot for years of merriment: Slim Jim each week manages to just outwit and outmaneuver his would-be captors. The hijinks take them all over the world, in cities and on farms, on airships and boats.

Frink, who signed only his surname to his work and left his first name a mystery to comic historians for years, died in 1912; had he lived longer, his name might have been remembered today as one of comics' greats instead of as a postscript. Strangely enough, his successor on *Slim Jim* is also an enigma. Raymond Crawford Ewer was a gifted penman who brought nearly as much inventiveness of art and ideas to the comics as Winsor McCay, and at about the same time.

Ewer was a comic strip innovator, even in those early days. He experimented with extra-long panels, bold colors, and treatments of the Sunday page as one

"Slim Jim," Raymond Ewer.

entity. His art was as funny as Frink's, but on a baroque, detailed order. His drawings looked like they came from sketchbooks, with many lines happily searching for the essence of a figure: Ewer's drawings were anatomically perfect and students can compare his work favorably, in terms of spirit, execution, and quality, with Heinrich Kley.

He brought a joyous spirit and some knockout visual excitement to *Slim Jim* but he, too, died young around Christmas 1913, after only one year of work on the strip. Ewer's last published drawings, except for *Slim Jim*, appeared in *Puck* magazine in the mid-1910s. Some earlier drawings—crude, on the verge of slick—appeared in *Judge*, but his *Puck* centerspreads in color are masterpieces of cartooning observation and delineation.

After Ewer, the World Company brought in Stanley Armstrong to continue *Slim Jim*. His work was pedestrian, suffering all the more from the shadows of excellence which preceded him. Jim took on a slightly crazed, funny expression and had more of a character under Armstrong, but overall, Armstrong's work was stiff.

Armstrong's service on the strip was strangely interrupted in 1915 when a succession of artists drew and signed it, each for a couple of weeks or so: Clarence Rigby, C. W. Kahles, Ernie McGee, and some reprinted Frink pages. But then Armstrong returned and continued on the strip which always enjoyed rural American popularity until the World Color Printing Co. itself died in 1937.

R.M.

SLYLOCK FOX AND COMICS FOR KIDS (U.S.) The usually uninspired genre of children's pages added a refreshing feature in 1986 with the introduction of *Comics for Kids*, by the son of *Moose* creator and King Features' bullpen artist, Bob Weber, Jr. Originally a Sunday only syndicated strip for foreign markets, King launched it domestically on March 31, 1987. Consisting of several regular interactive features, an early component was a hog family named *The Pigglys*, since replaced by the visual puzzle *Find Six Differences*, accompanied by an elemental *How to Draw* lesson and a multiple-choice question panel. *Bonnie and Boo-Boo* is a strip within a strip, featuring a team of siblings that

"Slylock Fox," Bob Weber Jr. © King Features Syndicate.

provides pure comedy drawn with a charming simplicity, differing from the familiar Weber style used throughout the other elements.

The strip's nucleus, though, is Slylock Fox, a shrewd detective who skillfully solves cases along with his diminutive and venerating sidekick, Max Mouse. Presented in one commanding panel, a crime is described simply while a hidden clue is pictured, inviting the reader to help deduce the situation caused by regular nemeses Count Weirdly, Shady Shrew, Wanda Witch, or Harry Ape, among others. Facts about nature, health, pet care, ecology, and self-esteem mix in with the brain teasers, resulting in an educational, entertaining, and informative package. All text and dialogue are captioned, giving the piece more the feel of children's book art than that of a comic strip. Drawings by young readers are regularly published; a fraction of the 150 to 200 drawings received each week. Weber, Jr., writes all the continuities but is assisted by his father on some of the artwork, especially since the advent of a daily version.

A fine card set, *Slylock Fox Brain Bogglers*, was produced recently, showcasing 90 of the cunning Reynard's best adventures. In 1994 the feature was retitled *Slylock Fox and Comics for Kids* and currently appears in 400 newspapers.

B.J.

SMILIN' JACK (U.S.) On October 1, 1933, Zack Mosley started *On the Wing* (changed to *Smilin' Jack* in December of the same year) as a Sunday feature for the *News-Tribune* Syndicate; a daily strip was added on June 15, 1936. Smilin' Jack Martin is a pilot and in the convention of the time, that means he does everything, from searching for lost explorers to solving bank rob-

beries. In his exploits he is aided and abetted by his boy companion Pinfeathers, his faithful cook and jack-of-all-trades Fat Stuff (a reformed headhunter whom he brought back from the South Seas), not to mention his associates, the blustering Velvet Harry and the rather sinister Downwind (whose face is always hidden from view).

Smilin' Jack's aerial adventures are only half as outlandish as his romantic entanglements. With all his other responsibilities he finds time to be a man around town (even growing a Clark Gable moustache for the purpose) with an endless string of girls around his neck: the loyal Mary, the fiery Dixie, the bitchy Gale (respectively blonde, redhead, and brunette) among others. This does not prevent him from marrying his boss Joy, who later presents him with a son nicknamed Jungle Jolly, before vanishing from his life. (During the war Jack was to find Joy who had lost her memory only to lose her again.)

The artwork on the strip is uniformly terrible, but in spite (or because) of it *Smilin' Jack* remained popular through the years due in part to the accuracy of its technical details, and in part to the cheerful absurdities of the plot. In the more demanding 1960s, however, *Smilin' Jack* gradually lost his appeal and he was finally grounded in 1973 after a 40-year career, the longest of any aviation strip.

The strip enjoyed its own comic book version in the 1940s, and in 1942 Universal released *The Adventures of Smilin' Jack*, the last movie serial based on a comic strip that they ever produced.

M.H.

SMITH, AL (1902-1986) An American artist born in Brooklyn, New York, on March 2, 1902, as Albert

"Smilin' Jack," Zack Mosley. © Chicago Tribune-New York News Syndicate.

Schmidt, his schooling was meager and a proclivity toward art was thwarted by lack of funds. In 1922 Smith got a job as copy boy on the old *New York Sun* but within a year he moved across Park Row to serve the *New York World* in the same capacity. It was here, in the manner so familiar to many of cartooning's greats, that the copy boy eventually was allowed to do some drawing on the stars' off days.

Smith's feature was *From 9 to 5*, a panel about office work, which had no connection with the later feature of the same name by Jo Fischer. This panel was picked up for a short time by United Feature Syndicate after the World folded. But the Depression rolled on and Smith resorted to jobs with the WPA in Closter and Demarest, New Jersey. In the early 1930s he did odd jobs with John Wheeler's Bell Syndicate, including Christmas spot drawings and a stint as ghost for sports cartoonist Bob Edgren.

In 1932 Wheeler and Bud Fisher contacted Smith about ghosting *Mutt and Jeff*, which, for approximately 14 years, had been ghosted by Ed Mack. Here began Smith's association with the classic strip which continues today and a tempestuous association with the volatile Fisher, who was notoriously tight and a heavy drinker.

Smith was forced to carry the strip without the troublesome guidance of Fisher. He soon made the strip more genteel than it had previously been; Mutt's married life was spent more by the hearth and less in the divorce court. Jeff, too, began to seriously court girls, including Encee (for n.c.: no comment) and Chlorine. Bruno the dog joined the Mutt family and *Cicero's Cat* became the Sunday top strip, borrowed from the office cat in *From 9 to 5*. Smith's art, too, was slicker and more slapstick than any of his predecessors who ghosted for Fisher (others included Billy Liverpool, Ken Kling, and George Herriman). After Fisher's death in 1954, Smith signed the strip himself, although ownership has remained in the hands of the Countess Aedita de Beaumont, Fisher's widow. He left *Mutt and Jeff* in the hands of George Breisacher after he retired in 1980; he died on November 24, 1986, in Rutland, Vermont.

In 1950 Smith founded the Smith Service, a syndicate serving weekly papers. His own features included *Rural Delivery* and *Remember When*, with other features drawn by Joe Dennett (*Down Main Street*) and George Wolfe (*Pops*).

Smith was very active in the National Cartoonists Society for many years, and served successively as founder of the placement service, general membership chairman, treasurer (nine years), and president from 1967 to 1969. In 1968 Smith won the Best Humor Strip award.

If *Mutt and Jeff* had lost its slapstick touch under Smith, it is but a reflection of the times; the strip remains a favorite with a large list of papers. Smith, in and out of the NCS, has been a help to many young cartoonists starting their careers.

R.M.

SMITH, ROBERT SIDNEY (1877-1935) Perhaps the most attentively read and relished American writer and artist of the first third of this century was born Robert Sidney Smith in Bloomington, Illinois, on February 13, 1877, almost 40 years before he was to publish the first episode of *The Gumps* in the *Chicago Tribune* on February 12, 1917; so began the great American family epic of the 1920s.

Smith's father was a dentist, and wanted his son to follow in the profession. The boy, however, showed early talent for drawing, developed it in grammar and high school, and was turning out local cartoons at the age of 18 for the *Bloomington Eye*. Within a year, college forgotten, Smith began a series of income-improving moves through a half-score of newspapers (from the *Indianapolis News* to the *Chicago Examiner*) with which he furthered his skills in sports and political cartooning. An immediate sports page hit with *Examiner* readers, Smith seized on his popularity to introduce his first comic strip there in 1908: *Buck Nix*. One of the first humanized animal strips, *Buck Nix* delighted Chicagoans, and led to his being hired by the *Chicago Tribune* in 1912 to continue the strip under a new name, *Old Doc Yak*. *Buck Nix* had been a daily strip; *Old Doc Yak* ran only on Sunday (with Smith doing sports cartoons as a daily stint), but Smith was about to undertake a regular seven-day-a-week strip.

Just after Christmas 1916, Joe Patterson, copublisher of the Tribune, outlined a strip idea to Smith that would feature a typical Chicago lower-middle-class family with problems and successes that would reflect those of the average *Tribune* reader. He remembered and liked the name, *Gump* (first used comically in L. Frank Baum's *The Land of Oz* (1904), but also an actual surname), and suggested it for Smith's new strip menage. Introduced by a short sequence of the first daily *Old Doc Yak* episodes, *The Gumps* began in February 1917. Two years later, public demand forced Smith to fold the Sunday *Old Doc Yak* and replace the still-popular strip with a Sunday *Gumps* in June 1919. By this time, *The Gumps* was being snapped up by newspapers across the country, alerted to the fact that Smith's family strip had greatly increased the *Tribune's* circulation.

The 1920s were the golden years for *The Gumps* and Robert Sidney Smith (who had begun his cartooning career with the signature "R. Sidney Smith," but soon dropped the first initial for the simple and famed "Sidney Smith"). Smith's personal fortune, of course, soared. By the early 1920s, he already owned an extensive estate, Shirland, near Trudehurst, Wisconsin, and a costly Chicago residence; commanded use of the topmost office in the Chicago Tribune tower; owned a fleet of cars, which he drove at top speeds along deserted country roads; and had hired the best talent he could find to work with him on *The Gumps* (Harold Gray, Sol Hess, Stanley Link, etc.).

The impoverishment of the country and the shattering of many dreams by the 1930s didn't seem to affect the popularity of *The Gumps*. In fact, Smith had so built the fame and value of his strip by 1935 that, on the expiration of the old contract with the *Tribune*, he was able to command a new one that would pay him a million dollars over the following three years, and he was given a Rolls-Royce as a bonus. Speeding back to his Wisconsin estate the morning after he had signed the new contract in Chicago (October 20, 1935) Smith collided with another driver at an isolated country point in Illinois and was killed instantly.

B.B.

SMITTY (U.S.) One of the few *Chicago Tribune-New York News* strips of the 1920s which was not in large part the idea of publisher Joe Patterson was Walter Berndt's *Smitty*, which first appeared daily on Monday, November 27, 1922, and Sunday on February 25, 1923 (in the *News* only). Derived to a great extent from Walter Hoban's *Jerry on the Job*, Berndt's first version of this famous strip ran in the *New York World* as *Bill the Office Boy* for a short time until Berndt was fired for insubordination. Taking the strip to the *News,* the young artist found Patterson to be interested. Having launched a strip about a working girl, *Winnie Winkle*, the publisher saw the use of one about a working kid with a similar office background, and was only inclined to change one thing: the hero's name. Trying a handy phone book for inspiration, Patterson hit the S's and found nothing but pages of Smiths. Giving up, he suggested "Smitty" as a nickname, pinpointed a cumbersome first name among the phone book Smiths, and told Berndt to get busy.

The first episode, captioned: "Meet Up With Augustus Smith," showed Smitty, a dapper little guy in cap and short pants, sauntering into a drugstore to phone his new boss, Mr. Bailey, and ask if the office boy job he had advertised the day before was still open. Told that it wasn't, and that the boy he had hired was satisfactory, the grinning Smitty strolled happily and securely out of the store, his worries over. Mr. Bailey, Smitty's genial, rotund boss, appeared in the following day's episode and costarred with the office boy hero through the ensuing 50 years of the strip.

"Smitty," Walter Berndt. © *Chicago Tribune-New York News Syndicate.*

A simple, but somehow always witty and amusing strip, *Smitty* had little in the way of plot in the daily strip (Smitty becomes a Golden Gloves boxer, gets involved in major league baseball, goes on camping trips with his boss, etc.) and featured only situation gags in the Sunday page, largely with the aid of Smitty's obstreperous kid brother, Herby, and his pet dog, a lop-eared mutt named Spot. Smitty's parents, Ma and Pa Smith, were the only other regular characters in the strip, until an Indian guide named George was introduced in the daily strip in the late 1930s, and Smitty (who grows infrequently over the years to young adulthood) meets a permanent girlfriend in the office named Ginny in the late 1950s, whom he eventually marries.

Never filmed in live action and animated only briefly by Pathé in 1928, *Smitty* appeared in a few worthwhile book collections in the late 1920s and early 1930s, as well as in some infrequent comic book collections a bit later, but otherwise has not been well reprinted. Berndt's only other strip work after launching *Smitty* was the addition of a four-panel Sunday companion strip named (despite his stardom in the larger part of the page) *Herby*, in 1930. Both strips were discontinued in 1973.

B.B.

SMOKEY STOVER (U.S.) What is probably one of the most outrageous comic strips ever devised saw the light of print (as a Sunday feature) on March 10, 1935: *Smokey Stover*, penned by the zany Bill Holman and distributed by the staid News-Tribune Syndicate.

Smokey Stover, as his name indicates, is a fireman and, along with his boss, Chief Cash U. Nutt, he turns the firehouse into a madhouse. Riding to the fires in a

"Smokey Stover," Bill Holman. © Chicago Tribune-New York News Syndicate.

red buggy, Smokey is likely to cause more mayhem than the cause of his alarm. The commotions are just as many within the firehouse as without: on occasion Smokey had the fire wagon outfitted with tank tracks (to tread softly) or equipped with chimes (more melodic than sirens).

Smokey Stover's chief sources of fun are the innumerable puns that Billy Holman regularly inflicts on his reading public ("carrying colds to Newcastle, the bottle of Bunker Hill, and for whom the belles toil are a few of them), and the cryptic signs which he liberally scatters throughout the strip (Notary Sojac, Foo, 1506 nixnix). Figuratively firing in all directions, Bill Holman was able to maintain a high level of spontaneity and hilarity for more than 40 years. *Smokey Stover* has had as many misses as hits, but its rapid-fire delivery and iconoclastic asides more than made up for the occasional clinkers and the inevitable duds. (For a long time *Smokey* had a companion strip, *Spooky*, about a cat as nutty as his master; when *Spooky* was discontinued, the cat became a permanent character in *Smokey*.)

Holman regrettably put an end to the zany exploits of his merry crew of firemen when he retired in 1973. *Smokey Stover* has been reprinted sporadically in the 1980s, most notably in an anthology of screwball comic strips published by Fantagraphic Books.

M.H.

SNAKE TALES (Australia) In October 1974 cartoonist Allan Salisbury (who signs "Sols") came up with *The Old Timer*, a comic strip featuring a beer-guzzling old codger, his sharpie pal the Con-Man, his nemesis the Flyin' Doc, and a couple of aborigines known as the Lost Tribesman and His Wife. The strip originated in Sydney's *Daily Telegraph* and was later syndicated all over Australia through Inter Continental Features. Sols kept adding new characters, like the Old Timer's secret admirer Lillie and Crazy Croc the lazy crocodile; and to crown it all, in 1976 Snake sneakily slithered in.

Snake is a pathetic reptilian whose only aim in his lonely and earthbound life is to acquire some friends along with a few limbs. Having once innocently asked what he didn't have that others did he got the obvious reply, "Fingers, thumbs, nails, knuckles, hands, wrists, elbows, legs, kneecaps, thighs," ad infinitum. As to his other failing, he has to resort to carrying a sign reading, "Give the snake a kiss," or to call upon a rent-a-friend service (for which he has to pay special rates).

All his shortcomings only served to endear Snake to the readers all the more, to such an extent that the feature was renamed *Snake Tales* in 1978.

Among the hallmarks of the strip almost from the beginning have been its puns. Some examples will suffice: "Why did so many turn up at the optician's party? He promised them all a spectacle." "Why did the drunk kamikaze pilot survive the war? He got smashed before he took off." "How do you stop your telly running all night? Make sure it has commercial brakes." While critics have excoriated the author for his incessant stream of bad puns, most readers appear to relish his corniness.

Sols's graphic style can charitably be characterized as minimalist, but it is nonetheless telling in its conciseness. Soon after *Snake Tales* became established, it met with growing success not only in Australia (where it has been reprinted into a number of paperbacks and has given rise to much merchandising) but also overseas, particularly in Scandinavia. In the United States it was syndicated by NEA from 1982 to 1991.

M.H.

SNOOKUMS *see* Newlyweds, The.

SNUFFY SMITH *see* Barney Google.

SOGLOW, OTTO (1900-1975) An American artist born in New York City on December 23, 1900, Soglow was educated in New York public schools and then trained at the Art Students League from 1919 to 1925 under, among others, John Sloan. Soglow's inspirations in art were Winsor McCay, George McManus, and George Herriman, although he aspired to a career in fine arts.

His first published drawing was an amateur submission to *Cartoons* magazine in 1919, but his professional career began in 1925 with Western illustrations for *Lariat* magazine. After breaking into the magazine field (Soglow had worked in New York at various odd jobs, including painting baby rattles), other sales followed, to the *New Yorker, College Humor, Life,* and *Judge.* In 1925 he also drew for the *New York World* "Metropolitan" section.

Soglow was a charter member of the zany *New Yorker* crew in those early days when camaraderie did so much to build that magazine into an institution. One can imagine the sessions when Soglow, Harold

Ross, S. J. Perelman, Thurber, E. B. White, and others thought up captions for Soglow's classic drawing of merely a city street with an open manhole; the cartoon ran literally dozens of times with different gags.

One such Soglow cartoon editor Harold Ross particularly liked, and he requested more of the Little King featured in it. Soon the Little King became as popular a magazine cartoon character as Henry, Little Lulu, or another generation's Hazel. And soon the eternal purchaser of comic genius, William Randolph Hearst, was in touch with Soglow.

Wily Ross, however, had a contract for the *Little King* full-page strips, so while Hearst waited for expiration, Soglow drew *The Ambassador* (very close to the King in flavor and style) in the Saturday feature section, with captions, and as a strip for King Features syndication. As a newspaper comic strip, *The Little King* began on Sunday, September 9, 1934. (Its companion strip was the equally funny *Sentinel Louie*.)

Soglow's stark, almost diagrammatic style, devoid of shading but always alive with action, has marked him as one of the most individualistic of modern strip artists. His contributions to the art have included services away from the drawing board. He was founder of the National Cartoonists Society, and he has been on frequent tours of bases in war and peacetime as well as devoting time and effort to other charitable causes. In recognition of his contributions he has received, among other awards, the NCS Reuben and the Elzie Segar Award.

Soglow retired from his weekly task of drawing spots for the *New Yorker*'s "Talk of the Town" in 1972 and continued to produce *The Little King* for a sadly diminishing list of Sunday papers, until his death on April 3, 1975.

R.M.

SOLANO LÓPEZ, FRANCISCO (1928-) Solano López is an Argentine artist born October 26, 1928, in Buenos Aires. The death of his father when he was eight delayed the future artist's avocation for drawing, which he had manifested at an early age. He briefly pursued law studies and later worked in advertising before definitively turning to comics in 1950. He worked for several publishers and later started his fruitful association with fabled editor and scriptwriter Hector Oesterheld; their first collaborative effort was *Uma-Uma* (1953) for the magazine *Rayo Rojo*. Soon afterward he took over *Bull Rockett*, which Oesterheld had created in 1952, and drew it until 1959; at the same time he also illustrated other Oesterheld creations, including *Ernie Pike* (on which Hugo Pratt was later to make his name), *Rolo, el marciano adoptivo* ("Rolo the Adopted Martian"), *Joe Zonda* (adventures in the South Seas), *Amapola Negra* ("The Black Poppy," a story of aerial war adventures), and especially *El Eternauta*. This series told the cataclysmic invasion of earth by extraterrestrial forces. Considered Oesterheld's masterpiece, it was later illustrated by Alberto Breccia in a new version that started in 1968. Oesterheld, however, wrote a sequel to the original version (just before his disappearance in 1977), which was also drawn by Solano López and which appeared in the magazine *Skorpio*.

In the late 1950s Solano López slowly developed a British market for his increased production. With the help of assistants he contributed for the next 15 years a flood of comic strips to IPC Magazines of London,

Francisco Solano López and Carlos Sampayo, "Evaristo." © the authors.

the most noteworthy being *Air Ace Library* (1959), *Kelly's Eye* (1963, in *Valiant*), *Galaxus* (1964, in *Buster*), *Toys of Doom* (1966, in *Buster*), *Raven on the Wing* (1968, in *Valiant*), *Adam Eterno* (1969, in *Lion*), and *Nipper* (1970, in *Tiger*). During his British phase he continued his collaboration with Oesterheld, drawing *Lord Pampa* (about a war pilot) for the magazine *Rayo Rojo* in 1963.

Solano López entered the latter phase of his career with a commitment to quality. It began with the second part of *Eternauta*, and continued with the artist's collaboration with writer Ricardo Barreiro. Together they produced *Slot-Barr*, a 1976 science-fiction series that aimed to bring more rational underpinnings to the genre, and especially *Ministerio*, set in a dictatorial society of the future, which debuted exactly 10 years later in the magazine *Fierro*. The duo's latest collaborative work has been *El Televisor*, a dystopian tale, also published in *Fierro*, starting in 1990.

In the interval Solano López worked for various European publishers, notably drawing *Historias tristes* ("Sad Stories") and *Ana* on texts by his son, Gabriel, between the late 1970s and mid-1980s. In collaboration with writer Carlos Sampayo, he came out in 1983 with *Evaristo*, which had as its protagonist a middle-age and disabused police commissioner in the Buenos Aires of the late 1950s and early 1960s. Building on Sampayo's splendid scripts, the visual rendition of *Evaristo* imparted to the work a climate of squalor, of things falling apart, deepening the sensation of hurt slowly oozed by the stories in their succession and foreshadowing the inexorable rotting away of life against a background of failure and defeat. Hailed internationally as a work of depth and significance, *Evaristo* is the artist's masterpiece to date.

J.C.

SOLDINO (Italy) In 1955 Renato Bianconi, a former editor of *Edizioni Alpe*, set up his own comic book publishing company in partnership with Giovanni Duga. The first title issued by this new house was *Trottolino*, followed in 1957 by *Soldino*.

Soldino was the creation of Giovanni Battista Carpi and Giulio Chierchini; they were followed first by Nicolino Del Principe, then by Tiberio Colantuoni, Motta, and more recently Dossi. Soldino is a little king, penniless but high-spirited, reigning over a mythical kingdom where thievery, corruption, trickery, and mischief are rampant. The monarch, however, is upstaged by his grandmother Abelarda, who often has to get her grandson out of some trouble of his own making. In spite of a decrepit body, Abelarda possesses unlimited strength; this super-grandma is able not only to knock out a whole gang of hoodlums, but also to split a mountain in two, lift a truck, or uproot a whole clump of trees like a hurricane. Abelarda is a highly colorful character who is the real star of the two comic books relating Soldino's mishaps: *Soldino Mensile* and *Soldino Super*. In the 1960s she was given her own *Abelarda* comic book in recognition of her popularity with the readers.

Another spin-off of *Soldino* is *Bongo*, an ape who frequently appeared in the company of Soldino and Abelarda. He has been recently promoted to full star status with an entire comic book devoted to his adventures. Soldino and company all ended their exploits in the early 1990s.

G.B.

SOLOVJEV, SERGEJ (1901-1975) Comics author Sergej Solovjev lived and worked in Serbia between the two World Wars. Born in 1901 in Kursk, Russia, Solovjev attended and finished Military Academy. As a cavalry officer he took part in combat against the Bolshevik forces during the civil war, and in 1920 escaped into Serbia. Just like many other Russians who decided not to return into the communist-controlled Russia, Solovjev opted to stay in emigration and become Yugoslav.

Solovjev worked as a manual laborer, then as a tax official, and started his studies at the Academy of Art in Belgrade. His first comic was a story of adventure and war, entitled *Legija prokletib* ("Legion of the Damned"); the first installment was in number 99 of *Mika Mis* ("Mickey Mouse") on May 21, 1937. Before the Nazi invasion of Serbia in April 1941, he had 31 comics printed in three different Serbian magazines. Some of these comics were later reprinted elsewhere. He signed most as "S. Solo" or "Moum Gey." The only Serbian comics artist more productive than he was Navojev. No less than 30 years after the end of World War II, one of Solovjev's comics episode was found and printed for the first time (in 1975), making his total production 32 comics.

At the beginning of 1939, *Mika Mis* editor Ignjačević had a conflict with Ivković and quit to establish a new magazine. Solovjev, unlike some others, continued to collaborate with both. The reason why he continued to work for Ignjačević is perhaps his good cooperation with scriptwriter Branislav Vidić. For nearly half of Solovjev's comics were scripted by Vidić; others, which were based on famous literature, may have been adapted by Vidić although they did not have his signature (including Dumas's *Three Musketeers* in 1938, Shakespeare's *Midsummer Night's Dream* in 1938,

Sergej Solovjev, "Ivanhoe." © Sergej Solovjev.

Scott's *Ivanhoe* in 1939, Shakespeare's *Romeo and Juliet* in 1939-1940, and *Robin Hood* in 1939). Whoever was responsible for the adaptations, they were done well with an emphasis on the most interesting key points, action sequences, plot overturns, and strong, dynamic characters.

Vidić actually signed only five scenarios for Solovjev's comics, in two different serials. *Crni ataman* ("Black Ataman") appeared on October 26, 1937. The serial's second episode was titled *Kapetan Leš* ("Captain Lash") in 1938, and the third episode was *Nevesta živog Bude* ("Bride of the Living Buddha") also in 1938. His settings included the mountainsides of the Caucasian Mountains, Turkmenistan, and Kirgizia. The plot involves a young cossack named Aljoša (pronounced *Alyosha*), who is falsely accused and expelled from his native village on the Caucasian Mountains and who decides it is payback time. His revenge is successful. Later he takes up the fight against injustices inflicted on others. This is an outstanding Serbian comics, extremely popular and important. According to an opinion poll taken in 1938, it was second in popularity after *The Phantom* but ahead of *Mandrake, Prince Valiant,* and *Flash Gordon*. The fourth episode, which was the last, was published without a special title. In it, Aljoša gets a loyal companion, Šućur (pronounced *Shootyur*). The other Vidić and Solovjev serial consisted of only two episodes, released in 1939. It was *Bufalo Bil*.

Vidić and Solovjev produced an excellent biographical serial, *Napoleon*, in three episodes, published in 1940. Also they produced the adventure serials *Black Mask—Lord Warwick* (1940), *Siberian Girl* (1940), and *Big Kid* (1940). Only Solovjev signed as author on three excellent comics *Put ka slavi* ("Road to Glory," 1940), *Ostrvo s blagom* ("Treasure Island" based on the novel by R. L. Stevenson) in 1941 but discontinued because of the onset of the war, reprinted entirely in 1951 in the magazine *Omladina* ("The Youth"), and *Carev štitonoša* ("Tzar's Shieldbearer") in 1940 to 1941. This last comic was strongly influenced by Foster's *Prince Valiant* and was the longest and most popular of the three. The time was the year 1330, setting medieval Serbia. Prince Dušan Nemanjić (pronounced *Dushan Nemanyich*), son of King Stefan the Third Dečanski, struggles after his father's death to ascend to the throne and remain on it. Through many adventures he is helped by his nephew, knight Miloš Vojinović.

The high quality of Solovjev's work was confirmed by publication abroad, mostly in France (*Three Musketeers, Tzar's Shieldbearer,* and others). His thematic range was wide. Solovjev took up all genres except science fiction and grotesque. He did Westerns, detective stories, historicals (mostly the early Russian and Serbian history), pirate stories, and biographies.

During the Yugoslav involvement in World War II Solovjev was not doing any comics. After the war he moved in 1945 to the city of Rijeka on the Adriatic coast, close to Italy; several years later (in 1953 or 1955, data on this are uncertain), he emigrated to Italy and stayed there, in the small town of Massa on the Mediterranean coast south of Genoa, for the rest of his life. After World War II many of his comics were reprinted in Serbia. Publisher and editor of the Serbian magazine *Pegaz* ("Pegasus"), Žika Bogdanović is one of the last Serbs who went to Massa and managed to talk to Solovjev there. The result of this conversation was that one of Solovjev's comics, unknown until then, *Pesma južnog vetra* ("Song of the Southern Wind"),

which he produced in 1945 but kept for himself, was printed in *Pegaz* number 3. This was in 1975, the same year as his death.

S.I.

SONOYAMA, SHUNJI (1935-   ) Sonoyama is a Japanese cartoonist born April 23, 1935, in Matsue, Shimane. While a junior at Waseda University, Sonoyama founded the Waseda University Cartoon Society, with Kineo Shitou and others. After graduation from the university and a short-lived (a few hours!) try at an advertising agency job, Sonoyama started his career as a professional cartoonist with *Ganbare Gonbe*, a humor strip that he created for the elementary school student newspaper *Mainichi Shōgakusei Shinbun* in 1958. In 1963 he published, at his own expense, a collection of gag cartoons, *Kokkyō no Futari*; in 1965 *Gyatoruzu* (his most famous adult strip, a kind of Japanese *B.C.*) appeared and was later adapted to animated film; followed in 1966 by *Hajimeningen Gon* ("Gon the Primitive Boy"), a children's version of *Gyatoruzu*. Among Sonoyama's other creations are *Hana no Kakarichō* ("The Office Chiefs Flower," 1969) and *Sasurai no Gambler* ("The Wandering Gambler," also 1969).

Sonoyama's greatest merit lies in his criticism of modern civilization, with such works as *Gyatoruzu, Hajimeningen Gon,* and the savage *Mayonakano Genshijin* ("The Primitive Man at Midnight"). In his view, primitive men were more human than modern people in that they were emotional, vital, and active, while modern people are only cogs in a huge and dehumanizing machine called the State. His strips tried to rediscover the human elements lost by modern man in our mechanized society. Those primitive men had to struggle against beasts and elemental forces in order to survive, and had to depend on their own skills for food, clothing, and shelter. Their sex urge was strong, but not perverted as in modern man and, while their lives were close to that of the animals, their human personalities came through with more strength and naturalness than the robotized humans of today.

Sonoyama is more noted for his writing than for his drawing. His graphic style is simple to the extreme, almost crude, but with a very warm and vibrant quality. In this regard he is not too dissimilar from Scott Adams, and like *Dilbert* in the United States, his "salarymen comics" (as they are called there) enjoy great success in Japan to this day.

H.K.

Shunji Sonoyama, "Gyatoruzu." © *Sonoyama.*

"Sor Pampurio," Carlo Bisi. © Corriere dei Piccoli.

SORANG (Spain) *Sorang*, Enric Sío's first color comic, conceived on an idea by Emili Teixidor and developed by Jaume Vidal Alcover, was originally designed for an adult and exclusive publication. The restrictions imposed by its actual vehicle, the weekly comic book series *Vector 2*, led to a complete overhaul of the script, which was taken over by Sío after page 25.

The theme of *Sorang*, which unfolded over a one-year period starting in October 1968, explores the possibility of a submarine society made up of the remnants of successive shipwrecks who regain life after a nuclear explosion. This aquatic group is ruled by Queen Materia, who has a matriarchal regime in which communication is not verbal, but telepathic and visual. Materia's henchmen abduct two land-dwellers from the beach—Max and Julio (the last one a scientist)—to work for the queen. Julio succeeds in isolating words through a scientific process, and converts each of them into an effective weapon in his struggle against the aquatic people. The original script ended with the elimination of Materia and the transformation of the denizens of *Sorang* into a normal people capable of communicating through different languages.

Sío, however, decided to change the ending and its implications; Julio realizes that he cannot fight effectively against those who dominate the image. His enemies do not use the language code and therefore are impervious to words. This situation forces him to give life to his own images, thus fighting the people of the abyss with their own weapons. In the resulting confusion, the people of Sarong destroy one another and the queen is disintegrated. In the final analysis, Julio has fought against a dead world that never existed, a world of ghosts.

Graphically *Sorang* meant total creative freedom for the author. He could eliminate perhaps for the first time in the history of the world's comics the black line which delineates the drawings, working exclusively with masses of color. Sio intended to adapt the techniques of advertising, design, and especially photography to the comics. The author's obsession with the photographic process known as pseudo-solarization is evident in the extraordinary color distortions which, while adding meaning to the language of the comics, have a double drawback: on the one hand Sío attempts to send a message in each page, conceived as a harmonic and plastic whole; on the other hand he obtains a demythifying, destructive, and antiheroic dimension.

In the ultimate pages of the strip, however, Sío rediscovered the value of black, which he had practically eliminated from his tonal range, contrasting it with collages of color photographs and monochromatic panels.

L.G.

SOR PAMPURIO (Italy) *Sor Pampurio*, created by Carlo Bisi, appeared in the pages of the *Corriere dei Piccoli* from 1929 to 1941. This illustration of the life and times of an upper-middle-class Italian family appeared in the period when it was still possible to think of the good life, before history and war had overtaken the Mussolini regime.

Pampurio, along with his wife, son, and maid Rosetta, is always looking for a new home. His frantic weekly chase not only represents the slightly mad aspects of house-hunting but symbolizes, on a higher level, everyman's dream of peace and quiet. Pampurio is always burdened with everyday problems, such as how to spend his free time, how to find money for the holidays, and how best to dispose of the old furniture in the country house. These problems are not very important, but in Pampurio's compulsive frenzy, we are reminded of our own tendencies to overblow the simple incidents of daily life.

Pampurio was sketched in a hasty, cartoony style by Bisi, who gave him an egg-shaped head surmounted by two wooly tufts instead of hair. His wife and son were similarly drawn in the linear, one-dimensional way that most befitted the protagonists' single-minded obsessions.

G.B.

SPECTRE, THE (U.S.) *The Spectre* was created by writer Jerry Siegel and artist Bernard Baily and made its first appearance in National's *More Fun* number 52 for February 1940. In a world populated with superpowered studs, even the Spectre was extraordinary. He was as close to God as the comic books got. He had the power of just about every superhero combined, and you could be killed just by staring into his skull-pupiled eyes.

The Spectre was really policeman Jim Corrigan. While trying to save his fiancée, Clarice Winston, he was encased in cement and drowned. He was returned to earth, however, and told he could not have eternal rest until he wiped out all crime on the planet. As a ghost, the Spectre could exist outside of Corrigan's body, which neatly handled the often-sticky alter ego problem. And incredibly enough, the Spectre could talk directly to God. Over the years, the Spectre and Jim Corrigan changed. After a while, his powers were reduced and other changes were developed in the Corrigan/Spectre relationship. Apparently, it was becoming impossible to write a strip about a demigod.

Artistically, *The Spectre* was a dark and ominous strip. His green and gray costume set the pace and Bernard Baily handled the feature ploddingly, letting the incredible Spectre's powers take the forefront.

The Spectre lasted in *More Fun* through February 1945, issue number 101. He also appeared in *All-Star* from the first issue, Summer 1940, through the 23rd issue (Winter 1945). In the 1960's rush to revive superheroes, *The Spectre* was one of the last reborn. After three outstanding Gardner Fox/Murphy Anderson issues of *Showcase*, however, he was awarded his own book in November 1967. The title did not sell, however, and it lasted only ten issues, through June 1969. True to form, the ghost did not die and was revived again in *Adventure*, beginning in January 1974, issue number 431. He later came back in his own title in 1987 to 1989; a third ongoing series started in December 1992.

J.B.

SPEED TARŌ (Japan) *Speed Tarō* was created by Sakō Shishido in late 1930 for the Yomiuri Sunday Manga, then passed to the Yamiuri-Shōnen Shinbun in May 1931 before being discontinued in early 1933.

Speed Tarō was a google-eyed Japanese boy with slanted eyebrows and an indomitable spirit. One day as he was driving in his favorite car, he came upon a gold-smuggling plot but was captured by the criminals. They were nationals of a foreign country, the fictitious Dorumania, and Tarō was secreted away to their country. There Tarō escaped and took an active part in the ensuing fight between Dorumania and its arch-rival Kurokodaya, in a plot thick with suspense, thrills, and unpredictable twists.

Sakō Shishido had studied art in the United States for about nine years (while working at the same time) before starting his career in comic strips in Japan. He had carefully studied and mastered the techniques of the great American comic strip artists and his strip, *Speed Tarō*, was like a breath of fresh air for Japanese children used to traditional plots and storytelling; Shishido used modern storytelling devices (framing, composition, space manipulation) and his trip ushered in the new age of Japanese comics.

H.K.

SPIDER-MAN (U.S.) *Spider-Man* was created by writer and editor Stan Lee and artist Steve Ditko and made his first appearance in Marvel's *Amazing Fantasy* number 15 in August 1962. Known alternately as the web slinger and your friendly neighborhood Spider-Man, the character is the embodiment of the comic book antihero and the best-known comic creation of the 1960s. By March 1963, the feature was appearing in its own title, and *Spider-Man* has been the strip Marvel has most often utilized in new formats and commercial ventures. *Spider-Man* symbolizes the Marvel philosophy of superhero comics: a super-powered individual, beset with personal problems and hang-ups, battles for truth, justice, and the American way, often questioning himself and what he is fighting to uphold.

As originally conceived by Lee and Ditko, Spider-Man (and alter ego Peter Parker) was just another hung-up high school student who happened to be bitten by a radioactive spider. And although the spider endowed Parker with superhuman abilities, it did not straighten out his personal drawbacks. Over the years, Spider-Man has been through a horde of lovers; has a cloying Aunt May who's had an infinite number of heart attacks; has been sought by police and J. Jonah Jameson, a newspaper publisher who, for some unexplained reason, hates Spider-Man; has grown six arms and later lost them; and even had a junkie friend whose father was his deadly enemy, the Green Goblin. Lee's scripts, loaded with action and inventive villains as well as pathos, were instant hits among teenaged readers. *Spider-Man* eventually became a symbol of the uncertainties of the youths of the 1960s.

The artistic contribution of Steve Ditko is hard to overestimate. His grotesque-looking characters, sharp layouts, and fast pacing made him a perfect illustrator for the strip. His superior renditions catapulted Ditko to prominence and many other achievements, but many consider his *Spider-Man* work the best of his long career. Ditko left the strip in the spring of 1966 and the assignment was given to John Romita. His version was much slicker and cleaner; he once said that Lee was never happy with his handsome version of Peter Parker and he drew the strip while it was at the height of his popularity.

Lee and Romita both left the strip early in the 1970s. Promoted to publisher in 1971, Lee handed the scripting chores to Roy Thomas and later to Gerry Conway. By 1970, Romita was assuming responsibility for Marvel's art direction and drew fewer and fewer *Spider-Man* stories. By late 1972, he was all but completely replaced by Gil Kane, Ross Andru, and others. Although the feature continued to sell well, much of the Lee-Ditko-Romita magic had disappeared.

As Marvel's premiere creation, *Spider-Man* has appeared in many other media. A record of *Spider-Man* adventures was released in 1973, and over the years, paperback books, posters, dolls, cartoons, and toys were also marketed.

Among the many artists who have worked on *Spider-Man* from the mid-1970s on, mention should be made of John Byrne, Steve Austin, Todd McFarlane, and Erik Larsen; while writers have included Roger Stern and Peter David. The character has also give birth to a number of spin-offs (*Spider-Man Adventures, Spider-Man Magazine, Spider-Man 2099*, even *Spider-Woman*).

"Spider-Man," Jim Mooney, John Romita. © Marvel Comics.

In addition the Register and Tribune Syndicate started distribution of the *Amazing Spider-Man* newspaper strip in 1977.

J.B.

SPIEGELMAN, ARTHUR (1948-) American cartoonist Arthur ("Art") Spiegelman, the son of two survivors from the Auschwitz concentration camp, was born in Stockholm, Sweden, on February 15, 1948, and immigrated with his parents to the United States in his early childhood. He studied cartooning in high school and became a professional at age 16, drawing illustrations and cartoons for the *Long Island Post*. Despite the opposition of his parents (who wanted him to become a dentist) he opted for an artistic career and majored in art and philosophy at Harpur College.

After he left college in 1968, he decided to join the burgeoning underground "comix" movement. Over the next decade he became a regular contributor to a number of underground publications, including *Young Lust, Real Pulp, Bizarre Sex,* and *Sleazy Scandals of the Silver Screen,* with such creations as "Ace Hole, Midget Detective," "Nervous Rex," and "Cracking Jokes" under a variety of pseudonyms ("Joe Cutrate," "Skeeter Grant," and "Al Flooglebuckle"). At the same time he drew bubblegum cards for Topps and cartoons for *Playboy.*

In parallel with his cartooning career Spiegelman edited several underground comic magazines: *Arcade* (with Bill Griffith) and, starting in 1980, *Raw,* with his wife Françoise Mouly. In the pages of *Raw* he published not only his works and those of other under-

ground cartoonists (Charles Burns, Gary Panter, Justin Green, and others) but also helped reveal to his comics-loving audience important talents from foreign shores (e.g., Ever Meulen from Belgium, Jacques Tardi of France, Joost Swarte from Holland, and Argentina's José Muñoz, among others).

Spiegelman's career really took flight with the publication of *Maus*. It originated in 1972 in the comic book *Funny Aminals* (sic) in the form of a three-page allegory in animal guise; drawing upon the experiences of his parents as concentration-camp survivors, it was a harrowing tale of cruelty, with the Jews represented as mice and the Germans depicted as cats. He later expanded this premise into a full-blown graphic novel, which he drew from 1980 to 1986 with the Jews again presented as mice and the Germans now called "the Katzies" (a bit of funnybook facetiousness, which in this context should have been resisted at all costs). Published in book form in 1986 as *Maus: A Survivor's Tale* by Pantheon, the work earned its author fame and a grant from the Guggenheim Foundation to complete the tale with *Maus II: From Mauschwitz to the Catskills,* which came out in 1991, again to great acclaim.

Basking in his newfound celebrity status, Spiegelman has considerably reduced his comics output since that time, aside from an occasional book review in comic strip form. He has illustrated one obscure novel and drawn a number of covers for the *New Yorker* (where his wife happens to work as cover art editor). To an interviewer he confided that he was looking for

Art Spiegelman, self-portrait.

Dan Spiegle, "Hopalong Cassidy." © Mirror Syndicate.

a "story worth telling" on a par with *Maus*. It remains to be seen.

M.H.

SPIEGLE, DAN (1920-   ) Dan Spiegle is an American cartoonist born December 10, 1920, in Cosmopolis, Washington. When he was 10 his family moved to northern California. In his second year of high school he sent a sample comic strip to King Features, which politely turned it down: from this moment Spiegle vowed to become a cartoonist. After graduation and a series of small art jobs, he enlisted in the navy at the start of World War II (he spent most of the war designing plane insignias and drawing cartoons for the base newspaper).

Discharged in 1946, Spiegle enrolled at the Chouinard Art Institute of Los Angeles on the G.I. bill. During his last year at Chouinard (1949), he was introduced to movie actor Bill Boyd who was looking for an artist to draw a projected strip based on his Hopalong Cassidy interpretation. Spiegle got the job and *Hopalong Cassidy* started appearing the same year, distributed by the Los Angeles Mirror Syndicate. *Cassidy* was sold to King Features in 1951, and Spiegle continued to draw the strip until its demise in 1955. He then tried his hand at a pirate strip, *Penn and Chris*, but it was rejected by all major newspaper syndicates (only in 1972 did it see the light of print in a small fanzine).

Spiegle then shifted to comic book work, and in 1956 he started his long collaboration with Dell Publications, working on a variety of comic book titles from *Maverick* (Spiegle's own favorite) to *Space Family Robinson* and *Magnus, Robot Fighter*. When Russ Manning left Dell to draw the *Tarzan* newspaper strip in 1967, Spiegle took over *Korak*. He has also done the comic

book versions of a number of Walt Disney movies and contributed many illustrations to *Mystery Comics Digest*. His credits in the 1980s and 1990s have included *Indiana Jones* for *Dark Horse*, *Crossfire* for *Eclipse*, and a number of Disney adaptations (*Pocahontas*, *Roger Rabbit*, etc.)

Dan Spiegle is a solid craftsman, unexciting but enjoyable, and his work displays an understated but obvious sense of fun.

M.H.

SPIRIT, THE (U.S.) Will Eisner created *The Spirit* on June 2, 1940, as a weekly seven-page feature, part of a comic book-sized Sunday supplement carried in the comic section of a score of American newspapers. *The Spirit*'s historical importance (as distinct from its artistic excellence) lies in its bridging of the gap between the comic book and the newspaper strip: the feature was distributed by the Register and Tribune Syndicate which also ran a *Spirit* strip in daily newspapers for about two years, from October 1941 to February 1944.

Eisner drew and wrote the feature from its inception till 1942 when he was called into service. During his four-year absence his work was carried on by Lou Fine and others. In 1946 Eisner took the strip back and was to draw it until 1950, when he decided to go into business for himself. *The Spirit*, now drawn by Wallace Wood, lingered a while longer before finally bowing out on September 28, 1952.

The Spirit covered the identity of Denny Colt, a criminologist whom everyone thought dead, and who used his disguise (a simple eye mask!) to fight crime from his hideaway in Wildwood Cemetery. At first he was not that distinguishable from the hordes of other hooded crime-fighters who were cluttering the comic pages. What made the Spirit unique was the depth of characterization and the sense of human involvement that Eisner was able to bring to his hero.

The Spirit's acolytes were more conventional: the harassed hapless Commissioner Dolan; his lovely blonde daughter Ellen, enamored (naturally!) of the hero; and Ebony White, the Spirit's sidekick, character-

"The Spirit," Will Eisner. © Will Eisner.

"Spirou," Jijé (Joseph Gillain). © Editions Dupuis.

ized midway between pathos and stereotype. On the other hand Eisner succeeded in delineating his auxilary characters, whether they be dyed-in-the-wool villains, slinky femmes fatales, or uncomprehending bystanders, with a sure hand and deft sense of humor, and graced them with Dickensian names such as Mortimer J. Titmouse, Humid S. Millibar, Carboy T. Gretch, Wisp O'Smoke, Sparrow Fallon, Plaster of Paris, and Autumn Mews.

The setting of the strip was Central City (in actuality New York), disquieting, squalid, but majestic in its formidable presence and its towering aloofness. In its seven-page narrative each *Spirit* episode constituted a self-contained short story, but the weekly unfolding of the tales revealed a peculiar rhythm, a cadence evoking not so much the prose narrative as the prose poem (even down to the suggestion of blank verse in the text). In this aspect *The Spirit* probably has few counterparts in comic history.

The Spirit was often reprinted in comic book form (in *Police Comics* in the 1940s, in its own book published by Quality Comics in the 1950s and by Harvey in the 1960s.) Since the late 1970s Kitchen Sink Press has been reprinting the old *Spirit* episodes with an occasional new story.

M.H.

SPIROU (Belgium) Spirou, created by the Frenchman Robert Velter (signing "Rob-Vel"), appeared in the first issue (April 21, 1938) of the comic weekly that bears its name.

Spirou was a bellboy at the Moustic Hotel and his adventures were not very remarkable at first. In 1939 he acquired an animal companion, Snip the squirrel, and together they underwent a series of adventures that took them all around the world. (Rob Vel was obviously trying to imitate the formula that had contributed to the success of Hergé's *Tintin*.) No less obviously the strip was floundering, and it temporarily disappeared in 1943 when the Germans banned the publication of *Spirou* magazine.

Spirou reappeared, along with the magazine, in October 1944, shortly after Belgium's liberation, under the signature of "Jijé" (Joseph Gullain). Jijé gave the strip a better visual organization and the benefit of his undeniable graphic qualities. He also provided Spirou with a sidekick, Fantasio, whose easygoing nature and levity were a welcome relief from the hero's earnestness.

But it was André Franquin who was to develop *Spirou* into a major feature. Succeeding Jijé in 1946, Franquin launched Spirou into his most unforgettable adventures, and created a gallery of secondary characters second only to Hergé's. One should mention Zantafio, Fantasio's megalomaniacal cousin, the eccentric inventor Count of Champignac, and best of all, the marsupilami, the most likable, versatile and fanciful animal ever to grace the comic page since Segar's jeep.

In 1969 *Spirou* was taken over by Jean-Claude Fournier who unfortunately possesses neither Franquin's graphic virtuosity nor his unbridled imagination. In 1979 he was replaced by Nicolas Broca and Raoul Cauvin who, in turn, were succeeded by Yves Chaland the next year. Chaland gave the spunky little bellboy a new, retro look that lasted only one story. Tome and Janry took over the character in 1981 and have been able to conserve him to this day.

Spirou's popularity steadily grew after World War II. Most of the episodes were reprinted in book form by Dupuis. *Spirou*, however, never enjoyed the success of *Tintin* or *Asterix*, partly because of a lack of direction (the series always hovered between humor, fantasy, and adventure without settling on any one theme), and partly because of the different (and sometimes incompatible) authors who worked on the strip.

M.H.

SPOOKY (U.S.) Bill Holman's Spooky, as a cat, appeared in the first Sunday *Smokey Stover* episode (called "Smokey") of March 10, 1935; *Spooky*, as a strip, first opened on April 7, 1935, as a four-panel gag row at the bottom of a *Smokey* full page, later becoming the half-page it remained for years on May 12, 1935. Spooky was a shaggy, shabby, black cat with white paws, whose red-bandaged tail was her trademark. (Her sex was established early, on May 12, 1935, when she presented a dismayed housewife with a brood of eight kittens.) Unlike Al Smith's equally female *Cicero's Cat*, Spooky never developed human-

"Spooky," Bill Holman. © Chicago Tribune-New York News Syndicate.

ized characteristics although it is evident from time to time that she can read and understand human speech and remained from first to last a fantasized feline who began her career in Cash U. Nutt's fire house, and then became a roving vagabond for the purpose of Bill Holman's often surrealistic slapstick.

Basically, *Spooky* was designed and distributed as a Sunday filler strip, something which could be conveniently dropped for the inclusion of advertisements in the Sunday sections. It is unlikely that any paper, even the feature's home papers, the *New York Daily News* and the *Chicago Tribune*, whose combined syndication circulated the strip at its outset, printed more than two-thirds of the episodes drawn, and most papers printed even less, although *Smokey Stover* itself ran regularly everywhere. Early in 1945, *Spooky* was dropped as a half-page, and was added to the *Smokey Stover* third-page as, once again, a single row of panels, making a full Holman half-page for those papers wishing to run it as such. In this last form, *Spooky* ran for another ten years, finally disappearing from print in the mid-1950s. An amusing gag strip, *Spooky* was not collected in any separate books but was reprinted in several comic books of the 1940s and 1950s.

B.B.

SPRANG, RICHARD (1915-   ) While certainly not an artist of the first rank—only a good journeyman purveyor of comic book fare—Dick Sprang is among those fortunate cartoonists who have lived long enough to see fame suddenly come to them thanks to a revived comic book market and the irresistible pull of nostalgia. Born in Fremont, Ohio, in 1915, he started his artistic career at age 15, painting signs, billboards, and movie posters in his hometown. Upon graduation from high school in 1934, he went to work as staff artist for the *Toledo News-Bee* daily newspaper, a position he held for two years.

Coming to New York City in 1936, he became a freelance artist, mostly illustrating pulp-magazine stories for the major publishers of the day. This led him almost naturally to comic book work, starting in 1941, when he was assigned by the editors at DC Comics to illustrate a *Batman* script. From that time on there was no looking back: for the next 20-odd years Sprang was

to draw countless comic book pages for DC, occasionally working on some *Superman* titles, but mainly concentrating on *Batman*.

After he took over *Batman*, Sprang did not tamper with the Caped Crusader's original image. "I didn't change him any more than that," he later stated. "Shortened his ears a little bit, and so on." His compositions, however, displayed a greater dynamism, and the action was depicted with a greater deal of telling detail. It was his covers that made him really stand out: these were crowd-pleasers portraying Batman and some of his more colorful foes, such as the Joker, Catwoman, and the Penguin, in unexpected settings (often having nothing to do with the story inside). Since Sprang labored in utter anonymity, like most of his comic book colleagues at the time, his budding renown went unnoticed by him.

In 1963 he left the comic book field, seemingly for good, and pursued a career as a rancher, guide, and surveyor in the West (he had moved to Arizona as far back as 1946). A chance encounter in the mid-1970s led to his rediscovery as one of the early pioneers of the medium. Soon he was making appearances at comics conventions and in 1987 was asked again to draw illustrations and covers for some of the *Batman* titles. Now in his eighties he is busier than ever turning out painted re-creations of his classic covers and limited-edition lithographs for the fan market, thereby illustrating the adage that everything old is new again.

M.H.

SPRINGER, FRANK (1929-   ) An American cartoonist born in New York City on December 6, 1929, Frank Springer is a master of realistic cartoon technique. After earning an art degree from Syracuse University in 1952, Springer served a tour in the U.S. Army. From 1955 to 1960 he served as George Wunder's assistant on *Terry and the Pirates*. He was also an assistant and influenced by the styles of Stan Drake on *The Heart of Juliet Jones* and Leonard Starr on the story strip *On Stage*.

Basically a freelance cartoonist, Springer has drawn a wide variety of adventure and action comic books for Dell, DC, and Marvel. He drew both sports and editorial cartoons for the *New York Daily News*. He worked on *Space Ghost*, a Hanna-Barbera Saturday morning animated television show. In 1979 he took over drawing Field Syndicate's *Rex Morgan, M.D.* for awhile bringing some of the most interesting artwork ever to that story strip begun in 1948. He collaborated with Marvel's Stan Lee and drew the syndicated soap opera strip *Virtue of Vera Valiant* for its year of existence. Springer, who has been president of the National Cartoonists Society, currently draws *The Adventures of Hedley Kase* for *Sports Illustrated for Kids*.

However, his most lasting fame is not from his excellent work in comic books, which were often unsigned, or comic strips, which he was usually ghosting for others, but for *The Adventures of Phoebe Zeit-Geist*. Influenced by the success in Europe of sexy cartoon albums, New York City's Grove Press not only published the American version of Jean-Claude Forest's *Barbarella* and Guy Pellaert's *Jodelle* in 1966, but launched its own sexy Perils of Pauline-style strip that year, *The Adventures of Phoebe Zeit-Geist*, which was serialized in its periodical *The Evergreen Review*.

Written by Michael O'Donoghue and drawn by Frank Springer, *The Adventures of Phoebe Zeit-Geist* in their entirety were published as a book by Grove Press in 1968. While sexy cartoon albums were not a novelty in Europe, *Phoebe Zeit-Geist* was a sensation in the United States. Springer used his realistic style to delineate in detail the brunette twenty-something Phoebe's vain attempts to keep her clothes on and virtue in place. She was successful at neither.

Although generally unknown outside the military, Wally Wood was at the same time writing and drawing his *Sally Forth* for the tabloid *The Overseas Weekly*, marketed exclusively to U.S. military personnel. Both Phoebe and Sally owe their inspiration to the success of *Barbarella*. Of the two, Sally, given Wood's years of being a *MAD* magazine veteran, was funnier and lacked the pretensions of O'Donoghue's script. However, Frank Springer's *Phoebe Zeit-Geist* art shows what the result would be when a master of newspaper story strip art takes a walk on the wild side. His *Phoebe* artwork also brought him story strip work published in *Playboy* and *National Lampoon*.

As distinguished as Springer's career has been, his place in history as a cartoonist will forever be linked with the often nude, bound, and spanked beauty Phoebe Zeit-Geist.

B.C.

SPY SMASHER (U.S.) Writer and editor Bill Parker and artists C. C. Beck and Pete Costanza created *Spy Smasher* in February 1940, and it first appeared in Fawcett's *Whiz* number 1. In reality rich playboy Alan Armstrong, Spy Smasher was a creature of the recently declared World War II. He was an undying patriot, an accomplished aviator, and, most importantly, a crusader. A larger-than-life Spy Smasher appeared on the cover of *Spy Smasher* number 2 proclaiming Death to Spies in America!

Most of the strips were typical of the patriotic overkill being churned out during the 1940s. Spy Smasher's sole desire was to search out and destroy the enemies of America. Fifth columnists and traitors were his prime targets. Strangely enough, the best stories in the series came when the character turned against the country and took on Captain Marvel. Brainwashed into hating America, Spy Smasher went on a rampage, kill-

Frank Springer and Michael O'Donoghue, "The Adventures of Phoebe Zeit-Geist." © the authors.

"Spy Smasher," Ken Bald. © Fawcett Publications.

ing, maiming, and destroying, all in an attempt to overthrow the country he once loved. He was eventually defeated by Captain Marvel, but the battle lasted four monumental issues (*Whiz* numbers 15 through 18). Spy Smasher was later pardoned for his crimes and sent back into the battle to protect America. Even though these stories took place in 1941, before the United States was officially involved in the war effort, it was novel to see an American hero allowed to turn traitor even temporarily, and even when brainwashed.

The artwork, while consistent, was never outstanding. The only other art of consequence besides creator Beck's was the work of Charles Sultan during 1941 and 1942. In fact, the most interesting artistic feature of *Spy Smasher* was his constant updating of uniform. Over the years he went from a World War I flying suit to a typical set of superhero's togs.

Spy Smasher ran into great trouble after the war years, however. A strip steeped in flag-waving patriotism during a time of crisis, the story line was lost without a foreign enemy to fight. After a brief attempt to rechristen the strip *Crime Smasher* and have the hero battle everyday criminals, the feature was dropped after its March 1953 appearance in *Whiz* number 83.

At the height of his popularity, however, *Spy Smasher* was an important member of the Fawcett stable. From 1941 to February 1943 he even had his own comic, *Spy Smasher*, which lasted 11 issues. Kane Richmond starred as Spy Smasher in a 1942 motion picture serial released by Republic Features.

J.B.

STANLEY, JOHN (1914-1993) American comic book writer and artist John Stanley was born March 22, 1914, in the Harlem district of New York City. Throughout his career, Stanley was a very private person and remained reluctant to discuss his past. As a result, information about him is sketchy and much of what comic book historians have written about him has since proven inaccurate. It is known, however, that Stanley attended two art schools, one of them the Art Students League, and that he began his career with various freelance cartooning jobs in New York, including selling several gag ideas to the *New Yorker* magazine.

In 1945, Stanley helped launch Western Publishing Company's *Little Lulu* comic, a feature with which he was affiliated for 14 years. Stanley wrote virtually all of the *Little Lulu* stories, drawing his scripts up in storyboard form. The penciled art for the comics, handled by others, was based on Stanley's layouts, a practice not uncommon in animation-type comic books. He usually did finished art, penciled and inked, for covers. Stanley's *Little Lulu* stories are fondly remembered for their simplicity and humor. Often, the simplest childhood problem would mushroom into a crisis of chaotic proportions. Stanley produced an incredible variety of stories featuring Lulu and the neighborhood youngsters.

While writing *Lulu*, Stanley also did stories and some art for a number of other Western publications including a regular feature, *Peterkin Pottle*, which ran in *Raggedy Ann* comics during the late 1940s. He kept no records of this work, which ranged from humor to adventure, and his fans have had a difficult time determining any further information.

In 1962 Western Publishing Company severed its affiliation with the Dell company and continued its books under the Gold Key logo. Stanley went with the newly formed Dell company and did stories and art for a variety of new comics including *Thirteen*, a teen comic, and *Melvin Monster* (1965-1966). He worked intermittently for Dell, also accepting some work doing storyboards for television cartoons. When the new Dell company cut back its titles and relied heavily on reprints, Stanley did some work for the Gold Key company: the first (and only) issue of *Choo Choo Charlie* (1969) and the first issue of *O.G. Whiz* (1971), a book about the exploits of a young boy who became president of a toy company.

O.G. Whiz was Stanley's last known work in comics. In subsequent years, he worked at a company that manufactures plastic rulers as head of the silk-screening department. He died from cancer on November 11, 1993.

M.E.

STARMAN (U.S.) *Starman* was created by writer Gardner Fox and artist Jack Burnley and first appeared in National's April 1941 issue of *Adventure Comics* (number 61). In reality playboy Ted Knight, Starman received his great powers from a magnetic wand that harnessed, as Fox put it in the original tale, the mysterious powers of the stars. Starman's costume was rather pedestrian: red and green tights. The costume's only variation was an odd cowl which covered only the back of his head.

Fox's scripts, though constantly competent and fast-paced, were never as original as many of his other efforts. In fact, *Starman* came across as just another superhero strip. His magic wand, which gave him the ability to fly, was never innovatively used.

On the other hand, artist Jack Burnley was one of the best artists in the National stable. Heavily influenced by Alex Raymond's work on *Flash Gordon*, Burnley's work was always smooth and refined. His draftsmanship was always excellent and his anatomy clean. While the astral avenger was never one of National's big heroes, he was always well-drawn. After Burnley departed to illustrate *Superman*, Mort Meskin (1942), Paul Reinman (1943), George Roussos (1942-1943), and others took his place.

A member of the Justice Society of America, *Starman* appeared in *All-Star Comics* from December 1941 through Winter 1945 and lasted in his solo feature through March 1946's *Adventure Comics* number 102.

When National authored a general revival of 1940s superheroes in the middle-1960s, *Starman* was exhumed and appeared in two issues of *Showcase* along with the *Black Canary*. It was revived twice again: in 1988 to 1992, and then in 1994 in a series that is still ongoing.

J.B.

STARR, LEONARD (1925-   ) An American artist born in Manhattan on October 28, 1925, Starr attended the High School of Music and Art and during World War II took courses at Pratt Institute. After the war Starr entered the comic book field, going to work for Fawcett and other publishers. Among his titles were *Human Torch*, *Sub-Mariner*, and *Don Winslow*; he rose from background work to inking and complete production.

Without the benefit of full training, the busy Starr grew proficient, fast, and slick but began to see deficiencies in his work that others may not have seen. He began studying with Frank Reilly at nights and concentrated on advertising work, with (inevitably) Johnstone and Cushing and other agencies. All the while he submitted story strip ideas to syndicates. In 1956 one of many was accepted and *On Stage* debuted in February of the following year, distributed by the Chicago Tribune-New York News Syndicate.

Contrary to publicity releases, Starr displayed no abnormal love of the theater while growing up. His preoccupation was art, and the work of his idols, Raymond and Caniff, is very clearly seen in his work. Starr's art is perhaps the most attractive and compelling of today's story strips. Tackiness and conformity are absent while a visual verve and mature story line consistently command attention. Starr has agonized no less than any of his fellows over the newsprint crunch and the decline of the story strip. Answering the first challenge, he has reluctantly resorted to street-scene wide angles and figure close-ups. And, in answer to the contemporary war against story strips, he experimented with humorous continuities for a period in the early 1970s.

Starr has won the Best Story Strip award from the National Cartoonists Society as well as its Reuben (1965). He has also served as vice president of the NCS. His work remains premier in his field and his integrity has never faltered.

Starr abandoned *On Stage* in 1979 to write and draw the revived *Annie* strip, to which he has given a more contemporary tone and a more visually appealing look. In 1980, in collaboration with Stan Drake, he developed the short-lived *Kelly Green* series of graphic albums; and in 1984 he acted as story and head writer of the *Thundercats* animated television show.

R.M.

STAR SPANGLED KID (U.S.) In the golden age of comic books during the 1940s, script writing was formularized, and one of the unbreakable rules of the business stated that the costumed hero was an adult and the sidekick was a teenager. Batman had the teen-aged Robin, Captain America had young Bucky, Toro rode the heated coattails of the Human Torch, and so on. About the only strip to break away from tradition was the *Star Spangled Kid* feature which premiered in National's *Star Spangled Comics* number 1 in October 1941. Created by writer Jerry Siegel, who helped create *Superman* several years earlier, and artist Hal Sherman, the hero of the strip was the Star-Spangled Kid, who in reality, was teenaged heir Sylvester Pemberton. His assistant was Pat Dugan, an ex-pugilist who had considerable mechanical skills and great strength. Together brainy Sylvester and the dim-witted Pat set forth to stop the Nazis, which was a formula Siegel chose not to break.

The duo had a unique origin, however. Sylvester Pemberton, a rich heir who had brains and strength, and Pat Dugan attended a patriotic movie together and helped break up an attempted Nazi disturbance. They learned of impending Axis plans for other domestic upheavals, and each set out separately to make the flag come alive. The Star-Spangled Kid came up with a red, white, and blue uniform, star-spangled of course, and Stripesy (Pat Dugan) managed a red, white, and blue striped costume. Each then set out independently to help destroy the fifth column activists and were rivals early on before they decided to team up to fight the Nazi menace. Sylvester hired Pat as his chauffeur, and Pat responded by modifying the Pemberton limousine into a 1940's version of a James Bond car. It had a bubble top, wings, rockets, and even helicopter blades—ludicrous, but well-conceived for the gimmicky strips of the 1940s.

Writer Siegel also populated the early strip with several exciting, if admittedly outlandish, villains. Among them were Moonglow, a scientist who was bombarded with moon rays and had his mind warped and his head turned into a type of light bulb; the Needle, a skinny ex-circus performer who used a deadly needle gun; and Dr. Weerd, a Jekyll-Hyde-type villain.

Artistically, the strip was never particularly outstanding, even though cocreator Sherman's work between 1941 and 1944 was above average for the war years. He was eventually succeeded by illustrators like Joe Kubert (1943), Lou Cazeneuve (1944-1945), Win Mortimer (1948), and several others.

In all, the *Star Spangled Kid* appeared in the first 81 issues of *Star Spangled Comics* until November 1948. The characters also appeared in *Leading* 1 (Winter 1942) through 14 (Spring 1945) as members of the short-lived *Seven Soldiers of Victory*, and in *World's Finest* issues 6 (Summer 1942) through 18 (Summer 1945).

J.B.

STAR WARS (U.S.) John Lucas's immensely successful *Star Wars* movie trilogy was largely based on comics iconology in general (and on *Flash Gordon* in particular), so it is not surprising that the comics would in turn make the theme their own.

Shortly after the first film's release Marvel came out with a *Star Wars* comic book, which lasted from 1977 to 1986. The first issues followed closely the plot of the original film, as Luke Skywalker, Han Solo, Princess Leiah, and their small band of freedom-fighters battled the evil Empire and its chief henchman, the black-helmeted Darth Vader. This adaptation, excellently illustrated by Howard Chaykin, proved very popular with the readers. The stories, initially written by Roy Thomas and later by Archie Goodwin, soon started to stray off-base, only following Lucas's original concept when the next two films in the trilogy (*The Empire Strikes Back* and *The Return of the Jedi*) were released in the early 1980s. Among the many artists who worked on the series, mention should be made of John Byrne, Frank Miller, Bill Sienkiewicz, Walt Simonson, and Al Williamson.

In 1991 Dark Horse started publishing a new line of *Star Wars* comic books. Mostly released as limited series (with such titles as *Dark Empire, Empire's End,* etc.), with Tom Veitch as principal writer and Cam Kennedy as main artist, these have enjoyed a fair amount of success so far.

A *Star Wars* newspaper strip also saw the light of print, distributed from March 1979 to March 1984 by the Los Angeles Times Syndicate. It was initially scripted by Brian Daley (the author of a number of *Star Wars* novels) and illustrated by Russ Manning and later by Alfredo Alcala. The duo of Archie Goodwin and Al Williamson took over in 1981. (The Goodwin-Williamson strips were reprinted by Russ Cochran in 1991, and as trade paperbacks by Dark Horse in 1994-1995.)

M.H.

STEEL STERLING (U.S.) *Steel Sterling* was created in February 1940 by artist and writer Charles Biro and made his first appearance in MLJ's *Zip Comics* number 1. The red-and-blue clad Man of Steel was really John Sterling, an experimenter who plunged his body into a cauldron of molten metal. Somehow, that gave Sterling the powers of invulnerability and flight. Whenever he ran or flew, the word zip would trail off from his boots.

Biro, one of the great creators of the 1940s, populated *Steel Sterling* with a coterie of fine supporting characters. Although girlfriend Dora Cummings was a run-of-the-mill love interest, Clancy, a fat, red-headed cop, and Louie, a skinny dimwit, soon developed into the Laurel and Hardy team of comic books. Later in the series, the fire-breathing Inferno was added as Steel Sterling's assistant. His popularity was so great, however, he was given his own feature after three issues. Artistically, Biro was famous for his inventive, but straightforward storytelling techniques.

After Biro's departure in 1942, the strip faltered despite the best efforts of artist Irv Novick and writers Otto Binder (1942-1944) and Bob Kanigher (1942). Throughout his career, Sterling fought an array of stereotyped Axis villains, but the particularly ruthless Baron Gestapo was popular enough to rate several return battles.

Steel Sterling appeared in *Zip Comics* until the Summer 1944 issue (number 47), and also appeared in all nine *Jackpot* comics from Spring 1941 to Summer 1943. Along with the other MLJ characters, *Sterling* was revived briefly in 1965.

J.B.

STERANKO, JAMES (1938-) American comic book artist and writer, James Steranko was born November 5, 1938, in Reading, Pennsylvania. A self-taught artist, Steranko entered the comics industry in 1966 while moonlighting as an ad agency art director (1964-1968) and movie illustrator (1966-1968); his first three creations the *Spyman, Gladiator,* and *Magicman* adventure features for Harvey were short-lived failures.

Steranko then moved to Marvel in December, 1966 and began working on *Nick Fury, Agent of S.H.I.E.L.D.* with writer-editor Stan Lee and artist Jack Kirby. After several issues of uninspired inking, Steranko improved and soon took over not only the penciling and inking, but also the writing and coloring. *S.H.I.E.L.D.* was set in the present and starred Nick Fury who was concurrently appearing in a World War II Marvel comic as the leader of a paramilitary, supersecret organization. The early stories were routine spy fare, but Steranko took the series away from its James Bondish orientation.

James Steranko, "Tower of Shadows." © Marvel Comics.

Building from his earlier material, which showed heavy influences of the Jack Kirby dynamic style, he added touches of Eisner, Krigstein, and many others and developed his own unique cinematic techniques which made *S.H.I.E.L.D.* possibly the best written and drawn strip of the decade. His innovative and intricate layouts, pop art-inspired drawings, and crisp storytelling captured the comic book world and netted him three fan-issued Alley awards in 1968. He was certainly on his way to becoming one of comic books' greatest illustrators. But, after the feature moved from *Strange Tales* to its own book in June 1968, Steranko's time-consuming work forced him to miss deadlines. He was finally taken off the book after December 1968's seventh issue, and the book folded a year later.

While drawing *S.H.I.E.L.D.* and for a time after he was removed, Steranko also created several well-received stories for *Captain America, X-MEN,* and for the horror and romance titles. But he continually had problems meeting the comic book industry's often oppressive deadline schedule, and all but abandoned the field in 1969. He formed the Supergraphics Publishing Company, and, in recent years, has produced two volumes on the comic book's history, many comic-oriented products, and introduced a magazine about the comics industry, *Comixscene.* The magazine gutted most of its comics material in 1973 and changed its name to *Mediascene.* He divided much of his time to the publication of the magazine (later renamed *Preview*). His last comic book work was on *Nick Fury vs. SHIELD* (1988), but he has done a number of covers, notably for *Ray Bradbury Comics.* He also produced two graphic novels, the movie-inspired *Outland* and the thriller *Red Tide.*

J.B.

STERRETT, CLIFF (1883-1964) The gifted creator of *Polly and Her Pals,* Cliff Sterrett, was born December 12, 1883, in Fergus Falls, Minnesota, into a middle-class family which put him through 12 years of school at Fergus Falls and nearby Alexander. Aware of his artistic ability, Sterrett left home to attend Chase Arts School in New York at 18. After two years of intense study there, he landed his first job in 1904 on the *New York Herald,* where he did spot news illustrations, decorative borders for photographs, sketches of interviewed celebrities—in fact, anything but cartoons, which were all the young Sterrett wanted to do. From the *Herald,* however, he went to the *New York Times* in 1908; after two dull years drawing visiting kings for the *Times,* and a further stint on the *Rochester Democrat and Chronicle,* Sterrett finally had his big chance—a job doing not one but four daily comic strips on the *New York Evening Telegram* in early 1911.

Sterrett's earliest *Telegram* strip was called *Ventriloquial Vag,* but he quickly added and developed three more: *When a Man's Married, Before and After,* and *For This We Have Daughters?,* drawing all of them for simultaneous publication in the six-day-a-week *Telegram,* like a one-man comic strip syndicate. The latter strip, about an avidly courted college-age girl and her deeply middle-aged parents, became the most popular with readers of the *Telegram's* syndicated comics across the country, and Hearst discerned a rising star in the young cartoonist, hiring him in late 1912 to work for his National News Syndicate.

Sterrett carried over the characters and concepts of *Daughters* into his new Hearst strip, first called *Positive Polly,* then a bit later *Polly and Her Pals,* which opened on the *New York Journal's* daily comic page on December 4, 1912. A year later, Hearst felt Sterrett had earned a Sunday page, and put his *Polly* in the four-color supplement of the *New York American.*

Sterrett added a second, one-row strip at the top of his weekly page on June 21, 1926, featuring a dog and a cat team called *Damon and Pythias* (the title being changed to *Dot and Dash* on September 5, 1926). This feature was replaced on July 1, 1928, by a quarter-page strip called *Sweethearts and Wives* (which was a resumption of Sterrett's old daily strip *Before and After,* and which took a humorously pessimistic view of man and woman trapped into marriage), the title of which was changed to *Belles and Wedding Bells* on June 22, 1930.

Sterrett's own domestic life seems to have been almost ideally happy, and it is obvious that he liked his family since he was one of the first Hearst strip artists who was permitted to draw at home rather than in the cartoonists' offices at the publisher's New York papers. Enlarging on this privilege, he moved to Ogunquit, Maine, in the early 1920s, where he and his family developed their taste for music by learning innumerable musical instruments.

One of the few strip artists (another was Roy Crane) honest enough not to sign his work when, because of illness or other problems, he had to have it ghosted, Sterrett dropped his signature from the daily *Polly* strip when he decided to cut his workload in half in 1935 and assigned the daily feature to another artist (as he had done a bit earlier with the Sunday *Belles and Wedding Bells*). He continued to draw the Sunday *Polly* until his complete retirement in 1958. After his wife's death in 1948, Sterrett went to live with his wife's sister, Dorothy, until his own death on December 28, 1964. Held by some to be second only to George Herriman as a graphic innovator on the comic page, Sterrett is inarguably one of the most important strip artists of all time.

B.B.

STEVE CANYON (U.S.) Shortly after leaving *Terry and the Pirates,* Milton Caniff created *Steve Canyon* for Field Enterprises as a synchronized daily/Sunday feature on January 13, 1947. The strip appeared simultaneously in 125 newspapers throughout the United States, a rare feat for a beginning feature.

As Caniff himself described him in a *Time* interview in December 1946, Steve Canyon was to be a sort of modern Kit Carson, the strong silent Gary Cooper plainsman type. . . . He'll have lots of gals, one at every port. True to his creator's word Steve Canyon cut a dashing figure from his first appearance. A former air force captain, now head of a shaky airline company Horizons Unlimited, Steve accepts the most dangerous missions. In his adventures, which take him to the most remote corners of the earth, he comes up against an assorted string of ruffians, gun-runners, drug traffickers, international spies, Nazi fanatics, and Communist agents. Many of them turn out to be women, eternally dangerous, and eternally in love with the hero, such as Copper Calhoun, the she-wolf of Wall Street, Steve's most relentless adversary and pursuer.

With the outbreak of the Korean war, Steve reenlists in the air force and, as Colonel Stevenson B. Canyon, he is sent to the hottest spots of the Cold War: from Korea to Turkey to Greece to Formosa to the Middle East, and in more recent years, Vietnam.

"Steve Canyon," Milton Caniff. © Field Newspaper Syndicate.

Another bevy of female enemies lay in wait for him: the one-armed Madame Hook, Captain Akoola of Soviet intelligence, Queen Taja, and others. In-between war adventures, there are more peaceful interludes, the heroine of which often is Poteet Canyon, Steve's pert and high-spirited ward. In April 1970, however, Steve married his old flame Summer Olson, and the strip has been floundering on the shoals of soap-opera melodramatics ever since. Following the end of the Vietnam war, Steve was seen more and more often out of uniform and many of the episodes were devoted to his marital woes (he eventually separated from his wife). Caniff continued to write the scripts but left penciling in the hands of his assistant, Dick Rockwell, reserving the inking to himself. The strip regained some of his erstwhile luster in 1986 with an adventure set in China, a nostalgic journey involving Steve with Caniff's heroes from an earlier era: Terry, Pat, and Connie. Steve Canyon was discontinued in June 1988, following its creator's death in April of that year.

As an example of Caniff's art, Steve Canyon reached its apex during the early and middle 1950s. But as a body of work, Steve Canyon cannot compare with Caniff's earlier and more inspired Terry though it generated a great deal of excitement in the first ten years of its existence, when Caniff's powers were at their peak.

Steve Canyon had its own comic book version in the 1940s and 1950s published by Dell and drawn by Ray Bailey, and it was adapted to the television screen for one season in 1958 to 1959, with Dean Fredericks in the role of Steve Canyon.

M.H.

STEVE ROPER (U.S.) One of the earliest brainchildren of Harold Anderson and Eugene Conleys at Publishers Newspaper Syndicate in Chicago was delayed because of the release of another brainchild, the George Gallup survey. But in the interim, the other creation, The Great Gusto, was taken in sample form to editors around the country and garnered an impressive advance sale.

But editors liked the half-pint Indian chief medicine man better than the title character, an admitted derivative of W. C. Fields. So The Great Gusto never became a comic strip; instead, Big Chief Wahoo was introduced, finally, in late 1936.

Allen Saunders, a cartoonist and writer, was the author, and Elmer Woggon, a cartoonist, the artist who proposed the strip. Both had ill-fated features with United Feature Syndicate: Woggon's Skylark aviation strip and Saunders's Miserable Moments, a copy of Clare Briggs's When a Feller Needs a Friend.

The Great Gusto ran a medicine show (the time setting changed from the 1890s to contemporary days with the title change) and Wahoo was his stooge. Eventually Wahoo became wiser and Gusto was phased out (the team of creators had once gone to Hollywood to receive congratulations from the real Fields, who was a fan of the strip). And a pretty Indian maiden, Minnie-Ha-Cha, a onetime nightclub singer in New York, entered the strip as his sweetheart.

The growing popularity of story strips and Publishers Syndicate's constant and excellent polling system to determine client's tastes in comics both led to the demise of Wahoo as a gag-a-day strip.

Steve Roper was introduced as a handsome blond photographer for a major news magazine; he parachuted into the reservation. At once he assumed the hero role, much to the chief's anoyance, especially when Minnie-Ha-Cha fell for Roper. Thereafter Wahoo became Watson to Roper's Holmes.

Finally, in 1953, comic artist and versatile ghost Bill Overgard was engaged, and he turned the strip into today's sleek, sexy, very attractive product. He introduced Mike Nomad, based on a character he had tried to sell in a strip, and found a gutsy counterpoint to the new Roper's urbane reserve. Mike drives a circulation truck for Proof.

"Steve Roper," Bill Overgard. © Field Newspaper Syndicate.

"Stonehenge Kit," A. J. Kelly. © Fleetway Publications.

Other major characters in the present-day *Roper* include: Major McCoy, head of the magazine empire; Steve's secretary Honeydew Mellon, a blonde Southerner; Crandall Mellon, Honeydew's uncle and a private eye; Mike's parents, Polish immigrants named Nowak; and Ma Jong, over whose restaurant Mike lives.

Overgard's art is as slick and dramatic as Woggon's was neat and funny. The story line, which has concentrated in recent years on frauds and racketeering, is still written by Overgard, with help from his son, John, a TV newscaster who once scripted *Dateline: Danger*. Today *Steve Roper*, in both story and art, is one of the foremost straight strips in the anemic genre.

Overgard brought in the character of Mike Nomad, a tough private eye in the Mike Hammer mold, in the late 1970s, and the newcomer soon took over the strip, now renamed *Steve Roper and Mike Nomad*. When Allen Sauders retired in 1979, he left the feature in the hands of his son John. Overgard left in his turn in 1983 to creade *Rudy*, and he was replaced by Fran Matera, an able if somewhat limited craftsman.

R.M.

STONEHENGE KIT THE ANCIENT BRIT (G.B.) This stone-age saga began in a small way—a half-page strip in the first issue of *Knockout* (March 4, 1939) but it quickly caught on, perhaps because of its novelty as a comic serial, and expanded into a full page. It later moved to the two-tone back cover.

The hero, a simple, loincloth-clad clod with three hairs on his head, spent his strip defending King Kongo (Kingy for short) of Kongo Kourt from G. Whizz the Wizard (Whizzy the Wizard for short), aided by Glam,

his gal pal. Whizzy used all manner of wacky inventions in his mad plan to usurp Kingy's crown: his Kit Kosher, his Wind Whizzer, his Trap Tripper, his Flea Flicker, not to mention his mighty musclemen, Brit Basher Number One and Brit Basher Number Two (terribly tough twins only identifiable by their attached paper labels). There was also the local fauna to consider: the Coal Chewing Fire Gobbler, the Brontowotsit, and the Crockerdilligator.

Norman Ward created *Stonehenge Kit* and added a new twist in 1942 by making all his characters speak in rhyme. A. J. Kelly took over from Ward on May 18, 1942, and the series continued until May 1944. After three years' retirement, *Kit and Kompany* were brought back by Kelly, and the series, which began again on February 1, 1947, was perhaps their best. "The Search for the Stolen Crown" was followed by the "Quest of the Magic Applecore," the "Kourt of King Arfer," and the "Prehistoric Puff-Puff." Kelly's early death robbed the series of genius, but Hugh McNeill, and later Denis Gifford, continued the strip until November 25, 1950.

D.G.

STONY CRAIG OF THE MARINES (U.S.) Don Dickson's *Stony Craig of the Marines* (also known as *Sergeant Craig*) started its career in the pages of the *Boston Traveler* in August 1937.

Sergeant Stony Craig and his subordinates, the loudmouthed Wise, the resourceful Fink, and the handsome Hazard, were U.S. Marines stationed in the American settlement in Shanghai. They seemed to be busier fighting the Japanese and their allies than protecting the American administrative headquarters. The similarities with Caniff's *Terry and the Pirates* are obvious (there is even a woman guerilla-fighter, half-Russian, half-Chinese, by the name of Tania). If anything, Dickson was even more emphatically anti-Japanese than Caniff, and he (correctly) foresaw the coming hostilities with Japan as early as 1939. To prepare for the day, Craig and his cohorts, in collusion with Intelligence Service officer Jeremy Blade (who looked like Clark Gable), did their best to harass the Japanese, blowing up their convoys, hijacking their arms shipments, and lending help to the guerillas. In between there were a few romantic interludes involving Hazard and his army nurse love, the blonde and demure Helen.

In 1940 (following the closing of all foreign settlements in China by the Japanese authorities) Craig and company returned to the United States to combat spies and fifth columnists until 1942 when the author left to join the marines. (With *Stony Craig* Don Dickson seemed to have found his métier in more ways than one; he later became the official artist of the Marine Corps and had his combat drawings published in *Life*, the *Saturday Evening Post* and *Collier's*, while his paintings were exhibited at the National Gallery in Washington.) The strip was continued for a while by Gerry Bouchard.

Obscure as it is, *Stony Craig* was an excellent (and prescient) action strip, well-plotted, straight-forwardedly written and drawn in a loose, punchy, and winning style. In a time when story strips are suffering from terminal anemia, it reminds us of how vital and robust the genre once was, before syndicate taboos and strictures started whittling it down.

M.H.

STRANGE WORLD OF MR. MUM, THE (U.S.) Irving Phillips's *The Strange World of Mr. Mum* started its career (as a daily panel, and later as a full-fledged comic strip) on May 5, 1958, for Publishers Syndicate.

Strange indeed is Mr. Mum's world. Browsers sprout wings on their heels to reach the upper shelves of libraries, Rodin's thinker takes time out for calisthenics, Oriental bazaar merchants hold discount sales on magic carpets, visitors from outer space have their spaceship refueled at the neighborhood gas station. Mr. Mum, small, bespectacled, and bald-headed, observes all these (and more) in bemused silence. (Neither does Phillips's protagonist intervene in the weird goings-on he is constantly witnessing—perhaps he is meant to symbolize the helplessness of the individual in a world of uncontrollable forces.)

Of course Phillips's trick consists in his abolishing (or suspending) the laws of time and space (in this he carries Virgil Patch's experiments one step further). We follow Mr. Mum into a fourth-dimensional world where the extraordinary is the commonplace and the exception becomes the norm.

Although often intellectual and sometimes esoteric, *Mr. Mum* is also one of the funniest inventions of the last two decades. It has been reprinted many times in paperback form, but was discontinued in 1974.

M.H.

STRIEBEL, JOHN H. (1891-1967) The noted cartoonist whose artwork on *Dixie Dugan* has been followed by tens of millions of readers for more than 40 years, John H. Striebel, was born on September 14, 1891, in Bertrand, Michigan, and moved a few years later to South Bend, Indiana, where he attended school and obtained his first cartooning job as the front-page

political artist for the *South Bend News* at age 14 (within the same week he had been fired as a newsboy by the *News* circulation manager). After attending Notre Dame for two years, Striebel moved on to Chicago, where he illustrated current fashions for the Meyer-Both Syndicate, then transferred his clothing talents to the Marshall Field Department Store, where he drew "Fashions of the Hour" for their advertising purposes. He also found a steady job, after some freelancing, with the *Chicago Tribune* art staff, where he illustrated current fiction in the *Tribune* weekly magazine section and drew the spot art for the new *Potters* weekly narrative feature by an old crony from the *South Bend News*, J. P. McEvoy. His drawing of McEvoy's chief characters, Ma and Pa Potter, and their daughter, Mamie, favorably impressed McEvoy and Striebel was asked to design the jacket for the 1923 book edition of the hit play McEvoy based on *The Potters*.

A few years later, after Striebel had introduced his daily anecdote feature, *Pantomime* (a paneled gag without recurrent characters or balloons, usually involving a child or animal), which ran through most of the 1920s, he was asked to illustrate a comic strip McEvoy planned to base on the heroine of his 1929 novel, *Show Girl*. The heroine, Dixie Dugan, like Mamie in *The Potters*, had parents called Ma and Pa, and McEvoy wanted them drawn just as Striebel had done the *Potter* characters. Striebel obliged, and the strip, called *Show Girl*, was launched in 1929. Slow in getting under way, it took off in the early 1930s. Its name changed to *Dixie Dugan*, the strip ultimately became one of the country's most widely read comic strips.

Also collaborating with McEvoy in illustrating *Show Girl* as a serial story for *Liberty* in 1929 (as well as its two sequels), Striebel continued to work on *Dixie Dugan* until the mid-1940s when McEvoy stepped off the strip and turned the scripting over to his son, Renny.

Following his hobbies of croquet, painting, and playing the violin, Striebel lived in Bearsville, New York, with his wife, Fritzi, and four daughters, until his death in 1967.

B.B.

STUPS (Germany) *Stups*, a creation of German comic artist Max A. Otto, was published in the newspaper *Grüne Post* from 1928 to 1929. The stories, trying to be on the safe side, used both verse below the pictures and speech balloons, speed lines, and other usual comic strip conventions. The strip holds up well even today and is proof of the much-neglected fact that a German comic production existed between the two world wars. Strangely enough, these strips rarely had the success they could have or should have had (with a few exceptions like *Vater und Sohn*), or were lost because of the paper drives of World War II.

Some of these strips were carried over into postwar years but, of course, with no mention of connections to an earlier era which everyone wanted to forget. Thus, Max Otto had another strip, titled *Stips*, in the postwar *Grünes Blatt*. In the 1950s he also drew *Jippi der Indianerboy* ("Yippi the Indian Boy"), a comic strip that for quite a while was included in *Pete*, a weekly dime novel series in a Western setting aimed at younger readers. In 1954 *Das Jippi-Buch* ("The Yippi Book") was published, featuring 48 pages of text and 46 pages of *Jippi* reprints.

"Stups," Max Otto. © Max Otto.

Neighboring Austria had seen an even longer running strip, *Tobias Seicherl*, drawn and written in Austrian dialect by Ludwig Kmoch and published in *Das kleine Blatt*. Originally opposed to fascism, the strip displayed nationalistic tendencies by the end of the 1930s. Nevertheless the strip disappeared just as all of the children's magazines (a number of them produced in Austria and distributed in Germany's department stores) disappeared by 1940. Most of these children's magazines were giveaways either for certain chains of department stores or for products like margarine. While filled with lots of text features, there were also a number of genuine comic strips in magazines like *Rama Post*, *Pa pa gei*, *Kiebitz*, or *Teddy Bär*. Some of them even featured reprints of foreign comic strips like *Prinz Waldemar* ("Prince Valiant") as late as 1939.

Stups may serve as a reminder that it will take a great deal of research to find the missing links of comics history in Germany.

W.F.

STURMTRUPPEN (Italy)

In 1968 the Roman newspaper *Paese Sera* sponsored a contest aimed at finding an original Italian daily strip. Franco Bonvicini (who signs his work simply as "Bonvi") won the contest with his comic creation *Sturmtruppen*.

Sturmtruppen was not the first Italian daily strip. One earlier effort was Marco Biassoni's *Prode Anselmo* ("Anselmo the Bold"), published in the newspaper *Il Giorno*; a whole batch of experimental features had also been sponsored by the Corriere Mercantile of Genoa, but none of those ever survived for more than a few months. While many Italian comics were very successful in the form of comic books or in weekly comic magazines, up to this time none of them had ever made it in a big way in the newspaper page. *Sturmtruppen*'s greatest merit lies in its success as a trailblazer; it was followed by a host of others (*Zio Boris*, *Gli Aristocratici*, *Santincielo*, *Et Voila*, *Olimpiastri*, *Pasquino*, *Animalie*, to name but a few). However, *Sturmtruppen* was the first and, in many ways, the most successful one.

The strip, featuring a cast of weird-acting German storm troopers (including a werewolf, a vampire, and several cannibals), takes place in an hallucinatory setting in the middle of World War II. It is replete with dumb Nazi officers and hapless soldiers bedeviled by race theories and blind obedience to their superiors. Of those none is more dumbfounded than Private Schultze on whose head are constantly heaped torrents of abuse and contradictory orders. *Sturmtruppen* not only satirizes militarism and the military mind like Jaroslev Hasek's *Good Soldier Svejk*, it is also a bitter, often sick, black comedy that indicts the whole human race.

Sturmtruppen has been reprinted in book form and was adapted to television by its author. In 1975 Bonvi abandoned the strip because he had grown tired of it (and he refused to have it ghosted), but a revival occurred in 1976. The feature ended for good with Bonvi's death in 1995.

G.B.

SUB-MARINER, THE (U.S.)

Created by Bill Everett in November 1939, *The Sub-Mariner* made its premiere appearance in Timely's *Marvel Comics* (later *Marvel Mystery*) number 1. The son of an American naval officer and Princess Fen of Atlantis, Prince Namor was perpetually angry at the human race. One of the first popular antiheroes, the character was awarded his own book in the Spring of 1941, and he also made appearances in *Human Torch*, *All Winners*, and a half-dozen other books.

He was against mankind, which culminated in several classic battles with the Human Torch in the *Marvel Mystery* and *Human Torch* books, which ended during the World War II years. He suddenly became a protector of America and made the seas a dangerous place for Axis aquatic travel. He even developed a love interest, Betty Dean, one of the few humans who

"Sturmtruppen," Bonvi (Franco Bonvicini). © Bonvicini.

"Sub-Mariner," Bill Everett. © Marvel Comics Group.

could reason with the wing-footed hybrid. She was later replaced by Namora, another undersea inhabitant. Prince Namor's phenomenal powers enabled him to fly and consult fish, and and he was equally effective on land and in water. This made him one of the most popular heroes of the 1940s.

Like the other stars of the golden age, however, the Sub-Mariner began floundering after the war. Never resuming his battle against humans, he took to fighting crooks and by 1949 was making his last appearances in *Marvel Mystery* (91, April) and *Sub-Mariner* (32, June). When Atlas began reviving superheroes in 1953, Namor was the most successful of the ill-fated trio of *Captain America, Human Torch,* and *Sub-Mariner.* Making his first reappearance in *Young Men* December 1953, number 24, he also appeared in several issues of *Human Torch* and *Men's Adventure. Sub-Mariner* was also revived, lasting from April 1954 (issue number 33) to October 1955 (issue number 42). When Marvel (formerly Timely and Atlas) reentered the superhero field in 1960, Namor was the first to be revived.

Making his re-reappearance in *Fantastic Four* number four, May 1962, the Sub-Mariner was once again cast as the enemy of society. Marvel returned him to his own feature in August 1965 in *Tales to Astonish* number 70, and he lasted in that book until it folded after April 1968 (issue number 101). The next month a new series of *Sub-Mariner* comics began with issue number 1, and that book lasted through September 1974 (issue number 72). During all these years, however, the Prince could never quite decide who or what he was

fighting for. He was comicdom's foremost schizophrenic.

The definitive artist on *Sub-Mariner* was the creator, Bill Everett. Handling the strip on-and-off between 1939 and 1973, his stylized artwork was always superior to other artists' interpretations. Everett always drew Namor with a triangular head and pointed eyebrows, and they became the character's trademark. Gene Colan, Marie Severin, Vince Coletta, Sal Buscema, and others have handled the strip over the years. Writers like Roy Thomas, Stan Lee, Otto Binder, Everett himself, and even novelist Mickey Spillane have all worked on Namor.

And although he now appears solely as a supporting character, the *Sub-Mariner* has had a long and illustrious career and will probably survive as long as superheroes do. Indeed the man from Atlantis has made his reappearance time and again in his own comic book: in 1984, from 1988 to 1989, and from 1990 to 1995.

J.B.

SUBURBAN COWGIRLS (U.S.) *Suburban Cowgirls* began Thanksgiving Day, 1987, in the newspapers of MPG Newspapers of Plymouth, Massachusetts. By the fall of 1989, after a number of syndicates looked at it, the strip's creators, Ed Colley, who draws, and Janet Alfieri, who writes, were offered a contract by Tribune Media Services. *Suburban Cowgirls* began international syndication October 1, 1990.

The lead characters in the strip are Maxine "Max" Marshall, a thirty-something single mother of two; Angelique, 13; Jesse, eight; and her best friend, Darlene Dillon, also thirty-something, who's been married 15 years and has no children.

The title *Suburban Cowgirls* hails from a night in the mid-1980s when writer Alfieri and a group of women friends decided to join a bowling league as a lark with that as the team's name. The idea was to get out of the house one night a week, away from husbands and kids. They never bowled, but it's a great title for a comic strip about relationships in sububia.

Janet Alfieri graduated from Emmanuel college, a Catholic women's college in Boston, in 1971 with a degree in sociology. Ed Colley earned both undergraduate and masters of fine arts degrees from Boston University; from 1962 until 1989 he was a high school art teacher. Colley drew editorial cartoons for the MPG Newspaper chain and Alfieri worked there as a features writer, reporter, and layout artist. After Colley put the word out that he was looking for a partner to develop a comic strip, Alfieri volunteered. As both have the shared experience of raising families in suburbia, the subject matter of *Suburban Cowgirls* was a natural for them.

In the strip Max wants nothing to do with her ex-husband. It's strongly implied that he was unfaithful in their marriage. She supports herself hosting the morning radio show on a small radio station WMOM-AM, "the radio station that rocks the hand that rocks the cradle." Her counterpoint is best friend Darlene Dillon whom she met in the back row of a low-impact aerobics class. Darlene works as assistant to the president of the local bank in their hometown of Tupperville outside a major city. Darlene's husband, Bob, is the top salesman for a plumbing supply company during the day, but off work he's become a television-addicted beer-drinking couch potato. He's more

"Suburban Cowgirls," Ed Colley and Janet Alfieri. © Tribune Media Services.

emotionally involved with his hound dog Bo than with Darlene. The couple are in marriage counseling.

Since the strip began, cartoonist Colley, as happens with all strips, has modified the appearance of the characters. If anything he has made the women more attractive and shapely. Max has a wild mop of blonde hair and the more conservative Darlene's brunette hair is perfectly groomed. Bob has remained constant from day one, beer-bellied and bald.

Max favors T-shirts with a message on the front. What started as a gimmick now is an integral part of the strip that fans look for. The daily from January 6, 1997, has no caption but plays off the T-shirts. Max and Darlene seen from the rear pass by a woman in a "Kiss Me I'm Irish" shirt and a man in a "Kiss Me I'm Polish" one. In the last panel Darlene is shown in her "Don't Touch Me I'm Waspish" T-shirt, and Max, the disc jockette, in her "KISS 1996 World Tour" shirt.

While Max turns heads, she searches in vain for a sensitive new-age guy. Darlene loves Bob but longs for romance to return to her marriage. In one daily she thinks he's snuggling up to her on the couch only to find out he's trying to get the TV program guide she's accidently sitting on. Many gags and short continuities revolve around Max's relationship with her kids. Janet Alfieri's writing and Ed Colley's cartoons have family humor and great design. Whether struggling to keep their figures at exercise class or discussing the ironies of life for thirty-something women, Max and Darlene are winners.

These Suburban Cowgirls just want to have fun and make you laugh. They have none of the victim quality of *Cathy* but rather are more everyday women such as the characters in *For Better Or For Worse*, *Gasoline Alley*, *Rose Is Rose*, or *Sally Forth*.

B.C.

SUGIURA, SHIGERU (1908-   ) Shigeru Sugiura is a Japanese comic book artist born in Tokyo on April 3, 1908. Sugiura's father was a doctor, as his older two brothers also went on to become, but the young Shigeru wanted to be an artist. He went to the Taiheiyō ga Kenkyujo school at Shimaya where he studied painting from 1926 to 1930. That same year his landscapes were accepted by Teiten (later Nitten), one of the most famous Japanese art exhibitions. But in spite of his artistic successes, Sugiura had trouble earning a living with his paintings in the Japan of the depression years, and he decided to become a comic strip artist, studying for one year with the celebrated comic artist Suihō Tagawa. Sugiura's first work of

Shigeru Sugiura, comic book illustration.

comic art appeared in the boys' magazine *Shōnen Kurabu*, in 1933.

After 18 years of relative obscurity (during which he contributed ephemeral cartoons to several magazines) Shigeru Sugiura burst upon the comic book scene with *Mohican Zokuno Saigo* ("The Last of the Mohicans"), his first best-selling strip. In 1953 he created the feature which he is best known for, *Sarutobi Sasuke*, a nonsensical comic strip about an inept secret agent by that name.

Sugiura's works are full of surprises which spring at the unsuspecting reader like jacks-in-the-box. In his strips he often makes use of American figures of comic art, screen, and fiction such as Tarzan, Laurel and Hardy, Popeye, the Marx Brothers, or Betty Boop. His art style, whimsical, weird, and almost surrealistic, has contributed to Shigeru Sugiura's appellation as the Japanese Basil Wolverton.

H.K.

SU LANG (1938-   ) Graduated from the Northwest Normal College in 1957 with a major in art, Su worked as a reporter and editor for the *Gansu Daily* in China between 1957 and 1985, and as a deputy general editor at Gansu (Province) People's Art Publishing House and deputy editor-in-chief of Gansu Pictorial between 1985 and 1995; since then he has been the deputy editor for Gansu People's Publishing House. He is a member of the Chinese Artist Association and of the Outstanding Committees of Chinese News Media Cartoon Research Society and Gansu Artist Association. As a nationally known cartoonist, he has been

President of Gansu Cartoonist Association. He is also a Researcher at the Museum of Gansu History.

Although all his cartoons and comics were made in his leisure time, which overburdened his life, Su never stopped making them after he started cartooning as a student in the 1950s. Several thousand cartoons, comics, and prints that were published in the past years were all made either at night or on holidays. His artworks were selected for national or international exhibitions many times, and his art often earned awards. In 1993 Su's cartoon received the highest award in Chinese cartoon circles—the Golden Monkey Award. In 1995 he was again awarded first prize in the National Newspaper Cartoon Competition; in the same year, he won first prize at the Second Black-and-White Cartoon Contest of Worker's Daily with his cartoon *The Shadow Troop*, which ridicules people eager to "serve" those who have power (the symbol of power is the seal in the hand of the man walking in front of the "troop"). The "services," however, are in various ways very convenient to different persons or personalities: some are always ready to light cigarettes for the boss and sing loudly flattering songs, and others are trying to please him with gifts and/or to serve him in bed.

Among Su's more than 10 cartoon and comics collections published, the comic book entitled *Legends Along the Silk Road* is the first of a seven-volume comic book series that was published in three languages (Chinese, English, and Japanese) by the Chinese Literature Publishing House in 1995. Illustrated with more than 500 drawings made by Su in two months, *Legends*

Along the Silk Road includes the history and natural scenery as well as the religions, arts, and numerous tales associated with the Silk Road, all based upon authentic historical records.

H.Y.L.L.

SULLIVAN, PAT (1887-1933) Pat Sullivan was an American cartoonist born in 1887 (or 1888, according to some sources) in Australia. Despite Sullivan's fame as the creator of the extravagantly successful Felix the Cat cartoon character, little seems to be known about his early life. After a disappointing stab at a cartooning career in a number of Australian papers, he left for England in 1908 and worked on the *Ally Sloper* feature for a time. In 1914 he emigrated again, this time to the United States. There he worked as a prize-fighter and vaudeville comedian while trying his hand at comic strips (creating *Pa Perkins* in 1914 and *Samuel Johnson* a little later), not too successfully.

Around 1915 Sullivan turned his sights toward animation, eventually establishing his own small studio: his first recorded effort in this field seems to have been an animated version of *Pa Perkins*. In 1917 Sullivan produced the first *Felix the Cat* short: the success was immediate and spectacular. By the time of Sullivan's death in 1933 more than 100 cartoons had been produced, *Felix* was appearing all over the world in many forms (as a comic strip since 1923), and a catchy little tune had everybody humming: Felix kept on walking/ Kept on walking still.

Pat Sullivan is only marginally connected with the comic strip field but, like Walt Disney after him, his work as an animator proved instrumental in many ways. And, of course, his *Felix the Cat* remains as a memorial to his imagination and talent.

M.H.

SUPERBONE (Italy) Feeling the need for a magazine aimed at the younger reader, Alceo and Domenico Del Duca, owners of the Casa Editrice Universo, decided to republish their old comic magazine, *Il Monello*, but in a more convenient pocket-size format. The first issue hit the newsstands in 1953 with a mixture of comic stories and illustrated tales with captions in octosyllabic verse. It was in this revamped version of *Il Monello* that, starting in issue number one, Erio Nicolo's *Superbone* ("Superbrat") appeared. It ran until the mid-1960s.

Drawn in a blend of realistic and grotesque graphic styles well suited to the spirit of the story, the feature starred an unruly young boy in the *Katzenjammer* tradition who liked to play pranks on parents, neighbors, and strangers alike. Unfortunately for him, however, each of his shenanigans ended up with his receiving a few good whacks of the broomstick wielded by his implacable aunt. Always wearing a pair of knickers and an unruly forelock falling on his eye, Superbone usually got in all kinds of scrapes with the other boys who lived in the village: he always tried to outwit them but they usually had the last laugh as they saw Superbone punished by his aunt.

The strip certainly does not come up to the quality of similar American series, but it is amusing and fresh, and the younger readers enjoy it immensely.

G.B.

SUPERGIRL (U.S.) *Supergirl* was created by editor Mort Weisinger and writer Otto Binder as a back-up feature for the *Superman* strip in Action Comics, com-

Su Lang, "Legends Along the Silk Road." © Su Lang.

mencing with issue number 252 (May 1959). The new feature was initiated after a tremendous reader response to an issue of *Superman*, a year earlier. The August 1958 issue of *Superman* carried a story, "The Girl of Steel," in which Jimmy Olsen used a magic totem pole to wish a Super Girl into existence. The character later sacrificed her life to save Superman's and, when that issue sold exceedingly well, it was decided to create a new Supergirl to be featured in *Action Comics*.

That Supergirl was the last remaining survivor (at the time) of Argo City, part of the planet Krypton. When the planet exploded, the original story explained, Argo City was hurled away on a large chunk of soil that soon turned into deadly Kryptonite. Lead sheeting was used to cover the ground but, years later, a meteor shower punctured the protective lead, unleashing the Kryptonite radiations. Scientist Zor-el (brother of Superman's father, Jor-el) sent his teenaged daughter, Kara, to earth, much as Jor-el had sent his son, Kal-el. In the intervening years, Kal-el had grown up into Superman. Since the new Supergirl was therefore Superman's cousin, it eliminated any possibility of a Superman-Supergirl romance, which would have interfered with the Superman-Lois Lane courtship.

The blonde, teenaged Supergirl was given a brown wig and the secret identity of Linda Lee, a resident of the Midvale Orphanage. For a time, the existence of a Supergirl on earth was carefully guarded, and Linda Lee scrupulously avoided being adopted. Finally, in August 1961, she was adopted by a Mr. and Mrs. Danvers (making her secret identity name Linda Lee Danvers) and, in February of the following year, Superman announced that her training period was over and that the world should know of her presence.

The first *Supergirl* story was drawn by Al Plastino, after which Jim Mooney became the permanent artist until 1968 when Kurt Schaffenberger took over. Stories were supplied by Binder, Leo Dorfman, Edmond Hamilton, and many others. Over the years, *Supergirl* also appeared frequently in all of the other magazines spun-off from the *Superman* feature, including her entry into the Legion of Superheroes. Linda Lee Danvers grew up and enrolled in college.

In June 1969, commencing with *Adventure Comics* number 381, *Supergirl* took over the whole magazine, abandoning the back-up slot in *Action Comics*. Schaffenberger and Winslow Mortimer illustrated the feature until the following year when Mike Sekowsky took over the editing, writing, and drawing. Linda Lee Danvers graduated from college at about this time and, shortly after, Sekowsky was replaced by a constantly changing crew of writers and artists, including Bob Oksner, Art Saaf, Vince Colletta, John Albano, Steve Skeates, and (later) Sekowsky again. In 1972, *Supergirl* left *Adventure Comics* and appeared in a new *Supergirl* magazine, beginning with number 1 (November 1972). It lasted ten issues, after which *Supergirl* became a rotating feature in *The Superman Family* comic book.

In 1982 the publishers revived the *Supergirl* comic book (as *The Daring Adventures of Supergirl*) with Gil Kane as the main artist, but it only lasted until 1984, the year that the *Supergirl* movie, starring Helen Slater, came out. In 1985 DC did the comic book adaptation. There also was a *Supergirl* miniseries in 1994.

M.E.

SUPERMACHOS, LOS (Mexico) *Los Supermachos de San Garabato Cuc*, more simply, *Los Supermachos* ("The Supermales"), is the Mexican comic feature that revolutionized that country's comic industry; it is without precedent or equivalent in other Spanish-speaking countries and stands as a symbol of what a successful political comic should be.

The strip's creator is the cartoonist Rius (pseudonym of Eduardo del Río), who in 1965, gave life to the inhabitants of the mythical town of San Garabato in a series of comic books published by Editorial Meridiano S.A. Following a dispute with the publisher in 1968 Rius left the series, and it passed into other hands. In the meantime, Rius devoted himself to the parallel collection, *Los Agachados*, with even more vigor and authenticity.

Through the characters of the inhabitants of this lost village of San Garabato, who spend their time arguing or taking siestas, Rius expounds subtle social criticism that is valid not only for Mexico but for all other countries where similar social conditions exist, as well. In the strip's vast dramatis personae a number of characters stand out, such as the politician Don Perpetuo del Rosal, and the Indians Chón Prieto and Juan Calzoncin. The latter vainly attempts to communicate his political ideas to his fellow villagers; at times he appears as the major character and gave his name to the movie inspired by the strip, *Calzoncin Inspector*. A stage play based *on Los Supermachos* was produced in Guadalajara.

L.G.

SUPERMAN (U.S.) 1—*Superman* was created by two 17-year-olds, writer Jerry Siegel and artist Joe Shuster, and made its first appearance in the premiere issue of National Comics' *Action* (June 1938). The quintessential comic book strip, *Superman* carried comic book's first costumed superhero and provided the impetus for the industry's boom in 1940 through 1945.

Based heavily on Philip Wylie's 1930 science-fiction novel *Gladiator*, Siegel's concept of the strip rested heavily on three now-clichéd themes: the visitor from another planet, the superhuman being, and the dual identity. As familiar as these themes were, however, the feature was originally rejected by every major newspaper syndicate in the country. M. C. Gaines eventually recommended *Superman* to publisher Harry Donnenfeld who bought it for $130 and repasted the strip into a 13-page comic book story. By 1941, *Superman* was being advertised as "The World's Greatest Adventure Strip Character" and was appearing in a half-dozen comic books and on radio.

Superman's origin is part of Americana: born on the doomed planet Krypton, Superman was launched into space just before the planet's collapse. Landing on earth, he was adopted by Jonathan and Martha Kent and discovered his Kryptonian heritage endowed him with great abilities. He later came to Metropolis, adopted the guise of a Daily Planet reporter and devoted his life to fighting for truth, justice, and the American way.

As the prototype of all comic book superhero features, *Superman* has received a great deal of psychological scrutiny. While the majority of his superheroic imitators were normal men transformed into superhumans, Superman was born super and adopted the alter ego of the somewhat craven Clark Kent. Critics are constantly analyzing the peculiar juxtaposition of

"Superman," © National Periodical Publications.

"Superman," Wayne Boring. © National Periodical Publications.

Superman, who could easily have been a king, and Clark Kent, who accepted a badgering boss (Perry White), an unceremonious attire, a less-than-brilliant companion (Jimmy Olsen), and the constant irony of being in competition with himself for the woman he loves (Lois Lane).

Despite the great powers originally given to him by Siegel, time strengthened the Man of Steel even further. He eventually developed the powers of flight and invulnerability and several types of x-ray vision. His powers became so immense, however, that green kryptonite was developed. Introduced by Bob Maxwell for the *Superman* radio show, and later incorporated into the comic books, green kryptonite were fragments of Superman's home planet that could kill him. In the 1950s, editor Mort Weisinger expanded the kryptonite concept to other colors (with varying effects) and added many other facets to the *Superman* feature. And it was Weisinger who considerably altered the tone of *Superman*'s adventures. Whereas Siegel's concept centered around a superhuman battling an almost equally endowed opponent, Weisinger's concept had a godlike Superman perplexed not by the second strongest man, but by fools (Mr. Mxyzlptlk), pranksters (Toyman), and gadgeted mad scientists (Lex Luther).

Artistically, Joe Shuster's crude, almost comedic version faded into oblivion after he left the feature, and, for many years afterwards, the publishers called his work too amateurish to reprint. Wayne Boring's later interpretations became more prevalent and his tight renderings, expressive faces, and stonelike figures made the feature a stalking ground of musclemen. In more recent years, however, the feature has been handled by Curt Swan and Murphy Anderson, and their version is slicker and more pristine than ever before.

The feature's fame has reached into other media, too. A fabulously successful radio show began in 1940 (featuring the voice of Bud Collyer), followed by several series of animated cartoons, a George Lowther novel (1942), several serials, a now-famous four-year television series starring George Reeves, and a Broadway play, *It's a Bird . . . It's a Plane . . . It's Superman!* An anthology, *Superman from the 30s to the 70s*, was published by Crown in 1971. Not to mention thousands of toys, games, giveaways, and a now-defunct museum, Metropolis, Illinois's Amazing World of Superman.

With the dawn of the 1970s, changes in the feature came at a terrifyingly rapid rate as Julius Schwartz assumed editorial control over several of the *Superman* family titles. Clark Kent even left the *Daily Planet* for a television job! But no amount of changes are likely to alter the importance of the *Superman* feature to modern American mythology.

The sinking fortunes of the Man of Steel were revived by the phenomenal success of the 1978 *Superman* movie starring Christopher Reeve. To capitalize on the film's momentum, the editors at DC called on a succession of talented artists, including John Byrne, Joe

Kubert, and Dave Gibbons, to revamp the character. In 1992 Superman died (for the umpteenth time), only to come back the following year; and in 1996 he finally hitched up with Lois Lane. (In 1997 he also changed his costume, but that gimmick only elicited yawns from a jaded public.)

Meanwhile the character's mediatization continued apace, with three more *Superman* movies coming out throughout the 1980s. In 1993 the television series *Lois and Clark: The New Adventures of Superman* started its long run on ABC. There have also been two more animated series, one on CBS-TV from 1988 to 1989, the other on the WB network, debuting in the fall of 1996. *Superman* even inspired a full-scale orchestral work, Michael Daugherty's five-movement *Metropolis Symphony*.

J.B.

2—*Superman* started his career in newspapers in 1939 (January 16, for the daily strip, November 5, for the Sunday page). Distributed by the McClure Syndicate, the feature was at first written and drawn by its creators, Jerry Siegel and Joe Shuster, before being taken over by Wayne Boring in 1940. The strip met with notable success in the 1940s, but its popularity declined in the 1950s and it was discontinued in 1967. It was revived 1977 to 1993.

The *Superman* newspaper strip was decidedly more adult than the comic book version. Its stories were more carefully plotted and its characterization somewhat better defined but, of course, the basic plot and situation remained unchanged.

M.H.

SUPERSNIPE (U.S.) The superhero explosion that did not begin until Jerry Siegel and Joe Shuster created *Superman* in 1938 had become an uncontrollable glut by 1942. Hundreds of titles showcasing hundreds of heroes many of them insufferable bores and uninspired imitations were flooding newsstands. But one company, Street and Smith, a top-notch pulp house turned comic producer, always looked at their comic book line differently. They marketed fewer titles than most, and spent most of their time pushing the comic reincarnations of pulp heroes like the *Shadow* and *Doc Savage*. And, starting in *The Shadow* number 6 for March 1942, began a delightful new series of adventures in a strip called *Supersnipe*.

Created by writer Ed Gruskin and illustrator George Marcoux, *Supersnipe* was actually a parody of the whole superhero craze and of comic books themselves. The strip featured Koppy McFad, an eight-year-old who lived in Yapburg and claimed to have more comic books than anyone in America. Or, as one cover blurb put it, He reads 'em, breathes 'em and sleeps 'em. Notwithstanding the fact that Koppy was only shown with the relatively small Street and Smith output, he did indeed have a lot of comics, and eventually assumed his Supersnipe alter ego to fight crime: real, imagined, and daydreamed. For a costume, Koppy wore red flannel underwear, his father's blue cape, and a domino mask. He never had any superpowers, save for once when a friend rigged up a flying rubber suit for him.

The character was an instant success, and, after an additional appearance in *The Shadow* and several other Street and Smith titles, *Supersnipe* comics began with October 1942's sixth issue. As the stories progressed, Koppy added a troupe of assistants. Among his friends were: Herlock Dolmes, a child who fancied checkered coats and a deerstalker cap and thought himself the youngest, greatest crimefighter in the world; Ulysses Q. Wacky, boy inventor; Wilferd Berlad, nicknamed Trouble, who lived a charmed life; and a self-proclaimed, self-styled girl guerilla named Roxy Adams. Together, Supersnipe and his rag-tag group went on to fight crime in Yapburg and around the world. Never forgetting, of course, that Koppy had the most comic books in the world!

Writer Gruskin who was also the *Street and Smith* comics editor wrote most of the stories in a deceptively simple manner. His characters never lost their charming curiosity, childish logic, and attractive sense of humor. They were simply children having fun, something rarely if ever successfully portrayed in comics. The artist, George Marcoux, originated the *Supersnipe* concept and illustrated the stories tastefully, often using a child's perception. Perhaps his most famous and often-seen cover appeared in June 1943 and depicted the barely four-foot Koppy in full dress holding a pin to a metal statuette of Hitler. Reflected in the mirror was a larger-than-life Supersnipe menacing the real Hitler with a giant stake.

Supersnipe outlasted many of the superheroes it lampooned, last appearing in August 1949's *Supersnipe* number 49. And although the strip has never been revived, it has become a legend of sorts.

J.B.

SUSKE EN WISKE (Belgium) *Suske en Wiske* is one of the longest running comic series to come out of Flemish Belgium. Originally created as *Rikki en Wiske* early in 1945, the first adventure did not see print until late in 1945, after the war had ended. *Rikki en Wiske* was published in the newspaper *De Nieuwe Gids*, later retitled *De Nieuwe Standaard*, finally *De Standaard*. *Rikki en Wiske* owed a lot to Hergé's *Totor* and *Tintin*, as

"Suske en Wiske," Willy Vandersteen. © Willy Vandersteen.

writer and artist Willy Vandersteen had always been a fan of these comics. The first episode plunged Rikki and Wiske, brother and sister, and their aunt Sidonie into a kidnapping affair, and the readers were pleased. Nevertheless, Vandersteen wrote Rikki out of the story because he was much older than Wiske and acted much like Tintin and, in the second story, introduced the orphan boy Suske, who is Wiske's age. Henceforth the series has been known as *Suske en Wiske*. The second story also introduced Professor Barabas, an ingenious if forgetful inventor who kept reappearing regularly.

In story number 31, another important addition to the cast was made in the person of Lambik, who was changed from plumber to private detective and was totally integrated into the adventurous lives of Suske and Wiske. Lambik represents the Belgian element in the comic strip. Besides his eccentricities and a penchant toward drinking, he has the proverbial heart of gold. The adventures of Suske and Wiske, taking place all over the globe, are drawn in a moderately funny style, much like the adventures of Tintin.

The success of the feature has led to reprints in album form starting in 1948. That same year, Vandersteen was asked to work for *Kuifje*, a Flemish edition of *Tintin* that was not doing too well. Hergé suggested that Vandersteen draw slightly more realistically and more detailed and should have style sheets for all his characters to facilitate a changeover to a ghost artist if necessary. *Suske en Wiske* has since spread to many European countries, making its humorous and moralizing tales an international phenomenon.

W.F.

SVIRČIĆ, ZDENKO (1924-   ) Zdenko Svirčić is a Yugoslav cartoonist and academic artist who was born in Split, on November 26, 1924. Svirčić's uncle was a photographer who took many pictures for different museums and reproduced the originals of famous Yugoslav artists. Svirčić was able to study art on these reproductions and to try something of his own. He was very busy painting and cartooning up to the age of 14, when he decided to quit and to try sculpture. World War II soon forced him to leave his new hobby, but after the war he studied at and graduated from the Academy of Plastic Arts in Zagreb.

After graduation he married and became concerned with supporting his family. He began to draw a few comic strip pages based on the famous *Salambo* novel and offered them to the Vjesnik publishing house in Zagreb. However, he got another job in the same house, and in 1954 his first comic strip was published. The scriptwriter was the noted Marcel Čukli. At that time Svirčić most admired Raymond's *Flash Gordon* and Foster's *Tarzan* and *Prince Valiant*. Immersed in comics and illustrations for different papers and books, he no longer had time for sculpture.

Many Yugoslav cartoonists usually drew (and still draw) both realistic and humor strips, but Svirčić has always done only the realistic ones. His most popular comics were *Gusari na Atlantiku* ("The Pirates of the Atlantic") and *U ledenoj pustinji* ("In the Ice Desert").

Svirčić left comics in 1967 because of his low income and because of the generally poor situation of comics in Yugoslavia. He now does mainly illustrations and front cover pictures for different publications.

E.R.

SWAB *see* Burgon, Sid.

SWAMP THING (U.S.) One of the few comic book characters bereft of superpowers to come out of the superhero-besotted 1970s, *Swamp Thing* made his appearance in July 1971 in the pages of DC Comics' *House of Secrets*. It was the creation of Len Wein, who wrote the texts, and Berni Wrightson, who contributed the artwork.

As these things stand, the protagonist's origins were fairly straightforward: Dr. Alec Holland was transmogrified into Swamp Thing when his laboratory, secreted deep in the Louisiana bayous, was bombed by foreign agents and he remained immersed in the marshes for days, only to reemerge as a creature half-vegetal, half-human, incapable of speech but remaining a sentient being under his exterior of roots, moss, and muck. The story caused enough of a sensation for *Swamp Thing* to get his own title in 1972.

Wein developed sensitive, intelligent scripts, dwelling at length on the plight of a human being trapped in an alien body. Other characters came into the story: Matt Cable, a government agent trying to solve the mystery of the swamp creature; Arcane, the obligatory mad scientist out to capture Swamp Thing for his own purposes; and Arcane's daughter Abigail, who fell for the handsome Cable. Interesting as these stories were, it was the artwork that arrested the reader's attention. Wrightson, who had honed his skills on the horror magazines published by Warren, created a mood of suspense, creepiness, and fear in a succession of chillingly evocative drawings. Unfortunately Wrightson left in 1974, followed later in the same year by Wein, and the title fell into the inept hands of David Michelinie, whose pedestrian plots not even Nestor Redondo's excellent artwork could redeem. *Swamp Thing* went into free fall, with the last issue appearing in 1976.

The title was revived in 1982 as *Saga of the Swamp Thing* under a number of artists, including Stephen Bissette, John Totleben, and Rick Veitch. In 1984 British writer Alan Moore took over the scripting, and in his retelling of the creature's origins he averred that Dr. Holland was in fact turned into a "plant elemental." Around this basic premise Moore constructed genuinely gripping tales, enhanced by a lyrical prose often reminiscent of Edgar Allan Poe and Mary Shelley, as in this opening to one of his stories: "At night you can almost imagine what it might look like if the swamp were boiled down to its essence, and distilled into corporeal form; if all the muck, all the forgotten muskrat bones, and all the luscious decay would rise up and wade on two legs through the shallows; if the swamp had a spirit and that spirit walked like a man." Despite its narrative and artistic brilliance, *Swamp Thing* met with only scant success. In 1993 it was transferred to DC's Vertigo imprint, a comic book line aimed at a more sophisticated audience.

M.H.

SWARTE, JOOST (1947-   ) Joost Swarte was born in 1947 in Hemstede, the Netherlands. While he studied industrial design at the academy of Eindhoven from 1966 to 1969, he became self-educated as an artist, especially in the field of comics. Swarte earned his fame as a graphic designer for his book and magazine illustrations as well as for his advertising art. They made him one of the most sought-after contemporary artists in the Netherlands, while his comic works have

"Swamp Thing," Len Wein and Berni Wrightson. © DC Comics.

Joost Swarte, self-portrait.

been few and for the most part have remained works that were at first only treated as of interest to insiders.

Swarte drew comic strips for various Dutch magazines between 1970 and 1980. These were finally collected for book publication under the prestigious title *Modern Art* in 1980. Each of the stories by Swarte is a little masterpiece in itself. The anarchic humor, which sometimes seems inspired by the Marx Brothers, time and again belies the seeming naiveté of his artwork.

Swarte in his regular as in his comic work shows strong influences of what has been termed the school of "ligne claire." In fact, he constantly refers to the epitome of ligne claire-ism, to Hergé. He not only takes this artistic style to its limits, he also uses the imagery of Hergé, even coming up with a very Tintin-like protagonist. One is wont to say he out-Hergés Hergé.

While Swarte obviously has been saturated with ligne claire comics, his storytelling turns what seems simple at first look into utmost ambiguity while at the same time being replete with all kinds of detail. Swarte's comics have long since gone from insider stuff to cult status as they playfully stretch the possibilities of the comics medium and reward readers with a refreshing joyfulness that is hard to find elsewhere.

Swarte also managed to become a regular guest in Art Spiegelman's *Raw* magazine. His art graces many products, books, and newspapers and can even be seen on Dutch postage stamps.

W.F.

SWEENEY AND SON (U.S.) Al Posen's *Sweeney and Son* started as a Sunday page in the same issue of the *Chicago Tribune* as Gaar Williams's famed *A Strain on the Family Tie*, an identical strip in theme, on October 1, 1933. Like the Williams strip, *Sweeney and Son* told of the weekly doings of father and son companions, sometimes at loggerheads, but more often in league together against the looming feminine world of propriety and discipline represented by the mother of the family. Both graphically and in an anecdotal story, Posen's strip was the lighter work of the two features, rarely rising above the simplified art and gag level of such strips as *The Little King* or *Reg'lar Fellers*, and it lacked virtually all of the sense of suppressed savagery and frantic desperation of domestic life that often surfaced in other father-and-son strips, such as Fera's *Elmer*, Crosby's *Skippy*, or Posen's fellow-starter, Williams's *Strain*.

It was a pleasant spot on the Sunday page, however, and the weekly escapades of Pop and Junior Sweeney usually provided a smile or two between the more attentively read *Dick Tracy* or *Little Joe*. Aside from the two protagonists, and Mom Sweeney, no other major characters entered the strip over the years, nor was there any narrative continuity of any consequence. Posen's style was attractive, with the same dancing movement that made his earlier daily strip, *Them Days Is Gone Forever*, so visually enjoyable. There were no separate book collections of the strip, although it ran in such News-Tribune published comic books as *Popular Comics, Super Comics*, and so on, in the 1930s and 1940s. The strip folded, almost without notice, in the late 1950s, as did its accompanying Sunday anecdotal feature, *Jinglet*.

B.B.

SWINNERTON, JAMES GUILFORD (1875-1974)

James Guilford Swinnerton was one of the two grand old men of American comics (the other was Harry Hershfield, 1885-1975). Guilford was instrumental in the creation of the American comic strip, and he is noted as the author of *Little Bears and Tykes, Little Jimmy*, and *Canyon Kiddies*. He was born in Eureka, California, on November 13, 1875, the son of Judge J. W. Swinnerton, founder of the *Humboldt Star*, a Northern California weekly newspaper. Raised in Stockton, California, where the elder Swinnerton presided as a judge before going on to Republican Party politics, Jimmy took his cartooning talent to San Francisco and landed a job at age 16 on William Randolph Hearst's first newspaper, the *San Francisco Examiner*, in 1892.

Here, the young cartoonist's tiny caricatured bear cubs, derived from the full-grown emblem on the California state seal and flag, and featured in small weekly panel drawings on the children's page in the Sunday *Examiner*, were an immense public hit. Although minisculely reproduced, the drawing was witty and eye-catching, while the bears' weekly antics (in the schoolroom, camping out, flying kites, etc.) tickled adults as much as the kids for whom they were intended. The addition of kids themselves to the bears' weekly feature led to the caption *Little Bears and Tykes*, for a short period. But Hearst wanted more out of his young employee than comic bears (although he learned from the popularity of the feature that a regularly repeated graphic feature could sell a lot of papers and by 1896, Swinnerton, signing "Swin," had become the *Examiner*'s political cartoonist, turning out huge drawings that often filled the paper's front and inside pages. At 21, Jimmy Swinnerton was a widely admired, well-paid success, and he remained so for the rest of his life.

Well established on the San Francisco scene, he was already a member, from August 28, 1895, of the city's honored Bohemian Club, and spent his life on its famed list of Fifty. Swinnerton felt obliged to pack up and leave for New York when his boss invited him to join the strip staff of the Hearst *New York Journal* at the close of the century. Here he dropped the *Little Bears* strip after a few scattered episodes and began to work

on two new features (all like the last few *Little Bears*, in the new comic strip art form style Hearst and his artists had developed in New York). The earliest, which ran under a number of individual weekly captions, was the first strip to introduce the Noah's Ark theme, involving its landed boatload of animals in many exquisitely drawn escapades, and could be called *Mount Ararat* after the term most frequently used in the strip captions. (Swinnerton later revived this theme in a Sunday page, temporarily replacing his *Jimmy* in 1918, and called it *In The Good Old Days*.) The second, developed a little later, featured humanized orange-and-black-striped felines which Swinnerton called lynxes, but which the public widely termed tigers; a series which shortly became the long-lived strip called *Mr. Jack*. Mr. Jack, a feline like his fellow characters, was a merry bachelor who continually lost out with the chorus girls and bathing beauties he pursued. Both strips were well established when he introduced his best-known and longest-running strip, *Jimmy* (later *Little Jimmy*), early in 1904.

Swinnerton was an enormously prolific and inventive strip artist, and managed to undertake a number of imaginative but short-lived strips from the early 1900s on. With *Mount Ararat*, which faded from sight in 1906, he fielded such titles as *Bad Mans, Anatole, Poor Jones, Professor Knix, The Great Scientist, Sweet Little Katy, Sam and His Laugh, Mr. Batch*, and an odd daily or two, notably *Clarissa's Chances* and *Mr. Nutt* (which he bylined "Guilford," using his middle name), all between the turn of the century and 1920. After 1920, however, his creative orientation turned almost entirely toward the theme of American desert life, a subject that had come to interest Swinnerton after he was sent to Arizona in 1902 to recuperate from incipient tuberculosis. (In the 1920s he moved to Los Ange-

James Swinnerton, "The Little Bears."

les where he could reach the desert easily and frequently.) Using the colorful subjects of the Navaho Indians and the desert wildlife, Swinnerton began to draw his famed *Canyon Kiddies* series (not a strip) for *Good Housekeeping* in the early 1920s. He developed his landscape painting at the same time, becoming one of the most famed Southwestern oil painters in the world. In addition, Swinnerton wrote numerous travel articles for newspapers and magazines, reviewed books in his field, and illustrated several volumes, from Annie Laurie's *The Little Boy Who Lived on the Hill* in 1895, to his own *Hosteen Crotchety* in 1965.

Still painting until his hands became too shaky to do the sort of work he demanded of them in 1965, Swinnerton retained his broad interest in art and life until his death at the considerable age of 98 on September 5, 1974, in a Palm Springs hospital.

B.B.

TAD *see* Dorgan, Thomas Aloysius.

TAGISAN NG MGA AGIMAT (Philippines) *Tagisan Ng Mga Agimat* ("The Sharpening of the Talismans") made its debut during the first anniversary issue of *Redondo Komix* on May 5, 1964. It ran consecutively for 31 issues and had more than 150 pages after completion.

This long, sequential novel deals with the ambitions of three men, Mando, Lauro, and Crispin, who were able to acquire superpowers through different methods. Mando won his talisman by leaping into the heart of a cyclone. Lauro gained his by following prescribed, traditional steps. At exactly midnight he had to cut off the tip of the heart of a special fruit located in the gloomiest part of the forest. Then he had to combat the nonhuman forces of the woods to succeed in his goal. Lastly, Crispin got his anting-anting ("talisman") by killing and burying a black cat and fulfilling certain superstitious beliefs in his attempt to gain his prize.

Each individual got involved with a series of adventures dealing with a witch, deadly creatures, cave people, and ordinary bandits and crooks. The focal point of the novel is the rivalry of the three men using their powers (specifically speed, strength, and invisibility) to battle each other in a variety of situations. The power that was gained by each individual somehow led to greedy desires. When one of them is pursuing an evil goal, another of them somehow finds out about it and tries to stop him. The novel culminates when the three have a head-on collision that causes havoc and destruction in the vicinity. Eventually the great powers that they hold cancel each other out and they finally become normal human beings again.

The novel, besides being an interesting and entertaining adventure story, provides the reader with a unique look into regional beliefs and superstitions. The lifestyles and the customs of the provincial natives are realistically portrayed with an intimate knowledge of the ways and mores of its inhabitants.

Virgilio Redondo, though known primarily as a writer, is the excellent artist who illustrated the strip for both Philippine and American publications. He has written numerous novels that have been drawn by many of the finest artists in the Islands, including himself. He has also done short stories that appeared in American comic books.

Redondo is considered by experts in the field to be one of the great draftsmen in the medium. As an artist, he was the most imitated in his homeland. His influence went beyond artistic technique since he was also responsible for discovering and training a new generation of artists.

O.J.

TAILSPIN TOMMY (U.S.) Created by Hal Forrest (artist) and Glen Chaffin (writer) in April 1928, *Tailspin Tommy* was distributed by Bell Syndicate. Building up slowly, the new strip soon gained newspapers from coast to coast and the following year the syndicate felt secure enough to release a Sunday version (October 1929).

Tailspin Tommy was the classic daredevil aviator, boyish and eager, ready to undertake any crazy stunt on a bet; his friend Skeeter was more of a wise kid and he provided most of the comic relief. Finally there was Betty Lou Barnes, an engaging and spunky brunette with a crush on Tommy, and a full-fledged aviatrix in her own right. The three companions were the

"Tagisan Ng Mga Agimat," Virgilio Redondo. © Redondo Komiks.

"Tailspin Tommy," Hal Forrest. © Bell Syndicate.

founders of a shaky airline company appropriately named Three-Point Airlines.

The plots of *Tailspin Tommy* were the garden-variety adventure-cum-aviation stories. The artwork was awful and the dialogues (always too verbose) specialized in aviation lingo ("ready for a three-point landing?, get your nose on the beam, let's make a 6-40 and land on his tail"). Yet there was enough authenticity in Tommy's air acrobatics to make this into the most popular aviation strip of the early 1930s. (In the middle 1930s Glen Chaffin left the strip and Hal Forrest assumed sole authorship—with no perceptible improvement in the writing.)

As was the custom with aviation strips of the time, *Tailspin Tommy* thrived not only on accuracy but on didacticism as well. The Sunday page opened with a single panel called "The Progress of Flight," which related (in some detail) the early efforts of such obscure pioneers as Charles Spencer and Alphonse Penaud, along with more established figures like the Wright brothers and Bleriot. In 1935, as the readers got tired of so much history, "The Progress of Flight" was replaced by *The Four Aces*, a strip dealing with the postwar adventures of a quartet of World War I air heroes.

By the end of the 1930s, *Tailspin Tommy* was seriously faltering and Forrest (who owned the feature) decided in 1940 to change syndicates. This proved of no avail, however, and within two years, *Tommy* was swept clean out of the skies (by that time newspaper readers were getting more demanding as to standards of draftsmanship, and furthermore the U.S. involvement in World War II made the strip's acrobatics into something of an anachronism).

Tailspin Tommy was profusely reprinted in comic books and in Big Little Books. In 1934 it had the distinction of being the first adventure strip to be made into a movie serial (produced by Universal and directed by Lew Landers who signed Louis Friedlander; it starred Maurice Murphy and Noah Beery, Jr). The serial was so successful that a sequel was produced the next year (with Ray Taylor directing, and Clarke Williams playing Tommy). In 1939 Monogram produced four more *Tailspin Tommy* serials with John Trent as Tommy, Marjorie Reynolds as Betty Lou, and Milburn Stone as Skeeter.

Ushered in at the end of the 1920s, snuffed out by the early 1940s, *Tailspin Tommy*, more than any other aviation strip, symbolized the romance of flight so prevalent in the depression decade. Less skillful (or less cunning) than some of his colleagues, Hal Forrest could not adapt to the changing times, and his strip did not long survive the spirit that brought about its birth.

M.H.

TALBOT, BRYAN (1952-   ) Bryan Talbot is a British artist born February 24, 1952, in Wigan, England. While studying at Preston Polytechnic in 1972, Bryan Talbot produced a weekly comic strip for the college newspaper in collaboration with a fellow student. After graduating with a degree in graphic design he worked for four years for the underground Alchemy Press, writing and drawing *Brainstorm Comix*. This was followed in 1978 by a space opera spoof, *Frank Fazakerly, Space Ace of the Future*; that same year he began his long-running saga, *The Adventures of Luther Arkwright*. In 1982 he started to work for the comic magazine *2000 AD*, notably producing *Nemesis the*

Warlock; at that time he also drew some *Judge Dredd* stories.

All this production attracted the notice of American publishers. In 1987 Valkyrie Press began the U.S publication of *Luther Arkwright* (it was later taken over by Dark Horse). Talbot's first original contribution to American comic books appeared in 1989 on DC Comics' *Hellblazer*; this in turn led to more work in the United States on such titles as *The Sandman, Batman*, and *The Nazz*. In 1994 to 1995 he produced *The Tale of One Bad Rat*, an original story that won him great acclaim. Then in 1995 to 1996 came his penciling of several issues of Neil Gaiman's *Teknophage*; he is currently at work on a new *Luther Arkwright* graphic novel.

Talbot has received a large number of comic book awards, has had several one-man shows of his works exhibited in London and New York, and is a frequent guest at comic festivals around the world.

M.H.

TALIAFERRO, CHARLES ALFRED (1905-1969) American comic strip artist born August 29, 1905, in Montrose, Colorado. His family later moved to Glendale, California, where he graduated as an art history major from Glendale High School and found work as a designer for a lighting fixture company. During his free hours, Taliaferro (who, by now, had assumed the nickname of "Al") pursued his art studies with correspondence courses, as well as attending lectures at the California Art Institute. On January 5, 1931, he joined the Walt Disney animation studio as an assistant artist.

One of Taliaferro's first jobs at Disney was inking some of the early *Mickey Mouse* newspaper strips, penciled by Floyd Gottfredson. In April 1932, Al began a seven-year run as penciler and inker of the *Silly Symphonies* Sunday comic strip. The strip, which adapted Disney shorts into panel form, occasionally featured Donald Duck and, when that character began his own strip, Taliaferro was chosen as the illustrator.

The *Donald Duck* newspaper strip began as a daily on February 7, 1938. A Sunday page was added (independent of the *Silly Symphonies* format) beginning December 10, 1939, by which time Taliaferro had abandoned the *Silly Symphonies* strip to Bob Grant. For most of its run, the *Donald Duck* strip was drawn completely by Taliaferro and written by Bob Karp.

The strip never attempted a continuity of the sort that appeared in the *Mickey Mouse* strip for a long time. Perhaps because of this, the *Donald Duck* strip soon became the most popular and widely circulated of all the Disney-based strips, reaching at one point a total of 322 newspapers or more than double the circulation of the *Mickey Mouse* strip. Along with Carl Barks's version in the comic books, Taliaferro's conception of Donald Duck became the standard version, especially after the studio ceased production of *Donald Duck* cartoons.

In 1965, Taliaferro relinquished the inking on the strip to other artists, although he carefully watched over their work to ensure its quality. He died on February 3, 1969.

During his 38-year career in comic art, the name Al Taliaferro appeared only once in a credit line when he did the drawings for a 1951 book, *Donald Duck and the Hidden Gold*.

M.E.

TANGUY ET LAVRDURE   *see* Michel Tanguy.

TANK MCNAMARA (U.S.)   In 1973 *Houston Chronicle*'s film critic and humor columnist Jeff Millar conceived the notion of a sports-based comic strip that would appeal equally to armchair athletes and to sport haters. For the drawing he turned to Bill Hinds, a 23-year-old freelance cartoonist, and the two men cobbled together six weeks of daily strips and three sample Sunday pages, which they sent to Universal Press Syndicate, which promptly accepted the project. The strip, christened *Tank McNamara* for its main protagonist, made its initial appearance on August 5, 1974.

Tank is a big, burly lug of a man, a former defensive tackle for the Houston Oilers, turned sports announcer. A master of misstatement and malapropism, he is only kept on because people keep betting on how many bloopers he will commit on any given broadcast (and because his lovable if bumbling personality proves appealing to the mother's instincts of the female viewers and to the killer instincts of the male audience). "St. Looie thirty, Cincinooti twoty," "And now ladies and gummelmen, here's the norts spews," and "Speaking from the women's shotput event, this is Mank Tanamara" are some of the tongue slips that earned him the affectionate nickname "Fumblemouth" and eventually got him canned (he was later reinstated due to public protest).

"Tank McNamara," Jeff Millar and Bill Hinds. © Millar/Hinds.

Around Tank there revolves a gallery of oddball characters: Sweatsox, the rabid sports fan who can name every player in the NFL but can't remember his kids' names; the psychopathic Dr. Tszap, professional therapist and demon inventor; Bush Bakert, the star NFL quarterback who spends more time in the television room pitching swimwear and dog food than on the gridiron playing ball; and Tank's airhead girlfriend, Barbi, are only a few of them.

The strip satirizes sports professionals, sports fans, and sports celebrities, and the culture from which they spring, but it is never biting or vicious. As Roger Staubach of the Dallas Cowboys stated in his foreword to the 1978 anthology, *The Tank McNamara Chronicles*, "It shows that all of us, professional players and fans alike, should take our games a bit less seriously."

M.H.

TANKU TANKURŌ (Japan)   Created by Gajō, *Tanku Tankurō* made its first appearance in the September

"Tanku Tankurō," Gajō. © Yōnen Kurabu.

1934 issue of the monthly children's magazine *Yōnen Kurabu*.

Tanku Tankurō was a kind of superman. Ensconced in a gigantic iron ball with eight windows, Tanku could, when faced with danger, pull his head, hands, and legs into the ball, like a turtle. He was also able to produce a number of implements out of his shell, such as a pistol, a machine gun, a sword, money, among other things. He could change into a tank (his name was derived from the word "tank"), an airplane, or a submarine. He could also liberate his alter ego, Mame Tankus ("Little Tanku"), to fight out of the shell.

In the course of his exploits, Tanku met plenty of challengers: Bozu the shaven-headed monster; the gigantic sumo wrestler Tenguyama; and Tsujigiri, the chief of a band of highwaymen. One of his more formidable enemies was the black-helmeted Kurokubato against whose army Tanku, his monkey companion Kiku, and their allies, had to fight a titanic battle, in the course of which they used such weapons as a cannon ball loaded with troops, a cyclone-gun, and other far-out inventions.

Tanku Tankurō, who is regarded as the oldest superhero in Japanese comics, made his last appearance in the December 1936 issue of *Yōnen Kurabu*.

M.H.

TARDI, JACQUES (1946-   )   Jacques Tardi is a French comics artist born August 30, 1946, in Valence, in southeastern France. Studies at art schools in Lyons and Paris led Tardi to try his hand at cartooning with a number of short stories published in the weekly *Pilote* at the beginning of the 1970s. His early efforts did not yet reveal a strong personality, as he flitted from political fiction (*Rumeurs sur le Rouergue*, the first of the so-called Today's Legends on a script by Pierre Christin, 1972) to lyrical fantasy (*Adieu Brindavoine*, which he wrote, also 1972) even to Western tales (*Blue Jacket*, 1973).

Tardi came into his own in the mid-1970s with a series of strongly felt tales, starting with *Un Episode Banal de la Guerre des Tranchées* ("A Banal Episode of Trench Warfare"), a powerful indictment of war; con-

Jacques Tardi, "La Bascule à Charlot." © Casterman.

tinuing with *Knock-Out*, an apology of pacifism; and culminating with *La Bascule à Charlot* ("Charlie's See-saw," a slang name for the guillotine), an impassioned denunciation of the death penalty. Those were followed by longer stories, *Polonius* (1976); *Adèle Blanc-Sec*, a political fantasy set in the Paris of *la belle époque* (also 1976); *Griffu*, a political thriller on a script by Jean-Patrick Manchette (1977); and *Ici Même*, yet another political fantasy on texts by Jean-Claude Forest this time (1977-1979).

The decade of the 1980s proved particularly prolific for Tardi. From 1981 on he unfolded his cycle of socio-political thrillers based on French mystery novelist Leo Malet's anarchistic private eye Nestor Burma. After *Brouillard au Pont de Tolbiac* ("Fog over Tolbiac Bridge") there came *120 Rue de la Gare* ("120 Station Street," 1986) and *Une Gueule de Bois en Plomb* ("A Lead Hangover," 1990). Each one of these stories is a suspenseful narrative in its own right, but taken together they present a disturbing view of French society. In addition the artist in this period turned out countless book and magazine illustrations, published several print portfolios, and held a gallery showing of his paintings.

Tardi's entire *oeuvre* has been dominated by his horror of war. On this theme he has written and/or illustrated an impressive number of stories, the most noteworthy being *Tueur de Cafards* ("Roach Killer," 1983), *Jeux pour Mourir* ("Games for Dying," 1992), and *C'était la Guerre des Tranchées* ("This Was Trench Warfare"), the definitive summing up of his thoughts on the subject, which he completed in 1993. His pacifist views have also led him to illustrate the novels of French writer (and convicted Nazi collaborator) Louis-Ferdinand Céline. It should be noted at this juncture that in his antiwar stories Tardi has almost exclusively dealt with World War I. He has carefully eschewed tackling the thornier issue of World War II in which pacifism (skillfully nurtured by Nazi propagandists such as Céline) was partly responsible for France's ignomini-

ous defeat in 1940 and the subsequent occupation of its territory by the Germans for four long years.

An author of undisputed power and intensity whose stories are more forcefully rendered in black and white (the artist is less persuasive in his use of color), Tardi is regarded as one of the foremost comics creators in his country. His almost exclusive devotion to French situations and concerns, to the detriment of more universal subjects, has largely prevented his fame from spreading beyond France's borders.

M.H.

TARÓ (Germany) *Taró* is one of the few adventure newspaper comic strips to come out of postwar Germany. *Taró* was created for *sternchen* ("starlet"), the children's supplement of *stern* ("star"), a weekly news magazine in the *Life* format, when the editors asked Fritz Raab, who had already written several novels for *sternchen*, to write a realistic adventure strip. In order to combine a contemporary setting with the romance of Indian stories, Raab picked a Latin American locale for his adventure strip. He also arrived at this decision because he had met the Swiss ethnologist Franz Caspar in the early 1950s and asked him about his experiences in living with an Indian tribe in the Mato Grosso area for six months.

Raab did extensive geographic and ethnographic research for *Taró*. Even Taró, the name of the hero, was carefully selected by Raab from a list of 50 possible names to ensure that the name was exotic and could be read and pronounced easily. *Taró* depicts the adventures of a highly trained, modern-day Latin American Indian working for the Brazilian Indian Protective Agency. Besides sheer adventure, *Taró* also had an occasional run-in with politics: in one episode the hero was pitted against a fascist organization. Raab's stories were aptly drawn by F. W. Richter-Johnsen, whose art (on textured paper), makes *Taró* into a highly satisfying strip. Writing and art blend into an outstanding example of modern-day comic strips. It comes as kind of a surprise therefore, that Raab and Richter-Johnsen met only four times during the nine years of *Taró*.

The first episode of *Taró* appeared on June 13, 1959; the last one on March 3, 1968. During that time, *Taró* lived through eight stories, the first one, "The Amulet," having 129 episodes published over a period of two years and six months. When *sternchen* was changed from a supplement to two normal pages in *stern* for technical and financial reasons, *Taró*'s reproduction size shrank considerably. Finally, the editors decided to end one of the comic strips. *Jimmy das Gummipferd*, having been included in *sternchen* from the very start, won out over *Taró*. Seventeen days after *Taró* ended, newspapers headlined atrocities of Brazilian Indian Protective Agencies, which would have been irreconcilable with the idealized comic strip activities. The end of the strip was therefore marked up to sheer luck.

Taró has never been reprinted in book or comic book form, but one of the stories, titled "Piranyas," was put on a long-playing record, a sign of the comic strip's success, a success made possible by excellent writing and art that make *Taró* one of the modern-day classics of the German comic strip.

W.F.

TARZAN (U.S.) 1—As a newspaper strip, *Tarzan* has known a long and complicated history. In 1928, Joseph H. Neebe, an executive of the Campbell-Ewald advertising agency, had acquired the comic strip rights to Edgar Rice Burroughs's creation and (after being turned down by *Tarzan* illustrator Allen St. John) had asked one of his staff artists, Harold Foster, to draw 60 daily strips to illustrate his condensation of Burroughs's *Tarzan of the Apes*. The Metropolitan Newspaper Service

then took over the syndication and sold the new feature on approval to a few newspapers. The first episode appeared from January 7 to March 16, 1929. This *Tarzan* version was enthusiastically received by the few readers who saw it and a sequel was decided upon. The second episode, "The Return of Tarzan" (also based on Burroughs's novel), debuted on June 17, 1929, drawn by Rex Maxon who had replaced Foster, and success continued unabated. (It should be noted at this juncture that British publication of Foster's *Tarzan* had anticipated American syndication by more than two months with the weekly magazine *Tit-Bits* starting serialization of the feature as early as October 20, 1928.)

In 1930, United Feature Syndicate absorbed Metropolitan Newspaper Service and immediately decided to launch a *Tarzan* Sunday page in addition to the daily strip. The first page appeared on March 15, 1931, drawn by Maxon who proved inadequate to the task. The syndicate then called back Foster, who took over the Sunday feature on September 27, 1931.

While Maxon ploddingly went on with the task of illustrating Burroughs's *Tarzan* novels (condensed by staff writers into a text running underneath the pictures—a definite throwback to the European picture story), Foster brilliantly developed his techniques in the Sunday page (where the narrative was enclosed within the frame of the picture, thus giving it more immediacy). Foster's style became more and more decisive and powerful, and was ultimately to achieve a graphic classicism which gave Tarzan his noblest and most serene incarnation. Foster's strip then became the most widely imitated of adventure strips.

In 1937, Foster went on to create *Prince Valiant*, and *Tarzan* passed into the hands of Burne Hogarth (his first signed page appeared on May 9). At first imitating his predecessor, Hogarth later developed his own style,

"Tarzan," Burne Hogarth. © ERB, Inc.

which made him into one of the most celebrated artists of the comics. Into *Tarzan* he poured all of his artistic knowledge, blending form and content into a single visual manifestation. *Tarzan* became a vast panorama of grandiose and jarring images, which stayed in the reader's mind long after Hogarth had abandoned the strip. Hogarth drew the Sunday adventures of the lord of the jungle until 1950, with a two-year interruption (1945-1947) during which the feature was done by Rubimor (Ruben Moreira).

The dailies, in the meantime, had remained in the hands of Maxon (except for a time in 1937-1938 when William Juhre had to take over the strip) until 1947. Then it was successively drawn by Hogarth (August-December 1947), Dan Barry (1947-1949), John Lehti (1949), Paul Reinman (1949-1950), Cardy (Nicholas Viskardy) later in 1950, Bob Lubbers (1950-1953), and John Celardo (1953-1967).

In 1967, Russ Manning (who had been doing the comic book version) was given the daily strip, and during the next year he took over the Sunday page as well, following Bob Lubbers (1950-1954) and John Celardo (1954-1968). Manning succeeded in restoring *Tarzan* to some of its erstwhile splendor. Unfortunately the daily strip was discontinued in 1973 (with old reprints being offered for syndication), while the Sunday page appeared in a pitifully small number of newspapers. After Manning left in 1979, the page was illustrated by Gil Kane and scripted by Archie Goodwin; in 1981 Mike Grell took over, succeeded in his turn by Gray Morrow (art) and Don Kraar (writing) in 1983.

The earlier *Tarzan* strips (notably those of Foster and Hogarth) have gone through a number of reprints in paperback and hardbound form, and in 1972 Watson-Guptill published an entirely new pictorial version of *Tarzan of the Apes* by Burne Hogarth followed in 1976 by *Jungle Tales of Tarzan*.

M.H.

2—When United Feature attempted to transfer *Tarzan* to the fast-growing comic book market, they began reproducing the comic strip version in their comic book titles. Reprints of the Hal Foster rendition appeared in *Tip Top* numbers 1 through 62 (April 1936-June 1941)

and in *Single Series* number 20 (1940). Rex Maxon's strips were reprinted in *Comics on Parade* numbers 1 through 29 (April 1938-August 1940). The second series of the *Sparkler* title carried reprints of Burne Hogarth material in issues 1 through 86 and 90 through 92 (July 1941—March 1950), while *Tip Top* numbers 171 through 188 carried reprints of Bob Lubbers material between November 1951 and September 1954.

3—In addition to the United Feature comic reprints, *Tarzan* was also appearing in books published by Dell, the first being *Black and White* number 5 (1938). That book carried reprints of Foster material, but two later Dell one-shots—*Color Comics* numbers 134 (1946) and 161 (1947)—contained original material. Dell also released *Tarzan* text stories with comic illustrations in *Famous Feature* number 1 (1938) and *Crackajack Funnies* numbers 15 through 36 (September 1939-June 1941).

Tarzan finally began appearing in its own original material comic book in January 1948, but writer Gaylord Dubois attempted to blend the Burroughs material with the currently popular motion picture version. What resulted was an unsatisfactory hybrid of Burroughs and movies: Tarzan's son was erroneously called Boy, Jane was a brunette, Tarzan lived in a treehouse, and covers sported photographs of Lex Barker or Gordon Scott from the movie *Tarzan*.

Jesse Mace Marsh's artwork was excellent, however. His renditions were uniquely angular, his layouts were clean and expressive, and he portrayed the jungle mood as well as any of the feature's more vaunted illustrators. He continued to draw *Tarzan* sporadically throughout the early 1960s, but his more frequent replacements were inferior and the book slipped sharply; by 1964, it was one of the poorest titles on the market.

Late that year, however, Charlton began issuing *Jungle Tales of Tarzan*, stories based on public domain Burroughs material. Although it lasted only four issues, it spurred Gold Key (the publisher had changed names in 1962) to upgrade their title. Russ Manning began illustrating *Tarzan* in November 1965, and he eventually became the best of the latter-day *Tarzan* artists. Manning eventually inherited the *Tarzan* newspaper strip in 1967 and dropped the comic book. After some inspired work by Doug Wildey, Paul Norris, and Mike Royer assumed the feature and the book collapsed into mediocrity.

Gold Key finally lost the rights to *Tarzan* and National began publishing the book in April 1972. Joe Kubert took over as artist, writer, and editor, and, relying on Burroughs adaptations and Foster's early *Tarzan* renditions, made the book solid once again. Already an accomplished jungle illustrator (he drew the *Tor* feature two decades before), Kubert will probably be ranked with the other great *Tarzan* artists.

National discontinued its *Tarzan* comic book in 1977. Marvel then took up the challenge and between 1977 and 1979 published a line of monthly *Tarzan* stories illustrated by such stalwarts as John Buscema and Rudy Nebres. The latest appearances of the apeman in comic books have happened in 1992, in a short-lived series issued by Malibu comics, and since 1996 in *Edgar Rice Burroughs's Tarzan* published by Dark Horse.

J.B.

"Tarzan," Harold Foster. © ERB, Inc.

TEDDY TAIL (G.B.) The Mouse that will make your children laugh. This was how *Teddy Tail* was trailered in the *Daily Mail* on Saturday, April 3, 1915, with a sketch initialed "C. F." C. F. was Charles Folkard, a children's book illustrator of considerable quality, and he fulfilled the paper's promise. On the following Monday, *Teddy Tail* appeared in not only the first British daily strip but the largest for many years to come—nine big panels, each with a five-line caption. Subtitled "The Diary of the Mouse in your House," Teddy's serial was swiftly under way, introducing the first of many regular characters, Dr. Beetle, in panel number 1.

By September 1915 Teddy was in his first book, a reprint of his daily strip with added tint in red ink; *The Adventures of Teddy Tail of the Daily Mail*, published by Adam and Charles Black, sold for a shilling. More collections followed: *T. T. in Nursery Rhyme Land* (1915); *T. T. in Fairyland* (1916); *T. T. in Historyland* (1917); *T. T.'s Fairy Tale* (1919); *T. T. at the Seaside* (1920); *T. T.'s Alphabet* (1921); *T. T. in Toyland* (1922); *T. T.'s Adventures in the A.B. Sea* (1926); and *T. T. Waddle Book* (1934).

The strip was taken over by Folkard's younger brother Harry, an artist of considerably less talent. Harry Folkard's Teddy decorated the original *Teddy Tail* League badge, and he also drew Teddy's full-page adventures for *Boys & Girls Daily Mail*, a colored comic supplement to the newspaper, starting April 8, 1933. By this time Teddy had become domesticated, and, instead of traveling into fantasies, he had homey adventures with his pals Piggy, Douglas the Duck, and Kittypuss the Cat, under the aegis of the widowed Mrs. Whisker (a large mouse).

A new turn in Teddy's tale came when Herbert Foxwell, the *Tiger Tim* artist, was brought over from Rainbow to redesign the strip. His first *Teddy* page was published on Saturday, November 4, 1933. An immediate success, the comic increased to three editions a week, then enlarged to full broadsheet format from September 14, 1935. A *Teddy Tail Annual* commenced Christmas publication from 1933 to 1941 (dated 1934 to 1942), the last two editions drawn by J. Michman and Ern Shaw.

From 1940 Teddy was dropped for the duration of the war but returned in about 1946. This time the artist was Spot (whose real name was Arthur Potts), and the style was slicker. All the old pals were present, including Dr. Beetle. The *Teddy Tail Annual* was revived and ran from 1948 to 1955, and some new reprints of the strip were issued in comic book form and printed in red and black as of yore: *T. T. and the Magic Drink*; *T. T. and the Pearl Thief*; *T. T. Goes West*; *Willow Pattern Story*; *T. T. and the Cave Men*; *T. T. and the Gnomes* (all 1950-1951). After the death of Potts, Edgar Spenceley took over, followed by Bill St. John Glenn, with Roland Davies in the *Annual*. The strip was finally discontinued on October 25, 1960, after an interrupted run of 46 years.

D.G.

TED TOWERS (U.S.) In 1934 King Features must have felt a need for another jungle strip besides the highly successful *Jungle Jim* (King's policy was to have at least two entries in every possible strip category) and they commissioned the noted explorer and animal trapper Frank Buck, author of the best-selling *Bring' em Back Alive* to create one for them. Thus on November 11, 1934, a new Sunday feature appeared under the heading: "Bring' em Back Alive Frank Buck Presents Ted Towers, Animal Master" (mercifully shortened to simple *Ted Towers* a short time later).

Glen Cravath was the first artist on this strip which he drew until February 1936; in the short span of four months (February to June) no fewer than three cartoonists tried for his succession: first an anonymous staff artist, then Joe King (probably a pseudonym), and later Paul Frehm. Finally the feature was taken over by Ed Stevenson, who carried on until its demise in May 1939. (For a few months in 1935 *Ted Towers* had a companion strip, *Animal Land*, about a young, Mowgli-like boy who consorted with jungle animals.)

Ted Towers was a wildlife trapper who worked for American zoos. Helped by his trusted Hindu assistant Ali and by his girl companion Catherine, he roamed the jungles of India in search of some rare or unusual specimen. Wild tigers and rogue elephants were not the only perils that Ted had to face: he also got to fight diamond smugglers and ivory hunters, and even, on one occasion, a villainous maharajah with a desire for Catherine.

Ted Towers's scripts were too often puerile (it is doubtful that Frank Buck ever wrote any of them), but the drawing was for the most part competent, and the jungle scenes convincingly handled. Today the strip has a period charm which makes it worth studying.

M.H.

TEENAGE MUTANT NINJA TURTLES (U.S.) One of the most meteoric—and most inexplicable—successes of the comics came about in 1984, when writer Kevin Eastman (then working as a short-order cook) and artist Peter Laird (then mostly unemployed) conceived a goofy parody of samurai and ninja comics, a faddish conceit in comic books of the time. Husbanding their talents they came up with the idea of a quartet of turtles living in the sewers who become mutated into humanoid beings and made superpowerful by radioactive waste floating in the waters. To add to their powers they later got training in the martial arts from Splinter, the pet rat of an assassinated ninja master. Thus were the Teenage Mutant Ninja Turtles born.

The four Turtles, facetiously named after celebrated Italian painters of the Renaissance and endowed with erect posture, three-fingered hands, and the ability to speak, are all differentiated by very human traits. Raphael is the wit of the foursome, coming up with quips and wisecracks in the teeth of danger; Michaelangelo is a fun-loving, laid-back character, fond of ice cream and pizza; while Donatello possesses the resourcefulness and cunning of a chess-player. The group is led by the swordmaster Leonardo, a cool customer who never loses his nerve or his purposefulness. In the course of the years the Turtles have battled a renegade ninja clan known as "the Foot," an international terrorist cell based in a tenement, and various other miscreants, human and animal.

Originally published by the creators in a print run of 3,000 black-and-white copies, *Teenage Mutant Ninja Turtles* would have died a quick death if by some fluke a United Press reporter hadn't written a piece about it. This twist of fate turned the mildly amusing spoof into a comic book version of the American Dream. Circulation by 1986 had skyrocketed to 130,000 copies per issue, and the title later received the full-color treatment as Archie Comics, and later Image, took over distribution. A successful animated version hit the television screen in 1988, and a theatrical film came out in 1990, quickly followed by a sequel in 1991. That same year a newspaper strip saw light of print under distribution by Creators Syndicate. The story continues. . . .

M.H.

TELESTRIP (G.B.) Trailed as The Craziest Cartoon in the business and Sheer Goonery in black and white, *Telestrip* arrived in the *London Evening News* on May 28, 1956. A series of lampoons on current television programs, complete with commercials, it opened with a three-week satire on *Dragnet* entitled "Dragnut," wherein Sgt. Friday and Fred Smith set forth on Crunday the Blunge of Foon, 1956 a.m., in search of the dreaded Facts, accompanied by much Dum-de-Dum-Dum on the overlapping soundtrack.

"Ye Adventures of Robbin' Hood (Ye Dab of Sherbet Forest)" followed, after a short plug for Baff. Then came "The Groove Family"; Kenneth McComfy's "Closed-Up," a film profile of Alan Lead; "Goon Law" with James Harness as Mick Gallon (changed from the artist's original Mutt Dullard by a nervous editor); "Ze Count of Monty Cristo"; "Ask Chuckles" (a burlesque on Ask Pickles, again censored from the artist's original Ask Giggles); and the final series, which was never published: "The Strange World of Planet Fred." The *Telestrip* was canceled before its six-month contract was completed. It had created too many headaches for the editor, with its parodies of products, and was the first casualty in the satire revolution which ultimately led to *Private Eye* magazine.

Denis Gifford, writer and cartoonist, completely switched styles for his first (and last) daily strip, clearly inspired by Harvey Kurtzman's *MAD* comic book and the new look cartoon films of U.P.A. He continued the *Telestrip* technique as *Teletoons*, drawing Davy Crackpot, Charlie Chump, Sea Weed (i.e., Sea Hunt), and even Mumbleman in Marvelman, T.V. Heroes, etc. (1960), and as Tellytoon (with the added spice of a per-

missive society) in Rex (1971): Star Wrek; The Virgin 'Un; The F.I.B.; Public Eye; etc.

D.G.

TENPEI TENMA (Japan) *Tenpei Tenma* was created by Taku Horie and made its first appearance in the June 1957 issue of the Japanese monthly *Shōnen Gahō*.

Tenpei Tenma is a *ronin* (a kind of roving samurai popularized by Kurozawa's films) of the Edo era, a master of sword, whip, and pistol, and a medicine man to boot. With the help of his favorite white stallion Tsukikage ("Moonlight") he battles against countless villains such as Sasori-dojin, Kaitō Ryuikitai, chief of a gang of mysterious thieves, the warlord Akugarō, and others.

The stories are highly entertaining as well as wildly imaginative. A kind of primitive James Bond, Tenma, when in a pinch, does not hesitate to resort to all kinds of gadgetry, firing a volley of shots from his whip, or laying a smoke screen to cover his escape. His adversaries are hardly less ingenious: Kaitō Ryukitai uses a movable bridge as his hiding place, stones fly out of a wall to meet the enemy, and so on.

Tenpei Tenma was Horie's first popular creation. It was particularly appreciated for its spectacular battle scenes pitching masses of armed warriors against one another in a manner reminiscent of *Prince Valiant*.

Tenpei Tenma made its last appearance in the March 1961 issue of *Shōnen Gahō*. Before then, however, it was made into a television series that lasted two years.

H.K.

TERRORS OF THE TINY TADS (U.S.) On October 15, 1905, the *New York Herald* came out with two brand new features: one was the celebrated *Little Nemo*

"Telestrip," Denis Gifford. © Denis Gifford.

"Tenpei Tenma," Taku Horie. © Shōnen Gahō.

"The Terrors of the Tiny Tads," Gustave Verbeck.

named creations such as the Trolleycaribou and the Hippopotamosquito, to the accompaniment of jingling verse reminiscent of Edward Lear, such as the following: His Falconductor takes the fare, five acorns a ride/ The Tiny Tads have paid for theirs, we see them all inside./And now they climb up mountains to the dizziest of heights/Then down again in valleys where they see most wondrous sights.

From 1910 on, the *Tads'* appearances in the *Herald* became more and more infrequent until they finally bowed out around 1915 to 1916.

M.H.

in Slumberland, the other, less well-known but of more than passing interest, was *The Terrors of the Tiny Tads* by Gustave Verbeck (or Verbeek).

The four tiny tads of the title are lost in a fantastic world of monsters and freakish creatures (this is a constant theme running all through Verbeck's not inconsiderable body of work). The animal, vegetal, and artificial meet and clash in such oddly shaped and oddly

TERRY AND THE PIRATES (U.S.) Milton Caniff created *Terry and the Pirates* for the Tribune-News Syndicate, which wanted to add an exotic adventure strip to its feature lineup. The daily strip version appeared first on October 22, 1934; a Sunday page was later added on December 9.

The strip, which took place in China, was not startingly original at first: it involved the same combination of a tall, handsome adventurer (Pat Ryan) and his youthful companion (Terry) that Caniff had already used in *Dickie Dare*; these two were soon to be joined by a comic Chinese relief nicknamed Connie. But the narrative gradually increased in interest as the settings became more and more authentic, the dialogue wittier and pithier, and the characters matured accordingly. A colorful gallery of rogues were to cross Pat's and Terry's path: the infamous Captain Judas, the perverted Pyzon, the barbarous general Klang, the sinister baron de Plexus, and others, while in the background hovered the ever-present Japanese menace. It was the

"Terry and the Pirates," Milton Caniff. © Chicago Tribune-New York News Syndicate.

women however who made the fortune of the strip: the voluptuous and deadly Dragon-Lady, the golden-haired, golden-hearted Burma, and the headstrong Normandie Sandhurst (nee Drake) vied for Pat's affections; while Terry was soon to acquire his own girl in the person of piquant, capricious April Kane.

When America entered World War II, Terry changed character. Terry, having finally passed the adolescent stage, became a pilot with the air forces in China, and his commanding officer, Colonel Flip Corkin, replaced Pat Ryan as the strip's father figure. Terry had finally become the star of the feature that bore his name, and the situation did not change after the war.

On December 29, 1946, following a contractual dispute with the syndicate, Caniff signed his last *Terry* page, and George Wunder took over the following week. Under Wunder's pen, *Terry* became obvious and heavy-handed. Most of the humor had gone, and the characters lost all personality. Terry himself became a major in the U.S. Air Force and a fierce upholder of the cold war philosophy (with none of Steve Canyon's redeeming graces). Wunder's Terry, to everyone's amazement, lasted for more than 25 years, until it was finally done in by a combination of bad plotting, poor characterization, stiff drawing, and a changed political atmosphere; it disappeared on February 25, 1973.

What everyone remembers is, of course, Caniff's *Terry*. It can be said that no other strip (not even Foster's *Tarzan*) was so widely imitated by so many people; its techniques of lighting, framing, and editing were assiduously studied not only by cartoonists but by moviemakers as well (the opening sequence and many of the shots, as well as the atmosphere of Lewis Milestone's *The General Died at Dawn* are clearly inspired by *Terry*).

Terry's popularity built up slowly and reached its peak during the war years. It had its own comic book version and was adapted to radio. In 1940 James W. Horne directed a movie serial of *Terry and the Pirates*, and in the 1950s the strip was also made into a television series.

Terry and the Pirates is one adventure strip that would not stay dead, however. Bucking the trend, it resurfaced in March 1995, distributed by Tribune Media Services, the successor to the News-Tribune Syndicate. The new version was set in a futuristic late-twentieth century, with Terry and Pat battling pirates, hijackers, and extortionists from their base in Hong Kong. Comic book writer Michael Uslan was in charge of the scripts, while the drawings were initially done by the brothers Tim and Greg Hildebrandt, who were replaced in 1966 by Dan Spiegle, a veteran of comic books and comic strips.

M.H.

TETSUJIN 28GŌ (Japan) *Tetsujin 28gō* was created by Mitsuteru Yokoyama in the April 1958 issue of the monthly magazine *Shōnen*, where it ran for approximately 10 years until 1966. Growing rapidly in public favor, *Tetsujin 28gō* for a long time competed with Tezuka's *Tetsuwan-Atom* for first position among adventure strips.

Tetsujin 28gō ("Iron Man no. 28") was a robot that had been created by Dr. Kaneda and Dr. Shikishima. These robots had been planned by the Japanese Secret Weapon Institute during the Pacific War (as the Japanese call World War II), but they were destroyed by the bombers of the U.S. Air Force. Dr. Kaneda and Dr.

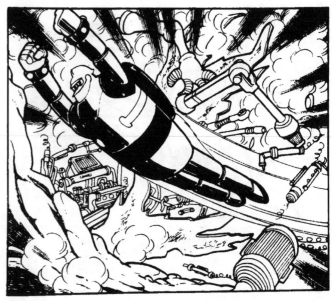

"Tetsujin 28gō," Mitsuteru Yokoyama. © Shōnen.

Shikishima did not give up their plans, however, and succeeded in producing *Tetsujin 28gō* in 1955. The robot was created not for war this time, but for peace, and was to assist the Japanese police in their fight against crime.

Tetsujin had a helmet-covered head, a rocket engine on its back, and a gigantic metallic body. The son of Dr. Kaneda, Shōtarō, manned the controls that directed Tetsujin. Tetsujin and Shōtarō battled criminals, other robots (evil ones), and monsters. Their arch-enemy was Dr. Franken, a mad scientist creator of a multiplicity of monsters and robots with which he was forever trying to smash in Tetsujin. At one point the control machine was stolen by a gang of criminals, and Tetsujin turned against Shōtarō and the police in an epic battle during which the controls were finally wrested from the evildoers.

Tetsujin 28gō has inspired a radio program and a series of television animated cartoons (in the United States it was released as "Gigantor"). The strip also gave rise to a spate of giant robot strips (*The Dai Machine, Giant Robot, King Robot,* and others).

H.K.

TETSUWAN-ATOM (Japan) Atom-Taishi ("Ambassador Atom") later called *Tetsuwan-Atom* ("Mighty Atom") was created by Osamu Tezuka in April 1951 for the Japanese comic monthly *Shōnen*. *Tetsuwan-Atom* soon developed into the most popular boy's strip of all time as well as one of the best of science-fiction strips.

Atom was a robot created by Dr. Tenma as a surrogate to Tenma's son who had been killed in a traffic accident. At first Dr. Tenma loved Atom as if he were his own son but came little by little to hate him, because Atom was a robot and as such could not grow up or mature. After being sold to a circus, Atom was adopted by kind, understanding Dr. Ochanomizu who infused him with a sense of purpose. Since then Atom has been fighting one enemy after another: the black-hearted robot Atlas; the Ice Men; the Hot-dog soldiers (cyborgs with the brains of dogs); and Satan, the giant monster robot.

From the first, Atom has been extraordinarily popular in Japan. Despite the fact that he is a robot, he displays human feelings, he can laugh, he can cry, he can

"Tetsuwan-Atom," Osamu Tezuka. © Shōnen.

get angry. But what has made him so beloved is that he is a friend of humanity, which he is able to protect from all kinds of dark menaces.

Tetsuwan-Atom was the longest-running strip in Japanese comic history up to that time (it lasted from April 1951 to March 1968). It is also one of the greatest and most famous creations of post-World War II Japanese comic books. *Tetsuwan-Atom* has inspired a series of animated cartoons (the first one was released in January 1963) which have been shown in more than 20 countries. (In the United States they were aired by NBC-TV under the title of *Astroboy*.)

H.K.

TEXAS SLIM AND DIRTY DALTON (U.S.) Easily the funniest of the Western strips before *Lucky Luke* was Ferd Johnson's little-seen but long-lived *Texas Slim and Dirty Dalton*, which began as a Sunday page titled simply *Texas Slim* in the *Chicago Tribune* on August 30, 1925. Launched in the midst of a group of already famed Sunday pages in the *Tribune* (*The Gumps, Gasoline Alley, Moon Mullins, Winnie Winkle,* etc.) at a time when most American Sunday papers ran only four pages a week, *Texas Slim* was not given a wide publication in the 1920s, but was enormously relished in Chicago and those few other areas where Johnson's broadly slapstick narrative of two cowboys in a big city (clearly Chicago) could be read. Johnson, an aide to Frank Williard on *Moon Mullins*, was given Sunday space by the *Tribune* so long as he felt he had time to draw the strip, but it was, sadly, not a priority item for the paper.

Texas Slim, and a boldly moustachioed, rather scurvy buddy named Dirty Dalton, veered from their boss, Mr. Akers's cattle spread in Texas to the Akers mansion in Chicago, where Texas was hamhandedly courting Jessie Akers during most of the early period of the strip. Dropped by the *Tribune* early in 1928, *Texas Slim* next surfaced as a short gag strip appearing Sunday at the bottom of Johnson's half-page *Lovey Dovey*, a new feature involving a typical married strip couple which ran for a few months in the middle of 1932 in the *Tribune*. Submerged again for half a decade, *Texas Slim* made its final, longest, and most successful

appearance as one of a number of strips included in a half-tabloid-size Comic Book Sunday section issued by the *Tribune* together with its regular Sunday comic section on March 31, 1940.

The *Tribune* Comic Book utilized several of the *Texas Slim* pages from the 1920s, together with two weekly pages of new material by Johnson. It was here that the *Texas Slim and Dirty Dalton* title was used for the first time, on August 18, 1940. Also for the first time, Johnson began serious week-to-week continuity, developing some excellent cliff-hanging comic suspense narrative, focusing initially on the grim doings of a cave-dwelling, hideously aged Joaquin Murrieta, then turning to other often hilariously inventive subjects. The 1940s were inarguably the high point of the *Texas Slim* strip, and it was clear that the public agreed: when the *Tribune* folded its Comic Book section due to paper shortages in April 1943, *Texas Slim and Dirty Dalton* continued as a generally distributed half-page feature for many years after, disappearing from sight only when Johnson took over the *Moon Mullins* strip upon Frank Willard's death in 1958.

B.B.

TEX WILLER (Italy) *Per tutti i diavoli, che mi siamo ancore alle costole?* ("By all the demons in Hell, are they still on my tail?"); thus did the protagonist of *Tex Willer* introduce himself to readers in the second panel of the first weekly comic book (September 30, 1948).

It proved to be the start of a phenomenal climb which, to this day, had suffered no setbacks. Twenty-six years went by since that time, but our hero, the only survivor among the multitudes of adventurous characters born in the postwar period, still rides into the sunset in 15 different editions published here and abroad. Tex has become a byname for two generations of readers because of its thematic and graphic qualities.

Credit for *Tex Willer*'s success should go to scriptwriter Giovanni Bonelli, who has authored some genuinely original stories built upon a meticulous historical and geographical documentation, and the artist Aurelio Galleppini, a master of the chiaroscuro and the photographic style. Bonelli and Galep (as the authors sign their pages) are as well known as their creatures.

DI PIU' NON POSSO DIR-TI, PERCHE' I GUERRIE-RI MANDATI SULLE LORO TRACCE, SO-NO STATI POI TRO-VATI GIA' SFIGU-RATI DAGLI AV-VOLTOI.

"Tex Willer," Aurelio Galleppini and Giovanni Bonelli. © Edizioni Araldo.

successes: *Lost World* (a science-fiction feature, 1948); *Metropolis* (also science fiction, 1949); *Jungle Tatei* (an animal strip, 1950); *Atom Taishi* (later changed to *Tetsuwan-Atom*, Tezuka's most famous creation, 1951); *Ribon no Kishi* ("Ribon the Knight," a girl strip, 1953); *Lemon Kid* (a Western, 1953); *Ogon no Trunk* ("The Golden Trunk," 1957); *Majin Garon* (science fiction, 1959); *O-Man* (1959); *Captain Ken* (1960); *Big X* (1963); *W 3* (1965); all of them science-fiction stories; then came *Vampire* (a tale of horror, 1966); *Hinotori* ("Phoenix," 1967); *Dororo* (an historical strip, 1967); *Buddha* (the life of Buddha adapted to strip form in 1972); *Black Jack* (a medical strip, 1973); and many others. Among his latter creations special mention should be given to *Adolf ni Tsugu* (1983-1985), an epic tale of World War II and beyond, and to *Hidamari no Ki* ("A Tree in the Sun," 1981), another medieval strip.

In 1961 Tezuka founded Mushi Productions which contributed a number of firsts to the Japanese animation field: the first television series of animated cartoons (*Tetsuwan-Atom*, 1963, known in the United States as "Astroboy") and the first color television series (*Jungle Tatei*, 1965). Tezuka also adapted *Ribon no Kishi* for television in 1967 and produced a number of movie cartoons from 1969 on.

Osamu Tezuka is the artist most directly responsible for bringing cinematic techniques to the Japanese comic strip. Before the war, Japanese comics were flat and cramped: Tezuka brought to them a sense of space and depth, a dynamic, pulsating rhythm, and an exciting story line. His strips are imaginative, fresh, and of

Tex, a Texas Ranger, is friend of the Navajo Indians, who call him Night Eagle. He is a champion of justice and a righter of wrongs with very unorthodox methods; he resorts to blows quite often, uses his Colts almost ceaselessly, and speaks in racy language. In his missions he is accompanied by Kit Carson (a very personal interpretation of the famous frontier scout), and by his own son Kit who has learned much from his dynamic and eternally youthful-looking father. (Tex, left a widower while still young, has stubbornly refused to remarry and has consistently shown his misogyny.)

While Bonelli still writes all the stories, the growing *Tex Willer* production has compelled Galleppini to seek help from a number of assistants (Mario Uggeri and Francesco Gamba in the beginning, now also Virgilio Muzzi, Erio Nicolo, Guglielmo Letteri, Giovanni Ticci, and Ferdinando Fusco).

Published initially by Edizioni Araldo, *Tex Willer* was later distributed by Daim Press in Milan. In 1985 Claudio Nizzi took over most of the scripting chores, while a long succession of artists, including Jesus Blasco, Fernando Fusco, Virgilio Muzzi, and Carlo Marcello, have also worked on *Tex Willer*, which is now being published by Sergio Bonelli, the creator's son.

G.B.

TEZUKA, OSAMU (1926-1989) Japanese comic book and comic strip artist born November 3, 1926, in Osaka, Osamu Tezuka created his first comic strip, *Māchan no Nikkichō* ("Machan's Diary") in 1946 for the children's magazine *Mainichi Shogakusei Shinbun*, while he was a student at Osaka University. In 1947 he produced his first best-selling comic book, *Shin Takarajima* ("New Treasure Island"), followed by a host of other

Osamu Tezuka, "Tetsuwan-Atom." © Shōnen.

epic proportions (especially his science-fiction stories). He has created hundreds of popular characters in all genres (science fiction, horror, fantasy, Western, animal, etc.) demonstrating his tremendous versatility and artistic range. Consequently his death from stomach cancer on February 9, 1989, at the relatively young age of 62 sent shock waves through the manga community.

Influenced in large part by Walt Disney (particularly in his animated films) and by old movies, Tezuka has in turn influenced countless numbers of Japanese cartoonists (Reiji Matsumoto, Shōtarō Ishimori, Fujio Fujiko, Hideko Mizuno, Shinji Nagashima, to name only his more famous disciples). Tezuka's works are being reprinted again and again, earning him the undisputed title of King of Japanese Comics. It can be said without exaggeration that Tezuka's career constitutes the capsule history of Japanese comic art since the end of World War II. After his death the National Museum of Modern Art in Tokyo organized a retrospective exhibition of his works in 1990; and in 1994 the city of Takarazuka, where he grew up, inaugurated the Osamu Tezuka Museum of Comic Art.

H.K.

THEIR ONLY CHILD *see* Newlyweds, The.

THEY'LL DO IT EVERY TIME (U.S.) Jimmy Hatlo's sports page gag-panel series, *They'll Do It Every Time*, first appeared on the daily comic page of Hearst's *San Francisco Call* on February 5, 1929. Uncopyrighted and unsyndicated, the weekday feature was used as a routine staff artist filler, Hatlo then being on the *Call* payroll. Hatlo's idea of making a satiric comment on the repeated bad habits and manners of people in general caught a ready response among the *Call* readers, however, and they began to send Hatlo suggestions. When Hatlo used these the first time was September 14, 1929, with "thanx to E. C. Thomas" he thanked the donor in print. These thanks later became the famed tip of the Hatlo hat to which millions of readers vied to obtain (especially since the original of the published drawing often went to the donor).

The paper's editors, watching its popularity grow, moved the small panel in a larger size to the *Call* sports page, and on May 4, 1936, *They'll Do It Every Time* went into national syndication via King Features. In the 1930s, Hatlo began to develop recurring characters in a family called the Tremblechins, with emphasis on their devilish daughter, Iodine. These characters were moved into Hatlo's first Sunday half-page called *Little Iodine*, which was released on July 4, 1943. Later, a second half-page, a weekly panel collection of gags with the same name as the daily panel, was syndicated by King Features on May 8, 1949. A noted subfeature of the Sunday *They'll Do It Every Time*, with an independent title and popularity, was Hatlo's *Inferno*, dealing with the desirable future torments of various obnoxious types. Large numbers of these daily and Sunday panels were collected into books from the late 1930s on, many in paperback format. On Hatlo's death, Bob Dunn carried on the daily and Sunday strips and features, with the aid of Al Scaduto and Hy Eisman. Since Dunn's death in 1989, Scaduto has been carrying the feature solo.

B.B.

"Thimble Theater," E. C. Segar. © King Features Syndicate.

THIMBLE THEATER (U.S.) 1—In 1919 W. R. Hearst noted with interest the work of one of his recent acquisitions, a cartoonist named Elzie Crisler Segar, and brought him to Manhattan to start work on a daily strip for the national Hearst chain. The new strip, to be called *Thimble Theater*, appeared to be a Hearst bid to maintain the format and content of Ed Wheelan's popular *Midget Movies*, which Hearst had just lost, along with Wheelan, to another syndicate.

The first *Thimble Theater* episode ran in the *New York Journal* on Friday, December 19, 1919, and appeared in other Hearst afternoon papers a few days later. Reader response was favorable, and Segar developed the interplay between his enlarged cast of characters, including a top-hatted villain called Willy Wormwood; the comic hero Harold Ham Gravy; his girlfriend, the ungracious Olive Oyl; and her irascible brother Castor Oyl.

Thimble Theater appeared in full Sunday color for the first time on the front page of the Saturday *Journal* on April 18, 1925. By then Segar had moved his daily *Thimble Theater* into the area of fantastic adventure *Continuity* with increasing audience interest. In the later 1920s he introduced *Continuity* into his Sunday pages, initiating one of the longest Sunday-page adventures in strip history with the desert trek that lasted from 1928 to 1930.

On January 17, 1929, the addition of the fabled Popeye figure to the strip made *Thimble Theater* into one of the most successful comic features of the 1930s. Popeye devastated readers everywhere: nothing like the fighting, wise-cracking, omnipotent sailor had ever been seen in the comics before. Then Segar created J. Wellington Wimpy the moocher who further delighted the public. A speedy succession of memorable characters followed: the Jeep, Toar, the Sea Hag, Alice the Goon, Swee'pea, and many others. Segar's ship had come in, laden with riches and fame: in a short time, artifacts based on the Popeye characters and his associates were on sale everywhere; a dozen books based on the *Thimble Theater* strip appeared and were sold out; Max Fleischer of Paramount Studios picked Popeye as the figure on which to move his animated film career to the greatest worldwide success this side of Disney (the Fleischer *Popeye* films began in 1932, and are still being made by other hands with continuing success). Popeye's famed spinach-eating for strength increased sales of spinach in the Depression era and earned Segar an enormous statue of Popeye in Crystal

City, Texas. In the midst of all this acclaim, Segar died on October 13, 1938.

So powerful, however, were the impressions his principal characters had made on the public imagination in less than a decade of brilliant narrative and inspired comedy that they managed to prosper in the lesser, ineptly imitative hands of Tom Sims, Bela Zaboly, and Bud Sagendorf for almost a generation after his death. Only in our time (so badly has the Segar heritage been mismanaged), have we seen *Popeye* disappear from most comic sections, vanish from theater and television screens, and continue to limp along only in a low-selling, infrequent comic book. But the fundamental genius of Segar remains as implicit in his totally unaged original strip work as that of Charles Dickens in his novels.

B.B.

2—*Thimble Theatre* (as it is most commonly spelled) or *Popeye* (as it was later renamed) was carried on by Bud Sagendorf, Segar's son-in-law and sometime assistant, from 1959 to the time of his death in 1994. From 1986 to 1992, however, he had to relinquish the dailies for former underground comix artist Bob London, who did a creditable job of revamping the venerable feature. His updating proved too radical for his antediluvian syndicate editors; and when he tried to present a pregnant Olive Oyl he was promptly fired for his pains. Since 1994 the Sunday page has been done by Hy Eisman, while the dailies have gone into reprints.

M.H.

THOMAS, ROY (1940-   ) 1—Roy Thomas is an American comic book writer and editor born November 22, 1940, in Missouri. Besides being one of the best writers and editors in the field today, Thomas is the most celebrated of the comic book fans who later became a professional in the field. Along with Dr. Jerry Bails, a Wayne State professor who is credited with beginning comic fandom, Thomas founded *Alter-Ego* in 1961. It was the first fanzine (fan magazine) devoted solely to the superhero comic (it had been preceded by some E. C. fanzines, but they were short lived) and is still considered one of the finest amateur magazines ever produced.

In it Thomas began to recount the careers of famous comic book features. In 1965 his proximity to the field brought him his first writing assignment, and he wrote several lacklustre superhero stories for the Charlton Publishing Company. Thomas deserted Missouri and his teaching career in 1965, moved to New York, and started working for National Comics, the home of Julius Schwartz, a man Thomas constantly touted as one of the greats in the field.

But his tour at National lasted only two weeks and he promptly moved to Marvel Comics, home of Stan Lee and the superhero-with-problems concept. After a stint writing non-superhero material, Thomas began to produce work on a broad range of superheroic titles, and it became quickly apparent that he was a talented writer. He had his most consistent success as the scripter of the *Avengers*, an ever-shifting conglomeration of Marvel heroes. Most of this *Avengers* work, and his other material as well, was well above the standard comic book fare. Thomas seemed to have an empathy for the superhero, and comic book critic Gary Brown once commented that Thomas understood the superhero psyche better than any other writer. On the other hand, however, he was also consistently attacked for

the plastic stereotypes of his women characters. Paty, a critic who later became a Marvel artist, once wrote that he does not know the workings of a woman's heart . . . and was often in terrible error.

His editing career also began to progress. He was made Marvel's associate editor shortly after his arrival and was soon their most valuable asset. When editor Stan Lee became publisher in 1972, it was Thomas who became the group's editor-in-chief. (The title was more symbolic than actual, however, since Thomas had been doing the bulk of the job for several years anyway.) Throughout his tenure as editor, the fan press constantly reported he had little impact on the corporate decisions or editorial directions of the company. And, although he angrily lashed out against anyone who reported this, he admitted that his abrupt resignation in 1974 stemmed mostly from an incapacity to affect high-level decisions. He remained with Marvel as a writer and editor of his own titles after he left the editorship.

In recent years, Thomas's best writing has come on the *Conan* feature and its many spin-offs. Adapting scripts from creator Robert E. Howard and later from other sword-and-sorcery sources, Thomas almost single-handedly made barbarian strips a force in the comic book industry. His writing and editing talents have won him many fan and industry awards.

J.B.

2—In the late 1970s Thomas moved to southern California where he unsuccessfully tried to write for television. He came back to DC in the early 1980s, scripting, among other titles, *All-Star Squadron, Infinity Inc., Plastic Man,* and the mini-series *The Ring of the Nibelung* (1989-1990). His work in the 1990s has been mainly for Topps Comics. After more than three decades writing for comic books (his efforts in other fields have all been failures), Thomas is now showing his age in the repetitiveness and predictability of his stories and the triteness of his dialogues.

M.H.

THOR (U.S.) There were few who could have predicted Marvel's dizzying rise to prominence after the 1961 debut of the *Fantastic Four*, least of all editor Stan Lee. Consequently, Marvel expanded not in a burst, but one feature at a time. After *The Hulk* and *Spider-Man, Thor* finally premiered in *Journey Into Mystery* number 83 (August 1962).

Originally plotted by Lee, written by brother Larry Lieber, and drawn by Jack Kirby, *Thor* was freely adapted from ancient Norse mythology. Feeble and frail Dr. Don Blake became the legendary god of thunder when he pounded a magical walking stick on the ground. The cane would instantly convert into an uru hammer, Blake's body would turn from Kirby-emaciated to Kirby-super-muscular, and thus meteorological. Most of the other old Norse gods eventually popped up, too: Odin, the god of gods and ruler of Asgard; Heimdall, guardian of the rainbow bridge; Balder, the brave; and later, Lady Sif, Thor's beloved. Also in attendance were a troupe of Norse villains, most notably Loki, Thor's half-brother and god of mischief.

Lee almost immediately assumed total script control, and they usually involved epic battles: Asgard would invade earth on occasion, with Thor fighting one side or the other half-heartedly; and Asgard seemed always to be under siege by some menace dug out of the

"Thor," © Marvel Comics Group.

Norse legends. Several times, Lee managed to write death itself into the script. But perhaps most unique in Lee's material was the patchwork grammar he supplied for the gods. Thor was always mangling some conjugation of "hath" or "thine" and phrases like: "if thou wilt permit me to charge yon frothy drink" were not uncommon. Lee also introduced another of his super-races, The Inhumans, here, and for several years, they appeared in a back-up feature along with the *Tales of Asgard* strip.

Kirby, already recognized as comic book's definitive artist, literally went wild in *Thor*. Epic battles were his forte and every god and goddess was drawn extravagantly. Many feel Kirby's best fantasy art appeared here because he was given free reign to draw not only earth, but heaven, hell, several netherworlds, and anyplace in-between. Whereas his *Fantastic Four* was enmeshed in machinery, *Thor* became a picture book of men in armor, well-endowed women, brandished swords, and super-fantasy worlds.

Given the monumental proportions of both script and art, *Thor* may have once been Marvel's finest feature. But Kirby (1970) and then Lee (1971) left the feature, and writer Gerry Conway and artists Neal Adams, John Buscema, and others could not stop the strip from becoming a shadow of its former self. It now runs in *Thor* comics, which replaced *Journey Into Mystery* in 1966. Among later illustrators of the series John Buscema, Gil Kane, and Walt Simonson have been the most prominent.

J.B.

THORNE, FRANK (1930-   ) American cartoonist and illustrator born in Rahway, New Jersey, on June 16, 1930, Thorne picked up his first comic book assignments in 1948 while in his freshman year at the Art Career School in New York City. At that time Standard Comics gave him several romance stories to pencil.

After graduation he was tapped by King Features to draw the *Perry Mason* newspaper strip (1951-1952), a stint that was followed by more comic book work, for Dell this time; he turned out a multitude of stories for *Flash Gordon, Jungle Jim, The Green Hornet, Tom Corbett,* and other of the company's titles in the 1950s alone.

Thorne returned to the newspaper field with *Dr. Guy Bennett*, a medical strip he produced for the Arthur Lafave Syndicate from 1957 to 1964. Shuttling back to comic books, he then contributed his talents to a number of titles for Gold Key (*Mighty Samson*), DC Comics (*Tomahawk, Enemy Ace, Tarzan, Korak*), and the ephemeral Atlas/Seaboard Company (*Sherlock Holmes, Son of Dracula, Lawrence of Arabia*).

His breakthrough came in 1975 when he was asked to draw the *Red Sonja* comic book for Marvel. Thorne perfected his mastery at the sword-and-sorcery genre with erotic undertones (soon to become overtones) in these tales spun off from Robert E. Howard's *Conan*. Under his expert guidance the red-haired Amazon (dubbed the "she-devil with a sword") attained heights of popular and critical acclaim that were hard to duplicate by his successors.

In 1978 the artist left *Sonja* to create his own barbarian woman warrior, Ghita of Alizzar, an indestructible blonde of unprecedented ferocity and unquenchable sexual drive. Set in an unspecified, long-forgotten past, the action was fast, the dialogue snappy; and the obligatory scenes of violence seemed to float in a fluid, almost balletic mise-en-scène. Best of all, the sexual shenanigans were liberally sprinkled with the salt of bawdy humor.

Since then there has been no stopping Thorne's vein of erotic fantasy. In the 1980s he produced *Lann* for *Heavy Metal, Moonshine McJuggs* for *Playboy*, and *Ribit!* for the Comico Company, all of these creations starring generously endowed females. They were followed in the 1990s by *The Iron Devil* and *The Devil's Angel*,

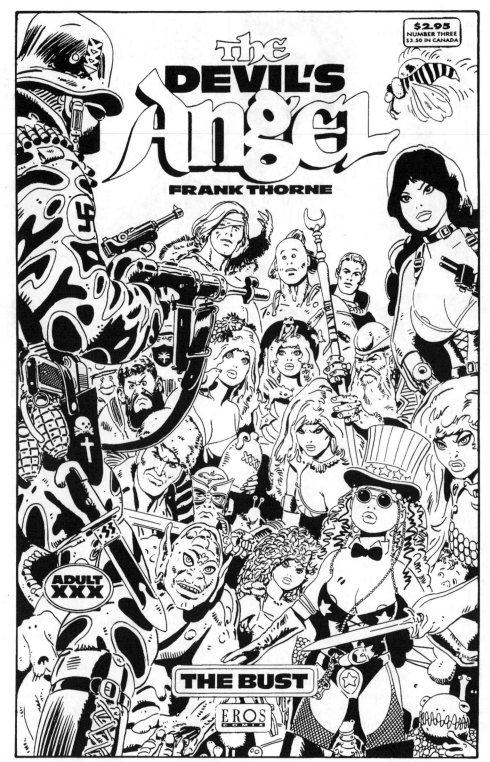

Frank Thorne, "The Devil's Angel." © Frank Thorne.

which continued to mine the erotic lode for which the artist had become famous.

In addition to his work in comics, Thorne has contributed numerous gag cartoons to *Playboy*, has done *The Illustrated History of Union County* (in New Jersey, where he was born), and has starred in touring humor and magic shows based on his comic book creations. As he recently declared, "I'm still having the best fun!"

M.H.

THUNDER AGENTS (U.S.) *THUNDER Agents* was the creation of Wallace Wood, Larry Ivie, and Leonard Brown, debuting in the first issue of the comic book of the same name, published by Tower in November

1965. The publication and its companion titles were never great successes, owing in large part to their 25-cent price at a time when most comic books sold for 12 cents. Although Tower offered twice as many pages in their books, they were unable to attract any sizable readership.

T.H.U.N.D.E.R. stood for The Higher United Nations Defense Enforcement Reserves, a secret espionage agency that employed men, equipped with superpower devices, to combat possible world dictators. Three agents were introduced in the first issue: Dynamo, a desk worker entrusted with a belt that bestowed super strength on its wearer; NoMan, an aging scientist who could transport his mind to a squad

"Tibor," Hansrudi Wäscher. © Hansrudi Wäscher.

of android bodies and hide in a cloak of invisibility; and Menthor, gifted with a mind-reading helmet. Also introduced in the first issue was the THUNDER Squad, a team of commando specialists. They, and each of the super-agents, had a strip in the *THUNDER Agents* comic book, usually all joining together for the finale of the issue.

The THUNDER Agents battled various organizations of evil and, during their brief run, gained and lost several agents. In the fourth issue, the *THUNDER Squad* feature was replaced by Lightning as one of that team's members received a costume that granted its wearer super-speed, à la Flash. In the seventh issue, Menthor was killed, to be replaced the following issue by Raven, a flying agent.

Although the comic failed to achieve great success, two spin-off magazines were tried. *Dynamo* got its own book, starting in August 1966, but it only lasted through four issues. There were two issues of *NoMan*, the first in November 1966. In addition, the book division of Tower issued several paperbacks reprinting early *THUNDER Agents* stories.

Many comic book fans highly prize their collections of *THUNDER Agents* because of the usually high standards of artwork, due mainly to the talents of main artist Wally Wood. Among the men who either wrote or drew (often both) for the series were Gil Kane, Reed Crandall, Steve Ditko, Mike Sekowsky, Dan Adkins, Steve Skeates, George Tuska, John Giunta, Manny Stallman, Ogden Whitney, Len Brown, Larry Ivie, Chic Stone, and Paul Reinman. The standards fell somewhat in the later issues which were published on an erratic schedule, once with an entire year between issues. The final issue of *THUNDER Agents*, number 20, was dated November 1969. The title was revived briefly by Archie Publications in 1983 to 1984.

M.E.

TIBET *see* Gascard, Gilbert.

TIBOR (Germany) Tibor is Germany's entry in the jungle hero field. He is a relative of Tarzan, if a distant one. The relation to the Italian vine-swinger, Akim, is a rather close one as the feature did evolve from the

Akim saga. *Akim Sohn des Dschungels* ("Akim Son of the Jungle") came to Germany in July 1953 in the oblong piccolo format of $2^{7}/_{8} \times 6^{5}/_{8}$ inches, which is somewhat like the format of the 1947 *Cheerio Premiums*. This first *Akim* was replaced in 1954 by *Herr des Dschungels* ("Lord of the Jungle"), written by Rasmus Jagelitz and drawn by Hansrudi Wäscher. Five issues later the feature reappeared as *Akim, New Adventures* after a second run-in with the Federal Office for Supervision of Literature Harmful to Young People. This run-in resulted in a blacklisting of the feature because of alleged excessive violence. The same office recently blacklisted a German edition of Warren's *Vampirella* and it is no longer in existence.

The *New Adventures of Akim*, drawn by Wäscher, lasted until 1959, with earlier stories reprinted in more regular-sized comic books. In September 1959 *Akim* was replaced by *Tibor, Sohn des Dschungels*. This piccolo-sized comic ceased publication after 187 issues in 1963 but continued in large-sized reprints until April 1968 when the publishers closed shop. The feature had a short comeback in 1971.

It is complicated enough to keep track of all the various editions of this particular jungle hero. To further complicate matters there actually are two origins for the *Tibor* character because some of the *Tibor* books of regular format are reprints of *Akim* tales, in which only the names have been changed. The *Tibor* piccolo comic book that replaced *Akim* in 1959 started with a new tale to make Tibor an original jungle hero. Instead of having a hero who has grown up in the jungle, now there is a young millionaire, Gary Swanson, who has crashlanded in the jungle and lost his memory. He is taught in the ways of the jungle by Kerak, a Great Ape, who he freed from a death trap. When Swanson-Tibor finally regains his memory, he learns that his cousin Chuck has spent the Swanson fortune and committed suicide. Finally, he learns that his fiancée has married another man. He decides to remain in the jungle to help protect his animal friends.

Like other comic books done by the prolific Hansrudi Wäscher, *Tibor* has gained a large following despite its somewhat wooden, relatively simple graphic style. The second *Tibor*, in order to differ from both

Tarzan and *Akim*, bends over backward to reverse all of its elements of origin. If it had not been played as a straight adventure series, this might have made quite a nice parody of the jungle genre with all of its standard elements of action. It is doubtful, however, that a parody would have had a comparable success. Reprints of the entire *Tibor* series were started in 1985 as a companion venture to reprints of *Sigurd, Akim, Nick, Tarzan,* and others.

W.F.

TIFFANY JONES (G.B.) Age: 19. Outlook: sunny. Heart: warm. A real switched-on, with-it girl of the sixties. Men will like her because she is the sort of girl every man dreams of meeting. Girls will like her because she is the sort of girl they can all identify with themselves. . . .

With these words Tiffany Jones was introduced to the readers of the *Daily Sketch* on Wednesday, November 11, 1964. Her daily strip began the following Monday. In an unprecedented plug for a cartoon, the *Sketch* trailered *Tiffany* in its full two-page centerspread, introducing not only her, but artist Pat Tourret and writer Jenny Butterworth, proudly presented as the first all-girl comic strip team in history. She's pert, lively, the bachelor girl, "every young man in a bed-sit will recognise at once," wrote Neville Randall. Jenny Butterworth commented, "She is the synthesis of all sixties girls, an all-systems-go girl. She has something of pop girl Marianne Faithfull. Something of an entrancing model girl whose career I have followed closely. And an appeal and character entirely of her own."

Tiffany Jones was conceived by Julian Phipps, a strip editor of the Associated Newspapers group, and he brought her artist and writer together for the first time. Jenny Butterworth, wife of comic page editor and writer Mike Butterworth and mother of three children, had a London University Bachelor of Arts degree in English. She had written stories for comics and pieces for her husband's weeklies for teenage girls. Pat Tourret, one of four artist sisters, also worked on strips and colored covers for the teenage weeklies. Together the two created a strip that quickly rose to the top in the British field. In May 1967 *Tiffany* reached her century: the *Chicago Sun Times* became the hundredth newspaper to acquire her syndicated adventures. She had reached 23 countries on five continents, with 55 newspaper outlets in America and Canada. When the *Daily Sketch* was discontinued, Tiffany moved to the *Daily Mail*, where she moved from the swinging 1960s into the 1970s, but was dropped in the 1980s.

Anouska Hempel played Tiffany in the 1973 film *Tiffany Jones*, directed by Peter Walker.

D.G.

"Tiger," Bud Blake. © King Features Syndicate.

TIGER (U.S.) *Tiger* was created by Bud Blake in May 1965 for King Features Syndicate, as one of King's perennial attempts to infuse new blood into the kid strip lineup. In this respect *Tiger,* while not outstanding by today's standards, was more successful than such doomed enterprises as *Nubbin* or *Dudley D.*

Tiger, with his cap falling over his eyes, his oversized sweater, and his idiot dog Strip, is a conventional comic strip kid, as is his younger brother Punkinhead, whose name evokes memories of *Reg'lar Fellers*. Tiger's best friend Hugo, the gluttonous dullard, also harks back to comic strip tradition—as far back as Feininger's *Kinder Kids*. The two girls in the strip, Bonnie and Suzy, are less well-defined, perhaps because Blake could not find any suitable comic strip model for them.

In the course of the strip's history, Blake has made a few timid forays into the field of social relevance, although *Tiger* is a far cry from *Peanuts* or even *Miss Peach*. Usually the daily and weekly gags revolve around the kids' innocent pranks, their musings, and their dreams. Not revolutionary, to be sure, not even mildly innovative, but a valiant and craftsmanlike effort at refurbishing an ancient and somewhat run-down genre. Relaxed, agreeable, and unassuming, *Tiger* (which won the NCS award for best humor strip in 1970) is proof that even the most worn-out comic strip formula can still work if it is done with integrity and skill. In 1995 it passed the 30-year mark and it is now published in more than 400 newspapers.

M.H.

TIGER TIM (G.B.) "Hooray! Mrs. Hippo has left the schoolroom! Now is our time to peep into that treacle jar!" cried Tiger Tim in his very first caption, thus setting the style of merry mischief that has been his code of behavior for 71 years. The oldest and longest-lived British comic hero, Tim is the ringleader of Mrs. Hippo's kindergarten, a strip of three oblong panels that also made history by being the first newspaper strip in England. It appeared on April 16, 1904, in the *Daily*

"Tiffany Jones," Pat Tourret and Jenny Butterworth. © Associated Newspapers Ltd.

"Tiger Tim," H. S. Foxwell. © Rainbow and Fleetway Publications.

Mirror, and was drawn by Julius Stafford Baker, who modeled his funny animals on the well-established style of American artist James Swinnerton. Unfortunately for history, the strip was not a continuing one at first, but was one of several, one-shot strips that appeared in the *Mirror* children's corner around that time. However, never one to lose sight of a good thing, Baker revived his kindergarten for *The Playbox*, one of the first British comic supplements. This children's section appeared as a color pullout to the monthly magazine, *The World and his Wife*, and *Tiger Tim* was its star from the start (November 1904). Upon the demise of the magazine in 1910, he was transferred, still in color, to *The Playhour* (later renamed *Playbox*), a supplement similar to another monthly magazine, *The New Children's Encyclopedia* (February 1910). With another change of title to *My Magazine*, Tim and his pals ran well into the 1930s.

The original Hippo Boys were Willy Giraffe, Peter Pelican, Billy Bruin, Jumbo Jim, Jacko the Monkey, and some unnamed animals: a fox, a leopard, a parrot (undoubtedly Joey), and a female goat. The cast changed slightly (as did the giraffe's name, to Georgie) when they all moved to page one of the new colored comic *Rainbow* (February 14, 1914). They found themselves at a new school, Mrs. Bruin's Boarding School, thus winning a new subtitle, "The Bruin Boys." An ostrich called Willie came in and the only girl went out. By mid-1914 a new artist had taken over, Herbert Foxwell, who remolded Baker's characters in his own superb style, making them the most popular in nursery comics. A second weekly began on June 1, 1919, called *Tiger Tim's Tales*, which soon converted itself into another colored comic, *Tiger Tim's Weekly* (January 31, 1920).

Meanwhile the good Mrs. Hippo had reopened her school. Her pupils were Tiger Tim's sister, Tiger Tilly, and the sisters of all the rest of the Bruin Boys, known collectively as the Hippo Girls. This strip appeared on the front page of yet another colored comic weekly, *The Playbox* (a revival of the old title), beginning on February 14, 1925. *Tiger Tilly* lasted until the paper merged with *Jack & Jill* (June 11, 1925), but *Tiger Tim* survived *Rainbow*'s merger with *Tiny Tots* (April 23, 1956). He continued in that nursery comic and after its demise reappeared in *Jack & Jill*, where he has been from 1966 to the present. Currently drawn in a revamped animated cartoon style by Peter Woolcock, the *Tiger Tim Annual*, published yearly from 1922 to 1957, was revived in 1973 as the *Tiger Tim Fun Book*. The strip was again dropped in the 1980s, but a revival is rumored.

D.G.

TILLIE THE TOILER (U.S.) Russ Westover created *Tillie the Toiler* for King Features Syndicate in January of 1921. As the title indicates, Tillie Jones was a working girl who labored (but not too hard) as secretary and part-time model in the fashion salon of Mr. Simpkins, alongside her sad-faced, pint-sized, gape-mouthed suitor Clarence MacDougall ("Mac") and under the watchful eye of Wally Whipple, her supervisor and Mac's hated rival.

Tillie was a dark-haired, wide-eyed, slender beauty whose brains were not on a par with her looks. She managed to get into all sorts of trouble of her own making, forever falling for handsome strangers with fast cars and faster schemes, only to be rescued in the nick of time by faithful, sober-headed Mac. Her relations to other men were flirtatious but innocent (in the

"Tillie the Toiler," Russ Westover. © King Features Syndicate.

convention of the times) and were aimed, more often than not, at triggering Mac's burning jealousy (although Tillie came close to getting married on a couple of occasions).

Tillie the Toiler's style was sketchy and almost crude, despite the fact that Westover employed some of the best ghost artists in the business (including a youthful Alex Raymond) once the strip had become established. One of the reasons for the strip's popularity was neither the writing nor the drawing but the fashions (to keep up to date Westover subscribed to every fashion magazine in the western world). When this aspect of the strip began to falter in the 1950s, Westover turned *Tillie* over to Bob Gustafson who prettied it up considerably, but to no avail. *Tillie* disappeared from the comic pages after marrying the long-suffering Mac, in April of 1959. (The syndicate listed Westover's retirement as their reason for killing the strip, but in fact the theme had gone out of style, and few readers at this point cared about Tillie's inane misadventures.)

In 1927 a movie of *Tillie the Toiler* was directed by Sidney Salkow, with Marion Davies as the heroine and William Tracy as Mac.

M.H.

TILLIEUX, MAURICE (1922-1978) A Belgian novelist, scriptwriter, cartoonist, and father of *Gil Jourdan*

César, Marc Lebut, and a natural daughter, Anne, Maurice Tillieux was born in Huy, in 1922. Tillieux's first job was with *Spirou*, where he illustrated the Fureteur column. Inspired by true events, Tillieux wrote the novels *Le Navire que tue ses capitaines* ("The Ship That Kills Its Captains") and *L'homme qui assassine* ("The Man Who's Killing"). In 1944 he started drawing 20 pages a month of the series, *Jeep*, for the journal, *Bimbo*. He also worked for *Heroïc Albums*, where he created a new feature, *Felix*.

Tillieux's *Gil Jourdan* appeared for the first time on September 20, 1956, in *Spirou* magazine; he had over a dozen of *Gil Jourdan*'s albums published. In the police adventures of Jourdan, his assistant, Libellule, and Inspector Crouton, Tillieux proved himself a top-flight scriptwriter and a good cartoonist. He became the most popular scriptwriter in the group of *Spirou* magazine of the time and collaborated with Roba on his comic strip, *La Ribambelle*, with Will on *Tif et Tondu*, with Francis on *Ford T*, and with some other cartoonists.

Tillieux's vocabulary was very original, brisk, and colorful; his sense of humor great. His drawing style, which would show his characters in surroundings typical of Atlantic France (the harbors, big cities, etc.), presented the adventures in often rainy and mysterious atmospheres, lending a mystic note to the police stories.

In order to stay closer to home, Tillieux produced the *César* strip for *Spirou*, giving complete freedom to his sarcastic humor. *César* is a brilliant caricature of a bachelor who is occupied with domestic problems. *Marc Lebut*, drawn by Francis, was also Tillieux's idea. The strip tells about two neighbors with different characters who experience hilarious adventures in the company of an old Ford Model T. Tillieux was a master of surprise, sarcasm, and nonsense. He died in a car crash in February 1978, but the characters he created live on.

E.R.

THE TIMID SOUL (U.S.) H. T. Webster's first drawing of Caspar Milquetoast, the titular hero of his *The Timid Soul* daily panel and Sunday page, appeared on several dates early in May 1924, in various papers subscribing to Webster's *New York World* gag panel series. Like a similar series of daily panels by Clare Briggs, on which Webster's strip was based, the *World* artist carried a number of continuing titles, used irregularly on various days, such as *Life's Darkest Moment, How to Torture Your Wife (Husband), The Thrill that Comes Once in a Lifetime*, and *The Events Leading Up to the Tragedy*. The new *Timid Soul* occasional title was the first Webster daily series to feature a recurrent character, however, and readers proved to be enthusiastic about the new, if infrequent, visitor to the comic page. Caspar Milquetoast, with his drooping white moustache, pince-nez, stooped shoulders, and lean, tired frame, was a new kind of comic figure among the rough and tough figures that generally populated the comics of the time (although a Milquetoast prototype, not followed up, appeared a few times in an earlier Webster series circa 1919 called *Are You One of these Spineless Creatures?*).

By the late 1920s, *The Timid Soul* had become so popular that it was appearing once a week in Webster's daily panels, and Caspar Milquetoast had been featured in a large volume of his own (published by Simon & Schuster in 1931, called *The Timid Soul*, and introduced by Ring Lardner). On Sunday, May 3, 1931, the first

"The Timid Soul," H. T. Webster. © New York Tribune.

concluded some time after Webster's death in April 1953, but were immediately pressed into a reprint series, together with his other daily panel features, for several years longer.

B.B.

TIM TYLER'S LUCK (U.S.) Lyman Young started *Tim Tyler's Luck* for King Features Syndicate as a daily strip on August 13, 1928, which was followed by a Sunday page in July 1931 (with Young's earlier creation *The Kid Sister* as its top piece).

Lyman Young grew up reading Horatio Alger stories and he was strongly influenced by them. The early *Tim Tyler* was drawn in silhouette and had a sentimental story line combined with a pseudo-Victorian atmosphere. Tim was an orphan who loved airplanes and the free life, and along with his pal Spud Slavins, this led him into some unlikely scrapes culminating in 1932 with their getting stranded in darkest Africa. In the course of their wanderings Tim and Spud came across the Ivory Patrol, a paramilitary organization set up to keep law and order in this part of Africa (1934). Tim and Spud soon joined the crack outfit and before long aviation was forgotten. Under the leadership of dark, handsome sergeant Paul Clark (later promoted to captain) and with the help of their pet black panther Fang, Tim and Spud performed their duties with creditable spirit.

In May of 1940 the two young heroes left the Ivory Patrol and went back to the United States where they eventually joined the Coast Guard. They did their best during the war in their fights against assorted groups of foreign spies and saboteurs. Soon after the war ended they went back to Africa and the Ivory Patrol (which had proved to be the strip's most popular attraction).

Tim Tyler's Luck is famed in comic strip circles for the number and quality of the ghosts who worked on the strip under the titular leadership of Lyman Young. Alex Raymond practically drew the daily strip and the Sunday page all by himself in 1932 and 1933 and he was followed by a number of others, including Charles Flanders and Burne Hogarth. Ever since 1952 the daily strip is officially credited to Lyman Young and his son Bob, while the Sunday page bears the signature of Tom Massey.

Be it as it may, *Tim Tyler's Luck* occupies an honorable position among adventure strips. The drawing is always competent and the story line very imaginative and sometimes inspired, which accounts for the tremendous success of the feature in Europe before World

Timid Soul Sunday page appeared, replacing Webster's preceding page dating from 1923, called *The Man in the Brown Derby* (which featured a considerably more aggressive and irascible hero than Caspar).

Timid Soul daily panels were reprinted everywhere and were featured in two more Webster collections, *Webster Unabridged* (1945) and *The Best of H. T. Webster* (1953). The generally accepted favorite seemed to be the 1928 drawing showing Caspar waiting in the pouring rain on a busy downtown street corner, his hat collapsed damply about his face, water puddling around his shoes, and saying firmly: Well, I'll wait one more hour for him, and if he doesn't come then he can go and borrow that $100 from someone else. *The Timid Soul* Sunday page and weekly black-and-white panel

"Tim Tylers's Luck," Lyman Young. © King Features Syndicate.

War II. In the United States the strip never reached such a high pinnacle but it was fairly popular. A series of *Tim Tyler* comic books were issued by Standard in the 1940s; in 1938 Ford Beebe directed a memorable movie serial of *Tim Tyler's Luck*, with Frankie Thomas in the starring role. The Sunday page was discontinued in July 1972. The daily strip continues, however, despite the death of its creator in 1984, and it is now the oldest adventure strip in existence.

M.H.

TINTIN (Belgium) Created by Hergé (Georges Rémi) in 1929, *Tintin* first appeared in *Le Petit Vingtième*, the weekly supplement of the Belgian daily *Le Vingtième Siècle*. It was a success from the first, and each of Tintin's adventures was later reprinted in book form, starting in 1930.

As with all original creations, Tintin's is a self-contained coherent fantasy world. The hero is a teenager and a reporter. In the conventions of the genre this means he does everything from detective work to space exploration, all assignments that Tintin carries out with characteristic aplomb and suitable humility. He is always flanked by his faithful fox terrier Milou (Snowy in the English version) already present in the first adventure ("Tintin in the Land of the Soviets"). Other unforgettable characters came to join Tintin and Milou in latter years. These included the twin detectives Dupont and Dupond (Thomson and Thompson) similarly black-attired and equally dimwitted, and the evil genius Rastapopoulos (they first appeared in 1934); in 1937 the incurable conspirator General Alcazar, and in 1939 the overbearing opera singer Bianca Castafiore. Captain Haddock, the irascible and rum-guzzling sailor,

made his appearance in 1941, followed in 1945 by the absentminded (and deaf to boot) Professor Calculus. These and dozens of others form an ever-changing gallery amidst whom our hero moves.

At the time of Hergé's death in 1983 there were 23 *Tintin* albums in print (the twenty-fourth, *Tintin and l'Alph Art*, was left unfinished): in the United States they are published by Little, Brown. *Tintin* has been brought to the screen numerous times (there have been two live features and countless animated cartoons) and has also appeared in a stage play. There have been many scholarly studies devoted to *Tintin* from the 1950s on, along with a flood of merchandising that reached a crescendo in the 1990s with the opening of a number of *Tintin* stores across Europe and even in the United States.

M.H.

TIRAMOLLA (Italy) Tiramolla, son of rubber and glue, is the creation of Roberto Renzi and Giorgio Rebuffi. He appeared first in the *Cucciolo* comic book of August 1952. Due to the success encountered by the character, a *Tiramolla* comic book was finally issued in July 1959. By then the character had been taken over with excellent results by Umberto Manfrin, while the texts continued to be scripted by Renzi.

Thanks to his particulate structure he is able to distend himself and assume all kinds of shapes, not unlike Plastic Man. *Tiramolla* is capable of performing the most extraordinary, impossible, and outlandish feats. To make up for his abilities, he is also extremely lazy. As his assistant he retains Saetta ("Lightning"), the butler. Tiramolla has overwhelmed a whole array of

"Tintin," Hergé (Georges Rémi). © Editions Casterman.

adversaries, the most outstanding being a science-fiction character named Mister Magic.

In the pages of the monthly *Tiramolla* have been featured many other series, such as *Ullao* by Umberto Manfrin, *Zeffy & Cerry* by Egidio Gherlizza, the long-lasting *Teddy Sberla* drawn by A. Terenghi, and *Robotman* by Franco Aloisi. *Whisky & Gogo* and *Pepito* have also been published in *Tiramolla*. The *Tiramolla* strip has had many scriptwriters and illustrators in addition to those already mentioned: Alfredo and Andrea Saio, Tiberio Colantuoni, M. L. Uggetti, Franco Frescura, Attilio Ortolani, and Carlo Chendi. The *Tiramolla* magazine was published up to the mid-1980s; an attempt to revive it was made in 1990 until 1993.

Tiramolla has also been published with great success in France, where it is known as *Elastoc*.

G.B.

TOBIAS SEICHERL (Austria) Created in 1930 by Ludwig Kmoch (actual name Ladislaus Kmochk) *Tobias Seicherl* was the first comic strip of Austrian origin. Kmoch (1897-1971) was a self-educated cartoonist who started working for the press after World War I. He worked for the satirical magazines *Muskete* and *Simplizissimus*, finally joining *Das kleine Blatt*, a social democrat newspaper, in 1929. For this paper he created the characters of Tobias Seicherl and his dog Struppi.

Tobias Seicherl first appeared on October 5, 1930. While the hero of the strip was a kind of typical loser, his dog was his better self, offsetting and commenting on his mistakes and prejudices. The most interesting thing about this strip is that it was always written in Viennese dialect which, apart from the strip content, made it a genuine Austrian strip. *Tobias Seicherl* presented readers with contemporary political satire commenting on current events of the day. The strip was obviously social democrat in outlook and propaganda. It criticized the Nazi movement, which also started cropping up in Austria. Kmoch achieved this by having the somewhat dense hero of his strip pick up Nazi

"Tobias Seicherl," Ludwig Kmoch. © Ludwig Kmoch.

ideas as his own and having the dog setting things straight. However, this was not the safest thing to do.

So when Kmoch felt he might get into hot water, he simply sent his hero on a number of world tours to avoid politics back home. In 1938, after the Austrian "anschluss," Tobias Seicherl changed fronts and henceforth propagated Nazi ideas. While Kmoch had visibly joined his former political enemies—whether of his free will or forcibly is open to debate—he seems not to have been too happy about this development. So he once more sent his hero on a world tour in 1939, afterward phasing out the series.

"Tiramolla," Giorgio Rebuffi. © Edizioni Alpe.

"Tobias Seicherl," Ludwig Kmoch. © Ludwig Kmoch.

After World War II the character of Tobias Seicherl was revived occasionally. Finally Kmoch was coaxed into doing new strips, which appeared from 1958 to December 23, 1961. Some of the early material has been reprinted, the historic background of the 1930 to 1933 strips has been commented and explained in a book publication which, however, did not explain Kmoch's collaboration. It is probable that he was exonerated fully or partially after the war or else his series might not have been revived.

Mention of *Tobias Seicherl* in an encyclopedia seems to be warranted only as the feature is of historic relevance as the first Austrian comic strip of note. However, its role in politics is so ambiguous that one would prefer the feature not to have had any historic relevance at all.

W.F.

TODANO BONJI (Japan) *Todano Bonji* ("Average Boy") was created by Yutaka Asō and made its first appearance in the evening newspaper *Asahi* in May 1933.

At the time the Great Depression was at its peak in Japan as well as in the United States, and there was a great deal of unemployment among college graduates, causing a great social problem. Todano Bonji was a mediocre boy who lived up (or down) to his name: he was faint-hearted, superficial, and conforming. After graduation from the university, Todano was unable to find a job. The story followed him as he sent out hundreds of résumés to no avail (he was so destitute at one point that he used the rejection notices to light his bamboo pipe). Finally Todano received a favorable answer, and he went to a nightclub in order to celebrate, got drunk, unknowingly insulted the president of the company that had just hired him, and got himself fired before he had even started on the job.

Other misadventures dogged Todano in search of the elusive job. Asō was able to express in very graphic terms the plight of the intelligentsia, and he won a great deal of sympathy for his luckless anti-hero. The popularity of *Todano Bonji* never reached, however, the heights of its creator's more famous work, *Nonkina Tousan*, and was discontinued in July 1934.

H.K.

TOKAI (Bangladesh) Bangladesh's most popular comic strip, *Tokai* was conceptualized in the late 1960s when the area was still part of Pakistan. The idea had to be shelved during the bloody civil war at the dawn of the 1970s and while its creator, Rafiqun Nabi (Ranabi), studied in Greece from 1973 to 1976. It finally saw print in the weekly *Bicitra*, beginning in 1977.

The exploits of a downtrodden street boy much in the tradition of *San Mao* in China, *Tokai* has had impacts throughout Bangladeshi society: Adults look to it for political messages and children view Tokai as the ideal character. Tokai was even introduced to the Bengali lexicon about 1990, when dictionaries included the word to describe the desperately poor.

The strip is purposively drawn in a very simple manner, a "bit illustrative, a bit realistic for our general readers who do not have an aesthetic richness," in the words of Ranabi. Attuned to the public's wants, Ranabi inserts messages into *Tokai*—"not direct political ones, but mixed with social commentary"—and occasionally allows readers to participate in the strip. For example, although Tokai is a Dhaka character, Ranabi has moved him to the countryside for short periods at the demands of readers. He said the strip for years has depicted current events and acted like a history of Bangladesh.

Ranabi started drawing cartoons on a regular basis in 1961, while an art student at the University of Dhaka. Throughout the decade, he joined other cartoonists in propaganda campaigns to liberate the territory from Pakistan, his works appearing in the *Weekly Forum* and as posters and leaflets. Besides drawing *Tokai*, Ranabi teaches full-time at the Institute of Fine Art, University of Dhaka, where he is also a painter.

J.A.L.

TOM AND JERRY (U.S.) The cartoon industry's most famous cat-and-mouse team was created by producer Fred Quimby and directors William Hanna and Joseph Barbera in 1939. The first *Tom and Jerry* short, *Puss Gets the Boot*, proved successful in theaters and began a series that lasted for well over a hundred films produced by M.G.M. in the next 25 years. The cartoons were characterized by an almost total dependence on slapstick sight gags, often bordering on the very violent, as the spunky mouse, Jerry, eluded Tom the cat. In 1942, Tom and Jerry and other M.G.M. properties were combined into a Dell/Western Publishing Company comic book named *Our Gang*. It was in this magazine that the format from the cartoons was expanded and modified into what became a highly successful comic book series for over 30 years.

"Tom Poes," Marten Toonder. © Marten Toonder.

The lead feature of the *Our Gang* comic book was a series, drawn by Walt Kelly, based on the Hal Roach *Our Gang* kid comedies. The popularity of *Tom and Jerry* soon eclipsed the lead feature and, as of issue 40, the cat and mouse received special cover billing. When a 1948 one-shot Dell Color Comic (number 193) starring Tom and Jerry sold extremely well, the feature took over the *Our Gang* comic completely, beginning with number 60 (1949).

For the comic books, Jerry the mouse was equipped with a cohort in the form of a small, gray, diapered mouse named Tuffy. Jerry and Tuffy lived in a mousehole in a home ostensibly guarded from mice by Tom. Some stories involved Tom's continuing efforts to evict the unwanted tenants; others concerned Tom's constant get-rich schemes which invariably failed. The best stories were usually those illustrated by Harvey Eisenberg, although many other artists rendered the feature from time to time.

In addition to the *Tom and Jerry* comic, the characters appeared in a number of Dell and Gold Key specials, published by Western, including comics such as *Tom and Jerry Summer Fun, Tom and Jerry Winter Carnival, Golden Comics Digest* and a promotional giveaway comic, *March of Comics.* Most of the specials also featured stories of other M.G.M. cartoon characters such as Barney Bear, Droopy, Wuff the Prairie Dog, and Spike and Tyke.

In 1961, the *Tom and Jerry* comic suspended publication for one year, resuming in 1962 and continuing until 1974 when it ceased publication with number 291. The title was picked up by Harvey Comics, which has been publishing it since September 1991 (mostly in the form of reprints of old episodes).

M.E.

TOM POES (Netherlands) Tom Poes ("Tom Puss") is the chef d'oeuvre of Dutch writer and artist Marten Toonder. Created in 1938, the strip was published in foreign newspapers until it was picked up by the Dutch newspaper *De Telegraaf* on March 16, 1941. This first run of the daily strip ended on November 20, 1944, and Toonder closed up shop for the rest of World War II. Finally, on March 10, 1947, the strip was reinstated in the newspaper *N.R.C.* The strip for quite some time has also been included in *Volkskrant* and, since story number 109, in daily newspapers like *Het Vaderland, Tijd-Maasbode,* et al. Thus far there have been more than 150 stories published in the daily strip version, which consists of pictures with narrative below them. The weekly version, with speech ballons and all the other comics trimmings, was started in *Ons Vrije Nederland* in 1945. New and reprint stories have since appeared in a number of weeklies including *Wereldkroniek, AVRO-bode, De kleine Zondagsvriend,* and *Revue.* Since 1955 the *Tom Poes* weekly version has been a welcome addition to the Dutch *Donald Duck* comic. Tom Poes also starred in his own weekly comics magazine, *Tom Poes Weekblad,* from November 1947 to June 1951. This magazine for children included various features, puzzles, and games. Many of the stories were also published in book form, others were originally created for books or in connection with advertising campaigns.

Tom Poes started out as a rather plump, cuddly cat. He got streamlined over the decades, walking upright into one comic adventure after another. The introduction of Heer ("Mr.") Olivier B. Bommel, a bear, in the third story of the series, provided a comrade and antagonist for Tom Poes. Bommel's popularity soon overshadowed that of Tom Poes.

The stories, originally written for a young audience, started changing when the strip returned to the newspapers after the war. Although plots and dialogue were still aimed at children, the humor of the strip was becoming more and more refined and establishment figures were being parodied. In the 1950s the stories became more intellectual, with an undertone of satire throughout the strip. The level was heightened even more in the 1960s and 1970s so that now the strip may very well be regarded as one of predominantly adult appeal. *Tom Poes* has grown up over the decades, along with the strip's readership. This, in part, explains its tremendous success in the Netherlands. The strip's intrinsic artistic and literary qualities have also helped to make it an international success. Hundreds of dailies and weeklies reprint the adventures of Mr. Bommel and Tom Poes. Some of the stories have also been produced as cartoons for television showing and for theatrical release.

W.F.

"Tony Falco," Andrea Lavezzolo and Andrea Bresciani. © Editoriale per Ragazzi.

TONY FALCO (Italy) *Tony Falco* appeared for the first time on December 11, 1948, as a weekly comic book published by Editoriale per Ragazzi. It unfolded over 48 issues (evenly divided in two parts), ending on November 5, 1949.

Tony Falco is doubtless Andrea Lavezzolo's masterpiece. It is a genuine novel in comic strip form and is of a literary value superior to that of most of Salgari's novels. The historical and costume details are always accurate. A dictionary, which did not limit itself to translating foreign dialogue but gave all necessary explanations concerning the ambience in which each story took place, was cleverly inserted within the panels of the strip.

As in a novel, the protagonist is surrounded by highly individualized characters: Babirousse represents shrewdness; Mohamed el Chelifa, generous strength; Haydee, delicate love, blindly loyal and mysterious. The drawings, meticulously rendered and artfully composed, were by Andrea Bresciani, a talented cartoonist who inexplicably and unfortunately disappeared from the Italian scene after the *Geky Dor* strip. (He is now reported to be living in Australia.)

G.B.

TOONDER, MARTEN (1912-   ) Marten Toonder, Dutch cartoonist, writer, and animator, was born May 2, 1912, in Rotterdam, Netherlands, where he grew up and went to high school and to the Rotterdam Academy of Art. There he learned the techniques of comic strips and of animated cartoons from a former Disney staffer, Dante Quinterno, from Buenos Aires.

During that time he made his debut as strip artist with Tobias (1931) and Bram Ibrahim (1932). From 1934 his strip *Uk en Puk* appeared in the weekly *Unicum*. In 1938 he started *Tom Poes*, a strip starring a cuddly pussycat that became more streamlined over the years. From 1938 to 1941 *Tom Poes* was published in Czechoslovakia and Argentina only, before being picked up by a Dutch newspaper. Over the years Toonder's creative genius came up with many more strips like *Japie Makreel* (1940), *Kappie* (1946), *Panda* (1946), *Koning Hollewijn* (1954), and many others. On the side he also produced comics for advertising.

At first, Toonder was assisted by his wife, Phiny Dick, his brother Jan Gerhard Toonder, by Piet Gertenaar, and Wim Lensen. The number of assistants grew with the number of strips created. This meant that, in the long run, roughly 80 percent of the Dutch comic artists have done work, at some time or other, for the Marten Toonder Studios that were founded in June 1942, originally to produce animated cartoons but soon including and branching out into comic strips. The Toonder strips' format ranges from strips of pictures with running narrative underneath them to full-blooded comic strips with balloons, and so on. At first, most work at the Toonder Studios was done by staff artists, then the studio relied more and more on freelancers.

Most of the Toonder animated cartoons and comic strips were financial successes. The comic strips are published in 15 countries. Marten Toonder isn't only a brilliant artist but also an excellent writer; he has added colorful expressions to the Dutch language. The Toonder style of doing funny comics has long influenced many comic artists in the Netherlands either directly through work for the studio or indirectly to stab at success through emulation.

For his eightieth birthday in 1992, Toonder was awarded the Tollens Prize, one of the most important literary awards of the Netherlands. Toonder commented that this showed that his work was definitively recognized as literary work. In the same year the first volume of his autobiography, *Toch is de aarde plat* ("But of course the earth is flat") was published.

W.F.

TOONERVILLE FOLKS (U.S.) Fontaine Fox's classic comic satire of rural life, *Toonerville Folks*, began as a daily gag panel distributed by the Wheeler Syndicate in early 1915 without running title or any thematic link beyond a vaguely country-suburban setting for most of the jokes. Many of the later famous characters emerged in these early panels (the Terrible-Tempered Mr. Bang, the Powerful Katrinka, Aunt Eppie Hogg, etc.), but they did not live in a specifically designated location, while other figures developed at this time (Thomas Edison, Jr., Uncle Peleg, etc.) were later dropped. The early occasional titles for the daily gags ("Pathetic Figures," "Pleasures of Light Housekeeping," etc.) included no reference to Toonerville, nor did the panel captions and dialogue.

"Toonerville Folks," Fontaine Fox. © McNaught Syndicate.

The famous Toonerville Trolley, name, skipper, twisted antenna and all, did not appear in the panel until 1916, while the other recurring characters were not linked in residence to the trolley's skipper until later. (The first authoritative unification of the Fox figures in one community came with the launching of Fox's Sunday page, *Toonerville Folks*, by the Bell Syndicate in 1920, at which time some papers gave the daily panel the running *Toonerville Folks* title, while others continued to use differing daily titles, as well as an earlier running title, *Life*.)

Virtually all of Fox's inimitable cast of characters: Mickey (Himself) McGuire, Tomboy Taylor, Wise-Cracker Wortle, Little Stanley, Willie Smith, the Dwarf, Old Man Flint, Stinky Davis, Suitcase Simpson, George Washington Smith, plus Katrinka, Mr. Bang, Eppie Hogg, and numerous others, were individually followed in the daily panel and Sunday page by the strip's millions of readers as if they were actual people. They were so recognizable that Fox could drop them in and out of the strip for weeks or months without using their names, with the full assurance that the readers would know who they were when they reappeared.

Most famed and admired of all Fox's inventions, however, was a trolley car and its living adjunct, the trolley skipper (never given a further name). This tall, angular, four-wheeled trolley with its interior stove and smokestack and its twisting miles of rural track was the delight of newspaper readers throughout the 1920s and 1930s; toys in its image were sold everywhere; and Educational Pictures' live-action *Toonerville Comedies* by Fontaine Fox of the early 1920s featured a replica of the trolley and its capped, bespectacled, and bearded skipper in every film. Various localities vied to lay claim to the original Toonerville trolley, and for decades every trolley line laid to rest across the country was called a Toonerville by local news writers.

Fox supplied little information about the line and its stops (although some were named from time to time in the strip: East Scurvee, etc.), although he did name its

founder occasionally, variously titled Captain and Colonel Silas Tooner, for whom the town was also named. But what happened on the line was hilariously documented in detail for 40 years including the grim period after World War II when the trolley was replaced by a bus, still jauntily and haphazardly operated by the old skipper.

Later in the 1920s, another Fox character, Mickey McGuire, was featured in a series of short live-action film comedies starring Mickey Rooney (who took his first name from the strip character). Several Toonerville strip collections by Fox were published in the late 1910s and early 1920s: Fontaine Fox's *Funny Folk*; *Cartoons*; and *Toonerville Trolley and Other Cartoons*, while a recent collection called *Toonerville Folks* was published by Scribner's in 1973. Fox himself folded the daily and Sunday strip in 1955 and retired to Greenwich, Connecticut, where he died in 1964.

B.B.

TOOTS AND CASPER (U.S.) Jimmy Murphy's gentle strip of family life and comic soap opera, *Toots and Casper*, first appeared in the *New York American* as a daily strip on July 8, 1919. It was launched as a Sunday strip on January 2, 1922. Syndicated by King Features, *Toots and Casper* began as a simple, domestic gag strip about a young middle-class couple with a baby in a big city. Never given a last name by Murphy (the point is routinely evaded in the strip by such statements as "A Mr. Casper to see you, Miss Jones."), the two reflect the mores of the postwar era with comic conflicts over Toots's daring clothes ("She's wearing a slit skirt and men's socks!") and Casper's interest in the good-looking baby-sitters hired to stay with their son, Buttercup.

The Sunday page continued the daily gags, and for some time the strip was a second-string filler feature for the Hearst daily and Sunday papers. In the mid-1920s, however, Murphy switched to a semi-serious continued story line on the order of that in *The Gumps*, complete with a rich bachelor uncle named Everett J. Chuckle, who drops in from money-making activities abroad long enough to get romantically involved and even married (just like Uncle Bim Gump), threatening the couple's hope of a plush inheritance. Other characters who emerged solidly in the developing narrative were Colonel Hoofer, a neighbor; Elsie Ferguson, Everett's long-lost love; Lemuel Plunkett, Casper's boss; Sophie Hoofer, the Colonel's wife; Danny Hoofer, the Colonel's son; Stella Klinker, a Mae West-type golddigger; Roger Kailerton; and Uncle Abner Chuckle, a second uncle (presumably poor, but actually rich also). A standby figure in the earlier gag episodes, a huge, bow-tied yellow dog companion for Buttercup named Spareribs, receded into the wings in later years.

Alternately half- and full-page, as advertising space dictated, the Sunday *Toots and Casper* page finally gained permanent full-page status once the continuing narrative became established and reader interest mounted. A single row of four panels was added as a weekly gag strip to the Sunday page and named *Hotsy-Totsy* on January 10, 1926; it featured an unnamed boy and girl couple romancing a la *Rosie's Beau*. On April 25, 1926, the permanent second Sunday strip, a third-page named *It's Papa Who Pays*, was added and focused on a middle-aged couple, simply called Mama and Papa, with four children of varying ages. A competent gag strip, this feature was routine filler material. (Later it was reduced in size to accommodate a highly popular series of cutouts featuring most of the Murphy characters in the early 1930s.)

Avidly read through the 1930s, *Toots and Casper* suffered a reduction in size and narrative complication during World War II, thus diminishing public interest. By the time the daily strip was discontinued on November 12, 1951, and the Sunday half-page on December 30, 1956, circulation of the strip had dropped radically. Attractively drawn and engagingly written, *Toots and Casper* was, with the daily *Gumps*, the best of the humorous, soap opera strips, and, in fact, of all soap opera strips.

B.B.

Sergio Toppi, illustration for the magazine Corto Maltese. © Milano Libri Edizione.

Rodolphe Töpffer,"M. Crépin."

TÖPFFER, RODOLPHE (1799-1846) French-speaking Swiss artist and writer born in Geneva in 1799, Rodolphe Töpffer was the son of well-known artist Wolfgang Adam Töpffer. Although he intended to be a painter like his father, Töpffer had to renounce his ambition because of poor eyesight. After studies in Paris he taught in several schools in Geneva, and was titular professor of rhetoric at the Geneva Academy of Belles-Lettres.

Töpffer Junior made a name for himself as a writer with charming and fanciful works such as *La Bibliothèque de mon oncle* ("My Uncle's Library," 1832), *Le Presbytère* ("The Presbytery," 1839-1846), both whimsical reminiscences about his childhood and youth; and *Voyages en Zigzag* ("Zigzagging Journeys," 1845), a description, with illustrations by himself, of his trips to the Swiss mountainside. His short stories, collected in 1841 in an anthology titled *Nouvelles Genevoises* ("Genevan Short Stories") also won him high praise.

But Töpffer's best-known and best-remembered works remain the more than half-dozen picture-stories, full of wit and mordancy, which he wrote in the course of his later years. These stories (much admired by Goethe) which anticipated the modern comic strip by some 50 years, were posthumously anthologized in the series of volumes published in 1846 to 1847 under the title *Histoires en Estampes* ("Stories in Etchings").

Rodolphe Töpffer who, along with Wilhelm Busch and Christophe, is regarded as one of the foremost precursors of the comic form, died in Geneva in 1846.

M.H.

TOPPI, SERGIO (1932-   ) Sergio Toppi is an Italian cartoonist and illustrator born October 11, 1932, in Milan. After high school Toppi decided to devote himself to illustration, and his first works were published in l954 in the *Enciclopedia dei Ragazzi Mondadori*. From 1957 to 1966 he worked for the Studios Pagot contributing to the realization of animated television spots. During the 1950s and the 1960s he illustrated several children's books and in 1960 he began contributing to the weekly *Corriere dei Piccoli* with illustrations, funny anecdotes, and war comics stories. For the new magazine *Corriere dei Ragazzi* (1972) Toppi drew many episodes of the series *Fumetti verità* and *I grandi del giallo*, both based on Mino Milani's scripts.

In 1974 he started drawing for the magazine *Messaggero dei Ragazzi* biographies of historical figures based on Milani's scripts and later collected in the volume *Uomini che non ebbero paura* ("Men who were not afraid," 1980). In these stories Toppi began to change his graphic style, breaking the traditional division of the page in regular panels and working on the whole page as a single unit. Here the size of the panels, and consequently of the characters, changed according to their narrative importance. Over the years this technique has been accentuated and has turned into Toppi's distinctive graphic mark, also characterized by strong cross-hatchings.

In the mid-l970s Toppi contributed to the magazine *Sgt. Kirk* with covers and a set of his own stories later collected in the volume *Cronache d'armi, di giullari, di briganti e militari* (1976). In 1976 Toppi started an ongoing collaboration with the weekly *Il Giornalino* for which he has drawn for stories by himself *I racconti della vita, Un giorno per caso* (both also collected in book form, the first in 1977 and the second in 1980), *Viso nascosto, Storie d'oro e di frontiera, I racconti del vento della sera*; for stories by G. Ramello the series *Il Vangelo sconosciuto*, and *La città*, a long sci-fi tale written by Gino D'Antonio.

During the 1970s Toppi also worked for Bonelli publishing house by drawing covers and the adventures *L'uomo del Nilo* (1976) and *L'uomo del Messico* (1977), based on Decio Canzio's scripts, and *L'uomo delle paludi* (1978), based on his own script. In the 1980s he wrote and drew for the monthly *Orient Express* the series *Il collezionista* ("The Collector") and these adventures have been collected in three volumes: *Il calumet di pietra rossa* (1984), *L'obelisco della terra di Punt* (1985), *La lacrima di Timur Leng* (1986) printed by L'Isola Trovata.

In the same period Toppi contributed to the magazine *Alter Alter* and then to *Corto Maltese* with his own stories, which later on have been partially reprinted by Milano Libri in the volumes *Sacsahuaman* (1980) and *Sharaz-De* (1984). Toppi's collaboration with the monthly *Comic Art* has produced a collection of stories reprinted in the volume *Myetzko e altre storie* (1992). Many of the comics created by Toppi, though drawn in perfect realistic style, are embued with a magical atmosphere that makes the reader wonder about the objective reality of things. Toppi has also collaborated with some foreign publishers. He drew some episodes of *L'histoire de France en B.D.* (1976) and of *La découverte du monde en B.D.* (1978). He also wrote and drew two long stories on the Spanish conquest of America published in book form in Spain (1992): *El Cerro de la Plata* and *Las fabulosas ciudades de Arizona*.

Toppi's artwork devoted to illustration consists of covers for the magazine *Tempo Medico* illustrations for E. Sotsass's volume *Ukiyo è Haiku & Suspençe*; for he has also worked the magazine *Corto Maltese*, for the nationwide daily *Corriere della Sera*, for the Italian edition of the *Reader's Digest* condensed books, and he did two packs of tarot cards. Toppi has been awarded in Lucca a Yellow Kid in 1975 and a Caran D'Ache for illustration in 1992.

G.C.C.

TORPEDO 1936 (Spain) In the early 1980s the Barcelona publisher Josep Toutain conceived the idea of a hero similar to those characters played by James Cagney, George Raft, or Humphrey Bogart in the classic American gangster movies of the 1930s that he had loved in his youth; thus was *Torpedo* born. Toutain entrusted the writing to Enrique Sanchez Abuli and for the art he turned to American Alex Toth. In February 1982, in the pages of the Spanish edition of *Creepy* magazine, the series, baptized *Torpedo 1936* (the vintage year was appended to situate the timeframe in a nutshell), finally saw light of print.

Luca Torelli was an orphan born in southern Italy in 1904 (as his police record indicated); immigrating to the United States as a child he grew up in the mean streets of an unnamed American city. Starting with petty theft and extortion, he progressively graduated to bank robbery and eventually attained the status of a hitman, which earned him the nickname *Torpedo* for his lethal efficiency. Tall and gaunt (the artist had playfully modeled him after his publisher), Torpedo showed no weakness or mercy in his errands of death, dispatching his victims with knife, gun, and bomb.

After only two episodes Toth quit, protesting the senseless violence.

He was replaced by Catalan artist Jordi Bernet who endowed these brutal tales with a stylized choreography of violence and an almost documentary sense of time and place. "One is struck, first of all and especially in Jordi Bernet's work, by the precise re-creation of period details," David H. Rosenthal wrote in his introduction to the first American edition of the series. "In this respect, *Torpedo 1936* recalls not the Thirties but films like Roman Polanski's *Chinatown*."

At first rendered exclusively in black-and-white, the series later received the full-color treatment. While color somewhat distracted from the pervasive atmosphere of blackness prevalent in the strip, it did not appreciably tone down the overall mood of nihilism, cynicism, and despair of the tales. An international hit (pun not intended) almost from the outset, *Torpedo 1936* has been extensively reprinted in this country by Catalan Communications.

M.H.

TORRES, DANIEL (1958-   ) Spanish cartoonist and illustrator born August 20, 1958, in Valencia, Spain, Daniel Torres started making himself known as a comics practitioner the same year he was getting his B.F.A. from the Valencia School of Fine Arts, in 1980. Since then his career has experienced a meteoric rise, first in Spain whence his fame spread rapidly to France, Belgium, Denmark, Italy, and the United States. A professional through and through, he could trace his roots to the so-called "Valencia School" of Spanish comics and to the international movement known as "the clear line" derived from Hergé, the creator of *Tintin*. Taking a post-modernist stance the "clear line" cartoonists prefer heavily black, hard-edged contours to the softer line, halftones, and shaded areas favored by most modern graphic artists.

At any rate Torres shows in his work a firm determination to assimilate a variety of concepts currently in fashion in a vast compilation of influences culled from the visual history of the twentieth century. In this he displays a highly personal and creative spirit, and he embellishes his experiments with stylistic flourishes that show he is an artist who enjoys his own creative discoveries. His vitality, at once adventurous and ironic, and the exquisiteness of his line succeed in bringing to life a very personal universe of characters, clothes, objects, places, and incidents.

Torres first made a name for himself in the pages of the magazine *El Vibora* in which the cult of the underground comix was nurtured along with an interest in the latest modes of graphic expression. There in 1980 he created his comic strip character Claudio Cueco and, with or without him, successively published from 1980 to 1983 *Asesinato a 64 imagenes por segundo* ("Murder at 64 Frames per Second"), *Alas y azar* ("Wings and Chance"), *El angel caido* ("The Fallen Angel"), and other stories. In the meantime he had started with *Opium* his long collaboration with *Cairo*, a monthly whose esthetic ideology was more in accordance with his own tastes.

After completing an original story, *Sabotage!*, for a Belgian publisher in 1982, he began the first of the adventures of his new hero, Rocco Vargas, *Triton*, later followed by *El misterio de Susurro* (1984), *Saxxon* (1985), and other titles. The saga of Rocco Vargas represents a trend currently much in fashion, a version (halfway

Daniel Torres, "Rocco Vargas," © Daniel Torres.

between parody and homage) of the space-opera genre, and it is replete with quotes, visual and textual, from works that have influenced the artist's personal mythos. As Armando Mistral, the protagonist is the owner of a nightclub, and a science-fiction writer to boot; as Rocco Vargas he doubles as a space hero. Humor is a fundamental element of the graphic line, the narrative, and the dialogues; joined to a deliberate blurring of the lines between different realities, the psychological instability of the characters, and the constant shifting of the situations, it adds depth and distancing to the ostensibly escapist plot. In 1984 *Heavy Metal* started serializing the Rocco Vargas stories in the United States.

While continuing to draw and write "the astral adventures of Rocco Vargas," Torres has also in recent years turned out several shorter tales, later anthologized in *El octavo dia* ("The Eighth Day," 1993). In 1997, in the pages of *Penthouse Comix*, he started *Aphrodite*, about the investigative and sexual exploits of a scantily clad female private eye.

J.C.

TORRES, ELPIDIO (1925-1973) A Filipino artist born September 2, 1925, in San Juan del Monte, Quezon City, Elpidio Torres came from a family of artists: his father was a sculptor; his brother, Jess, is a painter; and his younger brother, Menny, is a cartoonist. Four of his eight children are also involved with art. Despite all the art influence in the family, Elpidio did not start drawing until the age of 20. He attended the University of the Philippines and took up fine arts. While there he met Larry Alcala, who had been doing comic books since he was a youngster.

In 1946 Torres landed his first art job with *Bulaklak*. Within a year he was promoted to art director for *Bulaklak* and for Philippine *Movieland* magazine. After he had been working for many years for these publications, a long strike occurred and Elpidio decided to transfer to Ace Publications. While at Ace he was teamed up with Mars Ravelo, who is considered by many to be the foremost writer in the Tagalog vernacular. Their first comic collaboration was *Roberta* for *Pilipino Komiks*. It was a success so the two continued to work together on many popular comic book series for various publications. Among their most famous strips were *Booma*, a jungle fantasy; *Dyesebel*, a dramtic novel about a beautiful mermaid and her relationship with people; *Bondying*, a humorous story about a mature male who retains his infantile behavior due to his unusual upbringing; *Gog*, a tongue-in-cheek comedy-horror story about a many-eyed, blob-type, monster; and *Dobol Trobol*, a situation comedy dealing with twins. Many of these were also made into motion pictures.

Toward the latter part of his career Torres wrote many of his own scripts. He did *Robina*, a jungle series for Craft Publications' *Redondo Komix*. *Planeta X*, which he did for PSG Publications, was a moody, science fantasy series dealing with aliens and supernatural beings. For Ares Publications he produced *Planet Eye*. *Planet Eye* was a very unusual strip in that it had an old pulp-type feeling to it, combined with a surrealistic approach in its storytelling.

Torres was one of the most popular of all the comic artists in the Philippines. He was respected and admired by his peers. His work has influenced many of the younger artists, particularly Abe Ocampo, who is now illustrating for National Periodicals (U.S.).

Of all the comic illustrators in the Philippines, Torres's artwork reflects the classical style typified by Fernando Amorsolo, the master of Philippine art. While many of his compatriots patterned their works after the popular American strips, he preferred to draw and create art that conveyed the spirit of his country. His pastoral scenes capture the lyrical imagery of the *barrio* ("countryside"), and his sensitive renderings of the typical *provinciana* ("country lass") illustrate his strong attachment to the traditional concepts of romanticism and chivalry that is lacking in today's comics. Elpidio Torres died in 1973.

O.J.

TOTH, ALEXANDER (1928-   ) American comic book artist born June 25, 1928, in New York City, Alexander Toth studied at the School of Industrial Arts in New York. In 1944, Toth began freelancing after school for Eastman Color/Famous Funnies Company. When that firm folded several titles in 1946, Toth was laid off. He completed his schooling and secured work under editor Sheldon Mayer at Superman-DC (later National) in 1947, commencing with *Dr. Mid-Nite* and *Atom*, then progressing on to *Green Lantern*. To each of these and other strips, Toth lent a powerful and graphic style, highly influenced by various illustrators, especially Noel Sickles. Toth's approach gained him considerable respect in the field and his style was frequently imitated in other National books, even after his departure.

In 1950, he moved to California to assist Warren Tufts on the *Casey Ruggles* newspaper strip for United Feature Syndicate. He left DC in 1952 to join Standard Comics for two years, also working on crime comics for Lev Gleason Publications and war comics for EC. In 1954, Toth was drafted into the army where he labored on the base newspaper and created his own adventure comic strip, *Jon Fury* in Japan.

Upon discharge in 1956, he joined Western Publishing Company (Dell) and worked on comic book versions of motion pictures and television shows (*The Land Unknown*, *The FBI Story*, *Zorro*, and others). In 1960, he began directing art on the *Space Angel* television series. This was followed by freelance work for

Alex Toth, "Thunderjet." © William M. Gaines, Agent, Inc.

National's romance and mystery books until he joined Hanna-Barbera studios in 1964 to do layout and character designs for Saturday morning animated shows. Toth and Joe Barbera designed superhero-oriented programs including *Space Ghost*, *The Mighty Mighter*, and *The Herculoids*. Designing model sheets for cartoon shows could not keep Toth away from comics; throughout the 1960s, he freelanced for National (on *Hot Wheels* and *The Witching Hour*, among other titles), Warren, and for black-and-white hot rod comic magazines such as *Big Daddy Roth* and *Drag CARtoons*.

In later years, Toth simplified his art style, concentrating on an economy of line and an emphasis on panel composition. His sense of layout and story continuity is generally considered to be among the finest in the field. Toth continued to work for Warren until the late 1970s. In the early 1980s he drew the first two episodes of *Torpedo 1936* for the Spanish publisher Toutain and *Bravo for Adventure* for an independent American publisher. He was reprinted in the 1986 *True Love* comic book that reproduced some of his old stories for Standard. Since the late 1980s he has devoted most of his talents to television animation (*Batman*, *Thunderbolts*, etc.).

M.E.

TRIPJE EN LIEZEBERTHA (Netherlands) *Tripje en Liezebertha* ("Tripje and Liezebertha"), while not the first comic strip to be created by Dutch cartoonist Henk Backer, remains his most successful creation. It appeared in the *Rotterdamsch Nieuwsblad* ("Rotterdam News") from 1923 to 1963, when Backer retired.

On April 1, 1921, Backer had started *Yoebje en Achmed* ("Yoebje and Achmed"), the daily newspaper strip considered by most experts to be the first of its kind to originate in the Netherlands. *Yoebje en Achmed* had also appeared in *Rotterdamsch Nieuwsblad*, the newspaper Backer had turned to after *De Telegraaf* had rejected him because they were already reprinting an English strip.

Like *Voorwaarts* ("Forward"), the Social Democratic party's newspaper that published Backer's second strip, *Hansje Teddybeer en Mimie Poezekat* ("Johnny Teddybear and Mimi Pussycat") in 1922, the *Rotterdamsch*

"Tripje en Liezebertha," Henk Backer. © Henk Backer.

"Les Trois Mousquetaires du Maquis," Marijac (Jacques Dumas). © Coq Hardi.

Nieuwsblad never regretted welcoming the young artist into its fold. Only one year (1924) after the start of *Tripje en Liezebertha*, a first book of *Tripje* was published and people had to stand in line to get a copy. *Tripje en Liezebertha*, because of its growing popularity, also sparked its own Buster Brown effect by endorsing a number of products from lollipops to chocolates to mouth organs.

Tripje en Liezebertha was so enthusiastically received by the public for a reason. For one thing, the stories offered a chance for an innocent escape into the realm of fantasy which appealed both to children and the young at heart. For another, the art was exquisitely simple-looking yet superbly animated. Reading the strip was like watching marionettes coming to life, acting out their whimsical, fairy-tale adventures in the never-never land of fantasy.

Backer's strip is proof of the fact that most early European comic strips were aimed at children, in the tradition of the Bilderbogen of the nineteenth century. Backer's work also proves that, while appealing to children, it is also possible to charm adults by allowing them fleeting glimpses at their own childhood fantasies.

W.F.

TROIS MOUSQUETAIRES DU MAQUIS, LES (France) During the German occupation, the prolific Marijac (Jacques Dumas) created his famous strip, *Les Trois Mousquetaires du Maquis* ("The Three Musketeers of the Maquis") in the Resistance newspaper *Le Corbeau Déchainé* as a humorous release from the extreme tensions of underground resistance and as a defiant satire on the occupation forces and their French collaborators. After France's liberation, *Les Trois Mousquetaires* was featured on the front page of *Coq Hardi*, a new illustrated newspaper published and edited by Marijac (October 1944).

The mechanics of the plot were very simple: three Resistance fighters (drawn from real life) and known as l'Avocat ("the Attorney"), Pinceau ("Paintbrush"), and la Torpille ("Torpedo") wage an unrelenting private

war against the German occupation forces. The action, however bloody it may appear on paper, is more slapstick than mayhem. A typical instance shows one of the three musketeers getting hired as chef in a hotel serving as headquarters for the Germans, and blowing up the entire staff by means of a bomb concealed in a birthday cake. On another occasion, one of the friends, disguised as a farm girl, leads a whole German company into a booby-trapped barn. In spirit the musketeers are first cousins to another famous trio of French rogues, the *PiedsNickeles*, whom they emulate in cunning, deviousness, and sheer effrontery.

The strip was drawn in Marijac's usual nondescript style, but in this particular case the draftsmanship was less important than the merry absurdities of the plot. Early in 1949, *Les Trois Mousquetaires du Maquis* underwent a radical transformation in outlook. By then anti-German feelings had somewhat abated and the three friends decided to devote their energies to fighting gangsters, racketeers, and black-market profiteers. These, however, proved less diverting enemies than the hated Germans and, on November 23, 1950, the strip was finally dropped.

Les Trois Mousquetaires du Maquis is not a highly remarkable strip. The drawings are atrocious and the continuity slapdash at best. Yet it immediately caught the French spirit of the postwar period. Nor was the strip trying to capitalize (as so many others of the time) on the French Resistance's real or imagined exploits. Marijac was a former underground fighter and never hesitated to depict the faults of the resisters as well as their virtues. When some of the episodes of *Les Trois Mousquetaires* were reprinted in book form 25 years later by Editions Albatros, they received a warm reception, not only from former *Coq Hardi* readers but also from many young people curious about a time and a state of mind which must have seemed very remote.

M.H.

TRUDEAU, GARRY (1948-   ) American cartoonist born 1948 in New York City, Garry Trudeau graduated from Yale University and the Yale School of Art and Architecture. According to the rather tongue-in-cheek biography released by his syndicate, Trudeau had, at one time or another, participated in the archaeological excavation of a small, but significant medieval village, cofounded and edited a trilingual magazine for the diplomatic corps in Washington, D.C., designed and constructed light murals for Mayor Lindsay's Ping-Pong room in Gracie Mansion, worked as a photographic researcher for *Time-Life*, acted as assistant to the original producer of the off-Broadway hit *Futz* , contributed to *New York Magazine*, and wrote and illustrated a well-received series of columns on the 1972 Conventions for the *Miami Herald*!

In addition to quoting verbatim from this biography to researchers looking into his professional career, Trudeau is also fond of another self-deprecating quote from his editor: "Garry Trudeau is a thoughtful, concerned, and highly creative young man who is out to make a fast buck." Any objective assessment of Garry Trudeau's position, however, is not so simple.

Of course, Trudeau is best known for *Doonesbury*, which he created (as *Bull Tales*) in the pages of the *Yale Record* when Trudeau was an undergraduate. In 1969 the strip moved up to the *Yale Daily News* where it attracted wide notice. Universal Press Syndicate gave the feature its new title and started distributing it nationally the following year. Since then, Trudeau's renown has soared: his work is often quoted and analyzed in the news media (the *Washington Post* once proclaimed him "the youngest and most successful of the new wave of comic strip artists appearing in today's newspapers"), his strip appears in more than 400 newspapers around the country, and the book he coauthored with Nicholas von Hoffman, *The Fireside Watergate* (Sheed and Ward, 1974), has become a best-seller. Garry Trudeau remains a basically shy and private individual, however; his interest in the art of the comics is genuine (he once wrote a somewhat fanciful, but entertaining, history of comic art in *New York Magazine*) and there can be no doubt that he is more concerned with recognition than with money.

Garry Trudeau's draftsmanship (or lack of it) has been duly noted in many quarters. It should be mentioned, however, that his drawing style, consisting of a line reduced to its simplest expression, perfectly suits the purpose of the strip which is literary and not visual. The analogy between Trudeau and Feiffer is obvious, but only on the surface. Trudeau's idea of political sophistication is to make jokes, half anti-Left, half anti-Right, without regard to more universal relevance. Unlike such otherwise divergent comic strip satirists as Al Capp and the aforementioned Feiffer, he lacks conviction. When Garry Trudeau finally saw fit to express a strong viewpoint (whether political, moral, aesthetic, or whatever else he might choose) he was able to take his place in the ranks of the foremost comic artists.

In his already long career Trudeau has fought in favor of many political and humanitarian causes, and he has been a strong advocate of cartoonists' rights. He was the first newspaper strip artist in modern times to take a prolonged sabbatical from his work (in 1983-1984). He received the Pulitzer Prize in 1975, and (after 16 unsuccessful nominations) he finally won the National Cartoonists Society's Reuben Award in 1996.

M.H.

TSUGE, YOSHIHARU (1937-   ) Japanese comic book artist born October 31, 1937, in Oshima, Tokyo, Yoshiharu Tsuge quit elementary school while in the fifth grade and worked at a variety of odd jobs. He made his comic book debut in 1953. Among his very prolific production some works stand out prominently: *Yottsu no Hanzai* ("Four Crimes") in 1956; *Koroshiya* ("A Killer") in 1958; *Fukuwajutsushi* (a fantastic story about a ventriloquist) in 1960; *Nazo* (a mystery strip) in 1961; *Mishiranu Hitobito* ("The Strangers") in 1964; *Nezumi* ("The Rats") in 1965; *Unmei* ("Fate") in 1965; *Akai Hana* ("The Red Flower") and *Sanshōuo* ("The Salamander"), both in 1967.

In his early strips Tsuge came under the influence (as did so many other comic book artists) of the masters Osamu Tezuka and Sanpei Shirato. He created a great many strips in many genres (mystery, thriller, horror, etc.) but these strips were only for entertainment and Tsuge did not feel satisfied with his commercial production; so in 1966 he created the short comic story *Numa* ("The Shallow Man"), which really shocked readers. In it Tsuge revolutionized the concept of the strip: he went from entertainment to total self-expression, using psychodramatic techniques. This strip and the following, also thoughtful and brooding, disconcerted the majority of readers, but aroused the enthusiasm of a small group of devotees of comic art. Yoshiharu Tsuge's later production, if small in output, is highly significant in style and concept. It may yet prove a landmark in the history of Japanese comic art. Prolonged bouts of depression have prevented Tsuge from producing many comics in the 1980s and 1990s, although he has illustrated records of his trips around Japan and of his dreams.

Yoshiharu's younger brother, Tadao Tsuge, is also a comic book artist.

H.K.

TSUKIOKA, YOSHITOSHI (1839-1892) Yoshitoshi Tsukioka was a Japanese Ukiyo-e artist born March 17, 1839, in Tokyo into a powerful samurai family. In 1850 Tsukioka became a pupil of the famous master Kuniyoshi Utagawa, and in 1853 he made his debut, illustrating a famous Heike story. In 1866 Tsukioka and his rival in fame, Yoshiiku Ochiai, created the *Eimei Nijuhasshuku* ("The Sadistic Collection of Blood") series. In 1866 Tsukioka worked on another Ukiyo-e series, *Kaidai Hyakusensō* ("The Collection of Death Art"), and in 1872 started *Ikkai Zuihitsu* ("The Collection of Monster Art"). After completing only a few etchings of the latter series, Tsukioka suffered a nervous breakdown which temporarily incapacitated him.

Tsukioka recovered his health in 1873 and resumed work, using the pen name "Taiso" (meaning "great revival" in Japanese). Many important works were to come out of Tsukioka's pen in the following years: *Ii Tairō Sōnanzu* ("Prime Minister Ii Met With Disaster," 1874); his series on the Seinan Sensō (the Japanese southwestern war) in 1877, which became a best-seller and made his name famous; *Dainihon Meishō Kagami* (a series of traditional Japanese art) in 1878, another best-selling work. In 1885 Tsukioka started on his life work *Tsuki Hyakusha* ("Collection of Tsuki's Masterpieces"), which seriously taxed his mental faculties. In 1891 he was committed to a mental institution where he died on June 9, 1892.

Yoshitoshi Tsukioka was the foremost Ukiyo-e artist and the last great one in the Meiji era. His style was influenced by his master Kuniyoshi Utagawa, but he was also influenced by the European copperplate etchings in his later works. He was very good at depicting monsters and fantastic and grotesque creatures. In turn Tsukioka influenced a number of Ukiyo-e artists who later became the leading practitioners of the art (Kiyokata Kaburaki, Shinsui Ito).

In the last days of the Meiji era (toward the end of the nineteenth century) there were no cartoonists in the real sense of the word. Rakuten Kitazawa was to be the first Japanese cartoonist; but Yoshitoshi Tsukioka, along with his colleagues Gyōsai Kawanabe, Kiyochika Kobayashi, and Yoshiiku Ōchiai, played an important role in the prehistory of Japanese comic art, until Kitazawa definitively established the form.

H.K.

TUFTS, WARREN (1925-1982) An American cartoonist born in Fresno, California, on December 12, 1925, Warren Tufts started to take an art course in his first year of high school, but locked horns with the instructor and at his invitation transferred to something else. When about 12, shortly after joining the Boy Scouts, Tufts was cast in a weekly radio program series about scouting and later developed his own dramatic mystery program series, writing the scripts and enacting all the roles. Tufts joined the navy in 1943 following high school graduation; first he drew survival adventure strips, then he was involved briefly in war bond promotions, then functioned as an artist and writer and finally an editor of Naval Air Station newspapers.

From the navy Tufts returned to radio and then, suddenly in 1948, he resigned from the field completely to devote three months to the development of the *Casey Ruggles* strip, which was syndicated following the strong recommendation of the *San Francisco Chronicle*. Five years later, as an outgrowth of disagreements with United Feature Syndicate over the handling of *Ruggles*, Tufts's new comic satire titled *The Lone Spaceman* was born. He wanted to syndicate it himself, and his father and brother joined him in the enterprise as his sales force. *Spaceman* was sold to some 30 papers in the United States, but was discontinued after four to six months.

Then *Lance* was created. *Lance* underwent development as a full-page art feature, weekly only, incorporating color treatment not attempted before or since in this country in comic strip regular production. The father/brother sales team again did well, placing *Lance* in three out of five cities contacted. The feature enjoyed premium rates, many noteworthy cover placements, and numbered select newspapers among its approximately 100 clients. However, the enterprise made arrangements with two Eastern U.S. syndicates for handling the feature. They did not perform well and argued that the addition of a daily strip was necessary. Tufts compromised his goals and added the daily strip. Then the two syndicates suffered internal problems and went out of business and Tufts was left without the representation he required and was overcommitted.

Since the conclusion of *Lance* in 1960 Tufts dabbled in several things as a freelancer: television and motion pictures as an actor, writer, and story director; television series design and development, film titles design, comic book production, magazine feature writing and illustration; and light aircraft design and development.

It was while flying an airplane of his own design that he died in a crash on July 6, 1982.

E.R.

"Tumbleweeds," T. K. Ryan. © King Features Syndicate.

TUMBLEWEEDS (U.S.) Tom K. Ryan's hilarious anti-Western *Tumbleweeds* made its appearance in 1965 distributed by the Register and Tribune Syndicate.

In the village of Grimy Gulch, on the farthest reaches of civilization, there lives the slow-witted, slow-moving Tumbleweeds, the most inept cowboy that ever plied the West, mounted on his equally anemic and faint-hearted hag grandiosely named Epic. Tumbleweeds would live happy, basking in the obscurity of his talents, were it not for the persistent Hildegard Hamhocker, the town spinster, who constantly tries to force her slobbering affections on him; and Hildegard's endless rounds of pursuing counteracted by Tumbleweeds's no less determined dodging are among the highlights of the strip.

Among Grimy Gulch's other denizens, there is Sopwell the town drunk, the irascible judge Frump and his gambling partner Ace, and Claude Clay the undertaker ("You plug'em, we plant'em"). The somnolence of the town is only disturbed by the periodic raids of Snake Eye, the resident outlaw, followed by the epic (but harmless) gunfights with the sheriff and his benumbed deputy Knuckles. There is also a neighboring tribe of hostile(?) Indians whose fecklessness and ineptitude are only matched by the incompetence of their adversary, Colonel Fluster, commander of the hapless garrison of Fort Ridiculous.

More than 20 *Tumbleweeds* books have been published since 1968. In the late 1970s the strip was adapted into a Saturday-morning television cartoon series. A stage production premiered in 1983, and a live musical show called *Tumbleweeds Gulch* has played at the MGM Grand in Las Vegas since 1993.

Tumbleweeds is a good representative of the modern humor strip, fast, witty, and irreverent. Several collections of reprints have been published in pocket book form. (The strip is now being distributed by King Features Syndicate.)

M.H.

TURNER, LESLIE (1899-1988) Leslie Turner, the talented sustainer of a classic comic strip cast of charac-

Leslie Turner, "Captain Easy." © NEA Service.

ters in his daily and Sunday *Captain Easy* strips for three decades, was born in Texas (like Roy Crane, whose work he carried on) in December, 1899: in the last week of the nineteenth century, as he puts it. A boyhood cartoonist and a four-year student at Southern Methodist University, Turner (again like Crane) hit the rails and high roads of foot-sore adventure in his early 20s, managing to sandwich in six weeks of intensive study at the Chicago Academy of Fine Arts. Returning to Dallas to marry and freelance (during which he sold a number of gag cartoons to the old *Judge* magazine), Turner went on to New York, and hit the big slick popular magazine illustration market with repeated sales of story art in the late 1920s to such typical titles as *Redbook, The Ladies' Home Journal, The Saturday Evening Post,* and others. Then he went to Colorado in 1929 to freelance again, while raising sheep.

A long admirer of Crane's work in the comics, Turner eventually met the creator of *Wash Tubbs,* and commenced working for him in 1937, at a time when Crane felt his work was slipping a bit, and took a long trip to Europe to recuperate from a too-long-sustained stint at the drawingboard. Crane was highly pleased with Turner's deft work on the strip, and worked closely with him from that date until he (Crane) left the daily and Sunday strips in June of 1943 to tackle his own original idea for King Features: a strip to be called *Buz Sawyer.*

Turner, continuing only with the daily *Tubbs,* published his first episode on June 1, 1943. The Sunday page, ghosted by other inept artists after Crane left (among whom was the ordinarily competent Walt Scott), was finally taken over by Turner on October 26, 1952, and drawn by him until January 31, 1960, when it was placed in the accomplished hands of Mel Graff. (Turner returned to the Sunday page once between February 19 and March 26, 1961; otherwise the page was carried on with fair competence, but with little of the Crane and Turner style or wit, by Graff.) Later the *Tubbs* daily changed its title permanently to *Captain Easy* (not surprisingly in view of the small part the married Wash was taking in the strip) in the late 1940s, the date varying from paper to paper. By the late 1960s, Turner tired of the daily routine, and retired, his last strip appearing on January 17, 1970. He died on February 28, 1988, in Orlando, Florida.

Turner is one of the great masters of the comic strip medium. His humorous suspense stories rank among the finest sustained strip comedies of all time: as fine in its frequent peaks as anything Frank Willard, Billy De Beck, Cliff Sterrett, or Crane himself ever did.

B.B.

TURNER, MORRIE (1923-   ) American cartoonist born December 11, 1923, in Oakland, California, Morrie Turner learned to draw in high school and he graduated just in time to be inducted in World War II. Upon his return to civilian life, Turner joined the Oakland police department as a civilian clerk, freelancing all the while as a cartoonist for various magazines. In 1964 he quit the force to devote himself fully to cartooning. With the help and encouragement of fellow cartoonist Charles Schulz and comedian Dick Gregory, he created *Wee Pals,* an engaging kid strip featuring a merry band of youngsters of varied races and backgrounds. The strip, first syndicated by the Lew Little Syndicate in 1965, is now being distributed by the Register and Tribune Syndicate.

Morrie Turner has an easygoing, pleasing style, with few surprises but a neat line and a lively sense of composition that are deceptively simple. His dialogues are down-to-earth and fairly radiate genuine warmth and sympathy. Since the inception of the strip, Morrie Turner has received a wide variety of humanitarian awards, including the Brotherhood Award of the B'nai Brith Anti-Defamation League. He animated his little band of urchins in a television show called *Kid Power* (1973-1976) and has also published a series of pamphlets on antidrug, anti-gang, and child safety themes.

Morrie Turner is not, as many believe, the first successful black cartoonist (E. Simms Campbell preceded him by some 20 years with his *Cuties*), but he is certainly the first black cartoonist to find success with a strip featuring black characters. His efforts have paved the way for other black cartoonists (Brumsic Brandon with *Luther* in 1968, Ted Shearer with *Quincy* in 1970, and others).

M.H.

TURNER, RON (193?-   ) Although for millions who were subscribers to *The Eagle* (1950) Dan Dare is the great hero of the British science-fiction strip and Frank Hampson the finest artist of this comic century, for many others who were boys in the 1950s and who still collect and appreciate space art of the smaller, independent comics, no artist can touch the comic work of Ron Turner. However, due to the man's shy personality and refusal to come out of the artistic shadows, his name remains unknown to many. His age, background, and life is equally unknown, and will, it seems, remain so. Even his name, when it did emerge after some years of unsigned artwork, was originally believed to be Rowland Turner, according to his editor and his agent, through whom Ron supplied all his work.

Ron's artwork emerged in the independent comic books of 1949, published by the minor Scion Ltd. His first character, Scoop Grainger, was a newspaper reporter who appeared on the first three pages of *Big Scoop*, a one-shot. Inside was a two-page episode of "The Atomic Mole," the beginning of a four-part sci-fi serial. Although this adventure of Rip Rivers and Co. and their voyage under the earth embraced a terrible flying lizard and other prehistoric monsters, it would be in the worlds of outer space that Ron would find his true forte. He soon abandoned earthbound adventures like *Big Mounty* (1949) for *Captain Sciento* and *Space Pirates* in *Star Rocket* (1950), then took a giant leap in mankind's or boykind's publishing world from the cheapo indies to George Newnes's superb series of paperback "library" comic books, published in harness with their adult magazine, *Tit-Bits*. This was the well collected and quite rare series, *Tit-Bits Science Fiction Comics* (six issues, 1953), which also carried Ron's first color work. He supplied the striking full-color covers as well as the main interior stories, including "Giants of the Second World" and "Terror of Titan."

In 1954 he began a series and sometimes serial, *Space Age* for *Lone Star Magazine*, which was so successful that the character won his own title from 1960 *Space Ace*. When the *Tit-Bits* series closed, Ron moved to the even more prestigious Amalgamated Press and began drawing for their pocketbook comic series, *Super Detective Library* (1954-1961), illustrating the 64-page adventures of Rick Random in *Kidnappers from Space*, *The Man Who Owned the Moon*, and many more. John Steele was another hero, this time more earthbound, which Ron started with *Gateway to Glory* (1960). Other "library" series followed, including *Times Five* for *Thriller Picture Library* (1962), *Claws of the Cat* for *Air Ace Picture Library* (1963), and entries for both *Battle* and *War Libraries* (1974).

Scoop Donovan, an echo of his earliest strip, began a long run of two-page strips in *Film Fun* (1961), and two fabled television sci-fi series were illustrated by him for T.V.: *Century 21*, *Stringray*, Anderson's underwater series, and *The Daleks*, a spin-off from *Doctor Who*

(1965-1966). Later came *Star Trek* for the same comic (1970). More junior serials were *Whizzer & Chips* from 1969, *The Space Accident*, and *Wonder Car* being the best remembered. Then he was back among more adult strips, drawing *Judge Dredd* for *2000 A.D.* and *Spinball Slaves* for *Action* (both 1977), and when the classic *Dan Dare* was revived for the new series of *Eagle* (1985), Ron took on his fabled rival.

D.G.

TUROK, SON OF STONE (U.S.) In 1954, tired of paying hefty fees for the licensed properties they were then publishing (*The Lone Ranger, Steve Canyon, Tarzan*, etc.), Western Publishing and its associates decided to put out some original titles of their own. Their first venture was *Turok, Son of Stone*, created by Western editor Matthew H. Murphy, which made its appearance in two stand-alone comic books in 1954 and 1955, before making it to its own title (starting with number 3) in March 1956.

Turok was an Indian warrior who, together with his youthful companion Andar, got lost in one of the limestone caverns that are so common in the American Southwest. That particular cavern happened to be the entrance to the Lost Valley, home of prehistoric tribesmen, legendary animals, and dinosaurs. The saga took off in earnest in 1957 with the arrival of Paul S. Newman as the main writer of the series. Under his guidance Turok and Andar fought fires and braved rapids, hunted dinosaurs and confronted hostile cavemen in their unending quest for an egress to the outside world. In their wanderings they also crossed paths with prehistoric pygmies, a lost Aztec tribe, and even had a close encounter of the third type with a flying saucer and its extraterrestrial occupants. The author was ably aided and abetted in his epic undertakings by Alberto Giolitti, an Italian-born artist whose vision of this lost world matched Newman's own in his sure delineation of even secondary characters and his depiction of relentless action.

The series ended in 1982; at that time the two protagonists were no closer to getting out of the Lost Valley than they had been after entering it. Exactly ten years later Valiant (now Acclaim) Comics acquired the rights to the character. After a dry run in *Magnus, Robot Fighter* number 12, he won his own comic book in June 1993. Since sales reports from Western had indicated that circulation had surged with those issues that happened to feature dinosaurs, the new publishers took note of the fact and altered the title to *Turok, Dinosaur Hunter*. They also gave the hero a disheveled look and brutish appearance that were clearly derived from *Conan the Barbarian*. This metamorphosis didn't quite meet with Newman's approval: In a letter to the trade magazine *Wizard* in 1995 he commented that the artist "was a graduate of the Blown-Hair-Across-Face School of Art;" later amplifying this statement (in a letter to this writer) by adding that he "would gladly drive a #2 pencil through the insensitive heart of this fly-by-night revampire of our comic heritage."

M.H.

TUTHILL, HARRY J. (1886-1957) Born in the slums of Chicago in 1886, the gifted, independently creative and personally reticent Harry J. Tuthill, who was to gain national fame with the wryly cynical but hilarious domestic fantasy strip, *The Bungle Family*, did not come naturally by such technical artistry as he developed.

Basically a storyteller and creator of characters, the young Tuthill strove to develop his gritty, grubby style of drawing sufficiently to carry his ideas into print.

Selling newspapers by the age of eight on the streets of Chicago, he went on the road in his early teens to sell picture frames, baking powder, soap, anything he could get into a pair of valises. Then he traveled with a medicine show from Oklahoma, a street carnival, and a larcenous corn doctor, finally winding up in St. Louis, Missouri, at 19. Here, working in a paint store, reading dime novels, and trying to perfect his dismal drawing style, he went on to toil in an ice house and a dairy before he landed a job on the *St. Louis Post-Dispatch* in 1910, where he worked as staff artist and went to art school nights on his new salary. From the *Post-Dispatch* he went to the *St. Louis Star*, continuing the political cartooning he had started on the *Post-Dispatch*.

Deciding to tackle the big city, he went to New York toward the close of World War I and was hired by the *New York Evening Mail* to begin a group of daily strips with varying titles and subjects, to be published on alternate days; one was called *Home, Sweet Home* and featured the characters and situations on which he was to build his later, famed strip about the Bungles.

When publisher Frank Munsey sold the *Evening Mail* to the *New York Telegram* in January 1925, Tuthill decided to try major syndication and launched *The Bungle Family* daily and Sunday through the McNaught Syndicate. Doing continuous narration here for the first time, Tuthill found his real talent and his long-deserved audience. Within a few years, he was earning an average of $150,000 a year, owned a vast estate in the Ozarks, a city house on Portland Place in St. Louis, and a nearby mansion in Ferguson, Missouri. He worked in the latter place, in a dark study surrounded by shelves and stacks of books, among which were the science-fiction pulp magazines on which he doted, and from which many of the fantastic themes of *The Bungle Family* were derived.

Tired of shaping much of his strip's content to syndicate demands, he folded *The Bungle Family* (which he owned) in mid-1942, then revived it eight months later to aid the war effort, doing the distribution on his own and writing the strip as he saw fit. Weary even of that by the close of the war, Tuthill once more folded his strip in June 1945, and lived out the remainder of his life quietly in Missouri, doing nothing more with the strip masterpiece which had won him the ardent devotion of millions of readers for 25 years. He died in St. Louis on January 25, 1957, one of the half-dozen finest narrative strip talents the comic strip has ever produced.

B.B.

U

UDERZO, ALBERT (1927-   ) A French cartoonist born in Italy in 1927, Albert Uderzo was taken to France by his parents while still a child. He grew up and received his schooling in the southeastern part of France, showing a drawing ability early in his childhood. In 1945 he moved to Paris and, the next year, became one of the first cartoonists on the newly created comic weekly *O.K.* His creations there include *Arys Buck*, the tale of an invincible Gaul, the forerunner of *Astérix*; *Prince Rollin*; and *Belloy l'Invulnérable* (1948).

After the demise of *O.K.* in the early 1950s, Uderzo became an advertising artist, though he never abandoned the hope of creating a successful comic feature. In 1955 he tried to revive *Belloy* without success, first in the Belgian daily *La Libre Belgique*, then in the short-lived *Pistolin* magazine. In 1956 he created *Tom et Nelly* in the weekly *Risquetout*, and in 1957 he teamed up for the first time with René Goscinny to produce *Benjamin et Benjamine* (a kid adventure strip featuring a brother and sister) for *Top-Magazine*. Neither of these ventures did too well, but the next year (1958) the Uderzo-Goscinny tandem proved luckier with *Oumpah Pah le Peau-Rouge* (Oumpah Pah the Redskin).

In 1959 the French comic weekly *Pilote* was founded by Goscinny and others. Uderzo started his collaboration in the first issue, drawing two features: the aviation strip *Michel Tanguy* (written by Jean-Michel Charlier), and *Astérix*, on texts by Goscinny. *Astérix* became extraordinarily successful, and in 1966 Uderzo left *Michel Tanguy* to devote his time to the feisty little Gaul. In the meantime he had tried (for the third time) to revive *Belloy* in *Pilote*, with Charlier as his scriptwriter. The strip lasted from 1962 to 1964 (in 1968-69 Uderzo made still another try at re-creating *Belloy*, this time in *L'Echo de la Mode*, a woman's magazine).

Unlike the egotistical and publicity-hungry Goscinny, Uderzo did not seem to have his head turned by *Astérix*'s success. He shuns interviews and devotes his time to what he likes best: drawing. Following Goscinny's death in 1977, he has assumed the writing of *Astérix* while continuing to draw the series, both with great success.

M.H.

ULYSSE (France) One of the most successful and enjoyable comic strips of the last 30 years is based on one of the oldest adventure tales known to man. In 1966 the Club Français du Livre—the French equivalent of the Book-of-the-Month Club—asked illustrator Georges Pichard and writer Jacques Lob for a comic strip adaptation of Homer's *Odyssey*. Pichard and Lob set to work, but the club turned down their version of the Homeric legend, judging it too farfetched. From that moment on *Ulysse* was to know almost as many vicissitudes as the legendary king of Ithaca. The first episode appeared in the Italian magazine *Linus* in July 1968; after an eight-month silence, the next seven sequences were published in the French monthly *Charlie* (February-November 1969); the final episodes saw the light of print only in October 1973 (until June 1974) in the magazine *Phénix*.

The first liberty that the authors took with the *Odyssey* was to restrict the narrative to the central songs of the epic, those which relate Ulysses' wanderings. Accordingly, the story opens with the Greek warriors embarking aboard ships bound for their homeland (among the returnees is Homer himself, former war correspondent on the Trojan front) and ends with Ulysses regaining his wife Penelope and his kingdom over the pretenders. Furthermore, Lob and Pichard supplied a new interpretation to the ancient legend, treating it as a science-fiction story: the gods are extraterrestrial beings, technologically more advanced

"Ulysse," Jacques Lob and Georges Pichard. © Lob and Pichard.

than the humans, and they dream up all of Ulysses' ordeals for their private amusement. Within this framework, Lob and Pichard gave free rein to their imaginations and infused new life into the old Achaean myths: thus Polyphemos the Cyclops is nothing more than an android with a deadly laser gun for his only eye; the mermaids are abducted maidens on whom Poseidon has grafted a fish tail; and the shadows that Ulysses and his companions see on their journey to Hades are pictures from the filmed archives of the history of the world.

Lob's dialogue and texts are at once respectful and whimsical, blending slang expressions with Homeric vocabulary. But it is Pichard's illustrations that best convey the sense of awe and wonder that these old legends still conjure in the hearts of modern readers. In a time when every comic book scribe claims to be a new Homer, Lob and Pichard masterfully demonstrate that there can be no greater weaver of tales than the blind poet of Hellas.

M.H.

UP FRONT (U.S.) Bill Mauldin's famed and beloved World War II panel cartoon series, *Up Front*, began with a series of cartoons about army life and routine that he drew for the *45th Division News* in 1940 while a trainee. Like the formally titled *Up Front* that followed, this early series was reprinted and paid for by the civilian press, namely the *Daily Oklahoman* (then owned by the colonel who published the *45th Division News*). Mauldin's first panel for his divisional newspaper featured the two draftees who became famous as Willie and Joe of *Up Front*. (Undated, this panel appears in Mauldin's autobiographical *The Brass Ring* on page 92.) A collection of these drawings then appeared in Mauldin's first book, published when he was 19: *Star Spangled Banter* (1941).

Continuing the *News* and *Oklahoman* work into 1942 and early 1943, and submitting other panel gags to *Yank*, Mauldin continued to develop the content and style of the later *Up Front*. Following his participation in the invasion of Sicily in his unit's first overseas action, Mauldin began to draw his powerful combat cartoons, still for the *45th Division News*, which was the first U.S. Army newspaper to be published on European soil during World War II. In the summer of 1943 a second Mauldin collection was printed in Palermo for G.I. sales: *Sicily Sketchbook*. By Christmas 1943, with Mauldin headquartered in Naples and his *News* cartoons beginning to appear in the official army newspaper, *Stars and Stripes*, he published a third book collection of cartoons: *Mud, Mules, and Mountains*.

Also in late 1943, Mauldin was transferred to the staff of *Stars and Stripes*; at about the same time, his cartoon work attracted the attention of United Feature Syndicate. Now his work could be printed daily, and the *Up Front* title came to the fore, together with the growing emphasis on the Willie and Joe characters as regulars in the panel. A final European collection of this work was published by *Stars and Stripes* in Italy in 1945; it was called *This Damn Tree Leaks*. His first professional stateside book, based on the United Feature releases, was printed by Henry Holt and Company, and called, simply, *Up Front*. (The best extant collection of all Mauldin's wartime work is found in a large volume titled *Bill Mauldin's Army*, published by William Sloane Associates in 1951.)

The end of the war led Mauldin to change the name of his popular daily panel from *Up Front* to *Sweatin' It Out* (June 11, 1945), referring to Willie and Joe awaiting their discharges. After their discharges, the panel title switched to *Willie and Joe* (July 30, 1945). When Mauldin decided to broaden his scope of comment, the title was altered once more, to *Bill Mauldin's Cartoon*, on November 19, 1945. The last few Willie and Joe gags ran here, then the two were seen no more until the Korean War led Mauldin to resurrect them briefly in another context. Effectively, *Up Front* ran in various forms and titles from late 1940 until early 1951, at least as far as the continuing Willie and Joe characters, which made the panel a comic strip feature, were concerned.

B.B.

UPSIDE DOWNS OF LITTLE LADY LOVEKINS AND OLD MAN MUFFAROO, THE (U.S.) From October 1903 to January 1905 the Dutch-American artist Gustave Verbeck (or Verbeek) produced in the Sunday supplement of the *New York Herald* one of the weirdest comic strips ever conceived, *The Upside Downs*

One day, Lovekins and Muffaroo come to a beautiful lake, just like a mirror, and on its shores they see a lovely palace, toward which they make their way.

Then he vanishes, and pretty soon they find the two mysterious closets. Muffaroo remembers the Genie's words.

"The Upside Downs," Gustave Verbeck.

of *Little Lady Lovekins and Old Man Muffaroo* (the title alone is characteristic of the whole enterprise).

The Upside Downs gave its readers two comic strips for the price of one; instead of ending with the last panel, the action of each weekly episode proceeded backwards, once the page had been turned upside down. The plot was very simple: Lady Lovekins and her mentor Muffaroo ventured forth into a fantastic universe inhabited by wild beasts, freaks, and monsters, where perils abounded and where the unusual became commonplace.

The Upside Downs was the product of an inventive but bizarre mind. Its innovative narrative technique was never emulated, and no wonder (as one critic pointed out: How Verbeek managed to work all this out without going mad passeth all understanding). Twenty-five of *The Upside Downs* weekly episodes were published in book form in 1905 by G. W. Dillingham, and 20 more were reprinted in a paperback edition by the Rajah Press in 1963.

M.H.

UTAGAWA, KUNIYOSHI (1797-1861) Japanese Ukiyo-e artist, born November 15, 1797, in Nihonbashi, Tokyo. Around 1811 Kuniyoshi Utagawa became a pupil of Tokuni Utagawa (no relation). In 1815 he illustrated his first book for Gobuji Chūshingura. All through the Bunsei era (1818-29) Kuniyoshi Utagawa labored in obscurity and often in want, until his Ukiyo-e series (Ukiyo-e refers to a series of traditional Japanese prints grouped around a central theme) *Suikoden Nishikie* (a collection of 108 pictures of illustrious heroes) made him famous as a master of Musha-e (warrior pictures).

After that time things went smoothly for Utagawa; other series followed: *Tōtō Meisho* (a group of famous landscapes) from 1832 or 1833 is probably the best known. Utagawa reached his height during the Kouka and Kaei eras (1844 to 1853), when he created *Miyamoto Musashino Kujirataiji* (a Musha-e), *Sōma no Furudairi* ("The Old Imperial Palace of Sōma"), *Myoukai Kou Goju Sanbiki* (a wordplay on the 53 coach stops along the Tokaido highway), as well as series depicting famous actors and battle scenes. Utagawa's *kyogas* (a kind of cartoon) also enjoyed great popularity in his time. Kuniyoshi Utagawa died on March 5, 1861.

Utagawa studied and mastered Western techniques along with the traditional techniques of Ukiyo-e art. He showed his versatility and inventiveness not only in his more celebrated print series, but also in his simple cartoons and many book illustrations. All of the next generation of Ukiyo-e artists (Tsukioka, Ochiai, Kawanabe, and other less famous ones) were greatly influenced by Utagawa's innovations, which directly led to the comic strip.

H.K.

V

VALENTINA (Italy) Valentina Rosselli made her appearance in the second issue of the Italian monthly *Linus* (May 1965) in a story called *La Curva de Lesmo* ("The Lesmo Curve"), drawn and written by Guido Crepax. Valentina was a sophisticated Milanese photographer, girlfriend of the enigmatic American art critic and criminologist Philip Rembrandt. Actually Rembrandt was none other than Neutron, a mutant endowed with superhuman powers, such as the ability to paralyze his enemies with a glance or to stop an engine from running. Valentina at first followed Neutron in his various adventures against the subterraneans, a race of extremely intelligent but sightless superhumans who tried at different intervals to subjugate the humans of the surface.

"Valentina," Guido Crepax. © Crepax/Milano Libri.

Little by little, however, Neutron disappeared from the story, and in 1968, in the short-lived magazine *Ali Baba*, Valentina appeared alone for the first time. The next year the strip was officially named *Valentina* in belated recognition of the heroine's dominant presence, and it soon veered away from primarily science-fiction themes toward pure fantasy, half oneiric, half hallucinatory.

In her dreams (nightmares? divagations?) of a troubling sadomasochistic nature, Valentina travels through space and time in a universe unbounded by rules or rationality. She meets, in turn, monocled Nazis, 17th-century pirates, and Czarist Cossacks, whose plaything she invariably becomes. Amidst a splendid and baroque background reeking of sensuality and decadence, Valentina is usually the victim of the most barbarous treatment: raped, whipped, quartered, impaled, hung by the thumbs, she always emerges phoenixlike from her ordeals, unmarked and apparently untouched. The author once stated that *Valentina* was an allegory of purity in the modern world. The resemblance to the Marquis de Sade's *Justine* is certainly striking and has been widely commented upon.

Valentina's remarkable story line is matched by an equally original and inventive graphic style. Crepax's compositions are greatly inspired by the author's incredibly catholic culture: side by side can be found flashes from Bergman's or Antonioni's movies, pointed reminiscences of famous paintings (Gericault's *The Raft of the Medusa*, Botticelli's *Primavera*), and tongue-in-cheek allusions to American strips (*Mandrake, Dick Tracy*). The images they conjure are also baroque in their profusion and intricacy, and the space is filled with architectonic devices and geometric precision which constantly remind the reader that this is a theatrical universe and that the protagonists are only a representation.

Valentina has been reprinted in a number of books published by Milano Libri in Italy and translated all over Europe and in the United States. In 1989-90 RAI-TV in Italy broadcast a series of *Valentina* telefilms.

M.H.

VALENTINA MELAVERDE (Italy) *Valentina Melaverde* ("Valentina Greenapple"), created by Grazia Nidasio in 1968 and one of the few Italian strips produced by a female cartoonist, was also one of the most popular features published by *Il Corriere dei Ragazzi*.

Valentina appeared as either protagonist or narrator of the adventures woven around her. She was surrounded by her family: her self-effacing parents, her brother Caesar (an automobile nut), her gossipy sister Steffi (a keen observer of Valentina's psychological and physical development), and her friends, neighbors, and people she met in everyday life. Grazia Nidasio is a sharp depicter of youth, and particularly of the world of adolescence, with its restlessness and easy enthusiasms. Valentina's vicissitudes resembled incidents in

"Valentina Melaverde," Grazia Nidasio. © Corriere dei Ragazzi.

feminine without being coy, she was warm and genuine and represented good qualities that exist in all of us. Nidasio's very original graphic style is ambiguous enough to leave many things to the reader's imagination. Nidasio received the award for best Italian cartoonist at the Lucca Comics Conference in 1972.

G.B.

VALÉRIAN (France) *Valérian, Agent Spatio-Temporel* ("Valérian, Spatio-Temporal Agent") appeared in issue 420 of the French comic magazine *Pilote* (November 1967). The strip was the product of the collaboration between cartoonist Jean-Claude Mézières and scriptwriter Pierre Christin (a professor of journalism at the University of Bordeaux who uses the pseudonym Linus).

The action takes place in 2720 A.D., at a time when the peoples of Earth have extended their power over the entire galaxy; Valérian and his lovely female assistant, Laureline, are crack operatives for the Terran Empire. Unlike the contemporary *Philémon* (which also runs in *Pilote*), *Valérian* is much more of a space-opera, with countless rocket flights, breathless escapes, and hair-raising chase and battle scenes. Linus's dialogues and scripts are inventive and entertaining, and Mézières's artwork displays a whimsical undertone (especially in the depiction of secondary characters and costumes) without being outré. There are no memorable protagonists in *Valérian* (aside from the two leading characters), but this in no way detracts from the solid construction of this fast strip.

A success almost from the start, *Valérian* has been reprinted in book form by Editions Dargaud. Still written by Christin and drawn by Mézières, it celebrated 30 years of uninterrupted publication in 1997.

M.H.

everybody's life and were made interesting enough to capture the reader's attention. She later grew up; and when she entered college she was succeeded by her kid sister Steffi in a new series of adventures starting in the 1980s in the *Corriere dei Piccoli*.

Valentina was a nice young girl with green eyes, red hair, and a freckled face. Loyal, honest, trusting, and

VALHALLA (Denmark) Valhalla, the home of the Norse gods, is the setting of *Valhalla*, a comic series that has been termed "the Astérix of the North." The series was created in 1979 by Danish comic artist Peter Madsen (born 1958) upon the initiative of Henning Kure. Along with writers Kure, Hans Rancke-Madsen, and Per Vadmand, Madsen has come up with record-

"Valérian," J. C. Mézières and Linus (Pierre Christin). © Editions Dargaud.

breaking, best-selling comic albums. The semi-humorous artwork ideally complements the well-thought-out ironic allegorical stories, which depict conflicts between very human gods and humans themselves.

The humorous epic has been exported to many European countries and even to Indonesia. From 1982 to 1986 an animated feature film based on Madsen's comics was produced. It was to become the most expensive animated feature ever produced in Denmark, costing some 30 million Danish kroner (about 7 million U.S. dollars). The film was judged the best animated feature at Cannes.

Both the albums and the movie produced spin-offs using the supporting character of Quark, a kind of troll. The comic strip *Quark* is produced by humorist Torben Osted. Swan Films, the producers of the feature film, spun off a slightly different series of animated *Quark* shorts for television. The latter were in turn spun off into a short-lived comic book version in Germany. However, the gods did not smile on the animated cartoon series. This had nothing to do with the visual quality of the shorts—the animation was impeccable—but involved content and, more important, copyright ownership of the character of Quark. The cartoon series was discontinued, though the *Quark* comic strip, which occasionally displayed a style reminiscent of Walt Kelly's *Pogo*, continued to be published.

Valhalla artist Peter Madsen was also successful with other types of comic albums, such as *Grönlandsk dagbog* ("Greenland Diary") and a realistic adaptation of the New Testament for the Danish Bible Society in 1994.

W.F.

VAMPIRELLA (U.S.) When Warren Publications decided to add a third black-and-white magazine, they broke away from the mold of their earlier *Creepy* and *Eerie* books and made the new entry a hero title of sorts. *Vampirella* number one premiered in September 1969 and introduced a character by the same name, a wench who just happened to be a beautiful vampiress. *Vampirella*'s creation was a group affair: publisher

"Vampirella," José Gonzales. © Warren Publications.

James Warren developed the character along the lines of French artist Jean-Claude Forest's *Barbarella*; writer Forrest Ackerman plotted the series' early direction; and artists Frank Frazetta (design), Trina Robbins (costume), and Tom Sutton (pencils and inks) brought the character to life.

Ackerman's origin story explained that the black-tressed Vampirella was a native of Drakulon, a dying planet where blood replaced water as a life-sustaining element. Vampirella took refuge on Earth to prey on human blood for survival, and most of her subsequent adventures have centered on her constant search for plasma or a suitable substitute. Artistically, the Frazetta-Robbins-Sutton team produced a lithe, raven-haired beauty of considerable proportions. She wore a skimpy red costume, a serpentine bracelet, black boots, and a gold bat insignia about her pubic area. A live bat, perilously perched atop her outstretched finger, was an occasional companion.

The early Ackerman scripts were heavily tongue-in-cheek, but Archie Goodwin later abruptly reversed the mood. He emphasized intrigue and human interaction over humor, his Vampirella always conscience-wracked whenever she took a life to survive. Goodwin also introduced Conrad and Adam Van Helsing, described as descendants of the Van Helsing in Bram Stoker's *Dracula*. Like their ancestor, the Van Helsings were vampire hunters, but Adam eventually fell in love with his quarry. After Goodwin's departure, John Cochran, T. Casey Brennan, and others handled the stories.

Tom Sutton handled most of the early *Vampirella* artwork in a crisp, fast-paced style that emphasized continuity before sex appeal. But when José Gonzales replaced him, the strip became more overtly sexual, an obvious attempt to entice Warren's considerable teen-aged male readership. Though he was a more accomplished illustrator than Sutton, Gonzales's work suffered because he was a poor storyteller and his ornate panels rarely helped the story's continuity.

J.B.

The last issue (number 112) of Warren's *Vampirella Magazine* appeared in March 1983. The title was then acquired by Harris Publications, which released issue number 113 in 1988; this turned out to be the last issue of the magazine. Since 1991 Vampirella has appeared in a number of miniseries published by Harris. Among the contributors have been artists Louis Small Jr., Joe Quesada, Rudy Nebres, and Jimmy Palmiotti, and writers Warren Ellis and James Robinson.

M.H.

VAN BUREN, RAEBURN (1891-1987) American artist, born January 12, 1891, in Pueblo, Colorado, the son of George Lincoln and Luella la Mar van Buren. The young van Buren, showing an early talent for drawing, joined the art staff of the *Kansas City Star* immediately after graduation from Central High School in Kansas City, Missouri, where the family had moved.

Van Buren called the *Star* the best school for pen-and-ink illustrators in the country at that time (1909) because its owner, Colonel Nelson, eschewed photographs and half-tone drawings. After four years as a sketch artist, van Buren traveled to New York to take courses at the Art Students League and do freelance illustrations.

The former endeavor ended after a few frustrating weeks; classes with Thomas Fogarty's father and oth-

Raeburn van Buren, magazine illustration.

ers seemed to be too slow-paced and rudimentary for the talented van Buren. Freelancing was more fertile and rewarding, however. Van Buren became a frequent contributor to *Life* (for which he had been drawing for several years already), *Puck, Judge,* and Street and Smith publications. The pulp publication *Smith's Magazine* was the first national periodical to use a van Buren illustration (his work for the humorous journals consisted of captioned cartoons).

Van Buren, whose early work betrayed no sign of his youth or relative lack of training, soon became one of the country's leading illustrators. His credits include 368 stories for the *Saturday Evening Post,* 127 for *Collier's,* and numerous others for *Redbook, Cosmopolitan, Green Book, Esquire, The New Yorker,* and *McCalls,* along with newspaper illustrations for King Features Syndicate and the McClure Syndicate.

In the mid-1930s, cartoonist Al Capp offered van Buren the drawing duties on a comic strip creation, and van Buren accepted on the strength of Capp's prediction that radio would kill the big magazines. Thus *Abbie an' Slats* was born in 1937, and van Buren added splendidly to the unfortunately small list of accomplished illustrators in the comics; Alex Raymond and Frank Godwin were brothers in this small band.

Van Buren's art was always distinctive, individualistic, and at home with the strictures and conventions of the comic strip. His adaptability was attributable in part to his professionalism and in part to the guidance of Capp, but mostly it reflected his overwhelming talent and genuine concern for *Abbie an' Slats.* His heroes were handsome and dashing; his heroines racy and winsome; and incidental characters were humorous or villainous to the extreme as the situation demanded.

Van Buren's long work in illustration gave the comic strip a constantly fresh, breezy, and narrative feel. Although some of his magazine work was in crayon, his medium was pen and ink, and he was a master of blocking, shading, vignettes, and close-ups.

He spent his last years in retirement, dividing his time between his homes in Florida and Great Neck, Long Island, where he died on December 29, 1987.

R.M.

VANCE, WILLIAM (1935-   ) Belgian cartoonist, born September 8, 1935, at Anderlecht, near Brussels. After three years of study at the Royal Academy of Fine Arts in Brussels, from which he graduated in 1956 with a first prize in drawing, William Vance started his career as a commercial artist for an advertising agency. In 1962 he began his collaboration with the comic weekly *Tintin,* to which he contributed a number of illustrations before creating his first comic strip, *Howard Flynn* (a sea-adventure story with a script by Yves Duval), in 1964. The next year, again for *Tintin,* Vance produced a Western, *Ray Ringo,* which met with only small success.

In spite of these false starts, William Vance had established himself as one of the more intriguing adventure strip artists, and in 1967 he started on the two series that he is most noted for: *Bruno Brazil* and *Bob Morane. Bruno Brazil* (written by Michel Regnier, alias Greg, under his pseudonym of Louis Albert) recounts the hair-raising exploits of a small group of dedicated crime-fighters, the "Cayman Commando"; *Bob Morane,* the comic strip adaptation of a popular series of adventure novels written by Henri Vernes, was first published in the woman's weekly *Femmes d'Aujourd'hui* before going over to the comic magazine *Pilote.* In 1984 he started doing, on texts by Jean Van Hamme, the spy thriller *XIII,* which is still ongoing; and in 1991 he took up the drawing of Gir's *Marshal Blueberry.*

William Vance's style is virile and vigorous, and his compositions, always to the point, make up in energy what they lack in subtlety. *Bruno Brazil,* particularly, has shown a marked improvement in recent times and can now be considered one of the top strips in its category.

M.H.

VANDERSTEEN, WILLY (1913-   ) Willy Vandersteen (full name: Willibrord Jan Frans Maria Vandersteen), Flemish-Belgian comic artist, writer, and producer, was born in 1913 in Antwerp, in the Flemish part of Belgium. He grew up in Antwerp and entertained his friends by drawing comics on the sidewalk, but they were always washed away by the rain, as they were drawn with chalk. He got his ideas from reading many books and comics of the time, like *Kindervriend* ("Children's Friend"), a kids' magazine that included reprints of English comic strips. In 1923 he was impressed by *Totor, chef de la patrouille des Hannetons,* Hergé's first comic strip. While still in school and dreaming of adventure, he started taking evening courses at the Antwerp Academy of Art at the age of 15 and continued until he was 24. (Some sources state that he started taking the courses at 13.) While working as decorator for the department store Innovation, he was doing a ladies' coats showcase when he read an American fashion magazine and there found an article titled "Comics in Your Life." This put him on the road toward creating comics, but before anything could come of it, he found himself in the role of ministerial statistician.

A chance meeting with an editor of the weekly *Bravo* led to his contributing comic strips to that magazine. He wrote and drew comics like *Sindbad de Zeerover* ("Sindbad the Pirate") and *Piwo* starting in 1943. In 1944 he added *Lancelot* and *Tori* to the comics published in *Bravo.* Early in 1945 he created another series, this time for newspaper publication. It did not begin until after the war had ended, however. Thus, *De Avonturen van Rikki en Wiske* ("The Adventures of Rikki and Wiske") started in late 1945 in the newspaper *De Nieuwe Gids*, which was later retitled *De Nieuwe Standaard* and still later, simply *De Standaard*. Despite the strip's success, it was felt that Rikki looked too much like Tintin and was therefore replaced by the orphan boy Suske. This also helped eliminate the age difference that had existed between Rikki and the girl Wiske. *Suske and Wiske* laid the groundwork for Vandersteen's success, which led to the Vandersteen studios and a number of comic strips, including *De familie Snoek* (1946), *Tijl Uilenspiegel* (1951), *Bessy* (1951), *Prinske* (1953), *De rode Ridder* (1959), *Karl May* (1961), *Jerom* (1963), *Biggles* (1964), and *Safari* (1969).

Vandersteen's style was largely influenced by Hergé, but over the years may have been hurt by over-industrialization. In part this may have been caused by foreign sales of his comics. Some of his features—for example, *Bessy*—have had more episodes printed in Germany than in his own country. It is understandable that putting out a comic book like *Bessy* week after week starts wearing both plots and art thin. On the whole, however, Vandersteen's work is a significant contribution to the history of European comic strips.

W.F.

"Vanilla and the Villains," Darrell McClure. © King Features Syndicate.

VANILLA AND THE VILLAINS (U.S.) The last of the major variants on the theme of top-hatted stage villainy in the comic strip, Darrell McClure's daily *Vanilla and the Villains* began in several Hearst newspapers on September 10, 1928. Unlike the relatively sober, almost straight *Hairbreadth Harry* and *Minute Movies* melodramas of the 1920s (Kahles had abandoned his earlier fantasy for *Cat and the Canary*-style antics, while Wheelan was only slightly exaggerating the content of current film shockers), McClure's *Vanilla and the Villains* was wild, all-out, farcical nonsense, in a Marx Brothers–*Mad* magazine vein. Introduced in the first panel, Vanilla Graingerfield is shown riding a white horse amid a throng of worshipful plantation darkies in an Old South setting. (They are, as we shortly see, regularly horsewhipped into worshipfulness by Vanil-

la's wicked stepfather, Bourbon Mash.) A villain, Lambert Leer, tempts the stepfather into selling Vanilla's plantation and darkies for a sack of gold, only to be thwarted by Vanilla's poetry-reading but heroic boyfriend, Stonewall, and a bit later the U. S. Marines. McClure's comic artistry and sense of narrative make great fun out of all this stereotyped twaddle, and his drawings of such bizarre concepts as Lambert Leer and the Sinister Six all inside an absurdly elongated horse disguise (with a broomstick tail) are as visually memorable as anything on the comic pages of the time.

The art and story line became increasingly surreal as the strip rolled through its first year (McClure's vision of Russia in the 19th century is as fancifully funny as Walt Kelly's in a *Pogo* skit on czarist Moscow 20 years later), but McClure's pace was not as furious as in the first months. It is hard to say whether, when the strip was folded at the end of 1929 (with McClure going on to undertake *Little Annie Rooney* for Hearst's King Features), it could have continued its inspired foolery indefinitely. But while it lasted, *Vanilla and the Villains* was a tiny epic of concentrated spice and deft idiocy. It was a lively slice across the face of the average comic page of the time (overladen as it often was with domestic bickering and shopgirl romance), and it anticipated the avalanche of serious adventure and suspense strips shortly to come.

B.B.

VATER UND SOHN (Germany) *Vater und Sohn* ("Father and Son") was created in 1934 by Erich Ohser under his pen name E.O. Plauen (combining the initials of his name with that of his hometown). Ohser had drawn cartoons for various newspapers and had illustrated the books of Erich Kästner. Having been introduced to the Berlin scene by Kästner ultimately led to Ohser's creating *Vater und Sohn* for publication in *Berliner Illustrirte*.

Vater und Sohn unquestionably belongs to the field of modern humorous drawing in Germany. Millions of readers followed the pranks and adventures of the bald-headed, mustachioed father and his round-headed, tousle-haired young son. Contemporary critics felt that Ohser's father-and-son stories were a humorous product of a specifically German nature, but they were proved wrong by the international appeal documented by reprints all over the world.

Ohser's work is a perfect example of the pantomime comic strip that does not make use of words except for subtitles. Thus, one strip from circa 1935, titled "Similarity (realization reached on visiting a zoo)," has father and son walking through the zoo. When a walrus lookalike breaks the surface of a pond, the flustered father ends the visit.

Father and son are full of love for each other and are devoid of any evil. Whenever dark clouds loom, they find the silver lining of easy reconciliation. Theirs is a quiet, sometimes wistful kind of humor that has lost none of its charm over the decades. *Vater und Sohn* was intended as a gift to youth, and children readily approved of it. They sent many enthusiastic letters, and when Erich Ohser occasionally visited a school, he was immediately surrounded by young admirers who asked him to give their regards to his real-life son Christian. As an introduction by Kurt Kusenberg in one of the *Vater und Sohn* books said: "Children realized that a kind man who loved nature, animals, pranks and the cunning little tricks just like they did was tending

"Vater and Sohn," E. O. Plauen (Erich Ohser). © Südverlag Constanz.

with loving care a corner of childhood paradise—their paradise that once also had been his."

Ironically, this gentle soul was driven to commit suicide in March 1944 after being arrested by the Gestapo following a denunciation for alleged defeatist remarks in an air-raid shelter. It makes the death of the quietly humorous creator of *Vater und Sohn* all the more deplorable.

W.F.

VELTER, ROBERT (1909-1991) One of the most prolific of French comics creators as well as one of the least celebrated, Robert Velter was born in Paris on February 9, 1909. He wanted to pursue art as a career, but family circumstances forced him to go to work at age 16, and he became a steward aboard an ocean liner of the French Line. He drew and painted during the long days and nights spent at sea; and his love of art and of the sea was to inform many of his later comics creations. It was during his many layovers in New York that he discovered the American newspaper strips—*Bringing Up Father, Barney Google, Moon Mullins*—that influenced his style. So enamored did he become with cartooning that he quit his seafaring job and in 1934-35 became an assistant to Martin Branner on *Winnie Winkle*.

His break came after his return to France in the mid-1930s. Under the pseudonym "Bozz," he created *Mr. Subito*, a daily newspaper strip distributed by the French syndicate Opera Mundi. The strip, about the

mishaps and contretemps suffered by a meek, middle-aged man always nattily attired in a black coat and wearing a bowler, was told in pantomime. It met with success from the start. The character's renown prompted the publisher of the newly established children's weekly *Le Journal de Toto* to call on Velter to create the paper's emblematic character: Toto, characteristically, was a spunky cabin boy who had many adventures at sea. Signed "Rob-Vel," the feature occupied the front page (in color) of the publication throughout its brief existence, from 1937 to 1940.

Again signing himself Rob-Vel, the artist created his most famous character, one that still lives today, Spirou, for the newfangled and eponymous Belgian weekly. The little hero was a bellboy this time, and the mix of humor and adventure proved irresistible to the paper's young readers. For the same publication Velter also originated *Bibor and Tribar*, about (what else?) the adventures of two rambunctious sailors.

Mobilized during World War II, Velter was wounded in 1940. Because of his wounds, which made it difficult for him to hold a brush, he sold the rights to *Spirou* in 1943. He resumed his cartooning career after the war, reviving *Mr. Subito* (which he had had to abandon in 1940) in January 1946. When his strip ceased publication in 1969, he went on to create a number of short-lived series. He then was asked to take over *Le Professeur Nimbus*, which he turned out under the house pseudonym "J. Darthel" from 1973 to 1977. He retired in the late 1970s, devoting his retire-

Robert Velter (Bozz), "M. Subito." © Opera Mundi.

ment to giving interviews and writing his lighthearted memoirs in order to counteract the oblivion into which his work had fallen. He died in 1991, feisty to the end.

M.H.

VERBECK (a.k.a. VERBEEK), GUSTAVE (1867-1937) American artist of either Dutch or Belgian origin, born in 1867 in Nagasaki, Japan. His father, Guido Verbeck, born in what is now Belgium at a time when it was a part of the kingdom of the Netherlands, was a missionary who headed the school in Tokyo that later became Japan's Imperial University. Gustave Verbeck grew up in Japan and later went to Paris to study art; while in Paris he worked as a cartoonist and illustrator for a number of European newspapers.

Around the turn of the century Verbeck immigrated to the United States, where an immigration officer miswrote his name as Verbeek on his official papers. Subsequently the artist signed his works with either name (his children were later officially named Verbeek), but Verbeck is the more commonly accepted spelling.

In the United States, Verbeck did illustration work for *McClure's*, *Harper's*, *American Magazine*, and *The Saturday Evening Post*. He later joined the staff of the *New York Herald*, for which he contributed three weirdly original series: *The Upside Downs of Little Lady Lovekins and Old Man Muffaroo* (1903), whose novel technique was never imitated; the nightmarish *Terrors of the Tiny Tads* (1905); and *The Loony Lyrics of Lulu* (1910), about a weird professor and his no-less-peculiar niece Lulu on a monster hunt.

In the 1920s Verbeck left the newspaper field and devoted himself to engraving and painting (several exhibitions of his works were held in New York and elsewhere). He died in New York in 1937.

Gustave Verbeck is one of the early comic strip artists whose work deserves to be saved from oblivion. His creations are full of a dark and sardonic humor that at times sounds curiously modern, and of a broad, fanciful penwork that seems deliciously passe.

M.H.

VERBEEK, GUSTAVE *see* Verbeck, Gustave.

VIC FLINT (U.S.) A routine detective strip, *Vic Flint* was introduced by NEA to its subscribing newspapers on Sunday, January 6, 1946 (the daily started the next day).

Flint was originally drawn by John Lane, with credit for the story line going to Michael O'Malley. O'Malley was in reality a cover name for the dozen or so writers who worked on the strip throughout its history. Lane was suceeded on July 31, 1950, by Dean Miller, who contributed some uninspired artwork. He, in turn, was followed by Art Sansom, who, fortunately for NEA, was as versatile with the pen as Russ Winterbotham was with his typewriter. The last artist to work on the feature was, ironically, the son of the first artist, John Lane.

The daily ended on January 7, 1956, exactly 10 years after its introduction, but the Sunday continued. On August 8, 1965, the title was changed to *The Good Guys*, with art by John Lane and a new, humorous angle and continuity by J. Harvey Bond (Russ Winterbotham). The feature expired on March 12, 1967.

Flint and *Good Guys*, especially the former, were designed as NEA's answers to other syndicates' successes in detective genre. But Flint was too routine, too

stereotyped, too much the actor in a plot without interesting costars, to last. The feature went virtually unsold in papers that were not in the Scripps-Howard chain or heavy subscribers to other NEA features.

R.M.

"Vic Jordan," Paul Norris. © Field Newspaper Syndicate.

VIC JORDAN (U.S.) On December 1, 1941, a new kind of adventure strip appeared in the newly founded New York City newspaper *PM*. It was written by two staff men under the pseudonym Payne, and its first artist was Elmer Wexler.

Vic Jordan was the first newspaper strip depicting the struggle of the underground movement in Europe against Nazi occupation. Vic was originally a press agent for a French show that was closed down by the Germans. Among the cast was a girl who doubled as a spy for the British, and soon Vic found himself involved in the fight against the Germans. Bridges were blown up, trains derailed, and occupation troops ambushed in these grim tales of sabotage, violence, and torture.

Several times the Gestapo tried to infiltrate the underground group now led by Vic, but they were always outsmarted. As the months passed (and the war deepened), the strip became more and more realistic, showing the horrors of the occupation as well as the acts of heroism of the resistance fighters.

In 1942 Wexler enlisted in the U.S. Marines and was succeeded by Paul Norris, who was himself drafted in 1943. There followed David Moneypenny, a staff artist, and finally Bernard Bailey. The drawing, however, was always incidental to the spirit of the strip, with its stated sympathy for the occupied peoples of Europe.

On April 30, 1945, *Vic Jordan* last appeared, with the following epitaph: "The victory in Europe has been reflected on our comic page. *Vic Jordan*, our first comic strip, which was devoted to dramatizing the fight against fascism in the underground of Europe, has bowed to the fact that military victory is at hand. In the Sunday paper Vic made his exit. He was wounded, you remember, and has come back home for a rest."

M.H.

"Vidocq," Hans G. Kresse. © Hans G. Kresse.

VIDOCQ (Netherlands) *Vidocq*, created by Hans G. Kresse, one of the big three among Dutch comic artists, was started in issue number 32 of the Dutch comics weekly *Pep* in 1965. Vidocq, the first detective in the world and founder of the French Sûreté, fits in nicely with Kresse's other historic heroes or, one should say, heroes whose adventures take place in a certain period of history, therefore making necessary extensive research if the artist wants to accurately re-create the mood of the times.

A lesser artist might get bogged down with all the research necessary for a historical strip like *Vidocq*. He might even feel tempted to draw the strip in a kind of academic realism that is sure to discourage a large part of the public. Not so Kresse. Although he can offer proof of the accuracy of details incorporated into *Vidocq*, he does not let himself get carried away with it. Instead, he concentrates on the storytelling and the dramatic effects. As might be expected, Kresse uses the interplay of light and shadow to perfection, just as in *Eric de Noorman*. Compared with *Eric de Noorman*, one cannot help but feel a kind of rejuvenation in Kresse's line work, and his use of speech balloons, unlike his earlier work, gives his art a somewhat changed look.

Nor does the writing fall behind the extraordinary artwork. One must even point out that Kresse has spiced the stories with humorous situations in order to fit in with the character of the French sleuth. The fact that the historic Vidocq is well known may have quickened the acceptance of the strip, and the Vidocq television series did not hurt it either.

The strip, which originally appeared in *Pep* magazine, was later reprinted in a comic book format, was published in other countries, and has since been reprinted in book form.

W.F.

VIRUS, IL MAGO DELLA FORESTA MORTA (Italy) Ten years after the appearance of *Buck Rogers*, the Italian comics produced their second science-fiction strip, *Virus, il Mago della Foresta Morta* ("Virus, the Magician of the Dead Forest"), written by the prolific scriptwriter Federico Pedrocchi, who, in 1937, had produced *Saturno Contro la Terra*. The artwork of Virus was done by Walter Molino, and the feature appeared in 1939 in the pages of the comic weekly *L'Audace*.

The chief character was a mad scientist, a not-uncommon figure in the fiction of the 1930s. Together with his mysterious Indu servant Tirmud, he schemed to conquer the world. This evil genius had his laboratory in the heart of a petrified forest. There, protected by an insurmountable electromagnetic barrier, Virus built a machine capable of calling the dead back to life. His plans were foiled by the handsome Italian hero Roberto and his youthful nephew Piero, who defeated Virus's army of ancient Egyptians.

Virus is one of the best-plotted and best-written science-fiction strips of the 1930s. Molino was especially brilliant in this tale of the strange and supernatural, his penwork rivaling the best efforts of the American cartoonists of the period in impact and intricacy. A second episode, "The Pole V," was published in 1940, after which the feature was suspended. In 1946, a third (and last) episode, "The Master of Darkness," appeared in the weekly *Topolino*, drawn this time by Antonio Canale. The effort was laudable but did not approach the high standard of the first two stories.

Considered today as one of the high points of Italian comic art, Virus's first two episodes have been amply reprinted: in the series *Albi d'Oro* in the 1940s, and more recently in the monthlies *Sgt. Kirk* and *L'Avventuroso*, as well as in the collection *Grandi Albi dell'Avventuroso*. In 1971 the definitive version of all three episodes of *Virus* appeared in the prestigious anthology *Le Grande Firme del Fumetto Italiano* ("The Great Names of the Italian Comics").

G.B.

VOIGHT, CHARLES A. (1887-1947) An American artist born in Brooklyn, New York, in 1887, Charles Voight was an accomplished illustrator and premier delineator of pretty women. Voight was primarily a cartoonist and is best remembered in comics for his long-running strip *Betty*.

The young Voight left school at 14 and joined the art staff of the *New York World*, where he eventually became sports cartoonist. His first strip was *Petey Dink*, which survived in different forms through the years but began in the *Boston Traveler* in 1908. He was later on the art staffs of the *Chicago Evening Post* and the *New York Evening Mail* before joining the New York Tribune Syndicate at its formation in 1919.

During his early period he was heavily involved with advertising art, refining his style and gaining a reputation; he appears to have been influenced by Wallace Morgan. He also drew a comic strip series for the old *Life* magazine in the late 1910s called *The Optimist*.

He contracted with the Tribune Syndicate to draw *Betty*, a pretty girl strip, evidently intended to compete with such entries as *Polly* and *Boots*. His work on the strip, like his work in advertising and his illustration in the major magazines, was impressive.

Voight's mastery of the pen inspires awe. His girls are the prettiest in the comics. If he had a flaw as a comic artist, it was his inclusion of panoramic scenes (usually a landscape of bathing beauties or café cuties) and the sublimation of the story progression. But this became a predictable device—also a trademark—and was forgivable because, though it might have interrupted the narrative, it was never visually offensive. Moreover, he had a real sense of humor (unlike such

"Voltar," Alfredo Alcala. © Alfredo Alcala.

other penmen as Gibson), and his pages were always lively and funny.

Voight left the Herald-Tribune Syndicate in 1942 to work independently. He died in Brooklyn on February 10, 1947.

R.M.

VOLTAR (Philippines) In the history of the comic book medium, most of the features that have become classics have been team efforts, with several people doing different facets of the production: scripting, breakdowns, pencilling, inking, lettering, publishing. The exceptions to this method, of course, are the underground comix, which are generally one-shot affairs slanted toward a specific audience. *Voltar* is unique in that it was a continuing series geared toward mass readership, yet it was written, laid out, pencilled, inked, lettered, and published by one man, Alfredo P. Alcala. The brush used to ink many *Voltar* pages was a special fountain-brush invented by Alcala, thus making the series even more noteworthy. Aside from the circumstances of its production, what makes the series stand out is the work itself. It is an astonishing display of sustained, artistic endeavor. Every chapter contains a spectacular center spread. Each panel is embellished in an etching style that rivals the works of the old masters. Inch for inch, it is probably the most detailed art ever to appear in comic books.

Voltar is the main character of Alcala's heroic epic. This graphic-novel encompasses elements of myths, legends, and actual history. It is high adventure dealing with extraordinary beasts and creatures such as winged unicorns, satyrs, and a white eagle. Ancient cities are sacked and plundered by wild tribesmen and barbarians, while young warriors perform deeds of bravery and valor. Love, hate, joy, sorrow, fear, and anger are expressed by the various characters in this tremendous saga. Plots and subplots are intertwined as the protagonist sets forth to seek his destiny.

The illustrations convey the feeling and mood of antiquity and bring to the viewer a glimpse of the beauty and splendor of the mythological past. The superb rendering of the young damsels and the youthful warriors provides a strong contrast to the withered and wrinkled rendition of the older characters. The brooding landscapes are filled with gnarled and twisted trees, ominous cliffs, mysterious caves, dark clouds, and the constant presence of vultures.

Voltar began in the first issue of *Alcala Fight Komix*, which appeared on July 9, 1963. With it were *Gagamba* ("The Spider"), by Virgilio and Nestor Redondo; *Virgo*, by Jim Fernandez; *Siopawman*, by Larry Alcala; *Alamid* ("Wild Cat"), by Tony Caravana; *Kagubatang Bato* ("The Rock of the Wilderness"), by Ruben Yandoc; *Kasalanan Daw* ("The Fault"), by Menny Martin; *Kapitan Limbas* ("Bird of Prey"), by Ding S. Castrillo; and *Ang Pagbabago Ng Mga San data* ("The Evolution of Weapons"), a three-page feature also by Alfredo Alcala.

For several years *Voltar* dominated the annual art awards presentation sponsored by the Society of Philippine Illustrators and Cartoonists. In 1971 a *Voltar* illustration was exhibited in a fantasy and science-fiction event that was held in the United States. The artwork took first place in the heroic fantasy division. And in 1974 *Voltar* was featured in *The Hannes Bok Memorial Showcase of Fantasy Art*, a book that compiled many of the finest works in the field of fantasy. It was edited by Emil Petaja. In the United States the feature appeared in the comic book *Rook* between 1979 and 1981, with texts by Bill Dubay.

O.J.

WAGS, THE DOG THAT ADOPTED A MAN (U.S.)

Billy Marriner, an emerging comic genius who cut his teeth on the pages of *Puck*, created *Wags, the Dog that Adopted a Man* for T. C. McClure in 1905.

McClure was one of a handful of protean syndicates that pre-printed sections of color comics for small hinterland papers, which bought them and surprinted their logotypes. Consequently, *Wags* and other Marriner strips achieved wide circulation in many markets.

Although another Marriner creation, *Sambo and His Funny Noises*, enjoyed greater longevity, *Wags* seems to have caught the public's imagination and deserves to be remembered for at least one contribution: It was among the first strips (*Buster Brown and Tige* was another) to have an animal, as an animal, talk.

Wags was a cute pup (all of Marriner's creations were cute without being syrupy) who attached himself to an animal-hater. Every week Wags succeeded in foiling My Nice Man's desperate efforts to lose him, or even to kill him. *Wags* was the only Marriner strip in which an adult figures prominently or permanently, and its style was in Marriner's striking mixture of thin, wispy lines; juxtaposition of blacks and masterfully used white space; and an enchanting atmosphere, of a slight distortion, that pervaded the whole work. *Wags* almost always ran full page.

Evidently Marriner tired of the one-gag strip and gave up *Wags* in 1908. But the public wouldn't have it, and Wags continued his efforts to adopt a master for several years thereafter, courtesy of boilerplate syndicates that reprinted old comic pages and distributed them to rural papers.

R.M.

WAKEFIELD, GEORGE WILLIAM (1887-1942)

British cartoonist and illustrator George William "Billy" Wakefield was born in Hoxton, London, in 1887. He was educated locally, winning a scholarship to Camberwell School of Arts and Crafts. He submitted cartoon jokes to Edwardian comic papers and was published in *Ally Sloper's Half Holiday* in 1906, then regularly in *Scraps* from 1907. He began to specialize in idealized girls, sweet yet saucy, and illustrated the spicy serial *Peggy the Peeress* in *Photo Bits* (1910). An interest in fairy-tale fantasy showed in his superbly detailed illustrations to *Prince Pippin*, a serial for *Young Folks' Tales* (1911). He also drew King Edward VII lying in state at Westminster Abbey for one of the illustrated papers (1910). His first strip, *Baron De Cuff and the Hon. Samuel Shiney* (1908), appeared in *The Comic Companion*, a pullout supplement to the weekly magazine *You and I*. This was followed by *Tap Room Tales* (1908) in *Scraps*. An introduction to Frederick Cordwell, an important editor at Amalgamated Press, led to an association with children's comics that lasted until his death.

Gertie Goodsort (1911), his first strip for Cordwell's new weekly, *Fun & Fiction*, featured the kind of flapper he drew so well, and this led to *Gertie and Gladys*, a flapper double-act, in *Merry and Bright* (1911). When

George Wakefield, "Laurel and Hardy." © Amalgamated Press.

Cordwell started *The Favorite Comic*, Wakefield contributed *Wott and Nott* (1913), then returned to girls with *Gertie Gladeyes* in *Firefly* (1914) and *Flossie and Phyllis the Fascinating Flappers* in *Favorite* (1914). In 1915 came a change of sex, and Wakefield illustrated the long-running *Boys Friend* serial *Rookwood*, by Frank Richards. He served in the 6th Lancers during World War I and was invalided out, returning to comics in 1917 with *Carrie the Girl Chaplin* for *Merry and Bright*. A number of new characters for this weekly and for *Butterfly* followed, until a new trend in his career was sparked in 1920.

Silent movies had so established themselves that Fred Cordwell combined them with comics and came up with a new weekly, *Film Fun*. Wakefield set the style of the paper, tapping an amazing ability to capture film stars' likenesses without resorting to caricature. He drew the strip adventures of *Baby Marie Osborne*, *Mack Swain*, and *Ben Turpin* for *Film Fun* (1920), then *Ford Sterling* and *Fatty Arbuckle* for *Kinema Comic* (1920), a companion paper, followed by *Jackie Coogan* (1921), some footballers for the short-running *Sports Fun* (1922), *Larry Semon* (1923), *Wesley Barry* (1924), *Grock* (1929), *Walter Forde* (1930), *Laurel and Hardy* (his best-remembered series, from 1930 to his death), *Joe E. Brown* (1933), *Wheeler and Woolsey* (1934), *Max Miller* (1938), *George Formby* (1938), and *Lupino Lane* (1939).

Other artists on the comics were required to model their style after Wakefield's, including his son, Terence "Terry" Wakefield, who took over many of his father's characters. Extremely prolific, yet extremely detailed and meticulous in finish, Wakefield also contributed melodramatic illustrations to stories in *Bullseye* (1931) and *Surprise* (1932), as well as adapting complete movies into strips for *Film Picture Stories* (1934), which were his only attempts at dramatic strips. He also drew the full-color series *The Jolly Rover* on the front page of *My Favourite* (1928), and *Freddie Flap and Uncle Bunkle* (1934) and *Teacher Trotter* (1935), both full pages, for *Sparkler* and *Comic Cuts*. In his spare time he executed excellent oil paintings. He died in Norwich Hospital in 1942 at the age of 54. For more than a decade his strips were reprinted in *Film Fun Annual*.

D.G.

WALKER, ADDISON MORTON (1923-   ) Mort Walker, one of America's most successful cartoonists by any yardstick, was born in El Dorado, Kansas, on September 3, 1923, and moved shortly thereafter with his family to Kansas City, Missouri.

A few lessons of the inevitable Landon Course was all the art training Walker received. Other schooling included elementary education in Kansas City public schools and enough various courses at Washington University and the University of Missouri to graduate with a B.A. in Humanities from the latter institution after World War II. Walker had been drafted out of college in 1943 and rose to the rank of first lieutenant, seeing action with the infantry in Italy.

After the war and college, he married and moved to New York as an editor with Dell. His experience as editor of the University of Missouri's *Show Me* humor magazine helped as Walker took charge of *1000 Jokes*, *TV Stars*, and a revived *Ballyhoo*, with another struggling cartoonist-editor, Charles Saxon.

Eventually his freelance cartooning superseded editorial activities and by the late 1940s he was recog-

nized as the most-published gag cartoonist. John Bailey, the *Saturday Evening Post*'s cartoon editor, suggested college kids as a theme and soon Spider, named after a fraternity brother of Walker's, was a regular character in his cartoons.

The syndication bug came to Walker in 1950, and he peddled *Spider* to King Features, which bought it—the last strip, in fact, personally approved by William Randolph Hearst. Two of the minor suggestions that Walker accepted, however, were taking Spider off the campus and putting him on an army base, and changing his name.

The name change was deemed necessary because King had just bought *Big Ben Bolt*, a major character of which was Spider Haines. Walker made an entomological switch and came up with Beetle. Soon the surname of the *Post* editor was added as a bow of gratitude and alliteration, and *Beetle Bailey* saw the light of day on September 3, 1950, Walker's 27th birthday. The Sunday page followed a year later.

The strip was an immediate success; Walker won the NCS Reuben award in 1954, the first of many other awards from NCS, the Banshees, and other organizations. He has served as NCS president and in other capacities, notably as editor of the newsletter, the magazine, and the periodic album.

Other efforts included his Museum of Cartoon Art in Greenwich, Connecticut, which opened in the summer of 1974. Another manifestation of Walker's life-long love of the art has been his association with other strips. He is the creator and author of *Hi and Lois*, *Mrs. Fitz's Flats*, *Sam's Strip*, and *Boner's Ark*.

Mort Walker's major contribution to the art is graphic, although his simple gags soon became the formula for many humor strips since the 1950s. He has always kept his artwork clean, stark, and simple. Many have criticized the lack of detail and seeming standardization of poses, but the success of *Beetle Bailey* speaks for itself.

The flavor of his strips can best be described as "stylized bigfoot"—modern and slick, but preserving the comic conventions of Frank Willard and other boyhood favorites of Walker's. The combined lists of Walker's various strips make him the most published comic strip artist in the world.

R.M.

Walker's latter creations have been *Sam and Silo* with Jerry Dumas (begun 1977); *The Evermores*, a historical feature done in collaboration with Johnny Sajem (1982-86); and *Gamin and Patches*, a kid strip he signed Addison and which Bill Janocha illustrated (1987-88). The International Museum of Cartoon Art, which Walker considers to be his greatest accomplishment, opened in Boca Raton, Florida, in March 1996. His sons Greg and Neal are also cartoonists.

M.H.

WALKER, BRIAN (1926-   ) One of the most successful comic strip artists to turn to the form late in life is Brian Walker, whose style—lively yet heavy in thick brushwork—has graced many comics since 1967, when Walker was 40. Previously he had been busy in many artistic fields, including calligraphy, painting, engraving, illustration, writing, and furniture design.

Brian Walker was born in Brislington, Somerset, on March 22, 1926. Her son's obvious affection for art prompted Walker's mother to enroll him in the Pitman's Press Art Course, a correspondence school, when he was 14. Finishing the course two years later, he left home for Bristol, where he applied for an art job on the *Evening World*. He drew war maps and joke cartoons while attending the West of England College of Art. After service in the Royal Air Force from 1944 to 1947, he was granted three pounds a week to return to the College of Art, from whence he won a *Punch* Scholarship. Soon he began writing articles for *Picture Post*, *Lilliput*, and *Cycling* (his favorite hobby), and in 1967 he illustrated a humorous book written by his friend George Haines, entitled *How to Be a Motorist*.

It was this book that changed the direction of Walker's artistic life. Upon seeing the book, the Scottish publishing house D.C. Thomson, one of two major children's comic publishers of the day, offered Walker trial work on several strips. Soon he was given the chance to take over the popular *I Spy* series. This he drew for some 130 weeks, but he later confessed that he had been unable to create story lines himself and that all his many pages for Thomson were scripted by a staff writer, Peter Clark. When Clark was promoted, his work for Walker fell off. A cartoonist friend of Walker's, Cliff Brown, was working for Amalgamated Press, a Thomson rival, and introduced him to Bob Paynter, editor of *Whizzer and Chips*. His first artwork for this weekly comic was *Three Story Stan* (1972), and the gruesome strain haunted many of his A.P. series from then on. There were *Fun Fear*, *Evil Eye*, and *Ghost Train* for *Whoopee*; *Misery Buckets* and *Plain Jane* for *Buster*; and *Wizards Anonymous* and *Old Boy* for *Whizzer and Chips*. His most popular was *Scream Inn*, an extremely Victorian strip laden with detail, which he drew for some 300 weeks (during its last period the title was changed to *Spooktacular Seven*). It also appeared in *Whizzer and Chips*.

His more recent work includes *Box-a-Tricks* in *Buster*, scripted by Roy Davis; and a newspaper strip, *Ar Little Uns*, in the *Bristol Evening Post*.

D.G.

WALLY AND THE MAJOR (Australia) Created by Stan Cross for the *Herald and Weekly Times Ltd.* in 1940, the strip was an offshoot of an earlier, unsuccessful strip, *The Winks*. Two of the characters from the strip, Wally (whose surname has never been given) and Mr. Winks (who became a major), were transferred to a new strip about army life that appeared daily in the *Melbourne Herald*. While not as blatantly Australian as *Bluey and Curley*, it was Australian in attitude and flavor and presented a far more subtle approach to digger-humor. It is, perhaps, this subtlety—often based on wordplay—that distinguished it from other areas of digger-humor.

In creating a strip about army life, Cross was determined to avoid the popular conception of the Australian soldier, much of which had been created by *Smith's Weekly*, where Cross had spent the previous 20 years. He went to great pains to see that his soldiers did not swill beer or have a cigarette dangling from their lips; where possible, they even avoided slang in preference to an educated vocabulary. By removing his characters from the firing line and making them part of a home-front army, Cross was able to leisurely unfold his humor, without the sense of active participation of other war strips.

The laconic, saturnine Wally made a limited contribution to the strip, particularly after the introduction of Pudden Benson as Major Winks' batman. The bald, tubby Pudden, when not playing the role of an obtuse buffoon, was often capable of flashes of cunning insight. More often than not, Pudden was the catalyst for the strip's punch line. He became a star in his own right, and when the Sunday page was published, it appeared in some states under the title of *Pudden*. The Major was a short, rotund, fatherly figure whose previous army experience qualified him for a commission. One suspects that his battle experiences were limited to wielding his pen in the war of red tape. He was a gentleman of the old school with a middle-class background, who had never come to grips with modern attitudes. He was constantly staggered by the assessments delivered by those around him. A highlight of the strip, under Cross, was the variety of expressions on the Major's face in the last panel. They ran the full gamut from anger, frustration, shock, disbelief, painful resignation, and, occasionally, beaming understanding. Cross was a master when it came to depicting an appropriate expression with an economy of line.

After the war, rather than take the characters back to city life, Cross located his team on the Queensland cane fields. With the Major still in charge, this locale was not very different from the army camp. However, it did allow greater scope for backblock/rural humor as well as the introduction of new characters such as Olsen, the thick-headed Swede. This shrewd relocation assisted the strip's continued popularity. When Cross retired in 1970, the strip passed to Carl Lyon, who had drawn the Sunday page for many years in addition to assisting Cross with the daily strip. Lyon never reached the level of skill and subtlety imparted by Cross, and *Wally and the Major* was retired in 1979.

J.R.

WANG SHUHUI (1912-1985) Wang had a profound knowledge of and skill in Chinese classical painting, being especially good at brushwork and at line drawings of Chinese women in ancient times. Her stylistic achievements came from blending images in paintings with the likenesses of real individuals from around her, as in her art for her tale based upon the well-known ancient novel *Xi Xiang Ji* ("The West Chamber"). It was made in 1958 and won the First Painting Award in the First National Comics Competition. "The West Chamber" is about the love between a poor young scholar, Zhang Sheng, and a girl from a rich family, Cui Ying-ying. Their love is thwarted by a powerful old woman, Cui's mother. But with the help of Cui's maid Hong Niang, the old mother is forced to accept their love.

At age 15, Wang began to learn drawing by copying the images from borrowed drawing books. Later in her artwork she mixed the skills she had studied with Western-style portraiture. Except during the Cultural Revolution (1966-76), when she was prohibited from doing artwork, she created comic books all her life. Most were based on stories written in ancient times: *Xi Xiang Ji*, *Yang Men Nu Jiang* ("Woman General in Yang's Family"), *Kong Que Dong Nan Fei* ("The Peacock Flies to the Northeast"), *Liang Shanbo yu Zhu Yingtai* (a tragic love story), *Meng Jiang Nu* (the story of a newly-wed whose husband is killed in battle), and many others. All of these stories are well known in literary form as well as in operas adapted from the books.

H.Y.L.L.

WANG XIANSHENG HE XIAO CHEN (China) Mr. Wang and Little Chen were two well-known figures in two respective comic strips, *Wang Xiansheng* ("Mr. Wang") and *Xiao Chen Liu Jing Wai Shi* ("Stories of Little Chen Staying in the Capital City"), which appeared at the same time and were created by Ye Qianyu (1907-1995). Both comic strips were initially published in *Shanghai Cartoons*, a large-size semimonthly cartoon magazine started in May 1928. In June 1930 the magazine was merged with *Time Pictorial*, and Ye's strips continued to be published there, as well as in such publications as *Time Cartoons, Liangyou Morning*, and *Nanjing Morning News*. Ye's *Mr. Wang* and *Little Chen* lasted for 10 years, from the first issue of *Shanghai Cartoons* until the Sino-Japanese War broke out in 1937 and the publication of all journals was suspended.

Five interrelated figures in *Mr. Wang* and *Little Chen* were preeminent: Mr. Wang, his wife Mrs. Wang, and their daughter Miss Wang; and Little Chen and his wife Mrs. Chen. Though the relationships among these five characters never changed, the status of Mr. Wang and Little Chen did change according to the stories. Sometimes they were bullied by others, sometimes they were the ones doing the browbeating. Mr. Wang was a city dweller, and the stories in his strip focused on urban behaviors and problems, in addition to husband-and-wife feuds and other family affairs. Little Chen was a low-ranking official, and the episodes in his strip concentrated on government corruption and the effects of inflation and economic depression on the lives of the poor, for whom Ye had deep sympathy. Ye stopped cartooning entirely with the establishment of the People's Republic of China.

H.Y.L.L.

WARD, NORMAN (1906-1959) The comic art of Norman Ward, although never signed, was easily recognized by the young readers of *Film Fun*, the strips of several famous movie stars, which Ward took over after the death of the comic's virtual designer, George William Wakefield. Ward modeled his style very closely on Wakefield's, and only his distinctive lettering truly differentiated his work from his predecessor's. His strips included the front-and-back-page adventures of *Stan Laurel and Oliver Hardy* from 1944, his best-remembered work; *Joe E. Brown* and *Old Mother Riley and Her Daughter Kitty* (Lucan and MacShane), both from 1940; and *George Formby*, about the top comedy star in British films of the forties (from 1942). Ward's great success is unusual in that he took up the comic-strip form so late. He was 31 years old before he tried his hand at it, but after that he never looked back.

Norman Yendell Ward was born on November 30, 1906, in Page Bank, a colliery village in County Durham. His father was a coal mine policeman who had served with the Coldstream Guards and fought in the Boer War. Norman was nine years old when his father was killed in action at Ypres during World War I. Although he won a scholarship to a grammar school, his mother's destitution led him to leave school at 14 to become a telegraph boy at the local post office. Unable to progress higher than a telegraph-pole lineman, Ward emigrated to Australia in 1925 under the so-called Big Brother scheme. Returning to England in 1932, he tried several get-rich-quick schemes without success before taking a correspondence course in cartooning.

In a short while he had some of his cartoons accepted by the weekly magazine *Tit-Bits* (1933) and then won a regular spot cartoon in *Detective Weekly* on the theme of criminals and convicts. (It has been said that he acquired the knowledge for this piece from unusually close contact with prisons and prisoners during the Australian era of his life.) His first comic strips were based on popular personalities of the period, a theme that would eventually lead him to a career at *Film Fun*. First came a strip based on a ventriloquist, *Arthur Prince and Jim*, in the boys' weekly *The Pilot* (1937), followed by *Wee Georgie Wood*, about a midget from the Music Halls, which was published in the new boys' paper *The Buzzer* (1937). Several of his strips turned up in the George Newnes/Arthur Pearson seasonal comics: *Unlucky Georgie* and *Dr. Hee-Haw* in *The Christmas Holiday Comic* (1937-38); *Dick's Quick Tricks* in *The Seaside Comic* (1938); *Milly and Billy* in *The Summer Comic* (1938); and *Ice Cream for All* in *Sunny Sands* (1939). He drew the front-page heroine *Jill Joy the Tomboy* in the short-lived comic supplement in *Favourite Weekly* (1938), then joined the new and instantly successful weekly *Knockout Comic*. For this quality comic book Norman supplied the silly serials *Stonehenge Kit the Ancient Brit* and *Sandy and Muddy* and filled in on Jos Walker's serial *Sandy's Steam Man* (all 1939). Later, he drew for the same comic book *Tough But Tender Tex* (1944) and took over the front-page Boy Scout strip *Deed-a-Day Danny* (1945). From 1940, however, he was best known as the leading *Film Fun* cartoonist, concluding his run of movie stars by drawing *Bud Abbott and Lou Costello* (1947).

Norman Ward continued to draw right up to his sudden and premature death at age 54 in 1959.

D.G.

WÄSCHER, HANSRUDI (1928-   ) German writer, artist, and graphic designer, born on April 5, 1928, in St. Gallen, Switzerland. While Hansrudi Wäscher's German parents lived in the Italian part of Switzerland, Wäscher learned Italian fluently. In 1936 he became acquainted with Italian comic books and was most impressed by *Tarzan, Mandrake*, and Alex Raymond's *Flash Gordon*. He also loved reading the novels of Italian writer Emilio Salgari. With his parents, he returned to Germany in 1940. After high school he became an apprentice decorator and completed his studies as a graphic designer at the Werkkunstschule in Hannover. He landed a job with the Hannover Municipal Transit Authority.

As early as 1950, Wäscher had drafted plans for German comic books. However, no publisher seemed interested. In 1953 Walter Lehning Verlag started publishing comic books in the pocket-sized Italian format of $6^{5}/_{8} \times 2^{7}/_{8}$ inches. Somewhat flustered that his idea of entering the German comics scene on his own had been taken up by a publisher, Wäscher went to the Lehning offices and immediately sold his *Sigurd* feature. Since then, he has been in the comic business, writing and drawing more than 1,100 comic books in the Italian, or piccolo, format and some 450 normal-sized comic books; translating Italian comics into German; and drawing innumerable covers for Walter Lehning. Except for the first 40 issues of *Sigurd*, he has written all of the stories of his comic series, which include *Falk, Tibor, Nick, Gert Jörg*, and others. He started his own two series, *Nizar* and *Ulf*, when Lehning ceased publication in 1968. Since 1969 he has been working on the *Buffalo Bill* comic book of Bastei Verlag.

As most of Wäscher's comics show, he has a marked predilection for jungle tales (*Tibor, Nizar*) and for adventures involving knights (*Sigurd, Falk, Ulf*). He also feels at home with pirates (*Gert*) and science fiction (*Nick*). Wäscher's style at first glance seems to be simple and wooden. In part this is due to the fact that he had to do all of the artwork on the Lehning books in the same size that they were to be printed. Nevertheless, Wäscher manages to tell his stories well. The almost unending adventures of his heroes in the piccolo format still hold up today and are very much sought after by German collectors trying to recapture their childhood dreams and fantasies, gleaned from pocket-sized comic books eagerly devoured week after week to the chagrin of many a teacher. Wäscher's comic books, despite some of their artistic shortcomings, have helped to firmly establish comics in postwar Germany.

With fan interest in Wäscher continuing unabated, most of his work has been reprinted by Hethke Verlag with new artwork and new comic books and albums done for some of the old series. Wäscher's comic heroes have also been put on a series of telephone cards.

W.F.

WASH TUBBS (U.S.) The classic adventure and humor strip *Wash Tubbs* (originally titled *Washington Tubbs II*), by Roy Crane, began publication as an NEA Syndicate daily feature on April 21, 1924. The strip's pint-size hero-to-be, George Washington Tubbs II, curly-haired and with saucer-rimmed spectacles and an enormous penchant for women larger than himself (most were), sallied forth on the comic stage working in a small-town grocery called the Crabtree Emporium, run by a cracker-barrel philosopher type whom Wash simply called Boss. For the first few months, Wash and Mr. Crabtree were the principal characters, while Wash

had trouble with a rival named Bertram Speed for the attentions of a peroxide blonde called Dottie. Then, unexpectedly, on August 8, 1924, a wildly fresh element of mystery leading to buried treasure in the South Seas shattered the strip's story pattern. Before long Wash was aboard a ship called the *Sieve*, faced with a scurvy rogue named Tamalio, his life in danger, his future dubious; readers were shaken at their coffee.

NEA was by no means convinced that Roy Crane's novel experiment was worth repeating, and after Wash had returned home rich, he was again confined to relatively mundane exploits (crashing the movies; wooing a girl; riding the rails) for two years before Crane was able to fling him into a rough-and-tumble Wild West story (in a hell-town called Cozy Gulch) on July 15, 1926. Shortly after (on November 15, 1926), Wash met his buddy-in-arms, Gozy Gallup, and (as the strip title changed to *Wash Tubbs* in most papers in mid-1926) became involved in a medicine-show swindle, a circus, and then a brutal imbroglio with bandits in Mexico. Next came an excursion to Santo Domingo and Wash and Gozy's first encounter with Bull Dawson, who was to become Wash's worst enemy and a recurrent figure in the strip throughout the years. (Dawson's unshaven villainy first shadowed the strip on March 10, 1928.) By now, of course, the story line was pure adventure, and it was apparent Crane knew he was writing a kind of comic epic. In another year, the two-fisted adventurer, Captain Easy, had slugged his way into the strip, at the peak of a story of revolution and murder in central Europe. Easy (who entered the strip on February 6, 1929) was a man of mystery, obviously adventuring under a pseudonym, whose real and tragic story was not revealed for a number of years. (His true identity was William "Billy" Lee, framed by a rival for robbery in a staid southern town.) He became Wash's new fellow swashbuckler, while Crane retired Gozy to

"*Wash Tubbs,*" Roy Crane. © NEA Service.

marriage and a family (a fate Wash was to share a few years later).

Easy was the hit of the strip. Although Wash continued as the central character (even adventuring a bit on his own, circa 1931-32), it was obvious that Easy had become the feature's true hero. And when NEA decided to give Crane a Sunday page on July 30, 1933, it was Easy who was the new strip's solo hero and source of the title: *Captain Easy*. (Ostensibly, the Sunday strip detailed Easy's escapades before he met Wash. A colorful, graphically freewheeling feature, *Captain Easy* quickly became the most eye-appealing page in the color comics, surpassing even the Foster *Tarzan* and Raymond *Flash Gordon* in the variety of layout and inventiveness of art. The story, simpler than the daily *Tubbs*, was still gripping and suspenseful.)

Then World War II split Wash and Easy for good. Tied down at home with a draft-exempting job and dependents, Wash had to watch Easy go into the service as a special agent behind enemy lines—which is where, after a number of graphically superb adventures, Crane left Easy when he turned the daily *Tubbs* and Sunday *Easy* over to his assistant, Leslie Turner, on June 1, 1943, to begin his *Buz Sawyer* strip for King Features.

Turner's work on the two strips differed materially from Crane's narrative approach, although his style was strikingly similar in its effective utilization of the basic Crane graphic techniques. Following the close of World War II, Turner developed an interesting narrative structure for the daily strip in alternating highly comic stories (involving such inventions of his own as the ghastly Kallikak Family and the master swindler J. Buckingham Ish, who never fails to hook J. P. McKee) and basically serious adventure stories, usually set in foreign locales and occasionally involving the old battler, Bull Dawson. The Sunday strip (which he turned over to Mel Graff for a long period of time) was generally humorous in tone when he drew it.

Essentially, however, Turner did a remarkable job of continuing a major strip without a really noticeable shift in style or story (aided in the transition, of course, by the watershed of World War II). After Turner retired, the daily and Sunday strips, now both called *Captain Easy*, were carried on by the team of Jim Lawrence and Bill Crooks. Theirs was a valiant effort, particularly in graphic style, but the result was a good deal further away from the Crane work than was Turner's rendition, without being interestingly innovative in its own right. *Wash Tubbs* finally ended its long run in 1988.

B.B.

WATCHMEN (U.S.) One of the most original and gripping stories to come out of the superhero genre in the last decade, *Watchmen* typically was the work of two British imports, the writer Alan Moore and the artist Dave Gibbons. It was published by DC Comics as a limited series over the span of 12 issues extending from September 1986 to October 1987.

Set in a parallel universe that took the reader back to the late 1950s, *Watchmen* opened on a murder mystery and closed on a nuclear holocaust. In this reinvented world superheroes did coexist with mere mortals and were the pawns (or perhaps the masters) of that society's power structure. The Watchmen were just such a group of superheroes, made up of the megalomaniacal Ozymandias, the paranoid Rorschach (whose face was

"Watchmen," Alan Moore and Dave Gibbons. © DC Comics.

a blot), the all-powerful Dr. Manhattan (who liked to move about stark naked), and a handful of others. After they came upon the body of their former associate, the Comedian, they realized that a sinister plot to start a world conflict was afoot, and they set out to save the planet from extinction in the 12 minutes remaining before the trigger point.

In every episode (each of which was posited to be only one minute in duration) there were radical shiftings of time frames, flashbacks within flashbacks, and enough plot twists to fill at least a score of ordinary comic books. The suspense was kept constant through different levels of storytelling (there was even a comic book within the comic book, a pirate series titled *Tales of the Black Freighter*, whose plot echoed some of the strands in the main story line). The oddly angled perspectives and asymmetrical compositions, as well as the surreal coloring, added to the mood of eeriness and dread.

Symbolism and irony abounded throughout the disturbing tales. In the course of an interview Moore averred, "What we were trying to do was to create something which has a structure that is multi-faceted enough and has enough layers to it so that each subsequent issue redefines bits of the ones that have come before." Rock-group covers were represented alongside snatches of classical paintings, and excerpts of Bob Dylan lyrics were juxtaposed with quotes from the

Bible. The work's title was itself based on a line by the Roman poet Juvenal, the author of the *Satires*, "Qui custodiet custodies?" ("Who watches the watchmen?").

Watchmen was a great (and unexpected) success as a comic book series, and it enjoyed even greater popularity when it was reprinted in paperback form. A unique tour de force, its excellence has never been replicated, and it lies like an erratic rock in the middle of the great comic book desert.

M.H.

WATSO *see* Mager, Gus.

WAUGH, COULTON (1896-1973) American artist, born in 1896 in Cornwall, England. Coulton Waugh's father, Fredrick J. Waugh, was a famous marine painter, and his grandfather, Samuel Bell Waugh, was the portrait painter of Presidents Lincoln and Grant. Coulton Waugh came back to the United States as a young man and worked variously as a textile designer, a newspaper and magazine illustrator, and a cartoonist in New York, while continuing to follow in his ancestors' footsteps as a painter. Waugh's hobby was sailing (he was once shipwrecked off Cape Hatteras), and he contributed articles and illustrations to various yachting magazines and to *Boy's Life*.

When the editors at Associated Press had to find a replacement for Milton Caniff on *Dickie Dare*, they selected Waugh, who started his long association with the strip in October 1934. In 1943 he married his assistant, Mabel Odin Burvik, to whom he had earlier relinquished the strip (her signature, Odin, started appearing in the spring of 1944). In 1945 Waugh started a new strip, *Hank*, about a war veteran, for the New York daily *P.M.*, but the experiment proved short-lived.

In 1947 Coulton Waugh published *The Comics*, a pioneering study of American comic art. From then on he divided his career almost equally among drawing, painting, writing, and teaching. From 1960 to 1970 he wrote and drew the daily *Junior Editors* panel for A.P.; taught art at Orange County Community College; had many one-man shows and participated in three Waugh family shows, along with eight other Waugh painters; served as first curator of the Storm King Art Center in Cornwall, New York; and wrote two art instruction books, *How to Paint with a Knife* and *Landscape Painting with a Knife*, both published by Watson-Guptill. Coulton Waugh died suddenly on May 23, 1973.

Waugh's fame now rests mainly upon his trailblazing study *The Comics*, still the most widely quoted work on the subject. His drawings for *Dickie Dare* exhibit an old-fashioned, easy charm reminiscent of more innocent days and youthful dreams.

M.H.

WEARY WILLIE AND TIRED TIM (G.B.) Weary Willy and Tired Tim, among the longest-lived of British comic strip heroes, were created by Tom Browne. They may be traced back to two prototype tramps identified by an anonymous caption writer as Weary Waddles and Tired Timmy in a strip entitled *Innocents on the River*, which filled the top half of the front page of *Illustrated Chips* number 298, dated May 16, 1896.

Intended for no more than a single appearance—standard strip practice of the period—the two complementary characters (one tall and thin, one short and

"*Weary Willie and Tired Tim*," Percy Cocking.

fat) caught the editor's attention, and he asked for more adventures. They reappeared five weeks later (number 303), then two weeks after that (number 305), and in another two weeks they filled the entire front page. Number 310 saw them rechristened *Willy and Tim* (the "Willie" came some time later), and from number 317 they became a front-page fixture until the final issue of *Chips*, number 2997, dated September 12, 1953.

Although there were regular comic characters before *Willie and Tim*, their success undoubtedly led to the establishment of the Victorian comic paper, and to the popularity of Tom Browne's style as a comic artist. His characters and style were widely copied by other cartoonists and editors hoping to cash in on the hobo bandwagon, and Browne was even paid well to imitate himself with *Little Willy and Tiny Tim* (the originals' nephews) and *Airy Alf and Bouncing Billy*, bicyclists in *Big Budget* (1898). Browne abandoned his "World Famous Tramps" in 1900, and other artists were tried, including Arthur Jenner. The strip finally was entrusted to the excellent pen of Percy Cocking around 1912, and he continued to draw it to the end, some 40 years later, happily retiring the characters at age 58 to the mansion of Murgatroyd Mump, Millionaire!

D.G.

WEB, THE (U.S.) *The Web*, created in July 1942, made its first appearance in MLJ's *Zip* number 27. Although its creators are not known, artists John Cassone and Irv Novick handled the bulk of the stories in the feature's short career. Making only a dozen short appearances, it was last seen in *Zip* 38 for July 1943. The character's appeal was his costume: a brilliant, half-green and half-yellow jumpsuit, a green domino mask, and a fascinating, weblike cape.

In his alter ego, the Web was really noted criminologist John Raymond, whose brother, Tim, was a criminal. After John helped police capture his escaping brother, he set out to avenge evil as the Web. Only Rosie Wayne, the strip's love interest, knew his secret. Despite his rather short tenure, the character managed to battle several inventive villains, including the Black Dragon, Captain Murder, and Count Berlin. Neither stories nor artwork on *The Web* was particularly outstanding, however, and MLJ quickly dropped the feature to concentrate on *Archie* and a horde of other humor concepts.

When MLJ (now Archie-Radio) made a short reentry into the superhero field in 1965, *The Web* made the most appearances, popping up in nine stories. And despite a rather inventive gimmick—Rosie Wayne had become John Raymond's wife, and she and her mother constantly nagged Raymond for coming out of retirement and resuming his career as the Web—the strip and the whole MLJ line collapsed the next year. Before it did, however, *The Web* appeared in a paperback, *High Camp Superheroes* (Belmont, 1966).

J.B.

WEBSTER, HAROLD TUCKER (1885-1953) The beloved creator of *The Timid Soul* and *The Man in the Brown Derby* was Harold Tucker Webster, born to middle-class parents in Parkersburg, West Virginia, on September 21, 1885. Tall at an early age (he stood six feet four as an adult), he moved with his parents to Tomahawk, Wisconsin, where he grew up, working at odd jobs while he went to school. To keep his mind off mathematics, which he hated, he began to draw at seven, persevered, and sold his first drawing, much to his amazement, to an outdoor magazine called *Recreation* in his teens. Deciding then to become a professional cartoonist, he saved his money and went off in 1901 to study at the Frank Holmes School of Illustration in Chicago, where Harry Hershfield and Roy Baldridge, the illustrator, were fellow students. The school went out of business 20 days after Webster enrolled, and the teenage artist, finding no interest in his work at the Chicago newspapers, followed a lead that took him first to the *Denver Republican*, then to the *Denver Post*, where he earned $15 a week drawing sports cartoons (which he later admitted were terrible).

Barely 20, he returned to Chicago and did freelance cartoon work for the *Chicago News* (illustrating the famed *Mr. Dooley* series for a time), then got a salaried job doing political cartoons for the front page of the *Chicago Inter-Ocean* at $30 a week. There he was spotted by an official of the *Cincinnati Post*, who hired him away from the Chicago paper at a princely $70 a week. Saving enough to take a European trip in 1911, Web-

ster did an illustrated account for the *Post*, which he thought impressive enough to get him a New York job. Arriving in New York in 1912, he met his future wife through cartoonist R. M. Brinkerhoff and promptly landed a fine job at the *New York Tribune*. At the *Tribune* he started the variously named series of daily cartoon gags (without continuing characters) on which his national reputation was quickly based.

Readers guffawed at such irregular series as *Poker Portraits* and *Life's Darkest Moment*, and Webster's syndicated fame mounted until he was hired away from the *Tribune* by the *World* in the early 1920s. There he continued the same daily cartoons and launched a Sunday page about a recurrent character and his wife, *The Man in the Brown Derby*. When the *World* collapsed in early 1931, the *Tribune* (now the *Herald-Tribune*) was glad to welcome Webster back, but suggested after a time that he base his Sunday page on the daily panel character who had become his most popular figure: the Timid Soul. So, in May 1931, the weekly *Timid Soul* page was launched.

Continuing to grow in wealth and reputation, Webster authored and/or illustrated a number of top-selling books through the 1920s and 1930s, among them *Our Boyhood Thrills* (1915), *Webster's Bridge* (1924), *Webster's Poker Book* (1926), *The Shepper Newfounder* (1931), *The Timid Soul* (1931*), To Hell with Fishing* (1945), and *Life with Rover* (1949). With his strips appearing in 125 papers, he was residing in a comfortable New England estate and still drawing his full output, with only minimal assistance from a coworker on the Sunday page, at the time of his death in 1953. Rather than having any of his intensely admired work continued by a ghost, the *Herald-Tribune* elected to circulate reprints of his earlier work to interested papers, where it continued to appear for several years. A really adequate memorial volume of Webster's still richly humorous work is long overdue.

B.B.

WEBSTER, TOM (1890-1962) British cartoonist and animator Gilbert Thomas Webster was born at Bilston, Staffordshire, on July 17, 1890. Educated at Wolverhampton, he started work as a booking clerk on the Great Western Railway at the age of 14. Although he received no formal art training (he drew in his pram as later publicity had it), he won a prize of five shillings offered by the *Birmingham Weekly Post* for comic drawings for six weeks in succession. His first sports drawing, a field he made his own, was a sketch of Bernard Wilkinson made while he and Aston Villa were playing on the Sheffield United football team. It was accepted by *Athletic News* for a guinea. He left the railway and joined the art staff of the *Birmingham Sports Argus*, where for four years he drew sports cartoons, evolving the running commentary style that became his worldwide trademark. Webster drew a form of strip, continuity with commentary, within a single, large-framed panel. Once established in the national press, his technique became widely copied and is still in use today.

Webster went to London in response to an advertisement for a political cartoonist and joined the *Daily Citizen*, a new paper, at six pounds a week, a considerable raise from his 50 shillings in Birmingham. He had eked out his living with experiments in cartoon film animation for a local company. Now he did freelance sports cartoons for *Golf Illustrated* and the

H. T. Webster.

Tom Webster, humor cartoon.

He retired in 1940, but chafed at enforced idleness. He joined the *Daily Sketch* in October 1944, then moved to the *News Chronicle* in 1953, retiring for the second, and final, time in 1956. He died in 1962 at the age of 71.

D.G.

WEE PALS (U.S.) For some time Morrie Turner, a black cartoonist, had an idea for an integrated strip, which he broached to Charles Schulz at a cartoonists' meeting in 1964. Schulz warmly endorsed the idea, as did black comedian Dick Gregory at a later meeting. Thus encouraged, Morrie Turner produced *Wee Pals* in 1965 for the Lew Little Syndicate (later merged into the Register and Tribune Syndicate).

As the title implies, the strip is concerned with a merry group of schoolchildren of all races and colors. Nipper is a bright black boy whose eyes disappear under the Confederate cap he is always wearing; Sybil, an enterprising, no-nonsense black girl. Their white companions are the long-haired, mischievous Wellington; the fat, bespectacled Oliver; Connie, the blonde tomboy; and Jerry, the Jewish intellectual. Special mention should be made of Polly, the culturally integrated parrot.

The setting is suburban, and the kids, when they do not feel self-conscious about their backgrounds, behave like any other bunch of high-spirited comic strip youngsters. Highly enterprising (Sybil tells fortunes, another black youngster spouts quotes for every occasion, and Jerry sells soul food from every nationality), they are also gregarious and hold regular meetings of the Rainbow Power Club. To sum it up, the Wee Pals are a cross between Schulz's *Peanuts* and Branner's *Rinkey-dinks*.

Wee Pals had the merit of presenting to the American public the thorny problems of black and white integration in an entertaining package. As Charles Schulz once stated: "When Morrie draws about children trying to find their way in an integrated community, the results show that Morrie has been more than a mere observer. Of course, the best part of it all is that *Wee Pals* is a lot of fun."

A number of *Wee Pals* strips have been reprinted in paperback form by Signet, starting in 1969. There have also been a number of *Wee Pals* animated cartoons; and in the 1980s a children's show called *Wee Pals on the Go* was broadcast on a local television station. Now distributed by Creators Syndicate, the strip enjoys a stable, if relatively small, circulation.

M.H.

evening paper *The Star*. By the outbreak of World War I, he was earning 20 pounds a week.

In 1916, stricken with rheumatic fever, he was so desperate for work that he slept on the Thames embankment. Finally, the *Evening News* took a cartoon of the Tommy Noble-Joe Symonds fight, and Tom Webster was back in print. Soon he had sketches in seven Sunday papers. Tom Marlowe of the *Daily Mail* signed him exclusively in 1919, starting at 2,000 pounds a year, and he never looked back. He became part of the London sporting aristocracy and incorporated real-life persons into characters in his cartoons; these included Inman the billiards champ and, most famous of all, Tishy the Racehorse who crossed her legs. He created fictional heroes, too: the Horizontal Heavyweight and George, the common man and all-purpose spectator.

In 1936 he painted a Cavalcade of Sport, 12 panels, for the Cunard-White Star liner *Queen Mary*, a job that demonstrated his inborn artistry and certainly took longer to execute than his classic Beckett-Goddard fight cartoon, drawn for a *Mail* deadline in 18 minutes flat! He also made a brief return to animation in the 1920s, working with Brian White on a series featuring *Tishy and Steve*. The first collation of his drawings, *Tom Webster Among the Sportsmen* (1919), sold out its 70,000 copies in 20 minutes! Thereafter the *Tom Webster Annual* was published every autumn until 1939.

"Wee Pals," Morrie Turner. © Register and Tribune Syndicate.

WEE WILLIE WINKIE'S WORLD (U.S.) The same year that saw the appearance of *The Kin-der-Kids*, Lyonel Feininger contributed a second feature to the *Chicago Tribune*. Taking its title from the well-known nursery rhyme (already used by Rudyard Kipling), *Wee Willie Winkie's World* first saw print on August 19, 1906.

Wee Willie Winkie is less turbulent and more lyrical than *The Kin-der-Kids*. In this strip Feininger does not make use of balloons but inserts a printed narrative, illuminated by allegorical, floral, or abstract motifs, between the panels.

The strip's diminutive hero is a winning and naive little boy named Wee Willie, who finds himself in the midst of an enchanted universe (the theme is not unlike *Little Nemo*'s) where inanimate objects spring to life, familiar landscapes take on fantastic shapes, in a whimsical symphony of lines, colors, and forms. A metamorphosis, at times gradual, at times sudden and startling, transforms trees and clouds, rocks and buildings into tentacular monsters and threatening demons, or conversely into benevolent genies and hospitable havens.

Wee Willie Winkie's is a world of fantasy and whimsy, of sweetness and shadows, of marvel and terror. The last page of this remarkable series was published on January 20, 1907, and with *Wee Willie's* disappearance Lyonel Feininger's promising career as a comic strip artist came to a premature end.

M.H.

WEISINGER, MORT (1915-1978) American comic book writer and editor, born April 25, 1915, in New York City. After several years as a pulp writer, magazine editor, and literary agent, Weisinger joined National Comics in 1940. Although he originated a slew of superhero strips like *Green Arrow* and *Airwave*, he is best known for his long tenure as editor of the *Superman* family of magazines (1940-70). More than creators Siegel and Shuster, it was Weisinger who fashioned what is now known as the Superman legend.

As originally conceived and executed, *Superman* was artistically crude and totally humorless. But Weisinger stepped in with a new direction; he made the Superman of the late 1940s and 1950s a super-powered slapstick artist. It was not odd for the Weisinger Superman to be perplexed by the most bizarre of villains. No longer would he allow Superman to battle and defeat the second strongest man in the world. Weisinger made him battle imps and frivolous ne'er-do-wells. Villains like the Toyman, the Prankster, and the fifth-dimensional Mr. Mxyztplk began to appear, launching attacks of toys, gags, novelties, magic, and anything but muscle in attempts to best the Man of Steel.

Weisinger also must be credited with securing numerous talented artisans to chronicle the character's adventures. Artistically, Weisinger leaned most heavily on Wayne Boring, Al Plastino, and Curt Swan for *Superman*, Jim Mooney for *Supergirl*, and Kurt Schaffenberger for *Lois Lane*, but Jack Burnley, Irwin Hasen, and others of merit were also used. For the text, writers like Otto Binder, Edmond Hamilton, Al Bester, Bill Finger, and Manly Wade Wellman were used.

It was under Weisinger's aegis that concepts like kryptonite were developed; he also expanded the list of survivors of Krypton considerably. Argo City, The Phantom Zone, and the bottled city of Kandor all survived the planet's destruction, along with Weisinger-conceived characters like Supergirl, MonEl, Krypto, and

Super-Robot. During the 1950s Weisinger was also responsible for overseeing the creation of the Fortress of Solitude, the Bizarro world, Lex Luthor, Brainiac, the Legion of Super-Heroes, and many other bits of Supermania. He personally scripted the Superman motion picture serials starring Kirk Alyn and acted as story editor for the Superman television program.

Weisinger left *Superman* and comics in 1970 to devote his full time to a burgeoning book and magazine writing career. His novel *The Contest* was purchased by Columbia Pictures, and Weisinger's byline appeared in *Esquire, Argosy, Reader's Digest*, and many other magazines. He died in June 1978.

J.B.

WELLINGTON, CHARLES H. (1884-1942) American artist, born in 1884 in St. Louis, Missouri. Duke Wellington's first published work appeared in the *St. Louis Post Dispatch* and *St. Louis Republic*. He accepted, in 1908, an offer to draw for the *Memphis News-Scimitar* and later moved to Nashville for a six-month stint on the *Tennessean*. Wellington's work, though crude, was just good enough to impress Colonel Henry Stoddard of the *New York Evening Mail*, who offered him a contract (a year earlier Stoddard had lured another young cartoonist, Rube Goldberg, to New York City). Wellington drew spots and editorial cartoons for the *Mail* and dabbled in short-lived strips.

Also at this time, for syndication, Wellington drew *Pa's Imported Son-in-Law* for the McClure service; he quit in 1914, and under Ed Carey it became *Pa's Family and Their Friends*, which briefly capitalized on the Charlie Chaplin rage, featuring that comedian. Meanwhile Wellington revived his characters in the *Tribune* (for Hearst's Newspaper Feature Service) under the title *That Son-in-Law of Pa's!* and, finally, *Pa's Son-in-Law*. Except for the oafish English son-in-law, the strip was patterned after Sterrett's earlier *Polly*. In 1920 Wellington switched to the Tribune Syndicate.

Pa's Son-in-Law became a staple of the *Tribune* (and later *Herald-Tribune*) comic section, along with *Mr. and Mrs. Peter Rabbit* and others. It was syndicated with steady but modest success through the years and continued to Wellington's death in 1942.

C. H. Wellington, "Pa's Son-in-Law."

Wellington's drawing style never progressed past the advanced amateur stage. His knowledge of anatomy was limited; figures were stiffly proper. Gags were always wordy and the humor subdued, if not obscure. The strip never progressed, in art or character development, beyond the level of its early days.

Wellington died of pneumonia in Hollywood, California, at the age of 58.

R.M.

WERNER (Germany) *Werner*, a creation of Brösel ("Breadcrumb"), whose real name is Rötger Feldmann, was a surprise success on the German comics market. Among the elements that might have been expected to hinder the strip's popularity, but didn't, are the fact that the strip originally appealed to an underground audience, that its main character is a beer-guzzling biker (somewhat of an alter ego of the artist), that it is done in a very loose graphic style, and that it is written in North German dialect. *Werner* was first adopted by a sturdy group of devoted biking fans, then spread out to a large mainstream following among comic readers from all walks of life. Strangely enough, part of the success of the series stems from its use of dialect instead of "high German." *Werner* (whose first print runs these days are in the neighborhood of 150,000 copies) may even have inspired the highly salable dialect editions of *Astérix*.

Werner was first published in 1981 by Semmel Verlach, a publishing house originally founded for publication of *Werner* comics. The success of the strip has been nothing short of phenomenal. In 1992 the album *Ouhauerha* ("Oopsy Daisy") was the best-selling book of the year. It was almost inevitable that *Werner* should hit the silver screen. A first animated motion picture,

"Werner," Rotger Feldmann ("Brösel"). © Rotger Feldmann.

Werner beinhart ("Werner Bone Hard"), was produced in 1990. It mixed animation with a real-life story contrasting Brösel's reality and Werner's fictional adventures. A second, broadly humorous feature film, *Werner, das muss kesseln* ("Werner, It's Gotta Hum"), this time all animation, was released in 1996. Like its predecessor it was successful at the box office and then did a brisk business on videocassette.

Brösel draws and coauthors the *Werner* comics, which, after first being published in book form, have subsequently been published in magazines. The work of plotting and writing the stories is shared by Brösel's brother, Andi Feldmann. Girlfriend Kirsten Staack serves as business manager. When Semmel Publishing got into financial trouble, the *Werner* line of comics went independent in 1991. It is now being published by Achterbahn Verlag, a venture Brösel is involved in personally.

Werner also is used in merchandising T-shirts, calendars, phone cards, and other items. There is even a beer that takes its name from the beer drunk by the protagonists: Bölkstoff ("burp stuff"). In 1988 Brösel raced a revved-up four-motor Horex motorcycle of the kind Werner drives in the strip. The event was witnessed by 200,000 fans, and a film of the media event was made. Although Brösel failed to win the race, *Werner* shot to new heights of popularity.

W.F.

WESTOVER, RUSSELL (1886-1966) The creator of one of the most successful working-girl comic strips of all time, *Tillie the Toiler*, Russell (Russ) Westover was born into a large, middle-class family in Los Angeles on August 3, 1886. Following his merchant business in Oakland, the elder Westover sent his son to school there at the turn of the century. Russ went on to art school in San Francisco in the early 1900s, and at the time of the 1906 quake and fire, he had already been sports cartoonist on the *San Francisco Bulletin* for two years. Subsequently, he worked on the *Oakland Herald*, the *San Francisco Chronicle*, and the *Post*. During this time, he developed a style very similar to that which Rube Goldberg had made famous in sports cartooning on the East Coast, often turning out work that was very funny and memorable in its context.

Moving to New York on the strength of his Bay Area success at the time of World War I, Westover joined the cartooning staff of the *New York Herald*, where he created his first nationally syndicated strip, the Sunday page *Snapshot Bill*, based on the early shutterbug craze. Freelancing in the early 1920s, he sold King Features Syndicate on the idea of *Tillie the Toiler*, which was released in 1921 in both daily and Sunday editions of a number of Hearst newspapers. Based in part on the experiences and appearance of Westover's wife, Jenesta, the strip quickly became a hit with readers (one midwestern madman literally fell in love with Tillie, and he wrote long letters begging her not to get involved with Mac, her office boyfriend, and to consider his own proposals of marriage). By the mid-1920s, numerous newspapers were printing the strip. Hearst himself thought highly of it, and his Cosmopolitan Pictures made a film of *Tillie the Toiler* in 1927 with Marion Davies, which was widely promoted in the Hearst papers. Cupples and Leon published a series of *Tillie* books at this time, too. In 1926 Westover added a family-squabble strip to his Sunday page; it was to become *The Van Swaggers* and would run weekly with *Tillie* until the 1950s.

Moving in the 1930s to California, Westover retired from King Features in 1954. His still-popular strip was continued by Bob Gustafson until 1959. Westover died in San Rafael, California, of heart failure, on March 6, 1966.

B.B.

WHEELAN, EDGAR (1888-1966) A major contributor to the concept of comic strip continuity and a great satirist of the movie serial, American artist Ed Wheelan was a product of San Francisco, California, as were so many other great cartoonists of the early years. Wheelan, a Cornell University graduate, was inspired to become a cartoonist by his mother, Albertine Randall, who drew a strip in the 1910s called *The Dumb Bunnies*. He first drew spot and editorial cartoons for the *San Francisco Examiner*, then transferred to another Hearst property, the *New York American*. In April 1918 he created *Midget Movies*. It lasted nearly two years and mimicked the dramatic format of movies of the time, just as Chester Gould, with *Fillum Fables*, and Elzie Segar, with *Thimble Theater*, were both to do for Hearst soon afterward.

Wheelan broke with Hearst around 1920 and would harbor a lifelong conviction that Hearst was bent on his destruction. Ron Goulart records that on his deathbed Wheelan saw the black hand of Hearst in every misfortune that overtook him. Leaving Hearst proved a profitable move, however: Wheelan's *Minute Movies*, created for the George Matthew Adams Service in 1921, was an instant hit. Readers cherished the chattiness of the feature, wrote fan letters to the characters, and followed the day-to-day continuity with unflagging devotion, to the delight of editors.

Wheelan's story line, until he adapted the classics, was puckishly self-effacing. His art was somewhat crude but drippingly melodramatic, in keeping with the tone of the feature. In later years, Nicholas Afonsky's art prettied the strip up and give it a bit more of a comic flavor; Jess Fremon was another ghost for the strip. In the late 1930s Wheelan drew a circus feature, *Big Top*, and carried *Minute Movies* to *Flash Comics*. He then faded into obscurity in his later years. Wheelan died at Ft. Myers Beach, Florida, in 1966.

R.M.

WHEN A FELLER NEEDS A FRIEND (U.S.) Clare Briggs's best-known daily cartoon feature was almost certainly the occasional gag panel series called *When a Feller Needs a Friend*, which ran between 1912 and 1929 in the *Chicago Tribune* and the *New York Tribune* (later the *Herald-Tribune*). This widely popular feature about individuals (usually boys, dogs, and businessmen) caught helplessly alone in embarrassing and threatening domestic situations appeared at weekly intervals, between such other Briggs standby features as *Kelly Pool*, *The Days of Real Sport*, *Oh Man*, *Ain't It a Grand and Glorious Feelin'*, and *Somebody's Always Taking the Joy Out of Life*. Without recurring characters or continuity, *Feller* was not a comic strip: in fact, only one of Briggs's daily panel features (which carried no day-to-day linking title of any kind) had a vestige of a reappearing character, and that was the always-unseen Skin-nay of *The Days of Real Sport*. *Feller* itself seems to

"When a Feller Needs a Friend," Clare Briggs. © New York Tribune.

have first appeared in the *Chicago Tribune* on November 28, 1912, but this cannot necessarily be called the first example drawn by Briggs, since subscribing papers of the time, including Briggs's syndicating paper, the *Chicago Tribune*, simply did not run all of the panels he drew for distribution at the rate of seven a week.

After publishing a hardbound collection of *Feller* in 1914 through the Volland Company, Briggs took his panels to the *New York Tribune* in 1917 and remained there until his death in 1929. (The *Chicago Tribune*, however, continued to run his work by buying the *New York Tribune* cartoons.) A posthumous volume of *Feller* was published in 1930 by William H. Wise and Company as part of a seven-volume memorial set bound in leather. Many of Briggs's panel series were reprinted in newspapers after his death without being labeled as such, so that it is difficult to assign his last *Feller* panel. Greatly popular during his lifetime, Briggs's work was a development of early George McCutcheon material and was reflected in the similar work of H. T. Webster, Gaar Williams, Frank Beck, and others.

B.B.

WHERE I'M COMING FROM (U.S.) In September 1991, Barbara Brandon became the first African-American female cartoonist ever to have her comic strip syndicated by a major American newspaper syndicate. That's when Universal Press Syndicate debuted her Sunday feature *Where I'm Coming From*.

The weekly feature had first appeared in the *Detroit Free Press* in 1989. It stars a cast of seven black women who drift in and out of the artwork, usually talking to each other on the phone about life, men, single parenthood, sexism, and racism. The format owes much to

"Where I'm Coming From," Barbara Brandon. © Universal Press Syndicate.

the style of characters speaking out of the strip directly to the reader, a style developed by Jules Feiffer.

Usually just the characters' heads and hands are shown. Brandon, a daughter of Brumsic Brandon Jr., the creator of *Luther*, has as one of her goals debunking stereotypes about African-American culture and black women in particular.

Where I'm Coming From is designed to deliver only the occasional belly laugh. Brandon works as a kind of visual columnist, presenting her take on social issues and life. While she usually puts this in a humorous context, Brandon does not suffer fools or injustice lightly. Several reprint collections of *Where I'm Coming From* have been published, and there has also been a line of greeting cards.

B.C.

WHITE, BRIAN (1902-1984) British cartoonist and animator Hugh Brian White was born in Dunstable, Bedfordshire, on April 4, 1902. Educated at local schools, he was self-taught as an artist. He joined the local newspapers *Luton Reporter* and *Luton News* as a sports cartoonist and caricaturist in 1916. In 1924 he joined G. E. Studdy and William Ward as an animator on the *Bonzo* cartoon films, moving to *Pathé Pictorial* to animate Sid Griffiths' *Song Cartoons* (1926) and Joe Noble's *Sammy and Sausage* series (1928). With Griffiths he produced animated advertisements for Superads (1929), then made a sound cartoon, *Topical Breezes* (1930), featuring *Hite and Mite*. His last cartoon, *On the Farm* (1932), from H. M. Bateman drawings, was made in the Raycol color system.

White's first strip was *Mr. Enry Noodle* (1924) in *Pearson's Weekly*; it was followed by *Jolly Jinky* (1931) in the same journal. His first daily was *Adam and Eva* in the 1930s in the *London Evening Standard*, followed by the *Weather Pup* panel (October 1932) in the *Daily Mail*. This led to the acceptance of his most successful strip, *The Nipper*, which began a long run in the *Mail* from August 30, 1933, and brought such ancillaries as postcards and annuals. With the wartime paper shortage the strip was discontinued, and White tried strips for children's comics, taking over *Deed-a-Day Danny* from Hugh McNeill and creating *Little Tough Guy*, both in *Knockout* (1942).

He did war service with the police in Liverpool and Luton (1942-44), and in 1945 formed a publishing company, B. & H. White Publications, with his cousin. He reprinted the *Nipper* strips in painting-book form and produced a new *Nipper* comic, *Careful Nippers*, about

Brian White, *"Double Trouble."* © Associated Newspapers Ltd.

road safety, and *Nipper's A-Z Animal Book*. In 1948 he published *Bernard Shaw Through the Camera*. He produced *Nipper* filmstrips for Pathé (1951) and illustrated the Focal Press series of books on how to animate (1955).

In 1955, in an unprecedented move, London agent Frank Betts bought the rights to Bill McLean's American strip, *Double Trouble*, then syndicated in *The Star*, and White was contracted to continue it in a completely British version. When *The Star* was purchased by the *Evening News*, the strip was continued from October 16, 1960, until 1967. White returned to drawing strips for D. C. Thomson's children's comics in 1956 with *Shorty* in *Beezer*, followed by a revival of Allan Morley's character *Keyhole Kate* in *Sparky* (1968-74), *Tich and Snitch* in *Buzz* (1973), and *Plum Duffy* in *Topper* (1974). Although less ingenious and inspired, White's later kid strips carried the stamp of his good-humored *Nipper*. He died on November 4, 1984.

D.G.

WHITE, HUGH STANLEY (1904-1984) British cartoonist Hugh Stanley White was born on October 6, 1904, at Kilburn, London. He was educated at Arlington Park College, Chiswick, and then studied art at evening classes at Chiswick Art School. After six months in advertising with the Gordon and Gotch Agency, a chance meeting with Walter Booth while sketching at the Natural History Museum led to his becoming Booth's assistant, first on weekends, then full-time. For two years he assisted Booth on inking, backgrounds, lettering, etc., on *Rob the Rover* and other adventure strips. When his mother died, he visited Norway on her legacy, sketching whaling, Viking history, and other themes. Upon his return he interested Frank Anderson, an editor at Amalgamated Press, in his work. In 1929 he did his first solo strip, a weekly complete picture-story for the nursery comic *Bo-Peep* (1929), expanding into serials with *Ranji's Ruby* (1932) and *In the Days of Drake* (1933).

He became a pioneer of the British newspaper comic section with his complete adventure strips for *Boys & Girls Daily Mail* (1933) and serials for *South Wales Echo & Express Supplement* (1933-34): *Jimmy in Java*, *Peter in Pygmy Land*, etc. When the Walt Disney organization instituted *Mickey Mouse Weekly* in Britain, White was in at the start, contributing two dramatic serials to the first issue (February 8, 1936): *Ginger Nick the Whaler* and *Ian on Mu*. Subtitled "Pioneer of the Mystery Planet," the latter was a landmark, the first British science-fiction serial (apart from individual episodes of *Rob the Rover*). Planet Mu, inhabited by Chinese pygmies, Viking giants, hollow robots, and a cute little six-legged Hexpod, was frankly inspired by the film *Metropolis* and by *Flash Gordon*, but White's curious blend of Victorian Jules Verneisms and years of drawing for very young readers made the strip unique. It ran 15 weeks.

In 1938 came *Phantom City*, *Flashing Through*, and *Oil and Claw*, for the same Disney weekly; all were similarly fantastic. In 1939 he returned to Amalgamated Press to draw the science-fiction serial *Into Unknown Worlds* for *Butterfly*, and *John Irons, Lone Fighter* for *Triumph*.

After war service in civil defense and the Royal Air Force, White joined forces in the printing trade with a wartime acquaintance to edit and publish *Merry Maker* (1946), a monthly comic using his own art and that of his old friends Walter Booth and Basil Reynolds. Then came two comic books in the American style, *Xmas Comic* and *Atomic Age Comic* (1948), for which he tried some superheroes: *The Bat-Man*, etc. He took on Bob Monkhouse's *Tornado* for *Oh Boy* (1951), then did episodes of *Young Marvelman* (1952) and a science-fiction series in *Space Comics* (1953), all for Mick Anglo. But his style had become too dated to appeal to modern tastes, and after a spell in Kenya during which he did advertising art, he returned home to retire. He died on September 21, 1984, aged 88.

D.G.

WHITE BOY (U.S.) A Sunday half-page strip first appearing in the *Chicago Tribune* for October 8, 1933, and shortly thereafter in the *New York Daily News*, Garrett Price's *White Boy* was a curious, stunningly drawn, often wildly imaginative narrative about a white boy captured by an Indian tribe in the late 19th century. Much of its potential was blunted by Price's obvious conformity to the syndicate stricture that the Sunday strip should appeal to young readers. The attendant naiveté of dialogue and situation seems to have been a burden for the sophisticated *New Yorker* cartoonist and magazine fiction illustrator.

Loved and succored by an Indian girl named Chickadee, the strip's hero is known only as White boy for much of the early continuity, even after a scout named Dan Brown enters the story and would logically have been privy to his true name. In between purely educational episodes about Indian ways and arts, and gag pages about White boy's pet bear cub, Whimper, Price managed to introduce a weirdly gripping story about a young white "Moon Queen" who ruled over the local Indians with a tyrannical hand and who lived in a cavern palace guarded by gigantic bobcats and a grizzly bear.

Following this genuinely enthralling story, however, Price turned to more juvenile gag material and adapted a less realistic style to introduce caricatured comic horses and Indians and then abruptly, on April 28, 1935, switched the theme and period of his strip to a dude ranch in the West of the 1930s. He gave White boy the name of Bob White, dropped Chickadee and all of the earlier strip's characters, and introduced a new heroine in the first episode, Doris Hale. The renovated strip, which was called *Whiteboy in Skull Valley* (reduced later to *Skull Valley*), dealt with tenderfoot joke material, rustlers, and similar continuity at first, then developed a visually exciting narrative about cavemen for a time. It finally subsided into tired gag routines until the strip folded on August 16, 1936. Price drew a small-paneled gag strip called *Funny Fauna* to accompany his half-page for a time. It was an animal pratfall vignette without recurrent characters.

B.B.

WIEDERSHEIM, G. *see* Drayton, Grace.

WILDEY, DOUG (1922-1994) American comic book and strip artist, born on May 2, 1922, in Yonkers, New York. Lacking formal art training, Wildey began cartooning for his base newspaper in the service during World War II. In 1949 he got his first professional art job, drawing *Buffalo Bill* for the Street and Smith comic book publishing house.

For the next 10 years, Wildey did freelance work for a wide variety of comic book publishers, including National, Lev Gleason, and Dell/Western. He was most often assigned Western stories and strips, such as *Hopalong Cassidy* and *Lash LaRue* for Fawcett and *The Outlaw Kid* for Atlas (later Marvel). Wildey's photographic art style, based heavily on his morgue of picture clippings, made *The Outlaw Kid* a popular feature. It originally ran for three years, from 1954 to 1957, and was revived in reprints by Marvel in 1970. The resurrected book proved so popular that Marvel attempted to introduce new stories by a new artist after exhausting the supply of reprints. The readers preferred the Wildey stories, however, and Marvel was forced to drop the new series and reissue the old ones for the third time.

In 1959 Wildey followed Bob Lubbers as artist of *The Saint* newspaper strip (New York Herald-Tribune Syndicate) and drew it until the strip folded in 1962. He then joined Hanna-Barbera studios and created the prime-time animated adventure series *Johnny Quest*. The series enjoyed a healthy afterlife in off-network reruns, and Wildey remained in the animation industry, doing layouts and art direction. He designed the *Sub-Mariner* cartoons for the Grantray-Lawrence *Marvel Super-Heroes* TV show and returned to Hanna-Barbera for layout work on such shows as *The Fantastic Four*, *The Mighty Mighter*, and *The Herculoids*. He was also involved in the creation of presentation pieces for projected shows and feature films, for Hanna-Barbera and for other studios.

Along with his television work, Wildey drew *Korak, Son of Tarzan* in 1966 and *Tarzan* in 1968-69 for Gold Key/Western. He did freelance work for National and Skywald before beginning a new syndicated strip of his own creation in 1972. The strip, *Ambler*, for the Chicago Tribune-New York News Syndicate, gained a loyal but insufficient following and ended at the beginning of 1974. Wildey then returned to comic books, drawing *Kid Cody* for Atlas/Seaboard and *Jonah Hex* and *Sgt. Rock* for National. The stark realism of his characters made him very much in demand for strips of a mysterious or historical nature.

M.E.

In 1977 Wildey was a contributor to Joe Kubert's short-lived comics magazine *Sojourn*. Between 1983 and 1992 he published several comic books starring a Western hero called Rio. During his last years he worked mostly for television, notably on the *Johnny Quest* animated series. He died in Van Nuys, California, in October 1994.

M.H.

WILDMAN, GEORGE (1927-   ) George Wildman was born in Waterbury, Connecticut, in 1927, two years before Popeye would make his first appearance in Elzie Segar's *Thimble Theatre*. However, it is Wildman's inspired work drawing the *Popeye* comic book that King Features licensed to Charlton Comics of Derby, Connecticut, that remains one of the enduring accomplishments in cartooning.

A graduate of Whitney School of Art (now Pairer Art School) in New Haven, Wildman served in the navy toward the end of World War II. He was recalled to active service for the Korean War and served on the battleship *New Jersey*. After leaving the navy he worked as an art director for several Connecticut advertising agencies for 16 years.

Wildman entered the comics field in 1969, when he joined Charlton Comics. Within a relatively short period of time, he had become Charlton's comics editor. Wildman recalls that the best part of the job was dealing with cartoonists on their way to making it big. Charlton was unique in that it both edited and printed its own comics, all under one roof. Its parent company also published a series of pulp and music magazines. It was a starting place for many cartoonists, including John Byrne, Pat Boyette, Mike Zeck, Phil Mendez, Warren Statler, and Joe Staton (whose creation of *E-Man* was one of the superhero high points of Wildman's tenure as editor). Wildman was also blessed with a series of talented assistant editors, including Nick Cuti, Bill Pearson, and John Wren.

For King Features, Charlton published *The Phantom*, *Beetle Bailey*, *Blondie*, *Sarge Snorkle*, and *Flash Gordon* comic books. Of these the comics written by Bill Pearson and drawn by Wildman for Popeye's 50th anniversary in 1979 stand out. Wildman's Popeye birthday-special drawing was picked up by King and used worldwide in publicity.

Charlton also published *The Flintstones*, *Yogi Bear*, *The Jetsons*, *Hong Kong Phooey*, *Top Cat*, and *Scooby Doo* for Screen Gems. Connecticut cartoonists Ray Dirgo and Frank Roberge were stalwarts in this endeavor. Wildman signed Neal Adams to draw *The Six Million Dollar Man*, which was issued as a black-and-white magazine, as were *The Bionic Woman* and *Space 1999*. He published John Byrne's *Rog: 2000*.

By the early 1980s, however, Charlton Comics was in decline. Wildman left in 1984 when the company was only publishing reprints of old stories, some over and over. What brought Charlton Comics down was a direct result of its magazine distribution operation. When girlie magazine publisher Larry Flynt needed national distribution for his fledgling *Hustler* magazine, he struck a deal with Charlton. A few years later he dropped Charlton, and the company never recovered. Charlton Comics closed shop about 1986.

Wildman went on to draw many freelance cartoon projects for Random House, including *The Popeye Pop-Up Book* and books featuring *Annie*, *The Smurfs*, *Nancy and Sluggo*, and *The Snorks*. He currently has a commercial art and animation studio in Connecticut with his son Karl.

B.C.

WILLARD, FRANK HENRY (1893-1958) The man who took a notion by Joe Patterson and slammed it over the left-field wall for a home run, Frank Willard—whose *Moon Mullins* was one of the great comic strip hits of all time—was born near Chicago on September 21, 1893, the son of a physician. His early life is obscure (Willard keeping it that way in interviews), but apparently there was no support from home when the young Willard worked nights in a Chicago department store to keep himself in art school during his early twenties. His talent, however, was marked, and he was placing humorous and political newspaper panels in Chicago papers by 1914, following this freelancing with a permanent job on the *Chicago Herald* in 1916 (where he worked side-by-side with the then-unknown E. C. Segar and Billy De Beck). While with the *Herald*, Willard drew a Sunday page about a bunch of school kids called *Tom, Dick, and Harry*. When the *Herald* was purchased by Hearst for consolidation with the Chicago *American*, Willard went along with Segar and De Beck to the new paper. After a stint in the Allied Expeditionary Force during World War I, Willard began a daily strip for King Features called *The Outta-Luck Club*, about a family man and office worker named Luther Blink who relaxes from personal pressures at his club. Not particularly inspired, this was nevertheless the strip that Captain Joseph Patterson, publisher of the *New York Daily News*, saw and liked before he called Willard in to do a strip for the *News* and *Chicago Tribune* about an opportunistic, jovial young roughneck who would wear a derby (as Blink did) and knock about a big city's suburbs after a quick buck. Willard liked the idea, the initial money, and the name Patterson suggested: *Moon Mullins*.

The sample episodes the News-Tribune Syndicate circulated in 1923 intrigued a number of newspapers from coast to coast, and *Moon Mullins* began with a sizable circulation outside of its parent papers. Once again, Patterson had brought the right man and strip idea together, and the ebullient Willard put much of his own raffish character into Moon and his poolroom associates in the strip. Working with a gifted assistant,

Frank Willard, "Moon Mullins." © Chicago Tribune-New York News Syndicate.

J. R. Williams, "Out Our Way." © NEA Service.

Ferd Johnson, from the mid-1920s, Willard quickly built *Moon Mullins* into the kind of strip people read first in a newspaper each morning. (Many small-town dailies in the 1920s ran no other strip.) Together, Willard and Johnson were able to turn out an almost invariably funny, witty, and captivating continuity for the strip, and all this time Willard put in endless, exhausting hours at his obsession, golf, while Johnson turned out a Sunday page of his own called *Texas Slim* (later *Lovey Dovey*).

By 1934, Willard was able to hold his enormous audience enthralled in comic suspense while he maneuvered two of his principal characters, Emmy Schmaltz and Lord Plushbottom, into a marriage held at the Chicago World's Fair. By this time his annual income was over $100,000, *Moon Mullins* was in more than 400 newspapers, and many *Moon Mullins* books were in print. Later in the 1930s, Willard moved west, but his true home remained the golf course, his unending game taking him to all parts of the country, where he drew, near deadline, strip episodes in hotel rooms (which were sometimes lost, forcing Johnson to draw others or the syndicate to substitute old episodes). During World War II, *Moon Mullins* was one of the few strips to steer clear of war involvement for its principals: Moon stayed a bum throughout, as did the other characters in the strip. Never filmed, *Mullins* did make the radio in 1940.

Willard's death in Los Angeles at the age of 64 was sudden: he died a week after a stroke in the Cedars of Lebanon Hospital on January 12, 1958. Ferd Johnson, of course, continued *Moon Mullins*, and is still drawing it.

B.B.

WILLIAMS, JAMES ROBERT (1888-1957) American cartoonist, born August 18, 1888, in Nova Scotia, Canada, to American parents. His father, an executive with a public utility company, moved his family to Detroit after finishing his temporary assignment in Canada. J. R. Williams was raised with an early understanding of the importance of holding a job. A husky kid, he was playing football at 14, had worked as a fireman on the Pennsylvania Railroad at 15, and felt more than able to make his own way when, stirred by a spirit of adventure, he ran away from home (with no ill feelings) in his mid-teens.

Working his way to Little Rock, Arkansas, he got his first independent job as a mule skinner on a railroad grading gang. A little later, in southern Kansas, Williams did menial work on a ranch, getting his first real taste of cowboy life. Moving on to Fort Sill, Oklahoma, he signed up with the U.S. Cavalry for a three-year hitch, again playing football on the cavalry team, with the young Lieutenant George Patton as a fellow player.

Discharged at Fort Sheridan, Illinois, Williams returned to his parents in Ohio, married, and went to work for a nearby crane manufacturing company, where he drew his first published work: a cover design for the company catalog. He stayed with the crane company for seven years, all the while seriously polishing his style and submitting strip ideas to syndicates everywhere. Finally, in 1921, NEA put Williams to work doing his basic panel idea—the *Out Our Way* that is still running today.

Asked by NEA to do a Sunday page in the mid-1920s, Williams felt that his small-town family group, named the Willits, would be the most widely appealing of his character groups, and *Out Our Way, With the Willits*, was then launched. Williams never cared for the extra chore of the multipaneled Sunday page, and several cartoonists worked on it for him, first George Scarbo, and later his ultimate replacement on the strip, Ned Cochran. Widely syndicated by the late 1920s, Williams followed up a boyhood ambition and bought his own ranch near Walnut Creek, Arizona, moving there from Cleveland (the location of NEA) in 1930.

After a long period of ill health, Williams died of a chronic heart ailment in Pasadena, California (where he had moved in 1941), on June 18, 1957. It can certainly be said of Williams, though of few other cartoonists, that there is not a single one of his professionally published drawings, whether done for *Out Our Way* or for advertising use (Sunday page aside), that does not merit permanent reprinting in a complete set of his work.

B.B.

WILLIAMSON, AL (1931-   ) American comic book and comic strip artist, born on March 21, 1931, in New York City. After growing up in Bogota, Colombia, Williamson returned to New York and trained with Burne Hogarth. His first comic book work appeared in Eastern's *Heroic* number 51 in 1948, and even then the heavy influences of Alex Raymond were

Al Williamson, EC Science Fiction Panel. © William M. Gaines, Agent, Inc.

evident. During his early years, Williamson worked for many comic book houses, among them ACG (1951-52), Eastern (1948-52), for which he drew *Buster Crabbe* with Frank Frazetta; and Toby (1950-53), for which he drew *Billy the Kid* and *John Wayne*. Although his illustrative approach was rapidly maturing, his work did not really begin to solidify until he joined the E.C. group in 1952.

The youngest artist in an incredibly talented stable that already included Davis, Wood, Kurtzman, Severin, Frazetta, and Ingels and that would later include Crandall and Krigstein, Williamson began improving immediately. His slick, photographic style developed rapidly, and he was assigned to E.C.'s much-heralded science-fiction stories. Often working with Frazetta and Krenkel, an older artist who drew the most intricate backgrounds in the field, Williamson became popular with the rabid E.C. fans.

When E.C. folded in 1955, Williamson moved on to Atlas and spent six years drawing war, romance, adventure, and horror tales. Also during this time, he freelanced for ACG (1958-59), Charlton, Dell, and Harvey (all 1958), and Prize (1955-58). Much of his work was erratic, however, and few of the stories showed the flair and verve his E.C. work had exhibited.

Williamson then became John Prentice's assistant on the *Rip Kirby* newspaper feature in 1961. His work here was mainly backgrounding, but Williamson picked up valuable composition and layout pointers from the slick, clean Prentice. He continued with Prentice until 1964, and then returned to comic books, contributing material to Warren's black-and-white horror books (1964-66), Dell (1965), and Harvey (1962-67), some of it with Jack Kirby. In 1966, he drew three issues of King's *Flash Gordon* comic book, and like his idol Raymond before him, Williamson produced Flash's stories with dynamic conception, brilliant draftsmanship, and an eye-pleasing layout. He won the NCS's 1967 Story Comic Book plaque for his efforts.

Perhaps because of his stellar *Flash Gordon* work, King offered him a chance to replace artist Bob Lubbers on the *Secret Agent X-9* syndicated strip, another old Raymond feature. The title was soon changed to *Secret Agent Corrigan*, and Williamson drew it for 13 years, beginning on January 20, 1967. His superb use of blacks and zip-a-tone, combined with his solid layouts and Archie Goodwin's scripts, made *Corrigan* one of the few high-quality adventure strips of the time.

J.B.

Williamson quit *Corrigan* in 1980. Aside from drawing the *Star Wars* newspaper strip from 1981 to 1984, he has devoted his career to comic books for the last decade and a half, starting with the adaptation of *The Empire Strikes Back* in 1980. Since that time his work has appeared in many more movie adaptations (*Return of the Jedi, Blade Runner,* etc.) and in graphic novels such as *Predator and Prey.* From the late 1980s on he has concentrated on the *Daredevil* and *Punisher* comic book titles.

M.H.

WILSHIRE, MARY (1953-   ) American illustrator and comic book artist, born in New Jersey in 1953. Her work in comic books is only one aspect of Mary Wilshire's career. She currently is doing more illustration than cartoon work and is regularly published in the National Geographic Society's children's magazine *GEO World.* The mother of two daughters, Wilshire is especially interested in artwork for children. She was one of the artists drawing *Barbie* for Marvel Comics; that comic book ended in 1995, by some accounts a good product that fell victim to poor marketing.

Wilshire planned on a career in commercial art and studied at the Pratt Institute of Art in Brooklyn, New York. Her comic book career developed first as a lark in underground comix. In 1978 she had a four-page story published in *Wet Satin #2*, the comix of women's erotica edited by Trina Robbins. She also contributed to the underground comix *Young Lust* and *After Shock*.

She had grown up a fan of *Mad* magazine and of animated and newspaper comics and was influenced by the work of Jack Davis, Stan Drake of *The Heart of Juliet Jones*, Alex Kotzky of *Apartment 3G*, and animator Chuck Jones. Her first work for Marvel Comics came around 1980, when she contributed to *Crazy*, the *Mad* clone that never really caught on. Larry Hama, with whom Wilshire had worked on *Crazy*, asked her to take over the drawing of one of Marvel's stars, the barbarian swordswoman created by pulp fiction writer Robert E. Howard, *Red Sonja: She-Devil with a Sword*. Wilshire, who loves drawing people best of all, knew little of Red Sonja but liked the concept of a beautiful battling barbarian in a chain-mail bikini.

The character of Red Sonja had been redefined in the mid-1970s by Frank Thorne's tour de force drawing and Roy Thomas's scripts. Cartoonist, writer, and *Elfquest* creator Wendy Pini had become the first woman creatively involved with *Red Sonja*, writing some scripts, but it was Mary Wilshire who captivated fans, often teenage boys, as the beautiful woman cartoonist who drew the beautiful woman warrior.

Wilshire brought her own interpretation to *Red Sonja* in a style that was less ornate than Thorne's. Her skill at drawing the human form was displayed in full flower. No matter what else she does in her career, her work on *Red Sonja* has won her a place in comic book history as the character's definitive artist.

Wilshire's other work for Marvel included drawing such titles as *Power Pack*, *Spider-Man*, *Ka-Zar*, *New Mutants*, and a four-book miniseries of *Firestar*, a superheroine from the children's *Spidey* animated television show. Her magazine illustration work includes pieces for *National Lampoon*, *Heavy Metal*, and general-interest publications such as *Good Housekeeping* and *Reader's Digest*. She has also done extensive licensed-product artwork for the World Wrestling Federation.

B.C.

WILSON, ROY (1900-1965)   British cartoonist Royston Warner Wilson was born in Kettering, Northamptonshire, on July 9, 1900. Educated at Norwich and trained at Norwich School of Art, he was apprenticed to Trevor Page as a furniture designer for three years, then appointed as a junior draftsman on the air board staff in London. Conscripted into the army on November 10, 1918, the day before the armistice, he served in the King's Royal Rifle Corps in Cologne until March 13, 1920.

A chance meeting in a pub led to his becoming assistant to Norwich cartoonist Donald Newhouse, who paid Wilson three pounds a week to help him pencil and ink the characters he drew for the comic papers published by Amalgamated Press. On the side, Wilson contributed single-joke cartoons and also painted some color postcards for Jarrold's (1923). Working in Newhouse's style, which followed that of the earlier Tom

Browne and G. M. Payne, Wilson soon passed his tutor and became the finest exponent of the traditional British comic style. His earliest work is difficult to identify, as Newhouse did all the lettering, but it is certain he worked on all Newhouse strips from 1920, including *Monk and Jaff*, an animal strip in *Comic Life*; *Cuthbert the Carpenter* in *Funny Wonder*; *G. Whizz* in *Jester*; and *Tickle and Tootle* in *Sparks*.

In 1921, for the new nursery comic *Bubbles*, he worked on *Pickles the Puppy*, *Bunny the Rabbit*, and *Micky the Mouse*, also doing *Jacko and Jerry* in *Comic Life*. Animals would, in the years ahead, play an important part in Wilson's work, and some of his finest series featured comic animals: *George the Jolly Gee Gee* (October 15, 1938) and *Chimpo's Circus* (October 8, 1938). The latter strip was his first designed for full color and ran on the front of *Happy Days*, the new gravure comic, making it the finest weekly of the golden age of British comics.

Wilson's other color work was confined to annuals, for which he often painted covers and frontispiece plates: *Chips Annual*, *Butterfly Annual*, etc. These minor masterpieces and *Chimpo* were the only works he was allowed to sign by his publisher, Amalgamated Press. (He worked for no other.) In his later years he drew many star personality strips for *Radio Fun*, *Film Fun*, and *T.V. Fun*, but although his likenesses were excellent, their style restricted his natural humor. He was better with the sheer slapstick of *Pitch and Toss* or the wild fantasy of *Stymie and his Magic Wishbone* (1938). Outside comics his only artwork was a weekly painting-competition panel for *Woman's Own*, which he drew from 1947 until his death at age 65 from lung cancer in June 1965. His last strip, *Morecambe and Wise*, was published on January 30, 1965.

His strips include: 1920—*Beside the Seaside*; Funny Films; 1921—*Jolly Jacko*; *Pretty Peggy*; *Reel Comedies*; *Phil and Bert*; *Roland Butter and Hammond Deggs*; *Willie Evergrow*; 1922—*Joyland Express*; *Peter the Pussy Policeman*; *Mossoo Marmalade*; *Pitch and Toss*; 1923—*Basil and Bert* (first full-page solo); *P. C. Blossom*; *Rosie and Rex*; 1924—*Good Knight Gilbert* and *Folio the Page*; 1925—*Oozee the Wonder Bird*; 1926—*Chip and Jerry*; *3 Jolly Sailorboys*; 1927—*Happy Family*; *Fred and Freda*; 1928—*Tango the Terrier*; 1929—*Sir Toby Tinribs*; 1930—*Steve and Stumpy* (the first official Wilson strip without Newhouse); *Fun and Frolic at Fitzpip Hall* (the first Wilson front-page series, in *Comic Cuts*); 1931—*Molly and Mick*; 1932—*Augustus Topping*; *Chief Chucklehead*; 1933—*Happy Harry* and *Sister Sue* (the first full-color front page); 1934—*Tiddlewink Family*; *Jerry Jenny and Joe* (the first adventure strip); 1935—*Jack Sprat and Tubby Tadpole*; *Twiddle and Nobb*; *Peanut and Doughboy*; 1936—*Lieut. Daring and Jolly Roger*; *The Captain, the Kid and the Cook*; *Robin Hood*; 1937—*Daydreaming Don*; *Honey Potts*; 1938—*Dimple and Dumpling*; 1939—*Vernon the Villain*; *Happy Andy and His Playful Pets*; 1941—*Tommy Handley*; 1944—*Billy Muggins*; 1946—*Sweet Rosie O'Grady*; 1947—*Dragamuffin*; 1948—*Wildflower and Little Elf*; 1949—*Jimmy Jolly's Magic Brolly*; *Hook Line and Singer*; 1953—*Keeper Nyon*; 1954—*Smarty*; 1955—*Reg Varney*; 1956—*Derek Roy*; 1957—*Jerry Lewis*; 1958—*Terry Thomas*; 1960—*Harry Secombe*; 1961—*Cloris and Clare*; 1962—*Bruce Forsyth*; 1964—*Morecambe and Wise*.

D.G.

WINNER, CHARLES H. (1885-1956)   American artist, born in 1885 in Perrysville, Pennsylvania. Doc Winner began drawing on clay slates on the family farm and soon decided on a career in cartooning. In his early twenties, after an unhappy stint in art school, Winner secured a position with the *Pittsburgh Post*, succeeding Will De Beck, who was to lose several jobs and establish a cartooning school in order to survive before creating *Barney Google*.

Winner drew for the *Post* for a few years, but attracted national attention through the re-publication of notable editorial cartoons (he also drew sports cartoons). In 1914 he left to dabble with animation (as many of his contemporaries did) and draw a series of women's suffrage cartoons on contract. In 1918 Winner accepted an offer from the Hearst organization to join its comic art staff, beginning a 38-year association with Hearst, which is his main contribution to comic history.

Winner was perhaps the most talented and certainly the most utilized of the King Features bullpen crew, which included such workhorses through the years as Paul Fung Sr., Joe Musial, Bob Naylor, Bud Sagendorf, Bela Zaboly, Vern Greene, Paul and Walter Frehm, Austin Briggs, Charles Flanders, Nicholas Afonsky, Lou Sayre Schwarz, and Paul Norris. Most of these men did creditable jobs filling in on established comics anywhere from one day to several years. There were exceptions (Musial, for example, was adequate on *Barney Google* but a butcher with *The Katzies*).

Winner filled in on *Thimble Theatre* during Segar's last days and approximated the artwork; other assignments included work on *Barney Google* and (after Knerr's death) *The Katzenjammer Kids*.

Besides *The Katzies*, Winner was permitted to sign one effort: *Elmer*. Having inherited the strip in 1926 from A. C. Fera, whose strip had been titled *Just Boy* (perhaps after James West's very funny book), Winner proceeded to do consistent, homey, and gently humorous work. Elmer, whose constant exclamation was "Crim-a-nentlies!", was a quiet but solid favorite of two generations of readers.

Winner's style was versatile, but his early newspaper work was more reserved and solid than the work of his conscious influence, De Beck. His syndicate work, too (as in *Popeye* and *The Katzies*), is a little stiff and uncomfortable; action was not his forte. Neither was expression; the faces in *Elmer* are all slightly empty. The top strips to this feature, *Daffy Doodles* and *Alexander Smart, Esq.*, showed a little more looseness. Winner died on August 12, 1956, of cancer.

R.M.

WINNETOU (Germany) Winnetou, the noble Apache chief, was originally the creation of the prolific German novelist Karl May (1842-1912), whose books over the decades have sold 50 million copies in Germany alone and have been translated into 25 languages. May first introduced the character of Winnetou in an 1879 novel, but he did not start the *Winnetou* trilogy until 1893. Although he did a lot of research on America, it was not until 1908 that he actually visited the United States. Nevertheless, several generations took May's Western novels for gospel truth, and these novels laid the groundwork for a German fascination with the Western genre, a fact attested to by, among other things, the large number of German cowboy clubs.

The success of the books beckoned comic artists to try their hands with the material. They were especially alerted to Winnetou when a series of Karl May movies hit the screens in the early 1960s. The *Winnetou* saga was done in one way or another by Juan Arranz, by Studio Vandersteen, and by Walter Neugebauer for a special Kauka album. The best of these, staying closest to the original novels, started in February 1963 and was produced by Lehning Verlag, with the able hand of Helmut Nickel providing the artwork. It is largely due to Nickel that the flavor of the novels was still felt in the comic strip version. As with other strips he had done (e.g., *Robinson, Hot Jerry, Peters seltsame Reisen* ["Peters Strange Journeys," a comics parody]), Nickel used realism with just an inkling of comic relief, a characteristic of his style.

After the publication of the first eight issues, the series was split up into two alternating ones. Besides Western adventures with Winnetou, there were also comic books with adventures in the Orient. Of these only the *Winnetou* artwork was worthwhile. It is too bad that Nickel withdrew from comics at the time because the story was spread thin over a large number of *Winnetou* issues until 1965. The strip has also been reprinted in foreign countries.

W.F.

WINNIE WINKLE (U.S.) Created by Martin Branner and distributed by the News-Tribune Syndicate, *Winnie Winkle, the Bread Winner* made its first appearance as a daily strip on September 20, 1920. Winnie was a vivacious young woman (modeled after Branner's own wife, Edith) who worked as a stenographer for one Barnaby Bibbs in order to support herself, her father Rip, and Ma. Winnie's daily vicissitudes on her job constituted the thick of the plot until April 2, 1922, when Winnie blissfully announced in the first panel of her newly created Sunday page: "Folks, I want you to meet my adopted brother Perry."

For the next 25 years, *Winnie Winkle* was to display a split personality (as was the case with many other newspaper strips of the 1920s and 1930s). During the week (as becomes a working girl), Winnie remained the heroine of the strip. She had a string of suitors with whom she flirted outrageously before finally marrying Will (Mr.) Wright in 1937 and settling into the dull felicity of many other domestic strips. Branner saw the trap, however, and Will mysteriously disappeared in the 1940s, leaving Winnie free again to play the field (after a suitable time during which she searched in vain for her vanished husband).

On the other hand, the Sunday page was almost entirely given over to the antics of Perry and his merry gang of pals known as the Rinkey-dinks. In the 1940's, unfortunately, Perry came to be gradually replaced by the newcomer Denny Dimwit (the name tells it all), and the charm of the Sunday feature faded along with him.

In the 1950s the strip (now shortened to simply *Winnie Winkle*) was devoted entirely to Winnie's romantic adventures, and Perry, all grown up now, made only intermittent appearances. In 1962, Branner retired and left the strip to his former assistant, Max van Bibber, who did it in the same soap-opera vein, giving Winnie a new rival in the person of her own daughter Wendy.

In 1980 Frank Bolle took over *Winnie Winkle* from the retiring van Bibber. In an attempt to make the feature more relevant to the times, he introduced continuities dealing with crime, corruption, and illicit drugs. Despite his efforts the strip only barely kept afloat during his 16-year tenure. Ironically, when it was finally

"Winnie Winkle," Martin Branner. © *Chicago Tribune-New York News Syndicate.*

discontinued on July 28, 1996, the syndicate gave as the reason for its demise the fact that Winnie was "not recognized as a contemporary role model for the '90s."

Winnie Winkle had her own comic book in the 1940s, but the strip was never popular enough to be made into a motion picture.

M.H.

WINTERBOTHAM, RUSSELL (1904-1971) An American writer and editor born on August 1, 1904, in Pittsburg, Kansas, Winterbotham was a speedy novelist and facile editor. During his career he turned out dozens of paperback novels under the name J. Harvey Bond.

He joined the Newspaper Enterprise Association of Cleveland as a book editor and soon found himself writing strips. His work on Walt Scott's Sunday *Captain Easy* was adequate, but not up to the level of Crane, Turner, or even the recent Crooks and Lawrence humorous stories.

But he did turn in solid comic strip storywriting on *Chris Welkin*, several years of *Red Ryder*, and *Vic Flint* (and *Flint*'s latter-day metamorphosis, *The Good Guys*) under the Bond name.

Winterbotham wrote the brief but classic pamphlet on comic production, *How Comic Strips Are Made*. He retired from NEA in February 1969 and died in 1971 after a long illness.

R.M.

WIZARD OF ID, THE (U.S.) Johnny Hart created *The Wizard of Id*, in collaboration with Brant Parker for the drawing, on November 9, 1964. Like Hart's earlier *B.C.*, *The Wizard* is distributed by Publishers-Hall Syndicate.

In the forsaken kingdom of Id there once lived a midget of a monarch, grouchy, greedy, cruel, nasty,

and craven. His greatest satisfaction in life lay in the debasement and exploitation of his equally unlovable, loutish subjects. He was flanked by his cowardly knight Brandolph and by the Wizard, a magician of dubious achievement, whose spells, as often as not, backfired lamentably when they worked at all. Yet, in the dark recesses of the royal palace, the Wizard experimented untiringly with formulas and potions, under the watchful eye of the spirit that he sometimes succeeded in conjuring. (The Wizard was, along with Bang, the inebriated jester, the only man who could play tricks on the diminutive king with impunity.)

The mood of the strip swings from black humor ("What is bread?" asks an unwashed prisoner when told he has been put on bread and water as punishment for some offense) to oft-repeated inside jokes ("The king is a fink!"—the populace's protest cry—appears in the most unlikely places and in the most outlandish forms) to verbal and visual puns (in answer to the king's peremptory order to bring rain, the Wizard calls forth a cloudburst just over the king's head).

Johnny Hart's unique brand of humor is precisely captured by Brant Parker's simple yet sophisticated style. Using the same graphic conventions as Johnny Hart on *B.C.*, Parker brings to his drawings a more rounded, more humanized look, and his visual depiction of the characters is well-nigh flawless.

The Wizard of Id has been reprinted in paperback form by Fawcett. There are now more than 30 collections in print. The Wizard and his acolytes have also been featured in a number of animation specials. The strip, now distributed by Creators Syndicate, received the Reuben Award in 1984.

M.H.

WOLINSKI, GEORGES (1934-   ) French cartoonist and writer, born in 1934 in Tunisia, of a Polish

"The Wizard of Id," Johnny Hart and Brant Parker. © Field Newspaper Syndicate.

father and an Italian mother. In 1946, Georges Wolinski's family moved to Briancon, in southeastern France, where the young boy attended grammar and high school. In 1952 he went to Paris and studied at the School of Architecture for a while (by his own admission, Wolinski stayed in school only to avoid being drafted and sent to Algeria). In 1960 he started his long collaboration with the satirical monthly *Hara-Kiri*, to which he contributed cartoons, illustrations, and a series of comic strips on political or erotic themes: *Ils Ne Pensent Qu'à Ca* ("They Only Think of One Thing"), an extremely funny and ribald variation on the eternal war between the sexes; *Histoires Inventées* ("Invented Stories"); *Hit-Parades* (in which Wolinski indulged his own sardonic views of men, women, politics, literature, history, and the arts).

Wolinski played an active role in the May 1968 student revolt, making speeches, issuing manifestos, and founding with his colleague *Siné L'Enragé* ("The Rabid One"), one of the most mordant satirical magazines born during this turbulent period, and the only one to survive. He also expressed his philosophy in a new comic strip series, *Je Ne Veux Pas Mourir Idiot* ("I Don't Want to Die an Idiot," 1968), in which the slogans of the Establishment were pitilessly dissected and lampooned, with the inevitable punch line: "I don't want to die an idiot." Later, disillusioned by the failure of the student movement, he created a new series, *Il N'y A Pas Que la Politique Dans la Vie* ("There Is More to Life Than Politics"), whose title says it all.

In 1969 Wolinski became the editor of the newly created comic monthly *Charlie*, and he made quite a reputation for himself as a playwright with several plays adapted from his comic creations (*Je Ne Veux Pas*

Georges Wolinski, magazine cartoon.

Mourir Idiot was one of the hits of the 1970-71 theater season in Paris).

Georges Wolinski has often been called the French Jules Feiffer, and there are a number of similarities. Both men use their comic strips as vehicles for social and political criticism, their drawings are reduced to their simplest expression, their characters are often abject, and their dialogues are bitter. They both enjoyed somewhat similar careers (cartoonist, editor, playwright). But, while Feiffer has always played it safe, Wolinski never hesitated to do as he preached, making his art and his life one. That this made Wolinski the superior artist (as some in France contend) is a dubious proposition.

Since 1977, when he became political cartoonist of the Communist daily *L'Humanité*, Wolinski has devoted most of his efforts to editorial cartooning. His drawings have appeared in a variety of publications, from the liberal daily *Libération* to the conservative weekly *Paris-Match*. He has also written skits for television and has continued to produce stage plays. His comic-strip output has become sporadic, principally appearing in the pages of the humor magazines *L'Echo des Savanes* and *Charlie Hebdo*.

M.H.

WOLVERTON, BASIL (1909-1978) American comic book artist and writer, born July 9, 1909, in Central Point, Oregon. Although Wolverton had no formal art training, he soon became one of the most respected and innovative creators in the comic book field. His work was so offbeat, intricate, and personalized that *Life* magazine's editors once called his material work from "the spaghetti and meatball school of design"; many underground cartoonists cite Wolverton as a profound influence on their style.

A former newspaper artist who sold his first cartoon to *America's Humor* in 1926, Wolverton saw his first comic book work appear in Globe's *Circus* number one (June 1938). His first major strip was a fantasy/science-fiction/superhero feature entitled *Spacehawk*, which premiered in Novelty Press's *Target* number five in June 1940. His early scripts were violent and brutal, with retribution being substituted for justice. Spacehawk, an interplanetary crime-fighter, was more likely to kill a captured criminal than to bind him over for proper punishment. Artistically, the feature showcased Wolverton's creative genius. Although some of the work was crude and cramped, it showed brilliant flashes of Wolverton's unsurpassed storytelling. The feature lost its fantasy base by editorial fiat in 1942, and the strip disappeared after December 1942's *Target* number 34.

By that time, however, Wolverton had already entered his humor period and created *Powerhouse Pepper* for Timely in April 1942. The strip was an instant success and appeared sporadically until 1948. Powerhouse Pepper himself was a near-perfect physical specimen with an eye for beautiful women; he was, however, somewhat lacking in mental prowess. Wolverton used a cast of grotesque-looking characters in the strip. This was to become his trademark, but he also utilized a textual device that has yet to be successfully duplicated: all the *Powerhouse Pepper* characters spoke in outrageously zany rhymes and alliterations. Combined with his exaggerated anatomy, Wolverton's rhymes made the strip one of the most cherished features of the 1940s. Wolverton created several other outstanding humor strips during this period, including *Scoop Scuttle* (Lev Gleason), *Mystic Moot and His Magic Snoot* (Fawcett), and *Inspector Hector the Crime Detector* (Timely). Then, after creating 17 outstanding science-fiction and mystery stories for Atlas between 1951 and 1953, Wolverton left comic books until 1973, when he began drawing covers of appropriately grotesque characters for National's weird humor book entitled *Plop*.

In 1946, United Feature sponsored a contest that invited *Li'l Abner* readers to submit drawings of Lower Slobbovia's ugly woman, Lena the Hyena. Wolverton won the contest handily with a patently repulsive drawing, and he began drawing a long series of highly detailed caricatures of important people of the day. Also during his career, Wolverton drew a handful of well-received features for *Mad*, was active in the commercial art field, and created a beautifully rendered adaptation of the Bible for Ambassador Press.

Graphic Story Magazine, a limited-edition magazine produced by comic art fan William Spicer, devoted two complete issues to Wolverton and his career in 1970 and 1971. In it, *Mad* associate editor Jerry DeFuccio commented that, in recognition of Wolverton's contributions, the ACBA awards should rightfully have been named the Basil. He died in Vancouver, Washington, in 1978.

J.B.

WONDER WOMAN (U.S.) Wonder Woman was created by writer William Moulton Marston (under the pen name Charles Moulton) and first illustrated by H. G. Peter for National Comics' *All-Star* number eight (December 1941). The next month she began appearing in *Sensation* (where she adopted her civilian identity of Diana Prince); and she began in *Wonder Woman* comics in the summer of 1942.

Marston was not a comic book writer but rather a well-known psychologist and inventor of the polygraph. He created *Wonder Woman* to express his theories about male-female relationships. The strip has received heavy scrutiny over the years, being adopted by the woman's liberation movement as an early manifestation of their philosophy. On the other hand, Dr. Fredric Wertham's controversial *Seduction of the Innocent* (Holt, Rinehart and Winston, 1953) saw *Wonder*

Basil Wolverton, "Lena the Hyena." © Basil Wolverton.

"Wonder Woman," William Moulton Marston. © National Periodical Publications.

Woman as a "crime comic . . . found to be one of the most harmful."

Wonder Woman's origin had several versions, but the most widely accepted claimed she was an Amazon princess and daughter of Queen Hippolyte. She lived on Paradise Island, where no men were allowed and ostensibly came to America to help fight the World War II. Wearing a star-spangled costume of red, white, blue, and yellow, she was almost omnipotent, unless her bracelets of submission were chained together by a male.

It would be impossible to cite all the various psychological interpretations scholars have drawn from *Wonder Woman*, but they include sadomasochism, lesbianism, and literally dozens of other allegedly aberrant "isms."

After Marston died in 1947, the strip began ignoring pseudo-psychology and became a straight adventure strip. More emphasis was placed on Wonder Woman's gadgets: her invisible robot plane, her golden lasso, and her bracelets. By the late 1960s, she was just another superheroine. One of the few interesting interpretations came when Denny O'Neil became the writer and editor. He stripped Wonder Woman of her powers and traditional costume and made her a disciple of I Ching. The change did not last, however; she was soon back at her former status.

She still appears in *Wonder Woman* comics, now having published over 200 issues. And besides her numerous comic book appearances, she has also had a short-lived newspaper strip, made cartoon appearances, and is a sought-after property.

The strip's greatest recent achievement, however, was the publication of the *Wonder Woman* hardback anthology (Holt, Rinehart, 1972). Besides reprinting several of the classic Marston-Peter strips, the book carried an outstanding introduction by Gloria Steinem, renowned journalist, feminist, and editor of *Ms.* magazine. Dr. Phyllis Chesler, a psychologist and feminist, contributed an interpretative essay that captures the character's original concept more faithfully than anything published after Marston's death.

J.B.

Wonder Woman in the late 1970s and the 1980s experienced a series of ups and downs (with a majority of downs), culminating in the cancellation of the title in February 1986. She came back to her roots in the miniseries *The Legend of Wonder Woman* (May to August 1986), leading to a reprise of the *Wonder Woman* monthly comic book in February 1987. George Perez ably guided the Amazon Princess through her paces for the first couple of years, but aside from a brief interim by John Byrne, the title has again become mired in mediocrity.

Wonder Woman has been the subject of a number of media adaptations through the years. Aside from the aforementioned newspaper strip (1944-45), there was a live-action series on ABC-TV (1976-77), later transferring to CBS (1977-79), with Lynda Carter in the title role.

M.H.

WONG, TONY (1950-   ) Born in Canton, Tony Wong moved to Hong Kong at the age of six. There he became familiar with the only comics available, those from Japan. At 14 he quit school to support his family, working as an office boy and, later, as an artist for several firms. At 20 he started the comics company Yuk Long ("Jademan"), which by 1972 had become Hong Kong's leading comic-book publisher, a position it retains to this day. Wong's books used kung fu, science-fiction, ghost, and humor stories. His first big hit was the kung fu book *Siulauman* ("Street Fighter"), whose title was changed in 1980 to *Dragon and Tiger Heroes*; it is still a best-seller.

By the mid-1980s Jademan controlled 70 to 90 percent of Hong Kong's comics trade, amassing a total circulation of 2.1 million for its 15 titles. A feature Wong adopted from the Japanese publishers was their factory style of operation; he refined the system, using five times more artists per book, tiering his art staff, and building in bonuses as incentives for high production.

Wong was at the height of his career in 1987-88, when he listed Jademan on the Hong Kong Stock Exchange, diversified into other ventures, and eyed a large overseas market. He bought parts of daily newspapers, magazines, and other properties and expanded his distribution networks deeper into Asia, the United States, and other English-speaking countries, before running into a series of troubles that saw him lose control of Jademan in 1989. Shortly after, he was convicted and sent to jail for fraudulent business practices.

Upon his release from prison in 1993, Wong launched a new comics company that attracted back some of his old audience, as well as some former Jademan employees. Jademan itself had continued to thrive, evolving into a holdings firm of 14 companies, 2 of which published up to 20 comics titles by 1992.

Among Wong's major contributions, aside from igniting the comics industry of Hong Kong, were highlighting the international marketing possibilities for Asian comics, creating the martial arts genre for which the colony became known, and training a number of excellent artists, including Ma Wing-shing and Chris Lau, who went on to start their own comics companies.

J.A.L.

WOOD, ROBIN (1944-) Although he is generally considered to be an Argentinian author, Robin Wood was actually born in 1944 in Nueva Australia, a colony founded in the jungles of Paraguay by Australian immigrants, and he lived and worked in Brazil, Argentina, and Italy before settling in Copenhagen, Denmark, in 1993. After a childhood not too dissimilar from that of the young narrator of Paul Theroux's *The Mosquito Coast*, he moved with his parents to Buenos Aires. His love of adventure led him to work successively as a prizefighter in Argentinian boxing rings and as a truck driver through Brazilian jungles.

His first foray into comics occurred in 1965 when he started work, first as a cartoonist, then as a scriptwriter, for Editorial Columba in Buenos Aires. His first success in the field came with *Nippur de Lagash*, an adventure strip he created in 1974 and continues to produce today. An incredible succession of titles followed, from *Gilgamesh* (an epic saga set in ancient Mesopotamia) to *Merlino* (recounting the exploits of the fabled wizard from the Arthurian legends).

The author's fame spread internationally, especially to Italy, where most of his series were published in the monthly *LancioStory*. There he confirmed his success in 1981 with *Dago*, drawn by Alberto Salinas. The protagonist is a Venetian aristocrat named Cesare Renzi, the only member of his family to survive a murderous conspiracy of Venetian noblemen and Saracen pirates. The hero crisscrosses medieval Europe, under the contemptuous nickname "Dago," in search of his family's killers. Along the way, he meets such worthy opponents as Vlad Tepes the Impaler, better known as Count Dracula. In addition to the titles he has done using his own name, Wood has, under a variety of pseudonyms (including Robert O'Neil, Carlos Ruiz, and Roberto Monti), written innumerable series, ranging from Gothic tales (*Dracula*) to military yarns (*Il Cosacco, Qui la Legione*) to romance stories (*Amanda*).

Wood has been the recipient of many distinctions and honors for his work, including the Lifetime Achievement Award from the 1996 International Comics Salon in Rome.

M.H.

WOOD, WALLACE (1927-1981) American comic book and comic strip artist and writer, born June 17, 1927, in Menahga, Minnesota. A self-taught artist, Wally Wood received his only professional training during short stints at the Minneapolis School of Art and Burne Hogarth's Cartoonists and Illustrators School. Breaking into comic art as a letterer, he did not see significant amounts of his artwork appear in print until 1949. His best early work came in 1950, when he drew three weeks of Sundays for Will Eisner's *The Spirit*. Entitled "Denny Colt in Outer Space," the episode gave the earliest indication of Wood's amazing ability to interpret science-fiction material.

Wood also entered the comic book field in 1949, freelancing for many groups, including Ziff-Davis, Avon, Charlton, and EC. He finally settled down with EC about the time Bill Gaines and Al Feldstein introduced the New Trend line in 1951 and became their main science-fiction illustrator. Wood had perfected his talent with science-fiction material: he drew intricate spaceships, startling monsters, and beautiful space scenes; he was a master of lighting; he created intriguing and innovative alien planet scenes; and he topped it all off by drawing luscious and incredibly well-endowed women. His page composition and tight line work made him the acknowledged dean of comic book science fiction. He later went on to illustrate for science-fiction digests like Galaxy.

At the same time, however, Wood was also contributing heavily to EC's irrepressible *Mad*. Along with Will Elder and Harvey Kurtzman, Wood was a pioneer in *Mad*'s cluttered panel technique, and one had to really strain to catch all the sight gags and jokes Wood crammed into each panel. He appeared in every *Mad* magazine and comic produced during the book's first 12 years.

After EC folded its non-*Mad* line in 1956, Wood branched out and started a successful advertising art career, but he also found time to assist on syndicated strips such as *Terry and the Pirates*, *Flash Gordon*, and *Prince Valiant*. On September 8, 1958, he and Jack Kirby began a well-received syndicated science-fiction strip entitled *Skymasters*, which ran for 18 months.

Wood has since gone on to work for almost every comic book company while continuing to do advertising art. In 1964, he did some highly acclaimed work on Marvel's *Daredevil* book, and he later worked for National, Warren, Gold Key, King, and several others. In 1965, he created the *THUNDER Agents* for Tower with the aid of artists Steve Ditko, Dan Adkins, Reed Crandall, Gil Kane, and others; though short-lived, it was one of the best features of the 1960s.

In 1966, Wood founded *Witzend*, a fanzine in which professional artists wrote and drew strips they normally could not produce for the mass-market-oriented comic book companies. Stricken with an incurable illness, he took his own life on November 3, 1981, in Los Angeles.

J.B.

WOOLFOLK, WILLIAM (1917-) American comic book writer, editor, and publisher, born in June 1917 on Long Island, New York. After attending New York University, Bill Woolfolk began his writing career in 1936 by contributing to some of the many small literary magazines of the time. He then moved on to bylined pieces at slicks such as *Liberty* and *Collier's*, became an advertising copywriter, and finally entered the comic book field in 1941 as a writer for the MLJ line.

Unlike most writers of the time, who simply wrote the story and dialogue and gave it to the artist, Woolfolk used a style that would eventually become prevalent at Marvel in the 1960s. He would first produce a plot synopsis, allow the artist to draw the plot (Marvel art director John Romita once called it a visual plot), and then add dialogue to the finished artwork.

More than anything else about Woolfolk's comic career, however, was the amazing number of top-notch strips he wrote for various publishers simultaneously. At MLJ, he was writing for the entire line, including major features like *Black Hood* and *Shield* when, in 1942, Warren King introduced him to Fawcett and *Captain Marvel* and *Captain Marvel Jr.*; the same year, Fawcett editor John Beardsley moved to Quality and introduced Woolfolk to *Blackhawk*; after a short stint in the army in 1943, he returned to comics and added Timely strips *Captain America, Human Torch*, and *Sub-Mariner*; and, finally, in 1944, Woolfolk added National to his accounts and started on *Superman* and others. During most of this time, his works were appearing on the five all-time best-selling strips.

His best work undoubtedly came on *Blackhawk* and *Captain Marvel*. For the latter, he created the villain Captain Nazi, a durable Axis menace who ranked just below Dr. Sivana and Mr. Mind as the Captain's greatest foe. On Quality's *Blackhawk*, Woolfolk teamed with artist Reed Crandall and guided the strip through its glorious years (1941-45). Unlike some of the feature's other writers, he concentrated on giving distinct characters to the seven Blackhawks, who frequently were allowed to fade in deference to their military hardware.

In 1946, Woolfolk started his own publishing company, O. W. Comics, with J. G. Oxton, but the effort was short-lived. After another fling at comics writing with Orbit, Woolfolk began another, non-comics publishing business. Several years later, he went to Hollywood and became a successful television writer, then a story editor on the then-popular *Defenders* show. He finally retired from television and has since been writing mainstream novels.

Wally Wood, "Weird Science." © *William M. Gaines, Agent, Inc.*

His wife, Dorothy Rubichek, is also a former comic book writer and editor.

J.B.

WROBLEWSKI, JERZY (1940-1991) Jerzy Wroblewski was born in 1940 in Bydgoszcz, Poland, where he was educated at the Fine Arts Gymnasium. His career in comics began in 1959, when he drew and wrote a strip for his hometown newspaper, *Dziennik Wieczorny*. In 1967 Wroblewski drew the police story *Risk*, which became Poland's longest serial, composed of 53 segments. A propaganda strip, *Risk* starred a superbrave, educated, and intelligent policeman.

In the early 1970s, Wroblewski worked on another propaganda piece, *Underground Front*, about the Polish resistance movement, and from 1973 he worked on *Captain Zbik*, another police adventure strip. Prolific as an artist, Wroblewski also contributed many stories to *Relax* magazine, which debuted in 1976, and later to *Awantura* magazine. In the 1980s, he published his own albums of adventure, historical, sensational, and Western-style comics. He was considered Poland's most popular comics artist during the Communist era.

Wroblewski died on August 10, 1991.

J.A.L.

WUNDER, GEORGE (1912-1987) American artist, born in New York City on April 24, 1912. While still a boy Wunder moved with his family to Kingston, New York. He received art training through correspondence lessons from the International Correspondence Schools. His early ambition was to become an illustrator or commercial artist, although he closely followed the comic strips of Martin Branner and George McManus.

On July 1, 1936, Wunder joined the Associated Press as a staff artist (he remembers a vow of poverty as a prerequisite) and worked beside Noel Sickles, Bert Christman, sports cartoonist Tom Paprocki, editorial cartoonist Hank Barrow, and others. His duties included sports spot drawings and photo retouching.

At the end of 1942, Wunder joined the army, serving until February 1946. Upon his discharge he was informed by AP friend Jay Alan (*Modest Maidens*) that the syndicate he was trying to crack, the Chicago Tribune-New York News Syndicate, was looking for a

George Wunder, "Terry and the Pirates." © Chicago Tribune-New York News Syndicate.

replacement for Milton Caniff on *Terry and the Pirates*. After a conference with comic editor Mollie Slott, Wunder was chosen over a field of competitors. His first *Terry* appeared on December 29, 1946.

Wunder maintained a consistently varied parade of characterizations. His dialogue (always written by himself) was among the most sophisticated, taut, and cinematic—albeit Grade B—of the story strips. The body of criticism about Wunder, however, has focused on his artwork. He definitely maintained the AP conventions of shading and backgrounds and even the wrinkles that are the trademark of AP graduates like Caniff, Sickles, Robbins, Toth, and so many others. Upper lips disappeared from virtually all of the *Terry* characters in a manner that annoyed many fans, and the seemingly mesmerized eyes on all of the faces also cast a sameness upon the strip.

Filling Milton Caniff's shoes would be an unenviable assignment for any artist, and to Wunder's credit, he never compromised details in art and the strip's traditional ideological appeal at a time when pressures to modify both were extreme.

The last *Terry* appeared on February 15, 1973. Wunder died in 1987.

R.M.

X-MEN (U.S.)

X-MEN (U.S.) *X-Men* first appeared in *X-Men* number one (September 1963), the creation of writer-editor Stan Lee and illustrator Jack Kirby. The story introduced a band of teenaged mutants, each gifted with a particular superpower. The wheelchair-confined Professor X, gifted with amazing mental powers, brought them together at his private school to guard against the schemes of evil mutants, notably of their arch-foe, Magneto. The X-Men consisted of Cyclops, whose eyes emitted a powerful blasting beam; The Angel, born with operative wings; Iceman, a reverse Human Torch, able to hurl snow and ice bombs; The Beast, an apelike being whose erudite speech was in marked contrast to his bestial appearance; and Marvel Girl, able to levitate objects and command a force-field.

Kirby was the artist for the first 11 issues and remained on layouts for several more. After one issue by Alex Toth, Werner Roth became the principal artist and remained in that post until 1969, despite fill-in art jobs by Jack Sparling, Barry Smith, Jim Steranko, Don Heck, Ross Andru, Dan Adkins, and George Tuska. In 1966, writer Roy Thomas joined Roth on the book to continue the tales of the mutant band and their encounters with others born with bizarre powers. Despite the best efforts of all involved, the book remained one of Marvel's least-noticed titles. In 1967 and 1968, various gimmicks were used to try and boost sales, such as new uniforms for the team and the death of Professor X. Scripting chores passed on to Gary Friedrich and Arnold Drake.

In May of 1969, Thomas returned to the writing and joined with artist Neal Adams in an attempt to bring about a new look for the X-Men. New supporting characters were brought in, but this did little good. In March 1970, with issue number 66, Marvel announced the book's discontinuation.

In December of that same year, the title was revived in reprint form, and the success of the old stories prompted talk of attempting new stories. The X-Men appeared in other Marvel comics, and a series starring the Beast (albeit in highly altered form) enjoyed a brief run in *Amazing Adventures*. But it wasn't until 1975 that the new stories were finally undertaken. A revamped team, featuring several new members, was introduced by artist Dave Cockrum, first in a one-shot *Giant-Size X-Men* and then, replacing the reprints, in the regular *X-Men* comic book beginning with number 94 (August 1975).

M.E.

The second version of *X-Men* really took off in 1977 when John Byrne was entrusted with the artwork and contributed some needed pyrotechnics to the title.

"X-Men," Jim Lee/Bob Wiacek. © Marvel Comics.

Since that time the comic book (retitled *The Uncanny X-Men* in 1981) has been the favorite playground of some of the best artists in the field, including Neal Adams, John Buscema, Walt Simonson, Barry Smith, and Jim Lee. There have also been a number of entertaining plot developments (often involving the destruction of entire worlds) and the addition of several interesting newcomers to the group, such as Phoenix, Nightcrawler, Storm, and Colossus. The series has become Marvel's most successful line of comics, with innumerable spin-offs, all starting with the letter *X* (*X-Factor*, *X-Terminator*, *X-Men Classic*, *X-Force*, ad nauseam).

M.H.

YEATS, JACK B. (1870-1957)
An Anglo-Irish cartoonist, author, and painter, John Butler Yeats was born in London on August 19, 1871, the son of the Irish painter John Butler Yeats, and the brother of the poet William Butler Yeats. He was educated in County Sligo, Ireland. His first published drawing appeared on April 7, 1888, and he became a regular contributor of horse sketches to the magazine *Paddock Life* (1891-93). He illustrated his brother William's book *Irish Fairy Tales* (1892), and the same year began drawing joke cartoons for *Cassells' Saturday Journal* and the boys' weekly *Chums*.

Several tries at gags in strip form led to his creation of the first regular character in the Alfred Harmsworth comic weeklies, a burlesque on Conan Doyle's *Sherlock Holmes*, which he titled *Chubb-Lock Homes*. His great detective was assisted by another burlesque character, Shirk the Dog Detective, a takeoff on *Dirk the Dog Detective*, a serial story in *Illustrated Chips*. Chubb-Lock Homes made his debut in *Comic Cuts* on June 16, 1894, and the character transferred to *Funny Wonder* in August of that year. Homes's adventures turned into a weekly serial from December 22, 1894, and after an interval reappeared in the same paper as a full front-page feature in 1897.

By that time Yeats's work had developed considerably and had a lively, sketchy quality, with an artistic use of solid black and white spaces that set him immediately apart from the followers of Tom Browne. His love for horses came out in *Signor McCoy the Circus Hoss*, a remarkable creation for *Big Budget* (June 19, 1897). For the same weekly he created *John Duff-Pie* (1897) and *Little Boy Pink* (1898) and revamped his detective character as *Kiroskewero the Detective* (1899). Meanwhile, for *Funny Wonder* he created *Mrs. Spiker's Boarding House* (August 22, 1896); a comic Yankee, *Hiram B. Boss* (December 18, 1897); a smuggler, *Ephraim Broadbeamer* (June 10, 1898); and *Convict 9999* (1899).

Jack Yeats, "Chubb-Lock Homes."

Yeats wrote and drew two children's books, *James Flaunty or the Terror of the Western Seas* (1901) and *The Bosun and the Bobtailed Comet* (1904), then returned to comics with a new, neater style, signing his strips "Jack," followed by either a small bee or a small black bird. For Harmsworth's first weekly comic in color, *Puck*, he created *Dr. Up-To-Dayte's Academy* and *Sandab the Sailor* (both 1904) and some new series for the revamped *Jester and Wonder: Skilly the Convict* and *Lick-etty Switch* (both 1904), *Fandango the Hoss* (1905), and *The Jester Theatre Royal* (1907). Also in 1907 he did *Dr. Patent* and *The Little Stowaways* for *Puck*; then in 1909 *Roly Poly's Tours* and a crazy creature, *The Whodidit*, for *Comic Cuts*. His interest in the stage emerged more fully through *Carlo the Jester* in *Comic Cuts* (1912), *Jimmy Jog the Juggler* (1914), *Eggbert and Philbert* (1915), and his last strip, *Bill Bailey* (1917). The last three were for *Butterfly*.

Yeats left comics to continue his career as a writer and painter. His books include *Sailing Sailing* (1933), *The Amavanthers* (1936), and *The Careless Flower* (1947). Among his plays are *Apparitions*, *The Old Sea Road*, and *Rattle*. His watercolors and paintings, famous for their color qualities, are collectors' items, and a London exhibition was staged in March 1975. He died on March 28, 1957, aged 86.

D.G.

YEH HUNG CHIA (1913-1990)
Although considered the giant of Taiwan's golden era of cartooning in the 1950s, Yeh Hung Chia did not gain widespread popularity until 1958, when the good times were already drawing to a close. During the 1940s, Yeh sneered at Taiwan's social conditions in political cartoons but quit doing them after the conflict between China and Taiwan in February 1947. For nine years he worked as a designer, until in 1956 he began cartooning Chinese folktales.

Yeh's big break in comics came in 1958, when he created *Chuko Szu-lang*, about a character with a mighty double-edged sword. It was based on two Chinese historical figures: Chuko Kung Ming, a sage in the Three Kingdoms Period (220-265), and Yang Szulang, national hero and dutiful son of the Northern Sung dynasty (960-1127). Both embodied loyalty and filial piety. The first installment of what would become 55 books appeared as *Chuko Szu-lang Struggles with Evil Party* in *Cartoon Weekly*. Yeh's character, which filled 32 of the periodical's 72 pages, quickly became popular. Eventually Yeh's comic books sold 100,000 copies weekly, while at the same time inspiring songs and films.

Yeh had the zeal of a teacher, using his books to educate about good and evil. Other Yeh stories were included in *Silang and Zhenping* and focused in part on a comic strip hero named after the Chinese-language characters for sincerity and honesty. Yeh handled his

"The Yellow Kid," R. F. Outcault.

stable of comics through Hung-Chia Publishers, which he established.

His career nosedived after 1960, when the government began looking at his work less favorably; a car accident in 1974 left him handicapped. During the latter part of his life, he reorganized his old scripts and sought loans to reprint them.

J.A.L.

YELLOW KID, THE (U.S.) The hero of the first true comic strip, R. F. Outcault's Yellow Kid first appeared in two gag panels, one in color and one in black and white, in the same issue of the Sunday *New York World* on May 5, 1895. The color panel was called *At the Circus in Hogan's Alley* and was one of several similar slum kid panels Outcault drew through the middle of 1895 for the *World*, with varying locales given in the titles: Reilly's Pond, Casey's Alley, Shantytown, etc. On the sidelines in both of the May 5 panels is a large-headed, jug-eared boy of about six or seven, clad in a plain dress or nightshirt smudged with dirty handprints; in the color panel the nightshirt is blue. In a number of subsequent back-street kid panels, the nightshirted kid, who acquired the bald head he would later be famed for, plays either a subordinate role or is altogether missing. By January 5, 1896, however, the kid is more noticeable, and he wears a yellow nightshirt for the first time. Since his prominence in the panel series and the first use of yellow more or less coincided, from the public's point of view, they began to talk about the otherwise nameless child who had caught their amused fancy as the yellow kid. Outcault, however, used *Ho-*

gan's Alley as a general running title for the weekly panels, and neither he nor the *World* ever referred to the feature figure as the Yellow Kid while Outcault was employed there.

The Kid himself began to talk to his public with his nightshirt, emblazoning saucy and irreverent messages more or less related to the theme of the week's other panel action, but he never spoke otherwise (although some minimal dialogue balloons appeared in the *World* panels from time to time). The last *World* panel in this form by Outcault appeared on May 17, 1896, just after Outcault's departure for William Randolph Hearst's *New York Journal*. (George B. Luks continued the panels for the *World*, using the *Hogan's Alley* running title and dropping the yellow nightshirt for other hues on several occasions.) Hearst immediately applied the popular *Yellow Kid* label to the panel, trumpeting his acquisition everywhere in New York and encouraging Outcault to abandon the gag-panel format in favor of progressive panel narration, which other Hearst cartoonists were using in different features in the *Journal*'s *American Humorist* Sunday section. Outcault did so later in 1896, and with the addition of relevant balloon dialogue vital to the point of the weekly anecdote, he formed what amounted to the definitive comic strip for the first time.

But Outcault was not happy with the Kid, despite the financial harvest he was reaping. He and his wife were sensitive to the views of the "better people" in New York, and these people regarded *The Yellow Kid* as a public disgrace, even applying the color of his nightshirt to the sensational "yellow journalism" they despised (then largely centered in the New York *World* and *Journal*). The furor kicked up by the widely publicized legal battle between the *World* and the *Journal* over the rights to the *Hogan's Alley* characters (which resulted in Outcault retaining the right to continue the characters and the *World* holding control of the *Hogan's Alley* name and figures as well) irked him also. He dropped the Kid (and Hearst) to return to freelancing in 1898, later joining the staff of the *New York Herald* to introduce *Poor Li'l Mose* and, in effect, begin a new career.

But the memory of *The Yellow Kid* lingered forcefully. Not only were there dozens of artifacts, buttons, statuettes, games, puzzles, a joke magazine with the strip name (but containing no strips), and books (one, *The Yellow Kid in MacFadden's Flats*, consisting of Hearst strip reprints with an accompanying text, constituted the first true comic book), but Outcault himself used the Kid figure in advertisements well into the new century (usually pairing the Kid with his pet goat), and drew him in various guises in his later *Buster Brown* strip. Curiously, however, there has never been a *Yellow Kid* collection in this century, despite the fact that the entire oeuvre would run to only about 125 pages. It is vital, and long overdue.

B.B.

YOKOYAMA, RYŪICHI (1909-   ) Japanese cartoonist, born May 17, 1909, in Kochi. After graduation from Kōchi Jōtō Chūgakkō of the former school system, Ryūichi Yokoyama went to Tokyo in order to take the entrance examination to the Art Academy, but he failed to gain entrance for two consecutive years (1927-28). In 1928 he became a pupil of the famous sculptor Hakuun Motoyama, while contributing cartoons to various magazines in order to support himself. On the advice of Motoyama, Yokoyama decided on a cartooning career, and before long he made a success of it.

In 1932 Yokoyama and some of his fellow cartoonists (Hidezō Kondō, Yukio Sugiura, Fukujirō Yokoi, Zenroku Mashiko, Ryū Osanai, and other Young Turks) founded the Shin Mangaha Shūdan ("New Cartoonists' Group") to fight against the older cartoon establishment (in 1945 the association dropped the "New" in its name to become simply the Manga Shudan). Yokoyama became the leader of the new group. In 1936 he created his first famous comic strip, *Edokko Ken-chan* ("Ken from Edo"); later the title was changed to *Fuku-chan*, and the title character became one of the most famous characters in Japanese newspaper strips. *Fuku-chan*'s success was followed by more famous creations: *The Beggar King* (1946); *Doshako* and *Peko-chan* (both 1947); and *Densuke* (195). Densuke had been a second banana in *Peko-chan*, but, like Fuku-chan earlier, he graduated to star status. Other Yokoyama creations of note are *Chakkari Densuke* (1953); *Yuki* (Courage , 1966); and *Hyaku Baka* (1968).

In 1955 Yokoyama established his own company, Otogi Pro, for the production of animated films. Among the many cartoons he produced, the more noted are *Onbu Obake* (1955); *Fukusuke* (1957); *Hyōtan Suzume* (1959); *Instant History* (1964); *Kokki* ("The National Flag," 1965); and *Dobutsu Gomanbiki* (1966). Yokoyama has also contributed many cartoons, illustrations, and covers to newspapers and magazines, and he has also created a number of picture books.

Ryūichi Yokoyama, "Fuku-chan." © Asahigraph.

Lyman Young, "Tim Tyler's Luck." © King Features Syndicate.

Ryūichi Yokoyama was greatly influenced by American films as well as by American and European comic strips, and he reflected these influences in his strips and cartoons, bringing a fresh outlook to the Japanese comic strip scene before the World War II. Yokoyama's influence played a great role in the shaping of younger cartoonists, beginning with Yokoyama's own brother Taizō.

H.K.

YOKOYAMA, TAIZŌ (1917-   ) Japanese cartoonist, born February 28, 1917, in Kochi. While on vacation from Kōchi Commercial School in 1931, Taizō Yokoyama went to Tokyo to pay a visit to his elder brother Ryūichi and decided to remain in the capital. While there, he attended Kyōko Commercial School during the day and Kawabata Art School at night. Called into the army, Yokoyama was sent to China in 1938 but returned to Japan in 1941. That year he entered Teikoku School of Fine Arts, graduating in 1944 and exhibiting at several national art shows during that time.

Yokoyama was again drafted in 1945, but the war ended before he saw any action. Soon after his discharge, he started to do illustrations for the daily *Shinyūkan* and became a professional cartoonist in 1946 for *Shinyūkan* (that same year he joined the Manga Shudan, the cartoonists' association founded by his brother in 1932). To *Shinyūkan* and other publications, such as the satirical magazine *Van* and the humor magazine *Hōpu*, Yokoyama contributed a great number of cartoons. In 1952 he created his famous newspaper strip *Pū-san* (later made into a motion picture). More successes followed: *Shakai Gihyō* (an editorial panel which he created in 1954 and which is still in existence); *Shinjinbutsu Gihyō* (in which he caricatures celebrities) in 1957; *Gihyō no Tabi* (an illustrated travelogue, 1963). In 1965 he expanded the adventures of Pu-san further into a weekly magazine format. In the meantime, he had been instrumental in the founding of *Ehe*, a satirical magazine run by professional cartoonists, and in 1965 he was named chairman of the cartoon department of the Tokyo College of Design. He is now retired.

Taizō Yokoyama revolutionized the art of the Japanese cartoon after World War II: he drew cartoons that were extremely stylized with a sharp and geometric line. His political cartoons were direct and to the point, in contrast to the shilly-shallying of editorial cartoons before the war. His graphic style was influenced more by Saul Steinberg than by any Japanese artist. In addition to his cartoons, Yokoyama has also done illustration, covers, and oil paintings.

H.K.

YOU AND ME *see* Potts, The.

YOUNG, LYMAN (1893-1984) American cartoonist, born in 1893 in Chicago. Along with his younger and more famous brother Murat ("Chic"), he showed an early talent for cartooning, and later went to the Chicago Art Institute. After service in World War I and a short stint as a salesman, Lyman Young, prodded by his brother, started his cartooning career in 1924 by taking over *The Kelly Kids*, a sister-and-brother strip that had been created by C. W. Kahles in 1919. In 1927 he created his first strip, *The Kid Sister* (an offshoot of *The Kelly Kids*) for King Features Syndicate. In 1928 his most famous feature, *Tim Tyler's Luck*, appeared as a daily strip, to be followed in 1931 by a Sunday version (with *The Kid Sister* as its top). In 1935 *Curley Harper*, a reporter-detective strip, replaced *The Kid Sister* on the Sunday page.

From then on Lyman Young's career was exclusively devoted to the production of his strips, with which he strongly identified. (Young himself stated in a 1942 interview that *Tim Tyler* was his attempt at recapturing his childhood dreams of thrilling adventures in faraway places.) Many ghosts labored under Young's direction, but however many the people involved in the strip's production, *Tim Tyler* (Young's most memorable creation) was unmistakenly one man's vision. In the late 1950s Young relinquished the daily strip to his son Bob and the Sunday page to Tom Massey and retired, first to Florida (where he lived next to his brother Chic), and then to California. He died in Port Angeles, Washington, on February 12, 1984.

M.H.

YOUNG, MURAT (1901-1973) American cartoonist, born in Chicago on January 9, 1901. Young's mother, a painter, encouraged her two sons (Murat and his brother Lyman, who was also to become a cartoonist) to pursue artistic careers. Murat Young studied art in Chicago, New York, and Cleveland. In 1920 he went to work for the Newspaper Enterprise Association, where he originated his first comic strip, *The Affairs of Jane*. Moving to the Bell Syndicate, he created, in 1922, *Beautiful Bab*, the comic adventures of a pretty blonde in a girls' school.

In 1924 Young joined King Features Syndicate as an assistant. At King he created another girl strip, *Dumb Dora*, in 1925 (it was then that he signed his now-famous nickname, "Chic"). In September 1930, having left *Dora*, he originated the widely acclaimed *Blondie*. Among Chic Young's other strips, mention should be made of *The Family Foursome*, which served as *Blondie*'s top and related the doings of a middle-class couple and their two teenaged children. In 1934, with Blondie start-

Murat (Chic) Young, "Beautiful Bab." © Bell Syndicate.

ing a family of her own, *The Family Foursome* was replaced by *Colonel Potterby and the Duchess*, an underrated strip, full of whimsy and a wry, lunatic humor.

From 1930 on, Chic Young devoted himself entirely to his comic strip work, making *Blondie* into the most popular strip of all time. In 1948 he received the Reuben Award, and throughout his career, he has been the recipient of many more citations and awards. His style has been widely copied, and his theme (the matriarchal family viewed with knowing sympathy and tender irony) has inspired countless other strips, not to mention scores of TV situation comedies.

Chic Young died on March 14, 1973, in St. Petersburg, Florida.

M.H.

YOUNG ALLIES (U.S.) Leo Gorcey and Huntz Hall made the 1937 motion picture *Dead End* a phenomenal success, and their Bowery Boys (née Dead End Kids) spawned a horde of imitators in all media. The comic books were no exception, and the very first kid group was premiered in Timely's *Young Allies* number one during the summer of 1941. Created by editors Jack Kirby and Joe Simon, writer Otto Binder, and artist C. Wostkoski, the Young Allies were Bucky, Captain America's sidekick; Toro, The Human Torch's sidekick; and a group of youths unendowed with superpowers who had originally appeared as the Sentinels of Liberty. These boys were Percival O'Toole, alias Knuckles, a ruffian who hailed from New York's Lower East Side; Jeff Sandervilt, who seemed to be nondescript as a profession; Henry Tubby Tinkle, the group's fat kid; and a most unfortunate black caricature, Whitewash Jones. Whitewash had the archetypal rolling eyes, zoot suit, and dialogue complete with drawl.

The group made its first appearance as the Young Allies in a battle against the dreaded Red Skull, and their inexperience necessitated the aid of Human Torch and Captain America, both of whom were added to hype sales just in case the buying public wasn't sure it

could identify with its peer group. But the book was moderately successful, lasting 20 issues until 1946. The team also made about a dozen other appearances in other Timely titles and even spawned a Timely takeoff, the ill-fated *Tough Kid Squad*.

Most of the scripts were written by Stan Lee and Otto Binder and concentrated on fast action; it was standard fare for the book-length story to be divided into several parts with the tide of battle switching from the good guys to the bad at the drop of a chapter change. But the most intriguing plot device surfaced when Toro and Bucky fought for control of the group. After six issues of haggling, Bucky finally prevailed.

Many fine artists contributed material to the strip, including Al Gabriele, Frank Giacoia, Mike Sekowsky, Syd Shores, Don Rico, and Alex Schomburg.

J.B.

YOUR UNCLE FEININGER *see* Feininger, Lyonel.

Yue Xiaoying, "Engrossed in Arithmetic." © Yue Xiaoying.

YUE XIAOYING (1921-1985) Born in Zhenhai, Zhejiang Province, in 1921, Yue studied commercial art in Zhenhai Business School in 1938, and, the next year, studied New Year's painting in Shanghai under Wu Guangzhi, a master of that specialized art form. Yue taught himself cartooning. After the founding of the People's Republic of China, he concentrated on comics for children. In the 1950s his comic strip *The Colorful Road* (coauthored with others) was awarded first prize at the First National Exhibition of Comic Art. As art editor for the *Little Friends* magazine and *Xinmin Evening News* in Shanghai, he was a member of the National Chinese Artists Association. His comics work was published in *Selected Comics for Children by Yue Xiaoying*.

Although some of Yue's political cartoons from the 1940s were quite critical of the government, in later years his comics mostly extolled the "new people and new scenes in new China." Children were always dear to Yue's heart, and children warmly welcomed his comics. He was called, with honor, "an old friend of the little friends."

H.Y.L.L.

Z

ZIG ET PUCE (France) One of the most important and influential of European comic strips, Alain Saint-Ogan's *Zig et Puce* first appeared in the pages of the French weekly *Dimanche Illustré* on May 3, 1925. *Zig et Puce* started as a last-minute editorial replacement and was not supposed to run for more than a few weeks, but to everyone's (including the author's) surprise the strip met with an enthusiastic reception and was soon to become the star attraction of *Dimanche Illustré* until 1937, when the feature was transferred to *Cadet-Revue*.

Zig and Puce are two enterprising young boys, one short and chubby, the other tall and skinny, whose love for adventure takes them to the far corners of the earth and into outer space. In the course of their adventures they successively meet the penguin Alfred, who becomes their mascot (and will nearly steal the strip from them); Dolly, the young American heiress whom they repeatedly save from the clutches of her criminal uncle Musgrave; Marcel, the bad-tempered but resourceful dray-horse; Princess Yette of Marcalance, who will name them cabinet ministers after they have saved her throne; and a host of lesser characters.

"Zig et Puce," Alain Saint-Ogan. © Alain Saint-Ogan.

During the war and the years after, *Zig et Puce* was to know a somewhat checkered existence, passing from one ephemeral publication to another. These included *Benjamin, France-Soir Junior, Ima, Zorro,* and its own short-lived *Zig et Puce.* Its success, challenged by newer, more suspenseful features, accordingly declined. In 1963 Saint-Ogan relinquished the characters to the Belgian cartoonist Greg, who tried to re-create the strip in the magazine *Tintin,* but he encountered only moderate success and finally abandoned it in the late 1960s.

Zig et Puce was the first European strip to make exclusive use of balloons to carry dialogue, and as such it heralded an important breakthrough in European comic art and storytelling. *Zig et Puce* upheld the tradition of quality in the French-language comic strip and provided the aesthetic link between Forton's *Les Pieds-Nickelés* and Hergé's *Tintin.*

"I have achieved many things in my life," Alain Saint-Ogan wrote in his memoirs. "I have created innumerable characters, like Prosper the bear. I have illustrated the book for the centennial of the Military Medal; but all that people want to talk about is Zig and Puce." The success of the strip in the 1920s and 1930s was phenomenal: all the stories were reprinted in book form by Hachette, the strip was made into a play and a series of animated cartoons, and it was adapted to the radio and later into a series of records. The characters themselves had their likenesses made into toys, key rings, and countless other gadgets.

M.H.

ZIGOMAR (Yugoslavia) Zigomar was a popular hero of Serbian comics between World War I and World War II; his tales were also translated into other languages and published abroad. He grew out of the rivalry between two publishers. Milutin S. Ignjačević was the editor of the most popular Belgrade comics magazine of the time, *Mika Miš* ("Mickey Mouse"), between 1936 and the beginning of 1939. Because of disagreements with the owner-publisher, Aleksandar J. Ivković, Ignjačević quit his job and started his own magazine, *Mikijevo carstvo* ("Mickey's Domain"), which debuted on February 23, 1939. As he had treated authors well, many continued to work for him.

Because Ivković held the rights to publish *The Phantom* in Yugoslavia, Ignjačević ordered his tried-and-true team of Branislav Vidić and Nikola Navojev to produce another masked hero. They did. The first page of the new serial, *Zigomar,* appeared in *Mikijevo carstvo* number 28, on May 28, 1939. Because they didn't want readers to know the strip was a domestic product, the name of the scriptwriter was omitted. The reader response was overwhelming.

There is no denying that the Phantom prompted the creation of Zigomar. The resemblances include the fact that both are masked, never reveal their true identity,

"Zigomar," Branko Vidić and Nikola Navojev. © Vidic and Navojev.

have no superhuman powers, and love women from New York high society. Zigomar rescues his beloved Laura Morgan from distress on the first page of his first episode. And it turns out that she was a schoolmate of the Phantom! But there are key differences between the two masked characters. To begin with, Zigomar is a modern urban hero. He has a permanent underground shelter in New York City, from which he monitors events and activates himself as necessary, sallying forth to fight evildoers in the Big Apple or abroad. Secondly, in his operational center he has some advanced technology at his disposal. Thirdly, while the Phantom is a loner whose main partners in action are a horse and a wolf, Zigomar has an associate, the little Chinese boy Yang.

In sum, Zigomar more resembles another masked hero, one at a higher stage of evolution than the Phantom: Batman. Though the resemblance is astonishing, plagiarism is out of the question; Superman started in the United States in June 1938 and was unknown in Serbia in 1939, and Batman started in the United States in the same month as Zigomar debuted in Serbia, May 1939.

Five Zigomar episodes were published. The first was titled simply "Zigomar." Next came "Zigomar versus Phantom," "Zigomar and the Bride of Gods," "Zigomar, the Whip of Justice," and "Zigomar and the Mysteries of Egypt." (The last two episodes appeared in 1940.) The stories (and their weaknesses) were typical of action-adventure comics of the 1930s: a rich heiress is kidnapped; secret plans of a new submarine are stolen from some ministry and the search for them begins;

a sect of mystics lives in the Himalayas; secret rituals are performed in Egypt. . . .

After Navojev's death on November 9, 1940, Vidić continued to write scripts for Zigomar. Episode six is Leteći Zigomar ("The Flying Zigomar"). The artwork was done single-handedly—and successfully—by Dušan (Duško Bogdanović). But Zigomar never completed his flight. The Luftwaffe bombarded Serbia in the early-morning hours of April 6, 1941, and in two weeks Serbia was defeated and occupied by the forces of the Third Reich. Publishing virtually ceased. The last issue of Mikijevo carstvo, number 217, had appeared on April 8.

During his short career (he was 27 at the time of his death) Navojev produced some other outstanding features. Among them were Dve sirotice ("The Two Orphan Girls"); Mladi Bartulo ("Young Bartulo"), a pirate story; Mali moreplovac ("Sailor Kid"), a seafaring tale; and Taras Bulba. On most of these titles he worked closely with scriptwriter Branislav Vidić.

S.I.

ZORAD, ERNÖ (1911-   ) Hungarian graphic artist, painter, and comic strip artist. After secondary school he attended the Hungarian School of Applied Arts, where his classmates included the well-known Hungarian artists Amerigo Tot and Michel Gyarmathy. He dropped out after two years to become a gallery painter and a painter of horses. After military service in World War II, he became a book illustrator.

He contributed illustrations to a number of magazines and newspapers, including Magyar Vasarnap, Pesti Izé, and Szabad Szaj. Later on the editor in chief of the newspaper for the Hungarian Pioneer (Communist) Association asked him to draw a picture-story about a badly behaved Pioneer who enjoyed comics too much. (During the 1950s up until the revolution of 1956, drawing and reading comics was forbidden.) Since 1957, Zorad has drawn comics almost continuously for the magazine Fules, using a unique collage technique.

The comics he has drawn for Fules and other magazines and for daily and weekly newspapers now total more than 300. Since each of these comics consists of at least 16 pages and there are at least five panels to a page, it has been calculated that Zorad has done a minimum of 3,800 pages and 19,000 drawings, an incredible number. His work has also been anthologized in two albums, he has been amply written about, and in 1993 he completed a successful volume of memoirs as told to an interviewer.

K.R.

ZOZO (Belgium) Zozo was an animal strip created in 1935 by C. Franchi (of whom nothing else is known) for an obscure children's paper, Le Journal de Francette et Riquet, published in Liège, Belgium. In all probability, the strip would never have attracted anyone's attention had it not been regularly reprinted in book form by Editions Touret in Paris, thereby reaching a wide audience all over France and in other French-speaking countries.

Zozo, a tar-black, monkey-like creature, and his human companion Croquefer, a bearded sailor of herculean strength, were a pair of freewheeling adventurers always ready to embark on some farfetched enterprise. In the first episode Zozo and Croquefer single-handedly captured a crew of pirates who had hijacked a millionaire's yacht on the high seas. Further

"Zozo," C. Franchi. © Editions Touret.

adventures took the duo to Mexico, Hollywood, Indochina, Ethiopia, and even the North Pole, where they rescued the members of a stranded scientific expedition. One of the most entertaining stories featured the invention of their friend Dr. Microbus: the autofish, an extraordinary all-purpose vehicle.

In all, seven albums of *Zozo* were published; the first six were reprints, but the seventh (released in 1942) was an original story. A paperback edition was also published after World War II, but around 1948 *Zozo* disappeared again, this time for good.

Zozo was aimed at a childish audience, and its plots were as unsophisticated as its drawing. The author was obviously inspired by the two strips of humorous adventure most popular in France at the time: *Mickey Mouse* and *Zig et Puce*; and while his efforts do not put Franchi on a par with either Gottfredson or Saint-Ogan, they certainly deserve to be noted here.

M.H.

Color in the Comics

Paradoxically, color comics came into existence well before the cheaper black-and-white variety. The Sunday color comic supplements started in the mid-1890s and were over 10 years old when the first daily strip (Mutt and Jeff) was successfully established in 1907.

The use of color in the comic books, as well as in the Sunday pages, adds a dramatic dimension to the proceedings and the plot. It can call attention to a special point in the narrative, highlight a twist in the action, or underscore the climax of a sequence; it can also provide a psychological link between different panels in a sequence by carrying the same tonal value from one frame to the next.

The illustrations reproduced herein will give the reader a good idea of the imaginative uses to which color has been put by cartoonists around the globe.

"Anibal 5," Alexandro Jodorowski and Manuel Moro Cid. The creation of filmmaker Jodorowski ("El Topo" and "The Holy Mountain"), the strip was peopled with weird, fantastic creatures. © Editorial Novaro.

"Andy Capp," Reginald Smythe. After making a hit with the British public, Smythe's tough little Cockney conquered the U.S. and the world. © Daily Mirror Ltd.

"Asterix," Rene Goscinny and Albert Uderzo. Europe's most popular strip featured Goscinny's clever dialogue, Uderzo's uncluttered line, and the imaginative, witty use of speech balloons (here filled with hieroglyphics). Since Goscinny's death in 1977, the strip has been done entirely by Uderzo. © Editions Dargaud.

"B.C.," Johnny Hart. Despite its serious intent, "B.C." is studded with rib-splitting slapstick, hilarious dialogue, and a delightful sense of the absurd. © Field Newspaper Syndicate.

Enki Bilal and Pierre Christin, "Partie de Chasse." Yugoslav-born Bilal and his usual accomplice Christin are known for their uncompromising treatment of contemporary political themes (in this case the power struggle between Soviet-bloc leaders at the time of the Cold War). © Dargaud Editeur.

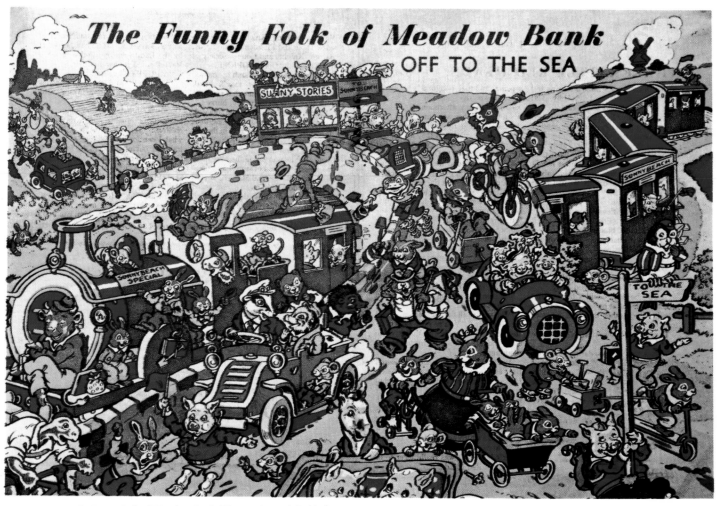

E. H. Banger, "The Funny Folk of Meadow Bank." Banger is noted for his fanciful renditions of animals in absurd situations. © Sunny Stories.

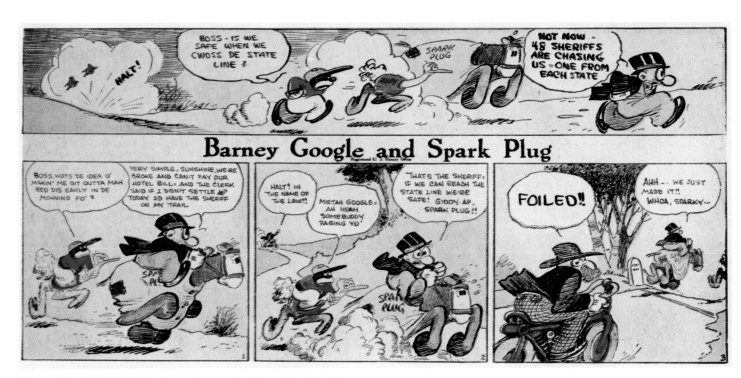

"Barney Google," Billy DeBeck. An earthy example of the traditional comic strip, "Barney Google" exhibits a good-natured humor and a graphic style that is the epitome of the well-crafted cartoon. © King Features Syndicate.

"Batman," Bob Kane. The hooded fighter for justice has achieved a renown
exceeded only by that of Superman. © D.C. Comics.

"Buster Brown," R. F. Outcault. This popular and enduring creation has
brought the image of Buster and his bulldog, Tige, to shoes, boy's suits, even
cigars and whiskey.

BLONDIE
Registered U. S. Patent Office

"Blondie," Chic Young. America's perennial favorite, "Blondie" has unrolled a merry chronicle of domestic life for over 60 years, and even the death of its creator has not dimmed its popularity. © King Features Syndicate.

"Bringing Up Father," George McManus. The most striking feature of this strip is its earthy theatricality, in which two lines of dialogue suffice to establish its theme. © King Features Syndicate.

"Beetle Bailey," Mort Walker. A lighthearted satire of military life, Walker's strip is drawn with a spirit and verve that even George Couteline has not surpassed. © King Features Syndicate.

"Buck Rogers," Phil Nowlan and Dick Calkins. The first science-fiction strip of worldwide fame has inspired countless imitations and rivals. © National Newspaper Syndicate.

"Blake et Mortimer," Edgar-Pierre Jacobs. Covering some of the most important themes of post-World War II science fiction, "Blake et Mortimer" often ranks with the best of American science-fiction strips. © Editions du Lombard.

"Brick Bradford," William Ritt and Clarence Gray. Without the futuristic vision of "Buck Rogers" or the epic grandeur of "Flash Gordon," "Brick Bradford" displayed undeniable qualities of fantasy, poetry, and imagination that equal its better-known rivals. © King Features Syndicate.

"Captain Marvel," C. C. Beck. In the 1940s Captain Marvel was Superman's most successful rival. © Fawcett Publications.

"Captain America," Joe Simon and Jack Kirby. During World War II Captain America and his boy companion, Bucky, were among the most persistent foes of the Axis and their allies. © Marvel Comics Group.

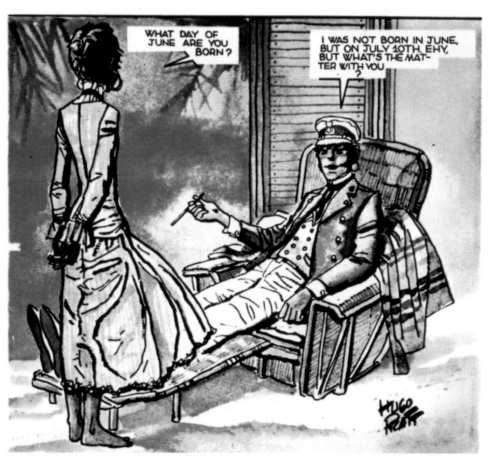

"Corto Maltese," Hugo Pratt. An atmospheric and exotic tale of adventure, *"Corto Maltese"* is set in the second decade of the 20th century. © Hugo Pratt.

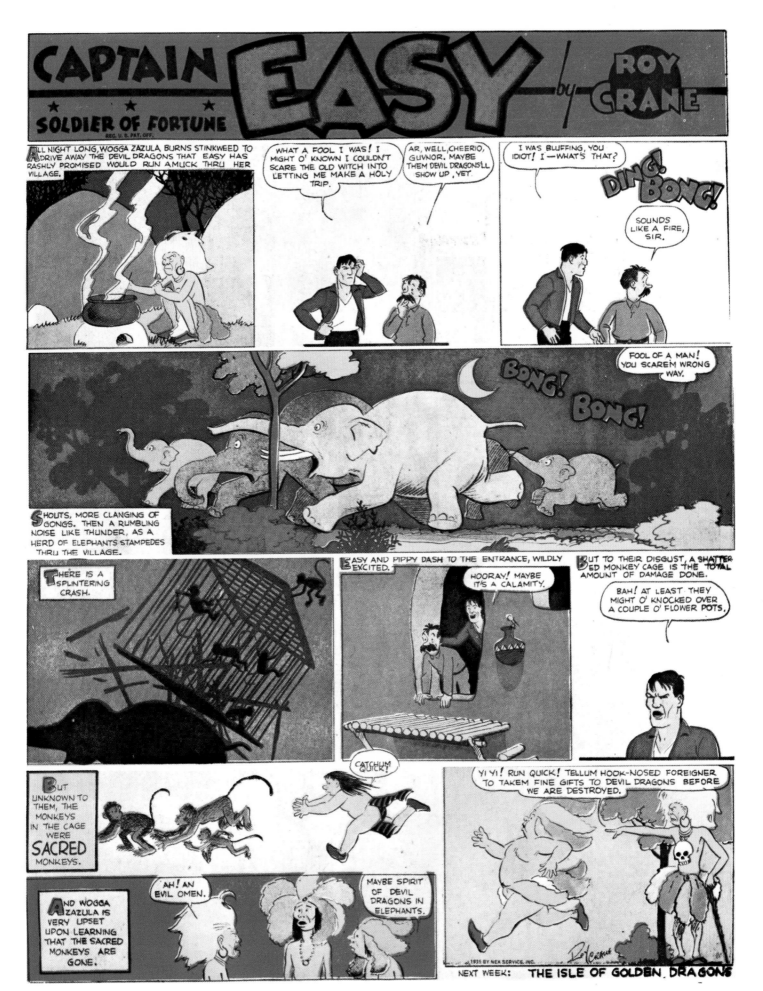

"Captain Easy," Roy Crane. Innovative layout, imaginative situations, and a brisk, unrelenting pace were the hallmarks of "Captain Easy." © NEA Service.

Fingering her jewels, the Nizerine Eleyn watched the Kündüke in their pursuit.

...energy trails binding and tripping the fugitive....

From the ledge above the entangled woman, Akbrum jumped down.

"They want this woman badly." Suddenly the Nizerine hurled her rings and broaches. They streaked through the rubble, leaving trails of energy, homing in on their prey....

...their touch painful as molten wire.

She tried to keep the crystal from him.

Howard Chaykin and Samuel Delany, "Empire." Chaykin was very active in the 1970s and 1980s in the field of science-fiction graphic novels. "Empire," based on the Samuel Delany novel, was one of his early (and most successful) essays in the genre. © Byron Preiss Visual Publications.

"Conan," Barry Smith. Robert E. Howard's fabled barbarian was given new life in a series of well-rendered tales. © Marvel Comics Group.

Richard Corben, "Cidopey." One of the most talented artists of the underground comics, Corben often draws very violently, but he can also be tender and lyrical. © Richard Corben.

"Connie," Frank Godwin. Frank Godwin's masterpiece blends outstanding draftsmanship, imaginative composition, and dramatic continuity. © Ledger Syndicate.

Robert Crumb, comic book cover. The best-known of underground cartoonists,
Crumb's choice of subject matter is often salacious. © Robert Crumb.

"Dan Dare," Frank Bellamy. One of England's best-known adventure strips, "Dan Dare" has seen the handiwork of many distinguished artists, Frank Bellamy foremost among them. © Odhams Press Ltd.

"Dzjengis Khan," Jos Looman. This chronicle of the life of the famed Mongol conqueror is one of the finest epic strips to come out of Europe. © Pep.

"Il Dottor Faust," Federico Pedroochi and Rino Albertarelli. Albertarelli provided remarkable artwork to complement Pedroochi's tasteful adaptation of the Faust legend. © Mondadori.

Du Jianguo, "The Little Rabbit Feifei." Du Jianguo is one of the foremost authors of children's comics in China, and "The Little Rabbit Feifei," based on a traditional folktale, is his most famous creation. © Du Jianguo.

"Dick Tracy," Chester Gould. The first detective strip to appear in print, "Dick Tracy" introduced crime and violence to the comic pages. © Chicago Tribune-New York News Syndicate.

"Doctor Strange," Roy Thomas and Gene Colan. One of the weirdest heroes to appear in comic books, Doctor Strange has known a checkered career, despite the talents of many of the people who worked on the feature. © Marvel Comics Group.

*"Donald Duck," Carl Barks. The supreme "duck artist," Barks's cover for one
of Donald's adventures is a classic. © Walt Disney Productions.*

"Dennis the Menace," Hank Ketcham. *"Dennis the Menace" renewed the tradition of the kid strip and became a part of the American idiom. © Field Newspaper Syndicate.*

"Fatty Finn," Syd Nicholls. *Modelled on the successful American strips, "Fatty Finn" was one of the funniest and most likable of Australian comic strips. © Syd Nicholls.*

Fernando Fernandez, "Zora." "Zora," with its striking drawings and innovative layouts, is one of Fernandez's most representative and most ambitious works.
© Fernando Fernandez.

"Felix the Cat," Otto Messmer. Of Felix's rare poetry and lyricism, French academician Marcel Brion said: "Felix is not a cat; he is the Cat. Or better to say yet, he is a supercat, because he does not fit in any of the categories of the animal kingdom." © King Features Syndicate.

"Flash Gordon," Alex Raymond. Universally regarded as the epitome of the adventure comics, Raymond's strip style has been widely imitated but never equalled. © King Features Syndicate.

"The Fantastic Four," Stan Lee and Jack Kirby. *A group of misfit superheroes, The Fantastic Four launched the highly successful line of Marvel comic books in the 1960s. © Marvel Comics Group.*

"Fred Bassett," Alex Graham. *Graham's philosophical dog is the most endearing canine this side of Snoopy. © Associated Newspapers Ltd.*

"Gaki Deka," Tatsuhiko Yamagami. Yamagami's *"boy-policeman,"* the most troublesome brat in Japanese comics, introduced a breath of fresh air into the stale tradition of Japanese child strips. © Shomen Chambion.

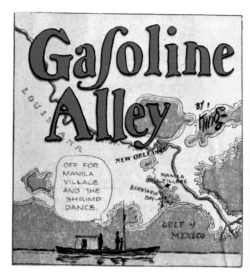  

"Gasoline Alley," Frank King. In "Gasoline Alley" King introduced a fundamental innovation: the characters in the strip grew old along with the readers. © Chicago Tribune-New York News Syndicate.

"The Gumps," Sidney Smith. For a long time "The Gumps" was the most popular of all comic strips, and it was the first to earn its author a million-dollar syndication contract. © Chicago Tribune-New York News Syndicate.

"Happy Hooligan," F. B. Opper. This forlorn hobo was a forerunner of Charlie Chaplin's "little tramp." © King Features Syndicate.

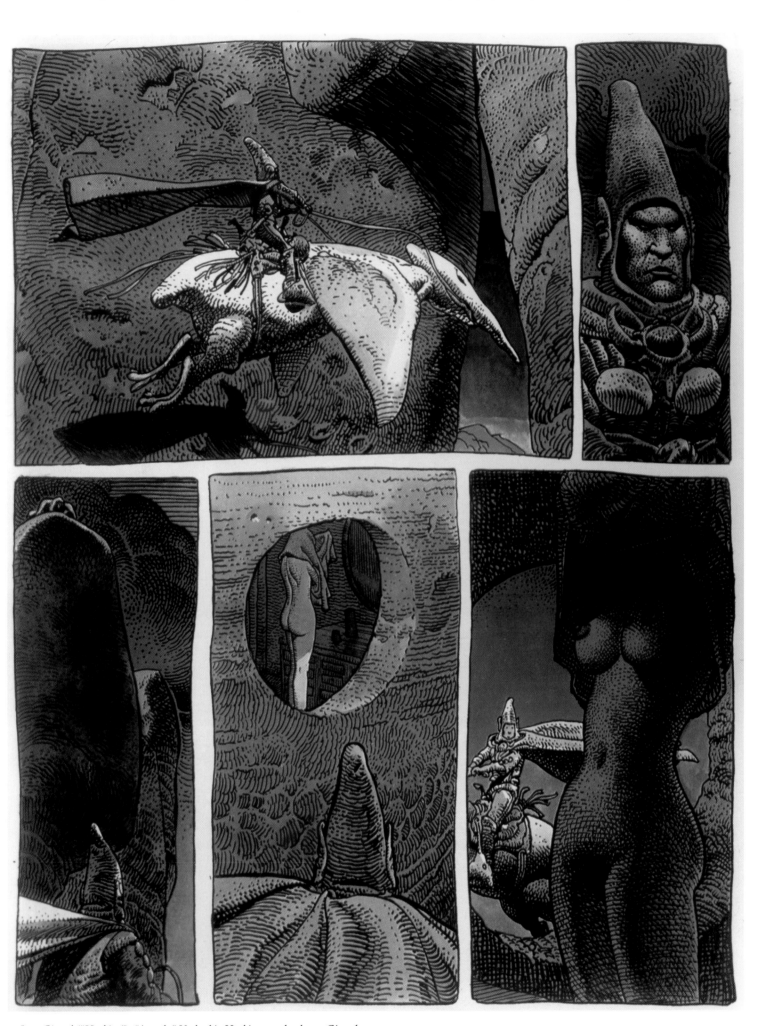

Jean Giraud ("Moebius"), "Arzach." Under his Moebius nomde plume, Giraud has produced some of the most acclaimed French comic stories of the last two decades. "Arzach" is probably his most representative creation, a fantasy tale realized entirely with visuals, without use of text or dialogue. © Humanoides Associés.

"Happy Days," Roy Wilson. Typical English whimsy was Wilson's stock-in-trade. © Amalgamated Press.

Frank Hampson, "The Road of Courage." Hampson was one of the most noted artists in the British tradition. © Odhams Press Ltd.

Harry Hargreaves, "Ollie of the Movies." Movie comedians were a staple of the English comic strip. © The Sun.

"The Hawkman." "The Hawkman" was one of the better-drawn and -written comic books in the National stable. © National Periodical Publications.

"Johnny Hazard," Frank Robbins. Unjustly neglected, "Johnny Hazard" was one of the better-drawn and more imaginatively plotted of the post-World War II adventure strips. © King Features Syndicate.

Hiroshi Hirata, "Katame no Gunshi." Hirata is an outstanding draftsman whose forte is the depiction of battle and war scenes. © Hiroshi Hirata.

"The Heart of Juliet Jones," Stan Drake. This strip is one of the best representatives of the soap-opera school of comic writing. © King Features Syndicate.

"The Katzenjammer Kids," Rudolph Dirks. This strip was the first genuine comic strip and is the oldest still in existence. © King Features Syndicate.

"The Katzenjammer Kids," Harold Knerr. Knerr took over the "Katzies" from Rudolph Dirks in 1914 but maintained the quality, high spirits, and unpredictability of the strip. © King Features Syndicate.

Koo Kojima, comic book illustration. One of Japan's leading illustrators, Kojima is particularly noted for his sexy, glamorous women. © Koo Kojima.

"Kozure Okami," Goseki Kojima. Kojima's strip is a grim tale of murder and revenge set in feudal Japan. © Manga Action.

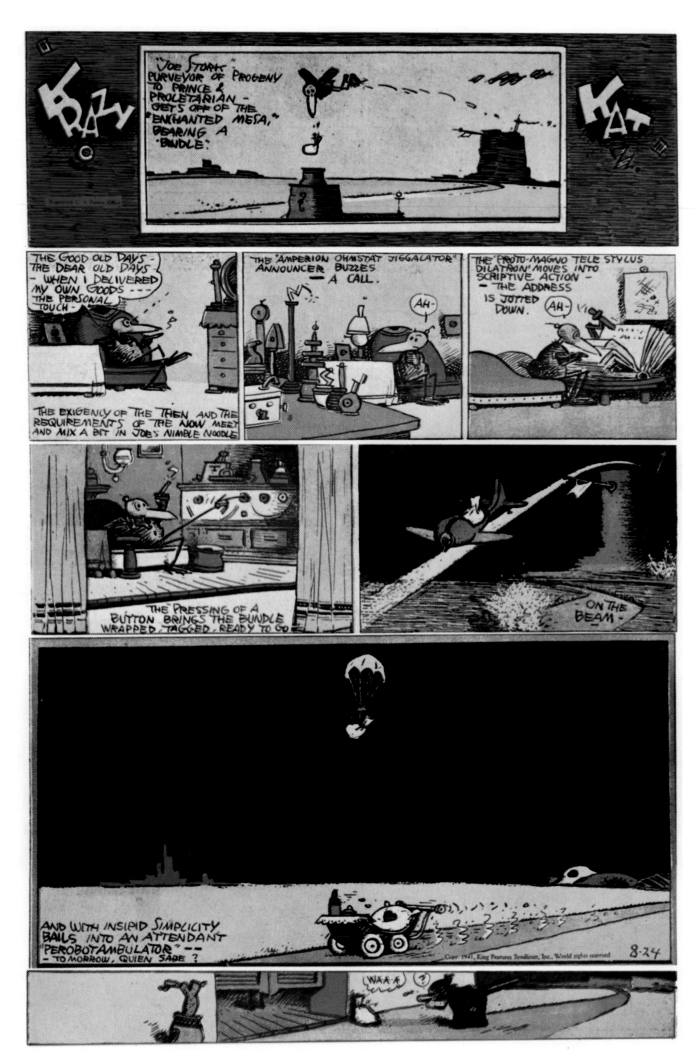

"Krazy Kat," George Herriman. Among the most celebrated comic strips of all time, "Krazy Kat" has earned its author the respect and admiration of intellectuals the world over. © King Features Syndicate.

"Lieutenant Blueberry," Jean-Michel Charlier and Gir (Jean Giraud). This French Western strip is noted for the quality of Gir's artwork. © Editions Dargaud.

"Li'l Abner," Al Capp. Li'l Abner and his hillbilly family and friends are now part of American folklore. © Chicago Tribune-New York News Syndicate.

"Little Jimmy," James Swinnerton. "Little Jimmy" is the best-remembered among Swinnerton's many comic strip creations. © King Features Syndicate.

"Little Orphan Annie," Harold Gray. Most noted for its author's ideological soap-boxing, "Little Orphan Annie" was also moody and suspenseful. © Chicago Tribune-New York News Syndicate.

"Little Nemo in Slumberland," Winsor McCay. *"Little Nemo"* is a masterpiece
of design, grace, and light.

"Lucky Luke," Rene Goscinny and Morris (Maurice de Bevere). This parodic Western is one of the funniest of European comic strips. © Editions Dargaud.

6. ...Ti sei preso (ahi', Marmittone!) molti giorni di prigione...

"Marmittone," Bruno Angoletta. An Italian "Sad Sack," Marmittone poked fun at Mussolini's military pretensions. © Corriere dei Piccoli.

"Mandrake the Magician," Lee Falk and Phil Davis. Mandrake, the master of magic and illusion, is a frequently imitated strip character. © King Features Syndicate.

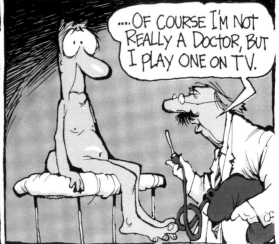

"Mallard Fillmore," Bruce Tinsley. "Mallard Fillmore" was created as a conservative counterpoint to "Doonesbury," with which it often appears on the editorial page of a number of newspapers. © King Features Syndicate.

Milo Manara, "The Wall." The fall of the Berlin Wall has inspired a number of comic-strip artists: here is Manara's exuberantly lyrical take on the event. © Carlsen Verlag.

Esteban Maroto, "Wolff." Maroto, who also works for American comic books, is one of the most famous contemporary Spanish cartoonists. © Buru Lan.

Lorenzo Mattotti, "Fuochi." The plot of "Fuochi" ("Fires") is quite simple: a battleship has been ordered to bomb out a little island, but one of the sailors, dazzled by the colors and creatures of the island, tries to prevent its destruction. The story's fascination lies in the artwork, midway between realism and abstraction, and in the narrative tension created by the images and the colors. © Lorenzo Mattotti.

Todd McFarlane, "Spawn." Todd McFarlane made a name for himself working on some of Marvel's most successful comic book titles. He has enjoyed his greatest hit, however, with a creation of his own, "Spawn," about a vengeful black superhero. © Todd McFarlane.

"Mickey Mouse," Floyd Gottfredson. Mickey Mouse began his joyful career in animated cartoons and was adapted into comic strips in 1930. © Walt Disney Productions.

*Attilio Micheluzzi, "Titanic." Micheluzzi's narrative talent is much in evidence
in this comicbook telling of the fabled ocean liner's doomed Atlantic voyage.
© Casterman.*

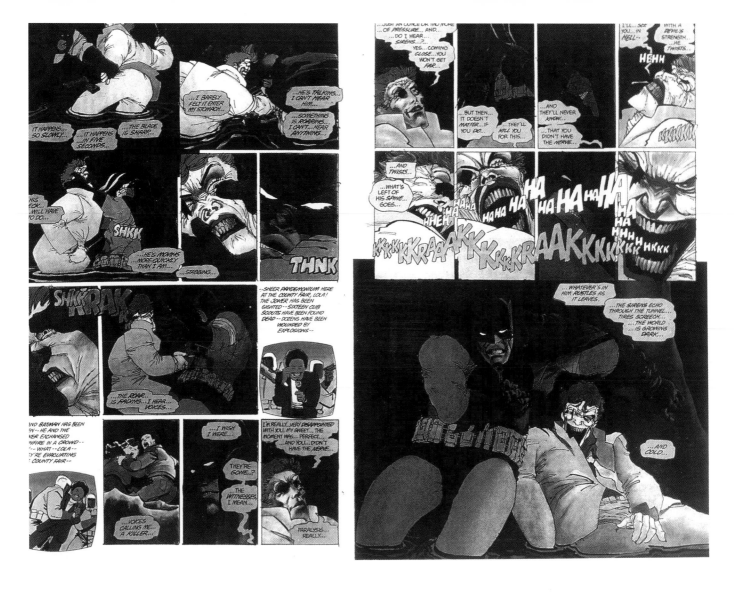

Frank Miller, "The Dark Knight Returns." Of all of Miller's achievements in the field of comic books, his most notable remains his successful revamping of the Batman character in the 1980s. © DC Comics.

"Over the Hedge," Michael Fry and T. Lewis. "Over the Hedge" features the bad boys of the animal world and has proved a huge success with the readers. The circulation of this dark-humored comic strip has grown consistently since its inception in 1995. © United Feature Syndicate.

c46

"Moon Mullins," Frank Willard. *Moon Mullins and his friends and relatives are some of the weirdest misfits ever to appear in the comic pages.* © Chicago Tribune-New York Times Syndicate.

*"Nus," Enric Sio. "Nus" is typical of Sio's avant-garde comic creations. ©
Salvat Editores.*

Pran, "Chacha Chaudhary." India's most popular comic book series. © Pran's Features.

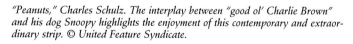

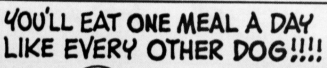

"Peanuts," Charles Schulz. The interplay between "good ol' Charlie Brown" and his dog Snoopy highlights the enjoyment of this contemporary and extraordinary strip. © United Feature Syndicate.

"Polly and Her Pals," Cliff Sterrett. Elements of surrealism and cubism were often incorporated into Sterrett's highly stylized strips. © King Features Syndicate.

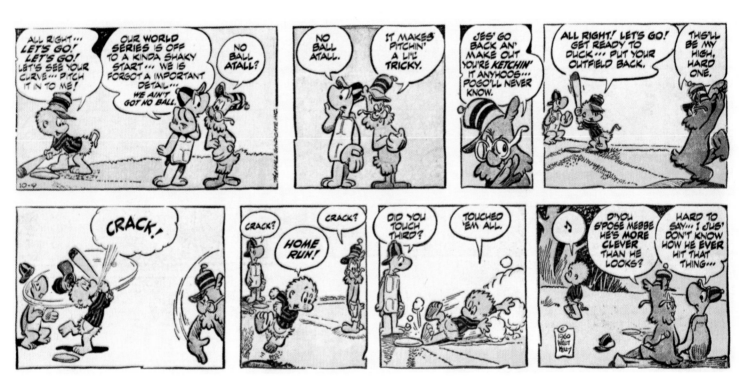

"Pogo," Walt Kelly. "Pogo" dealt with some of the most important moral, social, and political themes of its time. © Walt Kelly.

"Prince Valiant," Harold Foster. A breathtaking exercise in virtuosity of draftsmanship, "Prince Valiant" is Foster's most outstanding achievement in comics.
© King Features Syndicate.

"Quadratino," Antonio Rubino. "Quadratino" is the best of Rubino's many comic creations. © Corriere dei Piccoli.

„Jetzt hab ich keine Zeit mehr! Her mit dem Werkzeug, Pelle!"

„Langsam, Petzi! Zuerst müssen wir gut überlegen."

„Du brauchst zuerst eine Zeichnung von dem Schiff!"

„Eine Zeichnung? Das trifft sich gut, ich zeichne auch gern."

„Petzi, wir wußten gar nicht, daß du so gut zeichnen kannst."

„Das bauen wir! Das ist ein schönes Schiff!"

"Rusmus Klump" ("Petzi"), Carla and Vilhelm Hansen. This strip, intended especially for young children, is one of the most endearing. © PIB.

c53

AT MULA SA MABANGIS NA MUKHANG SING-TIGAS NG BATO NA PINAGKUKUYUMAN NG DAM-DAMING IBIG SUMAMBULAT SA MATINDING SA-MA NG LOOB, AY NAMALISBIS ANG DALAWANG BUTIL NA LUHA, NA HINDI NA MAKAYANG PIGILIN...

LUBOS ANG KAGALAKAN NG HARI NANG IABOT NA MULI ANG SANGGOL SA KA-MAY NG DAMA, AT TINUNGO ANG SILID NA KINAHIHIMLAYAN NG MAHAL NA KA-BIYAK...DATAPUWA'T... PARANG PINAG-SUKLUBAN NG LANGIT AT LUPA ANG BUONG KATAUHAN NG KILABOT NANG TUMAMBAD SA KANYANG PANINGIN ANG KAHAMBAL-HAMBAL NA ANYO NG ASAWA NA WALA NANG MALAY AT ISA NANG MALAMIG NA BANGKAY...

SANDALING NAMAGITAN ANG ISANG NAKABIBINGING KATAHIMIKAN SA PANA-HON NG PAGKAKALUHOD NG KILABOT NA HARI. TIIM ANG MGA BAGANG AT NANLILISIK ANG MGA MATA'Y DAHAN-DAHANG TUMINDIG, AT...

IGINALA ANG KANYANG PANINGIN SA MGA MUKHANG NA-ROROON AT HINAHANAP ANG MANGGAGAMOT NA KAN-YANG INATASANG MANGALAGA SA KALIGTASAN NG MAHAL NA REYNA, AT...

NAGIMBAL ANG LAHAT SA MADUGONG WAKAS NA SINAPIT NG MANGGAGAMOT. AT HARI, SA TINIG NA LIPOS NG HINANAKIT AT PAGDARAMDAM: —WALA PANG SINUMANG NAGDULOT SA AKIN NG GANITONG KASAKLAP NA KABIGUAN...

NANG MAKITA ANG KANYANG HANAP AY BINU-NOT ANG TA-BAK NG PINAKA-MALAPIT NA KABIG AT WALANG PA-KUNDANGANG...

SA Susunod **Ang hula**

Jesus Jodloman, "Ramir." Inspired by "Prince Valiant," "Ramir" is one of the best comic strips from the Philippines. © Halaklak.

"Rose Is Rose," Pat Brady. "Rose Is Rose" is an endearing family strip that has
gained great favor with the public since its humble beginnings in 1984.
© United Feature Syndicate.

COMPLAINTE DES LANDES PERDUES

DUFAUX — ROSINSKI

Rosinski, dessinateur de *Thorgal*, et Dufaux, l'un des meilleurs scénaristes actuels, nous font découvrir l'univers de Sioban, princesse sans royaume mais animée d'une extraordinaire soif de vengeance et de reconquête ! Un récit d'inspiration celtique empreint d'une ambiance fantastique et d'un souffle légendaire parfaitement servi par un dessinateur au sommet de son art. En l'espace de trois albums cette série fait déjà partie des indispensables.

3 titres disponibles (voir p. 64)

* SIOBAN * SELECTIONNÉ PARMI LES 30 INDISPENSABLES D'ANGOULÊME 94.

Gregor Rosinski and Jean Dufaux, "La Complainte des Landes Perdues."
Polish-born Rosinski became noted for the comic stories he contributed to
Warsaw magazines from the late 1960s to the mid-1970s. Moving to the West
he then demonstrated his graphic mastery in a number of comic series, of which
this is one of the most breathtaking. © Dargaud Editeur.

"Roy Tiger." A revived German comic strip industry produced "Roy Tiger."
© *Bastei Verlag.*

"Rusty Riley," Frank Godwin. Godwin's last creation is a nostalgic and beautiful paean to youth. © *King Features Syndicate.*

"Sandman," Neil Gaiman and Sam Kieth. One of the most original of contemporary comic book writers, Gaiman could take even an old warhorse like DC's Sandman and make it seem new. © DC Comics.

Matthias Schultheiss, "Them." Schultheiss is a German comics creator who is better known in France and the U.S. than in his native country. He has published several highly dramatic graphic novels and a number of shorter stories, of which "Them," built around the destruction of the Berlin Wall, is one. © Carlsen Verlag.

c59

"Sheena, Queen of the Jungle," W. Morgan Thomas. Sheena was the first in a
long line of sexy, scantily clad comic book heroines. © Fiction House.

"Sturmtruppen," Bonvi (Franco Bonvicini). Set during World War II, this strip
was a satire on military life and an example of black, even sick, humor.
© Franco Bonvicini.

"Il Signor Bonaventura," Sto (Sergio Tofano). This simple tale of a Good
Samaritan is beloved among Italian strips. © Corriere dei Piccoli.

"Sjors," Frans Piet. Begun as the Dutch version of the "Winnie
Winkle" Sunday page, "Sjors" later became the most popular kid
strip in the Netherlands. © Het Sjorsblod.

"Les Schtroumpfs," Peyo (Pierre Culliford). A race of gentle, civilized,
and utterly winsome elves, the schtroumpfs are involved in the most
improbable adventures. © Editions Dupuis.

HE WON'T JUMP THROUGH THE HOOP!

OFFER HIM CANDY

HE STILL WON'T!

I WILL!

One of these suspects stole an Egyptian sculpture from the Forest Museum. Slylock Fox is holding a box that contains physical evidence dropped by the thief at the crime scene. What do you think is in the box, and which suspect do you believe is guilty?

E-Mail: SLYLOCK F @ AOL.COM

WEBER

One of the raccoon's coat buttons is gone. The box contains his missing button. Slylock suspects the raccoon is the thief.

Find six differences between these two panels.

Answer – Cork, earring, air hose, crab leg, fish fin, octopus tentacle.

True or False

CLICK!

Electric lights can cause cats to shed.

True. Even the illumination of a television is enough to trigger shedding.

HOW TO DRAW a dinosaur

Your Drawing

This week's artist, Taylor Santos, age 9, of Pawtucket, RI, receives a free **SLYLOCK FOX BRAIN BOGGLERS** game.

Send your drawings (b&w) to Slylock Fox and Comics for Kids c/o this newspaper.

"Slylock Fox," Bob Weber Jr. Slylock Fox, a Sherlockian sleuth in vulpine guise, is the star of "Comics for Kids," the highly successful activity strip created by Bob Weber Jr., son of "Moose" creator Bob Weber. © King Features Syndicate.

c62

Reg Perrott, "Song of the Sword." Perrott was an early English adventure strip artist. © Amalgamated Press.

"Spider-Man," Stan Lee and John Romita. Also known as the "web slinger" and "your friendly neighborhood Spider-Man," this character epitomizes the comic book antihero and is the best-known comic creation of the 1960s. © Marvel Comics Group.

"The Spectre," Murphy Anderson. "The Spectre" was one of the more interesting superhero features. © National Periodical Publications.

"The Spirit," Will Eisner. "The Spirit" was the historical bridge between the comic book and the newspaper strip. © Will Eisner.

"Steve Canyon," Milton Caniff. "Steve Canyon" was one of the few contemporary continuity strips to exhibit some of the spirit and élan of the old adventure stories. © Field Newspaper Syndicate.

"Superman," Wayne Boring. Despite imitations and variations, since 1938 Superman has been the uncontested champion of the costumed superhero league. © National Periodical Publications.

"Tarzan," Harold Foster. More than any other, "Tarzan" established the adventure strip as an autonomous genre. © Edgar Rice Burroughs, Inc.

"Tarzan," Burne Hogarth. After taking over the strip from Harold Foster, Hogarth fashioned "Tarzan" into one of the most celebrated adventure strips in comics history. © Edgar Rice Burroughs, Inc.

CONTINUED ON 3RD PAGE FOLLOWING

"Swamp Thing," Alan Moore and Rick Veitch. Moore constructed genuinely gripping tales around the premise of a scientist turned into a "plant elemental" following the bombing of his laboratory. He was helped in his task by Veitch's often brilliant visuals. © DC Comics.

"Terry and the Pirates," Milton Caniff. More faithfully than any other comic strip, "Terry" reflected the American attitude after Pearl Harbor. © Chicago Tribune-New York News Syndicate.

"Tetsuwan-Atom" ("Astroboy"), Osamu Tezuka. This is Tezuka's most widely circulated comic feature. © Shonen.

"Thimble Theater" ("Popeye"), Elzie Segar. "Thimble Theater" reached its
peak of popularity in 1929, when the invincible one-eyed sailor, Popeye, and
the intellectual moocher, Wimpy, were introduced. © King Features Syndicate.

"Thor," Stan Lee and Jack Kirby. Thor is another of the superheroes made
popular by the dynamic duo, Lee and Kirby. © Marvel Comics Group.

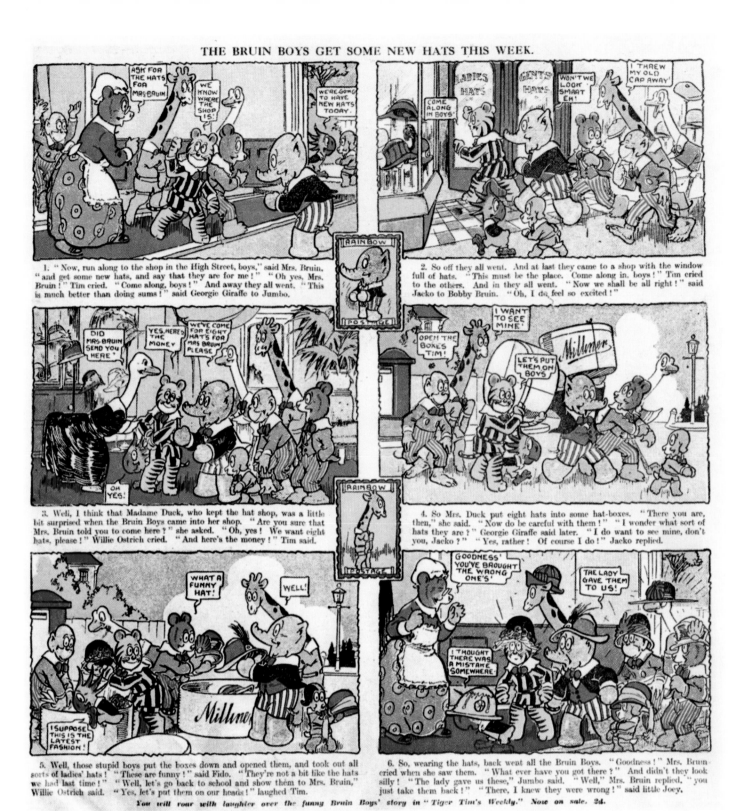

1. "Now, run along to the shop in the High Street, boys," said Mrs. Bruin, "and get some new hats, and say that they are for me!" "Oh yes, Mrs. Bruin!" Tim cried. "Come along, boys!" And away they all went. "This is much better than doing sums!" said Georgie Giraffe to Jumbo.

2. So off they all went. And at last they came to a shop with the window full of hats. "This must be the place. Come along in, boys!" Tim cried to the others. And in they all went. "Now we shall be all right!" said Jacko to Bobby Bruin. "Oh, I do feel so excited!"

3. Well, I think that Madame Duck, who kept the hat shop, was a little bit surprised when the Bruin Boys came into her shop. "Are you sure that Mrs. Bruin told you to come here?" she asked. "Oh, yes! We want eight hats, please!" Willie Ostrich cried. "And here's the money!" Tim said.

4. So Mrs. Duck put eight hats into some hat-boxes. "There you are, then," she said. "Now do be careful with them!" "I wonder what sort of hats they are?" Georgie Giraffe said later. "I do want to see mine, don't you, Jacko?" "Yes, rather! Of course I do!" Jacko replied.

5. Well, those stupid boys put the boxes down and opened them, and took out all sorts of ladies' hats! "These are funny!" said Fido. "They're not a bit like the hats we had last time!" "Well, let's go back to school and show them to Mrs. Bruin," Willie Ostrich said. "Yes, let's put them on our heads!" laughed Tim.

6. So, wearing the hats, back went all the Bruin Boys. "Goodness!" Mrs. Bruin cried when she saw them. "What ever have you got there?" And didn't they look silly! "The lady gave us these," Jumbo said. "Well," Mrs. Bruin replied, "you just take them back!" "There, I knew they were wrong!" said little Joey.

You will roar with laughter over the funny Bruin Boys' story in "Tiger Tim's Weekly." Now on sale. 2d.

"Tiger Tim" ("The Bruin Boys"), H. S. Foxwell. The dean of British animal strips, "Tiger Tim" has entertained several generations of young readers. © Fleetway Publications Ltd.

"Tintin," Hergé (George Rémi). "Tintin" has been the most acclaimed comic creation in Europe for more than 65 years. © Editions Casterman.

Daniel Torres, "Triton." This is an episode in the "astral adventures of Rocco Vargas,"
Torres's half-parody, half-homage to the space-opera genre. © Daniel Torres.

"Valhalla," Peter Madsen. "Valhalla" is a tongue-in-cheek retelling of the old Norse myths and legends. © A/S Interpresse.

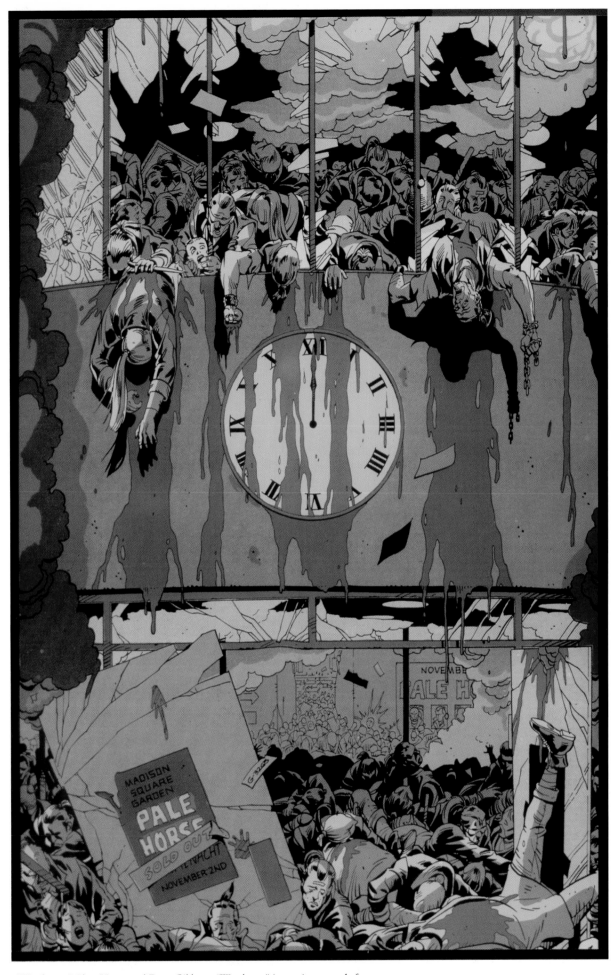

"Watchmen," Alan Moore and Dave Gibbons. *"Watchmen"* is a unique tour de force whose excellence has not been replicated so far. It lies like an erratic rock in the middle of the great American comic book landscape. © DC Comics

"Wee Willie Winkie's World," Lyonel Feininger. Feininger skillfully created a world of fantasy and whimsy, of sweetness and shadows, of marvel and terror.

"Winnetou," Helmut Nickel. Inspired by Karl May's popular novels, "Winnetou" is the only German Western strip of note. © Walter Lehning Verlag.

"The Wizard of Id," Johnny Hart and Brant Parker. This strip, with its weird cast of characters, can only be called a "black" fairy tale. © Field Newspaper Syndicate.

"Wonder Woman," William Moulton Marston. Hailed in some quarters as a champion of women's liberation, Wonder Woman spent an inordinate portion of her time in chains. © National Periodical Publications.

"White Boy," Garrett Price. "White Boy" was a handsome and offbeat Western whose qualities were unappreciated by readers. © Chicago Tribune-New York News Syndicate.

"The Yellow Kid," Richard Felton Outcault. Not yet a genuine comic strip in 1895, "The Yellow Kid" ushered in the era of the modern Sunday newspaper supplement and was of pivotal importance to the development of the American comic strip.

More About the Comics

A History of Newspaper Syndication
by Richard Marschall

"The Comic Paper in America"
by William Henry Shelton

"The Humor of the Colored Supplement"
by Ralph Bergengren

Glossary of Comic Strip Terms

A History of Newspaper Syndication
By Richard Marschall

The newspaper syndicate has been of inestimable value to the acceptance, growth, and development of the comic strip. It has served simultaneously as showcase and sounding board for the creators, and the syndicate business itself—although frequently subordinating creativity to commercialism—has given birth to almost all of the formats, conventions, devices, and techniques used in the modern comic strip. And it is to a handful of syndicate giants from the days of journalistic moguls that the whole experience known as the newspaper comic strip is most indebted.

Briefly, the syndicate concept started with the thirst for fast news about important events. In 1841 Moses Y. Beach of the *New York Sun* had messengers deliver President John Tyler's inaugural address to his pressroom, where he ran off pre-prints for local papers throughout New York State. Six years later the *Staten Islander* bought whole sections ("insiders") from the *Sun* for inclusion in its own editions.

In 1861 Ansel Nash Kellogg of the *Baraboo* (Wisconsin) *Republican* bought pre-printed war news from the *Wisconsin State Journal*, a practice capitalized on by the latter as it began the first large-scale regular distribution of newspaper material, including advertising. Kellogg himself picked up the idea and, in 1865, founded the first real syndicate, the A. N. Kellogg News Co., which originated features and jokes for subscribers.

Much of this activity was centered in Chicago, and hundreds of papers throughout the Midwest suffered when Chicago burned in 1871. But in the recovery the first continued stories appeared, the first illustrated syndicated articles came in 1872, and the first stereotyped plates ("boiler plates"), whereby papers could fit preset type into a page, debuted in 1875.

Most of the primitive syndicate activity to that time was confined to rural papers unable to offer their own feature material. But in the 1880s, distributed material went to town. Irving Bacheller sold big-name interviews to major papers and established the New York Press Syndicate, later contracting famous writers. Major Orlando Jay Smith in Chicago operated similarly in 1882. *The New York Sun* again shone by syndicating its fiction around the country, and the *New York World* sent Bill Nye, the most popular humorist of the day, and cartoonist Walt McDougall around the country to sell their reports to other papers.

Unable to persuade his employers to syndicate material from *Century* and *St. Nicholas* in 1884, S. S. McClure decided to establish his own syndicate. On a shoestring he did so, with one paper receiving material free in exchange for galley proofs, which were sent to other subscribers. Soon McClure had the biggest names in fiction and public life in his stable.

It was at that point that a now-obscure group of men introduced comic strips, just at their birth in the mid-1890s, to the syndicate process. As color was added to newspapers, major cities generally kept their comic sections to themselves,

George Herriman, "Major Ozone." (1906)

835

Clarence Rigby, "Little Ah Sid, the Chinese Kid." (1906)

but enterprising preprint and boiler-plate syndicates introduced the nation to the comic strip.

Following is a list of the major syndicates and their features. The comics often changed artists; some cartoonists were idea men, originating features and letting others continue them. Today, these old sections are delights—abounding in features, some in color, all with a freer and sometimes more amateurish look than their big-city counterparts, Hearst and Pulitzer. Familiar names of later greats often appear, too, mass-produced with large audiences in client papers such as the *Bellefontaine* (Ohio) *Index-Repository*, instead of in New York or Chicago papers.

Foremost among these concerns was the World Color Printing Co. of St. Louis, no relation to the *New York World*. It was the longest-lived of its contemporaries, supplying rural Sunday papers with preprinted color comics until 1937. Its president was Robert Sterling Gravel, and often artists—as they switched from feature to feature—would sign his middle name to a strip as an umbrella nom de plume.

The World Company's stable was the largest and most talented of any; its star idea man for years was George Herriman; its preeminent strip was *Slim Jim*. Herriman created and drew, among others, *Butch Smith, the Boy Who Does Stunts*; *Bud Smith* (continued by Bart and later Johnny Gruelle); *Major Ozone, the Fresh Air Fiend* (continued by Clarence Rigby, Bart and Ray Nottier); *Handy Andy* (continued by Gruelle); *Bruno and Pietro* (later drawn by Rigby); and *Alexander the Cat*, on which he was succeeded by Rigby and Alexander, among others.

Clarence Rigby was also prolific, contributing his own features, including *Little Ah Sid, the Chinese Kid* and *Pinky Prim the Cat*. George Frink drew Herriman's *Rosy Posy—Mama's Girl*, in addition to *Circus Solly* and *Slim Jim*. Dink (Dink Shannon) had a style similar to James Swinnerton's and produced *Sammy Small* and two comics taken over by Jack Rogers, *Uncle Ned* and *Mooney Miggles*. The classic *Hairbreadth Harry*, begun in the *Philadelphia Press*, was first syndicated by the World Company.

Raymond C. Ewer, "Things as They Ought To Be." (1909)

Other creations and their artists were *Mr. Smarty* by Collins, *Foolish Questions* by Rutledge, *The Almost Family*, *Jingling Johnson the Poet*, and *Fitzboomski the Anarchist* by Bradford (he later became a radical himself), *Brown the City Farmer* by Raymond Crawford Ewer, *Sleepy Sid* by Paul Plashke (who became an editorial cartoonist), *Cousin Bill from the City* and *Jocko and Jumbo* by Goewey (*Cousin Bill* was originated by Jack Farr, later a cartoonist for *Judge* and comic books), *Mama's Girl—Daddy's Boy* by Bart, *Willie Westinghouse Edison Smith* and *Muggsy* by Frank Crane, and *Teacher's Pet*, among a host of strips created by Carl Anderson of later *Henry* fame. Most of the foregoing were created before 1915.

The mainstay of T. C. McClure Syndicate's bullpen was Billy Marriner. He created *Wags, the Dog that Adopted a Man*, *Sambo and His Funny Noises*, and *Mary and Her Little Lamb*, among others. After Marriner's death, Pat Sullivan, who drew *Fadder und Mamma Lade* for McClure, continued some of his work before entering animation with *Felix the Cat*. Bray, another pioneer animator, drew an absentminded character, and Kate Carew, sister of Gluyas Williams, drew *Handy Andy*.

Simon Simple was one of the most popular early strips; its creator, Ed Carey, was paid more than $500 a page in 1905. The redoubtable C. W. Kahles drew *Clarence the Cop*, *Billy Bounce*, and many other strips for McClure (for various services he once had seven strips running simultaneously). Pioneer Walt McDougall drew *Hank the Hermit* and *Hank and His Animal Friends*, and A. D. Reed drew *Uncle Pike* and other farmer strips. J. A. Lemon drew perhaps the first henpecked-husband strip, *How Would You Like to Be John?*, for McClure.

From the *Philadelphia Inquirer*, Otis Wood ran the Keystone service and the syndicate that bore his name. Marriner contributed heavily to its offerings: *Irresistible Rags*, a black character; *Mr. George and Wifey*, continued by Jack Gallagher and Ernie McGee; and *The Feinheimer Twins*, a copy of Hans and Fritz that Marriner drew between 1902 and 1905 and which was then drawn, until 1914, by H. H. Knerr.

Other graduates of this class included Charles Payne, who drew *Bear Creek Folks*, *The Little Possum Gang* (later taken over by Joe Doyle and Jack Gallagher),

Billy Marriner, "Sambo and His Funny Noises." (1909)

C. W. Kahles, "Billy Bounce." (1904)

and *Kid Trubbel*, foreshadowing his later *S'Matter, Pop?*; Sidney Smith; Clare Victor Dwiggins (Dwig); and two Hearst favorites, Rudolph Dirks and R. F. Outcault. Dirks drew *The Terrible Twins*, an obvious approximation of his *Katzies*, for a handsome sum until Hearst made him stop, and Outcault, while still with the *Herald* between stints with Hearst, moonlighted on *Barnyard Fables* in Philadelphia.

Some larger cities had their own comic sections and made modest efforts to distribute them in the hinterlands. *The Boston Globe*, for instance, introduced *Kitty and Percy* by George H. Blair and *That Li'l Rascal Rastus* by Maginnis. *The Boston Herald* came out with *Bolivar* and *The Kid Klub* by Hal Coffman and Wallace Goldsmith respectively; both artists later became successful editorial cartoonists. Also from Boston came very handsome newspaper versions of Peter Newell's charming children's stuff, *Polly Sleepyhead*, and Palmer Cox's *Brownies*.

The *Philadelphia North American* was active in the early comic field, and Walt McDougall, already a veteran in the first two decades, was a mainstay. He drew *Handsome Hautrey, Fatty Felix, Peck's Bad Boy, Absent-Minded Abner* (daily), and perhaps the first continuity strip, *The Wizard of Oz*, for four months in 1904. The fine magazine artist W. O. Wilson drew *Madge, the Magician's Daughter*, and the great Zim (Eugene Zimmerman) drew two strips, one about two Dutch boys and another about a luckless reporter.

The *Philadelphia Record* presented Ernie McGee's *Mechanical Toys*, and the *Philadelphia Press* introduced Hugh Doyle's *Lazy Lew Casey*.

Other comics from the early days abound: Everett E. Lowry, later an editorial cartoonist, drew *Binnacle Jim* for T. C. McClure; Carl Anderson's first of many strips for McClure was *Spiegleburger*; Dink drew *Jones—His Wife Can't Boss Him* for the World Company and was followed by Armstrong before he worked on *Slim Jim*; Louis Dalrymple, a *Puck* magazine veteran, drew for the *Boston Post*; Karl's *Dem Boys* was a straight imitation of *The Katzenjammer Kids* between 1914 and 1917. At the same time, both Dirks and Knerr were drawing the kids in their own versions—and Hearst was also reprinting original Dirks pages from a decade before!

The *Chicago Tribune* thrived with its own comic section for years, kicking off with Lyonel Feininger's classic surrealist creations showcasing such names as Clare Briggs and F. M. Howarth (after the latter was fired by Hearst), and culminating in the pre-*Gasoline Alley* comic creations of Frank King just before syndicate organization.

Other titles, proving that the development of strips was not a slow process, include *Mrs. Rummage* and *Mr. Gouch and His Beautiful Wife* by Hy Gage; *Isador*

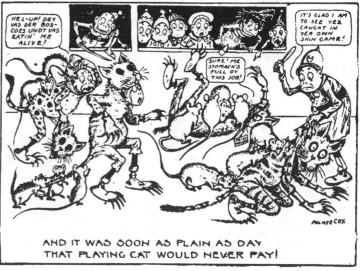

Palmer Cox, "The Brownies." (1907)

Walt McDougall, "Peck's Bad Boy." (1906)

Knobb Almost Keeps a Job by Honhorst; *Grandma's Girl* (yet another Herriman creation) by C. H. Wellington; Rigby's *Imaginative Clarence*; *Doubting Thomas* and *Pretending Percy*, two more from the active C. W. Kahles; and *Brainy Bowers*, another Ed Carey classic.

The early preprinters and boiler-plate syndicates served as valuable training grounds for both themes and artists. And, in the first two decades of this century, broad segments of the American public may have only vaguely known *Alphonse and Gaston* and *Foxy Grandpa*, but they warmly identified with *Hairbreadth Harry*, *Slim Jim*, and *Simon Simple*.

Back in the big cities, comparatively slow progress was being made with syndication. In 1895 the *New York Herald* was selling its features; later *Little Nemo* was an offering. The same year Hearst began distribution when the *Pittsburgh Press* requested reprint rights to certain features. But it was not until 1915 that Hearst consolidated all of his various syndicate operations into a large-scale syndicate. In that year the Newspaper Feature Service, International News Features, King Feature Syndicate, Premier Syndicate, and the Star Company, among others, were combined under the autocratic Moses Koenigsberg, with King Features the sales agent.

Of course, William Randolph Hearst's personal affection for and involvement with comics is well documented. He was a guiding genius who found, bought, and developed talent; he and his lieutenants displayed an uncanny knack for finding formulas and hitting popular tastes. Before syndicate operation, Hearst comics were seen around the nation in his many newspapers and in limited preprint offerings. Before 1920 Hearst's biggest stars were R. F. Outcault, Rudolph Dirks, F. B. Opper, James Swinnerton, Bunny (Carl Schultze), Winsor McCay, Cliff Sterrett, and George McManus.

The *New York World*, never far behind Hearst, began its syndicate operation in 1898. Of course many of its artists were bought away by Hearst (including Outcault and McManus), but by the 1910s the *World*'s publisher, Joseph Pulitzer, had lured Bud Fisher and Rudolph Dirks to his side. The early *World* offerings constituted a merry bunch of comic strips: R. W. Taylor's *Yens Yenson, Yanitor* and *Uncle Mose*; Gene Carr's long-running *Lady Bountiful* and *Stepbrothers*; Dwig's *Ophelia and Her Slate* and *Willie Fibb*; William J. Steinigans's *Splinters the Clown* and *The Bad Dream that Made Bill a Better Boy*; the talented F. M. Follett's *See-See Kid*; and the ubiquitous Kahles's *Billy Bragg*—all danced happily across the *World*'s pages with a wide array of McManus creations.

By the 1910s Pulitzer was heavily involved with preprints, starring *The Original Hans and Fritz—by the Creator of the Katzenjammer Kids*. When the *World* folded in 1931, its syndicate, the Press Publishing Co., merged with Max Elser's Metropolitan Features into United Feature Syndicate, an outgrowth of United Press's

W. O. Wilson, "Madge the Magician's Daughter." (1906)

literary agency, founded in 1891. When Hearst's International News merged with UP, Hearst received part ownership of United Feature.

In 1901 Robert F. Paine of the *Cleveland Press* founded the Newspaper Enterprise Association and then in 1909 the NEA Service—the service sells complete packages of comics rather than offering and contracting individual strips to client papers. It remained the last vestige of the boiler-plate system and provided many rural papers (and ultimately the affiliated Scripps-Howard chain) with quality comics. *Doings of the Duffs, Freckles and His Friends, Mr. Skygack from Mars, Everrett True,* and *Adolph and Osgar* were early favorites.

In 1907 George Matthew Adams signed big names to report on big events and contracted famous writers to produce short works that he syndicated. The early syndicate ventures were very successful, with Edwina Dumm and Ding Darling as two of his stars. Later the George Matthew Adams Service was absorbed by the Washington Star Syndicate, which in turn affiliated with King Features. The Central Press of Cleveland, founded in 1910 by V. V. McNitt, was a local feature service also ultimately swallowed by Hearst. However, McNitt was later the main drive (with Charles McAdam) behind the McNaught Syndicate, founded in 1922. In 1912 Victor Lawson of the *Chicago Daily News* arranged for Adams to establish The Associated Newspapers, composed of several large-city dailies. As a syndicate it later merged with Consolidated News Features and Bell and North American Newspaper Alliance. All finally merged with the McClure Syndicate, only to sell out to United Feature.

Bell Syndicate was the creation of John Wheeler, the father of modern syndication, who perfected many of the technical and sales aspects of the business. By sheer audacity, talent, and force of personality this former sports reporter was able to lure Bud Fisher away from Hearst and got the *New York World* to guarantee $50,000 a year for *Mutt and Jeff.* Fisher, Fontaine Fox, Charles Payne, Gluyas Williams, and Wally Carlson worked for Bell.

The Ledger Syndicate of Philadelphia was organized in 1915 to distribute features from the *Saturday Evening Post* and *Ladies' Home Journal; Hairbreadth Harry* and Frank Godwin's strips were its mainstays.

In 1919 Joseph M. Patterson of the *Chicago Tribune* started selling his paper's features on an active basis and moved to New York to establish the *Daily News.* Comics were created for the paper's debut and for distribution by the new Tribune-News Syndicate; soon the distributors had the most well-rounded and consistent offerings of any syndicate until the 1940s. Captain Patterson was an unequalled genius. He often took average artists, suggested titles, changed characters, and outlined themes to create classic comics. In the stable were Harold

Gray, Chester Gould, Frank King, Frank Willard, Sidney Smith, and, later, Milton Caniff.

Also in 1919 in Chicago Eugene P. Conley founded Associated Editors, which provided teenage features. In 1925 he joined with H. H. Anderson and launched Publishers Syndicate; it soon became a leader in the story-strip field as *Apple Mary* and *Chief Wahoo* turned serious. In 1962 Publishers was bought by Field Enterprises, which had entered the syndicate field as the Chicago Sun-Times Syndicate and had only recently bought up the Herald-Tribune Syndicate. The latter had an anachronistic offering, with old wheezes like *Mr. and Mrs.*, but also had new comics like *B.C.* and *Miss Peach*. It was itself the combination of two great namesake syndicates and was beginning to show signs of creativity when its parent newspaper died.

Field Enterprises went on to acquire the Hall Syndicate in 1967. Bob Hall, a former United salesman, had founded his syndicate in 1949 with the help of the *New York Post*, and he quickly compiled a list of such hits as *Pogo, Dennis the Menace*, and *Andy Capp*. Publishers-Hall (now Field Newspaper Syndicate) has since become one of the largest modern-day syndicates, and it still employs H. H. Anderson's techniques of polling and scientifically planning features and continuities.

Today the major syndicates have whittled down to five in number: King, United Media Services (regrouping United Feature and NEA), Tribune Media Services, Universal Press Syndicate, and Creators Syndicate. But, as various independent attempts have shown, syndicates are necessary for the distribution of an artist's work. It remains to be seen in these days of newspaper mortality whether syndicates will accommodate just one more time—this time with realism—and explore new outlets for the comic strip.

Richard Marschall

REPRINTED FROM *CRITIC*, SEPTEMBER 1901, 227-34

The Comic Paper in America
By William Henry Shelton

My past recollection of an American comic paper is of a sheet somewhat larger than *Puck*, printed on very coarse paper with grotesque figures in outline on the cover, which used to appear in the fifties in the window of Aldrich & Fairchild's bookstore in Canandaigua, along with *Gleason's Pictorial* and *Ballou's Dollar Monthly*. I was not much interested in the comic paper and have quite forgotten its name, but *Gleason's Pictorial*, with the shipping in Boston harbor at the head of the first page, was in high favor with a little coterie of us who met one evening of each week to copy its fascinating pictures.

In the autumn of '71 I came to New York to set up as an artist with no training whatever.

My very first commission was for a page in *Wild Oats*, then published in Beekman Street by Winchell & Small. The firm soon became Collier & Small, the last-named being the editor under the pen name of "Bricktop," which, it is needless to say, referred to the color of his hair. The page consisted of imaginary heads of Brigham Young's wives and was drawn in pencil over India ink washes, on a block of boxwood, glued and bolted together, of many small pieces. The engraving was of the coarsest and the drawing of the weakest. Times were good, however, and the public not over-critical. *Wild Oats* paid as high as $25 for a full-page drawing and $20 for a front page, which was about half the minimum prices ruling at Harper's.

Among the draughtsmen whom I met at that time in the little office in Beekman Street a few are living, but more are dead. Frank Bellew, who signed his drawings with a triangle, was a middle-aged Englishman of polished manners, and rather seedy dress, resulting from too convivial habits. "Mike" Woolf, genial and bubbling over with brilliant jokes, dropped in with as many comic sketches of children as he might have left after supplying the joke market at Harper's and Frank Leslie's. Tom Worth did the darkies sleigh-riding in dry-goods boxes behind grotesquely spavined horses. Sol. Ettynge also did darkies about Christmas time, but I never remember to have seen him, only hearing that he lived somewhere in Jersey and had a famous thirst with all his cleverness. Howard, who made comic valentines for a firm of lithographers in Nassau Street, and may do so still, was among the contributors, and there was also a small man, whose name I have forgotten, with premature gray hair, who got in a drawing occasionally and who was reputed to be particularly hard up. I had almost forgotten Wales, who was quite the most successful of us all in securing boxwood block from *Wild Oats*.

It was whispered at the time that he was on familiar drinking terms with Bricktop in a neighboring saloon. Wales was a cartoonist of much originality, whose professional career was cut short a few years later as a result of intemperance. Collier was the member of the firm with whom we bargained for our work. He was so easily imposed upon that it often became necessary for Bricktop to cut in with a veto from his office window behind which he ground out editorials and railway jokes. In '74 *Wild Oats* published a German edition, under the name of *Snedderadaugg*.

Phunny Phellow was a comic paper of the same period, published, if I remember, by Street & Smith, which afforded a convenient market for some of the cartoons that were not available elsewhere. "Not available," by the way, was a formula much in use by Mr. Parsons, then at the head of the art department at Harper's.

Another comic sheet which lived a short life and not a very merry one while *Wild Oats* was at the height of its prosperity, was the *Fifth Avenue Journal*. It was published during its troubled career from a bleak office in Newspaper Row by a

" YANKEE NOTIONS"

"VANITY FAIR"

young man who sported very large cuffs and paid his bills in very small installments. His was an early and fatuous attempt to intrude the comic paper, with suitably tempered jokes, upon the exclusive circles of the smart set.

The comic papers that have preceded the successes of to-day have strewn the literary prairie with their whitened bones since the early forties. A year and a fraction has compassed the ordinary span of a comic paper's life. In going over the lists of failures we find the names of men now famous in literature, art, and journalism associated with a curious crowd of notables-in-their-day.

Mr. Brander Matthews, in the *American Bibliopholist* for August, 1875, mentions thirty-four comic papers that had been started in this city previous to that date.

In the December number of the same publication Mr. L. W. Kingman adds eight more to the list. Mr. Matthews's list included the Galaxy, which had a humorous department, and the *Salmagundi*, edited by David Longworth, and written by William and Washington Irving and J. K. Paulding, which appeared as a periodical on Saturday, January 24, 1807, and ended with the twentieth number.

Excluding these two, and adding Mr. Matthews's list to Mr. Longworth's, we find that forty comic papers had been started in New York before 1875. The year 1872 seems to have been a banner year for such ventures, as no less than twelve were launched here, including *Wild Oats*, before mentioned, and its ephemeral predecessor, *The Brickbat*.

The Pictorial Wag, published about 1842, by Robert H. Elton, a wood engraver, and edited by Thomas L. Nichols, a water-cure doctor, has the honor of being the pioneer of comic periodicals in the city of New York.

Mr. Elton's unpopularity is said to have been too heavy a load for the *Wag* to carry, and the paper only published a few numbers. Mr. Elton afterwards went into real estate and built Morrisania and Eltonia.

Yankee Doodle appeared in 1845, as a sixteen-page quarto, published by Cornelius Matthews, whose funny name was "Puffer Hopkins." G. G. Foster, known as "Gaslight" Foster, Richard Grant White, and others were interested in the publication. Horace Greeley, then a young man of twenty-four, was at the same time a contributor and an object of caricature. N. P. Willis was another contributor, and the artist was one Martin. Puffer Hopkins was a man of wealth, but with all the talent enumerated his paper expired within the year.

Judy, an imitation of *Punch*, made its appearance a few weeks after *Yankee Doodle*. Its publisher was George F. Nesbitt, then known as the "Nassau Street Punster." Harry Grattan Plunkett, an actor, who was equally well known as Harry Plunkett Grattan, was editor, assisted by Dr. W. K. Northall, from the Olympic Theatre Company. One of the chief artists was a Mr. Wolfe, afterwards leader of the orchestra of Burton's Theatre. Over-burdened with comedians *Judy* came to a tragic end a few weeks before *Yankee Doodle*.

Following *Judy*, *The Bubble* appeared and burst after the second number.

The New York *Picayune*, started in 1847, lasted until 1858. Its phenomenal longevity is accounted for by the fact that it was published by a Dr. Hutchings to advertise his patent medicines. Its editor until 1854 was Joseph A. Scoville, an erratic character who quarrelled with the proprietor and started *The Pick*, which lived a little over a year.

Robert H. Levison, one of the subsequent editors of the *Picayune*, added to the reputation of the paper by publishing "The Comic Sermons of Julius Caesar Hannibal." In 1858 Frank Bellew, "The Triangle," who had been the artist of *The Reveille*, another short-lived periodical, became the editor of the *Picayune*, and associated with him appeared Mortimer Thompson,—G. K. Philander Doesticks.

In 1852 Dr. Hutchings started a second comic paper, *The Lantern*. At one period of its short career Jno. Broughton was its editor, assisted by one Thomas Powell, an Englishman, who was said to have been the original of both Mr. Pecksniff and Mr. Micawber. FitzJames O'Brien and Charles Seymour, theatrical critic of the *Times*, were contributors. With so many wags in control *The Lantern* did well to keep its light burning for eighteen months. This is evidently the same paper that appears in some lists as conducted by John Brougham, who was a persistent promoter of comic journalism, under the name of "Diogenes hys Lanterne."

Young Sam had had a career of twelve months following *The Lantern*, and *Young America*, started in 1853, existed a few months longer. Jno. McLennan, who drew comics for *Harper's Monthly*, and Hoppin, who made curious book illustrations in outline in Darley's time, were the artists.

Vanity Fair, started in 1859, lived eight years, and brought to the front some new names in literature, such as Richard Henry Stoddard, Edmund Clarence Stedman, Artemus Ward, Thos. Bailey Aldrich, and William Winter.

Momus was started in 1860, as a comic daily, and after a few numbers it was changed to a weekly and died.

Mrs. Grundy, started July 15, 1865, expired with the eleventh number.

Punchinello was born in April, 1870, and died in December. Among its contributors were Orpheus C. Kerr and W. L. Alden, the veteran editor of *Harper's Monthly*.

The Thistle was published for a short time in 1872 by S. M. Howard. The articles were signed by various names, but all were written by the poet Francis S. Saltus.

Among the comic papers were the various publications by Frank Leslie: *Champagne*, *The Cartoon*, *Budget of Fun*, *Jolly Joker*, and others. Of various nomenclature there is mention of a paper called the *Innocent Weekly Owl*, *The Phunniest of Phunny Phellows*, and, in Philadelphia, *John Donkey*.

The first great success in comic journalism, in New York, was that of *Puck*, which began its career at No. 13 William Street in the spring of 1877. Keppler and Schwarzmann were the owners of the new paper, and Sydney Rosenfeld was the first editor. He was succeeded during the first summer by H. C. Bunner, who kept the editorial chair until his death in 1896.

Mr. Joseph Keppler left Leslie's in the summer of 1876 and began making his arrangement to start *Puck*. He was so fearful, however, of adding another to the long list of failures in comic journalism that at the last moment he offered to remain in the employ of Frank Leslie if his salary were raised from fifty to fifty-five dollars a week.

Mr. Leslie indignantly refused, asserting that *Puck* could not live six months. The Kepplers, father and son, have been the cartoonists, and C. J. Taylor was for a long time the dean of the artist staff.

Puck was not only an evolution from failure to success, but from black and white to color. This striking innovation was of itself enough to ensure the triumph of the venture. It caught the popular fancy at once, and the paper has made fortunes for its owners.

Judge, published by Arkell and Co., took the field during the candidacy of James G. Blaine, to offset the political influence of *Puck*, and has achieved a permanent success on the same lines as its great rival.

The first number of *Life* appeared on January 3, 1883, at 1155 Broadway. This second great success in the comic field was inaugurated by J. A. Mitchell and Andrew Miller. Mr. Mitchell has distinguished himself as an author, but before he became an editor he was best known as an artist of cherubs.

His contributions to the exhibitions of the Etching Club were invariably cupids and he continued to draw cupids for *Life* until the little god turned on him and landed him in the usual way.

Charles Dana Gibson has been closely identified with *Life* from his first appearance in its pages.

Van Schaick has been affixing his familiar signature, "Van," to society drawings for about the same length of time. Mike Woolf was a frequent contributor. Charles Howard Johnson did some of his cleverest work for *Life*, and "Chip," the younger Bellew, before his death, formed a peculiar link between the old and the new in comic journalism.

The Lenox Library is the custodian of files, more or less complete, of several of these old comic periodicals. The only publication of this class, preserved at the Library, not mentioned in the foregoing list, is *Yankee Notions*, which, strange to relate, appears in the familiar cover of my boyish recollection in the window of the Canandaigua bookstore. It was pleasant once more to watch the pendent figures on the side of this old cover, clinging desperately to each other above the blade of a huge jack-knife still patiently waiting to receive them.

" LIFE "

The Lenox collection includes, furthermore, six volumes of *Yankee Doodle, six* of *Vanity Fair*, two of *Momus*, three of John Brougham's *Lantern*, and one each of *Judy* and *Mrs. Grundy*.

The cover of *Mrs. Grundy* was by Thos. Nast and consists of a broad-backed old woman with an umbrella and a cat, who is lecturing an audience of celebrities, crowding the interior of a theatre, which suggests the old Academy of Music on 14th Street.

Some of these publications, as *Yankee Notions* and *Momus*, are illustrated with sketchy drawings of the Sir John Gilbert school, then so much in vogue, cut in facsimile in the best manner of that period. Excellent examples of this school may be found in the *New York Ledger* of the fifties and in the comics in the back of *Harper's Monthly*. It was the best result at that time of the combined efforts of the draughtsman and the wood-engraver, and more artistic and sincere than the style adopted by the American Tract Society, which was a labored cross-sketching in imitation of steel engraving. Most of the comic papers of those early days are amusing because of the coarseness of the woodcuts and by reason of the deadly cheapness of the jokes.

Yankee Doodle covers the Mexican war period, and one of its cartoons shows Henry Clay brandishing a sword in front of an open cupboard in which a tiny Mexican is cowering among the shelves and the rats, with the legend below, "I smell the blood of a Mexican and I'll have it, too." The references to old New York as well as to old national issues are interesting in the extreme, and new surprises come upon you with the turning of every leaf. Henry J. Raymond appears "Trying to go ahead with the Times" against a contrary wind, and Wm. H. S--d rides through Washington seated beside Fred'k D--s in a barouche drawn by four horses having human heads—which may have been portraits.

REPRINTED FROM *ATLANTIC MONTHLY*, AUGUST 1956, 269-73.

The Humor of the Colored Supplement
By Ralph Bergengren

Ten or a dozen years ago,—the exact date is here immaterial, an enterprising newspaper publisher conceived the idea of appealing to what is known as the American "sense of humor" by printing a so-called comic supplement in colors. He chose Sunday as of all days the most lacking in popular amusements, carefully restricted himself to pictures without humor and color without beauty, and presently inaugurated a new era in American journalism. The colored supplement became an institution. No Sunday is complete without it,—not because its pages invariably delight, but because, like flies in summer, there is no screen that will altogether exclude them. A newspaper without a color press hardly considers itself a newspaper, and the smaller journals are utterly unmindful of the kindness of Providence in putting the guardian angel, Poverty, outside their portals. Sometimes, indeed, they think to outwit this kindly interference by printing a syndicated comic page without color; and mercy is thus served in a half portion, for, uncolored, the pictures are inevitably about twice as attractive. Some print them without color, but on pink paper. Others rejoice, as best they may, in a press that will reproduce at least a fraction of the original discord. One and all they unite vigorously, as if driven by a perverse and cynical intention, to prove the American sense of humor a thing of national shame and degradation. Fortunately the public has so little to say about its reading matter that one may fairly suspend judgment.

For, after all, what is the sense of humor upon which every man prides himself, as belonging only to a gifted minority? Nothing more nor less than a certain mental quickness, alert to catch the point of an anecdote or to appreciate the surprise of a new and unexpected point of view toward an old and familiar phenomenon. Add together these gifted minorities, and each nation reaches what is fallaciously termed the national sense of humor,—an English word, incidentally, for which D'Israeli was unable to find an equivalent in any other language, and which is in itself simply a natural development of the critical faculty, born of a present need of describing what earlier ages had taken for granted. The jovial porter and his charming chance acquaintances, the three ladies of Bagdad, enlivened conversation with a kind of humor, carefully removed from the translation of commerce and the public libraries, for which they needed no descriptive noun, but which may nevertheless be fairly taken as typical of that city in the day of the Caliph Haroun.

The Middle Ages rejoiced in a similar form of persiflage, and the present day in France, Germany, England, or America, for example, inherits it,—minus its too juvenile indecency,—in the kind of pleasure afforded by these comic supplements. Their kinship with the lower publications of European countries is curiously evident to whoever has examined them. Vulgarity, in fact, speaks the same tongue in all countries, talks, even in art-ruled France, with the same crude draughtsmanship, and usurps universally a province that Emerson declared "far better than wit for a poet or writer." In its expression and enjoyment no country can fairly claim the dubious superiority. All are on the dead level of that surprising moment when the savage had ceased to be dignified and man had not yet become rational. Men indeed, speak freely and vaingloriously of their national sense of humor; but they are usually unconscious idealists. For the comic cut that amuses the most stupid Englishman may be shifted entire into an American comic supplement; the "catastrophe joke" of the American comic weekly of the next higher grade is stolen in quantity to delight the readers of similar but more economical publications in Germany; the lower humor of France, barring the expurgations demanded by Anglo-Saxon prudery, is equally transferable; and the average American often examines on Sunday morning, without knowing it, an international loan-exhibit.

Humor, in other words, is cosmopolitan, reduced, since usage insists on reducing it, at this lowest imaginable level, to such obvious and universal elements that any intellect can grasp their combinations. And at its highest it is again cosmopolitan, like art; like art, a cultivated characteristic, no more spontaneously natural than a "love of nature." It is an insult to the whole line of English and American humorists—Sterne, Thackeray, Dickens, Meredith, Twain, Holmes, Irving, and others of a distinguished company—to include as humor what is merely the crude brutality of human nature, mocking at grief and laughing boisterously at physical deformity. And in these Sunday comics Humor, stolen by vandals from her honest, if sometimes rough-and-ready, companionship, thrusts a woe-begone visage from the painted canvas of the national sideshow, and none too poor to "shy a brick" at her.

At no period in the world's history has there been a steadier output of so-called humor,—especially in this country. The simple idea of printing a page of comic pictures has produced families. The very element of variety has been obliterated by the creation of types,—a confusing medley of impossible countrymen, mules, goats, German-Americans and their irreverent progeny, specialized children with a genius for annoying their elders, white-whiskered elders with a genius for playing practical jokes on their grandchildren, policemen, Chinamen, Irishmen, negroes, inhuman conceptions of the genus tramp, boy inventors whose inventions invariably end in causing somebody to be mirthfully spattered with paint or joyously torn to pieces by machinery, bright boys with a talent for deceit, laziness, or cruelty, and even the beasts of the jungle dehumanized to the point of practical joking. *Mirabile dictu!*—some of these things have even been dramatized.

With each type the reader is expected to become personally acquainted,—to watch for its coming on Sunday mornings, happily wondering with what form of inhumanity the author will have been able to endow his brainless manikins. And the authors are often men of intelligence, capable here and there of a bit of adequate drawing and an idea that is honestly and self-respectingly provocative of laughter. Doubtless they are often ashamed of their product; but the demand of the hour is imperative. The presses are waiting. They, too, are both quick and heavy. And the cry of the publisher is for "fun" that no intellect in all his heterogeneous public shall be too dull to appreciate. We see, indeed, the outward manifestation of a curious paradox: humor prepared and printed for the extremely dull, and—what is still more remarkable—excused by grown men, capable of editing newspapers, on the ground that it gives pleasure to children.

Reduced to first principles, therefore, it is not humor, but simply a supply created in answer to a demand, hastily produced by machine methods and hastily accepted by editors too busy with other editorial duties to examine it intelligently. Under these conditions "humor" is naturally conceived as something preëminently quick; and so quickness predominates. Somebody is always hitting somebody else with a club; somebody is always falling down stairs, or out of a balloon, or over a cliff, or into a river, a barrel of paint, a basket of eggs, a convenient cistern, or a tub of hot water. The comic cartoonists have already exhausted every available substance into which one can fall, and are compelled to fall themselves into a veritable ocean of vain repetition. They have exhausted everything by which one can be blown up. They have exhausted everything by which one can be knocked down or run over. And if the victim is never actually killed in these mirthful experiments, it is obviously because he would then cease to be funny,—which is very much the point of view of the Spanish Inquisition, the cat with a mouse, or the American Indian with a captive. But respect for property, respect for parents, for law, for decency, for truth, for beauty, for kindliness, for dignity, or for honor, are killed, without mercy. Morality alone, in its restricted sense of sexual relations, is treated with courtesy, although we find throughout the accepted theory that marriage is a union of uncongenial spirits, and the chart of petty marital deceit is carefully laid out and marked for whoever is likely to respond to endless unconscious suggestions. Sadly must the American child sometimes be puzzled while comparing his own grandmother with the visiting mother-in-law of the colored comic.

Lest this seem a harsh, even an unkind inquiry into the innocent amusements of other people, a few instances may be mentioned, drawn from the Easter Sunday output of papers otherwise both respectable and unrespectable; papers, moreover, depending largely on syndicated humor that may fairly be said to have reached a total circulation of several million readers. We have, to begin with, two rival versions of a creation that made the originator famous, and that chronicle the adventures of a small boy whose name and features are everywhere familiar. Often these adventures, in the original youngster, have been amusing, and amusingly seasoned with the salt of legitimately absurd phraseology. But the pace is too fast, even for the originator. The imitator fails invariably to catch the spirit of them, and in this instance is driven to an ancient subterfuge. To come briefly to an unpleasant point, an entire page is devoted to showing the reader how the boy was made ill by smoking his father's cigars. Incidentally he falls down stairs. Meantime, his twin is rejoicing the readers of another comic supplement by spoiling a wedding party; it is the minister who first comes to grief, and is stood on his head, the boy who later is quite properly thrashed by an angry mother,—and it is all presumably very delightful and a fine example for the imitative genius of other children. Further, we meet a mule who kicks a policeman and whose owner is led away to the lockup; a manicured vacuum who slips on a banana peel, crushes the box containing his fiancée's Easter bonnet, and is assaulted by her father (he, after the manner of comic fathers, having just paid one hundred dollars for the bonnet out of a plethoric pocketbook); a nondescript creature, presumably human, who slips on another banana peel and knocks over a citizen, who in turn knocks over a policeman, and is also marched off to undeserved punishment. We see the German-American child covering his father with water from a street gutter, another child deluging his parent with water from a hose; another teasing his younger brother and sister. To keep the humor of the banana peel in countenance we find the picture of a fat man accidentally sitting down on a tack; he exclaims, "ouch," throws a basket of eggs into the air, and they come down on the head of the boy who arranged the tacks. We see two white boys beating a little negro over the head with a plank (the hardness of the negro's skull here affording the humorous *motif*), and we see an idiot blowing up a mule with dynamite. Lunacy, in short, could go no farther than this pandemonium of undisguised coarseness and brutality,—the humor offered on Easter Sunday morning by leading American newspapers for the edification of American readers.

And every one of the countless creatures, even to the poor, maligned dumb animals, is saying something. To the woeful extravagance of foolish acts must be added an equal extravagance of foolish words: "Out with you, intoxicated rowdy," "Shut up," "Skidoo," "They've set the dog on me," "Hee-haw," "My uncle had it tooken in Hamburg," "Dat old gentleman will slip on dem banana skins," "Little Buster got all that was coming to him," "Aw, shut up," "Y-e-e-e G-o-d-s," "Ouch," "Golly, dynamite am powerful stuff," "I am listening to vat der vild vaves is sedding," "I don't think Pa and I will ever get along together until he gets rid of his conceit," "phew." The brightness of this repartee could be continued indefinitely; profanity, of course, is indicated by dashes and exclamation points; a person who has fallen overboard says "blub;" concussion is visibly represented by stars; "biff" and "bang" are used according to taste to accompany a blow on the nose or an explosion of dynamite.

From this brief summary it may be seen how few are the fundamental conceptions that supply the bulk of almost the entire output, and in these days of syndicated ideas a comparatively small body of men produce the greater part of it. Physical pain is the most glaringly omnipresent of these *motifs*; it is counted upon invariably to amuse the average humanity of our so-called Christian civilization. The entire group of Easter Sunday pictures constitutes a saturnalia of prearranged accidents in which the artist is never hampered by the exigencies of logic; machinery in which even the presupposed poorest intellect might be expected to detect the obvious flaw accomplishes its evil purpose with inevitable accuracy; jails and lunatic asylums are crowded with new inmates; the policeman always uses his club or revolver; the parents usually thrash their offspring at the end of the performance; household furniture is demolished, clothes ruined, and unsalable eggs broken by the dozen. Deceit is another universal concept of humor, that combine easily with the physical pain 'motif'; and mistaken identity, in which the juvenile idiot disguises himself and deceives his parents in various ways, is another favorite resort of the humorists. The paucity of invention is hardly less remarkable than the willingness of the inventors to sign their products, or the willingness of editors to publish them. But the age is notoriously one in which editors underrate and insult the public intelligence.

Doubtless there are some to applaud the spectacle,—the imitative spirits, for example, who recently compelled a woman to seek the protection of a police department because of the persecution of a gang of boys and young men shouting "hee-haw" whenever she appeared on the street; the rowdies whose exploits figure so frequently in metropolitan newspapers; or that class of adults who tell indecent stories at the dinner table and laugh joyously at their wives' efforts to turn the conversation. But the Sunday comic goes into other homes than these, and is handed to their children by parents whose souls would shudder at the thought of a dime novel. Alas, poor parents! That very dime novel as a rule holds up ideals of bravery and chivalry, rewards good and punishes evil, offers at the worst a temptation to golden adventuring, for which not one child in a million will ever attempt to surmount the obvious obstacles. It is no easy matter to become an Indian fighter, pirate, or detective; the dream is, after all, a daydream, tinctured with the beautiful color of old romance, and built on eternal qualities that the world has rightfully esteemed worthy of emulation. And in place of it the comic supplement, like that other brutal horror, the juvenile comic story, that goes on its immoral way unnoticed, raises no high ambition, but devotes itself to "mischief made easy." Hard as it is to become an Indian fighter, any boy has plenty of opportunity to throw stones at his neighbor's windows. And on any special occasion, such, for example, as Christmas or Washington's Birthday, almost the entire ponderous machine is set in motion to make reverence and ideals ridiculous. Evil example is strong in proportion as it is easy to imitate. The state of mind that accepts the humor of the comic weekly is the same as that which shudders at Ibsen, and smiles complacently at the musical comedy, with its open acceptance of the wild oats theory, and its humorous exposition of a kind of wild oats that youth may harvest without going out of its own neighborhood.

In all this noisy, explosive, garrulous pandemonium one finds here and there a moment of rest and refreshment,—the work of the few pioneers of decency and decorum brave enough to bring their wares to the noisome market and lucky enough to infuse their spirit of refinement, art, and genuine humor into its otherwise hopeless atmosphere. Preëminent among them stands the inventor of "Little Nemo in Slumberland," a man of genuine pantomimic humor, charming draughtmanship, and an excellent decorative sense of color, who has apparently studied his medium and makes the best of it. And with him come Peter Newell, Grace G. Weiderseim, and Conde,—now illustrating *Uncle Remus* for a Sunday audience,—whose pictures in some of the Sunday papers are a delightful and self-respecting proof of the possibilities of this type of journalism. Out of the noisy streets, the cheap restaurants with their unsteady-footed waiters and avalanches of soup and crockery, out of the slums, the quarreling families, the prisons and the lunatic asylums, we step for a moment into the world of childish fantasy, closing the iron door behind us and trying to shut out the clamor of hooting mobs, the laughter of imbeciles, and the crash of explosives. After all, there is no reason why children should not have their innocent amusement on Sunday morning; but there seems to be every reason why the average editor of the weekly comic supplement should be given a course in art, literature, common sense, and Christianity.

Glossary of Comic Strip Terms

Action strip A comic strip whose chief appeal is adventure and suspense rather than humor or human interest. Synonym of adventure strip.

Adventure strip A comic strip featuring a hero (or a group of heroes) involved in exciting and usually exotic adventures. Classifiable into a number of subcategories: the *aviation strip* features a pilot-hero in situations related (often remotely) to airplanes and flying (e.g., *Scorchy Smith*, *Barney Baxter*, and *Michel Tanguy*); the *science-fiction strip* uses themes that are grounded in scientific conjecture or implausibility, such as interplanetary expeditions and time travel (e.g., *Buck Rogers*, *Jeff Hawke*, and *Saturno contro la Terra*); the *detective strip* deals with stories of crime, detection, and suspense (e.g., *Dick Tracy*, *Secret Agent X-9*, and *Buck Ryan*); the *Western strip* takes place in the American West (e.g., *Red Ryder*, *Lieutenant Blueberry*, and *Tex Willer*); and the *superhero* strip stars a protagonist who is naturally or artificially endowed with superhuman powers (e.g., *Superman*, *Cyborg 009*, and *Garth*).

adventure strip: *"Dickie Dare,"* Coulton Waugh. © AP Newsfeatures.

Animal strip A comic strip with an animal, or a group of animals, as its main protagonist. Animal strips are of two types: one completely excludes people from its cast, but presents what are essentially human characters in animal guises (e.g., *Tiger Tim*, *The Pussycat Princess*, and *Pogo*); also known as "funny animal strips"; the other features recognizable animals in identifiable human environments (e.g., *Napoleon*, *Fred Basset*, and *Cubitus*).

Animal strip: *"Pogo,"* Walt Kelly. © Walt Kelly.

MORE ABOUT THE COMICS

Assistant   A person hired to help a comic strip artist with such tasks as lettering, inking, laying color, etc.

Backgroundman   An assistant who draws the backgrounds of a comic strip.

Balloon   An enclosed white space issuing from the lips of comic characters, generally used to convey dialogue, but can also enclose a variety of signs and symbols. (A discussion of the role of the balloon in comics can be found in the analytical summary contained in this work.)

Ben day (or benday)   **1.** A transparent screen, usually dotted or crosshatched, pasted over a panel to add shading. **2.** The process itself: to benday a drawing.

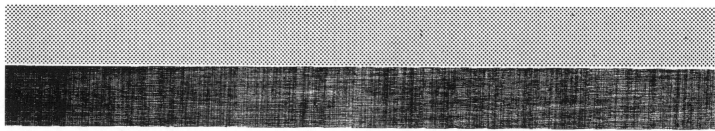

benday: *two screen patterns.*

Cartoon   (from the French *carton*, a sketch or study on pasteboard) A drawing of political, satirical, or humorous intent, containing within one frame a self-explanatory scene or composition accompanied by a caption or brief text. *Animated cartoon:* a series of drawings photographed on film and shown like a motion picture. (A detailed discussion of the animated cartoon can be found in the analytical summary contained in this work.)

Cartooning   The art of drawing cartoons; the art of doing comics.

Cartoonist   **1.** An artist who draws cartoons. **2.** A comic strip or comic book artist.

Cartoon strip   (British) Synonym for comic strip.

Color scheme   Indications given by a cartoonist for the coloring of a comic strip or page.

Comic art   The comics considered as an art form.

Comic book   An individual magazine, usually printed in color on pulp paper, containing stories or gags in comic strip form. A comic book may reprint previously published comic strips (reprint comic book) or original material.

Comicdom   **1.** An ensemble of those people (cartoonists, publishers, editors, etc.) engaged in the creation, production, and distribution of comics. **2.** The world of comics treated as a separate and self-contained entity.

Comic magazine (or comics magazine)   **1.** (U.S.) The official name for a comic book. **2.** (Europe) A magazine (usually weekly or monthly) featuring gag strips, story strips, and other comic material.

Comics   A narrative form containing text and pictures arranged in sequential order (usually chronological). Name derived from the first examples of the form, which were all of a humorous nature; it has since become a misnomer, since the comics now encompass narratives that are not primarily comical but involve suspense, adventure, human interest, etc. The term "comics" applied to the form has also proven unwieldy, as it does not easily lend itself to grammatical derivatives (e.g., there is no comic equivalent to the word "cinematic"). The Italians use the word *fumetto* (literally "little cloud," the traditional term for balloon), from which they have been able to derive such neologisms as *fumettare* (to arrange in comic strip form), *fumettologo* (a student or scholar of the comics), and *fumettistico* (pertaining to the comics). It would be a great advance in the study of the form if such a simple word (preferably from a Greek root) could be coined in the English language.

Comic strip **1.** A comic sequence arranged in strip form (e.g., horizontally); synonym of daily strip. **2.** Synonym of newspaper strip. **3.** Any story told in comic terms. **4.** Synonym of comics in general.

Comic supplement A separate section of a newspaper, usually published in color on Sundays, containing a number of comic features; also called a Sunday or weekly supplement.

Continuity Comic strip plot that unfolds over more than one installment.

Continuity strip A comic strip featuring day-to-day and/or week-to-week action.

Crossover The appearance of one character in another character's comic-book title.

Daily strip A comic feature appearing across a daily newspaper page, usually in a horizontal arrangement of panels. *Mutt and Jeff* is usually considered the first daily strip of any significance.

daily strip: "Peanuts," Charles Schulz. © United Feature Syndicate.

Doubletone Chemically pretreated paper consisting of two imperceptible patterns of lines or points, more or less widely spaced and regular, according to the model. A yellowish developer can then be applied to the paper with brush or pen to bring out both patterns, or a different solution can be applied that will reveal only one of the patterns. Roy Crane is acknowledged as the master of this delicate technique.

Drop Panel in a Sunday page designed to be discarded to accommodate a limited layout.

Drybrush Use of a nearly dry brush in order to achieve a gray, rather than a black, quality.

Episode **1.** A complete plot occurring in a continuity strip. **2.** A single installment (daily, weekly, or monthly) of a comic feature.

Family strip A comic strip centering on the adventures of a fictitious family group (e.g., *The Gumps, Blondie,* and *The Potts*).

doubletone effects: "Buz Sawyer," Roy Crane. © King Features Syndicate.

family strip: *"Blondie,"* Chic Young. © King Features Syndicate.

Fandom   Term used to describe the group of devotees of a particular form, medium, or activity; specifically, enthusiasts of the comic medium.

Fantasy strip   A comic strip whose main purpose is to appeal to the readers' imaginations or fancies (e.g., *Little Nemo*, *Krazy Kat*, and *Barnaby*).

Fanzine   Amateur publication (often of a cultish nature) devoted to some aspect of popular culture; specifically, a publication aimed at comic enthusiasts. Contraction of "fan magazine."

Feature   Any comic story (whether appearing in newspapers, magazines, or comic books) with a separate and continuing title. Synonym of comic strip.

Funnies   Synonym of comics. (While still widely used, the term is generally shunned by specialists and has acquired a slightly pejorative meaning.)

Funny strip   Synonym of humor strip.

Gag man   Writer who contributes gags or situation ideas to cartoonists.

Gag strip   Humor strip that makes a different point in each installment, without recourse to continuity (e.g., *Hagar the Horrible*, *Sturmtruppen*, and *Andy Capp*).

gag strip: *"Old Doc Yak,"* Sidney Smith. © Chicago Tribune-New York News Syndicate.

Ghost   Person who draws and/or writes a comic strip for a cartoonist who gets the public credit. Unlike an assistant who only does well-defined chores, a ghost carries a strip in its entirety. One of the most contemptible practices in the comics, it is particularly widespread among syndicated strip cartoonists (comic books usually do not pay enough to allow their practitioners to hire a ghost). In Europe the practice is illegal, and there is some question of its legality in the United States. The practice seems to violate the "truth in advertising'' laws because the actual author of the strip is not the one advertised in the byline.

Girl strip A comic strip featuring the (usually romantic) adventures of a young and unmarried girl or a group of young girls (e.g., *Tillie the Toiler, Winnie Winkle, Dot and Carrie*, and *Apartment 3-G*).

girl strip: "Connie," Frank Godwin. © Ledger Syndicate.

Graphic novel An extended comics narrative published in book form.

Humor strip A comic strip whose staple is comedy—slapstick or burlesque—and which makes its point in one installment (gag strip) or uses continuity (e.g., *Alley Oop, Tintin*, and *Patoruzú*).

Illustrated strip A comic strip whose drawings are related to illustration rather than to cartooning.

Inker Person who inks over the pencilled drawings of another cartoonist.

Kid strip Comic strip having a child, or a group of children, as its protagonist. From *The Katzenjammer Kids* to *Dennis the Menace*, the kid strip has been one of the staples of the comic medium.

Letterer Person who does the lettering in a comic strip.

Lettering The handwritten dialogues and/or text contained in a comic strip. Lettering is more important to the overall effect of a particular comic strip than it superficially appears; it should harmonize with the style of the specific comic strip for which it is devised. Some cartoonists, conscious of this prerequisite, do their own lettering (e.g., Charles Schulz).

Logo The distinctive word or group of words formed by the title of a comic strip. Contraction of logotype.

Manga Japanese word for comics; by extension, a comic story following Japanese conventions of narrative and style.

Miniseries (or **limited series**) A comic-book title published in a finite number of issues.

Montage panel A series of space-unrelated pictures arranged or superimposed within one comic strip panel.

kid strip: "Zig et Puce," Alain Saint-Ogan. © Saint-Ogan.

MORE ABOUT THE COMICS

Narrative **1.** Plot line or story line of a comic strip. **2.** Synonym of continuity.

Newspaper strip Any comic feature carried by a newspaper.

One-shot Comic book title issued only once (usually for tryout purposes).

onomatopoeia: *"Broom Hilda,"* Russ Meyers. © Chicago Tribune-New York News Syndicate.

Onomatopoeia Imitative sound words (e.g., vroom, bang, zap, gasp, argh) widely used in the vocabulary of the comics.

Open panel Any panel not enclosed within a frame; also called borderless panel.

open panel: *"Pedrito el Drito,"* Antonio Terenghi. © Universo.

Page A weekly newspaper comic feature usually printed in color (few Sunday comics are now full-page size, but the name is still traditionally used, regardless of actual format); also called weekly or Sunday page.

Panel 1. A single drawing, most often enclosed in a rectangular or square frame, that is part of a comic strip or page. 2. A daily or weekly gag feature consisting of just one panel (e.g., *Out Our Way* and *Our Boarding House*); sometimes called a panel strip.

panel (*definition 2*): "Outdoor Sports," Tad (T. A. Dorgan). © King Features Syndicate.

Pantomime strip 1. Comic strip in which no dialogue is used; silent strip. 2. Comic strip in which the protagonist remains mute, although dialogue may occasionally be used by secondary characters (e.g., *The Little King* and *Henry*).

Penciler Person who sketches the drawings of a comic strip in pencil.

Presentation strip A specially prepared strip that serves to introduce the feature's characters to new readers; also called an introduction strip.

Reprint A run of newspaper or comic book features issued after the date first published. Reprints may appear either in the original format or (more often) in magazine or book form.

Scripter 1. Synonym of scriptwriter. 2. Person hired to write the dialogue and/or narrative of a comic strip on a synopsis provided to him by the strip's author, syndicate, or comic book company.

Scriptwriter Person who writes the continuity and/or dialogue of a comic strip. (Lee Falk and Allen Saunders are two of the best-known American scriptwriters.)

Sequence 1. A chronological grouping of comic strips. 2. Synonym of episode.

Silent strip A comic strip using only pictures to the exclusion of dialogue or narration (e.g., *Adamson* ["Silent Sam"], *Max*, and *Ferdinand*).

silent strip: "Ferd' nand," H. Dahl Mikkelsen. © PIB.

MORE ABOUT THE COMICS

Splash panel   A large panel appearing at the beginning of a comic-book story; also called a bleed panel.

Sports strip   A comic strip built around some facet of the sports scene (e.g., *Joe Palooka*, *Michel Valiant*, and *Kyojin no Hoshi*).

Story strip   Comic strip that tells a story over a number of installments. Synonym of continuity strip. Story strip plots vary widely from burlesque (*Li'l Abner*) to soap opera (*Mary Worth*) to adventure (*The Phantom*).

Strip   **1.** A single installment of a daily strip. **2.** Synonym of comic strip.

Sunday page   A newspaper feature appearing only once a week, usually on Sunday.

Syndicate   An organization involved in the distribution of individual features (comics, columns, news items, etc.) to subscribing newspapers. (For more information, see "The History of Newspaper Syndication" included in this work.)

Thought balloon   Device used to convey the unspoken thoughts or musings of a character. (This kind of balloon is traditionally scalloped with tiny bubbles issuing up from the character's head.)

thought balloon: *"Carol Day,"* David Wright. © Associated Newspapers Ltd.

Vignette   A comic strip drawing fading out of its space, with no definite border.

Zip tone   **1.** Shading effect obtained by a series of parallel strokes of the brush. **2.** Synonym of doubletone.

U.S. Senate Hearings

Official Facsimile
Excerpts from the Record
U.S. Senate Subcommittee
of the Committee on the Judiciary
to Investigate Juvenile Delinquency

April 21, 22, and June 4, 1954
New York, New York

U.S. SENATE HEARINGS

**Hearings before the Subcommittee to Investigate Juvenile Delinquency
of the Committee on the Judiciary
United States Senate, Eighty-Third Congress,
Second Session, pursuant to S.190**

*Investigation of Juvenile Delinquency in the United States
April 21, 22, and June 4, 1954*

United States Government Printing Office
Washington 1954

Judiciary Committee

JUVENILE DELINQUENCY
(Comic Books)

WEDNESDAY, APRIL 21, 1954

UNITED STATES SENATE,
SUBCOMMITTEE OF THE COMMITTEE ON
THE JUDICIARY, TO INVESTIGATE JUVENILE DELINQUENCY,
New York, N. Y.

The subcommittee met at 10 a.m., pursuant to call, in room 110, United States Courthouse, New York, N. Y., Senator Robert C. Hendrickson (chairman of the subcommittee), presiding.

Present: Senators Hendrickson, Kefauver, and Hennings.

Also present: Herbert J. Hannoch, chief counsel; Herbert Wilson Beaser, associate chief counsel; and Richard Clendenen, executive director.

The CHAIRMAN. This meeting of the Senate Subcommittee on Juvenile Delinquency will now be in order.

Today and tomorrow the United States Senate Subcommittee Investigating Juvenile Delinquency, of which I am the chairman, is going into the problem of horror and crime comic books. By comic books, we mean pamphlets illustrating stories depicting crimes or dealing with horror and sadism. We shall not be talking about the comic strips that appear daily in most of our newspapers.

And we shall be limiting our investigation to those comic books dealing with crime and horror. Thus, while there are more than a billion comic books sold in the United States each year, our subcommittee's interest lies in only a fraction of this publishing field.

Authorities agree that the majority of comic books are as harmless as soda pop. But hundreds of thousands of horror and crime comic books are peddled to our young people of impressionable age.

You will learn during the course of these hearings that we shall also not be speaking of all crime comic books. Some of the types of crime and horror comic books with which we are concerned have been brought into the hearing room for your attention.

I wish to state emphatically that freedom of the press is not at issue in this investigation. The members of this Senate subcomittee—Senator Kefauver, Senator Hennings, and Senator Langer—as well as myself as chairman, are fully aware of the long, hard, bitter fight that has been waged to achieve and preserve the freedom of the press, as well as the other freedoms in our Bill of Rights which we cherish in America.

We are not a subcommittee of blue-nosed censors. We have no preconceived notions as to the possible need for new legislation. We want to find out what damage, if any, is being done to our children's minds by certain types of publications which contain a substantial degree of sadism, crime, and horror. This, and only this, is the task at hand.

Since last November the subcommittee has been holding many public hearings into the various facets of the whole problem of juvenile delinquency. The volume of delinquency among our young has been quite correctly called the shame of America. If the rising tide of juvenile delinquency continues, by 1960 more than one and a half million American youngsters from 10 through 17 years of age, will be in trouble with the law each year.

Our subcommittee is seeking honestly and earnestly to determine why so many young Americans are unable to adjust themselves into the lawful pattern of American society. We are examining the reason why more and more of our youngsters steal automobiles, turn to vandalism, commit holdups, or become narcotic addicts.

The increase in craven crime committed by young Americans is rising at a frightening pace. We know that the great mass of our American children are not lawbreakers. Even the majority of those who get into trouble with our laws are not criminal by nature.

Nevertheless, more and more of our children are committing serious crimes. Our subcommittee is working diligently to seek out ways and means to check the trend and reverse the youth crime pattern.

We are perfectly aware that there is no simple solution to the complex problem of juvenile delinquency. We know, too, that what makes the problem so complex is its great variety of causes and contributing factors. Our work is to study all these causes and contributing factors and to determine what action might be taken.

It would be wrong to assume that crime and horror comic books are the major cause of juvenile delinquency. It would be just as erroneous to state categorically that they have no effect whatsoever in aggravating the problem. We are here to determine what effect on the whole problem of causation crime and horror comic books do have.

From the mail received by the subcommittee, we are aware that thousands of American parents are greatly concerned about the possible detrimental influence certain types of crime and horror comic books have upon their children.

We firmly believe that the public has a right to the best knowledge regarding this matter. The public has the right to know who is producing this material and to know how the industry functions.

Our work during this investigation will be to determine the possible delinquency producing effect upon children of certain types of crime and horror comic books, and whether or not there are certain offshoots growing out of the industry.

This phase of our investigation is but the first of several into questionable, or, should I say, disturbing phases of the mass media fields.

At a later date, the subcommittee will be attempting to determine what negative effects, if any, upon children, are exerted by other types of publications, by the radio, the television, and the movies. This is not to say that juvenile delinquency is wholly or even substantially the result of certain programs and subject matters presented by the mass media. But there can be no question that the media plays a significant role in the total problem.

I will now ask the assistant counsel to call the first witness.

Senator KEFAUVER. Mr. Chairman, before we call the first witness, I just want to compliment the chairman upon a very excellent statement of the purposes of this subcommittee and of this hearing here.

I would like to reemphasize that I feel that congressional hearings must be related to something that the Federal Government has jurisdiction of. This subcommittee is looking into the violations of various Federal laws, such as the Dyer Act, Mann Act, violations of the interstate commerce, and in connection with the subject matter under investigation we, of course, do have a postal statute which prohibits the mailing or using the mails for the distribution and dissemination of indecent and scurrilous literature which will be part of the subject matter of this hearing.

The CHAIRMAN. That is correct, Senator.

Senator KEFAUVER. I think it is also important to point out that Mr. J. Edgar Hoover's report of yesterday shows that whereas the increase in population last year was 5 percent, crime had gone up 20 percent and the particularly large increase was in connection with burglary and stealing of automobiles.

The interesting point is that a large part of the burglaries was committed by juveniles. Also juveniles, according to the FBI report, comprise 53.6 percent of those arrested for stealing automobiles.

As the chairman said, we do not have all the answers, but I think that it is important to look into the various matters which Mr. Hoover and other experts do bring out in connection with the increase in juvenile delinquency; and certainly as to horror and crime comics, not the good kind as the chairman said, but the various small part, most all the witnesses do have something to say about these.

We are not going into this hearing with the idea of condemning anybody or censoring the press or impairing the freedom of the press and bringing out in relation to a Federal statute something so that all of these experts on juvenile delinquency are talking about.

That is my understanding.

The CHAIRMAN. The Senator from Tennessee is entirely correct and the Chair wishes to congratulate and commend the Senator for his contribution.

Now, will counsel call the first witness?

Mr. BEASER. Mr. Richard Clendenen.

The CHAIRMAN. Do you solemnly swear that the testimony you will give before this subcommittee of the Senate Committee on the Judiciary, will be the truth, the whole truth, and nothing but the truth, so help you God?

Mr. CLENDENEN. I do.

The CHAIRMAN. The Chair with pleasure announces the presence of the distinguished Senator from Missouri, Senator Hennings.

TESTIMONY OF RICHARD CLENDENEN, EXECUTIVE DIRECTOR, UNITED STATES SENATE SUBCOMMITTEE TO INVESTIGATE JUVENILE DELINQUENCY

Mr. BEASER. For the record will you state your name, your address, and your present occupation?

Mr. CLENDENEN. My name is Richard Clendenen, 1445 Ogden Street NW., Washington, D.C.

I am executive director of the Senate Subcommittee to Investigate Juvenile Delinquency.

Mr. BEASER. Mr. Clendenen, will you outline briefly your education and experience in the field of juvenile delinquency?

The CHAIRMAN. Before Mr. Clendenen answers that question, I would like to say that the Senate Subcommittee on Juvenile Delinquency feels that we have a very able staff director.

Mr. CLENDENEN. Thank you.

Prior to coming to my present position I had worked in the United States Children's Bureau for a period of 7 years, and held there the position of Chief of the Juvenile Delinquency Branch.

Prior to that time I had served in administrative capacities in institutions for emotionally disturbed children and delinquent children and also have had experience as a probation officer in a juvenile court.

Mr. BEASER. You are a trained social worker?

Mr. CLENDENEN. I am.

Mr. BEASER. Speaking on behalf of the staff, have you conducted an investigation into the comic-book industry?

Mr. CLENDENEN. Yes sir, we have. Our investigation into the comic-book industry has been almost exclusively limited to those comics which themselves center about horror and crime.

The particular type of comics to which I refer present both pictures and stories which relate to almost all types of crime and in many instances those crimes are committed through extremely cruel, sadistic, and punitive kinds of acts.

Now, in connection with that question, I should like to make it perfectly clear that our investigation has not been concerned with other types of comics, many of which all authorities seem to agree represent not only harmless, but many times educational entertainment.

I should also add that even within that type of comic books known as the horror crime comics, there are gradations within this group, too. That is, some are much more sadistic, much more lurid, than others in the same class or category.

Now, although our investigations have been limited to this particular segment of the comic-book industry, we should not give the impression that this is a small portion of the comic-book industry.

According to estimates which were provided us by the Audit Bureau of Circulations and the Controlled Circulation Audits, the two firms that publish circulation figures, there were about 422 different kinds of comic or comic-book titles on the newsstands in March 1954.

About one-fourth were of the crime and horror variety.

Now, as far as all comic books are concerned, although exact figures are lacking, most authorities agree that there are probably somewhere between 75 million and 100 million comic books sold in this country each month.

If one-quarter of these are of the crime variety of comics, this means that there are some 20 million comic books, crime comic books placed on the newsstands of this country each month.

Mr. BEASER. When you say crime and horror comics could you be more specific in describing what you are talking about?

Mr. CLENDENEN. Well, we have prepared a certain number of slides which show pictures taken from comic books of the type to which we have addressed ourselves.

Now, I would like, for the purpose of illustration, to relate very briefly in summary fashion 6 stories, together with pictures illustrating these 6 stories which will give you a sampling of the type of comic books that we are talking about here.

Now, in presenting these I would like to say that while it is not a random sampling actually it is a deliberate sampling in trying to present the various types of stories and pictures that appear.

These are not typical, rather they are quite typical of the stories and pictures which appear in this type of publication. The first such crime comic is entitled "Black Magic."

This is a picture showing the cover or title page of this comic. Now, one story in this comic is entitled "Sanctuary," and the cover shots relate to this particular story.

You will note that this shot shows certain inhabitants of this sanctuary which is really a sort of sanitarium for freaks where freaks can be isolated from other persons in society.

You will note 1 man in the picture has 2 heads and 4 arms, another body extends only to the bottom of his rib. But the greatest horror of all the freaks in the sanctuary is the attractive looking girl in the center of the picture who disguises her grotesque body in a suit of foam rubber.

The final picture shows a young doctor in the sanitarium as he sees the girl he loves without her disguise.

The story closes as the doctor fires bullet after bullet into the girl's misshapen body.

Now, that is an example of a comic of the horror variety.

The next slide, the second story, is the cover shot of a comic entitled "Fight Against Crime."

One story in this particular issue is entitled "Stick in the Mud." This is a story of a very sadistic schoolteacher who is cruel to all of the children in her classroom with only one exception. The one exception is the son of a well-to-do man who has lost his wife. Through her attentions to the son the teacher woos and weds the father.

The following picture shows the schoolteacher as she stabs her husband to death in order to inherit his money. She then disguises her crime by dragging his body into a bullpen where his corpse is mangled and gored.

The small son, suspecting his stepmother, runs away so that she will chase him into the woods where a bed of quicksand is located.

Our last picture shows the stepmother sinking into the quicksand and crying for help. The small son gets the stepmother to confess that she murdered his father by pretending he will go for help if she does so.

After her confession he refuses to go for help and stays to watch his stepmother die in the quicksand.

The next comic is entitled "Mysterious Adventures." This particular issue of which this is a cover shot contains a total of 6 stories in which 11 people die violent deaths.

One story, I think, in this particular issue, has to do with a confirmed alcoholic who spends all his wife can earn on alcohol.

As a result their small son is severely neglected. On the day the small son is to start in the first grade in school the mother asks his father to escort him to the school. Instead the father goes to his favorite bootlegger and the son goes to school by himself. En route he is struck and killed by an automobile.

Informed of the accident, she returns to find her husband gloating over his new supply of liquor.

This next picture shows the mother killing her alcoholic spouse with an ax. She then cuts up his body into small pieces and disposes of it by placing the various pieces in the bottle of liquor her husband had purchased.

If you will look at the picture in the lower right-hand panel, you will see an ear in one bottle, an eye in another, and a finger in another, and so forth.

Senator HENNINGS. I wonder if Mr. Clendenen has any figures on the relative circulation or sale of this character of things as against the more innocuous kind of comics? To what extent, in other words, do these appeal to the children to a greater or less degree than the kind we are all more or less familiar with, the harmless comic strips?

Mr. CLENDENEN. Well, about one-fourth of the total comic-book titles, that is the different comic books are of the crime and horror variety.

Now, perhaps not all of those are as rough as some of these that are shown.

On the other hand, this does constitute a not insubstantial segment of the comic-book industry.

Mr. BEASER. It is about 20 million a month, Senator Kefauver suggests.

Mr. CLENDENEN. That is right; 20 million a month of the crime and horror variety.

The CHAIRMAN. The Senator from Tennessee.

Senator KEFAUVER. Do I understand, Mr. Chairman, the 20 million per month is the number sold or placed on sale? How do you get that figure, Mr. Clendenen?

Mr. CLENDENEN. That is a circulation figure which refers to sales.

The CHAIRMAN. Distribution and sales?

Mr. CLENDENEN. Yes, sir.

Senator KEFAUVER. Is that from the industry itself?

Mr. CLENDENEN. No sir; those figures, Senator, are from Audit Bureau of Circulations and the Controlled Circulation Audits.

The two organizations are companies that collect and issue data on circulation of various kinds of magazines.

Senator KEFAUVER. Thank you, Mr. Clendenen.

The CHAIRMAN. Does the Senator from Missouri have any more questions?

Senator HENNINGS. I just wanted to ask Mr. Clendenen another question and I do not want to break into his fine presentation of this—The Yellow Kid was the first comic strip, was it not?

Mr. CLENDENEN. Yes, sir.

Senator HENNINGS. Then we went into the Happy Hooligan and Katzenjammers and the ones we used to think were funny as youngsters.

At any rate, the funnies we knew were really funny, there were things in them that were calculated at least to amuse. The daily papers throughout the country nowadays carry more and more of the so-called serials, whether they deal with crime or whether they deal with romance or whether they deal with one thing or another, they are more stories now and less of the old comic-strip variety.

Have you any material on that transition and any observations to make as to why obviously that must appeal to the public, or they would not run these syndicated strips in the papers as they do.

What is your view of that, Mr. Clendenen? Why has public taste changed apparently? Are we advancing or progressing in that sort of thing, or is it the obverse?

Mr. CLENDENEN. There really, of course, are not research base data on which an answer to your question could be founded. I am not sure whether the public taste has changed or not.

Certainly the comic-book industry which was born in and of itself during the depression years of the thirties, the latter thirties, represented perhaps rather than reflected any change in the taste of the public, represents a new idea, that is, to put the comics up in book form of this kind.

Just exactly why you have had a transition from the type of comics—and now I refer to comic strips, which appeared in an earlier day and on which each separate day represented a separate episode and were funny to the serious type of strip—I don't have any idea and no opinion on it.

I am not at all sure I said, and if I failed to say, I would like to say, that our investigation has not pertained at all to the comic strips appearing in the daily newspapers but rather the comic books.

Senator HENNINGS. Thank you.

Mr. CLENDENEN. The next slide, the next comic that we would like to present to you is entitled "Crime Must Pay the Penalty." This particular comic has 4 stories in which 27 people meet a violent death. One story in this particular issue called "Frisco Mary" concerns an attractive and glamorous young woman who gains control of a California underworld gang. Under her leadership the gang embarks on a series of holdups marked for their ruthlessness and violence.

Our next picture shows Mary emptying her submachine gun into the body of an already wounded police officer after the officer had created an alarm and thereby reduced the gang's take in a bank holdup to a mere $25,000.

Now, in all fairness it should be added that Mary finally dies in the gas chamber following a violent and lucrative criminal career.

Now, this is strictly of the crime variety.

The next comic book is entitled "Strange Tales" and has five stories in which 13 people die violently. The story actually begins with a man dying on the operating table because the attending doctor is so absorbed in his own troubles that he pays no attention whatsoever to his patient.

It develops that this is the story of a promising young surgeon who begins to operate on wounded criminals to gain the money demanded by his spendthrift wife.

After he has ruined his professional career by becoming associated with the underworld, the criminal comes to get help for his girl friend who has been shot by the police. When the girl is placed upon the operating table the doctor discovers that the criminal's girl friend is none other than his own wife.

This picture shows the doctor, first of all, as he recognizes his wife, and as he commits suicide by plunging a scalpel into his own chest.

His wife also dies on the operating table for lack of medical attention.

The next comic, The Haunt of Fear, has 4 stories in which 8 people die violently. One story entitled "Head-Room" has to do with a spinster who operates a cheap waterfront hotel. The renter of one room is a man she would like to marry.

To win his favor she reduces his rent by letting his room, during daytime hours, to an ugly and vicious appearing man. This shot shows her renting the room to that individual.

Meanwhile there are daily reports that a murderer is loose in the city who cuts off and carries away his victim's heads.

The hotelkeeper suspects the vicious appearing daytime roomer and searches his room where she discovers six heads hanging on hooks in the closet.

She is discovered there by her favorite roomer who is returning to the hotel for the night.

It develops that he is the murderer and the next picture shows the hotelkeeper's head being added to the closet collection.

From a psychological point of view, however, there is another story in this same issue which is really even more perturbing. This is the story of an orphan boy who is placed from an orphanage to live with nice-appearing foster parents.

The foster parents give excellent care and pay particular attention to his physical health, insisting that he eat nourishing food in abundance.

A month later the boy discovers the reason for their solicitude when they sneak into his room late at night and announce they are vampires about to drink his rich red blood.

It might be said that right triumphs in the end, however, since the boy turns into a werewolf and kills and eats his foster parents.

The final story is one entitled "Shock Suspense Stories." It contains 4 stories in which 6 persons die violently.

One particular story in this issue is called "Orphan." This is the story of a small golden-haired girl named Lucy, of perhaps 8 or 10 years of age, and the story is told in her own words.

Lucy hates both her parents. Her father is an alcoholic who beats her when drunk.

Her mother, who never wanted Lucy, has a secret boy friend. The only bright spot in Lucy's life is her Aunt Kate, with whom she would like to live.

Lucy's chance to alter the situation comes when the father entering the front gate to the home meets his wife who is running away with the other man. Snatching a gun from the night table, Lucy shoots her father from the window.

She then runs out into the yard and presses the gun into the hands of her mother who has fainted and lies unconscious on the ground.

Then through Lucy's perjured testimony at the following trial, both the mother and her boy friend are convicted of murdering the father and are electrocuted.

This picture shows, first, "Mommie" and then "Stevie" as they die in the electric chair.

The latter two pictures show Lucy's joyous contentment that it has all worked out as she had planned and she is now free to live with her Aunt Kate.

The last two comic books I mentioned are published by the Entertaining Comic group and I mention it because the publisher of Entertaining Comic group will be appearing here later this morning.

Now, that completes the illustration of the type of comics to which we are addressing ourselves.

Mr. BEASER. Just one point, Mr. Clendenen. In talking about the child who is placed in a foster home, turned into a werewolf, you said that psychologically that was disturbing. Why do you say that?

Mr. CLENDENEN. Let me refer back to the time that I was operating an institution for emotionally disturbed children. Any child who is not able to live, continue to live, with his own family and who is disturbed and goes into an institution and then later is facing foster-home placement has a great many fears both conscious and unconscious regarding the future. That is, he is very much afraid, very fearful about going out and living with the family.

He has met them, to be sure, but he does not know them and he is a very insecure individual to begin with. This is the type of material that I myself would feel would greatly increase a youngster's feeling of insecurity, anxiety, and panic regarding placement in a foster-family home.

Mr. BEASER. Mr. Clendenen, you produced a number of comic books with different titles. Are they all, each one of them, produced by a different company?

Mr. CLENDENEN. No, they are not. The organization of the publishers in the comic-book industry is really a very complex type of organization.

I would like to refer here to the Atlas Publishing Co., or Atlas publishing group as an example. Atlas represents one of the major publishers in the comic-book field and, incidentally, there will be a representative of the Atlas Co. appearing also at these hearings. The Atlas Co. is owned by a man-and-wife team, Mr. and Mrs. Martin Goodman.

Now, the Atlas Publishing Co. publishes between 49 and 50 different comic titles. However, this number of comic titles, the 45 or 50 comic titles, are produced through no less than some 25 different corporations.

The Atlas organization also includes still another corporation through which it distributes its own publications. This particular exhibit shows 20 of the different groups of crime and weird comics they produce through 15 corporations.

Now, although several of the other publishers who are in the business of publishing comic books are smaller, the patterns of organization are essentially the same.

In other words, many times they organize themselves in forms of 2, 3, 4 or more different corporations. The end result of this type of corporation is that while there are many corporations involved in the publishing of comic books, the entire industry really rests in the hands of relatively few individuals.

Mr. BEASER. When you say they organize into different companies, do they organize into companies that produce nothing but comic books or do they produce other types of literature?

Mr. CLENDENEN. No, they also produce other types of literature. Many of them produce different kinds of magazines in addition to producing comics.

Now, not only may a particular organization be engaged in producing comics, both comic and magazines, but many times they will produce both comics and magazines through one individual corporation within the group.

In this exhibit, for example, this particular comic, which is produced once again by Atlas—and we are using Atlas merely as an example—these particular publications are not only both produced by the Atlas, but they are produced by a single corporation within the Atlas group.

Mr. BEASER. You say Atlas group. That is a trade-mark?

Mr. CLENDENEN. Yes, all their publications carry the Atlas trademark.

Mr. BEASER. In the course of your investigation has your staff had occasion to review scientific studies which have been made on the effect of crime and horror comics upon children and the relationship to juvenile delinquency?

Mr. CLENDENEN. Yes, we have. That is, we have reviewed virtually all of the surveys and studies that have been made; that is, we have reviewed all that we have been able to find.

I might say that it probably is not too surprising that the expert opinions and findings of these studies are not wholly unanimous. That is, there is certain diversity of opinion regarding the effects of these materials on youngsters even among these individuals whom we might properly qualify as experts.

Now, in this connection, I would like to submit to the subcommittee a few items here which relate to this matter of effects of these materials upon youngsters. One of these is a survey that was made at our request by the Library of Congress which summarizes all of the studies that they could locate having to do with the effects of crime comics upon the behavior of youngsters.

The CHAIRMAN. Is it your desire that this material be put in the record, or made a part of the subcommittee's files?

Mr. CLENDENEN. The latter, I believe.

The CHAIRMAN. I think that would be preferable.

Mr. CLENDENEN. I also would like to submit a letter which we received from Dr. Robert Felix, Director of the Institute of Mental Health, to whom we submitted samples of these materials and this is his reply to us indicating his feelings on the effects of these materials.

The CHAIRMAN. Without objection, that will be made a part of the record. Let that be exhibit No. 1.

* * * * * * * *

We just do not know. We are trying to learn.

I, for one, appreciate the spirit in which you have come here today.

Mr. SCHULTZ. Thank you, sir.

The CHAIRMAN. Mr. Schultz, the Chair certainly appreciates the spirit of your testimony. You have been very helpful. I think I speak for every member of the subcommittee when I say we are grateful.

Senator KEFAUVER. Mr. Chairman, may I ask one more question?

The CHAIRMAN. Senator Kefauver.

Senator KEFAUVER. Those who carry the seal of the code, do they advertise inside the magazine that they are complying with the code of the Comic Magazine Publishers Association?

Mr. SCHULTZ. I know of no such specific advertisement, other than the impression of the seal itself on the cover.

Senator KEFAUVER. How do people know what that seal means, then?

Mr. SCHULTZ. I really don't know. Most of the publishers who are nonmembers develop seals of their own. You find a whole series of seals which say "Good clean reading," and everything else, so that the seal has lost its imprint and its value in many ways anyhow, except for somebody who takes the trouble to look very closely at that little legend that might have some meaning to it.

Other than that I think it has no value.

Senator KEFAUVER. Thank you very much.

The CHAIRMAN. The subcommittee will stand in recess until 2 o'clock this afternoon.

(Thereupon, at 12:20 p.m., the subcommittee recessed, to reconvene at 2 p.m., same day.)

AFTERNOON SESSION

The subcommittee reconvened at 2 o'clock p.m., upon the expiration of the recess.

The CHAIRMAN. The hearing will be in order.

The first witness this afternoon will be Dr. Frederic Wertham.

Doctor, will you come forward and be sworn, please.

Do you solemnly swear that the testimony you will give this subcommittee of the Committee on the Judiciary of the United States Senate, will be the truth, the whole truth, and nothing but the truth, so help you God?

Dr. WERTHAM. I do.

TESTIMONY OF DR. FREDERIC WERTHAM, PSYCHIATRIST, DIRECTOR, LAFARGUE CLINIC, NEW YORK, N. Y.

The CHAIRMAN. Doctor, do you have a prepared statement?

Dr. WERTHAM. I have a statement of about 20 or 25 minutes.

The CHAIRMAN. All right, Doctor, you proceed in your own manner.

Dr. WERTHAM. Thank you.

The CHAIRMAN. Doctor, do you have copies of your statement?

Dr. WERTHAM. It is not written out. I have a statement of my credentials.

The CHAIRMAN. I wonder if you could not in your own way summarize this for the record. Of course, the whole statement may go in the record in its entirety.

Without objection, that will be so ordered.

(The document referred to is as follows:)

FREDERIC WERTHAM, M.D., NEW YORK, N. Y.

Specializing in neurology and psychiatry since 1922.

Certified as specialist in both neurology and psychiatry by the American Board of Psychiatry and Neurology. Have also served as examiner on the board in brain anatomy and psychiatry.

Director, Lafargue Clinic, New York City.

Consulting psychiatrist, department of hospitals, Queens Medical Center, New York City.

Psychiatric consultant and lecturer, Juvenile Aid Bureau of the New York City Police Department.

Director, Psychiatric Services and Mental Hygiene Clinic, Queens General Hospital, 1939-52.

Consulting psychiatrist, Triboro Hospital, New York City, 1939-52.

Director, Quaker Emergency Service Readjustment Center (functioning under the magistrates court), 1948-51.

Senior psychiatrist, New York City Department of Hospitals, 1932-52.

In 1932 organized and became director of the Psychiatric Clinic of the Court of General Sessions in New York, first clinic of its kind in the United States.

1933-36, assistant to the director of Bellevue Hospital; in charge of prison ward; in charge of children's psychiatric ward; in charge of alcoholic ward.

1936-39, director of the Mental Hygiene Clinic of Bellevue Hospital.

1929-31, fellow of the National Research Council of Washington, D. C., to do research in neuropathology and neuropsychiatry. First psychiatrist ever to receive this fellowship.

1922-29, psychiatrist at Phipps Psychiatric Clinic, Johns Hopkins Hospital and Johns Hopkins University.

1926-28, chief resident psychiatrist, Johns Hopkins Hospital.

1926-29, assistant in charge of the Mental Hygiene Clinic, Johns Hopkins Hospital.

Taught psychiatry, psychotherapy, and brain anatomy at Johns Hopkins Medical School.

Postgraduate studies in London, Vienna, Paris, and Munich. Invited to read scientific papers at the Medical-Psychological Society of Paris and the Research Institute of Psychiatry in Munich.

President of the Association for the Advancement of Psychotherapy, 1943-51; coeditor of the American Journal of Psychotherapy.

Member of the Committee on Ethics of the American Academy of Neurology.

Lectured at Yale Law School, New York University Law School, Massachusetts Institute of Technology, on psychiatry, criminology, and related subjects.

Reviewed books for law reviews of New York University, Buffalo Law School, Northwestern Law School, etc.

Psychiatric consultant to the Chief Censor of the United States Treasury Department.

Only psychiatrist ever employed by the city of New York who is a member of all three national neuropsychiatric associations: American Neurological Association, American Psychiatric Association, American Association of Neuropathologists. Fellow of the New York Academy of Medicine, of the American Academy of Neurology, of the American Medical Association, etc.

PUBLICATIONS

The Brain as an Organ (Macmillan, 1934), used in medical schools throughout the world, a textbook of brain pathology.

Dark Legend. A study in murder. New York, 1941, and London, 1948.

The Show of Violence (Doubleday, 1949).

The Catathymic Crisis (1937), description of a new mental disorder now included in the leading textbooks of psychiatry.

Seduction of the Innocent (Rinehart, 1954).

Articles and papers on psychology, psychiatry, neurology, brain anatomy, etc.

Dr. WERTHAM. I have practiced psychiatry and neurology since 1922. I taught psychiatry and brain pathology and worked in clinics at the Johns Hopkins Medical School from 1922 to 1929.

In 1929 I was the first psychiatrist to be awarded a fellowship by the National Research Council to do research on the brain. Some part of my research at that time was on paresis and brain syphilis. It came in good stead when I came to study comic books.

From 1932 to 1952 I was senior psychiatrist at the New York City Department of Hospitals.

I was first in charge of the Psychiatric Clinic of the Court of General Sessions examining convicted felons, making reports to the court.

In 1936 I was appointed director of the Mental Hygiene Clinic in Bellevue.

In 1939 I was appointed director of psychiatric services at the Mental Hygiene Clinic at Queens General Hospital.

In 1946 I organized and started the first psychiatric clinic in Harlem, a volunteer staff. A few years later I organized the Quaker Emergency Mental Hygiene Clinic, which functioned as a clinic for the treatment of sex offenders under the magistrates court of New York.

These are my main qualifications. I have taught psychiatry in Hopkins and New York University.

I have written both books and papers and monographs. I have reviewed psychiatric books for legal journals, like the Buffalo School Journal.

I have lectured at the Yale Law School, at the Massachusetts Institute of Technology, and in other places.

I am a fellow of the New York Academy and a member of the three national neuropsychiatric associations, the American Psychiatric Association and American Neurological Association and American Association of Neuropathologists.

I am testifying at your request on the influence of crime and horror books on juvenile delinquency.

My testimony will be in four parts. First, what is in comic books? How can one classify them clinically?

Secondly, are there any bad effects of comic books?

I may say here on this subject there is practically no controversy. Anybody who has studied them and seen them knows that some of them have bad effects.

The third problem is how farreaching are these bad effects? There is a good deal of controversy about that.

A fourth part is: Is there any remedy?

And being merely a doctor, about that I shall say only a few words.

My opinion is based on clinical investigations which I started in the winter of 1945 and 1946. They were carried out not by me alone, but with the help of a group of associates, psychiatrists, child psychiatrists, psychoanalysts, social workers, psychiatric social workers, remedial reading teachers, probation officers, and others.

In addition to material seen at the clinic both at Queens and Lafargue, we have studied whole school classes, whole classes of remedial reading clinics, over 300 children in a parochial school and private patients and consultations.

To the best of my knowledge our study is the first and only individual large-scale study on the subject of comic books in general.

The methods that we have used are the ordinary methods used in psychiatry, clinical interviews, group interviews, intelligence tests, reading tests, projective tests, drawings, the study of dreams, and so on.

This study was not subsidized by anybody. None of my associates got any money, ever. I myself have never spoken on the subject of comic books and accepted a fee for that.

This research was a sober, painstaking, laborious clinical study, and in some cases, since it has been going on now for 7 years, we have had a chance to follow for several years.

In addition to that we have read all that we could get hold of that was written in defense of comics, which is almost a more trying task than reading the comic books themselves.

What is in comic books? In the first place, we have completely restricted ourselves to comic books themselves. That leaves out newspaper comic strips entirely.

I must say, however, that when some very harmless comic strips for children printed in newspapers are reprinted for children in comic books, you suddenly can find whole pages of gun advertisements which the newspaper editor would not permit to have inserted in the newspaper itself.

There have been, we have found, arbitrary classifications of comic books according to the locale where something takes place.

We have found that these classifications don't work if you want to understand what a child really thinks or does.

We have come to the conclusion that crime comic books are comic books that depict crime and we have found that it makes no difference whether the locale is western, or Superman or space ship or horror, if a girl is raped she is raped whether it is in a space ship or on the prairie.

If a man is killed he is killed whether he comes from Mars or somewhere else, and we have found, therefore, two large groups, the crime comic books and the others.

I would like to illustrate my remarks by western comic books by giving you an example. This is from an ordinary western comic book. You might call it the wide open spaces.

This is from an ordinary western comic book. You see this man hitting this girl with a gun. It is a sadistic, criminal, sexual scene.

We have also studied how much time children spend on crime comic books and how much money they spend. I should like to tell you that there are thousands of children who spend about $60 a year on comic books.

Even poor children. I don't know where they get the money. I have seen children who have spent $75 a year and more, and I, myself, have observed when we went through these candy stores in different places, not only in New York, how 1 boy in a slum neighborhood, seemingly a poor boy, bought 15 comic books at a time.

Now, people generalize about juvenile delinquency and they have pet theories and they leave out how much time, and, incidentally, how much money children spend on this commodity alone.

Now, as far as the effects on juvenile delinquency are concerned, we distinguish four groups of delinquency:

Delinquencies against property; delinquency associated with violence; offenses connected with sex; and then miscellaneous, consisting of fire setting, drug addiction, and childhood prostitution.

I may say the latter is a very hushed-up subject. I am not referring to what young girls do with young boys, but I am referring to 10-, 11-, 12-, 13-year-old girls prostituting themselves to adults.

Now, nobody versed in any of this type of clinical research would claim that comic books alone are the cause of juvenile delinquency. It is my opinion, without any reasonable doubt, and without any reservation, that comic books are an important contributing factor in many cases of juvenile delinquency.

There arises the question: What kind of child is affected? I say again without any reasonable doubt and based on hundreds and hundreds of cases of all kinds, that it is primarily the normal child.

Mr. Chairman, American children are wonderful children. If we give them a chance they act right. It is senseless to say that all these people who get into some kind of trouble with the law must be abnormal or there must be something very wrong with them.

As a matter of fact, the most morbid children that we have seen are the ones who are less affected by comic books because they are wrapped up in their own phantasies.

Now, the question arises, and we have debated it in our group very often and very long, why does the normal child spend so much time with this smut and trash, we have this baseball game which I would like you to scrutinize in detail.

They play baseball with a deadman's head. Why do they do that?

The CHAIRMAN. Doctor, do you want to put this up here on exhibition and explain it?

Dr. WERTHAM. Yes, sir.

Mr. Chairman, I can't explain for the reason that I can't say all the obscene things that are in this picture for little boys of 6 and 7. This is a baseball game where they play baseball with a man's head; where the man's intestines are the baselines. All his organs have some part to play.

The torso of this man is the chest protector of one of the players. There is nothing left to anybody's morbid imagination.

Mr. BEASER. That is from a comic book?

Dr. WERTHAM. That is from a comic book.

I will be glad to give you the reference later on. It is a relatively recent one.

Senator HENNINGS. Mr. Chairman, may I ask the doctor a question at that point?

The CHAIRMAN. The Senator from Missouri.

Senator HENNINGS. Doctor, I think from what you have said so far in terms of the value and effectiveness of the artists who portray these things, that it might be suggested implicitly that anybody who can draw that sort of thing would have to have some very singular or peculiar abnormality or twist in his mind, or am I wrong in that?

Dr. WERTHAM. Senator, if I may go ahead in my statement, I would like to tell you that this assumption is one that we had made in the beginning and we have found it to be wrong. We have found that this enormous industry with its enormous profits has a lot of people to whom it pays money and these people have to make these drawings or else, just like the crime comic book writers have to write the stories they write, or else. There are many decent people among them.

Let me tell you among the writers and among the cartoonists they don't love me, but I know that many of them are decent people and they would much rather do something else than do what they are doing.

Have I answered your question?

Senator HENNINGS. Yes, thank you.

Dr. WERTHAM. Now, we ask the question: Why does the normal child do that? I would say that psychology knows the answer to that.

If you consult, as we have done, the first modern scientific psychologist who lived a long time ago, you will find the answer. That psychologist was St. Augustine. This was long before the comic book era, of course, but he describes in detail how when he was a very, very young man he was in Rome and he saw these very bloody, sadistic spectacles all around him, where the gladiators fought each other with swords and daggers, and he didn't like it. He didn't want any part of it.

But there was so much going on and his friends went and finally he went and he noticed, as he expresses it, that he became unconsciously delighted with it and he kept on going.

In other words, he was tempted, he was seduced by this mass appeal, and he went.

I think it is exactly the same thing, if the children see these kinds of things over and over again, they can't go to a dentist, they can't go to a clinic, they can't go to a ward in a hospital, everywhere they see this where women are beaten up, where people are shot and killed, and finally they become, as St. Augustine said, unconsciously delighted.

I don't blame them. I try to defend them or I try to understand them.

Now, it is said also in connection with this question of who reads comic books and who is affected by them, it is said that children from secure homes are not affected.

Mr. Chairman, as long as the crime comic books industry exists in its present forms there are no secure homes. You cannot resist infantile paralysis in your own home alone. Must you not take into account the neighbor's children?

I might give one more example of the brutality in comic books. This is a girl and they are about to rip out her tongue. Now, the effect of comic books operates along four lines. While in our studies we had no arbitrary age limit, I am mostly interested in the under 16 and the first effect that is very early manifested is an effect in general on the ways of living with people.

That is to say, on theoretical development. One of the outstanding things there is in crime comic books—let me say here subject to later questions that in my opinion crime comic books as I define them, are the overwhelming majority of all comic books at the present time. There is an endless stream of brutality.

I would take up all your time if I would tell you all the brutal things. I would like to draw your attention to one which seems to be specific almost with this literature that I have never found anywhere else, that is injuring people's eyes.

In other words, this is something now which juvenile delinquents did which I never heard of years ago. They shoot people in the eye and they throw stones and so on.

As an example, I would give you a book which nobody would testify is a crime comic book if you had not read it. You all know the novels of Tarzan which you all saw in the movies, but the comic book Tarzan which any mother would let come into her home has a story which a little boy brought me in which 22 people are blinded.

One of the 22 is a beautiful girl. They are all white people who are blinded and the man who does it is a Negro, so in addition to that it causes a great deal of race hatred.

How old are the children to whom such things are given? Dell Publishing Co., which publishes this book, boasts that this story is being read aloud to a little girl who—she is 2 years old—now, of course, many other crime comic books have this injury to the eye motive.

In other words, I think that comic books primarily, and that is the greatest harm they do, cause a great deal of ethical confusion.

I would like to give you a very brief example. There is a school in a town in New York State where there has been a great deal of stealing. Some time ago some boys attacked another boy and they twisted his arm so viciously that it broke in two places, and, just like in a comic book, the bone came through the skin.

In the same school about 10 days later 7 boys pounced on another boy and pushed his head against the concrete so that the boy was unconscious and had to be taken to the hospital. He had a concussion of the brain.

In this same high school in 1 year 26 girls became pregnant. The score this year, I think, is eight. Maybe it is nine by now.

Now, Mr. Chairman, this is what I call ethical and moral confusion. I don't think that any of these boys or girls individually vary very much. It cannot be explained individually, alone.

Here is a general moral confusion and I think that these girls were seduced mentally long before they were seduced physically, and, of course, all those people there are very, very great—not all of them, but most of them, are very great comic book readers, have been and are.

As a remedy they have suggested a formal course of sex instruction in this school.

The CHAIRMAN. What is the population of this community, Doctor?

Dr. WERTHAM. I don't know the population of the community. I know the population of the school, which is about 1,800. The town itself I don't know, but I shall give it to counsel.

The CHAIRMAN. The Senator from Tennessee.

Senator KEFAUVER. Is there something confidential about the name of the town?

Dr. WERTHAM. Yes. Publicly I don't like to give it, but I have knowledge of it, but I will give it to counsel for the information of the committee.

The CHAIRMAN. That will be in order.

Dr. WERTHAM. Now, they tried to start a course of sex instruction in this school. They have not done it. They have not started it. I wonder what they are going to do. Are the teachers going to instruct the pupils, or are the pupils going to instruct the teachers?

One reason I don't want to mention this town is because the same kind of thing happens in many other places nowadays. Maybe not quite so much, maybe a little more.

Many of these things happen and it is my belief that the comic book industry has a great deal to do with it. While I don't say it is the only factor at all, it may not be the most important one, it is one contributing factor.

I would like to point out to you one other crime comic book which we have found to be particularly injurious to the ethical development of children and those are the Superman comic books. They arose in children phantasies of sadistic joy in seeing other people punished over and over again while you yourself remain immune. We have called it the Superman complex.

In these comic books the crime is always real and the Superman's triumph over good is unreal. Moreover, these books like any other, teach complete contempt of the police.

For instance, they show you pictures where some preacher takes two policemen and bang their heads together or to quote from all these comic books you know, you can call a policeman cop and he won't mind, but if you call him copper that is a derogatory term and these boys we teach them to call policemen coppers.

All this to my mind has an effect, but it has a further effect and that was very well expressed by one of my research associates who was a teacher and studied the subject and she said, "Formerly the child wanted to be like daddy or mommy. Now they skip you, they bypass you. They want to be like Superman, not like the hard working, prosaic father and mother."

Talking further about the ethical effects of comic books, you can read and see over and over again the remark that in crime comic books good wins over evil, that law and order always prevails.

We have been astonished to find that this remark is repeated and repeated, not only by the comic books industry itself, but by educators, columnists, critics, doctors, clergymen. Many of them believe it is so.

Mr. Chairman, it is not. In many comic books the whole point is that evil triumphs; that you can commit a perfect crime. I can give you so many examples that I would take all your time.

I will give you only one or two. Here is a little 10-year-old girl who killed her father, brought it about that her mother was electrocuted. She winks at you because she is triumphant.

I have stories where a man spies on his wife and in the last picture you see him when he pours the poison in the sink, very proud because he succeeded.

There are stories where the police captain kills his wife and has an innocent man tortured into confessing in a police station and again is triumphant in the end.

I want to make it particularly clear that there are whole comic books in which every single story ends with the triumph of evil, with a perfect crime unpunished and actually glorified.

In connection with the ethical confusion that these crime comic books cause, I would like to show you this picture which has the comic book philosophy in the slogan at the beginning, "Friendship is for suckers! Loyalty—that is for Jerks."

The second avenue along which comic books contribute to delinquency is by teaching the technique and by the advertisements for weapons. If it were my task, Mr. Chairman, to teach children delinquency, to tell them how to rape and seduce girls, how to hurt people, how to break into stores, how to cheat, how to forge, how to do any known crime, if it were my task to teach that, I would have to enlist the crime comic book industry.

Formerly to impair the morals of a minor was a punishable offense. It has now become a mass industry. I will say that every crime of delinquency is described in detail and that if you teach somebody the technique of something you, of course, seduce him into it.

Nobody would believe that you teach a boy homosexuality without introducing him to it. The same thing with crime.

For instance, I had no idea how one would go about stealing from a locker in Grand Central, but I have comic books which describe that in minute detail and I could go out now and do it.

Now, children who read that, it is just human, are, of course, tempted to do it and they have done it. You see, there is an interaction between the stories and the advertisements. Many, many comic books have advertisements of all kinds of weapons, really dangerous ones, like .22 caliber rifles or throwing knives, throwing daggers; and if a boy, for instance, in a comic book sees a girl like this being whipped and the man who does it looks very satisfied and on the last page there is an advertisement of a whip with a hard handle, surely the maximum of temptation is given to this boy, at least to have fantasies about these things.

It is my conviction that if these comic books go to as many millions of children as they go to, that among all these people who have these fantasies, there are some of them who carry that out in action.

Mr. BEASER. Doctor, may I interrupt you just a moment to go back to your Grand Central story?

Assume that is read by an otherwise healthy, normal child, with a good homelife, no other factors involved would you say that that would tempt him to go and break into a locker in Grand Central, or must there be other factors present already to give him a predisposition to steal from somebody else?

Dr. WERTHAM. I would answer that this way: I know of no more erroneous theory about child behavior than to assume that children must be predisposed to do anything wrong. I think there is a hairline which separates a boy who dreams about that, dreams about such a thing, and the boy who does it.

Now, I don't say, and I have never said, and I don't believe it, that the comic-book factor alone makes a child do anything.

You see, the comic-book factor only works because there are many, many other factors in our environment, not necessarily the homelife, not necessarily the much-blamed mother, but there are many other things; the other boys in school, the newspaper headlines where everybody accuses the other one of being a liar or thief.

There are many, many other factors in our lives, you see.

Now, actually, the answer should be put in this way: In most cases this factor works with other factors, but there are many cases that I know where such crimes have been committed purely as imitation and would have never been committed if the child hadn't known this technique.

In other words, I want to stress for you what we have found, that the temptation, and, of course, we know it from our ordinary lives—that temptation and seduction is an enormous factor. We don't have to be materially bad to do something bad occasionally, and, moreover, these children who commit such a delinquency, they don't do that because they are bad. They don't even necessarily do it to get the money or to get even, but it is a glorious deed.

You go there, you show how big you are. You are almost as big as these people you read about in crime comic books.

You see, the corruption of the average normal child has gone so far that except for those who follow this it is almost unbelievable to realize.

I would like to give you one more example. This is one I would like you to keep in mind, that the minimum edition of such a book, I think, is 300,000; probably this is distributed in a 650,000 edition.

Senator KEFAUVER. I did not understand.

Dr. WERTHAM. The minimum is 300,000.

Senator KEFAUVER. Is that a month?

Dr. WERTHAM. This is only one comic book. In order to make any kind of profit the publisher must print about 300,000 copies.

In other words, when you see a comic book you can always assume that more than 300,000 copies of this particular comic book have been printed.

In other words, you would not go far wrong if you assumed that this comic book is read by half a million children, for this reason, that when they are through with it and have read it, they sell it for 6 cents and 5 cents and then sell it for 4 cents and 2 cents.

Then you can still trade it.

So these comic books have a long, long life. We have studied this market. We know there is a great deal of this trading going on all over.

Now, this is a heroine. This is a woman who kills a man. You see, he has blood coming all over the man's face and she says, "I want you to suffer more and more and more and more."

Then the final triumph, she takes this man's organs and serves them up as dishes like a housewife and you see her "famous fried brains, famous baked kidneys, famous stuffed heart."

Next to that is the remainder of this man.

All I say is that quite apart from the disgust that it arouses in us—and I am a doctor, I can't permit myself the luxury of being disgusted—I think this kind of thing that children see over and over again causes this ethical confusion.

Senator KEFAUVER. That seems to be the end of that comic book story.

Dr. WERTHAM. Yes. I should add that it says here, "The End." "The End" is this glorious meal, cannibalism.

Senator KEFAUVER. So it did not have a very happy ending.

Dr. WERTHAM. Well, the comic book publishers seem to think it did. They made a lot of money.

Mr. Chairman, we have delinquency of the smallest kind. I have seen children who have stolen a quarter. I have seen children who stole $30,000. And they have to know some technique; they have to, for that.

But there are other crimes which you can commit in which you can take the ordinary kind of violence, for instance, there is an awful lot of shooting, knifing, throwing rocks, bombs, and all that, in combination.

On the Long Island Railroad at present I think three times a day children throw rocks through the windows.

Recently an innocent man was hit in the head and had a concussion of the brain and had to be taken to a hospital.

I have been for 12 years in Queens. I know these kids. I have seen quite a number of them who threw rocks. I can't see why we have to invoke highfalutin psychological theories and why we say these people have to have a mother who doesn't give them enough affection.

If they read this stuff all the time, some of them 2 and 3 hours a day reading, I don't think it is such an extraordinary event if they throw a stone somewhere where it may do some harm.

I want to add to this that my theory of temptation and seduction as I told you, is very, very vague. That is known to the comic-book publishers, too. They don't admit it when it comes to delinquency, but when it comes to selling stuff to children through the advertisements in comic books, then they have these enormous advertisements. This is from the Superman comic book. It says, "It is easier to put a yen in a youngster."

You see, I am still answering your question. It is easier to put a yen in a youngster when he comes from a normal thing. It is easier to go and commit some kind of delinquency.

Certainly it is easier to commit some kind of sexual delinquency.

Now, this leads me to the third avenue where they do harm. That is, they do harm by discouraging children. Mr. Chairman, many of these comic books, crime-comic books, and many of the other ones have ads which discourage children and give them all kinds of inferiority feelings. They are threatened with pimples. They worry the pre-adolescent kids about their breaths. They sell them all kinds of medicines and gadgets and even comic books like this one, and I am very conscious of my oath, even comic books like this have fraudulent advertisements, and I am speaking now as a medical physician. The children spend a lot of money and they get very discouraged, they think they are too big, too little, or too heavy. They think this bump is too big, or too little.

These discouraged children are very apt to commit delinquency as we know and have known for a long time.

Now, the fourth avenue I shall not go into in detail because that includes not only the crime-comic books, but that includes all comic books.

We have found—and in response to questions I will be glad to go into that—we have found all comic books have a very bad effect on teaching the youngest children the proper reading technique, to learn to read from left to right. This balloon print pattern prevents that. So many children, we say they read comic books, they don't read comic books at all. They look at pictures and every once in a while, as one boy expressed it to me, "When they get the woman or kill the man then I try to read a few words," but in any of these stories you don't have to have any words.

There is no doubt this is blood and this man is being killed. There is no doubt what they are going to do to this girl, you know, too.

In other words, the reading is very much interfered with.

The CHAIRMAN. Doctor, the original of all of those are in color?

Dr. WERTHAM. Yes, these are photostats I had made for your benefit.

Now, it is a known fact, although it is not sufficiently emphasized, that many delinquents have reading disorders, they can't read well. There have been estimates as to how many delinquents have reading disorders.

We have found over and over again that children who can't read are very discouraged and more apt to commit a delinquency and that is what Mr. Beaser meant, if there is another factor.

There is another factor.

Mr. BEASER. Many other factors.

Dr. WERTHAM. Yes, many other factors. We have isolated comic books as one factor. A doctor tries to isolate one factor and see what it does and tries to correlate it with other factors which either counteract it or help it or run parallel.

Now, Mr. Chairman, I have put the results of this investigation into several documents. One of them is an article in the Ladies Home Journal which gives a number of cases.

Another one is an article in the Reader's Digest which came out today.

The third one is a book.

I would like, Mr. Chairman, to draw your attention to the illustrations, but I would like to say that I am perfectly willing inasmuch as I have written this book with the greatest scientific care and checked and rechecked, and I am perfectly willing to repeat every word in there under oath.

The CHAIRMAN. Doctor, these documents will be made a part of the subcommittee's permanent file, without objection. Let that be exhibits Nos. 10a, 10b, and 10c.

(The documents referred to were marked "Exhibits Nos. 10a, 10b, and 10c," and are on file with the subcommittee.)

Dr. WERTHAM. Mr. Chairman, I would like to point out to you in conclusion that mine, in my own opinion, is not a minority report. I don't feel that way.

I would like to tell you that the highest psychiatric official in the Federal Government, who is also consulted when psychiatric problems come up in the Federal Government, Dr. Winfred Overholser, the Superintendent of Saint Elizabeths, has written that the evidence in my book is incontrovertible evidence of the pernicious influences on youth of crime comic books.

Prof. C. Wright Mills, a famous sociologist, a professor at Columbia, similarly agreed.

I would like to read you a word from the director of the juvenile delinquency project of the Children's Bureau in Washington, who has written:

In comic books we have a constant stream of garbage that cannot fail to pollute the minds of readers. After reading Dr. Wertham's book I visited my local newsstand and found the situation to be exactly as he reported it.

Senator KEFAUVER. Who is it that wrote that?

Dr. WERTHAM. Mr. Bertram M. Peck, the director of the current juvenile delinquency project in Washington.

The CHAIRMAN. He was before the subcommittee earlier in the hearings.

Dr. WERTHAM. Now, there are quite a number of other people who feel the same way. I would like to quote to you what the Minister of Justice of Canada said. In the beginning of this month they had two long sessions in the House of Commons, devoted almost entirely to my report on comic books and the Minister of Justice said:

I doubt if there is a single member of the House of Commons who dissents from disapproval of crime comic books.

In Canada, of course, they have the same situation. They get American comic books, not only directly, but they get them in plates. They can't help themselves.

Senator KEFAUVER. Dr. Wertham, while you are on the Canadian matter, Canada, of course, has a law, which was probably passed largely on the testimony you gave the House of Commons in Canada, which bans the shipment of certain horror and crime books.

What has been their experience with the reflection, or the result of that law upon juvenile delinquency? When was the law passed first?

Dr. WERTHAM. I am not quite sure. Maybe 1951. The information I have is based on the present official report of these debates on April 1 and 2. I judge from that that the law didn't work; that they made a list of crime comic books and they didn't know how to supervise it, in fact, they couldn't, and I doubt it can be done in that form.

They have more bad crime-comic books than they ever had. They never could get them off the stand.

The latest proposal on the 2d of April that I have is that they want to put the crime comic-book publishers in jail, but they can't do that, for one thing—we have them.

I don't think that would work. So that experiment is not yet completely evaluated. All I know is that they are very much worried about the effect of comic books on delinquency, that they have not been able by this one amendment to the criminal code to curb this situation.

Stating that mine is not a minority report, Mr. Chairman, I would like to quote one more critic, Mr. Clifton Fadiman, who says that he senses the truth in my presentation as he sensed the truth in Uncle Tom's Cabin.

I don't know the man personally.

Now, what about the remedy? Mr. Chairman, I am just a doctor. I can't tell what the remedy is. I can only say that in my opinion this is a public-health problem. I think it ought to be possible to determine once and for all what is in these comic books and I think it ought to be possible to keep the children under 15 from seeing them displayed to them and preventing these being sold directly to children.

In other words, I think something should be done to see that the children can't get them. You see, if a father wants to go to a store and says, "I have a little boy of seven. He doesn't know how to rape a girl; he doesn't know how to rob a store. Please sell me one of the comic books," let the man sell him one, but I don't think the boy should be able to go see this rape on the cover and buy the comic book.

I think from the public-health point of view something might be done.

Now, Mr. Chairman, in conclusion, if I may speak in seriousness about one suggestion that I have, I detest censorship. I have appeared in very unpopular cases in court defending such novelties as the Guilded Hearse, and so on, as I believe adults should be allowed to write for adults. I believe that what is necessary for children is supervision.

But I would like to suggest to the committee a simple scientific experiment, if I may, in great brevity.

I am not advocating censorship, but it is the comic-book industry which at the present moment tries to censor what the parents read. This enormous industry at present exercises a censorship through power. Ever since I have expressed any opinion about comic books based on simple research done in basements on poor children whose mothers cried their eyes out, ever since then I have been told by threats, by libel suits, of damages; it is a miracle that my book was published considering how many threatening letters these lawyers and people have written to my prospective publishers. They have even threatened with a libel suit the Saturday Evening Post and even the National Parent Teachers, which is a nonprofit magazine.

Senator KEFAUVER. While you are on that subject, Dr. Wertham, may I see that thing, anybody who opposes comic books is a Red?

Dr. WERTHAM. Yes; that is part of it.

Senator KEFAUVER. I have read a number of your writings. I have read your Seduction of the Innocent. You remember a number of years ago I had several visits with you and you told me about the pressure they tried to apply on you in connection with this.

But I noticed here this thing, that anyone who opposes comic books are Communists. "The group most anxious to destroy comics are the Communists."

Then they have here the statement:

This article also quoted Gershon Legman (who claims to be a ghost writer for Dr. Frederick Wertham, the author of a recent smear against comics published in the Ladies Home Journal). This same G. Legman, in issue No. 2 of Neurotica, published in autumn 1948, wildly condemned comics, although admitting that "The child's natural character must be distorted to fit civilization * * *. Fantasy violence will paralyze his resistance, divert his aggression to unreal enemies and frustrations, and in this way prevent him from rebelling against parents and teachers * * * this will siphon off his resistance against society, and prevent revolution."

This seems to be an effort to tie you up in some way as Red or Communist. Is that part of a smear?

Dr. WERTHAM. This is from comic books. I have really paid no attention to this. I can tell you that I am not a ghost writer. Like this gentleman who criticized it severely, they know I don't have a ghost writer.

Gershon Legman is a man who studied comic books. He is a man who tried to do something against comic books, so they tried to do something about him.

That is just one of the ordinary kinds of things. But, Mr. Chairman, they do something quite different which is much more serious. The comic-book industry at the present moment and this is the experiment. I would like to suggest to you the comic-book industry at the present moment interferes with the freedom of publications in all fields. They have their hands on magazines, they have their hands on newspapers, they threaten the advertisers; they continually threaten libel suits and action for damages.

The experiment I suggest to you is the following: My book has been selected, Seduction of the Innocent, which is nothing but a scientific report on comic books in that I tried to make in understandable language, that is what it is except that it includes areas other than juvenile delinquency.

This group was selected by a group of men of unimpeachable integrity, Christopher Morley, Clifton Fadiman, Loveman, Dorothy Canfield Fisher, John P. Marquand; they selected this book on account of its truth, and I suppose its writing, and it has been announced all over the country that it is a Book of the Month Club selection.

The contracts have been signed. The question I would like to put to you is this: Will this book be distributed or will the sinister hand of these corrupters of children, of this comic-book industry, will they prevent distribution? You can very easily find that out and then you can see how difficult it is for parents to defend their children against comic books if they are not allowed to read what they contain.

Thank you.

The CHAIRMAN. Senator Kefauver, do you have any questions?

Senator KEFAUVER. Yes, I have one or two, Mr. Chairman.

Dr. Wertham, I assume more than any other psychiatrist in the United States—perhaps I should not be asking this—but you, over a long period of time, have interviewed children, you worked in hospitals, clinics, and schools, observing the reaction to crime and horror comic books.

Could you give us any estimate of how many children this study has been made from—from which you derive your conclusions?

Dr. WERTHAM. Yes. I figured out at one time that there were more than 500 children a year come to my attention, or did come to my attention during the bulk of this investigation.

Now, I cannot say, however, that every one of these children had as complete a study as I think they should have. I mean, some of them I saw a few times; some have all kinds of tests, good social services; some had been before the court; some I saw privately and considered in great detail, but by and large I would say that we have seen hundreds and hundreds of children.

Senator KEFAUVER. Any way it runs into many thousands?

Dr. WERTHAM. Some thousands. I would not say many thousands.

Senator KEFAUVER. You have actually asked and tried to develop from many of these children how it was they happened to try to commit, or how it was they happened to commit this, that, or the other crime; is that correct?

Dr. WERTHAM. Senator, that is not exactly correct. For instance, if I have a child sent to me—I remember the commissioner of the juvenile aid bureau of the police once came to visit me to see how I examined a child because he had a good report of my clinic in Queens. This was a child who had committed some delinquency. I spent an hour talking to this child. I didn't even mention the delinquency. I didn't say a word about it.

The commissioner asked me afterwards, "Why didn't you mention it?"

I said, "I don't want to put him on his guard. I don't want to tempt him to lie to me. I want to understand this child. I want to understand the whole setting."

The judgment that these comic books have an effect on children, that is not the children's judgment. They don't think that. The children don't say that this does them any harm, and that is an interesting thing because it has been so misrepresented by the comic-book industry and their spokesmen in all the biased opinions that they peddle and that they hand out to unsuspecting newspaper editors.

They say I asked the child, "Did you do that because you read a comic book?"

I don't ask the child "Why do you have the measles?", or "Why do you have a fever?" No child has ever said to me this excuse, "I did this because I read it in the comic book. I figured that out."

The children don't say that. Many of these children read the comic books and they like it and they are already so corrupt that they really get a thrill out of it and it is very difficult.

What you can get out of them is this, "For me, this does not do any harm to me, but my little brother, he really should not read it. He gets nightmares or he gets wrong ideas."

The actual proof that a child can say, "I did this because of so and so," that is not at all how my investigation worked.

Senator KEFAUVER. I do remember you showed me one example of a horror book with a child with a hypodermic needle and you related that to some crime that you had known something about.

Dr. WERTHAM. I have known children, in fact, if I may say, Your Honor, I notice in the room the reporter who brought to my attention one of the earliest cases of children—may I say who it is—Judith Crist, who works for the New York Herald Tribune. She brought to my attention a case in Long Island where children stuck pins in girls or something. I told her then that I have found where they stuck pins in much worse places than the arm.

I told her of the injury to the eyes. You can very rarely say that the boys said exactly, "That is what I did because this is what I wanted to do."

I have had children who told me they committed robberies. They followed the comic book, but they said, "That is not good enough, the comic books say you go through the transom."

"But," they said, "you go through the side door."

Children nowadays draw maps and say, "This is the street where the store is we are going to rob; this is where we are going to hide and this is how we are going to get away."

That is in many comic books, and they show me in comic books that is how they are going to do it.

I would not say in such a case this is the only reason why this child committed delinquency, but I will say that is a contributing factor because if you don't know the method you can't execute the act and the method itself is so intriguing and so interesting that the children are very apt to commit it.

Senator KEFAUVER. In some of the comic books the villain made one mistake, he almost committed the perfect crime, but he made one mistake and he got caught. We found some cases where they are trying to eliminate the one mistake so that they can make the perfect crime.

Dr. WERTHAM. That is absolutely correct. That is the whole philosophy of comic books. The point is don't make any mistakes. Don't leave the map there. Don't break the light aloud, put a towel over it.

Senator KEFAUVER. Would you liken this situation you talk about, showing the same thing over and over again until they finally believed it, to what we heard about during the last war of Hitler's theory of telling the story over and over again?

The CHAIRMAN. The "big lie" technique?

Dr. WERTHAM. Well, I hate to say that, Senator, but I think Hitler was a beginner compared to the comic-book industry. They get the children much younger. They teach them race hatred at the age of 4 before they can read.

Let me give you an example of a comic book which I think is on the stand right now. It may have disappeared the last few days.

You know at the present moment New York City and other cities have a great social problem in integrating immigrating Puerto Ricans. It is very important to establish peace in these neighborhoods where friction may arise, or has arisen.

This particular comic book that I am referring to now has a story in which a derogatory term for Puerto Ricans, which I will not repeat here, but which is a common derogatory term, is repeated 12 times in one story. This greasy so and so, this dirty so and so. It is pointed out that a Spanish Catholic family moved into this neighborhood—utterly unnecessary.

What is the point of the story? The point of the story is that then somebody gets beaten to death. The only error is that the man who must get beaten to death is not a man; it is a girl.

Senator KEFAUVER. I think we ought to know the name of the comic book.

Dr. WERTHAM. I shall be glad to give it to your counsel.

Senator KEFAUVER. Can you tell us?

Dr. WERTHAM. I don't have it in my head.

Senator KEFAUVER. I am sure that Dr. Wertham is one who could tell about this, but I have heard it told that some people feel that comic books are harmless and respectable and don't pay much attention to them because they are certified to, and in some cases even recommended by high-sounding committees, with, of course, good names on the committees who give them an excellent bill of health.

Did you not make some investigation into whether or not a great many of the people on these so-called nonpartisan committees were actually in the pay of the comic book industry itself?

Dr. WERTHAM. Senator, I would have to mention individuals but I think it is to be assumed, and I suppose one knows that people whose names are on these comic books are paid—there are people who say, "Well, they are paid, they are biased."

I have a hard time understanding how any doctor or child expert or psychologist can put his name to that. That is not the important point, because the names usually are not known anyway.

What happens is that in Kalamazoo, or in North Dakota, or in the little village in Pennsylvania where I spend part of my time, they read the names of these institutions which sound very well, the so and so association, or so and so university. That is what influences the people.

Of course, these same people write articles which I have tried very hard to take at their face value. But when I found that they have misstatements, when they say articles sent out by one of the associations, the person who writes it and endorses these books for money, when they write a survey of all the comic books, you see all kinds of little ones, nothing of the real ones, it misleads the people.

But I think that is not as important a problem, Senator, as the problem right now that the industry itself is preventing the mothers of this country from having not only me, but anybody else make any criticism.

This tremendous power is exercised by this group which consists of three parts, the comic book publishers, the printers, and last and not least, the big distributors who force these little vendors to sell these comic books. They force them because if they don't do that they don't get the other things.

Mr. HANNOCH. How do you know that?

Dr. WERTHAM. I know that from many sources. You see, I read comic books and I buy them and I go to candy stores.

They said, "You read so many comic books." I talk to them and ask them who buys them. I say to a man, "Why do you sell this kind of stuff?"

He says, "What do you expect me to do? Not sell it?"

He says, "I will tell you something. I tried that one time."

The man says, "Look, I did that once. The newsdealer, whoever it is, says, 'You have to do it'."

"I said, 'I don't want to.'"

"'Well', he says, 'you can't have the other magazine'."

So the man said, "Well, all right, we will let it go."

So when the next week came, all the other magazines were late. You see, he didn't give them the magazines. So he was later than all his competitors, he had to take comic books back.

I also know it another way. There are some people who think I have some influence in this matter. I have very little. Comic books are much worse now than when I started. I have a petition from newsdealers that appealed to me to help them so they don't have to sell these comic books.

What they expect me to do, I don't know. Of course, it is known to many other people. It also happens in Canada.

I know it for more reasons. I don't want to mention journalists, but I can tell you of big national magazines, the editors of which would very much like to push this question of comic book problems. They can't do that because they are themselves being distributed by very big distributors who also do comic books, and then they suffer through loss of advertising.

That is why I gave you one example of the Book of the Month Club because I think that could nail it down once and for all, what these people do deliberately.

The CHAIRMAN. Senator Hennings, have you any questions?

Senator HENNINGS. Thank you, Mr. Chairman. I have no questions.

The CHAIRMAN. Mr. Hannoch, do you have any questions you want to ask?

Mr. HANNOCH. No questions.

Senator HENNINGS. I must say that I have the doctor's book, and I am reading it with great interest.

The CHAIRMAN. Doctor, we are very grateful to you for appearing here this afternoon.

Dr. WERTHAM. Thank you.

Mr. BEASER. William Gaines.

The CHAIRMAN. Will you come forward, Mr. Gaines?

Will you be sworn?

Do you solemnly swear that the testimony you will give to this subcommittee of the Committee on the Judiciary of the United States Senate, will be the truth, the whole truth, and nothing but the truth, so help you God?

Mr. GAINES. I do.

TESTIMONY OF WILLIAM M. GAINES, PUBLISHER, ENTERTAINING COMICS GROUP, NEW YORK, N.Y.

The CHAIRMAN. You may proceed in your own manner.

Mr. GAINES. Gentlemen, I would like to make a short statement. I am here as an individual publisher.

Mr. HANNOCH. Will you give your name and address, for the record?

Mr. GAINES. My name is William Gaines. My business address is 225 Lafayette Street, New York City. I am a publisher of the Entertaining Comics Group.

I am a graduate of the school of education of New York University. I have the qualifications to teach in secondary schools, high schools.

What then am I doing before this committee? I am a comic-book publisher. My group is known as EC, Entertaining Comics.

I am here as a voluntary witness. I asked for and was given this chance to be heard.

Two decades ago my late father was instrumental in starting the comic magazine industry. He edited the first few issues of the first modern comic magazine, Famous Funnies. My father was proud of the industry he helped found. He was bringing enjoyment to millions of people.

The heritage he left is the vast comic-book industry which employs thousands of writers, artists, engravers, and printers.

It has weaned hundreds of thousands of children from pictures to the printed word. It has stirred their imagination, given them an outlet for their problems and frustrations, but most important, given them millions of hours of entertainment.

My father before me was proud of the comics he published. My father saw in the comic book a vast field of visual education. He was a pioneer.

Sometimes he was ahead of his time. He published Picture Stories from Science, Picture Stories from World History, and Picture Stories from American History.

He published Picture Stories from the Bible.

I would like to offer these in evidence.

The CHAIRMAN. They will be received for the subcommittee's permanent files. Let that be exhibit No. 11.

(The documents referred to were marked "Exhibit No. 11," and are on file with the subcommittee.)

Mr. GAINES. Since 1942 we have sold more than 5 million copies of Picture Stories from the Bible, in the United States. It is widely used by churches and schools to make religion more real and vivid.

Picture Stories from the Bible is published throughout the world in dozens of translations. But it is nothing more nor nothing less than a comic magazine.

I publish comic magazines in addition to picture stories from the Bible. For example, I publish horror comics. I was the first publisher in these United States to publish horror comics. I am responsible, I started them.

Some may not like them. That is a matter of personal taste. It would be just as difficult to explain the harmless thrill of a horror story to a Dr. Wertham as it would be to explain the sublimity of love to a frigid old maid.

My father was proud of the comics he published, and I am proud of the comics I publish. We use the best writers, the finest artists; we spare nothing to make each magazine, each story, each page, a work of art.

As evidence of this, I might point out that we have the highest sales in individual distribution. I don't mean highest sales in comparison to comics of another type. I mean highest sales in comparison to other horror comics. The magazine is one of the few remaining—the comic magazine is one of the few remaining pleasures that a person may buy for a dime today. Pleasure is what we sell, entertainment, reading enjoyment. Entertaining reading has never harmed anyone. Men of good will, free men, should be very grateful for one sentence in the statement made by Federal Judge John M. Woolsey when he lifted the ban on Ulysses. Judge Woolsey said:

It is only with the normal person that the law is concerned.

May I repeat, he said, "It is only with the normal person that the law is concerned." Our American children are for the most part normal children. They are bright children, but those who want to prohibit comic magazines seem to see dirty, sneaky, perverted monsters who use the comics as a blueprint for action.

Perverted little monsters are few and far between. They don't read comics. The chances are most of them are in schools for retarded children.

What are we afraid of? Are we afraid of our own children? Do we forget that they are citizens, too, and entitled to select what to read or do? We think our children are so evil, simple minded, that it takes a story of murder to set them to murder, a story of robbery to set them to robbery?

Jimmy Walker once remarked that he never knew a girl to be ruined by a book. Nobody has ever been ruined by a comic.

As has already been pointed out by previous testimony, a little, healthy, normal child has never been made worse for reading comic magazines.

The basic personality of a child is established before he reaches the age of comic-book reading. I don't believe anything that has ever been written can make a child overaggressive or delinquent.

The roots of such characteristics are much deeper. The truth is that delinquency is the product of real environment in which the child lives and not of the fiction he reads.

There are many problems that reach our children today. They are tied up with insecurity. No pill can cure them. No law will legislate them out of being. The problems are economic and social and they are complex.

Our people need understanding; they need to have affection, decent homes, decent food.

Do the comics encourage delinquency? Dr. David Abrahamsen has written:

Comic books do not lead into crime, although they have been widely blamed for it. I find comic books many times helpful for children in that through them they can get rid of many of their aggressions and harmful fantasies. I can never remember having seen one boy or girl who has committed a crime or who became neurotic or psychotic because he or she read comic books.

The CHAIRMAN. Senator Kefauver.

Senator KEFAUVER. Is that Dr. David Abrahamsen?

Mr. GAINES. That is right, sir. I can give you the source on that, if you like. I will give it to you later.

The CHAIRMAN. You can supply that later.

(The source is as follows:)

Abrahamsen, Dr. David, Who Are the Guilty, New York: Rinehart & Co., Inc., page 279.

Mr. GAINES. I would like to discuss, if you bear with me a moment more, something which Dr. Wertham provoked me into. Dr. Wertham, I am happy to say, I have just caught in a half-truth, and I am very indignant about it. He said there is a magazine now on the stands preaching racial intolerance. The magazine he is referring to is my magazine. What he said, as much as he said, was true. There do appear in this magazine such materials as "Spik," "Dirty Mexican," but Dr. Wertham did not tell you what the plot of the story was.

This is one of a series of stories designed to show the evils of race prejudice and mob violence, in this case against Mexican Catholics.

Previous stories in this same magazine have dealt with antisemitism, and anti-Negro feelings, evils of dope addiction and development of juvenile delinquents.

This is one of the most brilliantly written stories that I have ever had the pleasure to publish. I was very proud of it, and to find it being used in such a nefarious way made me quite angry.

I am sure Dr. Wertham can read, and he must have read the story, to have counted what he said he counted.

I would like to read one more thing to you.

Senator Hennings asked Dr. Peck a question. I will be perfectly frank with you, I have forgotten what he asked him, but this is the answer because I made a notation as he went along.

No one has to read a comic book to read horror stories.

Anyone, any child, any adult, can find much more extreme descriptions of violence in the daily newspaper. You can find plenty of examples in today's newspaper. In today's edition of the Daily News, which more people will have access to than they will to any comic magazine, there are headline stories like this:

Finds he has killed wife with gun.
Man in Texas woke up to find he had killed his wife with gun. She had bullet in head and he had a revolver in his hand.

The next one:

Cop pleads in cocktail poisoning.
Twenty-year-old youth helps poison the mother and father of a friend.
Court orders young hanging. Man who killed his wife will be hung in June for his almost-perfect murder.

Let us look at today's edition of the Herald Tribune.

On the front page a criminal describes how another criminal told him about a murder he had done. In the same paper the story of a man whose ex-wife beat him on the head with a claw hammer and slashed him with a butcher knife.

In the same paper, story of a lawyer who killed himself.

In another, a story of that man who shot his wife while having a nightmare.

Another, a story of a gang who collected an arsenal of guns and knives. These are very many stories of violence and crime in the Herald Tribune today.

I am not saying it is wrong, but when you attack comics, when you talk about banning them as they do in some cities, you are only a step away from banning crimes in the newspapers.

Here is something interesting which I think most of us don't know. Crime news is being made in some places. The United Nations UNESCO report, which I believe is the only place that it is printed, shows that crime news is not permitted to appear in newspapers in Russia or Communist China, or other Communist-held territories.

We print our crime news. We don't think that the crime news or any news should be banned because it is bad for children.

Once you start to censor you must censor everything. You must censor comic books, radio, television, and newspapers.

Than you must censor what people may say. Then you will have turned this country into Spain or Russia.

Mr. BEASER. Mr. Gaines, let me ask you one thing with reference to Dr. Wertham's testimony.

You used the pages of your comic book to send across a message, in this case it was against racial prejudice; is that it?

Mr. GAINES. That is right.

Mr. BEASER. You think, therefore, you can get across a message to the kids through the medium of your magazine that would lessen racial prejudice; is that it?

Mr. GAINES. By specific effort and spelling it out very carefully so that the point won't be missed by any of the readers, and I regret to admit that it still is missed by some readers, as well as Dr. Wertham—we have, I think, achieved some degree of success in combating anti-Semitism, anti-Negro feeling, and so forth.

Mr. BEASER. Yet why do you say you cannot at the same time and in the same manner use the pages of your magazine to get a message which would affect children adversely, that is, to have an effect upon their doing these deeds of violence or sadism, whatever is depicted?

Mr. GAINES. Because no message is being given to them. In other words, when we write a story with a message, it is deliberately written in such a way that the message, as I say, is spelled out carefully in the captions. The preaching, if you want to call it, is spelled out carefully in the captions, plus the fact that our readers by this time know that in each issue of shock suspense stories, the second of the stories will be this type of story.

Mr. BEASER. A message can be gotten across without spelling out in that detail. For example, take this case that was presented this morning of the child who is in a foster home who became a werewolf, and foster parents—

Mr. GAINES. That was one of our stories.

Mr. BEASER. A child who killed her mother. Do you think that would have any effect at all on a child who is in a foster placement, who is with foster parents, who has fears? Do you not think that child in reading the story would have some of the normal fears which a child has, some of the normal desires tightened, increased?

Mr. GAINES. I honestly can say I don't think so. No message has been spelled out there. We were not trying to prove anything with that story. None of the captions said anything like "If you are unhappy with your stepmother, shoot her."

Mr. BEASER. No, but here you have a child who is in a foster home who has been treated very well, who has fears and doubts about the foster parent. The child would normally identify herself in this case with a child in a similar situation and there a child in a similar situation turns out to have foster parents who became werewolves.

Do you not think that would increase the child's anxiety?

Mr. GAINES. Most foster children, I am sure, are not in homes such as were described in those stories. Those were pretty miserable homes.

Mr. HANNOCH. You mean the houses that had vampires in them, those were not nice homes?

Mr. GAINES. Yes.

Mr. HANNOCH. Do you know any place where there is any such thing?

Mr. GAINES. As vampires?

Mr. HANNOCH. Yes.

Mr. GAINES. No sir; this is fantasy. The point I am trying to make is that I am sure no foster children are kept locked up in their room for months on end except in those rare cases that you hear about where there is something wrong with the parents such as the foster child in one of these stories was, and on the other hand, I am sure that no foster child finds himself with a drunken father and a mother who is having an affair with someone else.

Mr. BEASER. Yet you do hear of the fact that an awful lot of delinquency comes from homes that are broken. You hear of drunkenness in those same homes.

Do you not think those children who read those comics identify themselves with the poor home situation, with maybe the drunken father or mother who is going out, and identify themselves and see themselves portrayed there?

Mr. GAINES. It has been my experience in writing these stories for the last 6 or 7 years that whenever we have tested them out on kids, or teen-agers, or adults, no one ever associates himself with someone who is going to be put upon. They always associate themselves with the one who is doing the putting upon.

The CHAIRMAN. You do test them out on children, do you?

Mr. GAINES. Yes.

Mr. BEASER. How do you do that?

Senator HENNINGS. Is that one of your series, the pictures of the two in the electric chair, the little girl down in the corner?

Mr. GAINES. Yes.

Senator HENNINGS. As we understood from what we heard of that story, the little girl is not being put upon there, is she? She is triumphant apparently, that is insofar as we heard the relation of the story this morning.

Mr. GAINES. If I may explain, the reader does not know that until the last panel, which is one of the things we try to do in our stories, is have an O. Henry ending for each story.

Senator HENNINGS. I understood you to use the phrase "put upon," and that there was no reader identification—with one who was put upon, but the converse.

Mr. GAINES. That is right, sir.

Senator HENNINGS. Now, in that one, what would be your judgment or conclusion as to the identification of the reader with that little girl who has, to use the phrase, framed her mother and shot her father?

Mr. GAINES. In that story, if you read it from the beginning, because you can't pull things out of context —

Senator HENNINGS. That is right, you cannot do that.

Mr. GAINES. You will see that a child leads a miserable life in the 6 or 7 pages. It is only on the last page she emerges triumphant.

Senator HENNINGS. As a result of murder and perjury, she emerges as triumphant?

Mr. GAINES. That is right.

Mr. HANNOCH. Is that the O. Henry finish?

Mr. GAINES. Yes.

Mr. HANNOCH. In other words, everybody reading that would think this girl would go to jail. So the O. Henry finish changes that, makes her a wonderful looking girl?

Mr. GAINES. No one knows she did it until the last panel.

Mr. HANNOCH. You think it does them a lot of good to read these things?

Mr. GAINES. I don't think it does them a bit of good, but I don't think it does them a bit of harm, either.

The CHAIRMAN. What would be your procedure to test the story out on a child or children?

Mr. GAINES. I give them the story to read and I ask them if they enjoyed it, and if they guessed the ending. If they said they enjoyed it and didn't guess the ending, I figure it is a good story, entertaining.

The CHAIRMAN. What children do you use to make these tests with?

Mr. GAINES. Friends, relatives.

Senator HENNINGS. Do you have any children of your own, Mr. Gaines?

Mr. GAINES. No, sir.

Senator HENNINGS. Do you use any of the children of your own family, any nieces, nephews?

Mr. GAINES. My family has no children, but if they had, I would use them.

The CHAIRMAN. You do test them out on children of your friends, do you?

Mr. GAINES. Yes.

Mr. BEASER. Mr. Gaines, in your using tests, I don't think you are using it in the same way that we are here. You are not trying to test the effect on the child, you are trying to test the readability and whether it would sell?

Mr. GAINES. Certainly.

Mr. BEASER. That is a different kind of test than the possible effect on the child. Then you have not conducted any tests as to the effects of these upon children?

Mr. GAINES. No, sir.

Mr. BEASER. Were you here this morning when Dr. Peck testified?

Mr. GAINES. I was.

Mr. BEASER. Did you listen to his testimony as to the possible effect of these comics upon an emotionally maladjusted child?

Mr. GAINES. I heard it.

Mr. BEASER. You disagree with it?

Mr. GAINES. I disagree with it.

Frankly, I could have brought many, many quotes from psychiatrists and child-welfare experts and so forth pleading the cause of the comic magazine. I did not do so because I figured this would all be covered thoroughly before I got here. And it would just end up in a big melee of pitting experts against experts.

Mr. BEASER. Let me get the limits as far as what you put into your magazine. Is the sole test of what you would put into your magazine whether it sells? Is there any limit you can think of that you would not put in a magazine because you thought a child should not see or read about it?

Mr. GAINES. No, I wouldn't say that there is any limit for the reason you outlined. My only limits are bounds of good taste, what I consider good taste.

Mr. BEASER. Then you think a child cannot in any way, in any way, shape, or manner, be hurt by anything that a child reads or sees?

Mr. GAINES. I don't believe so.

Mr. BEASER. There would be no limit actually to what you put in the magazines?

Mr. GAINES. Only within the bounds of good taste.

Mr. BEASER. Your own good taste and salability?

Mr. GAINES. Yes.

Senator KEFAUVER. Here is your May 22 issue. This seems to be a man with a bloody ax holding a woman's head up which has been severed from her body. Do you think that is in good taste?

Mr. GAINES. Yes, sir; I do, for the cover of a horror comic. A cover in bad taste, for example, might be defined as holding the head a little higher so that the neck could be seen dripping blood from it and moving the body over a little further so that the neck of the body could be seen to be bloody.

Senator KEFAUVER. You have blood coming out of her mouth.

Mr. GAINES. A little.

Senator KEFAUVER. Here is blood on the ax. I think most adults are shocked by that.

The CHAIRMAN. Here is another one I want to show him.

Senator KEFAUVER. This is the July one. It seems to be a man with a woman in a boat and he is choking her to death here with a crowbar. Is that in good taste?

Mr. GAINES. I think so.

Mr. HANNOCH. How could it be worse?

Senator HENNINGS. Mr. Chairman, if counsel will bear with me, I don't think it is really the function of our committee to argue with this gentleman. I believe that he has given us about the sum and substance of his philosophy, but I would like to ask you one question, sir.

The CHAIRMAN. You may proceed.

Senator HENNINGS. You have indicated by what—I hope you will forgive me if I suggest—seems to be a bit of self-righteousness, that your motivation was bringing "enjoyment"—is that the word you used?

Mr. GAINES. Yes, sir.

Senator HENNINGS. To the readers of these publications. You do not mean to disassociate the profit motive entirely, do you?

Mr. GAINES. Certainly not.

Senator HENNINGS. Without asking you to delineate as between the two, we might say there is a combination of both, is there not?

Mr. GAINES. No question about it.

Senator HENNINGS. Is there anything else that you would like to say to us with respect to your business and the matters that we are inquiring into here?

Mr. GAINES. I don't believe so.

Senator KEFAUVER. I would like to ask 1 or 2 questions.

The CHAIRMAN. You may proceed, Senator.

Senator KEFAUVER. Mr. Gaines, I had heard that your father really did not have horror and crime comics. When he had the business he printed things that were really funny, and stories of the Bible, but you are the one that started out this crime and horror business.

Mr. GAINES. I did not start crime; I started horror.

Senator KEFAUVER. Who started crime?

Mr. GAINES. I really don't know.

Senator KEFAUVER. Anyway, you are the one who, after you took over your father's business in 1947, you started this sort of thing here. This is the May edition of Horror.

Mr. GAINES. I started what we call our new-trend magazines in 1950.

Senator KEFAUVER. How many of these things do you sell a month, Mr. Gaines?

Mr. GAINES. It varies. We have an advertising guaranty of 1,500,000 a month for our entire group.

Senator KEFAUVER. That is for all the Entertaining Comics, of which Shock is one of them? How do you distribute these, Mr. Gaines?

Mr. GAINES. I have a national distributor. There are roughly 10 individual national distributors which handle roughly half of the magazines. The other half is handled by American News.

The 1 of the 10 that I have is Leader News Co.

Senator KEFAUVER. That is a distributor. Then do they sell to wholesalers?

Mr. GAINES. They in turn sell to seven-hundred-odd wholesalers around the country.

Senator KEFAUVER. The wholesalers then pass it out to the retailers, the drug stores, and newsstands; is that right?

Mr. GAINES. That is right.

Senator KEFAUVER. They are all sold on a consignment basis?

Mr. GAINES. They are all returnable.

Senator KEFAUVER. So your magazines along with what other wholesaler may be handling, are taken in a package to the retailer and left there and he is supposed to put them on his stand and sell them?

Mr. GAINES. Yes.

Senator KEFAUVER. And if he does not sell them, or does not display them, then he is liable to get another retailer?

Mr. GAINES. No, we cover every retailer as far as I know.

Senator KEFAUVER. You don't like things to be put back and resold. You would like them to be sold.

Mr. GAINES. I would prefer it. Comics are so crowded today, I think there are some 500 titles, that it is impossible for any retailer to give all 500 different places.

Senator KEFAUVER. I notice in this edition of May 14 the one in which you have the greasy Mexican the first page has apparently two shootings going on at the same time here, then on the next page is an advertisement for young people to send a dollar in and get the Panic for the next 8 issues. Is that not right?

Mr. GAINES. That is right.

Senator KEFAUVER. This says the editors of Panic, 225 Lafayette Street. That is you?

Mr. GAINES. That is right.

Senator KEFAUVER. Then the attraction here is "I dreamed I went to a fraternity smoker in my Panic magazine," you have dice on the floor and cigarettes, somebody getting beer out, somebody laying on his back taking a drink. Do you think that is all right?

Mr. GAINES. This is an advertisement for one of my lampoon magazines. This is a lampoon of the Maiden-Form brassiere ad, I dreamed I went to so-and-so in my Maiden-Form brassiere, which has appeared in the last 6 years in national family magazines showing girls leaping through the air in brassieres and panties.

We simply lampoon by saying "I dreamed I went to a panic smoker in my Panic magazine."

Senator KEFAUVER. I mean, do you like to portray a fraternity smoker like that?

Mr. GAINES. This is a lampoon magazine. We make fun of things.

The CHAIRMAN. You think that is in good taste?

Mr. GAINES. Yes, sir.

Senator KEFAUVER. I have looked through these stories. Every one of them seems to end with murder, practically. I have looked through this one where they have the greasy Mexican and the Puerto Rican business. I can't find any moral of better race relations in it, but I think that ought to be filed so that we can study it and see and take into consideration what Mr. Gaines has said.

The CHAIRMAN. Mr. Gaines, you have no objection to having this made a part of our permanent files, have you?

Mr. GAINES. No, sir.

The CHAIRMAN. Then, without objection, it will be so ordered. Let it be exhibit No. 12.

(The magazine referred to was marked "Exhibit No. 12," and is on file with the subcommittee.)

Senator KEFAUVER. Is Mr. Gaines a member of the association that we talked about here this morning?

Mr. GAINES. No longer. I was a member for about 2 or 3 years and I resigned about 2 or 3 years ago.

Senator KEFAUVER. How did you happen to resign, Mr. Gaines?

Mr. GAINES. Principally for financial reasons.

Senator KEFAUVER. It only has $15,000 a year for the whole operation?

Mr. GAINES. At that time my share would have been $2,000. At that time, also, about 10 percent of the publishers were represented. I was a charter member of the association. I stuck with it for 2 or 3 years.

The theory was that we were going to get all the publishers into it and then the burden of financial—

Senator KEFAUVER. Did you have any argument about censorship, about this gentleman, Mr. Schultz, who was here, not liking the kind of things you were publishing?

Mr. GAINES. No sir. Mr. Schultz and I frequently had disagreements which we would iron out and I would make the changes he required until I decided to resign.

The CHAIRMAN. Did you have any part, Mr. Gaines, in preparing that code?

Mr. GAINES. No, the code was prepared by, I believe, the first board of directors of the association. I was on the board of directors later on, but not at first.

The CHAIRMAN. Did you subscribe to the code?

Mr. GAINES. Yes, sir.

The CHAIRMAN. Did you think that publishing a magazine like this for example would still be within the code?

Mr. GAINES. No, sir.

Senator KEFAUVER. You admit none of this would come within that code?

Mr. GAINES. Certain portions of the code I have retained. Certain portions of the code I have not retained. I don't agree with the code in all points.

Senator KEFAUVER. The code that you have here, none of your stories would come in that code. You could not print any of these if you complied with the full code we read here this morning.

Mr. GAINES. I would have to study the story and study the code to answer that.

Senator KEFAUVER. How much is your monthly income from all your corporations with this thing, Mr. Gaines?

Mr. GAINES. You mean by that, my salary?

Senator KEFAUVER. No. How much do you take in a month from your publications?

Mr. GAINES. I wouldn't know monthly. We figure it annually.

Senator KEFAUVER. Let us say gross.

Mr. GAINES. I don't know.

Senator KEFAUVER. What is your best estimate annually?

Mr. GAINES. I would say about $80,000 a month gross.

Senator KEFAUVER. How many books did you say you printed a month?

Mr. GAINES. A million and a half guaranteed sale. We print about two, two and a half million.

Senator KEFAUVER. How much net do you make a month out of it, that is, the corporations?

Mr. GAINES. Last year it came to about $4,000 a month.

Senator KEFAUVER. Do you have several corporations, Mr. Gaines?

Mr. GAINES. Yes, sir,

Senator KEFAUVER. How many corporations do you have?

Mr. GAINES. I have five.

Senator KEFAUVER. Why do you have five corporations?

Mr. GAINES. Well, I don't really know. I inherited stock in five corporations which were formed by my father before his death. In those days he started a corporation, I believe, for every magazine. I have not adhered to that.

I have just kept the original five and published about two magazines in each corporation.

Senator KEFAUVER. Do you not think the trouble might have been if one magazine got in trouble that corporation would not adversely affect the others?

Mr. GAINES. Oh, hardly.

Senator KEFAUVER. You did get one magazine banned by the attorney general of Massachusetts, did you not?

Mr. GAINES. The attorney general of Massachusetts reneged and claims he has not banned it. I still don't know what the story was.

Senator KEFAUVER. Anyway, he said he was going to prosecute you if you sent that magazine over there any more.

Mr. GAINES. He thereafter, I understand, said he never said he would prosecute.

Senator KEFAUVER. That is the word you got through, that he was going to prosecute you?

Mr. GAINES. Yes.

Senator KEFAUVER. When was that?

Mr. GAINES. Just before Christmas.

Senator KEFAUVER. Which magazine was that?

Mr. GAINES. That was for Panic No. 1.

Senator KEFAUVER. Just one other question. There is some association that goes over these things. Do you make any contribution to the memberships of any associations?

Mr. GAINES. No.

Senator KEFAUVER. Any committee that supervises the industry?

Mr. GAINES. No. There is no such committee or organization aside from the Association of Comic Magazine Publishers.

Senator KEFAUVER. You said you had a guaranteed sale of a million and a half per month.

Mr. GAINES. We guarantee the advertisers that much.

Senator KEFAUVER. So that you do have some interest in seeing that the distributor and wholesaler and retailer get your magazines out because you guarantee the advertisers a million and a half sales a month?

Mr. GAINES. I have a very definite interest. Unfortunately, I don't have a thing to do with it.

Senator KEFAUVER. Thank you, Mr. Chairman.

Mr. HANNOCH. Could I ask one or two questions?

The CHAIRMAN. Mr. Hannoch.

Mr. HANNOCH. What is this organization that you maintain called the Fan and Addict Club for 25 cents a member?

Mr. GAINES. Simply a comic fan club.

Mr. HANNOCH. You advertise the children should join the club?

Mr. GAINES. Yes.

Mr. HANNOCH. What do they do? Do they pay dues?

Mr. GAINES. No.

Mr. HANNOCH. What do they send 25 cents in for?

Mr. GAINES. They get an arm patch, an antique bronze pin, a 7 by 11 certificate and a pocket card, the cost of which to me is 26 cents without mailing.

Mr. HANNOCH. After you get a list of all these kids and their families and addresses, what do you do with the list?

Mr. GAINES. I get out what we call fan and addict club bulletins. The last bulletin was principally made up of names and addresses of members who had back issues they wanted to trade with other members.

Mr. HANNOCH. Did anybody buy that list from you and use it?

Mr. GAINES. No, sir; I have never sold it.

Mr. HANNOCH. Do you know anything about this sheet called, "Are you a Red dupe?"

Mr. GAINES. Yes, sir; I wrote it.

Mr. HANNOCH. How has it been distributed?

Mr. GAINES. It has not been distributed. It is going to be the inside front cover ad on five of my comic magazines which are forthcoming.

Mr. HANNOCH. And it is going to be an advertisement?

Mr. GAINES. Not an advertisement. It is an editorial.

Mr. HANNOCH. Do other magazines have copies of this to be used for the same purpose?

Mr. GAINES. No, sir.

Mr. HANNOCH. You haven't made this available to the magazines as yet?

Mr. GAINES. No, sir; and I don't intend to.

Mr. HANNOCH. You believe the things that you say in this ad that you wrote?

Mr. GAINES. Yes, sir.

Mr. HANNOCH. That anybody who is anxious to destroy comics are Communists?

Mr. GAINES. I don't believe it says that.

Mr. HANNOCH. The group most anxious to destroy comics are the Communists?

Mr. GAINES. True, but not anybody, just the group most anxious.

The CHAIRMAN. Are there any other questions?

Mr. HANNOCH. No.

Mr. BEASER. I have some questions.

The CHAIRMAN. Mr. Beaser.

Mr. BEASER. Just to settle the point which came up before, Mr. Gaines, who is it that gets the idea for this, for one of your stories, you, your editor, the artist, the writer? Where does it come from?

Mr. GAINES. Principally from my editors and myself.

Mr. BEASER. Not from the artists?

Mr. GAINES. No.

Mr. BEASER. He just does what he is told?

Mr. GAINES. He just followed the story and illustrates it.

Mr. BEASER. He is told what to do and how to illustrate it?

Mr. GAINES. No, our artists are superior artists. They don't have to be given detailed descriptions.

Mr. BEASER. He has to be told what it is?

Mr. GAINES. It is lettered in before he draws it.

Mr. BEASER. He knows the story pretty much, so he knows what he can fit in?

Mr. GAINES. Yes.

Mr. BEASER. You said that you had a circulation of 5 million Bible storybooks.

Mr. GAINES. Yes.

Mr. BEASER. How many years is this?

Mr. GAINES. Twelve years, since 1942.

Mr. BEASER. In other words, in little over 3-1/2 months you sell more of your crime and horror than you sell of the Bible stories?

Mr. GAINES. Quite a bit more.

Mr. BEASER. They seem to go better?

Mr. GAINES. This is a 65-cent book. The crime-and-horror book is a 10-cent book. There is a difference.

Mr. BEASER. No further questions, Mr. Chairman.

The CHAIRMAN. Thank you very much, Mr. Gaines.

Mr. GAINES. Thank you, sir.

The CHAIRMAN. Will counsel call the next witness?

Mr. BEASER. Mr. Walt Kelly.

The CHAIRMAN. Mr. Kelly, do you have some associates?

Mr. KELLY. I have, sir.

The CHAIRMAN. Do you want them to come up and sit with you?

Mr. KELLY. I think I would enjoy the company.

The CHAIRMAN. Fine. We would enjoy having them up here. I will swear you all at one time.

Do you solemnly swear that the testimony you will give to this subcommittee of the Committee on the Judiciary of the United States Senate, will be the truth, the whole truth, and nothing but the truth, so help you God?

Mr. KELLY. I do.

Mr. Caniff. I do.

Mr. Musial. I do.

TESTIMONY OF WALT KELLY, ARTIST, CREATOR OF POGO, AND PRESIDENT, NATIONAL CARTOONISTS SOCIETY, NEW YORK, N.Y.; MILTON CANIFF, ARTIST, CREATOR OF STEVE CANYON, NEW YORK, N.Y.; AND JOSEPH MUSIAL, EDUCATIONAL DIRECTOR, NATIONAL CARTOONISTS SOCIETY, NEW YORK, N.Y.

Mr. Hannoch. Will you give your name, sir?

Mr. Kelly. Walt Kelly, 2 Fifth Avenue, artist, drawer of Pogo, New York City.

Mr. Beaser. Have you a title, Mr. Kelly, in the association?

Mr. Kelly. I am the president of the National Cartoonists Society. I forgot about that. I just took office last night.

Mr. Caniff. Milton Caniff, New York City, N.Y. I draw Steve Canyon for Chicago Sun-Times Syndicate, and King Features Syndicate.

Mr. Musial. Joseph Musial. I am educational director for the King Features Syndicate. I am director for King Features Syndicate and educational director for the Cartoonists Society.

I live in Manhasset, Long Island, N.Y.

The Chairman. Thank you very much, gentlemen, you may be seated.

Mr. Counsel?

Mr. Beaser. You have a set method that you want to proceed in?

Mr. Kelly. We thought we would do a little commercial work here and show you some of the ways we proceed in our business.

However, before we get into that, I just want to take a moment to acquaint you in some degree at least with my own experience and I think it might be of use or value if the other gentleman would give you somewhat of their background.

The Chairman. I am sure it would be very helpful.

Mr. Kelly. I have been in the newspaper business and animated cartoons and cartooning generally since about 13 years of age. I regret to say that constitutes about 28 years now.

I got into the comic-book business at one time back in 1940 or 1941 and had some experience with its early days as before the 1947 debacle of so many crime magazines and so on.

In those days there was even then a taste on the part of children for things which are a little more rugged than what I drew. So that I was faced with the problem of putting into book form, into comic form, comic-book form, things which I desired to make popular, such as an American fairy story or American folklore type of stories.

I found after a while that this was not particularly acceptable.

The Chairman. Would you raise your voice just a little.

Mr. Kelly. I decided I would help clean up the comic-book business at one time, by introducing new features, such as folklore stories and things having to do with little boys and little animals in red and blue pants and that sort of thing.

So when my comic book folded, the one I started doing that with, I realized there was more to it than met the eye.

Perhaps this was the wrong medium for my particular efforts. Since then I have been in the strip business, the comic-strip business which is distinguished from the comic books.

We have found in our business that our techniques are very effective for bringing about certain moral lessons and giving information and making education more widespread.

Despite the testimony given before, I would say right offhand that cartoonists are not forced by editors or publishers to draw any certain way. If they don't want to draw the way the publisher or editor wants them to, they can get out of that business.

We have about 300 members of our society, each one of whom is very proud of the traditions and I think small nobility of our craft. We would hesitate, any one of us, to draw anything we would not bring into our home.

Not only hesitate, I don't think any one of us would do it. That is about all I have to say in that regard.

I would like very much to give one statement. May I do that now?

The CHAIRMAN. You may.

Mr. KELLY. This group here endorses a particular statement by the National Cartoonists Society. That statement is this:

The National Cartoonists Society views as unwarranted any additional legislative action that is intended to censor printed material. The society believes in local option. We believe that offensive material of any nature can be weeded from the mass of worthwhile publications by the exercise of existing city, State, and Federal laws.

Further, we believe that the National Cartoonists Society constitutes a leadership in the cartoon field which has previously established popular trends. We therefore will restrict any action we take to continually improving our own material and thus influencing the coattail riders who follow any successful idea.

We believe good material outsells bad. We believe people, even juveniles, are fundamentally decent. We believe, as parents and as onetime children ourselves, that most young people are instinctively attracted to that which is wholesome.

Our belief in this sound commercial theory is only in addition to our belief in free expression and the noble traditions of our profession. Our history abounds in stalwarts of pen and pencil who have fought for freedom for others. For ourselves as artists and free Americans we too cherish freedom and the resultant growth of ideas. We cannot submit to the curb, the fence, or the intimidating word. The United States of America must remain a land where the Govoernment follows the man.

Mr. BEASER. You are not saying that it is not possible to put into comics, crime comics and horror comics, what we have been talking about, things that might have some harmful effect?

Mr. KELLY. I think it is even entirely possible, sir. I think it is the duty of the creator of the material to see that this sort of thing does not get in there.

The creator, apart from the producer or the publisher, is personally responsible for his work.

I somewhat question the good doctor's statement before when he said in response to your question, sir, that perhaps the originators of this material might be under scrutiny, should be, as to their psychiatric situation.

We in the cartoon business sort of cherish the idea that we are all sort of screwball. We resent the implication that any man putting out that kind of stuff is not a screwball. That is another thing we fight for.

Senator HENNINGS. I would like to say to Mr. Kelly that I think your statement is admirable. I am a frustrated cartoonist myself. I wanted to be one when I was a boy and I got off the track. I have noticed the chairman of our committee doing a good deal of sketching during some of the hearings. He is really a very fine artist.

Without asking you to be invidious or to pass upon any thing ad hominem here with respect to any other publication, is it your opinion that there are certain publications being circulated and calculated to appeal to children in their formative years, their immature years, and from your understanding of the profession—and I call it one because it is; your strip is clean and enlightening as is Mr. Caniff's; the very best in the business—do you not deplore, do you gentlemen not deplore some of these things that you see purveyed to the children and in a sense pandering to the taste, or do you think those things will right themselves? Do you think sooner or later that the harm, if such exists, is outweighed by a good many other things?

Mr. KELLY. I think basically that is our position; yes, sir.

Senator HENNINGS. You realize, of course, the great danger of censorship?

Mr. KELLY. I realize, too, sir, the great danger of the magazines in question.

Senator HENNINGS. So it is a rough problem; is it not?

Mr. KELLY. We are put in a rather unpleasant position.

We don't like to be put in a position to defend what we will defend to the last breath.

The CHAIRMAN. Mr. Caniff do you feel the same way?

Mr. CANIFF. Yes, sir; but if I may, I would like to point out here because it has not been done, we first of all represent the newspaper strip as contrasted with the comic book. It is a fact, of course, as you all well know, that the newspaper strip is not only censored by each editor who buys it, precensors it, which is his right, but by the syndicate's own editors, who are many, and highly critical, and then this censorship includes the readers themselves, who are in a position to take the editor to task for printing your material and they are quick to respond.

So we are never in doubt as to our status. There will never be any question after the fact. You almost know by the time it hits the street whether or not your material is acceptable to the reader.

So we are in this white-hot fight of public judgment, which is as it should be.

For instance, Walt's strip runs in 400 newspapers. Mine in 350, Blondie in 1,300 out of the 1,500 dailies. That means we have a daily circulation of 55 or 75 million. So that we are in front of the pack all the time and highly vulnerable, as a result.

I bring this in here because I think it is germane on this principle alone, that we also have comic books publishing our material so that we are in this field as well.

It is pointed toward perhaps a little audience in the simple sense that we hope to sell to the daily audience that reads the 10-cent book.

But we are in effect as responsible as well. Insofar as deploring individual books, that is a matter of individual taste. Some books I like which you wouldn't like. I can't say blanketly, for instance, that I dislike all crime comics or I think they are bad. I think they are only good or bad as they affect you, the individual, and by the same token the individual reader of any age group is affected relatively rather than as a group and cannot be condemned I believe, as a group.

The CHAIRMAN. That is a very fine statement.

Mr. CANIFF. Thank you very much. Would you like to add anything, Mr. Musial?

Mr. MUSIAL. I am supposed to be educational director. I can see I have to give my job over to Mr. Caniff. He presented my thoughts better than I could.

I would like to say, I think cartoons are of a sort and instead of making a speech at this particular time I brought in an editorial drawing which I made, which I think germane to the situation. I would like to place this on the board, with your permission.

The CHAIRMAN. Would you please do that.

Mr. KELLY. Mr. Chairman, we would appreciate very much showing you a few of the things that we have been doing, one of which is a series of talks that I personally have been giving before journalism students, newspaper groups, luncheon clubs, and other respectable bodies and people in search of some sort of education, trying to point out what is the basis of the philosophical workings of the comic strip.

I think I can use my own strip as an example, and you can see what thought goes into what we do and how we do it.

[Demonstrating.] In the first place, in every one of our strips we have a central character around whom we base most of our plotting and action.

In my case it happens to be a character who is supposed to look like a possum, in effect; he is a possum by trade, but he doesn't really work at it because actually he happens to be related to most of the people that read comic strips.

Now, he looks a little bit like a monster. This little character actually looks a little bit like a monster.

On the other hand, he is supposed to be a possum and he had this turned-up, dirty nose and a rather innocent expression on his face which is indicative of a little boy because we usually have more readers that are little boys than are possums.

With this innocent, sweet character are a number of rather disreputable characters. The reason I bring up most of these is that each one represents a certain facet of one man's personality, unfortunately mine.

Here is an alligator who at one time worked as a political expert for Pogo. Pogo ran for the Presidency of the United States, and, of course, didn't make it. Now, he, we thought, would make an excellent political type because he has a sort of thick alligator skin and some say a head to match, and so on. He is the sort of character that stands around street corners and smokes cigars.

Along with that character are several other unfortunate people who got into the swamp. One is a dog who is very proud of being a dog. Of course, those of you who have been dogs in your time understand his position in that.

Senator KEFAUVER. You are not talking about a doghouse, now?

Mr. KELLY. No, I am staying away from that. This particular dog is the kind of dog who feels that he knows all the answers and has a great deal of respect for his own judgment and we all know people like that.

One other character who is probably pertinent to the kind of work I try to do is a little character known as the porcupine. Now, this character is a very grumpy sort of character. He looks like most of us do when we get up in the morning. He has generally a sort of sour-faced kind of philosophy. It is a long time after lunch and I am drawing these from the side, so they may have a sort of lean to them.

He is very sour about everything, but he says, "You never should take life very seriously because it ain't permanent." These are the sources of things that go into comic strips.

When I talk before journalism people I try to tell them these are various facets of one man's personality, mine, yours, that everyone has in him the ability to be all of the cruel, unkind, unpleasant, wonderful and pitiful people that exist in the world.

That is my message to young journalism students, because they are in search of the truth. They sometimes fight it and sometimes are able to report on it.

For myself, I have never received any intimidation nor have I been dropped by editor or publisher for anything I wanted to say.

All I have ever been dropped for is because I was lousy.

This character here, for example, is known as the deacon. He is one of those busybodies who assumes that everything he has to say is of such importance that I have to letter his script in a gothic type, which is sometimes readable and sometimes not. I assure you when you can't read it, it is not because I am hiding anything; it is because I can't letter very well.

That man is willing to prescribe for everyone and whatever he believes in very firmly, having borrowed it from someone else. He is out to do you good whether it kills you or not. That is not his concern.

Then every cartoonist being somewhat dishonest—cartoonists are very much like people—we sometimes introduce into our strips things which we hope will be cute and will get the ladies to write in and say "Ah." This is a little puppy dog who shows up every once in a while, and the ladies do write in and think he is very cute.

I won't continue with this because we will run out of paper. Milt won't have any room.

But I would like to just say that in delivering a serious lecture, one which involves trying to make these young people feel that it is possible in our newspapers as they exist today to express themselves, that we still have a great heritage of freedom in our press, one which we want to keep, one which if you are good enough you can make daily use of.

Young people are somewhat intimidated before they become actual journalists so that they are a little frightened. They think that publishers and editors are going to bring great pressure to bear on them; they are not going to be able to say what they would like to say, so a word coming from a silly cartoonist on the outside, a man who has grown at least to the point where he can buy his own cigars, they are refreshed by this sort of experience.

We find as cartoonists that using our simple techniques of making drawings and making statements that the two somehow become entwined, the people are willing to listen because we are making pictures largely, but willing to listen also because we do have, I believe, a great tradition of trying to express the truth in a decent and sometimes, we hope, humorous way.

We believe that this is the way of America. We think it will continue.

I am sure you gentlemen are as much concerned with it as I. I know that is why we are here.

The CHAIRMAN. Speaking as one member of the committee, Mr. Kelly, I can say that you cartoonists do make a great contribution to this country.

Mr. KELLY. Thank you, sir.

The CHAIRMAN. I am sure my colleagues will agree with that statement.

Mr. KELLY. I would like to add one thing to probably clear up what I was doing here. It probably escaped a lot of us. It escaped me.

I was trying to show here the different facets of personality. It is my belief that each one of us contains all these horrible things which we sometimes see in crime books, not in any enlarged form, but way back in there are things. That is why I try to bring out and Milt tries to bring out and 300 other cartoonists in our society try to bring out other things which are much better than that. We believe as people read comic strips they will get to realize that all other people are very much like ourselves and that they will be rather patient and understanding in trying to judge their fellow men.

The CHAIRMAN. Thank you very much, Mr. Kelly. That is a fine presentation.

Mr. CANIFF. Mr. Chairman, I would like to follow with this: As you can see, we are attempting not to debate with Dr. Wertham, whose opinion we value very highly, but rather to make this point, that the newspaper comic strip does two things, and we think this is extremely important.

First, it is to entertain, as you saw in the case of Walt's presentation, just the presentation is entertaining, aside from his message.

Second, the public servant aspect of this thing which we want to put on the record, because the horrible stuff is much more fascinating than the good stuff, but I think you agree with us that the good stuff should be on the record, too.

Many of these are simply incidents in our daily lives, because we spend almost as much time doing the public service kind of thing as our regular strips; in fact, it becomes an enormous problem.

In this instance you will see, for instance, Mr. Musial here with Governor Dewey during a New York State Department of Health mental hygiene campaign to which he gave a great amount of time, and other artists involved in the society as well.

This is Dagwood Splits the Atom, which was prepared with the scientific views of Leslie Grove, General Dunning, and so forth.

This has to do with the bond sale during the war, the use of the comic strips.

This is a bulletin, rather a booklet, which was prepared for boys who are sent to Warwick School, to the New York State Reformatory.

This is to tell them not how to get in the reformatory, but how to get out of it on the assumption they have read comic books.

This is to show if they conduct themselves properly they will get paroled back to their parents.

This obviously is to get kids to brush their teeth, using Dennis the Menace; of course he is not a menace; the title is apocryphal. These are simply incidents of the same thing.

All the people know the Disney comics. The widest selling comic book in the whole country and in Canada is Donald Duck. It outsells every magazine on the stand; that includes Life, the Saturday Evening Post.

As a matter of fact, the Dell comic books constitute 30 percent of the comic books published. They think it is too much that they even dropped Dick Tracy because it was a crime comic.

These pictures with General Dunning, General Eisenhower, President Truman had to do with the bond campaigns in which we participated. This is in this case Steve Canyon's Air Power. It so happens, speaking of people condoning comic books or endorsing them, this is endorsed by General Doolittle.

The CHAIRMAN. I might add it is endorsed by the junior Senator from New Jersey, too.

Mr. CANIFF. Thank you, Senator. I hope just for the simple business of letting you know how the other half live, shall we say, that we will do some good with the very medium which is fighting for its life, if you will, and we think very highly of the industry as such, because of its enormous potential.

Thank you.

The CHAIRMAN. Thank you very much, Mr. Caniff.

Are there any questions, Senator Kefauver?

Senator KEFAUVER. I wondered, Mr. Kelly and Mr. Caniff, how do you feel you can get at this sort of thing? I know you don't think this is a good influence, some of these horror comics that you see and none of us like. How do you get at a situation like this?

Mr. KELLY. I don't know. I have no idea, sir. My personal philosophy on such a thing would be that we must educate people to not like that sort of thing or to at least not produce it.

How we can do that, I don't know. It does seem to me that this is a manifestation of a particularly bad world situation at this time, that these are not in themselves the originators of juvenile delinquency so much as juvenile delinquency is there and sometimes these are the juvenile delinquents' handbooks.

I would be frightened at doing anything about it, sir.

Senator KEFAUVER. Who are the men drawing these cartoons? Are they members of your society?

Mr. KELLY. If they are, and doing it under assumed names, and in very bad style—they are not very good drawings actually—when a man is admitted to our society we don't just assume he can draw.

Senator KEFAUVER. As a member of your society, is there a code that he is not supposed to draw obscene and horror stuff of this kind?

Mr. KELLY. Yes, sir; our statement of things that we believe in encompasses anything that a decent man would be proud to sign his name to.

The CHAIRMAN. You have an established code, Mr. Kelly?

Mr. KELLY. We have, sir.

The CHAIRMAN. I wonder if we could have a copy of that.

Mr. KELLY. I will be delighted to send it to you.

The CHAIRMAN. That will be filed with the subcommittee's permanent file. Let it be exhibit No. 13.

(The document referred to was marked "Exhibit No. 13," and is on file with the subcommittee.)

Senator KEFAUVER. In substance what is your code?

Mr. KELLY. In substance our code is that if any man chooses to take advantage of his position, a unique position, where he has learned to draw and so influence other people, if he wants to take advantage of that to spread indecency or obscenity or in any way prove himself to be an objectionable citizen, we don't have room for him in the society.

Senator KEFAUVER. Now, this picture here of the woman with her head cut off seems to be by Johnny Craig. Do you know him?

Mr. KELLY. I don't know him, sir.

Senator KEFAUVER. Do you think these may be assumed names?

Mr. KELLY. I would doubt it. There are so many markets for our work that it takes a man who is interested in that sort of thing to pick up the job, I would say. None of our members need the work.

Senator KEFAUVER. None of your members do things of this kind?

Mr. KELLY. I haven't examined all their work, and I can't truthfully swear they don't, but I will be surprised and we will take action if they do.

Senator KEFAUVER. What would you do if you found they did?

Mr. KELLY. They would violate our code.

Senator KEFAUVER. What would you do about it?

Mr. KELLY. I don't know. Maybe invite them outside.

Senator KEFAUVER. This one seems to be by Geans.

Mr. KELLY. There was an astronomer—not, it couldn't be him.

Senator KEFAUVER. Here is another one by Jack Davis.

Mr. KELLY. We don't know them, really.

Senator KEFAUVER. I think we all commend you gentlemen on having an organization of this kind in which you do promote ethical procedure and try to get your members to only paint wholesome pictures and ideas.

Mr. KELLY. Thank you.

The CHAIRMAN. Mr. Musial had something he wanted to add.

Mr. MUSIAL. I wanted to present all the Senators with a copy of that drawing which interprets my feeling about what can be done. When the Senator asked about what we can do, I think the important thing that can be done and must be done and the only thing that can be done, is that once the American public is aware of the things that this committee is aware of, if we can get that over to the American people, then under our kind of democracy I think action will follow in a certain direction which will guarantee results.

I hate to say this, but I suggest that the committee solicit our services.

The CHAIRMAN. We do that.

Mr. MUSIAL. Here is a story in the New York Times of last Saturday. We have already contributed a book. I would like that included in the record, if I may.

The CHAIRMAN. It will be included. Let it be exhibit No. 14.

(The information referred to was marked "Exhibit No. 14," and reads as follows:)

EXHIBIT NO. 14

(From the New York Times, April 17, 1954)

COMIC BOOKS HELP CURB DELINQUENCY

STATE SCHOOL ADOPTS IDEA TO ALLAY INMATES' FEARS—JUDGE BACKS USE

(By Murray Illson)

Comic books, often accused of causing juvenile delinquency, also can be used to help cure it, in the opinion of A. Alfred Cohen, superintendent of the State Training School for Boys at Warwick, N.Y.

Mr. Cohen was in the city yesterday with a batch of comic books that had been printed by youths committed to the institution. The books have been endorsed by John Warren Hill, presiding justice of the domestic relations court. He called them "a very helpful and constructive step."

Justice Hill has been concerned with the increase of juvenile delinquency over the years, and has made many speeches trying to get people aroused enough to do something about it.

STORY OF THE SCHOOL

The comic books that Mr. Cohen had were all alike. He presented one for inspection. It was drawn by Charles Biro, chairman of the child welfare committee of the National Cartoonists Society, which has taken a special interest in the Warwick State Training School. The book's 8 pages, printed in color, told the story of the school.

Mr. Cohen explained that the purpose of the book was to allay the fears of boys who were being committed to the school, which is in Orange County, 55 miles from New York. Probation officers in the city's children's courts, which are part of the domestic relations' court, give the books to boys who are being sent to Warwick for rehabilitation.

Warwick, Mr. Cohen noted, is 1 of the State's 2 institutions for delinquent boys. Consisting of 40 buildings and 800 acres, it now has 476 boys between the ages of 12 and 16. Ninety-nine percent of them are from New York. Sixty youngsters are in the city's detention center at Youth House, awaiting placement at Warwick.

"We get the boys who are judged by the courts to be seriously delinquent," Mr. Cohen explained. "We maintain a clinic serviced by a psychiatrist, a psychologist and caseworkers who decide when a boy is ready to be sent home. The superintendent, however, has the final decision. The average stay for younger boys is about 14 months; for the older boys it's about 11 months."

Mr. Cohen said that when he went to Warwick 9 years ago the school was getting "the gang-type youngster" who was characterized by loyalty to a gang but who was, for the most part, "normal" in that he did not have serious emotional disturbances.

TODAY'S TYPE DESCRIBED

The type now going to Warwick was described by Mr. Cohen as the "lone wolf, who is very disturbed, very suspicious, can't form relationships with people, feels the world is against him, has never known the meaning of love, and has only experienced failure." He went on to say:

"Many of these kids literally have never had a hot meal before they came to Warwick, never had a full night's sleep and have known only real conflict in the home. The amazing thing is that they behave as well as they do.

"I have never met a youngster among the 8,000 who have passed through Warwick in the time I have been there who hadn't been beaten physically by experts—drunken parents, psychotic parents, or sadistic relatives. We know from first hand that the woodshed doesn't work."

Warwick, Mr. Cohen said, is an "open institution" that does not believe in confinement. It offers boys an academic education, vocational training in farming, and various recreational activities."

Comparatively recently, five boys at the institution were admitted to the local high school, Mr. Cohen said. All completed their courses. One went on to take a premedical course, and another won a college scholarship.

Mr. MUSIAL. I got a big kick out of it, the New York Times printing comics. If any of the press want this, it is available.

Again, like the Chinese who say 1 picture is worth 10,000 words, I would like to add this to it, 1 comic artist supplies more cheer than 10,000 doctors.

The CHAIRMAN. Thank you very much, Mr. Musial.

Does counsel have any further witnesses?

Mr. BEASER. No further witnesses.

The CHAIRMAN. The subcommittee will stand in recess until 10 o'clock tomorrow morning.

(Thereupon, at 4:30 p.m., a recess was taken, to reconvene at 10 a.m., Thursday, April 22, 1954.)

* * * * * * * *

(The subcommittee reconvened at 2:30 p.m., upon the expiration of the recess.)

The CHAIRMAN. This session of the subcommittee will be in order.

The subcommittee is highly honored today by the presence of a distinguished member of the Canadian Parliament, Mr. Fulton.

Mr. Fulton has had considerable experience with the problem which presently confronts the committee. If Mr. Fulton will come forward, we would like to hear the story as you have experienced it in your great country and our great neighbor, Canada.

You may be seated, Mr. Fulton.

I am going to depart from our usual procedure here in your case. We have been swearing witnesses, but we are not going to swear a member of the Canadian Parliament. You are one of us.

STATEMENT OF HON. E. D. FULTON, MEMBER, HOUSE OF COMMONS, CANADA

Mr. FULTON. I appreciate that very much.

Perhaps for the introductory words, I might stand, because I think it would be appropriate while I express on my behalf the feeling of deep appreciation I have for the honor of this invitation. I hope that my presentation may be of some assistance to you as indicating the course which your neighbor, Canada, followed in attempting to deal with this problem.

As a problem of concern in equal measure to both our countries, I assure you that although I am not a member of the government in Canada, I am quite certain that I speak for all our representatives in Parliament and for Canada as a whole when I say that they appreciate the honor of the invitation and the opportunity to come down and discuss with you these problems of such great mutual concern.

I think it is proper to suggest that this is one more example of the friendship and good neighborliness between our two countries.

I want to express to you, sir, and your colleagues on this subcommittee, my appreciation for the honor of this invitation and the opportunity to come here.

The CHAIRMAN. Thank you. We are grateful to you and grateful to Canada.

Now, Mr. Fulton, you may proceed to present your case in whatever manner you choose and think best.

Mr. FULTON. Mr. Chairman, I have first, two apologies to make. I was late this morning, owing to weather conditions over the airport here. I trust that my delay did not inconvenience your proceedings.

The second apology I have to make is that while I accept the responsibility for it myself, I should have been able to do it, I found that I didn't have sufficient notice to prepare a text, but I have made fairly extensive notes.

If it meets with your convenience, I would be prepared to make a statement outlining our approach to the problem and at the conclusion of that perhaps we could discuss it by way of any questions you might have.

The CHAIRMAN. That procedure will be entirely satisfactory to the subcommittee.

Mr. FULTON. There is one other matter I should explain. Your counsel, Mr. Beaser, asked me if it would be possible for me to arrange to have somebody from either our Federal Department of Justice or a provincial attorney general's office to be available to discuss with you the questions of enforcement of the law which we have in Canada. I regret that again owing to the time factor I was not able to arrange to have any such official with me.

The CHAIRMAN. For the record, the Chair might state that Mr. Fulton refers specifically to the law covering crime comics.

Mr. FULTON. That is correct. But I don't want the fact that no one else is here with me from any of the executive branch of government to be taken as an indication that they would not have liked to come had they been able to arrange it. The attorney general's department of the Province of Ontario expressed their regrets they could not make available a witness in the time at their disposal.

I thought perhaps at first I might make a few general remarks regarding the similarity of the problem as it appears to exist in our two countries.

But before I do so, there is one other introductory remark I would like to make, and that is as to my own position. I think in fairness it should be stated that I am not a member of the Government of Canada; nor, as a matter of fact, am I a member of the majority party.

I am a member of the opposition party. Therefore, I think I should say that nothing I say should be taken as necessarily indicating the views of the Government of Canada.

I will try, however, to the best of my ability, to summarize what I think to be the views of the Government of Canada with respect to this matter.

When I come to subjects or aspects of it in which I feel that it is not safe to indicate that this might be the general view, I shall try to remember to indicate to you that this is my own personal view. But in everything I say I think I should make it clear I am not here in a position to speak for the Government of Canada, but simply as an individual member of Parliament interested in this problem.

I think it goes probably without saying that we, our two countries, find themselves very much in the same situation with respect to this problem of crime comics and their influence on the matter of juvenile delinquency. Our two civilizations, our standards of living, our method of life, are very similar. Our reading habits are by and large similar to yours. Indeed, speaking generally, probably the majority of the reading material in the form of publications, that is, periodicals as distinguished from daily newspapers, have their origin here.

With respect to crime comics, I don't wish to be taken as saying that it is by any means one-way stream of traffic, because I understand some of those published in Canada find their way here and present you with a problem, but I think by and large with respect to the movement across the border of crime comics that is one thing where the balance of trade is somewhat in your favor.

Those features indicate that the problem is similar in both countries.

The CHAIRMAN. It would be safe to say that the balance of trade is largely in our favor in this case, would it not?

Mr. FULTON. That is my impression. You will appreciate that as much as we have enacted legislation which makes it a criminal offense to publish or sell a crime comic, there are not official statistics available as to the volume of these things published in Canada or sold in Canada because it is obvious that people trafficking in an illegal matter are not called upon and if they were, would not furnish the statistics they might be asked for.

We have in Canada examples which we feel indicated pretty clearly that crime comics were of similar nature to those circulating here have an adverse effect upon the thinking and in many cases on the actions of young boys and girls. I am not going to weary your committee with a complete catalog of cases. You probably have had many similar cases referred to you here, but there stands out in my mind a particular case which arose in Dawson Creek in the Yukon territory. One might have thought that that rather remote part of that country might be as insulated as any place might be against crime comics, but there was a case there in which one James M. Watson was murdered by two boys, ages 11 and 13.

At the trial evidence was submitted to show that the boys' minds were saturated with comic book reading. One boy admitted to the judge that he had read as many as 50 books a week, the other boy, 30.

The conclusion which the court came to after careful consideration of the evidence was that the exposure of these children to crime comics had had a definite bearing on the murder. There was no other explanation why the boys should have shot and killed the man driving past in his car. They probably didn't intend to kill him. They were imitating what they had seen portrayed day after day in crime comics to which they were exposed.

The other one is a case of more recent occurrence, reported in a local newspaper on March 11 of this year. I would like to read you the newspaper report. It originated at Westville, Nova Scotia:

Stewart Wright, 14, Wednesday told a coroner's jury how he shot his pal to death March 2, while they listened to a shooting radio program and read comic books about the Two-Gun Kid. The jury returned a verdict of accidental death and recommended that comic books of the type found at the scene be banned.

That, you appreciate, Mr. Chairman, is a case that occurred since the passage of our legislation, which indicates that we have not yet found the complete answer to this problem.

I would like everything I say to be taken subject to that understanding. I am not suggesting that the legislation we have passed is the complete answer.

I do suggest that it is a beginning in the effort to deal with this problem.

If we had the same general situation prevailing in Canada as you have in the United States, that is, a widespread body of opinion to the effect that this type of literature has a harmful influence on the minds of the young, we also had a similar conflict of opinions to that which I understand exists here. The publishers, particularly those engaged in the trade dealing with crime comics and other periodicals and magazines, as I think might be expected, were found on the whole to be on the side which held that these things were not a harmful influence on the minds of children.

I think that the explanation for that, sir, is readily available. They have an interest in the continuation of this stream of traffic. I am not saying, I don't wish to suggest, that they are all acting from improper motives. I am suggesting really that there is an obvious explanation as to why the majority of those concerned in the trade should be found on the one side, that is, on the side which says that these are not harmful.

I also have to confess that many experts and impartial experts in the field of psychiatry were found on the side of those who held that crime comics and similar publications were not harmful to children, but merely provided a useful outlet for what they called their natural violent instincts and tendencies.

Those generally were on the one side and as against them there were by and large all the community organizations, the parent-teacher associations, the federations of home and school, and similar organizations of a general community nature and those more particularly dealing with welfare work.

I would like to take this opportunity of paying here my tribute to the work that many of those organizations in Canada in arousing our people to an awareness of the problem, even if they didn't suggest in producing, as I say, a unanimous opinion as to how it should be dealt with. I say that because I believe that similar organizations here are assisting in that work.

Also on the side of those who came to the conclusion that these things were a harmful influence were the majority of our law-enforcement organizations. I think particularly of our own Federal Department of Justice where back in 1947 and 1948 when the matter was first discussed in Parliament in a concrete form, the Minister himself, speaking for the Government, expressed the view that these crime comics, of which he had been provided with samples, could have no other effect than a harmful one on the minds of young boys and girls.

That was even before we had taken any positive action to deal with the problem.

I also would like to pay my tribute to a noted expert in your own country, and, indeed, in your own city of New York, Dr. Frederic Wertham. I have read extensively from Dr. Wertham's articles and, of course, I read with great interest his latest book, Seduction of the Innocent. I have had considerable correspondence with Dr. Wertham and I think it is fair and accurate to say that insofar as I, myself, made any contribution to this matter and to the enactment of our legislation that I used and found Dr. Wertham's opinions, his quotations, of great assistance and I found they were generally accepted as authoritative in our country in a discussion of this matter.

I am not again saying that opinion was unanimous, but I think it is fair to say that Dr. Wertham's views were given great weight in our country.

The CHAIRMAN. Mr. Fulton, I might interrupt you at this point and, for the record, state that I received this morning upon my arrival here a communication from Dr. Wertham that was hand-delivered and that that communication will be made a part of the subcommittee files.

If at the conclusion of your testimony you would like to examine that letter, you may have that privilege.

Mr. FULTON. I shall be very much obliged, sir. I am looking forward, I might say, to meeting Dr. Wertham later on today.

That that survey of the general field in Canada, I would like to come to a more particular examination of the background of the present Canadian legislation.

We have had for many years—I see I am getting a little ahead of myself. There is another matter which I think I should mention, Mr. Chairman, to give you the full background picture and that is the constitutional position.

Here, I should say that although I am chairman of our own party organization, that is our own caucus committee of the Canadian Parliament dealing with matters having to do with law and law enforcement, I don't wish to pose as an expert lawyer.

The CHAIRMAN. That would compare to our Judiciary Committee, would it not?

Mr. FULTON. Yes, except that this is a committee into which our own party has organized, an opposition party, for the purpose of examining any legislation introduced by the Government having a bearing on those matters. It is because of my interest in that subject, and, to some extent, of my position in my own party, that I have been a spokesman on this matter. I mention that merely to make my position clear. I don't want to be taken as an expert.

I do now want to turn to a consideration of the constitutional position in Canada. I think I stated it correctly but I do so to some extent as an amateur. I mention it because there may be some difference in the constitutional position as between our two countries, particularly when it comes to the subject of law enforcement.

In Canada, broadly speaking, under our Constitution, which is the British-North America Act, all general criminal matters are reserved exclusively to the Federal Parliament, whereas on the other hand, all matters of local law enforcement are left exclusively to the jurisdiction of the provincial government.

When it comes to enacting criminal law, the Federal Parliament alone can act.

When it comes to enforcing that law the responsibility and the authority rests exclusively with the province. No province could enact as part of the criminal law any provision having exclusively application to its own territory.

On the other hand, everything enacted in the realm of general criminal law by the Federal Parliament is equally applicable all across the country.

As to the background of the legislation that we have, there has existed under the criminal code of Canada, which is a statute covering matters of general criminal law, for many years a section dealing with the general problem of literature, obscene literature, indecent objects, indecent exhibitions, and so on. That is found in section 207 of our criminal code.

And I should point out I have here with me a bill which has just this year been passed by the House of Commons, bill 7, which is an act entitled "An Act Respecting the Criminal Law." That is a general revision and recodification of the criminal code for the purpose of consolidating in one fresh statute the original statute, plus all the amending acts which have been passed over a period of some 50 years, since the last general revision. There are only, in a few cases, changes in principle.

Section 207, as it exists in the code now, is reenacted and will be found as section 150 in the bill, which is in the possession of your counsel. This bill has not yet become law because it has not yet passed our Senate, but it is my impression there will not be any changes in the present provisions of section 150 as passed by the House of Commons.

Section 150 incorporates section 207 of the old code, but until 1949 section 207 contained no reference to crime comics as such.

It was concerned exclusively with the matter of obscene objects, or obscure literature, indecent exhibitions, and so on.

I think it was after the last war—this is our experience at any rate—that the problem of crime comics as such came into existence. It seems to me by and large a postwar development. I am not saying it didn't exist before, but on the scale we now have it seems to be a postwar development which is probably the reason why our criminal law didn't refer to it before.

As a result of the emergency of the crime comics and the factors which I have reviewed already as to the public opinion which grew up about it, there was evidenced a considerable demand that something should be done to deal with this problem created by the crime comic. There was a campaign originated by such organizations as I have already mentioned, the Canadian Federation of Home and Schools, various service clubs organized themselves on a nationwide basis, put on a campaign pressing for some effective action to deal with the problem of crime comics and obscene literature generally.

Parent-teachers' associations joined in this effort. There was in addition considerable work done on it in our House of Commons.

I have already mentioned that in 1947 and 1948, when the matter was drawn to the attention of the Minister of Justice he expressed himself as holding the opinion that it was desirable to do something, although he said up to that time they had not yet been able to figure out any effective measures.

In the course of the discussion as to what should be done, the usual problem arose, and that was to reconcile the conflicting desires to have on the one hand freedom of action, freedom of choice, and on the other hand to prevent the abuse of that very freedom.

The problem is, are you going to have complete freedom of action, or are you going to have a measure of control.

The measure of control, it was generally agreed, divided itself into two alternatives: One, direct censorship; the other, legislative action, legislative action which would lay down the general standards and leave it to the courts to enforce rather than by direct censorship imposed from above by any governmental body.

Just as background, I might say that in Canada there exists no federal censorship as such. There is only in one Province that I am aware of any extensive censorship of literature, and that is in the Province of Quebec.

The majority of our Provinces, if not nearly all, have a form of censorship of movies under the authority of the provincial government. But by and large I think it would be fair to say that the majority opinion in Canada is opposed to the idea of censorship of literature.

I am not saying that that feeling is unanimous, but that seemed to be the feeling that if possible we should avoid bringing in direct censorship. That was my feeling with regard to the matter, not only my individual feeling, but it was my impression of the stated public opinion and, therefore, I felt if we were to get anywhere with it the approach should be by way of legislation to amend the criminal law so as to create an offense on the basis that society regards the continued publication of this material as a danger to society itself, and that society, therefore, through its instrument, its elected representatives, taking cognizance of the problem, is entitled to decide whether it is of sufficient seriousness and danger that the problem is to be dealt with in the usual way under our principle of justice by the elected representatives defining the problem constituting the offense, providing the penalty, and then leaving it to the individual who knows the law, knows what is there, to decide whether he wishes to run the risk, if you like, of continuing in that course of action with the knowledge if he does he may expose himself to the penalty.

In other words, to some extent you might say it is the process of imposing on the individual the obligation of self-censorship instead of imposing it on him by direction from above.

So that was the course that was followed in Canada.

I should perhaps mention one another feature which we have. That is a measure of control at the customs points. I don't know whether you have it, or not. I don't want to go into this in any great detail because I know you have a busy session before you. I will try to summarize it.

In our customs law, and under the tariff items which are approved by Parliament to apply that law there is an item 1201, tariff item 1201, which reads as follows:

> It prohibits the entry into Canada of books, printed paper, drawings, prints, photographs, or representations of any kind of a treasonable or seditious or immoral or indecent character, on the grounds that our criminal code makes those an offense in the country; therefore, we are not going to permit them to come into the country while it is an offense under our law.

That tariff item has not been amended with respect to crime comics, but, by and large, I am informed that the officers of the border points, if they are of the opinion that a particular comic magazine would be an offense under the new revision in the criminal code, they will exercise their own discretion in prohibiting its entry, or, if they are in doubt, they will refer it to the department at Ottawa for a ruling as to whether it is admissible or not.

Mr. BEASER. Are the crime comics which go into your country printed in this country, or are the plates sent to Canada for printing?

Mr. FULTON. I am informed it is done in both ways. In some cases the finished article is imported. In other cases the plates are sent over and they are printed in Canada.

Mr. BEASER. You do not know which method predominates, do you?

Mr. FULTON. My impression is that the finished article predominates. Perhaps we could go into that a little more fully later. There is a real problem confronting the customs officials in that we have not had yet very much jurisprudence built up. There have not been many actions in our courts under the new sections with regard to crime comics and the customs officials are loath to set themselves up as censors. They have no hesitation if a particular subject or article has been declared offensive by a court decision in prohibiting its entry, but they find themselves under great difficulty when it comes to saying as to whether or not an article, which has never been the subject of any judicial process, is in fact prohibited under our criminal law.

That is one difficulty.

The other is that the volume of these things moving across the border makes it difficult for them to enforce their own regulations 100 percent, and I think it would be fair to say that customs officers exist mainly for the purpose of collecting duties, customs, and excises, and not for the purpose of indulging in any form of quasi-censoring of literature.

It is an obligation under the tariff item which they willingly undertake, but it is not their main task.

Senator HENNINGS. It may be of interest, perhaps Mr. Fulton is very well aware of this, but Assemblyman James A. Fitzpatrick told me during the recess today that many people come over the border from Canada to Plattsburg, N.Y., which happens to be his home, for the purpose of procuring some of the American published comic or horror books and that they take them back across the border, smuggling them or bootlegging them across, as it were.

Mr. FULTON. That may be so, Senator. The only comment I could make on that is that I regret to say that these things circulate with sufficient freedom in Canada that I am surprised that they find it necessary to come down here for that.

Senator HENNINGS. Like carrying coals to Newcastle.

Mr. FULTON. I think it must be a very incidental purpose of their visit. I am not in any way questioning that it does take place.

What I want to avoid is giving the impression of saying that we have dealt with this effectively in Canada and it is only you that have the problem.

My attitude toward it is that it is still a mutual problem although we have made a beginning.

Senator HENNINGS. You are certainly eminently fair, and I am sure want to be very careful in having made that statement not to cause any misunderstanding on that point.

Thank you, sir.

Mr. FULTON. That, then, in brief, is the background of the situation with respect to the nature of the problem and the actual legislation, or lack of it, up to 1949.

In the fall session of our Parliament in 1949, I introduced a bill, of which I regret I have no longer copies left in my file. There is only one copy left in the file of the Department of Justice. There are plenty of copies of the statute in the annual volume of statutes, but of the bill itself, an individual bill, there is only one copy left readily available. So I had our Department of Justice prepare typewritten facsimiles of the bill as introduced.

I shall be glad to give them to your counsel or your clerk for filing at the end of my presentation. This is as best as can be done, a reproduction of the bill with the front page. This was the inside page, explanatory notes and the back page was blank. It was a short bill. It was introduced by way of an amendment to section 207 of the code.

I think it is short enough that I can read it to you and you can understand then our approach to the problem of trying to find the method of dealing with this subject.

I won't read the introductory words, except as follows:

BILL 10

AN ACT To amend the Criminal Code (Portrayal of Crimes)

His Majesty, by and with the advice and consent of the Senate and House of Commons of Canada, enacts as follows:

Subsection 1 of secton 207 of the Criminal Code, chapter 36 of the Revised Statutes of Canada, 1927, is amended by adding thereto the following:

"(d) prints, publishes, sells, or distributes any magazine, periodical, or book which exclusively or substantially comprises matter depicting pictorially the commission of crimes, real or fictitious, thereby tending or likely to induce or influence youthful persons to violate the law or to corrupt the morals of such persons."

Section 207 in its introductory sections provided that:

Every person shall be guilty of an offense who

and then the introductory sections (a), (b), (c), cover obscene literature, obscene exhibitions and I was adding section (d) to make it a violation to print, sell, distribute a crime comic as a crime.

I would like to read an explanatory note which was submitted at the same time and forms part of the printed material with the bill:

This act is designed to amend the Criminal Code to cover the case of those magazines and periodicals commonly called crime comics, the publication of which is presently legal, but which it is widely felt tend to the lowering of morals and to induce the commission of crimes by juveniles.

The purpose is to deal with these publications not by imposing a direct censorship or by blanket prohibition, but rather by providing in general terms that the publication and distribution as defined in the act shall be illegal and thus leaving it for decision by the court and/or jury, in accordance with the normal principles prevailing at a criminal trial to determine whether or not the publication in question falls within the definition.

That bill was introduced as a private member's bill and given first reading on September 28, 1949. In the debate which followed, after I had outlined my argument in support of the legislation, the Minister of Justice, speaking for the Government, stated that the Government was anxious to take effective action to deal with this problem, they welcomed the introduction of the bill.

However, it raised certain questions with respect to enforcement and, therefore, they asked if it might be stood for the time being while they communicated its contents to the provincial attorneys general to get the benefit of their views as to whether it was necessary; if so, whether it was enforcible in its present suggested form, or whether they themselves would like to see some amendments to make it more workable.

That was done. As a result of the views and opinions offered by provincial attorneys general when the debate was brought on again in committee the bill as introduced was quite extensively amended and in effect given the form of a complete revision and reenactment of the whole of section 207.

In other words, instead of just adding a new clause they incorporated the suggestion into the clause and made it a more workable whole.

It had one more effect which I would like to mention. The amendment to the bill, in that under section 207 in its previous form it was a defense to anyone accused of committing the crime of printing or publishing any obscene literature or crime comic after the amendment carried. It was a defense to the accused person to show that he did not have any knowledge of the indecent content or nature of the publication complained of.

It was felt, particularly with respect to crime comics—you say the specimens on the board this morning—that it would be really pretty ridiculous for anyone to try to plead "Well, I don't know the nature of this thing." The nature is self-evident. It was felt by the attorneys general if we were going to make this section effective not only with respect to crime comics, but with respect to offensive literature generally, really this defense of lack of knowledge of the contents of the articles complained of should be removed.

It would still be the onus on the Crown to prove intent in the general sense of that onus under the criminal law.

Senator HENNINGS. May I ask Mr. Fulton one question? You may have suggested this earlier in your statement.

Does this relate to the publisher, the distributor, and the newsdealer?

Mr. FULTON. Yes, sir; it includes the whole field.

Senator HENNINGS. I take it it is announced in the statute in the subjunctive; is that correct?

Mr. FULTON. Yes.

Senator HENNINGS. They may be joined, in other words, they may be coindictees, they may be individually indicted?

Mr. FULTON. Or they may be proceeded against separately. One may be proceeded against without the other.

I shall have something to say on that a little later. That is an interesting legal point. I mean with respect to the matter of dealing more effectively with the publisher.

I should like, if time permits and you think it important, to say something on that later. But that defense was removed as a result of this amendment.

I have also a facsimile copy of the bill as it was amended in committee as a result of the Government's own suggestions. I shall be glad to file that.

Mr. BEASER. Mr. Fulton, am I wrong in believing that the bill as finally passed was different than the one you introduced in that it made it an offense to print, circulate, and so forth, a crime comic to anyone; whereas, as you read your original bill I got the impression it was aimed at distribution which had as its purpose the influencing of youthful people; is that right?

Mr. FULTON. You are correct. In my initial draft of the bill as first moved the words "thereby tending or likely to induce or influence youthful persons to violate the law or to corrupt the morals of such persons" was included.

Mr. BEASER. Was that for enforcement purposes?

Mr. FULTON. I think so on the basis that the nature of these things and their tendency is self-evident.

Senator HENNINGS. That becomes a jury question.

Mr. FULTON. No; those words are not included in section 207 at the present time. The crime comic as defined in the bill, bill 10, as it eventually passed, was defended as follows:

(7) In this section "crime comic" means a magazine, periodical or book that exclusively or substantially comprises matter depicting pictorially (a) the commission of crimes, real or fictitious—

Now, sir, the only defense as such which is open to an accused under our law, under this bill, is the following:

No one shall be convicted of any offense in this section mentioned if he proves that the public good was served by the acts that are alleged to have been done and that there was no excess in the acts alleged beyond what the public good required.

If he can prove to the satisfaction of a judge or magistrate or judge and jury that the crime comic in fact served the public good, then there is no conviction.

Senator HENNINGS. That is somewhat then in parallel to your English libel law that you require not only that as defense one need establish not only truth as in the United States, but that it be for the public benefit.

Mr. FULTON. I think that, sir, is in the realm of criminal liability only.

Senator HENNINGS. I meant criminal liability, of course.

Mr. FULTON. Yes.

Senator HENNINGS. It must be for the public benefit under the British law, is it not?

Mr. FULTON. I think it might be going perhaps a little beyond, but it must not go too far beyond. There must be some public interest to be served, yes. I think that would be a fair statement.

Now, when the bill came back in its amended form, as I have indicated it in the summary here, it passed the House unanimously. The House of Commons adopted it without any dissenting vote.

It then went to our Senate and there by that time the periodical publisher or some of those engaged in the trade—I shall put it that way—perhaps had only just awakened to what was going on; maybe they thought it would never pass the House of Commons.

What the reason was, I don't know, but at any rate, they made no representation to the House. They didn't ask for its reference to a committee. It goes through the Committee of the Whole House, but they didn't ask for reference to a special committee on the bill and they made no formal presentation.

Then it got to the Senate, having passed the House; they asked to be allowed to appear and make representations. So the Senate referred it to one of its standing committees.

There the publishers appeared and they made representations which took the form of some of the submissions which I have read in the newspaper comment, at any rate on your own proceedings from time to time down here, namely, that these things were not harmful to juveniles; in fact, to some extent they formed a harmless outlet for their natural violent instincts.

Senator HENNINGS. I take it, sir, in defining crime you mean felony. That is in section 7, "crime comic" means a periodical or book that exclusively or substantially comprises matter depicting pictorially the commission of crimes.

Mr. FULTON. There is another amendment I was going to come to, Senator, but I will be glad to deal with that point now.

Senator HENNINGS. I do not mean to distract and divert you.

Mr. FULTON. You are concerned with the definition given to the word "crime"?

Senator HENNINGS. Yes sir; whether you mean felony, misdemeanor; what classification of crime, if any?

Mr. FULTON. I don't think that point has come before our courts.

Senator HENNINGS. For example, if an embezzlement is depicted in a crime comic, a bank teller, let us say, taking money from his employer, or involuntary manslaughter, would, in your judgment, that sort of thing depicted in a comic book constitute a crime within the meaning and purview of your statute?

Mr. FULTON. I would not care to express an opinion on that. I think that would be a matter of individual interpretation by the courts. To my knowledge the point has not arisen.

I think it may be a very important point. I would have to say this, that in my mind in drafting and submitting the original legislation I had in contemplation the crime of violence, what you might call the crime of violence, but taking it over to amend it and amending it, the Government deleted the reference to that type of definition and I had no objection whatever. They had consulted with the law-enforcement officers and the law-enforcement officers felt that a too narrow definition might create obstacles which might create difficulties in the way of its enforcement and no substantial representations against the broadening of the definition were made and so it went through in that form.

I would not care at the moment to express an opinion as to whether the court, looking at it, would say, "Well, the intention of the legislature was to confine it to crimes of violence," or not.

Senator HENNINGS. We would have a most interesting situation, would we not, bearing in mind that the crime of carrying a concealed weapon is a felony in most of our States, having portrayed in a comic a representation indicating that someone was carrying a concealed weapon by verbiage, but the weapon could not be seen.

That would still be carrying it along the line. I certainly do not want to be frivolous or to attempt to make light of part of it but to attempt to present the difficulty this field presents.

Mr. FULTON. I would express this purely as an offhand opinion, that the wording of the statute is wide enough to cover anything which is made a crime by our criminal code. Anything covered in there whether fraud or embezzlement is covered in the criminal code then on the face of it an illustration of a crime of that nature is included in section 207.

It might be an interesting point for defense counsel to raise that as defense the section didn't contemplate that type of crime. Then the court would have to decide what was the intent of the legislature as gathered from the words they used.

So far that point has not come before our courts.

I was mentioning that when it came before our Senate it was referred to a standing committee and the representatives of the trade appeared and made representations against the bill.

Dr. Wertham has an interesting passage in his book in which he records it as having been the opinion expressed that they appeared to be making progress until they made the mistake of producing to the Senators some examples of their wares, that when that was done their case was out of court.

I can't read the minds of our Senators. All I know is that in the result the standing committee reported the bill back to the Senate without amendment and it passed the Senate as a whole by a vote of 92 to 4.

Having passed the Senate, it then passed both Houses of our Parliament and was proclaimed and became law.

Now, our subsequent experience has been somewhat as follows and here I must say I am speaking on the basis of opinion for the reason, as I have said, statistics on this matter are hard to obtain but it is my impression, and I know this view is shared by the majority of those interested in the problem, the crime comic as such pretty well disappeared from the Canadian newsstands within a year or so following the enactment of this legislation.

But within about the same period of time alternative forms of comic magazines began to appear. Speaking in general terms, these took the form initially of an increase in the number of love and sex and girlie comics which began to hit the newsstands. And that as an interesting comment gave rise to a separate study launched by our Senate on the subject. They set up a committee to look into the sale and distribution of, I think the word they used was salacious literature.

One of the reasons why the demand for that rose so rapidly was the rapid increase in the circulation of that type of pulp magazine following the virtual disappearance of the crime comic.

I mention that merely as an interesting aside.

Then there crept back into circulation in Canada the crime comic again in its original form, but it also began to appear in other alternative forms and there the alternative form I have in mind is what I think you have described generally as the horror comic. I would venture the opinion that the reason the crime comic to a lesser extent and the horror comic to a greater extent reappeared and began to appear respectively, was in part because of the lack of prosecution of any publisher or printer or vendor under the new crime comic section. There were no prosecutions until about a year ago. And partly perhaps due to the fact that the public and myself and other similar interested persons included may have felt, now we have done our job, we can sit back and relax, with the result that there wasn't the same vigilant supervision of the newsstands to pick out offensive publications, bring them to the attention of the authorities and demand prosecution.

Whatever the reasons, anyway, the crime comic in its original form began to reappear and the horror comic in a much exhilarated form—I mean it is now circulating to an extent even greater than the present circulation of the crime comic and it is in Canada at any rate relatively newer in form and appearance. It has made its appearance later than crime comics. I think it would be fair to say it made its appearance only after the enactment of legislation in 1949.

But I have to express it again as my personal opinion that even the horror comic was in fact adequately covered by the legislation which we had enacted in 1949 because that legislation refers by definition to the commission of crimes, real or fictitious.

Now, again, it might be an interesting legal point as to whether the courts would say that a fictitious crime means merely a crime committed by a human being, the crime had not taken place in fact, whether they would confine it to that or whether it would be broad enough to cover the case of a crime committed by these fantastic beings, ghoul of the swamp and the Batman, those creatures that can have no existence in reality, but, nevertheless, commit what, if committed by a human being, would be crime.

It is interesting to speculate whether the words "crime, real or fictitious" would apply.

Senator HENNINGS. That would apply perhaps to a crime committed by Mickey Mouse, for example, a more innocuous kind of comic character.

Mr. FULTON. Yes, sir. Again it is a question, of course, whether the courts interpret the intent of the legislature as gathered from the words of the statute.

Mr. BEASER. Assuming you are able to find out how the American crime comics are getting into Canada, are you able under your statute to proceed against the publisher or distributor?

Mr. FULTON. In the United States?

Mr. BEASER. Yes.

Mr. FULTON. No. He is beyond our reach. His crime is not committed in Canada, you see. Unless he were to come and surrender himself voluntarily to the jurisdiction of our courts, I don't think there is any way; I don't think extradition proceedings would lie.

My understanding is that unless he came to Canada and committed the crime and came back here we could not use extradition proceedings.

Mr. BEASER. The question is whether under the Canadian statute Canada is able to proceed against an American publisher who publishes in this country crime and horror comics which then get into Canada, or whether they can proceed against a distributor who sends them into Canada.

Mr. FULTON. I think the first.

Senator HENNINGS. They would have no jurisdiction in the matter in the first place.

Mr. FULTON. Unless he submitted himself voluntarily to the jurisdiction of our courts, which I can't see him doing.

Senator HENNINGS. You would have no venue then?

Mr. FULTON. I think if he voluntarily submitted himself to jurisdiction we would. I think the execution of the sentence might, of course, present some interesting problems, but in effect I don't think it arises. In effect my opinion is—and I take it Senator Hennings concurs—that the first person we can deal with is the man who first imports it in Canada and there is no suggestion that we should proceed against the American publisher.

If we deal with the man who brings it in we are dealing effectively with it from our point of view. What is done here is a matter entirely for your own determination.

Mr. BEASER. Are you able to get the distributor; is it known or —

Mr. FULTON. It can be ascertained. I have to say with regret, in my view we are not proceeding sufficiently vigorously in our own country against the distributors, against the man who first puts this offensive material into circulation.

I would like to deal with that at greater length a little later.

I think that is one defect not only in our laws which exist, but in the enforcement of our law.

Now, I just was mentioning that these things have reappeared, although I think again it would be fair to say they don't circulate to the same extent as they did previous to the enactment of the legislation, but they circulate or have been circulating recently to an extent sufficient to give rise to genuine concern.

Then I would like to say a word in consequence of that about the courts and enforcement. I have expressed, I think, already the opinion that our legislation is adequate.

I would say, I think, by that opinion, unless the case comes before the courts in which the prosecution is dismissed then we would know whether or not the law was adequate, but I can see no reason why it should not cover it so I would like to discuss the problems of the courts and enforcement.

I think that first one should state what is probably a general proposition applicable equally in both our countries, that, generally speaking, one of the reasons for what I have called lack of vigorous enforcement may be the inherent dislike of taking measures which appear to be repressive with respect to the written word, with respect to literature.

Our law-enforcement authorities are reluctant, and I think properly reluctant, to launch prosecution against those in the printing and publishing business and in the distribution of literature. It is a reluctance which I think must and should be overcome where the case warrants it, but I used the words "I think it is a proper reluctance" and it is one which I think we must take into account.

In any event, there have been very few prosecutions in Canada, although this material is circulating in certainly greater quantity than I would like to see.

I would like then to refer to one or two specific cases which came before our courts. You will appreciate from your reading of the section as lawyers that there are two alternative methods of proceeding. One is by indictment in which case it comes up before a court with a judge.

The other is by what we call summary procedure or on summary conviction, which means it comes up before a magistrate.

The principle, of course, applicable in both courts are exactly the same as to proof and so on, but the powers of the respective courts with respect to imposition of penalties are quite different. The penalty which the higher court can impose on the more formal indictment procedure is much larger than that which can be imposed by a magistrate on a summary conviction.

The first case I should like to mention came up before a magistrate in the Province of Alberta. Being in a magistrate court, it is not a reported case, but it was the case which gave us the greatest concern because the facts as I understand them were something like this: That the magazine or crime comic complained of illustrated everything right up to the actual moment of the delivery of the death blow, omitted that, and then continued with all the gruesome details immediately following that. That was the presentation at any rate as I understand it, given by the defending attorney.

The legislation refers to the commission of crimes. This does not illustrate the actual commission of the crime and, therefore, the accused is not guilty.

The magistrate dismissed the case on that ground. That looked as though we would have to amend our legislation if we wished it to be effective because you will appreciate so far as the juveniles are concerned if you are going to say everything which falls short of the actual commission of the crime at the moment of death, shall I say, that everything of that sort is all right, then you haven't really got an effective act from the point of view of what we want to accomplish.

So reconsideration was immediately given to introducing the necessary amendment. That has been done. There is a slight modification in bill 7 in the proposed section 150 over and above what there was in bill 10, which I shall come to, but even before we in the House of Commons enacted bill 7, there was another case, *Regina* v. *Rohr*.

As you know, in our country all criminal prosecutions are brought in the name of the Queen, or whoever happens to be wearing the Crown at the time being, be it the King or the Queen. *Regina* v. *Rohr*, a Manitoba case, in which the same defense was raised before the magistrate. The magistrate, however, convicted in this case.

So as a test case it was appealed to the Court of Appeals of the Province of Manitoba. The appeal court stated, after looking at the words of the statute, they were clearly of the opinion that the intent of the legislature as clearly to be gathered from those words, was to cover all these incidental arrangements for and consequence of the crime and that, therefore, the prosecution was properly launched.

I am not going to weary you with it here, but if any member of your committee might be interested in the discussion of the effect of that decision, it may be found in the Canadian Bar review for December 1953 at page 1164, where the case and its implications are discussed by the Deputy Attorney General for British Columbia, Mr. Eric Peppler.

That decision seemed to dispose of the fears which we had that the whole statute might be rendered ineffective, but nevertheless there was this amendment which had been contemplated which was still carried forward for the sake of greater certainty.

It is not a very important or far-reaching amendment, but I think it does substantiate my point that these words are now sufficient to cover even the horror comic because the definition of crime comic as it previously appeared in section 207 was in this form:

Crime comic means in this section any magazine, periodical, or book which exclusively or substantially comprises matter depicting pictorially the commission of crimes, real or fictitious.

Now, it reads in this section:

Crime comic means a magazine, periodical, or book that exclusively or substantially comprises matter depicting pictorially:
A. The commission of crimes, real or fictitious, or
B. Events connected with the commission of crimes, real or fictitious, whether occurring before or after the commission of a crime.

Mr. BEASER. You would say, Mr. Fulton, that the statute itself seems to be sufficient. The difficulty lies in the enforcement?

Mr. FULTON. In the enforcement; that is my point.

Mr. BEASER. You think if there were effective enforcement the problem that Canada faces with respect to crime and horror comics would no longer be there?

Mr. FULTON. I don't suppose it will ever disappear entirely, but it would be effectively dealt with; yes.

To conclude in a very few words, I would like to say a word or two with regard to our present experience. Our present experience is, it must be confessed, that printers and publishers still defy the laws because comics are still on our stands, whether publishers in the sense of those who actually print them in Canada, or in the sense of those who put them into circulation after they are imported from your country.

That is the view I know of our Government, that the law is there; what is necessary now is vigorous and complete enforcement.

I did suggest in a recent debate, and it is still my view, that there should be a differentiation in the penalty so that a stiffer penalty would be provided for those who, as I see it, carry the greater responsibility for putting this offensive material into circulation, what you might call gently at the printer and publisher level; that there should be a stiffer minimum penalty, one that he will really feel, one which will not be, and what so often they are, merely license fees to continue in business.

Mr. BEASER. However, if the majority of these crimes and horror comics are coming in from the United States, that sort of stiffening of penalty would not be effective, would it?

Mr. FULTON. I think it could be made effective because I am convinced an adequate definition could be worked out to cover the case of the initial distributor.

Mr. BEASER. The initial distributor would be included?

Mr. FULTON. Yes. I don't suggest for a moment you can absolve from responsibility the individual news vendor or the retail distributor. I do think they carry a very much lesser degree of responsibility for this thing than the others.

I think, therefore, there should be a lesser penalty for them, that the penalty should be in the discretion of the court and in our jurisdiction it runs an average of anywhere from $5 to $50 for the individual vendor, but I feel there should be heavy penalties for those higher up in the scale.

And that until, in fact, my view in conclusion really is that until you take effective action to deal with those who first put these things into circulation you are not going to deal with the problem.

As I have said, I do not for a moment suggest that the individual vendor and retail distributor can be absolved from responsibility. He is a very minor factor in the chain of responsibility.

I would like to see and have in fact suggested that our own code be amended to make that differentiation, but that suggestion was not accepted by the House of Commons and by the Government.

So that remains at the moment my own opinion and that of certain of my colleagues in the House.

There are a couple of cases I would like to mention, just to finish. There is one case in Canada where a publisher has been prosecuted, the Queen against the Peer Publisher, Ltd., of Toronto, and William Zimmerman, who is the man who is the principal of that firm, resulted in conviction and fine of a $1,000 and costs against the company and suspended sentence for Zimmerman. No notice of appeal has yet been served.

That was a conviction again by way of summary procedure by magistrate which may account for the relatively low fine.

There was another case against Kitchener News Co., Ltd., distributor, again in the magistrate court. They were fined $25. They appealed.

The appeals court quashed the conviction on technical ground that the indictment was incorrectly drawn. The attorney general informs me that he is proceeding with a new trial on a fresh indictment. That is, so far as I have been able to ascertain, the record of court cases dealing with this new law, relatively new law, in Canada.

I believe that the court cases show that the law is workable and effective and the problem is enforcement with, as my personal opinion, a desirability of providing heavier penalty and really effective penalties for those at the top who have the greatest responsibility in the chain of circulation.

One other interesting and encouraging result which has flowed from our legislation is that in a number of cities in Canada, particularly after the last discussion, when the amended criminal code came up before the House and we had extensive and quite interesting debate on that section, as a result of that publicity, at least I think it is partly as a result of that publicity, a number of both wholesale and retail distributors are approaching citizens' committees in some of our cities and saying, "We don't want to break the law in the first place and we certainly don't want to run the risk of prosecution. We would like you to cooperate with us by suggesting to us the offensive titles and if you will do that we would like you to get a representative committee so that it does not just reflect the minority viewpoint. If you will do that we will agree to withdraw those titles from circulation."

I think that springs in some measure from the existence of the legislation.

As I say, I regard it as a quite encouraging indication that this legislation can and will produce beneficial results in Canada, although I am afraid again I must confess that I am not suggesting that it is the complete answer or that it has yet provided a complete elimination of this type of undesirable publication.

That, Mr. Chairman, concludes the statement which I have to make.

I appreciate your having listened to me so patiently. I apologize for having taken rather lengthy time. I am very much interested in this subject.

If I have abused your hospitality by going on too long, that is because of my interest in the subject.

The CHAIRMAN. You have been very helpful and you have made a contribution.

Senator HENNINGS. I, too, want to thank you very much and apologize in turn. I was asked by some representatives of the press to get an exhibit of one of the things that was in evidence this morning. I was engaged in that effort during the latter part of your statement. I shall read with great interest the record.

The CHAIRMAN. I might add it was a very able statement, well presented.

Mr. FULTON. Thank you very much.

The CHAIRMAN. I think that Canada is fortunate in having such an able representative in its Parliament.

Counsel, do you have any questions?

Mr. BEASER. Just one, Mr. Chairman.

As you notice, this morning I have been asking a number of witnesses as to the effect on our country's relationships with other countries of these crime and horror comics.

Would you care to comment on what impression and what effect crime and horror comics in Canada are having on the children's ideas of what the United States of America is like?

Mr. FULTON. I would say that their effect in that regard is not very serious in Canada. We live too close to you not to know that our way of life and yours are very much the same.

It would be my opinion, therefore, that a Canadian child reading this type of magazine would not—reaction on him would not be what dreadful things go on in the United States of America as distinct from what goes on in Canada.

Rather, the undesirability from our point of view certainly is that it portrays these as natural and everyday occurrences.

In other words, our objection to them is not that it portrays the United States as a country, which has lower standard of moral values than our own. It is merely that they portray human society as having an entirely distorted and unreal sense of value and of moral standards.

Besides that, I would make no, I certainly wouldn't express any opinion that they have a derogatory effect on the opinion of our children toward America as such because as I have pointed out, although to a considerable lesser degree, many publications of the same type are published in Canada, a sufficient number to be alarming and disturbing.

Mr. BEASER. I have no further questions, Mr. Chairman.

The CHAIRMAN. It is your considered judgment that this statute has been extremely helpful, is it not?

Mr. FULTON. Yes, it is, Senator, although I must again repeat that I feel it has not been used to the fullest possible extent.

The CHAIRMAN. Senator Hennings?

Senator HENNINGS. I have nothing further, Mr. Chairman. Thank you.

The CHAIRMAN. Thank you again, Mr. Fulton, very much indeed.

Mr. FULTON. Thank you, Mr. Chairman.

*   *   *   *   *   *   *   *

The CHAIRMAN. The chairman wishes to announce that today's hearing does not terminate the subcommittee's investigation into the field of crime and horror comic books. We shall continue to collect on this subject matter in this area, and if necessary further hearings will be scheduled at a later date.

All data thus far presented, plus all future facts compiled, will be studied most carefully before the subcommittee draws up its conclusions and recommendations.

The subcommittee will issue a special report upon this subject at an appropriate time, or we may make the report a part of our final report.

I think I speak for the entire subcommittee when I say that any action on the part of the publishers of crime and horror comic books, or upon the part of distributors, wholesalers, or dealers with reference to these materials which will tend to eliminate from production and sale, shall receive the acclaim of my colleagues and myself. A competent job of self-policing within the industry will achieve much.

We will adjourn now until 10 o'clock tomorrow morning.

(Thereupon, at 5 p.m., the subcommittee recessed, to reconvene at 10 a.m., Saturday, June 5, 1954.)

[Editor's Note: The hearings were never reconvened.]

Still More About the Comics

Selected Bibliography
Notes on the Contributors

Selected Bibliography

Abel, Robert H., and David Manning White, eds. *The Funnies: An American Idiom.* New York: The Free Press of Glencoe, 1963.

Aldridge, Alan, and George Perry. *The Penguin Book of Comics.* Harmondsworth, England: Penguin Books, 1967.

Becker, Stephen. *Comic Art in America.* New York: Simon & Schuster, 1959.

Berger, Arthur Asa. *The Comic-Stripped American.* New York: Walker and Company, 1974.

Couperie, Pierre, and Maurice Horn. *A History of the Comic Strip.* New York: Crown, 1968.

Craven, Thomas. *Cartoon Cavalcade.* New York: Simon & Schuster, 1943.

Daniels, Les. *Comix: A History of Comic Books in America.* New York: Outerbridge and Dienstfrey, 1971.

Davidson, Sol. *Culture and the Comic Strip.* New York: New York University Press, 1959. Ph.D. thesis.

Estren, Mark. *A History of Underground Comics.* San Francisco: Straight Arrow Books, 1974.

Feiffer, Jules. *The Great Comic Book Heroes.* New York: Dial Press, 1965.

Gifford, Denis. *The British Comic Catalogue 1874-1974.* London: Mansell, 1975.

―――. *Happy Days! One Hundred Years of Comics.* London: Jupiter Books, 1975.

―――. *Stap Me! The British Newspaper Strip.* Aylesbury, England: Shire Publications, 1971.

Goulart, Ron. *The Adventurous Decade.* New Rochelle, N.Y.: Arlington House, 1975.

Hirsh, Michael, and Patrick Lambert. *The Great Canadian Comic-Books.* Toronto: Peter Martin, 1971.

Horn, Maurice. *75 Years of the Comics.* Boston: Boston Book & Art, 1971.

Kempkes, Wolfgang, ed. *International Bibliography of Comics Literature.* New York: R.R. Bowker, 1974.

Lee, Stan. *Origins of Marvel Comics.* New York: Simon & Schuster, 1974.

Lupoff, Richard, and Donald Thompson, eds. *All in Color for a Dime.* New Rochelle, N.Y.: Arlington House, 1970.

―――. *The Comic-Book Book.* New Rochelle, N.Y.: Arlington House, 1973.

Murrel, William A. *A History of American Graphic Humor* (2 vols.). New York: Macmillan for the Whitney Museum of American Art, 1933 and 1938.

Reitberger, Reinhold, and Wolfgang Fuchs. *Comics: Anatomy of a Mass Medium.* Boston: Little, Brown, 1972.

Robinson, Jerry. *The Comics: An Illustrated History of Comic Strip Art.* New York: Putnam, 1974.

Sheridan, Martin. *Comics and Their Creators.* Boston: Hale, Cushman and Flint, 1942 (paperback edition: Luna Press, 1971).

Steranko, James, ed. *The Steranko History of Comics.* Reading, Pa.: Supergraphics (2 vols), 1970 and 1972.

Waugh, Coulton. The Comics. New York: Macmillan, 1947 (paperback edition: Luna Press, 1974).

Wertham, Frederic. *Seduction of the Innocent.* New York: Rinehart and Co., 1954.

Books in Other Languages

Blanchard, Gérard. *La Bande Dessinée.* Verviers, Belgium: Editions Marabout, 1969.

Bono, Gianni. *Appunti sul Fumetto Italiano del Dopoguerra.* Genoa, Italy: Gli Amici del Fumetto, 1972.

Caen, Michel, with Jacques Lob and Jacques Sternberg. *Les Chefs d'Oeuvre de la Bande Dessinée.* Paris: Planète, 1967.

Caradec, François. *I Primi Eroi.* Milan: Garzanti, 1962.

Carpentier, André, ed. *La Bande Dessinée Kébécoise.* Bois-des-Filion, Qué.: La Barre du Jour, 1975.

Della Corte, Carlo. *I Fumetti.* Milan: Mondadori, 1961.

Gasca, Luis. *Los Comics en España.* Barcelona: Editorial Lumen, 1969.

———. *Los Comics en la Pantalla.* San Sebastian, Spain: Festival Internacional del Cine, 1965.

Lacassin, Francis. *Pour un le Art, la Bande Dessinée.* Paris: Union Générale d'Editions, 1971.

Lipscyc, Enrique. *La Historieta Mundial.* Buenos Aires: Editorial Lipscyc, 1958.

Marny, Jacques. *Le Monde Etonnant des Bandes Dessinées.* Paris: Editions du Centurion, 1968.

Moliterni, Claude, ed. *Histoire de la Bande Dessinée d'Expression Française.* Paris: Editions Serg, 1972.

Peignot, Joseph. *Les Copains de Votre Enfance.* Paris: Denoël, 1963.

Strazzula, Gaetano. *I Fumetti.* Florence: Sansoni, 1970.

Welke, Manfred. *Die Sprache der Comics.* Frankfurt a/Main: Dipa Verlag, 1958.

An Additional Bibliography
1976-1997

Only books dealing with some important aspect of the comics have been listed. Most are in the English language, but some foreign works of note have also been included. For a more comprehensive bibliography, refer to John A. Lent's four-volume *International Bibliography* mentioned below.

Aurrecoechea, Juan Manuel, and Armando Bartra, *Historia de la Historieta en Mexico.* 5 volumes. Mexico City: Grijalbo, 1990-1997.

Baron-Carvais, Annie. *La Bande Desinée.* Paris: Presses Universitaires de France, 1985.

Benton, Mike. *The Comic Book in America.* Dallas, Tex.: Taylor Publishing, 1990.

Blackbeard, Bill. *A Century of Comics.* 2 volumes. Northampton, Mass.: Kitchen Sink Press, 1995.

Blackbeard, Bill, and Martin Williams, eds. *The Smithsonian Collection of Newspaper Comics.* New York: Abrams, 1978.

Coma, Javier, and Roman Gubern. *Los Comics en Hollywood.* Barcelona: Plaza & James, 1988.

———. *Diccionario de los Comics.* Barcelona: Plaza & James, 1991.

Coma, Javier, and Roman Gubern, eds. *Historia de los Comics.* Barcelona: Toutain Editor, 1994.

Fossati, Franco. *I Fumetti in 100 Personaggi.* Milan: Longanesi & C., 1977.

Gasca, Luis, and Roman Gubern. *El Discurso del Comic.* Madrid: Catedra, 1988.

Gaumer, Patrick, and Claude Moliterni. *Dictionnaire Mondial de la Bande Dessinee.* Paris: Larousse, 1994.

Gifford, Dennis. *The International Book of Comics.* London: Deans International Publishing, 1984.

———. *American Comic Strip Collections.* New York: G.K. Hall, 1990.

Goulart, Ron, ed. *The Encyclopedia of American Comics.* New York: Facts on File, 1990.

———. *The Funnies: 100 Years of American Comic Strips.* Holbrook, Mass.: Adams, 1995.

———. *Ron Goulart's Great History of Comic Books.* Chicago: Contemporary Books, 1986.

Harvey, R.C. *The Art of the Funnies: An Aesthetic History of the Comic Strip.* Jackson, Miss.: University Press of Mississippi, 1995

Herner, Irene. *Mitos y Monitos.* Mexico City: Editorial Nueva Imagen, 1979.

Horn, Maurice. *Comics in the American West.* New York: Winchester Press, 1977.

Horn, Maurice, ed. *100 Years of American Newspaper Comics.* Avenel, N.J.: Gramercy, 1996.

———. *Sex in the Comics.* New York: Chelsea House, 1985.

———. *Women in the Comics.* New York: Chelsea House, 1977.

Inge, M. Thomas. *Comics as Culture.* Jackson, Miss.: University Press of Mississippi, 1990.

Jones, Gerard, and Will Jacobs. *The Great Comic Book Heroes. Revised edition.* Rocklin, Calif.: Prima, 1997.

Lent, John A. *An International Bibliography of Comic Art.* 4 volumes. Westport, Conn.: Greenwood Press, 1994-96.

Marschall, Richard. *America's Great Comic-Strip Artists*. New York: Abbeville Press, 1989.

Moya, Alvaro de. *Historia da Historia em Quadrinhos*. Saõ Paulo, Brazil: L & PM Editora, 1986.

————. *Shazam!* Saõ Paulo, Brazil: Editora Perspectiva, 1977.

O'Sullivan, Judith. *The Great American Comic Strip*. Boston: Little, Brown, and Company, 1990.

Robbins, Trina. *A Century of Women Cartoonists*. Northampton, Mass.: Kitchen Sink Press, 1994.

Ryan, John. *Panel by Panel: An Illustrated History of Australian Comics*. Melbourne: Cassell Australia, 1979.

Sabin, Roger. *Comics, Comix, and Graphic Novels*. London: Phaidon Press, 1997.

Schodt, Frederik. *Manga! Manga!: The World of Japanese Comics*. New York: Kodansha International, 1983.

————. *Dreamland Japan*. San Francisco: Stone Bridge Press, 1996.

Scott, Randall W. *Comic Books and Strips*. Phoenix, Ariz.: Oryx Press, 1988.

Tomic, Svetozar. *Strip, Poreklo i Znacaz*. Novi Sad, Yugoslavia: Forum Market-print, 1985.

Wood, Art. *Great Cartoonists and Their Art*. Gretna, Louisiana: Pelican Publishing, 1987.

Notes on the Contributors

Maurice Horn

Maurice Horn, the editor of this encyclopedia, is an internationally recognized authority on comics and cartoons. He was co-organizer of the first exhibition held at a major museum, "Bande Dessinee et Figuration Narrative," at the Louvre in Paris. He also organized the exhibition "75 Years of the Comics" at the New York Cultural Center.

He has lectured on comics and cartoons at universities worldwide, and his European series of lectures in 1973-74 was printed in *Information et Documents*, the official publication of the American Center in Paris. He has written hundreds of articles on the subject for American and foreign magazines, and has contributed to *Collier's Encyclopedia* and to *The International Encyclopedia of Communications*. He has edited a number of reprints of classic American and European comic strips, and has received many awards and honors in the field.

Many of the books he has authored or edited have become standard reference works in their field. In addition to *The World Encyclopedia of Comics*, he has edited *100 Years of American Newspaper Comics* and the multivolume *Contemporary Graphic Artists*. He is coauthor of *A History of the Comic Strip* and author of *75 Years of the Comics, Women in the Comics, Comics of the American West*, and *Sex in the Comics*. He is currently at work on an update of *The World Encyclopedia of Cartoons*.

Manuel Auad

A native of the Philippines, Manuel Auad currently resides in California. His knowledge of the Philippines comics scene has enabled him to bring many fine Filipino artists to the attention of American comic book publishers.

Bill Blackbeard

Bill Blackbeard, a Californian, has written a number of science-fiction novels, as well as articles and stories on a variety of subjects. In 1967 he founded the San Francisco Academy of Comic Art, which is devoted to the study and preservation of the comics and other forms of popular culture.

Blackbeard is the author of *Comics* (1973), the two-volume anthology *A Century of Comics* (1995), and many articles on the subject. He edited *The Smithsonian Collection of Newspaper Comics* (1978) and has organized several exhibits in the Bay Area.

Gianni Bono

Born in Genoa, Italy, in 1949, Gianni Bono has been a comics fan since he was a child. Together with Nino Bernazzali, he founded the club "Gil Amici del Fumetto" in 1967. An editor of the fanzine *Comics World* from 1967 to 1972, Bono has written articles on the comics for such publications as *Il Secolo XIX* and *Eureka*, and is the author of *Appunti sul Fumetto Italiano del Dopoguerra* ("Observations on the Postwar Italian Comics"). Bono wrote many scripts for adventure comics, especially war comics, and edited *If*, a quarterly magazine devoted to the comics world.

Joe Brancatelli

Joe Brancatelli remembers that his first comic book was bought at the expense of an egg cream that his father had offered to buy for him. He has been reading them ever since, which is why he was qualified to contribute the bulk of the American comic book entries.

A graduate of New York University's School of Journalism, Brancatelli has been writing professionally since he was 16. He became the managing editor of *The Monster Times*, a children's horror and comics tabloid, at age 18 and went on to found *Inside Comics*, the first professional magazine about comic art in America, at age 20. Concentrating primarily on behind-the-scenes news, *Inside*

Comics quickly became a controversial publication. After leaving *Inside Comics*, Brancatelli served short stints at UPI and on a New Jersey daily newspaper before turning to freelance writing.

Mary Beth Calhoun

Mary Beth Calhoun is an associate at an Ohio research and consulting firm, as well as a freelance writer and editor. Previously she was employed as an editorial assistant for a scientific journal. While growing up, she followed the comics in the *Pittsburgh Press*, and having maintained her interest in the field since that time has contributed a number of entries to the *World Encyclopedia of Comics*, as well as to other comics-related reference works.

Javier Coma

Javier Coma has written extensively on film, jazz music, and the comics. He is the editor of the acclaimed *Historia Mundial de los Comics*, and has written a series of articles, *Comics, classicos y modernos*, for the influential daily newspaper *El Pais*. Among his many other books on the subject have been *Del gato Felix al gato Fritz, Los comics: Un arte del siglo XX, Diccionario de los comics*, and *Los comics en Hollywood* (with Roman Gubern). In 1996 he published an important study on Western movies, *La gran caravan del western*, and he is currently working on a book about Hollywood's war movies.

He also contributed to *Contemporary Graphic Artists* and has written for many other publications in the United States, Great Britain, France, Italy, and Argentina. He has received many international honors in recognition of his contributions to the field.

Bill Crouch Jr.

Bill Crouch Jr., a Connecticut Yankee, has written about cartooning since he was first published in *Cartoonist Profiles* in 1974. For that magazine he interviewed Harold Foster, Noel Sickles, and Norman Mingo (the first artist to paint Alfred E. Neuman in full color for the cover of *Mad*). He edited *Dick Tracy, America's Most Famous Detective*, and coauthored a Dick Tracy collectibles book. In addition, he was a contributor to *The World Encyclopedia of Cartoons* and *100 Years of American Newspaper Comics*. He has also written scripts for syndicated comics and humorous comic books, specifically *Yogi Bear, Top Cat, Hong Kong Phooey*, and *The Flintstones*.

Giulio Cesare Cuccolini

Giulio Cesare Cuccolini, a native of Corregio (Emilia), studied at institutions in Italy, the United States, England, and France. He has been a member of the faculty at the University of Bologna, where he taught philosophy and history, and he has written and lectured extensively on comics in Italy and abroad. He is a past president of Associazione Nazionale degli Amici del Fumetto, and has long been associated with the International Comics Salon in Lucca and with Expo-Cartoon in Rome. He wrote the introductory material to the Italian edition of *The World Encyclopedia of Comics*.

Mark Evanier

Born in 1952 in Los Angeles, California, Mark Evanier began reading at a surprisingly early age, interspersing comic books with all kinds of books and magazines. Gradually, an interest in communications developed, with emphasis on movies, television, and, of course, comic books. He became president of a local comic book collector's society and was a frequent contributor to comic book and film fanzines. In the summer of 1969 Evanier began freelancing for various magazines.

While attending the University of California at Los Angeles, Evanier worked for Marvelmania International, a mail-order firm producing Marvel Comics character merchandise, and produced four issues of the company's fanzine. He quit to work as Jack Kirby's assistant on Kirby's comics for National Periodicals (later DC), but continued freelancing magazine pieces and special material for Walt

Disney Studios. In 1972 he began writing "funny animal" stories for such Gold Key comics as *Super Goof, Mickey Mouse, Bugs Bunny, Porky Pig, Daffy Duck, Beep Beep the Road Runner, The Beagle Boys, Looney Tunes,* and *Moby Dick.*

Mark Evanier has also written underground comix scripts, foreign comic albums, ghost comics, film reviews, and book reviews. Among his recent works have been *Comic Handbuch* and *San Francisco* (with Gerhard Muller).

Wolfgang Fuchs

Wolfgang Fuchs, born in 1945, grew up and went to school in and around Munich, Germany. While attending university courses in American cultural history, journalism and communications, and English literature, Fuchs participated in a university project that led to his coauthorship of *Comics: Anatomie eines Massenmediums.* A number of assignments for television, audiovisual aids and articles followed.

Fuchs gained valuable experience in the comics field by translating a number of comics and editing a German *Peanuts* comic book in 1974-75; he has since translated *Comics: The Art of the Comic Strip* for *Graphis.* He is currently a contributing editor of *Shock!*, a regular contributor to *Jugend, Film, Fernsehen,* and is preparing special projects for both. Recently he coauthored a series of articles on comics and advertising in *werben & verkaufen.* Among his recent works are *Comic Hardbuch* and *San Francisco* with Gerhard Müller.

Luis Gasca

Luis Gasca is a native of San Sebastian, Spain, and a graduate of Saragossa Law School (1955). He has been the manager of several advertising agencies and has taught at the School of Tourism of San Sebastian.

The writer of a number of books on a variety of subjects, his publications in the field of comic art include: *Los Comics en la Pantalla* ("Comics on the Screen"), *Imagen y Ciencia Ficción* ("Image and Science Fiction"), and *Los Comics en España* ("The Comics in Spain").

Gasca has been extremely active in the fields of comics and the movies; in fact, he is an executive board member of the San Sebastian Film Festival and of various comics conventions. He is currently the general editor of *Pala*, a San Sebastian-based publishing house specializing in books of and about comics.

Denis Gifford

Denis Gifford, the contributor of the entries about British comic characters and cartoonists in this encyclopedia, is Britain's leading authority on the comics. A collector of comics since the age of three, Gifford now has over 20,000 comics. His first ambition was to draw and edit comics, so at age 12 he printed and published his own comic, *Junior.* He turned professional at 14, drawing *Sammy and His Sister* for *All Fun Comic,* and then he took over such standing characters as *Pansy Potter* in *Beano* and *Our Ernie* in *Knockout.* His first regular job was as a junior cartoonist on the Sunday paper *Reynold's News.* During national service in the RAF (1946), he freelanced, drawing superheroes in the American style for *Streamline Comics* (1947).

Gifford has edited a series of comic books for Modern Fiction, including *Amazing Comics* (1949); he created *Steadfast McStaunch* (1950) and *Flip and Flop* (1954), among others, and was one of the artists on *Marvelman* (1955). In 1956 he created the daily *Telestrip*, the first newspaper strip to satirize current television shows. In 1960 he drew the complete *Classics Illustrated of Baron Munchausen.*

Gifford changed careers to take up writing and show business in the 1960s. He created a nostalgic panel game for BBC radio called *Sounds Familiar* (1966-74) and a television version, *Looks Familiar,* in 1972. Another of his ideas was the first panel game for cartoonists, *Quick on the Draw* (1974). Gifford has also written several books on the comics: *Discovering Comics* and *Stap Me! The British Newspaper Strip* (1971); *Six Comics of World War One* (1973, reprint); *Victorian Comics, The British Comic Catalogue,* and *Happy Days: One Hundred Years of Comics* (1975). Gifford is also the author of the acclaimed *British Film Catalogue.* Among his recent works are *The International Book of Comics* and *American Comic Strip Collections*.

Robert Gerson

Robert Gerson is a book designer and painter whose creative influences are drawn from the comic art medium. In 1970 he published and edited the limited-edition art magazine *Reality*. Devoted to comic book art and fantasy illustration from the artist's perspective, *Reality* featured the early works of artists Jeffrey Jones, Michael Kaluta, Kenneth Smith, and Howard Chaykin. Robert has collected original comic book, comic strip, and illustration art since 1970. His collection features artwork dating back to 1893.

As a book designer his most notable work is the 1987 edition of Ansel Adams's *The Mural Project*. He studied at the School of Visual Arts in Manhattan and the Pennsylvania Academy of the Fine Arts in Philadelphia. Robert paints in the fantasy art tradition reminiscent of the period of art known as the "golden age of illustration." He currently lives in the Brandywine River valley in Pennsylvania.

Paul Gravett

Born in Chelmsford, Paul Gravett completed studies in the law at Cambridge University. He edited the magazine *Escape* with Peter Stanbury, and has written many articles on the comics and lectured at comics conventions in Europe and the United States. He is the director of the Cartoon Art Trust in London.

Peter Harris

Peter Harris of Toronto is the editor of one of the largest weekly magazines in Canada, *Star Week*, the TV and entertainment supplement of the *Toronto Star*. At the same time, he was also the editor of the smallest, *Captain George's Penny Dreadful*, a nostalgia-oriented newsletter issued every Friday by the Vast Whizzbang Organization for many years.

Hongying Liu-Lengyel

Hongying Liu-Lengyel was born in Beijing, China, and graduated from Anhui University in Hefei in 1982. After marrying an American in the mid-1980s she moved to the United States, where she received a Ph.D. in communication from Temple University. She has written on comic art for various Chinese journals and has done a great number of book reviews on Chinese cartoons and comics for the U.S. publications *Wings* and *WittyWorld*.

She has lectured widely on the subject at Chinese and American universities. She has authored several books, including *Chinese Cartoons as Mass Communication: The History of Cartoon Development in China* (1993).

Pierre L. Horn

Pierre L. Horn is professor of French at Wright State University in Dayton, Ohio, where he also holds the Brage Golding Distinguished Professorship in Research. He has written extensively on French literature and civilization, and his works include biographies of Louis XIV and Lafayette. In addition, he has lectured on popular culture and contributed numerous entries to *The World Encyclopedia of Cartoons*, the multivolume series *Contemporary Graphic Artists*, and *100 Years of American Newspaper Comics*. He also edited the *Handbook of French Popular Culture*, and is the advisor for the multivolume *Guides to the World's Cinema*, published by Greenwood Press.

In 1978 he was decorated with the rank of Chevalier dans l'Ordre des Palmes Académiques by the French government.

Slobodan Ivkov

Born in 1959 in Subotica (northern Serbia), Slobodan Ivkov pursued postgraduate studies at the Faculty of Philosophy in Belgrade. He has been drawing comics and cartoons since 1977, and has also written scripts for many eminent

Yugoslav authors. He has published a number of comic books and has been comics editor for several publications. He has also been active in cartoons and graphic design, and has participated in some 70 exhibitions in Yugoslavia and abroad.

He is the organizer of the great retrospective exhibition "60 Years of Serbian Comics (1936-1995)," and the author of the accompanying 320-page catalogue. He has written articles on comics and cartoons for every leading magazine in Serbia and for many publications abroad. He has had a book of his cartoons, *Zid* ("The Wall"), and a collection of his science-fiction stories, *At Book's Edge*, published. He is a member of the Association of Applied Artists and of the Association of Journalists of Yugoslavia, and is the recipient of many honors and awards for his works in the field of comics.

Bill Janocha

Bill Janocha is a freelance artist who has been studio assistant to Mort Walker on *Beetle Bailey* since 1987. He has contributed articles to *Nemo, Inks,* Comicana books, and *Mad* magazine. Editor of the 1988 and 1996 editions of *The National Cartoonists Society Album,* Janocha helped with the development of the 1995 "Comic Strip Classics" U.S. postage stamps and with exhibitions for the Newspaper Features Council and for the International Museum of Cartoon Art. He was also a contributor to *100 Years of American Newspaper Comics.*

Orvy Jundis

A native of the Philippines, Orvy Jundis was born in 1943 and came to the United States in 1954, where he attended San Francisco Junior College, San Francisco State, and the University of San Francisco. An active leader in the Philippine American Collegiate Endeavor (PACE, a group responsible for originating and establishing Asian-American study programs), Jundis received a special commendation from the California state legislature and the Philippine Consulate.

Jundis was the first Filipino to promote and exhibit Philippine comic art outside of the Philippines. Actively involved in comics, science fiction, and fantasy fandom, Jundis founded the Philippine Comic Archives in 1968. In 1971 he returned to the Philippines to do extensive research on Filipino comics, but three years later he was back in the United States working with Marvel Comics and founding the Philippine Science-Fantasy Society. That same year (1974) Jundis brought the Philippines' talented Alex Niño to the United States.

A very prolific writer, editor, and artist, Jundis has written newspaper articles for the *San Francisco Phoenix,* the *Philippine News,* and the *Mabuhay Republic,* and his fanzine articles have appeared in *Jasoomian* and *Destiny.* He has contributed artwork to *Amra, ERBania, Collector's Showcase,* and *Stoned,* and his poetry has been published in *Kapatid, Kalayaan International, Filipino Heart-Throbs, Liwanag* (where he is an art editor), and *Time to Greeze* (an anthology of Third World arts and writing). He was a collaborator in *The Showcase of Fantasy Art,* edited by Emile Petaja, with an introduction by Ray Bradbury.

Hisao Kato

Hisao Kato was born in Oiso, Japan, on December 16, 1951. After graduation from the College of Foreign Studies in 1970, he entered the Tokyo Academy of Design, where he studied basic editorial design. In 1972 Kato attended the Japanese School for Editors and, after graduation in 1973, started on a promising editorial career.

A knowledgeable student of the comics, Kato has written several articles on the subject, as well as scripts for comic book companies. He read and carefully studied a great number of comic books, magazines, graphic publications, newspapers, and Ukiyo-e books as background material for the Japanese entries to this encyclopedia.

John A. Lent

Dr. John A. Lent, a professor at Temple University, has authored or edited 49 books, including *Asian Popular Culture* and *An International Bibliography of Comic*

Art, a four-volume reference work. He is chair of the Comic Art Working Group of the International Association for Mass Communication Research, the Asian Popular Culture Group of the Popular Culture Association, and the Asian Cinema Studies Society; he is also the editor of *Asian Cinema* and *Berita*, and the managing editor of *WittyWorld*. He has interviewed cartoonists and lectured on comic art on every continent, and was a contributor to *100 Years of American Newspaper Comics*.

Lent's nearly 40-year career includes a Fulbright scholarship to the Philippines, directorship of the first academic program in mass communication in Malaysia, pioneering research in Asia and the Caribbean, and study at universities in Norway, Mexico, Japan, and India.

Richard Marschall

Richard Marschall has devoted his life to the study and collection of comic strips and cartoons. His collection includes more than 3,000 original drawings, bound runs of the early humor magazines, and voluminous amounts of published and unpublished miscellany about cartoons and cartoonists.

Born in 1949 in Ridgewood, New York, he started drawing cartoons at an early age, and formed friendships with many cartoonists. He received degrees in American Studies and History from the American University in Washington, D.C., writing his master's thesis on the early American humor and cartoon magazines. While in school he began freelancing editorial cartoons to many of the nation's leading conservative journals.

In 1972 Marschall joined the staff of the Palisades Newspapers in Englewood, New Jersey, as a reporter and cartoonist. He shifted later in the year to the *Connecticut Sunday Herald* in Norwalk and served in the same capacities before rising to the positions of feature editor and magazine editor. Thereafter followed brief stints as associate editor of United Feature Syndicate and associate editor for comics of the Chicago Tribune-New York News Syndicate. In September 1975 he assumed his duties at Field in Chicago.

Marschall has exhibited major portions of his collection and has spoken on the comics extensively, as well as having assisted on several books on the subject. His areas of specialization are early magazine cartoons, early humor strips, American illustration, and the political cartoon. He credits his father's interest in cartoons with exciting his own proclivities.

He is now a freelance writer, and his works on the comics include *America's Great Comic-Strip Artists* (1989).

Alvaro de Moya

Alvaro de Moya is the foremost Brazilian authority on comics and cartoons. He has organized a number of important exhibitions of comic art in Brazil and South America, and has lectured extensively on the subject in America and in Europe. He has been a member of numerous international juries. Among the books he has written are *Shazam!*, *Historia da Historia em Quadrinhos*, and *O Mundo de Disney*.

Kalman Rubovszky

Born in Kisvarda, in northeastern Hungary, in 1942, Kalman Rubovszky is a professor at Debrecen University. He started research in the comics in the 1980s and gave a series of lectures on Hungarian comics at the International Comics Salon in Lucca, Italy, in 1982. He has also organized scientific conferences on comics. He has written many essays on the comics and has published two books on the subject, *Apropos comics!* (1988) and *A képregény* ("Novels in Pictures," 1989).

Ervin Rustemagić

Born in Ilidž, Yugoslavia, in 1952, Ervin Rustemagić worked as an illustrator for the children's newspaper *Male novine* in Sarajevo after his graduation from high school. In November 1971 he founded the comics magazine *Strip Art*, which he also edited for two years.

Rustemagić regularly attends many international comics conventions as the head of the Yugoslav delegation and a member of the juries of Angoulême (France) and Gijon (Spain). He is the author of the first book on comic art ever published in Yugoslavia, *The Professional Secrets of the Comics*. His lecture, which he presented at Angoulême 1, "La Bande Dessinée Yougoslave," was the first lecture on Yugoslav comics ever given anywhere.

John Thomas Ryan

A collector of vintage comics and original artwork, John Thomas Ryan was born in 1931 in Cowra, N.S.W., Australia. He contributed many articles, including some for the well-known *Bid gee* series, to amateur magazines relating to the comics.

In 1964 Ryan published Australia's first comic fanzine, *Down Under*, and its lead article, "With the Comics Down Under," won the Alley Award for the best article. In 1979, he published *Panel by Panel: An Illustrated History of Australian Comics*, the definitive work on the subject. He died in 1980.

Matthew Allen Thorn

Matt Thorn is a cultural anthropologist, writer, and translator who lives and works in Kyoto, Japan. He has translated thousands of pages of Japanese comics into English for Viz Comics, including Hayao Miyazaki's *Nausicaä of the Valley of Wind*, Rumiko Talahashi's *Mermaid* saga, and Hagio Moto's *They Were Eleven*. The author of numerous articles and essays on *shojo manga*, or Japanese girls' and women's comics, he is currently working on an ethnographic book on the subject. He also maintains a World Wide Web site known as "The Shojo Manga Home Page."

Dennis Wepman

Dennis Wepman has taught English at the City University of New York and held the post of cultural affairs editor of the *New York Daily News*. The holder of a graduate degree in linguistics from Columbia University, he is the author of 12 volumes of biography and has contributed to numerous publications in linguistics, literature, art, and popular culture, as well as to several standard reference books on cartooning. He has been a contributor to the multivolume *Contemporary Graphic Artists*, to *The Encyclopedia of American Comics*, and to *100 Years of American Newspaper Comics*. He is the chief review editor of *WittyWorld*, the international cartoon magazine.

Appendices

Code of the Comics Magazine Association of America

Institutions

In general, recognizable national, social, political, cultural, ethnic and racial groups, religious institutions, and law enforcement authorities will be portrayed in a positive light. These include the government on the national, state, and municipal levels, including all of its numerous departments, agencies, and services; law enforcement agencies such as the FBI, the Secret Service, the CIA, etc.; the military, both United States and foreign; known religious organizations; ethnic advancement groups; foreign leaders and representatives of other governments and national groups; and social groups identifiable by lifestyle, such as homosexuals, the economically disadvantaged, the economically privileged, the homeless, senior citizens, minors, etc.

Socially responsible attitudes will be favorably depicted and reinforced. Socially inappropriate, irresponsible, or illegal behavior will be shown to be specific actions of a specific individual or group of individuals, and not meant to reflect the routine activity of any general group of real persons.

If, for dramatic purposes, it is necessary to portray such a group of individuals in a negative manner, the name of the group and its individual members will be fictitious, and its activities will not clearly be identifiable with the routine activities of any real group.

Stereotyped images and activities will not be used to degrade specific national, ethnic, cultural, or socioeconomic groups.

Language

The language in a comic book will be appropriate for a mass audience that includes children. Good grammar and spelling will be encouraged. Publishers will exercise good taste and a responsible attitude as to the use of language in their comics. Obscene and profane words, symbols, and gestures are prohibited.

References to physical handicaps, illnesses, ethnic backgrounds, sexual preferences, religious beliefs, and race, when presented in a derogatory manner for dramatic purposes, will be shown to be unacceptable.

Violence

Violent actions or scenes are acceptable within the context of a comic book story when dramatically appropriate. Violent behavior will not be shown as acceptable. If it is presented in a realistic manner, care should be taken to present the natural repercussions of such actions. Publishers should avoid excessive levels of violence, excessively graphic depictions of violence, and excessive bloodshed or gore. Publishers will not present detailed information instructing readers how to engage in imitable violent actions.

Characterizations

Character portrayals will be carefully crafted and show sensitivity to national, ethnic, religious, sexual, political, and socioeconomic orientations. If it is dramatically appropriate for one character to demean another because of his or her sex, ethnicity, religion, sexual preference, political orientation, socioeconomic status, or disabilities, the demeaning words or actions will be clearly shown to be wrong or ignorant in the course of the story. Stories depicting characters subject to physical, mental, or emotional problems or with economic disadvantages should never assign ultimate responsibility for these conditions to the characters themselves. Heroes should be role models and should reflect the prevailing social attitudes.

Substance abuse

Healthy, wholesome lifestyles will be presented as desirable. However, the use and abuse of controlled substances, legal and illicit, are facts of modern existence, and may be portrayed when dramatically appropriate.

The consumption of alcohol, narcotics, pharmaceuticals, and tobacco will not be depicted in a glamourous way. When the line between the normal, responsible consumption of legal substances and the abuse of these substances is crossed, the distinction will be made clear and the adverse consequences of such abuse will be noted.

Substance abuse is defined as the use of illicit drugs and the self-destructive use of such products as tobacco (including chewing tobacco), alcohol, prescription drugs, over-the-counter drugs, etc.

Use of dangerous substances both legal and illegal should be shown with restraint as necessary to the context of the story. However, storylines should not be detailed to the point of serving as instruction manuals for substance abuse. In each story, the abuser will be shown to pay the physical, mental, and/or social penalty for his or her abuse.

Crime

While crimes and criminals may be portrayed for dramatic purposes, crimes will never be presented in such a way as to inspire readers with a desire to imitate them nor will criminals be portrayed in such a manner as to inspire readers to emulate them. Stories will not present unique imitable techniques or methods of committing crimes.

Attire and Sexuality

Costumes in a comic book will be considered to be acceptable if they fall within the scope of contemporary styles and fashions. Scenes and dialogue involving adult relationships will be presented with good taste, sensitivity, and in a manner which will be considered acceptable by a mass audience. Primary human sexual characteristics will never be shown. Graphic sexual activity will never be depicted.

Administrative Procedure

I

All comics which member publishers wish to bear the Comics Code Seal will be submitted to the Code administrator for review prior to publication. The administra-

tor will review them according to the guidance he has received from the permanent committee and will either approve them to bear the seal, or return them to the publisher with his comments. The responsible editor from the publisher will either revise the comic, in accordance with those comments, or discuss with the administrator the concerns raised with him and reach agreement on how the comic can properly bear the Code Seal either without being revised or with a mutually agreeable set of alternative revisions. In the event no agreement can be reached between the editor and the

administrator, the matter will be referred to the permanent committee, which will act promptly to determine if, or under what conditions, the comic in question can bear the Code Seal. Decisions of the permanent committee will be binding on the publishers, who agree not to place the Code Seal on any comic on which it is not authorized.

II

The members of the Comics Magazine Association of America include publishers who elect to publish comics that are not intended to bear the Code Seal, and that therefore need not go through the approval process described above. Among the comics in this category may be titles intended for adult readers. Member publishers hereby affirm that we will distribute these publications only through those distribution channels in which it is possible to notify retailers and distributors of their content, and thus help the publications reach their intended audiences. The member publishers agree to refrain from distributing these publications through those distribution channels that, like the traditional newsstand, are serviced by individuals who are unaware of the content of specific publications before placing them on display.

III

Recognizing that no document can address all the complex issues and concerns that face our changing society, the member publishers have established a permanent committee composed of the senior editor of each member's staff. This committee will meet regularly to review those issues and concerns as they affect our publications, and to meet with and guide the administrator of the Comics Code, and will replace the previous written guidelines of the Comics Code.

Appendix B
Reuben Award Winners

In April of each year the National Cartoonists Society awards the Reuben—so named in honor of Rube Goldberg, the NCS's first president—to an outstanding cartoonist for his or her achievements during the preceding year. (From 1946-53 it was called the Billy DeBeck Award.)

1946: **Milton Caniff**
1947: **Al Capp**
1948: **Chic Young**
1949: **Alex Raymond**

1950: **Roy Crane**
1951: **Walt Kelly**
1952: **Hank Ketcham**
1953: **Mort Walker**
1954: **Willard Mullin**
1955: **Charles Schulz**
1956: **Herbert Block (Herblock)**
1957: **Hal Foster**
1958: **Frank King**
1959: **Chester Gould**
1960: **Ronald Searle**

1961: **Bill Mauldin**
1962: **Dik Browne**
1963: **Fred Lasswell**
1964: **Charles Schulz**
1965: **Leonard Starr**
1966: **Otto Soglow**
1967: **Rube Goldberg**
1968: **Johnny Hart and Pat Oliphant (tied)**
1969: **Walter Berndt**
1970: **Alfred Andriola**
1971: **Milton Caniff**
1972: **Pat Oliphant**
1973: **Dik Browne**
1974: **Dick Moores**
1975: **Bob Dunn**
1976: **Ernie Bushmiller**
1977: **Chester Gould**
1978: **Jeff MacNelly**

1979: **Jeff MacNelly**
1980: **Charles Saxon**
1981: **Mell Lazarus**
1982: **Bil Keane**
1983: **Arnold Roth**
1984: **Brant Parker**
1985: **Lynn B. Johnston**
1986: **Bill Watterson**
1987: **Mort Drucker**
1988: **Bill Watterson**
1989: **Jim Davis**
1990: **Gary Larson**
1991: **Mike Peters**
1992: **Cathy Guisewite**
1993: **Jim Borgman**
1994: **Gary Larson**
1995: **Garry Trudeau**
1996: **Sergio Aragones**

Appendix C
Directory of Newspaper Syndicates

Chronicle Features
870 Market Street
San Francisco, CA 94102

Creators Syndicate
5777 W. Century Boulevard, Suite 700
Los Angeles, CA 90045

Editors Press Service
330 W. 42nd Street
New York, NY 10036

King Features Syndicate
235 E. 45th Street
New York, NY 10017

Los Angeles Times Syndicate
218 S. Spring Street
Los Angeles, CA 90012

Newspaper Enterprise Association
200 Madison Avenue
New York, NY 10016

Toronto Star Syndicate
1 Yonge Street
Toronto, ON M5E 1E6
Canada

Tribune Media Services
435 N. Michigan Avenue, Suite 1500
Chicago, IL 60611

United Feature Syndicate
200 Madison Avenue
New York, NY 10016

Universal Press Syndicate
4520 Main Street, Suite 700
Kansas City, MO 64111-7701

Washington Post Writer's Group
1150 15th Street NW
Washington, DC, 20071-9200

Appendix D
Directory of Comic Book Publishers

Acclaim Entertainment
One Acclaim Plaza
Glen Cove, NY 11542-2708

Caliber Comics
225 N. Sheridan Road
Plymouth, MI 48170

Comico Comics
119 W. Hubbard Street
Chicago, IL 60610

Dark Horse Comics
10956 SE Main Street
Milwaukie, OR 97222

DC Comics
1700 Broadway
New York, NY 10019

Fantagraphics
7563 Lake City Way NW
Seattle, WA 98113

Harris Comics
1115 Broadway
New York, NY 10010

Image Comics
1440 N. Harbor Boulevard, Suite 305
Fullerton, CA 92635

Kitchen Sink Press
320 Riverside Drive
Northampton, MA 01060

Marvel Entertainment Group
387 Park Avenue South
New York, NY 10016

Topps Comics
One Whitehall Street
New York, NY 10004

Warp Graphics
43 Haight Avenue
Poughkeepsie, NY 12601

Indices

A: Proper Name Index
B: Title Index
C: Media Index
D: Contributors Index
E: Geographical Index
F: Illustration Index
G: Subject Index

Index A
Proper Names Index

Index A
Proper Names Index

Chapman, Steve, 209
Charlebois, J., 607
Charlier, Jean-Michel, 159, 196, 241, 345, 396, 476-77, 529, 647, 781
Charteris, Leslie, 686
Chartier, Albert, 196-97
Chatterton, George, 631
Chatto, Keith, 82
Chaulet, George (pseud. Georges, François), 217
Chaykin, Howard, 40, 197-98, 212, 726
Chayrin, Jerome, 149
Chendi, Carlo, 149, 198, 228, 587, 606, 644, 765
Chen Ping, 674
Chéret, André, 638-39
Chiaverotti, Claudio, 273
Chiba, Akio, 199, 370
Chiba, Tetsuya, 38, 101, 198-99
Chierchini, Giulio, 587, 715
Chiletto, Franco, 143, 266, 549
Chmielewski, Henryk Jerzy (pseud. Chimel), 200
Christensen, Bert, 684
Christensen, Don, 122, 162, 231, 625
Christiansen, Anne, 346
Christiansen, Arthur, 210
Christin, Pierre (pseud. Linus), 131, 527, 745, 786
Christman, Bert, 200, 673, 820
Christophe. *See* Colomb, Georges (pseud. of)
Chu, Ronald (pseud. of Chu Teh-Yung), 200-201
Chua, Enrie, 212
Chu Hsiang-chun, 393-94
Chung-chien, Lu, 345
Chu Teh-Yung (pseud. Chu, Ronald), 200-201
Cifre, Guillermo, 202
Cilino, Frank, 309
Cimpellin, Leone, 162, 202-3, 602, 603
Cinco, Terry, 418
Ciocca, Walter, 203, 481
Clampett, Bob, 162, 625
Claremont, Chris, 397, 568
Clark, George, 354
Clark, Jim, 386
Clark, Peter, 797
Class, Alan, 236
Coching, Francisco V., 32, 350, 400, 462
Cochran, John, 787
Cochran, Ned, 592, 810
Cochran, Russ, 401
Cocking, Percy (pseud. Daw, Jack), 205-6, 801
Cockrum, Dave, 821
Coelho, E. T., 215
Cohl, Emile, 501, 567, 616

Colan, Eugene (pseud. Austin, Adam), 104, 118, 182, 183, 206, 233, 260, 395, 403, 534, 732
Colantuoni, Tiberio, 227, 715, 765
Cole, Jack (pseud. Johns, Ralph), 26, 206, 364, 471, 621-22
Coletta, Vince, 732
Coll, Charles, 557, 693
Colletta, Vince, 735
Colley, Ed, 732-33
Collins, Dennis, 608
Collins, Max Allan, 489
Collins, Ray (pseud. Zappietto, Eugenio), 239, 249, 441, 552
Colomb, Georges (pseud. Christophe), 12, 206-8, 290, 292, 399, 770
Colquhoun, Joe, 208-9
Combe, William, 663
Comés, Didiet, 211
Condre, J., 438
Conleys, Eugene, 728
Connell, Del, 485
Connelly, Joe, 485
Conner, Dale, 518-19
Connolly, Joseph, 638
Connor, Dale, 677
Conselman, Bill, 280-81
Conte, Brigitte, 346
Conti, Oscar (pseud. Oski), 213
Conway, Gerald, 233, 397, 404, 718, 757
Cooke, Brian, 468
Cooper, Robert St. John, 468
Corbella, Ferdinando, 132, 562, 659
Corben, Richard Vance, 213-14
Corbett, Bertha, 271, 632
Cordwell, Frederick, 795
Cores, Carlos, 480-81
Coria, Francisco, 141
Cornelius, Cosper, 87, 300
Corno, Andrea, 459
Cornwell, Bruce, 232
Cornwell, Dean, 87
Corteggiani, François, 191
Cortez, Jayme, 215
Cory, Fanny Young, 215-16, 348, 632
Cosgriff, Jack, 122
Cossio, Carlo, 161, 216, 228, 246-47, 327, 659
Cossio, Vittorio, 216, 247
Costanza, Pete, 120, 723
Coulson, Juanita, 135, 693
Counihan, Bud, 129
Coutelis, Alexandre, 529
Covarrubias, Miguel, 187
Cowan, Denys, 356
Cox, Erle, 592
Cox, Palmer, 441, 628
Craenhals, François (pseud. Hals, F.), 36, 198, 217-18
Craft, Jerry, 218
Craig, Chase, 162, 218-19, 625
Craig, John, 219, 331, 404

Crammond, Harry, 574
Crandall, Reed, 136, 219-20, 260, 303, 308, 331, 364, 379, 400, 401, 458, 471, 587, 759, 818, 819
Crane, Royston Campbell (Roy), 27, 158, 169-70, 220, 322, 727, 777, 799-800
Cravath, Glen, 749
Craveri, Sebastiano (pseud. Pin-Tin), 221
Crawford, Arthur, 150
Crawford, Mel, 270
Crenshaw, George, 685
Crepax, Guido, 37, 39, 61, 221-22, 627, 785
Cretti, Glauco, 245
Crooks, Bill, 800
Crosby, Leo, 740
Crosby, Percy Leo, 222-23, 325, 552, 647, 707-8
Cross, Stanley George, 223, 625, 666, 797
Crouch, Bill, 635
Crowley, Wendell, 183, 223
Cruikshank, George, 223-24
Crumb, Charles, 323
Crumb, Robert, 36, 39, 91, 224-26, 284, 289, 323-24, 449, 463, 481, 540-41, 694
Cruse, Howard, 40, 226-27
Cruz, Gemma, 659
Cubbino, Mario, 190
Cubie, Alex, 666
Cueto, Francisco, 348
Cuidera, Chuck, 136, 219, 622
Čukli, Marcel, 738
Culliford, Pierre (pseud. Peyo), 36, 228, 318, 680
Culliford, Thierry, 680
Cusso, Miguel, 94
Cuti, Nick, 809
Cutrate, Joe. *See* Spiegelman, Arthur (pseud. of)
Cuvelier, Paul, 214

D

Daix, Andre, 630
Dale, Allen. *See* Connor, Dale; Saunders, Allen (pseud. of)
Daley, Brian, 726
Dallis, Nicholas, 32, 97, 231-32, 424-26, 454, 649-50
Dalmasso, Giacomo, 111
Dalton, Cal, 162, 315
D'Ami, Rinaldo (pseud. D'Amy, Roy), 510
Damiani, Damiano, 103
Damonte Taborda, Raul, 232
Daniel, Vincent, 657
D'Antonio, Gino, 118, 602, 771

Index A
Proper Names Index

Elder, William W., 237, 278, 319, 331, 378, 463, 481, 690
Eleuteri Serpieri, Paolo, 278-79
Elias, Leopold, 78, 135, 185, 280, 307
Ellis, Frank, 411
Ellis, Warren, 787
Ellison, Harlan, 397
Ellsworth, Whitney, 117, 434
Elrod, Jack, 513
Elworth, Lennart, 282, 314
Embleton, Ronald S., 282, 518
Englehart, Steve, 104, 260, 397, 519
Ernst, Kenneth, 263, 285, 519, 677
Ernsting, Volker, 285, 533-34
Erwin, Will. *See* Eisner, Will (pseud. of)
Escher, Reinhold, 169, 285-86, 525, 648
Escobar, Josep, 186
Esposito, Mike, 689
Essegesse (pseud. of Sinchetto, Sartoris, Guzzon), 177, 446-47
Estrada, Ric, 308, 690
Estren, Mark, 224
Evanier, Mark, 122, 162, 231, 625
Evans, George, 81, 204, 219-20, 286-87, 331, 686, 690
Everett, Bill (pseud. Blake, Everett; Blake, William), 26, 90, 131, 166, 206, 233, 260, 287, 731-32
Ewer, Raymond Crawford, 19, 709
Ezquerra, Carlos, 424

F

Facciolo, Enzio, 245
Fagarazzi, Daniele, 190
Fago, Vincent, 611
Fajardo, Perez, 311
Falk, Lee, 24, 238, 290-91, 321, 361, 399, 508-9, 611-12, 677
Fallberg, Carl, 162
Fasani, Angelo, 587
Fauche, Xavier, 493
Faustinelli, Mario, 102, 627
Fawcett, Gene, 185
Fawcett, Robert, 87, 267
Fawkes, Wally (pseud. Trog), 29, 310
Fazekas, Attila, 294
Feiffer, Jules, 33, 62, 295-96, 775, 807, 816
Feign, Larry, 296-97
Feininger, Lyonel, 14, 16, 19, 63, 71, 297, 444-45, 525, 628, 804
Feldmann, Andi, 805
Feldmann, Rötger (pseud. Brösel), 805
Feldstein, Al, 126, 237, 297, 331, 400, 401, 458, 818
Fenderson, Mark, 499
Feng Zikai, 300
Fera, A. C., 281-82, 740, 813

Ferdinand, Ron, 242, 441
Ferguson, Fred, 370
Fernandez, Fernando, 41, 301, 793
Fernandez, Jim, 32, 343
Ferrer, Manuel, 239
Ferrier, Arthur, 301-2
Ferro, Ted, 113, 474
Figueras, Alfonso, 102, 302
Filho, Manoel Victor, 83
Filippucci, Lucio, 517
Fine, Louis (pseud. Berold, Basil; Cortez, Jack; Lectron, E.; Lewis, Kenneth), 26, 77, 86, 92, 133, 135-36, 303, 364, 379, 400, 471, 622, 720
Finger, Bill, 117, 303, 357, 434, 656, 804
Finne, Jalmari, 604
Fischer, Ludwig, 305
Fischer, Margot, 497
Fisher, Hammond Edward, 179, 255, 303-4, 420, 478, 531
Fisher, Harry Conway (Bud), 16-17, 66, 98, 201, 304-5, 419, 555-56
Fisher, William, 317
Fitzgerald, Owen, 316
Flagg, James Montgomery, 347, 395
Flanders, Charles, 306-7, 446, 490, 686, 763, 813
Flax (pseud. of Palacio, Lino), 263, 595
Fleischer, Dave, 309
Fleischer, Max, 129, 309, 755
Fleisher, Michael, 424
Flessel, Craig, 673
Fletcher, Frank, 155, 249, 309
Fletcher, Rick, 489, 582
Fletcher, Wendy, 279-80
Flinders, Evelyn, 309-10, 704
Flinton, Ben, 104
Flooglebuckle, Al. *See* Spiegelman, Arthur (pseud. of)
Florese, Rudy, 462
Floyd, Dick, 617-18
Flynt, Larry, 809
Fogelberg, Ola (pseud. Fogeli), 603-4
Fogelberg-Kalia, Toto, 604
Folkard, Charles (pseud. C. F.), 18, 317, 749
Folkard, Harry, 749
Folwell, Arthur, 538
Forest, Jean-Claude (pseud. Valherbe, Jean), 36, 39, 110-11, 313, 722, 746, 787
Forman, Tom, 379, 551
Formhals, Henry, 140, 320, 420
Forrest, Hal, 24, 743-44
Forsythe, Vic, 419-20
Fortess, Karl, 61
Forton, Louis, 22, 130, 141-42, 256, 313-14, 615, 829
Forza, John, 314
Fosgrave, Les, 563
Fossati, Franco, 672

Foster, Bob, 261
Foster, Harold, 23, 71, 86, 125, 147, 213, 215, 220, 287, 315, 347, 348, 374, 389, 400, 411, 427, 457, 460, 467, 510, 524, 525, 554, 628-29, 645, 662, 678, 716, 738, 747, 748, 752
Foster, Warren, 315
Fournier, Jean-Claude, 721
Foust, Felix, 429
Fox, Fontaine Talbot, Jr., 316, 600, 647, 768-69
Fox, Fred, 218, 281
Fox, Gardner (pseud. Cooper, Jefferson; Sommers, Bart), 78, 104, 117, 212, 257, 307, 316-17, 319, 357, 374, 376, 422, 429, 430, 673, 683, 718, 724
Fox, Gil, 136, 267, 673
Foxwell, Herbert, 22, 317, 749, 761
Fradon, Ramona, 152, 154, 527
Franchi, C., 830-31
Francis, Stephen, 503
Francisco, Carlos, 32
François, André, 559
François, Jacques. *See* Dumas, Jacques (pseud. of)
Franićević, Andra, 256
Franklin, Robert. *See* Goodwin, Archie (pseud. of)
Franquin, André, 318-19, 337, 339, 721
Frazetta, Frank, 160, 212, 220, 308, 319-20, 331, 337, 401, 432, 481, 587, 787, 811
Fredericks, Fred, 509
Fredericks, Harold, 321
Fred (pseud. of Aristides, Othon), 36, 527, 613
Freeman, Don, 161, 544
Freghieri, Gianni, 273
Frehm, Paul, 749, 813
Frehm, Walter, 813
Freixas, Carlos, 579, 619-20
Freixas, Emilio, 177, 197
Freleng, Fritz, 162, 231, 625
Fremon, Jess, 806
Frescura, Franco, 228, 765
Freyse, Bill, 322, 590
Friedrich, Gary, 338, 397, 404, 689
Friedrich, Mike, 430
Frink, George, 709
Frise, James Llewellyn, 322-23
Frollo, Leone, 111
Frost, A. B., 499
Fry, Christopher, 208
Fry, Michael, 593-94
Fuchs, Erika, 324-25
Fuchs, Wolfgang, 680
Fuente, Victor de la, 37, 343, 375
Fuji, Bob, 443
Fujiko, Fujio, 755
Fujitani, Bob, 222, 368
Fukui, Eiichi, 83, 399

Index A
Proper Names Index

Index A
Proper Names Index

Index B
Title Index

Index B

Title Index

Index B
Title Index

Index C
Media Index

Brancatelli, Joe

Index D
Contributor's Index

Index D

Contributor's Index

Index G
Subject Index